Mexican Political Biographies, 1935–1993

 Special Publication

Institute of Latin American Studies
University of Texas at Austin

Mexican Political Biographies, 1935–1993
Third Edition

by Roderic Ai Camp

 University of Texas Press, Austin

Third Edition, 1995

Requests for permission to reproduce material from this work should be sent to Permissions, University of Texas Press, P.O. Box 7819, Austin, Texas 78713-7819.

⊗ The paper used in this publication meets the minimum requirements of American National Standard for Information Sciences—Permanence of Paper for Printed Library Materials, ANSI Z39.48–1984.

Library of Congress Cataloging-in-Publication Data

Camp, Roderic Ai.
    Mexican political biographies, 1935–1993 / by Roderic Ai Camp.—
3rd ed.
        p.   cm. — (ILAS special publication)
    Includes bibliographical references (p.   ).
    ISBN 0-292-71174-3 (alk. paper). — ISBN 0-292-71181-6 (pbk. : alk. paper)
    1. Politicians—Mexico—Biography. 2. Statesmen—Mexico—Biography.
3. Mexico—Biography. I. Title. II. Series: Special publication (University of Texas at Austin.
Institute of Latin American Studies)
F1235.5.A2C35 1995
972'.0099—dc20   95-840
[B]

To
William H. Beezley,
William P. Glade,
and Richard E. Greenleaf,
who have devoted their lives
to understanding Mexico

Contents

A Note to the Reader

Designed to carry out a more specific function than a general *Who's Who*, this volume contains the biographies of public figures, living or deceased, who have been prominent in Mexican political life from 1935 to mid 1993. In 1968 when I began research on career patterns of Mexican public figures, I found both a lack of available information and, when biographical data were available, contradictory information. Errors ranged from six different birth dates for a single person to the crediting of individuals with positions they did not hold. Not only did errors appear rather frequently in Mexican sources, they were repeated in many of the English-language reference works and scholarly studies of Mexico by North Americans. And they in turn were repeated by other scholars. In addition to the most accurate information available about the career patterns of numerous public figures, this volume contains appendixes of the most important elective, appointive, and party positions in Mexico, with the names of the persons who have held them and their tenure in office. By having lists of positions as well as biographies of persons who have held them, the reader who does not have a person in mind will be able to find information about someone who has held a specific position in Mexican government without knowing his or her name. Thus, the book will also provide scholars with a selective version of a government organizational manual for Mexico from 1935 to 1993.

This book was compiled with the purpose of alleviating a dearth that has existed since 1946, when Ronald Hilton edited the last volume of *Who's Who in Mexico*. Even though the 1946 edition and the two that preceded it were typical of the standard of *Who's Who*, they were scholarly and accurate and provided researchers with the only English language source for biographical information on living Mexicans who had distinguished themselves in all fields. Unfortunately, that series was terminated with the third edition, and no single comprehensive and detailed biographical reference work on Mexico was published until my own *Who's Who in Mexico Today* in 1988. The biographical essay following the appendixes will make clear the limitations of available works in Spanish that have been published in Mexico.

This revised and enlarged edition contains significant changes. The information in the first and second editions, current through 1981, has been completely updated, both in the appendixes and the biographies themselves. Of the original 1,350 biographies, more than half have undergone significant additions or changes to one or more categories, while many others have had minor changes. Furthermore, six hundred new biographies have been added, increasing the coverage of political leaders prominent in the period covered by the earlier editions, in addition to biographies of prominent officeholders in the administrations of José López Portillo, Miguel de la Madrid, and Carlos Salinas de Gortari.

In response to several suggestions made by colleagues and critics, beginning with the second edition, I added information about family ties, especially the names of spouses, where available. Also, I added several new categories to the appendixes, most notably the names of *oficiales mayores*, the third-ranking cabinet position as well as the names of other important party presidents, several new ambassadorial positions, and union leaders. Biographies of these persons, where possible, were included in the biographical section, as were additional biographies of leftist political activists who may not have held formal government posts.

The arrival of Carlos Salinas de Gortari's (1988–1994) generation to the presidency, and the leading contenders for the official party presidential nomination in 1993, provides further evidence of recent trends in the career patterns of those who rise to the top of the Mexican political system. Salinas, as well as his closest collaborators, whose biographies appear in this edition, follows the pattern of his predecessor, Miguel de la Madrid, representing the Mexican public figure who has made his career in the federal bureaucracy, never having held an elective post or having been an active militant in the official party. Furthermore, although Salinas retains close ties to his northern roots, he is truly a product of Mexico City, like Luis Echeverría, López Portillo, and De la Madrid. Regionalism, which long has played a significant role in Mexican politics, is fast disappearing from the scene. Moreover, the continued dominance of the National University, especially the National School of Law, on the professional education, socialization, teaching experience, and early political recruitment of political leaders has begun to wane. Salinas is the first president in Mexican history to have an economics degree, although from the National University, and a doctorate in economics from Harvard, from the United States. Nearly all of the leading members of the Salinas cabinet have studied abroad, and economists for the first time equal lawyers in top political posts. Many of his collaborators studied and taught at private secular or religious schools, the first generation of leaders from such origins to have reached important national offices. The majority of those who will be designated as the closest collaborators of the next president, and will have had similar career experiences, regardless of party affiliation, are also likely to be included in this volume. Thus, the incremental changes in Mexican public careers and political recruitment patterns are fully documented, from generation to generation, in the biographies of this book.

Acknowledgments

A book of this sort relies upon the goodwill and assistance of many people, but especially those whose biographies it contains. I owe a debt to librarians, government officials, scholars, and relatives of the biographees. Among the first groups, I would like to express thanks to the late Nettie Lee Benson and to Lutie L. Higley, of the University of Texas and the University of Arizona Libraries, respectively, for their invaluable assistance. Further, I would like to thank the staffs of the Hispanic Section of the Library of Congress, the Columbus Memorial Library of the Pan American Union, the University of Iowa Library, the Howard-Tilton Library of Tulane University, the Woodrow Wilson Center for International Scholars of the Smithsonian Institution, the Ibero-American University Library, the Carlos Menendez Library in Mérida, Yucatán, the U.S. Department of State Library, and the Library of the Supreme Court of Justice of Mexico.

The number of Mexican government officials, at both the state and national levels, who have helped with this work are too numerous to mention. I would like to single out Miguel Basáñez and Manuel Carrillo, who have taken more than a passing interest in this research project and have made sources of information far more accessible.

For helpful suggestions along the way, I wish to thank Ronald Hilton, the late Stanley R. Ross, and James Wilkie, all pioneers in Mexican written and oral biography and bibliography, and Clifton E. Wilson, for early editorial suggestions. Without the assistance of several other colleagues, this work would be far less complete. In particular, Peter H. Smith provided supporting data for both the appendixes and numerous biographies in the original edition from his own vast biographical study of Mexico, and helpful source suggestions and encouragement along the way. Paul Kelso supplied me with critical biographical data from a personal note file extending back many years. Rudy de la Garza provided the majority of data for the appendixes on federal deputies, especially data on committee assignments, through 1970. And last, Donald Mabry shared information on opposition party leaders in the 1970s.

The Roger Stone Thayer Center for Latin American Studies of Tulane University and a Tinker Foundation Grant in Mexican Policy Studies made the completion of this third edition possible. I relied very heavily on the editorial assistance of Scott Pentzer, Meg Mitchell, and Sallie Hughes. Additionally, I would like to thank Alejandro Spíndola for his assistance in obtaining additional information to complete the appendixes; Luis Medina, Sergio Aguayo, and Lorenzo Meyer, for easy access to library material in the Colegio de México; and Jorge Carpizo for access to the Universidad Nacional Autónoma de México archives. Finally, Virginia Hagerty's and Carolyn Palaima's special devotion and enthusiasm for this project added immensely to its quality.

How to Use This Book

The author has adhered to the Mexican custom of using the father's surname followed by the mother's maiden name for biographees' names. When the biographee's second surname is not commonly used in other printed sources, it appears in parentheses. The date of death, when known, follows the name. Because no obituary index for Mexican newspapers is available, and therefore correct information was not always accessible, all persons for whom no death date is given are not necessarily alive, although it can be presumed that the majority of them are. Further information is usually available in the issues of the major Mexican newspapers and *El Tiempo* near date of death. The biographical information in the entries is divided into twelve categories, each denoted by a boldfaced letter. Where no code letter appears, no substantiated information was available. The word *none* indicates that the biographee has no representation in that category, such as no major political position, no military career, or no pursuit of formal education. When an office is italicized in a biography, the individual and his position are also listed in the appendixes. When the name of a supervisor, teacher, relative, or mentor is italicized within a biography, that individual has his or her own biographic entry or is listed in the appendixes. The categories are:

(a) Date of birth.

(b) Geographical location of birthplace: city or municipality, and state. All municipal names and spellings follow the 1970 edition of the *Diccionario Porrúa*.

(c) Education: primary, secondary, and preparatory education, and professional and college education with the dates of attendance and graduation, if possible. The most complete biographies will give thesis titles as well. Also included at the end of the educational category are teaching positions, whether they are on the primary, secondary, or college level, and other educational positions.

(d) Elective positions: any positions that at least nominally are attained through the electoral process, from council member to president. (Legislatively appointed governors are not included in this category, but rather under the governmental positions category.)

(e) Party positions: both formal and informal positions that persons have held for any political party or campaign in Mexico. Party candidates for public office are also included. The word *none* indicates that the person has not held any position on the National Executive Committee of the PRI, or the equivalent of that position for other political parties, from June 18, 1935, to 1993.

(f) Governmental positions: the most important appointive governmental positions on the local, state, and national level. They generally follow in chronological order, and it is not unusual for a person to hold more than one of these positions simultaneously, especially advisory positions in the federal bureaucracy.

(g) Interest group activity: rather broadly defined as union positions and positions in numerous professional and student organizations that have politically oriented activities in Mexico, such as the National Student Federation.

(h) Other positions: lesser governmental positions, private positions that the person may have held, or self-employment, such as his or her own medical or legal practice. This category also includes authorship, significant professional offices, and unusual awards.

(i) Parents, spouses, and friends: relevant personal data, including parents' occupations, when known, as well as information about relatives and friends who may have held governmental positions. Readers should note that any person serving as a private secretary or a secretary general of government has been appointed by a person who has considerable confidence in him or her and, therefore, the mentor should be a significant career contact. These persons, however, appear in the government positions category and their names are not repeated here.

(j) Military experience: career information, with the exception of high-level appointive positions normally thought of as bureaucratic positions in the Secretariat of National Defense (these offices appear in the governmental positions category). An attempt has been made to give the highest rank achieved by the person and the date when he received promotion. This category also includes information about the person's Revolutionary activities, if any.

(k) Miscellaneous information: specifics about the biographee's career from various sources, whether they are strictly informative, complementary, or critical. The author does not necessarily agree with all statements, favorable or unfavorable, presented in this section, but the sources for these statements will be indicated or will be cited in the source section. The purpose of this category is to give the reader more insight into the career of each individual than can be obtained through a perusal of biographical facts, and to repeat evaluations made by official government publications such as *El Nacional* and such highly critical publications as *Por Qué!* or *Proceso.* Also included in this section are statements about any unusual aspects of the biographee's political career.

(l) Additional sources: books, reference works, data banks, government directories, newspapers, and magazines in which additional information about the individual can be found. Most biographical monographs about an individual are not cited, since these are more commonly known and readily available to the reader. Newspaper dates are included because they may indicate that additional information about that person might be found in other newspapers of a corresponding date. The word *letter* indicates that some or all information in the biography was confirmed by the biographee personally, a government agency, or a friend or relative of the biographee, which is true of more than four hundred biographies.

How Persons Were Selected for Inclusion

The two criteria for inclusion were Frank Brandenburg's top six levels of political prestige, with some modifications, as outlined in *The Making of Modern Mexico* (Prentice-Hall, 1964, pp.158–159), and cross-referencing of biographical data in a minimum of two sources, preferably an official government source as well as a private source. Using Brandenburg's categories, the author has concentrated on those positions that are stepping-stones to even more influential positions in Mexico.

As Brandenburg makes quite clear in his classic work, his prestige ladder includes only those persons with *political* prestige; it does not include, for example, business people and religious leaders, although some prominent business people who have become involved in politics are included. Brandenburg includes the following in his list:

1. The Head of the Revolutionary Family. While this person, by Brandenburg's own analysis, may or may not be the President of Mexico, since 1935 every person who has held this position has been President before, during, or after his tenure as Head of the Family.

2. The President of Mexico.

3. Members of the Inner Circle and factional leaders of the Revolution. Persons in this high-prestige category have at one time or another held one of the formal governmental positions making up the following three categories. All persons whom Brandenburg classifies as Inner Circle leaders are labeled as such in the biographies, and all of them are included in this directory.

4. Cabinet members, including the Governor of the Federal District, the Military Chief of Staff, the Private Secretary to the President, managers of major state industries, and directors of large semiautonomous agencies, commissions, banks, and boards. An attempt has been made, where information is available, to include all of these individuals in the biographical section.

5. Governors of the larger states and the federal territories, ambassadors in prestigious posts, regional strongmen not in the Inner Circle, the two presidential legislative spokesmen in the respective Houses of Congress, Military Zone Commanders, and the official-party president.

6. Supreme Court Justices, Senators, Undersecretaries of cabinet minis-

tries, and Assistant Directors of large state industries, commissions, boards, and dependencies; the Secretary General and sector heads of the official party; leaders of major oppositional parties; and the Secretaries General of the major unions. Although senators do not belong in the same categories as undersecretaries, many are included in this book. Entries since the second edition have been selected more carefully based on other career positions, or on their potential for obtaining influential future posts.

The author has broadened his coverage to include other influentials not falling within Brandenburg's categories. Included in both the biographical section and the appendixes are two positions that Brandenburg omits entirely, the rectors of the two major universities in Mexico City, the National Autonomous University (UNAM) and the National Polytechnic Institute (IPN). A number of cabinet-level individuals have held these positions, as well as the directorships of the major schools at UNAM (Law, Economics, and Medicine), either on the way up, between other positions, or after service in the cabinet.

A majority of the individuals who have served as *oficial mayor*, the third-ranked position in cabinet agencies, have been included. Many of the biographees have held an *oficial mayor* position immediately before moving up to a Subsecretaryship, as in the case of President Luis Echeverría Alvarez, who was *oficial mayor* both of Public Education and of the official party, PRI, before becoming Subsecretary of Government in 1958. *Oficiales mayores* may well be filling some of the cabinet positions in later administrations, and, therefore, a concentrated effort has been made to include many of them.

In addition to the broad coverage given to the official party, PRI, and despite a critical lack of information, an attempt was made to include candidates from other parties for higher elective offices. The only opposition parties listed in the appendices are the National Action Party (PAN), the Democratic Revolutionary Party (PRD), the Cardenista Front for National Reconstruction (FNCR), the Authentic Party of the Mexican Revolution (PARM), the Mexican Democratic Party (PDM), and the Popular Socialist Party (PPS). However, presidential candidates and party leaders who have provided opposition to the official party since 1934 and precandidates for president within PRI have been included. All official party presidents have been included in the biographical section.

The appendixes include a large section on Federal Deputies, which Brandenburg relegates to category 9. Because of the rubber stamp function that most Mexicanists attribute to Congress, there has been a tendency to underrate the position of Federal Deputy, even though it provides an important training ground for persons moving up the prestige ladder through elective positions. The author has concentrated on persons who have held a deputyship more than once, or who have held other positions of considerably higher prestige after holding a deputyship. An examination of the biographies included will show that recruitment to Brandenburg's levels 4 and 5 often occurs because of contacts made in the Chamber of Deputies. Deputies definitely rank higher than Ambassadors, Ministers, and Consuls General, which Brandenburg has placed in a lower category, equated with Governors of small and medium-sized states. I also made a special effort to include women in the first two editions, even if they had not achieved quite the same level of political experience as their male counterparts. This is no longer necessary for female deputies or judges, although they still reach fewer top executive posts.

Other positions included in the appendixes are those that appear most often in the career paths of persons reaching the top four categories, positions that serve as stepping-stones to the highest offices in Mexico. For example, with the exception of the Ambassadorship to the United States (a stepping-stone to Secretary of Foreign Relations or Secretary of the Treasury) and the Ambassadorship to the United Kingdom, no specific ambassadorship has consistently had any significance in the career path of public figures. These included such recently important posts as Japan or the European Economic Community. Instead, they have been interim positions for influentials who are on the out or sinecures for persons leaving more influential positions. However, because they have been held repeatedly by high-level government officeholders, ambassadors to the Organization of American States and the United Nations have been added to the third edition. Regional strongmen and Military Zone Commanders who have become Governors, Senators, Deputies, or Cabinet Secretaries have been included. Governors of all states, large and small, have been included in the appendixes, and an attempt has been made to include as many as possible in the biographical section, even though Brandenburg places Governors of small and medium-sized states in category 7.

The second criterion, the cross-referencing of factual data, dictated that no person was included in the biographical section unless the major positions held were cross-referenced in a minimum of two sources, preferably an official government source, as well as a private source. This does not mean that the information contained in the biographies and the appendixes is infallible, since even government sources proved to be inaccurate on occasion, but that no biographical data or listings of positions were included unless the information could be substantiated from other sources. As a result of this and the simple lack of information on some people and positions, more than two hundred people who fitted the political criteria for inclusion in this directory were rejected because of incomplete or unsubstantiated biographies. No biography is included if information was missing for three or more of the career categories. For approximately half of the people in this directory, conflicting information exists about their careers, and the author has had to judge to the best of his ability which facts are the most valid ones.

Source Abbreviations

Academia de Artes	Academia de Artes, *Curricula* (Mexico City: Academia de Artes, 1977)
Acción	*Acción* (Mexico City)
Aguirre	Celso Aguirre Bernal, *Compendio histórico-biográfico de Mexicali, 1539–1966* (Mexicali, 1966)
Alcazar	Marco Antonio Alcazar, *Las agrupaciones patronales en México* (Mexico: El Colegio de México, 1970)
Almanaque	Series of state almanacs published by Almanaque de México, Mexico City, 1981-1982
Alonso	Jorge Alonso, *La Dialéctica Clases-Elites en México* (Mexico: Centro de Investigaciones Superiores del INAH, 1976)
Análisis Político	*Análisis Político*
Anderson	Roger C. Anderson, "The Function of the Governors and Their States in the Political Development of Mexico," unpublished Ph.D. dissertation, University of Wisconsin, 1971
Annals	*Annals of the American Academy of Political and Social Sciences*
Anuario Fin.	*Anuario Financiero* (various years)
Arriola	Carlos Arriola, "Las organizaciones empresariales contemporáneos," in Centro de Estudios Internacionales, *Lecturas de política mexicana* (Mexico: El Colegio de México, 1977)
Baker	Richard D. Baker, *Judicial Review in Mexico* (Austin: University of Texas Press, 1971)
Balboa	Praxedis Balboa, *Apuntes de mi vida* (no publisher)

Basáñez	Miguel Basáñez, *La lucha por la hegemonía en México, 1968–1980* (Mexico: Siglo XXI, 1981)
BdM	Banco de México, *Programa de becas y datos de los becarios* (Mexico, 1961)
Beltrán	Enrique Beltrán, *Medio siglo de recuerdos de un biólogo mexicano* (Mexico: Sociedad Mexicana de Historia Natural, 1977)
Bermúdez	Antonio J. Bermúdez and Octavio Vejar Vázquez, *No dejes crecer la hierba* (Mexico: Costa Amic, 1969)
Bezdek	Robert R. Bezdek, "Electoral Opposition in Mexico: Emergence, Suppression, and Impact on Political Processes," unpublished Ph.D. dissertation, Ohio State University, 1973
Blanco	Félix Blanco, *Poetas mexicanos* (Mexico: Editorial Diana, 1967)
Boletín Bibliográfico	Porrúa, *Boletín Bibliográfico* (various years)
Brandenburg	Frank Brandenburg, *The Making of Modern Mexico* (Englewood Cliffs, N.J.: Prentice-Hall,1964)
Bravo	José Bravo Ugarte, *Efraín González Luna* (Mexico: Acción Nacional, 1968)
Bremauntz	Alberto Bremauntz, *Setenta años de mi vida* (Mexico: Ediciones Jurídico Sociales, 1968)
Cadena Z.	Daniel Cadena Z., *El candidato presidencial, 1976* (Mexico, 1975)
Cambio	*Cambio* (Mexico City weekly)
Campa	Valentín Campa, *Mi Testimonio* (Mexico: Ediciones de Cultura, 1978)
Cardona	Alfredo Cardona Peña, *Semblanzas mexicanas, artistas y escritores del México actual* (Mexico: Libro-Mex, 1955)
Casasola V	Gustavo Casasola, *Seis siglos de historia gráfica de México*, vol. 6 (Mexico: Editorial Gustavo Casasola, 1971)
Castillo	Isidro Castillo, *Indigenistas de México* (Mexico, 1968)
CB	*Current Biography*
C de D	*Directorio de la Cámara de Diputados* (Mexico: Imprenta de la Cámara de Diputados, various years)
C de S	*Directorio* (Mexico: Cámara de Senadores, various years)
CH	*Current History*

Chumacero	Rosalia d'Chumacero, *Perfil y pensamiento de la mujer mexicana* (Editores Mexicanos Unidos, 1974)
Cline	Howard F. Cline, *The United States and Mexico* (New York: Atheneum, 1965)
CN	Colegio Nacional, *Memorias* (various years)
Cole	Ricard R. Cole, "The Mass Media of Mexico," unpublished Ph.D. dissertation, University of Minnesota, 1972
Colín	Mario Colín, *Semblanzas de personajes del estado de México* (Mexico, 1972)
Contreras	Sergio Contreras Cruz, *Mi partido* (Mexico: Ediciones Organización, 1978)
Correa	Eduardo J. Correa, *El balance de Avila Camacho* (Mexico, 1946)
Correa41	Eduardo J. Correa, *El balance de Cardenismo* (Mexico, 1941)
Covarrubias	Ricardo Covarrubias, *Los 67 gobernantes del México independiente* (Mexico: PRI, 1968)
Crowson	Benjamin Franklin Crowson, *Biographical Sketches of the Governors in Mexico* (Washington, D.C.: Crowson International Publishers, 1951)
CyT	Enrique Cordero y Torres, *Diccionario biográfico de Puebla*, 2 vols. (Mexico, 1972)
Daniels	Josephus Daniels, *Shirt-Sleeve Diplomat* (Chapel Hill: University of North Carolina Press, 1947)
DAPC	Presidencia de la República, *Directorio de la administración pública centralizada, 1977* (Mexico, 1977)
DBC	Octavio Gordillo y Ortiz, *Diccionario biográfico de Chiapas* (Mexico: Costa Amic, 1977)
DBGM	Presidencia de la República, *Diccionario biográfico del gobierno mexicano* (Mexico, 1984)
DBGM87	Presidencia de la República, *Diccionario biográfico del gobierno mexicano* (Mexico, 1987)
DBGM89	Presidencia de la República, *Diccionario biográfico del gobierno mexicano* (Mexico, 1989)
DBGM92	Presidencia de la República, *Diccionario*

	biográfico del gobierno mexicano (Mexico, 1992)
DBM68	*Diccionario biográfico de México (1966–1968)* (Monterrey: Editorial Revesa, 1968)
DBM70	*Diccionario biográfico de México (1968–1970)* (Monterrey: Editorial Revesa, 1968)
D de C	*Directorio de la Cámara de Diputados, 1976–79*
D del S	*Diario del Sureste* (Mérida, Yucatán)
D del Y	*Diario del Yucatán* (Mérida, Yucatán)
DEM	Aurora M. Ocampo, *Diccionario de escritores mexicanos* (Mexico: UNAM, 1967)
DGF47	Mexico, Dirección Técnica de Organización, *Directorio del gobierno federal, 1947*
DGF50	Mexico, Dirección Técnica de Organización, *Directorio del gobierno federal, 1950*
DGF51	Mexico, Dirección Técnica de Organización, *Directorio del gobierno federal, 1951*
DGF56	Mexico, Dirección Técnica de Organización, *Directorio del gobierno federal, 1956*
Directorio	Cámara de Diputados, unpublished biographical directory of members, (various years, 1964–1988)
Directorio, 1970–1972	*Directorio general de presuntos diputados al XLVII Congreso de la Unión* (unpublished)
DJBM	*Directorio jurídico biográfico mexicano, 1972* (Mexico: Sociedad Mexicana de Información Biográfica Profesional, 1972)
DNED	*Directorio nacional de economístas* (Mexico, 1959)
DP64	*Diccionario Porrúa* (Mexico: Editorial Porrúa, 1964)
DP70	*Diccionario Porrúa* (Mexico: Editorial Porrúa, 1970)
DPE61	*Directorio del poder ejecutivo, 1961* (Mexico, 1961)
DPE65	*Directorio del poder ejecutivo, 1965* (Mexico, 1965)
DPE71	*Directorio de poder ejecutivo federal, 1971* (Mexico: Secretaria de la presidencia, 1971)
Dromundo	Baltasar Dromundo, *Rojo Gómez* (Mexico, 1946)
Dulles	John W. F. Dulles, *Yesterday in Mexico* (Austin: University of Texas Press, 1961)

EBW46	*Biographical Encyclopedia of the World* (New York: Institute for Research in Biography, 1946)
ELD	Mexico City, *Escuela Libre de Derecho aniversario de su fundación, 1912–22* (Mexico, 1922)
El Día	*El Día* (Mexico City)
El Informador	*El Informador* (Guadalajara)
El Nacional	*El Nacional* (Mexico City)
El Universal	*El Universal* (Mexico City)
Enc. Mex.	*Enciclopedia de México* (Mexico: various years)
Enc. Mex87	*Enciclopedia de México* (Mexico, 1987)
Encinas Johnson	Luis Encinas Johnson, *La alternativa de México* (Mexico: Ediciones Sonot, 1969)
En de E	Mexico City, UNAM, *Escuela Nacional de Economía, Anuario, 1959* (Mexico: UNAM, 1959)
Este País	*Este País* (Mexico City)
Excélsior	*Excélsior* (Mexico City)
Ezcurdia	Mario Ezcurdia, *Miguel de la Madrid* (Mexico: Manuel Porrúa, 1982)
Fuentes Díaz	Vicente Fuentes Díaz, *Los partidos políticos en México* (Mexico: Editorial Altiplano, 1969)
Func.	Sergio Serra Domínguez and Robert Martínez Barreda, *México y sus funcionarios* (Mexico: Litográfico Cárdenas, 1959)
Garrido	Luis Garrido, *El tiempo de mi vida* (Mexico: Porrúa, 1974)
Gaxiola	Francisco Javier Gaxiola, Jr. *El Presidente Rodríguez* (Mexico: Cultura, 1938)
Gaxiola 2	Francisco Javier Gaxiola, *Memorias* (Mexico: Editorial Porrúa, 1975)
G de M	Ricardo Covarrubias, *Los 67 gobernantes del México independiente* (Monterrey, 1965)
G de NL	Ricardo Covarrubias, *Gobernantes de Nuevo León* (Monterrey, 1961)
G de S	Francisco R. Almada, *Diccionario de historia, geografía y biografía sonorenses* (Chihuahua: Empresora Ruiz Sandoval, 1952)
Gil	Carlos Gil, *Hope and Frustration* (Wilmington: Scholarly Resources, 1992)
Glade	William P. Glade Jr. and Charles W. Anderson, *The Political Economy of Mexico* (Madison:

	University of Wisconsin Press, 1963)
Glade & Ross	William P. Glade and Stanley R. Ross, eds. *Críticas constructivas del sistema político mexicano* (Austin: Institute of Latin American Studies, 1973)
G of M	Marvin Alisky, *The Governors of Mexico*, Southwest Studies, Monograph 12 (El Paso: Texas Western College, 1965)
G of NL	Marvin Alisky, *Government of the Mexican State of Nuevo León* (Tempe: Arizona State University, 1971)
G of S	*Guide to the Government of the Mexican State of Sonora* (Tempe: Arizona State University, 1971)
Gómez Maganda	Alejandro Gómez Maganda, *Bocetos presidenciales* (Mexico: Editorial Joma, 1970)
González Navarro	Moises Gónzalez Navarro, *La Confederación Nacional Campesina* (Mexico: Costa Amic, 1968)
Grayson	George Grayson, *The Politics of Mexican Oil* (Pittsburgh: University of Pittsburgh Press, 1980)
Greenberg	Martin H. Greenberg, *Bureaucracy and Development: A Mexican Case Study* (Lexington, Mass.: Heath, 1970)
Gruening	Ernest Gruening, *Mexico and Its Heritage* (New York: D. Appleton-Century, 1928)
Guerra Leal	Mario Guerra Leal, *La grilla* (Mexico: Editorial Diana, 1978)
HA	*Hispano Americano* or *Tiempo*
Haddox	John H. Haddox, *Antonio Caso, Philosopher of Mexico* (Austin: University of Texas Press, 1971)
HAHR	*Hispanic American Historical Review*
HAR	*Hispanic American Report*
Hayner	Norman S. Hayner, *New Patterns in Old Mexico* (New Haven: College and University Press, 1966)
Hernández Chávez	Alicia Hernández Chávez, *Historia de la revolución mexicana, 1934–1940*, vol. 16 (Mexico: El Colegio de México, 1979)
Heroic Mexico	William Weber Johnson, *Heroic Mexico* (New York: Doubleday, 1968)
Hoy	*Hoy*

Hurtado	Javier Hurtado, "Familias, política y parentesco: Jalisco, 1919–1991," unpublished manuscript, University of Guadalajara, 1993.
IEPES	IEPES of PRI, unpublished campaign biographies, 1981
Illescas	Francisco R. Illescas and Juan Bartolo Hernández, *Escritores veracruzanos* (Veracruz, 1945)
Ind. Biog.	Arturo R. Blancas and Tómas L. Vidrio, *Indice biográfico de la XLIII Legislatura Federal* (Mexico, 1956)
Inf. Please	*Information Please!* (New York: Macmillan, various years)
Informe	State of the Union addresses by governors, published by the state government for each year in office
IWW	*International Who's Who* (London: Europa Publications, various years)
Johnson	Kenneth F. Johnson, *Mexican Democracy, A Critical View* (New York: Praeger, 1971)
Johnson, 1978	Kenneth F. Johnson, *Mexican Democracy, A Critical View*, 2nd ed. (New York: Praeger, 1978)
JSH	Jesús Silva Herzog, *Biografías de amigos y conocidos* (Mexico: Cuadernos Americanos, 1980)
Justicia	*Justicia* (legal review) (Mexico City) 1967–1968
Kirk	Betty Kirk, *Covering the Mexican Front* (Norman: University of Oklahoma Press, 1942)
Kirshner	Alan M. Kirshner, "Tomás Garrido Canabal and the Mexican Red Shirt Movement," unpublished Ph.D. dissertation, New York University, 1970
Krauze	Enrique Krauze, *Caudillos culturales en la revolución mexicana* (Mexico: Siglo XXI, 1976)
LAD	*Latin American Digest*
La Jornada	*La Jornada* (Mexico City)
La Nación	*La Nación* (National Action Party publication)
LAT	*Los Angeles Times*
Latin America	*Latin America* (London)
Lehr	Volker G. Lehr, *Manual biográfico del*

	Congreso de la Unión, LII Legislatura (Mexico: UNAM, 1984)
Lemus	George Lemus, "Partido Acción Nacional: A Mexican Opposition Party," unpublished MA thesis, University of Texas, 1956
Letters	Indicates correspondence concerning the biographee from a friend, relatives, state or federal agency, or the biographee himself
Libro Azul	*Blue Book of Mexico* (Mexico, 1901)
Libro de Oro	H. Ruiz Sandoval Jr., *El Libro de oro de México* (Mexico: 1967–1968)
Lieuwen	Edwin Lieuwen, *Mexican Militarism: The Political Rise and Fall of the Revolutionary Army* (Albuquerque: University of New Mexico Press, 1968)
Linajes	Torsten Dahl, ed., *Linajes en México* (Mexico: Casa Editorial de Genealogía Ibero Americana, 1967)
López	José López Escalera, *Diccionario biográfico y de historia de México* (Mexico: Editorial del Magistrado, 1964)
Loret de Mola	Carlos Loret de Mola, *Confesiones de un gobernador* (Mexico: Editorial Grijalbo, 1978)
Loret de Mola, 91	Carlos Loret de Mola, *Los ultimos 91 días* (Mexico: Editorial Grijalbo, 1978)
Mabry	Donald J. Mabry, *Mexico's Acción Nacional* (Syracuse: Syracuse University Press, 1983)
McAlister	Lyle N. McAlister, *The Military in Latin American Socio-Political Evolution: Four Case Studies* (Washington, D.C.: Center for Research in Social Systems, 1970)
Maldonado	Braulio Maldonado, *Baja California, comentarios políticos* (Mexico: Costa-Amic, 1960)
Maples Arce	Manuel Maples Arce, *Soberana juventud* (Madrid: Editorial Plentitud, 1967)
Medina, 20	Luis Medina, *Historia de la revolución mexicana, periodo 1940–1952,* vol. 20 (Mexico: El Colegio de México, 1979)
Mexico Journal	*Mexico Journal* (Mexico City)
Mexiquenses	*Los mexiquenses* (Mexico: Quién es Quién en México, no date)
Meyer, No. 12	Lorenzo Meyer et al., *Historia de la revolución mexicana, periodo 1928–1934,* vol.

	12 (Mexico: El Colegio de México, 1978)
MGF	Mexico, Secretaria de la Presidencia, *Manual de organización del gobierno federal, 1973* (Mexico, 1973)
MGF69	Mexico, Secretaria de la Presidencia, *Manual de organización del gobierno federal, 1969–1970* (Mexico, 1970)
Michaels	Albert L. Michaels, *The Mexican Election of 1940* (Buffalo: Council on International Studies, State University of New York, 1971)
Millon	Robert P. Millon, *Mexican Marxist, Vicente Lombardo Toledano* (Chapel Hill: University of North Carolina Press, 1966)
Moncada	Carlos Moncada, *Años de violencia en Sonora, 1955–1976* (Mexico: Editorial V Siglos, 1977)
Morton	Ward Morton, *Woman Suffrage in Mexico* (Gainesville: University of Florida Press, 1962)
Navarrete	Alfredo Navarrete Martínez, *Alto a la contra-revolución* (Mexico, 1971)
News	*The News* (Mexico City)
Nicholson	Irene Nicholson, *The X in Mexico: Growth within Traditionalism* (London: Faber and Faber, 1965)
Noriega	Raúl Noriega, *Discursos doctrinadas en el congreso constituyente de la revolución mexicana* (Mexico: Instituto Nacional de Estudios Históricos de la Revolución, 1967)
Nov de Yuc	*Novedades de Yucatán* (Mérida, Yucatán)
Novo	Salvador Novo, *La vida en México en el periodo presidencial de Miguel Alemán* (Mexico: Empresas Editoriales, 1967)
Novo35	Salvador Novo, *La vida en México en el periodo presidencial de Lázaro Cárdenas* (Mexico: Empresas Editoriales, 1964)
NYT	*New York Times (The)*
Pacheco	Ciriaco Pacheco Calvo, *La organización estudiantil en México* (Mexico, 1934)
Padgett	L. Vincent Padgett, *The Mexican Political System* (Boston: Houghton Mifflin, 1966)
PdM	*Personalidades de Monterrey* (Nuevo León: Vega y Asociados, 1967)
Peral	Miguel Angel Peral, *Diccionario histórico, biográfico, geográfico e industrial de la*

	república (Mexico: Editorial PAC, 1945?)
Peral47	Miguel Angel Peral, *Diccionario histórico, biográfico, geográfico e industrial de la república* (Mexico: Editorial PAC, 1947)
Peral60	Miguel Angel Peral, *Diccionario histórico, biográfico, geográfico e industrial de la república* (Mexico: Editorial PAC, 1960)
Pérez López	Abraham Pérez López, *Diccionario biográfico hidalguense* (Mexico: Imprenta *Polémica* (April 1969)
Polémica	*Polémica* (April 1969)
Política	*Política*
Por Qué	*Por Qué?*
Proceso	*Proceso*
Protag.	*Los protagonistas* (Mexico: Quién es Quién en México, no date)
PS	Peter Smith, unpublished files
Punto	*Punto*
Q es Q	Carlos Morales Díaz, *Quién es quién en la nomenclatura de la Cuidad de México* (Mexico: Coast Amic, 1971)
Q es QAP	*Quién es quién en la administración pública* (Mexico: Secretaria de la Presidencia, 1982)
Q es QY	*Quién es quién: diccionario biográfico peninsular* (Mérida: Editorial Marina, 1971)
Quién Será	Arturo Gómez Castro, *¿Quién será el futuro presidente de México?* (Mexico, 1963)
Raby	David L. Raby, *Educación y revolución social en México* (Mexico: Secretaria de Educación Pública, 1974)
Rev. de Ejer.	*Revista de Ejercito y Fuerza Aerea*
Richmond	Patricia Richmond, "Mexico: A Case Study of One-Party Politics," unpublished Ph.D. dissertation, University of California, Berkeley, 1965
Ríos	Mario Ríos Villegas and Alexander N. Naime, *Los grupos empresariales en el estado de México* (Toluca: Gobierno del Estado, 1983)
Rodríguez Barragán	Nereo Rodríguez Barragán, *Biografías potosinas* (San Luis Potosí: Biblioteca de Historia Potosina, 1976)
Romero Flores	Jesús Romero Flores, *Maestros y amigos* (Mexico: Costa Amic, 1971)
Ronfeldt	David Ronfeldt, *Atencingo, The Politics of*

	Agrarian Struggle in a Mexican Ejido (Stanford: Stanford University Press, 1973)
Schers	David Schers, "The Popular Sector of the Mexican PRI," unpublished Ph.D. dissertation, University of New Mexico, 1972
Scott	Robert E. Scott, *Mexican Government in Transition* (Urbana: University of Illinois Press, 1964)
Semblanzas	Antonio Armendáriz, *Semblanzas* (Mexico, 1968)
Siempre	*Siempre*
Simpson	Leslie Byrd Simpson, *Many Mexicos* (Berkeley: University of California Press, 1964)
Skirius	John Skirius, *José Vasconcelos y la cruzada de 1929* (Mexico: Siglo XXI, 1978)
Strode	Hudson Strode, *Timeless Mexico* (New York: Harcourt, Brace, 1944)
STYRBIWW	*International Yearbook and Statesmen's Who's Who* (by year)
Tiempo	*Hispano Americano* (Mexican version)
Tiempo Mexicano	Carlos Fuentes, *Tiempo mexicano* (Mexico: Joaquín Mortiz, 1972)
Tirado	Ricardo Tirado Segura, *Las organizaciones empresariales mexicanas* (Mexico: Instituto de Investigaciones Sociales, UNAM, 1979)
Tucker	William P. Tucker, *The Mexican Government Today* (Minneapolis: University of Minnesota Press, 1957)
Urióstegui	Pindaro Urióstegui Miranda, *Testimonios del proceso revolucionario de México* (Mexico: Argrin, 1970)
UTEHA	*Diccionario Enciclopedia UTEHA* (Mexico: UTEHA, 1950)
Vázquez de Knauth	Josefina Vázquez de Knauth, *Nacionalismo y educación en México* (Mexico: El Colegio de México, 1970)
Villaseñor	Victor Manuel Villaseñor, *Memorias de un hombre de izquierda*, 2 vols. (Mexico: Editorial Grijalbo, 1976)
Villaseñor, E.	Eduardo Villaseñor, *Memorias-Testimonio* (Mexico: Fondo de Cultura Económica, 1974)
WB48	*World Biography* (New York: Institute for Research in Biography, 1948)
WB54	*World Biography* (New York: Institute for

	Research in Biography, 1954)
Wences Reza	Rosalio Wences Reza, *El movimiento estudiantil* (Mexico: Editorial Nuestro Tiempo, 1971)
Weyl	Nathanial Weyl and Sylvia Weyl, *The Reconquest of Mexico* (New York: Oxford University Press, 1939)
Wilkie	James Wilkie and Edna Wilkie, *México visto en el siglo XX* (Mexico: Instituto Mexicano de Investigaciones Económicos, 1969)
WNM	Lucien F. Lajoie, *Who's Notable in Mexico* (Mexico, 1972)
Womack	John Womack Jr., *Zapata and the Mexican Revolution* (New York: Knopf, 1968)
WSJ	*Wall Street Journal*
WWLA35	*Who's Who in Latin America* (Stanford: Stanford University Press, 1935)
WWLA40	*Who's Who in Latin America* (Stanford: Stanford University Press, 1940)
WWM45	*Who's Who in Latin America: Mexico* (Stanford: Stanford University Press, 1935)
WWM87	*Who's Who in Mexico* (Washington, D.C.: Worldwide Reference Publications, 1987)
WWMG	Marvin Alisky, *Who's Who in Mexican Government* (Tempe: Arizona State University, 1969)
WWW70-71	*Who's Who in the World, 1970–71*
Zevada	Ricardo J. Zevada, *Calles el presidente* (Mexico: Editorial Nuestro Tiempo, 1971)

Abbreviations Used in the Text

ACJM	Catholic Association of Mexican Youth
CEMLA	Center for Monetary Studies of Latin America
CEN	National Executive Committee
CEPES	Center of Economic, Political and Social Studies (local and regional versions of IEPES)
CNC	National Farmers' Confederation
CNOP	National Federation of Popular Organizations
CONASUPO	National Company of Public Commodities
CONCAMIN	Federation of Chambers of Industry of Mexico
CONDUMEX	Conduit of Mexico
CORDEMEX	(Government enterprise that produces henequen)
CROC	Revolutionary Federation of Workers and Farmers
CROM	Regional Federation of Mexican Workers
CTM	Mexican Federation of Laborers
DTyTF	Federal District and Federal Territories
FSTSE	Federation of Government Employees' Unions
IEPES	Institute of Economic, Political and Social Sciences
IMSS	Mexican Institute of Social Security
IPN	National Polytechnic Institute
ISSSTE	Institute of Security and Social Services for Federal Employees
ITAM	Autonomous Technological Institute of Mexico
ITESM	Monterrey Technological Institute of Higher Studies
NAFIN	Nacional Financiera
NOTIMEX	Mexican News and Information Agency
PAN	National Action Party

PCM	Mexican Communist Party
PDM	Mexican Democratic Party
PEMEX	Petroleos Mexicanos
PFCRN	Cardenist Front for National Reconstruction Party
PIPSA	Producer and Importer of Paper
PMT	Mexican Workers Party
PNR	National Revolutionary Party (1929–1938)
PPS	Popular Socialist Party
PRD	Democratic Revolutionary Party
PRI	Institutional Revolutionary Party
PRM	Party of the Mexican Revolution (1938–1946)
PST	Socialist Workers Party
SITMMRM	Independent Union of Metallurgical Mining Workers
SNTE	National Union of Educational Workers
STFRM	Mexican Railroad Workers Union
STPRM	Mexican Petroleum Workers Union
SUTDDF	Union of the Workers of the Federal District
UNAM	National Autonomous University or National University of Mexico

Mexican Political Biographies, 1935–1993

A

Abarca Alarcón, Raimundo
a-Mar. 4, 1906. b-Chilpancingo,
Guerrero. c-Medical degree, Military
Medical School, Mexico City; Professor of Physics, Chemistry, and
Psychology. d-Mayor of Iguala,
Guerrero, 1949-50; *Governor of
Guerrero*, 1963-69. e-President of PRI
in Iguala, Guerrero; Secretary General
of CNOP of PRI in Guerrero.
f-Director of the Hospital of Iguala.
g-Secretary General of the National
Medical Federation. h-Physician for
the National Railroads of Mexico;
surgeon for the ISSSTE; Chief of
Medical Services for the 27th Military
Zone, Acapulco, Guerrero; President
of the Iguala Red Cross. j-None.
k-None. l-WWMG, 5; DBM68, 1; HA,
10 June 1974, 13.

Abaroa Zamora, América
a-May 11, 1933. b-Colima. c-Primary
studies at the Dr. Miguel Galindo
School, Colima, Colima; public
accounting degree, Autonomous
University of Mexico, Toluca, México.
d-*Plurinominal Deputy* from the PST,
1979-82. e-None. f-None. g-President
of the Executive Council of the Union
of Popular Colonies of Naucalpan,
A.C. j-None. k-None. l-C de D, 1979-
82; Romero Aceves, 681; Protag., 9.

Abascal, Salvador
a-1910. b-Morelia, Michoacán.
c-Primary and secondary studies at
seminary; law degree from the School
of Law, University of Michoacán,
Morelia. d-None. e-Joined the
National Sinarquista Movement, 1934;
head of the National Sinarquista
Union, 1940-41. f-Judge in Ayutla,
Guerrero, 1931-32. g-None. h-None.

i-From an old family of landowners and
miners; father a large landholder and
lawyer. j-None. k-Dismissed as a judge
in 1932 because he tried to uphold the
rights of claimants against the local
bosses. l-Meyer, 40.

Abúndez (Chávez), Benigno
(Deceased 1958) a-Feb. 13, 1880.
b-Xochipala, Jojutla, Morelos. c-Early
education unknown; no degree.
d-*Senator* from the State of Morelos,
1934-40; *Federal Deputy* from the State
of Morelos, Dist. 2, 1955-58, member of
the Committee on Natural Resources,
the Committee on Social Welfare, and
the Committee on National Lands.
e-Founding member of the PNR, 1929;
President of the PNR in Morelos;
President of the Zapatista Front.
f-None. g-Founder of the League of
Agrarian Communities in Morelos.
h-Farmer for many years. j-Joined
Emiliano Zapata's forces under General
Francisco Mendoza Palma, 1911; fought
with Zapata in Morelos until 1918;
reached rank of General under the
Zapatistas; joined the federal army in
1920; rank of Brigadier General, 1920;
incorporated in the First Division under
the command of General *Genovevo de
la O*; commander of the 48th, 51st, and
53rd battalions; commander of the
Legionnaire Division of Morelos.
k-Precandidate for governor of Morelos,
1938. l-Peral, 11; DP70, 4; IndBiog., 7.

Aceves Alcocer, Gilberto
a-June 10, 1921. b-Tototlán, Jalisco.
c-Completed primary, secondary, and
preparatory studies; took some commercial courses, no degree; never taught.
d-*Federal Deputy* from the Federal
District, Dist. 5, 1967-70, member of
the Public Works and the Rules Committees; *Federal Deputy* from the state
of Jalisco, Dist. 7, 1973-76. e-None.

f-Head of the second shift of the guard house, Department of the Federal District, Mexico City. g-Secretary General of the Union of Workers of the Federal District; Secretary of Bureaucratic Action, National Federation of Popular Organizations in the Federal District; Secretary of Social Action of the FSTSE; Secretary of Bureaucratic Action, National Executive Committee, CNOP, 1974-75; *Secretary General of the FSTSE*, 1970-75. i-Married Consuelo Velasco Lara. j-None. k-None. l-HA, 27 Dec. 1971, 24; MGF69, 90; *Excélsior*, 13 Mar. 1973, 13; C de D, 1973-76, 12.

Aceves de Romero, Graciela
a-Sept. 6, 1931. b-Guadalajara, Jalisco. c-Primary studies at the Colegio Calasars, Guadalajara; secondary studies and normal teaching certificate, Eastern Normal School, Guadalajara; completed preparatory studies in premedicine, Preparatory School No. 2, Guadalajara; degree in education, Pedagogical University, Mexico City; teacher at the Rafael Ramírez School, the Chapultepec School, the Michoacán School, the Republic of Uruguay School; Director of the Villanueva School and the Dr. Cruz Gómez Tagle School; Director of the Republic of Birmania School, 1981. d-*Federal Deputy* (Party Deputy from PAN) from the Federal District, Dist. 12, 1967-70; *Federal Deputy* (Party Deputy from PAN) from the Federal District, Dist. 12, 1973-76; *Plurinominal Deputy* from the PAN, 1979-82, member of the Federal District Committee, the Library Committee, the Special Committee for Regulation of Private Schools, and the Foreign Relations Committee. e-Member of PAN, 1950; won first place in PAN oratory contest; candidate of PAN for city council of Guadalajara, 1954; member of regional council of PAN, the

Federal District, 1960; candidate for alternate federal deputy from Dist. 12, the Federal District, 1961, 1964; Secretary of Electoral Affairs of the National Council of PAN. f-None. g-None. i-Married Humberto Romero C., teacher and lawyer. j-None. k-None. l-C de D, 1967-70; C de D, 1973-76; C de D, 1979-82; Aceves Romero, 687-84; Protag., 9.

Aceves Parra, Salvador
a-Apr. 4, 1904. b-La Piedad, Michoacán. c-Primary studies in Guadalajara, Jalisco; secondary studies, Mexico City; preparatory studies at the National Preparatory School in Mexico City, 1920-24; medical degree, National School of Medicine, UNAM; graduate fellow in cardiology, United States (many times); Professor of Medical Pathology, National School of Medicine, UNAM, 1933-69; adviser to many state universities; member of the Governing Council of UNAM, 1964. d-None. e-Active supporter of José Vasconcelos in 1929 presidential campaign. f-Chief of Medical Services, General Hospital, Mexico City, 1938-44; Chief of Medical Services, National Institute of Cardiology, 1944-61; Director of the National Institute of Cardiology, 1961-65; *Subsecretary of Assistance*, 1964-68; *Secretary of Health*, 1968-70. g-President of the Mexican Academy of Medicine. h-Assistant at the Medical Clinic, UNAM, 1934; Director of the Medical Clinic, UNAM, 1934; intern, General Hospital, Mexico City, 1933-36; medical adviser for Internal Medicine, General Hospital, Mexico City, 1936-38. i-Professor of Medicine with *Rafael Moreno Valle* at UNAM; attended UNAM with a number of members of the *Alemán* Generation, including *Manuel Gual Vidal*, Salvador Azuela, *Rogerio de la Selva*, and *Antonio Dovalí*

Jaime; close friend of *Antonio Armendáriz* at UNAM; married Carmen García Cuadra; son of José M. Aceves, a farmer, and María Parra. j-None. k-None. l-DBM68, 3-4; *Hoy,* 25 Oct. 1969, 17; HA, 7 Aug. 1944, 7; letters.

Aceves Saucedo, Angel
a-Nov. 12, 1940. b-Izúcar de Matamoros, Puebla. c-Early education unknown; economics studies at the National School of Economics, UNAM, 1961-65, graduating with an honorary mention, 1967; MA in economics, New York University, Magna Cum Laude, on a United Nations Scholarship, 1969; Ph.D. in economics, New York University, Magna Cum Laude, 1970; Professor of Finances and Economic Development, National School of Economics, UNAM, 1966-67; Coordinator of Economics, School of Business and Administration, UNAM, 1970-71; Coordinator of the Seminar of Public Sector Economics, National School of Economics, UNAM, 1972-74. d-*Federal Deputy* from the State of Puebla, Dist. 1, 1979-82; *Senator* from the State of Puebla, 1982-88; *Plurinominal Federal Deputy,* 1991-1994. e-Subdirector of the IEPES of the CEN of PRI, 1981-82; *Secretary of the IEPES of the CEN of PRI,* 1982-88. f-Chief of Statistical and Mathematical Analysis, Secretariat of the Treasury, 1965-66; general adviser, Oficial Mayor, Secretariat of Industry and Commerce, 1970-71; adviser, Secretariat of Industry and Commerce, 1971; general coordinator, Oficial Mayor, Department of the Federal District, 1971-72; general coordinator, Department of the Federal District, 1988-91. g-President of the League of Revolutionary Economists, 1980-82. h-None. i-Son of businessman Angel Aceves Ayala and Celia Saucedo García; married Gloria Hernández Cota.

j-None. k-None. l-DBGM87, 424; Lehr, 376; C de D, 1979-82; C de S, 1982-88; DBGM, 459; DBGM89, 15.

Aconsta Reyes, Ricardo Guadalupe
a-Dec. 12, 1951. b-Mexico City. c-Early education unknown; economics degree from the Higher School of Economics, IPN; Professor of the Economic History of Mexico and Social Science Methods, IPN; Technical Subdirector, Department of Applied Economics, IPN; Director, Department of Applied Economics, IPN. d-None. e-Joined the Mexican Communist Party (PCM), 1977; cofounder of PSUM delegation, education committee; candidate of the PSUM for federal deputy from the Federal District, Dist. 8, 1982. f-None. g-None. h-None. j-None. k-None. l-*El Día, Metropoli,* 26 May 1982, 6; HA, 19 Apr. 1982, IV.

Acosta García, Isauro
a-June 11, 1899. b-Ursulo Galván, Municipio de San Carlos, Veracruz. c-Completed primary studies; no degree. d-Local Deputy to the 32nd State Legislature of Veracruz; *Senator* from the State of Veracruz, 1952-58; member of the Committee on Industries and the Committee on Small Agricultural Properties; alternate member of the Economy and Statistics Committee. e-None. f-None. g-Began agrarian activities as an organizer in Chixicastle, Municipio de Puente Nacional, Veracruz, 1918; organizer for agrarian unions, 1918-20; cofounder with Ursulo Galván of the League of Agrarian Communities, 1923; cofounder of the National Peasant League with Ursulo Galván and leader of that organization, 1926-30; President of the League of Agrarian Communities of Veracruz, 1928-30, 1943-44; representative of the League of Agrarian Communities of Veracruz before the Mixed Agrarian

Commission. h-Campesino at the age of 16. j-Soldier in the 86th Line Battalion in opposition to the Adolfo de la Huerta rebellion, 1923. k-Elected as the alternate senator but replaced *Roberto Amoros* who resigned his senate seat to become director general of the National Railroads, 1952. l-DGF56, 8, 10, 11, 14; Ind. Biog., 8.

Acosta Jiménez, Fermín
a-Dec. 5, 1925. b-San Luis Potosí, San Luis Potosí. c-Primary studies in San Luis Potosí and Cuautla, Morelos, 1931-38; secondary studies in Mexico City and Cuernavaca at a private school, 1940-43; student at the Military Aviation School, graduating as a corporal in aviation mechanics, May 1, 1946; enrolled Military Aviation School, 1947, graduating as a pilot and 2nd Lieutenant, Aug. 1, 1949; enrolled Higher War College, 1954, graduating with a diploma in staff and command, Feb. 5, 1956; advanced course, Higher War College, 1975; Professor of Logistics, Higher War College, 1967; Professor, Air College, 1975; Director, Special Military Air Force School, 1971-77. d-None. e-None. f-*Director, Department of the Air Force*, 1988-91. g-None. h-None. i-Son of Simón Acosta Badillo, self-employed worker, and Ana María Jiménez Movsiváes; married Enriqueta Cortés Munguía. j-Joined the 1st Battalion, 8th Infantry Regiment, Jan. 1944; Corporal of Conscripts, Mar. 1, 1944; member of the 205th squadron, 1950-54; rank of 1st Lieutenant, Nov. 20, 1953; rank of 2nd Captain, Nov. 20, 1956; attached to the Air Force staff headquarters, 1956-58; rank of 1st Captain, Nov. 20, 1959; member of the 1st Air Group, 1958-59; attached to the Air Force staff headquarters, 1959-60; Commander of 205th air squadron, 1960-61; Commander of the 202nd jet squadron, 1961-65; rank of Major, Nov.

20, 1963; Chief, Section Four, Air Force Staff, 1965-69; rank of Lt. Colonel, Nov. 20, 1965; Assistant Chief of Staff, Air Force, 1969-71; rank of Colonel, Nov. 20, 1971; rank of Brigadier General, 1977; Commander of the 9th Air Base, 1978; Commander of the 4th Air Group, 1978-79; rank of Brigade General, 1979; Commander of the 2nd Air Base, Ixtepec, Oaxaca, 1979-81; of the 7th Air Base, Piedela Cuesta, Guerrero, 1981-83; of the 5th Air Base, Zapopan, Jalisco, 1983-84; and of the 8th Air Base, Mérida, Yucatán, 1985-88; rank of Division General, 1985. k-None. l-Rev. de Ejer., Nov. 1971, 40; Rev. de Ejer., Nov. 1975, 85; DBGM89, 16; Rev. de Ejer., Dec. 1979, 68.

Acosta Lagunes, Agustín
a-Dec. 31, 1929. b-Paso de Ovejas, Veracruz. c-Primary studies at the Enrique C. Rebsamen School, Jalapa, Veracruz; secondary and preparatory studies at the Preparatory School of Jalapa; economic studies at the National School of Economics, UNAM, 1952-58, completing his thesis on "Considerations over and Economic Analysis of Enterprises," Jan. 25, 1966; postgraduate work at New York University and in Geneva, Switzerland, in administration and control over state and private enterprises on a United Nations Fellowship; Professor of International Trade, National School of Economics, UNAM, 1958-66; director of a seminar on foreign trade, National School of Economics, UNAM, 1965-67. d-*Governor of Veracruz*, 1980-86. e-None. f-Analyst, Economic Studies Department, National Bank of Mexico and the Bank of Mexico, 1959-64; Controller General, National Bonded Warehouses; Subdirector of Control, Board of Governors, Decentralized and State Agencies, Secretariat of Government Properties, 1964-66; Director

General of Acquisitions, Inspection Department, Secretariat of Government Properties, 1966-71; adviser to *José López Portillo*, Subsecretary of National Patrimony, 1971-72; general manager of Light and Power of the Center, S.A., 1972-74; fiduciary delegate of NAFIN, 1977-79; Director General of the Mint, Secretariat of the Treasury, 1978-79; *Subsecretary of Investigation of the Secretariat of the Treasury*, 1979-80. g-Adviser to the Busdrivers Alliance. h-Economist and consultant to Cementos Anahuac, S.A., 1974-76. i-Member of the "Gónzalez Aparicio" Group under *Emilio Mújica Montoya* at UNAM; married Esperanza Azcón; brothers, Rafael and Florencio, cattle ranchers. j-None. k-None. l-*Excélsior*, 8 Apr. 1980, 23A; Almanaque de México, 421; *Excélsior*, 7 June 1979, 5; letter; *Proceso*, 1 Feb 1982, 13-15; Protag., 10.

Acosta Romo, Fausto
a-Oct. 20, 1915. b-Sonora. c-Primary studies in Hermosillo; normal degree; law degree National School of Law, UNAM, 1937, with a thesis on "The Strike Law and Obligatory Arbitration in Our Social Law." d-*Senator* from the State of Sonora, 1952-58, member of the Committee on Immigration, the Health Committee, the Third Labor Committee, the Second Balloting Committee; substitute member of the Tax Committee, the National Waters and Irrigation Committee, and the Livestock Committee. e-PRI campaigner; President of PNR in Sonora; general delegate of PRI to Jalisco and Querétaro; directed *Juan C. Gorráez's* gubernatorial campaign, 1955. f-*Assistant Attorney General of Mexico* (2), 1964-66; Secretary General of Government of the State of Sonora under Governor *Ignacio Soto*, 1949-52; Acting Governor of Sonora, Aug.-Sept. 1951; Gerente of Comisiones and Servicios, S.A., an agency of

CONASUPO. g-None. h-Practicing lawyer, El Aguila Petroleum Company; Director of the Legal Department, Director of the Trust Department, National Bank of Ejido Credit, Ciudad Obregón, Sonora; lawyer for PEMEX, 1938. i-Classmate of *Antonio Rocha Cordero*. j-None. k-Precandidate for governor of Sonora on the PRI ticket, 1961 and 1967; according to Roger Anderson he was the choice of national PRI leaders for governor in 1961, but was unpopular among state leaders. l-WWMG, 5; DPE65, 209; HA, 21 Dec. 1964, 10; DGF51, I,92; Anderson, 112-3; Ind. Biog., 9-10; Moncada, 56.

Acosta Velasco, Ricardo
(Deceased Jan. 13, 1978) a-May 11, 1908. b-Molango, Hidalgo. c-Engineering agronomy degree, National School of Agriculture, San Jacinto, Federal District, 1927; studied at the TVA, United States, 1947-51; advanced studies in irrigation at the National School of Agriculture, Chapingo, México. d-*Federal Deputy* from the State of Guanajuato, Dist. 3, 1940-43; member of the Great Committee of the Justice Committee. e-Technical adviser to *Octaviano Campos Salas* for the IEPES of PRI and author of special projects for PRI; in charge of developing an agricultural program for presidential candidate *Adolfo Ruiz Cortines*; collaborated in developing an agricultural program for presidential candidate *Gustavo Díaz Ordaz*. f-Member of the Technical Board, National Irrigation Commission, 1929; Director of the Technical Board of the CNI for the State of Morelos, 1929-33; Director of the National Office of Agrarian Organizations of the Federal District, 1933-34; Director General of the Mexican Agrarian Organizations, Department of Agrarian Affairs, 1934; delegate of the Department of Agrarian Affairs, 1938;

delegate of the Department of Agrarian Affairs in San Luis Potosí, 1939; organizer and Technical Director of the National Maíz Commission, 1946-47; technical adviser, National Sugar Cane Commission, 1951-52; Director General of Agriculture, Secretariat of Agriculture and Livestock, 1952-59; technical adviser to Psytonsyo del Maguey, 1961; *Subsecretary of Agriculture*, 1964-70. g-None. h-Author of several articles on agrarian subjects. i-Father-in-law of Joaquín Pría Olavarrieta, president of CANACINTRA, 1978; married to Emma Brambila. j-None. k-None. l-WWMG,5; DGF56, 224; DBM68, 5-6; HA, 4 Jan. 1965, 28; DGF50, 160; DGF51,II,231.

Adato de Ibarra, Victoria
a-Feb. 11, 1929. b-Tuxpan, Veracruz. c-Early education unknown; law degree, National School of Mexico, UNAM, with an honorable mention, 1962; Professor of Procedural Law, National School of Law, UNAM, 1960-63, 1966-83; Professor of Procedural Law, Anahuac University, 1970-83; Professor of Procedural Law, Technical Institute of the Attorney General of the Federal District, 1971-74. d-None. e-None. f-Agent of the Ministerio Público, Attorney General of the Federal District, 1963-65; Agent of the Ministerio Público, 8th Judicial District, Federal District, 1965-66; Penal Judge, 10th Judicial District, Federal District, 1969-74; Subdirector of the Technical Institute, Attorney General of the Federal District, 1971-73; Subdirector of Training, Prison Personnel Center for the Federal District, 1973-74; Judge of the Higher Tribunal of Justice of the Federal District, 1974-76, 1982; 2nd Assistant Attorney General of the Federal District, 1976-82; *Attorney General of the Federal District*, 1982-85; *Justice of the Supreme Court*, 1985-

88, 1988- . g-None. h-None. i-Daughter of José Adato Ynsunza, businessman, and Consuelo Green Sosa. j-None. k-None. l-Informe, 75-76; *Excélsior*, 1 Dec. 1982, 34; *The News*, 2 Dec. 1982; HA, 13 Dec. 1982, 18; DBGM89, 587; DBGM, 17.

Agramont Cota, Félix
a-1917. b-La Paz, Baja California del Sur. c-Primary studies at the Escuela Emiliano Zapata; secondary and normal studies at the Escuela Normal Rural de Todos Santos, 1933-37; agricultural engineering degree, Aug. 1945, National School of Agriculture, 1939-45; received recognition as one of the outstanding students in the field of agricultural research. d-*Governor of Baja California del Sur*, 1970-75. e-None. f-Technical Subdirector of the Productora Nacional de Semillas, 1961-70; General Agent for the Secretary of Agriculture and Livestock in Jalisco, 1958-60; Administrator of the National Commission of Maíz. g-None. h-Worked on the ejido "El Pescador" as a child; recipient of a Rockefeller Foundation Study Grant for research on seed production, 1947. j-None. k-President *Echeverría* was present at Governor Agramont Cota's first state of the union message in 1972. l-*Hoy*, 26 Dec. 1970, 5; HA, 13 Dec. 1971, 35; HA, 7 Dec. 1970, 20; letter.

Aguilar Alvarez, Ernesto
a-Jan. 25, 1910. b-Tacubaya, Federal District. c-Primary studies at the Colegio Luz Saviñón; secondary studies at the Colegio Francés Morelos; preparatory at the National Preparatory School, Mexico City; law degree, National School of Law, UNAM, Aug. 10, 1933; Professor of Civic Education, National Preparatory School, 1938-66; Professor of Mercantile Law, School of Commerce and Administration, UNAM, 1938-66;

Professor of Amparo, UNAM, 1938-66. d-None. f-Executor Judge, Ninth District, Dec. 1, 1933; Judge of the Higher Tribunal of Justice, State of Veracruz; Judge of the First Instance; Magistrate of the Higher Tribunal of Justice of the Federal District; President of the Higher Tribunal of Justice of the Federal District; Magistrate of the Collegiate Tribunal, First Circuit; *Justice of the Supreme Court*, 1966-77. g-None. h-Member of the Mexican delegation to the United Nations Meeting, San Francisco, 1945. i-Knew *Antonio Luna Arroyo* at the National School of Law; attended secondary school with President *López Mateos*. j-None. k-None. l-*Justicia*.

Aguilar (Castillo), Magdaleno
a-July 22, 1900. b-Rancho de la Reforma, Municipio de Juamave, Tamaulipas. c-Completed second grade at a rural primary school, no degree. d-Local Deputy to the State Legislature of Tamaulipas, 1938; *Senator* from Tamaulipas, 1946-52; member of the Gran Comisión, member of the Committees on the Agrarian Department and Agricultural Development, member of the First Balloting Committee and substitute member of the Committee on Foreign and Domestic Commerce; *Governor of Tamaulipas*, 1940-45; *Senator* from Tamaulipas, 1964-70. e-Member of the 1929 delegation from Tamaulipas to select a presidential candidate; *Secretary of Agrarian Action of the CEN of PRI*, 1953-59, 1959-64; chief of *Alemán*'s campaign for President in the state of Tamaulipas, 1945. f-None. g-President of the Executive Agrarian Committee responsible for receiving presidential resolutions for the ejidos of La Libertad and La Misión, 1925; First Secretary of the League of Agrarian Communities and Farmer Unions of Tamaulipas, 1926; President

of that union, 1927-28, 1934; Secretary of Organization of the CNC. h-Adviser to the National Bank of Agricultural Credit, 1928-29. i-Political supporter of *Emilio Portes Gil* early in his career; son of Gil Aguilar, an ejidatario, and Marcelina Castillo. j-None. k-Considered for Secretary General of the CNC, 1962. l-HA, 26 Nov. 1943, 15; HA, 18 Aug. 1942, 14; HA, 15 Dec. 1944, IV; DBM68, 9; DGF51, I, 89, 10-12; Enc. Mex., I, 214; WWMG, 5; Peral, 18; letter; López 23; Navarro, 232.

Aguilar Chávez, Salvador
b-Zacatecas, Zacatecas. c-Engineering degree, National School of Engineering, UNAM, 1936. d-None. e-None. f-Subdirector of Construction, Director of Construction, National Irrigation Commission; Director of Fincas in the Secretariat of Public Works; Director of Railroads in the Secretariat of Public Works; Comptroller General of the Secretariat of Hydraulic Resources, 1952-58; *Subsecretary of Hydraulic Resources*, 1964-70. g-None. h-Construction engineer, public works projects; Assistant to the Superintendent of Construction, Marte R. Gómez Dam; President of the Mexican Association of Engineers and Architects, 1973-74. i-Married Elvira Leal. j-None. k-None. l-HA, 21 Dec. 1964, 4; DGF56, 413; HA, 26 Mar. 1973, 25.

Aguilar González, Francisco
(Deceased Mar. 17, 1972) a-1895. b-Ixmiquilpan, Hidalgo. c-Early education unknown; graduated, Heroic Military College; professor, Heroic Military College. d-None. e-None. f-Minister to Japan and China, 1935-38; *Ambassador to France*, 1940-42; Ambassador to Portugal, 1944-45; Ambassador to Sweden, 1945-46; Ambassador to China, 1947-52; Ambassador to Brazil; Ambassador to Argen-

tina, 1956-58; rank of Special Ambassador. g-None. h-None. i-First cousin of Francisco I. Madero. j-Career army officer; joined army 1920; observer, French Army; Military Attaché to Washington, D.C.; Military Attaché to Stockholm, Sweden; Military Attaché to Rome, Italy; Subdirector, Department of the Navy; rank of Brigade General, Nov. 1940; rank of Division General, 1950. k-None. l-Perez López, 21; PS.

Aguilar Hernández, Francisco
a-July 10, 1924. b-Pachuca, Hidalgo. c-Primary studies in the Melchor Ocampo School, Hidalgo; secondary studies at the University of Guanajuato; preparatory studies at the National Preparatory School; medical degree from the National School of Medicine, UNAM. d-*Senator* from the State of Morelos, 1970-76, President of the Small Agricultural Property Committee and the Third Labor Committee, Second Secretary of the Insurance Committee, First Secretary of the Health Committee. e-Secretary of Popular Action of PRI in Morelos; Delegate of PRI. f-Representative of the IMSS in Morelos; President of the IMSS, Cuernavaca, Morelos. g-Secretary General of the CNOP in Morelos; delegate of the SNTSE; leader of CNOP in the State of Hidalgo. h-Employee of the Green Cross, 1949-50; practicing physician. j-None. k-None. l-C de S, 1970-76, 71.

Aguilar Irungaray, José I.
a-1908. b-Palau, Coahuila. c-Early education unknown; no degree. d-Mayor of Chihuahua, Chihuahua, 1940-41; Mayor of Hidalgo del Parral, Chihuahua, 1952-53; *Federal Deputy* from the State of Chihuahua, Dist. 2, 1961-64, member of the Committee on Mines; *Senator* from the State of Chihuahua, 1970-76, member of the Gran Comisión, President of the First

Committee on Mines, Second Secretary of the Colonization and First Tariff and Trade Committees, First Secretary of the Government Properties Committee, and alternate member of the Immigration Committee. e-President of PRI in State of Chihuahua; general delegate of the CEN of PRI. f-Director of the state penitentiary of Chihuahua, 1956-58; President of the Federal Arbitration Board, Chihuahua, 1965-70. g-Secretary General of the Miners Union, 1942-43. h-None. k-None. l-PS; C de D, 1961-63, 5, 69; C de S, 1970-76, 9, 69.

Aguilar Marañón, Hesiquio
a-Feb. 4, 1918. b-Córdoba, Veracruz. c-Primary studies in Córdoba; studied briefly at the Heroic Military College, Mexico City; law degree, National School of Law, UNAM, 1942; special studies in labor law, Sorbonne, Paris. d-*Federal Deputy* from the State of Veracruz, Dist. 8, 1955-58, member of the Colonization Committee, the Legislative Studies Committee (first year), the Military Justice Committee, and the Foreign Relations Committee; *Federal Deputy* from the State of Veracruz, 1967-70. e-Participant in the presidential campaign of *Adolfo Ruiz Cortines*. f-Agent of the federal Ministerio Público; Judge of the First Instance, Veracruz, Veracruz; Private Secretary to *Cándido Aguilar* as Senator, 1934-40; member of the Mexican delegation to the United Nations, 1950-52; Director, Department of Statistics and Publicity, State of Veracruz. g-None. h-Trained as an airline pilot; graduated from the Air Academy, Los Angeles, California; prominent columnist, *Excélsior*. i-Nephew of *Cándido Aguilar*, son-in-law of President Carranza; son of Silvestre Aguilar, constitutional deputy from Veracruz; son, *Hesiquio Aguilar de la Parra*, served as federal deputy

from Veracruz, Dist. 8, 1979-82; married Guadalupe de la Parra López. j-Rank of Lt. Colonel in the military justice system. l-PS; DGF56, 29, 31, 33, 35, 37; MGF69, 96; Ind. Biog., 11; Protag., 12; DBGM, 19.

Aguilar Olvera, Belisario
a-July 10, 1938. b-Jacala, Hidalgo. c-Secondary studies at the Prevocational No. 2, IPN; vocational studies at Vocational School No. 2, IPN; engineering degree, Higher School of Mechanical and Electrical Engineering, IPN, 1960-64; professor, IPN, 1976-79. d-*Federal Deputy* (PPS Party Deputy), 1973-76; *Plurinominal Deputy* from the PPS, 1979-82, 1988-91. e-Joined the PPS, 1959; Director of the Popular Socialist Youth in the Federal District, 1961-62; Secretary of Organization of the Popular Socialist Youth, 1962; Secretary General of the Popular Socialist Youth, 1966; candidate for federal deputy from the State of Hidalgo, Dist. 5, 1966; Member of the Central Committee of the PPS, 1970-89; Oficial Mayor of the Central Committee of the PPS, 1970; Director of the PPS in the Federal District, 1970-89; candidate for senator from the Federal District, 1976. f-None. g-Student leader, 1948-55, IPN. h-Unknown. i-Son of Juan Aguilar Castillo, businessman, and Salustia Olvera Trejo; married Beatriz Eugenia Fernández Vázquez, normal teacher. j-None. k-None. l-Protag., 13; Directorio, 1973-76; C de D, 1979-82; DBGM89, 389.

Aguilar Pico, Rigoberto
(Deceased June 27, 1974) a-June 2, 1906. b-Mazatlán, Sinaloa. c-Primary studies in Mazatlán; medical degree, National School of Medicine, UNAM, 1930, with a specialty in pediatrics; specialized studies in pediatrics, Paris, Bordeaux, Hamburg, and Berlin;

Professor of Clinical Pediatrics, National School of Medicine, UNAM. d-None. e-None. f-*Substitute Governor of Sinaloa*, Feb. 28, 1953, to Dec. 31, 1956. g-None. h-Founding Director, Dolores Sáinz Infant Hospital; Chief of Services, Infant Hospital of Mexico, 1937-57. i-Son of General José Aguilar B.; brother of Saúl Aguilar Pico, law graduate of the National School of Law, 1932, and Superior Court Justice of Sinaloa, 1950s to 1970s; married Clotilde Bernal. j-None. k-He was not a militant party member when selected as governor to replace *Enrique Pérez Arce*. l-DGF56, 100; HA, 2 Sept. 1953, 18; HA, 26 Sept. 1952; HA, 6 Mar. 1953, 12-13; Peral 60, 149; *Excélsior*, 29 June 1974, 2; WNM, 3.

Aguilar Talamantes, Rafael
a-Oct. 24, 1940. b-Mulegé, Santa Rosalia, Baja California del Sur. c-Early education unknown; studies in economics, National School of Economics, UNAM, 1958-62; studies in law, National School of Law, UNAM, 1971-76; no degree. d-*Plurinominal Federal Deputy* from the PST, 1982-85; *Plurinominal Federal Deputy* from the PFCRN, 1988-91. e-Principal organizer and Director of the National Center of Democratic Students of the Mexican Communist Party; member of the People's Electoral Front; member of the PCM; founder and ideologue of the PST, 1978; Secretary General of the PST, 1975-76; President of the PST, 1979-87; President of the Cardenista Front for National Reconstruction Party (PFCRN), 1988-f-None. g-Involved in various student movements in Baja California del Sur, Chihuahua, Durango, Puebla, and Michoacán. i-Son of Marino Mercante, railroad fireman; mother a miner's daughter. j-None. k-Convicted of property damage to the nation, 1966; imprisoned in Morelia,

Michoacán; expelled from the presidency of the PST, 1987. l-Directorio, 1982-85; C de D, 1982-85; *Excélsior*, 24 June 1981, 12B; HA, 11 Apr. 1987, 18; DBGM89, 389; Lehr, 569.

Aguilar (Vargas), Candido
(Deceased Mar. 19, 1960) a-Feb. 12, 1888. b-Congregación de Palma y Monteros, Veracruz. d-Governor of Veracruz, June 20, 1914, to June 24, 1917; Deputy to the Constitutional Convention of 1917; First Vice President of the Convention; *Senator* from Veracruz, 1934-40; *Federal Deputy*, Dist. 8 from Veracruz, 1943-46. e-President of the Party of the Revolution, 1951. f-Secretary of Foreign Relations from Feb. 4, to Nov. 9, 1918; Confidential Ambassador to the United States and Europe, 1919. g-Founder of the League of Agrarian Communities in Veracruz. h-Milkman before the Revolution. i-Son-in-law of President Carranza; married Virginia Carranza; brother of *Silvestre Aguilar*; uncle of *Hesiquio Aguilar Marañón*, federal deputy from Veracruz, 1967-70; great-uncle of *Hesiquio Aguilar de la Parra*, federal deputy from Veracruz, l979-82. j-Joined the anti-Reelectionist movement under Francisco I. Madero in 1910, served under General Gavira and became a Constitutionalist in 1913; served as a Chief of Operations, but left the army after President Carranza was killed; rank of Division General, 1944; Commander of the Legion of Honor, 1950. k-Remained loyal to Carranza; joined the de la Huerta rebellion in 1923 and was exiled; lived in San Antonio, Texas, 1920-25; publicized the corruption in the PRM and was thrown out of the official party on June 10, 1944; went into self-exile in Cuba and El Salvador, 1952-54; imprisoned for political reasons in Veracruz, 1952. l-Peral 47, 5-6, DP70, 35, letter, Gruening, 584, UTEHA, 284; Correa, 238; López, 21.

Aguilar (Vargas) Jr., Silvestre
(Deceased 1955) a-1914. b-Córdoba, Veracruz. c-Primary studies in Córdoba, Veracruz, and San Antonio, Texas; secondary studies in St. Louis and Chicago; law degree, School of Law, University of Veracruz, Jalapa. d-Deputy to the Constitutional Convention from the State of Veracruz, Dist. 11, 1916-1917; *Federal Deputy* from the State of Veracruz, Dist. 9, 1937-40; *Federal Deputy* from the State of Veracruz, Dist. 6, 1943-46; *Federal Deputy* from the State of Veracruz, Dist. 9, 1949-51, member of the Committee on Forest Affairs, the Library Committee, the First Balloting Committee, and Executive Secretary of the First Instructive Committee for the Grand Jury. e-None. f-Employee of the Secretariat of Government; Oficial Mayor of the State of Veracruz under Governor *Jorge Cerdán*, 1940-43; Treasurer of Veracruz, 1946. i-Brother of *Cándido Aguilar*, son-in-law of Venustiano Carranza, and Senator from Veracruz, 1934-40; son, *Hesiquio Aguilar Marañón*, was a federal deputy from Veracruz, 1967-70; grandson, *Hesiquio Aguilar de la Parra*, was a federal deputy from Veracruz, 1979-82. k-In exile in the United States and Cuba, 1920. l-Peral, 20; C de D, 1937-40, 5; C de D, 1943-46, 5; C de D, 1949-51, 61; DGF51, 26, 30, 34.

Aguilar y Maya, Guillermo
b-Guanajuato. c-Law degree, National School of Law, UNAM, Nov. 1935, with a thesis on a critique on crimes pursued in guerrilla warfare. d-*Federal Deputy*, State of Guanajuato, Dist. 7, 1943-44. e-None. f-Justice of the Higher Tribunal of Justice of the Federal District, 1946-52; *Attorney General of the Federal District and Federal Territories*, 1952-56; President of the National Council of Unrenewable Resources, 1956-58. g-None. i-Brother of *José*

Aguilar y Maya; father was a small landowner. j-None. k-None. l-DGF56, 502; D de Y, 2 Dec. 1952, l; DGF51, I, 487; HA, 10 Dec. 1956, 5; HA, 5 Nov. 1956.

Aguilar y Maya, José
(Deceased Nov. 30, 1966) a-July 28, 1897. b-Jerécuaro, Guanajuato. c-Primary, secondary, and preparatory; Seminario de Morelia, Michoacán, and Colegio de Guanajuato; law degree, National School of Law, UNAM; Professor of Spanish and Literature, Preparatory School, Guanajuato; Professor of General Theory and of Public Law, UNAM, for ten years, during which he gained national recognition; head, Department of Justice and Public Instruction, Guanajuato. d-Federal Deputy, State of Guanajuato, 1924-26, 1926-28, 1928-30; *Federal Deputy*, State of Granajuato, Dist. 7, 1937-40; *Governor of Guanajuato*, 1949-55. e-None. f-Attorney General of DFyTF, 1928; Attorney General of DFyTF, 1930-32; *Attorney General of Mexico*, 1940-46, 1955-58. g-None. h-Director General of Seguros de México, S.A., 1948; author of many works and emergency war legislation for President *Avila Camacho*. i-Brother of *Guillermo Aguilar y Maya*; friend of Senator Enrique Colunga, who was governor of Guanajuato, 1923-27, and minister of government under President Obregón; married María Tinajero; father was a small landowner. j-None. k-Attributes his nomination as governor of Guanajuato to teaching students who later became pivotal men in the Mexican political system; leader of political faction in Guanajuato known as the "Reds"; supported candidacy of *Ernesto Hidalgo* as governor, 1943. l-WWM45, 1; HA, 18 Feb. 1957, 6; HA, 28 Sept. 1953; DP, 38; Gruening, 429; DGF51, I, 89, 487; Peral, 18-19; STYRBIWW54, 573; Enc. Mex., I, 214-

15; UTEHA, 286; WWLA35, 16; López, 25; Anderson, 85-86.

Aguilar y Salazar, Manuel
(Deceased 1959) a-1892. b-Sitacoyoapan, Oaxaca. c-Primary at Sitacoyoapan; secondary studies in Puebla; law degree, Institute of Arts and Sciences in Oaxaca, Oaxaca; Professor of Law at the Institute of Arts and Sciences; director of various private schools. d-Deputy to the Constitutional Convention, 1917; *Federal Deputy* from Oaxaca, Dist. 3, 1952-55, member of congressional committees on livestock and the Second Committee on Justice. f-Agent of the Ministerio Público for the Federal Attorney General in Oaxaca; Chief of the Department of Justice of the State of Oaxaca; consulting lawyer to the state government of Oaxaca. g-None. h-Practicing lawyer. j-None. k-Member of the National Action Party. l-C de D, 1952-54; Morton, 67; DP70, 2360.

Aguilera Alvarez, Cosme
a-Sept. 1, 1900. b-Puebla, Puebla. c-Primary, secondary, and preparatory studies, Puebla; accounting degree. d-Local deputy to the state legislature of Puebla (twice); *Federal Deputy* from the State of Puebla, Dist. 4, 1943-46; *Federal Deputy* from the State of Puebla, Dist. 5, 1967-70. e-Member of PRI. f-Tax collector; director, Department of Government and Justice, State of Puebla; Treasurer General of the State of Puebla; General Coordinator of the literacy program, Puebla. g-None. h-None. i-Married Bertha Davis. j-First Captain, Constitutional Army. k-Companion of *Gustavo Díaz Ordaz* as a federal deputy, 1943-46. l-MGF69, 94; PS, C de D, 1943-46, 5.

Aguilera Dorantes, Mario
a-Aug. 15, 1907. b-Oaxaca, Oaxaca. c-Teaching credential, Escuela Nacional de Maestros, 1927, with a thesis on

"Education and Democracy"; graduate studies in primary education at Pennsylvania State University, 1945, with a thesis on "Education in Mexico"; professor of secondary and normal schools in the Federal District, including Progreso No. 6, San Lucas and Coyoacán, d-None. e-Joined PNR, 1934. f-Normal school director, Federal District; Director of Federal Education, Secretariat of Public Education; Director General of Pilot Project for the Secretariat of Public Education, 1951; Director General of Agricultural and Rural Normal Instruction, Secretariat of Public Education; Director General of Agricultural Education; Coordinator of Indigenous Affairs, Secretariat of Public Education; *Oficial Mayor, Secretariat of Public Education*, 1961-64, 1964-70; President, National Technical Council of Education, 1970-73, 1988-93; Coordinator General of Literacy and Extracurricular Education, Secretariat of Public Education, 1977. g-Peasant organizer, Sonora, 1932-34. h-Author of several works on education. i-Married Teodosia Martínez y de Armas, normal teacher; son of Mariano Aguilera Cerdas, military, and Carlota Dorantes Torrentera. j-None. l-DBM70, 8-9; DGF51, I, 294; DPE61, 97; DBM68, 12; Enc. Mex., I, 161-162; HA, 25 Apr., 1977, F; DAPC, 1977, 1; DBGM89, 19-20.

Aguilera Gómez, Manuel
a-July 27, 1936. b-Orizaba, Veracruz. c-Early education unknown; preparatory studies at the National Preparatory School, 1952-53; studies in economics at the National School of Economics, UNAM, 1954-58, degree Dec. 18, 1962, with a thesis on economic development in San Luis Potosí; Professor of Macroeconomics and Economic Dynamics, Economic Theory and Development Policy, and the Theory of Economic

Planning, University of San Luis Potosí, 1964-67; Dean, School of Economics, University of San Luis Potosí, 1964-67; Director, Institute of Economic Investigations, University of San Luis Potosí, 1964-67; professor at the National School of Economics, UNAM, 1969- ; Director of the Seminar on Economic Development and the Economic Structure of Mexico, National School of Economics. d-*Senator* from the Federal District, 1991- . e-None. f-Secretary General of Advancement, State of San Luis Potosí. 1960-61; Director of Economic and Social Planning, State of Guanajuato, 1962-63; Director, Department of Regional Planning, Presidency of Mexico, 1970; Subdirector and Director General of Economic Studies, Secretariat of Industry and Commerce, 1971-72; Coordinator General of the Border and Free Zone National Development Program, 1977-78; Director General of the Mexican Institute of Coffee, 1978-82; Director General of Popular Housing Renovation, Department of the Federal District, 1986-88; *Secretary General of Government*, Department of the Federal District, 1988-91. g-President of the National College of Economists, 1979-80. h-Founder and Director General of Tobaccos Mexicanos, S.A.; chairman of the board of Tobaccos Aztecas. i-Son of Salvador Aguilera Carbajal, self-employed, and Emma Gómez Serrano; married Celina Verduzco Vázquez. j-None. k-None. l-Letter; DBGM89, 20; DBGM92, 409.

Aguilera Noriega, Jorge
a-May 20, 1931. b-Ciudad Victoria, Tamaulipas. c-Early education unknown; economics degree, National School of Economics, UNAM, 1951-55, with a thesis on "Public Finances in the State of Tamaulipas." d-None. e-Joined PRI, 1948; Oficial Mayor of the IEPES of

PRI, 1969-70; President of the PRI in the State of Tamaulipas, 1986-88. f-Department head, Exchanges, Small Business Bank, Mexico City, 1955-57; Treasurer General of Tamaulipas, under Governor *Norberto Trevino Zapata,* 1958-63; Subdirector of Delegations, CONASUPO, 1973-76; *Oficial Mayor of the Secretariat of Trade,* 1978-82; Coordinator of the National Food Committee, Secretariat of Programming and Budgeting, 1983-85; *Oficial Mayor of the Secretariat of Agriculture and Hydraulic Resources,* 1988-90. g-Secretary of Youth Action of the CNOP of Tamaulipas, 1959-61; President of the Sports Committee of CNOP of Tamaulipas, 1959-61. h-Member of the Board of various enterprises associated with CONASUPO, 1971-76. j-None. k-None. l-Protag., 13; DBGM89, 20.

Aguirre Alegría, Francisco
a-Apr. 20, 1912. b-Acayucán, Veracruz. c-Primary, secondary, and business studies in Jalapa, Veracruz; preparatory studies in Mexico City; completed first three years of law studies at the National School of Law, UNAM; studies in political and social sciences, UNAM. d-*Federal Deputy* from the Federal District, Dist. 11, 1955-58; member of the First Treasury Committee, the Health Committee, and the Department of the Federal District Committee; *Federal Deputy* from the Federal District, Dist. 15, 1961-64, member of the Health Committee and alternate member of the First Labor Committee. e-Secretary of Action of PRI in the Federal District, 1955. f-None. g-Secretary General of the Union of Coordinated Health Services (became Local 12 of the National Union of Health Workers), 1937; Secretary of Labor and Conflicts, National Union of Health Workers; Secretary of Organiza-

tion of the FSTSE, 1943-46; Secretary General of the Union of Health Workers, 1947-50, member of the CEN of the FSTSE, 1949-53; *Secretary General of the FSTSE,* 1953-56. h-None. i-Collaborator of *Ruffo Figueroa.* j-None. k-None. l-Sirvent, 174; Ind. Biog., 11-12; DGF56; C de D, 1961-63, 5.

Aguirre Andrade, Patricio
a-May 27, 1907. b-Federal District. c-Primary, secondary, and preparatory studies at the Colegio de Estado of Aguascalientes; medical degree, National School of Medicine, UNAM, with a thesis on blood transfusions from cadavers to living persons; specialty in the field of the conservation of tissues. d-*Alternate Federal Deputy* from the Federal District, Dist. 3, 1952-55; *Federal Deputy* from the Federal District, Dist. 3, 1955-58; member of the Sugar Industry and the First Section of the General Means of Communications Committees. e-Founding member of PAN, 1939; official of the PAN Regional Committee of the Federal District; member of the National Council of PAN, 1952-56. f-None. g-None. h-Practicing physician, 1947; surgeon, Streetcar Company of Mexico; laboratorian, Hospital Inglés, 1940-46; owner, textile industry, 1947-55. i-Son of Gustavo Aguirre Ortiz, revolutionary major and veterinarian. j-None. k-None. l-DGF56, 22,34,37; Ind. Biog., 12-13.

Aguirre Beltrán, Gonzalo
a-Jan. 20, 1908. b-Tlacotalpan, Veracruz. c-Primary studies in Tlacotalpan, 1915-21; preparatory studies at the National Preparatory School, Mexico City, 1926-27; medical degree, National School of Medicine, UNAM, 1931; Rockefeller Fellow, Northwestern University; Rector of the University of Veracruz, 1956-63. d-*Federal Deputy*

from the State of Veracruz, Dist. 12, 1961-64, member of the Committee on Bellas Artes and the Second Committee on Public Education; member of the Gran Comisión; member of the Inter-parliamentary Delegation to the United States. e-None. f-Head of the Sanitary Unit for Huatusco, Veracruz, 1939-40; head, Department of Demography, Secretariat of Government, 1942-51; Director General of Indigenous Affairs, Secretariat of Public Education, 1946-52; Director of the Coordinating Indigenous Center for the Tzeltal-Tsotzil Region, 1951-53; *Subsecretary of Cultural Affairs, Secretariat of Public Education,* 1970-76; Director General of the National Indigenous Institute, 1971-72. g-None. h-Intern, General Hospital, Mexico City, 1931-32; biologist, Department of Demography, Secretariat of Government, 1942; practicing physician, Veracruz, 1938-41; Secretary General of the Mexican Society of Anthropology; Director of the Inter-American Indigenous Institute, 1966-70; author of many scholarly works on history, agriculture, and Indians; recog-nized scholar in the field of anthropol-ogy. i-Married Judith Avendano; son of Gonzalo Aguirre Beltrán and Pilar Beltrán Luchichi. j-None. k-Received the Belisario Domínguez Award, 1991. l-WWM45, 2; DGF47, 172; HA 20 Sept. 1971,22; HA 14 Dec. 1970, 22; DGF50, II, 465; DGF51, I, 68; II, 636; WB48, 60; WWW70-71.

Aguirre (del Castillo), Vicente
a-Oct. 1907. b-Ixmiquilpan, Hidalgo. c-Primary studies in Ixmiquilpan; preparatory studies in Mexico City; law studies at the National School of Law, UNAM, 1928-32, law degree, 1933. d-*Federal Deputy* from the State of Hidalgo, Dist. 4, 1937-40; *Senator* from the State of Hidalgo, 1940-46; *Governor of Hidalgo,* 1946-51. e-President of the

PRM in Hidalgo. f-Chief of Political Control, State of Hidalgo; Private Secretary to *Javier Rojo Gómez* as candidate for and governor of Hidalgo, 1936-37. g-First President of the Patronato of Maguey; Vice-president of the National Union of Sugarcane Producers, 1978. h-Practicing lawyer, 1951-78. i-Brother of *Victor M. Aguirre,* federal deputy from Hidalgo, 1943-46 and 1949-52; relative of *Javier Rojo Gómez;* law school classmate of *Carlos Ramírez Guerrero.* j-None. k-Sup-ported *Javier Rojo Gómez's* precandi-dacy for President of Mexico, 1946. l-Peral, 60, 166-67; HA 13 Dec. 1946, 6; Correa, 7; letter; Gaxiola, 318; Pérez López, 23.

Aguirre (del Castillo), Víctor M.
a-Mar. 24, 1914. b-Ixmiquilpan, Hidalgo. c-Primary studies in Ixmiquil-pan; secondary studies in Mexico City; studies in agricultural engineering, National School of Agriculture, Chapingo, no degree. d-Mayor of Tula, Hidalgo; Mayor of Pachuca, Hidalgo; *Federal Deputy* from the State of Hidalgo, Dist. 3, 1943-46; *Federal Deputy* from the State of Hidalgo, Dist. 3, 1949-52, member of the Gran Comisión, the 4th Ejido Committee, and an alternate to the War Materiels Committee. g-None. i-Brother of *Vicente Aguirre,* governor of Hidalgo, 1946-51. j-None. k-None. l-DGF51, 22, 29, 32, 35; Peral, 60, 167; C de D, 1943-46; C de D, 1949-52.

Aguirre (Palancares), Norberto
a-Sept. 7, 1906. b-Pinotepa Nacional, Oaxaca. c-Agricultural engineering degree, National School of Agriculture, Chapingo; Professor of Economy at the National School of Economics, UNAM. d-*Federal Deputy,* State of Oaxaca, Dist. 7, 1943-46, 1949-52, member of the Agriculture and Development Commit-

tee and the Second Treasury Committee; *Federal Deputy*, State of Oaxaca, 1961-64; member of the Small Agricultural Properties Committee, the Committee of Legislative Studies (Agricultural Section), the Administration Committee, and the Gran Comisión; *Federal Deputy* from the State of Oaxaca, Dist. 8, 1979-82. f-Director of Agrarian Laws, 1943-46, Department of Agrarian Affairs; Director of the National Commission of Maíz, 1949-53; Rector of the University of Sonora, 1953-56; Secretary General of Government, State of Oaxaca, 1956-61; *Head of the Department of Agrarian Affairs and Colonization*, 1964-70. g-Secretary General of the League of Agrarian Communities and Farmers Union, State of Oaxaca. h-Agricultural engineer in charge of agrarian reform projects, 1929-43; founding member of the National Commission of Maíz (Vocal); adviser to the Mexican delegation at the Inter-American Conferences at Chapultepec in 1945 and Caracas in 1942; adviser to the Mexican delegation to the United Nations, 1946. i-Married Pilar Salazar; relative Amando Baños Díaz was a precandidate of PARM for federal deputy from Oaxaca. j-None. k-Expelled from the League of Agrarian Communities in Oaxaca for supporting General *Henríquez Guzmán*, 1952. l-DBM70, 12-13; HA, 13 May 1968, 7; DBM68, 14; DGF50, II, 159; C de D, 1949-51; C de D, 1961-63; DGF51, I, 24, 30, 32-33; II, 231; HA, 10 July 1972, 10; WWW70-71; WB48; Correa, 366; HA, 4 Oct. 1976, 15; *Excélsior*, 14 Dec. 1978, 9.

Aguirre (Samaniego), Manuel Bernardo
a-Aug. 20, 1903. b-Parral, Chihuahua. c-Some primary studies at the Colegio Palmore, Parral, and in Ciudad Juárez, Chihuahua; secondary studies in the Federal District; primarily self-educated. d-Mayor of Chihuahua, Chihuahua, 1947-49; *Federal Deputy* from the State of Chihuahua, Dist. 4, 1940-43; Secretary to the President of the Chamber of Deputies, 1940; President of the Gran Comisión, 1940-43; member of the Committee on National Waters and Irrigation and the Committee on Highways; *Federal Deputy* from the State of Chihuahua, Dist. 1, 1961-64, President of the Chamber of Deputies, Nov. 1961; member of the Gran Comisión; member of the Committee on Public Works, the Indigenous Affairs Committee, the Committee on Forest Affairs, and the Library Committee; *Senator* from Chihuahua, 1964-70; President of the Senate, Nov. 1966; President of the Gran Comisión, 1967; *Governor of Chihuahua*, 1974-80. e-Founding member of the PNR, 1929; director of the presidential campaign for Plutarco E. Calles, Parral and Ciudad Juárez, Chihuahua, 1924; Director of PRI in Chihuahua, 1944-45; first Oficial Mayor of the CNOP of PRI, 1945-46; delegate of the CEN of PRI to nineteen different entities; *Secretary of Political Action of the CEN of PRI*, 1964. f-Head of the Federal Office of the Secretariat of the Treasury for the First District, Mexico City, 1957-60; *Secretary of Agriculture and Livestock*, 1971-74. g-None. h-Ticket taker, Alcazar Theater, Parral, Hidalgo; legal representative for American Smelting and Refining and for West Mexico Mines. i-Brother, Salvador Aguirre, was an engineer; married Paula Aún. j-None. k-None. l-WWMG, 5; HA, 25 Jan. 1971, 28; EBW46, 42; DGF61, 46; WWW70-71; WB48, 61; HA, 24 Dec. 1973, 24-25; *Excélsior*, 8 Jan. 1974; HA, 8 July 1974, 32; *Excélsior*, 16 Dec. 1973, 1; Enc. Mex., 1977, Annual, 542-43.

Aguirre Soria, María Guadalupe
a-June 14, 1933. b-Villahermosa, Tabasco. c-Early education unknown;

preparatory studies from the National
Preparatory School; law degree; civics
teacher at Williams School, Mexico
City. d-*Federal Deputy* from the
Federal District, Dist. 22, 1967-70.
e-None. f-Private Secretary to *Juan
Orozco González* as Oficial Mayor of
the Secretariat of National Patrimony,
1958-64; Subdirector of Methods and
Systems, Secretariat of National
Patrimony, 1964-66. g-Secretary of the
Alliance of Mexican Women. h-Author.
i-Father a surgeon; unmarried. j-None.
k-None. l-MGF69, 91; DPE61, 55;
DPE65, 85; PS.

Aguirre (Velázquez), Ramón
a-Sept. 21, 1935. b-San Felipe, Guanajuato. c-Primary studies in San Felipe;
secondary studies in Celaya; certified
public accounting studies, National
School of Business and Administration,
UNAM, 1953-57, graduating in 1962,
with a thesis on the "Cost System and
Structural Steel Industry"; numerous
graduate courses in finance, public
budgeting, public administration, and
marketing, Mexico and abroad; professor, National School of Business and
Administration, UNAM, 1963-70, and
the National Institute of Public Administration, 1972-75. d-Governor-elect of
Guanajuato, 1991. e-Joined the PRI,
1956; precandidate of PRI for federal
deputy from Guanajuato in 1979, but
was replaced by *Ignacio Vázquez Torres*
at the last moment. f-Auditor, Income
Tax Division, Secretariat of the Treasury; Chief of Auditors, Income Tax
Division, Secretariat of the Treasury,
1956-60; Technical Subdirector of
Expenditures, Secretariat of the Treasury, 1970-71; Director General of
Expenditures, Secretariat of the Treasury, 1971-75; *Subsecretary of Expenditures, Secretariat of the Treasury*, 1976;
*Subsecretary of Budgeting, Secretariat
of Programming and Budgeting*, 1979-

81; *Secretary of Programming and
Budgeting*, 1981-82; *Head of the
Department of the Federal District*,
1982-88; Director of the National
Lottery, 1988-91. g-None. h-Director
General of the Mexican Mortgage
Association, 1977; Vice-President of
Planning and Finance, Somex, 1978-79.
i-Collaborator of Miguel Rico Ramírez,
subsecretary of budgeting, 1976, early in
his career; close ties to *Miguel de la
Madrid*; son of Francisco Aguirre Valle,
an engineer, and Martina Velázquez;
married Clara Luz Bizzuett Manteca.
j-None. k-Removed from the governorship of Guanajuato before taking office
by President Salinas because of political
difficulties over widespread accusations
of electoral fraud. l-HA, 19 Oct. 1981,
31; MGF73, 225; *Excélsior*, 4 Feb. 1976,
1 Dec. 1982, 36A; HA, 13 Dec. 1982, 18;
HA, 27 Dec. 1982, 27-30; DBGM89, 21-
22; DBGM, 22.

Ahuja Fuster, Héctor Vicente
a-Jan. 22, 1932. b-Cosamaloapan,
Veracruz. c-Primary studies at the Juan
Enríquez School, Tlacotalpan, Veracruz,
1939-45; secondary studies at Secondary
No. 3, Orizaba, Veracruz, 1947-49;
business school studies, Tlacotalpan,
Veracruz, 1945-56; cadet, Military
Aviation School, 1950-1952, graduating
as a pilot September 16, 1952; diploma
in staff and command, Higher War
College, September 1, 1973; courses in
the T-33, Randolph Field, Texas, and in
advanced artillery, Nellis Air Force
Base, Las Vegas, Nevada. d-None.
e-None. f-*Chief of the Air Force*, 1991-
g-None. h-None. i-Son of Romeo
Ahuja Castro and Juana Fuster Aguirre;
married Hilda Fricke Rivera. j-Career
Air Force officer; joined the Air Force as
a cadet, February 6, 1950; operations
officer, various air squadrons; executive
officer, Squadron 206, 201 and 200; test
pilot; commander of Air Squadron 205;

Adjutant General and Commander of Cadets, Air College; Chief of Staff and Course Director, Air Force Higher War College, 1974; rank of Colonel, 1974. k-None. l-Rev. de Ejer., Aug. 1974, 130; DBGM92.

Ahumada, Herminio
(Deceased July 1, 1983) a-Oct. 7, 1899. b-Soyopa, Sonora. c-Primary and secondary studies at the Nogales, Arizona, public school; outstanding student, completed five grades in two years; law degree, National School of Law, UNAM. d-*Federal Deputy* from the State of Sonora, Dist. 2, 1943-46, President of the Chamber of Deputies, 1944; answered President *Manuel Avila Camacho's* state of the union address, 1944. e-Executive Secretary of the National Anti-Reelectionist Party of Sonora, 1926; Private Secretary to José Vasconcelos, opposition candidate for president, 1929. f-Judge, Higher Tribunal of Justice, State of Sonora; Justice of the Higher Tribunal of Justice of the Federal District, 1940-43. g-President of the National Student Congress, Oaxaca, Oaxaca, 1926. i-Son-in-law of José Vasconcelos. j-None. k-Asked Obregón as a student leader not to run for president a second time. l-HA, 10 July 1983, 6; C de D, 1943-46.

Ahumada Padilla, Alberto Javier
a-Oct. 8, 1925. b-Colima, Colima. c-Early education unknown; engineer studies, National School of Engineering, UNAM, 1945-49, graduating in 1949. d-*Federal Deputy* from the State of Colima, Dist. 1, 1979-82; *Senator* from the State of Colima, 1982-88; *Plurinominal Federal Deputy*, 1988-91. e-Joined PRI, 1949; member of the Revolutionary Youth of PRI, 1951. f-Supervisor of Publicity, National Lottery, 1948-52; various positions in the Department of Studies and Projects, Secretariat of the

Navy, 1952-56. g-President of the National Federation of Small Property Owners, 1983-88. h-Practicing engineer, 1944-47. i-Son of Jesús Ahumada Orozco, lawyer and public notary, and María Padilla Estrada; married Rosa María Medina Vidriales. j-None. k-None. l-DBGM87, 478.

Ainslie (Rivera), Ricardo
a-1897. b-Guerrero, Coahuila. c-Primary education at public schools in Guerrero and Piedras Negras; no degree. d-Local deputy to the state legislature of Coahuila, 1924; Federal Deputy from Coahuila, 1930-32, 1932-34, member of the Gran Comisión; *Alternate Senator* from the State of Coahuila, 1946-52. e-President of the Railroad Union's Party in Coahuila, 1919. f-Provisional Governor of Coahuila, Oct. 25, 1925 to Nov. 30, 1925; *Interim Governor of Coahuila*, 1947-48; Treasurer General of Coahuila (eight years). g-None. i-Father a British immigrant. j-Joined the Revolutionary Army in 1913; reached the rank of Major. k-Forced to resign as governor of Coahuila in Mar. 1948, as a result of a dispute over his successor with leaders of the PNR. l-Anderson; HA 6 Feb. 1948, 8; letter; DGF47, 19; DGF51, 5; Enc. Mex., 1977, II, 530.

Alamillo Flores, Luis
a-Dec. 27, 1904. b-Fortín de la Flores, Veracruz. c-Primary studies at public school in Puebla, Puebla; military studies at the University of Puebla; enrolled at the Heroic Military College, 1923, graduating as a 2nd Lieutenant of cavalry, Jan. 11 1924; Staff and Command Diploma, Higher War College, 1928-31; advanced studies at the Sorbonne, the Military Engineering School of Versailles, Paris, and George Washington University. d-None. e-None. f-Military Attaché, Mexican Embassy, Washington, D.C., 1943-45;

military adviser, Mexican delegation to the United Nations, San Francisco, 1945; Military Attaché, Mexican Embassy, Paris; Assistant Chief of Staff, Pacific Military Region; Director, Higher War College, 1932-34; Director, Heroic Military College, 1945-48; Chief of Staff, Pacific Military Region; Chief of Staff, Secretariat of National Defense. g-None. h-None. i-Married Herlinda Landín. j-Joined the army as an infantry soldier, July 1, 1919; member of the 6th Battalion, 1924; rank of 2nd Captain, Apr. 1, 1924; rank of Major, Jan. 1, 1932; fought in seven battles against the Zapatistas, Teocalli, Puebla; member of the escort squadron of General Agustín Maciel, 1924; rank of Colonel, May 1, 1940; rank of Brigadier General, Aug. 1, 1942; rank of Brigade General, Sept. 16, 1946; Commander of the 4th Military Zone, Hermosillo, Sonora, 1966-68; Commander of the 24th Military Zone, 1972; retired, 1976; rank of Division General, Sept. 20, 1952. k-None. l-NYT, 7 Sept. 1945, 5; WWM45, 2; DBM68, 15; Rev. de Ejer., Sept 1976, 133; Rev. de Ejer., Dec. 1962, 29.

Alanís Camino, Fernando

a-Feb. 17, 1934. b-Federal District. c-Early education unknown; law degree, National School of Law, UNAM, 1955-59, with a thesis on "Studies of Constitutional Law and Political Science, the Relation between Church and State in Mexican Constitutional Law," 1959; professor, National School of Law, UNAM, 1961-63; professor, Banking and Business School, Ibero-American University, 1956-57; Professor, National Institute of Public Administration, 1975-76. d-None. e-Joined PRI, 1960; Coordinator of Sports, Recreation and Tourism, *Miguel de la Madrid* presidential campaign, 1981-82. f-Adviser, Director General of Credit, Secretariat

of the Treasury, 1960-61; Adviser, Director General of Internal Taxes, Secretariat of the Treasury, 1961-62; technical adviser to the IMSS, 1962-64; Secretary of the Administrative Board of Pemex, 1977-82; *Subsecretary of Sports*, Secretariat of Public Education, 1982-85. g-None. h-Practicing lawyer. i-Son of Fernando Alanís Bretón, bank official, and María Luisa Camino Gutiérrez, civil servant; married Constanza Uribe Ahumada, teacher. j-None. k-None. l-HA, 20 Dec. 1982, 12; Q es QAP, 301; DBGM, 23; DBGM87, 21.

Alanís Fuentes, Agustín

a-Feb. 19, 1930. b-Federal District. c-Primary studies at the José Enrique Rodó and El Pensador Mexicano; secondary studies at Secondary School No. 4; preparatory studies at the National Preparatory School; legal studies at the National School of Law, UNAM, 1948-52, degree, 1953, with a thesis on criminal confessions, for which he received an honorable mention; professor at the National Preparatory School, Mexico City, 1950, subjects included civics; professor at the National School of Law, 1964- ; Professor of History at UNAM, 1966, member of the University Council of UNAM, 1952; Professor of Labor Law, UNAM, 1968. d-None. e-Auxiliary general delegate of the CEN of PRI to Guanajuato, 1969-70. f-Administrative official of the Higher Tribunal of Justice of the Federal District and Federal Territories, 1947-50; administrative official of the Secretariat of National Patrimony, 1947; Agent of the Ministerio Público of the Attorney General of the Federal District and Federal Territories, 1951-53; Head of the Evaluation Section of the Department of Social Welfare of the Secretariat of Labor, 1958-63; Subdirector of the Department of Social Welfare of the Secretariat of Labor, 1963-65; Director of the Department of Social Welfare of the Secretariat of Labor, 1965-70; *Subsecretary B of the Secretariat of Labor, 1970-76; Attorney General of the Federal District, 1976-82;* Secretary General of Government of the State of Morelos, 1985-88; Director General of Labor and Social Welfare, Department of the Federal District, 1988-93. g-Student leader at the National Preparatory School and the National Law School. h-Technical adviser to the Mexican Institute of Social Security, 1967-70. i-Son of Angel Alanís Fuentes, lawyer and attorney general of the Federal District, and Angela García; married María Judith Figueroa Gallardo. j-None. k-None. l-DPE65, 156; HA, 14 Dec. 1970, 23; *El Día*, 1 Dec. 1976, 10; HA, 7 Mar. 1977, 24-25; DBGM92, 21; DBGM89, 22.

Alarcón, Alfonso G.
(Deceased 1953) a-June 25, 1884. b-Chilpancingo, Guerrero. c-Primary and secondary studies at the Colegio de Puebla; medical degree, University of Puebla, 1910; Rector, University of Puebla; Director, Department of Pediatrics and Infant Hygiene, National School of Medicine, UNAM. d-*Federal Deputy* from the State of Guerrero, Dist. 1, 1914-16; *Senator* from the State of Guerrero, 1952. e-None. f-Delegate of the Department of Health; Director of the Office of Infant Hygiene, Department of Health, 1935; Secretary General of the Department of Health; Director of the Office of Infant Hygiene, Puebla; Governor of Guerrero (appointed by the Local Legislature), 1933. g-None. h-Practicing pediatrician in Tampico (twenty-five years); Director of *Labor Médica* and the *Gaceta Médica* of Tampico; author of many works. j-Precursor, 1910 Revolution; partici-

pant, 1910 Revolution. k-None. l-DGF56, 6; PS; WWM45, 2; Enc. Mex., I, 194.

Alatriste (Abrego) Jr., Sealtiel
a-1904. b-Libres, Puebla. c-Primary studies in Mexico City; preparatory studies at the National Preparatory School; accounting degree (certified public accountant), UNAM, 1925; economics degree, National School of Economics, UNAM, Dec. 20, 1938, with a thesis on Mexican banks; professor at the National School of Commerce and Administration, UNAM; professor at the National School of Law; administrator of the National Polytechnic Institute. d-None. e-None. f-Treasurer of the Federal District, 1947-52; member of the Administrative Council of the Small Business Bank of the Federal District, 1951; *Subsecretary of Government Properties, 1959-64; Director General of the Mexican Institute of Social Security, 1964-66.* g-Vice-President of the National College of Economists; President of the National Institute of Accountants. h-Worked as a private accountant in the firm of Roberto Casas Alatriste; accountant in the National Workers Bank; translator of many economic works; author of three technical books and many articles on economics and accounting; practicing accountant, 1967-78. i-Son of Sealtiel L. Alatriste, member of the prerevolutionary Liberal Clubs in Mexico; grandson of General Miguel Cástulo de Alatriste, an important Liberal in the 1850s and governor of Puebla; cousin of Carmen Serdán Alatriste, wife of Aquiles Serdán, revolutionary precursor; son Eduardo, director general in hydraulic resources. j-None. k-Forced to resign in the midst of an anticorruption campaign he was conducting at IMSS in 1966. l-*El*

Universal 1 Dec. 1964; DGF4, 97;
IWW66, 16; DP70, 54; DGF51, II, 507,
577, 679; Johnson; letters.

Alavéz Flores, Rodolfo
a-Apr. 18, 1915. b-Oaxaca, Oaxaca.
c-Primary studies at the public school
in Oaxaca; secondary studies at the
Institute of Arts and Sciences of
Oaxaca; preparatory studies at the
Institute of Arts and Sciences; law
degree from the Institute of Arts and
Sciences and from the National School
of Law, UNAM. d-Local Deputy to the
State Legislature of Oaxaca, 1944-47;
Alternate Federal Deputy from Oaxaca,
Dist. 8, 1949-51; *Federal Deputy* from
the State of Oaxaca, Dist. 7, 1964-67;
Vice-President of the Chamber, Nov.
1966, member of the Second Eijdo
Committee and the Pharmaceutical-
Chemical Industry Committee; *Federal
Deputy* from the State of Oaxaca, Dist.
2, 1970-73, member of the Arid Zones
Committee, the Indigenous Affairs
Committee, the Legislative Studies
Committee, Sixth Section on Agrarian
Affairs, and the Gran Comisión;
Alternate Senator from the State of
Oaxaca, 1976-82, but replaced Senator
Eliseo Jiménez Ruiz, 1977. e-President
of the State Committee of PRI, Oaxaca.
f-Counselor, Federal Board of Concilia-
tion and Arbitration; assistant to the
Federal Board of Conciliation and
Arbitration of the Federal District;
agent of the Ministerio Público of the
Attorney General's Office; Subsecretary
of Government of the State of Oaxaca;
Oficial Mayor of Oaxaca, 1951.
g-Secretary of Press and Publicity of the
National Committee of the CNC;
Secretary of the League of Agrarian
Communities of Oaxaca. h-None.
j-None. l-Directorio, 70-72; C de D,
1964-66, 82, 87; C de D, 1970-72, 99; C
de D, 1949-51, DGF51, 91.

Alayola Barrera, César
(Deceased) a-June 30, 1892. b-Cam-
peche, Campeche. c-Primary studies in
Mérida, Yucatán; secondary studies at
the Instituto Literario; law degree,
School of Law, University of Yucatán,
June 12, 1920; Professor of Spanish
Etymology, 1916-23, Mixed Normal
School of Yucatán; Professor of Private
International Law, School of Law,
University of Yucatán; Professor of First
Year Philosophy, Instituto Literario,
Mérida, Yucatán, 1927-30. d-Federal
Deputy from the State of Yucatán,
1928-30; Senator from the State of
Yucatán, 1930-34; *Governor of Yucatán*,
1934-36. e-Member of Southeast
Socialist Party; joined the PNR. f-Agent
of the Ministerio Público attached to
the Second Criminal Judicial Division,
Yucatán; First Justice of the Peace,
Mérida, Yucatán; Third Criminal Judge;
Assistant Attorney General of Yucatán;
Secretary General of Government of the
State of Yucatán; Interim Governor of
Yucatán. g-None. h-Practicing lawyer;
consulting lawyer to the United
Railroads of Yucatán, S.A., 1924. i-Son
of Professor José Alayola Preve. j-None.
k-Took a leave of absence from the
governorship, then resigned for reasons
of health, Feb. 1936. l-HA, 12 June
1942, 30; Peral, 30; letter.

Alba Leyva, Samuel
a-Dec. 12, 1928. b-Durango, Durango.
c-Primary studies at the Florencio M.
del Castillo public school; secondary
studies at Secondary School No. 4,
Mexico City; preparatory studies at the
National Preparatory School, Mexico
City; studies in law at the National
School of Law, UNAM, 1947-51, law
degree, Nov. 28, 1952, with a thesis on
family patrimony, received the Justo
Sierra medal for the second highest
grade point average of his law genera-

tion. d-None. e-None. f-Supervisory Judge, Department of the Federal District, 1955-58; Agent of the federal Ministerio Público; Agent of the Ministerio Público of the Assistant Attorney General's Office, 1962; advisory lawyer to the federal tax attorney, 1968; Director, Department of Plea Control, Attorney General's Office; Subdirector and Director of the Central Office of Investigatory Preparations, Attorney General's Office; Private Secretary to *Julio Sánchez Vargas*, Attorney General of Mexico, 1969-71; Director of the Docket Office, Attorney General of Mexico, 1971-72; Inspector General of the Attorney General of Mexico, 1972-73; Coordinator General of the Anti-Narcotics Campaign, 1976; *Assistant Attorney General of Mexico* (2), 1974-76, 1976-82; Director General of Criminal Proceedings, Attorney General of Mexico, 1985-87; *Justice of the Supreme Court*, 1987- . g-None. h-None. i-Married to Esther Martínez Mendoza; son of Feliciano Alba Avila, railroad worker, and Esther Leyva Favela; classmate in high school and preparatory of *Agustín Alanís Fuentes*. j-None. k-None. l-HA, 14 Jan. 1974; HA, 13 Dec. 1976, 10; letter; Protag., 16; DBGM92, 632.

Alcalá de Lira, Alberto
a-Apr. 23, 1917. b-Rancho La Reforma, Municipio of Aguascalientes, Aguascalientes. c-Primary studies in Aguascalientes; teaching certificate, Matías Ramos Colony School, Zacatecas, 1941; school teacher. d-Member of the City Council of Aguascalientes, 1954-55; Local Deputy to the State Legislature of Aguascalientes, 1959-62; *Federal Deputy* from the State of Aguascalientes, Dist. 1, 1955-58, member of the Sugar Industry Committee and the Agrarian Department Committee; *Senator* from the State of Aguascali-

entes, 1964-70; *Federal Deputy* from the State of Aguascalientes, Dist. 2, 1985-88. e-Joined PRI, 1945; president of a polling station; representative of the Agrarian Sector to the National PRI Assemblies. f-Delegate of the Secretariat of Agrarian Reform to the State of Aguascalientes, 1982. g-Secretary General of the League of Agrarian Communities, 1954-56, 1968-71. h-Returned to farming as an ejidatario after teaching for several years. i-Son of Francisco Alcalá Arbilla, farmer, and María Guadalupe de Lira Aguilas; married Leonor Aguilar. j-None. k-None. l-Ind. Biog., 13-14; DGF56, 21, 32, 34; C de D, 1955-58; C de S, 1964-70; MGF69; letter; DBGM87, 429-30.

Alcalá Ferrera, Ramón
a-Jan. 17, 1912. b-Champotón, Campeche. c-Primary studies in Champotón; secondary and preparatory studies at the Instituto Campechano, Ciudad del Carmen, Campeche; graduated from the Naval Academy at Veracruz, Veracruz. d-*Federal Deputy* from the State of Campeche, Dist. 1, 1967-70; *Senator* from the State of Campeche, 1970-76, member of the Gran Comisión, President of the First Naval Committee, First Secretary of the War Materiels Committee, Second Secretary of the National Defense and the Military Health Committee. e-Founding member of PRI, 1946. f-Director of Social Security, Secretariat of the Navy, 1965. g-None. h-None. i-Married Esperanza Guadarrama; cousin of Raúl Alcalá Martínez, Director General, Secretariat of Navy, 1984. j-Career Naval officer; rank of Vice Admiral, Nov. 4, 1971; Chief of Aides to the Commanding General of the Fleet, *Antonio Vázquez del Mercado*, 1956. k-None. l-C de S, 1970-76, 69; DPE65, 53; DGF56, 386; C de D, 1967-70; Q es QAP, 94.

Alcalá Quintero, Francisco
a-Jan. 31, 1912. b-Federal District.
c-Accounting degree (certified public
accountant), School of Business and
Administration, UNAM; degree from
the Graduate School of Business and
Administration, UNAM, postgraduate
studies abroad; professor at UNAM and
IPN. d-None. e-None. f-Joined the
Bank of Mexico, 1927; Subgerente of the
National Bank of Foreign Commerce,
1946-52; *Subdirector General of the
National Bank of Foreign Commerce,
1953-58; Subdirector General of the
National Bank of Foreign Commerce,
1958-65; Subsecretary of Revenues of
the Secretariat of the Treasury, 1965-70;
Director General of the National Bank
of Foreign Commerce, 1970-76, 1976-
79;* joined the diplomatic corps, May 25,
1979; Ambassador to Spain, 1979-83.
g-None. h-Member of the Administrative Council of the National Bonded
Warehouses. j-None. k-None.
l-DGF56, 4222; D de Y, 2 Dec. 1970;
DGF51, II, 571, 586; HA, 7 May 1979,
19; *Excélsior*, 1 Dec. 1976, 1; HA, 9 Apr.
1979, 9; *Uno Más Uno*, 26 Feb. 1983, 2.

Alcantar Enríquez, Enrique
a-July 12, 1928. b-San Pedro Lagunillas,
Nayarit. c-Early education unknown;
completed primary studies; studies in
business adminstration; no degree;
completed course in English, YMCA
Community College, Chicago.
d-*Plurinominal Federal Deputy* from
the PDM, 1982-85. e-Member of the
PAN youth group, 1964-70; coordinator
of the PDM political campaigns in
Jalisco, Colima, Baja California, and
Durango, 1966; candidate of the PDM
for local deputy, Dist. 1, Nayarit, 1979;
candidate for governor of Nayarit;
national adviser to the PDM, 1972.
f-None. g-Founder and President,
Union of Businessmen, 1946-50; Vice-
President, Chamber of Commerce,

Tepic; founder and President, Alliance
of Businessmen. h-Owner of Raymundo
Travel Agency; in sales and promotion
in the travel industry for 12 years. i-Son
of Anastasio Alcantar Sauceda, businessman, and Carmen Enríquez Soto;
married Ana María Ibarra. j-None.
k-None. l-Directorio, 1982-85; C de D,
1982-85; Lehr, 651.

Alcántara Miranda, Jesús
a-Dec. 25, 1922. b-Acambay, México.
c-Preparatory studies at the Colegio
Cervantes, Mexico City, 1939-42; no
degree. d-Mayor of Acambay, México,
1958-61; Local Deputy to the State
Legislature of México, Dist. 8, 1961-64;
Federal Deputy from the State of
México, Dist. 32, 1979-82; *Federal
Deputy* from the State of Mexico, Dist.
9, 1985-88; *Senator* from the State of
México, 1988-91. e-Joined PRI, 1949;
President of PRI in Acambay, 1949-51.
f-Syndic of Acambay, México, 1952-55.
g-Secretary of Relations, National
Chamber of Communications and
Transportation, 1981-83. h-President of
the Board, Flecha Roja Buslines, 1967-
87; President of the Board, Occidente
Buslines, 1980-87. i-Son of Manuel
Alcántara Flores, businessman, and
María Luis Miranda Flores, public
accountant; married Margarita Alcalá
Ordaz. j-None. k-None. l-DBGM89,
392; C de D, 1985-88; C de D, 1979-82;
C de S, 1988-91.

Alcérreca García Peña, Luis Gonzaga
a-Feb. 9, 1899. c-Primary and secondary
studies at public schools in Mexico
City; studies at the National School of
Agriculture on a scholarship from the
State of Veracruz, 1915; engineering
degree, National School of Agriculture,
1919-24; Director, School of Engineering, University of Michoacán, 1928-35.
d-None. e-None. f-Engineer, Local
Agrarian Commission of Michoacán,

official of the state government of Michoacán, 1928-32, under General *Cárdenas*; Director, Technical Department, Secretariat of Agriculture, 1935; delegate of the Department of the Federal District, 1936; senior member of the Agricultural Adviser Office, Secretariat of Agriculture, 1943-64; Director of Advisory Section No. 2, Secretariat of Agriculture, 1951-64; *Secretary General of the Department of Agrarian Affairs and Colonization*, 1964-70. g-None. h-Author of various books. i-Parents from the lower-middle class; nephew of General Angel García Peña, Secretary of War under Madero; married Josefina Ramírez. j-Joined the Constitutional Army, Nov. 15, 1915, under General Pablo González. k-None. l-DPE61, 127; DGF51, 466; *Justicia*, Feb. 1972; MGF69, 355.

Alcocer Villanueva, Jorge
a-Apr. 3, 1955. b-León, Guanajuato. c-Early education unknown; economics degree from the National School of Economics, UNAM, 1978; MA in economics, National School of Economics, UNAM, 1981; Professor of Economics, National School of Economics, UNAM, 1977-89; researcher, Graduate School, National School of Economics, UNAM, 1978-79. d-*Plurinominal Federal Deputy* from PSUM, 1985-88. e-Coordinator of Parliamentary Advisers, PSUM, 1979-83; member of the Political Committee, Central Committee, PSUM, 1984-87; Secretary of Finances, Central Committee, PSUM, 1984-85; member of PRD, 1988-91. i-Son of Armando Alcocer Alba and María Luisa Villanueva Rodríguez; married Gloria Olmos Juárez. j-None. k-None. l-Exámen, Feb. 1991, 27; C de D, 1985-88.

Aldrete, Alberto V.
(Deceased 1959) a-Mar. 6, 1892. b-Ensenada, Baja California del Norte.

c-Primary and secondary in Ensenada; preparatory studies in Los Angeles; none. d-Mayor of Ensenada, 1926-27; *Governor of Baja California del Norte*, 1946-47, resigned from office. e-None. f-Administrator of the *Periódico Oficial*; Treasurer General of Baja California del Norte, 1920-24. g-None. h-Wheat rancher, installed the first flour mill in Mexicali Valley, founder of the Cía. Mexicana de Malta, S.A.; founder and owner of the Cervecería Tecate, S.A. i-Personal friend of President *Miguel Alemán*. j-None. k-Anderson says he resigned because of reaction to his imposing municipal officials; declared bankruptcy, 1948; fled to Spain, 1951, after a warrant was issued for his arrest. l-DP70, 63; HA, 27 Dec. 1946; letter; Anderson; Aquirre, 491.

Aldrett Cuéllar, Pablo
a-1903. b-Matehuala, San Luis Potosí. c-Early education unknown; none. d-Councilman for Matehuala, San Luis Potosí, 1930; Mayor of Matehuala, 1932; Local Deputy to the State Legislature of San Luis Potosí, 1939; *Federal Deputy* from the State of San Luis Potosí, Dist. 2, 1943-46; Local Deputy to the State Legislature of San Luis Potosí, 1946; *Alternate Senator* from the State of San Luis Potosí, 1946-52; *Federal Deputy* from the State of San Luis Potosí, 1952-55; *Senator* from the State of San Luis Potosí, 1958-64, member of the Committees on Administration, Colonization, and the Agrarian Department, and also a member of the First Ejido Committee and the Second Balloting Group. e-Founding member of the PNR, 1929; campaigned for *Lázaro Cárdenas*, 1934. f-None. g-Secretary General of the Agrarian Communities and Agrarian Unions of San Luis Potosí (twice); Secretary of Interior of the CNC. h-None. i-Parents were peas-

ants. k-None. l-Func. 340; C de D, 1952-54; C de D, 1943-45; C de S, 1958-64, 30, 33, 35-36, 46, 49, 51.

Alegría (Escamilla), Rosa Luz
b-Federal District. c-Primary studies at the Rosa de Luxemburg School, Mexico City, 1950-57; secondary studies from Secondary School No. 18 Soledad Anaya Solorzano, Mexico City, 1957-60; preparatory studies from the National Preparatory School, 1960-62; studies at the National School of Architecture, UNAM, 1963-64; BS degree in theoretical physics, National School of Science, UNAM, 1968; courses in National School of Philosophy, UNAM, 1964-68; MS in sciences, UNAM, 1969; postgraduate studies in science, French Petroleum Institute; postgraduate studies in econometrics, Colegio de Francia and UNAM, Ph.D. in econometrics from both institutions, 1970; Professor of Mechanical Structures, National School of Architecture; Professor of Mathematics, National School of Economics, UNAM; researcher in basic elementary and higher education; researcher for the Mexican Institute of Petroleum; assistant researcher and Professor of Quantum Mechanics, French Petroleum Institute. d-None. e-None. f-Researcher for Pemex; coordinator of expression and communication section, Free Textbook Commission, 1971-76, primary education level; scientific adviser, National Population Council; scientific adviser, Secretariat of Public Education, 1970-76; member of the Executive Committee of the National Technical Council of Education, 1970-76; *Subsecretary of Evaluation,* Secretariat of Programming and Planning, 1976-80; *Secretary of Tourism,* 1980-82. g-None. i-Former daughter-in-law of Luis Echeverría. j-None. k-First woman to become a cabinet minister. l-HA, 31 Oct. 1977, 6;

letter; HA, 3 Mar. 1980, 8; *Excélsior,* 14 Aug. 1980, 10; HA, 30 Nov. 1981, 30; Romero Aceves, 336.

Alejo (López), Francisco Javier
a-Dec. 30, 1941. b-Salvatierra, Guanajuato. c-Primary and secondary studies in Mexico City; economic studies from the National School of Economics, UNAM, 1959-63, graduating with a thesis on "The Strategy of Economic Development in Mexico from 1920-1970," 1969; advanced courses in developmental economic planning, United Nations Institute of Latin American Planning, Santiago, Chile, 1963; work toward a Ph.D. in economics, Oxford University, 1965; Professor of Economic Development, Mexican Economic Policy, and Lineal Programming, National School of Economics, UNAM, 1962-71; full-time researcher, Colegio de México, 1969-71. d-None. e-Joined PRI, 1962. f-Economist for Nacional Financiera; economist for the National Bank of Foreign Commerce; economist for the Secretariat of Industry and Commerce; economist for the Secretariat of the Presidency; Director General of the Fondo de Cultura Económica, 1971-74; *Subsecretary of Income,* 1974-75; *Secretary of National Properties,* 1975-76; Director General of the Ciudad Sahagún Industrial Complex, 1976-78; Director General of Diesel Nacional, 1978-79; Ambassador to Japan, 1979-82; adviser, Secretariat of the Treasury, 1982-84; Director General of National Warehouses, 1988-91; Ambassador to Italy and the Food and Agricultural Organization, United Nations, 1991- . g-None. i-Student of *Horacio Flores de la Peña,* whom he replaced as Secretary of National Properties; son of Ramón Alejo Arrizabalaga and Dolores López Vital; married Armonía Ocaña, public official. j-None. k-Resigned as Director General

of the Ciudad Sahagún Industrial Complex, June 29, 1978, after the government announced an administrative reorganization of the major industries. l-HA, 21 Oct. 1974, 21; HA, 13 Jan. 1975, 8; *Excélsior*, 29 June 1978, 4; DBGM92, 24-25; DBGM89, 24.

Alemán (Valdés), Miguel
(Deceased May 14, 1983) a-Sept. 29, 1900. b-Sayula, Veracruz. c-Not permitted to study in the Sayula schools because of father's political beliefs; primary and secondary studies in Acayucan, Coatzacoalcos, and Orizaba; preparatory studies at the National Preparatory School, Mexico City, where he founded the newspaper *Eureka*, 1920-25; law degree from the National School of Law, 1925-28, with a thesis on occupational diseases and accidents among workers. d-*Senator* from the State of Veracruz, 1934-36; *Governor of Veracruz*, 1936-39; *President of Mexico*, 1946-52. e-President of the Unifying Committee of Plutarco Elias Calles in Veracruz, 1933; national head of the presidential campaign for *Avila Camacho*, 1939-40. f-Justice of the Higher Tribunal of Justice of the Federal District, 1930-35, member of the Federal Board of Conciliation and Arbitration, 1930; legal adviser to the Secretary of Agriculture and Livestock, 1928-30; *Secretary of Government*, 1940-45; Director General of the National Tourism Commission, 1958-83. g-None. h-Fluent in English; practiced law in Mexico City, 1928-30, specialized in cases involving compensation for miners and railroad employees; worked as an assistant to a geologist during the summers, 1925-28. i-As a law student at UNAM, knew *Angel Carvajal, Manuel Sánchez Cuen, Hector Pérez Martínez, Andrés Serra Rojas, Manuel Ramírez Vázquez, Luis Garrido Diaz, Antonio Carrillo Flores,*

Alfonso Noriega, Antonio Dovalí Jaime, and *José Castro Estrada*; father, Miguel Alemán, was originally a storekeeper and then a Revolutionary General, later serving as a federal deputy, 1927-28; he was killed in 1929 opposing the reelection of Obregón; son, *Miguel Alemán Jr.*, served as PRI finance secretary, 1990s; married Beatriz Velasco. j-None. k-Leader of the right wing of PRI after his presidency; major investor in several industries, owns the Continental Hotel. l-DP70; 64-65; Covarrubias, 96; DBM68, 23-24; WWMG, 6; WWM45, 3; letters; DGF50, II, 149; DGF47; DGF51, I, 47; DP70, 64; CB, Sept. 1946, 3-5; CN Sept. 1946, 3-5; UTEHA, 421; Q es Q, 13; Wise, 58; Scott, 218.

Alemán Velasco, Miguel
a-Mar. 18, 1932. b-Veracruz, Veracruz. c-Primary studies in Jalapa and Mexico City; secondary studies in San Antonio, Texas, and at the Colegio México; preparatory studies at the Centro Universitario México; law degree, National School of Law, UNAM, July 1954, with a thesis on international legal problems of air law; international law studies, Sorbonne, Paris, 1953; studies in air law, Rome, 1954. d-*Senator* from the State of Veracruz, 1991-. e-*Secretary of Press and Public Relations of the CEN of PRI*, 1968; *Secretary of Finances of the CEN of PRI*, 1992- . f-Adviser to the Secretary of Communications and Transportation, 1960; Ambassador at Large, 1989-91. g-Editor of student paper, *Vox Legis*, 1947-49; founder and director of *Voz*, 1950-53. h-Practicing lawyer; editor of *Ambiente*, 1957; lawyer for Lockheed; television producer, 1960s; General Coordinator, Telesistema Mexicana, S.A., 1966-69; Director of News, Telesistema Mexicana, S.A., 1969-70; First Vice-President, Radio News Chamber, 1970; First Vice-President, Panamerican

Publishers, 1971; Executive Vice-President, Televisa, 1973-83; Vice-President and Subdirector General of Novedades Editores, S.A., 1981- ; member of the board of Telesistema Mexicana, S.A., 1982-89; President of Televisa, 1985-89. i-Son and heir to the fortune of ex-president *Miguel Alemán Valdés* and of Beatrice Velasco; father reputed to have been among the wealthiest men in Mexico; married Christianne Magnani, French actress and Miss Universe. j-None. k-Sold his 17percent interest in Televisa to Emilio Azcárraga. l-HA, 30 July 1979, 9; WNM, 5-6; Protag., 19; letter.

Alessio Robles (Fernández), Miguel
a-June 16, 1929. b-Federal District. c-Primary and secondary studies in Mexico City; law degree, National School of Law, UNAM, 1954; course in business management, Pan American Institute of Higher Management; professor, Ibero-American University, 1957-60. d-None. e-None. f-Legal adviser to the Arbitration Commission on the sugarcane conflict, 1947; Subdirector of Internal Taxes, Secretariat of the Treasury, 1955-59; Director General of Sidermex, 1982-86. g-Manager, National Association of Beer Manufacturers; manager, Chamber of Beer and Malt Industries; first Vice-President of the National Chamber of Industries; President of Coparmex; President, National Chamber of Beer and Malt Industries; President of Concanaco, 1970-71. h-Manager of *Nuevo Mundo*, 1950-54; Director General of the Mining Consortium B.J.-Peña, 1971-82; member of the board of Latin American Insurance, International Bank, and the Fundidora de Monterrey. i-Son of Miguel Alessio Robles, Secretary of Industry and Commerce, 1922, and Josefina Fernández Almendaro;

nephew of Vito Alessio Robles, former senator, opposition party leader, and intellectual; married Beatriz Landa Verdugo; classmate of *Miguel de la Madrid* at UNAM. j-None. k-None. l-WNM, 7; IEPES; DBGM, 27; Q es QAP, 525.

Almada López, Carlos Fernando
a-Aug. 26, 1951. b-Guasave, Sinaloa. c-Early education unknown; graduated from the University of Sinaloa, 1974; MA in public administration, International Institute of Public Administration, Paris, France; Ph.D. in public administration, University of Paris, 1979; professor, Regional Technical Institute, Culiacán, Sinaloa, 1972-74; Professor of Political Science, Graduate School, Political Science, UNAM, 1980-81; professor, Autonomous University of the State of México, 1982-83. d-None. e-Subdirector of the IEPES of the CEN of PRI, 1983-86. f-Director of Publicity and Social Communication in Culiacán, 1972-74; Secretary of Publicity and Social Communication in Culiacán, 1974-75; Coordinator of Industrial Development, Secretariat of Industry and Commerce, 1975-76; Executive Secretary of the National Institute of Public Administration, 1979-80; Subdirector of the Workers Bank under *Alfredo del Mazo González*, 1979-81; Secretary of Administration of the State of México, 1981-86; *Oficial Mayor of the Secretariat of Energy, Mines and Government Industries*, 1986-88. g-None. h-None. i-Son of Cosme Almada Trapero, civil engineer, and María Dolores López Angulo; married María de los Milagros Calvo; political disciple of *Alfredo del Mazo González*. j-None. k-None. l-HA, 13 May 1986, 17; *Mexiquenses*, 9-10; DBGM87, 25.

Alonso Sandoval, José Luis
a-Feb. 24, 1937. b-San Pedro, Coahuila.
c-Primary studies in the Francisco
Sarabia Public Rural School, El Compas,
Durango; secondary studies in the Rural
Normal School of Tamatan, Tamau-
lipas; normal certificate from the
Normal School, Saltillo, Coahuila,
1951-55; preparatory studies at the
Night Preparatory School of the State of
Coahuila; law degree, National School
of Law, UNAM, 1958-64; teacher,
primary school, 1957-67. d-*Federal
Deputy* from the Federal District, Dist.
3, 1970-73, member of the Department
of the Federal District Committee, the
Desert Zones Committee, and the
Forest Affairs Committee; *Plurinominal
Federal Deputy* from the PFCRN, 1988-
91. e-Secretary of Organization of the
PRI in the Federal District, 1973-75;
President of the Third District Commit-
tee of PRI for the Federal District;
President of PRI in the Federal District,
1979-80; *Secretary of Organization* of
the CEN of PRI, 1980-81; joined the
Cardenista Front for National Recon-
struction Party (PFCRN), 1988.
f-Auxiliary Secretary to the Secretary
General of Olympic Games Organizing
Committee; Private Secretary to the
Director General of Higher Education,
Secretariat of Public Education; Admin-
istrative Subdirector of the Land Tenure
Commission, Secretariat of Agrarian
Reform, 1981-82; Delegate of the
Secretariat of Public Education, Tamau-
lipas, 1983-84; Delegate of the Depart-
ment of the Federal District, Gustavo
Madero, 1985. g-Secretary of Organiza-
tion of the CEN of CNOP, 1972-73;
President of the Society of Students of
the School of Law, UNAM, 1962.
h-None. i-Married María Elena
Valencia Chávez, normal teacher; son of
José Luis Alonso de la Rosa and Petra
Sandoval Rodríguez, normal teachers.

j-None. k-Opposed *Jesús Reyes Heroles*
and *Agustín Alanís Fuentes* for dean of
the Law School as a student leader,
1961; expelled from the National
University, 1962. l-*Excélsior*, 10 Feb.
1979, 14; Directorio, 1970-72; C de D,
1970-73, 100; DBGM89, 394.

Alonso y Prieto, Rafael
a-Sept. 6, 1917. c-Early education
unknown; public accounting degree,
National School of Business and
Administration, UNAM; Professor and
chairman, Department of Economics,
University of Monterrey, 1977-79;
Director, Cervantes Social Work School,
Monterrey. d-*Plurinominal Deputy*
from PAN, 1979-82. e-Member,
Regional Committee of PAN, Nuevo
León. f-Controller General of the Board
of Administration and Vigilance of
Foreign Properties, 1943-44. g-Founder
and President of the Institute of Public
Accountants, 1950-52, 1956-57; Presi-
dent of the National Council of the
Mexican Institute of Public Accountants, 1967-69. h-Practicing public
accountant. j-None. k-None. l-C de D,
1979-82; Protag., 21.

Alpuche Pinzón, Graciliano
(Deceased Dec. 2, 1990) a-Apr. 2, 1919.
b-Mérida, Yucatán. c-Early education
unknown; enrolled in the Heroic
Military College as a cadet, June 1,
1936; graduated as a 2nd Lieutenant in
artillery; diploma from the Higher War
College in staff and command training,
1944-47; Instructor in tactics and
combat information, Heroic Military
College. d-*Senator* from the State of
Yucatán, 1976-82; *Governor of Yucatán*,
1982-84. e-None. f-None. g-None.
h-None. i-Married María Eugenia Viejo;
brother, Juan, reached rank of Colonel,
1971. j-Career army officer; volunteer,
36th Infantry Battalion; junior officer,

1st Artillery Regiment, 3rd Artillery
Battalion; staff officer, 2nd Infantry
Division, National Military Service;
Section Chief, staff, 1st Infantry
Division (volunteers), Military Camp
No. 1; Chief, planning subsection of S-1,
staff, Secretariat of National Defense;
Director of the Black Powder Plant,
Santa Fe; Subchief of Staff of the 15th
and 32nd Military Zones; Chief of Staff
of the 32nd Military Zone, Yucatán;
Adjutant General to *Juan Flores Torres*,
Subsecretary of Defense, 1958-64;
Military Attaché to Argentina; Director,
Department of Recruitment and
Personnel, Secretariat of National
Defense; Director General of Artillery,
Secretariat of National Defense, 1974;
rank of Lt. Colonel, Nov. 20, 1960; rank
of Brigadier General, Nov. 20, l971.
k-Beat out*Víctor Cervera Pacheco* for
PRI gubernatorial nomination; not
favored for the governorship by his
predecessor, *Francisco Luna Kan*;
resigned as governor because of serious
problems with henequen workers and
accusations of "inexplicable wealth"
among his collaborators. l-Rev. de Ejer.,
Jan. 1974, 86; Rev. de Ej., Nov. 1971, 38;
HA, 24 Aug. 1981; *Excélsior*, 16 Aug.
1981, 6; HA, 27 Feb. 1980, 32; *Excélsior*,
5 Jan. 1983, 23; MGF72-73, 175; DPE61,
32; *El Nacional*, 3 Dec. 1990, 5.

Altamirano, Manlio Fabio

(Deceased Jan. 25, 1936) a-Oct. 12,
1892. b-Jalapa, Veracruz. c-Primary
studies in Misantla, Veracruz; preparatory studies at the National Preparatory
School, law degree from the National
Law School, UNAM. d-Federal Deputy
from the State of Veracruz (five times),
1916-25; *Senator* from Veracruz, 1934-
35; *Governor-elect* of Veracruz, 1936.
e-Member of the Obregonista Party;
signer of the Declaration by General
Calles setting forth the formation of the
National Revolutionary Party, Dec. 1,

1928. f-Director of Talleres Gráficos de
la Nación; Gerente of the government
daily newspaper *El Nacional.* g-Member of the radical groups supporting the
Casa del Obrero Mundial. j-None.
k-Assassinated as governor-elect before
he could take office, an event that
opened up the governorship to *Miguel
Alemán*, launching his national career.
l-DP70, 78; Peral, 43; Gruening, 480;
Gaxiola, 303, 23; Enc. Mex. I, 168;
González Navarro, 128-19; Q es Q, 17-
18; López, 45.

Altamirano Herrera, Rafael

(Deceased) a-July 25, 1908. b-Queré-
taro, Querétaro. c-Primary studies in
Querétaro, Querétaro; secondary studies
in Mexico City; preparatory studies in
Mexico City; law degree from the
National School of Law, UNAM, 1932,
with a specialization in penal law;
Professor by Opposition of Roman Law,
National School of Law, UNAM, 1944-
53. d-*Senator* from the State of Que-
rétaro, 1958- . e-None. f-Penal Judge in
Aguascalientes, Aguascalientes, 1932-
34; Judge of Civil and Treasury Matters,
Aguascalientes, 1934-35; Juvenile Court
Judge, 1935-41; Judge of the Eleventh
Civil Judicial District, 1941; Auxiliary
Secretary to the 5th Division of the
Higher Tribunal of Justice of the Federal
District; Justice of the Higher Tribunal
of Justice of Querétaro; Private Secre-
tary to the Director General of Pensions, 1953. g-None. j-None. k-None.
l-Func., 330; C de S, 1958-64, 10.

Alvarado, José

(Deceased Sept. 23, 1974) a-Sept. 21,
1911. b-Lampazos, Nuevo León.
c-Secondary studies in Monterrey;
preparatory studies at the Colegio Civil,
Monterrey; completed studies in law,
National School of Law, UNAM, but
never completed his thesis for a degree;
Professor of Literature and Philosophy,

National Preparatory School; professor at the University of Nuevo León; Rector of the University of Nuevo León, 1961-63. d-Candidate for Federal Deputy from the Popular Party, 1952. e-Supporter of José Vasconcelos for President, 1929; member of the CEN of the Popular Party, 1948. f-None. g-Secretary of the National Student Federation, 1933. h-Writer for *Barandal*; collaborator with the Spanish exiles on *Romance* and *Futuro*; wrote for *El Popular* in the 1940s; journalist for *El Nacional* until 1948; wrote for *Combate* and from the 1950s until 1974 was a writer for *Excélsior*. i-Friend of *Eduardo Livas* since primary school days, recommended him for rector as Governor of Nuevo León; friend of *Alejandro Gómez Arias* since 1929 in Monterrey; companion of *Enrique Ramírez y Ramírez* as a writer for *Claridad*, 1930; his father was a professor and secretary of the University of Nuevo León; married Cándida Pérez. j-None. k-Resigned from the rectorship of the University of Nuevo León after being attacked as a communist by certain interest groups. l-*Excélsior*, 26 Sept. 1974, *Excélsior*, 24 Sept. 1974; HA, 7 Oct. 1974; letter.

Alvarado (Alvarado), Silverio Ricardo
a-Feb. 7, 1917. b-Ozuloama, Veracruz. c-Primary studies in Veracruz; completed rural normal certificate, Rural Normal School, Ozuloama, Veracruz, 1929-30; no degree. d-*Alternate Federal Deputy* from the State of Veracruz, Dist. 2, 1943-46, under *Rafael Murillo Vidal*; member of the City Council of Tuxpan, Veracruz, 1943-46; Local Deputy to the State Legislature of Veracruz, 1950-53, 1962-65; *Federal Deputy* from the State of Veracruz, Dist. 2, 1967-70; *Federal Deputy* from the State of Veracruz, Dist. 1, 1973-76; *Senator* from the State of Veracruz,

1976-82; *Federal Deputy* from the State of Veracruz, Dist. 18, 1982-85. e-Joined the PRM, 1937; President of the PRM in Tuxpan, Veracruz, 1940-42; Subsecretary of Labor Action, CEN of PRI, 1975-80. f-None. g-Secretary of Organization of the Federation of Workers and Peasants of Northern Veracruz, 1941; Secretary of Organization of the Only Union of Workers of Veracruz, 1947; Secretary General of the Only Union of Workers of Veracruz, 1950; Secretary of Organization of the Revolutionary Federation of Workers and Peasants (CROC) of Veracruz, 1952-55; Secretary General of CROC in the State of Veracruz, 1958-61, 1964-67; Secretary of Technical and Economic Affairs of CROC, 1968-70; President of CROC, 1970-71; Secretary of Political Action, Revolutionary Federation of Mexican Workers (CROM), 1983-86. h-None. i-Married Celestina Roldán Casados; son of Tomás González Guillermo, a carpenter and in the military, and Eva Alvarado Sobrevilla. j-None. k-None. l-C de D, 1943-46; C de D, 1967-70; C de D, 1973-76; C de S, 1976-82; Directorio, 1982-85.

Alvarado Arámburo, Alberto Andrés
a-Feb. 4, 1925. b-La Paz, Baja California del Sur. c-Primary and secondary studies in Baja California del Sur; preparatory studies in biological sciences, National Preparatory School; completed two years of medical studies, National School of Medicine, UNAM. d-*Alternate Federal Deputy* from the State of Baja California del Sur, Dist. 1, 1961-64, under *Antonio Navarro Encinas*; *Federal Deputy* from the State of Baja California del Sur, Dist. 1, 1964-67; *Senator* from Baja California del Sur, 1976-81; *Governor of Baja California del Sur*, 1981-87. e-Youth Director of PRI; Director of Social Action of PRI; general delegate of the CEN of PRI to

Baja California del Sur; Subsecretary of the CEN of PRI; Special Delegate of the CEN of PRI to Sonora, Yucatán, Chihuahua, and Tlanepantla; *Secretary of Organization of the CEN of PRI,* 1976. f-Director of the Office of the Federal Electric Commission in Baja California del Sur; Director of the Office of Population, State of Baja California del Sur; Director of Property Control, State of Baja California del Sur; Delegate of the City of La Paz, 1954-56. g-None. h-None. i-Cousin of *Angel Mendoza Arámburo,* governor of Baja California del Sur, 1975-81 j-None. k-None. l-C de D, 1961-64, 6; C de D, 1964-67, 45; PS.

Alvarado González, Agustín
a-June 2, 1912. b-Martínez de la Torre, Veracruz. c-Primary studies at the Benito Juárez School; no secondary or college studies. d-Local Deputy, State Legislature of Veracruz; *Alternate Federal Deputy,* State of Veracruz, Dist. 4, 1952-55; *Federal Deputy,* State of Veracruz, Dist. 5, 1970-73, member of the Committees on National Lands, Agricultural Development, and the Ejido (Third Accounts). e-None. f-Director of the Department of Indigenous Affairs, Director of Agriculture, State of Veracruz. g-Secretary General of the League of Agrarian Communities of the State of Veracruz. h-None. j-None. k-None. l-C de D, 1952-54; Directorio, 1970-72, 100.

Alvarez Acosta, Miguel
a-Sept. 29, 1907. b-San Luis Potosí, San Luis Potosí. c-Primary studies in San Luis Potosí, teaching certificate, Normal School of San Luis Potosí, 1925; law degree, University of San Luis Potosí, 1931; Professor of Sociology, Civics, History, and Political Economy, Normal School of San Luis Potosí; Director of Primary School, San Luis

Potosí; Director of the Higher School of Xilitla. d-None. e-None. f-Technical adviser to the Secretariat of Foreign Relations; Consul to the United States and to Central America; Career Consul, 1939; Agent of the Ministerio Público of the Office of the Attorney General; Judge of the First Instance, Matehuala, San Luis Potosí; Magistrate of the Superior Tribunal of Justice of the State of San Luis Potosí; Substitute Governor of San Luis Potosí, 1938; representative to the Food and Agriculture Organization; Judge of the Federal Tax Court, 1942-54; Director General of the National Institute of Bellas Artes, July 29, 1954-58; Director General of Organizations for the International Promotion of Culture; rank of Ambassador in the Mexican Foreign Service; *Subsecretary of Broadcasting,* Secretariat of Communications and Transportation, 1972-76. g-Secretary General of the National Teachers Union, 1958. h-Began working at odd jobs at age 10; author of many novels and articles; legal adviser to the National Mixed Agrarian Commission. i-Son of Cirilo Alvarez Aldape, who died when he was a child; mother, María Macedonia, earned a living sewing. j-None. k-None. l-DEM,. 15; HA, 23 Oct. 1972, 18; HA, 9 Aug. 1954, 5; MGF69, 179; O'Campo, 15-16.

Alvarez Alvarez, Luis Héctor
a-Oct. 25, 1919. b-Camargo, Chihuahua. c-Primary studies in Camargo; secondary studies in Ciudad Juárez and at El Paso High School, El Paso, Texas; studied at University of Texas; engineering degree. d-Mayor of Chihuahua, Chihuahua, 1983-86. e-Candidate for governor of Chihuahua, National Action Party, 1956; joined PAN about 1953; member of the CEN of PAN; presidential candidate of PAN, 1958; *President* of PAN, 1986-93. f-None.

g-None. h-Involved in agricultural enterprises, 1942-46; textile manufacturer in Chihuahua, 1946-57; Director General of the Compañía Industrial Río Bravo, 1957; President of the Educational Center for Ciudad Juárez; textile manufacturer; retired, 1983. i-Son of an industrialist, merchant and rancher. j-None. k-Led PAN negotiations with PRI to support the 1989 electoral reforms. l-Scott, 184, 240; HAR, 12 Dec. 1957, 645-46; HA, 2 Dec. 1957; Morton, 105-06; Johnson, 33; Mabry, 155, 215, 55; *Proceso*, 22 Dec. 1986, 20-21; letter.

Alvarez Amézquita (Chimalpopoca), José
a-Aug. 4, 1911. b-Federal District. c-Primary and secondary studies at the Colegio Francés de Morelos; preparatory studies at the National Preparatory School (evening sessions) in Mexico City; medical degree, National School of Medicine, UNAM, 1935; Professor of Medicine and of specialized courses, National School of Medicine, UNAM, 1938-58. d-None. e-None. f-Chief of Surgical Services, Juárez Hospital, Mexico City, 1948; Director General of Medical Services, Secretariat of Labor, 1956-58; *Secretary of Health and Public Welfare*, 1958-64. g-President of the National Association of Surgeons, 1952. h-Intern, Juárez Hospital, Mexico City, 1933-34, 1935-39; Director General of Medical Assistance, Secretariat of Health and Public Welfare, 1949-52; founder of the Mexican Hospital Society. i-Attended secondary school with *Adolfo López Mateos*; son of José Alvarez Amézquita, a physician. j-None. k-None. l-HA, 9 Nov. 1964, 15-16; WWMG, 6; IWW66, HA, 8 Dec. 1955, 8, 28; DBM68, 28-29; DGF51, 340; *Quién Será*, 128; Func, 183; WWW70-71, 24.

Alvarez Borboa, Teófilo
(Deceased 1962) a-Jan. 8, 1891. b-Villa de Higueras de los Monzones, Badirahuato, Sinaloa. c-Primary studies in Villa de Higueras; secondary studies in the Federal District; teaching certificate from the Normal School, 1910. d-*Senator* from the State of Sinaloa, 1958-64, President of the Committee on Military Justice, member of the Second Naval Committee. e-None. f-Oficial Mayor of Government under *Juan de Dios Bojórquez*, 1934-35. g-None. h-None. i-School companion with *José Angel Ceniceros*. j-Joined the Revolution under General Obregón, Apr. 9, 1914, with the rank of 2nd Lieutenant; Commander of the 51st Battalion, 1925-26; Commander of the 42nd Battalion; Director of Justice for the 1st Military Zone; Brigade General, Nov. 1934; Supreme Chief of the Military Tribunal; Director of Infantry, Secretary of National Defense; Commander of the 7th Military Zone, Sonora and Sinaloa, 1951-57; rank of Division General, 1958. k-None. l-Func, 350; C de S, 1961-64, 51; DGF56, 201; DGF51, 103; DP70, 88-89.

Alvarez de la Fuente, Francisco
a-May 7, 1951. b-Río Grande, Zacatecas. c-Early education unknown; law degree, University of Tamaulipas, 1972-77; Professor of Economics and Sociology, Normal School of Tamaulipas; Professor of Economics, Teachers Education School; Professor of Law, José Vasconcelos Preparatory School, Tamaulipas; Professor of Experimental Methods and Structure, Ponciano Arriaga Preparatory School. d-*Plurinominal Federal Deputy* from the PDM, 1982-85. e-Legal adviser, PDM in Tamaulipas, 1979-80; Secretary of Organization of the PDM in Tamaulipas, 1980-81; President of the PDM in Tamaulipas, 1981-85; candidate of the

PDM for federal deputy from the 4th district of Tamaulipas, 1982. f-Employee, Forestry and Fauna Division, Secretariat of Agriculture; Agent of the Ministerio Público in the 10th Mixed Judicial District, Tula, Tamaulipas, 1979-81; Secretary of the Mixed Penal District, 1st Instance of the 11th Judicial District, Tamaulipas, 1978-79; Agent of the Ministerio Público, Jaunabe, Tamaulipas. g-None. h-Journalist. j-None. k-None. l-Directorio, 1982-85; C de D, 1982-85; Lehr, 628.

Alvarez del Castillo (Labastida), Enrique
a-Nov. 23, 1923. b-Guadalajara, Jalisco. c-Early education unknown; law studies from the National School of Law, UNAM, 1942-47, graduating 1947; LLD from the National School of Law, UNAM, 1950-51, graduating with an honorable mention; Professor of Labor Law, National School of Law, UNAM, 1953-78. d-*Federal Deputy* from the State of Jalisco, Dist. 25, 1976-79, member of the Section on Higher Education of the Educational Development Committee, the Section on Amparo of the Legislative Studies Committee, the Third Labor Committee and the Public Budget Committee; *Governor of Jalisco*, 1983-89. e-Joined PRI, 1944; *Subsecretary General of the CEN of PRI*, 1978. f-Department head, Division of Labor Relations, IMSS; *Secretary General of the Mexican Institute of Social Security*, 1965-66; Oficial Mayor of the Organizing Committee for the Olympic Games; *Supernumary Justice of the Supreme Court*, 1979-82; *Justice of the Supreme Court*, 1982; *Attorney General of Mexico*, 1988-91; Director General of Public Works Bank, 1991- . g-None. h-Administrative Director of Mexican Power and Light, 1970-73; legal counsel to ASARCO, San Luis Potosí; author of

many articles and books on labor law. i-Married Virginia Baeza; son of Antonio Alvarez del Castillo, journalist, and Berta Labastida; student of and close friend to *Mario de la Cueva*; nephew of Luis and Juan Manuel Alvarez del Castillo Velasco, secretary general of the Federal District, 1915, and federal deputy; cousin of *José Juan de Olloquí y Labastida*. j-None. k-Removed as Attorney General because of continued human rights abuses and drug trafficking. l-DBM68, 29-30; D de C, 1976-79, 21, 53, 78; C de D, 1976-79; *Proceso*, 20 Sept. 1982, 22-25; *Excélsior*, 12 Aug. 1982, 21; DBGM89, 29.

Alvarez González, Manuel
a-Jan. 6, 1914. b-Federal District. c-Completed secondary studies in Mexico City, 1929; graduated as a master mechanic from technical school, Mexico City. d-*Federal Deputy* from the Federal District, Dist. 10, 1961-64, 1967-70; *Federal Deputy* from the Federal District, Dist. 29, 1982-85. e-President of the Executive Committee of the 10th Electoral Committee, Federal District. f-None. g-Secretary General of the Meatworkers Union; Treasurer of the CTM, 1978-80; Assistant Secretary of Organization, CTM, 1981. h-Chief of Butchering, Central Foodstuffs, Federal District, 1939-82. j-None. k-None. l-Directorio, 1982-85; PS; Directorio, 1967-70; MGF69, 90; C de D, 1961-64, 6, 70; Lehr, 147.

Alvarez López, Manuel
(Deceased June 27, 1960) a-Sept. 15, 1885. b-Colima, Colima. c-Primary and secondary studies at the Seminario Conciliar of Colima; no degree. d-*Federal Senator* from the State of San Luis Potosí, 1946-52, member of the Health Committee and alternate member of the Second Ejido Commit-

tee; *Governor of San Luis Potosí*, 1955-59. e-None. f-Consul General in Buenos Aires; Consul General in Brazil. g-None. h-Industrialist. i-Part of *Gonzalo N. Santos* clique. j-Joined the Revolution, 1911, supported Francisco Madero. k-Anderson reports that he was forced out of the governorship of San Luis Potosí in Jan. 1959 because of close ties with *Gonzalo Santos*. l-DGF56, 99; NYT, 26 Oct. 1958, 19; HA, 3 Oct. 1955, 20-21; Anderson; DGF51, 7, 11, 14; PS.

Alvarez Nolasco, Ernesto
a-Mar. 20, 1920. b-Ahome, Sinaloa. c-Completed primary and secondary studies; preparatory studies from the University of Guadalajara, 1935-37; no degree. d-*Federal Deputy* from the State of Sinaloa, Dist. 1, 1961-64, member of the Waters and National Irrigation Committee and the National Properties Committee; *Federal Deputy* from the State of Sinaloa, Dist. 4, 1967-70. e-Joined PRI, 1952; general delegate of the CEN of PRI to Campeche, Yucatán, 1961-64; Regional Delegate of the CEN of PRI to Nayarit, Sonora, and Baja California, 1967-70; *Subsecretary of Press and Publicity of the CEN of PRI*, 1971-76. f-Director of the Federal Treasury Office, Los Mochis, Sinaloa, 1959-61; Director General of Information, Secretariat of the Government, 1976-79; Director General of Public Relations for the President of Mexico, June 6, 1979-82; Director General of Information and Public Relations, Secretariat of Public Education, 1982-85. g-Secretary General of CNOP in Sinaloa, 1964-67. h-Journalist, 1939- ; Editor, *Novedades, Diario de la Tarde*, 1939-58. i-Married Felisa Valdés; son of Cosme Alvarez Almada, teacher, and Margarita Nolasco. j-None. k-None. l-C de D, 1961-64, 70; C de D, 1967-70; PS; Q es QAP, 302; DBGM, 30.

Alvarez Ponce de León, Griselda
a-Apr. 5, 1913. b-Guadalajara, Jalisco. c-Normal teaching certificate; advanced studies at the Specialization Normal School, Secretariat of Public Education; degree in Spanish letters, UNAM; professor at the Specialization Normal School, 1951; primary school teacher. d-*Senator* from Colima, 1976-79; *Governor* of Colima, 1979-85. e-None. f-Subdirector of the Division of Social Action, Secretariat of Public Education, 1959-61; Director, 1961-64; Director of the Division of Social Work, Secretariat of Health; head of the Department of Social Work and Inspection, INDECO; Chief of Archives, Secretariat of Health; Director of Social Welfare Services, IMSS, 1976. g-None. h-Author and poet. i-Daughter of Miguel Alvarez García, governor of Colima; great-granddaughter of Manuel Alvarez, the first governor of Colima; niece of Higinio Alvarez, senator, deputy, and acting governor of Colima; father of *Antonio Toledo Corro*, governor of Sinaloa, 1980-86, administered her grandfather's hacienda in Sinaloa; close friend of *Victoria Adato de Ibarra*. j-None. k-First woman governor in Mexican history. l-HA, 10 May 1976, 12-13; DPE61, 103; Latin America, 26 Jan. 1979, 20; *Excélsior*, 7 Jan. 1979, 12; Enc. Mex., I, 1977, 163.

Alzalde Arellano, Ricardo
a-Apr. 3, 1907. b-Torreón, Coahuila. c-Early education unknown; no degree. d-*Federal Deputy* from the State of Baja California del Norte, 1949-52, Dist. 1, member of the Library Committee, the Hunting and Fishing Committee, the Second Ejido Committee, the Social Welfare Committee, and the Gran Comisión; *Federal Deputy* from the State of Baja California del Norte, 1958-61, Dist. 1, member of the Hunting and Fishing Committee, the National Lands

Committee, and the Budget and Accounts Committee. e-None. f-Director of Agrarian Affairs, Baja California del Norte, 1965. g-Peasant leader in Baja California del Norte, 1937; Secretary General of the League of Agrarian Communities of Baja California del Norte, 1948-49. h-Ejidatario. j-None. k-Moved to Baja California del Norte in 1937 as a peasant. l-DGF51, 19, 29, 30, 31, 32, 35; C de D, 1958-61, 69; C de D, 1949-52, 6, 63; Aguirre, 492; Func., 124.

Amador Amador, Jorge
a-Nov. 21, 1947. b-San Martín Hidalgo, Jalisco. c-Early education unknown; law degree, University of Guadalajara, 1970; graduate studies, Colegio de México, 1973-76; preparatory school teacher; professor, Colegio de México; professor, University of Guadalajara. d-*Plurinominal Federal Deputy* from PST, 1979-82; *Plurinominal Federal Deputy* from PST, 1985-88. e-Joined PST, 1973. f-None. g-None. h-None. i-Son of Jesús Amador Robles and Esther Amador Ortega; married Mica-Claire Gambrill Ruppert. j-None. k-None. l-C de D, 1985-88; C de D, 1979-82.

Amaro (Domínguez), Joaquín
(Deceased Mar. 15, 1952) a-Aug. 16, 1889. b-Hacienda Corrales de Abrego, Sombrerete, Zacatecas. c-Primary studies, Sombrerete, Zacatecas; no degree. d-None. e-None. f-Subsecretary of the Secretariat of National Defense, 1924; Secretary of National Defense, Dec. 30, 1924, to Nov. 30, 1928; Secretary of National Defense, Nov. 30, 1928, to Mar. 2, 1929; Secretary of National Defense, May 20, 1930, to Oct. 15, 1931; Director of the National Military College, 1931-35; Director of Military Education, 1935-36. g-None. h-None. i-Married Elisa Izaguirre; son of Antonio Amaro and

Angela Domínguez, peasants; father killed in the Revolution. j-Joined the Revolution as a private, Feb. 28, 1911, serving under Gertrudis Sánchez; fought against the forces of Bernardo Reyes, 1911; fought against the forces of Emiliano Zapata, 1913; participated in the battle of Celaya, 1915; joined Plutarco Calles and Alvaro Obregón in support of the Plan of Agua Prieta against Venustiano Carranza, 1919; rank of Division General, 1920; Commander of the 5th Division of the North, 1920; fought against the forces of Adolfo de la Huerta in the Bajio region, 1923; Director of the military prison camps, 1924; Commander of the military zones of Chihuahua, Durango, Nuevo León, Coahuila, and San Luis Potosí; Commander of the 28th Military Zone, Oaxaca, Oaxaca, 1947-50; Commander of the 18th Military Zone, Hidalgo, 1950-52. k-Precandidate for president of Mexico, 1939. l-Libro de Oro, 1935-36, 21; Enc. Mex., I, 1977, 277-78; DP70, 94-95; López, 52; NYT, 18 Feb. 1940, 23; WWM45, 4; Rev. de Ejer., Sept. 1976, 127.

Amaya Brondo, Abelardo
a-Apr. 19, 1918. b-Ciudad Juárez, Chihuahua. c-Agricultural engineering degree, National School of Agriculture, 1941; studies in Israel in irrigation. d-None. e-None. f-Engineer, Department of Studies and Projects, National Irrigation Commission, 1941-42; Engineer, Lower Salamanca Canal, Guanajuato, National Irrigation Commission, 1942-43; Engineer, San Juan River Irrigation District, Tamaulipas, National Irrigation Commission, 1943-48; Engineer, Morelos Dam, Colorado River, Secretariat of Hydraulic Resources, 1948-50; Engineer, Río Bravo Irrigation District, Secretariat of Hydraulic Resources, 1950-58; Gerente General of Hydraulic Resources in the

State of Nuevo León, 1959-61; Subdirector General of Irrigation Districts of the Secretariat of Hydraulic Resources, 1961-64; Director General of Irrigation Districts of the Secretariat of Hydraulic Resources, 1964-70; *Subsecretary B of Hydraulic Resources*, 1970-76; *Subsecretary of Agriculture and Operations*, 1978-82. g-None. i-Brother, Mario, was director of public works in Baja California del Norte for many years; married Alicia Enderle. j-None. k-None. l-D de Y, 2 Dec. 1970; DGF69, 302; DPE65, 130; HA, 14 Dec. 1970, 22; BCN, 492; Protag., 27.

Amaya Rodríguez, Federico
a-Mar. 2, 1902. b-Villa de Iturbide, Nuevo León. c-Early education unknown; graduate of the Heroic Military College, Jan. 1, 1922, as a 2nd Lieutenant in administration; professor, Higher War College, 1936. d-*Senator* from the State of Nuevo León, 1976-82; member of the Gran Comisión, the Military Health Committee, the National Defense Committee, the Consular Service Committee, and the National Defense Committee. e-None. f-Chief of the Department of Licensing and Public Meetings, Department of the Federal District, 1945-46; technical adviser to the Director General of Pemex, 1946-48; Ambassador to Yugoslavia; Ambassador to Paraguay, 1953; Director of Traffic, Department of the Federal District; Director General of the Institute of Social Security of the Armed Forces, 1977-78. g-None. h-None. i-Married Carmen Rodríguez Morales; son Federico Amaya Rodríguez, director general in Secretariat of Agrarian Reform and graduate of Heroic Military College. j-Career army officer; served with the 1st Battalion, Secretary of War, 1922-29; Assistant Chief of Staff, Querétaro Military Zone; Assistant Chief of Staff,

Presidential Staff; Chief of Staff, Presidential Staff; Military Attaché, various Central American countries; Commander of the Mechanized Brigade, Military Camp No. 1, 1952-53; Military Zone commander of San Luis Potosí, Durango, Nuevo León, and Jalisco. k-None. l-Protag., 27; C de S, 1976-82.

Amezcua Dromundo, Cuauhtémoc
a-July 4, 1938. b-Mexico City. c-Self-educated; communications degree, UNAM; secondary teacher, foreign languages; principal, various secondary schools. d-*Plurinominal Federal Deputy* from the PPS, 1979-82; *Plurinominal Federal Deputy* from the PPS, 1985-88; *Alternate Senator* from the Federal District, 1988-91; *Plurinominal Federal Deputy* from the PPS, 1991-94. e-Joined the PPS, 1957; member of the executive committee of the PPS in the Federal District, 1968- ; member of the Central Committee of the PPS, 1973- ; Secretary General of the PPS in the Federal District, 1979-84; member of the National Directorate of the PPS, 1982- ; Press Secretary of the PPS, 1984-85; International Relations Secretary of the PPS, 1985-88; Organization Secretary of the PPS, 1988. f-None. g-None. h-None. i-Son of Artemio Amezcua López and Noema Dromundo; married María de Lourdes Orellana. j-None. k-None. l-DBGM87, 434; letter.

Amezcua Gudiño, Leticia
a-Oct. 12, 1941. b-Sahuayo, Michoacán. c-Early education unknown. d-Secretary of the City Council of Sahuayo, 1978; *Federal Deputy* from the State of Michoacán, Dist. 11, 1979-82. e-Member of *Luis Echeverria*'s campaign committee in Michoacán, 1969; President of the PRI in Sahuayo, Michoacán, 1972-75; general delegate of the CEN of PRI in Michoacán, 1976; general delegate of the CEN of PRI,

local elections, Michoacán, 1977;
Coordinator for the mayoralty campaign
of Sahuayo, Michoacán, 1977. f-None.
g-President of the Municipal Student
Committee, 1960; correspondent of the
University Student Council of San
Nicolás de Hidalgo, 1959; Secretary of
Women's Action of the Municipal
League of CNOP, 1972. h-None.
i-Daughter of Carlos Amezcua Ramírez
and Julia Gudiño Galvéz. j-None.
k-None. l-Romero Aceves, 685-86; C de
D, 1979-82.

Amilpa (y Rivera), Fernando
(Deceased Jan. 18, 1952) a-May 30,
1898. b-Jojutla de Juárez, Morelos.
c-Primary and secondary studies in
public schools in Morelos; no degree.
d-*Federal Deputy* from the State of
Morelos, Dist. 6, 1937-40; Vice President of the Gran Comisión, 1939;
Secretary of the Gran Comisión, Sept.
1937. *Senator* from Morelos, 1940-46;
Federal Deputy from the Federal
District, Dist. 8, 1946-49, member of
the Committee on Labor, the Committee on General Communication Lines;
President of the Chamber of Deputies,
Nov. 1948. e-Candidate for governor of
Morelos, 1945. f-None. g-Member of
the Confederation of Mexican Workers;
worked with labor movement under
General Obregón; represented the labor
unions when the government established the first Board of Conciliation
and Arbitration; member of the Secretariat of the Union of Bus Drivers of the
Federal District; labor representative on
the Municipal Council of the Federal
District; member of the Secretariat of
the Transportation Union Workers of
the Department of Transportation of
the Federal District; Secretary General
of the General Federation of Workers
and Peasants, 1935-36; *Secretary
General of the Confederation of
Mexican Workers*, 1946-50. h-Truck
driver, Department of Sanitation,

Department of the Federal District.
i-Three of his daughters became active
as leaders in the CTM; helped *Vicente
Lombardo Toledano* and *Fidel
Velázquez* organize the CTM. j-Fought
with Emiliano Zapata in Morelos, 1915.
k-Precandidate for governor of Morelos,
1945. l-EBW46, 48; DP70, 100; Novo35,
130; C de D, 1946-49, 64; *Excélsior*, 31
Mar. 1947; WB48, 167; González
Navarro, 141; Enc. Mex., I, 285.

Amorós (Guiot), Roberto
(Deceased Aug. 14, 1973) a-June 8,
1914. b-Coatepec, Veracruz. c-Primary
studies in Jalapa; secondary studies in
Veracruz; law degree, School of Law,
University of Veracruz, Jalapa, Apr. 17,
1935; fellowship in economics, University of Rome. d-*Senator* from Veracruz,
1952. e-Active in *Avila Camacho*'s
presidential campaign, 1940; Director of
the Office of Policy Coordination and
Technical Affairs, *Ruiz Cortines'*
campaign, 1952. f-Oficial Mayor of the
Presidency, June 9, 1943, to July, 1946;
Secretary of the Presidency, July, 1946,
to Nov. 30, 1946; *Oficial Mayor of the
Presidency*, Dec. 1, 1946, to Jan. 1,
1948; *Subsecretary of the Presidency*,
Jan. 1, 1948, to Nov. 13, 1951; *Director
General of the National Railroads of
Mexico*, 1952-58; *Director General of
CONASUPO*, 1958-64; Auxiliary
Secretary to the President of Mexico,
1964-70. g-Secretary General of the
National Union of Educational Workers, 1939. h-Director of the Department
of Conventions, Secretariat of Labor,
1940; President of the Board of Directors of PIPSA; legal consultant to the
Secretariat of the Presidency; Director
of Editoral Ruto; President of the
National Council of Sugar, Secretariat
of Labor; government representative to
the National Printing Office, 1970-73;
author of several books on law and
articles on decentralized government
agencies. i-Collaborated professionally

with *Benjamín Méndez Aguilar* and *Carlos Hank González*; married Karin Riekfol. j-None. k-None. l-*Hoy*, 29 Apr. 1967, 60; DGF56, 8; DGF47; D del S, 5 Dec. 1946, l; DGF50, II, 189, 355, 361; DGF51, I, 55; II. 510; Enc. Mex. I, 390; Func. 107; *Quién Será*, 152; HA, 2 July 1956, 42; Novo, 657; *Excélsior*, 15 Aug. 1973, 2B; HA, 20 Aug. 1973; Illescas, 745.

Anaya Ramírez, Rafael
a-Aug. 17, 1910. b-Molango, Hidalgo. c-Primary studies in Molango; rural teaching certificate from the Regional Normal School, Apr. 7, 1926; normal studies, Normal School of Pachuca, 1945-50, certificate, Apr. 24, 1951; rural school teacher; primary urban school teacher; director of an elementary school; primary school inspector, Hidalgo. d-Local Deputy to the State Legislature of Hidalgo, Dist. 8, 1957-60; *Alternate Senator* from the State of Hidalgo for *Raúl Lozano Ramírez*, 1970-75; *Senator* from the State of Hidalgo, Sept. 1, 1975, to Aug. 31, 1976. e-None. f-Representative of the General Coordinator's Office, Secretariat of Public Education, 1960; educational inspector for State of Hidalgo, 1969; Director of Adult Education, State of Hidalgo, 1969-78; President of National Committee of Adult Education Administrators, Secretariat of Public Education, 1969-77. g-Secretary of Finances of Local 15 of the SNTE, 1951-54; Secretary General of Local 15 of the SNTE, 1954-58; Secretary General of the State Coordinating Committee of the FSTSE, 1963-69; President of the National Committee of Public Teachers of the SNTE, 1964-67. h-None. i-Has known *Raúl Lozano Ramírez* since childhood. j-None. k-Part of a group of prominent Hidalgo politicians who advanced their careers inside the SNTE. l-MGF73, 65; C de S, 1970-76, 11; López Pérez, 521-22.

Anchondo Fernández, Rebeca
a-Jan. 29, 1926. b-Casas Grandes, Chihuahua. c-Primary studies, Regional Women's Institute, Chihuahua, Chihuahua; secondary studies at the Nuevo Casas Grandes Business School, Chihuahua. d-Member of the City Council of Nuevo Casas Grandes, 1956-59; Alternate Mayor of Nuevo Casas Grandes, 1971-74; Local Deputy to the State Legislature of Chihuahua, 1974-77; *Federal Deputy* from the State of Chihuahua, Dist. 9, 1979-82. e-Secretary of PRI of Nuevo Casas Grandes, 1951-58. f-Scribe, First Officer and Secretary of First Appeals Judicial District, 1941-62; Secretary of the City Council of Nuevo Casas Grandes, 1962-74. g-Secretary of Feminine Action of Nuevo Casas Grandes, 1946-48, 1959-71; Secretary General of CNOP of Nuevo Casas Grandes, 1959-62. h-None. i-Daughter of Jesús María Anchondo Terrazas and Carmen Fernández Guzmán; married Rafael Rodríguez Acuna. j-None. k-None. l-Romero Aceves, 687-88; C de D, 1979-82.

Anderson Nevárez, Hilda
a-Oct. 10, 1938. b-Mazatlán, Sinaloa. c-Primary studies at the Escuela Josefa Ortiz de Domínguez, Mazatlán; secondary studies at the Secondary School No. 4, Federal District; National Normal School, Mexico City (2 years); female literacy course, International Labor Organization, Geneva, Switzerland; studied at St. John's College, Maryland; intensive course on female labor, Ebert Foundation; Bonn, Germany; studies at the University of Wisconsin in radio, television, and feminist labor, 1961. d-*Federal Deputy* from the Federal District, Dist. 13, 1964-67, Secretary, 1965; member of the Social Action Committee, the Radio Industry Committee, and the Mexican-United States InterParliamentary Congress; *Federal Deputy* from the Federal District, Dist.

19, 1970-73, member of the Department of the Federal District Committee, and the Foreign Relations Committee; *Senator* from Sinaloa, 1976-82, President of the Chamber, Dec. 1976; *Federal Deputy* from the Federal District, Dist. 13, 1982-1985; *Federal Deputy* from the Federal District, Dist. 13, 1988-91, Delegate to the Federal District Assembly, Dist. 13, 1991-94. e-General Delegate of the CEN of PRI to Yucatán and Sonora, and to Dist. 13 of the Federal District, 1967-68; Secretary General of ANFER, National Revolutionary Woman's Group of PRI; *Secretary of Women's Action of the CEN of PRI*, 1972. f-None. g-President of the Women's Subcommittee for the Labor Congress; Secretary General of the Workers Federation of Women's Organizations of the Mexican Revolution of the CTM; Secretary of the Institute of Worker's Education, CTM; Secretary of Relations for the Radio Industry Workers Union. h-None. i-Daughter of Roberto F. Anderson Renero, an engineer, and Hilda Nevárez, a teacher. j-None. k-None. l-Directorio, 70-72; C de D, 1964-66, 77, 87; C de D, 1970-72, 100; HA, 20 Dec. 1976, 43; Directorio, 82-85; Romero Aceves, 369-70; DBGM89, 397-98; DBGM92, 608.

Andrade de (del Rosal), Marta
a-Feb. 7, 1920. b-Nogales, Sonora. c-Secondary studies at the Rural Normal School in Actopan, Hidalgo, 1936; education studies at the National School of Teachers in Mexico City; studies in social science at the Superior Normal School in Mexico City, 1940; teaching certificate for secondary schools; studied social policy at Claremont College, California, 1941; rural school teacher at age 16 in Actopan, Hidalgo; teacher of civics, Spanish literature, history, and other subjects in the secondary schools of the Federal District. d-*Federal Deputy* from the

Federal District, Dist. 6, member of the Social Welfare Committee (1st year), member of the Second Government Committee, 1958-61; *Federal Deputy* from the Federal District, Dist. 12, 1964-67, member of the Committee on the Diplomatic and Consular Service, the Second Public Education Committee, and the Library Committee (1st year); *Federal Deputy* from the Federal District, Dist. 21, 1976-79, member of the Social Action Committee, the Middle Education Section of Educational Development, Development of Tourism Committee, Housing Development Committee, and Federal District Committee; *Alternate Senator from the Federal District*, 1982-88; Representative to the Federal District Assembly, Dist. 38, 1988-91. e-Member of the Confederation of Mexican Youth, Mexican Revolutionary Party, 1936; head of Policy Inspection for the Confederation of Mexican Youth; member of the National Directive Committee for *Avila Camacho*, 1934-40; head of the Department of Women's Action of the Youth Activities Section, 1936; organized the first Women's Committee, 1939; Secretary of the Organization of the Mexican Revolutionary Party, 1939; organized the National Women's Committee in favor of *Ruiz Cortines* for President, 1951; Secretary of the National Women's Committee of Political Action of the National Executive Committee of PRI, 1952; Secretary of the Organization of the Women's Council of the Executive Regional Committee of the Federal District, 1952-53; Director of Women's Action of the Regional Committee of PRI in the Federal District, 1953; official orator of PRI, 1953; official orator in the *Díaz Ordaz* campaign, 1964; state delegate of PRI to Mexico, Veracruz, Hidalgo, and the Federal District; member of the National Women's Council of the CNOP of PRI;

Oficial Mayor of PRI in the Federal District, 1976; Secretary General of PRI in the Federal District, 1977. f-Head of the Nursery Department, Secretariat of Public Education, 1946-47; Director of Social and Cultural Action, 1979-81; Subdirector of Social Services, ISSTE, 1982. g-Organized the first nursery for the children of employees of the Secretariat of Public Education in the Federal District. h-Author of articles on women in Mexico. i-Daughter of Angel Alfonso Andrade Córdoba and Luz Guzmán Rivero, teachers; married Juan José del Rosal Paulín, lawyer. j-None. k-Members of the female sector of PRI opposed her candidacy in 1957-58 as a federal deputy from the Federal District because of her campaign trip through the state of Puebla, which caused considerable dissension; candidate for federal deputy from the ninth district of the Federal District, 1955. l-C de D, 1958-60; C de D, 1964-66; DBM68, 188-90; DGF47, 171; Morton, 87, 100-01, 107-08; Func., 181; D de C, 1976-79, 4, 20, 41, 44, 47; DBGM 89, 564; DAPC, 6.

Andrade Ibarra, José Luis
a-May 27, 1939. b-Amatlán, Jalisco. c-Primary studies begun at the age of eight and completed at age fourteen; secondary studies in La Paz, Baja California del Sur, and in Mexicali; normal certificate, Mexicali; special studies in civics and pedagogy, Superior Normal School of Jalisco; three years of studies in mathematics; secondary school teacher, Mexicali. d-*Federal Deputy* from Baja California, Dist. 1, 1979-82. e-*Secretary of Social Action of the CEN of PRI,* 1979-80; *Secretary of International Affairs of the CEN of PRI,* 1981; precandidate for senator from Baja California, 1981. f-None. g-Secretary of Labor and Conflicts, Local 37 of the SNTE, Mexicali; Secretary General of various sections of the SNTE; Secretary General of Local 37 of the SNTE;

Secretary General of the SNTE, 1977-80; President of the Congress of Labor, 1980. h-As a child worked in the fields. j-None. k-None. l-HA, 3 Apr. 1978, 8; *Excélsior,* 3 Feb. 1980, 6; *Excélsior,* 26 Dec. 1981, 16; Protag., 29.

Andreu Almazán, Juan
(Deceased Oct. 9, 1965) a-May 12, 1891. b-Olinalá, Guerrero. c-Primary studies in Olinalá; preparatory studies at the Colegio del Estado de Puebla, 1903-08; medical studies, Colegio del Estado de Puebla, 1908-10, no degree. d-None. e-None. f-Secretary of Communications and Public Works, 1930-32. g-None. h-Director of the Anáhuac Construction Company. i-Parents were wealthy landowners; friend of Revolutionary precursor, Aquiles Serdán; brother of *Leonides Andreu Almazán.* j-Joined the Revolution in 1910 under Madero; fought under Emiliano Zapata, 1911; rank of Brigadier General, May 3, 1911; joined General Huerta, 1913; opposed Madero, 1912-13; fought against Rómulo Figueroa; opposed Carranza, 1915-20; one of the youngest Revolutionary generals; joined Obregón, 1920; rank of Division General, Jan. 1, 1921; Commander of the 5th Military Zone, Monterrey, Nuevo León, 1924-34; appointed Chief of Staff to Carranza, but never served in that position; commander of a military column against General Escobar, 1929; Commander of the 6th Military Zone, Torreón, Coahuila; fought against de la Huerta, 1923. k-Went into exile after General Huerta was defeated; resigned from the Army in 1939 to become a presidential candidate of the Revolutionary Party of National Unification; after defeat went into exile in Panama, Cuba, and the United States, 1940-47, but later returned to Mexico; Brandenburg considers him in the Inner Circle from 1935-40; was one of the wealthiest men in Mexico. l-DP70, 107; Kirk,

233ff; Enc. Mex. I, 407; Brandenburg, 80; CB, 27 July 1940, 14-16; NYT, 1 Aug. 1938; CH, Apr. 1940, 36; Michaels, 25-30; WB54, 136; Daniels, 80-81; Peral, 55; Bermúdez, 141; NYT, 11 Oct. 1965, 39.

Andreu Almazán, Leonides
(Deceased Jan. 18, 1963) a-Aug. 8, 1896. b-Olinalá, Guerrero. c-Preparatory studies in Puebla; medical degree from the National School of Medicine, UNAM, 1923; hygienist at the University of Paris; Professor of Medicine at the Military Medical School. d-Governor of Puebla, 1929-33, resigned shortly before completion of term. e-None. f-Ambassador to Great Britain, 1935; Minister to Germany, Oct. 27, 1935, to 1938; *Head of the Department of Health*, 1938-39. g-None. h-Chief of the Clinic of the Necker Institute in Mexico, D.F.; Chief of Urological Services of the Military Hospital in Mexico, D.F.; Chief of the Pharmacy Department of the Mexican Institute of Social Security; adviser to the Mexican Institute of Social Security. i-Brother of *Juan Andreu Almazán*, resigned as head of the Health Department to direct brother's campaign for president, 1939; related to *Miguel Andreu Almazán*, federal deputy from Guerrero, Dist. 4, 1937-39. j-Fought with Emiliano Zapata during the Revolution. l-Peral, 55; D del S, 17 Jan. 1938; DP70, 106-07.

Anguiano (Equihua), Victoriano
(Deceased 1958) a-1908. b-Michoacán. c-Early education unknown; law degree, University of Michoacán; Professor of Law, University of Michoacán; Rector, University of Michoacán, 1940; Professor of Law and History, UNAM. d-Federal Deputy from the State of Michoacán, Dist. 7, 1935-37; *Federal Deputy* from the State of Michoacán, Dist. 5, 1946-49, member of the Immigration Committee and the Library Committee. e-Supporter of José Vasconcelos, 1929; Secretary General of the National Independent Democratic Party, 1946, which supported *Ezequiel Padilla* for president of Mexico; Assistant Secretary General of the Popular Party, 1947; Secretary General of the Popular Party, 1948-49; Member of the National Coordinating Committee of the Popular Party, 1947. f-Agent of the Ministerio Público of the Attorney General's Office; Secretary General of Government of the State of Michoacán; Justice of the Superior Tribunal of Justice of the State of Michoacán, 1951-58. g-None. i-Mother, a Tarascan Indian; nephew, Hermenegildo Anguiano Martínez, federal deputy, 1988-91; brother Luis Anguiano Equihua, an agronomist. j-None. k-Resigned as Secretary General of the Popular Party after he was criticized for his denunciation of *Lázaro Cárdenas* as a cacique in Michoacán; political enemy of *Lázaro Cárdenas*. l-*Excélsior*, 14 Nov. 1949; Villaseñor, II, 120; DGF47, 9; C de D, 1946-49; Enc. Mex., 1977, I, 309-10; DBGM89, 598

Angulo, Mauro
(Deceased 1948) a-1894. b-Santa Ana Chiautempan, Tlaxcala. c-Law degree from the Colegio del Estado de Puebla, 1915. d-Local Deputy to the State Legislature of Tlaxcala (twice); Federal Deputy from the State of Tlaxcala, Dist. 3, 1920-22; Federal Deputy from the State of Tlaxcala, Dist. 1, 1928-30; Provisional Governor of Tlaxcala, 1933; *Senator* from Tlaxcala, 1934-40; *Federal Deputy* from the State of Tlaxcala, Dist. 1, 1943-44; *Interim Governor of Tlaxcala*, 1944-45; *Senator* from Tlaxcala, 1946-48. f-Legal adviser to the State of Tlaxcala, 1920; Attorney General of Justice of the State of Puebla; Secretary General of Government of the State of San Luis Potosí. g-None.

h-None. j-None. k-Assassinated in
Mexico City in 1948. l-DP70, 111;
letter; Peral, 56; DGF47, 22.

Angulo (Gallardo), Melquiades
(Deceased 1966) a-July 26, 1889. b-Hacienda de San José de Porras, Municipio
de Allende, Chihuahua. c-Degree in
engineering from the College of Mining,
1917. d-None. e-None. f-Oficial Mayor
of the State of Chihuahua, 1918-19;
Secretary of Government of the State of
Chihuahua, 1919-20; Provisional Governor of Chihuahua, 1919-20; *Subsecretary of Public Works*, 1938-39; *Secretary of Public Works*, 1939-40; Chief of
the Department of Railroads of the
Secretariat of Public Works, 1934-38.
g-None. h-Involved in developing new
plan for the city of Querétaro, 1918;
employed for many years by the Secretariat of Public Works; became a rancher in Jalisco, 1940. i-Son of Melquiades Angulo and Concepción Gallardo.
j-None. k-Did not support the Plan of
Agua Prieta, 1920. l-DP70, 111; D de Y,
6 Apr. 1938, 1; Almada, 543-44.

Apodaca Osuna, Francisco
a-Apr. 2, 1910. b-Rosario, Sinaloa.
c-Law degree, National School of Law,
UNAM, 1940-45; advanced studies in
law, University of Paris, 1947-48;
advanced studies in economics, London
School of Economics, 1950-53; Professor
of Law at the National Law School,
UNAM, 1946-47. d-None. e-None.
f-Subdirector General of Credit, Secretariat of the Treasury, 1954-58; scientific investigator for the Department of
Credit, Secretariat of the Treasury,
1957-58; executive adviser to the
Council on Foreign Commerce attached
to the Secretariat of Foreign Relations;
head of the council 1961-64; *Ambassador to France*, 1965-70, g-None. h-First
job as a lawyer for the Secretariat of the
Treasury, 1945; scientific investigator

for the Secretariat of the Treasury, 1946;
Subdirector General for the Secretariat
of National Patrimony, 1947; subdelegate to Europe for the Secretariat of
National Patrimony, 1948; investigator
for the Institute of Comparative Law,
1949; scientific investigator for the
Secretariat of the Treasury, 1950.
i-Married Beatriz Nájera. j-None.
k-None. l-DGF56, 163; BdM, 60-61;
DPE61, 19; MGF69, 181.

Aponte Robles Arenas, Francisco Javier
a-Nov. 26, 1919. b-Federal District.
c-Primary, secondary, and preparatory
studies in Mexico City; no degree.
d-*Federal Deputy* (Party Deputy from
the PAN), 1967-70, member of the
Rural Electric, Sugar Industry, Public
Works, Tourism, and Public Housing
Committees; *Plurinominal Deputy*
from the PAN, 1979-82. e-Joined PAN,
1966; Delegate of the CEN of PAN to
Mérida, Yucatán, 1967; adviser to the
CEN of PAN, 1970; President of the
Regional Committee of PAN in
Morelos, 1970; campaign coordinator
for PAN in Baja California, 1977.
f-None. g-Member of the Mexican
Electricians Union. i-Married Marina
Maysse. j-None. k-None. l-Directorio,
1967-70, C de D, 1967-70, 65, 74, 81, 90,
91; Protag., 30-31.

Aragón Rebolledo, Eliseo B.
a-June 14, 1887. b-Axochiapan, Morelos. c-Primary studies in Morelos;
secondary and preparatory studies in
Mexico City; law degree from the
National School of Law, UNAM.
d-City councilman; Local Deputy to the
36th State Legislature, of Morelos;
Federal Deputy from the State of
Morelos, Dist. 2, 1943-46; *Senator* from
the State of Morelos, 1958-64, President
of the Special Tourist Affairs and the
Special Legislative Studies Committees;
member of the Gran Comisión; and the

Protocol, Migration, Rules, and First Foreign Relations Committees. e-Founding member of the PNR, PRM, and the PRI. f-Appeals court judge. g-None. h-Author. j-None. k-None. l-Func., 280; C de S, 1958-64, 9, 51.

Aranda del Toro, Luis
a-1901. b-Tepic, Nayarit. c-Secondary and Preparatory Studies at the University of Guadalajara; medical degree, School of Medicine, University of Guadalajara. d-*Federal Deputy* from the State of Nayarit, Dist. 1, 1937-40; *Senator* from the State of Nayarit, 1940-46, President of the Economy and Statistics Committee, First Secretary of the Colonization Committee and Prosecretary of the Senate, 1946. e-None. f-Chief of Medical Services, Department of Pensions. g-None. h-Practicing physician. i-His friendship with *Miguel Alemán* launched his public career in 1937. j-None. k-None. l-C de S, 1940-46; Libro de Oro, 1946, 5; PS; C de D, 1937-40.

Aranda Osorio, Efraín
a-Nov. 17, 1905. b-Motozintla de Mendoza, Chiapas. c-Primary studies in Motozintla; secondary in Mexico City; preparatory studies at the National Preparatory School, Mexico City; law degree, National School of Law, UNAM, 1932. d-*Federal Deputy* from the State of Chiapas, Dist. 4, 1937-40, President of the Chamber of Deputies, President of the Political Control Committee; *Governor of Chiapas* 1952-57; *Senator* from the State of Chiapas, 1946-52. e-Chief of *Miguel Alemán's* presidential campaign in the State of Chiapas, 1945-46. f-Judge of Soconusco, Veracruz; Civil Judge, Tapachula, 1933, Chiapas; Civil Judge of the Federal District, 1935; lawyer attached to the Office of the Attorney General of Mexico; Judge of the Superior Tribunal of the Federal District, 1941-43; Private

Secretary to the Governor of Chiapas, 1932; Secretary General of Government of the State of Chiapas, 1944-46; Ambassador to Guatemala, 1958-61. g-None. h-Working own cattle ranch, 1958. i-Nephew, Antonio Aranda Osorio, was a Federal Deputy, 1970-73; brother-in-law of Octavio Cal y Mayor. j-None. k-Candidate for Governor of Chiapas, 1943. l-HA, 6 Feb. 1948, 9; HA 29 Oct. 1943, 14; *Siempre*, 28 Jan. 1959, 6; DGF47, 19; DGF56, 91; letter, DGF51, 5; WB48, 233; DPE61, 22; HA, 4 Nov. 1955, 18; DBC, 10.

Araujo (y Araujo), Emilio
(Deceased Oct. 23, 1953) a-Aug. 9, 1892. b-Tuxtla Gutiérrez, Chiapas. c-Law degree, National School of Law, UNAM, 1913-17. d-Represented the State of Chiapas at the Constitutional Congress, 1916-17; Mayor of Tuxtla Gutiérrez; Federal Deputy and President of the Chamber of Deputies, 1917-20; *Federal Deputy* from State of Chiapas, Dist. 3, 1937-40; *Interim Governor of Chiapas*, 1938; *Senator* from Chiapas, 1940-46; President of the Senate, 1942; President of the First Justice Committee, Secretary of the Constitutional Affairs, Foreign Relations, and Consular and Diplomatic Service Committees, and member of the First Balloting Group. f-Judge of the lower court in Chiapas; legal adviser to the Department of the Federal District; legal adviser to the Mexican delegation at the United Nations Conference in San Francisco, 1945; Secretary General of Government of the State of Chiapas (twice). g-None. h-Member of various commercial and scientific commissions in Europe, 1920-37; lawyer for the Mexico City Chamber of Commerce in Europe, 1927. i-Close to President Carranza during constitutionalist movement, fled with Carranza in 1920; law partner with *Ezequiel Padilla*; married Eloísa Ana Mónica Mendizábal

Gutiérrez; son, Roberto Araujo Mendizábal, is a lawyer with the firm of Padilla and Araujo. j-None. k-President of the Mexican Democratic Party, which ran *Ezequiel Padilla* for president in 1945-46. l-WWM45, 5; DP70, 129; Peral, 61; letter; Medina, No. 20, 61.

Arellano Belloc, Francisco
(Deceased Mar. 9, 1972) a-Feb. 9, 1900. b-Rioverde, San Luis Potosí. c-Law degree, founder of the Michoacán Academy of Science, Letters, and Poetry. d-*Federal Deputy* from the State of San Luis Potosí, Dist. 3, 1937-40. f-Oficial Mayor of Government of the State of Michoacán, 1924; Judge of the First Instance in the State of Veracruz; Secretary General of Government under *Lázaro Cárdenas*; Secretary of Resolutions of the Supreme Court of Justice; Acting Governor of the State of Sonora; Judge of the Superior Tribunal of Justice of the Federal District and Federal Territories; chief of the legal department of Petróleos Mexicanos; legal adviser to Petróleos Mexicanos, 1972. g-None. h-Founder of the magazine *Mastiles*, published poetry with *Jaime Torres Bodet*, 1918; member of United Nations' missions to Latin America to establish petroleum legislation. j-None. k-None. l-HA, 20 Mar. 1972, 24; Peral, 62; Novo35, 235.

Arellano Tapia, Alicia
b-Magdalena, Sonora. c-Primary and secondary studies in Magdalena; preparatory studies at the University of Guadalajara; medical degree as a dental surgeon, School of Medicine, University of Guadalajara, 1952; Professor of Oral Pathology, School of Medicine, IPN; Chief of Dental Services, IPN. d-*Alternate Federal Deputy* from the State of Sonora, 1958-61; *Federal Deputy* from the State of Sonora, Dist. 2, 1961-63, member of the Public Health and Library Committees;

Senator from the State of Sonora, 1964-70; Mayor of Magdalena, Sonora, 1974-77; Mayor of Hermosillo, Sonora, 1979-81. e-Director of Women's Action of PRI in Sonora; Director of a Free Dental Clinic for the poor for PRI; Auxiliary Secretary of the CEN of PRI, 1966. f-None. g-National Coordinator of the CEN of CNOP. h-Practicing dentist. i-Married Dr. Pavolich. j-None. k-First woman senator, along with *María Lavalle Urbina*, in Mexico. l-*Excélsior*, 8 July 1979, 18; WWMG, 7; PS; G of S, 34; *Excélsior*, 9 Apr. 1979, 14; HA, 7 Mar. 1966, 17.

Arévalo Gardoqui, Juan
a-July 23, 1921. b-Federal District. c-Early education unknown; enrolled as a cadet at the Heroic Military College, 1940, graduating as a 2nd Lieutenant in the Cavalry, 1943; completed cavalry course at the Applied Military School, 1944; graduated from the Higher War College, 1947-50; officer of cadets, Heroic Military College, 1945; instructor, Higher War College. d-None. e-Director of security in the *Adolfo López Mateos* presidential campaign, 1957-58. f-*Secretary of National Defense*, 1982-88. g-None. h-None. i-Son of Divison General Gustavo Arévalo Vera and Magdalena Gardoqui; married María del Carmen LaMadrid. j-Career army officer; First Cadet and Corporal of Cadets, Heroic Military College; junior officer, 16th and 18th Cavalry Regiments; Chief of Section 1, Staff, 2nd Military Region, El Cipres, Baja California; Chief of Section 1, Staff, 3rd Military Region, Mérida, Yucatán; Chief of Section 1, Staff, Secretariat of National Defense; Chief of 3rd and 4th Sections, Staff, extinct Mechanized Brigade, 1951-54; Chief of 3rd and 4th Sections, Presidential Guards, 1954-57; Chief of Adjutants to President *Adolfo López Mateos*, 1958-64; rank of Colonel, 1964; Assistant Chief of Staff, Military

Parade, 1969; rank of Brigadier General, Nov. 20, 1970; Commander of the 4th, 10th, and 16th Cavalry Regiments in Tenancingo, México, Aguascalientes, Aguascalientes, and Torreón, Coahuila, respectively; Director General of Cavalry, Secretariat of National Defense, 1972-76; rank of Brigade General, Nov. 20, 1974; Chief of Staff of the Military Column, Chihuahua, Chihuahua, 1976-81; Commander of the 5th Military Zone, Chihuahua, Chihuahua, 1976-81; rank of Division General, 1979; Commander of the 1st Military Zone, Federal District, 1981-82. l-HA, 13 Dec. 1982, 11; Rev. de Ejer., Nov.-Dec. 1974, 98; Rev. de Ejer., Nov.-Dec. 1973, 94-95; Rev. de Ejer., Nov.-Dec. 1970, 26; Rev. de Ejer., July 1979, 54; MGF72-73, 175; *Excélsior,* 2 Dec. 1982, 34; Q es QAP.

Argil Camacho, Gustavo
a-Nov. 6, 1901. b-Federal District. c-Primary and secondary studies in Mexico City; medical degree, National School of Medicine, UNAM, Mar. 22, 1923, with a thesis on renal failure; Professor of Clinical Medicine and Pathology, National School of Medicine, UNAM, 1933-70; Professor of Pathology, 1927. d-None. e-None. f-Laboratory doctor, General Hospital, Mexico City, 1926-40; Director of the General Laboratories, General Hospital, Mexico City, 1941-52; President of the Technical-Sanitation Council, Papaloapan Commission, 1948-52; Director of the Department of Clinical Investigations, National School of Medicine, UNAM, 1934-46; Director of the National School of Medicine, UNAM, 1942-44; *Oficial Mayor of the Secretariat of Health,* 1946-48; *Subsecretary of Health,* 1948-52. g-None. h-Founder and Director of the *Revista Médica,* 1920-70, when he was a fourth-year medical student; author of two basic medical texts with *Fernando Ocaranza* as well as other medical works.

i-Graduated from UNAM with *Rafael P. Gamboa.* j-None. k-None. l-Letter, DGF51; DGF47, 197; Peral, 47, 31; DGF50, II, 445; DGF51, I, 335.

Armendáriz (Cárdenas), Antonio
a-Sept. 29, 1905. b-Palo Blanco, Coahuila. c-Primary in Mexico City; secondary at the Superior School of Commerce, 1920-22, Mexico City; preparatory at the National Preparatory School in Mexico City, 1923-27; law degree, National School of Law, UNAM, 1928-33; Professor of Sociology and Economy at UNAM, 1930-60. d-None. e-None. f-Secretary for the National Commission of Economic Studies, 1933; lawyer for the National Banking Commission, 1933-34; Director of Securities for the Bank of Mexico, 1933; Secretary General of UNAM, 1933-34; Director General of Secondary Education of the Secretariat of Public Education, 1941-45; *Subsecretary of the Treasury,* 1952-58; *Ambassador to Great Britain,* Sept. 1960 to Feb. 1965; *Director General of the Bank of Foreign Commerce,* 1965-70; Director General of the National Bonded Warehouses, 1970-75. g-None. h-Legal adviser to the Bank of London, National Ejido Bank, and many other banks; Director, Legal Department, La Provincial Insurance Co.; President of the National Securities Commission, 1949-52; private law practice, 1943-53; editorialist for the two Mexican newspapers, *Excélsior* and *Novedades,* 1940-70; Editor of *Comercio Exterior,* official publication of the National Bank of Foreign Commerce. i-Knew *Antonio Carrillo Flores, Andrés Serra Rojas, Alfonso Guzmán Neyra, Manuel Gual Vidal, Agustín García López, Antonio Ortiz Mena, Angel Carvajal,* and others as students at the National School of Law; father, Anastasio Armendáriz, a peasant; son, *Manuel Armedáriz Etchegaray,* was subsecretary of foreign investment,

Secretariat of Commerce, 1982-88; daughter, Mercedes, is married to *Anastasio González Martínez*, supreme court justice, 1977-90. j-None. k-None. l-WWM45, 6; DBM68, 40-41; DBM70, 46; letters; *Semblanzas*; DGF50, II, 57, 211, 273; DGF51, 65; Enc. Mex., I, 263; DBGM, 42

Armendáriz Etchegaray, Manuel Benito
a-Jan. 1, 1940. b-Federal District. c-Early education unknown; law degree, National School of Law, UNAM, with a thesis on economic policy objectives; graduate studies in economic theory, London School of Economics; MA in economics, Yale University; professor, National School of Economics, UNAM, 1966-73; professor, ITAM, 1966-73; professor, Colegio de México, 1966-73. d-None. e-Joined PRI, 1969. f-Various positions in the Bank of Mexico, 1958-74; Representative to the Food and Agricultural Organization, Rome, 1975-76; Representative to the International Organizations, Geneva, Switzerland, 1976-77; Director-in-Chief of International Economic Affairs, Secretariat of Foreign Relations, 1977-78; economic adviser, Secretariat of Foreign Relations, 1979-80; Subdirector of Planning, Mexican Institute of Foreign Trade, 1980-82; *Subsecretary of Regulation of Foreign Investment and Technology Transfer*, Secretariat of Industry and Commerce, 1982-88. g-None. h-None. i-Son of *Antonio Armendáriz Cárdenas*, subsecretary of the treasury, 1952-58, and Ana María Etchegaray Ortiz; married Guadalupe Morales Rodríguez; brother-in-law of *Anastasio González Martínez*, supreme court justice. j-None. k-None. l-DBGM 87, 41; letters.

Armienta Calderón, Gonzalo
a-Jan. 10, 1924. b-Culiacán, Sinaloa. c-Early education unknown; law degree, University of Sinaloa, 1942-46, with a thesis on "The Coercive Economic

Power," 1948; LLD degree, National School of Law, UNAM, 1958-59; professor, University of Sinaloa, 1948-58, 1970-72; professor, Autonomous Technological Institute of Mexico, 1963. d-None. e-None. f-Agent of the Ministerio Público and Judge of the First Instance, Culiacán, Sinaloa, 1948-50; Assistant Attorney General of the State of Sinaloa, 1951-52; Judge, Superior Tribunal of Justice of Sinaloa, 1956-58; Secretary of Resolutions, 2nd Divison, Tax Court, 1958-63; Secretary of the City Council of Mazatlán, Sinaloa, 1960; Special Fiduciary Agent, department head, and Assistant Director of the Legal Department, Somex, 1963-68; Special Fiduciary Agent, Housing Fund, 1969; General Counsel and Chief of the Contracts Department, Fovisste, 1972-78; *Subsecretary of the Secretariat of Agrarian Reform*, 1978-81; Chief of Advisers, Secretary of Labor, 1982; General Coordinator of Delegates, Secretary of Urban Development and Ecology, 1982-84; President and Judge, Federal Tax Court, 1986-88; Director General of Legal Affairs, Secretariat of Government, 1988. g-None. h-Public Notary, Sinaloa, 1951; secretary of various administrative boards, including Embotelladora Garcí Crespo, S.A. and Sosa Texcoco, S.A., 1970. i-Considered to be part of *Antonio Toledo Corro*'s group; son of Fernando Armienta Urrea, telegrapher, and Aurora Calderón Félix; married Susana Hernández Campos; son, Gonzalo Manuel Armienta Hernández, was assistant tax attorney, Secretariat of the Treasury, 1992. j-None. k-None. l-Q es QAP, 276; *Excélsior*, 17 June 1978, 10, 25 June 1978, 1; DBGM89, 36; DBGM92, 40.

Arrayales de Morales, Aurora
a-June 28, 1918. b-Mazatlán, Sinaloa. c-Early education unknown; teaching certificate from the Normal School of

Culiacán, Sinaloa; specialist in abnormal children; founded a home for abnormal children; teacher for many years; professor at the Preparatory School and the Normal School of Mazatlán, Sinaloa. d-Councilwoman of Mazatlán, Sinaloa 1955; *Federal Deputy* from Sinaloa, Dist. 4, 1958-61, member of the Social Action Committee, the Second Public Education Committee, and the Second Instructive Committee for the Grand Jury; member of the Gran Comisión; Local Deputy to the State Legislature of Sinaloa, Dist. 3, 1962-64. e-President of Women's Social Action of PRI in Mazatlán; Director of Women's Action of the CEN of PRI, 1958; General Delegate of the CEN of PRI numerous times; organized the National Women's Congress of PRI, 1960. f-Subdirector of Social Services of the ISSTE; Director of Social Welfare Department, IMSS, 1970-76; Delegate of the Department of the Federal District to Xochimilco, 1977. g-Leader, teachers' union, Culiacán and Mazatlán. h-None. j-None. k-None. l-C de D, 1958-61, 70; Func., 355; Romero Aceves, 374-75.

Arreguín (Vélez) Jr., Enrique
a-Aug. 6, 1907. b-Morelia, Michoacán. c-Primary and secondary at the Escuela Oficial Miguel Hidalgo, Morelia; preparatory at the Colegio San Nicolás, Morelia, 1917; medical degree from the University of Michoacán, June 8, 1928; Professor of Hygiene, Secondary School of Coyoacán, Mexico City; Professor of Geology, Paleontology, and Zoology at the Colegio de San Nicolás; Professor of Medicine, History, General Biology, General Pathology, and Medical Pathology at the University of Michoacán; Rector of the University of Michoacán, 1934-35. d-None. e-None. f-Member of the Council of Superior Education and Scientific Investigation, 1936-37; Secretary of the Presidential Studies Commission, 1937; President of the

Presidential Studies Commission, 1938; *Subsecretary of Public Education*, 1940-41. g-None. h-Director of the Central Office of Professional Liabilities of the Mexican Institute of Social Security, 1950-64; Director of the Department of Professional Liabilities of the Mexican Institute of Social Security, 1964-70; Chief of the Bacteriology Section and the Clinical Laboratory Analysis of the General Hospital, Mexico City i-Son of Enrique Arreguín, Sr., who was local deputy to the State Legislature of Michoacán in 1912, director of the State of Michoacán Pawnshop, and professor for twenty years at the Colegio de San Nicolás. j-None. k-Head of the Vanguardias Nicolaitas; resigned from the Secretariat of Public Education because of adverse political pressures against the implementation of a socialist education program. l-D del S, 2 Dec. 1940, 1, 6; DGF69, 6633; DGF50, 109.

Arriaga Rivera, Agustín
a-1925. b-Michoacán. c-Preparatory studies from the Colegio de San Nicolás, Morelia; economics degree from the National School of Economics, UNAM, Dec. 14, 1951, with a thesis on Social Security in Mexico; graduated with a perfect grade point average; Professor at the University of Michoacán, 1952-54; professor at the University of Tamaulipas, 1955-58; professor at the National School of Economics, UNAM, 1949-51. d-*Federal Deputy* from the State of Michoacán, 1952-55, member of the Social Welfare Committee, the First Balloting Committee, the Legislative Studies Committee (2nd year), and the Permanent Commission; *Governor of Michoacán*, 1962-68. e-Member of the National Committee of PRI, 1949-51; *Secretary of Youth Action of CEN of PRI*, 1950-51; General Delegate of the CEN of PRI to Oaxaca, 1978. f-Adviser to the Mexican delegation to the United Nations, 1945;

Secretary of the Director General of the Sugarcane Trust, 1946-47; Subdirector of Social Action of the Secretariat of Public Education, 1949-53; Chairman of the Board for Material and Moral Improvement, Nuevo León, 1955-59; Director General of the National Bank of Cinematography, 1959-62; Director General of Port Development Fund, Secretary of Communications and Transportation, 1989- . g-President of the National Federation of University Students of Mexico, 1949; President of the 1946 student generation at the National School of Economics; Director of the National Institute of Mexican Youth, 1959-62. h-Stockholder and board member in various corporations. i-Initially served with *Luis Echeverría* and *Hugo Cervantes del Río* as a youth member of the National Committee of PRI under the tutelage of *Rodolfo Sánchez Taboada*; student at UNAM with *Luis Echeverría*; son of Agustín Arriaga Díaz Barriaga, lawyer, a professor at the Colegio de San Nicolás, and Mercedes Rivera Hinojosa; married María Guadalupe Díaz González Cosío. j-None. k-Confronted with a major student riot as Governor of Michoacán in 1966; considered to be the first governor of Michoacán after 1940 not handpicked by *Lázaro Cárdenas*. l-WWMG, 7; DBM68, 44; DGF56, 437; Díaz Fuentes, 265; DGF51, I, 291; C de D, 1952-54, 52, 57; HA, 12 Jan. 1959, 14; DPE61, 108; *Excélsior*, 17 Dec. 1974, 4; NYT, 20 May 1962, 30; NYT, 30 June 1962, 17; Enc. Mex., 1977, I, 428-29; DBGM92, 41-42.

Arrieta, Domingo
(Deceased Nov. 18, 1962) a-Aug. 4, 1874. b-Municipio de Candelas, Durango. c-Early education unknown; none. d-Constitutional Governor of Durango, Aug. 1, 1917 to May 24, 1920; *Senator* from Durango, 1936-40. e-None. f-Governor and military commander of Durango, 1914-16. g-None. h-Before joining the Revolution was a miner and a muleteer in Durango. i-Brother of Mariano Arrieta, who was an early Revolutionary leader in the State of Durango, became Governor of Durango for several months in 1915, and continued career as a military officer; father of *Atanasio Arrieta García*, senator from Durango, 1946-52. j-Joined the Revolution under Madero, 1910; commander of the garrison of Durango, 1911-13; fought against Huerta in 1913; general of the Revolutionary forces that took Durango, 1913; became military commander of Durango, 1913-14; fought against Francisco Villa, 1914-16; Constitutionalist, 1916-20; fought against General Obregón, 1920-24; became a Division General on Nov. 16, 1940; retired from the army Aug. 1, 1944. k-Remained faithful to Carranza when he fled the presidency; pardoned by Obregón, May 7, 1924; rejoined the army Sept. 11, 1927. l-DP70, 149-50; Peral, 72; Q es Q, 43-45; Enc. Mex., Annual, 1977, 478-79.

Arrieta García, Atanasio
b-Durango. c-Primary studies only; no degree. d-*Senator* from the State of Durango, 1946-52, member of the National Properties Committee, the Indigenous Affairs Committee, the Second Ejido Committee, and the First Mining Committee. e-None. f-None. g-None. h-Businessman. i-Son of General *Domingo Arrieta*, senator from Durango, 1934-40. j-None. k-Precandidate for governor of Durango, 1949, but lost to *Enrique Torres Sánchez*. l-DGF51, I, 6, 10, 11, 13; C de S, 1946-52.

Arrieta M., Darío L.
a-Dec. 26, 1901. b-Iguala, Guerrero. c-Engineering degree, National School of Agriculture, 1934; Professor, National School of Agriculture. d-None. e-None. f-Director General of Agricul-

ture, Secretariat of Agriculture, 1943-49; Executive Coordinator of Agricultural Investigation, 1949; Director of Agricultural Defense, 1954; *Substitute Governor of Guerrero*, 1954-57; Director General of Agricultural Defense, 1958-61. g-None. h-Technical adviser to the Secretariat of Agriculture, 1954, j-None. k-None. l-DPE61, 72; HA, 31 May 1954, 5; DGF56, 93; *Siempre*, 14 Jan. 1959, 6.

Arriola Molina, Rafael
b-Veracruz. c-Early education unknown; teaching certificate. d-*Federal Deputy* from the State of Veracruz, 1946-49, member of the Budget and Accounts Committee; *Senator* from Veracruz, 1970-76. e-*Secretary of Political Action of the CEN of PRI*, 1949-51; President of PRI in the State of Veracruz, 1968. f-Subdirector of Government, State of Veracruz, 1955. g-None. h-None. j-None. k-Considered to be powerful in state politics. l-PS; C de D, 1946-49, 40, 65; Romero, *Mis Seis Años*.

Arroyo Ch., Agustín
(Deceased Apr. 24, 1969) a-Aug. 28, 1891. b-Irapuato, Guanajuato. c-Primary studies at Pueblo Nuevo, secondary at private schools in Guanajuato; no degree. d-Local deputy, State of Guanajuato, Federal Deputy from Guanajuato, 1919-24; Governor of Guanajuato, 1927-31. f-*Subsecretary of Government*, 1935-36; first Director of the Department of Press and Publicity (which became PIPSA), 1936-40; *Secretary of Labor and Social Welfare*, 1940; President of the Administrative Council of PIPSA, 1958-62; publisher of the official government newspaper *El Nacional*, 1962-68; member of the Board of PIPSA, 1967-69. g-None. h-Post office employee, Celaya, Guanajuato, 1915; worked in the department of General Provisions, under *Francisco Múgica*.

i-Close personal friend of Governor Enrique Colunga of Guanajuato 1923-27, who imposed *Arroyo Ch.* as governor; also a friend of Governor Antonio Madrazo, 1920-23; early supporter of *Francisco Múgica* as president, 1939-40; political adviser to *Lázaro Cárdenas*; married Carolina Damián; son, *Agustín*, was a federal deputy from Guanajuato, 1955-58 and 1964-67. j-Joined the Revolution while quite young. k-He and Colunga controlled state politics in Guanajuato. l-Dulles; WWMG, 7; *Hoy*, 10 May 1969, 8; HA, 29 Dec. 1958, 8; Peral, 73; Gruening, 427, 487-88; Kirk, 3; Enc. Mex. I, 303; NYT, 21 Jan. 1940, 21; Michaels, 21.

Arroyo Damián, Agustín
a-Mar. 12, 1919. b-Celaya, Guanajuato. c-Early education unknown; medical degree, National School of Medicine, UNAM, with a specialty as a surgeon in ophthalmology; postgraduate work at various universities in the United States; Professor of Chemistry, National School of Medicine, UNAM. d-*Federal Deputy* from the State of Guanajuato, Dist. 8, 1955-58, member of the Mail and Telegraph Committee, the Sugar Industry Committee, and the Committee on Health; *Federal Deputy* from the State of Guanajuato, Dist. 8, 1964-67, member of the Public Health Committee and the Military Health Committee. e-None. f-None. g-None. h-Practicing surgeon; founder of the Beatriz Velasco de Alemán Ophthalmology Clinic, Celaya, Guanajuato; Chief of Ophthalmological Services, French Hospital. i-Son of *Agustín Arroyo Ch.*, secretary of labor, 1940. j-None. k-None. l-DGF56, 24,32,34,37; C de D, 1955-58; C de D, 1964-67, 45; Ind. Biog., 17.

Arroyo de Yta, Fernando
a-Dec. 17, 1937. b-Federal District. c-Early education unknown; civil engineering degree, National School of

Engineering, UNAM, 1963; studies in engineering administration, University of California, Los Angeles; professor, National School of Engineering, UNAM, 1975; professor, National School of Architecture, UNAM, 1977. d-None. e-Joined PRI, 1964. f-General Supervisor, Public Works, Bank of Mexico, 1966-71; head of Department of Financial Evaluation, Infonavit, 1972-82; *Oficial Mayor of the Secretariat of Urban Development and Ecology*, 1982-84; *Subsecretary of Housing*, Secretariat of Urban Development and Ecology, 1984-85. g-None. h-Coordinator of Prefabricated Homes, Spancrete Enterprises, 1971-82. i-Son of Juan Arroyo Ocampo and Carmela de Yta Calderón; married Victoria Sobreyva Castaños. j-None. k-None. l-Q es QAP; DBGM84, 44.

Arroyo Marroquín, Romarico
a-Dec. 13, 1942. b-Tulancingo, Hidalgo. c-Early education unknown; civil engineering degree, National School of Engineering, UNAM, 1961-65; MA degree in science with a specialization in economic engineering systems, Stanford University, 1970; professor, School of Engineering, UNAM, 1969; professor, National School of Architecture, UNAM, 1972; professor, School of Continuing Education, UNAM. d-None. e-None. f-Chief of Analysts, Calculations Center, Secretariat of Hydraulic Resources, 1967-68; Assistant Director General, Fonatur (Fund for the Guarantee and Promotion of Tourism), 1973-76; Director General of Fonatur, 1976-77; adviser to the Subsecretary of the Secretariat of the Treasury, 1977-78; *Subsecretary of State Industries*, Secretariat of Energy, Mines, and Parastate Industries, 1982-87; Director General of Astilleros Unidas, Secretariat of Communications and Transportation, 1987-89. g-None. h-Director, Division of Planning and Transportation, Ipsea

Consultores, S.A., 1971-73; Director General of Cia. Minera de Cananea, S.A., 1978-82. i-Brother of Orlando Arroyo Marroquín, director of communications systems for the CEN of PRI; son of Daniel Arroyo Bengoa, pilot, and María de los Angeles Marroquín Perea; married Brunhilde Schoener Freytag. j-None. k-None. l-*Excélsior*, 4 Dec. 1982, 35; Q es QAP, 68; IEPES; DBGM, 44; DBGM89, 38.

Arteaga y Santoyo, Armando
a-Oct. 26, 1906. b-Monterrey, Nuevo León. c-Primary and preparatory studies at the Colegio Civil, Monterrey; began law studies at the University of Nuevo León; law degree, National School of Law, UNAM, 1925-32; summer school, University of Texas, Austin. d-*Federal Deputy* from the State of Nuevo León, Dist. 2, 1946-49, member of the Gran Comisión and the Committee on Administration; *Federal Deputy* from the State of Nuevo León, Dist. 4, 1961-64, member of the Gran Comisión, the Domestic and Foreign Commerce Committee, the Legislative Studies Committee (Labor), and the Permanent Commission, 1963; Vice-President of the Chamber, Sept. 1962; Secretary of the Preparatory Council, 1961-63; *Senator* from Nuevo León, 1964-70. e-*Director of the IEPES of the CEN of PRI*, 1946-52; *Director of the IEPES of the CEN of PRI*, 1953; *Secretary of Political Action of the CEN of PRI*, 1965; representative of the New Advisory Council of the IEPES of PRI in charge of structural reforms, June 28, 1972; general delegate of the CEN of PRI more than twenty-five times. f-Agent of the Ministerio Público of the Attorney General of Mexico in the Federal District, 1935-41; Oficial Mayor of the State of Nuevo León, 1941-43; Secretary General of the Government of the State of Nuevo León, 1943-44; Private Secretary to the Governor of the

State of Nuevo León, *Arturo B. de la Garza*, 1944-45; Administrator of CEIMSA, 1958; Oficial Mayor of the Chamber of Deputies, 1976-79. g-None. h-Practicing lawyer in Mexico, D.F., 1970-73. i-*Santiago Roel* was his political disciple; father in legal work in Monterrey. j-None. k-None. l-WWM45, 6; *Siempre*, 4 Feb. 1959, 6; letter; HA, 10 July 1972, 10; Almanaque de N.L., 105.

Artigas Fernández, Mario
a-Nov. 6, 1917. b-Tuxpan, Veracruz. c-Early education unknown; geographic engineer, Heroic Naval College, 1938-43; continental defense studies, Inter-American Defense College; professor, Heroic Naval College, 1960-75; professor, Center for Higher Naval Studies, 1960-75. d-None. e-None. f-*Oficial Mayor of the Navy*, 1976-82. g-None. h-None. j-Career naval officer; Director of Naval Weapons and Armaments, Secretariat of the Navy, 1968-69; Assistant Chief and Interim Chief of Staff, Secretariat of the Navy, 1969-70; Director General of Services, Secretary of the Navy, 1970-74; Chief of Staff, Secretariat of the Navy, 1974-76. k-None. l-Protag., 36.

Asiain, Rodolfo
(Deceased 1963) a-1907. b-Tula, Hidalgo. c-Primary and secondary in Hidalgo, preparatory at the Literary Institute of Hidalgo, law degree from the National School of Law, UNAM, 1917-22. d-None. e-None. f-Secretary General of Government of the State of Hidalgo under Governor Amado Azuara, 1921-23; Correctional Judge of the Federal District, 1925; Penal Judge of the Federal District, President of Disputes and Magistrate of the Tribunal Superior of Justice; *Justice of the Supreme Court*, 1936-40; consulting lawyer to the Tariff Commission of Electricity and Gas, chief of the Legal

Department of the Tariff Commission of Electricity and Gas. g-None. h-None. k-Played a prominent role in the Supreme Court decision on the expropriation of the oil companies in 1938. l-DP70, 158; letter; DGF50, II, 239; DGF51, II, 338.

Aspe (Armella), Pedro Carlos
a-July 7, 1950. b-Federal District. c-Primary studies at the Instituto Patria, Mexico City, 1956-62; secondary studies at the Instituto Patria, 1962-64; preparatory studies at the Instituto Patria, 1964-66; economics degree, Autonomous Technological Institute of Mexico, with a thesis on migration, expectations and probability of employment, 1974; Ph.D. in economics, Massachusetts Institute of Technology, with a thesis on international transmission mechanisms, 1978; Secretary of Academic Services and Coordinator of Economics Research, ITAM, 1973-74; instructor in macroeconomics, MIT, 1977-78; professor, CEMLA, 1978; Director, economics curriculum, ITAM, 1978-82. d-None. e-Joined PRI, 1980; adviser to the director general of the IEPES of PRI, *Carlos Salinas*, 1982. f-Coordinator of economic advisers, Secretariat of the Treasury, 1978-82; *Subsecretary of Planning*, Secretariat of Programming and Budgeting, 1985-87; *Secretary of Programming and Budgeting*, 1987-88; *Secretary of the Treasury*, 1988- . g-None. h-Author of several books on income distribution. i-Son of Pedro Aspe Sais, lawyer, professor at the Free Law School, and director general of the Palacio de Hierro, and Virginia Armella Maza; married Concepción Bernal Verea, historian and daughter of distinguished anthropologist and diplomat, Ignacio Bernal y García Pimental; met *Carlos Salinas* in 1978 while at MIT; student of *Francisco Gil Díaz*, *Manuel Cavazos Lerma*, and *Carlos Sales Gutiérrez* at ITAM;

student and friend of *Leopoldo Solís.*
j-None. k-A leading precandidate for
the PRI presidential nomination, 1993.
l-DBGM, 45-46; DBGM87, 44;
DBGM89, 39; Q es QAP, 134; *Proceso,*
31 Aug. 1992, 15.

Aubanel Vallejo, Gustavo
a-July 23, 1904. b-Guadalajara, Jalisco.
c-Primary and secondary studies at
public schools in Guadalajara; prepara-
tory studies from the University of
Guadalajara; medical degree, University
of Guadalajara. d-Mayor of Tijuana,
Baja California del Norte, 1954-56;
Federal Deputy from the State of Baja
California del Norte, Dist. 2, 1961-64,
member of the Indigenous Affairs
Committee and the First Balloting
Committee; *Federal Deputy* from the
State of Baja California del Norte, Dist.
2, 1967-70, member of the Gran
Comisión, the Pharmaceutical and
Chemical Industry Committee, and the
Social Welfare Committee; *Senator*
from the State of Baja California del
Norte, 1970-76, member of the Gran
Comisión and the First Balloting
Committee; Second Secretary of the
Second Foreign Relations Committee,
the National Properties Committee, and
the Tax Committee; First Secretary of
the Social Welfare Committee and
President of the Public Assistance
Committee, member of the Interparlia-
mentary Committee, 1973. e-Joined the
PNR, 1931. f-*Substitute Governor of
Baja California del Norte,* Dec. 19,
1964, to Nov. 30, 1965. h-Coauthor of
the constitution for Baja California del
Norte; operated a medical clinic in
Tijuana, 1931-76. j-None. k-Appointed
by the state legislature as Governor of
Baja California del Norte. l-C de D,
1967-69, 76; C de D, 1961-63, 71;
MGF69, 89; HA, 28 Dec. 1964, 14; C de
S, 1970-76, 7, 70.

Avila Bretón, Rafael
(Deceased) a-Feb. 15, 1893. b-Tlaxcala,
Tlaxcala. c-Preparatory and legal
studies at the Colegio del Estado de
Puebla; law degree, National School of
Law, UNAM; Professor of Industrial
Law and Civil Procedure, National
School of Law, UNAM. d-*Senator* from
the State of Tlaxcala, 1940-46; *Governor
of Tlaxcala,* 1946-51. e-None. f-Public
Defender, 1917; Penal Judge, Pachuca,
Hidalgo, 1918-20; Auxiliary Agent,
Ministerio Público of the Federal
District; Judge of the Civil Division,
Federal District; Justice, Superior
Tribunal of Justice of the State of
Tlaxcala. g-None. h-Public welfare
attorney. i-Married Herlinda Hoyos.
j-None. k-Investigated for illicit land
dealings, 1971. l-STYBIWW544, 593;
LAD, 14 Oct. 1971; HA, 15 Nov. 1946,
11; letter; WB54, 323.

Avila Camacho, Manuel
(Deceased Oct. 13, 1955) a-Apr. 24,
1897. b-Teziutlán, Puebla. c-Primary
education in Teziutlán, secondary
studies in accounting at Liceo
Teziuteco, 1912; studied at the National
Preparatory School; no degree.
d-*President of Mexico,* 1940-46.
e-Secretary and stenographer to José I.
Novelo, President of the Cooperativist
Labor Party, 1919. f-Oficial Mayor of
the Secretariat of National Defense,
1933-34; *Oficial Mayor of the Secretariat of National Defense,* 1934-36;
Subsecretary of National Defense in
charge of the Secretariat, 1936-37;
Secretary of National Defense, 1937-39.
g-Secretary of the local agrarian of the
Sierra in Puebla. h-None. i-Close
friend of *Lázaro Cárdenas* since 1920;
childhood friend of *Vicente Lombardo
Toledano;* brother *Maximino Avila
Camacho* was governor of Puebla; and
brother *Rafael Avila Camacho* was an
army general and governor of Puebla,
1951-57; son of Manuel Avila Castillo

and Eufrosina Camacho, middle-class ranchers; nephew of *Andrés Figueroa*, secretary of national defense, 1935-36; married Soledad Orozco. j-Joined the Army Dec. 23, 1913, under General Antonio Medina, first as a civilian then with the rank of 2nd Lieutenant; Major in 1916; Colonel, 1920; supported the Agua Prieta rebellion, 1920; Chief of Staff of the 1st Sonora Brigade, State of Michoacán under *Lázaro Cárdenas*, 1920; fought Yaquis in Sonora, 1920; Chief of Military Operations, Isthmus, 1920; Commander of the 79th cavalry regiment, 1923; fought against the Cristeros; fought against the de la Huerta Rebellion in Michoacán, 1924; Commander of the 38th Cavalry Regiment, 1924; rank of Brigadier General in 1924; fought under General *Cárdenas* against the Escobar Rebellion, 1929; rank of Brigade General, Sept. 1, 1929; chief of military operations in Colima, 1929-31; Commander of the Military Zone of Tabasco, 1932-33. k-One of his biographers says he was born in Martínez de la Torre, Veracruz, not in Puebla. l-WWM45, 6; DP70, 179-80; Peral, 76; *Hoy*, Dec. 1940, 19-21; NYT, 3 Nov. 1939; Kirk; UTEHA, 1222; WB48, 323; Enc. Mex. I, 410-11; Q es Q, 48; Gaxiola, 2, 254; Blanco, 134; HA, 28 May 1979, VI.

Avila Camacho, Maximino
(Deceased Feb. 17, 1945) a-Aug. 23, 1891. b-Teziutlán, Puebla. c-Primary studies in Teziutlán; cadet at the National Military College; no degree. d-Governor of Puebla, 1937-41. e-None. f-Chief of Political Police, Secretariat of Government, 1925; *Secretary of Public Works*, 1941-45. g-None. h-Post office employee; farmer; sales agent for the Singer Sewing Machine Company; cowboy; professional bullfighter; horse breeder; cattleman; owned several ranches by 1940; his wealth was esti-mated at 2 to 3 million pesos. i-Brother

of President *Manuel Avila Camacho* and *Rafael Avila Camacho*, governor of Puebla, 1951-57; son of Manuel Avila Castillo and Eufrosina Camacho, middle-class landowners. j-Joined the Revolution in 1914; Brigadier General, 1929; military caudillo of Puebla during the late 1920s and early 1930s, Chief of the 51st Cavalry, in charge of prison where Vasconcelistas were murdered; Assistant Inspector General of the Army; Acting Inspector General of the Army; rank of Division General, 1940. k-Leader of the right wing of the National Revolutionary Party. l-DP70, 180; HA, 28 May 1943, 9; DGF56, 98; Scott, 122; Kirk, 93, 245; UTEHA, I, 1222; Morton, 49; Peral, 77; Q es Q, 48; Wilkie; Skirius, 188; NYT, 5 May 1941, 8; CyT, 64.

Avila Camacho, Rafael
(Deceased Mar. 20, 1975) a-Dec. 14, 1905. b-Teziutlán, Puebla. c-Primary studies in Teziutlán; graduated from the National Military College, 1925, as a 2nd lieutenant in the cavalry; enrolled in the Applied Military College, 1934; Director of the National Military College, 1948-50. d-Federal Deputy from the State of Puebla, Dist. 9, 1934-37, member of the Gran Comisión; Mayor of Puebla, Puebla, 1939-41; *Governor of Puebla*, 1951-57. e-President of the State Committee of the PRM, Puebla. f-*Oficial Mayor of Industry and Commerce*, 1942-45; administrative manager of PEMEX, 1945; *Subsecretary of Public Works*, 1945-46. g-None. h-Retired to private life as a rancher, 1958-75. i-Brother of *Maximino* and *Manuel Avila Camacho*; longtime friend of *Alejandro Gómez Maganda*; son of Manuel Avila Castillo and Eufrosina Camacho, ranchers; nephew of *Andrés Figueroa*. j-Career army officer; aide to Commander of the 13th Military Zone; stationed with the 51st cavalry regiment; participated in 21

battles; chief of staff of the 13th Military Zone, 1931; stationed with the 38th cavalry regiment; Chief of Staff of the 29th Military Zone; member of the presidential staff; aide to the Oficial Mayor and the Subsecretary of War; rank of Lt. Colonel, 1940; rank of Colonel, 1943; rank of Brigadier General, 1946; rank of Division General, 1961. k-None. l-DGF56, 98; DGF51, II, 679; Peral, 77; Gómez Maganda, 105; CyT, 64-65; Excélsior, 21 Mar. 1975, 4; HA, 31 Mar. 1975, 21; RdE, Sept. 1976, 134; Rev. de Ejer., Sept. 1976, 134.

Azar García, Jorge Salomón
a-Dec. 20, 1952. b-Campeche, Campeche. c-Early education unknown; agricultural engineering degree with a specialty in technical zoology, School of Agricultural Engineering, Monterey Institute of Higher Studies, 1972-78; MA in public administration, School of Business, Autonomous University of Nuevo León, 1978-79. d-Governor of Campeche, 1991- . e-Joined PRI, 1971. f-Administrative Chief, Regional Delegation, Zone 8, Secretariat of Health, 1974-79; Director, Forestry and Agricultural Products Development, State of Campeche, 1980-85; Delegate of the Secretariat of Agriculture and Hydraulic Resources, 1986-88; adviser, Subsecretary of Forestry and Agro-Industrial Development, 1988; Delegate of the Secretariat of Programming and Budgeting to Tuxtla Gutiérrez, 1989-91. i-Son of Abraham Azar Farah, ophthalmologist and delegate of the IMSS in Campeche, and Teresa García Mejenes; married Lydia León Gamboa, architect; related by marriage to Patrocinio González Garrido, secretary of government; friend of Ernesto Zedillo, secretary of public education; attended ITESM with Luis Donaldo Colosio. j-None. k-None. l-DBGM92, 724; Proceso, 18 Mar. 1991, 26-29.

Aznar Zetina, Antonio J.
a-June 12, 1904. b-Campeche, Campeche. c-Primary and secondary studies in Campeche; preparatory studies at the Campeche Normal School; degree from the Naval College in Veracruz; advanced studies at the Higher War College, Mexico, D.F. d-None. e-None. f-Naval Attaché to the Mexican Embassy, Paris; Naval Attaché to the Mexican Embassy, Washington, D.C..; Subsecretary of the Navy, 1965-70. g-None. h-None. i-Son of Luis Aznar Cano, a lawyer; uncle Tomás Aznar Cano served as a senator and governor. j-Commander of the coast guard ship 24; Director of the Naval College; Chief of Staff of the Navy, 1958-61; Commander of the Transport Progreso; Commander of the Destroyer Guanajuato; Commander of the 2nd Naval Zone; Vice Admiral, 1965; rank of Admiral. k-None. l-DBM68; 50; DBM70; 56; DPE65, 48; DE61, 39; Q es Q, 30.

Azuara, Juan Enrique
(Deceased 1958) a-July 15, 1895. b-Tampacán, San Luis Potosí. c-Primary studies in Tampacán; secondary and preparatory studies at the Scientific and Literary Institute of San Luis Potosí; law degree, Scientific and Literary Institute of San Luis Potosí, 1922. d-Federal Deputy from the State of San Luis Potosí, Dist. 11, 1926-28, 1928-30; Senator from the State of San Luis Potosí, 1958, died in office. e-None. f-Public defender; Judge of the First Instance in Ciudad Valles, 1922; District Judge of Toluca, México, 1947; Magistrate of the Collegiate Circuit Tribunal of the Federal District; President of the Collegiate Circuit Tribunal, 1952-58. g-None. h-None. i-Son, Enrique Azuara Salas, oficial mayor of the treasury. j-Civilian employee in the Revolution. k-None. l-DP70, 192; C de S, 1958-64; Func., 341; MGF47, 49.

Azuela Guitrón, Mariano
a-Apr. 1, 1936. b-Federal District.
c-Early education unknown; legal
studies at the National School of Law,
UNAM, 1954-58, with a thesis on legal
themes and the state in contemporary
church doctrine, 1958; Professor of Law,
Ibero-American University, 1963-83.
d-None. e-None. f-Special Investigator,
Income Tax Department, Secretariat of
the Treasury, 1957-59; Coordinator of
Insured Clubs, Social Loans Department, IMSS, 1958-60; Secretary of
Studies and Accounts, Supreme Court,
1960-71; Judge, Federal Tax Court,
1971-83; President, Federal Tax Court,
1981; *Justice of the Supreme Court*,
1981-90. g-None. h-None. i-Son of
Mariano Azuela Rivera, supreme court
justice, and María de los Dolores
Guitrón Machaen; married Consuelo
Bohigas Lomelín; grandson of notable
novelist Mariano Azuela; nephew of
historian Salvador Azuela Rivera;
brother of intellectual Arturo Azuela;
brother of María Antonieta, circuit
court judge, 1984. j-None. k-None.
l-Q es QAP; letters; DBGM87, 600;
DBGM89, 592.

Azuela (Rivera), Mariano
a-Mar. 15, 1904. b-Lagos de Moreno,
Jalisco. c-Primary studies in Lagos de
Moreno and Guadalajara; preparatory
studies at the National Preparatory
School, Mexico City; law degree,
National School of Law, UNAM, 1928;
LLD, UNAM; professor at the Univer-
sity of San Luis Potosí and the Univer-
sity of Monterrey; Senior Professor,
course in amparo, National School of
Law; Professor of Public Law, Graduate
School, National School of Law,
UNAM; Professor of Guarantees and
Amparo, National School of Law,
UNAM, 1930-58. d-*Senator* from the
State of Jalisco, 1958-60. e-None.
f-Judge of the Federal Tax Court of
Mexico, 1937-51; President of the

Federal Tax Court of Mexico, 1949-51;
Justice of the Supreme Court, 1951-57,
1960-64, 1964-70, 1970-71. g-None.
h-Worked for a Federal District judge as
a student, 1927; practiced law with
Manuel Gómez Morín, 1930-35,
member of the Commission for Legal
Studies, Office of the Attorney General;
author of various articles on amparo.
i-Son of author Mariano Azuela; friend
of *Antonio Luna Arroyo*; married
Dolores Guitrón; son, *Mariano Azuela
Guitrón*, became a supreme court justice, 1981; daughter María appointed to
the federal circuit court, 1984. j-None.
k-Was not a member of PRI while
serving on the Supreme Court. l-Libro
de Oro, 1967, xlvi; Func, 238; *Excélsior*,
6 Apr. 1971, 1, 14; DGF51, 468; C de S,
1961-64, 13; letters; DBGM89, 591-92

B

Badillo (García), Román
(Deceased) a-Feb. 24, 1895. b-Otumba,
México. c-Primary studies in Mexico
City; preparatory studies at the Na-
tional Preparatory School; law degree
from the National School of Law,
UNAM. d-None. e-Leader at the Anti-
Reelectionist Party Convention, 1934,
considered a supporter of Antonio Díaz
Soto y Gama as a presidential candidate
of that party. f-Agent of the Ministerio
Público, 1926-27; criminal judge in
Veracruz; Judge of the Superior Tribunal
of Justice of Veracruz, 1927; Secretary
General of Government of the State of
Querétaro; adviser to the president of
Mexico, 1940-46; *Oficial Mayor of the
Department of Agrarian Affairs*, 1958-
62. g-None. h-Practicing lawyer.
i-Practiced law with Antonio Díaz Soto
y Gama. j-None. k-None. l-López, 75;
Balboa, 95; DPE61, 126.

Baeza (Meléndez), Fernando
a-Jan. 21, 1942. b-Ciudad Delicias,
Chihuahua. c-Preparatory studies from
the Jesuit Regional Institute, Chihuahua; legal studies, Ibero-American
University, 1960-64, law degree from
the National School of Law, UNAM,
with a thesis on "Natural and Positive
Law in Their Naturalism Tradition,"
1967; professor, public preparatory
school, Delicias, Chihuahua, 1965-71.
d-*Federal Deputy* from the State of
Chihuahua, Dist. 6, 1985-86; head of
the PRI delegation from the State of
Chihuahua; *Governor of Chihuahua*,
1986-91. e-General Coordinator of *Luis
Echeverría's* presidential campaign,
Ciudad Delicias, Chihuahua, 1969-70.
f-Secretary of the Board of Water and
Sanitation, Ciudad Delicias, Chihuahua, 1968-71; Private Secretary to
Governor *Oscar Flores* of Chihuahua,
1971-74; Oficial Mayor of the Attorney
General of Mexico, *Oscar Flores
Sánchez*, 1976-82; *First Assistant
Attorney General of Mexico*, 1982-86.
g-None. h-Practicing lawyer, 1965-68.
i-Son of Florencio Baeza Morales,
rancher and PAN founder, and María de
los Angeles Meléndez; married Blanca
Margarita Gómez Ortiz; student of
Rafael Preciado Hernández at Ibero-
American University. j-None. k-None.
l-IEPES; Q es QAP, 460; *Proceso*, 6 July
1987, 10; HA, 7 Jan. 1986, 18; DBGM89,
662; DBGM, 50.

Baeza Somellera, Guillermo
a-June 20, 1937. b-Guadalajara, Jalisco.
c-Primary studies at the Institute of
Sciences, Guadalajara, 1945-51; secondary studies at the Institute of Sciences,
1951-53; preparatory studies at the
Institute of Sciences, 1952-54; law
degree, University of Guadalajara, 1954-
59. d-Candidate for Federal Deputy
from Jalisco, 1967; candidate for
Councilman of Guadalajara, 1964;
Federal Deputy (PAN party deputy),

1970-73, member of the Legislative
Studies Committee (1st year) on
General Affairs. e-Joined PAN, 1951;
Secretary General of the Regional
Committtee of National Action for
Jalisco; President of PAN for Jalisco,
1970; member of the National Council
of PAN, 1971. f-None. g-None.
i-Married Villanueva; brother, Jorge,
was a PAN party deputy, 1973-76.
j-None. k-None. l-Directorio, 70-72; C
de D, 70-72, 102; Mabry.

Balboa Gojón, Praxedes
(Deceased Oct. 10, 1980) a-1900.
b-Ciudad Victoria, Tamaulipas. c-Primary studies at the Normal School
Annex, Ciudad Victoria, 1907-12;
secondary and preparatory studies at the
Colegio Civil of Monterrey, Nuevo
Leon, 1914-1919; law degree from the
National School of Law, UNAM, 1925.
d-Federal Deputy from the State of
Tamaulipas, 1928-30; Federal Deputy
from the State of Tamaulipas, Dist. 4,
1930-32; Federal Deputy from the State
of Tamaulipas, Dist. 4, 1934-37;
Governor of Tamaulipas, 1963-69.
e-Member of the Constitutional
Convention of the PNR, 1929; President
of the PNR in Tamaulipas; campaign
manager for Antonio Villarreal as
Governor. f-Agent, Department of
Labor, Secretariat of Industry and
Commerce, 1924; head of the Concilia-
tion and Arbitration Committee for
Tamaulipas, 1925-28; Chief, Depart-
ment of Labor, Secretariat of Industry
and Commerce, 1929-30; Federal
Conciliator, Mixed Commission of the
National Railroads of Mexico, 1929;
Director of the Legal Department of
Petróleos Mexicanos, 1938; head of
Legal Department, PEMEX in Mata
Redonda, 1938-40; lawyer for Legal
Department, PEMEX, 1940-52; *Admin-
istrative Subdirector of Petróleos
Mexicanos*, 1952-58, 1958-62. g-Stu-
dent leader at UNAM, organized a

group in support of Plutarco Calles as president, 1923. h-Had an active role in the formulation of the Federal Labor Law and the Agrarian Reform Law which modified the original 1915 legislation. i-Attended the National Law School with *Eduardo Bustamante* and *Agustín García López*; grandson of General Juan Gojón, governor of Tamaulipas; father a doctor; originally member of *Emilio Portes Gil's* camarilla, but later a political enemy. j-None. k-Removed as a federal deputy by *Lázaro Cárdenas*, Sept. 12, 1935; became a political enemy of *Emilio Portes Gil*. l-WWMG, 7-8; letters, *Excélsior*, 24 Jan. 1973, 19, 11 Oct. 1980, 20A.

Ballesteros Prieto, Mario
a-Nov. 1912. b-Oaxaca, Oaxaca. c-Early education unknown; graduated from the Heroic Military College, Jan. 1, 1934; advanced studies, Higher War College, 1939-42; instructor, Higher War College; advanced studies, Command and Staff School, Ft. Leavenworth, Kansas. d-None. e-None. f-Chief of Staff of the Secretariat of National Defense, 1964-67. g-None. h-None. j-Career army officer; 2nd Lieutenant, Tenth Cavalry Regiment; various staff positions, Chief of Staff, Secretariat of National Defense, 1964-70; Chief of Staff of the 15th Military Zone, 1964; rank of Brigadier General, Nov. 20, 1964; rank of Brigade General, 1968; rank of Division General, 1972; Military Attaché to Chile and Peru, 1972. k-None. l-HA, 21 Dec. 1964, 10; DPE65, 33; Rev. de Ejer., Nov. 1972, 39; Rev. de Ejer., Dec. 1964, 24.

Baltázar Barajas, Angel
a-Sept. 21, 1926. b-Morelia, Michoacán. c-Early education unknown; law degree, University of Michoacán; professor, School of Law, University of Michoacán; Secretary of the Governing Board of the University of Michoacán. d-*Federal*

Deputy from the PPS (party deputy), 1967-70. e-Founding member of the PPS. f-Agent of the Ministerio Público, Mechaupan, Michoacán, 1959-67. g-None. i-Married Eva Chávez Martínez. j-None. k-None. l-PS, C de D, 1967-70.

Bandala, Bernardo
a-Aug. 20, 1893. b-Teziutlán, Puebla. c-Early education unknown; no degree. d-Federal Deputy from the State of Puebla, Dist. 2, 1932-34, Secretary of the National Revolutionary Bloc in the Chamber of Deputies; *Senator* from the State of Puebla, 1934-40. e-President of the PNR in the State of Puebla. f-None. g-None. i-Brother, Homero Bandala, was a federal deputy from Puebla; grew up in Teziutlán at the same time as the *Avila Camacho* family. j-Officer in the Constitutional Army; member of the Chief of Staff under President Carranza. k-None. l-C de D, 1932-34; C de S, 1934-40; PS, 0539; CyT, 72.

Banuelos, Félix
(Deceased Sept. 2, 1948) a-Oct. 1, 1878. b-Monte Escobedo, Zacatecas. c-No formal education. d-*Governor of Zacatecas*, 1937-40. f-Governor of Quintana Roo, 1931-32. g-None. h-Farmer. i-Parents were peasants; cousin of General Santos Banuelos. j-Joined the Revolution, 1910-11, serving under Luis Moya in Puente de Comatlán; rose to rank of Captain, 1911, returned to farming, 1911-13; joined *Pánfilo Natera* as a 1st Captain, 1913; Commander of the 1st Banuelos Brigade; rank of Lt. Colonel, 1913; rank of Colonel, 1914; rank of Brigadier General, 1914; supporter of Francisco Villa, 1914-1920; supported the government against de la Huerta in 1923; Brigadier General on May 30, 1923; retired from the army on Jan. 1, 1944. k-In June 1939, while governor of Zacatecas, the press alleged that he was trying to leave the Party of

the Mexican Revolution (PRM), but two days later he claimed to have made no such statement. l-Peral, 86; D de Y, 20 June 1939, 1.

Baranda (García), Alfredo
a-Nov. 11, 1944. b-Federal District. c-Early education unknown; law degree, National School of Law, UNAM, 1964-69; MA in economics, Colegio de México, 1969-71; MA in business administration, Harvard University; Professor of the Seminar on Political Science and Public Administration, UNAM; Professor, Central Bank course, Autonomous Technological Institute of Mexico; professor, CEMLA. d-None. e-Joined PRI, 1965; Coordinator of Economic Studies, *Alfredo del Mazo González*'s campaign for governor, 1982; Special Delegate of the CEN of PRI to Tlalnepantla and Atizapan, México; member of the CEPES of PRI, State of México. f-Various positions, Bank of Mexico, 1971-80; Director of Financial Policy System, Secretariat of the Treasury, 1980-81; Director of Finances, State of México, 1981-86; *Substitute Governor* of México, 1986-87; Ambassador to Spain, 1987-91; Federal Attorney for the Consumer, 1991- . g-None. h-None. i-Married Lucía Sáenz Viezca; son of Alfredo Baranda Carsolio, lawyer, and Alicia García de la Torre; brother of Pedro Baranda García, Oficial Mayor of Tourism, 1986-88. j-None. k-None. l-DBGM87; HA, 13 May 1986; Mexiquenses, 23; DBGM92, 47.

Barba González, Silvano
(Deceased Aug. 1967) a-Nov. 29, 1895. b-Valle de Guadalupe, Jalisco. c-Primary studies in Catholic schools in Tepatitlán, Jalisco, and San Juan de Los Lagos, Jalisco; secondary studies in San Juan de Los Lagos; preparatory studies in Guadalajara; law degree from the University of Guadalajara, Jalisco, Oct.

2, 1920; Rector of the University of Guadalajara, 1927-28. d-Local deputy to the legislature of Jalisco, 1920 (for two successive terms); Federal Deputy from Jalisco, Dist. 8, 1926-28; *Governor of Jalisco*, 1939-43; *Senator* from Jalisco, 1952-58; member of the Foreign Relations Committee, the Mail and Telegraph Committee and President of the Migration Committee. e-Private Secretary to *Lázaro Cárdenas* during 1934 presidential campaign; *President of the CEN of PRI*, Aug. 20, 1936, to Apr. 2, 1938. f-Attorney General of the State of Jalisco, 1922-24; Secretary General of the Government of Jalisco, 1925; Provisional Governor of Jalisco, 1926-27; district court judge of Guadalajara, Tepic and Monterrey, 1928-34; *Oficial Mayor of the Secretariat of Government*, 1934-35; *Secretary of Labor*, 1934-35; *Secretary of Government*, June 18, 1935, to Aug. 20, 1936; *Head of the Department of Agrarian Affairs and Colonization*, 1944-46; political adviser to the President of Mexico, 1965-67. g-Cofounder of the Association of Catholic Youth, 1918. h-Author of the Labor Law of Jalisco; author of a biography on the Mexican caudillo Manuel Luzada. i-Friend and political supporter of José Guadalupe Zuno, governor of Jalisco, 1923-26; tied to *Margarito Ramírez*'s political faction after Zuno left office; relative of Marcelino Barba González, federal deputy from Jalisco, Dist. 3, 1937-39; longtime supporter of *Lázaro Cárdenas*; married Esther Padilla, sister of Adalberto Padilla Ascencio, justice of the Supreme Court, 1961-66; nephew, Adalberto Padilla Quiróz, was a federal deputy; parents were wealthy landowners and cattle ranchers. j-Fought against the Cristeros, 1926-28, and against the military uprising in Sonora, 1929. k-None. l-DBM68, 87; DGF56, 6; DP70, 219; *Polémica*, 68; Gruening, 444, 448; Wilkie, 192; Kirk, 126-27; Ind. Biog., 20-

21; Hernández Chávez, 26; Hurtado, 271.

Barberena (Vega), Miguel Angel
a-Aug. 4, 1928. b-Jesús María, Aguascalientes. c-Primary, secondary, and preparatory at the Autonomous Institute of Sciences, Aguascalientes; graduate in engineer from the Heroic Naval College, Veracruz, 1947-51; fellowship to study at the University of Michigan, 1955-57; mechanical engineering degree, University of Veracruz, 1957; MA degree in nuclear engineering, University of Michigan, 1957-1958; postgraduate studies, economic development, National School of Economics, UNAM, 1962; Director, School of Science, University of Veracruz, 1961-62; Director, National Calculating Center, IPN, 1964; Director of Workshops, IPN, 1963-64; Member of the University Council of the University of Veracruz, Jalapa, Veracruz, 1958-63. d-*Alternate Senator* from Aguascalientes, 1970, but replaced *Gómez Villanueva*, 1971-76, member of the Second Section of the Legislative Studies Committee, First Secretary of the Second Consular and Diplomatic Service Committee, Second Secretary of the Railroad Committee; *Governor of Aguascalientes*, 1986-92. e-Joined PRI, 1947; Secretary of Organization of the CEN of PRI, 1973-74; *Secretary General of the CEN of PRI*, 1974-75; general delegate of the CEN and of the IEPES of PRI, 1959-70; general delegate of the CEN of PRI to Coahuila, 1970; general delegate of CEN of PRI to Baja California, 1973. f-Member of the delegation from Mexico to UNESCO in Italy; President of the Coordinating Committee on Transportation, Secretariat of Communication and Transportation, 1969; Director General of Railroads, Secretariat of Communication and Transportation, 1964-71; *Subsecretary of Communication and Transportation,*

1976-80; member of the Presidential Staff, Secretariat of the Navy, 1989. g-None. i-Collaborator of *José Antonio Padilla Segura* at IPN and the Secretariat of Communication and Transportation; son of Ernesto Barberena López, farmer, and Marina Vega López; married Mirian Cruz Valdés. j-Career naval officer; rank of Rear Admiral, 1984. k-Precandidate for senator from Aguascalientes, 1981. l-C de S, 1970-76, 70; DAPC,6; MGF69, 277; *Excélsior*, 26 Dec. 1981, 16A; DBGM89, 663.

Barbosa Espinosa, María Albertina
a-Apr. 8, 1942. b-Canatlán, Durango. c-Secondary and normal teaching certificate, Basic Normal School of Durango; special courses in Atlanta, Georgia, and New York; primary teacher, Durango, 1961-64; professor, Normal School of Durango, 1975-80. d-*Alternate Federal Deputy* from the State of Durango, Dist. 5, 1979-82; *Federal Deputy* from the State of Durango, Dist. 3, 1982-85, member of the Human Dwelling and Public Works Committee; *Federal Deputy* from the State of Durango, Dist. 4, 1988-91, member of the Foreign Relations Committee. e-Subdirector of the Center for Political Education of PRI, Durango, 1979-80; Director of the Center for Political Education of PRI, 1980-81. f-None. g-Secretary of Education of the National Women's Revolutionary Group (ANFER), 1979-80; Secretary General of the National Women's Revolutionary Group for Durango, 1981-91. h-None. i-Daughter of Alberto Barbosa Ayala, chauffeur, and María del Carmen Espinosa Simentel; widow. j-None. k-None. l-Directorio, 1982-85; C de D, 1979-82; Lehr, 166; DBGM89, 403.

Barbosa Heldt, Antonio
(Deceased Sept. 18, 1973) a-1908. b-Colima. c-Primary and secondary studies in Colima; teaching certificate

in rural education from the Normal School of Colima; graduate work in normal and technical training, Graduate Teachers College; teacher at the Progreso Primary School, Mexicali, 1927; rural teacher in Colima and Baja California del Sur. d-*Governor-elect of Colima*, 1973. e-None. f-Director General of Education in the Cuenca de Papaloapan, 1953; Subdirector General of Primary Education, Calendar B, Secretariat of Public Education, 1961-65; Director General of Education for the Cuenca del Grijalva and the Cuenca del Fuerte; Federal Inspector, Mexicali Valley, Sonora; Administrator, Plan Chontalpa; Director General of Primary Education, Dist. 4, Federal District, Secretariat of Public Education, 1965-70; *Oficial Mayor of Public Education*, 1970-73. g-Secretary General of the Union of Teachers of Baja California del Sur. h-Director General of the Scholastic and Physical Education Department of the Secretariat of Hydraulic Resources. i-Married to Francisca Stevens; brother, Humberto, was treasurer of Colima and a precandidate for governor, 1978. j-None. k-Considered to be an apostle of rural education in Mexico; committed suicide because he contracted a fatal disease. l-HA, 26 Mar. 1973, 38; *Excélsior*, 12 Mar. 1973, 12; HA, 14 Dec. 1970, 23; DPE61, 99; *Excélsior*, 8 Mar. 1973, 14; HA, 26, Mar. 1973, 38; *Excélsior*, 11 Nov. 1978, 23; Romero Aceves, 25-27.

Bárcena (Ibarra), Alicia Isabel
a-Mar. 5, 1952. b-Federal District. c-Early education unknown; biology degree, School of Science, UNAM, 1971-75, with a thesis on "Herbal Vegetation of Coatlán del Río, Morelos," 1977; MA studies in science, UNAM, 1975-79; MA in ecology and biotic resources, National Institute of Research on Biotic Resources, Jalapa, 1979-82; MA in public administration,

Harvard University, 1987-88; professor, School of Science, UNAM, 1974-75; professor, Autonomous Metropolitan University, Ixtapalapa campus, 1975-79; researcher, National Institute of Research on Biotic Resources, 1978-82. d-None. e-Coordinator of the Southeast Plan, IEPES of PRI, 1982; Technical Secretary of the Committee on Ecology and Environment, IEPES, 1982. f-Director of the Yucatán Flora Project, National Institute of Biotic Resources, 1980-81; Director of the Regional Office, National Institute of Biotic Resources, 1981-82; *Subsecretary of Ecology*, Secretariat of Urban Development and Ecology, 1982-86; Director General of the National Fishing Institute, 1988-91. g-None. h-None. i-Daughter of Agustín Bárcena Montañez, lawyer and translator, and Alicia Ibarra Vega, magazine editor. j-None. k-None. l-Q es QAP, 273; DBGM, 52; DBGM89, 44.

Barocio Barrios, Alberto
(Deceased 1966) a-1890. b-Montemorelos, Nuevo León. c-Preparatory in Mexico City; engineering degree from the National School of Engineering, UNAM, 1914; graduate studies at Columbia University, New York; professor at the Higher School of Mechanical and Electrical Engineering (18 years); Professor of Hydraulics, National School of Engineering, UNAM, 1941; Director of the National School of Engineering, UNAM; professor at the Constructors School. d-None. e-None. f-Subinspector of Ports, Secretariat of Communication; Chief of the Photo-Topographical Department of the National Irrigation Commission; Chief of the Water Section, Secretariat of Public Health; Director of the Department of Bridges, Secretariat of Communication; *Subsecretary of Government Properties*, 1953-58. g-None. h-Chief of the Laboratory, National School of Engineering, UNAM; engineering

specialist, Department of the Federal District; specialist in material costs for Petróleos Mexicanos; held many positions in Petróleos Mexicanos until 1966. j-Engineer for the Division of the North, 1915; Captain of the Engineers for General Benjamín Hill, 1916. k-Important member of Masonry in Mexico. l-DGF56, 431; DP70, 224; DGF47, 271.

Barra García, Félix
a-Sept. 26, 1934. b-Castillo de Teayo, Veracruz. c-Primary studies in the María Enriqueta Article 123 School, Poza Rica de Hidalgo, Veracruz; secondary at the Salvador Díaz Mirón School, Poza Rica de Hidalgo, 1948-50; preparatory at the National Preparatory School, 1951-52; began studies at the National School of Political Science, UNAM, graduated with a thesis on "The Traditional and Newer Forms of Intervention"; Professor of Social, Economic, and Political Problems of Mexico, National School of Political Science, UNAM, until 1974; instructor in literacy classes, IMSS. d-None. e-None. f-Director of the Institute of Socio-Economic Research, UNAM, 1958-70; Director General of Orientation and Social Services, UNAM, 1970-72; *Secretary of Agrarian Reform*, 1975-76. g-None. i-Classmate of *Augusto Gómez Villanueva* at UNAM. j-None. k-Arrested and charged with criminal fraud in 1977. l-HA, 6 Oct. 1975, 8; *Excélsior*, 27 Sept. 1977, 1; *Proceso*, 18 Dec. 1976, 9-10.

Barragán Camacho, Salvador
a-Oct. 14, 1932. b-Ciudad Madero, Tamaulipas. c-Completed secondary studies only. d-*Federal Deputy* from the State of Tamaulipas, Dist. 5, 1965-67; *Senator* from the State of Tamaulipas, president of the 2nd Navy Committee. e-None. f-None. g-President, Revolutionary Group of Local 1, National Petroleum Workers Union

(STPRM); Secretary General of Local 1 of the STPRM, 1971-73; *Secretary General of the STPRM*, 1980-84. h-Chief, Coquizadora Plant, Pemex, Ciudad Madero. i-Son of Desiderio Barragán Chalres, railroad worker, and Nicolasa Camacho Montalvo; married Lorenza Macías Rodríguez. j-None. k-None. l-DBGM87, 437; Lehr, 467.

Barragán (Rodríguez), Juan
(Deceased Sept. 28, 1974) a-Aug. 30, 1890. b-Ríoverde, San Luis Potosí. c-Primary and secondary studies in San Luis Potosí; preparatory studies at the Scientific and Literary Institute of San Luis Potosí; completed fourth year of law school. d-Federal Deputy from the State of San Luis Potosí, Dist. 6, 1917-18; Senator from the State of San Luis Potosí, 1918-20; *Federal Deputy* from the State of San Luis Potosí, 1964-67, Dist. 1, member of the Military Industry Committee, the Military Justice Committee; *Federal Deputy* from the State of San Luis Potosí, Dist. 10, Party Deputy for PARM, 1970-73, member of the Department of the Federal District Committee, the Legislative Studies Committee, General Means of Communication and Transportation, and the Public Security Committee. e-*President of the Authentic Party of the Mexican Revolution*, 1965-74. f-None. g-None. i-Great-grandfather, Miguel Francisco Barragán, was interim president of Mexico in 1836; grandfather was a senator under Benito Juárez; son of Juan Francisco Barragán Anaya, a rancher, served as mayor of Ciudad del Maíz; sister, María, married to *Mariano Moctezuma*, subsecretary of industry and commerce, 1936-38; intimate collaborator of *Jacinto B. Treviño*, cofounder of PARM; married to Teresa Alvarez; son, Juan, was a candidate for federal deputy from the PARM, 1967. j-Joined the Revolution in 1913, served under *Jesús Agustín Castro*; Lt. Colonel

in 1920; Chief of Staff for President Carranza, 1920; career army officer, rank of General; incorporated back into the army by President *Cárdenas.* k-Organized a strike at the Scientific and Literary Institute of San Luis Potosí in support of Madero; imprisoned after the murder of Venustiano Carranza, 1920; escaped into exile in the United States and Cuba; supported the Serrano-Gómez Rebellion in 1927. l-IIA, 28 May 1973, 9; C de D, 1970-72, 102; C de D, 1964-66, 87; letter; DP70, 566; Cockcroft, 38; Pindaro Urióstegui, 191-92; HA, 7 Oct. 1974, 11; López Esc., 85.

Barraza Allande, Luciano
a-July 19, 1940. b-Gómez Palacio, Durango. c-Agricultural engineering degree, National School of Agriculture, Chapingo, 1956-62, with a thesis on "Production and Consumption of Ajonjoli"; Master of Science in Economics, University of Wisconsin, Madison, 1963; Ph.D. in Economics, University of Wisconsin, Madison, 1964-66, with a thesis on "Econometric Model for the Mexican Economy"; Professor of Econometrics, Graduate College, National School of Agriculture; Professor of Economic Development and Theory, Colegio de México. e-Joined PRI, 1962. f-Analyst, Department of Economic Studies, Bank of Mexico, 1966-70; adviser to the Second United Nations Seminar on Developmental Problems, Amsterdam; Director General, Agricultural Economy, Secretariat of Agriculture, 1970-72; *Oficial Mayor of the Secretariat of Agriculture and Livestock,* Aug. 3, 1972, to Aug. 25, 1972; Director General of Guanos and Fertilizers, Aug. 25, 1972-76; Director General, Division of Agricultural Projects, Inter-American Development Bank, 1977-82; Secretary of Rural Development, State of Michoacán, 1986-87; regional delegate, Secretariat of Programming and Budgeting,

1987-88; Director of Administration and Finances, Federal Highways and Bridges, 1989. g-Secretary of the Student Society, National School of Agriculture. h-Author of ten books. i-Brother, Enrique, was director general of border affairs, 1989; son of Luciano Barraza Núñez, cattle rancher, and Luz Allande Pérez; married Martha Carreño Manjarrez. j-None. k-None. l-*Excélsior*, 26 Aug. 1972, 1, 9, 4 Aug. 1972, 19; HA, 4 Sept. 1972, 30; IEPES; DBGM89, 46.

Barreiro Pereda, Mario
a-Mar. 23, 1945. b-Federal District. c-Actuary degree, UNAM, with a thesis on "Studies of the Primary School Population in Mexico, 1968-71"; Chief of Electronic Processes, Statistics Department, UNAM, 1969-71; adviser, Technical Planning Committee, UNAM, 1970-71; Chief of Planning and Programming, National School of Medicine, UNAM, 1971-72. d-None. e-None. f-Director of Educational Section, Division of Public Investment, Secretariat of the Presidency, 1972-74; Chief of Statistics and Basic Data, Division of Public Investment, Secretariat of the Presidency, 1974-75; Chief of the Department of Investment Development, Division of Public Investment, Secretariat of the Presidency, 1975-76; Director of Control of Tax Incentives, Division of Tax Development, Secretariat of the Treasury, 1976-79; Executive Coordinator, Subsecretary of Programming, Secretariat of Programming and Budget, 1979-82; *Subsecretary of the Government Transformation Industry,* Secretariat of Energy, Mines, and Government Industry, 1982-86. g-None. h-None. i-Son of Ernesto Barreiro Sánchez, engineer and public official, and Olga María Perea Sánchez; married María Leticia Castellanos Guzmán; brother, Octavio, chief of quality control, IMSS, 1991. j-None. k-None.

l-Q es QAP, 168-69; DBGM, 53; DBGM92, 49.

Barrera Fuentes, Florencio
a-Aug. 23, 1920. b-Saltillo, Coahuila. c-Primary studies at the Colegio Roberts, Saltillo; first year of secondary at the Ateneo Fuente, Saltillo; completed secondary at the National Preparatory Night School, Mexico City; preparatory studies at the National Preparatory School, Mexico City; law degree from the National School of Law, UNAM, Mar. 25, 1950. d-*Alternate Federal Deputy* from the State of Coahuila, Dist.1, 1949-52; *Federal Deputy* from the State of Coahuila, Dist.1, 1958-61, member of the Gran Comisión, President of the Chamber of Deputies, Oct. 1960, and member of the Legislative Studies Committee, Library Committee, and President of the Second Constitutional Affairs Committee; member of the Mexican delegation to the First InterParliamentary Conference of Mexico and the United States, 1961; *Senator* from the State of Coahuila, 1964-70, President of the Senate, 1967, President of the Legislative Studies Committee, the Second Treasury Committee, and the Electrical Industry Committee; representative of the Senate to the Federal Electoral Commission, 1970. e-Joined PRM, Oct. 15, 1940, as a member of the labor sector; Auxiliary Secretary of the CEN of PRI, 1961-63; general delegate of the CEN of PRI to municipal elections in the states of México, Oaxaca, Nayarit, Morelos, Coahuila, Nuevo León, Guanajuato, Hidalgo, and Durango; general delegate of the CEN of PRI to federal deputy elections in Colima and Chihuahua. f-Typist, section head, National Lottery, 1936-44; Private Secretary to *Nazario Ortiz Garza*, Director General of CONASUPO, 1944-46; Private Secretary to *Nazario Ortiz Garza*, Secretary of Agriculture, 1946-49; Director Gen-

eral of Administration and Accounting, Secretariat of Agriculture, 1949-51; *Oficial Mayor of Agriculture*, 1951-52; Assistant to the Director of the Federal Electric Commission, Manuel Moreno Torres, 1961-64. g-None. h-Writer for many newspapers, including *El Universal*. i-Son of Federico Barrera Cuéllar, a physician, and Enriqueta Fuentes. j-None. k-None. l-Func., 140; C de D, 1949-52; C de D, 1958-61; DGF51, 19; C de S, 1964; PS, 0580.

Barrientos (Esparza), Javier A.
a-Feb. 3, 1917. b-Federal District. c-Early education unknown; mechanical and electrical engineering degree, Higher School of Mechanical and Electrical Engineering, IPN; special studies in Stafford, England; practical studies in Lyon, France; professor at the Higher School of Mechanical and Electrical Engineering, IPN (eleven years). d-None. e-None. f-Representative of Mexico to the Latin American Free Trade Association, 1967; *Subsecretary of Communications and Transportation*, 1970-71. g-None. h-Founder of various private firms. j-None. k-None. l-HA, 4 Oct. 1971, 36; HA, 14 Dec. 1970, 22.

Barrios (Castro), Roberto
a-Mar. 19, 1910. b-Atlacomulco, México. c-Primary studies in Atlacomulco; teaching certificate, Normal School of Toluca, México; educator and secondary school teacher. d-Local deputy to the State Legislature of México during the governorship of *Isidro Fabela*, 1942-45; *Federal Deputy* from the State of México, Dist. 1, 1952-55, member of the Credentials Committee and the Library Committee. g-General delegate of PRI for various states during the campaign of *Adolfo Ruiz Cortines*, 1951-52; general delegate of the CEN of PRI to the States of Tabasco and Chiapas; Chief of the campaign of

Alfredo del Mazo Vélez for governor of México, 1945; director of *Miguel Alemán*'s campaign for president in the State of México, 1946. f-Representative of the federal government on the Advisory Council of the National Bank of Ejido Credit, 1950; Subdirector of the Department of Literacy, Secretariat of Public Education; Director of Colonization, Cuenca de Papaloapan; *Head of the Department of Agrarian Affairs and Colonization*, 1958-64. g-Founding member of the National Confederation of Campesinos (CNC), 1938; Secretary General of the League of Agrarian Communities and Agricultural Unions of the State of México; *Secretary General of the CNC*, 1947-50; founder of the National Autonomous Union of Teachers, member of the Valle de Bravo Teacher's Association. h-None. i-Disciple of *Graciano Sánchez*, longtime labor leader; active in union movement with *Adolfo López Mateos*; married Luz María del Valle. j-None. k-Involved in a scandal over ejido lots that was accomplished with the forged signature of *Adolfo López Mateos*. l-*El Universal*, 2 Dec. 1958; HA, 8 Dec. 1958, 30, 32; C de D, 1955, 6; DGF50, II, 139; *Quién Será*, 132-33; *Excélsior*, 13 May 1963; *Por Qué*, 11 Sept. 1969, 35; González Navarro, 256-57; Func., 93; Medina, 20, 183.

Barros Sierra, Javier
(Deceased Aug. 15, 1971) a-Feb. 25, 1915. b-Federal District. c-Primary studies, Colegio Francés Alvarado, Mexico City, 1928; secondary studies, Public School No. 3, 1931; preparatory studies, National Preparatory School, Mexico City, 1934; civil engineering degree, National School of Engineering, UNAM, 1940; Master of Science in Mathematics, School of Science, UNAM, 1947; Professor of Mathematics, UNAM, 1938-58; Director of the National School of Engineering,

UNAM, 1955-58. d-None. e-None. f-President of the Permanent Commission of UNAM; Director of the Mexican Institute of Petroleum; *Secretary of Public Works*, 1958-64; *Rector of UNAM*, 1966-70. g-None. h-Investigator for the Institute of Mathematics, UNAM, 1943-57; Secretary of the Mexican Society of Mathematics, 1943-57; adviser in mathematics to the National Preparatory School; adviser, School of Science, UNAM; adviser to the National Chamber of Industries; Manager of Estructuras y Construcciones, S.A. i-Brother of *Manuel Barros Sierra*; grandson of Justo Sierra Méndez, secretary of justice, 1905-11; student at UNAM of *Antonio Dovalí Jaime*; nephew, Carlos J. Sierra Bravota, was Private Secretary to *Carlos Sansores Pérez* as governor of Campeche; son, *Javier Barros Valero*, was Private Secretary to *Fernando Solana* as secretary of public education and subsecretary of foreign relations, 1988; close friend of *Fernando Espinosa Gutiérrez*; married María Cristina Valero Rosell; son of José Barros Olmedo and María de Jesús Sierra; nephew of Miguel Lanz Duret and María Concepción Sierra. j-None. k-Submitted his resignation as rector of UNAM in 1968 but more than 1,000 students asked him to remain; one of the few rectors in recent years to complete his term at UNAM. l-HA, 8 Dec. 1958, 28, 30; *Hoy*, 4 Apr., 1970; HA, 23 Aug. 1971, 15; WWMG, 8 Func. 75; *El Universal*, 2 Dec. 1958, 8; Enc. Mex. I, 530; letter.

Barros Sierra, Manuel
(Deceased 1967) a-1916. b-Federal District. c-Primary and secondary studies, Mexico City; preparatory, National Preparatory School, Mexico City; law degree, National School of Law, UNAM, 1940; with a thesis on the "Problems of Expert Testimony and Its Value in Civil Law." d-None. e-None.

f-Assistant to the Director of the Banco Nacional Hipotecario Urbano y de Obras Públicas, 1953-54; Manager of the Trust Department of the Banco Nacional Hipotecario Urbano, 1954-61; *Subdirector of Finances of Petróleos Mexicanos*, 1964-67; Executive Director of the Inter-American Development Bank, 1963-66. g-General Subdirector of the National Union of Sugar Producers, 1962-64. h-Member of the administrative councils of the Industrial Complex of Sahagún City, the Mexican Institute of Petroleum, and others; member of the Mexican delegation to the Regional Conference of the International Organization of Labor in Buenos Aires, 1958, World Conference on Trade and Development, 1964. i-Brother of *Javier Barros Sierra*, secretary of public works, 1958-64; grandson of Justo Sierra Méndez, secretary of justice, 1905-11; son of María de Jesús Sierra Mayarola and José Barros Olmedo; nephew of Miguel Lanz Duret, federal deputy. j-None. k-None. l-HA, 4 Jan. 1965, 27; DP70, 2365, letter.

Barros (Valero), Javier
a-Apr. 26, 1949. b-Federal District. c- Early education unknown; studies in politics and public administration at the National School of Political and Social Sciences, UNAM, 1968-72, graduating in 1972 with a thesis on "Public Enterprises, the Case of Mexico"; MA in politics and public administration, University of London, 1973-74; researcher, National School of Political and Social Sciences; professor, National School of Political and Social Sciences; Director, Department of Public Administration, UNAM, 1974-75. d-None. e-Joined PRI, 1970. f-Executive Secretary of the National Institute of Public Administration, 1976; Private Secretary to *Fernando Solana*, secretary of commerce, 1976-77; Private Secretary to *Fernando Solana*, secretary of education, 1977-78; Director General of Adult

Education, Secretariat of Public Education, 1978; Director General of Publications and Libraries, Secretariat of Public Education, 1979-82; Director General of the National Institute of Fine Arts, 1982-87; Consul General in San Francisco, 1987-88; *Subsecretary C*, Secretariat of Foreign Relations, 1988-92. g-None. h-None. i-Son of *Javier Barros Sierra*, rector of UNAM, and María Cristina Valero Rosell; grandson of Justo Sierra, secretary of public education; grandson of María de Jesús Sierra and José Barros Olmedo; nephew of *Manuel Barros Sierra*, subdirector of Pemex. j-None. k-None. l-HA, 2 Aug 1982, 10; Q es QAP, 304; DBGM, 55; DBGM89, 48; *Excélsior*, 20 Jan. 1982, 17A; HA, 1 Feb. 1982, 22; IEPES; letter.

Bartilotti (Perea), Pedro Luis
a-May 4, 1936. b-Villahermosa, Tabasco. c-Primary studies in the Federal District; medical degree, National School of Medicine, UNAM, 1954-57; economics degree, National School of Economics, UNAM, 1958-62; Professor of Industrial Design, Ibero-American University, 1970-80. d-*Alternate Federal Deputy* from the Federal District, Dist. 15, 1964-67; *Federal Deputy* from the Federal District, Dist. 1, 1967-70, 1982-85. e-Joined PRI, 1952; member, National Council of PRI, 1964-67; general delegate of the CEN of PRI to 16 states, 1967-70; Subdirector of the National Youth Organization of PRI, 1959-60; Director of Youth of PRI in the Federal District, 1960-61; *Secretary of Finances of the CEN of PRI*, 1968-70; Coordinator of *José López Portillo's* presidential campaign in Tabasco, 1976; Secretary of Publicity of PRI, Federal District, 1981-82; general delegate of the CEN of PRI to Sonora, 1983; general delegate of the CEN of PRI to Chihuahua, 1985. f-Director of Public Relations, State of Tabasco, 1980-82; Director of the DIF and FONAPAS,

Tabasco, 1977-80; Director General of the Small Business Bank, 1970-76; Oficial Mayor of the Chamber of Deputies, 1964-67; Delegate of the Department of the Federal District, Gustavo Madero, 1988; Coordinator of Advisers, Subsecretary of Operations, Secretariat of Tourism, 1988-92; Secretary of Industrial Development, Tabasco, 1992- . g-Secretary General of the Medical Students University Federation, 1954; Director of Publicity, CNOP, *Gustavo Díaz Ordaz* presidential campaign, 1964; Director of the National Youth Organization of CNOP, 1961-63. h-None. i-Son of Pedro Bartilotti Quintero, treasurer general of the State of Tabasco under *Francisco Trujillo Gurría*, and Guadalupe Perea Romero. j-None. k-None. l-Bulnes, 605; C de D, 1964-67; C de D, 1967-70; Directorio, 1982-85; DBGM89, 48-49; DBGM92, 727.

Bartlett (Bautista), Manuel

(Deceased Apr. 24, 1963) a-Dec. 23, 1893. b-Tenosique, Tabasco. c-Primary studies, Tenosique; secondary studies, Colegio de Tenosique and the Mexican Methodist Institute of Puebla; preparatory studies, the Juárez Institute of Villahermosa, Tabasco, 1909-15; law degree, UNAM, Apr. 17, 1920, with a thesis on "The Advancement of the Defense"; editor of student paper *El Estudiante*. d-Local Deputy to the Legislature of the State of Tabasco, 1921-22; *Governor of Tabasco*, 1953-55, did not complete constitutional term. f-Consulting lawyer for the Council of Mexico City, 1920; public defender for the military, 1922; consulting lawyer for the Secretariat of the Treasury, 1924-28; chief of the legal department of the Secretariat of the Treasury, 1929; judge of the district court in the States of Veracruz, Puebla, and México; Judge of the First District Court (Administrative Affairs); *Justice of the Supreme*

Court, 1941-52. g-President of the Free Student Association, Juárez Institute, 1913. h-Practicing attorney, 1920; lawyer for the Office of Common Jurisdiction, Federal District, 1923. i-Son, *Manuel Bartlett Díaz*, was secretary general of the CEN of PRI and secretary of government, 1982; father, Gabriel Bartlett Cámara, was a businessman; wife, Isabel Díaz Castilla, was the daughter of rebel Salvador Díaz Mirón; paternal grandfather was Dr. Bartolomew Bartlett. j-None. k-Active in revolutionary movements in 1914-15; led a student protest strike on the death of Madero and was expelled from the Juárez Institute, 1913; candidate for governor of Tabasco three times before winning the nomination; asked state legislature for a leave of absence after the federal government pressured him to resign following numerous riots against his administration as governor. l-DP70, 232; DGF47, 29; WWM45, 9; WB48, 459; Scott, 276; EBW46, 421; NYT, 18 Mar. 1955, 15; NYT, 24 Mar. 1955, 11.

Bartlett (Díaz), Manuel

a-Feb. 23, 1936. c-Early education unknown; law degree, with an honorable mention, National School of Law, UNAM, 1959, with a thesis on state obligations to societal damages; courses in public administration toward a Ph.D., Victoria University, Manchester, England, as a fellow of the British Council, 1967-68; studies in law, School of Law, Paris, France, 1959-61, on a fellowship from the French government and UNAM; diploma from the School of International Comparative Law, Strasbourg, France, 1963-64; Ph.D in political science, School of Political and Social Sciences, UNAM, 1967-68; Professor of General Theory of the State and of Political Ideas, National School of Law, UNAM, 1962-66; Professor of Mercantile Law, School of Business and

Administration, UNAM. d-*Governor of Puebla*, 1993- . e-Auxiliary Secretary to *Carlos Madrazo* as President of the CEN of PRI, 1964-65; general delegate of the CEN of PRI to Sinaloa during confrontation between *Madrazo* and *Leopoldo Sánchez Celis*, 1964-65; Director General of *La República*, official organ of PRI, 1963; organized the Revolutionary Youth Movement of PRI patterned after the Spanish Falange; adviser to *Miguel de la Madrid* on relations with PRI during his presidential campaign, 1981; *Secretary General of the CEN of PRI*, 1981-82. f-Adviser to the Director of Treasury Studies, Secretariat of the Treasury, 1962-63; adviser to the Director General of Credit, Secretariat of the Treasury, 1962-64; Subdirector of Government of the Secretariat of Government, 1969-70; Auxiliary Secretary to *Mario Moya Palencia*, Secretary of Government, 1969-70; Subdirector General of Government, Secretariat of Government, 1970; Secretary of the Federal Electoral Commission, 1970-76; Director General of Government of the Secretariat of Government, 1970-76; Director in Chief of Political Affairs, Secretariat of Foreign Relations, 1977-79; adviser to *Miguel de la Madrid* as Secretary of Planning and Budgeting, 1979-81; *Secretary of Government*, 1982-88; *Secretary of Public Education*, 1988-92. g-Auxiliary Secretary to *Jorge Rojo Gómez* as Secretary General of the CNC, 1962-63. h-None. i-Son of *Manuel Bartlett Bautista*, former governor of Tabasco; mother, Isabel Díaz Castilla, daughter of noted rebel Salvador Díaz Mirón; remained with *Lauro Ortega* after *Madrazo* left the presidency of PRI; supported *Mario Moya Palencia* for the presidency, 1975; married Gloria Alvarez Miaja. j-None. k-None. l-HA, 3 May 1982, 11; *Excélsior*, 9 Nov. 1981, 18A; DPE71, 5; DAPC, 77, 7; HA, 28 Dec. 1964, 4; *Excélsior*, 29 Sept. 1981,

23A; MGF73, 205; *Excélsior*, 15 Oct. 1981, 1A; Informe, 44-45; Almanaque de México, 16-17; *Excélsior*, 1 Dec. 1982, 20, 36A; HA, 13 Dec. 1982, 10; HA, 3 Jan. 1983, 11.

Bassols, Narciso
(Deceased July 24, 1959) a-Oct.22, 1897. b-Tenango del Valle, México. c-Preparatory studies, National Preparatory School, Mexico City, 1911-15; law degree, National School of Law, UNAM, May 29, 1920; Professor of Ethics, Logic, and Constitutional Law at the National School of Law, UNAM, 1920-31; Director of the National School of Law, UNAM, 1928-29. d-None. e-Founder of the League of Political Action with *Vicente Lombardo Toledano*; founder and Vice-President of the Popular Party, 1947-49. f-Secretary General of Government of the State of México under Governor Carlos Riva Palacio, 1925-26; Secretary of Public Education, 1931-34; Secretary of Government, 1934; Secretary of the Treasury, 1934-35; *Ambassador to Great Britain*, 1935-37; delegate to the League of Nations, 1937; *Ambassador to France*, 1938-39; Ambassador to Russia, 1944-46; adviser to *Adolfo Ruiz Cortines*, 1952-54. g-None. h-Founder of the National School of Economics, UNAM; author of the Agrarian Law of 1927; author of many articles. i-Longtime friend of *Vicente Lombardo Toledano*; student with *Gilberto Loyo* and *Rafael de la Colina* at the National Preparatory School and at UNAM; studied sociology under *Antonio Caso* at UNAM; father, Narciso Bassols, was a judge; great-nephew of Sebastian Lerdo de Tejada; mentor to *Ricardo J. Zevada* and *Víctor Manuel Villaseñor*; married Clementina Batalla. j-None. k-Participated in the gubernatorial campaign in Aguascalientes, 1919, writing campaign speeches; Calles considered him as a successor to Ortiz

Rubio as president of Mexico, 1932; ran for federal deputy from the State of México and lost; resigned as director of the Law School after a student rebellion against the introduction of a trisemester system; considered one of the most brilliant law professors at UNAM. l-WWM45, 9; DP70, 235; letters, EBW46, 212, Kirk, 222, 269-70; Peral, 96; Enc. Mex., II, 533; *Excélsior*, 14 Nov. 1949; NYT, 17 Oct. 1954, 16.

Bastarrachea Sabido, Jorge
a-Aug. 15, 1949. b-Mérida, Yucatán. c-Early education unknown; certified public accounting degree, School of Accounting and Business Administration, UNAM, 1965-69, with a thesis on the role of private banks in enterprise development; postgraduate studies, School of Political and Social Sciences, UNAM, 1970-74, with a degree in sociology; MA in finance, Higher Institute of Technological Studies of Monterrey, 1976-77; professor, Mount Sinai Preparatory School, 1973-75; professor, Autonomous Technological Institute of Mexico, 1976-78. d-None. e-Joined PRI, 1970. f-Assistant Treasurer of Financial Resources, IMSS, 1978-80; Treasurer General of IMSS, 1980-82; *Oficial Mayor of Labor*, 1982-88; Executive Secretary of State Workers Housing Fund, 1988-91. g-None. h-Subdirector of the Payments Section, Bank of Commerce, 1968; officer, Division of Fixed Income Bonds, Bank of Commerce; credit analyst, Bank of Commerce; Assistant Manager, San Bartolo Branch, Bank of Commerce; Manager, Avila Camacho Branch, Bank of Commerce; Account Executive, Diana Branch, Bank of Commerce; Zone Subdirector, Bank of Commerce, 1978. i-Son of Roberto Bastarrachea Solís, businessman, and María Luisa Sabido Sosa; married Nohemí Elizabeth Gutiérrez Vargas. j-None. k-None. l-Q es QAP, 360; DBGM, 56; DBGM89, 49.

Bátiz Vázquez, Bernardo
a-Sept. 14, 1936. b-Federal District. c-Primary studies in the State of Chiapas and the Federal District; secondary studies at Diurna No. 1, Mexico City; preparatory studies at the National Preparatory School, Mexico City; law degree from the National School of Law, UNAM, 1954-58; teacher at the Benito Juárez Night Preparatory School and the Hispano-American Institute; Professor of Law, National School of Law, UNAM, 1961-63; Professor of Sociology at the Ibero-American University, 1962-72. d-*Alternate Federal Deputy*, Party Deputy, 1967-70, Federal District; *Federal Deputy* from the Federal District, Dist. 16, 1970-73; member of the Department of the Federal District Committee, the Ejidal No. 1 Committee and the Money and Credit Institutions Committee; *Plurinominal Federal Deputy* from PAN, 1982-85, coordinator of the PAN delegation; *Plurinominal Federal Deputy* from PAN, 1988-91. e-Joined PAN, 1962; President of the Regional Committee of PAN for the Federal District, Dist. 16, 1964-67; member of the Regional Committee of PAN for the Federal District, 1968, 1981; *Secretary General of PAN*, 1972-75; member of the National Council of PAN, 1972-85; Secretary of Organization of CEN of PAN, 1980; *Secretary General of PAN*, 1983. f-None. g-None. h-Consulting lawyer to BANAMEX, 1967; practicing lawyer, 1975- . i-Married to Dulce María Zavala Cisneros; son of José Bátiz Grajales, bank official, and Esther Vázquez Espejel. j-None. k-None. l-Directorio, 1970-72; letter; C de D, 1970-72, 103; HA, 19 Feb. 1979, vii; Directorio, 1982-85; DBGM89, 405.

Bautista (Castillo), Gonzalo
(Deceased Oct. 7, 1952) a-Jan. 1, 1896. b-Puebla, Puebla. c-Primary at the Escuela Ventanas in Puebla; secondary

studies in Puebla; preparatory and beginning of professional studies in Puebla; medical degree from the National School of Medicine, UNAM. d-Local Deputy to the Legislature of the State of Puebla, 1920; Federal Deputy from the State of Puebla, 1922-28, 1920-34; *Senator* from the State of Puebla, 1934-40; Mayor of Puebla, 1940-41; *Governor of Puebla*, 1941-46. e-Member of the League of Professionals and Intellectuals of the Mexican Revolutionary Party. f-None. g-Student delegate to the 2nd National Student Congress with *Leonides Andreu Almazán*, 1921. h-Author. i-Father of *Gonzalo Bautista O'Farrill*; married María O'Farrill, from a wealthy Puebla family; *Gustavo Díaz Ordaz* served under him as secretary general of government; parents were from the middle class. j-Joined the Revolution in 1910. k-President *Avila Camacho* personally attended his inauguration ceremonies as governor of Puebla. l-Correa47, 20; DP70, 238; letter, Peral, 98; Enc. Mex., I, 536.

Bautista O'Farrill, Gonzalo
a-Apr. 16, 1922. b-Puebla, Puebla. c-Primary studies in Puebla; secondary studies at Secondary School No. 1, Mexico City; preparatory studies at the National Preparatory School, 1939-40; medical degree from the University of Puebla, 1947, with a thesis on the "Significance of Metabolical Determinants on the Glucose Curve of Tolerance"; Professor of Bacteriology, School of Medicine, University of Puebla, 1950-53; Rector of the University of Puebla, 1953-54; Professor of Virology of the School of Medicine at the University of Puebla, 1957-60. d-*Federal Deputy* from the State of Puebla, Dist. 5, 1961-64; President of the Editorial Committee, President of the Committee on Health and Welfare, member of the Child Assistance and Social Security

Committee, President of the Interparliamentary Committee, President of the Complaints Committee; *Senator* from the State of Puebla, 1964-70; Oficial Mayor of the Gran Comisión, President of the Administrative Committee, President of the Committee on Social Security; Secretary of the First Committee on Tariffs and Foreign Trade; Secretary of the First Committee on Public Education; *Interim Governor of Puebla*, Apr. 1972, to Mar. 8, 1973; Mayor of Puebla, 1970-72. e-Director of Economic and Social Planning for the presidential campaign of *Adolfo López Mateos* in Puebla, 1958; general delegate of PRI to Veracruz, Sonora, Jalisco, Baja California del Norte, Sinaloa and Nayarit. f-None. g-None. h-Resident in the Hospital of Nutritional Illnesses, 1948; investigator at Columbia University, New York, on scholarship, 1954; worked in the Laboratory of Viral Investigations, Columbia University, 1955-56. i-Son of *Gonzalo Bautista (Castillo)*, former governor of Puebla, and María O'Farrill, from a wealthy Puebla family. k-Resigned governorship under pressure. l-HA, 24 Apr. 1972; DBM68, 62-63; *Hoy*, 6 May 1972, 60-61; *Excélsior*, 26 Dec. 1974,12; Cole, 161; CyT, 82-83; MGF69, 106.

Bay, Alejo R.
a-1891. b-Alamos, Sonora. c-Early education unknown; no degree. d-Constitutional Deputy from the State of Sonora, Dist. 3, 1917-18; Local Deputy to the State Legislature of Sonora, 1919-21; Federal Deputy from the State of Sonora, Dist. 3, 1920; Governor of Sonora, 1923-27; Senator from the State of Sonora, 1928-30; *Senator* from the State of Sonora, 1940-46. e-None. f-Director of Customs in Veracruz, Veracruz, 1920-23; Treasurer General of the State of Sonora, 1939-40. g-None. i-None. j-Joined Victoriano Huerta's forces but changed sides 7 days later to

the Constitutionalists under José J. Obregón; signed the Plan of Agua Prieta, 1920; signer and supporter of the Hermosillo Plan, 1929. k-Exiled to the United States, 1929; repatriated by *Lázaro Cárdenas.* l-Almanaque de Sonora, 1982, 128; López Esc., 102; C de S, 1940-46; C de D, 1920.

Baylon Chacón, Oscar
a-Apr. 24, 1927. b-Chihuahua, Chihuahua. c-Early education unknown; engineering degree, Escobar Brothers School of Agronomy, Chihuahua. d-Mayor of Tecate, Baja California; Local Deputy from Tijuana to the State Legislature of Baja California; *Alternate Senator* from Baja California, 1976, but in functions as Senator, 1977-82, replacing *Roberto de la Madrid.* e-Secretary General of PRI in Baja California. f-Director General of Public Works, State of Baja California; Director General of the Property Census, State of Baja California; Oficial Mayor of the State Government of Baja California; President of the Board of Moral and Material Improvement, Secretariat of Government Properties; *Interim Governor of Baja California,* 1989. g-Secretary General of CNOP in Chihuahua; Secretary of Electoral Action of CNOP. h-None. j None. k-None. l-Protag., 46-47; C de S, 1976-82.

Baz (de Prada), Gustavo
(Deceased Oct. 12, 1987) a-May 1, 1894. b-Tlalnepantla, México. c-Primary and secondary studies, Guadalajara; preparatory studies, Scientific and Literary Institute of Toluca, México; began professional studies at the Military Medical School, 1913, on a scholarship; medical degree from the National School of Medicine, UNAM, Mar. 1, 1920; graduate studies in the United States at Harvard University, Boston University, and the Agustana Hospital in Chicago; studies in Europe on a private scholarship; Director, National School of Medicine, UNAM, 1935-36; Professor of Medicine at the National School of Medicine, UNAM, 1920-46; *Rector of UNAM,* 1939-40. d-*Governor of México,* 1957-63; *Senator* from the State of México, 1976-82. e-Member of the League of Professionals and Intellectuals of the Party of the Mexican Revolution, 1939, member of the Advisory Committee of the IEPES of PRI, 1972. f-Chief of Medical Services, Juárez Hospital, Mexico City, 1925; *Secretary of Health and Public Welfare,* 1940-46; Director of Jesús Hospital, 1952-57; Chairman of the Trust Fund of Jesús Hospital, 1964-70. g-President of the Student Society at the National School of Medicine. h-Director of the Military Medical School, 1936-39; created the Social Service for Medical Students in Mexico, 1938; initiated the standard method of medical documentation in Mexico, 1925; practicing physician. i-Personal friend of *Manuel Gual Vidal;* married Elena Díaz Lombardo; son, Gustavo, married the daughter of *Pasqual Gutiérrez Roldán;* was the personal physician to *Manuel Avila Camacho* before he became president. j-Joined the Revolution, 1914-15; served as a Colonel under Emiliano Zapata; rank of General; Military Governor of the State of México, 1918. k-Donated salary to maternal and child welfare centers when he served as Secretary of Health. l-HA, 2 Nov. 1959, 19; WWMG, 8; WWM45, 10; Hayner, 24546; Peral, 98-99; HA, 4 Aug. 1944, 7; HA, 22 Sept. 1944, 6; WB48, 492; *Excélsior,* 13 July 1972, 19; DGF51, II, 687; letter; *Excélsior,* 8 June 1978, 12.

Becerra Gaytan, Antonio
a-Apr. 19, 1933. b-Chihuahua, Chihuahua. c-Private accounting degree, Colegio Palmore, Chihuahua; MA in psychology, José R. Medrano Higher Normal School; primary and higher

normal teacher, 1953-75; university professor. d-*Plurinominal Deputy* from the leftist coalition, 1979-82. e-Member of PRI, 1958-61; joined the PCM, 1961; candidate for Senator from the Peoples Electoral Front, Chihuahua; Secretary General of the PCM in Chihuahua, 1964-79; joined the PCM Central Committee, 1979. f-None. g-Student leader at the Higher Normal School; Secretary General of Delegation No. 1, Local 40, SNTE; director of the Revolutionary Teachers Movement, 1958-59; member of the organizing committee of the Independent Peasant Federation, Chihuahua. h-None. j-None. k-None. l-Protag., 47; C de D, 1979-82.

Bécker Arreola, Juan Guillermo
a-Aug. 30, 1931. b-Canatlán, Durango. c-Early education unknown; studies at the National School of Economics and the National School of Law, UNAM; law degree, National School of Law, UNAM; Professor of Economic Theory, School of Business and Administration, UNAM. c-None. e-None. f-Joined the Secretariat of Industry and Commerce, 1952; Director of the Office of Radio, Telephone, and Television, Secretariat of Communications, 1955; Director of the Office of Autotransportation, 1959; Subdirector and Director, Department of Special Studies, Division of Trade, Secretariat of Industry and Commerce, 1959-61; Director General of Industries, Secretariat of Industry and Commerce, 1961-64; Director General of Standards, Secretariat of Industry and Commerce, 1965-67; Director General of Industries, 1967-74; *Subsecretary of Industry and Commerce*, 1974-76; Financial Subdirector of INFONAVIT, 1976-82; Director General of Diesel Nacional, 1982-85; Director General of Sidermex, 1986-91; Director General of the Mining Development Commission, Secretariat of Energy and Mines, 1991- . g-None.

i-Studied under *Agustín López Munguía*; son of Juan Bécker Krueger, stockbroker, and María Arreola; married Concepción Rodríguez González; brother, Maximiliano, member of Tabamex board, 1982. j-None. k-None. l-HA, 28 Jan. 1974, 18; DPE65, 96; Q es QAP, 507; DBGM, 57; DBGM92, 52.

Bellizzia Castañeda, Pascual
a-Oct. 22, 1933. b-Frontera, Tabasco. c-Primary studies at the Tomás Garrido School, Tabasco; secondary studies at the Palavicini School, Tabasco; law degree, National School of Law, UNAM, postgraduate studies in law, Sorbonne, Paris, France. d-Local Deputy to the State Legislature of Tabasco, 1961-64; *Senator* from the State of Tabasco, 1970-76, First Secretary of the First Committee on Mines, President of the Livestock Committee; Mayor of Villahermosa, Tabasco, 1980-82. e-Joined PRI, 1955; member of the Technical Advisory Council of PRI; general delegate of the CEN of PRI to Nuevo León, Yucatán, and Morelos. f-None. g-Leader of the Farmer and Rancher's Association, Tabasco; Secretary of Labor for the CEN of CNOP; adviser to the CEN of CNOP. i-From a peasant background. j-None. k-None. l-C de S, 1970-76, 70; PS, 0630; Protag., 48.

Bello, Daniel J.
a-Sept. 28, 1908. b-Puebla, Puebla. c-Preparatory studies at the National Preparatory School, member of the "Casa de la Troya" group; law degree, National School of Law, UNAM, 1928-31; student assistant at UNAM; Professor of Mercantile Law, National School of Law, UNAM, 1934-65. d-None. e-None. f-Secretary of the Federal Electric Commission, 1950-51; Manager, Bank of Mexico, 1951-70; *Subdirector General of the Bank of Mexico*, 1971-

78; adviser to the director general of the Bank of Mexico, 1978-82. g-None. j-None. k-None. l-Dromundo, 33; letter; DGF50, II, 245; DGF51, II, 9, 345.

Beltrán Beltrán, Amando
a-Feb. 11, 1905. b-Tantoyuca, Veracruz. c-Primary studies at the Gabino Barreda School, Tampico; preparatory at the National Preparatory School; law studies from 1928-32 at the National School of Law, UNAM, degree, Apr. 13, 1934; Professor of World History at the National Preparatory School No. 2, 1936-72; member of the University Council of UNAM, 1943-44, 1953-56; lecturer, Center for Cultural Diffusion for Workers, UNAM, 1936-42; Director of the National Preparatory School No. 2, 1939-48. d-None. e-None. f-Agent for the Ministerio Público, 1949-50; Secretary of Group Five, Federal Board of Conciliation and Arbitration, 1933; President of Group Five, Federal Board of Conciliation and Arbitration, 1936; Director of the Strike Department, Secretariat of Labor, 1941-43; Director of Social Welfare, Secretariat of Labor, 1947; Alternate President of the Federal Conciliation and Arbitration Board, 1944; President of the Federal Conciliation and Arbitration Board, 1945-46; head of the Labor Office for Auxiliary Agents, Office of the Attorney General, 1951; Secretary of the Board of Directors of the National Railroads of Mexico, 1951; Oficial Mayor of the National Railroads of Mexico, 1952-59; Director of Personnel, National Railroads of Mexico, 1969; Subdirector of Administration, National Railroads of Mexico, 1969-73. g-None. h-Practicing lawyer. i-Collaborator of *Francisco Trujillo Gurría*, secretary of labor, 1943-46; son of lawyer Francisco Beltrán; married Rosa Leonor Valles Patoni. j-None. k-None. l-Letter; MGF69, 588; DGF51, I, 536; WNM, 20.

Beltrán Brown, Francisco
c-Early education unknown; medical degree, National School of Medicine, UNAM; professor, National School of Medicine, UNAM. d-None. e-None. f-Director of the Children's Hospital, National Institute of Pediatrics, 1977; Director General of the National Pediatrics Institute of the National System for Integral Family Development, 1980; *Subsecretary of Welfare*, 1980-82. g-President of the Mexican Society of Pediatrics. h-Various positions in the Infant Hospital, Mexico City, 1946-54; Chief of Surgery, Infant Hospital, Mexico City, 1954-76. j-None. k-National prize for surgery, 1963. l-HA, 7 July 1980, 12; DAPC, 1981, 88.

Beltrán (Castillo), Enrique
a-Apr. 26, 1903. b-Federal District. c-Secondary studies at the Pablo Moreno Secondary School, Federal District, 1916; preparatory studies at the National Preparatory School; bachelor of science in Zoology, UNAM; Sc.D. from UNAM, 1926; Ph.D. in Zoology, Columbia University, 1931-33; Professor of Natural Sciences, UNAM, 1922-26; Professor of Zoology, National School of Agriculture, 1934-38; Professor of Biology and Zoology, National Preparatory School, 1931-58; Professor of Protozoology, Graduate School, UNAM, 1946-50; Assistant in Botany, UNAM, 1922-26; Professor of Zoology, Higher Normal School, 1936-58; Professor of Protozoology, National School of Biological Sciences, 1940-58; Professor of Biological Education, National Teachers School, 1935-47; Professor of Parasitology, School of Health and Hygiene, Secretariat of Agriculture, 1945-46. d-None. e-Founder of the Revolutionary Anti-Clerical Group, 1929; member of the Communist Party, 1930-31. f-Assistant, Museum of Natural History, Secretariat

of Agriculture, 1923; Microbiologist, Division of Biological Studies, Secretariat of Agriculture, 1924-25; Founder and Director, Marine Biological Station of the Gulf, 1926-28; member of the Reorganization Committee for the Secretariat of Agriculture, 1933; Founder and Director, Biotechnical Institute, Secretariat of Agriculture; Chief, Department of Secondary Instruction, Secretariat of Public Education, 1937-38; Director, Department of Protozoology, Institute of Health and Tropical Diseases, Secretariat of Health, 1939-51; *Subsecretary of Forest Resources and Fauna*, Secretariat of Agriculture, 1958-64. g-None. h-Director, Mexican Institute of Renewable Natural Resources, 1952-79; author of hundreds of articles and books on conservation and biology. i-Professor of *Luis Echeverría, Emilio Martínez Manautou, Renaldo Guzmán Orozco,* and *Guillermo Soberón.* j-None. k-None. l-Enc. Mex., I. 552; HA, 22 Dec. 1958; DPE61, 69; WWW70-71, 80-81; letter.

Beltrones Rivera, Manlio Fabio
a-Aug. 30, 1952. b-Villa Juárez, Sonora. c-Early education unknown; economics degree, National School of Economics, UNAM, 1970-74, with a thesis on agriculture in Mexican economic development; Professor, National School of Economics, UNAM, 1975. d-*Federal Deputy* from the State of Sonora, Dist. 4, 1982-85, member of the government and constitutional affairs committees; *Senator* from the State of Sonora, 1988; *Governor of Sonora,* 1991-. e- Joined PRI, 1968; Assistant Secretary of the CEN of PRI, 1983-86; President of PRI in Sonora, 1987-88; Secretary of Promotion, CEN of PRI, 1987-88. f-Chief, Department of Delegations, National Registry of Electors, 1975-76; Auxiliary Secretary of the Subsecretary of Government, *Fernando Gutiérrez Barrios,* 1976-77;

Private Secretary to the Subsecretary of Government, *Fernando Gutiérrez Barrios,* 1977-82; General Coordinator of Advisers, Secretariat of Communications and Transportation, 1983; Secretary of Government of the State of Sonora, 1985-87; *Subsecretary of Government, Political Development and Human Rights,* Secretariat of Government, 1988-91. g-None. h-None. i-Married Sylvia Sánchez Estrada, psychologist; political disciple of *Rodolfo Félix Valdés* and *Fernando Gutiérrez Barrios.* j-None. k-None. l-DBGM89, 52; letter; *Proceso,* 11 Mar. 1991, 17; *El Nacional,* 23 Oct. 1991, 11.

Benítez Claveli, Vicente L.
b-Federal District. c-Primary and secondary studies, Mexico City; college degree, Mexico City. d-Federal Deputy from the State of Aguascalientes (twice); *Senator* from Aguascalientes, 1934-40; precandidate for Governor of Aguascalientes, 1941. e-None. f-Ambassador to Nicaragua, 1941-43; special post in the Secretariat of Foreign Relations, 1943; Ambassador to Venezuela, Dec. 1943 to Feb. 1945; Ambassador to Guatemala, July 1945 to 1948; Ambassador to Argentina, 1954; Ambassador to Yugoslavia, 1958-61. g-None. h-Journalist. j-Participated in the Revolution. k-None. l-EBW46, 23; DPE61, 25; WB54, 547; IYBSTWW54, lxxviii, 609.

Berber, Alberto F.
(Deceased June 30, 1956) a-June 12, 1885. b-Chilpancingo, Guerrero. c-Primary studies, Chilpancingo; no degree. d-Mayor of Acapulco, 1934; Federal Deputy from the State of Guerrero, Dist. 5, 1935-37; *Governor of Guerrero,* 1937-41. e-None. g-None. j-Career army officer; Commander of the Garrison, Acapulco, 1932-33; rank of Brigadier General, June 1, 1941; rank of Division General. k-Removed as Governor Feb. 19, 1941, because he

tried to continue his political power by imposing his half-brother, Francisco Carreto. l-letter; D de Y, 2 Nov. 1940, 1; Peral, 105; Anderson, 79-80; Rev. de Ejer., July 1956.

Bermúdez (Dávila), Carlos Humberto
a-Mar. 27 1932. b-Primary, secondary, and preparatory studies in San Luis Potosí; graduated, Heroic Military College, 2nd Lieutenant of artillery; diploma in military administration from the Higher War College, 1957-60; counterinsurgency studies, United States. d-None. e-Auxiliary Secretary to the President of the CEN of PRI, 1963-64; Director of Security for the presidential campaign of *Miguel de la Madrid*, 1981-82. f-Chief of Aides, President *Luis Echeverría*, 1970-76; Presidential Chief of Staff, 1982-88. g-None. h-None. i-Son of Francisco Bermúdez Landa, lawyer and officer, and Angela Dávila; married Blanca Chagoya García. j-Career army officer; joined Army, Jan. 1950; staff officer, Section 5 (Plans), Staff, Secretariat of National Defense; Chief, Section 1, Staff, 12th Military Zone, San Luis Potosí, San Luis Potosí; Commander, Instruction and Operations Section, 1st Artillery Battalion; Commander, Section 2 (Intelligence), Presidential Staff; 2nd in command, 1st Artillery Regiment, Presidential Guards; Assistant Chief of the Presidential Staff, 1976-81; rank of Brigadier General, Nov. 20, 1979. k-None. l-HA, 13 Dec. 1982, 20; Q es QAP, 17; DBGM87, 56; DBGM, 59.

Bermúdez (Jaquez), Antonio J.
(Deceased Feb. 10, 1977) a-June 13, 1892. b-Chihuahua, Chihuahua. c-Secondary studies from the Los Angeles Business College; no degree. d-Mayor of Ciudad Juárez, Chihuahua, 1942-45; *Senator* from Chihuahua (never served in the position), 1946. f-Treasurer of Ciudad Juárez, Chihuahua, 1945-46;

Director General of Petróleos Mexicanos, 1946-58; Ambassador to Arab countries, 1958-61; Director of the National Frontier Program, 1961-65. g-None. h-Founded his own business in Chihuahua while very young, later became a very wealthy businessman after founding a whiskey factory in Ciudad Juárez; his career in local politics was noted for increasing revenues as treasurer and fighting vice in Ciudad Juárez. i-Parents, well-to-do landowners; married to Hilda Mascarena. j-None. k-Precandidate for president of Mexico, 1951-52; did not accept a salary as Director of PEMEX. lHA, 18 Mar. 1949, 26; DGF47, 20; DGF50, II, 279, 80; DGF51, II, 383-84, I, 6; HA, 21 Feb. 1977, 13; *Proceso*, 19 Feb. 1977, 29; NYT, 28 July 1957, 2; NYT, 30 July 1951, 5; NYT, 17 Aug. 1950, 6.

Bermúdez Limón, Carlos Gerardo
a-July 14, 1935. b-Tampico, Tamaulipas. c-Economics degree, National School of Economics, UNAM, 1954-58; thesis, 1960, on "Public Works and Economic Development in Mexico"; graduate studies at Yale University on a United Nations and Secretariat of the Treasury Fellowship; graduate studies at the U.S. Department of the Treasury, Washington, D.C.; Professor of Mexican Economic Problems, School of Economics, National Polytechnic Institute, and the Autonomous Technological Institute of Mexico, 1962-68. d-None. e-Adviser to the CEPES for the Valley of Mexico. f-Adviser and Analyst, Department of Treasury Studies, Secretariat of the Treasury; Subdirector, Department of Economic Studies, Secretariat of the Treasury; Director of the Center for Development Studies; Director General of PIPSA, 1970-74; 1982-89. g-President of the League of Revolutionary Economists of Mexico; President of the National College of Economists; Vice-President of the 1954 Generation,

National School of Economics.
h-Author of various articles; Director of
the Center for Economic Studies of the
Private Sector; on the board of 6 major
corporations, 1980; economic consultant. i-Attended college with *Jesús Silva
Herzog F.*, *Agustín Olachea Borbón*,
Eliseo Mendoza Berrueto; married Silvia
Pacheco (deceased, 1980); son of Carlos
Bermúdez Lacayo, chemical engineer,
and María de Jesús Limón Alatorre.
j-None. k-None. l-*Hoy*, 10 June 1972,
13; letter; *Latin America*, 12 Mar. 1976,
83; *Excélsior*, 26 Apr. 1980, 18A;
DBGM87, 57.

Bernal de Piña de Badillo, Zorayda
a-Feb. 25, 1934. b-Oaxaca. c-Early
education unknown; graduate of the
Latin American Hospital, Puebla, in
nursing; advanced studies in social
work in Rumania and Peru; courses on
labor law, Academy of Law and Social
Welfare. d-*Federal Deputy* from the
State of Oaxaca, Dist. 7, 1976-79, mem-
ber of Railroad Section of the General
Means of Communication Committee,
the Economic, Cultural, and Social
Development of Peasant Women
Section of the Agrarian Affairs Commit-
tee, the Artisan and Small Industries
Development Committee, the Mail and
Telegraph Section of the Development
of Means of Communication, the
Isthmus Section of the Regional
Development Committee, the Infant
and Maternal Welfare Section of the
Social Security and Public Health
Committee and the National Properties
Committee. e-None. f-None.
g-Secretary General of the Political
Committee of the National Railroad
Workers Union; Vice-President of the
Congress of Female Workers. i-Married
Dr. Jesús Badillo Chávez. j-None.
k-None. l-C de D, 1976-79, 5; D de C,
1976-79, 8, 14, 22, 28, 34, 40, 63;
Excélsior, 27 Aug. 1976, 1C.

Bernal Miranda, Benito
(Deceased Oct. 21, 1974) a-1892.
b-Alamos, Sonora. c-Early education
unknown. d-Mayor of Navajoa, Sonora;
Senator from Sonora, 1970-74, member
of the Gran Comisión, president of the
Third National Defense Committee,
First Secretary of the Military Health
and the Pensions and Military Retirement Committees, Second Secretary of
the Livestock Committee and member
of the Fishing Committee. e-Activist in
the Anti-Reelectionist Party, 1910.
f-None. g-None. h-None. i-Married
Carlota Domínguez; son, *Benito Bernal
Domínguez*, was a federal deputy from
Sonora, 1958-61. j-Joined the Revolution, 1910; fought in various battles
under Captain Lucas Girón, 1910; 2nd
Lieutenant in the 5th Sonoran Irregulars
under Lt. Colonel Jesús Chávez
Camacho, 1912; served under Alvaro
Obregón, 1913; Chief of Staff for General Obregón; career officer, reached the
rank of Division General, Mar. 1, 1962.
k-None. l-*Excélsior*, 22 Oct. 1974; HA,
28 Oct. 1974, 14; C de S, 1970-76, 15.

Bernal (Tenorio), Antonio
a-1911. b-Toluca, México. c-Law
degree, National School of Law,
UNAM; professor at the Worker's
University; teacher in various secondary
schools; professor at the National
Preparatory School, Mexico City.
d-*Federal Deputy* from the State of
México, Dist. 8, 1967-70, member of
Committee on Motor Transportation,
First Committee on National Defense
and the Third Section on Criminal Law
of Legislative Studies. e-First Secretary
of the Political Commission of the
Federation of the Union of Workers of
the Federal Government (FSTSE),
assisting in the campaign of *Miguel
Alemán*, 1946; Secretary General of
Disputes of the National Confederation
of Popular Organizations of PRI, 1965-
66; Alternate Secretary of Popular

Action of the CEN of PRI, 1968-70.
f-Adviser to the President of Mexico,
1946-52; adviser to the President of
Mexico, 1952-58; *Director General of
Federal Highways and Bridges and
Adjacent Entrances and Exits, 1970-76.*
g-Member of the Judicial Workers
Union; Secretary General of the Mexi-
can Chauffeurs Union; candidate for
Secretary General of the FSTSE, 1946;
Secretary of Organization of the FSTSE,
1946-48; Secretary of Labor and Conflicts, FSTSE, 1961-65; *Secretary General of the FSTSE, 1965-67;* President of
the Congress of Labor, 1966; Secretary
General of the Union of Federal Judicial
Workers, 1977. h-Employee of the
Fourth Division of the Supreme Court;
one of the founders of the magazine
Futura. j-None. k-Ran for alternate
federal deputy with *Víctor Manuel
Villaseñor,* 1943, as a militant leftist.
l-HA, 15 Nov. 1946, 4; HA, 7 Dec. 1970,
27; Villaseñor, II, 33; Sirvent, 175.

Bernard, Miguel
(Deceased Oct. 25, 1939) a-1873.
b-Brownsville, Texas. c-Engineering
degree, National Military College,
Mexico City, 1893-97, graduated as a
Lieutenant of Artillery, Nov. 1897;
Professor of Math, Physics, and Me-
chanics, National Military College;
Professor of Applied Mechanics,
National Military College, 1904;
studied construction in France; Profes-
sor of the School of Artillery, National
Military College; Organizer and Direc-
tor of the School of Mechanical and
Electrical Engineering. d-None.
e-None. f-Chief of the Department of
Technical, Industrial, and Commercial
Instruction, Secretariat of Public
Education; *Oficial Mayor of the
Secretariat of Industry and Commerce,
1937-38; Director General of the
National Polytechnic Institute, 1939.*
g-None. h-Chairman, technical military commissions in the United States,

Europe, and Japan. i-Son of Miguel
Bernard and Rosa Perales. j-Commander of the 2nd Co. of Cadets, 1904;
1st cadet, 1892; rank of Corporal, Dec.
1892; rank of 2nd Sgt. and 1st Sgt.,
1893; rank of 2nd Captain, 1897; rank of
1st Captain, 1901; rank of Major, 1904;
rank of Lt. Colonel, 1909; served in the
1st. Artillery Battalion, 1897-98; fought
Zapata under General Angeles, as his
Chief of Staff, 1912-13; Military Attaché
to Japan, 1913; rank of Colonel, June,
1912; rank of Brigadier General, Oct. 19,
1913; Commander of the 1st Infantry
Brigade; Chief of Staff of the Zozaya
Division, and later Commander;
Director of the Higher War College.
k-None. l-DP70, 257; Enc. Mex. I, 561;
Q es Q, 71; SofW, 1914, 27.

Berrueto Ramón, Federico
(Deceased Jan. 15, 1980) a-Oct. 2, 1900.
b-Sabinas, Coahuila. c-Teaching
credential from the Normal School in
Coahuila, 1921; teaching credential
from the Normal School of Mexico,
Nov. 18, 1937, with a thesis on adoles-
cent problems; professor at Texas State
College for Women; professor at the
Higher School of Agriculture; professor
at Normal School in Mexico City, and
Secondary School in Coahuila.
d-*Federal Deputy* from the State of
Coahuila, Dist. 1, 1946-49, member of
the Gran Comisión, the Second Com-
mittee on Public Education, and the
Budget Committee; *Senator* from
Coahuila, 1958-64; member of the Gran
Comisión, President of the Committee
on Indigenous Affairs, First Vocal of the
Second Committee on Public Education
and the Committee on Electrical
Industry. e-Representative on the
National Advisory Council of PRI from
the National Confederation of Popular
Organizations, 1946; State Committee-
man for PRI from Coahuila; President of
PRI in Coahuila. f-Director of the
Department of Public Education for

Coahuila, 1953; Director of the Normal
Schools for Coahuila; Subdirector of
Primary Schools in Saltillo, Coahuila;
Subsecretary of Public Education, 1964-
70. g-Founding member of the Federation of Teachers' Unions in Coahuila,
Secretary General of the Federation of
Teachers' Unions in Coahuila, 1933.
h-Educational consultant to the Secretariat of Public Education. i-Brother,
Professor *Mauro Berrueto Ramón,*
served as a federal deputy, 1964-67.
j-None. k-Precandidate for governor of
Coahuila, 1963 and in 1969. l-WWMG,
9; DBM68, 72; DBM70, 82; D del S, 22
Jan. 1946, 1; Func., 138; Enc. Mex., II,
106; *Excélsior,* 16 Jan. 1980, 12.

Berrueto Ramón, Mauro
a-Feb. 7, 1908. b-Sabinas, Coahuila.
c-Primary studies in Nava and Lampa-
citas, Coahuila; secondary and normal
studies, Normal School of Coahuila,
Saltillo, Coahuila, with a normal certificate, 1928; studies at the Higher Normal School and the School of Philosophy and Letters, UNAM, 1933-34; MA
degree in social science from UNAM.
d-*Federal Deputy* from the State of
Coahuila, Dist. 4, 1964-67, member of
the Television Industry Committee.
e-Secretary of Organization of the State
Committee of PRI, Coahuila; general
coordinator of *Gustavo Díaz Ordaz's*
campaign in Coahuila, 1964. f-Federal
school inspector, Monterrey, Nuevo
León, 1935-39; federal school inspector,
Nogales, Sonora, 1939-40; federal school
inspector, State of Coahuila, 1940-47;
Syndic, city council of Saltillo, Coahuila, 1943-45; agent of the National
Ejido Credit Bank, Coahuila, 1948-52;
Director of Agriculture and Livestock,
State of Coahuila, 1952-54. g-None.
h-Operated own cattle ranch in Coahuila since 1948. i-Brother of *Federico
Berrueto Ramón,* subsecretary of public
education, 1964-70. j-None. k-None.
l-C de D, 1964-67, 46, 87.

Berthely, Lylia C.
b-Tlacotalpan, Veracruz. c-Certificate
in upper primary education; MA in
Spanish language and literature; MA in
geography; MA in science education;
Ph.D. in pedagogy with a specialization
in psychology; teacher at various secondary and vocational schools; Professor
of Spanish, Spanish Literature, General
Psychology, and Pedagogy, National
Teachers School and the Higher Normal
School, Mexico City; Professor and
Director of the psychology courses, IPN
(nine years). d-*Federal Deputy* from
Veracruz, Dist. 8, 1973-76. e-Joined
PNR, 1936; Youth Delegate to PNR in
Veracruz, 1938; National Coordinator of
Professional and Intellectual Women of
the IEPES of PRI, 1969-70. f-Chief of
the Office of State Delegates of Mexico
to UNESCO, 1949-51; Director of the
Technical Office, Department of Private
Secondary School Incorporation,
Secretariat of Public Education, 1951-
52; Subdirector, Department of Private
Secondary School Incorporation,
Secretariat of Public Education, 1952-
54; Subdirector of the Division of
Literacy and Extrascholarly Education,
Secretariat of Public Education, 1954;
Director General of the Division of
Literacy and Extrascholarly Education,
1954-59; Director General of Expert
Services, Attorney General of the
Federal District, 1959-64; Director,
Department of General Inspection,
Secretariat of Communications and
Transportation. g-None. h-None.
j-None. k-None. l-Romero Aceves,
293-300; C de D, 1973-76, 293-300.

Betancourt Pérez, Antonio
a-June 13, 1907. b-Mérida, Yucatán.
c-Primary studies at the Escuela
Modelo, Mérida; preparatory at the
Literary Institute of Yucatán; normal
studies at the Escuela Rodolfo Menéndez de la Peña; studied social science at
the Lenin Institute, Moscow. d-*Federal*

Deputy from the State of Yucatán, Dist. 3, 1940-43, member of the Second Balloting Committee, the First Public Education Committee and the Protocol Committee; Vice-President of the Chamber of Deputies, Nov. 1942; member of the Permanent Commission, 1941. e-None. f-Director of the Department of Public Education, State of Yucatán; Director of Federal Education, State of Yucatán; Director General of *Diario del Sureste*, Mérida, Yucatán, 1972-73. g-None. h-Employee of the Department of the Federal District; employee of the Secretariat of Public Education; author of numerous articles on history and education. j-None. k-None. l-C de D, 1940-42, 6, 47, 49.

Beteta (Monsalve), Mario Ramón
a-July 7, 1925. b-Federal District. c-Primary and secondary studies in Mexico City, law degree from the National School of Law, UNAM, Dec. 4, 1948, with a thesis on the responsibility for illegal acts; professor at Secondary Schools Nos. 8 and 10, Mexico City, 1945-48; Professor of Introductory Economics, National School of Economics, 1954-56; Professor of Monetary Theory, National School of Economics, UNAM, 1951-59; Master of Arts in Economics, University of Wisconsin, June 16, 1950, with a thesis on the institutional focus of economic planning. d-*Governor of México*, 1987-89. e-Member of the New Advisory Council of the IEPES of PRI, in charge of structural reforms of the party June 28, 1972. f-Adviser to the Office of the Director General of the Bank of Mexico; assistant to the Manager of the Bank of Mexico; Submanager of the Bank of Mexico, 1957; Manager of the Bank of Mexico, 1960-63; Director General of Credit of the Secretariat of the Treasury, 1964-70; *Subsecretary of the Treasury*, 1970-75; *Secretary of the Treasury*, 1975-76; President of the SOMEX Group, 1977-

82; *Director General of PEMEX*, 1982-87; Director General of COMERMEX, 1989-90. g-None. h-Investigator of the Department of Economic Studies of the Bank of Mexico, 1948; Mexican delegate to major international monetary conferences. i-Nephew of *Ramón Beteta*, former secretary of the treasury, 1946-52; son of General Ignacio Beteta Quintana, Chief of Staff during the presidency of *Lázaro Cárdenas* and well-known Mexican artist; married Gloria Leal Kuri. j-None. k-None. l-BdeM, 72-73; *Hoy*, 24 June 1967, 26; HA, 14 Dec. 1970, 20-21; HA, 29 Mar. 1976; LAD, 5 Dec. 1975, 379; HA, 6 Oct. 1975, 9; *Excélsior*, 27 Sept. 1975, 22.

Beteta (Quintana), Ramón
(Deceased Oct. 5, 1965) a-Oct. 7, 1901. b-Federal District. c-Primary and secondary studies in Mexico City; preparatory studies at the National Preparatory School; attended UNAM, 1919-20; degree in economics from the University of Texas, 1920-23; law degree from the National School of Law, 1925-26; Ph.D. in Social Sciences from UNAM, 1934 (first Ph.D. in this field); Professor of Economics at the National School of Economics, UNAM, 1924-42; Professor of Law at the National Law School, UNAM; professor at the National Preparatory School in Mexico City, 1925-28; professor at secondary schools in Mexico City. d-None. e-Member of the League of Professionals and Intellectuals of the Mexican Revolutionary Party, 1939; director of *Miguel Alemán*'s campaign for president, 1945-46. f-Legal consultant to the Agricultural Bank, 1926-28; Private Secretary to the Secretary of Public Education (*Ezequiel Padilla*), 1928-29; legal adviser to the Secretary of Public Education, 1929-30; head of the Department of Education and Social Services, Department of the Federal District, 1930-31; head of the Department of

Securities, Secretariat of Industry and Commerce, 1931-32; Oficial Mayor of the Secretariat of Industry and Commerce, 1932-33; Director General of the Department of National Statistics, Secretariat of Industry and Commerce, 1933-35; technical adviser to President *Lázaro Cárdenas*, 1935; *Subsecretary of Foreign Relations*, 1936-40; *Subsecretary of the Treasury*, 1940-45; *Secretary of the Treasury*, 1946-52; Ambassador to Italy, 1952-55; Ambassador to Greece, 1955-58. g-None. h-Minor administrator of the Secretariat of the Treasury, 1924; member of the Mexican delegation to the Inter-American Peace Conference in Buenos Aires, 1936; editor of the *News* and *Novedades*, 1958-64. i-Personal adviser to *Lázaro Cárdenas*; professor of *Antonio Armendáriz* and *Hugo B.Margaín* at UNAM; close friend of Moisés Sáenz; brother of General Ignacio Beteta Quintana, director of military industry and chief of staff under President *Cárdenas*; uncle of *Mario Ramón Beteta*; son of Enrique Beteta Méndez, a lawyer, and Sara Quintana, from a wealthy landowning family. j-None. k-Precandidate for president of Mexico, 1951, but too strongly identified with the right wing of PRI; actually born in Hermosillo, Sonora, but registered his birth in the Federal District. l-*Hoy*, 4 Nov. 1939, 18; DBM68, 72-73; IWW66, 111; EBW46, 125; WWM45, 13; DGF56, 126-27; Scott, 214; letters.

Biebrich Torres, Carlos Armando
a-Nov. 19, 1939. b-Sahuaripa, Sonora. c-Preparatory studies in humanities, University of Sonora; law degree, University of Sonora, 1963 (fifth person to graduate in law); thesis on labor law; Professor of Labor Law, School of Business and Administration, University of Sonora, 1964-66. d-*Federal Deputy* from the State of Sonora, Dist. 4, 1967-70, member of the Gran

Comisión, the Committee on Taxes, the Committee on Constitutional Affairs, the Committee on the Budget, and the Seventh Section on Commerce and Credit of the Legislative Studies Committee; *Governor of Sonora*, 1973 to Oct. 25, 1975. e-State Director of PRI in Sonora; Auxiliary Secretary to *Luis Echeverría* during his presidential campaign, 1970; gave two hundred speeches during the *Echeverría* campaign; general delegate of the CEN of PRI to Zacatecas, 1979. f-Secretary of the City Council of Ciudad Obregón, 1961-63, under Mayor *Faustino Félix Serna*; Secretary of the City Council of Cajeme, Sonora; Auxiliary Secretary to the Governor of Sonora, 1964-67; *Subsecretary of Government*, 1970-73. g-President of the Federation of University Students of the University of Sonora, 1958; active journalist for student newspapers; winner of the National Oratory Contest of PRI, 1963; organized the Assembly for the Political Orientation of Youth for PRI, 1958. h-None. i-From modest middle class background; friend of *Luis Encinas Johnson*, whom he supported for governor in 1961; supporter of *Mario Moya Palencia* for president, 1975; married Socorro Gandara, related to one of the wealthiest families in Sonora. k-Resigned from the governorship after internal political struggle with collaborators of *Luis Echeverría*. l-*Hoy*, 19 Dec. 1970, 60; HA, 14 Dec. 1970, 19-20; HA, 1 Jan. 1973, 29; HA, 10 Sept. 1973, 40; *Excélsior*, 26 Oct. 1975, 1, 13 Nov. 1975; letter.

Blanco Cáceres, Othón P.
(Deceased Oct. 18, 1959) a-Mar. 7, 1868. b-Ciudad Victoria, Tamaulipas. c-Preparatory studies at the National Preparatory School until 1885; National Military College, 1885-89, graduating as a 1st Lieutenant, Jan. 31, 1889; Subdirector of the Naval College, 1909.

d-None. e-None. f-Head of the Department of the Navy in the Secretariat of War, 1918-20; Inspector General of the Fleet, 1927-28; Head of the Department of the Navy, 1929-32; officer in the Inspector General's Office, 1933-39; *Subsecretary of the Navy*, 1940-46. g-None. h-None. i-Son of Francisco Blanco and Juana Núñez de Cáceres; mother was a descendant of Dr. José Núñez de Caceres, liberator of Santo Domingo. j-Member of the Inspection Committee for the Corvete Zaragoza training ship, 1890-93; Corvete Lieutenant, Dec. 20, 1893; 2nd Lieutenant, July, 1896; Com-mander of the Chetumal, 1897-99; Chief of Naval Forces in the Southeast of Yucatán, 1899; 2nd in command of the Bravo, 1905; participated in the campaign against the Mayan uprising, 1907; Commander of the Transport Progreso, 1907-08; captain of a frigate, 1909; Full Captain of the Navy, 1913, and in 1912, Com-mander of the *Guerrero*; Commodore and then Vice Admiral in 1914; Chief of Naval Forces in the East of the Yucatán Peninsula, 1899-12; Commander of the *Bravo*, 1908-09, 1910-11; not on active duty, 1914-23; Commanding General of the Gulf Fleet, 1923; rank of Admiral, Oct. 16, 1943; retired from active duty, July 31, 1944. k-None. l-D de Y, 5 Dec. 1940, 1; DP70, 268; letter; Peral, 110-111.

Blanco Fuentes, Argentina
a-1903. b-Muzquiz, Coahuila. c-Primary studies in Muzquiz; secondary at St. Mary's College, Notre Dame, Indiana; received teaching certificate; language teacher. d-*Federal Deputy* from the State of Coahuila, Dist. 4, 1964-67. e-Member of PARM; campaigned for *Rafael Sánchez Tapia* during the 1939 presidential campaign. f-Employee, Regulations Department, Secretariat of Industry and Commerce; employee, Secretariat of Agriculture;

employee, Department of Agrarian Affairs; employee, Department of Social Affairs, Department of the Federal District. g-None. j-None. k-None. l-C de D, 1964-67, 46; PS.

Blanco Mendoza, Herminio Alonso
a-July 25, 1950. b-Chihuahua, Chihuahua. c-Early education unknown; economics degree from the Monterrey Institute of Higher Studies, 1966-71; MA in economics, University of Chicago, 1973; Ph.D. in economics, University of Chicago, 1973-78, with a dissertation on investment and uncertainty; professor, University of Texas, Austin, 1980-85. e-Joined PRI, 1985; Assistant Coordinator for Foreign Trade, IEPES, 1988. f-Adviser, Secretary of the Treasury, 1978-80; adviser, President of Mexico, 1985-88; *Subsecretary of Foreign Trade*, Secretariat of Commerce, 1988-90; Head Negotiator for the North American Free Trade Agreement, 1990-93. g-None. h-None. i-Son of Arturo Blanco Valenzuela, immigration agent, and Ortensia Mendoza Rosas; married Ana Elena Gutiérrez. j-None. k-None. l-DBGM89, 53.

Blanco Sánchez, Javier
a-Dec. 18, 1926. b-Guadalajara, Jalisco. c-Primary studies in Orfanatorios de Morelia, Michoacán and Celaya, Guanajuato; secondary studies at the Conciliar Seminary of Mexico; studies at the School of Philosophy and Letters, Ibero-American University, Mexico City, 1947-50; legal studies at the Escuela Libre de Derecho and the National School of Law, UNAM, 1952-56. d-*Federal Deputy* from the Federal District, Dist. 3, 1961-64, member of the Fine Arts Committee; *Federal Deputy* from the Federal District, Dist. 9, 1967-70, member of the Fine Arts Committee; *Federal Deputy* from the Federal District, Dist. 13, 1973-76; *Plurinominal Federal Deputy* from

PAN, 1982-85. e-Joined the youth
sector of PAN, 1948; youth director for
the 11th electoral district, 1948; member of the regional committee of PAN
for the Federal District, 1949; Secretary
of Organization of the National Youth
Sector of PAN, 1949-52; adviser to the
National Council of PAN, 1949-78;
Secretary of the regional committee of
PAN for the Federal District, 1953-58;
candidate of PAN for Federal Deputy
from Dist. 7, Federal District, 1955;
candidate of PAN for Federal Deputy
from Dist. 8, Federal District, 1958;
Secretary of the PAN delegation, 1958-
60; candiate of PAN for Senator from
the Federal District, 1964; member of
the CEN of PAN, 1950-79. f-None.
g-Founding member of the Student
Youth Front, 1950; member of the
Executive Committee of the National
Student Federation, 1951; Secretary
General of the Center for Mexican
Journalists. h-Journalist; correspondent
to the Chamber of Deputies, 1955-61.
i-Married Elena Zepeda, 1959; son of
Jesús Blanco Estrada, career military,
director of defense for Los Reyes and
Periban de Ramos, Michoacán, and
mayor of Periban, and Josefina Sánchez.
j-None. k-One of the few PAN members to have been elected federal deputy
three times from a district. l-C de D,
1967-70, 56, 1961-64, 7; Directorio,
1973-76, 7; C de D, 1973-76, 7; letter;
PS; Lehr, 60; DBGM, 476.

Blas Briseño (Rodríguez), José
a-Aug. 28, 1938. b-Zitacuaro, Michoacán. c-Primary, secondary, and preparatory in the Federal District; teaching
certificate from the Higher Normal
School, Mexico City, with a specialty in
pedagogy; accounting degree from the
Autonomous Technological Institute of
Mexico; master of arts in business and
administration. d-*Alternate Federal
Deputy* from the Federal District, Dist.
9, 1964-67; *Federal Deputy* from the

National Action Party (Party Deputy).
e-Joined PAN in 1955. f-None. g-None.
h-Operates consulting firm specializing
in the administration of construction
firms. j-None. k-None. l-C de D, 1970-
73, 145, 1964-67.

Bobadilla Peña, Julio
a-1918. b-Progreso, Yucatán. c-Primary
studies in Yucatán; secondary and
preparatory studies in Mérida, Yucatán;
no degree. d-Local Deputy to the State
Legislature of Yucatán, 1963; *Federal
Deputy* from the State of Yucatán, Dist.
2, 1967-70, member of the Gran
Comisión. e-General delegate of the
CEN of PRI in Colima, Campeche, and
Yucatán; member of the State Commit-
tee of the PRM, Yucatán; Secretary of
Popular Action of PRI in Yucatán, 1963;
*Secretary of Popular Action of the CEN
of PRI,* 1971. f-Agent of the National
Lottery in Yucatán; Director, Depart-
ment of Cooperatives, Division of
Agriculture, State of Yucatán; Secretary
General of Government of the State of
Yucatán, 1964; Oficial Mayor of the
State of Yucatán; *Oficial Mayor of the
Secretariat of Communications,* 1973-
76; Delegate of the Department of the
Federal District, 1976-78. g-Student
leader in the Federation of University
Students and the Unified Socialist
Youth of Mexico; Secretary General of
CNOP in Yucatán, 1963; member of the
CEN of CNOP, 1971; *Secretary General
of CNOP,* 1971-72. h-None. i-Father a
modest employee of Yucatán Railroads
and founder of the Socialist Party of the
Southeast; later mayor and president of
the Federation of Labor Leagues of
Progreso; son, Julián Bobadilla Novelo,
was a precandidate for federal deputy,
1979. j-None. k-Schers says he was
chosen as secretary general of CNOP
because of close relation to *Luis
Echeverría*; lost as a precandidate for
governor of Yucatán, 1975. l-Schers, 27;
C de D, 1967-70; PS, 695.

Bobadilla Romero, Manuel
(Deceased July 16, 1978) a-Sept. 23, 1909. b-Bacubirito, Sonora. c-Primary studies in Los Mochis, Sinaloa; no degree. d-Local Deputy to the State Legislature of Sonora; *Federal Deputy* from the State of Sonora, Dist. 3, 1964-67, member of the Desert Zones Committee and the Military Justice Committee; *Federal Deputy* from the State of Sonora, Dist. 3, 1970-73, member of the First Railroads Committee, the First Balloting Committee, and the Small Agricultural Property Committee. e-None. f-None. g-Secretary General of the Union of Workers (CTM) of Sonora, 1937-78; Secretary of Agriculture of the CTM, 1978. h-None. i-Married Carlota Icedo; son of Bauterio Bobadillo and Vicenta Romero. j-None. k-Assumed the directorship of the Sonora CTM while in jail as a labor agitator in Ciudad Obregón. l-Directorio, 1970-72, 22; *Excélsior*, 18 July 1978, 12; C de D, 1964-67, 89, 96; C de D, 1970-73, 103.

Bojórquez, Juan de Dios
(Deceased 1967) a-Mar. 8, 1892. b-San Miguel Horcasitas, Sonora. c-Agricultural engineering degree, National School of Agriculture, San Jacinto, Federal District, 1912; Professor of Mexican History, Normal School, Hermosillo, Sonora, 1918. d-Deputy to the Constitutional Convention at Querétaro, 1916-17; Federal Deputy from the State of Sonora, 1918-20; *Senator* from Sonora, 1964-67. f-Governor of Baja California del Sur; Subsecretary of Agriculture, 1914; Minister to Honduras; Minister to Guatemala, 1922; Minister to Cuba, 1926; Head of the Department of Statistics, 1926-32; Head of the Department of Labor, 1932-34; Secretary of Government, 1934-35; Director General of the Small Business Bank of the Federal District, 1950-52; Director

General of Maíz Industrializado, 1964-67. g-Organized the Local Agrarian Commission of Sonora, 1916; Secretary of the Local Agrarian Commission of Sonora; founder and President of the Intellectual Workers' Block. h-Author of many biographies; agricultural engineer in Sonora, 1913; Administrator of the Secretariat of Industry and Commerce, 1914; Director of the government newspaper, *El Nacional.* j-Participated in the Revolution as a Constitutionalist, 1913. k-Worked in Los Angeles, California, 1913. l-DP70, 273; WWM45, 13-14; DGF50, II, 414; Gaxiola, 92ff; Peral, 115; Morton, 7; Enc. Mex., II, 128; Gómez, 148-58.

Bolaños Cacho (Guendeláin), Raúl
a-June 21, 1916. b-Oaxaca, Oaxaca. c-Early education unknown; law degree, School of Law, Institute of Arts and Sciences of Oaxaca, 1940; special studies in history and sociology; Professor of General Theory of the State and of Mexican History, Benito Juárez University, Oaxaca. d-*Federal Deputy* from the State of Oaxaca, Dist. 3, 1955-58; *Senator* from the State of Oaxaca, 1964-70; President of the Chamber of Deputies, 1955; President of the state legislature of Oaxaca, 1982. e-President of PRI in Oaxaca, 1956-66; general delegate of the CEN of PRI to Nuevo León and Jalisco. f-Director of the Cultural Department of Youth Affairs, State of Oaxaca, 1947-50; Director of Education, Secretariat of Public Education, for the State of Oaxaca, 1951-55; Syndic of the City Council of Oaxaca, Oaxaca. g-Secretary General of CNOP of Oaxaca. i-Son, *Raúl Bolaños Cacho Guzmán*, was a federal deputy from Oaxaca, 1976-79; cousin, *Demetrio Bolaños Espinosa*, was a federal deputy from Oaxaca, 1934-37, 1940-43; nephew of Miguel Bolaños Cacho, lawyer and governor of Oaxaca; great-grandson of Aurelanos Bolaños, governor of Oaxaca; grandson of Dr.

Ramón Bolaños. j-None. k-None. l-C de S, 1964; C de D, 1955-58; DGF56; Peral, 115; Almanaque de Oaxaca, 1982, 25; Ind. Biog., 26-27.

Bolaños Espinosa, Demetrio

b-Oaxaca, Oaxaca. c-Primary studies at the Institute of Arts and Sciences, Oaxaca; engineering degree from the National School of Agriculture. d-Federal Deputy from the State of Oaxaca, 1934-36; *Federal Deputy* from the State of Oaxaca, Dist. 4, 1940-43, member of the Securities Committee; member of the city council of Mixcoac, 1926. e-Director of the PRM radio station, Mexico City, 1937. f-Founder and Director of the Office of Economic Information for States and Federal Territories, 1938-46; founder and first Director of *Proa*, first newspaper of the Mexican congress, 1934; editor of *El Universal*, 1946. g-None. h-Journalist since 1920; editor of *El Universal Ilustrado*; author and translator under the name of Oscar Leblanc. i-Nephew of Miguel Bolaños Cacho, lawyer and governor of Oaxaca; cousin, *Raúl*, served as a federal deputy from Oaxaca, 1955-57. j-None. k-None. l-EBW46, 60; Peral, 115; C de D, 1940-42, 48.

Bonfil, Ramón G.

a-Feb. 10, 1905. b-Tetepango, Hidalgo. c-Teaching certificate in elementary level education; elementary teacher in the Normal School for Men; started legal studies at UNAM but left to continue rural teaching; higher studies in Geneva, 1956, and in Paris, 1958, 1960; director of various primary and normal schools. d-*Federal Deputy* from the State of Hidalgo, Dist. 2, 1943-46. e-Founding member with *Carlos Madrazo* and *Lauro Ortega* of the National Confederation of Popular Organizations of PRI (CNOP), Jan. 18, 1942. f-Director of Federal Education, Jalisco, 1932; Director General of

Literacy of the Secretariat of Public Education, 1964-68; Director General of Teachers' Education of the Secretariat of Public Education, 1969-70; *Subsecretary General of Public Education*, 1970-76; Secretary General of the Free Textbook Commission, 1978-82. g-First Secretary General of the Mexican Federation of Teachers, 1932-33. h-Worked for the Regional Center of Fundamental Education of UNESCO in Patzcuaro. i-Married Guadalupe Castro; father of *Alfredo V. Bonfil*; friend of *Adolfo López Mateos* since 1933. j-None. k-Supported the candidacy of *Javier Rojo Gómez* for secretary general of the CNC, 1945; precandidate for governor of Hidalgo, 1974. l-DPE65, 140; HA, 14 Dec. 1970; *Excélsior*, 20 Oct. 1974, 9; Raby, 70; Enc. Mex., II, 140-41; Pérez López, 68.

Bonfil (Pinto), Alfredo V.

(Deceased Jan. 25, 1973) a-Nov. 28, 1936. b-Querétaro, Querétaro. c-Primary and secondary studies at the Escuela Anexa a la Normal, Saltillo, Coahuila; preparatory studies at the Ateneo Fuente, Saltillo; law degree, National School of Law, UNAM, 1954-58; Professor of World History, Mexican History, and Social Studies, National Preparatory School, 1959-67. d-*Federal Deputy* from the State of Querétaro, Dist. 2, 1970-73, member of the Gran Comisión, the Agrarian Affairs Committee, the Second Government Committee, the Sugar Industry Committee, and the Second Constitutional Affairs Committee. e-Campaigned for *Francisco López Serrano* as a precandidate for governor of Coahuila; Director of Youth for PRI, Federal District; Secretary of Agrarian Action of PRI for the Federal District; Director of Citizen Education for the National Institute of Mexican Youth, 1964-70; campaign coordinator of the CNC for *Luis Echeverría*, 1970; *Secretary of Agrarian*

Action of the CEN of PRI, 1970-73; member of the Program and Ideology Committee of the New Advisory Commission to PRI, 1972. f-Private Secretary to *Francisco López Serrano*, Secretary General of the Department of Agrarian Affairs, 1959-64; Director General of the New Centers of Population, Department of Agrarian Affairs. g-Member of the Governing Board of the Student Association of the National Preparatory School No. 1, 1952-53; member of the Technical Board of the CNC, 1964; Oficial Mayor of the CNC, 1967-68; Secretary of Organization of the CNC, 1968-70; *Secretary General of the CNC*, 1970-73. h-None. i-Intimate friend of *Augusto Gómez Villanueva*; served with *Enrique Soto Izquierdo*, *Pedro Vázquez Colmenares*, and Pindaro Urióstegui as leaders of the Student Society of the National Preparatory School, 1952-53; close friend and collaborator with Pindaro Urióstegui; son of *Ramón G. Bonfil*, subsecretary of education, 1970-76; married Yolanda Ojeda. j-None. k-Lost as a precandidate for governor of Querétaro, 1973; badly injured by a bus while leading a student strike against increased fares, 1958; many Mexicans believe the plane in which Bonfil crashed was purposely sabotaged. l-HA, 26 Apr. 1971, 8, 10 Jul. 1972, 10; Directorio, 1970-72; *Excélsior*, 6 Feb. 1973, 18, 29 Jan. 1973, 11; HA, 12 Nov. 1973, 10; Basáñez, 199.

Bonilla, Adolfo
(Deceased) a-June 24, 1880. b-Tlaxco, Tlaxcala. c-Primary education in Huamantla, Tlaxcala; no college degree. d-*Governor of Tlaxcala*, 1933-37. e-None. f-President of the Military Tribunal in Puebla, 1927. g-None. h-None. i-Father of *Ignacio Bonilla Vázquez*, who served as his inspector of police and himself became Governor; political enemy of *Luciano Huerta Sánchez*. j-Became active in the anti-

reelectionist movement in 1910 and joined the Revolution in 1911; reached the rank of General in the Army, Nov. 17, 1915; fought with Francisco Villa and Emiliano Zapata until 1920; Commander of the 98th Regiment against the de la Huerta rebellion. k-Dissolved the Puebla State Legislature, Nov. 15, 1935. l-Peral, 116; D de Y, 1 Jan. 1936, 4.

Bonilla Cortés, Roberto T.
a-May 28, 1893. b-Tetela de Ocampo, Puebla. c-Primary education in Puebla; secondary education at the Normal School in Puebla, 1908, and the Normal School in Mexico City; law degree, Escuela Libre de Derecho, May 2, 1925, with a thesis on the public jury in Mexico; teacher in the Normal School of Puebla; normal school teacher, 1915-26; professor at the Military College, 1924; professor at the National Polytechnic Institute, 1925-41; Professor of Law at the National School of Law, UNAM, 1937-39. d-None. e-None. f-Military Judge, 1927-35; Judge of the Supreme Tribunal of Military Justice, 1935-40; Attorney General of Military Justice, 1940-41; *Subsecretary of Public Education*, Sept. 9, 1941, to 1943; Secretary General of Government of the State of Puebla, 1951-56. g-None. h-Military adviser, 1925-26. i-Friend of *Rafael Avila Camacho* and *Lauro Ortega*; brother of *Javier Bonilla Cortés*, federal deputy, 1955-58; joined the Revolution as a normal school student with *José A. Ceniceros* and *Jesús González Lugo*. j-Served in the Revolution, 1914; rank of Brigadier General of the Army, 1941. k-None. l-WWM45, 14; *Hoy*, 20 Sept. 1941, 3; DGF56, 98; Correa, 46, 77; Kirk, 150; DGF51, 91.

Bonilla Díaz de la Vega, Pedro
a-Apr. 10, 1933. b-Patzcuaro, Michoacán. c-Early education unknown; medical degree, UNAM, 1956-62. d-*Federal*

Deputy (Party Deputy from the PPS), 1973-76; *Plurinominal Deputy* from the PSUM, 1982-85. e-Joined the PCM, 1978; candidate of the PCM for Federal Deputy from Veracruz, Dist. 3, 1979; member of the Party of the Mexican People (PPM), 1977-81; member of the State Committee of the PSUM in Veracruz, 1981; member of the Central Committee of the PSUM, 1981; candidate of the PSUM for Federal Deputy from Veracruz, Dist. 3, 1982; candidate of the PPS for mayor of Poza Rica, Veracruz, 1976; candidate of the PPS for senator from Puebla, 1970. f-Physician, PEMEX, 1966-67. g-None. h-Practicing physician. j-None. k-None. l-Directorio, 1982-85; C de D, 1973-76, 1982-85; Lehr, 626.

Bonilla García, Jesús Javier
a-Nov. 11, 1937. b-Federal District. c-Early education unknown; economics degree, Autonomous Technological Institute of Mexico, 1956-60, with a thesis on "Census Information and Structural Changes in Mexican Industry," 1962; postgraduate work in economic planning, Institute of Social Studies, The Hague, Holland, 1962-63; Professor of Economic Theory, National School of Economics, UNAM; Professor of Political Economy, School of Anthropology, Ibero-American University. d-None. e-Joined PRI, 1961. f-Director, Office of Basic Economic Statistics, Secretariat of Industry and Commerce, 1960; Director, Office of Industrial Census, Secretariat of Industry and Commerce, 1959-60; Director, Technical Department, Secretariat of Industry and Commerce, 1960-64; Subdirector of Statistics, Secretariat of Industry and Commerce, 1964-71; Director General of Economic Statistics, Secretariat of Industry and Commerce, 1972-73; Director of the National Commission on Minimum Wages, 1973-77; *Subsecretary of Educational Planning*, Secretariat of Public Educa-

tion, 1976-78; Executive Adviser to the Director General of Infonavit, 1977-78; Subdirector of Institutional Services, IMSS, 1978-82; President of the National Commission on Minimum Wages, Secretariat of Labor, 1982-88; *Subsecretary B of Labor*, 1988-91; *Director General of Conasupo*, 1991- . g-None. h-Office worker, Legal Department, PEMEX, 1954-59. i-Son of Anselmo Bonilla Esevan, lawyer, and Elena García Piña, secretary; married Margarita Castañeda Santibáñez; son, Javier Bonilla Castañeda, was director general of international affairs, Secretariat of Foreign Relations, 1992. j-None. k-None. l-*Excélsior*, 29 Sept. 1978, 14; Q es QAP, 359; DBGM, 62; DBGM87, 59; *El Nacional*, 3 Jan. 1991, 1, 5.

Bonilla Vázquez, Ignacio
(Deceased Jan. 19, 1970) a-1901. b-Apizaco, Tlaxcala. c-Early education unknown; no degree. d-*Senator* from the State of Tlaxcala, 1964-68; *Governor of Tlaxcala*, 1969-70. e-None. f-Inspector of Police for the State of Tlaxcala; Director General of Fishing and Related Industries, Secretariat of the Navy, 1952-58; Chief of Purchasing for the Secretariat of National Defense, 1959-63. g-None. h-None. i-Son of *Adolfo Bonilla*; collaborator of *Rodolfo Sánchez Taboada* as president of PRI where he met *Luis Echeverría*. j-Career army officer; rank of Brigadier General; retired from active duty. k-*Por Qué?* claims he made a personal fortune as Chief of Purchasing for National Defense; fought a bitter campaign against *Luciano Huerta Sánchez* for governorship of Tlaxcala, 1968. l-WWMG, 9; DGF56, 383; DP70, 280; *Por Qué?*, 4 July 1969, 15.

Borge Martín, Miguel
a-Oct. 30, 1943. b-Cozumel, Quintana Roo. c-Early education unknown; aeronautical engineering degree, IPN,

1962-65; MA degree, Brown University, 1971-73; Ph.D., University of Paris, 1978-80; professor, IPN, 1970; professor, Ibero-American University, 1969-70, 1973-74; Professor of Engineering, Graduate School, National School of Engineering, UNAM, 1974. d-*Senator* from the State of Quintana Roo, 1982-87; *Governor of Quintana Roo*, 1987-93. e-Member of PRI. f-Adviser, governor of Quintana Roo, 1974-75; Director General of Livestock, Quintana Roo, 1975-78; Secretary, Economic Development, Quintana Roo, 1981-82. g-None. h-None. i-Son of Cecilio Borge Sade, businessman, and Margarita Martín Vázquez; married Rosalia Janetti Díaz. j-None. k-None. l-DBGM89, 666; HA, 4 Nov. 1986, 12; C de S, 1982-88.

Borrego Estrada, Genaro
a-Feb. 28, 1949. b-Zacatecas, Zacatecas. c-Early education unknown; degree in industrial relations, Ibero-American University, 1966-69, with a thesis on worker participation in management. d-*Federal Deputy* from the State of Zacatecas, Dist. 1, 1982-85; *Governor of Zacatecas*, 1986-92. e-Founding member of the National Revolutionary Youth Movement of PRI, 1973; Auxiliary Secretary to *Miguel de la Madrid*, presidential campaign, 1981-82; General Delegate of the CEN of PRI to Colima, 1983; *Oficial Mayor of the CEN of PRI*, 1982-86; *President of the CEN of PRI*, 1992-93. f-Private Secretary to the Director General of the National Ejido Credit Bank, *José Rodríguez Elías*, 1968-72; Director General of Personnel, IMSS, 1973-76; Private Secretary to the Subsecretary of the Control of Government Properties, *Ricardo García Sainz*, 1976-77; Private Secretary to the Secretary of Planning and Budgeting, *Ricardo García Sainz*, 1977-79; Director General of Administration, Infonavit, 1979-80; Director General of Administration and Planning, DINA, 1980-81;

Director General of the Ciudad Sahagún Trust, 1982. g-None. h-None. i-Son of Genaro Borrego Suárez, lawyer, and Olga Estrada Padres; married Elizabeth Hoffmann Atkinson; attended Ibero-American University with *Emilio Gamboa Patrón*, whom he invited to be his auxiliary secretary during *Miguel de la Madrid*'s campaign; *José Rodríguez Elías* helped him attend Ibero-American University when Borrego's father died in 1967. j-None. k-Forced to leave the presidency of PRI after numerous problems with state and local PRI leaders. l-DBGM, 477; DBGM89, 667; *Proceso*, 13 Apr. 1992, 9-11; Lehr, 533; HA, 25 Mar. 1986, 25; C de D, 1982-85; *Proceso*, 7 Jan. 1991, 27-28.

Borunda, Teófilo R.
a-Dec. 22, 1912. b-Chihuahua, Chihuahua. c-Primary, secondary, and preparatory studies in Chihuahua; no degree. d-Mayor of Ciudad Juárez, Chihuahua, 1940-42; *Federal Deputy* from the State of Chihuahua, Dist. 3, 1943-46, 1949-52, President of the Gran Comisión; *Alternate Senator* from the State of Chihuahua, 1946-52; *Senator* from the State of Chihuahua, 1952-56, member of the Gran Comisión, member of the Committee on Taxes, the First Committee on Government and the Special Commission on Tourist Affairs; substitute member of the First Committee on Petroleum; *Governor of Chihuahua*, 1956-62. e-*Secretary General of the National Executive Committee of PRI*, 1946-50. f-Ambassador to Argentina, 1971. g-First Secretary of Educational Action of the CNOP, 1943. h-Leading cattleman in Chihuahua with holdings in Santa Isabel and on the Hacienda de Encinillas. i-Friend of *Rodolfo Sánchez Taboada*; relative, who was mayor of Ciudad Juárez, was killed by a bomb in a political feud, 1938; longtime friend of *Luis Echeverría*; son of Cleófas Borunda and

Aurelia Ortiz, farmers; ties to Dr. Mariano Samaniego's family, political boss of El Paso from the 1860s to 1905; father-in-law of *Fidel Herrera Beltrán*, federal deputy from Veracruz; married Hortensia Flores. j-None. k-Answered *Miguel Alemán*'s 5th state of the union address, 1951; precandidate for senator from Chihuahua, 1970, 1982, but did not win the nomination. l-*Hoy*, 21 Mar. 1971, 4; DGF47, 22; DGF56, 6; D del S, 6 Dec. 1946, 1; HA, 9 May 1955, 3; DGF51, 6, 20, 27, 29; C de D, 1949-51; Ind. Biog., 22-28; Loret de Mola, 26; Wasserman, 6, 13-14; *Excélsior*, 26 Dec. 1981, 16A; *Proceso*, 8 Mar. 1982, 6-9.

Bosques Saldívar, Gilberto
a-July 20, 1892. b-Villa de Chiahutla, Puebla. c-Primary studies in Chiahutla, completed his studies at the Normal Institute of the State of Puebla; continued his studies in 1911; teaching certificate; professor at the Normal Institute of Puebla; teacher at the primary and secondary level in Puebla; Professor of Spanish, Higher School of Construction, Secretariat of Industry and Commerce. d-Federal Deputy from the State of Puebla to the Constitutional Convention at Querétaro, 1917; Federal Deputy from the State of Puebla, Dist. 7, 1922-24; Federal Deputy from the State of Puebla, Dist. 6, 1934-37, President of the Chamber of Deputies. e-*Secretary of Press and Publicity for the CEN of the PRM*, 1937-39. f-Employee of the Department of Technical Education for Women, Secretariat of Public Education; employee of the Press Department, Secretariat of the Treasury, 1929; Director General of *El Nacional*, 1938; First Consul General, Paris, France, 1938-42; Chargé d'affaires, Vichy, France, 1939-42; Minister to Portugal, 1946-50; Minister to Finland, 1950-53; *Ambassador to Cuba*, 1953-64; retired from the Foreign Service, 1967. g-President of the Executive Committee of

the Association of Normal Students, 1910; Director of the Maderista student movement of the State of Puebla, 1910. h-Journalist, Mexico City, 1920. i-Participated in the Aquiles Serdán conspiracy; organized students and teachers against Victoriano Huerta, 1913; good friend of *Narciso Bassols*; grandson of Antonio Bosques, who fought Maximilian; son of Cornelio C. Bosques, merchant, and María de la Paz Salvídar. k-Prisoner in Germany, 1942-44; precandidate for governor of Puebla, 1949. l-DBP, 721-22, letter; Casasola, V; CyT, 115; *Excélsior*, 7 Oct. 1984, 11, 26A.

Bracamontes (Gálvez), Luis Enrique
a-June 22, 1923. b-Talpalpa, Jalisco. c-Preparatory at the National Preparatory School, Mexico City; engineering degree from the National School of Engineering, UNAM, Aug. 22, 1946, with a thesis on "Planning Civil Engineering Works"; MA in physical science, UNAM, 1942-45; professor at the National Preparatory School, Mexico City, 1940-47; professor at the National School of Engineering, UNAM, 1944-52, in the field of topography. d-None. e-Joined PRI, 1938. f-Head of the University City construction in Mexico City, for the Secretariat of Public Works, 1950-55; *Subsecretary of Public Works*, 1952-58; *Subsecretary of Public Works*, 1958-64; Director General of the National Commission of Secondary Roads, 1952-64; *Secretary of Public Works*, 1970-76; Director General, Mexican Transportation Institute, Secretariat of Industry and Commerce, 1989- . g-None. h-Construction engineer on urban projects in the Federal District and other parts of Mexico, 1946-49; engineer for the University City project; adviser to the National Railroads, 1953-58, the National Urban Mortgage Bank, and the Secretariat of Public Works, 1953-64; Director General of the Mexican Company of

Engineering Consultants, S.A., 1965-70;
Director General of the Ciudad Industrial del Valle de Cuernavaca, 1966-70;
president of consulting firm, 1977-88.
i-Friend of *Carlos Lazo*; student of
Antonio Dovali Jaime at the National
School of Engineering; son of Enrique
Bracamontes Torres, accountant, and
Emma Galvéz Gutiérrez; married María
Beatriz Manero Sastre. j-None. k-One
of the youngest men ever to become a
subsecretary in a Mexican Cabinet;
precandidate for president of Mexico,
1975. l-HA, 7 Dec. 1970, 25; DBM68,
78; DGF56, 251; letters; Cadena, 34;
Enc. Mex., II, 153; DBGM89, 55-56;
DBGM92, 60-61.

Brasdefer Hernández, Gloria
a-Mar. 21, 1939. b-Federal District.
c-Early education unknown; law degree,
National School of Law, UNAM, 1959-
64; courses in public administration,
Buenos Aires, Argentina, 1967-69;
Professor of Administrative Law, School
of Political and Social Sciences, UNAM,
1969-82. d-Delegate to the Assembly of
the Federal District, Dist. 3, 1988-91;
Federal Deputy from the Federal
District, Dist. 3, 1991-94. e-Member of
the Advisory Council of the IEPES of
PRI. f-Lawyer, Division of Legal and
Legislative Affairs, Secretariat of the
Presidency, 1965-69; analyst, Technical
Section, Public Administration Commission, Secretariat of the Presidency,
1969-71; Chief of the Department of
Compilation and Analysis, Division of
Administrative Studies, Secretariat of
the Presidency, 1971-74; Technical Secretary of the Advisory Technical Com-
mittee on Legal Norms for the Public
Sector, Secretariat of Labor, 1971-74;
Director General of Programs, Organization, and Information, Secretariat of
Labor, 1977-78; *Oficial Mayor of Labor*,
1978-82; *Oficial Mayor of Fishing*,
1982-88. g-None. h-None. i-Daughter
of Guillermo Brasdefer Tamayo, white

collar worker, and Ana María Hernández Perezcano; married Raúl Corres
Ricárdez, lawyer; sister, Graciela,
director general of programming,
BANRURAL, 1989. j-None. l-IEPES; Q
es QAP, 409; Protag., 56; DBGM, 64;
DBGM89, 565; DBGM92, 429.

Brauer Herrera, Oscar
a-Dec. 14, 1922. b-Jalapa, Veracruz.
c-Primary and secondary studies in
Jalapa; agricultural engineering degree
with a specialty in parasitic plants,
National School of Agriculture, 1952;
master of science, University of California, Davis, 1954-55; Ph.D., Georg Aug.
University, Gottingen, Germany, 1960-
62; Professor of Genetics, Graduate
School, National School of Agriculture,
1959-60, 1962-69; Research Professor,
1959-65; Director of the Graduate
School, National School of Agriculture,
1965-69. d-None. e-None. f-Investigator of horticulture, Office of Special
Studies, Secretariat of Agriculture,
1952-58; Researcher on hybrid corn for
the Rockefeller Foundation, 1954-63;
Director of the Center for Agricultural
Investigations, Central Plateau, Office
of Special Studies, Chapingo, México,
1958; Director of the Center of Agricultural Investigations, Sinaloa, 1969-70;
Director, National Institute of Agricultural Research; *Subsecretary of Agriculture*, 1972-74; *Secretary of Agriculture*,
1974-76. g-None. h-Agronomist,
Anderson Clayton, Matamoros, 1951-
52; author of many technical books and
articles; speaks four languages and reads
seven. j-None. k-None. l-letter; HA,
30 Oct. 1972, 30, 14 Jan. 1974, 14.

Bravo Aguilera, Luis
a-Apr. 30, 1935. b-Federal District.
c-Early education unknown; economics
degree, National School of Economics,
UNAM, 1953-57, with a thesis on "The
Capital Market in Mexico," 1958; graduate studies at Columbia University,

1959-61; MA in economics, Harvard University, 1961; Professor of Economic Theory, National School of Economics, UNAM, 1962-66; Professor of Monetary Theory, Ibero-American University, 1962. d-None. e-Joined PRI, 1963; Auxiliary Coordinator of the IEPES of PRI, 1963-64. f-Director General of Industries, Secretariat of Industry and Commerce, 1964-70; Subdirector General of Tariffs and International Affairs, Secretariat of the Treasury, 1970-76; Director General of Tariffs and Border Affairs, Secretariat of the Treasury, 1976; Director General of Tariffs, Secretariat of Commerce, 1977-82; *Subsecretary of Foreign Trade*, Secretariat of Commerce, 1982-88; Director, Board, Bancomer, 1988-90. g-President of the National School of Economics 1953-57 generation. h-None. i-Protégé of *Octaviano Campos Salas*; son of Alfredo Bravo Carranza, mechanic, and María Luisa Aguilera García; married Carolina Rangel Ortiz. j-None. k-None. l-IEPES; Q es QAP, 189; Protag., 57; MGF69; DBGM, 64; DBGM89, 57.

Bravo Ahuja, Rodrigo
a-June 23, 1913. b-Tuxtepec, Oaxaca. c-Business administration studies; private accounting degree. d-*Alternate Federal Deputy* from the State of Oaxaca, Dist. 4, 1961-64; *Federal Deputy* from the State of Oaxaca, Dist. 4, 1967-70, 1976-79. e-Member of PRI. f-None. g-None. i-Brother of *Víctor Bravo Ahuja*, secretary of public education, 1971-76; son of Rodrigo Bravo and Carmen Ahuja. j-None. k-PAN has accused him of being a cacique in Oaxaca. l-*Excélsior*, 8 Dec. 1975, 17; C de D, 1967-70; C de D, 1976-79.

Bravo Ahuja, Víctor
a-Feb. 20, 1918. b-Tuxtepec, Oaxaca. c-Primary studies in the Alfonso XIII Spanish Institute, Tacubaya, Federal District; preparatory studies at the Higher School of Mechanical and Electrical Engineering, IPN; degree in aeronautical engineering from the School of Engineering, National Polytechnic Institute, Aug. 20, 1940; studies at the Heroic Military College, 1938-44; postgraduate work in science at the National University, Cal Tech, 1943-44, and University of Michigan, 1944-45; MS, Cal Tech, 1944; Professor of Aviation Mechanics at the Military School of Aviation, 1938-39; Professor of Physics at the School of Sciences, UNAM, 1941-42; Professor of Engineering, National Polytechnic Institute, 1941, 1945-68; professor at the Graduate School of the Technical Institute of Monterrey; professor at the Military College, 1942-43; member of many educational advisory boards in Mexico; President of the Center of Investigations and Advanced Studies, 1961-68; founder and Director of the Institute of Industrial Investigation of Monterrey, 1950-59; Director of Summer Sessions of the Technical Institute of Higher Studies of Monterrey, 1951-55; Director of the Engineering School of the Technical Institute of Higher Studies of Monterrey, 1955-58; Secretary General of the Technical Institute of Higher Studies of Monterrey, 1948-49; Rector of the Technical Institute of Higher Studies of Monterrey, 1950-58. d-*Governor of Oaxaca*, 1968-70. e-None. f-Chief, Office of Engineering, Aeronautical Shops, Mexican Air Force; *Subsecretary of Technical and Vocational Education*, 1958-64; *Subsecretary of Technical and Graduate Education*, 1964-68; *Secretary of Public Education*, 1971-76. g-None. h-Consultant to UNESCO, 1958-68; author of many articles in his professional field. i-Brother of *Rodrigo Bravo Ahuja*, federal deputy from Oaxaca, 1967-70, 1976-79; son of Rodrigo Bravo and Carmen Ahuja. j-None. l-HA, 7 Dec. 1970, 25; WWMG, 9; GdNL, 17;

letter; HA, 21 Dec. 1964, 6, 22 Feb. 1971, 17; *Excélsior*, 8 Dec. 1975, 17; Enc. Mex. II, 162.

Bravo Carrera, Luis
a-Nov. 1, 1902. b-Oaxaca, Oaxaca. c-Primary education in Oaxaca; preparatory at the Institute of Arts and Sciences in Oaxaca; graduated from the Naval College at Veracruz, Nov. 16, 1924. d-None. e-None. f-Naval Attaché to the Mexican Embassy in Rome; *Secretary of the Navy*, 1970-76. g-None. h-None. i-Married Graciela Román. j-Career naval officer; Subdirector of Naval Boat Construction, Spain; Commander of the Sixth Naval Zone; rank of Corvette Captain, June 1, 1941; Director of the Naval School of the Pacific, Mazatlán, Sinaloa, 1947; rank of Rear Admiral, 1952; Commander of the Third Naval Zone, Veracruz, 1956; Chief of Staff of the First and the Third Naval Zones; Director of the Naval College at Veracruz; Chief of Staff of the Navy; Director General of the Fleet, 1958-61; rank of Admiral, Nov. 20, 1963; Oficial Mayor of the Navy. k-Was on the retired list when he was appointed secretary of the navy. l-DGF47, 234; D de Y, 6 Dec. 1970, 2; HA, 7 Dec. 1970, 24; DGF56, 386; DPE61, 39; *Excélsior*, 8 Dec. 1975, 17; HA, 21 June 1976, 11.

Bravo Hernández, Mayo Arturo
a-May 14, 1938. b-Federal District. c-Primary and secondary studies in the Federal District; accounting degree in the Federal District. d-*Federal Deputy* from the Federal District for PAN (Party Deputy), 1970-73. e-Joined PAN, 1965; member of the Regional Committee of PAN for the Federal District; Chief of the Regional Committee of PAN for Dist. 20 of the Federal District. f-None. g-None. i-Married María Emma Hernández. j-None. k-None. l-C de D, 1970-73, 145.

Bravo Izquierdo, Donato
(Deceased Aug. 21, 1971) a-Oct. 22, 1891. b-Coxcatlán, Tehuacan, Puebla. c-Primary and secondary studies in public and private schools in the State of Puebla and in Orizaba, Veracruz; no degree. d-Deputy to the Constitutional Congress of Querétaro from the State of México, Dist. 15, 1916-17; Federal Deputy from the State of México, Dist. 15, 1918-20; Federal Deputy from the State of Puebla, Dist. 11, 1928-30; Provisional Governor of Puebla, 1928; *Senator* from Puebla, 1958-64, President of the War Materiels Committee; member of the Railroad Committee; substitute member of the Military Justice Committee, the Second Petroleum Committee, and the First Balloting Committee. f-None. g-None. h-Worker at the Thread and Fabric Factory, Ciudad Mendoza, Veracruz, 1909. i-Son of José María Bravo Omos and Aurelia Izquierdo. j-Career military officer; joined the Revolution in 1913 under the command of General Barbosa; Zone Commander of the First Military Zone, Federal District; Inspector General of the Army of the Third Inspection Commission; supported General Obregón against Carranza, 1920; fought against de la Huerta, 1923; fought against Escobar, 1929; Commander of the 25th Military Zone, Puebla, Puebla, 1948, 1957; rank of Brigadier General, 1942. k-Involved in antigovernment activities, 1909. l-WWM45, 15; McAlister, 224; Peral, 118; C de S, 1961-64, 52; Func., 316; Dávila, 112; Rev. de Ejer., Oct. 1957, 40.

Bravo Silva, José
a-1926. b-Morelia, Michoacán. c-Early education unknown; studies in economics from the School of Economics, Technological Institute of Mexico, Mexico City, 1946-50; received economics degree in 1953 with a thesis on "An Essay on the Administrative Control of

Prices." d-None. e-None. f-Subdirector, Department of Prices, Division of Prices, Secretariat of Industry and Commerce, 1955; *Subdirector General of the National Bank of Foreign Commerce*, 1970-76. g-None. i-Supported *Carlos Torres Manzo* for governor of Michoacán, 1974. j-None. k-None. l-letter; DNED, 46; *Excélsior*, 19 Jan. 1974, 8.

Bravo Valencia, Enrique
a-1909. b-Jiquilpan, Michoacán. c-Primary and secondary studies in Jilquilpan; completed second year of secondary; no degree. d-Mayor of Jiquilpan, Michoacán; *Federal Deputy* from the State of Michoacán, Dist. 4, 1946-49, member of the Mail and Telegraph, Indigenous Affairs, and Social Action Committees; local deputy to the State Legislature of Michoacán; Mayor of Morelia, Michoacán; *Senator* from Michoacán, 1952-58, member of the National Properties and Resources Committee, the Second Ejido Committee, the First Mines Committee, and the First Balloting Group. e-Secretary General of the Regional Committee of PRI in the Federal District; President of PRI in Michoacán, 1952; Secretary of Organization in the campaign of *Dámaso Cárdenas* for governor of Michoacán, 1950. f-President of the Federal Board of Moral and Civic Improvement, Morelia; Director of the Federal Treasury Office, No. 17, 1964-70, No. 4, 1971-76. g-None. h-None. j-None. k-Precandidate for governor of Michoacán in 1956, 1962, 1968, and 1974. l-Ind. Biog., 28; *Excélsior*, 20 Dec. 1973, 9; C de S, 1952-58; C de D, 1946-49, 6.

Bremauntz, Alberto
(Deceased Dec. 9, 1978) a-Aug. 13, 1897. b-Morelia, Michoacán. c-Primary studies in Morelia, Uruapan, and Ciudad Hidalgo; studies at the Colegio de San Nicolás, 1910; graduated from the Normal School of Michoacán, 1916;

law degree from the University of Michoacán, 1929, with a thesis on participation in utilities and salaries in Mexico; Professor of Economics at the University of Michoacán; secondary teacher at various schools; professor and Director, School of Business, University of Michoacán; Rector of the University of Michoacán, 1963-66. d-Mayor of Morelia, 1929; Federal Deputy from the State of Michoacán, 1932-34; *Alternate Senator* from Michoacán, 1934-40. e-Secretary General of the PNR for Michoacán; founding member of the Socialist Party of Michoacán; Secretary General of *Francisco J. Mújica's* campaign for governor of Michoacán, 1920. f-Stenographer for *Francisco Mújica*, Department of General Provisions, Federal District Department, 1918-20; Private Secretary to *Francisco Mújica*, 1920; Judge of the First Penal Court, Federal District, 1934; Justice of the Superior Tribunal of Justice of the Federal District, 1935-63. g-Founder of the Socialist Front of Mexican Lawyers, 1934. h-Founded several newspapers in Michoacán; agent of the Ministerio Público in Michoacán; public defender; consulting lawyer to *Agustín Lenero*, secretary general of government, Michoacán, 1929-30; consulting lawyer to *Lázaro Cárdenas* and *Dámaso Cárdenas*. i-Father a musician and pharmacist; uncle of *Ernesto Soto Reyes*, senator from Michoacán, 1934-40; uncle of *José María Mendoza Pardo*, governor of Michoacán, 1944-49. j-None. k-President of the Education Committee of the Chamber of Deputies that presented the revision of Article 3 to include socialist education, 1933. l-Garrido, 201; Bremauntz.

Bremer Martino, Juan José
a-May 22, 1944. b-Federal District. c-Early education unknown; law degree, National School of Law, UNAM, Oct. 2, 1967, honorable mention, with a thesis

on international law; received a 9.6 grade average out of 10 for all courses at law school. d-*Federal Deputy* from the Federal District, Dist. 23, 1985-88. e-Professor of Analysis of the Mexican Constitution, Institute of Political Education, PRI; President of the Cultural Committee of the IEPES of PRI, 1981; *Secretary of Ideology of the CEN of PRI, 1987.* f-Personal Secretary to the Private Secretary, *Ignacio Ovalle Fernández,* of the President of Mexico, 1970-72; Private Secretary to President *Luis Echeverría, 1972-75, Subsecretary of the Presidency, 1975-76;* Director General of the Institute of Fine Arts, 1976-82; Ambassador to Switzerland, 1982; *Subsecretary of Culture,* Secretariat of Public Education, 1982-85; *Ambassador to the Soviet Union, 1988-90;* Ambassador to Germany, 1990- . g-Leader of 1966 student strike; President of the 1962 Generation of Law Students, 1963. i-Son of Juan José Bremer, well-known law professor at UNAM, and Cristina Martino; married Ana María Villaseñor Cusi; grandson of Roberto A. Bremer, a businessman, and Julián Barrera; uncle, Guillermo Bremer Barrera, was a member of PAN; *Miguel de la Madrid* worked for his father, 1957-60. j-None. k-None. l-HA, 25 Sept. 1972, 1; DAPC, 77, 9; Q es QM, 1952, 30-32; HA, 26 Apr. 1982, 10; *Excélsior,* 17 Apr. 1982, 4A; Enc. Mex., 2, 164; López Esc., 125; DBGM, 66-67; DBGM92, 62.

Brena Torres, Rodolfo
a-May 16, 1911. b-Ejutla, Oaxaca. c-Secondary and preparatory studies at the Benito Juárez University of Oaxaca; preparatory studies continued at the National Preparatory School, UNAM; studied at the National School of Law, UNAM, but discontinued studies due to lack of money in 1931; law degree from the Scientific and Literary Institute of the State of México, 1949. d-*Senator*

from the State of Oaxaca, 1958-62; President of the Gran Comisión; head of the Committee on Foreign Affairs and Tariffs; head of the Committee on National Properties and Resources; member of the First Committee on Petroleum and the Second Committee on Labor; *Governor of Oaxaca, 1962-68.* e-None. f-Agent of the Ministerio Público for the Federal Attorney General's Office in the State of México, 1950; public defender in the State of México, 1950; delegate of the Mexican Economic Commission to the Organization of American States, 1959. g-Attorney for the Mexican Petroleum Workers Union, 1940. h-Practicing attorney in Mexico City, in the field of labor law. j-None. k-None. l-G of M, 10; DBM68, 80; letter; Func. 302.

Brito Foucher, Rodulfo
(Deceased May 15, 1970) a-Nov. 8, 1899. b-Villahermosa, Tabasco. c-Primary studies in private school, Villahermosa, 1907-12; preparatory education at the Institute of Tabasco, 1913-17, and at the National Preparatory School, 1917-18; law degree from the National School of Law, UNAM, Dec. 28, 1923; attended New York University, Columbia University, and the University of Berlin; Professor of General Theory at the National School of Law, UNAM, 1927-35; Director of the National School of Law, UNAM, 1932-33. d-None. e-None. f-Subsecretary of Foreign Relations and Subsecretary of Government, de la Huerta Rebellion, 1923; later became Secretary, 1923; served as Governor of Campeche before his forces were defeated, 1923; *Rector of UNAM, 1942-44.* g-President of the Student Federation; delegate to the First National Student Congress, 1921. h-President of the White Cross in Mexico City, 1942-68; practicing attorney in private law firm in Mexico City, 1940-70, at time of death. i-Friend

of *Agustín García López*, when both were students at the National School of Law; father, a close collaborator of the governor of Tabasco; cousin of *Andrés Iduarte*; grandfather was governor of Tabasco; married Esperanza Moreno. j-None. k-An active Mason; headed punitive expedition to Villahermosa during the reign of Garrido Canabal that cost the lives of his brother and several other followers on July 14, 1935. The killings caused an outcry in the press that eventually produced the fall of the Garrido Canabal regime. In exile, 1924-27, New York; in exile in Berlin, Washington, D.C., and New York, 1936-40. l-DBM68, 82; DBM70, 90; WWM45, 15; Simpson, 354; Kirk, 155; letter; HA, 4 Aug. 1944, 7; DP70, 295; Peral, 121; Balboa, 110-12.

Brito Rosado, Efraín
a-Sept. 2, 1912. b-Mérida, Yucatán. c-Primary studies in Mérida; secondary studies in Mexico City; preparatory studies at the National Preparatory School; law degree from the National School of Law, UNAM, Dec. 17, 1936, with a thesis on "The Significance of Politics"; Professor of World History and the History of Art. d-*Federal Deputy* from the State of Yucatán, Dist. 2, 1943-46; *Federal Deputy* from the State of Yucatán, Dist. 3, 1949-52, member of the Inspection Committee of the General Accounting Office; *Senator* from the State of Yucatán, 1952-58, member of the Foreign and Domestic Trade Committee, the First Government Committee, the Electrical Industry Committee and the Legislative Studies Committee; substitute member of the Health Committee. e-Orator for the National Anti-reelectionist Party, 1927; supporter of José Vasconcelos in the 1929 campaign; orator and Secretary General of the Revolutionary Party of National Unification, 1940; orator for *Miguel Alemán*, 1946. f-President of

the Legislative Studies Commission, Secretariat of Public Education; Founder and Director of the School for Citizenship Training, Secretariat of Public Education; Director of Social Action, Department of the Federal District; First Secretary of the Legation to Spain, 1936; Chargé d'affaires, Brazil. g-Student leader of the autonomy movement at UNAM, 1929; President of the Federation of University Students, 1930-31; National Oratory Champion, 1928. h-Columnist and editorialist for *Crítica* (Buenos Aires). i-Friends with *Miguel Alemán* and *Adolfo López Mateos* during student days; nephew of Dr. Manuel Mestre Ghigliazza, governor of Tabasco, 1911-13; nephew of Eduardo Mestre Ghigliazza, federal deputy from Puebla, 1910-12. j-None. k-Fled Mexico with *José Castro Estrada* with the help of *Agustín García López* after supporting *Juan Andreu Almazán*, 1940; remained in exile several months; precandidate for governor of Yucatán, 1951. l-Letter; C de S, 1952-58; DGF56, 8, 10, 11, 12, 14; C de D, 1943-45, 7; C de D, 1949-51, 65; Casasola, V; Ind. Biog., 29-30.

Buchanan (López), Walter Cross
(Deceased Sept. 21, 1977) a-Apr. 29, 1906. b-San Luis de la Paz, Guanajuato. c-Engineering degree from the Higher School of Mechanical and Electrical Engineering, National Polytechnic Institute, 1931; professor at the School of Engineering, UNAM, 1931-55; professor specializing in steam powered machinery and railroads at the National Polytechnic Institute, 1931-35; Director of the Higher School of Mechanical and Electrical Engineering at the National Polytechnic Institute, 1944; founder of the major in communication and electronics at the National Polytechnic Institute, 1937. d-None. e-None. f-Head of the Department of Control for Industrial Electricity, Secretariat of

Public Works, 1951; *Subsecretary of Public Works, 1952-55; Secretary of Public Works, 1955-58; Secretary of Communications and Transportation,* 1958-64. g-None. h-President of the Board of Directors of Radio Aeronautica Mexicana, S.A., 1965-77. i-Son of Walter C. Buchanan, an engineer. j-None. k-None. l-HA, 4 Aug. 1958, 11; HA, 8 Apr. 1957; DGF56, 251; Func. 77; NYT, 10 Nov. 1955, 2.

Bucio Alanís, Lauro
a-Aug. 18, 1928. b-Ciudad Hidalgo, Michoacán. c-Early education unknown; agricultural engineering degree, National School of Agriculture, July 25, 1954; MS, Iowa State University, Sept. 1955; Bank of Mexico fellowship to Iowa State University, 1955; Ph.D. in genetics, University of Birmingham, 1963-66; Director, Department of Genetics, National School of Agriculture; Dean, Graduate School, National School of Agriculture, 1972. d-None. e-None. f-Agronomist, Office of Special Studies, Secretariat of Agriculture; Field Director, Agricultural Experiment Station, Jaloxtoc, Morelos; Director of the Maíz Germinating Plasma Bank; Director of Maíz Improvement Program, Tamaulipas and Bajio, National Maíz Commission; Director of the Basic Seeds Department, National Maíz Commission; *Oficial Mayor of Agriculture,* 1972-76. g-None. i-Nephew of Emilio Alanís Patiño. j-None. k-None. l-BdM, 77-78.

Bueno Amezcua, José de Jesús
(Deceased 1969) a-Oct. 10, 1930. b-Guadalajara, Jalisco. c-Law degree, University of Guadalajara, 1955. d-*Federal Deputy* from the State of Jalisco, Dist. 8, 1967-70, member of the Legislative Studies Committee. e-Student member of the Revolutionary Youth group of the PRI; participated in the founding of the Middle Class

League, a basic sector of the National Confederation of Popular Organizations of PRI in Jalisco, 1952; headed different political commissions for PRI, 1953-59; member of the Economic Planning Council of PRI for the campaign of *Adolfo López Mateos,* 1958; participated in the mayoralty campaign of *Francisco Medina Asencio,* 1962; participated in the campaigns of *Francisco Medina Asencio, Agustín Yáñez,* and *Juan Gil Preciado* for governor of Jalisco. f-Private Secretary to the mayor of Guadalajara, 1962-64; Private Secretary to the governor of Jalisco, 1965-67. g-Held many positions in the Federation of University Students of the University of Guadalajara. h-Official of the Legal Department of CONASUPO; First Officer of the Administrative Section of CONASUPO. i-Friend of *Francisco Medina Asencio,* governor of Jalisco, 1965-69. j-None. k-None. l-DBM68, 83-84; letter; C de D, 1967-69.

Buenrostro Ochoa, Efraín
(Deceased Mar. 11, 1973) a-Oct. 28, 1896. b-Jiquilpan, Michoacán. c-Primary education in Jiquilpan; secondary in Guadalajara, Jalisco; three years of engineering school at the Liceo de Varones in Guadalajara; no degree. d-None. e-None. f-Vice consul in various cities of the United States, 1918-28; Secretary General of Government of the State of Michoacán, 1928-32; Assistant Treasurer General of Mexico, 1932-34; *Subsecretary of the Treasury,* 1934-39; *Secretary of Industry and Commerce,* 1939-40; *Director General of Petróleos Mexicanos,* 1940-46; Director General of Cía. Industrial de Atenquique, 1964-70. g-None. i-Intimate friend of *Lázaro Cárdenas;* became friends with Cárdenas during his first five years of primary education in Jiquilpan, Michoacán; married Carmen Araiza; son, a physician, in Mexico City. j-None. k-None.

l-DBM68, 84; HA, 6 Oct. 1944, 28; Dulles 608; *Excélsior*, 13 Mar. 1973.

Burgos García, Enrique
a-Apr. 20, 1946. b-Querétaro, Querétaro. c-Early education unknown; law degree, University of Querétaro, 1963-67; LLD, National School of Law, UNAM, 1974-76; professor, University of Querétaro, 1978-89. d-Mayor of San Juan del Río, Querétaro, 1970-73; Local Deputy to the State Legislature of Querétaro, 1985-88; *Senator* from the State of Querétaro, 1988-91; *Governor* of Querétaro, 1991- . e-Secretary of Youth Action of PRI, Querétaro, 1966; Secretary of Political Action of PRI, Querétaro, 1985-88. f-Agent of the Ministerio Público, 1969-70; Secretary of Government, State of Querétaro, 1982. g-None. h-Practicing lawyer, 1973-76; notary public, 1976-88. i-Son of Enrique Burgos Mondragón, federal employee, and Emilia García Vargas; married Yolanda Hernández Ontiveros. j-None. k-None. l-DBGM89, 408; C de S, 1988-91.

Burguete Farrera, Ezequiel
(Deceased Oct. 7, 1975) a-Mar. 7, 1907. b-Tuxtla Gutiérrez, Chiapas. c-Primary studies in Tuxtla Gutiérrez; preparatory studies at the National Preparatory School, 1920-24; law degree, National School of Law, UNAM, Mar. 8, 1929; Professor of Civics and Economics, University Preparatory School; Professor of Penal Law at the National School of Law, Jan. 1, 1939, to 1972. d-None. e-None. f-Representative of the Federal Treasury (estates) in Tuxtla Gutiérrez, 1929-30; Court Clerk of the Chiapas District Court in charge of civil and penal sections, 1930-31; consulting lawyer to the Office of the Attorney General of Mexico, June 1932 to Feb. 1933; agent of the Ministerio Público of the Consulting Department of the Attorney General, Jan. to Sept. 1933;

special agent of the Ministerio Público of the Attorney General in the investigation of the role of Father Jiménez in the death of President Obregón, 1933-34; agent of the Ministerio Público in charge of preparatory investigations, 1934-35; head of the Department of Preparatory Investigations of the Office of the Attorney General, 1934-35; Attorney "C" of the Legal Department of the Secretariat of the Treasury, Jan. to Dec. 1935; head of the Legal Department of the National Bank of Ejido Credit in charge of the Nationalization of Properties Section, July 1939 to Aug. 1941; representative of Capital (Group VII) on the Federal Board of Conciliation and Arbitration, 1942-47; adviser to the Secretary of the Presidency; *Supernumerary Justice of the Supreme Court*, May 2, 1966, to June 27, 1967; *Justice of the Supreme Court*, 1967-75. g-None. h-Private law practice, 1943, 1947-66; attorney for Petróleos Mexicanos. i-Knew *Antonio Carrillo Flores* at the National School of Law; son of Ezequiel Burguete, landowner, Federal Deputy under Madero and a federal judge; married to María Santaella; grandfather, large landowner. j-None. k-Representative of the Federation of People's Parties to the Federal Electoral Commission; candidate of the Federation of People's Parties in Michoacán, 1952. l-Letter; DBM68, 86; DGF50, II, 347; Morton, 63; HA, 6 Jun. 1952, 8; *Excélsior*, 7 Oct. 1975, 5; *Justicia*, Aug. 1968.

Bustamante (Vasconcelos), Eduardo
a-Oct. 12, 1904. b-Oaxaca, Oaxaca. c-Primary studies at the Colegio Unión, Oaxaca, 1910-15; preparatory at the Colegio Unión and the Institute of Arts and Sciences of Oaxaca, 1917-22; law degree, National School of Law, UNAM, Oct. 6, 1926; Professor of Public Finance at the National School of Economics, UNAM, 1947-60. d-None. e-None. f-Technical consult-

ant to the Technical Fiscal Department of the Secretariat of the Treasury, 1928, and head of that department in 1932; financial adviser to the State of Nuevo León, 1927-31; Director General of Revenues of the Secretariat of the Treasury, 1934; Director General of the Bank of Industry and Commerce, 1942-45; Private Secretary to the secretary of public education, Puig Casauranc, 1930-31; Private Secretary to the Secretary of Industry and Commerce, Aaron Sáenz, 1931; *Subsecretary of the Treasury,* 1946-49; Mexican delegate to the United Nations with *Adolfo López Mateos,* 1951; *Secretary of Government Properties,* 1958-64; member of the Advisory Council of the Bank of Commerce and the Bank of Industry and Commerce, 1965-70. g-None. h-Private law practice, 1934-46; first employment as Fourth Official of the Technical Fiscal Department of the Secretariat of the Treasury, 1925; author of articles on law; attended numerous conferences on economics. i-Friends with *Mario Ramón Beteta, Miguel Alemán, Manuel Gual Vidal, Jaime Torres Bodet, Antonio García López, Antonio Carrillo Flores,* and *Alfonso García González* since college days at the National School of Law; father, a self-made businessman; relative of *Juan I. Vasconcelos,* federal deputy from Oaxaca, 1964-67; brother of *Miguel E. Bustamante,* subsecretary of health, 1960-64; married Refugio Dávila. j-None. k-None. l-Letter; WWM45, 16; HA, 3 June 1963; HA, 5 Oct. 1959; DBM68, 88; HA, 8 Dec. 1958, 30.

Bustamante (Vasconcelos), Miguel E.
a-May 2, 1898. b-Oaxaca, Oaxaca. c-Primary and secondary studies in Oaxaca; preparatory studies at the Institute of Arts and Sciences in Oaxaca, 1914-19; medical degree from the National School of Medicine, UNAM, 1925; Ph.D. in Public Health,

Johns Hopkins University, 1928; Professor of Hygiene at the National School of Medicine, UNAM, 1931-52; special lecturer, U.S. universities, 1942-43; Director of the Department of Social and Preventive Medicine, 1956-58. d-None. e-None. f-Director of the Health Training Station at Xochimilco, Secretariat of Public Health; Assistant Head of the Federal Health Bureau of the Secretariat of Public Health, 1931; Head of the Federal Health Bureau, 1932-35; Director of the Cooperative Health Unit in Veracruz, 1930; Supervisor of Foreign Health Missions, 1938; Director General of the Institute of Health and Tropical Diseases of the Secretariat of Public Health, 1942-43, 1946-47; Secretary General of the Sanitation Bureau, Pan American Union, 1947-56; Director General of Health Services, Secretariat of Health, 1958-59; *Subsecretary of Public Health and Welfare,* Jan. 27, 1960, to 1964; Secretary General of the National Council of Health, 1965. g-None. h-Intern, General Hospital of Mexico City, 1924-25; Fellow of the Rockefeller Foundation, 1926-28; Epidemiologist of the Institute of Health and Tropical Diseases of the Secretariat of Public Health, 1939-41; author of numerous articles and papers on public health that have appeared in North American journals. i-Brother of *Eduardo Bustamante,* secretary of government properties, 1958-64; father, a self-made businessman; cofounder of the Institute of Health and Tropical Diseases with *Manuel Martínez Báez,* 1937; married Alicia Connolly. j-None. k-None. l-D de Y, 10 Dec. 1964, 20; DGF47, 199; *Annals,* Mar. 1940, 161; WWM45, 16; WWW70-71; letter; Enc. Mex. II, 178.

Bustani Hid, José
a-Oct. 18, 1935. b-Federal District. c-Early education unknown; economics degree, National School of Economics,

UNAM, 1954-58, with a thesis on "The Costs of Federal Investment," 1961; courses in computing, 1960, mechanized accounting, 1966, and economics and social planning, 1968; postgraduate studies, Pan American Institute of Management Studies, 1973-74. d-None. e-None. f-Subdirector of the Department of Budgeting Control of Decentralized Organizations and Enterprises, Secretariat of the Treasury, 1965-68; Subdirector of Studies and Budget Planning, Secretariat of the Treasury, 1971-74; Director General of Administration, Secretary of Labor, 1974-75; Director General of Inspection of Funds and Stock, Secretariat of the Treasury, 1975-76; Director General of Administration, Attorney General of the Federal District, 1976-77; Oficial Mayor of the Attorney General of the Federal District, 1977-78; Director of Acquisitions and Services, SOMEX, 1979; Director General of Administration of Personnel, Secretariat of Programming and Budgeting, 1979-81; *Oficial Mayor of Programming and Budgeting,* 1981-82; *Oficial Mayor of the Department of the Federal District,* 1982-84; *Secretary of Social Development,* Department of the Federal District, 1984-86. g-None. h-None. i-Son of Abdo Bustani Jaraschy, businessman, and María Hid Andrew; married Ivonne Moukarzel Said; student of *Mario Ramón Beteta.* j-None. k-HA, 26 Oct. 1981, 28; HA, 20 Dec. 1982, 28; IEPES; Q es QAP, 427; DBGM, 69.

C

Caamano Muñoz, Enrique
a-July 13, 1911. b-Federal District. c-Early education unknown; degree in business administration; certified public accountant. d-None. e-None. f-Accountant, Controller General,

National Finance Bank, 1936-46; Director General of Expenditures, Secretariat of the Treasury, 1949-58; *Subsecretary of Expenditures,* Secretariat of the Treasury, 1958-64; *Subsecretariat of Expenditures,* 1964-70. g-None. h-Member of the board of directors of various companies, including Mexican Light and Power; Treasurer of the Mexican Tube Company, 1947-49. i-Married Isabel Rico. j-None. k-None. l-D del S, 2 Dec. 1964; DPE51, 147; DGF56, 164; *Siempre,* 14 Jan. 1959, 6; WNM, 30; DPE61, 40.

Caballero, Luis G.
a-1877. b-Morelia, Michoacán. c-Preparatory studies at the Colegio de San Nicolás, Morelia; law degree, Colegio de San Nicolás, 1912. d-None. e-None. f-Public Defender, Superior Tribunal of Justice of the State of Michoacán; agent of the Ministerio Público; adviser to General Alfredo Elizondo, Governor of Michoacán, 1915-17; Attorney General of the State of Michoacán, 1917-20; Second Judge, 1st Civil Court, Morelia, 1922-23; member of the Committee to Reform the Civil Code, Michoacán, 1924; Secretary of the Superior Tribunal of Justice of Michoacán, 1926-27; Judge of the Superior Tribunal of Justice of Michoacán, 1927-28; district court judge, Nayarit and México, 1928; Judge, 2nd District Court, Mexico City; district court judge, Hidalgo; Judge, 5th Circuit Court, Puebla, Puebla; *Justice of the Supreme Court,* 1938-41; Judge, 2nd District Court, Mexico City, 1941; Judge, 5th Circuit Court, Puebla, Puebla, 1960. g-None. h-None. i-Son of prominent judge and ten-time federal deputy, Luis G. Caballero, and Isabel Escobar. j-None. k-Presided over the arraignment of Daniel Flores, attempted assassin of President Pascual Ortiz Rubio. l-DP70, 309-10; Rice, 232-33; Dicc. Mich., 61-62.

Caballero Aburto, Raúl
b-Ometepec, Guerrero. c-Primary studies in Ometepec; secondary at the National Military College; diploma in staff and command, Higher War College, 1933-36. d-*Governor of Guerrero*, 1957-61. d-None. f-Military attaché to El Salvador, Costa Rica, and Nicaragua, 1962-65. g-None. h-None. j-Joined Francisco Madero, 1910; fought in the Constitutionalist Army during the Revolution; rank of Brigadier General; career army officer; Zone Commander of the 26th Military Zone, Jalapa, Veracruz, 1956. k-Caballero Aburto's powers as governor were removed by the federal government after a student revolt and *Adolfo López Mateos* sent in federal troops; he was accused of corruption and opposed by the Civic Association of Guerrero of which *Genaro Vázquez Rojas* was a member; *Hispano Americano* accused him of putting 60 relatives into state offices as governor; the secretary general of the CNC in Guerrero claimed he held illegal large landholdings in Guerrero in Aug. 1972. l-NYT, 31 Dec. 1960, 1; NYT, 5 Jan. 1961, 9; NYT, 15 Apr. 1959, 8; *Excélsior*, 29 Aug. 1972, 27; DGF56, 202; G of M, 19-20; HA, 14 Apr. 1958, 10; HA, 14 Feb. 1972, 15.

Caballero (Caballero), Arquimides
a-Oct. 21, 1918. b-Tampico, Tamaulipas. c-Primary teaching certificate, Normal School, Ciudad Victoria, 1934-37; primary school teacher, Tampico, 1937-39, Mexico City, 1939-41; completed preparatory studies, Ciudad Victoria; teaching certificate in mathematics, Higher Normal School, Mexico City, 1940-43; primary and secondary school teacher; Director of Oral Normal School, 1948-49; Secretary of the Institute of Teacher Training, 1948-49; Professor of Mathematics, Higher Normal School, Mexico City, 1947-57;

Director of the Higher Normal School, Mexico City, 1957-66. d-None. e-None. f-Director of Secondary Night Schools, Secretary of Public Education, 1950-57; Chief of Mathematics Classes, Private Secondary Schools, Secretariat of Public Education, 1966-70; Director General of Middle Education, Secretariat of Public Education, 1970-71; Director General of Basic Education, Secretariat of Public Education, 1971; President of the National Technical Council of Education, 1976-80; *Subsecretary of Basic Education*, 1980; *Subsecretary of Middle Education*, 1980-82, 1982-88. g-None. h-Vice-President of the Committee of Experts for Teacher Education, UNESCO; adviser to the National Free Textbook Commission, 1958. i-Married Elsa Yolanda Gutiérrez, Sept. 14, 1945; son of Arquimedes Emiliano Caballero Caballero and Santos Caballero. j-None. k-None. l-DAPC81, 90; DAPC71, 11; DPE, 71, 106; MGF73, 188; HA, 21 July 1980, 10; *Excélsior*, 9 July 1980; *Uno Más Uno*, 9 July 1980, 3; WNM, 30; Q es QAP, 299; Protag., 60; DBGM. 70.

Caballero Escamilla, Raúl
a-May 31, 1919. b-Marín, Nuevo León. c-Early education unknown; law degree, School of Law and Social Sciences, University of Nuevo León, 1945. d-Local Deputy to the State Legislature of Nuevo León, Dist. 3, 1949, 1970; member of the City Council of Monterrey, Nuevo León, 1969, 1974; *Federal Deputy* from the State of Nuevo León, Dist. 3, 1976-79; *Senator* from the State of Nuevo León, 1982-88; *Federal Deputy* from the State of Nuevo León, Dist. 11, 1988-91. e-Joined PRI; Secretary of Labor Action of PRI, State of Nuevo León, 1971-83. f-Agent of the Ministerio Público, 1957-58; President of the Local Arbitration and Conciliation Board, Nuevo León, 1943-48. g-Student leader; Secretary of

the CTM of Nuevo León, 1971-89.
h-None. i-Son of Andrés Caballero
Moreno, blue collar worker, and Alberta
Escamilla Martínez; married Ana María
García Ordóñez. j-None. k-None.
l-DBGM89, 408; Lehr; C de D, 1976-79;
C de D, 1988-91.

Cabañas (Barrientos), Lucio
(Deceased Dec. 1974) a-Dec. 15, 1939.
b-El Porvenir Ejido, San Vicente de
Benítez, Guerrero. c-Completed fifth
grade, Cayaco, Atoyac; teaching
certificate, Normal School, Ayotzinapa,
1963; primary school teacher, Mexcal-
tepec, Guerrero; sixth grade teacher in
Atoyac, Guerrero. d-None. e-Member
of the Civic Association of Guerrero
with *Genaro Vázquez Rojas*; leader of
Vázquez Rojas's guerrilla band after his
death in 1972. f-None. g-Rural normal
school leader, 1959; leader, National
Federation of Peasant Societies, Guerrero. h-Teacher, 1960-67. i-*Nabor A.
Ojeda* took him to Mexico City as a
young child; left teaching in 1967 when
his brother was killed in a teachers'
strike in Atoyac de Alvarez, Guerrero;
son of Cesáro Cabañas and Rafaela
Barrientos Gervacio, peasants. j-None.
k-Led a band of guerrillas that rescued
Genaro Vázquez Rojas from prison,
Apr. 1968; attacked army patrols in
Guerrero, June and Aug. 1971; allegedly
kidnapped gubernatorial candidate
Rubén Figueroa of Guerrero, 1974;
killed under somewhat mysterious
circumstances after the army attacked
his group to rescue *Figueroa*. l-HA, 17
June 1974, 14; HA, 10 June 1974, 12;
HA, 9 Dec. 1974, 6-7.

Cabrera Carrasquedo, Manuel
(Deceased 1955) a-Aug. 6, 1885.
b-Oaxaca, Oaxaca. c-Primary studies in
Oaxaca; preparatory and professional
studies at the Institute of Arts and
Sciences in Oaxaca; engineering degree
from the Military College at Chapul-

tepec, Mexico City, 1908; Professor at
the Military College. d-*Governor of
Oaxaca*, 1952-55, replacing Governor
Manuel Mayoral Heredia who was
removed from office by the federal
government. e-None. f-Assistant Head
of the Commission of Military Studies
of the Secretariat of National Defense;
*Oficial Mayor of the Secretariat of
National Defense*, 1946-52. g-None.
h-None. j-Joined the federal army in
1908; member of the general staff of
General Felipe Angeles; reached the
rank of Brigadier General in 1939. k-In
exile in the United States after the
defeat of Victoriano Huerta, 1914.
l-WWM45, 17; DP70, 315; DGF47, 109;
Peral, 130; HA, 10 Oct. 1955, 15; NYT,
5 Aug. 1952, 4.

Cabrera Muñoz Ledo, Jesús
a-Apr. 20, 1928. b-Apaseo de Grande,
Guanajuato. c-Preparatory studies in
Celaya, Guanajuato; law degree, National School of Law, UNAM; advanced
studies at the School of Law and Econo-
mic Sciences, Paris, France, 1950-52;
special studies in international relations
at the Institute of International Studies,
Paris, France, 1949-52, with a thesis on
"The Principle of International Public
Law"; special studies in international
organization, Switzerland and the
United States on fellowships from the
French government and the United
Nations, 1952; professor at the Colegio
de México, 1965-75. d-*Senator* from
Guanajuato, 1976-80, President of the
Foreign Relations Committee. e-Joined
PRI, 1953; adviser to the CEN of PRI in
international affairs, 1976-80. f-Career
foreign service officer, joined 1953;
reached rank of ambassador; Assistant
Permanent Delegate to UNESCO;
Subdirector General of International
Organizations, Secretariat of Foreign
Relations, 1965; Director General of
Cultural Relations, Secretariat of For-
eign Relations, 1969; Director-in-Chief

of Cultural Affairs, Secretariat of Foreign Relations, 1970-75; Ambassador to Austria, 1981-86; Ambassador to Costa Rica, 1986-90. g-Secretary of Ideological Education, CNOP, 1978-80. h-None. i-Son of Jesús Cabrera Velásquez, farmer, and Margarita Muñoz Ledo Primo; married Muriel del Olmo Tappan, teacher. j-None. k-None. l-MGF69, 179; DPE71, 6; MGF73, 339; BdM, 79; *Excélsior*, 9 July 1980, 22A; Almanaque de Guanajuato, 32; DBGM89, 61.

Cal y Mayor (Sauz), Octavio
a-Dec. 14, 1920. b-Pozo Colorado Cintalapa, Chiapas. c-Primary studies at the Escuela Benito Juárez, Cintalapa (three years), and in the Federal District (three years); secondary education at Public School No. 3, Federal District; preparatory at the Preparatory School for Children of Workers, Coyoacán (two years); medical degree, National School of Medicine, UNAM (six years); Professor of World History; Professor of Medicine, UNAM. d-*Federal Deputy* from the State of Chiapas, Dist. 6, 1970-73; member of the Public Assistance Committee, the Indigenous Affairs Committee, and the Foreign Relations Committee. e-Vice-President of *Efraín Aranda Osorio*'s campaign for governor of Chiapas, 1952; Secretary of Political Action for CNOP in Chiapas, 1952; Director of Public Commissions for the 1952 presidential campaign in Chiapas. f-Director of Otoneurology, General Hospital, Mexico City. g-None. h-Founding member of the Mexican Society of Neurological Sciences; author of several books. i-Half-brother of Rafael Cal y Mayor; son of General Rafael Cal y Mayor. j-None. k-None. l-Directorio, 1970-72; C de D, 1960-72, 104.

Calcáneo, Tito Livio
a-Dec. 7, 1902. b-Villahermosa, Tabasco. c-Primary and secondary studies at the Juárez Institute and the Simon Sarlat School, Tabasco; preparatory studies up to the fourth year, Colegio de Tabasco; no degree. d-Local Deputy to the State Legislature of Tabasco, 1937-38; *Alternate Federal Senator* (replaced the regular Senator) from Tabasco, 1940-46. e-None. f-First Director for Fiscal Services of the State of Tabasco. g-None. h-Director of the Machinery Department, National Irrigation Commission, 1935. j-Joined the navy, 1916; active in the army during the Revolution; rank of Colonel in the army, 1927. k-One of the leaders in the Senate in favor of impounding Axis property in Mexico. l-EBW46, 66; Peral, 133; C de S, 1940-46.

Calderón, Cecilio Carlos Rubén
a-June 5, 1943. b-Temax, Peto, Yucatán. c-Completed secondary studies; teacher certificate, Normal Rural School, Yucatán, 1961-64; graduated, Higher Normal School, Mexico City, 1972-77, with a thesis on the Cuban Revolution; primary school teacher, 1964-78; researcher at the Higher Normal School, Mexico City, 1972-77; principal, various primary schools, Yucatán. d-Mayor of Peto, Yucatán, 1968-70; Local Deputy to the State Legislature of Yucatán, 1971-73; *Federal Deputy* from the State of Yucatán, Dist. 2, 1976-79, Dist. 3, 1982-85, Dist. 2, 1988-91. e-Joined PRI, 1960; President of PRI in Peto, Yucatán, 1975; Secretary of Agrarian Action of PRI, Yucatán, 1977-82. f-None. g-Secretary of the Regional Peasant Committee, Peto, Yucatán, 1977-82; Secretary General of the Agrarian Communities and Peasant Organizations of Yucatán, 1982; Secretary of Colonization of the CEN of the CNC, 1978; Secretary of Conflicts, Student Circle of the Rural Normal School, Yucatán; active in the teachers union in Yucatán. h-None. i-Son of Carlos Calderón Avilés, farmer, and Hermelinda Cecilio Abud; married

Aurelia Sabido Calderón, normal teacher. j-None. k-None. l-Directorio, 1982-85; C de D, 1976-79; Lehr, 525; DBGM89, 409.

Calderón, Esteban B.
(Deceased Mar. 29, 1957) a-May 6, 1876. b-Santa María del Oro, Nayarit. c-Primary in Ixtlán del Río, secondary and preparatory studies; assistant in the Higher School of Tepic, Nayarit; director of a boys' school, Buenavista, Sonora, 1911; rank of 2nd Lieutenant from a military school, 1902. d-Deputy to the Constitutional Convention, 1916-17, coauthor of Article 123; Provisional Governor of Nayarit, 1928-29; Senator from Jalisco, 1918-20; Senator from Nayarit, 1930-34; *Senator from Nayarit, 1952-58,* member of the Rules Committee, First Secretary of the Second National Defense Committee, the First Navy Committee, and the Social Welfare Committee. e-Co-founder with General Manuel Diéguez of the Liberal Union of Humanity in Cananea, Sonora, which was affiliated with the Flores Magon brothers, 1906. f-Governor and Military Commander of Colima, 1914-15; Director General of Taxes, State of Jalisco; Director of Customs in Nuevo León, 1929; President of the National Claims Commission, 1918; President of the Federal Board of Material Improvement, 1925-27; Director of the Purchasing Department, National Railroads of Mexico, 1937. g-Leader of the Cananea mining strike, 1906; sentenced to 15 years in prison, 1909; imprisoned with Manuel Diéguez in San Juan de Ulloa. h-Worked in the mining fields of Sonora, 1904-06. i-Son of Jesús B. Calderón and Vita Ojeda, from the middle class. j-Organizer of volunteers to oppose Victoriano Huerta, 1913; fought under General Obregón; fought against Villa, 1915; rank of Brigade General, Apr. 27, 1917; rank of Division General, 1939. k-Opposed

Venustiano Carranza's imposition of a successor in 1920. l-DGF56, 7, 9-12; Ind. Biog., 30-32; Morales Jiménez, 55-59; Dávila, 111.

Calderón Corona, Esvelia
a-Nov. 18, 1944. b-Morelia, Michoacán. c-Primary studies at the José María Morelos School, Morelia; secondary at the Adolfo López Mateos School, Villa Jiménez, Michoacán. d-Alternate Local Deputy to the State Legislature of Michoacán; *Federal Deputy* from the State of Michoacán, Dist. 3, 1970-73, member of the Child Welfare Committee, the Second Section of the Agrarian Affairs Committee, the Colonization Committee, and the Rural Electrification Committee. e-None. f-None. g-Secretary of Women's Action of the Agrarian Communities of Michoacán; Alternate Secretary of Women's Action of the CEN of the CNC. j-None. k-None. l-C de D, 1970-73, 105; Directorio, 1970-72.

Calderón Martínez, Antonio
a-Oct. 12, 1930. b-Parras, Coahuila. c-Economics degree from the National School of Economics, UNAM, 1952; attended the English Language Institute of the University of Michigan, 1954-55; worked on national income studies at the U.S. Department of Commerce, 1955; graduate studies at American University, Washington, D.C., on a Bank of Mexico scholarship, 1955-56, MA degree, 1956; Professor of Foreign Trade, Ibero-American University; Professor of Economics, UNAM. d-None. e-None. f-Head of the Department of Latin American Trade, Bank of Mexico, 1959-65; Director General of Statistics, Bank of Mexico, National Center of Information on Foreign Trade, Mortgage Bank of Public Works; *Subdirector of the National Bank of Foreign Commerce,* 1965-70; Director General of Trade, Secretariat of Industry and

Commerce, 1970-76; Technical Director of the Center for Specialization for International Trade, 1976. g-None. h-Economist, National Urban and Public Works Mortgage Bank, 1952, Bank of Mexico, 1952-54, 1956-57, and economist for the Secretariat of the Treasury, 1957-59; author. i-Son of Antonio Calderón Lopéz, surgeon, and Aurora Martínez Rodríguez, business women; brother, Guillermo, was ambassador to Sweden, 1971-74. j-None. k-None. l-DBM68, 92-93; BdM,80; Enc. Mex., II, 230; DPE71, 52.

Calderón Rodríguez, Enrique
b-Durango. c-Early education unknown; no degree. d-*Governor of Durango*, 1936-40. f-Assistant Chief of Police of the Federal District, 1934-35; Consul General of the Mexican Foreign Service in San Francisco, California, 1940-43. g-None. h-None. i-Brother, *Ernesto Calderón Rodríguez*, was a Federal Deputy from Durango, 1937-40. j-Joined the Constitutional Army in 1916; career army officer; rank of Colonel, 1927; rank of Brigadier General, Oct. 1, 1943. k-Protests in the Mexican press against his being appointed consul general because of alleged crimes he committed while serving as governor of Durango; presidential candidate in 1945, receiving a minor number of votes; reported by the *New York Times* to being held on charges of fraud by Mexican authorities, 1953. l-WWM45, 17; Peral, 47, 64; Correa 46, 68-69; NYT, 27 Sept. 1953, 23.

Calderón Velarde, Alfonso G.
a-Sept. 19, 1913. b-Calabacillas, Chihuahua. c-Primary studies in San José de Gracia and Los Mochis, Sinaloa, 1920-27; no degree. d-*Federal Deputy* from the State of Sinaloa, Dist. No. 1, 1946-49, member of the First Ejido Committee, the Development of Cooperatives Committee, and the Sugar

Industry Committee; Mayor of Ahome, Sinaloa, 1962-65; *Federal Deputy* from the State of Sinaloa, Dist. No. 1, 1967-70, member of the Second Labor Committee and the First Treasury Committee; *Senator* from the State of Sinaloa, 1970-74; President of the Hydraulic Resources Committee, First Secretary of the Industries Committee, Second Secretary of the Development of Cooperatives Committee and member of the First Balloting Group; *Governor of Sinaloa*, 1975-81. e-Treasurer of PRI in Sinaloa, 1951; President of PRI in Sinaloa, 1951-57. f-*Subsecretary of Fishing Development*, 1982-85. g-Co-founder of the CTM, Sinaloa, 1936; Secretary of the Executive Committee of Local 53 of the Union of Mechanics and Similar Occupations of Mexico, 1931; Secretary of the Union of Workers and Laborers of Northern Sinaloa, 1934; founding member of the Union of Sugar Industry Workers of Mexico, 1937; Secretary General of Local 12 of the Sugar Industry Workers Union, Los Mochis; Secretary of Conflicts and Head of Medical Services, Sugar Industry Workers Union, Los Mochis, 1943-45; Assistant to the Secretary of Political Affairs of the CTM, 1946-49; Assistant to the National Committee of the CTM, 1960-62; Secretary General of the CTM of Sinaloa, 1966-67, 1974; Secretary of Organization of the CEN of the CTM, 1974. h-Electrician, United Sugar Company, Los Mochis, 1931; coauthor of the constitution for the Union of Workers and Farmers of Sinaloa. i-Father was a carpenter. j-None. k-Unexpected choice for PRI candidate for governor, 1974. l-MGF73, 66; C de S, 1970-76, 71; C de D, 1946-49, 67; C de D, 1967-70, 69, 73; DGF47, 11; MGF69, 95; HA, 14 Oct. 1974, 33; *Excélsior*, 22 May 1978, 16; Enc. Mex., Annual, 1977. 550.

Calleja García, Juan Moisés
a-Sept. 4, 1915. b-Federal District.
c-Primary studies in public schools in
the Federal District; secondary studies
at Secondary School No. 5, Federal
District, 1929-31; preparatory studies at
the National Preparatory School, 1931-
33; legal studies, National School of
Law, UNAM, 1933-38, graduating with
a thesis on labor law, 1941; Professor of
Labor Process, National School of Law,
UNAM, 1941-44; professor at the
National Polytechnic Institute, 1942-72;
secondary school teacher, 1942-72.
d-*Federal Deputy* from the Federal
District, Dist. 10, 1964-67, 1970-73,
member of the Department of the
Federal District Committee, the Labor
Section of the Legislative Studies
Committee, the First Government
Committee, the General Accounting
Office Committee, and the First Labor
Committee; *Federal Deputy* from the
Federal District, Dist. 29, 1985-88.
e-Joined the PNR, 1931; President,
District Committee of PRI, Dist. 10,
Federal District, 1966-68, 1970-76.
f-*Justice of the Supreme Court*, June 17,
1975-76, 1976-82, 1982-84. g-Adviser to
the CTM; adviser to the National
Union of Radio and Television Workers;
adviser to the National Electricians
Union; representative of labor to the
Federal Board of Conciliation and
Arbitration; delegate to the International Labor Organization; Chief, Legal
Department, various CTM unions,
1946-75; Secretary General of Delegation 3, Local 10, SNTE, 1973-75.
h-Helped in rewriting reforms for
Article 127 of the Constitution.
i-Married Socorro Castañón; son of Juan
Calleja Benítez, businessman, and
Brigada García Flores. j-None. k-None.
l-*Excélsior*, 18 June 1975, 18; Directorio,
1970-72, 30; DBGM, 641; DBGM87,
446.

Calles (López Negrete), Mario
a-Nov. 9, 1921. b-Federal District.
c-Early education unknown; medical
degree from the National School of
Medicine, UNAM. d-None. e-None.
f-Subdirector of Infant and Maternal
Welfare, Secretariat of Health, 1970;
Director of Medical Services, Federal
Electric Commission; *Subsecretary of
Health*, 1976-80; *Secretary of Health
and Welfare*, 1980-82. g-Adviser to the
ISSSTE. h-Physician, Children's
Hospital, Los Angeles; physician,
Children's Hospital, Mexico City;
physician, Spanish Sanatorium. i-Son of
engineer of Francisco Calles González;
great-nephew of President Plutarco E.
Calles; childhood friend of *José López
Portillo* and *Luis Echeverría*. j-None.
k-None. i-HA, 16 June 1980, 25;
DAPC81, 90; DAPC77, 11; DPE, 115;
Excélsior, 23 Jan. 1980, 2B; *Proceso*, 16
july 1984, 9; *Proceso*, 16 July 1984, 9.

Calles Pordo, Aureo Lino
(Deceased Nov. 20, 1957) a-Sept. 23,
1887. b-Huimanguillo, Tabasco. c-Primary studies in Huimanguillo; no
degree. d-*Interim Governor of Tabasco*,
1935-36. f-Municipal judge of Huiman-
guillo, 1911-13; Director of Infantry of
the Secretary of National Defense,
1946-49; Commander of the Legion of
Honor of the Secretariat of National
Defense; *Subsecretary of National
Defense*, 1949-52. g-None. h-None.
i-Son of peasants Agustín Calles and
Eleodora Pardo; first cousin of Lauro,
José, and Gonzalo Acuña Pardo; brother,
Aquiles, died in the battle for Paraiso,
Tabasco, 1914; married Linda Ramírez;
son, Homero, a naval captain; son,
Aureo, an air force major; and son,
Aquiles, a physician. j-Joined the
Revolution as an enlisted man under his
uncle, General Pedro Cornelio Colorado
Calles, 1913; served in the Constitu-
tional Army, 1913-15; joined General
Salvador Alvarado, 1915; became a

career army officer, Commander of the 20th military zone, Colima, Colima, 1935; Commander of the 30th military zone, Villahermosa, Tabasco, 1937; Military Zone Commander of Yucatán; rank of Brigadier General, 1915, rank of Brigade General, July 16, 1932; reached rank of Division General, July 16, 1942. k-None. l-DGF56; Peral, 136; DP70, 333; DGF51, I, 177; NYT, 24 July 1935, 6; Bulnes, 585-86; López, 141; Almanaque de Tabasco, 154; Dávila, 113.

Caloca, Lauro G.
(Deceased Oct. 17, 1956) a-Aug. 18, 1884. b-San Juan Bautista del Teul, Zacatecas. c-Primary studies in Zacatecas, Zacatecas; law degree from the Institute of Sciences of Zacatecas on a fellowship; professor at the Institute of Sciences of Zacatecas; Director of the library, Institute of Sciences of Zacatecas. d-Federal Deputy from the State of Zacatecas, Dist. 6, 1924-26; Senator from Zacatecas, 1928-30, 1932-34; *Senator* from Zacatecas, 1952-56. e-None. f-Secretary General of Government of the State of Puebla; Interim Governor of Zacatecas; Provisional Governor of Puebla; adviser to the Secretary of Agriculture, 1920-24. g-None. h-Cofounder of the rural school program in Mexico, 1921; Director of *La Voz* of Zacatecas, 1913; Director of *El Independiente* of Zacatecas, 1920; writer for *El Universal*, Mexico City; poet and short story writer. i-Brother of General José R. Caloca; worked as a peasant and carpenter to support mother. j-Fought in the Revolution under Francisco Villa and Emiliano Zapata. k-None. l-DGF56, 8; López, 142; Enc. Mex. 1977, II, 236; Q es Q, 91.

Calzada, Antonio
a-Sept. 9, 1931. b-Querétaro, Querétaro. c-Primary studies at the Instituto Querétaro, Querétaro; secondary and preparatory studies at the Colegio Civil

of Querétaro; architecture degree, School of Architecture, UNAM. d-Mayor of Querétaro, 1970-73; *Governor of Querétaro*, 1973-79. e-Director of the CEPES in Querétaro, 1968-70; accompanied *Luis Echeverría* on his 1969 presidential campaign in Querétaro; delegate of the IEPES of PRI to various cities; Secretary of the CEPES of PRI in Quintana Roo, 1962-64; Delegate to the General Assembly of PRI, 1968. f-Delegate of the Institute of Social Security in Querétaro, 1965-70; Manager of the Federal Potable Water Service, Cozumel, 1962-64; President of the Federal Board of Civil and Moral Improvements, Chetumal and Cozumel, Quintana Roo, 1960-64. g-None. h-Employee of the Secretary of Public Works; employee of the Secretariat of National Patrimony; Manager of the Mexican Works Construction Company, 1958-60. i-Impressed *Echeverría* with his organizational abilities during the 1969 presidential campaign; married to Teresa Rovirosa. j-None. k-None. l-HA, 15 Oct. 1973, 47; Enc. Mex., Annual, 1977, 548-49.

Camacho Guzmán, Rafael
a-Nov. 16, 1916. b-Querétaro. c-Preparatory studies at the Colegio Civil of Querétaro; completed first year of studies in agricultural engineering at the School of Agriculture, Roque, Guanajuato. d-*Senator* from the State of Querétaro, 1976-79; *Governor of Querétaro*, 1979-85. e-Founding member of the PRM. f-None. g-Founding member of the Radio Network Workers Union; member of the Labor Section, Mexican–North American Commission; Secretary of Organization, Congress of Labor; delegate to the International Labor Organization (several times); Secretary General of the Radio, Television, and Related Industries Union, 1961-79; Secretary of Relations of the CEN of the CTM, 1974-80. h-None.

j-None. k-Candidate of *Fidel Velázquez* for the gubernatorial nomination; *Latin America* claims he was imposed by the CTM on *José López Portillo*. l-LA, 26 Jan. 1979, 30; Almanaque de México, 396; C de S, 1976-82.

Camacho López, Aaron
a-July 1, 1908. b-Tulyehualco, Federal District. c-Primary studies in the Federal District; studied at the Normal School, Federal District; law degree, National School of Law, UNAM. d-*Alternate Federal Deputy* from the Federal District, Dist. 12, 1937-40; *Federal Deputy* from the Federal District, Dist. 12, 1940-43, member of the Department of the Federal District Committee; *Federal Deputy* from the Federal District, Dist. 11, 1949-52, member of the Social Action Committee (second year), and alternate member of the First Public Education Committee and the Electric Industry Committee. e-None. f-Inspector General of Delegations, Department of the Federal District; Director of Control of Delegations, Department of the Federal District. g-None. j-None. k-None. l-Peral, 136; C de D, 1937-39; C de D, 1940-42, 48; C de D, 1949-51, 11; López, 143.

Camacho Solís, Víctor Manuel
a-Mar. 30, 1946. b-Federal District. c-Primary studies, Instituto Cumbres, 1954-59; secondary studies, Instituto Cumbres, 1960-62; preparatory studies, Instituto Cumbres, 1963-65; economics degree, National School of Economics, UNAM, 1966-70; MA in Public Affairs, Princeton University, 1972; professor, various subjects, Colegio de México; professor, National Teachers College, 1979-80; Professor of the Mexican Political System, National School of Political and Social Science, UNAM, 1978, and Latin American Studies School, UNAM, 1979. d-None. e-Secretary of Relations, National Youth

Directorate of PRI, 1965; Subdirector of Political Studies, IEPES of PRI, 1981-82; *Secretary General of the CEN of PRI,* 1988. f-Assistant researcher, Department of Economic Studies, Bank of Mexico, 1969; Analyst, Coordinator of Economic and Social Planning, Secretariat of the Presidency, 1972-73; Private Secretary to the Subsecretary of Commercial Planning, *Leopoldo Solís,* 1977; adviser to the Director General of the National Finance Bank, 1979; adviser to the Director General of Economic Policy, Secretariat of Programming and Budget, 1980; *Subsecretary of Regional Development,* Secretariat of Programming and Budget, 1982-86; *Secretary of Urban Development and Ecology,* 1986-88; *Head of the Department of the Federal District,* 1988-93; Peace Commissioner to Chiapas, 1994. g-None. i-Son of Dr. and General Manuel Camacho López, career military officer, and Luz Solís Echeverría; married Guadalupe Velazco Siles (deceased), daughter of *Manuel Velasco Suárez,* governor of Chiapas, 1970-76; father in pharmaceutical business with *Manuel Velasco Suárez* and *Jesús Lozoya Solís,* governor of Chihuahua and personal physician to Salinas family; close student friend of *Emilio Lozoya* and *Carlos Salinas* at UNAM; original disciple of *Leopoldo Solís.* h-None. j-None. k-Leading precandidate for PRI presidential nomination, 1993. l-Q es QAP, 134; *Proceso,* 19 Oct. 1987, 10; *Proceso,* 20 Jan. 1988, 21; DBGM89, 64-65; DBGM, 75.

Camarena Adame, Lidia
a-July 15, 1939. b-Federal District. c-Completed third through sixth grade at the Republic of El Salvador Primary School, Mexico City; secondary studies at the Secondary School No. 6, Mexico City; preparatory studies at the National Preparatory School No. 4; studies in economics at the National School of

Economics, UNAM, 1957-62, economics degree May 2, 1968, with a thesis on development administration; studies in public administration, School of Political and Social Science, UNAM, 1961-63; postgraduate course in personnel administration, Institute of Higher Studies of Monterrey, 1967; studies toward a Ph.D., UNAM; postgraduate work in public administration in Berlin, Germany, and the University of Leeds, England; scholarship from the Secretariat of Public Education; professor, IPN; professor, School of Political and Social Sciences, 1965-82. d-*Federal Deputy* from the Federal District, Dist. 8, 1979-82. e-Coordinator of Logistics for the IEPES during *José López Portillo's* presidential campaign, 1976; Subsecretary of Organization of the CEN of PRI. f-Supervisor, Secretariat of Public Works, 1963-64; Director, Administrative Office, Division of Legal Affairs, Secretariat of Public Works, 1964-65; Director of Organization, Personnel Division, PEMEX, 1968-70; technical adviser, Oficial Mayor of the Secretariat of Human Dwellings and Public Works, 1970-72; adviser, Secretariat of Human Dwellings and Public Works, 1972-73; technical adviser, Subsecretary of Expenditures, Secretariat of the Treasury, 1974-75; Director of Administration and Finance, Productos Pesqueros Mexicanos, 1977-79. g-None. h-Joined the government bureaucracy, Aug. 16, 1963. i-Daughter of Jesús Camarena Ibarra, commander of the central barracks, Mexico City, 1920, and Elena Adame Sánchez. j-None. k-None. l-C de D, 1979-82; Romero Aceves, 689-91.

Camarena Medina, Ramón
a-Dec. 14, 1907. b-Chihuahua, Chihuahua. c-Preparatory studies, Ciudad Juárez; agricultural engineering degree. d-*Federal Deputy* from the State of Veracruz, Dist. 10, 1940-43, member of

the Administration Committee; *Federal Deputy* from the State of Veracruz, Dist. 6, 1946-49, member of the Committee on National Waters and Irrigation, alternate member of the First Ejido Committee. e-None. f-Delegate of the Department of Agrarian Affairs in Chiapas; Director of the Ejido Credit Bank, Veracruz. g-None. j-None. k-None. l-Peral, 37; C de D, 1940-42; C de D, 1946-48, 67.

Camargo Figueroa, Héctor
a-Jan. 6, 1907. b-Federal District. c-Primary studies at Public School No. 47, advanced primary at Antonio Alzate Public School, Mexico City; completed three years of vocational training in mechanical-electrical engineering; enrolled in the Heroic Military College, Feb. 7, 1924, graduating as a 2nd Lieutenant in infantry, July 1, 1927; completed staff and command course and chief of staff course, Higher War College, 1934-37; officer of students, 1st Company, Heroic Military College, 1930-31; professor, Higher War College; Chief of Instruction, Military Medical College. d-None. e-None. f-*Subsecretary of National Defense*, 1975-76. g-None. h-None. i-Father, Angel Camarago, was an accountant; member of the same cadet generation as Jorge Castellanos Domínguez, military zone commander. j-Career army officer; fought in various campaigns against the Cristeros and the supporters of General Escobar (20 battles) in Jalisco, Chihuahua, Durango, Coahuila, and Sonora; junior officer, 51st and 47th Infantry Battalions; 1st Lieutenant, 29th and 37th Infantry Battalions; Subchief of Staff, 31st military zone, Tapachula, Chiapas, 1st Military Zone, Mexico City; and 27th Military Zone, Acapulco, Guerrero; Chief of Staff of the 24th, 22nd, and 5th Military Zones; Commander, 3rd Inspection Committee, Inspector General of the Army; Com-

mander of the 26th Infantry Battalion;
garrison commander, Matamoros,
Tamaulipas; Commander of the 11th
Military Zone, Zacatecas; Commander
of the 25th Military Zone, Puebla, 1973-
75; rank of Division General. l-Rev. de
Ejer., Jan. 1973, 90; Rev. de Ejer., Oct.-
Nov. 1976, 142-43; *Excélsior*, 17 May
1975, 21; Rev. de Ejer., June-Aug. 1982,
53.

Camarillo Ochoa, Elezar
a-June 5, 1923. b-Atlixco, Puebla.
c-Secondary studies at the Workers
Center, Atlixco, Puebla, 1933-37; no
degree. d-Alternate Local Deputy to the
State Legislature of Puebla, 1957-60;
Alternate Federal Deputy from the
State of Puebla, Dist. 4, under *Antonio
J. Hernández*; Local Deputy to the State
Legislature of Puebla, 1966-69, 1975-78;
Federal Deputy from the State of
Puebla, Dist. 4, 1970-73, 1979-82, 1985-
88. e-Joined PNR, 1940; Secretary of
Political Action of PRI, State of Puebla,
1970-73. f-None. g-None. h-Laborer.
j-None. k-None. l-DBGM87, 448; C de
D, 1970-73; C de D, 1979-82; C de D,
1985-88.

Campa (Salazar), Valentín
a-Feb. 14, 1904. b-Monterrey, Nuevo
León. c-Primary studies in Torreón,
Coahuila, 1910-16; completed first year
of secondary; no degree. d-Candidate of
the Workers Bloc for Governor of
Nuevo León against Plutarco Calles Jr.
and General Zuazua, 1934; candidate of
the Mexican Communist Party for
president of Mexico, 1976; Plurinominal
Deputy from the PCM, 1979-82.
e-Member of the Mexican Communist
Party. f-None. g-Cofounder of the
Unitary Mexican Federation of Workers;
attended the International Red Unions
Meeting, Moscow, 1931; member of the
Executive Committee of STFRM, 1943-
47. h-Employed by La Corona, subsid-
iary of Royal Dutch Shell, Tampico,

1920-21; office worker, National
Railroads of Mexico; shipping clerk,
National Railroads of Mexico, Hipólito,
Coahuila, 1922; employee, National
Railroads of Mexico, Ciudad Victoria,
1927. j-None. k-Imprisoned numerous
times by the Mexican government for
his leadership in railroad strikes and
political opposition, including Lecumberri prison, 1930, 1949-52, and Lecumberri and Santa María prisons for the
1958-59 Railroad Strike, 1960-70.
l-Campa; HA, 14 June 1946, 41-42.

Campero, José
a-Oct. 1893. b-Colima, Colima. c-Early
education unknown; no degree. d-Senator from the State of Colima, 1932-34;
Provisional Governor of Colima, Aug.
24, 1935, to Nov. 1, 1935, appointed by
the Senate to replace Governor Saucedo
until new elections could be held;
Federal Deputy from the State of
Colima, Dist. 1, 1937-40. f-Secretary
General of Government of the State of
Colima, 1931-32; Oficial Mayor of the
Senate, 1936-37. g-None. h-Newspaper
reporter in San Luis Potosí, Chihuahua,
and other parts of Mexico. j-Joined the
Constitutionalist Army in Sonora, 1913.
k-Remained loyal to Carranza in 1920.
l-Peral 47, 67-68; letter; Correa 41, 47;
González Navarro, 117.

Campillo Sáinz, Carlos
a-Aug. 7, 1919. b-Federal District.
c-Primary and secondary in the Federal
District; medical degree from the
National School of Medicine, UNAM;
postgraduate work in hospital administration at the World Health Organization; special studies at the National
Institute of Cardiology, Mexico City;
studies in virology in Boston and at the
University of California at Berkeley,
1946-47, 1952-53; received a Pan American Union scholarship for his studies in
Boston; Professor of Infectious Diseases
at the National School of Medicine,

UNAM, 1947-60; Professor at the School of Public Health of the Secretariat of Health and Public Welfare, 1947-68; Professor of Virology at the National School of Medicine, UNAM, 1962-66; Rockefeller scholarship for virology studies at the University of California, 1946-47; Director of the School of Medicine, UNAM, 1968-70. d-None. e-Member of the New Advisory Council of the IEPES, 1972. f-Director of the Laboratory of Virology of the Secretariat of Health and Welfare, 1968; member of the Investigating Committee on Health, Secretariat of Health and Public Welfare; *Subsecretary of Health*, 1970-76. g-None. h-Doctor for IMSS; scientific investigator for IMSS and the Secretariat of Health and Public Welfare; specialist in malaria for the Institute of Health and Tropical Diseases of the Secretariat of Health and Public Welfare; recipient of the U.S. Department of Health award for studies on polio, 1965; recognized specialist and author of over sixty scientific works. i-Brother of *José Campillo Sáinz*; married Haydée Serrano; father, an engineer. j-None. k-None. l-DGF69, 756; letter; HA, 20 Sept. 1971, 48; DBM68, 97-98; BdM, 81; DPE61, 111.

Campillo Sáinz, José
a-Oct. 9, 1917. b-Tlalpan, Federal District. c-Primary and secondary education in the Federal District; legal studies at the Escuela Libre de Derecho; law degree from the National School of Law, UNAM, 1941; specialized studies in Italy, 1938; Professor of Law at the National School of Law, UNAM, 1942-79. d-None. e-None. f-President of the National Center of Productivity; President of the Coordinating Committee of the International Activities of Private Enterprise in Mexico; Mexican representative to the United Nations for industrial development; *Subsecretary of Industry*, Secretariat of Industry and Commerce, 1970-74; *Secretary of Industry and Commerce*, 1974-76; Director General of INFONAVIT, 1976-82; 1982-88, 1988-91. g-Director of the Mining Chamber of Mexico; President of the National Federation of Industrial Chambers (CONCAMIN), 1966-68. h-Director of Legal, Economic, and Social Affairs for the Companía Fundidora de Fierro de Monterrey, 1962-70. i-Son of mining engineer and industrialist, José G. Campillo Rioloza, and María Elena Sáinz Cordero; brother of *Carlos Campillo Sáinz*; married Luz García de la Torre; *Mario de la Cueva*, head of his thesis committee; professor of *Miguel de la Madrid* at UNAM; son, José Ignacio, served as technical secretary of foreign trade cabinet group, 1989. j-None. k-None. l-DBM68, 98; HA, 14 Dec. 1970, 21; DPE71; *Excélsior*, 18 Jan. 1974, 1, 13; HA, 28 Jan. 1974, 16; Romero Aceves, 556-57; DBGM87, 71-72.

Campillo Seyde, Arturo
(Deceased May 25, 1958) a-Aug. 14, 1884. b-Paso del Macho, Orizaba, Veracruz. c-Primary studies in Córdoba, Veracruz; no degree. d-Federal Deputy from the State of Veracruz, Dist 11, 1920-22; Federal Deputy from the State of Veracruz, Dist. 14, 1922-24, 1924-26; Federal Deputy from the Federal District, Dist. 4, 1926-28; Senator from Veracruz, 1928-32, leader of the National Revolutionary Bloc, Secretary of the Permanent Committee of Congress; Federal Deputy from the State of Veracruz, Dist. 10, 1935-37. f-Governor of Quintana Roo, 1930-31; federal customs official, Reynosa, 1952. g-None. i-Close friend of General *Miguel Alemán*, helped *Miguel Alemán's* legal career. j-Supporter of Félix Díaz during the Revolution; joined Obregón against Carranza, 1920; rank of Brigadier General, Jan. 1, 1924; zone commander of Tlaxcala and Querétaro.

k-Expelled from the PNR in 1930 as a leader of the "Whites" on the permanent committee of Congress. l-Peral, 138; DP70, 342; López, 147; Meyer, No. 12, 114, 125; Alvarez Corona, 115; Dávila, 194.

Campos Gutiérrez, Rosa María
a-Feb. 8, 1941. b-Jalapa, Veracruz. c-Early education unknown; degree in science and techniques of information, Women's University of Mexico; Professor of Introductory Journalism, Women's University of Mexico; graduate in theater and set design from the Centro Universitario de Teatro. d-*Federal Deputy* from the State of Veracruz, Dist. 22, 1979-82, member of the Editorial Affairs Committee, the Radio, Television, and Film Committee, and the Information and Complaints Committee. e-Director of Public Relations during the gubernatorial campaign of *Rafael Hernández Ochoa* in Veracruz, 1974; delegate of the Press and Publicity Secretary of the CEN of PRI to Veracruz during *José López Portillo*'s presidential campaign, 1976; adviser to Women's Action of PRI in the Federal District, 1977-79. f-Director of Press and Public Relations for the Metro, 1976-78. g-Executive Secretary of the National Union of Editorial Writers, 1977-78. h-Reporter for *Ovaciones*, 1964-78; columnist for *Ovaciones*, 1978-81; news reporter on the Zabludowsky 24-hour show, 1964-75; various television programs, 1973-75, including Nescafe News and Luis Spota's program. i-None. j-None. k-None. l-Directorio, 1979-82, 18; Almanaque de México, 65, 70, 71; Romero Aceves, 692-94.

Campos Ortiz, Pablo
(Deceased 1963) a-Mar. 17, 1898. b-San Juan del Río, Querétaro. c-Preparatory at the National Preparatory School, Mexico City; studies in law from the National Law School, 1916-18; law

degree from the University of Rio de Janeiro, 1919-22; Professor of International Law at the National School of Law, UNAM. d-None. e-None. f-Joined the Mexican Foreign Service, Third Secretary of the Mexican legation in Brazil, 1921-23; Assistant to the Head of Protocol, Secretariat of Foreign Relations, 1923; Third Secretary to the Mexican legation in Spain, 1925-26; First Secretary and adviser to the Embassy in Washington, D.C.; Chargé d'affaires of the Embassy in Honduras, 1925; Chargé d'affaires in Madrid, Washington, The Hague, Nicaragua, and Chile; Director General of Political Affairs for the Secretariat of Foreign Relations, 1943-44; *Oficial Mayor of the Secretariat of Foreign Relations*, 1944-46, 1952-56; *Ambassador to Great Britain*, 1957-61; *Subsecretary (2) of Foreign Relations*, 1961-63. g-None. h-None. i-Knew *Rafael de la Colina* at the National Law School as a student; married Ivonne Lynch; son, Pablo, an engineer; son of lawyer Pablo Campos Aguilar and Dolores Ortiz; sister, Esperanza, married businessman Alberto Hubbe Patron. j-None. k-None. l-WWM45, 18; DGF56, 123; DP70. 344-45; letter, EBW46, 25; Peral, 139-40; DPE61, 15; WB48, 962; DPE61, 15.

Campos Salas, Octaviano
a-Mar. 22, 1916. b-San Luis Potosí, San Luis Potosí. c-Primary studies in San Luis Potosí; attended Normal School in San Luis Potosí, 1926-32; economics degree from the National School of Economics, UNAM, 1940-44, with a thesis on the "Intervention of the State in the Wheat and Flour Market"; award for outstanding student in economics, 1942; graduate work in economics on a scholarship at the University of Chicago, 1944-47, and in the State of California, 1948; rural teacher, San Luis Potosí; inspector of rural schools, State of San Luis Potosí, 1934; Director of

Elementary Schools of the Federal Government for the Federal District and for the States of San Luis Potosí, Guanajuato, and Coahuila, 1940; in the field of education from 1931-44; most distinguished student of the U.S. Department of Commerce course on national income, 1950; Professor of Economics, National School of Economics, UNAM; Professor of Public Administration in Costa Rica, 1955; Director of the National Schools of Economics, UNAM, 1963-64. d-None. e-Director of the Institute of Political, Social, and Economic Studies of PRI, 1963-64. f-Director General of Statistics of the Secretariat of Industry and Commerce; head of the Department of Economic Studies for the Bank of Mexico, 1953; head of the Balance of Payments Department of the International Monetary Fund, 1950-52; Subdirector of Census and Statistics, Secretariat of the Treasury, 1942-49; Director General of Trade, Secretariat of Industry and Commerce, 1962-64; Manager, Bank of Mexico, 1953-64; *Secretary of Industry and Commerce,* 1964-70; Ambassador to West Germany, 1979-82. g-*Secretary General of the Mexican Teachers Union,* 1938-40. h-Assistant economist for the Secretariat of the Treasury; adviser to the Secretary of Industry and Commerce; economist for the United Nations; economist for the Center for Monetary Studies of Latin America, 1949; author of numerous articles on economic subjects; member of numerous economic commissions. i-Student of *Eduardo Bustamante* at the National School of Economics; friend of *Jorge Espinosa de los Reyes* at UNAM. j-None. k-Marxist as a student and normal teacher; supported *Narciso Bassols'* candidacy as a federal deputy in 1943. l-WWMG, 10; HA, 7 Dec. 1964, 19; DBM68, 99-100; Correa 41, 536; Por Qué, 16 Oct. 1969, 14-17; Enc. Mex., 1977, II, 311-312; *Excélsior,* 28 July 1979.

Campos Vega, Juan Gualberto
a-Apr. 15, 1950. b-Mérida, Yucatán. c-Early education unknown; economics degree, IPN, 1972-77; professor, National School of Political Education, PPS, 1981. d-Alternate Local Deputy to the State Legislature of Yucatán, Dist. 3, 1970-73; *Plurinominal Federal Deputy* from the PPS, 1982-85; Local Deputy to the State Legislature of Yucatán, 1988-90; *Plurinominal Federal Deputy* from the PPS, 1991-94. e-Joined the PPS, Feb. 1972; member of the Popular Socialist Youth, 1969-73; Youth Director of the PPS in the Federal District, 1973; Secretary of Finances of the Popular Socialist Youth, 1973-78; representative of the PPS to the National Voter Registration Committee, 1978; Secretary General of the Popular Socialist Youth, 1978-81. f-Administrative employee, IMSS, 1974-78. g-Leader of the Student Federation of the South East. h-Economist. i-Son of Gualberto Campos Alarcón, merchant, and Ninfa Mirey Vega Sabido, teacher; married Griselda Tibui Ortiz Pérez. j-None. k-None. l-Directorio, 1982-85; C de D, 1982-85; Lehr, 618; DBGM, 482; DBGM92, 434.

Canale (Muñoz), Eleazar
a-1906. b-Sonora. c-Early education unknown; law degree from the Escuela Libre de Derecho, Mexico City, Oct. 29, 1929. d-*Federal Deputy* from the State of Hidalgo, Dist. 1, 1937-40. f-Member of the Federal Board of Conciliation and Arbitration, Federal District; labor arbitrator for the Secretariat of Labor; head of the Legal Department of the Federal District, 1946-48; *Subsecretary of Labor,* 1948-52; Judge of the Fourth Chamber of the Federal Tax Court, 1952-70. g-None. h-Legal adviser to the Department of the Federal District. i-Brother of Senator *Antonio Canale,* 1946-52; served on Federal Board of conciliation with *Manuel Ramírez*

Vázquez. j-None. k-None. l-HA, 15 Oct. 1948, 3; DGF56, 557; DGF69, 389; DPE51, 399.

Canales Najjar, Tristán Manuel
a-May 24, 1951. b-Federal District. c-Early education unknown; law degree, National School of Law, UNAM, professor, Institute of Political Education, CEN of PRI. d-*Federal Deputy from the Federal District, Dist. 38, 1979-82.* e-Coordinator of the National Committee of Civic Action and Voter Education of PRI; representative of the CEN of PRI to the Technical and Vigilance Committee of the National Voters Registration Commission; Subsecretary General of the CEN of PRI, 1978; *Secretary of Finances of the CEN of PRI, 1976-78;* Private Secretary to the President of the CEN of PRI, *Carlos Sansores Pérez,* 1978. f-Private Secretary to the Director General of Industrial Property, Secretariat of Industry and Commerce, 1973; Treasurer of the Chamber of Deputies, 1973-76; Oficial Mayor of the Senate, 1976. g-President, 1974 Law Generation, graduate law program, UNAM. h-None. i-Son of *Tristán Canales Valverde,* subsecretary of labor, 1964-70; political disciple of *Carlos Sansores Pérez.* j-None. k-None. l-Protag., 64; C de D, 1979-82.

Canales Valverde, Tristán
(Deceased 1970s) a-1909. b-Veracruz, Veracruz. c-Early education unknown; preparatory studies at the Veracruz Institute; law degree from the National School of Law, UNAM, 1933. d-None. e-None. f-Appeals judge of Matamoros, Tamaulipas, 1934; Secretary General of Government of the State of Tamaulipas; head of the Department of Legal Complaints for the Federal District, 1951; Director General of the Division of Government, Secretariat of Government, 1952-62; *Oficial Mayor of the Secretariat of Labor,* 1964; *Subsecretary*

B of Labor, 1964-70. g-First Secretary General of the Workers Union of the Office of the Attorney General of the Federal District and Federal Territories, 1939. h-Practicing lawyer; Assistant Secretary of the Federal Electricity Commission; technical adviser to the Mexican Social Security Institute; held numerous judicial posts. i-Father of *Tristán Canales Najjar,* federal deputy from the Federal District, 1979-82, and Secretary of Finances of the CEN of PRI, 1976; married Angelina Najjar. j-None. k-Candidate for governor of Veracruz. l-*Hoy,* 25 May 1968, 60; DGF56, 83; DGF51, 479; HA, 21 Dec. 1964, 10; DPE61, 12; Pasquel, 54.

Candia (Galván), Isidro
a-May 2, 1897. b-Sanctorun, Tlaxcala. c-Primary studies at Calpulalpan, Tlaxcala; teaching certificate. d-Local deputy to the State Legislature of Tlaxcala, 1934; Mayor of Tlaxcala; *Governor of Tlaxcala,* 1937-41. e-None. f-Director of the Department of Indigenous Affairs, 1941. g-None. j-Joined the Revolution under the Zapatista forces, 1912; Colonel in the Army. k-Under investigation in 1971 by the government for alleged illicit land dealings in Tlaxcala. l-LAD, Oct. 1971; letter; D de Y, 3 Dec. 1940, 6; Peral, 142; PS, 0931.

Cañedo Benítez, Alejandro
a-Feb. 25, 1939. b-Early education unknown; public accounting degree, ITAM, 1957-62, with a thesis on internal control and fraud; professor, Autonomous University of Puebla, 1967-69. d-*Federal Deputy* (Party Deputy from PAN), 1973-76; *Plurinominal Federal Deputy* from PAN, 1985-88. e-President of PAN, State of Puebla, 1982-84. f-None. g-None. h-Public accountant. i-Son of Roberto Cañedo and Josefina Benítez. j-None. k-None. l-DBGM87, 449; C de D, 1985-88; Lehr; C de D, 1973-76.

Cañedo Vargas, Jorge
a-Sept. 5, 1947. b-Morelia, Michoacán.
c-Primary and secondary studies in
Michoacán; teaching certificate, Higher
Normal School of Puebla, 1966-68; law
degree, School of Law, University of
Michoacán, 1970-74; primary school
teacher, various schools, Morelia.
d-*Federal Deputy* from the State of
Michoacán, Dist. 2, 1973-76, 1982-85.
e-Secretary of the Youth Organization
of PRI in Michoacán, 1970-73; President
of the Youth Organization of PRI in
Michoacán, 1971-73; delegate of the
National Youth Organization of PRI to
various states; President of the National
Council of Revolutionary Youth of PRI,
1973-76; participated in *José López
Portillo*'s presidential campaign, 1976;
Subsecretary of Social Action of the
CEN of PRI, 1981-82. f-Private Secretary of the Director General of the
ISSSTE, 1973-75; representative of the
State of San Luis Potosí in Mexico City,
1982. g-Member of the SNTE; President
of the Generation of lawyers of Michoacán; Director of Youth Organization of
the FSTSE in Michoacán, 1970-71;
general adviser, SNTE, 1980-82.
h-National oratory champion. i-Son of
Simón Canedo de la Vega, printer, and
Sara Vargas, normal teacher. j-None.
k-None. l-C de D, 1983-76; C de D,
1982-85; Directorio, 1982-85; Lehr, 299;
DBGM, 482.

Cano Escalante, Francisco
a-Aug. 9, 1931. b-Esperanza, Puebla.
c-Early education unknown; public
accounting degree, School of Banking
and Administration, UNAM, 1950-54.
d-None. e-None. f-President of the
Board, National Sugar Finance Bank,
1972-76; General Coordinator, Unified
Program for Basic Products, Secretariat
of the Presidency, 1980-82; *Subsecretary of Regulation and Foodstuffs*,
Secretariat of Trade and Industrial
Development, 1982-85. g-President,
National Chamber of Commerce of
Mexico City, 1966-67; President of
Concanaco, 1968-69; President, Na-
tional Sugar Industry Union, 1972-76.
h-Director General of Impusora de
Cuenca de Paploapan, 1970-72. i-Son of
Francisco Cano Sansebastian, industri-
alist and businessman, and Emilia
Escalante Vallejo; married Ana Rangel
Campos. j-None. k-None. l-Q es QAP,
191; DBGM, 79.

Canto Carrillo, Nicolás
a-Dec. 7, 1917. b-Hecelchacan, Cam-
peche. c-Primary studies in Hecel-
chacan, Campeche; secondary studies in
Campeche, Campeche; rural teaching
certificate from the Normal Rural
School, Campeche; teacher in Calkini,
Campeche and other towns. d-Mayor of
Calkini, Campeche, 1942-44; Local
Deputy to the State Legislature of
Campeche, 1947-50; Mayor of Calkini,
1952; *Senator* from the State of Cam-
peche, 1958-64, Secretary of the Gran
Comisión (1st year), President of the
Development of Cooperatives Commit-
tee, Second Secretary of the Second
Naval Committee and the Insurance
Committee, alternate member of the
Second Labor Committee, the National
Properties Committee, and the Special
Legislative Studies Committee. e-Pre-
sident of PRI in the State of Campeche,
1956-58; general delegate of the CEN of
PRI in Campeche, 1958. f-None.
g-Active member of the CTM; Secretary
General of the League of Agrarian
Communities, State of Campeche.
h-Began teaching in 1934. i-Parents
were peasants. j-None. k-None.
l-Func., 133; C de S, 1961-64, 14, 53.

Canto Echeverría, Humberto
a-1900. b-Mérida, Yucatán. c-Primary
studies in Mérida; professional studies
from Rensselaer Polytechnic Institute
and from the Brooklyn Polytechnic
Institute; courses from Ohio Northern

University; engineering degree. d-*Governor of Yucatán*, 1938-42. e-None. f-Director, Department of Public Works, State of Yucatán, 1930-34. g-None. h-Manager of a sugar plantation in Cuba; business manager for a newspaper, 1931. i-Father a prominent attorney and public notary in Mérida. j-None. k-None. l-HA, 12 June 1942, 30.

Cantu Estrada, José
(Deceased Nov. 28, 1938) a-1904. b-Nuevo Laredo, Tamaulipas. c-Primary studies in Nuevo Laredo; preparatory studies in Ciudad Victoria; law degree, National School of Law, UNAM, 1928. d-*Federal Deputy* from the State of Tamaulipas, Dist. 1, 1937-38, President of the Chamber of Deputies; answered President *Cárdenas'* 3rd state of the union address. e-None. f-Member of the Advisory Council to the President of Mexico; President of the Federal Conciliation and Arbitration Board, 1933; Chief of the Office of Publications, Secretariat of Foreign Relations; *Subsecretary of Labor*, 1935-37. g-None. j-None. k-None. l-*Excélsior*, 24 Aug. 1979, 14A; C de D, 1935-37; PS, 954.

Cantú Jiménez, Esteban
(Deceased 1966) a-Nov. 27, 1880. b-Linares, Nuevo León. c-Primary studies in Linares, Nuevo León; special classes in Morelia, Michoacán; enrolled in the National Military College, 1897. d-*Senator* from the State of Baja California del Norte, 1952-58, President of the Second Naval Committee, Second Secretary of the Military Health Committee, member of the Second Balloting Group. e-None. g-None. i-Brother of José T. Cantú, federal deputy from Baja California, 1917-18. j-Career Army officer; served in the 7th Cavalry Regiment, Mexico City; Instructor in the Second Army Reserve, Chihuahua, Jalisco, and Zacatecas, 1902-03; fought

against the Yaquis in Sonora, 1903-06; rank of Major, 1911; fought in the Cuesta del Gato, Chihuahua; supported Villa, 1914; Constitutionalist nominally, but really independent, 1915; Chief of the Federal Garrison, Mexicali, 1914-17; Governor and Military Commander of Baja California del Norte, 1917-20; reached the rank of Colonel. k-Had to flee to the United States in 1914 for opposing the assassination of Madero; lived in Los Angeles, California, during the 1920s and 1930s. l-Ind. Biog., 32-33; DGF56, 5, 8, 10-13; DP70, 354.

Cantú Peña, Fausto
a-May 12, 1941. b-Monterrey, Nuevo León. c-Economics degree, Technical Institute of Higher Studies, Monterrey, Mar. 6, 1964; Eisenhower Fellowship in the United States for studying the theory and practice of industrial, agricultural, and tourist development, 1967; studies at the National Center of Productivity; Professor of General Economics and Business Economics, Technical Institute of Higher Studies, Monterrey. d-None. e-Director of the CEPES of PRI for Nuevo León. f-Economic investigator for the National Minimum Wage Commission; Director of the Commission for Industrial Growth and Economic Development of the State of Nuevo León, 1970; Gerente, Nacional Financiera; Director General of the Mexican Coffee Institute, 1971-77. g-Treasurer of the College of Economists for Nuevo León. h-None. i-Married María Felicitas. j-None. k-Convicted of fraud committed while Director General of the Mexican Coffee Institute, 1978. l-DBM68, 109; HA, 5 Nov. 1973, 21; DBM70, 111.

Canudas Orezza, Luis Felipe
(Deceased Oct. 21, 1978) a-Sept. 8, 1911. b-Campeche, Campeche. c-Primary studies at the Public School Modelo No. 3, Ciudad del Carmen;

preparatory studies at the Liceo Carmelita, Ciudad del Carmen, and at the National Preparatory School, 1928; law degree from the National School of Law, UNAM, Dec. 20, 1934 (honorable mention), with a thesis on "Lesions in Civil Law"; LLD from the National School of Law, UNAM, Apr. 10, 1950; Professor of General Theory of the State and Constitutional Law, UNAM, 1938-68; professor of graduate courses in law for the LLD, UNAM, 1950-68; guest professor at various state universities. d-None. e-None. f-Judge of the Second District, Civil Section, Federal District, 1932-34; Agent of the Ministerio Público, Office of the Attorney General, 1935; auxiliary agent, Office of the Attorney General, 1936-37; Director, Office of Amparo, Department of the Federal District, 1938-40; Subdirector of the Advisory Office of the Attorney General of Mexico, 1941-44; Director of the Advisory Office of the Attorney General of Mexico, 1944-49; *Assistant Attorney General of Mexico (2)*, 1949-51; *Assistant Attorney General of Mexico (1)*, 1951-52; Director, Legal Department, National Railroads of Mexico, 1953-56; Director of the Office of Amparo, Secretariat of the Treasury, 1959-65; Director General of the Legal and Advisory Department, Office of the Attorney General, 1965-68; *Supernumerary Justice of the Supreme Court*, 1968-70; *Subsecretary General of Legal Affairs of the Department of Agrarian Affairs and Colonization*, 1971-75 (first appointee to this position); *Supernumerary Justice of the Supreme Court*, 1976-78. g-None. h-Judicial Porter, Third District, Federal District; Scribe and Section Chief for Amparos, Sixth District, Federal District; author of many articles and codes. i-Attended college with *Antonio Luna Arroyo*; brother, Eduardo, a surgeon; son of Eduardo Canudas Sánchez and Carmen Orezza. j-None. k-None. l-HA, 26 July

1971, 16; DGF51, 535; DGF47, 309; DGF69, 120; DPE65, 210; D de Y, 26 July 1971; *Justicia*, 1968; *Excélsior*, 26 Oct. 1978, 22A.

Cárdenas (del Río), Dámaso
(Deceased Feb. 4, 1976) a-1898. b-Jiquilpan de Juárez, Michoacán. c-Early education unknown, no degree. d-*Senator* from the State of Michoacán, 1932-34; *Governor of Michoacán*, 1950-56. e-None. f-Interim Governor of Michoacán, 1930; Oficial Mayor of the Secretariat of the Treasury, 1934-35. g-None. h-Director of a construction firm. i-Son of Dámaso Cárdenas, a small groceryman, and Felicitas del Río; grandfather, Francisco Cárdenas, was a soldier in the Reform; brother of President *Lázaro Cárdenas*; married Baby Castellanos. j-Participated in the Revolution; reached rank of Division General. k-Declined the nomination for governor, 1939. l-Strode, 302; Romero Flores, 72; Novo35, 339; DGF56, 96; Michaels, 8; DPE51, I, 90; *Excélsior*, 5 Feb. 1976.

Cárdenas (del Río), Lázaro
(Deceased Oct. 19, 1970) a-May 21, 1895. b-Jiquilpan de Juárez, Michoacán. c-Primary studies in Jiquilpan de Juárez; no formal education after 1909. d-Governor of Michoacán, 1928-32, with numerous leaves of absence; *President of Mexico*, 1934-40. e-President of the CEN of the PNR, 1930-31. f-Interim Governor of Michoacán, 1920; Secretary of Government, Aug. 28, 1931 to Oct. 15, 1931; Secretary of War and Navy, 1933; Secretary of National Defense, 1942-45; Executive Director of the Cuenca del Tepalcatepec, 1947-60; Executive Director of the Cuenca del Río Balsas, 1960-70. g-None. h-Worked as a printer, 1911-13. i-Brother of *Dámaso Cárdenas*; married Amalia Solorzano; son of Dámaso Cárdenas Piñedo, a small grocer, and Felícitas del

Río Amezcua; father of *Cuauhtémoc Cárdenas Solorzano.* j-Joined the Revolution, 1913, under the forces of General Guillermo García Aragón as a 2nd Captain and member of his staff; fought under General Obregón against Emiliano Zapata, 1914; Major in charge of a detail of the 22nd Cavalry Regiment; fought under the forces of Lucio Blanco, 1914; fought the forces of Francisco Villa under General Plutarco Calles, 1915; fought against the de la Huerta rebellion during which he was captured by *Enrique Estrada,* 1923; rank of Brigadier General, 1924; Commander of the military zone of Tampico, 1925; rank of Division General, 1928; fought against the Cristeros, 1928; Commander of the 19th Military Zone, Puebla, Nov. 1, 1933 to Jan. 1, 1934; Commander of special Pacific Defense Zone, 1941-42. k-Saved General *Enrique Estrada* from a military execution, 1924, who later served as a federal deputy during his presidency; active in the National Liberation Movement in the 1960s; leader of one of the largest political groups in Mexico until his death. l-WWM45, 18-19; DBM68, 114; EBW46, 29; DGF56, 414; *Hoy,* 31 Oct. 1970, 15-16; DP70, 362-63; 2374-75; Strode, 302; DGF50, II, 451; WB54, 162; IWW40, 172; Q es Q, 100-01; *Annals,* Mar. 1940; Morton, 88; Enc. Mex., 1977, II, 361-67; NYT, 20 Oct. 1970; *Justicia,* June 1970.

Cárdenas García, Virgilio
a-Oct. 31, 1914. b-Monterrey, Nuevo León. c-Early education unknown; no degree. d-Member of the City Council of Monterrey; *Federal Deputy* from the State of Nuevo León, Dist. 3, 1961-64, member of the First Railroad Committee and alternate member of the Second Labor Committee; *Federal Deputy* from the State of Nuevo León, Dist. 3, 1967-70, member of the Electric Industry Committee. e-Member of PRI. f-None. g-Union leader. h-Private accountant.

i-Married María Esther Aguillen. j-None. k-None. l-Directorio, 1967-70, 75; C de D, 1961-64, 73.

Cárdenas González, Enrique
a-1927. b-Ciudad Victoria, Tamaulipas. c-Primary studies in Ciudad Victoria; secondary studies in Ciudad Victoria; engineering studies at the Escobar Brothers Agricultural School, Ciudad Juárez, Chihuahua. d-Mayor of Ciudad Victoria, 1969-70; *Senator* from the State of Tamaulipas, 1970–72, President of the Second Petroleum Committee, Second Secretary of the Industries and the Public Works Committees, member of the First Balloting Committee, member of the Fishing Committee and Secretary of the First Instructive Section of the Grand Jury; *Governor of Tamaulipas,* 1975-81. e-President of the Local Electoral Committee, Ciudad Victoria, 1963; *Secretary of Social Action of the CEN of PRI,* 1971-72; general delegate of the CEN of PRI to Baja California del Sur, 1971-72. f-*Subsecretary of Tax Investigation,* 1972-74. g-None. h-Owner of several radio stations. i-Boyhood friend of *Luis Echeverría* in Ciudad Victoria where Echeverría's father worked; brother, Jorge, federal deputy, 1985-88 and member of PARM. j-None. k-Lost as a precandidate for governor of Tamaulipas to *Manuel Ravize,* 1967. l-*Excélsior,* 1 June 1974, 16, 12 Nov. 1973; Enc. Mex., Annual, 1977, 551; *Novedades de Yucatán,* 19 Jan. 1972, 1; HA, 31 Jan. 1972, 19; Loret de Mola, 91, 146; DBGM87, 449; *Excélsior,* 4 Dec. 1983, 20.

Cárdenas Huerta, Gustavo
a-1905. b-Saltillo, Coahuila. c-Primary studies in Saltillo, Coahuila; preparatory studies at the Ateneo Fuente School, Saltillo; legal studies, National School of Law, UNAM, 1924-28, graduating 1930. d-*Senator* from the State of Coahuila, 1952-58, President of

the Committee on Water and National Irrigation, First Secretary of the Federal District Committee, Secretary of the First Justice Committee, member of the Second Balloting Committee and the Special Legislative Studies Committee, and First Secretary of the Second Instructive Group of the Grand Jury. e-*Secretary General of the CEN of the PRM*, 1940. f-Agent of the Ministerio Público in the Federal District, 1930-36; Public Defender, 1936-37; Agent of the Ministerio Público, 1937-38; Defense Attorney for Labor, 1938-39; Justice of the Superior Court of Justice of the Federal District, 1940-46; *Oficial Mayor of Hydraulic Resources*, 1946-52. g-None. h-Worked way through law school; author of several books. i-Political disciple of *Antonio Villalobos*; son of Fernando de Cárdenas and Adelaida Hurtado. j-None. k-None. l-Ind. Biog., 34-35; DGF56, 5, 9-11, 13-14; DGF51, I, 413.

Cárdenas Rodríguez, Antonio
(Deceased 1969) a-Oct. 6, 1903. b-Hacienda la Trinidad, Municipio General Cepeda, Coahuila. c-Early education unknown; enrolled in the National Military College, 1923; transferred to the Military Aeronautics School, graduating as an aviator in 1927; combat courses and air staff courses, United States, 1944. d-None. e-None. f-*Chief of the Mexican Air Force*, 1946-52. g-None. h-Flew for the Air Mail Service, 1927. i-Married Xóchitl Zamora; son of Sabino Cárdenas and María M. Rodríguez. j-Career Air Force officer; pilot of the Good Neighbor flight from San Francisco to Buenos Aires, 1940; observer of the Mexican government attached to the U.S. forces in North Africa, 1943; Commander of the Mexican Expeditionary Air Forces, Squadron 201, 1945; participated in combat operations in the Pacific, 1945; rank of Brigadier General, 1952.

k-None. l-DP70, 363; DGF51, 180; Enc. Mex., 1977, II, 368; WWM45, 19.

Cárdenas (Solorzano), Cuauhtémoc
a-May 1, 1934. b-Federal District. c-Preparatory studies at the National Preparatory School; Civil Engineering degree, National School of Engineering, UNAM, Jan. 22, 1957; special training at the Ministry of Reconstruction, Paris, France, 1957-58, and at Electricity of France, Paris, 1957-58; Bank of Mexico fellowship to work for Krupp in Germany, 1958; special studies in regional and urban planning. d-*Senator* from the State of Michoacán, 1976; *Governor of Michoacán*, 1980-86. e-Member of the National Executive Committee of the National Liberation Movement, 1961-62; student supporter of the presidential campaign of General Miguel Henríquez, 1951; joined PRI, 1967; member of the IEPES of PRI, *Luis Echeverría*'s presidential campaign, 1970; cofounder of the Democratic Current, PRI, 1986; presidential candidate of the PFCRN, PARM, PMS, PPS, 1988; *President of the PRD*, 1989-93; presidential candidate of the PRD, 1993. f-Planner, Río Balsas, Secretariat of Hydraulic Resources, 1964-69; Director, Public Trust Fund of Lázaro Cárdenas City, 1971-76; Subdirector of Las Truchas, 1969-74; *Subsecretary of Forest Resources and Fauna*, Secretariat of Agriculture, 1976-80. g-None. h-Director of Constructora Indé, S.A., 1956-57; practicing engineer, 1960. i-Son of President *Lázaro Cárdenas*; nephew of Roberto Ruiz del Río, secretary general of government in Michoacán; nephew of *Dámaso Cárdenas*, governor of Michoacán, 1950-56; in business with *Heberto Castillo*, 1956-57; business partner of *Gonzalo Martínez Corbalá*. j-None. k-Some observers believe he won the 1988 presidential election. l-BdM, 84; C de S, 1976-82; HA, 18 Aug. 1980, 31; Almanaque of México, 367; letters.

Cardiel Reyes, Raúl
a-Nov. 1, 1915. b-Saltillo, Coahuila.
c-Primary studies at the Colegio
Roberts and the school attached to the
State Normal School, 1921-26; secondary education at the Ateneo Fuente del
Saltillo, 1927, and at the University of
San Luis Potosí, 1933-34; preparatory
studies at the University of San Luis
Potosí, 1934-35; law degree, University
of San Luis Potosí, Dec. 12, 1939;
philosophy studies at UNAM, 1946-49;
MA in philosophy, 1961, magna cum
laude; audited courses in law and
political science from the University of
Southampton, England, 1953; Professor
of the History of Philosophical Doctrines, University of San Luis Potosí,
1939-44; Professor of Logic, National
Preparatory School, 1947-62; Professor
of Administrative Law at the School of
Public Health, 1950; Professor of World
History and of Political Theory, School
of Political and Social Sciences, UNAM,
1956-72; Professor of Law, National
School of Law, UNAM, 1958-61; many
other teaching positions. d-None.
e-None. f-Secretary General of the
Board of Conciliation and Arbitration of
the State of San Luis Potosí, 1934-38;
consulting lawyer to the State of San
Luis Potosí, 1940; Chief of Public
Defenders for the State of San Luis
Potosí, 1941; legal adviser, Movie
Directors Union, 1945-48; Secretary of
Scholarly Services of UNAM, 1954-56;
Director General of Scholarly Services
of UNAM, 1956-61; Private Secretary to
the Subsecretary of the Presidency,
1962-63; legal adviser to the Subsecretary of the Presidency, Feb. to Sept.
1962; Private Secretary to the Secretary
of Public Education, 1964-70; cultural
adviser to the Secretary of Public
Education, 1971-76; Director General of
Channel 13 (Government television
station), 1978. g-Secretary of Labor and
Strikes of the National Union of Employees of the Secretariat of National

Patrimony, 1951-54; founder and Auxiliary Secretary of the Executive Committee of the National Association of
Universities and Institutions of Higher
Learning. h-Lawyer for the Legal Department of the Secretariat of National
Patrimony, 1947-48; lawyer for the Secretariat of National Patrimony, 1948-
54; practicing lawyer, San Luis Potosí,
1939-45; practicing lawyer, Federal
District, 1945-49. i-Friend of *Agustín
Yáñez*; father, Felipe Cardiel Reyes, a
small businessman; married María del
Socorro Ramírez. j-None. k-None.
l-DPE70, 102; DBM68, 114-15; DGF47,
264; DBM70, 116-17; Enc. Mex., IV,
225; Enc. Mex., II, 162-63; letter.

Carpizo (McGregor), Jorge
a-Apr. 12, 1944. b-Campeche, Campeche. c-Primary studies at the Justo
Sierra Méndez Primary School, Campeche, 1951-56; secondary studies at the
Instituto Campechano, Campeche,
Campeche, 1956-59; preparatory studies
at La Salle University, Federal District,
1961-62; law degree from the National
School of Law, UNAM, with a 9.9 GPA
and honorable mention, 1962-67; MA in
law, University of London; LLD,
National School of Law, UNAM, with
an honorable mention; Secretary of the
Institute of Juridical Research, UNAM,
1967-69; adviser to the Auxiliary
Secretary General of UNAM, 1970-71;
Secretary of the University Tribunal,
1973-77; General Attorney of UNAM,
1973-77; Coordinator of the Humanities, UNAM, 1977-78; Director of the
Institute of Juridical Research, UNAM,
1978-84. d-None. e-None. f-*Rector of
UNAM*, Jan. 2, 1985-88; *Justice of the
Supreme Court*, 1990; Director, Human
Rights Commission, Secretariat of
Government, 1990-92; *Attorney
General of Mexico*, 1992-94; *Secretary
of Government*, 1994. g-None.
h-Expert on constitutional law. i-Son of
Oscar Carpizo Berrón, businessman, and

Luz María MacGregor Dondé; brother Oscar worked in the secretariat of the treasury, 1989. j-None. k-None. l-HA, 17 Dec. 1984, 14; letters; *Excélsior*, 6 Dec. 1984, 1; DBGM89, 71.

Carrancá y Trujillo, Raúl
(Deceased 1968) a-Aug. 27, 1897. b-Campeche, Campeche. c-Preparatory studies from the Literary Institute of Yucatán; law degree from the University of Madrid, Spain, on a private scholarship; LLD from the University of Madrid, 1925; studies at the University of Paris; professor, National School of Economics, UNAM; professor, National School of Law, UNAM, 1926-60; Dean, School of Political and Social Science, UNAM, 1953. d-None. e-Supporter of José Vasconcelos for president, 1929. f-Agent of the Ministerio Público of the Federal District, 1928-29; Assistant to the Attorney General of the Federal District; Judge of the 8th Penal Court, Federal District, 1930; Justice of the Superior Court of the Federal District, 1940; First District Court Judge, 1944; Director of Cultural Dissemination, UNAM, 1948-52; *Secretary General of UNAM*, 1952-53, under Rector *Luis Garrido*; Chief, Legal Department, National Savings Bonds, 1953. g-None. h-Legal adviser to the president of Mexico; author of numerous works on penal law; cofounder of the review *Criminalia* with *Luis Garrido*, 1933. i-Friend and collaborator of *Luis Garrido* for many years; son of Camilo Carrancá y Vusquets and Narcisa Trujillo. j-None. k-None. l-WWM45, 19-20; DP70, 372; Casasola, V, 2422; Enc. Mex., 1977, II, 382; Garrido.

Carranza Hernández, Rafael
a-Apr. 28, 1919. b-Federal District. c-Primary studies in Mexico City; engineering studies in Philadelphia, Pennsylvania, civil engineering degree. d-*Federal Deputy from the State of*

Coahuila, Dist. 1, 1952-55, member of the Gran Comisión, the Budget and Accounts Committee, the Foreign Relations Committee, and the Administration Committee; Secretary of the Preparatory Committee; *Alternate Senator* from the State of Coahuila, 1958-60; *Senator* from the State of Coahuila, 1960-64, President of the Colonization and the Public Works Committees, Second Secretary of the Consular and Diplomatic Service Committee and First Secretary of the Special Hydraulic Resources Committee; *Federal Deputy* (Party Deputy from PARM), 1979-82. e-Member of the Presidium of PARM; Treasurer of the CEN of PARM, July 3, 1977-79. f-*Secretary General of the Department of Agrarian Affairs*, 1955-58; Director General of the Agricultural Bank of the North West, 1965-68; General Adviser to the Director of the National Agricultural Bank, 1968-70; Coordinator General of the Agricultural Program for the Central Zone of the State of Coahuila, 1971-74. g-None. i-Son of Venustiano Carranza, President of Mexico. j-None. k-Replaced Senator *Vicente Dávila Aguirre* who died in office, 1960. l-DGF56, 453; C de S, 1961-64; C de D, 1952-55, 7; HA, 26 Feb. 1979, V; *Excélsior*, 16 Apr. 1979, 16.

Carranza (Palacios), José Antonio
a-Aug. 2, 1941. b-Oaxaca, Oaxaca. c-Early education unknown; engineering degree, Technological Institute of Higher Studies, Monterrey, 1963; MA degree in science; professor, School of Engineering, University of Veracruz; professor, School of Architecture, University of Oaxaca; professor, School of Business and Administration, University of Oaxaca; professor, Graduate School of Administration, Technological Institute of Higher Studies of Monterrey; Rector of the Regional Technological Institute of

Oaxaca. d-None. e-None. f-Director General of Projects and Inspection, State of Oaxaca; Director General of Education, Health, and Social Welfare, State of Oaxaca; Director of the Technological Institute, Secretariat of Public Education, 1968-70; Director General of Planning, Secretariat of Public Education, 1970-76; Director of Primary Education for Everyone Program, Secretariat of Public Educaton; Director General of Programming, Secretariat of Public Education, 1978-79; *Subsecretary of Education and Technical Investigation*, Secretariat of Public Education, 1979-82; Subdirector General, Institutional Services, IMSS, 1982. g-None. h-Regional Manager, Instructora Athens, S.A., 1963. i-Member of *Víctor Bravo Ahuja*'s political group; studied under *Víctor Bravo Ahuja*. j-None. k-None. l-HA, 9 July 1979, 20, 20 Dec. 1982, 14; Protag., 71.

Carrasco Gutiérrez, Víctor Manuel
b-Toluca, México. c-Normal certificate from the Normal School of Toluca; medical studies at the National Polytechnic Institute; medical degree; primary school teacher in rural schools and in night workers schools; high school teacher; normal school teacher; Professor of the History of the Mexican Labor Movement, Workers University, Mexico City. d-*Federal Deputy* from the State of México, Dist. 11, 1976-79. e-Member of the Central Committee of the CEN of PRS. f-None. g-Official of the SNTE in the State of México. i-Married Rosa Luz Fuentes R. j-None. k-None. l-D de C, 1976-79, 9; HA, 30 Apr. 1979, IV.

Carrasco Palacios, Diódoro
a-Apr. 9, 1927. b-Huajuapan de León, Oaxaca. c-Business studies, Institute of Arts and Sciences, Oaxaca, 1942-45; no degree. d-Mayor of Cutlatán, Oaxaca, 1953; Local Deputy to the State Legisla-

ture of Oaxaca, 1953-56; *Federal Deputy* from the State of Oaxaca, Dist. 5, 1967-70; *Alternate Senator* from the State of Oaxaca under *Gilberto Suárez Torres*, 1970-76; *Federal Deputy* from the State of Oaxaca, Dist. 5, 1973-76, 1988-91; *Governor of Oaxaca*, 1992- . e-None. f-Chief of Agro-Industry, Conasupo, 1980-82. g-Secretary of the League of Agrarian Communities, Oaxaca, 1968-73; Secretary of Agrarian Action of the Revolutionary Federation of Workers and Peasants (CROC), 1970-74. h-Unknown. i-Son of Diódoro Carrasco Oropeza and María Amelia Palacios Vázquez; married Alma Altamirano Vázquez. j-None. k-None. l-DBGM89, 412; C de D, 1967-70, 1988-91, 1973-76.

Carreño Gómez, Franco
a-May 16, 1898. b-Alaquines, San Luis Potosí. c-Primary studies in Alaquines; law degree from the National School of Law, UNAM, 1923; LLD, National School of Law, UNAM, 1961; Professor of Law, National School of Law, UNAM; professor at Night School, Mexico City, 1921. d-None. e-None. f-Consulting lawyer for the Department of the Federal District; consulting lawyer for the Secretariat of Communications; consulting lawyer for the National Agrarian Commission; Assistant Attorney General of the Federal District, 1929; Secretary General of Government of the State of San Luis Potosí under Governor *Genovevo Rivas Guillén*, 1938-39; *Justice of the Supreme Court*, 1941-46, 1947-52, 1953-58, 1959-64, President of the Administrative Division, 1943, 1948, 1953, 1958, and 1963. g-Co-founder of the Student Society of the National Preparatory School, 1915; Secretary General of the Union of Lawyers of the Federal District, 1935-37; President of the Society of Friends of Cuba, 1952-60. h-Student author for *México Nuevo*; practicing lawyer with

Luis Garrido, 1922-23; writer for *El Monitor Republi-cano*, 1924; practicing lawyer with *Manuel Moreno Sánchez*; author of numerous books on law. i-Close personal friend of *Luis Garrido* since law school days; married Lucía García Valencia. j-None. k-Worked for many years to remove *Gonzalo Santos'* political influence in San Luis Potosí. l-WNM, 35; NYT, 26 Oct. 1958, 19; Garrido; DGF56, 567.

Carrillo Arena, Guillermo

a-Feb. 4, 1941. b-Federal District. c-Early education unknown; architectural degree, National School of Architecture, UNAM, 1958-62. d-None. e-General Delegate of the CEN of PRI to Oaxaca, 1982. f-President of the Board of Material and Moral Improvements, San José del Cabo, La Paz, and Santa Rosalia, Baja California del Sur, 1965-66; Director General of the Health Engineering and Construction Commission, Secretariat of Health, 1967-70; Chief of Projects, IMSS, 1970-76; Technical Subdirector of Infonavit, 1975-78; Director General of the Acapulco Trust, Secretariat of Housing and Public Works, 1979-82; Subdirector of Works and Property, IMSS, 1982-85; *Secretary of Public Works and Human Dwellings*, 1985-86. g-President of the College of Mexican Architects, 1974. h-Practicing architect, 1962-65, 1978-79. i-Son of Marcos Carrillo Cárdenas, lawyer, and Rosario Arena Sáinz; married María Amparo Quijano Campbell. j-None. k-None. l-*Excélsior*, 12 Mar. 1985, 7; DBGM, 85-86.

Carrillo Arronte, Ricardo

a-Aug. 9, 1939. c-Ciudad Juárez, Chihuahua. c-Early education unknown; Ph.D. in economics, National School of Economics, UNAM; Director of the Center of Applied Economics, UNAM, 1978-79; Subdirector of the Division of Graduate Studies, National

School of Economics, UNAM, 1971-72. d-None. e-Joined PRI, 1962; organizer in Ciudad Juárez for *Gustavo Díaz Ordaz* presidential campaign, 1963-64; organizer of events for the IEPES of PRI, *Luis Echeverría* campaign, 1969-70; *Secretary of Ideological Divulgation of the CEN of PRI*, 1982-84. f-Mana-ger, Regional Development, NAFIN, 1972-74; Director General of Plan Lerma Technical Assistance, 1972-76. g-Secretary of the Exterior, National College of Economists, 1973-75; Coordinator of the National Committee of Economic Planning Studies, League of Revolutionary Economists, 1976-78. h-President of CIDE, 1983-84. i-Married Jacqueline Lammns. j-None. k-None. l-HA, 6 Feb. 1984, 10, 12.

Carrillo Castro, Alejandro

a-Oct. 20, 1941. b-Federal District. c-Early education unknown; legal studies, National School of Law, UNAM, 1959-63, graduating in 1965 with a thesis on "Regulating Foreign Investment in Mexico"; Ph.D. in public administration, UNAM, 1971-73, with a thesis on the methodology for analyzing and reforming public administration; professor, National School of Law, UNAM, 1972-76; professor, School of Political and Social Sciences, UNAM, 1977-88; professor, Colegio de México, 1985, 1987-88. d-None. e-Joined PRI, 1959; Secretary of International Relations, Youth Committee of CEN of PRI, 1964; Subdirector of Planning, IEPES of PRI, 1975; member of the advisory council of the IEPES of PRI, 1981-86. f-Lawyer, Division of Juridical Affairs, Secretariat of the Presidency, 1964-65; Private Secretary to the Oficial Mayor of the Secretariat of the Presidency, 1965-70; Technical Secretary, Commission of Public Administration, 1967-70; Director General of Administrative Studies, Secretariat of the Presidency, 1971-73; Secretary General of Conacyt,

1973-76; adviser to the Subsecretary of Expenditures, *Carlos A. Isoard*, 1975-76; General Coordinator of Administrative Studies, Secretariat of the Presidency, 1977-82; *Director General of the ISSSTE*, 1982-88; Consul General in the United States, 1988-92; *Ambassador to the Organization of American States*, 1992-94. g-None. h-Author of several books on public administration. i-Son of *Alejandro Carrillo Marcor*, Governor of Sonora, 1975-79, and Aurea Castro Valle; grandfather served as consul general in London. j-None. k-None. l-IEPES; Q es QAP, 513.

Carrillo Durán, Ricardo
a-Nov. 20, 1904. b-Zitácuaro, Michoacán. c-Law degree, National School of Law, UNAM, May 8, 1929. d-Federal Deputy from Zitácuaro, Michoacán, 1932-34; *Federal Deputy* from the State of Chihuahua, Dist. 3, 1961-64; member of the Second Committee on Government, alternate member of the Committee on Taxes and the Committee on Public Works; Secretary of the Chamber of Deputies, 1962; *Alternate Senator* from the State of Chihuahua, 1964-70. e-President of PRI in Ciudad Juárez, 1957-61. f-Attorney General of the State of Michoacán, 1935; Judge of the First Instance, Ciudad Juárez, 1936-45; Secretary of the City Council of Ciudad Juárez, 1936-45, 1957-61; Subdirector of Loans and Pensions of the Institute of Security and Social Service for Federal Employees, 1964-70; *Administrative Subdirector of Petróleos Mexicanos*, 1970-76. g-None. h-Practicing lawyer in Mexico City, 1947-57. i-Classmate of *Miguel Alemán*, *Antonio Carrillo Flores*, and *Hector Pérez Martínez*; son of Francisco Carrillo and Fortimata Durán. j-None. k-None. l-Letter, DGF69, 623, 106.

Carrillo Flores, Antonio
(Deceased) a-June 23, 1909. b-Coyoacán, Federal District. c-Primary education in Mexico City, three years in New York City, 1914-17; preparatory at the National Preparatory School, 1921-24; law degree from the National School of Law, UNAM, Mar. 21, 1929; honorary LLD, UNAM, 1950; Professor of Administrative Law, National Law School, UNAM, 1936-52; Professor of General Theory, National School of Law, 1932-34; member of the Governing Council of UNAM, 1947-52; Director of the National School of Law, 1944-45; Professor of special courses on "The State in Economic Life," Rector of the Autonomous Technological Institute of Mexico, 1971-72. d-*Federal Deputy* from the Federal District, 1979-80. e-None. f-Agent of the Ministerio Público of the Federal Attorney General, 1930-31; head of the Legal Department of the Attorney General of Mexico, 1931-32, 1934-35; Secretary of the Supreme Court of Justice, 1933; head of the Department of Legal Affairs of the Secretariat of the Treasury, 1935-36; adviser to the Consulting Department of the Bank of Mexico, 1938-41, 1946-52, 1971-72; *Director General of Nacional Financiera*, 1945-52; Founding President of the National Securities Commission, 1946-47; *Secretary of the Treasury*, 1952-58; *Ambassador to the United States*, 1958-64; *Secretary of Foreign Relations*, 1964-70; Director General of Fondo de Cultura Económica, 1970-72; Founding Judge of the Federal Tax Court, 1937-38; Mexican Governor of the International Bank for Reconstruction and Development; *Ambassador to the Soviet Union*, 1980-82; Director General of Banco Comercial, 1982. g-None. h-Author of banking legislation and several books and numerous articles on law and economics; coauthored a book with *Ezequiel Burguete* in 1935; practicing

lawyer, 1976. i-Formed early friendships at the National School of Law with *Miguel Alemán, Ezequiel Burguete, Antonio Ortiz Mena, Alfonso Noriega, Angel Carvajal, Antonio Armendáriz, José Castro Estrada, Salomon González Blanco, Manuel Ramírez Vázquez, Ernesto Uruchurtu, Manuel Sánchez Cuen,* and *Andrés Serra Rojas;* studied at the National School of Law under *Luis Garrido Díaz;* son of the distinguished Mexican composer Julian Carrillo, discoverer of sound number 13 on the musical scale; brother of *Nabor Carrillo,* Rector of UNAM, 1952-61; son, *Emilio Carrillo Gamboa,* was director general of Teléfonos de México, 1982-87, and ambassador to Canada, 1987. j-None. k-None. l-DBM68, 121-22; letter; *El Universal,* 2 Dec. 1964; *Hoy,* 11 Oct. 1969; WWMG, 11; Brandenburg, 113; HA, 5 Dec. 1952, 9; DGF56, 161; IWW, 197-98; Tucker, 437, Baker; NYT, 28 July 1957, 2; *Excélsior,* 5 Sept. 1982, 20.

Carrillo (Flores), Nabor
(Deceased) a-Feb. 23, 1911. b-Coyoacán, Federal District. c-Primary and secondary education in the Federal District; preparatory at the National Preparatory School and at George Washington High School, New York City; began university studies in New York; continued engineering studies at UNAM, 1929-32; engineering degree, National School of Engineering, UNAM, 1932, with an honorable mention; MA in science from Harvard University, 1941; Ph.D. in science from Harvard University, 1942; Guggenheim Fellow; student assistant in math, 1932; professor at the National Preparatory School; Professor of Math at UNAM, 1932-53. d-None. e-None. f-Employee, National Irrigation Commission, 1934-36; Chief of Engineers, National Irrigation Commission, 1936-45; member of the Mexican Commission of Scientific

Investigation, 1943-45; Mexican representative to the atomic site on Bikini Island, 1946; *Rector of UNAM,* 1952-61; Director of the Atomic Energy Center in Mexico; executive member of the National Commission of Nuclear Energy; Director of the Mexican–North American Institute of Cultural Relations, Mexico City, 1966-67. g-None. h-Internationally famous specialist in underground mechanics; promoter of the Atomic Energy Center in Mexico. i-Brother of *Antonio Carrillo Flores;* son of Julian Carrillo, distinguished Mexican composer and discoverer of sound number 13 on the musical scale; author of many scientific articles; uncle of *Emilio Carrillo Gamboa,* ambassador to Canada, 1987. j-None. k-None. l-WWM45, 21; *Excélsior,* 21 Aug. 1971, 7A; DP70, 380; Hayner, 169; DP70, 378-79; DGF50, II, 207; DGF51, II, 299; HA, 27 Feb. 1953, 35.

Carrillo Gamboa, Emilio
a-Oct. 16, 1938. b-Federal District. c-Early education unknown; legal studies from the National School of Law, UNAM, 1954-59, graduating in Aug. 1959 with a thesis on "Tax Problems of Federalism"; studies at Georgetown University. d-None. e-Joined PRI, 1962. f-Director, Department of Financial Studies, Teléfonos de México, 1960; Assistant to the Director General of Teléfonos de México, 1960-62; Secretary of the Board of Teléfonos de México, 1962-67; Subdirector General of Teléfonos de México, 1967-75, Director General, 1975-87; Ambassador to Canada, 1987-88. g-None. h-None. i-Son of *Antonio Carrillo Flores,* secretary of foreign relations, and Fanny Gamboa Farrera; nephew of *Nabor Carrillo Flores,* Rector of UNAM; brother Nabor was coordinator of advisers, Subsecretariat, Secretariat of Commerce, 1985. j-None. k-None. l-*Excélsior,* 1 June 1975, 1; Q es QAP, 527; DBGM87, 79.

Carrillo (Marcor), Alejandro
a-Mar. 15, 1908. b-Hermosillo, Sonora.
c-Primary studies in Hermosillo,
Sonora; secondary studies in San
Antonio, Texas; winner of the state
contest in English, 1927; scholarship to
study at the University of Texas,
Austin, and at Southern Methodist
University; attended Tulane University,
1929; law degree, National School of
Law, UNAM, 1934; professor at the
National Preparatory School, Mexico
City, 1930-60; Dean of the School of
History, National War College; profes-
sor at UNAM, 1930-33; professor at the
National War College, 1933-63; Direc-
tor of Preparatory School Gabino
Barreda, 1933-35; member of the
National Board of Higher Education,
1935-39; Secretary of the Workers
University, 1936-43; Assistant Director
of the Workers University, 1943.
d-*Federal Deputy* from the Federal
District, Dist. 7, 1940-43, member of
the Economy and Statistics Committee,
the Social Works Committee, the Labor
Committee, and the Editorial Committee; *Federal Deputy* from the Federal
District, Dist. 17, 1964-66, member of
the Second Committee on the Treasury,
the Committee on Taxes, and the
Committee on Budgets and Accounts;
President of the Chamber of Deputies,
Dec. 1966, and member of the Permanent Commission; *Senator* from Sonora,
1970-75; President of the First Foreign
Relations Committee, First Secretary of
the Federal District Department and the
Second Constitutional Affairs Committee. e-Joined the PNR, 1933; directed
the national publicity for *Miguel
Alemán*'s campaign for president, 1946;
cofounder of PPS, 1948; joined the PRM,
1951, member of the National Council
of PRI, 1972. f-*Secretary General of the
Federal District*, 1946-51; head of
special mission to Trinidad, 1962,
accompanied *Adolfo López Mateos* to
Asia, 1958; publisher of the daily

government newspaper *El Nacional*,
1968; Ambassador to the United Arab
Republic, 1958-61; *Interim Governor of
Sonora*, 1975-79. g-Member of the Executive Committee of the Mexican Federation of Workers, 1943-45. h-Adviser
to PIPSA; publisher of the daily newspaper *El Popular*, 1943; journalist, *El
Popular*, 1938-45; *El Nacional*, 1968;
author of many books on politics and
economics. i-Close personal friend of
Vicente Lombardo Toledano; son of
Alejandro P. Carrillo, consul general of
Mexico in San Antonio, Texas, and
María Luisa Marcor; cousin of *Adolfo
de la Huerta O*; married Aurea Castro;
son, *Alejandro Carrillo Castro*, close
adviser to *José López Portillo* and
Director General of the ISSSTE, 1982.
j-None. k-Precandidate for federal
deputy, 1933; candidate for senator on
the Popular Party ticket, 1952; answered the state of the union address in
1941; resigned as Secretary General of
the Federal District to support *Vicente
Lombardo Toledano*, 1951. l-HA, 28
Feb. 1972; DGF47, 293; DGF51; HA, 24
Apr. 1972; Correa 46, 71; Millon, 141;
DBM68, 121; WWM45, 20; DPE61, 20;
Kirk, 91; DGF51, 471; DGF50, II, 77,
317, 413; Peral, 154; HA, 12 Dec. 1947;
Enc. Mex., 1977, II, 395; *Excélsior*, 4
Aug. 1978, 15; C de S, 1970-76, 75;
Excélsior, 13 Oct. 1980, 23A, 26 Oct.
1975, 13A; Cadena Z., 144.

Carrillo Olea, Jorge
a-Nov. 19, 1937. b-Jotutla, Morelos.
c-Early education unknown; graduated
from the Heroic Military College, 1954-
57, as a 2nd Lieutenant in infantry, best
student of his class; graduated from the
Applied Military School, 1960; degree in
military administration, Higher War
College, 1962-65; graduated from
armored car course, Ft. Knox, 1967-68;
professor at the Heroic Military College,
1958-61; professor at the Higher War
College, 1965-70. d-None. e-Joined

PRI, 1962. f-*Subsecretary of Tax Investigation*, Secretariat of the Treasury, 1975-76; *Subsecretary of Government (3)*, 1982-88; Director of National Security and Research Center, Secretariat of Government, 1988-90; Coordinator of Health Crimes (Drug Task Force), Attorney General of Mexico, 1990-93. g-None. h-None. i-Son of Angel Carrillo Mellado, businessman, and Rebeca Olea Martini, teacher; married Hilda María Enríquez Andrade; good friend of General *Jesús Castañeda Gutiérrez* at the Heroic Military College. j-Commander of the 3rd Cadet Company, Heroic Military College, 1959-62; Chief of Section 2, Intelligence, Chief of Staff, Secretariat of National Defense, 1970-75; Director of the Unified Drydocks, 1976-82; Technical Secretary of the National Coordinating Commission of Navy Industry, 1977; rank of Colonel. k-The only army officer to hold a subsecretaryship outside the defense secretariats in 1982; saved *Luis Echeverría* from a violent student demonstration at UNAM in 1975. l-*Excélsior*, 27 Feb 1976, 4; HA, 8 Mar. 1976, 21; Q es QAP, 26; DBGM87, 79; DBGM92, 78; *Proceso*, 9 Nov. 1987, 18; Q es QAP, 26.

Carrillo Salinas, Gloria
a-Mar. 20, 1940. b-Zumpango, México. c-Primary studies in public schools, Mexico City; no degree. d-*Alternate Federal Deputy* from the Federal District, Dist. 10, 1973-76; *Federal Deputy* from the Federal District, Dist. 10, 1976-79. e-Joined PRI, 1966; participated in *Luis Echeverría's* campaign for president, 1970; Secretary of Social Action of PRI in District No. 10, Federal District. f-None. g-Secretary of Relations of the Federation of Women Workers Organizations of the CTM, 1976; President of Women's Action of the CEN of the National Meatworkers Union, 1976. h-Employee

in a meatworkers' industry; stenographer. j-None. k-None. l-*Excélsior*, 18 Aug. 1976, 19; D de C, 1976-79, 4; HA, 24 May 1976, 10, 12.

Carrillo Torres, Francisco
(Deceased 1952) a-June 1896. b-Comala, Colima. c-Primary studies in Comala; no degree. d-*Governor of Colima*, 1935. f-Subdirector of the Department of Aviation, Secretariat of National Defense; Chief of Aviation for the North-East region. g-None. h-Responsible for the construction of federal airports at Ensenada and La Paz; miner at Cananea before the Revolution. j-Joined the Revolution in 1913 under Obregón, aviator for the Secretariat of National Defense, 1923, fought against the Cristeros; fought with *Saturnino Cedillo*; rank of Colonel in the air force. k-Removed from the office of governor by the federal government because of political ties with Calles. l-DP70, 381-82.

Carrillo Zavala, Abelardo
a-Dec. 5, 1939. b-Palizada, Campeche. c-Primary studies at the Justo Sierra Méndez School, Campeche; private accounting graduate, Longinos de Apolinar Business School, Campeche; teacher of writing and correspondence. d-Member of the City Council, Campeche, Campeche; Alternate Local Deputy to the State Legislature of Campeche; *Federal Deputy* from the State of Campeche, Dist. 2, 1970-73; Dist. 1, 1976-79; Dist. 2, 1982-85; *Governor of Campeche*, 1985-91. e-Orator in *José López Portillo's* presidential campaign in Campeche, 1976; Secretary of Organization of PRI in Campeche, Campeche. f-Secretary of the Department of Information and Tourism, State of Campeche; accounting assistant, Treasurer General of Campeche. g-Member of the Constitutive Session of the Federation of Youth

Organizations of the CTM, 1962; Assistant Secretary of Relations of the CEN of the CTM; special delegate of the CTM to Morelos, Yucatán, Nuevo León, Tabasco, Veracruz, Quintana Roo, Sonora, Guerrero, and Jalisco; Secretary General of Local 21, National Union of Music Workers; Secretary General of the State Workers of Campeche, 1970; Secretary General of the Only Union of Philharmonics of Campeche, 1961-66; Assistant Secretary of Production and Supplies, CEN of the CTM, 1982. h-Practicing accountant. i-Son of Azcanio Carrillo Vázquez, career navy, and María del Carmen Zavala; married Luz del Alba Delgado Mendicuti, social worker. j-None. k-Has served more times as a federal deputy since 1970 from the State of Campeche than any other individual. l-Directorio, 1982-85; Directorio, 1970-72; C de D, 1976-79; Lehr, 58; *Excélsior*, 18 Jan. 1985, 12, 15; DBGM, 484; DBGM89, 67.

Carrión Rodríguez, Eugenio Pacelli
a-Feb. 20, 1950. b-Federal District. c-Primary studies, 1956-61, secondary studies, 1962-64, and preparatory studies, 1965-67, all at the Colegio Franco Inglés, Mexico City; business administration degree, UNAM, 1968-72, with a thesis on Mexican exports to Latin America; MA, Colegio de México, 1973-75, with a thesis on energy price policies; MA in economic theory, University College, London, 1976-77; Ph.D. in energy economics, University of Grenoble, France, 1980; professor, School of Business Administration, UNAM, 1972-73; professor, National School of Political Studies, Acatlán campus, UNAM; professor, Autonomous University of Azcapotzalco; Assistant Secretary, Colegio de México, 1979. d-None. e-None. f-Analyst, petroleum sector, Secretariat of Government Properties, 1977-78; Subdirector of Economic Studies, Secretariat of

Government Properties, 1979; Assistant Director of Economic Studies, Pemex, 1983-86; Director General of the Technical Unit on Prices, Secretariat of the Treasury, 1986-88; *Oficial Mayor of Commerce*, 1988-89; *Subsecretary of Internal Trade*, Secretariat of Commerce, 1989- . g-None. h-Administrator of warehouses, Siemens Mexicana, 1971. i-Son of José Trinidad Carrión Gómez and Guadalupe Rodríguez Gómez; married Beatriz de Negri Cazales, interpreter. j-None. k-None. l-DBGM89, 74.

Carvajal (Bernal), Angel
(Deceased Jan. 27, 1985) a-1900. b-Santiago Tuxtla, Veracruz. c-Secondary studies at the National Preparatory School; preparatory studies at the National Preparatory School, 1921-24; studied law at the National School of Law, UNAM, 1925-27, degree in 1928, with a thesis on presidential resolutions on the agrarian question, which became a classic work; adviser at National Preparatory School; formed the Vasco de Quiroga Society to campaign against illiteracy; Director of a National Student Campaign, Secretariat of Public Education, 1923; professor, Law School, University of Veracruz, 1944-50; teacher in secondary and normal schools, 1944-50; professor at the National Preparatory School, 1930-44; Professor of Law, National School of Law, UNAM; Director of the Escuela de Iniciación Universitaria, 1938-42. d-None. e-President of the Student Association at the National Preparatory School; delegate to the student congress, 1928. f-Director of the Department of Prices, Secretariat of Communication and Public Works, 1934; Director of the Department of Administration, Secretariat of Public Education; Private Secretary to the Secretary of Public Education; agent of the Ministerio Público attached to the Supreme Court;

chief of the auxiliary agents of the Criminal Division of the Attorney General of Mexico; *Assistant Attorney General of Mexico*, 1936-40, 1940-44; *Justice of the Supreme Court*, 1944; Secretary General of Government of the State of Veracruz, 1944-46; *Subsecretary of Government Properties*, 1946-47; *Governor of Veracruz*, 1948-50; *Secretary of Government Properties*, 1951-52; *Secretary of Government*, 1952-58; *Justice of the Supreme Court*, 1958-72 (retired). g-None. h-Lawyer, Department of Public Health; Secretary of the Intersectoral Board for Enemy Properties and Businesses, 1942. i-Friendships with *Antonio Carrillo Flores, Miguel Alemán, Adolfo Zamora, Alfonso Noriega, Ezequiel Burguete,* and *José Castro Estrada* at UNAM; close friend of *Adolfo Ruiz Cortines*; married Magda Moreno; son *Gustavo Carvajal Moreno* was subsecretary of labor, 1976-78, and selected president of the CEN of PRI, 1979; father, a small rancher. j-None. k-Precandidate for president, 1958, opposed by Cardenists; supported José Vasconcelos for President, 1929. l-HA, 5 Dec. 1952, 9; DGF56, 83; HA, 10 Aug. 1951, 14; WWMG, 12; D del Y, 2 Dec. 1952, 1; Scott, 222; Dulles, 473; letters, Morton, 92; *Justicia; La Jornada,* 28 Jan. 1985, 5.

Carvajal (Moreno), Gustavo
a-Oct. 29, 1940. b-Santiago Tuxtla, Veracruz. c-Primary studies in Arnulfo Navarro, Jalapa, and Veracruz, Veracruz and in the Chapultepec School, Mexico City; secondary studies at Secondary School No. 3, Mexico City; preparatory studies at the National Preparatory School No. 1; law degree from the National School of Law, UNAM, Jan. 21, 1963; business administration degree from the School of Business and Administration, UNAM, 1964; Professor by Opposition of Civics, 1964-92, Professor by Opposition of Sociology,

1964-92, and Professor of Political, Social, and Economic Problems of Mexico, all at National Preparatory School; Professor of Political Society of Contemporary Mexico, School of Political and Social Sciences, UNAM, 1970-73; Professor of Constitutional Law, National School of Law, UNAM, 1967-68; Director of the National Preparatory School Antonio Caso, No. 6, 1966-70; Director General of Information and Relations, UNAM, 1970-73. d-*Federal Deputy* from the State of Veracruz, Dist. 22, 1991-94. e-Joined PRI, 1958; Private Secretary to *José López Portillo* during presidential campaign, 1976; *Secretary General of the CEN of PRI,* Aug. 11, 1978-79; *President of the CEN of PRI,* 1979-81. f-Consulting lawyer to the Legal Consulting Office of the Secretariat of the Presidency, 1963-65; lawyer for the Department of Disputes of the Federal Tax Attorney's Office, 1960-62; lawyer, Department of Disputes for the Federal Income Tax Division, 1962-63; Agent of the Auxiliary Ministerio Público of the Attorney General of the Federal District, 1963-64; Subdirector of Investigations of the Attorney General of the Federal District, 1964-65; aide to the Attorney General of Mexico, 1967; Private Secretary to the Attorney General of Mexico, 1967-68; Legal Subdirector of Guanos and Fertilizers, 1973-75; *Subsecretary (A) of Labor,* 1976-78; *Secretary of Agrarian Reform,* 1981-82; Director General of Tabamex, 1988-90; Director General of the Public Works Bank, 1990-91. g-None. h-Director General of Carvajal Moreno and Associates, 1986-88. i-Son of *Angel Carvajal,* secretary of government, 1952-58, and precandidate for president of Mexico, 1958; married Sofia Isunza. j-None. k-None. l-Letter; *Excélsior,* 11 Aug. 1978, 1; HA, 19 Feb. 1979, 12-13; DBGM92, 439.

Casas Alemán, Fernando

(Deceased Oct. 30, 1968) a-July 8, 1905. b-Córdoba, Veracruz. c-Primary and secondary studies in Córdoba; preparatory in Córdoba, law degree, National School of Law, UNAM, 1921-25. d-*Provisional Governor of Veracruz*, 1939-40; *Senator* from the State of Veracruz, 1946-52 (never held office). e-Personal representative and director of *Miguel Alemán's* campaign for President, 1945-46. f-Secretary of the Board of Conciliation and Arbitration, Dist. 5, 1930; agent of the Ministerio Público in the State of Veracruz, 1926; judge in the State of Veracruz; consulting lawyer on the Labor Law for the Secretariat of Industry and Commerce, 1929; Secretary General of Government of the State of Veracruz, 1936-39; *Head of the Federal District*, 1946-52; *Subsecretary of Government*, 1940-45; Ambassador to Italy, Greece, China, 1953-64; Ambassador to Japan, 1964-68. g-None. h-Practicing lawyer in Veracruz, 1935-36. i-Intimate friend of *Miguel Alemán*; practiced labor law with *Miguel Alemán* and *Gabriel Ramos Millan*; was a professor of *Miguel Alemán* at the Law School; son, Miguel, married daughter of *Gilberto Limón*, secretary of national defense, 1946-52. j-None. k-*Miguel Alemán's* personal choice for the PRI candidate for President in 1946; rejected because of charges of excessive corruption in the Federal District. l-DPE65, 28; HA, 13 Oct. 1950, 15; DBM68, 125; G of M, 14; Greenburg, 24-25; DP70, 389; DGF47, 22; HA, 28 Feb. 1947, 11; DGF50, II, 317, 329; Q es Q, 108-09; López, 173.

Casillas Hernández, Roberto

a-Sept. 22, 1930. b-Aguascalientes, Aguascalientes. c-Early education unknown; law degree, National School of Law, UNAM, 1953; LLD degree, National School of Law, UNAM; Professor of Constitutional Law, National School of Law, UNAM; professor emeritus, School of Law, Bauro, São Paulo, Brazil. d-*Senator* from the State of Aguascalientes, 1982-88. e-None. f-Lawyer, Division of Securities and Finances, Secretariat of the Treasury, 1952; President, Board of Material and Moral Improvement, Chetumal, Quintana Roo, 1959-60; Subdirector, External Control, Department of Material and Moral Improvement Boards, Secretariat of Government Properties, 1963; Director General of the National Warehouses, 1977-78; *Private Secretary to the President*, 1978-82. g-None. h-Author of many books. i-Son of Celestino Casillas Huerta and Jovita Hernández Ramírez; married Liliana Mendieta Fernández. j-None. k-None. l-Protag., 74; *Excélsior*, 16 Dec. 1978, 4; HA, 24 Aug. 1981; C de S, 1982-88; DBGM87, 450; Lehr, 31; DBGM, 185.

Casillas Ontiveros, Ofelia

a-Jan. 11, 1937. b-Toluca, México. c-Rural primary teaching certificate; studies at the Oral School, Teacher Education Institute, 1962-64; rural primary teacher, 1957; studies toward an education degree. d-*Federal Deputy* from the Federal District, Dist. 3, 1973-76; Prosecretary of the Chamber, 1973-76; Vice-President of the Chamber, Dec. 1974; *Federal Deputy* from the Federal District, Dist. 31, 1979-82; Dist. 21, 1985-88. e-Joined PRI, 1957; Women's Coordinator of PRI in the Federal District, 1975-77; alternate member of the National Council of PRI; Director of Advertising for PRI, Federal District, 1980-81; Subsecretary of Electoral Action, CEN of PRI, 1982. f-None. g-Member of the Student Society, Institute of Teacher Education, 1963-64; Women's Youth Director of the CNC; Subsecretary of Social Action of CNOP, 1965-65; Women's Secretary of CNOP, 1967-77; representative of the National Revolutionary Women's Association to the Federal District, 1977-79; Secretary of Political Action of the National Revolutionary Women's Association (ANFER); Secretary General of ANFER, 1977-79, 1984-87; National Women's Coordinator of CNOP, 1980. h-None. i-Daughter of Antonio Casillas and Ana María Ontiveros García, primary school teacher; married *Manuel Orijel Salazar*, federal deputy from the Federal District and lawyer. j-None. k-None. l-Aceves Romero, 695-96; Protag., 74; C de D, 1973-76, 1979-82; DBGM87, 450-51; DBGM89, 566.

Caso Lombardo, Andrés
a-Sept. 16, 1924. b-Federal District. c-Primary studies at the Colegio Gordon District; secondary studies at Secondary School No. 3; preparatory studies at the National Preparatory School; economics degree, National School of Economics, UNAM; professor at the National School of Economics, UNAM. d-None. e-None. f-Director, Department of Personnel, Secretariat of Public Works, 1953-55; Director General of Administration, Secretariat of Public Works, 1956-58; technical adviser and Director of Administrative Services, Secretariat of Public Works, 1959-64; Director of Personnel, Petróleos Mexicanos, 1966-70; *Oficial Mayor, Secretariat of Public Works*, 1970-76; Controller General of the Federal Electric Commission, 1976-80; adviser to the administrative reform program, Secretariat of the Presidency, 1977-82; Director General of Productora Mexicana de Tubería, 1980-82; Director General of Airports and Auxiliary Services, Secretariat of Communications and Transportation, 1982-85; *Subsecretary of Communications and Transportation*, 1985-86; Director General of the National Railroad System, 1986-88; *Secretary of Communications and Transportation*, 1988-93. g-None. h-Executive Secretary, Technical Commission on General Means of Communication, Secretariat of Public Works, 1965; President of the Institute of Public Administration; Mexican representative to various international conferences on public administration. i-Son of *Alfonso Caso*. j-None. k-One of the two negotiators representing President *Gustavo Díaz Ordaz* in negotiations with the students, 1968; precandidate for secretary general of CNOP, 1974; forced to resign as secretary of communications because of bribery scandal involving IBM. l-HA, 14 Dec. 1970, 22; HA, 9 Oct. 1972, 12; *Excélsior*, 13 Apr. 1977, 1, 8 Dec. 1974, 23; IEPES; DBGM92, 81.

Caso (y Andrade), Alfonso
(Deceased Nov. 30, 1970) a-Feb. 1, 1896. b-Federal District. c-Primary and secondary studies in Mexico City; preparatory studies at the National Preparatory School, Mexico City; law degree, National School of Law, UNAM, 1919; Professor of Epistemology, 1918-28, Professor of Mexican Archaeology, 1929-43, and Professor of General Ethnology, 1930-33, all at School of Philosophy and Letters, UNAM; Professor of the Philosophy of Law, National School of Law, 1918-39; Professor of Mexican Archaeology, National School of Anthropology, UNAM, 1939-43; professor at the University of Chicago, 1943; Director General of Graduate Studies and Scientific Investigation, UNAM, 1944; Director of the National Preparatory School, 1928-30. d-None. e-Joined the Mexican Labor Party founded by *Vicente Lombardo Toledano*, 1919. f-Lawyer, Legal Department, Secretariat of Industry and Commerce, 1922-27; Director of Explorations at Monte Albán, 1931-43; head of the Department of Archaeology of the National Museum, 1930-33; head of the Welfare Section of the National Agrarian Commission; Private Secretary to the Secretary of Industry and Com-

merce; Director of the National Institute of History and Anthropology, 1939-
44; *Rector of UNAM*, 1944-45; *Secretary of Government Properties*, Dec.
1946 to Dec. 31, 1948 (first appointee to
this position); Director of the National
Indigenous Institute, 1949-70. g-None.
h-Lawyer, Legal Department, Department of the Federal District, 1919;
Oficial Mayor of the Department of the
Federal District, 1920; Editor, *Mexican
Journal of Historical Studies*; author of
numerous books and articles on
indigenous peoples of Mexico. i-Taught
Miguel Alemán at the National School
of Law; son of engineer Antonio Caso
and brother of the distinguished philosopher Antonio Caso; son, *Andrés Caso
Lombardo*, was oficial mayor of Public
Works, 1970-76, and secretary of communications, 1988-92; brother-in-law of
Vicente Lombardo Toledano; married
María Lombardo Toledano (1898-64);
married Aida Lombardo Toledano, 1966;
daughter, Beatriz, is a sculptress; son-in-
law, Carlos Solorzano, is a dramatist
and novelist. j-None. k-Appointed
Rector of UNAM in 1944 to supervise
the writing of a new governing code and
to settle campus disorders. l-Nicholson,
251; Simpson, 354; IWW, 201; HA, 25
Aug. 1944; 28 May 1956, 12; WWM45,
21-22; DP70, 2375; Hayner, 266-67;
WB48, 1017; WB54, 174; Enc. Mex.,
1977, II, 409.

Castañeda Gutiérrez, Jesús
a-Apr. 1, 1921. b-Federal District.
c-Early education unknown; enrolled in
the National Military College, 1936;
graduated from the Heroic Military
College, Jan. 1, 1941, as a 2nd Lieutenant; first place awards as an outstanding
student; professor, National Military
College; professor, Higher War College;
special studies, Fort Leavenworth,
Kansas; staff and command diploma
from the Higher War College, 1949-52.
d-None. e-None. f-Chief of the Presi-

dential Staff, 1970-76. g-None. h-None.
i-Married María de la Luz Monter.
j-Career army officer; Commander of
the 1st Company of Cadets, Heroic
Military College, 1946; rank of Lt.
Colonel, 1960; rank of Colonel, 1965;
Commander of the 1st Batallion of
Presidential Guards, 1964-70. k-None.
l-*Excélsior*, 1 Dec. 1970; WNM, 37; Rev.
de Ejer., Oct. 1960, 19.

Castañeda Guzmán, Luis
a-Dec. 14, 1914. b-Oaxaca, Oaxaca.
c-Early education unknown; public
notary degree; law degree, Rector of the
University of Oaxaca. d-*Plurinominal
Federal Deputy* from PAN, 1979-82.
e-Secretary General of PAN in Oaxaca;
candidate for Federal Deputy from PAN;
for senator from PAN; for governor of
Oaxaca from PAN; founding member of
PAN, 1939. f-None. g-None. h-Lawyer
and notary public. j-None. k-None.
l-*La Nación*, 16 Sept. 1981, 11.

Castañeda O'Connor, Salvador
a-Oct. 14, 1931. b-Tepic, Nayarit.
c-Early education unknown; law degree,
National School of Law, UNAM, 1952-
56; Professor of Labor Law, Workers
University of Mexico, 1957-62; Professor of History, Normal School of
Nayarit, 1965-69. d-*Federal Deputy*
(Party Deputy from the PPS), 1973-76;
Plurinominal Federal Deputy from the
PSUM, 1982-85. e-Candidate for federal
deputy from the PPS from the Federal
District, 1961, 1970; Secretary of the
CEN of the PPS; candidate for Secretary
General of the PPS, 1974; candidate of
the PPS for mayor of Tepic, Nayarit,
1975; candidate of the PPS for senator
from Nayarit, 1976; founder and
director of the Mexican Peoples Party,
1977-81; Secretary of Legal Affairs of
the National Committee of the
UGOCEM, 1960-62; member of the
PPS, 1952-81; Secretary of Electoral
Affairs, Central Committee of the

PSUM, 1981; member of the Political Committee of the Central Committee of the PSUM. f-Chief, Office of Presidential Resolutions, Department of Agrarian Affairs, 1955-59; Secretary, City Government of Tepic, 1973. g-None. h-Practicing lawyer. j-None. k-None. l-Directorio, 1982-85; C de D, 1973-76; Lehr, 563.

Castañeda (y Alvarez de la Rosa), Jorge
a-Oct. 1, 1921. b-Federal District. c-Early education unknown; legal studies, National School of Law, UNAM, 1938-42, graduating in 1943 with a thesis on legal acts; Professor of Law at the National School of Law, UNAM, Professor of Law, Escuela Libre de Derecho, 1958; Professor at the Colegio de México, 1966-67, 1969-70. d-None. e-None. f-Career foreign service officer, joined, 1950; legal adviser to the Secretariat of Foreign Relations, 1955-58; rank of minister, 1959-62; Director General of International Organizations, Secretariat of Foreign Relations, 1959-62; Alternate Representative of Mexico to the United Nations, 1961-62; Ambassador to Egypt, 1962-65; Director-in-Chief of the Secretariat of Foreign Relations, 1965-70; Permanent Representative of Mexico to the United Nations and International Organizations in Geneva, 1970-76; *Subsecretary of Studies and Special International Affairs,* Jan. 12, 1976-79; *Secretary of Foreign Relations,* 1979-82; Ambassador Emeritus, 1982; *Ambassador to France,* 1982-88. g-None. h-None. i-Son of Jorge Castañeda Rendón, lawyer, and Carmen Alvarez de la Rosa Kraus, normal teacher; married Alicia Cabrera; son, Jorge Castañeda, is a prominent intellectual and critic of PRI. j-None. k-First appointee to this new subsecretaryship established in 1976; only Mexican in recent years to receive the appointment of ambassador emeritus except for *Antonio Carrillo Flores* and

Luis Padilla Nervo. l-HA, 18 Jan. 1976, 14; *Excélsior,* 13 Jan. 1976, 4; DPE65, 18; *Excélsior,* 9 Jan. 1976, 18, 17 May 1979, 9; HA, 20 Sept. 1982, 10; *Excélsior,* 22 Jan. 1983, 5, 8 A; DBGM87, 82.

Castañón León, Noé
a-Apr. 15, 1948. b-Berriozábal, Chiapas. c-Early education unknown; preparatory studies at the Institute of Arts and Sciences of Chiapas; law degree, National School of Law, UNAM, 1967-70, with a thesis on amparo; Professor of Law, National School of Law, UNAM, 1979-82; founding professor, Supreme Court Judicial Institute, 1978-79, 1982-83. d-None. e-Joined PRI, 1965; Secretary of Political Action of PRI, Chiapas, 1965-66. f-Judge, 1st District, Civil Court, Federal District, 1968-74; adviser, Department of Tourism, 1973-74; Secretary of Studies and Accounts, Supreme Court, 1974-79; Secretary of Agreements, Supreme Court, 1980-85; *Justice of the Supreme Court,* 1985-88, 1988- . g-Secretary General of the Student Society of the Institute of Arts and Sciences of Chiapas, 1965-66. h-None. i-Son of Wilfrido Castañón Lira, elementary school teacher, and Amparo León León; married María Elena Ramírez Iñguez, lawyer; brother Wilfrido a district court judge. j-None. k-None. l-DBGM89, 597; DBGM87, 607; DBGM92, 642.

Castaños Martínez, León Jorge
a-Jan. 31, 1938. b-Durango, Durango. c-Early education unknown; agricultural engineering degree, with a specialty in forestry, National School of Agriculture, Chapingo, 1953-59, with a thesis on "An Analysis of the Efficiency of the Supply Operations of a Forest Industry Firm in Chihuahua," 1963; MA degree in forestry, Oregon State University, 1964. d-None. e-None. f-Subdirector, Department of Forestry, National School of Agriculture, 1963-

65; adviser, Forestry Division, Secretariat of Agriculture and Hydraulic Resources, 1966-71; Director of the Working Group in Planning and Development, Subsecretary of Forestry and Fauna, 1971-72; Director General of Reforestry Development, Secretariat of Agriculture and Hydraulic Resources, 1980; *Subsecretary of Forestry and Fauna*, 1982-85; Executive Secretary of the National Forestry Committee, Secretariat of Agriculture, 1985-88. g-None. h-Directed various projects, Division of Forestry Development, Secretariat of Agriculture and Hydraulic Resources, 1980-81. i-Son of Manuel Castaños Valiente, agronomist, and Magdalena Martínez Lara, normal teacher; married Matilde Leticia Núñez, lawyer; brother, Carlos Manuel, was rector of the National School of Agriculture, 1989. j-None. k-None. l-Q es QAP, 213; DBGM, 91; DBGM89, 79.

Castaños Patoni, Fernando
a-Aug. 5, 1921. b-Durango, Durango. c-Primary studies in public and private schools; secondary studies at Secondary School No. 3, Mexico City; engineering degree, National School of Engineering, UNAM; studies in economics. d-None. e-None. f-Topographer, Department of the Federal District; planner, National Irrigation Commission; local engineer, National Railroads of Mexico; Director, Department of Planning and Promotion of Industrial Development, State of Querétaro; Director General of the Potable Water System, Secretariat of Hydraulic Resources; *Oficial Mayor of the Secretariat of Hydraulic Resources*, 1970-76. g-None. h-Director General of various private enterprises. i-Studied under *Brito Foucher* and *Gustavo Baz* at UNAM; classmate of *Luis Echeverría* at secondary school. j-None. k-None. l-HA, 14 Dec. 1970, 22; DPE71; letter; *Excélsior*, 16 June 1976, 4.

Castellano (Jiménez) Jr., Raúl
a-Nov. 3, 1902. b-Las Esperanzas, Coahuila. c-Primary and secondary studies at the Colegio Internacional, Monterrey, Nuevo León, 1912-17; secondary and preparatory studies, Colegio Civil, Monterrey, 1917-22; legal studies, School of Law, University of Guadalajara, 1923-28; law degree, Jan. 8, 1929; professor, Practical Medical School, Guadalajara, Jalisco, 1923-24; National School of Law, UNAM; and at University of Michoacán. d-*Senator from the State of Coahuila*, 1982-88. e-Leader of the movement supporting General *Miguel Henríquez Guzmán* for President, 1952. f-Scribe, Second Civil Division, Monterrey, Nuevo León; public defender, Guadalajara, Jalisco; Secretary of the First District, Guadalajara; Secretary of the Superior Court of Justice, Morelia, Michoacán, 1929; Justice of the Civil Division of the State Superior Court of Michoacán, 1929-31; attorney for the Secretariat of the Treasury, 1932-34; Oficial Mayor of Baja California del Sur, 1931; *Attorney General for the Federal District and Federal Territories*, 1934-37; Private Secretary to President Cárdenas, 1938-39; *Head of the Federal District*, 1939-40; Ambassador to Panama, 1942-46; *Supernumerary Justice of the Supreme Court*, 1963-72; adviser to the Governor of Michoacán, 1980-82; political adviser to *Miguel de la Madrid*, 1981-82; *Ambassador to Cuba*, 1989-90. g-None. h-Practicing lawyer in Mexico City, 1943-62, 1973-76; delegate to the Eighth Pan American Conference. i-Knew *Antonio Martínez Báez* at UNAM; married Consuelo Martínez Báez, sister of *Antonio Martínez Báez*; son, Raúl Castellano Martínez, served as Federal Deputy from Michoacán, 1985-88; son of Manuel Castellano Rodríguez, career military and public servant, and Rosa Jiménez Rodríguez, normal teacher. j-None. k-None. l-Letter, D del Y, 4

Jan. 1938, 1; D del Y, 2 Dec. 1935;
EBW46, 161; *Justicia*; WB48, 1022;
Excélsior, 28 July 1972, 1, 24 Feb. 1973,
17; *Hoy*, Nov. 1, 1939; *Excélsior*, 17
Mar. 1983, 14; DBGM89, 80; DBGM87,
451-52; Lehr, 63.

Castellanos, Everardo Milton
a-Mar. 23, 1920. b-Copainalá, Chiapas.
c-Primary and secondary studies at
Tuxtla Gutiérrez, Chiapas; preparatory
studies at the National Preparatory
School, Mexico City; law degree,
National School of Law, UNAM, 1943,
with a thesis on insufficient guarantees
for individual public rights. d-Local
Deputy to the State Legislature of
Chiapas; *Federal Deputy* from the State
of Chiapas, 1949-52, member of the
Economy and Statistics Committee and
the First Balloting Committee; *Alternate Senator* for Baja California del
Norte, 1964-70; *Governor of Baja
California del Norte*, 1971-74. e-Joined
PRI, 1946, President of the Regional
Executive Committee, Chiapas;
President of the State Committee of
PRI, Baja California del Norte, 1952-58;
Director of *Adolfo Ruiz Cortines'*
campaign in Baja California del Norte,
1952; Director of *Braulio Maldonado
Sánchez's* campaign for governor, 1953;
Director of *Eligio Esquivel Méndez's*
campaign for governor, 1959; adviser to
the Regional Committee of PRI and the
CEPES, 1965-70. f-Director of the Legal
Department, Secretariat of the Navy,
1952; President, Superior Tribunal of
Justice, Baja California del Norte, 1960;
Director General, Agricultural Credit
Bank, 1965-70. g-None. h-Private law
practice, Mexicali, 1953; founder of the
*Judicial Bulletin of Baja California del
Norte*. i-Personal representative of *Luis
Echeverría* at the polls, 1970. j-None.
k-CCI accused him of fraud as governor
in Jan. 1978; precandidate for senator
from Baja Calfornia, 1981. l-DGF69,
105; C de D, 1949-51, 66; DGF51, 20,

31, 34; HA, 18 Oct. 1971; letter;
Excélsior, 27 Jan. 1978, 12, 26 Dec.
1981, 16A.

Castellanos Coutiño, Horacio
a-July 7, 1929. b-Venustiano Carranza,
Chiapas. c-Primary studies in Veracruz, secondary and preparatory studies
in Mexico City; law degree, National
School of Law, UNAM, 1950-54, graduated July 1955 with a thesis on the
rule-making function of Mexican administrative law; Professor by Opposition,
Constitutional Law and Administrative
Law, National School of Law, UNAM.
d-*Senator* from the State of Chiapas,
1976-82, President, Nov. 1976. e-Delegate of the IEPES of PRI to Tamaulipas
and Hidalgo, 1970. f-Director General
of Legal Affairs and Legislation, Secretariat of the Presidency, 1970-72;
*Attorney General of the Federal
District and Federal Territories*, 1972-
76. g-None. h-Practicing lawyer, 1955-
70; author. i-Classmate at UNAM with
Jorge de la Vega Domínguez. j-None.
k-Assisted in helping to settle the 1966
student strike at UNAM. l-HA, 25 Dec.
1972, 40, 15 Apr. 1974, 32; C de S, 1976-
82; DBC, 32-33; Almanaque de Chiapas,
38; DP70, 397.

Castellanos Domínguez, Absalón
a-Oct. 2, 1923. b-Federal District.
c-Early education unknown; cadet,
Heroic Military College, July 1, 1939, to
July 1, 1942, graduated as a 2nd Lieutenant in infantry; 2nd Sergeant of cadets,
Heroic Military College; section and
company commander courses, Infantry
Center, Mar. to June 1943; course in
arms, Higher War College, Feb. to July
1960; Professor of Infantry Tactics and
Methods of Instruction, Heroic Military
College; cadet commander, Heroic Military College; Director of the Mariano
Matamoros Military School, 1972-75;
Director of the Heroic Military College,
1976-80. d-*Governor of Chiapas*, 1982-

88. e-None. f-None. g-None. h-None. i-Son of Matias Castellanos Castellanos and Hermila Domínguez Cebadua; married Elsy Herrerias Novelo; grandson of Senator Belisario Domínguez; uncle of *Jorge de la Vega Domínguez*, president of the CEN of PRI, 1987-88; cousin of distinguished woman of letters, Rosario Castellanos; disciple of *Marcelino García Barragán*, secretary of national defense, 1964-70, who taught him at the Heroic Military College. j-Career army infantry officer; Section Commander, 53rd Battalion; Section Commander, 3rd Battalion, 6th Regiment, 2nd Infantry Division; Assistant Adjutant and Inter-im Commander, 46th Infantry Battalion; Section Commander, machine gun company, 46th Infantry Battalion; Commander of the 1st Fusiliers Battalion; second in command of the 4th Infantry Battalion; Chief of Instruction, 2nd Infantry Battalion, Presidential Guards; Commander of the 1st Mixed Arms Group, Presidential Guards; Commander of the 1st 81mm Mortar Group, Presidential Guards; Commander of the 4th Infantry Battalion; Commander of the 15th Infantry Battalion; Commander of the 150th Infantry Brigade; rank of Lt. Col., Nov. 20, 1961; Garrison Commander, Manzanillo, Colima; rank of Brigadier General, 1970; Commander of the 18th Military Zone, Pachuca, Hidalgo, 1975; rank of Division General, Nov. 20, 1979; Commander of the 33rd Military Zone, Nayarit, 1982. k-Beat *Rafael Gamboa Cano* and *José González Blanco Garrido* for the PRI nomination for governor. l-Almanaque de Chiapas, 40; Rev. de Ejer., Dec. 1979, 68, Jan. 1975, 119-20, Dec. 1965, 60; *Proceso*, 13 Mar. 1989.

Castellanos Jr., Francisco
a-1893. b-San Nicolás, Tamaulipas. c-Law degree. d-Governor of Tamaulipas, 1931; *Senator* from the State of Tamaulipas, 1934-40. f-Agent of the Ministerio Público in Tamaulipas; Judge of the First Appellate Court, Tamaulipas; Attorney General of Tamaulipas; member of the Advisory Council to the President of Mexico; Secretary of the Presidency, 1940-41; *Attorney General of the Federal District and Federal Territories*, 1941-46; Administrator of Customs for Matamoros, Tamaulipas, 1952-58. g-None. i-Parents were peasants. j-None. k-President of the Opposition Socialist Party of Tamaulipas; split with state political boss *Emilio Portes Gil* after *Portes Gil* wanted to run for governor a second time. l-*Hoy*, 20 Sept. 1941, 3; DGF56, 162; Correa, 77; NYT, 12 Sept. 1941, 8.

Castellanos Tena, Fernando
a-June 3, 1917. b-Zamora, Michoacán. c-Early education unknown; law degree, UNAM, 1939-43, with a thesis on constitutions; LLD, National School of Law, UNAM, 1956-67; professor, School of Political and Social Sciences, UNAM, 1951-57; Director, National Preparatory School No. 8, 1965-68; Director, Graduate Studies, National School of Law, UNAM, 1970-73. d-None. e-Joined PNR, 1935. f-Administrative official, Secretariat of Public Health, 1935-44; Agent of the Ministerio Público, Attorney General of the Federal District, 1945-48; Private Secretary to the Subsecretary of the Treasury, *Angel González de la Vega*, 1949-50; technical adviser, Secretariat of the Treasury, 1951-52; Agent of the Ministerio Público, Attorney General of Mexico, 1955-57; Secretary of Studies and Accounts, Supreme Court of Justice, 1957-68; Federal Circuit Court Judge, 1968-74; *Justice of the Supreme Court*, 1976-82, 1982-85. g-None. h-Practicing lawyer, 1948-49, 1953-54. i-Son of Fernando Castellanos Gutiérrez, lawyer, and Carmen Tena Herrera. j-None. k-None. l-DBGM, 643.

Castellot Madrazo, Gonzalo
a-Feb. 20, 1922. b-Campeche, Campeche. c-Primary studies at the Colegio Francés, Mexico City, 1928-33; secondary studies at Secondary School No. 3, Mexico City, 1934-36; preparatory studies at the National Preparatory School, 1937-38; legal studies from the National School of Law, UNAM, 1939-45, graduating with a thesis on salaries, Mar. 26, 1949. d-*Federal Deputy* from the Federal District, Dist. 7, 1961-64, member of the Committee on Radio and Television Industry and the Editorial Committee; *Federal Deputy* from the Federal District, Dist. 9, 1979-82; *Federal Deputy* from the Federal District, Dist. 37, 1985-88. e-Official Orator for the PRI during the presidential campaigns of *Adolfo López Mateos* and *Gustavo Díaz Ordaz*. f-Head of the Department of Radio, Television, and Movies of the Department of Information and Public Relations of the Office of President of Mexico, 1964-70. g-Founded the workers' union for Station XEX, 1947; Secretary General of the National Industrial Union of Television Actors and Workers, 1955- . h-Radio and television announcer; director of documentary movies and television programs. i-Classmate of *José López Portillo* at UNAM; son of José Castellot Paullada, diplomat and journalist, and Ernestina Madrazo Torres, sister of Manuel F. Madrazo Torres, director of the department of health, 1934. j-None. k-None. l-DBM68, 131; C de D, 1961-63, 74; DBGM87, 452.

Castillo Ayala, Javier
a-Oct. 2, 1945. b-Federal District. c-Early education unknown; economics degree, National School of Economics, UNAM, 1963-67, with a thesis on the "Analysis of the Evolution of Accounting in the Public Sector"; special studies in monetary and financial subjects, CEMLA, Mexico City, 1972-73; studies in public finance at the United Nations and the International Monetary Fund. d-None. e-Joined PRI, 1971. f-Subdirector, Department of Economic Studies, Director General of Credit, Secretariat of the Treasury, 1974-75; Chief of the Unified Financial Program, Director General of Credit, Secretariat of the Treasury, 1975-76; adviser to the Secretary of the Treasury, 1977-78; Director of Financial Statistics, Division of Financial Planning, Secretariat of the Treasury, 1978-79; Director General of Unified Public Finances, General Coordinator of Budget Control, Secretariat of Planning and Programming, 1979-81; Director General of Budget Policy, Subsecretary of Budgeting, Secretariat of Programming and Budget, 1981-82; *Subsecretary of Budget Control and Accounting*, Secretariat of Programming and Budget, 1982-85; adviser, Controller General of Mexico, 1985-86; Director of Corporate Planning, Sidermex, 1986-88; Director General of Azufrera Panamericana, 1989-90. g-None. h-None. i-Political disciple of *Miguel de la Madrid*; son of José Guadalupe Castillo Martínez, laborer, and Gracia Ayala Martínez Salinas; married Guadalupe Amezcua Magaña, social worker. j-None. k-None. l-Q es QAP; DBGM89, 81.

Castillo Castillo, Fernando
a-Mar. 20, 1920. b-Oaxaca, Oaxaca. c-Primary studies at the Colegio Unión, Oaxaca, 1920-25; secondary and preparatory at the Institute of Arts and Sciences, Oaxaca; law degree from the Autonomous Institute of Arts and Sciences, Oaxaca; Professor of Sociology and General Theory, School of Law, Benito Juárez University, Oaxaca. d-Local Deputy to the 41st and 45th State Legislatures of Oaxaca; *Alternate Federal Deputy* from the State of Oaxaca, Dist. 9, 1961-64, 1967-70; *Federal Deputy* from the State of

Oaxaca, Dist. 7, 1970-73, member of the Third Ejido Committee and the Naval Committee. e-President of the local electoral committee of Oaxaca, 1958-60; delegate of PRI from Oaxaca to the national PRI conventions. f-Director of the Office of Investigations, Department of Agrarian Affairs; Civil and Criminal Judge of the First Instance, Ejecutla and Juchitlán, Oaxaca; agent of the Ministerio Público (Criminal Division) in Oaxaca. g-None. h-None. j-None. k-None. l-Directorio, 1970-72; C de D, 1970-72; C de D, 1961-64; C de D, 1967-70; MGF69, 94.

Castillo Fernández, Guillermo
a-June 25, 1902. b-Teziutlán, Puebla. c-Primary and secondary studies in Teziutlán; normal studies at the Normal Institute of Puebla on a scholarship from the governor of Puebla, 1917-20; completed teaching certificate in Mexico City; teacher for seventeen years; director of primary and secondary schools; rural missionary teacher. d-Local Deputy to the State Legislature of Puebla; *Senator* from the State of Puebla, 1952-58, President of the First Tariff Committee and the Foreign Affairs Committee; First Secretary of the Indigenous Affairs Committee; member of the First Public Education Committee and the Consular Service and Diplomatic Committee. e-Secretary General of *Rafael Avila Camacho's* campaign for governor of Puebla, 1950. f-Federal Inspector of Education, Tlaxcala, Puebla, Oaxaca, Chihuahua, Coahuila, Durango, and Chiapas; agent of the Secretariat of Agriculture in Puebla, Tlaxcala, Oaxaca, and Veracruz; Oficial Mayor of the National Pawnshop; Director General of the National Pawnshop; Information Officer for the Mexican–North American Commission on Hoof and Mouth Disease; Oficial Mayor of the State of Puebla under Governor *Rafael Avila Camacho*, 1951-

52. g-None. k-Knew *Rafael Avila Camacho* since they were children in Teziutlán. j-None. k-None. l-DGF56, 7, 9-13; Ind. Biog., 40.

Castillo Hernández, José
a-Nov. 28, 1918. b-León de los Aldama, Guanajuato. c-Primary and secondary studies in Guanajuato; medical degree. d-Mayor of León, Guanajuato; *Federal Deputy* from the State of Guanajuato, Dist. 2, 1967-70; *Senator* from the State of Guanajuato, 1970-76, President of the National Properties and Resources Committee, First Secretary of the Foreign and Domestic Trade Committee, Second Secretary of the Industries, the Second Mines, and the Health Committees. e-Member of PRI. f-Secretary General of Government of the State of Guanajuato. g-Secretary General of CNOP in Guanajuato. i-Married Celia Río de Castillo. j-None. k-None. l-C de S, 1970-76, 74; C de D, 1967-70; PS, 1135.

Castillo Lanz, Angel
a-Nov. 1, 1898. b-Isla de Champoton, Campeche. c-Primary studies in Champoton; law degree, School of Law, University of Campeche. d-Governor of Campeche, 1923-27; Federal Deputy from the State of Campeche, Dist. 2, 1928-30, member of the Gran Comisión, Secretary of the Chamber; Federal Deputy from the State of Campeche, Dist. 1, 1930-32, member of the Gran Comisión; Federal Deputy from the State of Campeche, Dist. 1, 1932-34, member of the Gran Comisión; *Senator* from the State of Campeche, 1934-40. e-None. f-Oficial Mayor of the Chamber of Deputies, 1934; Director, Accounting Office, Chamber of Deputies, 1951-56. g-None. j-None. k-Some sources considered him to have been the political boss of Campeche. l-Enc. de Mex., II. 301; DGF56, 38; DGF51, I, 28; C de S, 1934-40; PS, 1138.

Castillo Larranaga, José

a-Feb. 5, 1899. b-Oaxaca, Oaxaca.
c-Primary and secondary studies in
Oaxaca, Oaxaca; preparatory studies at
the Institute of Arts and Sciences of
Oaxaca (four years) and completed at
the University of Puebla and the
National Preparatory School; law degree
from the National School of Law,
UNAM, May 24, 1922; Professor of
Procedural Law, 1935 to 1960s, Profes-
sor of Amparo and Guarantees, 1942,
and Professor of Agrarian Law, 1940 to
1960s, all at the National School of
Law, UNAM; adviser to the University
Council of UNAM; Director of the
Division of Law, Postgraduate School,
UNAM; Dean, National School of Law,
UNAM, 1949-51. d-Federal Deputy
from the State of Oaxaca, 1924-26,
President of the Justice Committee,
president of the political bloc. e-None.
f-Actuary, 4th Supernumerary District,
Federal District; Agent of the Ministerio
Público of the Attorney General of
Tamaulipas; Secretary of the Third
Correctional Judicial District, Federal
District; First Supernumerary Judge of
the District Court of Puebla; lawyer,
Secretariat of Government, 1951;
Justice of the Superior Tribunal of
Justice of the Federal District and
Federal Territories, 1951-52, 1953-58.
g-None. h-Student scribe for the Second
Justice of Peace of the Higher Military
Tribunal; practicing lawyer, 1927-51;
author of numerous legal codes and
books. j-None. k-None. l-López, 180;
DGF51, I, 487; DGF56, 513.

Castillo Ledón, Amalia

(Deceased June 3, 1986) a-Aug. 18,
1902. b-San Jeronimo, Tamaulipas.
c-Teaching certificate at the Normal
School for Women, Ciudad Victoria,
Tamaulipas; studies in the humanities
at the graduate school, UNAM, with a
degree in letters; studies, National
Conservatory, Mexico City; teacher at a
girls' school in Ciudad Victoria, 1918;
teacher at the Normal School for Men,
Mexico City, 1925-29. d-None.
e-National Association for Child
Welfare, 1929; founder of the Child
Welfare Committee in Tepic, Nayarit,
1930; head of the Bureau of Educational
Activities, General Administration of
Civic Action, Mexico City, 1933-45;
adviser to the Mexican delegation to the
United Nations Conference on International Organizations in San Francisco,
1945; Ambassador to Finland and
Sweden, 1956; adviser to the Secretary
of Foreign Relations, 1957; *Subsecretary
of Public Education*, 1958-64; Ambassador and head of the permanent delegation to the International Organization
of Atomic Energy, 1964-70; Ambassador
to Austria, 1967. g-Founder of the
Mexican Alliance for Women, 1953;
President of the Revolutionary Federation of Women. h-Statistician of the
Bureau of Education, State of Tamaulipas, 1918; joined the Foreign Service in
1953; President of the Inter-American
Commission of Women; author of many
dramatic works and numerous articles
on the theater. i-Wife of the Mexican
historian Luis Castillo Ledón, 1879-
1944, who was governor of Nayarit,
1930-31. j-None. k-First woman to
address the Mexican Senate on women's
suffrage; first woman to be appointed to
a subsecretary position in the Mexican
cabinet. l-WWMG, 12; WWM45, 2223;
DGF56, 126, 129; Correa 46, 332; HA,
23 Feb. 1959, 17; Enc. Mex., II, 210; HA,
17 June 1986, 41; O'Campo, 143-44.

Castillo López, Jesús

a-May 16, 1905. b-Cuernavaca, Morelos. c-Law degree, National School of
Law, UNAM, 1928-32. d-*Senator* from
Morelos, 1940-42; *Governor of Morelos*,
1942-46. e-None. f-Secretary General
of Government of the State of Morelos,
1938-39; Director General of Cinematography, Secretariat of Government,

1951. i-Protégé of General *Elpidio Perdomo*. j-None. k-None. l-HA, 15 May 1942, 3; HA, 18 Jan. 1946, IV; Peral, 162; DGF51, I, 69.

Castillo (Martínez), Heberto
a-Aug. 23, 1933. b-Ixhuatlán de Madero, Veracruz. c-Primary studies in public school, Mexico City; secondary studies from Secondary School No. 4, Mexico City; civil engineering degree; professor at UNAM and at IPN. d-*Plurinominal Federal Deputy* from the Mexican Workers Party, 1985-88, member of the Government Commit- tee. e-Coordinator of the National Liberation Movement, 1963; Secretary General of the Mexican Workers Party (PTM), 1982-84; formed a coalition with the Revolutionary Workers Party (PRT), 1986; presidential candidate of a leftist coalition, 1987, but withdrew in favor of *Cuauhtémoc Cárdenas*, 1988; candidate for president of the Demo- cratic Revolutionary Party (PRD), 1993; withdrew from the PRD, 1993. f-None. g-None. h-President of the Indé Construction Company, 1956-58. i-Son of Felipe Gregorio Castillo, mule driver in highland Otomi Indian region, and Graciano Martínez; married María Teresa Juárez Carranza; *Cuauhtémoc Cárdenas* managed his company, 1956- 57; accompanied General *Lázaro Cárdenas*, 1954-61. j-None. k-Invented the Tridilosa structural construction method; protested U.S. intervention in Guatemala, 1956; arrested and incarcer- ated as a political prisoner for participa- tion in the student movement, 1968-70. l-HA, 3 Oct. 1983, 7; Protag., 77; Gil, 246; letter.

Castillo Mena, Ignacio
a-July 31, 1929. b-Durango. c-Primary studies at the Justo Sierra School, Monterrey, and Secondary School No. 3, Mexico City; preparatory studies at the National Preparatory School; law

degree, National School of Law, UNAM, July 9, 1951, with an honorable mention and a 9.6 average; Professor of History and Literature, National Preparatory School. d-*Alternate Senator* from the State of Durango, 1964-67; *Federal Deputy* from the Federal District, Dist. 6, 1967-70, member of the Legislative Studies Committee, Second Section (Civil Law), Secretary to the President of the Legislative Studies Committee for the first year; member of the Federal District Committee; *Senator* from Durango, 1976-82; *Plurinominal Federal Deputy* from the Party of the Democratic Revolution, 1988-91. e-Official orator for PRI, 1950-52, active during the presidential campaign of *Adolfo Ruiz Cortines*, 1952; *Director of Youth Action for PRI*, 1954-59; Sub- director General of Professions for PRI, 1949-61; Director of Legal Affairs for PRI, 1961-64; state committeeman from Durango to PRI, 1952-70; Private Secretary to the President of the CEN of PRI, 1966-68; resigned from PRI and joined the Cardenista Front for National Reconstruction Party, 1987; joined the PRD, 1988; coordinator of the PRD in Michoacán and member of the CEN of the PRD. f-Secretary to the President of the Superior Court of Justice of the Federal District and Federal Territories; Director of Public Relations for the Secretariat of Industry and Commerce; President of the Local Board of Concilia- tion and Arbitration, 1971-75, for the Federal District; Ambassador to Ecuador, 1991-94. g-President of the 1947 Generation of Law School stu- dents. h-None. i-Collaborator of *Lauro Ortega Martínez*; married Alicia Valdez López; son of *Mariano Castillo Nájera*, senator from Durango, 1946-52, and Clementina Mena. j-None. k-Accused by PRD members of being a turncoat for accepting ambassadorial appointment, 1991. l-HA, 2 Aug. 1971, 62; WWMG,

12; letter; C de D, 1967-69; DPE61, 101; MGF69, 105; C de S, 1964-70; *Excélsior*, 6 Apr. 1973, 10; *Justicia*, Oct. 1973; HA, 27 Oct. 1975, 23; DBGM92, 85.

Castillo Nájera, Francisco
(Deceased 1954) a-Nov. 25, 1886. b-Durango, Durango. c-Primary and secondary studies in Durango; preparatory at the Juárez Institute of Durango; medical degree from the National School of Medicine, UNAM, 1903; advanced studies at the University of Paris and the University of Berlin; Professor of Urology at the Military Medical College, 1917-27; Professor of Forensic Medicine at the National School of Medicine, UNAM, 1920-22, Medicine, UNAM, 1927; Professor of Urology for postgraduate students, UNAM, 1927. d-None. e-None. f-Director of the Juárez Hospital, Mexico City, 1918-19; Director of the Military Medical College, 1920; head of the Council of Legal Medicine for the Federal District, 1919-21; Minister to China, 1922-24; Ambassador to Belgium, 1927-30; Ambassador to Holland, 1930-32; head of the Department of Health and Welfare, 1932; Ambassador to Sweden, 1932, to France, 1933-35, and to the League of Nations, 1934; *Ambassador to the United States*, 1935-45; *Secretary of Foreign Relations*, 1945-46; President of the National Securities Commission, 1946-54. g-None. h-Founding member of the Mexican Medical Association, President of the National Academy of Medicine. i-Close personal friend of *Lázaro Cárdenas*; brother, *Marino Castillo Nájera*, was federal deputy from Durango, 1943-45; and Senator, 1946-52; son, Francisco, was a Captain in the Navy and subdirector of the Naval Medical Center; son, Guillermo, was head of the Department of Security of the General Administration of the Consular Service of the Secretariat of

Foreign Relations; brother, José, died in the Revolution, 1914; son of Rosa Nájera and Romualdo Castillo, political boss of Indé, Durango; married Eugenia Dávila Zayas; nephew, *Ignacio Castillo Mena*, was senator from Durango, 1976-82. j-Career army medical officer; Lt. Colonel and surgeon, Oct. 11, 1915; director of medical services, Laveaga Brigade; director of the military hospitals in León and Torreón, 1915; director of sanitary services, Sonora, 1915; director of sanitary services, Baja California, 1915-17; rank of Colonel, July 21, 1916; Brigadier General, Jan. 21, 1921; and Brigade General, Jan. 11, 1939; retired from the military, July 16, 1951. k-Precandidate for president, 1939. l-DP70 403; Strode, 370; Peral, 162-63; DGF50, 83; EBW46, 34; DGF47, 20; DPE65, 19; DBM68, 133; Enc. Mex., II, 420; DGF51, II, 105; Kirk, 210-11; Michaels, 3; HA, 29 Mar. 1946; O'Campo, 72-73; Medina, 20, 11; Gómez, 103.

Castillo Nájera, Marino
a-July 18, 1890. b-Durango, Durango. c-Primary studies in Durango; preparatory studies at the National Preparatory School, Mexico City; law degree, National School of Law, UNAM. d-Federal Deputy from the State of Durango, 1918-20; Federal Deputy from the State of Durango, Dist. 1, 1922-24; *Federal Deputy* from the State of Durango, Dist. 3, 1943-45; *Senator* from Durango, 1946-52. e-None. f-Consulting lawyer to the Secretariat of Agriculture; Director of the Legal Department of the Department of the Federal District; Justice of the Superior Tribunal of Justice of the Federal District, 1940-42. g-None. h-Practicing lawyer. i-Brother of *Francisco Castillo Nájera*, secretary of foreign relations, 1945-46; father of *Ignacio Castillo Mena*, senator from Durango, 1976-82; son of Rosa Nájera and Romualdo Castillo, political boss of Indé, Durango.

j-Supported Obregón as of Jan. 4, 1920.
k-None. l-Peral; DGF47, 20; C de S,
1946-52; DGF51, I, 6, 9, 11, 12, 14;
Gómez, 103.

Castillo Peralta, Ricardo
a-Mar. 11, 1939. b-San Luis Río
Colorado, Sahuaripa, Sonora. c-Primary
and secondary studies in Sonora; law
degree, University of Sonora, 1959-63.
d-*Federal Deputy* from the State of
Sonora, Dist. 1, 1976-79, coordinator of
the deputies from the CNC; *Federal
Deputy* from the State of Sonora, Dist.
5, 1982-85. e-Member of the IEPES of
PRI, 1975-78; general delegate of the
CEN of PRI to Campeche, 1982.
f-Director of Coordinators, Rural Credit
Bank; Director of Coordinators, Secre-
tary of Agriculture and Hydraulic
Resources; Private Secretary to *Alfredo
Bonfil*, Secretary General of the CNC,
1970-73. g-Coordinator in the CNC;
delegate of the CNC to various states;
Secretary General of the Leagues of
Agrarian Communities and Peasant
Unions of Sonora; President of the
Student Federation of Sonora, 1959-60;
President, Political Committee, CNC,
1977-80. i-Married Beatriz Solís.
j-None. k-None. l-Directorio, 1982-85;
C de D, 1976-79; Lehr, 448; DBGM, 486.

Castillo Peraza, Carlos Enrique
a-Apr. 17, 1947. b-Mérida, Yucatán.
c-Early education unknown; philosophy
degree, UNAM, 1968-71; special studies
in Greek philosophy, Freiburg University, Switzerland, 1972-76; teacher,
Centro Universitario Montejo, Mérida,
1976-78; professor, La Salle University,
1972-82, 1987-89. d-*Plurinominal
Federal Deputy* from PAN, 1979-82,
1988-91. e-Joined PAN, 1967; Director,
National Institute of Studies and
Political Training, PAN, 1979; Secretary
of International Relations, CEN of
PAN, 1979-82; National Adviser to
PAN, 1979- ; *President of PAN*, 1993- .

f-None. g-None. h-Self-employed,
1976-89. i-Son of Julio Enrique Castillo
González, businessman and Isela Peraza
Casares, dental surgeon; married Julieta
López Morales, economist. j-None.
k-None. l-DBGM89, 415.

Castillo Solter, Manuel
(Deceased) a-Mar. 1, 1894. b-Jalisco.
c-Primary studies at the liceo for boys;
engineering degree, National School of
Engineering, UNAM. d-Member of the
City Council, Mexico City, 1927-28;
Federal Deputy from the State of
Morelos, Dist. 1, 1958-61, alternate
member of the Tax Committee and
member of the First Balloting Commit-
tee. e-Member of PARM. f-Director of
Telecommunications Service, Secre-
tariat of Communications and Public
Works, 1931; Private Secretary to the
Secretary of Communications and
Public Works, 1931; zone chief, Agricul-
tural Credit Bank, 1934; Director of
Technical Engineering, Sanitation
Engineering Division, Secretariat of
Health, 1938; Secretary of Land Office
Boards, Secretariat of the Treasury,
1944. g-None. h-None. j-Joined the
Revolution, 1913; reached rank of Lt.
Colonel; member of the Legion of
Honor. k-None. l-Func., 282; C de D.,
1958-61, 73.

Castillo Tielemans, José
(Deceased July 3, 1990) a-1911. b-San
Cristóbal de las Casas, Chiapas.
c-Primary studies in San Cristobal de
las Casas; preparatory at the National
Preparatory School, Mexico City; law
degree, National School of Law,
UNAM, 1937, with a thesis on repara-
tions for damage in criminal law;
professor, University Extension of the
Military College. d-*Senator* from the
State of Chiapas, 1958-64; Secretary of
the Senate, 1959; President of the
Committee on Immigration, President
of the Third Committee on Labor; First

Executive Secretary of the Second Committee on Justice and a member of the Special Committee on Legislative Studies; *Governor of Chiapas*, 1964-70. e-Active in the CEPES in support of *Manuel Avila Camacho* for President, 1940; Private Secretary to *Gabriel Leyva Velázquez*, President of PRI, 1952-56; Private Secretary to *Agustín Olachea Aviles*, 1956-58, President of PRI; member of the Regional Committee of PRI, Chiapas. f-Attorney General of the State of Hidalgo; agent of the Ministerio Público attached to the Penal Courts, Federal District; Investigator, Secretariat of Agriculture; Substitute President of the Board of Conciliation and Arbitration for the Federal District. g-Delegate to the 5th National Student Congress, 1928; President of the National Law School Student Association, 1936; founder of an organization of Chiapan residents in Mexico City. i-Son of Miguel Castillo and Manuela Tielemans. j-None. k-None. l-WWMG, 12; C de S, 1958-64, 54; DPE51, II, 210, 213; Func., 152.

Castillo Torre, José
(Deceased) a-1891. b-Mérida, Yucatán. c-Law degree, University of Yucatán, 1914; member of the University of the Southeast Council, 1922. d-Councilman for Mérida, Yucatán, 1918; Federal Deputy from the State of Yucatán, 1918-24; President of the Chamber of Deputies, 1919; *Senator* from the State of Yucatán, 1926-30, President of the Senate, 1926; *Senator* from the State of Yucatán, 1940-46, Secretary of the Senate; President of the First Public Education Committee, President of the Second Foreign Relations Committee; *Federal Deputy* from the State of Yucatán, 1949-52, member of the Legislative Studies Committee (1st and 2nd years), the First Committee on Government, and the Foreign Relations

Committee; member of the Gran Comisión. e-None. f-Member of the State Commission to Revise the Legal Codes of Yucatán, 1916; assistant lawyer for the Secretary General of Government of the State of Yucatán, 1917; representative of the State of Yucatán in Mexico City, 1922; President of the Editorial Commission of the Secretariat of Foreign Relations; legal adviser to the Mexican delegation to the United Nations Conference on International Organizations, San Francisco, 1945. g-None. h-Consulting lawyer to the State Government of Yucatán, 1918, 1924; lawyer for Railroads of Yucatán in Mexico City, 1922, for the Secretariat of Foreign Relations, 1934, 1937, for the Consulting Office of the Attorney General of Mexico, 1938-39; author of many legal articles. j-None. k-None l-WWM45, 23; C de D, 1949-51, 67; DGF51, 27, 29, 32, 33, 36; Enc. Mex., II, 210; Peral, 164; WB48, 1026.

Castillón Coronado, María Refugio
a-Mar. 24, 1929. b-Guadalajara, Jalisco. c-Early education unknown; no degree. d-Councilwoman of the City Council of Guadalajara, 1956-58, under Mayor *Juan Gil Preciado*, and 1971-73, under Mayor *Guillermo Cosío Vidaurri*; *Federal Deputy* from the State of Jalisco, Dist. 7, 1976-79, member of the Social Action Committee, the Agricultural Development Committee, Section Three of the Education Development Committee, the Development of Natural and Energy Resources Committee, the Forest and Fauna Development Committee, and the Maternal and Infant Section of the Development of Social Security and Public Welfare Committee. e-None. f-None. g-Member of the League of Small Industries of the City of Guadalajara, 1947; Secretary General of the Union of Unsalaried Workers of Jalisco; active feminist in Jalisco. j-None. k-None. l-*Excélsior*, 24 Aug. 1976, 18;

Enc. Mex., 1977, IV, 579; D de C, 1976-79, 4, 11, 18, 19, 23, 31, 40.

Castorena Monterrubio, Saúl
a-Aug. 22, 1942. b-Huejutla, Hidalgo. c-Studies at the Autonomous University of Puebla, law degree; studies toward an MA in education from the National Center of Industrial Technical Teaching. d-*Federal Deputy* from the Federal District, Dist. 15, 1976-79; Minority Coordinator of his party in the chamber, 1976-77. e-Representative of PARM to the Federal Electoral Commission; delegate of PARM to every state in Mexico; Coordinating Secretary of Legislation of the CEN of PARM, 1976-77. f-None. g-None. h-Practicing lawyer, notary, and actuary. i-Married María de los Angeles Hidalgo. j-None. k-None. l-D de C, 1976-79, 12; HA, 30 Apr. 1979, VIII.

Castorena (Zavala), José de Jesús
a-Nov. 6, 1901. b-Jaripito, Guanajuato. c-Early education unknown; law degree, National School of Law, UNAM, 1925, with a thesis on strike law in Mexico; Professor of Labor Law, UNAM. d-None. e-None. f-*Oficial Mayor of Labor*, 1940; President of the Federal Conciliation and Arbitration Board; *Provisional Governor of Guanajuato*, 1947-48. g-None. h-Practicing lawyer; author of several legal works. i-Attended UNAM with *Antonio Martínez Báez*; protégé of *José Aguilar y Maya*; married to Luisa Bringas. j-None. k-Considered an outstanding authority on labor law; replaced *Vicente Lombardo Toledano* as professor of this subject at UNAM. l-DBM68, 134; HA, 16 Jan. 1948, 3-4; HA, 20 Feb. 1948, 11-12; Anderson; López, 183.

Castrejón y Chávez, Gustavo
a-June 11, 1910. b-Hacienda de San Pedro Jorullo, Municipio de la Huacana, Michoacán. c-Studied at the Colegio de

San Nicolás de Hidalgo (University of Michoacán) and the University of LaSalle, Chicago. d-*Federal Deputy* from the Federal District, Dist. 2, 1946-49, member of the First Committee on Public Education, the Second Committee on Elections, and the Tourism Committee; member of the Social Welfare Committee, 1947. f-Tax representative of the State of México; *Oficial Mayor of the Secretariat of Hydraulic Resources*, 1958-61. g-None. h-Cashier of the National Irrigation Commission; accountant for the National Irrigation Commission; Director General of National Schools in Los Angeles, California; Director General of the Radio Technical Institute of Mexico, S.A., 1966-68. i-Married Carmen Ulloa. j-None. k-None. l-DBM68, 134; C de D, 1946-48; DPE61, 90; WB48, 1028.

Castro Cabrera, Samuel
a-1917. b-Los Mochis, Sinaloa. c-Early education unknown; no degree. d-*Federal Deputy* from the State of Sinaloa, Dist. 1, 1958-61, member of Development of Cooperatives Committee and alternate member of the Sugar Industry and Navy Committees; *Federal Deputy* from the State of Sinaloa, Dist. 1, 1964-67, member of the Foodstuffs and Second Labor Committees. e-Member of the PNR, PRM, and the PRI; participant in the 1952, 1958, and 1964 presidential campaigns in Sinaloa. f-None. g-None. h-Employee, Ingenio of Los Mochis. i-Collaborator of *Gabriel Leyva Velázquez*, president of the CEN of PRI and powerful regional leader in Sinaloa. j-None. k-None. l-C de D, 1958-61, 74; 1964-67, 47, 94.

Castro Elías, Miguel
a-Aug. 31, 1910. b-Tochtepec, Puebla. c-Primary studies at the José Manzo Institute, Puebla, Puebla; no degree. d-Local Deputy, State of Veracruz, Dist. 8, 1959-62; *Federal Deputy* from the

State of Veracruz, Dist. 9, 1964-67, member of the Second Labor Committee; *Federal Deputy* from same, 1979-82. e-None. f-Representative of labor on the Board of Conciliation and Arbitration, State of Veracruz, 1957-58. g-Secretary General of the Union of Workers and Artisans of the Beer Industry (4 times); Secretary General of the Federation of Unions of Beer Workers of the Mexican Republic of CROC; Secretary of Conflicts of CROC for Orizaba, Veracruz, 1968-70; Secretary General of CROC in the State of Veracruz, 1961-64, 1971-74; President of the Political Committee of CROC, State of Veracruz, 1975-79; Secretary of Economics and Technical Affairs, CROC, 1976-80; President of CROC, 1978-79. h-Employee in the Río Blanco Thread and Textile Factory, Veracruz, 1926-36; master mechanic, Cervecería Moctezuma, S.A., Orizaba, Veracruz, 1936-79. j-None. k-None. l-C de D, 1979-82, 17; C de D, 1967-70, 26; Protag., 77.

Castro Estrada, José
(Deceased Dec. 1, 1980) a-Dec. 29, 1908. b-Morelia, Michoacán. c-Primary and secondary education in Morelia under Professor Vargas; preparatory in the National Preparatory School in Mexico City; law degree from the National School of Law, UNAM, Dec. 16, 1929; Professor of Administrative Law at the National School of Law, UNAM, for thirteen years; adviser to and member of the Governing Board of UNAM, 1962-72. d-None. e-Supporter of *Juan Andreu Almazán* for president, 1940. f-Secretary of the Review Board for Fiscal Infractions, Secretariat of the Treasury, 1929; agent of the Ministerio Público of the Criminal Courts; *Subsecretary of Forest Resources of the Secretary of Agriculture*, 1952 (first appointee); *Justice of the Supreme Court*, 1952-67; Director General of

Forest Products of Mexico, 1968-70. g-Founding member of the Socialist Lawyers Front, 1936. h-Adviser to financial institutions; adviser to the National Lottery; adviser to Latin American Life Insurance Company, S.A.; head of legal affairs for private charity; author of articles on legal and economic subjects; member of several committees in charge of writing new federal codes; practicing lawyer in Mexico City, 1970-72. i-Friend of numerous members of the 1929 generation of lawyers at the National Law School, including *Miguel Alemán, Antonio Carrillo Flores, Angel Carvajal, Andrés Serra Rojas, Manuel Gual Vidal, Antonio García López, Manuel Sánchez Cuen,* and *Carlos Franco Sodi;* father was a lawyer and grandfather was a justice of the Supreme Court; son, José, was director general of Mexican consulting in Engineering and Development, S.A.. j-None. k-Briefly in exile after the 1940 election. l-Letter, DBM68, 135; WWMG, 12; DGF69, 129; DGF51, 203; *Justicia,* Feb. 1967; *Excélsior,* 2 Dec. 1980, 17.

Castro Leal, Antonio
(Deceased Jan. 8, 1981) a-Mar. 2, 1896. b-San Luis Potosí, San Luis Potosí. c-Primary, secondary, and preparatory studies in Mexico City; member of the 1915 "Seven Wise Men" generation; law degree, National School of Law, UNAM; LLD, National School of Law, UNAM; Ph.D., Georgetown University; Professor of Spanish Literature, National Preparatory School; Professor of Mexican and South American Literature, Graduate College, UNAM; Professor of Public International Law, UNAM, 1929; Rector of UNAM, Dec. 9, 1928 to June 21, 1929. d-*Federal Deputy* from the Federal District, Dist. 18, 1958-61, member of the Editorial Committee (first year), the Legislative Studies Committee (4th Section), the

Cinematography Development Committee, and the Foreign Relations Committee. e-None. f-Private Secretary to the Rector of UNAM, 1920; First Secretary to Chile, 1920, 1923; Chargé d'Affaires, Chile, 1922, 1924-25; First Secretary and adviser to Mexican Embassy, Washington, D.C., 1925; inspector, Mexican Consulates in the United States, 1926; legal adviser, Commercial Aviation Commission, Washington, D.C., 1927; Secretary General and technical adviser, Mexican delegation to the Inter-American Conference, Havana, Cuba, 1928; official adviser to the League of Nations, 1930-31; Diplomatic Counselor to France, 1929; Mexican delegate to the First Conference on the Codification of International Law, The Hague, 1930; adviser to the Mexican Ambassador to Spain, 1931; Director, Department of Bellas Artes (first appointee), 1934; Director General, Cinematographic Supervision, Secretariat of Government, 1947; Ambassador to UNESCO, 1949-52. g-None. h-Founder and Director of the *Revista de Literatura Mexicana*, 1940; author and editor of many books. i-Knew *Jaime Torres Bodet* and *Luis Garrido Díaz* at the National Preparatory School; married María Rafaela Espino. j-None. k-None. l-DEM, 75; DGF47, 72; Enc. Mex., II, 213-14; Peral, 167; C de D, 1958-60, 74; Func., 193; Novo, 389; WWLA35, 88; López, 185; HA, June, 1958; Enc. Mex., 1977, II, 425-26; *Excélsior*, 8 Jan. 1981, 4.

Castro (Rivera), Jesús Agustín
(Deceased Mar. 22, 1954) a-Aug. 15, 1887. b-Rancho de Eureka, Ciudad Lerdo, Durango. c-Primary in the public schools of Durango, had to leave school for economic reasons; no degree. d-*Senator* from the State of Durango, 1924-28; Governor of Durango, 1921-24. e-None. f-Governor of Chiapas, 1914-15; Governor of Oaxaca, 1915-16;

Subsecretary of National Defense, 1917-18, in charge of the Secretaryship; *Secretary of National Defense, 1939-40.* g-None. h-Conductor for a streetcar company, 1910. i-Son of José F. Castro, a middle class rancher; close friend of Enrique Nájera, who followed *Jesús Castro* as governor of Durango, 1924-27, when he was military commander of the state; Castro's personal political organization supported Nájera. j-Led 127 men against the Díaz government, Nov. 20, 1910; joined the Revolution, 1911, serving under General Pablo González; rank of Colonel, 1911; fought under Madero; joined Carranza, 1913; rank of Brigade General, Oct. 17, 1914; Division General, 1920; Military Commander of Tlaxcala, Puebla, and Veracruz, 1918; Commander of the 10th Military Zone, Durango, 1935-36; Commander of the 5th Military Zone, Chihuahua, Chihuahua, 1936-37. k-Ran for president of Mexico, 1946. l-Lieuwen, DP70, 406; Gruening, 423-25; Peral, 166-67; D de Y, 24 Jan. 1939, 1; EBW46, 1133; Q es Q, 115-16; Enc. Mex., II, 423; López, 184; NYT, 28 Jan. 1946, 9; Dávila, 81-82.

Castro Sánchez, Juventino
a-1921. b-Amealco, Querétaro. c-Early education unknown; accounting degree. d-Local Deputy to the State Legislature of Querétaro, 34th legislature; Mayor of Querétaro, 1961-64; Local Deputy to the 41st State Legislature of Querétaro, 1964-65; *Governor of Querétaro, 1967-73.* e-President of PRI of the State of Querétaro. f-Director of Traffic, Querétaro, 1946-49; Director of Transportation, State of México, 1974. g-Secretary General of the Union of Millers, Querétaro, 1939-41; Secretary of Labor Conflicts, Federation of Mexican Workers in Querétaro, 1941-43; Secretary of Finances, CTM in Querétaro, 1943-46; Secretary of Interior, Federation of Bus Companies, Mexico, 1949-

54. h-Started career as a millstone cutter for a private milling company; operated own bus company, 1954-61. j-None. k-*Por Qué* accused his gubernatorial administration of being dishonest; *Excélsior* said in 1974 that Governor Castro Sánchez and his secretary general of government were ordered to appear in court on charges of fraud involving 700,000 pesos. l-WWMG, 12; *Excélsior*, 28 Feb. 1974, 4, 1 Oct. 1974, 16; *Por Qué*, 4 Dec. 1969, 21.

Castro Villagrana, José
(Deceased 1960) a-Mar. 10, 1888. b-Zacatecas, Zacatecas. c-Primary and secondary studies in Zacatecas, Extension School of the Normal School of Zacatecas, preparatory at the Institute of Sciences at Zacatecas; medical degree from the National School of Medicine, UNAM, 1914, with a thesis on the treatment of acute peritonitis; Professor of Anatomy, National School of Medicine, UNAM, 1912-22; Professor of Therapeutics and Surgery, Juárez Hospital, Mexico City; professor at the National School of Medicine, 1944-50; Director of same, 1950-54. d-None. e-None. f-Director of the Juárez Hospital, 1929-39; Head of Medical Services for the Union of Mexican Electricians, 1937-46; *Subsecretary of Health*, 1958-60. g-None. h-Intern, Juárez Hospital, 1914; preparer of cultivation mediums, Bacteriological Institute, Mexico City, 1913-15; assistant at the Clinical Laboratory, National School of Medicine, 1915-18; Prosector of Topographical Anatomy, National School of Medicine, 1919-22; surgeon at Juárez Hospital, 1946; President and cofounder of the Mexican Academy of Surgery, 1942-46; editor of the medical journal *Postoperative and Preoperative*; responsible for introducing televised instruction at the National School of Medicine; author of numerous articles on therapeutics and surgery. i-Son, Xavier, a

doctor in Mexico City. j-None. k-None. l-HA, 22 Dec. 1958, 7; Peral 47, 81; EBW46; DP70, 409; HA, 4 Aug. 1944, 7; Enc. Mex., II, 214; WB48, 1029.

Castro y Castro, Fernándo
a-Mar. 18, 1925. b-Federal District. c-Early education unknown; legal studies from the National School of Law, UNAM, 1943-46, graduating in 1949 with a thesis on "The Legal Fundamentals in the Relations between Church and State"; graduate studies from the School of Philosophy and Letters, UNAM; course in general administration from the Mexican Association of Scientific Administration; courses in budgeting and costs and organization of office work from the Center of Industrial Productivity; Professor of Sociology of the National School of Law, UNAM, 1962-64. d-None. e-Adviser to the President of PRI, Federal District, 1953-58; Secretary General of the 39th District Committee, Federal District, 1979. f-Legal adviser to the Department of the Federal District, 1948-50; legal agent for PIPSA, 1949-52; Private Secretary to the Secretary of Public Health, 1951-52; Subdirector of the National Bank of Small Businesses, 1960-64; Secretary of the Council for the Institute of Social Security for Federal Employees, 1960; Secretary of the National Advisory Commission of Fishing, 1962-64; *Oficial Mayor of the Secretariat of Navy*, 1964-70; Director in Chief of the Secretariat of Foreign Relations with the rank of Ambassador, 1970; Director General of International Affairs, Secretariat of Labor, 1970-76; Director General of FERTICA, 1977-79; Manager of Advertising and Information, 1979-82; *Subsecretary of Fishing Infrastructure*, 1982-88. g-None. h-Technical adviser to the Mexican Institute of Social Security, 1956; legal adviser to the Subsecretary of Credit of the

Secretariat of the Treasury; member of the law firm Castro and González Guevara, 1948-66; lawyer for the Legal Department of the National Lottery, 1957-58; technical adviser to CONASUPO, 1961. i-Friend of *Rafael P. Gamboa*, secretary of public health, 1946-52; married Elena Estrada Viesca; son of Federico Castro Olea, banker, and Mercedes Castro Chauvert; brother, Juventino, was director general of legal affairs, Attorney General of Mexico, 1982. j-None. k-None. l-DBM68, 135-36; DPE71, 6; letter; DBGM, 85.

Catalán Calvo, Gerardo Rafael
(Deceased) a-Oct. 3, 1894. b-Chilpancingo, Guerrero. c-Preparatory studies in Chilpancingo; industrial engineering degree, National School of Agriculture and the National Military College, 1923; studied in the United States, 1930-32; Professor of Math and Ballistics at the National Military College, 1926-27; Director of Military Studies, 1933-34. d-*Governor of Guerrero*, 1941-45. e-None. f-None. g-None. h-Technical consultant to the National Military College. i-Brother, Felipe, was Treasurer of the Federal District. j-Joined the Revolution in 1914; career army officer; rank of Lt. Colonel, 1930; Brigadier General, Oct. 1, 1943; Commander of various military units, 1934-40. k-President *Manuel Avila Camacho* personally attended his inauguration as governor of Guerrero. l-WWM45, 241; HA, 28 May 1943, 16; Peral, 169; HA, 15 Sept. 1944, ix; Correa, 51; EBW46, 60; WB48, 1030; *Excélsior*, 18 Feb. 1976, 5.

Cavazos Cortés, Gerardo
a-Jan. 8, 1942. b-Villa de Santiago, Nuevo León. c-Secondary studies in Mexico; completed technical training in mechanics, Technological Institute of Nuevo León; instructor in basic education, Federal Electric Commis-

sion. d-*Federal Deputy* from the State of Nuevo León, Dist. 3, 1973-76; *Federal Deputy* from the State of México, Dist. 2, 1982-85. e-President of PRI, Villa de Santiago, Nuevo León; Assistant Secretary General of PRI, State of Nuevo León; General Delegate of the CEN of PRI. f-Technician, Federal Electric Commission, 1963-82; Director of Industrial Development, State of Nuevo León. g-Organizer of 14 unions in Nuevo León; representative of the CEN of SUTERM in Nuevo León; Secretary of Labor and Organization of the Union of Electrical Workers of the Federal Electric Commission, Villa de Santiago, Nuevo León; Secretary of Organization of SUTERM, State of Nuevo León, 1977-83. h-Designer, Medalla de Oro Textile Co., 1958-60; designer, Trailers de Monterrey, S.A., 1960-63. i-Son of Francisco Cavazos Villarreal and Francisca Cortés Silva; married Dora Caballero. j-None. k-None. l-Directorio, 1982-85; C de D, 1973-76; Lehr, 2; DBGM, 487.

Cavazos Lerma, Manuel
a-Mar. 3, 1946. b-Matamoros, Tamaulipas. c-Early education unknown; economics degree from the Monterrey Institute of Higher Studies, 1963-68; MA degree and studies toward a Ph.D., London School of Economics, 1969-72; Professor of Economic Geography, ITESM, 1968; Professor of Economics, Autonomous Technological Institute of Mexico, Mexico City, 1972-80. d-*Federal Deputy* from the State of Tamaulipas, Dist. 8, 1982-85, 1988-91; *Senator* from the State of Tamaulipas, 1991-93; *Governor of Tamaulipas*, 1993- . e-Joined PRI, 1972; adviser to the IEPES of PRI, 1973-74; Subdirector of Development Projects, IEPES of PRI, 1981-82. f-Analyst, Bank of Mexico, 1968-69; Chief of Monetary Studies, Bank of Mexico, 1972-76; adviser, International Economics, Bank of

Mexico, 1977-78; collaborator, Global Development Plan, Secretariat of Programming and Budgeting, 1979; Director of International Economic Policy, Secretariat of Programming and Budgeting, 1980-82; *Oficial Mayor of Government*, 1985-88. g-Secretary of Development Planning, CNOP, 1982-84. h-None. i-Son of Manuel Cavazos Rodríguez, chauffeur, and Clara Lerma Sánchez. j-None. k-First graduate of the ITESM to reach the post of oficial mayor in the federal executive branch. l-DBGM89, 416; DBGM92, 442; *Excélsior*, 13 Jan. 1985, 27A; DBGM, 488; DBGM87, 88; Lehr, 475.

Cebreros (Murillo), José Alfonso
a-Jan. 15, 1946. b-Culiacán, Sinaloa. c-Primary and secondary studies in Culiacán; economic studies (two years) in Culiacán; economics degree from the National School of Economics, UNAM, 1965-67, with a thesis on "External Disequilibrium, the Task of Development and Economic Policy." d-None. e-Coordinator of Advisers, CEN of PRI, 1987-88. f-Economist, Department of Petrochemicals, Division of Control and Inspection of Decentralized Agencies, Secretariat of Government Properties, 1966-68; Head, Department of Petrochemicals, Secretariat of Government Properties, 1968-69; Assistant to the Director of Control and Inspection, Secretariat of Government Properties, *Horacio Flores de la Peña*, 1969-70; Private Secretary to the Secretary of Government Properties, *Horacio Flores de la Peña*, 1970-74; Director General of Studies and Projects, Secretariat of Government Properties, 1974-76; *Subsecretary of Government Properties*, 1976; Secretary General of the Department of Fishing, 1977-78; *Subsecretary of Programming*, Secretariat of Programming and Budgeting, 1978-79; Director General of BANPESCA, 1980-82; Coordinator of the National Food

Committee, Secretariat of Programming and Budgeting, 1984-87; Coordinator of Advisers, Secretariat of Agriculture and Hydraulic Resources, 1988-90. g-None. h-Member of the Technical Planning Committee, UNAM, 1968-70; author of various books and articles on economics. i-Student of *Horacio Flores de la Peña*; son of José Alfonso Cebreros Loaiza, public official, and María Luisa Murillo; married Azalea Zurita Ojeja. j-None. k-None. l-Letter, *Excélsior*, 6 Sept. 1977, 26 Jan. 1978; DBGM89, 84.

Cedillo, Saturnino
(Deceased Jan. 11, 1939) a-1890. b-Rancho de Palomas, San Luis Potosí. c-Completed only primary school. d-Governor of San Luis Potosí, 1927-31. e-Active member of the National Agrarian Party; Head of the Agrarian Sector of the National Revolutionary Party, 1934. f-Secretary of Agriculture, 1931; *Secretary of Agriculture and Livestock*, 1935-37. g-None. h-Auxiliary judge in Palomas San Luis Potosí, 1912. i-Brothers, Magdaleno and Cleofas, both fought with *Saturnino* under Emiliano Zapata and were killed during the Revolution; longtime friend of *Gildardo Magaña* since they were companions fighting under Zapata; tried to persuade *Magaña* to support him in his fight against President *Cárdenas*; parents, Amadeo Cedillo and Pantaleona Martínez, were peasants. j-Joined the Revolution in 1911; supported the Plan of Agua Prieta, 1920; Commander of Military Operations in San Luis Potosí, 1920-27; fought against the de la Huerta rebellion in 1923; supported the government against Escobar, 1929; Commander-in-Chief of the Central Division, 1926; Division General, 1928; Commander of Military Operations in San Luis Potosí, 1935. k-Imprisoned by Victoriano Huerta, 1912-14; supporter and later political enemy of Governor Aurelio Marique,

1924-25; gave *Lázaro Cárdenas* the decisive help of the agrarian sectors, 1934-35; resigned his cabinet post to protest governmental policies and become head of a rebellious military movement, 1938; killed in the fighting, 1939; member of the Inner Circle, 1934-37. l-D de S, 17 June 1935, 1; Gruening, 311; DP70, 417; Kirk, 40, 66-67; Dulles; Brandenburg, 80; González Navarro, 150-51; Weyl, 234; Novo35; Daniels, 259-60; Q es Q, 117-18.

Celis Campos, Jesús
(Deceased) a-Aug. 26, 1895. b-Bamoa, Sinaloa. c-Primary studies in Alamos and in Navajoa, Sonora; no degree. *Senator* from the State of Sinaloa, 1952-58, First Secretary of the First National Defense Committee, the Military Health Committee, and the First Instructive Section of the Grand Jury; Second Secretary of the Military Justice Committee, member of the First Balloting Group, and President of the War Materiels Committee. e-None. f-Military Attaché, Special Mission to Peru, 1921; Military Attaché, Guatemala, 1922-23; Director of the Military Prison of Santiago Tlaltelolco, 1925; Commander of Infantry, Federal District Police; Subdirector of the Federal District Police, 1932; Director of Traffic in the Federal District; Ambassador to the Dominican Republic and Haiti. g-None. j-Joined the army, 1913; 2nd Lieutenant on the General Staff of Benjamín Hill, Sept. 13, 1913; career officer; rank of Lt. Colonel, 1921; rank of Lt. Colonel in Artillery awarded by the Peruvian government, 1921; fought against the de la Huerta rebellion as subdirector of the Department of Cavalry, Secretary of War, 1923; commander of various cavalry companies, 1932-42; commander of various military zones. k-None. l-Ind. Biog., 41-42; DGF56, 7, 9-13.

Ceniceros, Severino
(Deceased June 15, 1937) b-Durango, Durango. c-Early education unknown; no degree. d-Senator from the State of Durango, 1920-22, 1932-34. e-None. f-*Interim Governor* of Durango, 1936. g-None. j-Revolutionary soldier; took part in taking Durango from the federal forces, 1911; joined Carranza, 1911; supported Madero, 1910-11; fought with Calixto Contreras in Cuencame; Governor and Military Commander of Durango, Sept. 28, 1914, to Oct. 13, 1915; officer under Francisco Villa; reached rank of Division General. k-None. l-Q es Q, 119; NYT, 17 Dec. 1935, 1.

Ceniceros (Andónequi), José Angel
(Deceased Apr. 24, 1979) a-June 8, 1900. b-Durango, Durango. c-Primary studies in Mexico City, 1906-11; normal studies from the National Normal School, Mexico City, 1912-15; teaching certificate from the National Normal School of Mexico, 1921; law degree from the Escuela Libre de Derecho, Apr. 25, 1925, with a thesis on "Penal Law of Bolshevik Russia"; doctor of law, National School of Law, UNAM, 1950; professor at the National Teachers School, 1921-40; professor at the National School of Law, UNAM, 1937-44, the Escuela Libre de Derecho, 1928-34, and at the Higher Normal School, Mexico City, 1928-34. d-None. e-Director of the PRI publication *El Nacional*, 1936. f-Agent of the Ministerio Público; public defender, Secretariat of National Defense; adviser, Secretary of the Navy; Oficial Mayor of the Secretariat of Foreign Relations; Attorney General of Military Justice, 1931-32; Assistant Attorney General of Mexico, 1932-34; *Subsecretary of Foreign Relations*, 1935-36; *Ambassador to Cuba*, 1944-47; *Secretary of Public Education*, 1952-58; Ambassador to Haiti, 1947. g-None. h-Adviser to Nacional Financiera; author of numerous articles; Director of

the Industrial Company of Atenquique, Guadalajara, 1941; President of Phillips Mexicana; practicing lawyer, 1970-79. i-Attended law school with *Ernesto Enríquez Coyro*; son of Felipe Cenicero Villarreal and Guadalupe Andónequi; married Amalia Hernández. j-Fought in the Revolution; joined Constitutionalist forces, 1914, as a normal school student with *J. Jesús González Lugo* and *Roberto T. Bonilla Cortés*; Captain of the Infantry, 1915. k-None. l-DBM68, 139; WWM45, 24-25; HA, 5 Dec. 1952, 9; DGF56, 299; HA, 13 Jan. 1958; HA, 25 Feb. 1956, 61; D de Y, 2 Dec., 1972; Enc. Mex., 1977, II, 450-51; Alonso, 227; HA, 7 May 1979, 11; Maples Arce, 161-62.

Cepeda Flores, Ramón
(Deceased 1973) a-Apr. 8, 1907. b-Saltillo, Coahuila. c-Primary studies from first through fourth grades under Josefina Calderón, Arteaga, Coahuila, 1917-21, and fifth and sixth grades were continued while living with his maternal grandparents in Saltillo, Coahuila, 1921-22; two years of preparatory at Ateneo Fuente, Saltillo; business studies at the Navarro Academy, Saltillo; no degree. d-Member of the City Council, Torreón, 1946-48; Mayor of Torreón, 1949-51; *Governor of Coahuila*, 1951-57. e-President of PRI in Torreón, Coahuila, 1944-45. g-None. h-Rancher, 1928-1937, in Arteaga; moved to Torreón, 1937. i-Great-grandfather, Juan Antonio de la Fuente, served as minister to France; uncle, Rafael Cepeda de la Fuente, was a brigadier general, constitutional deputy, 1916-17, and governor of San Luis Potosí; father, Ramón Cepeda de la Fuente, rancher and colonel in the Revolution, was persecuted by Victoriano Huerta; mother, Elena Flores, whose brother Mariano Flores fought under her husband during the Revolution, reached the rank of brigadier general, and served as governor of San Luis Potosí; mother is the great-

niece of Mucío and Pedro Martínez, major figures in nineteenth-century Coahuilan politics; uncle, Abraham Cepeda de la Fuente, was killed in action during the Revolution; Ramón is a cousin of *Ignacio Cepeda Dávila*. j-None. k-None. l-HA, 3 Dec. 1956, 12; DGF56, 91; HA, 29 Nov. 1954; López, 192; Rodríguez Barragán; Moreno, 113-17.

Cerdán (Lara), Jorge
(Deceased 1959) a-July 23, 1897. b-Jalapa, Veracruz. c-Primary and secondary studies at the Liceo Hidalgo, under Professor Joaquín Vázquez Trigos, Jalapa, Veracruz; preparatory studies at the preparatory school of the University of Veracruz, Jalapa; law degree from the University of Veracruz, specializing in finance, June 7, 1935. d-Local Deputy to the State Legislature of Veracruz, 1930-32; *Governor of Veracruz*, 1940-44. f-Director of the Treasury of the State of Veracruz, 1916; Treasurer General of Veracruz, 1936-39. g-None. h-Employee, Treasury Department, State of Veracruz, 1911-13; practicing lawyer, Mexico City, 1945-59. i-Son of Alfredo Cerdán and Elena Lara, a teacher; member of *Maximino Avila Camacho*'s political group. j-Office worker for the revolutionaries, 1914-16. k-None. l-WWM45, 25; DP70, 424; Peral, 174; EBW46, 74; WB48, 1042; López, 193; Pasquel, Jalapa, 125-26.

Cerecedo López, Felipe
a-Feb. 5, 1921. b-Chicontepec, Veracruz. c-Primary studies at the Rafael Valenzuela Primary School, Chicontepec; secondary studies at the National Teachers School; teaching certificate, Normal School of Chiapas; primary school teacher. d-*Federal Deputy* from the State of Veracruz, Dist. 2, 1970-73, member of the Public Assistance Committee, the Agrarian Affairs Committee, the Second Ejido Committee, the Railroads Committee, and the Commit-

tee on Subsistence and Supplies; *Federal Deputy* from the State of Veracruz, Dist. 2, 1976-79, member of the Ejido and Communal Section of the Agrarian Affairs Committee. e-Founder and Coordinator General of the PPS in Veracruz. f-None. g-Founder and Secretary General of the Alliance of Farmers Groups of Northern Veracruz. h-Director of a primary boarding school (22 years). i-Married Ernestina Díaz. j-None. k-None. l-C de D, 1970-72; Directorio, 1970-72; D de C, 1976-79, 12.

Cervantes Corona, José Guadalupe
a-May 24, 1924. b-Teúl, Zacatecas. c-Teaching certificate, Zacatecas; law degree, School of Law, University of Zacatecas; primary school teacher, 1940-50; Professor of Pedagogy and Logic, Manuel Avila Camacho Normal School, Zacatecas. d-*Federal Deputy* from the State of Zacatecas, Dist. 3, 1961-64; *Senator* from the State of Zacatecas, 1976-80; *Governor of Zacatecas*, 1980-86. e-General Delegate of the CEN of PRI to many states; delegate of the CEN of PRI to Campeche, 1974. f-Director of Public Education, State of Zacatecas, 1950-53; Director of Press, State of Zacatecas, 1953-56; Oficial Mayor of Zacatecas, 1956-57; Secretary General of Government of the State of Zacatecas; administrative official of the Department of the Federal District, 1970-71. g-Secretary of Organization of the CEN of the CNC, 1979. h-Editor-in-chief of *Providencia*, Zacatecas, 1953-60. i-Considered close to the political group of *Oscar Ramírez Mijares*. j-None. k-Precandidate for Governor of Zacatecas, 1974; selection as gubernatorial candidate in 1980 seen as a stimulus to politicians following PRI party careers. l-*Excélsior*, 17 Dec. 1979, 18; HA, 17 Mar. 1980, 25; *Excélsior*, 25 Feb. 1980, 22A, 19 July 1979, 19A; C de D, 1961-64; C de S, 1976-82; Almanaque de México, 430.

Cervantes Delgado, Alejandro
a-Jan. 24, 1926. b-Chilpancingo, Guerrero. c-Teaching certificate, National Teachers College; economics degree, National School of Economics, UNAM, 1944-48, degree, June 26, 1958, with a thesis on "Aspects of Public Expenditures and Taxation in Mexico"; Professor of the Theory of Finance and Public Finance, National School of Economics, UNAM; primary school teacher. d-*Federal Deputy* from the State of Guerrero, Dist. 3, 1973-76; *Senator* from Guerrero, 1976-80, Secretary of the Gran Comisión, 1976-80; *Governor of Guerrero*, 1981-87. e-*Director General of the IEPES of the CEN of PRI*, 1978-80. f-Subdirector of Planning, National Railroads of Mexico, 1972-73; Controller General of National Railroads of Mexico, 1972-73; Director of Treasury and Economy, State of Guerrero, 1963-65; Director, Office of Fiscal Policy, State of Guerrero, 1953-56; Director of Technical and Economic Studies, Secretariat of Government Properties, 1959-63; Subdirector of Fishing Economic Affairs, Secretariat of Industry and Commerce, 1966-70; Technical Subdirector, Division of Internal Taxes, Secretariat of the Treasury, 1970-71. g-None. i-Classmate of *Emilio Mújica Montoya* in the "González Aparicio" group at UNAM; married Graciela Rocha. j-None. k-None. l-HA, 26 Mar. 1979, V; DPE71, 37; C de S, 1976-82; D de C, 1973-76; Almanaque de México, 1982, 510; *Excélsior*, 29 Feb. 1980, 13A.

Cervantes del Río, Hugo
a-July 4, 1927. b-Federal District. c-Primary studies at the Central School of Mexico, Mexico City; secondary studies at the National University Initiation School; preparatory from the National Preparatory School, 1944-46; law degree from the National School of Law, UNAM, 1951, with a thesis on agrarian

labor and the 1917 constitution; Professor of Constitutional Law at the National School of Law, UNAM, 1960-65; Professor of Mexican History, National Preparatory School, 1950-59. d-*Senator* from the Federal District, 1976. e-Interim Head of the Legal Department of PRI, 1952; active in youth movement in PRI with *Luis Echeverría*, 1946-52; President of PRI in the Federal District, 1975-76. f-Private Secretary to *Rodolfo Sánchez Taboada*, Secretary of the Navy, 1952-54; Director of Accounting of the Secretariat of the Navy, 1954-55; Customs Administrator for Sonoita, Sonora; *Director General of Federal Highways and Bridges and Adjacent Entrances and Exits*, 1959-65; *Governor of Baja California del Sur*, 1965-70; *Secretary of the Presidency*, 1970-75; *Director General of the Federal Electric Commission*, 1976-80. g-Student leader in secondary, the National Preparatory School, and at UNAM. h-Treasurer of Mexican Railroads, 1956-59; Director of Customs, Sonoita, Sonora, 1955-56. i-Friend of *Luis Echeverría* and *Rodolfo Sánchez Taboada*; studied under *José López Portillo* at UNAM; married María Luisa Vallejo. j-None. k-Winner of the Lanz Duret Prize as the Best Student of Constitutional Law, 1949. l-HA, 7 Dec. 1970, 26; WWMG, 13; *Hoy*, 19 Dec. 1970; D de Y, 5 Dec. 1952, 1; HA, 29 Jan. 1973, 22; *Excélsior*, 18 Feb. 1977, 12 Mar. 1976; Cadena Z., 19-36; *Excélsior*, 10 Oct. 1975, 20; Enc. Mex., 1977, II, 467.

Cervantes (Hernández), Anselmo
a-Apr. 13, 1908. b-Texcoco, Tlaxcala. c-Preparatory studies at the National Preparatory School; law degree from the National School of Law, UNAM; professor at the National Normal School, Mexico City. d-Local Deputy to the State Legislature of Tlaxcala, 1947-59; *Alternate Senator* from the State of Tlaxcala, 1952-58; Local Deputy to the State Legislature of Tlaxcala, 1955-56; *Federal Deputy* from the State of Tlaxcala, Dist. No. 1, 1961-64, member of the Gran Comisión, the Third Labor Committee, and alternate member of the Social Welfare Committee; *Governor of Tlaxcala*, 1963-69. e-General delegate of the CEN of PRI. f-Oficial Mayor of the State of Tlaxcala, 1951-53. g-None. j-None. k-None. l-WWMG, 13; DGF56, 8; C de D, 1961-63.

Cervera Pacheco, Víctor
a-Apr. 23, 1936. b-Mérida, Yucatán. c-Primary and secondary studies at the Colegio Americano, Mérida, Yucatán; preparatory studies at the University of Yucatán; no degree. d-Local Deputy to the State Legislature of Yucatán, 1960-62, Dist. No. 3, 1968-70; Mayor of Mérida, Yucatán, 1971-73; *Federal Deputy* from the State of Yucatán, Dist. No. 1, 1973-76; *Senator* from the State of Yucatán, 1976-82; *Federal Deputy* from the State of Yucatán, Dist. 1, 1982-85. e-Campaigner for *Luis Torres Mesías* and *Agustín Franco Aguilar* during their gubernatorial campaigns in Yucatán; youth delegate of PRI to CNOP. f-*Substitute Governor of Yucatán*, 1984-88; *Secretary of Agrarian Reform*, 1988- . g-Secretary General of the Society of Preparatory Students, University of Yucatán, 1953; President of the Society of Preparatory Students, 1954; Secretary General of the University Student Federation of Yucatán; delegate of the University Student Federation to the National Convention, Jalapa, Veracruz, 1956; Secretary General of the League of Agrarian Communities and Peasant Unions of Yucatán, 1967-70; Secretary of Health and Social Services, CEN of the CNC, 1968; *Secretary General of the CNC*, 1980-83. h-Owns ranch; administrator of a printing company; adviser to ejido credit associations. i-Bitter political opponent of *Carlos Loret de Mola*,

governor of Yucatán, 1970-76; son of
Juan Cervera and Francisca Pacheco
Solís; married Amira Hernández Guerra.
j-None. k-Political infighting with
Loret de Mola precipitated a public
battle between the state and local government in Mérida. l-C de D, 1973-76;
Q es Qy, 77-78; C de S, 1976-82; Loret
de Mola; HA, 1 Mar. 1982, 13, 27 Feb.
1984, 31-32; DBGM92, 91; DBGM89,
87; Lehr, 523.

Chapital, Constantino
(Deceased 1943) a-Feb. 12, 1897.
b-Oaxaca, Oaxaca. c-Early education
unknown; no degree. d-Federal Deputy
from the State of Oaxaca, Dist. 11,
1934-36; *Governor of Oaxaca*, 1936-40.
e-None. f-Director of the Santiago
Tlatelolco Military Prison. g-None.
h-None. j-Career army officer; Constitutionalist; fought Victoriano Huerta
under General Fernando Dávila;
accompanied President Carranza on his
flight to Veracruz, 1920; rank of
Brigadier General; Chief of Mounted
Police in the Federal District; Chief of
Judicial Police in the Federal District;
Chief of Staff of the 6th Military Zone;
Military Attaché to London, England.
k-Smith says he was separated from the
military under an indictment for the
disappearance of jewels under his
jurisdiction while director of the
Judicial Police. l-PS; C de D, 1934-37.

Charis Castro, Heliodoro
(Deceased) a-July 9, 1896. b-Juchitán,
Oaxaca. c-Early education unknown;
no degree. d-Federal Deputy from the
State of Oaxaca, Dist. 17, 1926-28;
Federal Deputy from the State of
Oaxaca, Dist. 1, 1937-40; *Senator* from
the State of Oaxaca, 1940-46; *Federal
Deputy* from the State of Oaxaca, Dist.
1, 1952-55. e-None. f-None. g-None.
j-Joined the Revolution in Oaxaca; rank
of Brigade General, Feb. 1, 1925;
supported the Escobar rebellion, 1929;

rank of Division General, Dec. 9, 1953.
l-López Esc., 253; Dávila, 132; C de S,
1940-46; C de D, 1926-28, 1937-40,
1952-55.

Chaurand Concha, Ricardo
a-Aug. 6, 1910. b-Celaya, Guanajuato.
c-Primary studies in Celaya; preparatory
studies from the Colegio San Borja,
Mexico City, and from the Colegio La
Salle, Havana, Cuba; teaching certificate; studies in philosophy and history,
School of Philosophy and Letters,
UNAM; career educator; Director of the
Colegio México, Celaya, 1944-67.
d-*Federal Deputy* from the State of
Guanajuato, Dist. 8, 1964-67, member
of the Second Section of the Agrarian
Affairs Committee. e-Member of PAN.
f-None. g-None. h-None. j-None.
k-None. l-C de D, 1964-67, 47, 78; PS,
1452.

Chávez (Amparán), Alfredo
(Deceased June 16, 1972) a-July 14,
1891. b-Hidalgo del Parral, Chihuahua.
c-Primary education in Parral, Chihuahua; attended a private agricultural
school in Ciudad Juárez, Chihuahua; no
degree. d-Local Deputy to the State
Legislature of Chihuahua; Interim
Governor of Chihuahua; *Senator* from
the State of Chihuahua, 1946-52,
member of the Gran Comisión; member
of the National Waters and Irrigation
Committee, the Second Committee on
Mines, and the Foreign and Domestic
Trade Committee; substitute member
of the Department of the Federal
District Committee; *Governor of
Chihuahua*, 1940-44. e-None. f-Tax
collector for Parral, Chihuahua; Interim
Governor under *Gustavo Talamantes*,
1936; Chief of State Police, Chihuahua,
1938. g-None. h-Began career as an
agriculturist; after retirement from
political activity, engaged in cattle
ranching in Villa Matamoros. i-Son,
Alfredo, served as federal deputy from

the state of Chihuahua, Dist. 5, 1958-60; son of Manuel Chávez Váldez, prominent cattle rancher; attended agricultural college with *Gustavo L. Talamantes*, governor of Chihuahua, 1936-40. j-Rank of Colonel in the Mexican army. k-None. l-HA, 31 July 1947, 16; letter; EBW46, 68; *Excélsior*, 17 June 1972; DGF51, I, 6, 9-11, 13; DGF47, 20.

Chávez Carrillo, Rodolfo

a-May 11, 1923. b-Colima, Colima. c-Primary studies and secondary studies in Colima; government scholarship recipient at the National Polytechnic School, 1938; attended Prevocational School No. 3, Mexico City, 1939; attended Vocational School No. 1, 1941; architectural engineering degree from the School of Engineering and Architecture, IPN, 1943-47, with an honorary mention; Professor of Mathematics, University of Colima. d-Mayor of Colima, 1952-54; *Governor of Colima*, 1955-61. e-None. f-Subdirector of Public Works, State of Colima, 1948-50; Director General of Public Works, State of Colima, 1950; Director of Puerto México, Tijuana, Baja California del Norte, 1963; Representative of the Secretariat of National Patrimony, Baja California del Norte, 1964-72; President of the Federal Board of Material Improvements, Tijuana, Baja California del Norte, 1963-73. g-None. h-Intern, Resident Architect, Guanos y Fertilizantes, S.A., Mexico City, 1947; planner and constructor of several building projects, 1961-62; President of the Mexican Society of Geography and Statistics, 1966-72. j-None. k-None. l-Letters; DGF56, 91.

Chávez Hernández, José Servando

a-1936. b-San Lucas, Michoacán. c-Early education unknown; degree in political science from the School of Political and Social Science, UNAM;

law degree from the National School of Law, UNAM, 1964. d-*Federal Deputy* from the State of Michoacán, Dist. 7, 1964-67, member of the Agrarian Section of the Legislative Studies Committee, the Petroleum Committee, and the Technical Section of the Ejido Committee. e-General delegate of the CEN of PRI to Guerrero, 1980. f-Secretary General of Government of Quintana Roo; Secretary General of Government of the State of Michoacán, 1968-71, under Governor *Carlos Gálvez Betancourt*; Interim Governor of Michoacán, 1971-74. g-Member of the CNC; Secretary of Agrarian Action of the CNC, 1980. h-Practicing lawyer. i-Parents were peasants; brother, Ausencio Chávez, was secretary general of government in Michoacán under Governor *Carlos Torres Manzo*. j-None. k-None. l-HA, 4 Oct. 1971, 45; C de D, 1964-67; *Excélsior*, 26 Nov. 1978, 6.

Chávez Martínez, Humberto

a-Feb. 3, 1934. b-Federal District. c-Early education unknown; architectural degree, National School of Architecture, UNAM. d-None. e-Joined PRI, 1968. f-Director, Technical Coordinator of the Housing Discount Trust, Bank of Mexico, 1964-65; Chief, Department of Housing Development, National Mortgage Bank, 1965-67; Assistant Manager of Housing, Public Works Bank, 1967-71; Manager, Housing and Urban Development, Public Works Bank, 1971-77; Director General of Popular Housing, Department of the Federal District, 1978; Subdirector of the Housing Discount Fund, Bank of Mexico, 1978-82; Director General of the Housing Discount Fund, Bank of Mexico, 1982-88; *Subsecretary of Housing*, Secretariat of Urban Development and Housing, 1988-91. g-None. h-None. i-Son of Carlos Chávez Holguín, engineer, and Eva Martínez García; married María López

Decaen. k-Resigned as subsecretary for
personal reasons, Apr. 4, 1991.
l-DBGM87, 103; *EL Nacional*, 5 Apr.
1991, 13; DBGM89, 96.

Chávez Orozco, Luis
(Deceased Sept. 16, 1966) a-Apr. 28,
1901. b-Irapuato, Guanajuato. c-Primary studies at the Instituto Sollano;
preparatory studies at the León Institute, Guanajuato; professor at UNAM;
professor for the Secretariat of Public
Education. d-None. e-None. f-Chief of
the Department of Publicity of the
Secretariat of Foreign Relations, 1930-
32; Head of the Department of Administration, Secretariat of Public Education,
1933-35; Head of the Department of
Libraries of the Secretariat of Public
Education, 1935-36; *Subsecretary of
Public Education*, 1936-38; Head of the
Department of Indian Affairs, 1939-40;
Ambassador to Honduras, 1941; First
President of the Institute of Mexican
and Russian Cultural Interchange, 1944;
adviser to the Presidency of Mexico.
g-First Secretary General of the National Teachers Union of Mexico.
h-Writer for the major daily newspaper,
Excélsior; prolific historian, author of a
twelve-volume history of Mexico and of
works on economic and diplomatic
history and education. j-None.
k-Noted for his anticlerical position in
the *Cárdenas* administration.
l-WWM45, 27; DP70, 592; Peral, 207;
WB48, 1079; Villasenor, II, 38; Casasol,
V; Raby, 52; López, 255-56; Enc. Mex.,
1977, II, 284; Michaels, 125.

Chávez Padrón de Velázquez, Martha
a-July 31, 1925. b-Tampico, Tamaulipas. c-Early education unknown;
studies in literature, School of Philosophy and Letters, UNAM; law degree,
National School of Law, UNAM, 1948;
Ph.D. in law, UNAM, 1954 (first
Mexican woman to receive a Ph.D. in
law); professor specializing in rural

sociology at UNAM, the National
School of Agriculture, and at the
Secretariat of Agriculture and the
Secretariat of Public Education.
d-*Senator* from Tamaulipas, 1976-82;
Federal Deputy from the State of
Tamaulipas, Dist. 9, 1982-85. e-Joined
PRI as a student activist, 1946; worked
for PRI, 1959; Director of Social Action
of the CEN of PRI, 1961; member of the
National Council of Women of PRI;
member of the Advisory Council to the
IEPES of PRI, 1972. f-Director General
of Agrarian Laws, Department of Agra-
rian Affairs; adviser to the Department
of Agrarian Affairs; *Subsecretary of the
New Centers of Ejido Populations*,
Secretariat of Agrarian Reform, 1970-76;
*Supernumerary Justice of the Supreme
Court*, 1985-88, 1988-94. g-Member of
the CEN of the CNC, 1976. h-Author
of several law texts. i-Student of
Agustín Yañez at UNAM; daughter of
Félix Chávez Padrón, mechanic, and
Josefina Padrón Martínez, nurse.
j-None. k-First female lawyer from
Tamaulipas; first female professor at the
National School of Law, UNAM. l-HA,
19 June 1972, 66, 20 Sept. 1971, 29;
DGF71, 129; HA, 21 Dec. 1970, 24, 7
June 1970, 11-13; Enc. Mex., Annual,
1977, 495; Romero Aceves, 352-54;
DBGM92, 645; Lehr, 475; DBGM87,
612; DBGM89, 602.

Chávez Peón Medina, Federico Daniel
a-Jan. 24, 1937. b-Federal District.
c- Early education unknown; MD from
the National Medical School, UNAM,
1955-62; intern, National Institute of
Nutrition, 1963-65; surgical intern,
National Institute of Nutrition, 1965-
67; specialist in cardiovascular surgery,
Massachusetts General and Harvard
Medical School, 1967-71; professor,
Harvard Medical School, 1968-70;
professor, Graduate School, National
School of Medicine, UNAM, 1971;
researcher, National Institute of

Nutrition, 1971-78; professor, La Salle, 1972-74. d-None. e-None. f-Executive Secretary, National Health Program, Conacyt, 1977-82; *Subsecretary of Health*, 1980-82. h-Director, Chemical Pharmaceutical Division, Fisomex, 1982-88. i-Son of Enrique Chávez Peón, director general of American Cyanmid of Mexico, and Sofía Medina Valdés; grandson of Daniel Chávez, lawyer, and Mercedes Peón Valdez. j-None. k-None. l-DBGM, 111-112.

Chávez (Ramírez), Eduardo
(Deceased May 28, 1982) a-May 16, 1898. b-Federal District. c-Early education unknown; preparatory studies at the National Preparatory School, 1912-16; engineering degree from the National School of Engineering, UNAM, 1922; Professor of Drawing at night school, 1912 d-None. e-None. f-Subchief of the Department of the Organization of Irrigation Systems; President of the Engineering Commission of the Secretariat of National Patrimony, 1947; Chief of Internal Projects for the Río Bravo project; Secretary and member of the Papaloapán Commission, 1947-50; Executive Secretary of the Tepalcatepec Commission, 1950-52; *Secretary of Hydraulic Resources*, 1952-58. g-None. h-Began work for the National Irrigation Commission, 1926; technician for hydraulic and irrigation construction materials; engineer on various construction projects for the Department of Public Works, 1933; worked on hundreds of projects from 1933-52 in the field of irrigation and hydroelectric projects. i-Married Margarita Barragán; brother of reknowned Mexican composer, Carlos Chávez; son of engineer Agustín Chávez and Juvencia Ramírez, a teacher; grandfather, a lawyer; great-grandfather, José María Chávez, governor of Aguascalientes; daughter, Margarita, married Alejandro Caso, son

of *Alfonso Caso*. j-Left school to support Carranza in Veracruz, 1913. k-Resigned as Secretary of Hydraulic Resources in 1958 because of disagreements with President *Ruiz Cortines* on the regional commission policies of the Secretariat of Hydraulic Resources. l-Greenberg, 25; *El Universal*, 2 Dec. 1958; DBM68, 167-68; DGF47, 256; HA, 5 Dec. 1952, 9; DGF56, 411; DGF50, II, 451; *Excélsior*, 2 Aug. 1972, 1, 16; NYT, 27 July, 1954, 10; Enc. Mex., III, 281-82; *Excélsior*, 29 May 1982; HA, 14 June 1982, 13.

Chávez (Sánchez), Ignacio
(Deceased July 12, 1979) a-Jan. 31, 1897. b-Zirándaro, Guerrero. c-Secondary studies in Morelia, Michoacán, at the Colegio de San Nicolás de Hidalgo; two years of professional studies in medicine at Morelia, at the Colegio de San Nicolás de Hidalgo, 1914-16; medical degree from the National School of Medicine, UNAM, May 4, 1920; Ph.D. in Biological Sciences from UNAM, 1934; instructor at the Colegio de San Nicolás, 1914-15; Professor of Cardiology at the National School of Medicine, UNAM, 1946-66, also at the Graduate School; Professor of Medicine, 1923-50; Rector of the University of Michoacán, 1920-22; postgraduate work in Paris, 1926-27; Director of the National School of Medicine, UNAM, 1933-34; President of the Union of Latin American Universities; professor at UNAM, 1966-70. d-None. e-Supporter of José Vasconcelos in 1929. f-Head of the Medical Clinic, UNAM, 1922-23; Director of the General Hospital of Mexico City, 1936-39; founder and Director of the National Institute of Cardiology, 1944-61; *Rector of UNAM*, 1961-66; Director of the National Institute of Cardiology, 1975-79. g-None. h-Author of numerous articles on medical subjects; Honorary Director of the National Institute of Cardiology,

1970-75. i-Brother of *Rodolfo Chávez
Sánchez*, justice of the Supreme Court,
1936-40; 1955-59; heart specialist to
President Calles; daughter, Celia,
married to poet Jaime García Térres;
son of Ignacio Chávez, small farmer,
and Socorro Sánchez; classmate of
Manuel Martínez Báez, Gabino Fraga,
and *Eduardo Villaseñor* at the Colegio
de San Nicolás. j-None. k-Resigned the
Rectorship of UNAM after a major
student strike. l-DBM70, 155-56;
DBM68, 168-69; WWM45, 26; Hayner,
269; IWW68, 220-21; Peral, 205-06,
WWW70-71, 174; DGF51, 342; *Justicia,*
May 1971; letters; HA 23 July 1979, 5-6.

Chávez (Sánchez), Rodolfo
(Deceased) a-May 8, 1895. b-Zirándaro,
Guerrero. c-Primary studies in Morelia,
Michoacán, 1904-07; preparatory
studies in the Colegio de San Nicolás,
Morelia; law degree from the Colegio de
San Nicolás, Morelia, Dec. 4, 1917.
d-None. e-None. f-Syndic of the City
Council of Morelia, 1918; Secretary to
the District Court of Tuxpán, Veracruz,
1924-25; consulting lawyer to the State
of Veracruz, 1924-27; Attorney General
of the State of Veracruz, 1928-36, under
Governors Adalberto Tejada and
*Gonzalo Vázquez Vela; Justice of the
Supreme Court,* 1936-40; 1955-59.
g-Student leader in support of Madero.
h-Author of the Legal Code of the State
of Veracruz. i-Brother of *Ignacio
Chávez,* rector of UNAM, 1961-66; son
of Ignacio Chávez and Socorro Sánchez,
small farmers; supporter of *Francisco
Múgica,* 1920s. j-Fought in the Revolution; served under General Obregón;
reached rank of Brigadier General.
k-None. l-Peral, 207; letters; DGF56,
567.

Chávez Silva, Roberto
a-Apr. 10, 1913. b-Morelia, Michoacán.
c-Early education unknown; no degree.
d-Member of the City Council of

Morelia, Michoacán, 1940-41; *Federal
Deputy* from the State of Michoacán,
Dist. 3, 1964-67, member of the Labor
Committee. e-Member of the PPS;
member of the Central Committee of
the PPS. f-None. g-Joined the Bakers
Union, CROM, 1926; Secretary General
of the Bakers Union of the Revolution-
ary Federation of Workers of Michoa-
cán, 1932; Secretary of Labor Conflicts,
CTM, State of Michoacán, 1938-39;
Secretary General of the Coalition of
Unions of Michoacán, 1939-40; Secre-
tary of Union Affairs of the CEN of the
General Union of Mexican Workers and
Peasants, UGOCM; Secretary General
of the UGOCM in Michoacán. h-Baker.
i-Parents were from the working class.
j-None. k-None. l-Directorio, 1964-67;
C de D, 1964-67, 47, 95.

Chávez Vázquez, Alfredo
a-June 4, 1918. b-Hidalgo del Parral,
Chihuahua. c-Primary studies at Public
School No. 99, Parral; studies in
business administration, Sánchez Celis
Academy. d-Local Deputy to the State
Legislature of Chihuahua, 1944-46;
Federal Deputy from the State of
Chihuahua, Dist. 5, 1958-61, member of
the Gran Comisión, the Indigenous
Affairs Committee, the Livestock
Committee, and the Inspection Com-
mittee for the General Accounting
Office. e-None. f-None. g-None.
h-Founder and owner of Bodegas de
Delicias, S.A.; owner of Construciones y
Trabajos Agriculturales, S.A. i-Son of
Alfredo Chávez, governor of Chihua-
hua, 1940-44. j-None. k-None. l-Func.,
168; C de D, 1958-60, 41, 76.

Chávez Velázquez, Bernardo
a-Dec. 1, 1900. b-Puebla, Puebla.
c-Preparatory studies in Puebla; professional studies at the Universidad
Palafoxiana, University of Puebla, and
the Military Medical College; medical
degree. d-Federal Deputy from the State

of Puebla, 1930-32, 1932-34; *Federal Deputy* from the State of Puebla, Dist. 3, 1940-43, member of the Foreign Relations Committee and the Committee on Social Assistance for Infants; *Federal Deputy* from the State of Puebla, Dist. 6, 1946-49, member of the Child Welfare and Social Security Committee and the Military Health Committee. f-Chief of Health Inspections, Department of Health of the Federal District; Inspector General of the Attorney General of Mexico; Consul of Mexico in various European countries and in the United States; Head of the Department of Justice and Government, State of Puebla; Director of the Federal Transit Department, 1946. g-None. h-Practicing surgeon. j-Lieutenant in the army, 1914; Director of the Sanitation Sections, 2nd Division. k-None. l-EBW46, 108; C de D, 1942; WB48, 1078; DGF47, 11; C de D, 1946-48.

Chavira Becerra, Carlos
(Deceased Sept. 20, 1983) a-Nov. 11, 1915. b-Camargo, Chihuahua. c-Completed primary studies. d-*Federal Deputy* from the State of Chihuahua, Dist. 6, 1961-64; *Plurinominal Federal Deputy from PAN*, 1982-85. e-Founding member of PAN, 1939; member of the Regional Committee of PAN, State of Chihuahua, 1940; regional adviser to PAN, State of Chihuahua, 1940; candidate of PAN for mayor of Ciudad Camargo, Chihuahua, 1944, for federal deputy from Chihuahua, Dist. 5, 1952, for local deputy to the State Legislature of Chihuahua, 1967, 1982; founding member of PAN, Ojinaga, Chihuahua, 1957; participated in a PAN campaign in Ojinaga, 1958; PAN candidate for senator from Chihuahua, 1964. f-None. g-Secretary General, Textile Workers Union, CROM, Ciudad Camargo, 1935; President, Catholic Association of Mexican Youth, 1935-40. h-Has worked at many occupations, including miner

and mechanic; textile worker, Florida and La Estrella Companies, 1929-34; administrator, hacienda, Parras, Coahuila, 1936-39; accountant, bank, Parras Coahuila, 1936-39; jeweler by profession; wrote for *Novedades* of Chihuahua. i-Son of Mauricio Chavira Legorreta and Magdalena Becerra Acosta; married Cruz Esperanza Rodríguez Alvarez. j-None. k-Directorio, 1982-85; C de D, 1961-64; Lehr; DBGM, 495.

Cházaro Lara, Ricardo
a-Jan. 26, 1920. b-Veracruz, Veracruz. c-Primary studies in the Justo Sierra School, Veracruz; secondary and preparatory studies at the Veracruz Institute, Veracruz; degree in mechanical engineering from the National Naval College, Veracruz, graduated as a Corvette Lieutenant, 1943; special course from the Subchaser Training Center, Miami, Florida, 1943; special course in electronics, Treasure Island, San Francisco, 1952. d-None. e-None. f-Assistant to President *Adolfo Ruiz Cortines*, 1953-58; *Subsecretary of the Navy*, 1970-76; *Secretary of the Navy*, 1976-82. g-None. h-None. i-Married to Luz del Alva Iza; longtime friend of *Adolfo Ruiz Cortines*. j-Rank of Coastguardsman, Sept. 1, 1942; Corvette Lieutenant, May 16, 1943; Frigate Lieutenant, Nov. 20, 1946; Naval Lieutenant, Nov. 20, 1949; Corvette Captain, Nov. 20, 1952; Frigate Captain, Nov. 20, 1956; Naval Captain, Nov. 20, 1961; Rear Admiral, Nov. 20, 1964; Vice Admiral, Apr. 21, 1971; Admiral, June 1, 1976; joined the Coast Guard ship *Guanajuato*, 1942; Chief of Machinery, Coast Guard ship 1, 1943-44; Chief of Machinery, Coast Guard ship 20, 1944-45; Chief of Fatigue Duty, *Querétaro*, 1945-47; Chief of Machinery, Coast Guard ship 2; Chief of Machinery, ship *Baranda*, 1951-52; Chief of Workshops for Naval Classes in Mazatlán, 1952; Subdirector of the

Drydocks, Salina Cruz, Oaxaca, 1952-53; Inspector General of Machinery, Pacific, 1964-66; Technical Subdirector of the Navy, PEMEX, 1966-70. k-Precandidate for governor of Veracruz, 1973. l-DPE61, 39; D del S, 2 Dec. 1970; HA, 6 Dec. 1976, 22, 4 Apr. 1977, 15; Excélsior, 1 Dec. 1976; El Dia, 1 Dec. 1976; 20.

Chico Goerne, Luis
(Deceased Jan. 16, 1960) a-Feb. 16, 1892. b-Guanajuato, Guanajuato. c-Primary and secondary education in Guanajuato; law degree from the University of Guanajuato, 1918; advanced studies in sociology in Paris, 1923; Professor of Law and Sociology at the Colegio de Guanajuato; Professor of Law at the Escuela Libre de Derecho; Professor of Sociology at the National School of Law, UNAM; Director of the National School of Law, UNAM, 1929-33. d-None. e-None. f-Judge of the Superior Military Court, 1920; Rector of UNAM, 1935-38; adviser to the Mexican legation in Paris, 1938-40; adviser to the President of Mexico, 1941-46; Justice of the Supreme Court, 1947-52, 1952-58, and 1958-60. g-None. h-Assisted with the writing of the 1929 and 1931 penal codes of Mexico; author of several books on law and sociology. i-Son of Joaquín Chico González and Francisca Ramírez, a wealthy Guanajuato family; father was a lawyer and great nephew of José María Chico y Linares, minister of justice under Hidalgo; father prominent in local politics, served as a deputy from 1894 to 1910; grandfather, Joaquín Chico Obregón, a well-known lawyer; married Clotilde Santa Coloma; son is an architect; professor of many prominent public men, including Antonio Armendáriz; Manuel Hinojosa Ortiz practiced law with him in 1935-36; married Clotilde Santa Coloma. j-None. k-None. l-HA, 8 Oct. 1943; 37-38; WWM45, 27;

DGF56, 567-68; DP70 598-99; Enc. Mex., III, 24; Peral, 208; WB48, 1098; Holms, 278.

Chirinos (Calero), Patricio
a-July 27, 1939. b-Panuco, Veracruz. c-Early education unknown; economics degree, National School of Economics, UNAM, 1959-64, with a thesis on "Economic Development and Social Change"; professor, School for Foreigners, UNAM, 1964-72; professor, Political Training Institute, PRI, 1972-75. d-Federal Deputy from the State of Veracruz, Dist. 4, 1973-76; Governor of Veracruz, 1992- . e-Joined PRI, 1962; Secretary of Policy Planning of the National Youth Directorate of PRI, 1964-65; Private Secretary to Rodolfo Echeverría Jr., Oficial Mayor of PRI, 1970-71; Auxiliary Secretary of the National Executive Committee of PRI, 1971-72; Subdirector of the IEPES of PRI, 1972-75; Special Delegate of the CEN of PRI to Baja California del Sur, Durango, Sonora, Tabasco, San Luis Potosí, and Veracruz; General Delegate of the IEPES of PRI to Querétaro, Guanajuato, Puebla, Nuevo León, Durango, and Tabasco, 1975-76; Coordinator of the Subdirectorate of Political Studies, IEPES of PRI, 1981-82. f-Auxiliary Secretary of the Head of the Department of the Federal District, Alfonso Corona del Rosal, 1968-70; Adviser, Secretary of Government, Jesús Reyes Heroles, 1976-77; Adviser, Subsecretary of Labor, Rodolfo Echeverría Jr., 1977-81; Director General of Delegations, Secretariat of Programming and Budgeting, 1982-88; Secretary of Urban Development and Ecology, 1988-92. g-Secretary of Social Action of CNOP, 1971-72. h-None. i-Son of Antonio Chirinos Gea, civil servant, and Catalina Calero Valdez; married Molly Brown Magruder, educator. j-None. k-None. l-DBGM87, 105; DBGM89, 96; C de D, 1973-76; Proceso, 21 Oct. 1991, 15.

Christlieb Ibarrola, Adolfo
(Deceased Dec. 6, 1969) a-Mar. 12, 1919. b-Federal District. c-Primary studies at Colegio Francés Puente de Alvarado and in Jalisco; secondary studies at the Colegio Francés Morelos; law degree from the National School of Law, UNAM, Aug. 27, 1941; studied at the School of Philosophy and Letters, UNAM, 1936-40; adviser to the School of Philosophy and Letters, 1937-39; Professor of Constitutional Law, National School of Law, UNAM, 1954-57; Professor of Mexican History, Colegio Francés Morelos, 1939-45. d-*Federal Deputy* from the Federal District, Dist. 23, 1964-67, member of the Foreign Trade Committee, the Legislative Studies Committee (Seventh Section of Credit and Trade), the Second Government Committee, and the Committee on Mines; leader of the National Action Party delegation to Congress, 1964. e-*President of the CEN of PAN*, 1962-68; PAN representative to the Federal Electoral Commission; joined PAN in 1942. f-None. g-None. h-Practicing lawyer, 1941-69; Director, Fiduciary Department, Regional Bank of the North, S.A., 1952; Secretary of the Mexican Bar Association. i-Lawyer in the firm of *Roberto Cossío*, a school friend and later secretary general of the CEN of PAN, 1939-51; son of Alfredo Christlieb Rappa and Paula Garrola; married Hilda Morales. j-None. k-None. l-DP70, 617; C de D, 1966; Enc. Mex., III, 97; WWMG, 13; HA, 7 Dec. 1964, 21; letter; Q es QM, 1952, 53.

Chuayffet (Chemor), Emilio
a-Oct. 3, 1951. b-Federal District. c-Early education unknown; preparatory studies at the Centro Universitario México; law degree, National School of Law, UNAM, 1970-74, with a thesis on the Federal District. d-Mayor of Toluca, México, 1982; *Governor of México*, 1993- . e-Joined PRI, 1969; president of

PRI, Toluca, 1976-78; president of the advisory council of the CEPES of PRI in México, 1983-87. f-Auxiliary Secretary of the Subsecretary of Labor, *Arturo Llorente González*, 1974-76; Delegate of the Department of the Federal District to Benito Júarez, 1976-81; Secretary of Education, State of México, 1983-87; Secretary of Government, State of México, 1987; Director, Federal Electoral Institute, 1991-93. g-None. h-None. i-Son of Emilio Chuayffet Chauyffet, surgeon, and Ruth Chemor Abraham; married Olga Guadalupe Soto Priego; grandfather a prosperous Toluca merchant. j-None. k-Raised by maternal grandmother when parents and sister were killed in an automobile accident. l-*Proceso*, 15 Feb 1993, 28-29; DBGM92, 102.

Chumacero Sánchez, Blas
a-Jan. 18, 1908. b-Puebla, Puebla. c-Primary and secondary studies in Puebla; studied labor law at night school in Puebla. d-*Federal Deputy* from the State of Puebla, Dist. 2, 1940-43, member of the Administration Committee (2nd year), the First Balloting Committee, and the Gran Comisión, 1942; *Federal Deputy* from the State of Puebla, Dist. 1, 1946-49, member of the Textile Industry Committee, the Committee on Credit, Money, and Credit Institutions, the First Credentials Committee, and the Health Committee; *Federal Deputy* from the State of Puebla, Dist. 1, 1952-55, Vice-President of the Chamber, Sept. 1952; Secretary of the Chamber, Sept. 1954, member of the Library Committee (2nd year), the Editorial Committee (1st year), and the Budget Committee; *Federal Deputy* from the State of Puebla, Dist. 1, 1958-61, member of the Second Government Committee, the Inspection Committee of the General Accounting Office (2nd year), the First Budget Committee, the Rules Commit-

tee, the Second Credentials Committee, and the Third Labor Committee; *Federal Deputy* from the State of Puebla, Dist. 1, 1967-70, member of the Legislative Studies Committee, Fifth Section on Labor and Ninth Section on General Affairs; the First Treasury Committee, the Steel Industry Committee, the Industries Committee, and the First Labor Committee; *Senator* from the State of Puebla, 1976-82, President of the Senate, Nov. 1976; *Federal Deputy* from the State of Puebla, Dist. 1, 1985-88; *Senator* from the State of Puebla, 1988- . e-*Secretary of Labor Action, CEN of PRI*, 1946; *Secretary of Labor Action, CEN of PRI*, 1964-82. f-None. g-Secretary General of the Union of the Industrial Plant of San Alfonso; Secretary General of the CTM for the State of Puebla, 1935-36, 1952-93; Secretary of Labor and Conflicts, National Council of the Federation of Laborers and Farmers, State of México; Secretary of Organization of the CTM, 1943-46; President of the Justice Committee of the CTM, 1955-62; Secretary of Labor of the CTM, 1946-49, 1962- . h-Representative for labor on the Board of Conciliation and Arbitration, Puebla. i-Son of Zenón Chumacero Bueno, laborer, and Joséfa Sánchez Serrano; married Aurelia Corona; Chumacero Sánchez worked for many years in textile plants in Puebla. j-None. k-As of 1979, had served as a federal deputy more times since 1940 than any other Mexican. l-C de D, 1946-48, 70, 1967-69, 66, 67, 73, 74, 1952-54; Func, 318; C de D, 1940-42, 9, 53, 1958-60, 76; *Excélsior*, 20 Jan. 1976, 5A; DBGM89, 425-26; DBGM92, 449-50.

Cicero Mackinney, Roger
a-May 14, 1929. b-Mérida, Yucatán. c-Early education unknown; journalism studies, Latin American University, 1947-49; teacher, Conciliar Seminary, Yucatán. d-*Plurinominal Federal*

Deputy from PAN, 1982-85, 1989-92, member of the Housing and Public Works Committee. e-Joined PAN, 1968; Secretary of Press and Publicity of the CEN of PAN; candidate for local deputy, federal deputy, and senator for Yucatán from PAN. f-Director of the Committee for Economic Development in Yucatán, Campeche, and Quintana Roo. g-None. h-Essayist for various newspapers and journals; regular contributor to *La Nacional*, the official paper of PAN. i-Son of Víctor José Cicero Cervera and Rita MacKinney Huerta; married Silvia Cáceres Piña. j-None. k-None. l-Directorio, 1982-85; DBGM89, 417-18.

Cisneros Molina, Joaquín (Francisco)
(Deceased Mar. 26, 1991) a-Aug. 1, 1907. b-Tlaxcala, Tlaxcala. c-Primary studies in Tlaxcala; preparatory studies at the National Preparatory School, Mexico City; teaching certificate in primary education from the National Teachers School, 1928; law degree from the National School of Law, UNAM, Nov. 3, 1936; primary, secondary, and preparatory education teacher; Director of Preparatory Education for the State of Tlaxcala, 1945. d-*Federal Deputy* from the State of Tlaxcala, Dist. 1, 1949-52, member of the Third Ejido Committee; member of the Gran Comisión; *Governor of Tlaxcala*, 1957-63. f-Director of Libraries for the Secretariat of the Treasury, 1935-36; Secretary General of the State of Tlaxcala, 1936; Secretary of the Federal Tax Court, 1937-38; Director of the Department of Legal Consultants, Secretariat of the Treasury, 1942; Secretary General of the Department of Indigenous Affairs, 1941-42; Secretary General of Government of the State of Tlaxcala, 1944; Secretary General of Government of the State of Tlaxcala, 1952-57; *Private Secretary* to President *Gustavo Díaz Ordaz*, 1964-70; delegate of the Secretariat of Public

Education to the State of Tlaxcala, 1978. g-None. h-None. i-Friend of *Gustavo Díaz Ordaz* since they served together in the Chamber of Deputies; son, Joaquín Cisneros Fernández, was alternate senator from Tlaxcala, 1976-82. j-None. k-None. l-DBM68, 144; Hayner, 211; C de D, 1949-51; *Excélsior*, 8 Dec. 1975, 22; Enc. Mex., II, 488; *Excélsior*, 19 July, 1978, 9, 26 Dec. 1981, 16A.

Coello (Ochoa), David
(Deceased 1959) a-Aug. 20, 1885. b-Alvarado, Veracruz. c-Degree from the Naval College of Veracruz, 1900. d-None. e-Cofounder of PARM, 1954. f-*Oficial Mayor of the Secretariat of the Navy,* 1948-49; *Secretary of the Navy,* 1948-49; Inspector of Fishing for Tuxpán, Nayarit, 1952-58. g-None. h-Considered an expert on naval warfare. j-Joined the navy in 1909; member of the merchant marine, 1917-27; rejoined the navy, 1927; career naval officer; rescued a North American ship off the coast of Mexico, 1924; commander of various naval ships; Commander of the 4th Naval Zone, 1939-40; rank of Commodore, 1940; Subdirector of the Navy, 1940; Secretary General of the Merchant Fleet, 1940-41; Director of the Fleet, 1941-42; Commander of the 1st Naval Zone, 1942-43; Acting Commander of the 4th Naval Zone, 1944-45; Commandant, Islas Margaritas Naval Base, 1945-46; rank of Vice Admiral, 1949. k-None. l-DGF47, 233; DP70, 459; DGF56, 384; D de Y, 5 Dec. 1940, 1; HA, 15 Oct. 1948, 3; *Excélsior*, 20 Oct. 1949; PS, 1258.

Coello Trejo, Javier
a-Oct. 22, 1948. b-San Cristóbal de las Casas, Chiapas. c-Early education unknown; law degree, University of Chiapas, 1967-70, with a thesis on the ministerio público against corruption. d-None. e-None. f-Agent of the Ministerio Público; Private Secretary to the Director of Federal Police of Chiapas; Private Secretary to the Attorney General of Chiapas; special agent of the Ministerio Público of the Attorney General of Mexico; Secretary General of Government of Chiapas, 1983-88; *Assistant Attorney General* of Investigation and Anti-Drug Trafficking, 1988-90. g-None. h-None. i-Son of Roberto Coello Lesieur, journalist, and María del Carmen Trejo Quevedo; married Jovita Zuarth Corzo. j-None. k-Resigned from his position as assistant attorney general after numerous complaints against his agents for sexual abuse and rape. l-DBGM89, 88.

Colín Sánchez, Mario
(Deceased Mar. 25, 1983) a-June 22, 1922. b-Atlacomulco, México. c-Primary studies at the public school, Atlacomulco; secondary studies at a public school, Toluca, Mexico, and Secondary School No. 4, Mexico City; preparatory studies at the National Preparatory School, 1940-41; law degree, National School of Law, UNAM, 1942-47, with a thesis on "The Municipality in Mexico"; Rector of the Scientific and Literary Institute of Mexico, 1951-52. d-Local Deputy to the State Legislature of México, 1947-50; *Federal Deputy* from the State of México, Dist. 4, 1955-58, alternate member of the Second Government Committee and the Rules Committee; *Alternate Senator* from México, 1958-64; *Federal Deputy* from the State of México, Dist. 5, 1964-67, member of the Tariff Committee and the First Ejido Committee; *Federal Deputy* from the State of México, Dist. 8, 1970-73, member of the Industries Committee, the Gran Comisión, the Cultural Affairs Committee, and the Editorial Committee (1st year). e-President of the Regional Committee of PRI, San Luis Potosí; delegate of PRI to various states. f-Private Secretary to

the Governor of México, 1945-47, *Alfredo del Mazo*; Judge of the First Instance; Head of the Public Registry, Tlalnepantla; Secretary of Education, State of México, 1981-83. h-Created the multivolume *Encyclopedia of the State of México*; winner of the 1942 oratory contest at the National Law School. i-Brother of author and lawyer Guillermo Colín Sánchez, justice of the Superior Tribunal of Justice of the Federal District; companion of *Luis Echeverría* at UNAM; married María Asúnsolo; nephew of *Alfredo del Mazo Vélez*, governor of México. j-None. k-Shot Mar. 5, 1983, in Cuernavaca, died after four operations. l-DGF56, 25, 33, 36, 398; C de S, 1961-64, 14; C de D, 1955-57, 54; Directorio, 1970-72; C de D, 1970-72, 107; letters; Enc. Mex., 1977, III, 22-23; C de D, 1964-67, 77, 82; Guerra Leal, 127; *Excélsior*, 26 Apr. 1983, 5A, 2 May 1983, 34A; HA, 28 Sept. 1981, 27; *Excélsior*, 27 Mar. 1983, 4A.

Colomo y Corral, José
(Deceased 1969) a-Oct. 6, 1894. b-Meoqui, Chihuahua. c-Secondary studies at the Scientific and Literary Institute of Chihuahua, 1907-12; degree in petroleum engineering, 1920, and Professor of Engineering, 1931-45, both at the National School of Engineering, UNAM. d-None. e-None. f-Subdirector of the Department of Petroleum, Secretariat of Industry and Commerce, 1927-37; Assistant Director of Mines and Petroleum, Secretariat of Industry and Commerce, 1939-40; Director, Department of Coordination and Technical Studies, Petroleos Mexicanos, 1941-45; *Subdirector of Production of PEMEX*, 1950-64; *Subdirector of Primary Production of PEMEX*, 1965-69. g-None. h-None. j-None. k-None. l-Letter, WWM45, 28; DGF50, II, 203, 279, 280; DGF51, II, 293, 383-84.

Colosio (Murrieta), Luis Donaldo
(Deceased Mar. 23, 1994) a-Feb. 10, 1950. b-Magdalena de Kino, Sonora. c-Primary at the Juan Fenochio School, Magdalena, 1957-62; secondary studies at Secondary School No. 3, Magdalena, 1963-65; preparatory studies at the University of Sonora, 1966-68; economics degree, Technological Institute of Higher Studies, Monterrey, 1968-72; MA in regional development and urban economics, on government scholarship, University of Pennsylvania, 1974-75; studied English several summers at the University of Arizona Center for English as a Second Language; Ph.D. studies in economics, University of Pennsylvania; professor, Autonomous University of the State of México, 1979, Colegio de México, 1979, National School of Political Studies, Acatlán, UNAM, 1979, Anáhuac University, 1979. d-*Federal Deputy* from the State of Sonora, Dist. 6, 1985-88, member of the Treasury Committee; *Senator* from Sonora, 1988-91. e-Member of the CEPES of PRI in the Federal District, 1981-82; *Oficial Mayor of the CEN of PRI*, 1987-88; *President of the CEN of PRI*, 1988-92; PRI presidential candidate, 1993-94. f-Adviser to Director General of Macro Economic and Social Policy, 1979-80, Subdirector of Regional and Urban Policy, 1980-82, both at Secretariat of Programming and Budgeting; Technical Secretary of the Development Planning Committee (Coplade), Federal District, 1982-83; Director General of Regional Programming and Budgeting, Secretariat of Programming and Budgeting, 1984-85; Secretary, Secretariat of Social Development, 1992-93. g-None. h-None. i-Son of Luis Colosio Fernández, meat packer and self-educated accountant, and Ofelia Murrieta, homemaker; classmate at ITESM of *Carlos Medina Plascencia*, governor of Guanajuato, José Luis Soberanes Reyes, subsecretary of urban

development; and *Rogelio Montemayor Seguy*; married Diana Laura Rojas, economist; obtained his first position under *Rogelio Montemayor Seguy*, governor of Coahuila; adviser to *Carlos Salinas de Gortari*, 1979. j-None. k-A leading candidate for the PRI presidential nomination, received the nomination of PRI, Nov. 28, 1993; assassinated while campaigning, generating difficulties for PRI and further pressures for reform. l-DBGM87, 456; DBGM89, 419; *Arizona Daily Star*, 28 May 1989, 3C; *Proceso*, 21 Aug. 1992, 15; letters; DBGM92, 93.

Conchello Dávila, José Angel
a-Sept. 1, 1923. b-Monterrey, Nuevo León. c-Law degree, National School of Law, UNAM; studied industrial development in Canada on a United Nations scholarship; Professor of Economics, School of Banking and Business Administration, UNAM; Professor of Journalism; professor, Ibero-American University. d-Candidate for federal deputy, 1955; *Federal Deputy* from the Federal District, Dist. 19, 1967-70, member of the Tariff Committee, the International Trade Committee, the Legislative Studies Committee, Seventh Section on Commerce and Credit, the Cinematographic Development Committee, the Television Industry Committee, and the Desert Zones Committee; *Federal Deputy* (PAN party deputy), 1973-76; head of the PAN delegation, 1974; member of the Tenth Interparliamentary Reunion, 1970; *Plurinominal Federal Deputy* from PAN, 1985-88; Representative to the Assembly of the Federal District, 1988-90. e-Joined PAN, 1955; national adviser to PAN, 1967-87; member of the National Executive Committee of PAN, 1969; *President of the CEN of PAN*, 1972-75; President of PAN in the Federal District, 1989. f-Administrative Director, National Council of Produc-

tivity. g-Director, Economic Studies Department, CONCAMIN; represented Mexican employers at the Administrative Council of the International Labor Organization, Geneva, 1953. h-Director of a private public relations firm, 1974; Director of Public Relations, Cerveceria Moctezuma; writer for *La Nación*, official publication of PAN; fluent in French, English, and Italian. i-Disciple of Federal Deputy *Antonio Rodríguez* when he joined PAN; *Jorge Garabito* and *Efraín González Morfín* supported him for the presidency of PAN; son of Andrés Conchello Meseguer, industrialist, and Clotilde Dávila Rodríguez; married Otilia Román Marx. j-None. k-Accused by dissident members of PAN of attempting to split the party, 1978; lost leadership of PAN delegation to Congress when he defied new party leadership; PAN candidate for governor of Nuevo León, 1979. l-Letter; *Excélsior*, 28 Feb. 1973, 19, 30 Mar. 1973, 22; HA, 18 Jan. 1973, 16, 21 Feb. 1972, 13; MGF69, 91; C de D, 1967-69, 61, 70, 72, 75; *Proceso*, 17 Apr. 1978, 10-16; HA, 9 Apr. 1979, VI; DBGM89, 568.

Contreras Camacho, Máximo
a-Sept. 7, 1913. b-Pichucalco, Chiapas. c-Primary studies at the public school, Pichucalco; secondary and preparatory studies at Secondary School No. 4, preparatory at the National Preparatory School, Mexico City; law degree, National School of Law, UNAM. d-*Alternate Federal Deputy* from the State of Chiapas, Dist. 1, 1958-61; *Federal Deputy* from the State of Chiapas, Dist. 4, 1961-64, member of the Budget and Accounts Committee and the Second Labor Committee; *Federal Deputy* from the State of Chiapas, Dist. 3, 1970-73, member of the Second Constitutional Affairs Committee, the Foreign Trade and Tariff Committee, the Fiscal Section of the Legislative Studies Committee, and

the Gran Comisión. e-Delegate of
CNOP; delegate of PRI in various states.
f-Administrator of Customs, Nuevo
Laredo; conciliator, Secretariat of Labor;
Director of Legal Affairs, Secretariat of
Health; Oficial Mayor of Government of
the State of Guerrero; district judge,
Guerrero; judge in the State of Chiapas.
g-None. h-Rector of the Institute of
Arts and Sciences, Chiapas. i-Brother,
Gregorio, was a justice of the Superior
Tribunal of Justice of the Federal
District; son, Máximo, was head of the
Legal Department of the Metro, 1974;
married Amparo Barrera. j-None.
k-Precandidate for senator from Chia-
pas, 1981. l-Directorio, 70-72; C de D,
1961-63, 75, 1970-72, 107, 1958-60;
Excélsior, 26 Dec. 1981, 16A.

**Contreras Martínez, María de los
Angeles**
a-May 5, 1933. b-Tarimoro, Guanajuato. c-Early education unknown;
teaching certificate; private accounting
degree. d-Member of the City Council
of Guanajuato, Guanajuato, 1958-60;
Federal Deputy from the State of
Guanajuato, Dist. 7, 1967-70. e-Participated in various deputy campaigns,
and the gubernatorial campaign in
Guanajuato, 1951; joined PRI, 1954;
Director of the women's section of PRI,
State of Guanajuato, 1954-66; Secretary
General of the State Committee of PRI
for Guanajuato, 1967. f-None.
g-Delegate of the CNC to various
national conventions. j-None. k-None.
l-Directorio, 1967-70; PS, 1288.

Coquet Laguna, Benito
a-Aug. 26, 1913. b-Jalapa, Veracruz.
c-Primary and secondary studies in
Jalapa; law degree from the University
of Veracruz, Jalapa, 1935, with a thesis
on labor legislation. d-*Federal Deputy*
from the State of Veracruz, Dist. 11,
1943-46, President of the Chamber,
Sept. 1945, 1946. e-Orator for the

presidential campaign of *Avila
Camacho*, 1940; participant in José
Vasconcelos' campaign for president,
1929. f-Agent of the Ministerio Público
in Coatepec, Veracruz; Chief of Legal
Affairs, Agricultural Credit Bank,
Veracruz, 1935-39; public defender,
Superior Tribunal of Justice of the State
of Veracruz, 1935-39; Director of the
National Institute of Bellas Artes, 1941-
43; Ambassador to Cuba, 1947-52;
*Oficial Mayor of the Secretariat of
Government*, 1946-47; *Subsecretary of
the Presidency*, 1952-56; *Secretary of
the Presidency*, 1956-58; *Director
General of the Mexican Institute of
Social Security*, 1958-64. g-Delegate
from Veracruz to the National Student
Congress in San Luis Potosí, 1933; Vice-
President and President, National
Student Federation, 1934. h-None.
i-Married Julia Ramos Larzen; son, Juan
Benito Coquet Ramos, director general
of the Department of the Federal
District, 1992. j-None. k-None. l-*El
Universal*, 2 Dec. 1958; HA, 8 Dec.
1958, 32; DGF56, 53; D del S, 3 Dec.
1952, 1; DGF51, I, 104; Gómez
Maganda, 106; *Quién Será*, 145; Func,
103; Enc. Mex., 1977, III, 138-39.

Cordera Campos, Rolando
a-Jan. 31, 1942. b-Colima. c-Early
education unknown; economics degree;
full-time professor. d-*Plurinominal
Federal Deputy* from PSUM, 1982-85.
e-Secretary of Studies of the PSUM;
member of the Political Committee of
the Central Committee of PSUM.
f-None. g-None. h-Educator; author of
books on economic policy. j-None.
k-None. l-Directorio, 1982-85.

Cordera (Ruiz), Miguel Angel
a-Oct. 10, 1912. b-Jalapa, Veracruz.
c-Early education unknown; law degree
from the School of Law, University of
Veracruz, Jalapa, 1935. d-None.
e-None. f-Consulting lawyer to the

State Government of Veracruz, 1940; President of the National Coffee Commission, 1954-59 (forerunner of the Mexican Institute of Coffee); Director General of the Mexican Institute of Coffee, 1959-66; Executive Coordinator of CONASUPO, 1976. g-None. h-Industrial farmer in coffee and tropical agricultural crops. i-Son of Miguel Angel Cordera Ruiz, a lawyer; practiced law with him as a student; married Carmen de Lascuráin. j-None. k-None. l-DBM68, 149.

Córdoba Montoya, Joseph Marie
a-June 1, 1950. b-Ciotat, France. c-Early education unknown; engineering degree, Ecole Politechnique, Paris, 1970-73; MA in philosophy, Sorbonne, 1970-73; Ph.D. studies in economics, Stanford University, with an unfinished thesis on "Prices and Quantities in the Planning Process," 1974-77; professor, University of Pennsylvania, 1978-79, Colegio de México, 1979. d-None. e-Joined PRI, 1980; adviser to the Director General of the IEPES of PRI, *Carlos Salinas*, 1982. f-Adviser to *Francisco Gil Díaz*, Director of Income, Secretariat of the Treasury, 1979-80; Director of Regional Planning, 1980-81; Director General of Social and Economic Policy, 1982-83, Chief of Advisers, 1983-85, Director General of Social and Economic Policy, 1985-87, all at Secretariat of Programming and Budgeting; special adviser to *Carlos Salinas*, 1987-88; Coordinator of the Office of Coordination of the Presidency, 1988-94. g-None. h-None. i-Son of José Córdoba Caparros, lawyer, and Dolores Montoya, Spanish exiles; father was an official in the Republican city government of Almería and was imprisoned in Spain, 1939-45, before escaping; married Sofia Urrutia Lazo, daughter of Oscar Urrutia Lazo, architect, and María Elena Lazo, writer; naturalized Mexican, May 10, 1985; roomed with *Guillermo Ortiz*

Martínez, subsecretary of the treasury, at Stanford; met *Rogelio Gasca Neri*, subsecretary of programming and budgeting, at Stanford. j-None. k-Participated in the student strike in Paris, 1968; according to *Proceso*, violated the Constitution when he joined PRI as a noncitizen. l-DBGM87, 94; DBGM89, 89; *Proceso*, 6 Apr. 1992, 8.

Corella Gil Samaniego, Norberto
a-July 24, 1927. b-Douglas, Arizona. c-Primary studies in Douglas, Arizona; secondary studies in Hermosillo, at the University of Sonora; degree in business administration from the Institute of Technology and Higher Education of Monterrey, Nuevo León, May 1950. d-*Plurinominal Federal Deputy* from PAN, 1988-91. e-President of the Executive Committee of the Regional Council of the National Action Party, 1963-65; Head of the National Action Party for the State of Baja California del Norte, 1968-70. f-None. g-Secretary of the Council of the National Chamber of Commerce of Mexicali, 1954-55; President of the National Chamber of Commerce of Mexicali, 1955-56; Founding President of the State Confederation of Chambers of Commerce of Baja California del Norte, 1956-59; Founding President of the Employer's Center of Baja California del Norte, 1958-63. h-Director of Sales, Cia. Maderera y Ganadera del Noroeste, Ciudad Juárez, Chihuahua, 1950; Subdirector of Proveedores de la Construcción, S.A., 1952-54; Director of Concretos de Mexicali, 1954; Director of Proveedores de la Construcción, S.A., 1954-70. i-Son of Alfredo Corella Barceló and Celia Gil Samaniego Freaner; brother, René, was oficial mayor of the state of Baja California, 1992. j-None. k-National Action Party candidate for governor of Baja California del Norte; precandidate for the PAN

candidacy for president, 1975.
l-DBM68, 150; Aguirre, 497; DBGM89,
421; DBGM92, 740.

Corella Molina, Emiliano
a-May 18, 1891. b-Banamichi, Sonora.
c-Self-educated; no degree. d-Mayor of
Banamichi, 1912-13, 1916-19; Alternate
Local Deputy to the State Legislature of
Sonora, 1919-21; Local Deputy to the
State Legislature of Sonora, 1924-26;
Federal Deputy from the State of Sonora, 1930-32; Senator from the State of
Sonora, 1932-36; *Federal Deputy* from
the State of Sonora, Dist. No. 2, 1955-
58, President of the Agricultural Development and Livestock Committee.
e-None. f-Interim Governor of Sonora,
1934-35. g-President of the Livestock
Union of Sonora, 1947; President of the
Lions Club of Banamichi. h-Business-
man; adviser to the Livestock and
Agricultural Bank of Sonora, 1956.
j-None. k-None. l-Ind. Biog., 44-45;
DGF56, 28, 33; C de D, 1955-58.

Coria (Cano), Alberto
(Deceased 1960) a-July 4, 1892. b-Para-
cho, Michoacán. c-Primary studies in
Paracho; secondary at the Colegio de
San Nicolás, Morelia; abandoned
studies in 1913 to fight against the
forces of Victoriano Huerta; law degree,
University of Michoacán, 1929; normal
professor, Colegio de San Nicolás, 1916;
Professor of Mathematics, Colegio de
San Nicolás, 1913-32 Rector of the University of Michoacán, 1929. d-Councilman of the City Council of Morelia,
1916-17, 1924; Local Deputy, State of
Michoacán, 1920-24; Federal Deputy
from the State of Michoacán, 1932-34.
e-None. f-Agent of the Ministerio
Público, 1928; Attorney General of the
State of Michoacán, 1931-32; Justice of
the Superior Tribunal of Justice of the
Federal District and Federal Territories,
1935-40; Justice of the Federal Tax
Court, 1951-58; Justice of the Federal

Circuit Court, Mexico City, 1959-60.
g-Cofounder of the World House of
Labor; First Secretary General of Labor,
Michoacán, under Governor *Lázaro
Cárdenas*. i-Close friend of *Alberto
Bremauntz* during the 1920s. j-Captain
in the Constitutionalist forces in
Michoacán, 1913-15. k-Coauthor of the
socialist revision of Article 3 of the
1917 Constitution with *Alberto
Bremauntz*. l-DGF56, 551; DP70, 521;
Enc. Mex., 1977, III, 152; DGF51, I, 549.

Corona, Gustavo
a-1899. b-Morelia, Michoacán. c-Primary studies in Morelia; secondary and
preparatory studies at the Colegio de
San Nicolás de Hidalgo, Morelia; law
degree from same, May 25, 1931.
d-Mayor of Morelia, 1929; Rector of the
University of Michoacán, 1934.
e-None. f-Secretary of the Local Board
of Conciliation and Arbitration, Morelia; Judge, 5th Civil District, Mexico
City; President of the Federal Board of
Conciliation and Arbitration, 1937-38;
*Secretary General of the Department of
the Federal District*, 1939-40; lawyer for
PEMEX, 1960. g-Student activist; member of the student Red Cross under Dr.
Jesús Díaz Barriaga, serving throughout
Michoacán. j-None. k-His arbitration
decision became the judicial basis of the
petroleum expropriation, 1938. l-Dicc.
Mich., 101.

Corona Bandín, Salvador
a-1912. b-Guadalajara, Jalisco. c-Primary, secondary, and preparatory studies in Guadalajara; language specialist;
Professor of English and French in the
Guadalajara schools. d-Local Deputy to
the State Legislature of Jalisco; *Federal
Deputy* from the State of Jalisco, Dist.
9, 1961-64, member of the Gran
Comisión; *Senator* from the State of
Jalisco, 1964-70. e-General Delegate of
the CEN of PRI to Veracruz, 1964;
President of PRI in Jalisco. f-Oficial

Mayor of the State Legislature of Jalisco; Director of the Complaints Department, Department of Agrarian Affairs, 1945-46; Private Secretary to *Silvano Barba González*, Head of the Department of Agrarian Affairs, 1944-45. g-None. i-Member of *Barba González's* political group. j-None. k-None. l-C de S, 1964-70; MGF69; C de D, 1964-70.

Corona del Rosal, Alfonso
a-July 1, 1908. b-Ixmiquilpán, Hidalgo. c-Primary studies in Mexico City; first year of preparatory at the National Preparatory School 1930-31; law degree with honorable mention, National School of Law, UNAM, Sept. 29, 1937; BS in biology from the National Military College and commissioned a 2nd Lieutenant in the Cavalry, 1921; Professor of Labor Law at the Secondary School for Workers No. 9; Professor of Political Economy at the National School of Law, UNAM; Professor of Military Morals at the National Military College, 1923-33. d-*Federal Deputy* from the State of Hidalgo, Dist. 5, 1940-43, member of the Committee on Libraries; *Federal Senator* from Hidalgo, 1946-52, member of the Committee on Legislative Studies, the Department of the Federal District Committee, the Special Forestry Committee, the First Justice Committee, the Second Balloting Committee, the First National Defense Committee, and the Military Justice Committee; substitute member of the First Committee on Constitutional Affairs; *Governor of Hidalgo*, 1957-58. e-Member of the Youth Section of the Mexican Revolutionary Party, 1938; Subsecretary of Military Action for the Mexican Revolutionary Party, 1938-40; member of the national publicity committee for *Avila Camacho*, 1939-40; President of the Regional Committee of the Federal District during the campaign of *Adolfo*

Ruiz Cortines, 1951-52; *President of the CEN of PRI*, 1958-64. f-Private Secretary to *Javier Rojo Gómez*, Head of the Federal District, 1943-46; Director General of the National Army-Navy Bank; Director of Labor and Welfare for the Federal District; *Secretary of Government Properties*, 1964-66; *Head of the Department of the Federal District*, 1966-70. g-Secretary of the Society of Students, UNAM. h-None. i-Friend of *Javier Rojo Gómez*; son of Germán Corona, a school teacher, and Aurora del Rosal; son, *Germán*, was a senator from Hidalgo, 1970-76; married Carmen Alvarez; friend of *Antonio Nava Castillo* since they were cadets at the National Military School. j-Career army officer; promoted to Lt. Colonel by *Manuel Avila Camacho* just before he left the presidency, 1946; participated in the campaigns of 1923, 1927, and 1929; Director of Military Industries, 1953-54; rank of Division General. k-Precandidate for president of Mexico, 1969. l-MacAlister, 223; DGF47, 20; HA, 7 Dec. 1964, 19; D del S, 1 Dec. 1940, 1; DBM68, 151; D del S, 3 Dec. 1946, 1; Scott, 31, 306; DGF51, I, 6, 11-14; Enc. Mex., 1977, III, 155; Pérez López, 101-02.

Corona del Rosal, Germán
a-Apr. 14, 1932. b-Ixmiquilpán, Hidalgo. c-Primary studies, 1941-46; secondary studies at Secondary School No. 4, Mexico City, 1947-48; studies at the Heroic Military College, 1950-53, graduating as a 2nd Lieutenant in the cavalry. d-*Senator* from the State of Hidalgo, 1970-76, Secretary of the Permanent Committee, Dec. 1973, President of the Indigenous Affairs Committee, and First Secretary of the First National Defense Committee; *Federal Deputy* from the State of Hidalgo, Dist. 1, 1985-88, Dist. 5, 1991-94. e-None. f-Treasurer, Local Highway Board, Hidalgo, 1957-58; Executive

Secretary of the Indigenous Property of the Quezquital Valley, 1956-69; Delegate of the Department of the Federal District, Gustavo A. Madero, 1976-81; Director General of Political and Social Research, Secretariat of the Government, 1981-82; delegate of the Secretariat of Programming and Budgeting, 1983-84. g-None. i-Son of General *Alfonso Corona del Rosal,* president of the CEN of PRI, 1958-64, and Raquel del Rosal Rodríguez; married María de los Angeles Vázquez Hale. j-Career army officer, reached rank of Captain. k-Precandidate for governor of Hidalgo, 1973 and 1978. l-C de S, 1970-76, 74; PS, 1222; *Excélsior,* 28 June 1974, 4; HA, 7 Jan. 1974, 12; Pérez López, 122-23; Directorio, 1985-88, 200-02; DBGM87, 458; DBGM92, 445.

Corona Mendioroz, Arturo
a-Dec. 18, 1915. b-Federal District. c-Early education unknown; graduated from the National Military College as a 2nd Lieutenant of Cavalry, Jan. 1935; graduated from the Applied Military School; staff and command diploma, Higher War College, 1942; attended the U.S. Command School; Professor of Cavalry Tactics at the National Military College; Professor at the U.S. Staff and Command School (Army), 1949; Professor of Spanish at the U.S. Military Academy, West Point, 1950. d-None. e-None. f-*Oficial Mayor of the Secretariat of National Defense,* 1970-72. g-None. h-None. j-Career army officer; Commander of the 13th Cavalry Regiment, Chief of Sections 2 and 4 of the General Staff of the Secretariat of National Defense, 1951; rank of Colonel, 1957; rank of Brigadier General, 1965; Director of the Higher War College, 1964-67; Commander of the 29th Military Zone, Minatitlán, Veracruz, 1976-77; Commander of the 7th Military Zone, Monterrey, Nuevo León, 1977; Commander of the 32nd

Military Zone, Mérida, Yucatán, 1978-79; Director General of Military Education, Secretariat of National Defense, 1981. k-None. l-HA, 14 Dec. 1970, 20; DBM68, 157; DAPC, 81, 30; R de E, Dec. 1965, 60; Rev. de Ejer., Jan 1958, 31; Rev. de Ejer., Dec. 1965, 60.

Coronado Organista, Saturnino
a-Feb. 19, 1892. b-Guadalajara, Jalisco. c-Primary and secondary studies in Guadalajara; preparatory studies in Guadalajara; law degree from the School of Law, University of Guadalajara; Professor of Civil and Administrative Law, School of Law, University of Guadalajara; Rector, University of Guadalajara. d-Member of the City Council of Guadalajara, 1946-47; Vice-Mayor of Guadalajara, 1947-48; *Federal Deputy* from the State of Jalisco, Dist. 1, 1949-52, member of the Gran Comisión, the Legislative Studies Committee, the Tax Committee, and the Insurance Committee; *Senator* from the State of Jalisco, 1952-58, member of the Gran Comisión, the Foreign and Domestic Trade Committee, the Second Government Committee, the First Constitutional Affairs Committee, and the Legislative Studies Committee. e-President of the State Electoral Committee, Jalisco, 1946; campaigned for *Miguel Alemán,* 1946. f-Interim Governor of Jalisco, 1947; Attorney for the State Planning Commission, Jalisco, 1947-51. g-None. h-In business, 1940-46. i-Held first political position under Governor *Marcelino García Barragán,* 1946; protégé of *J. Jesús González Gallo.* j-None. k-None. l-DGF51, 22, 29, 32, 33, 36; C de D, 1949-52, 68; DGF56, 6, 9-12, 14; Enc. Mex., 1977, V, 579; Ind. Biog., 45-46.

Corral Martínez, Blas
(Deceased Apr. 29, 1947) a-Feb. 11, 1883. b-Presidios, Durango. c-Early education unknown; no degree. d-*Gov-*

ernor *of Durango*, 1944-47. e-None.
f-*Oficial Mayor of the Secretariat of
National Defense, 1936-38; Subsecre-
tary of National Defense, 1938-39;
Oficial Mayor of the Secretariat of
National Defense, 1941.* g-None.
h-None. i-Fought with *Jesús Agustín
Castro* during the Revolution; married
Josefina Ramírez. j-Joined the Revolu-
tion, 1911; fought against Huerta, 1913-
14; organized the 21st Rural Guard;
Governor and Military Commander of
Chiapas, 1914; rank of Brigadier
General, 1916; President of the Superior
Military Tribunal; rank of Division
General, Apr. 1, 1938. k-None. l-D de
Y, Jan. 1938; letter; Peral, 188; Q es Q,
135; Cadena, 139.

Corral Romero, Octavio
a-July 20, 1922. b-Chihuahua, Chihuahua. c-Primary studies at the Niños
Heroes School No. 318, Chihuahua,
Chihuahua; secondary and preparatory
studies at the Scientific and Literary
Institute of Chihuahua; medical degree
from the National School of Medicine,
UNAM; completed all studies except
for thesis in philosophy, University of
Chihuahua. d-*Federal Deputy* (Party
Deputy from PAN), 1967-70, member of
the Public Health Committee and the
Special Education Committee. e-President of PAN in Chihuahua, Chihuahua,
1957-59; member of the Regional
Committee of PAN, 1960-70; member
of the National Council of PAN, 1960;
President of the State Committee of
PAN for Chihuahua (8 years). f-None.
g-None. i-Father, Jesús J. Corral, was a
mining engineer and senator, 1920-24.
j-None. k-Letter; C de D, 1967-70, 57.

Corrales Ayala (Espinosa), Rafael
a-Sept. 14, 1925. b-Guanajuato,
Guanajuato. c-Law degree, National
School of Law, UNAM, with a thesis on
"The State and the Nation in Mexico";
professor at the National School of Law,

UNAM, 1930s-1960s. d-*Federal Deputy*
from the State of Guanajuato, Dist. 1,
1949-52, member of the Gran Comisión, the Committees on Legislative
Studies (1st and 2nd year), Budgets and
Accounting (2nd year) and Vice President of the Chamber, Nov. 1949;
Alternate Senator from the State of
Guanajuato, 1952-58; *Federal Deputy*
from the State of Guanajuato, Dist. 1,
1955-58; member of the Committee on
Money, Credit and Credit Institutions,
and the Committee on Foreign Relations; Secretary of the Introductory
Council; President of the Chamber,
Sept. 1956; *Federal Deputy* from the
State of Guanajuato, Dist. 1, 1979-82;
Governor of Guanajuato, 1985-91.
e-*Secretary General of the CEN of PRI*,
1956-58; precandidate for senator from
Guanajuato, 1981; General Delegate of
the CEN of PRI to Querétaro, 1982.
f-*Assistant Attorney General of Mexico
(1),* 1946-47; Chief of Press Relations,
UNAM, 1948-49; Chief of the University Extension Department, UNAM,
1949; Head of the Press Department,
Presidency of Mexico, 1953-54; Director
of Information, Secretariat of Government, 1954-55; President of the Arbitration Tribunal for Federal Workers, 1960-
62; *Secretary General of the Department of Tourism, 1962-64;* Director
General of the National Lottery for
Public Welfare, 1964-70; adviser to the
Secretary of the Treasury, 1976-82;
*Oficial Mayor of the Secretariat of
Government, 1982-85.* h-Director of
the *Universidad de México,* 1948-52.
i-Part of the group recruited to PRI by
Rodolfo Sánchez Taboada; son of Rafael
Corrales Ayala, a lawyer who adminis-
tered German property for the Mexican
government during World War II, and
Luz Espinoza Castañon; brother of
Salvador Corrales Ayala, Director
General of Social Communication,
Secretary of Urban Development and
Ecology, 1983; uncle of Rafael Corrales

Ayala, federal circuit court judge;
married Gloria Favela Icaza. j-None.
k-Oratory champion, 1930s; responded
to the 4th state of the union address of
Adolfo Ruiz Cortines; precandidate for
governor of Guanajuato, 1978; precandidate for senator from Guanajuato, 1981.
l-DGF47, 309; DGF56, 6; *Siempre*, 7
Sept. 1956, 6; DGF69, 680; *Tiempo
Mexicano*, 56; DGF51, 21, 29, 32, 35,
36; *Excélsior*, 26 Dec. 1981, 16A, 11
Dec. 1982, 23A; Guerra Leal, 123;
QesQAP, 280; HA, 7 Feb. 1983, 22;
DBGM89, 600, 675; *Excélsior*, 27 July
1984, 20.

Correa Racho, Víctor Manuel
(Deceased 1978) a-Oct. 18, 1917.
b-Mérida, Yucatán. c-Primary studies
in Mérida; secondary studies at the
Bucareli School; preparatory studies at
the Francés Morelos School, Mexico
City; law degree, Law School, University of Yucatán, Dec. 1940; special
studies in contract law. d-Mayor of
Mérida, Yucatán, 1966-70. e-Head of
the regional committee for the National
Action Party in the State of Yucatán;
adviser to the National Executive
Committee of PAN, 1972-73. f-None.
g-Vice President of the College of
Lawyers of Yucatán. h-Notary Public in
Mérida; lawyer for the National Chamber of Commerce in Mérida; founder
and first director of the Trust Department, Bank of the Southeast, Mérida;
practicing lawyer, 1972-78; Director
General of Mutual Previsora Banhiner.
A.C., 1972-73. i-Married Elvira Mena
Peniche. j-None. k-Candidate of the
National Action Party for federal
deputy, Dist. 1, Yucatán, 1949; candidate of the National Action Party for
governor of Yucatán, 1969, in a highly
disputed election; praised by *Loret de
Mola* as an honest mayor. l-DBM70,
146-47; letters; Loret de Mola, 47.

Cortés Herrera, Vicente
(Deceased 1963) a-July 10, 1889.
b-Guanajuato, Guanajuato. c-Preparatory studies at the University of Guanajuato; engineering degree from the National School of Engineering, UNAM,
1913. d-Federal Deputy, 1926-28.
e-None. f-Director of National Works,
Department of the Federal District;
Director of Buildings and Monuments,
Department of the Federal District,
1922-24; Director of Public Works in
Mexico City, 1925-28; President of the
National Commission of Highways,
1931-33; *Subsecretary of Public Works*,
1935-38; *Director General of Petróleos
Mexicanos*, 1938-40; *Subsecretary of
Public Works*, 1940-41; Head of the
Sixth Zone for the Secretariat of Public
Works, 1946-52, 1952-58. g-None.
h-Author of works on civil engineering
in Europe. i-Brother, Manuel, served as
rector of the University of Guanajuato,
1936-43; married Luz Estrada. j-None.
k-Came to the attention of *Lázaro
Cárdenas* after building a road through
Michoacán, 1932. l-D de Y, 19 Apr.
1938, 1; letter; WWM45, 31; DGF56,
257-58; D del S, 2 Dec. 1940, 1, 6;
DGF51, I, 255; Peral, 190; DP70, 535;
López, 237.

Cortés Lobato, Viterbo
a-Sept. 4, 1926. b-Jalapa, Veracruz.
c-Early education unknown; veterinary
medical degree, School of Veterinary
Medicine, UNAM, 1945-50; Professor of
Genetics and General Zoology, UNAM,
1954-77; Professor of Genetics and
Biostatistics, National School of
Agriculture, Chapingo, 1954-77;
Professor of Zoological Divisions and
Classifications, National School of
Agriculture. d-Member of the City
Council of Veracruz, Veracruz; *Federal
Deputy* from the Federal District, Dist.
21, 1970-73; *Plurinominal Federal
Deputy* from the PPS, 1982-85. e-Can-
didate for federal deputy from the State

of Veracruz, Dist. 6, from the PPS, 1961; candidate for federal deputy from the Federal District, Dist. 21, from the PPS, 1964; candidate for federal deputy from the Federal District, Dist. 19, from the PPS, 1967; candidate for senator from Veracruz from the PPS, 1976; member of the Central Committee of the PPS. f-Regional veterinarian, Division of Animal Health, Secretary of Agriculture, 1953-55; Director of Aviculture Department, Secretariat of Agriculture, 1956-68, 1975-78; Director of the Livestock Center, Secretariat of Agriculture, Federal District, 1968-75. g-None. h-Author of several books. i-Son of Vicente Cortés Lobillo, laborer, and Taurina Lobato Lobato; single. j-None. k-None. l-C de D, 1982-85; Lehr, 617; C de D, 1970-73; DBGM, 492.

Cortés Muñiz, Roberto A.
a-May 31, 1915. b-Monterrey, Nuevo León. c-Primary and secondary studies in Monterrey; no degree. d-Local Deputy to the State Legislature of Nuevo León, Dist. 2, 1946-49; *Senator* from the State of Nuevo León, 1952-58 (elected as an alternate, but replaced *Rodrigo Gómez*), member of the Gran Comisión, the Mail and Telegraph Committee, the Rules Committee, the First Labor Committee, the First Petroleum Committee, the First Balloting Committee, and Secretary of the First Instructive Section of the Grand Jury. e-Joined the PNR youth section, 1935; President of the youth section for Nuevo León, 1939; Official Orator for the *Alemán* and *Ruiz Cortines* campaigns in Nuevo León; President of the State Committee of PRI of Nuevo León, 1947-52; President of PRI in Tabasco; delegate of the CEN of PRI in Tampico, Nayarit. f-Oficial Mayor of the City Council of Monterrey, 1941-42; Oficial Mayor of the State of Nuevo León, 1949-52; Subdirector General of the National Border Program, 1965-69; President of the Na-

tional Commission of Medical Services, 1964-69. g-Secretary General of Local 67 of the Miners Union; President of the Mixed National Commission of Medical Services for Sugar Cane Workers, 1959-64. h-Employee of the Cia. Fundidora de Fierro y Acero, Monterrey, 1933-56. i-Son of Abundio Cortés and Lucia Muñiz. j-None. k-None. l-Letters; DBM68, 153-54; DGF56, 7, 9, 11; Ind. Biog., 46.

Cortés Silva, Porfirio
a-Aug. 27, 1930. b-Guadalajara, Jalisco. c-Primary studies at public school, Guadalajara, 1939-45; secondary studies at public school, Guadalajara, 1945-48; preparatory studies at the University of Guadalajara, 1948-50; law degree from the School of Law, University of Guadalajara, with a thesis on civil process; Professor of Political Economy, University of Guadalajara. d-Secretary of the City Council of Guadalajara; Local Deputy to the State Legislature of Jalisco (44th and 49th legislatures); *Federal Deputy* from the State of Jalisco, Dist. 3, 1958-61, Assistant Secretary of the Chamber, 1958, member of the Fifth Section of the Legislative Studies Committee, the Tax Committee, the First General Means of Communication Committee, and the Industries Committee; *Federal Deputy* from the State of Jalisco, Dist. 4, 1970-73, member of the Legislative Studies Committee, Fifth Section, and the First Labor Committee; *Federal Deputy* from the State of Jalisco, Dist. 4, 1976-79, member of the First Labor Committee, the First Section of Constitutional Affairs, the Section on Transformation and on the Automotive Industry of the Industrial Development Committee, the Border Zone Section of the Regional Development Committee, and the Constitutional, Administrative, and Labor Sections of the Legislative Studies Committee; Mayor of Tlaquepaque,

Jalisco, 1982-84; *Federal Deputy* from the State of Jalisco, Dist. 4, 1985-88. e-Secretary of Social Action, State Committee of PRI, Jalisco, 1976-82. f-Agent of the Ministerio Público; Justice of the Peace, Jalisco; lawyer, state government of Jalisco, 1973. g-Joined the CTM, 1937; President of the Student Society of the Law School, University of Guadalajara. i-Married Mclida García; son of Porfirio Cortés Mancilla and Amada Silva Romero; son, José Cortés García, was a federal deputy; nephew of Francisco Silva Romero, founder of CROC and mayor of Guadalajara, 1941-42. j-None. k-None. l-C de D, 1970-73, 108; D de C, 1976-79, 21, 26, 27, 36, 50-51, 54, 73; C de D, 1976-79, 13, 1958-61, 75, 98; Func., 242; DBGM87, 458; Directorio, 1985-88, 206-08; *Excélsior*, 1 Mar. 1985, 13.

Cosío Vidaurri, Guillermo
a-Sept. 4, 1929. b-Jalisco. c-Primary studies in Guadalajara, 1936-42; secondary studies in Secondary Night School for Workers No. 1, Guadalajara, 1942-45; preparatory studies, Night Preparatory School, University of Guadalajara, 1945-47; legal studies from the University of Guadalajara, 1948-53, law degree, 1953; Professor of Law, School of Law, University of Guadalajara, 1957-66. d-Local Deputy to the State Legislature of Jalisco, 1959-61; *Federal Deputy* from the State of Jalisco, Dist. 12, 1967-70, member of the Fourth Ejido Committee, the Fiscal Section of the Legislative Studies Committee, the First Tax Committee, and the General Means of Communication Committee; Mayor of Guadalajara, 1971-73; *Federal Deputy* from the State of Jalisco, Dist. 1, 1976-79, Secretary of the Gran Comisión, member of the Administration Committee; *Governor of Jalisco*, 1989-92. e-Joined PRI in 1949; Secretary of Political Action of PRI in Jalisco, 1959-61; General Del-

egate of the CEN of PRI to Baja California del Norte, Coahuila, Chihuahua, Yucatán; precandidate for governor of Jalisco, 1981; President of PRI in the Federal District, 1984-85. f-Auxiliary President of the 3rd Group of the Board of Conciliation and Arbitration, 1950; actuary of the Agent of the Ministerio Público attached to the Chief of Police, Guadalajara, 1951-52; Treasurer of Zapopán, Jalisco, 1953-54; Judge of the 1st Instance, Ameca, Jalisco, 1954-55; legal adviser to the League of Agrarian Communities, Jalisco, 1959-65; Director of Public Education, State of Jalisco, 1962-64; Secretary General of Government of the State of Jalisco, 1964-65; Director General of Administration, Secretariat of Agriculture, 1966-67; *Subsecretary of Organization*, Secretariat of Agrarian Reform, 1980-81; *Subsecretary B of Labor*, 1981-82; Director General of the Metro, Department of the Federal District, 1982-84; *Secretary General* of the Department of the Federal District, 1985. g-President of the Preparatory Night School Student Association, 1946; President of the Student Society of the School of Law, University of Guadalajara, 1952; auxiliary delegate of the CNC to the regional agrarian committee, 1955-56; special delegate of the CNC for Jalisco, 1960-61. i-Married Idolina Gaona; son of Salvador Cosío Castillo, a journalist, and María Magdalena Vidaurri, teacher. j-None. k-Forced to resign as governor in aftermath of PEMEX explosions in Guadalajara. l-D de C, 1976-79, 5; C de D, 1967-70, 65, 70, 73, 90; Enc. Mex., 1977, IV, 579; *Excélsior*, 3 Sept. 1976, 1C, 26 Dec. 1981, 16A; DBGM87, 98; DBGM89, 676; Q es QAP, 440; HA, 23 Apr. 1984, 6, 5 Nov. 1985.

Cossío y Cossío, Roberto
a-Feb. 13, 1904. b-Federal District. c-Early education unknown; law degree from the National School of Law,

UNAM, 1929, with a thesis on the "Influence of Francisco Cosentini on the New Civil Code"; Professor of Mercantile and Civil Law, National School of Law, UNAM, 1930-74. d-None. e-Member of the National Council of PAN, 1939; member of the CEN of PAN, 1939; *Secretary General* of the CEN of PAN, 1939-51. f-None. g-None. h-Lawyer for many small businesses; lawyer for the Chamber of Commerce of Mexico City. i-Son of José Lorenzo Cossío, lawyer and judge, and Victoria Gabucio, from Palma de Mallorca, Spain; brother, José Lorenzo Cossío y Cossío, was director of legal affairs, PNR, and secretary to *Antonio Villalobos*, president of the CEN of the PNR; close friend of *Manuel Gómez Morín* since law school days; grandson of José L. González de Cossío, lawyer, and Josefa Cossío y González. j-None. k-None. l-Letter; *Excélsior*, 27 Sept. 1975, 1-2B.

Costemalle (Botello), José Ernesto
a-Mar. 20, 1938. b-Chihuahua, Chihuahua. c-Early education unknown; public accounting studies, School of Accounting and Administration, UNAM, 1956-60, graduating with a thesis on "Import Substitution, the Case of Mexico," 1961; economic studies, National School of Economics, UNAM, 1956-60, graduating with a thesis on "Inflation and Its Effects on the Interpretation of Financial Conditions," 1966; Professor of Accounting and Finances, UNAM, 1962-65, 1968-70; Professor of Finances, Ibero-American University, 1960; member of the Board of UNAM, 1983. d-None. e-Joined PRI, 1967. f-Tax inspector, Federal Treasury Office, Secretariat of the Treasury, 1960-61; adviser, Subdirector of the Income Tax Division, Secretariat of the Treasury, 1961-62; Coordinator of External Auditing, Division of Control of State Enterprises,

Secretariat of Government Properties, 1967-69; Subdirector of Control and Inspection of State Enterprises, Secretariat of Government Properties, 1970; Director of Finances, CONASUPO, 1971-76; Subdirector of Administration and Finances, CONASUPO, 1976-82; *Director General of CONASUPO*, 1982-88. g-None. h-General accountant, Reynolds Aluminum of Mexico, 1962-66; partner of de la Paz and Costemalle, CPAs, 1982; member of the trustees of UNAM, 1983. i-Son of Ernesto Costemalle Ponce de León, bank official, and Enriqueta Botello Gutiérrez; married Bertha Arzola Cárdenas. j-None. k-None. l-*Excélsior*, 3 Dec. 1982, 21A; IEPES; HA, 7 Mar. 1983, 10; QesQAP, 505; DBGM87, 98; DBGM, 105.

Cota, Eduardo Armenta
a-May 2, 1920. b-Empalme, Sonora. c-Early education unknown; special studies in business administration, Guadalajara, 1945-48; no degree. d-None. e-Joined PRI, 1967. f-Assistant to the Subdirector of Traffic, 1951-52, General Assistant Passenger Agent, 1953-61, General Passenger Agent, 1961-63, all with Railroads of the Pacific; Assistant to the Subdirector of Traffic, National Railroads of Mexico, 1963; General Fleet Agent, Railroads of the Pacific, 1964-70; Chief of the Freight Traffic Department, National Railroads of Mexico, 1970-73; Assistant Manager of Traffic, National Railroads of Mexico, 1973-82; *Director General of the National Railroads of Mexico*, 1982-86. g-None. h-Employee, Supplies Warehouse, Transportation Department, Southern Pacific Railroad of Mexico, 1935-46; employee, Traffic Department, Southern Pacific Railroad of Mexico, 1946. i-Son of Pedro Cota Rodríguez, railroad employee, and Valvaneda Armenta Velarde; married Lydia Medina Peña. j-None. k-None. l-QesQAP, 509; DBGM, 106.

Coudurier (Sayago), Luis
b-Federal District. c-Primary and
secondary studies in Mexico City;
preparatory studies in Mexico City; law
degree from the National School of Law,
UNAM, 1947, with a thesis on industrial property. d-None. e-None.
f-Auxiliary Secretary to the Head of the
Department of the Federal District,
Ernesto P. Uruchurtu, 1953-64; member
of the Mixed Planning Commission of
the Department of the Federal District;
*Oficial Mayor of the Department of the
Federal District*, 1964-66. g-None.
h-Practicing lawyer, Mexico City, 1942-
52, 1967- . i-Married Ana María
Lascuraín. j-None. k-None. l-HA, 21
Dec. 1958, 10; Libro de Oro, 1972, 54;
DPE65, 191.

Coutiño (de Cos), Amador
(Deceased Mar. 6, 1966) a-Apr. 30,
1895. b-Chiapa de Corzo, Chiapas.
c-Primary studies in Chiapa de Corzo;
preparatory studies in San Cristóbal de
Las Casas, Chiapas; law degree from the
National School of Law, UNAM.
d-Federal Deputy from the State of
Chiapas, Dist. 4, 1934-37. e-None.
f-Interim Governor of Chiapas, 1928;
Judge, Seventh Civil Court District,
Mexico City; President of the Superior
Tribunal of Justice of the State of
Chiapas; *Interim Governor of Chiapas*,
Sept. 23, 1936 to Dec. 14, 1936; *Attorney General for the Federal District and
Federal Territories*, 1938-40. g-None.
k-None. l-DBC, 51-52; Casasola, V,
2258; Navarette, 201; D de Y, 4 Jan.
1938, 2; Correa, 60.

Coutiño Ruiz, Oralia
a-Dec. 4, 1930. b-Chiapa de Corzo,
Chiapas. c-Early education unknown;
law degree, National School of Law,
UNAM, 1949-53, with a thesis on
agrarian reform; MA in labor law,
UNAM, 1970-72; MA in private
international law, University of Madrid,

1975; Professor of Law. d-*Federal
Deputy* from the State of Chiapas, Dist.
4, 1982-85. e-Joined PRI, 1966. f-Direc-
tor of the Social Security Centers Xola
and Tepeyac, IMSS; Director of the
Department of Social Work, IMSS.
g-Joined ANFER, 1966; Secretary of
Women's Action of the Chiapas Colony,
Mexico City; National Women's
Director of the FSTSE, 1980-83; Secre-
tary of Legal Affairs of CNOP, 1976-79;
Secretary General of the National
Union of Workers of the Secretary of
Labor, 1979-82. h-None.
i-Daughter of Lisandro Coutiño Ruiz,
druggist, and María Antonieta Ruiz
Corzo. j-None. k-None. l-Directorio,
1982-85; C de D, 1982-85; Lehr, 88;
DBGM, 492-93.

Covarrubias Gaitán, Francisco
a-Aug. 27, 1944. b-Federal District.
c-Early education unknown; architecture degree, National School of Architecture, UNAM, 1963-67, with a thesis
on "Adjacent Housing in Gasca,
Guanajuato," 1967; MA in urbanism,
Division of Higher Studies, UNAM,
1968-70; special studies, University of
London, 1974; member of the University Council of UNAM; Coordinator of
Extension Courses, Division of Gradu-
ate Studies, National School of Architecture, 1972-73. d-None. e-None.
f-Coordinator of Alterations, 19th
Olympic Games, Mexico City, 1967-68;
Director General of Urban and Housing
Equipment, Secretariat of Human
Dwellings and Public Works, 1976-82;
Subsecretary of Urban Development,
Secretary of Urban Development and
Ecology, 1983-88, 1988-92. g-None.
i-Son of Francisco Covarrubias García,
lawyer, and María Trinidad Gaitán
Medina, businesswoman; married Flora
Patiño García. j-None. k-None. l-HA,
14 Feb. 1983; Q es QAP, 274; DBGM87,
99; DBGM89, 91; HA, 20 May 1986, 20.

Covián Pérez, Miguel
a-Feb. 8, 1930. b-Mérida, Yucatán.
c-Early education unknown; law degree,
National School of Law, UNAM, 1956,
with a thesis on "Crises of Law and
Revolution"; Professor of Theory of the
State and Constitutional Law, UNAM.
d-*Federal Deputy* from the Federal
District, Dist. 21, 1964-67. e-Secretary
of Popular Action of the PRI in the
Federal District; Subsecretary of Organization of the CEN of PRI, 1975-76;
*Secretary of Organization of the CEN of
PRI, 1976; Oficial Mayor of the CEN of
PRI, 1976-78;* General Delegate of the
CEN of PRI to various states. f-Agent of
the Ministerio Público, Attorney Gener-
al of the Federal District, 1959; consult-
ing lawyer to the Secretariat of Labor;
adviser to the Head of the Department
of the Federal District, 1971; Administrative Subdirector of the ISSSTE, 1979;
Ambassador to Cuba, 1967-70; delegate
from Gustavo Madero to the Depart-
ment of the Federal District, 1982-84.
g-Secretary of the CNOP of PRI in the
Federal District. i-Son of lawyer José
María Covián Zavala and María Aurora
Pérez; political disciple of *Alfonso
Martínez Domínguez;* married Migdalia
García Mateo. j-None. k-None. l-C de
D, 1964-67; *Proceso,* 8 Mar. 1982, 6-9; Q
es QAP, 432; DBGM, 107.

Cravioto, Alfonso
(Deceased Sept. 11, 1955) a-Jan. 24,
1883. b-Pachuca, Hidalgo. c-Primary
studies at the Fuentes y Bravo School,
Pachuca; preparatory studies at the
Scientific and Literary Institute of
Pachuca and at the National Prepara-
tory School, Mexico City; law degree,
National School of Law, UNAM.
d-Federal Deputy from the State of
Hidalgo, Dist. 6, 1911-13; Federal
Deputy from the State of Hidalgo, 1922-
24; Deputy to the Constitutional
Convention of Querétaro from Hidalgo,
Dist. 7, 1916-17; Federal Deputy from

the State of Hidalgo, Dist. 7, 1917-18;
Senator from the State of Hidalgo, 1922-
24; *Senator* from the State of Hidalgo,
1952-58. e-Active in the anti-reelectionist movement. f-Secretary of the
City Council of Mexico City, 1911;
Director of the University Section of
the Council on Higher Education, 1914;
Director General of Fine Arts, 1914;
Oficial Mayor of Public Education,
1915; Secretary of Public Education,
1915-17; Ambassador to Guatemala,
1925-26, 1927; Ambassador to Chile,
1926-27, 1928-32; Ambassador to Belgium, 1932-34; *Ambassador to Cuba,*
1934-38; Ambassador to Bolivia, 1939-
43. g-None. h-Cofounder of several
important magazines including *Savia
Moderna* with Luis Castillo Ledón,
1906. i-Son of General Rafael Cravioto,
prominent liberal officer and politician,
and governor of Hidalgo, 1895, and
Laura Mejorada; married Elena Vázquez
Sánchez. j-None. k-Imprisoned in
Belem for articles that attacked President Díaz. l-WWM45, 32; Peral, 193;
DGF56; C de S, 1952-58; DP70.

Cravioto Cisneros, Oswaldo
a-Mar. 17, 1918. b-Pachuca, Hidalgo.
c-Enrolled in the National Military
College, 1935; graduated from the
National Military College, Feb. 1, 1939,
as a 2nd Lieutenant; staff officer
diploma, Higher War College, Jan. 16,
1948; professor, National Military
College; Professor of World History at
the University of Oaxaca and at the
University of Chiapas. d-*Senator* from
the State of Hidalgo, 1964-70, Secretary
of the Gran Comisión. e-General
Coordinator of *Gustavo Díaz Ordaz's*
campaign in Hidalgo, 1958; *Secretary of
Organization of the CEN of PRI,* 1965-
68. f-Chief of Security Services, State of
Hidalgo, under Governor *Corona del
Rosal,* 1957-58; Oficial Mayor of the
State of Hidalgo under Governor *Corona del Rosal,* 1958; *Interim Governor of*

Hidalgo, 1958-61; *Substitute Governor of Hidalgo*, 1961-63; Manager, National Army-Navy Bank, 1970-76. g-None. h-None. i-Protégé of *Alfonso Corona del Rosal*; related to *Alfonso Cravioto*, *Rafael Cravioto Muñoz*, federal deputy from Hidalgo, 1973-76, and to *Aldalberto Cravioto Menenses*, federal deputy from Hidalgo, 1967-70. j-Career army officer; joined the 1st Battalion of Sappers, Dec. 10, 1934, as an ordinary soldier; rank of Corporal, May 6, 1935; joined the Morelos Group, May 28, 1940; rank of Major, Nov. 20, 1952; reached rank of Colonel; assigned to the 28th Military Zone, Pachuca, Hidalgo, 1949; served in various Infantry Battalions; cadet officer at the National Military College. k-None. l-WWMG, 14; HA, 15 Dec. 1958, 15-16, 7 Mar. 1966, 17; MGF69, 105; *Excélsior*, 16 July 1972, 22; Pérez López, 110.

Cravioto Meneses, Adalberto
a-Jan. 19, 1913. b-Pachuca, Hidalgo. c-Primary studies in Zempoala and the Benito Juárez Schools, Pachuca; secondary and preparatory studies from the Scientific and Literary Institute of Hidalgo, graduated, 1932; received a scholarship from the State of Hidalgo to study at the National School of Medicine, UNAM, medical degree, Sept. 23, 1938. d-*Alternate Federal Deputy* from the State of Hidalgo, Dist. 1, 1958-61; Mayor of Pachuca, Hidalgo, 1964-66; *Federal Deputy* from the State of Hidalgo, Dist. 1, 1967-70, member of the Military Health Committee. e-Joined PRI, 1940; campaigned in Hidalgo during the 1940, 1946, 1952, and 1958 presidential campaigns; delegate of the CNOP to PRI, 1952, 1968. f-Joined the Department of Health, 1939; internship, Ejido Hospital, Torreón, Coahuila; Director of the Ejido Hospital, Torreón; Director of the Cooperative Rural Medical Services, Lagunera of Durango and Coahuila,

1941; Director General of Cooperative Rural Medical Services, Secretariat of Health and Public Welfare, 1953-59; Director of Medical Services of the ISSSTE, Hidalgo, 1961; Director General of Coordinated Medical Services of State of México, 1976. g-President of the 1932-37 medical student generation, UNAM. h-Physician, Secretary of Communications and Transportation; physician, General Hospital, Mexico City; practicing physician, Mexico City, 1970. i-Father achieved only a primary education, fought in the Revolution 1914-18 and later served as a local deputy in Hidalgo (twice) and as a federal deputy from the same state; married María del Carmen Galindo. j-None. k-None. l-Pérez López, 112-113; Directorio, 1967-70; letter; DGF56, 337; C de D, 1958-61, 8, 1967-70, 87.

Creel de la Barra, Enrique
a-Mar. 31, 1927. b-Federal District. c-Early education unknown; law degree, National School of Law, UNAM, 1944-48; studies at the School of Philosophy and Letters, UNAM, 1944-48, in modern French letters; studies in international labor law, International Labor Organization, Switzerland, 1950-51; Professor of Law and Cultural History. d-None. e-Adviser to the IEPES of PRI, 1975-76. f-Director General of Development, Department of Tourism, 1962-64; Financial Subdirector of FOVI, 1964-70; Director of Credit Institutions and Auxiliary Agencies, National Banking Commission, 1971-76; President of the National Banking Commission, 1976-82; Director General of the Public Works Bank, 1982-85. g-None. h-Employee, Department of Public Debt, Secretariat of the Treasury; Secretary General of Representatives of the Mexican Chamber of International Commerce, Inter-American Council of Trade and Production. i-Son of Enrique Creel Terrazas, and Leonor León de la Barra y

Torres, niece of President Francisco León de la Barra, 1911; grandson of Enrique C. Creel, secretary of foreign relations, 1910-11, and major Chihuahuan entrepreneur; cousin of *Enrique Creel Luján*, treasurer of PAN. j-None. k-None. l-Q es QAP, 499; Protag., 88; DBGM, 107; Linajes, 145-47.

Creel Luján, Enrique
b-Chihuahua. c-Early education unknown; architecture degree, School of Architecture, UNAM; MA degree in architecture, University of Notre Dame. d-None. e-Joined PAN, 1958; member of the CEN of PAN, 1959-75; Treasurer of PAN, 1959-75. f-None. g-None. h-Practicing architect. i-Grandson of Enrique Creel, ambassador to the United States and secretary of foreign relations, 1910-11; brother-in-law of *Hugo B. Margáin*; married Celia Charles Sierra; cousin of *Enrique Creel de la Barra*, director of the public works bank, 1982. j-None. k-None. l-Mabry, 237; DBM68, 157-58.

Cruickshank García, Gerardo
a-Dec. 25, 1922. b-Tehuantepec, Oaxaca. c-Early education unknown; civil engineering degree, National School of Engineering, UNAM, 1929-33; studies, CEMLA, Santiago, Chile, 1956; professor, School of Engineering, Autonomous University Benito Júarez of Oaxaca, 1948-49; professor, UNAM, 1968-70. d-None. e-Joined the PNR, 1934. f-Chief of Studies and Projects, Bolivia Irrigation Districts, 1939-42; General Supervisor, Miguel Alemán Hydraulic Systems, Federal Electric Commission, 1950-52; chief engineer, Secretariat of Hydraulic Resources, 1953-54; chief engineer, Valle de México, Secretariat of Hydraulic Resources, 1958; Subdirector of Projects and Laboratories, Secretariat of Public Works, 1964-65; Subdirector General of Projects, Secretariat of Public Works,

1965-66; Director General of Projects and Land Routes, Secretariat of Public Works, 1967-70; *Subsecretary of Planning*, Secretariat of Hydraulic Resources, 1971-76; *Subsecretary of Planning*, Secretariat of Hydraulic Resources, 1977-80; Executive Secretary, Texcoco Lake Commission, Secretariat of Hydraulic Resources, 1980-85. g-None. h-Engineer, dam construction, 1943-45; Chief, Civil Works, Colimilla Electric Company, Jalisco, 1945-49. i-Son of Gerald Cruickshank Bonito, mechanical engineer, and Marina García Márquez; married María de la Paz Villanueva Toltentino; brother of *Jorge Cruickshank*, senator. j-None. k-None. l-DBGM, 108; DPE71, 38; DPE65, 117; *Excélsior*, 11 Mar. 1980, 4.

Cruickshank García, Jorge
(Deceased Jan. 1989) a-July 29, 1915. b-Tehuantepec, Oaxaca. c-Primary studies at the Escuela Morelos y Veracruzano, Veracruz; secondary and preparatory at the Secondary and Preparatory School of Veracruz; secondary teaching certificate; studied at the Superior School of Mechanical and Electrical Engineering and at the Municipal Engineering School; engineering degree. d-*Federal Deputy* from the State of Oaxaca, Dist. 1, 1964-67, member of the Cultural Affairs Committee, the Second Railroads Committee and the Second General Means of Communication Committee; *Federal Deputy* (PPS party deputy), 1970-73, member of the Department of the Federal District Committee, the Government Committee, the Social Security Committee and the Fish and Game Committee; *Senator* from Oaxaca, 1976-82; *Plurinominal Deputy* from the PPS, 1982-85, coordinator of the PPS delegation; *Plurinominal Federal Deputy* from the PPS, 1988-89. e-Director of Communist Youth, 1939-40; founding member of the Popular

Party, 1948; member of the Central
Committee of the PPS, 1960-82;
Secretary of International Relations of
the PPS, 1962-63; Secretary of Press and
Publicity of the PPS, 1963-65; Secretary
of Organization of the PPS, 1965-68;
Interim Secretary of the National
Central Committee of the PPS, 1968;
Secretary General of the PPS, 1969-79,
1979-81. f-None. g-Secretary General
of Local 10, National Union of Educa-
tional Workers (SNTE), 1943-49, 1954-
64; Auxiliary Secretary of the National
Committee of Unified Socialist Youth
of Mexico, 1938-39; cofounder of the
National Union of Educational Work-
ers; Secretary of Labor and Conflicts,
SNTE; Secretary of Acts, SNTE;
Secretary of Union Education, SNTE;
Secretary of Foreign Relations, SNTE.
h-None. i-Brother of *Gerardo
Cruickshank García*, Subsecretary of
Hydraulic Resources, 1970-76; son of
Gerald Cruickshank Bonito, technician,
and Marina García Márquez. j-None.
k-Candidate for federal deputy from
Oaxaca, 1949, for the Popular Party;
candidate for federal deputy from the
Federal District, Dist. 17, from the PPS,
1958; candidate for governor of Oaxaca,
1968, for the PPS; critics accused him of
accepting PRI support as a candidate for
senator from Nayarit in exchange for
recognizing the defeat of the PPS
candidate *Gascón Mercado* for governor
of Nayarit, 1975. l-Directorio, 1970-72;
HA, 4 June 1973, 4; C de D, 1970-72,
108, 1964-66, 78, 84, 95; *Latin America*,
11 Nov. 1977, 349; *Directorio*, 1982-85;
Lehr, 616.

Cruz (Castillejos), Wilfrido
(Deceased Aug. 26, 1948) a-Apr. 29,
1898. b-Espinal, Juchitán, Oaxaca.
c-Primary and secondary studies at the
Veracruz Institute; preparatory studies
at the Veracruz Institute; law degree
from the National School of Law,
UNAM, Apr. 23, 1921; Professor of Law,

University of Oaxaca; Professor of Law,
University of Puebla; rural school
teacher, 1916. d-Federal Deputy from
the State of Oaxaca, Dist. 4, 1930-32,
Dist. 11, 1932-34; *Senator* from the
State of Oaxaca, 1934-40. e-None.
f-Judge in the Federal District; judge in
Oaxaca; judge in Hidalgo; Judge of the
Superior Court of Puebla, 1926; Attor-
ney General of the State of Oaxaca,
1927-28; Judge and President of the Su-
perior Tribunal of Justice of the Federal
District and Federal Territories, 1940-
43. g-None. h-Author of several books;
author of the reform of Article 27 of the
Constitution. j-None. k-Member of the
Executive Committee of the National
Pre-Electoral Center for *Manuel Avila
Camacho*, 1939; favored women's
suffrage while a senator. l-WWM45, 32;
Peral, 197; Morton, 32; Novo, 286;
Casasola, V, 2422; López, 243.

Cruz Chávez, Fernándo
a-1906. b-Mixquiahuala, Hidalgo.
c-Early education unknown; agricultural engineering degree. d-*Alternate
Senator* from the State of Hidalgo, 1940-
45, for *Vicente Aguirre*, in functions as
Senator, 1945-46; *Federal Deputy* from
the State of Hidalgo, Dist. 5, 1946-49,
member of the Gran Comisión, the First
Government Affairs Committee, and
the Complaints Committee. e-*Secretary of Agrarian Affairs of the CEN of
the PRM*, 1943. f-None. g-Member of
the Political Bureau of the CNC;
Secretary General of the CNC of
Hidalgo. j-None. k-None. l-PS, 1396;
D de S, 1940-46; C de D, 1946-49, 69.

Cruz de Mora, Aurora
a-June 22, 1931. b-Ejido Buenos Aires,
Municipio Altamira, Tamaulipas.
c-Early education unknown; no degree.
d-Mayor of Altamira, 1961-62; Local
Deputy to the State Legislature of
Tamaulipas, 1973; *Federal Deputy* from
the State of Tamaulipas, Dist. 4, mem-

ber of the Foreign Relations Committee, the Second Labor Committee, the Sugar Cane Products and the Social, Economic and Cultural Development of Peasant Women sections of the Agrarian Affairs Committee, the Section on Sugar of the Industrial Development Committee, the Social Security and Public Health Development Committee, and the Gran Comisión. e-None. f-None. g-Secretary of Women's Action of the Regional Farmers Committee of the Altamira Ejido Zone, of the League of Agrarian Communities of the State of Tamaulipas, and of the CNC. j-None. k-None. l-*Excélsior*, 21 Aug. 1976, 1C; D de C, 1976-79, 4, 8, 13, 26, 38, 71, 74.

Cubría Palma, José Luis
a-May 11, 1927. b-Jalapa, Veracruz. c-Completed primary through preparatory school; enrolled in the Naval College, 1942, graduated, 1945; MA degree in marine engineering and naval architecture, MIT, Cambridge, Massachusetts, 1955-58; professor, School of Engineering, University of Veracruz, 1959-60. d-None. e-None. f-Director General of Dry Docks, Salina Cruz, Oaxaca, 1966-68; Director of Naval Construction, Secretariat of the Navy, 1968-70; Director General of the Dry Docks of Veracruz, S.A., 1970; *Oficial Mayor of Navy*, 1970-76; representative of the National Highways and Roads Committee to Japan; Director General of Supplies, Federal Electric Commission, 1976-80; Director General of Federal Fishing Delegations, Secretariat of Fishing, 1981-88; Director General of Ports and Merchant Marine, Secretariat of Communication and Transportation, 1988-90. g-None. h-None. i-Son of Luis Cubría López and María Palma Camarillo; married Elsy Lizárraga Hernández. j-Career naval officer; rank of Captain, 1968; rank of Vice-Admiral. k-Precandidate for governor of the State of Veracruz, 1973. l-HA, 14 Dec. 1970;

PS, 1410; Q es QAP, 412; DBGM, 109; DBGM87, 101; DBGM89, 93.

Cué de Duarte (Sarquís), Irma
a-May 7, 1938. b-Tierra Blanca, Veracruz. c-Early education unknown; law degree, National School of Law, UNAM, 1955-59, with a thesis on writs; Professor of Public Administration, UNAM, 1959-. d-*Federal Deputy* from the State of Veracruz, Dist. 12, 1982-85, Secretary of the Budget and Programming Committee. e-Member of the Advisory Council of the IEPES of PRI, 1982; *Secretary General of the CEN of PRI*, 1984-87. f-Agent of the Ministerio Público; Assistant to the Director General of Treasury Studies of the Secretariat of the Treasury, 1967-73; Director of the Legal Consultation Department, CONACYT, 1974-76; Director General of Legal-Administrative Studies, Coordinator General of Administrative Studies, Presidency, 1976-82; Subdirector General of Legal Affairs, ISSSTE, 1987-88; *Justice of the Supreme Court*, 1988- . g-Member of the Advisory Council of CNOP, 1981. h-None. i-Daughter of Alvaro Cué Cambero, druggist, and Teresa Sarquís Carriedo. j-None. k-Answered President *de la Madrid*'s first State of the Union address, 1983; first woman to hold the position of Secretary General of the CEN of PRI. l-Directorio, 1982-85; HA, 5 Sept. 1983, 6; C de D, 1982-85; Lehr, 503; DBGM, 494; DBGM89, 601; DBGM92, 646.

Cué Merlo, Eduardo
a-Dec. 13, 1909. b-Puebla, Puebla. c-Primary education from the Ignacio Ramírez School, Puebla; studies in business administration, El Portalillo School, Puebla; no degree. d-First Councilman of Puebla; Mayor of Puebla, 1960-63; *Senator* from Puebla, 1964-70. e-Secretary of Finances of the State Committee of PRI of Puebla,

1963-64. f-Executive Secretary of the Board of Public Welfare, Puebla, 1951-60; President of the Savings Fund of Employees and State Officials of Puebla, 1960-67; Treasurer of the City Council of Puebla, 1960. g-None. h-Industrialist. j-None. k-Donated salary as mayor and councilman of Puebla to charitable causes. l-C de S, 1964-70; MGF69, 106; CyT, 198-200.

Cuéllar Abarca, Crisanto
a-Feb. 15, 1901. b-Atlangatepec, Tlaxcala. c-Primary studies in Tlaxcala, 1906-13; secondary studies at the Scientific and Literary Institute of Tlaxcala, 1914-15; no degree. d-Local Deputy to the State Legislature of Tlaxcala, 1945, 1951; *Federal Deputy* to the State of Tlaxcala, Dist. 2, 1958-61; member of the Indigenous Affairs Committee, the Tourism Committee, the Textile Committee, and the Library Committee. e-President of the State Committee of PRI, Tlaxcala, 1946, 1957. f-Joined the judicial branch, 1923; actuary, judicial district, Tlaxcala; Director of the Department of Tourism, Culture and Civic Action, State of Tlaxcala; Coordinator of the Federal Board of Material and Civic Improvements, State of Tlaxcala; Director of Libraries and Museums, State of Tlaxcala; Director of the Cultural Institute of Tlaxcala; Oficial Mayor of the State of Tlaxcala; Secretary General of the Government of the State of Tlaxcala; Private Secretary to the Secretary of Tourism; Private Secretary to the Governor of Tlaxcala, *Isidro Candia*, 1937-40; Private Secretary to the Director of the Department of Indigenous Affairs, *Isidro Candia*, 1941-45; Delegate of the Department of Tourism, Tlaxcala, 1956-58; *Interim Governor* of Tlaxcala, Jan. to Apr. 1970. g-None. h-Writer; journalist; author of thirteen books. i-Father a school teacher, white collar worker, business-

man. j-Served as a telegrapher in the Constitutional army. k-None. l-Func., 383; DGF56, 86; C de D, 1958-61, 8, 75.

Cuenca Díaz, Hermenegildo
(Deceased May 17, 1977) a-Apr. 13, 1902. b-Puruandiro, Michoacán. c-Primary studies from father; preparatory studies at the National Polytechnic Institute; graduated in engineering from the Higher School of Mechanical and Electrical Engineering of the Military College with the rank of 2nd lieutenant, Feb. 1, 1922; graduated from the Higher War College, May 1942; military instructor, Military Agricultural School, Chapingo. d-*Senator* from the State of Baja California del Norte, 1964-70. e-None. f-Chief of Staff of the Secretariat of National Defense, 1951-52; *Secretary of National Defense*, 1970-76. g-None. h-Author of various military works. i-Parents, Luis Cuenca Pérez and Elena Díaz Rodríguez, were rural school teachers; married Rosario Acosta. j-Career army officer; fought in more than fifty battles, 1924; liaison officer between Mexico and the United States, San Antonio, Texas; served in the 34th and 44th Infantry Battalions; commander of the troop school for the 44th Infantry Battalion; Assistant Chief of Staff of the 17th Military Zone, Head of the Special Intelligence Service of the Presidential Staff, 1940-46; rank of Colonel, Feb. 12, 1946; Brigadier General, 1947; Chief of Staff of the 3rd Division; Brigade General, Nov. 1952; Commander of the 23rd Military Zone in Tlaxcala, Tlaxcala, 1956; rank of Division General, Dec. 1, 1958. k-Formed part of the cadets who accompanied Carranza when he fled Mexico City to Veracruz, 1920; PRI candidate for governor of Baja California del Norte when he died, 1977. l-HA, 7 Dec. 1970, 23; *Hoy*, 14 Dec. 1970; DGF56, 202; DGF, 69; HA, 12 Dec. 1952, 6; DBM68, 160-61; *Excélsior*, 18

May 1977, 1, 11; Rev. de Ejer., Oct.–
Nov. 1976, 139-40.

Cueto Fernández, Fernándo
a-Dec. 30, 1896. b-Puebla, Puebla.
c-Primary studies in Hidalgo, Puebla (6
years); secondary studies in San Pedro y
San Pablo, Puebla (2 years); attended the
National Military College; no degree.
d-Local Deputy to the State Legislature
of San Luis Potosí, 1939-41; *Federal
Deputy* from the State of Puebla, Dist.
7, 1955-58, member of the Second
National Defense Committee, the First
Balloting Committee, and the Budget
and Accounting Committee (2nd year),
Vice-President of the Chamber; *Federal
Deputy* from the State of Puebla, Dist.
6, 1970-73, member of the First National Defense Committee and the
Military Industry Committee. e-None.
f-Treasurer General of San Luis Potosí,
1939-40; Department Director, Federal
District Police Department, 1947;
Director General of Traffic, State of
Puebla, 1951; Oficial Mayor of the State
of Puebla, 1954-55. g-None. i-Disciple
of *Rafael Avila Camacho*; son of Jesús
Cueto Rodríguez. j-Joined the army at
age thirteen under Colonel Epigmenio
Martínez; 1st Sgt., 1913; fought in fifty-
six battles during the Revolution, 1910-
14; career army officer; Chief of Staff of
the 25th Military District, Puebla,
Puebla, 1956; rank of Brigadier General,
1953. k-None. l-Directorio, 1970-72; C
de D, 1955-57, 48, 62; C de D, 1970-72,
108; CyT, 200-201; Ind. Biog., 47-48.

Cueto Ramírez, Luis
(Deceased Jan. 16, 1977) a-1901.
c-Early education unknown; distinguished cadet at the National Military
College, 1924-28. d-None. e-None.
f-Chief of Police of the Federal District,
1958-64, 1965-69. g-None. h-None.
i-Married Graciela García; son, Jorge,
was medical subdirector of IMSS.
j-Career army officer; joined the

Revolution at age fourteen; fought
against the Escobar rebellion, 1929;
Commander of the 8th Military Zone,
Tamaulipas, 1952-57; rank of Division
General, Nov. 18, 1964. k-Removed as
Police Chief after 1968 student move-
ment demanded his resignation.
l-DGF56, 201; DPE61, 141; *Proceso*, 22
Jan. 1977, 34; DPE65, 201.

Cuevas Canciano, Francisco
a-May 7, 1921. b-Federal District.
c-Law degree from the Escuela Libre de
Derecho, 1943; graduate studies at
McGill University, Montreal, graduating with an MA in civil law, 1946; studies in Ottawa, London, and at Columbia University, New York; professor at
Mexico City College and at the Escuela
Libre de Derecho; Director of the
Center of International Studies at the
Colegio de México. d-None. e-None.
f-Joined the Foreign Service, 1946; Third
Secretary of the Mexican Embassy in
London, 1946-49; adviser to the Secretary of Foreign Relations, 1954; Subdirector of International Organizations
for the Secretariat of Foreign Relations,
1957; Consul General in Paris, 1959-60;
legal adviser to the Mexican delegation
to the United Nations, 1960; Subsecretary General of the Mexican delegation
to the Third General Assembly of the
United Nations; *Ambassador to the
United Nations*, 1965-70, 1976-79;
Ambassador to Brazil, 1979-80; to
UNESCO, 1970-76; to Belgium, 1980-
82; *Ambassador to the United Kingdom*, 1982-86; Ambassador to Austria,
1986-88. g-None. h-Author of many
articles on legal subjects and foreign
affairs. i-Collaborator of *Luis Padilla
Nervo* for many years; son of José Luis
Cuevas and Sofía Cancino; married
Esmeralda Arboleda. j-None. k-None.
l-DGF69, 184; DBM68, 161-62;
WWW70-71, 209; *El Universal*, 14 Sept.
1965; *Excélsior*, 13 Jan. 1983, 4; HA, 13
Oct. 1980, 64; DBGM, 109-110.

Cuevas Mantecón, Raúl
a-Aug. 26, 1918. b-Federal District.
c-Early education unknown; law degree,
National School of Law, UNAM, 1936-
40, with a thesis on inadmissibility of
evidence based on false assertions;
professor, National School of Law,
UNAM, 1952-72; member of the
Technical Council, National School of
Law, UNAM, 1938. d-None. e-None.
f-Secretary of Studies and Accounts,
Supreme Court, 1959-60; Subsecretary
of Accounts, Supreme Court, 1960-65;
Secretary General of Supreme Court,
1966-72; *Justice of the Supreme Court*,
1973-83. g-None. h-Practicing lawyer,
1941-50. i-Married María Cristina
Viveros Ortega. j-None. k-None.
l-DBGM, 646-47; *Excélsior*, 21 Feb.
1973, 22. Court, 1973-83.

D

Danzos Palomino, Ramón
a-Oct. 15, 1918. b-Bacadehuachi,
Sonora. c-Primary studies in Bacade-
huachi; secondary studies in Hermosillo, Sonora; rural teaching certificate.
d-*Plurinominal Federal Deputy* from
the PCM, 1979-82; from the PSUM,
1985-88. e-Joined the Mexican Communist Party, 1939; Alternate Member
of the Central Committee of the Mexican Communist Party, 1954; joined the
PSUM, 1981. f-None. g-Began union
and agrarian activities in Sonora, 1938;
member of the Executive Committee of
the Federation of Workers of Southern
Sonora, 1958; Secretary General of the
Independent Farmers Central (CCI).
h-Teacher, Ciudad Buenavista, Sonora.
i-Son of Francisco Danzos Medina and
Luisa Palomino Gutiérrez; married Dora
Estela Ibarra Portillo. j-None. k-Candidate for federal deputy from Sonora,
Dist. No. 5, 1949, on the Popular Party
ticket; candidate for federal deputy from
Sonora, Dist. No. 3, on the Popular

Party ticket; imprisoned in the 1960s
for his political activities and leadership
of peasant strikes; precandidate for
governor of Sonora on the PRD ticket,
1991; candidate of the Mexican Communist Party for federal deputy from
Sonora, Dist. No. 7, 1979. l-*Excélsior*,
24 Nov. 1974, 4; Johnson, 1978, 94;
Excélsior, 2 May 1979, 23A; DBGM87,
461; *El Nacional*, 25 Mar. 1991, 9.

Dávila, José María
a-Apr. 21, 1897. b-Mazatlán, Sinaloa.
c-Secondary and preparatory education
at the Literary and Scientific Institute of
San Luis Potosí; graduated from the
National Military College. d-Federal
Deputy from the State of Baja California, Dist. 1, 1930-32, member of the
Gran Comisión; Federal Deputy from
the Federal District, Dist. 8, 1932-34;
Senator from the Federal District, 1934-
40, member of the Gran Comisión.
e-None. f-Head of the Office of Immigration of the Secretariat of Government, 1922-30; Mexican Ambassador
to Guatemala, 1940; Mexican Ambassa-
dor to Brazil, 1940; member of the
Administrative Council of the National
Bonded Warehouses, 1946-52; Director
General of the National Bank of
Agricultural and Livestock Credit,
1946-52. g-None. i-Son of Dr. José M.
Dávila. j-Joined the Revolution in 1914;
rank of Captain, 1915; fought under
Cedillo against General Escobar, 1929.
k-Precandidate for governor of Sinaloa,
1944. l-EBW46, 70; letter; DGF47, 356;
DGF50, II, 130, 409; DGF, II, 166;
WB48, 1361; Peral, 211; DGF49, 468;
Kirk, 126; López, 263.

Dávila Aguirre, Vicente
(Deceased 1960) a-Oct. 13, 1893.
b-Ramos Arizpe, Coahuila. c-Primary
and secondary studies in Ramos Arizpe;
studied at the National Military College
(3 years); degree in mechanical engineering, United States. d-Local Deputy

from Monclova to the State Legislature of Coahuila, 1912, and 1935; *Senator* from the State of Coahuila, 1958-60. e-None. f-Provisional Governor of San Luis Potosí, 1915; Secretary General of Government of the State of Coahuila, 1935. g-None. h-Practicing engineer. j-Career army officer; supported Madero in the Revolution, 1912-13; fought under General Maclovio Herrera, 1914, assumed command of his men when Herrera died, and supported Carranza; rank of Brigadier General, June 1, 1942; Commander of the Military Zones of Chihuahua, Guanajuato, and Sinaloa. k-Abandoned studies at the National Military College to fight in the Revolution; member of the State Legislature of Coahuila that disavowed Huerta as legal president of Mexico after the death of Madero, 1914; supported the de la Huerta rebellion, 1923. l-DP70, 624; C de S, 1961-64, 14; Peral, 212; Func., 139; López, 264.

Dávila Mendoza, Miguel Angel
a-Aug. 2, 1934. b-Federal District. c-Early education unknown; public accounting degree, Higher School of Business Administration, IPN, 1963; MA in administrative sciences, Higher School of Business Administration, IPN, 1964; Ph.D. degree, IPN, 1965; professor at the Graduate School of Administrative Sciences, IPN. d-None. e-Joined PRI, 1972. f-Director of Corporate Financial Planning, SOMEX; Subdirector General of Budget Control, Secretariat of the Treasury, 1971; Subdirector General of Expenditures, Secretariat of the Treasury, 1971-74; Director General of Expenditures, Secretariat of the Treasury, 1975-76; Director General of Budget Policy, Secretariat of Programming and Budget, 1978-81; *Subsecretary of Budgeting*, Secretariat of Programming and Budget, 1981-82; Director General of FERTIMEX, 1982-88; Delegate of the Department of the Federal District,

Magdalena Contreras, 1988-90. g-None. h-Finance director of various companies in the private sector, 1958-70; Assistant Director General of the Mexican Mortgage Association, 1977-78. i-Classmate of *Ramón Aguirre Velázquez* at UNAM; served with him in several positions; married Patricia Guzmán Sañudo; son of Alfonso Dávila Aguila, industrialist, and María de los Angeles Mendoza. j-None. k-None. l-HA, 26 Oct. 1981, 28; IEPES; Protag., 97; DBGM89, 97; DBGM87, 106; DBGM, 115.

Dávila Narro, Jesús
a-Oct. 8, 1947. b-Monterrey, Nuevo León. c-Early education unknown; legal studies, School of Law, University of Coahuila, 1965-70, graduating with a thesis on Mexican democracy, 1971; degree in Spanish language and literature, Higher Normal School of Coahuila, 1965-69; founding Professor in Constitutional Law, National School of Political Studies, Acatlán campus, UNAM, 1978- ; Professor of Constitutional Theory, Institute of Political Education, PRI. d-*Federal Deputy* from the State of Coahuila, Dist. 1, 1973-76. e-Joined PRI, 1969; Oficial Mayor of PRI, Coahuila, 1969-70; adviser, Secretary General of the CEN of PRI, 1982. f-Director, Department of Legal Affairs, Director General of Government, Secretariat of Government, 1970-73; adviser to the Director in Chief of Political Affairs, Secretariat of Foreign Relations, *Manuel Bartlett Díaz*, 1976-79; adviser to the Coordinator of Federal Delegations of the Secretariat of Planning and Budgeting, 1979-81; Director of the Editorial Board, Attorney General of Mexico, 1979-82; General Manager of FONATUR, National Finance Bank, 1980-82; *Subsecretary of Government*, 1982-85. g-None. h-None. i-Served under *Manuel Bartlett Díaz* in several posts, member of his political group; married Bertha Alicia Cardona García;

son of José Dávila de la Fuente, cattle rancher, and Lilia Narro Tehar. j-None. k-None. l-Q es QAP, 25; *Excélsior*, 27 July 1984, 20.

de Alba, Pedro
(Deceased Nov. 10, 1960) a-Dec. 17, 1887. b-San Juan de los Lagos, Jalisco. c-Primary in San Juan de los Lagos, Jalisco; secondary and preparatory studies at the Institute of Sciences, Aguascalientes; medical degree from the National School of Medicine, UNAM, graduated as a surgeon; studies in medicine at the Medical-Military Practical School of the Army, 1913; diploma in ophthalmology in Paris; Professor of General History and of Spanish Literature at the National Preparatory School and the School of Philosophy and Letters, UNAM; commissioned by the Secretary of Public Education of the State of Nuevo León to organize the University of Monterrey, 1933. d-Federal Deputy from the State of Aguascalientes, Dist. 1, 1920-22; Senator from Aguascalientes, 1922-26, President of the Senate, member of the Foreign Relations Committee; *Senator* from the State of Aguascalientes, 1952-58, member of the Gran Comisión, the Public Welfare Committee, the First Public Education Committee and the Health Committee. f-Counselor of Public Education in Aguascalientes, 1917; Director of the Health Service in Aguascalientes, 1918; Director of the Preparatory School in Aguascalientes, 1919; Director of the Institute of Sciences of Aguascalientes; Director of the National Preparatory School, 1929-33; member of the Technical Advisory Council to the Secretariat of Public Education, 1935; Assistant Director of the Pan American Union, 1936-47; Ambassador to Chile, 1947; Ambassador to the International Organization of Labor, 1948-51; Delegate to UNESCO, 1951. g-None.

h-Author of several books. i-Nephew, *Alfonso de Alba Martín*, served as a federal deputy, 1967-70, from Jalisco; father, Lamberto de Alba, was a partner in cattle ranching business; grandfather, Bas de Alba, was a small rancher; maternal grandfather was a general under Porfirio Díaz. j-Major in the Mexican army. k-None. l-WWM45, 3; DP70, 54; DGF56, 5, 8, 9, 10, 12; DGF51, 110, 117; WB48, 1383; IWW40, 22; Ind. Biog., 49-50.

de Alba Arroyo, Miguel
a-Sept. 20, 1908. b-Guadalajara, Jalisco. c-Primary at private schools until 1921; preparatory studies in sciences, University of Guadalajara, 1921-25; medical studies, University of Guadalajara, 1925-27, 1929-31, completed only second year of professional studies. d-Alternate Councilman, Guadalajara, 1943-46; *Alternate Federal Deputy* from the State of Jalisco, Dist. 1, 1952-55, for *Rodolfo González Guevara*; Alternate Councilman, Guadalajara, 1953-54, in functions, 1954-55; Local Deputy to the State Legislature of Jalisco, 1956-59; *Federal Deputy* from the State of Jalisco, Dist. 2, 1961-64, member of the Second Balloting Committee and the Vehicular Transport Committee; *Federal Deputy* from the State of Jalisco, Dist. 2, 1967-70, member of the Mail and Telegraph Committee and the Film Development Committee. e-None. f-Assistant to the Attorney in Defense of Labor, Department of Labor, State of Jalisco, 1937-38; Defender of Labor Interests, Department of Labor, 1938-40; Labor Inspector, State of Jalisco, 1940-41; Administrator of the Market, Guadalajara, 1943-55. g-Secretary General of the Workers Federation of Jalisco, 1934-46; Oficial Mayor of the CTM of Guadalajara, 1941; Secretary General of the Organization of Workers, Guadalajara, 1947-60; Secretary of Social Welfare of the CTM, Guadalajara,

1948-51; Secretary of Organization of the CTM, Guadalajara, 1951-54; Secretary General of the CTM of Jalisco, 1954-58; Assistant Secretary of the CTM of Jalisco, 1958. h-Worked in industry, 1927-28; businessman, 1929-46. j-None. k-None. l-Directorio, 1967-70; PS, 1523; C de D, 1967-70, 61, 1961-63, 10, 75.

de Dios Bátiz, Juan
(Deceased May 20, 1979) a-Apr. 2, 1890. b-Zataya, Sinaloa. c-Early education unknown; began engineering studies in Culiacán, completed at the National Military College, 1908-12; cadet, 1st Company. d-Federal Deputy from the State of Sinaloa, Dist. 1, 1922-24, member of the Gran Comisión; Federal Deputy from the State of Sinaloa, Dist. 3, 1924-26, Dist. 2, 1930-32; Senator from the State of Sinaloa, 1932-34. e-Treasurer of the CEN of the PNR, 1931. f-Interim Governor of Sinaloa, 1926-27; Director of Technical Education, Secretariat of Public Education, 1934-36; founder of the IPN, 1936; Director of Social Welfare, Secretary of Labor, 1936-40; Director General of the National Mortgage Bank, 1940-46. g-None. h-Manager of various private firms, 1946-70. i-Married Laura Pérez de Bátiz; son Juan de Dios was a director general in the Secretariat of Industry and Commerce, 1961; brother-in-law of *Lázaro Cárdenas*. j-Participated in the Revolution; served in the 1st Artillery Regiment under Col. Felipe Angeles; participated in the battle for Nazas, Durango, 1912; fought against Orozco, 1912; rank of 2nd Captain, Feb. 10, 1913; officer, 3rd Artillery Regiment; fought in Torreón in the Nazas Division under General J. Refugio Velasco; Commander in the 3rd Artillery Regiment; rank of 1st Captain, 1914; rank of Major, 1914; joined the Constitutionalists, 1915; Military Governor of Nayarit. k-President Cárdenas allegedly

offered him the position of Secretary of Public Education in 1934, but he turned it down in order to found the IPN. l-HA, 28 May 1979, 14; *Excélsior*, 21 May 1979, 4; Peral, 97; *Excélsior*, 22 May 1979, 30; DPE61, 66.

de Garay y Arenas, Fernando
a-June 25, 1943. b-Federal District. c-Early education unknown; mechanical engineering degree, Higher School of Mechanical and Electrical Engineering, IPN, 1961-64, with a thesis on urban transportation; professor, IPN, 1965-72. d-None. e-Member of the National Youth Executive Committee of PRI, 1962-67; Technical Secretary, IEPES of the CEN of PRI, 1975-76; member, Advisory Council, IEPES of PRI, 1981. f-Private Secretary to the Director of Traffic, Department of the Federal District, 1967-70; Director, Department of Planning, Division of Transportation Services, Secretariat of Communications and Transportation, 1971-72; Subdirector of Transportation Services, Division of Federal Transportation, Secretariat of Communications and Transportation, 1972-76; Director General of Federal Transportation, Secretariat of Communications and Transportation, 1976-81; *Subsecretary of Operations*, Secretariat of Communications and Transportation, 1981-82, 1983-85; Director General of Aeromexico, 1985-87; Director General of Route 100, Department of the Federal District, 1988-89. g-None. h-Analyst, Consólida, S.A., 1963; employee, Department of Machinery and Equipment, Division of Railroads, Secretariat of Communications and Transportation, 1966-67. i-Son of Francisco de Garay de la Garza, accountant, and Luz María Arenas Canales, public official; married Ana Elena Zamarripa López. j-None. k-None. l-Q es QAP, 250-51; DBGM, 158; DBGM89, 130; HA 17 Sept. 1985, 24.

de Ibarola Aznar, Antonio
a-July 28, 1909. b-Federal District.
c-Early education unknown; law degree,
National School of Law, UNAM, 1933.
d-None. e-Candidate for federal deputy
from PAN, 1955; member of the
National Council of PAN. f-None.
g-None. h-Practicing lawyer; author of
several books on law. i-Son of Alfonso
María de Ibarrola y Vertíz and Manuela
Aznar; married María Nicolín Martínez
del Campo. j-None. k-None. l-WNM,
56-57.

de Icaza (y León), Francisco A.
a-Dec. 31, 1905. b-Berlin, Germany.
c-Secondary studies in Madrid, Spain;
law degree, National School of Law,
UNAM, 1928; studies in political
science, Catholic University, Louvain,
Belgium, 1948-49; studies in art,
Academy of Fine Arts, Brussels, 1949-
50. d-None. e-None. f-Fourth official
of the Secretariat of Foreign Relations,
1926, Third official, 1926; Third
Secretary in charge of trade, Costa Rica,
1929, El Salvador, 1930; Third Secretary
to the legation in Havana, Cuba, 1931;
First Secretary, Berlin, Germany, 1936-
38; Counsellor to Argentina, 1940-41, to
Guatemala, 1942; Ambassador to
Lebanon, 1947-49, to Belgium and
Luxemburg, 1949-52; *Ambassador to
Great Britain*, 1952-55, to Guatemala,
1956-58, to Argentina, 1964-70.
g-None. h-None. i-Son, *Antonio de
Icaza*, is a career foreign service officer;
son of Francisco A. de Icaza, poet and
diplomat serving in various European
posts, including positions in Spain and
Germany, 1863-1925, and Beatriz León;
married María González; son, Carlos
Alberto, was a director general of the
Secretariat of Foreign Relations.
j-None. k-None. l-DGF56, 126; DPE65,
23; Peral, 404; DP70, 1050; DGF51, 107-
08; STYRBIWW, 1951, 692; DPE61, 20.

de la Colina (Riquelme), Rafael
a-Sept. 20, 1898. b-Tulancingo, Hidalgo. c-Preparatory studies at the National Preparatory School; BS from
UNAM, 1916; MS from UNAM; never
taught because of foreign service career.
d-None. e-None. f-Member of the
Consulate in Philadelphia, Pennsylvania, 1918-22; Vice-Consul, St. Louis,
Missouri, 1922, and Eagle Pass, Texas,
1922-23; Chief of the Administrative
Department of the Consular Division of
the Secretariat of Foreign Relations,
1923-24; Consul, Boston, 1924-25, New
Orleans, 1925-28, Laredo, Texas, 1928-
30, and Los Angeles, 1930-32; Head of
the Consular Department, Secretariat of
Foreign Relations, 1932-33; Head of the
License Bureau, Federal District,
Secretariat of Foreign Relations, 1933;
Consul General, San Antonio, Texas,
1934-35, New York, 1936-43; Minister,
Washington, D.C., 1943-44; rank of
Ambassador, 1944; *Ambassador to
the United States*, 1949-52; *Ambassa-
dor to the United Nations*, 1952-58;
Ambassador to Canada, 1958-62;
Ambassador to Japan, 1962-64; *Ambas-
sador to the Organization of American
States*, 1965-76, 1976-82, 1982-85.
g-None. h-Assistant Secretary General
at the Inter-American Conference on
War and Peace, 1945; technical adviser
of the Mexican delegation to the United
Nations, San Francisco, 1945; envoy
attached to the Mexican Embassy,
Washington, D.C., 1946; delegate
from Mexico to the First General
Assembly of the United Nations,
1947. i-Attended National Preparatory
School with several members of the
famous "Seven Wise Men of Mexico"
which included *Lombardo Toledano*,
Teófilo Olea y Leyva, *Alfonso Caso*,
also knew *Jaime Torres Bodet, José
Gorostiza, Pablo Campos Ortiz,
Narciso Bassols*, and Daniel Cosío
Villegas; father, Manuel de la Colina, a
school teacher and supporter of Madero;

mother, María Riquelme Palacio; grandfather, Rafael B. de la Colina, founder of the Scientific and Literary Institute of Hidalgo; mar-ried Ruth Rosecrans. j-Private Secretary to General *Cándido Aguilar*, 1917-18, reached rank of Lieutenant. k-None. l-Letter; WWM45, 28; Inf. Please, 189, 201 (1950-51); DGF56, 128; Peral, 179; DPE61, 20; DGF51, 105; WB48, 1417-18; STYRBIWW54, 693; WB54, 278; WWW70-71, 191; HA, 7 Oct. 1974, 6ff; NYT, 29 Dec. 1948, 9; López, 273; Enc. Mex., 1977, III, 23; DBGM, 101.

de la Cueva (y de la Rosa), Mario
(Deceased Mar. 6, 1981) a-July 11, 1901. b-Federal District. c-Primary studies at the Florencio María del Castillo School, first prize, 1908; preparatory studies at the National Preparatory School, 1918-21; enrolled in the National School of Medicine; changed curriculum to legal studies on the advice of *Manuel Gómez Morín*, law degree, National School of Law, UNAM, 1925; advanced studies in philosophy and law, University of Berlin, 1932-33; Professor of Introduction to the Study of Law, Theory of the State, Labor Law and Constitutional Law, UNAM, 1929-70; professor emeritus, UNAM; Dean, National School of Law, UNAM, 1952-54; Coordinator of Humanities, UNAM, 1962-66. d-None. e-None. f-Secretary of Studies and Accounts, Labor Division, Supreme Court, under Justice *Alfredo Iñárritu; Secretary General of UNAM*, 1938-40, under *Gustavo Baz; Rector of UNAM*, 1940-42; Director of the Legal Department, Secretary of Industry and Commerce, 1944-46; President of the Federal Board of Conciliation and Arbitration, 1946; Director General of the National Cinematographic Bank, 1946-52. g-None. h-Author of a classic work on Mexican labor law; author of many books; began a successful law practice,

1925; traveled in Europe for two years. i-Professor of *Alfonso Pulido Islas, José Juan de Olloqui, Mario Colín Sánchez, Miguel de la Madrid, Jesús Reyes Heroles, Fernando Zertuche Muñoz*, and many other public figures; student friends in the 1920s included *José Ricardo Zevada, Manuel Gual Vidal*, and *Antonio Martínez Báez*; son of Ricardo de la Cueva, a surgeon, and María de a Rosa y Berriozábal, a descendant of General Berriozábal; grandfather a physician; lived with uncle Arturo de la Cueva, a lawyer. j-None. k-One of the most influential professors for three generations of lawyers and public figures at UNAM; recipient of the National Prize in History, Social Sciences and Philosophy; turned down offer from two presidents to become a supreme court justice. l-*Hoy*, 21 Mar. 1970, 20; DGF47, 351; DGF51, II, 65, 421; DGF50, 292; Peral, 47, 96; letter; Enc. Mex., 1977, III, 227; WNM, 57-58; Boletín-Bibliográfico, Mar.-Apr. 1981, 1-6; HA, 16 Mar. 1981, 6.

de la Flor Casanova, Noé
a-May 29, 1904. b-Teapa, Tabasco. c-Primary studies in Teapa; preparatory studies at the Juárez Institute, Villa-hermosa, Tabasco, 1920, and on a scholarship from José Vasconcelos at the National Preparatory School; law degree from the National Law School, UNAM, Mar. 21, 1930, with a thesis on the "Delinquent Politician and Political Delinquents"; professor at the National Law School, UNAM, 1937-42. d-*Governor of Tabasco*, 1943-46. e-None. f-Secretary of the Criminal Courts in the Federal District, 1930-36; Justice of the Peace, 1937-39; Judge of the Superior Tribunal of Justice of the Federal District and Federal Territories, 1940-42, 1946-58. g-Founding member of the Socialist Lawyers Front, 1936. h-Author. i-Son of Manuel de la Flor

Hernández and Elodia Casanova; from
extremely poor family; *Carlos Pellicer*
helped him obtain a scholarship from
José Vasconcelos for all of his preparatory and professional studies; classmate
of *Adelor Sala* at the Juárez Institute;
law committee included *Brito Foucher,
Franco Carreño* and *Raúl Carrancá
Trujillo.* j-None. k-Removed from the
office of governor in Feb., 1946.
l-DGF56, 513; HA, 14 May 1943, 13;
HA, 28 Sept. 1945, xii; WWM45, 42;
EWB46, 174; López, 362; Casasola, V,
2422; Peral, 274-75.

de la Fuente Rodríguez, Juan Antonio
(Deceased 1979) a-Nov. 10, 1913.
b-Saltillo, Coahuila. c-Primary studies
at the Miguel López School, Saltillo,
Coahuila; secondary studies at the
Ateneo Plaza de San Francisco, Saltillo;
studies at the National Military
College, 1931-35, graduated as a 2nd
Lieutenant of cavalry, Jan. 1, 1935;
studies in biology, National Preparatory
School, 1936-37; course in cavalry
tactics, School of Applied Military
Studies, 1939-40; attended the Staff and
Command School, Higher War College,
1941-44; special studies in armored
vehicles, Fort Knox, Kentucky, 1950-51;
instructor in armored vehicles, Higher
War College; Director of the National
Military College; Director of the Higher
War College. d-None. e-None.
f-Military Attaché, Santiago, Chile;
Director of Military Education, Secretariat of National Defense; *Subsecretary
of National Defense*, 1976-79. g-None.
h-None. i-Classmate of *Félix Galván
López* at the National Military College
and the Higher War College; married
María Teresa Escobar; son, Gonzalo,
was director general in the Secretariat of
Agriculture and Hydraulic Resources.
j-Career army officer; fought against
rebel groups in Jalisco, 1935-36; fought
against rebel groups in Putla, Oaxaca,
1940; lst Lieutenant, June 1940; 2nd

Captain, Jan. 1944; lst Captain, Nov. 20,
1947; Major, Nov. 20, 1950; Lt. Colonel,
Nov. 20, 1956; Colonel, Nov. 20, 1959;
Section Chief, Presidential Staff;
Commander of the 18th Cavalry
Regiment; Commander of the Mazatlán
Garrison; rank of Division General,
Nov. 20, 1975. k-Strongest precandi-
date for governor of Coahuila before his
death in a helicopter crash. l-Enc. Mex.,
Annual, 1977, 535; *Excélsior*, 16 Mar.
1980, 21; Rev. de Ejer., Dec. 1979, 55-
56; DBGM, 152.

de la Fuente (Sanders), Fernando
(Deceased 1965) a-Feb. 10, 1889.
b-Tampico, Tamaulipas. c-Law degree;
National School of Law, UNAM, 1915.
d-None. e-Member of the Social Democratic Party, 1937; Secretary of Interior
of the CEN of the National Independent
Party, 1938. f-Penal judge, 1924; Judge
of the Superior Tribunal of Justice of the
Federal District and Federal Territories;
Justice of the Supreme Court, 1929-34;
Justice of the Supreme Court, 1940-46
and 1946-52. g-None. h-Assisted in
writing the monetary law, 1930-31;
helped to create the Bank of Mexico
with *Manuel Gómez Morín*; founder of
the Pension Department. i-Descendant
of the titled family of the Marquis of
Fuenclara y Montemayor; married
María de la Cruz Cárdenas Pérez;
daughter, Hayde Virginia, married
prominent lawyer Armando Herrerías
Tellería; son of Federico de la Fuente
and Adela Sanders. j-None. k-Appointed Director of the National School
of Economics, but never accepted the
position. l-Enc. Mex., IV, 478; DP70,
795; letter; DGF47; DGF51, I; Novo35,
76; Linajes, 120-21.

de la Fuentes Rodríguez, José
a-Apr. 20, 1920. b-General Zepeda,
Coahuila. c-Early education unknown;
law degree from the National School of
Law, UNAM, 1939-44; completed all

studies but dissertation for an LLD in penal law; Professor of Penal Law, Civics, and Economic and Social Problems; Rector of the University of Coahuila, 1967-70, d-Local Deputy to the State Legislature of Coahuila; *Federal Deputy* from the State of Coahuila, Dist. 1, 1967-70, member of the Administration Committee (2nd year), Penal Section of the Legislative Studies Committee, Second Justice Committee, Petroleum Committee and the Public Security Committee; *Federal Deputy* from the State of Coahuila, Dist. 1, 1976-79, member of the Gran Comisión, Section Four of the Educational Development Committee, the Higher Education Committee, the Electrical Section of the Industrial Development Committee, the Development of Natural and Energy Resources Committee, the Rural and Arid Zone Industry Section of the Regional Development Committee, the Development of Social Security and Public Health Committee, the Social Welfare Section of the Social Security and Public Health Committee, the Penal Section of the Constitution Studies Committee, the Government Committee, the Justice Committee, and the Foreign Relations Committee; *Governor of Coahuila*, 1981-87. e-President of the State Committee of PRI of Coahuila; General Delegate of the CEN of PRI to Baja California del Norte; *Secretary of Popular Action of the CEN of PRI*, 1976-79; *Secretary General of the CEN of PRI*, 1979-80. f-Criminal Judge of the Federal District; agent of the Ministerio Público; Attorney General of the State of Coahuila. g-*Secretary General of the CNOP*, 1976-79. i-Classmate of *José López Portillo* at UNAM; married Elsa Hernández, lawyer. j-None. k-None. l-C de D, 1967-70, 56, 66, 79, 87; D de C, 1976-79, 19, 21, 25, 31, 32, 34, 38, 51, 56, 61, 71; *Excélsior*, 21 Aug. 1976, 1C; MGF69, 89; Directorio, 1967-70.

de la Garza (González), Arturo
a-Aug. 1, 1936. b-Monterrey, Nuevo León. c-Primary studies at the Simón de la Garza Melo School, Monterrey (6 years); secondary at the Moisés Saenz School; preparatory at the Colegio Civil, Monterrey; studied law and social sciences at the University of Nuevo León, 1954-55. d-Local Deputy to the State Legislature of Nuevo León, 1961-66; *Federal Deputy* from the State of Nuevo León, Dist. 8, 1970-73, member of the Gran Comisión, the Livestock Committee, the Small Agricultural Properties Committee and the Hydraulic Resources Committee; *Federal Deputy* from the State of Nuevo León, Dist. 6, 1991-94. e-Joined PRI, 1954; General Delegate of the CEN of PRI to Coahuila, 1970; President of PRI in Guadalupe, Nuevo León, 1969-70. f-Adviser to the National Agricultural Credit Bank of Nuevo León. g-Delegate from Nuevo León to the National Livestock Federation; adviser to the National Livestock Federation; President of the Regional Livestock Union for Nuevo León; Secretary of the Council for the Promotion of Livestock, Nuevo León. h-Rancher. i-Son of former Governor of Nuevo León and cattle rancher, *Arturo B. de la Garza*; married De la Luz Tijerina. j-None. k-None. l-Directorio, 1970-72; C de D, 1970-72, 109.

de la Garza Gutiérrez, Jesús B.
a-Oct. 1, 1895. b-Monterrey, Nuevo León. c-Primary in Nuevo León; secondary at the Colegio Civil, Monterrey; preparatory studies at the National Preparatory School; attended the Mining School of Mexico, Mexico City; degree in military construction, Military College, 1917; degree in civil engineering, National School of Engineering, UNAM, 1920. d-*Federal Deputy* from the Federal District, Dist. 11, 1940. e-None. f-*Subsecretary of Public*

Works, 1940; *Secretary of Public Works,* 1940-41; Director General of War Materiels for the Secretariat of National Defense, 1941-46; Director General of Military Social Security, Secretariat of National Defense, 1964-70. g-None. h-None. i-Married María Casas. j-Career army officer; cadet at the National Military College, 1909; joined the Revolution as a Maderista in 1910; Inspector General of Police, Monterrey; Head of Military Education, Secretariat of National Defense; Director of Agricultural Schools, Secretariat of National Defense; President of the First War Committee; rank of Brigadier General, 1940; rank of Division General, 1970. k-Attended the Convention of Aguascalientes, 1914-15; precandidate for governor of Nuevo León, 1943. l-DGF65, 44; WB48, 1419; EBW46, 1133; *Hoy,* 7 Dec. 1940, 3-4; Peral, 323; WWM45, 48; Rev. de Ejer., 25 Dec. 1970.

de la Garza Ollervides, Eulogio
a-Jan. 29, 1905. b-Sierra Mojada, Coahuila. c-Primary studies in five different schools in Coahuila and Chihuahua; preparatory studies at the Scientific and Literary Institute of Chihuahua, Chihuahua; engineering degree from the National School of Agriculture, Chapingo; professor at the National Forestry School, Coyoacán, Federal District; Director of the Institute of Higher Forestry Education, Los Molinos, Perote, Veracruz. d-None. e-None. f-Inspector General of the Forestry Service, 1936; Inspector General in the Southeast, 1937; Alternate Director of the National Museum of Flora and Fauna, Chapultepec, Mexico City, 1938; General Agent of the Secretariat of Agriculture in Toluca, México, 1940; Chief of Services, Secretariat of Agriculture, 1941; Head of the Legal Department, Secretariat of Agriculture, 1943; Head of the Technical Forestry Council, 1945; Technical

Director of the Department of Forests and Game, 1949; Director General of the Department of Forests and Game, Secretariat of Agriculture, 1949-51; adviser to National Railroads of Mexico, 1953; *Subsecretary of Forests and Fauna of the Secretary of Agriculture,* 1970 to June 7, 1972. g-Adviser to the National Chamber of Forest Industries; Head of the Technical Union of the National Chamber of Industries (Cultivating Forests). h-Leave of absence to work for the National Urban Mortgage Bank of Public Works, 1947; consulting engineer to the Papaloapán Commission, 1957; practicing engineer in the Office of Private Forests, 1927-36; began career as a practicing student at the South East Forest Station, Xochimilco, Federal District, 1927; author of several articles on trees. j-None. k-Resigned from the subsecretary position for personal reasons. l-Letter; HA, 14 Dec. 1970, 21; *Excélsior,* 8 June 1972, 1; DGF51, I, 204-05.

de la Huerta Oriol Jr., Adolfo
a-Jan. 3, 1910. b-Guaymas, Sonora. c-Primary studies in Guaymas and in the Federal District; preparatory studies in Los Angeles, California; no degree. d-*Senator* from Sonora, 1976-82. e-None. f-Private Secretary to Adolfo de la Huerta, Inspector General of Consulates, Secretariat of Foreign Relations, 1936-43; Vice-Consul, Tucson, Arizona, 1955-56; Director of the Department of Passports for the Secretariat of Foreign Relations, 1956-64; *Secretary General of Tourism,* 1964-70, and 1970-74. g-None. h-Worked for a newspaper in Los Angeles, California; joined the Foreign Service, 1943; reached the rank of First Chancellor; visited all consulates in the United States as private secretary to his father. i-Son of the former Mexican President Adolfo de la Huerta; cousin of *Alejandro Carrillo M.,* governor of Sonora, 1975-79. j-None.

k-None. l-DGF56, 141; DPE70, 136; DPE65, 178; HA, 21 Dec. 1964, 9; letter; DPE61, 16; *Excélsior*, 4 Aug. 1978, 15; Almanaque de Sonora, 1982, 30-31.

de la Madrid (Hurtado), Miguel
a-Dec. 12, 1934. b-Colima, Colima. c-Primary and secondary studies in Mexico City; preparatory studies from the Cristóbal Colón School; law degree with honorable mention from the National School of Law, UNAM, 1952-57, thesis on "Economic Thought of the 1857 Constitution"; second highest GPA of his law school generation (9.9); MA in public administration from Harvard University, 1964-65; Professor of Constitutional Law at the National School of Law, UNAM, on leave since 1968. d-*President of Mexico*, 1982-88. e-Member of PRI since 1963. f-Adviser to the Administration of the Bank of Mexico, 1960-65; Subdirector General of Credit of the Secretariat of the Treasury, 1965-70; *Subdirector of Finances of Petróleos Mexicanos*, Dec. 1970 to Apr. 1972; Director General of Credit of the Secretariat of the Treasury, May 4, 1972 to 1975; *Subsecretary of Credit* of the Secretariat of the Treasury, 1975-76; 1976-79; *Secretary of Planning and Programming*, 1979-82; Director General of the Fondo de Cultura Económica, 1988- . g-Oratory champion of all Mexico City secondary schools, 1949; Vice-President of the Law Student Society, UNAM, when *Porfirio Muñoz Ledo* was president. h-Employed in the Legal Department of the National Bank of Foreign Commerce, 1953-57; worked briefly for the Mining Chamber of Mexico with *José Campillo Sainz*; secretary of the Mexican delegation to the First Annual Reunion of the Inter-American Economic and Social Council of the Organization of American States, 1962; attended many international economic conferences, 1963-69; author of various articles. i-Studied general

theory of the state at UNAM under *José López Portillo*; closest friend at law school was Raúl Garza Padilla; thesis committee included *Mario de la Cueva, Jesús Reyes Heroles, Antonio Martínez Báez,* and *Adolfo Christlieb Ibarrola*; uncle, Alfonso de la Madrid, is the grandson of Porfirista governor of Colima, Enrique O. de la Madrid; cousin of *Fernando Fernández Hurtado*, his political mentor; son of lawyer and notary Miguel de la Madrid Castro and Alicia Hurtado; married Paloma Cordero Tapia, daughter of lawyer Luis Cordero Bustamante and Delia Tapia Labardini; first political mentor was *José Ricardo Zevada*, who recruited him to public life; student of John Kenneth Galbraith, Calvin Blair, Don K. Price and Arthur Smithies at Harvard; nephew Carlos de la Madrid Vírgin was Governor of Colima. j-None. k-None. l-Letters; HA, 15 May 1972; *Excélsior*, 4 May 1972, 4, 6 July 1981, 10A; HA, 5 Oct. 1981, 4; NYT, 2 Dec. 1982, 3; *Excélsior*, 11 July 1982, 8, 6 Oct. 1981, 8, 10, 26 Sept. 1981, 13A; Ezcurdia, 18; *Excélsior*, 4 Dec. 1982, 14; HA, 31 May 1982, 47; Análisis Político, May 1982, 22; HA, 28 May 1979, 13; NYT, 26 Sept. 1981, 4; *Excélsior*, 17 May 1979, 9.

de la Madrid Romandia, Roberto
a-Feb. 3, 1922. b-Caléxico, California. c-Primary studies in the Cuauhtémoc Elementary School, Mexicali; secondary at Southeast Junior High School, Nestor, California, and at Sweetwater Union High School, National City, California; degree in business administration from the Sweetwater Evening High School. d-*Senator* from Baja California del Norte, 1976; *Governor of Baja California del Norte*, 1977-83. e-Member of the Advisory Council of *Adolfo López Mateos'* presidential campaign, 1958; Coordinator of the Socio-Economic Study Groups, *Milton Castellanos'* campaign for Governor of

Baja California, 1971; Secretary General of the CEPES of PRI in Tijuana and Tecate during the *Luis Echeverría* campaign, 1970; Chief of the Administrative Department of the IEPES of the CEN of PRI, 1975-76. f-President of the Federal Board for Moral and Material Betterment, Baja California del Norte, 1970-75; Director of Economic Development, Baja California del Norte, 1971; President of the Committee of Inter-Governmental Affairs, 1971; Director General of the National Lottery, 1976-77. g-President of the Federation of Border Towns, 1970-75. h-Employee of the National Chamber of Commerce and Industry, Tijuana, 1936; employee of the Bank of the Pacific, S.A., Assistant Cashier, Bank of Baja California; distributor for PEMEX, for Richfield Oil and Pennzoil, 1942-74; Vice-President of the San Diego Planning Commission; member of the Knights of Columbus, 1951-53. i-Longtime friend of *José López Portillo*; son of Miguel de la Madrid Aguilar and Elena Romania; married Elena Victoria; son, Roberto, served as director of state enterprises during his father's administration; cousin, Alejandro Roasa, served as attorney general of Baja California; another cousin, Consuelo Fontes, was his private secretary. j-None. k-Pre-candidate for governor of Baja California del Norte, 1976; lost to General *Cuenca Díaz*, but became the PRI candidate when *Cuenca Díaz* died during the campaign; became a naturalized Mexican Feb 26, 1969. l-HA, 30 May 1977, 21, 14 Nov. 1977, 25; C de S, 1976-82; *Proceso*, 13 Feb. 1978, 23; *Excélsior*, 1 Dec. 1976, 19 May 1977, 10; Enc. Mex., Annual, 1977, 540; *Ovacions*, 1 Mar. 1983, 2.

de la Peña Porth, Luis
(Deceased Apr. 30, 1979) a-1923. b-Tlapán, Federal District. c-Primary studies at the Ignacio L. Vallarta School,

Tlapán, Federal District; secondary studies at Secondary School No. 4, Mexico City; preparatory studies at the National Preparatory School, 1938-39; engineering degree from the National School of Engineering, UNAM, 1943; professor, Higher School of Mechanical Engineering, IPN, 1954-61; Professor of Science, UNAM, 1958-61; researcher, Institute of Physics, UNAM, 1965-68. d-None. e-None. f-Program Director, Mining Development Commission, Saltillo and Hermosillo, 1956-58; Director General of Unrenewable Resources, Secretariat of Government Properties, 1958-60; Director General of Mines and Petroleum, Secretariat of Government Properties, 1965-66; Director of Engineering, Mining Development Commission, 1967-70; *Subsecretary of Renewable Resources*, 1970-73. g-None. h-Worked for a North American company, 1944-47; hydraulic geologist, Mexican government, 1947-52, 1952-54; operated own cotton farm, 1954-56; representative of international firm in Mexico, 1960-63; adviser to private and government firms, 1973-76; Director General of Roca Fosfórica Mexicana, 1977-79. i-Student companion of *Manuel Franco López*, Secretary of National Patrimony, 1964-70; student of *Mariano Moctezuma*, Subsecretary of Industry and Commerce, 1938-42; father was a mining and civil engineer; grandfather had a medical degree but went into mining. j-None. k-Resigned from subsecretaryship in 1973 after a heart attack. l-Letters; DPE65, 83; HA, 14 Dec. 1970, 21; HA, 12 Mar. 1973, 21; *Excélsior*, 2 May 1972, 2; HA, 14 May 1979, 22.

de Lara Isaacs, Alfredo
a-Nov. 14, 1919. b-Calvillo, Aguascalientes. c-Preparatory studies at the National Preparatory Night School; law degree, National School of Law,

UNAM, 1946. d-*Alternate Federal Deputy* from the State of Aguascalientes, Dist. No. 2, 1955-58; *Senator* from the State of Aguascalientes, 1958-64, Secretary of the Senate, 1958, President of the Protocol Committee; Executive Secretary of the Military Justice Committee; Second Secretary of the First Labor Committee and the Special Legislative Studies Committee. e-Official of the CNOP, 1953-58. f-Youth Delegate of the Youth Section of the Department of the Federal District, 1938; Director of the Federal Prosecutors Office for the Defense of Labor, Secretariat of Labor; Director of the Department of Inspection, Secretariat of Labor. g-Vice-President of the Federation of Intellectuals of the Federal District; student leader in the Law School Society, UNAM. h-Journalist; writer for *La Batalla*; editor; edited *La Universidad* with *Salvador Pineda* as a student. j-None. k-None. l-Func., 116; C de S, 1961-64, 54; DGF56, 21.

de Lascuraín Obregón, Javier
a-Nov. 16, 1919. b-Federal District. c-Law degree from the Escuela Libre de Derecho, Aug. 20, 1945. d-None. f-None. g-None. h-Joined the Cia. de Fianzas Lotonal, S.A., 1945; head of the criminal agency for that firm, 1945-47; head of the criminal agency for the Cia. General de Fianzas, 1947; Subdirector of Fianzas Modelo, 1954-66; Director of Fianzas Modelo, 1966-70. i-Son of engineer Angel de Lascuraín. k-Member of the National Action Party; candidate for federal deputy from the Federal District, Dist. 23, 1961, for the National Action Party. l-DBM70, 84.

de la Selva y Escoto, Rogerio
(Deceased 1967) a-1900. b-León, Nicaragua. c-Studies at the Brother of Christ School, Nicaragua; fellowship to study in Mexico, 1921; law degree, National School of Law, UNAM, 1929-

33; professor at the National School of Law, UNAM. d-None. e-Member of the first National Advisory Council of the National Confederation of Popular Organizations of PRI, 1944. f-Agent of the Ministerio Público, 1931; Private Secretary to *Miguel Alemán* as justice of the State Supreme Court of Veracruz, 1934-36; Private Secretary to *Miguel Alemán* as governor of Veracruz, 1936-40; Private Secretary to *Miguel Alemán* as secretary of Government, 1940-45; *Secretary of the Presidency*, 1946-52; Judge of the Military Court; Private Secretary to *Miguel Alemán* as president of the National Council of Tourism, 1964-67. g-None. h-None. i-Longtime personal friend of *Miguel Alemán* since college days at the National School of Law; knew *Salvador Aceves Parra* at UNAM. j-Not a career officer; received a presidential appointment as a General in order to serve as a justice on the military court. k-Became a naturalized citizen of Mexico, one of the few naturalized citizens ever to hold such a high public office in Mexico; in exile in New York City, 1927-31; accused by Senator *David Franco Rodríguez* of trying to divide the PRI, 1954. l-DP70, 1976; D de S, 3 Dec. 1956, 1; HA, 6 Dec. 1946, 6; DGF47; DGF51, I, 55; Brandenburg, 102; Letters; *Excélsior*, 2 Aug. 1949; NYT, 30 July 1954, 3; Villaseñor, II, 100.

de la Torre Grajales, Abelardo
(Deceased Apr. 22, 1976) a-Dec. 4, 1913. b-Chiapa de Corzo, Chiapas. c-Primary and secondary studies in San Cristobal de las Casas, Chiapas; no degree. d-Local Deputy to the State Legislature of Chiapas; Mayor of San Cristóbal de las Casas; *Federal Deputy* from the State of Chiapas, Dist. 2, 1952-55; member of the Second Committee of the Treasury and the Committee on Budgets and Accounts; *Senator* from the State of Chiapas, 1958-64, member of

the Gran Comisión, the First Petroleum Committee, the First Labor Committee, and the First Balloting Committee; President of the First Instruction Section of the Grand Jury. e-Joined the PNR, 1931; candidate of the CNOP of PRI for Senator, 1958; *Secretary of Organization of the CEN of PRI*, 1959-64, 1964-65. f-*Oficial Mayor of the Secretariat of National Patrimony*, 1964-68; *Subsecretary of Government Properties*, 1968-70; Director General of Services, IMSS, 1970-76. g-Occupied various union positions, 1930s; Secretary General of the National Union of Treasury Workers; *Secretary General of the FSTSE*, 1952-58. h-Employee of the Secretariat of the Treasury, 1930s. i-Friend of *Alfonso Corona del Rosal*; married Juanita Delgado. k-PRI candidate for senator from Chiapas, 1976, died prior to the election. l-C de S, 1964, 55; *Siempre*, 5 Feb. 1959, 6; DPE65, 76; HA, 21 Dec. 1964, 11; HA, 28 Dec. 1964, 4; DBM68, 185; C de D, 1955, 9; Scott, 165; Func., 153; *Excélsior*, 23 Apr. 1976, 10; DBdeC, 245.

de la Torre Padilla, Oscar
a-Feb. 8, 1932. b-Guadalajara, Jalisco. c-Primary studies at the Horace Mann School, Mexico City; secondary studies at Secondary School No. 14, Mexico City; preparatory studies at the Centro Universitario de México; degree in political science, School of Political and Social Science, UNAM, 1951-56; Diploma in Tourism, International University of Official Tourist Organizations; degree in tourism, University of Guadalajara, 1968-72. d-Councilman, Guadalajara, Jalisco; Local Deputy to the State Legislature of Jalisco; *Federal Deputy* from the State of Jalisco, Dist. No. 9, 1970-73, member of the Crafts Committee, the Immigration Committee and the Tourism Committee. e-Joined PRI, 1951; general delegate of the CEN of PRI to Baja California del

Sur and Nuevo León, 1981; *Secretary of Organization of the CEN of PRI*, 1982; President of PRI, State of Jalisco, 1988-89. f-Federal delegate of the Department of Tourism to the State of Jalisco; Director of Tourism for the State of Jalisco; *Secretary General "C" of the Department of the Federal District*, 1970-73; *Secretary General of the Department of Tourism*, 1974-76; customs official, Secretariat of the Treasury, Guadalajara, 1977; Secretary of Tourist Development, State of Jalisco, 1989. g-None. i-Married Mary Ann Grillo. j-None. k-None. l-HA, 21 Jan. 1974, 14; Directorio, 1970-72; DBGM89, 747.

de la Vega Domínguez, Jorge
a-Mar. 14, 1931. b-Comitán, Chiapas. c-Primary studies at the public school Belisario Domínguez, Comitán, Chiapas, 1940-45; secondary education in Comitán, 1946-48; preparatory at the National Preparatory School, 1949-50; degree in economics with honorable mention from the National School of Economics, UNAM, 1958, with his thesis on "Petroleum Industry in Mexico: Some Aspects of Its Development and Financial Problems"; Professor of third year engineering at the Technological Institute of Ciudad Madero, Tamaulipas, 1957-58; Professor of the Theory of Public Finance at the National Polytechnic School, 1960-65; Director of the Graduate School of Economics, National Polytechnic School, 1963-64; President of his generation at the National Preparatory School and of the 1955 Generation of the National School of Economics. d-*Federal Deputy* from the State of Chiapas, Dist. 3, 1964-67, member of the Committee on National Properties and Resources and the Committee on Budgets and Accounts; member of the Interparliamentary Delegation to the United States; *Governor of Chiapas*,

1976-77. e-Director of the Institute of Economic, Political and Social Studies of PRI, 1968-70; adviser to the IEPES of PRI during the national platform meeting, 1963; *President of the CEN of PRI, 1986-88.* f-Economist for the Secretariat of Industry and Commerce, 1951-55; General Manager of the Tampico Branch of the Small Business Bank, 1956-58; Subdirector of Diesel Nacional, S.A., 1959-61; Subdirector of the Small Business Bank, 1962; Head of the Department of Public Expenditures, Secretariat of the Presidency, 1963-64; Subdirector in charge of sales, CONASUPO, 1965-68; *Director General of CONASUPO, 1971-76; Secretary of Trade, 1977-82; Secretary of Agriculture and Hydraulic Resources, 1988-90.* g-President of the College of Economists of Mexico, 1961-63. h-Organized the first Congress of Economics Students in Latin America, 1956; author of many articles and pamphlets. i-Attended the National School of Economics, UNAM, with *Julio Faesler*, Director of the Mexican Institute of Foreign Trade, 1970-76, and *Carlos Torres Manzo*; nephew of Belisario Domínguez, the Mexican Senator who publicly accused General Huerta of the murder of Francisco Madero; first helped in public career by his professor and mentor, *Gilberto Loyo*; son of Jaime de la Vega Culebro, farmer, and Lesvia Domínguez Mandujano; married Hermilia Grajales Román. j-None. k-Representative of President *Díaz Ordaz* to student leaders of the 1968 strike; precandidate for senator from Chiapas, 1981. l-Letter; C de D, 1964-66; *Excélsior*, Dec. 1970, 16 Dec. 1977, 6, 15 Apr. 1975, 7, 13 Apr. 1977, 1, 14, 10 Dec. 1977, 1, 13, 26 Dec. 1981, 16A; WNM, 61; DBGM89, 366.

del Castillo Franco, Armando
a-Aug. 27, 1920. b-Canatlán, Durango. c-Primary studies at a public school in Durango; secondary and preparatory studies in Mexico City; law degree, National School of Law, UNAM, 1943. d-*Federal Deputy* from the State of Durango, Dist. 4, 1949-52, President of the Chamber, Sept. 1949, member of the Film Industry Committee and the Legislative Studies Committee; answered *Miguel Alemán*'s 3rd state of the union address, 1949; *Federal Deputy* from the State of Durango, Dist. 3, 1979-80, President of the Administration Committee; *Governor of Durango, 1980-86.* e-Director of the National Youth Sector of the CEN of PRI, 1946-49; Secretary General of the Unified Revolutionary Front, supporting *Miguel Alemán* for president, 1946. f-Director of Public Defenders for the Department of the Federal District, 1946; Director of Civic Action and Popular Orientation, Department of the Federal District, 1946; Secretary General of the State of Durango, 1951; Director of Social Action of the Department of the Federal District, 1946; Director of Educational Action of the Department of the Federal District, 1946. g-Coordinator of Federal Deputies of CNOP for Durango, 1979; Secretary of Legislative Promotion of CNOP, 1980. i-Nephew, Carlos del Castillo Arguelles, served as director of urban works; first cousin, Manuel Guzmán Franco, was director of ISSSTE j-None. k-Politically inactive during most of the 1960s and 1970s. l-DGF51, I, 22, 32, 33; C de D, 1949-52, 66; *Excélsior*, 19 Feb. 1980, 4; Almanaque de México, 345; *Proceso*, 1 Feb. 1982, 13-15.

de León García, María Eugenia
a-Jan. 4, 1954. b-Tampico, Tamaulipas. c-Early education unknown; economics degree, Autonomous Technological Institute of Mexico, 1971-75; MA in administration, ITAM, 1976-77; courses in Turin, Italy, 1983, Lima, Peru, 1984, and Madrid, Spain, 1985; professor, ITAM, 1974-76; professor, Ibero-

American University, 1978-80. d-None.
e-None. f-Director of Acquisitions, Airports and Auxiliary Services, 1983; Subdirector of Administration, Airports and Auxiliary Services, 1984-85; Coordinator of Advisers, Subsecretary of Operations, Secretariat of Communications and Transportation, 1985-86; Director General of Finances, National Railroads of Mexico, 1987-88; *Oficial Mayor of the Secretariat of Communications and Transporation,* 1988-92. g-None. h-None. i-Daughter of Carlos de León González, and Socorro García Delgado. l-DBGM89, 198; DBGM92, 206.

Delgado, Alfredo
a-Dec. 1, 1890. b-El Fuerte, Sinaloa.
c-Primary studies in Oakland, California; no degree. d-*Governor of Sinaloa,* 1937-40. e-None. f-Chief of the Mounted Police, Federal District, 1920-24. g-None. h-None. j-Fought in the Revolution; career army officer; held various commands; rank of Brigadier General, June 1, 1941. k-None. l-Peral 47, 102; letter.

Delgado Ramírez, Celso Humberto
a-Oct. 29, 1942. b-Tepic, Nayarit.
c-Primary studies at the Gabriel Leyva School; secondary studies at the Secondary Boarding School of Secondary School No. 1, Tepic; preparatory studies at the Institute of Science and Letters of Nayarit; law degree, National School of Law, UNAM, 1966; Assistant Professor, World History, National Preparatory Night School, 1968. d-*Federal Deputy* from Nayarit, Dist. 2, 1970-73, member of the Legislative Studies Committee and the 9th Section of the General Affairs Committee, President of the Chamber; *Senator* from the State of Nayarit, 1982-87; *Governor of Nayarit,* 1987-93. e-General delegate of the CEN of PRI to Guanajuato and Chiapas, 1979; Director of PRI in the Federal District, 1981-82. f-Employee, Promo-

tion Department, Division of Social Welfare, Secretariat of Labor, 1966; lawyer, Legal Department, National Agricultural Credit Bank, 1966-68; inspector, Cooperative Education Department, Secretariat of Public Education, 1968-69; Ambassador to Egypt, 1972-73, to Argentina, 1973-75; *Ambassador to Cuba,* 1975-76. g-Vice-President and founder of University Oratory, 1962; Secretary of Cultural Action, Youth Action of the CNC, 1962-68; Secretary of Political Action of the CEN of the Federation of Mexican Youth, 1965-68; President of the CEN of the Federation of Mexican Youth; Secretary of Press and Publicity of the CEN of the CNC, 1971-72. h-None. i-Married María Trinidad Ramírez, social worker; son of Celso Delgado Barreras, composer and musician, and María Trinidad Ramírez, ejidatario. j-None. k-Answered *Luis Echeverría's* 2nd state of the union address, 1972. l-Directorio, 1970-73; C de D, 1970-73, 9, 48, 109; C de S, 1982-88; DBGM87, 461; DBGM89, 679; HA, 20 Jan. 1987, 18.

Delgado Severino, Rodolfo
a-May 20, 1914. b-Acayucán, Veracruz.
c-Early education unknown; graduated as a 2nd Lt. in the cavalry, Heroic Military College; staff diploma, Higher War College; professor, National School of Agricluture, Chapingo, 1939-49; Professor of Military History, Heroic Military College and Applied Military School. d-*Plurinominal Federal Deputy* from PARM, 1979-82. e-Joined PNR; supported *Manuel Avila Camacho* during his presidential campaign, 1940; adjutant and Chief of Security, *Miguel Alemán's* presidential campaign, 1946; Chief of Security, *Gustavo Baz* gubernatorial campaign, 1957; joined the PARM; Secretary of Organization of PARM; Secretary of Social Promotion of PARM. f-Director of Judicial Police, Baja California; Director of Public

Safety, Baja California. g-None.
h-None. i-Member of the "Morelos"
Group headed by *Alfonso Corona del
Rosal*; member of the "Hidalgo" Group
headed by *Antonio Nava Castillo*.
j-Career army officer; member of the
presidential guard during the military
campaign against General Escobar,
1929; Assistant Chief of Staff, Presidential Staff, 1946-52; Military Attaché to
the United States, 1952; Military
Attaché to Argentina, 1952; Commander of the 31st Military Zone,
Tuxtla Gutiérrez, Chiapas, 1966;
Commander of the 19th Military Zone,
Ciudad Ixtepec, Oaxaca, 1971-73;
Commander of the 8th Military Zone,
Tampico, Tamaulipas, 1973-76; Commander of the 6th Military Zone,
Saltillo, Coahuila, 1976. k-None.
l-Protag., 98; C de D, 1979-82.

Delgado Valle, José
a-July 12, 1927. b-Tlalnepantla,
México. c-Primary at the Centro
Escolar of the State of Michoacán,
Mexico City; secondary studies from
Secondary School No. 5, Mexico City;
special course in mechanics from
Vocational School No. 2, Mexico City;
no degree. d-Local Deputy from Dist. 6
to the State Legislature of México;
Federal Deputy from the State of
México, Dist. 2, 1970-73, member of the
Public Welfare Committee, the Tube
Industry Committee and the First
Balloting Committee; *Federal Deputy*
from the State of México, Dist. 3, 1976-
79; *Federal Deputy* from the State of
México, Dist. 15, 1985-88. e-Secretary
of Political Action of PRI in the State of
México, 1966-69. f-Syndic of the City
Council of Tlalnepantla, México, 1961-
63; Treasurer of Nezahualcóytl, México,
1967-69, 1976. g-Assistant Secretary of
Industrial Development, CTM, 1962-68;
Secretary of Political Action of the
Union of Workers of the State of
México, 1976-80; Secretary General of

the CTM of Tlalnepantla, México;
member of the Tube Workers Union;
Secretary of Organization of the CTM of
the State of México, 1983-86. h-Indu-
strial maintenance employee. i-Married
Jacoba López Doñez; son of Agapito
Delgado Escamilla and Rafaela Valle
Vargas. j-None. k-None. l-C de D,
1970-73, 109; Directorio, 1970-72; D de
C, 1976-79, 16; DBGM87, 462.

del Mazo González, Alfredo
a-Dec. 31, 1943. b-Toluca, México.
c-Primary studies in Toluca; preparatory
studies at the Mary Brothers School,
Centro Universitario México; business
administration degree, UNAM, 1966,
with a thesis on the international
division of a savings bank; studies in
finance and economics, England; MA in
administration, Mar. 1969; Professor of
Administration and Finances, School of
Business Administration and Finances,
UNAM, 1967; Professor of International
Finance, ITAM, 1975; Professor of
International Banking, Ibero-American
University, 1969-70. d-*Governor of
México*, 1981-86. e-Joined the PRI,
1962; researcher, IEPES of PRI, 1970-76.
f-Coordinator of the External Debt,
Secretariat of the Treasury, 1971;
Director General of the Public Debt,
Secretariat of the Treasury, 1976-78;
Vice President of the National Securi-
ties Commission, 1976-78; Director of
the National Institute of Credit, 1978-
79; Director General of the Workers
Bank, 1979-81; *Secretary of Energy,
Mines and Government Industries*,
1986-88; Ambassador to Belgium and
the European Economic Community,
1988-90. g-None. h-Began banking
career at the Banco Comercial Mexicano, 1963, where he became assistant
manager, branch mananger and subdirector; Director, International Division,
1972-73; Director General of the
Mercantile and Mining Bank, 1973-76.
i-Son of former Governor *Alfredo del*

Mazo Vélez and Margarita González; cousin of *Mario Colín Sánchez*. j-None. k-Nominated as governor to stop the influence of *Carlos Hank González's* group; one of the three leading pre-candidates for the PRI presidential nomination, 1987. l-*Excélsior*, 5 Mar. 1981, 21a; HA, 28 Sept. 1981, 27; *Almanaque de México*, 526; letters; *Proceso*, 7 Mar. 1988, 28; HA, 29 Apr. 1986, 9, 1 Sept 1987, 48.

del Mazo Vélez, Alfredo
(Deceased Dec. 19, 1975) a-Aug. 21, 1904. b-Atlacomulco, México. c-Primary studies in Atlacomulco, México; secondary in Mexico City; professional schools in Mexico City; no degree. d-*Governor of México*, 1945-51; *Senator* from the State of México, 1952-58, member of the Gran Comisión, the Colonization Committee, the Secondary Money, Credit, and Credit Institutions Committee, the Department of the Federal District Committee and substitute member of the Committee on the Consular and Diplomatic Service; President of the Senate, Oct. 1954. e-Assisted PRI in the presidential campaign of *Adolfo Ruiz Cortines*, 1952; Political Secretary to *Adolfo López Mateos* during his campaign, 1958; general delegate of the CEN of PRI to Sonora, Yucatán, Veracruz and Puebla, 1952-58. f-Director of the Administrative Department of the National Irrigation Commission, 1940-42; Director of Warehouses for the National Highway Commission, 1932-33; Director of Warehouses for the National Irrigation Commission, 1933; Treasurer of the State of México, 1942-43; Secretary General of Government of the State of México, 1943-45, under Governor *Isidro Fabela*; *Secretary of Hydraulic Resources*, 1958-64. g-None. h-Worked as an agricultural laborer; general laborer for the National Irrigation Commission, 1926. i-Father and grandfather both served as mayors of

Atlacomulco; son of Manuel del Mazo Villasante, small rancher, and Mercedes Vélez Díaz; married Margarita González; political disciple of *Isidro Fabela*; personal friend of *Adolfo López Mateos*; son, *Alfredo*, was governor of México, 1981-86. j-None. k-Ran against *Francisco J. Gáxiola* and *Alfredo Navarrete* for the PRI nomination for governor, 1944; early precandidate for president, 1963. l-HA, 30 Nov. 1969, 21, 8 Dec. 1958, 30; DGF56, 6, 9, 10; Greenberg, 26; Scott, 282; DGF51, I, 90; Colín, 201-31; HA, 14 Sept. 1951, 4 June 1948, 29 Dec. 1975, 14; Func., 89; letters.

del Olmo Martínez, Joaquín
a-Aug. 16, 1904. b-Federal District. c-Primary studies in public schools, Mexico City; completed secondary; no degree. d-*Alternate Federal Deputy* from the Federal District, Dist. No. 4, 1955-58; *Federal Deputy* from the Federal District, Dist. No. 2, 1958-61, member of the Traffic Committee and the Library Committee; *Federal Deputy* from the Federal District, Dist. No. 18, 1967-70, member of the Department of the Federal District Committee and the Pharmaceutical Industry Committee; *Federal Deputy* from the Federal District, Dist. No. 18, 1973-76. e-None. f-Representative of Labor to Special Group No. 4, Federal Board of Conciliation and Arbitration, 1961. g-Secretary of Organization and Statistics of the CTM, 1961. h-Auto mechanic. i-Married María Luisa Díaz; son a precandidate for federal deputy. j-None. k-None. l-Func., 177; DGF56, 22; C de D, 1955-58, 1958-61, 9, 1967-70, 62, 75, 1973-76, 18; *Excélsior*, 7 Dec. 1978, 21.

de los Reyes, José María
a-Mar. 19, 1902. b-Tula, Hidalgo. c-Primary studies in the Federal District, 1918-21; preparatory at the Escuela Preparatoria Libre de Homeopatia, 1921-22, and at the National Preparatory

School, 1923-27; law degree from the National School of Law, UNAM, 1928-32; founder of the National Preparatory Night School and other secondary schools in Mexico; Professor of economic and social geography of Mexico (thirty-five years). d-*Federal Deputy* from the State of Hidalgo, Dist. 3, 1952-55, member of the Budget and Accounts Committee (3rd year) and the Legislative Studies Committee (2nd year). e-Supporter of José Vasconcelos, 1929; Secretary of Political Education of PRI for the Federal District, 1975. f-Subdirector General of the National Preparatory School, 1936; Secretary of the National Preparatory School, 1930-35; Director General of Administration, UNAM, 1946-47; Technical adviser to the Rector, UNAM, 1948-60; Director of the Home School for Boys, Secretariat of Government, 1938-42; Director, Office of Cinematography and National Films, Secretariat of Public Education, 1943-46; Director of the publication *Educación*, Secretariat of Public Education, 1946-49; Director of the National Preparatory Night School, 1924-55; member, National Technical Council of Education, 1957-63. g-President of the Student Society of the National Preparatory Night School; active student leader in the 1926, 1927, 1928 and 1929 Student Congresses; member of the National Strike Committee, for the National School of Law, UNAM, 1929. h-Assistant to Colonel Leónardo Torres during the Revolution. i-Attended primary school with *Román Badillo*; father, José María de los Reyes, was a small farmer. j-None. k-Participant in Cuban Revolutionary activity, 1917-18. l-C de D, 1952-55, 52, 63; letter.

del Pozo (Rangel), Efrén C.
(Deceased May 14, 1979) a-Sept. 11, 1907. b-San Luis Potosí, San Luis Potosí. c-Preparatory studies at the University of San Luis Potosí with specialty in science, 1929; medical degree, with a specialty in surgery, National School of Medicine, UNAM, 1936; lab assistant in chemistry, 1928-29, lab assistant in botany and zoology, 1929-30, Secretary, 1927-29, all at University of San Luis Potosí; Professor of Botany and Zoology, Colegio de San Luis Potosí, 1928-30; Professor of Physiology, National School of Biological Sciences, IPN, 1936-46; Research Fellow, Harvard Medical School, 1940-43; Guggenheim Fellow, 1941-43; Dean, National School of Biological Sciences, IPN, 1943-44; Director, Department of Physiology, Institute of Biomedical Sciences, UNAM, 1943-79; *Secretary General of UNAM*, 1953-61; researcher emeritus, UNAM, 1974-79. d-None. e-None. f-Director, Physiology and Pharmacology Laboratories, Institute of Health and Tropical Diseases, Secretariat of Public Health, 1944-46. g-Secretary General of the Union of Latin American Universities, 1961-79. h-Researcher, National Institute for Medical Research, London, 1947; scientific consultant, Merck Institute, 1948-79. i-Collaborated with *Nabor Carrillo Flores* at UNAM; son of Francisco C. del Pozo and Romana Rangel; married Carmen Ramírez. j-None. k-Candidate for the rectorship of UNAM, but did not receive sufficient votes from the governing board. l-WNM, 63; JSH, 303-05; letter.

del Rincón Bernal, Jorge
a-Nov. 27, 1930. b-Guaymas, Sonora. c-Preparatory studies at the Scientific Institute of Guadalajara, Jalisco; professional studies in business administration at the Ibero-American University; law degree, National School of Law, UNAM, 1950-55; professor at the University of Sonora. d-None. e-Member of PAN. f-None. g-General Manager of the Employers' Center of Sinaloa, 1961-65; President of the Employers' Center

of Sinaloa, 1965-68; member of the Board, Employers' Federation of the Republic of Mexico, 1966; adviser to the Chamber of Commerce. h-Manager of Inmuebles y Condominio, S.A., Mexico City, 1956-57; employee, Sears Roebuck of Mexico, 1957-58; Director, Legal and Personnel Department, Companía Comercial del Noroeste, S.A., 1958-60; President of the Board, Companía Comercial de Guasave, S.A., 1965-70. i-Married Elisa Jarero; son of Francisco Rincón Rodríguez and Cristina Bernal. j-None. k-Headed a civic movement in Culiacán which forced the federal government to expropriate the Sinaloa Electric Company; candidate for federal deputy from the Federal District, Dist. 2, as a member of the National Action Party. l-DBM70, 176; WNM, 63.1

del Río Rodríguez, Carlos Antonio
a-May 10, 1929. b-Federal District. c-Early education unknown; law degree, National School of Law, UNAM, 1947-1954; LLD degree, National School of Law, UNAM, 1965; professor, National School of Law, UNAM, 1959-82; professor of the Institute of Social, Economic and Administrative Science, 1956. d-None. e-None. f-Chief of the Customs, Pensions and Treasury Studies, Department of Disputes, Federal Tax Attorney's Office, 1954-60; Chief, Department of Disputes, Federal Tax Court, 1960-63; Judge, Federal Tax Court, 1963-65; President, Federal Tax Court, 1965-69; *Justice of the Supreme Court*, 1969-85; *Chief Justice of the Supreme Court*, 1986-91; President, Second Division, Supreme Court, 1970. g-None. h-Practicing lawyer; author of several books. i-Son of Francisco del Río Canedo, diplomat, and María Rodríguez Martínez; married to Silvia Chiriboga Vázquez. j-None. k-Resigned from the Supreme Court under pressure. l-Protag., 291; letter; DBGM, 682; DBGM87, 655; DBGM89, 637.

del Valle, Alberto
a-Dec. 15, 1890. b-Aguascalientes, Aguascalientes. c-Primary studies in Aguascalientes; secondary studies at the Institute of Sciences of Aguascalientes, 1911-14; studied medicine at the Medical School of the University of San Luis Potosí (two years); medical degree from the National School of Medicine, UNAM, 1917; Professor of Chemistry at the Scientific Institute of Aguascalientes. d-Local Deputy to the State Legislature of Aguascalientes, 1928-30; Mayor of Aguascalientes, 1937-38; *Senator* from Aguascalientes, Sept. 1934 to Aug. 1936; *Governor of Aguascalientes*, 1940-44. f-Founder and Director of the Anti-Venereal Clinic, 1920-21; Director of Education for Aguascalientes, 1917-20; Director of the Preparatory School for the State of Aguascalientes. g-None. h-Began career as a practicing surgeon, 1917. i-Son of Genaro del Valle. j-Head of the Sanitary Section of the Brigade Luis Moya, 1915. k-None. l-EBW46, 55; WWM45, 120; WB48, 1436; Peral, 825.

de María y Campos, Mauricio
a-Oct. 13, 1943. b-Federal District. c-Early education unknown; economics degree, National School of Economics, UNAM, with a thesis on "Technology Transfer, Dependency and Economic Development," 1968; MA in economic development, University of Sussex, 1970; Professor, International Economics Seminar, National School of Economics, UNAM, 1970-73. d-None. e-None. f-Adviser to the Capital Goods Program, National Finance Bank, 1972-73; Secretary of Evaluation, Division of Technology Transfers, Secretariat of Industry and Commerce, 1973-74; Director General of Foreign Investments, Secretariat of Industry and Commerce, 1974-76; Director General of Tax Incentives, Secretariat of the Treasury, 1976-79; Subdirector General of Fiscal

Promotion, Secretariat of the Treasury, 1979-82; Director General of Fiscal Promotion, Secretariat of the Treasury, 1982; *Subsecretary of Industrial Development*, Secretariat of Commerce and Industrial Development, 1982-88; Director of Strategic Planning, SOMEX, 1988-90. g-None. h-None. i-Son of Mauricio de María y Campos Algara, architect, and María Teresa Castelló Yturbide, ethnologist and art historian; married Patricia Meade García de León, chemical engineer; brother, Alfonso, was director general of cultural affairs, Secretariat of Foreign Relations. j-None. k-None. l-*Excélsior*, Dec. 4, 1982, 35; Q es QAP, 191; DBGM89, 216; DBGM92, 223; DBGM87, 235; DBGM, 267.

de Olloqui Labastida, José Juan
a-Nov. 5, 1931. b-Federal District. c-Primary and secondary studies in the Federal District; law degree from the National School of Law, UNAM, Aug. 1956; MA in economics, George Washington University, 1970; graduate work in law, National School of Law, UNAM; Professor by Competition, History of Economic Thought, National School of Law, UNAM, 1964-66; Professor of Economic Problems of Mexico and Economic Theory, UNAM and Ibero-American University; attended the English Language Institute, University of Michigan, 1957; member of the Patronate of UNAM, 1983. d-None. e-Joined PRI, 1959. f-Director of the Department of Currency, Banking and Investment, Secretariat of the Treasury, 1958-66; Deputy General of Credit, Secretariat of the Treasury, 1966-70; President of the National Securities Commission, 1970-71; Executive Director of the Inter-American Development Bank, 1966-70; *Ambassador to the United States*, 1971-76; *Subsecretary (A) of the Secretariat of Foreign Relations*, 1976-79; *Ambassador to Great*

Britain, 1979-82; Director General of Banco Serafín, 1982-88, 1988-91; Director General of the Workers Housing Institute (INFONAVIT), 1991-93. g-President and founder of the Miners Association of Zacatecas, Zacatecas and Parral, Chihuahua, 1963-71. h-Joined the Bank of Mexico, 1951; author and translator of books, articles and reviews; member of the Patronato of UNAM, 1983. i-Son of Fernando de Olloqui Iñíguez, a banker, manager of the Bank of Mexico in Monterrey, and Margarita Labastida González Rubio; grandson of General José Juan de Olloqui; second cousin of *Oscar Flores Sánchez*; sister, Margarita de Olloqui Labastida, is married to Ambassador Roberto de Rosensweig Díaz. j-None. k-None. l-Letters; DPE65, 54; BdM, 102; DPE61, 41; NYT, 2 Dec. 1976; HA, 7 Mar. 1983, 10; *Excélsior*, 5 Sept. 1982, 20A; HA, 7 Mar. 1983, 10; DBGM87, 343; *Excélsior*, 27 July 1984, 20.

Díaz Arias, Julián
c-Economics degree from the National School of Economics, UNAM, Nov. 28, 1946; Professor and Superintendent of Technical Education at the National Polytechnic Institute, 1938-58; professor at the National School of Economics, UNAM, 1945-65; professor at the Scientific Institute, 1952-53; professor at the Higher Normal School, 1945-47. d-None. e-None. f-Head of the Department of Banks, Secretariat of the Treasury, 1947-51; President of the Executive Board of the Administration of Pensions, 1952-53; head of the Department of Properties and Construction of the Mexican Institute of Social Security, 1953-58; *Oficial Mayor of the Secretariat of Industry and Commerce*, 1959; *Subsecretary of Industry and Commerce*, 1959-61; business administrator and general attorney for Nacional Financiera, 1960-62; Director General of Financiera Nacional Azucarera, 1962-

65; *Subdirector of National Finance Bank*, 1965-70, 1970-72; Director General of Financiera Nacional Azucarera, May 1972, to 1976; Director of Collective Transportation, Department of the Federal District, 1976-82. g-Participant in a student conference with *Luis Echeverría*, 1945. h-Attended conference in Central America. i-Friend of *Jorge Espinosa de los Reyes* at UNAM; married Isabel Gómez. j-None. k-None. l-HA, 15 May 1972, 31; letters; DBM66, 194-95; DGF50, II, 35, 409, 413; DGF51, II, 146, 570, 577, 43; DAPC, 1981, 7.

Díaz Ballesteros, Enrique
a-July 13, 1916. b-Morelia, Michoacán. c-Early education unknown; law degree, National School of Law, UNAM, 1935-39, with a thesis on the constitution. d-None. e-Joined PRI, 1935; adviser, IEPES of PRI, 1968-70. f-Legal Agent, Department of Agrarian Affairs, 1938-40; lawyer, National Railroads of Mexico, 1941-45; Chief, Administrative Law, Legal Department, National Railroads of Mexico, 1948-54; Director of Legal Services, National Railroads of Mexico, 1955-61; Consulting Attorney to the Attorney General of Mexico, 1943-54; Director of Legal Services, Emiliano Zapata Mill, 1952-59; General Counsel to the Director General of the National Railroads, 1961-64; Manager of the Administrative Division, CONASUPO, 1961-65; Subdirector of Operations, CONASUPO, 1971-75; *Director General of CONASUPO*, 1976; Director General of Metropolitan Services of the Federal District, 1977; *Subsecretary of Commercial Planning*, Secretariat of Trade, 1978; *Subsecretary of Regulations*, Secretariat of Trade, 1978-79; *Director General of CONASUPO*, 1979-82; *Subsecretary of Foodstuffs and Internal Trade*, Secretariat of Commerce, 1988-89. g-Secretary of Education of the National Union of Employees and Workers of the Department of Agrarian

Affairs and Colonization, 1938-39. h-Practicing lawyer, 1938-61. i-Son of Luis Díaz Castillo, public servant, and María Ballesteros Izquierdo; married Isabel Anaya Azpiroz. j-None. k-None. l-*Excélsior*, 5 May 1979, 1, 10; DPE71; DAPC; DBGM87, 107; DBGM89, 99.

Díaz Cerecedo, Cándido
a-Feb. 2, 1927. b-Sierra de Chicontepec, Veracruz. c-Completed secondary studies in Jalapa; normal studies in Jalalpa on a scholarship from the Secretariat of Public Education, 1949-51; preparatory studies at night school, Veracruz, Veracruz; legal studies at the National School of Law, UNAM, 1955-59, law degree, 1960; teacher, Federal District, 1955-71; founder of the Institute for Adult Education, Tamiahua, Veracruz; founder of the Secondary Night School for Workers, Tamiahua, Veracruz; professor, Federal Institute of Teacher Training, 1962-71. d-Mayor of Chicontepec, Veracruz, 1975-77; *Plurinominal Federal Deputy* from the PST, 1982-85. e-Joined PRI, 1955; joined the PST, 1979; candidate for federal deputy from the PRI, 1979; candidate of the PST for governor of Veracruz, 1980; presidential candidate of the PST, 1981-82. f-None. g-Founder of several unions as mayor of Chicontepec, Veracruz. h-Worked as a milkman, blacksmith, charcoal maker. i-From a very poor Nahuatl family; married María Refugio Zabalza Covarrubias, normal teacher. j-None. k-Left the PRI because of the imposition of *Manuel Ramos Gurrión* as the PRI candidate for federal deputy. l-Análisis Político, May 1982, 34; Almanaque, 14-15; DBGM, 497; Lehr, 620.

Díaz de Cossío (Carvajal), Roger
a-Dec. 5, 1931. b-London, England. c-Engineering degree from the National School of Engineering, UNAM, 1953; MS in civil engineering, 1955-57, Ph.D.

in engineering, 1958-60, researcher, 1958-60, all at University of Illinois; Director of Graduate Studies, School of Engineering, UNAM, 1961-66; Director of the Engineering Institute of UNAM, 1966-70; Coordinator of the Sciences, UNAM. d-None. e-Joined PRI, 1978. f-*Subsecretary of Planning of the Secretariat of Public Education*, 1971-76; Director General of Studies and Projects, Secretary of Commerce, 1977-78; Director General of Publications and Libraries, Secretariat of Public Education, 1978; *Subsecretary of Culture and Recreation*, 1978-82; Subdirector General of Social and Cultural Services, ISSSTE, 1982-88; Director General of Scientific Cooperation, Secretariat of Foreign Relations, 1988-90; Director General of Mexican Communities Abroad, Secretariat of Foreign Relations, 1991-94. g-None. h-Assistant on construction works to Engineer González Fernández, 1953-54; calculator for the Division of Bridges, National Railroads of Mexico, 1955. i-Son of Martín Díaz de Cossío Calero, businessman, and Isabel Carbajal Bolandi, normal teacher. j-None. k-None. l-DPE71, 103; BdM, 106; DGF69, 756; HA, 27 Nov. 1978, 17-18; DAPC, 1977, 21; DBGM89, 100.

Díaz de León, Humberto
a-Jan. 30, 1928. b-Mexico City. c-Preparatory studies; technical studies in railroads. d-*Federal Deputy* from the State of Puebla, Dist. 9, 1967-70, member of the Legislative Studies Committee and the General Means of Communications and Transportation Committee. e-Member of PARM. f-None. g-None. i-Married Guillermina del Pozo. j-None. k-None. l-Directorio, 1967-70; C de D, 1967-70, 68.

Díaz Díaz, Daniel
a-Mar. 17, 1934. b-Huandacareo, Michoacán. c-Early education unknown; civil engineering studies,

National School of Engineering, UNAM, 1951-54, degree, 1960; MA in economic programming, Center for Economic Programming, France, 1963-64; course in public administration, Center for Industrial Development, United Nations; Professor of Planning, National School of Engineering, UNAM, 1965-82; professor, National School of Architecture, 1975. d-None. e-Joined PRI, 1956. f-Department head and office chief, Division of Planning and Programming, Secretariat of Public Works, 1959-63; Director of Research Department, Division of Planning and Programming, Secretariat of Public Works, 1964-66; Director General, Division of Planning and Programming, Secretariat of Public Works, 1966-72; Director General of Programming, Secretariat of Public Works, 1972-76; Director General of Investment Analysis, Secretariat of Public Works, 1977-82; *Subsecretary of Public Works*, 1982-84; *Secretary of Communication and Transportation*, 1984-88. g-President of the College of Civil Engineering of Mexico, 1982-84; Executive Secretary of the Alumni Society of the School of Engineering, UNAM. h-None. i-Son of Daniel Díaz Ortiz, printer, and Enriqueta Díaz García; married Graciela Alatriste Ortiz. j-None. k-None. l-IEPES; Q es QAP, 250; *Excélsior*, 1 Dec. 1984, 1; DBGM, 111; DBGM87, 108.

Díaz Duran, Fernando
a-Nov. 4, 1905. b-Gómez Palacio, Durango. c-Secondary studies at the Escuela Zaragoza, Zacatecas, Zacatecas; graduated as an accountant from the Institute of Sciences, Zacatecas; licensed public accountant. d-Secretary of the City Council of Irapuato, 1928; Mayor of Irapuato; Local Deputy to the State Legislature of Guanajuato; *Federal Deputy* from the State of Guanajuato, Dist. 4, 1943-46, Secretary of the

Chamber of Deputies, *Federal Deputy from the State of Guanajuato, Dist. 5, 1958-61,* member of the Administration Committee (2nd year); *Federal Deputy from the State of Guanajuato, Dist. 4, 1967-70,* member of the Public Education Committee and the Rules Committee. e-Secretary General of CNOP of PRI for Guanajuato; *Secretary of Political Action of the CEN of PRI, 1959; Secretary of Organization of the CEN of PRI, 1964-65; Secretary General of the CEN of PRI, 1965-68.* f-Secretary of Education for the State of Guanajuato, 1940-43; Director of the Department of Labor, State of Guanajuato; President of the Board of Conciliation and Arbitration, Guanajuato. g-None. h-Employed in various positions by the Secretariat of the Treasury. i-Political disciple of *Enrique Fernández Martínez* during early political career; married Enriqueta Aranda. j-None. k-Secretary of the Federation of Political Parties of Guanajuato. l-Peral, 220; C de D, 1943-45, 1958-60, 76; Func., 212; C de D, 1967-69, 64, 86.

Díaz Infante, Luis
a-Sept. 20, 1896. b-León, Guanajuato. c-Early education unknown; law degree, National School of Law, UNAM, 1923; Professor of Civil Law at the Escuela Libre de Derecho. d-*Federal Deputy from the State of Guanajuato, Dist. 2, 1946-48,* member of the Library Committee (1st year) and the First Committee on Balloting; President of the First Instructive Section of the Grand Jury, member of the Committee on Constitutional Affairs, substitute member of the Treasury Committee and the First Committee on General Channels of Communication. e-None. f-Judge of the First Civil Court; Judge of the Superior Tribunal of the Federal District and Federal Territories; President of the Superior Tribunal of the Federal District and Federal Territories; *Justice of the*

Supreme Court, 1948 and 1950-58; *Interim Governor of Guanajuato,* 1948-49. g-None. h-Member of the national commission charged with the writing of new civil codes. i-Related to Miguel Díaz Infante, federal deputy from Guanajuato, 1912. j-None. k-Member of the Sinarquista movement in Mexico; Simpson claims he was the first antirevolutionary governor of Mexico. l-HA, 7 Oct. 1949, xxii; Peral 222; DGF47, 568; Simpson, 337; C de D, 1946-48, 70; DGF51, 568.

Díaz Infante Aranda, Ernesto
a-Jan. 6, 1930. b-Federal District. c-Early education unknown; law degree, University of San Luis Potosí, 1950-54; Subdirector, School of Economics and Administration, Autonomous University of Baja California, 1961-65; professor, Autonomous University of Baja California, 1965-69. d-None. e-None. f-Secretary, Judicial District of Tijuana, Baja California, 1959-65; Secretary of Studies and Accounts, Supreme Court of Justice, 1965-66; Judge, First District, Chihuahua, Chihuahua, 1967-68; Judge, First Appeals Court in Civil Matters, 1968-79; *Justice of the Supreme Court,* 1979-82, 1982-88; President of the Supernumerary Justices of the Supreme Court, 1982. g-None. h-None. i-Son of Eduardo Díaz Infante y Mejía, public official and federal labor inspector, and Concepción Aranda de la Parra; grandson of Miguel Díaz Infante y Aranda, physician, and Teresa Mejía; married Zulema Reyes Cunningham, lawyer; brother Raúl was a circuit court judge, 1992; brother Eduardo a federal judge. j-None. k-None. l-DBGM87, 615.

Díaz Lombardo, Antonio
(Deceased Nov. 8, 1992) a-Jan. 8, 1903. b-Federal District. c-Primary and secondary studies at the English-French School and the English School Mexico City; preparatory at the National

Preparatory School in Mexico City; studied at the Higher School of Mechanical and Electrical Engineering of the National Polytechnic Institute. d-None. e-Assisted *Miguel Alemán* during his presidential campaign, 1946. f-Director General of the Bank of Transportation, 1943-46, 1953; *Director General of the Mexican Institute of Social Security*, 1946-52. g-Secretary General of the Alianza de Camioneros of Mexico. h-Employed by El Aguila; employed by Aeronaves de Mexico; President of the Latin American Bank; President of the Central Savings Bank, 1945-72; principal stockholder of El Popo, 1931. i-Father a well-known engineer. j-None. k-The *New York Times* claims he was forced to resign as Director of the Bank of Transportation because of a conflict of interest arising from his financial control over bus companies; one author claims he started his career in transportation as a driver on the Peravilo-Cozumel bus line. l-HA, 21 May 1943, 9, 6 Dec. 1946, 6; WWM45, 35; Enc. Mex., III, 236; Scott, 250; DGF50, II, 103; Brandenburg, 102; NYT, 12 July 1953, 26; López, 291; Blanco, 323; Alonso, 219.

Díaz Muñoz, Vidal
a-Mar. 21, 1900. b-Las Puentes, Veracruz. c-Primary and secondary education at public schools; no degree. d-*Senator* from Veracruz, 1940-46, member of the National Properties and Resources Committee, the Public Works Committee, First Secretary of the Third Labor Committee and President of the Electrical Engineering Committee; *Federal Deputy* from the State of Veracruz, Dist. 11, 1946-49, Secretary of the Chamber, Sept. 1946, member of the Second Committee on the Treasury, the Committee on Taxes, the Committee on the Sugar Industry and the Inspection Committee of the General Accounting Office (2nd year).

e-Expelled from the PRI for joining the Popular Party, 1946; member of the Popular Socialist Party; member of the Finance Committee of the Popular Party, 1947; Secretary of the Electoral Affairs Committee, Popular Party, 1948; founder of the Veracruz Socialist Party in 1957. f-None. g-Active in union organizations of the Regional Federation of Mexican Labor, 1925-32; served with the Federation of Latin American Workers, 1932-43; prominent leader of the sugar cane workers. j-Member of the Mexican army, 1910-25; reached the rank of Lt. Colonel, 1925. k-Split with *Vicente Lombardo Toledano* in 1957 to found his own party with the support of sugar cane workers; supported *Adolfo López Mateos* in the 1958 presidential election. l-EBW46, 37; Correa, 75; C de D, 1946-48, 70; Scott, 190-91; Morton, 104; Peral, 223; WB48, 1494.

Díaz Ordaz, Gustavo
(Deceased July 15, 1979) a-Mar. 11, 1911. b-Ciudad Serdán (San Andrés), Puebla. c-Primary studies in Oaxaca, Oaxaca, and in Guadalajara, Jalisco; preparatory studies at the Institute of Arts and Sciences, Oaxaca, Oaxaca; studied law at the University of Guadalajara and at the Institute of Arts and Sciences, Oaxaca; law degree from the University of Puebla, Feb. 8, 1937; Professor of Law at the University of Puebla; Vice Rector of the University of Puebla, 1940-41. d-*Federal Deputy* from the State of Puebla, Dist. 1, 1943-46; *Senator* from Puebla, 1946-52, member of the Administrative Committee, the Legislative Studies Committee, the Second Petroleum Committee, the First Government Committee, the First Constitutional Affairs Committee and the Second Foreign Relations Committee; *President of Mexico*, 1964-70. e-None. f-Prosecuting Attorney for Tehuacán, Puebla; President of the Arbitration and Conciliation Board of

Puebla; Agent of the Ministerio Público for Tlatlahuqui, Puebla, 1943; Justice of the Superior Court of the State of Puebla; Secretary General of Government of the State of Puebla under *Gonzalo Bautista,* 1941-45; Director General of Legal Affairs of the Secretariat of Government, 1953-56; *Oficial Mayor of Government,* 1956-58; *Secretary of Government,* 1958-64; Ambassador to Spain, 1977. g-None. h-Employed as an office boy in the Palacio de Gobierno of Puebla; practicing attorney, 1937. i-Father, Ramón Díaz Ordaz, was an accountant and his mother, Sabina Bolanos Cacho, a school teacher; brother-in-law of Guillermo Borja Osorno, justice of the state superior court of Puebla; great-grandfather, José María Díaz Ordaz, a lawyer, a general, and governor of Oaxaca; father-in-law of *Salim Nasta,* formerly his private secretary, 1964; married Guadalupe Borja. j-None. k-Resigned from ambassadorship to Spain after strong protests from important political figures, 1977. l-D de Y, 1 Dec. 1964, 1; Enc. Mex., III, 237-38; DGF56, 83; G of S, 14; WWMG, 14; DBM68, 197-98; HA, 8 Dec. 1958, 24; DP70, 2386-87; Covarrubias, 116; DGF47; C de D, 1943-45, 9; DGF51, I, 7, 10-13; NYT, 2 Dec. 1964, 16; IWW64-65; HA, 11 Apr. 1977, 7, 23 July 1979, 8-9.

Díaz Palacios, Socorro
a-Feb 16, 1949. b-Pueblo Juárez, Colima. c-Primary studies at the Benito Juárez Rural Public School, Pueblo Juárez, Colima, 1955-61; secondary studies at Secondary School No. 8, Colima, 1961-64; preparatory studies at the University of Colima, 1964-66; degree in journalism, Carlos Septién García School of Journalism, 1966-70; Professor of Journalism at the School of Political and Social Sciences, UNAM, 1978-81; Professor of Journalism at the Institute of Political Education, PRI, 1976.

d-*Senator* from the State of Colima, 1982-88, member of the Gran Comisión; *Federal Deputy* from the State of Colima, Dist. 1, 1988-91, President of the Chamber, 1991. e-Joined PRI, 1969; adviser to the State Committee of PRI in Colima; Treasurer of PRI, Comalá, Colima, 1969; member of the Advisory Council, IEPES of PRI, 1980-82. f-None. g-None. h-Reporter, 1970-71, Chief of Information, 1972-73, Chief of Editors, 1973-75, columnist, 1975-80, editorial writer, 1971-76, 1979-80, Subdirector, 1977-80, all at El Día; Director of the Sunday Supplement, Channel 13 Television, 1974-80; Editor of El Día; Director-in-Chief of El Día, 1981-85. i-Protégé of *Enrique Ramírez y Ramírez*; daughter of Francisco Díaz Ballesteros, merchant, and María Palacios Vargas. j-None. k-None. l-IEPES; C de S, 1982-88; Directorio, 1982-88; Lehr, 76; *Excélsior,* 27 July 1984, 20; DBGM87, 464; DBGM89, 428-29.

Díaz Rodríguez, Roberto
a-Dec. 12, 1910. b-Aguascalientes, Aguascalientes. c-Primary studies only. d-Local Deputy to the State Legislature of Aguascalientes (3 times); *Alternate Senator* from Aguascalientes, 1976-80, in functions as Senator, 1980-82. e-Labor adviser on various IMSS committees for PRI. f-None. g-Delegate of the CTM to Geneva, 1972; Secretary General of the CTM of Aguascalientes. h-None. j-None. k-None. l-Letter; Almanaque de México, 58.

Díaz Serrano, Jorge
a-Feb. 6, 1921. b-Nogales, Sonora. c-Early education unknown; mechanical engineering degree from the Higher School of Mechanical and Electrical Engineering, IPN, 1941; MA degree in the history of art and Mexican history, School of Philosophy and Letters, UNAM, 1972-74; fellowship student to the United States to study internal

combustion engines at private firms, 1943-45. d-*Senator* from Sonora, 1982-83. e-None. f-*Director General of PEMEX*, 1976-81; *Ambassador to the Soviet Union*, 1981-82. g-None. h-Inspector, National Irrigation Commission, 1941-43; Director of the Diesel and Locomotive Department, Fairbanks Morse, 1946-56; founded numerous companies, 1956-65; supervisor of a drilling company, Veracruz, 1962-64; Director and owner of the Golden Lane Drilling Company, 1965-70; representative of General Motors in electrical diesel engines and generators, 1969-73. i-Personal friend of *José López Portillo* for many years; friend of *Octavio Senties*; nephew Luis Bojórquez Serrano, a precandidate for federal deputy from Sonora, 1979. j-None. k-Considered an international authority on the perforation and exploitation of petroleum; lost his immunity as a senator and tried for fraud as PEMEX director, 1983. l-*El Día*, 1 Dec. 1976; *Excélsior*, 18 Mar. 1977, 6, 8; HA, 21 Mar. 1977, 12.

Díaz Soto y Gama, Antonio
(Deceased 1967) a-1880. b-San Luis Potosí, San Luis Potosí. c-Primary studies in a public school in San Luis Potosí; law degree, Scientific and Literary Institute of San Luis Potosí, 1900; Professor of the History of the Mexican Revolution, National Preparatory School, 1933; Professor of Agrarian Law, National School of Law, UNAM, 1930s. d-Federal Deputy from the State of San Luis Potosí, Dist. 2, 1920-22, 1922-24, Dist. 4, 1924-26, Dist. 2, 1928-30. e-Founding member of the Liberal Club Ponciano Arriaga; organizer of the first Liberal Congress of Mexico, 1901; active in the Liberal Party, 1904-1912; cofounder of the National Agrarian Party, 1920, in reality, a personal movement; supported Alvaro Obregón as a campaign propagandist, 1927-28; supported *Juan Andreu Almazán* for

president, 1940; Vice-president of the Mexican Democratic Party which ran *Ezequiel Padilla* for president, 1945; representative of the PDM to the Federal Electoral Commission, 1946. f-None. g-None. h-Wrote for *Renacimiento* and *El Universal*. i-Related to Valentín Gama, prominent educator at UNAM; son of lawyer Conrado Díaz Soto, a supporter of Sebastián Lerdo de Tejada. j-Joined Emiliano Zapata's forces, 1914-20; represented Zapata at the Convention in Mexico City, Jan. 1915. k-Notable orator during congressional debates in the 1920s; in exile in the United States for opposing the Díaz regime, 1902-04; named Secretary of Justice but refused appointment, 1915. l-Letters; Medina, 20, 61; DP70, 2015; Enc. Mex., XI, 500; Cockcroft, 71; Rivas, 3, 25; Meyer, 13, 245; López, 296.

Domenzáin Guzmán, Hugo
a-July 14, 1933. b-Federal District. c-Early education unknown; medical degree, National School of Medicine, UNAM, 1951-56; orthopedic residency, Barberton Citizens Hospital, 1957-60. d-*Senator* from the State of Morelos, 1988-91. e-Joined PRI, 1963. f-Chief of Orthopedics, Inguarán Children's Hospital, Department of the Federal District, 1964-70; Director, Topilejo Hospital, Department of the Federal District, 1970-72; Coordinator of Orthopedics, Infant Hospitals, Department of the Federal District, 1972-73; Director of the Coyoacán Xoco Emergency Hospital, Department of the Federal District, 1973-78. g-Secretary of Social Security of CNOP, 1979-80; Secretary of the CEN of CNOP, 1986-89; Secretary General of the Union of the ISSSTE, 1978-81; *Secretary General of the CEN of the FSTSE*, 1989-94. h-None. i-Son of Hugo Domenzaín Ordóñez and Luz María Guzmán; married Elia Martínez Ortega, surgeon. j-None. k-None. l-DBGM89, 429-30.

Domínguez (Canabal), José Agapito
(Deceased Apr. 19, 1970) a-Oct. 23,
1913. b-Montecristo, Tabasco.
c-Completed primary, secondary and
preparatory studies, attended the
National Polytechnic Institute, no
degree. d-*Federal Deputy* from the
State of Tabasco, Dist. 2, 1955-58,
member of the Gran Comisión, the
Library Committee, and the First
Committee on Balloting; *Federal
Deputy* from the State of Tabasco, Dist.
2, 1967-70, member of the Gran Comi-
sión and the Committee on Budgets and
Accounts (2nd year). e-Various posi-
tions in PRI; General Delegate of PRI to
Yucatán. f-Adviser to the Secretary of
Public Health; Head of the Department
of Health of the Department of the
Federal District; Inspector General of
the National Urban Mortgage Bank;
adviser to the Secretary of Government;
Head of the Federal Office of the
Treasury in San Luis Potosí, Yucatán
and Tabasco. g-Organized the First
Congress of National Students in
Frontera, Tabasco; First President of the
National Federation of Technical
Students at the National Polytechnic
Institute. i-Nephew of the Tabascan
political leader Garrido Canabal.
j-None. k-Elected governor of Tabasco
in 1970, but died of a heart attack before
taking office. l-DGF56, 28; DP70, 663;
C de D, 1955-57, 42, 47, 56, 1967-69;
DGF51, 337; Ind. Biog., 51; Almanaque
de Tabasco, 160.

Domínguez Cota, Isidro
a-May 15, 1907. b-Cananea, Sonora.
c-Attended the National Military
College. d-*Federal Deputy* from Baja
California del Sur, 1940-43. e-None.
f-Private Secretary to the Governor of
Baja California del Sur, 1932-37.
g-None. h-Employed by the Light and
Power Company of the Isthmus of
Tehuantepec; author of articles on Baja
California. i-Brother of Governor *Juan*

Domínguez Cota. k-None. l-Peral, 229;
C de D, 1940-42, 9.

Domínguez Cota, Juan
(Deceased) a-Dec. 16, 1888. b-La
Purisima, Baja California. c-Early
education unknown; no degree.
d-None. e-None. f-Secretary General of
Baja California del Norte under *Luis I.
Rodríguez; Governor of Baja California
del Sur*, 1935-37. g-None. h-Miner.
i-Brother of *Isidro Domínguez Cota*;
from a poor family; compadre of *Luis I.
Rodríguez.* j-Joined the Revolution,
1910; fought against Huerta and Orozco,
1912-14; fought against Villa, 1914-15;
fought against de la Huerta, 1923;
commander of military operations in
Morelos, 1927; fought against the
Cristeros, 1928; supported the government against General Escobar, 1929;
rank of Division General, May 16, 1929;
Commander of the 3rd Military Zone,
La Paz, Baja California, 1936.
k-Participated in the Cananea mining
strike, 1906; commander of the troops
who captured and executed General
Serrano and his companions. l-Peral,
229; D de Y, 5 Sept. 1935; letter;
Gómez, 121.

Domínguez Fermán, Serafín
a-Dec. 15, 1939. b-San Andrés Tuxtla,
Veracruz. c-Early education unknown;
law degree, National School of Law,
UNAM, 1957-61, with a thesis on
constitutional principles and Mexican
foreign policy; Professor of Law,
National School of Law, UNAM, 1971-
72; Professor of Law, National School of
Political Studies, UNAM, Acatlán,
1979-82. d-*Federal Deputy* from the
State of Veracruz, Dist. 13, 1973-76,
Dist. 22, 1982-85. e-Joined PRI, 1960;
Legal Director, CEN of PRI, 1964-65;
Subdirector of International Affairs of
the CEN of PRI, 1976-77; Subsecretary
of Ideological Divulgation of the CEN of
PRI, 1978; Coordinator, Basic Plan of

Government of PRI, 1976-82. f-Agent of the Ministerio Público, 1963-68; Chief, Electoral and Political Department, Secretariat of Government, 1966-70; Technical Subdirector of the National Institute of Youth, 1971-72; delegate of the Secretariat of Planning and Budgeting to Colima, 1982; assistant to the Director General of Government, Secretariat of Government, 1982. g-None. h-Practicing lawyer. i-Son of Serafín Domínguez Cadena, businessman, and Edelmira Fermán Morales, rural teacher. j-None. k-None. l-Directorio, 1982-85; C de D, 1973-76, 1982-85; Lehr, 514.

Dondé Escalante, Pedro
a-Dec. 18, 1938. b-Federal District. c-Early education unknown; economics degree, Autonomous Institute of Mexico, with a thesis on "Foreign Trade as an Institution of Economic Development," 1963; studies toward a Ph.D in economics, Harvard University, 1964-66; Professor of Economic Theory, Department of Economics, Autonomous Institute of Mexico, 1969-72; Professor, School of Business and Administration, UNAM, 1971; program for private sector management, Pan American Institute, 1973-74. d-None. e-None. f-Analyst, Income Tax, Department of Economic Studies, Secretariat of the Treasury, 1959-61; analyst, Department of Economic Studies, Bank of Mexico, 1962-63; Chief of the Office of Economics, FOMEX, Bank of Mexico, 1963-64; office chief, INFRATUR, Bank of Mexico, 1968-72; Subdirector of the Foundation for the Promotion of Tourist Infrastructure (INFRATUR), Bank of Mexico, 1972-74; Manager of Planning and Economic Studies, National Finance Bank Fund, 1974-76; Manager of Projects of Baja California del Sur, National Fund for Tourism Development, 1976-77; Manager, Economic Analysis Section, Bank of Mexico, 1977-82; *Subsecretary*

of Planning, Secretary of Tourism, 1982-85; Director General of Trusts, Bank of Mexico, 1985-88; Director General of the Industrial Equipment Fund, Bank of Mexico, 1988-89. g-None. h-Researcher, banking costs, Bank of Commerce, 1961-62; economist, Division of Economic and Social Development, Inter-American Development Bank, 1966-67. i-Son of Rafael Dondé Gorozpe, civil engineer, and Julia Escalante Ortega; married Susana Mayer Romero, psychologist. j-None. k-None. l-Q es QAP, 395; DBGM, 124; DBGM87, 112; DBGM89, 102.

Dorado Baltázar, Emilia
a-Aug. 11, 1909. b-Guadalajara, Jalisco. c-Primary studies at the Three Friends School, Guadalajara, 1918-24; secondary studies, Normal School of Jalisco, Guadalajara, 1924-27; teaching certificate, Normal School of Jalisco, 1927-30; school teacher. d-*Federal Deputy* from the State of Jalisco, Dist. 3, 1970-73, member of the Social Action Committee (1st year), the Protocol Committee, the Sugar Industry Committee and the Social Welfare Committee (1st year). e-Member of the PPS. f-None. g-Member of the SNTE. i-Married León Fernandez Caudillo; daughter of Juan Dorado Albino and Martina Baltázar. j-None. k-None. l-C de D, 1970-72, 111; Directorio, 1970-72.

Dorantes Segovia, Luis José
a-Mar. 17, 1934. b-Tula de Allende, Hidalgo. c-Early education unknown; law degree, National School of Law, UNAM, 1955-59. d-*Federal Deputy* from the State of Hidalgo, Dist. 2, 1976-79; *Senator* from Hidalgo, 1982-88, President of the Social Welfare Committee, Secretary of the 1st Labor Committee. e-Secretary of Finances, National Youth of PRI, 1959-60. f-Tax auditor, Department of the Federal District, 1960-61; tax actuary, Depart-

ment of the Federal District, 1961-63; lawyer, Director General of Expenditures, Secretariat of the Treasury, 1963-77; lawyer, Director General of Credit, Secretariat of the Treasury, 1977-82. g-Founding member of the Revolutionary University Student Group, 1953; Secretary General of the Student Society of the National Preparatory School No. 1, 1954-55; Secretary of Relations, 1955 Law Generation, UNAM; Secretary of Labor and Conflicts, Local 15, National Union of Treasury Workers, 1966; Secretary General of Local 15, National Union of Treasury Workers, 1966-69; Secretary of Social Services, National Union of Treasury Workers, 1969-72; Secretary of Housing, FSTSE, 1971-73; Secretary General of the National Union of Treasury Employees, 1975-78; Secretary of Labor and Conflicts, FSTSE, 1977-80; *Secretary General of the FSTSE*, 1980-83. h-None. i-Son of Roberto Dorantes Benicia, industrialist, and Carmen Segovia Gómez. j-None. k-None. l-C de D, 1976-79; C de S, 1982-88; Lehr, 212; DBGM87, 465-66.

Dovalí Jaime, Antonio
(Deceased Nov. 11, 1981) a-Oct. 3, 1905. b-Zacatecas, Zacatecas. c-Preparatory studies at the National Preparatory School in Mexico City, 1920-23; engineering studies at the National School of Engineering, UNAM, 1924-28; engineering degree, UNAM, June 18, 1930; Professor of Engineering (Bridges) at the National School of Engineering, UNAM, 1937-67; Director of the National School of Engineering, UNAM, 1959-66; member of the Governing Council of UNAM; Professor of Bridges at the Military College, 1954. d-None. e-None. f-Resident Subdirector of Construction of the Calles Railroad, Tamaulipas, 1929; Subdirector General of Railroad Construction, Secretariat of Public Works,

1941-42; Director General of Railroad Construction, Secretariat of Public Works, 1943-48; *Subsecretary of Public Works*, 1949-52; Director of Construction for the Chihuahua-Pacific Railroad, 1952-58; Director of the National Institute of Petroleum, 1966-70; *Director General of Petróleos Mexicanos*, 1970-76. g-None. h-Engineer of six different projects for the National Highway Commission, 1930-36; construction engineer for the National Railroads of Mexico, 1936-38. i-Brother of Alberto Dovalí Jaime, a Mexican engineer who used innovative preformed concrete construction for public works projects; established numerous friendships during education at UNAM, including those with *Miguel Alemán, Antonio Carrillo Flores, Antonio Ortiz Mena, Raul López Sánchez, Adolfo Orive Alba, Angel Carvajal, Javier Barros Sierra, Alfonso Guzmán Neyra, Leopoldo Chávez, José Hernández Terán, Gilberto Valenzuela,* and *Luis E. Bracamontes*; son, Antonio Dovalí Ramos, was director general of planning, Department of the Federal District, 1978. j-None. k-None. l-*Hoy*, 23 Jan. 1971, 10; DGF47, 143; Enc. Mex., III, 304; letter; HA, 22 Mar. 1971, 25; DP70, 668; DGF50, II, 377, 389; *Excélsior*, 31 Oct. 1978, 16, 13 Nov. 1981, 38A; HA, 23 Nov. 1981, 18.

Duahlt Kraus, Miguel
a-Jan. 16, 1917. b-Córdoba, Veracruz. c-Early education unknown; law degree; courses in administration. d-None. e-None. f-Manager of Trade and Exports, UMPASA; Coordinator of Engineers, National Finance Bank; Manager, Administrative Division, CONASUPO; *Oficial Mayor of Industry and Commerce*, 1977-80; adviser to the Secretary of Public Education, 1982. g-None. h-Author of several technical works on administration. j-None. k-None. l-HA, 2 June, 1980; IEPES.

Ducoing Gamba, Luis Humberto
a-May 15, 1937. b-San Luis de la Paz, Guanajuato. c-Primary studies at the San Luis Rey School, San Luis de la Paz (4 years); secondary studies at the Querétaro Institute, Querétaro, the Internado México, Federal District and the Lux Institute, León, Guanajuato; preparatory studies at the León Preparatory School, León; law degree with a specialty in administrative appeal, University of Guanajuato, 1960; Professor of Mexican History, World History, and the Philosophy of History at the Preparatory School and University of Guanajuato, 1958-62. d-*Federal Deputy* from the State of Guanajuato, Dist. 6, 1964-67, member of the Bellas Artes Committee, the Sugar Industry Committee, and the First Instructive Section of the Grand Jury Committee; *Federal Deputy* from the State of Guanajuato, Dist. 9, 1970-73, Secretary of the Gran Comisión, member of the First Section (Constitutional) of the Legislative Studies Committee, the First Government Committee, and the First Constitutional Affairs Committee; *Governor of Guanajuato*, 1973-79. e-Youth Director of PRI, Guanajuato; Secretary General of PRI, Guanajuato; special delegate of PRI to the municipal elections of Romita and Comonfort, 1960; general delegate of the CEN of PRI to Aguascalientes, Guerrero and Veracruz; Auxiliary Secretary to *Luis Echeverría* during presidential campaign, 1969-70; *Secretary of Political Action of the CEN of PRI*, 1970-73. f-Public Defender, Guanajuato; labor inspector for Guanajuato. g-President of the 1956-60 generation of lawyers, University of Guanajuato; student leader at the León Preparatory School; special delegate of the CNC to Veracruz, Sonora and Nayarit; member of the National Committee of the CNC for Michoacán, Yucatán, Campeche and Quintana Roo; Private Secretary to the Secretary Gen-

eral of the CNC; Secretary of Education Action, CEN of the CNC; President of the Political Committee of the CNC, 1972. h-None. i-Married Martha Nieto; son of Luis Ducoing Media and Rebeca Gamba. j-None. k-Answered *Luis Echeverría*'s first State of the Union address, 1971. l-C de D, 1964-66, 79, 87, 89; Directorio, 1970-72; *Excélsior*, 27 Feb. 1973, 12; C de D, 1970-72, 111; HA, 24 Sept. 1973, 32, 34, 36; Enc. Mex., Annual, 1977, 544.

Dufoo López, Carlos
a-Nov. 4, 1912. b-Puebla, Puebla. c-Early education unknown; teaching certificate. d-*Federal Deputy* from the Federal District, Dist. 8, 1973-76; *Federal Deputy* from the Federal District, Dist. 1, 1979-82. e-None. f-President of the Cuauhtémoc Delegation Neighborhood Board, Mexico City. g-Secretary of Organization of the Truckdrivers Alliance; Oficial Mayor of the Truckdrivers Alliance; Secretary of Transportation of the CEN of CNOP. j-None. k-None. l-Protag., 106; C de D, 1979-82, 1973-76.

Dupré Ceniceros, Enrique
a-1913. b-Durango. c-Engineering degree, National School of Engineering, UNAM, 1932-36. d-*Federal Deputy* from the State of Durango, Dist. 2, 1952-55; member of the Committee on National Waters and Irrigation, the Committee on the Agrarian Department, and the Committee on Social Welfare; *Senator* from the State of Durango, 1958-62; member of the Gran Comisión, President of the Senate (1st year); President of the First Committee on Government; President of the Special Committee on Forests and member of the Second Committee on Ejidos; *Governor of Durango*, 1962-66. e-Inactive in PRI since 1967. f-Employed in the Department of Agrarian Affairs; regional coordinator of the Secretariat of Agriculture, 1978.

g-Member and official of the CNC.
h-Attended the Inter-American Conference on Conservation, Washington,
D.C., 1948; author of a pamphlet on
Mexican forest problems published by
the U.S. Department of State, 1949.
j-None. k-Resigned from the governorship, Aug. 4, 1966. l-G of M, 10; C de
D, 1952-54, 9; C de S, 1964, 55; Func.,
198; NYT, 6 Aug. 1966, 3; *Excélsior*, 14
Dec. 1978, 9.

Durán Solís, Leonel
a-Dec. 14, 1931. b-Federal District.
c-Early education unknown; legal studies, National School of Law, UNAM,
1952-54; studies in Anthropology,
National School of Anthropology and
History, UNAM, 1952-54, graduating
with a thesis on the social and economic characteristics of the Cuenca del
Río Balsas, 1967; postgraduate studies at
the École Pratique des Hautes Etudes de
L'Amerique Latine, University of Paris,
France, 1968-70; Assistant Researcher,
National Museum of Anthropology and
History, 1953-54. d-None. e-Joined
PRI, 1964. f-Researcher, National
Indigenous Institute, 1954-59; researcher, Río Balsas Commission, 1959-
61; anthropologist, Río Balsas Commission, Lázaro Cárdenas Steel Complex,
1962-73; Coordinator of Social Studies,
Río Balsas Commission, 1962-67;
anthropologist and Chief of Projects,
Department of Ethnology and Anthropology, National Institute of Anthropology and History, 1970-77; Subdirector of
Popular Cultures, Secretariat of Public
Education, 1978-81; *Subsecretary of
Culture and Recreation*, Secretariat of
Public Education, 1985-86; Director
General of the Center of Graduate Studies in Social Anthropology, Secretariat
of Public Education, 1986-88, 1988- .
g-None. h-None. i-Son of Raymundo
Longinos Durán, public official, and
María Solís Valles; married Silvia Ortiz
Echaníz, anthropologist. j-None.

k-None. l-HA, 18 Mar. 1985, 15-16; Q
es QAP, 311; DBGM, 127; DBGM87,
114; DBGM89, 103.

Dzib Cardozo, José de Jesús
a-Jan. 12, 1921. b-Campeche, Campeche. c-Preparatory studies at the
National Preparatory School in Mexico
City, 1940-44; law degree from the
National School of Law, UNAM;
studied French at the Alianza Francesa
in Mexico City; Professor of Law,
French, and Spanish Language and
Literature at the University of Campeche; Professor of Oceanography,
Meteorology, and Fishing Legislation,
Campeche Practical School of Fishing;
Professor of Spanish and Spanish
Literature, Women's University of
Veracruz; Rector of the University of
Campeche, 1961-62. d-None. e-Precandidate of PRI for senator from
Campeche, 1981. f-Private Secretary to
Rafael Matos Escobedo, Justice of the
Supreme Court of Mexico; Director of
the Office of Regulation and Administration of Goods and Chattels, Secretariat of National Patrimony; Director
of the Department for the Inspection of
Goods and Chattels, Secretariat of
National Patrimony; Agent of the
Ministerio Público (Auxiliary) of the
Attorney General of Mexico, 1962-64;
Secretary General of Government of the
State of Campeche under Governor
Trueba Urbina, 1955-61; Assistant
Attorney General of the Federal District
and Federal Territories (2), 1964-70,
and 1970-76. g-None. h-Author of
several articles; librarian during student
days in the Department of Social
Action, Department of the Federal
District. i-Father of *Jorge Dzib Sotelo*,
federal deputy from Campeche, Dist. 1,
1982-85; married Xenio Sotelo. j-None.
k-None. l-DPE70, 162; DBM68, 206;
letter; DGF56, 90; *Excélsior*, 26 Dec.
1981, 16A; Directorio, 1982-85.

E

Echeverría Alvarez, Luis

a-Jan. 17, 1922. b-Federal District. c-Primary studies in Mexico City (grades 1-3); 4th grade at the "Pen" Institute, Ciudad Victoria, Tamaulipas; 5th and 6th grades at Lauro Aguirre School, Ciudad Victoria; secondary in Mexico City; preparatory at the National Preparatory School, 1938-40; special studies in Chile, Argentina, Paris, and the United States on a scholarship, 1941; law studies from the National School of Law, UNAM, 1940-44; law degree, Aug. 1945, with a thesis on "The Balance of Power System and the Society of Nations"; Professor of Legal Theory at the National School of Law, UNAM, 1947-49. d-*President of Mexico*, 1970-76. e-Joined PRI in March 1946; Private Secretary to the President of the National Executive Committee of PRI, *Rodolfo Sánchez Taboada*, Dec. 1946; Assistant Secretary to the Regional Director of PRI for the Federal District, *Rodolfo Sánchez Taboada*, Mar. to Dec. 1946; Platform Adviser to PRI, 1946; *Secretary of Press and Publicity of the CEN of PRI*, 1946-52; General Delegate of the CEN of PRI, 1948; President of the Regional Committee of the State of Guanajuato; Representative of the CEN of PRI to *Salvador Sánchez Colín*'s campaign for governor of México, 1951; *Oficial Mayor of PRI*, 1957-58. f-Director of Accounts for the Secretariat of the Navy, 1952-54; *Oficial Mayor of the Secretariat of Public Education*, 1954-57; *Subsecretary of Government*, 1958-63; *Subsecretary in Charge of the Secretariat of Government*, 1964; *Secretary of Government*, 1964-70; Ambassador to UNESCO, 1977-78, to Australia, 1978-79, at large, 1979. g-Student delegate to the Free World Youth Association, 1943; founder of Students for Revolutionary Action, 1947. h-None. i-Son of Rodolfo Echeverría Gayou, army paymaster, and Catalina Alvarez Gayou; brother, Eduardo, was a member of the Advisory Council of the IEPES of PRI and President of the Technical Council of the Subsecretary of Public Health, 1974; brother, *Rodolfo*, was Director General of the National Cinema Bank; nephew, *Rodolfo Echeverría Jr.*, was Oficial Mayor of PRI and a Federal Deputy; son, Rodolfo, was Director of Industrial Development of the Secretariat of Agriculture at the time of his death in 1983; political disciple of *Rodolfo Sánchez Taboada*, who commanded the forces where Echeverría's father worked; studied under *Alfonso Noriega* and *Luis Garrido Díaz* at the National University; knew *Luis M. Farías* as a student at UNAM; son-in-law of José Zuno Hernández, former governor of Jalisco. j-None. k-Delivered the nomination speech for *Adolfo López Mateos* before PRI, Nov. 17, 1957. l-Enc. Mex., III, 354; DPE65, 13; G of S, 14; Fuentes Díaz, 265; DGF56, 299; WWMG, 15; DBM70, 191; HA, 17 Dec. 1964, 18; DPE61, 11; Morton, 93; LA, 27 Oct. 1978, 330; *Excélsior*, 18 Feb. 1977, 6, 30 Apr. 1983, 1; letters; HA, 26 Jan. 1988, 45.

Echeverría Alvarez, Rodolfo

a-Sept. 24, 1917. b-Federal District. c-Law degree from the Escuela Libre de Derecho, Oct. 4, 1940, with a thesis on the intervention of the state in the functions of credit institutions; law degree from the National School of Law, UNAM, 1944. d-*Federal Deputy* from the Federal District, Dist. 18, 1952-55, Vice-President of the Chamber of Deputies, Oct. 1953, member of the First Labor Committee, the Second Balloting Committee, the Film Industry Committee, and the Committee on Bellas Artes (3 years); substitute member of the Radio and Television Industry Committee; *Federal Deputy* from the Federal District, Dist. 6, 1961-64, President of the Chamber of Deputies, member of the Fifth Section of the Legislative Studies Committee (Labor), the Film Industry Committee; substitute member of the First Constitutional Affairs Committee; *Alternate Senator* for the Federal District, 1964-70. e-Member of the Advisory Council for Ideology and Program of the IEPES of PRI, 1972. f-Director General of the National Cinema Bank, 1970-76; Private Secretary to *Ernesto P. Uruchurtu.* g-Director General of the Mexican Actors Union. h-Professional actor, worked under the name Rodolfo Landa; cofounder of the University Theater at UNAM. i-Brother of President *Luis Echeverría*; father of *Rodolfo Echeverría Jr.,* oficial mayor of PRI; student of *Alfonso Noriega* at UNAM; father, Rodolfo Echeverría Esparza, a government employee; married Avelina Ruiz Vázquez; son of Rodolfo Echeverría Esparza and Catalina Alvarez Gayou. j-None. k-None. l-C de D, 1954, 9, 1961-63, 76; G of Nl, 17; DBM68, 368; letter; *Excélsior,* 16 Mar. 1973, 22.

Echeverría Castellot, Eugenio
a-Nov. 19, 1924. b-Ciudad del Carmen, Campeche. c-Primary studies at the Technical, Industrial, and Business School No. 22, Campeche; secondary and preparatory at Vocational School Nos. 1 & 2, National Polytechnic Institute; degree in petroleum engineering, National Polytechnic Institute, 1947, with a thesis on the "Cost of Building a Petroleum Pipeline from the Teapa, Tabasco, Oil Fields to Campeche." d-Mayor of Campeche, 1959-61; *Governor of Campeche,* 1979-85. e-Joined PRI, 1957. f-Began governmental career, 1947; Director of Public Works for the State of Campeche, 1951-57. g-None. h-None. i-Distinguished student of *María Lavalle Urbina*; student suppor-

ter of *Carlos Sansores Pérez* when the latter was president of the Campeche Student Federation; *Rafael Rodríguez Barrera*, Governor of Campeche, 1973-79, was Private Secretary to Echeverría Castellot as mayor of Campeche. j-None. k-Precandidate for governor of Campeche, 1961 and 1967. l-*Excélsior,* 19 Dec. 1978, 22; *Latin America,* 26 Jan. 1979, 30; *Excélsior,* 6 Jan. 1979, 1, 11; Almanaque de México, 324.

Echeverría Ruiz Jr., Rodolfo
a-June 19, 1946. b-Federal District. c-Law degree from the National School of Law, UNAM; postgraduate work in the fields of politics and economics, London, England; professor, Higher War College, 1976-77. d-*Federal Deputy* from the Federal District, Dist. 24, 1973-76. e-Joined PRI, 1961; Director of the Youth Section for the sixth electoral district of the Federal District of PRI; Secretary of Social Action of Youth of PRI for the Federal District; Director of the Youth Section of PRI for the Federal District; official orator for the *Díaz Ordaz* campaign, 1964; Auxiliary Secretary to the National Executive Committee of PRI attached to the IEPES, 1969-70; *Director of the National Youth Sector of the CEN of PRI,* 1965; *Oficial Mayor of PRI,* 1970-76. f-Representative of the State of Hidalgo in Mexico City, 1969-70; Secretary to Senator *Sánchez Vite* on the Federal Electoral Commission; Coordinating Secretary of the Gran Comisión of the Senate; *Subsecretary of Government (2),* 1976-78; *Subsecretary of Labor,* 1978-81; *Ambassador to Cuba,* 1982-85; Technical Subdirector of Pemex, 1985-87; Secretary General of Metropolitan Coordination, Department of the Federal District. g-None. h-Second place award for oratory, 1963. i-Son of *Rodolfo Echeverría Alvarez* and Avelina Ruiz; nephew of *Luis Echeverría;* married María de los Angeles Andrade, psycho-

logist. j-None. k-None. l-HA, 21 Dec. 1970, 21; G of NL, 17; *Excélsior*, 28 Feb. 1973, 19, 16 Mar. 1973, 22, 21 July 1973, 12; DBGM89, 105; DBGM, 128.

Elías Ayub, Alfredo
a-Jan. 13, 1950. b-Federal District. c-Primary studies at the Colegio México, 1956-62; secondary and preparatory studies at the Colegio México, 1962-68; civil engineering degree, School of Engineering, Anáhuac University, 1968-73; MA in business administration, Harvard University, 1973-75. d-None. e-None. f-Director General of Coordination and Programs, National Fund for Social Activities (FONAPAS), 1977-79; Subdirector General of the National Fund for Social Activities, 1980-81; Director General of FONAPAS, 1981-83; Executive Coordinator, Secretariat of Urban Development and Public Works, 1983-85; Private Secretary to the Governor of México, *Alfredo del Mazo*, 1985-86; Private Secretary to the Secretary of Mines, Energy and Government Industries, *Alfredo del Mazo*, 1986; Coordinator of Advisers, Secretariat of Mines, Energy and Government Industries, 1986-88; *Subsecretary of Mines and Basic Industries*, Secretariat of Mines, Energy and Government Industries, 1988- . g-None. h-None. i-Son of Alfredo Elías Aiza, businessman, and Silvia Ayub Kuri; married Amelia Urdaneta Casas; student at Harvard University at the same time as *Carlos Salinas Gortari*. j-None. k-None. l-DBGM89, 106; letter.

Elías Calles (Alvarez), Fernando
a-May 30, 1940. b-Hermosillo, Sonora. c-Early education unknown; law degree, National School of Law, UNAM, with a thesis on "Foreign Investment in Mexico"; Professor of Constitutional Law, National School of Political Studies, Acatlán, UNAM, 1975-81. d-*Federal Deputy* from the State of Sonora, Dist.

3, 1973-76, Secretary of the Chamber of Deputies, 1975. e-Joined PRI, 1959; Secretary of Youth Action of the CEN of PRI, 1959-61; Auxiliary Secretary of the President of the CEN of PRI, *Alfonso Corona del Rosal*, 1961-64; Private Secretary to the Secretary General of the CEN of PRI, *Enrique Olivares Santana*, 1969-70; Delegate of the CEN of PRI to San Luis Potosí, 1968-69, Querétaro, 1968-69, Quintana Roo, 1974-75, Aguascalientes, 1972-73, Jalisco, Tamaulipas, 1968-69, and Campeche, 1975-76; Administrative Director of the CEN of PRI, 1966-68. f-Chief of Planning of the Division of Standards, Secretariat of Industry and Commerce, 1960-61; Chief of Auditors, Secretariat of Government Properties, 1964-66; Director of Delegates, Secretariat of Public Education, 1978-82; Director General of Government, Secretariat of Government, 1983-85; *Subsecretary of Government*, Secretariat of Government, 1985-88; *Subsecretary of Educational Coordination*, Secretariat of Public Education, 1988-92; Director General of the National Free Textbook Commission, 1992-94. g-Coordinating Secretary of State Federations of CNOP, 1975-76. h-None. i-Son of Alfredo Elías Calles Chacón, rancher, and Elena Alvarez Murphy; married Patricia Romo Quevedo; nephew of Plutarco Elías Calles Chacón Jr., federal deputy, 1930-32, 1934-37; nephew of Rodolfo Elías Calles, secretary of commerce, 1934-35; grandson of president Plutarco Elías Calles, 1924-28. j-None. k-None. l-DBGM, 130; DBGM89, 106; DBGM92, 113; C de D, 1973-76; HA, 21 Jan. 1985, 16.

Elizondo (Lozano), Eduardo Angel
a-Dec. 7, 1922. b-Monterrey, Nuevo León. c-Primary studies at the Colegio Justo Sierra, the Colegio Monterrey and the Colegio Félix Escamilla, 1928-34, Monterrey; secondary studies from Secondary No. 1, 1934-37; preparatory

studies at the Colegio Civil, Monterrey, 1937-39; law degree from the University of Nuevo León, 1945; professor at the University of Nuevo León, 1945-50; professor at the Institute of Technology and of Higher Education, Monterrey; Rector of the University of Nuevo León, 1965-67. d-*Governor of Nuevo León*, 1967-70. e-None. f-Agent of the Ministerio Publico, 1945-46; public defender, 1944; Treasurer General of the State of Nuevo León, 1961-65; Judge of the Superior Tribunal of Justice of the State of Nuevo León, 1973-74. g-None. h-Adviser to various industries in the field of taxation, 1945-67; practicing lawyer in the firm of Santos de la Garza, 1950; President of the Regional Banks of the North (Garza-Sada chain); President of Argon of Monterrey and Productores Oxigena; member of the board of many banks, including Banco Mercantil de Monterrey. i-Father, Eduardo Elizondo González, was an accountant and banker. j-None. k-Resigned from the governorship of Nuevo León after students rioted in opposition to his choice of rector of the University of Nuevo León; son-in-law of Manuel L. Barragán, major entrepreneurial figure. l-PdM, 104; DBM68, 212-13; DBM70, 195; G of NL, 15; *Excélsior*, 12 Jan. 1973, 28, 24 Feb. 1967, 16; letter.

Elizondo, Juan Manuel
a-1905. b-Monterrey, Nuevo León. c-Primary studies in Monterrey; law student at UNAM, 1930s, but did not complete his studies. d-*Senator* from Nuevo León, 1946-52, member of the First Balloting Group, the Second Labor Committee, and the Immigration Committee, alternate member of the Social Welfare Committee; *Plurino-minal Federal Deputy* from PPS, 1979-82. e-One-time member of the Mexican Communist Party; member of the Executive Committee of the Popular Party (later the PPS), 1947. f-Delegate

from Mexico to the International Labor Organization conference; adviser to the Mexican Labor delegation in Geneva, 1947. g-Secretary General of the Union of Metallurgical Miners. i-Friend of *Vicente Lombardo Toledano*; father, a local politician in Monterrey. j-None. k-Tried to introduce agricultural reforms as a senator, but opposed openly by *Rodolfo Sánchez Taboada*, president of the CEN of PRI, 1946-52; expelled from PRI in Jan. 1946 for joining the Popular Party. l-*Excélsior*, 17 Nov. 1949; DGF47, 21; DGF51, 7, 13, 14; Morton, 59-60; C de S, 1946-52, 36; HA, 10 Oct. 1947, 5; *Excélsior*, 16 Nov. 1974, 9; letter; *Excélsior*, 15 Apr. 1979, 16; Medina, 20, 138.

Elorduy (García), Aquiles
(Deceased Aug. 5, 1964) a-Sept. 20, 1875. b-Aguascalientes, Aguascalientes. c-Primary studies at the Liceo Fournier, Sombrerete, Zacatecas; secondary studies at the Colegio Franco-Español, Mexico City; preparatory at the National Preparatory School; law degree from the National School of Law, UNAM, Sept. 28, 1903; professor at the National School of Law, UNAM; Director of the National School of Law, UNAM, 1925, 1927-29. d-Federal Deputy from the State of Zacatecas, Dist. 4, when the Chamber was dissolved by Victoriano Huerta, 1912-14; Local Deputy to the state legislature of Zacatecas; *Federal Deputy* from the State of Aguascalientes, Dist. 1, 1946-49, member of the Committee on the Diplomatic Service; *Senator* from the State of Aguascalientes, 1952-58, member of the Second Committee on Justice and the Second Group of the Balloting Committee, and substitute member of the Colonization Committee and the First Committee on Tariffs and Foreign Trade. e-One of the few Mexican congressmen to be elected to the Congress on different party tickets,

having been the candidate of the PAN as federal deputy and candidate of the PRI as senator; joined PAN, 1940; founder of the anti-reelectionist center in Mexico City, 1909. f-Delegate to the Sixth Pan American Conference in Havana, Cuba, 1928. g-None. h-Wrote for *Siempre* and *Excélsior*, author of a three-act comedy, 1931; founder of the magazine *La Reacción*. i-Student of Justo Sierra; professor and friend of many prominent political leaders, including *Miguel Alemán, Mariano Ramírez Vázquez, Antonio Carrillo Flores*, and *Alejandro Gómez Arias*. j-None. k-Donated salaries as a federal deputy and senator to the school system in Aguascalientes. l-WWM45, 36; C de D, 1946-48, 71; DGF56, 9, 10, 11, 13; DP70, 700; Enc. Mex., III, 417; Morton, 54-56, 73-75; HA, 26 Sept. 1976, 25.

Encinas Johnson, Luis
a-Oct. 23, 1912. b-Hermosillo, Sonora. c-Teaching certificate, 1922; law degree from the National School of Law, UNAM, June, 1935; Rector of the University of Sonora, 1956-61. d-Local Deputy to the state legislature of Sonora, 1956; Mayor of Ciudad Obregón, Sonora; *Governor of Sonora*, 1961-67. e-President of the Regional Committee of PRM for the State of Sonora. f-Director of the State Department of Labor, State of Sonora; Deputy Prosecuting Attorney for the State of Sonora; Attorney General of Sonora; Justice of the Superior Tribunal of Justice of Sonora; Secretary General of Government of the State of Sonora under Governor *Ignacio Soto*, 1950-55; member of the Federal Board of Conciliation and Arbitration for the Federal District; Director General of the National Bank of Agricultural Credit, 1970-75. g-None. h-Practicing attorney, 1967-70; author of several books on political and social problems in Mexico. i-Father, Luis Encinas, was Mayor of

Hermosillo, 1921-22; married Lourdes González. j-None. k-Retired from public life midway during his career because of health; defeated Fausto Acosta Romo for the PRI gubernatorial nomination, 1967; *Proceso* accused him of representing the interests of large landowners in Sonora. l-G of S, 23; DGF56, 100; HA, 14 Dec. 1970, 25; Tucker, 429; WWMG, 16; letter; Anderson, 112-13; HA, 29 Apr. 1974, 13; NYT, 24 Mar. 1967, 2; NYT, 27 Mar. 1967, 8; *Excélsior*, 11 Jan. 1975, 1; *Proceso*, 7 Aug. 1978, 17; Moncada, 12ff.

Enríquez Coyro Jr., Ernesto
a-Nov. 29, 1901. b-Federal District. c-Primary studies in Mexico City; secondary studies at the Technical Institute in Mexico City; attended the University of Cataluña; Bachelor of Science from the University of Barcelona, Spain, 1918; studied law at the Escuela Libre de Derecho, 1919-24, graduating Nov. 8, 1924, with a thesis on the state of labor; Professor of Music History and of Aesthetics at UNAM, 1931-44; Professor of International Public Law at the National School of Law, UNAM, 1941-50; participated in organizing the new faculty of music at the UNAM, 1930; founder and Director of the School of Political and Social Sciences, UNAM, 1950-52; Professor of the History of Political Ideas, 1961. d-None. e-None. f-Consultant to the Diplomatic Department of the Secretariat of Foreign Relations, 1938-40; adviser to the Secretary of Public Education; Head of the Department of Legal Affairs of the Secretariat of Foreign Relations, 1941-45; *Oficial Mayor of the Secretariat of Public Education*, 1945-46; Director of Administrative Inspection of the Secretariat of National Patrimony; in charge of the reorganization of the Secretariat of National Patrimony, 1950; Subdirector (Administrative) of the Mexican

Institute of Social Security, 1952-58; *Subsecretary of Public Education*, 1958-64. g-None. h-Private law practice, 1925-40; represented Mexico at various international conferences; assistant agent for the Mexican-United States Claims Commission, 1935-38; author of many books on international law and on Mexico. i-Attended the Escuela Libre de Derecho with *Javier Gaxiola* and *José Angel Ceniceros*; practiced law with *Ceniceros*, who helped him obtain his first job as an agent for the Mexican–United States Claims Commission; grandfather was governor of México and a senator under Porfirio Díaz; served in various positions under *Jaime Torres Bodet*; father, Ernesto Enríquez, a lawyer; married Alejandrina Rubio; father of *Ernesto Enríquez Rubio*, subsecretary of agriculture, 1990. j-None. k-None. l-Letter; HA, 22 Dec. 1958, 7; D de Y, 3 Dec. 1958, 10; Peral, 244; DGF47, 269; WWM45, 37; DBM68, 215-16; DBM70, 196-97; ELD, 57.

Enríquez (Rodríguez), Enríque A.
(Deceased Mar. 22, 1974) a-July 15, 1887. b-Toluca, México. c-Primary studies at the Annex to the Normal School, Toluca; preparatory studies at the Scientific and Literary Institute of México, Toluca; law degree from the National School of Law, UNAM, Nov. 8, 1913; Professor of Law at the Scientific and Literary Institute of México, Toluca (nineteen years); Director of the Scientific and Literary Institute of México, 1923-25. d-Local Deputy to the State Legislature of México; Deputy to the Constitutional Convention from the State of México, Dist. No. 14, 1916-17; Federal Deputy from the State of México, Dist. 1, 1926-28. e-None. f-Secretary of the Mexican legation to Colombia and Uruguay; Chargé d'Affaires of the Mexican Embassy in Argentina; Agent of the Ministerio Público; Minister to Costa Rica; Justice of the

Superior Court of the Federal District and Federal Territories, 1956. g-Delegate of the School of Law at the first National Student Congress, Mexico City, 1910. h-None. i-Married María de Jesús Escallón; son of Valente Enríquez, a lawyer, and Mercedes Rodríguez. j-Career army officer; fought in the Army of the Northwest, 1914-16; rank of Captain, 1914; rank of Colonel, 1916; military judge; reached rank of Brigadier General, 1947; retired 1957; member of the Legion of Honor. k-None. l-HA, 1 Apr. 1974; DGF56, 514.

Enríquez Rubio, Ernesto
a-Aug. 8, 1945. b-Federal District. c-Primary studies at the Instituto Alonso de la Veracruz, Mexico City, 1952-57; secondary studies, 1958-60; preparatory studies, Colegio Alemán, Mexico City, 1961-62; law degree, Free School of Law, 1963-67, with a thesis on "A Legal Point for Economic Integration in Latin America," degree in business administration from Autonomous Technological Institute of Mexico, 1964-67; MA in international relations, University of the Americas, 1968; MA in government, American University, 1969-71; postgraduate work in public finance, UNAM, 1971-72; postgraduate work in planning and systems engineering, La Salle University, 1978; professor at the Escuela Libre de Derecho and the Institute of Public Administration, 1972-76. d-None. e-None. f-Director of Small and Medium Institutional Units, Bank of Mexico, 1972; Chief of Financial Advisers, Bank of Mexico, 1972-73; Subdirector of Official Negotiations, Bank of Mexico, 1973-74; Subdirector of the Development Banks Division, Bank of Mexico, 1974-78; Assistant Director of the Mexican Institute of Foreign Trade, 1979-80; *Oficial Mayor of the Secretariat of Agriculture*, 1982-84; Executive Director, SOMEX, 1985; Subdirector General, National Railroads

of Mexico, 1986-88; *Subsecretary of Livestock*, Secretariat of Agriculture and Hydraulic Resources, 1988-90; *Subsecretary of Agriculture*, Secretariat of Agriculture and Hydraulic Resources, 1990- . g-None. h-None. i-Son of *Ernesto Enríquez Coyro*, subsecretary of education, 1958, and Alejandrina Rubio Vivanco. j-None. k-None. l-Q es QAP, 214; DBGM92, 113.

Enríquez Savignac, Antonio
a-Aug. 17, 1931. b-Federal District. c-Preparatory studies, Colegio Americano, Mexico City; degree in business administration from Ottawa University, June 5, 1955; MBA degree, Graduate School of Business Administration, Harvard University, June 1957; studies on a Bank of Mexico Fellowship. d-None. e-Joined PRI, 1969. f-Subdirector, Department of Economic Studies, Bank of Commerce, 1955; divisional manager, Bank of Mexico; adviser to the Director General of the Bank of Mexico, 1964-73; Director of Industrial Development, Bank of Mexico, 1967-69; Director General of the National Foundation for the Development of Tourism, (FONATUR) 1969-76; *Subsecretary of Tourism and Planning*, 1976-77; *Subdirector General of Finances*, PEMEX, 1981-82; *Subsecretary of the Treasury*, 1982; *Secretary of Tourism*, 1982-88. g-None. h-Subdirector of Public Relations, American Smelting, New York, 1957-60; Director of Research and Marketing, Young and Rubicon, S.A., 1960; loan officer, Inter-American Development Bank, Washington, D.C., 1960-63. i-Son of Manuel Enríquez Simoní, publicist, and Cecelia Savignac; son Juan Enríquez Cabot was director general in the Department of the Federal District, 1989; married Marjorie Cabot Lewis, of the Cabot Lodge family in Boston; attended Harvard at the same time as *Miguel de la Madrid*. j-None. k-None. l-BdM,

108; HA, 14 Nov. 1977, 22; *News*, 2 Dec. 1982, 8; *Excélsior*, 1 Dec. 1982, 34A; DBGM, 131; DBGM87, 117.

Escobar Muñóz, Ernesto
(Deceased) a-1902. b-Federal District. c-Primary studies in Mexico City; law degree from the National School of Law, UNAM, 1928-32. d-*Governor of Morelos*, 1946-52. e-None. f-Secretary General of Government of the State of Morelos, 1942-46, under Governor *Jesús Castillo López*. g-None. h-Practicing lawyer. i-Classmate at UNAM of *Jesús Castillo López*; classmate of *Fausto Galván Campos*, his Secretary General and Senator from Morelos. j-None. k-None. l-Letters; DGF51, 90; López, 320.

Escofet Artigas, Alberto
a-Nov. 9, 1933. b-Barcelona, Spain. c-Early education unknown; electrical engineering degree, National School of Engineering, UNAM, 1951-55, with a thesis on "Nondestructive Dielectrical Proofs," 1956. d-None. e-None. f-Director of the Technical Office, Laboratory Department, Federal Electric Commission, 1956-59; Electrical Superintendent, Northeast Division, Federal Electric Commission, 1959-60; Director of the Office of Electrical Engineering, Federal Electric Commission, 1961-63; founder and Director of Systems Operations, Federal Electric Commission, 1963-70; Director, Department of Engineering Systems, Federal Electric Commission, 1970; Subdirector of Programs and Control, Federal Electric Commission, 1971-72; Subdirector General of Production, Federal Electric Commission, 1973-74; Subdirector General of Operations, Federal Electric Commission, 1977-80; *Director General of the Federal Electric Commission*, 1980-82; Director General of URAMEX, 1982-83; *Subsecretary of Mines*, Secretariat of Energy, Mines, and

Government Industries, 1987-88; *Subsecretary of Energy*, 1988-91. g-None. h-Technical Subdirector of Applied International Techniques, S.A., 1974; adviser to the executive secretariat of the National Engineering Commission, 1975-76. i-Son of José Escofet Andréu, businessman, and Josefa Artigas Font; married María Eugenia Cedeño Blanquet, pharmacologist. j-None. k-First technician in the electrical industry to head the Federal Electric Commission. l-HA, 21 July 1980, 25; Almanaque de México, 43; Q es QAP, 529; Protag., 111; HA, 11 Apr. 1987, 30.

Escudero Alvarez, Hiram
a-Oct. 11, 1935. b-Morelia, Michoacán. c-Primary studies at the Instituto Patria, Federal District, 1943-49; secondary and preparatory studies, Instituto Patria, 1949-51, 1951-53; studied at the School of Philosophy, UNAM, 1953-55; studied law at Escuela Libre de Derecho, 1954-58, degree in 1960 with his thesis on "The Confession in Criminal Cases"; graduate studies in psychology; Professor of Penal Law. d-*Alternate Federal Deputy* from the Federal District, Dist. 2, 1964-67; *Federal Deputy* (Party Deputy for PAN), 1970-73, member of the Cultural Affairs Committee; the Legislative Studies Committee (Seventh Section on Commerce and Credit), and the Small Agricultural Properties Committee; *Plurinominal Deputy* from PAN, 1979-82. e-Member of PAN; President of the National Youth Section of PAN. f-None. g-None. h-Practicing lawyer specializing in banking matters; fluent in English. i-Father, an engineer; married Silvia Mendoza. j-None. k-None. l-C de D, 1970-72, 14; Directorio, 1970-72; DJBM, 41.

Esparza Reyes, J. Refugio
a-Aug. 23, 1921. b-Villa Juárez, Aguascalientes. c-Early education unknown; graduate of the Normal School of San

Marcos, Zacatecas, 1938-43; advanced studies at the Higher Normal School in technical education; rural school teacher for many years; professor at the Normal School of San Marcos; Director of Rural Boarding School students. d-Local Deputy to the State Legislature of Aguascalientes, 1962; *Federal Deputy* from the State of Aguascalientes, Dist. 2, 1967-70, member of the First Balloting Committee; *Governor of Aguascalientes*, 1974-80. e-Secretary General of PRI for the State of Aguascalientes, 1962-68. f-Private Secretary to *Augusto Gómez Villanueva*, secretary general of the CNC, 1968-70; *Oficial Mayor of the Department of Agrarian Affairs and Colonization*, 1970-74. g-Secretary of the Third Delegation of Local 1 of the SNTE, 1946-48; Secretary of Social Action of Local 1, SNTE, 1948-50; Secretary General of Local 1, SNTE, 1950-52; Secretary of the National Inspection Committee, SNTE, 1966-68; President of the Political Committee of the SNTE, 1963-65; member of the Executive Council of the SNTE, 1970-74. h-None. i-Parents were peasants. j-None. k-None. l-C de D, 1967-69, 77; *Excélsior*, 30 Jan. 1974, 1; HA, 11 Feb. 1974, 38; MGF69, 89; HA, 21 Dec. 1970, 24; *Excélsior*, 17 July, 1978, 1, 18-20; Enc. Mex., Annual, 1977.

Esperón, Roberto
a-1957. b-Puebla, Puebla. c-Primary and secondary studies; studies in the technical science of information; preparatory school teacher. d-None. e-Joined the Socialist Workers Party, 1974; Director of *El Insurgente Socialista* (official PST paper); Information, Political Education, and Publicity Secretary of the Executive Committee of the PST; President of the National Committee of Electoral Affairs of the Executive Committee of the PST, 1979; member of the Central Committee of the Executive Committee of the PST,

1979. f-None. g-None. h-Journalist; editorial writer for *Excélsior*. j-None. k-None. l-HA, 30 Apr. 1979, IX.

Espino de la O., Everardo
a-Aug. 5, 1938. b-Chihuahua, Chihuahua. c-Early education unknown; law degree from the National School of Law, UNAM; MA in economics and public administration, Harvard University. d-None. e-Subdirector of the IEPES of the CEN of PRI, 1975-76, under *Julio Rodolfo Moctezuma Cid*. f-Official of the International Monetary Fund; Subdirector of Finances, PEMEX; Subdirector of Credit, Secretariat of the Treasury; Adviser to the National Sugar Commission and to the Secretariat of the Treasury; Director General of the National Rural Credit Bank, 1976-82. g-None. i-Brother, Francisco, an industrialist; son of Francisco Espino Baca and María de la O. j-None. k-Precandidate for senator from Chihuahua, 1981; convicted of fraud, 1983. l-*Excélsior*, 1 Dec. 1976, 17 May 1983, 5A; DBM66, 220.

Espinosa de los Monteros, Antonio
(Deceased Sept. 19, 1959) a-Jan. 15, 1903. b-Sinaloa. c-Preparatory at Gettysburg Academy, Pennsylvania; Sacred Heart College, Denver, Colorado; Bachelor of Science from Gettysburg College, 1925; MA from Harvard University, 1927; Professor of Economics, 1927-31; professor at the National University, 1929-34. d-None. e-None. f-Head of the Economics Library and Archives, Secretariat of the Treasury, 1929-30; Head of the Department of Alcohol for the Secretariat of the Treasury, 1931-32; Chief of the Department of Economic Studies for the Secretariat of Industry and Commerce, 1933-36; Manager of Nacional Financiera; *Director General of the National Finance Bank*, 1935-40 and 1940-45; *Subsecretary of the Treasury*, 1940;

Ambassador to the United States, 1945-48. g-None. h-Economist, Secretariat of the Treasury, 1927-28; economist, Bureau of Statistics, 1928-29, 1932-33; one of the founders of Nacional Financiera; major investor in Altos Hornos, 1947; important investor with Monterrey industrialists, 1940s; one of the founders of the National School of Economics, UNAM; author of several books. i-Father a druggist; roomed together at Harvard with *Daniel Cosío Villegas*; close friend of *Jesús Silva Herzog*. j-None. k-Director of General *Henríquez Guzmán*'s campaign for president of Mexico, 1951-52. l-WWM45, 37-38; DP731; HA, 21 Sept. 1945, 6; Enc. Mex., III, 532; Novo, 652; NYT, 9 Sept. 1940, 5, 29 Dec. 1948, 9, 15 July 1944, 11; López, 326; Alonso, 227, 231, 167-68.

Espinosa de los Reyes Sánchez, Jorge
a-June 20, 1920. b-Federal District. c-Economics degree from the National School of Economics, UNAM, 1940-44; London School of Economics, 1945-47; Professor of Economics at Mexico City College, 1948-49, 1952-53, at UNAM, 1949, 1951-55, at the Autonomous Technological Institute of Mexico, 1953-54; professor at CEMLA, 1954-59. d-None. e-None. f-Subchief of the Department of Credit in the National Bank of Agricultural Credit, 1953-54; Program Director for the National Investment Commission, 1954-58; Subdirector of the Investment Commission for the Secretariat of the Presidency, 1958-59; Director General of Industries, 1959-61; *Oficial Mayor of the Secretariat of Industry and Commerce*, 1961-64; *Subdirector of Petroleos Mexicanos*, 1965-70, 1971-76; Subdirector General of the Bank of Mexico (2), 1976-77; *Director General of the National Finance Bank*, 1977-82; *Ambassador to the United States*, 1982-88. g-None. h-Assistant Economist, Bank of Mexico,

1942-44; economist for the Department of Economic Statistics, Bank of Mexico, 1947-48; economist and investigator for the Department of Financial Studies, Nacional Financiera, 1948-51. i-Friend of *Octaviano Campos Salas, Alfredo Navarrete,* and *Julián Díaz Arias* at the National School of Economics; brother of *Mario Espinosa de los Reyes;* married Sofia Dávila; son of Isidro Espinosa de los Reyes, physician, and Amparo Sánchez; son, Jorge, was director general of Development Banks, Secretariat of the Treasury, 1988. j-None. k-None. l-Enc. Mex., III, 532; HA, 4 Jan. 1965, 27; letters; DPE61, 66; BdeM, 115; WWMG, 16; DGF56, 59; DGF69; *Excélsior,* 24 Nov. 1977, 15, 23 Dec. 1982, 10A; DBGM89, 109.

Espinosa Gutiérrez, Fernando
(Deceased Apr. 3, 1966) a-Nov. 10, 1919. b-Querétaro, Querétaro. c-Primary and secondary studies in Querétaro, Querétaro; preparatory studies at the National Preparatory School, 1936-37; civil engineering degree from the National School of Engineering, UNAM, 1942; studies toward an MA in mathematics, 1942; Professor of Laboratory Physics, National Preparatory School, 1938-42; Professor of Trigonometry, Analytical Geometry, and Calculus, National Preparatory School, 1940-44; professor at the School of Engineering, UNAM, 1943-48; Professor of Mechanics and Fluids, School of Engineering, UNAM, 1944. d-*Alternate Senator* from the State of Querétaro, 1964. e-None. f-Engineer, Office of Experimental Engineering, National Irrigation Commission, 1942-44; Director General of Highways, Secretariat of Public Works, 1953; Technical Adviser to the Subsecretary of Public Works, 1954-55; Director of Technical Advisers, Secretariat of Public Works, 1956-58; Director General of Projects and Laboratories, Secretariat of Public

Works, 1959-64; *Subsecretary of Public Works,* Dec. 23, 1964, to 1966. g-None. h-Engineer, Director of Construction, Manager of Roads, Bridges, and Railroads for Ingenieros Civiles, S.A., 1944-53. i-Friend of *Javier Barros Sierra* and *Fernando Hiriart Balderama* at UNAM; son Enrique Espinosa worked for the Bank of Mexico. j-None. k-None. l-Letter; HA, 4 Jan. 1965, 7; *Libro de Oro,* xxiv; DPE65, 116; DPE61, 84; MGF69, 106; WWMG. 16; DGF56.

Espinosa Michel, J. Jesús
(Deceased 1959) a-1901. b-Ranchería Agua Zarca, Coquimatlán, Colima. c-Early education unknown; none. d-Local Deputy to the state legislature of Colima; Mayor of Coquimatlán, 1935; *Federal Deputy* from Colima, Dist. 2, 1940-43, member of the First Balloting Committee; *Federal Deputy* from Colima, Dist. 2, 1946-49, member of the Petroleum Committee, substitute member of the Second Ejido Committee. e-None. h-Ejidatario for many years, retired from politics in 1949 to work his farm. g-None. f-Inspector General of Police, Colima. j-Fought with Francisco Villa during the Revolution; fought against the de la Huerta rebellion under General Higinio Alvarez in 1923. l-Enc. Mex., III, 532; C de D, 1946-48, 71, 1940-42; DP70, 731; DGF47, 6.

Espinosa Porset, Ernesto
(Deceased July 25, 1972) a-May 3, 1887. b-Zinapecuaro, Michoacán. c-Early education unknown; no degree. d-None. e-None. f-Auditor General of the Department of Pensions, Secretariat of the Treasury, 1932; Head of the Credit Department of the Bank of Mexico, 1932-38; *Subdirector General of the Bank of Mexico,* 1938-40, 1940-46, 1946-52, 1952-58, 1958-64, and 1964-70; Secretary of the Administrative Council of the Bank of Mexico, 1947-68.

g-None. h-Probationer for the Central Bank of Mexico, 1904; Assistant in the Accounts and Checking Department, Central Bank of Mexico, 1906; Head of the Department of Checks, Secretary to the Director, Assistant Accountant, and Bookkeeper, all at El Descuente Español, S.A.; Cashier, Banco Español Refaccionario; adviser to Financiera Bancamex, 1970-72; author of several books on banking in Mexico. j-None. k-None. l-Letter; DGF50, II, 10-11, 211, 197; DGF51, II, 585, 467; DBM68, 22-23.

Espinosa Rivera, José
a-1927. b-Federal District. c-Certified Public Accountant, degree from the National University. d-None. e-*Secretary of Finances for the National Executive Committee of PRI*, 1964-69. f-Head of the Department for Regional Economic Investment for the Secretariat of the Treasury, 1970-72. g-None. h-Investigator for the Department of Treasury Studies, Secretariat of the Treasury; Fiscal Investigator for the Department of Treasury Studies; Head of the Economic Studies Department for the Patronato del Valle Mezquital; tax adviser to the state governments of Durango, Sonora, Chihuahua, Tamaulipas, San Luis Potosí, Campeche, Tabasco, and Nayarit. j-None. l-HA, 21 Dec. 1964, 10; DPE70, 35; WWMG, 16.

Espinosa Sánchez, Juventino
(Deceased) a-Jan. 26, 1891. b-Tecuala, Nayarit. c-Early education unknown; no degree. d-*Governor of Nayarit*, 1938-41. e-None. f-Substitute Governor of Nayarit, 1931. g-None. h-None. i-Son, Juventino Jr., served as an alternate federal deputy for Nayarit, Dist. 1, 1952-55. j-Joined the Revolution, 1913; career military officer; Brigadier General, May 16, 1929; Military Zone Commander in the Northeast; Commander of the 14th Military Zone,

Aguascalientes, Aguascalientes, 1956; Rank of Division General. l-Peral, 253; DGF56, 202; Enc. Mex., III, 531; C de D, 1952-54, 10; López, 327; Dávila, 131.

Espinosa Villarreal, Oscar
a-Nov. 23, 1953. b-Federal District. c-Early education unknown; business administration degree, School of Accounting and Administration, UNAM, 1972-79, with a thesis on tourism; professor, Anáhuac University, 1990. d-Local Deputy to the State Legislature of México, 1984-87; *Alternate Federal Deputy* from the State of México, Dist. 2, 1988-91. e-Joined PRI, 1975. f-Director of the Treasury, State of México, 1982-84; Director General of Treasury and Credit, State of México, 1984-86; Private Secretary to the Governor of México, *Alfredo Baranda*, 1986-87; Director, Investment Banks, National Finance Bank, 1987-89; President, National Stock Exchange Commission, 1989-91; *Director General of the National Finance Bank*, 1991-94. g-Director General, Mexican Association of Stock Exchanges, 1980-81. h-Supervisor, Insurance Agents, La Comercial Insurance Company, Atlántico Insurance Company, and Tepeyac Insurance Company, 1973-75; stockbroker, 1977-80. i-Son of Francisco Espinosa Figueroa, and Rosa María Villarreal Martínez, public official; married María de los Angeles Mijares Reyes Spíndola. j-None. k-None. l-*El Nacional*, 3 Jan. 1991, 1, 5; DBGM89, 110; DBGM92, 115.

Esponda, Juan M.
a-1901. b-Comitán, Chiapas. c-Primary studies in Tapachula; secondary studies in Tuxtla Gutiérrez; agricultural engineering degree, National School of Agriculture, Chapingo, 1925. d-Federal Deputy from Chiapas, Dist. 1, 1928-30; Federal Deputy from the State of Chiapas, Dist. 2, 1930-32, 1932-34;

Senator from the State of Chiapas, 1934-40; *Federal Deputy* from the State of Chiapas, Dist. 2, 1943-44; *Governor of Chiapas*, 1944-46. e-None. f-Director of the Office of Presidential Affairs under General Obregón, 1920-24; Judge of the Superior Tribunal of Justice of the State of Chiapas; Secretary General of Government of the State of Chiapas, 1940-43, under Governor *Rafael P. Gamboa.* g-None. j-Joined the Constitutionalists in 1915 under General *Jesús A. Castro;* served under *Blas Corral Martínez.* k-Did not complete term as governor; Anderson suggests he resigned because of protests over his imposing municipal appointments. l-HA, 7 Dec. 1946, 30, 15 Dec. 1944, viii; letter; C de D, 1943-45; HA, 29 Oct. 1943, 14; DBdeC, 79; Enc. Mex., 1977, III, 310; Anderson.

Esquer Apodaca, Salvador
a-Nov. 16, 1917. b-Guasa, Sinaloa. c-Primary studies in the Francisco I. Madero Rural School, Choix, Sinaloa; no degree. d-*Federal Deputy* from the State of Sinaloa, Dist. 1, 1970-73, 1979-82, 1985-88; *Senator* from the State of Sinaloa, 1988-94. e-Joined PRI, 1952. f-None. g-Secretary General of Local 12, Sugar Industry Workers of the Mexican Republic (STIAS), 1950-52; Secretary of Conflicts of the STIAS, 1954-57; Secretary of Labor of the STIAS, 1957-81; Secretary General of the STIAS, 1981-87. h-Laborer, sugar industry. i-Son of Francisco Javier Esquer Robles, artisan, and Rosario Apodaca Acosta; married María Ninfa Coronel Estrada. j-None. k-None. l-C de D, 1970-73, 1979-82, 1985-88; DBGM87, 468.

Esquivel de Quintana, Josefina
a-Mar. 19, 1918. b-Valle de Bravo, México. c-Primary studies in the Valle de Bravo; completed 4th grade; no degree. d-*Federal Deputy* from the State of México, Dist. No. 2, 1976-79,

member of the Second Section of the Social Action Committee, and member of the Section of Women's Peasant Development of the Agrarian Affairs Committee. e-None. f-None. g-Began participating in peasant organizations in 1932; Secretary of Women's Action of the League of Agrarian Committees, State of México; Secretary of Women's Action of the Regional Peasant Committee, Valle de Bravo, 1963-70. i-Parents were peasants. j-None. k-None. l-D de C, 1976-79, 4, 8; *Excélsior*, 22 Aug. 1976, 29; C de D, 1976-79, 21.

Esquivel Méndez, Eligio
(Deceased Dec. 17, 1964) a-1908. b-Mérida, Yucatán. c-Engineering degree from the National School of Engineering, UNAM, 1933. d-*Governor of Baja California del Norte*, 1959-64. e-None. f-Director of Construction on the Morelos Dam, the Matamoros Dam, and other projects; engineer on hydro-electric project in Bolivia; Director of the engineering commission to provide South America with technical assistance, 1939-40; head of the Mexicali Irrigation District, including the Colorado River, for the Secretariat of Hydraulic Resources, 1943-57. g-None. h-None. j-None. k-Retired from 1957-59 for medical treatment resulting from a heart attack in 1957; won PRI nomination because of expertise with the irrigation problems in his state and his ties with ranchers' associations. l-G of M, 15-16; DP70, 733-34; DGF51, I, 434; Enc. Mex., III, 537; HA, 28 Dec. 1964, 14; NYT, 11 Aug. 1959, 8, 2 Nov. 1959, 28.

Estefan Acar, Joseph
a-Dec. 15, 1934. b-Tehuantepec, Oaxaca. c-Primary studies at the Istemena Private School, Tehuantepec, Oaxaca; secondary studies from the Miguel Hidalgo Public School, Tehuan-

tepec; preparatory studies, Instituto Libanés Mexicano; no degree. d-*Federal Deputy* from the State of Oaxaca, Dist. 1, 1970-73; *Alternate Federal Deputy* from Oaxaca, 1979-82; *Federal Deputy* from the State of Oaxaca, Dist. 10, 1982-85. e-Joined PRI, 1967; President of PRI in Tehuantepec. f-Director of Public Relations, State of Oaxaca, 1980-81; Federal Delegate of Tourism to Oaxaca, 1974-80; adviser to the Oficial Mayor of the Secretariat of Public Education, 1973-74; President of the Board of Moral and Civic Improvements, Tehuantepec, 1969-82. g-Secretary General of CNOP in Oaxaca, 1969. h-Industrialist; Manager of Isthmus Motors, S.A., 1970-78. i-Son of Jorge Estefan Letayf, businessman, and Rosa Acar Zaffa; married Michelle Chidiac Acar. j-None. k-None. l-Directorio, 1970-72, 1982-85; C de D, 1970-73, 1982-85; Lehr, 370.

Estrada Iturbide, Miguel
a-Nov. 17, 1908. b-Morelia, Michoacán. c-Preparatory studies and some law at the Colegio Libre del Derecho, Morelia; law degree, Colegio Civil of Guanajuato, Guanajuato, May 1932; founder, director, and professor of the Technical Academy of Business Instruction, 1936; professor, Workers Society, Michoacán, 1926. d-Candidate for federal deputy from Michoacán, 1943; Candidate for senator from Michoacán; *Federal Deputy* from the State of Michoacán, Dist. 5, 1964-67. e-Founder of PAN in Michoacán; founding member of PAN, 1939; member of the National Council of PAN; Director of the Regional Committee of PAN for the State of Michoacán, 1939-56; precandidate for the presidential nomination of PAN, 1964. f-None. g-Founder and member of the National Union of Catholic Students, 1931. h-Practicing lawyer; founding partner of General Hipotecaria, S.A.; distinguished orator. i-Des-

cendant of Agustín Iturbide; members of his family from Michoacán for generations; active in Catholic student organizations with *Manuel Ulloa Ortiz.* j-None. k-None. l-*Excélsior,* 7 Nov. 1963, 1, 16; Mabry; letter.

Estrada Reynoso, Enrique
(Deceased Nov. 11, 1942) a-1889. b-Mayahua, Zacatecas. c-Studied in Guadalajara; almost completed studies in civil engineering; no degree. d-*Federal Deputy* from the State of Zacatecas, Dist. 3, 1937-40; *Senator* from the State of Zacatecas, 1940-42. e-None. f-Governor of Zacatecas, 1920; Subsecretary of War, 1921; Secretary of War, 1922; *Director General of the National Railroads of Mexico,* 1941-42. g-None. h-None. i-Brother of *Roque Estrada Reynoso, President of the Supreme Court,* 1952. j-Joined the Revolution under General Rafael Tapia, 1910; Constitutionalist Chief of Operations in Michoacán and Colima, 1923; career army officer reaching rank of Division General. k-Joined the de la Huerta rebellion as a principal leader in 1923, when he was serving as Chief of Military Operations in Jalisco; defeated by General Obregón in Ocotlán and exiled to the United States; supported the Escobar rebellion in 1929, during which he captured the future president of Mexico, *Manuel Avila Camacho,* but allowed him to go free; one of the most prominent examples in recent Mexican politics of an opposition leader co-opted back into the system. l-C de D, 1937-39; C de S, 1946; DP70, 739; Michaels, 11; Enc. Mex., 1977, 563; Peral, 255-56; Q es Q, 200.

Estrada Reynoso, Roque
(Deceased Nov. 27, 1966) a-Aug. 16, 1883. b-Moyahua, Zacatecas. c-Primary studies in Moyahua; secondary at the Martín Sousa School, Guadalajara; preparatory studies in Guadalajara,

Jalisco; attended law school, forced into exile, but later completed his law degree at the University of Guadalajara, 1906. d-Federal Deputy from the State of Zacatecas, 1920-22. e-Member of the Anti-Reelectionist Center, 1909; *Secretary of Press and Publicity of the CEN of PRI*, June 19, 1935. f-Provisional Secretary to Francisco Madero, 1910; Private Secretary to Carranza, 1914; General Peace Delegate of Jalisco, 1911; Provisional Governor of Aguascalientes, 1915; Secretary of Justice, 1915-16; Temporary Secretary to Francisco Madero when he returned to Mexico; *Justice of the Supreme Court*, 1941-46 and 1946-51; *President of the Supreme Court*, 1952. g-Organized workers in a socialist party, 1904. i-Brother of General *Enrique Estrada Reynoso*, senator from the State of Zacatecas; son of Camillo Estrada and Micaela Reynoso; brother-in-law of Ignacio Ramos Praslow, governor of Jalisco, 1920. j-Participated in the Revolution; orator for Madero; Commanding Officer of the 2nd Cavalry Brigade, Western Division, 1914-15; rank of Brigadier General. k-Jailed with Francisco Madero in San Luis Potosí, 1909; turned down candidacy for governor of Jalisco because he did not meet the constitutional age requirement; Candidate for president of Mexico against General Obregón, 1920; joined brother in support of the de la Huerta rebellion, 1923; exiled to the United States, 1923; 1927-29. l-Enc. Mex., III, 564; DP70, 740; D del S, 19 June 1935, 1; DGF51, I, 568; WB48, 1695; Peral, 257; López, 334.

Estrada Rodríguez, Amado
a-1920. b-Culiacán, Sinaloa. c-Primary, secondary, and preparatory studies in Culiacán; law degree, University of Sinaloa, Culiacán; Professor of Labor Law, Social University of the Northeast (9 years). d-Local Deputy from the State

of Sinaloa, 1956-59; Mayor of Culiacán, 1960-62; *Senator* from the State of Sinaloa, 1964-70. e-Oficial Mayor of the PNR in Sinaloa, 1938; President of PRI in Culiacán; Secretary General of the State Committee of PRI. f-Agent of the Ministerio Público, Sinaloa; agent of the Ministerio Publico, Culiacán; President of the State Board of Conciliation and Arbitration (8 years); Attorney General of the State of Sinaloa, 1962-64. g-Organizer, agricultural and labor unions; organizer for youth organizations in Sinaloa; President of the Student Society, University of Sinaloa; delegate of the students to the University Council, University of Sinaloa; President of the Federation of University Students. h-None. j-None. k-None. l-*Mis Seis Años*; MGF69, 106.

Etiene Llano, Pedro René
a-Sept. 26, 1950. b-Ciudad Victoria, Tamaulipas. c-Early education unknown; economics degree, National School of Economics, UNAM; law degree, School of Law, Ibero-American University. d-*Plurinominal Deputy* from the PST, 1979-82; *Plurinominal Deputy* from the PST, 1988-91. e-Joined the PST, 1973; member of the National Organizing Committee of the PST; Secretary of Political Education of the PST; Political Comissar of the Northern Zone, PST; member of the Central Committee of the PST, 1975-82; Secretary of the Labor Union Committee of the PST. f-None. g-None. j-None. k-None. l-Protag., 115; C de D, 1979-82; DBGM89, 434.

Ezeta Uribe Remedios, Albertina
a-Aug. 7, 1907. b-Toluca, México. c-Primary and secondary studies in Toluca; preparatory studies from the Scientific and Literary Institute of Mexico, Toluca; law degree from the National School of Law, UNAM; Professor of Law and Sociology, Autono-

mous University of the State of México; Professor of Law and Sociology, School of Business and Administration, UNAM. d-*Federal Deputy* from the State of México, Dist. 6, 1955-58, member of the Tariff Committee, the Foreign Trade Committee, the Public Welfare Committee, the Legislative Studies Committee, and the First Justice Committee. e-Member of the popular sector of PRI. f-Juvenile Court Judge, State of México; public defender; judge, District 2, Toluca, México, 1943-52; Notary Public No. 2, Toluca, Mexico, 1952-72. g-None. h-Practicing lawyer, 51 years. j-None. k-She was the only female public notary in Mexico in 1955. l-Ind. Biog., 57; C de D, 1955-58.

F

Fabela (Alfaro), Isidro

(Deceased Aug. 12, 1964) a-June 28, 1882. b-Atlacomulco, México. c-Primary studies in Mexico City; preparatory at the National Preparatory School, Mexico City; law degree from the National School of Law, UNAM, 1908; Professor of History, National Institute, Chihuahua, 1911-13; Professor at the Literary Institute of Chihuahua, 1912-13; Professor of International Public Law, National School of Law, UNAM, 1921. d-Federal Deputy from the State of México, Dist. 9, 1912-14, 1922-23; *Governor of México*, 1942-45; *Senator* from México, 1946, but resigned to accept appointment to the International Court of Justice. e-None. f-Chief Public Defender for the Federal District, 1911; Adviser to and Director of the Federal Penitentiary, Federal District, 1911; Oficial Mayor and Secretary General of Government of the State of Chihuahua, 1911-13; Oficial Mayor and Secretary General of Government of the State of Sonora, 1913; Secretary of Foreign Relations, 1913-15; Special

Diplomat to Italy and Spain, 1915; Minister to Argentina, Brazil, Chile, and Uruguay, 1916; Special Ambassador to Argentina, 1918-20; Judge for the Italian-Mexican International Arbitration Commission, 1928-32; Technical Commissioner, Secretariat of Foreign Relations, 1933; Legal Adviser to the French Legation in Mexico, 1933; President of the First Agricultural Conference, 1938; Mexican Delegate to the International Office of Labor, League of Nations, 1937-40; Judge of the International Court of Justice, 1946-52. g-None. h-Founded the newspaper, *La Verdad*, 1910, and *El Puebla*, 1914; practicing lawyer, 1921-28; attorney for several private companies, including Cauum Oil Company. i-Established early friendships with José Vasconcelos, *Alfonso Caso* and *Luis Castillo Ledón*; married Josefina Eisenmann; son of Francisco Trinidad Fabela and Guadalupe Alfaro, members of the upper middle class; daughter, Josefina, is a historian. j-None. k-One of the founders of the Ateneo de la Juventud, 1901; Kirk claims *Fabela* was very critical of *Ezequiel Padilla* as Secretary of Foreign Relations, because he himself did not receive the Secretaryship; in exile in Cuba, 1913; in exile in California, 1923; his home has been turned into a public library in San Angel, Federal District. l-HAHR, Feb. 1972, 124-25; Kirk, 207; DP70, 747; Enc. Mex., III, 593; Peral, 258; EBW46, 71; WWM45, 38-39; letter, WB48, 1711-12; WB54, 350.

Fabre del Rivero, Carlos

a-Sept. 20, 1937. b-Puebla, Puebla. c-Primary and secondary studies at private schools in Puebla and Mexico City; law degree from the University of Puebla, Mar. 29, 1962, with a thesis on the ISSTE; studied at the National Center of Productivity; Professor of Economic Problems of México and of Industrial Development (3rd and 5th years), School of Business Administration, University of Puebla; Professor of Public Administration, University of Puebla, 1964-67. d-Substitute Mayor of Puebla, 1969-70. e-Joined PRI, 1955; state oratory champion, 1956 and 1957; third-place winner of the national PRI oratory contest, 1957; participated in *Luis Echeverría's* campaign in Puebla, 1969-70; member of the CEPES of PRI in Puebla, 1963-68; Auxiliary Secretary to *Luis Echeverría* during presidential campaign, 1970; general delegate of the CEN of PRI to Quintana Roo and Querétaro, 1981-82; Director of the Youth Section of PRI, Puebla. f-Director General of Industrial and Commercial Development, State of Puebla, 1963-69; *Oficial Mayor of Industry and Commerce*, 1970-76; Delegate from Cuauhtémoc to the Department of the Federal District, 1982-84. g-Student leader at the University of Puebla. h-Practicing lawyer, Puebla, 1961-63; author of several works. i-Married Artemia Zarandona Sasíu; son of Carlos Oscar Fabre Baños, career military, and Ana María del Rivero. j-None. k-Precandidate for governor of Puebla, 1974. l-HA, 14 Dec. 1970, 21; letter; *Excélsior,* 9 May 1974, 19.

Faesler Carlisle, Julio
a-May 10, 1930. b-Chihuahua, Chihuahua. c-Primary studies at a Jesuit School; secondary studies at the Regional Institute, Chihuahua, Chihuahua; preparatory studies from a Jesuit school; law degree from the National School of Law, UNAM, 1955, thesis on "The Most Favored Nation Clause and International Treaties"; economics degree from the National School of Economics, UNAM, 1956, thesis on "The Intervention of the State in Economic Life"; Professor of Economic Theory and the History of Economic Doctrines, National School of Law, UNAM; Professor of Mexican Economic

Problems, University of the Americas; Professor of Economic Theory, Escuela Libre de Derecho; Professor of Business Finance, Ibero-American University; Director of the Ph.D. Seminar in Foreign Trade, IPN. d-None. e-None. f-Assistant Economist, National Price Commission, 1952; Private Secretary to the Subsecretary of the Treasury, *Antonio Armendáriz,* 1952-57; Commercial Attaché, London; Commercial Attaché, Brussels, 1964; Subdirector General of Trade, International Economic Affairs, Secretariat of Industry and Commerce, 1965-67; Director General of Latin American Economic Integration, Secretariat of Industry and Commerce, 1967-70; Director General of the Mexican Institute of Foreign Trade, 1970-76; Director General of Exports of Mexico, 1977-82. g-None. h-Self-employed, 1968-70. i-Attended UNAM with *Jorge de la Vega Domínguez, Mario Moya Palencia,* and *Carlos Torres Manzo;* parents from the middle class. j-None. k-None. l-Letters; HA, 21 Mar. 1977, 19.

Farell (Cubillas), Arsenio
a-June 30, 1921. b-Mexico City. c-Primary studies at the Centro Escolar Benito Juárez, Mexico City, 1929-34; secondary studies at Secondary School No. 3, Heroes de Chapultepec, Mexico City, 1935-37; preparatory studies from the National Preparatory School, 1938-39; legal studies from the National School of Law, UNAM, 1940-44, graduating May 9, 1945, with a 9.8 GPA and a thesis on the civil code of the Federal District; recieved an honorable mention in his studies towards an LLD degree, 1950-51; Professor by Competition in Civil Law, 1966, Civil Legal Process, 1956, and Forensic Law, National School of Law, UNAM; Professor, 2nd course in labor law, National School of Law, UNAM, 1949-50; Professor of Civil Law, School of

Law, Ibero-American University, 1967. d-None. e-None. f-Secretary of the Trustees of the National University, 1966; *Director General of the Federal Electric Commission*, May 29, 1973-76; *Director General of the Mexican Institute of Social Security*, 1976-82; *Secretary of Labor*, 1982-88, 1988-94. g-Consulting lawyer to the Society of Authors and Composers, to the Union of Cinematographic Production Workers, to the Mexican Union of Aviation Pilots, and to the National Actors Association. h-Adviser to the Chapala Electric System Company; President of the National Chamber of Alcohol and Sugar Industries, 1973. i-Practiced law with *Rodolfo Echeverría*; classmate at the National Preparatory School and National School of Law of *Jose López Portillo* and *Luis Echeverría*; compadre of *Rodolfo Echeverría*; *Luis Echeverría* worked in his law office before graduating; grew up in same neighborhood as *Luis Echeverría* and *José López Portillo*; son of Enrique Farell Solá and Consuelo Cubillas Gutiérrez; married Rosa María Campa; brother, Luis Farrell Cubillas, air force general. j-None. k-None. l-HA, 4 June 1973, 16, 3 June 1974, 24; *Excélsior*, 30 May 1973, 13; Guerra Leal, 124; HA, 13 Dec. 1982, 15; DBGM, 138; Q es QAP, 357.

Farías (Martínez), Luis Marcelino
a-June 7, 1920. b-Monterrey, Nuevo León. c-Primary studies in Monterrey; secondary studies in Mexico City, Eagle Pass, Texas, and Torreón, preparatory studies at the National Preparatory School, 1939-41; studied law at the National Law School, UNAM, 1941-45, degree, 1947, with a thesis on the 1950 constitutional reforms on amparo; Professor of Philosophy at the National Preparatory School, Mexico City; Professor of Philosophy at UNAM, 1954. d-*Federal Deputy* from the Federal District, Dist. 16, 1955-58;

member of the Committee on Bellas Artes, the Legislative Studies Committee, the Committee on the Radio and Television Industry; *Federal Deputy* from the State of Nuevo León, Dist. 2, 1967-70; President of the Gran Comisión, PRI Majority Leader in the Chamber of Deputies, member of the First Committee of Government, the First Constitutional Affairs Committee; *Senator* from Nuevo León, 1970, 1973-76, member of the permanent committee, Executive Secretary of the Second Government and Justice Committees; *Federal Deputy* from the State of Nuevo León, Dist. 6, 1979-82, President of the Gran Comisión; Mayor of Monterrey, Nuevo León. e-Active in the Youth Action of PRUN in support of *Juan Andreu Almazán* for president, 1939-40; joined PRI in 1951; general delegate of the CEN of PRI to Sinaloa, 1973. f-Translator for Presidential Conferences, 1961; Oficial Mayor of the Department of Tourism, 1964-67; Director General of Information, Secretariat of Government, 1958-64; *Substitute Governor of Nuevo León*, 1970-73. g-President of the National Federation of University Students, 1941-42; President of the Student Generation of UNAM, 1941; founder and First Director of the National Association of Announcers, 1951-52; founder and first President of the Inter-American Association of Announcers, 1952-53; Secretary General of the Union of Artists and Workers of Station XEW, 1945-53, 1955-64; President of the Nuevo León Center, Mexico City, 1955-59. h-Television commentator, 1951-58; radio commentator, 1946-58; author of several books on politics in Mexico. i-Friendship with Francisco Venegas, important Catholic student leader in the 1940s; married María Emilia Mackey; good friend at preparatory with *Mario Colín Sánchez*; his preparatory generation included many important political leaders; daughter *María Emilia* was federal deputy from the Federal District, 1985-88; cousin of *Adrián Lajous*. j-None. k-Senator from Nuevo León before he was appointed governor to replace *Eduardo Elizondo* in 1970. l-Enc. Mex., IV, 13-14; DBM68, 227; WWMG, 16; DGF56, 23, 31, 33-34; LAD, Oct. 1971, 2; G of NL, 16; PdM, 110-12; DBM70, 200; C de D, 1957, 1967-69; Ind. Biog., 57-58; *Excélsior*, 3 July 1980, 18A; letters.

Faz Riza, Paz
a-Apr. 18, 1893. b-Coahuila. c-Early education unknown, no degree. d-Federal Deputy from the State of Puebla, Dist. 11, 1932-34. e-None. f-*Provisional Governor of Coahuila*, Mar. to June 1948. g-None. j-Joined the Revolution; fought under General Fortunato Maycotte in Hidalgo and Puebla; supported the Plan of Agua Prieta; joined the de la Huerta rebellion, 1923; rank of Brigadier General, 1941. k-Replaced *Ricardo Ainslie* as governor until a special election could be held in which *Raúl López Sánchez* was selected as governor. l-López, 339; Peral, 260.

Félix Serna, Faustino
(Deceased Apr. 17, 1986) a-May 14, 1913. b-Pitiquito, Sonora. c-Primary at the Colegio Sonora, Hermosillo; teaching certificate from the State of Sonora Normal School. c-First Councilman of the City of Cajeme, Sonora, 1952; Interim Mayor of Cajeme, 1953; Mayor of Ciudad Obregón, Municipio of Cajeme, 1961-63; *Federal Deputy* from the State of Sonora, Dist. 2, 1964-67, member of the Gran Comisión, the Public Works Committee, the Agricultural Development Committee, and the First Committee on Taxes; *Governor of Sonora*, 1967-73. e-President of PRI during the gubernatorial campaign, 1961. f-None. g-Secretary General of the Agricultural Credit Union of

Cajeme, 1936-40; President of the Agricultural Credit Union of Cajeme; President of the Political Revolutionary Group of Sonora, 1977. h-Private accountant for a local bank in Ciudad Obregón; operated trucking service in Sonora; founded the Sindicato de Fleteros del Valle del Yaqui, 1936; organized the company of Algodón y Semillas de Caborca. i-Friend of Rodolfo Elías Calles, Mayor of Cajeme, 1952; son of Félix Serna, mayor of Cajeme; son-in-law, *Javier R. Bours*, was a federal deputy from Sonora, 1970-73, and precandidate for governor of Sonora, 1978; married Lilian Escalante. j-None. k-*Proceso* accused him of representing the interests of large landowners in Sonora. l-Letter; C de D, 1964-66; WWMG, 17; *Excélsior*, 7 June, 1977, 23, 10 Sept. 1978, 14; *Proceso*, 7 Aug. 1978, 12-14; Moncada, 60.

Félix Valdés, Rodolfo
a-May 22, 1922. b-Nacozari, Sonora. c-Degree in civil engineering, National School of Engineering, UNAM, 1947; Professor of General Topography, National School of Engineering, UNAM, 1954; member of the University Council, UNAM, 1962-66; Auxiliary Secretary of the School of Engineering, 1954-59; Director of Planning, Graduate School of Engineering, UNAM. d-*Governor of Sonora*, 1985-91. e-Member of the IEPES of PRI, 1963-83. f-Engineer, Secretariat of Public Works, 1945-58; adviser to the Department of the Federal District on earthquake damaged buildings, 1952-58; Head of the Department of Planning, Secretariat of Public Works, 1959-61; Director General of Planning and Programming, Secretariat of Public Works, 1961-64, 1964-66; *Subsecretary of Public Works*, 1966-70, 1970-76; 1977-82; *Secretary of Communications and Transportation*, 1982-84. g-President of the Student Society of the School of Engineering. h-Held many

positions in the Department of the Federal District, the Secretariat of Hydraulic Resources, and the Secretariat of National Defense. i-Married Gloria Flores Pérez Sandi; son of Jesús Felíx Vázquez, farmer, and Margarita Valdés Salido. j-None. k-Precandidate for governor of Sonora, 1978. l-HA, 14 Dec. 1970, 22; DPE65, 117; DPE61, 84; letter; *Excélsior*, 23 Nov. 1977, 18; PS, 6150; *Excélsior*, 1 Dec. 1982, 34; HA, 13 Dec. 1982, 14; *News*, 2 Dec. 1982, 8; *Excélsior*, 27 July 1984, 20; Q es QAP, 249; DBGM89, 683; DBGM, 140.

Fernández, Rafael

a-1940. b-Federal District. c-Early education unknown; sociology degree. d-None. e-Cofounder of the first National Committee to form an opposition political party; cofounder of the Socialist Workers Party, 1973; member of the Central Committee and the Executive Committee of the Socialist Workers Party. f-None. g-None. h-Writer for *El Universal*; writer for *Uno Más Uno*. i-Parents were Spanish Republicans who emigrated from Spain; grandfather an Austrian miner. j-None. k-First became politically active in 1971. l-HA, 12 Feb. 1979, 20.

Fernández Aguirre, Braulio

a-Nov. 21, 1912. b-San Pedro de las Colonias, Coahuila. c-Primary studies in San Pedro de la Colonias; secondary in Saltillo; degree in business administration from the Zaragoza Academy, Monterrey, Nuevo León. d-Mayor of Torreón, Coahuila, 1945-48; *Alternate Federal Deputy* from the State of Coahuila, Dist. 2, 1949-52; Mayor of Torreón, Coahuila, 1958-60; *Federal Deputy* from the State of Coahuila, Dist. 2, 1961-63, member of the Gran Comisión, the Waters and Irrigation Committee and the Sugar Industry Committee, Vice-President of the Chamber, Nov. 1961; *Governor of*

Coahuila, 1963-69; *Senator* from the State of Coahuila, 1970-76, member of the Gran Comisión, President of the First Treasury Committee and the Small Agrarian Property Committee, First Secretary of the First Tariff and Foreign Trade Committee, and Second Secretary of the Second Government Committee; member of the Permanent Committee, Jan. 1973. e-General delegate of the CEN of PRI, 1970; member of the Political Action Committee of the New Advisory Council to PRI, 1972. f-Employee, Traffic Department, Torreón; inspector, State Treasury Office, Coahuila, Treasurer of Torreón; President of the National Arid Zones Committee, 1970. g-None. h-Left public life to farm grapes with his father. i-Father a rancher; son, *Braulio Fernández Aguirre*, was a federal deputy from Coahuila, 1985-88; married Lucía Aguirre Elguezábal. j-None. k-The CNC of Coahuila opposed his nomination as the PRI gubernatorial candidate, 1963. l-GofM, DGF51, I, 20; C de D, 1949-52; C de S, 1970-76, 73; HA, 10 July 1972, 10; Moreno, 109-110; *Proceso*, 1 Feb. 1982, 13-15.

Fernández Albarrán, Juan

(Deceased Mar. 27, 1972) a-Jan. 10, 1901. b-Toluca, México. c-Primary studies at the Colegio Hispano-Mexicano, Toluca; secondary and preparatory studies from the Scientific and Literary Institute of México, Toluca; law degree, National School of Law, UNAM, graduating with an honorable mention. d-Mayor of Toluca, México; *Federal Deputy* from the State of México, Dist. 7, 1943-46; *Senator* from the State of México, 1952-58, member of the Committee on Mines, the Second Balloting Committee; substitute member of the Committee on Foreign and Domestic Commerce, the Committee on Cooperative Development, and the Committee on Labor; *Governor of México*, 1963-69.

e-Representative to PRI from Toluca; *Secretary General of PRI*, 1959-63, under *Alfonso Corona del Rosal*. f-Agent of the Ministerio Público, Mexico City; judge, Mexico City; Oficial Mayor of the State Legislature of México; Secretary General of Government of the State of México, 1937-41, under Governor *Wenceslao Labra*; member of the Federal Electoral Commission, 1946; *Oficial Mayor of the Department of Agrarian Affairs*, 1946-52; Judge of the Superior Tribunal of Justice of the State of Veracruz and of the State of Durango. h-None. i-Related to *Juan Albarrán*, alternate federal deputy from México, Dist. 10, 1937-40; son of Juan Fernández, pharmaceutical chemist and professor, and María del Refugio Albarrán. j-None. k-None l-DGF51, I, 465; DGF56, 6, 10-13; letter; DBM68, 230; Correa, 447; WWMG, 17.

Fernández del Cevallos, Diego
a-Mar. 16, 1941. b-Federal District. c-Early education unknown; law degree, National School of Law, UNAM, 1960-64, with a thesis on criminal law; professor, Ibero-American University, 1964- . d-*Plurinominal Federal Deputy* from PAN, 1991-94, member of the Government and Constitutional Affairs Committee, head of the PAN delegation to the Chamber of Deputies. e-Joined PAN, 1959, but began speaking at PAN rallies in 1952; president of National PAN Youth; member of the National Council of PAN; member of the CEN of PAN; PAN candidate for president, 1993. f-None. g-None. h-Practicing lawyer, 1964- . i-Son of José Fernández de Cevallos, founding member of PAN, 1939, and rancher, and Beatriz Ramos Iñigo; married Claudia Gutiérrez Navarrete; aligned with *Luis Héctor Alvarez* and *Carlos Castillo Peraza* in PAN. j-None. k-Father jailed in 1940 for political activities; Diego jailed for distributing PAN literature. l-*El*

Financiero International, 18 Oct. 1993, 20; DBGM92, 458-59; C de D, 1991-94.

Fernández Doblado, Luis
a-Apr. 9, 1925. b-Tuxpan, Veracruz. c-Early education unknown; law degree, National School of Law, UNAM, 1944-48, with a thesis on culpability and error; professor, National School of Law, UNAM, 1958-87, Graduate School of Law, UNAM, 1971-78, Law School, University of Nuevo León, 1970, Free School of Law, 1959-60, and at Institute of Judicial Specialty, Supreme Court of Justice, 1979-83. d-None. e-None. f-Lawyer, Secretariat of the Treasury, 1944-48; Secretary of Agreements, Superior Tribunal of Justice of the Federal District, 1956-58; Secretary of Studies and Accounts, Supreme Court of Justice, 1960-67; Agent of the Ministerio Público, 1962-63; District Judge, State of México and Nuevo León, 1967-71; Circuit Court Judge, Federal District, 1978-81; *Supreme Court Justice*, 1981-91. g-None. h-Practicing lawyer, 1948-60. i-Married Martha Tovar Ardavin. j-None. k-None. l-DBGM, 653; DBGM89, 608; DBGM87, 618.

Fernández Fernández, Aurora
b-México. c-Primary and secondary studies at the Colegio Sara L. King; teaching certificate; preparatory studies from the National Preparatory School; degree in political science from the School of Political and Social Sciences, UNAM (second woman to receive this degree from the National University). d-*Federal Deputy* from the Federal District, Dist. 9, 1970-73, member of the Infant Welfare Committee, the Department of the Federal District Committee, and the Second Balloting Committee. e-Joined the PNR, 1933; Oficial Mayor of the Women's Sector of the PNR; Secretary of Organization of the Women's Sector of PRI; Secretary General of the Women's Sector of PRI;

Secretary of Organization of the Women's Sector of the PRI in the Federal District, 1937. f-Delegate of the Department of the Federal District to Milpa Alta, 1947-50; Head of the Office of Women's Action, Department of the Federal District, 1950-69. g-Delegate of the Women's Section of the Federal District before the National Women's Committee, 1937; Representative of the Women Farmers of the State of México, 1939; Secretary of Women's Action, League of Agrarian Communities and Peasant Unions, 1939-42; cofounder of the National Women's Alliance during the *Miguel Alemán* presidential campaign, 1945-46; Secretary of Women's Action, Mexican Federation of Labor, 1951; cofounder of the Mexican Alliance of Women, 1952. i-Mother was a rural school teacher; father died when she was a month old. j-None. k-None. l-Chumacero, 66-70; Directorio, 1970-72; C de D, 1970-73, 10, 39, 113; DGF51, I, 484; DGF56, 469; DPE61, 146; DPE65, 195.

Fernández Flores, Manuel
a-Sept. 16, 1933. b-Nogales, Veracruz. c-Early education unknown; no degree. d-None. e-Joined the Popular Socialist Party, 1952; member of the Central Committee of the PPS; Secretary of Labor Policy, Central Committee, PPS, 1979. f-None. g-Delegate of the Mexican Electricians Union to international conferences; Secretary of External Affairs, Central Committee, Mexican Union of Electricians, 1979. h-Laborer in the electrical industry, 1953- . j-None. k-None. l-HA, 12 Mar. 1979, V.

Fernández Gomez, Rubén
a-May 13, 1910. b-Federal District. c-Early education unknown; veterinary medical degree, UNAM, 1931; professor, UNAM. d-None. e-None. f-Director of Veterinary Hygiene, Secretariat of

Health, 1942; Director of Health in the Federal District, Secretariat of Health, 1942-46; Director General of the Milk Industry, Secretariat of Agriculture, 1952-58; adviser to the National Agricultural Bank and the National Rural Credit Bank, 1965-75; *Subsecretary of Forest Resources and Fauna*, 1976-81. g-None. h-None. j-None. k-None. l-Protag., 118.

Fernández Hurtado, Ernesto
a-Nov. 19, 1921. b-Colima, Colima. c-Preparatory studies at the National Preparatory School, 1939-40; degree in economics, National School of Economics, UNAM, 1941-45; MA in public administration from Harvard University, June 1948, with a thesis on "Income Elasticity of Foreign Commerce in Latin American Countries"; specialized economic studies at the International Monetary Fund, 1948-49; Professor of Money and Banking at Mexico City College; Professor of Money and Banking and International Trade at the National School of Economics, UNAM; Professor of International Trade at the Technological Institute of Mexico, 1956-59; Professor in the field of central banking at the Center for Monetary Studies of Latin America. d-None. e-None. f-Assistant economist, Bank of Mexico, 1941-44; Head, Balance of Payments Section, Department of Economic Studies, Bank of Mexico, 1948-55; Manager of the Department of Economic and Foreign Studies, Bank of Mexico, 1955-60; technical adviser to the Director General, *Rodrigo Gómez*, 1954; Subdirector of the Bank of Mexico, 1960-70; *Director General of the Bank of Mexico*, 1970-76; Director General of Banco BCH, 1978-82; Director General of Bancomer, 1982. g-None. h-Member of the Board of Metalver, 1982. i-Student of *Eduardo Bustamante* at the National School of Economics; married Evelyn

Terovane; mentor to *Miguel de la Madrid*; son of Mariano Fernández Morales, lawyer, and Guadalupe Hurtado Vizcaíno. j-None. k-Pre-candidate for governor of Colima, 1977; was *Rodrigo Gómez's* choice to succeed him; considered a representative of the extreme ideological right. l-*Hoy*, 17 Apr. 1971, 12; letters; B de M, 119-20; WNM, 76; *Excélsior*, 6 July 1981, 1, 10A; DBGM, 142.

Fernández MacGregor, Genaro
(Deceased Dec. 22, 1959) a-May 4, 1883. b-Federal District. c-Primary and secondary education at the Instituto Científico, Mexico City; preparatory studies at the Colegio de Mascarones, 1897-1900, Mexico City; law degree from the National School of Law, UNAM, 1901-07; Professor of International Private and Public Law at the National Law School, UNAM, 1918-25; Professor of Spanish Literature and General History, National Preparatory School, 1912-16; *Rector of UNAM*, Mar. 1945 to Feb. 1946. d-None. e-None. f-Private Secretary to the Secretary of Industry and Commerce, 1908-09; Assistant Director of the Office of Patents, 1909-11; Director of International Affairs, Secretariat of Foreign Relations, 1911-14; legal adviser to the Secretariat of Foreign Relations, 1917-24; member of the United States-Mexican Claims Commission, 1924-36; member of the International Tribunal of Arbitration, The Hague. g-None. h-Author of many novels; Founder and Director of the *Mexican Journal of International Law*. i-Father, Genaro R. Fernández Becerra, a mining engineer who administered Genaro Fernández's grandfather's affairs; mother, Concepción MacGregor; married Ana María MacGregor; brother of Luis Fernández MacGregor, member of the Mexican Foreign Service; the Fernández MacGregor family has figured prominently in the history of

the Mexican Foreign Service; related to *Eduardo Hay*; practiced law with Alejandro Quijano; close friend of Antonio Caso through ties between their two fathers; related to José María Piño Suárez, Vice President of Mexico under Madero; nephew of Justo Sierra; cousin of *Manuel J. Sierra*, Oficial Mayor of the Treasury. j-None. k-Student strike in Nov. 1945 was instrumental in bringing about his resignation as Rector of UNAM three months later. l-DP70, 762; Hayner, 269; Peral, 269; Correa, 50; Enc. Mex., IV, 117; EWB46, 546; IWW40, 333; WB48, 1759.

Fernández Manero, Víctor
a-Nov. 17, 1898. b-Villahermosa, Tabasco. c-Primary and secondary studies in Villahermosa; preparatory studies at the Juárez Institute, Villahermosa; medical degree, with a specialty as a surgeon, National School of Medicine, UNAM. d-Federal Deputy from the Federal District, Dist. 5, 1934-36; *Governor of Tabasco*, 1936-39. e-Leader in *Avila Camacho's* campaign for president, 1939-40. f-Head of the Department of Hygiene, Secretariat of Public Education, 1930-31; attaché to the Mexican Embassy in Paris, 1931; *Head of the Department of Health*, 1940-43 (last director); *Ambassador to France*, 1946-51; and to Yugoslavia. g-None. h-Mexican representative to the International Medical Congress, Washington, D.C., 1930. i-Married Alicia Islas. j-None. k-Wealthiest member of the *Avila Camacho* cabinet in 1940 with over one million pesos in assets. l-D de Y, 1940; Correa 41, 2, 70; DGF51, 105, 109; Enc. Mex., IV, 117; Peral, 269.

Fernández Martínez, Enrique
a-June 15, 1897. b-San Felipe Torres Mochas, Guanajuato. c-Early education unknown; no degree. d-Federal Deputy from the State of Guanajuato, Dist. 9, 1920-22, Dist. 2, 1924-26, 1928-30,

president of the Gran Comisión; Federal Deputy from the State of Guanajuato, Dist. 1, 1930-32, member of the Gran Comisión; Federal Deputy from Guanajuato, Dist. 10, 1934-35; became *Interim Governor of Guanajuato*, Dec. 13, 1935, to 1937, replacing *Jesús Yáñez Maya; Governor of Guanajuato*, 1939-43. g-None. h-None. i-Friend of governors Enrique Colunga and *Arroyo Ch.*; intimate friend of *Luis I. Rodríguez;* son, *Enrique Fernández Martínez Arce*, federal deputy from Guanajuato, 1982-85, and secretary general of CNOP. j-None. k-Brandenburg gives him Inner Circle status; critics considered him an unconstitutional governor since he was the interim governor before being elected in 1940. l-Dulles, 662; Peral, 269; Gruening, 428; Correa 41, 78-79; Brandenburg, 80; NYT, 29 Apr. 1935, 8, 17 Dec. 1935, 1; López, 497-98.

Fernández Martínez Arce, Enrique
a-Mar. 4, 1938. b-Guanajuato, Guanajuato. c-Early education unknown; law degree, National School of Law, UNAM, 1957-62. d-*Alternate Federal Deputy* from the State of Guanajuato, Dist. 5, 1961-64; *Federal Deputy* from the State of Guanajuato, Dist.1, 1982-85, Secretary of the Gran Comisión. e-Joined PRI, 1957; Secretary General of PRI, Irapuato, Guanajuato, 1962-63; Auxiliary Secretary of the CEN of PRI, 1963; Secretary General of PRI in the Federal District, 1964-69. f-Secretary, City Council, Irapuato, 1962-63. g-National Delegate of the CNOP to the presidential campaign, 1963-64; *Secretary General of the CNOP*, 1983-87. h-None. i-Son of *Enrique Fernández Martinez*, governor of Guanajuato, 1940-43. j-None. k-None. l-*Excélsior*, 27 July 1984, 20; *Proceso*, 2 July 1984, 8; Lehr, 178; *El Heraldo*, 19 Jan. 1983; C de D, 1982-85, 1961-64; DBGM, 504.

Fernández Robert, Raúl
a-1905. b-Tulancingo, Hidalgo. c-Primary and secondary studies in Pachuca, Hidalgo; preparatory and part of professional studies in Pachuca; completed law degree at the National School of Law, UNAM, 1929; professor at the National Polytechnic Institute. d-*Senator* from the State of Hidalgo, 1952-58, Secretary of the Economics and Statistics Committee, Second Secretary of the Second Mines Committee, President of the Military Justice Committee, member of the Gran Comisión, and member of the Second Balloting and the Legislative Studies Committee. e-None. f-Consulting lawyer to the Chief of Police of the Federal District, 1932-37; Attorney General of Military Justice, 1946-52; Director of the Federal Custom's Office, Ciudad Juárez, Chihuahua, 1961; Director of the Federal Custom's Office, Tampico, Tamaulipas, 1965. i-Classmate of *Miguel Alemán* at UNAM. j-Career officer in military justice; reached rank of Brigade General. k-Prominent athlete; member of the Mexican Olympic Basketball Team, 1936. l-Ind. Biog., 60-61; MGF47, 110; DGF51, I, 178; DGF56, 6, 8, 10-14, DPE61, 45; DPE65, 58.

Fernández Varela (Mejía), Héctor
a-Aug. 12, 1933. b-Federal District. c-Early education unknown; MD degree with a thesis on "Pain in Urology" from the National School of Medicine, UNAM, 1956; professor at the National School of Medicine, UNAM, 1958-82, La Raza Medical Center, IMSS, 1965-73, General Hospital of Mexico, 1969-71, IPN, 1968-82, and at Children's Hospital, Mexico City, 1973-82; Dean, National School of Professional Studies, Iztacala. d-None. e-None. f-Auxiliary Secretary of Scholarly Medical Services, UNAM, 1958-63; General Physician and Pediatrician, IMSS, 1959-64; pediatri-

cian, General Pediatrics Hospital, Secretariat of Health, 1963-82; medical adviser to the Medical Subdirector of IMSS, 1975-82; medical adviser to ISSSTE; *Subsecretary of Health*, 1982-85; Director General, National Pediatrics Institute, 1985-88, 1988- . g-None. h-Pediatrician, Juárez Hospital, 1962-63; Director, Villa Gustavo A. Madero Children's Hospital, 1973-74; Director of San Juan de Aragón Children's Hospital. j-None. k-None. l-Q es QAP, 331; DBGM, 143-44; DBGM89, 117.

Fierro Fierro, Santiago
a-Oct. 29, 1921. b-Durango, Durango. c-Early education unknown; MD degree. d-*Plurinominal Deputy* from the Leftist Coalition Party, 1979-82. e-Joined the PPS, 1960; candidate for mayor of Durango, 1970; candidate for federal deputy (several times); Secretary General of the PPS in Teziutlán, Puebla, 1964-66; Secretary General of the PPS in Durango; alternate member of the Central Committee of the PPS, 1970-75; member of the Executive Committee of the Central Committee of the Mexican Popular Party. f-None. g-None. h-Practicing physician. j-None. k-None. l-Protag., 119; C de D, 1979-82.

Fierro Villalobos, Roberto
a-Nov. 7, 1897. b-Ciudad Guerrero, Chihuahua. c-Primary studies in Ciudad Guerrero; graduated from the Military Aviation School as a First Captain of Auxiliary Cavalry; Director of the Military Aviation School, 1932. d-None. e-None. f-Chief, Department of Civil Aviation, 1930; Director of Military Aviation, 1935-36; Interim Governor of Chihuahua, 1931-32; Director of Military Aviation, 1940; Military Attaché to China and Japan, 1936-38; Chief of the Mexican Air Force, 1959-64. g-None. h-Employed at various jobs in his youth, including at a pharmacy, as a railroad lineman, a

chauffeur, and an auto mechanic; businessman, 1941-59. i-Friend of *Marcelino Garcia Barragán* since 1921, when he was an instructor at the National Military College; married Carmen Jasso; father, a street vendor, and mother washed clothes to support his family in El Paso during the Revolution. j-Joined the Revolution in 1913, under the forces of General Jesús María Ríos; rejoined the Revolution in 1917, fighting under General Enríquez until 1920; fought against de la Huerta, 1923; fought against Escobar, 1929; Chief, First Air Regiment, 1929-30; rank of Brigadier General, 1938; reached rank of Division General. k-Worked in El Paso, Texas, 1911, at the Pierson Lumber Company; worked in Hollywood, California, 1913, as a movie extra; set world speed record flying from New York to Mexico City, 1930. l-Enc. Mex., IV, 1977, 168-69; DPE61, 33; DBM68, 218; WWM45, 42; letter; Almada, 578-79.

Figueroa, Andrés
(Deceased Oct. 17, 1936) a-Jan. 13, 1884. b-Chaucingo, Municipio de Huitzuco, Departamento de Hidalgo, Guerrero. c-Primary studies at the Morelos Institute and the Pape Carpentier Institute in Cuernavaca; no degree. d-Member of the City Council of Quetzalapa; Mayor of Quetzalapa; member of the City Council of Huitzuco, Guerrero. e-None. f-*Secretary of National Defense*, 1935-36. g-None. h-Agricultural laborer, 1907. i-Brother, Rómulo, fought in the Revolution with Andrés; son of small landowners; uncle of *Manuel Avila Camacho*. j-Joined the Revolution in Aug. 1910; supported Madero against Zapata; formed the "Figueroa Brigade" under General Obregón; fought against Carranza; commander of various military zones, 1920-35; fought against the Cristeros, 1926-29; Commander of the 22nd

Military Zone, Toluca, México; Commander of the 31st Military Zone, Chiapas, 1935. k-None. l-DP70, 770; D de S, 19 June 1935, 1; Enc. Mex., IV, 402; Q es Q, 207; HA, 28 May 1979, VI.

Figueroa Balvanera, Ignacio L.
(Deceased Dec. 5, 1959) b-Querétaro, Querétaro. c-Primary studies in Querétaro; secondary studies at the Normal School of Querétaro, 1908-12, graduating two years early with a teaching certificate, June 16-17, 1913. d-*Senator* from Querétaro, 1934-40. e-None. f-Involved with numerous irrigation projects in Querétaro; Assistant Director of the National Agrarian Commission, 1920-21; Director of National Properties, Secretariat of the Treasury, 1933-34. g-None. h-None. i-Political disciple of *Marte R. Gómez*, and later, *Emilio Mújica*; son of Ignacio L. Figueroa, director of the Normal School of Querétaro; brother of *José Figueroa Balvanera*, senator from Querétaro, 1952-58. j-None. k-None. l-Muñoz, 193-95; C de S, 1934-40.

Figueroa Balvanera, José
b-Querétaro, Querétaro. c-Primary studies in Querétaro; secondary and preparatory studies at the Colegio Civil, Querétaro; veterinary studies, National School of Agriculture, 1908-14, veterinary degree, 1914; postgraduate studies in Europe, Canada, Brazil, Argentina, and the United States. d-*Senator* from Querétaro, 1952-58, member of the Balloting Committee; First Secretary of the Special Committee on Livestock and the Committee on Health; President of the Agricultural and Development Committee and the Military Health Committee. e-None. f-Director General of Livestock, Secretariat of Agriculture and Livestock, 1951. g-None. i-Son of Ignacio L. Figueroa, distinguished teacher and director of the

Normal School of Querétaro; brother of *Ignacio Figueroa Balvanera*, senator, 1934-40. j-None. k-None. l-DGF51, I, 208; DGF56, 7, 9-10, 12-14; Ind. Biog., 61-62; Gómez, 196.

Figueroa Figueroa, Rubén
(Deceased Mar. 18, 1991) a-Nov. 9, 1908. b-Huitzuco de los Figueroa, Guerrero. c-Primary studies in Huitzuco; secondary studies in Mexico City; preparatory studies at the National Preparatory School; self-educated as a librarian and bibliographer, National Library of Mexico; degree in topographical and hydrological engineering, National Engineering School, UNAM. d-Alternate Federal Deputy from the State of Guerrero, Dist. No. 4, 1934-36; *Federal Deputy* from the State of Guerrero, Dist. No. 2, 1940-43, member of the Editorial Committee (1st year), the Tax Committee, and the General Means of Communication Committee; *Federal Deputy* from the State of Guerrero, Dist. No. 2, 1964-67, member of the Tariff Committee, the Automobile Transportation Committee, and the First General Means of Communication Committee; *Senator* from the state of Guerrero, 1970-74, member of the Gran Comisión, President of the General Means of Communication Committee, and the Public Works Committee; *Governor of Guerrero*, 1975-81. e-Delegate from Guerrero to the Constitutional Convention of the PNR, 1928; delegate to the PNR National Convention, 1933; General delegate of the CEN of the PRM to Quintana Roo, 1943. f-Porter, National Library, Mexico City; Assistant Librarian, National Library; Director, José E. Rodó Public Library; Assistant Director, Ibero-American Library, 1932; member, Mixed Agrarian Commission of Guerrero; topographical engineer, Guerrero; Inspecting Engineer, Railroad Department, Secretariat of Public Works, 1936-39; Sanitation

Engineer, Secretariat of Public Health; Executive Director, Cuenca del Balsas Commission, 1974. g-Student representative of the first year engineering students; member of the Mixed Agrarian Commission in Guerrero; member of the CNC committee in Chihuahua, 1942; President of the Truckers Alliance of Mexico, 1955-79. h-Director General of *Voz*; started own oil essence firm, 1944-50. i-Parents, Nicasio Figueroa Fuentes and Eufenia Mata, were peasants; married Lucía Alcocer, also the daughter of peasants; uncles were murdered during the initial stages of the Revolution; brother of *Ruffo Figueroa*; political ally of *Carlos Duffo*, federal deputy, 1973-76; son, Rubén Figueroa Alcocer, was the federal deputy from the Federal District, Dist. No. 17, 1979-82, and governor of Guerrero, 1993. j-None. k-Kidnapped by Guerrero guerrilla leader, *Lucio Cabañas*, May 30, 1974, and rescued by the Army on Sept. 8, 1974. l-*Excélsior*, 16 Mar. 1973, 22, 17 Aug. 1972, 5; C de D, 1964-66, 1940-42, 10, 48, 51; HA, 10 June 1974, 15-16; *Hoy*, 14 Mar. 1970, 4; *Excélsior*, 1 Feb. 1975, 6, 26 Dec. 1981, 16A; Latin America, 30 Mar. 1979, 99; *Excélsior*, 7 July 1980, 33A; DBGM89, 435; *Proceso*, 25 Mar. 1991, 20-23.

Figueroa Figueroa, Ruffo
(Deceased July 25, 1967) a-Nov. 10, 1905. b-Huitzuco de los Figueros, Guerrero. c-Completed primary studies; two years of secondary; no degree. d-*Federal Deputy* from the Federal District, Dist. 4, 1943-46; *Senator* from Guerrero, 1946-52, member of the Committees on Public Welfare and Social Security, and substitute member of the Economy and Statistics Committee. e-*Secretary General of the National Confederation of Popular Organizations*, 1964-65; important representative of the bureaucratic sector in PRI delegations. f-Subdirector of the ISSSTE,

1952-58, 1959-64; *Governor of Quintana Roo*, 1965-67. g-Delegate of Local 17 of the Union of the Workers of the Federal District (SUTDDF), 1935; Action Secretary of Local 17; Secretary of Interior, SUTDDF; Secretary General of Local 17, SUTDDF; Secretary of Labor and Strikes of the Popular Sector of the Federal District; Secretary of Bureaucratic Action of the National Federation of Popular Organizations, 1943; *Secretary General of the FSTSE*, 1943-46. h-Assistant librarian, 1922; librarian in the Jose Enrique Rodó Library. i-Brother *Rubén Figueroa* was a union leader of transportation workers, a federal deputy from Guerrero in 1940-42, 1964-66, and a senator from Guerrero, 1970-74; married Ilusión Cobian Sáinz; son, Rómulo Andrés, was a director general in the Secretariat of Communications and Transportation, 1982; nephew, Rubén Figueroa Alcocer, was governor of Guerrero, 1993. j-None. k-The Figueroa brothers are from a revolutionary family in Guerrero, their uncle, Ambrosio, initiated the Revolution in their native region and was shot by General Huerta; precandidate for governor of Guerrero, 1957, lost to *Raúl Caballero Aburto*. l-HA, 10 Dec. 1962, 21, 19 Jan. 1959, 11, 15 Nov. 1946, 5; DGF47, 20; DP70, 771; G of M, 10; Alvarez Corral, 153-54; DBGM, 146.

Figueroa Velasco, Juan
a-June 24, 1909. b-Coixtelhuaca, Puebla. c-Primary studies in the Benito Juárez School, Puebla; three years of secondary studies, University of Puebla; first year of preparatory studies at the University of Puebla; no degree. d-Local Deputy to the State Legislature of Puebla; *Federal Deputy* from the State of Puebla, Dist. 2, 1961-64, 1970-73, member of the Mines and the National Lands Committees. e-None. f-None. g-President of the National Committee of CROC; Secretary of Technical and

Economic Affairs of the National Committee of CROC; Secretary General of CROC in Puebla; director of *Resurgimiento*, the official paper of CROC in Puebla. i-Married Guadalupe Becerra. j-None. k-None. l-Directorio, 1970-72, 72-73; C de D, 1970-73, 114, 1961-64.

Flores Betancourt, Dagoberto
a-Jan. 20, 1906. b-Silacayoapan, Oaxaca. c-Primary studies in Silacayoapan and Mexico City; secondary studies in Mexico City, 1925-27; normal teaching certificate from the National Teachers School, Mexico City, 1928-30; preparatory studies at the National Preparatory School, Mexico City, 1930-31; law degree from the National School of Law, UNAM, 1932-36; school teacher. d-*Alternate Federal Deputy* from the State of Oaxaca, Dist. 10, 1937-40; *Federal Deputy* from the State of Oaxaca, Dist. 6, 1967-70, member of the Gran Comisión. e-None. f-Agent of the Ministerio Público. g-Leader in the National Union of Educational Workers. i-Father a peasant. j-None. k-None. l-D de Y, 4 Dec. 1970; C de D, 1967-70; MGF69, 94.

Flores Castellanos, Petronilo
(Deceased Apr. 4, 1957) a-May 31, 1890. b-Union de Tula, Hidalgo. c-Primary and secondary studies in public schools, Guadalajara, Jalisco; no degree. d-None. e-None. f-*Governor of Baja California del Sur*, 1956-57. g-None. h-None. j-Joined the Revolution in 1913, under General Diéguez; career army officer; rank of Brigadier General, Feb. 16, 1914; Chief of Staff of the 3rd Military Zone, La Paz, Baja California del Sur, 1939-56; Chief of Staff of the 28th Military Zone, Oaxaca, Oaxaca; commander of various military zones; Commander of the 3rd Military Zone, La Paz, Baja California del Sur, 1956-57. k-Served as Chief of Staff under *General Olachea Aviles* from 1946-56.

l-*Siempre*, 19 Sept. 1956, 10; DP70, 781; Peral, 276; Casasola, V.

Flores Curiel, Rogelio
a-Mar. 3, 1923. b-Tepic, Nayarit. c-Primary studies at the Juan Escutia School, Tepic, and the Fernando Montaño School, Nayarit; secondary studies at the Institute of Science and Letters of Nayarit; preparatory studies from the National Military College; graduated from the National Military College, 1941-44, graduated with distinction from the Staff School of the Higher War College, Mexico City; professor and Chief of Curriculum at the Higher War College, Mexico City, 1964-67; Subdirector of the National Military College, 1968-69. d-*Alternate Senator* from the State of Nayarit, 1964-70; *Senator* from Nayarit, 1970, 1971-75, member of the Gran Comisión, President of the Military Justice Committee, member of the permanent committee, 1974; *Governor of Nayarit*, 1975-81. e-Joined PRI, 1951; Auxiliary Secretary of the State Committee of PRI for Baja California; Delegate of the CEN of PRI to CNOP, 1975; special delegate of PRI to Chiapas, Durango, and Nuevo León. f-Member of the Mexican delegation to the Inter-American Defense Board, 1953; Military Attaché to El Salvador, 1959-61; Private Secretary to the Secretary of National Defense, 1961-64, *Agustín Olachea Aviles*; member of the Mexican Delegation to the International Air and Space Reunion; Chief of Police for the Federal District, 1970-71. g-Secretary of Legislation, CEN of CNOP, 1975-76. h-Scribe, Nayarit Department of Public Works. i-Wedding compadre of *Luis Echeverría*. j-Career army officer, 1st Sgt. of the Cadet Honor Squad at the National Military College; rank of Colonel. k-Removed from his position as Chief of Police after student riots in Oct. 1971. l-HA, 14 Dec. 1970, 25; MGF69-70; C de S, 1964-70;

Excélsior, 21 Feb. 1975, 12, 21 Mar. 1975, 4; Enc. Mex., Annual, 1977, 547.

Flores de la Peña, Horacio
a-July 24, 1923. b-Saltillo, Coahuila. c-Primary and secondary studies in Saltillo; preparatory studies at the Ateneo Fuente, Saltillo; degree in economics from the National School of Economics, UNAM, Dec. 13, 1955, with an honorary mention for his thesis on "Obstacles to Economic Development"; postgraduate work at American University, Washington, D.C., 1947-49; Professor of Modern Economic Systems, National School of Economics, 1956-63; Professor of Theories of Economic Development, National School of Economics, 1964-66; Director of the National School of Economics, UNAM, 1965-66; Executive Coordinator of the Technical Planning Commission of UNAM, 1967-70. d-None. e-Technical adviser to the IEPES of PRI. f-Member of the Mexican delegation to the United Nations, 1951-53; Director of Administration and Inspection of Decentralized Agencies and Enterprises, Secretariat of Government Properties, 1959-70; *Secretary of Government Properties*, 1970-75; *Ambassador to France*, 1977-82; *Ambassador to the Soviet Union*, 1982-88; Ambassador to Italy, 1989. g-None. h-Head of the Tariff Committee, 1944-47; employee of the Secretariat of the Treasury, 1950; employee of the Ejido Credit Bank, 1959; employee of the Agrarian Credit Bank, 1953-58. i-Student of *Eduardo Bustamante* at the National School of Economics, UNAM; attended UNAM with *Raúl Salinas Lozano* and *Octaviano Campos Salas*; married Alena Justic; member of *Emilio Mújica Montoya*'s group at UNAM; son of José Flores Dávila, farmer, and Concepción de la Peña Meléndez. j-None. k-None. l-DGF69, 238; DPE61, 58; HA, 7 Dec. 1970, 24; letter; *Hoy*, Dec. 1970; HA, 13 Jan. 1975, 7-8; LA, 17 Jan. 1975,

20; *Excélsior*, 13 Jan. 1983, 4A; Silva Herzog, 128-29; *Excélsior*, 29 Feb. 1980, 13A; DBGM87, 131; DBGM, 146.

Flores (Fernández), Edmundo
a-Nov. 20, 1918. b-Federal District. c-Early education unknown; degree in economics and agricultural engineering, National School of Agriculture, 1940; MS degree, University of Wisconsin, 1947; Ph.D. in economics, University of Wisconsin, 1948; visiting professor, Princeton University, 1962-63; visiting professor, University of Texas, 1957-58; Fellow, Mathematics Institute of Economic Research, UNAM, 1967; Professor of Agricultural Training, United Nations, Santiago, Chile, 1963; Professor of Agricultural Economics, National School of Economics, UNAM 1953-80; Professor of Economic Development, National School of Economics, UNAM, 1964-80. d-None. e-None. f-Agricultural economist, Rural Economics Division, Secretariat of Agriculture, 1950-52; Mexican Representative to the Food and Agricultural Organization, Rome, 1973-74; Special Ambassador to Cuba, 1975; Director General of the National Council of Science and Technology, 1976-82. g-None. h-Economist, United Nations, 1953. i-Son of Edmundo Flores and Paz Fernández; married Karin Schimmelpfeng; good friend of *Jesús Silva Herzog*, prominent economist, intellectual, and subsecretary of the treasury. j-None. k-Contributor to many newspapers and journals. l-JSH, 127-28; Enc. Mex., IV, 328; WNM, 77; Protag., 121.

Flores Fuentes, Raymundo
a-Mar. 15, 1913. b-Chalma, Veracruz. c-Normal teaching certificate; primary school teacher, Veracruz, 1933; secondary school teacher; professor at the Night Institute for Workers, Jalapa, Veracruz. d-Local deputy to the State Legislature of Veracruz; city council

member of Jalapa; *Federal Deputy* from the State of Veracruz, Dist. 1, 1955-58, President of the Administration Committee, member of the Second Government Committee. e-President of PRI in the State of Veracruz. f-Director of Population, Secretariat of Government, Reynosa, Tamaulipas; founder and President of the Board of Civic and Moral Improvement, Reynosa; President of the Electoral Committee for Baja California del Norte; Director of Customs, Tampico. g-Secretary General of the Teachers Union of Jalapa; Secretary General of Local 30 of the Union of Education Workers of Mexico (STERM); Secretary General of STERM, 1940; Secretary General of the CTM in the State of Veracruz; Secretary of Education of the CTM; Executive Secretary of the Southern Zone for the CNC, 1975; *Secretary General of the CNC*, 1957-59. i-Son, *Raymundo Flores Bernal*, was federal deputy from the State of Veracruz, 1970-73; relative of *Guilbaldo Flores Fuentes*, federal deputy from the State of Veracruz, 1976-79; married Etna Bernal Romero. j-None. k-None. l-Ind. Biog., 62-63; *Excélsior*, 5 Jan. 1957; DGF56, 28, 30, 34; Navarro, 220; *Directorio*, 1970-72; DBGM87, 131.

Flores Granados, Roberto
a-July 25, 1931. b-Ixtapalapa, Federal District. c-Primary studies at a private school in the Federal District; secondary and preparatory studies at the National Preparatory School No. 2, 1947-52; degree in dentistry from the School of Dentistry, UNAM, 1953-58; Professor of Surgical Techniques, UNAM; Secretary of the School of Odontology, UNAM, 1970. d-*Alternate Federal Deputy* from the Federal District, Dist. No. 21, 1967-70; *Federal Deputy* (from PAN Party), 1970-73. e-Joined PAN, 1948; Secretary of the PAN Committee for Dist. No. 21, Federal District, 1960; regional adviser to PAN, 1973. f-None. g-None. h-Practicing dentist. i-Married María Eugenia Hernández. j-None. k-Candidate for alternate federal deputy from the Federal District, 1961. l-Directorio, 1970-72; MGF69, 91.

Flores M., Alfonso
a-Aug. 3, 1907. b-Ixtlahuaca, México. c-Studies at the Scientific and Literary Institute of México, Toluca; no degree. d-*Federal Deputy* from the State of México, Dist. 7, 1937-40; *Senator* from the State of México, 1940-46, President of the Tariffs and Foreign Trade Committee, First Secretary of the Development of Cooperatives Committee, member of the Gran Comisión, First Secretary of the Tax Committee, President of the Public Works Committee, First Secretary of the Second Petroleum Committee, and Second Secretary of the Foreign Relations Committee. f-Manager of the Workers Clothing and Equipment Cooperative, 1947-52. g-None. h-None. k-None. l-PS, 2112; Libro de Oro, 1946, 6; DGF51, I, 504; C de S, 1940-46; C de D, 1937-40.

Flores Mazari, Antonio
a-1908. b-Jojutla, Morelos. c-Studies at the School of Mechanical Engineering, Mexico City; studies in journalism at the Methodist Institute; completed preparatory studies; no degree. d-*Senator* from the State of Puebla, 1964-70. e-None. f-None. g-Secretary General of the National Union of Newspaper Editors, 1964. h-Journalist; sports editor, *La Afición*; sports editor, *El Popular*; editor, *El Universal*. i-Member of *Emilio Riva Palacio*'s group. j-None. k-Outstanding football player on the champion Express Team, 1926. l-C de S, 1964-70; MGF69.

Flores Muñoz, Gilberto
(Deceased Oct. 6, 1978) a-May 4, 1906. b-Compostela, Nayarit. c-Studied at a military school in Guadalajara, Jalisco;

no degree. d-Federal Deputy from the State of San Luis Potosí, 1930-32, 1935-37; *Senator* from the State of San Luis Potosí, 1940-46, President of the Second Public Education Committee, the General Means of Communication Committee; Executive Secretary of the Second Foreign Relations Committee and the Securities Committee; *Governor of Nayarit*, 1946-51. e-Campaign manager for *Reynaldo Pérez Gallardo* for governor, 1939; Secretary of Labor Action, CEN of PNR, 1934-35; *Secretary of Education Action*, CEN of PNR, 1936-37; *Secretary General of the PNR*, 1937; National Coordinator of *Adolfo Ruiz Cortines'* campaign for president of Mexico, 1951-52. f-Labor Inspector for the State of San Luis Potosí, 1930; President of the Federal Conciliation and Arbitration Board, San Luis Potosí, 1928; *Secretary of Agriculture and Livestock*, 1952-58; Director General, National Sugar Industry Commission, 1977-78. g-None. h-Stock in La Moderna and Santa María tobacco companies. i-Good friend of *Rodolfo Sánchez Taboada*; political disciple of *Gonzalo Santos*; son, Gilberto Flores Izquierdo, was medical subdirector of IMSS in 1978; mentor of *Emilio González*; uncle was chief of operations in San Luis Potosí; supported *Luis Morones Prieto* for president. j-Joined the Army in 1923; supported the de la Huerta rebellion, captured and imprisoned in San Luis Potosí; Captain of the Cavalry, 1928; member of the General Staff of Carrera Torres. k-Precandidate for the PRI presidential nomination, 1957; offered the position of secretary of agriculture in the López Mateos administration; imposed *José Limón Guzmán* and *Francisco García Montero* as governors of Nayarit. l-D de Y, 2 Dec. 1952, 1; Brandenburg, 112; HA, 5 Dec. 1952, 9; DGF56, 223; DGF51, I, 91; Peral, 47, 123; EBW46, 93; Enc. Mex., IV, 336; D del S, 2 Dec. 1952; HA, 9 May 1955, 3;

WB54, 379; *Excélsior*, 12 Aug. 1977, 6; NYT, 28 July, 1957, 2; *Excélsior*, 11 Dec. 1969, 11 Mar. 1981, 23.

Flores Olea, Víctor

a-Aug. 24, 1932. b-Toluca, México. c-Primary and secondary studies in Mexico City; preparatory studies at the National Preparatory School; legal studies, National School of Law, UNAM, 1950-54, graduating Apr. 5, 1956; studies in history, School of Philosophy and Letters, UNAM, 1950-52; postgraduate work at the School of Law and Political Science, University of Rome, 1956-57, and at the Institute of Political Studies, Paris, 1957-58; MA and Ph.D. in political science, UNAM, 1968-69; postgraduate work at the London School of Economics, 1969-70; Professor of Political and Social Sciences, School of Political and Social Sciences, UNAM, 1959-75; professor at the National School of Economics, UNAM, 1960-62; Dean, School of Political and Social Sciences, UNAM, 1970-75. d-None. e-None. f-*Ambassador to the Soviet Union*, 1975-76; *Subsecretary of Popular and Extracurricular Education*, 1976-78; *Subsecretary of Culture and Recreation*, Secretariat of Public Education, 1978; Ambassador to UNESCO, 1978-82; *Subsecretary of Multilateral Affairs*, Secretariat of Foreign Relations, 1982-88; President, National Council of Culture and Arts, 1989-90. g-Supporter of the 1968 student movement. h-Author of several books on Marxism and socialism; practicing lawyer in the law firm of Oscar Morineau; lawyer for American Smelting and Refining, 1953-56. i-Published *Medio Siglo* with *Porfirio Muñoz Ledo, Arturo González Cosío*, and *Genaro Vázquez Colmenares*; thesis committee at UNAM included *Mario de la Cueva, José López Portillo, Enrique Velasco Ibarra*, and *José Campillo Sáinz*; son of Florencio Flores

Flores, industrialist, and María Teresa Olea Muñoz. j-None. k-None. l-HA, 17 Feb. 1975, 18; Excélsior, 7 Feb. 1975, 13; Enc. Mex., 1977, IV, 336; BdM, 123-24; HA, 27 Nov. 1978, 17-18; Silva Herzog, 132-33; Testimonios, 113; IEPES; DBGM89, 120.

Flores (Sánchez), Oscar
(Deceased Nov. 20, 1986) a-June 22, 1907. b-Chihuahua, Chihuahua. c-Primary, secondary, and preparatory studies in Chihuahua; law degree, National School of Law, UNAM, 1930. d-Senator from the State of Chihuahua, 1952-58, member of the Committees on Agricultural Development, Legislative Studies, Livestock, General Routes of Communication, and the First Ejido and Second Petroleum Committees; Governor of Chihuahua, 1968-74. e-None. f-Attorney for Labor, Chihuahua, 1931; Public Defender, Chihuahua; member of the Administrative Council of the National Bank of Agricultural and Livestock Credit, 1951; Director of the North American–Mexican Commission for the Eradication of Hoof and Mouth Disease, 1947-51; Subsecretary of Livestock, 1946-52; Attorney General of Mexico, 1976-82. g-None. h-Practicing lawyer, Chihuahua. i-Second cousin of José Juan de Olloqui. j-None. k-Precandidate for senator from Chihuahua, 1981. l-HA, 10 Aug. 1951, 15; DGF59, 149; DGF51, I, 203; II, 165, 219; HA, 5 Apr. 1949, iii; DGF47, 123; DGF56, 6, 10-14; Ind. Biog., 63-64; Excélsior, 1 Dec. 1976; López, 366; Excélsior, 26 Dec. 1981, 16A; letter.

Flores Tapia, Oscar
a-Feb. 5, 1917. b-Saltillo, Coahuila. c-Primary studies in Saltillo; teaching certificate; secondary teacher. d-Senator from the State of Coahuila, 1970-74, President of the Protocol Committee, First Secretary of the Second Public Education Committee and the Second Treasury Committee; Governor of Coahuila, 1975-81. e-Founder and President of the organization known as Culture and Political Science, which advocated Luis Echeverría for president of Mexico, 1968-70; President of PRI in Coahuila (twice); President of the Editorial Committee of the CEN of PRI, 1972-73; Secretary of Popular Action of the CEN of PRI, 1973. f-Director of Public Relations, Coahuila; Director of the Historical Archives, Coahuila; Director of Printing, City of Saltillo; Private Secretary to the Governor of Coahuila. g-Secretary General of the National Federation of Popular Organizations (CNOP), Nov. 9, 1972-75. h-Poet, historian, and author of numerous books on Mexico; traffic cop, Saltillo; he and his family own more than 30 businesses. i-Son, Francisco Flores Flores, was director of public works, Arteaga, Coahuila, 1978; daughter, Julia Isabel Flores Dávila, was a department head in his administration. j-None. k-Founding member of the National Liberation Movement in Mexico; resigned from the governorship under federal pressure; found guilty of "unexplicable wealth" by a congressional grand jury. l-C de S, 1970-76; HA, 20 Nov. 1972, 13; letter; Enc. Mex., 1977, III, 336; HA, 24 Feb. 1975, 14, 13 Jan. 1975, 29; Excélsior, 6 Jan. 1975, 7, 26 May 1978, 20, 8 Aug. 1981, 17-18A.

Flores Torres, Juan
a-Jan. 31, 1896. c-Early education unknown; no degree. d-None. e-None. f-Subsecretary of National Defense, 1958-61; Director General of Personnel, Secretariat of National Defense, 1964-70. g-None. h-None. j-Joined the Revolution; career army officer; rank of Brigadier General, May 1, 1938; commander of various military zones; Commander of the 3rd Infantry Division for the State of México and the Federal District; rank of Division

General. k-None. l-DPE61, 32; D del S,
1952; MGF69, 196; DPE65, 43; Peral,
47, 123; HA, 29 Dec. 1958, 8; *Siempre,* 7
Jan. 1959, 6; DGF47, 110.

Flores Valdés, Jorge Andrés
a-Feb. 1, 1941. b-Federal District.
c-Early education unknown; degree in
physics, School of Science, UNAM,
1958-62, with a thesis on "Theoretical
Analysis of Energy Levels of 201bi";
Ph.D. in physics, School of Science,
UNAM, 1962-65, with a thesis on the
theory of groups; postdoctoral studies,
Princeton University, 1965-67; post-
doctoral studies in nuclear theory at the
International Center of Theoretical
Physics, Trieste, Italy, 1969; professor,
UNAM, 1962; visiting professor,
Institute of Nuclear Physics, University
of Paris, Orsay; Dean, Physics Institute,
UNAM, 1974-82. d-None. e-None.
f-Coordinator of the Physics Science
Committee, Conacyt, 1974-78; *Subsecretary of Higher Education and Scientific Research,* Secretariat of Public
Education, 1982-85. g-President of the
Mexican Physics Society, 1973-75.
h-Director, *Mexican Review of Physics,*
1962- . i-Son of Jorge Flores Espinosa,
physician, and María de Jesús Valdés,
teacher; married Jacqueline Roux López,
biologist. k-None. l-HA, 20 Dec. 1982,
12; Q es QAP, 300; DBGM, 149.

Flores Zaragoza, Reyes Rodolfo
a-Oct. 18, 1929. b-Ayotlán, Jalisco.
c-Early education unknown; law degree,
University of Guadalajara, 1949-54,
graduating with a thesis on delin-
quency; special studies in public law,
University of Paris, 1954-55; Director,
Preparatory School No. 3, Guadalajara,
1958-70; professor, School of Economics
and Law, University of Guadalajara.
d-*Federal Deputy* from the State of
Jalisco, Dist. 1, 1973-76; *Alternate Federal Senator* from the State of Jalisco,
1976-79, in functions, 1979-82; *Federal*

Deputy from the State of Jalisco, Dist.
8, 1979, 1985-88. e-Joined PRI, 1951;
Director of State Youth of PRI, Jalisco,
1958; Director of the CEPES of PRI in
Jalisco, 1970; General Delegate of the
CEN of PRI in Puebla, 1973-75, Yucatán, 1975-76, Veracruz, 1980; Guerrero,
1980-81, Michoacán, 1981-84, and Campeche and Veracruz, 1984-86; President
of PRI in Jalisco, 1976-80; Subdirector of
the IEPES of PRI, 1980. f-Oficial Mayor
of the State Legislature of Jalisco, 1962-
68; Oficial Mayor of the City of Guadalajara, 1968-70. g-None. h-Practicing
lawyer, 1955-70. i-Son of Rodolfo Flores
Gutiérrez, primary teacher, and Consuelo Zaragoza Padilla, primary teacher;
married Leticia Márquez Gutiérrez.
j-None. k-None. l-DBGM87, 473; C de
D, 1973-76, 1979-82; 1985-88.

Foglio Miramontes, Fernando
a-Dec. 8, 1906. b-Temosachic, Chihuahua. c-Preparatory studies at the
Escuela Particular de Agricultura,
Ciudad Juárez, Chihuahua; engineering
degree in agronomy from the Escuela
Particular de Agricultura, 1925. d-*Governor of Chihuahua,* 1944-49. e-None.
f-Chief, Department of Agriculture,
Department of Agrarian Affairs, 1934-
35; Assistant Director General of
National Statistics, 1935-36; Director
General of National Statistics, Jan.,
1936, to Jan. 4, 1937; *Subsecretary of
Agriculture,* Jan. 5, 1937, to 1940; *Head
of the Department of Agrarian Affairs
and Colonization,* 1941-43; Agrarian
Adviser for the Department of Agrarian
Affairs, Consultant No. 2, 1964-65.
g-None. h-Regional agronomist, 1926;
author of works on the geography and
agriculture of Michoacán. j-None.
k-Precandidate for governor of Chihuahua, 1940, opposed by *Alfredo Chávez*
and ex-Governor *Gustavo Talamantes;*
competed for the PRI nomination for
senator from Chihuahua, 1970;
González Navarro states that he had

over 30,000 hectares of his own land in Laguna de Palomas, Chihuahua; supported *Javier Rojo Gómez* for president, 1946. l-DPE65, 171; EBW46, 48; Enc. Mex., IV, 343; Strode, 403; D de Y, 5 Jan. 1940, 1; *Hoy*, 21 Mar. 1971, 4; WWM45, 42; STYBIWW54, 738; González Navarro, 268; Anderson, 75-76; López, 367; Gaxiola, 318.

Foncerrada Moreno, Juan
a-Mar. 9, 1935. b-Federal District. c-Early education unknown; studies in economics, National School of Economics, UNAM, 1953-57, graduating in 1960 with a thesis on "Productivity of Manual Labor in Transformation Industries"; special courses in economics at the Organization of American States, 1972, and at the Inter-American Development Bank, 1975; Adjunct Professor, General Economic History and Economic Industrialization, National School of Economics, UNAM, 1960-63. d-None. e-None. f-Coordinator of Regional Delegates of Infonavit; Director of Analysis and Financial Evaluation, Secretariat of the Treasury; Representative of Mexico to the World Bank; adviser to the Executive Director of the World Bank, 1980-82; adviser to the Secretary of the Treasury, *Jesús Silva Herzog*, 1982; Director General of the Banco Refaccionaro of Jalisco, 1982; *Oficial Mayor of the Secretariat of the Treasury*, 1982-86. g-None. h-None. i-Son of businessman Miguel Foncerrada Basave and María Luisa Moreno Ruffo; grandson of engineer Carlos Foncerrada; married Beatriz Berumen Riquelme. j-None. k-None. l-*Excélsior*, 29 Dec. 1982, 18; QesQAP, 110; WNM, 79-80.

Fonseca Alvarez, Guillermo
a-June 22, 1933. b-San Luis Potosí, San Luis Potosí. c-Primary studies at a public school in Mexico City; secondary studies at "San Luis" Secondary School,

San Luis Potosí; preparatory studies at the University of San Luis Potosí; law degree, University of San Luis Potosí; teacher in history, geography and Spanish grammar, Professor of the General Theory of the State, Introduction to the Study of Law and Sociology, School of Law, University of San Luis Potosí. d-*Federal Deputy* from the State of San Luis Potosí, Dist. 4, 1967-68; Mayor of San Luis Potosí, 1968-69; *Senator* from San Luis Potosí, 1970-73; *Governor of San Luis Potosí*, 1973-79; *Federal Deputy* from the Federal District, Dist. 17, 1985-88. e-President of the Regional Committee of PRI of the State of San Luis Potosí; general delegate of the CEN of PRI; directed a San Luis Potosí committee to support *Luis Echeverría's* candidacy for President, 1969; *Director General of the IEPES of PRI*, 1979-80; President of PRI for the Federal District, 1980. f-Agent of the Ministerio Público of the Office of the Attorney General; Clerk for the Board of Conciliation and Arbitration of the State of San Luis Potosí; President of the Board of Conciliation and Arbitration of the State of San Luis Potosí; *Subsecretary of Agrarian Affairs*, Secretariat of Agrarian Reform, 1981-82; General Manager of Federal School Construction Program, Secretariat of Public Education, 1988-92; *Oficial Mayor of Agriculture*, 1992-94. g-Secretary of the Law Students Society of the University of San Luis Potosí; Secretary General of the Federation of University Students of San Luis Potosí; *Secretary General of CNOP*, 1987. h-Participant in various oratory contests in San Luis Potosí. i-Met *Luis Echeverría* as a federal deputy; son of Ignacio Fonseca Macías and Pilar Alvarez. j-None. k-None. l-HA, 22 Jan. 1973, 37-38; C de D, 1967-69; HA, 1 Oct. 1973, 30; Enc. Mex., Annual, 1977, 549-50; DAPC, 81, 57; DBGM89, 122; DBGM92, 128; DBGM87, 473; HA, 27 Jan. 1987, 10.

Fonseca García, Francisco
b-Federal District. c-Medical degree
from the National School of Medicine,
UNAM, 1925; professor, School of
Medicine, UNAM, 1964. d-*Federal
Deputy* from the Federal District, Dist.
4, 1949-52, member of the Child Wel-
fare and Social Services Committee, the
Legislative Studies Committee and the
Health Committee. e-None. f-Director
of the General Hospital of Mexico City;
head of Medical Services for the Insti-
tute of Social Security for Government
Employees, 1963; Subdirector General
(Medical) of the Institute of Social
Security for Government Employees,
1964-70. h-Surgeon in the General
Hospital, Mexico City, 1925. j-None.
k-None. l-HA, 21 Dec. 1964, 10;
DGF51, I, 21, 30, 32, 36; MGF69, 623.

Fox Cruz, Miguel Angel
a-Feb. 2, 1939. b-Los Mochis, Sinaloa.
c-Early education unknown; certified
public accounting degree, School of
Business and Administration, UNAM,
1958-62, with a thesis on "Implantation
of a Mechanized System for the Control
of Warehouses and Inventories."
d-None. e-Delegate of the IEPES of PRI
to Sinaloa, 1980-82. f-Auditor, Chief of
Auditors and General Supervisor,
National Warehouses, 1963-65; Director
of Auditing and Controller General,
Secretariat of Hydraulic Resources,
1965-70; Subdirector of Expenditures,
Secretariat of the Treasury, 1972-76;
Subdirector General of Public Expenditures, Secretariat of Planning and
Budgeting, 1977-78; Director General of
Administration, Secretariat of Agrarian
Reform, 1978-80; Secretary of Adminis-
tration, State of Sinaloa, 1981-82;
Director General of the North East
Bank, 1982; *Oficial Mayor of the Secre-
tariat of Agrarian Reform*, 1982-86.
g-None. h-Controller General, Perfora-
dor México, S.A., Fomento Inmobiliario,

S.A. and other private firms. i-Son of
Miguel Angel Fox Ibarra, farmer, and
Consuelo Cruz Muñoz; married Mary
Muller de la Lama. j-None. k-None.
l-Q es QAP, 379; DBGM, 151;
DBGM87, 135; DBGM89, 122.

Fraga (Magaña), Gabino
(Deceased July 27, 1982) a-Apr. 19,
1899. b-Morelia, Michoacán. c-Primary
studies in Morelia; secondary studies at
the Colegio Primitivo de San Nicolás de
Hidalgo, Morelia, 1910-13; law degree
from the National School of Law,
UNAM, 1920; LLD from the National
School of Law, UNAM, 1950; Professor
of Administrative Law, National School
of Law, UNAM, 1925-64; member of
the Governing Board of UNAM.
d-None. e-None. f-Consulting lawyer
to the Secretariat of the Treasury, 1920;
Oficial Mayor of the Secretariat of the
Treasury, 1920; head of the Consultative Department, Secretariat of the
Treasury; head of the Legal Department,
Secretariat of Labor, 1924; head of the
Legal Department, Secretariat of
Industry and Commerce, 1930; head of
the Department of Consultation and
Legislation, Secretariat of Agriculture
and Livestock, 1930; President of the
National Banking Commission, 1935-
38; *Justice of the Supreme Court*, 1941-
44, and President of the Second Chamber; *Subsecretary of Foreign Relations*,
1964-70. g-None. h-Practicing attorney
in Mexico City, 1920; practicing
attorney, 1938-41; member of various
commissions for new legal codes;
founding member of the Institute of
Public Administration; author of
numerous legal works. i-Professor of
numerous public figures at UNAM,
including *Hugo B. Margáin, José Castro
Estrada*, and *Manuel R. Palacios*; law
partner with *Antonio Martínez Báez* for
many years; son, *Gabino Fraga Mouret*,
appointed secretary general of IMSS,

1982. j-None. k-None. l-DPE65, 17; HA, 21 Dec. 1974, 4; DBM66, 244-45; WWM45, 42; Enc. Mex., IV, 392; *Justicia*, Sept. 1966; DAPC, 1977, 3.

Fraga Mouret, Gabino
a-Feb. 13, 1943. b-Federal District. c-Early education unknown; law degree, National School of Law, UNAM, 1962-68, with a thesis on "State Intervention in Economic Matters." d-None. e-General delegate of the CEN of PRI. f-Private Secretary to *Jesús Reyes Heroles*, President of the CEN of PRI, 1972-75; Private Secretary to *Jesús Reyes Heroles*, Director General of IMSS, 1975-76; Director of Government, Secretariat of Government, 1976-79; Coordinator of the Mexican Committee to Aid Refugees, Secretariat of Government; General Coordinator of the Committee on Energy, Plan of Government, 1982-88, 1981-82; *Secretary General of IMSS*, 1982-85; *Subsecretary of Housing*, Secretariat of Urban Development and Ecology, 1985-88; *Secretary of Urban Development and Ecology*, 1988. g-None. h-None. i-Son of *Gabino Fraga Magaña*, subsecretary of foreign relations, 1964-70, and Renée Mouret; married Anne Marie Hilaire. j-None. k-None. l-HA, 20 Dec. 1982, 14; DBGM, 151.

Fragoso Fragoso, Marco Antonio
a-June 13, 1943. b-Coacalco, México. c-Early education unknown; degree in romance languages; postgraduate studies in theology (1961) and language (1961-63) at St. John's University, Minnesota, on a fellowship; university professor. d-*Plurinominal Federal Deputy* from PAN, 1982-85. e-Member of PAN Central Committee, Tehuacán, Puebla, 1978-81; coordinator for PAN campaign for mayor of Tehuacan, 1979-80. f-None. g-None. h-Translator, Olympic Games, 1968; founding

member of the Cultural and Historical Center of Tehuacan, Puebla, 1977; founder of the Explorers Club of Mexico, Puebla, 1973; announcer for Radio XEWJ, Puebla; technical translator in English, French and Italian, 1961-67. i-Ignacio Fragoso Fragoso, businessman, and Isaura Fragoso Ramírez; married Andrea Faure Larrieu. j-None. k-None. l-Directorio, 1982-85; DBGM, 504; Lehr, 553.

Franco Bencomo, Joaquín
b-Yucatán. c-Agricultural engineering degree, National School of Agriculture, Chapingo. d-None. e-None. f-Adviser to the Department of Agrarian Affairs; Chief of Agricultural Advisory Service, Dist. 8, for Oaxaca, Michoacán, Tlaxcala, Department of Agrarian Affairs, 1952-58; Chief of Agricultural Advisory Service, Dist. 8, 1958-64; *Secretary General (2) of the Department of Agrarian Affairs and Colonization*, 1964-70. g-None. h-Agricultural engineer for the Department of Agrarian Affairs, 1930; member of various agrarian commissions. i-Married Teresa Góngora. j-None. k-None. l-HA, 11 Jan. 1965, 9; DGF56, 454; DPE61, 128.

Franco Díaz, Efrén
a-July 6, 1946. b-Federal District. c-Early education unknown; degree in mechanical and electrical engineering, UNAM, 1964-69, with a thesis on industrial diagnostics; MA studies in administrative sciences, Graduate School of Business and Administration, IPN; secondary teacher, 1964-69; Professor of Statistical Methods, Graduate School of Business, UNAM, 1970-72. d-None. e-Joined PRI, 1970. f-Technical Coordinator, Technological Activites, Secretariat of Public Education, 1968-73; Director of Project Administration, Organization and Method Unity, Federal Electric Com-

mission, 1971-72; Chief of the Office of Reception, Requests and Payments, Federal Electric Commission, 1973; Assistant Subdirector of Central Power and Light, 1973-76; Administrative Subdirector of Operations, Federal Electric Commission, 1976; Director General of Prices, Secretariat of Commerce, 1976-81; *Subsecretary of Internal Trade,* Secretariat of Commerce, 1981-82, 1982-85; Technical Director, National Price Commission, 1986-88; Oficial Mayor of the Secretariat of Fishing, 1988-89. g-None. h-None. i-Son of Efrén Franco Lugo, lawyer, and Catalina Díaz Lailson; married María de los Angeles Cañal Pickering. j-None. k-None. l-DAPC81, 23; Q es QAP, 190; DBGM, 151.

Franco López, Manuel
a-Apr. 10, 1921. b-Federal District. c-Preparatory studies from the National Preparatory School; engineering degree in mines and metallurgy from the National School of Engineering, UNAM, 1944; Professor of Geology and Mining Exploitation, School of Engineering, UNAM, 1954. d-None. e-None. f-Member of the National Council on Natural Resources, Secretariat of Government Properties; *Subsecretary of Unrenewable Resources of the Secretariat of Government Properties;* 1964-66; *Secretary of Government Properties,* 1966-70. g-President of the Association of Mining, Metallurgy and Geological Engineers of Mexico. h-Superintendent, Empresa Dos Estrellas, S.A.; Subdirector and Superintendent, Cia. Minera, S.A. and Concepción Carmen and Annexes, S.A., Guerrero; geologist for the Secretariat of Hydraulic Resources; General Manager, Metalúrgicas de Guadalupe, S.A., Zacatecas; Director, Department of Technical Studies, Mexican Society of Industrial Credit, S.A.; engineer, New Light Mine, Guanajuato; consulting engineer and contractor on many

projects. i-Classmate of *Luis de la Peña Porth;* father a mining engineer. j-None. k-None. l-D del S, 21 Sept. 1966; DPE65, 76; DBM66, 245; Enc. Mex., 1977, IV, 402; letter.

Franco Pérez, Víctor Manuel
a-July 28, 1918. b-Guanajuato, Guanajuato. c-Early education unknown; law degree, National School of Law, UNAM, 1939-43; LLD, National School of Law, UNAM, 1950-51; professor, National School of Law, UNAM, 1969. d-None. e-None. f-Secretary General of Agreements, Federal Tax Court, 1945-51; Secretary of Studies and Accounts, Supreme Court, 1951-67; Judge, First Circuit Court in Criminal Affairs, 1968-82; *Justice of the Supreme Court,* 1982-88. g-None. h-None. i-Son of Florencio Franco Vázquez, businessman, and Josefina Pérez Ramírez; married Aurora Pellotier Flores. j-None. k-None. l-DBGM, 654; DBGM87, 619.

Franco Rodríguez, David
a-Apr. 10, 1915. b-Pajacuarán, Michoacán. c-Primary studies in Pajacuarán; secondary and preparatory studies at the Colegio de San Nicolás; legal studies, National School of Law, UNAM; legal studies, Colegio de San Nicolás, 1935-39, graduating in 1940; Professor of law, University of Michoacán; Secretary, University of Michoacán. d-*Federal Deputy* from Michoacán, Dist. 4, 1949-51, member of the Gran Comisión, the Second Government Committee, the National Waters and Irrigation Committee, and the Legal Complaints Committee; *Senator* from Michoacán, 1952-58, member of the Gran Comisión, 1954, substitute member of the First and Second Committees on Credit, Money, and Credit Institutions and the Second Government Committee; member of the Small Private Farms Committee and the First Petroleum Committee; *Governor of Michoacán,*

1956-62. e-Joined the PNR, 1930; General delegate of the CEN of PRI many times. f-Agent of the Ministerio Público, Michoacán, 1938; Appeals Court judge, Cacomán, Tacámbaro, and Marauatío, Michoacán, 1940-42; consulting lawyer to the Secretary of Agriculture and the National Irrigation Commission, 1945-46; Director of the Consulting Department, Secretariat of Hydraulic Resources; *Assistant Attorney General (1) of Mexico*, 1964-70; *Assistant Attorney General of Mexico*, 1970-73; *Justice of the Supreme Court*, 1973-76, 1976-82, 1982-85. g-None. i-Grandfather, David Franco, was a local deputy in Michoacán and orator; son of David Franco Reyes, lawyer, and María Rodríguez Mora; married María de Jesús Bautista; uncle, Daniel Franco López, was judge of the superior court of justice of the Federal District. j-None. k-None. l-DPE65, 209; DGF51, I, 23, 30, 33; Enc. Mex., IV, 402; DGF56, 6, 9-12, 14; HA, 24 Sept. 1962, 28; DP70, 789; Ind. Biog., 64-65.

Franco Sodi, Carlos
(Deceased Apr. 16, 1961) a-1904. b-Oaxaca, Oaxaca. c-Primary studies in Oaxaca; preparatory at the Institute of Arts and Sciences of Oaxaca; law degree from the National School of Law, UNAM; Professor of Penal Law and the Penal Process, National School of Law, UNAM; Honorary Doctor of Laws, UNAM. d-None. e-None. f-Assistant Agent of the Ministerio Público of the Attorney General's Office for the Federal District; Director of the *Diario Oficial* of the Federal Government; Judge of the Criminal Court, Pachuca, Hidalgo; Director of the Federal Penitentiary in the Federal District, 1935-36; Judge of the First Instance; *Attorney General of the Federal District and Federal Territories*, 1946-52; *Attorney General of Mexico*, 1952-56; *Justice of the Supreme Court*, 1956-58 and 1958-

61. g-Member of the National Center of Anti-Reelectionist Students, National School of Law, UNAM, 1927, opposed to Obregón's election. h-Expert on criminal law; author of numerous books on legal subjects; editor of *Criminology*. i-Friend of *José Castro Estrada* and *Miguel Alemán* from college years. j-None. k-None. l-*El Universal*, 2 Dec. 1958; DGF51, I, 487; DGF47, 294; Peral, 282; DP70, 790; Enc. Mex., IV, 403; DGF56, 539; D del S, 2 Dec. 1946, 1; López, 369; Villaseñor, I, 264.

Franco Urías, Salvador
a-Jan. 15, 1890s. b-Durango. c-Early education unknown; law degree, National School of Law, UNAM. d-Federal Deputy from the State of Durango, Dist. 3, 1920-22, member of the Gran Comisión; Federal Deputy from the State of Durango, Dist. 3, 1922-24, member of the Gran Comisión; *Senator* from the State of Durango, 1940-46, President of the Military Justice Committee, First Secretary of the Physical Education Committee, Second Secretary of the Development of Cooperatives Committee and member of the Gran Comisión. e-Elected Federal Deputy as a member of the Cooperatist Party. f-None. g-None. h-Director of *El Continental*, El Paso, Texas; journalist for many years; friend and political patron to *Jorge Prieto Laurens*, secretary general of the National Democratic Party, 1945-46. i-Son of Jesús Franco Ugarte and Carmen Urías. j-Supported Adolfo de la Huerta against the government, 1923; supported the Escobar rebellion, 1929. k-None. l-Peral, 282; C de S, 1940-46; L de O, 1946, 6.

Fritsche Anda, Oscar
(Deceased 1965) a-Apr. 10, 1906. b-Guanajuato, Guanajuato. c-Primary studies in Guanajuato; preparatory in Mexico City; graduated from the

National Naval College, Jan. 1927;
spent several years at the National War
College, Mexico City; professor at the
Naval College; Director of the Naval
College of the Pacific. d-None. e-None.
f-Chief of Naval Services for the
Commander of the Navy, 1955-58;
Naval Attaché to Italy, 1958-61;
Subsecretary of the Navy, 1964-65.
g-None. h-Author of *Nomogramos
Astronómicos*. j-Career naval officer;
member of the Coast Guard, 1928-29;
head of the Department of Information,
Navy Department, 1933-34; Commander of the "Progreso," 1934-35;
commander of various naval zones
including the 3rd for Baja California,
1940-46; Commander of the 5th Naval
Zone, Ciudad del Carmen, Campeche,
1951. k-Shipped arms to Republican
Spain during the Civil War. l-DGF51, I,
389; Enc. Mex., IV, 414; DP70, 793-94;
DGF47, 234; DGF56, 386; HA, 21 Dec.
1964, 9.

Fuentes, Carlos
a-Nov. 11, 1928. b-Federal District.
c-Primary studies in Washington, D.C.,
1934-40; secondary studies at the
Grange School, Santiago, Chile; completed secondary in Washington, D.C.,
1946; preparatory studies at the Colegio
Francés Morelos, Mexico City; started
law studies at Catholic University,
Washington, D.C., 1948, and completed
his law degree from the National School
of Law, UNAM, with a thesis on "The
Rebus Sic Stantibus Clause in International Law," 1951; studies at the
Institut des Hautes Etudes, France;
fellowship from the Mexican Center for
Writers, 1956-57, lectured in the United
States; fellow at the Woodrow Wilson
Center for International Scholars,
Washington, D.C., 1973-74. d-None.
e-Joined the Mexican Communist Party,
1952; resigned 1962. f-Secretary of the
Mexican Delegation to the International
Law Commission of the United Na-

tions, 1950-52; member and secretary of
the Mexican Delegation to the International Labor Office, 1950-52; Cultural
Attaché to Geneva, Switzerland, 1950-
52; Assistant Director, Press Department, Secretariat of Foreign Relations,
1954; Press Secretary, United Nations
Information Center, 1954; Secretary and
Assistant Director, Cultural Department, UNAM, 1955-56; Director, Department of Cultural Affairs, Secretariat
of Foreign Relations, 1957-59; *Ambassador to France*, 1975-77. g-None.
h-Author of numerous best-selling
novels; cofounder and editor of *Revista
Mexicana de Literatura*, 1955-58; coedi-
tor of *El Espectador*, 1959-61, *Siempre*,
1959-60, and *Política*, 1960. i-Grandson
of Rafael Fuentes y Velez, a banker; son
of career diplomat and ambassador to
Italy, Rafael Fuentes Boettiger, and
Bertha Macías; became friends with
Octavio Paz, 1950; close friends in
student days with *José Campillo Sáinz*;
student of *Mario de la Cueva*, who
helped sponsor *Tierra Nueva* and *Medio
Siglo*; first wife, actress Rita Macedo;
second wife, Sylvia Lemus; first Mexican professor was *Hugo B. Margaín*.
j-None. k-Lived in self-imposed exile in
Europe, 1965-69; *Proceso* claims he
resigned as ambassador to France
because of differences with *Santiago
Roel*. l-IWW, 79-80, 411; CB, Oct. 1972,
10; Testimonios, 119; *Excélsior*, 23 Oct.
1975, 4; O'Campo, 120-22.

Fuentes del Bosque, Jesús G.
(Deceased 1960) a-June 9, 1893. b-Saltillo, Coahuila. c-Early education
unknown; no degree. d-None. e-None.
f-Chief of Staff, Secretariat of National
Defense, 1958-60. g-None. h-None.
i-Son of Julio Fuentes and Florentina del
Bosque. j-Joined the army Jan. 14, 1914,
under General Francisco Coss; staff
officer to Generals Pablo González and
Jesús Dávila Sánchez; rank of Colonel,
1924, for actions during a campaign;

rank of Brigadier General, Jan. 1, 1939; rank of Brigade General, Sept. 16, 1946; Commander of the 11th Infantry Battalion; Commander of the 1st and 2nd Artillery Regiments; Chief, Sections 2 and 3, Department of Artillery; Chief of Staff, 24th military zone; Commander of the garrison in Manzanillo, Guaymas, and Piedras Negras; Director of the Artillery Department, Secretariat of National Defense, 1958. k-Champion shooter, Central American Games, 1926; national champion in shooting, 1927. l-Rev. de Ejer., 1960.

Fuentes Díaz, Vicente
a-May 6, 1920. b-Chilpancingo, Guerrero. c-Primary studies in Chilpancingo; secondary studies from the National Teachers School; teaching certificate, National Teachers School, 1939. d-*Alternate Federal Deputy* from the State of Guerrero, Dist. 1, 1961-64; *Federal Deputy* from the State of Guerrero, Dist. 1, 1964-67, member of the Gran Comisión, President of the Chamber, Oct. 1965; member of the Cultural Affairs Committee, the Editorial Committee, the First Treasury Committee, and the Legislative Studies Committee on General Affairs; *Senator* from the State of Guerrero, 1970-76, President of the Editorial and Library Committee, Secretary of the First Foreign Relations and the First Tariff and Foreign Trade Committees; Secretary of the Gran Comisión; *Plurinominal Federal Deputy* from PRI, 1988-91. e-Member of the Mexican Communist Party, expelled, 1943; Secretary of Press and Propaganda for the Popular Socialist Party; editor of *El Popular*, the PPS paper; left the PPS in 1957; cofounder of the Youth Sector of PRI, 1938; member of the Regional Committee of PRI for the Federal District, 1954-61; Director of the National Editorial Commission of the CEN of PRI, 1969; *Secretary General of the CEN of PRI*, 1970-72.

f-None. g-Delegate to the Constitutional Congress of the Mexican Federation of Youth, 1938; Director of Press for the CNOP, 1963-64. h-Author of many books on politics and history; journalist since 1941. i-Friend of *Enrique Ramírez y Ramírez*. j-None. k-None. l-Scott, 181; Enc. Mex., IV, 487; C de D, 1964, 66; letters; HA, 8 Jan. 1973, 11; *Política*, Nov. 1969; WNM, 83; IEPES; DBGM89, 436.

Fuentes Martínez, Enrique
a-Mar. 3, 1918. b-Hermosillo, Sonora. c-Completed primary school, business school, and three years of professional studies in electrical mechanics; never taught. d-*Federal Deputy* from the State of Sonora, Dist. 2, 1967-70, member of the Vehicular Transportation Committee, the First Ejido Committee, the Livestock Committee, the Mines Committee, and the Fishing and Hunting Committees. e-Member of PAN. f-None. g-None. i-Married Amalia Rodríguez. j-None. k-Speaks English. l-MGF69, 95; C de D, 1967-70, 59, 64, 80; Directorio, 1967-70.

G

Galeano Sierra, Adalberto
(Deceased 1957) b-Campeche, Campeche. c-Primary studies in Campeche, Campeche; law degree, School of Law, Instituto Campechano. d-Senator from the State of Campeche, 1924-28. e-None. f-Secretary of the District Court, Campeche; Judge of the Superior Tribunal of Justice of the State of Campeche; Attorney General of Campeche; Secretary General of Government of the State of Campeche; Justice of the Superior Tribunal of Justice of the Federal District and Federal Territories, 1929-57. g-None. j-None. k-None. l-DP70, 803; Casasola, V, 2442; DGF56, 513; DGF51, I, 486.

Galguera Torres, Hilario
a-Mar. 26, 1928. b-Federal District.
c-Architecture degree, National School
of Architecture, UNAM, 1946-50;
Professor of Composition, Universidad
Femenina Motolinia; Assistant in
Composition, National School of
Architecture; Professor of Urbanism,
School of City Engineers, 1955; Professor of Composition, Universidad Ibero-
Americana, 1961. d-*Federal Deputy*
from the Federal District, Dist. 23,
1967-70, member of the Cultural Affairs
Committee and the Department of the
Federal District Committee. e-Director
of *Luis González Aparicio*'s campaign
for senator, 1964. f-Architectural
foreman, National Hospital Commission, 1956; Head of the Planning Subcommittee for Huixquilcuán, México;
Head of the Technical Works Division
for Nonoalco, 1960; Director General of
Projects for the Construction Commission of the Secretariat of Health, 1965.
g-President of the Student Association
of the National School of Architecture,
1948; Secretary of the Federation of
University Students and representative
before the Gran Comisión. h-Adviser to
UNESCO; foreman for Mario Pani and
Enrique del Moral, architects; supervisor of the construction of the rectory of
the National University. j-None.
k-None. l-DBM68, 249; C de D, 1967-
69, 58; MGF69, 91.

Galindo Arce, Marcelina
a-Nov. 30, 1920. b-Pichucalco, Chiapas.
c-Primary and secondary studies;
preparatory studies; normal teaching
certificate; school teacher. d-*Federal
Deputy* from the State of Chiapas, Dist.
4, 1955-58, member of the Promotion
and Development of Sports Committee,
the Child Welfare Committee, the
Social Security Committee, and the
Social Action Committee. e-None.
f-None. g-None. h-Journalist. j-None.
k-First female deputy elected from the

State of Chiapas. l-Ind. Biog., 65-66;
DGF56, 22, 30, 31, 36.

Galindo Ochoa, Francisco
a-Mar. 8, 1913. b-Tamazula de Gordi-
ano, Jalisco. c-Early education unknown; no degree. d-*Federal Deputy*
from the State of Jalisco, Dist. 7, 1949-
52, Secretary of the First Instructive
Section of the Grand Jury and member
of the First Balloting Committee;
Federal Deputy from the State of
Jalisco, Dist. 11, 1955-58, member of
the Second Balloting Committee and
the Editorial Committee (first year).
e-Adviser to the PRM; Director of the
Office of the Popular Sector of the PRM;
Treasurer of PRI during the Ruiz
Cortines presidential campaign, 1952;
President of PRI in the Federal District;
*Secretary of Political Action of the CEN
of PRI*, 1956-58; *Secretary of Press and
Publicity of the CEN of PRI*, 1958.
f-Director General of the Department of
Fishing; Director General of Press and
Publicity, Presidency of Mexico, 1965.
g-Secretary of Organization of CNOP,
Federal District; Secretary of the CEN
of CNOP. i-Son, Francisco Galindo
Musa, Secretary of the CEN of PRI,
1990-91, and Federal Deputy from
Jalisco; married Helena Musa Choaro.
j-None. k-None. l-DPE65, 11; Ind.
Biog., 66-67; DGF56, 25, 32, 334;
DGF51, I, 22, 34; DBGM89, 438.

Gallardo Dávalos, Salvador
a-July 9, 1893. b-Rio Verde, San Luis
Potosí. c-Preparatory studies at the
Scientific and Literary Institute of San
Luis Potosí, 1910; began medical studies
at the Scientific and Literary Institute of
San Luis Potosí, but abandoned his
studies to join the Revolution; completed medical studies at the National
School of Medicine, UNAM, 1915-18,
receiving his degree July 30, 1918;
professor, military teaching hospital,
1915; Professor of Literature, Institute

of Science and Literature, Aguascalientes; normal and preparatory school professor, Aguascalientes; founder of the Military Medical School, 1916. d-*Alternate Senator* from the State of Aguascalientes, 1946-52, but replaced *Edmundo Games Orozco* from 1950-52, member of the Gran Comisión. e-Founding President of the PNR, Aguascalientes, 1929; President of PRI in Aguascalientes, 1956; coordinator of the presidential campaign of *Adolfo Ruiz Cortines* in Zacatecas, 1952. f-Physician for the Secretariat of Health, Mexico City, 1933-35; physician for the National Rural Credit Bank, 1935-37; Coroner, State of Aguascalientes (30 years); physician, Justo Sierra Rural School, Cañada Honda, Aguascalientes. g-None. h-Lived in Aguascalientes, 1928-33; author of many plays and poems. i-Longtime friend of *Jesús Silva Herzog.* j-Joined the Revolution as a medical student; 2nd Captain, 1915; fought under Colonel Nieto, and Generals *Jara* and *Cándido Aguilar* in Veracruz; Major, medical corps, under General Fortunato Maycotte; fought in the forces of General Alberto Carrera Torres. k-None. l-DGF51,I, 5, 9; JSH, 140-43.

Gallardo González, Celia
a-1924. b-Morelia, Michoacán. c-Primary studies at the Mariano Jiménez Public School, Morelia; secondary at the University of Michoacán; normal teaching certificate, Normal School, University of Michoacán; preparatory studies in the social sciences, University of Michoacán; normal school teacher. d-Member of the City Council of Morelia, Michoacán, 1957-59; Local Deputy to the State Legislature of Michoacán, 1959-62; *Federal Deputy* from the State of Michoacán, Dist. 1, 1964-67, member of the Infant Welfare and the Fine Arts Committees. e-Secretary of Women's Action of the

State Committee of PRI, Michoacán; Secretary General of the State Committee of PRI of Michoacán, 1964. f-None. g-Secretary of Women's Action of the Federation of University Students of Michoacán; Secretary of Women's and Social Action of the State Federation of Workers of CNOP, 1944; member of the National Women's Council of CNOP, 1967. i-Father, a music teacher. j-None. k-None. l-C de D, 1964-67, 78, 79.

Gallástegui, José S.
a-Nov. 11, 1929. b-Federal District. c-Law degree. d-None. e-None. f-Career foreign service officer; attached to the Mexican Embassy in France; Director General of Legal Affairs for the Secretariat of Foreign Relations; Director General of the Diplomatic Service, of International Organizations, of the Consular Service, and of Migratory Workers; Head of the Office of Technical Advisers, Secretariat of Foreign Relations; Private Secretary to the Secretary of Foreign Relations under *Manuel Tello, José Gorostiza,* and *Antonio Carrillo Flores,* 1958-65; *Oficial Mayor of the Secretariat of Foreign Relations,* 1965-70; *Subsecretary of Foreign Relations,* 1970-76; Inspector General of the Diplomatic Missions, Secretariat of Foreign Relations, 1976-82. g-None. h-Joined the Foreign Service, June 1, 1947; rank of Ambassador. i-Married Luisa Paredes; served as Auxiliary Secretary to *Ernesto P. Uruchurtu* as Subsecretary of Government, 1952. j-None. k-None. l-DPE71, 6; DPE65, 17; DPE61, 15; HA, 14 Dec. 1970, 20.

Galván (Bourel), Ferrer
a-1920. b-Veracruz. c-Agricultural engineering degree, School of Agriculture, Ciudad Juárez, Chihuahua, 1937. d-Local Deputy to the State Legislature of Veracruz. e-None. f-Agronomist,

Department of Agriculture, State of
Veracruz, 1938; engineer, National
Highway Department; *Subsecretary of
Agrarian Action*, Secretariat of Agrarian
Reform, June 19, 1978-82. g-Chief of
the Agrarian Brigade, Acayucán, Veracruz; Substitute Secretary General of
the Agrarian Commission of Veracruz,
1948; Alternate Secretary General of the
CNC, 1952; *Secretary General of the
CNC (substitute)*, 1952-53. h-None.
i-Son of a distinguished Mexican
agrarian leader, Ursulo Galván, who
was a carpenter by profession; mother
worked in the Civil Hospital of Veracruz; grandparents were landless
peasants; mother, Irene Bourel, was a
federal deputy from Veracruz, 1961-64.
j-None. k-None. l-HA, 1 Feb. 1952, 8-9;
Enc. Mex., 1977, V, 74; *Excélsior*, 17
June 1978, 1, 10; Meyer, No. 13, 271.

Galván Campos, Fausto
a-1909. b-Cuernavaca, Morelos. c-Pri-
mary and secondary studies in Mexico
City; preparatory studies completed in
Mexico City, 1926; law degree, National
School of Law, UNAM, June 3, 1932,
with a thesis on the reforms in Article
One, of the Jan. 6, 1915 Agrarian Law.
d-*Senator* from the State of Morelos,
1952-58, President of the Agrarian
Department Committee, member of the
Second Balloting Committee, President
of the Second Instructive Section of the
Grand Jury, First Secretary of the
Special Forest Committee, and Second
Secretary of the Agricultural Develop-
ment Committee. e-President of PRI in
Morelos, 1952. f-Director of the
Congressional Library; Judge of the Fifth
Penal Court, Mexico City; President of
the Superior Tribunal of Justice of the
State of Morelos; Secretary General of
Government of the State of Morelos,
1951, under Governor *Ernesto Escobar
Muñoz*. g-Cofounder of the CNC;
founder of the League of Agrarian
Communities of the State of Morelos.

i-Classmate at the National School of
Law of *Ernesto Escobar Muñoz* and
Jesús Castillo López, governor of
Morelos, 1942-46. j-None. k-None.
l-Ind. Biog., 67; DGF51, I, 90; C de S,
1952-58; DGF56, 6, 9, 10, 11, 13, 14.

Galván López, Félix
a-Jan. 20, 1913. b-Villa de Santiago,
Guanajuato. c-Primary studies in Villa
de Santiago; preparatory studies in
Mexico City and in Querétaro; enrolled
at the National Military College, Jan. 7,
1930, graduated as a 2nd Lieutenant in
the Cavalry, Jan. 1, 1934; distinguished
cadet, served as a sergeant of the cadets;
graduated from the Staff and Command
School, Higher War College, 1941-44;
course in military arms from the
Applied Military School, 1937; lecturer
at the Inter-American Defense College,
Washington, D.C. d-None. e-None.
f-Member of the Presidential Staff,
1946-52; Assistant to the Military
Attaché, Washington, D.C., Jan. 1, 1952
to Apr. 30, 1953; Assistant to the
Inspector General of the Army, Oct. 1,
1959 to Aug. 15, 1965; Private Secretary
to the Secretary of National Defense,
Marcelino García Barragán, Aug. 16,
1965 to Jan. 15, 1969; Chief of Staff of
the Secretariat of National Defense, Jan.
16, 1969 to Nov. 30, 1970; *Secretary of
National Defense*, 1976-82. g-None.
h-None. i-Married Elisa Juárez; his
mentor was *Marcelino García Barragán*,
who opposed *Luis Echeverría* for the
presidency; parents owned a printing
shop. j-Career army officer; served in
the 20th, 13th, and 35th Regiments,
1934-40; fought against the rebellion of
Saturnino Cedillo in San Luis Potosí,
1939; Section Chief of the 3rd Infantry
Division, 1946; rank of 2nd Captain,
1946; rank of Colonel, Nov. 16, 1952;
rank of Brigade General, Nov. 20, 1968;
rank of Division General, Nov. 20,
1970; Commander of the 6th Military
Zone, Torreón, Coahuila, 1970-72;

Commander of the 16th Military Zone, Irapuato, Guanajuato, 1973-74; Commander of the 5th Military Zone, Chihuahua, Chihuahua, 1974-76. k-Founded the first school for the Huichole Indians, Jalisco, 1939; *Acción* claims he was selected to represent a balance between *Luis Echeverría* and *Ricardo Cházaro*. l-HA, 6 Dec. 1976, 22; *El Día*, 1 Dec. 1976; DPE65, 34; Enc. Mex., Annual, 1977, 536-37; *Excélsior*, 1 Dec. 1976, 13; Acción, 18 Jan., 1982, 8.

Galván Maldonado, Rafael
(Deceased July 3, 1980) a-Nov. 7, 1919. b-Uruapán, Michoacán. c-Primary studies in Jacona and Zamora, Michoacán; secondary and preparatory studies from the Colegio de San Nicolás, Morelia, Michoacán, and from Vocational School No. 2 of the IPN and the National Preparatory School No. 1; two years of studies at the Higher School of Mechanical and Electrical Engineering, IPN; four years of studies at the National School of Economics, UNAM. d-*Senator* from the State of Michoacán, 1964-70, member of the Gran Comisión. e-Founding member of the PRM. f-None. g-Student leader; founder of several student newspapers; began union actvities in the National Federation of Electric Industry Workers, 1939; Secretary General and founder of the Union of Electrical Workers of the Mexican Republic (STERM), 1952-72; his union joined the National Union of Electricians and Related Occupations (SUTERM), 1972; President of the National Industrial Workers Central. h-Employee of the Radio and Electric Industry; worked as a porter for years; employee of the La Boquilla, Chihuahua Electric Plant; wrote for *Excélsior*. i-Married Laura Chávez. j-None. k-His senatorial nomination surprised most observers; expelled from SUTERM, 1975; antagonized PRI leadership because of his independent union

leadership. l-PS, 2199; C de S, 1964-70; MGF69; *Excélsior*, 4 July 1980, 4, 30; HA, 14 July 1980, 16.

Gálvez Betancourt, Carlos
a-Feb. 14, 1921. b-Jiquilpán, Michoacán. c-Preparatory studies from the National Preparatory School, 1939-40; law degree, National Law School, UNAM, 1946, with a special mention; Professor of Logic and Ethics, National Preparatory and Normal School, 1949-64; Professor of Constitutional Law and the Philosophy of Law, National School of Law, UNAM. d-*Governor of Michoacán*, 1968-70. e-Joined the PRM, 1940. f-Subdirector of the Department of Professions, Secretariat of Public Education, 1950-56; Subdirector of the Department of Physical Education, Secretariat of Public Education, 1956-58; Subdirector and Director of Immigration, Secretariat of Government, 1958; Subdirector General of Government, Secretariat of Government, under *Tristán Canales Valverde*, 1958-61; Director General of Legal Affairs, Secretariat of Government, 1964; *Oficial Mayor of Government*, 1964-65; *Subsecretary of Government*, under *Luis Echeverría Alvarez*, 1965-68; *Director General of the Mexican Institute of Social Security*, 1970-75; *Secretary of Labor*, 1975-76. g-Secretary General of the Association of Professors and Intellectual Workers. h-Worked for the Department of Professions, Secretariat of Public Education, 1945-48. i-Student with *Alfonso Noriega Jr.* at the National University; collaborator of *Luis Echeverría* in various positions, 1954-68; uncle of *Ignacio Gálvez Rocha*, federal deputy from Michoacán, 1970-73; son of Ignacio Gálvez Hijar and Carlota Betancourt Quiroz. j-None. k-None. l-DPE61, 12; DPE65, 13; HA, 7 Dec. 1970, 26; DGF56, 302; HA, 21 Dec. 1964, 4; HA, 6 Oct. 1975; Cadena, 38; *El Nacional*, 1 Mar. 1990.

Gálvez Rocha, Ignacio
a-June 22, 1940. b-Jiquilpán, Michoa-
cán. c-Primary studies at the Federal
School Francisco Madero, Jiquilpán,
1949-54; preparatory studies at the
National Preparatory School No. 2,
Mexico City, 1955-60; medical degree,
National School of Medicine, UNAM,
1961-67. d-*Federal Deputy* from the
State of Michoacán, Dist. 5, 1970-73,
member of the Public Assistance
Committee, the Social Welfare Com-
mittee (1st year), and the Health
Committee. e-Delegate of the CNOP of
PRI during *Gustavo Díaz Ordaz's*
campaign for president, 1964; Secretary
of Political Action and Vice-President of
the National Committee of CNOP;
Delegate for Internal Affairs, CNOP;
Secretary of Social Action, CEN of
CNOP, 1974. f-Director of Medical
Services for Sports, Secretariat of Public
Works; Auxiliary Secretary to Governor
Carlos Gálvez Betancourt, 1968-70.
g-Secretary of Political Action of the
Mexican Federation of University
Students. h-None. i-Nephew of *Carlos
Gálvez Betancourt*. j-None. k-None.
l-Directorio, 1970-72; C de D, 1970-72,
114; *Excélsior*, 20 Oct. 1974.

Gama (y Cruz), Valentín
(Deceased 1942) a-1868. b-San Luis
Potosí, San Luis Potosí. c-Secondary
and preparatory studies at the Scientific
and Literary Institute of San Luis
Potosí; degree in engineering, National
School of Engineering, 1893; professor,
National School of Engineering, 1904-
15; Dean, National School of Engineering. d-None. e-Cofounder of PAN,
1939. f-Member of the International
Boundary Commission between Mexico
and the United States, 1891-96; Subdirector of the National Observatory,
1903-10; Director of the National
Observatory; Rector of UNAM, Sept. to
Dec. 1914 and Apr. to June 1915.
g-None. h-None. i-Son of Dr. Ignacio

Gama, Rector of the Scientific and
Literary Institute of San Luis Potosí.
j-None. k-None. l-DP70, 810; López,
385.

Gamboa Cano, Rafael P.
a-Sept. 16, 1930. b-Tapachula, Chiapas.
c-Early education unknown; economics
degree, National School of Economics,
UNAM. d-*Federal Deputy* from the
State of Chiapas, Dist. 1, 1961-64, 1979-
82. e-President of PRI in Chiapas; general delegate of CNOP to various states;
President of PRI in the Federal District;
active in the presidential campaign in
Nuevo León, 1981-82; General Delegate
of the CEN of PRI (14 times), General
Delegate of the CEN of PRI to Sinaloa,
1983; *Secretary of Organization of the
CEN of PRI*, 1966; Assistant Secretary
of the CEN of PRI, 1985, 1988. f-General Manager, Companía Exportadora y
Importadora de México, 1956-58; Director General of the Industrial de Abastos,
1970-76; General Manager of Airports
and Auxiliary Services, 1986; Director
General of Social Communication,
Secretariat of Labor, 1992-94. g-None.
h-None. i-Son of *Rafael Gamboa
Pascasio*, president of the CEN of PRI,
1946, and Carmen Cano; cousin,
Humberto Gamboa Pascasio served as a
federal deputy, 1943-45; uncle, Dr. Noé
Gamboa Pascasio, was a local deputy,
Chiapas; married María Inés
Castellanos Vázquez. j-None. k-None.
l-*Excélsior* 30 Sept. 1983, 2A; Protag.,
130; DBGM92, 135.

Gamboa Pascasio, Rafael
(Deceased Aug. 2, 1979) a-May 20,
1897. b-Tuxtla Gutiérrez, Chiapas.
c-Primary studies in Tuxtla Gutiérrez;
secondary studies at the Prevocational
and Industrial School; medical degree
from the National Medical School,
UNAM, 1923; studies in medicine in
France; professor at the University of
Chiapas. d-*Federal Deputy* from the

State of Chiapas, Dist. 2, 1937-40; *Governor of Chiapas*, 1940-44. e-General Coordinator of *Miguel Aleman's* campaign for President; first President of the reorganized CEN of PRI, Jan. 19 to Dec. 5, 1946. f-Director General of Pensions of the Union of Government Bureaucrats, 1945; Secretary General of Government of the State of Chiapas, 1939-40, under Governor *Efraín Gutiérrez; Secretary of Public Health*, 1946-52. g-None. h-Practicing physician in Tuxtla Gutiérrez, 1923-35; entered state politics, 1935. i-Father-in-law of *Emilio Rabasa*, secretary of foreign relations, 1970-75; son *Rafael P. Gamboa Cano* was a federal deputy from Chiapas, 1961-64, 1979-82; married Carmen Cano; uncle of Humberto Gamboa Pascasio, federal deputy from Chiapas, 1943-45. j-None. k-Was imposed by *Miguel Alemán* as the president of PRI alienating other party leaders. l-*Polémica*, Vol. I, No. 1, 1969; *Hoy*, 21 Dec. 1940, 78; DGF50, II, 485; DPE51, I, 733, 335; DPE51, II, 713, etc.; *Excélsior*, 2 Dec. 1946; HA, 6 Dec. 1946, 6; Enc. Mex., V, 106-07; HA, 13 Aug. 1979, 11.

Gamboa Pascoe, Joaquín
a-May 30, 1922. b-Federal District. c-Secondary studies at Secondary No. 4, Mexico City; preparatory studies from the National Preparatory School; law degree, National School of Law, UNAM, 1939-44; Professor of Labor Law, National School of Law, UNAM. d-*Alternate Senator* from the Federal District under *Fidel Velázquez Sánchez*, 1958-64; *Federal Deputy* from the Federal District, Dist. 18, 1961-64, member of the Labor Section of the Legislative Studies Committee and the First Constitutional Affairs Committee; *Federal Deputy* from the Federal District, Dist. 13, 1967-70, member of the Administration Committee, the Second Instructive Section of the Grand Jury, the Budget and Accounts Committee (second year), and the Second Labor Committee; *Senator* from the Federal District, 1976-82, President of the Gran Comisión, 1976-82. e-Auxiliary Secretary to the CEN of PRI, 1966-68; Assistant Secretary of the CEN of PRI, 1968-70. f-None. g-Secretary of Political Action of the Union of Workers of the Department of the Federal District, 1962-70; lawyer, Legal Office, Union of Workers of the Department of the Federal District, 1946; legal adviser of the Union of Workers of the Department of the Federal District, 1946-70; Secretary General of the Union of Workers of the Department of the Federal District, 1973-78; Secretary General of the CTM in the Federal District, 1977-82. i-Longtime friend of *Jesús Yurén*, whom he met at the Legal Office of the Union of Workers of the Department of the Federal District; son-in-law of *Fidel Velázquez*; son, Joaquín Gamboa Enríquez was a precandidate for federal deputy, 1979; father a businessman; classmate of *José López Portillo* at UNAM. j-None. k-PRI candidate for federal deputy from the Federal District, 1973, but defeated by *Javier Blanco Sánchez* of PAN. l-C de D, 1961-64, 78, 1967-70, 55, 79, 83; *Proceso*, 18 Dec. 1976, 8-9, 11 Dec. 1976, 20-21.

Gamboa Patrón, Emilio
a-Aug. 23, 1950. b-Federal District. c-Early education unknown; studies in industrial relations at Ibero-American University, 1970-74; received his degree in 1979 with a thesis on a development program for workers in a decentralized government agency. d-None. e-Member of the advisory council to the IEPES of PRI; member of PRI. f-Administrative assistant, Director of Projects, IMSS, 1969-71; adviser, Director of the Department of Personnel Development, IMSS, 1971-73; Subdirector, Depart-

ment of Personnel Development, IMSS, 1973-76; Private Secretary to the Technical Subdirector of Workers Housing Fund, 1976; adviser, Subdirector of Collective Transportation Service, Metro, Secretariat of Transportation, 1978; Private Secretary to *Miguel de la Madrid*, Secretary of Planning and Budgeting, 1979-82; *Private Secretary to President de la Madrid*, 1982-88; Director of Federal Workers Housing Insitute, 1988-91; *Director General of the IMSS*, 1991-93; *Secretary of Communications and Transportation*, 1993-94. g-President of the Student Society of Ibero-American University. h-None. i-Political disciple of *Miguel de la Madrid*; classmate of *Genaro Borrego* at Ibero-American University; *Borrego* invited him to be auxiliary secretary to *de la Madrid*; son of Emilio Gamboa Martínez, businessman, and Josefina Patrón Méndez; married María Angélica Miner de la Concha; brother, Jorge Antonio, was delegate of the Secretariat of Tourism, 1993. j-None. k-None. l-*News*, 29 Nov. 1982; HA, 13 Dec. 1982, 20; Q es QAP, 17; DBGM, 157-58; *El Nacional*, 4 Jan. 1991, 1-5; DBGM92, 136.

Games Orozco, Edmundo
(Deceased 1953) a-Feb. 28, 1902. b-Aguascalientes, Aguascalientes. c-Primary studies in Aguascalientes; teaching certificate from the San Carlos Academy, Mexico City, 1919-23; secondary school teacher; Professor of Pedagogical Studies, 1936. d-*Senator* from the State of Aguascalientes, 1946-52, member of the First Committee on Tariffs and Foreign Commerce, the Agrarian Department Committee, the First Committee on Public Education, the Consulate and Diplomatic Service Committee, and the Protocol Committee; substitute member of the National Railroads Committee; *Governor of Aguascalientes*, 1950-53. e-None. f-Director General of Education, State of

Aguascalientes, 1934-36; Secretary of the Federal Department of Education, Secretariat of Public Education; Director of Federal Schools in the State of Aguascalientes; Federal Inspector for the Secretariat of Public Education, State of Coahuila, 1937; Federal Inspector, Secretariat of Public Education, Ojo Caliente, Zacatecas, 1937-40; Federal Inspector, Secretariat of Public Education, Juchilpila, Zacatecas, 1941-44; Director of Education in Zacatecas for the Secretariat of Public Education, 1944-46. g-Director of the Teachers Union, 1940. i-Parents descendants of a long line of Spaniards in Mexico. j-None. k-None. l-DGF47, 19; Enc. Mex., V, 109; DGF51, I, 5, 10, 11, 14, 88; C de S, 1946-52; DP70, 812; Anderson.

Gámiz Fernández, Everardo
a-Apr. 13, 1924. b-Durango, Durango. c-Primary and secondary studies in Durango; normal certificate, Normal School of Durango, 1938-40; preparatory studies in Mexico City; began professional studies in civil engineering, but left to work, 1939; taught at Thomas Edison and Justo Sierra Institutes, 1949-52. d-*Federal Deputy* from the Federal District, Dist. 5, 1964-67, member of the Public Housing Committee, the Editorial Committee, and the Department of the Federal District Committee; *Federal Deputy* from the Federal District, Dist. 21, 1982-85, 1991-94. e-Joined the judicial division of the PRM, 1937; general delegate of the CEN of PRI, 1959; President of PRI in the Federal District, 1963-66, 1970-71. f-Employee of the Department of the Federal District, 1939; Manager, Learning Centers, CONASUPO, 1976-82; Delegate of the Department of the Federal District to Venustiano Carranza, 1985-88. g-Secretary General, Executive Committee, Local 11, Department of the Federal District Union, 1946-55; Secretary of Organiza-

tion, Labor, and Conflicts, Local 11, Department of the Federal District Union, 1949-63; other posts on the Executive Committee of the Department of the Federal District Union; Secretary of Organization of the CEN of the FSTSE, 1967; Secretary General of the Department of the Federal District Union, 1964-67, 1982-85. h-None. i-Son of Everardo Gámiz Olivas, teacher and peasant, and Luz Fernández Rosa; brother of *Salvador Gámiz Fernández*, senator from Durango, 1970-76; brother of *Máximo Gámiz Fernández*, federal deputy from Durango, 1952-55; married Concepción Larnoa. j-None. k-None. l-PS, 2223; C de D, 1964-67, 81; Lehr, 139; Directorio, 1982-85; DBGM, 503.

Gámiz Fernández Jr., Salvador
a-July 9, 1922. b-Durango, Durango. c-Primary studies in Durango; secondary studies at a public school in Durango; medical degree, IPN. d-*Senator* from the State of Durango, 1970-76, member of the Gran Comisión, President of the Health Committee, member of the First Balloting Group, First Secretary of the First Foreign Relations Committee, Second Secretary of the Public Welfare Committee. e-Joined PRI, 1958; aide to the President of the CEN of PRI, 1960-65; President of PRI in Durango; general delegate of the CEN of PRI, 1964; *Secretary of Political Action of the CEN of PRI*, 1970-71; *Subsecretary of Political Action of the CEN of PRI*, 1973. f-Physician, Secretariat of Health, 1960-69; Director, ISSSTE Clinic; *Interim Governor of Durango*, Dec. 13, 1979-1980. g-Member of the Technical Council of the CNC; President of the Medical Association of the IPN; President of the National Association of Graduates of Schools for Workers' Sons. i-Father, a peasant; brother, *Máximo Gámiz Fernández*, was secretary general of PRI in the Federal District and a federal deputy from Durango, 1952-55;

brother, *Everardo Gámiz Fernández*, was a federal deputy from the Federal District, 1964-67; originally a political disciple of *Vicente Lombardo Toledano*; member of *Jesús Robles Martínez*'s political group at IPN; precandidate for rector of IPN, 1982. j-None. k-None. l-*Excélsior*, 16 Dec. 1979, 18; HA, 24 Dec. 1979, 10; C de S, 1970-76, 75; *Excélsior*, 4 Dec. 1982, 4A.

Gandarilla Avilés, Emilio
a-Feb. 6, 1923. b-Federal District. c-Completed primary and secondary studies; no degree. d-*Federal Deputy* from the Federal District, Dist. 8, 1958-61, member of the Department of the Federal District Committee, the General Accounting Office Committee, and the Budget and Accounts Committee; *Federal Deputy* from the Federal District, Dist. 8, 1964-67, member of the Department of the Federal District Committee, the Complaints Committee, and the Foreign Relations Committee. e-President of PRI for the Eighth District, Federal District. f-Adviser to the Director of Pensions; President of the National Housing Committee; Private Secretary to *Rómulo Sánchez Mireles*, president of the Gran Comisión, 1964-67. g-Secretary of Interior of Section Fifteen, the Department of the Federal District Union, 1947; Press Secretary of the Department of the Federal District Union; Secretary of the Pension Fund of the Department of the Federal District Union; Secretary General of CNOP in the Federal District, 1964. h-Journalist; photographer; graphic editor of *El Universal*. j-None. k-None. l-Func., 183; C de D, 1958-60, 77, 1964-67, 81, 92, 93; PS, 2231.

Garabito Martínez, Jorge
a-Mar. 29, 1915. b-Guadalajara, Jalisco. c-Primary and secondary studies in Guadalajara; preparatory studies in Guadalajara; law degree, School of Law,

University of Guadalajara; studies in
economics and philosophy. d-*Federal
Deputy* from the Federal District, Dist.
16, 1964-67, member of the Penal
Section of the Legislative Studies
Committee; *Federal Deputy* from the
Federal District, Dist. 1, 1970-73,
member of the Department of the
Federal District Committee, Social
Security Committee, Fish and Game
Committee, and the Cinematographic
Development Committee; *Federal
Deputy* from the Federal District, Dist.
12, 1976-79. e-Founding member of
PAN, 1939; represented PAN before the
Federal Electoral Committee; President
of PAN in the Federal District; member
of the CEN of PAN. f-None. g-None.
h-Practicing lawyer; entrepreneur in the
glass industry. i-Married María Teresa
Yáñez. j-None. k-None. l-C de D,
1976-79, 23, 1964-67, 83; Directorio,
1970-72; C de D, 1970-73, 115; Mabry.

Garate (Legleu), Raúl
a-Sept 11, 1892. b-Matamoros, Tamaulipas. c-Primary studies at a public
school, Matamoros; secondary studies
in the United States; no degree.
d-Deputy to the Constitutional Convention from the State of Tamualipas, Dist.
3, 1916-17; Federal Deputy from the
State of Tamaulipas, 1917-18; *Senator*
from the State of Tamaulipas, 1952-58,
member of the General Means of
Communication Committee, the War
Materiels Committee, and the Third
National Defense Committee. e-President of the Revolutionaries Club,
Brownsville, Texas, 1913. f-Inspector
General of Police, Mexico City, 1919-
20; Director of Public Charities, Federal
District, 1919; *Subsecretary of National
Defense*, 1946-47; *Provisional Governor
of Tamaulipas*, 1947-51. g-None.
h-None. i-Friendship with *Manuel
Avila Camacho* helped career; political
enemy of *Emilio Portes Gil*; from a
wealthy family. j-Joined the Revolution

in 1913 under General Lucío Blanco as a
1st Captain; Governor and Military
Commander of Tamaulipas, 1914-16;
remained loyal to Carranza, 1920; taken
prisoner at Tlaxcalantongo by
Obregón's forces; inactive, 1920-23;
rejoined the army, 1923; Subdirector of
the Revisory Committee on Military
Papers, 1923; Brigadier General, 1924;
Chief of Staff, 22nd Military Zone,
Toluca, México, 1930-31; Commander
of the Garrison at Tapachula, Chiapas,
1929-30; Chief of Staff of the 17th
Military Zone, Querétaro, Querétaro,
1927-28; rank of Brigade General, Sept.
1, 1929; Commander of the 2nd Cavalry
Regiment, Tehuacán, Puebla, 1932-37;
rank of Division General, 1941; Com-
mander of Military Camp No. 1, 1942;
Commander of the 22nd Military Zone,
Toluca, México, 1942. k-Imposed by
Miguel Alemán as governor over the
protests of local leaders and citizens;
precandidate for governor, 1945,
defeated by *Hugo González*; opposed by
Emilio Portes Gil and *Magdaleno
Aguilar* for provisional governor;
imprisoned by Victoriano Huerta in the
Canoa Barracks, Mexico City, 1913.
l-HA, 6 Sept. 1971, 19; Peral, 302; HA, 6
Oct. 1950, xiv; DGF56, 8, 10, 12, 13;
Brandenburg, 103; NYT, 10 Apr. 1947,
5; Anderson, 348; López, 391; Rev. de
Ejer., Nov.–Dec. 1974, 205; Torrea, 24;
Dávila, 183-84.

García Abunza, Antonio
a-Jan. 17, 1909. b-Federal District.
c-Early education unknown; studies at
the Heroic Military College, 1915-24,
graduated as a 2nd lieutenant; advanced
studies, School of Military Education,
1936; diploma from the Higher War
College, 1940-44; special studies at Ft.
Benning, Georgia, 1947-48. d-None.
e-Oficial Mayor of the CEN of PARM,
1977-81. f-None. g-None. h-None.
j-Career army officer; commander of the
29th and 40th Infantry Battalions; chief

of Section 1, Staff, 7th military zone; Chief of Staff of the 31st and 5th military zones. k-Champion shooter at the Olympics, Berlin, Germany, 1936. l-Protag., 132.

García Aguilar, Horacio
a-June 19, 1919. b-Salvatierra, Guanajuato. c-Early education unknown; agricultural engineering degree, National School of Engineering, Chapingo. d-None. e-Member of the advisory council of the IEPES of PRI, 1981-82; member of the National Technical Executive Committee of PRI. f-Subdirector, Trust Fund Department, Trust Fund of Agriculture and Agricultural Development (FIRA), Bank of Mexico, 1948; Director, Trust Fund Department, FIRA; Subdirector General of FIRA, 1965; Director General of FIRA, 1965-82; Subdirector, Bank of Mexico, 1981-82; *Secretary of Agriculture and Hydraulic Resources*, 1982-84. g-None. h-Employee in the Secretariat of Agriculture, the National Ejido Credit Bank, and the National Foreign Trade Bank, 1941-47. j-None. k-None. l-Q es QAP, 211; *Excélsior*, 1 Dec. 1982, 34; HA, 13 Dec. 1982, 13-14; *News*, 2 Dec. 1982, 8.

García Aguilar, José Dolores
a-Mar. 16, 1894. b-Campeche, Campeche. c-Completed primary studies only. d-Local Deputy to the State Legislature of Campeche (twice); *Alternate Senator* from the State of Campeche, 1958-64, under Senator *Nicolás Canto Carrillo*; *Federal Deputy* from the State of Campeche, Dist. 2, 1964-67, member of the National Properties Committee, the Welfare Committee and the Railroad Committee. e-Cofounder of the Socialist Agrarian Party of Campeche, 1920; member of the PNR, the PRM, and the PRI. f-None. g-Cofounder of the first Maritime and Laborers Union, Campeche, Campeche; Secretary

General of the Maritime and Laborers Union, Campeche, Campeche; Secretary General of the CTM in Campeche, 1956. h-Typographer; maritime worker. j-Supported Madero. k-None. l-PS; C de D, 1964-67, 49, 80, 84; MGF69; C de S, 1961-64, 16.

García (Aguirre), Trinidad
(Deceased Feb. 2, 1981) a-Dec. 11, 1895. b-Federal District. c-Secondary studies from the Institute of Science and Letters of Mexico; preparatory studies at the Institute of Science and Letters of México, Toluca, 1910-14, and at the National Preparatory School, 1914; law degree from the National School of Law, UNAM, Dec. 11, 1919; honorary LLD, National School of Law, UNAM, 1950; professor at the National Preparatory School; professor at the School of the Brothers of Mary; Professor of Civil Law, Mercantile Law, and International Public Law, National School of Law, UNAM, 1919-70; Professor of Civil Law, LLD Program, National School of Law, UNAM, 1950-70; member, Board of Governors, UNAM, 1932-40; Dean of the National School of Law, UNAM, 1934-35. d-None. e-Founding member of the National Council of PAN, 1939; founding member of the CEN of PAN, 1939. f-General counsel for UNAM. h-Practicing lawyer, Mexico City. g-Represented the petroleum companies in labor-management disputes, 1938. i-Son of lawyer and historian Genaro García and Concepción Aguirre; grandfather, a distinguished scientist, educator, and public man; married Elisa Térres, daughter of prominent physician José Térres; son, Jaime García Térres, a prominent poet and former Director of the Fondo de Cultura Económica; close friend of *Manuel Gómez Morín*. j-None. k-*Emilio Portes Gil* offered him an appointment as justice of the Supreme Court in 1929, but he declined; participant in the 1929 Autonomy

Movement at UNAM. 1-WWM45, 44; letter; WNM, 87; López, 410; DBM70, 242; Novo35, 423; Enc. de Mex., V, 177.

García Alba Iduñate, Pascual
a-June 19, 1948. b-Ciudad Lerdo, Durango. c-Early education unknown; industrial engineering degree, Regional Technical Institute La Laguna, 1968-72; MA in economics, Colegio de México, 1973-75, with a thesis on dual economic models; MA in philosophy, Yale University, 1977; Ph.D. in economics, Yale University, 1975-78, with a thesis on value added tax in Mexico; professor, Colegio de México, 1978, 1983-84, National School of Political Studies, Acatlán, UNAM, 1979-86, Autonomous Metropolitan University of Azcapotzalco, 1979-88. d-None. e-Joined PRI, 1978. f-Adviser, Division of Political and Industrial Research, Secretariat of Government Properties, 1978-80; advsier, Secretary of the Treasury, 1980-82; Coordinator of Social and Economic Policy, Secretariat of Programming and Budgeting, 1983; economic adviser, President of Mexico, 1985-87; Director General of Economic and Social Policy, Secretariat of Programming and Budgeting, 1987-88; *Subsecretary of Development and Budget Control*, Secretariat of Programming and Budgeting, 1988-92; *Subsecretary of Educational Coordination*, Secretariat of Public Education, 1992-94. g-None. h-None. i-Son of Pascual García Alba Fernández, rancher, and María Angélica Iduñate Acosta; married Marcela Garciadiego Ojeda, historian; classmate at Yale University of *Ernesto Zedillo*, secretary of programming and budgeting, 1988-92. j-None. k-None. 1-DBGM92, 139; DBGM89.

García Barragán, Marcelino
(Deceased Sept. 3, 1979) a-June 2, 1895. b-Rancho "Los Aguacates," Cuauhtitlán, Jalisco. c-Primary studies in the Primary School of Autlán; military studies at the National Military College, 1920; 1st Sgt. of Cadets, 1920; Adjutant General of the National Military College, 1926-29; Director of the National Military College, 1941-42. d-*Governor of Jalisco*, 1943-46. e-President of the Federation of People's Parties, 1950-52. f-*Secretary of National Defense*, 1964-70. g-None. h-None. i-Friend of General *Matías Ramos Santos*, Secretary of National Defense, 1952-57, and of *Francisco L. Urquizo Benavides*, Secretary of National Defense, 1945-46; close friend and companion of *Roberto Fierro* at the National Military College; son, *Javier García Paniagua* was senator from Jalisco, 1970-76 and subsecretary of government, 1978; brother of *Sebastián García Barragán*; son of Luis García and Virginia Barragán; son, Marcelino was director of customs in Ciudad Juárez, 1980; political enemy of *J. Jesús González Gallo*. j-Participated in the Revolution as an enlisted man, 1913; joined the Juárez Brigade, Division of the North, as a 2nd Lieutenant, May 14, 1915; rank of Major, 1921; military mission to Brazil and Argentina, 1921, 1924; Lt. Colonel, 1924; fought 5 battles in the cavalry, 1924-26; Colonel and Commanding Officer of the 11th Cavalry Regiment, 1928; member of the 3rd Cavalry Regiment, 1930-41; Commander of the 42nd cavalry regiment; attached to the 21st military zone, 1947; rank of Brigadier General, 1940; not in the army, 1950-58; reincorporated into the army in 1958 by *President López Mateos*; commander of various military zones including the 11th and 17th; Commander of the 22nd Military Zone, 1962-64; rank of Division General; attached to the 15th military zone. k-Leader of the candidacy of General *Henríquez Guzmán* for President, 1951; example of the political co-optation process in Mexico; forced

out of the governorship for not putting into effect the constitutional six year term, Feb. 17, 1947. l-Lieuwen, 147; Enc. Mex., V, 178; HA, 7 Dec. 1964, 18; EWB46, 123; McAlister, 224; WB48, 1921; DPE65, 33; WWW70-71, 335; *Siempre*, 4 Feb. 1959, 6; NYT, 18 Feb. 1947, 15; *Excélsior*, 14 Sept. 1976, 4, 17 Aug. 1978, 17, 5 Sept. 1979, 19; HA, 10 Sept. 1979, 27; Rev. de Ejer., Sept. 1976, 132; Medina, No. 20, 97.

García Barragán, Sebastián
a-Aug. 8, 1899. b-Autlán de Navarro, Coatillán, Jalisco. c-Primary studies in Autlán, Jalisco (only 4 years); no degree. d-Vice-Mayor of Guadalajara, 1943-44; Mayor of Autlán, 1931; City Council member of Guadalajara, 1947-48; Local Deputy to the State Legislature of Jalisco (twice); *Federal Deputy* from the State of Jalisco, Dist. 10, 1958-61, member of the Social Action Committee; *Federal Deputy* from the State of Jalisco, Dist. 11, 1967-70, member of the Agrarian Section of the Legislative Studies Committee, the Military Health Committee, the Sugar Industry Committee, and the Small Agricultural Property Committee. e-Joined PNR, 1930. f-Income tax official, Autlán. g-President of the Ejido Committee, Autlán; Secretary of the Agricultural Association of the League of Agrarian Communities and Peasant Unions of Jalisco, 1967. i-Brother of *Marcelino García Barragán*, Secretary of National Defense, 1964-70; married Elena Guerrero. j-None. k-None. l-C de D, 1958-61, 77; Enc. Mex., 1977, V, 579; C de D, 1967-70, 69, 74, 82; Func., 249; PS, 2273.

García Carranza, Francisco
b-Guanajuato, Guanajuato. c-Primary and secondary studies in Guanajuato; preparatory studies at the National Preparatory School; completed two years of legal studies, National School

of Law, UNAM, 1914-16; professor at the Institute of Science and Literature of Chihuahua; Rector of the Scientific and Literary Institute of Chihuahua. d-Federal Deputy from the State of Chihuahua, Dist. 2, 1924-26, Dist. 3, 1937-40; Local Deputy to the State Legislature of Guanajuato, 1940-42; Mayor of Silao, Guanajuato, 1942-43; *Federal Deputy* from the State of Guanajuato, Dist. 6, 1943-46, Dist. 4, 1949-52, member of the Second Instructive Section of the Grand Jury, the First Balloting Committee, the Third Labor Committee, and the Second General Means of Communication Committee; *Senator* from the State of Guanajuato, 1952-58, President of the Railroad Committee, First Secretary of the Treasury and the Labor Committees, and Second Secretary of the Department of the Federal District Committee. e-None. f-President of the State Board of Arbitration and Conciliation, Chihuahua. g-None. h-Became a journalist, 1920; Director of *Orientación* of Guanajuato; Director of *El Diario* and *La Voz de Chihuahua* in Chihuahua. j-Joined the Revolution under General *Jesús Agustín Castro*, 1916; served until 1919. k-None. l-C de D, 1943-46, 1949-52, 72, 1924-26, 33; Ind. Biog., 68; MGF56, 6, 8, 10, 11, 13.

García Correa, Bartolomé
(Deceased 1978) a-Apr. 2, 1893. b-Umán, Yucatán. c-Primary studies at a private night school; secondary studies from the Literary Institute of Yucatán; primary school teacher; professor at the Modelo School. d-Deputy to the Constitutional Convention of Querétaro, 1916-17; Mayor of Umán, Yucatán; Mayor of Mérida, Yucatán; Local Deputy to the State Legislature of Yucatán, 1917; Senator from the State of Yucatán, 1928-30; Governor of Yucatán, 1930-34; *Senator* from the State of Yucatán, 1934-40. e-Member of

the Anti-Reelectionist Party, 1910;
Secretary of the Benito Juárez Political
Club, 1913; founder and Vice-President
of the Socialist Party of the Southeast,
1918; member of the organizing committee to establish the PNR, Dec. 1928.
f-Interim Governor of Yucatán (3 times);
Private Secretary to Felipe Carrillo
Puerto as Mayor of Mérida. g-Founder
of the Mutualist Workers Unions, 1913.
h-Laborer in a harness factory. j-Supported the Constitutionalists; opposed
to Adolfo de la Huerta, 1923. k-Jailed
for political activities; retired from
politics in Cerro de Ortega, Tecomán,
Colima, since 1940. l-PS, 2283; C de S,
1934-40; Loret de Mola, Caciques, 102.

García Cruz, Miguel
(Deceased 1969) a-Oct. 13, 1909.
b-Cuanana, Oaxaca. c-Primary studies
in Cuanana; preparatory studies at the
Central Agricultural School El Mexe,
Hidalgo, 1927-29; engineering degree
from the National School of Agricul-
ture, Chapingo, 1936; Professor of Social
Security, Demography, and Population
Policy at the National School of
Economics, UNAM, 1950-54. d-*Federal
Deputy* from Oaxaca, Dist. 7, 1952.
e-None. f-Section Chief and Cashier of
the National Agricultural Credit Bank,
1935-36; Head of the Department of
Social Security, Secretariat of Labor,
1941-42; President of the Editorial
Committee for the new Social Security
Law, 1941-42; *Secretary General of the
Mexican Institute of Social Security*,
1943-46, 1946-52, 1952-58. g-Member
of the National Farmers Federation;
member of the Political Action Committee of the Mexican Agronomy
Society, 1953. h-Economist, National
Ejido Credit Bank, 1936-37; economist,
Department of Economic Studies, Bank
of Mexico, 1937-38; economist, Techni-
cal Department, National Bank of
Foreign Commerce, 1938; economist,

Office of the Six Year Plan, 1939;
technical adviser, National Urban
Mortgage Bank, 1945; delegate to the
Inter-American Conference on Social
Security, 1942; President of the Social
Welfare Commission, 1953; author of
several books on social security in
Mexico and over 265 articles. j-None.
k-Joined PRI in 1945, two years after he
was appointed to a subcabinet level
position. l-Enc. Mex., IV, 183; DGF47;
WB45, 411; WWM45, 45; WB48, 1921;
DGF51, II, 103-04.

García de Alba (Larios), Esteban
(Deceased 1959) a-1887. b-Tecolotlán,
Jalisco. c-Primary studies in Tecolotlán
and Ciudad Guzmán; secondary and
preparatory studies at the Liceo for
Boys, Guadalajara; law degree from the
University of Guadalajara, Jalisco, 1910.
d-Local Deputy to the State Legislature
of Jalisco (twice); Federal Deputy from
the State of Jalisco, Dist 15, 1926-28,
1928-30, Dist. 6, 1930-32, member of
the Gran Comisión; *Senator* from the
State of Jalisco, 1940-46, President of
the Senate, 1942, member of the Gran
Comisión, President of the Second
Government Committee and the First
Foreign Relations Committee, and
member of the First Balloting Group.
e-*Secretary General of the PNR*, 1936-
37; *Secretary General of the PRM*, 1938.
f-*Oficial Mayor of the Secretariat of
Government*, 1935-40; Subsecretary of
Labor; Ambassador to Colombia and
Venezuela; *Director General of the
ISSSTE*, 1946-52. h-Auxiliary notary,
Castaños Firm. i-Son of physician
Rafael García de Alba and Policarpa
Larios. j-None. k-Precandidate for
governor of Jalisco (twice). l-DGF51, II,
113; DGF50, II, 40; I, 91; DGF47, 392; D
de Y, 24 June 1937, 1, 28 Aug. 1936, 1, 1
Jan. 1936, 3; D del S, 2 Dec. 1946, 1;
WWM45, 45; C de S, 1940-46; DP70,
823; Enc. Mex., 1977, V, 184.

García Escamilla de Santana, Consuelo
a-June 18, 1930. b-Federal District.
c-Primary studies in Mexico City;
secondary studies in Mixcoac, Mexico
City; normal school in Toluca, México;
two years of study in social work at
UNAM. d-*Federal Deputy* from the
State of Querétaro, Dist. 1, 1970-73,
member of the Infant Welfare Committee, the Fine Arts Committee, and the
Consular and Diplomatic Service
Committee. e-None. f-None. g-None.
j-None. k-None. l-C de D, 170-73, 115;
Directorio, 1970-72.

García (Estrada), Francisco E.
a-June 4, 1920. b-Zacatecas, Zacatecas.
c-Early education unknown; law degree
from the Scientific and Literary Institute of Zacatecas, 1949; professor, Scientific and Literary Institute of Zacatecas; professor, Normal School of Zacatecas; Director of the Normal School of
Zacatecas, 1955. d-Local Deputy to the
State Legislature of Zacatecas, 1947-50;
Governor of Zacatecas, 1956-62.
e-President of the Federation of Revolutionary Youth of Zacatecas, 1943-47;
director of the PRI youth organization
of Zacatecas, 1948-52. f-President of
the State Board of Conciliation and
Arbitration of Zacatecas, 1950; Private
Secretary to *José Minero Roque*,
governor of Zacatecas, 1951; Oficial
Mayor of the State of Zacatecas, 1952-
53; Secretary General of Government of
the State of Zacatecas, 1953-54; Ambassador to the Philippines, to Poland, to
the Dominican Republic. g-Secretary of
the Mixed Agrarian Committee of
Zacatecas, 1947-50. h-Director of
Provincia, Zacatecas, 1947-52. i-Son of
Ursulo Estrada, a teacher, and Dolores
Estrada; married Concepción Medina
Ordaz. j-None. k-Member of *Leobardo
Reynoso's* political group. l-HA, 8 Dec.
1958, 42; DGF56, 103; HA, 24 Sept.
1956; WNM, 87.

García Flores, Margarita
a-July 4, 1925. b-Monterrey, Nuevo
León. c-Primary studies in the Serafín
Peña Institute, Monterrey, Nuevo León;
secondary studies in the Secondary
School, No. 1, Monterrey; law degree
from the School of Law, University of
Nuevo León, Monterrey, 1945, with a
thesis on the legal and economic
situation of the working woman;
advanced studies in social work and
political economy; Professor of Economics, Ethics, and Domestic Education,
University of Nuevo León. d-Member
of the City Council of Monterrey, 1951-
52; *Federal Deputy* from the State of
Nuevo León, Dist. 4, 1955-58, member
of the Social Action Committee, the
Legislative Studies Committee, the
First Balloting Committee, the First
Section of the Grand Jury, and the First
Constitutional Affairs Committee;
Alternate Senator from the State of
Nuevo León, 1958-64; *Federal Deputy*
from the State of Nuevo León, Dist. 1,
1973-76. e-Secretary of Women's
Action, PRM, State of Nuevo León,
1950; *Secretary of Women's Action of
the CEN of PRI*, 1946-52; 1952-58.
f-Department Head in the Division of
Rural Communities, State of Nuevo
León, 1947-48; lawyer, League of
Agrarian Communities, State of Nuevo
León, 1949-52; Director of the Depart-
ment of Social Services, Mexican
Institute of Social Security, 1958;
Delegate of the Department of the
Federal District to Cuajimalpa, 1976-80.
g-Representative of Mexican Women's
Organizations to the International
Labor Organization, 1954; Secretary of
Women's Activities, CEN of CNOP,
1974-75. i-Daugher of Feliciano García,
a career officer, and Celia Flores.
j-None. k-None. l-Chumancero, 94-97;
Ind. Biog., 69; DGF56, 26, 30, 33-36; C
de D, 1973-76, 16.

García García, José Luis
a-June 26, 1933. b-Lerma, México.
c-Early education unknown; legal
studies, Autonomous University of the
State of México, Toluca, 1953-58,
graduated 1964. d-*Alternate Federal
Deputy* from the State of México, Dist.
4, 1973-76; *Federal Deputy* from the
State of México, Dist. 10, 1976-79;
Mayor of Nezahualcoyotl, México,
1978-81; *Federal Deputy* from the State
of México, Dist. 22, 1982-85. e-Joined
PRI, 1958; Secretary General of PRI in
State of México, 1971-79. f-Agent of the
Ministerio Público; delegate of the State
of México to the Federal Voter Registry,
1970-72. g-Secretary of Political Action
of CNOP, State of México, 1968;
National Coordinator of CNOP, 1976-
79; Secretary General of CNOP, State of
México, 1982. h-Practicing lawyer,
1960-70. i-Son of Félix García Garduño,
farmer, and María García Bernal;
married Celina Garduño Castro.
j-None. k-None. l-Directorio, 1982-85;
C de D, 1976-79, 1982-85; DBGM, 506;
Lehr, 278.

García González, Alfonso
(Deceased Dec. 2, 1961) a-Mar. 19,
1909. b-Toluca, México. c-Primary
studies at the Colegio Legorreta and the
Colegio San José, Toluca, México;
secondary studies at the Scientific and
Literary Institute of the State of México;
preparatory studies at the National Preparatory School, Mexico City; law degree, National School of Law, UNAM,
1931. d-*Governor of Baja California del
Norte*, 1952-53. e-None. f-Ambassador
to Colombia, 1956-58; appointed
Governor of Baja California del Norte,
1947-52, by *Miguel Alemán; Director
General of Tourism*, 1959-61; President
of the Mexican Sports Federation, 1958.
h-Practicing lawyer, 1931-47; Scribe,
Eighth Correctional Court, Federal
District; Public Defender, Tijuana, Baja

California del Norte. i-Personal friend
of *Miguel Alemán* who was present at
García González's bedside when he
died; married Dolores Cacho. j-None.
k-Winner of the Heavyweight Boxing
Championship of the State of México;
member of the Boxing Team at UNAM,
1926-29; attended the Central American
Games and the Ninth Olympics as a
boxer, 1927; first constitutionally
elected governor of Baja California del
Norte, 1952-53; precandidate for
senator, 1958. l-DP70, 827, 2386; Enc.
Mex., V, 188; HA, 5 Jan. 1959, 7;
DGF51, I, 88; DPE61, 129; *Tiempo,* 11
Dec. 1961, 38; STYRBIWW54, 748;
Novo, 677-80; Villaseñor, 267.

García Gutiérrez, Lino
a-Sept. 23, 1926. b-Apizaco, Tlaxcala.
c-Completed primary school; some
secondary studies, Melchor Ocampos
School, Atlixco, Puebla, 1939-41; no
degree. d-*Federal Deputy* from the
State of Puebla, Dist. 5, 1973-76, Dist.
4, 1982-85. e-None. f-None. g-Secre-
tary of CROM, Atlixco, Puebla; Secre-
tary General of the Chamber of Labor of
CROM; Secretary of Interior of CROM,
Atlixco, Puebla, 1969-70; Secretary of
Education of the El Volcán Textile
Workers Union; Treasurer of the El
Volcán Textile Workers Union Bank;
Secretary General, 1952-69, and
Treasurer, 1982, of the El Volcán
Textile Workers Union, Atlixco, Puebla.
h-Textile worker, El Volcán Textile
Factory, 1952-69. i-Son of Calixto
García García, peasant, and Refugio
Gutiérrez Millán. j-None. k-None.
l-Directorio, 1982-85; C de D, 1973-76,
1982-85; Lehr, 381; DBGM, 506.

García Leal, Dionisio
(Deceased) a-Nov. 1, 1894. b-China,
Nuevo León. c-Primary studies only; no
degree. d-Federal Deputy from the State
of Nuevo León, Dist. 3, 1932-34;

Federal Deputy from the State of Nuevo León, Dist. 3, 1937-40; *Senator* from the State of Nuevo León, 1940-46, President of the First Tariff and Foreign Trade Committee and Credit Institutions Committee, and Second Secretary of the Treasury Committee. e-None. f-None. g-None. j-None. k-None. l-Libro de Oro, 1946, 7; PS, 2313; C de D, 1932-34, 1937-40; C de S, 1940-46.

García Lizama, José
a-July 6, 1932. b-Mérida, Yucután. c-Completed secondary studies; studies toward a degree in public accounting, graduated as a private accountant, Universal Academy, Mérida, 1945-48; no degree. d-*Plurinominal Federal Deputy* from PDM, 1982-85. e-Secretary of Relations of the National Sinarquista Movement, 1981- ; member of the National Board of the National Sinarquista Movement, 1978; Director of the National Sinarquista Movement in the Federal District, 1980; President, PDM, 18th District, State of México, 1976; representative of the PDM before the Federal Electoral Commission, 1980-81; Secretary of Finances, PSM, 1980-82; Secretary of Relations, PDM, 1981. f-None. g-Member of various Christian family movements in Naucalpán, Tlanepantla, Federal District, and in Pachuca. h-Office worker; real estate developer, 1972; agent, Fletes Flecha, 1954-64; agent, Plataformeros de Progreso, 1964-66; agent, Flete Directo, 1966-76; manager, transportation business; apartment manager. i-Son of Jesús García Figueroa, businessman, and María Lizama Manzanilla. j-None. k-None. l-Directorio, 1982-85; C de D, 1982-85; Lehr, 595; DBGM, 507.

García López, Agustín
(Deceased Jan. 15, 1976) a-May 24, 1901. b-Toluca, México. c-Primary and secondary studies in Toluca; elementary studies at the Normal School and the Mariano Riva Palacio School, both in Toluca; preparatory studies at the Scientific and Literary Institute, Toluca; law degree from the National Law School, UNAM, 1923; LLD; professor at the Inter-American Institute of Constitutional Law, Cuba; Professor of Introduction to Law and Obligations and Contracts, National Law School, UNAM; Professor of Comparative Law, University of Washington; Dean of the National School of Law, UNAM, 1938-39; Director of the School of Comparative Law, UNAM, 1956-72; Professor Emeritus of UNAM. d-None. e-Director of the Revolutionary Unification Front of PRI; Secretary of Statistics for the presidential campaign of *Miguel Alemán.* f-Consulting lawyer to the Secretariat of the Treasury, 1924; technical adviser to the Mexican Institute of Social Security; Secretary of the Penal Division of the Supreme Court, 1929-31; Agent of the Ministerio Público of the Attorney General in the State of México; *Secretary of Public Works,* 1946-52. g-None. h-Assistant lawyer to the Revenue Division, 1921-22; member of the Mexican delegation to UNESCO. i-Friends with *José Castro Estrada, Antonio Arméndariz, Rodolfo Brito Foucher, Eduardo Bustamante,* and *Luis Garrido Díaz* at UNAM; student assistants included *Raúl Martínez Ostos* and *Nicolás Pizarro Suárez;* professor of *Miguel Alemán;* married Julieta Galindo; son of Alberto García del Río and María López de la Fuente. j-None. k-Member of the De la Huerta group; founded a free law office to defend students and professors from government persecution, 1923. l-DBM68, 261; HA, 14 Oct. 1949, 23 June 1950; Enc. Mex., V, 192; letter; DGF51, I, 239; II, 523, 553; DGF50, II, 377, 395; HA, 26 Jan. 1976; *Excélsior,* 16 Jan. 1976; *Justicia,* Sept. 1973.

García Máynez (y Espinosa de los Monteros), Eduardo
a-Jan. 11, 1908. b-Federal District. c-Preparatory studies at the National Preparatory School; law degree, National School of Law, UNAM, June 26, 1930; studies at the School of Philosophy and Letters, UNAM, 1926-30; studies at the University of Berlin and in Vienna, 1932-33; LLD degree, National School of Law, UNAM, Apr. 10, 1950; Professor of Ethics, Introduction to the Philosophy of Law, and Juridical Philosophy, National School of Law, UNAM; Dean, National School of Philosophy and Letters, UNAM, 1940-42; *Secretary General* of UNAM, 1944-45; Rector of Autonomous Technological Institute of Mexico, 1946-52; founder and director of the Center for Philosophic Studies, 1945-65; Emeritus Researcher, Institute of Philosophic Research, UNAM, 1974. e-None. f-None. g-Member of the National College, 1957- . h-Director of the magazine *Philosophy and Letters*, 1940-54; winner of the National Prize in Letters, 1976. i-Son of Antonio García Maynez and Loreto Espinosa de los Monteros; married María Elena Cervantes; student of Antonio and *Alfonso Caso*; influential professor of many student generations at the National University. j-None. k-None. l-Enc. Mex., IV, 223; Enc. Mex., V, 192; letters; WNM, 88-89; López, 404.

García Murillo, Manuel
a-June 10, 1945. b-Federal District. c-Early education unknown; degree in informational sciences, UNAM. d-None. e-*Secretary of Press and Publicity of the CEN of PRI*, 1980-81. f-Director, Documentation Department, UNAM, 1973-74; Interim Director General of Information, UNAM, 1975; Director, Department of Radio, Division of Information, Presidency of Mexico, 1974-76; Media Adviser, Director of Channel 13 Television, 1974-76; Gen-

eral Coordinator of Publicity, National Public Works Bank, 1976; Subdirector of Information, Secretariat of Government, 1980. g-None. h-None. i-Tied to *Gustavo Carvajal*'s group. j-None. k-None. l-*Excélsior*, 21 Mar. 1980, 18.

García Paniagua, Javier
a-Feb. 13, 1935. b-Casimiro Castillo, Jalisco. c-Primary and secondary studies; completed preparatory studies; no degree. d-*Senator* from the State of Jalisco, 1970-76, President of the First Credit, Money and Credit Institutions Committee, Second Secretary of the Agricultural and Development Committee, the Economic and Statistics Committee, and the First National Defense Committee. e-Member of PRI; *Subsecretary General of the CEN of PRI*, 1970; general delegate of the CEN of PRI to fifteen states; *President of the CEN of PRI*, 1981. f-General agent of CEIMSA, Colima, 1958-59; Director, Seguro Agrícola of Colima, 1958-65; Director of the Agricultural Bank, Michoacán, 1965-70; Director of the Department of Federal Security, Secretariat of Government, 1976-78; *Subsecretary (3) of Government*, 1978-80; *Secretary of Agrarian Reform*, 1980-81; *Secretary of Labor*, 1981; Police Chief of the Federal District, 1988-91; Director General of the National Lottery, 1991-94. g-None. h-None. i-Son of General *Marcelino García Barragán*; nephew of *Sebastián García Barragán*; a longtime friend of *Lázaro Cárdenas*. j-None. k-None. l-*Excélsior*, 17 Aug. 1978, 7, 16 Aug. 1978, 1, 27 Apr. 1980, 20; C de S, 1970-76, 75; DAPC; HA, 11 Jan. 1982, 17; *Excélsior*, 30 Dec. 1981, 1, 10A; Guerra Leal, 25; *El Nacional*, 9 Mar. 1991, 11; DBGM92, 144.

García Pérez, Gabriel
a-Mar. 24, 1948. b-Federal District. c-Early education unknown; medical degree, National School of Medicine,

UNAM, and National School of Biological Sciences, IPN, in medical bacteriology, 1965-69; Ph.D. in biochemical sciences, University of Nice, France, 1973-78; professor and researcher, UNAM, IPN, and the Autonomous Metropolitan University. d-None. e-None. f-Coordinator of Medical Bacteriology, La Raza Hospital, IMSS, 1970-71; Director General of Administration, Secretariat of Health, 1986-88; *Oficial Mayor of the Secretariat of Health*, 1988-92. g-None. h-None. i-Son of José Cruz García González, and Esperanza Pérez Sangines, businesswoman; married Alicia Zamora García, bacteriologist. j-None. k-None. l-DBGM89, 136.

García Pérez, Rodolfo
a-Nov. 9, 1915. b-Federal District. c-Early education unknown; completed preparatory studies; no degree. d-*Federal Deputy* from the Federal District, Dist. 12, 1961-64, and Dist. 2, 1982-85. e-Subsecretary of Labor of the CEN of PRI, 1970-73; President of the 3rd District Committee of PRI, Federal District. f-None. g-Secretary of Political Action of the CEN of the Revolutionary Workers Federation; Secretary of Social Security of the CEN of the Revolutionary Workers Federation; Treasurer of the CEN of CROC; Secretary General of the Union of Soft Drink Workers; Secretary General of the National Union of Bottle Industry Workers of Mexico, 1970-85. i-Son of Luis García, career military officer, and Luz Pérez; married Teresa Estrada. j-None. k-None. l-Directorio, 1982-85; C de D, 1961-64, 1982-85; Lehr, 120; DBGM84, 507.

García (Pujou), León
(Deceased Jan. 12, 1972) a-Nov. 22, 1903. b-San Luis Potosí, San Luis Potosí. c-Primary studies in San Luis Potosí; no degree. d-Local Deputy to the State Legislature of San Luis Potosí; Federal

Deputy from the State of Zacatecas, Dist. 4, 1928-30; *Federal Deputy* from the Federal District, Dist. 12, 1937-40; Secretary of the Permanent Commission, 1939; *Senator* from the State of San Luis Potosí, 1940-46, President of the Second Ejido Committee, member of the Gran Comisión and the Second Balloting Group and First Secretary of the Industry and the Agricultural Development Committee. e-Member of the National Agrarian Party headed by *Aurelio Manrique*; head of the Zapatista Front; *Secretary of Agrarian Action of the CEN of the PRM*, 1938. f-Executive Director of the National Colonization Commission, 1952-58; President of the Federal Board of Conciliation and Arbitration; Director of the Office of Legal Complaints, Secretariat of the Presidency, 1958-64; General Coordinator for the Secretariat of Agriculture and Livestock, 1964-72. g-Cofounder with *Graciano Sánchez* of the National Farmers Federation (CNC) in 1938; first Oficial Mayor of the CNC, 1938; Alternate Secretary General of the CNC. h-Mechanic before entering politics. i-Political supporter of *Aurelio Manrique*, former governor of San Luis Potosí, 1923. j-None. k-Precandidate for governor of San Luis Potosí, lost to *Gonzalo Santos*; precandidate for Secretary General of the CNC, 1941, 1957, 1966; involved in a land scandal in the Federal District, 1964. l-Peral, 314; HA, 24 Jan. 1972, 16; C de D, 1937-39, 11; González Navarro, 256, 266, 137, 168; *Excélsior*, 28 June 1942; Libro de Oro, 1946, 7.

García Ramírez, Sergio
a-Feb. 1, 1938. b-Guadalajara, Jalisco. c-Primary and secondary studies in Guadalajara; preparatory studies in Mexico City; law degree from the National Law School, UNAM, 1955-59, received honorary mention for his thesis on "Repression and Penitentiary

Treatment of Criminals," 1961; advanced studies in law at the National Law School, 1963-64; advanced studies of penal systems in Europe; LLD degree from the National Law School, UNAM, Apr. 24, 1971, on the subject of prisons without bars; Professor of Penal Law, National School of Law, UNAM, 1965-93, 1970; Professor of Advanced Studies in Penitentiary Law, 1970; researcher, Institute of Juridical Research, UNAM, 1966-76; researcher, National Institute of Criminal Sciences, 1976-79. d-None. e-None. f-Delegate of the Social Welfare Department to the Federal District Penitentiary, 1961-63; Judge of the Guardian Council for the Guardian School for the Rehabilitation of Children; Director General of the Central Penitentiary, Mexico City; Head of the Department of Political Investigations, Secretariat of Government; Subdirector General of Government, Secretariat of Government, 1970; *Attorney General of the Federal District and Federal Territories*, 1970-72; *Subsecretary of Government Properties*, Aug. 9, 1972-73; *Subsecretary of Government*, Apr. 30, 1973-76; *Subsecretary of Youth, Recreation and Sports*, Secretariat of Public Education, 1976-78; *Subsecretary of State Industry*, Secretariat of Property and Industrial Development, 1978-81; *Secretary of Labor*, 1981-82; *Attorney General of Mexico*, 1982-88; President of the Agrarian Court, 1992-94. g-None. h-Founder of the first prison without bars in Mexico; investigator of the Institute of Comparative Law, 1965-70; author of nine books; considered an outstanding expert on penal institutions in Mexico. i-Worked under *Luis Echeverría* before he became president; student of César Sepúlveda at UNAM; son of Alberto García Balda, public official, and Italia Ramírez Corona Salem, official interpreter of Presidents *Gustavo Díaz Ordaz, Luis Echeverría,* and *José López Portillo*; married María

Concepción Gómez Rivera. j-None. k-None. l-HA, 7 Dec. 1970, 26; *Hoy*, 8 May 1971, 12; letter; *Excélsior*, 10 Aug. 1972, 10; HA, 21 Aug. 1972, 13, 7 May 1973, 23, 6 Feb. 1978, 15, 17 May 1976, 12, 11 Jan. 1982, 17, 6 Feb. 1978, 15; *Excélsior*, 30 Dec. 1981, 1, 10A; *Proceso*, 20 July 1987, 9; Hurtado, 65; DBGM, 165; DBGM92, 145.

García Reynoso, Plácido
c-Primary and secondary studies unknown; studies at the National Teachers' College, Mexico City; law degree, National School of Law, UNAM, 1927-35; professor, National Teachers' College, 1932. d-None. e-None. f-Private Secretary to the Secretary of the Treasury, *Narciso Bassols*, 1935; Head of the Legal Department, 1946-49, Head of the Credit and Trust Department, 1950, Manager and Second Subdirector, 1951-52, and Manager, 1952-58, all at the Bank of Mexico; *Subsecretary of Industry and Commerce (A)*, 1958-64, 1964-70; Director General of the Asociación Hipotecaria Mexicana, S.A., 1971-72; Ambassador and Permanent Delegate to the International Organizations in Geneva, Switzerland, 1979-81; Ambassador to Japan, 1981-82. g-Director of the First Convention of Socialist Teachers, 1935. h-Official, Secretariat of Public Education, 1935; Head of the Permanent Mexican Delegation to LAFTA, Montevideo, Uruguay, 1965; Director General of Azúcar, S.A. i-Married Alicia Corona. j-None. k-None. l-D de Y, 10 Dec. 1964, 1; DGF50, II, 12, 57, 413, 433; DPE61, 64; DGF51, 8; DPE65, 29; Justicia, Dec. 1971; HA, 28 Dec. 1981, 21, 13 Aug. 1979, 13, 28 Dec. 1981, 21.

García Robles, Alfonso
(Deceased Sept. 2, 1991) a-Mar. 20, 1911. b-Zamora, Michoacán. c-Primary studies in Zamora; secondary and

preparatory studies in Guadalajara; law studies, National School of Law, UNAM, 1931-33; continued legal studies at the University of Paris, 1934-36; law degree, Faculty of Law, University of Paris, 1936, in international law with honors; graduate studies at the National Law School, UNAM and diploma from the Academy of International Law, The Hague; LLD degree. d-None. e-Member of the IEPES advisory council of PRI, 1972. f-Career Foreign Service officer; joined the Foreign Service, 1939; rank of Third Secretary, 1939; member of the delegation to Sweden, 1939-41; Director General of Political Affairs and the Diplomatic Service, Secretariat of Foreign Relations, 1941-46; Mexican representative to the United Nations, 1946-57; Director of the Political Affairs Division, United Nations, 1946-57; Head of the Department of International Organizations; rank of Ambassador, 1957; Director in Chief of the European, Asian, and African Department, Secretariat of Foreign Relations, 1957-61; Ambassador to Brazil, 1962-64; *Subsecretary of Foreign Relations, 1964-70; Ambassador to the United Nations, 1971-75; Secretary of Foreign Relations, 1975-76;* Head of the Mexican Delegation to the United Nations Committee on Disarmament, 1976-82, 1982-88; Ambassador Emeritus, 1982. g-None. h-Delegate to over forty international conferences; President of the Association for the Denuclearization of Latin America, 1964-67; author of 20 books and over 300 articles on foreign affairs and international law; awarded the Nobel Peace Prize, 1982. i-Son of Quirino García and Teresa Robles; married Juana María Szyszb. j-None. k-None. l-Enc. Mex., V; *Polémica*, I, 1969, 81; WWW70-71, 335; IWW66, 425; DBM70, 239-40; DBM68, 262-63; DPE65, 17; DPE61, 15; WWM45, 46; *Excélsior*, 30 Dec. 1975,

11; HA, 25 Oct. 1982, 9-10; WNM, 89-90; *El Nacional*, 6 Sept. 1991, 11.

García Rojas, Antonio
a-Dec. 9, 1914. b-Tampico, Tamaulipas. c-Primary studies; business studies as a stenographer; no degree. d-*Federal Deputy* from the State of Tamaulipas, Dist. 2, 1961-64; *Senator* from the State of Tamaulipas, 1964-70. e-Joined the PRM, 1937; President of the Avila Camacho Youth Group, Tampico, Tamaulipas, 1939-40. f-Syndic of the City Council of Reynosa, Tamaulipas; Director of Public Works, Reynosa, Tamaulipas, 1952-54; Director of Administration, PEMEX, Reynosa; member of the Administrative Council of PEMEX, 1959-61. g-Founder and Director of Local 36, Petroleum Workers Union; adviser to the STPRM. i-Son of Cruz García Rojas Avila, a lawyer; great-great-grandson of a foun-der of Tampico. j-None. k-Resigned as Director of Public Works of Reynosa because of a disagreement with Governor *Treviño Zapata*. l-C de S, 1964-70; MGF69; C de D, 1961-64; PS, 2347.

García Rojas (Barrios), Jorge Gabriel
a-Nov. 24, 1931. b-Pinos, Zacatecas. c-Early education unknown; law degree, National School of Law, UNAM, 1957; LLD degree, National School of Law, UNAM, 1960; professor of law, UNAM, 1958; professor, Ibero-American University, 1966. d-*Senator* from the State of Zacatecas, 1976-82. e-Candidate for the PRI gubernatorial nomination for Zacatecas. f-Private Secretary to the Private Secretary of the President of Mexico, *Joaquín Cisneros Molina*, 1968-70; President of Administrative Suits, Tribunal of the Federal District, 1971-72; adviser, Secretary of Labor, 1974-75; Director General of Legal Affairs, Secretariat of Labor, 1975; Private Secretary to the President of the CEN of PRI, *Jesús Reyes Heroles*; Di-

rector of the National Pawnshop, 1982.
g-None. h-Official, Mining Chamber of
Mexico. i-Son of *Jorge Gabriel García
Rojas*, justice of the Supreme Court,
1952-61, and Ana María Barrios Gómez;
brother, Fernando, was general coordinator of the Pathology Department,
National Indigenous Institute, 1982.
j-None. k-None. l-HA, 9 May 1983, 28;
Protag., 137; C de S, 1976-82.

García Rojas (Salazar), (Jorge) Gabriel
(Deceased) a-May 12, 1893. b-Pinos,
Zacatecas. c-Primary studies in San
Luis Potosí; secondary studies in
Aquascalientes; law degree from the
National School of Law, UNAM, 1919;
LLD, National School of Law, UNAM,
1950; Professor of the General Theory of
Obligations and Contracts, the Theory
of Juridical Acts, the System of Private
Law; Legal Methods, National School of
Law, UNAM, 1920-77; Professor of the
2nd, 3rd, and 4th Civil Law Course, Na-
tional School of Law, UNAM, 1936-37;
Professor of the Philosophy of Law, Na-
tional School of Law, UNAM, 1942-50;
Director of the Seminar of Private Law,
National School of Law, UNAM; Profes-
sor of Civil Law and Judicial Methodol-
ogy, LLD Program, National School of
Law, UNAM, 1977; Dean of the Law
School Professors, UNAM, 1977;
Professor Emeritus, UNAM. d-*Federal
Deputy* from the Federal District, Dist.
6, 1949-51, member of the Gran Comisión, the Department of the Federal
District Committee, the Legislative
Studies Committee, and the First
Justice Committee. e-None. f-Secre-
tary of the City Government of Mexico
City, 1919; President of the Editorial
Committee to Revise the Civil Code of
the Federal District and Federal Territo-
ries, 1931-32; *Supernumerary Justice of
the Supreme Court, 1951-52; Justice of
the Supreme Court*, 1952-58, 1959-61.
g-President of the Mexican Institute of
Process Law, 1947-50; President of the

Association of City Councils, 1921-23.
i-Father of *Jorge Gabriel García Rojas*,
senator from Zacatecas, 1976-82; his
relationship with *José López Portillo*, as
his student, helped his son's career;
married Ana María Barrios Gómez; son
of José García Rojas and Concepción
Salazar. j-Participated in the Revolution. k-None. l-López, 408; DGF51, 21,
29, 31, 34; C de D, 1949-51, 72; *Excélsior*, 28 Mar. 1977, 4, 17 Dec. 1979, 18,
1 July 1980; Enc. Mex., V, 197.

García Ruiz, Ramón
a-Aug. 27, 1908. b-Guadalajara, Jalisco.
c-Teaching certificate from the Normal
School of Jalisco, 1926; certified as an
expert in rural education by the Na-
tional School of Philosophy, Superior
Normal School, UNAM, 1928; educa-
tional adviser to the National Commis-
sion of Free Textbooks, 1959-64.
d-*Federal Deputy* from the State of
Jalisco, Dist. 4, 1952-55, member of the
Library Committee (2nd year), the
Editorial Committee (1st year), the
Second Public Education Committee,
and the First Section of the Credentials
Committee. e-None. f-Director of
Inspection, Secretariat of Public
Education, for the States of Mexico,
Morelos, and Jalisco, 1931-36; Inspector
General, Secretariat of Public Educa-
tion, 1937; Director General of Primary
Education, 1942-43; Private Secretary to
the Governor of Jalisco, *Jesús González
Gallo*, 1947-52; Coordinator General of
Services for Preschool and Primary
Education; Coordinator General of
Secondary and Normal Education,
Secretariat of Public Education, 1961-
64; Codirector of the Center of Funda-
mental Education for Community
Development in Latin America,
UNESCO, 1964-70. g-None. h-First
employment as an inspector, 1929-30;
author of numerous books and articles
on rural education. j-None. k-None.
l-DBM68, 263-64; C de D, 1952-54, 45,

47, 49; WWM45, 47; DPE61, 108; Enc. Mex., V, 1977, 198.

García Sáinz, Ricardo
a-June 9, 1930. b-Federal District. c-Law degree from the National Law School, UNAM, Mar. 1954; professor, School of Business Administration, UNAM. d-None. e-None. f-Secretary of the Qualifying Committee of the Income Tax, 1952-56, under Director *Hugo B. Margaín*; Administrative Subdirector of CONDUMEX, 1956-58; Director General of CONDUMEX, 1958-60; Subdirector General of Administration of the Mexican Institute of Social Security, 1966-70, 1970-76; *Subsecretary of Control of Government Properties and Industrial Development*, 1976-77; *Secretary of Planning and Programming*, 1977-79; Director General of Diesel Nacional (DINA), 1981-82; *Director General of IMSS*, 1982-88, 1988-90; Director General of Mexicana Airlines, 1991-93. g-Vice-President of the National Chamber of Industries; member of the Coordinating Committee of International Activities of Private Enterprise; President of the National Association of Imports and Exports, 1960-63. h-Worked for the Department of Commercial Revenues, 1951-52. i-Son-in-law of lawyer Jorge Luna y Para; married Georgina Luna y Parra, grandaughter of Pascual Luna y Parra, subsecretary of the treasury, 1913; son of Ricardo García Sáinz, public official, and Dolores Lavista, businesswoman. j-None. k-None. l-HA, 14 Dec. 1970, 25; DGF56, 168; HA, 7 Mar. 1966, 13; MGF69; HA, 28 Nov. 1977, 16, 13 Dec. 1976, 9; *Excélsior*, 17 Nov. 1977, 11; WNM, 90; Linajes, 149-50; DBGM, 169.

García Santacruz, J. Jesús
a-Dec. 28, 1910. b-Michoacán. c-Primary studies in Michoacán; engineering degree from the National School of Agriculture. d-*Federal Deputy* from the State of Michoacán, Dist. 9, 1964-67; *Senator* from the State of Michoacán, 1970-76, member of the Gran Comisión and the First Balloting Group, President of the National Waters and Irrigation Committee, Second Secretary of the Second Ejido Committee, the First Petroleum Committee, and the Third Labor Committee. e-Joined the PNR, 1936. f-Agent, Ejido Credit Bank; Executive Secretary, Regional Agricultural Committee, Sinaloa; Chief General Agent, Secretary of Agriculture, Sinaloa; Secretary, Forest Commission, Michoacán; Vice-President, National Agricultural Bank; General Agent, Secretary of Agriculture; Executive Secretary, Collective Society of Ejido Credit. g-None. h-None. j-None. k-None. l-C de D, 1964-67; C de S, 1970-76, 75; PS, 2352.

García Sierra, Aurelio
a-Sept. 18, 1918. b-Ejido Laguna Larga, Municipio de Penjamo, Guanajuato. c-Primary studies in Penjamo, secondary and preparatory studies in Guanajuato; economics degree from the Higher School of Economic Science, University of Guanajuato. d-Local Deputy to the State Legislature of Guanajuato; Mayor of Penjamo; *Federal Deputy* from the State of Guanajuato, Dist. 4, 1958-61, member of the Agrarian Affairs Department Committee, the First Balloting Committee, and the Insurance Committee; *Federal Deputy* from the State of Guanajuato, Dist. 5, 1976-79, member of the Agrarian Affairs Committee. e-President of PRI in the State of Guanajuato. f-Justice of the Peace, Guanajuato. g-Secretary General of the League of Agrarian Communities, State of Guanajuato, 1962; Oficial Mayor of the National Farmers Federation, 1965. j-None. k-None. l-*Excélsior*, 19 Aug. 1976, 18; Func., 211; C de D, 1958-61, 78; D de C, 1976-79, 7.

García Solís, Iván
a-July 19, 1937. b-Federal District.
c-Early education unknown; secondary
studies in economics; teaching certificate; studies in economics, National
School of Economics, UNAM, no
degree; studies in Philosophy and
Letters, UNAM, no degree; primary and
secondary school teacher in civics.
d-*Plurinominal Federal Deputy* from
PSUM, 1982-85. e-Joined the PCM,
1960; candidate of the PCM for Federal
Deputy from the Federal District, Dist.
12, 1979; member of the Central
Committee of PSUM, 1981-88; member
of the Political Committee of PSUM,
1981-88; candidate of PSUM for Federal
Deputy from the Federal District, Dist.
12, 1982; member of the Mexican Revolutionary Movement. f-None. g-Involved in workers' and teachers' strikes;
official of Local 9, National Teachers
Union; member of the CEN of the
SNTE, 1966, 1977. h-Journalist; Director *Así Es* weekly. j-None. k-None.
l-Directorio, 1982-85; C de D, 1982-85.

García Téllez, Ignacio
a-May 21, 1897. b-León, Guanajuato.
c-Primary studies from Petra Durán and
Pedro Rojas' Schools, León; secondary
and preparatory studies from the
Colegio de Guanajuato, León; law
degree from the National School of Law,
UNAM, Mar. 5, 1921, with a thesis on
taxes in Mexico; first Rector of UNAM,
1929-32. d-Federal Deputy from León,
Guanajuato, 1922-24; Interim Governor
of Guanajuato, 1924; *Senator* from
Guanajuato, 1934. e-Secretary of the
Campaign Committee for the presiden-
tial campaign of Lázaro Cárdenas, 1933;
Secretary General of the CEN of PRI,
1935-36. f-Attorney for the Technical
Commission on Legislation, 1926;
Oficial Mayor of the Secretariat of
Government, 1924-28; Acting Subsecre-
tary of Government, 1928; Secretary of
Public Education, 1934-35; Private

Secretary to President *Lázaro Cárdenas*,
1937-38; *Secretary of Government*, Jan.
4, 1938 to 1940; Head of the Department of Credit, Secretariat of the
Treasury, 1925; *Secretary of Labor*,
1940-43; *Director General of the
Mexican Institute of Social Security*,
1944-46; Private Secretary to *Lázaro
Cárdenas*, 1948; practicing lawyer,
1970. g-None. h-None. i-Personal
friend of *Lázaro Cárdenas*, with whom
he worked from 1934 until Cardenas'
death; married Manuela Madrazo
Basauri; son of Ignacio García Peña and
Genoveva Téllez González. j-None.
k-Candidate of the Unified Guanajuato
Front for governor in 1943, lost to
Ernesto Hidalgo; shifted cabinet-level
positions in 1944 to bring IMSS out of
financial disaster. l-WWM45, 47; Peral,
319; Kirk, 337; Strode, 302; DBM68,
265; Enc. Mex., V, 199-200; D del S, 19
June 1935, 1; letter; NYT, 4 Jan. 1944,
31, 24 Jan. 1943, 4; WNM, 90; WWM40,
212; Meyer, No. 12, 287.

García Toledo, Anastasio
b-Oaxaca. c-Law degree. c-Federal
Deputy from the State of Oaxaca, 1930-
32; *Governor of Oaxaca*, 1934-36.
e-None. f-Oficial Mayor of the Secretariat of Government; Head of Infractions Section of the Transportation
Department of the Federal District,
1944; Head of the Public Registry Office
for Property and Commerce, Federal
District Palace Office, Department of
the Federal District, 1951. g-None.
j-None. k-None. l-Peral, 319; DPE51, I,
483.

García Villalobos, Ricardo
a-Feb. 11, 1904. b-Ciudad Jiménez, Chihuahua. c-Preparatory studies from the
National Preparatory School; law degree, National School of Law, UNAM,
May 19, 1931; LLD degree, National
School of Law, UNAM, Sept. 7, 1951;
member of the Technical Council,

Professor of Civil Law, 1937-62, and Dean, 1958-62, all at National School of Law, UNAM. d-None. e-None. f-Director, Federal Automobile Registry, 1930; Director, Tax Office, Secretariat of the Treasury, 1937-47; Judge, Federal Tax Court, 1947-51; President, Federal Tax Court, 1951-53; Director General of Business Revenues, Secretariat of the Treasury, 1953-58, 1963-70; delegate from Iztapalapa to the Department of the Federal District, 1976-82. g-President of the Federation of University Students, 1929-30; delegate to the 5th National Student Congress with *Andrés Serra Rojas* and *Angel Carvajal* from the Federal District. h-None. i-Married Guadalupe Gálvez; son of Juan García Villalobos and Enriqueta Espinos. j-None. k-None. l-HA, 30 Sept. 1957, 57; DAPC, 77, 29; WNM, 91; MGF69; Pacheco, 30-32.

García y González, Vicente
a-1909. b-Pénjamo, Guanajuato. c-Primary and secondary studies in Pénjamo and Guanajuato. d-*Senator* from the State of Guanajuato, 1958-64, member of the Gran Comisión, First Secretary of the Cooperative Development Committee, Second Secretary of the Social Security Committee, and President of the Second Labor Committee. e-None. f-None. g-Founder of the Federation of Workers Unions of Irapuato, Guanajuato; militant strike leader in the labor movement. h-Journalist; writer for *El Nacional*. i-Parents were from the working class. j-None. k-None. l-Func., 206; C de S, 1961-64, 55-56.

Garduño Canizal, Leopoldo
a-Mar. 7, 1910. b-Celaya, Guanajuato. c-Enrolled in the Naval College, Jan. 17, 1925, completed his cadet studies; completed studies at the Applied Military School, 1934-35; completed staff and command course, Higher War College, 1938-41; completed preparatory courses

in armored vehicles, Fort Leavenworth, Kansas; completed preparatory course in military arms, graduated 5th in his class, Fort Knox; instructor, Heroic Military College, the Military Command School, and the Zaragoza Military Academy. d-None. e-None. f-*Oficial Mayor of the Secretariat of National Defense*, 1976. g-None. h-None. i-Married Debora Espinosa. j-Commander of the 2nd Battalion, 27th Infantry Division, National Military Service; Group Commander, 37mm Anti-tank Group, 1st and 2nd Infantry Divisions, National Military Service; Chief of Instruction and second in command, 12th Mechanized Cavalry Regiment; Military Attaché to Guatemala, 1973; Chief of Staff and Accidental Commander, 16th military zone; Chief of Staff of the 26th Military Zone; Commander of the 33rd Infantry Group, Rural Defenses; Commander of the 4th Infantry Battalion; Commander of the 5th Infantry Brigade, 1968; Commander of the 2nd Infantry Brigade, 1973; rank of Brigade General, 1974; Commander of the 32nd Military Zone, Mérida, Yucatán, 1977. k-None. l-Rev. de Ejer., Oct.–Nov. 1976, 144-45; DBM68, 267; Rev. de Ejer., Apr. 1973, 95.

Garfías Magaña, Luis
a-June 21, 1931. b-Ciudad Guzmán, Jalisco. c-Early education unknown; joined the Heroic Military College as a cadet, Jan. 1, 1948, graduated as a 2nd lieutenant in the artillery, Jan. 1, 1951; staff and command diploma, Higher War College, 1954-57; advanced artillery courses, Ft. Sill and Ft. Bliss; staff and command diploma, Ft. Leavenworth, Kansas, 1964-65; professor, Heroic Military College, 1965-65; professor, Chief of Teaching and Chief of Courses, Higher War College, 1962-70; Coordinator of the National Defense College, 1980-82. d-*Federal Deputy from the State of Jalisco, Dist. 6, 1982-*

85. e-None. f-Ambassador to Paraguay, 1986-89. g-None. h-None. i-Son of Colonel Luis Garfías Espinosa de los Monteros, career military engineer, and Estela Magaña; married Francisca Roberts. j-Junior officer, 105mm Mortar Group, Mechanized Brigade and in the Transportation Battalion, Presidential Guards; Chief, Section 1 and Section 3, Staff, Presidential Guards; Commander of the 120mm Mortar Battalion, 2nd Artillery Battalion, 2nd Infantry Brigade; Assistant Chief of Staff, 11th Military Zone, Zacatecas, Zacatecas; Group Chief, Military Schools, Division of Military Education, Secretariat of National Defense; Assistant Miltary Attaché to the United States, Washington, D.C., 1973-75; Assistant Chief of Staff, Secretariat of National Defense, 1972-73; rank of Colonel, 1973; Chief of Staff, 12th Military Zone, San Luis Potosí, San Luis Potosí, 1977-78; Chief of Staff, 25th Military Zone, Puebla, Puebla, 1980-81; rank of Brigadier General, 1977; Director General of Archives, Secretariat of National Defense, 1986; President of the Second War Council, 1989-90; Garrison Commander, Tecate, Baja California, 1991; Rector of the Army and Air Force University, Secretariat of National Defense, 1991-92; Commander of the 23rd Military Zone, Tlaxcala, Tlaxcala, 1993-94. k-None. l-Rev. de Ejer., Nov. 1977, 70, Nov.–Dec. 1973, 39; Mar. 1976, 154; Directorio, 1982-85; DBGM89, 140; DBGM, 509; DBGM87, 149; Lehr, 231; DBGM92, 148; letter.

Garizurieta (Ehrenzweig), César
(Deceased 1961) a-July 19, 1904. b-Tuxpan, Veracruz. c-Law degree, National School of Law, UNAM, 1931. d-*Federal Deputy* from the State of Veracruz, Dist. 3, 1940-43, member of the Budget and Accounting Committee (1st year) and the Tourism Committee; substitute member of the Constitu-

tional Affairs Committee; *Federal Deputy* from the State of Veracruz, Dist. 3, 1949-52, member of the Protocol Committee, the Library Committee, and the Agrarian Department Committee, and substitute member of the First Justice Committee. e-None. f-Judge of the First Appeals Court, 1931-40; Judge of the Tribunal Superior of Justice of Veracruz; presidential adviser; Consultant for Area 6 of the Department of Agrarian Affairs, 1947; *Oficial Mayor of the Department of Agrarian Affairs*, 1952-58; Ambassador to Haiti and Honduras, 1958-61. g-Founding member of the Socialist Lawyers' Front, 1936; leader in the 1929 strike movement of UNAM. h-Started private law practice in Mexico City, 1931; author of many novels. i-Brother, Miguel, served as an administrator in the Agrarian Department, 1956; father, José L. Garizurieta, was a well-known normal school teacher in Jalapa. j-None. k-Author of the saying, "To live outside the budget is to live in error." l-EBW46, 35; Peral, 47, 138; DGF47, 280; DPE51, I, 26, 30, 31, 34; DP70, 835; DGF56, 453; C de D, 1940-42, 1949-51, 73; DEM, 135; Enc. Mex., 1977, 208.

Garrido Díaz, Luis
(Deceased Oct. 19, 1973) a-May 15, 1898. b-Federal District. c-Primary studies at the Colegio Fournier and the Pablo Moreno School in Mexico City; preparatory studies at the National Preparatory School, Mexico City; law degree from the National School of Law, UNAM, 1922; LLD degree from the National School of Law, UNAM, 1942; Professor of Forensic Law, National School of Law, UNAM, 1929-72; Professor of Economic Doctrines, UNAM, 1929-72; Professor at the Colegio de San Nicolás de Hidalgo, Morelia; cofounder of the Mexican Association of Universities and Institutions of Higher Education; Professor of

the History of Economic Doctrines, Graduate School, UNAM, Rector of the University of Michoacán, 1924; Director of the Faculty of Law, University of Michoacán, 1924. d-None. e-Member of the New Advisory Council for the IEPES of PRI, 1972. f-Auxiliary agent of the Ministerio Público for the Federal District for the Office of the Attorney General, 1929-30; Prosecuting Attorney for the State of Michoacán, 1924-25; Head of the Diplomatic Department for the Secretariat of Foreign Relations, 1935-36; Penal Judge for the Federal District, 1930-34; Director of Seguros de México, S.A., 1939-48; Executive Secretary of National Savings Bonds; *Rector of UNAM*, 1948-52; Subdirector of *El Nacional*, government daily newspaper, 1936; President of the Superior Court of Michoacán, 1925-28. g-None. h-President of the National Lawyers Association, 1970-72; prolific author, coauthored a book with *José Ceniceros*. i-As a student at National Preparatory School and UNAM, knew *Jaime Torres Bodet* and *Manuel Gómez Morín*; friend of *Franco Carreño* for many years; son of Domingo Garrido, who worked for Wells Fargo, and Carolina Díaz. j-None. k-None. l-WWM45, 47; IWW66-67, 428; DGF47, 381; EBW46, 422; WB48, 431; WB54, 414; DBM70, 253-54; letter.

Garza Caballero, Manuel
a-Jan. 12, 1929. b-Monterrey, Nuevo León. c-Early education unknown; engineering studies, 1957-61, Higher School of Engineering and Architecture, IPN, graduating with a thesis on cardboard tubing, 1963; MA in administration, Graduate College, Technological Institute of Higher Studies of Monterrey, 1976; postgraduate work, 1968-81; professor, Director General of Organization and Methods, 1979-82, and Technical Secretary, 1980-82, all at IPN. d-None. e-None. f-Delegate,

Tamaulipas and Jalisco, Department of Agrarian Affairs, 1965-66; Director, Center of Technical industrial Studies of Monterrey, Nuevo León, 1966-67; Subdirector, Agricultural Technical Schools, Secretariat of Public Education, 1969-70; Director General of Technical, Industrial, and Commerical Education, Secretariat of Public Education, 1970-76; General Coordinator, Rural Programs, IMSS, 1977-78; Assistant Director General of Adult Education, Secretariat of Public Education, 1978-79; *Director General of the IPN*, 1982-85. g-None. h-None. i-Son of Eleuterio Garza Garza, milkman, and María de Jesús Caballero González; married María del Pilar Amaro Peniche, teacher. j-None. k-None. l-Q es QAP, 312-13; *Excélsior*, 7 Dec. 1982, 29; DBGM, 172

Garza Cárdenas, Fortino Alejandro
a-Sept. 4, 1917. b-Monterrey, Nuevo León. c-Early education unknown; no degree. d-*Federal Deputy* from PARM (Party Deputy), 1970-73; member of the Second National Defense Committee, the Hunting and Fishing Committee, and the Plaints Committee; *Federal Deputy* from PARM (Party Deputy), 1976-79. e-*President of the CEN of PARM*, 1980-83; Secretary of Social Action of the CEN of PARM, 1983. f-Employee of the State of Nuevo León, 1935-36, of the Secretariat of Health, Nuevo León, 1938-40, and of the Police Department, Federal District, 1940-46; employee of the Secretary of Agriculture and Captain of the Federal Forest Police, 1947-58; Commandant in the Customs Department, 1960-61; employee of the Secretariat of Communications, 1963-68, and of the Department of Fishing, Secretariat of Industry and Trade in Monterrey, Nuevo León, 1968-70. g-None. i-Son of Colonel Fortino Garza Campos; married Ernestina Rodríguez; originally part of *Luis M. Farías*'s political group. j-None.

k-None. l-Directorio, 1970-72; C de D, 1970-73, 115; D de C, 1976-79; Guerra Leal, 283.

Garza Tijerina, Julián
(Deceased 1976) a-Jan. 28, 1900. b-General Bravo, Nuevo León. c-Primary studies in General Bravo; fifth and sixth years plus preparatory studies at Colegio Civil, Monterrey, Nuevo León; medical degree from the Military Medical School, Federal District, 1925, with the rank of Major; Professor of Internal Pathology. d-Local Deputy to the State Legislature of Nuevo León; *Senator* from the State of Nuevo León, 1934-40, member of the permanent committee, 1938; *Federal Deputy* from the State of Nuevo León, Dist. 2, 1943-46. e-Secretary of Exterior and Labor Action, PNR, 1933; Secretary of the Federal District of the PNR, 1933; Director of the IEPES of the PNR, 1936. f-Director of Medical Services, Monterrey; Subdirector of the Military Hospital, Monterrey; Director of Medical Services for the Green Cross, Federal District; Director General of Hygiene and Welfare in States and Territories, Secretariat of Health, 1946. g-None. h-Author of books on medical subjects and Nuevo León history. i-Studied under *Francisco Castillo Nájera* and *Fernando Ocaranza*; married Isabel Alejandro Méndez; son, Luis Félix, was director general of cultural development, Secretariat of Public Education. j-Participated in various military battles; rank of Lt. Colonel in the Medical Military Service. k-None. l-Peral, 324; C de D, 1943-45; C de S, 1934-40; letters; MGF47, 197.

Garza Zamora, Tiburcio
(Deceased Dec. 13, 1973) a-1900. b-Rancho el Mezquite, Reynosa, Tamaulipas. c-Primary studies in Ciudad Victoria; no degree. d-*Federal Deputy* from the State of Tamaulipas,

Dist. 1, 1958-61, member of the Gran Comisión, the First National Defense Committee, the General Accounting Office Committee, and the Military Justice Committee. e-None. g-None. h-None. i-Married Francisca Guajardo de Garza. j-Joined the Revolution, 1915; rank of Colonel, 1920; career army officer; rank of Brigade General, 1964; reached rank of Division General; Commander of the 26th Military Zone, Veracruz, Veracruz; Commander of the 20th Military Zone, Colima, Colima; Commander of the 5th Military Zone, Chihuahua, Chihuahua; Commander of the 7th Military Zone, Monterrey, Nuevo León, 1970; retired from active duty, 1970. k-None. l-*Excélsior*, 14 Dec. 1973, 21; Func., 374; C de D, 1958-61, 79; Rev. de Ejer., Dec. 1964, 23.

Garzón Santibáñez, Alfonso
a-Aug. 4, 1920. b-Ejido el Salto, Mazatlán, Sinaloa. c-Preparatory studies, Ignacio Zaragoza School, Mazatlán, Sinaloa, 1934-36; no degree. d-*Alternate Federal Deputy* from the State of Baja California del Norte, Dist. 1, 1961-64; *Federal Deputy* from the State of Baja California del Norte, Dist. 3, 1970-73, member of the Agricultural Committee, the Waters and Irrigation Committee, and the First Balloting Committee; *Federal Deputy* from the State of Baja California del Norte, Dist. 3, 1976-79, member of the Ejido and Communal Organization Section of the Agrarian Affairs Committee, member of the Agricultural Committee, and the Committee for the Development of Marine Resources; *Senator* from Baja California del Norte, 1982-88; *Plurinominal Federal Deputy* from the PRI, 1988-91. e-Joined the PNR, 1936; *Agrarian Subsecretary of the CEN of PRI*, 1980-89. f-None. g-Began activities in the agrarian union movement, 1936; President, El Salto Ejido, 1940-42; Ejido Comisariat, Eréndira, Baja Cali-

fornia, 1945-48; Secretary of Agrarian Acts, League of Agrarian Communities and Peasant Unions, Mexicali, 1952; cofounder of the CCI with Humberto Serrano and *Ramón Danzos Palomino*, 1960; Secretary General of the Independent Peasant Federation (CCI), 1963-86. i-Son of Valentín Garzón Tisnado and María Santibáñez Lizárraga, peasants; married María Guadalupe Martínez Cruz. j-None. k-Ran for mayor of Mexicali as a militant of the Alliance of Free Voters of Baja California, 1962; left PRI from 1960 to 1964; split with *Ramón Danzos Palomino* Oct. 2, 1964, to support PRI. l-*Excélsior*, 21 Aug. 1976, 1C; C de D, 1976-79, 25, 1970-73, 116; D de C, 1976-79, 6, 12, 31; C de D, 1961-63, 12; DBGM89, 445; Lehr, 39.

Gasca, Celestino
(Deceased Apr. 6, 1981) a-May 17, 1893. b-Cuitzeo de Abasolo, Guanajuato. c-Early education unknown; no degree. d-Deputy to the Constitutional Convention, 1916-17; *Federal Deputy* from the State of Guanajuato, Dist. 2, 1937-40; *Senator* from the State of Guanajuato, 1940-46, President of the First National Defense Committee, member of the First Balloting Group, President of the Second Labor Committee and Second Secretary of the First Mines Committee. e-Secretary of Labor Action of the Pro Avila Camacho Committee, 1939-40; supporter of General *Miguel Henríquez Guzmán* for President, 1951-52. f-Governor of the Federal District, 1921-23. g-Joined the House of the Workers of the World, 1913; active in the Red Labor Battalions that supported General Obregón; Secretary General of the Shoeworkers Union; important leader of CROM. h-Worked as a saddle maker before the Revolution of 1910; employee of United Shoe Leather. i-Father was a peasant and shoemaker. j-Joined the Revolution, 1910; supporter of Francisco

Madero; fought de la Huerta's forces in Tabasco, Veracruz, and Hidalgo, 1923; Quartermaster General of the army, 1929; fought against the Escobar rebellion, 1929; rank of Brigadier General. k-Founder of the Federal Board of Conciliation and Arbitration as governor of the Federal District; national government candidate for governor of Guanajuato, but lost to *Agustín Arroyo Ch.* backed by powerful state machine, 1927; precandidate for governor of Guanajuato, 1935; precandidate for secretary general of the CTM; accused by the government of supporting a leftist insurrection against President *Adolfo López Mateos*, 1962, and briefly imprisoned. l-Peral, 326; C de D, 1937-39, 11; C de S, 1940-46; López, 414; Casasola, V; Enc. Mex., V, 1977, 277-78; HA, 20 Apr. 1981, 12; Guerra Leal, 37; Meyer, 99.

Gasca Neri, Rogelio
a-Nov. 7, 1942. b-Federal District. c-Primary studies at the Emiliano Zapata Primary School, Mexico City, 1948-53; secondary studies at the Prevocational School No. 4, IPN, 1954-56; preparatory studies at the Vocational School No. 5, IPN, 1957-58, in chemical engineering; degree in industrial chemical engineering, IPN, 1959-63; Ph.D. in science, Stanford University, 1966-70; MA in business administration, Stanford University, 1973-75; Chief, Department of Sciences, Materials and Metallurgy, Graduate School of Physics and Mathematics, IPN, 1970-73. d-None. e-None. f-Director of Finances, Aeromexico, 1986-87; Director General of Aeromexico, 1987-88; *Subsecretary of Programming, Budgeting, and Industrial Development*, Secretariat of Programming and Budgeting, 1988-92; *Subsecretary of Programming and Budgeting*, Secretariat of the Treasury, 1992-94. g-None. h-None. i-Son of José Gasca Franco and Angelina

Neri Orozco; married Barbara Beumont. j-None. k-None. l-DBGM89, 142; DBGM92, 150.

Gascón Mercado, Alejandro
a-Mar. 1932. b-Aután, Nayarit. c-Primary studies at the Francisco Madero Public School, Tepic, Nayarit; secondary studies at the Secondary Boarding School for Workers' Children, 1947-49; preparatory studies at the National Preparatory Night School, 1950-51. d-*Federal Deputy* from the State of Nayarit, Dist. 1, 1970-73, member of the Agriculture Committee, the Rural Electricity Committee, the Money and Credit Institutions Committee, and the Rules Committee; Mayor of Tepic, Nayarit, 1975; *Plurinominal Deputy from the PPS*, 1979-82; *Plurinominal Federal Deputy* from the PSUM, 1985-88. e-President of the Youth Division of the PPS for the Federal District, 1953; President of the National Committee of the Youth Division of the PPS, 1954-56; Auxiliary Secretary to *Vicente Lombardo Toledano*, 1961-67; Secretary of Press and Publicity, National Central Committee of the PPS; Secretary of Organization, National Central Committee of the PPS; Secretary of Economic Studies of the National Central Committee of the PPS; Oficial Mayor of the PPS; Secretary General of the PPS, 1975; founder of a splinter party from PPS called the Party of the Mexican People (PPM), 1976-81. f-Ambassador to Venezuela, 1978-79. g-President of the National Federation of Boarding Schools for Workers' Children, 1949; Secretary General of the Union of Workers and Peasants of Mexico, 1984-86. i-Brother of *Julián Gascón Mercado*, governor of Nayarit, 1964-70; parents were peasants. j-None. k-Candidate of the PPS for governor of Nayarit; lost to Rogelio Flores Curiel in what *Latin America* and critics termed a rigged election. l-C de D, 1970-72, 116;

Directorio, 1970-72; LA, 11 Nov. 1978, 349-50; *Excélsior*, 21 Feb. 1975, 12; *Proceso*, 24 Apr. 1978, 23.

Gascón Mercado, Julián
a-Jan. 28, 1925. b-Ejido de Trapichillo, Tepic, Nayarit. c-Primary studies in Tepic; secondary studies on a peasant scholarship at the Socialist School for Workers in Tepic; medical degree from the National School of Medicine, UNAM, 1947-52, with a thesis on "The Importance of Medical Services in Rural Areas"; professor, National School of Medicine, UNAM, 1972. d-*Governor of Nayarit*, 1964-70; *Senator* from Nayarit, 1988-91. e-Joined PRI, 1950. f-Head of the Medical Services for the National Chemical and Pharmaceutical Industry, 1958-62; Director of the Hospital of the National University; Coordinator General of the Hospital de Jesús, Mexico City, 1971-73. g-Member and official of the National Farmers Federation. h-Surgeon at the Hospital de Jesús, 1955-63, under the administration of *Gustavo Baz*; Head of Social Work for the Center for Private Assistance in the Federal District and Territories, 1960-61; author of three books in the medical field. i-Coauthored a book on surgery with *Gustavo Baz*; brother of *Alejandro Gascón Mercado*, federal deputy from Nayarit, 1970-73; son of Anselmo Gascón and Victoria Mercado, peasants. j-None. k-Elected on the PPS and the PRI ticket; supported by the Cardenistas for governor, but opposed by local PRI leaders. l-WWMG, 18; Enc. Mex., V, 228; *Por Qué*, 25 Sept. 1968, 41; Anderson, 114; *Excélsior*, 22 May 1973, 22; DBGM89, 446.

Gastélum Salcido, Juan José
(Deceased May 3, 1981) a-July 2, 1895. b-Hermosillo, Sonora. c-Early education unknown; no degree. d-*Senator* from the State of Sonora, 1976-81. e-None. f-*Subsecretary of National*

Defense, 1964-70. g-Active Mason; Vice-president of the Scottish Rite; Grand Commander of Spanish Masonry. h-None. i-Son, José de Jesús, retired Captain; married Manuela Morales. j-Career army officer; joined the Revolution in 1911 as a supporter of Madero; served under the Constitution-alists with General Benjamín Hill; Commander of the military zones of Querétaro, Querétaro, Tuxpán, Vera-cruz, and Oaxaca; rank of Brigadier General, Feb. 1, 1930; Commander of the 30th Battalion, 1937; rank of Brigade General, Mar. 1, 1942; Director General of Social Services of the army, Secre-tariat of National Defense, 1946-48; Inspector General of the army, 1951-52; Commander of the 4th Military Zone, Hermosillo, Sonora, 1956; Director of the National Military College; rank of Division General. k-Last three-star general from the 1910 Revolution on active duty. l-DGF56, 201; DGF51, I, 180; DPE65, 33; HA, 21 Dec. 1964, 9; Peral, 47, 141; C de S, 1976-82; Davila, 192; HA, 11 May 1981, 11.

Gavira, Gabriel
(Deceased July 15, 1956) a-Mar. 18, 1867. b-Orizaba, Veracruz. c-Primary studies in the Lancasterian system; stu-dies at the National Vocational School; self-educated in French, English, Geo-metry, Chemistry. d-None. e-None. f-President, Higher Tribunal of Military Justice; *Governor of Baja California del Norte*, 1936. g-Active in the labor movement in Orizaba; cofounder of the Mutualist Liberal Circle, Orizaba, Veracruz, 1892. h-Carpenter for many years. i-Son of Moisés Eduardo Gavira, an accordion player, and Pilar Castro. j-Joined the Revolution under the Maderistas, Nov. 20, 1910; fought under Generals Diéguez, Murguía, Obregón, and Aguilar in San Luis Potosí and Durango; Commander of expeditionary forces in Sinaloa and Sonora; attended the Convention of Aguascalientes, 1914-15; Governor and Military Commander of San Luis Potosí, 1915, and Durango, 1916-17; supported General Obregón in 1920; Chief of Staff, Secretary of War, 1925-27; reached rank of Brigade General. k-Led a rebellion against the authorities of Veracruz before the Revolution, imprisoned in San Juan De Ulloa; losing candidate for governor of the State of Veracruz; President of the Council of War that sentenced Felipe Angeles to death. l-López, 414; letter; Enc. Mex., V, 247.

Gaxiola Urías, Marcario
(Deceased 1953) a-1890. b-Angostura, Sinaloa. c-Early education unknown; no degree. d-Governor of Sinaloa, 1929-32; *Senator* from the State of Sinaloa, 1952-53. e-None. f-None. g-None. h-Miner before the Revolution. j-Joined the Revolution; Constitutionalist; fought against Victoriano Huerta, 1913; commander of the 1st Battalion under General Obregón, 1913-14; Brigadier General, Army of the Northeast, under General Obregón; supported the Plan of Agua Prieta. k-None. l-C de S, 1952-58; DGF56; PS, 2444.

Gaxiola (Zendejas) Jr., Francisco Javier
(Deceased Aug. 3, 1978) a-Sept. 6, 1898. b-Toluca, México. c-Primary studies at the School of Señorita Esther Cano and the Pestalozzi School, Toluca; second-ary studies at the Scientific and Literary School of Toluca and the Liceo Fournier, Mexico City; preparatory stu-dies at the National Preparatory School in Mexico City, 1912-16; law degree from the Escuela Libre de Derecho, Apr. 15, 1922, with a thesis on "Jurisdic-tional Invasions in Constitutional Opinions"; Professor of Political Econo-my at the Escuela Libre de Derecho, 1923-28, where he won prizes as a stu-dent. d-None. e-None. f-Representa-tive of the Secretariat of the Treasury to

the State of México, 1919; Envoy to the
Spanish American Congress, Madrid,
1920; Agent of the Ministerio Público
(Auxiliary) for the Attorney General in
the Federal District; Assistant District
Attorney for the Federal District, 1926;
Acting Governor of Baja California del
Norte, 1929; Governor of Baja California del Norte, 1930-32; Private Secretary to President *Abelardo Rodríguez*,
1932-34; President of the Council of
Arbitration and Conciliation for the
Secretariat of Industry and Commerce,
1932; Secretary General of Government
of Baja California del Norte, 1929-30;
manager of the private fortunes of
Abelardo Rodríguez, 1934-40; *Secretary
of Industry and Commerce*, 1940-44;
personal representative of *Manuel Avila
Camacho* to Franklin D. Roosevelt,
1942. g-None. h-Founder of the Mexican Bar Association, 1923; Secretary
General of the Mexican Bar Association,
1928; Oficial Mayor of the First Legal
Congress, 1921; President of the Illustrious and National College of Lawyers,
1957-72; private law practice with son,
Francisco, 1945-78; founder of the
National Bank of Cooperative Development; coauthor with *Rodrigo Gómez* of
the reform of Article 27. i-Attended the
Escuela Libre de Derecho with *Emilio
Portes Gil* and *Ezequiel Padilla*, and
taught *Felipe Tena Ramírez, Vicente
Sánchez Gavito*, and *Abel Huitrón y
Aguado*; father, a well-known author,
lawyer, and diplomat, who served as a
local deputy and as governor of México,
1919-20; brother, Jorge, an adviser to
Jaime Torres Bodet as secretary of
public education, and general counsel
for *Abelardo Rodríguez*; son, *Franciso J.
Gaxiola Ochoa*, a federal deputy from
the Federal District, 1979-82; married
Clotilde Ochoa. j-None. k-Resigned as
secretary of industry to run for governor
of México; defeated for the nomination
by *Alfredo del Mazo*, 1944. l-DP70,
843; DBM68, 282-83; WWM45, 48; Enc.

Mex., V, 245; WB48, 1940; EBW46, 531;
Peral, 328; letters; Strode, 370; HA, 11
June 1943, 38.

Gerstl Valenzuela, José
a-Sept. 9, 1935. b-Federal District.
c-Early education unknown; engineering studies, Higher School of Mechanical and Electrical Engineering, IPN,
1954-57, with a thesis on laboratory
systems for IPN, 1960; Ph.D. in science,
Royal Technological Institute of
Stockholm, Sweden, 1965; professor of
the Center for Research and Advanced
Studies, IPN, 1965- . d-None. e-None.
f-Director of Electronic Controls, Altos
Hornos, 1957-58; Director of Planning,
Teléfonos de México, 1973; *Director
General of IPN*, 1973-76; adviser,
Director General of Teléfonos de
México, 1977-82; adviser, Subsecretary
of Education and Technological Re-
search, 1982; Director General of the
National College for Professional
Technical Education, Secretariat of
Public Education, 1983. g-None.
h-Employee, Industrias Logo, 1955-56;
Director of Maintenance, Plásticos,
S.A., 1957; Supervisor, Teléfonos de
México, S.A., 1960. i-Son of José Gerstl,
geological engineer, and Carmen Araceli
Valenzuela; married Diana Irene
Solórzano Cantú, economist. j-None.
k-None. l-HA, 24 Dec. 1973, 14; Q es
QAP, 313; DBGM, 176.

Ghigliazza García, Sergio A.
a-Jan. 19, 1933. b-Federal District.
c-Early education unknown; economics
degree, National School of Econonmics,
UNAM, 1952-56; MA degree, Yale
University, 1961; courses in economics,
Graduate School, Columbia University,
1959; courses in public finance, Yale
University, 1959-60; professor, CEMLA;
professor, National School of Economics, UNAM, 1960-70; professor, Institute of Banking and Finances, 1981-82.
d-None. e-None. f-Subdirector General

of the Bank of Mexico, 1982-85; Assistant Director General, Bank of Mexico, 1985-88, 1988-90. h-Economist, Center for the Study of Economics of the Private Sector, 1963-64. i-Son of José Francisco Ghigliazza, banker, and Bertha García Román; married María Esther Alicia Ramos Talancon; classmate of *Miguel Mancera Aguayo* at Yale, 1959-60, director general of the Bank of Mexico, 1988-94. j-None. k-None. l-DBGM, 176; DBGM89, 144.

Gil Díaz, Francisco
a-Sept. 2, 1943. b-Federal District c-Early education unknown; economics degree, Autonomous Technological Institute of Mexico, 1962-66; Ph.D. in economics, University of Illinois, Chicago, 1967-72; Coordinator of Economics, ITAM, 1973-78; professor at ITAM, 1970-76; professor at the Colegio de México, 1970-84. d-None. e-None. f-Chief of Economic Projects, Presidency of Mexico, 1971; economist, Bank of Mexico, 1973; Director General of Economic-Treasury Studies, Secretariat of the Treasury, 1976; Head, Organization and Analysis of Economic Information, Bank of Mexico, 1977-78; Director General of Income Policy, Secretariat of the Treasury, 1978-82; Subdirector, Bank of Mexico, 1982-85; Director of Economic Research, Bank of Mexico, 1985-88; *Subsecretary of Revenues*, Secretariat of the Treasury, 1988-94. g-None. h-None. i-Son of Francisco Gil Arias, businessman and fisherman, and Ana María Díaz Perches; married Margarita White de la Peña; studied under *Miguel Mancera Aguayo* at ITAM; professor of *Pedro Aspe*, secretary of the treasury, 1988-93; political disciple of *Leopoldo Solís*. j-None. k-None. l-DBGM92, 152; DBGM89, 144.

Gil Elorduy, José Ernesto
a-Sept. 18, 1943. b-Federal District. c-Early education unknown; law degree,

National School of Law, UNAM, 1962-66, with a thesis on "Political Integration in Latin America." d-*Federal Deputy* from the State of Hidalgo, Dist. 2, 1979-82; Mayor of Pachuca, Hidalgo, 1985-88; *Federal Deputy* from the State of Hidalgo, Dist. 3, 1991-93. e-Joined PRI, 1962; general delegate of the CEN of PRI to the states of Morelos, Chiapas, Sinaloa, Campeche, and Hidalgo, 1977-81; active in *Guillermo Rossell de la Lama*'s gubernatorial campaign in Hidalgo, 1980; President of PRI in the State of Hidalgo, 1982-83. f-Lawyer, Legal Department, Secretariat of Industry and Commerce, 1962-65; lawyer, Legal Department, Federal Automobile Registry, Secretariat of the Treasury, 1965-67; Assistant Treasurer and Director of the Amparo Section, City of Naucalpán, Mexico, 1967-69; legal adviser to the Secretary General of the Department of the Federal District, *Octavio A. Hernández*; Director, Administrative Department, Benito Juárez International Airport, Mexico City, 1970-72; Appointments Secretary to the private secretary of the president of Mexico, *Ignacio Ovalle Fernández*, 1973-75; *Private Secretary to the President of Mexico, Luis Echeverría*, 1975-76; Representative of the State of Hidalgo in Mexico City, 1981-82; Secretary General of Government, State of Hidalgo, 1988-91. g-None. h-None. i-Son of Pedro Gil García, lawyer, and Julieta Elorduy Delgado; married Hortensia Elorduy Arriola, painter. j-None. k-None. l-letter; *Excélsior*, Mar. 1982, 21; DBGM92, 470.

Gil Guillén, Clementina
a-Jan. 5, 1938. b-Federal District. c-Early education unknown; law degree, National School of Law, UNAM, 1954-58; Professor of Law, National School of Law, UNAM, 1962-74. d-None. e-Joined PRI, 1959. f-Judicial official, 8th Division, Superior Tribunal of

Justice of the Federal District, 1958;
lawyer and adviser, Telecommunications Division, Secretariat of Communications and Transportation, 1959-67;
Auxiliary Secretary, Supreme Court of
Justice, 1967-69; Secretary, 7th Division, 1969-71, Family Judge, 1971-76,
Judge, 1976-82, and President, 1982-88,
all of the Superior Tribunal of Justice of
the Federal District; *Justice of the
Supreme Court*, 1989- . g-None.
h-None. i-Daughter of Eduardo Gil
Martínez, graphic artist, and María de la
Luz Guillén Gallegos; married David
Lester Green, teacher. j-None. k-None.
l-DBGM89, 611; DBGM92, 657.

Gil Preciado, Juan
a-June 26, 1909. b-Juchitlán, Jalisco.
c-Primary studies in Juchitlán; education degree from the Guadalajara International School; Professor of Mathematics, University of Guadalajara; secondary school principal, Ocotlán, Jalisco,
1927-28; Professor of Civics for the
Federal army, 32nd Regiment, 1929;
founder and Director of the Workers
and Farmers' School, 1935; Director of
Extension, University of Guadalajara,
1936; Secretary General of the Polytech-
nical School of the University of Guadalajara. d-Local Deputy to the State
Legislature of Jalisco, 1955-56; *Federal
Deputy* from the State of Jalisco, Dist.
13, 1940-43, member of the Tourism
Committee; Secretary of the Chamber,
Sept. 1940; Mayor of Guadalajara, 1956-
58; *Governor of Jalisco*, 1959-64.
e-Committee Chairman for the PNR,
1938; President of the State Committee
of the PRM for Jalisco; first Secretary of
Organization of CNOP, 1943; member
of the first council of the CNOP of the
PRM, 1944; General Delegate of the
CEN of PRI, 1978. f-Executive Secre-
tary for General García de Alba,
Governor of Baja California del Sur;
Oficial Mayor and Secretary General of

Government, Baja California del Sur;
Director of Planning for the Department
of Agrarian Affairs, 1943; Director of
Information, United States–Mexican
Commission on Hoof and Mouth
Disease, 1946-52; Private Secretary to
the Subsecretary of Agriculture, *Oscar
Flores Sánchez*, 1948-52; *Secretary of
Agriculture*, 1964-70. g-Student leader
at the Second Congress of Socialist
Students, 1935. h-Owned a sausage
shop. i-Married Aida Elizondo; son,
Juan Rodolfo Gil Elizondo, delegate of
the Department of the Federal District,
1993; son of Anselmo Gil Lomelí,
Mayor of Juchitlán, and María de la Luz
Preciado. j-Major, 32nd Regiment,
1929. k-Precandidate for president of
Mexico, 1970; precandidate for federal
deputy, 1978. l-Enc. Mex., V, 372-73; *El
Universal*, 1 Dec. 1964; WWMG, 18;
HA, 7 Dec. 1964, 19; DGF51, II, 220;
DPE65, 98; Peral, 330; DGF51, I, 203;
DGF56, 95; HA, 4 Aug. 1944; Johnson,
193; *Excélsior*, 15 July 1977, 12; NYT, 6
Oct. 1969, 16; *Excélsior*, 12 Nov. 1978,
18; Contreras, 138; DBGM92, 152.

Gil Ryathyga, Jesús
a-Nov. 1, 1915. b-Culiacán, Sinaloa.
c-Primary studies at a public school,
Culiacán, completed 1925; secondary
studies at Culiacán; normal school
studies at the Colegio Civil Rosales;
scholarship from the State of Sinaloa to
study at the National School of Teachers, graduated with a teaching certificate, Apr. 25, 1934; studies at the
National School of Economics, UNAM,
no degree. d-Local Deputy to the State
Legislature of Sinaloa under Governor
Pablo Macías Valenzuela; *Alternate
Senator* from the State of Sinaloa, 1952-
58, but replaced Senator *Macario
Gaxiola Urías* in 1953, member of the
Second Public Works Committee, First
Secretary of the Cooperative Development Committee, Secretary of the

Social Welfare Committee and President of the Second Public Education Committee. e-None. f-Inspector of Public Education, Sinaloa; General Inspector of School Construction, Secretariat of Public Education; general agent of CIEMSA in Sinaloa. g-Organizer, FSTSE in Sinaloa; organizer, Jacobo Gutiérrez Agrarian League. h-None. j-None. k-None. l-Ind. Biog., 371-72; DGF56, 7, 9-12.

Giner Durán, Praxedes
a-Feb. 15, 1893. b-Santa Rosalia de Conchos, Camargo, Chihuahua. c-Educated in public schools; no degree. d-Federal Deputy from the State of Chihuahua, Dist. 5, 1928-30, member of the Permanent Committee; Senator from the State of Chihuahua, 1930-34, President of the Senate; *Governor of Chihuahua*, 1962-68. e-President of the Administrative Commission of the Chamber of Deputies in charge of organizing a national political party, PNR; founding member of the PNR. f-None. g-None. h-None. k-Joined the Revolutionary forces, 1911; Chief of Staff under the forces of Francisco Villa; Chief of Staff of the 6th Brigade, Monclova, Coahuila, 1918; Chief of Staff of the 4th Military Zone, Hermosillo, Sonora, 1934; Subchief of Staff for the Federal District, 1935; Chief of Staff of the 6th Military Zone, Torreón, Coahuila, 1943; Chief of Staff of the 5th Military Zone, Chihuahua; Commander of the 2nd Military Zone, Mexicali, Baja California del Norte, 1953, of the 17th Military Zone, Querétaro, Querétaro, 1953, of the 18th Military Zone, Pachuca, Hidalgo, 1953-55, of the 27th Military Zone, 1955-59, Acapulco, Guerrero, and of the 5th Military Zone, Chihuahua, 1959-61; rank of Division General. l-WWMG, 17; DBM68, 284-85; DGF56, 202; Peral, 330-331; HA, 6 Sept. 1971, 19; Meyer, No. 12, 131.

Godínez Bravo, Miguel Angel
a-Apr. 4, 1931. b-Puebla, Puebla. c-Primary studies at the Manuel Avila Camacho School, Tezuitlán, Puebla; secondary studies at the Oriente Institute, Puebla; preparatory studies at the University of Puebla; graduated from the National Military College, 1953, as a 2nd Lieutenant of Cavalry; diploma in staff and command, Higher War College, 1957-60; Professor of General Staff Materiels and Tactics, Higher War College. d-None. e-None. f-Chief of Section Four, Presidential Staff; Subchief of the Presidential Staff; Chief of the Presidential Staff, 1976-82. g-None. h-None. i-Son of Miguel Angel Godínez, a school teacher, and Rebeca Bravo. j-Career army officer; officer in the 6th Cavalry Regiment, Atlixco, Puebla, in the 9th Cavalry Regiment, San Andrés Tuxtla, Veracruz, in the 13th Cavalry Regiment, Hacienda Echegaray, and in the 12th Armored Regiment of the Presidential Guards; Commander of the First Armored Squadron, Presidential Guards; rank of Colonel, 1974; rank of Brigade General, 1979; Commander of the 31st Military Zone, Tuxtla Gutiérrez, Chiapas, 1990-94. k-None. l-*El Día*, 1 Dec. 1976; Rev. de Ejer., Nov.–Dec. 1976, 14; *Excélsior*, 1 Dec. 1976, 14; *Proceso*, 12 Apr. 1993, 7.

Gomar Suástegui, Jerónimo
(Deceased Jan. 21, 1972) a-Sept. 30, 1908. b-Ayutla, Guerrero. c-Secondary education at the School of Administration, 1925; attended the Vocational School of the National Military College; graduated from the National Military College as a 2nd Lieutenant in the Infantry, Jan. 1930; graduated from the Higher War College, Mar. 1936, with a diploma in military staff administration; instructor, Applied Military School, 1941; training at the U.S. Department of Defense, 1947; training

at the Panama Canal Zone, 1962.
d-*Alternate Senator* from the State of
Guerrero, 1964-70. e-None. f-Director
of the Heroic Military College, 1958-64;
Director of the Department of Military
Industry, 1964-70; *Subsecretary of
National Defense*, 1970-72. g-None.
h-None. i-Son of Rafael Gomar and
Natalia Suástegui; married Alicia
Hernández Román. j-Career army
officer since Apr. 14, 1925; Subchief of
Staff of the 1st and 2nd Infantry Divi-
sions; Commander of the 8th Battalion
of Infantry, 1952; head of the Inspection
Commission for the Inspector General
of the army; Military Attaché to
Guatemala and Central America, 1945;
rank of Division General. k-None.
l-DPE70, 113; DPE65, 35, 45; letter; HA,
26 Jan. 1939, 8, 31 Jan. 1972, 14;
MGF69, 568; HA, 14 Dec. 1970, 20;
Rev. de Ejer., Jan. 1972, 19; WNM, 96.

Gómez (Alvarez), Pablo
a-Oct. 21, 1946. b-Federal District.
c-Early education unknown; economics
degree, National School of Economics,
UNAM, 1966-68, 1971-73, graduating
with a thesis on "Democracy and
Political Crisis in Mexico"; department
head, National School of Economics,
UNAM, 1975-76; professor, UNAM,
1974-79. d-*Plurinominal Federal
Deputy* from the PCM, 1979-82, 1988-
91, member of the Government and
Constitutional Affairs Committee.
e-Joined the Mexican Communist Party
in high school; member of the Central
Committee of the PCM, 1972-81;
member of the Political Committee of
the PCM, 1977-81; member of the
National Council of the PMS, 1987-89;
Secretary General of the Unified
Socialist Party of Mexico (PSUM), 1982-
87; member of the National Council of
the PRD, 1989. f-None. g-Member of
the Student Strike committee, UNAM,
1968; member of the Coordinating
Committee of Academic Employees,

UNAM, 1975-76. h-Economist. i-Son
of Benito Gómez Unda, public official,
and María de Jesús Alvarez Frausto;
married María Elvira Concheiro
Bórquez, sociologist. j-None. k-Imprisoned by government in Lecumberri
Prison for activities in 1968 student
movement, 1968-71; self-exile, 1971.
l-HA, 29 Mar. 1982, 8; DBGM89, 448.

Gómez Arias, Alejandro
(Deceased Mar. 3, 1990) b-Oaxaca,
Oaxaca. c-Early education unknown;
preparatory studies at the National
Preparatory School, 1926-29; law degree
cum laude from the National School of
Law, UNAM, 1933, with a thesis on
Hans Kelsen; professor at the National
Preparatory School; professor at UNAM.
d-None. e-Orator for José Vasconcelos's
presidential campaign, 1929; Vice-
President of the Popular Party (later the
PPS), 1947; cofounder of the Mexican
Civic Front of Revolutionary Affirma-
tion, 1963. f-Private Secretary to
Secretary of Public Education, *Octavio
Vejar Vázquez*, 1941-43. g-President of
the Student Federation of the Federal
District, 1928; President of the National
Student Federation, 1928-29.
h-Cofounder of the National College;
National Oratory Champion, 1928;
member of the 1925 Committee to
Reorganize the National University;
author; editor of *Política*, 1963; writer
for *Siempre*. i-Knew *Miguel Alemán*
and *Salvador Novo* at UNAM; met
Adolfo López Mateos at night school;
father a physician, revolutionary, and
federal deputy, 1920; preparatory school
boyfriend of Frida Kahlo; married Teresa
Salazar Mallén. j-None. k-None.
l-Letters; HA, 10 Oct. 1947, 5; HA, 27
Sept. 1976, 25; *Excélsior*, 29 Feb. 1960;
Proceso, 13 Mar. 1989, 54; *El Nacional*,
4 Mar. 1990, 1, 4.

Gómez Esparza, José
a-1898. b-San Santomo, Hidalgo. c-Primary studies in San Santomo; secondary studies in San Santomo; medical degree, National School of Medicine, UNAM; special studies in medicine in France. d-Federal Deputy from the State of Hidalgo, Dist. 2, 1934-37; *Alternate Federal Deputy* from the State of Hidalgo, Dist. 3, 1940-43, but replaced the deputy; member of the First Balloting Committee; President of the Chamber of Deputies, Dec. 1942; *Senator* from the State of Hidalgo, 1946-52, member of the Gran Comisión, the Indigenous Affairs Committee, and the First Balloting Committee. e-*Secretary General of the CEN of PRI*, 1952, 1953. f-Ambassador to China (never went because of WWII), 1944; Ambassador to Bolivia, 1944-46; *Oficial Mayor of Government Properties*, 1953-58; Ambassador to El Salvador, 1958-59. g-None. j-None. k-Author of a PNR petition in Congress, June 14, 1935; precandidate for governor of Hidalgo, 1945. l-C de D, 1940-43, 53; DGF51, I, 9, 10, 11, 14; DGF56; PS, 2498; Pérez López, 175.

Gómez (Gómez), Rodrigo
(Deceased Aug. 14, 1970) a-May 18, 1897. b-Linares, Nuevo León. c-Secondary studies in accounting at the General Zaragoza Commercial Academy, Monterrey, 1913-14, graduating as a private accountant. d-*Senator* from Nuevo León, Sept. to Nov. 1952. e-None. f-Head of the Exchange Department, Bank of Mexico, 1933; First Manager of the Bank of Mexico, 1941-47; *Subdirector General of the Bank of Mexico*, 1947-52; *Director General of the Bank of Mexico*, 1952-58, 1958-64, 1964-70. g-None. h-Employee of an electrical company, Monterrey, Nuevo León; accountant for various private businesses, 1915-18, including a general store in Linares; employee of the Compañía Fundidora de Fierro, Mon-

terrey, 1918-19; Assistant Manager of the Branch Office of Lacuad and Co., Monterrey, 1919-20, Mérida, Yucatán, and Tampico, Tamaulipas, 1921-22; head of the Department of Exchanges, Mercantile Bank, Monterrey, 1922-32; Executive Director of the International Monetary Fund for Mexico and Central America, 1946-48. i-Son of Manuel María Gómez and Elena Gómez; brother Salvador was director of agricultural development, Secretariat of Agriculture. j-None. k-Prominent in the Mexican movement to join the Latin American Free Trade Association in 1960 with *Plácido García Reynoso*; went to San Antonio, Texas, as a bracero, 1914. l-DGF51, II, 11, 63, etc.; DP70, 880-81; D del S, 5 Dec. 1952, 1; IWW67, 451; DGF56, 7; HA, 5 May 1954, 5 June 1957; DBM68, 293-94; letter.

Gómez Guerra, Enrique
a-Aug. 10, 1917. b-León, Guanajuato. c-Secondary and preparatory studies in León, Guanajuato; teaching certificate in social sciences, UNAM, 1929-33; law degree, National School of Law, UNAM, 1934-38; school teacher; Director of the Preparatory School, 1964, Director of Secondary, and Professor of Civic Culture and Greek and Latin, all at University of Guanajuato. d-Local Deputy to the State Legislature of Guanajuato, 1953-55; Mayor of León, 1955-57; *Alternate Federal Deputy* from the State of Guanajuato, Dist. 2, 1946-49, under *Luis Díaz Infante*, but in functions as deputy 1948-49; *Federal Deputy* from the State of Guanajuato, Dist. 2, 1958-61, member of the First Section, Legislative Studies Committee, the Second Treasury Committee, the First Constitutional Affairs Committee, the Complaints Committee, and the Consular and Diplomatic Affairs Committee; *Federal Deputy* from the State of Guanajuato, Dist. 7, 1964-67, member of the Administrative Section,

Legislative Studies Committee, the
Textile Industry Committee, and the
Budget and Accounts Committee;
Federal Deputy from the State of
Guanajuato, Dist. 2, 1976-79. e-General
Delegate of the CEN of PRI to the State
of Veracruz, 1965; President of PRI,
State of Guanajuato, 1974-75. f-Judge,
1947; Attorney General of the State of
Guanajuato, 1979-82. g-Secretary
General of the CNOP of the State of
Guanajuato, 1952-54. h-None. j-None.
k-None. l-C de D, 1964-67, 83, 87, 91,
1958-61, 79; Func., 209; C de D, 1946-
49; Almanaque de Guanajuato, 29.

Gómez Gutiérrez, Juan Manuel
b-Federal District. c-Early education
unknown; law degree from the National
School of Law, UNAM; professor, National School of Law, UNAM. d-None.
e-Joined the Mexican Communist Party,
1950; organizer, Mexican Peace Movement; organizer, National Liberation
Movement. f-None. g-Organizer, Independent Union Front; adviser to various
labor unions and housing groups.
h-Practicing lawyer. j-None. k-Candidate for federal deputy from the Federal
District, Dist. 7, of the Leftist Coalition, 1979; lawyer for various political
prisoners. l-HA, 23 Apr. 1979, VI.

Gómez Maganda, Alejandro
(Deceased Sept. 14, 1984) a-Mar. 3,
1910. b-Arenal de Gómez, Galeana,
Guerrero. c-Primary studies in Acapulco; secondary and preparatory studies
from the Colegio of San Jacinto; cadet,
National Military College; graduated
from the National Teachers School; law
degree, National School of Law, 1933.
d-Federal Deputy from the State of
Guerrero, Dist. 6, 1934-37, president of
the government bloc of deputies, Sept.
1936; *Federal Deputy* from the State of
Guerrero, Dist. 4, 1946-49, member of
the Library Committee, the Second
Balloting Committee, the Second

Instructive Section for the Grand Jury,
and the Gran Comisión, 1946; President
of the Chamber of Deputies, Sept. 1947;
Governor of Guerrero, Apr. 1, 1951 to
1954. e-Prominent orator in the
presidential campaigns from 1934 to
1952; Coordinator for the Frente Cívico
Mexicano de Afirmación Revolucio-
naria, 1961-65. f-Private Secretary to
General *Matías Ramos Santos*; Private
Secretary to socialist Juan R. Escudero,
governor of Guerrero, 1933; member of
the Technical Study Commission of the
Secretary of the Presidency, 1939-40;
Director General of Social Action for
the Federal District, 1941-43; Administrator of Maritime Customs, Acapulco,
Guerrero, 1944-45; Private Secretay to
Gabriel Leyva Mancilla, Governor of
Guerrero, 1946; adviser to the Presidency; Consul in Los Angeles, California, 1930s; Consul General in Spain and
Portugal during the Spanish Civil War;
Ambassador to Panama, 1965; Ambassador to Jamaica, 1968; Oficial Mayor of
the National Council of Tourism under
Miguel Alemán, 1971-76. g-President of
the Second Congress of Student Cooperative Representatives, 1926; President
of the National Student Convention in
Morelia, Michoacán, 1933. h-Author of
numerous historical works. i-Longtime
collaborator of *Miguel Alemán*; father,
General Tomás Gómez, was a Revolutionary; grandfather, Alejandro Gómez,
a peasant; married Joséfina Bermeo
Córdoba; first political mentor was *Luis
I. Rodríguez*, with whom he served an
internship; daughter, *Guadalupe
Gómez Bermeo*, served as a federal
deputy from Guerrero, 1979-82. j-Participated with irregular forces in the
Costa Chica, 1920s. k-Term as governor of Guerrero ended in 1954, when
the Senate dissolved his powers after
complaints of widespread corruption in
the state; declared persona non grata as
consul in Los Angeles for agitating the
braceros; answered *Miguel Alemán*'s

first state of the union address, 1947.
l-DPE65, 30; Scott, 275; Morton, 56;
DGF51, I, 89; Enc. Mex., V, 445; Peral,
338; Brandenburg, 103; NYT, 23 May
1954, 37; *Excélsior*, 15 Sept. 1984, 22.

Gómez Maganda de Anaya, Guadalupe

a-Apr. 20, 1945. b-Acapulco, Guerrero.
c-Primary studies at the First Congress
of Anáhuac School, Chilpancingo, 1951-
56; preparatory studies at the Women's
University of Mexico, 1957-61, receiving a gold medal for scholastic achieve-
ment; studies in law, National School of
Law, UNAM, 1962-66, graduating with
an honorable mention, Aug. 15, 1967;
course in French civilization, Sorbonne,
Paris, 1978. d-*Federal Deputy* from the
State of Guerrero, Dist. 4, 1979-82,
Secretary of the Permanent Committee,
1980, member of the Trade, Radio and
Television, Tourism, and Justice Committees, member of the Grand Jury;
Senator from the State of Guerrero,
1982-88; *Federal Deputy* from the State
of Guerrero, Dist. 4, 1988-91. e-Em-
ployee, Press Secretary, PRI Committee
of the Federal District, 1974. f-Aide to
the Agent of the Ministerio Público of
the 8th Delegation, Attorney General of
the Federal District, 1962-64; lawyer for
the ISSSTE, 1964-66; Assistant Director,
Legal Department, and adviser, National Council of Tourism, 1969-79;
President of the Superior Tribunal of
Justice of Guerrero, 1975; Secretary
General of Government of the State of
Guerrero, under *Javier Olea Muñoz*,
1975. g-Director of Advertising and
Public Relations, National Council of
Social Tourism, CNOP, 1980; General
Delegate of ANFER to the State of
Tlaxcala, 1980. h-None. i-Daughter of
Alejandro Gómez Maganda, Governor
of Guerrero, 1951-54, and Josefina
Bermeo Córdoba, normal teacher; grand-
daughter of General Tomás Gómez,
veteran of the Revolution; great-
granddaughter of Alejandro Gómez, a

peasant. j-None. k-None. l-*Excélsior*,
27 Feb. 1975, 13; Romero Aceves, 697-
99; Protag., 145; Lehr, 194; C de S, 1982-
84; DBGM, 511; DBGM87, 480.

Gómez Maqueo, Roberto

(Deceased) a-1892. b-Orizaba, Veracruz. c-Engineering degree specializing
in engineering mechanics, National
Naval College, graduated as a captain,
Nov. 1, 1929; professor at the National
Naval College. d-*Federal Deputy* from
the State of Veracruz, Dist. 9, 1952-54,
member of the Administrative Committee (1st and 3rd years), the First Committee on National Defense, the Budget
and Accounts Committee, and the
Naval Committee; Vice President of the
Chamber of Deputies, Nov. 1952;
Senator from Veracruz, 1958-64,
member of the Second Section of the
Balloting Committee and the General
Means of Communication Committee;
President of the Naval Committee.
e-None. f-Head of the autonomous
Navy Department, 1940; *Secretary of
the Navy*, 1955-58. g-None. h-Author
of many technical engineering studies.
j-Career naval officer; Commodore,
1939; Chief of Staff for the Pacific
Regiment, 1941-45; Commander of the
Destroyers "Veracruz," "Democracia,"
and "Morelos"; Inspector General of the
Navy, 1951; Intendant General of the
army; rank of Admiral, Oct. 27, 1959.
k-None. l-DGF51, I, 380;
STYRBIWW58, 415; DGF56, 381; HA, 2
Jan. 1956, 6; letter; C de S, 1961-64;
Func., 386.

Gómez Mont, Felipe

(Deceased 1970) a-Feb. 19, 1916.
b-Federal District. c-Kindergarten,
Colegio Español; primary studies at the
Colegio Giosso; secondary studies at the
Colegio Francés San Borja; preparatory
studies from the Colegio Francés
Morelos; law degree, Escuela Libre de
Derecho, Aug. 24, 1939, with a thesis

on "The Mentally Ill under Criminal Law"; Professor of Penal Law at the Escuela Libre de Derecho, 1941-52; Professor of Law at the Ibero-American University; visiting professor at the University of Miami; Professor of Penal Law in the United States, France, and Europe. d-*Federal Deputy* from the Federal District, Dist. 3, 1952-55, member of the Child Welfare and Social Security Committee, the Legislative Studies Committee, the First Balloting Committee, and the Second Constitutional Affairs Committee; *Federal Deputy* from the Federal District, Dist. 3, 1958-61, Dist. 2, 1964-67, member of the Department of the Federal District Committee and the First Justice Committee. e-Member of PAN. f-Participated in writing the reforms of the federal penal codes. g-President of the National Association of Catholic Lawyers. h-Adviser to the National Bank of Mexico; opened law firm with Raúl F. Cárdenas in Mexico City; conducted penal law studies for Interpol; writer for Mexican and foreign magazines and newspapers. i-Brother, Francisco, a medical doctor, served as director of instruction, General Hospital, National Medical Center; law partner Raúl F. Cárdenas appointed rector of the Escuela Libre de Derecho, 1972. j-None. k-Distinguished congressional debater. l-DP70, 887; Morton, 69; C de D, 64-66, 81, 89, 1952-54, 43, 51-53, 65, 1958-60.

Gómez Morín, Manuel
(Deceased Apr. 19, 1972) a-Feb. 27, 1897. b-Batopilas, Chihuahua. c-Primary studies at the Colegio del Sagrado Corazon in León, Guanajuato, 1906-10; started preparatory studies at the Instituto María Inmaculada, León 1910-13, and completed at the National Preparatory School in Mexico, 1913-15; law degree from the National Law School, UNAM, 1918; member of the genera-

tion of the National Preparatory School known as the Seven Sages, which included *Narciso Bassols, Vicente Lombardo Toledano, Alfonso Caso, Octavio Medellín Ostos,* and *Teófilo Olea;* courses in economics, Columbia University, New York, 1921; Professor of Law, UNAM, 1919-38. d-None. e-Supporter of José Vasconcelos, 1929; founder and *President of the CEN of PAN* (National Action Party), 1939-49. f-Member of the Governing Council of UNAM; Secretary of the National Law School, UNAM, 1918-19; Oficial Mayor of the Secretariat of the Treasury, 1919-20; Subsecretary of the Secretariat of the Treasury in charge of the Secretariat, 1920-21; financial agent for the Federal Government in New York City, 1921-22; Dean of the National School of Law, UNAM, 1922-24; founder and first Chairman of the Board of the Bank of Mexico, 1925; Rector of UNAM, 1933-34. g-President of the Student Society of the National Law School. h-Editor of *La Vanguardia,* 1915; Scribe of the 4th Correctional Court, Mexico City, 1915; official of the Department of Statistics, Secretary of Development, 1916; practicing lawyer, 1918-19, 1921-72; lawyer, Soviet Trade Delegation, Mexico City, 1928; author of legislation creating the Bank of Mexico; author of the first reform of Credit Institutions 1931; major investor in the Bank of London and Mexico, 1941, and Cervecería Modelo, 1943; author of several books. i-Longtime personal friendships maintained with *Alfonso Caso* and *Vicente Lombardo Toledano* despite different political views; married Lydia Torres; father a miner; father-in-law of *Juan Landerreche Obregón;* son, *Juan Manuel Gómez Morín* served as secretary general of PAN, 1969-72. j-None. k-Candidate for federal deputy on the PAN ticket, 1946, 1958; considered by some scholars to have been a secret supporter of Adolfo de la Huerta, 1923.

l-Kirk, 310-12; WWM45, 50; Padgett, 67-70; WB48, 2014-15; *Hoy,* 29 Apr. 1972, 3; DBM68, 292; HA, 24 Apr. 1972, 21; letters; Justicia, Jan. 1973; Alonso, 232, 229, 222, 213.

Gómez Morín Torres, Juan Manuel
a-Oct. 31, 1924. b-Federal District. c-Primary studies in Mexico City; secondary studies at the Colegio Francés Morelos; law degree from the National School of Law, UNAM; attended Law School, Harvard University; Professor of Mercantile Law, Ibero-American University. d-*Federal Deputy* from the Federal District, Dist. 23, 1967-70, member of the Federal District Department Committee, the Legislative Studies Committee (4th Section, Administrative, and 8th Section, Fiscal) for the 1st year; member of the Legislative Studies Committee (2nd Section, Civil) for the 2nd year; member of the United States–Mexican Interparliamentary Conference, 1968. e-Member of the Youth Section of PAN, 1939; Prosecretary of the National Committee of PAN, 1952; member of the Regional Committee for PAN for the Federal District, 1955; member of the CEN of PAN, 1959-70; Secretary of the Regional Committee for PAN for the Federal District, 1960-66; President of the Regional Committee for PAN for the Federal District, 1966; *Secretary General of the CEN of PAN,* 1969-72, 1974-75; Secretary of Promotion, CEN of PAN, 1975. f-None. g-None. h-Practicing lawyer. i-Son of *Manuel Gómez Morín,* founder and president of PAN; married Casilda Martínez del Río. j-None. k-None. l-DBM70, 259; C de D, 1967-69, 62; MGF69-70; letter.

Gómez Ortega, Miguel Angel
a-Nov. 25, 1917. b-Orizaba, Veracruz. c-Early education unknown; enrolled at the Heroic Naval College, 1937, graduated Feb. 17, 1942, as a coast-

guardsman; courses in antisubmarine warfare, San Diego, California, 1962; continental defense course, Inter-American Defense College, Washington, D.C., 1964-65; diploma, staff and command, Naval War College, Newport, Rhode Island, 1962-63; advanced course, Higher War College, 1986; professor, Heroic Naval College, 1946. d-None. e-None. f-*Secretary of the Navy,* 1982-88. g-None. h-None. i-Son of Angel Gómez Ortiz, businessman, and Modesta Ortega Ortega; married María Antonieta Gómez Candiani. j-Career naval officer; rank of Corvette Lieutenant, 1943; rank of Frigate Lieutenant, 1946; Naval Lieutenant, 1950; rank of Corvette Captain, 1953; rank of Frigate Captain, 1956; rank of Naval Captain, 1961; rank of Rear Admiral, 1967; rank of Vice Admiral, 1972; commander of the 3rd Naval Zone; Naval Attaché to Brazil; Assistant Chief of Section Six, Fleet Staff; Chief of Section Six, Fleet Staff; rank of Admiral, June 1, 1976; Chief of Staff, 2nd Naval Zone; Chief of Section Five, Fleet Staff; commander of the 5th Naval Zone; Chief of Staff of the Fleet; Commander General of the Fleet, 1982. k-None. l-*Excélsior,* 2 Dec., 1982, 34; *News,* 2 Dec. 1982; HA, 13 Dec. 1982, 12; DBGM87, 158; Q es QAP, 91.

Gomezperalta Damirón, Manuel
a-July 29, 1938. b-Federal District. c-Primary studies at the English School, Mexico City, 1945-41; secondary studies at the Instituto Mexicano Universitario, Mexico City, 1952-55; preparatory studies at the Antonio Caso Preparatory School, Mexico City, 1955-57; law degree, National School of Law, UNAM, 1957-63, with a thesis on legal medicine. d-None. e-Joined PRI, 1963; Secretary General of the 10th District of PRI, Federal District, 1963; adviser to the Electoral Division of the CEN of PRI, 1967. f-Adviser to the Secretary of

Labor, 1973-74; President of the Special Federal Board of Arbitration and Conciliation, 1974-78; adviser to the Secretary General of the IMSS, *Fernando Zertuche Muñóz*, 1977; Chief of Documentation, IMSS, 1977; Chief of Orientation Services and Complaints, IMSS, 1977-82; President of the Federal Arbitration and Conciliation Board, 1982-85; *Subsecretary of Labor*, Secretariat of Labor, 1985-88, 1988-94. g-None. h-None. i-Son of Mauro Gomezperalta, lawyer, and Clemencia Damirón Díaz; married Anna Rosa Casali Kadmonoff. j-None. k-None. l-DBGM92, 156; DBGM, 182; HA, 29 Oct. 1985, 10; DBGM87, 160.

Gómez Reyes, Roberto
a-Apr. 18, 1918. b-Ixtlán del Río, Nayarit. c-Primary studies at a public school, Ixtlán del Río; rural normal certificate, Normal School of Jalisco, Nayarit, 1934-36; teaching certificate, National Teachers College, 1937-40; preparatory studies in economics, National Preparatory School, 1942-43; degree in economics from the National School of Economics, UNAM, 1944-49; instructor in world history and teaching, secondary schools in Nayarit, 1941; primary school teacher, 1942-49; Professor of Economic Thought, 1960-63, Professor of the History of Economic Doctrines, 1964-65, and Professor of Public Finances, 1978, all at National School of Economics, UNAM; Professor of Economic and Social Problems, University of the Valley of Mexico, 1978. d-*Federal Deputy* from the State of Nayarit, Dist. 1, 1967, President of the First Treasury Committee and First Secretary of the Budget Committee; *Governor of Nayarit*, 1970-76. e-Joined the PRM, 1942. f-Economist, Secretariat of the Treasury, 1950-59; Director, Technical Office, Merchandise Division, Secretariat of Government Properties, 1954-58; Head of the

Registration and Certificate Control Department, Secretariat of Government Properties, 1959-62; Head of the Department of Temporary Import Permits, Secretariat of Government Properties, 1963-64; Head of the Receiving Department, Division of Automobile Registration, 1965-77; Secretary General of Government of the State of Nayarit under Governor *Julián Gascón Mercado*, 1967-70. g-Secretary General of the Student Society of the Normal School of Jalisco, Nayarit, 1935; Secretary of Labor Action, Federation of Mexican Youth, 1940; Secretary General of Delegation 78, Local 9, Teachers Union of the Federal District, 1944-45; Auxiliary Secretary of the CEN of the SNTE, 1946-47. h-None. i-Student of *Alfonso Pulido Islas* at UNAM; father a peasant. j-None. k-Precandidate for governor of Nayarit, 1963; precandidate from the Popular Sector for senator from Nayarit, 1964. l-HA, 28 Aug. 1967, 5; DPE61, 40; DPE65, 70; *Excélsior*, 21 Feb. 1975, 12; Loret de Mola, 91, 194.

Gómez Robleda, José
a-July 24, 1904. b-Orizaba, Veracruz. c-Early education unknown; medical degree, National School of Medicine, UNAM, 1929; professor of biology, legal medicine and psychology, National School of Medicine, UNAM, 1930-52; Secretary, National School of Medicine, UNAM, 1934; Director, Institute of Statistical Research, UNAM, 1950. d-None. e-Member of the Coordinating Committee of the Popular Party, 1947; Secretary General of the Popular Party, 1947. f-Director, Department of Medical Biological Studies, National School of Medicine, UNAM, 1942; Director, Department of Scientific Research, Secretariat of Public Education, 1940-41; Secretary of the Technical Studies Committee, Secretariat of Public Education, 1948; *Subsecretary of*

Education, 1952-54. g-None. h-Author of numerous books. i-Student of *Octavio Véjar Vázquez* with whom he collaborated in the Secretariat of Public Education and the Popular Party; married Victoria Trujillo; son of José Gómez Mont and Concepción Robleda. j-None. k-Candidate for federal deputy from the Federal District, Dist. 4, 1949, for the Popular Party. l-HA, 10 Oct. 1947, 5; WWM45, 51; Villaseñor, II, 118; NYT, 20 Feb. 1953, 6; Beltrán.

Gómez Robledo, Antonio
a-Nov. 7, 1908. b-Guadalajara, Jalisco. c-Law degree, University of Guadalajara; Ph.D. in philosophy, UNAM; special studies, School of Law, Paris, the Academy of International Law, The Hague, Fordham University, New York, and the University of Rio de Janeiro; professor, National School of Law, UNAM, and the Institute of Advanced Studies at Monterrey. d-None. e-None. f-Career Foreign Service Officer, joined the foreign service, 1936; member of the Ninth Inter-American Conference, Bogotá, 1948; alternate Mexican representative to the Organization of American States, 1949-51; Legal Adviser to the Mexican Embassy, Washington, D.C., 1951-54; rank of Ambassador, 1959; Ambassador to Brazil, 1959-61; member of the Permanent Delegation to International Organizations, Geneva, 1965; Mexican representative to the Disarmament Committee, Geneva, 1964-66; Ambassador to Italy, 1967-70; Legal Adviser to the Secretary of Foreign Relations, 1971-74, replacing Oscar Rabasa; Ambassador to Greece, 1974-76; Ambassador to Switzerland, 1977. g-Representative of Mexico to the Ibero-American Convention of Catholic Students, 1931, elected president of the National Federation of Catholic Students of Mexico; representative of Mexico to the Ibero-American Catholic Student Secretariat, Rome, Italy, 1933.

h-Author of many diplomatic and legal works; member of the National College, 1960- ; National Prize in Letters, 1976. i-Wrote for *Agustín Yáñez's Bandera de Provincias*; Private Secretary to *Ezequiel Padilla*, Rio Conference. j-None. k-None. l-HA, 22 Feb. 1971, 31; DPE61, 20; DPE65, 29; *Excélsior*, 29 Nov. 1974; Fuentes Díaz, 37; Enc. Mex., V, 448-49; López, 432; WNM, 98.

Gómez Sada, Napoleón
a-May 22, 1914. b-Municipio de Cadereyta, Nuevo León. c-Completed secondary studies; no degree. d-Member of the City Council, Monterrey, Nuevo León, 1952-54; *Alternate Senator* from the State of Nuevo León, 1958-64; *Senator* from the State of Nuevo León, 1964-70, 1976-82; *Plurinominal Federal Deputy* from PRI, 1988-91. e-Joined PNR, 1934. f-None. g-Secretary General, Local 64, Union of Mining and Metallurgical Industry Workers of Mexico, 1950-60; Alternate Secretary General of the Union of Mining and Metallurgical Industry Workers of Mexico (SITMMRM), 1958-59; Secretary General of the SITMMRM, 1960-91. h-Employee of Metalúrgica de Peñoles, S.A. i-Son of Manuel Gómez Pérez, farmer, and Francisca Sada; married Eloísa Urrutia Lozano; son, Napoleón Gómez Urrutia, was director of the Mint, 1987. j-None. k-None. l-MGF69, 106; C de S, 1961-64, 16, 1964-70, 1976-82; *Excélsior*, 3 June 1979, 21; PS, 252; DBGM, 180; DBGM87, 159; DBGM89, 450.

Gómez Sandoval, Fernando
a-1930. b-Oaxaca, Oaxaca. c-Primary studies at the Pestalozzi School, Oaxaca; secondary studies at the Institute of Arts and Sciences, Oaxaca (presently known as the Benito Juárez University); law degree from the Institute of Arts and Sciences, 1950; Director of the Preparatory School of

the Benito Juárez University (twice);
Professor of Sociology and Philosophy of
Law, Benito Juárez University; Rector of
the Benito Juárez University, 1959-62,
1977. d-*Alternate Federal Deputy* for
the State of Oaxaca, Dist. 3, 1956-59;
Local Deputy to the 43rd State Legisla-
ture of Oaxaca; *Substitute Governor of
Oaxaca*, 1970-74 replacing *Víctor Bravo
Ahuja*, who became Secretary of Public
Education. e-Secretary General of the
State Executive Committee of PRI,
Oaxaca (twice). f-Agent of the Mini-
sterio Público of the Attorney General's
Office; Assistant Attorney General for
Oaxaca; Penal and Civil Judge in the
State of Oaxaca; Inspecting Judge of the
Superior Tribunal of Justice of the State
of Oaxaca; Private Secretary to Gover-
nor *José Pacheco Iturribarría*, 1955-56;
legal adviser to the Federal Electric
Commission; Secretary General of
Government under Governor *Víctor
Bravo Ahuja*, 1968-70. g-None. h-Prac-
ticing lawyer, 1957-58. i-Father, an
accountant; mother, a teacher; married
Martha Audiffred Flores; compadre of
Víctor Bravo Ahuja and *Manuel Zárate
Aquino*. j-None. k-Precandidate for
senator from Oaxaca, 1976. l-DGF56,
26; letter; *Excélsior*, 8 Dec. 1975, 17.

Gómez (Segura), Marte Rodolfo
(Deceased Dec. 16, 1973) a-July 4, 1896.
b-Ciudad Reynoso, Tamaulipas. c-Pri-
mary studies in Aguascalientes and at
the Escuela Anexa a la Normal de
Maestros, Mexico City; no secondary or
preparatory studies; agricultural
engineering studies from the National
School of Agriculture, San Jacinto,
1909-14, degree, Sept. 1917; helped
organize the Escuela Libre Ateneo
Ceres; attended the Free Social Science
School, Paris, 1916-17; Professor of
Rural Economy, National School of
Agriculture; Director of the National
School of Agriculture, 1923-24. d-Local
Deputy to the State Legislature of

Tamaulipas, 1927; Federal Deputy from
the State of Tamaulipas, Dist. 2, 1928-
30, President of the Chamber of
Deputies, 1928; Senator from the State
of Tamaulipas, 1930-32, President of the
Senate, 1932; *Governor of Tamaulipas*,
1937-40. e-None. f-Topographer for the
Agrarian Commission of Yautepec,
Morelos, 1915; Director of the Depart-
ment of Ejido Improvements, 1917-22;
Auxiliary Director of the National
Agrarian Commission, 1917-22;
Subgerente of the National Agrarian
Credit Bank, 1926-28; Secretary of
Agriculture, Nov. 30, 1928, to Feb. 5,
1930; Subsecretary of the Treasury,
1933; Secretary of the Treasury, 1933-
34; Gerente of the National Railroads of
Mexico, 1934; *Ambassador to France*,
1935-36; *Secretary of Agriculture*, 1940-
46; Ambassador to the League of
Nations, 1935-36; President of the
Council of Development and Coordination of National Productivity, 1954-56.
g-President of the Local Agrarian
Commission of Tamaulipas, 1925,
appointed by *Emilio Portes Gil*. h-President of Worthington of Mexico, S.A.,
1950-66; author of many books on
Mexican agriculture. i-Political
associate of *Emilio Portes Gil* since
1920; close friend of General Jesús M.
Garza, who graduated from the National School of Agriculture; father,
Rodulfo Vidal Gómez, was a colonel
and graduate of the National Military
College; mother was a teacher in a
private school; son is a physician for
IMSS; knew *Alfonso González Gallardo*
at the National School of Agriculture;
close friend of *Jaime Torres Bodet* since
1935, when he served under Gómez in
France; married Hilda Leal. j-Joined the
Revolution in Morelos, 1915, served in
the forces of Zapata. k-Brandenburg
considered him a member of the Inner
Circle, 1940-46; important leader of the
Calles bloc in the Chamber of Deputies,
1928-30. l-IWW67, 450-51; WWM45,

50; EBW46, 189; DBM68, 290; Brandenburg, 80; DGF56, 63; Peral, 338; WB48,
2015; Strode, 323-24; HA, 8 Sept. 1944,
27; Enc. Mex., V, 438-39; Kirk, 121-22;
letter; HA, 24 Dec. 1973, 8; *Justicia*,
Feb. 1973; Wilkies, 77; Media, No. 20,
11; Meyer, No. 12, 27.

Gómez Velasco, Antonio
a-Sept. 3, 1897. b-Sayula, Jalisco. c-Primary studies in Mexico City; completed
business studies; no degree. d-*Federal
Deputy* (from PARM Party), 1979-82.
e-*President of the CEN of PARM*, 1975-
79. f-Director of Physical Education
and Premilitary Education, Secretariat
of National Defense; Subdirector of
Cavalry, Secretariat of National
Defense, 1935-36; Chief of Foot Police,
Department of the Federal District;
Director of Traffic, Department of the
Federal District, 1948-67. g-None.
h-None. i-Son of Magdaleno Gómez
and Cecilia Velasco; married Delores
Gutiérrez López. j-Career army officer;
joined the Constitutional army, June 11,
1913, as a 2nd Captain of Cavalry in the
3rd Brigade of General Mariano
Arrieta's forces; aide and secretary to
General Mariano Arrieta, Chief of
Instruction of the Escolta Brigade, under
General Pablo González; Chief of Staff,
4th Brigade, 21st Division, under
General *Jesús Agustín Castro*; Chief of
Staff, 2nd Division of the Army of the
Northeast, under General *Enrique
Estrada*; Chief of Staff under General
Roberto Cruz; Chief of Staff to General
Joaquín Amaro in Michoacán; Com-
mander of the Bravos Battalion, 2nd
Brigade, 21st Division; rank of Brigade
General, Feb. 9, 1924; fought Cedillo,
1939; commander of military garrisons
in Tlalnepantla, México; Chalchimo-
mula, Puebla; Esperanza, Puebla and
Veracruz, Veracruz, 1939-40; Com-
mander of the 30th Cavalry Regiment,
1932-34; Zone Commander of the 5th
and 29th military zones; Director, Civil

Defense, Regional Guards and the
Reserves, Secretariat of National
Defense, 1940-46; Commander of the
2nd Infantry Division; reached rank of
Division General. k-Resigned as
president of PARM under disputed
circumstances. l-DBM66, 295; HA, 28
May 1979, x, 5 Aug. 1949, 6; Rev. de
Ejer., May 1975, 127.

Gómez Villanueva, Augusto
a-July 23, 1930. b-Aguascalientes,
Aguascalientes. c-Primary studies in
the Jesús Díaz de León Public School,
Aguascalientes; secondary studies in
Durango in the Boarding School for the
Children of Peasants and Laborers No.
6; preparatory studies at the National
Preparatory Night School; political
science degree from the National School
of Social and Political Science, UNAM,
1965; professor at the National School
of Social and Political Science, UNAM;
professor at the Autonomous Institute
of Sciences, Aguascalientes. d-*Federal
Deputy* from the State of Aguascalientes, Dist. 2, 1964-67, member of the
Consular Service Committee, the
Editorial Committee, the Second
Balloting Committee, the Legislative
Studies Committee (Agrarian Section),
and the Gran Comisión, President of
the Chamber of Deputies, Sept. 1965,
answered President *Gustavo Diaz
Ordaz's* first State of the Union Address, 1965; *Senator* from Aguascalientes, 1970, 1975-76; *Federal Deputy*
from the State of Aguascalientes, 1976-
77, President of the Gran Comisión,
1976-77; *Federal Deputy* from the State
of Aguascalientes, Dist. 2, 1988-91.
e-Joined PRI, 1956; representative of the
Agrarian Sector on the National
Political Council of PRI; Director of
Publications for the CEN of PRI;
member of the National Council of PRI;
Technical Secretary of the IEPES of PRI;
Technical Director of the preelection
campaign of *Enrique Olivares Santana*

for governor of Aguascalientes, 1961-62; Director of the Editorial Department of the Youth Sector of PRI; *Secretary of Agrarian Action of the CEN of PRI, 1968-70,* when *Olivares Santana* was Secretary General of PRI; *Secretary General of the CEN of PRI, 1975-76.* f-Coordinator of Planning Projects for the State of Aguascalientes; Head of the Department of Publicity, State of Aguascalientes; Director of the Information Bulletin of the Secretariat of Communication and Transportation; Head of the Office of Personnel Analysis, Secretariat of Communication and Transportation; Private Secretary to the Governor of Aguascalientes, *Enrique Olivares Santana, 1962-64; Secretary of the Department of Agrarian Affairs and Colonization, 1970-75;* Ambassador to Italy, 1977. g-Vice-President of the Federation of Univerity Students; President of the Society of Secondary Students of Durango; Secretary General of the Preparatory School Students of the Federal District; Secretary of Organization of the National Farmers Federation, 1967-68; *Secretary General of the National Farmers Federation, 1968-70.* h-Worked as a laborer on the National Railroads of Mexico. i-Student of *Ernesto Enríquez Coyro* at the National School of Social and Political Science, UNAM; son of Macario J. Gómez, peasant, railroad worker, and candidate for Federal Deputy from Aguascalientes sacrificed by PRI, and María Eugenia Villanueva Escobar; dedicated thesis to his political mentor, *Enrique Olivares,* and his wife, Belém; numerous contacts with prominent politicians from his boarding school and preparatory and professional school days; lived at the National Military College with cadets who became prominent generals. j-None. k-Accused of fraud, Second Judicial District, Mexico City, 1977. l-*Hoy,* 7 Dec. 1970, 26; WWMG, 19; HA, 11 Jan. 1971, 31; DPE71, 129; C de D, 1964-66; letters;

LA, 12 Mar. 1976, 83; HA, 24 Oct. 1977; LA, 11 Nov. 1977, 349; Loret de Mola, 68; *Excélsior,* 23 May 1983, 20A, 22 May 1983, 23A; WNM, 98: DBGM, 181; DBGM89, 451.

Gómez Zepeda, Luis

a-Dec. 18, 1905. b-Aguascalientes, Aguascalientes. c-Primary studies in Aguascalientes; attended the Industrial School for Orphans; no degree. d-*Senator* from the State of Aguascalientes, 1964-70. e-Coordinator of Social Affairs for the CEN of PRI, 1969; Secretary of Organization of the CEN of PRI, 1970. f-Director General of the Workers Cooperative Society of Clothing and Equipment, 1970-73; *Director General of the National Railroads of Mexico, 1973-76, 1976-82.* g-Cofounder of the Railroad Workers Union of the Mexican Republic, 1933; Secretary of Organization of Local 17 of the Railroad Workers Union, 1933-36; Secretary of Organization and Education of the Union of Mexican Railroad Workers, 1940; Secretary of Conflicts of the CTM, 1940, 1944; Secretary General of the Union of Mexican Railroad Workers, 1944, 1962-64, 1965-68; member of the CEN of the Revolutionary Federation of Farmers and Workers (CROC), 1952-56; Secretary General of CROC, 1953-54, 1961-62. h-He became a railroad worker on the Constitutionalist railroads, 1917-18; messenger, Buenavista telegraph office, 1918; sold chocolates as a boy; worked for a butcher at age eleven; mimeographer, 1917-18; i-Distantly related to *Adolfo López Mateos,* grandfather, a physician; father, Luis Gómez Reyna, a bookkeeper; friend of *Alfonso Corona del Rosal* since youth. j-None. k-Imprisoned in the Federal District for labor activities, 1948; attempted to become Secretary General of the STFRM, 1942; precandidate for senator from Aguascalientes, 1982. l-HA, 8 Apr. 1974, 16-17; *Excélsior,* 5 July 1973, 15;

HA, 7 Dec. 1970, 27-28, 14 May 1973, 25; C de S, 1964-70; MGF69; *Proceso*, 18 Dec. 1976, 18-21; Villaseñor, II; WNM, 98; *Excélsior*, 26 Dec. 1981, 16A.

González, Jesús B.

(Deceased 1955) a-July 14, 1888. b-Zacalica, Zacatecas. c-Early education unknown; left school in 1900 to work; completed part of his preparatory; no degree. d-Federal Deputy from Zacatecas, Dist. 2, 1920-22, member of the Gran Comisión; Federal Deputy from Zacatecas, Dist. 1, 1922-24; *Senator* from Zacatecas, 1946-52, member of the Gran Comisión, the Second Committee on Tariffs and Foreign Trade, the Second Instructive Section of the Grand Jury Committee and the Securities Committee. e-None. f-Secretary of the Administration of the National Railroads of Mexico; Subdirector of PIPSA; Secretary of the Advisory Council of PIPSA; administrative official of National Patrimony. g-None. h-Worked in a bakery; clothing store employee; employee of a branch office of the national bank; founded the newspaper *El Canonazo*, 1904; poet; founded the weekly *La Revista de Zacatecas*; newspaper reporter; writer for *Excélsior* and *Revista de Revistas*. i-Orphaned at eight; great-uncle supported his family. j-None. k-Exiled from the State of Zacatecas by General Luis Medina Barrón, 1914. l-*Excélsior*, 11, May 1972; DP70, 891; DGF51, I, 8-10, 12, 14; letter; López; DGF47, 10, 12, 14, 22.

González Aparicio, Luis

(Deceased Sept. 23, 1969) a-Feb. 22, 1907. b-Jalapa, Veracruz. c-Preparatory studies from the Colegio Preparatoria of Jalapa; architecture degree, National School of Architecture, 1933; Professor of Architecture, National School of Architecture, UNAM. d-*Senator* from the Federal District, 1964-69. e-Director of the Center of Economic, Political,

and Social Studies of PRI. f-Head of the reconstruction project of the State Palace, Hermosillo, Sonora; constructed experimental agricultural stations in the Valle del Yaqui; constructed Workers Housing Projects on the Emiliano Zapata Ejido, Zacatepec, Morelos; Director of the Planning Commission for the Papaloapan Commission, 1950; instituted the Modern Market Construction Program for the Federal Government in Mexico City; Executive Secretary of the Papaloapan Commission, 1951-52; President of the Western Zone Planning Committee for the Valley of Mexico, 1958-59. g-None. h-President of the National College of Architects, 1959. i-Son of Enrique González Montalvo and Rosa Aparicio; father worked for the Exploratory Geographic Commission; mother worked for her brother, lawyer Manuel Aparicio Guido; married María Luisa González; brother of the notable economist and adviser to *Lázaro Cárdenas*, Enrique González Aparicio. j-None. l-Enc. Mex., V, 454; Correa, 105; DGF51, II, 615; DP70, 895; Pasquel, 259-61.

González Avelar, Miguel

a-Mar. 19, 1937. b-Durango, Durango. c-Early education unknown; law degree, National School of Law, UNAM, with a thesis on the national electrical industry; Professor of Constitutional Law, National School of Law, UNAM, 1965-82; Professor of Public Administration, National School of Economics, UNAM, 1965-67; professor at the Higher Normal School, 1962-65; Director General of Professorate, UNAM, 1966-70. d-*Senator* from the State of Durango, 1982-85, President of the Gran Comisión, 1982-85; *Plurinominal Federal Deputy* from PRI, 1991-94. e-Joined the PRI, 1962; commissioned by *José María de los Reyes*, Secretary General of PRI in the Federal District, to restructure the 3rd electoral district in the Federal District;

Secretary of Information and Publicity, *CEN of PRI*, 1981-82. f-Private Secretary to the Secretary of Labor, 1970-71; Subdirector General of Higher Education and Scientific Research, Secretariat of Public Education, 1964-66; adviser to *Rafael Hernández Ochoa*, Subsecretary of Government, 1970; Director General of Social Welfare, Secretariat of Labor, 1971-72; representative of the Permanent Technical Committee of Labor Affairs to the Organization of American States; Subdirector of the Legal Department of INFONAVIT, 1972-76; Subdirector General of INDECO, 1976-79; Director General of Information and Public Relations, Secretariat of Programming and Budget, 1979-81; *Secretary of Public Education*, 1985-88; Director General of the Matías Romero Foreign Service Institute, Secretariat of Foreign Relations, 1988-91. g-Member of the National College of Lawyers; member of the Association of Professionals of Durango. h-Auxiliary of the Federal Electric Commission. i-Classmate of *Miguel de la Madrid* at the National School of Law; son of Medardo González Peña, career military, and María Avelar Durán; brother, Víctor, was a federal deputy from the State of Coahuila; brother, Raúl, was director general in the Secretariat of Energy, Mines, and Government Industries. j-None. k-None. l-HA, 16 Aug. 1982, 7; DPE71, 120; DPE65, 141; HA, 27 Sept. 1982, 11-12; *Proceso*, 4 Oct. 1982, 16; DBGM, 812; Lehr, 162; DBGM92, 473.

González Azcuaga, Pedro
a-Nov. 11, 1945. b-Palizada, Campeche. c-Early education unknown; degree in political science, National School of Political and Social Sciences, UNAM; degree in Accounting, School of Business Administration, UNAM; studies in international relations, Colegio de México; Professor of History, Autonomous University of the State of México, 1971-

75. d-*Federal Deputy* from the Federal District, Dist. 24, 1976-79; Vice-President of the Chamber of Deputies, 1976; member of the Permanent Committee. e-Joined PARM, May 1971; *President of PARM*, Feb. 1973 to May 1975; member of the Federal Electoral Commission. f-Various posts in the Secretariat of Public Works, 1968-73; adviser to the Director of Production of PEMEX, 1970; delegate of the ISSSTE to the State of Hidalgo. g-None. i-Married Rita H. Sozaya Gallegos; son of Francisco González Reynoso and Elena Azuaga. j-None. k-None. l-HA, 12 Feb. 1979, 19; D de C, 1976-79, 28; letter.

González Beytia, José
a-June 17, 1908. b-Yucatán. c-Teaching certificate from the Rodolfo Menéndez de la Peña Normal School, Mérida; studies at the National Teachers' College, Mexico City; attended the University of Yucatán; teacher of Spanish, Agustín Vadillo Cicero School; secondary school teacher in Mexico City; Secretary of the Preparatory School for Children of Workers, Coyoacán, Federal District. d-Local Deputy to the State Legislature of Yucatán, 1943-46; *Governor of Yucatán*, 1946-51. e-None. f-Private Secretary to the Governor of Yucatán, *Ernesto Novelo Torres*, 1940-43. g-Representative of the Yucatán Socialist Students to the National Student Congress, Ciudad del Carmen; student leader in the first and second Socialist Student Congresses, 1934-35. h-None. i-Married Blanca Rosa Rodríguez Barrera; protégé of the Novelo Torres political clique. j-None. k-Resigned as governor in 1952 in an attempt to prevent the imposition of *Tomás Marentes* as his successor; his attempt failed. l-STYBIWW54, 758; Anderson, 94; C de D, 1943-46; HA, 16 Feb. 1951, 9; D de S, 22 Jan. 1946, 1; DPE51, I, 93; HA, 8 Feb. 1946, 3.

González Blanco, Alberto
(Deceased Nov. 1, 1974) b-Tuxtla Gutiérrez, Chiapas. c-Primary studies in the State of Chiapas; preparatory studies at the National Preparatory School, 1920-24; law degree, National School of Law, UNAM, Oct. 24, 1927; LLD, National School of Law, UNAM, 1958 (honorary mention); first thesis on the agrarian problem and LLD thesis on sexual crimes in Mexican doctrine and positive law. d-None. e-None. f-Consulting lawyer for the National Agrarian Commission; Director of the Department of Colonization, Secretariat of Agriculture; consulting lawyer, Secretariat of Agriculture; Secretary, First Civil Judicial District, Federal District; Sixth Judge, Second Penal Court, Federal District, 1941; Justice of the Superior Tribunal of Justice of the Federal District; Secretary of Studies, Supreme Court of Justice; District Court Judge, Yucatán and Querétaro; *Supernumerary Justice of the Supreme Court*, 1963-64, 1964-67. g-None. i-Brother of *Salomón González Blanco*, secretary of labor, 1958-70; brother of *Alfonso González Blanco*, federal deputy from Chiapas, 1964-67; close friend of *Antonio Luna Arroyo* at graduate school; son of Miguel González, a lawyer, and Patrocinia Blanco Corzo; cousin, Esteban Corzo Blanco, was mayor of Palenque, 1973-76. j-None. k-None. l-*Justicia*; letter; *Excélsior*, 22 Aug. 1979, 15.

González Blanco, Salomón
(Deceased Mar. 17, 1992) a-Apr. 22, 1902. b-Playa de Catozaja, Chiapas. c-Primary studies in Salto de Agua, Tapachula, and Tuxtla Gutiérrez, Chiapas; preparatory studies at the National Preparatory School, Mexico City; first three years of legal studies, Escuela Libre de Derecho, 1922-24; law degree from the National Law School, UNAM, May 16, 1927, with a thesis on

the social evolution of unions; LLD from the National Law School, UNAM; Professor of Labor Law, National School of Law, UNAM (15 years); professor at the Escuela Libre de Derecho; Director of the Juárez Institute, Tabasco, 1931-32. d-*Alternate Senator* from Tabasco, 1934-40; *Senator* from the State of Chiapas, 1976-78, member of the Gran Comisión, and President of the Chamber, Sept. 1977. e-None. f-Second Auxiliary Secretary of the Fourth Division of the Superior Tribunal of Justice of the Federal District, 1927-30; Judge of the First Appeals Court, Villahermosa, Tabasco, 1930; Magistrate of the Superior Tribunal of Justice for the State of Tabasco, 1931; Commissioner of the Agricultural Department of the National Agrarian Commission; Assistant Auditor, General Accounting Office, Secretariat of the Treasury; Magistrate of the Superior Tribunal of Justice of the Federal District and Territories, 1941-47; Director General of Conciliation, Secretariat of Labor, 1947; *Oficial Mayor of the Secretariat of Labor*, Sept. 20, 1947, to Dec. 31, 1952; *Subsecretary of Labor*, 1953-57; *Subsecretary in Charge of the Secretariat of Labor*, 1957-58; *Secretary of Labor*, 1958-64, 1964-70; *Substitute Governor of Chiapas*, Dec. 9, 1978-80. g-None. h-Author of numerous works on labor law. i-Friend of *Antonio Carrillo Flores* and *Manuel Ramírez Vázquez* at the National Law School, UNAM; son, *José González Blanco*, served as secretary general of the Department of the Federal District; married Josefa Garrido; brother-in-law of Tomás Garrido Canabal; brother, Alberto, was justice of the supreme court, 1963-67; cousin Esteban Corzo Blanco, served as mayor of Palenque, 1973-76; son of Miguel González, a lawyer, and Patrocinia Blanco Corzo; father-in-law of of Patricia Ortiz Salinas, daughter of *Antonio Ortiz*

Mena and cousin of *Carlos Salinas.*
j-None. k-Precandidate for president of
Mexico, 1963. l-EGF56, 397; Enc. Mex.,
V, 455; HA, 6 Feb. 1948, 10; IWW67,
452; WWMG, 19; DBM68, 296-97; HA,
8 Dec. 1958, 26; DPE61, 115; DPE65,
154; DGF51, I, 399; HA, 7 Dec. 1964,
20; Func., 87; Richmond, 375; *Excélsior,*
22 Aug. 1979, 15: *El Nacional,* 8 Mar.
1992, 16; *Proceso,* 25 Jan. 1988, 24.

**González Blanco (Garrido), José
Patrocinio**
a-May 18, 1934. b-El Paraíso, Municipio de Catazajé, Chiapas. c-Law degree
from the National School of Law,
UNAM, Apr. 26, 1956; MA in law and
economics at Trinity Hall, Cambridge
University, 1957-59, graduated Nov.
1961; professor at secondary schools;
Professor of Law, Anáhuac Branch,
UNAM, 1972-78. d-*Federal Deputy*
from the State of Chiapas, Dist. 6, 1967-
70, member of Industries Committee,
the Fiscal Committee, the Tariff
Committee, and the Gran Comisión;
Senator from Chiapas, 1982-88; *Gover-
nor of Chiapas,* 1988-92. e-General
Delegate of the CEN of PRI to Oaxaca,
1968, Jalisco, 1969, and Guanajuato,
1969. f-Chancellor, Mexican Embassy,
London, 1957-59; Secretary of the
Directive Council of the ISSSTE, 1960;
Subdirector of the Department of Public
Investments, Secretary of the Presi-
dency, 1960-61; Director of Public
Investments, Secretariat of the Presi-
dency, 1961-64; Assistant Director of
the National Lottery, 1965; *Secretary
General (B) of the Department of the
Federal District,* 1970-73; delegate of
the Department of the Federal District
to Miguel Hidalgo, 1976-78; Director
General of the Commission for Urban
Development of the Department of the
Federal District, 1978-82; *Secretary of
Government,* 1992-94. g-Student leader
and President of the 1952 Generation of
Lawyers. h-Practicing lawyer, 1960-65,

1972-76. i-Son of *Salomon González
Blanco,* secretary of labor, 1958-70;
classmate of *Miguel de la Madrid;* son-
in-law of *Antonio Ortiz Mena;* nephew
of Garrido Canabal; wife, Patricia Ortiz
Salinas, is a cousin of *Carlos Salinas.*
j-None. k-Forced to resign after
Chiapan guerrilla uprising. l-HA, 14
Dec. 1970, 24; BdM, 135; DPE61, 124;
DPE70; *Proceso,* 25 Jan. 1988, 24-27;
Lehr, 83-84; DBGM89, 690.

González Bustamante, Juan José
a-May 16, 1899. b-Matehuala, San Luis
Potosí. c-Primary studies in San Luis
Potosí; preparatory studies in Mexico
City; law degree from the Escuela Libre
de Derecho, Jan. 8, 1929; LLD from the
National School of Law, UNAM, 1950;
Professor of Penal Law and the Legal
Process, National School of Law,
UNAM, 1937-78. d-*Senator* from San
Luis Potosí, 1964-70, President of the
Senate. e-None. f-Third Judge of the
First Penal Court, 1935-36; Magistrate
of the Superior Tribunal of Justice of the
State of San Luis Potosí, 1938; Judge of
the Ninth Penal Court, 1941-46;
Assistant Attorney General of Mexico,
1946-47; Judge of the First District
Criminal Court, 1947-52; *Secretary
General of UNAM,* 1948-52; *Supernu-
merary Justice of the Supreme Court,*
1958; *Justice of the Supreme Court,*
1959-64; President of the First Division
of the Supreme Court, 1959-64.
g-None. h-Journalist for many years;
author of numerous articles, writer for
Excélsior since 1928. i-Son of Cruz
Antonio González and María
Bustamante; son, Juan José González
Suárez, was a judge in the Fourth Penal
District of the Federal District, 1969;
married María de Jesús Suárez Trujillo;
friend of *Luis Garrido* for many years.
j-Joined the Revolution, 1915; fought in
Tampico. k-None. l-MGF69, 106;
DGF51, I, 591; DGF47, 47; C de S, 1964-
70; DBM68, 297; Correa, 60; *Por Qué,*

13 Nov. 1969, 17; Casasola, V; WNM, 98; Garrido, 266, 336; Peral, 343; Enc. Mex., V, 457; *Mis Seis Años*, 265.

González Casanova, Pablo
a-Feb. 11, 1922. b-Toluca, México. c-Preparatory studies at the National Preparatory School, 1939-40; studies from the National School of Law, UNAM, 1940-42; MA degree in history, 1943-46, on a scholarship from the National School of Anthropology; Ph.D. in sociology from the University of Paris, 1947-50, with a thesis on French ideology toward Latin America; scholarship from the French government; scholarship from the Colegio de México to study in Paris, 1947-50; Professor of Sociology, National School of Political and Social Science, UNAM, 1952-66; Professor of Historical Sciences, UNAM; Professor of Sociology, National School of Economics, UNAM, 1954-58; Researcher, Institute of Social Investigations, UNAM, 1950-52, 1972-77, Colegio de México, 1950-54, and at Institute for Research in Economics, UNAM, 1954-56. d-None. e-None. f-Director of the Center for Development Studies, 1965-66; Dean, National School of Political and Social Sciences, UNAM, 1957-65; Director of the Institute of Social Investigations, UNAM, 1966-70; *Rector of UNAM*, 1970-72; Director of the Institute of Social Investigations, UNAM, 1977- . g-None. h-Author of works on sociology and Mexican politics. i-Son of Pablo González Casanova, linguist and Professor of Anthropology at UNAM, who resigned in protest in 1935; originally a disciple of Lucio Mendieta y Núñez at UNAM. j-None. k-Resigned from rectorship Dec. 1972, after numerous strikes; first Mexican graduate with a Ph.D. in sociology. l-Correa, 340; DP70, 896; DBM70, 263; Enc. Mex., V, 460; WNM, 99.

González Cavazos, Agapito
a-Dec. 22, 1915. c-China, Nuevo León. c-Early education unknown; no degree. d-*Federal Deputy* from the State of Tamaulipas, Dist. 3, 1970-73, member of the Second Railroad Committee, the Petroleum Committee, and the Second Public Housing Committee; *Federal Deputy* from the State of Tamaulipas, Dist. 3, 1976-79, member of the Agrarian Affairs Committee, the Small Property Section of the Agricultural Development Committee, the Industrial Development Committee, the Housing Development Committee, and the Committee for Social and Economic Development Planning. e-Campaigner for PRI in many electoral campaigns. f-None. g-Joined the Union of Industrial Employees and Workers, 1932; member of Local 16 of the Union of Oil Industry Workers. i-Married Eva Benavides. j-None. k-None. l-C de D, 1970-73, 116, 1976-79, 28; D de C, 1976-79, 5, 7, 13, 27, 45, 66.

González Cortázar, José de Jesús
a-Aug. 12, 1934. b-Guadalajara, Jalisco. c-Law degree from the University of Guadalajara; postgraduate work at the City of London College. d-*Federal Deputy* from the State of Jalisco, Dist. 7, 1961-64, member of the Second Balloting Committee and the Committee on Foreign Relations and substitute member of the Small Agricultural Property Committee; member of the Mexican Congressional Delegation to the Second, Third, and Fourth Interparliamentary Conferences between Mexico and the United States. e-Adviser to the Legal Studies Section and Historical Studies Section of the IEPES of PRI, 1968; delegate of PRI to Colima for the 1964 Presidential elections. f-Technical adviser to the Mexican Institute of Social Security; member of the Development Commission for the Chapala Lake Region.

g-President of the Law School Student Association of the University of Guadalajara, 1953. h-Lawyer for PEMEX; President of the Agricultural and Industrial Credit Union of the West; Vice-President of the Fourth Inter-American Consular Reunion. i-Son of J. Jesús González Gallo, governor of Jalisco, 1947-53. j-None. k-Tried to oppose the political control of former Governor José Guadalupe Zuno Hernández. l-DBM68, 306-07; C de D, 1961-63, 70; Enc. Mex., V, 466.

González Cosío, Manuel
a-Apr. 15, 1915. b-Querétaro, Querétaro. c-Primary studies in Querétaro; secondary and preparatory studies at the Colegio Francés and University of Querétaro; degree in chemical engineering from the School of Science, UNAM. d-Alternate Federal Deputy from the State of Querétaro, Dist. 1, 1946-49; Federal Deputy from the State of Querétaro, Dist. 1, 1949-52, member of the Gran Comisión, the National Waters and Irrigation Committee, the First and Second Legislative Studies Committee, the Industries Committee, the Public Works Committee, and the General Accounting Office Inspection Committee (2nd year); Senator from the State of Querétaro, 1952-58; member of the Gran Comisión, the Second Ejido Committee, and the Forestry Committee; Governor of Querétaro, 1961-67; Senator from Querétaro, 1976. e-None. f-Director General of Desert Zones for the Federal Government, 1950-52; Director General of La Forestal, 1958-61; Ambassador to Venezuela, 1968-70; President of the Administrative Council of the National Laboratories of Industrial Development, 1971-72; Director General of Alimentos Balanceados de Mexico, S.A., 1968-71; Director General of CONASUPO, 1976-79. g-Secretary General of the Union of Federal Employees for Querétaro, 1940-43; Presi-

dent of the Confederation of University Students for the Federal District, 1934; Secretary General of the National Union of Workers of the Secretary of Agriculture; Secretary of Conflicts and Technical Problems, FSTSE; President of the Student Society of the School of Chemical Sciences, UNAM. i-From a longtime politically active family in Querétaro; grandfather was a federal deputy and governor of Querétaro; married María de la Trinidad Septién, daughter of prominent lawyer, Manuel María Septién y González de Cosío. j-None. k-None. l-Enc. Mex., V; DGF50, 9, 10, 14; DGF51, I, 204, 25, 29-35; C de D, 1949-51; C de S, 1952-58; Peral, 344; Excélsior, 15 Apr. 1977, 6; Ind. Biog., 74.

González Cosío (Díaz), Arturo
a-May 3, 1930. b-Federal District. c-Legal studies from the National Law School, UNAM, 1948-52, graduating with a thesis on "Political Parties in Mexico," Sept. 27, 1954; Ph.D. from Cologne, Germany, 1954-56, with a thesis on writs; professor, National School of Law, UNAM, 1962-89, Colegio de México, 1966, and at the Sorbonne, Paris, France, 1971-74. d-Federal Deputy from the Federal District, Dist. 22, 1973-76. e-Member of the Political Committee of the New Advisory Council of the IEPES of PRI, 1972; Secretary of Political Education of the CEN of PRI, 1972-76; Oficial Mayor of the CEN of PRI, 1981; Subdirector of the IEPES of PRI, 1987-88. f-Private Secretary to the Director of Ciudad Sahagún Industrial site, 1959-62; head of publicity and studies for the Private Secretary of the President of Mexico, Humberto Romero Pérez, 1962-64; Auxiliary Secretary to the head of the Department of the Federal District, Ernesto P. Uruchurtu, 1964-66; Director General of Copyrights, Secretariat of Public Education, 1968-70; Director General of Industrial Property, Secretary

of Industry and Commerce, 1970-73; Subdirector of Delegations, CONASUPO, 1976-79; *Oficial Mayor of the Secretariat of Agrarian Reform*, 1980-82; adviser to the Secretary of Labor, 1983-88; Coordinator of Advisers to the Head of the Department of the Federal District, 1988-93. g-Secretary General of the Association of University Professors of Mexico. h-Employee of the National Securities Commission, 1951-52. i-Published a literary review with *Víctor Flores Olea, Porfirio Muñoz Ledo* and others at UNAM, 1950s; son of Arturo González Cosío, military medical officer and a longtime friend of General *Miguel Henríquez Guzmán*, and María Díaz de la Garza; married Berenice Montes Angeles. j-None. k-None. l-HA, 21 Dec. 1964, 10, 10 July 1972, 10; DPE70, 62; B de M, 135; *Excélsior*, 16 Mar. 1973, 27, 28 Feb. 1973, 19; Enc. Mex., V, 460; Guerra Leal, 316; DBGM92, 157.

González de Aragón, Arturo
a-July 15, 1943. b-Federal District. c-Early education unknown; degree in public accounting, National School of Business and Administration, UNAM, 1962-66, with a thesis on controlling budgeting techniques; Director of Scholarly Planning, School of Business and Administration, UNAM, 1968-69. d-None. e-Subsecretary of Finances, CEN of PRI, 1981-82. f-Director General of Budgeting, Administration, and Finance, Secretariat of Programming and Budgeting, 1980-81; Corporate Director, Somex, 1978-79; Subdirector of Expenditures, Secretariat of the Treasury, 1975-76; *Subsecretary General "B" of the Department of the Federal District*, 1982-84; *Secretary of Planning and Evaluation, Department of the Federal District*, 1984-88. g-None. h-Director, Mexican Mortgage Association, 1977-78; Controller General, Papelería y Maquinaría San Agustín,

S.A., 1969-70; President, Advisory Committee on Administration and Budget Affairs, Organization of American States, 1980-82. i-Son of Ezequiel González de Aragón, office worker, and Victoria Ortiz Díaz; married Josefina Rodríguez Flores. k-None. l-HA, 20 Dec. 1982, 28; Q es QAP, 426;

González de la Vega (Iriarte), Angel
a-Sept. 26, 1895. b-La Paz, Baja California del Sur. c-Preparatory studies at the National Preparatory School; law degree from the National School of Law, UNAM, June 28, 1919. d-None. e-None. f-Agent of the Ministerio Público of the State of Veracruz, 1919-20; Secretary of the Correctional Judicial District, Mexico City, 1920-22; Secretary of the Criminal Judicial District, Mexico City, 1923-26; Agent of the Ministerio Público of the Attorney General of Mexico, 1926-32; Second Assistant Attorney General of Mexico, 1932-35; Director, Bureau of International Taxes, Secretariat of the Treasury; President of the Revisory Committee on the federal income tax; Subdirector General of Revenues, Secretariat of the Treasury, 1935; Director, Economic Archives, Secretariat of the Treasury, 1936; founding Justice of the Federal Tax Court, 1936; *Subsecretary of the Treasury*, 1949-50; *Supernumerary Justice of the Supreme Court*, 1951-52, 1952-58; *Justice of the Supreme Court*, 1958-65. g-None. i-Brother of *Francisco González de la Vega*, attorney general of Mexico, 1946-52; son of lawyer Angel González de la Vega; mother, Rebecca Iriarte, ran a boarding house for students at the National Preparatory School and the National University; classmate of *Ramón Beteta* at UNAM; father's sister, Josefa González de la Vega y Hornedo, married José María Zevada, uncle of *Ricardo José Zevada*; grandfather, Angel González de la Vega, was a mining engineer; grandson, René

González de la Vega, was assistant attorney general of the Federal District. j-None. k-None. l-DGF51, 568; WNM, 99; Linajes, 294.

González de la Vega (Iriarte), Francisco (Deceased Mar. 3, 1976) a-Dec. 3, 1901. b-Durango, Durango. c-Studied at the National School of Law, UNAM, 1917-20, law degree, 1923; LLD in penal sciences from the School of Law, University of Veracruz; Professor of Penal Law, Escuela Libre de Derecho; professor at the National School of Law, UNAM, 1921-23; member of the Commission of Legal Studies, UNAM, 1944-45; founder of the University of Durango, 1957. d-*Senator* from the State of Durango, 1952-57, member of the Second Balloting Committee, the Legislative Studies Committee, and the First Committee on Credit, Money, and Credit Institutions; substitute member of the Department of the Federal District Committee; *Governor of Durango*, 1957-61. e-Supported José Vasconcelos, 1929. f-Correctional Judge, 1929; Assistant Attorney General of Mexico, 1930-31; Penal Judge, 1931-38; President of the Legislative Commission on Education, 1942-43; *Attorney General of Mexico*, 1946-52; Director General of PIPSA, 1952-56; *Head of the Department of Tourism*, 1961-64; Ambassador to Argentina, 1969-70. g-None. h-Practiced law, Durango, 1923-29; President of the Mexican Academy of Penal Sciences; author of over fifteen books on penal law. i-Studied with *Luis Garrido Díaz* at UNAM; during his career as a professor of law, he taught the last four Mexican presidents who attended the National Law School, *Miguel Alemán, Adolfo López Mateos, José López Portillo*, and *Luis Echeverría*; son of Angel González de la Vega y Hornedo, a judge, and Rebecca Iriarte; grandson of mining engineer Angel González de la Vega; brother of *Angel González de la*

Vega, justice of the Supreme Court, 1951-65; married Angelita Zevada, sister of *Ricardo José Zevada*; great-uncle of René González de la Vega, assistant attorney general of the Federal District, 1991. j-None. k-Hayner considered him to be an extremely honest governor; offered rectorship of UNAM in 1948 but remained as the attorney general. l-Letter; Hayner, 221; Peral, 47, 148-49; DGF51, II, 653; I, 535; DGF50, II, 481; WWM45, 41; MGF69; DGF56, 6, 13, 14; HA, 8 Dec. 1948; *Quién Será*, 140; HA, 15 Mar. 1976, 17; Ind. Biog., 74-75; DBGM92, 158.

González Fernández, José Antonio a-Mar. 8, 1952. b-Federal District. c-Early education unknown; law degree, Free School of Law, 1970-75, with a thesis on federal intervention in the states; MA, Warick University, 1975-77; professor, Free School of Law, 1977- ; professor, Autonomous Metropolitan University, Azcapotzalco, 1977- . d-None. e-Joined PRI, 1972; Technical Secretary, National Meetings, IEPES of PRI, 1981-82. f-Private Secretary to the Director of National Voter Registry, Federal Electoral Commission, 1974-75; Chief, Department of Urban Development, General Credit Division, Secretariat of the Treasury, 1978; Delegate of the Secretariat of Public Education, Guerrero, 1981; Assistant Director General of Personnel, Secretariat of Public Education, 1982; Director General of Legal Affairs, Secretariat of Health, 1982-83; *Oficial Mayor of the Secretariat of Health*, 1983-85. g-President, Free Law School Student Society, 1973-74. h-None. j-None. k-None. l-DBGM, 183.

González Fernández, Vicente (Deceased 1959) a-Jan. 17, 1885. b-Ocotlán de Morelos, Oaxaca. c-Attended the Escuela de Aspirantes, for military cadets, Mexico City; no degree. c-*Gov-*

ernor *of Oaxaca*, 1940-44. e-None.
f-Chief of Police for the Federal District,
1934-39; Director of the Department of
Artillery, Secretariat of National
Defense. g-None. i-From a middle class
family; personal friend of *Lázaro
Cárdenas* since they served in several
military campaigns together. j-Career
military man; joined the Revolution,
1910; served in the Federal Army under
General Carlos Tejada; served under
General Pablo González; staff officer
under Venustiano Carranza; rank of
Brigadier General, 1920; rank of
Division General, Nov. 16, 1940; Chief
of Military Operations in Guerrero;
fought against the Escobar Rebellion,
1929, under General *Cárdenas*; fought
against the de la Huerta revolt in
Tabasco, 1922-23, under General
Cárdenas; Commander of the 25th
Military Zone, Puebla; Commander of
Military Operations in Michoacán
under Governor *Cárdenas*; Commander
of the 1st military zone, Mexico City,
1939-40. k-None. l-DP70, 899; Enc.
Mex., V, 464; Peral, 353; *Hoy*, 21 Dec.
1940, 68; D de Y, 1 Nov. 1940, 2.

González Gallardo, Alfonso
a-Jan. 21, 1891. b-Lagos de Moreno, Jalisco. c-Primary studies in Guadalajara;
secondary studies at the Liceo of Guadalajara; engineering studies in agronomy
and hydraulics, National School of Agriculture, San Jacinto, 1909-13, degree,
July 1, 1913; assistant in physics, 1910;
Professor of Geology, Mineralogy, and
Topography at the National School of
Agriculture, Chapin-go. d-None.
e-None. f-Second Engineer and Chief of
Soil Department, Secretary of Agriculture, 1921-22; head of the Technical Department, National Agricultural Credit
Bank, 1926-28; employee of Oficial
Mayor of Agriculture, 1928-30; Oficial
Mayor of Agriculture, 1930-32; Oficial
Mayor of the Treasury, 1933-34; Sub-
secretary of the Treasury, 1934; in

charge of many Mexican delegations to
international agricultural conferences;
Subsecretary of Agriculture, 1940-46;
Director of the Institute for the Improvement of Sugar Production, 1964-
70. g-None. h-Began career as an engineer in the National Irrigation Works,
1913-20, with jobs in Ayotla, Oaxaca,
Colima, Guanajuato, Hidalgo, and
Michoacán; helped to bring the Rockefeller Foundation to Mexico; founded
the Institute for the Improvement of
Sugar Production, 1949; Director of the
the Office of Agricultural Experimenta-
tion Stations of UNPA, S. A., 1949-66;
author of many publications on the
sugar industry in Mexico. i-Student
with *Marte R. Gómez* and *Luis L. León*
at the National School of Agriculture;
collaborator of *Marte R. Gómez* for
many years; married Eva Karg; son of
Dr. Eudoxio González Aguirre. j-None.
k-None. l-D del S, 2 Dec. 1940, 1, 6;
letter; WB48, 2018; DBM68, 302; Peral,
345; Gómez, 251-53.

González Gallo, J. Jesús
(Deceased Aug. 17, 1957) a-Sept. 12,
1902. b-Yahualica, Jalisco. c-Primary
studies in Yahualica; studies for the
priesthood at the Catholic Seminary in
San Juan de Lagos; preparatory studies
at the University of Guadalajara; law
degree from the University of Guadalajara, 1923. d-Local Deputy from the
State of Jalisco, 1922-24; Federal Deputy
from Jalisco, Dist. 3, 1930-32; *Senator*
from Jalisco, 1934-40. e-President of the
Revolutionary Party of Jalisco, part of
the PNR; editor of the PNR newspaper
for Jalisco, *El Jalisciense*; President of
the PNR regional committee for the
State of Jalisco, 1932-34. f-Judge of the
First Instance, Jalostotitlan, Jalisco,
1923; Secretary of the Fifth Division of
the Superior Tribunal of Justice, Jalisco;
Criminal and Civil Judge, Guadalajara;
Secretary of the Federal Council of
Conciliation and Arbitration; Subdirec-

tor of the Department of Government of
the Federal District, 1927-30; *Private
Secretary to the President of Mexico,
Manuel Avila Camacho,* 1940-46.
g-None. h-None. i-Son, *José de Jesús,*
was a federal deputy from Jalisco, 1961-
64; married Paz Cortázar; knew *Efraín
González Luna* and *Agustín Yáñez* from
student days in the Mexican Association of Catholic Youth in Guadalajara;
uncle of Rigoberto González Quezada,
federal deputy from the State of Jalisco;
great-uncle of Julián Orozco González,
federal deputy from the State of Jalisco.
j-None. k-Political rival of *Marcelino
García Barragán;* close friend of Soledad
Orozco, wife of *Manuel Avila
Camacho,* since childhood; from a
middle class family of farmers; compadre of *Leobardo Reynoso.* l-DP70,
899; letter; Enc. Mex., V, 464-65;
DGF51, II, 699; I, 90; Hurtado, 177.

González Gálvez, Sergio
a-July 11, 1934. b-Toluca, México.
c-Early education unknown; political
science degree, University of Nuevo
León, 1956; MA in law, University of
Michigan, 1956-57, with a thesis on due
process; LLD, Georgetown University
Law School, 1957-58, with a thesis on
new sources of international law.
d-None. e-None. f-Chief of the Inter-
American System Department, Division
of Internation Organizations, Secretariat
of Foreign Relations, 1960-61; Third
Secretary, Mexican Embassy, Brazil,
1962-64; Assistant Subdirector General,
1964-66, Subdirector General, 1966-72,
Director General, 1972-74, Director in
Chief, Ambassador rank, 1975-79, and
legal adviser, 1979-83, all at Secretariat
of Foreign Relations; Ambassador to
Japan, 1983-88; *Subsecretary A of the
Secretariat of Foreign Relations,* 1988-
91; Ambassador to Japan, 1992-94.
g-None. h-None. i-Son of Ernesto
González Valdés, businessman, and
María Elena Gálvez Vázquez; married

Carolina Díaz Garduño, political
scientist. j-None. k-None. l-DBGM89,
153; DBGM92, 159.

González Gollaz, Ignacio
a-Oct. 1929. b-Amatitlán, Jalisco.
c-Primary studies, Guadalajara, Jalisco;
completed second year of legal studies,
Autonomous University of Guadalajara,
before dropping out to become a full-
time activitist in the National Sinarquista Union. d-Candidate of the
Mexican Democratic Party for president, 1982. e-Directed the first campaign against *Gonzalo N. Santos* in the
State of San Luis Potosí, 1952; youth
leader as a teenager of the National
Sinarquista Union; Director General of
the National Sinarquista Union, 1959- ;
first President of the Mexican Democratic Party, 1975-78, 1984-86, 1987.
f-None. g-None. i-Father was a small
farmer, mother a school teacher who
gave him lessons. j-None. k-Detained
by the attorney general of Mexico
because of conflicts with the governor
of Guanajuato, 1964. l-Análisis Político, May 1982, 13; Carlos Gil.

González Guevara, Rodolfo
a-Dec. 22, 1918. b-Mazatlán, Sinaloa.
c-Primary, secondary, and preparatory
studies in Guadalajara; law degree,
University of Guadalajara. d-Secretary
of the City Council of Guadalajara,
1947-52; *Federal Deputy* from the State
of Jalisco, Dist. 1, 1952-55, member of
the Legislative Studies Committee (1st
and 2nd years), the Balloting Committee, and the Administrative Committee
(3rd year); President of the Chamber of
Deputies, Dec. 1954; *Federal Deputy*
from the Federal District, Dist. No. 13,
1976-79, President of the Gran Comisión, 1977-79. e-Member of the
Ececutive Committee of PRI, State of
Jalisco, 1946-52; *Secretary of Political
Action for the CEN of PRI,* 1955; President of the PRI in the Federal District,

1955-59, 1959-64; *Secretary General of the CEN of PRI*, 1964; member of the New Advisory Council of the IEPES of PRI, the Ideology and Program Commission, June 28, 1972; General Delegate of the CEN of PRI to Sonora, 1972; Director of the CEPES of PRI of the Federal District, 1976; leading figure in the "Democratic Current" movement of PRI; resigned from PRI to join the PRD, 1991. f-Director of the General Office for the Secretariat of Industry and Commerce, Guadalajara, Jalisco, 1948-52; *Subsecretary of Government Properties*, 1964-66, under *Corona del Rosal*; *Secretary General of the Federal District Department*, 1966-70, under *Corona del Rosal*; *Subsecretary of Government*, May 25, 1979-82; Secretary General of the ISSSTE, 1982-83; Ambassador to Spain, 1983. g-Secretary General of the Federation of Socialist Students of the West, 1934; lawyer, Legal Division, CTM, Jalisco, 1941-52. i-Collaborator of *Alfonso Corona del Rosal* since 1958; married Elisa Macías; brother, *Héctor González Guevara*, a federal deputy from Sinaloa, 1979-82; son of Antonio González Lie, businessman, and Leonor Guevara Morales, teacher. j-None. k-Participated in the creation of the Popular Party; resigned as the general delegate of PRI in protest to *Carlos Biebrich*'s selection as Governor of Sonora, 1973; answered *José López Portillo*'s second state of the union address, 1978. l-DGF51, I, 268; C de D, 1952-54; HA, 10 July 1972, 10; *Siempre*, Jan. 3, 1959, 6; Enc. Mex., V, 579; DPE65, 76; MGF69; HA, 21 Dec. 1964, 7; Johnson, 1978, 181; *Excélsior*, 30 July 1978, 23; *Uno Más Uno*, 26 Feb. 1983, 2; Hurtado, 309; DBGM, 184-85; letter.

González Herrera, Saúl
a-Nov. 4, 1915. b-Ciudad Guerrero, Chihuahua. c-Early education unknown; law degree, National School of Law, UNAM, 1938-43, with a thesis on administrative law. d-Local Deputy to the State Legislature of Chihuahua, 1950-53; *Federal Deputy* from the State of Chihuahua, Dist. 1, 1964-67; *Senator* from the State of Chihuahua, 1988-94. e-Member of the youth groups of the PRM; President of PRI, State of Chihuahua, 1965-66; General Delegate of the CEN of PRI, Coahuila, 1966-67; Special Delegate of the CEN of PRI, Chiapas, 1967; Assistant Secretary General of the CEN of PRI, 1987-88; *Secretary of Organization of the CEN of PRI*, 1986-87. f-Judge of the First Instance, Ciudad Guerrero, 1944-45, and Benito Juárez, 1945-46, both in Chihuahua; Director General of Tarahumara Forest Products, 1972-76; *Substitute Governor of Chihuahua*, 1985-86. h-Notary Public, Benito Juárez, Chihuahua, 1949-50; Notary Public, Morelos, Chihuahua, 1968-89. i-Son of Simón González Amaya and Enedina Herrera Casavantes; married Delia Jaimes Beiza. j-None. k-None. l-DBGM89, 453-54; DBGM92, 477.

González Hinojosa, Manuel
a-Jan. 28, 1912. b-San Luis Potosí, San Luis Potosí. c-Primary, secondary, and preparatory studies, San Luis Potosí; law degree from the School of Law, University of San Luis Potosí; member of the University Council of the University of San Luis Potosí; Professor of Agrarian Law, National School of Law, UNAM; Professor of Agrarian Law, Ibero-American University; preparatory school teacher. d-*Federal Deputy* from PAN (party deputy), 1967-70, 1973-76. e-Founding member of PAN, 1939; adviser to the National Council of PAN, 1940-70; President of the Regional Committee of PAN for San Luis Potosí, 1940s; President of the Regional Committee of PAN in the Federal District, 1955; member of the CEN of PAN, 1952-69; *President of the CEN of PAN*, 1969-72. f-None. g-Member of the

Catholic Action organization. h-Practicing lawyer in the Federal District; multilingual. i-José G. Minondo, secretary general of the CEN of PAN, was a political disciple of *González Hinojosa*; son, Alejandro, was a candidate for federal deputy for PAN in 1979, but resigned before the election; father, a rancher; married Ana María Alcocer. j-None. k-His opposition party activities forced him to leave San Luis Potosí in the 1950s; candidate of PAN for federal deputy from San Luis Potosí, 1943, 1949, for senator, 1952, for federal deputy from the Federal District, 1958, for federal deputy in 1979 but resigned before the election. l-*Excélsior*, 28 Feb. 1973, 19; Mabry, 81, 153; C de D, 1973-76, 29, 1967-70; letter; HA, 2 Apr. 1979, V; *Excélsior*, 29 Apr. 1979, 14.

González López, Guillermo
a-1946. b-Nuevo León. c-Early education unknown; law degree, National School of Law, UNAM, 1950. d-None. e-None. f-Lawyer, Legal Office, Department of Traffic and Highway Police, Secretariat of Communication and Transportation, 1950; Director, Legal Office, Department of Traffic and Highway Police, 1953; Private Secretary to the Director of the Department of Traffic and Highway Police, 1953-59; Director, Department of Consulting, Secretariat of Public Works, 1960-63; Director, Department of Legal Affairs, Secretariat of Public Works, 1963-76; *Subsecretary of Social Welfare*, Secretariat of Labor, 1976-82. g-None. h-None. j-None. k-None. l-Protag., 152.

González (Lugo), Hugo Pedro
b-Nuevo Laredo, Tamaulipas. c-Secondary studies at the Colegio Civil; law degree from the National School of Law, UNAM, 1928-32, degree, Feb. 1933. d-*Federal Deputy* from the State of Tamaulipas, Dist. 1, 1940-43, member of the Gran Comisión, the Committee

on Government, the Budget and Accounts Committee, and the Second Constitutional Affairs Committee; *Governor of Tamaulipas*, 1945-47. e-Secretary of the Center for his father's gubernatorial campaign, 1927. f-Scribe, 3rd Division of the Superior Court of Tamaulipas, 1927-28, 5th Civil District Court, Mexico City, 1928, 3rd Civil Court, Mexico City, 1931-32, and 6th Penal Court, Mexico City, 1932-33; Judge of the Superior Tribunal of Justice of the Federal District, 1943; General Manager of the National Bonded Warehouses, 1949-52; Director General of Legal Services for the Department of Tourism, 1958-61; Ambassador to Bolivia, 1966-70; Ambassador to Indonesia, 1970-71. g-President of the Student Society of the National Preparatory School; Secretary of the Law School. h-Practicing lawyer, Tamaulipas, 1933. i-Father, a lawyer and prominent politician in Tamaulipas, having served as senator, state attorney general, and secretary general of government. j-None. k-Removed from the governorship of Tamaulipas on the pretext that he allowed the murderer of the most outspoken critic of his administration, newspaper editor Vicente Villasaña of *El Mundo*, to get away from the authorities after he was seen in the Governor's home in Ciudad Victoria; the murderer was the police chief of Ciudad Victoria and a member of his administration; according to Medina, the real reason for his removal was his loyalty to *Emilio Portes Gil* and his sympathy to the presidential candidacy of *Javier Rojo Gómez* in 1945. l-*Excélsior*, 7 Apr. 1947, 9; DGF51, II, 572; MGF69, 180; DGF50, 410; DPE61, 129; NYT, 10 Apr. 1947, 5; Anderson; letter; Medina, 20, 98-99.

González Lugo, J. Jesús
(Deceased 1965) a-Dec. 27, 1892. b-Colima, Colima. c-Primary studies in Colima, secondary studies at the Nor-

mal School of Mexico City; teaching certificate, 1914; Director of the School for Dependents of the Army. d-*Governor of Colima*, 1949-55. e-None. f-Director of the 2nd Inspection Committee of the Army, 1937; Chief of Staff for the Secretariat of National Defense, 1940-46; *Subsecretary of National Defense*, 1946-49. g-None. h-None. i-Political protégé of *Miguel Alemán*. j-Career army officer; joined the federal army under President Huerta as a cadet, Oct. 4, 1913, and served until Aug. 28, 1914; rank of 2nd Captain, 1914; rank of Brigadier General, Dec. 11, 1920; fought against Carranza until May 7, 1920, his troops were incorporated into the Constitutional Army under de la Huerta; rank of Brigade General, Apr. 1, 1925; rank of Division General. k-As governor of Colima, became one of the rare cases in recent Mexican political history, in which a governor was deprived of his powers by the local legislature for alleged corruption and illegal procedures; the Secretary of Government, *Adolfo Ruiz Cortines* sent the Oficial Mayor to investigate the legislature for not observing the proper legal procedures; the local legislature changed its mind and recalled González Lugo to the governorship; he retired from politics in 1955. l-DP70, 901; DGF51, I, 89; letter; DGF47, 109; Enc. Mex., V, 468; HA, 30 Mar. 1951, 10-11; Moreno, 98-101; Arriaga Rivera, 357; *Excélsior*, 18 Mar. 1951; NYT, 22 Mar. 1951, 11; Dávila, 118.

González Luna, Efraín
(Deceased Sept. 10, 1964) a-Oct. 18, 1898. b-Autlán, Jalisco. c-Primary studies at the Instituto del Sagrado Corazón in Autlán, 1906-08; secondary studies at the San José Institute, 1908-11, and at the Morelos University, 1911-14; preparatory studies in Guadalajara, 1915-16; law degree from the University of Guadalajara, 1916-20, degree, Oct. 19, 1920; Professor of Law at the University

of Guadalajara; Professor of Law at the National School of Law, UNAM. d-None. e-Founded the National Action Party (PAN) with *Manuel Gómez Morín*, 1939. f-None. g-Joined the Catholic Association for Mexican Youth (ACJM), 1921; orator for and President of the ACJM. h-Author of many articles on social and political subjects; participated in the National Catholic Conference on Social Problems in the United States, 1942; private law practice in Guadalajara, 1923-64. i-Son, *Efraín González Morfín*, served as a federal deputy from the PAN, 1967-70; son, Ignacio, a practicing attorney in Guadalajara and a graduate of the 1949 Law School Generation of UNAM; son, Adalberto, a Jesuit and professor with a Ph.D. in theology; father, Mauro H. González, was a lawyer; *Jesús González Gallo* and *Agustín Yáñez* were also members of the ACJM at the same time as González Luna; married Amparo Morfín; related to Enrique González Martínez, subsecretary of public education, 1913-14; brother, *Ramiro González Luna*, served as a federal deputy from PAN, 1967-70. k-Presidential candidate of PAN, 1952. l-DP70, 901; WWM45, 52; WWMG, 19; Morton, 63-64; Enc. Mex., 1977, V, 468; Padgett, 67-70; letter; Mabry, 36; DJBM, 57; Meyer, 59.

González Luna, Ramiro
a-Nov. 17, 1911. b-Guadalajara, Jalisco. c-Early education unknown; began medical studies at the University of Guadalajara; medical degree, National School of Medicine, UNAM; postgraduate work in Los Angeles, New York, and Boston. d-Candidate for local deputy, State of Jalisco, 1949; *Federal Deputy* (Party Deputy from PAN), 1967-70, member of the Military Health Committee, the Social Welfare Committee, the Agricultural Committee, the Public Welfare Committee, and the Pharma-

ceutical Industry Committee. e-Member of PAN; resigned from PAN Sept. 27, 1968. f-None. g-Participated in the student movement of Jalisco, 1933. i-Brother of *Efraín González Luna*, cofounder of PAN; son of lawyer Mauro H. González and Rosaria Luna; married Delfina Sauza. j-None. k-None. l-C de D, 1967-70, 56, 57, 76, 84, 87.

González Martínez, Aida
a-June 21, 1939. b-Federal District. c-Early education unknown; degree in international relations, School of Political and Social Sciences, UNAM, 1960-63; law degree, Free Law School, 1973-75. d-None. e-Joined the PRI, 1973; member of the Advisory Council of PRI, 1986-90. f-Joined the Foreign Service, 1957; Private Secretary to *Alfonso García Robles*, Director of the European, Asian, and African Department, Secretariat of Foreign Relations, 1957-61; Private Secretary to *José Gorostiza*, Subsecretary of Foreign Relations, 1961-64; Private Secretary to *Antonio Carrillo Flores*, 1964-70; Assistant Subdirector General of International Organizations, Secretariat of Foreign Relations, 1971-74; Subdirector General of International Organizations, Secretariat of Foreign Relations, 1975-77; Director General of International Affairs, Secretariat of Labor, 1977-78; Ambassador, in charge of International Labor Affairs, International Labor Organization, 1977-79; *Oficial Mayor of Foreign Relations*, 1979-82; Inspector General, Secretariat of Foreign Relations, 1982-88; Director-in-Chief, Migratory Affairs and Human Rights, Secretariat of Foreign Relations, 1989-90. g-None. h-None. j-None. k-None. l-*Excélsior*, 26 June 1979, 18; Protag., 152.

González Martínez, Atanasio
a-Sept. 8, 1934. b-Piedras Negras, Coahuila. c-Early education unknown; legal studies, National School of Law,

UNAM, 1953-57, graduating in 1960; postgraduate studies at King's College, Cambridge University, 1960, and at the Academy of International Law, The Hague, Holland, 1960-62; Professor of Law, National School of Law, UNAM, 1963-67; professor, Graduate School, IPN, 1969-71. d-None. e-None. f-Adviser, Director General of Income Tax, Secretariat of the Treasury, 1963-65; Chief of Utilities Sharing, Secretariat of the Treasury, 1965; Judge, Federal Tax Court, 1969-73; President, Federal Tax Court, 1973-76; *Supernumerary Justice of the Supreme Court*, 1976-77; *Justice of the Supreme Court*, 1977-82, 1982-88, 1988-94. g-None. h-Secretary of the Board of Casa of Coahuila, 1965-74; President of the Board of Casa of Coahuila, 1974-79. i-Son of Atanasio González Sánchez, farmer, and María Martínez González; married Mercedes Armendáriz Etchegaray, daughter of *Antonio Armendáriz*, Subsecretary of the Treasury. j-None. k-None. l-Protag., 153; DBGM92, 659; DBGM89, 613; DBGM, 658.

González Morfín, Efraín
a-June 5, 1929. c-Primary and secondary studies at the Institute of Sciences, Guadalajara, Jalisco, 1936-48; preparatory studies, Institute of Sciences, Guadalajara; studied Greek and Latin in the United States, 1948-51; studied philosophy at the University of Innsbruck, Austria, 1955; studied economics, political science, and sociology at the Sorbonne, Paris, 1956-58; taught philosophy for four years. d-*Federal Deputy* from the Federal District, Dist. 8, 1967-70, member of the Department of the Federal District Committee, the Second Taxes Committee, and the Money and Credit Institutions Committee. e-Joined PAN, 1959; member of the National Executive Committee of PAN; member of the PAN youth group as a student; member of the studies com-

mission of PAN; Regional Director of PAN for the Federal District, 1969; Presidential candidate for PAN, 1969-70; *President of the CEN of PAN*, 1975. f-Professional translator for a series on economic development for CEMLA. g-None. h-Author of an administrative document for PAN approved at the 20th Annual Convention; author of numerous articles for National Action, official PAN publication; speaks eight languages. i-Son of *Efraín González Luna*; godson of *Manuel Gómez Morín*; married Mónica Marseille; nephew of Enrique González Martínez, subsecretary of public education, 1913-14. j-None. k-None. l-Letter; C de D, 1967-69, 62, 74, 81; Enc. Mex., 1977, V, 471.

González (Parra), Emilio M.
a-May 23, 1913. b-Ixtlán del Río, Nayarit. c-Primary and secondary studies completed; some preparatory and special courses; no degree. d-*Federal Deputy* from the State of Nayarit, Dist. 2, 1940-43; Local Deputy to the State Legislature of Nayarit, 1945-48; *Federal Deputy* from the State of Nayarit, Dist. 2, 1949-52, member of the Industries Committee, the First Balloting Committee, and the Complaints Committee; *Senator* from the State of Nayarit, 1952-58, President of the Social Action Committee, First Secretary of the Second Labor Committee; Secretary of the Second Instructive Section of the Grand Jury and member of the Second Balloting Group; *Federal Deputy* from the State of Nayarit, Dist. 2, 1967-70, member of the Gran Comisión, member of the First Balloting Committee; *Senator* from the State of Nayarit, 1970-76, President of the Mail and Telegraph Committee, First Secretary of the Cooperative Development Committee, Second Secretary of the National Resources and Properties Committee, and member of the Fishing Committee; *Federal Deputy* from the State of

Nayarit, Dist. 2, 1979-82; *Senator* from Nayarit, 1988-94, President of the Gran Comisión. e-President of the Regional Committee of PRI for the State of Nayarit, 1957-61; *Secretary of Political Action of the CEN of PRI*, 1988. f-Telegrapher and Radio Telegrapher, Secretariat of Communications and Public Works, 1929. g-Leader in the Union of Workers of the Secretariat of Communications and Public Works; First Secretary General of the Coordinating Committee of the Federation of Workers of the State of Nayarit; Secretary General of the Federation of Workers of the State of Nayarit, 1937-38; Secretary General of the Mexican Federation of Labor of the State of Nayarit, 1938-79; Secretary of Political Action of the CTM, 1979-81; Alternate Secretary General of the CTM, 1988-94. h-Has financial interest in the Escuinapa Packing Co. i-Member of *Gilberto Flores Muñoz*'s political group, 1946; son of Emilio González Ramírez and Gonzala Parra Aguilar; married Sofía Acosta (deceased); second wife, Verónica Valdez Sojo, social worker. j-None. k-One of the few Mexican politicians to have become senator and deputy six times since 1935; order for his arrest issued in 1944 for assault and violation of a minor; *Excélsior* accused him of extortion. l-C de D, 1967-70, 77; Ind. Biog., 75-76; *Excélsior*, 29 Dec. 1978, 12; C de D, 1940-43; C de S, 1970-76, 76; C de D, 1949-52, 74; *Excélsior*, 11 June 1979, 15, 11 Mar. 1981, 23, 31; DBGM92, 478.

González Pedrero, Enrique
a-Apr. 7, 1930. b-Villahermosa, Tabasco. c-Primary studies at the Daniel Delgadillo School, Mexico City; secondary studies at the public Secondary School No. 22, Acapulco; preparatory studies at the National Preparatory School; law degree from the National School of Law, UNAM, 1950-56, degree,

Oct. 25, 1957; studies at the University of Paris in economics and political and social sciences, 1953-54; Professor of the Sociology of Religion, 1956-58, Professor of the Sociology of Political Parties, 1959-61, Professor of the Theory of the State, 1960-70, and Director, 1965-70, all at the National School of Political and Social Sciences, UNAM. d-*Senator* from the State of Tabasco, 1970-74, member of the Gran Comisión, President of the Second Committee on the Consular and Diplomatic Service, First Secretary of the Second Foreign Relations Committee, and First Secretary of the First Public Education Committee; *Governor of Tabasco*, 1983-89. e-Member of PRI, 1949; founder of the National Liberation Movement (MLN) in Mexico; lawyer for the MLN, 1962; adviser to the IEPES of PRI, 1970; member of the Commission of Political Training for the IEPES of PRI, 1972; *Secretary General of the CEN of PRI*, 1972-74; participated in *Luis Echeverría's* campaign for president; Director of Political Training of PRI (preparing 200 young men in political speaking and policies), 1971-72; Coordinator of the Advisory Council for the IEPES of PRI, 1982. f-Adviser to the Directorship of PEMEX under *Jesús Reyes Heroles*; investigator for the Commission of Planning Studies (University), Secretariat of Public Education, 1961; lawyer for the Department of Mercantile Income, Secretariat of the Treasury; Director General of the Mexican Corporation of Radio and Television, 1974-76, President of the National Textbook Commission, 1979-82. g-None. h-Secretary of the magazine *El Trimestre Económico*; member of the Technical Department, *El Trimestre Económico*; founder of the magazine, *Política*; author of six books and translator of over a dozen books; Vice-President of the Siglo XXI publising

firm, 1966. i-Married Julieta Campos, important contemporary author; friend of *Mario de la Cueva*; knew *Miguel de la Madrid* at UNAM; brother, José, served as director general of Fisheries Development, Department of Fishing, 1977-79; close friendship with *Fernando Solana* instrumental in his appointment as president of the National Textbook Commission; son of Ramón González Vega, public official, and Rosa Pedredo Focil. j-None. k-Critic for many years of PRI and active political leftist; interceded during the 1968 repression of students to get various professors and students released. l-B de M, 137-38; HA, 28 Feb. 1972, 13; Análisis Político, 3 July 1972, 4; *El Día*, 22 Feb. 1972; MGF69, 756; HA, 10 July 1972, 10, 21 Jan. 1974, 58; Enc. Mex., 1977, V, 473; *Excélsior*, 12 Jan. 1974, 12, 16 Nov. 1979, 20, 25 July 1982, 21A; HA, 23 June 1980, 10; IEPES; DBGM89, 156.

González Rivera, Abraham
(Deceased) a-1893. b-Jalisco. c-Early education unknown; no degree. d-*Senator* from the State of Jalisco, 1940-46; *Federal Deputy* from the State of Jalisco, Dist. 9, 1946-49, member of the First Government Committee and alternate member of the Credit, Money, and Credit Institutions Committee; *Federal Deputy* from the State of Jalisco, Dist. 5, 1952-55, member of the Forest Affairs Committee and the Economics and Statistics Committee. e-None. f-None. g-None. h-Large landholder and cattle rancher. j-None. k-None. l-C de D, 1946-49, 73, 1952-55, 11, 43, 48; C de S, 1940-46.

González Roa, Fernando
(Deceased 1936) a-1880. b-Salamanca, Guanajuato. c-Primary studies in Salamanca; secondary in Guanajuato; law degree, University of Guanajuato, 1904; Professor of Law, National School of Law, UNAM; Professor of Law at the

Escuela Libre de Derecho; Director, School of Commerce, UNAM. d-None. e-None. f-Civil Judge, Guanajuato, 1904-05; Judge of the Correctional Courts, 1905; Secretary General of Government of the State of Guanajuato; Director of Government for the Federal District; Secretary of Justice, 1910-13; Judge of the Superior Tribunal of Justice, Federal District and Territories; Subsecretary of Government; adviser to the Secretary of the Treasury; President of the Executive Board of the Bank of Mexico; Mexican delegate to the World Monetary Conference, 1933; Ambassador to the United States, 1934; *Secretary of Foreign Relations*, June 17, 1935, to Nov. 30, 1935; Ambassador to Guatemala, 1935. g-None. h-Practicing attorney, 1906-09; author of several books on the Mexican agrarian problem. i-Students included *Emilio Portes Gil*, *Eduardo Villaseñor*, and *Eduardo Bustamente*; married Edme Gutiérrez Zamora. j-None. k-Never functioned in the position of Secretary of Foreign Relations because of poor health; appointed Ambassador to Belgium, 1936, but died before holding post. l-Enc. Mex., V, 474; WWLA35, 179; DP70, 905; DP64, 629; D del S, 27 June 1935, 1; Daniels, 98-99; Peral, 352.

González Rubio, Ignacio
a-May 24, 1917. b-Ciudad Guzmán, Jalisco. c-Early education unknown; law degree, National School of Law, UNAM, Aug. 12, 1933; LLD degree, National School of Law, UNAM, with an honorable mention, Dec. 16, 1952; Professor of Law, National School of Law, UNAM, 1953-55, 1958-60, 1964. d-*Federal Deputy* from the State of Jalisco, Dist. 1, 1955-58, Dist. 9, 1967-70, member of the Budget and Accounts Committee, the General Accounting Office Committee, and the Section on General Affairs of the Legislative Studies Committee; *Federal Deputy*

from the State of Jalisco, Dist. 7, 1979-82. e-Joined PRI, 1955; Secretary of Publicity and Civic Orientation of the CEN of PRI, 1959-61. f-Adviser to the National Colonization Commission, 1952; general attorney for UNAM; adviser to the State Government of Jalisco, 1958-64; adviser to the Secretary of Agriculture, 1958-64; Mexican delegate to the United Nations Safety of Life at Sea Conference, London, 1960; Director, Legal Department, National Ejido Credit Bank, 1961-67. g-None. h-None. i-Son of Refugio Vergara and José González Rubio, lawyer, federal deputy from the State of Jalisco, Dist. 19, 1912-14, and judge of the Superior Tribunal of Justice of Jalisco; married Dora L. j-None. k-Speaks French and English. l-Letter; C de D, 1979-82, 1967-70, 70, 73, 1955-58.

González Sáenz, Leopoldo
a-Feb. 6, 1924. b-Cienega de Flores, Nuevo León. c-Primary studies at the Antonio L. Treviño School, Cienega; secondary studies in Cienega; law degree, School of Law, University of Nuevo León, 1946; Professor of Juridical Law, School of Law, University of Nuevo León. d-Mayor of Monterrey, Nuevo León, 1961-63; 1974-76; *Federal Deputy* from the State of Nuevo León, Dist. 1, 1958-61, member of the Gran Comisión; President of the Chamber of Deputies, Sept. 1959; Secretary of the Preparatory Council of the Chamber of Deputies, 1958, member of the Foreign Relations Committee (4th Section); *Federal Deputy* from the State of Nuevo León, Dist. 1, 1964-67, member of the Gran Comisión and the Credentials Committee (4th Section); *Federal Deputy* from the State of Nuevo León, Dist. 4, 1973-74. e-Adviser to the National Council of PRI; adviser to the CNOP of PRI; State Director of the CNOP of PRI in Nuevo León; Secretary of Conflicts of the CEN of CNOP of

PRI; Auxiliary Secretary of *Alfonso Corona del Rosal*, president of the CEN of PRI, 1964; *Secretary of Organization of the CEN of PRI*, 1975-76. f-Agent of the Ministerio Público, 1942; Scribe of the Juvenile Court, Criminal and Civil Divisions; Secretary, State Board of Conciliation and Arbitration of Nuevo León; Judge in Nuevo León; Assistant Director of Legal Affairs of the State of Nuevo León; Head of Legal Affairs for the State of Nuevo León; Secretary of the City Council of Monterrey; Director of Construction for the Metro in Mexico City, 1968. g-None. i-Married Consuelo Elena Villarreal; son of Camilo González and Nicolasa Sáenz. j-None. k-Answered the presidential state of the union address of *Adolfo López Mateos*, 1958; considered by political observers to be a very powerful political leader in Nuevo León; precandidate for governor of Nuevo León, 1978. l-DBM68, 315; PdM, 176-77; C de D, 1958-60, 42; *Excélsior*, 2 Apr. 1973, 13; C de D, 1964-66, 42, 66; HA, 25 Dec. 1972, 42, 26 Nov. 1973, 34; Func., 294.

González Salas (Petricioli), Marcela
a-Nov. 18, 1947. b-Federal District. c-Early education unknown; economics degree, Autonomous Technological Institute of Mexico, 1971-75, with a thesis on "Social Development in an Urban Population"; postgraduate work, Ibero-American University, 1977; studies in the history of art, Davies School of London, England, and the Catholic Institute, France, 1964-65; professor, ITAM, 1972-74; teacher, Adult Literacy Program, Guerrero, 1976; professor, IPN, 1978-79. d-Local Deputy to the State Legislature of Mexico, 1981-83, President of the Committees on Legal Affairs and Social Development, and Vice-President and President, Chamber of Deputies, 1982; *Federal Deputy* from the State of México, Dist. 30, 1985-88. e-Member,

Advisory Council, IEPES of PRI, 1982; Subdirector of Popular Organization Studies, IEPES of PRI, 1982. f-*Oficial Mayor of Programming and Budgeting*, 1982-85. g-None. h-Involved in private activities, State of México, 1966-81; active in feminist publications, 1974-82. i-Daughter of Armando González Salas Hernández, electrical engineer, and María Teresa Petricioli Mercado. j-None. k-None. l-Q es QAP, 135; DBGM, 193; DBGM87, 485.

González Salazar, Roque
a-June 13, 1931. b-General Terán, Nuevo León. c-Early education unknown; legal studies, School of Law and Social Science, University of Nuevo León, 1948-53, law degree, with a thesis on "Tax Law, Naturalism and Characteristics," 1954; postgraduate work in international relations, Institute of Political Studies, University of Paris, France, 1960-62, at Indiana University, 1962-63, and at the University of London, 1963-65; professor, Center of International Studies, Colegio de México, and at the School of Policy and Social Studies, UNAM, 1967-69; Secretary General of the University of Nuevo León, 1957-59; Interim Rector, University of Nuevo León, 1959; Director of the Center for International Studies, Colegio de México, 1969-72; General Coordinator, Academic Affairs, Colegio de México, 1978. d-None. e-Private Secretary to the President of PRI, Nuevo León, 1952-54; Subsecretary of Planning, Secretary of Organization, CEN of PRI, 1981-82. f-Public Defender, Monterrey, Nuevo León, 1954-55; Secretary, 4th Civil District, Monterrey, Nuevo León, 1955-56; First Judge, Civil District, Monterrey, Nuevo León, 1956-57; adviser, Mexican Embassy in Moscow, 1965-66; *Ambassador to the Soviet Union*, 1973-75; Ambassador to Argentina, 1975-77; Subdirector General of International

Financial Affairs, Secretariat of the Treasury, 1977-78; Director General for East Europe and the Soviet Union, Secretariat of Foreign Relations, 1979-82; *Oficial Mayor of Foreign Relations,* 1982-88; Ambassador to Portugal, 1989-91; Ambassador to Paraguay, 1991-94. g-None. h-Director, *Foro Internacional,* Colegio de México, 1969-72. i-Son of Miguel González González, farmer, and Magdalena Salazar González; married Rosamaría Aktories Grigoleit. j-None. k-None. l-Q es QAP, 50; DBGM, 188-89; DBGM89, 157; DBGM92, 165.

González Schmal, Jesús
a-Nov. 6, 1941. b-Federal District. c-Primary studies, Delicias, Chihuahua, and Mexico City; secondary studies, Alexander Von Humboldt School, Mexico City; law degree, National School of Law, UNAM, 1968; MA in sociology, UNAM; degree in industrial relations, Ibero-American University; professor, Institute of Educational Sciences. d-*Plurinominal Deputy* from PAN, 1979-82, 1985-88, Coordinator of the PAN delegation. e-Joined PAN, 1964; member of the Youth Secretariat of PAN; member of the National Council of PAN; Secretary of Youth of the CEN of PAN, 1969; Secretary of Internal Affairs of the CEN of PAN, 1986. f-None. g-None. i-Brother of *Raúl Jaime González Schmal,* secretary general of PAN, 1975-78, 1981-84; son of Raúl González, small rancher and founder of Delicias, Chihuahua, 1931, and Bertha Schmal; married María Concepción Contró; influenced by professor Miguel Mansur to become politically active, 1962. j-None. k-None. l-C de D, 1979-82; Carlos Gil, 99-100; DBGM87, 486.

González Schmal, Raúl Jaime
a-1940. b-Federal District. c-Primary studies at Colegio Franco Español; completed secondary studies at the Colegio Franco Español; law degree. d-None. e-President of the National Youth Organization of PAN; member of the CEN of PAN; *Secretary General of the CEN of PAN,* 1975-78; *Secretary General of the CEN of PAN,* 1981-83. f-None. g-None. h-Practicing lawyer. i-Brother of *Jesús González Schmal,* plurinominal deputy from PAN, 1979-82; son of Raúl González, rancher and founder of Delicias, Chihuahua, 1931, and Bertha Schmal; studied political science under *José González Torres.* j-None. k-Candidate for federal deputy from PAN, Federal District, Dist. 11, 1970. l-*Excélsior,* 6 Apr. 1975, 9; *La Nación,* 14 June 1970, 11; *Excélsior,* 30 Mar. 1975, 4; Protag., 154.

González Sosa, Rubén
a-Aug. 24, 1922. b-Zacatlán, Puebla. c-Primary studies at the Ramón Marquez School, Zacatlán, Puebla; secondary studies in Mexico City; preparatory studies at the National Preparatory School; law degree, National School of Law, UNAM, 1942-46; advanced studies at the Graduate Institute of International Studies, Geneva; professor, National School of Law, UNAM, 1953-54. d-None. e-None. f-Vice-consul, San Francisco, California, 1946; Minister to England; Secretary of a Special Mission to the Chief of States Reunion, Panama, 1956; Ambassador to the OAS, 1957-58; in charge of the Mexican Embassy, London, 1965; rank of Ambassador, 1969; Director General of Legal Affairs, Secretariat of Foreign Relations, 1969-70; Director in Chief of the Secretariat of Foreign Relations, 1970-71; *Subsecretary of Foreign Relations,* 1971-76; Ambassador to the Dominican Republic, 1979-82. g-President of the first law generation of the class of 1942. h-Career Foreign Service officer; joined the Foreign Service, Apr. 1946; held posts in Geneva, Switzerland, and Spain. i-Friend of *Luis*

Echeverría since youth; married Patricia Flavell; son of Antonio González López and Enedina Sosa. k-Precandidate for governor of Puebla, 1974. l-DPE70, 6; letter; HA, 14 Dec. 1970, 20; MGF69, 179; CyT, 307-08; *Excélsior*, 12 Sept. 1974, 4, 12 Sept. 1979, 4.

González Torres, José
a-Sept. 16, 1919. b-Cotija, Michoacán. c-Primary studies at the Colegio Jalisco, Guadalajara; secondary studies at the Colegio Salesiano, Guadalajara; preparatory studies at the Institute of Sciences, Guadalajara; law degree from the National School of Law, UNAM, Aug. 20, 1945, with a thesis on tax powers; Professor of History at the Escuela Libre de Derecho; studied for a doctorate. d-*Plurinominal Deputy from PAN*, 1982-85. e-*Secretary General of PAN*, 1956-58; *President of the CEN of PAN*, 1959-62. f-None. g-President of the Catholic Association of Young Mexicans, 1940-44; President of National Catholic Action, 1949-52; International President of Pax Romana; Secretary General of the National Union of Parents, 1954-56. h-Representative of Catholic intellectuals in many international conferences. i-Father a prosperous rancher; recruited to PAN by *Manuel Ulloa Ortiz* and *Rafael Preciado Hernández*, 1941. j-None. k-Candidate for federal deputy for the Eighth District in the Federal District, 1955; candidate for president of Mexico, 1963-64, on the National Action ticket; candidate for federal deputy from PAN for the Federal District, 1967. l-Scott, 185; HA, 2 Dec. 1963, 7; *El Universal*, 2 Mar. 1964, 1; HA, 15 Apr. 1949, 5; Mabry, 155; *La Nación*, 29 Mar. 1959, 19; HA, 5 Mar. 1979, III; Lehr, 549; DBGM, 516.

González Torres, Roberto
a-Apr. 28, 1939. b-Federal District. c-Early education unknown; law degree, National School of Law, UNAM, 1961.

d-*Alternate Federal Deputy* from the Federal District, Dist. 19, 1967-70. e-None. f-Subdirector of Cultural Action, ISSSTE, 1979-80; *Oficial Mayor of the Secretariat of Health*, 1980-82. g-Secretary General of the National Union of Workers of the Attorney General of Mexico, 1962-65; Secretary of Cultural Action of the CEN of the SNTE, 1965-68; adviser to the SNTE before the ISSSTE, 1968-71; representative of the SNTE before the Federal Tribunal of Conciliation and Arbitration, 1977-79. h-None. j-None. k-None. l-Protag., 152; C de D, 1967-70.

González Varela, José
a-Aug. 15, 1911. b-Zacatecas, Zacatecas. c-Primary studies at Colegio Margíl, Zacatecas; secondary studies at Secondary School No. 2, Mexico City, and in Zacatecas; preparatory studies at the National Preparatory School; medical degree from the Military Medical College, 1932-36; advanced studies in physiotherapy, Northwestern University, 1942; advanced studies in electroencephalography, Illinois Neuro Psychiatry Institute; professor at the Military Medical College. d-*Senator* from the State of Zacatecas, 1964-70. e-Joined the PNR, 1936; campaigned for *José Elías Rodríguez* for governor, 1962. e-General delegate of the CEN of PRI to Querétaro during *Luis Echeverría*'s presidential campaign, 1970; Director of the CEPES of PRI in Zacatecas, 1964. f-Director of Medical Services for the Department of Agrarian Affairs; Secretary of Finances of the FSTSE; Director of the Military School for Nurses; Director of the Central Military Hospital. g-Secretary General of the Union of Workers of the Department of Agrarian Affairs; Director of Social Promotion of the CEN of CNOP; Secretary of Legislative Promotion of CNOP. i-Compadre of *José Elías Rodríguez*; father followed a military

career. j-Colonel in the medical corps, 1962. k-None. l-C de S, 1964-70; PS, 2678; MGF69; *Mis Seis Años*; Rev. de Ejer., Dec. 1962, 30.

González Villarreal, Fernando Jorge
a-May 7, 1941. b-Santa Barbara, California. c-Early education unknown; civil engineering degree, National School of Engineering, UNAM, 1959-63; MS degree, University of California, Berkeley, 1966-67; Ph.D. in engineering, University of California, Berkeley, 1967-68; professor and researcher, National School of Engineering, UNAM, 1968-78. d-None. e-None. f-General Coordinator of the National Hydraulic Plan, Secretariat of Agriculture and Hydraulic Resources, 1972-76; Executive Secretary of the National Hydraulic Plan, 1976-82; *Subsecretary of Hydraulic Infrastructure*, Secretariat of Agriculture and Hydraulic Resources, 1982-88; Director General, National Water Commission, 1988-90. g-President of the Mexican Hydraulic Association, 1976. h-Private consultant to Ingenieria y Procesamiento Electrónico, S.A., 1968-70. i-Son of Fernando González y González and Alicia Villarreal Villarreal; married Martha Julia Cañez Félix. j-None. k-None. l-IEPES; Q es QAP, 211; DBGM89, 158; DBGM, 190; DBGM87, 169.

González Villarreal, Marciano
(Deceased 1970) a-Nov. 2, 1885. b-Cerralvo, Nuevo León. c-Studied in Ciudad Victoria, Tamaulipas, and Mexico City; no degree. d-Federal Deputy from the State of Nuevo León, Dist. 2, 1916-18, Dist. 6, 1918-20; *Federal Deputy* from the Federal District, Dist. 19, 1964-67, member of the National Defense Committee (2nd), the Editorial Committee, and the Committee on Mines. e-Member of PARM. f-Comptroller General of Mexico; Inspector General of Nuevo

León; high official of the Secretariat of the Treasury, 1935-37; *Oficial Mayor of the Federal District*, 1937-38; *Oficial Mayor of the Secretariat of National Defense*, 1939-40, in charge of the Subsecretary of National Defense, 1939-40; Director General of the Manufacturing of Supplies; Secretary General of Government of Quintana Roo; Secretary General of Government of the State of Puebla. g-None. h-None. i-Nephew of a former president of Mexico, General Manuel González. j-Constitutionalist; rank of Lt. Colonel, 1914; Secretary of the Revolutionary Convention of Aguascalientes, represented General Teodoro Elizondo, 1914-15; accompanied Carranza to Tlaxcalantongo, 1920; supported the de la Huerta rebellion, 1923; career army officer; rank of Division General. k-Exiled from Mexico after the death of Carranza; jailed in 1907 for attacking President Díaz in a speech; candidate for governor of Nuevo León. l-Peral, 354; DP70, 907-08; C de D, 1964-66, 49.

Gordillo de Anda, Gustavo
a-April 25, 1947. b-Federal District. c-Early education unknown; economics degree, National School of Economics, UNAM, 1965-68; postgraduate studies in planning and development, 1969-70, and Ph.D. in planning and development, 1970-72, Ecole Practique des Hautes Etudes, France, with a dissertation on the growth model and social conflict in Mexico, 1934-40; professor, National School of Economics, 1972-73, researcher, 1973-75, and Coordinator of Research, 1977-78, 1979-82, all at UNAM. d-None. e-Joined PRI, 1988. f-*Subsecretary of Policy*, Secretariat of Agriculture and Hydraulic Resources, 1988-92; *Subsecretary of Organization and Agrarian Development*, Secretariat of Agrarian Reform, 1992-94. g-None. h-Coordinator of the weekly section on peasants and rural areas, *El Día*, 1984-

86. i-Son of Gustavo Gordillo Paniagua, military physician, and Tuchee de Anda Ramírez; married María Patricia Pensado Leglise, economist. j-None. k-None. l-DBGM89, 159; DBGM92, 166-67.

Gordillo Morales, Elba Esther
a-Feb. 6, 1945. b-Comitán, Chiapas. c-Teaching certificate, Federal Institute of Teacher Education, 1963; studies in history, National Normal School, Mexico City, 1966; rural primary teacher, Chiapas, 1960; primary school teacher, Ciudad Netzahualcoyotl, Mexico, 1964; secondary history teacher, Tlalpan, Federal District, 1965; Professor of History, Institute of Political Education, PRI, 1977. d-*Federal Deputy* from the Federal District, Dist. 26, 1979-82, Dist. 2, 1985-88. e-Joined PRI, 1960; presidential campaign coordinator for the CEN of PRI, 1975; coordinator, senatorial campaign for PRI, San Luis Potosí, 1975; Subsecretary of Organization (Teaching) of the CEN of PRI, 1984. f-None. g-Joined the SNTE, 1960; held several positions in Delegation 21, SNTE, 1971-75; Secretary of Relations, Sectional Executive Committee, SNTE, 1974-77; Secretary General of Local 36, Valle de México, SNTE, 1977-80; Alternate Secretary of Labor and Conflicts, Pre-School Division, 1977-80, Secretary of Labor and Conflicts, Pre-School Division, 1980-83, and Secretary of Finances, 1983-86, all with the CEN of the SNTE; Secretary General of the SNTE, 1989-94. h-None. i-Daughter of Daniel Gordillo Pinto and Estela Morales Ochoa, teacher. j-None. k-None. l-Romero Aceves, 700-01; C de D, 1979-82; DBGM87, 486.

Gorostiza (Alcalá), Celestino
(Deceased Jan. 11, 1967) a-Jan. 31, 1904. b-Villahermosa, Tabasco. c-Secondary studies at the Institute of Sciences, Aguascalientes, Aguascalientes, and at the Colegio Francés, Mexico City; preparatory studies at the National Preparatory School, Mexico City; professor at and Director of the School of Dramatic Art, Institute of Fine Arts. d-None. e-None. f-Director of the Department of Fine Arts, Secretariat of Public Education; Director of the Department of Theater, Secretariat of Public Education, 1952-58; Director of the National Institute of Fine Arts, 1958-64; Secretary of the National Conservatory, Secretariat of Public Education. g-None. h-Distinguished Mexican author; member of the *Contemporáneos*, 1928-31; created the Teatro de Ulises with Xavier Villaurrutia and *Salvador Novo*, 1927-28; founder of the Teatro Orientación, 1932. i-Brother of *José Gorostiza* and friend of *Jaime Torres Bodet*; son of Celestino Gorostiza and Elvira Alcalá; nephew, Francisco Javier, was a subdirector in the Secretariat of Communications and Transportation, 1991. j-None. k-None. l-DP70, 909; DPE61, 107; Peral, 354; DGF56, 305; DEM, 155-56; letter; Enc. Mex., 1977, V, 478.

Gorostiza (Alcala), José
(Deceased Mar. 16, 1973) a-Nov. 10, 1901. b-Villahermosa, Tabasco. c-Primary studies in Querétaro, Querétaro, and Aguascalientes, Aguascalientes; preparatory studies at the National Preparatory School, Mexico City, and the Colegio Francés de Mascarones; degree from UNAM; Professor of Literature at UNAM, 1929; Professor of Modern History, National School of Teachers, 1932. d-None. e-None. f-First Chancellor, Mexican Embassy, London, 1927; Secretary of the Department of Fine Arts, Secretariat of Public Education, 1932-35; head of the Department of Publicity, Secretariat of Foreign Relations, 1935-37; Third Secretary in Copenhagen, 1937; Private Secretary to the Secretary of Foreign Relations

Eduardo Hay, 1937-39, with the rank of Second Secretary; First Secretary, Mexican Embassy, Rome, 1939-40; First Secretary in Guatemala, 1940-41; First Secretary in Havana, Cuba, 1942; adviser in Cuba, 1942-44; Director General of Political Affairs, Secretariat of Foreign Relations, 1944; adviser to the Mexican Delegation to the United Nations Conference, San Francisco, 1945; adviser to the Mexican Delegation, First Session of the United Nations, New York, 1946; Director General of the Diplomatic Service, Secretariat of Foreign Relations, 1946-49; delegate to the Río Conference, 1947; delegate to the Inter-American Conference, Bogota, 1948; Ambassador to Greece, 1950-51; Alternate Permanent Representative of Mexico under *Padilla Nervo* to the United Nations, 1951-53; *Subsecretary of Foreign Relations*, 1953-58, 1958-64; *Secretary of Foreign Relations*, 1964; head of the National Commission of Nuclear Energy, 1965-70. g-None. h-Distinguished Mexican writer and poet; published his first book of poems at age 24; member of the famous literary group, the *Contemporáneos*. i-Brother of *Celestino Gorostiza*, head of the Department of Theater, Secretariat of Public Education, 1952-58, Director of the National Institute of Fine Arts, 1958-64, and one of Mexico's distinguished writers and intellectuals who also was a member of the *Contemporáneos*; knew *Rafael de la Colina* at UNAM and served with him in the Foreign Service; friend of *Jaime Torres Bodet* at the National Preparatory School and at UNAM; married Josefina Ortega; son of Celestino Gorostiza and Elvira Alcalá; nephew, Francisco Javier, was a subdirector in the Secretariat of Communications and Transportation, 1992. j-None. k-None. l-DP70, 909; DPE61, 107; DGF56, 305; letters; DPE61, 15; WWM45, 53; DBM68, 320;

DGF51, I, 110; DGF56, 123; DGF47, 89; *Libro de Oro*, xli; Peral, 354-55; *Justicia*, 6 May 1973; HA, 26 Mar. 1973, 11; *Excélsior*, 17 Mar. 1973, 11.

Govea, Salvador G.
a-Aug. 6, 1898. b-Colima, Colima. c-Completed primary studies only, Colima. d-*Alternate Senator* from the State of Colima, but replaced *Rafael S. Pimentel* from 1954-58, Secretary of the Tax Committee and President of the General Means of Communication Committee. e-None. f-Secretary General of the Government of the State of Colima under Governor *Salvador Saucedo*, 1930-34; Treasurer General of the Government of the State of Colima under Governor *J. Jesús González Lugo*, 1949-51. g-None. j-Joined the Revolution, 1914; served in the Army of the Northeast under General *Juan José Rios*, served in the security forces for the National Railroads under Colonel Salvador Herrejón. k-None. l-Ind. Biog., 1977-78; DGF56, 5, 9, 11, 13.

Gracia, Ezequiel M.
b-Calpulalpan, Tlaxcala. c-Early education unknown; degree in agricultural engineering, National School of Agriculture, San Jacinto, Federal District, 1909-14, on a scholarship from the State of Tlaxcala. d-Local Deputy to the Constitutional Convention of the State of Tlaxcala, 1918; Local Deputy to the State Legislature of Tlaxcala, 1919-23, 1943-45; *Alternate Senator* from the State of Tlaxcala, 1946-48; *Senator* from the State of Tlaxcala, 1948-52, replacing *Mauro Angulo*. e-None. f-Commissioned to do topographical surveys of lands donated to his home village, 1915; auxiliary engineer, Department of Agrarian Indemnification, 1920-30; agent of the National Bank of Agricultural Credit, 1934; agent of the National Bank of Ejido Credit, Nayarit, 1935-38; official, Central Office, National Bank

of Ejido Credit, 1938-40; agent of the
Secretariat of Agriculture, Zacatecas,
Morelos, and Tlaxcala, 1940-43; Director of the Agricultural Department of
the State of Tlaxcala, 1952; agent of the
National Ejido Credit Bank, Tlaxcala,
1952. g-Secretary of the Agrarian Committee of Calpulalpan, 1915. h-Worked
with Miguel Schultz in surveying the
hacienda of ex–Secretary of Agriculture,
Antonio Tamariz, 1914. i-Ties to *Marte
R. Gómez* from college days; father,
mayor of Calpulalpan and longtime teacher; daughter *Alma Inés Gracia Torres*
was a federal deputy from Tlaxcala,
1982-85. j-None. k-None. l-Gómez,
264-69; C de S, 1946-52; DBGM, 517.

Gracia de Zamora, Alma Inés
a-Jan. 21, 1937. b-Santa Ana, Chiautempan, Tlaxcala. c-Early education
unknown; completed preparatory, 1954-
56. d-Local Deputy to the State
Legislature of Tlaxcala, 1977-80;
Federal Deputy from the State of
Tlaxcala, Dist. 2, 1982-85. e-Director of
Social Action of PRI, Tlaxco, Tlaxcala,
1977-80; Director of Women's Action of
PRI, State of Tlaxcala, 1968-73. f-None.
g-Secretary General of ANFER, State of
Tlaxcala, 1981-82; Auxiliary Secretary
of Women's Action of the CNC. h-Executive secretary. i-Daughter of Senator
Ezequiel M. Gracia, agricultural
engineer, and Rebeca Torres Martínez;
married Roberto Zamora Pérez, farmer;
grandfather was mayor of Calpulalpan,
Tlaxcala. j-None. k-None. l-Directorio, 1982-85; C de D, 1982-85; Lehr, 483.

Grajales (Godoy), Francisco J.
a-Aug. 1, 1898. b-Chiapa de Corzo,
Chiapas. c-Studies at the Military
School, Tuxtla Gutiérrez, Chiapas,
construction engineering degree from
the Heroic Military College, graduating
as a lieutenant, 1924; aide to the
Director of the Heroic Military College;
professor at the Heroic Military College;

professor at the Higher War College;
Director of the Heroic Military College,
1955-58; studied in France and Germany before World War II. d-*Governor
of Chiapas*, Dec. 1, 1948, to Nov. 30,
1952. e-None. f-Military Attaché in
Berlin; Military Attaché in Austria and
Czechoslovakia; Subchief of Staff of the
Secretariat of National Defense; Chief
of Staff of the Secretariat of National
Defense, 1946-47; Director of the
Higher War College, Secretariat of
National Defense, 1958-64. g-None.
h-Author of several books on military
strategy. i-Brother, Jorge, a brigadier
general, defeated for the governorship of
Chiapas, 1943; nephew of former Governor Victorio Grajales; son of Emilio
Grajales and Margarita Godoy. j-Joined
the Revolution as a 1st Sergeant, 1914;
participated in the first and second
battles for Tuxtla Gutiérrez, 1917-18;
various battles, 1919-20; career army
officer; Subchief of Staff, 28th Military
Zone; fought under General Francisco
Urbalejo against the Cristeros, 1929;
Subchief of Staff for the Isthmus
Military Zone, 1941-45; reached rank of
Division General; retired, 1976.
k-Precandidate for governor of Chiapas,
1943. l-DGF51, I, 89; HA, 6 Feb. 1948,
10, 29 Oct. 1943, 14; DGF47, 109; HA,
10 Nov. 1950, 12-16, 26 Jan. 1959, 8;
DBdeC, 108; Rev. de Ejer., Sept. 1976,
137.

Granados Roldán, Otto
a-Nov. 24, 1956. b-Aguascalientes,
Aguascalientes. c-Early education unknown; law degree, National School of
Law, UNAM, 1975-78; MA in political
science, Center of International Studies,
Colegio de México, 1979-81, with a thesis on peasant organizations in Mexico;
professor, National Institute of Public
Administration, 1981-82. d-*Governor* of
Aguascalientes, 1992- . e-Joined PRI,
1973; Auxiliary Secretary of the Oficial
Mayor of the CEN of PRI, 1981. f-Chief

of the Department of Analysis, Center of Documentation and Information, Chamber of Deputies, 1977-78; Coordinator of Publications, Center for Political Documents, Secretariat of Government, 1978-79; Private Secretary to the Secretary of Education, *Jesús Reyes Heroles*, 1982-85; adviser to the Ambassador to Spain, *Rodolfo González Guevara*, 1985-86; *Oficial Mayor of the Secretariat of Programming and Budgeting*, 1986-88; Director General of Social Communications of the Presidency of Mexico, 1988-92. g-None. h-Writer for *Proceso, Uno Más Uno, Sabado.* i-Son of Claudio Granados Gutiérrez, businessman, and María Guadalupe Roldán Gándara; married María Teresa Franco Sevilla. j-None. k-None. l-DBGM89, 161; *Proceso*, 11 Jan. 1988, 20

Grant Munive, María de los Angeles
a-Mar. 10, 1929. b-Tlaxco, Tlaxcala. c-Primary studies at the Colegio Esparza, Puebla; secondary studies at the Carlos González Vespertina Cooperative School, Tlaxco; studies in art and music at the Colegio Esparza, Puebla; secondary school teacher in art and music. d-Local Deputy to the State Legislature of Tlaxcala; Mayor of Tlaxco, Tlaxcala; *Federal Deputy* from the State of Tlaxcala, Dist. 2, 1970-73, member of the Gran Comisión. e-Director of the Women's Section of PRI, Tlaxcala. f-None. g-Secretary of Municipal Promotion, CNOP. i-Daughter of Carmine James Grant and Concepción Munive; widow. j-None. k-None. l-Directorio, 1970-72; C de D, 1970-73.

Grimm González, Guillermo
a-July 19, 1938. b-Federal District. c-Early education unknown; business administration degree, Ibero-American University; Professor of Marketing and Advertising, Ibero-American University,

1965-67. d-None. e-None. f-Subdirector of Marketing, Somex Bank, 1978-79; *Subsecretary of Recreation*, Secretariat of Tourism, 1982-88. g-None. h-Director of Marketing and Supervisor of Accounts, Stanton Pritchard-Wood, S.A., 1965-67; Manager of New Products, Vick-Mexico, Division of Richardson-Merrill, S.A., 1965; founded Advising and Counseling, S.A., 1972; external consultant, National Fund for Tourism Development, 1972-78; Director of Marketing, Concord, S.A., 1979-80; Director General of Omnia Services, S.A., 1980-82. i-Son of Guillermo Grimm Esquer, industrialist, and Josefina González Casillas. j-None. k-None. l-Q es QAP, 396; DBGM, 196; DBGM87, 172.

Guajardo Hernández, Gonzalo
a-May 16, 1919. b-Cuautla, Morelos. c-Preparatory studies at the University of Nuevo León, Monterrey; medical degree with a specialty in pediatrics, National School of Medicine, UNAM, 1943-48, degree in June 1949; Temporary Assistant Professor of Pediatrics, University of Nuevo León, 1955. d-None. e-Head of the Regional Committee for the National Action Party of the State of Nuevo León, 1980; Secretary of the State Committee, 1968. f-None. g-None. h-Practicing physician in pediatrics. i-Attended school with *Javier de la Riva Rodríguez*, federal deputy from PRI and medical director of the ISSSTE; and with Rafael Campos, member of the PPS and Mayor of Teziutlán, Puebla, 1972; son of Gonzalo Guajardo. j-None. k-Candidate for federal deputy from the Federal District for PAN, 1949; candidate for federal deputy from Nuevo León for PAN, 1955 and 1961; candidate for senator from Nuevo León for PAN, 1964; precandidate for governor of Nuevo León for PAN, 1973. l-Letter; DBM68, 324-25; PdM, 183; Almanaque de N.L., 123.

Gual Castro, Carlos

a-Oct. 16, 1927. b-Villahermosa, Tabasco. c-Early education unknown; graduated as a surgeon, National School of Medicine, UNAM, 1945-51; resident, 1951-55; Professor of Endocrinology, Diabetes, and Nutrition, National Institute of Nutrition and the Graduate Division, National School of Medicine, UNAM, 1972-82; postgraduate studies in biochemistry of steroids, Clark University and the Worcester (Mass.) Foundation for Experimental Biology; Professor of the Biology of Human Reproduction, Graduate Division, National School of Medicine, UNAM, 1959- ; Professor of Clinical Endocrinology, National School of Medicine, UNAM, 1978- . d-None. e-None. f-Full-time researcher, 1959, and Director of Endocrinology Laboratory, 1960, of Department of Endocrinology, 1975-76, of Research Division, 1965-76, and of Department of Reproductive Biology, 1976, all at the National Institute of Nutrition; *Subsecretary of Assistance*, 1976-80; Director of the National Institute of Nutrition "Salvador Zubirán," 1980-82; Coordinator of the National Medical Center of the IMSS, 1982. g-None. h-None. i-Son of Carlos Gual del Rivero and Graciela Castro; married Beatriz Berlanga. j-None. k-None. l-Letter; DAPC, 33; WNM, 105; IEPES; *Excélsior*, 17 June 1982, 21A; HA, 28 June 1982, 21.

Gual Vidal, Manuel

(Deceased Jan. 21, 1954) a-June 9, 1903. b-Campeche, Campeche. c-Primary studies in Campeche, but completed primary and secondary studies in Tampico; preparatory at the National Preparatory School, completed in 1920; law degree from the National School of Law, UNAM, 1926; Professor of Contract and Civil Law, National School of Law, UNAM, 1926-45; Director, National Law School, 1939-41; *Secretary General of UNAM*, 1938-39; *Interim Rector of UNAM*, 1944. d-None. e-None. f-Adviser to the Secretary of Agriculture, 1926-28; Secretary of the Civil Division of the Supreme Court, 1929-30; adviser to the Bank of Mexico, 1935; technical adviser, Department of General Credit, Secretariat of the Treasury, 1935; President of the Patrons of the National Lottery, 1944-46; *Secretary of Education*, 1946-52. g-Manager of the National Association of Bankers, 1941-45. h-Practiced law for a private firm in New York, 1936-38; attorney for a group of electric companies, 1931-45; private law practice, 1934-35; author of many articles on education. i-Went to the National University with *José Castro Estrada, Antonio Armendáriz,* and *Eduardo Bustamante;* personal friend of *Gustavo Baz;* brother, *Rafael Gual Vidal,* was a lawyer and a judge for the Superior Tribunal of the Federal District and also served as head of the Legal Department for the oficial mayor of the PRM; Rafael served under Manuel as head of the Legal Department for the Federal Committee on the Construction of Schools, 1950; taught *Miguel Alemán* at UNAM; practiced law with *Antonio Martínez Báez;* son of León Gual Victoria and Rosario Vial. j-None. k-None. l-HA, 21 Apr. 1950, 5; WWM45, 53; DP70, 929; DGF51, II, 445; DGF51, I, 285; WB48, xvii; DGF50, II, 329, 455.

Gual Vidal, Rafael

a-Jan. 7, 1898. b-Campeche, Campeche. c-Primary studies at the Colegio of the State of Campeche, preparatory studies at the National Preparatory School and at Tulane University; law degree from the National School of Law, UNAM; studies in languages; Professor of Sociology and Economic Policy, UNAM. d-None. e-Director of the

Legal Department, Oficial Mayor's Office, PRM. f-Agent of the Ministerio Público Militar; local judge; Judge of the First Appellate Court; Justice of the Superior Tribunal of Justice of the Federal District and Federal Territories; Director, Legal Department, National Committee for School Construction, Secretariat of Public Education. g-None. h-Coauthor of the Civil Code. i-Married María Aguilar; brother of *Manuel Gual Vidal*, secretary of education, 1946-52; son of León Gual Victoria and Rosario Vidal. j-None. k-DBM70, 281-82.

Gudiño Canela, Baltasar
a-Jan. 25, 1900. b-Jiquilpan, Michoacán. c-Primary studies at the public school in Jiquilpan; no degree. d-Mayor of Jiquilpan, 1935; *Federal Deputy* from the State of Michoacán, Dist. 6, 1937-40; Local Deputy to the State Legislature of Michoacán, 1942-44; *Federal Deputy* from the State of Michoacán, Dist. 5, 1958-61, member of the Fourth Ejido Committee and the First Balloting Committee, and substitute member of the First Instructive Section of the Grand Jury. e-Joined the Partido Democrático Jiquilpense (Socialist) in 1926; founding member of the PNR, 1929. g-Organized peasant groups for the Partido Democrático Jiquilpense; leader of the Agrarian Ejido Association, 1936. j-Joined the Revolution, 1916; left the army as a 1st Captain, 1924. k-None. l-Func., 272; C de D, 1958-60, 80, 1937-39, 11.

Gudiño (Díaz), Manuel
(Deceased Oct. 11, 1971) a-1895. b-Colima, Colima. c-Primary studies in Colima; secondary studies at Normal School; normal certificate from the Porfirio Díaz Normal School of Colima; law degree, National School of Law, UNAM; secondary school teacher.

d-Alternate Federal Deputy from the State of Colima, 1922-24, under Rubén Vizcarra, but replaced him; *Senator* from the State of Colima, 1934-40, member of the Gran Comisión; *Federal Deputy* from the State of Colima, 1940-43, member of the Second Government Committee and the Second Justice Committee, President of the Chamber, 1942; *Governor of Colima*, 1943-49. e-*Secretary of Organization of the CEN of the PNR*, 1936. f-Judge in the State of Colima; Secretary General of Government of the State of Colima, 1931, 1935; President of the Superior Tribunal of Justice of the State of Colima, 1971. g-President of the Third National Student Congress. h-Librarian in Colima; journalist; Director of the literary journal *Alborada*; principal stockholder in the Bank of Colima. i-Brother, J. Trinidad Gudiño, was a military engineer who served as director of public works during his administration. j-None. k-Rival of *Daniel Cosío Villegas* for leader of the Second National Student Congress; answered *Manuel Avila Camacho's* 2nd state of the union address. l-HA, 19 Nov. 1943, 14; D del S, 1 Dec. 1940, 1; letter; C de D, 1940-42; Peral, 367; Moreno, 94ff.

Guel Jiménez, Francisco
a-Dec. 16, 1915. b-Aguascalientes, Aguascalientes. c-Primary studies in Aguascalientes, secondary and preparatory studies at the Preparatory School, Aguascalientes, 1930-34; medical studies at the National School of Medicine, UNAM, 1935-40, graduated as a surgeon, 1941. d-Member of the City Council of Rincón de Romos, Aguascalientes, 1954-56; Mayor of Aguascalientes, 1963-65; *Federal Deputy* from the State of Aguascalientes, Dist. 1, 1967-68, member of the Gran Comisión and the General Accounting Office Inspection Commit-

tee; *Governor of Aguascalientes*, 1968-74. e-Director of the CEPES of Aguascalientes, 1962. f-Treasurer of the Board of Material and Moral Improvements, Pabellón, Aguascalientes, 1948; Director of the IMSS Hospital, Aguascalientes, 1958-62; Director General of the National Arid Zones Commission, 1976-82. g-Secretary of Economic and Agricultural Affairs, CEN of CNOP, Aguascalientes, 1949; Secretary General of the ISSSTE Union of Aguascalientes, 1961; adviser to CNOP, 1965; Secretary General of CNOP of Aguascalientes, 1966. h-Began medical practice in Pabellón de Arteaga, Aguascalientes, 1941. j-None. k-Precandidate for senator from Aguascalientes, 1981. l-C de D, 1967-70, 78; MGF69, 89; *Excélsior*, 1 Dec. 1976, 26 Dec. 1981, 16A.

Guerra Castaños, Gustavo

a-Sept, 10, 1926. b-Coahuila. c-Primary studies at the Apolonio M. Aviles School; secondary studies at the Lucio Blanco Secondary School, Múzquis, Coahuila; preparatory studies from the San Ildefonso Night School, Mexico City; law degree, School of Law, University of Coahuila. d-Local Deputy to the State Legislature of Coahuila; *Federal Deputy* from the State of Coahuila, Dist. 1, 1970-73; *Senator* from the State of Coahuila, 1976-82. e-Youth Director of PRI in Coahuila; Director of the IEPES of PRI in Coahuila; special delegate of the CEN of PRI to Durango. f-Adviser to the Treasury General of Coahuila; President of the State Electric Commission of Coahuila, 1963-69. g-Secretary General of CNOP in Coahuila; President of the National Federation of Small Property Owners, 1974. h-Lawyer; fruitgrower. i-Married Concepción de Luna; son of Gustavo Guerra Flores and Julia Castaños. j-None. k-Precandidate for the gubernatorial nomination of PRI in Coahuila, 1974. l-*Excélsior*, 30 Dec.

1974, 13; Directorio, 1970-72, 92; C de D, 1970-73.

Guerra Leal, Mario

a-1919. c-Studied secondary at the Colegio México (Brothers of Mary), Mexico City; preparatory studies at the National Preparatory Night School while working at the National Bank of Mexico, Mexico City; law degree from the National School of Law, UNAM. d-None. e-Lawyer for the Federation of the Parties of the Mexican People, 1953-58; President of the Federation of the Parties of the Mexican People; President of the Parties of the Mexican Republic in the Federal District; Secretary General of PARM; President of the National Anti-Communist Party, but later expelled; Director of PARM in the Federal District; *President of the CEN of PARM*, 1983-86. f-Private Secretary to General *Miguel Henríquez Guzmán*; Private Secretary to General *Juan Barragán*. g-Winner of an oratory contest at secondary school. i-Son of Jorge Guerra Leal, a lawyer; uncle, Benito Guerra Leal, was second-in-command of the Mexico City Police Department under General *Roberto Cruz*; uncle, Antonio Guerra Leal, practiced law with *Alfonso Corona del Rosal*; student of *Hugo B. Margáin* at Colegio México; studied under *Agustín Yáñez* at the National Preparatory School; studied under many politicians at UNAM, including *José Campillo Saínz*. j-None. k-Imprisoned for political reasons, 1970s. l-Guerra Leal.

Guerra (Olivares), Alfonso

(Deceased Oct. 1967) a-1897. b-Tepic, Nayarit. c-Studied on a scholarship in Switzerland, Germany, and Europe in the fields of politics and economics. d-*Senator* from the State of Nayarit, 1964-67. e-None. f-Fourth Consul in Guatemala, 1923; rank of Vice Consul; Vice Consul, Zurich, 1923; Consul,

Hamburg, Germany, 1924; Director General of the Consular Service, Secretariat of Foreign Relations, 1946; *Oficial Mayor of the Secretariat of Foreign Relations*, 1946-51; *Subsecretary of Foreign Relations*, 1951-53; Ambassador to Germany, 1953-58, 1958-64. g-None. h-Career Foreign Service Officer. j-None. k-None. l-*Hoy*, 28 Oct. 1967, 13; DGF51, II, 585; DGF51, I, 97; DGF50, II, 421; DPE61, 20; Peral, 360; DP70, 945; DGF56, 124.

Guerrero, Silvestre
(Deceased 1968) a-Dec. 10, 1892. b-Acámbaro, Guanajuato. c-Primary studies in Acámbaro, Guanajuato; secondary studies in Morelia, Michoacán; preparatory studies at the National Preparatory Schoool; law degree, National School of Law, UNAM. d-Federal Deputy from the State of Michoacán, Dist. 5, 1924-26, 1926-28; Senator from the State of Michoacán, 1930-34. e-Secretary General of the CEN of PNR, 1930-31. f-Private Secretary to *Lázaro Cárdenas*, 1920; Secretary General of Government in the State of Michoacán, 1928-30, under *Lázaro Cárdenas; Attorney General of Mexico*, 1934-36; *Secretary of Government*, 1936-37; *Secretary of Health and Welfare*, 1939-40. g-None. i-Close friend of *Lázaro Cárdenas*; son of Silvestre Guerrero and Gregoria Martínez. j-None. k-None. l-Peral, 364; D de Y, 24 Jan. 1939, 1; DP70, 949; Enc. Mex., V, 44; *Excélsior*, 2 Dec. 1934; DBM68, 364.

Guerrero Briones, Alfonso
a-1915. b-San Luis Potosí, San Luis Potosí. c-Preparatory studies at the University of San Luis Potosí; law degree from the National School of Law, UNAM, professor at UNAM and at IPN. d-*Federal Deputy* from the State of San Luis Potosí, Dist. 1, 1961-64, member of the Civil Section, Legislative Studies Committee, and of the Consular and Diplomatic Service Committee. e-Member of PAN. f-None. g-Prominent student leader at the University of San Luis Potosí; President of the National Student Federation, of the Federation of Students of the Federal District, and of the Student Society of the National Preparatory School. j-None. k-Candidate for federal deputy for Dist. 4, State of San Luis Potosí, for PAN, 1970. l-*La Nación*, 14 June 1970, 26; C de D, 1961-64, 13, 70; *Excélsior*, 28 May 1979, 27.

Guerrero del Castillo, Eduardo
a-Feb. 26, 1929. b-Federal District. c-Early education unknown; degree in diplomatic sciences, UNAM, 1957; degree in political science, School of Political and Social Sciences, 1958; postgraduate work in Latin American economics, Brazil and at UNAM. d-None. e-Subsecretary of Finances of the CEN of PRI; *Secretary of Finances of the CEN of PRI*, 1979-81. f-Director General of Organization and Methods, Secretariat of Agrarian Reform; Technical Subdirector of the Division of Internal Affairs, Secretariat of Public Education. g-None. h-Positions in the private sector. j-None. k-None. l-Protag., 157.

Guerrero Esquivel, Fernando
b-Toluca, México. c-Preparatory studies from the National Preparatory School, Mexico City; law degree from the National School of Law, UNAM, with an honorary mention. d-*Federal Deputy* from the State of México, Dist. 5, 1946-49, member of the Budget and Accounts Committee (second year); *Federal Deputy* from the State of México, Dist. 3, 1952-55, member of the Legislative Studies Committee and the First Balloting Committee; *Federal Deputy* from the State of México, Dist. 4, 1958-61, member of the First Treasury Committee, the First Balloting Committee,

the First Credentials Committee, and the Foreign and Domestic Trade Committee. e-Participated in *Lázaro Cárdenas's* presidential campaign, 1934. f-Private Secretary to *Ernesto P. Uruchurtu*, Head of the Federal District Department, 1955-58; administrative posts in the Department of Agrarian Affairs and Colonization; delegate of the Department of the Federal District to Villa Obregón, 1961. g-Posts in the CTM. j-None. k-None. l-C de D, 1952-55, 51, 57, 63, 71; Func., 259; C de D, 1958-61, 80, 1946-49, 73.

Guerrero (Guajardo), Anacleto
(Deceased Feb. 10, 1980) a-Aug. 5, 1892. b-Hacienda del Porvenir, Nuevo León. c-Early education unknown; no degree. d-*Governor of Nuevo León*, 1936-38; *Senator* from the State of Nuevo León, 1952-58, member of the Agricultural Development Committee, the War Materiels Committee, the Second Committee on National Defense, and the Administrative Committee (1st year). e-None. f-Head of the Department of Cavalry, Secretariat of National Defense; Chief of Staff of the Secretariat of National Defense, 1933. g-None. i-Son, Pedro Armando Guerrero Garate, was an agent of the Secretariat of Agriculture. j-Joined the Revolution, Nov. 27, 1910, fought under the forces of Major Celedonio Villarreal; career army officer; head of the 21st Regiment of the Constitutional Army; fought against the Escobar rebellion, 1929; head of the Army Garrison at Ciudad Juárez; Commander of the 82nd Infantry Battalion, of the 1st Infantry Battalion, Guanajuato, of the 3rd, 6th, 21st, 24th, and 71st Calvary Regiments, of the 5th Military Zone, Chihuahua, Chihuahua, 1936, of the 15th Military Zone, Guadalajara, Jalisco, 1939, of the 30th Military Zone, Tampico, Tamaulipas, 1952, and of the 20th Military Zone, Colima, Colima; rank of Brigadier

General, 1929; reached rank of Division General. k-Candidate for governor of Nuevo León, 1931. l-DGF56, 7, 9-11; Dulles, 646; Peral, 362; Brandenburg, 80; Ind. Biog., 78-79; Dávila, 135; Almanaque de N.L., 12.

Guerrero López, Euquerio
(Deceased Mar. 1, 1990) a-Feb. 20, 1907. b-Guanajuato. c-Early education unknown; preparatory studies at the University of Guanajuato, 1920-24; law degree, University of Guanajuato, Nov. 16, 1929; Professor of Law, Law School, University of Guanajuato, at the National School of Law, UNAM, at Ibero-American University, and at the Higher War College; Rector, University of Guanajuato, 1967-70; Secretary General of the University of Guanajuato under Rector *Luis I. Rodríguez*, 1930-31. d-*Senator* from the State of Guanajuato, 1976-82. e-None. f-Agent of the Ministerio Público in Guanajuato, 1931-32; Judge of the Superior Tribunal of Justice, State of Guanajuato, 1931, 1933, 1934-37; Chief of the Advisory Department of the Private Secretary to the President of Mexico, 1936-37; Director of the Department of Government, Secretariat of Government, 1938; Alternate President of the Federal Board of Conciliation and Arbitration, 1940-43; President of the Federal Board of Conciliation and Arbitration, 1943; *Supernumerary Justice of the Supreme Court*, 1970-73; *Justice of the Supreme Court*, 1973-76; *President of the Supreme Court*, 1974-76; Director General of the National Institute of Senility, 1979-90. g-None. h-Director, Department of Labor, Mexican Light and Power Company, 1943-54; Administrative Subdirector, Mexican Light and Power Company, 1954-70; lawyer with Baker, Botts and Miranda, 1961-67; author of many books. i-Student with *Luis I. Rodríguez, Manuel Moreno,* and Antonio Madrazo at the University of

Guanajuato; longtime collaborator with *Luis I. Rodríguez*; married Alicia Reynoso; son of lawyer Nicéforo Guerrero, interim governor of Guanajuato, 1903, and María de Jesús López, a teacher; brother of *Nicéforo Guerrero, Jr.*, justice of the Supreme Court, 1940-57; son, Nicéforo, was a director general of the Secretariat of Government. j-None. k-None. l-HA, 7 Jan. 1974, 26; *Excélsior*, 18 Nov. 1974; Almanaque de Guanajuato, 32; DBGM, 89, 162-63.

Guerrero (López) Jr., Nicéforo
(Deceased 1969) a-1897. b-Guanajuato, Guanajuato. c-Law degree from the National School of Law, UNAM, 1924. d-*Alternate Senator* from the State of Guanajuato, 1934-37; *Senator* from the State of Guanajuato, acting as replacement for *Ignacio García Téllez*, 1937-40, member of the Permanent Committee, 1938. e-None. f-Secretary of the Supreme Court of Mexico; Oficial Mayor of the State of Guanajuato; Secretary General of Government of the State of Guanajuato; Private Secretary to President Pascual Ortiz Rubio; Attorney General of the Federal District, Feb. 5, 1930, to July 1, 1931; *Justice of the Supreme Court*, 1940-46, 1946-52, 1952-57; *Provisional Governor of Guanajuato*, 1946-47 (on leave from the Supreme Court). g-None. h-Assistant lawyer in Mexico City; practicing lawyer. i-Son of a distinguished Mexican lawyer Nicéforo Guerrero and teacher María de Jesús López; brother of *Euquerio Guerrero López*, justice of the Supreme Court, 1973-76; nephew, Nicéforo Guerrero Reynoso, was director general in the secretariat of government. j-Volunteered to fight against the North American invasion of Veracruz, 1914. k-Anderson says he resigned because of a split in the state party, Aug. 1947; resigned from the PRM in May 1940 because of Guanajuato election. l-DP70, 950; Morton, 32;

DGF56, 567; DGF51, I, 567; HA, 18 Jan. 1946, 1, 25 Jan. 1946, 8; letter; Peral, 363-64; Anderson, Casasola, V.

Guerrero Martínez, Pedro
a-Sept. 16, 1905. b-Campeche, Campeche. c-Primary studies at the Colegio Manuel R. Samperio and at the Model School No. 1, Campeche; preparatory studies at the Campeche Institute of Science and Letters; law degree, University of Campeche, Mar. 5, 1932; professor, School of Law, University of the Southeast, Mérida, Yucatán. d-*Alternate Federal Deputy* from the State of Campeche, Dist. 1, 1937-40; *Federal Deputy* from the State of Campeche, Dist. 1, 1943-46; *Senator* from the State of Campeche, 1946-52, member of the Gran Comisión, the National Property and Resources Committee, the Legislative Studies Committee, the First Constitutional Affairs Committee, and the First Balloting Committee; substitute member of the Tax Committee. e-None. f-Secretary of the City Council of Campeche, 1927-28; agent of the Ministerio Público (Criminal Division) in Campeche, 1929-30; Director of the Public Defender's Office, Campeche, 1931-32; Attorney General of the State of Campeche, 1932; Auxiliary Secretary of the First Judicial District of the Federal District, 1933; Treasurer General of the State of Campeche, 1936-38; Director, Department of Legal Affairs for the State of Campeche, 1940-42; Director, Public Registry of Property and Trade, Federal District, 1955-57; Judge of the Superior Tribunal of Justice for the Federal District, 1957-59; President of the Superior Tribunal of Justice for the Federal District, 1959-63; *Justice of the Supreme Court*, 1963-74. g-None. h-None. i-Political disciple of *Héctor Pérez Martínez*; son of Pedro Guerrero Perneu and Francisca Martínez Alomía. j-None. k-None.

l-C de D, 137-39, 11, C de D, 1943-45;
Justicia, July 1968; DGF51, 5, 9-15.

Guerrero (Mendoza), Marco Antonio
a-Sept. 28, 1919. b-Tucson, Arizona.
c-Early education unknown; graduated
as a 2nd Lieutenant in the infantry,
Heroic Military College, 1939-42;
instructor, Higher War College, 1946,
1950; diploma, staff and command,
Higher War College, 1946-49; studies in
armoured cars, United States, 1955-56;
studies at the Inter-American Defense
College, Washington, D.C., 1964;
Subdirector of the Higher War College,
1967-69; Subdirector of the Heroic Military College, 1973-76; Director of the
Higher War College, 1978-80. d-None.
e-None. f-*Subsecretary of National Defense,* 1982-88. g-None. h-None. i-Son
of Rómulo Guerrero Ramírez, public
official, and María Mendoza Méndez;
married Rosa Mónica Corona Guzmán.
j-Career army officer; joined the army as
a regular soldier, 47th Infantry Battalion, 1938; officer, 3rd Mortar Regiment,
1942; officer, 5th Military Zone, 1946-
49; Chief of Section 3, Staff, Secretariat
of National Defense, 1955, 1956-57; attached to 1st Armored Reconnaissance
Group, Presidential Guard, 1958-59;
officer, 2nd Artillery Battalion, Infantry
Brigade, 1959-61; aide, Military Attaché,
Mexican Embassy, United States and
Canada, 1961-63; Assistant Chief of
Staff, 28th Military Zone, 1964-65; rank
of Artillery Colonel, 1965; Chief of
Section 1, Staff, Secretariat of National
Defense, 1965-67; rank of Brigadier
General, 1971; Commander of the 1st
Artillery Battalion, Presidential Guards,
1970-71; Chief of Staff, Presidential
Guards, 1971; rank of Brigade General,
1975; Director General of Artillery,
Secretariat of National Defense, 1976-
80; rank of Division General, 1979;
Military Attaché to the Soviet Union,
Poland, and East Germany, 1980-82.
k-Held highest position in 1982 by a

career officer from enlisted origins. l-Q
es QAP, 71-72; Rev. de Ejer., Nov. 1975,
84, Dec. 1965, 61, Nov. 1971, 40;
DBGM, 198; DBGM87, 173.

Guerrero Mier, Angel Sergio
a-Aug. 18, 1935. b-Durango, Durango.
c-Early education unknown; law degree,
Juárez University of Durango, 1954-58.
d-Local Deputy to the State Legislature
of Durango, 1968-70; *Federal Deputy*
from the State of Durango, Dist. 1,
1976-79, Dist. 5, 1985-88; *Senator* from
the State of Durango, 1991-97. e-President of PRI, State of Durango, 1974-79;
*Secretary of Ideological Divulgation of
the CEN of PRI,* 1980-81; General
Delegate of the CEN of PRI to Tlaxcala,
1983; General Delegate of the CEN of
PRI to México, 1984. f-Chief of Press
and Publicity, State of Durango, 1956-
57; Head, Department of Government,
State of Durango, 1959-66; Oficial
Mayor of the State of Durango, 1966;
Secretary General of Government of the
State of Durango, 1970-74; Chief of Ad-
visers, Secretariat of Agrarian Reform,
1981-82. g-Director of CNOP, Durango,
Durango, 1955; Secretary General of
CNOP, State of Durango, 1966-70;
Coordinator of CNOP, 1976. h-None.
i-Son of Salvador Guerrero Díaz and
Angela Mier; married Margarita Guerra.
j-None. k-None. l-DBGM89, 488; C de
D, 1985-88; C de S, 1991-97.

Guerrero Ortiz, Arturo
a-Sept. 7, 1911. b-Acámbaro, Guanajuato. c-Primary studies from the
Benito Juárez Public School, Acámbaro;
secondary studies from the Colegio
Civil of Querétaro, 1926-29; preparatory
studies from the Colegio de San
Nicolás, Morelia, Michoacán, 1929-31;
medical degree, School of Medicine,
University of Michoacán, 1937; residency in Oklahoma, United States.
d-*Federal Deputy* from the State of
Querétaro, Dist. 1, 1964-67, member of

the Gran Comisión; *Senator* from the State of Querétaro, 1970-76, President of the Development of Cooperatives Committee, Second Secretary of the National Properties and the Second Labor Committees, member of the Gran Comisión and of the First Balloting Group. e-Secretary of the CEPES of PRI in Querétaro. f-Director of Medical Services of the IMSS in Querétaro, 1970; Director of the IMSS Hospital, Querétaro, Querétaro, 1970. g-Joined the Union of Health and Welfare Workers, 1938; Secretary General of Local 32 of the Union of Health and Welfare Workers; Adviser to the League of Agrarian Communities in Aguascalientes; Secretary of Organization of CNOP in Querétaro, 1970. h-Lived in Querétaro since 1926. i-None. k-None. l-C de S, 1970-76, 76; C de D, 1964-67; PS, 2746.

Guerrero Villalobos, Guillermo
a-Nov. 29, 1935. b-Federal District. c-Early education unknown; civil engineering studies, Higher School of Engineering and Architecture, IPN, 1956-59, graduating in 1960; graduate courses in construction engineering at UNAM, 1962-63; professor, Division of Graduate Studies, UNAM, 1965, 1975; Professor of Stability, Higher School of Engineering and Architecture, IPN, 1966; Professor of Earthquake Repairs and Tunnels, School of Engineering, UNAM, 1975. d-None. e-None. f-Director General of Hydraulic Works, Department of the Federal District; Director General of Hydraulic Operations, Department of the Federal District, 1978-82; *Subsecretary of Works and Services*, Department of the Federal District, 1982-84; adviser, Secretary of the Controller General, 1984-86; Assistant Director of Construction, Department of the Federal District, 1986-87; General Counsel, Department of the Federal District, 1987-88; *Director General of the*

Federal Electric Commission, 1988-94. g-None. h-Calculist and designer, Estructuras y Cimentaciones, S.A., 1956-59; Manager of Structures and Supervisor, DIRAC, S.A., 1963-67; director of various construction projects, Mexico City, 1968-71. i-Son of Francisco Guerrero Vizcaya, public official, and Magdalena Villalobos Rodríguez; married María Elena Alcaraz Preciado. j-None. k-First member of the de la Madrid subcabinet to resign; resigned over controversy surrounding Metro line 8. l-HA, 20 Dec. 1982, 28; Q es QAP, 426; *Proceso*, 9 Jan. 1984, 30; DBGM89, 164; DBGM92, 170.

Guevara Bautista, Julieta
a-Dec. 10, 1940. b-Pachuca, Hidalgo. c-Early education unknown; political science degree, National School of Political and Social Sciences, UNAM, 1960-64; professor at the National School of Political Studies, Acatlán campus, UNAM;, 1970-78; Director, Center of Public Administration Research, UNAM, 1973-75; Director, Division of Social and Economic Studies, National School of Political Studies, Acatlán campus, UNAM, 1975-78. d-*Federal Deputy* from the State of Hidalgo, Dist. 2, 1982-85, President, Public Education Committee; *Senator* from Hidalgo, 1988-91; *Federal Deputy* from the State of Hidalgo, Dist. 1, 1991-94. e-Joined PRI, 1962; member, Administrative Council, IEPES of PRI; Director of Education, ANFER of PRI, 1981. f-Delegate of the Secretariat of Public Education, State of México, 1979-81; Director of the Center for Research in Public Administration. g-None. i-Daughter of Evaristo Guevara Vivar, industrialist, and María de la Luz Bautista Tovar; married Mario Martínez Silva, political scientist. j-None. k-None. l-Directorio, 1982-85; Lehr, 214; DBGM, 517-18; DBGM89, 450; DBGM92, 483.

Guevara (y Orihuela), Gabriel R.
(Deceased) a-Mar. 13, 1887. b-Chilpancingo, Guerrero. c-Early education unknown; no degree. d-*Governor of Guerrero, 1933-35; Governor of Quintana Roo, 1940-46.* e-None. f-None. g-None. h-Worked as an aide to the subdirector of a mining camp in the Morado fields. i-Longtime friend of *Manuel Avila Camacho.* j-Career army officer; joined the Constitutionalists as a private under General Gertrudis G. Sánchez, 1913; fought under General Sánchez the entire Revolution; military commander of various zones; rank of Brigadier General, Jan. 1, 1928; returned to active duty, 1935; Director of the 5th Inspection Committee of the Army, 1937. k-When Governor of Guerrero, his powers were dissolved by the state legislature in order to replace Guevara with a governor loyal to President Cárdenas. l-Peral, 366; D de Y, 7 Nov. 1935, 1; Gómez Maganda, 100; Alvarez Corral, 135; Dávila, 119.

Guillot Schiaffino, Alejandro
(Deceased 1966) a-1913. b-Apizaco, Tlaxcala. c-Secondary education from the Methodist Institute of Puebla; engineering degree from the Superior School of Engineering, IPN, Mexico City, 1937. d-None. e-None. f-Head of the Laboratory for the Superior School of Engineering; head of Special Instruction for the Federal District; head of the Laboratory Department for the National Polytechnic School; *Director General of the National Polytechnic School, 1948-50;* adviser to the Mexican Institute of Social Security; Director General of Technical, Industrial, and Commercial Education, Secretariat of Public Education, 1958-66. g-None. h-Founder of the College of Electrical and Mechanical Engineering. j-None. k-None. l-DP70, 953; DPE61, 105; DPE65, 140.

Guinart López, Modesto A.
(Deceased Aug. 30, 1977) a-June 15, 1897. b-Veracruz, Veracruz. c-Early education unknown; no degree. d-*Federal Deputy from the State of Veracruz, Dist. 10, 1963-76.* e-Director of Administrative Services of the CEN of PRI, 1976. f-*Subsecretary of National Defense, 1952-58.* g-None. i-Son, Adolfo Guinart, an army captain. j-Career army officer; joined the Revolution under General *Cándido Aguilar,* 1914; rank of Brigadier General, Sept. 16, 1943; Commander of the 27th Military Zone, Acapulco, Guerrero, 1946; Chief of Staff of the 1st Division, 1946; Commander in Chief of the 2nd Division, 1947; Director General of the Army; rank of Division General; Commander of the 16th Military Zone, 1968. k-Accompanied Carranza on his flight from Mexico City, 1920. l-Peral, 47, 155; DGF47, 110; DGF56, 199; HA, 12 Dec. 1952, 6; D del Y, 2 Dec. 1952, 1; *Excélsior,* 8 Mar. 1973, 14, 30 Aug. 1977, 9 Dec. 1976; Casaola, V.

Gurría Ordóñez, Manuel
a-Oct. 31, 1931. b-Cunduacán, Tabasco. c-Primary studies in Tabasco; secondary studies in public schools in Mexico City; preparatory studies at the National Preparatory School; law degree, National School of Law, UNAM, 1956; Professor of Labor Law, National School of Law, UNAM, 1969- ; Professor of Ethics, Benito Juárez University Preparatory School, Tabasco, 1950s. d-*Federal Deputy from the State of Tabasco, Dist. 1, 1964-67,* member of the Gran Comisión; answered *Adolfo López Mateos*'s 6th state of the union address, 1964; *Federal Deputy from the Federal District, Dist. 1, 1985-88; Senator from Tabasco, 1991-92.* e-Subdirector of Electoral Action of the CEN of PRI, 1970; General Delegate of the CEN of PRI to Sonora, 1965, 1973. f-Subsecre-

tary of Government of the State of Tabasco, 1955-58; Secretary General of the State of Tabasco under Governor *Carlos Madrazo*, 1959-64; legal adviser to the Head of CONASUPO 1967-70; Director General of Government, Department of the Federal District, 1970-73; adviser to the Head of the Department of the Federal District, 1973-76; *Secretary General (B) of the Department of the Federal District*, 1978-79; *Secretary of Government of the Department of the Federal District*, 1979-82; *Subsecretary of Operations*, Secretariat of Tourism, 1988-91; *Interim Governor of Tabasco*, 1992-94. g-Student adviser to UNAM. i-Nephew of *Francisco Trujillo Gurría*, secretary of labor, 1943-46; cousin of Angela Gurría, prominent sculptress and wife of *Marcelo Javelly Girard*, secretary of urban development and ecology, 1982; son of Jorge Manuel Gurría Martínez de Escobar, engineer, and Ninfa Ordóñez Madrazo; married Soledad Hernández Sastre; son, Manuel Gurría Hernández, was director general of administration, Secretariat of Agriculture, 1992. j-None. l-*Excélsior*, 29 Aug. 1979, 14; C de D, 1964-67; DAPC81, 5; DBGM89, 164-65; DBGM92, 769-70.

Gurría Treviño, José Angel
a-May 8, 1950. b-Tampico, Tamaulipas. c-Primary studies at the Colegio Americano, Tampico, 1955-56, and the Escuela Moderna Americana, Mexico City, 1957-60; secondary studies at the Escuela Moderna Americana, 1961-63; preparatory studies at the Escuela Moderna Americana, 1965-66, and at the La Salle University, Mexico City, 1966-67; economics degree, National School of Economics, UNAM, 1968-72; graduate studies in engineering, Leeds University, England, 1973-74; courses at Harvard University, 1975, and the University of Southern California, 1977-78. d-None. e-Joined PRI, 1968; Secretary

of International Relations of the CEN of PRI, 1994. f-Private Secretary to the Director of Finances, National Finance Bank, 1970-75; Permanent Delegate to the International Coffee Organization, 1976-78; Subdirector of the Public Debt, Secretariat of the Treasury, 1978-79; Director General of External Financing, Secretariat of the Treasury, 1979-82; Director General of Public Credit, Secretariat of the Treasury, 1982-88; *Subsecretary of International Financial Affairs*, Secretariat of the Treasury, 1989-94. g-None. h-None. i-Son of Francisco José Gurría Lacroix, public official and director general of Banoro, and Carmen Treviño Humana; married Lulú Ululani Quintana Pali, eye surgeon. j-None k-None. l-DBGM89, 165; letter; DBGM92, 173; letter.

Gurza Falfán, Alfonso
(Deceased 1965) a-1905. b-Durango, Durango. c-Enrolled at the National Military Academy, 1922, graduating as 2nd Lieutenant of Infantry, Oct. 1, 1925; graduated from the Higher War College; Subdirector of the National Military College; Director of the Higher War College. d-None. e-None. f-Military Attaché to Canada; Military Attaché to the United States; *Oficial Mayor of the Secretariat of National Defense*, 1965. g-None. h-None. i-Son of Jaime Gurza, Subsecretary of the Treasury under President Madero. j-Career military officer; attached to the 14th Infantry Regiment, French Army, 29th Infantry Battalion, U.S. Army; member of the 1st Air Regiment, 2nd Belgium Army; attached to the Lancers, 6th Artillery, 2nd Belgium Army; Chief of Staff of the 201st Mexican Air Squadron; Chief of Staff of the Secretariat of National Defense; Chief of Military Details for the Chief of Police of the Federal District, 1950; rank of Brigade General, 1957. k-None. l-DP70, 954; DGF51, I, 486.

Gurza Villarreal, Edmundo
a-Nov. 2, 1927. b-Coahuila. c-Early
education unknown; civil engineering
degree, National School of Engineering,
UNAM, 1949-56; teacher, La Laguna
French Institute, 1961-63; teacher, Carlos Pereyra Preparatory School, 1964-72;
professor, School of Engineering, Higher
Institute of Science and Technology of
Coahuila, 1975-80. d-Member of the
City Council of Torreón, 1966-67; May-
or of Torreón, 1978-79; *Plurinominal
Federal Deputy* from PAN, 1979-82.
e-Joined PAN, 1961; candidate of PAN
for federal deputy, Coahuila, 1964.
f-None. g-President of the French Alliance, La Laguna, 1977-80. j-None.
k-None. l-Protag., 159; C de D, 1979-82.

Gutiérrez Barrios, Fernando
a-Oct. 26, 1927. b-Veracruz, Veracruz.
c-Early education unknown; graduated
from the Heroic Military College, 1943-
47. d-*Governor of Veracruz*, 1986-88.
e-None. f-Civilian employee and
Control Officer, Federal Security Police,
Secretariat of Government, 1950-58;
Subdirector of the Federal Security
Police, Secretariat of Government,
1958-64; Director, Federal Security
Police, 1964-70; *Subsecretary of
Government*, 1970-76, 1976-82; *Director General of Federal Highways and
Bridges*, 1982-86; *Secretary of Government*, 1988-92. g-None. h-None. i-Son
of Fernando Gutiérrez Ferrer, military
officer who reached the rank of colonel,
and businessman, and Ana María
Barrios Bravo; married Divina María
Morales Espinosa. j-Career army
officer; administrative position, south-
eastern Mexico; officer, Presidential
Assault Guards Battalion, 1948-49;
officer, Mechanized Brigade, 1949-50;
resigned from the army, 1950; reached
rank of 1st Captain. k-Cleared Fidel
Castro of charges in Mexico, 1950s,
paving the way for his return to Cuba.
l-DPE71, 2; DPE61, 14; DBGM, 201;

HA, 6 May 1986, 7; *Mexico Journal*, 16
Dec. 1988, 16; DBGM92, 173.

Gutiérrez Cázares, Jesús
(Deceased 1959) a-Oct. 28, 1895.
b-Huatabampo, Sonora. c-Primary and
secondary studies in Huatabampo,
Sonora; no degree. d-*Governor of
Sonora*, Dec. 17, 1935, to Jan. 1937.
e-None. f-None. g-None. i-Son of Jesús
Gutiérrez Cázares and Angela Cázares.
j-Career army officer; joined the Constitutional Army under General Guillermo
Chávez, 1913; fought General Villa,
1915-17; fought Yaquis in Sonora, 1918;
fought in the Huastecas against Peláez,
1919; Commander, Nogales Garrison,
1930-32; fought against the de la Huerta
rebellion, 1923; Commander of the 7th,
9th, 13th, 16th, 46th, 60th, and 64th
army regiments; Chief of Staff of the
Expeditionary Column to Sonora under
Manuel Avila Camacho, 1920; reen-
tered the Army Reserves, 1938; Commander of the 4th Military Zone,
Sonora, 1939; rank of Division General,
Oct. 11, 1955. k-None. l-Peral, 369;
HA, 15 May 1942, 15; D de Y, 1 Jan.
1936, 4; NYT, 17 Dec. 1935, 1, 6; Enc.
Mex., 1977, VI, 333; PS, 2788;
Hernández Chávez, 95; de Parodi, 55-60.

**Gutiérrez de Velasco y Aranda, Manuel
León**
a-Mar. 26, 1921. b-Federal District.
c-Early education unknown; legal
studies, National School of Law,
UNAM, 1937-41, graduating with a
thesis on "Crimes of Social Dissolution," 1943; MA in letters, School of
Philosophy and Letters, UNAM; studies
toward an MA in economics, National
School of Economics, UNAM; professor,
Benito Juárez University, Durango,
1947-48; professor, University of Aguascalientes, 1959-60; professor, University
of Guanajuato, 1960-78. d-None.
e-Joined PRI, 1949. f-Judge of the First
Instance, Criminal and Civil Division,

Piedad and Puruandaro, Michoacán, 1945-46; agent of the Ministerio Público, Durango, 1947-48; Secretary of Agreements, Board of Conciliation and Arbitration, Federal District, 1949-52; Secretary, 4th Division, Superior Tribunal of Justice of the Federal District, 1954-56; Judge, First District Court, Jalisco, Chiapas, and Aguascalientes, 1956-61; Judge of the Collegiate Circuit Court, 1961-78; *Supernumerary Justice of the Supreme Court,* 1979-82, 1982-87; President, Supernumerary Division, Supreme Court, 1979. g-None. h-None. i-Son of Manuel Gutiérrez de Velasco Mena, engineer, and Luz Arranda Castillo; married Elena Romo Gutiérrez; son, Hector, was a federal circuit court judge. j-None. k-None. l-Protag., 160; DBGM89, 615; DBGM87, 626.

Gutiérrez Gurría, Alfonso
a-Mar. 27, 1902. b-Teapa, Tabasco. c-Primary studies in Tabasco; no degree. d-*Federal Deputy* from the State of Tabasco, Dist. 1, 1937-40, member of the Gran Comisión; *Senator* from the State of Tabasco, 1940-46, President of the First Credit, Money, and Credit Institutions Committee, First Secretary of Foreign and Domestic Trade and the First Petroleum Committees, Second Secretary of the Economics and Statistics and the Tax Committees and member of the Second Balloting Group. e-President of the PRM in Tabasco. f-None. g-None. i-Cousin of *Francisco Trujillo Gurría,* governor of Tabasco, 1939-43; related to *Manuel Gurría Ordóñez.* j-None. k-None. l-Libro de Oro, 1946, 7; C de S, 1940-46; C de D, 1937-40; PS, 2797.

Gutiérrez Hernández, Arnaldo
a-1920. b-Guerrero, Chihuahua. c-Primary studies in Guerrero, Chihuahua; no degree. d-Member of the City Council of Guerrero; *Federal Deputy* from the State of Chihuahua, Dist. 4,

1958-61, member of the Fishing and Hunting Committee and the Budget and Accounts Committee; *Federal Deputy* from the State of Chihuahua, Dist. 5, 1964-67, member of the Livestock Committee; *Senator* from the State of Chihuahua, 1970-76, President of the Second Ejido Committee, First Secretary of the National Properties Committee, the Department of Agrarian Affairs Committee, and the Forest Committee. e-General Delegate of the CEN of PRI to Chihuahua; campaigned for *Teófilo Borunda* for governor of Chihuahua, 1956. f-None. g-Leader of the League of Agrarian Committees, Chihuahua. h-Farmer and small businessman. i-Parents were campesinos; collaborator of *Teófilo Borunda.* j-None. k-None. l-Func., 167; C de D, 1958-61, 80, 1964-67, 50, 85; C de S, 1970-76, 76.

Gutiérrez Herrera, Magdaleno
a-July 22, 1918. b-Suchitepec, Oaxaca. c-Primary studies at the Public School of Suchitepec, 1927-28; secondary studies at the Public School for Children of Agricultural Industry Workers, 1929-32, and at Tehuacán, Puebla; Secondary Night School for Workers No. 15, Federal District, 1947-49; vocational studies at Vocational School No. 3, IPN, 1950-51; studies at the Higher School of Commerce and Administration, IPN, 1952-55; Professor of Applied Costs, Higher School of Commerce and Administration, 1959-70; taught at the University of Veracruz. d-*Federal Deputy* from the Federal District, Dist. 14, 1970-73, member of the Agrarian Affairs Committee (1st Section), the Department of the Federal District Committee, and the Electric Industry Committee. e-Joined PAN in 1940; adviser to PAN; candidate for federal deputy from Oaxaca, 1952; candidate for senator from Oaxaca, 1958. f-None. g-None. j-None. k-None. l-C de D, 1970-72, 118; Directorio, 1970-72.

Gutiérrez Lascuráin, Juan
(Deceased Mar. 5, 1959) a-1911.
b-Federal District. c-Engineering degree
from the National School of Engineering, UNAM. d-*Federal Deputy* from the
Federal District, Dist. 7, 1946-49, member of the Second Committee on the
Treasury and the Industries Committee.
e-Joined PAN, 1943; member of the National Council of the National Action
Party, 1956-59; *President of the CEN of
PAN*, 1949-56. f-None. g-Active
member of the Catholic Association of
Mexican Youth. h-Practicing engineer.
j-None. k-As a federal deputy, proposed
reform projects for Articles 27 and 115
of the Constitution, including amendments providing women with rights of
suffrage. l-DP70, 960; Morton, 56-57; C
de D, 1946-48; DGF47, 7; Mabry, 51.

Gutiérrez Oropeza, Luis
a-July 12, 1919. b-Puebla, Puebla.
c-Early education unknown; graduated
from the Heroic Military College as a
2nd Lieutenant in Artillery, July 1,
1942; diploma in staff and command,
Higher War College. d-None. e-None.
f-Presidential Chief of Staff, President
Gustavo Díaz Ordaz, 1964-70. g-None.
j-Career army officer; joined army 1938;
rank of Artillery Colonel, 1964; rank of
Brigadier General, 1968; rank of Brigade
General, 1972; Director General,
Department of Military Industry,
Secretariat of National Defense, 1970-
76. k-None. l-DGF69, 157; R de E, Dec.
1964, 24; WNM, 108; HA, 7 Dec 1970,
26.

Gutiérrez (Rincón), Efraín A.
a-Aug. 24, 1897. b-Tuxtla Gutiérrez,
Chiapas. c-Primary studies from the
Industrial Military School, Tuxtla
Gutiérrez; engineering degree from the
National School of Agriculture, 1912-
14, 1916-18. d-*Governor of Chiapas*,
1937-40. e-None. f-Director General of
Waters, Lands, and Colonization,

Department of Agrarian Affairs; adviser
to the Department of Agrarian Affairs;
Secretary General of the Department of
Agrarian Affairs; Director General of
the National Bank of Agricultural
Credit. g-None. h-Member of the
Administrative Council of Inmobiliaria
Fénix, S.A. i-Brother, Gustavo, was a
local deputy and state treasurer during
Efraín's governorship, and later became
a precandidate for governor of Chiapas,
1943. j-Fought in the Revolution under
General Emiliano Zapata in Morelos;
rank of Captain, 1915; returned to
Mexico City to finish studies in 1916.
k-None. l-DP70, 1845; DBM68, 330-31;
HA, 29 Oct. 1943, 14; Gómez, 279.

Gutiérrez Roldán, Emilio
(Deceased Jan. 20, 1977) a-May 8, 1905.
b-Tlalpujahua, Michoacán. c-Engineering degree from the National School of
Agriculture; Director of the De la
Huerta Agricultural School, Michoacán.
d-*Federal Deputy* from the State of
Puebla, Dist. 11, 1940-43, member of
the Committee on Credit, Money, and
Credit Institutions, and the Polling
Committee for the Election of a senator
from the Federal District; Secretary of
the Gran Comisión, Sept. 1942; member
of the Permanent Commission, 1940;
President of the Chamber of Deputies.
e-None. f-Member of the Executive
Council of the National Ejido Credit
Bank; Agent of the National Agricultural Bank; Director General of National Seed Production, Secretariat of
Agriculture and Livestock, 1964-70;
Director of Agents for the National Ejido Credit Bank. g-Secretary of Political
Control for the CNC. h-Author of
articles on ejido credit; Secretary
General of the Mexican Economic
Society. i-Brother of *Pascual Gutiérrez
Roldán*, director general of PEMEX,
1958-64. j-None. k-None. l-DBM68,
287-88; DPE65, 102; C de D, 1940-42,
47, 50; MGF69, 264; Peral, 373.

Gutiérrez Roldán, Pascual
(Deceased June 19, 1979) a-May 29, 1903. b-Mazatlán, Sinaloa. c-Secondary studies at the Colegio Francés until 1918; preparatory studies at Forestry School, 1918-21; engineering degree in agronomy and forestry, National School of Agriculture, 1925; degree in economics, National School of Economics, UNAM, 1935; Ph.D. in economics in the United States; Professor of Monetary Theory and Credit, National School of Economics, UNAM, 1938-42; professor at the National School of Banking, 1937. d-None. e-None. f-Subchief of the Department of Agricultural Organizations, National Agrarian Commission, 1929; Agricultural Attaché to the Mexican Embassy, Washington, D.C., 1930-31; Office of Economic Investigations, 1932, Director General of Credit, 1933-34, technical adviser, 1934-35, and Director General of Credit, 1936-40, all at the Secretariat of the Treasury; Director General of the Bank of Popular Credit, 1935-36, and of the Savings Promotion Bank, 1941-45; *Director General of National Steel Industry*, 1952-58; *Director General of PEMEX*, 1958-64. g-None. h-Organized the National Mortgage Bank of Public Works, 1935; vice-president of a private firm, 1977; President of the Board of Hules Mexicanos, S.A., 1979; member of the Board of Siemens, S.A., 1979. i-Brother *Emilio Gutiérrez Roldán* was a federal deputy, 1940-43; daughter married to *Gustavo Baz*'s son; married Elisa Saldívar; son of Pascual Gutiérrez C. and Concepción Roldán. j-None. k-None. l-HA, 4 Jan. 1960, 41; IWW66, 484; WB48, 2106; EBW46, 408; HA 5 Oct. 1945, xxvi; DGF51, II; *Quién Será*, 148-49; WNM, 108.1

Gutiérrez Ruiz, David Gustavo
a-Dec. 25, 1939. b-Villahermosa, Tabasco. c-Economics degree from the National School of Economics, UNAM, with a thesis on "The Policy of Agricultural Development in the State of Tabasco"; special postgraduate studies at the Institute of Economic Development, Paris; special studies in the rural provinces of France and at the University of Paris, the National Agricultural Bank of France, and the Regional Agricultural Credit Bank of France on agricultural credit; Professor of Economic Problems of Mexico, National School of Economics, UNAM; professor, School of Business Administration and School of Engineering, University of Tabasco. d-*Senator* from Tabasco, 1976. e-*Secretary General of the CNOP*, 1975-76. f-Technical adviser in the National School of Economics, UNAM, 1960-63; technical adviser to the IMSS, 1960-63; represented Mexico before the Common Market, 1963; Private Secretary to *Manuel R. Mora*, Governor of Tabasco, 1965-68; Treasurer of Tabasco, 1968-69; Secretary General of Government of the State of Tabasco, 1970-71; *Governor of Quintana Roo*, 1971-75; Director General of Guanos and Fertilizers, 1976-82. g-President of the Tabascan University Circle, Mexico City, 1959-60. h-Assistant in the IMSS, 1958. i-Son of David Gutiérrez Aldecoa and Daisy Ruiz León; grandson of Santiago Ruiz Sobredo, governor of Tabasco, 1924-1926; disciple of *Manuel R. Mora*; married Luz León Estrada. j-None. k-None. l-*Excélsior*, 8 Dec. 1974, 23, 30 Jan. 1975, 13; HA, 24 Feb. 1975, 14; Bulnes, 785-86; Alvarez Corral, 165-66.

Gutiérrez Treviño, Eulalio
(Deceased Jan. 14, 1977) a-Oct. 23, 1916. b-Saltillo, Coahuila. c-Primary and secondary studies from the Colegio Robert, Saltillo; agricultural engineering degree from the Antonio Narro Agricultural School, Saltillo, 1937. d-Mayor of Saltillo, Coahuila; *Senator* from the State of Coahuila, 1964-70; *Governor of Coahuila*, 1970-76. e-None. f-Director

of Agriculture, Papaloapan, Veracruz; President of the Board of Material and Moral Improvements, Saltillo. g-None. h-Director, Noche Buena Mining Company, Ramos Arizpe, Coahuila; involved in the mining construction business, 1976-77. i-Son of General Eulalio Gutiérrez, interim president of Mexico, 1914, and Petra Treviño; son, Mario Eulalio Gutiérrez Talamás, was mayor of Saltillo. j-None. k-His successor, Governor *Oscar Flores Tapia*, accused him of misusing more than 500 million pesos as governor; his nomination as the PRI gubernatorial candidate in 1969 came as a surprise since *Federico Berrueto Ramón* was thought to be the nominee. l-WWMG, 20; DGF69, 105; *Excélsior*, 15 Jan. 1977, 27; *Proceso*, 22 Jan. 1977, 34.

Gutiérrez (y Gutiérrez), José Luis
(Deceased 1967) a-1900. b-Guanajuato, Guanajuato. c-Primary and secondary studies in Guanajuato; preparatory studies in Guanajuato; law degree from the University of Guanajuato. d-None. e-None. f-Penal Judge in Mexico City; Judge of the Superior Tribunal of Justice of the Federal District and Federal Territories; Secretary General of Government of the State of México, 1941-45; *Acting Governor of Mexico*, 1942, after *Alfredo Zárate* was assassinated; Assistant Attorney General of the Federal District under Attorney General *Franco Sodi*, 1946-52; *First Assistant Attorney General of Mexico*, 1952-58; *Supernumerary Justice of the Supreme Court of Mexico*, 1964-67. g-None. h-None. j-None. k-None. l-DGF56, 539; DP70, 960; letter; DGF51, I, 487.

Gutiérrez Zorrilla, Felipe
a-Aug. 21, 1923. b-Monterrey, Nuevo León. c-Early education unknown; law degree from the University of Nuevo León, 1942-48; MA degree in Comparative Law, New York University, New York City, 1948-49; Professor of Constitutional and Mercantile Law, Technological Institute of Higher Studies, Monterrey, 1953-66. d-*Federal Deputy* from the State of Nuevo León, Dist. 1, 1967-70, member of the Committee on Agricultural Development and the Committee on Small Agricultural Property; *Plurinominal Federal Deputy* from PAN, 1982-85. e-Joined PAN, 1940; Secretary of the Regional Committee of PAN, Nuevo León, 1970; regional adviser to PAN in Nuevo León, 1970. f-None. g-None. h-Secretary of the Institute of Social Studies, Monterrey; private law practice, Monterrey. j-None. k-Candidate for federal deputy on the PAN ticket, 1970. l-DBM68, 332; C de D, 1967-69; MGF69, 94; *La Nación*, 14 June 1970, 21; Directorio, 1982-85; Lehr, 615.

Guzmán, Martín Luis
(Deceased Dec. 22, 1976) a-Oct. 6, 1887. b-Chihuahua, Chihuahua. c-Primary studies in Tacubaya, Federal District; preparatory studies at the National Preparatory School, Mexico City; law degree from the School of Law, Jan. 7, 1909, Professor of Graduate Studies, 1911, and professor at the School of Commerce, 1911, all at UNAM; Professor of Spanish, University of Minnesota, 1917. d-Federal Deputy from the Federal District, Dist. No. 6, 1922-23; *Senator* from the Federal District, 1970-76. e-Member of the Political Education Section of the New Advisory Council of the IEPES of PRI, 1972. f-Librarian at the National School of Graduate Studies, 1911; Chancellor of the Mexican Consulate, Phoenix, Arizona, 1909-10; adviser to the Secretary of War, 1914-15; Ambassador to the United Nations, 1941; President of the National Commission on Free Textbooks, 1959-76; Executive Member of the National Planning Commission for Hospitals, 1961. g-None.

h-Secretary of the Popular University, 1912; Director of the National Library; member of the Literary Group El Ateneo, 1911; Director of *El Gráfico* in New York, 1917; Chief of the editorial section of *El Heraldo de México*; founded the Mexico City evening paper *El Mundo*, 1922; director of various newspapers, 1925-34; worked for *El Universal*, 1936-41; cofounder with *Adolfo López Mateos* and *Pascual Gutiérrez Roldán* of the publishing firm that is today Librería Cristal, S.A.; founder and Director of the magazine *Tiempo*, 1942-76; winner of the National Prize in Literature, 1958; author of *The Memoirs of Pancho Villa* and the autobiographical book of the Revolution, *El aguila y la serpiente*. i-Close friend of *Adolfo López Mateos*; son of Colonel Martín Luis Guzmán; married Anita West Villalobos; daughter-in-law, Dolores Ferrer Garralda, is the daughter of Spanish vice-admiral Manuel Ferrer Antón, the granddaughter of José Ferrer Pérez, adjutant to King Alfonso XIII, and great-granddaughter of Fernando Calderón, secretary of the Court of Ministers to Isabel II. j-Joined the Revolution in 1911 under Francisco Madero; attached to the forces of *Ramón F. Iturbe*, 1913-14; joined Francisco Villa, 1914; carried out numerous assignments as a civilian; reached rank of Colonel. k-Jailed briefly, 1914; exiled in Spain, 1915-16, 1924-36; and in the United States, 1916-20; delegate of the Progressive Constitutional Party. l-Letters; DBM68, 333-34; DPE61, 113; WWM45, 54-55; Strode, 215; DPE70, 104; DPE65, 136; WB54, 467; WB48, 2109; *Proceso*, 1 Jan. 1977, 77; HA, 3 Jan. 1977, 523; *Excélsior*, 27 Dec. 1976, 2B; Enc. Mex., 1977, VI, 339-40.

Guzmán Araujo, Roberto

(Deceased 1969) a-1911. b-Guanajuato, Guanajuato. c-Primary studies in Guanajuato; law degree from the National School of Law, UNAM; studies in Paris. d-*Senator* from the State of Guanajuato, 1946-52, member of the Mail and Telegraph Committee, the Second Justice Committee, the Military Justice Committee, the Second Mines Committee, and the Committee on the Consular and Diplomatic Service. e-Orator for *Manuel Avila Camacho*, 1940. f-Mexican delegate to the Brussels Peace Conference, 1936; Assistant Attorney General of the Federal District and Federal Territories, 1941-45; *Oficial Mayor of the Secretariat of Government*, June 18, 1945, to Feb. 15, 1946; adviser to the president of Mexico, 1966-69. g-Representative of the Federal District to the Cárdenas Student Youth Group, 1933; Secretary of Publicity, Cárdenas Student Youth Group, 1933. h-Director of the *Revista América*, 1942-59; founder with Pablo Neruda of *Nuestro España*; author of numerous plays, novels, and books on history. i-Married María del Carmen Pandal Montes de Oca; son, Roberto, was director general of legal affairs, Secretariat of Labor, 1987; daughter-in-law, Susana Merigo Melo, is a lawyer; son, Gerardo, was director general of agreements, Secretariat of Labor, 1987 j-None. k-None. l-DGF47, 20; Peral, 47, 158; Correa, 360; DGF51, I, 6, 10, 12-14; DP70, 963-64; C de S, 1946-52; Gómez Maganda, 106; Enc. Mex., 1977, VI, 344; DBGM92, 177.

Guzmán Bracho, Roberto

a-Feb. 15, 1932. b-Federal District. c-Primary, secondary, and preparatory studies in Mexico City, law degree from the National Law School, UNAM, 1954. d-None. e-None. f-Auxiliary lawyer to Public Notaries No. 10, No. 71, Mexico City; Private Secretary to the Subsecretary of Unrenewable Resources, Secretariat of National Patrimony, *Manuel Franco López*, 1964-66; Private Secretary to the Secretary of Government Properties, *Manuel Franco López*, 1967-70; *Oficial Mayor of Government Properties*, 1970-75; Director General of Tracto-Sidena, S.A., 1975-76. g-None. h-Practicing attorney in firm of Guzmán Bracho and Ruiz, Mexico City j-None. k-None. l-HA, 14 Dec. 1970, 20-21; DPE70, 44; HA, 24 Feb. 1975, 30, 21 Apr. 1975, 31.

Guzmán Cabrera, Sebastian
a-Feb. 26, 1928. b-Civela, Ixtaltepec, Oaxaca. c-Early education unknown; teaching certificate, Rural Normal School, Comitacillo, Oaxaca, 1940-44. d-Local Deputy to the State Legislature of Veracruz, 1969-71, 1973-76; *Federal Deputy* from the State of Veracruz, Dist. 14, 1979-82, 1985-88; *Plurinominal Federal Deputy* from the State of Veracruz, 1991-94. e-Secretary of Labor Action, PRI, State of Veracruz, 1978. f-None. g-Secretary General, Local 10, National Petroleum Workers Union (STPRM), 1984-85; *Secretary General of the STPRM*, 1989-92, 1992-95. h-Unknown. i-Son of José Guzmán and Guadalupe Cabrera; married Gabina García Blas. j-None. k-None. l-DBGM87, 48; DBGM92, 483-84; *Proceso*, 6 Jan. 1992, 30; *El Nacional*, 27 Aug. 1991, 7; C de D, 1979-92, 1985-88.

Guzmán Cárdenas, Cristóbal
a-Mar. 2, 1898. b-Santa María del Oro, Durango. c-Primary studies in Santa María; secondary studies in Santa María and Mapimi, Durango, completed secondary in Parral, Chihuahua; graduate of the Higher War College; special studies in artillery, Fort Sill, Oklahoma; Director of the Higher War College. d-*Senator* from Durango, 1964-70. e-*Secretary of Political Action of the CEN of PRI*, 1964-70. f-Director General of Military Education, 1958-61; Chief of Staff of the Secretariat of National Defense, 1944-46; Military Attaché to the Mexican Embassy,

Washington, D.C., 1938; Military Adviser to the Mexican Delegation to the United Nations, 1945; Military Attaché to the Mexican Embassy, Washington, D.C., 1941-42, 1957; Director of the Department of Military Industry; special ambassador to Venezuela; Ambassador to Yugoslavia. g-None. h-Author of several works on artillery. i-Married Carmen Cházaro. j-Career army officer; joined the army as a 2nd Lieutenant, 1913; commander of an artillery regiment, 1938-40; rank of Colonel, 1938; commander of a mechanized brigade, 1943-44; rank of Brigadier General, 1942; Commander of the 21st Military Zone, Morelia, Michoacán, 1948; reached rank of Division General, 1953. k-Supported General *Henríquez Guzmán*'s presidential campaign. l-WWM45, 55; C de S, 1964-70; DPE61, 33; MGF69, 105; Peral, 373; *Mis Seis Años*.

Guzmán Guzmán, Carlos
a-Nov. 26, 1903. b-Mascota, Jalisco. c-Primary studies in Mascota, 1909-15; preparatory studies at the University of Guadalajara, 1917-21; law degree from the University of Guadalajara, 1926, with a thesis on amparo. d-Local Deputy to the Fortieth State Legislature of Jalisco, 1930-32; Federal Deputy from the State of Jalisco, Dist. 11, 1934-37; *Federal Deputy* from the State of Jalisco, Dist. 4, 1958-61, member of the Second Section of the Legislative Studies Committee, the Second Constitutional Affairs Committee, and the First Credentials Committee. e-None. f-Secretary of the Judiciary, Jalisco, 1927-30; Judge of the Superior Tribunal of Justice of the State of Jalisco, 1938; Agent of the Ministerio Público of the Office of the Attorney General in the Federal District; Secretary to the Chief of Police of the Federal District; Secretary General of Government of the State of Jalisco, 1932-34; Private Secretary to

the Private Secretary of the President of Mexico, J. *Jesús González Gallo*, 1940-46; Oficial Mayor of the Presidency, 1946. g-None. j-None. k-None. l-Func., 243; C de D, 1958-60, 80.

Guzmán Neyra, Alfonso
a-1906. b-Panuco, Veracruz. c-Primary studies in Panuco, completed in Tampico; preparatory studies at the National Preparatory School, Mexico City; law degree from the National School of Law, UNAM, 1929-33, with his thesis on "Insurance against Unemployment"; Professor of Labor Law, School of Law, University of Veracruz, Jalapa. d-Local Deputy to the State Legislture of Veracruz. e-President of the 6th Electoral District of the PNR for Veracruz, 1932; Director of *Manuel Avila Camacho*'s campaign for president in the State of Veracruz, 1939; Director of *Miguel Alemán*'s campaign for president in the State of Veracruz, 1945-46; President of the Regional Committee of PRI for the Federal District, 1951-52. f-Agent of the Ministerio Público in the State of Aguascalientes, 1934; President of the Superior Tribunal of Justice of the State of Veracruz; consulting lawyer to the Secretariat of Public Works; President of the Federal Council of Conciliation and Arbitration, 1947-50; Director General of Labor and Social Welfare, Department of the Federal District, 1951; Director General of Public Works, Department of the Federal District, 1952; *Justice of the Supreme Court of Mexico*, 1952-58, 1965-69; *President of the Supreme Court of Justice*, 1959-64, 1969-74. g-Student participant in the 1929 Autonomy Movement; representative of the National Law School, 1930; founder of the regional peasant committee No. 1, Panuco, Veracruz. h-Practicing attorney, 1946-49; President of the Administrative Council of Braniff Airlines, 1940-46. i-Father, a pharmacist and a graduate of the National

Medical School, became a small cattle rancher and a supporter of Madero; family has resided in the Panuco area since 1750; knew *Antonio Armendáriz* and *Antonio Dovalí Jaime* at UNAM; related to *Manuel Guzmán Willis*, senator from Tamaulipas, 1952-58. j-None. k-None. l-Letter; DGF56, 568; *Hoy*, 17 Jan. 1970, 53; IWW66, 485; WWW70-71, 300; DGF51, I, 481; *Justicia*, Jan., 1967; *Excélsior*, 11 Dec. 1978, 18.

Guzmán Orozco, Guillermo
a-Nov. 10, 1923. b-Federal District. c-Early education unknown; law degree, National School of Law, UNAM, 1942, with a thesis on the concept of sovereignty. d-None. e-None. f-Judicial official, 1945; Secretary of Studies and Accounts, Supreme Court of Justice, 1961-64; Subsecretary of Accounts, Supreme Court of Justice, 1964-68; Federal Circuit Court Judge, 1968-82; *Justice of the Supreme Court*, 1983-88, 1988-94. g-None. h-Practicing lawyer. i-Son of Jesús Guzmán Vaca, lawyer, and Julias Orozco Herrera; married Ana María González Alonso. j-None. k-None. l-DBGM, 660; DBGM89, 615; DBGM92, 662.

Guzmán Orozco, Renaldo
a-June 7, 1920. b-Arandas, Jalisco. c-Medical degree from the National School of Medicine, UNAM; postgraduate work at the Children's Hospital, University of Iowa. d-*Federal Deputy* from the Federal District, Dist. 20, 1961-64, member of the Social Security and Child Welfare Committee and the Editorial Committee; *Federal Deputy* from the State of Jalisco, Dist. 7, 1967-70, member of the Second Treasury Committee, the Social Security Committee, the Gran Comisión, and the Public Welfare Committee; *Alternate Senator* from the Federal District, 1964-67; *Senator* from Jalisco, 1970. e-Presi-

dent of the National Political Action Committee of the CNOP of PRI, 1962-64; Subsecretary of Popular Action of the CEN of PRI, 1964-65; *Secretary of Popular Action of the CEN of PRI, 1964-70; Secretary General of the National Confederation of Popular Organizations of PRI,* 1965-70. f-Surgeon in IMSS hospitals; *Subsecretary of Health,* 1970-76. g-Administrative positions in the IMSS Workers Union; Treasurer of the IMSS Workers Union, 1955-59; Secretary General of the Union of IMSS Workers. h-None. i-Married Dolores García Jurado; student of *Enrique Beltrán.* j-None. k-None. l-MGF69, 105; C de D, 1967-69, 57, 1961-64; letter; *Hoy,* 31 Jan. 1971, 4; WWMG, 20; HA, 14 Dec. 1970, 23; Schers, 23.

Guzmán Rubio, Jesús
a-June 23, 1924. b-Villa Juárez, Oaxaca. c-Early education unknown; graduated as a 2nd Lieutenant, Heroic Military College; law degree, National School of Law, UNAM. d-*Alternate Federal Deputy* from the State of Oaxaca, Dist. 8, 1958-61; *Federal Deputy* (Party Deputy from PARM), 1973-76. e-Vice-President and National Coordinator of PARM, 1976; delegate of PARM, Conference on the Renovation of City Government in Oaxaca, 1977; *President of PARM,* 1979-80. f-Member of the Presidential Staff, 1949-52; ballistics expert, Attorney General of Mexico; official, Topographical Engineering Group, Department of Agrarian Affairs. g-None. h-None. i-Married to *Arcelia Sánchez de Guzmán,* plurinominal deputy, 1976-79. j-Career army officer; commander of the Rural Defense Forces, Soconusco. k-None. l-*Excélsior,* 10 July 1980, 1; Protag., 161; C de D, 1958-61, 1973-76, 1976-79.

Guzmán Willis, Manuel
(Deceased May 13, 1973) a-Aug. 19, 1900. b-Panuco, Veracruz. c-Primary

studies in Tampico and Mexico City; secondary studies at the Williams Institute, Tacubaya, Federal District; preparatory studies at the National Preparatory School, Mexico City; no degree. d-Mayor of Tampico, 1948-50; *Senator* from the State of Tamaulipas, 1952-58, member of the Gran Comisión, 1954, the Committee on National Property, and the First Committee on Mines, substitute member of the Second Committee on the Navy and the Agricultural and Development Committee. e-One-time member of PAN. f-Representative of the Secretariat of National Patrimony on the Federal Board for Material Improvement, Tampico, Tamaulipas (15 years); Delegate of the Technical Inspection Office of the Secretariat of National Patrimony, Tampico, 1951; *Subsecretary of Livestock,* 1965-70. g-Founder of the Regional Union of Cattle Ranchers of Huastecas; President of the Livestock Association of Cebu Cattle Ranchers. h-Operated father's business at age 20; organizer of the Second Pan American Games; discus champion of Central America, 1926; President and founder of the Livestock Bank of Tampico. i-Father, an entrepreneur in petroleum and cattle; married Maltilda Maya; related to *Alfonso Guzmán Neyra.* j-None. k-Defeated *Emilio Portes Gil's* candidate for mayor of Tampico, 1948. l-DGF56, 9, 8, 11-13, 437; DGF51, 456; letter; *Excélsior,* 14 May 1973, 2; *El Universal,* 14 Sept. 1965; HA, 14 Mar. 1955; Ind. Biog., 80-81; Medina, No. 20, 188.

H

Haddad Interian, José
a-June 23, 1922. b-Oxkutzcab, Yucatán. c-Completed secondary school at the Academia Comercial Marlene, Mérida, Yucatán; private accounting degree. d-Alternate Party Deputy from PAN,

1973-76; *Plurinominal Federal Deputy* from PAN, 1982-85. e-Joined PAN, 1955; candidate for federal deputy from PAN, 1967; National adviser to PAN, 1973; Secretary of Finance, Regional Committee of PAN, Yucatán, 1978. f-Secretary of the Commander General of the Fleet, Secretariat of the Navy. g-Secretary of Acts of the Mexican Catholic Union, Yucatán, 1946-55; taught courses in Christianity in the Family Christian Movement, 1955-62. h-Practicing accountant; Chief of Sales, Miraflores Development, 1967-74; columnist, *Diario de Yucatán.* i-Son of Sood Haddad Mattar and Máxima Interian; married María Addi Barquet Iza. j-None. k-None. l-Directorio, 1982-85; C de D, 1982-85, 1973-76; Lehr, 613; DBGM, 519.

Hank González, Carlos
a-Aug. 28, 1927. b-Tiangustenco de Galeana, México. c-Primary studies at the Benito Juárez School, Tiangustenco, 1935-40; secondary studies at the Normal School of México, Toluca, 1941-46; teaching certificate from the Superior Normal School of Mexico, Mexico City, 1947-50, with a field specialty in biology and history; Professor of Primary Education, 1941-46; secondary teacher in Atlacomulco, México, 1947-51. d-Mayor of Toluca, 1955-57; *Federal Deputy* from the State of México, Dist. 6, 1958-61, member of the Editorial Committee (1st year), Secretary of the Chamber (2nd year); *Governor of México,* 1969-75. e-Member of PRI since 1944; head of the state delegation from CNOP to the PRI Convention, 1952; delegate of PRI to the State of Tabasco, 1961; delegate of CNOP in San Luis Potosí, 1961; member of the Policy Committee of the CEN of CNOP; Assistant to the President of the CEN of PRI. f-Director of the Department of Secondary Education, Toluca, México, 1952; Director of the Board of Material

and Moral Improvements, Toluca, México, 1952; Treasurer of Toluca, 1954; Director General of Government of the State of México, 1957-58; Subdirector of Sales, CONASUPO, 1961-64; *Director General of CONASUPO,* 1964-69; *Head of the Department of the Federal District,* 1976-82; *Secretary of Tourism,* 1988-90; *Secretary of Agriculture,* 1990-. g-President of the Student Association of the Normal School of Mexico; head of the "Ideal Republic Club" in Atlacomulco; Secretary General of the Youth Federation for the State of México, PRM, 1944; Secretary General of the 27th Delegation of the National Union of Teachers, 1947-51. h-Wealthy businessman; started out with a candy factory; owner of the White Truck Company; has real estate interests. i-Father, Jorge Hank Weber, an officer in the German army, colonel in the Mexican army under General Amaro, but died in 1929; mother, Julia González; stepfather, Trinidad Mejía Ruiz, was a shoemaker and small store owner; disciple of *Isidro Fabela, Adolfo López Mateos,* and *Alfredo del Mazo;* supported *Mario Moya Palencia* for President, 1975; son, Carlos Hank Rhon, directs a large family industrial empire. j-None. k-None. l-HA, 21 Dec. 1964, 9; C de D, 1958-60; HA, 31 Jan. 1972, 31, 34; WWMG, 20; letter; Func., 261; LA, 3 Dec. 1976; Enc. Mex., 1977, VI, 636-64; HA, 20 Dec. 1976, 22; LA, 12 Mar. 1976, 83; *Excélsior,* 28 Feb. 1974, 13 Dec. 1974; HA, 24 June 1974, 38; *Excélsior,* 22 Apr. 1977, 6; DBGM92, 177-78.

Hay (Fortuño), Eduardo
(Deceased Dec. 27, 1941) a-Jan. 29, 1877. b-Federal District. c-Primary, secondary, and preparatory studies in Mexico City; engineering degree from the University of Notre Dame, 1901. d-Federal Deputy, 1914-16, 1916-18. e-None. f-Inspector General of Consulates for Europe, Secretariat of Foreign

Relations, 1911-12; Inspector General of Police, 1912-13; Confidential Agent to Brazil, Peru, and Colombia, 1914, to Venezuela, 1914-15; Subsecretary of Agriculture and Development, 1916; Minister to Italy, 1918-23,to Japan, 1924-25; Subsecretary of Trade and Public Works, Aug. 27, 1927 to Dec. 1, 1928; Director General of Public Welfare for the Federal District, 1928-29; Ambassador to Guatemala, 1929; Director General of Customs, 1932-33; Consul General, Paris, 1933-34; *Secretary of Foreign Relations,* 1935-40. g-None. h-Author; Chief of the Engineering Firm of Schonduke and Neubuder. i-Close friend of President Carranza and General Obregón; married Angelina Sais; son of engineer Guillermo Hay and Josefina Fortuño; son, Eduardo Jr., was consul in Paris, France; daughter married architect Adolfo Mariscal. j-Joined the Revolution in Jan. 1911; Chief of Staff for Francisco Madero, 1911; Chief of Staff under General Villarreal and General *Ramón Iturbe,* 1913; rank of Brigadier General, 1913. k-None. l-DP70, 968; Peral, 377; WWLA40, 239; Daniels, 105ff; Enc. Mex., 1977, VI, 368; López, 486-87; Garrido, 213.

Hedding Galeana, Benjamín
a-Feb. 6, 1945. b-Federal District. c-Early education unknown; public accounting degree, Oregon State University, 1970, with a thesis on the public accountant profession; MA in administration, Monterrey Institute of Higher Studies, 1982; professor, Business and Administration School, IPN, 1965; Dean, Graduate School of Business Administration, IPN, 1971-73. d-Representative to the Assembly of the Federal District, 1988-91. e-Joined PRI, 1974. f-*Oficial Mayor of the Secretariat of Public Education,* 1973-76; Director General of Boletrónico, Department of the Federal District, 1978-82; Adminis-

trative Director of Administration and Finances, National College of Professional Technical Education, 1983-88. g-None. h-Accountant, Petroleum Club of Mexico, 1960-63; accountant, Mexican Institute of Chemical Engineers, 1963-65; auditor, Price Waterhouse, 1965-67; accountant, Ejidal Packing Corporation, 1968-69. i-Son of Marcelo Hedding García, public accountant, and Elvira Galeana Resendiz; married Blanca María Ver Guerra. j-None. k-None. l-DBGM89, 570.

Hegewisch Fernández Castelló, Adolfo Enrique
a-Dec. 14, 1932. b-Federal District. c-Early education unknown; law degree, Free School of Law, 1955, with a thesis on article 74 of the amparo; professor, Free Law School. d-None. e-None. f-Adviser, Department of International Affairs, IMSS; Director, Legal Department, National Advisory Fishing Council; Private Secretary to the Subsecretary of the Treasury; Subdirector General, Federal Electric Commission; *Subsecretary of Regulation of Foreign Investment and Technology Transfer,* Secretariat of Trade and Industrial Development, 1982-87; Ambassador to West Germany, 1987-90; Ambassador to the European Economic Community and Belgium, 1990-94. g-None. h-Legal Director, Grupo Somex; Executive Vice President, Banco Mexicano Somex. i-Son of Adolfo Hegewisch Quijano and Ana Fernández Castelló; married Marcela Reguero Alarcón, graduate in international relations. j-None. k-None. l-DBGM, 206; DBGM89, 169; DBGM92, 178.

Henestrosa (Morales), Andrés
a-Nov. 30, 1906. b-Ixhuatán, Oaxaca. c-Primary studies in the public school of Juchitlán, Oaxaca; teaching certificate; preparatory studies in science from the National Preparatory School; started

legal studies at the National School of
Law, UNAM, no degree; Professor of
Mexican Literature and Spanish
American Literature, Higher Normal
School and the National Preparatory
School, Mexico City; advanced studies
in linguistics, United States, on a
Guggenheim fellowship. d-*Federal
Deputy* from the State of Oaxaca, Dist.
1, 1958-61, member of the Protocol
Committee, the Indigenous Affairs
Committee, the Editorial Committee
(1st year), the Tourism Committee, and
the Inspection Committee of the
General Accounting Office; *Federal
Deputy* from the State of Oaxaca, Dist.
1, 1964-67, member of the Committee
on Fine Arts, the Library Committee
(1st year), the Protocol Committee, and
the Television Industry Committee;
Senator from the State of Oaxaca, 1982-
88; *Plurinominal Federal Deputy* from
PRI, 1988-91. e-Member of the Cultural
Committee of the Popular Party, 1947;
Secretary of Press and Publicity of the
Popular Party, 1948. f-Director of the
Special Tax Department, Department of
the Federal District, 1937-43; Chairman, Department of Literature, National Institute of Fine Arts, 1952-58;
Director of the Press for the Senate,
1964. g-None. h-Director of *El Libro y
el Pueblo* and *Letras Patrias*; well-
known author of short stories. i-From a
very poor family; orphaned as a baby;
son of Martina Henestrosa Pineda and
Arnulfo Morales Nieto, peasant.
j-None. k-Participated in the 1929
strike at the National University with
Adolfo López Mateos; campaigned for
José Vasconcelos in 1929 along with
Angel Carvajal. l-C de D, 1958-60, 81,
1964-66, 79, 80, 87; Enc. Mex., 1977, VI,
378; López, 487; Lehr, 360.

Henríquez Guzmán, Miguel
(Deceased Aug. 29, 1972) a-Aug. 4, 1898.
b-Piedras Negras, Coahuila. c-Began
studies as a cadet at the Military

College, Mexico City; engineering
degree, 1913. d-None. e-None. f-None.
g-None. h-None. i-Friend of Madero
family. j-Career army officer; joined the
Revolution, 1914, as a 2nd Lieutenant,
10th Army Brigade of the Army of the
Northeast under General Andrés
Saucedo; member of the General Staff of
the 2nd Division, Army of the Center,
1914; fought under General Jesús
Carranza, 1914; Chief of Staff of the 1st
Infantry Brigade under General *Vicente
González Fernández*, 1920; rank of Lt.
Colonel, 1920; Chief of Staff to General
Vicente González Fernández, Tabasco,
1923-25; Commander of the Foot Police,
Mexico City, 1926-27; Temporary
Commander of the 24th Military Zone,
Cuernavaca, Morelos; Temporary
Commander of the 27th Military Zone,
Guerrero; Commander of the 74th
Cavalry Regiment; rank of Brigadier
General, May 16, 1929; Chief of Staff for
Lázaro Cárdenas in Michoacán, 1929;
Commander of the 30th Military Zone,
Villahermosa, Tabasco, 1935-36, of the
13th Military Zone, Nayarit, 1936, of
the 10th Military Zone, Durango, 1936-
37, of the 4th Military Zone, Hermosillo, Sonora, 1937, of Military Operations for the State of San Luis Potosí,
1938, of the 7th Military Zone, Monterrey, Nuevo León, 1940, and of the
15th Military Zone, Guadalajara, Jalisco, 1943; Head of the 4th Army Regiment; rank of Division General, Aug. 1,
1942. k-Member of the group of cadets
who protected President Madero on his
trip from Chapultepec Castle to the
National Palace during the Félix Díaz
uprising, Feb. 1913; supported President
Cárdenas during the *Cedillo* revolt in
San Luis Potosí, 1938-39; precandidate
for president of Mexico, 1946; candidate
for president of Mexico, 1952, for the
Federation of People's Parties of Mexico; expelled from PRI in 1951 for his
premature campaigning for president.
l-WWM45, 56; Scott; Padgett, 66; HA,

11 Sept. 1972, 16; Peral, 377; Enc. Mex., 1977, VI, 386; López, 487.

Heredia Ferráez, Jorge
c-Law degree, National School of Law, UNAM, May 30, 1947. d-None. e-None. f-Agent of the Ministerio Público of the Attorney General of Mexico, Tampico, Tamaulipas; Head of the Technical Department of the Division of Professions; Legal Adviser to the National Housing Institute; Director General of Legal Affairs, Secretariat of Government, 1968; *Oficial Mayor of Government*, 1968-70; Oficial Mayor of the Federal Electric Commission, 1970-73. g-None. h-Attorney for PEMEX. j-None. k-None. l-HA, 14 Dec. 1970, 25.

Hernández, Pablo Mario
(Deceased Jan. 8, 1974) a-July 1, 1894. b-Lagos de Moreno, Jalisco. c-Primary and secondary education at Morenci and Clifton, Arizona; no degree. d-None. e-None. f-Chief of Trains, National Railroads of Mexico; Assistant Director General of the Railroads of Mexico, 1941; *Acting Director General of the National Railroads of Mexico*, 1941; Assistant Director General of the National Railroads, 1943-45; *Director General of the National Railroads of Mexico*, 1945-46. g-None. h-Joined the National Railroads as a laborer; machinist; superintendent of various divisions in the National Railroads of Mexico, 1921-41. i-Married Graciela Treviño; son of Rafael Hernández and Dolores Muñoz. j-None. k-None. l-WWM45, 56; *Excélsior*, 9 Jan. 1974, 14; HA, 21 Dec. 1945.

Hernández Alvarez, Enrique
(Deceased Nov. 2, 1938) a-June 24, 1892. b-Ciudad González, Guanajuato. c-Primary studies in Ciudad González; secondary studies in León, Guanajuato; medical degree, National School of

Medicine, UNAM, 1917; student professor at the Guanajuato Studies Center, 1917. d-Federal Deputy from the State of Guanajuato, Dist. 16, 1920-22, 1922-24, 1928-30, 1930-31; Governor of Guanajuato, 1931. e-President of PNR in Guanajuato and the Federation of Revolutionary Parties of Guanajuato. j-President of the Board of Directors for Public Welfare; representative of the federal government before the Henequen Cooperative; *Secretary of Health and Public Welfare*, Jan. 3, 1938, to Nov. 2, 1938. g-None. i-Classmate at the Guanajuato Studies Center of *Ignacio García Téllez*, secretary of government, 1938-40, and of *Luis Díaz Infante*, governor of Guanajuato, 1948-49; supported for governor by *Agustín Arroyo Ch.* and *Enrique Fernández Martínez*. k-First Secretary of the Secretariat of Health; removed from the governorship of Guanajuato after the Congress declared his powers dissolved, June 4, 1931; this movement was led by a political faction of Manuel Ortega. l-D de Y, 3 Nov. 1938, 1; *Hoy*, 12 Nov. 1938, 17; Peral, 47, 161; Novo, 35, 195.

Hernández Barrón, María del Rosario
a-Dec. 24, 1948. b-Culiacán, Sinaloa. c-Primary studies at the Agustina Ramírez School, Culiacán, Sinaloa; secondary and preparatory studies, University of Sinaloa; law degree, School of Law, University of Sinaloa; professor, Preparatory School, University of Sinaloa. d-*Federal Deputy* from the State of Sinaloa, Dist. 8, 1979-82. e-Secretary of Electoral Education, local PRI committee. f-Chief of Public Defenders, State of Sinaloa. g-Secretary General of the National Revolutionary Association of Women, Sinaloa. h-None. i-Daughter of engineer Isidro Hernández Moreno and María Luisa Barrón; married lawyer Roberto Emilio Armenta Cárdenas. j-None. k-None. l-Romero Aceves, 702-03; C de D, 1979-82.

Hernández Cervantes, Héctor
a-Dec. 31, 1923. b-Federal District. c-Early education unknown; economics degree from the National School of Economics, UNAM, 1941-45; studies in England, 1946-48; MA in economics from the University of Melbourne, Australia, 1949-50; postgraduate fellowship, social sciences, El Colegio de México; Assistant Professor of Economic Theory, National School of Economics, UNAM, 1958; Professor at CEMLA. d-None. e-None. f-Economist, Bank of Mexico, 1946-47; Assistant to the Director of the National Committee to Control Imports, 1947-48; Secretary of the Committee on Export Prices, 1951-52; Subdirector of Economic Research, National Finance Bank, 1952-54; Subdirector of Economic Studies, Secretariat of the Treasury, 1955-58; Director General of Trade, Secretariat of Industry and Commerce, 1961-64; Director General of International Studies, Secretariat of the Treasury, 1970-76; *Subsecretary of Trade*, Feb. 24 to Nov. 30, 1976; *Subsecretary of Foreign Trade*, Secretariat of Commerce, 1976-82; *Secretary of Commerce*, 1982-88; Director General of BANCOMER, 1988-90. g-None. i-Classmate at UNAM of *Octaviano Campos Salas* and *Horacio Flores de la Peña*; son of Benjamín Hernández Pichardo, career military, and María de la Luz Cervantes; married Raquel García de León. j-None. k-None. l-B de M, 146; DGF61, 66; EN de E, 1958, 108; *Excélsior*, 25 Feb. 1976, 4; HA, 8 Mar. 1976, 26, 13 Dec. 1982, 13; IEPES; *Excélsior*, 1 Dec. 1982, 34A; Q es QAP, 189; DBGM, 208.

Hernández Cházaro, Eduardo
(Deceased Nov. 23, 1957) a-May 4, 1898. b-Tlacotalpán, Veracruz. c-Early education unknown; no degree. d-Federal Deputy from the State of Vera-cruz, 1918-20; *Federal Deputy* from the State of Veracruz, Dist. 12, 1940-43, member of the Gran Comisión, the First National Defense Committee, and the Second Credentials Committee; Secretary of the Political Control Committee. e-Member of the Executive Committee of the National Pre-Electoral Center of *Avila Camacho*, 1939. f-Member of the Chief of Staff, President Obregón, 1920-24; Assistant Chief of Staff to President Calles, 1924-28; Chief of Staff for President Ortiz Rubio, 1928-29; Secretary to President Ortiz Rubio, 1929-30; Head of the Department of the Federal District, 1930; Consul in San Antonio, Texas, 1931-35; Inspector of Military Attachés, 1930-31. g-None. h-None. i-Son, Eduardo, an engineer and director of several construction firms; married Sofia Lemus. j-Joined the army, May 23, 1914, as a 2nd Lieutenant of Cavalry; 2nd Captain, 1915; 1st Captain, 1920; Major, 1924; Lt. Colonel, 1927; Brigadier General, 1944; Brigade General, 1949; Commander of the 23rd Military Zone, Tlaxcala, Tlaxcala, 1950-51; Commander of the 22nd Military Zone, Toluca, México, 1951-57; rank of Division General, 1952. k-Precandidate for governor of Veracruz, 1936. l-DP70, 980; C de D, 1940-42; Peral, 379; letter; Novo35, 286; Rev. de Ejer., Nov. 1957, 52.

Hernández Corzo, Rodolfo
a-Oct. 4, 1909. b-Comitán, Chiapas. c-Primary studies in Chiapas; secondary studies at the Chiapas State Normal and Preparatory School, graduated as a normal teacher, Mar. 1928; BS in biology, National Preparatory School, 1934; MS, Northwestern University, 1939-40; degree in chemistry, IPN, Nov. 19, 1940; Ph.D., Stanford University, 1949-52, with a dissertation on the biogenesis of itacomic acid; normal teacher, 1928-31; assistant professor in Higher Technical Education; professor in Graduate School; Professor of Cine-

matography, Military Communications School; founder and organizer of courses in applied mathematics in chemistry and biology, IPN, 1940-49; Professor of Chemical and Physical Biology, 1940-49; originator of the Microbiology Warfare Course, Higher War College, 1940-49; Director General of the National School of Biological Sciences, IPN, 1952-55. d-None. e-None. f-Scientific adviser to the federal government; adviser to the Bank of Mexico; adviser to UNESCO; *Director General of IPN*, 1953-56; Director General of Standards, Secretariat of Industry and Commerce, 1961; Director General of the Division of Wild Fauna, Secretariat of Agriculture and Livestock, 1964-70. g-None. h-Investigator for the Radon Emanation Corporation, 1940-41; author of numerous technical and scientific works. i-Brother, Antonio, professor and investigator for the National School of Biological Sciences, IPN. j-None. k-None. l-DGF56, 304; B de M, 147-48; DGF65, 101; MGF69, 264; Enc. Mex., 1977, VI, 406-07.

Hernández Delgado, José
a-Sept. 7, 1904. b-Guanajuato, Guanajuato. c-Law degree, School of Law, University of Guanajuato, Feb. 20, 1926; Professor of Law, National School of Law, 1931-34. d-*Federal Deputy* from the State of Guanajuato, Dist. 3, 1937-40. e-None. f-Auxiliary Agent of the Attorney General of the Federal District and Federal Territories, Mar. 29, 1930, to Mar. 30, 1931; Second Assistant Attorney General of Mexico; Oficial Mayor of the Secretariat of the Presidency, 1934-37; Attorney General of the Federal District and Federal Territories, July 13, 1931, to Sept. 4, 1932; Director General of the National Workers Bank, 1941-42; President of the Liquidating Committee for the National Workers Bank, 1942-44; Director General of the

National Bank of Cooperative Development, 1944-46, 1946-52; *Director General of Nacional Financiera*, 1952-58, 1958-64, and 1964-70. g-None. i-Brother, *Herculano Hernández Delgado*, was a federal deputy from Guanajuato, 1952-55, and a founder of the Sinarquista movement; father served as oficial mayor of health under *Enrique Hernández Alvarez*. j-None. k-None. l-Letter; DGF50, II, 190; DGF51, II, 278; DGF47, 364; D de Y, 5 Dec. 1952, 1; C de D, 1937-39, 12; *Justicia*, Jan. 1966; Michaels, 102; Enc. Mex., 1977, VI, 402.

Hernández Enríquez, César Rubén
a-Sept. 1, 1943. b-Querétaro. c-Early education unknown; social science degree, National School of Political and Social Science, UNAM, 1970; Professor of Sociology, UNAM, 1970-71; Technical Director of the Colegio Cambridge, 1973-74; professor at the National School of Political Studies, UNAM, Acatlán campus, 1979; adjunct professor, Labor Institute, Secretariat of Labor. d-*Senator* from the State of Querétaro, 1976-82. e-Auxiliary Secretary of the Oficial Mayor of PRI in the Federal District, 1969; personal representative of *Luis Echeverría* to the 17th Electoral District, Federal District, 1970; Director of Recruitment for PRI, Federal District, 1971; special delegate of the CEN of PRI to Veracruz. f-Chief of Section A, Community Development, Michoacán, Secretariat of Public Education, 1968; adviser, Chamber of Deputies. g-General delegate of the CNOP of PRI to Aguascalientes, 1975; Alternate Secretary of the CNOP of PRI to Guerrero, 1976. i-Son of Salvador Hernández Rivera, surgeon, and Laura Enríquez González; sister *Silvia Hernández Enríquez* was senator from Querétaro, 1991-94. j-None. k-None. l-Protag., 166; C de S, 1976-82; DBGM, 520.

Hernández Enríquez (de Galindo), Silvia
a-Sept. 12, 1951. b-Querétaro, Querétaro. c-Early education unknown; degree in political science and public administration, School of Political and Social Sciences, UNAM, 1967-70; MA degree in public administration, London School of Economics, 1971-73; postgraduate studies at the Sorbonne, Paris, in French and French civilization. d-*Alternate Federal Deputy* from the Federal District, Dist. 7, 1973-76; *Federal Deputy* from the Federal District, Dist. 16, 1976-79; *Senator* from the State of Querétaro, 1982-88, 1991-94. e-Joined PRI in secondary school in 1962; *Secretary of Organization of the CEN of PRI*, 1981-82; *Secretary of Popular Action of the CEN of PRI* (changed to United Citizens in Movement), 1989-93. f-Employee of the Assistant Secretary to the Governor of the State of Guanajuato; Assistant Secretary to *Oscar Flores Tapia*; adviser to the Chamber of Deputies; Director General of the National Institute of Mexican Youth (INJUVE), 1976-82. g-Founder of the National Insurgency of Women; adviser to the Mexican delegation to the World Conference of Women. h-Fluent in French and English. i-Brother, *César Rubén Hernández*, became senator from Querétaro, 1979-82; daughter of Salvador Hernández Rivera, surgeon, and Laura Enríquez González; married Jesús Humberto Galindo Zárate. j-None. k-First woman in Mexican history to hold a regular secretaryship on the CEN of PRI; youngest senator elected from Querétaro. l-C de D, 1973-76, 7; HA, 31 Oct. 1977, 7; *Excélsior*, 29 Aug. 1976, 26; C de D, 1976-79; *Excélsior*, 27 Dec. 1981, 17A, 26 Dec. 1981, 16A; Romero Aceves, 385-86; *Excélsior*, 27 July 1984, 20; DBGM87, 492; Lehr, 395; DBGM, 520.

Hernández Galicia, Joaquín
a-1922. b-Veracruz, Gulf. c-Early education unknown; no degree. d-None. e-None. f-None. g-Member of Local 1, Union of Petroleum Workers of the Mexican Republic (STPRM); Secretary of Labor of the Majoritarian Unification Group, Local 1, STPRM; Secretary General of the Majoritarian Unification Group; President of the Majoritarian Unification Group; *Secretary General of the STPRM*, 1962-64; unofficial administrator of social works, Local 1, STPRM. h-Welder. i-Father was a petroleum worker and union member. j-None. k-One of the most powerful figures in the petroleum union; arrested on orders of President Carlos Salinas, 1989; supported *Cuauhtémoc Cárdenas*'s presidential campaign, 1988. l-Grayson.

Hernández Gómez, Tulio
a-May 26, 1938. b-Tlaxcala, Tlaxcala. c-Early education unknown; law degree, National School of Law, UNAM, 1962. d-*Federal Deputy* from the State of Tlaxcala, Dist. 1, 1964-67, member of the Gran Comisión; *Governor of Tlaxcala*, 1981-87. e-Joined the Youth Sector of PRI, 1953; member of the Youth Leadership of PRI, Federal District, 1954; Director of Youth of PRI, Tlaxcala, 1957-60; Subdirector of National Youth of the CEN of PRI, 1959-64; Auxiliary Secretary of the CEN of PRI, 1968-70. f-Director of the Department of Citizen Education, National Institute of Mexican Youth, 1959-64; Coordinator of Housing, National Institute of Mexican Youth, 1962; adviser to the Director of the National Institute of Mexican Youth, 1964; adviser to the State Government of México, 1971-75; adviser to the Secretary of the Treasury, 1975-76; Delegate of Azcapotzalco to the Department of the Federal District,

1976-79; *Oficial Mayor of Government,*
1979-80. g-Member of the Youth Sector
of the CNC, 1960-61. i-Part of *Enrique
Olivares Santana's* political group; son
of *Francisco Hernández y Hernández,*
secretary general of the CNC, 1959-62.
j-None. k-None. l-C de D, 1964-67;
Excélsior, 19 July 1979, 19, 17 Dec.
1979, 18, 6 May 1980, 4; Almanaque de
México, 602; *Proceso,* 30 June 1980, 29;
Excélsior, 26 Dec. 1981, 16A.

Hernández (González), Amador
a-May 14, 1925. b-Ranchería de Nicolás
Bravo, Tehuacán, Puebla. c-Primary
studies in Actzingo and Ciudad Mendoza, Puebla; secondary studies in
Jalapa; preparatory studies in Jalapa.
d-Local Deputy to the State Legislature
of Puebla, 1951-54; *Federal Deputy*
from the State of Puebla, Dist. 6, 1955-
58, member of the Second Ejido Committee and the Editorial Committee;
Federal Deputy from the State of
Puebla, Dist. 6, 1961-64, member of the
First Ejido Committee and the Agriculture and Development Committee;
Federal Deputy from the State of
Puebla, Dist. 6, 1979-82. e-Coordinator
of the State Political Committee for
Miguel Alemán for President, 1946;
Secretary General of the State Commit-
tee for *Adolfo Ruiz Cortines* for Presi-
dent, 1952; Secretary General of PRI for
Puebla, 1953-55; *Secretary of Agrarian
Action of the CEN of PRI,* 1965-68.
f-None. g-Secretary of Health and
Social Security of the CEN of the CNC,
1956-59; Coordinating Secretary of the
League of Agrarian Communities of the
CNC, 1960-65; *Secretary General of the
CNC,* Aug. 28, 1965, to Sept. 21, 1967;
general delegate of the CNC to Baja
California del Norte, 1977. h-Worked
as an ejidatario in Tehuacán, Puebla.
j-None. k-Johnson suggests he resigned
as secretary general of the CNC under
pressure from President *Díaz Ordaz*
after armed clashes among CNC

members; *Excélsior* accused him of
being a cacique in Tehuacán in 1978;
split PRI into two factions in Tehuacán,
1977; removed as federal deputy from
Puebla, Dist. 6, before serving in 1967,
allegedly for threatening a policeman
with a gun while drunk. l-*Excélsior,* 11
Nov. 1978, 23; Ind. Biog., 82; Navarro
González, 267; Johnson, 35; D de Y, 29
Aug. 1965, 1; *Excélsior,* 8 Sept. 1977; C
de D, 1961-64, 80; DGF56, 27, 32.

Hernández (González), Octavio Andrés
a-Nov. 10, 1917. b-Federal District.
c-Primary studies in Mexico City;
studied at the School of Banking and
Commerce, 1939-41; accounting degree;
law degree from the National School of
Law, UNAM, 1946, with special
mention; LLD degree from the National
School of Law, UNAM, 1950-52;
academic posts, 1938. d-*Federal Deputy*
from the Federal District, Dist. 4, 1967-
70, member of the Gran Comisión,
President of the Legislative Studies
Committee. e-Member of PRI and the
PRI sponsored National Conference on
Political and Ideological Analysis of the
Revolution. f-Notary Public No. 10,
Mexico City; Private Secretary to the
Secretary of Industry and Commerce,
Gustavo P. Serrano, 1944-46; Private
Secretary to the Secretary of Industry
and Commerce, *Antonio Ruiz Galindo,*
1946-48; legal adviser to the Secretary of
Industry and Commerce, 1948-52; Head
of the Department of Social Security,
Secretariat of Industry and Commerce,
1952-58; Head of the Department of
Minimum Salaries, Department of the
Federal District; legal adviser to the
Head of the Federal District, *Corona del
Rosal;* attorney for the Mexican Insti-
tute of Social Security; legal adviser to
the Oficial Mayor of the Secretariat of
Public Works, 1966-67; Legal Manager
of the National Bank of Public Works,
1966-67; *Secretary General of the Department of the Federal District,* 1970-

76, 1976-79; Director General of the
Public Works Bank, 1979-82. g-President of the Student University Federation at the National University which
opposed *Chico Goerne* as rector, 1938.
h-Practicing lawyer; lawyer for
CONCAMIN. i-Second nephew of
Francisco Madero; father, Lorenzo L.
Hernández, was the former treasurer
general of Mexico, 1923-31, 1932-33,
head of the Department of the Federal
District, Oct. 31, 1931, to Jan. 20, 1932,
and founder and first gerente of Nacional Financiera, 1934; student of *Alfonso
Noriega* at the National University;
author of many works on international
law and economic and banking problems in Mexico; received second place
in a contest for private accountants
among over six thousand competitors,
1943. j-None. k-None. l-DGF51, I,
265, II, 56; DPE65, 117; DGF56, 285;
MGF69, 517, 90; HA, 1 Nov. 1946, 6, 22
Nov. 1971, 23; DBM70, 306; DBM68,
40-41; DBM68, 339-40; WWM45, 56;
DPE61, 18; letters; C de D, 1967-69;
Enc. Mex., 1977, VI, 404.

Hernández Haddad, Humberto
a-July 19, 1951. b-Villahermosa,
Tabasco. c-Early education unknown;
law degree, National School of Law,
UNAM, July 10, 1972, with a thesis on
"Constitutional Analysis of the Reform"; courses, Center for International
Affairs, Harvard University, 1977-82;
MA degree in International Economics,
Johns Hopkins, 1981-82; Professor of
Constitutional Law, National School of
Political Studies, Acatlán Campus,
UNAM, 1976; professor, School of
Business, University of Texas, San
Antonio, 1989-94. d-*Federal Deputy*
from the State of Tabasco, Dist. 2, 1973-
76, Dist. 9, 1979-82, President of the
Science and Technology Committee;
Senator from the State of Tabasco,
1982-88, President of the Foreign
Relations Committee. e-Secretary of

Cultural Action of the PRI National
Youth, 1967; Political Delegate of the
PRI National Youth to Yucatán, 1972-
73; General Delegate of the CEN of PRI
to Guerrero, 1974, Quintana Roo, 1976;
General Coordinator of the IEPES of the
CEN of PRI, *Miguel de la Madrid*
presidential campaign, 1981-82; *Secretary of International Affairs of the CEN
of PRI*, 1983-87. f-Lawyer, Personnel
Department, PEMEX, 1971-73; Consul
General, San Antonio, Texas, 1989-94.
g-Member of student group, *Andrés
Iduarte*, Columbia University, New
York, 1965; President of the Federation
of Tabasco Students in the Federal
District, 1968; Delegate of the CNOP to
Nuevo León and Campeche, 1978;
National Coordinator of CNOP, 1978.
h-None. i-Son of Antonio Hernández
Caro, businessman, and Tirsa Haddad
Gallegos; came to the attention of
president *Gustavo Díaz Ordaz*, during a
speech in which Haddad condemned the
U.S. occupation of the Dominican
Republic, 1965. j-None. k-None. l-C
de D, 1973-76, 21; DBGM87, 492;
letters; HA, 5 Aug. 1974, 46-47; C de D,
1979-82, 2; HA, 1 Mar. 1982, 13.

Hernández Hernández, Manuel
a-Oct. 18, 1909. b-San Miguel Tixac,
Oaxaca. c-Primary studies in Tlaxiaco,
Oaxaca; preparatory studies in Oaxaca,
Oaxaca; medical degree, National
School of Medicine, UNAM; Professor
of Philological Studies, National Preparatory School No. 2 and 5. d-*Alternate Federal Deputy* from the State of
Oaxaca, Dist. 7, 1955-58; *Federal
Deputy* from the State of Oaxaca, Dist.
7, 1958-61, member of the Library and
the Military Health Committees;
Federal Deputy from the State of
Oaxaca, Dist. 7, 1967-70, member of the
Indigenous Affairs Committee. e-None.
f-Employee, Secretariat of Public Health
in Coahuila, Hidalgo, Michoacán, and
Mexico; Chief of Surgical Clinic,

National School of Medicine, UNAM.
g-Founder and President of the Coalition of the Mixtec Oaxacan People,
1951-70. i-Married Clemencia Palacios.
j-None. k-None. l-Func., 310; C de D,
1958-61, 81, C de D, 1967-70, 59.

Hernández (Jiménez), Antonio J.
a-Jan. 6, 1904. b-San Jerónimo Tequi-
napa, Municipio of Cholula, Puebla.
c-Primary and secondary studies in the
Madero Institute, Puebla; no degree.
d-Member of the City Council of
Atlixco, Puebla; *Federal Deputy* from
the State of Puebla, Dist. 3, 1943-46;
Dist. 4, 1955-58, member of the First
Balloting Committee; 1961-64, member
of the Mail and Telegraph Committee,
1967-70, member of the Textile Industry Committee, Dist. 3, 1976-79.
e-*Subsecretary of Labor of the CEN of
PRI*, 1978. f-Employee of the Board of
Material and Moral Improvements,
Atlixco, Puebla. g-Delegate of the
Central Committee of CROM to the
states of Puebla and Tlaxcala; member
of the Union of Revolutionary Workers
of Omtepec; Secretary General of the
Federation of Workers and Farmers of
Puebla (later CTM), 1935-82; Secretary
General of CROM, 1983. h-Worked as a
youngster in the Covadonga Thread
Factory; employee of the Metepex
Textile Factory. i-Father was an
employee in the Hercules Textile
Factory, Querétaro. j-None. k-Antonio
Hernández has repeated as a federal
deputy more times since 1943 than
almost any other Mexican public figure.
l-DGF56, 27, 33, 74; C de D, 1967-70,
76; *Excélsior*, 20 Aug. 1976, 1C; Ind.
Biog., 83; C de D, 1961-64, 80.

Hernández Juárez, Francisco
a-Oct. 16, 1925. b-Tlacochahuaya,
Oaxaca. c-Primary studies at the Felipe
Carrillo Puerto School, Tlacochahuaya;
secondary studies at the Rural Normal
School, Comitancillo, Oaxaca, 1944-45,

and at the Rural Normal School El
Mexe, Hidalgo, 1946; teaching certificate, National Teachers School, 1947-
49; preparatory studies at the National
Preparatory School, 1950-51; studied
law, National School of Law, UNAM,
1952-57; primary school teacher,
Federal District, 1950-58; secondary
teacher at the Isthmus of Tehuantepec
Secondary and Preparatory School,
1962-87; Professor at the Regional
Technological Institute of the Isthmus
of Tehuantepec, Oaxaca (2 years).
d-*Federal Deputy* from the State of
Oaxaca, Dist. 1, 1970-73, member of the
Waters and Irrigation Committee, the
Second Public Education Committee,
the Second Justice Committee, and the
Legislative Studies Committee, Ninth
Section on General Affairs; *Federal
Deputy* from the State of Oaxaca, Dist.
1, 1976-79, member of the Section on
Commercialization and Industrialization of the Agrarian Affairs Committee
and member of the Higher Education
Section of the Educational Development Committee; *Plurinominal Federal
Deputy* from the PPS, 1985-88, 1991-94.
e-Joined PPS, 1948; Secretary General of
the PPS in Oaxaca, 1964-78; member of
the National Central Executive Committee of PPS, 1968-94; Secretary of
International Relations of the CEN of
the PPS, 1968-85; Secretary of Organization of the CEN of the PPS, 1985-87.
f-None. g-Director of the National
Teachers School Student Association;
Secretary of National Relations, SNTE,
1985-86; Secretary of International
Relations, SNTE, 1986-87; organized
the Union of Construction Workers of
Juchitán, Oaxaca. h-Practicing attorney. i-Married María Guadalupe Silva
Arteaga, surgeon; son of Ricardo
Hernández Pérez, peasant, and
Raymunda Juárez Martínez. j-None.
k-Candidate of the PPS for governor of
Oaxaca, 1980. l-C de D, 1970-72, 119;
Directorio, 1970-72; D de C, 1976-79, 7,

21; HA, 5 Mar. 1979, V; *Excélsior*, 28 July 1980, 23A; DBGM87, 492; DBGM92, 480.

Hernández Labastida, Miguel
a-Sept. 5, 1935. b-Veracruz, Veracruz. c-Primary studies at the Republic of Guatemala Primary School, Coyoacán, Federal District; secondary studies at the Columbus (N. Mex.) Grammar School, and Deming (N. Mex.) High School; Certified Public Accountant, with a degree from the Public Accountants School, 1954-58, with a thesis on "The Social Functions of Public Accounting"; taught courses in accounting. d-*Alternate Federal Deputy* from the Federal District, Dist. 22, 1967-70; *Federal Deputy* from the Federal District, Dist. 22, 1970-73, member of the Auto Transportation Committee and the Livestock Committee; Dist. 12, 1976-79, member of the Foreign Relations Committee and the Insurance and Finance Section of the Treasury Committee; *Plurinominal Federal Deputy* from PAN, 1988-91. e-Member of the National Organizing Commission of PAN, 1973-91; member of the Regional Committee for the Federal District of PAN, 1972-91; Director of PAN for the 12th District, Federal District, 1963-70; joined PAN, 1954; Secretary of Organization of PAN in the Federal District, 1970-76; President of PAN in the Federal District, 1981-87. f-None. g-President of the Mexican Youth Catholic Action (ACJM), 1957-59; President of the Union of Mexican Catholics, 1957-60; President of Catholic Action, 1960-63. h-Public accountant; controller, Litolámina, 1955-59; manager, Química Hércules, 1960-79. i-Married Ana María Meixueiro; son of Manuel Hernández Esqueda and Margarita Labastida Arteche. j-None. k-Candidate for federal deputy, 1967. l-C de

D, 1970-72, 119; Directorio, 1970-72; C de D, 1976-79, 33; D de C, 1976-79, 71, 59, 57; DBGM89, 460

Hernández Loza, Heliodoro
(Deceased May 30, 1990) a-July 3, 1898. b-Tepatitlán, La Barca, Jalisco. c-Primary studies completed in La Barca, Jalisco; no degree. d-Local Deputy to the State Legislature of Jalisco, 1934-35, 1939-41, 1950-52, 1969-71, 1975-77; Mayor of Guadalajara, 1948-49; *Federal Deputy* from the State of Jalisco, Dist. 3, 1943-46; Dist. 2, 1964-67, member of the First Railroads Committee, the First Labor Committee, and the First Public Housing Committee; *Senator* from the State of Jalisco, 1982-88. e-Joined PNR, 1929; President of the PNR, Guadalajara, Jalisco, 1935; general delegate of the CEN of PRI to Michoacán, 1965. f-Subdirector of the Department of Transportation, Guadalajara, 1928. g-Founder, Only Union of Mechanics of Jalisco, 1920; founder, Transportation Federation of Jalisco, 1932; Secretary of Organization of the CTM, 1954-56; Assistant Secretary General of the CTM, 1961-66; Secretary of Statistics of the CTM, 1967-72; Assistant Secretary of the CEN of the CTM, 1973-77. h-Mechanic; chauffeur. i-Married to *María Guadalupe Martínez Hernández*, federal deputy from Jalisco, 1958-61 and 1970-73. j-None. k-Critics call him the "Fidel Velázquez of Jalisco" and accuse him of amassing a fortune as a union leader. l-C de D, 1964-67, 50, 84, 95, 96, 1943-46, 12; HA, 19 Apr. 1982, VI; PS, 2927; Basurto; Lehr, 224; *Excélsior*, 3 Jan 1983, 18; DBGM87, 493; DBGM, 521.

Hernández Mendoza, Leónardo M.
(Deceased Aug. 30, 1966) a-Nov. 6, 1888. b-Atotonilco el Grande, Hidalgo. c-Primary studies in Atotonilco el Grande; no degree. d-Local Deputy to the State Legislature of Hidalgo, 1922-

24; Federal Deputy from the State of Hidalgo, Dist. 3, 1924-26; *Federal Deputy* from the State of Hidalgo, Dist. 2, 1940-43, member of the Gran Comisión, the Inspection Committee of the General Accounting Office, and the Social Welfare Committee; *Senator* from the State of Hidalgo, 1958-64; Executive Secretary of the Colonization Committee, member of the First Committee on National Defense and the Second Committee on Mines, and substitute member of the Committee on Taxes. e-None. f-Chief of Social Defense, Atotonilco el Grande, 1923; Director of Public Welfare for the State of Puebla, 1927-28. g-None. h-Involved in cattle ranching and agriculture. i-Son of Mateo Hernández. j-Joined the Revolution as a noncommissioned officer, served under Gabriel Hernández; supported Venustiano Carranza, 1913; career army officer; commander of military zones in Coahuila, Sonora, Hidalgo, and Jalisco; rank of Division General. k-None. l-EBW46, 56; C de D, 1940-42, 54, 58; letter; C de S, 1961-64, 57; Func., 228; Pérez López, 200.

Hernández Netro, Mateo
(Deceased 1946) a-1890. b-San Luis Potosí. c-Early education unknown; no degree. d-*Governor of San Luis Potosí*, 1935-38. e-None. f-None. g-None. h-Involved in ranching after 1938. i-Longtime friend and supporter of *Saturnino Cedillo*. j-Joined the Revolution in 1910; fought with *Saturnino Cedillo*, 1913; fought against Victoriano Huerta, 1914; fought under Zapata; career army officer; supported Plan of Agua Prieta, 1920; supported the de la Huerta rebellion, 1923; fought against the Escobar rebellion, 1929; rank of Colonel in the army. k-Abandoned the governorship of San Luis Potosí, May 22, 1938, to support the *Cedillo* rebellion against the government; received amnesty from President *Cárdenas* after

General *Cedillo's* death, 1938. l-Peral, 47, 163; DP70, 982; D de Y, May 22, 1938, 1; Peral, 382; Meyer, 319.

Hernández Ochoa, Rafael
(Deceased May 18, 1990) a-June 4, 1915. b-Municipio Vega de la Torre, Ranchería Santa Gertrudis, Veracruz. c-Primary studies in the Enrique C. Rebsamen Public School, Jalapa, Veracruz; secondary and preparatory studies in Jalapa; law degree from the National School of Law, UNAM, 1944, thesis on state intervention; attended the University of Veracruz. d-*Federal Deputy* from the State of Veracruz, Dist. 5, 1973-74; *Governor of Veracruz*, 1974-80. e-Joined PRI, 1959. f-Municipal Judge, Veracruz; Agent of the Ministerio Público of the Office of the Attorney General; Subdirector, Legal Department, Electric Industry of Mexico, 1948-52; Chief of Labor Relations, Electric Industry of Mexico, 1953; Director of the Legal Department of the State of Veracruz; Subdirector General of Administration, Secretariat of Government, 1962; Subdirector of Population, Secretariat of Government, 1958-61; Auxiliary Secretary to *Luis Echeverría*, 1958; Director of Political and Social Investigations, Secretariat of Government, 1964; *Subsecretary of Government*, 1964-70; *Secretary of Labor*, 1970-72; *Subsecretary of Forestry*, Secretariat of Agriculture and Hydraulic Resources, 1989-90; adviser to *Carlos Hank González*, 1990. g-President of the National Livestock Federation. h-Practiced law, 1944-77; member of the National Council of Tourism. i-Student of *Alfonso Noriega* at UNAM; married Teresa Peñafiel; son of Fernando Hernández Carrasco, cattle rancher, and Elvira Ochoa Hernández, teacher. j-None. k-Resigned from the post of secretary of labor, Sept. 11, 1972, after two operations; his popularity among PRI members in Veracruz as a

candidate for federal deputy in 1973 surprised many PRI officials; precandidate for PRI Majority Leader of the Chamber of Deputies, 1973. l-D de Y, 1 Dec. 1970, 2; DPE61, 13; DPE65, 13; *Hoy*, 21 Dec. 1964; HA, 7 Dec. 1970, 3 May 1971, 12, 18 Sept. 1972, 10-11; *Excélsior*, 8 Mar. 1973, 14; HA, 7 Jan. 1973, 12; *Excélsior*, 18 Dec. 1973, 15; HA, 6 May 1974, 39-40; Enc. Mex., 1977, VI, 410; *El Nacional*, 19 May 1990, 5; DBGM89, 172.

Hernández Partida, Leopoldo
a-Aug. 26, 1908. b-Guadalajara, Jalisco. c-Primary studies in Guadalajara; preparatory studies at the National Preparatory School; law degree from the National School of Law, UNAM, 1928-32. d-*Federal Deputy* from the Federal District, Dist. 12, 1943-46; *Federal Deputy* from the State of Jalisco, Dist. 5, 1967-70, member of the Indigenous Affairs Committee and the Money and Credit Institutions Committee; *Federal Deputy* from the State of Jalisco, Dist. 5, 1982-85. e-Director of *Revolución*, publication of the PNR, 1930; joined the PNR, 1932; *Secretary of Popular Action of the CEN of the PRM*, 1938-40; *Secretary of Agrarian Action of the CEN of PRI*, 1964; Interim President of PRI for the Federal District; general delegate of the CEN of PRI to Jalisco, 1965-66; general delegate of the CEN of PRI to Quintana Roo, 1970. f-Secretary of the 1st Judicial District in Administrative Matters, Federal District, 1935-36; Private Secretary to the Director of the Department of Indigenous Affairs, 1936-37; Attorney General of the State of Hidalgo under Governor *Javier Rojo Gómez*, 1937-38; Private Secretary to *Javier Rojo Gómez*, Head of the Federal District Department, 1940-45; Administrator of the regional office of the IMSS, Jalisco, 1953-59; Director General of Central Agricultural Bank, 1974-76; Private Secretary to the Director of the Department of Indigenous Affairs, First Administrative District, Federal District, 1982. g-Student supporter of General Alvaro Obregón for president, 1928; founding member of the Federation of Workers and Peasants of Hidalgo, 1930; joined the Mexican Peasant Federation, 1933; founding member of the CNC, 1938; Private Secretary to Graciano Sánchez, Secretary General of the CNC, 1938-40; Member of the CEN of the CNC, 1961-63; Private Secretary to *Javier Rojo Gómez*, Secretary General of the CNC, 1962-63. h-Campaigned for General Obregón with *Luis I. Rodríguez* and *Alfonso Pulido Islas*. i-Son of Alberto Hernández Martínez, public accountant and auditor for the secretary of the treasury, and Guadalupe Partida Rivera; related to *Wenceslao Partida Hernández*, federal deputy from Jalisco, 1943-46; married Amparo González Navarro. j-None. k-None. l-Letter, C de D, 1967-70, 59, 81, 1943-46; MGF69, 92; Lehr, 230; DBGM, 522.

Hernández Pinzón, Carolina
a-Feb. 19, 1949. b-Veracruz, Veracruz. c- Primary studies at the Benito Juárez and Federico Frobel Schools, Veracruz, 1956-61, best student in her class; studies in public speaking at public schools, 1961-63; secretarial studies, 1962-64, and preparatory studies in humanities, 1965-66, both at Ilustre Institute of Veracruz; studies in law, School of Law, University of Veracruz, Jalapa, 1967-71; law degree, Feb. 11, 1972; language studies in French, Italian, and English, School of Languages and Philosophy & Letters, University of Veracruz, 1968-69; Professor of Roman Law, University of Veracruz, Jalapa, 1972; Professor of Hispanic American Literature, Preparatory School of Veracruz, 1973; Professor of Legal Sociology, University of Veracruz, 1975. d-Second Syndic of the City Council of Veracruz, Veracruz,

1973-74; Local Deputy from Dist. 12 to the State Legisature of Veracruz, 1974-77; *Federal Deputy* from the State of Veracruz, Dist. 21, 1979-82. e-Delegate of the Local Committee of PRI of Jalapa to Youth Sector of CNOP, 1965; Secretary of Women's Action of the Youth Sector of PRI, State of Veracruz, 1969-71; Secretary of Civic Action of the State Committee of PRI, Veracruz, 1975; President of the State Committee of PRI, Veracruz, 1975-77; delegate of the CEN of PRI to various state and local elections. f-Social worker, Second Judicial District, Court of First Instance, Jalapa, Veracruz, 1970-71. g-Secretary General of the ANFER for the State of Veracruz. h-None. i-Daughter of lawyer Fulgencio Hernández V. and Margarita Pinzón. j-None. k-Assistant Champion, National Children's Public Speaking Contest, 1962. l-C de D, 1979-82, 38; Romero Aceves, 704-05.

Hernández Posadas, Mario
a-Oct. 9, 1929. b-Jalapa, Veracruz. c-Completed secondary school; agronomy degree, Escobar Brothers Higher School of Agriculture, Ciudad Juárez, Chihuahua, 1944-50. d-*Federal Deputy* from the State of Veracruz, Dist. 6, 1964-67, Coordinator of the CNC delegation; *Federal Deputy* from the State of Veracruz, Dist. 12, 1976-79; *Senator* from the state of Veracruz, 1982-88, President of the Agricultural Development Committee. e-Joined PRI, 1955; Special Delegate of the CEN of PRI to various states; Subsecretary of Agrarian Action of the CEN of PRI, 1965-68. f-Assistant Manager, National Ejido Credit Bank, Veracruz; Director, Department of Publicity, Conasupo; regional agronomist, Department of Agriculture, State of Veracruz; Coordinator of the Southern Region of Veracruz, Department of Agrarian Affairs and Colonization; Supervisor of Delegations of the Agrarian Advisory Group,

Secretariat of Agrarian Reform. g-Secretary of the Agrarian Communities of Veracruz, 1964-67; Secretary of Agrarian Action of the CNC, 1965-68; *Secretary General of the CNC*, 1983-86. h-None. i-Son of Pablo Hernández Hernández, topographical engineer, and Dina Posadas Salas; married Lina Sara Córdoba Ladrón de Guevara, normal teacher. j-None. k-None. l-DBGM87, 493; Lehr, 491; C de D, 1976-79, 1964-67; C de S, 1982-88.

Hernández Rivera, Onofre
a-Jan. 19, 1943. b-Zacualtipán, Hidalgo. c-Early education unknown; completed secondary studies; normal teaching certificate, National Normal School, 1959-61; teaching degree, Pedagogical University, 1979-82; primary school teacher and principal, 1962; Professor of Physical Education, Sports Federation, 1964-66. d-*Alternate Federal Deputy* from the Federal District, Dist. 14, 1970-73; *Federal Deputy* from the Federal District, Dist. 14, 1973-76; *Federal Deputy* from the State of Hidalgo, Dist. 4, 1982-85. e-President of PRI, District 14, Federal District; Special Delegate of the CEN of PRI to San Luis Potosí, 1976; Special Delegate of the CEN of PRI to Chihuahua, 1979; *Secretary of Social Action of the CEN of PRI*, 1977-79. f-None. g-Student leader at the National Teachers' School; Secretary of Press, Local 9, SNTE; Secretary of Organization, Local 9, SNTE; member of the CEN of the SNTE, 1979-82; Secretary of Acts of the CEN of the SNTE; Secretary of Organization of the CEN of the SNTE. h-None. i-Son of Salvador Hernández Arteaga, businessman, and Dolores Rivera García; married Rosa Portillo Ortiz, normal teacher. j-None. k-None. l-Perez López, 524; HA, 19 Apr. 1982, VIII; C de D, 1973-76, 7; Directorio, 1982-85; Lehr, 216; Directorio, 1970-73; DBGM89, 461.

Hernández Rojas, Jesús
a-June 25, 1914. b-Hacienda de Estafia-
yuca, Tlaxcala. c-No formal education.
d-Mayor of Mariano Arista, Tlaxcala,
1953; Local Deputy to the State Legislature of Tlaxcala, 1967-70; *Senator* from
the State of Tlaxcala, 1976-82. e-None.
f-President of the Vigilance Committee,
Mariano Arista, Tlaxcala, 1943-47;
representative from Mariano Arista to
the Federal Board of Potable Water,
1956-61; delegate, Agricultural Credit
Bank, 1959. g-President, National
Chamber of Pulque Industries, 1965-66;
Treasurer, National Chamber of Pulque
Industries, 1967; Secretary General of
the League of Agrarian Communities of
Tlaxcala, 1971-82. j-None. k-None.
l-C de S, 1976-82; Protag., 167.

Hernández Téllez, Sabino
a-Oct. 29, 1940. b-León, Guanajuato.
c-Early education unknown; teaching
certificate, Tepic Normal School, 1959;
degree in history, Higher Normal
School of Nayarit, 1964; history teacher,
middle school, 1959-82; Professor of
History and Philosophy, Normal
School; Professor of History and
Philosophy, Higher Normal School,
1965- . d-Local Deputy to the State
Legislature of Nayarit, 1975; *Plurino-*
minal Deputy of the People's Party of
Mexico, 1979-82, member of the
Fishing, Editorial Affairs, Federal
Transportation, and Distribution of
Consumer Goods Committees. e-Joined
the PPS, 1963; member of the Central
Committee of the PPS, 1968-76;
Secretary General of the PPS in Nayarit,
1972-75; member of the Committee in
the Defense of the Party, 1976; founder
and member of the Central Committee
of the PPM, 1977; Coordinator of the
Secretariat of the Central Committee of
the PPM, 1980. f-Syndic, City of Tepic,
1973-75. g-Member, 1st State Committee of the Federation of Students of
Nayarit, 1952-54; Secretary General of

the Normal Student Society, 1959;
delegate to the 15th Student Congress,
Moscow, 1966. h-Wrote for *Vida*
Nueva, Nayarit, 1975-77. j-None.
k-Resigned from post as Local Deputy
to protest against fraud, 1975. l-C de D,
1979-82; Protag., 167.

Hernández Terán, José Mann
a-Dec. 15, 1921. b-Mérida, Yucatán.
c-Primary studies in Saltillo, Coahuila;
Mexico City; and Mérida, Yucatán;
secondary studies at the Evening
Extension School, UNAM, Mexico City;
engineering degree, National School of
Engineering, UNAM, 1946. d-None.
e-None. f-Secretary of Public Works for
the Chihuahua-Pacific Railroad, 1960;
joined the National Irrigation Commission, 1944; Project Chief for the Office
of Structural Engineering, Secretariat of
Hydraulic Resources; manager of the
Río Yaqui, Naucalpán-Zaragoza-
Tlalnepantla projects; Director of
Construction for the Río Yaqui;
technical adviser to the Federal Electric
Commission for the 27th of Sept.
Hydroelectric Plant, 1958-60; Director
of Construction, Río Yaqui; Executive
Secretary of the Río Fuerte Commission, Secretariat of Hydraulic Re-
sources; Director of the Río Fuerte
Commission, 1955-64; *Secretary of*
Hydraulic Resources, 1964-70.
g-President of the Executive Council of
the College of Mexican Civil Engineers.
h-Arbitrator for the El Aguila Construc-
tion Company with the Government of
El Salvador; engineering consultant,
1971. i-Student of *Javier Barros Sierra*
and *Agustín Yáñez* at the National
Preparatory School; student of *Antonio*
Dovalí Jaime at UNAM; knew *Leandro*
Rovirosa Wade, Manuel Franco López,
Gilberto Valenzuela, and *Luis Enrique*
Bracamontes at UNAM. j-None.
k-None. l-Letter; WWMG, 21; D de Y, 2
Dec. 1964, 2; IWW70-71, 423; *El*
Universal, 2 Dec. 1964; *Libro de Oro*,

1967, xxxiv; DPE65, 126; *Excélsior*, 21 Aug. 1973, 1.

Hernández Torres, José de Jesús
a-June 4, 1944. b-Federal District. c-Early education unknown; business administration degree, School of Business and Administration, UNAM; MA in economics, IPN, 1971-73. d-None. e-Adviser, Secretary General of the CEN of PRI, 1981. f-Director General of Government, Secretariat of Government, 1971; Assistant Director, Acapulco Trust, 1976; Director General of Radio, Television, and Film, Secretariat of Government, 1982-88; *Oficial Mayor of Public Education*, Secretariat of Public Education, 1988-92. g-None. h-Vice-President, Consorcio Aristos, 1970-75; Director General and President, Viva Turística Corporation, 1976-79; Director General, Factible Company, 1979-80. i-Son of Daniel Hernández Méndez, businessman, and María del Refugio Torres López; married Milagros Montero Zubillaga, psychotherapist. j-None. k-None. l-DBGM89, 174.

Hernández Vela, Salvador
a-Dec. 31, 1908. b-Zaragoza, Coahuila. c-Primary studies at the Juan Antonio de la Fuente School, Zaragoza, Coahuila; secondary studies at the Ateneo Fuente, Saltillo, Coahuila; studied at Harvard Medical School, Walter Reed Hospital, and Brook Medical Center; medical degree; graduated from the Staff School of the Higher War College, 1933-36; professor at the Military Medical School; Head of the Teaching Council at the Military Medical School. d-*Alternate Senator* from Coahuila, 1958-64; *Federal Deputy* from the State of Coahuila, Dist. 4, 1970-73, member of the First Committee on National Defense and the Committee on Military Health. e-None. f-Subdirector General of Military Health, Secretariat of National Defense; member of the

Directive Council of the Chief of Staff, Secretariat of National Defense. g-None. h-Founded the *Magazine of Military Health*; author of numerous books and articles. j-Career army medical officer; rank of Brigadier General, Nov. 27, 1953; rank of Brigade General, 1960; member of the Legion of Honor. k-None. l-C de D, 1970-72, 12, 120; C de S, 1961-64; DBM68, 343; Directorio, 1970-72; Rev. de Ejer., Oct. 1960. 16.

Hernández y Hernández, Francisco
a-1908. b-Calpulalpan, Tlaxcala. c-Teaching certificate; school teacher. d-*Federal Deputy* from the State of Tlaxcala, Dist. 2, 1949-52, member of the Indigenous Affairs Committee, the First Public Education Committee, the Legislative Studies Committee, and the Second Balloting Committee; President of the Second Instructive Section of the Grand Jury and President of the Chamber of Deputies, Dec. 1949; *Senator* from the State of Tlaxcala, 1958-64, member of the Gran Comisión, the Indigenous Affairs Committee, the National Lands Committee, and substitute member of the Agrarian Department Committee. e-None. f-Director of the *Diario Oficial*; Director of the Congressional Library; Director General of the National Ejido Credit Bank, 1964. g-*Secretary General of the CNC*, 1959-62. h-Author of articles on peasants. i-Supported for the position of secretary general of the CNC by *Roberto Barrios*, *Raymundo Flores Fuentes*, and *Gabriel Leyva Velázquez*; father of *Tulio Hernández Gómez*, oficial mayor of the Secretariat of Government, 1979. j-None. k-Critical of local agrarian leaders who had held their positions for more than twenty years; changed 445 of the 480 regional committees of the CNC; precandidate for senator from Tlaxcala, 1981. l-*Excélsior*, 27 Aug. 1959; C de D, 1949-51, 75; C de S. 1961-

64, 57; Func., 380; González Navarro, 266; Ronfeldt, 193; *Excélsior*, 26 Dec. 1981, 16A.

Herrera, Enrique
a-Oct. 2, 1938. b-Federal District. c-Degree in political science from the National School of Political and Social Sciences, UNAM, 1963; postgraduate studies abroad in mass communications; Professor of the Sociology and Philosophy of Law, National School of Law, UNAM; Professor of Economic and Social Analysis, Ibero-American University, Mexico City; Professor of Economic Analysis, National Polytechnic Institute. d-None. e-None. f-President of the National Broadcasting Commission, 1969-70; Subdirector of Information, Secretariat of Government, 1967-70; *Subsecretary of Broadcasting*, Secretariat of Communications and Transportation, 1970-71. g-None. h-Founder and Director of the Mexican News and Information Agency (NOTIMEX), 1968-70. j-None. k-Resigned because of ties to *Alfonso Martínez Domínguez*. l-HA, 14 Dec. 1970, 22; DPE71.

Herrera, María Guadalupe Calderón de
a-Feb. 14, 1938. b-Morelia, Michoacán. c-Primary studies in a public school and the Plancarte Institute; preparatory studies from the Colegio San Nicolás de Hidalgo; law degree from the School of Law and Social Science, University of Michoacán; criminology course from the Office of the Attorney General of the Federal District; Professor of Economic Policy at the School of Industrial Engineering, University of Michoacán. d-*Federal Deputy* from the State of Michoacán, Dist. 1, 1967-70, member of the Inspection Committee of the General Accounting Office, the Social Action Committee (1st year), the Public Welfare Committee, the Editorial Committee (2nd year), the Legisla-

tive Studies Committee (Third Section on Penal Affairs), and the Subsistence and Supplies Committee. e-Director of the Women's Sector of PRI for Michoacán, 1963-70. f-Official of the Attorney General's Office; agent of the Ministerio Público of the Attorney General in the State of Michoacán, 1961-63; laboratory expert in criminal cases for the Attorney General of Michoacán; Director of the Social Security Center for Family Welfare, Institute of Social Security, 1966-67. g-None. h-Pianist for a nursery school; social worker for the Mexican Institute of Social Security, 1964-66. i-Father, a bank employee. j-None. k-None. l-DBM68, 344; C de D, 1967-69, 55, 57, 63, 66, 78, 88; MGF69; PS, 0854; letter.

Herrera Beltrán, Fidel
a-Mar. 7, 1949. b-Nopaltepec, Cosamaloapán, Veracruz. c-Primary studies in the Francisco I. Madero School, Tuxtepec, Oaxaca; secondary at public secondary school, Ciudad Alemán, Veracruz; preparatory at Preparatory School Article 3, Jalapa; three years of legal studies at the School of Law, University of Veracruz, 1967-69; completed degree at UNAM, Feb. 23, 1971, with a thesis on the theory and reality of the division of powers in the Mexican political-juridical structure; MA in political science and public administration, London School of Economics and Political Science, 1971-73; diploma in languages and French literature, French Alliance; diploma, Polytechic Institute, London; diploma, International Institute of Human Rights, Strasbourg. d-*Federal Deputy* from the State of Veracruz, Dist. 12, 1973-76, Dist, 16, 1979-82, Dist. 12, 1991-94. e-Auxiliary Secretary and Orator, *Rafael Murillo Vidal* campaign for governor, 1968; Youth Director of PRI, Veracruz; orator, *Luis Echeverría* campaign, 1970; Secretary General of

the National Revolutionary Youth Movement of PRI, 1973; Coordinator, *Rafael Hernández Ochoa* gubernatorial campaign, 1974; *Secretary of Organization of the CEN of PRI*, 1974-75; general delegate of the CEN of PRI to Colima, 1976; general delegate of the CEN of PRI to Chihuahua, Coahuila, and Durango; Secretary General of the PRI in the Federal District, 1977; President of PRI in the Federal District, 1977-79; Subsecretary General of the CEN of PRI, 1979; General Coordinator of Planning, IEPES of PRI, 1982. f-Auxiliary Secretary to Governor *Rafael Murillo Vidal*, 1968-73; President of the Board of Material and Moral Improvement, Veracruz; Technical Secretary of the General Coordinator of Student Social Services, Higher Education Institutions, Secretariat of Programming and Budget, 1982; Oficial Mayor of the Gran Comisión, Chamber of Deputies, 1985-88; *Oficial Mayor of the Secretariat of Ecology and Urban Development*, 1988. g-Director of Youth Action of the Executive Committee of CNOP, Veracruz; Coordinator, Federation of Students of Veracruz; President of the Student Society of Preparatory School Article 3, Jalapa; President of the Student Society of Secondary School, Ciudad Alemán. h-None. i-Son-in-law of *Teófilo Borunda*; son of Fidel Herrera Osorio, businessman, and María Beltrán Vallecillo; married Rosa Margarita Borunda Quevedo. j-None. k-None. l-IEPES; Q es QAP, 150; C de D, 1973-76, 1979-82; DBGM, 213; DBGM92, 488.

Herrera Gómez Tagle, Gildardo
a-Feb. 21, 1935. b-Tenango del Valle (San Francisco Tepexoxuca), México. c-Early education unknown; legal studies, Autonomous University of the State of México, 1953-56, no degree. d-*Alternate Federal Deputy* from the State of México, Dist. 3, 1964-67; Local Deputy to the State Legislature of

México, 1969-72; *Federal Deputy* from the State of México, Dist. 1, 1976-79, Dist. 15, 1982-85. e-Joined PRI, 1963. f-None. g-President of the National Society of Aguamiel Producers; Secretary of Rural Housing and Community Development of the CEN of the CNC, 1980-82; Secretary General of the League of Agrarian Communities and Peasant Unions, State of México, 1980. h-Lawyer. i-Son of Delfino Herrera Nava, farmer, and Catalina Gómez Tagle Franco; married María de la Luz. j-None. k-None. l-Directorio, 1982-85; C de D, 1976-79, 1982-85.

Herrera y Lasso, Manuel
(Deceased) a-June 13, 1890. b-San Luis Potosí, San Luis Potosí. c-Primary studies in San Luis Potosí; began his secondary studies in 1900 at the Conciliar Seminary, San Luis Potosí; preparatory studies completed at the Scientific and Literary Institute of San Luis Potosí; studies in law at the National School of Law, UNAM; studies in law completed at the Escuela Libre de Derecho, Mexico City, July 24, 1912 to Mar. 17, 1914, law degree from the Escuela Libre de Derecho, June 29, 1915, with a thesis on the Constitution; Professor of Spanish, National Preparatory School, 1914; Professor of Sociology, 1914-22, Professor of Constitutional Law, 1930-52, and Professor Emeritus, 1966, all at the Escuela Libre de Derecho. d-None. e-Cofounder of PAN, 1939. f-Private Secretary to Eduardo Tamaríz, Secretary of Agriculture, 1914; consulting lawyer to the City Government of Mexico City, 1919; adviser to the President of Mexico, 1947-64; adviser to the Chamber of Deputies, 1964-67. g-Student cofounder of the Escuela Libre de Derecho, 1912. h-Practicing lawyer with Agustín Rodríguez, 1914-19. i-Son of engineer Manuel Herrera y Raso and Guadalupe Lasso de la Vega; married Raquel Méndez Armendáriz; student of

Emilio Rabasa; professor of *Emilio Portes Gil*. j-None. k-Recruited many future leaders of PAN from his students; candidate for federal deputy, 1917; lived in Cuba two years. l-Enc. Mex., VI, 421; Lemus, 38; ELD, 65; DBM66, 345; DP70, 988; Grimaldo, 28-32.

Herrera y Tejeda, Ignacio
(Deceased) a-Oct. 21, 1893. b-Querétaro, Querétaro. c-Preparatory studies at the Conciliar Seminary, Querétaro, 1911-12; studies in medicine, National School of Medicine, UNAM, 1912-13; studies at the University of California, Berkeley, 1919; law degree from the School of Law, Colegio Civil of Querétaro, 1928; professor at the Normal School for Women, 1921-22; professor at the Colegio Civil of Querétaro, 1929; secondary school teacher, Guanajuato, 1930; professor at the Preparatory School of Celaya, 1930; professor at the Conciliar Seminary of Querétaro, 1946-50. d-None. e-None. f-Official of the Mexican Embassy in Guatemala, 1922-23; official of the Mexican Embassy in Peru, 1924-26; Interim Governor of Veracruz; judge in the State of Querétaro and the State of Guanajuato, 1929-31; Judge of the Superior Tribunal of Justice of the Federal District and Federal Territories, 1935-40. g-None. i-Son of Doctor Ponciano Herrera y Fuentes and María Tejeda Mirón. j-Joined the Revolution as a student; fought with Emiliano Zapata, 1913-14; fought with Francisco Villa, 1914-15. l-WNM, 115-16.

Hidalgo, Ernesto
(Deceased 1955) a-Aug. 5, 1896. b-San José Iturbide, Ciudad Obregón, Guanajuato. c-Early education unknown; no degree. d-Federal Deputy from the State of Guanajuato, Dist. 5, 1926-28, Dist. 18, 1928-30, Dist. 8, 1930-32; *Governor of Guanajuato*, 1943-46. e-None. f-Press attaché in the United States for the Mexican Foreign Service, 1916; Mexican delegate to a commercial congress in Argentina, 1917; Private Secretary to Secretary of the Treasury, Luis Cabrera, 1915; *Oficial Mayor of the Secretariat of Foreign Relations*, 1936-40, 1940-42; Minister to Poland, 1946-52. g-None. h-Journalist; wrote for *El Imparcial*; Director of *El Universal Gráfico*, 1921-36; writer for *Excélsior*; author of a book criticizing federal intervention in the states. i-Part of *José Aguilar y Maya*'s political clique in Guanajuato. j-None. k-Was removed from the governorship on Jan. 8, 1946, after a riot occurred on Jan. 2, 1946, in which many people were killed; Scott claims he was removed to placate public opinion that reacted strongly against the killing of many rioters in León by troops called in by the governor; the cause of the riots was attributed to rigged elections; *Hidalgo* wrote a book defending his position. l-DP70, 992-93; Peral, 389; Scott, 138; Simpson, 337; DGF51, I, 108; NYT, 9 Jan. 1946, 10; Anderson, 85-86; Enc. Mex., 1977, VI, 426.

Highland Gómez, Mario
a-Sept. 26, 1922. b-Federal District. c-Early education unknown; CPA degree, Higher School of Business and Administration, IPN; Subdirector General of IPN. d-None. f-Chief of Auditors, Fraud Department, Treasury Division, Department of the Federal Distrct, 1947-54; Subdirector General of the Income Tax Division, Secretariat of the Treasury, 1959-60; Subdirector General of the Federal License Registry, 1967-71; Controller General of CONASUPO, 1972-73; Coordinator of Banks, National Agricultural and Ejido Credit Banks, 1974-76; Subdirector General of IMSS, 1965-66; Subdirector of the National Rural Credit Bank, 1974-76; *Oficial Mayor* of the Secretariat of Agriculture and Hydraulic

Resources, 1976-80; *Subsecretary of Planning*, Secretariat of Agriculture and Hydraulic Resources, 1980-82. g-None. h-Administrative Manager of CIMEX, S.A., 1954-58. i-Son of John Phillip Highland and Luz Gómez y Vallejo; brother, Juan, is president of many firms. j-None. k-None. l-*Excélsior*, 11 Mar. 1980, 4; WNM, 116; Protag., 169.

Hinojosa (Hinojosa), Juan José
a-Sept. 3, 1921. b-General García Treviño, Nuevo León. c-Completed primary and secondary studies; special courses in personnel, Institute of Higher Studies of Monterrey; no degree. d-*Federal Deputy* from the State of Nuevo León, Dist. 3, 1949-52, member of the Industries Committee and the Cooperative Development Committee; *Federal Deputy* (Party Deputy from PAN), 1967-70; *Federal Deputy* from the Federal District, Dist. 11, 1973-76; *Plurinominal Federal Deputy* from PAN, 1982-85. e-Joined PAN, 1940; member, Regional Committee of PAN, Nuevo León, 1940-50; Treasurer General of the CEN of PAN; Secretary of the CEN of PAN (several times), 1950-80. f-None. g-None. h-Practicing lawyer; manager, National Distributor Company, Mexico City; Sales Director, Vidriera Monterrey, S.A., 1972; editorial writer for *Excélsior*, 1973-76; editorial writer for *Proceso*, 1976-82; writer for *Expansión*, 1981-82. i-Son of José Hinojosa, peasant, and María Hinojosa; married María del Socorro L. j-None. k-One of the first members of PAN to win a seat in the Chamber of Deputies. l-C de D, 1949-52, 76, 1973-76, 7; Enc. Mex., VI, 532; Directorio, 1973; DGF51; WNM, 116; López, 511; Directorio, 1982-85; Lehr, 557.

Hinojosa Jr., Cosme R.
(Deceased Dec. 1965) a-1879. b-Tacupeto, Sonora. c-Early education unknown; no degree. d-Local Deputy to the State Legislature of Sonora, 1911-13. e-Member of the Anti-Reelectionist Party with Benjamín Hill. f-Director of Mails, Hermosillo, Sonora; Director General of the Mails, 1920-28; Director General of the ISSSTE, 1928-34; Director General of the Mails and Telegraph, 1934-35; *Head of the Department of the Federal District*, 1935-38; Consul in San Antonio, Texas, in Naco, Arizona, 1951, in Tucson, Arizona, 1956-58; President of the Patronate of the National Pawnshop. g-None. h-Traveling salesman for La Fama; involved in the private banking field, 1938. j-Joined the Revolution in 1910; fought against Carranza in 1920. k-As Secretary of the State Legislature of Sonora, led the vote to not recognize Victoriano Huerta's government, 1913. l-Q es Q, 283; DP70, 1001; DGF56, 141; Peral, 393-94; DGF51, I, 128; López, 511; Enc. Mex., 1977, VI, 532.

Hinojosa Ortiz, Manuel
a-1910. b-Parangaricutiro, Michoacán. c-Primary and secondary studies at private schools in Michoacán; preparatory studies at the Colegio San Nicolás de Hidalgo, in physics at the National Preparatory School, 1931, and in chemical engineering, 1932; studies in law, literature, and philosophy, UNAM, 1932-36; law degree, National School of Law, UNAM, with an honorable mention, 1937, and a thesis on administrative action; Professor of Civics, secondary school in the Federal District; Professor of Constitutional Law, University of Michoacán, 1951. d-*Federal Deputy* from the State of Michoacán, Dist. 6, 1952-53, member of the Legislative Studies Committee, the Budget and Accounts Committee, and the Credentials Committee; *Senator* from the State of Michoacán, 1958-64, President of the Committee on National Waters and Irrigation, member of the Second Balloting Committee, the

Special Forestry Committee, member of the Special Hydraulic Resources Committee; substitute member of the Third Committee on Labor and the Consular and Diplomatic Service Committee. e-General coordinator for the gubernatorial campaign of *Dámaso Cárdenas*, 1949-50; Director of Legal Affairs, PRI, 1948-49; lawyer for PRM, 1937. f-Lawyer for the Department of Agrarian Affairs, 1937-43; Secretary General of Government of the State of Aguascalientes, 1944-47, Secretary General of Government of the State of Michoacán under *Dámaso Cárdenas*, 1950-52; *Subsecretary of Forest Resources, Secretary of Agriculture*, 1953-58; Secretary of Colonization, Department of Agrarian Affairs, 1958; Representative of CORDEMEX in Mexico City, 1965-70; Director General of Forest Industry and Production, State of México, 1970-71. g-Secretary of Planning and Organization of the CEN of the CNC, 1961-64. h-Author of many books on agricultural problems; practicing lawyer, 1937-43, 1972-80. i-Political protégé of *Dámaso Cárdenas*; father a small businessman; practiced law with *Luis Chico Goerne*, 1935-36. j-None. k-Recognized expert on Mexican forestation problems; favored the women's suffrage proposal as a federal deputy. l-Letters; C de S, 1961-64, 57; D de Y, 12 Dec. 1964; Morton, 70-71; DGF51, I, 90; Func., 266; DGF56, 223; *Hoy*, 17 Jan. 1970, 4; C de D, 1952-54, 12.

Hiriart Balderrama, Fernando
a-Oct. 21, 1914. b-Santa Barbara, Chihuahua. c-Primary and secondary studies in Santa Barbara; preparatory studies from the National Preparatory School, 1932-34; studies in civil engineering, National School of Engineering, UNAM, 1934-37, graduated with a thesis on experimental hydraulic design, 1938; Professor of Engineering, UNAM and IPN; Director, Engineering

Institute, UNAM, 1955-58; member of the Governing Board of UNAM, 1963-71. d-None. e-None. f-Project designer, National Irrigation Commission, 1938-40; Subdirector of the Engineering Labs, National Irrigation Commission, 1940-41; Chief Engineer, Federal Electric Commission, 1950-53; Director General of Hydraulic Works, Department of the Federal District, 1953-58; Technical Director of Construction, ISSSTE Clinics, 1959-63; Subdirector General of the Federal Electric Commission, 1959-70; adviser to *José López Portillo*, Director General of the Federal Electric Commission, 1972-73; Director of Public Investment, Secretariat of the Presidency, 1971-76; adviser to the Federal Electric Commission, 1976-77; *Subsecretary of Decentralized Industry of the Secretariat of Patrimony and Industrial Development*, 1977-82; *Director General of the Federal Electric Commission*, 1982-88; *Secretary of Energy, Mines, and Government Industries*, 1988-94. g-None. h-Author of many articles; Technical Director of Hydraulic Resources, ICA, S.A., 1942-50; technical consultant to the IMSS, 1955-66. i-Father of *Humberto Hiriart Urdanivia*, federal deputy from Jalisco, 1970-73; son of Pedro Hiriart Vázquez, businessman, and María Balderrama Madariaga. j-None. k-None. l-HA, 5 Dec. 1977, 28; *Justicia*, Oct. 1977; MGF69, 537; *Excélsior*, 2 Dec. 1982, 22A; DBGM, 216; DBGM92, 186.

Hiriart Urdanivia, Humberto
a-Oct. 31, 1939. b-Federal District. c-Primary studies in the Benito Juárez School, Mexico City; secondary studies at Secondary School No. 3, Mexico City; preparatory studies at the National Preparatory School, economics degree from the National School of Economics, UNAM. d-*Federal Deputy from the State of Jalisco, Dist. 5, 1970-73*, member of the Tax Committee, the

General Accounting Office Committee, the Money and Credit Institutions Committee, and the Budget and Accounts Committee. e-*Subsecretary of Political Action of the CEN of PRI*, 1973. g-None. i-Son of Engineer *Fernando Hiriart Balderrama*, Subsecretary of Decentralized Industry, 1977. j-None. k-None. l-C de D, 1970-73, 120; Directorio, 1970-73.

Hirschfield Almada, Julio
a-Feb. 11, 1917. b-Federal District. c-Most of his primary and secondary studies in the Federal District; studied at the University of Michigan and the National School of Engineering, UNAM; no degree. d-None. e-None. f-Director General of Airports and Auxiliary Services, 1970-73; *Head of the Tourism Department*, 1973-76. g-None. h-Sales agent, Vice-President, and General Manager of H. Steel Company, S.A., 1949-64; President and Director General of Productos Metálicos Steel, S.A., 1964-70. i-Married to Dora Sáenz, daughter of the important Sonoran politician Aarón Sáenz; son, Julio, is married to Patricia Torreblanco Calles, granddaughter of President Calles. j-None. k-Kidnapped on Sept. 27, 1971; released by the Frente Urbano Zapatista after they were paid a 3 million peso ransom that the group supposedly wanted to distribute to the urban poor in Mexico City; Carlos Fuentes commented on the possibility of the group's being a front organization for right-wing officials in the *Echeverría* administration. l-HA, 7 Dec. 1970, 28, 4 Oct. 1971, 22, 7 Feb. 1972, 33-34; LAD, Jan. 1972, 2.

Hori Robaina, Guillermo
a-Oct. 16, 1932. b-Villa Flores, Chihuahua. c-Primary and secondary studies at the Williams School; preparatory studies at the University Center of Mexico; law degree at the National Law

School, UNAM, 1952-56; studied social security systems in Europe under PEMEX and the Secretariat of Labor; MA in industrial relations, Cornell University, 1962-63; Professor of Labor Law at the School for the Education of Workers of the Regional Confederation of Mexican Workers; Professor of Personnel Administration, School of Commerce and Administration, UNAM, 1965-70. d-None. e-None. f-Clerk, 1952-54, Secretary of Hearings, 1954-57, and counsel, 1957-58, of the Federal Board of Conciliation and Arbitration; Head of the Department of Social Security, Secretariat of Labor, 1959-60; Head of the Federal Department of Labor Inspection, Secretariat of Labor, 1961-63; Substitute President of the Federal Conciliation Board, 1963-64; *Oficial Mayor of the Secretariat of Labor and Social Welfare*, Jan. 18, 1965, to 1970; labor adviser, PEMEX, 1970-74; labor adviser, Tax Auditor Division, Secretariat of the Treasury, 1974-77; Oficial Mayor, National Lottery, 1982-86; Subdirector General of the National Lottery, 1986-88. g-None. h-Representative of the president before many labor conventions. i-Son of Mario D. Hori, physician, and Piedad Robaina Oteiza; married María Teresa Fojaco Sumobano. j-None. k-None. l-DBM68, 349; DPE61, 154; *Libro de Oro*, xxxvi; MGF69; DBGM, 217.

Hoyos Schalamme, Myrna E.
a-Sept. 15, 1944. b-Merida, Yucatán. c-Early education unknown; law degree, School of Law, University of Yucatán; advanced courses in human communications and human relations. d-*Federal Deputy* from the State of Yucatán, Dist. 1, 1976-79; *Senator* from the State of Yucatán, 1982-88, President of the Tourism Committeee, Secretary of the Health Committee. e-Subdirector of Electoral Action of PRI in the Federal District; general delegate of the CEN of

PRI to Jalisco, 1979; Subsecretary of
Social Action, CEN of PRI, 1977-79;
Subsecretary of Organization, CEN of
PRI, 1981-82; President, National
Committee of Cultural Development,
CNOP of PRI, 1980-83. f-Scribe, 2nd
Civil Court District, Mérida, Yucatán,
1964-67; assistant to Senator *Francisco
Luna Kan*, 1970-76; Director, Office of
General Studies, Division of Fares,
Secretariat of Communications and
Transportation, 1973-76; Director
General of Agrarian Development,
Secretariat of Agrarian Reform, 1988-94.
g-Secretary General of the Gómez Farías
Association, Federal District, 1974-75.
h-Lawyer, Peniche-Bolio Pinzón Firm,
Mérida, 1962-64. i-Married to agrono-
mist José Alberto Navarrete; daughter of
Luis H. Villanueva, health education
teacher and local PRI leader, and María
Schlamme Vargas. j-None. k-None.
l-D de C, 1976-79, 35; *Excélsior*, 28 Aug.
1976, 1C; Q es Qy, 130-31; C de S,
1982-88; Lehr, 520; DBGM92, 187-88.

Huerta Sánchez, Luciano
(Deceased) a-Jan. 7, 1906. b-Ixtenco,
Tlaxcala. c-Primary studies at the
Colegio Pensador Mexicano, Tlaxcala;
preparatory studies at the National
Preparatory School, 1920-24; medical
degree from the National School of
Medicine, UNAM, 1931; Professor of
Clinical Surgery, National School of
Medicine, UNAM, 1937-70; Director of
Medical Services, UNAM, 1958-66,
under Rector *Nabor Carrillo Flores*.
d-*Senator* from the State of Tlaxcala,
1964-70; *Governor of Tlaxcala*, 1970-76.
e-Entered politics in 1956; State
committeeman for PRI. f-Physician,
National School for the Deaf and Blind;
Intern, General Hospital, Mexico City;
Subdirector of the Hospital of the Secre-
tariat of the Treasury; Director of Medi-
cal Services, Constructora Industrial,
Ciudad Sahagún; Director of Medical
Services, Secretariat of the Treasury,

1954-58. g-Physician, National Sugar
Workers Union. i-Knew *Antonio
Armendáriz* and *Antonio Carrillo Flores*
while a student at UNAM; father was a
businessman and Mayor of Ixtenco.
j-None. k-None. l-MGF69, 106; letter;
C de S, 1964-70; PS, 3025.

Huitrón y Aguado, Abel
(Deceased Apr. 19, 1980) a-July 20,
1908. b-Jilotepec, México. c-Primary
studies at a public school, Federal
District; attended the Normal School of
Toluca on an academic scholarship;
secondary and preparatory studies at the
Colegio Francé Morelos, Mexico City;
law degree, Escuela Libre de Derecho,
Oct. 24, 1934, with a thesis on the new
law in Mexican criminal legislation;
law degree, National School of Law,
UNAM, Aug. 14, 1935, with a thesis on
resolutions in punitive law; Professor of
Amparo and Constitutional Law,
National School of Law, UNAM (12
years). d-Local Deputy to the State
Legislature of México; *Federal Deputy*
from the State of México, Dist. 7, 1949-
52, member of the Credit, Money, and
Credit Institutions Committee and
substitute member of the Rules Com-
mittee; *Senator* from the State of
México, 1958-64, President of the
Department of the Federal District
Committee, member of the Second
Labor Committee, the First Industries
Committee, and the Second Committee
on Tariffs and Foreign Trade, substitute
member of the Second Committee on
Credit, Money, and Credit Institutions,
Vice-President of the Senate (twice), and
Secretary of the Senate, 1962. e-General
delegate of PRI to Oaxaca, Puebla, and
Nayarit. f-Agent of the Ministerio
Público, Toluca, México; Justice of the
Superior Court of the State of México;
Director of Social Action, State of
México, 1942-44; Secretary General of
Government of the State of México,
1944-51; Director of the Legal Depart

ment of the Department of the Federal District, 1952-58; *Justice of the Supreme Court*, 1964-70 and 1970-75; President of the First Division of the Supreme Court, 1966. g-None. h-Practiced law for ten years; consulting lawyer to the State of México. i-Personal friend of *Adolfo López Mateos* since secondary school days; studied under *Francisco Javier Gaxiola* at the Escuela Libre de Derecho; brother *Manuel Huitrón y Aguado*, was an alternate senator from the State of México, 1970-76. j-None. k-None. l-Letter; C de D, 1949-51; DGF56, 468; DGF51, I, 23, 31, 36, 90; C de S, 1961-64, 16; *Justicia*; Func., 254; *Excélsior*, 22 Apr. 1980.

I

Ibarra de Piedra, Rosario

a-Feb. 24, 1928. b-Saltillo, Coahuila. c-Preparatory studies at the Colegio Civil of Nuevo León, 1943-45; no degree. d-*Plurinominal Federal Deputy* from the PRT, 1985-88. e-Presidential candidate of the Revolutionary Workers Party, 1981-82, 1987-88; party lost registration, 1988. f-None. g-Founder and Director of the National Front against Repression, 1979; cofounder of the National Committee for Prisoners, Persecuted, Disappeared, and Political Exiles, 1978. i-Son, Jesús, accused of belonging to the 23rd of September Communist League; interviewed *Luis Echeverría* numerous times to obtain release of her son from the Military Camp No. 1; husband, professor and physician Valdemar Ibarra Ramírez, detained and tortured for political activities; daughter of Jesús Piedra Rosales, agricultural engineer, and Concepción de la Garza Villarreal. j-None. k-First female presidential candidate. l-Análisis Político, May 1982, 26; Almanaque de México, 15-16; DBGM87, 496.

Ibarra Herrera, Manuel

a-Jan. 8, 1932. b-Tampico, Tamaulipas. c-Early education unknown; law degree, National School of Law, UNAM, 1955-59, graduating 1960 with a thesis on "Los Esposales"; Professor of Agrarian Law, National School of Law, UNAM, 1962. d-None. e-None. f-Director, Office of Reconsideration of Minor Cases, Income Tax Division, Secretariat of the Treasury, 1956-60; head of the Department of Presidential Resolutions, Department of Agrarian Affairs, 1961-62; Subdirector, Office of Agrarian Rights, Department of Agrarian Affairs, 1962-64; Private Secretary to the Subsecretary of Government, *Rafael Hernández Ochoa*, 1964-66; Director General of Political and Social Investigations, Secretariat of Government, 1966-70; *Oficial Mayor of the Secretariat of Government*, 1970-76; Director of Traffic and Purchases, Supervisor of Warehouses, Manager of Production and General Counsel, Mexican Publishing Organization, 1977-78; Director General of the Federal Judicial Police, Attorney General of Mexico, 1982-84. g-President of the 1955 Generation of Law Student Alumni, National School of Law. h-Employee of the Office of the Attorney General of Mexico, 1949-52; employee of the Secretariat of the Treasury, 1952; employee of the Income Tax Division, Secretariat of the Treasury, 1953-56; employee, Department of Agrarian Affairs, 1960; Director of *El Sol de Toluca*. j-None. k-Precandidate for governor of Tamaulipas, 1974. l-HA, 14 Dec. 1970, 20; DPE65, 13; DPE71, 2; Q es QAP, 463.

Ibarra (Ibarra), Guillermo

(Deceased Apr. 17, 1980) a-Nov. 28, 1911. b-Alamos, Sonora. c-Normal and preparatory studies in Hermosillo, Sonora; teaching certificate, Hermosillo, 1928; law degree, National School of

Law, UNAM, 1937; teacher, 1928-43; founder and Director, School for Children of Workers, Culiacán, 1937; Director of the Preparatory School of Coyoacán for Children of Workers, 1941. d-*Senator* from the State of Sonora, 1958-64, member of the Gran Comisión, President of the Second Committee on Public Education; member of the First Committee on National Defense, the First Committee on Constitutional Affairs, the Special Committee on Legislative Studies, and the Second Committee on Credit, Money, and Credit Institutions. e-None. f-Director General of Secondary Education, Secretariat of Public Education, 1940-41; President of Group No. 10 of the Federal Board of Conciliation and Arbitration, 1942; Judge of the Federal Tax Court, 1943-48; Director of the official government newspaper, *El Nacional*, 1948-56; Gerente General of PIPSA, 1956-58; *Oficial Mayor of the Secretariat of Hydraulic Resources*, 1964-70. g-President of the National Student Federation of Mexico, 1933; representative of the Mexican Federation of Labor in Santiago, Chile, 1939; member of the National Executive Committee of STERM, 1938-40; Editor of the STERM newspaper. h-Member of the Administrative Board of PIPSA, 1951-56; author of numerous articles. i-Son, Guillermo Ibarra Grijalva, was subdirector of Diesel Nacional, 1980. j-None. k-None. l-C de S, 1961-64, 58; *Libro de Oro*, xxxv; DBM68, 354; DGF51, II, 495; DPE65, 126; *Hoy*, 31 Jan. 1970, 4; Func., 358; HA, 19 Nov. 1956, 15; Enc. Mex., 1977, VII, 108-09; *Excélsior*, 19 Apr. 1980, 2.

Ibarra Muñoz, David
a-Jan. 14, 1930. b-Querétaro, Querétaro. c-Early education unknown; studies in auditing and public accounting, UNAM, 1947-51, public accounting degree,

1952, with a thesis on internal accounting; economics degree, National School of Economics, UNAM, 1953-57; Ph.D. in economics, Stanford University, 1959-61; Professor of Finance Math, School of Business Administration, UNAM, 1955-56; Professor of Financial Analysis, National School of Economics, 1955-56; Secretary of Social Services, UNAM, 1955-57; Researcher, Planning Committee, University Student Association of UNAM, 1957-58; Professor of Techniques of Economic Research, National School of Economics, UNAM, 1957; Professor of Methods of Planning, Secretariat of Public Works, 1959; Professor of Applied Economics, UNAM, 1961-62; Professor of Theory and Methods of Planning, National School of Economics, UNAM, 1964-70; Director of Graduate Studies, National School of Economics, UNAM, 1967-69. d-None. e-None. f-Auditor, Bank of Mexico; economist, Economic Commission for Latin America (ECLA), Santiago, Chile, 1958-59; Chief of the Development Section, ECLA, Mexico City, 1961-63; Coordinator of Research, ECLA, Mexico City, 1964-66; Assistant Director of ECLA, Mexico City, 1966-66; Director of ECLA, Mexico City, 1970-73; Assistant Director of the National Finance Bank, 1974-76; *Subdirector General of the National Finance Bank*, 1976; *Director General of the National Finance Bank*, 1976-77; *Secretary of the Treasury*, Nov. 17, 1977-82; Director General of the National Bank of Mexico (BANAMEX), 1982. g-None. h-Chief of auditors, *Manuel Gómez Morín*'s law firm. i-Son of Engineer David Ibarra; married Olga Cardona. j-None. k-Fired as secretary of the treasury, Sept. 1982. l-B de M, 153; *El Día*, 1 Dec. 1976; *Excélsior*, 17 Nov. 1977, 11, 28 Nov. 1977, 16; HA, 19 July 1976, 32; *Excélsior*, 5 Sept. 1982, 20A.

Ibarrola Santoyo, Eugenio
a-Sept. 8, 1923. b-Morelia, Michoacán.
c-Secondary studies at the Escuela
Apostólica y Escoldasticado de los
Misioneros del Espiritú Santo, 1935-45;
legal studies at the Escuela Libre de
Derecho, 1947-51, graduating Apr. 30,
1953, with a thesis on political power.
d-*Federal Deputy* from the Federal
District, Dist. 11, 1952-55, member of
the Rules Committee, the Legislative
Studies Committee (1st year), and the
First Balloting Committee. e-None.
f-Candidate for notary public, 1958-59;
Notary Public No. 122 of the Federal
District, 1959-80. g-Member of the
Council of Notaries of the Federal
District, Jan. 1, 1964, to Dec. 31, 1965.
h-Businessman in Morelia, Michoacán;
member of the Board of Directors of
Mutualidad Notarial, A.C., 1965-69.
i-Brother, Roberto, is an architect,
professor at UNAM, and was head of
projects for the Office of Buildings and
Monuments, Department of the Federal
District; married María Bertha Urqui-
aga; son of Gabriel Ibarrola and María
Santoyo. j-None. k-None. l-DBM68,
355-56; C de D, 52-54, 51, 66; DJBM, 70.

Icaza y López Negrete, Xavier
(Deceased 1969) a-Oct. 2, 1892. b-Durango, Durango. c-Preparatory studies
at the National Preparatory School; law
studies from the Escuela Libre de
Derecho, 1912-16, graduating Aug. 10,
1917, with a thesis on constitutional-
ism; Professor of Law and Literature,
University of Veracruz, Jalapa; Professor
of History and Literature, UNAM;
Director of the School of Labor Law,
1939; member of the Board of Directors
of the Workers University. d-None.
e-None. f-*Justice of the Supreme Court*,
1935-40. g-None. h-Attorney for many
private firms in Mexico, including
Financiera de México and the Compania
Mexicana de Petróleo El Aguila, 1919;
representative of El Aguila to the state

government of Veracruz, 1922. i-Married Ana Guido; son of Xavier Icaza and
Dolores López Negrete; classmate of
José Ortiz Tirado, justice of the Supreme Court; practiced law with Carlos
Díaz Dufoo, Jr. j-None. k-Refused to
review the Arbitration Board findings in
the well-known petroleum case, 1938.
l-WWM45, 58; Kirk, 164; DP70, 2403;
IWW40, 525; Peral, 404; ELD, 85-86.

Iduarte Foucher, Andrés
(Deceased Apr. 16, 1984) a-May 1, 1907.
b-Villahermosa, Tabasco. c-Primary
studies in Villahermosa and in Mexico
City, Dr. Hugo Topf's School; secondary
studies at the Colegio Mexicano,
Mexico City; preparatory studies at the
National Preparatory School, Mexico
City, 1922-26; studied at UNAM, 1926-
28, 1930-32; studied at the University of
Paris, 1928-30; law degree from the
University of Madrid, 1935; LLD degree,
1936; Ph.D. from Columbia University,
1944; LLD from the National School of
Law, UNAM, 1953; Professor of General
History, National Preparatory School;
Professor of History at UNAM, 1930-32,
1953; member of the University
Council of UNAM, 1930-32; Secretary
of the Ibero-American Section, Ateneo
of Science and Literature of Madrid,
1933-36; Professor of Spanish American
Literature, Columbia University, 1939-
72; instructor at Barnard College, 1941-
45; professor at the University of California, Berkeley, 1947, at the University
of Caracas, 1945, and at the University
of the Oriente, 1955. d-None. e-None.
f-Director General of the National Institute of Fine Arts, 1952-54. g-Editor of
student paper *Angora*, National Preparatory School, 1924; writer for student
magazine, *Avalanche*, 1923. h-Author;
Editor, *Universidad de México*. i-From
a very important political family in
Tabasco; father, Andrés Iduarte, was a
judge; cousin of *Rodulfo Brito Foucher*;
Manuel Bartlett was a close friend and

student of his father's; intimate friend of Herminio Ahumada; also close to *Pedro de Alba* and *Gabriel Ramos Millán*; married Graciela Frías-Amescua. j-None. k-Scott says that Professor Iduarte was dismissed from his position as Director General of Fine Arts in 1954, for permitting a Communist flag to be draped over the coffin of the Mexican painter Frida Kahlo as her body lay in state at the Institute. l-Scott, 335; DEM, 180; letter; Lochner, 33-36, 531-32; JSH, 197; WNM, 119.

Iglesias (Hernández), Serafín
a-Oct. 12, 1914. b-Veracruz, Veracruz. c-Completed preparatory studies in Veracruz; no degree. d-*Federal Deputy from the State of Veracruz, Dist. 7, 1964-67.* e-*Secretary of Press of the CEN of the PRM,* 1939-40. f-Director of leftist publishing, Chamber of Deputies, 1942-43. g-Secretary General of the CTM of Veracruz, 1934-38. h-Political journalist, 1936-40; director of various magazines, 1944-64; businessman. j-None. k-None. l-C de D, 1964-67.

Iguíniz González, Manuel
a-Oct. 4, 1921. b-Jalisco. c-Early education unknown; no degree. d-*Plurinominal Federal Deputy from PAN, 1982-85.* e-Candidate of PAN for local deputy, State of Puebla; candidate for alternate senator from Puebla from PAN; candidate for governor of Puebla from PAN, 1980; Director of PAN, Parras, Coahuila; member of the Regional Committee of PAN, State of Puebla; President of PAN, State of Puebla. f-None. g-None. h-Textile technician. j-None. k-None. l-Directorio, 1982-85; C de D, 1982-85.

Iñárritu (y Ramírez), Jorge
a-Apr. 27, 1916. b-Tacubaya, Mexico City. c-Primary studies in Mexico City; legal studies, National School of Law, UNAM, 1934-38, graduating Nov. 13,

1939. d-None. e-None. f-Head of the Judicial Section, Supreme Court, 1945; Subdirector and Director of the *Judicial Weekly* of the Supreme Court, 1945-58; Oficial Mayor of the Supreme Court, 1958-59; Subsecretary of Resolutions, Supreme Court, 1959-60; Secretary General of Resolutions, Supreme Court, 1960-64; *Justice of the Supreme Court,* 1964-70, 1970-76, 1977-82; *President of the Supreme Court,* 1983-86. g-None. h-Author of many works on amparo; consulting lawyer to the Secretariat of Communications and Public Works and to the Secretariat of Health and Public Assistance. i-Married Holda Rodríguez; son of Silverio Iñarritu Flores, public official, and María de la Luz Ramírez de Aguilar. j-None. k-None. l-*Justicia,* Oct. 1968; letter; WNM, 119; *Excélsior,* 4 Jan. 1983, 2A; DBGM, 662; Protag., 174.

Iñurreta (de la Fuente), Marcelino
a-June 29, 1901. b-Cunduacán, Tabasco. c-Primary studies in Oaxaca; secondary studies in Oaxaca, received a private accounting degree; preparatory studies at the National Preparatory School; enrolled in the National Military College, but left without completing studies to join the Revolution. d-*Federal Deputy from the Federal District, Dist. 2, 1943-46,* elected as an Alternate but replaced *Carlos Madrazo* when he was suspended; *Senator from the State of Tabasco, 1952-58,* member of the Rules Committee, the National Lands Committee, the Second National Defense Committee and the Balloting Committee. e-None. f-Subdirector of the Military Judicial Police; presidential adviser on public health; Paymaster General of the Federal District Police Department, 1943; first Director of the Federal Department of Security, Secretariat of Government 1946-52. g-None. h-Champion in various sports; expert pistol shot. i-Personal assistant to

General Obregón. j-Joined the Juan Antonio de la Fuente Brigade as a private; rank of 1st Captain, 1916; rank of Colonel, Oct. 13, 1949; rank of Brigadier General, Sept. 28, 1951; reached rank of Brigade General, Dec. 30, 1955. k-President *Alemán* violated the promotion law in promoting him to brigadier general. l-Ind. Biog., 88-89; DGF51, 69; DGF56, 7, 9, 10, 12, 13.

Ireta (Viveros), Félix
(Deceased Oct. 26, 1978) a-Nov. 20, 1893. b-Zinapécuaro, Michoacán. c-Primary studies in Zinapécuaro; none; no degree. d-*Senator* from the State of Michoacán, 1946-52; *Governor of Michoacán*, 1940-44. e-None. g-None. i-Fought with the *Avila Camacho* brothers during the Revolution. j-Joined the Revolution; Constitutionalist, 1913; commander of various military zones; fought against the Escobar Rebellion, 1929; rank of Brigade General, Dec. 27, 1938; Commander of the 21st Military Zone, Morelia, Michoacán, 1952-56; Commander of the 21st Military Zone, Morelia, Michoacán, 1969. k-Strongly attacked in the press for various abuses committed by his government in Michoacán. l-DGF56, 202; DGF51, 6; Peral, 406; HA, 22 May 1942; HA, 25 Sept. 1942, 9; C de S, 1946-52; Gómez Maganda, 102; *Excélsior*, 28 Oct. 1978, 2; López, 536.

Islas Bravo, Antonio
(Deceased 1949) a-1885. b-Atlixco, Puebla. c-Law degree, National School of Law, UNAM, 1910. d-Federal Deputy, 1924-26. e-None. f-Agent of the Ministerio Público; civil judge, Chihuahua; consulting lawyer to the Secretary of Agriculture; Head of the Legal Department of the Secretariat of Agrarian Affairs; *Justice of the Supreme Court of Mexico*, 1940-46 and 1946-49; President of the Third Division of the Supreme Court, 1944. g-None. h-Author of the

book *Presidential Succession in 1928*. j-Joined the Revolution; supporter of Francisco Madero; fought under General Villa, 1914-18. k-Opposed the reelection of General Obregón. l-Letter; DP70, 2406; López, 539.

Islas Olguín, Guillermo
a-June 25, 1928. b-Federal District. c-Primary studies at the Francisco Figueroa School, Tacuba, Federal District, 1934-40; secondary studies at the Manuel Acosta School, Tacuba, 1941-43; preparatory studies at the National Preparatory School, San Ildefonso, Mexico City, 1944-46; medical degree, National School of Medicine, UNAM, 1948-53, with a thesis on "My Social Service in Coyotepc, México"; special studies in gynecology and obstetrics, UNAM and IMSS, 1959-62. d-*Federal Deputy* from the Federal District, Dist. 19, 1970-73, member of the Fine Arts Committee, the Small Industries Committee, and the Health Committee; *Federal Deputy* from the Federal District, Dist. No. 19, 1976-79, Dist. 29, 1988-91. e-Joined PAN, 1951; Director of PAN for the Federal District, 1952-54. f-None. g-Member of the Mexican Academy of Sciences. h-Practicing physician. i-Married Lydia León Amézquita; son of Matías Islas Vargas, public accountant, and Luis Olguín Morales. j-None. k-Candidate for alternate federal deputy, Federal District, 1958. l-C de D, 1970-72, 121; Directorio, 1970-72; DBGM89, 464.

Isoard (Jiménez de Sandi), Carlos Alfredo
a-Sept. 19, 1921. b-Federal District. c-Early education unknown; CPA degree, Higher School of Business and Administration, IPN, 1948-52, with a thesis on the "Eras of Auditing," 1952; professor at UNAM, 1957-61; professor at the Pan American Institute of Business, 1957-82. d-None. e-None.

f-Employee, Bank of Mexico, 1939-45; Director, Department of Technical Studies, Income Tax Division, Secretariat of the Treasury, 1952-54; Director of Evaluation Board, Income Tax Department, Secretariat of the Treasury, 1954-58; Subdirector of the Income Tax Department, Secretariat of the Treasury, 1959; *Subsecretary of Expenditures*, Secretariat of the Treasury, 1970-76; adviser to the Secretary of the Treasury, 1976; general auditor, Secretariat of Public Education, 1977-82; Coordinator of Planning, Secretariat of Health, 1982; *Subsecretary of Planning*, Secretariat of Health, 1982-83; adviser, Secretariat of Health, 1983-84; Executive Director of Programs and Evaluation, National Finance Bank, 1984-88. g-Manager, National Union of Sugar Producers, 1959-60. h-Auditor, Mancera Brothers, 1945-50; Controller, United Shoe and Leather, S.A., 1950-51; Director General, General Chemical, S.A., 1961-67; Director General of Laboratories, John Deere, S.A., 1967-68; Vice-President, Affiliates of Telephones of Mexico, S.A., 1969-70. i-Son of José Luis Isoard Megy, white collar worker, and Concepción Jiménez de Sandi y Hallen; married Yolanda Viesca y Viesca; son, Carlos Enrique, was director general in the Bank of Mexico, 1992. j-None. k-None. l-*Excélsior*, 4 Feb. 1976; Q es QAP, 332; DPE71, 27; DGF56, 168; HA, 3 Apr. 1972, 7; DBGM87, 190; DBGM92, 193.

Ituarte Servín, Alfonso
a-Oct. 30, 1914. b-Tacubaya, Federal District. c-Primary studies at Luz Saviñón School and at a public school, both in Mexico City; two years of study in business school; private accounting degree, School of Banking and Business, 1936; CPA degree, National Polytechnic School. d-*Federal Deputy* from the Federal District, Dist. 17, 1955-58, member of the First Balloting Commit-

tee and the Second General Means of Communication Committee; *Federal Deputy* (Party Deputy from PAN), 1967-70, member of Trade and Credit Section and the Tax Section of the Legislative Studies Committee, the First Government Committee, the Industries Committee, the Second Balloting Committee and the Small Industries Committee. e-Member of PAN; *President of the CEN of PAN*, 1956-57. f-None. g-Member of various religious defense groups; propagandist for the League for Religious Defense; founder and President of the Civic Center of the Federal District; member of the CNIT; President of Catholic Action. h-Accountant. i-Son of Daniel Ituarte Esteva and María Servín; married Josefina Soto de Iduarte. j-None. k-Candidate of PAN for federal deputy from the Federal District, Dist. 17, 1952. l-DGF56, 23, 34, 37; Ind. Biog., 89; *La Nación*, 29 Mar. 1959, 18; C de D, 1967-70, 67, 70, 72, 76, 77, 81.

Iturbe, Ramón F.
(Deceased 1970) a-Nov. 7, 1889. b-Mazatlán, Sinaloa. c-Primary and secondary studies in Culiacán Seminary, Sinaloa; studies at the California Military School, Los Angeles; studies in civil engineering, United States, 1912-13; no degree. d-*Federal Deputy* from the State of Sinaloa, Dist. 3, 1937-40, President of the Chamber. e-Founder of the Mexican Constitutional Front to support a presidential candidate in 1939. f-Provisional Governor of the State of Sinaloa, 1917-20; Director of the Cooperative Development, Secretariat of Industry and Commerce, 1936; Military Attaché to Japan, 1941-42; Commander of the Mexican Legion of Honor, Secretariat of National Defense, 1958-64, 1964-66. g-None. h-Merchant before the Revolution; managed a small general store, Alcoyonque. i-Son of Adolfo Fuentes and Refugio Iturbe; married Mercedes Acosta. j-Career

army officer; joined the Revolution in 1910; member of rebel group under Juan Bardes, Culiacán, 1910; fought Orozco, 1912; commander of irregular forces in Sinaloa, 1912, of military operations in Sinaloa, 1913, of the forces that captured Mazatlán, 1914, of the military zones of Nayarit, Sinaloa, and Sonora, 1914-15, of the 3rd division, Constitutional Army, and of the forces that captured Culiacán under General Obregón, 1913; rank of Brigadier General, 1912; Brigade General, Oct. 28, 1913; Commander of Military Operations in Jalisco, Colima, 1916; rank of Division General. k-Supported the Escobar movement, 1929; in exile in the United States, 1929-35; expelled from the PRM for his activities in support of the candidacy of General *Almazán* for president, 1938-39; later supported the candidacy of *Rafael Sánchez Tapia* in the 1940 campaign for president; received the Belisario Domínguez Medal from the Mexican Senate, 1966. l-DPE65, 42; DPE61, 34; C de D, 1937-39; *El Universal*, 18 Jan. 1939; Michaels, 22; *Annals*, Mar. 1940, 21; DP70, 2406; Peral, 407; Novo35, 271; Enc. Mex., VII, 1977, 363; EBW46, 1141.

Iturriaga (Sauco), José E.
a-Apr. 10, 1914. c-Preparatory studies at the National Preparatory School; studies in law at the Escuela Libre de Derecho; studies in philosophy and history, School of Philosophy and Letters, UNAM; economic studies at the National School of Economics, no degree; fellow at the Colegio de México, 1944; Professor of the History of the Mexican Revolution, Colegio de México, 1949. d-None. e-Member of the Advisory Council to the IEPES of PRI, 1972. f-Employee of the National Finance Bank, 1934-64; official of the Historical Archives of the Secretariat of the Treasury, 1943-46; Director, Institution and Agency Inspection

Department, Secretariat of National Patrimony, 1947-48; adviser to the President of Mexico, 1952-58, 1958-64; Subdirector of the National Finance Bank, 1959-64; *Ambassador to the USSR*, 1965-66; adviser to *Luis Echeverría*, 1971. g-None. h-Editorial writer, *Novedades*; editorial writer, *Mañana*. i-Son of María Eugenia de la Fuente; son, Renato, was a director general in the Secretariat of Public Education, 1987. j-None. k-Candidate for federal deputy for the Popular Party (later the PPS) with *Narciso Bassols* and *Víctor Manuel Villaseñor*, 1943. l-*Siempre*, 28 Jan. 1959, 6; DGF47, 269; DPE65, 31; Villaseñor, II, 33; Enc. Mex., VII, pp.365-66; DBGM87, 190.

Iturribarría (Martínez), Jorge Fernando
a-Apr. 5, 1902. b-Oaxaca, Oaxaca. c-Secondary education at the Institute of Arts and Sciences, Oaxaca; teaching certificate; professor of normal school; professor at the Institute of Arts and Sciences. d-*Federal Deputy* from the State of Oaxaca, Dist. 3, 1967-70, member of the Library Committee (2nd year). e-None. f-Oficial Mayor of the Legislature of the State of Oaxaca. g-None. h-Director and editor of various newspapers; author of many books on the history of Oaxaca. i-Related to Governor *José Pacheco Iturribarría*. j-None. k-None. l-WWM45, 59; C de D, 1967-69, 60; Peral, 410.

J

Jara (Rodríguez), Heriberto
(Deceased Apr. 17, 1968) a-July 10, 1884. b-Orizaba, Veracruz. c-Primary and secondary studies, Escuela Modelo, in Orizaba; secondary studies at the Scientific and Literary Institute of Hidalgo; attended the Escuela Naval de Antón Lizardo. d-Federal Deputy from the State of Veracruz, 1912-13; Deputy

to the Constitutional Congress from the State of Veracruz, 1916-17; Senator from the State of Veracruz, 1920-24; Governor of Veracruz, Dec. 18, 1924, to Oct. 31, 1927. e-Member of the Constitutional Party, 1913; *President of the CEN of PRI*, 1939-40. f-Minister to Cuba, 1917-20; Governor of the Federal District, 1914; *Secretary of the Navy*, 1941-46. g-None. h-Writer for many magazines and newspapers at the beginning of his career and after his retirement in 1946. i-Married Ana María Avalos; from very humble background. j-Career military officer; rank of Colonel, 1913; Brigadier General, 1914; directed the Cadets against the North American invasion of Veracruz, 1914; rank of Brigade General, 1915; Division General, 1924; joined the Revolution in 1910, fighting under General Camerino Mendoza; Commander of the 26th Military Zone, Veracruz, Veracruz, 1935-37; Assistant Inspector General of the Army, 1935; Inspector General of the Army, 1935; Commander of the 28th Military Zone, Oaxaca, Oaxaca, 1938; Director General of Military Education, Secretariat of National Defense, 1938-39. k-Participated in the Río Blanco Mill Strike when he was a bookkeeper, 1907; voted against the renunciation of Madero and Piño Suárez as a federal deputy, 1913; one of the extreme radicals at the Constitutional Convention; opposed the candidacy of *Angel Carvajal* for president in an open letter signed by *Silvano Barba González* and *Luis I. Rodríguez*; manager for *Avila Camacho*'s campaign for president, 1940; his appointment as secretary of navy strongly criticized by naval officers who felt a navy rather than an army officer should have been appointed; newspapers were also critical, calling Jara "General of the Ocean Cavalry." l-D de Y, 20 June 1939, 1; Daniels, 89; Peral, 414-15; D de Y, 1 Jan. 1936, 4; Kirk, 239-40; Morton, 41-42,

92; *Polémica*, Apr., 69, 70; DGF51, II, 699; DP70, 1110; *Hoy*, 27 Apr. 1968, 4; WWM45, 60; Enc. Mex., VII, 1977, 450.

Jaramillo González, Cándido

(Deceased 1970) a-1910. b-Zongolica, Veracruz. c-Primary studies in Jalapa, Veracruz; teaching certificate in Veracruz; normal teacher in the State of Veracruz. d-None. e-Founder of the Popular Socialist Party with *Vicente Lombardo Toledano*, 1947. f-Comptroller General of the Secretariat of Industry and Commerce. g-Director General of the Mexican Federation of Teachers, 1937-38; *Secretary General of the FSTSE*, 1940-42. i-Brother, Julio, was a Mexican musician. j-None. k-None. l-DP70, 1112; Correa, 12; Raby, 76.

Javelly Girard, Marcelo

a-Jan. 18, 1927. b-Jalapa, Veracruz. c-Early education unknown; legal studies, National School of Law, UNAM, 1944-48, graduating Nov. 3, 1949, with a thesis on legal responsibility; courses in the United States. d-None. e-Joined PRI, 1952. f-Lawyer, 1950-52, Subdirector, 1952-57, and Director of the Auxiliary Office of Credit, 1958-65, all at Division of Credit, Secretariat of the Treasury; Director of Operations and Banking, Discount Housing Fund, Bank of Mexico, 1965-71; Vice-President of the Banking and Insurance Commission, 1971-72; adviser to the Director General, *Jesús Silva Herzog Flores*, of INFONAVIT, 1974-76; Director of the Liquidation Trust of Auxiliary Organization and Credit Institutions, 1977-82; Director General of Aboumrad Bank, 1982; *Secretary of Public Works and Human Settlements*, 1982-85; Ambassador to Switzerland, 1988. g-None. h-Lawyer, firm of José María Gurría Urgell, 1946-50; practicing lawyer, 1974-76. i-Wife, Angela Gurría, prominent sculptress; son-in-law of distinguished lawyer and professor, José

María Gurría; son of Juan Javelly
Olivero, businessman, and Emilie
Girard Suzan. j-None. k-None.
l-Letters; HA, 7 Feb. 1983, 23; Informe,
66-67; IEPES; *Excélsior*, 1 Dec. 1982, 34
A; *The News*, 8 Dec. 1982, 8; HA, 13
Dec. 1982, 15; letters.

Jiménez Cantú, Jorge
a-Oct. 27, 1914. b-Villa del Carbón,
México. c-Primary studies at the
Centro Escolar Belisario Domínguez,
Mexico City, 1922-28; secondary at
Secondary School No. 1 and No. 7,
Mexico City, 1929-31; preparatory
studies in biological sciences, National
Preparatory School, 1932-33; medical
degree, National School of Medicine,
UNAM, 1940; Professor of Clinical
Surgery, National School of Medicine,
UNAM, 1941-57; Professor of Biology,
Instituto México and the Centro
Universitario México. d-*Governor of
México*, 1975-81. e-None. f-Secretary
of Organization for the National
Commission of the Campaign for
School Construction, 1948-51; Adminis-
trative Committee of the Federal School
Construction Program, 1951; adviser to
the National Institute of Youth, 1952-
57; Director General of Medical
Services, Secretariat of Public Works,
1952-56; Secretary General of Government of the State of México, 1957-63,
under Governor *Gustavo Baz*; Manager
of CONASUPO, 1964-68, under *Carlos
Hank González*; Secretary General of
Government of the State of México,
1969-70, under Governor *Hank
González*; *Secretary of Health and
Welfare*, 1970-75. g-President of the
Student Society of the National School
of Medicine; President of the Federation
of University Students; student member
of the University Council, 1937-38.
h-Secretary General of the Commission
of CONASUPO to promote rural
improvements; founder of the College
Military Pentathlon, 1938, commander

of this organization. i-Married Luisa
Isabel Campos; son of Jesús Jiménez
Gallardo and Guadalupe Cantú. j-None.
k-None. l-DPE71, 113; MGF69, 551;
HA, 7 Dec. 1970, 25; DGF56, 259;
DPE51, II, 446; *Hoy*, Dec. 1970; HA, 3
Feb. 1975, 34; Cadena Z., 41-42; HA, 6
Oct. 1975, 35, 28 Jan. 1980, 31.

Jiménez Cárdenas, Simón
a-May 16, 1909. b-Armadillo, Mazatlán,
Sinaloa. c-Primary studies at the José
María Morelos School, 1919-25; secon-
dary studies at the Federal Teacher
Education Institute, 1952-54, 1954-57;
teaching certificate from the Higher
Normal School of Nayarit, 1963, with a
specialty in Mexican and world history;
Professor of Geography in the Public
Secondary School, Mazatlán; Professor
of Civics, Public Secondary School of
Guamuchil, Sinaloa. d-*Federal Deputy*
(Party Deputy from the Popular Social-
ist Party), 1970-73, member of the
Waters and Irrigation Committee, the
First Section of the Agrarian Affairs
Committee, the Cultural Affairs
Committee, and the Securities Com-
mittee. e-Member of the Central
Committee of the PPS; Secretary of
Electoral Affairs, Regional Committee
of the PPS for Sinaloa; representative of
the PPS on the Sinaloa Electoral
Commission. f-Director of Rural
Schools; Director of Urban Schools;
Federal Inspector of Primary Education.
g-Secretary General of the Workers and
Farmers Federation of the South of
Sinaloa. h-None. j-None. k-None. l-C
de D, 1970-72, 121; Directorio, 1970-72.

Jiménez (Delgado), Ramón
(Deceased) a-Dec. 21, 1895. b-San Luis
Potosí, San Luis Potosí. c-Educated at
the Model School of San Luis Potosí; no
degree. d-*Interim Governor of San Luis
Potosí*, 1941-43. e-None. f-Head of the
Federal Judicial Police for the Office of
the Attorney General of Mexico, 1965.

g-None. h-None. j-Career army officer; supported the federal government against the Cristero Revolt, 1927; Commander of the 4th Army Regiment (Cavalry); Director of the Military Hospital, Mexico City; Commander of the 15th Military Zone, Guadalajara, Jalisco, 1946-52; Commander of the 17th Military Zone, Querétaro, Querétaro, 1952-55; rank of Brigadier General, Aug. 1, 1942. k-None. l-HA, 7 May 1943, 12; DPE65, 210; Peral, 415; DGF56, 202; NYT, 20 Aug., 1941; Casasola, V.

Jiménez del Prado (Becerra), Salvador
a-Dec. 2, 1907. b-Querétaro, Querétaro. c-Early education unknown; law degree. d-Local Deputy, State Legislature of Querétaro, 1946; *Senator* from the State of Querétaro, 1970-76. e-President of PRI in the Federal District. f-Consulting lawyer, Department of the Federal District, 1945; Director of the Legal Department, Channel 13 Television Station, 1973; Director, Department of Legal Affairs, Department of Fishing, 1977-82. g-Coordinator of Small Businessmen of Mexico; Oficial Mayor of the CNOP. h-Practicing lawyer. j-None. k-None. l-PS; C de S, 1970-76.

Jiménez de Palacios, Aurora
(Deceased) a-Dec. 9, 1922. b-Tecuala, Nayarit. c-Primary studies at a public school, Mazatlán; scholarship student in 1937 at the Secondary School for Children of Workers, Culiacán, Sinaloa, graduated with honorable mention; preparatory at the Mixed Boarding School for Children of Workers, Coyoacán, Federal District; economics degree from the School of Economics, University of Guadalajara, 1941-46; graduated in 1947 with a thesis on "Social Welfare in Mexico"; Executive Secretary, University of Guadalajara; Executive Secretary, Technical Council, University of Guadalajara. d-*Federal Deputy* from Baja

California del Norte, Dist. 2, 1954-55. e-None. f-Executive Secretary, Social Security Institute, Guadalajara; Director of Clinic No. 1, IMSS, Guadalajara. g-None. i-Married lawyer José Cruz Palacios. j-None. k-First female federal deputy in Mexico, elected in the special election for Baja California, 1954. l-ENE, 118; C de D, 1952-55; Bulnes, 656; Romero Aceves, 387-88.

Jiménez Espirú, Javier
a-July 31, 1937. b-Federal District. c-Early education unknown; degree in electrical and mechanical engineering, National School of Engineering, UNAM; courses in industrial refrigeration, Paris, France, 1961; studies in medical electronics, Paris, 1968-71; Chair, Mechanical and Electrical Engineering Department, 1968-70, professor, National School of Engineering, 1962-82, Auxiliary Secretary General, 1973-76, Administrative Secretary, 1977-78, and Dean, School of Engineering, 1978-82, all at UNAM. d-None. e-Joined PRI, 1958. f-Official of the National Transportation and Communications Commission; Director General of Machinery and Transportation, Secretariat of Public Works, 1972-73; Manager of Halero, S.A., 1963-67; *Subsecretary of Communications and Technical Development*, Secretariat of Communication and Transportation, 1982-88; Subdirector (Commercial) of PEMEX, 1990-94. g-None. h-Author of many books. i-Son of Javier Jiménez Segura, director general of military industry and division general, and Rosa Espirú Herrera; married Elisa Margarita Gutiérrez Saldívar; brother, Enrique, was a director general in the Secretariat of Industry and Commerce. j-None. k-None. l-*Excélsior*, 4 Dec. 1982, 35A; IEPES; Q es QAP, 250; DBGM92, 194; Protag., 177; DBGM, 226; DBGM87, 194.

Jiménez Lazcano, Mauro
a-July 10, 1942. b-Federal District.
c-Early education unknown; economics
degree from the National School of Economics, UNAM, 1962-67, with a thesis
on "Principal Obstacles to Economic
Integration of Latin America"; Assistant
Professor of Economic Problems of
Latin America, National School of
economics, UNAM; Ph.D. studies in
economics, Colegio de México, 1977;
Professor of Planning and Development,
National School of Economics, 1967-68.
d-None. e-Adviser to the Secretary
General of PRI, *Manuel Bartlett Díaz*,
1981-82. f-Director of Information and
Public Relations for the President of
Mexico, 1970-76; *Subsecretary of the
Presidency*, Feb. 26 to Nov. 30, 1976;
Director General of Information, Secre-
tariat of Government, 1982-84. g-None.
h-Reporter for *El Mexicano*, attached to
the presidency, 1961-63; reporter on
political affairs for the newspaper *La
Prensa*, 1964-69; General Manager of
Asesoria Económica, S.C., 1977-82;
Director of the magazine, *Económica*.
i-Son of Mauro Jiménez Mora, public
official, and Sara Lazcano; married
Margarita Romero, teacher. j-None.
k-Press assistant for *Luis Echeverría*
during his campaign for president, 1969-
70. l-HA, 14 Dec. 1970, 23; DPE71, 124;
Excélsior, 27 Feb. 1976, 4; HA, 8 Mar.
1976, 6; Q es QAP, 32; DBGM, 227.

Jiménez Méndez, María del Carmen
a-Nov. 5, 1928. b-Federal District.
c-Early education unknown; chemical
engineering degree, National School of
Chemical Sciences, UNAM; professor,
Technical Institute of Parral, Chihuahua. d-Secretary of the City Council of
Parral, *Plurinominal Federal Deputy*
from PAN, 1979-82, 1985-88. e-Member of the National Council of PAN.
f-None. g-None. h-Unknown.
i-Daughter of Guillermo Jiménez and
Esperanza Méndez. j-None. k-None.

l-DBGM87, 498; C de D, 1979-82, 1985-
88.

Jiménez Morales, Guillermo
a-Dec. 2, 1933. b-Huauchinango,
Puebla. c-Primary studies at the Benito
Juárez Public School, Huauchinango,
1940-45; secondary studies at Cristóbal
Colón School, 1946-48; preparatory stu-
dies at the Instituto Vasco de Quiroga,
Mexico City, 1949-50; legal studies,
National School of Law, UNAM, 1951-
55, graduating 1957; Professor of Civics,
Police Academy, Federal District; Pro-
fessor of Economic Problems of Mexico,
School of Science and Administration,
UNAM. d-*Federal Deputy* from the
State of Puebla, Dist. 10, 1973-76, Dist.
11, 1979-80; *Governor of Puebla*, 1981-
87. e-Secretary General of PRI of the
State of Puebla, 1957-58; member of the
National Council of PRI; President of
PRI in Puebla, 1973; delegate of the
IEPES of PRI during the presidential
campaign in Yucatán, Campeche, and
Quintana Roo, 1975-76; general delegate
of the CEN of PRI to the States of
Coahuila, San Luis Potosí, Nuevo León,
Tamaulipas, and Zacatecas, 1979;
President of PRI in the Federal District,
1988. f-Agent of the Ministerio Público
of the Attorney General of the Federal
District, 1958; lawyer for the Secretariat
of Health, 1959; Secretary of the
Infractions Evaluation Committee,
Secretariat of Health, 1959; Director of
Personnel and Social Welfare Depart-
ment, office of the Construction and
Sanitation Engineering Committee,
1967; Private Secretary to the Director
General of Public Works, Department of
the Federal District, 1968-70; Administrative Subdirector of Public Works,
Department of the Federal District,
1970-73; Director General of Citizen
Participation of the Attorney General of
the Federal District; auxiliary member
of the Federal Electoral Commission,
Secretariat of Government; *Secretary of*

the Secretariat of Fisheries, 1991-94.
g-General delegate of the CNC to various states, 1965-67; Secretary of Organization of the CNOP, 1980. h-None.
i-Son of Alberto Jiménez, farmer, and Estela Morales Cruz Cid; married Laura Elena Betancourt Betancourt; stepbrother of *Julio Rodolfo Moctezuma*; attended high school with *Miguel de la Madrid.* j-None. k-None. l-*Almanaque de Puebla*, 25; *Excélsior*, 3 July 1980, 4A; C de D, 1973-76, 1979-82; DBGM92, 195-96.

Jiménez O'Farrell, Federico
(Deceased) a-Dec. 20, 1890. b-Chalchicomulca, Puebla. c-Early education unknown; law degree; graduate studies at UNAM; Professor of Civics, Common Law, and Political Economy, University of Puebla. d-None. e-None.
f-Career Foreign Service Officer; Director of the Federal Office of the Treasury, Puebla; Librarian, UNAM; Private Secretary to the Secretary of Foreign Relations, 1919; Chargé d'affaires, San José, Costa Rica, and Managua, Nicaragua, 1921; *Ambassador to Great Britain*, 1945-51; *Ambassador to France*, 1951-54. g-Member of the Agrarian Commission of Puebla. i-Brother, Alberto, served as a military surgeon during the Revolution. k-None. l-DGF51, I, 105; Novo35, 37; STYRBIWW54, 817; Peral, 418; DP70, 1122.

Jiménez Rueda, Julio
(Deceased June 25, 1960) a-Apr. 10, 1896. b-Federal District. c-Preparatory studies from the National Preparatory School; law degree, National School of Law, 1919, Ph.D. in letters, School of Philosophy and Letters, 1935, Dean of the School of Philosophy and Letters, 1942-44, 1953-54, Professor Emeritus, School of Philosophy and Letters, Dean of the National School of Archeology, Director of Summer School, 1928-32, and Secretary General, 1932-33, all at

UNAM; *Secretary General of UNAM*, 1944. e-None. f-Secretary of the Mexican Delegation to Buenos Aires, 1921-22; Secretary of the Mexican Delegation to Montevideo, 1920; Director of the School of Theatrical Arts, Secretariat of Public Education, 1917-20; Director of the National Archives, 1943-52. g-Prominent in the Knights of Columbus; member of the National League of Catholic Students with Jorge Prieto Laurens and *Manuel Herrera y Rivera*, 1914; Director of *El Estudiantil*, 1913; Editor of the *Bulletin of Archeology*, 1943-52; Director of the Center for Mexican Writers, 1955-60; writer for many newspapers; novelist and dramatist. i-Student of poet Luis Urbina; son of engineer Arturo Jiménez and Eloisa Rueda; married Guadalupe Ortiz de Montellano, sister of poet Bernardo Ortiz de Montellano; son, Bernardo Jiménez Montellano, was a successful poet and writer; students at the National Preparatory School included *César Sepúlveda* and *Clemente Bolio.* j-None. k-None.
l-DP70, 1122-23; WWM45, 60; DEM, 183-85; letter; Carreño, 356-57; Arriaga y Rivera, 359; O'Campo, 183-85.

Jiménez Ruiz, Eliseo
a-Nov. 8, 1912. b-Xiacui, Ixtlán de Juárez, Oaxaca. c-Primary studies in Xiacui; secondary studies in Oaxaca; cadet at the National Military College, 1931-34, graduated as a 2nd Lieutenant in Infantry, Jan. 1, 1935; studies at the Applied Military School, 1937; graduated from the Higher War College as a 2nd Captain, 1942-45; instructor, Higher War College, 1947-48. d-*Federal Deputy* from the State of Oaxaca, Dist. 2, 1964-67, member of the Indigenous Affairs Committee and the First National Defense Committee; *Senator* from the State of Oaxaca, 1976-77. e-None. f-Command Chief, Federal Highway Police; Subdirector and

Director of Public Safety, State of Guerrero; Director of the Traffic Inspection Division, Department of the Federal District; *Interim Governor of Oaxaca*, Mar. 3, 1977-80. g-None. h-Worked as an agricultural laborer and miner in the Natividad Mine. i-Married Paz Migueles Navarro; brother, Fidel, was director of public works, State of Oaxaca, 1978; daughter, Ana María Jiménez, was a precandidate for federal deputy from Oaxaca, 1979. j-Career Army officer; 2nd Lieutenant, 28th Armed Battalion, 1935-36; Commander, machine gun company, 48th Battalion, 1938-42; 2nd Captain, staff of a mechanized brigade; rank of 1st Captain, Aug. 1, 1948; rank of Major in the Infantry, Jan. 1, 1951; Commander, Light Mechanized Brigade, 1951-53; rank of Lt. Colonel, 1952; Chief of Staff, 18th Military Zone, 1960; Commander, 20th Infantry Battalion, Tapachula, Chiapas, 1961-63; Military Attaché to Guatemala and Honduras, 1968-71; rank of Brigadier General, July 1, 1970; Chief of Staff, 7th Military Zone, Monterrey, Nuevo León, 1971-72; Commander of the 35th Military Zone, Chilpancingo, Guerrero, 1972-74; Commander of the 27th Military Zone, Acapulco, Guerrero, 1974-76; rank of Brigade General, 1974. k-Promoted to Brigadier General for helping to rescue the Guatemalan Foreign Secretary from kidnappers; according to government sources, he commanded the forces who rescued *Rubén Figueroa* from *Lucio Cabañas*, 1974, but critics claim the government paid the ransom without a military rescue. l-HA, 14 Mar. 1977, 22; C de D, 1964-67, 79, 81; Enc. Mex., Annual, 1977, 548; *Excélsior*, 11 Aug. 1978, 4, 10 Nov. 1978, 12; Protag., 178.

Jiménez Segura, Javier
a-Nov. 13, 1905. b-Federal District. c-Primary and secondary studies in the public schools of Mexico City; enrolled

at the National Military College, Feb. 10, 1920, graduating as an Artillery Lieutenant, Dec. 21, 1924, and as a military industrial engineer, Oct. 1, 1925; professor at IPN. d-None. f-Chief, Proving Section, Mexican Air Force; Chief, Mechanical Laboratories, Military Industry; Director of the Army Cartridge Factory; Inspector of Army Warehouses and Parks; Oficial Mayor of Military Industry; Secretary General of Military Industry, 1966-71; Director General of War Materiels, Secretariat of National Defense, 1971-73; Director General of Military Industry, July 16, 1973-76, 1976-82. g-President of the National Military College Association; President of the College of Military Engineers. h-None. i-Son, *Javier Jiménez Espirú*, was subsecretary of communications, 1982; son, Enrique, was a director general in the Secretariat of Industry and Commerce; married Rosa Espirú Herrera; brother, Luis, a career army officer. j-Career Army officer; rank of 2nd Captain, Aug. 1, 1936; officer, 3rd Artillery Regiment; officer, artillery battery, National Military College; rank of Captain, Aug. 16, 1941; rank of Major, Mar. 16, 1944; rank of Lt. Colonel, Sept. 16, 1946; rank of Colonel, Nov. 20, 1950; rank of Brigadier General, Nov. 20, 1953; rank of Brigade General, Nov. 20, 1965; rank of Division General, Nov. 20, 1972. k-None. l-*El Día*, 1 Dec. 1976, 10; DGF56, 529; Rev. de Ejer., Dec. 1964, 23; Rev. de Ejer., Jan. 1958, 32.

Joaquín Coldwell, Pedro
a-Aug. 5, 1950. b-Cozumel, Quintana Roo. c-Primary studies at the Benito Juárez School, Cozumel, 1956-61; secondary studies from the Andrés Quintana Roo School, Cozumel, 1961-63; preparatory studies at the Franco Español Preparatory School, Mexico City, 1963-65; law degree, Ibero-American University, 1966-71; professor, Center

of Scientific and Technical Studies, Cozumel. d-Deputy to the Constitutional Convention of Quintana Roo, Dist. 6, 1974, president of the convention; *Federal Deputy* from the State of Quintana Roo, Dist. 1, 1979-80, coordinator of the delegation of CNOP deputies, 1980; *Governor of Quintana Roo*, 1981-87. e-None. f-Secretary General of Government of the State of Quintana Roo, 1975-79, under Governor *Jesús Martínez Ross*; Director General of the National Fund for Tourism Development, Secretariat of Tourism, 1988-90; *Secretary of Tourism*, 1990-93. g-Secretary of Organization of the CNOP, 1979-80; coordinator of the deputation of CNOP deputies to the Chamber of Deputies, 1979-80. h-None. i-Son of Nassim Joaquín Coldwell Ibarra, businessman, and Miguelina Coldwell Fernández; married Nahima Amar Dorantes; attended Ibero-American University with *Emilio Gamboa*. k-Youngest constitutional governor in Mexican political history; first Mexican governor to have graduated from Ibero-American University and from any major private university. l-DAPC, 1981, 94; C de D, 1979-82, 14; letter; *Excelsior*, 19 Oct. 1980, 4A, 16 Aug. 1982, 27A; DBGM89, 186; DBGM92, 196.

Joffre Vázquez, Sacramento
a-May 12, 1906. b-San Francisco Cuautlacingo, Puebla. c-Primary and secondary studies in Ciudad Serdán; no degree. d-Mayor of Ciudad Serdán, Puebla, 1933-36; *Alternate Federal Deputy* from the State of Puebla, Dist. 8, 1937-40; Local Deputy to the State Legislature of Puebla, 1939-42, 1962-65; *Federal Deputy* from the Federal District, Dist. 11, 1943-46; *Federal Deputy* from the State of Puebla, Dist. 5, 1976-79, member of the Social Action Committee, the National Defense Committee, the Chontalpa Southeast Zone Section of the Regional Develop-

ment Committee, the Disaster Zone Section of the Regional Development Committee, the National Properties Committee, and the Committee for Civic Programs and Special Acts; *Federal Deputy* from the State of Puebla, Dist. 14, 1982-85. e-Delegate of the CEN of PRI to all national conventions, 1929-85; joined the PNR, 1929; *Secretary of Agrarian Action of the CEN of the PRM*, 1940. f-None. g-Ejido organizer in Puebla, 1922; founder of the Union of Agrarian Communities of Ciudad Serdán, Puebla; Secretary of the League of Agrarian Communities of Puebla; President of the Ejido Directorate of Chalchicomula, Puebla; cofounder of the CNC; Secretary of Finances of the CNC, 1938-41, 1976-79; Secretary General of the Old Guard Agraristas. h-Worked as a peasant and small businessman. i-Son of Sacramento Joffre García, peasant and ejido organizer, and María de Jesús Vázquez; married Rosario Velázquez; son, Oscar, was rector of IPN, 1988. j-None. k-The government initiated criminal charges against him and *Carlos Madrazo* as an attack on the left, 1944. l-D de C, 1976-79, 4, 10, 36, 37, 63, 67; *Excélsior*, 22 Aug. 1976, 29; C de D, 1937-40, 1943-46. Medina, 20, 19; *Excélsior*, 4 June 1979, 22; Directorio, 1982-85; Lehr, 391; DBGM89, 186; Lehr, 391; DBGM, 530.

Jonguitud Barrios, Carlos
b-Coxcatlán, San Luis Potosí. c-Teaching certificate, Normal Rural School, Tenería, México; preparatory studies at the National Preparatory School; studies in law at the National School of Law, UNAM; no degree; primary school teacher; civics teacher, Toluca, México; history teacher, secondary schools and the prevocational school of IPN; Professor of Law at the Autonomous Technological Institute of Mexico. d-*Alternate Federal Deputy* from the Federal District, Dist. 14, 1967-70;

Senator from the State of San Luis
Potosí, 1976-77; *Governor of San Luis
Potosí*, 1979-85; *Senator* from the State
of San Luis Potosí, 1988-91. e-*Secretary
of Organization of the CEN of PRI*,
1970; *Secretary of Social Action of the
CEN of PRI*, 1976. f-*Director General
of the ISSSTE*, 1976-78. g-Student
leader in the Normal Rural School,
Teneria, México; representative of the
Normal Rural School of Ozuluoma to
the National Congress of the Federation
of Socialist Students; Secretary General
of the Federation of University Students
at UNAM; President of the Society of
Students at the National Preparatory
School; Auxiliary Secretary of the
Secretary of Organization of the SNTE;
Secretary of Press and Publicity, Local
9, SNTE; Private Secretary to *Manuel
Sánchez Vite*, 1952-55; Secretary of
Labor and Conflicts, Local 15, SNTE;
Secretary General of the Thirty-First
Delegation of Local 9, SNTE; Auxiliary
Secretary of Labor and Conflicts of the
CEN of the SNTE; Director General of
Publishing of the CEN of the SNTE;
President of the Congress of Labor.
h-Worked in Poza Cercado ejido,
Veracruz. i-Political disciple of *Manuel
Sánchez Vite*; longtime admirer of
Vicente Lombardo Toledano; father-in-
law of *Ramón Martínez Martín*,
senator; son of Jonguitud Alvarez, cattle
rancher, and Modesta Barrios Hernán-
dez; married María Guadalupe Rodea
García, teacher. j-None. k-Reputedly
remained with *Luis Echeverría* when he
and his mentor *Manuel Sánchez Vite*
split politically. l-*Excélsior*, 21 Dec.
1978, 29, 15 July 1977, 6, 8; LA, 15 Dec.
1978, 388; *Excélsior*, 17 May 1983, 22A;
DBGM89, 468; Hurtado, 403.

Joublanc Rivas, Luciano
(Deceased 1959) a-Feb. 21, 1896. b-Federal District. c-Primary and preparatory in Mexico City; no degree. d-None.
e-None. f-Career Foreign Service

officer; joined the Foreign Service, 1923;
Second Scribe, Sweden, 1923; Third
Secretary, July 1, 1926; Third Secretary,
in charge, Peru, 1926-27; Third Secretary, Guatemala, 1928-29; Second Secretary, Guatemala, 1929; Second Secretary, Diplomatic Department, Secretariat of Foreign Relations, 1929-30; Second Secretary, Washington, D.C., 1930;
First Secretary, Poland, 1934; Chargé
d'affaires, Poland, 1934-38; Chargé
d'affaires, Sweden, 1941-44; Ambassador
to Portugal, 1944-45; Ambassador to
Poland, 1945-46; *Ambassador to the
Soviet Union*, 1946-48; Ambassador to
the United Nations, 1956-57. g-None.
h-Author of many works; poet; founder
and Director of *El Fifi*, San Luis Potosí;
wrote for *El Universal Illustrado*.
i-Son, Luciano Joublanc, chemical engineer; grandson, Luciano Joublanc Montaño, ambassador and director general,
Secretariat of Foreign Relations, 1988.
j-None. k-None. l-Q es Q, 302; letter;
Dir. Soc, 1935, 280; DBGM89, 187.

Juárez Carreño, Raúl
a-July 14, 1928. b-Federal District.
c-Primary studies at the Emiliano
Zapata Public School, Mexico City,
1935-40; secondary studies at Secondary
School No. 1, Mexico City, 1941-43;
preparatory studies, National Preparatory School, 1943-44; graduated from
the Heroic Military College as a 2nd
Lieutenant, 1945-48; engineering
degree, National School of Engineering,
UNAM, 1950-54; staff and command
diploma, Higher War College, 1954-57;
English courses, Mexico–North American Institute of Cultural Relations,
1959-61; counterinsurgency course, Fort
Bragg, North Carolina, 1961; information and public relations course, Fort
Slocum, New York, 1961; psychological
warfare course, Fort Bragg, 1965;
professor, Higher War College, 1959-62.
d-None. e-None. f-*Oficial Mayor of the
Secretariat of National Defense*, 1988-

94. g-None. h-None. i-Son of Artemio Juárez Fragoso and Adela Carreño Medina; married Ana Ofelia Villanueva Hernández. j-Career army officer; joined the army as a cadet at the Heroic Military College, May 1, 1945; attached to the 5th Regiment, 2nd Infantry Division, 1948-49; member of the 1st Battalion, 35th Regiment, 12th Infantry Division, 1949-52; rank of 1st Lieutenant, 1950; member of the 52nd Infantry Battalion, 1952; rank of 2nd Captain, 1955; rank of 1st Captain, 1958; member of the 2nd Infantry Battalion, Presidential Guards, 1958; rank of Major, 1964; Chief of Instruction, 47th Infantry Battalion, 1964; rank of Lt. Colonel, 1965; member of Section 1A, Staff, Secretariat of National Defense, 1965-69; Chief of Subsection 1A, Staff, Secretariat of National Defense, 1969-70; Chief of Section 1, Secretariat of National Defense, 1970-72; Commander, 4th Infantry Battalion, 1972-75; rank of Colonel, 1972; attached to the 15th military zone under general *Federico Amaya Rodríguez*, 1975-76; rank of Brigadier General, 1975; Commander of the 11th Infantry Battalion, 1976-77; attached to Staff, Secretariat of National Defense, 1977-79; Chief of Laws, Staff, Secretariat of National Defense, 1979; Military Attaché, Venezuela, 1979-81; rank of Brigade General, 1979; Commander of the 6th Military Zone, Saltillo, Coahuila, 1981-82; Group Commander, Presidential Guards, 1982-85; Commander of the 8th Military Region and the 28th Military Zone, Oaxaca, Oaxaca, 1985-87; Commander of the 12th Military Zone, San Luis Potosí, San Luis Potosí, 1987-88. k-None. l-Rev. de Ejer., Dec. 1988, 15-16; DBGM92, 197-98.

Juárez Carro, Vicente
a-June 24, 1924. b-Panotla, Tlaxcala. c-Primary and secondary studies in Puebla; preparatory studies from the National Preparatory School; law degree, National School of Law, UNAM. d-*Senator* from the State of Tlaxcala, 1970-76, member of the Gran Comisión, President of the Military Justice Committee and the National Lands Committee, Second Secretary of the First Justice Committee and member of the Fourth Section of the Legislative Studies Committee. e-Joined the PRM, 1950; Director of the CEPES of PRI in Tlaxcala, 1962-64; Director of the magazine *Justicia Social* of PRI, 1956-57; President of the Assembly of the National Council of PRI, 1957. f-Public Defender, 1954-56; Judge of the Mixed Court of Appeals, Tlaxcala, 1957; Public Defender, Federal Jurisdiction, Tlaxcala, 1957-59; Consulting Lawyer, City Council of Tlaxcala, 1958-61. g-Secretary General of the College of Lawyers of Tlaxcala; Secretary General of CNOP in Tlaxcala, 1957; delegate of CNOP, 1957. h-Employee of the Secretariat of the Treasury, 1946-53. j-None. k-None. l-C de S, 1970-76, 77; PS, 3155.

Junco (Voigt), Alfonso
a-Feb. 25, 1896. b-Monterrey, Nuevo León. c-Primary and secondary studies at the Institute of the Sacred Heart; degree in accounting. d-None. e-Cofounder of PAN, 1939. f-None. g-None. h-Weekly contributor to *El Universal*, 1928; weekly contributor to *Excélsior*, 1926-28; poet and author of numerous works; general accountant, Veracruz Industrial Company; practicing accountant until 1954, when he retired to conduct full-time research; director of *Abside*. i-Son of Celedonio Junco de la Vega, noted poet and playwright and Wlisa Voigt; brother, Humberto, was mayor of Garza García, Nuevo León, 1964-66, a PAN activist, and an employee of the Monterrey group; brother, Rodolfo, was director of *El Sol* newspaper in Monterrey; married Mercedes

Palacio. j-None. k-Candidate of PAN
for federal deputy numerous times.
l-Lemus, 38; López, 563; WWM45, 61;
Carreño, 357-58; WNM, 122; WWM40,
259; Enc. Mex., 7, 543; Velázquez, 141-
42; DBM66, 363-62.

K

Kehoe Vincent, Heriberto

(Deceased 1977) a-Sept. 14, 1931.
b-Tampico, Tamaulipas. c-Completed
primary studies; two years of secondary;
no degree. d-*Federal Deputy* from the
State of Veracruz, Dist. 3, 1967-70.
e-Member of PRI. f-PEMEX employee.
g-Many union positions, STPRM;
Secretary General of the STPRM, 1977.
i-Married María del Carmen Amezcua.
j-None. k-None. l-C de D, 1967-70.

Kiehnie (Mutzenbecher), Bruno

a-Apr. 19, 1958. b-Federal District.
c-Early education unknown; business
administration degree, School of
Accounting and Administration,
UNAM, 1976-80; diploma in political
science, Graduate Institute, Pforzheim,
Germany, 1980-81. d-None. e-Joined
PRI, 1975; Private Secretary to the
Director General of the IEPES of the
CEN of PRI, *Carlos Salinas de Gortari*,
1981-82; Subsecretary of Finances of the
CEN of PRI, 1987-88. f-Analyst,
INFONAVIT, 1976-77; adviser, Secretariat of Agrarian Reform, 1977-78;
adviser, Secretariat of Commerce, 1978-
79; Private Secretary, Construction
Committee, Secretariat of Health, 1980-
81; Assistant Controller General, Secretariat of Health, 1981; Private Secretary
to the Secretary of Programming and
Budgeting, Secretariat of Programming
and Budgeting, 1982-87; Technical
Secretary of the Internal Group, Secretariat of the Treasury, 1989-90; Oficial
Mayor of Tourism, 1990-91; *Subsecretary of Promotion and Development*,

Secretariat of Tourism, June 7, 1991-93.
g-None. h-None. i-Son of Constantine
Kiehnle Nanne, public accountant, and
Imelda Mutzenbecher Zúñiga; married
Ana María Garza Vargas. j-None.
k-None. l-DBGM92, 199.

Kumate Rodríguez, Jesús

a-Nov. 12, 1924. b-Mazatlán, Sinaloa.
c-Primary studies in Public School No.
1 and No. 5, Mazatlán, 1930-35; secondary and preparatory studies, Preparatory School of Mazatlán, 1935-40; medical degree from the Military Medical
School, 1941-46; intern, Central Military Hospital, 1947-48; Ph.D. in biochemistry, IPN, 1948-50, 1961-63; professor, Military Medical School, 1948-
54; professor, National School of Medicine, 1955-94; Professor of Immunology,
School of Biological Sciences, UNAM,
1964- ; academic staff, Children's
Hospital, Mexico City, 1953-66; Fellow,
Boston University, 1981. d-None.
e-None. f-Coordinator, National Institutes of Health, Secretary of Health,
1983-85; *Subsecretary of Health*, 1985-
88; *Secretary of Health*, 1988-94.
g-Member of the National College,
1974- . h-Researcher, 1953-61, Coordinator of Research, 1961-79, and Director, 1979-80, all at Children's Hospital,
Mexico City. i-Son of Efrén Kumate
and Josefina Rodríguez; married Bertha
Guerra. j-None. k-None. l-QesQAP,
342; DBGM87, 198; DBGM89, 189.

Kuri Breña, Daniel

c-Preparatory studies at the National
Preparatory School; law degree, National School of Law, UNAM; Professor
of the Philosophy of Law, National
School of Law, UNAM. d-None.
e-Member of the CEN of PAN, 1939-49.
f-None. g-President of the National
Federation of Students, 1934-35;
cofounder of the National Federation of
Catholic Students of Mexico, 1926.
h-Manager of the Industrial Bank, 1948;

author of many books and contemporary Catholic philosopher. i-Catholic student leader with *Manuel Ulloa Ortiz* and *Carlos Septién García*, comembers of the CEN of PAN, 1939. j-None. k-None. l-López, 569; Mabry, 21.

L

Labastida (Muñoz), Horacio

a-1918. b-Puebla, Puebla. c-Early education unknown; law degree from the University of Puebla, 1942; special studies at the School of Philosophy and Letters, UNAM, 1952-54; graduate studies at the University of California, Berkeley, 1963; Director of the Preparatory School, University of Puebla, 1945; Rector, University of Puebla, 1946-50; adviser to the Rector of UNAM, 1951; founding Professor of the History of Sociology, School of Political and Social Sciences, UNAM, 1954; professor at the National Preparatory School, 1951-55; professor at the Escuela Libre de Derecho, 1951-55; professor at ITAM, Mexico City, 1951-55. d-*Federal Deputy* from the State of Puebla, Dist. 9, 1973-76; *Senator* from the State of Puebla, 1976-79; *Plurinominal Federal Deputy* from PRI, 1988-91. e-*Director of the IEPES of the CEN of PRI*, 1972-75. f-Director of Cultural Diffusion, *Universidad de México*, UNAM, 1952; Director of Scholarly Services, UNAM, 1953; Director of Social Services, UNAM, 1954; Secretary, District Court, Puebla; local judge, Puebla; Judge of the Superior Tribunal of Justice of the State of Puebla; Director of Information, Secretariat of Public Works, 1959-63; Director of Information, Secretariat of Communications, 1966-70; Director of Planning, Secretariat of Agrarian Reform, 1970-72; Ambassador to Nicaragua, 1979-82. g-None. h-None. i-Son of Roberto Labastida Meza, lawyer and interim governor of Puebla, 1921-22, and María Muñoz Encijo; married María Almedaro. j-None. k-None. l-HA, 5 Mar. 1979, I; Enc. Mex., 7, 568; DPE, 1961, 86, 1965, 110; WNM, 124; *Excélsior*, 7 Aug. 1979, 1.

Labastida Ochoa, Francisco

a-Aug. 14, 1942. b-Los Mochis, Sinaloa. c-Primary studies at the Colegio Madrid; economics degree, National School of Economics, UNAM, 1964, with a thesis on "Tax Policy in Underdeveloped Countries"; postgraduate work in evaluation of education projects and planning, CEPAL, Santiago, Chile; professor, UNAM; professor for PRI. d-*Governor of Sinaloa*, 1986-92. e-Joined PRI, 1960; General Coordinator of Projects, Subdirector of Planning, IEPES of PRI, 1975-76. f-Analyst, Secretary of the Treasury, 1962; Chief, Income Section, Department of Regional Tax Studies, Financial Studies Division, Secretariat of the Treasury, 1965; economic researcher, Federal Institute of Teacher Education, Secretariat of Public Education, 1965-66; Director, Office of Truck Transportation, Division of Taxes, Secretariat of Communications and Transportation, 1966-67; Chief, Department of Social Welfare, Division of Public Investment, Secretariat of the Presidency, 1968-72; Subdirector, Division of Public Investment, Secretariat of the Presidency, 1972-75; Director General of Fiscal Development, Secretariat of the Treasury, 1976-79; *Subsecretary of Programming*, Secretariat of Planning and Budgeting, 1979-82; *Secretary of Government Properties*, 1982-86. g-None. h-None. i-School companion and friend of *Andrés de Otezya*; disciple of *Fernando Hiriart Balderrama*, grandson of Francisco Labastida Izquierdo, interim governor of Jalisco, 1920; son of Eduardo Labastida Kofhal, surgeon, and Gloria Ochoa Sánchez; married Rosa Elena Gómez de la Torre.

j-None. k-None. l-*Excélsior*, 1 Dec. 1982, 34a; HA, 13 Dec. 1982, 12-13; Informe, 53-54; Hurtado, 309; *Proceso*, 20 July 1987,10; DBGM, 230.

Labra (García), Wenceslao
a-Sept. 28, 1895. b-Zumpango, México. c-Attended the Military Preparatory Academy, graduate of the National Military College as a 2nd Lieutenant of Cavalry, Mar. 10, 1913. d-Local Deputy to the State Legislature of México; Federal Deputy from the State of México, Dist. 14, 1922-24, 1924-26, 1926-28, Dist. 7, 1928-30; *Senator from México*, 1934-37; *Governor of México*, 1937-41. e-*Secretary of Organization and Statistics of the CEN of PRI*, 1936-37. f-Director of the National Lottery. g-One of the founders of the National Farmers Federation, 1938; considered as a candidate for secretary general of the CNC, 1941. i-Relative, *Armando Labra Manjarrez*, was a federal deputy, 1976-79; son-in-law of Filiberto Gómez, prominent politician in the State of México; married Rita Gómez Hernández; from a middle class family. j-Joined the Revolution; 2nd Lieutenant of the Cavalry, 27th Irregular Regiment, 1913; rank of Colonel, 1940. k-Brandenburg considered *Labra* in the Inner Circle status as Governor of México; supported *Miguel Henríquez Guzmán* for President, 1951. l-Brandenburg, 80; Peral, 426-27; *Hoy*, 21 Dec. 1940, 64-65, 13 Jan. 1940, 8-9, 60-61; González Navarro, 168; *Excélsior*, 27 Feb. 1933, 11; Hernández Chávez, 22.

Laguna (García), José
a-Feb. 28, 1921. b-Federal District. c-Early education unknown; medical degree from the National School of Medicine, UNAM, with a thesis on "Medical Health Report on Social Service in San Blas, Nayarit," 1937-43; residency, General Hospital, Mexico City, 1943-44; advanced studies, Harvard University, 1948; advanced studies, Rowell Animal Nutrition Institute, Aberdeen, Scotland, 1950; professor, National School of Medicine, UNAM, 1944-70; Director, Biochemistry Department, School of Medicine, UNAM; Dean, National School of Medicine, UNAM, 1971-75; Director of Technological Education, University Center for Health. d-None. e-None. f-Researcher, Institute of Health and Tropical Medicine, Secretariat of Health, 1944-46; adviser in gastroenterology, National Institute of Cardiology, 1944-47; Director of Biochemistry Labs, Nutritional Illnesses Hospital, 1951-54; Director, Multinational Biochemistry Project, OAS, 1970-72; *Subsecretary of Planning, Secretariat of Health*, 1977-80; adviser, Coordinator of Health Services, Presidency, 1981-82; *Subsecretary of Assistance, Secretariat of Health*, 1982-85. g-None. h-Director of Labs, Biochemistry, Bhering Institute, 1952-60. i-Professor of many prominent political leaders who were medical students; son of Pedro Laguna González, businessman, and Clementina García Clerge; married Julieta Calderón, surgeon. j-None. k-None. l-Q es QAP, 332; Protag., 185; letters; DBGM, 231.

Lajous Martínez, Adrián René
a-Jan. 24, 1920. b-Buenos Aires, Argentina. c-Early education unknown; law degree, National School of Law, UNAM, 1949; postgraduate work in economics, New York University, 1956. d-None. e-None. f-Counselor, Mexican Embassy, Washington, D.C.; representative of the Mexican government to the International Sugar Negotiations, 1965-73; Executive Director, World Bank, Washington, D.C., 1970-72; Director, Fund for Industrial Development, 1974-76; Director General of the Mexican Institute of Foreign Trade, 1976-79; *Director General of the National Bank of Foreign Trade*, 1979-82. g-Manager,

Inter-American Cotton Federation, 1959-63; President, International Sugar Council. h-Manager, Radio Programs of Mexico, S.A.; various positions, National Bank of Foreign Trade, 1953-58; director of the Legal Department and the Credit Department, National Savings Bank, 1950-52; member, International Coffee Organization, London, 1963-64; Manager of Export Department, National Sugar Growers Association, 1965-67. i-Son of Adrián René Lajous, engineer and vice-president of Ford Motor Company in Mexico, and Evangelina Martínez; married María de la Luz Vargas Burgos, daughter of Plácido Vargas Páez, an accountant; son, Adrián, appointed Subdirector of Production of PEMEX, 1982, and married to Soledad Loaeza, distinguished academic and intellectual; daughter, *Luz Lajous Vargas* served as a federal deputy from the Federal District, 1982-85, and is married to *Ignacio Madrazo Reynoso*, subsecretary in the secretariat of the treasury, 1982; daughter, *Roberta Lajous Vargas*, served as director general of Northern Affairs, Secretariat of Foreign Relations, 1982, and is married to *Fernando Solana Morales*, Secretary of Foreign Relations, 1993; daughter Alejandra was official historian of the presidency, 1982-88. j-None. k-Resigned from the National Bank of Foreign Trade, Sept. 2, 1982, because he disagreed with the nationalization of the banks. l-Letter; Linajes, 276-77; *Excélsior*, 5 May 1979; Protag., 185-86; Q es QAP, 58.

Lajous Vargas, Luz

a-Nov. 19, 1945. b-Federal District. c-Early education unknown; actuary degree, UNAM, 1963-68, with a thesis on Mexican pension plans; postgraduate work at Institute of Higher Studies of Monterrey, London School of Economics, and Sorbonne. d-*Federal Deputy* from the Federal District, Dist. 32,

1982-85, President of the Department of the Federal District Committee; *Plurinominal Federal Deputy* from PRI, 1988-91. e-Joined the CNOP of PRI, 1975; Executive Secretary of the IEPES of PRI, 1981-82; Subsecretary of Organization, CEN of PRI, 1981-82; Assistant Secretary of the IEPES of PRI, 1985-87. f-Adviser to the Advisory Group of the Secretariat of Planning and Budget; General Coordinator of Management Control, Secretariat of Planning and Budget, 1979-81. g-Oficial Mayor of CNOP, 1985. h-Assistant actuary, La Comercial Insurance Company, 1967-69; pension actuary, Phillips and Associates, 1971-73; consultant, McKinski and Company, 1973-77. i-Daughter of *Adrián Lajous Martínez*, director general of the National Bank of Foreign Trade, 1979-82, and Luz Vargas Burgos; married *Ignacio Madrazo Reynoso*, subsecretary in the secretariat of the treasury, 1982; sister of Adrián Lajous Vargas, Subdirector of Production of PEMEX, 1982; sister, *Roberta Lajous Vargas*, was a director general in the Secretariat of Foreign Relations, and is the wife of *Fernando Solana Morales*, Secretary of Foreign Relations, 1993; sister Alejandra was the Official Historian of the Presidency; sister-in-law of Soledad Loaeza, leading intellectual and academic, Colegio de México. j-None. k-None. l-Directorio, 1982-85; Lehr, 150; DBGM89, 190-91; DBGM, 531.

Lajous Vargas, Roberta

a-Feb. 6, 1954. b-Federal District. c-Early education unknown; degree in international relations, Colegio de México, 1971-75, with a thesis on Mexico's participation in the North American sugar market; MA in political science, Stanford University, 1975-77, with a thesis on the Latin American economic system; professor, School of Political and Social Sciences, UNAM, 1977-83; professor, Colegio de México,

1985- . d-None. e-Member of PRI;
_Secretary of International Affairs of the
CEN of PRI_, 1990, 1993. f-Subdirector
of Cultural Exchange, Secretariat of
Public Education, 1977-79; Subdirector
of Regional Cooperation, 1979-80,
Subdirector of Multilateral Economic
Relations, 1980-82, Director General of
North America, 1982-86, and Director
General for Western Europe, 1986-88,
all at Secretariat of Foreign Relations.
g-None. h-None. i-Daughter of _Adrián
Lajous Martínez_, director general of the
foreign trade bank, and Luz Vargas
Burgos; sister of Adrián Lajous Vargas,
PEMEX official; sister-in-law of Soledad
Loaeza Tovar, leading intellectual and
academic at the Colegio de México;
married to _Fernando Solana Morales_,
secretary of foreign relations, 1988-94;
sister of Luz Lajous Vargas, federal
deputy, 1988-91; sister of Alejandra
Lajous Vargas, chronicler of the presidency of Mexico; sister-in-law of
Ignacio Madrazo Reynoso, subsecretary
of tax investigation, 1982. l-DBGM87,
199-200; DBGM92, 200; letter.

Lamadrid (Sauza), José Luis
a-Feb. 22, 1931. b-Guadalajara, Jalisco.
c-Preparatory studies in Guadalajara;
law degree from the University of
Guadalajara, 1949-54; professor at the
Preparatory School of Guadalajara;
professor at the School of Law, Philoso-
phy, and Liberal Arts, University of
Guadalajara, 1956-71; professor,
National School of Law, National
School of Economics, and School of
Philosophy and Letters, UNAM, 1969-
70; Director of the Seminar on Political
Theory, School of Political and Social
Sciences, UNAM, 1969; Professor of the
Seminar on Political Thinkers, UNAM,
1969; member of the University
Council of UNAM. d-_Federal Deputy_
from the State of Jalisco, Dist. 1, 1961-
63, member of the Legislative Studies
Committee (First Section on Constitu-

tional Affairs), the First Treasury
Committee, and the First Justice
Committee; _Federal Deputy_ from the
State of Jalisco, Dist. 11, 1973-76, Dist.
1, 1982-85; _Plurinominal Federal
Deputy_ from PRI, 1988-91; _Senator_
from Jalisco, 1991- . e-Oficial Mayor of
the CEN of PRI; representative of PRI
before the Local Electoral Committee,
1955; founder of the Revolutionary
Youth of Jalisco; _Secretary of Press and
Publicity of the CEN of PRI_, 1964;
Assistant Secretary of the CEN of PRI,
1972-73; _Secretary of Social Action of
the CEN of PRI_, 1973-75; representative
of PRI on the Federal Electoral Commission, 1975-76. f-Director of Public
Relations of the Department of the
Federal District, 1966-67; Oficial Mayor
of the Department of Education, State
of Jalisco, 1959-61; _Oficial Mayor of the
Secretariat of Government_, 1976-78;
Subsecretary of Government, Aug. 14,
1978, to May 24, 1979. g-President of
the Federation of University Students of
Guadalajara, 1954-55. h-None. i-Son of
Rosendo Lamadrid Vega, industrialist,
and Rosalía Sauza Corona; related to
Governor Ramón Corona. j-None.
k-None. l-HA, 21 Dec. 1964; C de D,
1961-63; 81; Excélsior, 13 July 1973, 4;
C de D, 19, 73-76, 13; HA, 13 Oct. 1975,
17; DBGM84, 531-32; Lehr, 226;
Directorio, 1982-85; DBGM89, 470;
Hurtado, 344.

Lameiras Olvera, Esteban
a-1947. b-Federal District. c-Early
education unknown; studies at the
School of Philosophy and Letters,
UNAM, but left because of the 1968
student strike; studies in communication; Professor of Communication,
College of Sciences and Humanities,
Ibero-American University. d-None.
e-Member of the PST since its founding;
member of the Central Committee and
the Executive Committee of the PST,
1975-76. f-None. g-None. j-None.

k-Candidate of the PST for federal deputy from Dist. 18, State of México, 1979. l-HA, 14 May 1979, VIII.

Lanche Guillén, Dámaso
a-Dec. 11, 1912. b-Ometepec, Guerrero. c-Early education unknown; normal teaching certificate; taught primary school, 1933-40; secondary school teacher, 1941-43; medical degree. d-*Federal Deputy* from the State of Guerrero, Dist. 5, 1952-55, Dist. 10, 1979-82, member of the Health and Welfare Committee and head of the Guerrero delegation. e-None. f-Chief of Medical Services, Mexican Institute of Social Security, Guerrero, 1955-63; Chief of Medical Services, IMSS, Federal District, 1963-73. g-President of the Regional Union of Agricultural Colonies of Costa Chica, Cuajinicuilapa; Permanent Secretary of the National Political Committee of the CNC, 1953; Secretary General of the League of Agrarian Communities and Peasant Unions, Guerrero. h-Cattle rancher and farmer. j-None. k-None. l-C de D, 1952-55, 1979-82; Protag., 187.

Landeros Gallegos, Rodolfo
a-Sept. 14, 1931. b-Calvillo, Aguascalientes. c-Early education unknown; no degree. d-*Senator* from the State of Aguascalientes, 1976-80; *Governor of Aguascalientes*, 1980-86. e-Director of Press for *José López Portillo*'s campaign for president, 1976; *Secretary of Press and Publicity of the CEN of PRI*, 1978-80. f-Employee, Press Department, Secretariat of Agriculture, 1951; Director, Press Department, IMSS, 1954-58; Director, Press Department, Secretariat of Industry and Commerce, 1958-64; Coordinator of Press, INFONAVIT, 1965-66; Director of Public Relations, Secretariat of the Treasury, 1966-68; Director of Press and Public Relations, President of Mexico, 1976-78; Adviser on Special Affairs, President *José López*

Portillo, 1977. g-None. h-Journalist; founder of *El Sol del Centro*, Aguascalientes; sports editor, *El Sol del Centro*, 1945; Political Affairs Editor, *El Sol del Centro*; journalist for *Siempre*, *Este*, and *Diario ABC*; worked in editorial offices of García Valseca chain. i-From three generations of peasants; considered himself to be a political disciple of *Antonio Ortiz Mena* and *Mario Ramón Beteta*; married Natalia Verdugo. j-None. k-None. l-*Excélsior*, 21 Mar. 1980, 18, 17 Dec. 1979, 19; *Hoy*, 12 Nov. 1977, 11; HA, 31 Mar. 1980, 26; C de S, 1976-82; DPE61; DPE65; MGF69; HA, 12 Oct. 1981, 6; Almanaque de Aguas., 13.

Landerreche Obregón, Juan
a-Nov. 1, 1914. b-Federal District. c-Secondary and preparatory studies at the Colegio Francés Morelos; law degree with honorable mention, National School of Law, UNAM, May 6, 1936, with a thesis on "Constitutional Theory and Real Estate"; LLD, with an honorable mention, June 24, 1955, with a thesis on "The Participation of Workers in Business Utilities." d-*Federal Deputy* from the Federal District, Dist. 8, 1964-67, member of the Committee on Money and Credit Institutions; *Federal Deputy* from PAN (party deputy), 1970-73, member of the First Section of the Legislative Studies Committee, the Second Government Committee, the Second Constitutional Affairs Committee, and the Tourism Committee; *Plurinominal Federal Deputy* from PAN, 1979-82. e-Candidate for federal deputy from PAN four times before winning in 1964; founding member of PAN, 1939; member of the Legislative Studies Committee of PAN; member of the National Committee of PAN, 1975; Secretary of Policy of the National Executive Committee of PAN, 1975. f-None. g-Active in the 1933 student movement; Director of the National

Catholic Student Union. h-Cofounder of *Jus*, a law and social science review; Director of *Jus*, 1941-57; employee of Serfin Banking Group; Vice-President of Moresa, 1981-82. i-Married Gabriela Gómez Morín, daughter of *Manuel Gómez Morín*; Catholic student leader with *Manuel Ulloa Ortiz*. j-None. k-None. l-Mabry; C de D, 1970-72, 121, 1967-69, 90.

Lang Islas, Jorge
a-Nov. 6, 1904. b-Texcoco, México. c-Primary studies in Texcoco; secondary studies at the Melchor Ocampo Center, Pachuca, Hidalgo; completed secondary studies at the Scientific and Literary Institute of Pachuca; graduated from the Naval Military College, as a coast-guardsman, Nov. 26, 1924; studied submarine warfare in Chile, 1938-40; advanced studies in engineering in Mexico; professor at the Naval College (4 years); Subdirector and Director of the Naval College of the Gulf, Veracruz, 1947. d-*Federal Deputy* from the State of Colima, Dist. 2, 1958-61, member of the Fish and Game Committee, the Second Committee on National Defense, and the Naval Committee. e-None. f-Commanding General of the Fleet, Secretariat of the Navy, 1964-65. g-None. h-None. j-Career naval officer; rank of Corvette Lieutenant, 1927; Commander of the Coast Guard cutter 28, 1940-41, of the destroyer *Guanajuato*, 1941-42, of the 1st Naval Zone, Tampico, Tamau-lipas, 1951, of the 6th Naval Zone, Manzanillo, Colima, 1955-58, and of the Attack Force, 1958; rank of Vice Admiral. k-None. l-HA, 21 Dec. 1964, 9-10; DGF51, I, 388; DPE65, 51; DGF56, 386; DGF47, 230; Func., 149.

Langle Martínez, Eduardo
a-Dec. 18, 1914. b-Puebla, Puebla. c-Early education unknown; law degree, National School of Law, UNAM, with a thesis on salaries. d-None. e-None.

f-Actuary, 1st Judicial District, Veracruz, Veracruz, 1942-43; actuary, 2nd Judicial District in Administration, Federal District, 1943-46; Private Secretary to the Governor of Tabasco, *Francisco J. Santamaría*, 1947-49; Secretary of Studies and Accounts, Supreme Court of Justice, 1949-50; District Court Judge, Piedras Negras, Coahuila, 1950-52; District Court Judge, Tijuana, Baja California, 1953-60; Judge, 2nd District Criminal Affairs, Federal District, 1960-64; Assistant Attorney General of the Federal District, 1964-66; *Subsecretary of State Industries*, Secretariat of Government Properties, 1966-68; *Justice of the Supreme Court*, 1971-72; Secretary General of Government of the State of Puebla, 1972-75; *Justice of the Supreme Court*, 1975-76, 1976-82, 1982-85. g-None. h-None. i-Son of Eduardo Langle Pérez, businessman, and Concepción Martínez Beltrán; married Rosa Luz Gómez Fernández. j-None. k-None. l-DBGM, 664; DGF65.

Lanz Duret, Fernando
a-Jan. 19, 1916. b-Campeche, Campeche. c-Preparatory studies at the National Preparatory School, Mexico City; law degree from the National School of Law, UNAM, 1940, with a thesis on the general subject of law. d-*Federal Deputy* from the State of Campeche, Dist. 1, 1952-55, member of the Permanent Committee, 1952, Vice-President, Dec. 1952, member of the Second Constitutional Affairs Committee, the Second Instructive Section of the Grand Jury and the Second Balloting Committee; *Senator* from the State of Campeche, 1958-64, member of the Foreign and Domestic Trade Committee, the Second Constitutional Affairs Committee, the Second Foreign Relations Committee, and the Special Legislative Studies Committee; President of the First Credit, Money and Credit Institutions Committee. e-Member of the Program

Committee of the PRI; PRI delegate to Guanajuato, 1955. f-Director General of the Department of Legal Affairs, Secretariat of Health, 1964-71. g-Member of the University Council, UNAM; President of the Student Association, UNAM. h-Newspaperman, 1941; writer for *El Universal*; war correspondent in England, 1942-45; correspondent on European Reconstruction, 1945-46. i-Father and grandfather well-known lawyers; father, Miguel Lanz Duret, served as a federal deputy from the Federal District; mother is María Concepción Sierra, daughter of Justo Sierra Méndez, secretary of justice; nephew of *Manuel J. Sierra*; classmate of *Rafael Moreno Valle* at the National Preparatory School. j-None. k-None. l-Func., 132; DPE71, 116; C de D, 1952-54, 60, 58, 52, 53, 51, 50; C de S, 1961-64, 58; DPE65, 163.

Lanz Galera, Joaquín
(Deceased 1965) a-1884. b-Campeche, Campeche. c-Primary and secondary studies in Campeche; law degree, School of Law, University of Campeche. d-Deputy from the State of Campeche to the Constitutional Convention, 1916-17; Federal Deputy from the State of Quintana Roo, Dist. 1, 1918-20; Senator from the State of Campeche, 1924-26. e-None. f-Secretary, local court of Campeche; Judge, First Circuit Court District, Federal District; Judge, District Court, Querétaro, Querétaro, 1951; Judge, Second Circuit Court District, Puebla, Puebla, 1956; Justice of the Superior Tribunal of Justice of the Federal District and Federal Territories. g-None. h-None. j-None. k-None. l-DP70, 1157; DGF51, I, 594; DGF56, 585.

Lara (Ramos), César Agusto
(Deceased Jan. 10, 1962) a-Nov. 24, 1896. b-Pichucalco, Chiapas. c-Primary studies in Pichucalco and in the Liceo of Chiapas, San Cristóbal de las Casas. d-Federal Deputy from the State of Chiapas, Dist. 6, 1918-20; Mayor of Arriaga, Chiapas; Mayor of Tuxtla Gutiérrez, Chiapas, 1926-27; Federal Deputy from the State of Chiapas, Dist. 6, 1930-32; Federal Deputy from the State of Chiapas, Dist. 5, 1934-37, member of the Gran Comisión; *Interim Governor of Chiapas*, 1947-48. e-None. f-Assistant Chief of Police, Federal District, 1938-40; Director, Department of Press and Tourism, State of Chiapas. g-None. h-Journalist and poet. j-Joined the Maderistas as a student under Colonel Ignacio Gutiérrez, 1910; fought against Pascual Orozco; reached rank of Brigadier General, 1924. k-Simpson credits him with ending pistolerismo in Chiapas. l-Simpson, 342; letter; Peral, 431; DBC, 132.

Larios Gaitán, Alberto
b-Colima, Colima. c-Teaching certificate from the Normal School of Colima, Sept. 1944; Professor of Math and Mexican History, and Subdirector, Secondary School of Manzanillo, Colima; teacher, 18th of March and Francisco Díaz Covarrubias Elementary Schools, Mexico City, 1946-60; Professor of Math and Mexican History, IPN, 1950-61; teacher, secondary schools, Mexico City. d-None. e-Member of the National Council of PRI, 1964-65. f-None. g-Student leader in Colima; Private Secretary to *Jesús Robles Martínez* and Lozano Bernal as Secretaries General of the SNTE, 1949-52; Secretary of Political Action of CNOP of PRI, 1961-65; Secretary General of the SNTE, 1961. h-Worked in night school and state penitentiary to complete teaching certificate. i-Father a school teacher. j-None. k-Established the first secondary school in Manzanillo, Colima. l-Romero Aceves, 100-02; DBGM89, 471-72.

Larios Ibarra, Jesús Salvador
a-Aug. 17, 1919. b-Hermosillo, Sonora.
c-Early education unknown; law degree,
School of Law, University of Sonora,
1975-80, with a thesis on electoral laws.
d-Treasurer of Hermosillo, Sonora,
1967-70; *Plurinominal Federal Deputy*
from PAN, 1982-85. e-Joined PAN, Apr.
1943; candidate for senator from PAN,
1958; regional adviser to PAN, 1967-80;
national adviser to PAN, 1970; candidate of PAN for alternate federal deputy
from Sonora, 1967; candidate of PAN
for local deputy, State Legislature of
Sonora, 1970, 1973; member of the
Regional Committee of PAN, Sonora;
Treasurer of the Regional Committee of
PAN, Sonora, 1948-50; Secretary General of PAN, Sonora; President of the
Regional Committee of PAN, Sonora,
1973-76. f-None. g-None. h-Practicing
lawyer; accountant, Banpaís, 1947-55,
Carta Blanca, 1955-61, Volkswagen,
Hermosillo, 1961-62. i-Son of Manuel
Larrios Soteb, topographical engineer,
and Luz Enriqueta Ibarra Almada, tea-
cher; María Dolores Gaxiola Gándara.
j-None. k-None. l-Directorio, 1982-85;
Lehr, 633; DBGM, 533.

Lastra Andrade, Adolfo
a-Aug. 9, 1923. b-Federal District.
c-Early education unknown; engineering degree, National School of Engineering, UNAM; Professor of Administration and Economics, National School of
Engineering, UNAM. d-None. e-None.
f-Assistant Manager of Supplies, 1973,
General Superintendent of Construction, 1973-74, and Executive Coordinator of Projects, 1974-76, all at Federal
Electric Commission; *Subdirector of
Production, PEMEX*, 1976-79; Subdirector of Exploitation, PEMEX, 1979-82.
g-None. j-None. k-None. l-Letter.

Lavalle Urbina, Eduardo J.
a-1910. b-Campeche, Campeche.
c-Secondary education at the Campeche

Institute, Campeche; law degree, Dec.
24, 1934. d-Mayor of Campeche;
Governor of Campeche, 1944-49.
e-President of the Regional Committee
of the PNR in Campeche. f-Agent of
the Ministerio Público of the Office of
the Attorney General (in civil affairs),
Campeche; Secretary of the Campeche
Board of Conciliation and Arbitration;
Judge of the Superior Tribunal of Justice
of the State of Campeche; Attorney
General of Campeche. g-None.
i-Brother of *María Lavalle Urbina*; son
of Manuel Lavalle y Covián, prominent
lawyer, journalist, and literary figure,
and Esperanza Urbina Alfaro. j-None.
k-Elected governor as the candidate of
the Popular Electoral Front of Campeche. l-HA, 7 Oct. 1949, xxviii; Peral,
436.

Lavalle Urbina, María
a-May 24, 1908. b-Campeche, Campeche. c-Primary studies in Campeche;
secondary studies in Campeche;
teaching certificate from the Normal
School of Campeche, 1927, in elementary and secondary education; law
degree, School of Law, Campeche
Institute, 1944; primary school teacher,
1927; Professor of the Science of
Education, Normal School of Campeche; primary school director, 1943.
d-*Senator* from the State of Campeche,
1964-70, President of the Senate, Dec.
1965 (first woman), and member of the
Permanent Committee. e-Director of
the National Feminine Organizations of
the CEN of PRI, 1965-70; precandidate
for senator from Campeche, 1981.
f-Director of the State Literacy Campaign, Campeche; Judge of the Tribunal
Superior of Justice of the Federal District, 1947-54 (first woman appointed to
this position); Director of the Department of Social Welfare, Secretariat of
Government, 1954-63; Director of the
Civil Registry, 1970-73; *Subsecretary of
Primary and Normal Education*, 1976-

80; President of the Free Textbook Commission, 1982-84. g-President of the Mexican Women's Alliance. h-None. i-Helped *Rafael Murillo Vidal* defend squatters' rights to colonize in a section known as the 201st Squadron; sister of *Eduardo J. Lavalle Urbina*; daughter of Manuel Lavalle y Covián, a lawyer, jouralist and literary figure, and Esperanza Urbina. j-None. k-First woman senator from Campeche. l-DPE61; DGF51, I, 487; Q es Q, 318; C de S, 1964-70; DGF56, 84; HA, 3 Feb. 1975, 9; Enc. Mex., VIII, 1977, 2; HA, 31 Oct. 1977, 8; letter; DBGM, 237.

Lazo (Barreira), Carlos Jr.
(Deceased Nov. 5, 1955) a-Aug. 19, 1914. b-Federal District. c-Primary studies at the San Borja Institute, Mexico City, 1921-27; studied carpentry at the Pape Carpentier Institute; secondary and business studies at the San Borja Institute; preparatory studies at the Colegio Francés Morelos; architecture degree from the National School of Architecture, UNAM, 1934-39, with a thesis on "Planning and Rural Architecture in Mexico"; studied planning in the United States, 1940-42, on a scholarship from the U.S. Department of Defense; studied Planning in Canada, 1942-43; Professor of Drawing, Instituto Bachillerato, 1934; professor at the School of Architecture, UNAM, and at the National Polytechnic Institute. d-None. e-Contributor to *Miguel Alemán*'s program of government during the 1945 presidential campaign. f-Adviser to the President of Mexico, 1949; *Oficial Mayor of the Secretariat of National Patrimony*, 1947, under *Alfonso Caso*; representative of the Secretariat of the Treasury to the Planning Commission for the Federal District, 1948; President of the Technical Architectural Commission, Secretariat of National Patrimony, 1947; President of the Federal Commission for Planning, Secretariat of Na-

tional Planning, 1947; Director General of the University City, 1950; *Secretary of Public Works*, 1952-55. g-None. h-Representative of the Society of Architects to the Congress of Social Assistance, 1938; architectural adviser to Catholic Action, 1937; professional architect for the University City Project, Mexico City, 1949-50; Codirector of the Congress for the Promotion of Popular Dwellings, 1946; author of several studies on planning; Codirector of the magazine *Construction Review*. i-Son of an architect and former director of the School of Architecture, UNAM, Carlos M. Lazo, and Luz Barreira; married Yolanda Margáin. j-None. k-Winner of many architecture prizes; died in an aviation accident. l-WWM45, 63; STYRBIWW54, 848, 1113; DGF47, 269; HA, 5 Dec. 1952, 9; DP70, 1165; López, 583; Enc. Mex., VIII, 1977, 5.

Lazos, Efraín
a-1906. b-Tuxtla Gutiérrez, Chiapas. c-Early education unknown; law degree, National School of Law, UNAM, 1930. d-Mayor of Tapachula, Chiapas; *Senator* from the State of Chiapas, 1946-52, member of the Legislative Studies Committee, the Public Welfare Committee and the Gran Comisión. e-None. f-Civil judge, Tapachula; Justice of the Superior Tribunal of Justice of Chiapas. g-None. i-Classmate of *Miguel Alemán* at UNAM. j-None. k-None. l-DGF51, I, 5, 9-11; PS, 3229.

Lecona Soto, Noé
(Deceased 1945) a-Dec. 6, 1903. b-Huachinango, Zacatlán, Puebla. c-Law degree from the National School of Law, UNAM. d-Local deputy to the 31st Legislature of the State of Puebla; *Senator* from the State of Puebla, 1940-45. e-None. f-Agent of the Ministerio Público of the Office of the Attorney General for the Federal District; Secretary of the Mixed Agrarian

Commission, Veracruz; head of the Legal Department of the Office of Public Works for the State of Puebla; Judge of the Civil Division in the State of Puebla; Secretary General of Government of the State of Puebla under Governor *Maximino Avila Camacho*, 1937-40. g-None. h-Author of a book on agrarian legislation, 1932. i-Son of Zapatista and Lt. Colonel, Reinaldo Lecona, who represented Emiliano Zapata at the 1915 Convention at Mexico City, and later supported de la Huerta, 1923. j-None. k-None. l-EBW46, 103; DP70, I, 1166; C de S, 1940-46; Peral, 438.

Ledón Alcaraz, Enrique
a-Oct. 18, 1911. b-Tecuala, Nayarit. c-Primary and secondary in Tepic, Nayarit; preparatory studies in Guadalajara. d-Mayor of Tuxpan, 1946-47; 2nd Councilman of Tuxpan, 1947-49; 1st Councilman of Tuxpan, 1949-52; Mayor of Tuxpan, 1952-54; *Senator* from the State of Nayarit, 1958-64. e-Member of PRI. f-Director, Department of Reforestation, Secretariat of Agriculture, 1955-58. g-Joined the CTM, 1931. h-Electrician. j-None. k-None. l-Func., 386; Basurto.

Leff Zimmerman, Gloria
a-Jan. 13, 1949. b-Federal District. c-Early education unknown; sociology degree, School of Political and Social Sciences, UNAM; MA from the Colegio de México; Ph.D. in the social sciences, Colegio de México; Professor and Coordinator of the Sociology Curriculum, Autonomous University of Mexico in Unidad Azcapotzalco. d-None. e-Member of the Executive Committee of the PST. f-None. g-Director of the Intellectual Workers Front, 1979. j-None. k-Candidate for federal deputy from the PST for Round III, 1979. l-HA, 7 May 1979, VI.

Leipen Garay, Jorge
a-June 18, 1937. b-Valencia, Spain. c-Early education unknown; economics degree, National School of Economics, UNAM, 1954-59, with a thesis on the "Textile Industry and Artificial Fibers," 1961; MA in business administration, Columbia University, 1961-62; professor, UNAM, 1960-62; professor, IPN, 1960. d-None. e-None. f-Subdirector of the Mining Development Commission; aide to the Director General of Industry, Secretariat of Industry and Development, 1959-60; adviser to the Subsecretary of Nonrenewable Resources, 1961; Private Secretary to the Subsecretary of Nonrenewable Resources, Secretariat of Government Properties, *Manuel Franco López*, 1965-66; Director General of Fosforitas Mexicanas, S.A., 1966-70; Director General of ZINCAMEX, S.A., 1970-71; Director General of the Mining Development Commission, 1971-73; *Subsecretary of Nonrenewable Resources*, Secretariat of Government Properties, 1973-76, 1976-78; Director General of Siderúrgica Lázaro Cárdenas–Las Truchas, Altos Hornos de México, and the Companía Fundidadora de Fierro y Acero, 1978-82; Director General of the Council of Mining Resources, 1982. g-None. h-Production Manager, American Textile, 1958; Director General of Phibro de México, S.A., 1961-64. i-Son of Helmut Leipen Fuerst, chemist, and Francisca Garay; married Elizabeth Linares Díaz. j-None. k-None. l-HA, 12 Mar. 1973, 21; *Excélsior*, 29 Jan. 1978, 1; Q es QAP, 505; DBGM, 239.

Leñero (Ruiz), Agustín
a-Dec. 5, 1904. b-Villamar, Michoacán. c-Preparatory studies, University of Guadalajara; law degree, School of Law, University of Guadalajara; professor, School of Law, University of Michoacán; Dean, School of Law, University of Michoacán, 1927-30. d-Federal Deputy

from the State of Michoacán, 1932-34. e-Director, Legal Department, PNR, 1930-31. f-Attorney General, State of Michoacán, 1927-28; President, Superior Court of Justice of the State of Michoacán, 1928-29; Secretary General of Government of the State of Michoacán under Governor *Lázaro Cárdenas*, 1929-30; Director, Legal Department, Secretariat of Government, 1931-32; General Consul of Mexico to Paris, France, 1935-37; Ambassador to Czechoslovakia, 1937-38; founder and Director, Legal Department, PEMEX, 1938-39; *Private Secretary* to President *Lázaro Cárdenas*, 1939-40; Ambassador to Argentina, 1940-42, to Sweden and Finland, 1958-62, to Costa Rica, 1964-70. g-None. h-Author of various works. i-Close friend of *Dámaso Cárdenas*; collaborator of *Lázaro Cárdenas* in numerous state and federal positions, 1927 to 1940; attended the University of Guadalajara with *Luis I. Rodríguez* and *Raúl Castellano*; married Milagros Bores Bustamante; befriended *Alberto Bremauntz* early in his career; son, Agustín Leñero Bores, was a federal deputy from the State of México, 1985-88; brother, Alfonso, was a federal deputy from the State of Michoacán, 1930-32. j-None. k-Supported General *Miguel Henríquez Guzmán* for president, 1951-52. l-Enc. Mex., 8, 18; D de Y, 25 Jan. 1939, 1; DPE61, 21; Daniels, 76; López, 588; WNM, 27-28; Cadena Z., 143.

León Bejarano Valadez, Armando
a-Apr. 11, 1916. b-Cuautla, Morelos. c-Early education unknown; graduated as a surgeon, National Medical School, UNAM, 1939; Professor of Clinical Medicine, Graduate School, National School of Medicine, UNAM, 1940-75; professor of special orthopedic courses, National School of Medicine, UNAM, 1940-75. d-*Governor of Morelos*, 1976-82. e-Joined PRM, 1940. f-Chief of Orthopedics and Traumatology, and Sub-

director, Central Hospital, Secretariat of Communications and Transportation, 1946-61; Assistant Coordinator of Medical Services, Secretariat of Communications and Transportation, 1958-61; Chief of Orthopedic Services and Subdirector, Balbuena Hospital, Mexico City, 1961-63; Director of the Clinical Department of Traumatology Instruction, National Medical Center, 1963-70; Director of the Department of Regulation of Food and Drink, Secretariat of Health, 1975-80. g-Founder and President of the Mexican Orthopedic and Traumatology Association of the IMSS. h-Author of many works. i-Daughter, Gloria, married Rafael Angel Calderón, son of ex-President Calderón Guardia of Costa Rica, and former secretary of foreign relations; son, Armando, was a state official of Morelos. j-None. k-None. l-Enc. Mex., Annual, 1977, 546-47; *Excélsior*, 8 Feb. 1975, 21; HA, 19 Jan. 1976, 15; Almanaque de México, 1981, 371; *Excélsior*, 14 May 1979, 14A.

León Brindis, Samuel
a-1896. b-Chiapas. c-Early education unknown; medical degree; professor, Institute of Arts and Sciences, Chiapas; Rector, Institute of Arts and Sciences, Chiapas. d-Federal Deputy from the State of Chiapas, Dist. 4, 1934-37, treasurer of the leftist bloc; *Governor of Chiapas*, 1958-64. e-None. f-Director of the Federal Office of Public Health, Chiapas, 1951-52. g-None. h-Practicing physician. j-None. k-Anderson suggests that he was very popular in Chiapas and was selected as the gubernatorial candidate in opposition to the national PRI choice. l-Anderson, 103; DGF51, 356; DBM, 375; Enc. Mex., 1977, III, 310.

León Murillo, Maximiliano
a-Feb. 13, 1925. b-Tecario, Michoacán. c-Primary studies at the Republic of Brazil Primary School, Mexico City,

1935-40; secondary studies at the National School of Teachers, 1941-46; preparatory at the National Preparatory School, Mexico City, 1953-54; teaching certificate in Mexican and World History, Higher Normal School, 1955-59; studied archaeology at the National School of Anthropology and History, 1960-65; primary and secondary school teacher, Federal District (25 years); professor at the National Preparatory School. d-*Federal Deputy* (PPS party deputy), 1970-73, member of the Indigenous Affairs Committee, the First National Defense Committee, the Television Industry Committee, the Petroleum Committee, and the Second Labor Committee. e-Member of the PPS. f-None. g-Leader of the SNTE. h-None. j-None. k-None. l-Directorio, 1970-72; C de D, 1970-72, 122.

León Orantes, Gloria
(Deceased Aug. 1984) a-June 6, 1916. b-Tuxtla Gutiérrez, Chiapas. c-Primary studies in Tuxtla Gutiérrez, Chiapas; secondary studies in Secondary School No. 6, Mexico City; preparatory studies (first year) at the Scientific and Literary Institute of México, Toluca, México, and at the National Preparatory School; law degree, National School of Law, UNAM, July 18, 1940, with a thesis on the social and legal functions of the federal agent. d-None. e-None. f-Lawyer attached to the Consulting Department of the Attorney General's Office, 1940-41; investigating agent of the Ministerio Público of the Attorney General of the Federal District, 1947-48; Agent of the Ministerio Público, attached to the penal division of the Superior Tribunal of Justice of the Federal District, 1948-51; Agent of the Ministerio Público, attached to the 8th and 9th Districts of the Third Penal Court and the 6th District of the Second Penal Court of Mexico City, 1952-53; Judge, First Court of Appeals (mixed

jurisdiction), Coyoacán, Federal District, 1953-54; Judge of the Superior Tribunal of Justice of the Federal District and Federal Territories, 1954-77; *Justice of the Supreme Court*, 1977-84. g-None. h-Practicing lawyer, 1941-43. i-Daughter of Juan José León, a lawyer, and Serafina Orantes; widow of engineer Francisco Pelaéz. j-None. k-Second woman ever to be appointed to the Mexican Supreme Court. l-DBM70, 325; DBC, 137-38; DGF56, 513; MGF73, 111; DBGM, 665; Protag., 192.

León (Uranga), Luis I.
(Deceased Aug. 1981) a-July 4, 1890. b-Ciudad Juárez, Chihuahua. c-First five years of primary studies in Ciudad Juárez; last year of primary in a normal school, Mexico City; enrolled in the veterinary program at the National School of Agriculture; agricultural engineering degree, National School of Agriculture. d-Alternate Deputy to the Constitutional Convention, 1916-17; Federal Deputy from the State of Sonora, 1918-20, from Chihuahua, 1920-22, 1922-24, from the Federal District, 1924; *Senator from the State of Chihuahua*, 1964-70. e-Orator and leader of Calles's campaign for governor of Sonora; orator and leader of the de la Huerta campaign for governor of Sonora; orator for General Obregón's presidential campaign, 1919-20; accompanied Plutarco Calles on presidential campaign, 1924; cofounder of the Mexican Civic Front for Revolutionary Affirmation, 1963. f-Director, Agricultural Department, State of Sonora, 1915-17; Subsecretary of the Treasury under Provisional President Adolfo de la Huerta, June 1 to Dec. 1, 1920; Secretary of Agriculture, Dec. 1, 1924, to Nov. 30, 1928; Secretary of Industry and Commerce, Feb. 5, 1928, to Oct. 30, 1930; Interim Governor of Chihuahua, 1929-30; Executive Director, Northern Zone, National Colonization Commission, Secretariat of

Agriculture, 1951. g-President of the local agrarian committee. h-Director of the Mexico City daily *El Nacional*, 1931. i-Son of Marcelo León, a Juarista who fought the French at age 16 and reached the rank of Lt. Colonel in the National Guard; later was director of customs in Ciudad Juárez and himself a federal deputy; mother, Dolores Uranga, was the granddaughter of a Juarista who was mayor of Paso del Norte and a military commander. j-Supported General Obregón against Venustiano Carranza, 1919. k-In exile, 1935-40. l-Cadena Z.; Enc. Mex., 8, 50; Dulles; Urióstegui, 477ff; DGF51, I, 210; Aldama, 571-73; Gómez, 326.

Leónel Posasa, Marcos
a-Oct. 8, 1938. b-Tampico, Tamaulipas. c-Early education unknown; no degree. d-None. e-Joined the Mexican Communist Party, Apr. 1956; member of the Central Committee of the PCM, 1964-79; member of the Executive Committee of the PCM, 1979; Director of *Oposición*, official newspaper of the PCM, 1973-78. f-None. g-Secretary General of the Mexican Communist Youth, 1965-70. h-Electrician in the petroleum industry. j-None. k-None. l-HA, 19 Mar. 1979, X.

Leyva Mancilla, Baltasar R.
a-Jan. 6, 1896. b-Chilpancingo, Guerrero. c-Early education unknown; preparatory studies at the National Preparatory School; enrolled at the National Military College, 1912, left when it closed. d-*Governor of Guerrero*, 1945-51; *Senator* from Guerrero, 1964-70. e-President of PRI in Guerrero. f-*Oficial Mayor of the Secretariat of National Defense*, 1952-56. g-None. h-None. i-Married Fermina V. Pitágoras. j-Joined the Revolution in the Aquiles Serdán Brigade, Puebla; Chief of Staff of General Antonio Guerrero in Chihuahua; Commander of the Military Zones of Guanajuato, San Luis Potosí, and Tamaulipas; career army officer; rank of Brigadier General, Apr. 1, 1941. k-Accused of illegal landholdings by the secretary general of the CNC of the State of Guerrero, 1972. l-DGF56, 199; letter; HA, 1 Nov. 1946; *Hoy*, 1 May 1971, 10; MGF69, 105; *Excélsior*, 29 Aug. 1972, 27; PS, 3281.

Leyva (Mortera), Xicoténcatl
a-Apr. 4, 1940. b-Jalapa, Veracruz. c-Primary and secondary at public schools, Tijuana; preparatory studies at a public school, Tijuana; law degree, National School of Law, UNAM; Professor of Administrative Law, UNAM, 1965-69. d-Mayor of Tijuana, 1977-80; *Governor of Baja California*, 1983-88. e-Joined the PRI as a youth leader, 1957; official of the Secretary of Press and Publicity of the CEN of PRI, 1969; Secretary General of PRI in Baja California, 1976. f-Director of the Department of Review of Minor Suits, Secretariat of the Treasury, 1965-70; Auxiliary Secretary of the Subsecretary of the Treasury, 1969; Administrative Subdirector of the National Institute of Youth; Delegate of the National Institute of Youth in Baja California, 1977; representative of the National Finance Bank, Washington, D.C., 1989. g-Member of the service professionals union, CTM. h-Public Notary No. 1, Baja California, 1983. i-Son of Xicoténcatl Leyva Alemán, former mayor of Tijuana and director of immigration in Baja California in 1942; father, cousin of *Miguel Alemán*; mother, Socorro Mortera, is sister of petroleum union leader and federal deputy, Porfirio Mortera; married María Elena Boeja; political enemy of *Roberto de la Madrid*. j-None. k-Removed from his position as governor for losing the state to *Cuauhtémoc Cárdenas* in 1988. l-*Excélsior*, 12 May 1983, 4, 20A, 13 May 1983, 21A; HA, 23 May 1983, 40; *Mexico Journal*, 6 Feb. 1989, 10.

Leyva Velázquez, Gabriel
a-June 30, 1896. b-Los Humayes, Municipio San Ignacio, Sinaloa. c-Primary studies at the Porfirio Díaz School, Culiacán, Sinaloa; studied at normal school in Mexico City, under a scholarship from President Madero, left studies in 1913 to fight Victoriano Huerta with many fellow students; no degree. d-*Federal Deputy* from the State of Sinaloa, Dist. 2, 1937-40; President of the Permanent Commission, Dec. 1940; Oficial Mayor of the Chamber of Deputies; *Senator* from the State of Sinaloa, 1940-46, President of the Administration Committee and the Department of Agrarian Affairs Committee; member of the Second Balloting Committee; *Governor of Sinaloa*, 1957-62; *Senator* from the State of Sinaloa, 1970-76, member of the Gran Comisión, President of the First National Defense Committee, President of the Military Retirement and Pension Committee, Executive Secretary of the Livestock Committee and member of the Second Balloting Committee. e-President of the Congressional electoral commission for the 1940 presidential election; *President of the CEN of PRI*, 1952-56; member of the Political Action Committee of the New Advisory Commission of PRI, 1972. f-*Provisional Governor of Sinaloa*, 1935-37. g-*Secretary General of the National Farmers Federation*, 1942-47. h-Author of several books. i-*Leyva* family were friends of the Maderos; Gabriel's father, a rural school teacher and court scribe in Culiacán, was a precursor of the Revolution and became the first martyr of the movement in Sinaloa, 1910; Gabriel's uncle, José María Leyva, also was a precursor of the Revolution, and active in the Cananea mining strike in Sonora; son, Gabriel, was a director general in the federal government; grandson, Gabriel, was a director general in the Secretariat of Fisheries;

married María del Rosario Ochoa y Arreola. j-Career army officer; commissioned by Francisco Madero, 1911; joined the forces of General Obregón as a 2nd Lieutenant on the staff of *Ramón Iturbe*, May 14, 1914; rank of 1st Lieutenant, Aug. 20, 1914; rank of 2nd Captain, Apr. 1, 1915; rank of 1st Captain, June 1, 1915; rank of Major, July 6, 1920; rank of Lt. Colonel, Mar. 21, 1924; rank of Colonel, 1927; rank of Brigadier General, Dec. 1934; rank of Brigade General, Sept. 16, 1946; reached the rank of Division General. k-Brandenburg considers *Leyva Velázquez* to have been one of the strongest regional leaders in Mexico as governor of Sinaloa; criticized by peasants who invaded his property in Sinaloa during the summer of 1972. l-WWM45, 63; letter; HA, 5 Nov. 1943, 35; Peral, 446-47; *Polémica*, Vol. 1, 1969, 74; McAlister, 223-24; Brandenburg, 108, 111, 151; EBW46, 200; HA, 10 July 1972, 10; *El Universal*, 1 July 1972; Morton, 77-78; Novo35, 235; Q es Q, 327; López, 590; HA, June 1945; WNM, 129-30; C de S, 1970-76, 80; Enc. Mex., VIII, 1977, 67; *Excélsior*, 20 Mar. 1985, 1, 9.

Liceaga Angeles, Jesús Ulises
a-Jan. 31, 1938. b-Federal District. c-Early education unknown; mathematics degree, National School of Science, UNAM; MA in psychology, Higher Normal School, 1964-65; Ph.D. in psychological pedagogy, Higher Normal School; primary and secondary teacher; Director, National School of Teachers, 1985-88. d-None. e-Joined PRI, 1981. e-None. f-Chief, Technical and Higher Education Department, Division of Normal Education, Secretariat of Public Education; adviser, Subsecretary of Education, Secretariat of Public Education; *Subsecretary of Middle Education*, Secretariat of Public Education, May 1989-92. g-None. h-None. i-Son of Jesús Liceaga García, surgeon, and

Alicia Angeles Martínez, public official; married Artemia Castro Linares, teacher. j-None. k-None. l-DBGM89, 199-200.

Liceaga Ruibal, Víctor Manuel
a-Sept. 11, 1935. b-La Paz, Baja California del Sur. c-Early education unknown; economics degree, National School of Economics, UNAM, 1956-60, with a thesis on "Fishing as a Factor in Development." d-*Alternate Senator* (in functions) from the State of Baja California del Sur, 1976-82, Secretary of the Great Committee; *Federal Deputy* from the State of Baja California del Sur, Dist. 1, 1985-86, head of the state delegation; *Governor of Baja California del Sur*, 1987-93. e-Joined PRI, 1958; Youth Director of PRI, 1964-65, Secretary General of PRI, 1969-70, and President of PRI, 1974-77, all in Baja California del Sur; General Delegate of the CEN of PRI to various states, 1978-82. f-Director of Tourism, Baja California del Sur, 1967; Representative of Baja California del Sur in the Federal District, 1971-73; Director, Press and Public Relations, Baja California del Sur, 1974; Delegate of Iztapalapa to the Department of the Federal District, 1982-85. g-None. h-None. i-Son of Víctor Manuel Liceaga Solares, military engineer, and Elena Ruibal Barrera, businesswoman; married Gloria Alicia Trueba Ochoa. j-None. k-None. l-C de D, 1985-88; C de S, 1976-82; DBGM89, 704; HA, 30 Sept. 1986, 21.

Licón Baca, Clemente
a-June 26, 1931. b-Parral, Chihuahua. c-Early education unknown; degree in business administration, Michigan State University, Lansing, 1946-50; courses in management, University of California, 1967-68; course in administrative objectives, Larry Wilson Institute, Chicago, Illinois, 1969; course in international trade, University of Pennsylvania, 1969.

d-None. e-General Coordinator, senatorial and gubernatorial campaigns, State of Chihuahua. f-Adviser, General Manager of the Import-Export Company of Mexico, 1952-56; adviser, Governor of the State of Chihuahua, 1956-62; Treasurer of Chihuahua, Ciudad Juárez, 1962-63; adviser to the Directors General of the Federal Electric Commission, 1973-76, of Complamar, 1976-82, and of the Department of Military Industry, 1978-82, and to Forestal, 1978-82; Manager of Commercial Operations, Candelilla Cera Trusts, National Rural Credit Bank, 1979; *Oficial Mayor of the Secretariat of Energy, Mines and Government Industries*, 1982-86. g-None. i-Son of Clemente Licón Fierro, businessman, and Delfina Baca Rodríguez; married Micaela Avila Núñez. j-None. k-None. l-Q es QAP, 169; DBGM, 244-45.

Liekens, Enrique
(Deceased) a-July 4, 1882. b-Juchitán, Oaxaca. c-Early education unknown; no degree. d-Federal Deputy from the State of Oaxaca, 1920-22, Dist. 2, 1930-32, Dist. 4, 1932-34. e-Member of the PNR. f-Employee, Department of Statistics, 1912; Assistant Consul General, San Francisco, California, 1920-21; Secretary of the Mexican Delegation to Rome, 1921-22; Assistant Consul General, Vienna, Austria, 1922-23; Assistant Consul General, Hamburg, Germany, 1923-24; Consul General, El Paso, Texas, 1927; *Director General of the ISSSTE*, 1935-40. g-None. h-Poet. j-Joined the Constitutional Army with a rank of Major, 1914; fought, 1914-17; rejoined the army, 1920, with a rank of Lt. Colonel. k-None. l-López, 601.

Liera B., Guillermo
a-Apr. 6, 1905. b-Ahome, Sinaloa. c-Agricultural engineering degree, College of Agriculture, Ciudad Juárez, Chihuahua. d-Federal Deputy from the

State of Chihuahua, Dist. 2, 1934-37. e-*Subsecretary of Political Action of the CEN of PRI*, 1962. f-Engineer, National Irrigation Commission; Director General of Agriculture, Secretariat of Agriculture; *Oficial Mayor, Secretariat of Agriculture*, 1940; *Subsecretary of Livestock*, Secretariat of Agriculture, 1940-46; Director, Department of Indigenous Affairs, 1946-49; Executive Secretary of the National Olive Commission, 1947-60. g-None. j-None. k-None. l-DGF51, II, 237; D de Y, 3 Dec. 1940, 1; DGF50, 163; Peral, 458; letter; HA, 26 Dec. 1952, 3; Maldonado, 92.

Limón de Muñoz, José de Jesús
a-1912. b-Guadalajara, Jalisco. c-Early education unknown; no degree. d-*Federal Deputy* from the State of Jalisco, Dist. 12, 1964-67. e-None. f-Director, Department of Education, State of Jalisco; Secretary General of Government of the State of Jalisco, 1959-64, under *Juan Gil Preciado; Governor of Jalisco*, 1964-65. g-None. h-Public notary, 1965-85. j-None. k-None. l-C de D, 1964-67.

Limón Guzmán, José
a-June 20, 1898. b-Amatlán de Cañas, Nayarit. c-Primary studies; studied accounting; degree. d-Secretary of the City Council of Tepic, Nayarit; Secretary of the City Council of Ixtlán, Nayarit; *Senator* from the State of Nayarit, 1946-52, member of the Gran Comisión, the Agricultural and Livestock Committee, the Legislative Studies Committee, the Social Welfare Committee, the First Balloting Committee, and the Special Committee on Tourist Affairs; *Governor of Nayarit*, 1952-56. e-Campaigner, presidential campaigns of *Lázaro Cárdenas* and *Manuel Avila Camacho*; paymaster for the Secretary of Administrative Action of the PNR. f-Oficial Mayor of the Legislature of the State of Nayarit.

g-Secretary General of the Union of Small Businessmen. h-Worked as a carpenter, scribe, and later a small businessmen. i-*Excélsior* says he was the political disciple of *Gilberto Flores Muñoz*, his gubernatorial predecessor. j-None. k-None. l-DGF51, I, 7, 9, 10, 11, 12-14; C de S, 1946-52; DGF56, 97; DGF47, 21; *Excélsior*, 21 Feb. 1975, 12.

Limón (Marques), Gilberto R.
(Deceased) a-Mar. 15, 1895. b-Alamos, Sonora. c-Secondary studies at the Colegio de Sonora; assistant, Talamantes School, Navajoa; no degree. d-None. e-None. f-*Subsecretary of National Defense*, 1945-46; *Secretary of National Defense*, 1946-52; adviser to the Secretary of National Defense, 1976. g-None. h-None. i-Daughter, Cristina, married the son of *Fernando Casas Alemán*; married María Manlay; son of Manuel M. Limón; brother, José A. Limón, commander of the Nogales garrison, 1951. j-Career army officer; joined the Revolution under General Obregón as a 2nd Lieutenant, Navajoa Volunteers, May 8, 1913, member of the 10th Sonoran Battalion, Army of the North, 1914; fought against Francisco Villa, 1914-15; Chief of Staff, 1st Infantry Brigade, 2nd and 5th Divisions, Army of the North East, under General Chávez, 1917; rank of Lt. Colonel, 1917; officer, 84th Infantry Battalion, Commander of the 44th line battalion; rank of Colonel, 1920; fought against the de la Huerta rebellion, 1923; rank of Brigadier General, 1924; head of the Presidential Guards, 1924-28; fought against the Escobar Rebellion, 1929; Director of the National Military College, 1931, 1942-46; head of the Department of Manufacturing Industries, 1932-34; Director of Military Education, Secretariat of National Defense, 1936-42; Brigade General, Oct. 11, 1927; rank of Division General, Aug. 1, 1942; President of the National

Unification of Revolutionary Veterans, 1979. k-None. l-WWM45, 63-64; Peral, 449; DGF51, I, 177, 184; STYRBIWW54, 856; López, 602; Enc. Mex., VIII, 1977, 96; *Excélsior*, 31 Mar. 1979, 10; Rev. de Ejer., Jan. 1975, 18, Sept. 1976, 26.

Limón Rojas, Miguel
a-Dec. 17, 1943. b-Federal District. c-Early education unknown; legal studies, National School of Law, UNAM, 1963-67, graduating with a thesis on "Revolutionary Law," 1968; postgraduate work, University of Aix-Marsella, France, 1968-69; professor, UNAM, 1970-72; professor, Metropolitan University, 1974-78; Director, Law Department, 1974, and of the Division of Social Sciences and Humanities, 1974-78, both at Metropolitan University, Atzcapotzalco campus; Academic Secretary, National Teachers University, 1978-81. d-None. e-Subdirector of Social Studies of the IEPES of PRI, 1981-82; coordinator of the Education Committee for the Plan of Government, 1982-88. f-Adviser, Secretary of Public Education, 1978; Director General of Professions, 1981-82, *Subsecretary of Planning*, 1982-83, and Director, National Indigenist Institute, 1983-88, all at Secretariat of Public Education; *Subsecretary of Population and Migratory Services*, Secretariat of Government, 1988-93. g-None. h-None. i-Collaborated on the electoral reforms with *Jesús Reyes Heroles*, 1977; son of Miguel Limón Díaz, notary public, and Ana Elena Rojas Guadarrama. j-None. k-None. l-Q es QAP, 297-98; DBGM89, 201; DBGM, 245; DBGM92, 208.

Ling Altamirano, Jorge Alberto
a-Apr. 19, 1942. b-Federal District. c-Secondary studies at the Cristóbal Colón School, Mexico City; engineering degree, National School of Engineering, UNAM, 1962-69; teaching courses in Germany; teacher at the Colegio Franco Inglés, 1968; teacher, Speed Reading Institute, 1973-76. d-Alternate plurinominal deputy, PAN, 1979-82; *Plurinominal Federal Deputy* for PAN, 1982-85. e-Joined PAN, 1958; member of the Regional Committee of PAN for the Federal District, 1977; adviser to the Regional Committee of PAN for the Federal District; adviser to the National Council of PAN, 1982; Subdirector of Studies and Political Education of PAN, 1979; member of the CEN of PAN, 1979. f-None. g-None. h-Essayist; Chief of Maintenance, Mexican Prefab Construction Company, 1964-66. i-Brother of Héctor Ling Altamirano, plurinominal deputy from PAN, 1979-82; brother of Ricardo Alfredo, plurinominal deputy from PAN, 1991-93; son of Guillermo Ling Altamirano, white collar worker, and Guadalupe Altamirano Lara, teacher; married Leticia Gómez. j-None. k-None. l-Directorio, 1982-85; Lehr, 556; DBGM92, 501; DBGM89, 473; DBGM, 536.

Livas Villarreal, Eduardo
a-Jan. 21, 1911. b-Monterrey, Nuevo León. c-Primary studies at Escuela Livas, Monterrey, 1918-23; secondary and preparatory studies from the Colegio Civil, Monterrey; law degree from the Escuela de Leyes, 1927-32, degree in 1933; one of the student members of an organization that founded the University of Nuevo León, 1933; member of the Board of Regents of the University of Nuevo León. d-*Senator* from the State of Nuevo León, 1958-61; President of the Committee on Industries, President of the Second Instructive Section for the Grand Jury; member of the Social Welfare Committee, the Social Security Committee, the Second Balloting Committee, and the First Constitutional Affairs Committee and substitute member of the Economics and Statistics Committee; *Governor of Nuevo León*,

1961-67. e-Director of the Council for Economic Planning in Nuevo León during the presidential campaign of *Adolfo López Mateos*, 1958. f-Agent of the Ministerio Público of the Office of the Attorney General in Nuevo León, 1933-35; Private Secretary to the Governor of Nuevo León, General *Bonifacio Salinas Leal*, 1939-43; Secretary General of Government of the State of Nuevo León under Governor *Arturo B. de la Garza*, 1943; Private Secretary to the Governor of Nuevo León, *Luis Morones Prieto*, 1949. g-Member of the Cárdenas Youth Group from Nuevo León, 1933. h-Practicing attorney, 1950-52; newspaperman, 1952; Director of *El Porvenir*, 1953-55. i-Son of Professor Pablo Livas, distinguished Nuevo León educator who operated the primary school that Eduardo attended, and Francisca Villarreal, also an educator; brother Alfredo, director of bus lines in Nuevo León; brother Enrique, a heart specialist, professor and former rector of the University of Nuevo León; and brother Juan, a businessman in Monterrey. j-None. k-Precandidate for governor of Nuevo León, 1949. l-DBM68, 378; DBM70, 327; PdM, 221; C de S, 1961-64, 59; G of Nl, 15; Func., 191; Enc. Mex. 1977, 123; González, II, 466-69; WNM, 130.

Llarena del Rosario, Xóchitl Elena
a-June 1, 1939. b-Veracruz, Veracruz. c-Early education unknown; medical degree, with a specialty in gynecology, National School of Medicine, UNAM, 1955-60. d-*Alternate Federal Deputy* from the Federal District, Dist. 27, 1976-79, under *Hugo R. Castro Aranda*; *Federal Deputy* from the Federal District, Dist. 27, 1982-85. e-Joined PRI, 1959; President of the 27th District Committee of the Federal District, 1977-80; Secretariat of Social Action of PRI, Federal District, 1980-82; coordinator of volunteers for social service, 27th

District Committee of PRI, Federal District; Subsecretary General of PRI in the Federal District, 1981. f-Specialist in obstetrics and gynecology, IMSS, 1961-62. g-None. h-Practicing physician. i-Daughter of Ramón Llanera Díaz, businessman, and Xóchitl del Rosario Bustamante; married David Guillén Abasolo, surgeon. j-None. k-Directorio, 1982-85; C de D, 1982-85, 1976-79; Lehr, 145.

Llorente González, Arturo
a-1920. b-Veracruz, Veracruz. c-Primary studies in Veracruz; secondary and preparatory studies at the Escuela Civil, Veracruz; law degree from the National School of Law, UNAM, 1944, with a thesis on the rights of authors, artists, and writers; Rector of the University of Veracruz, 1946-50. d-*Federal Deputy* from the State of Veracruz, Dist. 9, 1958-61, member of the Editorial Committee and the Gran Comisión; President of the Legislative Studies Committee (first and second years); *Senator* from Veracruz, 1964-70; Mayor of Veracruz, 1953-55. e-None. f-Legal adviser to the Secretary of Public Works, 1943-46; legal adviser to the head of the Department of the Federal District, 1943-46; Director General of the Coordinating Division of the Boards of Civic, Moral, and Material Improvements, Secretariat of Government, 1955-56; *Oficial Mayor of the Federal District*, 1956-58; Director General of Professions, Secretariat of Public Education, 1961-64; *Subsecretary of Labor (A)*, 1970-76; Delegate of the Department of the Federal District to the Benito Juárez Delegation, 1976-79. g-President of the Student Society of the National School of Law, UNAM. h-His law thesis was one of the first on that topic in Mexico and was published as a monograph; practiced law, 1943-46. i-Student of *Alfonso Noriega* and *Mario de la Cueva* at the National Law

School; married Bertha Lilia Martínez. j-None. k-Precandidate for governor of Veracruz, 1974; precandidate for federal deputy from Veracruz, 1976. l-DPE70-71, 119; WWMG, 22; DGF56, 89; HA, 14 Dec. 1970, 223; letter; Morton, 124; Func., 396; *Excélsior*, 13 Mar. 1973, 11, 8 Dec. 1975, 17; Enc. Mex., Annual, 1977, 575.

Loaeza (Tovar), Enrique M.
a-May 10, 1944. c-Early education unknown; law degree, National School of Law, UNAM, 1966; MA degree in international law, University of London; diploma in air space law, London Institute of World Affairs. d-None. e-Adviser to presidential candidate, *José López Portillo*, 1975-76. f-Auxiliary Secretary to the Subsecretary of the Presidency, *José López Portillo*, 1970-71; Auxiliary Secretary to the Subsecretary of Government Properties, *José López Portillo*, 1971-72; Auxiliary Secretary to the Director General of the Federal Electric Commission, *José López Portillo*, 1973-75; Director General of Airports and Auxiliary Services, 1976-80; Director General of Aero Mexico, 1980-82. g-None. h-None. i-Son of lawyer Enrique M. Loaeza, representative of Mexico to the International Civil Aviation Organization, 1951; distant nephew of *José López Portillo*; sister married *José López Portillo*'s son, 1980; brother of Soledad Loaeza Tovar, leading intellectual and wife of Adrián Lajous Vargas. j-None. k-None. l-HA, 23 Jan. 1978, 17; Smith, 301; DGF51, I, 111; HA, 7 Apr. 1980.

Loaiza, Rodolfo Tirado
(Deceased Feb. 20, 1944) a-Dec. 18, 1894. b-San Javier, Sinaloa. c-Educated in the public schools of San Javier, San Ignacio and Mazatlán, Sinaloa; no degree. d-Federal Deputy from the State of Sinaloa, Dist. 4, member of the Gran Comisión, 1934-36; *Senator* from the

State of Sinaloa, 1936-40, member of the permanent committee, 1938; *Governor of Sinaloa*, 1940-44. e-*Treasurer of the CEN of PRI*, June 19, 1935. f-Assistant Chief of Staff of the Secretariat of National Defense, 1929-32; Chief of Staff of the Secretariat of National Defense, 1932-33. g-None. h-Author of several economic and social projects. i-From a lower middle class background; son was active in the 1929 student strike at UNAM. j-Joined the Revolution as a private, 1911; Paymaster General of the Army; reached the rank of Colonel. k-Assassinated at the Hotel Belmar, Mazatlán, Sinaloa. l-Peral, 451; D de S, 19 June 1935, 1; letter; EBW46, 145; DP70, 1196.

Lombardo de Gutiérrez, Marcela
a-Mar. 20, 1926. b-Federal District. c-Primary teaching certificate; secondary teaching certificate, National Teachers School, 1941-43; studies in French and French literature; studies at the National School of Economics, UNAM, 1944-48; diploma in arts and sciences, McGill University, 1944-45; Director, Department of Publications, Workers University of Mexico, 1950-68; member of the governing board and General Coordinator of the Vicente Lombardo Toledano Center for Philosophical, Economic, and Political Studies, 1978-91. d-*Federal Deputy* from the Federal District, Dist. 15, 1976-79, Dist. 38, 1988-91. e-Founding member of the Popular Party, 1948; member of the Central Committee of the PPS, 1957-91. f-Adviser, Technical Committee, National Indigenous Institute, Secretariat of Public Education, 1973-76. g-Founder of the Popular Youth. h-Interpreter, Olympic Committee, 1967-68. i-Daughter of *Vicente Lombardo Toledano* and Rosa María Otero; niece of *Luis Lombardo Toledano*, federal deputy from Puebla; married Raúl Gutiérrez; member of the *Emilio*

Mújica Montoya Group at UNAM. j-None. k-None. l-HA, 19 Mar. 1979, III; C de D, 1976-79, 40; *Excélsior*, 29 Feb. 1980, 13A; DBGM89, 473-74.

Lombardo Toledano, Vicente
(Deceased Nov. 19, 1968) a-July 16, 1894. b-Teziutlán, Puebla. c-Primary education at the Liceo Teziuteco in Teziutlán; preparatory studies at the National Preparatory School in Mexico City, 1911-15; law degree from the National School of Law, UNAM, 1919; MA, UNAM, 1919, with a thesis on public law and new philosophical currents; Ph.D., UNAM, 1933; professor at the National Preparatory School, 1922-23; founder and Director of the Gabino Barreda University, 1934; professor at the Gabino Barreda University, 1933-50; founder and Director of the Workers University of Mexico, 1936-68; Professor of Law at the National Law School, UNAM, 1918-33; Secretary of the School of Law, UNAM, 1919; Director of the National Preparatory School, 1922; founder and Director of the National Preparatory School Night Classes, 1923. d-Member of the City Council of the Federal District, 1924-25; Federal Deputy from the State of Puebla, Dist. 13, 1924-25, 1926-28; *Federal Deputy* from the State of Puebla, Dist. 8, 1964-67, member of the Legislative Studies Committee (1st Section on Constitutional Affairs), and the Cultural Affairs Committee. e-Member of the Mexican Labor Party, 1921-32; leading organizer of the PRM, 1938; founder and *President of the Popular Party*, 1948-68, which later became the Popular Socialist Party, 1960. f-Oficial Mayor of the Department of the Federal District, 1921; head of the Department of Libraries, Secretariat of Public Education, 1921; Interim Governor of Puebla, 1923. g-Secretary General of the League of Professors of the Federal Distrct, 1920; alternate delegate of the Student University Federation to the First International Student Congress, 1921; member of the Central Committee of the Revolutionary Federation of Mexican Workers, 1923-32; Secretary General of the National Federation of Teachers, 1927; organizer and Secretary General of the General Federation of Workers and Peasants of Mexico, 1933; organizer and *Secretary General of the Federation of Mexican Workers*, 1936-40; organizer and President of the Latin American Federation of Workers, 1938-63; Secretary General of the Federation of Labor Unions of the Federal District, 1932; Secretary General of the Mexican Socialist League, 1944. h-Founder of many literary magazines and reviews; author of many articles. i-Son of a wealthy industrialist ruined by the Revolution; father was mayor of Teziutlán and an alternate deputy, 1912; brother, *Luis Lombardo Toledano* served as a federal deputy from Puebla, Dist. 11, 1937-40; daughter, *Marcela Lombardo de Gutiérrez*, was a PPS party deputy, 1976-79; longtime friend of *Manuel Avila Camacho, Manuel Gómez Morín*, and *Alejandro Carrillo*; friend of *Rafael de la Colina* at the National Preparatory Scool and at UNAM. j-None. k-Expelled from the National University for his radical views, 1933; member of the "Seven Wisemen" generation of the National Preparatory School; had Inner Circle status 1934-38; presidential candidate on the Popular Party ticket, 1952. l-WWM45, 65; DP70, 1199; Peral, 453; NYT, 19 Nov. 1968, 40; *Annals*, Mar. 1940, 54; Padgett, 73-79; Millon, 199-203; Strode, 288-89, 324-25; IWW40, 686; DBM68, 380-81; Johnson, 83-84; Brandenburg, 82-85; Scott, 141-42, 190-91; letter; Kirk, 84-96; Enc. Mex., VIII, 1977, 128.

López, José Dolores

a-Mar. 31, 1939. b-Fresnillo, Zacatecas. c-Early education unknown; no degree. d-None. e-Joined the PCM, 1958; Secretary General of the PCM for the State of Zacatecas, 1965-73; member of the Executive Committee of the PCM, 1979. f-None. g-Secretary of Union Action of the Independent Central of Agricultural Workers and Peasants (CIOAC), 1979. h-Worked as an agricultural laborer until he was 16. j-None. k-Imprisoned for political reasons, 1964, 1969, 1970. l-HA, 2 Apr. 1979, VII.

López Aparicio, Alfonso

(Deceased 1985) a-Dec. 30, 1922. b-León, Guanajuato. c-Early education unknown; law degree, National School of Law, UNAM, with a thesis on the Mexican labor movement; professor, National School of Law, UNAM, 1952-70. d-None. e-None. f-Lawyer, Legal Department, Secretariat of Labor, 1953-58; Director General of Social Welfare, Secretariat of Labor, 1959-64; adviser, Secretariat of Labor, 1965-69; President, Federal Board of Conciliation and Arbitration, 1970; *Justice of the Supreme Court*, 1970-76, 1976-82, 1982-85. g-None. h-None. i-Son of Alfonso López Pérez, businessman, and María del Refugio Aparicio Valdés. j-None. k-None. l-DBGM, 666; HA, 7 Jan. 1986, 9.

López Arías, Fernando

(Deceased July 3, 1978) a-Aug. 8, 1905. b-Zuchilapán, Coatzacoalcos, Veracruz. c-Law degree, National School of Law, UNAM, 1929-34. d-Local deputy to the State of Veracruz, 1943-46; *Federal Deputy* from the State of Veracruz, Dist. 7, 1940-43, member of the First Justice Committee, the Second Balloting Committee, and the Library Committee (2nd year); *Senator* from Veracruz, 1946-52, member of the Gran Comisión, the National Waters and Irrigation Committee, the Naval Committee, the First Committee on Constitutional Affairs, the Second Labor Committee, and the First Balloting Committee; *Governor of Veracruz*, 1962-68. e-Youth leader of PRI; *Secretary of Political Action of the CEN of PRI*, 1946-48. f-Agent of the Ministerio Público of the Office of the Attorney General of Mexico in Coatzacoalcos, Veracruz; Judge in Coatzacoalcos; Judge of the Superior Tribunal of Justice of Veracruz; President of the Superior Tribunal of Justice of Veracruz; Secretary of Acts and Permits, Supreme Court of Mexico; Oficial Mayor of the Senate, 1943-45; *Oficial Mayor of the Department of the Federal District*, 1952; *Oficial Mayor of the Secretariat of Government Properties*, 1952-53; *Subsecretary of Government Properties*, 1953; *Attorney General of Mexico*, 1958-62. g-Cofounder of CNOP; Secretary of Acts of CNOP (first one), 1943; Secretary General of the Socialist Lawyers Front, 1938. h-Author of articles on Veracruz. i-Father, a peasant; married Carmen Bouzas; knew *Adolfo López Mateos* at UNAM; son, Fernando López Valenzuela, was interim president of PRI in the city of Veracruz. j-None. k-Student supporter, along with *Adolfo López Mateos*, of José Vasconcelos for president, 1929. l-DGF47, 22; HA, 23 Jan. 1948, 15; D de Y, Dec. 2, 1958, 7; *El Universal*, 2 Dec. 1958, 8; HA, 8 Dec. 1958, 30; WWMG, 23; letter; DGF51, I, 8-10, 12-14; Func., 87; *Excélsior*, 4 July 1978, 4, 7 Feb. 1950, 1, 21 Apr. 1973, 1, 18 Jan. 1980, 1.

López Avelar, Norberto

a-June 6, 1900. b-Totolapán, Morelos. c-Primary studies in the public schools of Totolapán and Mexico City; secondary in the army; no degree. d-*Federal Deputy* from the State of Morelos, Dist.

2, 1949-51, member of the Gran
Comisión and the Second Committee
on National Defense; *Senator* from the
State of Morelos, 1952-58, member of
the Gran Comisión, the Third Committee on National Defense, the War
Materials Committee, and the Electric
Industry Committee; substitute
member of the Military Health Committee; *Governor of Morelos*, 1958-64.
e-*Secretary of Political Action of the
CEN of PRI*, 1952. f-Inspector General
of Police; Delegate of the government of
Baja California del Norte to Ensenada
and Tijuana; Oficial Mayor of the State
of Baja California del Norte under
Rodolfo Sánchez Taboada. g-None.
h-Parents were peasants. j-Joined the
Revolution; fought with the Constitutionalists; reached the rank of Colonel;
assistant to *Rodolfo Sánchez Taboada*.
k-Scott indicates that there was strong
opposition to López Avelar's nomination as governor because of his supposed connection with the assassination of Zapata; one of Zapata's daughters spoke in his defense. l-Scott, 235;
C de D, 1949-51, 77; DGF51, I, 23, 29,
31; letter; DGF56, 6, 9-12; HA, 8 Dec.
1958, 42; Ind. Biog., 91-92.

López Bermúdez, José
(Deceased July 19, 1971) a-Dec. 19,
1910. b-Moroleón, Guanajuato. c-Engi-
neering degree from the Agricultural
School of Ciudad Juárez, 1933. d-*Feder-
al Deputy* from the State of Chihuahua,
Dist. 4, 1946-49, member of the Credits
Committee, the Agrarian Department
Committee, the Livestock Committee,
and the Inspection Committee for the
General Accounting Office (first year);
Federal Deputy from the State of
Guanajuato, Dist. 6, 1955-58, member
of the Agrarian Department Committee
and the Inspection Committee for the
General Accounting Office; President of
the Preparatory Council; President of
the Chamber of Deputies, Dec. 1946;

Alternate Senator from Guanajuato,
1958-61; *Federal Deputy* from the State
of Guanajuato, Dist. 8, 1961-64, member of the Legislative Studies Committee (Agrarian Section), the Foreign
Relations Committee, and the Protocol
Committee. e-*Secretary General of
PRI*, 1949-52; Director of Orators for
PRI in the presidential campaign of
Adolfo Ruiz Cortines. f-Rural organizer
for Cultural Missions, Secretariat of
Public Education, 1934-36; Private
Secretary to *Alfredo Chávez*, Governor
of Chihuahua, 1943-44; Director "D" of
the Department of Railroad Construc-
tion, Secretariat of Communications
and Public Works, 1936-40; Assistant
Director of Planning, Department of
Agrarian Affairs, 1940-43; technical
adviser to the Secretary of Agriculture
and Livestock; Oficial Mayor of the
Secretariat of Hydraulic Resources;
*Secretary General of the Department of
Agrarian Affairs and Colonization*,
1952-55. g-None. h-Started government career working in the Cultural
Missions Program, Secretariat of Public
Education; author of numerous books
and biographies of Mexican leaders;
member of the Mexican delegation
under *Jaime Torres Bodet* to the Inter-
American Assembly, 1947. j-None.
k-Precandidate for governor of Guana-
juato, 1955. l-Peral, 454; *Polémica*, Vol.
I, 1969, 21; *Siempre*, Dec. 3, 1958, 6; C
de D, 1946-48, 76; letter; DGF47, 6;
DGF56, 24, 30, 32, 35; HA, 26 July
1971, 72; C de D, 1961-63, 81, 1956-58;
Excélsior, 11 Aug. 1947; González
Navarro, 213; López, 608; Enc. Mex.,
VIII, 1977, 135; Ind. Biog., 92-93.

López Bretón, Guadalupe
a-Dec. 7, 1935. b-Puebla, Puebla. c-Primary and secondary studies in Puebla;
teaching certificate, Normal Institute of
Mexico, Puebla, 1950-53; professor,
Higher Normal School, 1954-55; teacher
in various schools in Puebla; Director,

Juan C. Bonilla Public School, Cholula, Puebla. d-*Alternate Senator* from the State of Puebla, 1970-73, but replaced Senator *Guillermo Morales Blumenkron*, 1973-76, President of the Second Credit Committee and the Money and Credit Institutions Committee, First Secretary of the Property and Natural Resources Committee, Second Secretary of the Second Consular and Diplomatic Services Committee; *Federal Deputy* from the State of Puebla, Dist. 7, 1976-79, member of the Agricultural Development Committee, the Section on Maternal and Infant Welfare of the Public Health Committee, the Second Government Committee, and the Immigration Committee; *Federal Deputy* from the State of Puebla, Dist. 3, 1985-88. e-Director of Women's Action of PRI, Puebla, 1969-75; general delegate of the CEN of PRI to Querétaro, 1976; general delegate of the CEN of PRI to Campeche, 1980; Subsecretary of Social Action of the CEN of PRI, 1981; President of PRI in Puebla, 1984. f-Director General of Welfare Programs, Secretariat of Labor, 1981; Director, Social Development, Puebla, Puebla, 1984-85. g-Secretary of Education Action of the CEN of CNOP, 1974; active in the SNTE of Puebla, Puebla. h-None. i-Daughter of Froylán López López, public official, and Carmen Bretón Carrión; married Angel Galindo Corcuera, businessman. j-None. k-First female senator from the State of Puebla. l-D de C, 1976-79, 11, 20, 38, 56, 62; *Excélsior*, 18 Aug. 1976, 29; C de S, 1970-76, 80.

López Cano y Aveleyra, Normal Silvia
a-Dec. 20, 1942. b-Federal District. c-Early education unknown; law degree, National School of Law, UNAM, 1961-65, with a thesis on "Evolution of Women's Agrarian Rights"; MA in public administration, University of Michigan, Ann Arbor, 1969; Ph.D. stu-

dies, UNAM, 1969; Professor of Agrarian Law, UNAM, 1965-73. d-*Federal Deputy* from the Federal District, Dist. 40, 1982-85. e-Special delegate of the CEN of PRI to various states; President of the 7th Committee of PRI, Federal District; Secretary of the Coordinating Committee of Meetings for the CEN of PRI. f-Agricultural adviser to the Department of Agrarian Affairs. g-Delegate of the CNC in Querétaro and in Puebla. j-None. k-None. l-Directorio, 1982-85; C de D, 1982-85.

López Cárdenas, Fernando
b-Yucatán. c-Early education unknown; law degree, School of Law, University of the Southeast, Mérida; Professor of Logic, National School of Law, UNAM. d-Federal Deputy from the State of Yucatán, Dist. 1, 1932-34; *Governor of Yucatán*, Oct. 5, 1935, to July 1, 1936. e-None. f-Secretary General of Government of the State of Yucatán under Governor *César Alayola Barrera*, 1934-35; *Justice of the Supreme Court of Mexico*, 1938-40. g-None. j-None. k-Resigned the governorship of Yucatán because of several violent workers' strikes. l-Daniels, 487; C de D, 1932-34.

López Contreras, Felipe
a-April 17, 1935. b-Pátzcuaro, Michoacán. c-Early education unknown; law degree, Free Law School, 1954-58, with a thesis on collective labor contracts; professor, Free School of Law, 1965-70, La Salle University, 1974-76, and University of Guadalajara, 1977-83. d-None. e-None. f-Secretary of Studies and Accounts, Supreme Court of Justice, 1965-71; Judge, 3rd Circuit Court 1971-76; Judge, 1st Circuit Court, 1976-83; *Justice of the Supreme Court*, 1984-88, 1988-94. g-None. h-None. i-Son of Roberto López Torres, industrialist, and María Concepción Quevedo Cortina. j-None. k-None. l-DBGM89, 621; DBGM87, 635; DBGM92, 671.

López Cortés, Francisco
(Deceased) a-1895. b-Ixtepec, Oaxaca.
c-Early education unknown; law degree.
d-Federal Deputy from the State of
Oaxaca, Dist. 16, 1924-26, 1928; Governor of Oaxaca, 1928-32; *Senator* from
the State of Oaxaca, 1934-40; *Federal
Deputy* from the State of Oaxaca, Dist.
6, 1943-46. e-None. f-Secretary of Government of the State of Baja California
del Sur, 1920. g-None. j-None.
k-None. l-C de D, 1924-26, 1928-30; C
de S, 1934-40; C de D, 1943-46, 14.

López Dávila, Manuel
(Deceased Oct. 1974) b-Ahualulco, San
Luis Potosí. c-Primary studies in San
Luis Potosí; secondary studies at the
Urban Normal School, San Luis Potosí;
teaching certificate; graduate studies in
psychology and educational administration; professor of secondary schools in
San Luis Potosí, Rector of the Scientific
and Literary Institute of Chihuahua.
d-*Alternate Senator* from Chihuahua,
1946-52, but replaced Senator *Antonio J.
Bermúdez* during the entire term;
member of the Second Committee on
Credit, Money, and Credit Institutions,
the National Properties Committee, the
Second Committee on Public Education, and the Second Petroleum Committee; *Governor of San Luis Potosí*,
1961-67. e-Representative of the CNOP
on the National Advisory Council of
PRI, 1946; State Committeeman for PRI
in San Luis Potosí. f-Director of Federal
Education, State of San Luis Potosí,
Secretariat of Public Education; Inspector General, Secretariat of Public
Education; Head of the Department of
Libraries, Secretariat of Public Education; Director General of Literacy and
Education, Secretariat of Public Education; Oficial Mayor of the Chihuahua
State Department of Public Education,
1958-61. h-None. i-Married María del
Carmen Chacón. j-None. k-Robert
Bezdek believes he lost the gubernatorial election to the PAN candidate.
l-WWMG, 23; DBM68, 383; DBM70,
332; DGF47, 20; DGF51, I, 6, 10, 11, 13,
294; D del S, 22 Jan. 1946, 1; letter;
Excélsior, 18 Nov. 1974; NYT, 3 July
1961, 2; Bezdek, 70-72.

López de Nava (y Baltierra), Rodolfo
(Deceased 1965) a-Dec. 1, 1893.
b-Cuernavaca, Morelos. c-Primary
studies at the Porfirio Díaz School,
Cuernavaca; secondary studies at the
Pape Carpentier Institute, Cuernavaca;
no degree. d-*Governor of Morelos*,
1952-58. e-None. g-None. h-Author of
a standard military text. i-Son, Rodolfo,
was in 1974 a department head in the
Secretariat of National Patrimony.
j-Career army officer; Commander of
the Military Zones of Jalisco and
Veracruz; Director of Army Supply
Warehouses; rank of Brigadier General.
k-None. l-DGF56, 96; DP70, 1207;
DPE71, 47; López, 615.

López Domínguez, José Dolores
a-Feb. 15, 1940. b-Fresnillo, Zacatecas.
c-Completed primary studies; no degree.
d-*Plurinominal Federal Deputy* of
PSUM, 1982-85; studied in Iron Curtain
countries. e-Member of the PCM, 1960;
Secretary General of the PCM in
Zacatecas, 1965-73; member of the
Constitutional Assembly of the Popular
Front of the State of Zacatecas, 1974;
member of the Central Committee of
the PSUM, 1981. f-None. g-Secretary
General of the Central Peasant Federation (CCI) of Zacatecas; activist in land
invasions of the Popular Front of Small
Property Owners; member of the
National Mineworkers Union, 1957-60.
h-Laborer until 1956; employee,
General Motors, 1961-62. j-None.
k-Imprisoned for political activities,
1964, 1969, 1970. l-Directorio, 1982-85;
C de D, 1982-85; Lehr, 591.

López Faudoa, Eduardo
a-Sept. 6, 1939. b-Ciudad Lerdo, Durango. c-Medical degree from the National School of Medicine, UNAM, 1963; Professor of Anatomy, National School of Medicine, UNAM; special studies in medicine for burns, England, 1970. d-*Federal Deputy* from the State of Durango, Dist. 2, 1979-82. e-Special representative of PRI to Nezahual-cóyotl, 1968, 1978-79. f-*Oficial Mayor of the Secretariat of Health*, 1970; *Secretary General of the Mexican Institute of Social Security*, Sept. 27, 1971, to Dec. 7, 1976. g-Adviser to the Secretary General of CNOP, 1965-69. h-Consultant for the Pascua Dermatology Center; Chief of Services for the Surgery Section for Burns Rehabilitation, Rubén Leñero Hospital. i-Personal physician to *Luis Echeverría* during his presidential campaign. j-None. k-Precandidate for governor of Durango, 1974; precandi-date for senator from Durango, 1981. l-DPE71, 113; HA, 14 Dec. 1970, 23, 4 Oct. 1971, 34, 20 Sept. 1971, 48; *Excélsior*, 29 Dec. 1973, 5, 26 Dec. 1981, 16A; Protag., 197.

López Flores, Arturo
a-Dec. 15, 1919. b-Tepic, Nayarit. c-Early education unknown; graduated from the Heroic Military College as a 2nd Lieutenant of Artillery, 1938-41; diploma, Higher War College, 1952-54; courses, Inter-American Defense College, Secretariat of National Defense, 1962-63; professor, Heroic Military College, 1963, 1965-66. d-None. e-None. f-*Oficial Mayor of the Secretariat of National Defense*, 1983. g-None. h-None. i-Served in the Mexican Embassy at the same time as General *Antonio Guerrero Mendoza*; served under General Luis R. Casillas as his Chief of Staff; cadet with Generals Tomás Mancera Segura and José Espejel Flores at the Heroic Military College; son of Francisco López Fregoso, photog-rapher, and Francisca Flores Sánchez, teacher; married María Luz Sánchez Tovar. j-Joined the army as an infantry soldier, 1937; junior officer, 1st Artillery Regiment, Division of War Materiels and Powder Manufacturing; served in the 4th Artillery Regiment, 1947; attached to the 13th Military Zone, Tepic, Nayarit; member of the Staff, Secretariat of National Defense; second in command, 3rd Artillery Regiment, 1958-59; officer, Staff, Secretariat of National Defense, 1959-61; aide to the Military Attaché to the Mexican Embassy in the United States and Canada, 1962-65; rank of Colonel, 1964; commander, infantry brigade, Staff, Secretariat of National Defense, 1965-70; rank of Brigadier General, 1969; attached to the Personnel Division, Secretariat of National Defense, 1970-71; aide, Director General of Military Education, Secretariat of National Defense, 1971-72; Chief of Staff, 26th Military Zone, La Boticaria, Veracruz, 1973-76; rank of Brigade General, 1973; Commander of the 29th Military Zone, Ciudad Ixtepec, Oaxaca, 1976. k-None. l-Rev. de Ejer., Nov. 1969, 47, Nov.-Dec. 1973, 38; QesQAP, 72; Rev. de Ejer., Dec. 1964, 24; DBGM87, 216; DBGM, 249.

López González Pacheco, Miguel
a-Oct. 2, 1925. b-Puebla, Puebla. c-Primary studies at the Colegio Benavente, Puebla; secondary studies at the Colegio Benavente, Puebla; preparatory studies at the Instituto Oriente, Puebla; law degree, University of Puebla; Professor of Private International Law and Mercantile Law, University of Puebla. d-*Federal Deputy* (Party Deputy from PAN), 1970-73, member of the Domestic Trade Committee and the Administrative Section of the Legislative Studies Committee. e-Director of the Youth Group of PAN, 1950; Director of the Study Commission of the Regional Committee of PAN; regional adviser to

PAN. f-Employers' representative before the Central Board of Conciliation and Arbitration of Puebla, 1953. g-President of the Student Association of the University of Puebla; coordinator of lawyers for the Bank of Puebla. h-Practicing attorney; attorney for the University of Puebla; Chief of the Legal Department, Bank of Puebla, 1974. i-Son of lawyer Miguel López y López and Carolina González Pacheco; married Marcela Arta Sánchez. j-None. k-Twice a candidate of PAN for federal deputy. l-Directorio, 1970-72; C de D, 1970-72, 122.

López Hernández, Manuel J.
a-Dec. 7, 1912. b-Campeche, Campeche. c-Primary and secondary studies in Campeche; preparatory studies in Campeche; law degree, Institute of Campeche, Oct. 8, 1938; Professor of World History, Institute of Campeche; Professor of Agrarian Law, School of Law, University of Campeche. d-*Federal Deputy* from the State of Campeche, Dist. 1, 1946-49, member of the Navy Committee, the Foreign Relations Committee, and the Protocol Committee; *Governor of Campeche,* 1949-55. e-None. f-Attorney for the Defense of Labor, State of Campeche; Director of the Coordinating Office of Labor Affairs, State of Campeche; Private Secretary to the Governor of Campeche; Secretary of the National Chamber of Deputies; President of the Superior Tribunal of Justice of the State of Chiapas. g-Founder of the CTM of Campeche, 1937. h-Practicing lawyer, Campeche, Campeche. j-None. k-None. l-DGF51, I, 88; DGF47, 5; HA, 7 Oct. 1949, xxviii; C de D, 1946-49, 76; Crowson.

López Lira, Jesús
(Deceased Sept. 2, 1961) a-Aug. 26, 1888. b-Salamanca, Guanajuato. c-Primary studies at Primitivo Soto's School; secondary studies at the University of Guanajuato; scholarship student to the

University of Guanajuato; preparatory studies in Mexico City; medical degree in dental surgery from the University of Puebla; professor of the Superior Normal School; secondary teacher in the Federal District until 1953. d-Mayor of Guanajuato; Local Deputy to the 40th State Legislature of Guanajuato; Federal Deputy from Guanajuato to the Constitutional Convention at Querétaro, 1916-18; Federal Deputy from the State of Guanajuato, Dist. 2, 1922-24; *Senator* from Guanajuato, 1958-64. e-None. f-Physician for the Secretariat of Health (ten years); adviser to the governor of the State of Guanajuato; Administrator of Customs, Nuevo Laredo, Tamaulipas, 1953-58. g-None. h-Practicing surgeon. i-Brother of *José López Lira;* son of physician Florentino López and Virginia Lira; collaborator of *José Siurob.* j-Fought in the Revolution, 1910; a Constitutionalist, under the forces of General Jesús Carranza, 1913; rank of Lt. Colonel, 1915. k-In the United States, 1927-31. l-Func., 207; C de S, 1961-64, 17; DGF56, 153; PS, 3382.

López Lira, José
(Deceased 1965) a-Oct. 7, 1892. b-Salamanca, Guanajuato. c-Primary and secondary studies in Guanajuato; law degree from the University of Guanajuato; Professor of Sociology, and Professor of Amparo and Guarantees, National School of Law, UNAM; Interim Rector of UNAM, Aug. 2 to Sept. 4, 1929; Secretary General of UNAM, 1930. d-None. e-None. f-First Head of the Advisory Department of the Office of the Attorney General, 1931; Attorney General of the State of Guanajuato; Justice of the Superior Tribunal of Justice of the State of Guanajuato; Assistant Attorney General of Mexico; *Oficial Mayor of Health,* 1938-40; Secretary General of Government of the State of Tlaxcala, 1942-45, under Governor *Manuel Santillán;*

Director of the Legal Department, Secretariat of Government, 1948-52; Prosecretary of the Board of Administration and Protection of Foreign Property, 1946; *Secretary of Government Properties*; 1952-58; *Justice of the Supreme Court of Mexico*, 1958-62. g-None. h-Administrative official of the Secretariat of Health and Welfare, 1938. i-Brother, Dr. *Jesús López Lira*, served as a senator from Guanajuato, 1958-64; son of Florentino López, a physician, and Virginia Lira. j-None. k-None. l-Peral, 458; HA, 5 Dec. 1958, 10; DGF56, 431; DGF51, I, 68; DP70, 1208; Enc. Mex., VIII, 1977, 147.

López Manzanero, Gonzalo
b-Yucatán. c-Early education unknown; no degree. d-Mayor of Mérida, Yucatán; Local Deputy to the State Legislature of Yucatán; *Senator* from the State of Yucatán, 1946-52, member of the Gran Comisión and the Industries Committee; alternate member of the First Labor Committee. e-None. f-Secretary General of Government of the State of Yucatán. g-President of the Union of Workers Leagues of Yucatán; cofounder and leader of the Truckdrivers Alliance of Yucatán, 1930. j-None. k-None. l-DGF51, I, 8-12, 14; PS, 3387.

López Mateos, Adolfo
a-May 26, 1910. b-Atizapán de Zaragoza, México. c-Primary studies on scholarship from the Dondé Foundation at the Colegio Francés, Mexico City; secondary studies in Toluca while working as a librarian at the Scientific and Literary Institute of México; preparatory and legal studies at the Scientific and Literary Institute of México, Toluca; completed preparatory from the National Preparatory School and the Scientific and Literary Institute of Toluca, 1924-25; law degree from the National School of Law, UNAM, 1929-34, with a thesis on crimes against

economic policy; Professor of World History and Ibero-American Literature at the Normal School of Toluca, 1927; professor at the Scientific and Literary Institute of México; Rector of the Scientific and Literary Institute of México, 1944-46. d-*Senator* from the State of México, 1946-52, replacing *Isidro Fabela* who resigned to join the International Court of Justice, member of the Gran Comisión, the First Committee on Credit, Money, and Credit Institutions, the Legislative Studies Committee, the Special Forestry Committee, the Treasury Committee, the Tax Committee, the First Balloting Committee, the Second Foreign Relations Committee and the First Section of the Instructive Committee for the Grand Jury. e-Delegate and student leader of the Socialist Labor Party, 1929; Secretary of the Regional Committee for the PNR in Toluca, México, 1931-34; orator for the presidential campaign of *Miguel Alemán*; Secretary General of the PNR for the Federal District; *Secretary General of PRI*, 1951-52; campaign manager for the presidential campaign of *Adolfo Ruiz Cortines*, 1952. f-Agent of the Ministerio Público of the Office of the Attorney General; Private Secretary to the Governor of Mexico, Colonel Filiberto Gómez, 1928; Private Secretary to Carlos Riva Palacio, President of the CEN of PRN, 1934; auditor of Government Printing Office for the National Workers Bank of Development, 1934; employee of the Popular Publications Committee of the Secretariat of Public Education, 1937; delegate of the National Workers Bank of Development to the Government Printing Office, 1938-40; Secretary General of the Division of Extracurricular and Aesthetic Education, Secretariat of Public Education, 1941-43; Assistant Director of the National Institute of Fine Arts, 1941-42, under Javier Icaza and *Benito Coquet*, Secretariat of Public Education; Chairman of the Mexican Delegation to the International Economic Convention, Geneva, 1951; member of the Federal Electoral Commission, 1952; *Secretary of Labor*, 1952-58; *President of Mexico*, 1958-64. g-Secretary General of the Teachers' Union. h-Worked in a library to support himself during secondary school; founded the magazine *Impetu*, 1927. i-Carlos Riva Palacio convinced him to join the official party; worked in the law firm of *Octavio Medellín Ostos* while a student at UNAM; son of a dentist, Dr. Mariano Gerardo López y Sánchez Román, who died when he was very young; his mother, Elena Mateos Vega, supported five children on a very small income; married Eva Sámano Bishop. j-None. k-As a student leader, supported José Vasconcelos in his campaign against Pascual Ortiz Rubio in 1929; traveled to Guatemala on foot with a group of students, 1926-1927; voluntarily went into exile in Guatemala, 1929; led a 136-day walk to Guatemala, 1926. l-HA, 28 Dec. 1964, 4; Cline, 162; HA, 19 Jan. 1959; DGF51, I, 6, 9-14; Scott, 214, 218-20; DP70, 1208-09; Brandenburg, 3-6, 113-18; HA, 12 Dec. 1952, 5; WWMG, 23-24; HA, 5 Dec. 1952, 9; DGF56, 397; Covarrubias, 140; Johnson, 32-35; letter; STYRBIWW60, 1210; Enc. Mex., VIII, 1977, 147-48; *Justicia*, Feb. 1970.

López (Mena), Héctor F.
(Deceased 1957) a-1880. b-Coahuayutla, Guerrero. c-Primary studies in La Huacana, Michoacán; enrolled in the Colegio de San Nicolás, Morelia; no degree. d-City councilman of Coahuayutla; Senator from the State of Guerrero, 1920-22; Governor of Guerrero, 1925-28. e-Director of General *Juan Andreu Almazán*'s campaign for president, 1940; Vice-President of the Revolutionary Party of National Unification, 1940; Vice-President of the Mexican Democratic Party, 1945, which

supported *Ezequiel Padilla* for president. f-Secretary of Government of the State of Michoacán, 1914; Subdirector, Department of Infantry, Secretariat of War; Subdirector, Chief of Staff, Secretariat of War; Interim Governor of Michoacán. g-None. h-Historian; geographer. i-Son of poet Arracleto López. j-Joined the Revolution, 1910; fought under General Gertrudis Sánchez in Michoacán, 1914; career army officer; military commander of Orizaba; rank of Brigade General. k-Jailed for opposing Díaz, 1909; accused of ordering the murder of General Silvestre Mariscal. l-DP70, 1209-10; Gruening, 432-433.

López Mendoza, Sergio
a-Sept. 27, 1932. b-Federal District. c-Early education unknown; civil engineering degree, National School of Engineering, UNAM, 1951-55, with a thesis on technical aspects of public works contracts; professor, National School of Engineering, UNAM, 1953-54, 1968, 1973-84. d-None. e-Joined PRI, 1960. f-Technical Auxiliary Secretary of the Subsecretary of Public Works, 1966-70; Private Secretary to Subsecretary A, Secretariat of Public Works, *Rodolfo Félix Valdés*, 1970-76; Director General of Cooperative Highways, Secretariat of Communications and Transportation, 1976-86; *Director General of Federal Highways and Bridges*, 1986-88. g-None. h-Resident engineer, Montaje, Estructuras Ligeras de México, 1953; resident engineer and manager, South-East Division, Constructora Morelos, 1960; Director General, Disimex, 1965. i-Son of Feliciano López de la Vega, accountant and businessman, and Ana Luisa Noriega Rodríguez. j-None. k-None. l-DBGM, 250; DBGM87, 218.

López Munguía, Agustín
a-Aug. 12, 1920. b-Federal District. c-Primary and secondary in Mexico City; preparatory at the National

Preparatory School; economics degree from the National School of Economics, UNAM, 1940-44; MA in public administration from Harvard University, 1950-51; advanced studies in budgetary problems at the London School of Economics and Political Science, University of London, 1956; attended the English Language Institute, University of Michigan, 1950; Professor of Money and Banking, Mexico City College, 1953-55; Professor of Public Finance, National Polytechnic School, 1959; Professor of the Theory of Public Finance, National School of Economics, UNAM, 1953-71. d-None. e-None. f-Economist for the Department of Economic Studies, Bank of Mexico, 1943-48; Head of Statistics, National Commission for the Control of Imports, 1943-48; Secretary of the Export Price Commission, 1949; Head of the Department of Economic Studies, 1952-58; Assistant Director General of Treasury Studies, Secretariat of the Treasury, 1959-76; Subdirector General of the Bank of Mexico, 1977-82; *Oficial Mayor of Trade*, 1982-88. g-None. h-None. i-Attended the National School of Economics with *Julián Díaz Arias, Jorge Espinosa de los Reyes*, and *Octaviano Campos Salas*; during his long teaching career, among those he taught were *Carlos Torres Manzo, Jorge de la Vega Domínguez*, and *Carlos Bermúdez Limón*; son of Rafael López Salgado, businessman, and Concepción Murguía Villaneuva, teacher; married María del Socorro Canales Lozano. j-None. k-None. l-Letter; DGF56, 164; BdM, 166; DPE65, 142; DPE71, 24, *Excélsior*, 21 Dec. 1977, 23; Informe, 35; DBGM87, 218.

López Padilla, Benecio
a-Aug. 23, 1888. b-Zaragoza, Coahuila. c-Early education unknown; no degree. d-*Governor of Coahuila*, 1941-45. e-None. f-Interim Governor of Tamaulipas, 1919-20; Head of the Department

of Archives, Correspondence, and History, Secretariat of National Defense, 1958-70. g-Organizer and Secretary General of the Mexican Mining Union, 1909. h-Employed as a miner in Nueva Rosita, Coahuila, before the Revolution. i-Married Carlota Duarte; son of Ramón López Patiño. j-Joined the Revolution as a private in the army of Arnulfo Gómez; Governor and Commander of Military Operations in the State of Tamaulipas, Dec. 9, 1923–Feb. 1, 1924; rank of Brigadier General, Sept. 1, 1922; fought against Carranza, 1920; Commander of the 18th Military Zone, Venta Prieta, Hidalgo, of the 21st Military Zone, Morelia, Michoacán, 1935, of the 11th Military Zone, Zacatecas, Zacatecas, 1936, of the 1st Military Zone, Mexico City, 1936-37, and of the 15th Military Zone, Guadalajara, Jalisco, 1938; Inspector General of the Army; rank of Division General, Oct. 16, 1937; k-None. l-WWM45, 66; DPE61, 32; HA, 14 Aug. 1942, 14; Peral, 453-54; MGF69, 196; DPE65, 45; López, 618; Dávila, 119; Hernández Chávez, 92.

López Portillo Brizuela, Arturo
a-July 7, 1908. b-Guadalajara, Jalisco. c-Primary studies at the Luis Silva School; Guadalajara; secondary studies at the Annex to the Normal School Guadalajara; preparatory studies at the Preparatory School of Jalisco; teaching certificate, Aguascalientes, 1930; economics studies, National School of Economics, UNAM, 1934-38, degree in 1944, with a thesis on "Commercial Refrigeration in Mexico"; member of the University Council of UNAM; teacher, 1928-45. d-*Federal Deputy* from the Federal District, Dist. 9, 1958-61, member of the First Section of the Legislative Studies Committee; *Federal Deputy* from the Federal District, Dist. 1, 1964-67, member of the Tariff Committee and the Second Treasury

Committee. e-General delegate of the CEN of PRI to the States of Hidalgo, Sinaloa, and Puebla. f-Official, Federal Income Tax Department, Secretariat of the Treasury; delegate of the national census department to the State of San Luis Potosí, 1939-40; Director of the Census Department, National Foreign Trade Bank, 1958. g-Delegate and President of the National Congress of Students, Mérida, Yucatán; President of the Student Society of the School of Economics; joined the Teachers Union of the Federal District, 1931; member of the Treasury Workers Union; Assistant Secretary of the Secretary General of the FSTSE; active in the Federation of Workers of the Federal District and the CTM, 1940-45; Secretary of Social Welfare, 1947, Secretary of Organization, and Secretary General, 1957-60, all of the National Treasury Workers Union; Secretary of Labor and Conflicts, FSTSE, 1959-61; Secretary of Statistics, FSTSE, 1961-65. h-Teacher, 1928-45. j-None. k-None. l-Func., 184; C de D, 1958-61, 83, 1964-67, 77, 86; DNE, 129; Sirvent, 177.

López Portillo (Pacheco), José
a-June 16, 1920. b-Federal District. c-Primary studies at the Benito Juárez Public School, Federal District; secondary studies completed in the Federal District, 1935; preparatory studies at the National Preparatory School, Mexico City, 1937; law degree from the University of Santiago, Chile, on a political science scholarship from the Chilean government, 1942-45; law degree from the National School of Law, UNAM 1946; LLD from the National School of Law, UNAM, 1950; Professor of Law at the National School of Law, UNAM, 1947-58; Founder of the University Extension Program; founding Professor of Political Science and Government Policy, Ph.D. Program in Administrative Sciences, Graduate School of Business

and Administration, UNAM. d-*President of Mexico*, 1976-82. e-Member of the Social and Economic Council during the presidential campaign of *Adolfo López Mateos*, 1958; member of the New Advisory Council of the IEPES of PRI, 1972. f-Technical adviser to the Oficial Mayor of the Secretariat of National Patrimony, 1959-60; member of the Revisory Committee of Article 3 of the Constitution, 1959; Director General of the Federal Boards of Material Improvement, Secretariat of Government Properties, 1960-65; Director of Legal Counsel to the Secretariat of the Presidency, 1965-68; *Subsecretary of the Presidency*, 1968-70; *Subsecretary of Government Properties*, 1970-72; *Director General of the Federal Electric Commission*, 1972-73; *Secretary of the Treasury*, May 29, 1973, to 1975. g-Member of the Almazanista Student Vanguard, 1939-40. h-Practicing lawyer, 1946-59; author of several books. i-*Pedro Ojeda Paullada* served as Subdirector of the Federal Boards of Material Improvement under *López Portillo*; friend of *Luis Echeverría* since grammar school days; grandson of José López Portillo y Rojas, Secretary of Foreign Relations under Victoriano Huerta and governor of Jalisco, 1911-13; son of engineer José López Portillo y Weber, historian and member of the Board of Directors of PEMEX; worked for many years in the law firm of *Gabriel García Rojas*; daughter, Paulina, married Pascual Ortiz Rubio Downey, grandson of former President Pascual Ortiz Rubio; cousin of Pedro Telo de Landero y Pacheco, director of the National Fruitgrowers Commission; son, *José Ramon López Portillo*, served as Subsecretary of Planning, 1980-81, and married María Antonieta García López, daughter of Ambassador Agustín García López Santaolalla; cousin, *Manuel López Portillo*, served as Subsecretary of Environmental Improvement, 1980-82;

cousin of prominent journalist Julio Scherer García. j-None. k-None. l-HA, 14 Dec. 1970, 21, 21 Aug. 1972, 12; DPE61, 61; *Excélsior*, 19 June 1970, 4; HA, 18 Nov. 1968; *Excélsior*, 10 Aug. 1972, 10; WWMG, 24; HA, 11 June 1973, 13-14; Latin America, 26 Sept. 1975, 297; HA, 29 Sept. 1975, 7; Enc. Mex., VIII, 1977, 154D-55; HA, 1 Jan. 1982, 13; Guerra Leal, 368; *Excélsior*, 7 June 1981; HA, 12 July 1982, 6; letter.

López Portillo (Romano), José Ramón
a-Feb. 2, 1954. b-Federal District. c-Early education unknown; economics degree, National School of Economics, UNAM, Anáhuac campus, best GPA of his generation; special studies at Stanford University and Cambridge University, 1976-77. d-None. e-Director of analysis, presidential campaign committee, 1975-76; member of campaign committee for *Miguel de la Madrid*, 1981-82. f-Director General of Documentation and Analysis, Secretariat of Programming and Planning, 1976-80; Technical Secretary of the Technical Committee of Government Studies of the Presidency, 1979; Technical Secretary of the Coordinating Committee of Social Services of the Secretariat of Programming and Planning, 1979; *Subsecretary of Programming and Budgeting*, 1980-81; Ambassador to the Food and Agricultural Organization, 1982-88. g-None. h-None. i-Son of President *José López Portillo* and Carmen Romano Nolk; student of *Carlos Tello*; married María Antonieta García López Loaeza, grandaughter of *Agustín García López*. j-None. k-None. l-*Excélsior*, 19 Aug. 1980, 15A; LA, 17 Sept. 1982, 6; *Excélsior*, 23 Dec. 1982, 20A.

López Portillo (y Ramos), Manuel
b-Guadalajara, Jalisco. c-Early education unknown; medical degree, National School of Medicine, UNAM, 1959; degree in sociology, UNAM, 1973.

d-None. e-None. f-Director of Emergency Hospital, Division of Medical Services, Department of the Federal District, 1970-76; Director of Medical Services, Rations Industry, 1973-76; Subdirector of Medical Services, Department of the Federal District; Subdirector of Medical Services, ISSSTE, 1976-80; *Subsecretary of Environmental Improvement*, Secretariat of Public Health, 1980-82. g-Active member of the International College of Surgeons. h-Began practice with IMSS, physician and researcher, 1963-71; neurosurgeon, General Hospital of Mexico; psychiatric expert; Attorney of the Federal District, 1964-71. i-Cousin of *José López Portillo*. j-None. k-Winner of the National Prize in Surgery, 1975. l-*El Informador*, 5 July 1980, 1-2; HA, 14 July 1980, 16; Protag., 199.

López Prado, Felipe
a-Sept. 13, 1916. b-El Salto, Jalisco. c-Completed first year of secondary school at the Revolutionary Union of Workers of Río Grande School; one year of medical studies. d-Alternate Member of the City Council of Guadalajara, 1957; Alternate Local Deputy, State Legislature of Jalisco, 1958-60; Local Deputy to the State Legislature of Jalisco, 1962-64; *Federal Deputy* from the State of Jalisco, Dist. 4, 1967-70, Dist. 19, 1979-82. e-None. f-None. g-Secretary of Acts and Labor, Vegetable Oil Workers Union, 1944-46; Secretary General of the Vegetable Oil Workers Union, 1947-50; President of the Parents Association of Secondary School No. 2 for Boys, Guadalajara, 1953-57; Secretary General of the Union of Chocolate and Candy Workers, 1958; President of the Parents Association of the Enrique González Martínez Primary School, 1967-69. i-Father a blue collar worker and businessman; grandfather, a policeman j-None. k-None. l-Directorio, 1967-70; C de D, 1979-82; letter.

López Ramos, Mariano
a-Jan. 6, 1946. b-Mascota, Jalisco.
c-Completed secondary studies; teaching certificate; medical degree, 1971-76; professor of medicine, National School of Medicine, UNAM; primary teacher, 1964-68. d-*Plurinominal Deputy* from the PST, 1982-85. e-Joined the PST, 1978; candidate for federal deputy from the PST, 1979; Secretary of Organization, PST in the Federal District, 1978-79; Secretary of Management and Transactions, PST, Federal District, 1980-81; Director, Cadres School, PST, 1981; member, Central Committee, PST, 1981-82; Subsecretary of Agrarian Workers, PST, 1982. f-None. g-Organized peasants in the State of Guanajuato; organized teachers and parents in Nezahualcóyotl; participant in the student movement, 1968; member, Revolutionary Teachers Movement, 1968-70; Subsecretary of the National Union of Agricultural Workers, 1982. h-Practicing physician, 1977-78. j-None. k-None. l-Directorio, 1982-85; C de D, 1982-85; Lehr, 571.

López Rea, Filomeno
a-July 5, 1909. b-La Puerta, Municipio of Tonantico, México. c-Self-educated; no degree. d-*Federal Deputy* from the State of Morelos, Dist. 2, 1970-73, member of the Sugar Industry Committee, the Second Balloting Committee, and the Supplies and Foodstuffs Committee; *Federal Deputy* from the State of Morelos, Dist. 2, 1976-79, Dist. 2, member of the Section on Sugar Cane Production of the Agricultural Development Committee; member of the Primary Products Section of the Development of Foreign Trade Committee; member of the Sugar Section of the Industrial Development Committee and of the Rural Industry and Arid Zones Section of the Development of Natural Resources Committee. e-None. f-President of the Administrative and the In-

spection Committees, Emiliano Zapata Mill, Cacatepec, Morelos. g-Secretary General of the League of Agrarian Communities and Agrarian Unions, 1963-71. j-None. k-None. l-D de C, 1976-79, 13, 16, 26, 34; *Excélsior*, 27 Aug. 1976, 1C; C de D, 1970-73, 48, 122.

López Sanabria, Juan Manuel
a-May 31, 1920. b-Angangueo, Michoacán. c-Primary studies at a private school in Morelia, Michoacán; preparatory studies at the University of Guanajuato; medical degree from the University of San Luis Potosí, Dec. 22, 1945; graduate studies at the General Hospital, Mexico City, under Dr. Fernando Latapí, 1947-48; studies at Mt. Sinai Hospital, New York, 1948-49; Professor in allergies at the School of Medicine, University of Guanajuato, 1950. d-*Federal Deputy* from PAN (party deputy), 1970-73, member of the Artisans Committee, the Legislative Studies Committee, the Tenth Section on General Means of Communication and Transportation, and the Chemical Pharmaceutical Industries Committee; Mayor of Ojuelos, Jalisco; *Plurinominal Federal Deputy* from PAN, 1979-82. e-Director of the Guanajuato State Committee of PAN; member of the National Executive Committee of PAN. f-None. g-None. h-Practicing dermatologist; Chief of the Dermatology and Allergy Service, Regional Hospital, León, Guanajuato, 1950; Chief of Dermatology and Allergy Service, Red Cross Hospital, León, Guanajuato, 1950-57, and at Central Hospital, León, Guanajuao, 1956-82. i-Son of engineer Maurilio López Muñoz and Elena Sanabría Rule. j-None. k-None. l-C de D, 1970-72, 122; DBM70, 338; Directorio, 1970-72; WNM, 132.

López Sánchez, Hermilo
a-1892. b-San Cristóbal, Chiapas. c-Early education unknown; preparatory

studies from the National Preparatory School; law degree, National School of Law, UNAM. d-None. e-None. f-District Judge; Criminal Judge; Interim Judge of the Superior Tribunal of Justice of the Federal District; Secretary of the Court of Justice of Tlalpán; Correctional Judge; Agent of the Ministerio Público of the Office of the Attorney General; *Justice of the Supreme Court*, 1935-40, 1940-46, and 1946-51. g-None. j-None. k-None. l-Novo35, 216; letter.

López Sánchez, Raúl
(Deceased Jan. 11, 1957) a-Dec. 28, 1904. b-Torreón, Coahuila. c-Primary studies at the Colegio Modelo de Elvirita Vargas, Torreón, 1910-16; preparatory studies from the National Preparatory School, 1916-20; law degree from the National School of Law, UNAM, 1923-29. d-*Federal Deputy* from the State of Coahuila, Dist. 3, 1943-46, President of the Gran Comisión; *Senator* from Coahuila, 1946-48, Secretary of the Gran Comisión. e-None. f-*Interim Governor of Coahuila*, June 1, 1948, to 1951; *Secretary of the Navy*, Feb. 7 to Nov. 30, 1952; Head of the Department of Labor for the State of Veracruz, 1936-39, under Governor *Miguel Alemán*. g-Alternate Secretary General of the CNC, 1952. h-Practicing attorney for labor unions, 1930-32; in law practice with *Miguel Alemán* and Abraham Castellanos, 1929-36. i-Son of General Mario López Ortiz; father formed a group of revolutionaries who included *Jesús Agustín Castro*; knew *Mariano Ramírez Vázquez, Gabriel Ramos Millán, Miguel Alemán,* and *Antonio Dovalí Jaime* at UNAM; attended school with *Salvador Novo*, who was a boyhood friend; son, Mariano López Mercado, was defeated for federal deputy from Dist. 2, State of Coahuila, 1979. j-None. k-None. l-DP70, 1212; HA, 15 Feb. 1952, 4; DGF51, I, 5, 88; Enc. Mex.,

5, 46; letter; C de D, 1946-48; C de S, 1946-52; DGF47, 22; Novo, 204; HA, 21 Jan. 1957; Enc. Mex., 8, 157.

López Sedano, Rigoberto
a-Jan. 5, 1932. b-Etzatlán, Jalisco. c-Completed primary and secondary studies; completed courses in business. d-*Federal Deputy* (Party Deputy from PAN), 1967-70. e-Member of PAN. f-None. g-None. h-Businessman. i-Married Teresa González. j-None. k-None. l-Directorio, 1967-70; C de D, 1967-70.

López Serrano, Francisco
a-Jan. 28, 1912. b-Monclova, Coahuila. c-Secondary at the Ateneo Fuente of Saltillo, Coahuila; law degree from the National School of Law, UNAM. d-*Federal Deputy* from the State of Coahuila, Dist. 1, 1943-46. e-Director of *Miguel Alemán*'s campaign for president in the State of Coahuila, 1946. f-Member of the UNAM Legal Committee sent to Tabasco to investigate student deaths, 1935; alternate member of the Federal Board of Conciliation and Arbitration, Federal District; Chief of the Public Defenders of the Federal District; President of the Central Board of Conciliation and Arbitration, Federal District; *Secretary General of Colonization*, Department of Agrarian Affairs, 1958-63. g-President of the Student University Federation, 1934. h-Author of several works on agrarian law and the University of Mexico. j-None. k-Pre-candidate for governor of Coahuila, 1963. l-*Siempre*, 4 Feb. 1959, 6; Correa, 363; DPE61, 126; Peral, 463.

López y López, Antonio
a-May 23, 1899. b-Puebla, Puebla. c-Primary studies at the Colegio of San Juan Bautista de la Salle, Puebla; degree in pharmacy, University of Puebla. d-Member of the City Council of Huajuapán de León, Oaxaca; Mayor of

Huajuapán de León; *Alternate Federal Deputy* from the State of Oaxaca, Dist. 6, 1955-58; *Federal Deputy* from the State of Puebla, Dist. 5, 1958-61. e-Member of PAN. f-None. g-Secretary of the Chamber of Commerce of the State of Puebla. j-None. k-None. l-Func., 322; C de D, 1955-58, 1958-61; DGF56.

Loret de Mola (Médiz), Carlos

(Deceased Feb. 11, 1986) a-July 30, 1921. b-Mérida, Yucatán. c-Primary and secondary studies in Mérida; preparatory studies at the Colegio Montejo of Mérida; degree in journalism from the University of Yucatán. d-*Federal Deputy* from the State of Yucatán, Dist. 3, 1961-63, Prosecretary of the Chamber, Sept. 1963; member of the Committee on the Radio and Television Industry, the Protocol Committee, the Inspection Committee of the General Accounting Office, and the Gran Comisión; *Senator* from the State of Yucatán, 1964-70; *Governor of Yucatán*, 1970-76. e-Member of the National Council of PRI; PRI delegate to the State of Durango, 1965. g-None. h-Journalist; began career with *Diario de Yucatán*, 1939; reporter for many newspapers; editor of *El Heraldo*, San Luis Potosí, 1951-55; *El Diario de Yucatán*, *Novedades*, Mexico City, 1946-51; and *El Mundo*, Tamaulipas, 1951-55; founder of *El Heraldo*, Aguascalientes; editor of *El Heraldo*, Chihuahua, 1955-57; Director of *Noticero Mexicano*, Mexico City, 1957-60; writer for *Excélsior*, 1976-86; author of numerous biographies and books on Mexican history. i-Son of Carlos Loret de Mola Medina, an agent of the Ejido Bank in Yucatán, and Loreto Médiz Bolio, sister of *Antonio Médiz Bolio*, senator from Yucatán, 1952-57; married Bertha Vadillo; *Adolfo López Mateos* initiated his career after meeting him during his presidential campaign, 1958. j-None.

k-Died in an automobile accident under mysterious circumstances. l-HA, 11 Jan. 1965, 8; DBM68, 388; D de Y, 1970; QesQY, 150-51; Enc. Mex., VIII, 1977, 160-61; Loret de Mola; López, 625.

Loyo (González), Gilberto

(Deceased Apr. 10, 1973) a-Feb. 4, 1901. b-Orizaba, Veracruz. c-Primary, secondary, and preparatory studies at the Preparatory School of Orizaba; degree in economics from the National School of Economics, UNAM; law studies at UNAM; degree in statistics, University of Rome, 1932; professor at the National School of Economics, UNAM 1936-53, 1958-66; Director of the National School of Economics, 1944-52; Professor of Statistics and Demography and founder of the first Professorship of Demography at UNAM; Professor of Economic History at the National Polytechnic School; Professor of Agricultural Economics at the National School of Agriculture; member of the Governing Board of UNAM, 1971-73. d-None. e-None. f-Director of the National Census, 1939-40; Director General of Credit and Statistics, Secretariat of Industry and Commerce, 1946-52; Director of Social Welfare; member of the First Mexican Delegation to the Economic Commission for Latin America, 1948; Director General of the Census, 1950; *Secretary of Industry and Commerce*, 1952-58; Chairman of the National Commission for Minimum Wages, 1963-72; Chairman of the Center for Agrarian Investigations, Department of Agrarian Affairs, 1968; adviser to the National Bank of Foreign Commerce; adviser to the Secretary of National Patrimony. g-None. h-Member of many statistical and census committees in the United States and Latin America; author of numerous books on economic and demographic subjects. i-Friends with many future public leaders in Mexico while studying at UNAM, including *Javier Rojo Gómez, Ignacio García Téllez, Narciso Bassols, Ramón Beteta, Jaime Torres Bodet, Rodulfo Brito Foucher* and *Salvador Novo;* longtime friend of *Jesús Silva Herzog.* j-None. l-Letter; WWM45, 66; DBM68, 388-89; HA, 5 Dec. 1952, 9; HA, 8 May 1972, 19; Peral, 465; DGF47, 155; DGF56, 277; DBM70, 339-40; HA, 10 July 1972, 10; Scott, 99; Brandenburg, 108; STYRBIWW54, 863; HA, 23 Apr. 1973, 36; *Excélsior,* 11 Apr. 1973, 16; Enc. Mex., VIII, 1977, 164-65; NYT, 27 July 1954, 10.

Lozano Ramírez, Raúl
a-Mar. 9, 1911. b-Molango, Hidalgo. c-Primary studies in Molango, Hidalgo; secondary at the Rural School of Molango; preparatory studies from the Scientific and Literary Institute of Pachuca, Hidalgo; law degree, National School of Law, UNAM, 1933, with a thesis on political theory of the state; graduated with an honorable mention; Professor of Law at the Scientific and Literary Institute of Pachuca and at the National School of Law, UNAM. d-Local Deputy to the State Legislature of Hidalgo; *Federal Deputy* from the State of Hidalgo, Dist. 4, 1943-46, 1964-67; *Senator* from the State of Hidalgo, 1970-76, member of the Gran Comisión, the Second Balloting Group, and the First Section of the Legislative Studies Committee; President of the National Lands and Resources Committee; Second Secretary of the Waters and National Irrigation and the Second Justice Committees. e-None. f-Private Secretary to the Governor of Hidalgo, *Javier Rojo Gómez,* 1937-40; Secretary of the State Board of Conciliation and Arbitration of Hidalgo; Oficial Mayor of the State of Hidalgo; Attorney General of the State of Hidalgo; Secretary General of Government of the State of Hidalgo under Governor *Otilio Villegas,* 1940-41; Private Secretary to the Gover-

nor of Hidalgo, *José Lugo Guerrero,* 1941-43; Justice of the Superior Tribunal of Justice of Hidalgo, 1945-57; *Provisional Governor of Hidalgo,* Apr. 29-Sept. 7, 1975; *Justice of the Supreme Court of Mexico,* 1975, 1976-81. g-None. h-Lawyer for the Blue Cross Cement and Bus Company, 1957-64; Director of Legal Services of the Blue Cross Cement Cooperative, 1964-75. i-Political disciple of *Javier Rojo Gómez;* has known *Manuel Sánchez Vite* since childhood in Molango. j-None. k-Precandidate for the gubernatorial nomination of PRI in Hidalgo, 1974, 1978. l-C de S, 1970-76, 78; HA, 12 May 1975, 41; HA, 5 May 1975, 43; *Excélsior,* 27 Oct. 1975, 19, 18 Oct. 1974, 1; C de D, 1943-46, 1964-67; Pérez López, 241-42; Protag., 201.

Lozoya Solís, Jesús
(Deceased May 22, 1983) a-Mar. 3, 1910. b-Parral, Chihuahua. c-Primary studies in Parral; preparatory studies at the Scientific and Literary Institute of Chihuahua; medical degree, Military Medical School. d-*Alternate Senator* from the Federal District, 1952-58. e-None. f-*Interim Governor of Chihuahua,* Aug. 10 to Oct. 3, 1955. g-None. h-Practicing physician; Director, Military Medical School; Director, Central Military Hospital, Mexico City. i-Married Susana Thalmann Richard; son, *Emilio Lozoya Thalmann,* appointed *Subsecretary of Labor,* 1982; son, Jorge, was a director general in the Secretariat of Foreign Relations, 1987; physician to *Carlos Salinas*'s parents; military physician with President *Salinas*'s uncle, Eduardo de Gortari Carbajal, and *Manuel Camacho*'s father, Manuel Camacho López. j-Career military medical officer; rank of Colonel, Nov. 8, 1949; rank of Brigade General, 1972. k-None. l-DGF56, 6, 92; *Excélsior,* 23 May 1983, 22A; *Proceso,* 11 Jan. 1993, 18; Rev. de Ejer., Nov. 1972, 49.

Lozoya Thalmann, Emilio
a-May 15, 1947. b-Federal District. c-Primary, secondary, and preparatory studies at the Colegio Alemán Alexander Von Humboldt, Mexico City, 1954-64; economics degree from the National School of Economics, UNAM, 1970, with a thesis on efficiency in sociopolitical contexts; MA degree in business administration, Columbia University, 1972; MA degree in public administration, Harvard University, 1974; professor at the School of Economics and Political Science, Colegio de México; professor at the National School of Economics and the Graduate School of Political and Social Sciences, UNAM. d-None. e-Director, International Relations, National PRI Youth, 1965; Executive Secretary of the IEPES of PRI, 1982. f-Analyst, Division of Economic Studies, Secretariat of the Presidency, 1972-73; adviser to the Subdirector General, Light and Power Company, 1974-75; Subdirector of Programming, Coordinating Committee of Industrial Policy, 1975-76; Treasurer General of IMSS, 1977-80; Administrative Subdirector of IMSS, 1980-82; *Subsecretary "B" of Labor,* 1982-88; Director General of the ISSSTE, 1988-92; *Secretary of Energy, Mines, and Government Industries,* Jan. 4, 1993- 94. g-None. h-Manager, Infan Labs, 1968-72; Manager, UME Establishments, 1968-72. i-Son of Dr. and General *Jesús Lozoya Solís,* interim governor of Chihuahua, 1955, and Susana Thalmann; father was a physician to the Salinas family; student companion of *Carlos Salinas* and *Manuel Camacho* at the university; father in business with *Manuel Camacho*'s father; brother, Jorge, was a director general in the Secretariat of Foreign Relations; married Gilda Margarita Austin Solís. j-None. k-None. l-*Excélsior,* 23 May 1983, 22A; IEPES; QesQAP, 358; *Proceso,* 19 Oct. 1987, 10-11; DBGM, 254; DBGM89, 208; DBGM87, 222.

Luévano Romo, Josefina
a-Jan. 22, 1926. b-Aguascalientes, Aguascalientes. c-Early education unknown; teaching certificate, Cañada Honda Normal School, Aguascalientes, 1935-37; secondary school teacher. d-Member of the City Council of Nezahualcóyotl, México, 1979-82; *Federal Deputy* from the State of México, Dist. 10, 1982-85. e-Member of PRI; President of the electoral board for state and national elections, 1970-78. f-None. g-None. i-Daughter of Hilario Luévano Heredía, farmer, and María Hilaria Romo Hernández; married Trinidad López Adame, businessman. j-None. k-None. l-C de D, 1982-85; Directorio, 1982-85; DBGM, 531.

Lugo, José Inocencio
(Deceased Nov. 25, 1963) a-Dec. 28, 1874. b-Santa Ana del Aguila, Municipio of Ajuchitlán, Guerrero. c-Primary and secondary studies in Morelia, Michoacán; preparatory studies at the Colegio de San Nicolás, Morelia; law degree from the School of Law, Colegio de San Nicolás, Morelia; professor at the National Military College. d-Deputy to the Constitutional Convention at Querétaro, 1916-17; Federal Deputy from the State of Guerrero, 1917-18; Federal Deputy from the State of Guerrero, Dist. 8, 1918-20. e-Member of the Anti-Reelectionist Party, 1909. f-Governor of Baja California del Norte; Governor of Guerrero, 1910-13; Subsecretary of Government, June 1 to Aug. 4, 1920; Secretary of Government, 1920; Head of the Department of Justice, Secretariat of War and Navy; *Interim Governor of Guerrero,* 1935-36, replacing Governor *Gabriel R. Guevara.* g-President of the Student Nicolaita Committee in rebellion against the reelection of the state governor, 1895. h-Practicing lawyer in Catalán, Guerrero. i-Son, *José Inocente Lugo Lagunas,* served as federal deputy from

Guerrero, Dist. 1, 1955-57, and President of the Fourth Division of the National Tax Court, 1964-70. j-Coordinated Revolutionary activities in Guerrero, 1910; imprisoned, 1910; joined the forces of General Gertrudis Sánchez, 1910; imprisoned by General Huerta; fought against Huerta in the forces of General Gertrudis Sánchez; rank of Brigadier General, Feb. 16, 1932; rank of Division General. k-Took an active part in writing Article 123 of the 1917 Constitution at the Querétaro Convention. l-D de Y, 6 Nov. 1935, 1; DP70, 1219-20; Peral, 468; DGF56, 24, 31, 33, 36; MGF69, 389; Enc. Mex., VIII, 1977, 170.

Lugo de Rueda León, Josefina
a-Dec. 29, 1917. b-Durango, Durango. c-Early education unknown; teaching certificate; teacher. d-Local Deputy to the State Legislature of Durango, 1959-61; *Alternate Federal Deputy* from the State of Durango, Dist. 1, 1964-67, but replaced *Angel Rodríguez Solórzano*, 1966-67. e-Campaigned for PRI in the 1946, 1952, 1958, and 1964 campaigns; Director of Women's Action of PRI in Durango, 1962-66. f-None. g-First Secretary of the Delegation of the Local 38 of the SNTE, 1953; delegate of the Teachers Congress of the SNTE, 1954, 1956; Secretary of Finances of the 38th Section of the SNTE, 1958; Secretary of Women's Action of the League of Agrarian Communities, 1958-61; delegate to the Teachers Congress of the SNTE, 1959. j-None. k-None. l-C de D, 1964-67.

Lugo Gil, Humberto Alejandro
a-May 4, 1937. b-Huichapán, Hidalgo. c-Preparatory studies at the National Preparatory School; law degree, National School of Law, UNAM. d-*Federal Deputy* from the State of Hidalgo, Dist. 5, 1967-70; *Senator* from the State of Hidalgo, 1976-82; *Federal Deputy*

from the State of Hidalgo, Dist. 5, 1982-85, President of the Gran Comisión, 1982-85; *Senator* from the State of Hidalgo, 1988-94. e-Delegate of the CEN of PRI to various states, 1957-58; President of PRI in Huichapán, Hidalgo, 1958-61; Director of the CEPES of PRI in Hidalgo, 1963; *Secretary of Press and Publicity of the CEN of PRI*, 1968, 1976-78; *Secretary of Organization of the CEN of PRI*, 1978; Oficial Mayor of the CEN of PRI, 1979; *Secretary of Popular Action of the CEN of PRI*, 1979-83; *Secretary General of the CEN of PRI*, 1986. f-Agent of the Ministerio Público, Pachuco, Hidalgo, 1957-58; Director of the Department of Preliminary Accusations, Attorney General of Hidalgo, 1958; Director of Economic Studies, Department of Treasury Studies, Secretariat of the Treasury, 1960; Director General of Offices and Apartments of the Chamber of Deputies, 1964; Private Secretary to the President of the Gran Comisión of the Chamber of Deputies, *Alfonso Martínez Domínguez*, 1965-67. g-President of the Student Society of the National Preparatory School, 1954; Vice-President of the 1957 Law School Generation; Secretary General of the Student Society of the National School of Law, UNAM, 1958; delegate of the CEN of CNOP to various states, 1963-65; Vice-President of the National Policy Committee of the CEN of CNOP, 1966; *Secretary General of the CNOP*, 1980-82. h-None. i-Son of *José Lugo Guerrero*, governor of Hidalgo, 1941-45; nephew of *Adolfo Lugo Guerrero*, federal deputy from Hidalgo, 1943-46; cousin of *Jorge Rojo Lugo*, governor of Hidalgo, 1975-76; nephew of *Javier Rojo Gómez*, governor of Hidalgo, 1937-40; married Luz del Carmen Guerrero. j-None. k-None. l-C de D, 1967-70; C de S, 1976-82; MGF69; C de D, 1982-85; Pérez López, 242-43; Directorio, 1982-85.

Lugo Guerrero, José
(Deceased Aug. 26, 1980) a-Sept. 17, 1899. b-Huichapán, Hidalgo. c-Primary in the public schools of Huichapán; secondary studies in Pachuca, Hidalgo; law degree, National School of Law, UNAM, 1926. d-Local deputy to the State Legislature of Hidalgo; Mayor of Huichapán; Mayor of Pachuca, Hidalgo; Federal Deputy from the State of Hidalgo, Dist. 5, 1932-34; *Federal Deputy* from the State of Hidalgo, Dist. 5, 1937-40; *Senator* from the State of Hidalgo, 1940-41; *Governor of Hidalgo*, 1941-45. e-None. g-Member of the CNC. i-Brother-in-law of *Javier Rojo Gómez*; parents were middle class merchants and farmers; son, *Humberto A. Lugo*, was a federal deputy from Hidalgo, 1967-70; brother, *Adolfo Lugo Guerrero*, was a federal deputy from Hidalgo, 1943-46; protégé of *Rojo Gómez*. j-Joined the Revolution under General Martínez y Martínez, 1915. k-None. l-HA, 12 Mar. 1943, 41; Peral, 468; González Navarro, 177; López, 629; Almanaque of México, 510.

Lugo Verduzco, Adolfo
a-Mar. 24, 1933. b-Huichapán, Hidalgo. c-Primary school in Mexico City; preparatory studies at the Cristóbal Colón School; law degree, National School of Law, UNAM, 1952-56; studies in certified public accounting, UNAM, 1956-59; postgraduate studies, University of Michigan, 1961; studies in public administration, the Hague, 1961-63; postgraduate studies in public administration, National School of Administration, Paris, France, 1963-65; studies in political science, UNAM, 1967-68; Professor of Public Administration, National School of Economics, UNAM, 1965-66; Professor of Public Administration, National School of Political and Social Sciences, UNAM, 1967; Professor of Planning, National School of Political and Social Science, UNAM, 1976.

d-*Senator* from the State of Hidalgo, 1982-87, member of the Gran Comisión, President of the Second Government Committee, President of the First Petroleum Committee and Secretary of the Second Constitutional Affairs Committee; *Governor of Hidalgo*, 1987-93. e-Secretary of Planning and Programming, IEPES of PRI, 1969; *Oficial Mayor of the CEN of PRI*, 1981-82; *President of the CEN of PRI*, 1982-86. f-Employee, Legal Department, Secretariat of the Navy, 1954-56; Head, Department of Acquisitions, IMSS, 1966-67; Head, Administrative Department of Acquisitions, IMSS, 1968-69; Subdirector of Affiliates, CONASUPO, 1970-73; General Manager of Distribution, CONASUPO, 1973-76; Director General of the National Consumer Institute, 1976-79; *Oficial Mayor* of the Secretariat of Programming and Budget, 1979-81. g-Member of the CNC. h-Employee, Krieger and Wolff, Accountants; lawyer, firm of Ramos and Lugo, 1959-60. i-Nephew of *José I. Lugo Guerrero*; son of *Adolfo Lugo Guerrero*, federal deputy from Hidalgo, and Magdalena Verduzco Andrade; cousin of *Humberto Alejandro Lugo Gil* and *Jorge Rojo Lugo*, governor of Hidalgo; has known *Miguel de la Madrid* since childhood at Cristóbal Colón school. j-None. k-None. l-*Proceso*, 4 Oct. 1982, 16; Lehr, 210-211; C de S, 1982-88; DBGM, 540.

Lúján Gutiérrez, Jesús
a-Apr. 26, 1934. b-Villa López, Chihuahua. c-Primary studies in Public School No. 192, Ciudad Juárez, Chihuahua, 1941-47; secondary studies at the Rural Normal School, Salaices, Chihuahua, 1951-53; teaching certificate, Higher Normal School, Chihuahua, Chihuahua, 1961-64; primary school teacher, 1954-60; secondary school teacher, 1960-70; director of various primary and secondary schools; professor, Higher

Normal School, Chihuahua, 1963-68; Professor of Engineering, University of Chihuahua, 1964-66. d-*Federal Deputy* (Party Deputy from the PPS), 1970-73, member of the Forest Affairs Committee, the Agricultural Development Committee, the Electric Industry Committee, and the Hydraulic Resources Committee; *Federal Deputy* from the Federal District, Dist. 14, 1976-79, member of the Physical Education Section of the Educational Development Committee, the Development of the Fishing Industry Committee, the Department of the Federal District Committee, and the Complaints Committee; *Plurinominal Federal Deputy* from the PPS, 1982-85, 1988-91. e-Joined the PPS, 1950; member of the Popular Socialist Youth, 1950-55; Secretary General of the Regional Committee of the PPS in Chihuahua, 1960-71; member of the Central Committee of the PPS, 1968-91; official of the Executive Secretariat of the PPS, 1973; Secretary of Electoral Policy of the PPS, 1979. f-Federal inspector of primary schools. g-Secretary of Education, Union of Workers and Peasants of Mexico, 1962-69; general delegate of the National Teachers Union (SNTE), 1957-59, 1960-62. i-Married Esther Ponce; son of Alfonso Lújan Escobedo, ejidatario, and María Gutiérrez Náñez. j-None. k-Candidate for federal deputy from the State of Chihuahua, 1964, 1967; candidate for governor of Chihuahua, 1968, 1974. l-C de D, 1970-73, 123, 146, 1976-79; D de C, 1976-79, 22, 42, 46, 48, 70; HA, 12 Feb. 1979, 22; DBGM, 540; DBGM89, 480.

Luna Arroyo, Antonio
a-June 13, 1910. b-Federal District. c-Primary and secondary studies in the Federal District; teaching certificate from the National Teachers College, 1929; law degree from the National

School of Law, 1933; LLD degree from the National School of Law, UNAM, 1955; professor of civics in secondary schools; director of curriculum in secondary schools; professor at the National School of Economics, 1937; professor at the National Teachers College, 1932-46. d-None. e-Secretary of Press and Publicity for the CEN of the PNR, 1935. f-Member of the Jury for Tax Infractions, Secretariat of the Treasury, 1935-36; President of the Publishing Commission, Secretariat of Education; Head of the Department of Economic Studies, Secretariat of Labor; adviser to the Secretariat of Education, 1935; member of the National Population Council, 1939; Assistant Attorney General of Mexico, 1939-42; adviser to President *Manuel Avila Camacho*; Secretary General of CONASUPO, 1946; Director General of the Advisory and Legislative Division, Secretariat of Agriculture and Livestock, 1946-52. g-None. h-Author of school texts; Director General of *La Justicia*. i-Knew *Salvador Mondragón Guerra, Enrique Martínez Ulloa, Maríano Ramírez Vázquez, Rafael Rojina Villegas*, and *Luis Felipe Canudas Orezza* at UNAM; brother of Francisco Luna Arroyo (Francisco Larroyo), a prominent educator; son of Feliciano Luna y Luna, and Ceferina Arroyo. j-None. k-None. l-EBW46, 516; DGF51, I, 206; DGF47, 123; Enc. Mex., VIII, 1977, 170; López, 630; WNM, 135.

Luna Estrada, Miguel
a-Sept. 15, 1923. b-Durango, Durango. c-Early education unknown; law degree. d-*Federal Deputy* (Party Deputy from the PPS), 1967-70. e-Member of the PPS; official of the PPS in Durango. f-Agent of the Ministerio Público; Judge of the First Instance, Durango. g-Organized unions for the PPS. i-Married Elisa Partida. j-None. k-None. l-C de D, 1967-70; Directorio, 1967-70.

Luna Kan, Francisco
a-Dec. 3, 1925. b-Noc-Ac Hacienda, Municipio of Mérida, Yucatán. c-Primary studies in the Juan N. Alvarez School, Mérida; two years of secondary studies at the Rural Normal School, Hecelchacán, Campeche, 1939-40; completed secondary at Public School No. 5, Mérida, 1943; studies at Vocational School No. 4, IPN, Mexico City, in biological sciences, 1944-51; medical degree, Higher School of Rural Medicine, IPN, with a thesis on epidemiology and social characteristics of tubercular patients, 1952; MA in health sciences, Secretariat of Health, Dec. 1953, with a thesis on "Health Zoning in Yucatán"; professor of health sciences at various institutions. d-*Federal Deputy* from the State of Yucatán, Dist. 3, 1964-67, member of the Library Committee; *Senator* from the State of Yucatán, 1970-75, President of the Senate, Dec. 1974, President of the Colonization Committee and First Secretary of the Public Welfare Committee; *Governor of Yucatán*, 1976-82. e-Agrarian subdelegate of the CEN of PRI to Yucatán, 1965; general delegate of the CEN of PRI to Yucatán, 1970; President of PRI in Yucatán, 1965-68; *Secretary General of the CEN of PRI*, 1984. f-Divisional Director, Coordinated Health and Welfare Services, Yucatán, 1953-55; Technical Adviser, Division of Experimental Studies, Secretariat of Health, 1956-60; Physician, Federal Services, State of Yucatán, 1956; Director of Coordinated Health and Welfare Services, State of Yucatán, 1960-63; Chief of the Department of Sanitation, State of Yucatán, 1967-68. g-Member of the Political Action Committee of the CEN of the National Union of Health and Welfare Workers, 1964; Secretary General of the CNC in Yucatán, 1971-74. j-None. k-None. l-Q es QY, 152-53; C de S, 1970-76, 78; Enc. Mex., Annual, 1977, 552-553; C de D, 1964-67, 79.

Luna Lugo, Arturo
b-Ascención, Municipio of Aramberri, Nuevo León. c-Early education unknown; teaching certificate, Nuevo León. d-*Federal Deputy* from the State of Nuevo León, Dist. 5, 1952-55, member of Colonization Committee and the First Ejido Committee and Vice-President of the Chamber, Dec. 1953; *Federal Deputy* from the State of Nuevo León, Dist. 5, 1976-79, member of the Agrarian Affairs Committee; member of the Agricultural Section of the Agricultural Development Committee; member of the Manufactured Products Section of the Foreign Trade Development Committee; member of the Transformation Section, Industrial Development Committee; member of the Mineral Section of the Natural Resources Development Committee; member of the Administrative Section of the Legislative Studies Committee and member of the Tax Section of the Treasury Committee. e-None. f-Agrarian Consultant, Department of Agrarian Affairs, 1971-82. g-Secretary of Organization, Revolutionary Agrarian Peasant Committee, Aramberri and Zaragoza, Nuevo León, 1941-43; Secretary of Youth Action, League of Agrarian Communities and Peasant Unions, Nuevo León; Alternate Secretary General of the CNC, 1953-54; *Secretary General of the CNC*, 1954-57. i-Parents were ejidatarios; married Estela Alvizo. j-None. k-None. l-*Excélsior*, 23 Aug. 1976, 8; C de D, 1952-55, 46, 50; D de C, 1976-79, 5, 12, 17, 24, 32, 51, 58; C de D, 1976-79, 43.

Luque Loyola, Eduardo
a-Sept. 5, 1910. b-Querétaro, Querétaro. c-Secondary and preparatory studies at the Colegio Civil of Querétaro; law degree from the National School of Law, UNAM, 1935; Professor of Industrial Law, Agricultural Law and Political Economy, University of Querétaro.

d-*Federal Deputy* from the State of Querétaro, Dist. 1, 1943-46; *Senator* from the State of Querétaro, 1946-52, member of the Gran Comisión, the Second Committee on Credit, Money, and Credit Institutions, the Agricultural Development Committee, and the Third Labor Committee; *Federal Deputy* from the State of Querétaro, Dist. 1, 1961-64, member of the Legislative Studies Committee, First Section on Constitutional Affairs and the Gran Comisión; *Senator* from the State of Querétaro, 1964-70, President of the Senate. e-President of the Regional Committee of PRI for the State of Querétaro; general delegate of the CEN of PRI to various states. f-Agent of the Ministerio Público; Attorney General for the State of Querétaro; lawyer for the IMSS; *Interim Governor of Querétaro*, 1949; Administrator of Customs, Chetumal, Quintana Roo, 1958-61; President of the Federal Board of Conciliation and Arbitration; Public Defender for Labor; Attorney General of Querétaro; Adviser to the Secretary of Government, 1977-79; delegate of the Secretariat of Agrarian Reform to Querétaro, 1981. g-Member of the National Campesino Federation; founder and First Secretary General of the Popular Sector Leagues Foundation; founder of the Federation of Workers of the CTM in Querétaro; founder of the Federation of Government Employees of Querétaro. h-None. i-Son, Ernesto, was a leader in the 1966 strike at UNAM and senator from Querétaro, 1988-91; son of peasant Rafael Luque and María Dolores Loyola; married Rebeca Feregrino. j-None. k-Precandidate for governor of Querétaro, 1979. l-DBM66, 393; C de S, 1964-70, 1946-52; C de D, 1961-63, 82; MGF69, 106; C de D, 1943-45; DGF51, I, 7, 9, 10, 12, 14; CyT, 91; DAPC81, 59; letter; DBGM89, 480.

Luque Salanueva, Víctor

a-Mar. 6, 1908. b-Tlacolula, Oaxaca. c-Early education unknown; public accounting degree, 1925-31. d-None. e-None. f-Director, Administrative Department, Department of the Navy, 1940; Director, Purchasing Department, Secretariat of Public Works, 1945-48; Director, Technical Section, Division of Expenditures, Secretariat of the Treasury, 1948-49; Director General of Expenditures, Secretariat of the Treasury, 1949-52; Director General of Accounts and Administration, Secretariat of the Treasury, 1956-57; *Oficial Mayor of the Navy*, 1958. g-None. h-President of the Board of Constructora Malta, S.A., 1964. i-Married María del Refugio Herrera Gámez; son of Luis E. Luque Tello and Herminia Salanueva Díaz. j-None. k-Involved in the Olympic Games organizing committees and the Pan American Games. l-DGF56; DGF51; WNM, 135.

M

Machiavelo Martín del Campo, Carlos

a-Mar. 12, 1934. b-León, Guanajuato. c-Early education unknown; MA degree in Hospital Administration, School of Hospital Administration, Secretariat of Health and Public Welfare and UNAM, 1961-62; medical degree, School of Medicine, University of Guanajuato, 1952-59; Professor of Hospital Administration in Morelia, Michoacán, 1961-62; professor, School of Medicine, University of Guanajuato, León, 1964-67. d-*Federal Deputy* from the State of Guanajuato, Dist. 2, 1973-76, 1982-85. e-Special delegate of the CEN of PRI, Salamanca, Guanajuato, 1974; Secretary of Electoral Action, State Committee of PRI, Guanajuato, 1973-76; special delegate of the CEN of PRI, Veracruz, Veracruz, 1977. f-Director of Unit A, Clinical Department, IMSS Hospital,

Chinampas, Chihuahua, 1971-73; Secretary General of Government, State of Guanajuato, 1979-81. g-Representative of the University Students of the State of Guanajuato to student congresses in Nuevo León and San Luis Potosí; President of the Student Society of the School of Hospital Administration, 1961-62. j-None. k-None. l-Directorio, 1982-85; C de D, 1982-85, 1973-76; DBGM, 542; Lehr, 179.

Macías Valenzuela, Anselmo
(Deceased Jan. 1965) a-Apr. 5, 1896. b-Agiabampo, Sonora. c-Primary studies in Alamos, Sonora; no degree. d-*Governor of Sonora*, Sept. 1, 1939, to Aug. 30, 1943. e-None. f-None. g-Member of the CTM. h-None. i-Son of Pablo Macías and Angela Valenzuela; brother of General *Pablo Macías Valenzula*, Secretary of National Defense, 1940-42. j-Joined the Revolution on Feb. 10, 1914, fighting with the 10th Battalion; fought against the Zapatistas, 1914-15; fought against Francisco Villa at Celaya, 1915; Commander of the 15th and 30th Cavalry Regiments; defended Morelia, Michoacán, 1924; Brigadier General, Sept. 1, 1929; opposed the Escobar rebellion, 1929; Commander of the 11th Military Zone, Zacatecas, Zacatecas, the 20th Military Zone, Colima, Colima, 1933, the 13th Military Zone, Tepic, Nayarit, the 27th Military Zone, Iguala, Guerrero, 1937, the 22nd Military Zone, Toluca, México, 1938, the 19th Military Zone, Villa Cuauhtémoc, Veracruz, 1945, and the 54th Battalion, 2nd Regiment of Presidential Guards. k-None. l-WWM45, 67; Peral, 474; López, 636; De Parodi, 37-43; Dávila, 124.

Macías Valenzuela, Pablo E.
(Deceased May 3, 1975) a-Nov. 15, 1891. b-El Fuerte, Las Cabras, Sinaloa. c-Early education unknown; no degree. d-*Governor of Sinaloa*, 1945-50.

e-None. f-*Secretary of National Defense*, 1940-42; Director of Military Pensions, Secretariat of National Defense, 1957-75. g-None. h-None. i-Personal friend of *Manuel Avila Camacho*; son of Pablo Macías and Angela Valenzuela; brother of General *Anselmo Macías Valenzuela*. j-Joined the Revolution under General Obregón as a Lieutenant in the 4th Battalion of Sonora, 1912; fought in eighty-six battles against the forces of Victoriano Huerta; fought against Pascual Orozco, 1912-13; fought Villa's forces as an officer in the 6th Sonoran Battalion, 1915; fought the Yaquis as Commander of the 8th Sonoran Battalion; Commander of the 23rd Cavalry Regiment, 1917-18; rank of Colonel, Dec. 15, 1915; rank of Brigadier General, Aug. 1, 1920; Commander of Military Operations, Baja California del Norte, 1922; Commander of Military Operations, Sinaloa, 1923; fought against the de la Huerta rebellion, 1923; rank of Brigade General, Jan. 16, 1924; fought against the Escobar rebellion, 1929; Commander of the 29th Military Zone, Ixtepec, Oaxaca, 1937; reached rank of Division General, Oct. 16, 1937; Commander of the 4th Military Zone, Hermosillo, Sonora, the 17th Military Zone, Querétaro, Querétaro, the 15th Military Zone, Guadalajara, Jalisco, 1940, the 7th Military Zone, Monterrey, Nuevo León, the Pacific Military Region, 1942-45, and the 1st Military Zone, Mexico City, 1951-56. k-Supposedly appointed as secretary of national defense to represent the interests of the veterans of the Revolution; awarded the Belisario Domínguez Award, 1973; Medina says the Left accused him of being the intellectual author of the murder of *Rodolfo T. Loaiza*, governor of Sinaloa, in 1945. l-Informe, 1949-50; *Hoy*, 7 Dec. 1940; WWM45, 67; DGF51, I, 182; Peral, 474; DGF56, 201; HA, 20 Dec. 1946, 9, 19 Jan. 1951, 13-16; *Excélsior*, 4 May 1975,

4, 32; Anderson, 341; HA, 8 Oct. 1973, 13; Medina, 20, 20; Rev. de Ejer., Dec. 1957, 25; Dávila 122; Hernández Ch., 103.

Maciel Salcedo, Ignacio
a-Sept. 29, 1910. b-Guadalajara, Jalisco. c-Primary studies in a public school, Guadalajara; secondary and preparatory studies in the Preparatory School, University of Guadalajara; law degree, School of Law, University of Guadalajara; Secretary General of the University of Guadalajara, 1953-59; Director of the School of Law, University of Guadalajara. d-*Senator* from the State of Jalisco, 1970-76, President of the Second Treasury and the First Consular and Diplomatic Service Committee; First Secretary of the First Government Committee, and member of the First Section of the Legislative Studies Committee. e-None. f-Assistant President of the Board of Conciliation and Arbitration, State of Jalisco; judge in Atotonelco de Alto, Jalisco; Assistant Attorney General of Jalisco; Judge, Traffic Department, Guadalajara, Jalisco; Legal Adviser to the Chief of Police, Guadalajara; Director, Department of Labor and Social Welfare, Jalisco. g-None. j-None. k-None. l-C de S, 1970-76, 79; PS, 3514.

Madero (Beldén), Pablo Emilio
a-Aug. 3, 1921. b-San Pedro de las Colonias, Coahuila. c-Early education unknown; chemical engineering degree, with a specialty in sugar and petroleum, National School of Chemical Sciences, UNAM, 1945. d-Candidate of PAN for mayor of Monterrey; candidate of PAN for federal deputy from Nuevo León; *Plurinominal Federal Deputy* from PAN, 1979-82; candidate of PAN for president of Mexico, 1981; *Plurinominal Federal Deputy* from PAN, 1991-94. e-President of PAN in Nuevo León, 1974-78; President of PAN in

Monterrey; Secretary of Organization of PAN in Nuevo León; joined PAN, 1939; adviser to the CEN of PAN, 1974-79; *President of the CEN of PAN*, 1984-86. f-None. g-Vice-President of the National Federation of Transformation Industries; President of the Latin American Association of Glass Producers. h-Industrialist in the glass industry in Monterrey. i-Nephew of Francisco I. Madero; son of Division General Emilio Madero González and Mercedes Beldén; married Norma Morelos Zaragoza, candidate for alternate federal deputy from Nuevo León, 1979; son, Pablo, was a candidate of PAN for federal deputy; cousin of *Francisco José Madero González*, federal deputy from Coahuila, 1979-81; nephew of *Raúl Madero González*. j-None. k-Adviser to the Mexico–North America Institute of Cultural Relations. l-*La Nación*, 16 Sept. 1981, 10; *Excélsior*, 16 Apr. 1979, 16; HA, 5 Oct. 1981, 9; Análisis Político, May 1978, 5; Almanaque de México, 15; HA, 20 Feb. 1984, 16.

Madero González, Francisco José
a-Oct. 16, 1930. b-San Antonio, Texas. c-Early education unknown; completed secondary studies; private accounting degree, Business Banking School, 1947-48. d-Mayor of Torreón, 1975-78; *Federal Deputy* from the State of Coahuila, Dist. 6, 1979-81; *Senator* from Coahuila, 1982-88. e-Joined PRI, 1956; Director General of the IEPES of PRI for Coahuila, 1967-69; Secretary General of PRI for Torreón, 1960-61; Interim President of PRI for Torreón, 1962-65. f-Director of the Board of Material Improvements for Torreón, 1965-79; Director of Public Registry of Property, Viesca, Coahuila, 1963-75; *Interim Governor of Coahuila*, Aug. 10 to Nov. 30, 1981. g-None. h-Businessman, 1953-57; insurance agent, 1957-61; Supervisor, La Comercial Insurance, Torreón, 1957-61. i-Son of former

Governor _Raúl Madero González_ and Dora González Sada; mother, niece of prominent Monterrey industrialist and subsecretary of the treasury in 1920, Francisco G. Sada; nephew of Francisco I. Madero; cousin of _Pablo Emilio Madero Beldén_, president of PAN, 1984. j-None. k-None. l-Almanaque de México, 1982, 475; _Excélsior_, 2 Oct. 1982, 9A, 11 Aug. 1981, 1A; Lehr, 62; DBGM84, 542; DBGM87, 507.

Madero (González), Raúl

(Deceased) a-Sept. 16, 1888. b-Parras, Coahuila. c-Early education unknown; no degree. d-_Governor of Coahuila_, 1957-63. e-Prominent member and cofounder of the Authentic Party of the Mexican Revolution (PARM), 1954. f-Provisional Governor of Coahuila, June 15-20, 1915; Governor of Nuevo León, Feb. 16 to May 18, 1915; member of the Board of the National Army-Navy Bank as a representative of the Secretariat of National Defense, 1952-57. g-Member of the Veterans of the Revolution who participated in honoring President _Echeverría_, 1971; Commander of the Legion of Honor, 1975-82. i-Brother of Francisco Madero; great-grandfather was governor of Coahuila, 1880-84; father was a millionaire; brother Emilio became a prominent Coahuilan industrialist; son, _Francisco Madero González_ was interim governor of Coahuila, 1981; married Dora González Sada, niece of Francisco G. Sada, secretary of the treasury, 1920; close friend of _Antonio I. Villarreal_. j-Joined the Revolution as a close collaborator of brother Francisco; involved in his brother's flight from Morelos, 1911; fought with Villa under Colonel Eugenio Aquirre Benavides in the Zaragoza Brigade, 1913-14; rank of Colonel, Nov. 16, 1914; rank of Brigadier General, Apr. 2, 1915; fought Obregón with Villa, 1914-15; rejoined Army as a Brigadier General, 1939; rank of Division General, Apr.

1, 1944; retired Apr. 21, 1961; Chief of Arms for Zapata's surrender. k-Noted in the Revolution for saving Francisco Villa's life from a firing squad, 1912; fled into exile in the United States, 1913; in exile, 1915; supported the de la Huerta rebellion, 1923; supported the Escobar rebellion, 1929; Scott suggests that Madero may have been given the PRI nomination for governor of Coahuila in return for PARM's recognition and support of _Adolfo López Mateos_ in 1958; last survivor of the revolutionary group of Nov. 20, 1910; received the Belisario Domínguez Award, 1982. l-DP70, 1230; Scott, 188; DGF, II, 35; HA, 17 Dec. 1962, 25, 10 Sept. 1971, 18; Michaels, 40; Dulles, 441; López, 640; _Excélsior_, 15 Apr. 1975, 16; Enc. Mex., Annual, 1977, 576; Almanaque of N.L., 101; HA, 11 Oct. 1982, 9-10, 18 Oct. 1982, 7; _Excélsior_, 2 Oct. 1982, 9A.

Madrazo (Becerra), Carlos A.

(Deceased June 4, 1969) a-1915. b-Villahermosa, Tabasco. c-Primary and secondary studies in Villahermosa; preparatory studies from the National Preparatory School; law degree from the National School of Law, UNAM, 1937; professor of history in secondary schools. d-_Federal Deputy_ from the Federal District, Dist. 2, 1943-46; President of the Chamber of Deputies, Sept. 1944; _Governor of Tabasco_, 1959-64. e-Founder of the National Federation of Popular Organizations (CNOP) of the PRM, Jan. 18, 1942, with _Ramón G. Bonfil_ and _Lauro Ortega_; principal leader of the Bloc of Revolutionary Youth of the Red Shirts under Garrido Canabal, 1933-35; director of the Federation of Mexican Youth, 1939; member of the First National Council of the CNOP, 1944; _President of the CEN of PRI_, 1954-65. f-Private Secretary to the Governor of Guanajuato, _Luis I. Rodríguez_, 1937-38; Private Secretary to the President of the CEN of the PRM, *Luis I. Rodríguez*, 1938-39; official of the Secretariat of Public Education, 1941; Head of the Department of Economic Statistics, Department of the Federal District; Director of Social Action of the Department of the Federal District, 1942-43; head of the Legal Department of the National Sugar Cane Commission. g-President of the Student Society of the National Preparatory School, 1933; President of the Federation of Mexican Youth, 1939; member of the Technical Council of Education of the Federation of Socialist Students of Tabasco, 1933-35. h-None. i-Son, *Carlos Madrazo Pintado*, was assistant secretary to *Alfonso Martínez Domínguez*, and became oficial mayor of public works, 1976-78; son, Roberto, important leader in the National Youth Sector of PRI and was senator from Tabasco, 1988; married Gabriela Pintado; cousin of General *Miguel Orrico de los Llanos*, governor of Tabasco, 1955-58; son of Pio Quinto Madrazo and Concepción Becerra, rural teacher. j-None. k-Involved in a major political scandal as a federal deputy and was forced to resign; Madrazo was later exonerated and was reinstated as a federal deputy; the reason for his involvement was attributed to his support of *Javier Rojo Gómez* for president, 1945; resigned as president of the CEN of PRI after failing to bring about reforms; many of his supporters believe that the airplane crash in which he died was the result of sabotage. l-WWMG, 25; DP70, 1232; Enc. Mex., V, 220; Johnson, 45-47; Correa, 36, 114, 118; HA, 26 Jan. 1945, 5; HA, 4 Aug. 1944; *Por Qué?*, 25 Sept. 1969, 12ff; Cadena Z., 129; NYT, 2 Sept. 1944, 9; CyT, 91; *Excélsior*, 5 June 1977, 4; Enc. Mex., VIII, 1977, 198.

Madrazo Pintado, Carlos Armando
a-Aug. 22, 1940. b-Federal District. c-Preparatory studies at the National Preparatory School; law degree, Na-

tional School of Law, UNAM, 1958-62, completed his thesis in 1963 on divestiture; postgraduate work at UCLA, 1979-80; professor of civics, National Preparatory School No. 1, 1964-66. d-*Federal Deputy* from the Federal District, Dist. 23, 1973-76. e-Member of the Youth Directorate of PRI, 1960; Auxiliary Secretary of the CEN of PRI, 1970; General Delegate of the CEN of PRI to the states of Chihuahua, Oaxaca, Guerrero, San Luis Potosí, Durango, Guanajuato, and Sinaloa; *Secretary of International Affairs of the CEN of PRI*, 1980. f-Lawyer, Customs Department, Tax Attorney's Office, 1960-63; lawyer, Financial Studies Division, Secretariat of the Treasury, 1963; aide to the attorney general of the Federal District, 1963-64; aide to the oficial mayor of Public Works, 1965; Subdirector of Labor, Secretariat of Labor, 1965-66; Auxiliary Secretary to *Alfonso Martínez Domínguez*, 1970-71; delegate of the Department of the Federal District to Alvaro Obregón, 1971-73; *Oficial Mayor of the Secretariat of Public Works*, 1976-78; Director General of Agrarian Delegates, Secretariat of Agrarian Reform, 1981-82; Oficial Mayor of the Attorney General of Mexico, 1982-84. g-Auxiliary Secretary to the Secretary General of the CNC, 1965-67. h-Practicing lawyer in the firm of Madrazo and De Buen, 1960-70. i-Son of *Carlos Madrazo*, president of the CEN of PRI, and Graciela Pintado Jiménez; married Judith María Kramer Rellstab; brother, Roberto, was a senator from Tabasco, 1988. j-None. k-None. l-*Excélsior*, 16 Mar. 1973, 22; DJBM, 83; *Hoy*, 14 Mar. 1970, 4; *Excélsior*, 28 Feb. 1973, 19, 21 Jan. 1975, 5; Protag., 205; Q es QAP, 461; DBGM, 258.

Madrazo Reynoso, Ignacio
a-Apr. 8, 1944. b-Federal District. c-Early education unknown; economics degree, National School of Economics,

UNAM, 1963-67, with a thesis on "The Necessity of Combining Industrialization and General Economic Development Policy," 1968; MA in economics, Cambridge University, 1974; Professor of Public Finance, National School of Economics, UNAM, 1972-73; Professor of Public Finance, School of Economics, Anáhuac University, 1972-73. d-None. e-None. f-Economist, Technical Section, Secretariat of Government Properties, 1971-72; Coordinator of the Subdirector of Analysis, Division of Control and Inspection, Secretariat of Government Properties, 1971; Director, Economic Studies Department, Secretariat of Government Properties, 1972; Subdirector of Acquisitions Inspection Department, Secretariat of Government Properties, 1972-73; Administrative Subdirector, 1974, Subdirector of Finance, 1974-76, and Director General of Credit, 1976-78, all at National Sugar Finance Bank; Director General of Customs, Secretariat of the Treasury, 1978-80; *Oficial Mayor of the Treasury*, 1980-82; *Subsecretary of Tax Investigation*, Secretariat of the Treasury, 1982-88; Director General of Azúcar, Secretariat of Agriculture and Hydraulic Resources, 1988-90; adviser to the Secretary of the Treasury, 1990-91; Director General of the National Savings Board, Secretariat of the Treasury, 1991-94. g-None. h-Analyst, Industrial Coordinators, S.A., 1966. i-Son of Luis Madrazo Basauri, lawyer, and Alicia Reynoso Pedroza; married *Luz Lajous Vargas*, federal deputy, 1982-85 and 1988-91; son-in-law of *Adrián Lajous*; brother-in-law of Roberta Lajous, director general in the Secretariat of Foreign Relations, and wife of *Fernando Solana Morales*, secretary of foreign relations; brother-in-law of Adrián Lajous Vargas, subdirector of production in PEMEX. j-None. k-None. l-Q es QAP, 109; *Excélsior*, 9 Apr. 1980, 22, 29 Dec. 1982, 18;

DBGM87, 226; DBGM89, 210; DBGM92, 218.

Magaña Cerda, Conrado
a-Mar. 13, 1900. b-Zamora, Michoacán. c-Early education unknown; no degree. d-Mayor of Los Reyes, Michoacán, 1936-37; Mayor of La Piedad, Michoacán, 1937-38; Mayor of Zamora, Michoacán, 1938-39; *Federal Deputy* from the State of Michoacán, Dist. 4, 1955-58. e-President of PRI, State of Michoacán, 1942-52. f-*Substitute Governor of Michoacán*, 1939-40; President of the Local Board of Coordinating Agricultural Statistics, Michoacán. g-President of the Federation of Small Landholders. i-Brother of *Gildardo Magaña*, governor of Michoacán. j-Fought in the Revolution; Zapatista; reached rank of Lt. Colonel. k-None. l-Ind. Biog., 97; C de D, 1955-58; Dicc. Mich., 249.

Magaña (Cerda), Gildardo
(Deceased Dec. 13, 1939) a-June 8, 1891. b-Zamora, Michoacán. c-Studied at the Colegio de Jacona seminary in Zamora; studied business administration in San Antonio, Texas; studied accounting at Temple College, Philadelphia, completed studies in private accounting, 1908; no degree. d-Federal Deputy from the State of Michoacán, Dist. 2, 1926-28; *Governor of Michoacán*, 1936-39. f-Governor of the Federal District and Secretary of Government during the Convention of Aguascalientes, 1914; *Governor of Baja California del Norte*, 1934-35. g-Secretary General of the Union of Small Property Owners; organizer of the National Agrarian Federation. h-Practicing accountant, Rojas and Taboada, Mexico City, 1908; author of a major work on Zapata and agrarianism in Mexico. i-Companion and longtime friend of *Saturnino Cedillo* since Revolutionary days under Zapata; precursor of the Revolution in a

group that included Camilo Arriaga, José Vasconcelos, and *Francisco Múgica*; father, a successful businessman and teacher; brother, Octavio Magaña, served as a federal deputy from Michoacán, 1924-1930. j-Joined the Revolution; instrumental in briefly uniting Villa and Zapata; became Chief of Staff of the Army of the South on the death of Zapata, 1919; Commanding General of the Liberating Army of the South, 1919; Commander, First Division, Army of the South, 1920; head of the Agrarian Settlement Program, 1920-24; rank of Division General, Jan. 1, 1921; career army officer, without assignment, 1924-34; Commander of the 24th Military Zone, Cuernavaca, Morelos; Commander of the 2nd Military Zone, Baja California, 1935-36. k-Important intellectual in the Zapatista movement; active in Tacubaya plot against the Díaz government; imprisoned in Mexico City, 1912-14; the son of General Domingo Arenas accuses Magaña of resonsibility in his father's murder; Brandenburg considered Magaña in the Inner Circle status as governor of Michoacán; precandidate for President of Mexico, 1939. l-Brandenburg, 90; Kirk, 86, 118; DP70, 1233; *Heroic Mexico*, 163, 173, 330; D de Y, 5 Sept. 1935; Michaels, 3; Bermúdez, 80-81; González Navarro, 150; Enc. Mex., VIII, 1977, 201-02; Raby, 215; López González, 123-27.

Magaña Negrete, Gumersindo
a-Dec. 5, 1939. b-Uruapan, Michoacán. c-Early education unknown; law degree, School of Law, University of San Luis Potosí; Professor of Civil Law, Legal Process, and Political Economy, School of Law, University of San Luis Potosí. d-*Purninomial Federal Deputy* from the PDM, 1979-82, member of the Agrarian Reform and Public Education Committees. e-Secretary of Information and Political Action, National Committee,

PDM; presidential candidate of the PDM, 1988; PDM lost legal party registration after 1988 election. f-None. g-Joined the Sinarquista Youth Movement, Uruapan, 1954; Youth Secretary of the National Sinarquista Union, San Luis Potosí; Chief of the National Sinarquista Union, San Luis Potosí; Secretary General of the *El Sol* Journalists Union, San Luis Potosí. h-Practicing lawyer; journalist. i-Grandmother a Sinarquista. j-None. k-None. l-*Proceso*, 22 Feb. 1988, 25; C de D, 1979-82; Directorio, 1979-82.

Magdaleno (Cardona), Mauricio
a-May 13, 1906. b-Villa de Refugio, Zacatecas. c-Primary and secondary studies in Aguascalientes, Aguascalientes; preparatory studies at the National Preparatory School, 1920-23; studied at the Graduate School of UNAM, 1923-25; studied at the University of Madrid, 1932-33; Professor of History and Literature, UNAM, 1934-35. d-*Federal Deputy* from the State of Zacatecas, Dist. 3, 1949-52, member of the Legislative Studies Committee (2nd year); *Senator* from the State of Zacatecas, 1958-64, member of the Gran Comisión, President of the First Committee on Public Education, member of the First Committee on Foreign Relations, the First Balloting Committee, the First Instructive Section of the Grand Jury; substitute member of the Tourist Affairs Committee and the Legislative Studies Committee. e-None. f-President of the Revisory Committee on Income Taxes, 1934-36, Secretariat of the Treasury; member of the Technical Council for Theaters, Mexico City, 1936-39; correspondent for the National Institute for the Investigation of Theaters; Head of the Library and Archives, Secretariat of the Treasury, 1936-45; writer for the newspaper *El Universal*, 1934-64; Director General of the Division of Social Action, Depart-

ment of the Federal District, 1952-58; *Subsecretary of Cultural Affairs of the Secretariat of Public Education*, 1964-70. g-None. h-Well-known author of numerous plays, books and movie scripts. i-Became friend of *Adolfo López Mateos* and *Manuel Moreno Sánchez* during Vasconcelos campaign, 1929; son of Vicente Magdaleno Redin, Liberal and Maderista, and María Cardona; brother, Vicente, a well-known poet; married Rosario Ríos. j-None. k-Campaign aide to José Vasconcelos, 1929. l-*Libro de Oro*, xxxv; DGF51, I, 27; C de D, 1949-51, 77; DPE65, 135; C de S, 1961-64, 59-60; DBM68, 399; DBM70, 349; C de S, 1964, 12; WWM45, 68; Strode, 415; DEM, 207-08; HA, 21 Dec. 1964, 4; Haddox, 8; Func., 410; letter; López, 642; Enc. Mex., VIII, 1977, 203; WNM, 137.

Maldonado, Víctor Alfonso
a-Sept. 19, 1906. b-San Luis Potosí. c-Early education unknown; law degree. d-*Federal Deputy* from the State of San Luis Potosí, Dist. 1, 1937-40; *Federal Deputy* from the State of San Luis Potosí, Dist. 3, 1943-46. e-None. f-Joined the Foreign Service, 1946; Ambassador to Bolivia, 1946-48, El Salvador, 1949-53, Ethiopia and Turkey, 1954-55, Angola, 1956-58, the United Arab Republic, 1959-60, Sweden, 1960-61, Ethiopia, 1962-65, and Honduras, 1965-66; *Ambassador to Cuba*, 1970-75. g-None. h-None. i-Son, *Víctor Alonso Maldonado Moroleón* served as a federal deputy from San Luis Potosí, 1976-79 and 1982-85; father an indigenous peasant. j-None. k-None. l-C de D, 1937-40, 1943-46; letter; DBGM89, 213.

Maldonado López, Carlos B.
a-Aug. 15, 1911. b-Hermosillo, Sonora. c-Primary studies in Hermosillo; some secondary studies in Hermosillo and in Mexico City; no degree. d-*Senator* from the State of Sonora, 1958-64, Second

Secretary of the Special Forestry Committee, alternate member of the First Petroleum, Special Livestock, and First Ejido Committees. e-Participated in the presidential campaign of General Alvaro Obregón, 1928; participated in the presidential campaign of *Adolfo López Mateos*, 1958; general delegate of the CEN of PRI to the states of Jalisco, Colima, Guanajuato, and Sonora. f-None. g-Founding member of the CTM, 1936; President of the CTM in the State of Sonora. h-Laborer for many years. j-None. k-None. l-C de S, 1961-64, 60; Func., 359.

Maldonado Moroleón, Víctor Alfonso
a-Oct. 14, 1936. b-San Luis Potosí, San Luis Potosí. c-Early education unknown; law degree, 1955-59, economics degree, 1955-59; and Ph.D. in economics, 1960-62, all from University of Paris; Professor of World Economic Structures, National School of Economics, UNAM, 1968-71; visiting professor, University of Quebec, Canada, 1968; visiting professor, Institute of Mexican Studies, Perpignan, France, 1976. d-*Federal Deputy* from the State of San Luis Potosí, Dist. 3, 1976-79, member of the Gran Comisión; *Federal Deputy* from San Luis Potosí, Dist. 1, 1982-85. e-Joined PRI, 1960; Subdirector of Political Studies of the CEPES of PRI, Federal District; adviser, Secretary General of the CEN of PRI, 1981-82. f-Director, Office of Trade Policy, Secretariat of the Treasury, 1963-64; Subdirector, Department of Economic Studies, Secretariat of the Treasury, 1964-68; Director General of Documentation, Presidential State of the Union Addresses, Secretariat of the Presidency, 1970-76. g-Secretary of Finances, League of Revolutionary Economists, 1976-78. h-Writer for many Mexico City newspapers and magazines. i-Son of *Víctor Alfonso Maldonado*, federal deputy from San Luis Potosí and

ambassador to Cuba, 1970-75, and
Manuela Moroleón Arriaga, teacher;
married Amparo Anso López, lawyer.
j-None. k-None. l-Directorio, 1982-85;
C de D, 1976-79; Lehr, 416; DBGM89,
213; DBGM, 543.

Maldonado Pereda, Juan
a-Feb. 11, 1934. b-Veracruz, Veracruz.
c-Early education unknown; law degree,
National School of Law, UNAM, with a
thesis on "The Mexican Revolution and
the Chamula Tribe"; Professor of the
History of Mexico, Graduate Institute of
Business Studies; Professor of Political
Parties, Electoral Law and General
Theory of the State, School of Political
Science, UNAM, Acatlán; Professor of
Social and Economic Doctrines, School
of Law, University of Tabasco; Secretary
General of the Juárez University of
Tabasco, 1963-64; Rector of the Juárez
University of Tabasco, 1964. d-*Alter-
nate Senator* from the State of Veracruz,
1970-76; Mayor of Veracruz, Veracruz,
1973-76; *Federal Deputy* from the State
of Veracruz, Dist. 11, 1979-82, 1985-88.
e-Director of Youth Action of PRI,
Federal District, 1955; Auxiliary
Secretary General of the CEN of PRI,
1965; Auxiliary Secretary of the
National Editorial Committee of the
CEN of PRI, 1968; President of PRI in
the Federal District, 1981-82. f-Judge of
the First Instance, Huimanguillo,
Tabasco, 1960; President of the Board of
Conciliation and Arbitration of Tabasco, 1961; Director of Publications,
UNAM; Private Secretary to *Rafael
Murillo Vidal*, Governor of Veracruz,
1968; *Subsecretary A of the Depart-
ment of the Federal District*, 1982-84.
g-None. h-Public notary, 1960-61.
i-Son of Eugenio Maldonado and
Evangelina Pereda; married Ana María
Hernández. j-None. k-None. l-HA, 20
Dec. 1982, 28; Q es QAP, 425; C de D,
1979-82; DBGM87, 508; HA, 2 Apr.
1984, 22.

Maldonado Pérez, Caritino
(Deceased Apr. 17, 1971) a-Oct. 5, 1915.
b-Tlalixtaquilla, Guerrero. c-Primary
studies in Alcozauca, Guerrero; teaching certificate, Rural Normal School of
Oaxtepec, Morelos, 1928-29; graduate,
National Teachers School, 1936-38;
preparatory studies, National Prepara-
tory School; school teacher, 1929-32;
teacher at the Regional Rural School,
Coyuca de Catalán, Guerrero, 1938-40;
primary and secondary teacher in public
and private schools, Mexico City, 1940-
44. d-Local Deputy to the State
Legislature of Morelos, 1944-45; *Federal
Deputy* from the State of Guerrero,
Dist. 5, 1949-51, member of the Gran
Comisión, the First Committee on
Public Education, and the Second
Balloting Committee; substitute
member of the Committee on Forest
Affairs; *Alternate Senator* from Gue-
rrero, 1952-58; *Senator* from the State of
Guerrero, 1958-64, President of the
Special Committee on Small Agricul-
tural Property, member of the First
Committee on Public Education,
substitute member of the Internal and
Foreign Trade Committee, the Protocol
Committee, and the Industries Committee; *Governor of Guerrero*, 1969-71.
e-President of PRI in the State of
Guerrero, 1948-49; *Secretary of Popular
Action of the CEN of PRI*, 1952-56.
f-Private Secretary to *Baltasar Leyva*,
Governor of Guerrero, 1945-48; Head of
the Department of Inspection, Secretariat of Labor, 1952-58; *Oficial Mayor
of the Secretariat of Health*, 1965-69.
g-Active in the SNTE, 1940; *Secretary
General of the CNOP of PRI*, 1952-58.
h-None. j-None. k-Considered a
cacique of the local region he represented in Guerrero; *Por Qué* states that
he was denounced in 1950 for being
connected with the murder of three
persons. l-C de S, 1961-64, 60; *Libro de
Oro*, xxxvi; DGF56, 6, 399; DPE65, 148;
C de D, 1949-51, 78; DGF51, I, 22, 30,

32, 34; *Siempre,* 19 Sept. 1956, 10; 21
Dec. 1964, 4; *Por Qué,* 4 Oct. 1968, 35;
HA, 10 June 1974, 13; Func., 218.

Maldonado Pinedo, Ana María Irma
a-Feb. 24, 1938. b-Zacatecas. c-Teaching certificate as a secondary teacher
from the Manuel Avila Camacho Normal School, Zacatecas, 1953-56; law degree, University of Zacatecas, 1959-61;
Director, Manuel Avila Camacho Normal School, 1980-82; Director, School of
Social Work, Zacatecas, 1978-82; professor, Normal School of Zacatecas, 1973-
80 at School of Social Work, Zacatecas,
1973-80 and at Manuel Avila Camacho
Normal School, 1965- . d-*Federal Deputy* from the State of Zacatecas, Dist.
5, 1982-85. e-Joined PRI, 1956. f-None.
g-Secretary of Acts and Agreements,
Local 58, SNTE, 1979-81; Secretary of
Relations, Local 58, SNTE, 1979-81.
h-Teacher. j-None. k-None. l-Directorio, 1982-85; Lehr, 537; DBGM, 544.

Maldonado Sánchez, Braulio
a-Aug. 21, 1902. b-San José del Cabo,
Baja California del Norte. c-Primary
studies in Baja California; secondary
studies in Mexico City; preparatory studies at the National Preparatory School;
special studies in the Army; enrolled in
UNAM, 1924; law degree 1940s. d-Alternate Federal Deputy from the State of
Baja California del Norte, Dist. 2, 1930-
32; Federal Deputy from the State of
Baja California del Norte, Dist. 1, 1932-
34; *Federal Deputy* from Baja California
del Norte, 1946-49, member of the Gran
Comisión, the Second Treasury Committee, the Second Balloting Committee, the Budget and Accounts Committee, and the First Constitutional Affairs
Committee; Secretary to the president
of the Preparatory Committee; *Federal
Deputy* from Baja California del Norte,
1952-53, member of the Third Section
of the Credentials Committee and the
Social Action Committee (1st year);

Governor of Baja California del Norte,
1953-59. e-Leader of the Popular
Electoral Front; cofounder of the Leftist
Socialist Party, 1931; Secretary General
of the Leftist Socialist Party; member of
the National Advisory Council of PRI;
attempted to found a new party, the
Coordinating Revolutionary Movement
of the Mexican Republic, 1977. f-Adviser to the Independent Farmers Central
(CCI), 1966. g-González Navarro states
that the CCI was financed by *Maldonado Sánchez;* active in the National
Students League. h-Worked as a laborer
in the United States; worked in a
butcher shop; author of a political
commentary on Baja California and his
regime. i-Former Federal Deputy
Leopoldo Sales Rovira was part of his
political organization in Baja California;
met *Miguel Alemán* at the National
Preparatory School; student of *Manuel
Gómez Morín;* daughter was PRD candidate for governor of Baja California,
1989. j-Rank of 2nd Sergeant in the army. k-Student participant in 1927 presidential campaign in support of General Serrano with *Miguel Alemán* and
Efraín Brito Rosado; deported as a result
of his supposed participation in the
Popular Electoral Front's attempt to
disrupt the *Díaz Ordaz* campaign, 1964;
Johnson and *Por Qué* claim his regime
as governor was characterized by extensive corruption and that he was responsible for the development of a huge
prostitution ring in Tijuana. l-C de D,
1946-48, 77, 1952-54, 14; Johnson, 134;
Por Qué, 2 July 1968, 2; DGF56, 90;
DGF47, 4; D del S, 22 Jan. 1946, 1; *Por
Qué,* 4 Oct. 1968, 46-48; González Navarro, 238, 241; HA, 28 Sept. 1953, 25;
Excélsior, 17 June 1977, 10; HA, 5 July
1954, 9; *Proceso,* 15 Dec. 1986, 11-13.

Maliachi (y Velasco), Eduardo
a-Oct. 24, 1941. b-Veracruz, Veracruz.
c-Secondary teaching certificate,
National Normal School, 1960; special-

ist in teaching, Higher Normal School, Mexico City, 1966; economics degree, with a thesis on "Criteria for Assigning Resources to Higher Education in Mexico," 1973; primary school teacher, 1961-67; secondary school teacher, 1967-73; professor, National School of Teachers of Industrial Workers, 1969; professor, National School of Economics, UNAM, 1972-73; Rector, National Teachers University, Secretariat of Public Education, 1986-88. d-None. e-None. f-Assistant to the Subsecretary of Planning and Educational Coordination, Secretariat of Public Education, 1971; Chief of Technical Activities in Secondary Schools, Federal District, 1972-73; Subdirector of Middle Education, Division of Improving Professional Teaching, Secretariat of Public Education, 1974-75; Director General of the National Institute of Educational Research, 1976; analyst, Education Section, Secretariat of Programming and Budget, 1977-78; Assistant Director General of Normal Education, Secretariat of Public Education, 1978-79; Director General of Normal Education, Secretariat of Public Education, 1979-80; *Oficial Mayor of the Secretariat of Public Education,* 1980-82, 1982-86. g-None. h-None. i-Son of Admiral Enrique Maliachi Arias and Carmen Velasco Uribe; married Elsa Villasaña Hernández, teacher. j-None. k-None. l-HA, 2 June 1980, 13; IEPES; Q es QAP, 301; DBGM, 261-62; DBGM87, 230.

Mancera Aguayo, Miguel
a-Dec. 18, 1932 b-Federal District. c-Primary and secondary studies at Brothers of Mary schools, Mexico City; preparatory studies at the Centro de Universitario Mexicano, Mexico City; economics degree, Autonomous Technological Institute of Mexico, 1951-56; MA in economics, Yale University, 1959-60; Professor of Political Economy, Escuela Libre de Derecho, 1957; Profes-

sor of International Trade, ITAM, 1958-64, and CEMLA, 1962-64. d-None. e-None. f-Employee, Public Investment Committee, Presidency, 1957-58; joined the Bank of Mexico as an economist, 1958-62; administrator, FOMEX, 1962-67; Manager, Department of International Affairs, 1967-71; Subdirector General of International Affairs, 1971-73, and Subdirector General of Finances, 1973-82, all at Bank of Mexico; *Director General of the Bank of Mexico,* 1982-88; 1988-96. g-None. h-Employee, Bank of Commerce, 1953-56; worked in the Bank of England and other English banks. i-Son of *Rafael Mancera Ortiz,* subsecretary of treasury, 1948-58, and María Luisa Aguayo Cendejas; brother, Gabriel, an accountant in Mancera Brothers; attended Yale with *Jesús Silva Herzog;* married Sonia Corcuera Corcuera; son, Carlos Mancera Corcuera, coordinator of advisers, Secretariat of Public Education, 1988; disciples include *Francisco Gil Díaz, Guillermo Ortiz Martínez,* and *Ernesto Zedillo.* j-None. k-Resigned as director general of the Bank of Mexico after the nationalization of the private banks, Sept. 2, 1982. l-IEPES; Q es QAP, 497; *Excélsior,* 18 Mar. 1982, 14; BdeM, 120; WSJ, 3 Sept, 1982, 3; *Mexico Journal,* 18 Dec. 1989, 16-21; DBGM, 263; DBGM92, 221; DBGM89, 213.

Mancera Ortiz, Rafael
(Deceased Sept. 30, 1968) a-Aug. 22, 1895. b-Federal District. c-Preparatory studies at the National Preparatory School, CPA degree from the National School of Business Administration, UNAM, 1917; Professor of Accounting at the Graduate School of Business and Administration, UNAM, 1932-36; and the School of Economics and Social Sciences, IPN, 1925-36. d-None. e-None. f-Oficial Mayor of the Controller General of Mexico, 1924-27; Oficial Mayor of the Secretariat of the Trea-

sury, 1927-30; Subsecretary of the
Treasury, 1930-32; adviser to Nacional
Financiera; *Subsecretary of Credit,*
Secretariat of the Treasury, 1948-52,
1952-58. g-First President of the
National Association of Public Accountants in Mexico, 1929-30, 1959-61.
h-Organized a private accounting firm
of Mancera and Sons; author of a book
on public administration and economic
development in Mexico, 1953. i-Son
Miguel Mancera was director general of
the Bank of Mexico, 1982; son Gabriel
is a CPA, managing the firm of Mancera
and Sons; married María Luisa Aguayo;
brother, Alfredo, a CPA, is married to
Rosa Aguayo, sister of María Luisa; son
of Alfredo Mancera y Pérez and Dolores
Ortiz y Córdova. j-Participated in the
Revolution, 1913-20. k-One of the
initiators of the certified public accounting system in Mexico. l-DGF47;
DGF51, II, 231, 303, 487, 359; DGF56,
161; DP70, 2413; HA, 12 Dec. 1952, 5;
WNM, 139; Enc. Mex., VIII, 1977, 239;
Libro Azul, 217; DBGM89, 213.

Manero, Antonio
(Deceased 1964) a-1885. b-Toluca,
México. c-Primary and secondary stu-
dies in Mexico City; Professor of Busi-
ness Organization, National School of
Economics, UNAM, 1945-48. d-Federal
Deputy from the State of México, Dist.
15, 1920-22; *Federal Deputy* from the
State of México, Dist. 2, 1943-46,
President of economic commissions as a
Federal Deputy, 1943. e-None.
f-Member of the Inspection and Regula-
tory Commission of the Banking
System; President of the Treasury and
Public Credit Commission, 1920;
member of the commission formed to
found the Bank of Mexico; founder and
Director General of the National Labor
Bank, 1929; financial adviser to the bloc
of senators from the official party, 1935;
Director of Finances for the Department
of the Federal District, 1939-40; founder

and President of the Industrial Bank of
the State of México, 1943; Director
General of PIPSA, 1940; Director of
Financial Studies of the Secretariat of
the Treasury, 1944. g-None. h-Author
of many books on Revolutionary
banking institutions. i-Father, a well-
known lawyer. j-Joined the Revolution,
1913; fought under Carranza. l-C de D,
1943-45, 15; DP70, 1246; López, 648;
Casasola, V; Enc. Mex., VIII, 1977, 242.

Manjarrez Moreno, Luis Cruz
b-Tochimilco, Municipio of Atlixco,
Puebla. c-Primary studies in Puebla,
Puebla; secondary and preparatory
studies in Mexico City; began studies at
the Higher School of Construction and
Engineering. d-Local Deputy to the
State Legislature of Puebla; *Federal
Deputy* from the State of Puebla, Dist.
2, 1949-52, member of the Editorial
Committee, the Cinematographic
Development Committee, and the
Complaints Committee; *Senator* from
the State of Puebla, 1952-58, member of
the Second Tariff and Foreign Trade
Committee, the Immigration Commit-
tee and the Special Legislative Studies
Committee. e-President of PRI in the
State of Puebla, 1952. f-Subdirector,
Office of Public Entertainment, Depart-
ment of the Federal District; Director of
Press and Publicity, Secretariat of
Communications; Director of Press and
Publicity, Secretariat of Agriculture and
Livestock. g-None. h-Journalist. i-Son
of *Froylán C. Manjarrez,* founding
editor of *El Nacional* (official govern-
ment paper) and federal deputy, and
Georgina Moreno Ortega; brother,
Héctor Cruz Manjarrez Moreno, was
ambassador to Turkey and Rumania.
j-None. k-Founder of the Casa del
Campesino, Atlixco, Puebla, 1935;
founder of the first Casa Materno-
Infantil, 1947. l-DGF51, I, 29, 31, 33; C
de D, 1949-51, 78; Ind. Biog., 99-100;
DGF56, 7, 9-12, 14; DBGM87, 232.

Manjarrez (Romano), Froylán C.
(Deceased Oct. 3, 1937) a-Oct. 5, 1894.
b-Tochimilco, Puebla. c-Early educa-
tion unknown; studies in business; no
degree. d-Deputy to the Constitutional
Convention from the State of Puebla,
Dist. 6, 1916-17, considered part of the
Jacobin group; Federal Deputy from the
State of Puebla, Dist. 6, 1917-18; Federal
Deputy from the State of Sonora, Dist.
1, 1920-22; Federal Deputy from the
Federal District, Dist. 15, 1922-24;
Federal Deputy from the State of
Puebla, Dist. 3, 1932-34; *Federal
Deputy* from the State of Puebla, Dist.
3, 1937. e-*Secretary of Publicity for the
CEN of the PNR*, 1934; Director
General of *El Nacional* of the PNR,
1934. f-Provisional Governor of Puebla,
1922-23. g-Collaborated in the Intellec-
tual Workers Bloc with *Adolfo Ruiz
Cortines, Gilberto Loyo*, and others.
h-Began journalistic career, 1910. i-Son
of Román C. Manjarrez and María
Romano; son, *Luis C. Manjarrez* served
as a senator from Puebla, 1952-58; son,
Héctor Cruz, was ambassador to
Turkey, 1986. j-None. k-Exiled to
Cuba, France, and Spain, 1920; sup-
ported de la Huerta rebellion, 1923;
exiled to Cuba and Spain, 1923-30;
Emilio Portes Gil brought him back to
Mexico; jailed in Madrid for involve-
ment in conspiracy against General
Primo de Rivera. l-Enc. de Mex., 8, 248;
Morales Jiménez, 287; Almanaque de
Puebla, 131; C de D, 1937-40; DBGM,
263; DBGM87, 232.

Manrique de Lara Hernández, Aurelio
(Deceased 1967) a-Apr. 27, 1891. b-San
Luis Potosí, San Luis Potosí. c-Primary
studies in the Scientific and Literary
Institute of San Luis Potosí, San Luis
Potosí; normal teaching certificate from
the National Teachers College, Mexico
City; completed 4th year of medical
studies; professor at the National
Preparatory School, 1912-17. d-Federal

Deputy from the State of San Luis
Potosí, Dist. 1, 1917-18, member of the
Gran Comisión; Federal Deputy from
the State of San Luis Potosí, Dist. 1,
1920-22, Secretary of the Gran Comisión; *Federal Deputy* from the State of
San Luis Potosí, Dist. 1, 1922-23;
Governor of San Luis Potosí, 1923-25;
Federal Deputy from the State of San
Luis Potosí, Dist. 14, 1928-30. e-Founder of the National Agrarian Party,
1920; orator for General Obregón, 1920;
President of the Revolutionary Federation of Independent Parties, 1933.
f-Director of Information of the Secretariat of Government, 1934-40; *Director
General of the ISSSTE*, 1940-46;
Ambassador to Sweden, 1946-51 and
1952-56, Norway, 1946-52, and Den-
mark, 1956; Director of the National
Library, Secretariat of Public Education.
g-None. h-Author of numerous articles.
i-Active in the precursor movement to
the Revolution with Ricardo Flores
Magón, Juan Sarabia, *Antonio Díaz Soto
y Gama, Juan Barragán,* and others;
jailed in San Luis Potosí during the
Porfiriato; boyhood friend of *Jesús Silva
Herzog*; son of well-known lawyer,
Aurelio Manrique; uncle, Felipe
Manrique, was mayor of San Luis
Potosí. j-Fought under Obregón against
Huerta, 1914. k-Rebuked President
Calles in answer to his state of the
union message; forced into exile, 1929-
33; supported the Escobar rebellion,
1929; known for his dramatic debates
with *Antonio Díaz Soto y Gama* in the
Federal Chamber of Deputies. l-B de M,
170-71; DP70, 1248; DGF51, I, 107;
DGF56, 125; López, 649; Enc. Mex.,
VIII, 1977, 250; Montejano, 204.

Mantilla Molina, Roberto
a-Dec. 9, 1910. b-San Juan Bautista
(Villahermosa), Tabasco. c-Secondary
studies in Tampico, Tamaulipas,
Mexico, and Veracruz; preparatory
studies at the Preparatory School of

Veracruz; law degree, National School
of Law, UNAM, 1934; completed
studies for a degree in philosophy,
School of Philosophy and Letters, 1930-
33, but did not take exam; secondary
school teacher, Secondary School Nos. 4
and 1, 1933-34; Professor of the History
of Philosophic Doctrines and Logic,
National Preparatory School, 1933-49;
Professor of Mercantile Law, National
School of Law, 1934-75, and School of
Business and Administration, 1935-50,
both at UNAM; professor, Mexican
Technological Institute, 1948; Professor
of Mercantile Societies, LLD Program,
UNAM; Member of the Governing
Board of UNAM, 1971-77; Professor
Emeritus, National School of Law,
UNAM; Director, National School of
Law, UNAM, 1954-58; Director,
Institute of Comparative Law, UNAM,
1959-66; *Secretary General of UNAM,*
1961-66. d-None. e-None. f-Agent of
the Ministerio Público, civil matters,
Córdoba and Orizaba, Veracruz;
Director, Legal Department, Secretary
of Industry and Commerce, 1946-47;
President, legislative committee,
Secretary of Industry and Commerce.
g-President of the Student Society of the
School of Philosophy and Letters,
UNAM, 1932-33; Secretary General of
the Mexican Bar Association, 1944.
h-Practicing lawyer, 1934-80; member
of the Board of Latin American Life
Insurance, 1974. i-Related to *Antonio
Ruiz Galindo,* secretary of industry and
commerce, 1946-48; son of Víctor M.
Mantilla Marín and Adelina Molina;
married Lucía Caballero. j-None.
k-None. l-Letters; López, 651; WNM,
139-40; Anuario Fin., 1974, 1240.

Manzanilla Schaffer, Víctor
a-Nov. 13, 1924. b-Federal District.
c-Primary studies at the Benito Juárez
School, Mexico City; secondary studies
at Public School No. 3, Mexico City;
preparatory studies, National Prepara-

tory School, Mexico City, 1940-41; legal
studies from the National School of
Law, UNAM, 1942-46, graduating with
an honorable mention, 1948; LLD
studies except the examination;
postgraduate work in sociology at the
New School for Social Research, New
York, 1949; Professor by Competitive
Appointment in Sociology, National
School of Law, UNAM, 1955-70; Profes-
sor of Civics for the National Farmers
Federation (CNC), 1963-64; Professor of
Agrarian Reform, Institute of Compara-
tive Law, UNAM, Professor of Eco-
nomic Problems, UNAM; Professor of
Introductory Law, School of Administration, National School of Economics,
UNAM; Professor of Mercantile Law,
School for the National Chambers of
Commerce. d-*Federal Deputy* from the
State of Yucatán, Dist. 3, 1967-69,
member of the First Section of the Agrarian Affairs Committee, the Legislative
Studies Committee (6th Section of
Agrarian Affairs), the Livestock Committee, the Constitutional Affairs Committee, and the Desert Zones Committee; President of the Chamber of Deputies, Sept. 1967, answered *Díaz Ordaz's*
third state of the union address; *Senator*
from the State of Yucatán, 1970-76,
member of the Gran Comisión, President of the Agriculture and Development Committee and the Agrarian Department Committee; *Federal Deputy*
from the State of Yucatán, Dist. 3, 1976-
79; *Senator* from the State of Yucatán,
1982-88; *Governor of Yucatán,* 1988-91.
e-*Secretary of Press and Publicity of the
CEN of PRI,* 1970-72; Assistant Secretary to the President of the CEN of PRI,
Jesús Reyes Heroles, 1972-74; President
of the National Revolutionary Coalition; adviser to the IEPES of PRI;
President of the National Commission
on Legislative Studies of PRI, 1963.
f-Lawyer for the Office of the Assistant
Attorney General of Mexico; Private
Secretary to *Rafael Matos Escobedo,*

Assistant Attorney General of Mexico, 1947-48; Legal Assistant to the International Division of Narcotics, United Nations, 1949-51; Director of the Department of the Press, Department of Agrarian Affairs, 1958-61; Director of Social Agrarian Action and Information, Department of Agrarian Affairs, 1962-65; agrarian adviser, Advisory Section, Department of Agrarian Affairs, 1966-67; Ambassador to China, 1980-82. g-President of the Junior Chamber of Commerce of Mexico City, 1954; President of the 1942 Generation of Law Students, National School of Law, UNAM, 1942-46. h-Writer for *La República*, official PRI magazine; author of numerous articles. i-Son of Víctor J. Manzanilla, a prominent lawyer and revolutionary leader in Yucatán, who served as a federal deputy and founder of the Anti-Reelectionist Party, and Rosa Schaffer; attended the same primary school as *José López Portillo*. j-None. k-*Por Qué* claims that he turned down the PRI nomination for governor of Yucatán in 1969 because he would accept only if he had direct control over the appointments of the directors of CORDEMEX and the Agricultural Bank of Yucatán; voted against a presidential sponsored amendment to Article 27, 1977. l-DBM68, 405-06; DPE65, 177; DPE61, 127; HA, 14 Aug. 1972, 11; C de D, 1967-69, 57, 67, 72, 84, 91; *Por Qué*, 23 Oct. 1969, 22; C de S, 1970-76, 79; Enc. Mex., VIII, 1977, 256; C de S, 1982-88.

Manzur Ocaña, Julián Alejandro
b-Tabasco. c-Primary and secondary studies in Villahermosa; preparatory studies at the National Preparatory School; medical degree from the National School of Medicine, UNAM; professor of medicine, School of Medicine, University of Tabasco. d-*Senator* from the State of Tabasco, 1958-64, President of the Public Welfare Committee,

member of the Treasury Committee and the Gran Comisión, Secretary of the First Navy Committee. e-None. f-Secretary General of Government of the State of Tabasco, 1964. g-None. h-Practicing physician for many years. j-None. k-None. l-Func., 366; C de S, 1961-64, 61; letter; Bulnes, 698.

Marcué Pardiñas, Manuel
a-July 14, 1916. b-Federal District. c-Early education unknown; agricultural engineering degree, National School of Agriculture, 1933-40; agricultural economics studies, National School of Economics, UNAM, 1940-43. d-*Plurninominal Federal Deputy* from the PRD, 1988-91. e-Cofounder of the National Liberation Movement; joined the PRD, 1988. f-Inspector of Credit, National Foreign Trade Bank, 1940-42; Editor, *Economic Studies*, Bank of Mexico, 1948. g-None. h-Director, *Problemas Agrícolas e Industriales de México*, 1945-60; Director of *Política*, 1960-68. i-Son of Manuel Marcué Sánchez, retailer, and Luis Pardiñas Tovar, retailer; married Concepción Mendoza. j-None. k-None. l-DBGM89, 482-83; C de D, 1988-91.

Mar de la Rosa, J. Refugio
a-July 4, 1924. b-Chihuahua, Chihuahua. c-Secondary studies at the Institute of Sciences and Letters, Chihuahua, 1938-40; no degree. d-Member of the City Council, Chihuahua, Chihuahua, 1960-63; Local Deputy to the State Legislature of Chihuahua, 1965-68; *Federal Deputy* from the State of Chihuahua, Dist. 6, 1970-73, member of the Second Instructive Section of the Grand Jury, the Second Labor Committee, and the Second General Means of Communication Committee; *Federal Deputy* from the State of Chihuahua, Dist. 6, 1976-79, member of the Machinery Section of the Industrial Development Committee, the Border

Zones Section of the Regional Development Committee, the Third Section of the Development of Social Security and Public Health Committee, the First Section of the Development of Tourism Committee, and the Labor Section of the Legislative Studies Committee; *Senator* from the State of Chihuahua, 1982-88. e-Joined PRI, 1942; Secretary of Labor Action of PRI, Chihuahua, 1957. f-None. g-Secretary General of Section 32 of the Union of Hotel and Restaurant Workers, 1955; Secretary General of the CTM of the State of Chihuahua, 1957, 1980-90; Assistant Secretary of Labor, CTM, 1962-68, 1968-74; Assistant Secretary of Organization, CTM, 1974-80; Assistant Secretary of Finances, CTM, 1980. i-Son of Juan Mar Nah, cook, and Zenaida de la Rosa Macías; married María de Jesús Hernández, secretary. j-None. k-None. l-D de C, 1976-79, 27, 36, 38, 41, 54; *Excélsior*, 28 Aug. 1976, 1C; C de D, 1970-73, 123; HA, 1 Mar. 1982, 13; Lehr, 98; DBGM, 545.

Marentes Miranda, Tomás
a-Apr. 1, 1904. b-Villa de Munucma, Yucatán. c-Early education unknown; no degree. d-*Governor of Yucatán*, 1952-53. e-None. f-Subdirector of the National Lottery, 1946-52. g-None. i-Protégé of *Miguel Alemán*; son, Pablo Francisco Marentes González, was director general of the Mexican Institute of Television; father-in-law of Patricia Lerdo de Tejada; married Alicia González Oropeza. j-None. k-Scott says he was imposed as governor of Yucatán over public protests; deposed by the state legislature, June 15, 1953, one of the rare cases of this occurring in Mexican politics; students and henequen producers sent complaints to President *Ruiz Cortines* about his performance as governor. l-Anderson; Scott, 276; DGF47, 410; DGF51, I, 657; HA, 29 June 1953, 10; letter; DBGM87, 234.

Margáin (Gleason), Hugo B.
a-Feb. 13, 1913. b-Federal District. c-Secondary studies at the Colegio Francés Morelos, Mexico City; preparatory studies at the National Preparatory School; law degree from the National School of Law, UNAM, 1938, with a thesis on "The Law and Reality in Mexico"; Professor of Constitutional Law, 1947, Professor of Constitutional Writs, 1951-56, National School of Law, UNAM; Professor of Fiscal Law, 1952-56, School of Business Administration, UNAM. d-*Senator* from the Federal District, 1982-88. e-None. f-Director General of the Federal Retail Merchants Tax Division, Secretariat of the Treasury, 1947-52; Director General of the Federal Income Tax Bureau, Secretariat of the Treasury, 1952-59; *Oficial Mayor of the Secretariat of Industry and Commerce*, 1959-61; *Subsecretary of Industry and Commerce*, 1961-64; Director General of the National Commission on Profit Sharing, 1963-64; executive member of the National Institute of Scientific Investigation, 1962-64; *Ambassador to the United States*, 1965-70; *Secretary of the Treasury*, 1970-73; *Ambassador to Great Britain*, 1973-76; *Ambassador to the United States*, 1976-82. g-None. h-Author of several books on fiscal law and public administration; practicing lawyer, 1938-47. i-Son of César R. Margáin, a well-known doctor and professor, and María Teresa Gleason; studied under *Antonio Carrillo Flores*, *Ramón Beteta*, and *Alfonso Noriega* at UNAM; married Margarita Charles; sister, María Luisa, married *Manuel Sandoval Vallarta*; brother-in-law of industrialist Carlos Phillips Olmedo, brother of *Alfredo Phillips Olmedo*; brother-in-law of Enrique Creel Luján, treasurer of PAN. j-None. k-Resigned as secretary of the treasury because of economic policy differences with President *Echeverría*. l-IWW67, 789; WWW70-71, 607; DPE61,

64; DGF51, I, 149; DPE65, 26; *Hoy*, Dec. 1970; DGF56, 168; HA, 4 Jan. 1971, 15; HA, 7 Dec. 1970; WWMG, 25-26; letters; *Justicia*, Aug., 1973; Enc. Mex., VIII, 1977, 271-72; C de S, 1982-88; DBGM87, 509.

Marín, Fausto A.

b-Sinaloa. c-Primary and preparatory studies, Culiacán, Sinaloa; law degree, National School of Law, UNAM, 1927. d-Local Deputy to the State Legislature of Sinaloa; Federal Deputy from the State of Sinaloa, Dist. 4, 1924-26; *Federal Deputy* from the State of Sinaloa, Dist. 2, 1943-46; *Senator* from the State of Sinaloa, 1946-52. e-Organizer, presidential campaign for *Manuel Avila Camacho* in Sinaloa, 1940; director of the presidential campaign for *Miguel Alemán* in Sinaloa, 1946. f-Private Secretary to General Angel Flores, Governor of Sinaloa, 1920-23; Private Secretary to the Secretary of National Defense, Angel Flores, 1923; Secretary of Government of the State of Sinaloa; Oficial Mayor of the State of Sinaloa; Secretary General of Government of the State of Sinaloa. g-None. j-None. k-None. l-C de D, 1943-46; C de S, 1946-52.

Marín Ramos, J. Ricardo

b-Tepic, Nayarit. c-Early education unknown; studies at the School of Cavalry, National Military College; Industrial Subdirector of the National School of Agriculture. c-*Alternate Senator* from the State of Nayarit, 1946-52; *Senator* from the State of Nayarit, 1964-70. e-Joined the PNR, 1929. f-Director of the Department of Rural Defenses, Secretariat of National Defense; Director General of Physical Education, Secretariat of Public Education, 1946-52. g-None. j-Career army officer; joined the Revolution as an ordinary soldier; fought in eighty-six battles; reached rank of Division General. k-Precandidate for the gubernatorial nomination of PRI in Zacatecas many times. l-C de S, 1964-70; DGF51, I, 7, 289; C de S, 1946-52; MGF69.

Márquez Jiménez de Romero Aceves, María del Carmen

a-July 8, 1935. b-Tijuana, Baja California del Norte. c-Primary and secondary studies at San Ysidro and San Diego, California; credential as a secondary English teacher from UNAM and the Mexican–North American Cultural Institute, Mexico City; preparatory studies, Our Lady of Peace Academy, United States, 1951-53; professor, Regional Technical Institute of Tijuana, 1974- . d-*Federal Deputy* from the State of Baja California, Dist. 5, 1979-82; *Senator* from the State of Baja California, 1982-88. e-Joined PRI, 1964; President of the Political Action Group of Baja California, 1975-76; President of the Women's Coordinating Council of Tijuana, *José López Portillo* presidential campaign, 1976. f-None. g-Subdirector of International Affairs of ANFER; General Delegate of ANFER to Sonora, Baja California del Sur, and Colima, 1980-81. i-Married to lawyer Ricardo Romero Aceves, syndic of Tijuana, 1960-62, and author of many books; daughter of Dr. J. Adriano Márquez and Esperanza Jiménez Ceballos. j-None. k-First female senator from Baja California. l-C de D, 1979-82; C de S, 1982-88; Romero Aceves, 707-09; DBGM, 546; DBGM87, 510.

Márquez Ortiz, Adelaida

a-Dec. 9, 1937. b-Zacatecas, Zacatecas. c-Primary and secondary studies in Zacatecas; accounting studies at the Colegio del Centro Institute; teacher of Spanish, Mathematics, and Accounting, Academia Sor Juana Inés de la Cruz, Zacatecas. d-*Plurinominal Federal Deputy* from the Partido Democratico Mexicano, 1979-82, member of the Human Dwellings and Public Works

Committee, the Radio and Television Committee, and the General Accounting Committee. e-Active in the PDM since its founding; activist, National Sinarquista Union; coordinator of the PDM in Zacatecas, Durango, and Aguascalientes; President of the PDM in Jalisco, 1978-81. f-None. g-None. j-None. k-None. l-C de D, 1979-82; Romero Aceves, 706.

Márquez Padilla, Tarciso
a-Dec. 15, 1915. b-Federal District. c-Enrolled in the National Military College, Jan. 1, 1933, graduating as a 2nd Lieutenant of Artillery, Jan. 1, 1937; graduate of the Applied Military School, 1938-39; preparatory studies at the National Preparatory Night School, 1938-39; law degree, National School of Law, UNAM, 1940-44. d-None. e-Secretary of Organization of Morelos Military Group, *Manuel Avila Camacho* presidential campaign, 1939-40. f-Adjutant, President of Mexico, 1940-41; Assistant Military Attaché, Mexican Embassy, Washington, D.C., 1941-45; Assistant Director, Legal Department, PEMEX, 1945-50; Military Adviser, Mexican Delegation, United Nations Conference on International Organizations, San Francisco, 1945; *Oficial Mayor of the Secretariat of Industry and Commerce*, 1948-52; *Justice of the Supreme Court*, 1979-82, 1982-85. g-None. h-None. i-Classmate of *José López Portillo* at the National School of Law; married Paz Consuelo García Rodríguez; son of Pablo Márquez, businessman, and María Padilla Muñoz. j-Career army officer; rank of Colonel, Oct. 13, 1949; rank of Brigadier General, Oct. 18, 1956; agent of the Military Ministerio Público, 1st Military Zone, 1961-62; Judge and President, Supreme Military Court, 1967-78; reached rank of Brigade General. k-None. l-HA, 8 Jan. 1979, 14; WWM45, 71; DGF51, I, 263; Protag., 212; DBGM, 668.

Marrero Ortiz, Rafael
b-Campeche, Campeche. c-Early education unknown; no degree. d-Member of the City Council of Campeche; Alternate Local Deputy to the State Legislature of Campeche; *Alternate Senator* from the State of Campeche, 1964-67, but in functions for *Carlos Sansores Pérez*, 1967-70. e-Member of PRI; Secretary of Labor Action of PRI, Campeche. f-Director of Personnel, Port of Veracruz; Oficial Mayor of Civil Defense, Port of Veracruz, 1941-45; tax collector, State of Campeche; Director of Control, Department of the Treasury of Campeche; Assistant to the Secretary of Labor and Conflicts, Secretary of Communication and Public Works. g-Secretary of Organization, Federation of Workers of Tampico; Secretary of Organization and Workers Education, CTM of Campeche; General Delegate of the CTM in Yucatán; member of the Union of Radio and Television Workers of Mexico. j-None. k-None. l-*Mis Seis Años*; C de S, 1964-70.

Martínez Adame, Arturo
(Deceased) a-Dec. 11, 1896. b-Ciudad Bravo, Guerrero. c-Preparatory studies at the National Preparatory School; law degree, National School of Law, UNAM, 1915-21. d-Federal Deputy from the State of Guerrero, Dist. 5, 1922-24; *Senator* from the State of Guerrero, 1940-46, President of the Third Labor Committee, First Secretary of the Second Government Committee, the First Mines Committee, the Railroad Committee, and the Administrative Committee; Second Secretary of the Second Justice Committee and member of the First Balloting Committee. e-None. f-Federal District Court Judge; President of the Federal Board of Conciliation and Arbitration, 1951; *Justice of the Supreme Court*, 1951-52, 1952-58, and 1958-61; *Provisional Governor of Guerrero*, 1961-63. g-Stu-

dent representative of the Federation of University Students to the First International Student Congress, Mexico City, 1921. h-Author of several works on labor and government administration. i-Brother, *Emigdio*, served as a secretary of the CEN of PRI; student of Antonio Caso; classmate of *Vicente Lombardo Toledano* and *Teófilo Olea y Leyva* at the National Preparatory School. j-None. k-None. l-Peral, 496; DGF56, 568; G of M, 20; DGF51, I, 482; C de S, 1940-46; Casasola, V.

Martínez Adame, Emigdio
a-Aug. 5, 1905. b-Chilpancingo, Guerrero. c-Primary studies in Chilpancingo; secondary studies in Mexico City; preparatory studies at the National Preparatory School, Mexico City; law degree from the National School of Law, UNAM, 1929; studies in economics from the School of Economics, University of London, 1935-36; law studies in Paris; studies at the National School of Economics, UNAM, 1931-32; Professor of Economics, National School of Economics, UNAM, 1937-44. d-*Senator* from the State of Guerrero, 1952-58, member of the Permanent Commission of Congress, 1954; member of the Gran Comisión, the Second Committee on Tariffs and Foreign Trade, the Protocol Committee, the Second Committee on Credit, Money, and Institutions of Credit, the First Constitutional Affairs Committee and the Legislative Studies Committee. e-*Secretary of Political Action of the CEN of PRI*, 1953-56. f-Director General of Expenditures, Secretariat of the Treasury, 1934-35; Chief, Department of Credit, National Ejido Credit Bank; Consulting Minister, Mexican Embassy in Moscow, under Ambassador *Narciso Bassols*, 1944-46; Postmaster General of Mexico, 1947-52; Director General of the National Commerce Bank, 1958-64; Director of the Techni-

cal Institute, Office of the Attorney General of Mexico, 1981. g-President of the Student Society of the National School of Economics, 1932. h-Cofounder of the Fondo de Cultura Económica with *Eduardo Villaseñor, Eduardo Suárez, Ramón Beteta,* and others, 1934; editor of the *Revista Trimestre Económico.* i-Brother, *Arturo,* served as a senator from Guerrero, 1940-46; student assistant to *Manuel Gómez Morín*; member of the *Combate* group under *Narciso Bassols* opposed to the government of *Manuel Avila Camacho,* 1940-42. j-None. k-Precandidate for governor of Guerrero, 1950. l-DGF51, I, 240; DGF47, 143; Correa, 59; *Excélsior,* 15 Aug. 1972, 7D; DGF56, 6, 8, 9, 10, 12, 14; D de Y, Dec. 1958; HA, 15 Dec. 1958, 5; C de S, 1952-58; HA, 28 Feb. 1947; Ind. Biog., 100-01; DAPC81, 13.

Martínez Aguilar, Rogelio
a-Mar. 16, 1941. b-Federal District. c-Economics degree from the National School of Economics, UNAM, 1958-62, with a thesis on capital accumulation in the Mexican public sector; postgraduate work in economic planning in developing countries, Central School of Planning and Statistics, Poland, 1963-64; Professor of Economic and Social Problems of Mexico, National School of Economics, UNAM, 1967-69, 1971-72; professor, Ibero-American University, 1967-69; professor, University of Costa Rica, 1973-74; professor, National School of Political Science, UNAM, Acatlán campus, 1968-69. d-None. e-None. f-Section head, Public Budget, Secretariat of the Presidency, 1965-67; department head, Public Budget, Secretariat of the Presidency, 1967-69; Subdirector of Credit, National Agricultural Credit Bank, 1969-70; Subdirector General of Administrative Affairs, Secretariat of the Presidency, 1970-72; Ambassador to Costa Rica, 1972-75;

Ambassador to Venezuela, 1975-76; *Ambassador to the Soviet Union*, 1977-80; Director General, Economic Affairs, Secretariat of Foreign Relations, 1980-82; Ambassador to the German Democratic Republic, 1982-88; Ambassador to Israel, 1989. g-None. h-Author of economic and social essays. i-Son of Ruperto Martínez Medina, lawyer, and Catalina Aguilar Hernández; married Elzbieta Nawotka Zelazkiewicz, anthropologist. j-None. k-None. l-HA, 14 Aug. 1972, 9; *Excélsior*, 1 Aug. 1972, 9; DAPC, 11; DBGM89, 217.

Martínez Báez, Antonio
a-July 18, 1901. b-Morelia, Michoacán. c-Primary studies in Morelia; preparatory studies at the Colegio Primitivo de San Nicolás de Hidalgo, Morelia, 1913-19; legal studies at the University of Michoacán, 1920; studied at the National School of Law, UNAM, 1921-15, law degree, July 21, 1926; Professor of Constitutional Law at the National School of Law, UNAM, 1929-48, 1953-67; professor at the National Preparatory School, 1928; professor of special courses at the Escuela Libre de Derecho, 1929-48; professor at the Colegio de México, 1944; professor of graduate law courses at the National University; LLD from the National School of Law, UNAM, 1950; professor, National School of Law, UNAM, 1950-91; Professor Emeritus, National School of Law, UNAM, 1966; member of the Governing Board of UNAM (Secretary), 1945-66; member of the Governing Board of the Colegio de México, 1961-86. d-*Federal Deputy* from the State of Michoacán, Dist. 3, 1973-76; *Senator* from the State of Michoacán, 1982-88; *Plurinominal Federal Deputy* from PRI, 1988-91. e-Chief, Legal Affairs, PRI, 1974-75; member of the Statutes Section of the Advisory Council to the IEPES of PRI, 1972. f-Consulting lawyer for the National Agrarian Commission;

head of the Legal Department for the National Urban Mortgage Bank, 1935-41; Head of the Department of Indemnifications, Secretariat of Agriculture, 1935-41; President of the National Banking Commission, 1941-43; Director General of the Financiera Industrial Azucarera, 1943-46; *Secretary of Industry and Commerce*, Oct. 21, 1948, to Nov. 30, 1952; President of the Economic Commission for Latin America in Mexico, 1951-53; Director General of Guanos and Fertilizers, 1952-54; Head of the National Securities Commission, 1953-59; member of the Permanent Tribunal of Arbitration, The Hague, 1965; arbitrator for LAFTA, 1968. g-President of the Mexican Bar Association, 1959-60. h-Practicing lawyer, in practice for many years with *Manuel Gual Vidal* and *Gabino Fraga*; author of many articles. i-Student at UNAM with *Eduardo Bustamante, Ramón Beteta, Manuel Gual Vidal, Carlos Novoa, J. Jesús Castorena, Ricardo J. Zevada*, and *Manuel Ramírez Vázquez*; father, Dr. Manuel Martínez Solorzano, served as director of the Michoacán Museum, 1900-20, was a deputy to the Constitutional Congress, 1916-17, and taught at the Colegio San Nicolás in Morelia for 15 years; mother, Francisca Báez; grandfather, Ramón Martínez Aviles, lawyer and noted composer; brother, *Manuel*, served as subsecretary of health, 1943-46; student assistant to *Narciso Bassols*, 1925; married Alicia Flores Magón. j-None. k-None. l-D de S, 21 Oct. 1948; D de Y, Oct. 1948, 1; HA, 29 Oct. 1948, 17; DGF51, I, 263; DGF51, II, 95, etc.; letters; Enc. Mec., VIII, 1977, 307-08; DBGM89, 484.

Martínez Báez, Manuel
(Deceased) a-Sept. 26, 1894. b-Morelia, Michoacán. c-Primary studies in Morelia; preparatory studies at the Colegio de San Nicolás, Morelia, 1911;

medical degree from the Medical School, Morelia, Jan. 2, 1916; graduate studies in Malaria at the University of Paris, 1934; Professor of Histology, Anatomy and Pathology at the University of Michoacán, Morelia, 1922-25; Secretary General of the University of Michoacán, 1922-24; Rector of the University of Michoacán, 1924-25; lab assistant in the School of Medicine, University of Paris, 1933-34; special studies in tropical diseases, Department of Public Health; Professor of Natural and Physical Sciences, National Teachers College, 1917-20; Assistant Professor of Clinical Medicine, National School of Medicine, UNAM, 1925-32; Professor of Parasitology, UNAM, 1933-40. d-None. e-None. f-Head of the Department of Publicity and Hygienic Education, Department of Public Health, 1926; First Director of the Institute of Tropical Diseases, Secretariat of Public Health, 1939, 1942-43, 1952-58; Director General of Epidemiology, Secretariat of Public Health, 1941-42; supervisory official, Secretariat of Health, 1943; *Subsecretary of Health*, 1943-46; Ambassador to UNESCO, 1946-47. g-None. h-Author of many articles on tropical diseases. i-Brother of *Antonio Martínez Báez*, secretary of industry and commerce, 1948-52; son of Dr. Manuel Martínez Solorzano; married Aurora Palomo González. j-None. k-None. l-EBW46, 693; Peral, 47, 205; WWM45, 72; Enc. Mex., VIII, 1977, 308-09; López, 662.

Martínez Chavarría, Joaquín
a-May 21, 1924. b-Torreón, Coahuila. c-Degree in architecture, 1947, National School of Architecture, UNAM, 1947; Professor of Architecture, National School of Architecture, UNAM, 1962-66. d-None. e-Coordinator of the National Reunion for the Study of Public Housing during the presidential campaign of *Luis Echeverría*, 1970,

sponsored by PRI. f-Director General of construction of the López Mateos Urban Center, 1960; Head of the Office of Construction, Department of Architecture and Planning, ISSSTE, 1962; member of the Commission for the Study of Housing and Social Interest (from the public sector), 1968; Director General of the National Institute of Housing, 1970-76. g-Member of the College of Architects. i-Son of *Joaquín Martínez Chavarría*, senator from Coahuila, 1940-46. j-None. k-None. l-HA, 7 Dec. 1970, 27.

Martínez Corbalá, Gonzalo
a-Mar. 10, 1928. b-San Luis Potosí, San Luis Potosí. c-Degree in civil engineering, National School of Engineering, UNAM, 1946-50; MA, 1963, and Ph.D., 1967–69, both in political science, National School of Political and Social Sciences, UNAM. d-*Federal Deputy* from the Federal District, Dist. 22, 1964-67, member of the Committee on National Properties and Resources, the Committee on the Department of the Federal District, the Committee on Public Works, and the Second Public Housing Committee; President of the Committee on Foreign Relations; *Senator* from the State of San Luis Potosí, 1982-88; *Federal Deputy* from the State of San Luis Potosí, Dist. 6, 1988-91, Secretary of the Gran Comisión. e-President of Section 28 of the District Committee of PRI, Federal District, 1963; President of the 22nd District Committee of PRI, Federal District, 1963; General Delegate of the CNOP of PRI to San Luis Potosí, 1965; President of the Regional Executive Committee of PRI in the Federal District, 1965; precandidate for senator from San Luis Potosí, 1976. f-Ambassador to Chile, July 31, 1972, to 1974; Special Ambassador for South American Affairs, 1974-75; Director General of the Sahagún Industrial Complex, 1975-76;

Subsecretary of National Properties, Secretariat of Public Works, 1976; Subsecretary of Property and Auditing, Secretariat of Public Works, 1977; *Ambassador to Cuba,* 1980-82; Director General of the National Workers Housing Institute (Infonavit), 1991; *Interim Governor of San Luis Potosí,* 1991-92; Director General of the ISSSTE, 1993-94. g-President of the Mexican Society of Engineers. h-Director of the magazine *Civil Engineering CIC;* President of the Mexican Planning Society. i-Had business partnership with *Cuauhtémoc Cárdenas;* early political mentor to President *Carlos Salinas;* son of Jesús Martínez Macías, civil engineer, and María de Jesús Corbalá; married María Teresa Ulloa. j-None. k-As a federal deputy, made the protest speech that aroused public opinion against *Ernesto P. Uruchurtu* as head of the Department of the Federal District, culminating in his resignation, 1966. l-HA, 14 Aug. 1972, 9; *Excélsior,* 1 Aug. 1972, 1, 9; C de D, 1964-66, 52, 81, 90; *Excélsior,* 5 Jan. 1977, 22, 1 Apr. 1977; HA, 5 May 1975, 20; Guerra Leal, 210; IEPES; DBGM, 547-48; DBGM89, 486; *La Nación,* 11 Oct. 1991, 3.

Martínez de Hernández Loza, Guadalupe
a-Feb. 11, 1906. b-Guadalajara, Jalisco. c-Primary studies at the Josefa O. de Domínguez School, Guadalajara; secondary studies at normal school; teaching certificate, normal school; studies in social work, University of Guadalajara (3 years); seminars on union education for women; primary school teacher; secondary school teacher; teacher at the Secondary Night School for Workers; Director of the 47th Urban School of Guadalajara. d-*Federal Deputy* from the State of Jalisco, Dist. 2, 1958-61, 1970-73, member of the First Public Education Committee and the Social Welfare Committee (1st year); President of the

State Legislature of Jalisco, 1979-80; *Alternate Senator* from the State of Jalisco, 1976-82. e-Director of Women's Action of PRI for the State of Jalisco; President of PRI in Jalisco. f-Oficial Mayor of the Cultural Department of the State of Jalisco. g-Secretary of Social Action of the Federation of Workers of Jalisco; Secretary of Press and Publicity of the CTM in Jalisco; Secretary of Political Action of the Women's Federation of the CTM of the Federal District. h-None. i-Husband *Heliodoro Hernández Loza* was a federal deputy from Jalisco, 1943-46. j-None. k-None. l-C de D, 1958-60; C de D, 1970-72, 124; Directorio, 1970-72; Func., 241; *Excélsior,* 31 Mar. 1979, 10.

Martínez de la Vega, Francisco
(Deceased Feb. 18, 1985) a-Aug. 26, 1909. b-San Luis Potosí, San Luis Potosí. c-Primary studies under the Castro López sisters in San Luis Potosí; primary and secondary studies at the Colegio Francés de Alvarado, Mexico City, 1918-22; preparatory studies at the National Preparatory School (distinguished student), 1923-27; no degree. d-*Federal Deputy* from the State of San Luis Potosí, Dist. 1, 1958-59, member of the Library Committee (1st year). e-Secretary General of the Popular Party (later PPS), 1951-55; joined PRI, 1957. f-Assistant to the Editor of *El Nacional,* 1930-43, 1944-46; Private Secretary to *Gonzalo N. Santos,* 1943-44; chief of the editorial staff, *El Nacional,* 1944-48; Private Secretary to *Vicente Lombardo Toledano,* 1945, to *César Martino Torres,* director general of the National Ejido Bank, and to General *Miguel Hernández,* 1952; *Provisional Governor of San Luis Potosí,* 1959-61. g-None. h-Writer and journalist, began his journalism career in 1930; sports correspondent in South America and the United States, 1931; cofounder of *Siempre* with José Pages Llergo, 1953,

with *Siempre* from 1953-83; political affairs writer for *Hoy*, 1948-53; political commentator, *El Día*, 1970-75. j-None. k-Expelled from the PPS for supporting *Enrique Ramírez y Ramírez*. l-HA, 2 Oct. 1961, 13; *Siempre*, 4 Feb. 1959, 6; Peral, 499; Func., 342; C de D, 1958-60, 83; Enc. Mex., VIII, 1977, 317; Montejano, 208; HA, 4 Mar. 1985, 22.

Martínez Delgado, José
a-May 26, 1921. b-Federal District. c-Early education unknown; law degree, National School of Law, UNAM, 1942-46, with a thesis on "The Historic Project of Social Rights"; LLD, National School of Law, UNAM, 1950-51. d-None. e-None. f-Auxiliary to the Oficial Mayor, Department of Agrarian Affairs and Colonization, 1948-49; Private Secretary to the 1st Assistant Attorney General of Mexico, 1949; Secretary of Studies and Accounts, Secretary of Agreements, Supreme Court of Justice, 1949-67; Judge, 1st Circuit Court, Labor Affairs, Federal District, 1968-85; *Justice of the Supreme Court*, 1985-88, 1988-94. g-None. h-Practicing lawyer, 1947-48. i-Son of Ernesto Martínez Romero, businessman, and Marina Delgado Pineda, nurse; married Eleonara Pérez González, lawyer. j-None. k-None. l-DBGM89, 624; DBGM87, 639.

Martínez Domínguez, Alfonso
a-Jan. 7, 1922. b-Monterrey, Nuevo León. c-Primary studies in Monterrey; secondary studies in Mexico City; Bachelor of Arts from the Franco-Mexican College, Mexico City d-*Federal Deputy* from the Federal District, Dist. 4, 1946-49, member of the Committee for the Department of the Federal District, the Second Balloting Committee, the Public Works Committee and the Securities Committee; *Federal Deputy* from the Federal District, Dist. 17, 1952-55, member of

the Legislative Studies Committee and the Tourism Committee; *Federal Deputy* from the State of Nuevo León, 1964-67, Dist. 4, President of the Chamber of Deputies, Dec. 1964; President of the Gran Comisión, member of the First Committee on Government, the Constitutional Affairs Committee; *Governor of Nuevo León*, 1979-85; *Senator* from the State of Nuevo León, 1988-91. e-Secretary of Organization for the Regional PRI Committee of the Federal District, 1955; *Secretary of Popular Action of the CEN of PRI*, 1962–64; *President of the CEN of PRI*, 1968-70; *Secretary General of CNOP of PRI*, 1961-65. f-Began governmental career as a clerk (5th category) in the Department of the Federal District, 1937; Chief Editor of the Department of Public Relations, Department of the Federal District, 1943; *Head of the Department of the Federal District*, 1970-71; Director General of Airports and Auxiliary Services, Secretariat of Communications and Transportation, 1987-88. g-Secretary General of the Union of Workers of the Department of the Federal District, 1943-46; *Secretary General of the FSTSE*, 1949-52; Coordinator General of the ISSSTE; Secretary General of Local 15 of the Union of Workers of the Department of the Federal District, 1942-43. h-Author of two books on history. i-Son of Alfonso Martínez de la Garza, physician, and Margarita Domínguez; grandson of Dr. Alfonso Martínez de la Garza and María del Refugio de la Garza; married María de Lourdes Campos Licastro; brother, *Guillermo Martínez Domínguez*, director general of Nacional Financiera, 1970-74. j-None. k-Resigned from the Department of the Federal District after the 1971 student riots in Mexico City; most observers see the resignation as a result of internal power struggles within the ruling circle rather than just the result of the riots; precandidate for governor of Nuevo León, 1972. l-C de D, 1952-54, 14; WWMG, 26; HA, 7 Dec. 1970, 26; *Hoy*, Dec. 1970; DBM70, 359-60; DGF47, 6; *Polémica*, I, 1969, 79; DBM68, 414-15; C de D, 1964-66, 52, 1946-48, 78; *Análisis Político*, 26 Aug. 1972, 7; *Excélsior*, 10 Dec. 1978, 18.

Martínez Domínguez, Guillermo
a-1924. b-Monterrey, Nuevo León. c-Degree in economics from the National School of Economics, UNAM; professor at the National School of Economics, UNAM, 1948-64; representative of the National School of Economics on the UNAM Council, 1954-56. d-None. e-None. f-Director of Prices, Secretariat of Industry and Commerce, 1952; Director General of the Small Business Bank, 1952-55; Oficial Mayor of the Federal Electric Commission, 1955-59; *Director General of the Federal Electric Commission, 1964-70; Director General of National Finance Bank, 1970-74.* g-President of the Student Society of the National School of Economics, 1947-48. h-Reporter for *Excélsior* and *La Prensa*, editorial writer for *Excélsior, La Prensa* and *Hoy*; President of the National College of Economists; winner of the National Prize for Journalism, 1953. i-Brother of *Alfonso Martínez Domínguez*, head of the Federal District, 1970-71; son of Dr. Alfonso Martínez de la Garza and Margarita Domínguez, but orphaned at a young age; studied under *Eduardo Bustamante* at UNAM. j-None. k-As a journalist, exposed a fraud in the IMSS, 1953; resigned from NAFIN, 1974. l-WWMG, 26; HA, 7 Dec. 1970, 27; *Hoy*, 10 Apr. 1971, 12; DBM70, 360; *Justicia*, Aug. 1971; WNM, 142.

Martínez García, Pedro Daniel
a-1906. b-Purépero, Michoacán. c-Primary studies at a school associated with the Normal School, Mexico City, 1912-

19; preparatory studies at the National Preparatory School, 1920-24; medical degree, National School of Medicine, 1929; advanced studies in pediatrics, Children's Memorial Hospital, Chicago; Professor of Pediatrics, National School of Medicine, UNAM; professor of the School of Health and Welfare; Professor of Public Hygiene, Johns Hopkins University, 1940; Director of the School of Health and Welfare, 1958-64; Professor of Infectious Diseases, National School of Medicine, UNAM, 1956-64; Professor of Pediatrics, National School of Medicine, UNAM, 1944-65. d-None. e-None. f-Subdirector and Director of the Children's Hospital of Mexico, Secretariat of Health, 1951; Director General of Maternal and Infant Hygiene, Secretariat of Health; Chief, Coordinated Health and Welfare Services, State of Michoacán; Subdirector of Education and Instruction in Public Health, Secretariat of Health, 1957; Director General of Education and Instruction in Public Health, 1958-64; Director of Services, Secretariat of Health; *Subsecretary of Health*, 1964-70; Medical Director, National Indigenous Institute, 1976. g-None. h-Health adviser to World Health Organization; member of expert committees on health. i-Friend of *Manuel Martínez Báez, Ignacio Chávez* and *Eduardo Villaseñor*. j-None. k-None. l-HA, 21 Dec. 1964, 4; DPE65, 148; DPE61, 110; DGF51, II, 699-700; DGF51, I, 342; letters; Enc. Mex., VIII, 1977, 306.

Martínez Gil, José de Jesús
a-1935. b-Tampico, Tamaulipas. c-Early education unknown; law degree; teacher, Patriotic Institute; high school business teacher. d-*Federal Deputy* (Party Deputy from PAN), 1973-76. e-Joined PAN, 1956; President of PAN in the Federal District; director of the presidential campaign for *Efraín González Morfín*, 1969-70; member of

the CEN of PAN, 1979; regional adviser to the CEN of PAN, 1979; Secretary of National Coordination of the CEN of PAN, 1979. f-None. g-None. h-Practicing lawyer. j-None. k-Candidate for federal deputy, 1970; candidate for senator, 1976; candidate for federal deputy, 1979; resigned from PAN during his campaign for deputy, Apr., 1979. l-*Excélsior*, 24 Apr. 1979, 10; C de D, 1973-76, 29; HA, 19 Mar. 1979, VII.

Martínez Gortari, Jesús
a-May 23, 1919. b-Aguascalientes, Aguascalientes. c-Primary studies in a public school in Aguascalientes; secondary studies in a public school in Aguascalientes; no degree. d-*Federal Deputy* from the State of Aguascalientes, Dist. 1, 1976-79, member of the Social Action Committee, the Machinery Section of the Industrial Development Committee, the Development of Social Security and Public Health Committee, the Development of Tourism Committee, and the Railroad Section of the Transportation and General Means of Communication Committee. e-Joined PRI, 1956. f-None. g-Director of the Cooperative of the Union of Mexican Railroad Workers (STFRM), Secretary General of Local 2, STFRM, 1968; Treasurer General of the STFRM, 1971-76; Secretary General of the STFRM, Aug. 28, 1976-79. h-Began railroad career as a laborer for the National Railroads of Mexico, 1936. i-Married Refugio Macías. j-None. k-None. l-*Excélsior*, 22 Aug. 1976, 29; D de D, 1976-79, 4, 38, 41, 76; C de D, 1976-79, 47.

Martínez Hernández, Ifigenia (Navarrete)
a-June 16, 1924. b-Federal District. c-Early education unknown; economics degree, National School of Economics, UNAM, 1946; MA in economics, Harvard University, 1949; researcher in economics, National School of Economics, UNAM, 1957-67; Professor of Economics, National School of Economics, UNAM, 1955-62; Director, National School of Economics, UNAM, 1967-70; Professor of Economics, CEMLA, 1955-62. d-*Federal Deputy* from the Federal District, Dist. 22, 1976-79, member of the Section on Improving Rural Living of the Agrarian Affairs Committee, the Section on Development of the Peasant Woman of the Agrarian Affairs Committee, the Committee of Agricultural Development, member of Section Three of the Educational Development Committee, the Television Section of the Development of the Means of Communication Committee, of the Social Welfare of the Development of Social Security and Public Health Committee, the Development of Housing Committee, the Department of the Federal District Committee and the Fiscal Section of the Legislative Studies Committee; *Senator* from the Federal District, 1988-91. e-Member of PRI, 1954-87; cofounder of the Democratic Current of PRI, 1986; joined the PRD, 1988. f-Economist, Economic Commission for Latin America, 1949-50; economist, Department of Economic Studies, Pan American Union, 1951-52; Subdirector, Department of Subsidies, Secretariat of the Treasury, 1953-56; Director of the Office of Fiscal Policy, Secretariat of the Treasury, 1953-56; Director of the Office of the Fiscal Analysis, Secretariat of the Treasury, 1956-58; adviser, Subsecretary of Revenues, Secretariat of the Treasury, 1961-65; Director of Economic Advisers, Secretariat of the Presidency, 1965-70; Director of Administrative Programs, Secretariat of the Treasury, 1972-76; Alternate Ambassador to the United Nations, 1980-82; Coordinator of Advisers, Subsecretary of Agrarian Organizations, 1983-84. g-None. h-None. i-Divorced from *Alfredo Navarrete Romero*,

subdirector of finances of PEMEX, 1972-76; daughter of Jesús Martínez Elizalde and Concepción Hernández Garduño. j-None. k-One of Mexico's most prominent female economists. l-C de D, 1976-79, 46; D de C, 1976-79, 6, 8, 11, 18, 21, 29, 38, 40, 44, 47; HA, 5 Apr. 1976, 10; Enc. Mex., VIII, 1977, 313; DBGM89, 488; letter.

Martínez Lavalle, Arnulfo
(Deceased 1967) a-1912. b-Federal District. c-Early education unknown; law degree, National School of Law, UNAM, 1937; Professor of Criminal Procedures, National School of Law, UNAM; Professor of Sociology, School of Political and Social Sciences, UNAM. d-None. e-None. f-Secretary of the District Court, Federal District; official of the Superior Tribunal of Justice of the Federal District; Director of Preparatory Investigations, Attorney General of Mexico; Director, Inspector General's Office, Attorney General of Mexico, 1951; Justice of the Superior Tribunal of Justice of the Federal District and Federal Territories, 1956-67. g-None. h-Alternate Delegate to the Narcotics Commission, UNESCO; author of many works. j-None. k-None. l-DP70, 1275; DGF56, 514; DGF51, I, 435.

Martínez Legorreta, Arturo
a-Feb. 2, 1938. b-Atlacomulco, México. c-Early education unknown; degree in business administration, School of Business and Administration, 1958-62, studies in public administration, 1962 and Professor of Business Administration, 1963–64, all at Autonomous University of the State of México. d-Local Deputy to the State Legislature of México; Mayor of Toluca, 1972-75; *Federal Deputy* from the State of México, Dist. 4, 1976-79; *Federal Deputy* from the State of México, Dist. 16, 1982-85. e-President of PRI, State of México, 1982-83. f-Adviser, Assistant Manager

of Administration, CONASUPO, 1963-64; Assistant Director and Director, Department of Control of Distribution of Goods, CONASUPO, 1965-67; Director of Sales, CONASUPO, 1967-69; Oficial Mayor, State of México, 1969-72; Director General of Administrative Services, Department of the Federal District, 1980-81; adviser to the Governor of México, 1989-91; Secretary of Development of the State of México, 1991. g-President of the Student Society of the School of Business and Administration, Autonomous University of the State of México. h-None. i-Son of Enrique Martínez Colín, public official, and Lorenza Alicia Legorreta Chimal; married María del Pilar Lara Torres. j-None. k-None. l-C de D, 1976-79; C de D, 1982-85; Lehr, 272; DBGM, 549-50; DBGM92, 791.

Martínez Manautou, Emilio
a-July 30, 1919. b-Ciudad Victoria, Tamaulipas. c-Primary and secondary studies in Ciudad Victoria; preparatory studies at the National Preparatory School, Mexico City, 1937-39; medical degree from the National School of Medicine, UNAM, 1944; postgraduate work in internal medicine in New York and Massachusetts. d-*Federal Deputy* from the State of Tamaulipas, Dist. 2, 1955-58, member of the Gran Comisión, the Committee on Forestry Affairs, the Inspection Committee for the General Accounting Office, the Committee on Public Works, and the Budget and Accounts Committee; member of the City Council of Matamoros, Tamaulipas, 1951; *Senator* from the State of Tamaulipas, 1958-64, member of the Public Welfare Committee, the Health Committee, the First Balloting Committee, and the First Naval Committee; alternate member of the Second Committee on National Defense; *Governor of Tamaulipas*, 1980-86. e-State delegate of the CEN of PRI; head

physician to *Gustavo Díaz Ordaz* during his presidential campaign, 1964. f-Chief of Medical Services, Chamber of Deputies, 1952-53; Private Secretary to *Norberto Treviño Zapata*, President of the Gran Comisión, 1953-55; *Secretary of the Presidency*, 1964-70; *Secretary of Public Health*, 1976-80. g-President of the Medical Association of Matamoros, 1951-52; Secretary General of CNOP in Matamoros. h-Director of the Civil Hospital, Matamoros, 1953; medical practice in Matamoros, 1946-55. i-Early political protégé of *Norberto Treviño Zapata*; son of Alfredo Martínez Saldívar, a local deputy under Governor *Emilio Portes Gil*, and María Guadalupe Manatou; brother, Alfredo, was secretary general of government in Baja California del Norte, 1965-71; brother, *Antonio Martínez Manatou*, served as a federal deputy from the Federal District, 1967-70; brother, *Federico Martínez Manatou*, served as an alternate senator, 1982-88; married Leticia Cárdenas Montemayor. j-None. k-Precandidate for governor of Tamaulipas, 1962; precandidate for president of Mexico, 1970. l-DPE65, 169; C de D, 1955-57; HA, 7 Dec. 1964, 20; Johnson, 183-84; D de Y, 2 Dec. 1964, 2; DGF56; C de S, 1961-64, 61; Func., 372; LA, 3 Dec. 1976; Ind. Biog., 101-02; *Excélsior*, 25 Feb. 1977, 6, 8, 4 July 1974, 15; BdM, 174; Q es QAP, 385; HA, 16 June 1980, 40.

Martínez Martín, Ramón
a-Oct. 22, 1938. b-Arandas, Jalisco. c-Early education unknown; teaching certificate, National Normal School, 1958; professor of primary education, Secretariat of Public Education, 1959-64; professor of Middle Education in English, Secretariat of Public Education, 1965-69; English teacher, North American-Mexican Cultural Institute, Mexico City; Director, Héroes de Cerro Prieto and Suave Patria Primary Schools, 1967-69. d-*Senator* from the State of Jalisco, 1982-88, president of the First Education Committee. e-Joined PRI, 1961; *Secretary of Social Action of the CEN of PRI*, 1981-82. f-Director of Primary Education, Secretariat of Public Education, 1965-67. g-Secretary General of Delegation 76 of Local 10, National Teachers Union (SNTE); aide to the secretary of labor and conflicts of the SNTE; Private Secretary to the Secretary General of Local 9, SNTE, 1972-75; Secretary General of Section 9, SNTE, 1975-78; Secretary of Finances of the CEN of SNTE, 1977-80; *Secretary General of the SNTE*, 1980-83. h-None. i-Son of José Concepción Martínez López, businessman, and Josefina Martín Guzmán; married María Pura Castellanos Castillo, teacher; related to *Carlos Jongitud Barrios*. j-None. k-None. l-Lehr, 225; DBGM, 550; C de S, 1982-88.

Martínez Martínez, Abel
a-Mar. 4, 1914. b-Tláhuac, Federal District. c-Early education unknown; law degree. d-*Federal Deputy* (Party Deputy from PAN), 1967-70. e-Member of PAN. f-Secretary, Federal Board of Conciliation and Arbitration, 1947; Assistant to the President, Federal Board of Conciliation and Arbitration; Secretary General of the Federal Board of Conciliation and Arbitration, 1953; Director of Personnel, Public Property Registry. g-None. j-None. k-None. l-C de D, 1967-70; Directorio, 1967-70.

Martínez Medina, Lorenzo
a-July 7, 1918. b-Saltillo, Coahuila. c-Early education unknown; engineering degree from the Antonio Narro Higher School of Agriculture, Saltillo, 1936; MS in agriculture, University of Iowa, 1941; doctorate in agricultural sciences, University of Minnesota, 1951; teacher in the regional peasant school, La Huerta, Michoacán; Subdirector of the Agricultural Voca-

tional School, Champusco, Puebla; Director, Division of Agricultural Research, Antonio Narro Higher School of Agriculture, 1947-49, 1952-57, 1964-69; Director of the Antonio Narro Higher School of Agriculture, 1952-58. d-None. e-None. f-Researcher, Agricultural Field Station, León, Guanajuato; Director General of Agriculture and Livestock, State of Coahuila; general agent of the Secretariat of Agriculture, Saltillo, Coahuila, 1970; President of the Board of Directors, Agricultural Credit Bank, Saltillo, Coahuila; Director General of National Seed Production, 1970-73; *Subsecretary of Agriculture*, Jan. 2, 1974-76; Director General of the National Center for Educational Rural Credit System, 1977-82. g-Secretary of Credit and Agicultural Institutions, CEN of the CNC, 1977. h-None. j-None. k-None. l-HA, 14 Jan. 1974, 15; Protag., 217.

Martínez Nájera, Humberto
a-Aug. 23, 1921. b-Tepeji del Río, Hidalgo. c-Early education unknown; graduated, Naval Military School of the Pacific, 1936-41; courses at the National Center of Productivity; professor, Nautical School, Tampico, Tamaulipas; professor of steam engines, diesel motors, and thermodynamics, 1948. d-None. e-None. f-*Subsecretary of the Navy*, 1982-88. g-None. h-None. i-Son of Francisco Martínez Díaz, public official, and Josefina Nájera Mercado; married Araceli Castellanos MacGregor. j-Career naval officer; aide, Subsecretary of the Navy, 1947-48; Chief of Machinery, Veracruz Dredging, 1948-49; Chief of Shops, 5th Naval Zone, Ciudad del Carmen, 1949-50; Chief of Shops, Guaymas, Sonora, 1951-52; Subdirector of Dry Docks, Salina Cruz, Oaxaca, 1952-55; Director of the National Arsenal, Veracruz, Veracruz, 1955-56; Inspector General of Dredging, Secretariat of the Navy, 1956-57; Director of

Docks, Acapulco, 1957-62; Chief of Dry Docks, Salina Cruz, Oaxaca, 1963-66; Chief of Naval Construction, Secretariat of the Navy, 1966-67; Subdirector General of Dredging, Secretariat of the Navy, 1967-68; Director General of Dredging, 1968-70; Inspector General of the Fleet, Pacific, 1970; Director General of Repairs, Secretariat of the Navy, 1976-82. k-None. l-Q es QAP, 91-92; DBGM87, 242.

Martínez Ostos, Raúl
(Deceased) a-Sept. 22, 1907. b-Tantoyuca, Veracruz. c-Law degree from the National School of Law, UNAM, 1932; Professor of Civil Contracts, National School of Law, UNAM, 1934-35. d-None. e-None. f-Consulting lawyer to the Secretary of Public Works, 1935; consulting lawyer to the Department of Credit, Secretariat of the Treasury, 1936-40; consulting lawyer to the Federal Electric Commission, 1937; Head of the Department of Credit, Bank of Mexico, 1940-45; Alternate Executive Director of the International Monetary Fund as a representative of Mexico, 1946-48; Director of Treasury Studies, Secretariat of the Treasury, 1949-50; *Subdirector of National Finance Bank*, 1945-46, 1952-58, 1958-64, 1964-65; Executive Director of the Inter-American Development Bank, 1960-63. g-None. h-Member of the Board of Pigmentos y Productos Químicos, 1982. i-Son of Federico Martínez, physician; student of and assistant to *Agustín García López*; married Martha Martínez de Castro Peiro; son, Raúl, was director of Mexican radio and television, Secretariat of Government, 1982 . j-None. k-None. l-Letter; DBM68, 419; Anuario Fin., 1982, 281; DBGM, 274.

Martínez Peralta, Francisco
(Deceased) a-Aug. 24, 1895. b-Aconchi, Sonora. c-Primary studies in Sonora; no degree. d-*Federal Deputy* from the

State of Sonora, Dist. 2, 1937-40; *Federal Deputy* from the State of Sonora, Dist. 1, 1946-49, member of the Second National Defense Committee and the Military Justice Committee, substitute member of the Foreign Relations Committee; *Senator* from the State of Sonora, 1940-46, President of the Second National Defense Committee, Second Secretary of the Ejido Committee, member of the Gran Comisión, and alternate member of the Railroad and the Government Committees. e-*Secretary of Agrarian Action of the CEN of PRI*, 1946; Director of Traffic, Department of the Federal District, 1962-65. h-None. i-Uncle of *Ernesto P. Uruchurtu*. j-Career army officer; joined, 1910; Paymaster of the Army; rank of Colonel, 1940; reached rank of Division General. k-None. l-C de D, 1946-48, 78, 1937-39, 14; Peral, 504; Libro de Oro, 1946, 9.

Martínez Rivero, Abraham
a-Dec. 17, 1922. b-Federal District. c-Completed secondary studies, Bank and Business School, 1945-50; four years of studies in public accounting; special studies, Union Education, Workers of the Federal District Union, 1953-55. d-*Federal Deputy* from the Federal District, Dist. 19, 1976-79; *Senator* from the Federal District, 1982-88; representative to the Assembly of the Federal District, 1988-91. e-Representative of PRI to the 6th Electoral District of the Federal District, 1976; joined PRI 1948. f-None. g-Founder of the Only Union of Workers of Sports City, 1946; Director, Local 4, Confederation of Workers of the Federal District, 1974; Alternate Secretary General, Confederation of Workers of the Federal District, 1982; representative of labor before the local arbitration board, 1957; Secretary General of the Iron Workers Union, Federal District, 1973. h-Joined the Workers of the Federal District Department, 1934.

i-Son of David Martínez Escobar, union leader, and Loreta Rivero Celís; married Cecilia Alcantar Ochoa. j-Rank of 1st Sergeant, army. k-None. l-*Excélsior*, 29 Aug. 1976, 26; C de D, 1976-79; C de S, 1982-88; Lehr, 118; DBGM87, 513-14; DBGM89, 575; DBGM, 550.

Martínez (Rodríguez), José Luis
a-Jan. 19, 1918. b-Atoyac, Jalisco. c-Primary studies at the Colegio Renacimiento, Ciudad Guzmán, Jalisco, 1924-30, and at the Francés La Salle de México, 1931; secondary and preparatory studies at the University of Guadalajara, 1932-37; studies in medicine, National School of Medicine, UNAM, 1938-39; degree in letters from the School of Philosophy and Letters, UNAM, 1938-43; Professor of Mexican Literature, National Preparatory School, 1940-43, 1947-50; Professor of Advanced Spanish, Summer School, UNAM, 1942-44; Professor of Spanish Literature, Higher Normal School, Mexico City, 1945-51. d-*Federal Deputy* from the State of Jalisco, Dist. 8, 1958-61, member of the Protocol Committee, the Editorial Committee, the Public Education Committee, the Railroads Committee, the Foreign Relations Committee and the Consular and Diplomatic Service Committee; *Federal Deputy* from the State of Jalisco, Dist. 14, 1982-85. e-None. f-Private Secretary to the Secretary of Public Education, *Jaime Torres Bodet*, 1943-46; Secretary of the National College, 1947-51; Private Secretary to the Director General of the National Railroads of Mexico, *Roberto Amorós*, 1952-53; Administrative Assistant to the Director General of the National Railroads of Mexico, 1953-55; Director of Public Relations, National Railroads of Mexico, 1955-58; adviser to PIPSA, 1956-61; Ambassador to Peru, 1961-62; Ambassador to UNESCO, 1963-64; Director General of the National Institute of

Fine Arts, 1965-70; Ambassador to Greece, 1971-76; Director General of the Fondo de Cultura Económica, 1977-82. g-None. h-Member of the Governing Board, Colegio de México, 1967- . i-Son of Doctor Juan R. Martínez Reynaga and Julia Rodríguez; married Lydia Baracs. j-None. k-National Prize in Literature, 1980. l-Func., 247; Enc. Mex., VIII, 304; letter; WWM45, 73; C de D, 1958-61, 84; DPE61, 24; JSH, 230-32; Lehr, 239.

Martínez Rodriguez, José María
(Deceased Mar. 19, 1983) a-Jan. 9, 1912. b-Hacienda de San Lázaro, Tamazula, Jalisco. c-Primary studies (4 years only); no degree. d-City Councilman, Guadalajara, Jalisco, 1944; Vice-Mayor of Guadalajara, 1945-46; Local Deputy to the State Legislature of Jalisco, 1943-44; *Federal Deputy* from the State of Jalisco, Dist. 9, 1958-61, member of the Sugar Industry Committee; *Federal Deputy* from the State of Jalisco, Dist. 10, 1964-67, 1970-73, member of the Sugar Industry Committee and the Second Labor Committee; *Senator* from the State of Jalisco, 1976-82. e-None. f-None. g-Secretary General of Local 80 of the Sugar Cane Workers Union; Secretary of Correspondence and Agreements, National Sugar Cane Workers Union, 1941-42; Secretary General of the Federation of Workers of the State of Jalisco, 1943-46; Secretary of Conflicts, National Sugar Cane Workers Union, 1951-53; Secretary General of the National Sugar Cane Workers Union, 1953-59, 1975-78, 1983; Secretary of Agrarian Affairs, CTM, Jalisco; Secretary of Industrial Development, CTM, 1962-68; Secretary of Labor, CTM, 1983; President of the Board, Workers Bank, 1983. h-Worked as a child in the Tamazula Mill; assistant to a mechanic. j-None. k-None. l-C de D, 1964-66, 52, 1958-60, 84, 1970-72, 124; Directorio, 1970-72;

Func., 248; *Excélsior*, 21 Mar. 1983, 1, 11; HA, 4 Apr. 1983, 9.

Martínez (Rodríguez), Miguel Z.
(Deceased) a-Sept. 29, 1888. b-Lampazos, Nuevo León. c-Primary studies in Lampazos; student at the National Military Cadet School, 1909. d-*Federal Deputy* from the State of Nuevo León, Dist. 2, 1937-40. e-None. f-Chief of Police for the Federal District, 1941-43. g-None. j-Constitutionalist during the Revolution; rank of Brigadier General, Nov. 16, 1940; Commander of the 10th Military Region, Irapuato, Guanajuato, 1952-56; reached rank of Division General. k-Candidate for governor of Nuevo León, 1943. l-EBW46, 185; C de D, 1937-39, 14; Peral, 504; NYT, 2 Apr. 1943, 6; López, 669; Rev de Ejer., June 1952, 140.

Martínez Rojas, Salvador
a-Apr. 20, 1919. b-San Luis Potosí, San Luis Potosí. c-Early education unknown; law degree, National School of Law, UNAM, 1946, with a thesis on individual rights; Professor of Law, National School of Law, UNAM, 1960-65. d-None. e-None. f-Minor Judge of the Federal District, 1946-47; agent of the Ministerio Público, Attorney General's Office, 1948-49; Judge of the First Instance, Criminal Division, Mexicali, Baja California del Norte, 1949-52; Judge of the Superior Tribunal of Justice of Baja California del Norte, 1952-53; Chief of Agents of the Ministerio Público, Criminal Courts, 1953-54; Judge, 5th Criminal Court, Federal District, 1954-63; Judge of the Superior Tribunal of Justice of the Federal District, 1963-76; President of the Superior Tribunal of Justice of the Federal District, 1977-82; *Justice of the Supreme Court*, 1982-85. g-None. h-None. i-Son of Teodoro Martínez García, surgeon, and Sofía Rojas Carrillo, secretary; married Rosa Souza Pardo, surgeon.

j-None. k-None. l-Almanaque de
México, 1982, 77; Protag., 218; letter;
DBGM, 669.

Martínez Ross, Jesús
a-May 8, 1934. b-Ciudad Chetumal,
Quintana Roo. c-Primary studies in the
Belisario Domínguez Socialist School,
Chetumal, 1942-48; secondary studies
at Public School No. 2 for Students of
Workers, Mérida, Yucatán, 1948-51;
preparatory studies at the National
Preparatory School No. 1, 1952-53; law
degree, National School of Law,
UNAM, 1954-58; Professor of the
History of Culture, Center of Techno-
logical and Agricultural Studies,
Chetumal; Professor of Language and
Literature, Center of Technological
Studies No. 62, Chetumal, 1968.
d-*Federal Deputy* from Quintana Roo,
Dist. 1, 1973-75, President of the
Administrative Committee, member of
the Agricultural Development Commit-
tee, the Tourist Development Commit-
tee, the First Balloting Committee, the
Naval Committee, and the Gran
Comisión; *Governor of Quintana Roo*,
Apr. 5, 1975-81. e-Secretary General of
PRI for Quintana Roo, 1968; President
of the Quintana Roo Committee of the
National Council for Voter Registra-
tion, 1969. f-Agent of the Ministerio
Público, Chetumal, 1965-71; Oficial
Mayor of Quintana Roo under Governor
David G. Gutiérrez Ruiz, 1971-72.
g-Secretary General of the Student
Society of Public School No. 2 Students;
founder of the Civic and Social Front of
Quintana Roo, 1955; Secretary of
Legislative Promotion of the CNOP of
Quintana Roo; founder of the Quintana-
roonian Fraternity, 1961; President of
the Mexican Association for the Promotion and Publishing of Music, 1958-65;
adviser to the Federation of Workers of
Quintana Roo of the CTM, 1969. h-Director General of the music publishing
firm Compas, 1958-65. i-Married Alicia

Márquez; *Pedro Coldwell* served as his
secretary of government, 1975; son of
Pedro Martínez Arzu and Adela Ross
Corzo. j-None. k-First constitutional
governor of the State of Quintana Roo.
l-*Excélsior*, 18 Jan. 1975, 4; HA, 14 Apr.
1975, 5; C de D, 1973-76, 19; Enc. Mex.,
Annual, 1977, 549; HA, 11 Dec. 1978,
38, 23 Feb. 1976, 31, 20 Jan. 1975, 29;
Almanaque de México, 1982, 399;
Alvarez Corral, 173-75.

Martínez Tornel, Pedro
(Deceased 1957) a-Oct. 29, 1889.
b-Jalapa, Veracruz. c-Preparatory studies at the National Preparatory School,
Mexico City; engineering degree,
UNAM, 1918; Professor of Engineering,
UNAM; Director of the National School
of Engineering, UNAM, 1942-46.
d-None. e-None. f-Engineering adviser
and technical inspector, Secretariat of
Public Works, 1919-22; Superintendent,
Port of Salina Cruz, Oaxaca, 1923; Head
of the Drainage Section, Secretariat of
Public Works, 1924, 1925-32; technical
inspector, Secretariat of Public Works;
Assistant Director, Ports and Tele-
graphs, Secretariat of Public Works,
1933-34; Assistant Chief Engineer,
National Railroads of Mexico, 1935-37;
Head of the Construction Department,
National Irrigation Commission, 1938-
40; Director General of Construction,
National Railroads of Mexico, 1941-43;
Subsecretary of Public Works, 1943-45;
Secretary of Public Works, 1945-46.
g-None. h-Member of the Board of the
Mexican Tube Company and other
firms. i-Son of Engineer Braulio
Martínez and Concepción Tornel;
married Rebecca Pacheco. j-None.
k-Director of *Juan Andreu Almazán*'s
campaign for president, 1940; supported
General *Miguel Henríquez Guzmán* for
president, 1951. l-WWM45, 74; DP70,
1277; D de Y, 3 Oct. 1941, 2; Correa,
319; López, 670; Enc. Mex., VIII, 324;
Pasquel, Jalapa, 427.

Martínez Ulloa, Enrique
b-Ixtlán del Río, Nayarit. c-Primary and
secondary studies in Guadalajara, Jalisco; preparatory studies at the Prepara-
tory School of the State of Jalisco; law
degree, University of Guadalajara;
Secretary, University of Guadalajara.
d-None. e-None. f-Actuary for the 2nd
Judicial District, Guadalajara; Secretary
of Studies and Accounts, Supreme
Court of Justice; consulting lawyer,
Secretariat of Communications and
Public Works, Secretariat of Industry
and Commerce, and the Secretariat of
Agriculture; fiscal attorney for the
Federal Government, 1948-49, 1960-64;
Director of the Department of Legal
Affairs, Institute of Social Security;
Justice of the Supreme Court, 1964-70,
1970-74. g-None. h-None. i-Married
Esperanza González; son, Carlos, was a
subdirector of the National Urban Bank,
1984. j-None. k-None. l-*Justicia*, June,
1967; DPE61, 53; DBGM, 274.

Martínez Vara, Andrés
a-Jan. 31, 1914. b-Puebla, Puebla.
c-Early education unknown; engineering degree; professor, Heroic Military
College, National Polytechnic Institute
and the Rafael Dondé School. d-None.
e-Joined PRI, 1938. f-Expert Evaluator,
PEMEX, 1938; engineer, Construction
Division, PEMEX, 1940; investment
analyst, Secretariat of the Presidency,
1969-73; Director, Department of
General Services, Federal Electric
Commission, 1973-76; Oficial Mayor of
the Federal Electric Commission, 1976-
82; *Private Secretary to President José
López Portillo*, 1982. g-None.
h-Employee, Equipo Eléctrico Metálicos
y Anodizados, S.A., 1946. j-None.
k-None. l-Letter.

Martínez Verdugo, Arnaldo
a-Jan. 12, 1925. b-Pericos, Mocorito,
Sinaloa. c-Early education unknown;
studied painting at La Esmeralda School

of Painting and Sculpture, Secretariat of
Public Education, 1944-46. d-*Plurinominal Federal Deputy* from the PCM,
1979-82; *Plurinominal Federal Deputy*
from the PSUM, 1985-88. e-Joined the
Mexican Communist Party, 1946;
Director, Organizing Committee of
PCM's Communist Youth, 1948-50;
member of the Regional Committee of
the PCM in the Federal District, 1952-
59; alternate member of the Central
Committee of the PCM 12th Congress,
1954; member of the Regional Committee of the PCM in the Federal District,
1959; member of the Organizing
Committee of the PCM 13th Congress;
member of the Secretariat of the
Central Committee of the PCM, 1960-
63; Secretary General of the PCM, 1963-
83; member of the Political Committee
the the PSUM, 1981-87; Secretary
General of the PSUM, 1981-82; presidential candidate of the PSUM, 1981-82.
f-None. g-Joined the Workers and
Peasants Alliance of Mexico, 1947;
member of the Executive Committee,
Local 4, National Union of Paper
Workers. h-Employee, industry, 1940-
43; moved to Mexico City to work as an
employee in the San Rafael Paper Co.,
1943. i-Son of Yssac Martínez Ortega,
peasant and agricultural industry
worker, and Silvina Verdugo Verdugo;
common-law marriage to Martha
Recasens Díaz de León. j-None.
k-Defeated *Alejandro Gascón Mercado*
for presidential candidacy of the PSUM,
1981. l-HA, 15 Nov. 1981, 16; Almanaque de México, 15; Análisis Político,
May 1982; HA, 12 Feb. 1979, 26; Protag., 218-19; *Excélsior*, 6 June 1981, 6, 8.

Martínez (Villicaña), José Luis
a-Apr. 1, 1939. b-Uruapán, Michoacán.
c-Early education unknown; degree in
agricultural engineering, National
School of Agriculture, 1956-62; graduate
studies in statistical methods, 1973;
Secretary, National School of Agricul-

ture, 1967. d-*Governor of Michoacán,* 1986–88. e-Coordinator of Agrarian Reform and Rural Development of the IEPES of PRI, 1979-81. f-Subdirector of Colonization, Department of Agrarian Affairs, 1962-63; Chief of Evaluation of Agricultural Projects for FIRA, Bank of Mexico, 1963-65; regional evaluator, FIRA, Mexico, Hidalgo, Morelos and Guerrero, 1965-67; Chief of Operations, FIRA, 1969-72; Administrative Director of Public Relations, Guanos and Fertilizers of Mexico, 1972-76; Director of Planning, Secretariat of Agrarian Reform, 1978-80; Assistant Director of Azufrera Panamericana and Cia. Exploradora del Istmo, 1980-81; *Subsecretary of Planning and Agrarian Infrastructure,* Secretariat of Agrarian Reform, 1981-82; *Secretary of Agrarian Reform,* 1982-86; *Director General of Federal Highways and Bridges,* 1988-93; Director General of Airports and Auxiliary Services, 1993. g-Secretary General of the College of Agricultural Engineers, 1975-77; President, Student Society of the National School of Engineering, 1956. h-None. i-Son of Jesús Martínez García, farmer, who worked with *Lázaro Cárdenas,* and Soledad Villicaña Baraja; married Erika Hinsen Martínez. j-None. k-Removed from the governorship after *Cuauhtémoc Cárdenas* won the state in the 1988 presidential elections. l-IEPES; Q es QAP, 377; Protag., 219; *Excélsior,* 1 Dec. 1982, 34; *The News,* 2 Dec 1982, 8; HA, 13 Dec. 1982, 16; DBGM, 273; DBGM92, 230; HA, 18 Feb. 1986, 13, 11 Feb. 1986, 23.

Martino Torres, César
(Deceased 1969) a-1905. b-Sacramento, Durango. c-Agricultural engineering degree, School of Agriculture, Ciudad Juárez, Chihuahua, 1927. d-*Federal Deputy* from the State of Jalisco, Dist. 9, 1937-40. e-*Secretary of Agrarian Action of the CEN of the PRM,* 1938. f-Member of the Cultural Missions

Program, Secretariat of Public Education, 1929-32; Director General of the Workers Bank, 1940; Director General of the National Bank of Agricultural Credit, 1940-46; Head of the 5th Advisory Office of the Department of Agrarian Affairs, 1964-69; adviser to the Presidency, 1969. g-Founding member of the National Farmers Federation; First Secretary of Union Action of the National Farmers Federation; founder and President of the Mexican Agronomy Society. h-Founder and Director General of Constructora el Guadiana, S.A.; writer for *Hoy, Siempre* and *Excélsior.* j-None. k-Precandidate for Secretary General of the CNC, 1941, 1962; supporter of General *Henríquez Guzmán* for president, 1952. l-DP70, 1277; DPE65, 171; González Navarro, 137, 168, 232; C de D, 1937-39; Cadena Z., 143; Casasola, V; Enc. Mex., VIII, 1977, 324.

Massieu, Wilfrido
(Deceased Mar. 26, 1944) a-Dec. 27, 1878. b-Tacubaya, Federal District. c-Primary studies at a private school; preparatory studies, National Preparatory School; engineering studies from the National Military College, 1896-04, graduating as a lieutenant of engineers, Dec. 4, 1904; Professor of Communications, Military Aspirants School, 1911; professor, National Polytechnic Institute. d-None. e-None. f-Director of the Military Industry College, San Luis Potosí, 1920-21; Director of the College of Railroad Workers, Secretariat of Public Education, 1921 (which became the Technical Industrial Institute and then the National Polytechnic Institute in 1937); *Director General of the National Polytechnic Institute,* 1940-42. g-None. h-None. i-Son *Guillermo* was Director General of IPN, 1964-70; close friend and colleague of José Vasconcelos; son of Luis Massieu and Clotilde Pérez; married María Helguera;

daughter María del Refugio Massieu Quintanilla, prominent poet; grandfather of *José Francisco Ruiz Massieu*, governor of Guerrero. j-Career army officer; rank of 2nd Lieutenant in Infantry, 1901; joined the War Ministry Staff, 1914; commander of a bridge-building company, 1910-11; officer in the Corps of Engineers, 1903-13; rank of 2nd Captain, Dec. 26, 1906; rank of 1st Captain, 1909; rank of Major, Apr. 28, 1911; rank of Lt. Colonel, Feb. 10, 1913; head of numerous engineering projects in the army; rank of Colonel, July 10, 1913; Chief of Staff, Military Column, under General Joaquín Maas Flores, Coahuila, 1913; served under General Huerta against Carranza; rank of Brigadier General, Feb. 12, 1914; opposed the Revolutionary forces of Pablo González in Monterrey, Nuevo León. k-Received appointment as Director of Industrial Military School in San Luis Potosí because of old friendship with governor Severino Martínez. l-DP70, 1280-81; Enc. de Mex., 8, 333; Rev. de Ejer., June 1971, 5-7; Cuevas, 356.

Massieu Berlanga, Andrés.
a-Feb. 17, 1949. b-Federal District. c-Early education unknown; accounting degree, School of Business Administration and Accounting, UNAM, 1968-70; degree in Industrial Relations, Ibero-American University, 1970-74, with a thesis on administrative salary system. d-None. e-None. f-Messenger, Personnel Department, Bank of Mexico, 1967; Calculator, Foreign Debt Department, Bank of Mexico; analyst, Technical Office of Loans, Bank of Mexico, 1974; Coordinator of Presidential Travel, 1983-85; Assistant Secretary to president Miguel de la Madrid, 1985-87; Personal Secretary to Carlos Salinas, 1987-88; *Private Secretary to the President*, Carlos Salinas, 1988-94. g-None. h-Manager, Industrial Relations, Coca

Cola of Mexico, 1974-79; Director of Personnel, Lanzagorta Group, 1979-82. i-Son of Luis Massieu Saénz de Sicilia, engineer, and Alicia Berlanga Sepúlveda; married María de los Angeles Fernández Perera; became friends with *Emilio Gamboa*, secretary of communications, 1993, at Ibero-American University. j-None. k-None. l-*Proceso*, 11 Jan. 1988, 20; DBGM87, 243; DBGM89, 222; DBGM92, 231.

Massieu (Helguera), Guillermo
(Deceased Feb. 28, 1985) a-Oct. 7, 1920. b-San Luis Potosí, San Luis Potosí. c-Primary studies at the Colegio Luis G. León and the Colegio San Borja, Mexico City, 1926-34; secondary and preparatory studies at Vocational School No. 1, 1935-40; engineering degree in chemical sciences, National School of Biological Sciences, IPN, with a specialty in Chemical Bacteriology, Nov. 21, 1946; graduate studies at Oxford, England, 1954-55; Ph.D. in Biochemistry, National School of Biological Sciences, IPN, 1963; Subdirector of the National School of Biological Sciences, IPN, 1956-57; professor at the National Polytechnic Institute, 1943-50; professor at the National University of Mexico, 1951-56; Professor of Medical Chemistry, UNAM, 1957-58. d-None. e-None. f-Head of Laboratories, National School of Medicine, UNAM, 1945-53; investigator, Department of Physiology, UNAM, 1947-53; head of the Laboratory, National Institute of Nutrition, 1956; investigator, Institute of Biology, UNAM, 1958-61; *Director General of the National Polytechnic School*, 1964-70; Director, Center for Research and Advanced Studies, IPN, 1970-77; *Subsecretary of Scientific Research and Education*, 1978-79. g-None. h-Author of hundreds of articles on the biological sciences. i-Son of *Wilfrido Massieu*, Director General of IPN, 1940-42, and

María Helguera; married Yolanda Trigo Mesta; uncle of *José Francisco Ruiz Massieu*, governor of Guerrero. j-None. k-None. l-*Hoy*, 21 Jan. 1967, 60; B de M, 175-78; HA, 21 Dec. 1964, 7; MGF69; Enc. Mex., VIII, 1977, 333-34; HA, 17 Apr. 1978, 10; HA, 8 Dec. 1975, 13; DAPC, 46; WNM, 144; *Excélsior*, 1 Mar. 1985, 25.

Matos Escobedo, Rafael
(Deceased 1967) a-July 28, 1893. b-Oxkutzcab, Yucatán. c-Primary and secondary studies in Oxkutzcab; preparatory studies in Yucatán; professional studies in law at the University of the Southeast, Mérida, Yucatán; law degree from the National School of Law, UNAM, Sept. 20, 1922; professor at the University of Veracruz; Professor of Penal Law, National School of Law, UNAM; Professor of Penal Law, Graduate Studies in Law, UNAM, 1964-67. d-*Senator* from the State of Yucatán, 1964-70. e-Active in Liberal Party of Yucatán. f-Oficial Mayor of the State Legislature of Yucatán; Secretary of the 3rd Civil Court, Mexico City, 1923; Judge of the 8th Correctional Tribunal, 1930; Judge of the 3rd Correctional Tribunal, 1930; Judge of the 6th Penal Court, 1931; District Judge of the State of Veracruz, 1941-46; *Assistant Attorney General of Mexico*, 1946-50; *Supernumerary Justice of the Supreme Court*, 1951-52, 1952-58; *Justice of the Supreme Court*, 1959-64. g-None. h-Author of numerous articles on penal law and a book on law. i-Graduated with *Francisco González de la Vega* from the National Law School, 1922; served with or under *González de la Vega* in many government positions; mentor to *Víctor Manzanilla Schaffer*; son of José E. Matos and Adoralida Escobedo. j-None. k-Pre-candidate for governor of Yucatán, 1963-64. l-DBM68, 424; DGF51, 568; DP70, 1285; MGF69, 106; WWMG, 26.

Mayagoitia Domínguez, Héctor
a-Jan. 7, 1923. b-Federal District. c-Primary studies in Gómez Palacio, Durango; Jiménez, Chihuahua; Torreón, Coahuila; secondary studies at the School for Workers' Children, Lerdo, Durango; preparatory studies at the National Preparatory School, Coyoacán, Federal District; attended the National Polytechnic Institute, 1942-46, chemistry degree in bacteriology and parasitology, IPN, 1946; soil chemistry studies, Rutgers University, 1948; Doctorate in Chemistry, IPN; Professor of Chemical Sciences, IPN, 1948-65; Subdirector of the National School of Biological Sciences, IPN, 1948-52; *Director General of IPN*, Dec. 14, 1979-82. d-*Governor of Durango*, 1974-79. e-Member of the Youth Action Committee of PRI; Secretary of External and Internal Affairs for the Federation of Mexican Youth, 1945; member of the IEPES of PRI. f-Founder and Director of the Chemical Laboratory for Soils and Plants, National School of Biological Sciences, IPN, 1949-64; Private Secretary to the Director General of IPN, 1964-66; Director General of Technological Instruction, Secretariat of Public Education, 1966-70; *Subsecretary of Technical Instruction and Graduate Studies, Secretariat of Public Education*, 1970-74; Director General of CONACYT, 1982-88. g-Secretary General of the Student Society of the National School of Biological Sciences, 1945; Secretary General of SNTE Delegation to IPN, 1951; Alternate Secretary General of Section Ten of the SNTE, 1958-60; Secretary of the Editorial Committee, CEN, SNTE, 1960-66. h-Representative of the Secretariat of Public Education on the National Commission of Productivity. i-Married María Luisa Prado; son of Luis Mayagoitia Alba, railroad worker, and Guadalupe Domínguez Pulido. j-None.

k-Defeated Senator *Gamíz Fernández* for the gubernatorial nomination; precandidate for senator from Durango, 1982. l-HA, 14 Dec. 1970, 22; *Excélsior*, 12 Mar. 1974, 12, 25 Jan. 1974; MGF69, 312; HA, 11 Mar. 1974, 36; Enc. Mex., Annual, 1977; HA, 24 Dec. 1979, 10; *Excélsior*, 26 Dec. 1981, 16; QesQAP, 505-06; DBGM, 275

Mayés Navarro, Antonio
a-Oct. 7, 1905. b-Jiquilpán, Michoacán. c-Early education unknown; secondary studies at the Colegio de San Nicolás; no degree. d-Federal Deputy from the State of Michoacán, 1934-37; President of the left wing of the Chamber of Deputies, 1935; President of the Permanent Committee of Congress, 1935-37; Local Deputy to the State Legislature of Michoacán; *Senator* from the State of Michoacán, 1940-46, President of the Insurance Committee, First Secretary of the National Properties and the Credit, Money, and Credit Institutions Committees and alternate member of the Waters and Irrigation Committee. e-*Secretary of Agrarian Action of the CEN of the PNR*, 1936; member of the Policy Directorate, Popular Party, 1949. f-None. g-None. h-Journalist. j-None. k-None. l-Libro de Oro, 1946, 9; López, 675-76; Casasola, V; Villaseñor, II, 175.

Mayoral Heredia, Manuel
a-1898. b-Oaxaca, Oaxaca. c-Primary and secondary studies in Oaxaca; preparatory studies in Oaxaca; engineering degree, University of Oaxaca; postgraduate studies at Stanford University. d-*Governor of Oaxaca*, 1950 to July 31, 1952. e-None. f-*Subsecretary of Public Works*, 1946-50. g-None. j-None. k-Resigned under pressure after an unpopular tax law caused a riot and a general strike resulting in the deaths of several people. l-DGF51, II, 523; Scott, 276; NYT, 3 July 1952, 5; NYT, 5 Aug.

1952, 4; DGF47, 143; DGF51, I, 91; Brandenburg, 103; Anderson.

Medellín, Jorge León
a-May 1916. b-Federal District. c-Architecture degree, National School of Architecture, UNAM, 1939. d-None. e-None. f-Architect for the Department of Prehispanic Monuments, Federal District, 1939; Head, General Protection Department, Secretariat of Labor, 1944-45; member, International Labor Organization, 1945-47; architect, National Railroads of Mexico, 1947-51; Director General of the Buenavista Project, National Railroads of Mexico, 1952-53; Director General, Planning Council, National Railroads of Mexico, 1953-55; Subdirector of Studies and Programs, National Railroads of Mexico, 1955-60; Director General of the Construction Commission for National Medical Centers, 1960-61; technical adviser, Conasupo, 1961-65; designer of highways in the Federal District; urban adviser to the Head of the Department of the Federal District; *Subsecretary of Government Properties*, 1966-70; head of construction for the Mexican Institute of Social Security, 1970-72. g-President of various architectural associations. h-None. i-Married Enriqueta Ortega, architect; son of *Roberto Medellín Ostos*, secretary general of health 1935-37, and María Teresa Sánchez; nephew of *Octavio Medellín Ostos*. j-None. k-None. l-DPE65, 76; DBM68, 426; DBM70, 372; HA, 21 Dec. 1970, 23; Enc. Mex., VIII, 1977, 395; WNM.

Medellín Ostos, Octavio
(Deceased 1952) a-July 9, 1896. b-Ozuluama, Veracruz. c-Preparatory studies in Jalapa and at the National Preparatory School; law degree, National School of Law, UNAM; Professor of Law at the National School of Law, UNAM; Professor of Economics at the

National School of Economics, UNAM; Professor of Ethics at the National Preparatory School; normal school teacher. d-None. e-Leader of the Vasconcelos party movement with *Adolfo López Mateos*, 1928-29. f-Secretary General of Government of the Department of the Federal District, 1945. g-None. h-Author of many works; director of the magazine *Social Action*; director of the law association magazine; practicing lawyer, 1925-52. i-Brother of *Roberto Medellín Ostos*, Secretary General of Health, 1935-37; practiced law with *Julio Rodolfo Moctezuma Cid*; uncle of *Jorge León Medellín*, subsecretary of government properties, 1964-70. j-None. k-Member of the "Seven Wisemen" Generation of the National Preparatory School and the National Law School; formed a campaign group to support the candidacy of *Adolfo Ruiz Cortines*; defended *Valentín Campa* against government indictment, 1947. l-DP70, 1296; WWM45, 75; Peral, 512; *Hoy*, 29 April 1972, 3; Enc. Mex., VIII, 1977, 395; Campa, 221; Illescas, 540.

Medellín Ostos, Roberto
(Deceased Mar. 5, 1941) a-Apr. 29, 1881. b-Finca Repartidero, Tantoyuca, Veracruz. c-Primary studies in Tantoyuca; preparatory studies at the National Preparatory School; engineering degree, National School of Engineering, UNAM, 1908; Professor of Chemistry, National Preparatory School; professor at the National School of Medicine, UNAM; Secretary of the National University; Professor of Graduate Studies, UNAM; Director of Natural Sciences at the National Preparatory School; Director of Technical Instruction, School of Chemical Sciences, UNAM; Secretary General and Rector, UNAM, Sept. 12, 1932, to Oct. 15, 1933; *Director General of IPN*, 1937. d-None. e-Supporter of José Vasconcelos, 1928-29. f-Prosector

of Botany, National Preparatory School; Head of the Chemistry Department, National Medical Institute; Oficial Mayor of the Secretariat of Public Education, 1934-35, under *Eduardo Vasconcelos*; Secretary General of the Department of Public Health, 1935-37. g-None. h-Author of numerous works on botany. i-Brother of *Octavio Medellín Ostos*; father of *Jorge Medellín León*, subsecretary of government properties, 1964-70; married María Teresa Sánchez. j-None. k-Organizer of the school breakfast program. l-WWLA40, 316; Gruening, 535; López, 678; Enc. Mex., VIII, 1977, 395; WWLA35, 244; Raby, 23; Skirius, 205; Illescas, 383-84.

Medina Alonso, Edgardo
a-July 13, 1913. b-Mérida, Yucatán. c-Primary studies in Mérida; preparatory studies in Mérida, 1927-32; medical degree, School of Medicine, University of Yucatán, 1933-39; member of the University Council of the University of Yucatán; Secretary, School of Medicine, University of Yucatán. d-Local Deputy to the State Legislature of Yucatán; *Senator* from the State of Yucatán, 1958-64, President of the Administrative Committee, First Secretary of the Health and the Military Sanitation Committees, President of the Insurance Committee, and member of the Second Balloting Group and the Special Legislative Studies Committees. e-None. f-Physician, Medical Services, Isla Mujeres, Quintana Roo, 1939-41. g-President of the Circle of Preparatory Students of Yucatán; cofounder of the Student Revolutionary Party of Yucatán; founder and director of the student newspaper, University of Yucatán, *El Preparatoriano*; President of the Circle of Medical Students, 1933-39. h-Department head, O'Horan Hospital, Mérida. j-None. k-None. l-Func., 402; C de S, 1961-64, 61.

Medina Asencio, Francisco

a-Oct. 22, 1910. b-Arandas, Jalisco. c-Preparatory studies at the University of Guadalajara; law degree, University of Guadalajara, 1933; teacher of secondary night school in the Federal District; professor at the School of Economics, University of Guadalajara; Director, Seminar of Finance Law, School of Law, University of Guadalajara; founding teacher of the Night School for Workers in the Federal District. d-Councilman of Guadalajara, Jalisco, 1956-58; Mayor of Guadalajara, 1962-64; *Governor of Jalisco,* 1965-71. e-None. f-Judge of the 3rd Court of Appeals, Guadalajara; Secretary of the 8th Judicial District, Federal District; Secretary of the First Division, Superior Tribunal of Justice of Federal District; lawyer for the Director of Pensions, ISSSTE; Secretary for the Arbitration Tribunal for Federal Employees, Federal District; Treasurer of Jalisco, 1953-56; Director of Pensions, State of Jalisco; Director of National Properties, Secretariat of Government Properties, 1958; Ambassador to Italy, 1971-75. g-Founding member of the Union of Workers of the Superior Tribunal of Justice of the Federal Ditrict; Secretary of Promotion, Union of Workers of the Superior Tribunal of Justice of the Federal District. h-Employed as a porter in the 1st Criminal Court of the Federal District; scribe of the 1st Criminal Court of the Federal District; practicing lawyer, 1977-80. i-Close personal friend of *Gustavo Díaz Ordaz.* j-None. k-None. l-WWW70-71, 630; Enc. Mex., 8, 415; *Siempre,* 14 Jan. 1959, 6; DBM70, 372-73; *Hoy,* 13 Mar. 1971, 10; DBM68, 427; DGF56, 95; *Excélsior,* 22 Aug. 1978, 22; *Proceso,* 21 July 1980, 26.

Medina de Márquez, Genoveva

a-Jan. 3, 1921. b-Oaxaca, Oaxaca. c-Early education unknown; no degree. d-Member of the City Council of

Oaxaca, 1962-65; Alternate Local Deputy, State Legislature of Oaxaca; *Alternate Federal Deputy* from the State of Oaxaca, Dist. 9, 1973-76; Local Deputy, State Legislature of Oaxaca (twice); *Federal Deputy* from the State of Oaxaca, Dist. 5, 1979-82. e-Represented the Union of Vendors of Public Markets of Oaxaca, *José López Portillo* presidential campaign, Oaxaca, 1976; Women's Secretary of CNOP of PRI for *Luis Echeverría* campaign, Oaxaca, 1970; Women's Secretary of CNOP of Oaxaca, 1981. f-None. g-Joined the Popular Movement of Oaxaca, 1953; Secretary General and founder of the Union of Vendors of Public Markets of Oaxaca. i-Married Angel Márquez Colmenares. j-None. k-None. l-C de D, 1973-76; C de D, 1979-82; Romero Aceves, 710-12.

Medina (Gaona), Hilario

(Deceased July 24, 1964) a-June 26, 1891. b-León, Guanajuato. c-Primary studies at the Porfirio Díaz Model School, León; preparatory studies from the Preparatory School of León and the National Preparatory School, 1918; law degree from the National School of Law, UNAM; Professor of History at the National Preparatory School; Professor of Constitutional Law, National School of Law, UNAM, 1930. d-Deputy to the Constitutional Convention from the State of Guanajuato, Dist. 8, 1916-17, considered a Jacobin; *Senator* from the Federal District, 1958-64, member of the Gran Comisión, the Committee on the Department of the Federal District, the Rules Committee; President of the Second Justice Committee; member of the First Committee on Government and the First Constitutional Affairs Committee. e-None. f-Subsecretary in charge of Foreign Relations, 1919-20; *Justice of the Supreme Court,* 1941-57; *Chief Justice of the Supreme Court,* 1953, 1957-58. g-None. h-Librarian during last year in law school to earn money to finish degree. i-Son of Romualdo Medina, a businessman, and Leovigilda Gaona García; brother, Francisco, a professor at UNAM; married Raquel Melendez. j-Active in the Revolution. k-Important member of the Carranza administration; his public career suffered after Carranza was murdered in 1920. l-DGF51, I, 568; C de S, 1961-64, 61; STYRBIWW, 54, 892; Enc. Mex., V, 36; Peral, 513; DGF47, 29; DP70, 1299; WWM45, 75; DGF56, 567; Func., 174; Enc. Mex., VIII, 1977, 414; Linajes, 173-74.

Medina Medina, Calixto
a-Jan. 22, 1923. b-Huanusco, Zacatecas. c-Primary studies in public schools in Aguascalientes and in Zacatecas; secondary studies at the Institute of Sciences of Aguascalientes; preparatory studies at the Institute of Sciences of Aguascalientes; medical degree, National School of Medicine, UNAM. d-Local Deputy to the State Legislature of Zacatecas; *Federal Deputy* from the State of Zacatecas, Dist. 1, 1967-70, member of the Gran Comisión; *Senator* from the State of Zacatecas, 1970-76, President of the Second Mines Committee, member of the Gran Comisión. e-Joined PRI, 1952; participant in various PRI campaigns. f-None. g-Secretary of Professional Action, CNOP, Zacatecas; Secretary of Organization of CNOP, Zacatecas; Secretary General of CNOP in the State of Zacatecas. h-Director of the Health Center, General Hospital, Jalapa, Zacatecas. i-Married Jovita Llamas. j-None. k-None. l-C de D, 1967-70; C de S, 1970-76, 79; PS, 3920.

Medina Muñoz, Alberto
a-Aug. 7, 1922. b-Zapotán, Municipio of Compostela, Nayarit. c-Primary studies in Compostela, Nayarit; normal studies in Guadalajara, Jalisco; teaching certificate. d-Mayor of Tepic, Nayarit;

Local Deputy to the State Legislature of Nayarit; *Senator* from the State of Nayarit, 1958-64, Secretary of the Gran Comisión, President of the Second Credit, Money and Credit Institutions Committee, Second Secretary of the Rules and the Foreign and Domestic Trade Committees. e-President of PRI in Nayarit. f-None. g-Secretary General of the League of Agrarian Communities of Nayarit; member of the National Committee of the CNC. h-Fisherman. j-None. k-None. l-Func., 287; C de S, 1961-64, 62.

Medina Neri, Héctor
a-Dec. 25, 1921. b-Federal District. c-Early education unknown; engineering degree. d-None. e-None. f-Director of Tourism Delegations, Toluca, México, 1961; Manager of Refrigeradora de Tepepán, Secretariat of Industry and Commerce; *Subsecretary of Fishing*, Secretariat of Industry and Commerce, 1970-76. g-None. h-Employee of *El Heraldo de México*. j-None. k-Helped to promote the development of fish products in Mexico. l-HA, 14 Dec. 1970, 21; DPE61, 131.

Medina Peña, Luis
a-May 31, 1945. b-Monterrey, Nuevo León. c-Early education unknown; law degree, University of Nuevo León, 1962-66, with a thesis on bipolar systems in tension, 1969; degree in international relations, Colegio de México, 1969; MA in Latin American government and politics, University of Essex, 1971, with a thesis on the student movement of 1968, 1972; Ph.D., Oxford University, 1976-77; professor and researcher, Colegio de México, 1972-82; Coordinator of the Center for International Studies, Colegio de México, 1972-76; Assistant Secretary, Colegio de México, 1977-79. d-*Federal Deputy* from the State of Nuevo León, Dist. 3, 1979-82, represented the Chamber of Deputies to

the Federal Electoral Commission. e-Member of the Legislative Promotion Committee of the CEN of CNOP, 1980; general delegate of CNOP to Querétaro, 1981; representative of the CEN of CNOP to the IEPES of PRI, 1981-82. f-Director of the Institute of Legislative Research, 1982; Director General of Scientific Research, Secretariat of Public Education, 1983; *Subsecretary of Educational Planning*, 1983-88. g-None. h-None. i-Son of Luis Medina Castillo, lawyer, and Elisa Peña Garza, normal teacher; married Blanca Torres Ramírez. j-None. k-None. l-C de D, 1979-82; HA, 19 Dec. 1983, 10; Q es QAP, 318; DBGM87, 246; DBGM, 277; letter.

Medina Plascencia, Carlos
a-Aug. 14, 1955. b-León, Guanajuato. c-Early education unknown; degree in chemical engineering administration, School of Chemical Engineering, ITESM, 1973-77; MA in business administration, ITESM and the Graduate School of Mexico City, 1978-80; professor, ITESM, León, Guanajuato campus, 1980-81. d-Member of the City Council of León, Guanajuato, 1986-88; Mayor of León, 1989-91. e-Joined PAN, 1985; Finance Manager, PAN campaigns for federal deputy, 1988; adviser, PAN, León, Guanajuato, 1990; National Adviser to PAN, 1991. f-*Interim Governor of Guanajuato*, 1991-95. g-Vicepresident, Entrepreneurial Center of León, Guanajuato, 1983-85; adviser, COPARMEX, 1983-85. h-Director General of the Grupo Suela Medina Torres, 1978-91; adviser, Banco Internacional and Banpaís, 1980-84. i-Son of Carlos Medina Torres, industrialist, and María del Carmen Plascencia Fonseca; married Martha Padilla Vega, social worker. j-None. k-None. l-DBGM92, 793.

Medina Romero, Jesús
a-Jan. 8, 1921. b-San Luis Potosí, San Luis Potosí. c-Primary and secondary studies in San Luis Potosí; preparatory studies in San Luis Potosí; law degree, University of San Luis Potosí; studies in Spanish letters, University of San Luis Potosí. d-*Federal Deputy from the State of San Luis Potosí, Dist. 4, 1946-49; Federal Deputy from the State of San Luis Potosí, Dist. 1, 1955-58*. e-None. f-Oficial Mayor of the Government of the State of San Luis Potosí, 1946-50. g-None. j-None. k-None. l-Ind. Biog., 102-03; C de D, 1955-58, 1946-49.

Medina Valdez, Gerardo
a-Sept. 17, 1926. b-El Oro, México. c-Early education unknown; completed primary; journalism degree, Carlos Septién García School of Journalism; Professor of Journalism, Carlos Septién García School of Journalism, 1954-58. d-*Federal Deputy* (Party Deputy from PAN), 1967-70; *Federal Deputy* (Party Deputy from PAN), 1973-76; *Plurinominal Federal Deputy* from PAN, 1982-85; *Plurinominal Federal Deputy* from PAN, 1988-91; Plurinomial Representative of PAN to the Federal District Assembly, 1991-94. e-Candidate of PAN for federal deputy, State of México, 1958; candidate of PAN for senator, Federal District, 1970; candidate for federal deputy from PAN from Dist. 20, Federal District (twice); candidate for federal deputy from PAN from Dist. 28, Federal District, 1979; candidate of PAN for federal deputy, Federal District, 1982; member of the Regional Council of PAN for the Federal District, 1979; member, political committee, PAN, 1972; member of the National Council of PAN, 1967-82; member of the CEN of PAN, 1969-82; Secretary of Press and Publicity of the CEN of PAN, 1963-81; Delegate of the CEN of PAN to Sinaloa; Director of *La Nación*, official paper of PAN, 1963-81. f-None. g-None. h-Author; laborer, Dos Estrellas Mining Co., El Oro, 1942-45; solderer, MacComber de México,

1954; laborer, Campos Hermanos, 1954. i-Married Celia González; son of Gabino Medina García and María Valdez. j-None. k-none. l-HA, 14 May 1979, X; C de D, 1982-85; Directorio, 1982-85; C de D, 1967-70; DBGM89, 492; DBGM92, 619; DBGM, 554.

Medina Valtierra, Emma
a-July 4, 1959. b-León, Guanajuato. c-Early education unknown; teaching certificate, Instituto América, 1973-77; primary school teacher, Kindergarten No. 38. d-*Plurinominal Federal Deputy* from PAN, 1982-85. e-Joined PAN, 1976; Director of Publicity Brigades for PAN; Secretary of Political Education of the Youth Committee of PAN, 1981-82. f-None. g-Coordinator, Women's Promotion Group, León, 1979. i-Daughter of Rodolfo Medina Tejada and Emma Valtierra Aceves. j-None. k-None. l-C de D, 1982-85; *Directorio*, 1982-85; Lehr, 585; DBGM, 554

Médiz Bolio (Contarell), Antonio
(Deceased Sept. 15, 1957) a-Oct. 13, 1884. b-Mérida, Yucatán. c-Primary studies in Mérida; secondary studies at the Seminario Conciliar Universitario de Mérida and the Colegio Católico de San Ildefonso; law degree from the School of Law, University of Yucatán, 1907, with a thesis on strikes. d-Federal Deputy from the State of San Luis Potosí, Dist. 4, 1912-14; Federal Deputy from the State of Yucatán, Dist. 1, 1928-30; *Senator* from the State of Yucatán, 1952-57, member of the Indigenous Affairs Committee, the First Public Education Committee, the First Foreign Relations Committee, the First Balloting Committee, and substitute member of the National Properties Committee; President of the First Instructive Committee for the Grand Jury. e-Director of Popular Culture, PNR, 1936. f-Private Secretary to the Governor of Yucatán, 1903; Secretary to the 2nd Civil Court

of Mérida, 1905; Director of the Bulletin of the Secretariat of Public Education and Bellas Artes of Yucatán, 1912-13, 1915-18; Director General of Fine Arts, State of Yucatán, 1918-19; Second Secretary of the Mexican legation in Spain, 1919; Chargé d'affaires, Mexican legation in Spain, 1920; Second Secretary and Chargé d'affaires, Colombia, 1921; First Secretary and Chargé d'affaires, Argentina, 1921-22; First Secretary, Sweden, 1923-24; Ambassador to Costa Rica and Nicaragua, 1925-32; Director of the Department of Civic Action, 1932-34; Director of the Archeology Department, National Museum, 1937-39. g-None. h-Important figure in the development of Yucatán theater. i-Married Lucrecia Cuartas; son of Tomás Médiz and María Bolio y Cantarell; uncle of *Carlos Loret de Mola*; grandson of lawyer Antonio Médiz y Chacón, justice of the supreme court, and lawyer Rafael Bolio Rivas. j-Supported Madero during the Revolution. k-Exiled by Huerta and lived in Havana, 1914-15. l-DP70, 130; WWM45, 75; DGF56, 8, 9, 10, 12, 13; Peral, 514-15; C de S, 1952-58; Novo, 543; López, 688; Enc. Mex., VIII, 1977, 416; Valdés, 3, 230-31.

Medrano (Valdivia), Federico
(Deceased 1959) a-Mar. 2, 1896. b-Unión de San Antonio, Jalisco. c-Primary studies in San Francisco del Rincón; preparatory studies at the Colegio de León, 1913-17; law degree from the National School of Law, UNAM, 1918-22; taught at the Studies Center, University of Guanajuato, 1917. d-Federal Deputy from the State of Guanajuato, Dist. 9, 1922-24, 1924-26, 1928-30, Dist. 2, 1930-32; Senator from the State of Guanajuato, 1932-34; *Senator* from the State of Guanajuato, 1936-40; *Federal Deputy* from the State of Guanajuato, Dist. 3, 1940-43, President of the Chamber of Deputies

and Party Majority Leader; *Senator* from the State of Guanajuato, 1946-52, member of the Gran Comisión, the First Petroleum Committee, the Second Balloting Committee, the Second Labor Committee, the Agricultural and Development Committee; substitute member of the First Committee on National Defense. e-Secretary of Education of the CEN of the PRM, 1934; Secretary General of the PRM, 1933. f-None. g-Student leader during preparatory school days. h-None. i-Close friend of *Octavio Véjar Vázquez* at Law School. j-None. k-Retired from politics in 1952 to raise race horses; political enemy of *Gonzalo N. Santos*, who prevented him from holding his position as federal deputy, 1926-28; precandidate for governor of Guanajuato, 1935; expelled from PNR by *Matías Ramos Santos*, 1935. l-WWM45, 76; DP70, 1301; C de S, 1946-52; DBM70, 376; Peral, 515; DGF51, I, 6, 9, 10, 11, 13, 14; HA, 20 Aug. 1943, 7-8.

Meixueiro Alexandre, Héctor
a-Mar. 12, 1900. b-Santiago Xiacui de Ixtlán de Juárez, Oaxaca. c-Graduated from the Naval College at Veracruz, Veracruz. d-None. e-None. f-*Oficial Mayor of the Secretariat of the Navy*, 1952-58; *Oficial Mayor in charge of the Secretariat of the Navy*, Apr. 7–Nov. 30, 1958. g-None. h-None. i-Related to *Jorge Meixueiro*, federal deputy 1937-40. j-Career naval officer; Subdirector of the Naval School of the Pacific; commander of various destroyers; Chief of Staff of the 2nd Naval Zone, Ciudad Carmen, 1947; Chief of Staff of the 4th Naval Zone, Guaymas, Sonora, 1951-52; Chief of Staff of the Secretariat of the Navy; Interim Director of the Fleet; reached the rank of Admiral, Oct. 20, 1959. k-None. l-HA, 8 Dec. 1958, 41; Enc. Mex., V, 47; HA, 14 Apr. 1958, 6; DGF51, I, 386; DGF56, 381; DGF47, 234.

Meixueiro (Hernández), Jorge
(Deceased Aug. 18, 1943) a-1907. b-Ixtlán de Juárez, Oaxaca. c-Primary studies in Ixtlán; preparatory studies in Oaxaca; law degree, Scientific and Literary Institute of Oaxaca. d-Federal Deputy from the State of Oaxaca, Dist 5, 1928-30; Federal Deputy from the State of Oaxaca, Dist. 3, 1930-32; *Federal Deputy from the State of Oaxaca*, Dist. 4, 1937-40. e-Oficial Mayor of the CEN of the PNR, 1930. f-None. g-None. i-Son of Guillermo Meixueiro, lawyer and interim governor of Oaxaca, 1914, and María Hernández, daughter of Fidencio Hernández, compadre of General Félix Díaz and chief of his forces in Oaxaca. j-None. k-When he failed to become the PNR candiate for federal deputy from Oaxaca in 1943, he addressed the Chamber of Deputies and committed suicide before the full body. l-Bulnes, 632; C de D, 1937-40, 1930-32, 1928-30.

Mejía González, Adolfo
a-Dec. 16, 1933. b-Uruapán, Michoacán. c-Early education unknown; law degree, University of Michoacán, 1958; professor, National School of Law, UNAM; professor, University of Michoacán; full-time professor, IPN. d-*Plurinominal Federal Deputy* from the PST, 1979-82. e-Member of the National Liberation Movement, 1961-63. f-None. g-Member of the World Council for Peace, 1975; member of the Mexican Movement for Peace, 1961. h-Secretary to *Lázaro Cárdenas*, 1963-64. j-None. k-None. l-Protag., 222; C de D, 1979-82.

Melgar, Rafael E.
(Deceased Mar. 21, 1959) a-Mar. 14, 1887. b-Yanhuitlán, Oaxaca. c-Primary studies in Yanhuitlán and in Seminary School, Oaxaca, Oaxaca; no degree. d-Federal Deputy from the State of Oaxaca, Dist. 8, 1924-26, 1926-28,

President of the Balloting Committee; Federal Deputy from the State of Oaxaca, Dist. 8, 1928-30, President of the Administrative Committee; Federal Deputy from the State of Oaxaca, Dist. 10, 1930-32; President of the Obregonista Bloc and Federal Deputy from the State of Oaxaca, Dist. 7, 1932-34; Local Deputy to the State Legislature of Oaxaca; *Senator* from the State of Oaxaca, 1952-58, member of the First Committee on National Defense, the Second Foreign Relations Committee, and the First Balloting Committee. e-Founding member of the PNR; member of the CEN of the PNR, 1931. f-*Governor of Quintana Roo*, 1935-40; Ambassador to Holland, 1946-48. g-None. h-Administrator, *El Economista Mexicano*, 1907; Second Paymaster, Secretariat of Development, 1911-12; First Paymaster, Secretariat of Development, 1912; special mission to the United States, 1918; President, Naviera Mexicana Company. j-Joined the Revolution, 1913; career army officer; reached the rank of Brigade General, 1916. k-Head of the Nationalist Campaign, 1930. l-DGF56, 7, 10, 12-14; Peral, 517; DP70, 1304; Daniels, 490; C de S, 1952-58; López, 683; Bremauntz, 116; Ind. Biog., 171-74; Alvarez Corral, 129.

Melgarejo Gómez, José
a-Sept. 8, 1912. b-Puebla, Puebla. c-Studied under a tutor, 1920; primary at the Colegio Francés de la Perpetua, 1921-22, the Colegio Luz Saviñón, 1923, and the Colegio Francés La Salle, 1924-25, in Mexico City; secondary and preparatory at the Colegio Francés La Salle, 1926-28, 1929-30; degree in chemistry from the School of Chemical Sciences, Tacuba, Federal District, 1931-33; Professor of Experimental Physics and Higher Algebra, University of San Luis Potosí (3 years). d-*Federal Deputy* (Party Deputy from PAN), 1970-73, member of the Artisans Committee

and the Subsistence and Supplies Committee. e-None. f-None. g-None. h-Businessman. j-None. k-Candidate of PAN for the 1st Councilman of Naucalpan, México. l-Directorio, 1970-72; C de D, 1970-72, 125.

Mena, Anselmo
(Deceased 1958) a-1899. b-Federal District. c-Early education unknown; law degree, National School of Law, UNAM; graduate studies in London and in Paris. d-None. e-Founding member of the Popular Party, 1947; Vice-President of the Popular Party. f-Director of the Consular Department, Secretariat of Foreign Relations; Ambassador to Honduras; Ambassador to Nicaragua; Director General of Political Affairs, Secretariat of Foreign Relations, 1937-42; Consul General to London, England; Ambassador to Czechoslovakia, 1956-58. g-None. h-Author of several books. i-Classmate of *Jaime Torres Bodet*, School of Law, 1918-19. j-None. k-None. l-DP70, 1305; Enc. Mex., VIII, 423; DGF56, 125; López, 684; DGF51, I, 131.

Mena Brito, Antonio
a-Feb. 22, 1919. b-Mérida, Yucatán. c-Primary studies in Mérida; secondary and preparatory studies in the Federal District; law degree, National School of Law, UNAM; Professor of Law, National Preparatory School and the University Extension, UNAM; Professor of Literature in public and private schools; Secretary General of the Night Program, National Preparatory School, Federal District. d-*Senator* from the State of Yucatán, 1958-64, Secretary of the Gran Comisión, member of the Foreign and Domestic Trade Committee, the Special Legislative Studies Committee, and the Tourist Affairs Committee; President of the Second Credit, Money, and Credit Institutions Committee; member of the Rules Com-

mittee; alternate member of the Second Constitutional Affairs Committee and the Second Committee on Tariffs and Foreign Trade. e-Active in the presidential campaign of *Miguel Alemán*, 1946; *Secretary of Youth Action of the CEN of PRI*, 1946-52; *Secretary of Popular Action of the CEN of PRI*, 1952-58; general delegate of the CEN of PRI to many states. f-Director General of the National Youth Institute, Secretariat of Public Education, 1952-58. g-Student leader in secondary school; President of the Federation of University Students of Mexico. j-None. k-None. l-Func., 403; C de S, 1961-64, 62; DGF56, 306; *Excélsior*, 30 Aug. 1981, 4.

Mena Córdoba, Eduardo R.
b-Campeche. c-Early education unknown; no degree. d-Federal Deputy from the State of Campeche, Dist. 1, 1922-24, member of the Gran Comisión; Federal Deputy from the State of Campeche, Dist. 2, 1924-26, member of the Gran Comisión; Federal Deputy from the State of Campeche, Dist. 2, 1926-28, member of the Gran Comisión; *Governor of Campeche*, 1935-39; *Senator* from the State of Campeche, 1940-46, President of the Industries Committee, First Secretary of the First Tariff and Foreign Trade Committee, and Secretary of the Gran Comisión. e-None. f-Director of the Federal Treasury Office, San Pedro de las Colonias, Coahuila, 1951. g-None. j-None. k-Raby says he had many problems with leftists and the teachers unions during his term as governor because of his conservative views; forced by President *Cárdenas* to enforce the agrarian legislation in Campeche; the *Diario del Sureste* believes that the loss of his candidate for the senate against *Carlos Góngora Gala* in 1936 was the first defeat for the official party in a senatorial race. l-Letter; D de Y, 1 Jan. 1936, 4; Daniels, 488; D del S, 24 Aug.

1936, 25, 27; Raby, 226; DGF51, I, 167, Libro de Oro, 1940, 9.

Mena Palomo, Víctor
b-Izamal, Yucatán. c-Teaching certificate; no degree. d-Local Deputy to the State Legislature of Yucatán; Secretary of the City Council of Mérida; *Federal Deputy* from the State of Yucatán, Dist. 2, 1937-40; *Alternate Senator* from the State of Yucatán, 1952-53. e-President of the Socialist Party of the Southeast. f-*Interim Governor of Yucatán*, 1953-58. g-None. h-Owner of a PEMEX station, Mérida. i.Married Esperanza López Vega; son, Héctor Ignacio, was consul general in Río de Janeiro, Brazil, 1983. j-None. k-None. l-HA, 29 June 1953; DGF56, 8, 102; C de D, 1937-39; C de S, 1952-58.

Méndez Aguilar, Benjamín
a-Nov. 10, 1886. b-Jerécuaro, Guanajuato. c-Primary and secondary studies in Guanajuato, Guanajuato; no degree. d-Federal Deputy from the State of Guanajuato, Dist. 15, 1918-20, 1924-26; Federal Deputy from the State of Guanajuato, 1926-28, 1930-32; *Federal Deputy* from the State of Guanajuato, Dist. 5, 1949-52, member of the First Committee on Railroads and the First Committee on General Means of Transportation. e-None. f-Telegrapher, Carneros, Coahuila, 1901; station master, Coahuila, 1901-03; telegrapher, Office of the Superintendent of Car Service, Federal District, 1904-08; first class telegrapher, 1908-09; dispatcher, 1909-17; chief of dispatchers, 1917-18; President of the Price Commission, Railroad Service, 1918-28; member of the Board of Directors, National Railroads of Mexico, 1918-28; Superintendent of Passenger Service, 1918-24; Director of the Railroad of Desague del Valle de Mexico, 1918-24; Oficial Mayor of the National Railroads of Mexico, 1918-24; Director of Traffic, National

Railroads of Mexico, 1943-51; Representative of the National Railroads in Texas, 1951-54; Director General of the Railroad of the Pacific, 1954-58; *Director General of the National Railroads of Mexico*, 1958-64. g-None. h-None. i-Son of a doctor; son Roberto, an engineer and collaborator of *Luis Gómez Z.*; son *Benjamín Méndez Luna, Jr.* served as a federal deputy from Puebla, 1961-64; formed a political group called "Los Compadres," 1958-64, including *Eufrasio Sandoval Rodríguez*. j-None. k-None. l-HA, 8 Dec. 1958, 32; DBM68, 429-30; D de Y, 2 Dec. 1958, 7; C de D, 1949-51, 79; DGF51, II, 451; DGF50, II, 390; Func., 105.

Méndez Docurro, Eugenio
a-Apr. 17, 1923. b-Veracruz, Veracruz. c-Engineering degree in electrical communications from the National Polytechnic Institute, 1948; MS from Harvard University, 1949; graduate studies at Harvard University on a scholarship from the Secretariat of Public Education; graduate studies at the School of Science, University of Paris, 1949-50; studies at the Royal College of Science and Technology, London, 1962-63; Subdirector General of the National Polytechnic Institute, 1950-53; *Director General of the National Polytechnic Institute*, 1959-62. d-None. e-None. f-Director General of Telecommunications, Secretariat of Communications and Transportation, 1953-59; *Subsecretary of Communications and Transportation*, 1964-70; *Secretary of Communications and Transportation*, 1970-76; Coordinator General of Scientific and Technical Education, Secretariat of Public Education, 1976-77; *Subsecretary of Education and Scientific Investigation*, 1976-78; Director General of the Mexican Institute of Communications, Secretariat of Communications and Transportation, 1989-94. g-None.

h-President of the Consulting Commission on Broadcasting; member of the Mexican Delegation to UNESCO, 1960; technical consultant, Systems and Components Company. i-Son of Eugenio Méndez Aguirre, a lawyer and leftist who served as a federal deputy in the 1930s, and Carmen Docurro; married Pastora Méndez Zorrilla; godson of *Miguel Alemán*. j-None. k-Precandidate for the governor of Veracruz, 1974; precandidate for federal deputy from Veracruz, 1976; prosecuted by the attorney general for fraud; found guilty, 1978. l-DGF56, 252; *Libro de Oro*, xxxiv; DPE65, 104; DBM68, 430; DGF51, I, 292; *Hoy*, Dec., 1970; HA, 7 Dec. 1970; *Excélsior*, 13 Apr. 1973, 11; Enc. Mex., VIII, 1977, 428; *Excélsior*, 8 Dec. 1975, 17; HA, 3 Apr. 1978, 11-12, 17 Apr. 1978, 10; DBGM89, 226; DBGM92, 235.

Méndez Hernández, Lucía
a-Jan. 7, 1932. b-Jalapa, Veracruz. c-Primary studies at the Luis J. Jiménez Primary School, Jalapa; secondary and normal from the Federal Institute of Teacher Training, Jalapa; rural teacher, Federal Rural School Ricardo Flores Magón, Misantla, Veracruz, 1948; teacher, Socrates Public Primary School, El Pozón, Misantla, Veracruz, 1959; teacher, Villa de Yecuatla, Veracruz, 1951; teacher, Benito Juárez Arroyo Hondo School, Misantla, Veracruz, 1952-65; teacher, Andrés Quintana Roo School, Las Lajas, Veracruz, 1969-72; federal school inspector, Veracruz, 1972-77. d-Alternate Local Deputy, State Legislature of Veracruz, Dist. 6, 1974-76; *Alternate Federal Deputy* from the State of Veracruz, Dist. 5, 1976-79; *Federal Deputy* from the State of Veracruz, Dist. 5, 1979-82. e-Member of PRI. f-None. g-Secretary of Organization of ANFER, Veracruz, 1974. h-None. i-Daughter of Francisco Méndez Pérez and Guadalupe Hernández Rodríguez.

j-None. k-None. l-C de D, 1979-82, 1976-79; Romero Aceves, 713-14.

Mendieta y Núñez, Lucío
(Deceased) a-Jan. 11, 1895. b-Federal District. c-Primary studies at the Normal School, Oaxaca, Oaxaca; secondary studies at the Institute of Oaxaca, 1909-10; preparatory studies at the National Preparatory School, 1911-15; law degree from the National School of Law, UNAM, May 1, 1920; LLD, National School of Law, UNAM, 1950; Professor of Agrarian Law, Administrative Law, and Sociology, UNAM (25 years); Professor of Sociology, Autonomous Technological Institute of Mexico, 1947-54; Director of the Institute of Social Investigations, UNAM, 1939-66; professor at the Institute of Social Investigations, UNAM, 1970; cofounder with *Luis Garrido Díaz* of the School of Political and Social Science at UNAM; founder of the School of Economics, UNAM. d-None. e-Director of the Institute of Social Studies for the PNR, 1935. f-Chief of the Department of Population, Bureau of Anthropology, Secretariat of Agriculture, 1921; Director of the Institute of Social Investigations, Bureau of Population, Secretariat of Agriculture, 1934; adviser to the Department of Indian Affairs, 1936; *Oficial Mayor of the Department of Agrarian Affairs and Colonization,* 1946-48; Director of Educational and Cultural Affairs, National Council of Tourism, 1976-82. g-None. h-Director of the magazine, *Social Policy,* 1935; Director of *Mexican Sociology Review,* 1939-46. i-Attended UNAM with *Manuel Gómez Morín,* Angel Alanís Fuentes, *Manuel Bartlett,* and Alberto Vázquez del Mercado; disciple of Manuel Gamio; married Josefina Escalante; son of Colonel Justino Mendieta. j-None. k-Outspoken critic of the Mexican bureaucracy; prolific author and authority on agrarian reform

and sociological studies of Mexico. l-DGF47, 285; WWM45, 76; Peral, 521; letters; Enc. Mex., VIII, 1977, 431-32.

Mendiola (de la Portilla), Carlos C.
a-Oct. 25, 1903. b-Matamoros, Tamaulipas. c-Studied at the Internado Nacional, 1918-19; studies from the La Salle Extension University, Chicago, Illinois, 1930-33; no degree. d-None. e-None. f-Banking inspector for the National Banking Commission; *Subdirector General of the National Bank of Foreign Commerce,* 1940-42; Subdirector General of the Bank of Commerce, 1942-46. g-President, Chambers of Commerce of Mexico City; President, National Chambers of Commerce of Mexico. h-Director General, Banco Comercio Mexicano. i-Half brother of *Mario Mendiola,* Subdirector General of the National Bank of Foreign Commerce, 1942-53; married Rosa Murga; son of Manuel M. Mendiola, civil engineer, and Anita de la Portilla. j-None. k-None. l-WWM45, 76; WNM, 146.

Mendiola (Miranda), Mario
a-Aug. 4, 1910. c-Professional studies in business administration, commerce and electrical engineering; no degree. d-None. e-None. f-*Subdirector General of the National Bank of Foreign Commerce,* 1942-46, 1946-52, 1952-53; Administrative Director of CONCAMIN, 1970; Director General of the National Savings Bank. g-None. i-Half brother of *Carlos Mendiola,* Subdirector General of the National Bank of Foreign Commerce, 1940-42; married Enriqueta Gedovius; son of Manuel María Mendiola, civil engineer, and Ana María Miranda. j-None. k-None. l-DBM70, 378; DGF51, II, 29, 95, 195, etc.

Mendívil Blanco, Julieta
a-June 5, 1952. b-Puebla, Puebla. c-Early education unknown; psychology degree, School of Psychology, UNAM.

d-*Federal Deputy* from the State of Puebla, Dist. 2, 1979-82; *Alternate Senator* from the State of Puebla, 1982-88; *Federal Deputy* from the State of Puebla, Dist. 3, 1991-94. e-Joined PRI, 1967; Secretary of Organization of CNOP of PRI of Puebla, 1981-83. f-Director of Public Relations, Puebla, Puebla, 1973-76; Director of Product Department, Division of Tax Information, Secretariat of the Treasury, 1976-77; Subdirector of Publications, Division of Social Communication, Secretariat of the Treasury, 1977; Delegate of the Department of the Federal District to Iztacalco, 1982-88; Regional Delegate of INFONAVIT, Puebla, 1988-91. g-Secretary of Public Relations, CNOP, Puebla, 1973-76; Director of the National Revolutionary Women's Group, Puebla. h-None. i-Daughter of Rafael Mendívil Landa, orthopedic surgeon, and Julieta Blanca Salvatori; married Alfonso del Río Pintado, agricultural engineer. j-None. k-None. l-Q es QAP; C de D, 1979-82; C de S, 1982-88; DBGM92, 515-16; DBGM87, 249; DBGM, 281.

Mendoza Arámburo, Angel César
a-Dec. 15, 1934. b-La Paz, Baja California del Sur. c-Primary studies in the Venustiano Carranza School, La Paz; secondary studies at the José María Morelos School, La Paz; preparatory studies at the National Preparatory School; law degree, National School of Law, UNAM, 1953-57. d-*Federal Deputy* from Baja California del Sur, Dist. 1, 1967-70, member of the General Affairs Section of the Legislative Studies Committee and member of the Hydraulic Resources Committee; *Governor of Baja California del Sur*, 1975-81. e-Secretary General of Youth of PRI in Baja California del Sur, 1950; Secretary of Political Action of PRI in Baja California del Sur, 1967-70, 1974; President of the Electoral Committee of Baja California del Sur, 1967-70, 1974;

Secretary of Popular Action of the CEN of PRI, 1982. f-Assistant to the President and judicial official of the Superior Tribunal of Justice of the Federal District, 1958-66; Private Secretary to the Secretary of Hydraulic Resources, *José Hernández Terán*, 1964-65; Secretary General of Government of Baja California del Sur, under Governor *Hugo Cervantes del Río*, 1965-67; Secretary General of Government of Baja California del Sur, Mar. to Jan. 1970; Secretary General of Government of Baja California del Sur, under Governor *Félix Agramont Cota*, Oct. 1974 to Jan. 1975; *Subsecretary of Tax Inspection*, Secretariat of the Treasury, 1984-85. g-President of the Southern California Student Society of Mexico, 1953; *Secretary General of CNOP*, 1982. h-Practicing lawyer. i-Cousin of *Alberto Alvarado Arámburo*, federal deputy from Baja California del Sur, 1964-67; married Luz Davis Garayza; son of Angel Mendoza Sabido, businessman, and Julia Arámburo. j-None. k-Defeated cousin for gubernatorial nomination, 1975; first constitutional governor of the State of Baja California del Sur. l-Enc. Mex., Annual, 1977, 540; C de D, 1967-70, 67, 85; DPE65, 125; *Excélsior*, 4 Jan. 1975, 3, 17 Jan. 1975, 5; HA, 15 Apr. 1975, 7; Almanaque de México, 321; *Excélsior*, 17 Jan. 1983, 22.

Mendoza Berrueto, Eliseo Francisco
a-Apr. 13, 1931. b-San Pedro, Coahuila. c-Teaching certificate; degree in economics from the National School of Economics, UNAM, 1962, with a thesis on "Regional Planning and Economic Development: The Case of Mexico"; graduate studies at the Institute of Social Studies, Holland, 1962, received a diploma; graduate studies in economic planning, integral planning, and national accounts at the National School of Economics, UNAM; graduate studies in regional planning in Paris;

visiting investigator to the Institute of
Economics, Holland, 1962; professor at
the National School of Economics,
UNAM; professor at the National Polytechnic School; professor at the School
of Economics, University of Guadalajara; professor at the Colegio de México;
professor at the School of Architecture
(graduate program), UNAM; Director of
the Center for Economic and Demographic Studies, Colegio de México,
1967-70. d-*Senator* from Coahuila,
1976-78; *Federal Deputy* from the State
of Coahuila, Dist. 1, 1985-87; *Governor
of Coahuila*, 1987-93. e-Technical
adviser to the IEPES of PRI; Coordinator
of the Advisory Council of the IEPES of
PRI, 1982. f-Head of the Statistics Section for the Cooperative Industries Administration, 1953-56; Economic Investigator for the National Bank of Foreign
Commerce, 1958-59; Head of Administrative Budgets for the National Bank of
Ejido Credit, 1959; Assistant Director of
the Administrative Department, National Ejido Credit Bank, 1960; adviser
to the National Chemical-Pharmaceuti-
cal Industry, 1963; Director of Economic and Social Planning for the Plan
Lerma, 1963-66; adviser to the Subsecretary of Industry and Commerce, 1956-
58; adviser to the government of the
State of Jalisco, 1965-66; *Subsecretary
of Commerce, Secretary of Industry and
Commerce*, 1970-76; *Subsecretary of
Higher Education, Science and Technology*, 1978-82; *Subsecretary of Mines
and Energy*, 1982-85. g-None. h-None.
i-Attended the National School of
Economics with *Carlos Bermúdez
Limón*; married María Guadalupe
Altamira; son of Emilio Mendoza
Cisneros, businessman, and Guadalupe
Berrueto Ramón. j-None. k-None.
l-HA, 14 Dec. 1970, 21; letter ; DPE71;
HA, 9 Jan. 1978, 13; HA, 9 Aug. 1982,
18; *Excélsior*, 12 July 1980; Q es QAP,
167-68; DBGM89, 717; DBGM, 281;
HA, 18 Aug. 1985, 2; DBGM92, 795.

Mendoza González, Octavio
a-Dec. 1, 1900. b-León, Guanajuato.
c-Primary and secondary studies in
León, Guanajuato; preparatory studies
at the University of Guanajuato, 1913-
18; law degree, National School of Law,
1918-22, with a thesis on administration and administrators, Aug. 29, 1923;
Assistant to the Secretary of the Preparatory School, León, Guanajuato, 1916.
d-Federal Deputy from the State of
Guanajuato, Dist. 1, 1928-29. e-None.
f-Secretary of the Justice of the Peace,
Dist. 8; Commissioner of the First
Justice of the Peace, 1917-19; secretary
of the first cooperative founded by
President Obregón, 1920; consulting
lawyer to the Secretariat of the Government, 1924; Secretary General of
Government of the State of Guanajuato,
1926; Interim Governor of Guanajuato,
1927; Subsecretary of Government,
1929-30, in charge of the Secretariat of
Government, 1931; Ambassador to
Germany and Austria, 1931-32; Oficial
Mayor of the Secretariat of Foreign
Relations, 1932-34; Secretary of the
Board of Private Welfare, 1934-36;
Director of the Legal Department,
Department of the Federal District,
1936-38; *Justice of the Supreme Court*,
1941-46, 1947-52, 1953-58, 1959-64,
1965-68. g-None. h-None. i-Great-
grandfather served as a federal deputy
under President Benito Juárez; married
Magdalena Causier. j-None. k-None.
l-*Justicia*; letter.

Mendoza Hernández, Raúl
a-May 5, 1941. b-Federal District.
c-Early education unknown; legal
studies, National School of Law,
UNAM, 1960-61; studies in publicity
and marketing, Marketing and Publicity
Institute, 1966. d-None. e-Joined PRI,
1961. f-Adviser and department head,
Subchief of Administration, Securities,
1966-78, Securities Manager, 1980-83,
General Manager of Securities, 1983-84,

and Director of Administration, 1984-86, all at National Finance Bank; *Oficial Mayor of the Secretariat of the Treasury*, 1986-88; *Oficial Mayor of Labor*, 1988-90. g-None. h-None. i-Son of Enrique Mendoza Ortiz and Soledad Mendoza Delgado; married Carmen Casasús López Hermosa, normal teacher. j-None. k-None. l-DBGM89, 227.

Mendoza Márquez, Miguel
a-Mar. 9, 1921. b-Federal District. c-Primary studies at the Justo Sierra Public School, Mexico City; secondary from Secondary School No. 10, Mexico City; preparatory studies at the National Preparatory School; enrolled Military Aviation School, Aug. 25, 1941, graduating as a pilot June 1, 1944, with the rank of 2nd Lieutenant. d-None. e-None. f-*Head of the Department of the Air Force*, 1982-88. g-None. h-None. i-Married Julia Babichoff Marazoff; son of Cristóbal Mendoza Mendoza, public official, and Eulalia Márquez Gutiérrez. j-Career air force officer; joined the 201st Air Squadron, 1944; rank of 1st Lieutenant, June 16, 1946; rank of 2nd Captain, Nov. 20, 1948; rank of 1st Captain, Nov. 20, 1950; Commander of 202nd Air Squadron, 1951; rank of Major, Nov. 20, 1952; rank of Lt. Colonel, Nov. 20, 1965; Commander of the Medical Air Transport Squadron of c-47s, 1965; rank of Colonel, Nov. 20, 1965; Chief of the 4th Maintenance Level; Section Chief and Adjutant General, Mexican Air Force, 1965-72; Interim Commander, 2nd Air Group; rank of Group General, Nov. 20, 1971; rank of Brigade General, Nov. 20, 1975; Commander, 6th Air Base, 1980-81; Commander, 1st Air Base, 1981-82. k-None. l-Rev. de Ejer., Dec. 1971, 40, Nov. 1975, 84; *Excélsior*, 4 Dec. 1982, 35; Rev. de Ejer., Dec. 1972, 82, Dec. 1965, 61; Q es QAP, 73; DBGM87, 250; DBGM, 282.

Mendoza Pardo, José María
b-Michoacán. c-Early education unknown; law degree, School of Law, Colegio de San Nicolás, Morelia, Michoacán, 1925-29; Professor of History, Colegio de San Nicolás. d-*Governor of Michoacán*, 1944-49. e-None. f-Secretary General of Government of the State of Baja California del Norte; Attorney General of the State of Michoacán under Governor *Lázaro Cárdenas*; Secretary General of Government of the State of Michoacán under Governor *Lázaro Cárdenas*; *Justice of the Supreme Court*, 1941-44. g-None. h-Practicing lawyer. i-As a student visited *Lázaro Cardenas*'s home as part of a regular discussion group; brother-in-law of *Alberto Bremauntz*, federal deputy from Michoacán, 1932-34. j-None. k-Resigned Aug. 26, 1949, as governor, because of difficulties resulting from student unrest at the Colegio de San Nicolás over government subsidies. l-HA, 21 Sept. 1945; letter; Anderson; Bremauntz, 93; Romero Flores, 267; NYT, 20 May 1962, 30; Bravo, 228.

Meraz Nevárez, Braulio
a-Feb. 9, 1911. b-Santiago Papasquiaro, Durango. c-Professional studies at the Agricultural School of Santa Lucía of Durango; attended the National Military College. d-*Federal Deputy* from the State of Durango, Dist. 3, 1940-43, member of the Gran Comisión, member of the Agricultural Development Committee; Local Deputy to the State Legislature of Durango, 1947; *Federal Deputy* from the State of Durango, Dist. 4, 1952-55, member of the War Materiels Committee; *Federal Deputy* from the State of Durango, Dist. 4, 1964-67, member of the Gran Comisión, the Second Committee on National Defense, the Hydraulic Resources Committee, and the Livestock Committee. e-None. f-Substitute Governor of Durango, 1947 (two days), following death of *Blas*

Corral; Subdirector of CEIMSA, 1958.
g-Secretary General of CNOP in
Durango. h-Accountant. j-Career army
officer; joined the army as an enlisted
man, 1931; Field Marshal for the Army
Veterinary Medical School; Captain of
the Cavalry; reached the rank of Major.
k-None. l-Peral, 525-26; C de D, 1940-
42, 10, 51, 1952-54, 61, 1964-66.

Mercado Chávez, María del Carmen
a-Dec. 9, 1938. b-Guadalajara, Jalisco.
c-Early education unknown; legal
studies, School of Law, University of
Guadalajara. d-*Alternate Federal
Deputy* from the State of Jalisco, Dist.
4, 1979-82; *Federal Deputy* from the
State of Jalisco, Dist. 4, 1982-85.
e-Campaign coordinator for PRI
candidates for federal and local deputies
in Jalisco; Secretary General of the local
PRI Committee of the 4th Electoral
District, Jalisco. f-None. g-Secretary
General of the Clothing Workers
Industry Union, CROC, Jalisco, 1975.
i-Son of Longinos Mercado Barba and
Serapia Chávez Benavides. j-None.
k-None. l-C de D, 1979-82, 1982-85;
Directorio, 1982-85; Lehr, 229.

Mercado Flores, Ignacio
a-Mar. 1, 1938. b-Federal District.
c-Early education unknown; agricultural engineering degree, National
School of Agriculture, 1954-60; MS in
agricultural sciences, University of
California, Davis, 1964-65; courses in
advanced administration, Graduate
School of Business Administration,
Harvard University, 1980; professor,
National School of Agriculture, 1960-
61; professor, Univerity of California,
1964-65. d-None. e-Joined PRI, 1961.
f-Inspector, Agricultural Trust Funds
(FIRA), Bank of Mexico, 1961; special
supervisor, FIRA; fruit specialist, FIRA,
1968; Director, Technical Agriculture
Department, FIRA, 1968-69; Technical
Coordinator, FIRA, 1969-70; aide to the

Director General of FIRA, 1971-73;
Director, Administrative Department,
FIRA, 1970-71; Subdirector of Technical
Services and Assistance, FIRA, 1973-80;
Subdirector General of FIRA, 1980-82;
*Subsecretary of Agriculture and
Operations*, 1982-84; Technical Director, FIRA, 1992-94. g-None. h-None.
i-Son of José Ramón Mercado de Anda,
public official, and Evangelina Flores;
married Laura Pérez Linares. j-None.
k-None. l-Q es QAP, 210; DBGM92,
237; DBGM, 283.

Merino Fernández, Aarón
(Deceased Dec. 1976) a-Mar. 31, 1908.
b-Ixcaquixtla, Puebla. c-Agricultural
engineering degree from the National
School of Agriculture, with a specialty
in irrigation; Professor of Topography,
UNAM, 1929. d-*Federal Deputy* from
the State of Puebla, Dist. 6, 1940-43,
substitute member of the First Justice
Committee, the Health Committee.
e-None. f-Engineer in the Department
of Agrarian Affairs, 1928-38; Director of
General Services for the Department of
the Federal District; delegate of the
Department of Agrarian Affairs in
Puebla, 1938-40; President of the
Agrarian Commission in Puebla, 1940;
Head of the Technical Consulting
Corporation, 1943; Director General of
Public Works, Secretariat of Public
Works; *Oficial Mayor of the Secretariat
of Public Education*, 1946-48; *Subsecre-
tary of Public Education*, 1948-52;
Governor of Quintana Roo, 1959-64;
Interim Governor of Puebla, 1964-69.
g-Secretary of the Mexican Agronomy
Society; founder of the Platform of
Professionals Group, which served as a
political base for *Mario Moya Palencia,
Antonio Calzada,* and *Pedro Ojeda
Paullada*'s careers. h-Author of a book
on agriculture in Puebla. i-Brother of
Jesús Merino Fernández, subsecretary of
agriculture and livestock, 1946-54.
j-None. k-One of the few examples in

recent Mexican cabinet history where two brothers simultaneously held subsecretary positions. l-HA, 16 Jan. 1948, 7; DGF51, I, 285; EBW46, 115; D de S, 1 Dec. 1940, 1; C de D, 1940-42, 16, 61; Peral, 527; DGF47, 171; CyT, 441; HA, 13 Dec. 1976, 49; López, 695.

Merino Fernández, Jesús
a-1905. b-Ixcaquixtla, Puebla. c-Early education unknown; studies in agricultural engineering, National School of Agriculture, 1922-27, degree, 1929, with a thesis on the "Regulation of the Río Coatzala Waters in Puebla"; Professor of Engineering, 1934-38; Professor of Agricultural Economics, School of Social Science, UNAM, 1934-37. d-None. e-None. f-Auxiliary engineer to the National Irrigation Commission, Morelos, 1928; Chief of Topography, Department of Agricultural Waters, La Laguna, Puebla and in Morelos, 1929; adviser to the Presidency, 1934-40; delegate of the Department of Agrarian Affairs and Colonization to Morelos, 1939-40; Director of Public Works, State of Morelos, 1939-40; Executive Secretary of the National Irrigation Commission, 1941; adviser to NAFIN, 1942-46; Director General of the National Resources, Secretariat of the Treasury, 1942-46; *Subsecretary of Agriculture*, 1946-52; 1952-54; Gerente General of the National Bank of Cooperative Development, 1969. g-President of the Mixed Agrarian Commission, Morelos, 1930-33. h-Author of agrarian laws; Secretary General of the Mexican Agronomy Society. i-Brother of *Aaron Merino Fernández*, governor of Puebla, 1964-69. j-None. k-None. l-DBP, 441-42; DGF56, 223; DP70, 213; DGF47, 123; DGF51, I, 203; CyT, 441-42.

Merino Mañón, José
a-July 6, 1936. b-Toluca, México. c-Early education unknown; public administration degree, School of Political Sciences, Autonomous University of the State of México, 1953-57, with a thesis on the flour industry; Professor of Public Finances, National School of Economics, UNAM, 1961-64; Professor of Finances, School of Business, UNAM, 1963-65; Director, Seminar on Labor Administration, UNAM, 1982. d-*Federal Deputy* from the State of México, Dist. 4, 1979-82. e-Joined PRI, 1959; Vice-President of the CEPES of PRI, State of México, 1970-76; active in IEPES of PRI during *José López Portillo*'s presidential campaign, 1976. f-Coordinator of Auditors, Secretariat of the Treasury, 1959-65; Director of Revenues, State of México, 1969-72; Subdirector of the Federal Electric Commission, 1972-74; *Oficial Mayor of Government Properties*, 1975-76; Director General of the National Railroad Car Construction Company, 1976-78; Secretary of Labor, State of México, 1982-84; Secretary of Economic Development, State of México, 1984-86; Secretary of Finances, State of México, 1986-87, 1989-93. g-None. h-Public accountant, Bedwell, Figueroa, Merino and Mijares, 1965-69; consultant, Inter-American Development Bank. i-Married Blanca Alicia Juárez Flores, public accountant; son of José Merino Legorreta, businessman, and Isabel Mañón Calderón. j-None. k-None. l-HA, 24 Feb. 1975, 30; Protag., 227; C de D, 1979-82; Mexiquenses, 120; DBGM87, 250-251; DBGM92, 797.

Merino Rábago, Francisco
a-1919. b-Irapuato, Guanajuato. c-Early education unknown; no degree. d-None. e-None. f-Rural Inspector, National Ejido Credit Bank, 1938; assistant to a zone director, National Ejido Credit Bank; adviser, Director of the National Ejido Credit Bank, 1938-54; Director of Credit, National Ejido Credit Bank, 1954-56; Subdirector, National Ejido Credit Bank, 1956-58;

Director of Credit, National Ejido Credit Bank, 1959-65; adviser, Secretary of Agriculture, 1959-60; Subdirector, National Ejido Credit Bank, 1968-70; Coordinator General of the National Ejido Bank, 1970-72; Manager, La Laguna Ejido Bank, 1972-74; Manager, Michoacán Ejido Bank, 1975; Subdirector General of the National Bank of Rural Credit, 1975; Director General of the National Bank of Rural Credit, 1975-76; *Secretary of Agriculture, 1976-82*; Director General of the National Seed Company, 1982. g-Joined the CNC, 1939. i-First political mentor was *Gilberto Flores Muñoz*, Secretary of Agriculture, 1952-58. j-None. k-None. l-*Excélsior*, 1 Dec. 1976, 1, 25 Mar. 1977, 8; HA, 6 Dec. 1976, 23; *El Día*, 1 Dec. 1976, 1; HA, 8 Aug. 1977, 18; *Excélsior*, 26 Dec. 1981, 16.

Mesa Andraca, Manuel
(Deceased) a-June 8, 1894. b-Chilapa, Guerrero. c-Primary studies in Guerrero; agronomy degree, National School of Agriculture, 1910-17, on a government fellowship, with a thesis on teaching and agrarian publicity; special studies in agricultural economics, Georgetown University, 1925-28; Professor of Agricultural Economics, National School of Agriculture, 1928-30; Professor of Agricultural Economics, National School of Economics, UNAM; Professor of Rural Sociology, School of Anthropology and History; Professor of Gardening, National School of Agriculture, 1923-24; Secretary and professor, Agricultural School of Yucatán, 1917; Secretary, National School of Agriculture, 1923-24, under *Marte R. Gómez*; Dean, National School of Agriculture, 1928-30. d-None. e-Member of the Popular Party, 1943; candidate of the Popular Party for federal deputy from Acapulco, 1943; Director of Finance, Popular Party, 1948; member of the National Liberation Movement;

member of the Committee to Organize an Independent Political Party (Mexican Workers Party), 1973-74. f-Employee, state government of Yucatán, 1917-18; agronomist, Local Agrarian Commission, Guerrero, 1921-22; ejido organizer, Local Agrarian Commission, State of Veracruz, 1924-25; attaché, Mexican embassy, Washington, D.C., 1925-28; Director of Agricultural Publicity, Secretariat of Agriculture, 1928; Director, Department of Agricultural Instruction and Rural Normal Schools, Secretariat of Public Education, 1932-33; Director General of the National Finance Bank, 1934-35; Director General of the National Agricultural Credit Bank, 1935-40. g-None. h-Employee, Mexican Gulf Oil, Tampico Tamaulipas, 1918-21; member, Permanent Agricultural Committee, International Labor Office, 1938-49; Director, Latin American Department, UNESCO, 1950-51; Director, Center for Agricultural Research, 1954; Director, Institute of Mexican-Russian Intercultural Exchange, 1956-66. i-Son of Nicolás Mesa, judge of the Superior Tribunal of Justice of Guerrero, 1896-1911, and Aurelia Andraca; secretary to *Lázaro Cárdenas* in the 1960s. j-None. k-He and *Marte R. Gómez* were fired by President Obregón in 1924 for articles they authored. l-JSH, 248; Hayner, 211; Novo, 150; Gómez, 376-85.

Mier y Terán Ordiales, Carlos
a-July 26, 1946. b-Federal District. c-Early education unknown; civil engineering degree, National School of Engineering, UNAM, 1965-69; MA in Planning, National School of Engineering, UNAM, 1969-70; MA, London School of Economics, 1973-74; Ph.D. in regional economics, London School of Economics, 1975-76; courses at MIT, 1980. d-None. e-None. f-Analyst, Transportation Investment, Presidency of Mexico, 1971-74; department head,

Public Investment Division, Presidency of Mexico, 1975-76; Subdirector of Evaluation, Division of Programming and Budgeting, Secretariat of Housing and Public Works, 1976-78; Subdirector of Communication and Transportation, Division of Public Investment, 1978-79, Director of Budgeting, Communications, and Transportation, 1980-82, Director General of Programming and Budgeting, Basic Infrastructure, 1982-85, and Director General of Programming and Budgeting, Infrastructure, 1985-88, all at Secretariat of Programming and Budgeting; *Subsecretary of Communication and Technological Development*, Secretariat of Communications and Transportation, 1988-92; General Coordinator of Port Authorities, Secretariat of Communications and Transportation, 1992-94. g-None. h-None. i-Son of Carlos Mier y Terán Rivera, public accountant, and Gloria Ordiales; married Eva Patricia López Sánchez Mateos. j-None. k-None. l-DBGM89, 230; DBGM92, 238.

Mijares Palencia, José
(Deceased 1965) a-Mar. 1, 1895. b-Villahermosa, Tabasco. c-Primary studies at the Colegio Ayala and the Colegio San Bernardo, Puebla, 1902-07; secondary studies at the Colegio San Pedro and the Colegio San Pablo, and at the La Salle Christian School, Puebla, 1907-10; Cadet at the National Military College, Chapultepec, 1910-11; graduated, 1912, as a 2nd Lieutenant of Infantry; founder and Director of the Ignacio Zaragoza School, Puebla, Puebla, which later became a military academy. d-*Governor of Puebla*, 1933-37. e-Campaign manager for *General Almazán*'s presidential campaign, 1940. f-Chief of Mounted Police for the Federal District, 1929-31; Director General of Agricultural Education, Secretariat of Public Education, 1946-52. g-None. h-Director of a private

military academy, 1946; author of an organizational manual for the federal government, 1936, and other works. j-Joined the Revolution as a 2nd Lieutenant, 1912; rank of Captain, 1914; Brigadier General, 1927; Brigade General, 1931; Commander of the 17th Military Zone, Querétaro, Querétaro; Commander of the 27th Military Zone, Acapulco, Guerrero. k-Founder of the first private military academy in Mexico. l-D de Y, 8 Nov. 1935, 5 Sept. 1935, 1; DGF51, I, 290; DGF47, 172; EBW46, 1136; CyT, 444-45; Enc. Mex., IX, 1977, 68; NYT, 21 Aug. 1940, 8; Almanaque de Tabasco, 163.

Millán Brito, Juan
a-May 5, 1936. b-Taxco, Guerrero. c-Early education unknown; completed part of preparatory studies. d-*Plurinominal Federal Deputy* from PAN, 1982-85. e-Joined PAN, 1957; President of the Committee for Economic Activities of PAN, Taxco, 1980; candidate of PAN for the city council of Taxco; candidate of PAN for mayor of Taxco, 1980; President of PAN in Taxco, 1980. f-None. g-Member of various parents associations; adviser, Chamber of Commerce, Taxco; adviser, Taxco Red Cross. h-Businessman; owner of Millán Silver Store, 1962-80; owner of Bungalows Vista Alegre, 1978- . j-None. k-None. l-C de D, 1982-85; Directorio, 1982-85; Lehr, 639; DBGM, 557.

Minero Roque, José
a-1907. b-Nochistlán, Zacatecas. c-Primary studies in Nochistlán; secondary and preparatory studies in Guadalajara, Jalisco; attended the Conciliar Seminary, Zacatecas; scholarship seminary student in Rome (two years); law degree. d-*Federal Deputy* from the State of Zacatecas, Dist. 3, 1949-50, member of the Library Committee; Local Deputy to the State Legislature of Zacatecas, 1946-47; *Governor of*

Zacatecas, 1950-56. e-None. f-Private Secretary to *Leobardo Reynoso,* Governor of Zacatecas, 1944-45; Oficial Mayor of Zacatecas, 1945-46; Secretary General of Government of Zacatecas, 1947-49. g-None. i-Political protégé of Governor *Leobardo Reynoso.* j-None. k-None. l-HA, 26 Sept. 1955, 10; DGF56, 103; HA, 29 Sept. 1950, xxiv, 1949-51, 80; DGF51, I, 27, 93.

Miramontes (Briseño), Candelario
a-July 2, 1902. b-Tepic, Nayarit. c-Primary education in Tepic; no degree. d-*Federal Deputy* from the State of Nayarit, Dist. 1, 1940-43, member of the Balloting Committee, and the Third Ejido Committee; *Alternate Federal Deputy* from the State of Nayarit, Dist. 1, 1937-40; *Governor of Nayarit,* 1942-46; *Senator* from the State of Nayarit, 1946-52, substitute member of the Labor Committee (2nd). e-None. f-None. g-Member of the National Chamber of Commerce. h-Merchant, 1924-40. i-Son of Agapito Miramontes; from a humble family. j-None. k-None. l-Letter; EBW46, 204; DGF51, I, 14; C de D, 1937-39, 14, 1940-42, 14, 53.

Miranda Andrade, Otoniel
a-1915. b-Hacienda de Quetzalpa, Municipio de Jacala, Molango, Hidalgo. c-Early education unknown; medical degree; advanced studies at St. Agnes Hospital, Baltimore, Maryland. d-*Governor of Hidalgo,* Apr. 1 to Apr. 29, 1975. e-None. f-Head physician to *Manuel Sánchez Vite,* Governor of Hidalgo, 1969-70, 1972-75; Coordinator, Institutions for the Protection of Children, State of Hidalgo; Director, Civil Hospital, Pachuca, Hidalgo; Director, ISSSTE in Hidalgo; Director, Medical Services for the Public Health Department, Hidalgo, 1974. g-Secretary General of CNOP in Hidalgo. h-Practicing physician, 1975; physician, Nonalco Clinic, ISSSTE; physician,

Londrés Clinic, Mexico City; physician, 20th of Nov. Hospital, Mexico City; Director, Bank and Industrial Police Clinic, Mexico City. i-Born in the same year and in the same village as his mentor, *Manuel Sánchez Vite.* k-Served as a constitutionally elected governor for the shortest period of any Mexican governor since 1935; deposed by the Permanent Committee of Congress in what some political observers considered a move to further discredit his mentor, *Manuel Sánchez Vite.* l-*Excélsior,* 12 Oct. 1974, 1; HA, 21 Oct. 1974, 40; LA, 9 May 1975, 141; HA, 5 May 1975, 42; López Pérez, 284.

Miranda Fonseca, Donato
a-June 28, 1908. b-Chilapa, Guerrero. c-Primary studies in Chilapa; secondary studies at a normal school; law degree from the Escuela Libre de Derecho, Apr. 12, 1935, with a thesis on "Public Liberties and Article Three." d-Local deputy to the State Legislature of Guerrero; *Federal Deputy* from the State of Guerrero, Dist. 5, 1943-46; *Senator* from the State of Guerrero, 1946-52, member of the Gran Comisión, the Third Committee on National Defense, the Legislative Studies Committee, the First Balloting Committee, substitute member of the Second Public Education Committee, and the Special Forestry Committee; Mayor of Acapulco, Guerrero. e-Head of *Miguel Alemán's* campaign for president in the State of Guerrero, 1946. f-Judge of the Superior Tribunal of Justice of Guerrero, 1947; Representative to Petrópolis, Brazil; Representative to Caracas, Venezuela; member of the Mexican delegation to the Inter-American Assembly of Mutual Defense, 1947, with *José López Bermúdez;* Justice of the Superior Tribunal of Justice of the Federal District and Federal Territories; President of the Superior Tribunal of Justice of the Federal District and Federal

Territories, 1956-58; *Secretary of the Presidency*, 1958-64; Special Ambassador, Secretariat of Foreign Relations, 1965. g-Student leader and founder of the National Organization of Normal Students, 1927. h-Practicing lawyer, 1935. i-Married María Luisa Acosta; son of Donato Miranda Castro and Petra Fonseca. j-None. k-Precandidate for president of Mexico, 1964, reportedly *López Mateos'* first choice; participated in 1929 student strike with *López Mateos*; spoke at the PRI nominating assembly for *Miguel Alemán* in 1946; precandidate for governor of Guerrero, 1956. l-D del S, 20 Jan. 1946; *Excélsior*, 11 Aug. 1947; CB, 13 May 1965; *Excélsior*, 8 May 1972, b-2; *El Universal*, 2 Dec. 1958, 1; HA, 2 Dec. 1958, 32; DGF56, 513; Func.; NYT, 11 Aug. 1963, 34; HA, 10 June 1974, 13.

Miravete, Manuel E.
(Deceased) a-1894. b-San Andrés Tuxtla, Veracruz. c-Primary studies at the Escuela Cantonal, San Andrés, Tuxtla; no degree. d-Local Deputy to the 23rd Legislature of the State of Veracruz; Federal Deputy from the State of Veracruz, 1920-22, 1922-24, 1930-32; *Federal Deputy* from the State of Veracruz, Dist. 1, 1937-40. e-Director of various gubernatorial campaigns in the State of Veracruz. h-None. j-Private secretary to various revolutionary leaders. k-None. l-Peral, 535; C de D, 1937-39, 15.

Moctezuma, Fernando
(Deceased) a-1895. b-Ciudad del Maíz, San Luis Potosí. c-Early education unknown; law degree, 1920; Professor of Law, School of Law, University of San Luis Potosí, 1922-25. d-Federal Deputy from the State of San Luis Potosí, Dist. 8, 1926-28, 1928-30, Dist. 4, 1930-32, Dist. 5, 1932-34; *Federal Deputy* from the State of San Luis Potosí, Dist. 4, 1943-46; *Senator* from the State of San

Luis Potosí, 1946-52, member of the Gran Comisión, the Legislative Studies Committee, the Second Government Committee, and the Tax Committee. e-Secretary General of the PNR, 1931-34. f-Legal adviser, Secretary of Public Health, 1952-58. g-None. h-Practicing lawyer, 1920-26. i-Brother of *Mariano Moctezuma*, subsecretary of industry and commerce, 1936-38; early political mentor of *Antonio Rocha*, who was his alternate as senator; his sister-in-law was the sister of *Juan Barragán*; great-uncle of *Pedro Moctezuma Díaz Infante*. k-None. l-López, 713; DGF51, I, 7-12; DGF56, 331; C de S, 1946-52; C de D, 1943-46, 1926-28, 1928-30, 1930-32, 1932-34.

Moctezuma, Mariano
(Deceased July 28, 1942) a-Feb. 15, 1877. b-Ciudad del Maíz, San Luis Potosí. c-Engineering degree in geology, Aug. 23, 1905, School of Mines; professor at the National School of Engineering, UNAM, 1936-42; Director of the School of Engineering, UNAM, 1915-23, 1929-33, 1938-42; Director of the National Mining School. d-None. e-None. f-*Subsecretary of Industry and Commerce*, 1936-38; Subsecretary of Public Works, 1932-34, in charge of the Secretariat, Nov. 1934; *Subsecretary of Public Education*, 1934-36; Director of the National Observatory, Tacubaya, Federal District. g-None. h-None. i-Brother, *Fernando*, served as a senator from San Luis Potosí, 1946-52; brother-in-law of General *Juan Barragán*; married Rosa Barragán; grandfather of *Pedro Moctezuma Díaz Infante*, subsecretary of government properties, 1970-76; great-grandfather of *Esteban Moctezuma Barragán*, oficial mayor of public education, 1992. j-None. k-None. l-DP70, 1372; Peral, 537; HA, 7 Aug. 1942, 40; López, 714; DBGM, 286; DBGM92, 239.

Moctezuma Barragán, Esteban
a-Oct. 21, 1954. b-Federal District.
c-Primary studies, Instituto México,
Mexico City, 1961-67; secondary studies, Instituto México, 1967-70; preparatory studies, Centro Universitario de
México, 1970-73; economics degree,
National School of Economics, UNAM,
1973-77, with a thesis on planning in
Mexico; law degree, National School of
Law, UNAM, 1976-81; MA in political
economy, Cambridge University, 1977-
78, with a thesis on public enterprise
and subsidy policies in Mexico; course
in planning, Japan, 1981. d-None. e-Secretary of Finances, PRI, State of Sinaloa, 1986-87; joined *Ernesto Zedillo's*
presidential campaign staff, 1994.
f-Analyst, Secretariat of Programming
and Budgeting, 1973; Chief, International Affairs Department, Secretariat of
Programming and Budgeting, 1975-76;
Chief of the Department of Programming, Secretariat of Programming and
Budgeting, 1976; researcher, Presidency
of Mexico, 1979; Subdirector of State
Development Plans, Secretariat of
Programming and Budgeting, 1979-80;
Subdirector of Regional Policy Instru-
ments, Secretariat of Programming and
Budgeting, 1980-81; Private Secretary to
the Subsecretary of Housing and Public
Works, 1981; Private Secretary to the
Secretary of Energy, *Francisco
Labastida Ochoa*, 1982-86; Secretary of
Administration, State of Sinaloa, 1987-
88; *Oficial Mayor of Programming and
Budgeting*, 1988-92; *Oficial Mayor of
Public Education*, 1992-93; *Subsecre-
tary of Educational Coordination*,
Secretariat of Public Education, Jan. 7,
1993-94. g-None. h-None. i-Son of
Pedro Moctezuma Díaz Infante,
subsecretary of government properties,
1970-76, and Narua Teresa Barragán
Alvarez; married Cecilia Barbara Mor-
fin; grandson of general *Juan Barragán
Rodríguez*, president of PARM; great
nephew of *Fernando Moctezuma*,

secretary general of the PNR; great
grandson of *Mariano Moctezuma*,
subsecretary of industry and commerce;
brother Gonzalo was director general of
legal affairs, secretariat of health, 1989;
political disciple of *Ernesto Zedillo*.
j-None. k-None. l-Letter; DBGM92,
239-40; DBGM89, 232.

Moctezuma Cid, Julio Rodolfo
a-1927. b-Federal District. c-Early
education unknown; preparatory
studies, National Preparatory School;
law degree, National School of Law,
UNAM; Professor of Political Science,
School of Political and Social Science,
UNAM. d-None. e-*Director General of
the IEPES of the CEN of PRI*, Jan. 1975
to Sept. 1976. f-Private Secretary to
Raúl Ortiz Mena, Subsecretary of the
Presidency, 1959-61; Subdirector of
Planning, Secretariat of the Presidency,
1964-65; Director of Public Investments, Secretariat of the Presidency,
1965-70; adviser to the Secretariat of the
Presidency, the Treasury and to
CONASUPO, 1971-73; *Oficial Mayor of
the Treasury*, 1974-75; *Secretary of the
Treasury*, 1976-77; Coordinator of
Special Projects, President of Mexico,
1979-81; *Director General of PEMEX*,
1981-82; Director General of SOMEX,
1982-88. g-None. h-Practicing lawyer
with *Octavio Medellín Ostos*; Director
of the consulting firm Preinversión de
México, 1971-73. i-Friend of *José López
Portillo* since the 1950s; son of Alberto
Moctezuma, farmer, and Adela Cid;
married Blanca Rosa Franco; stepbrother
of *Guillermo Jiménez Morales*. j-None.
k-Fired by *López Portillo* because of his
inability to settle policy disagreements
with *Carlos Tello Macías*. l-DPE61,
124; *El Día*, 1 Dec. 1976; *Excélsior*, 17
Nov. 1977, 11; LA, Nov. 1977; *Excélsior*, 1 Dec. 1976; HA, 6 Dec. 1976, 22;
MGF69, 345; *Excélsior*, 7 June 1981, 1;
HA, 15 July 1981, 27.

Moctezuma Coronado, Javier
a-May 8, 1946. b-Federal District.
c-Early education unknown; public
accounting degree; professor, University
of Baja California. d-*Plurinominal
Federal Deputy* from PAN, 1982-85.
e-Joined PAN, 1972; Secretary of PAN,
Tijuana; Treasurer of PAN, Tijuana.
f-None. g-None. h-Accountant, Uva-
Casa Company. j-None. k-None. l-C
de D, 1982-85.

Moctezuma Díaz Infante, Pedro
a-Aug. 24, 1923. b-San Luis Potosí.
c-Architecture degree; National School
of Architecture, UNAM, 1950; Professor
of the Theory of Architecture, National
School of Architecture, UNAM, 1948-
59; Professor of Program Analyses,
Ibero-American University, 1957-58.
d-None. e-None. f-Engineer for the
Department of the Federal District;
Head of the Architecture Department,
Secretariat of Public Works; member of
the Commission for Colonial Monuments, National Institute of Anthropology and History; Head of the Department of Urbanism and Architecture,
Secretariat of Public Works, 1960-65;
worked with *Mario Moya Palencia*,
subsecretary of government, 1969-70;
*Subsecretary of Real Property and
Urbanism, Secretariat of Government
Properties*, 1970-76. g-None. h-Prac-
ticing civil engineer; built the central
office of PRI, Mexico City, 1968; constructed the Rectory of the University
of Tamaulipas, 1967, and many other
well-known public buildings. i-Son of
Beatriz Infante Torres and Pedro
Moctezuma Barragán; grandson of
Maríano Moctezuma, subsecretary of
industry and commerce, 1936-38, and
Rosa Barragán, sister of General *Juan
Barragán*; great-nephew of *Fernando
Moctezuma*, secretary general of the
PNR; son, *Esteban Moctezuma
Barragán*, was subsecretary of educa-
tion, 1993. j-None. k-None. l-HA, 4

Oct. 1971, 9; HA, 14 Dec. 1970, 21;
DPE71, 44; Enc. Mex., IX, 1977, 108-09;
DBGM89, 231-32.

Moguel Cal y Mayor, José
a-July 22, 1919. b-Cintalapa, Chiapas.
c-Early education unknown; graduated
as a 2nd Lieutenant in the artillery,
Heroic Military College, 1936-39; staff
and command diploma, Higher War
College, 1947-50. d-None. e-None.
f-*Oficial Mayor of the Secretariat of
National Defense*, 1980-83. g-None.
h-None. i-Cousin of Octavio Cal y
Mayor Sauz, federal deputy from
Chiapas, 1970-73; nephew of General
Rafael Cal y Mayor; great-nephew of
General Benigno Cal y Mayor, senator,
1928-32; son of Alfonso Moguel Cal y
Mayor, career military, and María Cal y
Mayor Moguel. j-Career army officer;
joined the army as a 2nd Sergeant, 1934;
served in the 2nd Artillery Regiment,
Guadalajara, Jalisco, 1939-40; served in
1st Artillery Regiment, 1940-41;
attached to the Technical Military
Division, Secretariat of National
Defense, 1941-42; member of the
Presidential Staff, 1942; officer, 4th 105
Mortars, Sappers Regiment, 1942-45;
attached to the Chief of Staff, Secretariat of National Defense, 1946; served
in the 4th Artillery Regiment, 1946-47;
attached to the 14th Military Zone,
Aguascalientes, 1950-52; attached to the
23rd Military Zone, Tlaxcala, 1952-53;
attached to the 13th Military Zone,
Tepic, Nayarit, 1953; rank of Colonel,
1960; Chief of Staff, 26th Military Zone,
1961; rank of Brigadier General, 1968;
Commander of the Army Garrison,
Ciudad Acuña, Coahuila, 1973-76; rank
of Division General, 1977; Commander
of the 3rd Military Zone, 1977-78; Director General of Artillery, Secretariat
of National Defense, 1978-79; Director
General of Personnel, Secretariat of
National Defense, 1979-80; Director of
the Social Security Institute of the

Armed Forces, 1983-88. k-None. l-Rev. de Ejer., Nov. 1968, 55, Nov. 1972, 49; Q es QAP, 79-80; Rev. de Ejer., Oct. 1960, 17, Nov. 1970, 70; DBGM87, 255.

Moguel Contreras, Idolina
a-Aug. 6, 1932. b-Oaxaca, Oaxaca. c-Early education unknown; degree in primary education, Higher Normal School, Mexico City, 1951, with a thesis on "Modern Theories of Learning"; MA in Spanish language and literature; Higher Normal School, 1948-51; Ph.D. in education, Higher Normal School, 1970-72; Ph.D. in linguistics, Colegio de México, 1977-79; various postgraduate courses; teacher, normal and private preparatory schools, 1955-71, Mexico City; professor, Higher Normal School, Mexico City, 1969-72. d-*Senator* from the State of Oaxaca, 1988-94. e-None. f-Subdirector, Secondary Day School, Federal District, 1965-70; Chief, Spanish Teaching Department, Division of Middle Education, Secretariat of Public Education, 1972; Secretary General of the National Technical Council of Education, 1971-76; Director General of Education and Professional Development, Secretariat of Public Education, 1977-79; Director General of Cultural and Self-teaching Materials, Secretariat of Public Education, 1979-82; *Subsecretary of Elementary Education*, 1982-88. g-None. h-None. i-Daughter of Arturo Moguel Camacho, military physician, and Bertha Contreras Sánchez; married Jesús Manuel Esparza Villarreal, military physician. j-None. k-None. l-HA, 20 Dec. 1982, 12; Q es QAP, 298; DBGM87, 255; DBGM89, 497; DBGM92, 519.

Moguel Esponda, Arturo
(Deceased July 14, 1980) a-1915. b-Cintalapa, Chiapas. c-Primary and secondary studies in Cintalapa; preparatory studies from the National Preparatory School; law degree, National

School of Law, UNAM, 1937. d-*Federal Deputy* from the State of Chiapas, Dist. 6, 1961-64, member of the Gran Comisión, Secretary of the Chamber; *Senator* from the State of Chiapas, 1964-70. e-None. f-Agent of the Ministerio Público, Federal District, 1938-42; Judge of the Superior Tribunal of Justice of the State of Chiapas, 1947-51; Private Secretary to *Rafael P. Gamboa*, Secretary of Health, 1952; adviser to the Secretariat of Agrarian Reform, 1980; Director, Advisory Board of the Secretariat of Agrarian Reform, Chiapas, 1980. g-None. i-Married Dora Díaz. j-None. k-None. l-C de S, 1964-70; MGF69; C de D, 1961-64; PS, 4086; *Excélsior*, 15 July 1980, 21; *Proceso*, 21 July 1980, 56.

Moheno Velasco, Rubén
a-May 14, 1910. b-Guadalajara, Jalisco. c-Primary studies at the Manuel M. Villaseñor School, Federal District; secondary and preparatory studies at public schools in the Federal District; studied law, National School of Law, UNAM (3 years); no degree. d-*Federal Deputy* from the State of Jalisco, Dist. 3, 1964-67, member of the Legislative Studies Committee (the Second Section on Civil Affairs), the First Railroads Committee, and the Electric Industry Committee; *Federal Deputy* from the State of Jalisco, Dist. 6, 1970-73, member of the Legislative Studies Committee (Nineteenth Section on General Means of Communication and Transportation, and the Second General Means of Communication Committee). e-Member of the National Committee of PRI; *Secretary of Political Action of the CEN of PRI*, 1965. f-Employee of the National Railroads of Mexico, 1925-73. g-Official of the Railroad Workers Union of the Federal District. h-None. i-Married Celia Verduzco. j-None. k-None. l-C de D, 1964-67, 52, 73, 87; C de D, 1970-73, 126; Directorio, 1970-72.

Molina Betancourt, Rafael
(Deceased Aug. 24, 1957) a-Nov. 16,
1901. b-Zacapoxtla, Puebla. c-Primary
studies at the public school in Zaca-
poxtla, 1913; secondary studies at the
Normal Institute of Puebla, 1918; teaching certificate from the Normal School
of Mexico City, June 1921; Professor of
Civics, Spanish, and World History.
d-*Federal Deputy* from the State of Puebla, Dist. 10, 1937-40. e-None. f-Director of Federal Schools, Chilpancingo,
Guerrero, 1928-33; Inspector General of
Federal Education, Celaya, Guanajuato,
1933-34; *Oficial Mayor of Public Education*, 1934-36; adviser to the Agricultural and Ejido Bank, 1936-37; Director
General of Population, Secretariat of
Government, 1941-47; Director General
of Primary Education, Secretariat of
Public Education, 1947-48; Director
General of Indigenous Affairs, 1948-50.
g-President of the Revolutionary
Fraternal Bloc; member of the SNTE,
1941-54; adviser to the National Union
of Technical Supervisors, 1952-54.
h-Author of various books on education;
Secretary General of the First Inter-
American Demographic Congress, 1946.
j-None. k-None. l-C de D, 1937-39;
DGF47, 171; DBP, 449-50; CyT, 449-50.

Molina Castillo, Eduardo José
a-Dec. 25, 1903. b-Mérida, Yucatán.
c-Primary studies in England and in
Europe; secondary studies in the United
States; no degree. d-*Federal Deputy*
from the State of Yucatán, Dist. 1, 1958-
61, member of the Second Section of the
Legislative Studies Committee, the
Textile Industry Committee, and the
Second Balloting Committee. e-President of the Regional Committee of PAN
for Yucatán; candidate for federal
deputy from PAN (twice). f-None.
g-None. h-Farmer; businessman;
Director of Cordeleros de México, S.A.,
1958. j-None. k-None. l-Func., 404; C
de D, 1958-60, 84.

Molinar (Simondy), Miguel
(Deceased Jan. 14, 1964) a-May 18,
1892. b-Chihuahua, Chihuahua.
c-Primary, secondary, and preparatory
studies at the Scientific and Literary
Institute of Chihuahua, Chihuahua; no
degree. d-None. e-None. f-*Oficial
Mayor of the Secretariat of Communications and Public Works*, 1941; Chief
of Police of the Federal District, 1952-
58; Director of Social Services of the
Army, 1959-64. g-None. i-Son of
Miguel Molinar and Carolina Simondy.
j-Career army officer; joined the
Revolution in the Huaxteco region,
1913; opposed the de la Huerta forces in
Morelia, Michoacán, 1924; rank of
Brigadier General, 1924; Commander of
the 13th Infantry Regiment; Com-
mander of the 16th Cavalry Regiment,
Los Tuxtlas, Veracruz; Commander of
the army garrison in Oaxaca, Oaxaca;
Veracruz, Veracruz; Celaya, Guana-
juato; and Saltillo, Coahuila; Chief of
Staff for the military zones of Mexico,
Guanajuato, Jalisco, Baja California del
Norte, Chihuahua, and Oaxaca; Chief of
Staff, 26th Military Zone, Veracruz,
1937; Zone Commander of Guadalajara,
San Luis Potosí, Veracruz and Queré-
taro; rank of Brigade General, Jan. 1,
1939; Zone Commander of Oaxaca,
Oaxaca, 1939-41; rank of Division
General, Mar. 1952. k-Saved General
Miguel Diéguez from being executed by
General Ramón B. Arnaíz. l-López, 717-
18; DP70, 1376; DGF61, 34; WWM45,
78; Almada, 1968, 341; Dávila, 182.

Mondragón (Guerra), Octavio S.
a-June 20, 1908. b-Querétaro, Querétaro. c-Primary studies in Querétaro;
secondary studies and preparatory
studies at the Colegio Civil, Querétaro,
1925; medical degree from the Military
Medical School, 1932; Director, Military Medical School, 1947-49. d-*Governor of Querétaro*, 1949-55. e-None.
f-*Oficial Mayor of the Department of*

Health, 1940-43, under *Fernández Manero*; *Oficial Mayor of the Secretariat of Health and Public Welfare*, 1943-45, under *Gustavo Baz*; personal physician to the President of Mexico, *Manuel Avila Camacho*, 1940-46; *Subsecretary of Health and Public Welfare*, 1946. g-None. h-None. i-Personal friend of *Andrés Serra Rojas*; married Alejandrina Gaytán; brother of *Salvador Mondragón Guerra*, justice of the Supreme Court, 1968-77; son of Antonio Mondragón Juárez and Josefina Guerra. j-Head of the Sanitary Division for the 34th Army Battalion, 1932-34; Director of the Infirmary, National Military College, 1934; Director of the Medical and Chemical Laboratory for the Army, 1935-39; attached to the Chief of Staff, Secretariat of National Defense, 1955. k-None. l-WWM45, 79; letter; DGF51, I, 91; HA, 29 Oct. 1943, 14; López, 718; WNM, 150.

Mondragón Guerra, Salvador
a-1905. b-Querétaro, Querétaro. c-Primary studies at the Luis Hernández and Benjamín Campa Schools, Querétaro; secondary and preparatory studies at the Colegio Civil of Querétaro; law degree, National School of Law, UNAM, Jan. 19, 1935; Professor by Competition of Mercantile Law (25 years), National School of Commerce and Administration; Professor of Mercantile Law, Ibero-American University, and University of Morelos. d-None. e-None. f-Secretary of Resolutions, Civil Division, Judge of the 1st Instance, Villa Obregón, Federal District; Auxiliary Secretary of the 5th Division, Superior Tribunal of Justice of the Federal District; Second Secretary of Resolutions, 4th Division, Superior Tribunal of Justice of the Federal District; First Secretary of Resolutions, 4th Division, Superior Tribunal of Justice of the Federal District; Judge of the 12th Civil District, Federal District; Judge of the Superior Tribunal of Justice

of the Federal District, 1943-56; President of the Superior Tribunal of Justice of the Federal District, 1945; Justice of the 1st Circuit Court of Appeals, Collegiate Tribunal of the Federal District, 1956; *Justice of the Supreme Court*, 1968-70, 1971-76; 1977. g-None. h-None. i-Classmate of *Antonio Luna Arroyo* at UNAM; brother of *Octavio S. Mondragón*, governor of Querétaro, 1949-55; son of Antonio Mondragón Juárez and Josefina Guerra. j-None. k-None. l-*Justicia*, Nov. 1968; letter.

Mondragón Hidalgo (Mora), Gustavo
a-Aug. 31, 1912. b-Federal District. c-Early education unknown; public accounting degree, National School of Business, 1933; professor at UNAM. d-None. e-None. f-Accountant and Internal Auditor, Federal Electric Commission, 1957-59; Controller, Federal Electric Commission, 1959-64; Manager of Finances, CONASUPO, 1965-69; *Substitute Director General of CONASUPO*, 1969-70; adviser, State of México, 1970-72; Director of the Cuatitlán-Izcalli Project, State of México, 1972-76; Comptroller General of the Department of the Federal District, 1976-79; *Secretary General "B"*, Department of the Federal District, May 30, 1979-82. g-President of the National College of Public Accountants. h-Auditor and accountant, private sector. i-Collaborator with *Carlos Hank González*, director general of CONASUPO, 1964-69, and governor of the State of México, 1970-74. j-None. k-None. l-*Hoy*, 19 Apr. 1969, 8; HA, 11 Sept. 1972, 54; DAPC, 1977, 48; Protag., 232; DAPC, 1981, 5.

Mondragón y Kalb, Manuel
a-Apr. 30, 1935. b-Federal District. c-Primary studies at the Instituto (Colegio) México, Mexico City, 1941-46; secondary studies at the Instituto

(Colegio) México, 1947-49; preparatory studies from the Centro Universitario México, 1950-51; medical degree, National School of Medicine, UNAM, 1952-57, with a thesis on pancreatic illnesses; MA in internal medicine and rheumatology, Hospital of Nutrition, 1958-59; many courses in public administration; professor, Juárez Hospital, Mexico City, 1968-73; professor, National School of Political Science, UNAM, Zaragoza campus, 1981. d-None. e-None. f-Chief of Rheumatology Service, Central Naval Hospital, 1965-71; Director of Medical Control, Subdirector General of Control, IMSS, 1971-74; Subdirector General of Operations, Subsecretariat of Environment, Secretariat of Public Health, 1974-76; Director General of Sports Development, Department of the Federal District, 1977-81; *Subsecretary of Sports*, Secretariat of Public Education, 1981-82. g-None. h-Interim Subdirector of the 20th of Nov. Hospital Center, 1963-64. i-Son of Manuel Mondragón Hidalgo, civil engineer, and Evelyn Kalb Rapport; married Martha Domínguez, businesswoman; nephew of *Gustavo Mondragón*, subsecretary of the Department of the Federal District, 1979-82; attended primary school with *Gustavo Reta Peterson*. j-None. k-None. l-Protag., 232; DAPC, 1981; DBGM87, 257-58; DBGM89, 235; DBGM92, 242.

Montaño Martínez, Jorge
a-Aug. 16, 1945. b-Federal District. c-Early education unknown; law degree, National School of Law, 1964-68, with a thesis on "International Law and the Vietnam War"; MA in politics and administration, London School of Economics, 1968-70, with a thesis on "Political Parties in Latin America"; Ph.D. in political sociology, London School of Economics, 1972-74; Secretary of the Graduate School of Political and

Social Science, UNAM, 1971-72; Head of the Department of Sociology, Autonomous Metropolitan University, Azcapotzalco campus, 1974-77; professor, School of Political and Social Sciences, UNAM, 1971; professor, Autonomous Metropolitan University, 1975; professor, Colegio de México, 1976. d-None. e-Joined PRI, 1971; adviser, Director General of the IEPES of the CEN of PRI, 1971-72, *Jorge de la Vega Domínguez*; Subsecretary of International Affairs of the CEN of PRI, 1981-82, 1987-88; adviser on international affairs to *Carlos Salinas* during his presidential campaign, 1988. f-Auxiliary Secretary to the Private Secretary of the President of Mexico, *Ignacio Ovalle Fernández*, 1970-71; Editorial Director, *El Trimestre Económico*, Fondo de Cultura Económica, 1975-76; Director of Higher Education Programs, Secretariat of Public Education, 1976-77; Subdirector General of the National Institute of Fine Arts, 1977-79; Director General of Specialized Organizations, United Nations, 1979-82; Director-in-Chief of Multilateral Affairs, Secretariat of Foreign Relations, 1982-87; *Ambassador to the United Nations*, 1989-92; *Ambassador to the United States*, 1992-94. g-None. h-None. i-Son of Jorge Montaño Quijas, merchant, and Paz Lucía Martínez Malpica; married Luz María Valdés, anthropologist. j-None. k-None. l-DBGM92, 244.

Montejo Sierra, José Manuel
a-June 7, 1920. b-Campeche, Campeche. c-Early education unknown; geographic engineering degree, Naval Military College, 1937-42; diploma, Inter-American Defense College, Washington, D.C., 1966; staff and command diploma, Center for Higher Naval Studies, 1971; Chief, Nautical Sciences Teaching Section, Naval Military College. d-None. e-None. f-*Subsecretary of the Navy*, 1976-82. g-None.

h-None. i-Son of Pedro Montejo Godoy, lawyer, and María Sierra de la Victoria; married Emma del Carmen Aguilar. j-Career naval officer; second-in-command and commander, many naval ships; Director General of Dredging, Secretariat of the Navy; Chief of Staff, 4th Naval Zone; Commander of the Naval Sector, Tuxpán, Veracruz; Chief of Section 1, Staff, Secretariat of the Navy; Director of Naval Education, Secretariat of the Navy, 1968-70; Commander of the 10th Naval Zone; Naval Attaché to Peru, with responsibility for Ecuador and Chile; Commander of the 4th Naval Zone; Subdirector General, Armed Forces Social Security Institute, 1982. k-None. l-Almanaque de México, 38; Protag., 233; DAPC, 77; DAPC, 81; DBGM, 289.

Montemayor (Seguy), Rogelio
a-Aug. 18, 1947. b-Federal District. c-Early education unknown; economics degree, Technological Institute of Higher Studies of Monterrey, 1965-69; psychology degree, Labastida University, Monterrey, Nuevo León, 1965-69; MA in administration, Technological Institute of Higher Studies of Monterrey, 1969-70; MA 1970-72, Ph.D., 1973-74, both in economics from University of Pennsylvania; professor, University of Pennsylvania, 1970-72; professor, Technological Institute of Higher Studies of Monterrey and the University of Nuevo León, 1974-76. d-*Federal Deputy* from the State of Coahuila, Dist. 4, 1988-91; *Senator* from the State of Coahuila, 1991-93; *Governor of Coahuila*, 1993- . e-Joined PRI, 1965. f-Subdirector of Macroeconomic Analysis, Monetary Affairs Division, Secretariat of the Treasury, 1977-78; Director of Economic Studies, Division of Planning, Secretariat of the Treasury, 1978-79; Subdirector General of Social and Economic Policy, 1979-80, Director General of Economic and Social Policy,

1981-82, and *Subsecretary of Programming*, 1982-85, all at Secretariat of Programming and Budgeting,; President of the National Institute of Statistics, Geography, and Information, Secretatiat of Programming and Budgeting, 1985-88. g-None. h-None. i-Son of Edilberto Edmundo Montemayor Galindo, businessman, and Lily Seguy Hernández; married Lucrecia Solano Martino; attended college with *Donaldo Colosio*; worked with *Carlos Salinas*, 1981-88. j-None. k-None. l-Q es QAP, 131; DBGM89, 499; *Proceso*, 22 Feb. 1993, 28-29.

Montes Alanís, Federico
(Deceased Dec. 1, 1950) a-Oct. 2, 1884. b-San Miguel de Allende, Guanajuato. c-Primary and preparatory studies in Querétaro, Querétaro; enrolled in the Military School, Jan. 3, 1905, graduated as a 2nd Lieutenant of artillery, Aug. 1, 1906. d-Federal Deputy from the State of Guanajuato, Dist. 14, 1917-18, 1918-20; Governor of Querétaro, 1919-20; Federal Deputy from the State of Guanajuato, Dist. 4, 1932-34. e-None. f-Chief of Police of the Federal District, May 1, 1938, to Aug. 15, 1939; *Oficial Mayor of the Secretariat of National Defense*, Nov. 1 to 30, 1940; Ambassador to Colombia, 1941-42; Ambassador to Cuba; Commander of the Legion of Honor, 1950. g-None. h-None. j-Career army officer; rank of 1st Lieutenant of Artillery, Mar. 18, 1909; rank of 2nd Captain, Sept. 12, 1911; member of the presidential staff, 1911; fought the Carrancistas under General Guillermo Rubio Navarrete in Candela, Coahuila, 1913; rank of 1st Captain, July 10, 1913; joined the Constitutionalists, Dec. 23, 1913; commander of a machine gun regiment, Northeast Division, 1914; rank of Colonel, Aug. 2, 1914; represented at the Convention of Aguascalientes by Major José Siurob, 1914-15; Commander of the 24th

Brigade of the Army of the Northeast, 1914-17; rank of Brigadier General, Dec. 1, 1914; rank of Brigade General, Nov. 25, 1916; reintegrated into the army, 1934; commander of various military zones, 1934-38; zone commander of the 31st Military Zone, Chiapas, 1935; rank of Division General, 1940; retired from active duty, 1950. k-As an aide to Madero, defended him by killing several officers when troops came to seize the president, 1913; imprisoned, 1913; accompanied Carranza to Tlaxcalantongo, 1920; imprisoned in Mexico City and accused of complicity in Carranza's murder, 1920-23. l-Enc. Mex., Annual, 1977, 580-81; López Escalera, 726.

Montes de Oca, Luis
(Deceased Dec. 4, 1958) a-1894. b-Federal District. c-Accounting degree; CPA; Superior School of Business, Administration, and Consular Affairs, Mexico City; Professor of Public Accounting, School of Business, UNAM, 1916-21. d-None. e-Campaigned for *General Almazán*, 1940. f-Consul General to El Paso, Texas; Hamburg, Germany; Paris; 1914-20; Comptroller General of Mexico, 1924-27; Secretary of the Treasury, 1927-32; *Director General of the Bank of Mexico*, 1935-40; presidential adviser to the National Banking Council. g-None. f-First employment as a public accountant for the federal government; financial agent to the United States for Carranza; author of the important 1931 monetary reform; founder and President of the International Bank of Mexico, 1958; founder with *Eduardo Suárez* of the National Bank of Foreign Commerce. j-Served in civilian posts as a consul during the Revolution. k-Opposed General Huerta as a student; initiated the use of CPAs in the comptroller's office; resigned from the directorship of the Bank of Mexico to support *General Almazán*, Sept. 7, 1940. l-HA, 15 Dec.

1958, 10; Kirk, 19, 39; Peral, 545; DP70, 1398; DP64, 964; WWM45, 80; DBM68, 545; Enc. Mex., IX, 1977, 171; NYT, 8 Sept. 1940, 28; Enc. Mex., IX, 1977, 171.

Montes (García), Antonio
a-Jan. 17, 1910. b-El Moral, Puebla. c-Early education unknown; no degree. d-Local Deputy to the State Legislature of Puebla; Federal Deputy from the State of Puebla, 1930-32; *Federal Deputy* from the State of Puebla, Dist. 3, 1952-55, member of the Fourth Ejido Committee; *Federal Deputy* from the State of Puebla, Dist. 3, 1976-79, member of the Ejido and Communal Organization Section of the Agrarian Affairs Committee, the Library Committee, and the Río Balsas Section of the Regional Development Committee. e-Joined the PNR, 1929; Secretary General of the Agrarian Party of Puebla, 1928. f-None. g-Secretary of Organization of the League of Agrarian Communities of the State of Puebla; Secretary General of the League of Agrarian Communities and Agrarian Unions of the State of Puebla, 1975. i-Married María Josefina Lezama. j-None. k-*Excélsior* considers him a peasant cacique in Puebla since the 1930s. l-*Excélsior*, 16 July 1978, 22; C de D, 1952-55, 51; D de C, 1976-79, 6, 9, 36; *Excélsior*, 21 Aug. 1976, 1C; C de D, 1976, 51.

Mora Aguilar, Manuel
c-Early education unknown; degree from the School of Political and Social Sciences, UNAM; professor. d-None. e-Member, Marxist Workers League, 1960; cofounder, Communist International Group, 1968; member of the Executive Committee, 4th International; Director, *Bandera Roja*, International Communist League; founder of the Revolutionary Workers Party, 1976; member of the Central Committee and the Political Bureau, Revolutionary Workers Party, 1981; Secretary General,

Revolutionary Workers Party, 4th International, 1981. f-None. g-Student leader of the Marxist Workers League. h-Writer for *Siempre*, *El Militante*, and *La Internacional*. j-None. k-Bombed the Bolivian Embassy with Salvador Lozano Pérez in retaliation for the death of Ché Guevara; participated in dynamiting the statue of Miguel Alemán at UNAM, 1966; jailed for conspiracy, 1976. l-Letter; 15 May 1981.

Mora (Martínez), Manuel R.
a-June 1, 1917. b-Villahermosa, Tabasco. c-Early education unknown; law degree. d-Member of the City Council of Villahermosa, 1944; Local Deputy to the State Legislature of Tabasco, 1944-46; *Federal Deputy* from the State of Tabasco, Dist. 1, 1961-64, member of the Gran Comisión; *Governor of Tabasco*, 1965-71. e-General delegate of the CEN of PRI. f-Private Secretary to the Governor of Tabasco, *Carlos Madrazo*, 1959-61. h-Poet. i-Mentor of *David Gustavo Gutiérrez Ruiz*; son of Manuel Mora Ascanio and Elena Martínez Godoy; great-grandson of Rafael Godoy Echegaray, senator, 1875-77, 1880-84; friend of *Rodulfo Brito Foucher*; opposed Garrido Canabal in Tabasco. j-None. k-None. l-Bulnes; Kishner; Almanaque de Tabasco, 155.

Mora Plancarte, Francisco
a-Mar. 21, 1907. b-Patzcuaro, Michoacán. c-Secondary studies at the Tridentine Seminary, Morelia; law degree, University of Michoacán, 1928. d-*Federal Deputy* from the State of Tlaxcala, Dist. 1, 1937-40, member of the Gran Comisión; *Federal Deputy* from the State of Michoacán, Dist. 2, 1946-49, member of the Gran Comisión. e-None. f-Secretary of the First Judicial District, Morelia; Judge of the First Judicial District, Morelia; Judge of the Superior Tribunal of Justice of Michoacán; agent of the Ministerio

Público, Puebla; Director of the National Lands Department, Secretariat of Agriculture; Counselor, Mexican Embassy, Havana, Cuba, 1942; Ambassador to El Salvador, 1942-43. g-None. i-Son of Ignacio Mora Plancarte, physician, and Carlota Pérez Girón; brother of *Norberto Mora Plancarte*, senator from Michoacán, 1970-76; longtime supporter of *Lázaro Cárdenas*; nephew of the bishop of Cuernavaca, Francisco Plancarte y Narvarette. j-None. k-None. l-C de D, 1947-40, 1946-49; letter.

Mora Plancarte, Norberto
a-May 23, 1923. b-Morelia, Michoacán. c-Primary studies at a public school, Morelia; secondary studies at Secondary School No. 8, Mexico City; preparatory studies at the National Preparatory School; law degree, National School of Law, UNAM, 1943-48; professor, UNAM, 1967-80. d-*Alternate Federal Deputy* from the Federal District, Dist. 14, 1961-63; *Federal Deputy* from the State of Michoacán, Dist. 7, 1967-70, member of the Gran Comisión, member of the Tariff Committee, the Forest Affairs Committee, the Administrative Section of the Legislative Studies Committee, and the Complaints Committee; *Senator* from the State of Michoacán, 1970-76, President of the Rules Committee, First Secretary of the Agricultural Development Committee, Second Secretary of the Indigenous Affairs and the Third National Defense Committees, and member of the Fishing Committee; *Federal Deputy* from the State of Michoacán, Dist. 3, 1976-79; *Senator* from the State of Michoacán, 1982-88, President of the Rules Committee. e-President of the Regional Committee of PRI, State of Michoacán. f-Administrative official of the Chamber of Deputies, 1937-64; Oficial Mayor of the Chamber of Deputies, 1964-67. g-Secretary of Pensions and Retirement, CEN of Library

Workers of the Chamber of Deputies; Secretary of Pensions and Retirement, CEN of the FSTSE, 1959-61; Secretary General of the Union of Employees of the Chamber of Deputies and the Senate; delegate of the FSTSE to the State of Michoacán; Secretary of Social Welfare of the CEN of the FSTSE, 1961-65; Secretary of Legislative Proposals of the CEN of CNOP, 1974. i-Son of Ignacio Mora Plancarte, physician, and Carlota Pérez Girón; brother, *Francisco Mora Plancarte*, was a federal deputy from Michoacán, 1946-49; married Dulce Aldaco Venegas. j-None. k-Precandidate for governor of Michoacán, 1974; precandidate for senator from Michoacán, 1981. l-C de D, 1967-70, 56, 58, 69, 85; DBM68, 444; *Excélsior*, 16 Sept. 1974; C de S, 1970-76, 80; C de D, 1976-79; *Excélsior*, 26 Dec. 1981, 16; Sirvent, 178; Lehr, 297; DBGM, 560.

Mora Ramos, Daniel
a-Aug. 4, 1908. b-Tanhuato, Michoacán. c-Primary studies at the Centro Escolar José María Morelos, Tanhuato, Michoacán (six years); secondary at the Urban Normal School of Morelia, Michoacán (three years); teaching certificate from the Urban Normal School of Morelia; advanced studies in language and literature from the Higher Normal School; Professor of the Science of Education, Oral Intensive Center No. 15 of the Federal Institute for Teacher Education. d-*Federal Deputy* from the State of Michoacán, Dist. 4, 1952-55, member of the Protocol Committee, the Editorial Committee (2nd and 3rd years), the First Public Education Committee and the First Balloting Committee; *Federal Deputy* from the State of Michoacán, Dist. 4, 1970-73, member of the Waters and Irrigation Committee, the Library Committee (1st year) and the First Public Education Committee. e-President of the State Committee of PRI for Michoacán;

Secretary of Social Action of PRI for Michoacán, 1970. f-Federal School Inspector for the Morelia, Michoacán, region; Director of Federal and State Education in Michoacán. g-Member of the SNTE. h-None. i-Cousin of *Luis Mora Tovar*; son of Lorenzo Mora Campos and Petra Ramos Vázquez; married Concepción Baca Barragán. j-None. k-None. l-C de D, 1970-72, 126; Directorio, 1970-72; C de D, 1952-54, 47, 49, 50, 57.

Mora Tovar, Luis
(Deceased Dec. 27, 1943) a-Aug. 25, 1895. b-Tanhuato, Michoacán. c-Primary and secondary studies at the Seminario Conciliar, Morelia, Michoacán, law degree. d-Local Deputy to the State of Michoacán; Federal Deputy from the State of Michoacán, 1934-36, head of the leftist bloc, President of the Chamber, 1935; *Senator* from the State of Michoacán, 1937-40. e-Founding member of the Michoacán Socialist Party, 1917. f-Secretary of the Agrarian Commission for the State of Michoacán; President of the Conciliation and Arbitration Board of the State of Michoacán. g-Cofounder of the League of Agrarian Communities in Michoacán; co-founder of the Revolutionary Federation of Labor of Michoacán. h-Poet; founder of *La Lucha*, Morelia, 1928. i-Cousin of *Daniel Mora Ramos*. j-Joined the Revolution. k-Jailed for political ideas. l-DP70, 1404; Peral, 548; Novo35, 29; Enc. Mex., IX, 1977, 360.

Morales Blumenkron, Guillermo
(Deceased Aug. 24, 1979) a-Apr. 27, 1908. b-Puebla, Puebla. c-Primary studies at the Escuela Pías and La Nueva Escuela, Puebla; secondary studies at the Colegio Inglés y Francés de San Borja; studies as a bookkeeper, Peralta and Berlitz Academies, Mexico City. d-*Federal Deputy* from the State of Puebla, Dist. 10, 1964-67; member of

the Television Industries Committee and the Cinematographic Industries Committee; *Senator* from the State of Puebla, 1970-73, 1974-76, President of the Second Committee on Credit, Money and Institutions of Credit, First Secretary of the National Property and Resources Committee and the Tax Committee. e-Joined PNR, 1932; national coordinator for radio during the *Díaz Ordaz* presidential campaign, 1964; Head of the official PNR radio station, XEFO, 1934-36; Secretary of Relations for CNOP, 1967. f-Covered the Presidential campaign for XEFO, 1933-34; covered the inauguration of President *Cárdenas*, 1934; originated the National Hour radio program for the federal government; *Provisional Governor of Puebla*, May 9, 1973, to 1974. g-President of the National Chamber of Broadcasting Industries, 1968; President of the Association of Mexican Publicity Agencies, 1952-54, 1957-59. h-Head of the Accounting Department, Bank of Monterrey, Puebla branch, 1923; involved in the private antique and furniture business, Mexico City, 1924-26; correspondent for Mexican newspapers in Havana, Cuba, 1927; began publishing the magazine *Reembolso*, 1927; publisher of *Variedades*, 1929; joined radio station XEW, 1938-49; owner of various Mexican radio stations, including XEQK and XEDA; founder and Director of the Morkron Publicity Agency, S.A., 1949-72; President of the Board of Cine Mundial, 1979. i-Married Josefina Montesinos; son of Ignacio Morales y Conde and María Blumenkron. j-None. k-None. l-DBM68, 440-42; C de S, 1970-76, 80; C de D, 196-66, 52, 85, 87, 88; HA, 21 May 1973, 25; *Excélsior*, 26 Dec. 1974, 12; WNM, 153.

Morales Espinosa, Eloy
a-Sept. 19, 1917. b-Ocozocoautla de Espinosa, Chiapas. c-Primary studies at the Emilio Rabasa School, Ocozo-

coautla; secondary teaching certificate, Rural Normal School, Cerro Hueco, Tuxtla Gutiérrez, Chiapas; teacher, Rural Normal School, Cerro Hueco. d-Local Deputy to the State Legislature of Chiapas, 1964-67; Alternate Mayor of Villa Comaltitlán, Chiapas, 1949-50; *Federal Deputy* from the State of Chiapas, Dist. 4, 1970-73; *Federal Deputy* from the State of Chiapas, Dist. 9, 1982-85. e-Joined the PRM, 1944; Secretary of Agrarian Action of the Regional Committee of PRI, Chiapas, 1956-70; President of PRI, Ocozocoautla, Chiapas, 1948-50; Secretary General of PRI in Chiapas, 1977-78. f-None. g-Secretary General of the League of Agrarian Communities in the State of Chiapas, 1963-73; Oficial Mayor of the CNC of Chiapas, 1960-63; Alternate Secretary General of the CNC, 1967. h-Tax collector. i-Son of Plácido Morales and Lucina Espinosa. j-None. k-None. l-Directorio, 1982-85, 1970-72; C de D, 1970-73, 1982-85; Lehr, 93; DBGM, 561.

Morales Farías, Carolina
a-Jan. 28, 1917. b-Monterrey, Nuevo León. c-Primary studies in Monterrey; secondary studies and accounting courses, Colegio de la Paz, Monterrey; studies in social work in Puerto Rico; certified public accountant. d-*Alternate Federal Deputy* from the State of Nuevo León, Dist. 4, 1958-61; *Federal Deputy* from the State of Nuevo León, Dist. 5, 1970-73, member of the Artesans Committee, the Second Ejido Committee and the Desert Zones Committee. e-None. f-Social worker, Secretariat of Agriculture. g-Secretary of Women's Action of the CNC; Secretary of Women's Action of the League of Agrarian Communities of the State of Nuevo León. i-Widow. j-None. k-None. l-C de D, 1958-61, 1970-73, 126.

Morales Lechuga, Ignacio
a-Jan. 6, 1947. b-Poza Rica, Veracruz.
c-Early education unknown; law degree,
Escuela Libre de Derecho, 1965-69, with
a thesis on notarial functions; professor,
Anáhuac University, 1971-74; professor,
Escuela Libre de Derecho, 1976-80;
professor, ITESM, 1976-80. d-None.
e-Joined PRI, 1980. f-Subsecretary of
Government, State of Veracruz, 1980-
81; Secretary General of Government,
State of Veracruz, 1981-84; President of
the Federal Electoral Committee,
Veracruz, 1981-84; Coordinator of the
National Program of Public Safety,
Secretariat of Government, 1984-88;
*Attorney General of the Federal
District*, 1988-91; *Attorney General of
Mexico*, 1991-93. g-None. h-Lawyer,
Orozco Morales Firm, 1970-74; Public
Notary No. 116, Federal District, 1974-
80. i-Son of Ignacio Morales Ponce,
merchant, and Enedi Lechuga Ríos;
married Jacqueline Broc; member of
Manuel Camacho's political group.
j-None. k-None. l-DBGM87, 260;
DBGM92, 247; *El Financiero Inter-
national*, 24 June 1991.

Morales Orozco, Crescencio
a-Sept. 13, 1935. b-Chucándiro, Michoacán. c-Early education unknown; law
degree, University of Michoacán, 1960-
65; professor, School of Nursing, University of Michoacán. d-*Plurinominal
Federal Deputy* from the PPS, 1982-85,
member of the National Defense
Committee; *Plurinominal Federal
Deputy* from the PPS, 1988-91. e-Joined
the PPS, 1959; Secretary of the PPS,
State of Michoacán, 1966; Secretary of
PPS in Morelia, 1959-65; candidate of
the PPS for local deputy, State Legislature of Michoacán, 1977; candidate of
the PPS for mayor of Morelia, 1979;
candidate of the PPS for federal deputy
from the State of Michoacán, 1982;
member of the Central Committee of
the PPS, 1975-90. f-Director, Legal

Department, Division of Education,
Secretariat of the Navy, 1972-75.
g-Secretary General of the National
Alliance of Workers in Michoacán,
1976. h-Practicing lawyer, 1965-70.
i-Son of Cresencio Morales Vallejo,
peasant, and Viviana Orozco Guzmán;
married María Guadalupe González
Botello. j-None. k-None. l-Directorio,
1982-85; Lehr, 654; DBGM89, 500.

Morales Ramos, Feliciano
a-July 12, 1916. b-Salinas, Coahuila.
c-Primary studies only; no degree.
d-Mayor of San Juan de Salinas, Coahuila; *Federal Deputy* from the State of
Coahuila, Dist. 4, 1952-55, 1967-70.
e-None. f-None. g-Official of the
National Miners Union. j-None.
k-None. l-C de D, 1967-70, 1952-55.

Morales Salas, Adrián
a-July 1, 1896. b-San Miguel de Mesqui-
tal, Zacatecas. c-Primary and secondary
studies in public schools; no degree.
d-*Senator* from the State of Zacatecas,
1940-46, Second Secretary of the First
Tariff and Foreign Trade Committee,
member of the Gran Comisión.
e-None. f-None. g-None. h-None.
j-Joined the Revolution in support of
Madero, 1911; 2nd Lieutenant, 1911; 1st
Lieutenant, 1913; Major, 1915; career
army officer, reached the rank of
Colonel, 1926. k-None. l-C de S, 1940-
46; EBW46, 178; Libro de Oro, 1946, 9.

Morales Sánchez, Gregorio
a-May 26, 1885. b-Salinas Victoria,
Nuevo León. c-Early education unknown; teaching certificate; teacher.
d-Federal Deputy from the State of
Nuevo León, Dist. 1, 1918-20, member
of the Gran Comisión. e-None. f-*Governor of Nuevo León*, 1935-36. g-None.
j-Participated in the Revolution;
supported General Pablo González,
1920; Commander of the 52nd Battalion
against General Escobar, 1929; rank of

Brigade General, Nov. 1, 1940. k-None. l-Peral; C de D, 1918-20.

Moreno Flores, Fausta
a-April 15, 1932. b-Puebla, Puebla. c-Early education unknown; law degree, National School of Law, UNAM, 1952-56. d-None. e-None. f-Lawyer, Secretariat of the Treasury, 1958-67; Secretary of Agreements, Federal Tax Court, 1967-69; Secretary of Studies and Accounts, Supreme Court of Justice, 1969-80; Judge, Third District Court in Administration, Federal District, 1978-82; *Justice of the Supreme Court*, 1983-88, 1988-94. g-None. h-None. i-Daughter of Eduardo Moreno del Callejo, chemical pharmacist, and Guadalupe Flores Limón; married Armando Corona Boza, lawyer. j-None. k-None. l-DBGM, 672; DBGM89, 628; DBGM92, 681.

Moreno Gómez, María Eugenia
a-Feb. 16, 1938. b-Federal District. c-Early education unknown; law degree, National School of Law, UNAM, 1955-60; diploma in political analysis, Ibero-American University, 1983. d-*Federal Deputy* from the Federal District, Dist. 25, 1979-82, President of the Social Security Committee. e-Joined PRI, 1968; adviser to the Secretary of Public Relations of the CEN of PRI, 1968; participated in the 1975-76 presidential campaign. f-Director of Social Welfare Services, IMSS, 1976-79; Delegate of the Department of the Federal District to Benito Juárez, 1982-88; Director of the Center of Higher Studies of Tourism, Secretariat of Tourism, 1989-94. g-President of the World Association of Women Journalists and Writers, 1973-78. h-Journalist; founder of the publishing firm Editorial Armonía, S.A., 1971; founder and Director of *Kena, La Mujer de Hoy*, and *Lupita*. i-Daughter of Eugenio Moreno Studelmann, public official, and Amparo Gómez Alcalde,

normal teacher. j-None. k-One of Mexico's leading feminists. l-Romero Aceves, 715-17; Protag., 238; C de D, 1979-82; DBGM92, 250.

Moreno Jiménez, Jesús
a-1913. b-Orizaba, Veracruz. c-Early education unknown; no degree. d-Local Deputy to the State Legislature of México; member of the City Council of Tlalnepantla, México; Mayor of Tlalnepantla, México; *Federal Deputy* from the State of México, Dist. 6, 1964-67, 1973-76. e-None. f-None. g-Secretary General of the Federation of Peasants of the State of México. j-None. k-None. l-C de D, 1964-67, 1973-76.

Moreno Mena, Margarita
a-June 16, 1943. b-Ciudad Juárez, Chihuahua. c-Primary studies at the Belisario Domínguez School, Chihuahua, and the Melchor Guaspe School, Chihuahua; secondary studies at the Secondary and Normal Night School, Chihuahua, 1956-63; studies at the Higher Normal School, Mexico City, 1966-68; studies in social studies, Porfirio Parra Higher Normal School, Mexico City, 1969-70; studies in psychology, Porfirio Parra Higher Normal School, Mexico City, 1971-73; rural school teacher, 1969-71; primary urban teacher, 1973-77; secondary vocational teacher, 1973-75; preparatory vocational teacher, 1975-77. d-*Federal Deputy* from the State of Chihuahua, Dist. 1, 1979-82. e-Secretary of Women's Action, PRI, City of Chihuahua; Secretary of Youth Action, PRI, City of Ciudad Juárez, 1958-60; Secretary of Organization of PRI, Granjas, Chihuahua, 1964-65; Secretary of Teacher Action, State Committee of the CNOP of PRI of Chihuahua. f-None. g-Secretary of Legislative Action, State Committee of ANFER; Secretary of Organization of the Coordinating Committee of the FSTSE; Secretary

General of Local 8, SNTE, 1976.
i-Daughter of Héctor Elpidio Moreno
and María del Refugio Mena. j-None.
k-None. l-Romero Aceves, 718-19.

Moreno (Moreno), Manuel M.
a-May 21, 1907. b-Guanajuato, Guana-
juato. c-Law degree, School of Law,
University of Guanajuato, 1931; MA in
history from UNAM, with a thesis on
"The Political and Social Organization
of the Aztecs"; Professor of Sociology
and History at the University of
Guanajuato. d-*Federal Deputy* from the
State of Guanajuato, Dist. 7, 1961-64;
President of the Legislative Studies
Committee; member of the Second
Constitutional Affairs Committee;
President of the Chamber of Deputies,
Oct. 1962; *Senator* from the State of
Guanajuato, 1964-67, President of the
Gran Comisión, 1965-67; *Governor of
Guanajuato*, 1967-73. e-President of
the Regional Committee of PRI for the
State of Guanajuato; Director of Legal
Affairs for PRI; head of the Consultative
Department, PRI, 1953; *Secretary of
Political Action of the CEN of PRI*,
1962-64; *Secretary General of the CEN
of PRI*, 1963-64. f-Director of Public
Education for the State of Guanajuato,
1934-35; Attorney General of the State
of Guanajuato, 1932-34; Secretary Gen-
eral of Government of the State of Guanajuato, 1935; Head of the Legal Office
for the Department of the Federal District, 1945; Director General of Labor,
Secretariat of Labor, 1953-58; Director
General of Professions, Secretariat of
Public Education, 1958-61; Head of the
Association Registration Department,
Secretariat of Labor, 1956-58. g-Leader
of the Student Union of Guanajuato,
1927. h-Worked as a porter and scribe
at the Superior Court of Justice of
Guanajuato as a student. i-Married
Carmen Contreras; son of Pablo Moreno
and Cresenia Moreno. j-None. k-None.
l-HA, Sept. 1971; C de D, 1961-63, 84;

DPE61, 101; C de S, 1964-70, 19;
DGF56, 398; DBM68, 445; HA, 9 Oct.
1972, 35; WNM, 153; *Excélsior*, 19 Oct.
1975, 1; Enc. Mex., IX, 1977, 257-58.

Moreno Rodríguez, Rodrigo
a-Sept. 7, 1947. b-León, Guanajuato.
c-Early education unknown; law degree,
School of Law, Ibero-American Univer-
sity, 1965-69; MA in law, UNAM, 1975;
LLD degree, National School of Law,
UNAM, with an honorable mention,
1975-76; courses in public administra-
tion, University of Manchester, 1974-
75; professor, Technological Institute,
León, Guanajuato, 1970-72; professor,
School of Political and Social Science,
UNAM, 1979- . d-*Alternate Federal
Deputy* from the State of Guanajuato,
Dist. 2, 1982-85. e-Joined PRI, 1967;
positions in the IEPES of PRI. f-Assi-
stant to the Director of Social Action,
Department of the Federal District,
1969; analyst, Division of Administra-
tive Studies, 1972-76, Subdirector of
Human Resources, 1976, Subdirector of
Legal Affairs, 1977, and Director
General of Administrative and Person-
nel Development, 1978-82, all at the
Secretariat of the Presidency; Delegate
of the Department of the Federal
District to Azcapotzalco, 1983-84;
*Secretary General of the Department of
the Federal District*, 1984-85. g-None.
h-Practicing lawyer, León, Guanajuato,
1970-72. i-Son of Rodrigo Moreno
Zermeño, lawyer, and Pura Rodríguez;
married Georgina González. j-None.
k-None. l-Q es QAP, 429; DBGM, 296;
HA, 5 Nov. 1985.

Moreno Sánchez, Manuel
Deceased a-July 11, 1908. b-Ranchería
Tierra Dura, Aguascalientes, Aguas-
calientes. c-Primary studies in Aguas-
calientes; preparatory studies at the
National Preparatory School, 1926; law
degree from the National School of Law,
UNAM, 1932, with a thesis on amparo;

Professor of International Public Law, UNAM, 1935-36; professor at the Institute of San Luis Potosí; professor at the University of Michoacán, 1933-34; Director of the School of Plastic Arts, UNAM, 1936; Secretary of the Institute of Aesthetic Investigations, UNAM, 1936-38. d-*Federal Deputy* from the State of Aguascalientes, 1943-46; *Senator* from the State of Aguascalientes, 1958-64, President of the Gran Comisión, President of the First Committee on Foreign Relations, President of the Committee on Foreign and Domestic Commerce, member of the First Committee on Tariffs and Foreign Trade, substitute member of the First Constitutional Affairs Committee. e-Orator for the 1940, 1946, and 1952 presidential campaigns; presidential candidate of the Social Democratic Party, 1982. f-Judge of the Superior Tribunal of Justice of the State of Michoacán, 1933-34; Judge of the Superior Tribunal of Justice of the Federal District, 1940-43; adviser to the state government of San Luis Potosí, 1939; Director, Legal Department, National Bank of Agricultural and Livestock Credit, 1946-52; Director of Traffic, Department of the Federal District, 1952. g-None. h-Author of many books and articles; practicing lawyer in the Federal District, 1943-58. i-Personal friend of *Adolfo López Mateos*; married Carmen Toscano; daughter Alejandra Moreno Toscano is married to Enrique Flores Cano and is secretary general of the Department of the Federal District, 1992; son Héctor Moreno Toscano, served as federal deputy from the State of México, 1979-82; daughter Carmen Moreno Toscano was ambassador to Costa Rica, 1992; practiced law with *Franco Carreño*; assistant to Professor Antonio Caso. j-None. k-Orator during the 1929 campaign with *Adolfo López Mateos*. l-C de S, 1961-64, 63; Brandenburg, 114;

Peral, 557; WWM45, 81; Enc. Mex., I, 104; C de D, 1943-45, 16; Func., 117; Gómez Maganda, 106; López, 741; HA, 1 Feb. 1952; Enc. Mex., IX, 1977, 261.

Moreno Torres, Manuel
(Deceased May 22, 1980) a-Feb. 22, 1912. b-Matehuala, San Luis Potosí. c-Primary and secondary studies in Matehuala; electrical engineering degree from the National Polytechnic Institute, 1935; studies in civil engineering, National School of Engineering, UNAM. d-*Federal Deputy* from the State of San Luis Potosí, Dist. 2, 1958-61, member of the Department of the Federal District Committee, the Fourth Section of the Legislative Studies Committee, the Electrical Industry Committee, the Public Works Committee, and the General Means of Communication Committee. e-None. f-Chief Engineer, construction of the Ferrocarril del Sureste Project, 1935-37; Director General of the Department of Public Works, Secretariat of Public Works, 1948-58; *Director General of the Federal Electric Commission*, 1958-64; Subdirector General of the Federal Electric Commission, 1976-80. g-Member of the Student Association of the National Polytechnic Institute. h-Many technical and administrative positions in public works. i-Married Cristina González; son of Anastasio Moreno Calvillo and Angela Torres. j-None. k-None. l-HA, 10 Dec. 1962, 3; DGF56, 467; C de D, 1958-60, 85; Func., 343; HA, 2 June 1980, 15; WNM, 153-54.

Moreno (Uriegas), María de los Angeles
a-Jan. 15, 1945. b-Federal District. c-Early education unknown; economics degree, National School of Economics, UNAM, 1962-66, with a thesis on "Women in the Mexican Economy," 1966; MA degree in socioeconomic planning, Institute for Social Studies, Netherlands University, Holland;

professor at UNAM, 1967-72. d-*Pluri-nominal Federal Deputy* from the PRI, 1991-94, and majority leader, 1993-94. e-Subdirector of Strategy and Development, IEPES of PRI, 1981-82. f-Economic analyst, Division of Muestreo, Secretariat of Industry and Commerce, 1964; sector census chief, Division of Statistics, Secretariat of Industry and Commerce, 1967-68; analyst, Department of Public Debt, Director General of Credit, Secretariat of the Treasury, 1969-72; office head, Director General of Credit, Secretariat of the Treasury, 1973-75; Subdirector of Studies on Income Distribution, Secretariat of Labor, 1975-76; Subdirector of Planning, Division of Employment, Secretariat of Labor, 1977-78; Subdirector of Planning, Division of Employment, UCECA, 1978-82; *Subsecretary of Evaluation,* Secretariat of Programming and Budgeting, 1983-88; *Secretary of Fisheries,* 1988-92. g-None. h-Economic consultant to Climas Perfectos, S.A., 1967-68. i-Daughter of Manuel Moreno Islas, surgeon, and Amalia Uriega Sánchez, surgeon. j-None. k-None. l-IEPES; Q es QAP, 133; DBGM, 297; DBGM87, 205; DBGM89, 243; DBGM92, 526.

Moreno Valle, Rafael
a-Aug. 23, 1917. b-Atlixco, Puebla. c-Primary studies in Atlixco; secondary and preparatory studies at the National Preparatory School; medical degree and military surgeon training from the Military Medical School, Dec. 9, 1940, graduating with the rank of Major; advanced studies, U.S. Department of Defense, 1941; Professor of Orthopedics at the National Medical School, UNAM (ten years); professor at the Military Medical School, 1944-64; studies in the United States. d-*Senator* from the State of Puebla, 1958-64, President of the Senate, member of the Gran Comisión, the Public Health Committee, the Second Foreign Relations Committee,

the Second National Defense Committee, substitute member of the Public Welfare Committee, President of the Military Health Committee; *Governor of Puebla,* 1969-72. e-*Secretary of Political Action of the CEN of PRI,* 1962-64. f-Head of Medical Services, Central Military Hospital, 1956; Director of the Central Military Hospital; *Secretary of Health and Public Welfare,* 1964-68. g-None. h-Founding member with *Salvador Aceves Parra* of the Mexican Orthopedic Society; president of many advisory health commissions. i-From a humble family background; son of Jesús Moreno and Engracia Valle de Moreno; brother, Jesús, served in the Revolution as a Lt. Colonel; supported *Emilio Martínez Manautou* for president, 1964. j-Career military medical officer; rank of Brigadier General, 1952. k-First graduate of the Military Medical School to become Secretary of Health; requested a leave of absence as governor of Puebla, Apr., 1972, and never returned to office. l-HA, 24 Apr. 1972, 53; *Libro de Oro,* xxxv; DPE65, 148; *El Universal,* 1 Dec. 1964; DBM70, 395-96; C de S, 1961-64, 64; HA, 7 Dec. 1964, 20; CyT, 475; *Excélsior,* 26 Dec. 1974, 12.

Morones Ochoa, Alejandro
a-Apr. 30, 1940. b-San Luis Potosí. c-Early education unknown; economics degree, University of San Luis Potosí, with a thesis on "The Copper Industry in Mexico"; course from the Pan American Institute of Higher Management. d-None. e-None. f-Economist, Department of Latin American Trade, Latin American Free Trade Section, Bank of Mexico, 1966-69; economist, Division of Economic Studies, Fund for the Promotion of Tourist Infrastructure, 1970-73; Finance Manager, National Tourism Fund, 1974-76; adviser to the Trust for the Liquidation of Auxiliary Organizations and Credit Institutions, 1978; *Subsecretary of Operations,*

Secretariat of Tourism, 1982-88. g-None. i-Son of Homero Morones Prieto, photographer, and Altagracia Ochoa Alemán; married Esperanza Tobías Hernández. j-None. k-None. l-Q es QAP, 396.

Morones Prieto, Ignacio
(Deceased Oct. 30, 1974) a-Mar. 2, 1900. b-Ciudad Linares, Nuevo León. c-Preparatory studies from the Colegio Civil of Monterrey and from the Scientific and Literary Institute of San Luis Potosí; medical degree from the University of San Luis Potosí, 1923; medical degree from the Sorbonne, 1923-28; Professor of External Pathology, University of San Luis Potosí, 1928-32; Professor of Clinical Surgery, University of San Luis Potosí, 1933-40; professor at the Scientific and Literary Institute of San Luis Potosí; professor at the Colegio Civil, Monterrey, Nuevo León; Dean of the School of Medicine, University of San Luis Potosí; Rector of the University of San Luis Potosí (6 years).
d-*Governor of Nuevo León*, 1949-52. e-None. f-*Oficial Mayor of the Secretariat of Health*, 1946; *Subsecretary of Health*, 1946-49; *Secretary of Health and Public Welfare*, 1952-58; *Ambassador to France*, 1961-65; *Director General of the Mexican Institute of Social Security*, 1966-70. g-None. h-Practiced medicine, 1928-45. i-Married Francisca Caballero; son of Ignacio Morones and Teresa Prieto; member of *Gonzalo N. Santos'* political group. j-None. k-Precandidate for president of Mexico, 1958. l-DPE65, 26; HA, 21 Sept. 1953, 7; *Libro de Oro*, xli; HA, 21 Sept. 1953; HA, 12 July 1954; WWMG, 27; HA, 5 Dec. 1962, 9; DGF56, 329, 331; DGF47, 197; DGF51, I, 91; G of NL, 15; DPE61, 22; López, 743; Enc. Mex., IX, 1977, 263; HA, 11 Nov. 1974, 11, WNM, 152; NYT, 28 July 1957, 2.

Mortera Prieto, Felipe L.
a-1911. b-Minatitlán, Veracruz. c-Primary studies in Minatitlán; completed part of secondary, Minatitlán; no degree. d-*Federal Deputy* from the State of Veracruz, Dist. 12, 1952-55, 1958-61. e-None. f-None. g-Many union posts; *Secretary General of the National Union of Petroleum Workers*, 1956-58. h-Began working in a refinery as a teenager. j-None. k-None. l-Func., 399; C de D, 1952-55, 1958-61.

Morúa Johnson, Mario
a-1922. b-Hermosillo, Sonora. c-Early education unknown; no degree. d-*Alternate Senator* from the State of Sonora, 1964-70, but in functions 1967-70 as a replacement for *Juan de Dios Bojórquez*. e-Director of Youth Action of the CEN of PRI, State of Sonora; representative of PRI in San Luis Río Colorado; campaigned for *Gustavo Díaz Ordaz* in Sonora, 1963-64. f-Commissioner, Sonoita, Sonora; Provisional Governor of Sonora, 1991. g-None. h-Businessman and cattle rancher. j-None. k-None. l-C de S, 1964-70.

Mota Sánchez, Ramón
a-Aug. 22, 1922. b-Federal District. c-Early education unknown; graduated as a 2nd Lieutenant of Artillery, Heroic Military College, July 1, 1941; diploma in staff and command, Higher War College, 1949-51; diploma in staff and command, U.S. Army, 1962-63; professor, Heroic Military College, 1946-49; Professor of Logistics and Strategy, Higher War College, 1951-65; professor, University of Nayarit, 1968-69. d-*Plurinominal Federal Deputy* from PRI, 1991-94. e-Joined PRI, 1952. f-Chief of Staff, Secretariat of National Defense, 1976-80; Director of Police and Traffic, Department of the Federal District, 1982-83; *Secretary of Protection and Traffic Routes*, Department of the Federal District, 1984-86. g-None.

h-None. i-Son of Julio Mota Ponce, career military, and Eloísa Sánchez López; married Mauría Magdalena Aguilar Palomino. j-Career army officer; Commander of Cadet Battery, Heroic Military College, 1946-47; rank of Colonel, 1967; Commander of the 1st Artillery Regiment; rank of Brigadier General, 1972; Commander of the Presidential Guards; Commander of the 21st Military Zone, Morelia, Michoacán; rank of Brigade General, 1976; Commander of the 25th Military Zone, Puebla, Puebla; Commander of the 31st Military Zone, Tuxtla Gutiérrez, Chiapas; Commander of the 15th Military Zone, Guadalajara, Jalisco, 1978-80. k-None. l-Rev. de Ejer., Nov. 1976, 67; Q es QAP, 444; Rev. de Ejer., Dec. 1967, 49, Nov. 1972, 50; DBGM, 298; DBGM92, 528.

Moya Palencia, Mario
a-1933. b-Federal District. c-Law studies at the National School of Law, UNAM, 1950-54, degree in 1955; graduate studies in Mexican history at the School of Philosophy and Liberal Arts, UNAM; Professor of Constitutional Law at the National School of Political Studies, Acatlán campus, UNAM, 1976-. d-None. e-Joined *Luis Donaldo Colosio's* presidential campaign staff, 1993–94. f-Assistant in the Office of Public Relations, National Railroads of Mexico, 1955-58; Subdirector of the Public Domain in the Division of Real Property, Secretariat of National Patrimony, 1959-61; Director General of the Bureau of Cinematography, Secretariat of Government, 1964-68; *Subsecretary of Government*, 1969-70, under *Luis Echeverría*; *Secretary of Government*, 1970-76; *Ambassador to the United Nations*, 1985-89; Ambassador to Japan, 1989-90; *Ambassador to Cuba*, 1990-93. g-President of the Platform of Mexican Professions, 1961-65. h-Cofounder of the magazine *Voz*

with Jorge Villa Treviño; editor, 1950-53; editor of *Ferronales*, 1954-57; wrote for *Novedades*, 1957-59. i-Student of *Alfonso Noriega* at UNAM; knew *Jorge de la Vega Domínguez* at UNAM; member of the student generation that included *Pedro Ojeda Paullada* and *Pedro Zorrilla*; married Marcela Ibáñez, lawyer; son of Mario Moya and Concepción Palencia. j-None. k-Precandidate for president of Mexico, 1976; precandidate for senator from the Federal District, 1981. l-HA, 7 Dec. 1970, 23; DPE65, 14; DPE61, 60; HA, 14 Aug. 1972, 12, 15 Jan. 1973, 10, 17 Oct. 1977, 12-13; Enc. Mex., IX, 1977, 272; *Excélsior*, 24 Jan. 1974, 14; *Proceso*, 8 Jan. 1977, 29; *Excélsior*, 26 Dec. 1981, 164; DBGM87, 266; DBGM89, 244.

Múgica, Francisco José
(Deceased Apr. 12, 1954) a-Sept. 2, 1884. b-Tinguindín, Michoacán. c-Primary and secondary studies at the Seminary of Zamora, Michoacán; school teacher; no degree. d-Deputy to the Constitutional Convention, 1916-17; Governor of Michoacán, 1920-22. e-Leader of *Lázaro Cárdenas's* campaign for president, 1934; Director of the leftist Constitutional Party, 1952. f-Head of the Port of Tampico, 1914; President of the Superior Tribunal of Justice, 1915; Governor and Military Commander of the State of Tabasco, 1916; Director of the Department of General Provisions, 1918-20; Director of the Federal Prison on Islas Marías, 1927-33; Head of the Administrative Department, Secretariat of National Defense, May, 1933; Secretary of the Secretariat of Industry and Commerce, 1934-35; *Secretary of Public Works*, June 18, 1935, to Jan. 23, 1939; *Governor of Baja California del Sur*, 1940-46. g-None. h-Tax collector, Chauinda, Michoacán, 1906; postal employee, Zamora, Michoacán; journalist; member of the Luis Cabrera law firm, 1924. i-Longtime

enemy of General Obregón and Melchor Ortega; close friend and supporter of *Lázaro Cárdenas*, 1925-39; father, a school teacher; married Matilde Rodríguez Cabo, psychiatrist; brother, Carlos Múgica, was oficial mayor of the Secretariat of War, 1920; members of his political group included *Luis Mora Tovar, Jesús Romero Flores* and *Agustín Arroyo Ch.*; son, Janitzio Múgica Rodríguez Cabo, was director of forests and ejidos, Secretariat of Agrarian Reform, 1979. j-Joined the Revolution under Madero, Nov. 20, 1910, as a 2nd Lieutenant; rank of 1st Captain, 1911; Captain of the Constitutional forces under General Lucio Blanco; rank of 2nd Captain, 1911; aide to Venustiano Carranza, 1911-13; rank of Colonel in the cavalry, 1914; rank of Brigadier General, 1914; Chief of Military Operations of various states; Brigadier General, 1932; Commander of the 32nd Military Zone, Mérida, Yucatán, 1933; Commander of the 21st Military Zone, Morelia, Michoacán, 1939; Commander of the 3rd Military Zone, La Paz, Baja Califonia del Sur, 1939-40; rank of Division General, 1939; without assignment, 1940-49; retired, 1949. k-Precandidate for president of Mexico, 1939; considered too radical; identified with León Trotsky, whom he helped bring to Mexico; Gruening states that Múgica was imposed over other candidates as governor of Michoacán, 1920; supported the candidacy of *Miguel Henríquez Guzmán* for president, 1952. l-Morton, 40; WWM45, 81-82; Kirk, 89, 118, 234; DP70, 1425-26; DP64, 985; Peral, 560-61; Gruening, 461; Michaels, 4, 32; Scott, 238-39; Brandenburg, 92-93, 80-82; Strode, 357-59; Enc. Mex., IX, 1977, 273; Q es Q, 401-02.

Mújica Montoya, Emilio
a-May 23, 1926. b-Federal District. c-Preparatory studies at the National Preparatory School, 1942-44; studies in economics, National School of Economics, UNAM, 1944-48, with an honorable mention for his thesis on economic cycles and economic development; Ph.D. in economics, Alexander Humboldt University, Berlin, Germany, 1956, with a thesis on Marxist analysis; Professor of the Theory of Economic Cycles, Economic Problems of Mexico, Mexican Foreign Trade, Planning and Development and International Economics, National School of Economics, UNAM, 1951-73; Coordinator of Studies on the Economy and Education, Colegio de México, 1972-73; Dean, National School of Economics, UNAM, 1959-63. d-None. e-Participant, PRI presidential campaigns, 1952, 1958, 1964; member of the Advisory Council of the IEPES of PRI, 1975-76; Coordinator of the Communications and Transportation Sections of the *José López Portillo* presidential campaign committees, 1976. f-Economist, Secretariat of Communications, 1948-50; economist, Secretariat of National Properties, 1950; economist, Secretariat of Industry and Commerce, 1951-52; economist, National Finance Bank, 1952-53; analyst, National Warehouses, 1953-58; Secretary of the Council of Advisers to the Director of CONASUPO, 1959-62; Director of Sectoral Planning, Secretariat of the Presidency, 1965-70; Director of Planning and Organization, National Railroads of Mexico, 1971; adviser to *José López Portillo*, Secretary of the Treasury, 1973-75; Executive Secretary of the Coordinating Committee of the Public Sector Industrial Policy, 1975-76; Director of the Public Sector, Secretariat of Government Properties, 1975-76; *Secretary of Communications and Transportation*, 1976-82; adviser to the Head of the Department of the Federal District, 1989-91; Director General of the Metro Transportation System, Department of the Federal District, 1991-93. g-None. h-Laborer, Waters

and Sanitation Division, Department of the Federal District, 1943-48. i-Some of his more prominent students at the National School of Economics include *Julio Faesler* and *Jorge Tamayo;* disciple of Professor Eduardo Botas; founded a political group of fellow students at UNAM called the Enrique González Aparicio Group; among its members were *Alejandro Cervantes Delgado, Marcela Lombardo, Agustín Acosta Lagunes, Nathan Warman,* and *Sergio Luis Cano;* rivalry with *Jorge de la Vega Domínguez* stems from their days as student activists at UNAM. j-None. k-None. l-*Excélsior,* 1 Dec. 1976; letter; HA, 6 Dec. 1976, 23; *El Día,* 1 Dec. 1976; HA, 25 July 1972, 17; DAPC, 49; *Excélsior,* 29 Feb. 1980, 13; DBGM92, 254.

Muñoz Cota, José
a-Jan. 21, 1907. b-Ciudad Juárez, Chihuahua. c-Primary studies at the New English School, Mexico City; preparatory studies at the National Preparatory School, Mexico City; law degree, National School of Law, UNAM. d-*Federal Deputy* from the Federal District, Dist. 1, 1937-40. e-Campaigned for José Vasconcelos in Oaxaca, 1929; campaigned for *Lázaro Cárdenas* for president, 1934; member of the Communist Party of Mexico; member of the extreme left group, LEAR. f-Director of Fine Arts, Secretariat of Public Education, 1934-37; Private Secretary to *Lázaro Cárdenas* as Commander of the Pacific Military Zone, 1941-43; Private Secretary to *Lázaro Cárdenas,* Secretary of National Defense, 1942-43; Ambassador to Honduras, 1943-46, Colombia, 1946-47, and Paraguay, 1947-50. g-Student leader; won the *El Universal* student oratory contest, 1926. i-Studied under Professor Horacio Zúñiga. j-None. k-None. l-López; Peral; C de D, 1937-40.

Muñoz Ledo (Lazo de la Vega), Porfirio
a-July 23, 1933. b-Federal District. c-Primary and secondary studies in Mexico City; preparatory studies at the National Preparatory School; law studies, National School of Law, UNAM, 1950-54, law degree, 1955; LLD, University of Toulouse, France, 1958; Lecturer in Hispanic Literature, University of Paris, 1959-60; professor at the National Preparatory School, 1950; professor at the Women's University of Mexico, 1950; studies in economics and political science, University of Paris, 1956-59; Professor of Mexican Political Institutions, Higher Normal School, 1962-63; Professor of the Mexican Political Process, Colegio de México, 1964- ; Professor of the Theory of the State, School of Political Sciences, UNAM, 1962-63. d-*Senator* from the Federal District, 1988-94. e-Adviser to the Section for Political Studies of the IEPES of PRI; member of the Section on Ideological and Political Analysis of the Mexican Revolution, PRI, 1972; *President of the CEN of PRI,* 1975-76; cofounder and national coordinator of the Democratic Current of PRI, 1986-87; supported *Cuauhtémoc Cárdenas* in the 1988 presidential campaign; cofounder of the PRD, 1988; *President of the PRD,* 1993- . f-Assistant in the Public Relations Office of the Secretariat of National Patrimony, 1950-53; adviser to UNESCO; technical adviser to the Presidency, 1960-64; Subdirector General of Graduate Education and Scientific Investigation, Secretariat of Public Education, 1961-65; cultural adviser to the Mexican Embassy, Paris, 1965; *Secretary General of the Mexican Institute of Social Security,* 1966-70; *Subsecretary of the Presidency,* 1970-72; *Secretary of Labor,* Sept. 12, 1972, to 1975; *Secretary of Public Education,* 1976-77; *Ambassador to the United Nations,* 1979-82; 1982-85. g-President of the Student Society of the National School of Law.

h-Author of legal articles; member of the Board of Fondo de Cultura Económica; adviser to the National Housing Institute. i-Political disciple of *Ignacio Morones Prieto*; student of *Mario de la Cueva*; first mentor was *Humberto Romero*; son of Ana Lazo de la Vega; father a school teacher. j-None. k-None. l-B de M, 87; HA, 14 Dec. 1970, 23, 18 Sept. 1972, 11, 22 Nov. 1971, 23; Enc. Mex., IX, 1977, 278; HA, 6 Dec. 1976, 23, 29 Dec. 1975, 7; *Excélsior*, 4 Feb. 1977, 6; LA, 3 Dec. 1976; *Excélsior*, 2 Aug. 1979; DBGM92, 529; letter.

Muñoz Mosqueda, Gilberto
a-Sept. 30, 1935. b-San Juan del Río, Guanajuato. c-Completed preparatory studies in Salamanca, Guanajuato; legal studies, no degree. d- Member of the City Council of Salamanca, Guanajuato, 1966-69; *Federal Deputy* from the State of Guanajuato, Dist. 6, 1973-76, 1979-82; *Senator* from the State of Guanajuato, 1982-88; *Federal Deputy* from the State of Guanajuato, Dist. 6, 1988-91. e-Joined PRI, 1958. f-None. g-Secretary General of Section 9, Union of Chemical and Petrochemical Workers of Mexico, 1962-68; Secretary of Industrial Development, CTM, State of Guanajuato, 1964-74; Secretary of Labor, Union of Chemical and Petrochemical Workers of Mexico, 1968-78; Secretary General of the Union of Chemical and Petrochemical Workers of Mexico, 1978-89. h-Employee, Salamanca Refinery, Salamanca, Guanajuato. i-Son of Carlos Muñoz Gómez, cattle rancher, and María Mosqueda Bravo; married Celia Olivares Rivera. j-None. k-None. l-DBGM89, 502; C de D, 1988-91; C de S, 1982-88; C de S, 1979-82; Directorio, 1979-82; C de D, 1973-76.

Muñoz Turnbull, Marco Antonio
a-Aug. 6, 1914. b-Jalapa, Veracruz. c-Primary studies at the Jalapa Kindergarden; preparatory studies at the University of Veracruz, Jalapa; law degree, School of Law, University of Veracruz, Jalapa, graduating in 1935 with the highest GPA of his class; civics and history teacher; Professor of Introduction to Philosophy, Private International Law and Labor Law, University of Veracruz. d-*Governor of Veracruz*, 1950-56; *Federal Deputy* from the State of Veracruz, Dist. 13, 1979-82, President of the Government Properties and Industrial Development Committee. e-Auxiliary Secretary to *Miguel Alemán* during the presidential campaign, 1946; cofounder of the Mexican Civic Front of Revolutionary Affirmation, 1963; general delegate of the CEN of PRI to Tlaxcala, 1978. f-Employee, Criminal Court; public defender; agent of the Ministerio Público; Director, Legal Department, State of Veracruz; Justice and President of the Superior Tribunal of Justice of the State of Veracruz, 1939-40; Subdirector, Department of Government, Secretariat of Government, 1940-46; *Oficial Mayor of Industry and Commerce*, 1947-49; Director General of the Emiliano Zapata Mill. g-Director General of the National Sugar Producers Union. h-None. i-Political disciple of *Miguel Alemán*; son of Francisco Javier Muñoz Landero and Leonor Turnbull; brother, Jorge, a physician and author. j-None. k-Precandidate for senator from Veracruz, 1976. l-Gómez, 197; DGF56, 102; HA, 8 Dec 1950, 14-16; D del S, 5 Dec 1946, 1; Cadena Z., 138; *Excélsior*, 8 Dec. 1975, 17; DGF50, 35; DGF47, 155; HA, 6 Dec l946, 6; Illescas, 691; Guerra Leal, 185; Almanaque de México, 66.

Muñoz Vázquez, Jesús
a-July 13, 1924. b-Federal District. c-Early education unknown; agricultural engineering degree, National School of Agriculture, 1940-47, with a thesis on irrigation, 1948; courses toward an MA in hydraulic and me-

chanical structures; professor in irrigation and foresty, National School of Agriculture, 1951-59; Dean, National School of Agriculture, 1957-59; Director and founder of the Graduate College of Agronomy, 1958-59. d-None. e-President of the Agricultural Committee of the IEPES of PRI. f-Subdirector, Department of Agrarian Organizations, Secretariat of Agriculture; Director of Irrigation Workers, Hidalgo, States of México and Querétaro, 1953-54; Director of Credit, National Ejido Credit Bank, 1960-64; Director of Credit, National Agribusiness Bank, 1964-68; Director of Agricultural Projects, Inter-American Development Bank, 1972-74; Director General of Agriculture, Secretariat of Agriculture and Hydraulic Resources, 1976-82; *Subsecretary of Hydraulic Planning*, Secretariat of Agriculture, 1982-84. g-President of the College of Agronomists of Mexico. h-Director General of the Modern Engineering Techniques Construction Firm. i-None. j-None. k-None. l-IEPES; Q es QAP, 212-13; Protag., 242.

Muñuzuri y Araña de Garivo, Rosa Martha
a-Mar. 6, 1946. b-Federal District. c-Early education unknown; journalism studies, University of Guerrero, 1965; medical degree, University of Puebla, 1965-69; anesthesiologist, UNAM, 1971. d-*Federal Deputy* from the State of Guerrero, Dist. 4, 1982-85; Local Deputy from the State Legislature of Guerrero, 1987-90. e-Secretary of Finances of PRI in Acapulco, 1981; adviser to the Technical Council of the CNOP of PRI, 1981. f-Chief of Sanitation Department, Acapulco, 1986-87; Secretary of Women, State of Guerrero, 1990- . g-None. h-Anesthesiologist, ISSSTE Hospital, Acapulco. i-Daughter of Enrique Muñuzuri Clark, surgeon, and Lilian Araña Ortega; married José Garibo Hernández, pediatrician.

j-None. k-None. l-Directorio, 1982-85; C de D, 1982-85; Lehr, 199; DBGM, 564-65; DBGM92, 803.

Murat (Casab), José
a-Mar. 19, 1949. b-Ixtepec, Oaxaca. c-Early education unknown; law degree, National School of Law, UNAM, with a thesis on the "Latin American Common Market"; professor, National School of Political Science, UNAM, Acatlán campus. d-*Federal Deputy* from the State of Oaxaca, Dist. 7, 1973-76; *Federal Deputy* from the State of Oaxaca, Dist. 1, 1979-82; *Alternate Senator* from the State of Oaxaca, 1982-88; *Federal Deputy* from the State of Oaxaca, Dist. 1, 1988-91, coordinator of the Oaxaca delegation. e-Joined PRI, 1971; Secretary of Political Action of the CNOP of PRI, 1974-75; *Secretary of Political Education of the CEN of PRI*, 1976-78; Secretary of Press and Publicity of the PRI, Federal District; general delegate of the CEN of CNOP of PRI to Nayarit and Oaxaca; President of PRI in Oaxaca, 1987-88; *Secretary of International Affairs of the CEN of PRI*, 1988-89. f-Representative of the State of Oaxaca in the Federal District, 1978-80. g-None. i-Son of José Tomás Murat, businessman, and Juana Margarita Casab; married María Guadalupe Hinojosa, economist. j-None. k-None. l-Protag., 242; C de D, 1973-76, 1979-82; letter; DBGM89, 502.

Murillo Karam, Jesús
a-Mar. 2, 1948. b-Real del Monte, Hidalgo. c-Early education unknown; law degree, School of Law, University of Hidalgo, 1967-70; department head, University of Hidalgo, 1972-74; professor, University of Hidalgo, 1972-74. d-*Federal Deputy* from the State of Hidalgo, Dist. 4, 1979-82; *Federal Deputy* from the State of Hidalgo, Dist. 6, 1985-88; *Senator* from the State of Hidalgo, 1991-93; *Governor* of Hidalgo,

1993- . e-Joined PRI, 1970; Secretary of Finance, Youth PRI, Hidalgo, 1971; President of PRI, Tulancingo, Hidalgo, 1972-73, 1975; Subsecretary of Organization of the CEN of PRI, 1980-81; General Delegate of the CEN of PRI to Durango, 1983-84; Secretary of Organization of PRI, Federal District, 1984-85; President of PRI, Hidalgo, 1987-88; General Delegate of the CEN of PRI to San Luis Potosí, 1988. f-Oficial Mayor of Tulancingo, Hidalgo, 1971-72; Municipal Secretary of Tulancingo, 1973-74; Assistant Attorney General of Hidalgo, 1975-76; Auxiliary Secretary of the Secretary of Agrarian Reform, 1976-77; Secretary General of Government of the State of Hidalgo, 1978-79; *Oficial Mayor of the Secretariat of Agrarian Reform*, 1989-91. g-None. h-None. i-Son of José Murillo Hamed, merchant, and María Karam Kuri; married María Guadalupe Ortega González. j-None. k-None. l-DBGM89, 246; DBGM92, 531; letter; C de D, 1979-82; Directorio, 1979-82; C de D, 1985-88.

Murillo Vidal, Rafael
a-Oct. 29, 1904. b-San Andrés Tuxtla, Veracruz. c-Primary studies in Córdoba; secondary and preparatory studies in Córdoba; law degree, National School of Law, UNAM, 1925; professor, School of Law, University of Veracruz. d-Local Deputy to the State Legislature of Veracruz, 1936-38; Mayor of Orizaba, Veracruz, 1938-40; *Federal Deputy* from the State of Veracruz, Dist. 2, 1943-46; *Federal Deputy* from the State of Veracruz, Dist. 4, 1949-52, President of the Chamber, Nov. 1949; member of the Legislative Studies Committee (2nd year); *Senator* from the State of Veracruz, 1964-67; *Governor of Veracruz*, 1968-74. e-Member of the National Advisory Committee to PRI from the CNOP, 1946; *Popular Secretary of the CEN of PRI*, 1946. f-Judge of the 1st Instance in Tuxpán, Veracruz, 1927;

Judge of the 1st Instance in Panuco, Veracruz; Justice of the Superior Tribunal of Veracruz; Oficial Mayor of the Senate, 1946-49; Secretary General of Government of the State of Veracruz; Director General of Government, Secretariat of Government, 1964-65; *Oficial Mayor of the Secretariat of Government*, 1965-68; Postmaster General of Mexico, 1953-64. g-Director of CNOP, Federal District; *Secretary General of CNOP*, 1946. h-None. i-Knew *Eduardo Bustamante* at UNAM. j-None. k-None. l-HA, 22 Dec. 1958, 7; D de S, 22 Jan. 1946, 1; DGF51, I, 26, 32; DPE61, 81; WWW70-71, 663; *Hoy*, 22 June 1958, 64; DGF56, 254; DGF47, 22; C de D, 1949-51, 80; Q es Q, 403-04.

N

Narro Robles, José Ramón
a-Dec. 5, 1948. b-Saltillo, Coahuila. c-Early education unknown; medical degree, National School of Medicine, UNAM, 1967-73; studies in community medicine, University of Birmingham, England, 1976-78; professor, National School of Medicine, UNAM, 1981- ; Director General of Planning, UNAM, 1982; Chief of the Department of Family Medicine, UNAM, 1979-81; Director General of Academic Extension, UNAM, 1981-82; *Secretary General of UNAM*, 1985-91. d-None. e-Joined PRI, 1973; Chief of Medical Services, Youth Sector of PRI, Federal District, 1972-73. f-Director General of Public Health in the Federal District, Secretariat of Health, 1982-84; Director General of Medical Services, Department of the Federal District, 1984; *Secretary General of the IMSS*, 1991-94. g-None. h-None. i-Son of José Narro González, surgeon, and María Magdalena Robles; married María del Carmen Lobo García, preschool teacher. j-None. k-None. l-DBGM92, 257; DBGM89.

Narváez Angulo, Fernando
a-1910. c-Early education unknown; law degree. d-None. e-None. f-Chief of the Board of Prior Investigations, Office of the Attorney General of the Federal District, 1947; Chief of Agents of the Ministerio Público, Criminal Division, Federal District; Private Secretary to the Attorney General of Mexico, *Carlos Franco S.*, 1952-58; official of the Supreme Court of Mexico; Director General of the Office of Prior Investigations, Office of the Attorney General of Mexico, 1968-76; *Attorney General of the Federal District*, 1976. g-None. j-None. k-None. l-DPE71, 160; MGF69, 329; *Excélsior*, 5 Mar. 1976, 16; DGF56, 539; MGF73, 429.

Nasta (Haik), Salim
a-Jan. 21, 1938. b-Federal District. c-Preparatory studies at the Centro Universitario Mexico, Mexico City; member of the 1957 generation at the National School of Law, UNAM, completing his thesis on Nov. 10, 1961, on the subject of welfare obligations under the law. d-None. e-Private Secretary to *Gustavo Díaz Ordaz* during his campaign for President, 1964; adviser to the IEPES of PRI. f-Head of the Legal Department for the Federal District Police; Assistant Private Secretary to the Secretary of the Presidency, 1963-64; Director General of Guanos and Fertilizers of Mexico, 1964-72. g-None. h-Fluent in French and English. i-Son-in-law of *Gustavo Díaz Ordaz*; married Guadalupe Díaz. j-None. k-*Nasta* resigned as Director General of Guanos and Fertilizers of Mexico on Aug. 25, 1972; Aguilar Monteverde considers his family to be among Mexico's wealthiest 1,000. l-HA, 7 Dec. 1970, 27; DJBM, 93; *Excélsior*, 26 Aug. 1972, 1; *Política*, Nov. 1969, 103; WNM, 158.

Natera (García), Pánfilo
(Deceased 1951) a-June 12, 1882. b-Hacienda de la Noria, Nieves, Zacatecas. c-No secondary education or degree. d-*Governor of Zacatecas*, 1940-44. e-None. f-None. g-None. h-Before the Revolution, Natera worked as a water carrier. i-Son of Francisco Natera, a Colonel in the Revolution, and *Pánfilo* fought under him, and Nestora García; son, *Pánfilo Jr.*, served as a federal deputy from Zacatecas during his father's term as governor, 1943-45. j-Served in the Revolution from 1910-11, 1913-15 under Generals Luis Moya and Francisco Villa; fought against Pascual Orozco, 1912-13; rank of Brigadier General, Dec. 20, 1913; delegate at the Convention of Aguascalientes, 1914-15; opposed General Villa, 1915; Provisional Governor and Military Commander of Zacatecas, 1915; no military commands, 1920-23; organized the 83rd Cavalry Regiment against de la Huerta, 1923; Head of the Army Inspection Commission, 1925; Alternate President of the Second Council of War; Commander of the 27th Military Zone, Acapulco, Guerrero; Commander of the 11th Military Zone, Zacatecas, Zacatecas, 1934-35; Commander of the 17th Military Zone, Querétaro, Querétaro, 1935-37; Commander of the 22nd Military Zone, Toluca, México, 1937-38; rank of Division General, Oct. 16, 1937. k-Retired to private life, 1945-51. l-DP70, 1450; Peral, 566; *Heroic Mexico*, 198-202, 25-06; D de Y, 7 Dec. 1940, 1; Enc. Mex., IX, 1977, 316-17; López, 758; Morales Jiménez, 173-75.

Nava, Alfonso L.
a-July 7, 1900. b-Iguala, Guerrero. c-Primary studies in Mexico City; secondary studies in business administration; professional studies in Boston, Massachusetts; no degree. d-Mayor of Iguala, Guerrero; Federal Deputy from the State of Guerrero, 1926-28; Federal

Deputy from the State of Guerrero, 1930-32; *Federal Deputy* from the State of Guerrero, Dist. 2, 1949-52, member of the Colonization Committee, the Fourth Ejido Committee, the General Accounting Office Committee and Vice-President of the Chamber of Deputies, Sept. 1950; *Senator* from the State of Guerrero, 1952-58, Second Secretary of the Development of Cooperatives Committee and the Second Instructive Section of the Grand Jury, member of the Second Balloting Committee. e-None. f-None. g-President of the Guerrero Society of Youth, 1923-26. h-Author of numerous articles. j-None. k-None. l-Ind. Biog., 107-08; C de D, 1949-52, 80; DGF56, 6, 10-14; C de S, 1952-58.

Nava Castillo, Antonio
(Deceased Mar. 29, 1983) a-Sept. 9, 1906. b-San Juan Ixcaquixtla, Puebla. c-Primary studies in San Juan Ixca- quixtla; secondary studies at the Colegio Lafragua, Puebla, Puebla; enrolled at the National Military College, 1921, graduated as a lieutenant, 1922; cadet, Military Aeronautical School, 1923, but left to fight against de la Huerta; Cadet Commander of the Cavalry Squadron, National Military College. d-Federal Deputy from the State of Puebla, 1935-37; *Federal Deputy* from the State of Puebla, Dist. 12, 1940-43, President of the Second Instructive Section of the Grand Jury, member of the Committee on the Electric Industry, the Second Commit- tee on National Defense, and the Gran Comisión; *Governor of Puebla*, 1963-64. e-*Secretary General of the National Federation of Popular Organizations of PRI*, 1944-46. f-Aide to President *Manuel Avila Camacho*, 1940-46; Director of the Federal Penitentiary, Federal District, 1955-58; Director General of Traffic, Department of the Federal District, 1961-63; Director of

Iron Works, Secretariat of Industry and Commerce, 1969. g-Cofounder of CNOP. h-Member of the Mexican Olympic Polo Team, 1936. i-Married María López; son of Manuel Nava Palacios and Delfina Castillo Gil. j-Career army officer; rank of Second Captain, 1923; junior officer, 77th Cavalry Regiment; fought against Generals Figueroa and Ocampo, 1923 rebellion; fought against Generals Aguirre and Gómez in Veracruz, 1927; opposed the Cristeros in Los Altos, Jalisco 1927; fought Generals Caraveo and Escobar in Ciudad Jiménez, Chihua- hua, 1929; rank of First Captain, 1929; rank of Major, 1936; aide to the Secre- tary of National Defense; commander of a mechanized brigade; aide to the Direc- tor, Heroic Military College; squadron commander, Presidential Guards; Commander of the 7th Military Zone; rank of Colonel, 1946; rank of Brigadier General, 1948; rank of Brigade General, 1952; rank of Division General, Nov. 20, 1960. k-Received a last-minute political promotion from *Avila Cama- cho*, along with *Corona del Rosal*, in Nov. 1946; forced to resign as governor of Puebla after student strikes brought pressure on the federal government to dissolve his powers in 1964; *Por Qué* claims he was involved in scandals in the meat-packing industry; supported *Miguel Henríquez Guzmán* for presi- dent, 1946. l-G of M, 31; DGF56, 466; Wences Reza, 55; HA, 27 Nov. 1961, 61; C de D, 1940-42, 17; DPE61, 145; D de Y, Jan. 1946, 1; D del S, 3 Dec. 1946, 1; *Por Qué*, 6 Nov. 1969, 10; *Excélsior*, 26 Dec. 1974, 12; CyT, 483; *Excélsior*, 5 June 1945; Medina, 20, 29; *Excélsior*, 30 Mar. 1983, 18; Rev. de Ejer., Aug. 1975, 142; HA, 11 Apr. 193, 6.

Navarrete (López), Jorge Eduardo
a-Apr. 29, 1940. b-Federal District. c-Early education unknown; teaching certificate, National Teachers College,

1955-57; economics degree, National School of Economics, UNAM, 1959-63, with a thesis on "Disequilibrium and Dependency, Mexican International Economic Relations in the 1960s"; special studies in export development, Switzerland, Norway, Denmark, Belgium, Sweden, and Israel; primary school teacher, Mexico City, 1959-61; professor, National School of Political and Social Sciences and the National School of Economics, UNAM, 1965-72. d-None. e-None. f-Analyst, Secretariat of the Treasury, 1960-62; economist, CEMLA, 1963-67; Director of the Department of Statistics and Information, National Foreign Trade Bank, 1967-72; adviser, Inter-American Development Bank, 1971; Ambassador to Venezuela, 1972-78; adviser to PEMEX, 1978; Ambassador to Yugoslavia, 1977-78; Alternate Representative of Mexico to the United Nations, 1978-79; *Subsecretary of Foreign Relations "D"*, 1979-82; *Subsecretary of Economic Affairs*, Secretariat of Foreign Relations, 1982-85; *Ambassador to England*, 1986-89; Ambassador to China, 1989-94. g-None. h-Economist, National Foreign Trade Bank; Director, *Comercio Exterior*. i-Son of Gabriel Navarette Pereira, normal teacher, and Lucrecia López Montelongo; married María Josefina Bolaños. j-None. k-None. l-HA, 14 Aug. 1972, 9; *Excélsior*, 1 Aug. 1972, 1, 9; HA, 11 June 1979, 9; Q es QAP, 49; IEPES; DBGM89, 248; DBGM, 302; DBGM92, 258.

Navarrete (Martínez), Alfredo
(Deceased) a-1893. b-Valle de Acambay, Morelos. c-Primary studies in Valle de Acambay; no degree. d-*Federal Deputy* from the State of México, Dist. 7, 1952-55, member of the First Railroad Committee, the Inspection Committee of the General Accounting Office (2nd year), the First Labor Committee, the Petroleum Committee, and the Social

Action Committee (3rd year). e-None. f-None. g-Early labor organizer and leader; member of the Railroad Workers Union, 1932; Secretary General of the Railroad Workers Union (STFRM), 1934-35; Head of the Transportation Workers Organization in the Zacatepec Mill, Morelos, 1938. h-At age 11, was working on an ejido in Morelos; moved to Mexico City, 1904, where he worked as a laborer at the San Lázaro Station, 1907-14; employed on the Interoceanic Railroad, 1910. i-Friend of *Ignacio García Téllez* and *Graciano Sánchez*, first Secretary General of the National Farmers Federation; married Martha Romero Ugalde; son, Víctor Manuel, was subdirector of the National Finance Bank, 1984. j-Train conductor during the Revolution. k-Participant in the precursor movement; member of the Club Reyes for a short time; joined the Anti-Reelectionist Club. l-Kirk, 93; C de D, 1952-54, 15, 41, 53, 62; DBGM, 302.

Navarrete (Romero), Alfredo
a-July 24, 1923. b-Federal District. c-Degree in economics from the National School of Economics, UNAM, 1942-46; MA in public administration, Harvard University, 1947; Ph.D. in economics from Harvard University, 1950; Professor, Advanced Economic Theory, National School of Economics, UNAM, 1953-61, and CEMLA, 1953-69. d-*Federal Deputy* from the State of México, Dist. 21, 1979-82. e-None. f-Economist for the Secretariat of the Treasury, 1944; economist for the Latin American Contributions Committee, United Nations, 1946; Alternate Executive Director of the World Bank, 1963-65; Director of the Department of Financial Research, National Finance Bank, 1953-58; manager of the National Finance Bank, 1959-61; Subdirector of the National Finance Bank, 1961-65; Director, the National Finance Bank,

1965-68; *Assistant Director General of the National Finance Bank*, 1968-70; Director General of the Financiera Nacional Azucarera, 1970-72; *Subdirector General of Finances of PEMEX*, May 4, 1972, to 1976; Director General of the Financiera Nacional Azucarera, 1976-82. g-None. h-Served on advisory commissions to Latin America for the Secretary General of the OAS; special adviser to the Secretary of the Treasury, 1953-70; winner of the National Prize in Economics, 1951. i-Formerly married to *Ifigenia Martínez*, senator and leader of the PRD; brother, Víctor, was head of economic investigations for Nacional Financiera, 1959; son of Alfredo Navarette Martínez, labor leader, and Martha Romero Ugalde; married Dolores Villarreal. j-None. k-None. l-DBM68, 453; DBM70, 405-06; B de M, 189; letter; *Excélsior*, 4 May 1972, 4; HA, 15 May 1972, 31; Enc. Mex., IX, 1977, 322; WNM, 158.

Navarro Cortina, Rodolfo

(Deceased 1958) a-Sept. 8, 1889. b-Durango. c-Early education unknown; no degree. d-None. e-None. f-*Governor of Baja California del Norte*, Aug. 16, 1936, to Feb. 22, 1937. g-None. h-None. i-Married Eleanor Mendoza; son, General Rafael Navarro Mendoza, served as assistant chief of staff, Air Force, 1972. j-Career army officer; joined the Revolution, 1913; no command positions, 1920-23; fought against the forces of General Adolfo de la Huerta, 1923; Commander of the Garrison, Morelia, Michoacán; fought against the forces of General Escobar as Chief of Staff, military column under General *Lázaro Cárdenas*, 1929; rank of Brigade General, May 16, 1929; Director of the General Artillery Warehouses; Director General of War Materiels, Secretariat of National Defense, 1934-35; Commander of the 1st Military Zone, Mexico City, 1935; Commander of the

2nd Military Zone, El Cipres, Baja California del Norte, 1935-37. k-Escorted ex-President Calles from Mexico during his forced departure by *Lázaro Cárdenas*, 1935; removed from the governorship by President *Cárdenas*. l-DP70, 1454; Casasola, V, 2342; López, 760; NYT, 23 Feb., 1937, 16; Rev. de Ejer., Dec. 1972, 81; Hernández Chávez, 93.

Navarro Diaz de León, Ginés

a-1917. b-Federal District. c-Early education unknown; medical degree as a surgeon, National School of Medicine, UNAM, 1940; professor, National School of Medicine, UNAM, eighteen years. d-None. e-None. f-Director General of Health for the Federal District, 1970-75; *Secretary of Health*, 1975-76. g-None. h-Secretary, Private Charities Board; various positions in the private sector; coauthor, National Health Plan. j-None. k-None. l-HA, 10 Mar. 1975, 16; *Excélsior*, 3 Mar. 1975, 4.

Navarro Encinas, Antonio

a-1910. c-Early education unknown; graduated from the National Military College, 1928-30; graduate of the Military Aviation School; special studies in Spain; professor, Military Aviation School. d-*Federal Deputy* from the State of Baja California del Sur, Dist. 1, 1946-49, member of the Gran Comisión; *Federal Deputy* from Baja California del Sur, Dist. 1, 1961-64, member of the Gran Comisión, Secretary of the Chamber. e-None. f-Member of the Chief of Staff under Secretary of National Defense, *Lázaro Cárdenas*, 1942-45; military attaché to various embassies. g-None. i-*Alberto Alvarado Arámburo* was his alternate deputy in 1961-64; co-student with General *Héctor Berthier Aguiluz*, Chief of the Air Force, 1976-82. j-Career Air Force officer. k-None. l-C de D, 1946-49, 1961-64; Rev. de Ejer., Mar. 1958, 29.

Navia Millán, Aurora
a-Aug. 15, 1912. b-Jerez, Zacatecas.
c-Teaching certificate from the Manuel
Avila Camacho Normal School, Zacatecas; teacher. d-Local Deputy to the
State Legislature of Zacatecas; *Federal
Deputy* from the State of Zacatecas,
Dist. 1, 1964-67; *Senator* from the State
of Zacatecas, 1970-76; *Federal Deputy*
from the State of Zacatecas, Dist. 5,
1979-82. e-Joined the PNR, 1936; Delegate to Yucatán of the CEN of the PNR;
Director of Women's Action of the State
Regional Committee of PNR, Zacatecas; general delegate of the CEN of PRI
to Yucatán; Secretary of Organization of
the CNOP of PRI in Zacatecas; Director
of the Regional Women's Committee of
PRI, Zacatecas, 1962-65; Director of
Women's Action of CNOP, 1963-70;
representative to the Federal Electoral
Commission from the PRI. f-Director
of Public Education, State of Zacatecas.
g-Secretary General of a local of the
SNTE. j-None. k-None. l-C de S, 1970-
76; Romero Aceves, 720-21; Protag.,
247; C de D, 1964-67, 1979-82.

Neme Castillo, Salvador José
a-Oct. 22, 1931. b-Villahermosa,
Tabasco. c-Early education unknown;
law degree, National School of Law,
UNAM, 1949-55; professor, National
School of Law, UNAM, 1967-68, 1972-
77, 1982-87. d-*Senator* from the State of
Tabasco, 1982-88; *Governor of Tabasco*,
1989-92. e-Assistant Secretary of Press,
PRI, Federal District, 1976. f-Legal
adviser, State of Tabasco, 1955; Secretary of the City Council, Villahermosa,
1956-58; legal adviser, Division of
Government, Department of the Federal
District, 1971-72; Secretary General of
Government, State of Tabasco, 1977-82.
g-None. h-Practicing lawyer, 1959-71.
i-Son of José Neme Hadna, businessman, and Aurelia Castillo Castillo;
married Celia Sastre López. j-None.
k-Removed from office by President

Salinas after widespread conflict over
disputed election results. l-DBGM89,
725; C de S, 1982-88.

Neri Arizmendi, Porfirio
(Deceased 1965) a-Feb. 28, 1894.
b-Tehuixtla, Morelos. c-No degree.
d-Federal Deputy from the State of
Morelos, 1926-28; Local Deputy to the
State Legislature of Morelos; *Federal
Deputy* from the State of Morelos, Dist.
1, 1940-43, member of the Gran Comisión, the Fifth Ejidal Commission; *Senator* from the State of Morelos, 1958-
64, member of the Agrarian Department
Committee, the Special Small Agricultural Property Committee, and substitute member of the Second Ejido Committee and the National Properties
Committee. e-None. f-Oficial Mayor of
the State of Morelos, 1936. g-Founding
member and President of the Zapatista
Front, 1965. h-None. j-Joined the Revolution, 1910; supported Madero; served
under Zapata; fought against Huerta;
attended the Convention of Aguascalientes, 1914; opposed Carranza; reached
the rank of Brigadier General, 1913.
k-None. l-DP70, 1464; C de S, 1961-64,
64; C de D, 1940-42, 17; Func., 281.

Nissan Rover, Simón
a-Aug. 25, 1941. b-Federal District.
c-Early education unknown; civil
engineering degree, National School of
Engineering, UNAM, 1959. d-None.
e-Adviser to the Committee on Fi-
nances and Evaluation of the CEN of
PRI, 1982. f-Adviser to the Subsecretary
of Budget and Planning, Secretariat of
Budget and Planning, 1981; Director
General of Evaluation of Works and
Services, Department of the Federal
District, 1983-84; *Secretary of Works
and Services*, Department of the Federal
District, 1984-85. h-Director of the
firm Construction and Structural
Design, 1965-68; Director and partner in
Simón Nissan and Associates, 1968-74;

director of many construction firms, 1975-79. i-Son of Moisés Nissan Mizrahi, businessman, and Esther Rovero; married Victoria Schoenfeld. j-None. k-None. l-HA, 16 Jan. 1984, 34; Q es QAP, 446; DBGM, 306.

Nochebuena (Palacios), Juvencio
b-Huejutla, Hidalgo. c-Early education unknown; no degree. d-Federal Deputy from the State of Hidalgo, Dist. 10, 1922-24; Federal Deputy from the State of Hidalgo, Dist. 6, 1924-26, member of the Gran Comisión; Federal Deputy from the State of Hidalgo, 1934-37; *Alternate Senator* from the State of Hidalgo, 1937-40; Mayor of Pachuca, 1940; *Federal Deputy* from the State of Hidalgo, Dist. 7, 1940-43; *Federal Deputy* from the State of Hidalgo, Dist. 4, 1946-49, 1952-55. e-None. f-Director of Traffic, Pachuca, Hidalgo. g-None. j-Fought in the Revolution under General Francisco de P. Mariel. k-None. l-Pérez López, 303-04; C de D, 1922-24, 1924-26, 1934-37, 1940-43, 1946-49, 1952-55.

Nogueda Otero, Israel
a-Jan. 16, 1935. b-Atoyac de Alvarez, Guerrero. c-Primary studies at the English Academy; secondary studies at the Colegio Williams; preparatory studies at the Centro Universitario México; degree in economics from the National School of Economics, UNAM, 160. d-*Federal Deputy* from Guerrero, Dist. 4, 1967-68; Mayor of Acapulco, Guerrero, 1969-71; *Substitute Governor of Guerrero*, 1971-75. e-Secretary of Professional-Technical Action, CNOP, PRI, 1967. f-Investigator for the Tariff Department, Secretariat of the Treasury; Chairman of the Minimum Wage Regulatory Commission; President of the Committee for the Sports Center, Acapulco, 1963-67. g-Vice-President of the Chamber of Commerce, Acapulco, Guerrero; President of the Chamber of Commerce, Acapulco. i-Knew *Jesús*

Silva Herzog F. at UNAM; brother-in-law of *Agustín Olachea Borbón*, head of the Department of Tourism, 1970-73; married Leticia Piñeda; political enemy of *Rubén Figueroa*. j-None. k-Campaign for federal deputy was in a hotly contested district; removed by the Permanent Committee of Congress as governor, Jan. 31, 1975. l-*Hoy*, 15 May 1971, 12; MGF69, 92; C de D, 1967-69; letter; HA, 10 Feb. 1975, 27-28; LA, 7 Feb. 1975, 45; *Excélsior*, 31 Jan. 1975, 1; Loret de Mola, *91*, 46.

Noguera Vergara, Arcadio
a-Jan. 12, 1907. b-Huautla, Hidalgo. c-Primary studies in Chicontepec, Veracruz; teaching certificate, Normal School, Chicontepec; teaching certificate, begun at the Normal School of Jalapa, completed at the National Normal School, Mexico City; primary school teacher, 1925-30; primary teacher, school affiliated with the National Teachers School, 1931-35; Subdirector, National Normal School, 1937-41; professor of world literature, National Preparatory School, 1940s and 1950s, retiring in 1964. d-None. e-Active in the presidential campaign of *Miguel Alemán*, 1946; *Secretary of Organization of the CEN of PRI, 1953-57.* f-Director of Literacy, Department of the Federal District, 1953-57; *Secretary General of the Department of Agrarian Affairs, 1958-64; Subsecretary of Elementary Education,* Secretariat of Public Education, 1981-82. g-Member of the Federation of Teachers, Federal District, 1934-35; Secretary of Promotion Committee of Teachers of the Federal District, 1936-37; First Secretary of Conflicts, SNTE, 1943-45. h-Prolific author; founder and Director of *México, Letras de Ayer y de Hoy.* j-None. k-Resigned from the National Normal School after being accused of being a communist, 1942. l-Pérez López, 304; D de Y, 12 Dec. 1964, 1; DPE61, 126.

Noriega (Cantú) Jr., Alfonso
(Deceased Jan. 16, 1988) a-Jan. 21, 1909.
b-Federal District. c-Primary studies at
the Colegio Francés Morelos (Perpetua
branch); secondary studies at the Colegio Francés Morelos (Puente de Alvarado
branch); preparatory studies from the
National Preparatory School; law degree
from the National School of Law,
UNAM, Dec. 27, 1929, with a thesis on
amparo; LLD, National School of Law,
UNAM; Professor of Law, National
School of Law, UNAM, 1939-71;
Professor Emeritus of Guarantees and
Appeals, UNAM, 1971-79; Professor of
Guarantees and Appeals, Ibero-American University; Professor of Constitu-
tional Law, Escuela Libre de Derecho;
professor at the National Preparatory
School; Director of the National School
of Law, UNAM, 1944-45; Secretary
General of UNAM, 1943-44; acting
Rector of UNAM, 1944; member of the
Governing Council of UNAM (12
years). d-None. e-None. f-Member of
the Advisory Council for the Depart-
ment of the Federal District, 1958-64;
Secretary of the Advisory Council of the
Department of the Federal District,
1964-70; Secretary General of the
Advisory Council of the Federal
District, 1970-72; Director General of
the Financiera Nacional Azucarera,
1953; Director General of Higher
Education and Scientific Research,
Secretariat of Public Education, 1946;
Director of the Tourism Trust, 1972.
g-Consultant for the Chamber of
Industries of the Federal District, 1956;
manager of CONCAMIN. h-Author of
articles and books on law; President of
the National Association of Lawyers,
1942. i-Knew *Antonio Carrillo Flores,
Manuel Ramírez Vázquez, Ernesto P.
Uruchurtu, Antonio Ortiz Mena, Angel
Carvajal, Manuel Sánchez Cuen,
Andrés Serra Rojas* at UNAM; studied
under *Alfonso Caso*; married María del
Carmen Fernández; son of Alfonso

Noriega Lazo and Sara Cantú. j-None.
k-National Prize in the Social Sciences,
1985. l-WWM45, 83; DGF56, 470;
Correa, 255; letter; DPE61, 134; *Excélsior*, 15 Jan. 1976; López, 769; WNM,
159; JSH, 270-71; HA, 2 Feb. 1988, 73.

Noriega (Ondovilla), Raúl
(Deceased Apr. 22, 1975) a-July 27,
1907. b-Federal District. c-Primary and
secondary studies in the Federal
District; preparatory studies at the
National Preparatory School, 1920-24;
law degree, National School of Law,
UNAM, 1924-28, receiving his degree
Mar. 1, 1947; Professor of the History of
Mexico, National Preparatory School,
1934-36; Professor of World History,
National Preparatory School, 1934-36.
d-*Federal Deputy* from the Federal
District, Dist. 17, 1967-70, member of
the Department of the Federal District
Committee, the Editorial Committee
(1st and 2nd year), the First Treasury
Committee. e-None. f-Alternate
Mexican delegate to the United Na-
tions, 1947-51; *Oficial Mayor of the
Secretariat of the Treasury*, 1951-58;
Director General of PIPSA, 1958-59;
Coordinator of Audiovisual Teaching,
Secretariat of Public Education, 1958-
64; Director of the Legal Department,
Altos Hornos, 1971-74; Director Gen-
eral of the Government Printing Office,
1974-75. g-None. h-Director of the
student newspapers *Agora, Policromias*
and *La Huelga*, 1920-29; editor of the
Sunday supplement, *El Nacional*, 1929;
Editor-in-Chief of *Izquierdas*, 1935-39;
Director of the Radio Station XEFO,
1935; founder and Director of the
Publishing House, Biblioteca del
Maestro; founder of the publishing
series, 20th Century Collection;
Director of *El Nacional*, 1938-47;
President of the Permanent Commission of the First Latin American Press
Congress, 1934-44; Director of the sup-
plement section to *Novedades*, 1961-70.

i-Friend of *Miguel Alemán* at the National Law School; son of José Noriega Robledo and Carlota Ondoville Ibáñez. j-None. k-None. l-MGF69, 91; DGF51, I, 145; DBM68, 456; WWM45, 84; letter; C de D, 1967-69, 62, 73; Novo, 746-47; Enc. Mex., IX, 1977, 403; HA, 12 Aug. 1974, 17; HA, 28 Apr. 1975, 11; *Excélsior*, 20 Oct. 1949; López, 769.

Noriega Pizano, Arturo
a-Apr. 10, 1915. b-Colima, Colima. c-Primary studies at the Gabino Barreda and the Benito Juárez Schools, Colima; secondary and preparatory studies, Normal School, Colima; law degree, School of Law, University of Guadalajara, June 1942, with a thesis on "Amparo before the State Supreme Courts on Articles 16, 18, 20 of the Federal Constitution"; secondary teacher in civics and economics, 1936; Professor of Sociology and Ethics, Normal School, Colima, 1944; Director of the Preparatory School of Colima. d-Mayor of Colima, Jan. 1, 1971 to Sept. 19, 1973; *Governor of Colima*, Jan. 1, 1974-80. e-None. f-Civil Judge and Director of the Public Property Registry, Colima, 1943-51; Public Notary, 1951-73; Judge of the Superior Tribunal of Justice of the State of Colima, 1951-52; President of the Superior Tribunal of Justice of the State of Colima, 1953-55; Attorney General of Colima, 1955-61; Secretary General of Government of the State of Colima under Governor *Pablo Silva García*, 1967-70. g-None. h-Practicing lawyer, 1961-66. i-Son of Bulmaro Noriega and Carmen Pizano; married Luisa María Campero. j-None. k-Elected governor in a special election after the governor-elect, *Antonio Barbosa Heldt*, committed suicide. l-Enc. Mex., Annual, 1977, 541-42; HA, 1 Oct. 1973, 35; *Excélsior*, 25 Sept. 1973, 4, 17 Dec. 1973, 6.

Norzagaray (Angulo), Bernardo
a-July 1, 1910. b-Guasave, Sinaloa. c-Preparatory at the French-English Institute, Mexico City; degree in agricultural engineering, Agricultural College, Ciudad Juárez, Chihuahua. d-*Federal Deputy* from the State of Sinaloa, Dist. 3, 1943-46; *Federal Deputy* from the State of Sinaloa, Dist. 4, 1952-55, member of the Waters and Irrigation Committee, the Second Credentials Committee, the Budget and Accounts Committee (1st year), and substitute member of the Agrarian Department Committee, the Properties and Natural Resouces Committee, and the Colonization Committee; Mayor of Ciudad Juárez, 1968-71. e-Representative of the National Farmers Federation on the CEN of PRI. f-Administrator of the Ejido Bank of Culiacán and Mazatlán, Sinaloa; Administrator of the Agricultural Bank of Culiacán; Director of Farm Loans of the Bank of Sinaloa; Head of the Department of Operations, National Army-Navy Bank, 1950-51; Head of the Agricultural Credit Department, National Army-Navy Bank; Secretary General of Government for the State of Sinaloa; President of the Federal Improvement Board, Ciudad Juárez, Chihuahua, 1958-64. h-None. j-None. k-*Por Qué* holds him responsible for the rapid expansion of prostitution in Ciudad Juárez during his term as mayor. l-C de D, 1952-54, 116, 46, 63; DGF51, II, 34; C de D, 1943-45, 17; WWMG, 28-29; *Por Qué*, 20 Nov. 1969; Peral, 574; DGF50, II, 36.

Novelo Torres, Ernesto
(Deceased 1968) a-1895. b-Valladolid, Yucatán. c-Studied for the priesthood in the Seminario Conciliar, Mérida; studied at the Literary Institute of Yucatán, Mérida, Yucatán. d-Mayor of Progreso, 1935; Local Deputy to the State Legislature of Yucatán, 1935-36; *Governor of Yucatán*, 1942-46; *Senator*

from the State of Yucatán, 1946-52, member of the Mail and Telegraph Committee, the Second Balloting Committee and the National Lands Committee. e-None. f-General accountant for National Telegraphs of Mexico, Mexico City, 1927; Head of Telegraph and Mail Office, Progreso, Yucatán; Treasurer General of Yucatán under Governor *Canto Echeverría*, 1938-40; Oficial Mayor of Yucatán, 1940-42. g-None. h-Telegrapher, Mérida, 1924-27; founder of the Fomento de Yucatán. i-Relative of José Inés Novelo, deputy to the Constitutional Convention, 1916-17; married Candelaria Serrano Cetina; son of Serapio Novelo and Encarnación Torres. j-None. k-*Novedades* claims he dominated the selection of Yucatán governors until 1963. l-DP70, 1478; WWM45, 84; HA, 12 June 1942, 30; DGF51, I, i, 10, 14; Informes, 1943, 1944; HA, 28 Apr. 1945, 23; Enc. Mex., IX, 1977, 408; *Novedades*, 5 Aug. 1963.

Novo (López), Salvador
(Deceased Jan. 13, 1974) a-July 30, 1904. b-Federal District. c-Primary studies in Chihuahua and Torreón, at the private Colegio Modelo and at a public school (6th year); secondary studies in Mexico City; preparatory at the National Preparatory School, 1917-20; began studies in law, UNAM, but changed to literature; MA, UNAM; Professor of Italian Literature, School of Philosophy and Liberal Arts, UNAM; Professor of Spanish, 1923-28; National Preparatory School; Professor of Spanish Literature, secondary schools; Professor of the History of Theater, National Conservatory, 1930-33; Professor of English, secondary schools. d-None. e-Member of the CEN of the Popular Party, 1947-48. f-Head of the Editorial Department, Secretariat of Public Education, 1924-28; Head of the Department of Publicity, Secretariat of Foreign Relations, 1930-34; Head of the Department of Theatrical Productions, National Institute of Fine Arts, 1946-52; Director of the School of Dramatic Art, National Institute of Fine Arts, 1956; Official Historian of Mexico City, 1965-74. g-None. h-Prolific author of poems, plays, and books; author of books on the *Alemán* and *Cárdenas* periods in Mexico; Director of the magazine, *Ulysses*, with the poet Xavier Villaurrutia, 1927-28. i-Boyhood friend of *Raúl López Sánchez*, governor of Coahuila, 1948-51; attended the National Preparatory School with *José Gorostiza, Raúl Noriega*, and *Mariano Ramírez Vázquez*; longtime friend of *Jaime Torres Bodet*; son of Andrés Novo Blanco, a prosperous Spanish businessman, and Amelia López Espino. j-None. k-Supported José Vasconcelos for president, 1928-29. l-DGF51, I, 293; DPE61, 107; WWM45, 84; DBM68, 458-59; letter; Novo, 749, 757-58; *Excélsior*, 15 Jan. 1974, 10; HA, 21 Jan. 1974, 9-10; Q es Q, 417-18; Enc. Mex., IX, 1977, 408; Velázquez, 198-200; O'Campo, 254-58; WNM, 159.

Novoa, Carlos
a-June 30, 1900. b-Federal District. c-Secondary at the Colegio de Mascarones (Jesuit); preparatory at the National Preparatory School, Mexico City; law degree from the National School of Law, UNAM, 1926; Professor of Money and Credit at the School of Commerce, UNAM, 1930-36. d-None. e-Founder of PAN, 1939. f-Consulting lawyer to the Secretariat of Treasury, 1926-35; President of the Public Debt Commission, 1932-33; President of the National Banking Commission, 1933; *Director General of the Bank of Mexico*, 1946-52. g-Director, 1937-41, and President, 1945-46, of the Bankers Association of Mexico. h-Director General of the Industrial Bank, 1940-46; Mexican delegate to the International

Monetary Fund, 1946-52; President of Patronage for UNAM, 1968. i-Knew *Antonio Martínez Báez* at the National School of Law; son of lawyer Eduardo Novoa, subsecretary of justice under Porfirio Díaz, and Margarita Roumagnac; married Eugenia Allard. j-None. k-Supported José Vasconcelos for president, 1928-29. l-*El Universal*, 2 Dec. 1946; DBM68, 458; WWM45, 84; DGF51, II, 6, 65, 77; DGF50, 71; Mabry, 35-36; letter; Skirius, 105; HA, 18 Apr. 1947, 30.

Noyola (Zepeda), J. Jesús M.
a-Sept. 7, 1898. b-Cerritos, San Luis Potosí. c-Primary and secondary studies in San Luis Potosí; preparatory studies at the University of San Luis Potosí; medical studies, Sorbonne, Paris; medical degree, University of San Luis Potosí; Director of the School of Medicine, University of San Luis Potosí, 1946-52; Rector of the University of San Luis Potosí, 1958-64. d-*Federal Deputy* from the State of San Luis Potosí, Dist. 6, 1949-52; *Alternate Senator* from the State of San Luis Potosí, 1952-58; *Senator* from the State of San Luis Potosí, 1964-70. e-None. f-None. g-None. i-Alternate senator under *Antonio Rocha*, 1952-58. j-None. k-None. l-C de D, 1949-52; DGF51, I, MGF69; C de S, 1952-58; DGF56; C de S, 1964-70.

Núñez Guzmán, Marina
a-Dec. 26, 1919. b-Tepic, Nayarit. c-Primary studies at the Amado Nervo School; stenographer from Taylor Academy, 1933. d-*Federal Deputy* from the State of Nayarit, Dist. 2, 1964-67. e-Director of Social Action of PRI, State of Nayarit; participated in the presidential campaign of *Gustavo Díaz Ordaz*, 1963-64. f-Employee, Department of Labor and Social Welfare, State of Nayarit, 1934-37. g-Typist, CTM of Nayarit, 1938-39;

employee, League of Agrarian Communities of the CTM of Nayarit; Secretary General of Feminine Action of the CTM; Secretary of Conflicts, Federation of Workers of Tepic. h-None. j-None. k-First female deputy from the State of Nayarit. l-C de D, 1964-67.

Núñez Jiménez, Arturo
a-Jan. 23, 1948. b-Villahermosa, Tabasco. c-Early education unknown; economics degree, National School of Economics, UNAM, 1966-70; professor, National School of Economics, UNAM, 1968-69; professor, School of Administration and Accounting, Autonomous Juárez University of Tabasco, 1971-72; Chief of Cultural Diffusion Department, Autonomous Juárez University of Tabasco, 1971-72; professor, National Institute of Public Administration, 1981-86; professor, National Institute of Public Administration, 1978-83. d-None. e-Joined PRI, 1969; Director of the CEPES of PRI, Tabasco, 1975-76; Private Secretary to the President of the CEN of PRI, *Adolfo Lugo Verduzco*, 1982-84; Assistant Secretary of the CEN of PRI, 1984-85; Secretary of Political Education of the CEN of PRI, 1985-88. f-Technical Budget Director, State of Tabasco, 1971-72; Private Secretary to the Governor of Tabasco, *Mario Trujillo García*, 1972-74; Delegate of the Program for Rural Economic Development Investment, Presidency of Mexico, 1974-76; Chief of Control, Subsecretary of Income, Secretariat of the Treasury, 1977-78; Subdirector of Administrative Coordination, Presidency of Mexico, 1978-82; Director General of Political Development, Secretariat of the Government, 1989-91; *Subsecretary of Government and Political Development*, Secretariat of Government, Mar. 13, 1991-1992; Director General of the Federal Electoral Institute, 1993-94. g-Secretary of Political Action and Ideological Orien-

tation, CNOP, Villahermosa, Tabasco. i-Son of Enrique Núñez García, geophysical engineer, and Olga Jiménez Pérez; married Martha Lilia López Aguilera, teacher. j-None. k-None. l-*El Nacional*, 14 Mar. 1991, 11; DBGM92, 262; DBGM89, 252; letters.

Núñez Urquiza, Carlos
a-Oct. 5, 1949. b-Federal District. c-Early education unknown; law degree, National School of Law, UNAM, 1968-70; administration degree, Ibero-American University, 1967-72; MA in administration, Stanford University, 1975-77; Dean, School of Administration, Ibero-American University, 1974-75. d-None. e-Joined PRI, 1974. f-Adviser, Oficial Mayor of Labor, 1974; Executive Secretary, National Council of Open Educational Systems, Secretariat of Public Education, 1978-80; Assistant Director General of Adult Education, Secretariat of Public Education, 1980-81; Director General, National Institute of Adult Education, Secretariat of Public Education, 1981-82; Director of Finances and Administration, Secretariat of Government, 1982-83; Director of Investment Banking, National Bank of Mexico, 1983-88; *Oficial Mayor of the Secretariat of Foreign Relations*, 1988-91. g-None. h-Director General of Plásticos and Novedades, 1972-74. i-Son of Carlos Núñez Chávez, surgeon, and Guadalupe Urquiza Jáuregui, teacher; married María del Carmen Jiménez. j-None. k-None. l-DBGM89, 252.

O

Obregón Padilla, Antonio
a-Mar. 4, 1933. b-León, Guanajuato. c-Primary studies at the Lux Institute, León; secondary studies at public secondary, León; preparatory at the Preparatory School, León; law degree,

Escuela Libre de Derecho. d-*Party Deputy* from PAN, 1967-70. e-Candidate for federal deputy from PAN, 1964; President of PAN for León, Guanajuato, 1965; member of the National Council of PAN, 1968; President of the Regional Committee of PAN, Guanajuato, 1968; representative of PAN to the Local Electoral Committee, Guanajuato, 1970. f-None. g-None. h-Lawyer. i-Father a businessman; married Gabriela Torres. j-None. k-Letter; C de D, 1967-70.

Obregón (Tapia) Jr., Alvaro
a-1916. b-Huatabampo, Sonora. c-Early education unknown; studies in business administration in the United States, 1936. d-*Governor of Sonora*, 1955-61. e-None. f-None. g-None. h-Rancher and businessman. i-Son of General and President Alvaro Obregón; brother, Francisco Obregón, served as President of the Civic Board of Moral and Material Improvement during *Alvaro*'s governorship; married Fernanda Luken j-None. k-Precandidate for mayor of Cajeme, Sonora, 1979; *Excélsior* alleges that Francisco was *Adolfo Ruiz Cortines'* candidate for governor, but because he was legally too young, *Alvaro* was given the post instead; accused of being a large landholder. l-WWM, 29; DGF56, 160; Almanaque de Sonora, 1982, 131; *Excélsior*, 2 May 1979, 4, 8 July 1979, 18; Moncada, 32.

Ocampo Noble Pérez, Federico
a-Oct. 4, 1903. b-Hidalgo, Pachuca. c-Primary and preparatory studies in Hidalgo; law degree, National School of Law, UNAM, 1928. d-*Federal Deputy* from the State of Hidalgo, Dist. 3, 1958-61; *Alternate Senator* from the State of Hidalgo, 1964-68, in functions, 1969-70, for *Manuel Sánchez Vite*. e-Joined PRI, 1936; general delegate of the CEN of PRI to Coahuila, Campeche and Guanajuato. f-Investigative Agent of the Ministerio Público of the Federal

District, 1935-37; representative of the Secretariat of the Treasury in the Federal District, 1937-45; tax attorney, State of Hidalgo; Secretary General of Government of the State of Hidalgo, under *Vicente Aguirre*, 1945-51; representative of the Central Zone of the National Arbitration Committee, Secretariat of the Treasury, 1953-58. g-None. h-Worked as a student in the Tax Department, Secretariat of the Treasury, 1924-26. j-None. k-None. l-Func., 232; C de D, 1958-61; C de S, 1964-70.

Ocaña García, Samuel

a-Sept. 7, 1932. b-Aribechi, Sonora. c-Primary studies at the J. Cruz Gálvez School, Hermosillo, Sonora; secondary and preparatory studies, Boarding School for the Children of Ejidatarios, Tepic Nayarit; medical degree, National School of Medicine, UNAM; specialist in pneumology, Higher School of Rural Medicine, IPN. d-Mayor of Navojoa, Sonora, 1973-75; *Governor of Sonora*, 1979-85. e-Joined PRI, 1959; Director of the CEPES of PRI, Navojoa, 1972; President of PRI in the State of Sonora, 1978-79. f-Subsecretary of Government of the State of Sonora, 1973-74; Secretary General of Government of the State of Sonora, 1976-77. g-Leader of the medical students at UNAM; president of the ex-fellowship students of the National Institute of Pneumology; founder of the Union of Textile Workers of Sonora, 1949. h-Textile worker, 1948-49; founder and director of the Regional Hospital of Pulmonary and Thoracic Surgery, Navojoa, Sonora. i-Collaborator of *Alejandro Carrillo M.*, governor of Sonora, 1975-79; father a peasant. j-None. k-Reportedly dismissed his entire police force as Mayor of Navojoa when a prisoner died under torture. l-LA, 26 Jan. 1979, 30; *Excélsior*, 18 Jan. 1979, 4, 18, 23, 17 Jan. 1979, 10; Protag., 251; Almanaque de México, 1982, 587.

Ocaranza Carmona, Fernando

(Deceased Feb. 12, 1965) a-May 30, 1876. b-Federal District. c-Secondary at the Scientific and Literary Institute of Toluca, México, and at the Colegio Hispano-México, Toluca; preparatory studies from the Scientific and Literary Institute of México, Toluca, 1890-94; medical studies at the National Medical School, UNAM, 1895-97; transferred to the Military Medical School, medical degree, May 8, 1900, graduating as a surgeon and Major in the army; professor at the Military Medical School, 1917; Professor of Physiology at the National School of Medicine, UNAM, 1915-46; secretary at the National School of Medicine, 1917-20, UNAM; Director of the National School of Medicine, UNAM, 1925-32, 1934; professor at normal schools; Professor of Clinical Medicine, UNAM, 1926-46; Rector of the Scientific and Literary Institute of Toluca, 1936-40. d-None. e-Founder of PAN, 1939. f-Director of the Municipal Hospital, Guaymas, Sonora, 1914-15; Head of the Department of Health, Guaymas, Sonora, 1908-10; emergency physician, Southern Pacific Railroads of Mexico, 1915; physician for the National Shipyards, 1916; Head of the Laboratory of Comparative Physiology, Institute of Biology, 1915-18; Director of the Institute of Hygiene, 1922-23; adviser to the Secretary of Health, 1921-24; *Rector of UNAM*, 1934-35; member of the General Health Council of Mexico, 1952-58. g-None. h-Surgeon, Red Cross, Tacubaya; author of many books and over 150 articles on medical subjects. i-Great-grandfather, Carlos de Mayo, was a colonel in the Spanish army of New Spain; married Loreto Esquer; son of Ramón Ocaranza and Antonia Carmona; students included *Maximiliano Ruiz Castañeda, Salvador Zubirán*, and *Julián Garza Tijerina*.

j-Head of the Military Hospital, Jalapa, Veracruz, 1904; Head of the 2nd Surgery Section, Military Hospital, Jalapa, Veracruz; joined the 19th Battalion, Sonora, 1900; left the army with the rank of Lt. Colonel to go into private practice in Sonora. k-None. l-DGF51, II, 687; DGF56, 329; DP70, 1499-1500; Peral, 581-82; DGF447, 199; DGF51, 333, 335; López, 784; Enc. Mex., IX, 543; Beltrán, 61; WWM45, 85.

Oceguera Ramos Gil, Rafael
a-Jan. 5, 1950. b-Esquinapa, Sinaloa. c-Early education unknown; normal teaching certificate, Regional Center of Normal Teaching, Ciudad Guzmán, Jalisco, 1968-69; law degree, National School of Law, UNAM and at the National School of Political Science, Acatlán, UNAM, 1977-81; studies in political science and public administration, UNAM, 1981; primary and secondary teacher, 1968-72. d-*Federal Deputy* from the State of Sinaloa, Dist. 3, 1976-79; *Federal Deputy* from the State of Sinaloa, Dist. 5, 1982-85, President of the Tourism Committee. e-Joined PRI, 1968; Secretary of Youth Action of PRI, Sonora, 1972-73; Secretary General of the National Movement of Revolutionary Youth of PRI, 1973-76; general delegate of the CEN of PRI in Nayarit and Durango, 1976-77. f-General delegate of the Secretariat of Public Education in Yucatán and Michoacán, 1979-80; Director General of Primary Education, Secretariat of Public Education, 1980-82. g-Director of Youth of Ciudad Obregón; Secretary General of the Student Revolutionary Youth Movement, Sonora, 1973-74. i-Son of Ramón Oceguera Verduzco, self-employed, and Elvira Ramos Celis; married Luisa María Espinosa de los Monteros, lawyer. j-None. k-None. l-Directorio, 1982-85; C de D, 1982-85, 1976-79; Lehr, 433; DBGM, 567.

Ochoa Campos, Moisés
a-Aug. 10, 1917. b-Chilpancingo, Iguala, Guerrero. c-Primary studies at the Public School of Chilpancingo; secondary studies at Colegio of Guerrero, Chilpancingo; degree in political science, National School of Political and Social Sciences, UNAM, May 1955, with a thesis on municipal reform; studied at the School of Political Science, Degli Studi University, Rome, 1955-56, and other studies in Rome; professor at the School of Political and Social Sciences, UNAM, 1957-59, in the field of theory; Director of the Seminar on Political Investigations, 1955-59. d-*Federal Deputy* from the State of Guerrero, 1958-61, Dist. 1, member of the Radio and Television Committee, the Budget and Accounts Committee (2nd year), substitute member of the Military Justice Committee; *Alternate Senator* from the State of Guerrero, 1964-70; *Federal Deputy* from the State of Guerrero, Dist. 1, 1970-73, member of the Cultural Affairs Committee, the Editorial Committee (1st year), the Money and Credit Institutions Committee, and the First Section of the Constitutional Affairs Committee. e-Private Secretary to the Director of Press and Publicity, CEN of PRI; *Secretary of Press and Publicity of the CEN of PRI*, 1952-58. f-Private Secretary to the Secretary of the Agrarian Department; Coordinating Director of the Civic Improvement Boards, Secretariat of Government, 1958; Assistant Director, Office of Intellectual Cooperation, Secretariat of Public Education; General Coordinator of Planning and Statistics, Secretariat of Public Education, 1965. g-None. h-Director of the periodical, *La República*, 1958; author of several works. i-Son of engineer Lorenzo Ricardo Ochoa and Luz Campos; marrried María Elena Castillo. j-None. k-First graduate of the School of

Political and Social Science, UNAM. l-B de M, 192; C de D, 1970-72, 127, 1958-60, 86; Func., 220.

Ochoa Palencia, Arturo
a-Feb. 25, 1911. b-Colima, Colima. c-Early education unknown; enrolled as a cadet, Heroic Military College, Jan. 1, 1930, graduating as a 2nd Lieutenant in Infantry, Jan. 1, 1934; diploma in communications, Military Communications School; completed Staff and Command course, Higher War College. d-None. e-None. f-*Oficial Mayor of the Secretariat of National Defense, 1976.* g-None. h-None. i-Married Francisca Francos. j-Career army officer; Section Commander, 37th Infantry Battalion; Commander of Communications, 2nd Cavalry Regiment; Chief of Communications, 29th Military Zone, Ciudad Ixtepec, Oaxaca; Chief of Section 1, Staff, 1st Infantry Division; Adjutant General, Higher War College; Assistant Chief of Staff, 27th Military Zone, Iguala, Guerrero; Chief of Section 1, Staff, Secretariat of National Defense; rank of Lt. Colonel, 1956; Commander, 47th Infantry Battalion; rank of Colonel, 1960; Chief of Staff, 1st Military Zone, Mexico City; rank of Brigadier General, 1967; Commander of the 32nd Military Zone, Mérida, Yucatán; rank of Division General, 1976. k-None. l-Rev. de Ejer., Oct. 1960, 17; Dec. 1967, 49, May 1957, 38, Oct.-Nov. 1976, 67; DAPC77, 12; Rev. de Ejer., Feb. 1975, 140.

Ochoa Toledo, Alfredo
a-Dec. 3, 1929. b-Tuxtla Gutiérrez, Chiapas. c-Primary and secondary studies, Tuxtla Gutiérrez; secondary studies, Special Secondary, Industrial, and Business Education No. 3, Tuxtla Gutiérrez; graduated as a 2nd Lieutenant in Artillery, Heroic Military College, 1948-51; diploma in administration, Higher War College, 1954-57; MA in mathematics, Higher Normal

School, 1968-72; Commander of Cadet Battery, Heroic Military College, 1959; Professor, Higher War College, 1958-59, 1966-71; Professor and Chief of Instruction, Heroic Military College, 1959-65; Subdirector, Heroic Military College, 1972-73; Subdirector of the Higher War College, 1975-76; Professor, IPN, 1977-79. d-None. e-Joined PRI. f-*Subsecretary of National Defense, 1988-94.* g-None. h-None. i-Son of Gilberto Ochoa Torres, school teacher, and Rosalia Toledo Pérez; married Beatriz Lazos Araujo. j-Joined the army as a cadet, Heroic Military College, 1948; officer, 2nd Artillery Regiment, 1951; rank of 1st Lieutenant, Jan. 1, 1953; rank of 2nd Captain, 1957; rank of 1st Captain, 1960; rank of major, 1963; officer, 2nd Artillery Battalion, 1965; rank of Lt. Colonel, 1966; second in command, 3rd Artillery Battalion, 1971-72; rank of Colonel, 1972; staff, Secretariat of National Defense, 1973; Commander, 4th Artillery Battalion, 1973-75; Chief of Staff, 10th Military Zone, Durango, Durango, 1975; Operations Officer, Garrison, Reynoso, Tamaulipas, 1975; rank of Brigadier General, Nov. 20, 1977; aide, Inspector General of the Army, 1977; Chief of Technical Section, Artillery Division, Secretariat of National Defense, 1977; Subdirector General of Artillery, Secretariat of National Defense, 1977-79; Interim Director General of Artillery, Secretariat of National Defense, 1979-81; Chief of the Technical Section, Artillery Division, Secretariat of National Defense, 1981-83; Director General of Military Education and the Army Air Force University, Secretariat of National Defense, 1983-85; rank of Brigade General, 1985; Military Attaché to Germany, France, Belgium, and Holland, 1985-86; Director General of Military Industry, Secretariat of National Defense, 1987-88; rank of Division General. k-None. l-QesQAP, 80; Rev. de Ejer., Nov. 1972,

50, Nov. 1981, 24; DBGM89, 253; DBGM87, 277; DBGM92, 263; Rev. de Ejer., Dec. 1988, 13-14.

Odorica Inclán, Fernando
b-Toluca, México. c-Primary and secondary studies in Toluca; law degree, National School of Law, UNAM; Rector of the Autonomous University of the State of México, Toluca. d-*Senator from the State of México, 1964-70*. e-None. f-Official of the Department of Alcohol, Secretariat of the Treasury. g-None. j-None. k-None. l-PS, 4453; C de S, 1964-70; MGF69.

Ogaz Pierce, José Abel
a-Nov. 16, 1949. b-Federal District. c-Preparatory studies at the National Preparatory School No. 7; studies in economics, National School of Economics, UNAM. d-None. e-Secretary of Political Education of the PPS in the Federal District, 1979; Director of the National Committee of Political, Economic and Social Studies of the PPS, 1979; Director, PPS Platform Committee, 1979. f-None. g-President of the Society of Students of the National Preparatory School No. 7; leader of the Popular Socialist Youth, 1970; delegate to the 7th Assembly of the World Confederations of Democratic Youth, 1970. j-None. k-None. l-HA, 26 Mar. 1979, I.

Ojeda, Carlos Darío
(Deceased) a-July 27, 1896. b-Veracruz. c-Early education unknown; no degree. d-Federal Deputy from the State of Veracruz, Dist. 9, 1930-32, Dist. 11, 1932-34. e-None. f-Joined the Foreign Service, 1935; Ambassador to Sweden, 1935-36, to Belgium, 1936-37, to Colombia, 1939-40, to Uruguay, 1940-43, to Costa Rica, 1946-48, to Italy, 1948-51, to Austria, 1952, to Italy, 1952-53, and to Peru, 1954-56; *Oficial Mayor of the Secretariat of Foreign*

Relations, 1957-64; Ambassador to Switzerland, 1965. g-None. h-None. i-Married María Teresa Maldonaldo Rojas; son, Carlos Darios, was consul general in Chicago, 1984 j-None. k-None. l-Letter; DBGM, 309.

Ojeda (Caballero), Nabor A.
a-June 12, 1894. b-Ometepec, Guerrero. c-Secondary studies at the Colegio Espiritu Santo, Oaxaca; preparatory studies at the Institute of Arts and Sciences, Oaxaca, Oaxaca; no degree. d-Local Deputy to the State Legislature of Guerrero, 1931-33; *Federal Deputy from the State of Guerrero, Dist. 5, 1937-40; Senator from the State of Guerrero, 1940-46*, President of the Indigenous Affairs Committee, member of the Gran Comisión, First Secretary of the Second National Defense Committee, Second Secretary of the Agrarian Affairs Department Committee; *Federal Deputy from the State of Guerrero, Dist. 2, 1967-70*, member of the Second National Defense Committee and the Military Justice Committee. e-None. f-Director of the Indigenous Zone, Valley of Mexico, 1935. g-First Secretary of Conflicts of the CNC, 1933-35; first Secretary General and founder, League of Agrarian Communities and Workers Union, Guerrero; director, ejidatario organization, Oaxaca. h-Author of federal laws dealing with communal lands and benefits for Revolutionary veterans. i-Son, *Nabor Gustavo Ojeda Delgado*, was a federal deputy from Guerrero, 1973-76; married Alicia Delgado, normal teacher. j-Joined the Revolution in support of Madero, 1911; rank of Captain, Feb. 1911; participated in 44 battles; rank of Brigade General. l-Peral states that the Mexican press published articles accusing Ojeda of responsibility for political murders in Guerrero. l-Peral, 584; C de S, 40-46; C de D, 1946-48, 81, 1937-39; González Navarro; López, 787.

Ojeda Delgado, Nabor Gustavo
a-June 6, 1947. b-Iguala, Guerrero.
c-Early education unknown; architectural engineering degree, National
Polytechnic Institute, with a thesis on
city buildings in Ixtepec, Oaxaca.
d-*Federal Deputy* from the State of
Guerrero, Dist. 6, 1973-76, Dist. 9,
1985-88, Dist. 7, 1991-94. e-Joined PRI,
1967; Special Delegate of the CEN of
PRI to Nayarit and Michoacán, 1975-76.
f-Director of Government, Acapulco,
1976; Manager of Organization, Mexican Coffee Institute, 1980; Subdirector
of International Relations, Secretariat of
Agriculture and Hydraulic Resources,
1984. g-Auxiliary Secretary to the
Oficial Mayor of the CNC, 1967-68;
Private Secretary to the Secretary
General of the CEN of the CNC, 1970;
Secretary of Rural Housing, CNC, 1971-
73; Oficial Mayor of the CNC, 1986-87;
Interim Secretary General of the League
of Agrarian Communities of Guerrero,
1987. h-None. i-Son of *Nabor Ojeda
Caballero*, brigade general and senator,
and Alicia Delgado, teacher; married
Reyna Concepción Lazcano Xoxotla.
j-None. k-None. l-DBGM87, 529;
DBGM92, 536.

Ojeda Paullada, Pedro
a-Jan. 19, 1934. b-Federal District.
c-Primary studies at the Escuela
Mexicano-Inglés, Mexico City, 1940-44;
secondary studies in Mexico City, 1945-
47; preparatory studies at the National
Preparatory School, 1948-49; studied at
the National School of Law, UNAM,
1950-54, law degree, 1955, with a thesis
on Federal Boards of Moral and Material
Improvement. d-*Plurinominal Federal
Deputy* from PRI, 1991-94. e-Joined
PRI, 1951; member, Organizing Committee of the National Program of PRI,
1962; representative of PRI to the
Electoral Commission for the 13th
District, Mexico City, 1963-64; delegate
of the IEPES of PRI to the CEPES of

Morelos, 1969; *President of the CEN of
PRI*, 1981-82. f-Merit employee,
Seventh Civil Judicial District, Federal
District, 1950-51; employee, Personnel
Department, PEMEX, 1952; legal intern,
Secretariat of Health and Welfare, 1953;
Subdirector General of the Federal
Boards for Material Improvements,
Secretariat of National Patrimony,
under *José López Portillo*, 1959-65;
adviser to the Chihuahua-Pacific
Railroad; Director General of Legal
Affairs, Secretariat of Communication
and Transportation; Director of the
Technical Advisory Commission of
General Means of Communication,
Secretariat of Communication and
Transportation, 1966-70; *Oficial Mayor
of the Presidency*, 1970-71; *Attorney
General of Mexico*, 1971-76; *Secretary
of Labor*, 1976-81; *Head, Department of
Fisheries*, 1982-88. g-Founder and
President of the Platform of Mexican
Professionals, 1961. h-Practiced law,
1955-59. i-Personal friend of *Luis
Echeverría*; knew *Jorge de la Vega
Domínguez* as a student at law school;
married Olga Cárdenas, lawyer; son of
lawyer Manuel R. Ojeda Lacroix,
director of the Legal Department,
Secretary of Health, and Adela
Paullada Preciat. j-None. k-None.
l-HA, 30 Aug. 1971, 10; MGF69, 278;
HA, 14 Dec. 1970, 23; DPE61, 61;
DPE71, 124; LA, 3 Dec. 1976; HA, 2
May 1977, 18; *Excélsior*, 1 Dec. 1976;
HA, 6 Dec. 1976, 23; *Excélsior*, 31 Jan.
1984, 4; Q es QAP, 407; *Excélsior*, 15
Oct. 1981, 1, 1 Dec. 1982, 34; Informe,
78; *Excélsior*, 31 Jan. 1984, 4; *Proceso*,
20 July 1987, 10; DBGM, 309; DBGM92,
536; letter.

Olachea Aviles, Agustín
(Deceased Apr. 13, 1974) a-Sept. 3,
1892. b-Todos Santos, San Venancio,
Baja California del Sur. c-No formal
education. d-None. e-*President of the
CEN of PRI*, Apr. 26 to Dec. 3, 1958.

f-Governor of Baja California del Sur, 1929-31; Governor of Baja California del Norte, 1931-35; *Governor of Baja California del Sur*, 1946-52, and 1952-56; *Secretary of National Defense*, 1958-64. g-None. h-Before the Revolution, worked as a miner. i-Parents were rural laborers; son, *Agustín Olachea Borbón*, was director of the Department of Tourism, 1970-73; married Ana María Borbón. j-Joined the Revolution as a private, 1913, under the forces of General Manuel Diéguez; head of Military Operations in Yucatán and Quintana Roo, 1925-26; fought the Yaquis in Sonora, 1926; rank of Brigadier General, May 16, 1929; fought against the Escobar rebellion, 1929; Commander of the 13th Military Zone, Tepic, Nayarit, 1940-45; Commander of the 15th Military Zone, Guadalajara, Jalisco, 1945-46; rank of Division General. k-Brandenburg considers Olachea Aviles in the Inner Circle of decision-making in Mexico from 1946 to 1958; as a young boy, he participated in the Cananea mining strike in 1906; supported *Lázaro Cárdenas* for president in 1934. l-*Hoy*, Dec. 1958; HA, 8 Dec. 1958, 25; DGF56, 103, 201; Brandenburg, 102; DGF51, I, 88; Scott, 171; Peral, 584; Morton, 93, 100, 110, 117-18; *Polémica*, Vol. 1, 1969, 75; Gaxiola, 177-78; Enc. Mex., IX, 1977, 569; *Excélsior*, 14 Apr. 1974, 4; HA, 22 Apr. 1974, 19; López, 787.

Olachea Borbón, Agustín
a-May 2, 1933. b-Tijuana, Baja California del Norte. c-Studied at the National School of Economics, UNAM, 1954-58, economics degree in 1960. d-None. e-Coordinator of Economic Advisers for the presidential campaign of *Adolfo López Mateos*, 1958, while his father was president of the CEN of PRI; precandidate for PRI senatorial nomination from Baja California del Sur, 1981. f-Member of the Advisory Commission

for the Mexican–United States Border; Director of Publications for the Bureau of Tourist Studies, 1966-70; *Head of Tourism Department*, 1970-73; Ambassador to Rumania, 1973. g-None. h-Employed in the Administration of Treasury Studies, Secretariat of the Treasury, 1954; author of many works on tourism in Mexico. i-Attended law school with *José Bermúdez Limón* at UNAM; son of *Agustín Olachea Aviles*, president of the CEN of PRI, 1956-58, and secretary of national defense, 1958-64; brother-in-law of *Israel Nogueda Otero*, governor of Guerrero, 1971-75; married María de los Angeles Nogueda. j-None. k-None. l-HA, 7 Dec. 1970, 26; *Hoy*, Dec. 1970; letter; *Excélsior*, 26 Dec. 1981, 16.

Olamendi Torres, Carlos
a-Oct. 17, 1955. b-Cholula, Puebla. c-Primary and secondary studies in Cuautla, Morelos; preparatory studies in Puebla, Puebla; studies in law at the University of Morelos, Cuautla, and at the National School of Law, UNAM. d-None. e-Secretary of Relations, Central Committee of the Socialist Workers Party; member of the Executive Committee of the Central Committee of the Socialist Workers Party, 1979. f-None. g-None. j-None. k-None. l-HA, 19 Mar. 1979, IV.

Olea Enríquez, Miguel Angel
a-Oct. 16, 1925. b-Chihuahua, Chihuahua. c-Early education unknown; public accounting degree, School of Banking and Business Administration, 1942-47. d-*Federal Deputy from the State of Chihuahua, Dist. 1, 1958-61, Dist. 10, 1982-85.* e-Joined PRI, 1947. f-Coordinator General of the General Commission on Prices, Secretariat of Commerce, 1977-82; Director General of CORDEMEX, 1964-71; Administrative Subdirector of Federal Automobile Registration, 1962-64. g-Treasurer and

Vice-President, Mexican Hotel Association, 1957-59; Vice-President of the Chamber of Commerce of Chihuahua, 1959. h-Manager, Hilton Hotel, Chihuahua, 1952-59; Director of Sales, Grupo Gruma Industrial, 1971-79. i-Son of Miguel Olea Siqueiros, businessman and industrialist, and Carmen Enríquez Alcalá; married Hortensia Sisniega Márquez. j-None. k-None. l-Directorio, 1982-85; C de D, 1958-61.

Olea Muñoz, Javier
b-Guerrero. c-Early education unknown; law degree, National School of Law, UNAM, 1954. d-None. e-None. f-Attorney General of the State of Guerrero under Governor *Raúl Caballero Aburto*, 1961; Private Secretary to the Governor of Guerrero; *Governor of Guerrero*, Jan. 31 to May 31, 1975; Ambassador to Japan, 1977-79. g-None. h-Practicing lawyer in criminal law, Mexico City. j-None. k-Resisted the Permanent Committee's decision to dissolve state powers under *Raúl Caballero*, 1961; held responsible by some for ordering the army to shoot student strikers in Guerrero, 1961; appointed Interim Governor of Guerrero by the Permanent Committee after *Israel Nogueda Otero*'s powers as governor were dissolved. l-DJBM, 99; HA, 11 Apr. 1977, 6; HA, 10 Feb. 1975, 27; *Excélsior*, 3 Feb. 1975, 9, 2 Feb. 1975, 9.

Olea y Leyva, Sabino M.
(Deceased 1950) b-Ajuchitlán, Guerrero. c-Early education unknown; preparatory studies at the Colegio de San Nicolás, Morelia, Michoacán; law degree, National School of Law, UNAM, 1907. d-None. e-None. f-Justice of the Superior Tribunal of Justice of the Federal District and Federal Territories; Justice of the Supreme Court, 1923-35, *Justice of the Supreme Court*, 1935-40. g-None. h-Poet. i-Father, an administrator of haciendas;

nephew of Agustín Aragón, the foremost positivist in Mexico in 1900; brother of *Teófilo Olea y Leyva*, justice of the Supreme Court, 1940-56. j-None. k-None. l-DP70, 1510; López, 788.

Olea y Leyva, Teófilo
(Deceased Sept. 5, 1956) a-Jan. 8, 1895. b-Miacatlán, Morelos. c-Preparatory studies at the National Preparatory School, Mexico City, 1911-15; law degree from the National School of Law, UNAM, Aug. 19, 1919; Ph.D. from the School of Higher Studies, UNAM; Professor of Logic, Ethics, Penal Law and Legal Procedures, School of Higher Studies and the Law School, UNAM; cofounder of the Popular University; Professor of Law, Escuela Libre de Derecho. d-Local Deputy to the State Legislature of Guerrero; President of the State Legislature of Guerrero, 1920. e-Prominent member of the National Action Party; supporter of General *Almazán*, 1939-40. f-Secretary General of Government of the State of Guerrero; Agent of the Military Ministerio Público; Justice of the Tribunal Superior of the Federal District and Territories; *Justice of the Supreme Court*, 1941-46, 1946-52, and 1952-56. g-Founder of the National Association of Legal Employees. h-Author of many major works on Mexican law; writer for *El Universal*. i-Classmate of *Trinidad García* at law school, who later became director of the law school, 1934-35; nephew of Agustín Aragón; father was an administrator of a hacienda; brother, *Sabino*, was a justice of the Supreme Court, 1935-40. j-Served in the Revolution. k-Part of the "Seven Wise Men" generation at National Preparatory School, which included *Manuel Gómez Morín*, founder and president of the National Action Party. l-Peral, 585; DP70, 1510; WWM45, 86; DGF56, 567; DGF51, I, 567; HA, 17 Sept. 1956, 15; Enc. Mex., IX, 1977, 570; López, 788; Krauze, 93; Cadena, 120.

Olguín Vargas, María Amelia
a-Jan. 5, 1946. b-Hidalgo. c-Primary
studies at the Centro Escolar 1940;
secondary studies at the Miguel Hidalgo
School, Actopán, Hidalgo; preparatory
studies at the National Preparatory
School; law degree, National School of
Law, UNAM. d-Local Deputy to the
State Legislature of Hidalgo, 1975;
Federal Deputy from the State of
Hidalgo, Dist. 3, 1979-82. e-General
delegate of the CEN of PRI to Morelos.
f-Secretary of Agreements, Local Board
of Conciliation and Arbitration,
Department of the Federal District,
1970-76; member, Local Board of
Conciliation and Arbitration, Department of the Federal District. g-Special
Delegate of the CNC to Michoacán,
1973; Secretary of Women's Action of
the League of Agrarian Communities of
the CNC of Michoacán, Quintana Roo,
Nuevo León, México, Oaxaca, Tabasco,
Chiapas, Sonora, Baja California del
Norte and Hidalgo; Secretary of Indigenous Action of the CEN of the CNC,
1974; Secretary of Union Action of the
CEN of the CNC, 1978. h-None.
i-Daughter of Ricardo Olguín Zamora
and Josefina Vargas Baños; widow.
j-None. k-None. l-Romero Aceves,
722; Protag., 255; C de D, 1979-82.

Olivares Santana, Enrique
a-Aug. 22, 1920. b-San Luis de Letras,
Rincón de Romos, Aguascalientes.
c-Primary and secondary studies in
Aguascalientes; secondary studies at the
Normal School, San Marcos, Zacatecas;
teaching certificate as a rural teacher,
Regional Peasant School, 1938; normal
teaching certificate, 1951; teacher at the
Escuela de Jesús María, Aguascalientes;
teacher at the Escuela de San José de
Gracia; group teacher, Secretariat of
Public Education. d-Local Deputy to
the State Legislature of Aguascalientes,
1950-53; *Federal Deputy* from the State
of Aguascalientes, Dist. 2, 1958-61,

member of the Administration Com-
mittee, the Legislative Studies Commit-
tee, the First Government Committee,
and the Foreign Relations Committee;
Governor of Aguascalientes, 1962-68;
Senator from the State of Aguasca-
lientes, 1970-76, President of the Gran
Comisión, the First Government Com-
mittee, and the First Constitutional
Affairs Committee. e-President of the
State Regional Committee of PRI in
Aguascalientes, 1952-53; delegate of the
CEN of PRI to San Luis Potosí, Yucatán,
and Colima, 1958-62; head of the State
Planning Council of Aguascalientes for
the presidential campaign of *Adolfo
López Mateos*, 1958; *Secretary General
of the CEN of PRI* under *Alfonso
Martínez Domínguez*, 1968-70; *Secre-
tary of Political Action of the CEN of
PRI*, 1972-74; member of the Political
Action Commission of the IEPES of
PRI, 1972; President, National Advisory
Committee on Ideology and Program,
José López Portillo presidential cam-
paign, 1976. f-Director of Group
Teachers, Secretariat of Public Educa-
tion; Federal Inspector for the Secre-
tariat of Public Education in Zacatecas
and Aguascalientes; Director General of
the National Public Works Bank, 1976-
79; *Secretary of Government*, 1979-82;
Ambassador to Cuba, 1985. g-Secretary
General of Local 1, National Teachers
Union; Secretary of Organization of the
National Teachers Union; leader of the
League of Agrarian Communities and
Farmers Unions, 1948. h-None.
i-Son of peasants; father, Teodoro
Olivares, an agrarian leader in Aguasca-
lientes; married Belén Ventura; *Augusto
Gómez Villanueva* was his private
secretary as governor; son, *Héctor Hugo
Olivares*, was oficial mayor of the
Department of Agrarian Affairs and
senator from Aguascalientes, 1976-82.
j-None. k-His accession to Secretary
General of the SNTE was blocked by
Jesús Robles Martínez and *Manuel*

Sánchez Vite's groups. l-HA, 18 Jan.
1971, 18; DBM68, 464; *Hoy,* 20 Feb.
1971, 10; DBM70, 414-15; C de S, 1970-
76; HA, 2 Jan. 1978; Func., 119; *Excélsior,* 7 June 1977, 6; HA, 10 July 1972,
10; *Excélsior,* 18 May 1979, 7; HA, 2
Jan. 1978; Func., 119; HA, 28 May 1979,
12-13; *Excélsior,* 23 May 1983, 18; HA 8
Apr. 1985.

Olivares (Ventura), Héctor Hugo
a-May 24, 1944. b-Pabellón de Arteaga,
Aguascalientes. c-Early education
unknown; secondary teaching certificate, Regional Normal Center, Ciudad
Guzmán, Jalisco, 1960-63; graduated
from the Higher Normal School,
Nayarit, with a specialty in geography,
1964-69; degree in political and social
science, National School of Political
and Social Science, UNAM, 1970-74.
d-*Senator* from the State of Aguascalientes, 1976-82; *Federal Deputy* from
the State of Aguascalientes, Dist. 2,
1982-85; *Senator* from the State of
Aguascalientes, 1988-94. e-Director of
Youth, Local Committee of PRI, Ciudad
Guzmán, Jalisco, 1962; Director of
Youth, Regional Committee of PRI, Jalisco, 1962; Director of Youth, Regional
Committee of PRI, Aguascalientes,
1969; Director of Youth, Regional Committee of PRI, Federal District, 1971;
*Secretary of Fishing Development of the
CEN of PRI,* 1977; *Secretary of Organization of the CEN of PRI,* 1984; *Secre-
tary of Agrarian Action of the CEN of
PRI,* 1986; *Oficial Mayor of the CEN of
PRI,* 1988. f-*Oficial Mayor of the
Department of Agrarian Reform,* 1974-
75. g-President of the first generation of
regional normal center students of
Ciudad Guzmán, Jalisco and Iguala,
Guerrero, 1963; Secretary of Organiza-
tion of Local No. 28, SNTE in Aguas-
calientes, 1967; Secretary of Press and
Publicity of the CEN of the CNC, 1970-
71; Secretary of Education Action of the
CEN of the CNC, 1971; delegate of the

CNC to the VI National Assembly of
PRI, 1971; Alternate Secretary General
of the CNC, 1974; Secretary of Organization of the CNC, 1980; *Secretary
General of the CNC,* 1986-88. i-Son of
Enrique Olivares Santana, secretary of
government, 1979-82, and Belén
Ventura Rodríguez; grandson of Teodoro
Olivares Calzada, first secretary general
of the League of Agrarian Communities
of Aguascalientes. j-None. k-None.
l-Almanaque de Aguascalientes, 21; HA,
26 Mar. 1984, 16; Directorio, 1982-85;
Protag., 255; C de D, 1982-85; C de S,
1976-82; HA, 26 Mar. 1984, 16;
DBGM92, 537; DBGM89, 507; Lehr, 34;
Protag., 255.

Olive, Issac
b-Paraíso, Tabasco. c-Early education
unknown; law degree, National School
of Law, UNAM. d-Federal Deputy from
the State of Tabasco, Dist. 3, 1922-24,
member of the Gran Comisión; Federal
Deputy from the State of Oaxaca, Dist.
11, 1918-20, member of the Gran Comisión; Federal Deputy from the State of
Oaxaca; Dist. 2, 1917-18. e-None.
f-Secretary of Government of the State
of Oaxaca; Judge, Criminal Jurisdiction,
Fifth Judicial District, Mexico City;
District Court Judge; *Oficial Mayor of
the Secretariat of Labor,* 1937-39.
g-None. i-Political collaborator of
Antonio Villalobos, Secretary of Labor,
1937-40. j-Joined the Constitutionalists
as a law school student. k-Supported
General Obregón in 1920. l-C de D,
1917-18, 1918-20, 1922-24; PS, 4430.

Oliver Bustamante, Mario
a-Sept. 22, 1924. b-Real del Monte,
Hidalgo. c-Early education unknown;
graduated as a 2nd Lieutenant in
Artillery, Heroic Military College, 1943-
47; diploma, staff and command course,
Higher War College, 1951-53; advanced
artillery courses, Ft. Sill and Ft. Bliss,
United States, 1955; instructor, U.S.

Army Caribbean School, Canal Zone, Panama, 1958-59; professor, Heroic Military College, 1962. d-None. e-None. f-Chief of Staff, Secretariat of National Defense, 1976; Military Attaché to Argentina, Uruguay, and Paraguay, 1978-81. g-None. h-None. j-Joined the army as a cadet, 1943; assigned to the 2nd Artillery Regiment, 1947-51; served with the 2nd Artillery Battalion, 1959; rank of Artillery Colonel, 1969; Chief, Section 3, Staff, Secretariat of National Defense, 1969-71; Chief of Staff, 16th Military Zone, Irapuato, Guanajuato, 1973-76, under General *Félix Galván López*, Secretary of National Defense, 1976-82; Chief of Staff, 5th Military Zone, Chihuahua, Chihuahua; rank of Brigadier General, 1974; Commander of the 5th Military Zone, Chihuahua, Chihuahua, 1981-83; Director General of Artillery, Secretariat of National Defense, 1983-86; Director General of Personnel, Secretariat of National Defense, 1986-88. k-None. l-Q es QAP, 80; Rev. de Ejer., 1969, 47, Nov-Dec. 1974, 99; DBGM87, 279; DBGM, 310.

Olivera Gómez Tagle, Mario C.
a-May 16, 1926. b-Toluca, México. c-Secondary and preparatory studies, Scientific and Literary Institute of México, Toluca; medical degree, National School of Medicine, UNAM, Sept. 1951; postgraduate studies, National Institute of Cardiology, 1956-58; Professor of Physiology, Pathology, and Cardiology, Dean, School of Medicine, and Rector, 1960, all at Autonomous University of the State of México, Toluca. d-*Senator* from the State of México, 1964-70. e-None. f-General physician, residency, National Railroads of Mexico, Toluca, 1952; general physician, IMSS Hospital, Toluca, 1961; general physician, ISSSTE, Toluca, 1962. g-Secretary General of the Union of Physicians of

the State of México. h-Radiologist, Toluca Hospital; physician. i-Married Celia Martínez; son of Dr. Mariano C. Olivera and Luz Gómez Tagle. j-None. k-None. l-WNM, 163; C de S, 1964-70.

Olivera Toro (y Cordero), Jorge
a-Aug. 18, 1917. b-Oaxaca, Oaxaca. c-Early education unknown; law degree, National School of Law, UNAM, 1941; Professor of Law, National School of Law, UNAM; professor at the Heroic Military College and the Higher War College. d-None. e-Joined PNR, 1932. f-Lawyer, Secretariat of the Treasury, 1942-43; Secretary of Agreements, Superior Tribunal of Justice of the State of Guerrero, 1943-45; Secretary, First Civil Judicial District, Mexico City, 1948; Director, Department of Social Security, Secretariat of Labor, 1959-60; Director General of Labor, Secretariat of Labor, 1961-63; technical adviser, Department of Tourism, 1966-69; adviser, Presidential Staff, 1957-68; adviser, Secretariat of National Defense, 1970-74; Subdirector of the Institute of Social Security of the Armed Forces, 1976; *Supernumerary Justice of the Supreme Court*, 1976-78; *Justice of the Supreme Court*, 1979-88. g-None. h-None. i-Son of Rafael Olivera Toro Martínez, businessman, and Carmen Cordero Martínez; married Juana Alonso García; son, Jorge Rafael Olivera Toro y Alonso, was a federal circuit court judge, 1990. j-None. k-None. l-Protag., 255-56; DBGM92, 685; DBGM87, 648; DBGM, 676.

Olivo Solís, Angel
a-Jan. 21, 1917. b-Tuxtla, Veracruz. c-Early education unknown; studies for a teaching certificate, 1938. d-*Federal Deputy* from the Federal District, Dist. 2, 1973-76, Dist. 2, 1979-82. e-Joined PRI, 1945; representative of the CEN of PRI to Michoacán and Guanajuato, 1969. f-Director, Office of Literacy,

Department of the Federal District, 1943; Assistant Director, Department of Labor, Department of the Federal District, 1945. g-Cofounder of the CTM, 1936; Secretary General of the Unión Lonas La Providencia, 1937; member of the executive board, the Federation of Workers, 1947; member of the executive committee, Federation of Working Groups, 1949; founder and leader of the National Revolutionary Coalition, 1950; director of the Revolutionary Federation of Workers, 1952; founder and leader of the Revolutionary Workers Federation, 1959; founder of the National Workers Central, 1960; Secretary General of the National Workers Central, 1963; founder of the Congress of Labor, 1966; Secretary General of the Revolutionary Workers Federation, 1967-84. j-None. k-None. l-HA, 10 July 1978, 9; C de D, 1973-76, 6; Protag., 256; PRI, 1983, 386.

Olmos (Hernández), Salvador
(Deceased July 10, 1978) a-1917. b-Jalapa, Veracruz. c-Teaching certificate. d-Councilman of Jalapa, Veracruz; Local Deputy to the State Legislature of Veracruz; *Federal Deputy* from the State of Veracruz, Dist. 5, 1958-61, member of the Colonization Committee, the Budget and Accounts Committee, the Securities Committee and the First General Means of Communication and Transportation Committee. e-None. f-Private Secretary to *Adolfo Ruiz Cortines*, Secretary of Government, 1946-52; *Private Secretary to the President of Mexico, Adolfo Ruiz Cortines*, 1952-58. g-Representative of the CTM. h-Personal Secretary to *Adolfo Ruiz Cortines*, 1961-73. j-None. k-None. l-DGF56, 67; C de D, 1958-60, 86; Func., 392.

Olvera Gámez, Domingo
a-May 9, 1902. b-Villa del Pueblito, Querétaro. c-Primary studies in the Colegio Arana, Querétaro, Querétaro;

secondary studies in the Colegio Civil of Querétaro; no degree. d-*Alternate Federal Deputy* from the State of Querétaro, Dist. 2, 1943-46; Local Deputy to the 36th Session of the State Legislature of Querétaro; *Federal Deputy* from the State of Querétaro, Dist. 1, 1955-58; *Senator* from the State of Querétaro, 1958-64, member of the Second Balloting Group, Second Secretary of the Second Ejido Committee and President of the Electrical Industry Committee. e-Oficial Mayor of PRI in Querétaro (twenty years). f-Oficial Mayor of the State Government of Querétaro, 1925; Secretary General of Government of the State of Querétaro; Treasurer of the City of Querétaro. g-None. h-Farmer until 1925. j-None. k-Elected as an alternate federal deputy in 1955 but replaced the regular deputy in 1956. l-Func., 331; DGF56, 27; C de S, 1961-64, 65.

Olvera Reyes, Alfonso
b-Ozumba, México. c-Early education unknown; law degree, National School of Law, UNAM, with a specialty in constitutional and administrative law. d-None. e-General delegate of the CEN of PRI to the municipal elections in Veracruz, Zacatecas and Nuevo León, 1976; general delegate of the CEN of PRI to the Sixth District, Puebla, during the elections for deputies, 1976; Subsecretary of Electoral Action of the CEN of PRI, 1978. f-Political Subdelegate and General Coordinator of the Alvaro Obregón Delegation, Department of the Federal District, 1967; adviser to the Department of Ejido and Communal Services, Secretariat of Agrarian Reform, 1977; Director of Governmental and Juridical Unity, Tlalpan Delegation, Department of the Federal District, 1977. g-President of the Federation of University Students, 1960-61. j-None. k-None. l-HA, 20 Nov. 1978, 21.

Oñate Laborde, Santiago
a-May 24, 1949. b-Federal District, c-Early education unknown; law degree, National School of Law, UNAM, with a thesis on legal process; diploma in law and sociology, Degli Studi di Pavia University, Italy, 1972-74; MA in economics and politics, London School of Economics, 1974-75; Ph.D. in legal sociology, School of Law, University of Wisconsin, 1981-82, with a thesis on labor disputes; professor, Law Department, Autonomous Metropolitan University, Azcapotzalco Campus, 1975-84; professor, National School of Law, UNAM, 1976. d-*Federal Deputy* from the Federal District, Dist. 25, 1985-88; Representative to the Assembly of the Federal District, Dist. 14, 1988-91. e-Joined PRI, 1974; Legal Director, CEN of PRI, 1987-89; *Secretary of Ideological Divulgation of the CEN of PRI*, 1990. f-*Ambassador to the Organization of American States*, 1991-92; Attorney for Environmental Protection, Secretariat of Social Development, 1992-94; Coordinator of the Office of Coordination of the Presidency, 1994. g-None. h-None. i-Son of Santiago Oñate Salemme, lawyer, and Clara Laborde Cancino; married María Laura Madrazo Cancino, lawyer. j-None. k-None. l-DBGM92, 267; letter.

Orduna Culebro, Alberto
a-Apr. 29, 1918. b-Tapachula, Chiapas. c-Primary and secondary studies in Tapachula; completed first year of business studies, Veracruz, Veracruz. d-*Federal Deputy* from the State of Chiapas, Dist. 5, 1964-67. e-Organized and founded of the Tapachultec Civic Party, 1945; candidate of PARM for federal deputy, 1952; member of PARM. f-Stenographer, federal government, 1937-47; Director of Personnel, Administrative Employees, Secretariat of Labor, 1947-48; tax administrator and General Inspector of finance, State of Chiapas, 1948-56; inspector of free ports; Inspector of Rules, Division of Government, Department of the Federal District; employee, Department of Agricultural Development, Department of Agrarian Affairs, 1959-64. g-None. h-Private affairs, 1957-59. j-None. k-None. l-C de D, 1964-67.

Orijel Salazar, Manuel
a-July 29, 1913. b-Federal District. c-Primary studies under Dr. Agustín Rivera, Mexico City, 1920-27; secondary studies at the Centro Escolar Revolucionario, Mexico City, 1941-43; preparatory studies at the National Preparatory School No. 3, 1944-45, and No. 1, 1957; law degree from the National School of Law, UNAM, 1958-62; professor at the National Preparatory School No. 2, Mexico City, 1963-66. d-*Federal Deputy* from the Federal District, Dist. 9, 1946-49, member of the Second Balloting Committee, the War Materiels Committee, the Third Labor Committee, the Second General Means of Communication Committee, and the Inspection Committee of the General Accounting Office; *Federal Deputy* from the Federal District, Dist. 8, 1964-67, member of the Administration Committee (1st year), the Department of the Federal District Committee, the 4th Section on Administration of the Legislative Studies Committee, and the Public Works Committee; *Federal Deputy* from the Federal District, Dist. 8, 1970-73, member of the Domestic Trade Committee, the Department of the Federal District Committee, the Seventh Section on Commerce and Credit of the Legislative Studies Committee, the Military Industry Committee, and the Rules Committee. e-Secretary of Bureaucratic Action, PRI; Secretary of the Youth Commission of the CEN of PRI; Secretary of Press and Publicity of the Regional Committee of PRI for the

Federal District; general delegate of the CNOP of PRI to various states; Treasurer and Secretary General of CNOP in the Federal District; member of the National Council of PRI; Director of Popular Action of PRI in the Federal District, 1976. f-Chief of Lawyers of the Board of Arbitration of the FSTSE; delegate of the Department of the Federal District to Ixtapalpa. g-Secretary of the National Policy Commission of the FSTSE; member of the Legal Studies Committee, FSTSE; Secretary of Resolutions, FSTSE. h-Special studies of public administration, union organizations, and labor relations in the United States. i-Married to *Ofelia Casillas Ontiveros*, federal deputy, 1973-76, 1979-82, 1985-88. j-None. k-None. l-C de D, 1946-48, 84, 1964-66, 63, 81, 83, 90, 1970-72, 128; Directorio, 1970-72.

Orive Alba, Adolfo
a-Dec. 9, 1907. b-Federal District. c-Primary and secondary studies in Mexico City; engineering degree from the National School of Engineering, UNAM, 1927; studied irrigation in the United States on a scholarship from the National Irrigation Commission, 1928; Professor of Engineering, UNAM, 1968. d-None. e-None. f-Subdirector of the Department of Hydraulic Resources, Secretariat of Public Works, 1929-31; Chief Engineer, National Irrigation Commission, 1932-35; engineer in charge of construction of the Rodríguez Dam, 1935-36; Director of Irrigation of the Rodríguez Dam, 1936-38; member of the United States-Mexican International Boundary and Waters Commission for the Colorado and Bravo Rivers, 1939-40; Executive Director of the National Irrigation Commission, 1940-46; *Secretary of Hydraulic Resources*, 1947-52; Director General of Siderúrgica las Truchas, S.A., 1969-78. g-None. h-Since 1932, author of numerous books and articles on irrigation in Mexico;

consulting engineer to Latin American countries, 1952; founded an engineering consulting firm, 1961, President of the irrigation consulting firm, CIEPS, 1966-68. i-Close friend of *Miguel Alemán*; knew *Antonio Dovalí Jaime* as a student at UNAM. j-None. k-Founder and first Secretary of the Secretariat of Hydraulic Resources. l-HA, 7 Aug. 1972; letter; DBM68, 466-67; HA, 21 Nov. 1952; DGF51, II, 615; Greenberg, 23; IWW67, 917; DGF50, II, 317, 455, etc.; DGF51, I, 413; Enc. Mex., Ix, 1977, 602.

Ornelas Kuckle, Oscar
a-Nov. 8, 1920. b-Chihuahua, Chihuahua. c-Preparatory studies at the Scientific and Literary Institute of Chihuahua; law degree, National School of Law, UNAM, July 10, 1944, with a thesis on legal decisions; founding professor of the School of Law, University of Chihuahua; Dean of the School of Law, University of Chihuahua; Secretary General of the University of Chihuahua; Rector of the University of Chihuahua, 1964-70, 1970-74. d-Mayor of Chihuahua, Chihuahua; *Senator* from the State of Chihuahua, 1976-80, representative of the Senate to the Federal Electoral Committee; *Governor of Chihuahua*, 1980-85. e-Secretary of the Local Electoral Committee, Chihuahua, 1952; Secretary of Educational Affairs of PRI, State of Chihuahua. f-Representative of the Federal Treasury Office, Chihuahua; Federal Public Defender, Chihuahua; Secretary of the Superior Tribunal of Justice of the State of Chihuahua. g-General delegate of the CNC to Veracruz. i-Has strong political ties to *Carlos Sansores Pérez*. j-None. k-None. l-*Excélsior*, 15 Feb. 1980, 16; C de S, 1976-82; DJBM, 101; Almanaque de México, 1981, 338, 1982, 489.

Orozco Alvarez, Pánfilo
a-June 1, 1936. b-Ojo de Agua de Poturo, Municipio Churumuco,

Michoacán. c-Early education unknown; teaching certificate, National
Normal School, Mexico City; primary
and secondary school teacher. d-*Party
Deputy* from the PPS, 1967-70. e-Member of the PPS. f-None. g-Member of
the SNTE. h-None. j-None. k-None.
l-C de D, 1967-70.

Orozco Camacho, Miguel
(Deceased 1945) a-May 5, 1886.
b-Zapopán, Jalisco. c-Primary studies in
Guadalajara; no degree. d-None.
e-None. f-Head of the Department of
Infantry, Secretariat of National
Defense, 1932-33; Head of the Depart-
ment of Engineers, Secretariat of
National Defense, 1934-35; Chief of
Staff of the Secretariat of National
Defense, 1936-37; *Oficial Mayor of the
Secretariat of National Defense*, 1937-
39; Director of the Federal Penitentiary,
1941-45. g-None. h-None. j-Joined the
Revolution, 1911; served under the
Constitutional Army of the North and
the Army of the West, 1913; rank of
Brigadier General, Mar. 21, 1925;
Commander of the 33rd Military Zone,
Campeche, Campeche, 1939-40; reached
rank of Division General. k-None.
l-DP70, 1549; López, 796; Dávila, 95.

Orozco Romero, Alberto
a-Apr. 1925. b-Guadalajara, Jalisco.
c-Primary studies at public schools,
Guadalajara; secondary studies at the
Secondary School No. 1 for Boys, Guadalajara; preparatory studies at the Preparatory School of Jalisco, Guadalajara;
law degree, School of Law, University of
Guadalajara, 1944-49, completed his
thesis in 1950; Professor of Private Law,
University of Guadalajara, 1953;
Professor of General Theory of Obligations, University of Guadalajara, 1954.
d-*Governor of Jalisco*, 1971-77. e-None.
f-Secretary of the 6th Tribunal of the 1st
Civil Court, Jalisco, 1951-52; 3rd Judge
of the 1st Civil Court, 1952-54; Judge of

the 6th Tribunal, 1st Civil Court, 1954-
58; Interim Judge of the 1st Division of
the Superior Tribunal of Justice of the
State of Jalisco, 1958-59; Alternate
Justice of the Superior Tribunal of
Justice of the State of Jalisco, 1959-60;
Justice of the 1st Division, Superior
Tribunal of Justice, Jalisco, 1960-65;
President of the Superior Tribunal of
Justice, Jalisco, 1965-67; *Supernumerary
Justice of the Supreme Court*, 1967-70;
Justice of the Supreme Court, 1970.
g-None. h-None. j-None. k-None.
l-Letter; G of NL, 42; *Justicia*, Sept.
1968; Enc. Mex., IX, 1977, 618.

Orozco Romo, David
a-Dec. 26, 1929. b-Federal District.
c-Early education unknown; law degree,
National School of Law, UNAM, 1947-
51; studies in philosophy, Ibero-
American University, 1979; Professor of
the History of Political and Social Ideas
and Professor in Mercantile Law, Ibero-
American University, 1965-81; Professor of the History of Administration,
Law and Accounting, Autonomous
Technological Institute of Mexico,
Mexico City, 1972-82. d-*Plurinominal
Federal Deputy* from the PDM, 1982-85,
coordinator of the PDM delegation.
e-Secretary of Political Action, 1955-70,
Secretary of Legal Affairs, 1955-70, and
Secretary of Student Action, 1955-70,
and President, 1961-64, all of the
National Sinarquista Union; precandidate for the presidential nomination of
the PDM, 1981; President of the PDM
in District No. 1, Federal District, 1981-
82. f-None. g-President of the Union of
Mexican Catholic Adults, Mexican
Catholic Action, 1971-74. h-Practicing
lawyer. j-None. k-None. l-C de D,
1982-85; Lehr, 566.

Orozco Rosales, Alfonso
a-Aug. 4, 1916. b-Guadalajara, Jalisco.
c-Primary studies at the Colegio Inmaculada Concepción, Guadalajara, 1923-

29; secondary studies at the Colegio del
Espíritu Santo, Guadalajara, 1929-32;
preparatory studies at the Notre Dame
des Anges, Espira de l'Agly, France,
1932-36; studies in mathematics,
National School of Engineering,
UNAM, 1937-42; Professor of Mathematics. d-*Federal Deputy* (Party
Deputy from PAN), 1970-73, member of
the Public Welfare Committee and the
Fiscal Section of the Legislative Studies
Committee. e-Member of PAN.
f-None. g-None. h-Businessman.
j-None. k-None. l-Directorio, 1970-72;
C de D, 1970-72, 128.

Orrico de los Llanos, Miguel
(Deceased) a-Sept. 18, 1894. b-Libertad
(Venustiano Carranza), Villahermosa,
Tabasco. c-Primary studies in Macus-
pana, Tabasco; graduated from the
National Military College. d-None.
e-None. f-Chief of Public Security,
State of Puebla; *Interim Governor of
Tabasco*, 1955-58. g-None. h-None.
i-Son of Italian, Miguel Orrico Bartilotty
and Adelaida de los Llanos; cousin of
Carlos A. Madrazo, president of the
CEN of the PRI; married Margarita
Carrillo. j-Fought under Carranza in the
6th North East Brigade during the
Revolution; became a member of his
staff; Chief of Staff of the 34th Military
Zone, Chetumal, Quintana Roo, of the
23rd Military Zone, Tlaxcala, Tlaxcala,
of the 17th Military Zone, Querétaro,
Querétaro, and of the 11th Military
Zone, Zacatecas, Zacatecas; Com-
mander of the 7th Military Zone,
Monterrey, Nuevo León, 1955; Com-
mander of the 4th Military Zone,
Hermosillo, Sonora; commander of the
garrison at Mexicali; Inspector of the 1st
Military Zone, Mexico City; rank of
Brigadier General, Nov. 1, 1940; rank of
Division General, Nov. 16, 1952.
k-None. l-Peral, 601; DGF56, 101; HA,
28 Mar. 1955, 5; Scott, 276; Bulnes, 693;
Almanaque de Tabasco, 155.

Ortega Cantero, Benjamín
a-Apr. 16, 1919. b-Coyoacán, Federal
District. c-Primary and secondary
studies at the Escuela Heroes de
Churubusco, Coyoacán; and at Secondary School No. 1, Mexico City; agricultural engineering studies in agricultural
parasitology, National School of
Agriculture, 1936-41, completed his
thesis in 1945, on the cotton plant;
fellowship student of the Rockefeller
Foundation and the Secretariat of
Agriculture, University of Minnesota,
MS degree in phytology, 1946. d-None.
e-None. f-Employee of the Secretariat
of Agriculture in the Office of Special
Studies, Rockefeller Foundation, 1944-
45; researcher, hybrid wheat seeds, Don
Martín, Coahuila, 1945; member of the
Committee to Increase Improved Seeds,
1946; Director, Northern Agricultural
Zone, Secretariat of Agriculture,
Torreón, Coahuila; representative of the
Lagunera Delegation for Vegetable
Cleanliness, Torreón, Coahuila, 1950-
25; representative of the Secretariat of
Agriculture to Comarca, 1952-58;
Manager, Secretariat of Hydraulic
Resources, 1958-72; Director General of
Vegetable Cleanliness, Secretariat of
Agriculture, 1972-76; *Subsecretary of
Agriculture and Operations*, 1976-78.
g-Organized Agricultural Defense
Groups, Coatzacoalcos, Veracruz.
j-None. k-None. l-Letter; DAPC, 54.

Ortega Hernández, Samuel
a-1905. b-Torreón, Coahuila. c-No
degree. d-*Federal Deputy* from the
State of Tlaxcala, Dist. 2, 1955-58,
member of the Library Committee (1st
year) and the Textile Industry Committee, substitute member of the First Railroad Committee; *Senator* from the State
of Tlaxcala, 1958-64, member of the
Railroad Committee and the General
Means of Communication Committee,
substitute member of the Indian Affairs
Committee and the Public Works

Committee; Local Deputy to the State Legislature of Coahuila. e-None. f-Secretary General of Government of the State of Coahuila, under *Pedro Rodríguez Triana*, 1940; President of the National Committee on Railroad Policy, 1956. g-Secretary General of the National Railroad Workers Union, 1956-58. h-Employee of the National Railroads of Mexico (30 years); author of several books. j-None. k-None. l-Func., 381; C de S, 65; DGF56, 28, 31, 33, 34; C de D, 1955-57; Ind. Biog., 109.

Ortega Martínez, Antonio
a-July 28, 1954. b-Aguascalientes, Aguascalientes. c-Early education unknown; completed secondary studies; studies toward a degree in engineering; no degree; instructor, Technical Institute of Aguascalientes. d-*Plurinominal Federal Deputy* from the PPS, 1982-85. e-President of the State Committee of the PST in Aguascalientes, 1977-80; Political Commissioner of the PST in San Luis Potosí, Aguascalientes, Durango and Zacatecas; First Housing Secretary of the PST, 1980; member of the Executive Committee of the Central Committee of the PST, 1980; candidate of the PST for federal deputy from Aguascalientes, 1979; President of the State Committee of the PST, Guanajuato, 1981. f-None. g-Student leader, Technical Institute of Aguascalientes. h-Industrial engineer. i-Son of Antonio Ortega Rodríguez, railroad worker, and Juan María Martínez Moreno; brother, *Jesús Ortega Martínez*, was a PRD federal deputy, 1988-91 j-None. k-Organized the Las Huertas Socialist Colony, Aguascalientes, Aguascalientes. l-Directorio, 1982-85; C de D, 1982-85; Lehr, 600; DBGM89, 508.

Ortega Martínez, Jesús
a-Nov. 5, 1952. b-Aguascalientes, Aguascalientes. c-Early education unknown; bacteriology chemistry

degree, National School of Biological Sciences, IPN, 1972-78. d-*Plurinominal Federal Deputy* from the PST, 1979-82; *Plurinominal Federal Deputy* from the PRD, 1988-91. e-Member of the PST; president of the PST in the State of México, 1977, Jalisco, 1983, Aguascalientes, 1986; Secretary General of the Central Committee of the PST, 1987; joined the PMS, 1987; Secretary of Political Education of the Central Committee of the PMS, 1987; joined the PRD, 1988; member of the National Council of the PRD, 1988- . f-Chemist, National Railroads of Mexico, 1974-76. g-None. h-Unknown. i-Son of Antonio Ortega Rodríguez, railroad worker, and Juana María Martínez Moreno; married Angélica de la Pe Gómez, political activist; brother of *Antonio Ortega Martínez*, federal deputy from the PPS, 1982-85. j-None. k-None. l-DBGM89, 508; C de D, 1979-82; C de D, 1988-91.

Ortega Martínez, Lauro
a-June 8, 1913. b-Federal District. c-Medical degree from the National School of Medicine, UNAM, 1935. d-*Federal Deputy* from the Federal District, Dist. 2, 1946-49, member of the Social Action Committee, the Child Welfare and Social Security Committee, the Foreign Relations Committee, the Military Health Committee, and the 3rd Section of the Credit Committee; *Federal Deputy* from the State of Morelos, Dist. 4, 1979-82, President of the Agrarian Reform Committee; *Governor of Morelos*, 1982-88. e-Secretary of Popular Action of PRM in the Federal District, 1929; cofounder of the CNOP of PRI with *Carlos Madrazo* and *Ramón Bonfil*, 1942; Secretary General of the CNOP of the Federal District, 1942-45; *Secretary General of the CEN of PRI*, 1964-65; *Interim President of the CEN of PRI*, 1965-68. f-Head of the Department of Psychology and Student Hygiene, Secretariat of Public Education,

1935-38; *Oficial Mayor of Health*, 1938-40; Assistant Treasurer of the Federal District, 1940-44; Subdirector and Director of the Mexican-United States Commission for the Eradication of Hoof and Mouth Disease, 1946-52; *Subsecretary of Agriculture and Livestock*, 1952-58; personal representative of President *Adolfo López Mateos* to the United States in the field of communication problems; adviser to the President of Mexico, 1976-79. g-Secretary General of the National Student Cardenista Party, 1933-34; Director of the Socialist Youth of Mexico in the Federal District, 1936. h-None. i-Close friend of *Fidel Velázquez Sánchez*, Secretary General of the Federation of Mexican Labor, 1949-81; knew *Carlos Madrazo* as a student leader in the 1930s. j-None. k-None. l-HA, 23 Dec. 1964, 4; *Polémica*, Vol. 1, No. 1, 28, 1969; DGF50, 149; Johnson, 68; C de D, 1946-48, 82; Fuentes Díaz, 281; DGF56, 223; Loret de Mola, 17; *Excélsior*, 25 Sept. 1981, 1.

Ortega Martínez, Noé Ricardo
a-Apr. 3, 1932. b-Jalapa, Veracruz. c-Primary studies at the Cayetano Rivera School, Veracruz, Veracruz; technical industrial studies, Technical Institute of Veracruz, Veracruz, 1946-47; completed all studies toward a law degree except thesis, University of Veracruz, Jalapa, 1965-69. d-*Federal Deputy* from the State of Veracruz, Dist. 2, 1970-73, Dist. 18, 1979-82. e-Delegate to the State Assemblies of PRI, Veracruz, 1962-70; delegate, Labor Sector, National Assembly of PRI, 1971, 1978; delegate of the State Committee of PRI to the 1st District, Veracruz. f-None. g-Secretary of Acts, Unity and Progress Union of Pipe and Steelworkers of Mexico, Veracruz, Veracruz, 1962-65; Secretary of Finances and Statistics, 1965-69, Secretary of Technical and Economic Affairs, 1968-71, and Secretary of Social Welfare, 1973-76, all of State Commit-

tee of CROC; Secretary General of CROC, State of Veracruz, 1971-73, 1975-79; Secretary General of the Central Political Committee of the Unity and Progress Union of Pipe and Steelworkers, Veracruz. j-None. k-None. l-Protag., 259; C de D, 1970-73, 1979-82.

Ortega (Olaza), Fausto M.
(Deceased Aug. 25, 1971) a-1905. b-Tezuitlán, Puebla. c-Primary studies in Tezuitlán; agricultural engineering degree, National School of Agriculture, San Jacinto. d-Local Deputy to the State Legislature of Veracruz, 1939-42, 1951-54; Mayor of Teziutlán, Puebla; *Alternate Federal Deputy* from the State of Puebla, Dist. 9, 1937-40; *Federal Deputy* from the State of Puebla, Dist. 7, 1946-49, member of the Gran Comisión and the Budget and Accounts Committee (1st year), substitute member of the Petroleum Committee; *Governor of Puebla*, 1957-62. e-None. f-Tax collector, Cholula, Zacapoaztla, Tepeaca, Tecamachalpeaca; Director, Federal Tax Office, Tecamachalco, Puebla; Secretary of the City Council of Teziutlán, Puebla; *Oficial Mayor of Communications and Public Works*, 1942-45; Director of the Tax Department, State of Puebla, 1951; Treasurer of the State of Puebla; Oficial Mayor of the State Government of Puebla, 1951-57, under Governor *Rafael Avila Camacho*. g-None j-None. k-Originally a close collaborator of *Rafael Avila Camacho* but broke with him after Ortega was elected governor. l-C de D, 1946-48, 82; HA, 6 Sept. 1971, 104; DGF56, 98; DGF51, I, 91; NYT, 5 Aug. 1961, 14; NYT, 22 Sept. 1961, 16; *Excélsior*, 26 Dec. 1974, 12; Almanaque de Puebla, 134.

Ortega Ortega, Manuel Valerio
a-July 19, 1930. b-Federal District. c-Early education unknown; studies in chemistry, National School of Biologi-

cal Sciences, IPN, 1948-52, graduating with a thesis on antibiotics, 1953; Ph.D. in biochemistry, MIT, with a thesis on nicotine acid in bacteria, 1960; Karl Taylor Compton Fellow, United States Nutrition Fund, 1956-58; Bank of Mexico Fellow, 1956-59; professor, MIT, University of Guadalajara, University of Nuevo León, University of Michoacán, 1955-77; Professor of Biochemistry, Department of Biochemistry, IPN, 1961-83; Professor of Chemistry, UNAM 1975-77; professor, School of Sciences, UNAM, 1975-77; Chief, Department of Biochemistry, Center for Research and Advanced Studies, IPN, 1964-66; Chief of the Department of Genetics and Cellular Biology, IPN, 1967-69; Director of the Center for Research and Advanced Studies, IPN, 1970-82. d-None. e-None. f-*Subsecretary of Educational and Technical Research*, Secretariat of Public Education, 1982-88. g-None. h-None. i-Son of Joaquín Ortega Echevarría and Elvira Ortega Espejo. j-None. k-None. l-QesQAP, 299; DBGM, 313; DBGM89, 283.

Ortega Villa, Margarita
a-May 5, 1951. b-Mexicali, Baja California. c-Early education unknown; sociology degree, Higher School of Political and Social Sciences, Autonomous University of Baja California, 1968-73; professor, Center of Higher and Technical Education, Autonomous University of Baja California, 1973-74; teacher, School of Higher Education, Autonomous University of Baja California, 1978-80; professor, Nursing School, Autonomous University of Baja California, 1968-73. d-*Alternate Federal Deputy* from the State of Baja California, Dist. 1, 1973-76, under *Federico Martínez Manatou*; Local Deputy to the State Legislature of Baja California, Dist. 3, 1974-77; *Alternate Federal Deputy* from the State of Baja California, Dist. 1, 1982-85; *Federal Deputy*

from the State of Baja California, Dist. 4, 1985-88; *Senator* from the State of Baja California, 1988-89. e-Director of the Women's Section, PRI, Baja California, 1971; Secretary General of ANFER of PRI, Baja California, 1974-80; President of PRI, Mexicali, 1981-82; Secretary of Organization of PRI, Baja California, 1983-84. f-Social Worker, Social Action Division, Mexicali, 1971; analyst, Institute for the Protection of Infants, Baja California, 1972; Director General of Real Estate Rolls, State of Baja California, 1983-85; Director General of the National Consumer Institute, 1989-94. g-Secretary of Women's Action of the CEN of CNOP, 1986-89. h-None. i-Daughter of Mario Ortega Cervantes, engineer, and Carmen Villa Aguilar; married José Jesús Romo Reynoso. j-None. k-None. l-DBGM87, 532-33; *Mexico Journal*, 10 Apr. 1989, 7; DBGM92, 272.

Ortiz Arana, Fernando
a-Oct. 26, 1944. b-Querétaro, Querétaro. c-Early education unknown; law degree, School of Law, University of Querétaro, 1963-67, with a thesis on the right to strike; preparatory teacher, University of Querétaro, 1963-65; Professor of Law, School of Law, University of Querétaro, 1968-69. d-*Federal Deputy* from the State of Querétaro, Dist. 1, 1979-82; *Federal Deputy* from the Federal District, Dist. 31, 1985-88; President of the Chamber of Deputies, December, 1985; Representative of the Assembly of the Federal District, 1988-91; *Federal Deputy* from the State of Querétaro, Dist. 1, 1991-94; President of the Gran Comisión, 1991-93. e-Joined the PRI, 1963; Coordinator of PRI Youth in the *Gustavo Díaz Ordaz* presidential campaign, Querétaro, 1964; Delegate of PRI to the State of Veracruz 17th District federal elections, 1980; General Delegate of the CEN of PRI, 1984-85;

Secretary of Electoral Action of the CEN of PRI, 1987; President of PRI in the Federal District, 1988-92; *President of the CEN of PRI*, 1993-94. f-Oficial Mayor of the State of Querétaro, 1973-76; Secretary General of Government of the State of Querétaro, 1976-79; Director of Property Registration, Secretariat of the Controller General, 1982-84. g-Student leader at the University of Querétaro; Secretary of Ideological Press, CNOP, 1981-83. h-Practicing lawyer in uncle's firm, 1967-73. i-Son of José Ortiz Antañana, real estate agent, and Virginia Arana Morán, teacher; married Susana Guadalupe Proal de la Isla; nephew of José Arana Morán, federal deputy and secretary general of government of Querétaro; brother of José Ortiz Arana, federal deputy. j-None. k-None. l-DBGM92, 539-40; *El Financiero*, 31 Mar. 1993, 54: C de D, 1979-82; Directorio, 1979-82; C de D, 1991-94.

Ortiz Armengol, Federico
a-Feb. 12, 1898. b-Oaxaca, Oaxaca. c-Primary studies in Oaxaca; secondary studies in Oaxaca; preparatory studies at the National Preparatory School; medical degree, National School of Medicine, Oct. 3, 1925, with an honorable mention; Professor of Physiology, National School of Medicine, UNAM; Rector, University of Oaxaca, 1954-58. d-*Federal Deputy* from the State of Oaxaca, Dist. 3, 1958-61, member of the Public Health Committee, the Fifth Section of the Legislative Studies Committee, the First Balloting Group and the First Instructive Section of the Grand Jury. e-None. f-Director, Anti-Rabies Institute, Mexico City, 1930-35; *Oficial Mayor of Labor*, 1935-36; delegate of the Secretariat of Health, Mérida, Yucatán, 1943-44; delegate of the Secretariat of Health, Durango, 1947; Director of Hygiene Center No. 3, Mexico City; Director of the General

Hospital, Oaxaca, Oaxaca, 1954-58. g-None. h-Practicing physician, 1925-30. j-None. k-Graduated from the National Medical School with the best grade point average of his class; answered *Adolfo Ruiz Cortines*' last state of the union address, 1958. l-Func., 306; C de D, 1958-61, 87; *Excélsior*, 29 Aug. 1979, 14.

Ortiz (Arriola), Andrés
(Deceased Jan. 18, 1945) a-Nov. 2, 1890. b-Chihuahua, Chihuahua. c-Primary and preparatory studies in Chihuahua; engineering degree in the field of hydraulics and topography, National School of Engineering, UNAM, Nov. 1913. d-Local Deputy in Chihuahua, 1917-18; Federal Deputy from the State of Chihuahua, Dist. 1, 1918; Provisional Governor of Chihuahua, Nov. 15, 1918, to Feb. 29, 1920; Governor of Chihuahua, Sept. 8, 1930, to Nov. 2, 1931. e-None. f-Chief and founder of the Department of Bridges and Highways, Secretariat of Communication, 1916-17; Director of the Trolley Company of Mexico City, 1918; *Director General of the National Railroads of Mexico*, 1944-45; member of the Committee for the Administration and Inspection of Foreign Properties, 1941-44. g-None. h-Author of the National Highway Law. i-Son of journalist Pablo Ortiz and Regina Arriola; grandson of Dr. Guillermo Ortiz, imperial prefect of the Department of Jiménez, Chihuahua. j-Remained loyal to Carranza. k-In exile in the United States, 1920; as provisional governor of Chihuahua put a price of 50,000 pesos for the capture of Francisco Villa; originally supported by *Luis León* for governor of Chihuahua, 1930, but betrayed León's political program. l-DP70, 1534; Peral, 596; HA, 10 Mar. 1944; López, 802; Enc. Mex., X, 1977, 10; Almada, 539; Almada, 1968, 383-84.

Ortiz Avila, José del Carmen

a-Mar. 4, 1919. b-Campeche, Campeche. c-Teaching certificate from the Rural Normal School, Hecelchakán, Campeche; graduated from the National Military College; completed advanced training, Applied Military School; diploma in staff and command, Higher War College; law degree, National School of Law, UNAM. d-*Federal Deputy* from the State of Campeche, Dist. 1, 1958-61, member of the Property and National Resources Committee, the Second Committee on National Defense, the Second and Sixth Sections of the Legislative Studies Committee, the Military Justice Committee, the Inspection Committee of the General Accounting Office (2nd year), and the First and Second Sections of the Credentials Committee; *Governor of Campeche*, 1961-66. e-None. f-None. g-None. i-Compadre of *Carlos Sansores Pérez*; son of a salaried peasant on the Hacienda Blanca Flor; long-time friend of *Eduardo Lavalle Urbina*; cadet in the same class as *Félix Galván López*. j-Career army officer; Assistant Chief of Staff of the 5th Military District, Chihuahua, Chihuahua, 1951, under General *Bonifacio Salinas Leal*; reached the rank of Brigadier General. k-Could not speak Spanish before the age of seven; early supporter with *Carlos Madrazo, José Torres Landa, Leopoldo Sánchez Celis* and *José Rodríguez Elías* of *Gustavo Díaz Ordaz* for president, 1964; supported precandidacy of *Antonio Ortiz Mena* for presidency, 1970. l-G of M, 8; DGF51, I, 183; C de D, 1958-60, 87; Func., 134; *Excélsior*, 18 Dec. 1973, 15.

Ortiz de Castañeda, Rosa María

a-June 16, 1921. b-Momax, Zacatecas. c-Certificate in primary education; school inspector. d-Interim mayor, community in Zacatecas; *Federal Deputy* from the State of Zacatecas,

Dist. 2, 1967-70. e-Director of CNOP of PRI, State of Zacatecas. f-None. g-None. i-Married Enrique Castañeda Leal. j-None. k-None. l-Directorio, 1967-70; C de D, 1967-70.

Ortiz Garza, Nazario S.

(Deceased Oct. 10, 1991) a-Dec. 31, 1893. b-Saltillo, Coahuila. c-Primary studies in Public School No. 2, Saltillo (completed 4th year); preparatory studies at the Ateneo Fuente, Saltillo; no degree. d-Councilman of Torreón, 1920, 1921-22; Mayor of Torreón, 1922; Mayor of Torreón, 1927-28; Local Deputy to the State Legislature of Coahuila, 1925; President of the State Legislature; Mayor of Torreón, Coahuila, 1927-28; Governor of Coahuila, 1930-34; *Senator* from the State of Coahuila, 1934-40. e-Campaign director for General Manuel Pérez Treviño for governor of Coahuila, 1924. f-Appointed Mayor of Saltillo, Coahuila, 1928; appointed Mayor of Torreón, 1926; *Director General of CONASUPO*, 1943-46; *Secretary of Agriculture*, 1946-52. g-President of the National Association of Winegrowers, 1954-63, 1969-71. h-Began working at age 14; businessman. i-Protégé of Manuel Pérez Treviño, President of the PNR; married María Teresa Baes de Benavides; brother, Francisco, was mayor of Torreón, 1931-32; son of Nazario Ortíz González, small businessman, and Guadalupe de la Garza y Garza. j-Fought with General Francisco Murguía without military rank, 1915-17; purveyor of military trains, Chihuahua, Chihuahua, 1917. k-Won election as federal deputy, 1923, but did not hold office; *New York Times* claimed the government expropriated his land holdings in Tampico in 1953 in a move against former Alemanistas. l-HA, 5 Nov. 1943, 34; DGF51, II, 165; DGF51, I, 203-04; Ha, 6 Dec. 1946, 5; HA, 26 Jan. 1951; Peral, 598; NYT, 25 June 1953, 17; letter; Enc.

Mex., X, 1977, 14-15; López, 804;
Justicia, Mar. 1973.

Ortiz Macedo, Luis
a-1933. b-Federal District. c-Early
education unknown; degree in architecture with honorable mention, National
School of Architecture, UNAM, 1960;
studied monument restoration in
France on a scholarship from the Bank
of Mexico and the French government;
founder and Director of the first
Institute of Monument Restoration at
the University of Guanajuato, 1963-67;
Professor of the History of Architecture,
National School of Architecture,
UNAM, 1955-66. d-None. e-None.
f-Executive Secretary of the Pro Guana-
juato Committee, 1963-66; Head of the
Department of Colonial Monuments,
National Institute of Anthropology and
History, 1966-68; *Subsecretary of
Cultural Affairs of the Secretariat of
Public Education*, 1969-70; Secretary
General of the National Institute of
Anthropology and History, 1968-69;
director of projects in Washington,
D.C., Rome and Guatemala; Director of
the National Institute of Anthropology
and History, 1970-72; Director General
of the Institute of Fine Arts, Jan. 11,
1972, to 1973. g-Representative of the
Mexican Architectural Society in Rio de
Janeiro, 1960. h-Author of many
historical works on art; member of
restoration groups for six different sites
in Mexico City. j-None. k-Received
world recognition for his restoration of
monuments. l-HA, 11 Jan. 1972; *Hoy*,
29 Apr. 1972, 62; *Excélsior*, 12 Jan.
1972, 9; D del S, 12 Jan. 1972, 1; DPE71,
108; Enc. Mex., X, 1977, 16.

Ortiz Martínez, Guillermo
a-July 21, 1948. b-Mexico City. c-Early
education unknown; economics degree,
National School of Law, UNAM, 1967-
72, with a thesis on the rice industry in
Mexico; MA in economics, Stanford

University, 1972-77; Ph.D. in monetary
theory, international economics and
econometrics, Stanford University,
1972-77; with a thesis on Mexican
capital accumulation and economic
growth; professor, Stanford University,
1975-76; professor, ITAM, 1977-83;
professor, Colegio de México, 1983.
d-None. e-None. f-Research assistant,
Presidency of Mexico, 1971-72; economist, 1977, Assistant Manager, 1980-82,
and Manager, 1982-84, all with Division
of Economic Research, Bank of Mexico;
*Subsecretary of the Treasury and Public
Credit*, 1988-94. g-None. h-Alternate
Executive Director of the International
Monetary Fund, 1984-86; Executive
Director of the International Monetary
Fund, 1986-88. i-Son of Leopoldo Ortiz
Sevilla, military officer, and Graciela
Martínez Ostos; married Margie Simon
Fine, environmental engineer; roomed
with *José Córdoba* at Stanford Univer-
sity. j-None. k-None. l-*Proceso*, 6 Apr.
1992, 8; DBGM92, 273.

Ortiz Mena, Antonio
a-Sept. 22, 1908. b-Parral, Chihuahua.
c-Primary studies at the Colegio
Alemán and the Colegio Franco-Inglés;
secondary and preparatory studies at the
National Preparatory School; law degree
from the National School of Law,
UNAM, 1925-28; studies in philosophy
and economics at UNAM. d-None.
e-None. f-Adviser, Department of the
Federal District, 1930-32; Head of the
Legal Department, Department of the
Federal District, 1932-36; Assistant to
the Director of the National Urban
Mortgage Bank, 1936-45; Head of the
Department for the Nationalization of
Properties, Office of the Attorney
General of Mexico, 1940-45; Subdirector
of the National Mortgage Bank, 1946-
52; First Director General of the Divi-
sion of Professions, Secretariat of Public
Education, 1945-46; *Director General of
the IMSS*, 1952-58; *Secretary of the*

Treasury, 1958-64, 1964-70; President of the Inter-American Development Bank, 1971-88; Director General of the National Bank of Mexico (BANAMEX), 1988-90. g-None. h-Founding Governor of the Inter-American Development Bank; Governor of the International Monetary Fund, 1959-70; member of the Revisory Committee on the Law of Enemy Properties and Businesses; member of the Political Defense Committee, 1940-45; practiced law upon graduating from law school, Mexico City. i-While attending the National Law School, 1925-28, knew Miguel Alemán, Antonio Carrillo Flores, Alfonso Noriega and Eduardo Bustamante; from well-to-do family; son of Antonio R. Ortiz, treasurer of the Federal District, and María Mena; grandfather, a miner and prefect of Alamos, Sonora; nephew of Eduardo Ortiz, subsecretary of public works; nephew of Carlos Ortiz, governor of Sonora; son-in-law of Antonio Mena, local deputy; brother of Raúl Ortiz Mena; son, Antonio Ortiz Salinas, was subsecretary of tourism, 1977-82; married Martha Salinas, Carlos Salinas's aunt; father-in-law of José P. González Garrido, secretary of government, 1993, and son of Salomón González Blanco; political disciple of Adolfo Ruiz Cortines. j-None. k-Precandidate for president of Mexico, 1970. l-HA, 27 Apr. 1964, 56; 8 Dec. 1958, 25; WWMG, 29; Hoy, 17 May 1969, 13; HA, 8 Mar. 1971, 43; DGF47, 352; DGF51, II, 65, 77, etc.; DGF50, 318; letters; Enc. Mex., X, 1977, 16-17; Justicia, Jan., 1971; NYT, 6 Oct. 1969, 16; letter; Excélsior, 26 Dec. 1981, 16; Proceso, 21 Dec. 1987, 24; Excélsior, 3 June 1984, 16.

Ortiz Mena, Raúl

a-Aug. 31, 1917. b-Federal District. c-Preparatory studies in the Federal District; economics degree from the National School of Economics, UNAM, June 5, 1942, with an honorable mention for his thesis on "Mexican Money, a Historical Analysis of the Causes in Its Fluctuations and Depreciations"; graduate studies in economics at Harvard University on a scholarship from the Bank of Mexico, 1943-44; advanced studies at the Department of Commerce, Washington, D.C., 1944; advanced studies at the Federal Reserve Bank, Washington, D.C., 1945; graduate studies at the University of Chicago, 1945. d-None. e-None. f-Intern in economics, Secretariat of Industry and Commerce, 1942; economist, Secretariat of Industry and Commerce, 1943; economist for the Secretariat of the Treasury and the Bank of Mexico, 1943; Head of the Department of Economic Studies, Bank of Mexico, 1946; Head of Financial Studies, Nacional Financiera, 1946-50; Director of the Department of Economic Investigations, Nacional Financiera, 1950-52; Director General of Credit, Secretariat of the Treasury, 1952-58; Subsecretary of the Presidency, 1958-61, 1964-68. g-None. h-Author of many articles on monetary subjects; Director of the Revista de Economia, Secretariat of Industry and Commerce. i-Brother of Antonio Ortiz Mena, secretary of the treasury, 1958-70; son of Antonio R. Ortiz, treasurer of the Federal District, and María Mena; uncles and grandfather prominent in politics; nephew, Antonio Ortiz Salinas, served as subsecretary of tourism, 1977-82; married Clementina García. j-None. k-The Ortiz Mena brothers are one of the few examples in recent Mexican cabinet history where two brothers have simultaneously held a secretaryship and subsecretaryship; Raúl resigned as subsecretary of the presidency for reasons of health, Nov. 6, 1968, and has assumed no public positions since that date. l-DGF56, 563; DGF51, II, 304; DGF50, II, B de M, 198; HA, 5 Jan. 1959, 4; WNM, 165-66.

Ortiz Mendoza, Francisco
a-Mar. 27, 1921. b-San Luis Potosí, San
Luis Potosí. c-Primary studies at the
Rodolfo Menéndez School, Federal
District (6 years); secondary studies at
the Prevocational School No. 1 and No.
3, IPN; preparatory studies at Vocational School No. 1 and No. 2, IPN, (5
years); electronic engineering degree
from the Higher School of Mechanical
and Electrical Engineering, IPN, 1947;
studied under a scholarship at the
University of Cuyo, Mendoza, Argen-
tina; Professor of Physics and Cultural
History, IPN; member of the Technical
Advisory Council of IPN. d-*Federal
Deputy* from the Federal District, Dist.
7, 1964-67, member of the Rural
Electrification Committee and the
Promotion and Development of Sports
Committee; *Federal Deputy* (Party
Deputy from the PPS), 1970-73, member
of the Department of the Federal
District Committee, the Constitutional
Section of the Legislative Studies
Committee, the General Means of
Communication and Transportation
Section of the Legislative Studies
Committee, the Livestock Committee,
the First Balloting Committee, the
Mines Committee, the Small Agricul-
tural Property Committee, and the
Second Constitutional Affairs Commit-
tee; *Federal Deputy* (Party Deputy from
the PPS), 1976-79; *Plurinominal Federal
Deputy* from the PPS, 1982-85, 1988-91.
e-Founding member of the PPS, 1948;
Secretary General of the Federaton of
Mexican Youth of the PPS, 1952-54;
Secretary General of the PPS for the
Federal District; Secretary of Political
Education of the National Central
Committee of the PPS, 1955; Secretary
of Press of the Central Committee of
the PPS, 1979. f-Chief Assessor,
Department of Telecommunications,
Secretariat of Communications and
Transportation. g-Member of the
Unified Socialist Youth of Mexico,

1937; Secretary General of the Student
Society of the Higher School of Electrical and Mechanical Engineering, IPN,
1947-48; Secretary General of the
Television Workers Union of Mexico,
1947; founder and Director General of
the Mexican Association of Electrical
Communications and Electronics, 1950-
60; member of the Executive Committee of Local No. 10 of the SNTE, 1968.
h-Engineer, Televisa, 1953-58; technical
head, Mexican Mercantile Company,
1958-62. i-Married Eva Pérez de Ortiz;
son of Francisco Ortiz Castillo and
Micaela Mendoza y Castilla. j-None.
k-None. l-C de D, 1964-66, 53, 83, 92,
1970-72, 129; Directorio, 1970-72; HA,
26 Feb. 1979, III; DBGM89, 509; Lehr,
572.

Ortiz Rodríguez, José
(Deceased 1962) a-Dec. 24, 1871.
b-Taretán, Penjamillo, Michoacán.
c-Primary studies under Juan Zacarías y
Mejía, public school, Taretán; secondary
and preparatory studies at the Zamora
Seminary, Morelia, Michoacán; completed preparatory studies at the
Colegio de San Nicolás, Morelia; law
degree, Colegio de San Nicolás, Morelia,
1897. d-Federal Deputy from the State
of Michoacán, Dist. 1, 1912-13, member
of the Renovation Group; Senator from
the State of Michoacán, 1920-24; Senator from the State of Michoacán, 1924-
28. e-Secretary General of the Peace
and Union Political Group, Morelia,
1912, the first revolutionary group in
Morelia. f-Secretary of Foreign Relations, Jan. 1915, under President Eulalio
Gutiérrez; Justice of the Superior Tribunal of Justice of Michoacán, 1930-31;
Justice of the Superior Tribunal of Justice of the Federal District and Federal
Territories, 1931-34, 1935-40, 1941-46,
1947-51. g-None. h-Established law
practice, Morelia, 1897. i-Son of
Urbano Ortiz and Sofía Rodríguez.
j-Supporter of Francisco Madero; served

in the Army of the Northeast under General Pablo González. k-Supported the candidacy of Miguel Silva with *Enrique Arreguín*, 1911; imprisoned by Victoriano Huerta, 1913, escaped and joined Carranza's staff; candidate for the governorship of Michoacán. l-DP70, 1539-40; Casasola, V, 2422; Dicc. Mich., 319; Andrade, 459-60.

Ortiz Salinas, Antonio
a-July 2, 1935. b-Federal District. c-Primary studies in the public schools of Mexico City; secondary studies from Secondary School No. 1, Mexico City; preparatory studies from the Vasco de Quiroga Institute, Mexico City; law degree, National School of Law, UNAM, 1958, with a thesis on the Mexican tax system; CEMLA fellow, 1958; United Nations Fellow, Harvard University, 1959-60, advanced studies in taxation and economic development, Harvard University and MIT, 1959-60. d-None. e-None. f-Lawyer, Legal Department, Mexican Institute of Social Security, 1953-56; lawyer, Ministerio Público, Attorney General of Mexico, 1957-58; economic researcher, Technical Office, Bank of Mexico, 1958-59; member, Committee on Fiscal Reforms, 1960; Assistant Manager, National Pawnshop Bank, 1961-63; Subdirector, Department of Economic Affairs and Statistics, Secretariat of the Treasury, 1964-67; Oficial Mayor of the Secretariat of Tourism, 1976-77; *Subsecretary of Tourism*, 1977-82. g-None. h-Engaged in private activities, 1970-76. i-Son of *Antonio Ortiz Mena*, secretary of the treasury, 1958-70; brother-in-law of *Patrocinio González Garrido*, secretary of government, 1993; cousin of President *Carlos Salinas*; nephew of *Raúl Ortiz Mena*. j-None. k-None. l-HA, 14 Nov. 1977; letter; DAPC, 54; *Excélsior*, 26 Dec. 1981, 16.

Ortiz Santos, Leopoldino
a-Nov. 16, 1929. b-San Luis Potosí, San Luis Potosí. c-Early education unknown; law degree, San Luis Potosí, 1948-52; professor, University of Juárez of Durango, 1967-69. d-Local Deputy from the State of San Luis Potosí, 1982-85. e-Joined the PRI, 1949; Secretary of Youth Action of PRI, 1949-52. f-Secretary General of the Federal Board of Conciliation and Arbitration, 1949-50; agent of the Ministerio Público and Assistant Attorney, Attorney General of Mexico, San Luis Potosí, 1951-52; District Court Judge, Puebla, Durango and Chetumal, 1965-70; Assistant Federal Tax Attorney, Secretariat of the Treasury, 1970-78; Circuit Court Judge, 1978; Federal Tax Attorney, Secretariat of the Treasury, Department of the Federal District, 1978-82; *Justice of the Supreme Court*, 1985-87; *Provisional Governor of San Luis Potosí*, May 25, 1987-91. g-Secretary of Finances, Judicial Workers Union, 1964-65; Secretary of Legal Affairs, CNOP, 1983-85. h-None. i-Son of Leopoldino Ortiz Ricavar, lawyer, and Concepción Santos Rivera; married Leticia González Escamilla. j-None. k-None. l-Lehr, 421; DBGM, 572; HA, 9 June 1987, 13; DBGM89, 729.

Ortiz Tirado, José María
(Deceased 1968) a-Aug. 8, 1894. b-Alamos, Sonora. c-Preparatory studies at the Colegio de Mascarones and the National Preparatory School, Mexico City; law degree, National School of Law, UNAM; Professor of Penal Law, UNAM, 1922-30. d-None. e-None. f-Public Defender, 1918-24; consulting lawyer to the Department of the Federal District, 1919; councilman, Mexico City, 1924; agent of the Ministerio Público of the Office of the Attorney General, 1924-29; Justice of the Tribunal Superior of Justice of the Federal District and Territories, 1929-

32, President, 1932-34; *Justice of the
Supreme Court of Mexico*, 1934-40,
1940-46, 1947, 1953-54, 1955-56; *President of the Supreme Court of Mexico*,
1954-55; Ambassador to Colombia and
Peru, 1948-52; *Subsecretary of Government*, 1952; President of the National
Commission of Nuclear Energy, 1956-
58. g-None. h-None. i-Parents were
wealthy; cousin, Alfonso Ortiz Tirado,
was a medical doctor and well-known
Mexican singer; married María
Antonieta Necchi; son, José Ortiz
Necchi, served as director of the federal
treasury office, Monterrey, 1965.
j-None. k-None. l-DP70, 1540; DGF51,
I, 106; WWM45, 88; HA, 15 Feb. 1952,
3; STYRIWW54, 933; Enc. Mex., X, 21;
López, 808; Parodi, 194.

Ortiz Walls, Eugenio
a-July 4, 1931. b-Oaxaca, Oaxaca.
c-Primary and secondary studies,
University of Oaxaca, Oaxaca; law
degree, University of Oaxaca, Oaxaca;
professor of sociology, law, literature,
and history at various institutions in
Mexico City. d-*Alternate Federal
Deputy* (Party Deputy from PAN), 1967-
70; *Federal Deputy* (Party Deputy from
PAN), 1973-76; *Plurinominal Federal
Deputy* from PAN, 1979-82, 1988-91.
e-Joined PAN, 1952; Oficial Mayor of
PAN; member of the CEN of PAN,
1969. f-None. g-Student leader.
i-Married María Teresa Castro de Ortiz.
j-None. k-Seen by some observers of
PAN as an ideologically progressive
Christian Democrat. l-C de D, 1973-76,
29; HA, 12 Feb. 1979, 17; C de D, 1979-
82; DBGM89, 509.

Ortuño Gurza, María Teresa
a-June 16, 1957. b-Torreón, Coahuila.
c-Early education unknown; economics
degree, Autonomous University of
Coahuila, 1973-78; philosophy studies,
University of Puebla, 1980-81; professor, Higher Institute of Technological

Studies of Monterrey, Laguna branch,
1979; professor, University of Puebla,
1980-81; professor, Higher Institute of
Science and Technology, Gómez
Palacio, Durango, 1982. d-*Plurinominal
Federal Deputy* from PAN, 1982-85,
1988-91. e-Joined PAN, 1970; candidate
of PAN for the city council, Torreón,
Coahuila, 1979. f-None. g-Director,
Employers Association. i-Daughter of
José Luis Ortuño Romo and Teresa
Gurza. j-None. k-None. l-Directorio,
1982-85; C de D, 1982-85; DBGM87,
572; DBGM89, 510.

Osorio Marbán, Miguel
a-Dec. 10, 1936. b-Chaucingo, Guerrero. c-Teaching certificate, National
Normal School, 1948-53; preparatory
studies in social sciences, National
Preparatory School, 1954-56; law degree,
National School of Law, UNAM,
graduated with the highest GPA of his
class; received an honorary mention for
his thesis on "Public Administration
and the Educational Obligations of the
State." d-*Federal Deputy* from the State
of Guerrero, Dist. 3, 1964-67, member
of the Second Ejido Committee, the
Second Constitutional Affairs Committee and the Complaints Committee;
Federal Deputy from the Federal
District, Dist. 39, 1985-88; *Plurinominal Federal Deputy* from PRI, 1991-
94. e-Joined PRM, Aug. 8, 1950;
participated in *Adolfo Ruiz Cortines'*
presidential campaign, 1952; Director of
the National Youth of PRI, 1959-64;
orator for the *Gustavo Díaz Ordaz*
presidential campaign, 1964; general
delegate of the CEN of PRI to Morelos
and Nayarit, 1964; President of PRI in
Nayarit, 1964; representative of PRI
before the Federal Electoral Commission, 1966-67; Private Secretary to
Lauro Ortega Martínez, President of the
CEN of PRI, 1966-68; Director of *José
López Portillo*'s campaign in the desert
zones of Coahuila, Nuevo León, San

Luis Potosí, Tamaulipas and Zacatecas, 1975-76. f-Technical adviser to the Director General of CONASUPO, 1968; Manager General of La Forestal, 1968-76; *Subsecretary of Agrarian Reform*, 1976-78. g-Secretary of Political Action of the Student Society of the National Teachers School, 1951-52; Secretary General of the Student Society of the National Teachers School, 1952-53; President of the Student Council of the National Preparatory School, 1955; Secretary General of the Federation of University Students, 1955-56; Representative of the National School of Law to the First National Congress of Law Students. h-Secondary school oratory champion, *El Universal* contest, 1950; Director of *Acción*, National Teachers School paper, 1950. i-Protégé of *Lauro Ortega Martínez*; son of Miguel Osorio Ramírez and María de la Luz Marbán, married Laura Ayllón. j-None. k-Pre-candidate for senator from Guerrero, 1981. l-Letter; *Proceso*, 12 June 1978, 25; C de D, 1964-67, 82, 92; DAPC, 54; *Excélsior*, 26 Dec. 1981, 16; DBGM92, 541; DBGM87, 534.

Osorio Palacios, Juan José
a-Jan. 21, 1920. b-Federal District. c-Primary and secondary studies in the Federal District; preparatory studies in the Federal District; studies at the National Conservatory of Music, 1938-45. d-*Federal Deputy* from the Federal District, Dist. 20, 1952-55, Vice-President of the Chamber of Deputies, Dec. 1952, member of the Department of the Federal District Committee, the Inspection Committee of the General Accounting Office (3rd year), and the First Labor Committee; *Federal Deputy* from the Federal District, Dist. 15, 1958-61, member of the Library Committee (1st year), the Fifth Section of the Legislative Studies Committee, the Second Section of the First Credentials Committee, and the Committee on Fine

Arts; *Federal Deputy* from the Federal District, Dist. 15, 1976-79, 1982-85, Dist. 34, 1988-91; Representative to the Assembly of the Federal District, 1991-94. e-Joined the PRM, 1938; *Secretary of Labor Action of the CEN of PRI*, 1974-75; Director of Political Action of PRI in the Federal District, 1976; *Secretary of Political Action of the CEN of PRI*, 1976-79, 1982-85, 1989. f-Member of the National Symphony Orchestra of Mexico, 1939-48. g-Joined the Music Workers Union, 1945; Secretary General of the Music Workers Union of Mexico, 1946; member of the Board of Directors of the Student Society of the National Conservatory of Mexico; Secretary of Organization of the CTM, 1956; Secretary of Social Action of the CTM; Secretary of Finance and Administration of the CEN of the CTM, 1982. h-Violinist; member of the orchestra at UNAM; member of the Classic Quartet and the Opera Orchestra of the National Symphony Orchestra; delegate to the International Music Congress, Geneva, 1954, 1957. i-Married Luz María Puente, concert pianist; son of Juan Enrique Osorio, lawyer, and Consuelo Palacios. j-None. k-Answered President *José López Portillo*'s state of the union address, 1977; precandidate for senator from the Federal District, 1981. l-Func., 190; C de D, 1958-60, 88, 1952-54, 48, 59, 69; *Excélsior*, 9 Dec. 1976, 20 Aug. 1976, 1C, 26 Dec. 1981, 16; DBGM92, 620

Osorio Ramírez, Miguel
a-1915. b-Xicohzingo, Tlaxcala. c-Primary studies in Xicohzingo; secondary studies at Secondary School No. 4, Mexico City; preparatory studies at the National Preparatory Night School; law degree, National School of Law, UNAM, Mar. 20, 1935; one year of advanced studies, School of Philosophy and Letters, UNAM; one semester of

studies toward an LLD degree. d-*Senator* from the State of Tlaxcala, 1952-58, President of the Administration Committee, Second Secretary of the Agrarian Department Committee, President of the Second Justice Committee, First Secretary of the First Petroleum Committee and Second Secretary of the Special Committee on Tourist Affairs. e-Secretary General of the CEN of PRI. f-Lawyer, Legal Office of Banks and Money, Secretariat of the Treasury; Director, Legal Office of Banks and Money; Secretary General of the Committee to Control Prices in the Federal District; Judge of the Superior Tribunal of Justice of the State of Tlaxcala; Director of Legal Affairs, Secretariat of Hydraulic Resources, 1958-61. g-None. h-Worked as an agricultural laborer on the San Jacinto, Cuacualoya, and Santa Agueda haciendas; textile worker in the Covadonga Factory, Puebla; weaver, La Tlaxcalteca Factory, Tlaxcala. i-Helped by *Alfonso Caso* as a law school student; worked under *Ricardo José Zevada* in the Legal Office of Banks and Money, 1930; son, Federico Osorio Espinosa, was a precandidate for federal deputy from Tlaxcala. j-None. k-None. l-DPE61, 95; *Excélsior*, 12 Nov. 1978, 14; Ind. Biog., 109-10.

Osorio y Carvajal, Ramón
a-1914. b-Valladolid, Yucatán. c-Preparatory studies South-East University, Mérida; medical degree, University of Yucatán, 1936; Ph.D. in psychology, School of Sciences, National Technical University of Cuba, 1947; Ph.D. in philosophy and letters, Latin American University of Havana, 1954; graduate studies in cancer at the University of Havana, in gynecology at the University of Havana, and in obstetrics at Tulane University; Professor of Medicine, University of Yucatán, 1936-43; Professor of Medicine, National Techni-

cal University of Cuba; Director of the School of Medicine, University of Yucatán, 1943-44; Rector of the University of Yucatán, 1943. d-*Federal Deputy* from the State of Yucatán, Dist. 1, 1952-55, member of the Library Committee, the Editorial Committee (3rd year); *Senator* from the State of Yucatán, 1967-70. e-Delegate of PRI to many districts; Secretary General of Social Action of the CEN of CNOP of PRI. f-Director of the National Naval Clinic, ISSSTE; representative of the Agrarian Department; Director General of Coordination, Department of Tourism; representative from the Department of Tourism to the Organization of American States, 1967; Delegate of the Department of the Federal District in Cuajimalpa de Morelos, 1971. g-None. h-Intern, O'Horan Hospital, Mérida; Director of the O'Horan Hospital, Mérida, Yucatán; Director of the sports section of the newspaper, *Voz*; author of many books. j-None. k-Originally elected as a Alternate Senator in 1964, but replaced *Matos Escobedo* when he died in 1967. l-*Hoy*, 21 Mar. 1970, 20; C de D, 1952-54, 16, 49; C de S, 1964-70; Enc. Mex., X, 1977, 24.

Osornio (Camarena), Enrique C.
(Deceased May 27, 1984) a-Sept. 1, 1897. b-Hacienda de Canada Honda, Aguascalientes. c-Early education unknown; medical degree; professor, Medical Military College; Director, Medical Military College. d-Senator from the State of Querétaro, 1928-30, 1930-32; *Governor of Aguascalientes*, 1932-36; *Senator* from the State of Aguascalientes, 1940-46, member of the Second Balloting Group, Second Secretary of the Foreign Trade Committee, the Social Welfare Committee, the Second Instructive Section of the Grand Jury and the Third Labor Committee, First Secretary of the Third National Defense Committee, and President of

the Military Health Committee.
e-None. f-Chief of Medical Services on
a special mission to Brazil, 1922; delegate of the Secretariat of Public Health
to Baja California and Aguascalientes,
1924-30; director of various hospitals.
g-Founder of the Socialist Revolutionary
Teachers Bloc, 1935. h-None. i-Brother, Javier Osornio Camarena, was
consul general in Chicago, 1961;
marrried Eva Saldamando. j-Career
army officer; joined the Constitutionalists under Manuel M. Diéguez, 1913;
fought under General Obregón in the
Army of the Northeast during the
Revolution; supported Plan of Agua
Prieta, 1920; rank of Brigade General;
Chief of the Medical Military Corps;
rank of Brigade General. k-Amputated
General Obregón's arm at the Battle of
Celaya; founder of the Practical Medical
Military College; the *New York Times*
alleges he was charged with the murder
of the manager of the state lottery,
1935; freed from prison, Jan. 31, 1944.
l-NYT, 27 July, 1935, 14; Libro de Oro,
1946, 9-10; D de Y, 5 Sept. 1935, 1;
Peral, 603; Almanaque de Aguascalientes, 104.

Osuna, Carlos F.
(Deceased) a-June 16, 1895. b-Saltillo,
Coahuila. c-Primary studies in Saltillo;
secondary studies at the Ateneo Fuente,
Saltillo; studies at the National School
of Agriculture; studies at Braughons
Business College, Nashville, Tennessee.
d-Federal Deputy from the State of
Nuevo León, Dist. 5, 1928-30; Senator
from the State of Nuevo León, 1930-32;
Federal Deputy from the Federal District, Dist. 6, 1934-37; *Federal Deputy*
from the State of Nuevo León, Dist. 3,
1943-46. e-None. f-Oficial Mayor,
Accounting Department, Secretariat of
the Treasury; officer in the consular
service. g-None. i-Son of General
Gregorio Osuna Hinojosa, large landholder and governor of Baja California

del Sur, 1913, and Paula Osuna; nephew
of Andrés Osuna Hinojosa, governor of
Tamaulipas, 1917-19; married Ofelia
Sáenz. j-None. l-WWM45, 89; Peral, C
de D, 1928-30; C de S, 1930-32; C de D,
1934-37, 1943-46.

Otal Briseño, Rigoberto
a-Jan. 4, 1905. b-Campeche, Campeche.
c-Primary studies in Campeche;
teaching certificate from the National
Normal School; graduated from the
Naval College, Veracruz. d-*Senator*
from the State of Campeche, 1952-58,
President of the First Naval Committee,
and First Secretary of the Public Works
Committee, of the Second Petroleum
Committee, and of the National
Defense Committee. e-None. f-Naval
Attaché to the Mexican Embassy in
Argentina; *Oficial Mayor of the Secre-
tariat of the Navy*, 1958-64. g-None.
h-None. j-Career naval officer; Coast-
guardman on the *Progreso*; fought the
Cristeros, 1928; Commander of the
Coastguard ship *G28*; rank of Captain,
Nov. 12, 1946; Commander of the
Mazatlán, of the *Querétaro*, and of the
transport ship *Durango*; Subdirector of
the National Fleet; Chief of Adjutants,
Secretariat of the Navy; Commander of
the 6th Naval Zone, 1951; rank of Rear
Admiral, Oct. 31, 1957. k-Regarded as a
hero during action against the Cristeros
when he saved numerous civilian
women and children. l-Ind. Biog., 111-
12; DGF51, I, 389; DPE61, 37.

Oteyza, José Andrés de
a-Nov. 21, 1942. b-Federal District.
c-Early education unknown; economics
degree from the National School of
Economics, UNAM, 1961-65, graduating with the best GPA in his class and
an honorary mention, Mar. 30, 1966;
MA in economics, Kings College, Cambridge University, 1966-68; Professor of
Economic Theory, Balance of Payments
and International Liquidity, National

School of Economics, 1968-71. d-None.
e-Coordinator of the Advisory Council
of the IEPES for *López Portillo's* presidential campaign, 1975-76. f-Economist
for the Department of Economic
Studies, Division of Control of State
Agencies and Enterprises, Secretariat of
National Patrimony, 1965-66; analyst,
Department of Economic Studies, Bank
of Mexico, 1968-70; Subdirector of
Analysis of Operations, Division of
Control of State Agencies and Enter-
prises, Secretariat of Government
Properties, 1970-71; Director of the
Division of Studies and Projects, Secre-
tariat of Government Properties, 1972-
74; Director General of the National
Sugar Industry Bank, 1974-75; *Secretary
of Government Properties,* 1976-82;
Ambassador to Canada, 1982-87; Direc-
tor General of Airports, Secretariat of
Communications and Transportation,
1988-93. g-President of the Society of
Latin American Students in Cambridge,
England. h-Author of several books.
i-Student of *Horacio Flores de la Peña.*
j-None. k-Youngest member of *José
López Portillo's* cabinet. l-Letter; *El
Día,* 1 Dec. 1976; HA, 13 Oct. 1975, 17;
HA, 7 Feb. 1977, 17; HA, 6 Dec. 1976,
22; DBGM89, 264; DBGM92, 274.

Ovalle Fernández, Ignacio
a-Feb. 7, 1946. b-Federal District.
c-Primary and secondary studies in
Mexico City; preparatory studies at the
National Preparatory School; studied
law, National School of Law, UNAM,
1962-66, graduating with a grade
average of 9.8 in 1968; Ph.D. in political
science, University of Belgrano, Argentina, 1983. d-None. e-Secretary of Cultural Action of the National Directorate
of Youth Action of PRI; Secretary of
Political Action of the National Directorate of Youth Action of PRI, 1965;
Auxiliary Secretary of Organization of
the CEN of PRI, 1966-67. f-Director,
Office of Sidewalk Vendors, Depart-

ment of the Federal District, 1967-68;
Private Secretary to *Rafael Hernández
Ochoa,* Subsecretary of Government
1968-69; Private Secretary to *Rodolfo
González Guevara; Private Secretary to
the President of Mexico,* 1970-72;
Subsecretary of the Presidency, Nov.
14, 1972, to 1975; *Secretary of the
Presidency,* 1975-76; Director, National
Indigenous Institute, 1977-82; Ambassa-
dor to Argentina, 1982-87; *Ambassador
to Cuba,* 1987-88; *Director General of
CONASUPO,* 1988-91. g-None. h-Won
first place in the 1967 National Literary
Contest sponsored by the National
Institute of Mexican Youth. i-Married
María Luisa Cavazos; second wife,
Ivonne Constanza Buentello Rebollo,
journalist; son of Inocente Ovalle
Fonseca, surgeon, and Gloria Fernández
Oroquieta. j-None. k-At age 28, *Ovalle
Fernández* became one of the youngest
subsecretaries in recent cabinet history.
l-HA, 7 Dec. 1970, 28, 25 Sept. 1972;
DPE71, 1; Enc. Mex., X, 1977, 38;
DAPC, 1977, 3; Protag., 263; DBGM89,
264; DBGM, 317.

P

Pacheco Iturribarría, José
(Deceased Nov. 15, 1981) a-Apr. 29,
1894. b-Oaxaca. c-Early education
unknown; no degree. d-*Senator from
the State of Oaxaca,* 1964-69. e-None.
f-*Substitute Governor of Oaxaca,* 1955-
56; Director General of the Administrative Division, Secretariat of National
Defense, 1965. g-None. h-None.
j-Joined the Revolution; head of various
army units; rank of Brigadier General,
Dec. 16, 1940; Chief of Staff to General
Miguel Henríquez Guzmán; rank of
Brigade General, September 28, 1948;
Commander of the 30th Military Zone,
Villahermosa, Tabasco, 1955; Commander of the 33rd Military Zone,
Campeche, Campeche, 1957-58; rank of

Division General, Oct. 20, 1959; Commander of the 16th Military Zone, Guadalajara, Jalisco, 1962-64. k-*Por Qué* claims he made 500,000 pesos a year in commissions in the purchase of military uniforms; took a leave of absence from his position as senator from Oaxaca. l-DGF56, 97; Peral 47, 246; DPE65, 40; MGF69, 106; *Por Qué*, 4 July 1969, 5 *Excélsior*, 16 Nov. 1981, 38.

Padilla Gutiérrez, Raúl
a-1924. b-Topatitlán, Jalisco. c-Early education unknown; law degree; Professor of Civil Law, School of Law, University of Guadalajara; Director, Department of Aesthetic Education, University of Guadalajara. d-Local Deputy to the State Legislature of Jalisco; *Federal Deputy* from the State of Jalisco, Dist. 1, 1964-67, e-President of the Regional Committee of PRI, Jalisco, 1964. f-Director of the Market, Guadalajara; Subsecretary General of the State of Jalisco; Private Secretary to *Rafael Moreno Valle*, Secretary of Health, 1966-68; *Oficial Mayor of Health*, 1968-70. g-None. h-Practicing lawyer. i-Son, Trinidad, was a student leader at University of Guadalajara, 1983-86; son, Raúl, was rector of the University of Guadalajara, 1989. j-None. k-None. l-C de D, 1964-67; MGF69; Hurtado, 260.

Padilla Nervo, Luis
a-Aug. 19, 1898. b-Zamora, Michoacán. c-Primary studies in Zamora; law degree, National School of Law, UNAM; attended the School of Economics and Political Science, University of London; attended the George Washington University, Washington, D.C.; studies at the School of Law and Social Science, University of Buenos Aires. d-None. e-None. f-3rd Assistant Protocol Officer, Foreign Service, 1918; Second Secretary to the Mexican Embassy in London, 1919; Assistant Secretary of the Mexican Legation to Buenos Aires, 1923; legal adviser to the Mexican Embassy in Washington, D.C., 1925-28; Second Secretary to the Mexican Embassy in Madrid, 1931; Oficial Mayor of the Secretariat of Labor; Subsecretary of Labor; Subsecretary of Education and Fine Arts, 1932; Secretary of the Mexican Legation to Buenos Aires; Chargé d'affaires, Havana; Minister to El Salvador, 1934-35; Minister to Panama, 1935-36; Minister to Uruguay, 1937-38; Minister to Denmark, 1939-40; adviser to the Mexican delegation to the United Nations Conference, San Francisco, 1945; President of the Mexican Delegation to the United Nations, 1945-52; *Secretary of Foreign Relations, 1952-58; Mexican Ambassador to the United Nations, 1958-63;* Justice of the International Court of Justice, 1963-73. g-None. h-President of the General Assembly of the United Nations, 1951-52; Chairman of the United States Disarmament Commission, 1959; adviser to many international commissions; member of the Board of the National Savings Bank. i-Married Cecilia Winston; nephew of Amado Nervo, a distinguished Mexican poet; son of Luis G. Padilla. j-None. k-Awarded the Belisario Domínguez award, 1980. l-*Excélsior*, 18 Aug. 1972, 15; WB54, 911; WWM45, 89; HA, 15 Jan. 1959; WWMG, 30; HA, 5 Dec. 1952, 9; WWW70-71, 675; DGF56, 123; HA, 5 Jan. 1959; IWW67, 925; DPE61, 25; Peral, 608; STYRBIWW54, 919; DGF51, I, 110; Enc. Mex., X, 1977, 74-75; López, 817; NYT, 27 July 1954, 10; HA, 13 Oct. 1980, 7; Libro Azul, 248.

Padilla (Peñalosa), Ezequiel
(Deceased Sept. 6, 1971) a-Dec. 31, 1890. b-Coyuca de Catalán, Guerrero. c-Secondary schooling at the Normal School, Chilpancingo, Guerrero; teaching certificate; preparatory studies at the National Preparatory School,

Mexico City; legal studies, National School of Law, UNAM, on a government scholarship; law degree, 1912; founding member of a group of students who formed the Escuela Libre de Derecho; studies at the Sorbonne, Paris, on a scholarship from the Secretary of Education, 1913-14; advanced studies, Columbia University, New York, 1916; Professor of Constitutional Law, UNAM, 1928. d-Federal Deputy from Coyuca de Catalán, Guerrero, 1922-24, 1924-26; Federal Deputy from the State of Guerrero, 1932-34; *Senator* from the Federal District, 1934-40; *Senator* from the State of Guerrero, 1964-70. e-State Delegate of PRI in Guerrero; candidate for president of Mexico for the Mexican Democratic Party, 1946. f-Minister to Hungary and to Italy, 1930-32; Attorney General of Mexico, 1928; Secretary of Public Education, 1928-30; *Secretary of Foreign Relations*, 1940-45. g-None. h-Author of several books. i-Knew *Francisco Gaxiola* and *Ernesto Enríquez Coyro* in preparatory school and at the Escuela Libre de Derecho; student companion of *Emilio Portes Gil* at the Escuela Libre de Derecho; son of Mariano Padilla, an impoverished lawyer in Coyuca de Catalán, and Evarista Peñalosa, a school teacher; married María G. Couttolenc; son, Ezequiel, was a subsecretary in the Secretariat of Tourism, 1988. j-Joined the Revolution; served under Emiliano Zapata as a common soldier; served as a secretary to several generals fighting under Francisco Villa; fled Mexico in 1916 after Villa's defeat. k-*Padilla* received government scholarships for all of his professional education, beginning with a scholarship to study at normal school, Chilpancingo, Guerrero; answered President Calles' state of the union address, 1925; precandidate for the PRI nomination for president, 1945; Brandenburg considers *Padilla* in the Inner Circle of influence in Mexico,

1940-45; self-exile in Cuba and the United States until 1922; *Padilla's* family accused of controlling excessively large plots of land in Guerrero by the secretary general of the state CNC, Aug. 1972. l-WWM45, 89; DBM68, 474; Morton, 47, 49, 51; EBW46, 14; Scott, 210; HA, 13 Sept. 1971, 21; Brandenburg, 80; letters; Kirk, 205-10; Strode, 381-88; CB, 1942; *Excélsior*, 29 Aug. 1972, 27; Daniels, 108ff; Peral, 607; Enc. Mex., X, 1977, 73; López, 817; HA, 8 Dec. 1944, 5; DBGM, 319.

Padilla Segura, José Antonio

a-Mar. 12, 1922. b-San Luis Potosí, San Luis Potosí. c-Primary studies in Aguascalientes, Aguascalientes, and in Mexico City; secondary studies at the Higher School of Mechanical and Electrical Engineering, Mexico City; degree in electrical engineering, National School of Engineering, UNAM, Aug. 1942; Ph.D. in science, UNAM; professor, School of Engineering, UNAM; Professor of Electrical Engineering, National Polytechnic Institute; Chief of Laboratories, Higher School of Mechanical and Electrical Engineering, IPN; Vice-President of the Research Center, National Polytechnic Institute. d-*Senator* from the State of San Luis Potosí, 1982-88. e-None. f-Engineer, National Irrigation Commission, 1942-45; *Director General of the National Polytechnic Institute*, 1963-64; *Secretary of Communication and Transportation*, 1964-70; *Director General of the National Steel Industry of Mexico, S.A.*, 1971-76; *Director General of the National Steel Industry of Mexico*, 1976-78; Director of the National College of Technical Professional Education, Secretariat of Public Education, 1979-82. g-None. h-Laborer, Mexican Electrical Laboratories, S.A., 1938; engineer, Cervecería Moctezuma, Orizaba; executive, Otto Deutz Motores, S.A., 1945-46; General Manager, Acosta y Padilla, 1946-57;

General Manager, Franco and Company. i-Married María Elena Longoría; father, José Padilla Romo, a white collar worker; mother, Antonia Segura y Gama, related to Antonio Díaz Soto y Gama, prominent politician in the 1920s; son, José Antonio, was a director general at the Secretariat of Communications and Transportation, 1982. j-None. k-Precandidate for senator from San Luis Potosí, 1976. l-DBM68, 476; WWMG, 30; HA, 7 Dec. 1964, 19; DPE65, 103; WNM, 169; HA, 1 Sept. 1975, 13; *Justicia*, Sept. 1971; HA, 23 May 1977, 64, 15 Jan. 1979, 10-11; Lehr, 414-15; C de S, 1982-88; DBGM, 319; DBGM89, 578.

Páez, Manuel M.
a-Apr. 5, 1885. b-Culiacán, Sinaloa. c-Early education unknown; teaching certificate. d-*Governor of Sinaloa, 1934-35.* e-None. f-Interim Governor of Sinaloa, 1927-28. g-None. h-Director of medical laboratories; purveyor for manufacturing companies. k-Powers as governor of Sinaloa were dissolved by the federal government because Páez was too friendly with President Calles. l-Dulles, 661; D de S, 10 Aug. 1935, 1; Peral, 608.

Páez Urquidi, Alejandro
a-Sept. 25, 1907. b-Goméz Palacio, Durango. c-Early education unknown; secondary studies at the Juárez Institute of Durango; engineering studies at the Mechanical and Engineering Institute of San Antonio, Texas, and at the National School of Engineering, UNAM; electrical engineering degree, UNAM, 1929; studied law and economics, UNAM, 1942-43. d-*Governor of Durango, 1968-74.* e-Representative of the CEN of PRI in Durango. f-*Director General of the Federal Electric Commission, 1946-52.* g-None. h-Technical positions in the Companía Impulsora de Empresas Eléctricas, S.A; President of the Board of

Alen, S.A., Ingenería Alen, S.C., Plásticos, Rex, S.A., Financiera Metropolitana; Autos y Equipos del Norte, and Diesel Mexicana, S.A. i-Married Alicia Aragón; son of Alejo Y. Páez and Dolores de Urquidi. j-None. k-None. l-DGF51, II, 345, 355; DGF50, 245; HA, 12 May 1950, 24; WNM, 169.

Palacios Alcocer, Mariano
a-May 27, 1952. b-Querétaro, Querétaro. c-Early education unknown; law degree, University of Querétaro, 1972-76; MA in public law, Autonomous University of the State of México, Toluca, 1977-79; professor of law, School of Law, University of Querétaro, 1974-79; Dean, School of Law, University of Querétaro, 1979; Rector, University of Querétaro, 1979-82. d-Local Deputy to the State Legislature of Querétaro, Dist 5, 1973-76; Mayor of Querétaro, 1976-79; *Senator* from the State of Querétaro, 1982-85; *Governor of Querétaro, 1985-91.* e-Joined PRI, 1971; Secretary of the National Revolutionary Youth Movement of PRI (MNJR) in Querétaro, 1973-76; President of the National Council of the MNJR, 1974-75; *Secretary of Political Education of the CEN of PRI. 1982-83.* f-None. g-None. h-None. i-Son of Samuel Palacios Borja, lawyer, and María de la Luz Alcocer Pozo; married Ana María González González. j-None. k-None. l-DBGM, 576; DBGM89, 730; Lehr, 396; *Excélsior*, 18 Jan. 1985, 12, 16 Jan. 1985, 22.

Palacios (Luna), Manuel R.
a-Nov. 1, 1906. b-Oaxaca, Oaxaca. c-Primary studies at the Relacimiento School, Oaxaca; secondary studies at the Institute of Arts and Sciences, Oaxaca, Oaxaca, 1916-19; preparatory studies at the Institute of Arts and Sciences, Oaxaca, 1919-21, and at the National Preparatory School, 1922; law degree from the National School of Law,

UNAM, Nov. 8, 1926, with a thesis on the church; Professor of Sociology, School of Commerce and Administration, UNAM, 1933; Professor of Revolutionary Legislation, National Teachers School, 1936-42; Professor of Sociology, Higher Normal School, 1938-46; Professor of Economic Policy, National School of Law, UNAM (31 years); cofounder of the Higher Normal School. d-*Senator* from the State of Oaxaca, 1946, but did not serve in the Senate. e-None. f-President of the Technical Commission, Secretariat of Public Education, 1935-37; Director, Department of Legal Affairs, Secretariat of Government, 1938-39; member of the Presidential Study Commission, 1937; Judge, Federal Board of Conciliation and Arbitration, 1938-39; President, Federal Board of Conciliation and Arbitration, 1941-43; adviser, Department of Social Welfare, Secretariat of Government, 1938-46; *Subsecretary of Labor*, 1943-46; *Director General of the National Railroads of Mexico*, 1946-52. g-President of the Alumni Association of the Students of the Institute of Arts and Sciences of Oaxaca. h-Adviser to the National Railroads of Mexico, 1943-46; founder and Director of the Seminar for Social Science for Workers, 1933; practicing lawyer, 1973. i-Published the student magazine *Eureka* at the National Preparatory School with *Miguel Alemán, Antonio Ortiz Mena, Gabriel Ramos Millán,* and *Adolfo Zamora;* father, Manuel Palacios y Silva, a well-known tinsmith; his uncle was a justice of the Supreme Court; married María del Carmen Sierra. j-None. k-Supported the candidacy of Gilberto Valenzuela for president, 1924; campaigned as an orator for José Vasconcelos, 1929, with *Adolfo López Mateos* and *Salvador Azuela.* l-Letter; Peral, 609; DGF51, I, 7; DGF51, II, 127, 529; WWM45, 90; DGF47, 21, 413; Enc. Mex., V, 45; Correa, 37; López, 819.

Palacios Vargas, J. Ramón
a-March 11, 1916. b-Puebla, Puebla. c-Early education unknown; law degree, University of Puebla, 1938; professor, Law School, University of Puebla, 1938-48, National School of Law, UNAM, 1949-51, University of Nuevo León, 1954-69, and at University of Querétaro, 1958. d-None. e-Joined PRI, 1940. f-Agent of the Ministerio Público, Tepeaco and Puebla, Puebla, 1941-43; Judge of the Superior Tribunal of Justice of Puebla and Monterrey, 1951-57; Circuit Court Judge, Querétaro and Monterrey, 1958-69; *Supernumary Justice of the Supreme Court,* 1970-77; *Justice of the Supreme Court,* 1977-86. g-None. h-Practicing lawyer. i-Son of Juan Palacios Marín, lawyer, and María de la Luz Vargas Fuentes; married Adelina Ortega Arreola. j-None. k-None. l-DBGM, 677; letter.

Paleta, Ignacio Cuauhtémoc
a-Feb. 1, 1921. b-Puebla. c-Early education unknown; law degree. d-*Federal Deputy* from the Federal District, Dist. 26, 1982-85. e-None. f-None. g-Labor adviser to the Mixed National Committee to Protect Salaries; Auxiliary Secretary of the Central Committee of CROM; President of CROM, State of Puebla; Vice-President of the National Mutual of Textile Workers; Secretary General of CROM; Secretary General of the National Textile Federation. j-None. k-None. l-Directorio, 1982-85; C de D, 1982-85.

Palomares (Navarro), Noé
a-Nov. 10, 1913. b-Alamos, Sonora. c-Primary studies in Alamos, Sonora; teaching certificate from the Normal School of Hermosillo; preparatory studies from the National Preparatory School, 1934-36; law degree from the National School of Law, UNAM, with a thesis on "Our Federal System and the Dissolution of Local Powers," 1940;

primary school teacher; Professor of
Law, National School of Law, UNAM.
d-*Alternate Senator* from the State of
Sonora, 1946-49; *Federal Deputy* from
the State of Sonora, Dist. 1, 1949-51,
member of the Gran Comisión, the
Second Legislative Studies Committee,
the First Government Committee, the
Securities Committee and the First Labor Committee; *Senator* from the State
of Sonora, 1952-58. e-State committee-
man for PRI; coordinator for the
presidential campaign of *Adolfo López
Mateos*, 1958. f-Lawyer, Legal Depart-
ment, Secretary of Agriculture, 1940-42;
Judge of the Superior Court of Justice of
Sonora; Director, Legal Department,
Secretariat of Government, 1948-49;
Private Secretary to the Secretary of
Government, *Héctor Pérez Martínez*,
1946-48, *Oficial Mayor of the Secre-
tariat of Government* under *Gustavo
Díaz Ordaz*, 1958-64; *Oficial Mayor of
Agriculture*, 1964-65; *Subsecretary of
Agriculture*, 1965-70. g-None. h-None.
i-Married Dolores Hilton. k-None.
l-HA, 8 Dec. 1958, 40; DPE61, 11; C de
D, 1949-51, 83; *Libro de Oro*, xxxiii;
WWMG, 31; DGF56, 7; DGF47, 21, 71;
HA, 22 Dec. 1958, 7; Ind. Biog., 113-14.

Pámanes Escobedo, Aurelio
a-Aug. 3, 1903. b-Ojo Caliente, Zacatecas. c-Early education unknown;
graduated as a major in engineering
from the National Military College,
1931; completed administrative course,
National Military College, 1933;
professor at the National Military
College; professor at the Higher War
College. d-*Federal Deputy* from the
State of Zacatecas, Dist. 1, 1940-43.
e-None. f-None. g-None. h-Director of
many conferences on engineering
tactics. i-Brother of *Fernando Pámanes
Escobedo*, oficial mayor of the Secretariat of National Defense, 1958-64.
j-Graduated as a career army officer.
k-None. l-C de D, 1940-42; Peral, 613.

Pámanes Escobedo, Fernando
a-Feb. 19, 1909. b-Ojo Caliente,
Zacatecas. c-Primary studies in Ojo
Caliente; cadet at the National Military
College, 1922-25, graduating as a 2nd
Lieutenant in Infantry, Nov. 1, 1925;
Captain of Cadets, National Military
College, 1931; graduated from the
Higher War College, 1932-36; professor
of military tactics, National Military
College. d-*Federal Deputy* from the
State of Zacatecas, Dist. 4, 1955-58,
member of the Committee on War
Materiels, the First Committee on
National Defense, the First Budget and
Accounts Committee; substitute mem-
ber of the Foreign Relations Committee;
President of the Chamber, 1957; *Alter-
nate Senator* from Zacatecas, 1964-70;
Governor of Zacatecas, 1974-80. e-PRI
delegate to Coahuila during the 1958
presidential campaign. f-Administrative Subchief of Staff of the Secretariat
of National Defense, 1953-54; *Oficial
Mayor of the Secretariat of National
Defense*, 1958-64; Military Attaché to
China, 1944-46; *Ambassador to Cuba*,
1964-67; Ambassador to Indonesia,
1967-69. g-None. h-None. i-Brother,
Aurelio Pámanes Escobedo, served as a
federal deputy from Zacatecas, 1940-43;
married Rafaela Beristáin j-Career army
officer; participated in thirty-one battles
in the Bajío region, 1925-31; rank of 2nd
Captain, May 16, 1929; rank of 1st
Captain, Aug. 1, 1936; stationed in
Guerrero, 1938-40; rank of Major, May
6, 1940; member of the military staff of
President *Avila Camacho*, 1942-43;
Director of Civil Defense, Secretariat of
National Defense, 1943; rank of Lt.
Colonel, May 5, 1944; Chief, Section 2,
Staff, Secretariat of National Defense;
rank of Colonel, 20 Nov. 1947; Chief of
Staff of the Second Infantry Division,
Guanajuato, 1947-49; Chief of Staff of
the First Volunteer Infantry Division,
1949-53; rank of Brigadier General, Nov.
1, 1951; Commander of the 39th

Battalion, Tampico; rank of Brigade General, Nov. 20, 1958; Commander of the 5th Military Zone, Chi-huahua, 1971-73; rank of Division Gen-eral. k-Most commentators did not be-lieve he could capture the gubernatorial nomination in Zacatecas. l-McAlister, 224; C de D, 1940-42, 59; DPE61, 32; Peral, 613; DPE65, 25; DGF56, 29, 32, 35, 36; MGF69, 106; *Excélsior*, 26 Dec. 1973, 4; HA, 4 Mar. 1974, 45-46; Enc. Mex., Annual, 1977, 553; HA, 19 Aug. 1974, 36; *Excélsior*, 5 Feb. 1974, 9.

Papé, Harold R.
a-Dec. 12, 1903. b-Fort Wayne, Indiana. c-Early education unknown; engineer-ing degree from Purdue University, Lafayette, Indiana, 1925. d-None. e-None. f-Technical representative and Vice-President for European Operations, ARMCO, Paris, France, 1926-44; *General Manager of National Steel Industry*, 1946-70. g-None. h-Engineer, American Rolling Mills Company (ARMCO), Hamilton, Ohio, 1925-26; adviser to the Mexican government on the construction of a new mint; princi-pal designer of Altos Hornos, 1941-44. j-None. k-Founder of the Papé Founda-tion, which has financed a children's hospital, a grammar school, and a school for mechanical and electrical engineers in Mexico; held the sub-directorship of a major decentralized agency longer than any other person in Mexico from 1935 to 1980. l-Letter; DGF51, II, 231, 327.

Páramo (Díaz), Juan José
a-Jan. 11, 1935. b-Federal District. c-Early education unknown; law degree, National School of Law, UNAM, with a thesis on "Retroactivity in Administra-tive Law"; studies in technical coopera-tion, decentralized agencies and organi-zation, Paris, France; professor, Na-tional School of Law, UNAM. d-None. e-None. f-Lawyer, National Railroads

of Mexico, 1955-62; adviser, Depart-ment of Administrative Legal Affairs, CONASUPO, 1960-64; Private Secre-tary to the Secretary of the Presidency, *Emilio Martínez Manatou*, 1966-70; Technical Secretary of the Mexican Food System, 1973-74; adviser, Sub-director and Director General of Oper-ations, CONASUPO, 1971-76; adviser, Department of Financial Investments, Division of Credit, Secretariat of the Treasury, 1974-76; Treasurer of Mexico, 1976-82; *Subsecretary of Budgeting*, Secretariat of Programming and Budget-ing, 1982-88; *Director General of the National Finance Bank*, 1988-91; Director General of Aseguradora Hidalgo, Secretariat of the Treasury, 1991-94. g-None. h-Practicing lawyer, 1955-63. i-Son of Juan José Páramo Castro, lawyer, and Guadalupe Díaz Ballesteros; married Beatriz Arias Staines. j-None. k-None. l-Q es QAP, 132; MGF69; DBGM, 322; DBGM89, 268; DBGM92, 280; DBGM87, 293.

Pardo Aspe, Emilio
(Deceased 1963) a-1889. b-Federal District. c-Studies in Belgium and France; law degree, National School of Law, UNAM; Professor of Penal Law, National School of Law, UNAM, 1932-35; Director of the National School of Law, UNAM, 1935-38. d-None. e-None. f-Agent of the Ministerio Público of the Office of the Attorney General of Mexico; *Justice of the Supreme Court*, 1941-46, 1947. g-None. h-Author of several legal studies; contributor to the magazine *Criminalia*. i-Son of Emilio Pardo Sabariego Jr., prominent lawyer, judge and federal deputy, and Enriquita Aspe; grandson of Francisco de P. Aspe, delegate to the Liberal Union Convention. j-None. k-As director of the Law School, was responsible for revising the curriculum and emphasizing public law. l-Letter; DP70, 1577.

Paredes Ramos, Higinio
a-Nov. 13, 1896. b-San Esteban
Tizatlán, Tlaxcala. c-Primary studies in
Tlaxcala, Tlaxcala; rural school teacher.
d-*Senator* from the State of Tlaxcala,
1952-58, member of the National
Properties and Resources Committee,
First Secretary of the Second Navy
Committee, Second Secretary of the
First Public Works Committee, member
of the First Balloting Group and President of the Second Ejido Committee.
e-None. f-Adviser to the National Bank
of Cooperative Development; Director
of the Cooperative Society of Maritime
Transportation. g-None. h-Peasant;
organized the Cooperative Society of
Maritime Transportation in Veracruz;
member of the Merchant Marine in
Veracruz. i-Married Bertha Rangel
Solís; daughter *Beatriz Elena Paredes
Rangel* was governor of Tlaxcala, 1986-
92. j-None. k-None. l-Ind. Biog., 115.

Paredes (Rangel), Beatriz Elena
a-Aug. 18, 1953. b-Tizatlán, Tlaxcala.
c-Primary, secondary and preparatory
studies, Tlaxcala; sociology degree,
School of Political and Social Science,
UNAM; professor, Institute of Political
Education, PRI. d-Local Deputy to the
State Legislature of Tlaxcala, 1974-77,
President of the State Legislature;
Federal Deputy from the State of
Tlaxcala, Dist. 2, 1979-82, 1985-86,
President of the Chamber of Deputies,
1986; *Governor of Tlaxcala*, 1986-92.
e-Secretary of Indigenous Action of the
CEN of the National Revolutionary
Youth Movement of PRI, 1973; Secre-
tary of Organization of the Regional
Committee of PRI, State of Tlaxcala,
1975-77; *Secretary General of the CEN
of PRI*, 1992. f-*Subsecretary of Agrar-
ian Organization*, Secretariat of
Agrarian Reform, 1982-85; *Subsecretary
of Government*, 1993. g-Secretary of
Planning and Family Orientation, CEN
of the CNC, 1977-80; Auxiliary Secretary of the League of Agrarian Communities and Peasant Unions of Tlaxcala;
Secretary General of the League of
Agrarian Communities and Peasant
Unions of Tlaxcala, 1977-79; Secretary
of Educational Action of the CEN of the
CNC, 1980-83. j-None. k-First woman
to answer a presidential state of the
union address. l-Romero Aceves, 723-
24; Q es QAP, 378; C de D, 1979-82;
DBGM89, 730; DBGM, 322; *El
Nacional*, 10 Apr. 1992, 9.

Parra (Gutiérrez), Manuel Germán
a-May 7, 1914. b-Federal District.
c-Primary studies in Mexico City;
preparatory studies at the National
Preparatory School, 1931; studied law at
the National School of Law, UNAM,
1932-34; degree in economics from the
National School of Economics, UNAM,
1935-37; Ph.D. in economics, National
School of Economics, UNAM, 1944-48;
professor at UNAM. d-*Federal Deputy*
from the Federal District, Dist. 11,
1979-82. e-None. f-President of the
National Convention for Technical
Education, 1940; head of a department,
Secretariat of Public Education, 1941;
economic adviser to the Presidency,
1943-46; *Subsecretary of Industry and
Commerce*, 1946-48, under *Antonio
Ruiz Galindo*; investigator under
Aguirre Beltrán for the Indigenous
Coordinating Center, Tzeltal-Tzotzil
Region, Chiapas, Secretariat of Public
Education, 1951; coordinator of the
Commission for Urban Development,
1972. g-Adviser to the Latin American
Federation of Labor, 1943; helped
organize the National Teachers Union.
h-Author of many books on education
and economics. i-Married Emilia Prado
Huante; son of Ignacio Parra Montes de
Oca; father of *Manuel Germán Parra
Prado*, director general of the FSTSE,
1983. j-None. k-Resigned from the
Secretariat of Industry and Commerce,
Jan. 7, 1948, when his superior, *Ruiz*

Galindo, also resigned. l-HA, 7 Feb. 1972, 21; DGF51, II, 636; HA, 23 Jan. 1948, 35, 27 Dec. 1946, 38; WWM45, 92; DGF47, 155; HA, 29 Oct. 1948, 1, 18 Apr. 1952, 42; López, 829; *Excélsior*, 24 Apr. 1979, 12.

Parra (Prado), Manuel Germán
a-May 28, 1939. b-Federal District. c-Primary studies at the Benito Juárez Primary School, Mexico City; sociology degree, National School of Political and Social Science, UNAM, 1957-61, with a thesis on the "Sociology of the Economic Structure of Society"; professor, Ibero-American University, 1985. d-*Federal Deputy* from the Federal District, Dist. 11, 1979-82, Dist. 26, 1985-88. e-Joined PRI, 1964. f-Researcher, National Finance Bank, 1962-64; Chief of the Corn Sales Department, CONASUPO, 1964-65; Executive Assistant to the Director General of CONASUPO, 1965-67; Subdirector General of Delegations, ISSSTE, 1988-94. g-Secretary of Promotion of the National Union of CONASUPO Workers; Secretary General of the National Union of CONASUPO Workers, 1971-74; Secretary of Educational Action and Literacy, FSTSE; Permanent Delegate of the FSTSE before the National Institute of Union Political Education, 1978-80; Secretary of International Relations, FSTSE, 1977-79; Secretary of the National Electoral Committee, FSTSE, 1979; President of the National Vigilance Committee, FSTSE; *Secretary General of the FSTSE*, 1983-86. h-None. i-Son of *Manuel Germán Parra*, subsecretary of Industry and Commerce, 1946-48, and Emilia Prado Huante; married María Luisa Pérez, teacher. j-None. k-Precandidate for the secretary general of the FSTSE, 1979. l-*Excélsior*, 24 Apr. 1979, 12; C de D, 1979-82; Protag., 268; DBGM87, 536; DBGM92, 281.

Parrés Guerrero, José G.
(Deceased July 5, 1949) a-Dec. 15, 1889. b-Real Mineral del Monte, Hidalgo. c-Primary studies in Real Mineral del Monte; secondary studies at Real Mineral del Monte and the Liceo Hidalgo, Pachuca, Hidalgo; preparatory studies at the Scientific and Literary Institute of Hidalgo, Pachuca; medical degree, National School of Medicine, UNAM, internship as a Zapatista, 1911-14; Director General of Rural Agricultural Schools. d-Governor of Morelos, 1920-23. e-None. f-Oficial Mayor of Agriculture, 1924; Subsecretary of Agriculture, 1924-27; Subsecretary in charge of the Secretariat of Agriculture, 1927-28; Subsecretary of Agriculture and Livestock, 1933-34; *Subsecretary of Agriculture and Livestock*, 1934-37; *Secretary of Agriculture and Livestock*, Aug. 16, 1937, to Nov. 30, 1940; adviser to the National Agrarian Council, 1932; President of the National Irrigation Commission; executive member of the National Irrigation Commission, 1940-46; adviser to President *Manuel Avila Camacho*, 1940-46. g-Secretary General of the Zapatista Front. h-Practicing physician, 1914. i-Son of Adrián Parrés and Concepción Guerrero. j-Joined Zapata's forces 1911; head of an Army Brigade in the Army of the South, 1916; Head of Sanitary Services for the Army of the South, 1916-18. k-Removed from the governorship of Morelos by a leading Zapatista, General De la O; resigned from post as subsecretary of agriculture to run for the governorship of Hidalgo, 1928, but not selected as the candidate; investigators from the Secretariat of Government considered *Parrés* an honest governor of Morelos. l-EBW46, 186; Womack, 367-81; Peral, 617; Enc. Mex., V, 44; DP70, 1088; Gruening, 659; Q es Q; Enc. Mex., X, 1977, 148-49; Pérez López, 341-42; López González, 195-96.

Pasquel Jiménez Unda, Leónardo
a-Oct. 6, 1910. b-Jalapa, Veracruz.
c-Early education unknown; law degree,
National School of Law, UNAM, 1940;
two years of study in literature; second-
ary school teacher. d-None. e-None.
f-Auditor, National Lottery; Assistant
Director of the Legal Department,
National Lottery; Director of Sales,
National Lottery; Director, Federal
Highway and Traffic Police; consulting
attorney, Governor of Tlaxcala; *Oficial
Mayor, Secretariat of Health*, 1945-46;
President, National Council of Wheat,
1947; Justice of the Superior Tribunal of
Justice of the Federal District and
Federal Territories, 1956; Research
Historian, Department of the Federal
District, 1959. g-None. h-Author of
many books. i-Married Alicia Lozano
Barrios; son of Salvador Pasquel y
Castilla and Luz Jiménez Unda. j-None.
k-None. l-WNM, 170-71; DGF56, 514.

Pastrana Castro, Gonzalo
a-Jan. 10, 1920. b-Tepocoacuilco,
Guerrero. c-Secondary studies, Guada-
lupita School, Cuernavaca, 1933-34; no
degree. d-*Alternate Senator* from the
State of Morelos, 1958-64; *Federal Deputy* from the State of Morelos, Dist. 1,
1964-67, Dist. 3, 1979-82; *Senator* from
the State of Morelos, 1982-88. e-President of PRI, Morelos, 1964; General
Delegate of the CEN of PRI to Campeche, Yucatán, Quintana Roo, and
Veracruz, 1966. f-Director General of
the National Agrarian Registry, Secretariat of Agrarian Reform, 1977-78.
g-Secretary General of Local 72, National Sugarcane Workers Union, 1951-
52; Secretary General of the CTM of
Morelos, 1958-75, 1978-88. h-Laborer.
i-Son of Eutimio Pastrana, farmer, and
Paz Castro Mejía; married Josefina Gómez Guerrero, wife. j-None. k-None.
l-DBGM87, 537; Directorio, 1979-82; C
de D, 1964-67; C de S, 1982-88.

Patiño Guerrero, Gustavo
a-Dec. 6, 1933. b-Cuernavaca, Morelos.
c-Primary studies at the Benito Júarez
School, Mexico City, 1941-46; secondary studies from the Fray Juan de
Zumárraga School, Mexico City, 1947-
49; preparatory studies from the
National Preparatory School, 1950-52;
CPA studies, Autonomous Technological Institute of Mexico, 1953-57,
graduating with a thesis on "Administrative Organization and Accounting in
the Agricultural Credit Bank," 1964.
d-None. e-None. f-General Accountant, National Agricultural Credit Bank,
1959-60; General Accountant, National
Bank of Ejido Credit, 1960-65; Director
of Budgeting, Secretariat of Public
Works, 1965-70; Assistant Controller of
the CFE, 1976-77; Director General of
Administration and Finances, Transportation Committee, Department of the
Federal District, 1977-80; *Oficial Mayor
of Communication and Transportation*,
1982-86; *Subsecretary of Transportation*, Secretariat of Communications
and Transportation, 1986-88, 1988-93.
g-None. h-Chief of Bull Computers and
assistant auditor, National Union of
Sugar Producers, 1957-59. i-Son of
Federico Patiño Romero, businessman,
and Ana María Guerrero; married
Georgina Durán Rueda. j-None.
k-None. l-Q es QAP, 251; DBGM87,
294; DBGM89, 270; DBGM92, 282.

Patiño Navarrete, Jesús
(Deceased 1970) a-1911. b-Tlalpujahua,
Michoacán. c-Agricultural engineering
degree, National School of Agriculture,
Chapingo. d-None. e-None. f-Admin-
istrator of the National Bank of Foreign
Commerce; Administrator of the
National Commission of Maíz; Assis-
tant Manager of the National Bank of
Ejido Credit; *Subsecretary of Agricul-
ture and Livestock*, 1958-64. g-None.
h-Subdirector of the National Bank of

Mexico, 1964-70. i-Married Elsa Nuñez. j-None. k-Considered to have been one of Mexico's experts on forestry problems; the National School of Agriculture twice named him the outstanding agronomist in Mexico. l-DP70, 1585; DPE61, 69.

Patiño Rodríguez, Julio
a-June 30, 1935. b-Jalapa, Veracruz. c-Early education unknown; law degree, National School of Law, UNAM, with a thesis on the "Islas Marías Prison"; professor, Higher School of Business and Administration, IPN, 1973-75. d-*Senator* from the State of Veracruz, 1988-91. e-Joined PRI, 1960; Director of Legal Affairs, PRI, Federal District, 1980; Legal Subdirector of the PRI Committee for Political, Social and Economic Studies, Veracruz, 1987-88. f-Investigative agent of the Ministerio Público; Subdirector General of Government, Secretariat of Government, 1964; Director General of Legal Affairs, Secretariat of Government, 1969-70; Director General of Legal Affairs, President of Mexico, 1971-72; Director of Legal Affairs and Legislation, Secretariat of the Presidency, 1973-74; *Oficial Mayor of the Secretariat of the Presidency*, 1974-76. g-None. i-Son of Julio Patiño García and Evangelina Rodríguez; married Martha Beckwith. j-None. k-None. l-DPE65, 15; MGF73, 303; DPE71, 5; HA, 17 June 1974, 9-10; MGF69, 161; DBGM89, 512.

Paulín Posada, Angélica
a-July 17, 1955. b-Querétaro, Querétaro. c-Early education unknown; business administration degree, University of Querétaro, 1973-78. d-*Federal Deputy* from the State of Querétaro, Dist. 1, 1982-85. e-Joined PRI, 1976; Secretary of Social Action of PRI, Querétaro, Querétaro, 1981; member of the Advisory Council of the CEPES of PRI, Querétaro, 1980-82. f-Director of

Administration and Finance, National Institute for Community Development and Popular Housing (INDECO), Querétaro, Querétaro, 1977-79; Delegate of INDECO to Querétaro, 1979-82. g-Adviser, CNOP, 1983. h-Reporter, 1973-76; Assistant Administrator, Metal Industrial Products, S.A., 1976-77. i-Daughter of José Ignacio Paulín Cossío, public official, and María del Carmen Posada Retana; granddaughter of Esteban Paulín y González, physician, and Angela González. j-None. k-None. l-DBGM, 577-78; Lehr, 397; Directorio, 1982-85; C de D, 1982-85.

Pavón Bahaine, Manuel
a-Sept. 14, 1907. b-Campeche, Campeche. c-Early education unknown; law degree; studied engineering and French; teacher in the primary, secondary and preparatory levels. d-Member of the City Council of Campeche; Alternate Mayor of Campeche; Local Deputy to the State Legislature of Campeche; *Alternate Senator* from the State of Campeche, 1952-58, to *Alberto Trueba Urbina*; *Federal Deputy* from the State of Campeche, Dist. 1, 1961-64, member of the Gran Comisión; *Federal Deputy* from the State of Campeche, Dist. 2, 1967-70, member of the Gran Comisión. e-Member of PRI. f-Consulting lawyer, State of Campeche; Oficial Mayor of the Government of the State of Campeche. g-Representative of the CTM to various congresses. i-Married Sara Flores. j-None. k-None. l-Directorio, 1967-70; C de D, 1964-67, 1967-70; C de S, 1952-58.

Pavón Vasconcelos, Franisco H.
a-May 27, 1920. b-Acayucán, Veracruz. c-Early education unknown; law degree, National School of Law, UNAM, 1944; LLD degree, National School of Law, UNAM, 1963; professor, National School of Law, UNAM, and many state universities. d-None. e-Joined PRM,

1938. f-Chief, Legal Department, Forestry and Hunting Division, Secretariat of Agriculture, 1942-49; agent of the Federal Ministerio Público, 1949-51; Chief of the Office of Prior Offenses, Attorney General of Mexico, 1951-53; Secretary of Studies and Accounts, First Division, Supreme Court, 1958-62; district judge in Zacatecas and Michoacán, 1961-64; Judge, First District Court, Civil Division, Federal District, 1965-67; Judge, Second District Court, Criminal Division, Federal District, 1967-68; Judge, 4th Circuit Court, Monterrey, Nuevo León, 1968-69; Judge, 6th Circuit Court, Puebla, Puebla, 1969-73; Judge, 2nd Circuit Court, Federal District, 1973-74; Judge, 1st Circuit Court, Federal District, 1974-76; *Supernumerary Justice of the Supreme Court*, 1976-77; *Justice of the Supreme Court*, 1978-90. g-None. h-None. i-Son of Francisco Pávon Moscoso, lawyer, and Teresa Josefa Vasconcelos; married María Elena Uribe Ramírez j-None. k-None. l-Letter; Protag., 269; DBGM, 678; DBGM89, 632.

Pawling (Dorantes), Alberto J.
(Deceased Nov. 26, 1955) a-July 25, 1887. b-Campeche, Campeche. c-Civil engineering degree, Naval College, Veracruz, Veracruz. d-None. e-None. f-Interim Oficial Mayor of Communications, 1930; Director General of the Department of the Navy; Director of Ports, Department of the Navy; *Subsecretary of the Navy*, 1946-49; *Secretary of the Navy*, Oct. 21, 1949, to Feb. 7, 1952. g-Manager of the Henequeneros de Yucatán. h-Author of various works on the construction of naval ports. i-Son, Alberto José Pawling Salazar, was a technician for the Department of Economic Studies, Bank of Mexico, 1961; married María de los Angeles Salazar Rosado. j-Career navy officer; 1st Captain for twenty-five years. k-Considered an expert on merchant marine problems in Mexico; constructed numerous naval projects to improve Mexico's port system. l-DGF51, I, 379; DP70, 1561; HA, 15 Oct. 1948, 3; STYRBIWW54, 944; *Excélsior*, 20 Oct. 1949; BdM, 203.

Paz Méndez, María Encarnación
a-April 21, 1943. b-Oaxaca, Tlacolula. c-Early education unknown; law degree, Benito Juárez University of Oaxaca, 1965-70; professor, School of Law, Benito Juárez University of Oaxaca. d-Alternate Local Deputy to the State Legislature of Oaxaca, 1970-73; *Federal Deputy from the State of Oaxaca*, Dist. 3, 1982-85. e-Member of the Advisory Council of the CEPES of PRI, State of Oaxaca; Oficial Mayor of the Regional Committee of PRI, Oaxaca, 1980-81; member of the Coordinating Committee for *Luis Echeverría*'s presidential campaign in Oaxaca, 1970; active in *José López Portillo*'s presidential campaign, 1976. f-Adviser to the Department of Agrarian Affairs in Oaxaca, 1973; Director, Department of Promotion and Social Service, Secretariat of Agrarian Reform, State of Oaxaca, 1972-73; Subdirector of the House of Culture of Oaxaca, 1973-74. g-Secretary General of CNOP, Juárez, Oaxaca, 1976-77. i-Daughter of Manuel Paz de la Cajiga, businessman, and María Méndez Luria. j-None. k-None. l-Directorio, 1982-85; C de D, 1982-85.

Paz Sánchez, Fernando
a-Sept. 23, 1932. b-Huichapan, Hidalgo. c-Early education unknown; economics degree, National School of Economics, UNAM, 1954-58, with a thesis on the structure and development of Mexican agriculture; diploma, World Bank, Washington, D.C., 1969; researcher, National School of Economics, UNAM, 1961-69. d-None. e-None. f-Subdirector General of Public Investment, Secretariat of the Presidency, 1966-76;

Subdirector of Planning, Secretariat of the Treasury, 1977; Auxiliary Coordinator of Projects, Secretariat of the Presidency, 1979-81; Director General of Special Programs, Secretariat of the Presidency, 1981-82; Director of Projects Division, SOMEX Bank, 1982-87; Secretary of Economic Development, State of Hidalgo, 1987-88; *Oficial Mayor of Energy and Mines*, Secretariat of Energy, Mines, and State Industries, 1988-94. g-None. h-None. i-Son of Arnulfo Paz Trejo, public official, and Dolores Sánchez Magos, teacher; married Agripina González Pompa; political disciple of *Fernando Hiriart Balderrama*, secretary of energy, 1988-94. j-None. k-None. l-DBGM92, 283; DBGM89.

Pedrajo, Rafael M.
a-July 5, 1896. b-San Luis Potosí. c-Primary and secondary studies in San Luis Potosí; graduated from the National Military College. d-Mayor of Morelia, Michoacán, 1930-32. e-None. f-Private Secretary to General *Lázaro Cárdenas* as Secretary of War, 1933; Head of Services for the Chief of Police, Department of the Federal District, 1933-34; Director of the Traffic Department, Department of the Federal District, 1934-37; *Governor of Baja California del Sur*, 1937-40. g-None. h-None. i-Close friend of *Abelardo L. Rodríguez*. j-Joined the Revolution, 1919; fought under *Lázaro Cárdenas*; career army officer; rank of Brigadier General. k-None. l-Peral, 621; *Hoy*, 21 Dec. 1946, 60-64; Cárdenas, 175.

Pellicer, Carlos
(Deceased Feb. 16, 1977) a-Nov. 23, 1899. b-Villahermosa, Tabasco. c-Primary studies in Mexico City; secondary studies at the Colegio del Rosario, Bogotá, Colombia; preparatory studies at the National Preparatory School; studies at the IPN and at institutions in Paris and Rome in history and art;

Professor of Modern Poetry, School of Philosophy and Letters, UNAM; secondary and preparatory teacher, Mexico City. d-*Senator* from the State of Tabasco, 1976-77. e-Supported José Vasconcelos for president, 1929. f-Director of the Department of Fine Arts, Secretariat of Public Education, 1942-45. g-None. h-Private secretary to painter Francisco Iturbe, Paris, 1927; renowned poet and author; winner of the 1964 National Prize in Literature; founder of various museums. i-Never married; nephew, Juan Pellicer López, was Ambassador to Iceland, 1977; son of Carlos Pellicer, Colonel in the Revolution and pharmacist, and Delfilia Cámara Ramo. j-None. k-Member of the innovative literary group, *Contemporáneos*, which included *Jaime Torres Bodet* and *José Gorostiza*; jailed for two months, 1930. l-HA, 28 Feb. 1977, 12; *Proceso*, 19 Feb. 1977, 28; Enc. Mex., X, 1977, 195; DAPC, 55; WNM, 172; Santamaría, 115-17.

Peña Ochoa, Juan C.
a-Jan. 27, 1897. b-Zamora, Michoacán. c-Completed primary studies; two years of business studies; no degree. d-Federal Deputy from the State of Veracruz, Dist. 9, 1932-34; Mayor of Querétaro; Mayor of Córdoba, Veracruz; *Federal Deputy* (Party Deputy from PARM), 1967-70. e-Founding member of the PNR; founding member of PARM; member of PARM. g-None. h-None. j-Career army officer; rank of Lt. Col. l-Directorio, 1967-70; C de D, 1932-34, 1967-70.

Peña Soto, Adrián
a-May 28, 1922. b-Ciudad Hidalgo, Michoacán. c-Completed primary studies; completed first year of secondary; two years of studies in journalism; no degree. d-*Federal Deputy* (Party Deputy from PAN), 1967-70. e-Representative of PAN, Local Electoral Committee,

1952; member of the 11th District Committee of PAN, Federal District, 1955; President of the 11th District Committee of PAN, Federal District, 1956; candidate of PAN for Alternate Federal Deputy, Federal District, 1958; candidate of PAN for Alternative Federal Deputy, Federal District, 1961; member of the Regional Committee of PAN, Federal District, 1964; member of the National Organizing Committee of PAN, 1967; candidate of PAN for senator from Michoacán, 1970. f-None. g-None. i-Married Esperanza Avila. j-None. k-None. l-Letter; Directorio de C de D, 1967-70; C de D, 1967-70.

Peniche Bolí, Francisco José
a-Apr. 23, 1926. b-Mérida, Yucatán. c-Primary and secondary studies at the Colegio Montejo, Mérida, Yucatán; preparatory studies at the Escuela Libre de Yucatán; law degree from the School of Law, University of Yucatán, Jan. 28, 1948, and law studies at the National School of Law, UNAM; LLD from the National School of Law, UNAM, Apr. 29, 1969; Professor by Competition of Introduction to the Study of Law, National School of Law, UNAM, 1964-79. d-*Federal Deputy* (Party Deputy from PAN), 1970-73, member of the Social Action Committee (1st year), the Tariff and Foreign Commerce Committee, the First Justice Committee, and the Sixth Agrarian Section of the Legislative Studies Committee; *Federal Deputy* (Party Deputy from PAN), 1976-79. e-Joined PAN, 1942; Secretary of the State Committee of PAN, Yucatán. f-Secretary of Studies, Circuit Collegiate Courts, Mexico City, 1968; Secretary of Studies, Supreme Court of Justice, 1969. g-None. h-Author of a basic text on law; practicing lawyer. i-Married Marilu Vázquez. j-None. k-Candidate for federal deputy from PAN, 1964. l-Directorio, 1970-72; C de D, 1970-72, 129-30; HA, 26 Feb. 1979, VI; C de D, 1976-79, 59.

Peraldi Ferrino, Laura
a-July 25, 1917. b-Cuatro Cienegas, Coahuila. c-Primary studies at La Corregidora, Saltillo, Coahuila (6 years); teaching certificate, Normal School, Saltillo; Teacher, Orientation of Family Activities, Mexican Institute of Social Security. d-*Federal Deputy* (Party Deputy from PARM), 1970-73, member of the Library Committee (1st year) and the Instructive Committee for the Grand Jury (2nd Section). e-Member of PARM. f-None. g-None. h-None. i-Daughter of General Fernando Peraldi; grandniece of President Venustiano Carranza; godchild of General *Juan Barragán Rodríguez.* j-None. k-None. l-Directorio, 1970-72; C de D, 1970-72, 130; Guerra Leal, 283.

Peralta y Díaz (Ceballos), Alejo
a-1917. b-Puebla. c-Early education unknown; mechanical electrical engineering degree, 1935; *Director General of IPN,* 1956-59. d-None. e-None. f-None. g-None. h-Founder of the Aztecs Baseball Team, 1953; founder of the Tigers Baseball Team, 1955; co-owner of Grupo Primer; President, Industrias Unidas, 1984- ; president of the board and major stockholder in numerous companies; ties to Mitsubishi of Japan. i-Son, Carlos Peralta Quintero, an investor in cellular phones and vice-president in father's firm. j-None. k-National Prize in Engineering, 1989. l-Protag., 271; letter.

Peraza Medina, Fernando
a-May 6, 1908. b-Tekax, Yucatán. c-Early education unknown; law degree, University of Yucatán, 1942; professor in the social sciences, IPN; professor, Federal Institute of Teacher Education; teacher in Yucatán and Mexico City. d-Member of the City Council of Mérida, Yucatán, 1938; *Federal Deputy* (Party Deputy from the PPS), 1967-70; *Plurinominal Federal Deputy* from

PSUM, 1979-82, member of the Tourism and Justice Committees. e-Member of the PCM, 1935-43; member of the Politburo, PCM, State of Yucatán, 1936-42; founder and militant of the Popular Party, 1948-60; militant of the Popular Socialist Party, 1960-71; member of the Central Committee of the PPS, 1968-71; candidate of the PPS for governor of Yucatán, 1969; founder and member of the Central Committee of the PPM, 1977. f-None. g-Cofounder, Unified Socialist Youth of Mexico, 1935; First Secretary of Educational Action, Unified Socialist Youth of Mexico, 1935-42; active member of the SNTE; delegate to the 50th Congress of the Communist League, Yugoslavia, 1968. i-Married Carmen Castro Canto. j-None. k-None. l-Directorio, 1967-70; C de D, 1967-70, 1979-82; Protag., 271.

Perdomo (García), D. Elpidio
a-Mar. 4, 1896. b-Tlaquiltenango, Morelos. c-Completed primary studies; no degree. d-*Alternate Senator* from the State of Morelos, 1934-38; *Governor of Morelos*, 1938-42; *Senator* from the State of Morelos, 1946-52, member of the Gran Comisión and the Military Health Committee, substitute member of the Public Welfare Committee and the First Credit, Money, and Credit Institutions Committee; *Federal Deputy* from Morelos, Dist. 2, 1967-70, member of the Military Industries Committee; *Senator* from Morelos, 1970-76, member of the Gran Comisión, President of the War Materiels Committee, First Secretary of the Second National Defense Committee. e-None. f-Inspector of Police, Monterrey, Nuevo León. g-None. h-None. i-Married Carmen Villareal. j-Joined the Revolution; Zapatista; career army officer; Commander of the 178th Regiment, 1924-25; Garrison commander, Piedras Negras, 1929-31; Commander of the 7th Regiment, 1932-34; rank of Brigadier

General, June 16, 1942; reached rank of Division General. k-His inauguration as governor was marked by violence. l-DGF51, 7, 9, 10, 11, 14; HA, 15 May 1942, 3; Peral, 627-28; MGF69, 93; C de D, 1967-69, 75; NYT, 3 May 1938, 10; C de S, 1970-76; Directorio, 1967-70.

Pérez Abreu Jiménez, Juan
c-Law degree from the National School of Law, UNAM, 1948. d-None. e-None. f-Private Secretary to *Hugo Rangel Couto*, Subsecretary of National Patrimony, 1950; Director of Primary Level Planning Studies, City of Campeche, 1951-52; representative of the Secretariat of Government in the Reorganization of Immigration Offices for the Northern Border, 1954; Director of the Division of the Boards of Material, Moral, and Civic Improvements, Secretariat of Government; investigator of Political Affairs, Secretariat of Government, 1958; Director of Publications, Senate of Mexico; Administrative Director of nine Interparliamentary Congresses between Mexico and the United States; *Oficial Mayor of Communication and Transportation*, 1970-73; Director General of the Workers Cooperative Society of Clothing and Equipment, 1973-76, 1976-82. g-Secretary General of the Student Society of the National Law School, 1945. i-Son of Juan Pérez Abreu de la Torre, Director General of Professions, 1947, and private secretary to *Hugo Rangel Couto*; father taught many politicians at UNAM. j-None. k-None. l-HA, 14 Dec. 1970, 22; DGF51, I, 443; DPE71, 73; HA, 14 May 1973, 25; *El Nacional*, 18 Oct. 1945; MGF47, 269.

Pérez Arce, Enrique
a-1888. b-El Rosario, Sinaloa. c-Secondary studies in Guadalajara; preparatory studies in Guadalajara and Mexico City; law degree. d-Federal Deputy from the State of Sinaloa, Dist. 4, 1932-34;

Governor of Sinaloa, 1951-53. e-None. f-Provisional Governor of Nayarit; Justice of the Superior Tribunal of Justice of the Federal District, 1940; Judge of the Superior Tribunal of Justice of the State of Sinaloa, 1949; *Justice of the Supreme Court*, 1949-50. g-None. i-Father a lawyer. j-None. k-Forced to resign from governorship because of disputes with the federal government over municipal elections and administrative incompetence, according to Scott and Anderson. l-Scott, 277; DGF51, I, 88; HA, 19 Jan. 1951, 13-16; *Hoy*, 7 Mar. 1943, 6-7; Anderson.

Pérez Cámara, Carlos
a-Jan. 22, 1922. b-Campeche, Campeche. c-Early education unknown; law degree, School of Law, University of Campeche. d-*Federal Deputy* from the State of Campeche, Dist. 1, 1964-67, member of the Gran Comisión; *Senator* from the State of Campeche, 1970-76; President of the National Properties Committee, First Secretary of the Second Tariff and Foreign Trade Committee, Second Secretary of the First Treasury Committee, member of the Fifth Section of the Legislative Studies Committee, and member of the Second Balloting Group; Mayor of Campeche, 1977-79. e-Joined PRI, 1940; General Delegate of the CEN of PRI to Nayarit, 1972; general delegate of the CEN of PRI to Puebla, 1976; Secretary of Electoral Action of PRI, Federal District, 1984-85. f-Treasurer of the State of Campeche; Secretary General of Government of the State of Campeche; Syndic of the City Council of Campeche; attorney, Department of Labor, State of Campeche; President of the Board of Conciliation and Arbitration, Campeche; *Interim Governor* of Campeche, 1973; Director General of Government, Department of the Federal District, 1986-88. g-Student leader of the Federation of Students of Campeche; President

of the Rotary Club; Assistant Director of the Legal Department of the SNTE, Campeche; Secretary of Political Action of CNOP, 1970; Secretary of Ideological Action of CNOP, 1973. h-Son of Genaro Pérez Méndez, public official, and Esperanza Cámara Ortegón; married Elsa Ortiz Osorio. j-None. k-Precandidate for the PRI nomination for mayor of Campeche. l-C de S, 1970-76, 83; C de D, 1964-67; DBGM87, 299.

Pérez Correa (Fernández del Castillo), Fernando
a-Nov. 26, 1942. b-Federal District. c-Early education unknown; law degree, National School of Law, UNAM, with a thesis on agricultural insurance; political science degree, France, 1967, with a thesis on contemporary political theory; philosophy degree, France, 1968; Ph.D. in politics, France, 1971, with a thesis on class ideology in the Mexican revolution; professor of political science, UNAM; professor, Colegio de México; visiting professor, Harvard University; Coordinator of the Center of Political Studies, UNAM; Coordinator of the College of Sciences and Humanities, UNAM; Coordinator of Humanities, UNAM; *Secretary General of UNAM*, 1972-81. d-None. e-Member of the Advisory Council of the IEPES of PRI, 1972-75, 1983; adviser to the president of the CEN of PRI, 1972-75. f-*Subsecretary 2 of Government*, 1984-88; Director of the National Institute for Adult Education, 1988-94. g-None. h-None. i-Son of Othón Pérez Correa, notary public, and Carmen Fernández del Castillo; married María Victoria González Cárdenas, public official. j-None. k-None. l-DBGM, 333; DBGM87, 300; DBGM89, 275; DBGM92, 287; letter.

Pérez Duarte, Constantino
(Deceased 1956) a-Mar. 11, 1886. b-Pachuca, Hidalgo. c-Engineering degree from the National School of

Engineering, UNAM. d-None. e-None. f-Technical consultant to the Secretariat of the Treasury, 1924-35; member of the Mexican delegation to the London Economic Conference, 1931; and to the Economic Conference, Montevideo, 1934; adviser to Altos Hornos de México, the National Railroads of Mexico; *Subsecretary of Industry and Commerce*, 1952-56. g-None. h-Metallurgist, Dos Estrellas Mining Company, 1911-14; Director of the Company Metalúrgica Atotonilco El Chico, 1914-19; General Manager of the Golden Girl Mine, 1935-45; organizer of major mining operations; President of the Compañía de Fomento Minero, S.A.; author of a book on silver mining. i-Son, Jorge Pérez Duarte Sellerier, was subdirector of the division of agriculture, Secretariat of Agriculture and Livestock, 1961; son of Julián Pérez Duarte; married Sara Sellerier. j-None. k-None. l-DP70, 1611; WWM45, 93; DPE61, 77; DGF51, II, 127.

Pérez Gallardo, Reynaldo
a-Sept. 16, 1896. b-Ciudad Fernández, San Luis Potosí. c-Early education unknown; no degree. d-*Governor of San Luis Potosí*, 1939-41. e-None. f-None. g-None. h-Author of many works. i-*Gilberto Flores Muñoz* was his campaign manager for governor; later, they became political enemies. j-Joined the Revolution; career army officer; rank of Brigadier General, May 1, 1938; fought against *Cedillo*, 1938. k-Removed from the governorship after a disastrous administration characterized by debts and accusations in the press of his being responsible for the murder of a sister of *Saturnino Cedillo*, Aug. 19, 1941. l-Letter; Peral47, 254-55; Correa41; Anderson, 332; NYT, 21 Aug. 1941, 8.

Pérez Gasca, Alfonso
(Deceased 1964) a-June 28, 1890. b-Pinotepa Nacional, Oaxaca. c-Pri-

mary studies in Oaxaca; secondary studies at the Institute of Arts and Sciences, Oaxaca; law degree from the Institute of Arts and Sciences, Oaxaca, 1912; professor at the Institute of Arts and Sciences, Oaxaca; Director of the Institute of Arts and Sciences, Oaxaca; Professor of Military Justice, National Military College. d-Federal Deputy from the State of Oaxaca, Dist. 15, 1920-22; *Federal Deputy* from the State of Oaxaca, Dist. 3, 1949-52, Secretary of the Gran Comisión, member of the Legislative Studies Committee (1st and 2nd year), the Second Constitutional Affairs Committee, President of the Chamber of Deputies, Oct. 1949; *Senator* from Oaxaca, 1952-56, member of the Gran Comisión, Second Secretary of the Second Government Committee; President of the First Constitutional Affairs Committee and Second Secretary of the Social Security Committee; *Governor of Oaxaca*, 1956-62. e-None. f-Public defender in Veracruz, 1915-18; Oficial Mayor of the Superior Tribunal of Justice of the Federal District; Secretary of the Auxiliary Claims Commission (War Damages), 1918-23; Judge of the 5th District of the Federal District; Assistant Attorney General of the Federal District; *Justice of the Supreme Court of Mexico*, 1933-38; Secretary of Resolutions for the Military Tribunal of Justice; member of various legislative commissions for the Federal District, the Secretariat of the Treasury, and the Secretariat of Industry and Commerce. g-None. h-Author of many literary and scientific articles. i-Brother, Flavio, served as a deputy to the Constitutional Congress, 1916-17, and later as a federal deputy from Oaxaca and Secretary General of the State. j-Assistant Director of the Department of Military Justice; Director of Military Justice during the Revolution; reached the rank of General in the army. k-None. l-DP70, 1612;

DGF56, 14; Peral, 632; C de D, 1949-51, 83; DGF51, I, 24, 27, 29, 32, 34; Peral, 633; Hayner, 211; Enc. Mex., X, 1977, 215; López, 845; Ind. Biog., 117-118.

Pérez H., Arnulfo
a-July 18, 1902. b-Chignahuapán, Alatriste, Puebla. c-Primary and secondary school in Chignahuapán; teaching certificate from the Normal School of Puebla, 1917; teacher in Puebla; MA degree in higher education; two years of law studies. d-Federal Deputy from the State of Puebla, Dist. 15, 1922-24, Federal Deputy from Tabasco, Dist. 1, 1932-34, member of the Gran Comisión. e-*Secretary of Labor Action of the CEN of the PNR*, 1936. f-*Oficial Mayor of the Secretariat of Agriculture*, 1935-38; *Oficial Mayor of Public Education*, 1938-40; *Oficial Mayor of the Department of Agrarian Affairs*, 1940-46; Director of Education, State of Tabasco; Director of Education, State of Puebla; Customs Director, Ciudad Juárez, 1948; Customs Director, Tampico, Nuevo Laredo and Nogales. h-Widely published poet in Mexico. i-Political collaborator of *Garrido Canabal* in Tabasco. j-None. k-None. l-DBP, 525-26; DGF51, I, 162; CyT, 525-26; PS, 4844.

Pérez Jácome, Dionisio
a-July 17, 1936. b-Coatepec, Veracruz. c-Early education unknown; CPA degree from the University of Veracruz, Jalapa, 1965; law degree, School of Law, University of Veracruz, Jalapa, 1959; Professor of Administrative and Tax Law, National School of Law, UNAM, 1968-69; Professor of Administrative and Tax Law, IPN, 1968-69. d-*Federal Deputy* from the State of Veracruz, Dist. 7, 1988-91. e-*Secretary of Information and Publicity of the CEN of PRI*, 1987-88; *Secretary of Political Associations of the CEN of PRI*, 1988. f-Agent of the Ministerio Público,

Attorney General of the Federal District, 1960-61; adviser, Secretary of Government Properties, 1967-70; adviser, Secretary of the Treasury, 1968-70; Delegate No. 8 of the Secretariat of the Labor to Veracruz, Veracruz, 1964-66; Assistant Manager of Foreign Trade, CONASUPO, 1970; Manager of Control, CONASUPO, 1976; Subdirector of Operations, CONASUPO, 1976-77; Subdirector, Sugar Industry, Secretariat of Government Properties, 1977; Private Secretary to the Director General of CONASUPO, *Jorge de la Vega Domínguez*, 1977-79; *Subsecretary of Regulation*, Secretariat of Commerce, 1979-82; Coordinator, National Food Program, Secretariat of Commerce and Industry, 1983-86; representative of the State of Veracruz in Mexico City, 1987-88; *Subsecretary of Civil Protection, Prevention and Social Readaptation*, Secretariat of Government, 1991-93. g-Director, Legal Department, National Coffeeworkers Agricultural Union, 1961-62. h-Various positions in the state government of Veracruz. i-Son of Dionisio Pérez Romera, farmer, and Margarita Jácome, normal teacher; married Gloria Friscione. j-None. k-None. l-*Excélsior*, 24 May 1979, 16; DGF65, 159; Protag., 272-73; DBGM92, 289; DBGM89, 516; *El Nacional*, 14 Mar. 1991, 11.

Pérez Martínez, Héctor
(Deceased Feb. 13, 1948) a-Mar. 21, 1906. b-Campeche, Campeche. c-Primary and secondary studies at the Instituto Campechano, Campeche; preparatory studies at the National Preparatory School, Mexico City, 1920; dental degree from the National School of Medicine, UNAM, 1928. d-*Federal Deputy* from the State of Campeche, Dist. 1, 1937-39; *Governor of Campeche*, 1939-44. e-None. f-Style rewrite man for *El Nacional*, Mexico City, 1929; reporter, 1929, Editor, 1931,

Director of Information, 1932, Secretary
of the Editorial Staff, 1935, Editor-in-
Chief, 1936, and Editor and Assistant
Director, 1937, all at *El Nacional*;
*Oficial Mayor of the Secretariat of
Government*, 1945; *Subsecretary of
Government*, June 18, 1945, to 1946;
Secretary of Government, 1946-48.
g-Member of the National Congress of
Youth, 1926. h-Wrote a column for
many years in the paper *El Universal*
under the directorship of *Manlío Fabio
Altamirano*; author of many books of
poetry and biographies of Mexican
leaders. i-*Miguel Alemán* knew *Pérez
Martínez* as a student at UNAM;
longtime friend of *Salvador Novo*; early
political mentor to *Pedro Guerrero
Martínez*, justice of the Supreme Court.
j-None. k-Considered by Brandenburg
to be in the Inner Circle from 1939-48;
defeated Senator *Góngora Gola* for the
governorship of Campeche, 1939.
l-EBW46, 179; WWM45, 93; DP70, 613;
Peral, 634; HA, 20 Feb. 1948, 3;
Brandenburg, 80, 102; Correa, 360;
Informes, 1941, 1942, 1943; Enc. Mex.,
X, 1977, 216-17; López, 848; Raby, 235.

Pérez Moreno, José
a-Jan. 20, 1900. b-Lagos de Moreno,
Jalisco. c-Secondary studies at the
Padre Guerra Liceo; preparatory studies
at the National Preparatory School;
studies at the Higher School of Business; pre-med studies at the National
School of Medicine, UNAM, 1919-22;
no degree; Professor of Human Geography at the Central School of Mexico and
the Motolinia School of Geography;
founder of the Technical Police Institute. d-*Federal Deputy* from the State
of Jalisco, Dist. 5, 1958-61, member of
the Fine Arts Committee, the Protocol
Committee, the Editorial Committee
(1st year), the First Public Education
Committee, and the Third Section of
the Legislative Studies Committee.
e-Oficial Mayor of PRI. f-Department

Head, Secretariat of Hydraulic Resources; Consul General, Milan, Italy;
Oficial Mayor of Hydraulic Resources,
1956-58. g-None. h-Became a journalist for *El Pueblo*, 1916; Director of the
México Nuevo; editor for *El Demócrata*,
1920-26; editor for *El Sol*, 1927; wrote
for *Hoy, Siempre, Mañana* and *La
Prensa*; editor for *El Universal*, 1927-52.
i-Son of Mariano Pérez Oropeza, a
teacher, and Elvira Moreno; married
Dolores Anaya Gutiérrez. j-None.
k-None. l-DGF56, 411; Func., 244; C de
D, 1958-60, 88; Enc. Mex., X, 1977, 217;
WNM, 174.

Pérez Ortiz, Basilio
a-June 10, 1904. b-Monterrey, Nuevo
León. c-Primary studies in Nuevo León
and Mexico City; cadet, Heroic Military
College, 1926-29, graduating as a 2nd
Lieutenant in Infantry, Jan. 1, 1929;
diploma, Applied Military School, 1934;
diploma, staff and command course,
Higher War College, 1940; studies in
military organization in Argentina,
Brazil, Chile, and Uruguay, 1947;
instructor, Applied Military School and
the Higher War College. d-None.
e-None. f-*Oficial Mayor of the Secretariat of National Defense*, 1964-70.
g-None. h-None. i-Son of Lt. Colonel
Jacinto Pérez Lozano and Virginia Ortiz;
brother of General Alberto Pérez Ortiz;
sons, Fernando and Tomás, are career
officers. j-Joined the army as a bugler,
Dec. 17, 1920; 1st Sgt., 23rd Infantry
Battalion; rank of 1st Captain, Dec. 1,
1943, as a staff officer, 2nd Military
Zone, Tijuana, Baja California del
Norte; rank of Major, Sept. 16, 1946, as
a staff officer, 2nd Military Zone; rank
of Lt. Colonel., Jan. 16, 1949; rank of
Colonel, Feb. 16, 1951; rank of Brigadier
General, Nov 20, 1963; Chief of Staff,
23rd Military Zone, Tlaxcala, Tlaxcala;
Chief of Staff, 25th Military Zone,
Puebla, Puebla; Chief of Staff, 6th
Military Region; Commander of the 8th

and 10th Infantry Battalions; Interim Chief of Staff, Secretariat of National Defense; Assistant Inspector General of the Army and Air Force; Commander of the Garrison, Ciudad Juárez, Chihuahua; commander of an infantry brigade; rank of Brigade General, Nov. 20, 1963; rank of Division General, Nov. 20, 1967; Commander of the 10th Military Zone, Durango, Durango 1972; Inspector General of the Army and Air Force, 1976. k-None. l-MGF69, 195; DPE65, 33; DAPC77, 12.

Pérez Ríos, Francisco
(Deceased Mar. 27, 1975) a-Aug. 14, 1908. b-Temascaltepec, México. c-Primary studies in Toluca and Mexico City; secondary and preparatory studies at the School of Mechanical and Electrical Engineering, IPN; completed fourth year of his professional studies in electrical engineering at IPN. d-*Federal Deputy* from the State of Mexico, Dist. 5, 1952-55, member of the Library Committee, the Editorial Committee, the Legislative Studies Committee, and the Electric Industry Committee; *Federal Deputy* from the State of México, Dist. 5, 1958-61; member of the Railroad Committee, the Electric Industry Committee, the Budget Committee, and the Labor Committee; *Federal Deputy* from the State of México, Dist. 2, 1964-67, member of the Agricultural Development Committee, the Electric Industry Committee, and the General Accounting Office Committee; *Senator* from the State of México, 1970-75, member of the Gran Comisión, First Secretary of the Second Committee on Credit, Money, and Credit Institutions, President of the Electric Industry Committee, Second Secretary of the First Navy and the Social Security Committees, and First Secretary of the General Means of Communication Committee. e-None. f-Chief of Machinery, National High-

way Commission; Chief of Machinery, National Irrigation Commission; Chief of Machinery, Federal Electric Commission; Magistrate of the Federal Board of Conciliation and Arbitration. g-Cofounder of the National Union of Government Electricians; Secretary General of the Union of Government Electricians; joined his union with the National Union of Electricians of Mexico, 1944; Secretary of Political Affairs of the CEN of the CTM, 1956-75; Secretary of Relations of the CEN of the CTM, 1950; *Secretary General of the National Union of Electricians,* 1944-72; *Secretary General of the Only Union of Electrical Workers* (SUTERM), 1972-75. h-Left IPN to work; one of the founding workers of the Federal Electric Commission, 1937. i-Close friend of *Fidel Velázquez;* married Rosa del Castillo; son of Julián Pérez and Concepción Ríos. j-None. k-Participated in several labor movements and strikes in Guerrero, 1930s. l-Func.; C de S, 1970-76, 81; *Excélsior,* 28 Mar. 1975, 1, 12; HA, 7 Apr. 1975, 12-13; C de D, 1964-67, 85, 89, 1958-61, 88, 1952-55, 46, 49, 52, 56.

Pérez Vela, Juan
a-Feb. 27, 1916. b-Celaya, Guanajuato. c-Primary studies, The Three Wars Institute, Celaya; secondary studies at the Colegio of Guanajuato; medical degree, National School of Medicine, UNAM, 1942. d-Mayor of Valle de Santiago, 1947-48; *Federal Deputy* from the State of Guanajuato, Dist. 6, 1961-64, member of the Committee on Fine Arts, the Fifth Section on Labor of the Legislative Studies Committee, the Agricultural Development Committee; *Senator* from the State of Guanajuato, 1964-70. e-General delegate of the CEN of PRI to Querétaro, 1963; President of the Regional Committee of PRI, State of Guanajuato, 1965-67; special delegate of the CEN of PRI to the National Voting

Council, 1970; general delegate of the CEN of PRI to the State of Veracruz, 1970. f-Director of the Center of Hygiene of the Regional Hospital, Valle de Santiago, 1944-49; _Oficial Mayor of Agriculture,_ 1970-72. g-None. h-None. i-Son of Jesús Pérez Vela, mayor of Celaya and federal deputy from Guanajuato, 1918-20. j-None. k-Resigned as Oficial Mayor of Agriculture, Aug. 2, 1972. l-HA, 14 Dec. 1970, 22; 14 Aug. 1972, 24; C de S, 1964-70; C de D, 1961-63, 87; DPE71, 63; letter.

Pérez (y Pérez), Celestino
(Deceased Mar. 27, 1982) a-Jan. 21, 1892. b-Tlacolula de Matamoros, Oaxaca. c-Primary studies at the Pestalozzi Normal School, Oaxaca; preparatory studies from the Institute of Arts and Sciences of Oaxaca; law degree, Institute of Arts and Sciences of Oaxaca, Aug. 1914; Rector of the Institute of Arts and Sciences of Zacatecas. d-Deputy to the Constitutional Convention from the State of Oaxaca, 1916-17; _Senator_ from the State of Oaxaca, 1970-76, President of the Second Constitutional Affairs Committee, Secretary of the Second Section of the Grand Jury, Second Secretary of the Second Treasury Committee, First Secretary of the Third Labor Committee, member of the Second Balloting Group, and member of the Third Section of the Legislative Studies Committee. e-Secretary General of the Anti-Reelection Party of Oaxaca; opposed Porfirio Díaz. f-Syndic of the First Revolutionary Government of Oaxaca, 1916; Agent of the Ministerio Público in Istmo, Oaxaca and elsewhere, 1918-30; Attorney General of Zacatecas; President of the Board of Conciliation and Arbitration, Baja California del Norte; Secretary of the Federal Board of Conciliation and Arbitration; General Counsel for the PEMEX employees, 1946-53; Judge of

the 1st Mixed Court of Appeals, Baja California del Norte; public defender, Zacatecas. g-Cofounder of the National Union of Petroleum Workers. i-Son of Celestino Pérez y Pérez and Faustina Pérez. j-Supported Madero, 1909. k-Precandidate for the PRI nomination for senator from Oaxaca, 1958; youngest deputy at the Constitutional Convention. l-C de S, 1970-76, 83; HA, 5 Apr. 1982, 14.

Pesqueira D'Endara, Manuel Eduardo
a-Dec. 18, 1901. b-Hermosillo, Sonora. c-Early education unknown; medical degree from the National School of Medicine, UNAM, 1920-25; Professor of Medicine, National School of Medicine, UNAM, 1931-52. d-None. e-None. f-Physician, General Hospital, Mexico City, 1931-52; _Subsecretary of Health,_ 1952-58. g-President of the Mexican Society of Urology, 1948-59. h-Author of numerous medical articles. i-Son of lawyer, José de Jesús Pesqueira, and Juana de Endara; married Carmen Olea; son _Eduardo Pesqueira Olea_ was secretary of agriculture, 1984-88. j-None. k-None. l-DGF56, 332; HA, 16 May 1955, 5; letter; WNM, 175.

Pesqueira Olea, Eduardo
a-July 20, 1937. b-Federal District. c-Early education unknown; law degree, National School of Law, UNAM, 1960; courses in administrative management, National Center of Productivity, 1961; courses in macro economics, George Washington University, 1977-78. d-None. e-None. f-Subdirector, Department of Banks, Secretariat of the Treasury, 1962-65; Director, Department of Investments, Secretariat of the Treasury, 1966-72; Assistant Subdirector of Credit, Secretariat of the Treasury, 1972-75; Director of Financial Investments, Secretariat of the Treasury, 1975-76; Representative of Mexico and Executive Director, World Bank,

Washington, D.C., 1977-78; General Coordinator of Delegates of the Secretariat of Planning and Programming, 1979-82; Director of Administration and Finances, Channel 13, 1982; Director General of the Agricultural Credit Bank, 1982-84; *Secretary of Agriculture and Hydraulic Resources*, 1984-88; Ambassador to the Food and Agriculture Organization, United Nations, 1989. g-None. h-None. i-Son of *Manuel Pesqueira D'Endara*, physician and subsecretary of health, 1952-58, and Carmen Olea Teja; married Mercedes Villegas Hermida, businesswoman. j-None. k-None. l-Q es QAP, 498; *Excélsior*, 19 July 1984, 1; DBGM87, 304; DBGM89, 279-80; DBGM, 334; *Proceso*, 4 Mar. 1991, 51.

Petersen-Biester, Alberto

a-Jan. 7, 1925. b-Guadalajara, Jalisco. c-Primary, secondary, and preparatory studies, Guadalajara; chemical engineering degree, Autonomous University of Guadalajara; Professor of Physics and Thermodynamics, Autonomous University of Guadalajara and the University of Guadalajara, 1944-48; Professor of Chemistry, Autonomous University of Guadalajara, 1947-52. d-Alternate Federal Deputy (Party Deputy from PAN), 1973-76; *Plurinominal Federal Deputy* from PAN, 1979-82. e-Joined PAN, 1952; Secretary of Finances of PAN, State of Jalisco, 1962-68; candidate of PAN for mayor of Guadalajara, 1967; Treasurer General of PAN, State of Jalisco, 1945-72; Secretary of the Treasury of the CEN of PAN, 1972-76; candidate of PAN for federal deputy from Jalisco, 1976. f-None. g-None. i-Son of Germán Petersen Biedenweg and María Biester Gaxiola; brother, Germán, was a federal deputy from PAN, 1991-94. j-None. k-None. l-C de D, 1973-76, 1979-82; *La Nación*; Protag., 274; DBGM92, 547-48.

Petricioli (Iturbide), Gustavo

a-Aug. 19, 1929. b-Federal District. c-Primary studies at the Colegio Franco Español, Mexico City; preparatory studies from the Technological Institute of Higher Studies of Monterrey, 1948-51; economics degree from the Autonomous Technological Institute of Mexico, with a thesis on "National Finance Organizations, the Banking System and the Stock Market," 1952; studies at the English Language Institute, University of Michigan, 1955; MA in economics, Yale University, 1955-58, on a fellowship from the Bank of Mexico; Professor of Monetary Theory, Autonomous Technological Institute of Mexico, 1959; Professor of Monetary Theory, UNAM. d-None. e-None. f-Assistant economist, Bank of Mexico, 1948; economist, Department of Economic Studies, Bank of Mexico, 1948-51; economist, National Price Commission, 1951-52; economist, Bank of Commerce, 1952-55; economist to the Director of the Bank of Mexico, 1958; Director of the Technical Office, Bank of Mexico; Manager, Bank of Mexico; Director General of Treasury Studies, Secretariat of the Treasury, 1967-70; *Subsecretary of the Treasury*, 1970 to Oct. 10, 1974; Subdirector of the Bank of Mexico, 1975-76; President of the National Securities Commission, 1976-82; Director General of the Multibanco Comercial del Norte, the Banco Comercial del Norte, and the Banco Comercial y Capitalizador, 1982; *Director General of the National Finance Bank*, 1982-86; *Secretary of the Treasury*, 1986-88; *Ambassador to the United States*, 1988-92; Director General of Highways and Auxiliary Roads, 1993-94. g-None. h-Member of the Board of Grupo Condumex, 1981. i-Married Rosa Morales. j-None. k-None. l-B de M, 210; HA, 14 Dec. 1970, 20; DPE71, 27; HA, 21 Oct. 1974, 21; *Excélsior*, 5 Sept. 1982, 20; IEPES; Q es QAP, 519; Ríos, 83; DBGM89, 280; DBGM, 335.

Phillips Olmedo, Alfredo
a-Sept. 2, 1935. b-Matamoros, Tamaulipas. c-Early education unknown; economics degree, National School of Economics, UNAM, 1957-60; public administration studies, Cambridge University, degree, University of London, 1965; graduate courses from American, George Washington, and Cambridge Universities; Professor of Economic Cycles and Negotiations, Ibero-American University. d-None. e-Joined PRI, 1961; Financial Coordinator of Development, Popular Consultation Program, IEPES of PRI, 1982. f-Loan officer, Inter-American Development Bank, Washington, D.C., 1965-66; Subdirector, Department of Banks, Money and Investment, Secretariat of the Treasury, 1964-65; Director, Department of Economic and Tax Programs, Division of Financial Studies, Secretariat of the Treasury, 1962-64; Alternate Executive Director, International Monetary Fund, 1966-68; Executive Director, International Monetary Fund, 1968-70; Manager, International Economic Affairs, Bank of Mexico 1970-75; Subdirector of International Affairs, Bank of Mexico, 1975-82; *Director General of the Foreign Trade Bank*, 1982-88; Ambassador to Canada, 1989-92; *Subsecretary of Urban Development and Infrastructure*, Secretariat of Social Development, 1992-93. g-None. h-None. i-Son of Howard S. Phillips, journalist and editor, and Dolores Olmedo, businesswoman. j-None. k-None. l-Libro Azul, 255; IEPES; Q es QAP, 498; letters; Protag., 274; DBGM, 335.

Piana Lara, Fernando
a-Nov. 22, 1919. b-Federal District. c-Early education unknown; cadet, Heroic Naval College, 1937-42; advanced studies in anti-aircraft artillery

and surface firing, Polígono de Tiro, Graves, Normandy, France; courses in human safety, London; course in nuclear energy legislation, Brussels; naval intelligence course, Panama; professor, Pacific Naval College and Heroic Naval College of the Gulf, 1947-50; Director of the Heroic Naval College. d-None. e-None. f-*Oficial Mayor of the Navy*, 1983-86. g-None. h-None. i-Son of Fernando Piana Almazán, naval officer, and Carmen Lara Terán; married Alicia Palazuelos Gómez. j-Career naval officer; executive officer and commander, various naval ships; aide to the Secretary of the Navy; aide to the President of Mexico; Naval Attaché to France; Subdirector of Naval Construction, Secretariat of the Navy, 1960-64; rank of Captain, October 4, 1962; Commander of the Transportation Squadron, Acapulco; Chief of the Second Section, Staff, Secretariat of the Navy; Commander of the 3rd Naval Zone; Director of Social Security, Secretariat of the Navy; Commander of the 12th Naval Zone, Acapulco; rank of admiral, 1976; Director General of Oceanography, Secretariat of the Navy, 1977-82. k-None. l-Q es QAP, 92; DBGM, 336.

Pichardo Pagaza, Ignacio
a-Nov. 13, 1935. b-Toluca, México. c-Primary studies from the Colegio Alemán, Mexico City, 1940-43, and the Colegio México, Mexico City, 1943-47; secondary and preparatory studies from the Centro Universitario México, Mexico City; legal studies, National School of Law, UNAM, 1953-58, graduating with a thesis on the "Juridical Bases of Planning in Mexico," 1965; degree in industrial relations, Latin American University; special studies, Dartmouth College, 1957-58; MA in administration and public finance, School of Economics, University of London. d-*Federal Deputy* from the State of México, Dist.

4, 1967-70, President of the Budget Committee; *Federal Deputy* from the State of México, Dist. 27, 1979-82, President of the Programming, Budgeting, and Public Accounts Committee. e-Editor of the newspaper for the PRI Youth Sector, 1958; participated in the 1964 presidential campaign; member of the IEPES of PRI; member of the Technical Council of Economists, CEN of PRI; Secretary of Press and Publicity of the National Youth Sector of PRI, 1959-61; Coordinator of IEPES events, presidential campaign, 1975-76; President of the CEN of PRI, 1994. f-Director, Department of Publications, National Foreign Trade Bank, 1964-67; Editor, *Comercio Exterior*, 1964-67; Director of the Department of Utilities, Secretariat of the Treasury; Subdirector, Income Tax Department, Secretariat of the Treasury; Director of the Treasury, State of México, 1969-71; Secretary General of Government of the State of México under Governor *Carlos Hank González*, 1971-75; *Subsecretary of Revenues, 1976-78; Subsecretary "A" of the Controller General of Mexico, 1983-87; Comptroller General of Mexico, 1987-88*; Director of the Institute for Consumer Protection, 1988-89; *Substitute Governor of México, 1989-93.* g-Member of the Technical Council of the CNC, 1966. h-Vice-President of Consultoria Externa de México, S.A., 1978-79. i-Son of Carlos Pichardo, lawyer and federal deputy from the State of México, 1934-36, and Carmen Pagaza Varela; married Julieta Lechuga Manternach. j-None. k-None. l-*Excélsior*, 18 Jan. 1978, 4; letter; Almanaque de México, 68; Protag., 275; Q es QAP, 155; Directorio, 1967-70; C de D, 1967-70, 1979-82.

Pimentel, Rafael S.
(Deceased 1954) a-1909. b-Colima. c-Teaching certificate; taught in Nayarit and Guanajuato. d-*Federal Deputy* from the Federal District, Dist. 1, 1949-52, member of the First Committee on General Means of Communication, the Committee on Cooperative Development, the Second General Accounting Committee, and the Auto Transportation Committee; *Senator* from the State of Colima, 1952-54. e-President of the National Transportation Commission for the campaign of *Adolfo Ruiz Cortines* for president. f-None. g-Secretary General of the Mexican Alliance of Truckdrivers; Secretary of Interior of the Mexican Alliance of Truckdrivers; President of the Mexican Alliance of Truckdrivers. h-None. j-One-time truck driver. k-None. l-DP70, 633; C de S, 1952-58; C de D, 1949-51, 84; DGF51, I, 20, 30, 33, 35, 36; Enc. Mex., X, 1977, 311.

Piña Olaya, Mariano
a-Mar. 29, 1933. b-Champusco, Puebla. c-Early education unknown; law degree, National School of Law, UNAM, 1952-56, with a thesis on labor law; advanced studies, Rafael Caldera Institute, Caracas, 1960-61, and Mario Deveali Institute, Buenos Aires, 1961-62; professor, National School of Law, UNAM, 1958- . d-*Federal Deputy* from the State of Puebla, Dist. 10, 1982-85; *Governor of Puebla, 1987-93.* e-General Delegate of the CEN of PRI. f-Private Secretary to the Secretary of the President of Mexico, 1959; Subdirector General of Afianzadora Mexicana, S.A., 1965-70; President of the Local Board of Conciliation and Arbitration, Federal District, 1971; Director General of Administration, Federal Electric Commission, 1973-76; Administrative Director of Aeromexico, 1977-80; Representative of Puebla in the Federal District, 1981-82. g-Director General of the National Chamber of Sugar and Alcohol Industries, 1972-73. h-Practicing laywer. i-Son of Mariano Piña García, normal teacher, and Julia Olaya

Hernández, normal teacher; married
Patricia Kurozyn Villalobos, lawyer.
j-None. k-None. l-DBGM89, 732;
Llehr, 387; DBGM92, 814.

Pineda (Pineda), Salvador
a-Jan. 1, 1916. b-Nucupétaro, Michoa-
cán. c-Early education unknown; prepa-
ratory studies at the National Prepara-
tory School; law degree, National
School of Law, UNAM; MA in history,
School of Philosophy and Letters,
UNAM. d-*Federal Deputy* from the
State of Michoacán, Dist. 6, 1949-52,
member of the First Public Education
Committee, the Legislative Studies
Committee, the Second Government
Committee, the Foreign Relations Com-
mittee, and the Gran Comisión; *Federal
Deputy* from the State of Michoacán,
Dist. 7, 1955-58, member of the Gran
Comisión and the Committee on Eti-
quette. e-*Secretary of Political Action
of the CEN of PRI*, 1952; *Oficial Mayor
of the CEN of PRI*, 1959-63. f-Subdirec-
tor of Civic Action, Department of the
Federal District; Private Secretary to the
Attorney General of Mexico; Subdirec-
tor of the National Institute of Fine
Arts; judge of the Federal Tax Court;
Ambassador to Greece, 1968. g-None.
h-Editor of *Universidad*. i-Son, *Raúl
Pineda Pineda*, elected as a federal
deputy from the State of Michoacán,
1979-82; classmate of *Alfredo de Lara
Issacs*. j-None. k-None. l-DGF51, I,
23, 29, 33, 34, 36; C de D, 1949-52, 84,
1955-58; DGF56; Ind. Biog., 121; HA, 23
July 1979, 30.

Piñón Reyna, Celia Martha
a-Nov. 5, 1949. b-Nogales, Sonora.
c-Primary studies at the Colegio
Medrano for Girls, Guadalajara; business studies at the Martínez Negrete
School, graduating as a private accountant and stenographer. d-Alternate Federal Deputy (Party Deputy from PAN),
1973-76; *Federal Deputy* from the State

of Jalisco, Dist. 7, 1976-79; *Plurinominal Federal Deputy* from PAN, 1979-
82. e-Secretary of Women's Action of
PAN, 4th Electoral District, Jalisco,
1971; Treasurer, Secretary of Acts, and
Secretary of Finance, Regional Committee of PAN, Jalisco, 1972-80; Oficial
Mayor of the Regional Committee of
PAN, Jalisco, 1973-77; Auxiliary
Delegate of PAN to Aguascalientes,
1974; member of the Regional Council
of PAN, State of Jalisco, 1976-82;
member of the National Council of
PAN, 1979-81; Delegate of PAN to the
State of Nayarit, 1979. f-None. g-None.
h-Assistant to an accountant, Guadalajara, 1964; social science teacher, Jalisco
Center of Productivity, Guadalajara,
1974-80; various positions, Cashier
Department, Serfín Banking Group.
i-Daughter of J. Encarnación Piñón Tapia, teacher, and Martha Reyna. j-None.
k-None. l-C de D, 1973-76, 1976-79,
1979-82; Romero Aceves, 725-26.

Pintado Borrego, Fausto
a-1921. b-Tacotalpa, Tabasco. c-Primary and secondary studies in Villahermosa, Tabasco; preparatory studies
at the National Preparatory School; law
degree from the National School of Law,
UNAM, 1948; teacher of civics in
secondary school; Professor of Administrative Law, School of Law, University
of Tabasco. d-*Senator* from the State of
Tabasco, 1964-70. e-None. f-First
Appeals Court Judge, Tenango de Doría,
Ciudad Teapa, Ciudad Hidalgo and
Frontera, Tabasco; legal adviser to the
State Government of Tabasco; Justice of
the Superior Tribunal of Justice of the
State of Tabasco; President of the
Superior Tribunal of Justice of the State
of Tabasco; Subdirector of Government
of the State of Tabasco, 1962-63.
g-None. h-Coauthor of the Legal Code
of Tabasco, 1959. i-Member of *Carlos
Madrazo*'s political group. j-None.
k-None. l-C de S, 1964-70; MGF69.

Pizano Saucedo, Roberto
a-Apr. 14, 1923. b-Colima, Colima.
c-Primary and secondary education at
the public schools, Colima; graduated as
a private accountant. d-*Alternate Federal Deputy* from the State of Colima,
Dist. 2, 1952-55; *Federal Deputy* from
the State of Colima, Dist. 2, 1955-58;
President of the Chamber of Deputies,
1957, member of the Gran Comisión,
the Fourth Ejido Committee; *Alternate
Senator* from the State of Colima, 1958-
64; *Senator* from the State of Colima,
1970-76; Mayor of Colima, 1978-79.
e-President of the State Regional Committee of PRI, Colima; Secretary General of the IEPES of PRI, Colima, Colima.
f-Employee, Federal Treasury Office,
Colima, 1937-39; Assistant Census Office, 1939-40; Secretary of the First Civil
Court District, Colima; Secretary of the
First Criminal Appeals Court, Colima;
Federal Delegate of the Secretariat of In-
dustry and Commerce; representative of
the ISSSTE in Colima. g-Member of the
National Union of Social Security and
Public Welfare Workers; Secretary of
Organization of Section 52 of the Union
of Workers of the Secretariat of Public
Works, 1944-47; representative of the
CEN of the CNC to the National Insti-
tute of Better Nourishment. h-Postal
Assistant, 1944-47; Telegrapher, 1947;
Director of the weekly newspaper, *La
Voz*, and *El Regional*, Colima; Director
General of the *Diario de Colima*. i-First
cousin of *Arturo Noriega Pizano*,
governor of Colima. j-None. k-None.
l-DBM68, 493-94; C de D, 1952-54, 17;
DGF56, 22, 30, 33; *Excélsior*, 4 Nov.
1978, 17; Ind. Biog., 121-22.

Pizarro Suárez (Mercado), Nicolás
a-Oct. 19, 1907. b-Federal District.
c-Primary studies at the Colegio Inglés,
Mexico City; secondary studies at the
Colegio México, Mexico City; preparatory studies at the National Preparatory
School; law degree, National School of
Law, UNAM, May 31, 1932, with a thesis on judicial value of damages; Professor of Civil and of Labor Law, National
School of Law, UNAM. d-None.
e-None. f-President of the Local Board
of Conciliation and Arbitration, Mérida,
Yucatán; *Director General of Civil
Pensions* (forerunner of ISSSTE), 1953-
60; *Director General of the ISSSTE*,
1960-64. g-None. h-Practicing lawyer,
1964-76; Manager of the Association of
Insurance Institutions; Assistant
Manager of La Nacional Insurance
Company, S.A.; author of several books.
i-Son of a lawyer, Ismael Pizarro Suárez,
and Alicia Mercado; married Victoria
Macías; student assistant to *Agustín
García López*. j-None. k-None. l-HA,
7 Mar. 1960, 9; *Siempre*, 4 Feb. 1959, 6;
HA, 10 Dec. 1962, 20-21; WNM, 176.

Ponce de León (Andrade), Xavier
a-Jan. 17, 1941. b-Morelia, Michoacán.
c-Early education unknown; business
administration degree, Autonomous
Technological Institute of Mexico,
1962-66; studies in systems information, Columbia University, New York
City, 1968. d-None. e-Joined PRI, 1959;
Subdirector of the IEPES of PRI, 1975-
76; Subsecretary of Finances of the CEN
of PRI, 1981-82. f-Systems analysts,
Bank of Mexico, 1959-70; Director of
Projects, Secretariat of the Presidency,
1969-73; Subdirector of Administrative
Studies, Secretariat of the Presidency,
1973-75; Director General of Coordination of Technical Assistance in Programming, Budget, Organization and
Information, Secretariat of the Treasury,
1976-81; adviser to the Plan of Government, 1976-82; Technical Secretary of
the Committee for Modernization of
Public Administration, Plan of Government 1982-88; *Oficial Mayor of the
Controller General of Mexico*, 1982-87;
Coordinator of Programs for Administrative Simplification, Secretariat of the
Controller General, 1987-88; Assistant

Director of Administration and Legal Affairs, National Finance Bank, 1989. g-None. h-None. i-Son of Joaquín Ponce de León, farmer, and Rosaura Andrade Gómez, teacher; married Julieta Inmán Campos, businesswoman. j-None. k-None. l-Q es QAP, 157; DBGM89, 285.

Porte Petit (Candavdap), Celestino
a-Nov. 2, 1910. b-Córdoba, Veracruz. c-Primary and secondary studies in Córdoba; began preparatory studies in Orizaba, completed in Mexico City; law degree, National School of Law, UNAM; Professor of Penal Law, National School of Law, UNAM; Professor of Penal Law, School of Law, University of Veracruz, Jalapa, Veracruz. d-None. e-None. f-Auxiliary Agent of the Ministerio Público, State of Veracruz; Judge of the First Instance, Córdoba, Veracruz; Agent of the Ministerio Público, Attorney General of Mexico; Judge of the Superior Tribunal of Justice of the State of Veracruz; Judge of the Superior Tribunal of Justice of the Federal District and Federal Territories. g-None. h-Editor of the *Revista de Jurisprudencia* and *Revista Jurídica Veracruzana*. i-Father of *Luis Octavio Petit Porte Moreno*, second assistant attorney general of Mexico, 1982; son, *Adalberto*, was a plurinominal federal deputy, 1988-91; married Isabel Moreno Henríquez. j-None. k-None. l-Enc. Mex., 10, 404; Illescas, 720-21; DBGM89, 517.

Porte Petit Moreno, Luis Octavio
a-June 1, 1938. b-Córdoba, Veracruz. c-Early education unknown; legal studies, National School of Law, UNAM, 1957-61, graduating with a thesis on "The Crime of Contraband," Oct. 3, 1962; Professor of the 2nd Course in Criminal Law, National School of Law, UNAM, 1967-70; Professor of the 1st Course in Criminal Law, National School of Law, UNAM, 1964-70. d-*Fed-*

eral Deputy from the State of Veracruz, Dist. 6, 1979-82. e-Private Secretary to the President of the CEN of PRI, *Carlos Madrazo*, 1965; Coordinator of the Popular Sector of PRI, 1980-81. f-Judicial official, Mixed Court of the First Instance, Federal District, 1958-60; lawyer, Tax Attorney's Office, Secretariat of the Treasury, 1960-61; lawyer, Tax Attorney, Income Tax Division, Secretariat of the Treasury, 1961-63; Auxiliary Agent of the Ministerio Público of the Attorney General of the Federal District and Federal Territories, 1963-64; Subdirector General of Investigation, Attorney General of the Federal District and Federal Territories, 1964; Chief, Office of Complaints and Investigation, Department of Health, Federal District, Secretariat of Health, 1966-70; agent of the Ministerio Público, Attorney General of the Federal District and Federal Territories, 1968-70; Director General of Prior Cases, Attorney General of the Federal District, 1970-73; Secretary General of Government of the State of Veracruz under Governor *Rafael Hernández Ochoa*, 1974-77; Director General of Control of Property, Federal Zone, Secretariat of Human Dwellings and Public Works, 1977-79; President, Federal Conciliation and Arbitration Board, 1982; *Assistant Attorney General of Mexico*, 1982-88, 1988-89. g-None. h-Assistant Manager, Compañía Operadora de Teatro of the Federal District, S.A., 1973; General Manager, Compañía Operadora de Teatro of the Federal District, S.A., 1973-74. i-Son of *Celestino Porte Petit*, judge of the Superior Tribunal of Justice of the Federal District, and Isable Moreno Henríquez; brother of *Adalberto Porte Petit Moreno*, plurinominal federal deputy, 1988-91. j-None. k-None. l-IEPES; Q es QAP, 460-61; Protag., 277; C de D, 1979-82; DBGM89, 286; DBGM, 339-40.

Portes Gil, Emilio
(Deceased Dec. 10, 1978) a-Oct. 3, 1890. b-Ciudad Victoria, Tamaulipas. c-Primary studies in Ciudad Victoria; secondary studies at the Normal School, Ciudad Victoria, 1906-10; law studies, Escuela Libre de Derecho, 1912-14, degree in 1915; professor of primary schools, Ciudad Victoria, 1910-12; Professor of Agrarian Legislation, School of Law, UNAM, 1930. d-Federal Deputy from Tamaulipas, 1916-17, 1921-22, and 1924-25; Governor of Tamaulipas, 1925-28. e-President of the CEN of PRI, Apr. 22, 1930, to Oct. 15, 1930; *President of the CEN of PRI*, June 15, 1935, to Aug. 20, 1936; founder of the Partido Socialista Fronterizo, Tamaulipas. f-First Official of the Department of War and Navy, 1914; Subchief of the Department of Military Justice, Department of War and Navy, 1915; Judge of the 1st Instance, Civil Section, Hermosillo, Sonora; Judge of the Superior Tribunal of Justice of Sonora, 1916; consulting lawyer to the Secretary of War, 1917; Secretary General of Government of the State of Tamaulipas, 1918-19; Provisional Governor of Tamaulipas, 1920; general lawyer for the National Railroads of Mexico, 1921-22; President of Mexico, 1928-30; Secretary of Government, 1928; Secretary of Government, 1930; Minister to France, 1931-32; delegate to the League of Nations, 1931-32; Attorney General of Mexico, 1932-34; Secretary of Foreign Relations, 1934-35; Special Ambassador to the Dominican Republic, 1944; Special Ambassador to Ecuador, 1946; First Ambassador from Mexico to India, 1951; President of the National Securities Committee, 1959; adviser to the Constructora Nacional de Carros de Ferrocarril, S.A., 1966; President of the Advisory Technical Committee, National Banking Commission, 1970. g-None. h-Author of books on the church, labor, and politics in

Mexico. i-Attended the Escuela Libre de Derecho with *Francisco Javier Gaxiola* and *Ezequiel Padilla*; son of Domingo Portes and Adela Gil; married Carmen García. j-Administrative positions during the Revolution. k-One of the founders of the Escuela Libre de Derecho. l-Letter; DBM68, 495-96; Gaxiola, 12, etc.; letter; Brandenburg, 80, 63; Peral, 648; WWM45, 94; Daniels, 43, 104; IWW40, 912; DP70, 1663-64; Strode, 28, 87; Dulles; Enc. Mex., X, 405-06; *Justicia*, Aug. 1970; HA, 18 Dec. 1978, 17-18.

Posada, Angel
(Deceased Mar. 12, 1938) a-1890. b-Parral, Chihuahua. c-Early education unknown; studies in agriculture, National School of Agriculture, San Jacinto, until 1914; agricultural engineering degree, Agricultural College, Ciudad Juárez. d-Federal Deputy from the State of Chihuahua, Dist. 5, 1932-34, member of the Gran Comisión; *Senator* from the State of Chihuahua, 1934-38. e-Secretary of Agrarian Action of the CEN of the PNR, 1934. f-Oficial Mayor of the State Government of Chihuahua; Oficial Mayor of the National Agrarian Commission, 1933-34; Director of the Agrarian Department, 1934. g-None. h-None. i-Father, an employee of the Bellavista Thread Factory, operated by Federico Sisniega, son-in-law of Luis Terrazas. j-None. k-Assassinated in Ciudad Juárez during his campaign for governor of Chihuahua. l-DP70, 1665; Peral, 650; C de S, 1934-40; Enc. Mex., X, 1977, 411; Goméz, 420-21.

Pozo, Agapito
(Deceased 1976) a-Apr. 21, 1899. b-Querétaro, Querétaro. c-Primary studies with the La Sallist Brothers; preparatory studies at the Colegio Civil of Querétaro; law degree from the Colegio Civil of the State of Querétaro,

1923; Rector of the University of Querétaro, 1970-72. d-*Senator* from the State of Querétaro, 1940-43; *Governor of Querétaro*, 1943-49. e-State committeeman for PRI. f-Agent of the Ministerio Público in León, Guanajuato, 1924-26; Civil Judge; Judge of the Superior Tribunal of Justice of the State of Guanajuato; Justice of the Superior Tribunal of the Federal District and Federal Territories, 1940; Secretary of the City Council of León, Guanajuato; Secretary of the City Council of Querétaro; Secretary of Government of the State of Querétaro; Director of the Administrative Office, Chief of Police for the Federal District; Private Secretary to the Chief of Police of the Federal District; Private Secretary to the Head of the Federal District; agent of the Ministerio Público of the Office of the Attorney General; *Justice of the Supreme Court of Mexico*, 1950-52, 1952-58, and 1958-64; *President of the Supreme Court*, 1958, 1964-68. g-None. h-Practicing attorney. i-Son of a lawyer. j-None. k-None. l-DBM68, 497; WWMG, 32; HA, 14 Apr. 1958, 8; DGF56, 568; Peral, 651-52; DGF51, I; Enc. Mex., X, 1977, 420; Casasola, V, 2422; *Justicia*, Aug. 1967.

Prado Mercado, María Elena
a-Feb. 3, 1955. b-Toluca, México. c-Primary studies at the 5th of May School, Colorines, México, 1961-66; secondary studies at the Benito Juárez School, Toluca, México, 1967-69; preparatory studies at the Adolfo López Mateos Preparatory School of the Autonomous University of the State of México, 1971-74; sociology degree, School of Political and Social Science, Autonomous University of the State of México, 1976-79. d-*Federal Deputy* from the State of México, Dist. 22, 1979-82. e-Joined the PRI youth, 1971; founding member of the National Movement of Revolutionary Youth of

PRI, 1973; delegate of the CEN of PRI to the Santo Tomás de los Plátanos, México, 1975; Secretary General of the National Movement of Revolutionary Youth of PRI, State of México, 1975. f-None. g-None. i-Daughter of Rodolfo Prado Torres and Alicia Mercado. j-None. k-None. l-Romero Aceves, 727-28; Protag., 278; C de D, 1979-82.

Prado (Proaño), Eugenio
(Deceased 1969) a-Nov. 12, 1897. b-San Buenaventura, Chihuahua. c-Primary studies at the public school attached to the State Normal School, Chihuahua; no degree. d-Local Deputy to the State Legislature of Chihuahua, 1934-35; Mayor of Chihuahua, 1935; *Federal Deputy* from the State of Chihuahua, Dist. 1, 1937-40; *Senator* from the State of Chihuahua, 1940-46, President of the Senate, President of the First Government Committee and the Treasury Committee, member of the Gran Comisión; *Federal Deputy* from the State of Chihuahua, Dist. 1, 1946-49, President of the Permanent Committee of Congress, 1949, member of the First Committee on Government, and the First Treasury Committee. e-None. f-Director of the Cooperative Sugar Mill of Zacatepec, Morelos; Director of the Cooperative Ejido Mill Emiliano Zapata, 1951; Interim Governor of Chihuahua. h-None. j-None. k-Answered *Manuel Avila Camacho*'s last state of the union address, 1946. l-C de D, 1946-48, 84; DGF51, II; WWMG, 94; Peral, 651; DP70, 1669; C de S, 1940-46; C de D, 1937-39, 17; López, 874; *Excélsior*, 8 July 1949; Enc. Mex., X, 1977, 420; HA, 16 Aug. 1946.

Preciado Hernández, Rafael
a-Apr. 29, 1908. b-Cucuciapa, El Grullo, Jalisco. c-Primary and preparatory studies, Guadalajara; law degree, University of Guadalajara, October 8, 1930; professor, Normal School for

Women, Guadalajara, Jalisco, 1930-32; Professor of Roman Law, University of Guadalajara, 1931-33; Professor of the General Theory of the State, Autonomous University of Guadalajara, 1934-35; Professor of the Philosophy of Law, Escuela Libre de Derecho, Mexico City, 1937-70; Professor of Philosophy of Law, National School of Law, UNAM, 1939-40; Professor of the Introduction of the State of Law, National School of Law, UNAM, 1941-70; Director, Seminar in the Philosophy of Law, UNAM, 1949-70. d-*Federal Deputy* (Party Deputy from PAN), 1967-70, member of the Department of the Federal District Committee, the Constitutional Affairs Section of the Legislative Studies Committee and the Second Balloting Committee. e-Representative to the Federal Electoral Commission from PAN, 1953-58, 1969-71; founding member of the National Council of PAN, 1939; member of the CEN of PAN, 1939, 1947-70; Director of the Regional Committee of PAN in the Federal District, 1943-46. f-Secretary, various divisions, Superior Tribunal of Justice of the State of Jalisco, 1931-32; Civil Judge, First Civil District, Guadalajara, 1933; Secretary of Studies and Accounts of the 3rd Division, Supreme Court, 1935-39. g-None. h-Practicing lawyer, 1931-35, 1939-70. i-Married Carmen Briseño; son of Severiano Preciado and María de Jesús Hernández, peasants. j-None. k-Responsible for recruiting many prominent members of PAN from his law classes. l-WNM, 178; Mabry; C de D, 1967-70, 62, 68, 77; letter.

Priego Ortiz, Luis
a-Aug. 19, 1929. b-Villahermosa, Tabasco. c-Early education unknown; law degree, National School of Law, UNAM; certificate in political science from the University of Paris; Professor at UNAM. d-*Federal Deputy* from the Federal District, Dist. 11, 1964-67,

member of the Forest Affairs Committee, the Government Committee, the Labor Section of the Legislative Studies Committee and the Constitutional Affairs Committee; *Federal Deputy* from the State of Tabasco, Dist. 1, 1976-79. e-General delegate of the CEN of PRI to Hidalgo and Michoacán; political adviser to the CEPES of PRI in the Federal District; member of the Editorial Committee to revise the declaration of principles of PRI. f-Delegate of Ixtapalapa, 1966-70; employee of the Secretariat of Agriculture. g-None. i-None. k-None. l-C de D, 1964-67, 79, 84, 92, 1976-79; D de C, 1976-79; *Excélsior*, 1 Sept. 1976, 1C.

Prieto Fortún, Guillermo
a-June 10, 1935. b-Federal District. c-Early education unknown; economics degree, National School of Economics, UNAM, 1953-57, graduating in 1960 with an honorable mention and a thesis on the "Development of Bridges and Public Highways over the Isthmus of Tehuantepec"; degree in business administration from the Pan American Institute of Higher Management (Opus Dei). d-None. e-Joined PRI, 1955. f-Economist, Income Tax Division, Secretariat of the Treasury, 1955; Subdirector of the Department of Technical Calculations, Secretariat of the Treasury, 1955-60; adviser to *Hugo B. Margáin*, Oficial Mayor of Industry and Trade, 1960-62; adviser to *Hugo B. Margáin*, Subsecretary of Industry and Trade, 1962-63; adviser to the First National Committee for the Participation of Workers in the Utilities Industry, 1963-64; economist, Department of Workers Participation in Utilities, Secretariat of Labor, 1964-70; Director General of the Income Tax Division, 1970-76; Director General of Tax Administration, Secretariat of the Treasury, 1976-78; *Subsecretary of Revenues*, Secretariat of the Treasury,

Jan. 17, 1978-82, 1982-86; Director General of the Multibanco Comermex, 1986-88, 1988-89; President of the National Banking Commission, Secretariat of the Treasury, 1989-94. g-None. h-None. i-Protégé of *Hugo B. Margáin*; son of Guillermo Prieto Pérez and María Luisa Fortún Aguilar; married Laura Meza. j-None. k-None. l-Letter; DAPC, 77, 57; Q es QAP, 108; DBGM87, 313; DBGM92, 298.

Prieto González, Luis Jesús
a-June 23, 1926. b-Monterrey, Nuevo León. c-Early education unknown; industrial engineering degree, Technological Institute of Higher Studies of Monterrey, 1944-48. d-Mayor of San Nicolás de los Garza, Nuevo León; *Plurinominal Federal Deputy* from PAN, 1982-85. e-Joined PAN, 1946; President of PAN, San Nicolás de los Garza, 1979; candidate for alternate mayor of Monterrey, Nuevo León, 1950; regional adviser of PAN, Nuevo León, 1972; national adviser to PAN, 1972; candidate of PAN for alternate federal deputy from Nuevo León, 1955; candidate of PAN for federal deputy from Nuevo León, 1982. f-None. g-Official, Catholic Action, 1947. h-Director, Human Resources, VISA Group, 1965-68; Director of Industrial Relations, HYLSA Steel Group, Monterrey, 1969-73; industrial engineer. i-Son of Ignacio Prieto Uranga and Elvira González Valenzuela. j-None. k-None. l-Directorio, 1982-85; C de D, 1982-85; Lehr, 605; DBGM, 582.

Prieto Laurens, Jorge
(Deceased) a-May 2, 1895. b-San Luis Potosí, San Luis Potosí. c-Primary studies in private Catholic schools, San Luis Potosí; preparatory studies at the National Preparatory School, 1909-13; no degree. d-Council member of the first City Council of the Federal District; Federal Deputy from the

Federal District, Dist. 11, (representing the Cooperatist Party), 1920-22; Federal Deputy from the State of San Luis Potosí, Dist. 5, 1922-21, member of the Gran Comisión, President of the Chamber of Deputies; Mayor of the Federal District, 1923; Governor of San Luis Potosí, 1923. e-President of the Cooperatist Party, 1923-24; political supporter (civilian) of the Adolfo de la Huerta rebellion, 1923; political supporter of José Vasconcelos for president, 1928-29; supporter (civilian) of the Escobar rebellion, 1929; President of the National Independent Party, 1938; Secretary General of the National Democratic Party, which supported *Ezequiel Padilla* for president, 1945-46. f-Department head, Secretary of Industry and Commerce, 1935. g-Student leader in 1910; led a student movement against Victoriano Huerta, 1913. h-Director of *La Tribuna*, Houston, Texas. i-Son of engineer, Antonio Prieto Trillo, and Emma Laurens. j-Fought in the Revolution with Zapata's forces; aide to the General Staff of General *Enrique Estrada*; military commander of Zacatecas; participant in taking the city of Guadalajara, 1920. k-In exile in the United States, 1923-33. l-López; C de D, 1922-24, 33; Casasola, V; Enc. Mex., V, 1977, 431.

Puente Leyva, Jesús
a-Sept. 24, 1937. b-Federal District. c-Primary and secondary studies in the Federal District; economic studies at the University of Nuevo León, 1958-63, economics degree in 1966; Professor of Economic Development and the Sociology of Development at the University of Nuevo León, 1966-69; postgraduate work in the field of general economic planning, the Latin American Institute of Planning of ECLA, 1964; studies at Harvard University, summer, 1965; MA in economics from Williams

College, in the field of economic development, 1965-66, degree, July 1966; Professor of Economic Development, National School of Economics, UNAM, 1969-72; Subdirector of the Center for Economic Studies, University of Nuevo León. d-*Federal Deputy* from the State of Nuevo León, 1976-79, member of the Gran Comisión. e-None. f-Economic investigator for the Center for Economic Investigations, University of Nuevo León, 1966-69; Research Specialist in Urban Economics, Office of Planning, State of Nuevo León, 1966-69; technical adviser to the Secretariat of Public Works, 1971-72; adviser to the Presidency; *Subdirector of the National Finance Bank*, 1972-76; Ambassador to Venezuela, 1981-86, to Peru, 1986-89, and to Argentina, 1989-93. g-None. h-Author of numerous articles and pamphlets on urban problems. i-Son of Jesús Puente, businessman, and Guadalupe Leyva Mena; married Blanca Treviño Garza, physician; student of *Raúl Rangel Frías* at the University of Nuevo León. j-None. k-Winner of the National Prize for Economics, 1968. l-HA, 15 May 1972, 31; letters; *Latin America*, 12 Mar. 1976, 83; Protag., 279; DBGM89, 288; DBGM92, 299-300.

Pulido Islas, Alfonso
(Deceased 1981) a-Aug. 13, 1907. b-Ixtlán, Nayarit. c-Primary studies in Ixtlán; secondary studies at the Catholic Seminary of Tepic and in Guadalajara; preparatory studies at the preparatory school of Jalisco at the University of Guadalajara; law studies at the University of Guadalajara; degree in economics from the National School of Economics, UNAM, Apr. 15, 1939, with a thesis on the "Cinematography Industry of Mexico"; professor at the National School of Economics, UNAM; Director of the National School of Economics, UNAM, 1942-44; professor at the National School of Law, UNAM; professor at the School of Philosophy and Letters, UNAM; professor at the National School of Commerce, UNAM; Director, Institute of Social Investigations, UNAM. d-None. e-Member of the League of Professionals and Intellectuals of PRI; member of the IEPES of PNR, 1933-39; founding member of PNR, 1929. f-Director, Office of Economic Statistics, Director General of Statistics, 1935-36; Oficial Mayor of PIPSA, 1937-39; Director of the Federal Department of Labor Inspection, 1939-40; Subdirector of the National Council of Economics, 1940-41; Subdirector General of the National Commission of Economic Planning, 1941-42; Director General of the Federal Board of Economic Planning, 1942; organizer and Director of the Small Business Bank, 1943-50; Director, Department of Alcohol, Department of the Federal District, 1950-53; Manager of Mexican Cinema, S.A., Secretariat of Government, 1953-58; Comptroller General of the Secretariat of National Patrimony, 1961-64; Subdirector of Administration, IMSS, 1964-65; adviser, Secretariat of the Treasury, 1965-74. g-Director of the Workers Federation of Jalisco, 1925-29; Secretary General of the Revolutionary Group "Claridad," 1934-44; Director of the League of Revolutionary Professionals, Popular Sector of PNR, 1935; founder and Director of the Front of Revolutionary Economists, 1936; organizer and President of the National Federation of Students for Obregón, 1927-28. h-Author of many books. i-Father, a campesino and laborer, became a self-educated artisan; attended UNAM with *Sealtiel Alatriste*. j-None. k-None. l-WWM45, 95; DPE61, 56; DGF51; DGF56; letters; López, 887; Enc. Mex., X, 1977, 566.

Q

Quevedo Moreno, Guillermo
a-May 6, 1911. b-Casas Grandes, Chihuahua. c-Early education unknown; no degree. d-Local Deputy to the State Legislature of Chihuahua; *Federal Deputy* from the State of Chihuahua, Dist. 2, 1937-40, Dist. 4, 1943-46, Dist. 5, 1955-58, member of the Gran Comisión, the Livestock Committee, and the Second National Defense Committee. e-None. f-None. g-None. i-Father, José Quevedo, a small businessman, rancher, and member of the State Legislature of Chihuahua, 1911-13; brother, Jesús, mayor of Casas Grandes; brother, José, mayor of Ciudad Juárez; brother of *Rodrigo Quevedo Moreno*, governor of Chihuahua, 1932-36, and senator from Chihuahua, 1958-64. j-None. k-None. l-Ind. Biog., 123-24; C de D, 1955-58; DGF56, 22, 30, 32, 33; C de D, 1943-46, 1937-40; Dávila, 93.

Quevedo Moreno, Rodrigo M.
(Deceased Jan. 18, 1967) a-Nov. 29, 1889. b-Casas Grandes, Chihuahua. c-Early education unknown; no degree. d-*Governor of Chihuahua*, 1935; *Senator* from the State of Chihuahua, 1958-64, member of the Gran Comisión, the Third Committee on National Defense, and the Agricultural Development Committee; substitute member of the Immigration Committee, the Second Committee on Mines, and the First Balloting Committee. e-None. f-None. g-None. h-None. i-Brother of *Guillermo Quevedo Moreno*, federal deputy from Chihuahua, 1943-46; father, José Quevedo, rancher and member of the first revolutionary state legislature of Chihuahua, 1911-13; brother, José, served a mayor of Ciudad Juárez; brother, Jesús, served as mayor of Casas Grandes and Ciudad Juárez. j-Joined the Revolution under Pascual

Orozco, 1911; fought with Orozco against Madero, 1912-13; recognized Victoriano Huerta, 1913; promoted to colonel by Huerta, June 23, 1913; fought under Juan G. Cabral; fought under Francisco Murguía; joined Villa's forces, 1917; rank of Brigadier General, 1917; fought with *Juan Andreu Almazán* against the Constitutionalists; supported the Obregón movement, 1920; fought against the de la Huerta rebellion, 1923; rank of Division General, Apr. 2, 1929; Commander of the 4th Cavalry Brigade under *Almazán* which fought against the Escobar Rebellion, 1929; Commander of the 25th Military Zone, Puebla, Puebla, 1936-38, of the 1st Military Zone, Federal District, 1941-45, of the 22nd Miliary Zone, Toluca, México, 1934, and of the 8th Military Zone, Tampico, Tamaulipas, 1951-56. k-Participated in the Flores Magón movement, 1908; *New York Times* reported that he was arrested in 1938 in connection with the killing of a state politician; Meyer reports that there was little local support for his selection as governor in 1935. l-D de Y, 5 Sept. 1935, 1; DGF56, 201; DGF51, I, 183; Peral, 658; C de S, 1961-64, 66; WWM45, 95; NYT, 27 July 1935, 14; NYT, 13 Mar. 1938, 28; Enc. Mex., XI, 1977, 3; Ind. Biog., 123-24; Almada, 581; Dávila, 93.

Quintanilla (Lerdo de Tejada), Luis
(Deceased Mar. 16, 1980) a-Nov. 22, 1900. b-Paris, France. c-Undergraduate and graduate studies in philosophy and letters at the Sorbonne, Paris; Ph.D. in political science; professor at the Dr. Mora Secondary School; Professor of English at the National Preparatory School; Professor of International Organizations and Political Parties at UNAM; lecturer at Johns Hopkins University, Williams College, the University of Virginia, and the University of Kansas; Professor of Political

Science, George Washington University, 1937-42; professor at the School of Political and Social Sciences, UNAM, 1968. d-None. e-None. f-Joined the foreign service, 1922; Second Protocol Assistant, 1922; Third Assistant for Protocol, 1924; Third Secretary, Guatemala, 1926; Second Secretary, Guatemala, 1926; Second Secretary, Brazil, 1927; Second Secretary, Washington, D.C.; General Secretary of the Mexican Delegation to the League of Nations, 1932; First Secretary, United States, 1942; Ambassador to the Soviet Union, 1942-45; Inspector General of Languages for Technical and Elementary Schools, Secretariat of Public Education; Chairman, Fact Finding Committee to Central America, 1948; Chairman, Inter-American Peace Commission, 1948-49; Ambassador to Colombia, 1945; delegate to the United Nations Conference, San Francisco, 1945; *Ambassador to the Organization of American States*, 1945-58; Director General of the National Housing Institute, 1958-64. g-None. h-Adviser to the Center for Study of Democratic Institutions, Santa Barbara; author of several books. i-From a wealthy family; father, Luis Quintanilla, an artist who lived in Paris, supported the denunciation of Victoriano Huerta by Mexican residents in France; married Ruth Stallsmith; good friend of *Antonio Rocha*. j-None. k-None. l-STYRBIWW, 54, 962; *Quién Será*, 1953-55; Kirk, 12; WWM45, 96; DGF51, I, 110; DGF56, 128; DBM68, 502-03; WWMG, 33; Enc. Mex., XI, 1977, 30; López, 897; NYT, 3 Dec. 1942; *Excélsior*, 14 May 1974, 18; NYT, 27 July, 1954, 10; *Excélsior*, 17 Mar. 1980, 17.

Quiroga Fernández, Francisco
a-Dec. 10, 1913. b-Federal District. c-Primary studies in a free private school and public school; secondary studies at a public school in the Federal District; preparatory studies at the National Preparatory School; medical degree, National School of Medicine, UNAM, 1940; special studies, Children's Hospital, Mexico City, 1945; professor at the National Teachers College, Mexico City. d-*Federal Deputy* from the Federal District, Dist. 1, 1964-67. e-Joined PAN, 1952; member of the National Committee of PAN, 1954-64; President of the Regional Committee of PAN in the Federal District, 1962-64. f-None. g-Member of the Catholic Association of Mexican Youth, 1929-46; member of the Mexican Catholic Union, 1946-64; President of the National Union of Parents, 1955-59. h-Delegate to the World Congress of Pax Romana, 1946. i-Married María Luisa Venegas; son of Santiago Quiroga Barrera and Francisca Fernández. j-None. k-None. l-C de D, 1964-67; PS, 4999.

Quiroga Treviño, Pablo
a-Jan. 25, 1903. b-Cienega de Flores, Nuevo León. c-Secondary studies at the Colegio Civil, Monterrey, Nuevo León, 1917-22; law degree from the National School of Law, UNAM, June 15, 1928; Professor of Law, University of Nuevo León, 1930-32. d-*Federal Deputy* from the State of Nuevo León, Dist. 1, 1949-52, member of the First Constitutional Affairs Committee, the Social Welfare Committee, the Consular and Diplomatic Committee, and the Child Welfare Committee. e-None. f-Agent of the Ministerio Público of the Office of the Attorney General; Judge of the District Court of Nuevo León, 1929; Oficial Mayor of the State of Nuevo León, 1930; Secretary General of Government of the State of Nuevo León, 1930-33; *Interim Governor of Nuevo León*, Dec. 27, 1933, to 1935; Judge of the Superior Tribunal of Justice of Nuevo León, 1943-49; Administrator of the Regional Cashier's Office of the

IMSS, Monterrey, 1952-58. g-None.
h-Scribe for the 3rd District Court,
Nuevo León; scribe for the Department
of Military Justice, Department of the
Navy; scribe for the 7th Judicial
District, Federal District; Notary Public
No. 24, Monterrey, Nuevo León, 1953-
74. i-Brother, Ambrosio, was a physician for IMSS. j-None. k-None.
l-DBM68, 503-04; WWM45, 96; P de M,
300-01; Peral, 662; C de D, 1949-51, 85;
HA, 12 Dec. 1952, 5; DGF51, I, 30, 35,
36; DGF51, II, 131; DJBM, 115.

Quiroz Miranda, Sergio
a-Mar. 30, 1946. b-Mexicali, Baja
California del Norte. c-Secondary
studies and a teaching certificate in
primary; primary school teacher; degree
from the Higher Normal School;
professor of primary, Tepic Academy,
Tepic, Nayarit; adviser in mathematics,
Pedadogical University; Professor of
Pedagogy, University of Baja California,
1976-80; Professor of Didactic Math-
ematics, National Teachers University,
Mexicali, 1980- . d-Local Deputy, State
Legislature of Baja California, 1980-82;
Plurinominal Federal Deputy from the
PPS, 1982-85. e-Joined the PPS, 1965;
Secretary General of the PPS, Mexicali;
Secretary of Press of the PPS, Baja
California; Secretary General of the
State Committee of the PPS, Baja
California, 1975-82; member of the
Central Committee, Popular Socialist
Party, 1976- ; candidate for mayor of
Mexicali, 1965. f-None. g-Leader,
National Teachers Union, Baja Califor-
nia, 1972-79. h-Primary school teacher.
i-Son of José Quiroz Hernández, ejida-
tario, and Margarita Miranda; married
Silvia Valdés Rivera, teacher. j-None.
k-None. l-Directorio, 1982-85; C de D,
1982-85; Lehr, 655; DBGM, 583.

R

Rabasa Gamboa, Emilio
a-May 12, 1949. b-Tuxtla Gutiérrez,
Chiapas. c-Early education unknown;
law degree, National School of Law,
UNAM, 1968-73; graduates studies,
London School of Economics, 1974-76;
professor, National School of Law,
UNAM, 1976-79. d-None. e-None.
f-Chief of Labor Relations, IMSS, 1968-
72; Auxiliary Secretary and adviser, Ad-
ministrative Subdirector, IMSS, 1972-
73; Subdirector, Evaluation System,
Administrative Studies, Secretariat of
the Presidency, 1977-78; legal adviser,
Oficial Mayor of the Secretariat of
Government, 1979-81; Subdirector and
Director of Government, Secretariat of
Government, 1981-82; Director of
International Affairs, IMSS, 1983-85;
Secretary General of the IMSS, 1985-88;
Subsecretary of Civil Protection,
Prevention and Social Readaptation,
Secretariat of Government, 1988-91.
g-None. h-Practicing lawyer, Rabasa
Firm, 1978-81. i-Son of *Emilio Oscar*
Rabasa, secretary of foreign relations,
and Socorro Gamboa Cano, daughter of
Rafael P. Gamboa, president of the
CEN of PRI; married Karen Kovacs
Strumpfner, social anthropologist;
grandson of of Oscar Rabasa Llanes,
ambassador; great-grandson of Emilio
Rabasa, federal deputy. j-None.
k-None. l-DBGM89, 289; DBGM.

Rabasa (Llanes), Oscar
(Deceased Feb. 26, 1978) a-Feb. 27,
1896. c-Preparatory studies at the
National Preparatory School; law degree
from the University of Pennsylvania,
1917; law degree, National School of
Law, UNAM, 1920; professor at the
National School of Law, UNAM, 1933-
34; professor at the Escuela Libre de
Derecho, 1928-29, 1931. d-None.
e-None. f-Legal adviser to the Secretary

of Communications and Public Works, 1922-25; consulting lawyer to the Assistant Attorney for the Mexican–United States Claims Commission, 1926-35; Director of the Department of Legal Affairs, Secretariat of the Treasury; Director General of Legal Affairs, Secretariat of Foreign Relations, 1946-51; Director General of the Diplomatic Service, 1951-56; Ambassador to Syria, 1956-60; Director-in-Chief of the Foreign Service and American Affairs, Secretariat of Foreign Relations, 1961; legal adviser to the Secretary of Foreign Relations, 1964-70; special adviser to the President of Mexico, 1971-76; rank of Ambassador in the Foreign Service. g-None. h-Author of numerous books on law and history in Mexico. i-Son of a distinguished Mexican jurist, Emilio Rabasa, who served as a Mexican representative at the 1914 Niagara Falls Conference, and as a federal deputy, 1922-24, and Mercedes Llanes; father of *Emilio Rabasa*, Secretary of Foreign Relations, 1970-75; married Lillian Mishkin; grandfather of *Emilio Rabasa Gamboa*, subsecretary of government, 1988-91. j-None. k-None. l-DGF50, II, 91; HA, 22 Feb. 1971, 31; DPE61, 15; WWM45, 97; DGF56, 124; DGF47, 97; DPE65, 17.

Rabasa (Mishkin), Emilio Oscar
a-Jan. 23, 1925. b-Federal District. c-Law degree, National School of Law, UNAM; LLD, National School of Law, UNAM; Professor of Law, National School of Law, UNAM (15 years), 1976- . d-None. e-None. f-Lawyer for the Banking Department, Secretariat of the Treasury; department head, UNAM, 1948; legal adviser to the Secretary of Health, *Ignacio Morones Prieto*, 1956; legal adviser to the Head of the Department of Agrarian Affairs; Head of the Department of Legal Affairs for the National Bank of Ejido Credit; Director General of Afianzadora Mexicana, S.A.; Director General of the Cinemato-

graphic Bank, 1965-70; *Ambassador to the United States*, 1970; *Secretary of Foreign Relations*, 1970-75. g-None. h-Author of several books on constitutional law. i-From a distinguished Mexican diplomatic family; grandfather, Emilio Rabasa, was a federal deputy, 1922-24, governor of Chiapas, 1891-94, and represented the Mexican government at the Niagara Falls Conference, 1914; father, *Oscar Rabasa*, a distinguished writer, professor of constitutional law, Ambassador in the Mexican Foreign Service, and special adviser to the President of Mexico; Emilio was a student of *Alfonso Noriega*, *César Sepúlveda* and *Luis Garrido Díaz* while attending law school at UNAM; son-in-law of *Rafael P. Gamboa*, President of the CEN of PRI; married Socorro Gamboa; son, *Emilio Rabasa Gamboa*, was subsecretary of government, 1988-91. j-None. k-Fought for the creation of the National School of Political and Social Sciences, UNAM; resigned as Secretary of Foreign Relations, Dec. 29, 1975. l-DGF56, 331; DPE70-71, 6; HA, 7 Dec. 1970, 23; *Hoy*, December, 1970; Loret de Mola, 91, 55.

Rafful Miguel, Fernando
a-1935. b-Ciudad del Carmen, Campeche. c-Early education unknown; degree in economics from the National School of Economics, UNAM; professor, National School of Economics, UNAM. d-*Senator* from Campeche, 1976. e-None. f-Adviser to the Department of Control and Inspection of Federal Decentralized Agencies and Businesses, Secretariat of Government Properties, 1965-66; Director, Department of Economic Studies, Secretariat of Government Properties, 1967-70; Director General, Department of Control and Inspection of Federal Decentralized Agencies and Businesses, 1970-73; *Subsecretary of Government Properties*, Apr. 30, 1973, to 1976; *Subsecretary of Fishing*,

Secretariat of Commerce, 1976-77; *Director General, Department of Fishing,* 1977-82. g-None. i-Protégé of *Horacio Flores de la Peña.* j-None. k-None. l-HA, 7 May 1973, 50; *Excélsior,* 2 May 1973, 5; Almanaque de México, 55.

Ramírez Acosta, Abel
(Deceased July 1, 1979) a-June 4, 1915. b-Molango, Hidalgo. c-Primary studies in Molango; studies at the Normal Rural Regional School, Molango until 1930, completed teaching certificate as a rural teacher, El Mexe, Hidalgo, 1934; normal teaching certificate, National Teachers School, Mexico City; law degree, National School of Law, UNAM; taught in Poza Rica, Veracruz; teacher, Alberto Correa School, Mexico City; teacher, Republic of Uruguay School, Mexico City; Professor of law, School of Law, University of Hidalgo. d-*Federal Deputy* from the State of Hidalgo, Dist. 4, 1970-73, member of the Lands and Natural Resources Committee and the First Public Education Committee. e-*Secretary of Finances of the CEN of PRI,* 1970-72. f-Oficial Mayor of the State of Hidalgo; Secretary General of the State of Hidalgo, under Governor *Manuel Sánchez Vite,* 1972-75; Treasurer General of Hidalgo under Governor *Otoniel Miranda,* 1975. g-Member of the SNTE; Secretary of Labor and Peasant Action, Local 15, SNTE, 1937; Secretary General of Local 9, SNTE; employee; Legal Department, Union of Railroad Workers of the Republic of Mexico; Secretary of Finances of the SNTE, 1955. h-Practicing lawyer, 1976-79. i-Cousin and political protégé of *Manuel Sánchez Vite;* married Natalina González. j-None. k-None. l-Directorio, 1970-72; C de D, 1970-72, 131; HA, 28 Nov. 1955, 13; Pérez López, 370-71.

Ramírez (Baños), Alfonso Francisco
(Deceased July 1, 1979) a-Nov. 15, 1896. b-Teposcolula, Oaxaca. c-Primary studies at a parochial school; secondary studies at the Colegio Unión, Oaxaca; preparatory studies at the Institute of Arts and Sciences, Oaxaca; law degree from the Institute of Arts and Sciences, Oaxaca, June 20, 1919; Professor of Spanish Language and Literature at the Institute of Arts and Sciences, Oaxaca; professor at the Superior School of Business Administration, Mexico City; Professor of Logic and Ethics; Professor of World History at the National Preparatory School. d-*Federal Deputy* from the State of Oaxaca, Dist. 12, 1922-24, Dist. 13, 1924-26, Dist. 16, 1926-28, Dist 12, 1930-32, Dist. 8, 1932-34, and Dist. 6, 1937-40. e-Founding member, PNR, 1929; orator for *Avila Camacho.* f-Judge of the 7th Correctional Court, Federal District, 1924-26; Judge of the 8th Correctional Court, 1926; Subdirector of the Legal Department for the Department of Federal Pensions; consulting lawyer to the Secretariat of Government, 1933; *Justice of the Supreme Court,* 1941-46, 1946-52, 1952-58. g-Student leader in Oaxaca, 1916; President of the Alumni Society of the Institute of Arts and Sciences of Oaxaca. h-Author of many works; contributor to *Hoy, Excélsior, El Universal;* poet. i-Son of Francisco Modesto Ramírez, a lawyer, Supreme Court Justice, and his professor at law school, and Concepción Baños; married Carmen Palacios Almont, daughter of lawyer José Palacios Roji. j-None. k-None. l-WWM45, 97; DGF56, 567; DGF51, I; C de D, 1937-39, 18; DBM68, 505; EBW46, 72; STYRBIWW54, 965; Peral, 665; HA, 25 Dec. 1972, 15; letters; López, 902; WNM, 183-84.

Ramírez Cuéllar, Héctor
a-July 17, 1947. b-Ciudad Juárez, Chihuahua. c-Early education unknown; studies at the School of Political and Social Sciences, UNAM, 1968-74; professor at Vocational School No.

1, IPN; professor at the Vicente Lombardo Toledano Workers University, Mexico City; professor, School of Political and Social Science, UNAM. d-*Federal Deputy* (Party Deputy from the PPS), 1976-79, member of the Permanent Committee; *Plurinominal Federal Deputy* from the PPS, 1982-85; Plurinominal Representative to the Assembly of the Federal District, 1988-91; *Plurinominal Federal Deputy* from the PPS, 1991-94. e-Joined the PPS, 1967; candidate for federal deputy from the 10th District, Federal District, 1973; member of the Central Committee of the PPS, 1969; Secretary of Organization of the Central Committee of the PPS, 1967; member of the National Directorate of the PPS, 1970-90; Secretary of Political Education of the Central Committee of the PPS, 1981; Secretary General of the Popular Socialist Youth, 1969-74; Secretary General of the PPS in the Federal District, 1979-87. f-Supervisor, Department of the Federal District, 1970-77. g-None. h-Writer for *El Día*. i-Son of Alfonso Ramírez Rodríguez, laborer, and Raquel Cuéllar Medrano; married Lilia Márquez Juárez. j-None. k-None. l-HA, 14 May 1979, IV; C de D, 1976-79; Directorio, 1982-85; Lehr, 598; DBGM89, 580; DBGM92, 550.

Ramírez Gamero, José
a-Dec. 6, 1938. b-Durango, Durango. c-Early education unknown; law degree, Juárez University of Durango, 1957-61, with a thesis on Pauliana action; studies in labor law, National School of Law, UNAM, 1969-70; studies, International Center of Professional and Technical Development, International Labor Organization, Turin, Italy, 1955; professor, School of Law, Juárez University of Durango, 1964-76. d-Mayor of Durango; Local Deputy to the State Legislature of Durango, 1972; *Federal Deputy* from the State of Durango, Dist. 4, 1976-79; *Senator* from the State of Durango,

1983-86; *Governor of Durango*, 1986-92. e-Joined PRI, 1955; Secretary of Political Action of PRI, Durango, 1983; Coordinator of Labor Sector of PRI, 1983-86. f-Chief, Legal Department, Planning and Urban Council, Durango; Chief, Legal Department, Treasurer General of Durango; Judge, 2nd Civil Court; Assistant Attorney of Collective Organizations, Attorney General for Consumers, 1979-82. g-Member of the CTM; General Delegate of the CTM, various states. h-Practicing lawyer, 1961. i-Son of José Antonio Ramírez Martínez, chauffeur and leader of the CTM of Durango for many decades, and Amelia Gamero Orozco; married María del Rosario Guzmán Hernández. j-None. k-None. l-*Proceso*, Oct. 1987; HA, 25 Feb. 1986, 21; Lehr, 163; DBGM, 584-85; DBGM89, 734.

Ramírez Garrido Abreu, Graco Luis
a-June 26, 1949. c-Early education unknown; law degree, National School of Law, UNAM. d-*Federal Deputy* (PST party deputy), 1979-82; *Plurinominal Federal Deputy* from the PST, 1985-88, Coordinator of the PST congressional delegation. e-Founding member of the PST, 1973; Secretary General of the PST. f-None. g-None. h-Practicing lawyer. i-Son of Air Force general Graco Ramírez Garrido Alvarado, and Elia Abreu; common-law marriage with Lourdes Alvarez Delgado; brother of brigadier general José Domingo Ramírez Garrido Abreu; grandson of division general José Domingo Ramírez Garrido, secretary of war. j-None. k-None. l-DBGM87, 544; C de D, 1979-82; Directorio, 1979-82; C de D, 1985-88.

Ramírez Genel, Marcos
a-Apr. 3, 1923. b-Villa Victoria, Michoacán. c-Agricultural engineering degree, National School of Agriculture, 1941-45, degree, 1947; MS, Cornell University, 1950-52; Ph.D. in agricultural

science, College of Agriculture, Cornell University (specialty in entomology), 1957; Professor of Graduate Studies at the National School of Agriculture, 1959; founding professor of the Graduate School, National School of Agriculture; Director of the National School of Agriculture. d-None. e-None. f-Investigator of the Office of Special Studies, Secretariat of Agriculture and Livestock, 1947-50, 1952-54; Head of the Department of Entomology, Graduate School, National School of Agriculture; Specialist in Entomology, Office of Special Studies, Secretary of Agriculture and Livestock; Coordinator General of Studies for the Plan Chapingo; Executive Director of the Plan Chapingo; Agricultural Attaché to the United States; *Subsecretary of Livestock*, 1970-72. g-None. h-Expert in agricultural investigations, International Bank for Reconstruction and Development; author of many scientific works. i-Married María Refugio Irigoyen. j-None. k-Studied at Cornell on a scholarship from the National Institute of Agricultural Investigations; resigned as Subsecretary of Livestock, Oct. 1972. l-DPE71, 63; B de M, 217-18; HA, 14 Dec. 1970, 21; letter.

Ramírez Guerrero, Carlos
a-Mar. 13, 1909. b-Pachuca, Hidalgo. c-Primary studies at the Julián Villagrán School, Pachuca; secondary and preparatory studies at the Scientific and Literary Institute of Hidalgo; law degree from the National School of Law, UNAM, 1928-32; professor at the Scientific and Literary Institute of Hidalgo; Director of the Scientific and Literary Institute of Hidalgo; Director of the Normal Schools of the State of Hidalgo. d-*Federal Deputy* from the State of Hidalgo, Dist. 3, 1955-58, member of the Economics and Statistics Committee, the Legislative Studies Committee (1st year), and the Second Justice Committee; *Alternate Senator*

from Hidalgo, but replaced *Julián Rodríguez Adame*, 1958-63, member of the Gran Comisión, the Mail and Telegraph Committee, and the Third Labor Committee; President of the Second Government Committee; substitute member of the Treasury Committee; *Governor of Hidalgo*, 1963-69. e-None. f-Federal tax attorney; agent of the Ministerio Público of the Office of the Attorney General; Municipal Judge for Pachuca, Hidalgo; Secretary General of Government of the State of Hidalgo under Governor Julio Guerrero; Oficial Mayor of the State of Hidalgo under Governor *Quintín Rueda Villagrán*, 1951-54; Assistant Attorney General of the State of Hidalgo; Director of the Department of Economy, State of Hidalgo; Secretary of State for Hidalgo; Judge of the Superior Tribunal of Justice of the Federal District, 1970. g-None. h-None. i-Classmate of *Vicente Aguirre*, governor of Hidalgo, 1946-51; son of poet Cecilio Ramírez Castillo, local deputy to the state legislature of Hidalgo, 1925-27. j-None. k-None. l-WWMG, 33; DBM68, 505-06; DGF56, 24, 32, 33, 35; C de S, 1961-64, 66; Ind. Biog., 126-27; López Pérez, 372-73.

Ramírez Guerrero, Ricardo
a-Feb. 6, 1906. b-Morelia, Michoacán. c-Early education unknown; no degree. d-*Federal Deputy* from the State of Michoacán, Dist. 1, 1943-46; *Senator* from the State of Michoacán, 1946-52, member of the Colonization Committee, the Third National Defense Committee, the War Materiels Committee and the Military Health Committee. e-None. f-Oficial Mayor of Baja California del Norte under Governor *Rodolfo Sánchez Taboada*, 1937-39. g-None. h-None. i-Married *Lázaro Cárdenas'* wife's sister. j-Military aide to President *Lázaro Cárdenas*. k-None. l-C de D, 1943-46; C de S, 1946-52; DGF51, I, 6, 10, 11, 13, 14.

Ramírez Ladewig, Carlos
(Deceased Sept. 12, 1975) a-Sept. 20, 1929. b-Guadalajara, Jalisco. c-Primary and secondary studies in Guadalajara; preparatory studies, law degree, School of Law, and professor, University of Guadalajara. d-*Federal Deputy* from the State of Jalisco, Dist. 7, 1955-58, member of the Administration and the Second General Means of Communication Committees; *Federal Deputy* from the State of Jalisco, Dist. 5, 1964-67, member of the Agricultural Committee, the Indigenous Affairs Committee, and the Rules Committee. e-Member of the PRM; President of the Youth Committee of PRI in Jalisco. f-Delegate of the IMSS to the State of Jalisco. g-Student leader at the University of Guadalajara; founder and Director of the Federation of Students of Guadalajara, 1950. i-Son of *Margarito Ramírez*, Governor of Quintana Roo, 1945-59; brother, Alvaro Ramírez Ladewig, was a candidate of the PPM for federal deputy, 1979, and candidate of the PSUM for federal deputy from Jalisco, Dist. 17, 1982. j-None. k-Youngest member of the Chamber of Deputies, 1955-58; in an interview he said that *Adolfo Ruiz Cortines* was directly responsible for selecting him as the PRI candidate for federal deputy from Jalisco, 1955; assassinated by his political opponents in Guadalajara. l-*Proceso*, 5 Feb. 1977, 6, 68, 12 Feb. 1977, 8; C de D, 1964-67, 77, 79, 93; Ind. Biog., 127-28; DGF56, 25, 30, 33, 37; *Excélsior*, 17 Sept. 1979, 15, 18 April 1982, 13.

Ramírez López, Heladio
a-May 11, 1939. b-Huajuapam de León, Oaxaca. c-Early education unknown; law degree, National School of Law, UNAM, 1960-64, with a thesis on armistices in international law; professor, National Preparatory School; Professor of Law, National School of Political Science, UNAM, Acatlán campus, 1977.

d-*Federal Deputy* from the State of Oaxaca, Dist. 6, 1976-79; *Senator* from the State of Oaxaca, 1982-86; *Governor of Oaxaca*, 1986-92. e-Founding member of the Youth Tribunal of PRI, 1959; Director of Youth of PRI, Federal District, 1966-70; President of the Regional Committee of PRI of Oaxaca, 1977-81. f-Official, Department of International Relations, National Institute of Youth; Director of Youth Centers, Youth Department, National Institute of Youth, 1970-72; Executive Director of the Puerto Vallarta Trust, 1973-76; Executive Director of the Cumbres de Llano Largo Trust, 1976-77. g-Agrarian Delegate of the CNC to Puerto Vallarta, 1972-77; Secretary of Union Acts of the CNC, 1981-82. h-None. i-Son of Antonio Ramírez Ramírez, peasant, and Hermelinda López; married Marcedalia Pineda Núñez, secretary. j-None. k-None. l-*Excélsior*, 29 Aug. 1976, 26; C de D, 1976-79; C de S, 1982-88; Almanaque de Oaxaca, 1982, 27; DBGM92, 819; DBGM89, 736; HA, 15 Apr. 1980; DBGM, 585.

Ramírez (Martínez), José Antonio
a-Nov. 6, 1910. b-San Felipe de Nombre de Dios, Durango. c-Primary studies only. d-Local Deputy to the State Legislature of Durango; *Federal Deputy* from the State of Durango, Dist. 4, 1961-64, 1967-70. e-Secretary of Labor Action of PRI in Durango. f-Director of Traffic, State of Durango; Director of the Department of Labor, State of Durango. g-None. j-None. k-None. l-C de D, 1961-64, 1967-70; MGF69.

Ramírez Mijares, Oscar
a-Jan. 12, 1922. b-Torreón, Coahuila. c-Teaching certificate. d-*Alternate Federal Deputy* from the Federal District, Dist. 19, 1958-61; *Federal Deputy* from the Federal District, Dist. 21, 1961-64, 1967-70; *Alternate Senator* from the State of Coahuila, 1976-77, but

replaced Senator *Eliseo Mendoza Berrueto*, 1978-82; *Federal Deputy* from the State of Coahuila, Dist. 5, 1982-85; *Senator* from the State of Coahuila, 1988-94. e-Secretary of the 1st Electoral District Committee of the PRM, Federal District; Director of Youth, *Manuel Avila Camacho* presidential campaign, Lagunera, 1940; Secretary General of President of the 19th Electoral District Committee of PRI, Federal Distirct, 1951-56; President of the 20th Electoral District Committee of PRI, Federal District, 1959-61; Secretary of Agrarian Action of PRI in the Federal District, 1964-66; general delegate of the CEN of PRI to various states, 1966-83; Secretary of Organization of PRI in the Federal District, 1966-67; *Secretary of Agrarian Action of the CEN of PRI*, 1977-80. f-None. g-Secretary General of the League of Agrarian Communities and Peasant Unions, Federal District, 1960-68; *Secretary General of the CNC*, 1977-80. h-None. i-Married Egla Millán de Ramos, a teacher; children Egla and Olga are both teachers; brother of José Ramírez Mijares, secretary general of government of the State of Coahuila and mayor of Piedras Negras; son of Nicolás Ramírez García, certified public accountant, and Juana Mijares Valdez. j-None. k-None. l-Letter; LA, 11 Feb 1977, 44; C de D, 1961-64, 1967-70; C de S, 1976-82; Directorio, 1982-85; *Excélsior*, 9 Aug. 1981, 21; C de D, 1982-85, 1958-61; DBGM89, 520; DBGM92, 552; DBGM, 585; Lehr, 68.

Ramírez (Miranda), Margarito
(Deceased Feb. 2, 1979) a-Feb. 22, 1891. b-Atotonilco el Alto, Jalisco. c-Primary studies in Guadalajara; secondary studies in Guadalajara; no degree. d-*Federal Deputy* from the State of Jalisco, 1924-26; *Federal Deputy* from the State of Jalisco, Dist. 11, 1926-28, Dist. 7, 1937; *Senator* from Jalisco, 1932-36. e-Founder and President of the Great

Revolutionary Party of Jalisco, 1927. f-Chief of Trains, National Railroads of Mexico, 1916-20; Superintendent of Trains, National Railroads of Mexico, 1920-27; Interim Governor of Jalisco, 1927-29; Superintendent of Trains, National Railroads of Mexico, 1929-32, 1936-37; Director of the Federal Penitentiary, Islas Marías, 1937-40; *Director General of the National Railroads of Mexico*, Oct., 1942-45; *Governor of Quintana Roo*, 1945-46, 1946-52, 1952-58, 1958-59. g-None. h-Started working on the railroad as a laborer, 1908; machinist; train conductor, 1911. i-Son, *Carlos Ramírez Ladewig*, was a federal deputy from Jalisco, 1955-58, 1964-67; son, Alvaro Ramírez Ladewig, was a precandidate of the PPM for federal deputy, 1979 and a candidate of PSUM for federal deputy from Jalisco, Dist. 17, 1982; married Ana Ladewig Camarena. j-None. k-Brandenburg considered him in the Inner Circle from 1942-46; saved the life of General Obregón, 1920. l-WWM45, 97; DGF56, 103; Peral, 670; Branden-burg, 102; C de D, 1937-39; DGF51, I, 91; López, 910; *Excélsior*, 13 Feb. 1979, 21; HA, 12 Feb. 1979, 72; *Proceso*, 5 Feb. 1977, 68; Enc. Mex., XI, 1977, 51-52; Alvarez Coral, 141-42.

Ramírez Oelrich, José Gustavo
a-July 26, 1939. b-Federal District. c-Early education unknown; law degree, National School of Law, UNAM, 1959-63, with a thesis on the centralized public sector; Treasurer, Autonomous Metropolitan University, 1974-76. d-None. e-Joined PRI, 1955. f-Director General of Administrative Control, Secretariat of Public Works, 1976-78; *Oficial Mayor of the Secretariat of Human Dwellings and Public Works*, 1978-82; Subdirector General of Administration, ISSSTE, 1982. g-None. h-Various positions under the Administrative Subdirector of the ISSSTE, 1960-64; Manager of Official Relations, Bank

of Industry and Commerce, 1965-69;
General Manager, Atlantic Bank Branch
7, 1972-74. i-Son of José Ramírez Ortiz,
lawyer, and María Alida Oelrich Espriú;
married María Cristina Ogarrio
Ramírez. j-None. k-None. l-Protag.,
285; DBGM, 343.

Ramírez Santiago, Melquiades
a-Oct. 10, 1903. b-Santo Tomás Jalieza,
Oaxaca. c-Early education unknown;
teaching certificate. d-*Federal Deputy*
from the State of Oaxaca, Dist. 4, 1943-
46, Dist. 5, 1955-58, member of the
First Public Education Committee and
the Indigenous Affairs Committee.
e-None. f-None. g-Secretary General of
the CTM of the State of Oaxaca, 1940-
51. h-Teacher. j-None. k-None. l-C de
D, 1943-46, 1955-58; Ind. Biog., 128.

Ramírez Ulloa, Carlos
(Deceased Jan. 1981) a-Nov. 6, 1903.
b-Guadalajara, Jalisco. c-Early education unknown; engineering degree,
National School of Engineering, 1924.
d-None. e-None. f-Adviser, Director
General of the Federal Electrical Commission; Director General of the Federal
Electric Commission, 1937-47; *Director
General of the Federal Electric Commission*, 1952-58; adviser, government
of the State of México. g-Founder, Mexican Hydraulic Association. h-None.
j-None. k-Considered a pioneer in the
electrical industry. k-None. l-Protag.,
285; HA, 12 Jan. 1981, 64; DGF50, II,
257; DGF51, II, 353; *Siempre*, 21 Jan.
1959, 6.

Ramírez Valadez, Guillermo
a-1909. b-Arandas, Jalisco. c-Primary
studies in Guadalajara; secondary
studies at the Normal School of
Guadalajara; preparatory studies at the
University of Guadalajara; studies in
economics, School of Economics,
University of Guadalajara, 1936-41,
graduating in 1945 with a thesis on

social welfare; law degree, National
School of Law, UNAM; Professor of
Penal Law, National School of Law,
UNAM; Rector of the University of
Guadalajara, 1955. d-Local Deputy to
the State Legislature of Jalisco; *Federal
Deputy* from the State of Jalisco, Dist.
6, 1949-52, member of the First Consti-
tutional Affairs Committee and Pro-
secretary of the Chamber; *Alternate
Senator* from the State of Jalisco under
Senator *Silvano Barba González*, 1952-
58; *Senator* from the State of Jalisco,
1958-64, Secretary, Second Secretary of
the Government Committee, President
of the Consular Service and Diplomatic
Committee and of the Special Legislative Studies Committee. e-President of
PRI in Jalisco. f-Justice of the Peace,
Jalisco; Agent of the Ministerio Público,
Jalisco; Representative of the Secretariat
of the Treasury, Jalisco; Manager,
Agricultural Bank of Guadalajara.
g-None. i-Great-uncle Antonio Valadez
Ramírez was governor of Jalisco, 1922-
23 and senator, 1926-32; Valadez
Ramírez was the longtime political boss
of Arandas according to *Excélsior*.
j-None. k-None. l-*Excélsior*, 27 May
1979, 18; EN de E, 196; DGF56, 6;
Func., 239; C de S, 1961-64, 66-67; C de
D, 1949-52, 85.

Ramírez Vázquez, Manuel
a-June 4, 1906. b-Federal District.
c-Primary studies in Guanajuato;
preparatory studies at the National
Preparatory School; law degree from the
National School of Law, UNAM, 1925-
29. d-None. e-None. f-President of the
Superior Tribunal of the State of
Veracruz, 1937; member of the Federal
Board of Conciliation and Arbitration,
No. 5; Federal Attorney for the Labor
Movement, 1946; *Subsecretary of
Labor*, 1946-48; *Secretary of Labor*,
January 12, 1948, to 1952. g-None.
h-Practicing lawyer, 1930, 1953-76;
author of articles on petroleum legisla-

tion. i-Studied under *Aquiles Elorduy* at UNAM; friend of and co-student with *Miguel Alemán, Antonio Carrillo Flores, Eduardo Bustamante, Alfonso Noriega,* and *Antonio Martínez Báez;* brother of *Mariano Ramírez Vázquez* and *Pedro Ramírez Vázquez;* father a bookstore owner. j-None. k-None. l-STYRBIWW54, 966; DGF50, II, 280; DGF51, II, 529; HA, 15 Oct. 1948, 3, 23 Jan. 1948; DGF47, 247; DGF51, I, 399.

Ramírez Vázquez, Mariano
a-Dec. 24, 1903. b-Federal District. c-Primary studies at a public school, Mexico City; preparatory studies at the National Preparatory School, 1920; law degree from the National School of Law, UNAM, June 8, 1926; Professor of Law, National School of Law, UNAM. d-None. e-None. f-Defense counsel, Criminal Division, Judicial District, Cuautla, Morelos; Judge, Civil Division, Judicial District, Cuernavaca, Morelos; Secretary of Justice for the Penal Division, Federal District; Director of the Department of Legal Services, Department of Labor; Secretary General of the Federal Board of Conciliation and Arbitration; Secretary General of the Department of Labor; *Assistant Attorney General of Mexico,* June 22, 1937, to 1940; Judge of the 14th Penal District, Federal District, 1941; *Justice of the Supreme Court,* 1947-49, 1954-58, 1958-64, 1964-70, and 1970-73; Director of the National Institute of Youth, 1950-52. g-None. h-None. i-Longtime friend of *Salvador Novo* since preparatory school days; longtime friend of *Antonio Luna Arroyo;* brother of *Manuel Ramírez Vázquez* and *Pedro Ramírez Vázquez;* father a bookstore owner. j-None. k-Retired from the Supreme Court, Dec. 12, 1973. l-D de Y, 22 June 1937, 2; DGF51, I, 568; Novo, 716-17, 746-47; DGF56, 567; STYRBIWW54, 966; Casasola, V; *Excélsior,* 12 Dec. 1973, 1C; *Justicia,* May, 1967.

Ramírez Vázquez, Pedro
a-Apr. 16, 1919. b-Federal District. c-Primary studies at the Annex to the National Normal School, Mexico City; secondary studies at Secondary School No. 4, Mexico City; preparatory studies at the National Preparatory School; architectural degree, National School of Architecture, UNAM, 1943, with a thesis on urban planning in Ciudad Guzmán, Jalisco; Professor of Architectural Composition and Urbanism, National School of Architecture, 1942-58; first Rector of the Metropolitan University, 1973-75. d-None. e-Technical adviser to the IEPES of PRI, 1969-70; *Secretary of Press and Publicity of the CEN of PRI,* 1975-76. f-First Zone Chief of the Federal Program for School Construction (CAPFCE) in Tabasco, 1944-47; Director of the Department of Building Conservation, Secretariat of Public Education, 1947-58; Director General of CAPFCE, 1958-64; founder and Technical Director of the Regional Center for School Construction for Latin America (UNESCO agency), 1964-66; President of the Mexican Organizing Committee of the Olympic Games, 1966-69, 1971-73; General Coordinator of Public Works, State of México, 1971-73; *Secretary of Public Works and Dwellings,* 1976-82. g-President of the National College of Architects. h-Practicing architect; codesigner of the National School of Medicine with *Carlos Lazo,* 1948; designed *Adolfo López Mateos'* home; architect for numerous public buildings, including the Secretariat of Foreign Relations, the Aztec Stadium, and the National Museum of Anthropology and History. i-Brother of *Manuel Ramírez Vázquez,* Secretary of Labor, 1948-52, and *Mariano Ramírez Vázquez,* Justice of the Supreme Court, 1947-73; father a bookseller; protégé of Professor *José Luis Cuevas* and *Carlos Lazo;* married Olga Campuzano Fernández; son, Pedro

Ramírez Campuzano, married Nelly Mota Velasco Torres Landa, niece of *J. José Torres Landa.* j-None. k-Considered for Subsecretary of Public Works, 1952, but lost out to *Enrique Bracamontes;* supported *Donato Miranda Fonseca* for president, 1964; recognized world-wide for many of his architectural works. l-*Excélsior,* 1 Apr. 1977, 6, 8; Enc. Mex., XI, 1977, 57-58; DBM68, 507; *Excélsior,* 1 Dec. 1976; *El Día,* 1 Dec. 1976; letters; Torres Martínez, 194-95; letter.

Ramírez y Ramírez, Enrique
(Deceased Aug. 14, 1980) a-Mar. 14, 1915. b-Federal District. c-Primary studies at the Florence del Castillo School, Mexico City; secondary studies at Secondary School Nos. 4 and 5, Mexico City; studies at the School of Plastic Arts, 1930-32, 1934-35, 1936-38; preparatory studies at the National Preparatory School; two years of legal studies, National School of Law, UNAM; no degree; professor at the Workers University, 1938; member of the Board of Directors, Workers University, 1945; professor at the Institute for Political Training, PRI, 1971-80. d-*Federal Deputy* from the Federal District, Dist. 3, 1964-67, member of the Protocol Committee, the Legislative Studies Commmittee (9th Section on General Affairs), and the Social Security Committee; *Federal Deputy* from the Federal District, Dist. 4, 1976-79. e-Supported José Vasconcelos for president, 1929; member of the Communist Party of Mexico, 1932-43, expelled in March, 1943; member of the National Directive Committee of the Popular Socialist Party, 1948-52, Treasurer of the PPS, 1948; Secretary of the CEN of the PPS, 1951-52; member of PPS, 1948-58; joined PRI, 1964; adviser to the CEN of PRI, 1967-70; Secretary of the Ideological Committee of the CEN of PRI, 1978. f-Private Secretary to *Vicente Lombardo*

Toledano, 1938-39, 1951-52. g-Student leader of the National Student Congress, San Luis Potosí; student leader at the Second Congress of Socialist Students, 1935; member of the Alliance of Revolutionary Writers and Students, 1930-32; member of CTM and leader of the Union of Graphic Arts Industry Workers; Director of the Unified Socialist Youth of Mexico, 1939; Secretary General of the Federation of Revolutionary Students, 1935. h-Author of many articles on social problems; founder and Director General of *El Día,* 1962-80; editorial writer for *El Popular,* 1938-46; began career in journalism, 1929. i-Son of Porfirio Ramírez, a blue collar worker, and Concepción Ramírez; married engineer Isabel Cisneros. j-None. k-*Adolfo López Mateos* invited him to join PRI; thrown out of the PCM because of disagreements wih Hernán Laborde. l-Peral, 671; Novo, 150-51, 214; C de D, 1964-66, 80, 84, 94; Enc. Mex., XI, 1977, 56-57; *Excélsior,* 24 Aug. 1978, 14, 31 Aug. 1976, C1, 17 Aug. 1980, B1, 8; HA, 25 Au. 1980, 9-10; *Excélsior,* 15 Aug. 190, 15, 24 Aug. 1978, 14.

Ramos, Ramón
(Deceased 1937) a-1894. b-Villa de Chinipas, Chihuahua. c-Agricultural engineering degree, National School of Agriculture. d-Federal Deputy from the State of Sonora, 1924-26; *Federal Deputy* from the State of Chihuahua, 1926-28; Senator from the State of Sonora, 1930-34; *Governor of Sonora,* 1935. f-Secretary of Government, 1931-32. g-None. h-None. k-Removed from the governorship because of loyalties to Calles. l-DP70, 1723; Dulles, 661.

Ramos Gurrión, Manuel
a-June 20, 1935. b-Coatzacoalcos, Veracruz. c-Early education unknown; legal studies, National School of Law, UNAM, 1958-62, law degree, with a

thesis on "The General Working Conditions of Federal Workers," Oct. 20, 1964; teacher, Preparatory School Article 3, Jalapa, 1965-66. d-Local Deputy to the State Legislature of Veracruz, 1968-71; *Federal Deputy* from the State of Veracruz, Dist. 15, 1973-76, Secretary of the Permanent Committee of Congress, 1975, President of the Chamber of Deputies, May 1976, member of the Administrative Committee; *Federal Deputy* from the State of Veracruz, Dist. 17, 1979-82; *Senator* from the State of Veracruz, 1982-88, member of the Gran Comisión and President of the Fishing Committee. e-Director of Youth of PRI, Veracruz, 1965-66; Secretary General of the CNOP of PRI, Veracruz, 1966; Secretary of Political Action, Regional Committee of PRI, State of Veracruz, 1969; Secretary of Organization, Regional Committee of PRI, State of Veracruz, 1969; Secretary General of the Regional Committee of PRI, State of Veracruz, 1970; President of the Regional Committee of PRI, State of Veracruz, 1971-75; general delegate of the CEN of PRI to Veracruz, 1975-76; general delegate and coordinator, *José López Portillo* presidential campaign, Veracruz, 1976; Secretary of Organization of the CEN of CNOP of PRI, 1976-79. f-Secretary of the City Council of Coatzacoalcos, Veracruz. g-Secretary of Labor and Conflicts of the Union of Workers of the Secretariat of Public Works, 1959-62. h-None. i-Son of Eduardo Ramos de los Santos, artisan, and Juana Gurrión; married Griselda Rella Cortés. j-None. k-None. l-C de D, 1973-76, 1979-82; C de S, 1982-88; Lehr, 490; DBGM87, 346; DBGM, 586-87.

Ramos Millán, Gabriel
(Deceased Sept. 26, 1949) a-Apr. 25, 1903. b-Ayapango, México. c-Preparatory studies at the National Preparatory School; law degree from the Escuela Libre de Derecho. d-*Federal Deputy* from the State of México, Dist. 9, 1943-46; *Senator* from the State of México, 1946-47, President of the Treasury Committee. e-None. f-Vice-President of the Administrative Council of Producción Agrícola, S.A.; adviser to Guanos y Fertilizantes de México, S.A.; founder and First President of the National Commission of Maíz, Jan. 6, 1947-49. g-Founder of the National Association of the Middle Class, 1945, to support *Miguel Alemán* for president. h-Defense lawyers for miners in Pachuca, Hidalgo. i-Longtime friend of *Miguel Alemán*, President of Mexico, 1946-52; held positions under *Miguel Alemán* as governor of Veracruz; parents were peasants. j-None. k-Known in Mexico as the "Apostle of Maíz" because of his campaign to improve the cultivation of corn and the development of new hybrid seeds; responsible for the first surplus production of corn since 1910. l-DP70, 1724-25; C de S, 1946-52; DGF51, I, 6; C de D, 1943-45, 19; Wise, 60, 139; Q es Q, 487; HA, 7 Oct. 1949, 6; López, 913; HA, 24 Jan. 1947, 34; Enc. Mex., XI, 1977, 61.

Ramos Santos, Matías
(Deceased Mar. 4, 1962) a-Feb. 24, 1891. b-San Salvador, Zacatecas. c-Primary and secondary studies in Concepción del Oro, Zacatecas; no degree. d-*Federal Deputy* from the State of Zacatecas, Dist. 8, 1918-20; *Governor of Zacatecas*, 1932-34, 1935-36. e-President of the CEN of PRI, Dec. 14, 1934, to June 15, 1935. f-Inspector of Railroads, Secretariat of Public Works, 1917; Oficial Mayor of the Secretariat of War, 1928-29; Subsecretary of War, 1929-30; *Secretary of National Defense*, 1952-58. g-None. i-Friend of *Marcelino García Barragán* and *Francisco Urquizo*; son, Ismael Ramos, served as 1st Captain of the Chief of Staff of the Secretary of National Defense, 1952; son of Ezequiel

Ramos, major in the federal army, and María Santos; married Dolores Arteaga. j-Joined the Revolution on Mar. 18, 1911 as a private; rank of Corporal, May 13, 1911; rank of 2nd Sergeant, Dec. 15, 1911; fought under Captain Gertrudis Sánchez, Mar. 18 to Aug. 20, 1911; rank of 1st Sergeant in the Cavalry, Apr. 15, 1912; fought under Major Eulalio Gutiérrez, Aug. 21, 1911 to Feb. 17, 1913; rank of 2nd Lieutenant, June 10, 1912; rank of Lieutenant, Aug. 30, 1912; rank of 2nd Captain, Feb. 18, 1913; rank of 1st Captain, Apr. 25, 1913; fought under Eulalio Gutiérrez, Division of the Center, Feb. 18, 1913 to June 30, 1915, against Victoriano Huerta; rank of Major, Sept. 3, 1913; rank of Lt. Colonel, Dec. 31, 1913; rank of Colonel, Mar. 7, 1914; rank of Brigadier General, Dec. 31, 1915; Commander of the El Rayo Brigade, 3rd Division of the Army of the Northeast, 1915-16, against Francisco Villa; 1916; wounded commanding the El Rayo and Félix Gómez Brigades, 1916; fought under General *Jacinto B. Treviño*; rank of Brigade General, May 20, 1916; ordered retired from the army, 1921-23; reactivated Dec. 18, 1923, to fight against the de la Huerta revolt; Commander of Military Operations, 11th Military Zone, Zacatecas, Zacatecas, 1923; Commander of Operations, 26th Military Zone, Tepic, Nayarit, 1923-24, 17th Military Zone, Querétaro, Querétaro, 1924-26, and 22nd Military Zone, Oaxaca, Oaxaca, 1926-27; Commander of Military Operations, 9th Military Zone, Tampico, Tamaulipas, 1927-28; fought against Escobar rebellion in the defense of Ciudad Juárez, 1929; Commander of Military Operations, 5th Military Zone, Chihuahua, Chihuahua, 1929; rank of Division General, May 16, 1929; Commander of Military Operations, 5th Military Zone, Chihuahua, Chihuahua, 1930-32; Commander of the 10th Military Zone, Durango, Durango,

1938-40, of the 22nd Military Zone, Toluca, México, 1940-41, of the 18th Military Zone, Pachuca, Hidalgo, 1941-43, of the 27th Military Zone, Acapulco, Guerrero, 1943-45, of the 12th Military Zone, San Luis Potosí, San Luis Potosí, 1945-46, and of the 7th Military Zone, Monterrey, Nuevo León, 1946-51. k-Retired from active service, 1959; one of a few officers to have commanded more than ten military zones in a career from 1923 to 1951. l-DGF56, 199; Peral, 673; *Polémica*, 1969, Vol. I, 67; McAlister, 223-24; DGF51, I, 183; D de Y, 3 Dec. 1952, 12; Q es Q, 487-88; Dulles, 635; López, 913-14; Enc. Mex., XI, 1977, 61; Rev. de Ejer., Apr. 1962, 50-52.

Rangel Couto, Hugo
a-1912. b-Guadalajara, Jalisco. c-Preparatory studies at the National Preparatory School, 1925-29; law degree, National School of Law, UNAM, 1929-34; economics degree, National School of Economics, UNAM, 1935-39, graduating June 20, 1939, with a thesis on democracy and communism in America; Secretary of the National School of Economics, 1937-38; researcher, Institute of Social Research, UNAM, 1934-38; Professor of the History of Economic Doctrines, National School of Law, UNAM; Director, Institute for Economic Research, UNAM, 1943-46. d-None. e-None. f-*Oficial Mayor of the Secretariat of Government Properties*, 1946-47; *Subsecretary of Government Properties*, 1947-49; *Subsecretary in Charge of the Secretariat of Government Properties*, 1949-51; *Subsecretary of Government Properties*, 1951-52. g-Secretary of the National School of Economics, 1936-38; member of the 1933 student strike committee. h-Author of numerous articles and books; economist, Workers Bank for Industrial Development, 1937-42; adviser to the Mexican Delegation to United Nations, 1946. i-Important

collaborator of *Alfonso Caso*, 1944-49; married Antonia Abreu. j-None. k-None. l-DGF47, 269; DGF51, I, 443; Enc. Mex., V, 46; HA, 10 Aug. 1951, 14; DGF51, II, 383; DGF50, II, 279; EN de E, 62; DNED, 200.

Rangel de la Fuente, Elvia
a-June 27, 1930. b-Ciudad Victoria, Tamaulipas. c-Early education unknown; teaching certificate; teaching certificate in psychology, Higher Normal School, Mexico City; teaching certificate in audiovisual education; primary school teacher; teacher of Mexican history and language and literature in secondary schools; Secretary of Finances, Higher Normal School. d-Member of the City Council of Ciudad Victoria, Tamaulipas; *Federal Deputy* from the State of Tamaulipas, Dist. 4, 1967-70. e-Director of Women's Action of PRI, Tamaulipas; Secretary of Social Action of the CEPES of PRI, Tamaulipas; Director of Women's Action of the CNOP of PRI, Tamaulipas. f-Director of Audio Visual Education, Tamaulipas. g-None. h-None. j-None. k-None. l-Directorio, 1967-70; C de D, 1967-70.

Rangel Frías, Raúl
a-Mar. 15, 1913. b-Monterrey, Nuevo León. c-Primary and secondary studies in Monterrey; preparatory studies at the Colegio Civil, Monterrey; law degree from the National School of Law, UNAM, 1933-38, with a thesis on Kelsen; member of the University Council of UNAM; Professor of the History of Philosophical Doctrines, National Preparatory School, Mexico City, 1936-38; Professor of Civics, secondary schools, Mexico City, 1936-38, and at the workers centers; Professor of Law, School of Law, University of Nuevo León, 1939-43; Rector of the University of Nuevo León, 1949-52, 1952-55. d-*Governor of Nuevo León*,

1955-61. e-None. f-Public relations officer, Department of the Federal District; Director of the Social Welfare Program, State of Nuevo León; Chief, Department of Social Action, University of Nuevo León, 1944; Oficial Mayor of the State of Nuevo León under Governor *Salinas Leal*. g-Member of the Alfonso Reyes group, 1929; President of the Student Society at the Colegio Civil of Nuevo León; delegate to the 7th National Student Congress, 1930. h-Practicing lawyer, 1970-79; member of the Board of the Fundidora de Acero de Monterrey, S.A.; member of the Board of Financiera Central, S.A. i-Son of Dr. Edelmiro Rangel Treviño and Josefina Frías Alcocer, sister of novelist Heriberto Frías; married Elena Hinojosa; attended law school with *Hugo B. Margáin* and *Alfonso Corona del Rosal*; student of *Manuel Moreno Sánchez*. j-None. k-Supported José Vasconcelos, 1929. l-*Excélsior*, 5 Oct. 1961; DBM68, 508-09; WWM45, 98; DGF56, 97; G of NL, 15; HA, 9 May 1955, 10; *Siempre*, 17 Sept. 1956, 6; PdM, 304; letters; López, 914; Enc. Mex., XI, 1977, 65; HA, 24 Aug. 1960; WNM, 185.

Rangel (Hurtado), Rafael
(Deceased Aug. 19, 1955) a-Oct. 31, 1888. b-San Francisco del Rincón, Guanajuato. c-Law degree, University of Guanajuato. d-Local Deputy to the State Legislature of Guanajuato, 1937-38; *Senator* from the State of Guanajuato, 1940-46, President of the Railroads Committee, Second Secretary of the Second Government Committee, member of the First Balloting Committee and the Gran Comisión; President of the Rules Committee and the Second Instructive Section of the Grand Jury. e-None. f-Secretary of the City Council of León, Guanajuato; Secretary General of Government of the State of Guanajuato, 1928-31; Private Secretary to the Governor of Guanajuato, 1931-32;

Secretary General of Government of the Territory of Baja California del Sur, 1934-37; *Interim Governor of Guanajuato*, 1938-39, during the leave of absence of *Luis I. Rodríguez* as President of the CEN of PRM. g-None. j-None. k-Leader of the "Green" Group in Guanajuato, 1943. l-Peral, 673-74; C de S, 1940-46; López, 914; *Libre de Oro*, 1946, 10; PS, 5086.

Rangel Meléndez, Enrique
(Deceased Jan. 8, 1969) a-July 15, 1904. b-San Luis de la Paz, Guanajuato. c-Primary studies only; no degree. d-*Federal Deputy* from the Federal District, Dist. 12, 1949-52; *Federal Deputy* from the State of Guanajuato, Dist. 9, 1961-64, 1967-69. e-None. f-None. g-Member of CROM, CNT and the CTM, 1928; founder of the Proletariat National Federation, 1952; leader of CROC; member of the Congress of Labor. h-Blue collar worker, shoe industry. i-Married Judith Zamora. j-None. k-None. l-Directorio, 1967-70; C de D, 1949-52, 1961-64, 1967-70.

Ravizé, Manuel A.
a-Sept. 20, 1910. b-Tampico, Tamaulipas. c-Primary studies at the San José Institute, Tacubaya; secondary and preparatory studies at the Colegio Francés "Centro Unión," and the Colegio Puente de Alvarado, Mexico City, in the field of commercial studies; studied engineering at the Atlanta Military Academy, Atlanta, Georgia; studied business administration in San Antonio, Texas; no degree. d-*Alternate Senator* from the State of Tamaulipas, 1958-64, under Senator *Emilio Martínez Manatou*; Mayor of Tampico, Tamaulipas, 1955-57; *Governor of Tamaulipas*, 1969-74. e-State committeeman for PRI in Tamaulipas; PRI delegate to Tampico; representative of precandidate for governor, Manuel Collado, 1943. f-Trustee of the City Council of Tam-

pico, 1943-45; Director of the Federal Office of the Treasury, 1958-64; President of the Federal Board of Material and Moral Improvements for Tampico, 1964-69. g-None. h-Businessman. i-Parents were fifth generation Tamaulipecos; father worked as a cashier for Ferrocarril del Golfo, 1897, and founded first petroleum company in the Tampico region, 1918; son Manuel is a businessman; married Teresa Matienzo Zubista; part of *Emilio Martínez Manatou's* political group. j-None. k-Precandidate for senator from Tamaulipas, 1976. l-Letter; *Excélsior*, 8 Dec. 1975, 17; Loret de Mola, 91, 143; Guerra Villarreal, 83.

Rea Carbajal, Raúl
a-Nov. 9, 1933. b-Tepic, Nayarit. c-Early education unknown; secondary teaching certificate, Higher Normal School, Tepic, Nayarit, 1961; teacher. d-Local Deputy to the State Legislature of Nayarit, Dist. 1, 1972-75; *Plurinominal Federal Deputy* from PSUM, 1982-85. e-Joined the PPS, 1961; Secretary General of the PPS, Nayarit, 1972; Secretary General of the Mexican People's Party, 1977-81; member of the Central Committee, PSUM, 1981; member of the Political Committee, PSUM, 1981; candidate of the PPS for local deputy to the State Legislature of Nayarit, 1966, 1969; candidate of the PCM for Mayor of Tepic, Nayarit, 1981; joined the PCM, 1981. f-None. g-Secretary of Conflicts, Local 49, National Teachers Union, 1961-64; leader, National Teachers Union, Nayarit, 1964-67. i-Son of Albino Rea Becerra, laborer, and Soledad Carvajal Cabezud, teacher; married Antonia Becerra Tapia, normal teacher. j-Served in the army; commander, machine-gun company. k-None. l-Directorio, 1982-85; C de D, 1982-85; Lehr, 646.

Real (Encinas), Carlos
a-Jan. 31, 1922. b-Federal District.
c-Primary and secondary studies in the
Federal District; preparatory studies in
the Federal District; law degree, Escuela
Libre de Derecho, July 20, 1944, LLD,
National School of Law, UNAM.
d-*Federal Deputy* from the State of
Durango, Dist. 2, 1949-52, member of
the Legislative Studies Committee, the
Second Balloting Committee, the
Second Committee on General Means
of Communication; Vice-President of
the Chamber of Deputies, Dec. 1949;
Federal Deputy from the State of
Durango, Dist. 1, 1955-58, member of
the External and Domestic Trade
Committee, the Budget and Accounts
Committee (1st year), and the Constitu-
tional Affairs Committee (1st year);
Secretary of the Chamber of Deputies,
1956; *Alternate Senator* from Durango,
1964-70. e-President of the Regional
Committee of PRI, Durango; President
of the Board for Material Improvements,
Ciudad Juárez and Nuevo Laredo, for
Adolfo Ruiz Cortines' presidential
campaign, 1951-52. f-Private Secretary
to *Ignacio Morones Prieto* as Director
General of IMSS, 1966-70; Director
General of Inspection of Domestic
Taxes, Secretariat of the Treasury, Feb.
1972; delegate of the Department of the
Federal District, 1976-77. g-None.
i-Son of *Carlos Real Félix*, senator from
Durango, 1958-64; brother of Dr.
Roberto Real Encinas. j-None. k-None.
l-HA, 14 Feb. 1972, 23-24; DGF56, 23,
31; DGF51, I, 21, 32, 34, 35, 36; C de D,
1949-51, 1955-57; C de S, 1964-70; Ind.
Biog., 128-29; DAPC, 1977, 59.

Real (Félix), Carlos
(Deceased Jan. 27, 1982) a-Nov. 17,
1892. b-Tamazula, Durango. c-Primary
studies in Durango, Durango; studies at
the National Military College; no
degree. d-*Governor of Durango*, 1932-

35; *Senator* from the State of Durango,
1958-64, President of the Second Committee for National Defense, member of
the Committee on the Electric Industry,
the War Materiels Committee, the Special Livestock Committee, the Second
Balloting Committee, and the Second
Instructive Committee for the Grand
Jury. e-Founding member of the PNR,
1929; *Oficial Mayor of the CEN of PRI*,
1956. f-Director, Telegraph Office,
Agiabampo, Sinaloa, 1913; Oficial May-
or of the Chamber of Deputies, 1946-49;
Gerente of the National Lottery, 1949-
52. g-None. h-Rancher, 1936-46. i-Son,
Carlos Real Encinas, served twice as a
federal deputy from Durango; son,
Roberto, president of Diteza, S.A.,
Robespierre, S.A., Turbotex, S.A., and
Atoyac Textil, S.A. j-Joined the Revolution as a 2nd Lieutenant, 1913; career
army officer; imprisoned by rebels,
1927, but escaped; Chief of Staff to Gen-
eral *Ramón F. Iturbe*; Commander of
Santiago Tlatelolco Prison, 1927; rank
of Brigadier General, 1932; Commander
of the 7th Military Zone, Monterrey,
Nuevo León; reached the rank of Divi-
sion General. k-Political boss of Durango during the early 1930s; removed from
the governorship because of loyalty to
Calles. l-DGF47, 13, 409; Dulles; C de
S, 1961-64, 67; *Siempre*, 14 Jan. 1959, 6;
Johnson, 32; D del S, 3 Dec. 1946, 1;
Func., 199; *NYT*, 17 Dec. 1935, 1; HA, 8
Feb. 1982, 17; *Excélsior*, 28 Jan. 1982.

Reboliedo Fernández, Mario G.
b-Jalapa, Veracruz. c-Early education
unknown; law degree from the School
of Law, University of Veracruz, July,
1935; Professor of Law, University of
Veracruz, 1945-50. d-None. e-None.
f-Agent of the Ministerio Público,
Veracruz; Assistant Auxiliary Attorney
General of the State of Veracruz; Judge
of the First Instance, State of Veracruz;
President of the Board of Conciliation

and Arbitration of the State of Veracruz; Secretary of the Superior Tribunal of Justice of the State of Veracruz; Director, Department of Government, State of Veracruz; Judge of the Superior Tribunal of Justice of the State of Veracruz; Attorney General of the State of Veracruz; Secretary General of Government of the State of Veracruz; Judge, Fifteenth Penal District, Federal District; Judge of the Superior Tribunal of Justice of the Federal District; *Justice of the Supreme Court of Mexico*, 1955-58, 1963-70, 1970-76; 1978-81; *President of the Supreme Court*, 1976-77, 1982-83. g-None. i-Professor of *Manlío Fabio Tapia Camacho*. j-None. k-None. l-*Justicia*, Apr. 1968; letter; *Excélsior*, 3 Mar. 1976, 1.

Rentería (Acosta), Daniel T.
(Deceased 1965) a-1897. b-Taretán, Michoacán. c-Preparatory studies at the Colegio de San Nicolás, Morelia, Michoacán; law degree, Colegio de San Nicolás. d-*Federal Deputy* from Michoacán, Dist. 3, 1958-61, member of the Transportation Committee. e-None. f-Treasurer of the State of Michoacán, 1934-40; Attorney General of Michoacán; Treasurer General of Mexico, 1934-46; General Cashier of the Rio de las Balsas Commission, 1961-65. g-None. h-None. i-Married María Acosta; father of *Héctor Rentería Acosta*, federal deputy from the State of Michoacán, 1970-73 and member of PARM; parents were of Indian ancestry; longtime collaborator of *Lázaro Cárdenas* since his term as governor of Michoacán, 1928-31. j-None. k-None. l-Func., 270; C de D, 1970-73, 1958-61, 89; Directorio, 1970-72; DP70, 1745; Anderson; *La Voz de Michoacán*, 16 Sept. 1949, 1.

Reta Martínez, Carlos Alfonso
a-Mar. 4, 1943. b-Morelia, Michoacán. c-Early education unknown; civil

engineering degree, National School of Engineering, UNAM, 1960-63; studies in political science and public administration, UNAM, 1967-70; MA and Ph.D. in public administration, UNAM, 1971-74; Graduate Professor of Federal Administration, Analysis of the Structure of Administration and Government Procedures, School of Political and Social Science, UNAM, 1974- ; Professor of Public Administration and the Para-State Sector in Mexico, Graduate School of Accounting and Administration, UNAM, 1974- . d-None. e-Youth Director of PRI in the Federal District, 1960-61; President of National Youth Committee of CNOP of PRI, 1962-68; Subdirector of the National Youth Organization of PRI, 1965-68; President of the Mexican Council of Youth; delegate of CNOP and PRI to various cities and states, 1963-68; Auxiliary Secretary of the CEN of PRI, 1968-70; founder and Director of *Polémica*, official publication of PRI, 1969-70; Secretary of Press and Publicity of the CEN of PRI, 1984-85. f-*Secretary General (C) of the Department of the Federal District*, 1970-71; Director General of Didactic and Cultural Materials, Secretariat of Public Education, 1978-79; Director of Public Relations, Department of the Federal District, 1985-88; Director of Public Relations, Secretariat of Foreign Relations, 1988-93. g-None. h-Assistant to the Resident Engineer of Estructuras y Cimentación, I.C.A., S.A.; Supervisor of Works, Estructuras y Cimentación, I.C.A., S.A., 1962-63; Investigator for the Fondo de Planeación Industria Azucarera; Director General of the Society to Promote Legal Establishments, S.A., 1973-76; Technical Director, Advisors & Consultants, S.C., 1974-91; Director General of the Latin American Institute of Educational Communicaton, 1978. i-Son of Rutilio Reta Ubasos and María Guadalupe Martínez Domínguez;

married Bertha Lira Hereford. j-None.
k-Student leader at UNAM. l-HA, 14
Dec. 1970, 24; DPE71; DBGM89, 294;
DBGM92, 309.

Reta Petterson, Gustavo Adolfo
a-May 26, 1937. b-Federal District.
c-Primary studies at the Instituto (Colegio) México, 1943-49; secondary studies
at the Instituto (Colegio) México, 1950-
52; preparatory studies at the Instituto
Vasco de Quiroga, 1953-54; medical
degree in veterinary medicine, UNAM,
1955-59; MS from the University of
Indiana, 1961-63, with a specialty in
livestock; professor at the School of
Veterinary Medicine, UNAM, 1976-80;
professor, University of Guadalajara,
1963-67. d-None. e-None. f-Director
of the agriculture section of the Experimental Fields of El Horno, Chapingo,
Secretariat of Agriculture, 1960-63;
Head of the Livestock Department for
the Plan Lerma, 1963-67; Director
General of Animal Health, Secretariat
of Agriculture and Livestock, 1967-72;
Subsecretary of Livestock, Feb. 23, 1972
to 1975; Director General of Projects,
Presidency of Mexico, 1980-82; Director
of Projects, Fomento Industrial SOMEX,
1983-88; Director General of Livestock
Policy, Secretariat of Agriculture and
Hydraulic Resources, 1989-90; Director
General of Animal Health, Secretariat
of Agriculture and Hydraulic Resources,
1990; *Subsecretary of Livestock*, 1990-
94. g-None. i-Son of Manuel Reta
Alducín, veterinarian, and Eloísa
Petterson Moriel; married Ana Cristina
Espinosa Morett. j-None. k-Resigned
as Subsecretary of Livestock, June 26,
1975; precandidate for federal deputy,
1975. l-HA, 6 Mar. 1972, 19; DPE71,
69; *Novedades*, 24 Feb. 1972, 1; HA, 21
Feb. 1972; MGF69, 264; *Excélsior*, 23
Feb. 1973, 5; *El Universal*, 27 June 1975;
DAPC81, 3; DBGM89, 294; DBGM92,
310.

Reyes Contreras, Alfredo
a-Dec. 7, 1947. b-Ixtlahuaca, México.
c-Early education unknown; law degree,
National School of Law, UNAM, 1965-
70; professor of law, Autonomous University of the State of México, 1977- .
d-Local Deputy, State Legislature of
México, 1975-77; *Plurinominal Federal
Deputy* from the PPS, 1982-85; *Federal
Deputy* from the State of México, 1988-
91. e-Candidate for Local Deputy to the
State Legislature of México, 1957;
joined the PPS, 1969; Secretary General
of the PPS, Toluca, México, 1974-75;
Secretary General of the PPS, State of
México, 1976-82; candidate of the PPS
for governor of the State of México,
1981; member of the Central Committee, Popular Socialist Party, 1978-88.
f-None. g-None. h-Member of the
editorial group of *Mazahua*, Ixtlahuaca,
México. i-Son of José Bernardo Reyes
Díaz, businessman, and Piedad
Contreras Ayala; married Carmen
Mercado Téllez, economist. j-None.
k-None. l-Directorio, 1982-85; C de D,
1982-85; DBGM, 589; DBGM89, 522.

Reyes Esparza, Diamantina
a-June 9, 1941. b-Villa Matamoros,
Chihuahua. c-Primary studies in Villa
Matamoros; completed secondary
studies and normal certificate at night
school; normal school teacher; Secretary
of the Parralance Institute. d-*Federal
Deputy* from the State of Chihuahua,
Dist. 2, 1970-73, member of the Social
Action Committee, the Immigration
Committee and the Small Industry
Committee. e-Youth Director of PRI in
Chihuahua; Director of the Women's
Sector of PRI in Chihuahua; Secretary
General of PRI in the State of Chihua-
hua. f-None. g-Secretary of Labor and
Conflicts of the Teachers Union of
Chihuahua; Secretary General of the
Teachers Union of Chihuahua. j-None.
k-None. l-Directorio, 1970-72; C de D,
1970-73, 132.

Reyes Heroles, Jesús
(Deceased Mar. 19, 1985) a-Apr. 3, 1921. b-Tuxpán, Veracruz. c-Primary studies at the Benito Juárez Public School; preparatory studies at the National Preparatory School; law degree with honorable mention from the National School of Law, UNAM, 1944; graduate studies at the University of La Plata and the University of Buenos Aires, 1945; Assistant Professor of Labor Law, National School of Law, UNAM, 1944-45; Professor of Economics and General Theory, UNAM, 1946-63; professor at the National Polytechnic Institute. d-*Federal Deputy* from the State of Veracruz, Dist. 2, 1961-64, member of the Committee on Tariffs and Foreign Trade, the Legislative Studies Committee (4th Section on Administration), the Permanent Commission, and delegate to the Interparliamentary Conference. e-Joined PRM in 1939 and began political career as Auxiliary Private Secretary to *Heriberto Jara*, President of the CEN of PRM; assistant to the Private Secretary of *Antonio L. Villalobos*, President of the CEN of PRM, 1940-44; member of the IEPES of PRI, 1949-51, 1960-61; adviser to the Technical Office for the presidential campaign of *Adolfo López Mateos*, 1958; adviser to the President of the CEN of PRI, *Gabriel Leyva Velázquez*, 1952; *President of the CEN of PRI*, Feb. 21, 1972, to 1975. f-Adviser to the Secretary of Labor, *Ignacio García Téllez*, 1944; Alternate President of the Special Group No. 1 of the Federal Board of Conciliation and Arbitration, 1946; Secretary General of the Mexican Institute of Books, 1949-53; adviser to the President of Mexico, *Adolfo Ruiz Cortines*, 1952-58; Director of Economic Studies for National Railroads of Mexico, 1953-58; Technical Subdirector General of IMSS, 1958-61; *Director General of PEMEX*, 1964-70; Director General of the Industrial Complex of

Ciudad Sahagún, Hidalgo, Dec. 1, 1970, to 1972; *Director General of the IMSS*, 1975-76; *Secretary of Government*, 1976-79; *Secretary of Public Education*, 1982-85. g-None. h-Author of six books and dozens of articles on political and economic problems; i-Attended the National Preparatory School with *Luis Echeverría*; attended primary school with *José López Portillo*; married Gloria González Garza, daughter of General Roque González Garza, president of the Convention Government, 1915; son Jesús, adviser to *Carlos Salinas*, 1982; son Federico, is a leading intellectual and author; son of Jesús Reyes Martínez, employee, and Juana Heroles Lombera. j-None. k-Losing candidate for the deanship of the National School of Law, UNAM, 1961; only member of the original de la Madrid cabinet to have held elective office. l-*Excélsior*, 22 Feb. 1971; *Novedades*, 21 Feb. 1972, 1; *El Universal*, 1 Dec. 1964; WWMG, 34; HA, 22 Dec. 1958, 8; HA, 7 Dec. 1964, 21; *Excélsior*, 21 Feb. 1972, 18; HA, 28 Feb. 1972, 12; D de Y, 2 Dec. 196, 2; IWW67, 1018; *Análisis Político*, 3 July 1972, 4; Enc. Mex., XI, 1977, 126; IEPES; Guerra Leal, 363; *Excélsior*, 10 Feb. 1979, 14; HA, 25 Mar. 1985, 15; letters.

Reyes López, Venustiano
a-Dec. 30, 1916. b-Ciudad Mendoza, Veracruz. c-Early education unknown; completed part of secondary; studies at the National Conservatory of Music, Mexico City, 1938-42; fellowship from the State of Veracruz to study directing at Julliard School of Music and Columbia University, New York City, 1942-46; professor, National School of Music and the National Conservatory, UNAM, 1946-82. d-*Federal Deputy* from the Federal District, Dist. 9, 1976-79, Dist. 6, 1982-85. e-Participated in the 1952, 1958, 1964 and 1970 presidential campaigns giving musical performances;

joined PRI, 1946. f-None. g-President of the Student Society of the National Conservatory of Music; member of the National Union of Musicians; Secretary General of the National Union of Musicians, 1961-82; Secretary of Press and Publicity, CTM. h-Textile worker, Santa Rosa, Veracruz; orchestra director. i-Married Teresa Reyes Ramírez. j-Performer at the front in World War II. k-None. l-Directorio, 1982-85; C de D, 1976-79, 1982-85; DBGM, 589.

Reyes Luján, Sergio
a-April 20, 1941. b-Federal District. c-Early education unknown; degree in physics, School of Sciences, UNAM, 1959-62; graduate studies, Uppsala, Sweden, 1964; Ph.D. studies in physics, UNAM, 1963, 1966, 1967; Chief of Physics Lab, School of Sciences, UNAM, 1964; full-time researcher, Physics Institute, UNAM, 1968-71; Auxiliary Secretary, School of Sciences, UNAM, 1969-71; Founding Director of the Instrument Center, UNAM, 1972-74; professor, School of Sciences, UNAM, 1960-74; professor, National School of Engineering, UNAM, 1968-70; Secretary of Autonomous Metropolitan University, Iztapalapa Campus, 1974-76; Secretary of Autonomous Metropolitan University, Xochimilco Campus, 1980-81; Secretary General of the Autonomous Metropolitan University, 1976-79; Rector of the Autonomous Metropolitan University, 1981-85. d-None. e-Joined PRI, 1986. f-*Subsecretary of Ecology,* Secretariat of Ecology and Urban Development, 1986-88, 1988-92; Director General of the National Ecology Institute, Secretariat of Social Development, 1992-93. g-None. h-None. i-Son of Víctor Manuel Reyes Martínez and María del Carmen Luján Garibay; married Ana María Gutiérrez Fernández. j-None. k-None. l-DBGM92, 311; HA, 15 Apr. 1986, 28; DBGM89, 296; DBGM87, 323.

Reyes Osorio, Sergio
a-Aug. 8, 1934. b-Federal District. c-Early education unknown; studies in agricultural engineering, National School of Agriculture, 1952-58, graduating with a thesis on "The State, Private Banks, and Agricultural Credit," 1962; MA in agricultural economics, University of Wisconsin, 1963-64, with a thesis on "Factors of Productivity in Mexican Agricultural Development"; Professor of Credit and Agricultural Economics, Graduate School, National School of Agriculture, 1965-66; Professor of Land Tenure, Graduate School, National School of Agriculture, 1968; Research Associate, Colegio de México, 1977- . d-None. e-None. f-Economist for the Securities and Development Fund for Agriculture; agricultural economist for FIRA, Bank of Mexico, 1959-65; member of the Advisory Board, Agricultural Center of Chapingo; Director of the Center of Agricultural Investigations, 1965-70; President of the Board, Center for Agricultural Investigations, 1973-82; *Subsecretary of the Department of Colonization and Agrarian Affairs,* 1970-74; *Subsecretary of Organization and Agricultural Development,* Secretariat of Agrarian Reform, 1974-76; Technical Secretary of the Agro-Business Cabinet, Presidency, 1977-82; General Coordinator of Special Programs, Secretariat of Agriculture, 1982-83; adviser to the Secretary of Programming and Budgeting, 1983-84; General Coordinator of Delegates, Secretariat of Agriculture, 1986-88; *Subsecretary of Agriculture,* 1988-90. g-Technical adviser, CNC, 1968-74. h-President of the National Institute of Agricultural Economics, 1982; editor of various agriculture magazines. i-Married Ofelia Flores; son of Fortunato Reyes Hernández and María Luisa Osorio Gómez. j-None. k-None. l-DPE71, 12 ; DBM68, 512; HA, 21 Dec. 1970, 24; IEPES; Q es QAP, 215; DBGM89, 296.

Reyes Spíndola (y Prieto), Octavio
(Deceased 1967) a-Aug. 24, 1892.
b-Federal District. c-Law degree. d-*Federal Deputy* from the State of Oaxaca, 1943-46, Dist. 5. e-None. f-Protocol Attaché, Independence Centennial, 1921; Chief Secretary to the Embassy in Brazil, 1922; Second Secretary, Guatemala, 1928; Second Secretary-in-Charge, Guatemala, 1929; Second Secretary to Spain, 1930; Second Secretary-in-Charge, Spain, 1930; First Secretary-in-Charge, Spain, 1931; Chargé d'affaires, Panama, 1934; *Ambassador to Cuba*, 1938-39; Ambassador to Chile, 1939-41; Ambassador to Argentina, 1942-43; Consul, Miami, Florida, 1956; alternate member of the Advisory Council for the Small Business Bank of the Federal District, 1950; adviser to the President of Mexico. g-None. h-Author of several articles. i-Son of Rafael Reyes Spíndola, Oaxacan journalist who founded the Mexico City newspaper *El Universal*, 1888, and *El Imparcial*, 1896. j-Participated in the European Front during World War I. k-Kirk claims that Reyes Spíndola was the foreign service officer who most avidly pushed the Revolution abroad. l-DGF51, II, 377; C de D, 1943-45, 19; Peral, 680-81; DP70, 1758; WWM45, 101; DGF56, 139; DGF50, II, 413; Q es Q, 495.

Reyes Velázquez, Pedro
a-1916. b-Lagos de Moreno, Jalisco. c-Secondary and preparatory studies at the Institute of Science, Guadalajara, Jalisco; professor, Institute of Higher Studies of Monterrey; Director of the Library, Institute of Higher Studies of Monterrey. d-*Federal Deputy* from the State of Nuevo León, Dist. 2, 1964-67. e-Member of PAN. f-None. g-None. h-Writer for *El Norte* and *El Porvenir*. i-Son of Mercado Velázquez and Pedro Reyes Vázquez; married María del Refugio Romo Portugal. j-None. k-None. l-C de D, 1964-67.

Reynoso (Gutiérrez), Brigido
b-Juchipila, Zacatecas. c-No formal education; self-educated. d-*Federal Deputy* from the State of Zacatecas, Dist. 3, 1943-46; *Senator* from the State of Zacatecas, 1952-58, member of the Special Legislative Studies Committee, First Secretary of the Second Government Committee, Second Secretary of the Public Education Committee, and First Secretary of the National Property and Resources Committee. e-None. f-None. g-None. h-Owner of La Mezquita Sugar Mill; was a peasant as a young man. i-Brother of *Leobardo Reynoso*, senator from Zacatecas, 1934-40 and governor, 1944-50; son of Brigido Reynoso. j-None. k-None. l-Ind. Biog., 130; C de D, 1943-46; C de S, 1952-58; DGF56.

Reynoso (Gutiérrez), Leobardo
a-Jan. 18, 1902. b-Zacatecas, Zacatecas. c-Primary studies, Zacatecas, self-educated; no degree. d-*Federal Deputy* from the State of Zacatecas, Dist. 3, 1932-34, member of the Gran Comisión; *Senator* from the State of Zacatecas, 1934-40, President of the Revolutionary Bloc in the Senate; Secretary of the Revolutionary Bloc; President of the Permanent Commission; *Federal Deputy* from the State of Zacatecas, Dist. 3, 1940-43, member of the Gran Comisión, President of the First Instructive Section of the Grand Jury; President of the Policy Control Committee (1st and 2nd years), *Federal Deputy* from Zacatecas, 1932-34; *Governor of Zacatecas*, 1944-50. e-Secretary of the CEN of PNR, 1935. f-Cashier for the Federal Senate, 1924-26; paymaster for the Mexican Senate, 1926-32; Ambassador to Portugal, 1958-61, to Guatemala, 1963-65, and to Denmark, 1965-70. g-None. h-Began career as a federal employee, 1920; son of Brigido Reynoso. i-Brother, *Brigido Reynoso*, served as federal deputy from Zacatecas, Dist. 3,

1943-46. j-None. k-Brandenburg considered him to be in the Inner Circle of influence in the 1940s. l-HA, 24 Sept. 1950, xxiv; HA, 28 Sept. 1945, x; DGF61, 24; C de D, 1940-42; C de S, 1934-40; letter; Brandenburg, 44-46, 80; *Excélsior*, 5 Sept. 1973, 18.

Riba y Rincón (Gallardo), Luis
a-Oct. 20, 1934. b-Federal District. c-Early education unknown; law degree, Escuela Libre de Derecho, Oct. 23, 1957, with a thesis on international double taxation; professor, National School of Business, UNAM; professor, course in taxes, Graduate School of Business Administration, UNAM. d-None. e-None. f-Tax investigator, Secretariat of the Treasury; Private Secretary to the Director of Income Taxes, Secretariat of the Treasury, *Hugo B. Margáin*, 1955-56, 1958-59; Private Secretary to the Oficial Mayor of Industry and Commerce, *Hugo B. Margáin*, 1959-61; Private Secretary to the Subsecretary of Industry and Commerce, *Hugo B. Margáin*, 1961-64; General Manager of the National Association of Automobile Distributors, A.C., 1965-69; *Oficial Mayor of the Secretariat of the Treasury*, 1970-75. g-None. h-None. i-Married María Guadalupe Fernández del Valle. j-None. k-None. l-HA, 14 Dec. 1970, 21; DPE71, 27.

Ricardo Tirado, José
(Deceased 1969) a-Nov., 1907. b-Cueltzalán, Teziutlán, Puebla. c-Primary studies in Teziutlán and Puebla, Puebla; no degree. d-*Federal Deputy* from the State of Puebla, Dist. 8, 1946-49, member of the Rules Committee; *Federal Deputy* from the State of Puebla, Dist. 9, 1952-55, member of the Complaints Committee and the Rules Committee; *Federal Deputy* from the State of Puebla, Dist. 8, 1958-61, member of the Administrative Committee; *Senator* from Baja California del Norte, 1964-69.

e-Representative of the CEN of PRI to the State of Puebla during the presidential campaigns of 1946, 1952; general delegate of the CEN of PRI to Baja California del Norte, 1953; President of the PRI in Baja California del Norte; *Secretary of Organization of the CEN of PRI*, 1968. f-Police Chief of Tijuana, 1931; Sub-director of Cooperative Development of Patents and Copyrights, Secretariat of Industry and Commerce; Director of the Federal Judicial Police; representative of Baja California del Norte in Mexico City, 1959-64. g-Ejido leader. j-None. k-None. l-Func., 325; C de D, 1946-49, 85, 1952-55, 18, 65, 66, 1958-61, 89; Aguirre, 513.

Rico Islas, Juan Felipe
(Deceased) a-Feb. 5, 1890. b-Federal District. c-Cadet at the National Military College, 1906; graduated from the National Military College as a 2nd Lieutenant, 1907. d-None. e-None. f-*Governor of Baja California del Norte*, Aug., 1944, to Dec., 1946. g-None. h-None. j-Inspector in the Army; fought in the Orozco campaign; fought against Félix Díaz in Veracruz, 1912; member of the Division of the North under the command of General Huerta; retired Colonel, 1914-20; returned to active service, fought against De la Huerta, 1923; fought against Escobar, 1929; Commander of the Garrison, Ciudad Juárez, Chihuahua, 1937; Division General, Sept. 1, 1942; Commander of the Military Zone for Baja California del Norte, 1946. k-None. l-Peral, 683; WWM45, 102; López; Dávila, 130.

Rincón Castillejos, Martha Luz
a-Mar. 7, 1933. b-Tonalá, Chiapas. c-Urban teaching certificate; secondary teaching certificate; secondary teacher. d-Interim mayor; *Alternate Federal Deputy* from the State of Chiapas, Dist. 1, 1964-67; 1; *Federal Deputy* from the State of Chiapas, Dist. 1, 1967-70.

e-Director of Women's Action of PRI, State of Chiapas. f-None. g-Member of Local 7, SNTE; President of the Teachers Ateneum of Chiapas. h-None. j-None. k-None. l-Directorio, 1967-70; C de D, 1964-67.

Rincón Coutiño, Valentín

(Deceased July 6, 1968) a-Oct. 8, 1901. b-Tuxtla Gutiérrez, Chiapas. c-Primary studies in Tuxtla Gutiérrez; preparatory studies at the National Preparatory School; law degree from the National School of Law, UNAM; Professor of Civil Law, National School of Law, UNAM; professor, School of Law, University of Jalapa. d-*Federal Deputy* from the State of Chiapas, Dist. 1, 1949-52, member of the Second Justice Committee. e-None. f-Judge of the 1st Instance; President of the Superior Tribunal of Justice of the State of Veracruz; President of the Superior Tribunal of Justice of the Federal District and Territories, 1940. g-Founder of the Social Front of Lawyers. h-Co-author of the Civil Code of Procedures for the State of Veracruz; President of the Mexican Society of Geography and Statistics, 1966-67; author of numerous articles on law and history. j-None. k-Mason; Grand Master of the Grand Lodge of the Valley of Mexico. l-DP70, 1763; DGF51, I, 34; C de D, 1949-51; Enc. Mex., XI, 1977, 133; DBC, 209-10.

Rincón Gallardo, Gilberto

a-May 15, 1939. b-Federal District. c-Early education unknown; law degree, National School of Law, UNAM, 1962; Professor of the Theory of the State, School of Political and Social Science, UNAM, 1963. d-*Federal Deputy* (Party Deputy from the Mexican Communist Party), 1979-82. e-Member of the MLN, 1961; joined the Mexican Communist Party, 1963; militant, Peoples Electoral Front, 1964; member of the Central Committee of the Mexican Communist

Party, 1972-81; representative of the Central Committee of the PCM to the Federal Electoral Commission, 1979; Secretary General of the PCM, Federal District, 1980. g-Member of the Independent Peasant Central (CCI). j-None. k-Imprisoned in Lecumberri Prison, July, 1968 to December, 1971, because of his participation in the 1968 student strike. l-HA, 26 Feb. 1979, IV; Protag., 291.

Rios Elizondo, Roberto

(Deceased Jan. 9, 1978) a-1912. b-Federal District. c-Preparatory studies at the National Preparatory School; law degree, National School of Law, UNAM; LLD from the National School of Law, UNAM; Professor of the first and second courses in Administrative Law, National School of Law, UNAM; Professor of Fiscal Legislation; Higher School of Commerce, National Polytechnic School; Professor of Fiscal Legislation, School of Commerce, UNAM. d-None. e-None. f-Subdirector of the Technical Fiscal Department, Treasury of the Federal District; Director of the Technical Fiscal Department, Treasury of the Federal District, 1947-50; Director of the Legal Department, Treasury of the Federal District, 1950-52; Fiscal Attorney for the Department of the Federal District; Assistant Treasurer, Department of the Federal District, 1952-64; *Oficial Mayor of the Secretariat of Public Works*, 1964-70; *Secretary General of the IMSS*, 1970-71; *Secretary General D of the Department of the Federal District*, 1971-73; *Secretary of Works and Services of the Department of the Federal District*, 1973-76; *Justice of the Supreme Court*, 1977-78. g-None. h-Delegate to the Department of the Federal District to the Secretariat of the Presidency; coauthor of the fiscal and administrative laws of the Department of the Federal District, 1947; author of many

articles and essays on administrative
law and fiscal subjects; President of the
Mexican Academy of Administrative
Law, 1966. i-Married Carmen Ferrer;
son Luis Roberto Rios Ferrer was a
director general in the Secretariat of
Communications and Transportation,
1987. j-None. k-None. l-*Libro de Oro*,
xxiv; DPE65, 116; DGF56, 487; DGF51,
I, 509; HA, 21 Dec. 1964, 10; DPE61,
146; DBM68, 516-17; HA, 22 Jan. 1973,
36; *Excélsior*, 10 Jan. 1978, 4; HA, 16
Jan. 1978, 10; DBGM87, 328.

Rios Zertuche, Antonio
(Deceased Oct. 19, 1981) a-1894.
b-Monclova, Coahuila. c-Early education unknown; no degree. d-None.
e-None. f-Director of the Department
of Cavalry, Secretariat of War; Inspector
of Police in the Federal District, 1929;
Ambassador to France, 1945-46.
g-None. h-Constructed military bases
in Tapachula, Chiapas and Puerto
Madero, Quintana Roo. j-Career army
officer; joined the army Jan. 5, 1914, as a
2nd Captain under General Jesús Dávila
Sánchez; Constitutionalist during the
Revolution; participated in 130 battles;
Chief of the 1st Regiment, Fieles
Brigade, Oaxaca; Commander of the 7th
Military Zone, Monterrey, Nuevo León;
Inspector General of the Army in
Sonora, Chihuahua, Zacatecas, Gue-
rrero, and Chiapas; rank of Division
General, December 31, 1943; adviser to
the Chief of Staff, Secretariat of Na-
tional Defense, 1981. k-Helped mecha-
nize the Mexican cavalry. l-López, 937;
letter; HA, 9 Nov. 1981, 24.

Rius Facious, Antonio
a-Sept. 23, 1918. b-Federal District.
c-Completed primary and secondary
studies; studies in Mexican history and
literature; no degree. d-None. e-Member of the National Committee of PAN,
1961-62; President of PAN, Federal
District, 1961; candidate of PAN for

federal deputy (twice). f-None. g-Director of the Mexican Catholic Action
Youth, 1940; founder of the Association
of Businesses of the Central District of
Mexico City. h-Journalist; Editor of *El
Norte*, Chihuahua, 1943-44; Editor of
España, 1955-60; manager of Almacenes
Cataluna, 1945-77; manager of Plastim-
presos, 1945-77; manager of Telas
Ahuladas, S.A.; poet and author of many
articles and books. i-Son of Magín Rius
Figueres and Pilar Facius, Spanish
immigrants; married Amalia Abbud.
j-None. k-None. l-Enc. Mex., XI, 1977,
141; WNM, 91.

Riva Palacio, Carlos
a-July 8, 1935. b-Texcoco, México.
c-Early education unknown; medical
degree, National School of Medicine,
UNAM, 1961; fellowship, labor medi-
cine, International Office of Labor,
Germany, 1962. d-*Federal Deputy* from
the Federal District, Dist. 3, 1976-79.
e-*Secretary of Popular Action of the
CEN of PRI*, 1979. f-None. g-President,
National Committee of Vigilance,
Union of Workers, Secretariat of Labor,
1963-66; Assistant Secretary of Labor
and Conflicts, 1969-72, Secretary of
Organization, Local 3, Secretary of
Planning and Statistics, 1972-73, and
Secretary General, 1973-78, all of the
Union of Workers of the ISSSTE;
President of the Subcommittee on Labor
and Legislation, 1977, President of the
Subcommittee on Organization, 1978,
and President of the National Commit-
tee on Labor and Legislation, 1978-79,
all of the FSTSE; *Secretary General of
the FSTSE*, 1977-80; *Secretary General
of CNOP*, 1979. j-None. k-None.
l-Almanaque of México, 57, 484;
Protag., 292; C de D, 1976-79.

Riva Palacio (López), Antonio
a-Apr. 26, 1928. b-Cuautla, Morelos.
c-Early education unknown; law degree,
National School of Law, UNAM, 1946-

51; Professor of Law, School of Law, Autonomous University of Morelos, 1964. d-*Federal Deputy* from the State of Morelos, Dist. 1, 1976-79; President of the Chamber of Deputies, 1977, 1979; *Senator* from the State of Morelos, 1982-87; President of the Gran Comisión, 1982-87; *Governor of Morelos*, 1988-94. e-Joined PRI, 1946; Secretary of Youth Action of the CEN of PRI, 1946; aide to the Youth Director of the CEN of PRI, 1957; *Secretary of Political Action of the CEN of PRI*, 1986. f-President of the Federal Board of Conciliation and Arbitration of Morelos, 1958-60; Secretary General of Government of the State of Morelos, 1960-64; adviser to the Subsecretary of Government, 1982. g-Delegate of the CNC in Michoacán, 1977; Secretary of Contracts of the CEN of the CNC, 1977-80. h-Practicing lawyer, 1949-58, 1964-76. i-Son of Mariano Riva Palacio San Vicente, businessman, and Purísima López Acosta; married Macaría Than Clemente; stepbrother *Enrique Riva Palacio* was a federal deputy from the State of México, 1982-85, 1988-91. j-None. k-None. l-DBGM, 590; Lehr; DBGM92, 820; DBGM89, 738; DBGM87, 551; HA, 1 Dec. 1987, 21.

Riva Palacio Morales, Rafael
a-June 3, 1913. b-Texcoco, México. c-Secondary studies at the Scientific and Literary Institute of México, Toluca; studies at the School of Business, UNAM, 1927-30; economics degree, National School of Economics, UNAM, 1933. d-*Federal Deputy* from the State of México, Dist. 3, 1970-73, member of the Radio Industry Committee, the Second Balloting Committee, and the Tourism Committee. e-None. f-Adviser for Publicity to President *Adolfo López Mateos*; Oficial Mayor of the Secretariat of the Presidency, 1963. g-President of the National Chamber of Broadcasting Industries. h-President of

the Mexican Association of Publicity Agents; General Manager of Publicity Salas, S.A., 1968. i-Descendant of Vicente Riva Palacio; son of Carlos Riva Palacio, President of the CEN of PNR, 1933-34, and Secretary of Government under Calles; brother of *Emilio Riva Palacio*, Governor of Morelos, 1964-70; *Adolfo López Mateos* served as private secretary to his father. j-None. k-None. l-C de D, 1970-72, 132; DBM68, 519.

Rivas Guillén, Genovevo
(Deceased 1947) a-Jan. 3, 1886. b-Rayón, San Luis Potosí. c-Primary studies at the public school No. 1, Tampico, Tamaulipas; no degree. d-None. e-None. f-*Provisional Governor of San Luis Potosí*, 1938-39, replacing *Mateo Hernández Netro*, who joined the *Cedillo* rebellion. g-None. h-Worked in a general store; worked in photography; self-employed farmer. i-Father, Francisco Rivas, was captured and shot by Victoriano Huerta during the Revolution, July 17, 1913; mother, Manuela Guillén. j-Joined the Constitutional Army as a private, Dec. 8, 1913, as a member of the 4th Squad, 25th Regiment, San Luis Potosí; as a Lt. Colonel, fought the North American troops under General Pershing, Carrizal, Chihuahua, 1916; fought the Cristeros, 1926-28; rank of Brigadier General, Apr. 1, 1928; rank of Division General, 1933; Commander of the 15th Military Zone, Guadalajara, Jalisco, 1937; Commander of the 12th Military Zone, San Luis Potosí, 1938; fought against Cedillo, 1938; Commander of the Military Zone of Querétaro, Oaxaca, and Sonora. k-None. l-DP70, 1770-71; WWM45, 102; D de Y, 27 May 1938, 1; Peral, 690; Q es Q, 500-01; Enc. Mex., XI, 1977, 144; López, 938.

Rivera Anaya, Manuel
a-Jan. 5, 1905. b-Chignahuapan, Puebla. c-Primary studies in Huanchingo, Villa

Juárez, Puebla, with some interruptions; preparatory studies at the University of Puebla; completed three years of legal studies, University of Puebla; no degree. d-Member of the city council of Puebla, 1930; Local Deputy to the State Legislature of Puebla (38th); *Federal Deputy* from the State of Puebla, Dist. 2, 1955-58, 1964-67. e-Joined the PNR, 1929. f-None. g-Student leader, Puebla, Puebla; joined the Federation of Unions of Workers and Peasants of Puebla, 1926; militant of the General Federation of Workers and Peasants of Mexico, 1933-36; joined the CTM, 1936; Secretary General of the Regional Federation of Workers and Peasants of Puebla, 1938; representative of labor on the Federal Board of Conciliation and Arbitration, Puebla; Secretary General of the National Workers Federation, 1942; Cofounder of CROC, 1952; President, National Political Control, CEN of CROC; President of CROC, 1956. h-Worked as a carpenter in youth to help support family. i-Son of Nemorio Rivero, revolutionary and Chief of Staff of the Francisco I. Madero Brigade, and a participant in the Convention of Aguascalientes, 1914. j-Served as an assistant to General Esteban Márquez, his father's superior officer, 1916. k-None. l-Ind. Biog., 131; C de D, 1955-58, 1964-67.

Rivera Crespo, Felipe
a-Oct. 9, 1908. b-Ciudad Jojutla, Morelos. c-Primary studies in Jojutla and in the Federal District; engineering degree in topography from the Superior School of Construction, Technical Industrial Institute (IPN), 1928. d-Trustee Attorney for the City of Cuernavaca, 1935; Mayor of Cuernavaca, 1955-57; *Alternate Senator* from the State of Morelos, 1952-58; Mayor of Cuernavaca, 1967-69; *Governor of Morelos*, 1970 to 1976. e-Secretary of Agrarian Action of the State Committee of the

PNR, Morelos, 1930; Secretary General of CNOP of PRI for the State of Morelos, 1954. f-Subdirector of Public Works for the State of Morelos, 1932; founder and President of the Local Highway Commission, 1935-70. g-Member of the Mixed Agrarian Commission of Morelos, 1929; President of the Association of Winegrowers of Morelos, 1966; President of the Lions Club of Morelos, 1955. h-President of the Board of Tourism for Morelos, 1960. i-Half brother, *Diodoro Rivera Uribe*, was a Senator from Morelos, 1964-70; son of Otilio Rivera. j-None. k-None. l-DGF56, 6; letter; *Hoy*, 20 May 1972, 62-63.

Rivera Marín, María Guadalupe
a-Oct. 23, 1924. b-Federal District. c-Early education unknown; economics degree, National School of Economics, UNAM, 1942-44; law degree, National School of Law, UNAM, 1942-47; LLD from the National School of Law, UNAM, 1952-54, with a thesis on colonial property rights; Professor of Labor Movements, School of Political and Social Science, UNAM; Professor of Economic Geography, of Mexican Sociology, 1965-67, and in School of Architecture, 1957, all at Ibero American University; professor, School of Business and Administration, UNAM, 1957; director general, El Colegio del Bajío, 1986-89. d-*Federal Deputy* from the Federal District, Dist. 22, 1961-64, member of the Penal Section of the Legislative Studies Committee and the Tax Committee; *Federal Deputy* from the Federal District, Dist. 9, 1979-82; *Alternate Senator* from Guanajuato, 1982-88, in functions, 1984. e-Joined PRI, 1961; Subsecretary of International Affairs of the CEN of PRI, 1983-84. f- Analyst of the Office of Insurance, Secretariat of the Treasury, 1944; analyst, Secretariat of Government Properties, 1947; researcher, writer, and adviser to the director general of the Nation-

al Finance Bank, 1949-54; Director of Investments, Housing Institute, 1958; technical adviser, Department of Rural Affairs, Department of the Federal District, 1967; Representative of Mexico to the International Labor Conference, Geneva, 1955; Chief, License Office, Department of the Federal District, 1966; Director General of Economic Studies, Department of the Federal District, 1970; Ambassador to the Food and Agriculture Organization, United Nations, Rome, 1977-79; Executive Secretary of the National Institute of Historical Studies of the Mexican Revolution, Secretariat of Government, 1989-93. g-None. h-Author. i-Daughter of painter Diego Rivera, cofounder of the Mexican Communist Party, and Guadalupe Marín Preciado, author; mother later married poet Jorge Cuesta; sister Ruth Marín, painter, married to painter Rafael Coronel; grandfather was a school teacher and her grandmother an obstetrician. j-None. k-First woman to win the National Prize in Economics, 1955. l-Enc. Mex., XI, 1977, 151; C de D, 1961-64, 88; López, 946; WWM45, 102; Romero Aceves, 729-80; *Excélsior*, 17 Sept. 1981, 5; HA, 22 Oct. 1979, 6; C de D, 199-82; DBGM92, 315.

Rivera Pérez Campos, José
a-Mar. 19, 1907. b-Celaya, Guanajuato. c-Primary studies in Celaya; preparatory studies at the National Preparatory School; law degree from the National School of Law, UNAM, 1931, with a thesis on the justification of the state; Professor of General History, National Preparatory School, 1929-35; Professor of the History of Philosophical Doctrines, National Preparatory School, 1932; Professor of the History of Political Thought, UNAM, 1932; Professor of Introduction to the Study of Law, National School of Law, UNAM, 1932-35; Professor of the General Theory of the State, National School of Law, UNAM,

1935-48; Secretary of the University of Guanajuato, 1936; *Secretary General of UNAM*, 1946; LLD, National School of Law, UNAM, 1951. d-*Alternate Senator* from Guanajuato, 1946-52; *Senator* from Guanajuato, 1970-76, member of the permanent committee, member of the Gran Comisión, President of the Second Justice committee, President of the Second Instructive Section of the Grand Jury, and First Secretary of the Constitutional Affairs Committee. e-None. f-Judge of the Superior Tribunal of Justice of the State of Guanajuato, 1936; Secretary General of PIPSA, 1937-39; *Oficial Mayor of Labor*, 1940; Judge of the Superior Tribunal of Justice of the State of Guanajuato, 1941-46; General Attorney for the Legal Department, National Railroads of Mexico, 1941-45, 1947; Director of the Department of Legal Affairs, PEMEX, 1948-52; *Justice of the Supreme Court*, 1954-58, 1958-64, 1964-70; Director of Legal Affairs, Secretariat of Government, 1979-80; *Subsecretary of Government (3)*, 1980-82. g-None. h-Author of many works; consulting lawyer to the Secretariat of Agriculture, 1932-34, and to the Secretariat of the Treasury, 1935. i-*Antonio Luna Arroyo*, a close family friend; brother Ricardo, a practicing lawyer and formerly director of the National Preparatory School; married Leticia Croche; began early career under *Enrique Fernández Martínez* in Guanajuato; important professor to *José López Portillo*. j-None. k-Outspoken critic of issues discussed in the Senate, 1974. l-DGF56, 567; DJBM, 120; DGF51, I, 6; DGF50, II, 281, 386; *Justicia*; C de S, 1946-52, 1970-76; WNM, 192; López, 9443; C de S, 1970-76, 84; Enc. Mex., XI, 1977, 152; *Excélsior*, 23 Sept. 1982, 4, 22; HA, 16 Oct. 1982, 15.

Rivera Silva, Manuel
a-1913. b-Federal District. c-Primary studies at public and private schools in

the Federal District; secondary studies at Secondary School No. 1, Federal District; preparatory studies at the National Preparatory School; law degree from the National School of Law, UNAM, 1937 (honorable mention), thesis published; Professor of Law, National School of Law, UNAM (twenty-three years). d-None. e-None. f-Delegate of the Office of the Attorney General to the Federal District, 1937; Minor Judge, Federal District; Criminal Judge of the 5th Criminal Court; Inspector General of the Office of the Attorney General; Assistant Fiscal Attorney for the Federal Government; Director General of the Division of Social Welfare, Secretariat of Labor, 1952-58; *Justice of the Supreme Court*, 1958-64, 1964-70, 1970-73. g-Student activist at the National Preparatory School; founder of the student intellectual magazine, *Barandal*, 1931. h-Practiced law, 1937. i-Son of lawyer Manuel Rivera Vázquez and Concepción Silva; married María Elvira Delgado; student of *Luis Chico Goerne* and *Francisco González de la Vega*. j-None. k-None. l-*Justicia*, July 1967; DGF56, 398; WNM, 192; *Excélsior*, 29 Feb., 1960.

Rivera Uribe, Diódoro
a-Dec. 19, 1916. b-Amacuzac, Morelos. c-Early education unknown; law degree, National School of Law, UNAM, Oct. 13, 1943; Professor at the Training Academy for Judicial Police of the Federal District; Founding Professor of Agrarian Law, University of Morelos. d-*Federal Deputy* from the State of Morelos, 1961-64, Dist. 1, President of the Sugar Industry Committee, the Editorial Committee, and the Fourth Interparliamentary Committee; *Senator* from the State of Morelos, 1964-70, member of the Agrarian Department Committee, the Indigenous Affairs Committee, the Legislative Studies Committee, the National Waters and Irrigation Committee, and

President of the Treasury Committee; Secretary and Vice President of the Gran Comisión. e-General delegate of PRI to Yucatán, Quintana Roo, Oaxaca, San Luis Potosí, Guanajuato, and Tlaxcala; Director of the IEPES of PRI for Morelos; President of the State Committee of PRI for Morelos. f-Investigator for the Institute of Historical Investigations, UNAM; Agent of the Ministerio Público of the Office of the Attorney General; Chief of Special Services of the National Railroads of Mexico; Chief of the Federal Fiscal Police; Assis-tant Director of the Federal Judicial Police; Director of the Campaign for the Control of the Drug Traffic in the North West; President of the Superior Tribunal of Justice of the State of Morelos. g-Secretary of Organization of the Federation of University Students; President, Student Society of the National School of Law, UNAM. h-Created the Social Service System for fourth and fifth year students in Federal Agencies. i-Half brother of *Felipe Rivera Crespo*, Governor of Morelos, 1970-76. j-None. k-Organized the private schools of the Federal District to support *Lázaro Cárdenas* during the petroleum expropriation, 1938. l-C de D, 1961-63; C de S, 1964-70; DBM68, 520-21.

Rivero Serrano, Octavio
a-July 15, 1929. b-Puebla, Puebla. c-Early education unknown; medical degree, National School of Medicine, UNAM, with an honorable mention, 1952; Professor in Neumology, Graduate School of Medicine, UNAM, 1968; professor, National School of Medicine, UNAM, 1955-77; Dean, National School of Medicine, UNAM, 1977-81; *Rector of UNAM*, 1981-85. d-None. e-None. f-Executive Secretary, Council of General Health, Secretariat of Health. g-None. h-Director, Department of Experimental Surgery, General Hospital, 1955-67; Medical Subdirector,

National Railroads of Mexico Hospital; Medical Subdirector, San Fernando Hospital; Director of Neumology, Secretariat of Communications Hospital, 1964-66; Director, Neumology Unit, General Hospital; Subdirector General, General Hospital. j-None. k-None. l-*Excélsior*, 4 Dec. 1980, 1; Protag., 294.

Riviello Bazán, Antonio

a-Nov. 21, 1926. b-Federal District. c-Primary studies at Efrén Valenzuela School, Mexico City; secondary studies at Secondary School No. 6, Mexico City; cadet, Heroic Military College, 1942-44, graduating as a 2nd Lieutenant; diploma, staff and command, Higher War College, 1950-52, graduating Jan. 1, 1953; Instructor, Higher War College, 1950, 1965; Subdirector, Heroic Military College, 1965-68. d-None. e-None. f-*Secretary of National Defense*, 1988-94. g-None. h-None. i-Son of Brigadier General Rodolfo Riviello Valdez and Concepción Bazán Peña; brother of General Rodolfo Riviello Bazán; married Victoria Vidrio Olivares. j-Joined the Army as a cadet, July 16, 1942; rank of 1st Lieutenant, July 1, 1946; officer, Motorized Brigade, 1944-49; officer, 32nd Infantry Battalion, 1949-50; attached to Staff, Secretariat of National Defense, 1953; officer, commando group, presidential guards, 1953; attached to Staff, Secretariat of National Defense, 1953; staff officer, 24th Military Zone, Cuernavaca, Morelos, 1953-57; rank of 1st Captain, Nov. 20, 1957; company commander and chief of instruction, 43rd Infantry Battalion, 1958-60; rank of Major, Nov. 20, 1959; assigned to the 22nd Military Zone, Toluca, México, 1959-60; Assistant Chief of Staff, 19th Military Zone, Villa Cuauhtemoc, Veracruz, 1960-62; second in command, 43rd Infantry Battalion, 1962-63; rank of Lt. Colonel, Nov. 20, 1963; rank of Colonel, Nov. 20, 1968; Commander, 4th Infantry Battalion,

1968-70; Assistant Chief of Staff, Secretariat of National Defense, 1970-73; rank of Brigadier General, 1973; Chief of Staff, 2nd Military Zone, El Cipres, Baja California, 1973; Commander of the 3rd Military Zone, La Paz, Baja California del Sur, 1973-76; Commander of the 21st Military Zone, Morelia, Michoacán, 1977-80; rank of Division General, 1977; Commander of the 25th Military Zone, Puebla, Puebla, 1980-82; Inspector General of the Army and Air Force, 1983-84; Military Attaché to Spain, 1985-86; Inspector General of the Secretariat of National Defense, 1987-88. k-None. l-Rev. de Ejer., Nov. 1983, 38, Feb. 1960, 22, Nov. 1968, 54; QesQAP, 84; DBGM, 356; Rev. de Ejer., Aug. 1975, 144; DBGM89, 300; DBGM87, 331; DBGM92; Rev. de Ejer., Dec. 1988, 11-12.

Rizzo García, Sócrates

a-Sept. 14, 1945. b-Linares, Nuevo León. c-Early education unknown; began studies in medicine but switched to economics, on a government scholarship, Autonomous University of Nuevo León, 1964-69, with a thesis on "The Primary Determinants of Monetary Demand and Supply in Mexico"; MA in economics, Colegio de México, 1969-71; Ph.D. in economics, University of Chicago, 1971-75; Professor of Economics, IPN and ITAM, 1975-76; Professor, Monterrey Technological Institute of Higher Studies and Autonomous Metropolitan University, 1977; Professor, UNAM, 1978-79; Professor, University of Chicago, 1978-82. d-*Federal Deputy* from the Federal District, Dist. 38, 1985-88, president of the Budget Committee; Mayor of Monterrey, Nuevo León; *Governor of Nuevo León*, 1991- . e-Joined PRI, 1960; President of PRI in Nuevo León. f-Adviser, General Coordinator of Social and Economic Programs, Secretariat of the Presidency (Programming and Budgeting), 1975-76;

Adviser, General Manager of Industrial Programs, National Finance Bank, 1976-77; Chief of Advisers to the Director General, National Finance Bank, 1970-79; Director of Treasury Policy Studies, Secretariat of the Treasury, 1979-81; Director, Macro Economic Analysis, Secretariat of Programming and Budgeting, 1982-83; Director General of Economic and Social Policy, Secretariat of Programming and Budget, 1982-85. g-Member of the Spartacus Leninist League as a student; Secretary of Planning and Development, CEN of CNOP of PRI, 1965-87. h-Worked as a ticket taker, Monterrey-Reynosa bus route, as a boy; fruit seller, Florida Market, Monterrey. i-Son of Agapito Rizzo Rizzo, public employee, who was often unemployed during son's childhood, and Jovita García Decanini; married Alma Elisa Reyes Martínez, economist; began political activities under Arturo de la Garza leftist study groups, 1962-63; political disciple of *Leopoldo Solís*, who arranged his first job in the secretariat of the presidency; longtime friend of *Carlos Salinas* since career in the secretariat of the presidency. j-None. k-None. l-*El Nacional*, 17 Mar. 1991, 7; *Proceso*, 25 Feb. 1991, 16; DBGM87, 552; DBGM92, 823.

Robledo Cabello, Luis
a-May 14, 1935. b-Saltillo, Coahuila. c-Early education unknown; civil engineering degree, National School of Engineering, UNAM, 1958-62; MA degree in public works planning, UNAM, 1966; professor, National School of Engineering and the National School of Economics, UNAM, 1959-66. d-None. e-Collaborator, IEPES of PRI, 1976; speaker, Popular Consultation Meetings, IEPES of PRI, 1982. f-Chief of the Division of Operations and Conservation of Potable Water, Secretariat of Hydraulic Resources, 1973-74; Subdirector General of Studies, Secretariat

of Hydraulic Resources, 1974-75; Executive Secretary of the Water Commission, Valle de México, 1975-80; Director General of Water Storage and Transfer, Secretariat of Agriculture and Hydraulic Resources, 1980-81; *Subsecretary of Hydraulic Infrastructure*, Secretariat of Hydraulic Resources, 1981-82. g-None. h-None. j-None. k-None. l-DAPC81.

Robledo Santiago, Edgar
a-Sept. 20, 1917. b-Motozintla, Chiapas (Colonia Belisario Domínguez). c-Primary studies at the Rural School of Motozintla, Chiapas, and at the Cuauhtémoc School of Huixtla, Chiapas; rural school teacher, 1934; studied on scholarship at the Rural Normal School, Cerrohueco, Chiapas, 1935; urban teaching certificate from the Normal Urban School, Tuxtla Gutiérrez, Chiapas, 1944-49; professor at the Institute of Arts and Sciences of Chiapas. d-*Federal Deputy* from the State of Chiapas, Dist. 3, 1967-70, member of the Cultural Affairs Committee; *Senator* from the State of Chiapas, 1970, 1975-76. e-None. f-Inspector of Rural Normal Schools, Secretariat of Public Education, 1952; *Director General of the FSTSE*, 1968-70; *Director General of the ISSSTE*, 1970-75. g-Secretary General of the National Union of Educational Employees, 1964-67. h-None. i-From very poor economic circumstances; alternated going to school with work as an agricultural laborer; married Cristina Brindis. j-None. k-None. l-HA, 7 Dec. 1970, 27; HA, 5 Apr. 1971, 14; WWMG, 34; C de D, 1967-69, 58; MGF69; DBC, 212-215; *Justicia*, Apr. 1973; WNM, 193; HA, 29 Sept. 1975, 10.

Robles, Gonzalo
(Deceased) a-1895. b-Cartago, Costa Rica. c-Primary studies at the Colegio de San Luis Gonzaga, Cartago, Costa

Rica; preparatory studies in Guadalajara, Jalisco; agricultural engineering studies, National School of Agriculture, 1909-11, 1912-13, on a fellowship, graduating as an agricultural engineer, July 1913; studied in the United States, 1911-12; degree in civil engineering, Valparaiso University, Indiana, 1917-21, revalidated in Mexico as an engineering degree in agronomy and hydraulics, 1922; Director, Central Agricultural Schools, 1925. d-None. e-None. f-Special mission to the United States to study agricultural colleges for Venustiano Carranza, 1916; adviser to the Secretary of Agriculture, 1922; technical adviser to President Calles, 1923; adviser to the Office of Economic Statistics, National Railroads of Mexico, 1932; Director General of the National Mortgage and Public Works Bank, 1933-35; *Director General of the Bank of Mexico,* 1935; founder and Director of the Department of Industrial Research, Bank of Mexico, 1946-52; Director General of the Agricultural Bank, 1935-38; adviser to the Bank of Mexico, 1938-79. g-Member of the Agrarian Commission in Veracruz. h-Participated in various agrarian congresses in Mexico City, 1921-22; worked for a private firm in Molango, Hidalgo, 1914-15. i-Grandfather was a physician; longtime friend of *Jesús Silva Herzog* and *Eduardo Villaseñor* since the 1920s; he and *Jesús Silva Herzog* attempted to create a system of ejido banks in 1926. j-None. k-Came to Mexico in 1909. l-Villaseñor, E. 92; Zevada, 117-18; Beltrán, 310-11; MGF47, 322; DGF51, II, 7, 293; DGF50, II, 11; DP, 2365; Villaseñor, II, 196; JSH, 336-38; Gómez, 442-443.

Robles León Martín del Campo, Jaime
a-1912. b-Jalisco. c-Secondary and preparatory studies in Guadalajara; law degree, Mexico City; Professor of Constitutional Law, Free School of Law, Mexico City, and Guadalajara; co-founder and supporter of the Autonomous University of Guadalajara. d-*Federal Deputy* from the State of Jalisco, Dist. 3, 1949-52, alternate member of the Consular Service and Diplomatic Committee. e-Member of PAN; cofounder of PAN with *Manuel Gómez Morín, Efraín González Luna* and others. f-None. g-None. h-Political commentator in newspapers and radios of Jalisco; practicing lawyer and notary. i-Son of Emiliano Robles León, lawyer and notary, and María del Refugio Martín; from three generations of lawyers; father of Martha Robles, well-known novelist; cousin of Ernesto Robles León, chief excutive officer of Bacardi. j-None. k-First candidate of PAN to run for governor of Jalisco; opposed *Agustín Yáñez* for the governorship in a hotly contested campaign in 1953; as a federal deputy fought for the revision of Articles 145 and 145bis of the federal Constitution. l-Letter; C de D, 1949-52; DGF51, I, 22, 36.

Robles Linares, Luis
a-Sept. 11, 1922. b-Ensenada, Baja California del Norte. c-Early education unknown; engineering degree from the National Polytechnic Institute, 1944; OAS scholarship to study agricultural planning and regional development in Tel Aviv, 1966. d-None. e-None. f-Chief of Resident Engineers, Obregón Dam, Sonora; Director of Construction, Cuauhtémoc Dam Irrigation zone; Chief of the Sonora Irrigation Zone, Secretariat of Hydraulic Resources; Chief of Construction, Small Irrigation Works, Sonora; Director of Potable Water, Sonora; Second Chief Engineer of Irrigation and Flood Control, Secretariat of Hydraulic Resources, 1968-70; *Subsecretary (A) of Hydraulic Resources,* 1970-76; *Subsecretary in Charge of Hydraulic Resources,* 1976; *Secretary of Hydraulic Resources,* 1976-77. g-None. h-None. i-Married María

de Jesús Gandara. j-None. k-Acquired Sonoran residency, 1946; precandidate for governor of Sonora, 1977. l-HA, 14 Dec. 1970, 22; DPE71, 88; _Excélsior_, 1 Dec. 1976; HA, 6 Dec. 1976, 23; _Excélsior_, 10 Sept. 1978, 12.

Robles Martínez, Jesús
a-Aug. 2, 1913. b-Colima, Colima. c-Engineering degree in electrical communications from the Higher School of Mechanical and Electrical Engineering, National Polytechnic Institute; Professor of Physics and Mathematics, National Polytechnic Institute; Director of Instruction, IPN; Subdirector General of IPN. d-_Federal Deputy_ from the State of Colima, Dist. 2, 1952-55, member of the Public Education Committee, the Credentials Committee, and the Consular and Diplomatic Service Committee, President of the Chamber, Sept. 1952; _Senator_ from the State of Colima, 1964-65. e-PRI state committeeman from Colima. f-_Secretary General of the FSTSE_, 1964-65; Director General of the National Bank of Public Works and Services, 1965-76. g-Leader of student groups at IPN, 1935; President of the National Federation of Technical Students, 1936; Secretary General of the National Union of Educational Employees, 1949-52. h-None. i-Brother Roberto was general manager of the National Public Works Bank, 1971-76; formed a powerful political clique with _Alfonso Martínez Domínguez_ and _Rómulo Sánchez Mireles_ in the FSTSE. j-None. k-Accused in the press of being a latifundista and using rich lands in San Luis Potosí for cattle raising; leader of the "Colima Group" in his home state; answered _Miguel Alemán_'s last State of the Union address, 1952. l-C de D, 1952-54, 18; MGF69, 516; WWMG, 34; HA, 7 Dec. 1970, 27; _Hoy_, 1 May 1971, 12; _Hoy_, 3 June 1972, 9; _Excélsior_, 26 June 1975, 4, 10 Dec. 1978, 18, 18 Mar. 1977, 12; HA, 8 Apr. 1974, 25.

Robles Quintero, Salvador
(Deceased June 29, 1992) a-Mar. 20, 1934. b-San Miguel Zapotitlán, Sinaloa. c-Early education unknown; economics studies, Higher School of Economics, National Polytechnic Institute, 1954-59, graduating with a thesis on "Credit to Small and Medium Industry in Mexico," 1962; MA in public administration, Harvard University, 1963-64. d-_Federal Deputy_ from the State of Sinaloa, Dist. 4, 1973-76, Dist. 6, 1985-88; _Federal Deputy_ from the Federal District, Dist. 39, 1992. e-Joined PRI, 1954; General Delegate of the IEPES of PRI to various states, 1969; Subsecretary of Organization of the CEN of PRI, 1981; Subsecretary of Information and Propaganda of the CEN of PRI, 1982. f-Economist, Division of Prices, Secretariat of Industry and Commerce, 1957-59; General Manager of the National Film Bank, 1970-76; Director of Theaters, Mexico City, 1977-78; Director General of Organization and Methods, Department of the Federal District, 1977; Director of Social Services, Department of the Federal District, 1977-78; Secretary of the Nomenclature Committee, Department of the Federal District, 1977-78; _Subsecretary of Planning and Organizational Infrastructure_, Secretariat of Agrarian Reform, 1983-85. g-Auxiliary Secretary of the CNC, 1965-76; Secretary of Programs, CEN of CNOP of PRI, 1973. h-None. i-Son of Lorenzo Montiel, peasant, and Rosa Estela Aguayo Carillo; married Esther Quintero Ruiz. j-None. k-None. l-Q es Q, 378; C de D, 1973-76; DBGM, 358; DBGM87, 554; DBGM92, 560; _El Nacional_, 30 June 1992, 9.

Robles Segura, Raúl
a-Nov. 7, 1933. b-Federal District. c-Early education unknown; CPA studies, School of Business and Administration, UNAM, 1951-54, graduating with a thesis on state financing, 1964;

professor, School of Accounting, Ibero-American University; professor, School of Accounting and Administration, UNAM. d-None. e-Vice-President of the Economic Reform Committee of the IEPES of PRI, 1981. f-Adviser to the Federal Electric Committee, 1965-70; Assistant Controller General of the Department of the Federal District, 1971-73; Director General of Taxation, Secretariat of the Treasury, 1976-82; *Subsecretary "B" of the Controller General of Mexico*, 1983-87; Subdirector of Trade, Pemex, 1987-90; Subdirector of Petrochemicals, Pemex, 1990-94. g-None. h-Accountant, Casas Alatriste and Manuel Resa, 1963-66, 1967-76. i-Son of José Robles Arenas, industrialist, and Amelia Segura Jaimese; married Irela Víctor y Carrión. j-None. k-None. l-Q es Q.

Rocha Bandala, Juan Francisco
a-Sept. 21, 1925. b-Tuxpan, Veracruz. c-Early education unknown; law degree, National School of Law, UNAM, 1949, with a thesis on bankruptcy; Professor of Civil Law, UNAM, 1960-66. d-None. e-Director of Electoral Action, Regional Committee of PRI, Federal District, 1964; General Coordinator of the Regional Committee of PRI, Federal District, 1969. f-General Counsel for the National Railroads of Mexico, 1950-52; Chief of Advisers, IMSS, 1957-59; Chief of Labor Attorneys, Secretariat of Labor, 1959-60; Subdirector, Department of Labor, Secretariat of Labor, 1959-62; Subdirector of Social Welfare, Secretariat of Labor, 1962-64; Subdirector General, Federal Property Registration, Secretariat of Government Properties, 1965; Chief of Labor Relations, IMSS, 1966-74; General Coordinator, Legal Affairs, National Ejido and Agricultural Credit Bank, 1975-76; President, Federal Board of Conciliation and Arbitration, 1976-79; *Oficial Mayor of the Secretariat of Agriculture and*

Hydraulic Resources, 1980-82; Subdirector, Legal Department, IMSS, 1982-88, 1988-89. g-Delegate of the CNOP in Chihuahua, Tabasco, and Veracruz, 1960-63. h-None. i-Son of Guillermo Rocha Sánchez, lawyer, and Raquel Bandala Sánchez; married Lucrecia Ladrón de Guevara. j-None. k-None. l-Protag., 295; DAPC81; DBGM89, 302; DBGM, 359.

Rocha (Cordero) Jr., Antonio
a-Apr. 6, 1912. b-Cerritos, San Luis Potosí. c-Primary studies, Ignacio Aguilar and Morelos School, under Fernando Vázquez; preparatory studies, University of San Luis Potosí; law degree, University of San Luis Potosí, June 13, 1935; Professor of Penal Law. d-*Alternate Federal Deputy* from the State of San Luis Potosí, Dist. 1, 1943-46; *Federal Deputy* from the State of San Luis Potosí, Dist. 1, 1949-52, member of the Library Committee (1st year), the First and Second Legislative Studies Committee, the Gran Comisión, and the Second Constitutional Affairs Committee; *Alternate Senator* from San Luis Potosí, 1946-49; *Senator* from the State of San Luis Potosí, 1952-58, member of the Gran Comisión, the Protocol Committee, the First Government Committee, President of the Second Constitutional Affairs Committee, member of the Third Labor Committee, and the Special Legislative Studies Committee; substitute member of the First Public Education Committee and the First Ejido Committee; *Governor of San Luis Potosí*, 1967-73; *Federal Deputy* from the State of San Luis Potosí, Dist. 1, 1979-82. e-None. f-Attorney, City Council, San Luis Potosí, 1939-41; Attorney, Department of Government, San Luis Potosí; Attorney General of San Luis Potosí, 1943-46; Secretary General of the State of San Luis Potosí, 1947-48; Attorney General of Tamaulipas, 1948; *Attorney*

General of Mexico, 1964-67; Justice of the Supreme Court, 1973-78. g-Delegate to the Seventh National Student Congress, San Luis Potosí, 1930. h-Practicing lawyer, 1935-43; founder and editor of the Penal Law Review, University of San Luis Potosí, 1939-43. i-Married Socorro Díaz del Castillo; Professor of Gustavo Carvajal; father was a pharmacist; brother Rafael served as Assistant Director of the Secret Service. j-None. k-Praised by Por Qué for his honesty as Governor of San Luis Potosí. l-El Universal, 1 Dec. 1964; WWMG, 34; DGF56, 7, 9-14; DGF47, 21; HA, 7 Dec. 1964, 21; DPE65, 209; DGF51, I, 7, 25, 29, 31, 32, 35; C de D, 1949-51, 88; Por Qué, 11 Dec. 1969; Enc. Mex., XI, 1977, 159; Ind. Biog., 132-33; Excélsior, 27 Feb. 1979, 14; Guerra Leal, 236.

Rocha Díaz, Salvador
a-Dec. 21, 1937. b-San Miguel de Allende, Guanajuato. c-Early education unknown; law degree, National School of Law, UNAM, 1954-58; diploma in comparative law, University of Strasbourg, France, 1963-65; professor, National School of Law, UNAM, 1964-72; professor, University of California, 1967; professor, Ibero-American University, 1967-74; professor, St. Mary's University, 1964. d-Federal Deputy from the State of Guanajuato, Dist. 9, 1982-85. e-Joined PRI, 1961. f-Secretary General of Government, State of Guanajuato, 1984-85; Director General of Legal Affairs, Secretariat of Government, 1985-88; Justice of the Supreme Court, 1989-92; Secretary of Government, State of Guanajuato, 1992- . g-Oficial Mayor of the CEN of CNOP, 1983-85. h-Senior partner, Rocha and Hegewisch, 1959-82. i-Son of Manuel Rocha Lassaulx, lawyer, and Carmen Díaz Sautto; married Eugenia Landero Flores. j-None. k-None. l-El Nacional, 23 June 1992; DBGM92, 824; C de D, 1982-85.

Rocha Garfias, Ramón
a-Sept. 8, 1906. b-Orizaba, Veracruz. c-Primary studies in Orizaba; preparatory studies in Mexico City; medical degree, National School of Medicine, UNAM, 1927; postgraduate work, Galveston, Texas. d-Federal Deputy from the State of Veracruz, Dist. 9, 1964-67. e-Founding member of the Popular Party, 1948; Secretary General of the PPS in Veracruz, 1964; member of the Central Committee of the PPS, 1964. f-Director of the Municipal Board of Public Welfare, Orizaba, 1944-46; Director of Medical Services, IMSS, Orizaba, 1947. g-None. h-Physician. i-Son of a lawyer. j-None. k-None. l-Directorio, 1964-67; C de D, 1964-67.

Rodríguez, Damian L.
(Deceased) a-June 6, 1887. b-Ramos Arizpe, Coahuila. c-Early education unknown; no degree. d-Federal Deputy from the State of Coahuila, Dist. 3, 1937-40; Senator from the State of Coahuila, 1940-46. e-None. g-None. h-None. j-Career army officer; rank of Brigadier General. k-Grand Master of the National Mexican Masonic Grand Lodge. l-Peral, 698; C de D, 1937-39, 19; C de S, 1940-46.

Rodríguez Adame, Julián
a-July 11, 1904. b-Pachuca, Hidalgo. c-Primary studies at the Benito Juárez School under Teodomiro Manzano, Pachuca, and the Annex to the Normal School; secondary studies at the Annex to the Normal School; preparatory studies at the Scientific and Literary Institute of Pachuca; engineering degree in agriculture from the National School of Agriculture, Chapingo; Director of the Central Agricultural School, Mexico, 1932-34; Professor of Agricultural Economics, National School of Economics, UNAM, 1939-56. d-Federal Deputy from the State of Hidalgo, Dist. 1, 1955-57, member of the Gran

Comisión, the Tariff and Foreign Trade Committee, and the First Treasury Committee; *Alternate Senator* from the State of Hidalgo, 1952-58, but replaced Senator Cravioto after he died, 1957-58; *Senator* from the State of Hidalgo, 1958-64, but never held office. e-Founding member of the PNR, 1929. f-Engineer in various technical positions for the National Agrarian Commission; Chief, Agrarian Department, Secretariat of Agriculture, 1934-35; Director of the Department of Credit, National Ejido Credit Bank, 1936; Director of the National Bank of Commerce, 1939; Manager, National Bank of Ejido Credit, 1938-39; *Secretary General of the Department of Agarian Affairs*, 1940-44; Director General of Prices, Secretariat of Industry and Commerce, 1946-55; *Director General of CONASUPO*, 1957-58; *Secretary of Agriculture and Livestock*, 1958-64; Ambassador to Japan, 1965-68; Ambassador to Pakistan, 1968-70. g-None. h-Adviser to various decentralized agencies; member of the Board of the National Savings Bank, 1974. i-Friends with *Mario Sousa* and *Adolfo López Mateos* since 1933; married Mercedes Santana; son of Julián S. Rodríguez, employee of the San Rafael Mining Company, who participated in the Revolution. j-None. k-*Por Qué* claims he was involved in a land deal with *Juan José Torres Landa* while serving as Secretary of Agriculture. l-HA, 28 Dec. 1951, 35; HA, 8 Dec. 1958, 28; DGF51, II, 29; DPE61, 69; DGF51, I, 263; *Por Qué*, 11 July 1969, 11; HA, 12 Dec. 1952, 6; *Excélsior*, 10 Nov. 1976.

Rodríguez Alcaine, Leónardo
a-May 1, 1919. b-Texcoco, México. c-Primary studies in Texcoco at the Colegio Juárez, completing his primary studies at the José Vicente Villada School, Mexico City; secondary studies at Secondary No. 7, Mexico City; completed two years at the School of Mechanical and Electrical Engineering, IPN; studies at the Customs Academy of the Secretariat of the Treasury. d-*Federal Deputy* from the Federal District, Dist. 8, 1955-58, member of the Electric Industry Committee; *Alternate Federal Deputy* from the State of México, Dist. 2, 1964-67; *Federal Deputy* from the State of México, Dist. 7, 1967-70, member of the Communications and Transportation Section of the Legislative Studies Committee; *Federal Deputy* from the State of México, Dist. 7, 1973-76; *Senator* from México, 1976-82, 1988-94. e-None. f-Subdirector of the General Warehouse, Federal Electric Commission. g-Secretary of Labor and Conflicts of Section 1, Union of Workers of the Federal Electric Commission, 1941-42; Secretary of Sports Action of the National Executive Committee of the Union of Workers of the Federal Electric Commission, 1942-45; Secretary of Organization of the CEN of the Union Workers of the Federal Electric Commission, 1945-51; Secretary of Organization and Publicity of the Union of Workers of the Federal Electric Commission, 1951-59; Secretary of Labor of SUTERM, 1975; *Secretary General of SUTERM*, Mar. 28, 1975- . h-First employed as a porter at the National Electric Commission, 1938. i-Longtime ally of *Francisco Pérez Rios* until his death in 1975; married Margarita Salazar Fernández. j-None. k-None. l-Ind. Biog., 134-35; *Excélsior*, 26 Mar. 1975, 4; DGF56, 25, 34; C de D, 1955-58, 1967-70, 70, 1964-67, 55; C de S, 1976-82; DBGM89, 526; DBGM92, 560.

Rodríguez Arcos, Ezequiel
a-Apr. 11, 1912. b-Champoton, Campeche. c-Early education unknown; teaching certificate; teacher. d-*Federal Deputy* (Party Deputy from the PPS), 1967-70. e-Member of the PPS; Secretary General of the PPS, State of Jalisco.

f-Federal school inspector. g-Member of the SNTE. h-None. i-Married Rosario Otal. k-None. l-C de D, 1967-70; Directorio, 1967-70.

Rodríguez Barrera, Rafael
a-Feb. 10, 1937. b-Guadalupe Barrio, Campeche, Campeche. c-Primary studies at the Justo Sierra Méndez Primary School, Campeche, 1942-48; secondary studies at the Instituto Campechano, 1948-53; studied law at the Instituto Campechano and completed his degree at the University of Campeche, Dec. 20, 1958; Professor of English, Spanish, Ethics, and Philosophy, Teachers Literacy Institute, Campeche; Professor of Constitutional Law, University of Campeche. d-Local Deputy to the State Legislature of Campeche, 1962; Mayor of Campeche, 1963-64; *Federal Deputy* from the State of Campeche, Dist. 1, 1970-73, member of the Gran Comisión, the Cooperative Development Committee, the Second Treasury Committee, the Fish and Game Committee, and the Second Constitutional Affairs Committee; *Governor of Campeche*, 1973-79. e-President of PRI in Campeche, 1962-64; *Secretary of Organization of the CEN of PRI*, 1972-73; member of the National Council of PRI; *Secretary of Internal Affairs of the CEN of PRI*, 1979-80; *Oficial Mayor of the CEN of PRI*, 1980-81. f-Public Defender, 1957-58; Secretary of the City Council of Campeche, 1958; Private Secretary to the Mayor of Campeche, *Eugenio Echeverría Castellot*, 1961-62; Director of Public Security and Traffic, Campeche; Secretary General of Government of the State of Campeche under Governor *Carlos Sansores Pérez*, 1967-69; *Subsecretary of Agrarian Organization*, Secretariat of Agrarian Reform, 1981-82; *Subsecretary of Agarian Affairs*, Secretariat of Agrarian Reform, 1982-86; *Secretary of Agrarian Affairs*, 1986-88. g-Manager,

National Chamber of Fishing Industries. h-Adviser, National Bank of Agricultural Credit. i-Son of Ramiro Rodríguez Aguayo, college professor, and Dolores Barrera Conde; married Socorro Cabrera, normal teacher; his cousin Sergio Mora Rodríguez was Oficial Mayor of the State Government of Campeche. j-None. k-Resigned as Mayor of Campeche because of grave differences with Governor *José Ortiz Avila*. l-Directorio, 1970-72; HA, 8 Jan. 1973, 34; C de D, 1970-72, 133; HA, 17 Sept. 1973, 40-43; Enc. Mex., Annual, 1977, 540-41; *Excélsior*, 6 Aug. 1978, 29; DBGM87, 335.

Rodríguez Cano, Enrique
(Deceased 1956) a-1912. b-Balcázar, Tuxpan, Veracruz. c-Early education unknown; no degree. d-Local Deputy to the State Legislature of Veracruz, 1944-45; Mayor of Tuxpan, Veracruz, 1936-38; *Federal Deputy* from the State of Veracruz, Dist. 2, 1949-52, member of the Gran Comisión, the National Waters and Irrigation Committee, the Agrarian Department Committee, and Vice-President for the Preparatory Committees. e-None. f-Tax collector, Alamo, Veracruz; Director of Printing, State Legislature of Veracruz, 1938-40; Director of the Library for the Federal Congress, 1940-42; Subsecretary of Government of the State of Veracruz, under *Adolfo Ruiz Cortines*, 1948; *Oficial Mayor of Government*, 1950-52, under Secretary *Adolfo Ruiz Cortines*; *Secretary of the Presidency*, 1952-56. g-Secretary General of the League of Agrarian Communities of the State of Veracruz, 1946, under Governor *Ruiz Cortines*. h-Began work in tax administration as a student. i-Personal confidant of *Adolfo Ruiz Cortines*; brother of engineer *Francisco Rodríguez Cano*, federal deputy from Veracruz, 1964-67; son of Enrique Rodríguez Rios and Francisca Cano Achaual. j-None.

k-*Ramón Beteta* has stated that *Ruiz Cortines* was not very much at ease with the college graduates of the *Alemán* administration, which is a reason why he placed so much confidence in *Rodríguez Cano* for many years. l-DGF51, I, 26, 29, 30, 31; C de D, 1949-51, 88; HA, 5 Dec. 1962, 10; DGF56, 53; DP70, 1788.

Rodríguez Canton, Juan de Dios
a-Feb. 20, 1942. b-Valladolid, Yucatán. c-Early education unknown; teaching certificate; principal, elementary school, 1962-64; professor, Higher Normal School, 1966-71. d-None. e-joined PRI, 1961. f-Chief, Technical Primary Education Department, Secretariat of Public Education, 1965-77; Private Secretary to the General Coordinator of Education of the Federal District Marginalized Zones, Secretariat of Public Education, 1977-78; Director General of Normal Education, Secretariat of Public Education, 1981-86; adviser, Oficial Mayor of the Secretariat of Public Education, 1987-88; *Subsecretary of Elementary Education*, Secretariat of Public Education, 1989-91. g-None. h-None. i-Son of Juan de Dios Rodríguez Heredia, teacher, and Esther Cantón Sáyago, teacher; married María Cristina Yáñez Loria. j-None. k-None. l-DBGM89, 303.

Rodríguez Claveria, José
(Deceased Mar. 19, 1958) a-May 30, 1892. b-Veracruz, Veracruz. c-Primary and secondary studies in Veracruz; no degree. d-*Federal Deputy* from the State of Veracruz, Dist. 9, 1949-52, member of the Second Treasury Committee, the Naval Committee, the Budget and Accounts Committee, the Insurance Committee, and the Tourism Committee; *Senator* from the State of Veracruz, 1952-57, President of the Gran Comisión, President of the First Committee on Credit, Money, and Cre-

dit Institutions and of the First Treasury Committee. e-None. f-Police Chief of Mérida under Salvador Alvarado; Director of Tourism, State of Veracruz; Director General of Tourism, Secretariat of Government, 1948-49. g-None. h-Founder of Financiera y Fiduciaria Veracruz, S.A.; Managing Director of Finanzas Mexicanas, S.A. i-Cofounded Financiera y Fiduciaria Veracruz with *Cosme Hinojosa*; helped *Adolfo Ruiz Cortines* become Oficial Mayor of the Department of the Federal District in 1935 after recommending him to *Cosme Hinojosa*. j-Joined the Revolution under General Salvador Alvarado; member of the General Staff of General Alvarado; rank of major; supported the de la Huerta rebellion, 1923. k-Exile in the United States, 1923. l-HA, 29 Oct. 1956; López, 970; Ind. Biog., 135-36; C de D, 1949-52, 88; DGF56, 8, 9, 10, 11.

Rodríguez de Campos, Gloria
a-Sept. 24, 1926. b-Federal District. c-Early education unknown; certificate in primary education, National Normal School, Mexico City; certificate as an education technician, Higher Normal School, Mexico City. d-*Federal Deputy* (Party Deputy from the PPS), 1967-70. e-Member of the PPS. f-None. g-None. i-Married Dr. Rafael Campos López. j-None. k-Directorio, 1967-70; C de D, 1967-70.

Rodríguez de Casas, Elizabeth
a-Oct. 28, 1948. b-Puebla, Puebla. c-Early education unknown; psychology degree, University of Puebla; postgraduate courses at various universities; studies toward an MA in public administration; professor at the University of Puebla; instructor, IMSS; instructor, course in television. d-Alternate Local Deputy to the State Legislature of Puebla; *Federal Deputy* from the State of Puebla, Dist. 7, 1979-82, member of the 3rd Labor Committee, the Foreign

Relations Committee, the Transportation Committee, the Tourism Committee, and the Complaints Committee. e-Coordinator of the Women's Section of the CNOP of PRI in Puebla during the presidential campaign of *José López Portillo*, 1976. f-Director, Department of Complaints, Consular Division, Secretariat of Foreign Relations. g-None. h-None. j-None. k-None. l-C de D, 1979-82; Romero Aceves, 731-33.

Rodríguez Elías, José
a-Dec. 21, 1919. b-San Pedro, Zacatecas. c-Primary studies in Santa Piedra Gorda; secondary and preparatory studies in Zacatecas, Zacatecas; engineering degree in topography, National School of Agriculture, Chapingo; Professor of Agriculture, Practical School of Agriculture, La Llave, Guerrero. d-*Alternate Federal Deputy* from the State of Zacatecas, Dist. 4, 1949-52; *Federal Deputy* from the State of Zacatecas, Dist. 1, 1952-55, Vice-President of the Chamber of Deputies, Nov. 1953, member of the Social Welfare Committee, the Securities Committee, and the Agrarian Department Committee; *Senator* from the State of Zacatecas, 1958-62, member of the National Waters and Irrigation Committee, the First Committee on Mines; President of the General Means of Communication Committee, member of the Second Balloting Committee and substitute member of the Special Committee on Small Agricultural Property; *Governor of Zacatecas*, 1962-67. e-President of the Regional Committee of PRI for the State of Zacatecas, 1954-58. f-Agricultural technician, Department of Indigenous Affairs, 1941; topographical engineer, Department of Agrarian Affairs, 1943-44; Subdirector of the Delegation of the Department of Agrarian Affairs, Zacatecas, 1945; Director of the Department of Agrarian Affairs, Zacatecas, 1946-47, 1949-52; Director General of

the National Bank of Ejido Credit, 1968-70. g-Secretary General of the League of Agrarian Communites and Unions, Zacatecas, 1948-49; member of the CEN of the CNC, 1942-58; Chairman of the Mexican Agronomy Society, 1955-58, 1959-62; Official of the CNC. h-None. i-Son of a rancher; father was mayor of San Pedro Piedra Gorda three times. j-None. k-*Por Qué* claims he was involved in a 100 million peso scandal as Director of the National Ejido Bank, 1969. l-*Por Qué*, 11 July 1969, 3; DGF51, I; C de D, 1949-51; G of M, 10; WWMG, 35; C de D, 1955-57, 18; C de S, 1961-64, 67; MGF69, 505; Func., 411; letter.

Rodríguez Familiar, Ramón
a-Sept. 27, 1898. b-Querétaro, Querétaro. c-Early education unknown; completed second year of preparatory studies at the Colegio Civil of Querétaro; diploma, staff and command course, Higher War College. d-*Governor of Querétaro*, 1935-39. e-None. f-Private Secretary to *Abelardo Rodríguez*, Governor of Baja California del Norte, 1929-30; Subchief of Staff, 1932-33, Chief of Staff, 1933-34, and Director General of Personnel, 1940-46, all at the Secretariat of National Defense. g-None. h-None. i-Brother José is an author; son of Ramón Rodríguez Perrusquia and Josefa Familiar Bardaguez; married María Luisa Fuentes. j-Career army officer; fought under General *Abelardo Rodríguez*; joined the army as an ordinary soldier, July 15, 1914; served under Generals Francisco Coss, Alvaro Obregón, *Juan José Rios*, and Plutarco Elías Calles; rank of Brigadier General, 1942; Assistant Chief of Staff of Military Operations, 2nd Zone; Subdirector General of Personnel, Secretariat of National Defense; rank of Brigade General, 1946; Commander of the 25th Military Zone, Puebla, Puebla, 1951; Intendant General of the Army, 1951;

Commander of the 14th Military Zone, Aguascalientes, Aguascalientes, 1959; head of military mission to Guatemala, 1962; rank of Division General, Nov. 8, 1956; Inspector General of the Army, 1970-72; Director of Military Pensions, Secretariat of National Defense, 1974. k-*Gaxiola* states that he was selected for the position of Chief of Staff because of his personal loyalty to *Rodríguez*, even though he was only a colonel. l-Peral, 700; WWM45, 104; DGF51, I, 181; DPE71, 14; Gaxiola, 93; Rev. de Ejer., Mar. 1974, 95, Aug. 1959, 23, July 1961, 29, July 1974, 104.

Rodríguez Flores, Jesús M.
a-Dec. 26, 1901. b-Tepezala, Aguascalientes. c-Primary studies in Chihuahua; engineering degree, Agricultural School of Ciudad Juárez, Chihauhua, 1928. d-*Federal Deputy* from the State of Veracruz, Dist. 5, 1937-40; *Governor of Aguascalientes*, 1944-50. e-None. f-Director, Local Road Commission, Chihuahua; topographical engineer, Local Agrarian Commission, Chihuahua; engineer, Puebla, San Luis Potosí, and Veracruz; Director of Agrarian and Agricultural Reorganization, Secretariat of Agriculture and the Department of Agrarian Affairs. g-None. h-Miner in youth. i-From a poor family; father a miner; worked way through school as a miner. j-None. k-Precandidate for governor of Aguascalientes, 1939. l-HA, 28 Sept. 1945, 9; letter; C de D, 1037-40.

Rodríguez Gómez, Francisco
a-Feb. 11, 1911. b-San Antonio, Ixtlahuacán del Río, Jalisco. c-Teaching certificate; law degree, School of Law, University of Guadalajara; postgraduate studies, 1942-43; Professor, School of Economics, University of Guadalajara, 1937-46. d-*Federal Deputy* from the State of Jalisco, Dist. 6, 1955-58, member of the Legislative Studies Committee (1st year), the Committee

on National Properties and Resources; Secretary of the Committee on Agrarian Law and Assistant Secretary of the Chamber of Deputies; *Federal Deputy* from the Federal District, Dist. 6, 1961-64, member of the Second Government Committee, Secretary of the Second Legislative Studies Committee; *Federal Deputy* from the State of Jalisco, Dist. 14, 1979-82. e-General Delegate of the CNOP of PRI to Baja California; General Delegate of the CEN of PRI to Hidalgo; General Delegate of the CEN of PRI to the Presidential campaign of *Adolfo López Mateos* in Guanajuato; General Delegate of the CEN of PRI in Guanajuato (3 years); Coordinator General of the Economic and Social Assembly during *Juan Gil Preciado*'s campaign for Governor; Coordinator of Presidential Campaigns in the State of México for *Gustavo Díaz Ordaz*, 1964. f-Director of the Normal School of Jalisco, 1937-39; Director of Secondary Education, State of Jalisco, 1942-43; Chief of the Education Department of Guadalajara, 1944; Secretary to the City Council of Guadalajara, 1944; President of the State Arbitration Board, Jalisco, 1944-45; Secretary General of the State of Jalisco under Governor *Marcelino García Barragán*, 1945-46; Director of Public Education in Jalisco, 1946-52; Legal adviser, State of Jalisco, 1952; Chief, Legal Department, National Agricultural Credit Bank, 1953-55; Attorney General of Justice of the State of Jalisco; *Oficial Mayor of Industry and Commerce*, 1964-70; *Interim Governor of Jalisco*, 1988-89. g-None. h-None. i-Married Graciela Orendain. j-None. k-None. l-DBM68, 529; DPE65, 88; C de D, 1961-63, 89; MGF69, 252; Ind. Biog., 136.

Rodríguez Jaime, Luis Dantón
a-Aug. 28, 1933. b-Guanajuato, Guanajuato. c-Law degree, National School of Law, UNAM, 1953-58, with a thesis on

"State Intervention in the Economy"; scholarship from the National Finance Bank to study at CEMLA, 1958-59; graduate studies, CEMLA, Venezuela, 1962; Professor of Sociology, School of Banking and Commerce, 1962-63; Director of Economic and Social Studies Seminar, Mexican Military Academy Preparatory School; Professor of Administrative Law, National School of Law, UNAM; Professor of Civics and Political Education, CNC; Professor of Public Law, Acatlán Branch, 1977-82. d-_Federal Deputy_ from the State of Guanajuato, Dist. 1, 1964-67; President of the Budget Committee and of the Tax Committee, member of the Money, Banking, and Credit Institution Committee; President of the Chamber of Deputies, Nov. 1966; _Federal Deputy_ from the State of Guanajuato, Dist. 1, 1973-76; President of the Executive Committee, Sept., 1973; _Federal Deputy_ from the State of Guanajuato, Dist. 8, 1982-85; _Plurinominal Federal Deputy_ from PRI, 1991-94. e-_Director of the IEPES of the CEN of PRI_, 1976-78; representative of the CEN of PRI to the Federal Electoral Commission, 1977; Technical Secretary of the Federal Electoral Commission, 1982. f-Law intern for National Finance Bank, 1955-57; Director, Legal Department, National Finance Bank, 1957-59; Director, Tax Stamp Department, Secretariat of the Treasury, 1959-60; Director, Alcohol Department, Secretariat of the Treasury, 1960-62; Director of Internal Taxes, Secretariat of the Treasury, 1962-63; General Manager of Rural Credit, Agrarian Bank of the Center, Celaya, Guanajuato, 1967-71; General Manager of Credit, National Agrarian Bank, 1971-73; Chief of Projects, Banrural, 1973-79; Director of Government, Secretary of Government, 1979-82; Ambassador to India, 1988-90. g-Member of the Technical Council of the CNC, 1965-68. h-Writer for many magazines. i-Son of _Luis I. Rodríguez_

Taboada, president of the PRM, and Eloísa Jaime Saucillo; married Erika Morrill Baumbach. j-None. k-Answered President _Echeverría_'s third State of the Union address; precandidate for Governor of Guanajuato, 1978; precandidate for senator from Guanajuato, 1976. l-DBM68, 530; DPE61, 43; C de D, 1964-66, 55, 90, 91; _Excélsior_, 28 Aug. 1973, 30 Apr. 1978, 26 Dec. 1981, 16; Directorio, 1982-85; letters; DBGM92, 562

Rodríguez (Luján), Abelardo L.
(Deceased Feb. 13, 1967) a-May 12, 1889. b-San José de Guaymas, Sonora. c-Primary education in Nogales, Sonora; no degree. d-President of Mexico, 1932-34; _Governor of Sonora_, 1943-48. e-None. f-Police Chief of Nogales, Sonora, 1912; Governor and Military Commander of Baja California del Norte, 1923-29; Governor of Baja California del Norte, 1929-30; Subsecretary of the Navy, 1931-32; Secretary of War and Navy, Aug. 2 to Sept. 2, 1932; Secretary of Industry and Commerce, Jan. 20 to Aug. 2, 1932; President of the Advisory Fishing Council, Secretariat of Industry and Commerce, 1961; General Coordinator of National Production, 1942-43. g-None. h-Wealthy businessman in the State of Sonora and Baja California del Norte; began investments in the 1920s; important shareholder in Banco Mexicano; cofounder of Empacadora del Norte, Navojoa, 1927; cofounder of Nacional de Productos Marinos, 1927; shareholder in National Portland Cement Company; coinvestor with _Javier Gaxiola_ in La Suiza; invested in Pesquera del Pacífico, 1937. i-Father, Nicolás Rodríguez, went bankrupt running several mule trains; worked in a hardware store with brother, Fernando; employed at Cananea Copper Mines; professional baseball player. j-Joined the Revolution, Lieutenant, 1913; rank of 1st Captain,

1914; fought against Huerta; rank of Major, 1914; rank of Lt. Colonel, 1915; Head of the 53rd Battalion under Obregón in the fighting against Villa; rank of Colonel, 1916; rank of Brigadier General, 1920; Military Commander of Baja California del Norte, 1921; chief of Military Operations in Oaxaca, 1923; rank of Brigade General, 1924; rank of Division General, June 11, 1928; Commander of the Military Zone of the Gulf, 1942. k-Resigned from the governorship of Sonora, April 1948, giving health as a reason. l-HA, 11 Dec. 1961, 3; Gaxiola, 57ff; NYT, 14 Feb. 1967, 43; Q es Q, 508; IWW40, 957; WWM45, 103; DP70, 1783; Covarrubias, 156; NYT, 26 Mar. 1943, 2; Anderson; *Justicia*, July, 1970.

Rodríguez Palafox, Ramiro
b-Santiago Papasquiaro, Durango. c-Early education unknown; graduated from the National Military College. d-*Federal Deputy* from the State of Durango, Dist. 3, 1946-49, member of the Gran Comisión; *Federal Deputy* from the State of Durango, Dist. 3, 1952-55. e-None. f-Assistant and Military Adjutant to *Miguel Alemán*, 1946. g-None. j-Career army officer. k-World champion horesback competitor in jumping and obstacle course. l-C de D, 1946-49, 1952-55.

Rodríguez Pérez, Francisco
a-June 1, 1939. b-Ciudad Juárez, Chihuahua. c-Early education unknown; economics degree, National School of Economics, UNAM, 1960-64; professor, National School of Economics, UNAM, 1964-66; professor, Autonomous University of Ciudad Juárez, 1967-70; Dean, School of Economics, Autonomous University of Ciudad Juárez. d-*Federal Deputy* from the State of Chihuahua, Dist. 3, 1973-76, Dist. 4, 1982-85, Secretary of the Trade Committee. e-Joined PRI, 1955; Youth

Director of Section 71 of PRI, Ciudad Juárez, Chihuahua, 1958-59; Secretary of Political Action, Youth Committee of PRI in the Federal District, 1966; Secretary General of the CEPES of PRI, Ciudad Juárez, Chihuahua, 1968-70. f-Tax inspector, Tax Division, Secretariat of the Treasury, 1967-69; controller, CONASUPO, 1970-73. g-Founder and President of the League of Revolutionary Economists of the State of Chihuahua, 1968-70; Secretary of Organization of Local 17 of the National Union of Treasury Workers, 1961-63; Secretary General of Local 17 of the National Union of Treasury Workers, 1965-67. h-None. i-Son of Francisco Rodríguez Lozada, public official, and Maura Pérez Peña, teacher; married Elisa Gil Martínez. j-None. k-None. l-Directorio, 1982-85; C de D, 1973-76; C de D, 1982-85; Lehr, 104.

Rodríguez Ramírez, Eliseo
a-Sept. 13, 1925. b-Ejido La Gavilana, Pénjamo, Guanajuato. c-Attended the Escuela Práctica de Agricultura de Roque, Celaya, Guanajuato, 1939-41; prevocational studies, Rafael Dondé School, Mexico City, 1942-43; cadet, Heroic Military College, 1944-45, serving as corporal of cadets, July 16, 1945; graduated as a 2nd Lieutenant in Administration, Jan. 1, 1946; secondary studies at Secondary Night School No. 14, Mexico City, 1946; preparatory studies from the National Preparatory School, 1947-48; legal studies from the National School of Law, UNAM, 1949-53, graduating June 27, 1955; professor, National School of Law, UNAM, 1959-61; professor, Heroic Military College, 1951-59. d-*Federal Deputy* from the State of Guanajuato, Dist. 5, 1961-64, member of the Second National Defense Committee, the Military Justice Committee, and substitute member of the First Justice Committee; *Alternate Senator* from the State of

Guanajuato, 1964-68, in functions as senator 1968-70; *Federal Deputy* from the State of Guanajuato, Dist. 5, 1985-88. e-Joined PRI, 1949; General Delegate of the CEN of PRI to Campeche, 1964; General Delegate of the CEN of PRI to Tlaxcala, 1969, 1970. f-Agent of the Ministerio Público, Civil Division, 1957; Agent of the Ministerio Público, 1957-58; adviser to the Private Secretary of the Attorney General of Mexico, 1960; Auxiliary Agent of the Ministerio Público of the Attorney General of Mexico, 1960-61, 1964; Oficial Mayor of the Senate, 1971-72; Subdirector of Migratory Services, Secretariat of Government, 1980. g-Founder of the Revolutionary Student Group of Guanajuato, 1947; member of the Revoluionary Student Group Ignacio Altamirano, National School of Law, 1949; Secretary General of the 1949-53 National Law School Generation; General Delegate of the CNC in Aguascalientes and Puebla, 1962; Secretary of Educational Action of the CEN of the CNC, 1962-65; Secretary General of the League of Agrarian Communities of the State of Guanajuato, 1966. h-Began working parcel of land left to him by his father, 1936. i-Son of Andrés Rodríguez and Francisca Ramírez, peasants who could not read or write. j-Career army officer; served in the 7th Administratve Section, 1946-47; rank of 1st Lieutenant, Jan. 1, 1949; rank of 2nd Captain, Sept. 1, 1952; rank of 1st Captain, Nov. 20, 1956; rank of Major, Nov. 20, 1959; department head, Secretariat of National Defense, 1977. k-None. l-C de D, 1961-63, 89; HA, 13 Sept. 1971, 13; letter; Rev. de Ejer., Apr. 1959, 28; C de S, 1964-70; DBGM, 591-92; Lehr, 104.

Rodríguez Roldán, Santiago
a-Oct. 6, 1922. b-Federal District. c-Early education unknown; law degree, National School of Law, UNAM, with a thesis on basic legal norms. d-None. e-None. f-First Secretary of Agreements, Second Judicial District, Veracruz, Veracruz; District Court judge, Tapachula, Chiapas and Acapulco, Guerrero; Judge, Circuit Court, Toluca, México, and Veracruz, Veracruz; Judge, Circuit Court, Federal District; *Justice of the Supreme Court*, 1979-82, 1982-88, 1988-93. g-None. h-None. i-Married Leonor Báez. j-None. k-None. l-DBGM, 683; DBGM89, 639; DBGM87, 656; DBGM92, 695.

Rodríguez Solórzano, Angel
a-May 31, 1919. b-Durango, Durango. c-Secondary and preparatory studies, law degree from the School of Law, 1947, and Professor of Biology, 1942-66, all at the Juárez Institute, Durango; Rector of the Juárez University of Durango (formerly Juárez Institute), 1953-64. d-*Federal Deputy* from the State of Durango, Dist. 1, 1964-67, member of the Cultural Affairs Committee, the Balloting Committee, and the First Public Education Committee. e-None. f-Secretary of the City Council of Durango, 1942-44; President of the State Board of Conciliation and Arbitration of Durango, 1944; Second Judge of the Civil Court of Durango; Assistant Attorney General of Durango; Attorney General of Durango; *Provisional Governor of Durango*, Aug. 4, 1966 to 1968. g-None. h-None. j-None. k-None. l-DBM68, 532; C de D, 1964-66, 55.

Rodríguez (Taboada), Luis Ignacio
(Deceased Aug. 28, 1973) a-Oct. 21, 1905. b-Silao, Guanajuato. c-Primary studies in Guanajuato; secondary and preparatory studies in Guanajuato; law degree from the University of Guanajuato, Apr. 29, 1929; Rector of the University of Guanajuato, 1929; Professor of Constitutional Law for many years. d-*Federal Deputy* from Baja California del Sur, 1934-36; local deputy to the

State Legislature of Guanajuato, 1929-30; *Governor of Guanajuato*, 1937-38, 1939-40; *Senator* from the State of Guanajuato, 1952-58, substitute member of the Protocol Committee, member of the First Justice Committee, the Rules Committee, the Second Balloting Committee, and the Legislative Studies Committee; president of the Foreign Relations Committee. e-*President of the CEN of PRM*, April 2, 1938, to June 19, 1939; founding member of the PRM. f-Superintendent of Education, State of Guanajuato, under Governor *Arroyo Ch.*, 1924; Chief Clerk, State of Guanajuato, under Governor *Arroyo Ch.*, 1926; Director of Popular Culture, State of Guanajuato, 1931-33; Oficial Mayor of Government of the State of Guanajuato, 1929-30; Secretary General of Government of the State of Guanajuato, 1927-28; Secretary General of Government and Interim Governor of Baja California del Sur under General *Juan B. Domínguez Cota*, 1932-34; *Private Secretary to the President of Mexico*, 1934-37, under *Lázaro Cárdenas*; Ambassador to France, 1939-40, to Chile, 1941-45, to Canada, 1946-50, to Guatemala, 1950-51, and to Venezuela, 1961-65. g-Student leader at the University of Guanajuato; president of the Revolutionary Convention of Ciudad Victoria, Tamaulipas, 1926. h-Owner, Kimberly Jewelry Shop, 1944. i-Father of *Luis Danton Rodríguez Jaime*; son of Victoriano Rodríguez and Jesusita Taboada; married Eloisa Jaime. j-None. k-Supported General Obregón for President, 1928; precandidate for President of Mexico, 1939; opposed *Angel Carvajal's* candidacy for the President of Mexico in 1952 in an open letter with *Heriberto Jara* and *Silvano Barba González*; member of the Inner Circle from 1934-40; first President of the revised PRM. l-DP70, 1232; *Polémica*, Vol. I, No. 1, 1969, 69; EBW46, 89; DGF56, 6, 10-14; Peral, 702; Brandenburg, 80; Morton, 74-75, 41, 92; Michaels, 3; HA, 3 Sept. 1973, 29; López, 953; Gómez, 106, 121; letters.

Rodríguez Triana, Pedro
(Deceased Feb. 26, 1960) a-1891. b-San Pedro, Coahuila. c-Primary studies only; no degree. d-*Governor of Coahuila*, 1938-41. e-Named delegate from Coahuila to the Mexican Liberal Party; Communist Party candidate for President of Mexico, 1929. g-Became an agrarian leader at age 14; agrarian adviser to the states of Durango, San Luis Potosí, Coahuila, Campeche, 1935; cooperative and ejido organizer, 1923. h-Peasant. j-Joined the Revolution, 1912; fought under Victoriano Huerta for a short time; Chief of Staff for General Benjamín Argumedo, 1915; fought against Venustiano Carranza, 1920; fought against Francisco Murguía, 1922. k-Remained in hiding after 1929 election in the mountains of northern Mexico, 1929-34; accused of mishandling funds as Governor of Coahuila; Brandenburg places him in the Inner Circle as Governor; removed two weeks before the end of his term as Governor for attempting to impose his own candidate, General Lucas González, as governor; Cuéllar Valdés says he was born in Zacatecas, and therefore, he violated the state constitution as Governor of Coahuila. l-DP70, 1792; Peral, 704-05; D de Y, 2 Nov. 1940, 1; Correa, 500-01; Brandenburg, 80; Anderson, 82-83; PS, 5363; Cuéllar Valdés, 238.

Rodríguez y Rodríguez, Jesús
a-Mar. 2, 1920. b-Federal District. c-Preparatory studies at the Colegio Francés Morelos, Mexico City; agricultural engineering degree, National School of Agriculture, 1939; law degree, National School of Law, UNAM, 1942, with his thesis on the "History and Politics of the Municipality in Mexico";

Professor of Administrative Law, National School of Law, UNAM, 1944-54; Professor of the State in Economic Life, National School of Economics, UNAM; Secretary of the School of Law under Dean *Mario de la Cueva*. d-*Senator* from the State of Morelos, 1988. e-Joined PRI, 1942. f-Lawyer, Office of Public Debt, Secretariat of the Treasury, 1942-43; Secretary, Federal Tax Court, 1943-44; Director, Department of Securities and Finance, Secretariat of the Treasury, 1945-46; Director, Office of Statistics, IMSS, 1943-47; alternate member of the National Price Commission, 1946-49; Vice President of the National Price Commission, 1950-52; Director of Services, Department of the Federal District, 1947-52; Private Secretary to the Director General of the IMSS, *Antonio Ortiz Mena*, 1953-58; Subdirector of Credit, Secretariat of the Treasury, 1958; *Subsecretary of the Treasury*, 1958-64; *Subsecretary of the Treasury*, 1964-70; Executive Director of the Inter-American Development Bank, 1971-78; President, Inter-American Committee of the Alliance for Progress, Washington, D.C.; President, Price Institute, 1980-82; Director General of the Bank of Credit and Services, 1982; Director of the National Lottery, 1982-88. g-None. i-Married Leonor Montero; political disciple of *Antonio Ortiz Mena*; son of Jesús Rodríguez de la Fuente, public official, and Margarita Rodríguez Tesorero. j-None. k-None. l-DPE61, 40; DGF50, II, 57; DGF51, II, 65; *Siempre*, 14 Jan. 1959, 6; HA, 22 Oct. 1973, 4 Aug. 1944, 7; letter; HA, 22 Oct. 1973, 23 Apr. 1984, 24-25; *Excélsior*, 5 Sept. 1982, 20; HA, 24 March 1980, 25; DBGM89, 527; DBGM92, 565-66.

Roel (García), Santiago
a-Dec. 4, 1919. b-Monterrey, Nuevo León. c-Primary studies at the Colegio Monterrey, Monterrey and the Colegio Americano, Monterrey; secondary studies at the Laurens Institute; preparatory studies from the University of Nuevo León and from the Ateneo Fuente, Saltillo, Coahuila; law degree from the University of Nuevo León; Professor of Agrarian and Tax Law, Guarantees and Amparo and Constitutional Law, School of Law, University of Nuevo León (twenty years); Professor of the History of Mexican Philosophy, School of Philosophy, University of Nuevo León; Director of the University Extension Program, University of Nuevo León. d-Alternate Local Deputy to the 46th State Legislature of Nuevo León; *Alternate Senator* from the State of Nuevo León, 1964-70, under *Armando Arteaga y Santoyo*; *Federal Deputy* from the State of Nuevo León, Dist. 1, 1970-73, President of the Foreign Relations Committee, member of the Legislative Studies Committee, President of the Chamber of Deputies. e-National Delegate of the IEPES of PRI; Coordinator of Speakers for the presidential campaign of *José López Portillo*, 1975-76; Subdirector of the Legal Department of the CEN of PRI. f-Legal adviser to the 7th Military Zone; Director of the Legal Department of the State of Nuevo León; adviser to the Secretary of the Treasury, 1973-75; *Secretary of Foreign Relations*, 1976-79. g-Lawyer for the Union of Workers of the National Railroads of Mexico in the State of Nuevo León. h-Practicing lawyer in Mexico City in the firm of Farell; author of various books. i-Son of lawyer Santiago Roel Melo, representative to the Constitutional Convention of 1917 and federal deputy and María Concepción García, a teacher; grandson of Secundino Roel, lawyer; close personal friend of *José López Portillo* and *Octavio Senties*; political disciple of *Alfonso Martínez Domínguez*. j-None. k-Early precandidate for Governor of Nuevo León, 1977; the

press claims he was fired as Secretary of Foreign Relations for his mishandling of the ministry and its policies. l-LA, 25 May 1979, 158; HA, 6 Dec. 1976, 22; *Excélsior*, 11 Mar. 1977, 6; HA, 17 Jan. 1977, 8; NYT, 2 Dec. 1976, 3; Directorio, 1970; WNM, 196; *Excélsior*, 1 Dec. 1976; *El Día*, 1 Dec. 1976.

Rojas (Gutiérrez), Carlos

a-Nov. 4, 1954. b-Federal District. c-Early education unknown; industrial engineering degree, National School of Engineering, UNAM, 1973-77, with a thesis on the tranformation of solar energy; professor, National School of Engineering, UNAM, 1976-78; researcher, Graduate School, National School of Economics, UNAM, 1977-79; professor, Institute for the Studies of Rural Maya Development, 1978-79. d-None. e-Joined PRI, 1979; Coordinator of Special Events, presidential campaign, 1987-88. f-Subdirector of the Coordinating Indigenous Center, Hopelchén, Campeche, National Indigenous Institute, 1979-80; Director of the Coordinating Indigenous Center, Huayacocotla, Veracruz, National Indigenous Institute, 1980-83; Director of Marginal Zones Program, Secretariat of Programming and Budgeting, 1983; Director of Southern Regional Operations, Secretariat of Programming and Budgeting, 1984; Coordinator of Advisers to the Subsecretary of Regional Development, *Manuel Camacho Solís*, 1985; Technical Secretary of Decentralization Program, Secretariat of Programming and Budgeting, 1986; *Subsecretary of Regional Development* and General Coordinator of "Solidarity," Secretariat of Programming and Budgeting, 1988-92, and Social Development, 1992-93; *Secretary of Social Development*, 1993-94. g-Technical adviser, CNC, 1984. h-None. i-Son of Crisóforo Rojas Esteves, businessman, and María Elena Gutiérrez Cervantes; married Dinorah Sotres

Narváez, political scientist; brother of *Francisco José Rojas Gutiérrez*, director general of Pemex. j-None. k-None. l-DBGM92, 323; DBGM89, 306.

Rojas (Gutiérrez), Francisco

a-Sept. 15, 1944. b-Federal District. c-Early education unknown; CPA degree, School of Business and Administration, UNAM, with a thesis on professional ethics; MA degree in planning and budgeting for economic and social development, Israel Center of Productivity, Tel Aviv; graduate studies in business management, Panamerican Institute for the Development of Higher Management (Opus Dei). d-None. e-Exective Secretary of the National Committee for Party Integration, CEN of PRI; *Secretary of Finances of the CEN of PRI*, 1981-82. f-Director, Office of Control of Budget, Controller General of the Department of the Federal District, 1971; Assistant Director of Finance, Controller General of Mexico City, Department of the Federal District, 1972; General Coordinator of Budget Control, Secretariat of the Treasury, 1973-74; Assistant Technical Director of Finance, Industry and Energy Sectors, Secretariat of the Treasury, 1974-75; Assistant Director of Budget Contol, Secretariat of the Treasury, 1975-76; Chief of Advisers to the Subsecretary of the Treasury, 1977-79; General Coordinator of Management Control of Budget, Secretariat of Programming and Budget, 1979-82; adviser to *Miguel de la Madrid* and coordinator of campaign finances and evaluation, 1981-82; *Controller General of Mexico*, 1983-87; *Director General of Pemex*, 1987-88, 1988-94. g-None. h-Accountant, Firm of Roberto Casas Alatriste and Manuel Resa. i-Son of Crisóforo Rojas Esteves, merchant, and María Elena Gutiérrez Cervantes; married María Elena Jiménez Alba; brother *Carlos Rojas Gutiérrez* was a subsecretary of social development, 1992. j-None. k-Was his idea to use national consultation as part of the 1982 presidential campaign. l-*Proceso*, 4 Oct. 1982; HA, 17 Jan. 1983, 22; *Excélsior*, 4 Jan. 1983, 15, 26; *The News*, 2 Dec. 1982; HA, 13 Dec. 1982, 18; Q es Q, 154; DBGM, 365; DBGM92, 323.

Rojas Rasso, Samuel Carlos
(Deceased Aug. 9, 1939) a-Dec. 23, 1891. b-Puebla, Puebla. c-Early education unknown; enrolled as a pilot Jan. 5, 1915, graduating as an aviator Feb. 22, 1918; aviation studies in Italy, 1922-23. d-None. e-None. f-*Chief of the Mexican Air Force*, 1938-38. g-None. h-None. i-Son of Ismael Rojas de Ita and Guadalupe Rasso; brother Manuel C. Rojas Rasso was a brigadier general. j-Career military pilot; fought in the Revolution; joined the Air Flotilla in Puebla under General Gustavo Salinas, Army of the East; flew combat missions in 1918, 1920; Chief of Pilots; fought General Villa in Sonora, 1919; rank of 2nd captain and pilot, Oct. 21, 1920; Commander of observation and bomber squadron; Air Attaché to the Mexican Embassy, Washington, D.C., 1923; prisoner of the rebel forces under de la Huerta, 1924; Commander of the Air Flotilla, 1924; Chief of the Advanced Air Groups; Commander of the 2nd Air Regiment; Director of the Heroic Military College, 1936; Director of Military Education, Secretariat of National Defense, 1936-37; Director, Department of Military Aeronautics, Secretariat of National Defense, 1938; Director, Department of Tactical Structures, Secretariat of National Defense; rank of Brigade General. l-Rev. de Ejer., Sept. 1976, 129; CyT, 2, 594-95.

Rojina Villegas, Rafael
b-Orizaba, Veracruz. c-Primary studies in Orizaba; secondary and preparatory studies at the National Preparatory

School, Mexico City; studied law at the National School of Law, UNAM, 1926-30, law degree, July 7, 1930, with honorable mention; LLD, National School of Law, UNAM, 1951; Professor of Civil Law and Introduction to the Study of Law, National School of Law, UNAM, 1934-64; Professor of Private Law, Graduate School, National School of Law, UNAM, 1954-64. d-None. e-None. f-Secretary of Studies, Supreme Court of Justice, 1945-51; Judge of the First Circuit Collegiate Court, 1951-58; *Justice of the Supreme Court*, 1962-64, 1965-70, 1971-76, 1976-77. g-None. h-Author of a 13-volume work on Mexican civil law; expert on the civil codes. j-None. k-None. l-*Justicia*; April, 1967; DGF56, 585.

Rojo Gómez, Javier
(Deceased Dec. 31, 1970) a-June 28, 1896. b-Hacienda de Bondojito, Municipio de Huichapan, Hidalgo. c-Primary studies in Huichapan and in the Federal District; preparatory studies at the National Preparatory School; law degree from the National School of Law, UNAM, 1924. d-Local Deputy to the State Legislature of Hidalgo, 1920-21, 1922-23, 1928-29; Federal Deputy from the State of Hidalgo, Dist. 2, 1926-28; Federal Deputy from the State of Hidalgo, 1932-33; *Governor of Hidalgo*, 1937-40. e-Adviser to PRI on farm policies, 1967. f-Secretary General of Government of the State of Hidalgo under General Antonio Azuara, 1923-24; Secretary General of Government of the State of Hidalgo, 1933-36; Judge of the First District, Federal District, 1936-37; *Head of the Federal District Department*, 1940-46; Ambassador to Indonesia, 1952-55; Ambassador to Japan, 1956-58; *Governor of Quintana Roo*, 1967-70. g-Lawyer for CROM after graduation; *Secretary General of the CNC*, 1962-66. h-Practiced law in the firm of *Emilio Portes Gil*; as a boy was

an agrarian laborer on the Hacienda of Tepeji del Río; Director General of Asegurador Agrícola Nacional, 1958; practiced law, 1958-64. i-Son of Juan Rojo and Petronila Gómez, agricultural laborers; father worked on the Bondosito hacienda; classmate of *Gilberto Loyo* at UNAM; brother-in-law of *José Lugo Guerrero*; father of *Jorge Rojo Lugo*; married Isabel Lugo; uncle of *Humberto Lugo Gil*, federal deputy from Hidalgo, 1967-70; related to Bartolome Vargas Lugo through marriage. j-None. k-One of the founders of the National Farmers Federation; formal complaint was brought against him in Oct. 1947 for illegal land sales as Head of the Federal District Department; ostracized by PRI but made a comeback; precandidate for President of Mexico, 1945; Inner Circle status from 1940-46; his candidacy for the Secretary General of the CNC was supported by the "Old Guard," including *Francisco Mújica, Heriberto Jara, Graciano Sánchez*, Luis Cabrera, and *Eduardo Suárez*; involved in a scandal as Secretary General of the CNC, along with *Roberto Barrios* and *León García*. l-Peral, 707; DP70, 2439-40; DBM68, 534-35; WWM45, 105; DGF56, 127; Nov. de Yuc., 29 Dec. 1971, 3; Correa, 345-52; Brandenburg, 80; *Por Qué*, 4 Oct. 1968, 36; Cline, 158; González Navarro, 233; letter; López, 958; *Excélsior*, 2 May 1975, 33, 29 June 1974, 17, 7 Sept. 1974, 17; Pérez López, 407-08; Chávez Hernández, 22.

Rojo Lugo, Jorge
a-June 18, 1933. b-Huichapan, Hidalgo. c-Primary and secondary studies in Mexico City; attended Cristóbal Colon School, Mexico City; preparatory studies from the National Preparatory School; law degree from the National School of Law, UNAM, 1958. d-*Federal Deputy* from the State of Hidalgo, Dist. 5, 1961-64, member of the Credit, Money, and Credit Institutions Com-

mittee, and the Agrarian Section of the Legislative Studies Committee; *Governor of Hidalgo*, 1975-76, 1978-81. e-General Delegate of the CEN of PRI to Aguascalientes, Tabasco and Chiapas, 1961-64; Auxiliary Secretary of the President of the CEN of PRI, *Alfonso Corona del Rosal*, 1961-63. f-Lawyer, Legal Section, Secretariat of Hydraulic Resources, 1959-60; assistant to the National Arbitration Commission of the Secretariat of the Treasury, 1960-61; Subdirector General of the National Agricultural Bank, 1965-70; Director General of the National Agricultural Bank, 1970-75; *Secretary of Agrarian Reform*, 1976-78. g-Member of the Advisory Council of the CNC. h-None. i-Married to García de Alba; cousin of *Humberto A. Lugo Gil*, senator from Hidalgo, 1976-82; son of *Javier Rojo Gómez*, governor of Hidalgo, 1937-40, and Isabel Lugo; nephew of *José Lugo Guerrero*, governor of Hidalgo, 1941-45; cousin of *Adolfo Lugo Verduzco*, president of the CEN of PRI, 1982; mother related to Bartolome Vargas Lugo. j-None. k-*Proceso* considered him a strong candidate for the presidency of the CEN of PRI in October, 1978. l-*Proceso*, 12 June 1978, 25; Enc. Mex., Annual, 1977, 545; *Excélsior*, 2 June 1978, 1; HA, 2 June 1975, 33, 6 Dec. 1976, 24, 28 Nov. 1977, 7; *Proceso*, 19 Mar. 1982, 6-9.

Rojo Pérez, Jesús
a-Jan. 2, 1938. b-Ocoyoacac, México. c-Primary studies at the Leóna Vicario School, Ocoyoacac; secondary studies at the Instituto García de Cisneros, Cholula, Puebla; preparatory studies at the Instituto García de Cisneros; secondary teaching certificate, Higher Normal School, Mexico City; courses in teaching English, Mexican–North American Institute of Cultural Relations; certified as a teacher of foreign languages, UNAM; secondary teacher at

Public School No. 2, Colegio Hernán Cortes, and the Marillac Institute. d-*Federal Deputy* (Party Deputy from the PAN) 1970-73, member of the Agricultural Development Committee and the Second General Means of Communication Committee. e-Member of PAN. f-None. g-None. h-None. i-Married María Elena Amaya Sedano. j-None. k-None. l-C de D, 1970-72, 134; Directorio, 1970-72.

Rolland, Modesto C.
(Deceased 1965) a-1881. b-La Paz, Baja California del Sur. c-Engineering degree. d-Deputy to the Constitutional Convention from Baja California, Dist. 2, 1916-17. e-None. f-Director of many government public works projects, including the Plaza México, Jalapa, Veracruz; *Subsecretary of Public Works*, 1934-40; *Subsecretary of Industry and Commerce*, 1940-46; Director General of Free Ports, 1946-52. g-None. h-Author of many technical works on ports and political tracts. j-None. k-None. l-DP70, 1796; HA, 6 Oct. 1950; DGF50, 474; DGF50, II, 645; NYT, 19 Dec. 1940, 6.

Román Celis, Carlos
a-Feb. 21, 1922. b-Coyuca de Catalán, Guerrero. c-Primary studies in the José María Morelos School, 1933, Coyuca de Catalán; secondary studies at the Ignacio M. Altamirano School, in Teloloapan, Guerrero, and in the Secondary Night School for Workers, No. 5, Mexico City, 1946; social science studies at the National Preparatory Night School, 1947-48; law degree from the National School of Law, UNAM, 1949-53; Professor of Literary Groups, Office of Literature, Department of the Federal District, 1945. d-*Alternate Federal Deputy* from the State of Guerrero, Dist. 3, 1952-55, *Federal Deputy* from the State of Guerrero, Dist. 3, 1955-58, member of the Radio and Television

Industry Committee, the Committee on Credit, Money, and Credit Institutions, the Second Labor Committee, and the Gran Comisión; *Senator* from Guerrero, 1958-64, member of the Gran Comisión, the Agriculture and Development Committee, the Third National Defense Committee, the National Lands Committee, the Second Balloting Committee, and the Special Legislative Studies Committee; President of the First Justice Committee; Secretary of the Second Instructive Section of the Grand Jury; substitute member of the First Government Committee and the National Railroads Committee. e-Official orator in the *Adolfo Ruiz Cortines* presidential campaign, 1952. f-Treasurer of the Board of Material Improvement, Coyuca, 1942; President of the Patriotic Board, Coyuca, 1943; Subdirector of Filmoteca Nacional, Secretariat of Public Education, 1947; Director of Press Relations, IMSS, 1953; Director of Legal Affairs, Secretariat of Health, 1976. g-President of the Student Association of the National Preparatory Night School. h-Worked in father's store as a youth; news agent in Coyuca; Editor-in-chief, *Revista Coyuca*, 1944; winner of the prize in physics and chemistry, secondary night school, Federal District, 1946; winner of prize for essay on Louis Pasteur, National Preparatory Night School, 1948; reporter for *Mañana* during the 1952 campaign. i-Father owned a general store. j-None. k-Precandidate for senator from Guerrero, 1981. l-Func., 219; C de D, 1952-54, 18; C de S, 1961-64, 68; DGF56, 30, 32, 37m, 34, 24; C de D, 1955-57; Ind. Biog., 139-40; *Excélsior*, 26 Dec. 1981, 16.

Román Lugo, Fernando
a-Jan. 16, 1916. b-Chilpancingo, Guerrero. c-Primary and secondary studies in Chilpancingo; preparatory studies in Chilpancingo; law degree; professor, School of Law, University of

Veracruz. d-None. e-Director General of the National Voters Registration, 1952. f-Secretary General of Government of the State of Veracruz, 1944-48, under governor *Adolfo Ruiz Cortines*; Judge of the Superior Tribunal of Justice of the State of Veracruz, 1952; *Oficial Mayor of the Secretariat of Government*, 1952-53; *Subsecretary of Government*, 1953-58; *Attorney General of the Federal District and Federal Territories*, 1958-64. g-Active in the Second Congress of Socialist Students, 1935. h-Practicing lawyer, Mexico City, 1964-80. i-Married Delia Cortés; taught law school with *Angel Carvajal*, University of Veracruz. j-None. k-None. l-HA, 8 Dec. 1958, 30; DGF56, 83; D de Y, 2 Dec. 1958, 7; HA, 27 Feb. 1953, 8-9; Func., 99.

Romandía Ferreira, Alfonso

a-July 28, 1901. b-Hermosillo, Sonora. c-Early education unknown; law degree from the National School of Law, UNAM, 1927. d-Federal Deputy from the Federal District, Dist. 7, 1928-30. e-Organizer of a student party in support of Calles' presidential campaign, 1923; leader of the pro-Obregón students, 1927. f-Oficial Mayor of Agriculture, 1932-33; special envoy to Paris, France; Director General of the Bank of Industry and Trade; Director, Credit Department, National Sugar Producers Organization, 1936-46; Director General of the Financiera Industrial Azucarera, 1946-53; Manager of the La Gloria Sugar Mill, 1951-70. g-None. h-None. i-Friend of *Miguel Alemán* since law school days; married Carmen Macías. j-None. k-None. l-Villaseñor, I, 264; Balboa, 23; DBM68, 535; WNM, 197.

Romero, Antonio

(Deceased) a-Feb. 26, 1893. b-Encinillas, Jilotepec, México. c-Early education unknown; no degree. d-Federal

Deputy from the State of México, Dist. 5, 1932-34; *Senator* from the State of México, 1934-40. e-None. f-None. g-None. h-None. j-Career army officer; Commander of the 14th Military Zone, Aguascalientes, Aguascalientes, 1959; Commander of the 6th Military Zone, Saltillo, Coahuila; rank of Brigadier General, June 1, 1941. k-None. l-C de S, 1934-40; Rev. de Ejer., Sept. 1961, 43; Rev. de Ejer., Sept. 1959, 16; C de D, 1932-34.

Romero, José Ruben

(Deceased 1952) a-Sept. 25, 1890. b-Cotija, Michoacán. c-Primary studies at the Pablo Barona School, Mexico City, 1897; studies in diplomacy; no degree. d-None. e-None. f-Private Secretary to Governor Miguel Silva, Michoacán, 1912; Private Secretary to Governor Pascual Ortiz Rubio, Michoacán, 1919; Inspector General of Communications, 1920-21; Director of Press and Information, Secretariat of Foreign Relations, 1921-22; Oficial Mayor of the Secretariat of Foreign Relations, 1924-30; Consul General to Barcelona, Spain, 1930-33; Director of the Civil Registry, Mexico City, 1933-35; Consul General in Spain, 1935-37; Ambassador to Brazil, 1937-39; *Ambassador to Cuba*, 1939-43. g-None. h-Businessman, Patzcuaro, Michoacán, 1913-15; tax collector, Puruandiro, Michoacán, 1911; well-known novelist. i-Son of Nemesio Romero, small businessman, and Refugio González. j-Supported Madero during the Revolution; Chief of Staff under General Salvador Escalante. k-Nearly executed during the Revolution. l-WWM45, 106; Peral, 1970, 1798; López, 960; letter; Cardona, 93.

Romero Alvarez, Humberto

a-Jan. 4, 1923. b-Villa de Ometepec, Guerrero. c-Early education unknown; civil engineering degree, National School of Engineering, UNAM, 1941-46;

MA in engineering, University of Michigan, 1947-48; professor, School of Public Health, UNAM, 1951-54. d-None. e-None. f-Director, Sanitation Engineering, Tepalcatepec Commission, Department of Hydraulic Resources, 1949-52; Executive Secretary of the National Committee to Eradicate Malaria, 1960-64; Chief Engineer of Potable Water, Secretariat of Hydraulic Resources, 1965-70; Subdirector General of Water and Sanitation, Department of the Federal District, 1973-76; *Subsecretary of Environmental Improvement*, Secretariat of Public Health, 1976-80; technical adviser, Secretariat of Agriculture and Hydraulic Resources, 1980-88; Director General of Environmental Health, Secretariat of Public Health, 1988-89. g-None. h-None. i-Son of Joaquín Romero López, public official, and Lucina Alvarez Alvarez; married Blanca Raquel Ordóñez de la Mora, surgeon. j-None. k-None. l-DBGM89, 307.

Romero Castañeda, David
b-México. c-Preparatory studies at the National Preparatory School; law degree, National School of Law, UNAM, 1936, with a thesis on arbitration in Mexican civil law. d-*Federal Deputy* from the State of México, Dist. 4, 1946-49, member of the Gran Comisión, the Second Government Committee and the General Accounting Office Committee. e-None. f-Supernumerary Justice of the Superior Tribunal of Justice of the Federal District and Federal Territories, 1940; Attorney General of the Federal Tax Office, 1958-60; *Subsecretary of Revenues* of the Secretariat of the Treasury, 1961-64. g-None. i-Cofounder of the student newspaper *Eureka* with *Miguel Alemán*; subsecretary of the treasury under classmate *Antonio Ortiz Mena*; married Elena Apis; son José Elías Romero Apis was assistant attorney general, 1992.

j-None. k-None. l-DPE61, 40; C de D, 1946-49, 86; *Libro de Oro*, 1959, xxxiii; DBGM92, 324.

Romero de Velasco, Flavio
a-Dec. 22, 1925. b-Ameca, Jalisco. c-Early education unknown; preparatory studies at the National Preparatory School; law degree, National School of Law, UNAM; special studies (five years) National School of Philosophy and Letters, UNAM. d-*Federal Deputy* from the State of Jalisco, Dist. 8, 1955-58, President of the Chamber, September, 1955; answered *Adolfo Ruiz Cortines'* 3rd State of the Union address, member of the Gran Comisión, member of the Library Committee, member of the Economy and Statistics Committee and member of the Foreign Relations Committee; *Federal Deputy* from the State of Jalisco, Dist. 3, 1961-64, member of the Credit, Money and Credit Institutions Committee and the Justice Committee; *Governor of Jalisco*, 1977-83. e-Joined PRI, 1950; orator during the *Adolfo Ruiz Cortines* presidential campaign, 1952; Secretary General of PRI in the Federal District; Director of the Committee for Ideological Dissemination during the *Adolfo López Mateos* campaign, 1958; General Delegate of the CEN of PRI to Tamaulipas, 1957, to Nayarit, 1964, to Nuevo León, 1976. f-Director of Social and Educational Action, Secretariat of Public Education; Administrator of Customs, Ciudad Juárez, 1965-71. g-Champion of Oratory in the Federal District, 1952. h-None. i-Initiated his career under the guidance of *Luis Echeverría*, 1946, serving as an assistant to *Rodolfo Sánchez Taboada*; nephew of *Rosendo Topete*, senator from Veracruz. j-None. k-None. l-Ind. Biog., 141; DPE61, 103; DGF56, 25, 30-32, 37; *Excélsior*, 18 Feb. 1977, 20 Feb. 1977; Almanaque of Mexico, 358.

Romero Flores, Jesús
a-Apr. 28, 1885. b-La Piedad, Michoacán. c-Teaching certificate from the University of Michoacán, Oct. 7, 1905; Director of the Normal School for the State of Michoacán, 1915. d-Deputy to the Constitutional Convention from the State of Michoacán, Dist. 16, 1916-17; local deputy to the State Legislature of Michoacán, 1922; Federal Deputy from the State of Michoacán, Dist. 17, 1922-24; *Senator* from the State of Michoacán, 1964-70. e-None. f-Director of Primary Schools, Valle de Santiago, Guanajuato; director, private school, Piedad Cabados; director of secondary schools, Piedad, Morelia; director of the School of Tangancicuaro de Artista, Zamora, Michoacán, 1910; Inspector General of Public and Private Schools, 1913-14; Director of El Pensador Mexicano Primary School, Mexico City, 1920; Director of Primary Education, Michoacán, 1930; Director of Public Education for the State of Michoacán, 1915-16; Director of Normal Schools, Morelia, 1925; Section Chief, Department of Primary Education, Department of the Federal District, 1918; Private Secretary to General *Francisco Mújica*, 1918; Director of the Public Library of Morelia, 1928; Historian for the National Museum of Mexico, 1935-45. g-None. h-Author of many works. i-Married Refugio Pérez; widowed, married María Pureco Rasso. j-None. k-None. l-C de S, 1964-70; MGF69; WWM45, 106; HA, 27 Nov. 1972, 11; Bremauntz, 65.

Romero Flores, José C.
a-1911. b-Tamaulipas. c-No formal education; self-educated. d-*Senator* from the State of Tamaulipas, 1970-76, member of the Gran Comisión, President of the Railroads Committee, First Secretary of the Electric Industry Committee, and Second Secretary of the Mail and Telegraph Committee.

e-None. f-None. g-Local Secretary of the STFRM; Prosecretary of the Mexican Alliance of Railroad Workers; Secretary General of Organization, Education and Statistics of the STFRM, 1962-65; President of the First World Railroad Workers Congress, Mexico City, 1969. h-Railroad employee. j-None. k-None. l-C de S, 1970-76, PS, 5421.

Romero Kolbeck, Gustavo
a-July 3, 1923. b-Federal District. c-Early education unknown; economics degree with an honorable mention from the National School of Economics, UNAM, 1946; graduate work at the University of Chicago and at George Washington University, 1947-48; Professor of Economics, UNAM, 1949; Professor of Economics, National School of Economics, UNAM, 1966-70; Director of the National School of Economics, 1967-69; member of the University Council of UNAM, 1967-69. d-None. e-None. f-Economist, Bank of Mexico, 1944-46; Researcher, Secretariat of Government Properties, 1948; Head, Department of Economic Studies, National Bank of Mexico, 1949-54; Subdirector of the National Research Committee, 1955-58; Director of Research, Secretariat of the Presidency, 1954-61; adviser to the presidency; Ambassador to Japan, 1971-73; *Director General of National Finance Bank*, Jan. 11, 1974-76; *Director General of the Bank of Mexico*, 1976-82; *Ambassador to the Soviet Union*, 1982-83. g-None. h-Founder of the Center for Economic Studies of the Private Sector, 1970. i-Married Leónor Martínez; son of Luis Romero González, public accountant, and Ana María Kolbeck; son Gustavo Kolbeck Martínez worked under him at the National Finance Bank. j-None. k-None. l-HA, 21 Jan. 1974, 16-17; letter; WNM, 198; HA, 18 Aug. 1975, 20; *Excélsior*, 15 Apr. 1982, 4.

Romero Pérez, Humberto
a-July 15, 1923. b-La Piedad, Michoacán. c-Primary studies in La Piedad;
secondary studies in the Federal
District; preparatory studies from the
National Preparatory School; law degree
from the National School of Law,
UNAM, 1950; Professor of Penal Law,
National School of Law, UNAM, 1951.
d-*Federal Deputy* from the State of
Michoacán, Dist. 4, 1979-82, President
of the Trade Committee. e-None. f-Private Secretary to *Francisco González de
la Vega*, Attorney General of Mexico,
1946-52; Director of Publicity for the
Secretariat of Labor under *Adolfo López
Mateos*, 1952; Alternate President, Federal Board of Conciliation and Arbitration, 1953; Director of Public Relations
for President *Adolfo Ruiz Cortines*,
1953-58; *Private Secretary to the President of Mexico, Adolfo López Mateos*,
1958-64; Chief of Advisers to Secretary
General "B" of the Department of the
Federal District, 1983; Director General
of Public Relations, Department of the
Federal District, 1983. g-President of
the Student Association, National
School of Law, UNAM; active in
student politics. h-Journalist; contributed to various newspapers and reviews;
practicing lawyer, Mexico City, 1964-
78. i-Student and political protégé of
Francisco González de la Vega; married
Alicia Gudiño Quiroz; son of Amador
Romero, public official, and Angelina
Pérez López. j-None. k-Precandidate
for Senator from Michoacán, 1981;
political enemy of *Gustavo Díaz Ordaz*.
l-DGF56, 53; DGF51, I, 535; HA, 8 Dec.
1958, 32; DPE61, 9; Func., 63; Libro de
Oro, 1959, xxv; *Excélsior*, 26 Dec. 1981,
16; *Excélsior* 8 July 1979, 18; HA, 9 May
1983, 32; Q es QAP, 450; Dicc. Mich.,
523.

Romo Gutiérrez, Arturo
a-Dec. 15, 1942. b-Fresnillo, Zacatecas.
c-Primary school teaching certificate,

National Normal School, 1960; law
degree, Free School of Law and the
National School of Law, UNAM, 1967-
72, with a thesis on the 1917 Constitution; diploma in labor economics,
Georgetown University, 1968-69;
professor, Institute of Political Education, PRI, 1978-80. d-*Alternate Federal
Deputy* from the Federal District, Dist.
9, 1970-73, to *Aurora Fernández*;
Alternate Senator from the State of
Zacatecas, 1976-82; *Federal Deputy*
from the State of Zacatecas, Dist. 1,
1979-82; *Senator* from the State of Zacatecas, 1982-88. e-Secretary of Political
Action of the National Revolutionary
Youth Movement of PRI; President, 9th
District of PRI in the Federal District,
1972-73; General Delegate of the CEN
of PRI to San Luis Potosí, 1975-76;
*Secretary of Ideological Difusion of the
CEN of PRI*, 1981-82; *Secretary of
Political Education of the CEN of PRI*,
1981; adviser to the President of the
CEN of PRI, 1982; member of the
Advisory Council of the IEPES of PRI.
f-Assistant Attorney General of the
Attorney General for Consumers, 1976-
79. g-Special delegate of the National
Institute of Youth, 1972-73; Assistant
Secretary of Education of the CEN of
the CTM; Chief of Union Education of
the CTM in the Federal District;
Secretary of Organization of the Union
of Construction Industry, Federal
District; Secretary of Education of the
CTM, 1983-86. h-Laborer, Cementos
Anáhuac, S.A., 1958-59. j-None.
k-None. l-IEPES; Protag., 301; C de S,
1982-88, 1976-82; C de D, 1979-82,
1970-73; Lehr, 531-32; DBGM87, 558;
DBGM, 592.

Rosado de Hernández, María Luisa
a-June 18, 1926. b-Tabasco. c-Primary
studies in Villahermosa, Tabasco;
teaching certificate, Normal School,
Villahermosa, Nov. 15, 1938; teacher for
many years. d-*Federal Deputy* from the

State of Tabasco, Dist. 1, 1958-61, member of the Second Public Education Committee, the Second Balloting Committee and the Fine Arts Committee. e-Member of PRI. f-Director of various public schools; consultant to the Secretariat of Public Education; adviser to UNESCO. g-None. h-None. i-Father participated in the Revolution. j-None. k-First female deputy from the State of Tabasco. l-Func., 368; C de D, 1958-61, 90.

Rosales Rodríguez de Fonseca, Leonor
a-July 1, 1930. b-Jalisco. c-Completed secondary studies; private accounting degree. d-Member of the City Council of Tijuana, 1978-81; *Alternate Federal Deputy* from Baja California, Dist. 2, 1979-82; *Federal Deputy* from the State of Baja California, Dist. 5, 1982-85. e-Secretary of Popular Action of ANFER of PRI in Baja California; Secretary of Organization of the CNOP of PRI in Baja California, 1976-80; Secretary of Political Action of the CNOP of PRI in Baja California; Secretary General of ANFER of PRI, Tijuana, 1976- ; Oficial Mayor of CNOP of PRI in Baja California, 1976-80; Subsecretary General of PRI, Baja California, 1979-81; President of La Venta Section of PRI, Baja California; Feminine Coordinator of local deputy campaigns, Baja California; President of Section No. 65 of PRI, Baja California; assistant to the Secretary General of PRI, Tijuana, 1963-66. f-Social worker, Department of Social Action, Secretariat of Labor, 1976-78. g-Secretary General of the Union of Colonies, Durango Colony. h-None. i-Daughter of Luis Rosales Torres, white collar worker, and Loreto Rodríguez Zavala; married Armando Fonseca Cervantes. j-None. k-None. l-Directorio, 1982-85; C de D, 1982-85, 1979-82; Lehr, 44; DBGM, 593.

Rosas Domínguez, Reynaldo
a-Nov. 6, 1937. b-Chihuahua. c-Early education unknown; studies in law, University of Chihuahua. d-None. e-Joined the Mexican Communist Party, January, 1961; member of the Central Committee of the PCM, 1973-79; Secretary General of the PCM in the Valle de México, 1979; member of the Executive Committee of the PCM, 1979. f-Employee of the Federal Electric Commission. g-Student leader; union organizer for the PCM. j-None. k-None. l-HA, 19 Feb. 1979, xi.

Rosas Magallón, Salvador
a-Aug. 9, 1916. b-Tepic, Nayarit. c-Primary studies in Reynosa, Tamaulipas; secondary studies in Jalisco; preparatory and two years of law at the University of Guadalajara, Guadalajara, Jalisco; law degree, National School of Law, UNAM, May 9, 1941. d-*Federal Deputy* from the State of Baja California del Norte, Dist. 2, 1964-67, member of the Hydraulic Resources Committee. e-Joined PAN, 1946; President of the Regional Council of PAN for Baja California del Norte (twice); adviser to the National Executive Council of PAN, 1969; member of the National Council of PAN, 1975. f-Judge in Tixtla, Guerrero, 1941; Agent of the Ministerio Público, Tlapa, Guerrero, 1942; Agent of the Ministerio Público, Los Mochis, Sinaloa, 1942-43. g-None. h-Began law practice, Baja California del Norte, 1945. j-None. k-Candidate for Federal Deputy from PAN, 1958; candidate for Governor of Baja California del Norte, 1959; precandidate for the PAN nomination for President, 1963, 1975; known in Baja California del Norte as the lawyer of the people. l-Letter, *Por Qué*, 4 Oct. 1968, 50; C de D, 1964-66, 55, 92.

Rosenblueth (Deutsch), Emilio
a-Apr. 8, 1926. b-Federal District. c-Early education unknown; civil

engineering degree, National School of Engineering, UNAM, 1947; MS degree in civil engineering, University of Illinois, 1947-48; MA degree, UNAM, 1949; Ph.D. in engineering, University of Illinois, 1948-51; lab assistant, University of Illinois, 1949-50; professor, Graduate Studies, School of Engineering, UNAM, 1959-82; Professor of Structures, National School of Engineering, UNAM, 1954; researcher, Geophysics Institute, UNAM, 1951-57; member, Governing Board, UNAM, 1972. d-None. e-None. f-Lab assistant, Secretariat of Hydraulic Resources, 1948; structural engineer, Secretariat of the Navy, 1954-55; structural engineer, Federal Electric Commission, 1952-54; Director, Engineering Institute, UNAM, 1959-66; Coordinator of Scientific Research, UNAM, 1966-70; adviser, Secretary General of UNAM, 1970-72; adviser, National Council of Science and Technology, 1971-76; adviser, Rector of UNAM, 1973-75; *Subsecretary of Educational Planning*, Secretariat of Public Education, 1977-82. g-Member of the National College, 1972- . h-Topographer, ICA, S.A., 1945-48; researcher, ICA, S.A., laboratories, 1951-55; Director General of Diseño Racional, S.C., 1956-70; President, DIRAC Industrial Group, 1970-77. i-Son of Emilio Rosenblueth and Charlotte Deutsch; nephew of distinguished scientist, Arturo Rosenblueth; married Alicia Laguette. j-None. k-Recipient of the National Prize in Science, 1974. l-Enc. Mex., 11, 192; WNM, 199-200; JSH, 352-53.

Rosenzweig Díaz, Alfonso de

(Deceased 1963) a-Jan. 2, 1886. b-Toluca, México. c-Law degree. d-None. e-None. f-Employee of the Mexican Consulate, St. Louis, 1907; Secretary of the Legation, China, 1910; member of the Mexican Legation, Japan, 1910;

Secretary of the Legation, Guatemala, 1912; Secretary in Brazil, 1918; Counselor in Brazil, 1921; Chargé d' Affairs, Colombia 1922, Holland 1923, Belgium 1924, Great Britain 1925; Counselor in France, 1925-26; Chief of Protocol, Secretariat of Foreign Relations, 1927; Minister to El Salvador, 1931; Ambassador to Sweden, 1933-34, to Bolivia and Paraguay, 1935-38, to Panama, 1939-40, and to Venezuela, 1941-42; rank of Ambassador, 1942; *Ambassador to Great Britain*, 1942-45; represented Mexico at the First General Assembly of the United Nations, 1945; *Ambassador to France*, 1946; Ambassador to Nicaragua, 1948-51; *Ambassador to the Soviet Union*, 1953-60. g-None. h-Author of a three-volume work on Mexico. i-Son *Alfonso Jr.* served as personal secretary to *Padilla Nervo*, when the latter was Secretary of Foreign Relations, and became Subsecretary (B) of Foreign Relations, 1976; son *Roberto*, was appointed Permanent Representative of Mexico to the United Nations, 1976; daughter, Carmen, a novelist; son of Fernando de Rosenzweig and Eudosia Díaz. j-None. k-Retired from the Foreign Service, 1960. l-Peral, 717; DGF51, I, 106; DP70, 1808; MGF69, 179; DGF56, 123, 129; WWM45, 106; NYT, 25 Oct. 1941, 3; López, 965; Enc. Mex., XI, 1977, 193; Romero Aceves, 472.

Rosenzweig Díaz (Azmitia) Jr., Alfonso

(Deceased Sept. 9, 1989) a-May 9, 1921. b-Río de Janeiro, Brazil. c-Early education unknown; legal studies, National School of Law, UNAM, 1940-44, graduating with a thesis on "The Chapultepec Treaty," 1946. d-None. e-None. f-Private Secretary to *Pablo Campos Ortiz*, Oficial Mayor of the Secretariat of Foreign Relations, 1945-46; joined the Foreign Service with the rank of Vice Consul, Apr. 1, 1946; official of the Political Affairs Office of the Department of Political Affairs, United Nations Security Council, Nov. 1946 to Oct.1951; Interim Director General of the Office of International Organizations, Secretariat of Foreign Relations, 1951-52; Private Secretary to *Manuel Tello*, Secretary of Foreign Relations, 1952-58; Director General of the Office of Legal Affairs, Secretariat of Foreign Relations, Dec.1958 to May 1961; Director General of the Diplomatic Service, May 1961 to May 1964; Director in Chief, Attached to the First Subsecretary of Foreign Relations, 1964-70; Director in Chief of Bilateral Political Affairs, Secretariat of Foreign Relations, 1970-75; legal advisor, Secretariat of Foreign Relations, 1975-76; *Subsecretary "B" of Foreign Relations, 1976-82; Subsecretary of Foreign Relations*, 1982-88. g-None. h-None. i-Son of *Alfonso Rosenzweig Díaz*, ambassador to Great Britain, 1942-45; brother of *Roberto Rosenzweig Díaz*, permanent representative of Mexico to the United Nations, 1976; married Olga Vázquez; second wife, Feodora Stancioff. j-None. k-None. l-HA, 20 Jan. 1975, 9; DPE65, 18; DPE71, 6; MGF69; *Libro de Oro*, 1967-68, xxiv; Q es QAP, 47-48; DBGM, 704

Rosenzweig Díaz (Azmitia), Roberto de
a-June 30, 1925. b-Amsterdam, Holland. c-Primary studies in Paris, France; degree in political and economic sciences, Oxford University. d-None. e-None. f-Joined the Foreign Service, 1946; Chargé d' Affaires, Brazil; Counselor, Mexican Embassy, Brazil; Secretary to the Mexican Embassy in Switzerland; Secretary to the Mexican Embassy in London, England; Counselor, Mexican Embassy, France; Director, International Treaty Department, Diplomatic Service; Director, United Nations Department, Division of International Organizations, Secretariat of Foreign

Relations; Ambassador to El Salvador, 1969-73, to Egypt, 1974-75, and to Syria, 1975-76; Permanent Representative of Mexico to the United Nations, 1976-77; Ambassador to German Federal Republic, 1977-79, to Low Countries, 1979-81, to Australia, 1981-86, and to Venezuela, 1987-88. g-None. h-None. i-Son of *Alfonso Rosenzweig Díaz*, Ambassador to Great Britain, 1942-45, and Elisa Azmitia Toriello; brother of *Alfonso Rosenzweig Díaz* Jr., Subsecretary "B" for Foreign Relations, 1976-82; sister Carmen an author and novelist; married Margarita de Olloqui Labastida, sister of *José Juan de Olloqui*, subsecretary of foreign relations. j-None. k-None. l-*Excélsior*, 9 Jan. 1976, 18; HA, 17 Feb. 1975, 17; *Excélsior*, 17 Aug. 1979, 4.

Rossell de la Lama, Guillermo
a-July 22, 1925. b-Pachuca, Hidalgo. c-Primary studies at the French-Spanish Institute; secondary studies at the Francés Morelos School and UNAM extension; preparatory studies from the Francés Morelos School; architecture degree from the National School of Architecture, UNAM, Oct. 4, 1951, with a thesis on "Planning of the New City of Guerrero"; Professor of Composition, National School of Architecture, UNAM. d-*Senator* from the State of Hidalgo, 1976, President of the Chamber, Sept. 1976; *Governor of Hidalgo*, 1981-87. e-Joined PRI, 1950; founding member of the IEPES of PRI; director of the Councils of Economic and Social Planning, *Adolfo López Mateos*' 1958 presidential campaign; personal adviser to the President of the CEN of PRI, 1957-63. f-Director of the Department of Tourism, Secretariat of Public Works, 1952; Director of Development and Planning, Secretariat of Public Works; *Oficial Mayor of the Secretariat of Government Properties*, 1958-59; *Subsecretary of Real Property and Urbanization*, 1959-

64; adviser to the National Housing Institute; President of the Regulatory Commission on Mexican-North American Border Cities; *Secretary of Tourism*, 1976-80. g-None. h-Practicing architect, 1964-75; employee of Carlos Obregón Santacilia and Enrique del Moral; chief of the workshop of Mario Pani. i-Protégé of *Carlos Lazo*, his professor and mentor in the Secretariat of Public Works; boss of *José López Portillo* as Subsecretary of Real Property and Urbanization; married Emilia Avitia; son Fernando was a precandidate for federal deputy from Hidalgo, 1979; son Guillermo was a precandidate for senator from Hidalgo, and married *Leandro Rovirosa Wade's* daughter, Haydee. j-None. k-None. l-HA, 6 Dec. 1976, 24; *Excélsior*, 4 Mar. 1977, 6; HA, 20 Feb. 1978, 8; *Excélsior*, 28 Feb. 1979, 22, *Excélsior*, 14 Aug. 1980, 1, 10; HA, 25 Aug. 1980, 34; Perez López, 418-19; letter; Almanaque de México, 1982, 514-15; *Excélsior*, 27 Dec. 1981, 17.

Rovirosa Pérez, Gustavo Adolfo
(Deceased 1970) a-1908. b-San Juan Bautista (Villahermosa), Tabasco. c-Primary studies at the Juárez Institute, Villahermosa; preparatory studies from the National Preparatory School; medical degree, School of Medicine, University of Puebla; Rockefeller Foundation Fellow in Public Health, Johns Hopkins University, 1936. d-*Senator* from the State of Tabasco, 1964-70. e-None. f-Director of Health and Social Welfare for the World Health Organization, Korea, 1950-57. g-President of the Association of Friends of Mexico and Korea. i-Son of engineer José N. Rovirosa, well-known Mexican scientist; related to *Leandro Rovirosa Wade*, Governor of Tabasco, 1977-83; brother, Carlos, famous pilot killed in a crash en route to Buenos Aires; son, Gustavo Rovirosa Renero, was special projects manager for PEMEX, 1992; married Inés

Renero Valverde. j-None. k-None. l-Enc. Mex., XI, 197; PS, 5459; C de S 1964-70; DBGM92, 327; DBGM89, 309.

Rovirosa Wade, Leandro
a-June 11, 1920. b-Villahermosa, Tabasco. c-Primary studies in Villahermosa; secondary and preparatory at the Instituto Veracruzano, Veracruz, 1933-37; civil engineering degree, National School of Engineering, UNAM, Nov. 15, 1943. d-*Governor of Tabasco*, 1977-83. e-None. f-Chief of Public Works, Ensenada, Baja California, 1942; Director of Hydraulic Works and Streets, Department of the Federal District, 1944-46; Director of Planning, Department of the Federal District, 1946-52; Director of the Department of Construction, Division of Maritime Works, Secretariat of the Navy, 1952-55; Director of Port Construction, Secretariat of the Navy; Director of the Malpaso Dam project; *Secretary of Hydraulic Resources*, 1970-76. g-President of the Alumni Society of the School of Engineering, UNAM, 1972; president of the National Chamber of the Construction Industry, 1965-67. h-Organized the construction firm of Raudals, S.A. i-Student of *Antonio Dovalí Jaime* at UNAM; friend of *Rodolfo Sánchez Taboada*; longtime friend of *Luis Echeverría*; compadre of *Hugo Cervantes del Río*; relative of *Gustavo Rovirosa Pérez*, senator from Tabasco, 1964-70; married Celia González; son of José Narciso Rovirosa Hernández and Haydee Wade Ives; father-in-law of Guillermo Rossell, son of *Guillermo Rossell de la Llama*. j-None. k-Accused of illicit personal gain as governor by *Excélsior*. l-HA, 7 Dec. 1970, 25; *Hoy*, Dec. 1970; DGF56, 383; HA, 1 Mar. 1971, 20; DGF51, I, 483; DPE71, 88; HA, 10 July 1972, 20; HA, 9 May 1955, 3; LA, 20 Aug. 1976; WNM, 200; Enc. Mex., XI, 1977, 197; *Excélsior*, 23 Dec. 1982, 10; Almanaque de Tabasco, 1982, 19-20.

Ruano Angulo, Luis Carlo
a-Aug. 29, 1927. b-Veracruz, Veracruz.
c-Primary studies, Republic of Bolivia
public school, Mexico City, 1933-36,
Francisco J. Clavijero public school,
Veracruz, Veracruz, 1937, and the
Veracruzana School, 1938-39; secondary
studies at the Veracruz Institute, 1940;
preparatory studies from the Francés
Morelos, Mexico City, 1941-42; cadet,
Antón Lizardo Naval School, Veracruz,
1942-45, graduating as a geographic
engineer; graduated from the Naval
School of the Pacific, Mazatlán, Sinaloa,
1945-47; staff and command diploma,
Higher War College, 1956-57, with a
thesis on defensive operations in a
theater of operations; MA in personnel
management, Fayol Institute, 1965; MA
in staff and command, Inter-American
Defense Board, 1966-67; MA in staff and
command, Center for Higher Naval
Studies, 1972, with a thesis on defensive operations in the Yucatán canal.
d. None. e-None. f-*Secretary of the
Navy*, July 18, 1990-94. g-None.
h-None. i-Son of Luis Ruano Milicia
and Olga Joaquina Angulo Márquez;
married Martha Elba Maldonado
Salcedo. j-Career naval officer; rank of
Marine Guard, 1948; rank of Corvette
Lieutenant, 1949; rank of Frigate
Lieutenant, 1952; rank of Navy Lieutenant, 1956; rank of Corvette Captain,
1961; rank of Frigate Captain, 1964;
rank of Naval Captain, 1969; rank of
Rear Admiral, 1974; rank of Vice
Admiral, 1979; rank of Admiral, 1986;
executive officer and captain, numerous
ships; Interim Naval Attaché, United
States, 1966-70; Inspector General of
Naval Arms, 1970-72; Chief of Naval
Forces, Gulf, 1975-77; Commander of
the Salina Cruz Naval Region; Commander of the Chetumal Naval Region,
1973-75; Interim Commander and Chief
of Staff, 1st Naval Zone, 1972-73;
Commander of the 10th Naval Zone,
San Blas, Nayarit, 1980-82, of the 6th

Naval Zone, Guaymas, Sonora, 1984-85,
and of the 1st Naval Zone, Tampico,
Tamaulipas, 1986-88; Section Chief No.
3, General Staff, Secretariat of the Navy,
1966; Chief of Adjutants, Subsecretary
of the Navy; Naval Attaché, France and
United Kingdom, 1982-83; Inspector
General of the Fleet, 1985-86; President
of the Admirals Board, 1989; Naval
Attaché to Peru, 1989-90. k-None.
l-DBGM89, 310; *El Nacional*, 20 July
1990, 3; letter; DBGM92, 328.

Rubio Félix, Lázaro
a-Jan. 6, 1917. b-Culiacán, Sinaloa.
c-Completed primary school; no degree.
d-Member of the City Council of
Mazatlán, 1940s; *Federal Deputy* (Party
Deputy from the PPS), 1967-70, member
of the Agrarian Affairs Committee, the
Department of the Federal District
Committee, the Second Government
Committee, the Small Agrarian Proper-
ties Committee and the Hydraulic
Resources Committee; *Federal Deputy*
(Party Deputy from the PPS), 1973-76;
Plurinominal Federal Deputy from the
PPS, 1979-82. e-Joined the PPS, 1948;
Secretary of Electoral Affairs of the
Central Committee of the PPS, 1952;
Secretary of Publicity of the Central
Committee of the PPS, 1979. f-None.
g-Member of the Union of Workers and
Peasants, Mazatlán, 1932; Secretary of
the Ejido Vigilance Committee, 1934;
Secretary of Organization of the
Regional Peasant Committee No. 1,
South Sinaloa, 1937; Secretary General
of the Regional Agrarian Committee of
Sinaloa, 1942-45; Secretary of Peasant
Affairs of the Mexican Association of
Workers and Peasants, 1952-62.
i-Married Lina Valdés; father was a rural
school teacher and fought in the
Revolution. j-None. k-Candidate for
governor of the State of Sinaloa (twice);
Confessed double agent and infiltrator
of the PPS and the CIA. l-HA, 2 Apr.
1979, IV; C de D, 1973-76, 30, 1967-70,

58, 61, 73, 82, 85; *Excélsior*, 19 Aug. 1979, 18; Medina, 20, 145; letter.

Rubio (Ortiz), Noradino
a-Apr. 20, 1896. b-Pisaflores, Hidalgo. c-Primary education in own home; attended superior schools; no degree. d-Mayor of Pisaflores, Hidalgo, 1918-19; Local Deputy to the State Legislature of Querétaro, 1927-29; *Federal Deputy* from the State of Querétaro, 1932-34; *Federal Deputy* from the State of Querétaro, Dist. 2, 1937-40; *Governor of Querétaro*, 1940-44. e-None. f-None. g-Member of the National Farmers Federation; active Mason. h-Farmer; wrote for various newspapers after 1944. i-Great-grandson of Independence leader Encarnación Ortiz; friend of *Saturnillo Cedillo*; son of Lorenzo Rubio. j-None. k-Simpson states that when Rubio was governor he employed an army of pistoleros under Saturnino Osorio to control Querétaro. l-Peral, 721; EBW46, 191; C de D, 1937-39, 19; Simpson, 342; Pérez Flores, 422.

Rubio Ruiz, Marcelo
(Deceased Jan. 6, 1977) a-1923. b-Santa Rosalia, Baja California del Sur. c-Teaching certificate; law degree. d-*Senator* from the State of Baja California del Sur, 1976-77, president of the Fishing Committee. e-President of the Regional Committee of PRI, Baja California del Sur. f-Director of Normal School, La Paz, Baja California del Sur; Delegate of the Secretariat of Public Education, Baja California del Sur; Secretary General of Government of Baja California del Sur. g-None. i-Father a miner. j-None. k-None. l-*Excélsior*, 7 Jan. 1977, 13; C de S, 1976-82.

Rueda Villagrán, Quintín
(Deceased Oct. 26, 1973) a-1905. b-Huichipan, Hidalgo. c-Early education unknown; economics degree; law degree; secondary school teacher;

professor at the National Polytechnic Institute. d-*Alternate Federal Deputy* from the State of Hidalgo, Dist. 2, 1946-49; *Federal Deputy* from the State of Hidalgo, Dist. 5, 1949-51, member of the Third Ejido Committee and the First Treasury Committee, president of the organizing committees; *Governor of Hidalgo*, 1951-57. e-None. f-Subdirector, National Ejido Bank; Controller General of the Secretariat of Agriculture; Director General of Information, Department of Paper Products; Director of Information, Secretariat of Government. g-None. j-None. k-*Villaseñor* claims Rueda Villagrán bought up lands for a government industry to make a personal profit; *Excélsior* suggests that *Miguel Alemán's* choice of Rueda Villagrán as governor was influenced by *Enrique Parra Hernández*. l-Villaseñor, II, 203; *Excélsior*, 24 Dec. 1978, 16-17; DGF51, I, 22, 32, 33, 90; DGF50, II, 409; DGF51, II, 571; C de D, 1949-52, 89; DGF56, 94; DGF47, 8, 360; HA, 6 Apr. 1951, 16-18; Pérez López, 427.

Ruffo Appel, Ernesto
a-June 25, 1952. b-San Diego, California. c-Primary studies in Ensenada; degree in business administration, Monterrey Institute of Technology and Higher Studies; teacher, Center of Higher Technical Training, Ensenada, Baja California, 1981-86. d-Mayor of Ensenada, Baja California, 1986-88; *Governor of Baja California*, 1989-95. e-Member of PAN; joined PAN, 1982; adviser, National Council of PAN, 1989- . f-None. g-President, Businessman's Coordinating Council, Ensenada, Baja California. h-Director of Personnel, Pesquera Zapata, 1976; Director General, Pesquera Zapata, 1986; stockholder in Aletas y Fibras, S.A. i-Son of Ernesto Ruffo Sandoval, fish packer, and Olga Appel Croswaith; married Margarita Sánchez MacFarland. j-None. k-First opposition party member, and

member of PAN, to be declared the winner in a gubernatorial race in the history of PRI, 1929 to present. l-DBGM89, 742; DBGM92, 827-28.

Ruiseco Avellaneda, Alfredo
a-Oct. 14, 1908. b-Veracruz, Veracruz. c-Primary studies from the Cantonal School of Veracruz and the Colegio Mexicano, Mexico City; preparatory studies from the National Preparatory School, 1925-29; law degree, National School of Law, UNAM, 1930-35; Professor of World History, National Preparatory School; Professor of Mexican History, National Preparatory School and the School of Plastic Arts, UNAM; Professor of Art History, School of Plastic Arts, UNAM; researcher, Institute for Social Research, UNAM; Professor of the History of Philosophical Doctrines, Normal School of Colima. d-*Federal Deputy* from the State of Colima, Dist. 2, 1961-64, member of the Gran Comisión, President of the Chamber, September, 1962; answered President *Adolfo López Mateos'* 4th State of the Union Address, President of the Permanent Committee; member of the Legislative Studies Committee, the Constitutional Affairs Committee, the Fine Arts Committee and the Editorial Committee; *Senator* from the State of Colima, 1964-70, President of the First Public Education Committee and the Second Instructive Section of the Grand Jury. e-Joined the PNR, 1932; member of the National Revolutionary Federation led by *Mario Souza*, which supported General Obregón for president, 1928; campaigned with *Adolfo López Mateos* during his presidential campaign in Aguascalientes, Durango, Zacatecas and Coahuila, 1958. g-Student leader of the Autonomy Movement at UNAM, 1929. h-Secretary General of Government of the State of Colima under Governor *José González Lugo*, 1951-56. i-Father

Alfredo Ruiseco Carbonell ran a shipping business in Manzanillo, 1920-70; married Concepción Rivera Silva. j-None. k-Moved to Manzanillo, Colima, 1920. l-Letter; C de S, 1964-70; MGF69; *Excélsior*, 29 Aug. 1979, 14.

Ruiz, Francisco H.
(Deceased 1958) a-1872. b-Jalisco. c-Primary and secondary studies in Guadalajara; preparatory studies in Guadalajara; law degree from the University of Guadalajara, 1899. d-None. e-None. f-Notary in Guadalajara; Judge and President of the Superior Tribunal of Jalisco; Judge of the First Instance in Jalisco; Civil Judge in various Mexican states including Colima, Zacatecas, México; Judge of the Superior Tribunal of Colima, Veracruz, and Jalisco; District Judge of the State of México; Secretary of the City Council of Guadalajara, 1918-19; Secretary General of Government of the State of Jalisco; Interim Governor of Jalisco; Justice of the Supreme Court, 1928-34; *Justice of the Supreme Court*, 1934-40. g-None. h-Author of law textbook. j-None. k-None. l-DP70, 1815; letter.

Ruiz Almada, Gilberto Sebastián
b-Sinaloa. c-Early education unknown; engineering degree, University of Sinaloa. d-*Senator* from the State of Sinaloa, 1976-82. e-None. f-Director of Public Works, Culiacán, Sinaloa, 1959; Subdirector of Administration of the Secretariat of Government, 1965; Director of Administration of the Secretariat of Government, 1969; *Oficial Mayor of the Secretariat of the Presidency*, 1970-74; *Subsecretary of Fiscal Investigation*, 1974-76. g-None. i-Supported *Leopoldo Sánchez Celis* as a precandidate for governor of Sonora, 1963; close friend of *Luis Echeverría*. j-None. k-None. l-DPE65, 13; MGF69, 161; C de S, 1976-82; *Excélsior*, 18 June 1974, 9, 23 Mar. 1980, 8.

Ruiz (Camarillo), Leobardo
(Deceased 1965) a-Jan. 18, 1892. b-Hacienda de Santiago, Pinos, Zacatecas.
c-Early education unknown; graduated from the National Military College, Dec. 24, 1914, as a 2nd Lieutenant in the Cavalry; Professor of Equitation, 1914, Assistant Director, 1928-31, and Director, 1953-54, all of the National Military College. d-None. e-None.
f-Member of a military study commission to Europe to study cavalry tactics, 1926; Director of the Department of Aeronautics, Secretary of War; Interim Governor of Zacatecas, 1932; Ambassador to Spain; Ambassador to Japan; Consul to Holland, 1935-37; *Chargé d' Affaires*, Mexican Embassy, Paris, France, 1937-38; Counselor of the Mexican Embassy, Paris, France, 1938; Director of Recruitment and Reserves, Secretariat of National Defense, 1941; *Oficial Mayor of the Secretariat of National Defense*, 1945-46; Military Attaché to the United States; Military Attaché to Canada; Ambassador to Peru, 1952-53; Director of Military Education, Secretariat of National Defense, 1954-58. g-Secretary of the Union of Apprentice Mechanics.
h-Worked on the railroad when he was a young man. i-Son of Eusebio Ruiz and Paula Camarillo; brother of Brigadier General Eladio Ruiz Camarillo, garrison commander, 1951; married Ofelia Pérez Escobar; son Leobardo Carlos was a Brigadier General; son *Rodolfo* was a federal deputy from Hidalgo, 1988-91.
j-Career army officer; joined the Revolution as a Captain in the artillery, Nov. 20, 1914; rank of major, 1915; fought in Hidalgo and Veracruz, 1915; colonel in the forces of Venustiano Carranza, 1920; accompanied Carranza to Veracruz, 1920; Commander of Artillery in the Army of the North East; rank of Brigadier General, 1940; rank of Division General, Sept. 4, 1947; Commander of the Third Military

Region, Mérida, Yucatán, 1951-52.
k-None. l-DP70, 1816; DGF56, 200; DGF51, 182; WWM45, 107; Rev. de Ejer., Sept. 1976, 136.

Ruiz Castañeda, Maximiliano
a-Dec. 5, 1900. b-Acambay, México.
c-Preparatory at the Scientific and Literary Institute of Toluca, México, 1912-16; medical degree from the National School of Medicine, UNAM, 1923; postgraduate work, University of Paris, 1924-25; instructor in Bacteriology and Immunology, 1932-36, and research fellow, Harvard Medical School, 1930-36. d-*Senator* from the State of México, 1958-64, member of the Gran Comisión, the Public Welfare Committee, the Second Petroleum Committee, and the Special Committee for the Belisario Domínguez Medal; President of the Second Foreign Relations Committee. e-None. f-Organizer and researcher, Department of Medical Research, General Hospital, Mexico City, 1937-70; Director of Central Laboratory, Children's Hospital, Mexico City, 1936-70. g-None. h-Author of medical works. i-Married Luisa Ochoa. j-None.
k-None. l-WWM45, 108; C de S, 1961-64, 68; letter; López, 970; MGF47, 198.

Ruiz Cortines, Adolfo
(Deceased Dec. 3, 1973) a-Dec. 30, 1890. b-Veracruz, Veracruz. c-Primary studies at La Pastora, Veracruz; studied at the Instituto Veracruzano for four years; no degree. d-*Federal Deputy* from the State of Veracruz, Dist. 3, 1937-40; *Governor of Veracruz*, 1944-48; *President of Mexico*, 1952-58. e-PRI Committeeman from Veracruz; campaign manager for the presidential campaign of *Miguel Alemán*, 1946; campaign treasurer for the presidential campaign of *Manuel Avila Camacho*, 1940.
f-Aide to Alfredo Robles Domínguez, Governor of the Federal District, 1914; member of Carranza's Secret Service,

1913; assistant to *Heriberto Jara,* Governor of the Federal District, 1914; private secretary to General *Jacinto B. Treviño,* Secretary of Industry and Commerce, 1920-21; employee, Office of Social Statistics, 1921-26; Director of the Office of Social Statistics, 1926-35; *Oficial Mayor of the Department of the Federal District,* 1935-37, under *Cosme R. Hinojosa;* Secretary General of Government of the State of Veracruz, 1939-40, under Governor *Fernando Casas Alemán; Oficial Mayor of the Secretariat of Government,* 1940-44; *Secretary of Government,* 1948-52; consulting economist to Nacional Financiera, 1959-67. g-None. h-Abandoned studies at age 16 to support family; employed in a textile mill; worked as an accountant. i-Father, a custom's agent, died when he was two months old; stepson, Mauricio Locken, was appointed 2nd Captain of the Chief of Staff, Secretariat of National Defense, 1952; helped by Alfredo Robles Domínguez, who was his civics teacher in Veracruz and was an important influence on his political career; influenced by Miguel Macías, one of his teachers at the Instituto Veracruzano, who later edited a pamphlet about *Ruiz Cortines* as Governor of Veracruz; friend of *Miguel Alemán* since 1935, when he was Oficial Mayor of the Federal District and *Alemán* was a Judge of the Superior Tribunal of Justice of the Federal District; formed friendship with *Adolfo López Mateos* when *López Mateos* represented México in the Senate and before the Secretariat of Government; married Lucia Carrillo, widowed, and married María Izaguirre. j-Joined the Army, 1914, in Veracruz; rank of 2nd Captain; aide to Robles Domínguez as Governor of Guerrero, 1914; administrative posts in the Paymaster General's Staff; served under General *Heriberto Jara;* recovered the federal treasury abandoned by Carranza, 1920; Paymaster of the Army of the East; administra-

tive posts in the Army, 1924; Paymaster General of the Brigade Mariel, 1915-16. k-Scott believes that the early contact and friendship between General *Treviño* and *Ruiz Cortines* was the reason why *Treviño's* political party, PARM, received government recognition. l-Cline, 160; *Heroic Mexico,* 352; Scott, 217-18; Gaxiola, 528; Q es Q, 525-26; *Libro de Oro,* liii; DBM68, 542; Morton, 88-89, 92; Covarrubias, 157; WWMG, 36; DGF56, 45; Brandenburg, 107-13; DP70, 1817; C de D, 1937-39, 19; Enc. Mex., XI, 1977, 206-09.

Ruiz de Chávez, Genaro
(Deceased June 3, 1958) a-June 12, 1892. b-San Cristóbal Las Casas, Chiapas. c-Primary and secondary studies in San Cristóbal; preparatory studies in San Cristóbal; law degree, 1915; professor of law, Graduate School of Business Administration, UNAM. d-Federal Deputy from the State of Chiapas, 1918-20. e-Cofounder of the Civic Front of Revolutionary Affirmation, 1963. f-Agent of the Ministerio Público; Judge of the Superior Tribunal of Justice, State of Chiapas; Oficial Mayor of the State of Chiapas; Judge of the 7th Penal Division, Federal District, 1940; Judge of the 19th Penal Division, Federal District, 1941; Judge of the Superior Tribunal of the Federal District, 8th Division, 1951-53; *Justice of the Supreme Court,* 1954-58. g-None. h-Director of *El Hijo del Pueblo,* 1909, in which he attacked Porfirio Díaz; author of various legal articles. j-None. k-None. l-DP70, 1819; DGF56, 567; DGF51, I, 487; Cadena Z., 1970; Casasola, V; DB de C, 224.

Ruiz de Chávez Guerrero, Manuel Hugo
a-Jan. 17, 1947. b-Federal District. c-Early education unknown; medical degree, National School of Medicine, UNAM, 1973; residency, National Medical Center, IMSS, 1974; MS in

sciences, University of London, 1977; professor, National School of Medicine, UNAM, 1973-81; Coordinator of Rural Health Program, UNAM, 1973-75; professor, National Preparatory School, Iztacala, 1979. d-None. e-None. f-Subdirector of Systems, Evaluation Division, Secretariat of Public Health, 1979-80; Director General of Evaluation and Control, 1983, of Sectoral Coordination, 1983-84, and of Assistance, Regional Coordination, 1985-86, all at the Secretariat of Public Health; *Subsecretary of Planning*, Secretariat of Public Health, 1986-88; Delegate A of the Secretariat of Controller General to the Secretariat of Public Health, 1988. g-None. h-None. i-Son of Manuel Ruiz de Chávez Salazar, lawyer, and Eva Guerrero Larrañaga; married Carmen Gutiérrez de Velazco, surgeon; cousin of *Arturo Ruiz de Chávez*, subsecretary of labor, 1981-82. j-None. k-None. l-HA, 2 Sept. 1986, 26; DBGM87, 347; DBGM89, 312.

Ruiz de Chávez Robinson, Arturo
a-June 22, 1937. b-Federal District. c-Early education unknown; law degree, National School of Law, UNAM, 1956-60, with a thesis on writs of amparo; professor, National School of Law, UNAM, 1976; professor, Institute of Labor Studies, 1979-82. d-None. e-Joined PRI, 1962. f-Coordinator of Oficial Mayor, Department of Tourism, 1965-66; Subdirector of Tourist Services, Department of Tourism, 1966-67; Oficial Mayor, Chamber of Deputies, 1967-73; Director General of Legal Affairs, Secretariat of Government, 1973-76; Director General of Conciliation, Secretariat of Labor, 1976-79; President of the Federal Board of Conciliation and Arbitration, 1979-81; *Subsecretary of Labor*, 1981-82; Corporate Director of Industrial Relations, SIDERMEX, 1982-85; Director General of Administration,

Secretariat of Agrarian Reform, 1986-88. g-Delegate of the CNOP to PRI, 1963. h-Member of the Ruiz de Chávez Correa Law Firm, 1956-63. i-Son of Arturo Ruiz de Chávez Salazar, lawyer, and Dorothy Robinson Bierbeck; married Cristina Magaña Méndez, dental surgeon; cousin *Manuel Ruiz de Chávez* was subsecretary of planning. j-None. k-None. l-DBGM, 376; DBGM87, 346.

Ruiz de la Peña, Francisco
a-Mar. 16, 1921. b-Federal District. c-Early education unknown; law degree, National School of Law, UNAM; Professor of International Administrative Law and Professor of Administrative Law, National School of Law, UNAM. d-None. e-None. f-Director, Department of Miscellaneous Deposits, National Finance Bank, 1962-64; Director of Industrial Relations and Control of Enterprises, National Finance Bank, 1964-65; Representative of the National Finance Bank, Washington, D.C., 1965-70; Treasurer, Secretariat of the Treasury, 1971-76; *Subdirector of Finances, Pemex*, 1976-82. g-None. j-None. k-None. l-DPE71, 42.

Ruiz Fernández, Daniel
a-Apr. 7, 1927. b-Madrid, Spain. c-Primary studies in Spain, 1933-49; secondary and preparatory studies, Academia Hispano Mexicana, 1941-45; civil engineering degree, National School of Engineering, UNAM, 1945-58, with a thesis on reinforced concrete; Director of the Engineering Institute, UNAM, 1970-74; Director General of Planning, UNAM, 1974-78. d-None. e-Joined PRI, 1965. f-Director General of Buildings, Secretariat of Public Works, 1965-70; General Manager of Federal School Construction Program, Secretariat of Public Education, 1978-88; *Secretary General of Public Works*, Department of the Federal District, 1988-93. g-None. h-Engineer, ICA,

S.A., 1948-53; superintendent, Estructuras y Cimentaciones de México, S.A.,
1953-54; Director of Estructuras y
Cimentaciones de México, S.A., 1964-
65. i-Son of Roberto Ruiz García, public
accountant, and Antonia Carrión,;
married Ana María Vilá Gimeno.
j-None. k-None. l-DBGM92, 333;
DBGM89, 315; letter.

Ruiz Galindo, Antonio
a-July 30, 1897. b-Córdoba, Veracruz.
c-Primary studies in Córdoba; secondary
studies at the Internado Nacional
(National Preparatory Boarding School);
studies at the School of Business and
Administration, UNAM; no degree.
d-None. e-None. f-*Secretary of
Industry and Commerce*, 1946-48.
g-None. h-Sales agent for General
Fireproofing; founded DM Nacional,
1929; built a new plant in 1937 after the
original factory was destroyed by fire;
organizer of a large-scale industrial city
on the outskirts of Mexico City, 1944-
46; President of the Board of Directors
of National Steel Industry; Director
General of DM Nacional, 1971-72.
i-Son, Antonio Jr., was Ambassador to
Germany; married Serafina Gómez
Sariol. j-Joined the Revolution under
Cándido Aguilar. k-Resigned from the
Secretariat of Industry and Commerce,
1948; DM Nacional was one of the first
Mexican firms to institute modern
automated facilities and methods of
mass production in Mexico. l-WWM45,
108; HA, 26 Dec. 1951; DBM68, 542-43;
DBM70, 490-91; Brandenburg, 102;
STYRBIWW54, 986; HA, 23 July 1956,
13, 28 Dec. 1951, 37.

Ruiz González, Pedro
a-May 25, 1928. b-Luis Moya, Zacatecas. c-Primary studies at the Escobar
Brothers School, Ciudad Juárez, Chihuahua; agricultural engineering degree,
National School of Agriculture.
d-*Federal Deputy* from the State of

Zacatecas, Dist. 4, 1964-67, member of
the Gran Comisión and the Fourth Ejido
Committee, Vice-President of the
Chamber, October, 1966; *Governor of
Zacatecas*, 1968-74. e-Secretary
General of PRI in Zacatecas, 1962-63;
President of PRI in Zacatecas, 1964.
f-Brigade Director, Hoof and Mouth
Disease Campaign, Secretariat of
Agriculture, 1949-51; Delegate of the
Agricultural Extension Service, Secre-
tariat of Agriculture; Zone Director,
National Agricultural Credit Bank,
1956; Subdirector of the Agricultural
Experiment Station, State of Zacatecas;
Irrigation administrator, Ejido Bank;
General Agent, Secretariat of Agricul-
ture, State of Zacatecas, 1959-64.
g-None. j-None. k-None. l-C de D,
1964-67, 83.

Ruiz Madero, Ramiro
a-Dec. 14, 1916. b-Torreón, Coahuila.
c-Early education unknown; no degree.
d-*Alternate Federal Deputy* from the
Federal District, 1961-64; *Alternate
Senator* from the State of Coahuila,
1976-82. e-None. f-Employee of the
Secretariat of Health and Welfare;
adviser to the Governing Board of the
ISSSTE, 1971-74. g-Secretary of
Organization of Local 39 of the Union
of Workers of the Secretariat of Health
and Public Welfare; Secretary General of
Local 39 of the Union of Workers of the
Secretariat of Health; Secretary of
Finances of the CTM in Torreon,
Coahuila; Secretary of Organization of
the Union of Workers of the Secretariat
of Health; Secretary General of the
Union of Workers of the Secretariat of
Health; Secretary of Budget, of Organi-
zation, 1956-59, of Labor Relations, of
Technical Problems, 1959-61, of
International Relations, 1961-65, of
Labor and Conflicts, 1965-68, and of
Finances, 1968-71, all of the CEN of the
FSTSE; founder and director of the
Finance Committee of the Congress of

Labor, 1974-75; General Coordinator of the Congress of Labor, 1978. h-Owner of many businesses. i-Son, Benjamín, served as Secretary General of the Congress of Labor. j-None. k-Accused of nepotism by *Excélsior* for employing five sons in the Congess of Labor. l-HA, 10 July 1978, 10; *Excélsior*, 13 Nov. 1982, 21; Sirvent, 180; C de D, 1961-64; C de S, 1976-82.

Ruiz Malerva, Demetrio
a-Aug. 6, 1941. b-Tuxpan, Veracruz. c-Primary, secondary, and preparatory studies in Tuxpan; law degree, National School of Law, UNAM, 1964-69, with a thesis on "A Juridical Sociological Essay on the Mexican Revolution;" Professor of Juridical Sociology, University of Veracruz; Professor of Political Publicity and Public Opinion, Institute of Political Education of PRI; secondary teacher in Mexican and twentieth-century history. d-*Federal Deputy* from the State of Veracruz, Dist. 2, 1973-76, 1979-82. e-Director of Youth Sector of PRI, Tuxpan, Veracruz, 1961-63; Coordinator of PRI Youth for the Northern Zone of Veracruz, 1961-63; joined PRI, 1967; President of PRI, Tuxpan, Veracruz, 1969-71; Secretary of Popular Action of the Regional Committee of PRI, Veracruz, 1971-73; Auxiliary Secretary of the CEN of PRI, 1974-75; Subdirector of Dialogue, Regional Committee of PRI, Veracruz, 1975; Director of *La República* of the CEN of PRI, 1977-78. f-Secretary of the Board of Material and Moral Improvement, Tuxpan, 1966-70; Second Syndic of the City Council of Tuxpan, 1967-70; consulting lawyer to the State Legislature of Veracruz, 1971; Oficial Mayor of the State Legislature of Veracruz, 1971-73; Director General of Information and Public Relations, Chamber of Deputies, 1979; Director of Social Communication, Secretariat of Programming and Budget, 1982. g-Secretary General of the Muni-

cipal League of CNOP of Tuxpan, 1968-69. h-None. i-Married Imelda Sordo; member of *Jesús Reyes Heroles'* group; son of Julio Ruiz Garma, public official, and Elia Malerva Garcés; political disciple of *Jesús Reyes Heroles*. j-None. k-None. l-Letter; Q es QAP, 136; C de D, 1979-82, 1973-76; Protag., 307.

Ruiz Massieu, José Francisco
(Deceased Sept. 28, 1994) a-July 22, 1946. b-Acapulco, Guerrero. c-Early education unknown; law degree, National School of Law, UNAM, 1965-69, with a thesis on "Legal and Political Characteristics of the LAFTA"; professor, National School of Law, UNAM, 1970-86. d-*Governor of Guerrero*, 1987-93. e-Secretary of the Housing Committee, IEPES of PRI, 1975-76; Subdirector General of Regional Coordination, IEPES of PRI, 1981; Secretary General of the CEN of PRI, 1994. f-Director of Orientation and Legal Services, Infonavit, 1972-79; agrarian adviser, Agrarian Advisory Body, Secretariat of Agriculture, 1979-80; Director General of Legal Affairs, Secretariat of Public Health, 1980-81; Secretary General of Government of the State of Guerrero, 1981-82; *Oficial Mayor of Health*, 1982; *Subsecretary of Planning*, Secretariat of Health, 1983-86; Director General of the Federal Workers Housing Institute, 1993-94. g-None. h-None. i-Son of Armando Ruiz Quintanilla, surgeon, and María del Refugio Massieu Helguera, editor, writer, and daughter of *Wilfrido Massieu*, rector of IPN; nephew of *Guillermo Massieu Helguera*, rector of IPN, 1964-70; married María Fernanda Riveroll Sánchez; brother Mario was technical secretary of the social welfare cabinet group; brother Armando was a director general in the secretariat of health; close ties to *Carlos Salinas's* group since law school. j-None. k-Prominent PRI politicians from Tamaulipas responsible for his

assassination. l-QesQAP, 333; DBGM, 374; HA, 26 Aug. 1986, 10; DBGM89, 742; DBGM92, 828.

Ruiz Soto, Agustín
a-Feb. 15, 1930. b-Canatlan, Durango. c-Early education unknown; law degree, School of Law, University of Durango; studies in English and sociology, University of Louisiana; Professor of World History, University of Durango. d-Local Deputy to the State Legislature of Durango; *Federal Deputy* from the State of Durango, Dist. 3, 1961-64, Dist. 1, 1967-70; *Senator* from the State of Durango, 1970-76, President of the Forestry Committee, Second Secretary of the Second Credit Committee and the National Lands Committee, and First Secretary of the Second Mines Committee. e-None. f-Subdirector of the Department of Multi-family Control and Administration, ISSSTE; Private Secretary to the Governor of Durango, *Francisco González de la Vega*, 1956-61. g-Legal adviser to the National Federation of Apple Growers; Secretary of Organization and Statistics of the CEN of CNOP. i-Married Magdalena Torres San Martín. j-None. k-None. l-C de D, 1967-70; C de S, 1970-76, 85; PS, 5512.

Ruiz Vasconcelos, Ramón
a-Sept. 16, 1913. b-Oaxaca, Oaxaca. c-Law degree. d-*Federal Deputy* from the State of Oaxaca, 1955-58, Dist. 9, Secretary of the Gran Comisión, member of the Legislative Studies Committee (1st year), the Livestock Committee, the Second Treasury Committee; *Senator* from the State of Oaxaca, 1958-64, member of the Second Government Committee, the First Mines Committee, the First Foreign Relations Committee, the Special Tourist Affairs Committee, and the Special Legislative Studies Committee; President of the Social Security Committee and substi-

tute member of the Securities Committee. e-President of the State Committee of PRI in Oaxaca. f-Lawyer, Secretariat of Public Works; Agent of the Ministerio Público of the Office of the Attorney General; Assistant to the Attorney General of Mexico; Chief of Preparatory Investigations, Attorney General of the Federal District; Ambassador to the Dominican Republic, 1965; Ambassador to Yugoslavia, 1969-70. g-None. h-Technical adviser to the IMSS. j-None. k-None. l-DPE65, 31; Func., 303; C de S, 1961-64, 69; DGF56, 26, 29, 33, 34, 30; Ind. Biog., 142.

Ruiz Vázquez, Guillermo
a-Nov. 5, 1919. b-La Barca, Jalisco. c-Primary, secondary and preparatory studies in Guadalajara, Jalisco; law degree, School of Law, University of Guadalajara, 1940. d-*Federal Deputy* from the State of Jalisco, Dist. 2, 1964-67; *Federal Deputy* (Party Deputy from PAN), 1970-73. e-Joined PAN, 1944; member of the Regional Committee of PAN, 1955; Secretary of Studies and Press Secretary, Regional Committee of PAN, Jalisco, 1955-60; President of the Regional Committee of PAN, Jalisco, 1960-64; national advisor to the CEN of PAN; candidate of PAN for local deputy to the State Legislature of Jalisco, 1955; candidate of PAN for federal deputy from PAN, 1946, 1955, 1958. f-None. g-President of the Catholic Association of Mexican Youth of Jalisco, 1942-43. h-Book seller; practicing lawyer. i-Married María Luisa Higuera. j-None. k-None. l-C de D, 1964-67, 1970-73; Mabry.

Ruiz Vega, Ofelia
a-June 20, 1940. b-Acambaro, Guanajuato. c-Primary studies at the Benito Juárez School and La Corregidora School; secondary studies at Dr. Benjamín Lara Secondary School; teaching certificate, Federal Institute of

Teaching; teaching certificate, Higher Normal School; teacher, Primary Urban School No. 1, Valle de Santiago, Guanajuato, 1956-66; Director, Primary Urban School No. 2, Valle de Santiago, Guanajuato, 1966-79. d-City council member, Valle de Santiago, 1974-76; *Federal Deputy* from the State of Guanajuato, Dist. 8, 1979-82. e-Leader of the CNOP of PRI in Guanajuato, 1975-78. f-None. g-Secretary of Labor and Conflicts, Local 15, National Teachers Union (SNTE), 1972-74; Secretary General of Local 15, National Teachers Union, 1975-78; Secretary of Health and Welfare, CEN of the SNTE, 1977-79. h-None. i-Daughter of Alfonso Ruiz Ojeda and Sofia Vega Ramírez. j-None. k-None. l-C de D, 1979-82; Romero Aceves, 734.

Ruiz Zavala, José María Leóncio
a-Apr. 30, 1904. b-San Luis Potosí, San Luis Potosí. c-Primary studies, Irapuato, Guanajuato; some secondary in various locations; no degree. d-*Federal Deputy* from the Federal District, Dist. 5, 1952-55; *Federal Deputy* from the Federal District, Dist. 5, 1958-61. e-None. f-None. g-Official, Transportation Workers Union. h-Employee. i-From a working class family. j-None. k-None. l-Func., 180; C de D, 1952-55, 1958-61.

Ruvalcaba Gutiérrez, Aurora
a-May 24, 1928. b-Colima, Colima. c-Primary studies in Sor Juana Inés de la Cruz, Colima; secondary in Colima, Colima; teaching certificate from the Normal School of Colima; degree in diplomacy from the School of Political and Social Sciences, UNAM. d-*Senator* from the State of Colima, 1970-76, President of the Second Foreign Relations Committee, Second Secretary of the Department of the Federal District Committee, and member of the First Section of the Legislative Studies Committee. e-Delegate of the Women's

Sector of PRI in Puebla. f-None. g-Secretary General of the SNTE in Colima; President of the Women's Sector of the SNTE, Colima; President of the Women's Sector of the CEN of SNTE; Women's Sector Director of the FSTSE; Vice-president of the Congress of Labor; President of the Congress of Labor. j-None. k-First female senator elected from Colima. l-C de S, 1970-76, 85; PS, 5519.

Ruvalcaba Sánchez, Filiberto G.
a-Feb. 4, 1905. b-Ixtlahuacán del Río, Jalisco. c-Primary studies; no further education. d-*Federal Deputy* from the State of Jalisco, Dist. 7, 1952-55, Dist. 8, 1961-64; *Senator* from the State of Jalisco, 1964-70. e-Joined the PNR, 1929. f-None. g-Organized the first agrarian workers in Jalisco; representative of Mexican labor to the International Labor Organization Conference, Geneva, Switzerland, 1954; representative of Mexican labor to the United Nations Labor Meetings, New York City, 1959; Secretary General of the National Miners and Metallurgical Workers Union; President of the Latin American Federation of Miners, 1960. h-Worked as a farm laborer; miner. j-None. k-None. l-C de D, 1952-55, 1961-64; C de S, 1964-70; MGF69.

S

Sabines Gutiérrez, Juan
a-1920. b-Tuxtla Gutiérrez, Chiapas. c-Primary and secondary studies in Tuxtla Gutiérrez; no degree. d-Mayor of Tuxtla Gutiérrez; *Federal Deputy* from the State of Chiapas, Dist. 3, 1952-55, member of the Second Balloting Committee and the Fourth Section of the Credentials Committee; *Federal Deputy* from the State of Chiapas, Dist. 1, 1958-61, member of the Colonization Committee, the Foreign and Domestic

Trade Committee, the Fifth Section of the Legislative Studies Committee, the Inspection Committee for the General Accounting Office (1st year), the Credentials Committee, substitute member of the Consular and Diplomatic Service Committee, and president of the Permanent Committee; *Senator* from Chiapas, 1970-76, member of the Gran Comisión, President of the Industries Committee, First Secretary of the Second Instructive Section of the Grand Jury and First Secretary of the Hydraulic Resources Committee; *Governor of Chiapas*, 1980-86. e-President of the State Regional Committee of PRI in Chiapas; General Delegate of the CEN of PRI to various states, 1964-67; *Secretary General of the CEN of PRI*, 1976-78. f-Representative of the State of Guanajuato in the Federal District, 1953-56; adviser to the President of Mexico, 1977-78. g-President of the Chamber of Commerce of Tuxtla Gutiérrez. h-Businessman. i-Brother, *Jaime Sabines Gutiérrez*, is a well-known poet and was a federal deputy from Chiapas, 1976-79; son of a Lebanese businessman; brother, Jorge, represents him before the national press. j-None. k-None. l-Func., 154; C de D, 1958-60, 90, 1952-54, 58; C de S, 1970-76; DB de C, 229; Almanaque of Chiapas, 29; *Proceso*, 1 Feb. 1982, 13-15.

Sala, Adelor D.
a-Jan. 28, 1897. b-Teapa, Tabasco. c-Primary and secondary studies from the Juárez Institute of Villahermosa; preparatory studies from the National Preparatory School; teaching certificate from the National Normal School, Mexico City, 1926; law degree, National School of Law, UNAM, 1934. d-*Senator* from the State of Tabasco, 1946-52, member of the Gran Comisión, the Legislative Studies Committee, the Second Tariff and Foreign Trade Committee and the First Petroleum Committee; member of the Permanent Committee, 1947. e-None. f-Judge of the Superior Tribunal of Justice of Tabasco; Judge of the 13th Civil Judicial District, Mexico City; Secretary General of Government of the State of Tabasco. g-None. j-None. k-None. l-C de S, 1946-52; DGF51, I, 7, 9-11, 13.

Salas, Ismael
a-May 2, 1897. b-San Luis Potosí. c-Early education unknown; studied accounting degree. d-Federal Deputy from the Federal District, Dist. 4, 1930-32, Dist. 5, 1932-34; *Federal Deputy* from the State of San Luis Potosí, Dist. 5, 1943-46; *Governor of San Luis Potosí*, 1949-55. e-*Treasurer of the CEN of the PRM*, 1941-43. f-Director, Federal Tax Office, Río Verde, San Luis Potosí, 1934-37; Director, Administrative Office, Department of Labor, 1937-40; Director, Federal Tax Office, Iguala, Guerrero, 1940-41; Treasurer General of the State of San Luis Potosí under *Gonzalo N. Santos*, 1946-48. g-None. i-Protégé of *Gonzalo N. Santos*; brother of *Herminio Salas*, Federal Deputy from the State of San Luis Potosí, 1940-43; brother-in-law of *Alberto Bremauntz*; father was a small shoestore owner. j-None. k-Member of the anti-clerical group of deputies in the 1932-34 legislature. l-Bremauntz, 109; C de D, 1943-46, 20, 1930-32, 1928-30; DGF51, I, 92; HA, 7 Oct. 1949, xxiii-xxvi.

Salazar Hurtado, Daniel
a-Aug. 27, 1911. b-Colima, Colima. c-Primary studies at the Colegio Cuauhtémoc, Guadalajuara; preparatory studies in Guadalajara; law degree, School of Law, University of Guadalajara, Dec. 13, 1934; studies in international, criminal and labor law, UCLA, 1928-29. d-None. e-None. f-Oficial Mayor, Penal Division, Supreme Court, 1934; Secretary of Studies and Accounts to Justice *Hermilo López Sánchez*, 1940;

Judge, Superior Tribunal of Justice of
the Federal District, 1940; President,
Third Arbitration Section, FSTSE
Arbitration Board, 1946. g-None.
h-None. i-Son of Daniel N. Salazar,
railroad dispatcher and an initiator of
the railroad nationalization in Colima,
and Estela Hurtado Vizcaíno. j-None.
k-None. l-Moreno, 148-49.

Salazar Martínez, Florencio
a-Dec. 31, 1931. b-San Luis Potosí, San
Luis Potosí. c-Primary studies at the
Colegio Inglés, San Luis Potosí; secondary and preparatory studies, University
of San Luis Potosí; law degree, School of
Law, University of San Luis Potosí;
Professor of Tributary Law, University
of San Luis Potosí. d-*Federal Deputy*
from the State of San Luis Potosí, Dist.
3, 1967-70; *Senator* from the State of
San Luis Potosí, 1970-76, member of the
Gran Comisión, President of the
Agriculture and Development Committee and the First Ejido Committee; First
Secretary of the First Justice Committee
and member of the Second Section of
the Legislative Studies Committee;
Governor of San Luis Potosí, 1985-91.
e-Joined PRI, 1956; Director of Legal
Development, PRI, San Luis Potosí,
1964-67; President of PRI in San Luis
Potosí, 1967; *Secretary of Finances of
the CEN of PRI*, 1981; General Delegate
of the CEN of PRI to Yucatán, 1984;
General Delegate of the CEN of PRI to
16 other states. f-None. g-President of
the Association of Lawyers of San Luis
Potosí, 1965-67. h-Founder of the
newspaper, *Plan de San Luis*. i-Son of
Florencio Salazar Méndez, federal
deputy from San Luis Potosí, 1940-43,
1946-49; married María del Socorro
Mendoza. j-None. k-None. l-C de D,
1967-70; C de S, 1970-76, 86; *Excélsior*,
27 July 1984, 20, 12 Jan. 1985, 17.

Salazar (Méndez), Florencio
a-1906. b-El Carmen, Tierra Nueva, San
Luis Potosí. c-Teaching certificate, on a
government scholarship, from the
Normal School of San Luis Potosí, 1925.
d-*Federal Deputy* from the State of San
Luis Potosí, Dist. 1, 1940-43, member of
the Gran Comisión; Local Deputy to
the State Legislature of San Luis Potosí,
1943-45; *Federal Deputy* from the State
of San Luis Potosí, Dist. 1, 1946-49;
Alternate Senator from the State of San
Luis Potosí, 1964-70. e-President of PRI
in San Luis Potosí, 1965. f-Director of
Public Education in the State of San
Luis Potosí. g-Founder of the Workers
Federation of the State of San Luis
Potosí; Secretary General of the CTM of
the State of San Luis Potosí. i-From a
humble background; father of *Florencio
Salazar Martínez*, federal deputy from
San Luis Potosí, 1967-70 and senator,
1970-76. j-None. k-Accompanied
Manuel Avila Camacho to Monterrey
for his meeting with Franklin D.
Roosevelt. l-López, 985; MGF69, 106; C
de D, 1940-43, 1946-49.

Salazar (Salazar), Antonio
a-Nov. 14, 1921. b-Villa de Alvarez,
Colima. c-Enrolled in the National
Military College 1939; graduated from
the National Military College as a 2nd
Lieutenant in the Infantry, July 1, 1942;
preparatory studies for law at the
National Preparatory Night School,
Federal District; law degree, National
School of Law, UNAM, Jan. 25, 1951,
with an honorable mention; Professor of
the General Theory of the State and
Military Law, University of Michoacán,
Morelia, 1951. d-*Federal Deputy* from
the State of Colima, Dist. 1, 1955-58,
member of the Military Justice Committee and the Second National Defense Committee; *Senator* from Colima,
1958-64, member of the Gran Comisión, the Second Tariff and Foreign
Trade Committee, the Second Constitu-

tional Affairs Committee, the Special Legislative Studies Committee; President of the Third National Defense Committee and substitute member of the War Materiels Committee; *Senator from Colima, 1976-82.* e-None. f-Agent of the Ministerio Público attached to the 21st Military Zone, Morelia, Michoacán; legal adviser to the Attorney General of Miliary Justice; Public Defender, First Judicial District, 1st Military Region; legal adviser to the Secretariat of National Defense; Chief of the Census Department, CNC. g-None. h-Worked as a farm laborer, age of 16. i-From a humble background. j-Joined the 17th Cavalry Regiment, Jan. 19, 1938, as a private; fought against *Saturnino Cedillo* in San Luis Potosí; Adjutant General of the 9th Infantry Regiment; Chief of Resolutions, Third Section, Department of Justice and Pensions, Secretariat of National Defense; career army officer; rank of Lt. Colonel. k-Precandidate for Governor of Colima three times. l-Func., 147; DGF56, 22, 32, 35; C de S, 1961-64, 69; *Excélsior*, 7 Jan. 1979, 12.

Salcedo Aquino, Roberto
a-Nov. 26, 1943. b-Federal District. c-Early education unknown; teaching certificate in language and literature, Higher Normal School; political science degree, School of Political and Social Sciences, UNAM; MA in political science, School of Political and Social Sciences, UNAM; Director of Political Science and International Relations, UNAM, 1979-83. d-None. e-Joined PRI, 1965; Auxiliary Secretary of the CEN of PRI, 1971-73; General Sub-Delegate of the CEN of PRI to Tabasco, 1978-80, 1982-83. f-Private Secretary to the Director General of the Mexican Corporation of Radio and Television, Secretariat of Government, 1974-76; Subdirector of the National Textbook Committee, Secretariat of Public Education, 1980-82; Regional Delegate

of the Secretariat of Programming and Budgeting to Tabasco, 1983-87; *Oficial Mayor of the Secretariat of Urban Development and Ecology, 1987-88; Oficial Mayor of the Department of the Federal District, 1988-93.* g-None. h-None. i-Son of Roberto Salcedo Ruiz, businessman, and María Apolonia Aquino Ramírez; married Teresa Cisneros Gudiño, sociologist. j-None. k-None. l-DBGM89, 320; DBGM92, 339.

Salcedo (Monteón), Celestino
a-July 26, 1935. b-Ocotlán, Jalisco. c-Teaching certificate; studied for agricultural engineering degree at the School of Agriculture, Navojoa, Sonora; agricultural engineering degree from the Antonio Narro School, Saltillo, Coahuila, 1957; rural school teacher. d-*Federal Deputy* from the State of Baja California del Norte, Dist. 3, 1967-70, member of the Hydraulic Resources Committee; *Federal Deputy* from the State of Baja California del Norte, Dist. 3, 1973-76; *Senator* from Baja California, 1976-82. e-*Secretary of Agrarian Action of the CEN of PRI, 1973.* f-Director of Colonies, Department of Agrarian Affairs, 1973; Director of National Lands, Department of Agrarian Affairs; Director of the National Agrarian Program, Department of Agrarian Affairs; Director General of FONAFE, 1977. g-Student leader in Navojoa and Saltillo; Secretary of the League of Agrarian Communities of Baja California del Norte, 1960-70; Ejido Commissioner, Mexicali, 1963-66; delegate of the CNC to Yucatán, 1970; *Secretary General of the CNC,* Feb. 15, 1973-74. h-Ejidatario in Mexicali. i-Father, Pedro Salcedo Rivera, was a peasant and agrarian leader who co-founded the League of Agrarian Communities in Baja California. j-None. k-None. l-*Excélsior*, 8 Mar. 1973, 14; *Excélsior*, 13 Mar. 1973, 11; C de D, 1967-69, 85; MGF69, 89; *Excélsior*, 15

Feb. 1973, 19; HA, 12 Feb. 1973, 11-13; *Excélsior*, 17 Feb. 1973; HA, 18 Mar. 1974; Loret de Mola, 38; *Excélsior*, 27 Jan. 1975, 16, 8 Dec. 1975, 22.

Saldaña Villaba, Adalberto
a-Apr. 30, 1908. b-Federal District. c-Primary and secondary studies in the Federal District; preparatory studies in the Federal District; law degree from the National Law School, UNAM. d-None. e-None. f-Legal adviser to PEMEX; Assistant to the Director of Nacional Financiera; *Director of National Finance Bank*, 1946-52; Manager of Legal Affairs, Altos Hornos de México, 1964-70. g-None. h-Adviser to Carlos Trouyet, S.A. i-Son of lawyer, Adalberto Saldaña, and Ignacia Villalba. j-None. k-None. l-DGF50, II, 57, etc.; DGF51, II, 77, etc.; DGF47, 344; MGF69, 443.

Sales Gasque, Renato
a-Mar. 26, 1931. b-Mérida, Yucatán. c-Early education unknown; law degree, National School of Law, UNAM, 1957-59; professor, School of Business, University of Campeche, 1966-68, Autonomous University of Hidalgo, 1971-72, University of Tabasco, 1973-75, and at University of Veracruz, 1976-77; Coordinator, Graduate Division, University of Campeche, 1980-82. d-*Senator* from the State of Campeche, 1982-85. e-Joined PRI, 1964; Special Delegate of the CEN of PRI to the Federal District, Nos. 7 and 16, 1965. f-Secretary of Agreements, Second District Court, Criminal Division, Federal District, 1964; Secretary of the the First District Court, Civil Division, Federal District, 1965; First Secretary, District Court, Campeche, 1966-68; Secretary of Studies and Accounts, Supreme Court of Justice, 1968-69; Judge, Second District Court, Tapachula, Chiapas, 1969-70; Judge, First District Court, Puebla, Puebla, 1970-71; Judge, District Court, Pachuca,

Hidalgo, 1971-72; Judge, 10th Circuit Court, Villahermosa, Tabasco, 1973-75; Judge, 7th Circuit Court, Veracruz, Veracruz, 1975-77; Judge, Administrative Division, Circuit Court, Federal District, 1977-80; President of the Superior Tribunal of Campeche, 1980-82; *Attorney General of the Federal District*, Dec. 27, 1985-88. g-Oficial Mayor of the National Federation of Workers and Peasants, 1984-85. h-None. i-Son of Raúl Sales Guerrero, lawyer, and Elia Gasque Espejo; married Ana Florencia Heredia Avila, normal teacher. j-None. k-None. l-DBGM89, 641; DBGM92, 697-98

Sales Gutiérrez, Carlos Enrique
a-Apr. 13, 1938. b-Federal District. c-Early education unknown; studies in economics, Autonomous Technological Institute of Mexico, 1961-66, graduating with a thesis on "The Structure of the Tax System in Mexico," 1967; Professor of Economics. d-*Senator* from the State of Campeche, 1991-97. e-None. f-Assistant economist, 1954-56, analyst, Foreign Trade, 1956-58, researcher, Economic Indicators Section, 1958-62, Chief of Income Section, 1961-65, Chief of the Public Debt Section, 1965-66, adviser, Division of Financial Studies, 1966-67, Chief, Office of Tax Policy, 1967-68, Director, Department of Economic Studies, 1969-70, Director General of Internal Taxes, 1975-76, and Director General of Tax Promotion and Internal Affairs, 1976, all at the Secretariat of the Treasury, General Manager, Finance Program, National Finance Bank, 1977-79; Subdirector General of Credit, Secretariat of the Treasury, 1979-82; *Subsecretary of National Banks*, 1982-86; Director General, National Public Works Bank, 1986-88; Treasurer of the Department of the Federal District, 1988-89; *Secretary General of Planning and Evaluation*, Department of the Federal District, 1990-91. g-None.

h-None. i-Son of Leopoldo Sales Rovira, public official, and Dolores Gutiérrez Presciat; married Jacqueline Arlette Sarra y Fabre; began his career under *Gustavo Petricioli.* j-None. k-None. l-Q es QAP, 108-09; IEPES; DBGM, 382; DBGM89, 321; DBGM92, 573.

Salgado Páez, Vicente
(Deceased) a-July 17, 1893. b-Valle de Santiago, Guanajuato. c-Primary studies in the Valle de Santiago and in the Villa de Uriangato, Guanajuato, 1900-06; engineering degree from the University of Guanajuato, 1909-15. d-*Federal Deputy* from the State of Guanajuato, Dist. 3, 1949-52, member of the Department of Agrarian Affairs and Colonization Committee, the First Balloting Committee and the Social Action Committee (1st year), President of the First Instructive Section of the Grand Jury; *Federal Deputy* from the State of Guanajuato, Dist. 6, 1958-61, member of the Agriculture and Development Committee, the Library Committee (1st year), the Plaints Committee, the Credentials Committee, and the National Lands Committee; *Federal Deputy* from the State of Guanajuato, Dist. 5, 1964-67, member of the First Section of the Agrarian Affairs Committee and the Livestock Committee. e-*Agrarian Secretary of the CEN of PRI,* 1952-53. f-Field agent, National Agrarian Commission, 1918; topographical engineer, National Agrarian Commission; agent of the National Ejido Credit Bank; Director of the New Centers for Agricultural Villages, 1937; Subdirector of Heneos de Yucatán, 1937-38; adviser to the Department of Agrarian Affairs and Colonization, 1940-49; Director of the Department of Credit, National Ejido Credit Bank, 1953-54; Director of the Department of Commerce, National Ejido Credit Bank, 1954-58. g-Founding member of the Local Agrarian Commit-

tees of Oaxaca and Guanajuato, 1916; topographer for the Agrarian Committee of Guanajuato, 1918; founder of the agrarian delegation of Querétaro. h-Worked in a soap factory, 1906-08; assistant stoker, Municipal Light Plant, Valle de Santiago, 1908; topographer, Guanajuato, Guanajuato. i-Father of engineer Felipe Salgado Pérez; married Carmen Pérez Espinosa. j-None. k-None. l-Func., 213; C de D, 1958-60, 91, 1964-66, 55, 78, 86; DGF51, 21, 31, 33, 34; C de D, 1949-51; WNM, 207.

Salgado Salgado, Alberto
a-Nov. 23, 1941. b-Teloloapan, Guerrero. c-Early education unknown; law degree, National School of Law, UNAM, 1960-64. d-*Plurinominal Federal Deputy* from the PST, 1982-85, member of the Justice and Rules Committees. e-Joined the PST, 1975; legal advisor to the PST. f-None. g-Legal adviser to various labor groups. h-Practicing lawyer. i-Son of Alberto Salgado Cuevas, lawyer, and Celia Salgado Lagunas, businesswoman. j-None. k-Candidate of the PST for federal deputy from Guerrero, Dist. 2, 1979. l-HA, 23 Apr. 1979, I; Lehr, 657; C de D, 1982-85.

Salido Beltrán, Roberto
a-Oct. 8, 1912. b-Alamos, Sonora. c-Early education unknown; enrolled in the National Military College, 1929, graduated as a tactical artillery officer, Jan. 1, 1932; graduate of the Military Aviation School as a Lieutenant of Aeronautics and a Pilot, Mar. 1, 1937; studies in air transport in the United States; diploma as an Air Force staff officer, Higher War College, 1948-53; Professor and founder of the course in air staff subjects, Higher War College; Professor of Aeronautical Tactics, Higher War College, 1941-43; Director of Teaching and Instructor in Air Tactics, Higher War College, 1952;

Professor of Aerodynamics, Military School of Aviation Mechanics, 1947; founder of the Air Force College; Director of the Military School of Aviation, 1959-64. d-None. e-None. f-Subdirector of the Mexican Air Force, 1953-55; Military Attaché to the Mexican Embassy, Washington, D.C., 1964-69; *Director of the Mexican Air Force,* 1970-76. g-None. h-None. i-Son of Division General Conrado C. Salido, zone commander, 1956; nephew of Brigadier General Francisco Salido; married Alejandrina Reyero. j-Career Air Force officer; rank of 2nd Captain for campaign merits, 1938; fought against *Saturnino Cedillo* in San Luis Potosí, 1939, rank of 1st Captain, 1943; rank of Major, Sept. 1, 1945; fought in World War II as a member of the 201st Squadron, 1945; rank of Lt. Colonel, 1947; rank of Colonel, 1950; rank of Brigadier General, 1952; rank of Brigade General, 1964; reached rank of Division General, Nov. 20, 1969. k-None. l-Enc. Mex., XI, 1977, 235; DPE71, 17; DGF56, 202; Enc. Mex., Annual, 1977, 596; Rev. de Ejer., Sept. 1972, 114.

Salinas Camiña, Gustavo A.
(Deceased 1964) a-July 19, 1893. b-Monclova, Coahuila. c-Primary studies in Monclova, Coahuila; secondary studies at the Moviles Military Academy, New York; graduated from the Moisant Aviation School, New York, as a pilot, September 24, 1912. d-None. e-None. f-Military Attaché to the Mexican Embassy, Paris, France, Brussels, Belgium, and London, England; Director of the National Artillery Foundry; Director, Department of Cavalry, Secretariat of National Defense; *Director, Mexican Air Force,* 1940; Director General of Military Aviation, 1940-45. g-None. h-None. i-Son of General Emilio Salinas Salamanca, provisional governor of Coahuila; nephew of Venustiano Carranza.

j-Joined the Revolution, 1912, fought against Pascual Orozco; rank of 2nd Lieutenant, July 25, 1912; fought against Victoriano Huerta; Chief of the 21st Artillery Regiment, 1915-20; rank of Brigadier General, 1924; supported General Escobar against the government, 1929; fought in World War II in the 201st Air Squadron, which he organized; reached rank of Division General. k-First Mexican to lead an aerial bombardment of a boat, the "Guerrero," during the Revolution; tried to save Francisco Madero by bombing rebellious troops in Mexico City, 1913. l-López, 987; DP70, 1840; Enc. Mex., XI, 1971, 235-36.

Salinas Carranza, Alberto
(Deceased 1970) a-Nov. 11, 1892. b-Cuatro Ciénegas, Coahuila. c-Secondary studies at Manlinos High School, United States; studied mechanics at the Rensselaer Polytechnic Institute, New York; studied aviation at the School of Aviation of Moisant, Garden City, New York, and Curtis Aviation School, Long Island, New York, 1911-12. d-*Senator from the State of Coahuila,* 1934-40. e-None. f-Founder and Director of the First Department of Aviation, Department of War, 1915; Director of the Cartridge Industry, Secretariat of National Defense; Director of Stores and Inventories, Secretariat of Public Works; Director of the Military Industry Department, Secretary of National Defense; Director and founder of the Civil Aviation Department, 1928, 1942-44, 1953-57, 1957-58; *Chief of the Mexican Air Force,* 1939-40; Military Attaché to Washington, D.C., to Rome, and to Belgrade; Military Attaché to France, 1959-60; adviser to the President of Mexico. g-President of the Veterans of the Revolution in the Service of the State. h-Author of various books. i-Nephew of President Carranza. j-Joined the first air squadron

under Carranza during the Revolution; career army officer; Brigadier General, July 1, 1942; Brigade General, Jan. 1, 1951. k-Founder of the first School for military pilots; promised the official party nomination for governor of Coahuila in 1957 by PRI president *Agustín Olachea Aviles*. l-Peral, 738-39; DP70, 2441; WWM45, 110; C de S, 1934-40; López, 987; *Excélsior*, 23 Dec. 1979, 18; Q es Q, 535-36.

Salinas de Gortari, Carlos
a-Apr. 3, 1948. b-Federal District. c-Primary studies at the Abraham Lincoln School, Mexico City, 1953-59; secondary studies from Secondary School No. 3, "Heroes de Chapultepec," Mexico City, 1960-63; preparatory studies from the National Preparatory School No. 1, "San Ildefonso," 1963-66; economics studies, National School of Economics, UNAM, 1966-69, graduating in 1971 with a honorable mention and a thesis on "Agriculture, Industry, and Employment, the Case of Mexico"; MA in public administration, 1972-73, MA in political economy, 1976, and Ph.D. in political economy and government, 1978, all at Harvard University, research assistant, Harvard University, 1974; Professor of Public Finance, Autonomous Technological Institute of Mexico, 1976; Professor of Fiscal Policy, CEMLA, 1978; adjunct professor, National School of Economics, UNAM, 1970-72; professor, Institute for Political Education of PRI. d-*President of Mexico*, 1988-94. e-Representative of the IEPES of PRI in diverse studies analyzing presidential state of the union addresses, 1973-79; Subdirector of Economic Studies of the IEPES of PRI, 1979; *Secretary of the IEPES of PRI*, 1981-82. f-Aide to *Gonzalo Martínez Corbalá*, 1966-68; adviser to the Subdirector of Public Finances, Secretariat of the Treasury, 1971-74; Director, Department of Financial Studies

and International Affairs, Secretariat of the Treasury, 1974-76; Subdirector of Economic Studies, Division of Economic and Treasury Studies, Secretariat of the Treasury, 1976; Technical Secretary, Internal Groups, Secretariat of the Treasury, 1976-77; Director of Economic Studies, Division of Treasury Planning, Secretariat of the Treasury, 1976-77; Subdirector General of Treasury Planning, Secretariat of the Treasury, 1978; Director General of Treasury Planning, Secretariat of the Treasury, 1978-79; Technical Secretary of the Economic Cabinet, 1979-81; Director General of Social and Economic Policy, Secretariat of Programming and Budget, 1979-81; *Secretary of Progamming and Budget*, 1982-88. g-None. h-None. i-Son of *Raúl Salinas Lozano*, secretary of Industry and Commmerce, 1958-64, and Margarita de Gortari Carvajal; married Yolanda Cecilia Occelli González; organized a group of friends, including *Manuel Camacho* and *José Ruiz Massieu*, into a civic association in 1971; nephew of *Antonio Ortiz Mena*, who is married to Martha Salinas; nephew of General Eduardo de Gortari and philosopher Eli de Gortari; brother, Raúl, was a director general in public works, 1977; thesis committee at UNAM included *David Ibarra* and *Jesús Silva Herzog*; early political patrons included *Hugo B. Margáin, Miguel de la Madrid*, and *Leopoldo Solís*. j-None. k-Youngest member of the 1982 cabinet. l-*Excélsior*, 2 Dec. 1982, 4; HA, 13 Dec. 1982, 12; Q es QAP, 131; *Proceso*, 4 Oct. 1981, 16; WSJ, 2 Dec. 1982; *The News*, 2 Dec. 1982, 8; DBGM87, 563; HA, 13 Oct 1987, 40, 20 July 1987, 10; *Proceso*, 25 Jan. 1988, 19.

Salinas Leal, Bonifacio
(Deceased Oct. 9, 1982) a-May 14, 1900. b-General Bravo, Nuevo León. c-Graduated from the National Military

College. d-*Governor of Nuevo León*, 1939-43; *Senator* from the State of Nuevo León, 1970-76, member of the Gran Comisión, president of the Second National Defense Committee, First Secretary of the Navy Committee, and Second Secretary of the Second Petroleum Committee. e-None. f-Inspector General of Police, Monterrey, Nuevo León, 1915; *Governor of Baja California del Sur*, 1959-65. g-None. h-None. i-Married Altagracia Cantú; related to the Sada Muguerza family, prominent Monterrey entrepreneurs, through his mother; early political patron of *Arturo B de la Garza, Eduardo Livas Villarreal*, and *José Ortiz Avila*. j-Career army officer; joined the army, 1913, fought under Carranza; rank of Major, 1918; rank of Brigadier General, 1929; Commander of the 3rd Cavalry Regiment, 1937, Silao, Guanajuato; Brigade General, June 1, 1938; Division General, Sept. 16, 1946; Commander of the 8th Military Zone, Tampico, 1946; Commander of the 5th Military Region, Guadalajara, Jalisco, 1951-56. k-Founder of the Nursery Schools for children of military men; the *New York Times* claims he resigned from the governorship of Baja California del Sur because he lost the support of labor and professional groups. l-DGF51, 183; Brandenburg, 80; Q es Q, 536; DBM68, 562; DBM70, 508; DGF56, 201; Casasola, V; NYT, 12 Apr. 1965, 11; González de la Garza, ii, 682-83; Rev. de Ejer., Jan. 1952, 137.

Salinas Lozano, Raúl
a-May 1, 1917. b-Monterrey, Nuevo León. c-Primary and secondary studies in Monterrey; preparatory studies in the Federal District; economics degree from the National School of Economics, UNAM, 1944, with a thesis on state intervention and prices; MA in public administration, American University, 1945; MA in economics, Harvard University, 1946, on a fellowship from the government; Professor of Economics, National School of Economics, UNAM, 1947-70, at Ibero-American University, and at the University of San Salvador, 1950-52. d-*Senator* from the State of Nuevo León, 1982-88. e-None. f-Economist, National Bank of Foreign Commerce; economist, CONASUPO; economist, Secretariat of the Treasury, 1946; Economic Coordinator, Secretariat of National Properties, 1947; Chief, Department of Economic Studies, Secretariat of the Treasury, 1948-50; tax consultant to the government of Honduras, 1950-52; economist; Technical Commission, Secretariat of National Patrimony, 1952-54; Director of Treasury Studies, Secretariat of the Treasury, 1952-54; Director of the National Investment Commission, 1954-58; Director of Economic Investigations, Secretariat of the Treasury, 1950-51, Alternate Governor of the International Monetary Fund, 1956-58; *Secretary of Industry and Commerce*, 1958-64; adviser to various public agencies, 1965-76; Technical Director of the National Price Commission, 1977-79; *Ambassador to the Soviet Union*, 1979-80; Director General of the Mexican Institute of Foreign Trade, 1980-82. g-None. h-Author of many books and articles. i-Student of *Eduardo Bustamante* at UNAM; attended UNAM with *Flores de la Peña*; married Margarita de Gortari; brother-in-law of general Eduardo de Gortari and philosopher Eli de Gortari; son of Carlos Salinas Reyna, bookkeeper, and María de Jesús Lozano Garza; son *Carlos Salinas Gortari* was president of Mexico, 1988-94; son Raúl was a government official. j-None. k-None. l-*El Universal*, 2 Dec. 1958, 1; HA, 8 Dec. 1958, 25-26; DGF56, 59; DGF51, I, 149; D de Y, 2 Dec. 1958, 7; Func., 79; Enc. Mex., XI, 1977, 236; *Excélsior*, 1 Nov. 1978, 22, 14 Nov. 1977, 9, 28 July 1979, 1; WNM, 207;

HA, 14 June 1982, 22; C de S, 1982-88; *Excélsior*, 27 Dec. 1981, 17; Lehr, 335-36; *Excélsior*, 27 July 1984, 20.

Salinas Ramos, Alberto
a-Apr. 8, 1905. b-Federal District. c-Secondary studies at the Vocational School of Mechanical Engineers; graduated from the Electrical-Mechanical Institute of San Francisco, California. d-None. e-Secretary of Rural Policy of the CEN of PARM. g-Delegate to the Constitutive Assembly of the CTM, 1936; founder and President of the Mexican Federation of Agricultural Organizations, 1979; Secretary General of the Inter-American Agrarian Organization, 1979. i-Collaborator of *Graciano Sánchez* in the CNC. j-None. k-None. l-HA, 2 Apr. 1979, II.

Salmorán de Tamayo, María Cristina
a-Aug. 10, 1918. b-Oaxaca, Oaxaca. c-Primary studies in Oaxaca; secondary studies at Public School No. 8, Mexico City; preparatory studies at the National Preparatory School, Mexico City; studies at the School of Humanities, UNAM; law degree, National School of Law, UNAM, 1945, with a thesis on "The Condition of Women under Labor Law"; LLD studies at the National School of Law, UNAM, 1951-52; studies in France at the International Labor Organization; founding teacher of Preparatory School No. 5, Coapa; Professor of the second course in Labor Law, National School of Law, UNAM, 1955-85; Professor of Agricultural Law, Superior School of Commerce and Administration, IPN. d-None. e-None. f-Employee for the Federal Board of Conciliation and Arbitration, 1941-42; Secretary of Hearings, Federal Board of Conciliation and Arbitration, 1942; Secretary of Resolutions, Federal Board of Conciliation and Arbitration; Assistant for Groups, under *Mario de la Cueva*, President of the Federal Board of

Conciliation and Arbitration, 1949; assistant member of the Federal Board of Conciliation and Arbitration, 1949-53, under *Manuel Ramírez Vázquez*; President of the Federal Board of Conciliation and Arbitration, Jan. 2, 1954, to May 12, 1961; *Justice of the Supreme Court*, 1961-64, 1964-70, 1970-76, 1976-82, 1982-85. g-None. h-Mexican delegate to the International Office of Labor. i-Student of *Alfonso Noriega*, Salvador Azuela, and *Mario de la Cueva*; married Alberto Tamayo, a lawyer. j-None. k-First woman member of the Supreme Court of Mexico. l-DGF56, 399; DPE61, 117; WWW70-71, 888; letter; *Justicia*, Mar. 1968; WNM, 206; Aceves Romero, 360-61; Chumacero, 210-13; DBGM, 680.

Salvat Rodríguez, Agustín
a-Oct. 23, 1908. b-Veracruz, Veracruz. c-Primary studies at the Escuela Benito Juárez, Salina Cruz, Oaxaca, and in Mexico City; preparatory studies at the Night Preparatory School, No. 5, 1934-35; law degree from the National School of Law, UNAM; Professor of World History, 1942-43. d-None. e-*Secretary of Finances of the CEN of PRI*, 1952-58; *Secretary of Finances of the CEN of PRI*, 1958-64; organized youth groups for the 1940 presidential campaign of *Avila Camacho*; personal representative of *Adolfo Ruiz Cortines* during his campaign for the presidency in the Federal District, 1952. f-*Head of the Department of Tourism*, 1964-70; Ambassador to the World Tourism Organization, 1979-81; Ambassador to Czechoslovakia, 1981-82. g-Foreign Secretary of the Mexican Union of Electricians, 1935. h-Employed by the Mexican Power and Light Company, 1924-39; author of numerous articles on technical subjects. i-Married Julieta Dorantes; son, Agustín Salvat Dorantes, is the manager of a public relations firm; son of Agustín Salvat, a street car

conductor, and Clotilde Rodríguez; grandfather a sea captain. j-None. k-Had to leave school at age 16 to support himself. l-HA, 29 Dec. 1958, 8, 7 Dec. 1964, 20-21; letter; WWW70-71, 794; DBM68, 565; *El Universal*, 1 Dec. 1964; DBM70, 509; *Excélsior*, 22 Aug. 1978, 22, 19 Aug. 1981, 14.

Samayoa (León), Mariano
(Deceased Mar. 16, 1960) a-Apr. 17, 1895. b-Chiapa de Corzo, Chiapas. c-Primary and secondary studies in Tuxtla Gutiérrez, Chiapas and in Mexico City; normal teaching certificate, Normal School of Mexico, Mexico City, 1914. d-Federal Deputy from the State of Chiapas, 1922-24; *Federal Deputy* from the State of Chiapas, Dist. 4, 1940-43, member of the Permanent Commission, the Second Committee on Public Education, the Second Balloting Committee, the Tourism Committee, and the Second Instructive Section of the Grand Jury; Secretary of the Chamber of Deputies, Sept. 1942. e-Founding member of the CNOP of PRI; member of the Cooperatist Party. f-Director of Public Education, State of Chiapas; Subdirector of Agricultural Education, Secretariat of Public Education; Director of Indigenous Affairs, Secretariat of Public Education, 1946-52; Secretary General of Government of the State of Chiapas under *Efraín Gutiérrez*, 1936-37; Interim Governor of Chiapas. g-None. h-None. j-Participated in the Revolution, but in nonmilitary affairs; Major in the Veterans of the Revolution. k-None. l-DGF51, I, 290; DGF51, II, 635; DGF50, II, 465; C de D, 1940-42, 49, 54, 55; Peral, 740; DP70, 1845; DBdeC, 231-32; López, 989; Contreras, 138.

San Pedro (Salem), Fernando
a-Feb. 14, 1902. b-Tampico, Tamaulipas. c-Primary studies at public school No. 1, Tampico; secondary

studies in New York, San Antonio, and Houston; no degree. d-Councilman for Tampico, 1928-29, and 1936; local deputy from the Tampico district to the State Legislature of Tamaulipas, 1943-45; Mayor of Tampico, 1946-48, and 1972-75; *Federal Deputy* from the State of Tampico, Dist. 5, 1976-79, member of the Government Properties Committee. e-Member of the Partido Socialista Fronterizo of Tamaulipas; member of PRI but elected mayor of Tampico, 1972, as PPS candidate; elected Federal Deputy as a representative of PARM. f-Traffic Inspector, Tampico, 1926; Alternate Councilman, Tampico, 1930-31; Director of the 9th Forestry District, 1931; head of the Office of Rents, State of Tamaulipas, 1934-35; adviser to the Board of Water and Drainage, 1959-61; adviser to the Federal Board for Material and Moral Improvement, Tampico (20 years); adviser to the Chamber of Commerce of Tampico, 1962-68; Vice President of the Chamber of Commerce of Tampico. g-None. h-Businessman in automobiles and trucks, 1918-56. j-None. k-None. l-Letter; C de D, 1976-79, 63.

Sánchez, Graciano
(Deceased Nov. 12, 1957) a-1890. b-San Luis Potosí, San Luis Potosí. c-Rural teaching certificate; no degree; rural school teacher. d-Local deputy to the State Legislature of San Luis Potosí; Federal Deputy from the State of Tamaulipas, Dist. 2, 1930-32; *Federal Deputy* from the State of Tamaulipas, Dist. 2, 1943-46. e-Supported *Miguel Henriquez Guzmán* in 1952. f-Head of the Department of Indigenous Affairs, Secretariat of Public Education. g-Founding member of the League of Agrarian Communities, State of Tamaulipas, during the governorship of *Emilio Portes Gil*; founder of the Mexican Peasant Federation, which supported *Lázaro Cárdenas*, 1933-34,

and eventually became the CNC; *Secretary General of the National Farmers Federation*, 1938-42. h-Worked on a hacienda in his youth. i-Longtime friend of *Portes Gil*; father a peasant. j-None. k-Member of the "Old Guard" of the CNC; Brandenburg places him in the Inner Circle of power from 1940-46. l-*Annals*, March, 1940; Brandenburg, 80; Peral, 743; DP70, 1907; C de D, 1943-45, 20; Kirk, 331; López, 992; Guerra Leal, 24; Castillo, 283; Michaels, 48-49.

Sánchez Acevedo, Antonio
(Deceased June 14, 1976) a-Sept. 17, 1899. b-Mérida, Yucatán c-Early education unknown; Adjutant General, Heroic Military College. d-None. e-None. f-Chief of Staff, Secretariat of National Defense, 1948-52. g-None. h-None. i-Son of Manuel Sánchez Tirado and Ana Elena Acevedo. j-Career army officer; joined the Army as an infantry lieutenant, Dec. 25, 1914; fought in fifty-one battles in Veracruz, Querétaro, Puebla, Jalisco, Chihuahua, Durango and Sinaloa, 1915, 1917-18, 1923-24, 1927, 1929 and 1935-40; officer, 4th and 5th Battalions, Division of the East, Constitutional Army; officer, 44th Infantry Battalion (later first Presidential Guard Battalion); Commander, 40th and 53rd Infantry Battalions of 2nd Group, Presidential Guards, of the 33rd Military Zone, Campeche, Campeche, of the 32nd Military Zone, Mérida, Yucatán, of the 18th Military Zone, Pachuca, Hidalgo, of the 4th Military Zone, Hermosillo, Sonora, of the 1st Military Zone, Mexico City, 1956-58; Inspector General of the Army, 1953; Director of Military Justice, 1961-64; adviser to the Secretary of National Defense, 1974; reached rank of Division General, Nov. 28, 1951. k-None. l-Rev. de Ejer., Oct. 1974, 128, June 1976, 136; DPE65, 41; DPE61, 34; DGF56, 201; Rev. de Ejer., July 1957, 39.

Sánchez Aguilar, Luis
a-1942. b-Torreon, Coahuila. c-Early education unknown; industrial engineering degree, Monterrey Institute of Higher Technological Studies; Ph.D. in political economy, University of Paris. d-None. e-Founding member of the Association of Community Political Activities, 1967; candidate of PARM for federal deputy, 1979; founder of the Social Democratic Party, 1981; presidential candidate of the PSD for president of Mexico, 1982. f-None. g-Adviser to Roberto Guajardo Suárez, president of the Employees Association of the Mexican Republic, 1970. h-Founded the Mexican Institute of Public Opinion; founder of SINTEMEX with Roberto Guajardo Suárez. i-Related to prominent entrepreneurial leader Roberto Guajardo Suárez. j-None. k-None. l-Letter.

Sánchez Cárdenas, Carlos
(Deceased Oct. 4, 1982) a-Aug. 31, 1913. b-Federal District. c-Early education unknown; preparatory studies in science and letters, National Preparatory School, 1932; no degree. d-*Federal Deputy* (Party Deputy from the PPS), 1967-70; *Plurinominal Deputy* from the PCM, 1979-82. e-Member of the Communist Youth of the PCM, 1932; joined the PCM, 1933-48; member of the Central Committee of the PCM, 1936; founder, Unified Socialist Youth of Mexico; cofounder and Secretary General of the Workers and Peasants Party, 1959-63; leader, Popular Socialist Party, 1967-70; left the PPS and founded the Action and Unified Socialist Movement (MAUS), 1970; member of the Central Committee and the Political Committee of the PSUM, 1982; Secretary General of the MAUS; representative of the MAUS before the Federal Electoral Movement, 1982. f-None. g-Founder, Federation of Working Students (later the Revolutionary Student

Federation), 1932; Director, *Tren
Blindado*, official paper of the Revolutionary Student Federation, 1933.
h-Director, *La Voz de México*, 1943-47;
founder and Director, *Noviembre*, 1948.
j-None. k-Arrested during May 1, 1952,
strike; first Mexican tried under the
social dissolution law; in prison, 1952-
54. l-*Excélsior*, 5 Oct. 1982, 4; Protag.,
316; C de D, 1967-70, 1979-82.

Sánchez Celis, Leopoldo
a-Feb. 14, 1916. b-Cosalá, Sinaloa.
c-Primary and secondary studies in
Cosalá; completed third year of secondary; no degree. d-Local Deputy to the
State Legislature of Sinaloa, 1950-52;
Federal Deputy from the State of
Sinaloa, Dist. 4, 1955-58, member of the
Gran Comisión, the Third Ejidal Committee, the Legislative Studies Committee (2nd year), the Instructive Committee for the Grand Jury, and the Balloting
Committee; *Senator* from the State of
Sinaloa, 1958-63, President of the
Second Naval Committee, member of
the Social Welfare Committee, and the
First Balloting Committee; *Governor of
Sinaloa*, 1963-67. e-Member of the
peasant sector of the PRM; Secretary of
Popular Action of the Regional Committee of the PRM in Sinaloa, 1941;
member of the National Council of the
PRM, 1944; general delegate of the PRM
to Jalisco, Zacatecas, Guanajuato,
Tamaulipas; President of the Regional
Committee of PRI, Sinaloa, 1950-56;
campaign coordinator for *Adolfo López
Mateos'* presidential campaign, 1957-58;
General Delegate of the CEN of PRI to
various states, 1959-62; *Secretary of
Political Action of the CEN of PRI*,
1959. f-None. g-Secretary General of
the First Youth Federation of Sinaloa,
1940; Secretary of Youth Action, League
of Agrarian Communities, 1941;
Secretary General of the Federation of
Popular Organizations of Sinaloa, 1942;
Chief of the Sinaloa Delegation to the

founding of CNOP, 1943; considered as
a precandidate for the Secretary Generalship of the National Farmers
Federation, 1962. h-None. i-Close
personal friend of *Amado Estrada*,
senator from Sinaloa, 1964-70; *Alfredo
Valdez Montoya* was Treasurer of
Sinaloa during his governorship and was
his candidate to succeed him; son,
Leopoldo Sánchez Duarte, was a
delegate of the Federal District Department to Coyoacán, later arrested on
fraud charges. j-None. k-One of the
PRI leaders most responsible for the
defeat of *Carlos Madrazo's* reform
program and the ouster of *Madrazo*
from the party leadership; peasants were
reported to be invading lands owned
illegally by Sánchez Celis in Sinaloa in
the summer of 1972. l-DGF56, 28; *El
Universal*, 1 July 1972; González
Navarro, 232; *Por Qué*, 25 Sept. 1969,
29; *Excélsior*, 1 Feb. 1974, 10; *Excélsior*,
30 July 1978, 23; Func., 351; DAPC77,
51; *Excélsior*, 24 Mar. 199, 4.

Sánchez Colín, Salvador
a-May 14, 1912. b-Atlacomulco, México. c-Primary studies in Atlacomulco;
secondary studies in Mexico City; studies at the Industrial Technical Institute; studied at the Central Agricultural
School of El Mexe, Hidalgo, under a
government scholarship; studied on a
scholarship from the Secretariat of
Agriculture at the National School of
Agriculture, 1930-35, and received an
agricultural engineering degree with a
specialty in agricultural industry from
the same institution in 1939; Professor
of Botany and Mathematics at the
Industrial Institute of Tijuana, Baja
California del Norte; advanced studies
in the United States in citrus fruit production. d-*Alternate Senator* from the
State of México, 1946-52; local deputy
from Texcoco to the State Legislature of
México, 1950; *Governor of México*,
1951-57. e-Member of the Technical

Advisory Commission on Agricultural Questions during *Alemán's* presidential campaign, 1946; cofounder of the Civic Front for Revolutionary Affirmation, 1963. f-Director of Agricultural Instruction, Department of Prevocational Education, Secretariat of Public Education, 1936-37; Chief of Instruction, Schools for Military Dependents, Secretariat of National Defense, 1937-38; Director of Agricultural Instruction, Industrial Institute of Tijuana, Baja California del Norte, 1939-40; Technical Inspector for the National Bank of Agricultural Credit, 1941-43; Scientific Investigator for the Department of Agriculture, Secretariat of Agriculture, 1944-46; Director General of Agriculture, 1946-51; adviser to the National Ejido Credit Bank, 1948; Technical consultant to the President, 1949; adviser to the Secretary of Agriculture, 1972. g-None. h-Founder of the magazine *Tierra*, 1946, official publication of the Secretariat of Agriculture; founder of the publishing house, Agrícola Mexicana; author of numerous technical studies. i-Son of peasants Silvano Sánchez Lobrera and María Colín Pérez; married María Trinidad Rodríguez Carrillo; worked in a print shop as a boy. j-None. k-Created a special variety of lemon known as the Colín lemon; the CCI accused him in 1979 of being one of the principal landholders in the state of México. l-Q es Q, 539-40; DGF51, I, 6, 206; DGF56, 95; DGF47, 20, 123; HA, 11 Sept. 1956, 17-20; DGF51, II, 181; DGF50, II, 139; letter; Colín, 242-51; WNM, 209; HA, 22 Oct. 1979, 29.

Sánchez Cono, Edmundo M.
(Deceased) a-Nov. 20, 1894. b-Oaxaca, Oaxaca. c-Early education unknown; medical degree from the Free School of Homeopathy of Mexico. d-*Governor of Oaxaca*, 1944-47. e-*Secretary of Social and Military Action*, CEN of the PNR, 1938-40. f-None. g-None. j-Career

army officer; returned to active duty, 1948; rank of brigadier general; director of schools for the children of army personnel. k-Precandidate for governor of Oaxaca, 1940; forced to resign as governor, Jan. 19, 1947, because of his financial policies and municipal political impositions. l-Anderson, 86-87; NYT, 20 Jan. 1947, 4; NYT, 26 Jan. 1947, 37; HA, 25 Aug. 1944, 23; Correa, 377.

Sánchez Cuen, Manuel
c-Preparatory studies from the National Preparatory School, 1920-24; law degree from the National School of Law, UNAM, May 18, 1928; professor at UNAM. d-None. e-None. f-Secretary, Judicial District, Tacubaya; Justice of the Peace, 1928; Secretary of Agreements, 3rd District, Mexico City, 1928-29; Secretary of the 4th Civil Court, Mexico City, 1929-30; Auxiliary Lawyer, Legal Department, Secretary of Industry and Commerce, 1930; Agent of the Ministerio Público in Mexico City, 1930; lawyer, Petroleum Department, Secretary of Industry and Commerce, 1930; Subdirector, Legal Department, Secretariat of Industry and Commerce, 1930-32; Director, Legal Department, Secretariat of Public Education, 1932-33; Director, Legal Department, Secretariat of Industry and Commerce, 1933-34; President, Committee to Revise the Trade Code, Secretariat of Industry and Commerce, 1934-35; Director, Tax Department, Secretariat of the Treasury, 1934-35; Subdirector of Revenues, Secretariat of the Treasury, under *Jesús Silva Herzog*, 1935-36; Judge, Federal Tax Court, 1936-38; *Oficial Mayor of Industry and Commerce*, 1939-40, under *Efraín Buenrostro*; Subdirector General of PEMEX, 1940-46, under *Efraín Buenrostro*; *Subsecretary of Industry and Commerce*, Oct. 23, 1948-52; Director General of the National Mortgage Bank, 1952-58. g-None. i-Attended UNAM with *José Castro*

Estrada, Antonio Carrillo Flores, Miguel Alemán, and *Alfonso Noriega;* student of *Antonio Martínez Báez* and *Eduardo Suárez;* son Luis was director general of Banco Sofimex; son Manuel was director general of Multibanco Comermex; married Elisa Lugo Angulo. j-None. k-None. l-D de Y, 23 Oct. 1948, 1; DGF51, I, 95; DGF50, II, 78; *Siempre*, 28 Jan. 1959, 6; letters; DBGM, 387.

Sánchez de Mendiburu, Fidela
a-May 10, 1909. b-Mérida, Yucatán. c-Primary and secondary studies in Mérida; normal teaching certificate, Rodolfo Menéndez Urban Normal School, Mérida, Dec. 30, 1931; certificate as an educator, 1945; special courses in mental hygiene, Superior Normal School, Federal District, 1955; diploma in Mental Hygiene, Maternal Center Manuel Avila Camacho, 1950; urban normal teacher. d-Member of the City Council of Mérida, 1956-58; *Federal Deputy* from the State of Yucatán, Dist. 1, 1964-67, member of the Social Action Committee (1st year), Public Welfare Committee, Second Public Education Committee, and Third Ejido Committee. e-Director of Feminine Action for PRI in Mérida, 1953-58, 1954-66; Director of Feminine Action, CNOP of PRI, 1959-64; member of the State Delegation; organizer of the Feminine Congress of CNOP, 1957. f-Director of the Federal School No. 5, Mérida, 1970. g-None. h-Director of various children's nurseries. j-None. k-Organized the first Civic Orientation Course for Women in Yucatán. l-C de D, 1964-66, 77, 78, 82; Q es QY, 231; Directorio, 1964-67.

Sánchez de Velasco, Abraham
a-1909. b-Hustla, Jalisco. c-Primary studies in the Episcopal Boarding School of Chilapa and the Colegio Francés, Mexico City; secondary studies in

Mexico City; preparatory studies at the National Preparatory School; economic studies, National School of Economics, 1929-33; economics degree, University of Guadalajara, 1936, with a thesis on tax policy; professor at the School of Law, the School of Economics, and the Business School, University of Guadalajara, 1935-61. d-None. e-None. f-Chief of Economic Archives, Secretariat of the Treasury, 1934-35; consultant to the General Archives, State Government of Jalisco, 1935-36; representative of the National Workers Industrial Development Bank, Jalisco, 1937-38; Secretary General of Government of the State of Jalisco, 1942-44; Chief of Economic Studies, Costal Planning Commission, Guadalajara, 1954-59; President of the Water Services Board, Guadalajara, 1959-64; Director of Economic Development, State of Jalisco, 1959-61; department head, Treasury Office, State of Guadalajara, 1961-64; President of the Popular Planning Assembly, 1964; *Oficial Mayor of the Secretariat of Agriculture,* 1964-70; Director of the Department of Statistics, IMSS, 1971-74, Subdirector of Personnel, IMSS, 1974-76. g-None. h-Consulting economist, 1942-44; President of the Committee for the Industrial Development of Jalisco, 1942-44; adviser to many private industries, 1940-55; adviser to the Chamber of Commerce and Industries, Guadalajara, 1939-41. j-None. k-None. l-Enc. Mex., XI, 1977, 341-42; EN de E, 228.

Sánchez Díaz, Raúl
a-Apr. 15, 1915. b-Guadalajara, Jalisco. c-Early education unknown; engineering degree from the National School of Engineering, UNAM. d-*Governor of Baja California del Norte,* 1965-71. e-None. f-Division Engineer, Sonora-Baja California Railroad; Director of the Campeche Division of the Southeast Railroad, 1949; Director of the Sonora-

Baja California Railroad, 1965. g-None. i-Student of *Antonio Dovalí Jaime*, Director General of PEMEX, 1970-76; father of Raúl Sánchez Díaz, Jr., Subsecretary of Education of Baja California, 1983. j-None. k-Moved to Baja California del Norte, 1942. l-Aguirre, 515; DPF65, 109; *Excélsior*, 28 Oct. 1983, 23.

Sánchez (García), Enrique Wenceslao
a-Sept. 28, 1911. b-Canatlán, Durango. c-Primary studies in Canatlán; secondary studies at the Conciliar Seminary of Durango; teaching certificate, Federal Institute of Teacher's Education and the Normal School of Mexico, 1928. d-President of the State Legislature of the Durango; *Federal Deputy* from the State of Durango, Dist. 3, 1958-61, member of the Library Committee, the Second Public Education Committee, the 6th Section of the Legislative Studies Committee and the Consular and Diplomatic Service Committee; *Federal Deputy* from the State of Durango, Dist. 3, 1964-67, member of the Library Committee and the First Public Education Committee. e-Secretary of Political Action of PRI in Durango, 1950-54. f-Director of the Tax Office, Canatlán, Durango, 1944. g-Secretary of the Federation of Teachers, 1936; joined the Union of Teachers of Durango, 1940; assistant to the Secretary of Conflicts and Organization, SNTE; Secretary of Labor and Conflicts of the FSTSE, 1956-59; Director, Department of Labor and Social Welfare, SNTE, Durango; Secretary of Educational Action, CTM, Durango; Secretary of Local 10 of the STERM; *Secretary General of the SNTE*, 1955-58. h-None. j-None. k-None. l-C de D, 1964-67, 82; Func., 202; C de D, 1958-61, 92.

Sánchez Gavito, Vicente
(Deceased Jan. 20, 1977) a-May 25, 1910. b-Federal District. c-Primary and secondary studies in the Federal District; completed preparatory studies at the National Preparatory School, 1928; law degree from the Escuela Libre de Derecho, Oct. 27, 1933, with a thesis on "The Place of Penal Law in the General Classification of Law." d-None. e-None. f-Joined the Foreign Service, 1935; career foreign service officer; consultant to the United States-Mexican Claims Commission; Director, North American Affairs, Secretariat of Foreign Relations, 1939-43; Counselor, Mexican Embassy, Washington, D.C., 1944-47; Director General of the Diplomatic Service, 1947-51; member of the United Nations Tribunal for the Libya and Eritrea Question, 1951-55; Minister to Washington, D.C., 1956-59; *Ambassador to the Organization of American States*, 1959-65; Ambassador to Brazil, 1965-70; *Ambassador to Great Britain*, 1970-73; Ambassador to Germany, 1974-77. g-None. h-Chairman and member of various international committees. i-Student of *Javier Gaxiola* at the Escuela Libre de Derecho; personal adviser to *Manuel Tello*; married María Murguía; grandson of Indalecio Sánchez Gavito, lawyer, and Antonio Beltrán; son of Vicente Sánchez Gavito Beteta, lawyer, and María Piña Aguayo; sister María Antonia was consul general in Milan; initmate friend of *Manuel Tello*. j-None. k-None. l-DPE61, 25; DPE65, 24; IWW67, 1072; letter; *Excélsior*, 8 May 1972, 2B; HA, 8 Apr. 1974, 13, 31 Jan. 1977, 15; *Excélsior*, 21 Jan. 1977, 4; DBGM, 390.

Sánchez Hernández, Tomás
(Deceased Sept. 24, 1980) a-Oct. 17, 1894. b-León, Guanajuato. c-Primary studies from the Sollano Institute and the Colegio de Guanajuato, León, Guanajuato; graduated from the National Military College, December 11, 1914, as a Lieutenant in artillery; industrial engineering degree, National Military

College, 1920-23; graduated from the Artillery School, Fontainblau, France, 1925-28; General Staff School, Paris, 1931-33; Director of the Higher War College, Secretariat of National Defense, 1934-40; Director of the National Military College, 1950-53. d-*Federal Deputy* from the State of Guanajuato, Dist. 4, 1973-76. e-None. f-Chief of Staff, Secretariat of National Defense, 1942-43; *Subsecretary of Public Education*, 1943-46; Military Attaché to France and Poland, 1947-50; Chief of Staff, Secretariat of National Defense, 1954-57. g-None. h-Author of many technical military articles. i-Married Jeannette Marle; son of Jesús Sánchez and Guadalupe Hernández; served under *Francisco Urquizo* in the cadet guard, 1913. j-Career army officer; rank of Major, 1920; rank of Lt. Colonel, 1923; Assistant Director of Technical Schools, Secretariat of National Defense, 1924; rank of Colonel, 1928; commander of a mountain artillery regiment, 1928-30; Director of the National Artillery Foundry, 1933-34; Technical Military Director, 1940-42; rank of Division General, 1950; Inspector General of the Army, June 16, 1953 to June 16, 1954; Director of the Military Industry Department, Secretariat of National Defense, 1958-60; Chief of the Mexican delegation to the United States-Mexican Defense Board during World War II. k-Member of President Madero's cadet guard during the Tragic Ten Days, 1913. l-WWM45, 111; DGF56, 199; Peral, 744; Kirk, 254; DPE61, 31; DGF51, I, 179; *Excélsior*, 13 Mar. 1973, 13; López, 993; Rev. de Ejer., Sept. 1976, 135, June 1953, 64.

Sánchez Juárez (Larque), Delfín
a-Oct. 6, 1916. c-Early education unknown; law degree. d-None. e-None. f-Director of Internal Affairs, IMSS, 1958; Special Ambassador of Mexico to the inauguration of President Rómulo

Betancourt, Caracas, Venezuela, 1958; *Secretary General of Tourism*, 1959-60; joined the Foreign Service, 1961; Ambassador to the Low Counries, 1964-65; Ambassador to Poland, 1965-66; Ambassador to Guatemala, 1966-70; Delegate of the Department of the Federal District to Cuauhtémoc, 1971-73. g-None. i-Married Mercedes Lazo Barreiro; son Delfín was a director general in the Secretariat of Commerce and Industrial Development. j-None. k-None. l-MGF73, 395; HA, 26 Feb. 1973, 27; DAPC, 66; *Siempre*, 14 Jan. 1959, 6, 18 Feb. 1959; MGF69, 182; DBGM, 390.

Sánchez López, Alberto
a-May 5, 1914. b-Federal District. c-Early education unknown; graduated from the Heroic Military College as a communications specialist; completed officer courses, Tacubaya Instructors Center; staff and command diploma, Higher War College, 1948-51; completed basic and advanced courses in armoured cars, Fort Knox, Kentucky, 1953. d-None. e-None. f-Chief of Staff, Secretariat of National Defense, 1972-76. g-None. h-None. j-Career army officer; joined the army as a private, 4th Infantry Battalion, Dec. 18, 1930; Assistant Chief of Staff, 30th Military Zone, Villahermosa, Tabasco; Assistant Chief of Staff, 33rd Military Zone, Campeche, Campeche; rank of Colonel, Oct. 20, 1964; Commander of the 12th Mechanized Cavalry Regiment; Adjutant to the Military Transportation Division, Secretariat of National Defense; Chief of Staff, 15th Military Zone, Guadalajara, Jalisco; Commander of the 20th Military Zone, Colima, Colima; rank of Division General, 1976; Commander of the 25th Military Zone, Puebla, Puebla, 1976-77, of the 19th Military Zone, Tuxpan, Veracruz, 1977-78, of the 18th Military Zone, Pachuca, Hidalgo, 1978-79, and of the 15th

Military Zone, Guadalajara, Jalisco, 1979-80. k-None. l-MGF, 1972-73, 175; Rev. de Ejer., Oct.-Nov. 1976, 67; Rev. de Ejer., May 1953, 65, Apr. 1972, 21-22.

Sánchez Madariaga, Alfonso
a-Nov. 15, 1904. b-Federal District. c-Completed primary and secondary studies; no degree. d-*Senator* from the Federal District, 1940-46, member of the Gran Comisión, president of the Department of the Federal District Committee, president of the First Labor Committee; *Federal Deputy* from the Federal District, Dist. 8, 1949-52, member of the Second Balloting Committee, the General Means of Communication Committee, and the Second Labor Committee; *Federal Deputy* from the Federal District, Dist. 5, 1955-58, president of the Child Welfare and Social Security Committee (1st year) and the First Labor Committee; *Senator* from the Federal District, 1970-76, president of the Senate, September, 1974. e-Secretary General of the PRM in the Federal District, 1937-38; *Secretary of Labor Action of the CEN of the PRM*, 1938-40; *Secretary of Labor Action of the CEN of PRI*, 1949-52. f-Member of the Advisory Council of the Department of the Federal District, 1929. g-Active in the labor movement, 1925; member of the Executive Committee of the Milkworkers Union; Representative of labor before the Federal Board of Conciliation and Arbitration, 1939; Secretary of Organization of the Union of Workers of the Federal District; Secretary General of the Union of Workers of the Federal District, 1945; Assistant Secretary General of the Inter-American Labor Organization, 1953-56; Secretary General of the Inter-American Labor Organization (ORIT), 1961; co-organizer of the Union of Workers of the Federal District, 1929; member of the Secretariat of the Federation of Regional

Workers and Farmers for the Federal District. h-Worked in a milk plant. j-None. k-Helped *Fidel Velázquez* form the Milkworkers Union, 1920s, which adhered to CROM, 1925; longtime labor leader who split with Luis Morones of CROM, 1929, to help form the CTM, 1936; candidate against *Joaquín Gamboa Pascoe* for Secretary General of the Workers Confederation of the Federal District, 1973. l-Brandenburg, 154; Peral, 745; DGF51, I, 21, 34, 36; DGF51, II, 127; DGF56, 23, 31, 33, 36, 37; C de D, 1949-51, 1955-57; C de S, 1940-46, 1970-76; López, 994.

Sánchez Meza de Solís (Ogarrio), Guillermina
a-Jan. 22, 1926. b-Federal District. c-Primary studies at the Benito Juárez School, Mexico City; secondary studies at Secondary School No. 11; preparatory studies at the National Preparatory School; economics studies from the National School of Economics, UNAM, 1942-46, graduating with a thesis on an economic interpretation of Latin America, 1950; degree in consular law and diplomacy, School of Political and Social Sciences, Feminine University of Mexico; graduate studies at the University of California at Berkeley and the University of Hawaii; Professor of Economic Geography and Credit Institutions, the Women's University of Mexico. d-*Federal Deputy* from the Federal District, Dist. 22, 1970-73, member of the Tariff and Foreign Trade Committee, the First Tax Committee, the Money and Institutions of Credit Committee and the Budget and Accounts Committee. e-Joined PRI, 1949; Coordinator of Professional Organizations of the IEPES of PRI; 1971-74; *Oficial Mayor of the CEN of PRI*, 1982-84. f-Economist, Department of Chemical Industries, Secretariat of Industry and Commerce; technical adviser, Secretariat of Industry and Commerce;

Private Secretary to the Oficial Mayor of the Federal Electric Commission, 1961-64; analyst, Secretariat of Industry and Commerce, 1965-68; Mexican representative to the United Nations Conference on Trade Organizations; Director of the Office of Regional Economic Organizations, Secretariat of Industry and Commerce; Director of the Office of Medicines, Secretariat of Industry and Commerce; Director General of Administrative Services, Department of the Federal District, 1973; *Oficial Mayor of the Secretariat of Foreign Relations*, 1976-78; *Subsecretary of Foreign Relations "D"*, 1978-79. g-Member of the Executive Council of the College of Economists; President of the League of Revolutionary Economists. h-Sales director, Abastos, S.A.; Subdirector of Factores Mexicanos, S.A., 1951. i-Classmate of *José López Portillo* in elementary and high school; married Jorge Solís Ogarrio, a lawyer. j-None. k-One of two Mexican women to have held both the position of oficial mayor and subsecretary in a cabinet agency prior to 1980; first female oficial mayor of PRI. l-*Excélsior*, 22 June 1979, 18; Directorio, 1970-72, 184-85; C de D, 1970-73, 136; EN de E, 239; d'Chumacero, 303-05.

Sánchez Mireles, Rómulo
a-1914. b-Coahuila. c-Preparatory studies at the Ateneo Fuente, Saltillo, Coahuila; law degree, National School of Law, UNAM. d-*Federal Deputy* from the Federal District, Dist. 8, 1952-55, member of the Department of the Federal District Committee, the Legislative Studies Committee, and the First Balloting Committee; *Federal Deputy* from the Federal District, Dist. 14, 1961-64; President of the Gran Comisión, member of the First Government Committee and the Constitutional Affairs Committee; President of the Chamber of Deputies, Sept. 1963; mem-

ber of the Inter-Parliamentary Congress of Mexico and the United States. e-Subsecretary of Popular Action of the CEN of PRI, 1952. f-*Director General of the ISSSTE*, 1964-70. g-Delegate to the National Convention of Preparatory Schools from the Ateneo Fuente; President of the Society of Law School Students and member of the University Council; first Oficial Mayor of CNOP, 1943; Director, Legal Department, FSTSE, 1943-46; Secretary of Finances of the FSTSE, 1946-49; *Secretary General of the FSTSE*, 1958-64. h-Author of an article on bureaucracy. j-None. k-Formed a political alliance with *Alfonso Martínez Domínguez* and *Jesús Robles Martínez* called the "Three Colonels." l-Padgett, 129; González Navarro, 118; WWMG, 37; C de D, 1961-63, 90, 1952-54, 19; *Hoy*, Dec. 1952; *Siempre*, 4 Feb. 1959, 6; *Excélsior*, 10 Dec. 1978, 18; PS, 5665; Sirvent, 181.

Sánchez Navarrete, Federico
a-Mar. 22, 1917. b-Federal District. c-Primary studies in the Colegio Francés de Mixcoac, Mexico City; studies at the National Contractors School; degree in agricultural engineering with a specialty in parasitology, National School of Agriculture, Feb. 6, 1943; studies at the English Language Institute, University of Michigan, 1948; MS, with a thesis on sugarcane diseases, Louisiana State University, 1949-50, graduating July 19, 1956, on a fellowship from the Bank of Mexico and the Secretariat of Agriculture; Ph.D. in agricultural sciences, Louisiana State University; Professor of Sugarcane Diseases, Veracruz Technological Institute of Sugarcane. d-*Federal Deputy* from the State of Morelos, Dist. 1, 1955-58. e-Member of PAN. f-Delegate to the State of Morelos, Secretariat of Agriculture, 1942-48; Zone Director, Secretariat of Agriculture; Technician, Secretariat of Agriculture, 1951-55; Director of the Agricul-

tural Experiment Station, Zacatepec, 1955; Technical Inspector, Institute for the Improvement of Sugar Production, 1956-57; Chief of the Sugar Cane Research Program, Institute of Agricultural Research, 1959. g-None. j-None. k-None. l-Ind. Biog., 147; DGF56, 26; C de D, 1955-58; BdM, 236-37.

Sánchez Ochoa, José de Jesús
a-1945. b-San Román, Jalisco. c-Early education unknown; degree in philosophy and religion, 1961-68; MA in history, Higher Normal School. d-*Federal Deputy* from the State of Jalisco, Dist. 4, 1973-76; Mayor of Zapopan, Jalisco, 1980-82; *Plurinomial Federal Deputy* from PAN, 1988-91. e-Secretary of Organization of PAN, State of Jalisco, 1973-76; Secretary of PAN, various states, 1976-80; President of PAN, Zapopan, Jalisco, 1980-87. f-None. g-None. h-Educator. i-Son of Enrique Sánchez Plascencio, cattle rancher; married Ruth Alina Guzmán Ramírez, normal teacher. j-None. k-None. l-C de D, 1973-76, 1988-91; DBGM89.

Sánchez Pérez, Daniel Angel
a-June 13, 1939. b-Uruapan, Michoacán. c-Early education unknown; law degree, School of Law, University of Michoacán, 1957-62, with a thesis on "Labor Conciliation." d-*Plurinominal Federal Deputy* from the PSUM, 1982-85. e-Originally a member of PRI; joined the PCM, 1978; candidate of the PCM for federal deputy from the State of Michoacán, 1979; candidate of the PCM for mayor of Apatzingan, Michoacán, 1980; joined the PSUM, 1981; candidate of the PSUM for federal deputy from the State of Michoacán, 1982; member of the Central Committee of the PSUM, 1982; member of the Political Committee of PSUM, Michoacán, 1982; member of the State Committee of PSUM, Michoacán, 1982; President of the PSUM, Apatzingan,

Michoacán. f-None. g-None. h-Practicing lawyer; writer for *Epoca*. i-Son of Daniel Sánchez Núñez, white collar worker, and María de los Angeles Pérez Solís; married María Inés García Díaz. j-None. k-None. l-Directorio, 1982-85; Lehr, 648; DBGM, 600.

Sánchez Piedras, Emilio
(Deceased June 13, 1981) a-Nov. 1, 1915. b-Tlaxcala, Tlaxcala. c-Primary and secondary studies in Tlaxcala; preparatory studies in the Federal District; law degree with honorable mention from the National School of Law, UNAM, Feb. 3, 1941. d-Local Deputy to the State Legislature of Tlaxcala (ten years); *Federal Deputy* from the State of Tlaxcala, Dist. 2, 1952-55, member of the Legislative Studies Committee, the Second Justice Committee, and the Consular Service Committee; substitute member of the Military Justice and Small Agricultural Property Committees; *Federal Deputy* from the State of Tlaxcala, Dist. 1, 1958-61, President of the Gran Comisión, member of the First Government Committee and the Rules Committee; *Governor of Tlaxcala*, 1975-81. e-Representative of *Adolfo López Mateos* during his presidential campaign in the State of Coahuila; general delegate of the CEN of PRI to Yucatán, Colima, Jalisco, and Coahuila. f-Agent of the Ministerio Público, Attorney General of the Federal District and Federal Territories, 1941-44; Consulting Lawyer, Department of Indigenous Affairs, under *Isidro Candia*, 1941-44; Director of Public Works, State of Tlaxcala, 1944-51; private secretary to Governors *Mauro Angulo* and *Rafael Avila Bretón*, 1945-51; president of the Committee for the Industrial Development of Tlaxcala, 1951-52; Director of Legal Affairs, Federal Electric Commission, 1965. g-Active in student politics; President of the Student Association at the National

School of Law, UNAM. h-Practicing
lawyer since he received his degree; tied
to the important industrial Pliana
Group and Industrias Polifil, S.A.
i-Married Elena Santiago; son of Emilio
Sánchez González, pulque rancher.
j-None. k-Caused the government of
Adolfo López Mateos diplomatic
difficulties with the United States after
making a speech favoring Cuba, 1960;
supposedly lost presidency of Gran
Comisión, Oct. 1960. l-Func., 382; C de
D, 1958-60, 92, 1952-54, 19, 52, 60, 69,
13 Nov. 1978, 6; *Excélsior*, 15 Nov.
1978, 23; HA, 14 June 1981, 4, 31.

Sánchez Pontón, Luis
(Deceased June 19, 1969) a-Aug. 5,
1889. b-Puebla, Puebla. c-Primary and
secondary education in public and
private schools in Puebla; preparatory
studies at the National Preparatory
School; law degree, National School of
Law, UNAM, 1912; Professor of Law
and Economics, UNAM, 12 years;
founder and President of the Council of
Primary Education, 1932-40. d-Federal
Deputy from the State of Puebla, Dist.
2, 1914-15; Constitutional Deputy from
the State of Puebla, Dist. 2, 1916-17;
Senator from the State of Puebla.
e-Member of the Constitutional Liberal
Party, 1916, but opposed Venustiano
Carranza for President. f-Secretary
General of Government of the Federal
District, 1914; Secretary General of
Government of Veracruz, 1915; Oficial
Mayor of the Secretariat of the Trea-
sury, 1930-31; Interim Governor of
Puebla, 1920-21; Director, Budget
Department, Secretariat of the Trea-
sury, 1928-29; Minister to Ecuador,
1942; *Ambassador to the Soviet Union*,
1946-47; Ambassador to Canada;
Ambassador to Switzerland; *Secretary
of Public Education*, 1940-41. g-Mem-
ber of the First Congress of Students,
1910. h-Author of education books;
President of the Financiera Hispano-

Mexicana, S.A.; member of the National
Council of Higher Education; Mexican
delegate to the Seventh Pan American
Conference. i-*Carlos Madrazo* and
Germán Parra were close collaborators
when he served as Secretary of Education; attended school with *Juan Andreu
Almazán*; married Ana María Garfías.
j-None. k-A distinguished student at
law school; asked for the resignation of
Porfirio Díaz as a student leader, 1910;
one of the first of the radical holdovers
from the *Cárdenas* period to be forced
out of a cabinet position. l-D de Y, 3
Dec. 1940, 6; Correa41, 96; *Hoy*, Dec.
1940, 3-4; EBW46, 516; Kirk, 137, 148;
Strode, 374; DP70, 1914; WWM45, 111;
Vázquez de Knauth, 200; Enc. Mex., XI,
1977, 340; López, 996.

Sánchez Taboada, Rodolfo
(Deceased May 2, 1955) a-1895. b-Te-
peaca (Hacienda de Macuila), Acatzingo,
Puebla. c-Primary studies in San
Sebastian Villa Nueva, Acatzingo,
Puebla; secondary studies at the Colegio
de San José and the Hospicio de Puebla,
Puebla; preparatory studies at the
Colegio del Estado de Puebla; completed
second year in a premedical program at
the Colegio del Estado de Puebla, but
terminated his studies in 1914; enrolled
in the National Military College to
become a 2nd Lieutenant in the Medical
Corp; no degree. d-None. e-President of
the Regional Committee of PRI for the
Federal District during the *Alemán*
presidential campaign, 1946; *President
of the CEN of PRI*, Dec. 5, 1946 to Dec.
1, 1952; one of the national directors of
Ruiz Cortines' presidential campaign,
1952. f-Assistant to President *Cárdenas*, 1935; Director of the Budget Office
for the Presidency, 1935; *Governor of
Baja California del Norte*, Feb. 22, 1937
to 1940; 1940-44; *Secretary of the Navy*,
1952-55. g-None. h-None. i-Brother
Ruperto was a federal deputy from Puebla, 1946-49; son *Rodolfo Sánchez Cruz*

was a federal deputy from Puebla, 1970-73 and a precandidate for governor of Puebla, 1974; close friend of *Teófilo Borunda*; married Emma Cruz; nephew *Germán Sierra Sánchez* was a federal deputy from Puebla, 1985. j-Career army officer; joined the Revolution as a 2nd Lieutenant under General Fortunato Maycotte, Nov. 10, 1914; fought Zapata in Morelos under Col. Jesús Guajardo; rank of Colonel, Oct. 4, 1939; rank of Brigade General, Nov. 1, 1952; reached rank of Division General. k-Brandenburg places him in the Inner Circle during the 1940s; *López Avelar* was his assistant in 1919; resigned from the Governorship July 31, 1944 because of the supposed discontent with the in-efficiency of his regime and the incompetent men he appointed; remained at the direct disposal of President *Avila Camacho*, Aug. 1, 1944 to Oct. 15, 1945; considered a benefactor to the University Pentathlon. l-Brandenburg, 80; HA, 9 May 1955; HA, 25 Aug. 1944; Morton, 59; HA, 5 Dec. 1952, 9; DP70, 1915; Peral, 749; *Polémica*, No. 1, 1969, 73; *Excélsior*, 3 Mar. 1974, 16; López, 998; *Excélsior*, 7 Nov. 1978, 13; Anderson; *Excélsior*, 3 Mar. 1974, 16; Enc. Mex., XI, 1977, 340-41; Loret de Mola, 76.

Sánchez Tapia, Rafael
(Deceased 1946) a-Sept. 24, 1887. b-Aguililllas, Michoacán. c-Primary studies in Morelos; secondary studies at the Conciliar Seminary of Zamora, Michoacán and in Spain; abandoned studies, 1911; completed equivalent of preparatory in arts and letters; no degree. d-Governor of Michoacán, Dec. 3, 1934 to June 30, 1935. e-None. f-Prefect of Jiquilpan, Michoacán; Prefect of Coalcoman, Michoacán; *Secretary of Industry and Commerce*, June 18, 1935 to Dec. 31, 1937. g-High-level member of the Cárdenas Schismatic Masonic Lodge. h-None. i-Married Dolores Revs.

j-Joined the Revolution, 1911; Brigadier General, 1915; opposed de la Huerta rebellion, 1923; rank of Division General, Apr. 1, 1938; Commander of the 1st Military Zone, Feder-al District, 1937-39; retired from active duty, 1940. k-Appointed governor of Michoacán by the state legislature after his predecessor was killed in an accident; precandidate for President of Mexico, 1939, but in the opinion of Bermúdez, had the least chance of receiving the official party nomination; ran for President on the Centro Unificador, 1939; Inner Circle status, 1934-37. l-Michaels, 3, 50; NYT, 12 Feb. 1939; Bermúdez, 88; Brandenburg, 80; Peral, 749; DP70, 1915; Lieuwen, 130; DP64, 1314; López, 998; Enc. Mex., XI, 1977, 341.

Sánchez Ugarte, Fernando de Jesús
a-Dec. 18, 1949. b-Federal District. c-Primary studies at Colegio Tepeyac, Mexico City, 1956-61; secondary and preparatory studies at Colegio Tepeyac, Mexico City, 1962-67; economics degree, Autonomous Technological Institute of Mexico, 1968-73; MA in economics, University of Chicago, 1974-75; Ph.D. in economics, University of Chicago, 1975-77, with a dissertation on tax incentives to promote industrialization; teacher, Colegio Tepeyac; professor, ITAM. d-None. e-None. f-Economist, Secretariat of the Presidency, 1972-73; adviser, Treasurer Economic Studies Unit, Secretariat of the Treasury, 1976-78; Area Director, Investment Policy Division, Secretariat of the Treasury, 1978-80; Subdirector General, Investment Policy Division, Secretariat of the Treasury, 1980-84; Director General, Investment Policy Division, Secretariat of the Treasury, 1986-88; *Subsecretary of Industry*, Secretariat of Trade and Industrial Development, 1988-94. g-None. h-Economist, International Monetary Fund, 1983-86. i-Son of Héctor Sánchez

Núñez, ophthalmologist, and María Guadalupe Ugarte Valdez; married Mary Anne Leenheer Simmons, translator. j-None. k-None. l-DBGM89, 327; DBGM92, 345.

Sánchez Vargas, Julio
a-Aug. 17, 1914. b-Ojo de Agua, Veracruz. c-Early education unknown; legal studies from the Escuela Libre de Derecho, 1931-35, graduating with a thesis on expropriation for the public good, May 18, 1936. d-None. e-None. f-Lawyer for the Legal Department of the Secretariat of Foreign Relations, 1936-37; lawyer, Office of Presidential Resolutions, Department of Agrarian Affairs, 1937-41; Attorney General of the State of San Luis Potosí under Governor *Reynaldo Pérez Gallardo*, 1940-42; Oficial Mayor of Government of the State of San Luis Potosí, 1942-43; Secretary General of Government of the State of San Luis Potosí under General *Ramón Jiménez*, 1943-44; secretary to the Chief of Police of the Federal District, 1944-46; Supernumerary Justice of the Superior Tribunal of Justice of the Federal District and Federal Territories, 1946-63; President of the Superior Tribunal of Justice of the Federal District and Federal Territories, 1963-67; *Assistant Attorney General of Mexico*, 1967; *Attorney General of Mexico*, 1967-70, 1970-71; *Justice of the Supreme Court*, 1977-83; Director General of the National Institute of Senility, 1990-94. g-None. h-Director General of the Mexican Society of Industrial Credit, 1971-76. i-Attended the Escuela Libre de Derecho with *Julio Santos Coy* and *Donato Miranda Fonseca*; married Rosa Beristáin Escobedo; son of Celedonio Sánchez Serna, lawyer, and Cristina Vargas Sánchez. j-None. k-Resigned from the Attorney General's office after student demonstration. l-*Excélsior*, 21 Aug. 1971, 1; DGF56, 514; DPE71, 160; HA, 7 Dec. 1970, 26; WNM, 212.

Sánchez Vázquez, Salvador
a-Oct. 21, 1940. b-Tepic, Nayarit. c-Early education unknown; public accounting degree, School of Accounting and Business Administration, UNAM, 1961-66, with a thesis on accounting as a technique for union control; professor, National School of Political Science, UNAM, Acatlán Campus, 1977-89; professor, National School of Law, UNAM, 1977-89; professor, Higher School of Business and Administration, IPN, 1978-82. d-*Federal Deputy* from the State of Nayarit, Dist. 1, 1988-91; *Senator* from the State of Nayarit, 1991- . e-General Delegate of the CEN of PRI, Durango and Hidalgo, 1979, Zacatecas, 1977-79, and Quintana Roo, 1969. f-*Director General of the ISSSTE*, 1975-77; Controller, Bridges and Federal Highways, 1982-88. g-Secretary General of the National Union of IPN Workers, 1965-68; Secretary of Acts, FSTSE, 1968-71; Secretary of Promotion, FSTSE, 1971-74; *Secretary General of the FSTSE*, 1974-75. h-Controller General, Dean Export Mexicana, 1967-70; Director, Consultores Mexicanos, 1977-82. i-Son of José Sánchez Arellano, public official, and Angela Vázquez López, public official; married María de los Angeles Medina Orozco. j-None. k-None. l-DBGM89, 539; DBGM92, 577; C de D, 1988-91; C de S, 1991-97.

Sánchez Vite, Manuel
a-Mar. 17, 1915. b-Molango, Hidalgo. c-Primary studies in Molango, Hidalgo; secondary studies at the Rural Normal School, Actopan, Hidalgo, 1931, and at Secondary School No. 4, Mexico City; rural teaching certificate from the Rural Normal School, El Mexe, Hidalgo, 1934; normal certificate from the National Teachers School, Mexico City, 1942-44; preparatory studies in social sciences from the National Preparatory School, 1945-46; law degree, National School of Law, UNAM, 1947-51; teacher in

various rural schools in El Mexe and Actopan, México. d-*Federal Deputy* from the State of Hidalgo, Dist. 2, 1955-58, member of the Social Action Committee, the Public Education Committee, the Third Ejido Committee, and the Committee on the Development and Promotion of Sports; *Senator* from the State of Hidalgo, 1964-69, Secretary of the Gran Comisión; *Governor of Hidalgo*, 1969-70, 1972-75. e-General Delegate of the CEN of PRI to Colima, Mexico and Veracruz; *President of the CEN of PRI*, 1970-72. f-Legal adviser to the National Teachers Union and to the ISSSTE; Attorney General of the State of Hidalgo, 1963-64; Oficial Mayor of the Controller of the Secretariat of the Treasury. g-Secretary of the National Teachers Union of Hidalgo, 1942-44; Secretary General of Local 9, SNTE, 1947-52; Secretary of Publicity of the CEN of the SNTE, 1949; Secretary General of Local 14, SNTE; Secretary of Youth Action of the CNOP; *Secretary General of the SNTE*, Nov. 19, 1952-55; President of the Political Committee of the SNTE, 1955. h-None. i-Married María Guadalupe Jiménez; *Abel Ramírez Acosta* part of his political group; son of Maximino Sánchez Vargas, a peasant, and María Trinidad Vite. j-None. k-As President of PRI, asked for three six-month leaves from the governorship of Hidalgo, making it possible for him to return as governor in May 1972 in a rather unusual fashion even by Mexican political standards; imposed his own successor as governor, 1975, but he remained in office only one month. l-HA, 15 Mar. 1971, 12; *Hoy*, 19 Dec. 1970, 4; MGF69; DBM70, 514; DGF56, 24; HA, 28 Nov. 1955, 10; WNM, 212; *Excélsior*, 24 Jan. 1975, 18; Pérez López, 440-41.

Sandoval Castarrica, Enrique
a-June 19, 1901. b-Federal District. c-Early education unknown; graduated as a 2nd Lieutenant, Heroic Military College; completed staff and command course, Higher War College, 1935; professor, chief of courses and Subdirector, Heroic Military College; professor, chief of courses and Subdirector, Higher War College. d-None. e-None. f-*Subsecretary of National Defense*, 1972-75. g-None. h-None. j-Career army officer; joined army as a 1st Sergeant in the Cavalry, Nov. 1, 1919, as a member of the staff of General Sidronio Méndez, Commander of the 14th Brigade; fought Zapatistas, 1919-20; fought in western Campeche, 1920; fought in Michoacán and Guanajuato, 1921; fought in Guerrero, 1927; fought Cristeros, 1927-29; Assistant Chief of Staff, Presidential Guards; Assistant Chief of Staff, Air Force Expeditionary Force to the Phillipines, 1945; Assistant Chief of Operations, General Staff, Secretariat of National Defense, 1953; Assistant Chief of Staff, Secretariat of National Defense under *Tomás Sánchez Hernández*, 1956; rank of Brigade General, 1961; Director, Department of Military Identification and Recruitment, Secretariat of National Defense, 1961; rank of Division General, 1968; Director of Military Transportation, Secretariat of National Defense, 1965-72. k-None. l-DGF69, 196; Rev. de Ejer., Jan. 1972, 22; DPE61, 34; Rev. de Ejer., Nov. 1968, 53, Nov. 1961, 68, June 1953, 65.

Sandoval López, Rodolfo
a-1912. b-Oaxaca, Oaxaca. c-Secondary studies from the Annex School, Normal School of Oaxaca, 1920-26; preparatory studies from the Institute of Arts and Sciences of Oaxaca; law degree, Institute of Arts and Sciences of Oaxaca, 1934-39; professor at the preparatory and law school Institute of Arts and Sciences of Oaxaca, 1929-42; fellowship student of the Center of Social Studies, Colegio de México, 1943-45. d-*Alternate Senator* from the State of Oaxaca,

1964-68, but replaced Senator *José Pacheco Iturribarría*, 1969-70. e-None. f-Employee of the Legal Department of the Petroleum Workers Union, 1946-50; employee of the Legal Department of the Federal Electric Commission, 1951-55; Interim Secretary General of Government of Oaxaca under General *José Pacheco Iturribarría*, 1956; Director of Aprovechamientos Forestales of Oaxaca, 1963-65; representative of the Secretariat of Industry and Commerce and the Hydroelectric Company of Oaxaca, 1957-65. g-None. h-Practicing lawyer in Oaxaca. j-None. k-None. l-C de S, 1964-70; MGF69; PS, 5689.

Sandoval Rodríguez, Eufrasio
a-Apr. 9, 1908. b-Ramos Arizpe, Coahuila. c-Engineering studies, National School of Engineering, UNAM, 1930-34, received degree in 1955. d-None. e-None. f-Began career with the National Railroads of México, 1934; worked as a leveler, assistant engineer, engineer, and supervisory engineer, 1934-43; principal engineer, Southern Zone, 1943-44; principal engineer, Northern Zone, 1944; conservation engineer, Tracks and Structures, 1954-55; Second Assistant of Studies and Projects of the Director General, 1955-58; Department head, Tracks and Structures, 1958-62; Subdirector of Tracks and Structures, 1962-64; *Director General of the National Railroads of México*, 1964-70. g-None. h-None. i-Member of a political clique called "Los Compadres" headed by *Benjamín Méndez Aguilar* as Director General of the National Railroads. j-None. k-None. l-WWMG, 37; DPE65, 109; *Excélsior*, Dec. 1964; PS, 5690.

Sandoval Vallarta, Manuel
(Deceased Apr. 18, 1977) a-Feb. 11, 1899. b-Federal District. c-Early education unknown; preparatory studies at the National Preparatory School,

1912-16; BS, Massachusetts Institute of Technology, 1921; Sc.D. in physics, 1924; Guggenheim Fellow, Berlin, 1927-28; Visiting Professor, University of Louvain, 1935-36; Lecturer, Harvard University, 1937; Lecturer, University of Toronto, 1937; Research Associate, MIT, 1923-26; Assistant Professor of Physics, MIT, 1926-30; Associate Professor of Physics, MIT, 1930-39; Professor, MIT, 1939; Resident Associate of the Carnegie Institute, Washington, D.C., 1939-43. d-None. e-None. f-Director of the Department of Scientific Research, UNAM, 1943-44; *Director General of the National Polytechnic Institute*, 1943-46; *Subsecretary of Public Education*, 1955-58; Director of the Mexican-North American Cultural Institute, 1961-66; member of the National Commission of Nuclear Energy, 1961-67. g-None. h-Author of many articles in the physical sciences; President of the Commission for the Promotion and Coordination of Scientific Cooperation in Mexico; member of the National College; recipient of the National Prize in Arts and Sciences, 1959. i-Brother-in-law of *Hugo B. Margáin*; married María Luisa Margáin; student of Albert Einstein; son of Pedro Sandoval Gual Vallarta and Isabel Lyon. j-None. k-None. l-WWM45, 111; DGF56, 299; EBW46, 876; DP70, 1076; *Libro de Oro*, 67-68, xvi; DGF51, I, 629; Peral, 750; DGF50, I, 455; HA, 9 Feb. 1954, 2 May 1977, 56; *Excélsior*, 30 Apr. 1977; letter; JSH, 367-69; *Proceso*, 23 Apr. 1977, 28.

Sandoval Zavala, Inocencio
a-Dec. 28, 1920. b-Puruandiro, Michoacán. c-Primary studies at the Escuela Maestro Vicente Lombardo Toledano, Mexico City (6 years); no secondary or preparatory education; no degree. d-*Federal Deputy* (Party Deputy from PAN), 1970-73, member of the Public Assistance Committee, the Rural

Electrification Committee, the Television Industry Committee, and the Second Section of the Instructive Committee of the Grand Jury. e-Member and District Director of PAN. f-None. g-None. h-Textile worker. j-None. k-Candidate for Federal Deputy from PAN (five times). l-C de D, 1970-72, 136; Directorio, 1970-72.

Sansores Pérez, Carlos
a-Dec. 25, 1918. b-Champotón, Campeche. c-Secondary studies, Instituto Campechano; law degree, School of Law, University of Campeche. d-*Federal Deputy* from the State of Campeche, Dist. 2, 1946-49, member of the Gran Comisión, the National Waters and Irrigation Committee, and the Hunting and Fishing Committee; *Federal Deputy* from the State of Campeche, Dist. 2, 1955-58, member of the Committee on Credit, Money, and Credit Institutions, the Legislative Studies Committee, and the Rules Committee; Vice President of the Chamber of Deputies, 1955; Secretary of the Chamber of Deputies, 1956; *Federal Deputy* from the State of Campeche, Dist. 2, 1961-64, Secretary of the Permanent Commission, 1963, member of the Treasury Committee, the Balloting Committee, the Instructive Committee for the Grand Jury, and the Budget and Accounts Committee; Vice President of the Chamber of Deputies, Dec., 1962; *Senator* from the State of Campeche, 1964-67; *Governor of Campeche*, 1967-73; *Federal Deputy* from the Federal District, Dist. 26, 1973-76, President of the Gran Comisión; *Senator* from the State of Campeche, 1976, President of the Gran Comisión, 1976. e-Founding member of PRI in Campeche; Secretary General of the Committee to elect *Miguel Alemán* in Campeche; founder of the Revolutionary Campeche Party, 1957; Auxiliary Secretary to the CEN of PRI, 1966;

delegate of PRI to Chihuahua, 1965; *Subsecretary General of the CEN of PRI*, 1973-74; *President of the CEN of PRI*, 1976-79. f-Secretary to the Penal Court, State of Campeche, 1941-43; Justice of the Penal Courts, State of Campeche; Chief of the Judicial Police, Campeche, 1943-44; Secretary General of Government of the State of Campeche, 1949-50, under *Manuel López Hernández*; agent of the Ministerio Público of the Federal District; Federal Defense Attorney for Labor, 1953-55; *Director General of the ISSSTE*, 1979. g-Delegate of the National Farmers Federation; President of the Campeche Student Federation, 1935-37. h-None. i-Supporter of *Carlos Hank González*; daughter, *Rosa María Martínez Denegri*, was a senator, 1976-82; son of Ulises Sansores; *Eugenio Echeverría Castellot* was his secretary when he was president of the student association; obtained position as Chief of the Judicial Police through the assistance of *María Lavalle Urbina*. j-None. k-Early supporter of women's suffrage in the Chamber of Deputies; resigned as Governor of Campeche to become Majority Leader of the Chamber of Deputies, 1973; accused of fraudulent business dealings and involvement in the murder of the president of PRI in Dzitbalché, 1961. l-*Hoy*, 4 Mar. 1967, 7; WWMG, 37; DGF56, 21; DGF47, 5; Morton, 55; HA, 1 Jan. 1965, 8; C de D, 1961-63, 91, 1946-48, 89; HA, 12 Mar. 1973, 31; *Excélsior*, 18 Dec. 1973, 15; HA, 27 Aug. 1973, 7; Ind. Biog., 148-49; *Proceso*, 10 Oct. 1977, 6-9; HA, 7 Jan. 1974, 12; *Proceso*, 11 Dec. 1976, 20, 19 June 1978, 29.

Santa Ana (García), Miguel
(Deceased Aug. 8, 1972) a-Nov. 5, 1896. b-Colima, Colima. c-Primary studies, Colegio San Luis Gonzaga; secondary, Liceo de Varones, Guadalajara, 1912. d-*Governor of Colima*, 1935-39; *Senator*

from the State of Colima, 1940-46, secretary of the Senate, member of the Gran Comisión, the Second Balloting Committee, First Secretary of the National Defense Committee, and Second Secretary of the Military Justice Committee. e-Candidate of the Reconstruction Party for governor of Colima, 1931; precandidate for federal deputy, 1946. f-None. g-None. h-None. i-Son *Cuauhtémoc Santa Ana* served as Federal Deputy from the Federal District, 1970-73, and was Secretary of the Gran Comisión and President of PRI in the Federal District, 1972. j-Joined the Revolution; fought under General Miguel Diéguez, 1914; career army officer; commander of various military zones; rank of Brigadier General. k-According to Moreno, directed a campaign against Governor *Torres Ortiz*, 1941-42; originally defeated by *Francisco Carrillo Torres* for governor, 1935. l-Peral, 751; D de Y, 8 Nov. 1935, 1; letter; *Excélsior*, 9 Aug. 1972, 10; Correa41, 76-77; Enc. Mex., II, 1977, 588; Moreno, 86-88.

Santa Ana (Seuthe), Cuauhtémoc
a-Oct. 10, 1938. b-Colima, Colima. c-Primary studies, Emiliano Zapata Primary School, 1944-49; secondary studies, Public Secondary School No. 16, 1950-52; preparatory studies at the National Preparatory School, 1953-55; law degree, National School of Law, UNAM, 1956-60; studied at the University of Geneva, 1963-64. d-*Federal Deputy* from the Federal District, Dist. 17, 1970-73, member of the Department of the Federal District Committee, the Second Government Committee, and the First Constitutional Affairs Committee; Secretary of the Gran Comisión. e-President of PRI in the Federal District, 1973-75; *Secretary of Political Action of the CEN of PRI*, 1970-73; Director of Publications for the National Youth sector of PRI. f-Sub-

director General of Government, Secretariat of Government; private secretary to the Subsecretary of Government; auxiliary secretary to the Oficial Mayor of Government, 1968-69; auxiliary secretary to *Luis Echeverría*, 1969-70; Delegate of the Department of the Federal District to Benito Juárez, 1976; Delegate of the Department of the Federal District to Cuauhtémoc, 1978; *Secretary General of Public Works and Services of the Federal District*, 1979-82; Coordinator of Administrative Simplification, Secretariat of the Controller General, 1984-87; Technical Administrative Subdirector of Pemex, 1987-94. g-Practicing lawyer for the CNC. h-None. i-Son of Governor *Miguel Santa Ana* and Martha Seuthe; married Urinda Angélica Otero Torres, art historian. j-None. k-Precandidate in 1973 for Governor of Colima, but lost the nomination; precandidate for Senator from Colima, 1981. l-*Directorio*, 1970-72; C de D, 1970-72, 136; DAPC, 1977, 66; *Excélsior*, 26 Dec. 1981, 16; DAPC81, 5; DBGM92, 347; DBGM89, 329; *Excélsior*, 27 July 1984, 20.

Santamaría, Francisco J.
(Deceased 1963) a-Sept. 10, 1889. b-Cacaos, Tabasco. c-Primary studies in Macuspana, Tabasco; secondary education, Instituto Juárez, Villahermosa; normal teaching certificate, Instituto Juárez, Tabasco, 1909; law degree, National School of Law, UNAM, Oct. 24, 1912, with a thesis on Article 91 of the 1917 Constitution; Professor of Mathematics, Instituto Juárez (University of Tabasco); director of the Porfirio Díaz Primary School; director of the Manuel Romero Rubio Secondary School. d-*Governor of Tabasco*, 1947-52. e-Orator for the candidacy of A. R. Gómez for Governor of the Federal District; campaigned for Generals Gómez and Serrano during their 1927 presidential campaign.

f-Penal Judge, Third District, Mexico City; Secretary General of Government of the State of Tabasco; consulting lawyer to the Mexican Embassy in Washington. g-Member of the National Student League, 1927. h-Member of the National Language Academy, 1954; author of numerous geographical, historical, and language dictionaries on Mexico, especially on the state of Tabasco; poet. i-Participated with *Miguel Alemán, Braulio Maldonado Sánchez* and *Efraín Brito Rosado* in the 1927 campaign; married Isabel Calzada; his nephews, Francisco and Joaquín Bates Caparroso, served in his administration. j-Constitutionalist; supported the Escobar movement, 1929; represented the movement abroad. k-The only survivor of a massacre at Huitzilac, Cuernavaca, 1927; in exile, 1927. l-Peral, 752-53; DP70, 1943; WWM45, 111-12; DGF51, 92; STYRBIWW54, 994-95; Dulles, 443; López, 1008; Bremauntz, 71; Enc. Mex., XI, 1977, 346-47.

Santana Benhumea, Graciela
a-Jan 15, 1941. b-Morelia, Michoacán. c-Primary studies at the Sor Juana Inéz de la Cruz School, Toluca, México; secondary studies at Secondary School No. 2, attached to the Normal School, 1953-55; teaching certificate, Normal Montesori School, Toluca, 1953-58; law degree, Autonomous University of the State of México, 1962-68; professor, Autonomous University of the State of México. d-Local Deputy to the Legislature of the State of México; *Federal Deputy* from the State of México, Dist. 15, 1979-82. e-None. f-Director, House of Artisans, State of México; Director of Artisan Development, State of México. g-Secretary of Women's Action of the CNC; Secretary General of Artisans of the State of México; Secretary of the Regional Peasant Committee, Santo Tomás, México. h-None. i-Daughter of Lauro Santana Martínez and Imelda

Benhumea Contreras. j-None. k-None. l-C de D, 1979-82; Romero Aceves, 735-36.

Santiago Ramírez, César Augusto
a-May 27, 1943. b-San Cristobal de la Casas, Chiapas. c-Early education unknown; law degree, School of Law, University of Chiapas; MA in law, Harvard University. d-*Federal Deputy* from the State of Chiapas, Dist. 9, 1979-82; *Federal Deputy* from the State of Chiapas, Dist. 2, 1985-88; Representative to the Assembly of the Federal District, Dist. 40. 1988-91; *Plurinominal Federal Deputy* from PRI, 1991-94. e-Oficial Mayor of the PRI, State of Chiapas; Subsecretary of Electoral Action of the CEN of PRI, 1987-88; Director of the Information and Electoral Studies System, CEN of PRI, 1988-89; *Secretary of Electoral Action of the CEN of PRI, 1989-92.* f-Consul in New England, 1974-76; Subsecretary General of Government of the State of Chiapas, 1976-77; Private Secretary to the Governor of Chiapas, 1978; adviser, Secretary of Commerce, 1981. g-Member of the advisory council of the CNC. h-None. i-Son of Filiberto Santiago Flores and Francisca Ramírez; married Elena Ruiz. j-None. k-None. l-DBGM92, 578; C de D, 1979-82; C de D, 1985-88.

Santillán (Osorno), Manuel
a-Sept. 29, 1894. b-Hacienda de Xalostoc, Tlaxcala. c-Preparatory studies in Jalapa, Veracruz; engineering degree from the National School of Engineering, UNAM; advanced studies in geology. d-*Governor of Tlaxcala,* 1941-44. e-None. f-Chief of Geologists for Mining and Petroleum, Secretariat of Industry and Commerce, 1929; Consulting Engineer to the Presidency, 1933; Chief Geologist of the Secretariat of Industry and Commerce, 1934; member of the Technical Commission of the

Presidency, 1935; Director of the
National Institute of Geology, 1929;
Subsecretary of Industry and Commerce, 1935-36, Director General of the
administration of petroleum, 1937-38;
Subsecretary of Public Works, 1939-40.
g-None. h-Began career as a mining engineer, Pachuca, Hidalgo, 1919; author
of several geology books. i-Married Luz
Gamper; son of Calixto Santillán.
j-None. k-Anderson says he was forced
to resign as governor because he tried to
oppose the national PRM leadership,
1933. l-WWM45, 112; EBW46, 1090;
Peral, 754; Anderson, 86; López, 1010.

Santos Cervantes, Angel
a-Sept. 1, 1905. b-Villa Aldama, Nuevo
León. c-Primary studies in Villa
Aldama; law degree from the University
of Nuevo León, 1929; Professor of Obligations and Conracts, School of Law,
University of Nuevo León. d-*Senator
from the State of Nuevo León, 1958-64*,
member of the Gran Comisión, President of the Second Tariff and Foreign
Trade Committee, First Secretary of the
Second Credit, Money and Credit Institutions Committee, President of the
Tax Committee, First Secretary of the
Insurance Committee, Second Secretary
of the Second Mines Committee, and
member of the First Balloting Group.
e-None. f-Secretary General of Government of the State of Nuevo León under
Governor Pablo Quiroga, 1935; President of the Water and Drainage Services
of Monterrey. g-None. j-None.
k-None. l-C de S, 1961-64, 70; Func.,
293.

Santos Coy Perea, Julio
a-July 18, 1909. b-Piedras Negras, Coahuila. c-Law degree from the Escuela
Libre de Derecho, June 21, 1922, with a
thesis on arbitration in the 1931 Legal
Code. d-None. e-None. f-Agent of the
Ministerio Público of the Office of the
Attorney General in the Isthmus of

Tehuantepec, 1934; federal agent of the
District Courts; assistant agent of the
Attorney General of Mexico; Director of
the Department of Preliminary Investigations, Department of the Federal
District; legal adviser to *Adolfo López
Mateos*, Secretary of Labor, 1952-56;
labor conciliator for the Secretariat of
Labor, 1956; Director of Conciliators,
Secretariat of Labor, 1956-58; *Subsecretary of Labor*, 1958-64; *Subsecretary (A)
of Labor*, 1964-70. g-None. h-Private
law practice, 1940-52. i-Son Julio Santos Coy, general and lawyer, and María
Petra Perea; married Angelina Cobo.
j-None. k-None. l-DPE65, 154; DGF56,
398; DBM68, 571-72; D de Y, 6 Dec.
1958; DPE61, 115; *Libro de Oro*, xxxvi.

Santos Guajardo, Vicente
(Deceased May 26, 1962) a-Feb. 9, 1895.
b-Villa de Progreso, Coahuila.
c-Primary studies in Villa Unión and
Múzquiz, Coahuila; preparatory studies
from the Ateneo Fuente, Saltillo, and
the National Preparatory School,
Mexico City; law degree, National
School of Law, UNAM, 1916-21;
Professor of Administrative Law,
National School of Law, UNAM;
Professor of Law, Ateneo Fuente, 1922.
d-Local Deputy to the State Legislature
of Coahuila, 1922-23; Federal Deputy
from Coahuila, 1924-26. e-None.
f-Director of the Legal Department,
Secretariat of Agriculture and Livestock; Judge of the Superior Tribunal of
Justice of the Federal District, 1928-34;
Assistant Attorney General of Mexico,
1934-37; *Subsecretary of Government*,
1937-40; *Subsecretary of Labor*, 1940-
43; *Director General of the Mexican
Institute of Social Security*, 1943-44;
Subsecretary of Foreign Relations, 1944;
Justice of the Supreme Court, 1944-52,
1952-57; President of the Supreme
Court, 1955-56. g-None. i-Collaborated
with *Ignacio García Téllez* in several
positions; met him at the National

School of Law; son of Antón Santos and Maximina Guajardo. j-Student leader during the Revolution. k-None. l-D de Y, 5 Jan. 1938, 2; DGF51, I, 568; DP70, 1342, 1953; Peral, 755; STYRBIWW57, 416; DGF56, 567; López, 1011; NYT, 4 Jan. 1944, 31.

Santos (Rivera), Gonzalo N.
(Deceased Oct. 17, 1978) a-1895. b-Villa Guerrero, San Luis Potosí. c-Early education unknown; no degree. d-Federal Deputy from the State of San Luis Potosí, Dist. 10, 1924-26, member of the Great Committee; Federal Deputy from the State of San Luis Potosí, 1926-28, answered the presidential State of the Union address, 1926, and served as majority leader as head of the Alliance of Socialist Parties; Federal Deputy from the State of San Luis Potosí, Dist. 10, 1928-30, member of the Great Committee; Federal Deputy from the State of San Luis Potosí, Dist. 3, 1930-32, member of the Great Committee; Federal Deputy from the State of San Luis Potosí, Dist. 6, 1932-34, member of the Great Committee; *Senator* from the State of San Luis Potosí, 1934-40; *Governor of San Luis Potosí*, 1943-49. e-Secretary of Affairs for the Federal District, CEN of the PRM, 1929; Secretary General of the CEN of the PNR, 1931. f-Custom's agent, 1917; Minister to Belgium, 1940; Director of Fishing, Secretariat of Industry and Commerce, 1959-61. g-None. h-None. i-Son Gaston Santos involved in San Luis Potosí politics; political enemy of *Federico Medrano.* j-Fought with Venustiano Carranza during the Revolution; rank of general in the army. k-Regional caudillo in San Luis Potosí; Brandenburg places him in the Inner Circle during *Alemán's* administration; his power in San Luis Potosí declined after the middle 1950s; accused of large-scale illegal land holdings in San Luis Potosí; important Callista congressional

leader and member of the "Reds" in congress; answered Calles' state of the union address, 1926. l-*Por Qué*, 4 Oct. 1968, 35; Hoy, 3 June 1972, 9; HA, 7 Oct. 1949, xxii; Peral, 755; Johnson, 32-33; HA, 28 Sept. 1944, VIII; DP70, 1581; Brandenburg, 80, 102; HA, 8 Oct. 1943, 13, 28 Aug. 1978, 20, 23 Oct. 1978, 18; *Excélsior*, 26 June 1975, 4; NYT, 7 Jan. 1959, 11; *Excélsior*, 28 Sept. 1976, 2 Sept. 1972, 11; NYT, 18 May 1958, 7, 4 Dec. 1958, 13; *Excélsior*, 23 Aug. 1978; Campa, 157.

Santoyo, Ramón Víctor
(Deceased July 12, 1957) a-Mar. 6, 1901. b-Guanajuato, Guanajuato. c-Law degree from the University of Guanajuato; Professor of Political Science, School of Political and Social Science, UNAM. d-Local Deputy to the State Legislature of Guanajuato; Federal Deputy from the State of Guanajuato, Dist. 9, 1928-30, Dist. 3, 1930-32; Federal Deputy from the State of Guanajuato, 1934-37, Secretary of the Chamber, Sept. 1936; *Federal Deputy* from the State of Guanajuato, Dist. 1, 1946-49, member of the Second Credentials Committee, the Budget and Accounts Committee, the Second Constitutional Affairs Committee, and the Inspection Committee of the General Accounting Office (1st year). e-None. f-Lower Court Judge; Judge of the Ministerio Público; Judge of the Superior Tribunal of Justice; Secretary General of Government of the State of Guanajuato; Oficial Mayor of Government of the State of Jalisco; Secretary General of Government of the State of Jalisco; Secretary General of Government of Baja California del Norte, 1931; head of Lawyers for the Department of the Federal District; *Assistant Attorney General of Mexico* (2), 1949-52; *Assistant Attorney General of México*, 1952-57. g-None. h-Representative of the Government on the Federal Board of

Conciliation and Arbitration, Federal District, 1957. i-Son, Ramón, a lawyer. j-None. k-None. l-DP70, 1953-54; DGF51, I, 535; DGF51; C de D, 1946-48, 89; Casasola, V; Aguirre.

Santoyo Feria, Vinicio
a-Dec. 26, 1932. b-Federal District. c-Early education unknown; cadet, Heroic Military College, 1949-51, graduating as a 2nd Lieutenant in Personnel Administration and Artillery; completed Applied Military School in artillery; diploma in military administration, Higher War College, 1963-66; professor, Military School Classes, 1954-57, and the School of Military Engineering, 1965-67; Director, 1st Year Course, Staff and Command Program, Higher War College, 1968-70; Professor of Staff and General Tactics, Higher War College, 1967-70; Subdirector, Heroic Military College, 1976-78; Subdirector, Higher War College, 1970-72; Director, National Defense College, 1981-82. d-None. e-None. f-Chief of Staff, Secretariat of National Defense, 1982-85. g-None. h-None. i-Married Socorro Cortés Cruz; son of Héctor Santoyo Galván, teacher, and Rosa María Fería Ugalde, nurse. j-Joined the army as a cadet, Jan. 1, 1948; section commander, 2nd Artillery Regiment; Chief of S-1, Staff, 2nd Infantry Brigade; Commander of the PMS Battery, 2nd Artillery Battalion; Chief, Pedagogical Section, Staff, Secretariat of National Defense; adviser, State of México, 1966-68; adviser, Director General of Police and Traffic, Department of the Federal District, 1969-71; rank of Colonel, 1972; Assistant Chief of Staff, 29th Military Zone, Veracruz, Veracruz, 1972-73; Chief of Staff, 30th Military Zone, Tabasco, 1973-74; Commander, 2nd 105 Artillery Battalion, 1974-76; rank of Brigadier General, 1977; Military Attaché to the Mexican Embassy in Brazil, 1978-80; Commander of the 15th Military

Zone, Guadalajara, Jalisco, 1985-89; Commander of the 26th Military Zone, La Boticaria, Veracruz, and the 6th Military Region, 1989-91; Director General of Military Education, Secretariat of National Defense, 1991-94. k-None. l-Rev. de Ejer., Nov. 1972, 50, Nov. 1977, 70; QesQAP, 73; HA, 25 MAr. 1985, 15; DBGM, 392; DBGM92, 349.

Santoyo Núñez, Hortensia
a-June 1, 1933. b-Acapulco, Guerrero. c-Teaching certificate; social work degree; completed studies as a private accountant. d-*Federal Deputy* from the State of Guerrero, Dist. 4, 1976-79. e-Organizer of the Women's Assemblies for PRI. f-Director of Center of Educational Action No. 36, Secretariat of Public Education. g-President of the Consumer Protection Committee, Acapulco. i-Married Emilio García Vélez. j-None. k-None. l-*Excélsior*, 27 Aug. 1976, 1C; C de D, 1976-79.

Sanz Cerrada, Jesús
a-Jan. 18, 1911. b-San Luis Potosí, San Luis Potosí. c-Primary, secondary, and preparatory studies, Colegio Francés; no degree. d-*Federal Deputy* from the State of Chihuahua, Dist. 3, 1955-58. e-Founder of PAN in Durango, 1939. f-None. g-Militant in the National Defense League for Freedom of Religion, 1934; organizer of employer organizations, various cities, 1940. h-Writer, *El Siglo de Torreón*; *El Tiempo*, Monterrey; *El Porvenir*, Monterrey; founder of *El Diario de Nuevo León*. j-Captain in the Cristero forces in Michoacán and Durango. k-Imprisoned for 9 months in Morelia, 1934; persecuted locally for membership in PAN; had to leave state, 1939. l-Ind. Biog., 149; C de D, 1955-58.

Sarmiento Sarmiento, Manuel
b-Sinaloa. c-Primary and secondary studies in Sinaloa; preparatory studies in Sinaloa; graduated as a 2nd Lieuten-

ant, National Military College. d-Local Deputy to the State Legislature of Sinaloa, 1944-46; Mayor of Guasave, Sinaloa, 1948; *Federal Deputy* from the State of Sinaloa, Dist. 2, 1961-64; *Senator* from the State of Sinaloa, 1964-70. e-None. f-None. g-Secretary of Finances of the CEN of the CNC, 1964. j-Career army officer; rank of Lt. Colonel. k-None. l-C de D, 1961-64; C de S, 1964-70; MGF69.

Sarro (Tresarrieu), Enrique
a-Sept. 14, 1905. b-Federal District. c-Primary studies, Mexico City; secondary studies, Colegio Alemán, Mexico City; professional studies at the National School of Law and Economics, UNAM; no degree; Professor of Economics, National School of Economics, 1934, 1938-39; Professor at the School of Commerce, UNAM; Professor at the National School of Law, UNAM. d-None. e-None. f-Assistant to *Jesús Silva Herzog*, Chief of the Library and Economic Archives, Secretariat of the Treasury, 1928; Assistant to *Jesús Silva Herzog*, Department of Economic Studies, National Railroads, 1932-33; Assistant Director of Economic Studies, Secretariat of Industry and Commerce, 1933-34; Director, Department of Special Taxes, Secretariat of the Treasury, 1935-37; Director, Department of Economic Studies, Bank of México, 1937-40; *Director of the National Finance Bank*, Feb. 21, 1941, to Nov. 15, 1945; *Director General of National Steel Industry*, 1946-52. g-None. h-Author of numerous works on economics. i-Coauthored several books with *Jesús Silva Herzog*; married María Teresa Pérez Pliego; son of Germán Sarro and María Teresa Tresarrieu; son, Enrique, an architect. j-None. k-Served as the first Director of Nacional Financiera. l-WWM45, 112; DGF51, II, 231, 327; DGF50, II, 225, 229; letter; López, 1014-15.

Saucedo (Pérez), Salvador
(Deceased Mar. 1963) a-Nov. 9, 1890. b-Colima, Colima. c-Early education unknown; no degree. d-Federal Deputy from the State of Colima, Dist. 1, 1917-18, member of the Great Committee; Federal Deputy from the State of Colima, Dist. 1, 1918-20, member of the Great Committee; Federal Deputy from the State of Colima, Dist. 1, 1920-22, member of the Great Committee; *Governor of Colima*, Nov. 20, 1931, to Aug. 21, 1935. e-Organizer and member of the Coliman Liberal Party. f-Director of Government Printing, 1914, under Governor J. Trinidad Alamillo, State of Colima; Director of the Federal Treasury Office, Zacatecas, Zacatecas, 1956, Tuxtla Gutiérrez, Chiapas; Tuxpan, Veracruz, and the Federal District; Director of the Federal Treasury Office, Colima, 1961-63. g-None. h-Became a printer in his youth; writer for the newspaper *La Revancha*; published the newspaper, *El Popular*, 1909; founded the *Colima Libre*, 1917; newspaper editor in Guadalajara. i-Brother, Miguel, was interim governor of Colima, 1935, and a local deputy; defeated General *Miguel Santa Ana* and Higinio Alvarez for governor, 1931; nephew, Carlos Pizano y Saucedo, was private secretary to *Jesús González Lugo*, 1949-51; nephew, Roberto Pizano Saucedo, was a federal deputy from Colima. j-Maderista during the Revolution. k-Removed from the office of Governor through a federal dissolution of powers because of friendship with Calles. l-Peral, 759; letter; DP70, 1958; DGF56, 168; Moreno, 83-85; Hurtado, 311-12.

Sáyago Herrera, Indalecio
a-Apr. 14, 1910. b-Meczalco, Altotonga, Orizaba, Veracruz. c-Completed primary and secondary studies; teaching certificate, Federal Institute for Teacher Education; primary school teacher. d-Local Deputy to the State Legislature

of Veracruz, 1977; *Federal Deputy* (Party Deputy from the PPS), 1967-70; *Plurinominal Federal Deputy* from the PPS, 1985-88. e-Founding member of the Popular Party, 1948; Secretary of Finances of the Popular Party, 1956; member of the Central Committee of the PPS, 1960-88; Secretary of Finances of the PPS, 1960-87. f-None. g-Secretary General of the Teachers Union (CROM), Zongolica, Veracruz, 1933; Secretary of Foreign Relations, Union of Intellectual Workers, CROM, Orizaba, Veracruz, 1936; Secretary General of the CTM, Orizaba, Veracruz, 1939; Secretary of International Relations, CEN of the SNTE, 1942; Secretary of Vigilance Committee, CEN of the SNTE, 1947; Secretary of National Relations, CEN of the SNTE, 1967. i-Married Sara Zúniga Herrera; common-law marriage with Manuela Vargas Godines; son of Ciro Sáyago García and Esther Herrera Carballo. j-None. k-None. l-Directorio, 1967-70; C de D, 1967-70; DBGM87, 566.

Schaufelberger (Alatorre), Luis F.
(Deceased Feb. 11, 1958) a-June 21, 1893. b-Puebla, Puebla. c-Primary and secondary studies in Puebla; graduated from the Naval College at Veracruz, as a coastguardsman. d-None. e-None. f-*Subsecretary-in-charge of the Secretariat of the Navy*, 1946-48. g-None. h-None. j-Career naval officer; Commander of the corvette *Zaragoza*, of the destroyer *Bravo*, of the Pacific Naval Zone, and of the Gulf Naval Zone; Inspector General; rank of Vice Admiral; Commander of the Naval Zone, Isla Margarita, Baja California. k-None. l-DGF47; DBP, 636-37; CyT, 636-37.

Scherman Leaño, María Esther de Jesús
a-Jan. 5, 1957. b-Guadalajara, Jalisco. c-Early education unknown; law degree, University of Guadalajara; secondary

and preparatory school teacher; professor, University of Guadalajara. d-Alternate Local Deputy to the State Legislature of Jalisco, 1983-85; *Federal Deputy* from the State of Jalisco, Dist. 3, 1985-88; *Senator* from the State of Jalisco, 1988-91; *Federal Deputy* from the State of Jalisco, Dist. 16, 1991-94. e-Joined PRI, 1979; Secretary of Promotion of PRI, State of Jalisco, 1983-86; Subsecretary of Electoral Action of the CEN of PRI, 1987; Assistant Secretary to the President of the CEN of PRI, 1989. f-None. g-Secretary of Women's Action, Student Federation of Guadalajara, 1977-80. h-Radio announcer, University Radio. i-Daughter of Jesús María Scherman y Guzmán, surgeon, and María Esther Leaño, executive secretary; married Sergio Torres Mariscal. j-None. k-None. l-DBGM89, 542; DBGM92, 580.

Schmill Ordóñez, Ulises
a-Apr. 4, 1937. b-Federal District. c-Early education unknown; law degree, National School of Law, UNAM, 1954-58; LLD, National School of Law, UNAM, 1961-62; Professor, UNAM, 1961-73, 1977-80; Researcher, Institute of Legal Research, UNAM, 1983-85. d-None. e-None. f-Secretary of Agreements, Federal Tax Court, 1960; Secretary of Studies and Accounts, Supreme Court, 1965; Judge, Federal Tax Court, 1968-70; Technical Subdirector, Income Tax Division, Secretariat of the Treasury, 1970; Ambassador to Germany, 1973; General Coordinator, Income Tax Division, Secretariat of the Treasury, 1977; *Justice of the Supreme Court*, 1985-90; *President of the Supreme Court*, 1991-94. g-None. h-Lawyer, Bremer, Quintana Firm, 1977-78; private practice, 1979-85. i-Son of José Schmill Sada, mechanical and electrical engineer, and Carmen Ordóñez Moralli; married Angels

Peralta di Gregorio. j-None. k-None.
l-*El Nacional*, 1 Jan. 1991, 1; DBGM87,
661; DBGM89, 643; DBGM92, 700.

Sentíes Echeverría, Yolanda Elisa
a-Jan. 1, 1940. b-Toluca, México.
c-Early education unknown; studies in
chemical pharmaceutical biology,
School of Chemical Sciences, UNAM,
1957-60, graduating with a thesis on the
measurement of carbon monoxide in
the blood of urban Mexico City drivers,
1961, for which she received an honorable mention; MA in public administration, Autonomous University of the
State of México, 1974-76; studies in
law, National School of Law, UNAM;
Professor of chemistry and physics,
Preparatory School of the Autonomous
University of the State of México, 1964-
71; founder and Technical Secretary,
School of Chemical Sciences, Autonomous University of the State of México.
d-Local Deputy to the State Legislature
of México, 1974-76; Mayor of Toluca,
México, 1976-78; *Federal Deputy* from
the State of México, Dist. 16, 1979-82,
member of the Gran Comisión; *Senator*
from the State of México, 1982-88,
President of the Health Committee,
Secretary of the 2nd Internal Trade
Committee, member of the First Public
Education Committee, the First
Balloting Committee, the First Section
of the Grand Jury Committee and the
Third Section of the Legislative Studies
Committee. e-Secretary of Cultural
Action of the PRI in State of México,
1971-72; Director of Promotion, CEN of
PRI, 1980-81; Assistant Secretary
General of the CEN of PRI, 1980-81.
f-Director General of Maternal Infant
Health, Secretariat of Health, 1988-94.
g-Coordinating Secretary of Population
Affairs, CNOP, State of México, 1970-
71; Secretary General of the National
Revolutionary Women's Association,
1981- . h-Active in social works;

founded many children's theaters in
Toluca. i-Daughter of *Octavio Sentíes*,
head of the Department of the Federal
District, 1971-76, and María del
Carmen Echeverría Mondragón; married
Dr. Carlos Ballesteros. j-None. k-Won
more than 70 percent of the votes as a
candidate for federal deputy; first female
mayor of Toluca and senator from the
State of México. l-HA, 21 Aug. 1972,
39; HA, 30 July 1979, 29; C de D, 1979-
82; Lehr, 254; C de S, 1982-88; Romero
Aceves, 732-34; Andrade, 37-40;
Excélsior, 25 Sept. 1981, 20; HA, 25
May 1981, 15; *Excélsior*, 1 Mar. 1982,
26; DBGM87, 567; DBGM89, 331;
DBGM92, 351-52; DBGM, 602-03.

Sentíes (Gómez), Octavio
a-Feb. 9, 1915. b-Veracruz, Veracruz.
c-Primary, secondary, and preparatory
studies in Veracruz; law degree from the
National School of Law, UNAM, Nov.
17, 1942, with a thesis on "Constitu-
tional Federalism and Economic
Centralism"; Temporary Professor of
Commercial Law, National School of
Law, UNAM, 1958; professor, National
School of Law, UNAM, 1981. d-*Federal
Deputy* from the State of México, Dist.
8, 1943-46; *Federal Deputy* from the
Federal District, Dist. 4, 1970-71,
president of the Gran Comisión, 1970-
71, member of the Department of the
Federal District Committee, the First
Government Committee, the Gran
Comisión, and the First Constitutional
Affairs Committee; President of the
Chamber of Deputies, Sept. 1970.
e-Member of the PNR. f-Private secretary to the Governor of México, *Wenceslao Labra García*, 1937-41; *Head of
the Federal District Department*, 1971-
76. g-Student leader of the Vasconcelos
movement in Veracruz, 1929; editor of
El Eco Estudiantil. h-Mexican delegate
to international conferences on motor
transportation; private law practice

with a specialty in transportation law,
1942, 1947-70. i-Student of *Alfonso
Noriega* at the National Law School,
UNAM; daughter, *Yolanda Sentíes
Echeverría*, was a senator from the State
of México, 1982-88; married to María
del Carmen Echeverría; related to
Roberto Mantilla Molina; wife related
to *Luis Echeverría*; son of Jorge Luis
Sentíes an Elisa Gómez; lawyer of
Rubén Figuroa, 1980; close to *Miguel
Alemán*. j-None. k-Precandidate for
Governor of Veracruz, 1979. l-HA, 21
Aug. 1972, 39; *Hoy*, 16 June 1971, 6;
Hoy, 27 Feb. 1971, 10; DPE71, 140; HA,
8 Jan. 1973, 29; C de D, 1970-72, 136;
Enc. Mex., XI, 1977, 378; WNM, 215;
Loret de Mola,*91*, 211.

Septién García, Carlos
(Deceased Oct. 19, 1953) a-Jan. 15,
1915. b-Querétaro, Querétaro. c-Pri-
mary studies at the Colegio Civil of
Querétaro and at a Catholic school;
preparatory studies at the Colegio Civil
of Querétaro; law degree, National
School of Law, UNAM, 1940; Director,
School of Journalism, Mexican Catholic
Action, 1951-53. d-None. e-Cofounder
of PAN, 1939; member of the CEN of
PAN, 1949; founder of *La Nación* of
PAN. f-None. g-Active leader of the
Catholic student organizations, 1930s.
h-Journalist; founder of *El Chinto*, 1927;
founder of *El Escolapia*, 1930; writer for
Excélsior; founder of the *Revista de la
Semana* of *El Universal*; editor of
Provincia, Querétaro, Querétaro; writer
for *Heraldo de Navidad*. i-Father,
Alfonso María Septién Díaz, a prominent lawyer in Querétaro and president
of the Mexican Bar Association, 1939;
great grandson of Colonel José Antonio
Septién. j-None. k-Catholic Action
journalism school named for him.
l-Mabry; Lemus, 38; Enc. Mex., XI,
1977, 379; DP70, 1978; Diaz, 120;
Carrasco Puente, 267.

Sepúlveda (Amor), Bernardo
a-Dec. 14, 1941. b-Federal District.
c-Early education unknown; law degree,
National School of Law, UNAM, 1964,
with a thesis on the "Constitutional
Debate in Mexico, 1821-24": MA in
International Law, Cambridge Univer-
sity, 1966; cofounder of the Center for
Studies of the United States, Colegio de
México; Professor of International Law,
Colegio de México, 1967-79; professor,
Division of Graduate Studies, School of
Political and Social Sciences, UNAM,
1971-75. d-None. e-*Secretary of
International Affairs of the CEN of PRI*,
1981-82. f-Adviser to *Miguel de la
Madrid*, 1966; Subdirector General of
Legal Affairs, Secretariat of the Presidency, 1968-70; adviser to the Secretary
of the Treasury, 1971-75; Director General of International Financial Affairs,
Secretariat of the Treasury, 1976-81;
adviser to *Miguel de la Madrid* in international affairs, 1981-82; *Ambassador
to the United States*, 1982; *Secretary of
Foreign Relations*, 1982-88; *Ambassa-
dor to Great Britain*, 1988-93. g-None.
h-Prolific author of books on interna-
tional affairs. i-Son of distinguished
physician and professor Bernardo
Sepúlveda and Margarita Amor de
Ferreira; nephew of *César Sepúlveda*;
great grandson of Dr. Adolfo
Schmidtlein, a military physician in
Maximillian's entourage and Gertrudis
García; grandson of Carolina
Schmidtlein and Emmanuel Amor de
Ferreira; mother's family wealthy
descendants of landowners in the
Porfiriato; wife is the granddaughter of
José Ives Limantour, secretary of the
Treasury, 1893-1911; brother, Jaime,
was a subsecretary of health, 1991.
j-None. k-None. l-*Excélsior*, 22 Dec.
1982, B1, 4; Linajes, 15-17; HA, 13 Dec.
1982, 10; IEPES; Q es QAP, 46; *Excél-
sior*, 1 Dec. 1982, 20, 34; HA, 12 Apr.
1982, 14; *Proceso*, 4 Oct. 1982, 16;
DBGM89, 332; DBGM92, 352-53.

Sepúlveda (Gutiérrez de Lara), César
a-1916. b-United States. c-Primary and secondary studies at the Colegio Hidalgo, Monterrey; preparatory studies at the University of Nuevo León, Monterrey, 1933-34, and at the National Preparatory School, 1934-39; law degree, National School of Law, UNAM, 1940-44; MA degree in history and letters, UNAM, 1943; Professor of International Public Law, National School of Law, UNAM; Professor of Law and International Relations, Colegio de México; Visiting Professor, School of Law, University of Michigan; Secretary of the National Preparatory School; Director, National School of Law, UNAM, 1962-66; Director, Institute of Comparative Law, UNAM. d-None. e-None. f-Director General of Scholarly Services, UNAM; adviser, Secretary of Foreign Relations, 1946-50; Director General of Industrial Property, Secretariat of Industry and Commerce, 1950-59; Director of the Diplomatic Studies Institute, 1970-76; Ambassador, 1976; Director of the Diplomatic Studies Institute, 1979-83; Ambassador to West Germany, 1983-85. g-Student leader; candidate for president of his law school class. h-Director, Inter-American Center for Social Security, 1977-79. i-Son of Ricardo A. Sepúlveda, self-made businessman, banker, and supporter of Madero and Villa during the Revolution; mother, Ana Gutiérrez de Lara, a teacher; married Alicia Núñez Ramírez; uncle of *Bernardo Sepúlveda Amor*; nephew, Jaime, was a subsecretary of health, 1991. j-None. k-None. l-DBM68, 578; DGF56, 284; letters; WNM, 215; *Excélsior*, 2 Aug. 1979, 1; *Uno Más Uno*, 26 Feb. 1983, 2; DBGM, 395.

Serdán Alvarez, María Isabel
a-Feb. 27, 1948. b-Puebla, Puebla. c-Early education unknown; chemical engineering degree, University of Puebla, 1965-70; special studies in chemistry, Trinity College, 1970-71; Professor of Chemistry and Engineering, University of Puebla, 1976-78. d-*Federal Deputy* from the State of Puebla, Dist. 7, 1982-85, member of the Health and Welfare Committee, the Social Security Committee, and the Tourism Committee. e-Member of the CNC; adviser to the CEPES of PRI in Puebla, 1980-81. f-Chemist, Secretariat of Health and Public Welfare, 1972-75; adviser to the Secretariat of Agrarian Reform, 1976-78; Director of the Nursery No. 1, IMSS, Puebla, 1977-79; chemist, Clinic No. 2, IMSS, Puebla. g-Secretary General of ANFER in Puebla, 1978-82; Secretary of Women's Action, CNOP, 1983. h-Chemist, private labs, 1969-72. i-Daughter of Aquiles Serdán del Valle, civil engineer, and María Isabel Alvarez Dávalos. j-None. k-None. l-Directorio, 1982-85; C de D, 1982-85; Lehr, 324; DBGM, 603.

Serna (Leal), Donaciano
a-1919. b-Molango, Hidalgo. c-Primary and secondary studies in Molango; teaching certificate in primary studies; CPA degree; studies for a Ph.D. in education; Ph.D. in pedagogy; professor, Univerity of Hidalgo; professor at the Regional Technical Institute and the Regional Normal Center, Hidalgo. d-Local deputy to the State Legislature of Hidalgo, 1960-63. f-Tax Collector, Pachuca; Treasurer General of the State of Hidalgo, 1969-70; *Interim Governor of Hidalgo*, 1970-72. g-Secretary General of Local 15 of the SNTE, 1959-62. h-Regular contributor to *Magisterio* and *El Heraldo de México*. j-None. k-Precandidate for Mayor of Pachuca, Hidalgo, 1972; precandidate for federal deputy from the State of Hidalgo, Dist. 4, 1973; appointed by the state legislature to replace *Manuel Sánchez Vite* when he took a leave to become President of the CEN of PRI. l-*Novedades*, 21 Feb. 1972, 13; *Excélsior*, 17

Mar. 1973, 13, 27 Mar. 1973, 12; HA, 20
Dec. 1971, 44; Pérez López, 449-50.

Serra Puche, Jaime José
a-Jan. 11, 1951. b-Federal District.
c-Primary studies at the Instituto Luis
Vives, Mexico City, 1956-62; secondary
and preparatory studies, Instituto Luis
Vives, 1962-68; degree in political
science, National School of Political
and Social Sciences, UNAM, 1969-73,
with a thesis on transnational corporations and power groups; MA in economics, Colegio de México, 1973-75, with a
neoclassical model of economic growth;
Ph.D. in economics, Yale University,
with a thesis on fiscal policies; Interim
Director and Director, Center of
Economic Studies, Colegio de México,
1981-82, 1983-85; professor and researcher, Center of Economic Studies,
Colegio de México, 1979-86; professor,
Stanford University, 1982. d-None.
e-Joined PRI, 1979. f-Analyst, Division
of Presidential State of the Unions,
Secretariat of the Presidency, 1972-75;
adviser, Secretariat of the Treasury,
1979-86; Chief of Advisers, Secretariat
of the Treasury, 1986; *Subsecretary of
Income*, Secretariat of the Treasury,
1986-88; *Secretary of Commerce and
Industrial Development*, 1988-94.
g-None. h-None. i-Son of Jorge Serra
Perayre and Carmen Puche Planas;
married Joanna Wright Abbott, economist; studied at Yale University with
Ernesto Zedillo, secretary of education,
1991. j-None. k-None. l-DBGM87,
366; DBGM89, 334; DBGM92, 354.

Serra Rojas, Andrés
a-Oct. 13, 1904. b-Pichucalco, Chiapas.
c-Primary studies in Veracruz, Veracruz;
preparatory studies, Instituto Veracruzano and the National Preparatory
School, 1924; law degree, National
School of Law, UNAM, 1928; LLD,
National School of Law, UNAM; Professor of Administrative Law, General

Theory of the State, Sociology, Political
Economy, and Mexican Economy,
National School of Law, UNAM;
professor at the National Polytechnic
Institute; professor at the National
Preparatory School. d-*Federal Deputy*
from the State of Chiapas, Dist. 1, 1943-
46; *Senator* from the State of Chiapas,
1964-70. e-Assistant Director of the
Institute for Social and Political Studies,
PNR, 1936; Official Orator in the presi-
dential campaign of *Miguel Alemán*,
1946. f-Agent of the Ministerio Público,
Attorney General's Office of the Federal
District, 1929-30; Director, Department
of the Nationalization of Property,
Office of the Attorney General of
Mexico, 1930; Assistant Attorney General of Mexico, 1933; Director General
of National Properties, Secretariat of the
Treasury, 1935; Private Secretary to the
Secretary of Health, *Gustavo Baz*, 1940-
42; *Secretary of Labor*, Dec. 1, 1946, to
Jan. 12, 1948; adviser, President of
Mexico, 1948; Director General of the
National Cinematography Bank, 1949-
52. g-Member of the executive commit-
tee of the Fifth National Student Con-
gress, 1928. h-Adviser to the Mexican
Delegation to the United Nations, 1945;
author of numerous works on adminis-
tration and law. i-Personal friend of
Octavio S. Mondragón, Subsecretary of
Health, 1946; friend of *Antonio Carrillo
Flores, Antonio Armendáriz, Alfonso
Noriega, José Castro Estrada, Miguel
Alemán*, and *Eduardo Bustamante* at
the National Preparatory School or at
the National Law School; protégé of
Emilio Portes Gil; grandson of Hipólito
Rojas, a revolutionary who fought
Victoriano Huerta; obtained first post
through his professor, José María Puig
Casaranc, Head of the Department of
the Federal District, 1929-30. j-None.
k-Was fired for not finding *Valentín
Campa* guilty on government charges,
1930; according to Valentín Campa,
Serra Rojas resigned as Secretary of

Labor because of intrigues by his subsecretary. l-WWMG, 38; WWM45, 112-13; HA, 6 Feb. 1948, 9; DGF50, 292; DGF50, I, 292; DGF51, I, 83; HA, 29 Oct. 1943, 14; DB de C, 235-37; Campa, 70-71; letter; Bulnes, 64; DBC, 235-37.

Serrano, Gustavo P.
(Deceased Sept. 10, 1979) a-Nov. 23, 1887. b-Altar, Sonora. c-Law degree, National School of Law, UNAM; member of the Board of Trustees, UNAM. d-Federal Deputy from Sonora, 1920-22. e-None. f-Secretary, Mexican Section, International Boundary Commission, 1922; President, International Boundary Commission, 1923; Secretary of Communication and Public Works, 1931-32; Ambassador to Guatemala, 1931-34; member of the Mexico-United States International Water Commission, 1935-38; Commissioner, Mexican-United States Agrarian Claims Commission, 1938-45; Executive Director of the National Irrigation Commission, 1939-44; *Secretary of Industry and Commerce*, 1944-46; adviser to the Administrative Council of the Federal Electric Commission, 1951. g-Member of the First Student Congress, UNAM, 1910; President of the National Chamber of Mining Industries, 1940. h-None. i-Father-in-law of Engineer José B. Zozaya, director of mining, Cía. Minería Autlán. j-None. k-None. l-DGF51, 345; DP70, 1088; WWM45, 113; DGF50, II, 245; EBW46, 132; HA, 7 July 1944, 7; Correa, 319; HA, 21 July 1944, 54; NYT, 2 July, 1944, 11; López, 1021; *Excélsior*, 12 Sept. 1979, 4.

Serrano Castro, Julio
a-Apr. 12, 1907. b-Tuxtla Gutiérrez, Chiapas. c-Primary studies in Juchitlan, Oaxaca; secondary studies in Tapachula, Chiapas; preparatory studies at the Institute of Arts and Sciences of Chiapas, Tuxtla Gutiérrez; law degree

from the National School of Law, UNAM, Oct. 31, 1930, with a thesis on agrarian reform. d-*Senator* from the State of Chiapas, 1949-52; *Senator* from the State of Chiapas, 1952-58, President of the Second Petroleum Committee, member of the Gran Comisión, the Third Labor Committee and the Special Legislative Studies Committee. e-None. f-Judge of the First Civil District Court of the Federal District; President of the Federal Board of Conciliation and Arbitration, 1946; Chief of the Office of Strikes and Conflicts, Secretariat of Labor; *Subsecretary of Labor and Social Welfare*, 1946; *Technical Subdirector of PEMEX*, 1946-50. g-President of the Socialist Front of Lawyers of the Federal District; represented workers in petroleum conflicts; President of the Union of Trucks and Buses of the Federal District, 1958. h-Specialist in labor law. i-Attended UNAM with *Miguel Alemán*. j-None. k-Precandidate for Governor of Chiapas, 1948. l-DGF47; DGF56, 5; HA, 5 Jan. 1959, 14; HA, 6 Feb. 1948, 10; DBC, 238; Ind. Biog., 149-51.

Serrano del Castillo, Nicanor
a-Nov. 1, 1918. b-Zacatelco, Tlaxcala. c-Primary studies in Tlaxcala; secondary studies at the School for Workers Children, Coyoacan, Federal District; preparatory studies from the National Preparatory School; economics degree, National School of Economics, UNAM. d-*Senator* from the State of Tlaxcala, 1970-76, President of the Foreign and Domestic Trade Committee, First Secretary of the Economics and Statistics Committee, and Second Secretary of the Electric Industry Committee. e-None. f-Archivist, Secretariat of the Treasury, 1941-45; General Manager of the Small Business Bank, 1952-55; economist, 1955-56, General Manager, 1965-67, and Oficial Mayor, 1968-70, all of the Federal Electric Commission.

g-None. h-Department head, Properties and Services, S.A., 1956-59; General Manager, Laminated Copper, S.A., 1960-64. j-None. k-None. l-C de S, 1970-76, 86; MGF69.

Serrano García, Ramón

a-Mar. 5, 1913. b-Colima, Colima. c-Completed primary studies, Miguel Hidalgo School, 1921-27; no degree. d-Member of the City Council of Colima, Colima; Local Deputy from the State Legislature of Colima; *Federal Deputy* from the State of Colima, Dist. 1, 1976-79, 1982-85, member of the Rules and the Labor and Social Welfare Committees. e-Joined PNR, 1935; Secretary of Labor Action, Colima PNR, 1938-41; Secretary of Labor Action, State of Colima PRI, 1941-83. f-None. g-Secretary of Organization of the CTM of Colima; Secretary of Cooperative Action of the CTM of Colima, 1937; Secretary of Political Action of the CTM of Colima; Attorney for the Defense of Labor in the Local Arbitration Board, Colima, 1954-75; Secretary of Labor and Conflicts of the CTM of Colima; Secretary General of the CTM of Colima, 1982. h-Laborer. i-Son of Federico Serrano Gaytán, small merchant, and Maximina García Cervantes; married Esther Ahumada Gutiérrez. j-None. k-None. l-Directorio, 1982-85; Lehr, 78; C de D, 1976-79, 1982-85; DBGM, 603.

Serrano Robles, Arturo

b-Tuxtla Gutiérrez, Chiapas. c-Early education unknown; law degree, National School of Law, UNAM, 1943; Professor of Guarantees and Amparo, National School of Law, UNAM, and University of Guanajuato. d-None. e-None. f-Judicial official, 2nd Judicial District, Administrative Law, Mexico City; actuary and secretary of 2nd Section of Accounts and Studies, Supreme Court; District Court Judge,

Guerrero, 1961-64; Circuit Court Judge, Puebla, 1964-69; Judge, 2nd Tribunal, Administrative Matters, 1st Circuit Court, Mexico City, 1969-73; *Supernumerary Justice of the Supreme Court*, 1973-74; *Justice of the Supreme Court*, 1975-81. g-None. h-None. k-Wrongly accused by the CCI of taking a 50-million-peso bribe; the CCI retracted the charges July 8, 1980, after an outcry in the press. l-*Excélsior*, 3 July 1980, 13, 8 July, 1980; Protag., 324.

Serrano (Tellechea), Raúl

a-May 28, 1908. b-Guaymas, Sonora. c-Engineering agronomy degree, Agricultural School of Ciudad Juárez. d-*Federal Deputy* from the State of México, Dist. 2, 1940-43, member of the Administration Committee (2nd year) and the National Waters and Irrigation Committee, substitute member of the Budgets and Accounts Committee; *Federal Deputy* from the State of México, Dist. 8, 1949-52, member of the Foreign and International Trade Committee. e-None. h-None. j-None. k-None. l-Peral, 764; DGF51, I, 23, 31; C de D, 1940-42, 43, 57, 1949-51, 90.

Servín Murrieta, Acela

a-Feb. 6, 1932. b-Totutla, Veracruz. c-Early education unknown; certificate in primary education; primary school teacher; Professor of Teacher Education, Enrique Rebsamen Normal School, Veracruz. d-*Federal Deputy* from the State of Veracruz, Dist. 7, 1967-70. e-None. f-None. g-Secretary of Radio Publicity for CNOP, Veracruz; Secretary General of the SNTE of Veracruz. j-None. k-None. l-Directorio, 1967-70; C de D, 1967-70.

Sierra Macedo, Manuel

a-Mar. 4, 1919. b-Federal District. c-Primary, secondary and preparatory studies at the Colegio Francés (presently the Colegio de México), Mexico City;

law degree, Free Law School, November 3, 1943, with a thesis on bills of exchange. d-*Federal Deputy* from the Federal District, Dist. 9, 1955-58, member of the Legislative Studies Committee and the Insurance Committee. e-Joined PAN, 1949; member of the National Executive Committee of PAN, 1944; Director of PAN for the Federal District, 1959. f-None. g-President of the Parents Association of the Colegio Franco-Inglés, 1963. h-Practicing lawyer, 1944- . i-Son of lawyer Manuel Sierra and Julia Macedo; married Margarita Arratia. j-None. k-Candidate of PAN for senator, 1958. l-Ind. Biog., 151-52; WNM, 216; ELD, 96; DGF56, 23, 33, 37; C de D, 1955-58.

Sierra (Mayora), Manuel J.
(Deceased 1970) a-Jan. 4, 1885. c-Early education unknown; law degree, University of Campeche; LLD, National School of Law, UNAM; Professor of History and International Public Law, National School of Law, UNAM, 1930; Director, Institute of Public International Law, UNAM. d-None. e-None. f-Director, Diplomatic Department, Secretariat of Foreign Relations, 1921; Director, Consular Department, Secretariat of Foreign Relations, 1921; representative on a special mission to the United States, 1924; Director of the Press Department, Secretariat of Foreign Relations; Director of the Diplomatic Department, Secretariat of Foreign Relations, 1927; Director, Department of Political Affairs, Secretariat of Foreign Relations, 1933; President of the Spanish-Mexican Arbitration Commission; Delegate to the Seventh Pan American Conference; *Oficial Mayor of Foreign Relations*, 1935-36; Director of Press and Publications, Secretariat of the Treasury, 1952-58; *Oficial Mayor of the Treasury*, 1959-64. g-None. h-Author of several books. i-Son of Justo J. Sierra, Justice of the

Supreme Court and Secretary of Public Education under Díaz, and Luz Mayora; uncle of *Javier Barros Sierra*; married Margarita Casasús; father-in-law, Joaquín de Casasús, was senator, banker and diplomat; uncle of Miguel Lanz Duret Jr.; became friends with *Adolfo López Mateos* during a regular breakfast gathering, 1933; professor of and mentor to *Manuel Tello*; grandson, Manuel Justo Sierra Noriega, was a director general in the Secretariat of Tourism. j-None. k-None. l-*Libro de Oro*, 1935-36, 258; Enc. Mex., XI, 1977, 387; Beltrán, 361; DGF56, 172.

Sierra Olivares, Carlos
a-July 8, 1939. b-Federal District. c-Early education unknown; degree in industrial relations, Ibero-American University, 1958-61, with a thesis on the evaluation of directive actions; professor, Anáhuac University, 1970-72; professor, Higher School of Business and Administration, IPN, 1968. d-None. e-None. f-Director of Administration and Finances, Institute of Urban Action and Social Integration, State of México, 1972-74; General Coordinator of Administration, Secretariat of the Treasury, 1977-78; Director General of Administration and Personnel Development, Secretariat of the Treasury, 1979-82; Director of the Modernization of Public Administration Unit, Secretariat of Programming and Budgeting, 1983-84; *Oficial Mayor of the Secretariat of Agriculture*, 1984-88; Director of Administration, Banrural, 1988-89. g-None. h-Manager, Advisory Group on Human Resources, Somatec, Grupo Somex, 1975-76. i-Son of Manuel Sierra Magaña, engineer, and Isabel Olivares Morales; married Juana Inés Abreu Santos, public official. j-None. k-None. l-QesQAP, 135; DBGM, 399; DBGM89, 335; *Uno Más Uno*, 18 July 1984, 4.

Sierra Rivera, Daniel
a-July 7, 1905. b-Orizaba, Veracruz.
c-Completed primary and secondary
studies, Workers Education Center,
Veracruz, 1918; no degree. d-Member of
the City Council of Orizaba, Veracruz,
1932-33; *Federal Deputy* from the State
of Veracruz, Dist. 7, 1946-49; Mayor of
Orizaba, 1952-54; *Federal Deputy* from
the State of Veracruz, Dist. 9, 1967-70;
Alternate Senator from the State of
Veracruz, 1970-76; *Federal Deputy* from
the State of Veracruz, Dist. 9, 1982-85,
member of the Labor and Social Welfare
and the Industrial Development Committees. e-Joined PRI, 1929. f-None.
g-Founding member of CROC; Secretary
General of the Union of Beer Workers of
CROC, Orizaba, Veracruz, 1940;
President of CROC, 1960. h-Employee
of Moctezuma Brewery, 1940- .
i-Married Alicia Alvarez Spíndola; son
of Rafael Sierra, peasant, and María
Rivera Blanco, seamstress. j-None.
k-None. l-Directorio, 1967-70; C de D,
1946-49, 1967-70, 1982-85; Lehr, 500; C
de S, 1970-76; DBGM, 603.

Silerio Esparza, Maximiliano
a-Mar. 14, 1939. b-Ejido Yerbabuena,
Rodeo, Durango. c-Primary studies in
Rodeo, began 1950; law degree, Benito
Juárez University, Durango, 1959-63.
d-Local Deputy to the State Legislature
of Durango, 1968-71; Mayor of Durango,
1971-74; Alternate Local Deputy to the
State Legislature of Durango, 1975-76;
Federal Deputy from the State of
Durango, Dist. 2, 1976-79; *Federal
Deputy* from the State of Durango, Dist.
4, 1982-85, member of the Gran Comi-
sión, the Government and Constitu-
tional Affairs Committees, the Agrarian
Reform Committee, and Secretary of
the Rules Committee; *Senator* from the
State of Durango, 1988-91; *Governor of
Durango*, 1992- . e-Joined PRI, 1959;
Youth Director of PRI in Durango,
1964-65; President of PRI in Durango,

Durango, 1965; President of PRI, State
of Durango, 1968; General Delegate of
the CEN of PRI to Veracruz, Chihuahua, Tamaulipas, Sonora, and Guanajuato, 1979-1982; General Delegate of
the CEN of PRI to Sonora, 1982.
f-Agent of the Ministerio Público;
Secretary General of Government of the
State of Durango, 1974-75. g-Secretary
of Organization of the League of Agrarian Communities of Durango, 1968-71;
Secretary General of the League of
Agrarian Communities of Durango,
1975-78; *Secretary General of the CNC*,
1991-93. i-Son of Maximiliano Silero
Arreola, ejidatario, and Blanca Elisa
Esparza; parents died when he was 12;
married Elvira Díaz Quiñones. j-None.
k-None. l-Lehr, 167; *Directorio*, 1982-
85; C de D, 1976-79, 1982-85; DBGM,
604; DBGM89, 544.

Silva García, Pablo
a-July 28, 1904. b-Colima, Colima.
c-Primary studies at the Ramón R. de la
Vega School, Colima, 1910-16; teaching
certificate, Normal School of Colima,
May 22, 1920; professor, Federal
Institute of Teacher Education; adviser
to the Papaloapan Commission on
education. d-*Governor of Colima*,
1967-73. e-None. f-Director of Federal
Education in Jalisco, 1951; Director of
Federal Education in Guanajuato, 1956;
Director General of Primary Instruction, Type B, States and Federal Territories. g-None. i-Student of Alberto
Larios Villalpando, secretary general of
the SNTE. j-None. k-None. l-DGF51,
I, 301; DPE61, 99; DGF56, 306; *Hoy*, 12
Sept. 1970, 63; letter; Romero Aceves,
165-66.

Silva Herzog, Jesús
(Deceased Mar. 13, 1985) a-Nov. 14,
1892. b-San Luis Potosí, San Luis
Potosí. c-Primary studies at a seminary
in San Luis Potosí, completed, 1905;
secondary studies at Paine Uptown

Business School, New York City, 1912-14; studies at the Graduate School, UNAM, 1919-23; economics degree from UNAM; founder of the National School of Economics, UNAM; Professor of Economic Policy, General Economic History and History of Economic Thought, National School of Agriculture, 1923-38; Professor of Literature and English, College for Primary Teachers, 1919-24; Professor of Economic Policy, National Teachers College, 1925-28; Professor Emeritus of UNAM, 1960; Professor of the History of Economic Thought, UNAM, 1931-59; Professor of Economic and Social Problems, School of Philosophy, UNAM, 1928-30; Director of the National School of Economics, UNAM, 1940-42. d-None. e-Writer during the campaign of *Aurelio Manrique* for Governor of San Luis Potosí, 1923; Secretary of Foreign Affairs, CEN of PNR, 1930. f-Employed in the Customs Office, San Luis Potosí, 1910-12; Director of Economic Statistics, National Statistics Department, 1926-27; Oficial Mayor of the Secretariat of Public Education, 1932; Subsecretary of Public Education, 1933-34; Founder and director of Economic Studies, the National Railroads of Mexico, 1931-32; Founder and director of the Department of Libraries and Economic Archives, Secretariat of the Treasury, 1928; Minister to the Soviet Union, 1928-30; economic adviser, petroleum conflict, 1937-38; General Manager of the National Petroleum Company, 1939-40 (before it became PEMEX); founder and Director of the Department of Financial Studies, Secretariat of the Treasury, 1942-45; *Subsecretary of the Treasury*, 1945-46; President of the Technical Council, Secretariat of National Patrimony, 1947-48. g-None. h-Reporter, 1914-15; businessman, 1916-17; author of major works on political and economic history; founder of the Mexican Insti-

tute of Economic Investigations, 1928; founder of several Revolutionary newspapers; adviser to the Secretary of National Patrimony, 1946-47; member of the Board of Governors, UNAM, 1945-62; Director of the magazine *Cuadernos Americanos*, 1948-81. i-Son of Joaquín Silva, an English teacher, and Estefania Herzog; boyhood friend of *Aurelio Manrique*; studied under *Antonio Caso*, Carlos Lazo, Ezequiel A. Chávez, and Alfonso Goldschmidt; son, *Jesús Silva Herzog Flores*, was secretary of the treasury. j-Accompanied Eulalio Gutiérrez during the Revolution as a reporter and supporter, 1914. k-Jailed in 1916 for four months. l-Wilkie, 634-35; Strode, 336-37; DGF59, II, 129; Peral, 769; DBM68, 582-83; Dulles, 934; WWM45, 113; López, 1029; Enc. Mex., XI, 1977, 394-95; *Excélsior*, 27 Jan. 1973, 9.

Silva Herzog (Flores), Jesús

a-May 8, 1935. b-Federal District. c-Primary and secondary studies in Mexico City; preparatory studies at the National Preparatory School; studied economics at the National School of Economics, UNAM, 1953-57; scholarship to study at CEMLA, 1958; economics degree with honorable mention from UNAM, 1959, with a thesis on "Considerations about the Petroleum Industry and Economic Development in Mexico;" Masters degree in economics from Yale University, 1960-62; Professor of Theory and Monetary Fiscal Policy at the Center of Economic and Demographic Studies, Colegio de México, 1964-69; Professor of International Economic Cooperation, National School of Economics, UNAM, 1963-69; Director of CEMLA, 1989-91. d-None. e-None. f-Economist, Department of Economic Studies, Bank of Mexico, 1956-60; Economist, Division of Economic Development, Inter-American Development Bank, 1962-63; Director of the Technical Office, Bank of Mexico, 1964-68; Coordinator for the Bank of Mexico, 1969-70; Director General of Credit, Secretariat of the Treasury, 1970-72; Director General of the National Institute of Housing, Apr. 24, 1972-76; General Manager in the Bank of Mexico, 1977-78; Director General of Credit, Secretariat of the Treasury, 1978-79; *Subsecretary of Credit*, May 22, 1979-82; *Secretary of the Treasury*, 1982-86; Ambassador to Spain, 1991-93; *Secretary of Tourism*, 1994. g-None. h-Delegate to Inter-American and International Economic Conferences; author of several articles and a book on economics. i-Son of *Jesús Silva Herzog*, Subsecretary of the Treasury, 1945-46, and Josefina Flores Villarreal; married María Teresa Márquez Díez-Canedo; friend of *Carlos Bermúdez Limón*, Director General of PIPSA, 1970-72, while both were students at UNAM. j-None. k-None. l-*Excélsior*, 30 Apr. 1972, 418; letter; HA, 7 May 1973, 17; *Excélsior*, 1 Dec. 1982, 36; Q es QAP; DBGM92, 357; letter.

Silva Nava, Carlos de
a-May 29, 1941. b-Federal District. c-Early education unknown; law degree, School of Law, Autonomous University of Guadalajara, 1959-64; professor, School of Law and Social Sciences, University of Guadalajara, 1965-67; professor, National School of Law, UNAM, 1968-72, 1978-81. d-None. e-None. f-Judicial official, 1965, Secretary, 1965-66, and First Secretary, Appeals Court, 1966-68, all with the Fourth Circuit Court, Guadalajara, Jalisco; Secretary of Studies and Accounts, Supreme Court, 1968-72; Third District Court Judge, Nuevo Laredo, Tamaulipas, 1972; Second Judge of the Administrative District, Federal District, 1972-77; Judge, Appeals Court, 10th Circuit, 1977-78; Judge, Second Appeals Court, First Circuit, Adminis-

trative Division, Federal District, 1978-84; *Justice of the Supreme Court*, 1984-88, 1988-94. g-None. h-None. i-Son of Alfonso de Silva Reynoso, lawyer, and Consuelo Nava Palacios; married Adriana Magallanes Medina. j-None. k-None. l-DBGM, 688; DBGM89, 644; DBGM87, 663; DBGM92, 702.

Siurob Ramírez, José
(Deceased Nov. 5, 1965) a-Nov. 11, 1886. b-Querétaro, Querétaro. c-Began studies in Querétaro; medical degree, National School of Medicine, UNAM, 1912. d-Constitutional Deputy from the State of Guanajuato, Dist. 13, 1916-17; Federal Deputy from the State of Querétaro, Dist. 3, 1918-20, Dist. 1, 1920-22; Federal Deputy from the State of Querétaro, 1922-24; Federal Deputy from the State of Querétaro, Dist. 3, 1924-26, Secretary of the Gran Comisión; President of the Congress (twice). e-Campaigned for Madero, 1909. f-Governor of Querétaro, 1914-15; Governor of Guanajuato, 1915-16; Governor of Quintana Roo, 1928-31; Director of Military Health, Secretariat of National Defense, 1934-35; *Secretary of the Department of Public Health*, June 19, 1935, to Jan. 4, 1938; *Head of the Department of the Federal District*, 1938-39; *Secretary of Health*, Aug. 5, 1939, to Nov. 30, 1940. g-None. h-Author of books on medicine and health in Mexico. i-Distant relative of Father Hidalgo. j-Joined the Revolution as a medical student in support of Madero, 1910; physician in the Northeast Medical Corps; career army officer; rank of Brigadier General, 1915; rank of Division General; Director of Military Health, Secretariat of National Defense, 1945; retired from the Army, 1945; Commander of the 17th Military Zone, Querétaro, Querétaro; Inspector General of the Army, 1932-34. k-One of the founders of the Army Bank; Brandenburg puts him in the inner circle of

influence, 1934-40. l-Peral, 771; DP70, 1996, 2022; Brandenburg, 80; D del S, 19 June 1935, 1; López, 1035; Enc. Mex., XI, 1977, 442; Alvarez Corona, 109-110.

Sobarzo (Díaz), Horacio
(Deceased Apr. 19, 1963) a-1896. b-Magdalena, Sonora. c-Primary studies at the Colegio de Estado, Sonora; secondary and preparatory studies in Hermosillo, Sonora; law degree, National School of Law, UNAM, 1925. d-None. e-Founding member of the National Council of PAN, 1939. f-Judge in Nogales, Sonora, 1928; Judge of the Superior Tribunal of the State of Sonora, 1929-37; Secretary General of Government of the State of Sonora, 1946-49; *Acting Governor of Sonora*, Apr. 1948, to Aug. 31, 1949, for General *Abelardo Rodríguez*. g-None. h-Author of several historical biographies. i-Father of *Alejandro Sobarzo Loaiza*, federal deputy and director general in the Secretariat of Government; married Julia Loaiza Lacy. k-None. l-DP70, 1997; Anderson; Mabry; Enc. Mex., XI, 1977, 443.

Sobarzo Loaiza, Alejandro
a-Feb. 16, 1934. b-Hermosillo, Sonora. c-Early education unknown; law degree, National School of Law, UNAM, April 24, 1965; LLD, Central University of Madrid; Professor of International Law, National School of Law, UNAM; Professor of International Relations, Political Science Graduate School, UNAM. d-*Federal Deputy* from the State of Sonora, Dist. 2, 1973-76; *Alternate Senator* from the State of Sonora, 1976-82, in functions 1981-82; *Federal Deputy* from the State of Sonora, Dist. 2, 1979-82, President of the Foreign Relations Committee, 1981; *Alternate Senator* from the State of Sonora, 1982-88, in functions, 1983-88. e-Private Secretary to the President of the CEN of PRI, *Jesús Reyes Heroles*,

1972-73; General Delegate of the CEN of PRI to Aguascalientes and Baja California, 1977-78; *Secretary of Organization of the CEN of PRI*, 1978; *Secretary of International Affairs if the CEN of PRI*, 1978-79; *Secretary of International Relations of the CEN of PRI*, 1987. f-Secretary of Studies and Accounts, Second Division of the Supreme Court, 1965-66; adviser to the Director General of Pemex, *Jesús Reyes Heroles*, 1966-70; Director General of Government, Secretariat of Government, 1982-83; Ambassador to Venezuela, 1989. g-None. h-Public Notary, Sonora, 1963-65; author of many articles and monographs. i-Son of *Horacio Sobarzo*, Interim Governor of Sonora, 1948-49, and Julia Loaiza Lacy; married María Dolores Morelos. j-None. k-Precandidate for governor of Sonora, 1978. l-HA, 19 Mar. 1979, I; *Excélsior*, 10 Sept. 1978, 12; C de D, 1973-76; C de S, 1976-82; C de D, 1979-82; C de S, 1982-88; HA, 11 May 1981, 11; Q es QAP, 39; DBGM89, 336-37; DBGM, 605; *Excélsior*, 25 July 1984, 20.

Soberanes Muñoz, Manuel
a-Feb. 11, 1911. b-La Paz, Baja California del Sur. c-Primary studies at the Melchor Ocampo School; preparatory studies at the National Preparatory School; graduated from the National Military College, 2nd Lieutenant of Infantry, 1929; law degree, National School of Law, UNAM, 1939; Professor of Military Ethics, National Military College. d-*Federal Deputy* from the State of Querétaro, Dist. 2, 1952-55; *Senator* from the State of Querétaro, 1964-70. e-Advisor to the Military Sector of the PNR; President of PRI in Querétaro; General Delegate of the CEN of PRI to various states. f-Private Secretary to the Governor of Hidalgo, *Alfonso Corona del Rosal*, 1957-58; Director of the Office of Business Revenues, Treasury of the Department

of the Federal District; Director of the Office of Infractions, Department of the Federal District; Director of the License Office, Department of the Federal District; Treasurer of the State of Querétaro. g-None. i-Son of a career army officer; brother, Urbano Soberanes Muñoz, was a colonel in 1959; brother, Gregorio, graduated from the National Military College in 1929; part of *Alfonso Corona del Rosal's* political group. j-Career army officer; rank of Colonel, Nov. 20, 1961; rank of Brigadier General, Nov. 20, 1972. k-None. l-C de D, 1952-55; C de S, 1964-70; MGF69; Rev. de Ejer., Nov. 1961, 11, Nov. 1972, 51; letter.

Soberanes Reyes, José Luis
a-May 18, 1950. b-Culiacán, Sinaloa. c-Early education unknown; civil engineering degree, Monterrey Institute of Technological and Higher Studies, 1966-71, with a thesis on water distribution systems; MA in urban planning and MA in operations research, University of Pennsylvania, 1973-76, University of Pennsylvania, 1973-76; professor at UNAM, 1978-80. d-None. e-Joined PRI, 1977; Coordinator of the Transportation Studies Committee, CEPES of PRI, Federal District, 1982; *Treasurer of the CEN of PRI*, 1990-92. f-Technical adviser in the Subsecretariat of Human Dwellings, Secretariat of Housing and Public Works, 1977-79; Coordinator of the Division of Regional Programming and Budgeting, Secretariat of Programming and Budgeting, 1983-85; Executive Coordinator and Director General of Policy Information, National Institute of Statistics, Geography and Information, Secretariat of Programming and Budgeting, 1985-88; Director of Urban Operations, Retail Distribution, Conasupo, 1988-90; *Subsecretary of Urban Development and Infrastructure*, Secretariat of Social Development, 1990-93. g-None. h-Technical Director

of Studies and Projects in Urban and Regional Planning, ACE Ingenieros Consultores, 1979-82. i-Son of José Luis Soberanes Cázares, rancher, and Aurora Reyes Medina; married Patricia Elvira Torres Nafarrate, lawyer; attended the Monterrey Institute of Higher Studies with *Luis Donaldo Colosio*; classmate of *Luis Donaldo Colosio* at the University of Pennsylvania; political disciple of *Luis Donaldo Colosio*. j-None. k-None. l-DBGM92, 357-58; letter.

Soberón (Acevedo), Guillermo
a-Dec. 29, 1925. b-Iguala, Guerrero. c-Primary and secondary studies, public schools, Mexico City; preparatory studies, National Preparatory School; medical studies from the National School of Medicine, UNAM, 1943-48, graduating 1949 with an honorable mention for his thesis on "Some Aspects of Paludism in Apatzingan, Michoacán"; Ph.D. in chemical physiology, University of Wisconsin, 1952-56, with a dissertation on the "Study of the Peroxidatic System of Leucocytes and Its Role in the Formation of Alloxan from Uric Acid"; full-time professor, Institute of Biomedical Research, UNAM, 1965-80; full-time researcher, Institute of Biomedical Research, UNAM, 1965-80, UNAM; professor at the Graduate School, IPN; visiting professor at various United States universities. d-None. e-None. f-Intern, 1950-51, Chief of the Department of Biology, 1956-65, Founder, Department of Bio-Chemistry, 1957, Director of Research, 1956-65, all at the National Institute of Nutrition; Director of Biomedical Research, UNAM, 1965-71; founder and coordinator of Scientific Research, UNAM, 1971-73; *Rector of UNAM*, Jan. 3, 1973-77, 1977-81; Coordinator of Health Services, Presidency of Mexico, 1981-82; *Secretary of Health*, 1982-88. g-Founding President of the Mexican Society of Bio-Chemis-

try. h-Author of numerous articles on medical subjects; employed as a medical expert by the United Nations; member of the National College, 1981. i-Studied under *Enrique Beltrán, Francisco Gómez Mont* and *Salvador Zubirán* at UNAM; brother of *Jorge Soberón Acevedo*, senator from Guerrero, 1976-82; son of *Galo Soberón y Parra*, prominent physician and federal deputy from Guerrero, 1937-40, and Carmen Acevedo. j-None. k-National Prize in Science, 1980. l-HA, 8 Jan. 1973, 18; letter; Enc. Mex., XI, 1977, 443; *Excélsior*, 1 Dec. 1982, 34; Q es QAP, 331.

Soberón Acevedo, Jorge

(Deceased Aug. 21, 1980) a-Oct. 6, 1921. b-Iguala, Guerrero. c-Early education unknown; medical degree, with specialized studies in cardiology, National School of Medicine, UNAM, 1946; Professor of Cardiology, National School of Medicine, UNAM, 1948-80. d-*Federal Deputy* from the State of Guerrero, Dist. 2, 1955-58, member of the Health Committee, the Budget Committee and the Instructive Section of the Grand Jury; *Alternate Senator* from the State of Guerrero, 1964-70; *Senator* from the State of Guerrero, 1976-80, member of the Permanent Committee, 1976-80. e-Became active in CNOP, 1948. f-Intern, Adjunct Physician, and Director of Clinical Services, all at the National Institute of Cardiology. g-Founder of the Mexican Association of Guerrero Residents, Mexico City. h-Founder of the *Voz del Sur* newspaper. i-Brother of *Guillermo Soberón*, Rector of UNAM, 1973-81; son of *Galo Soberón y Parra*, federal deputy from the State of Guerrero, 1937-40, and Carmen Acevedo; married Carmen Silva. j-None. k-None. l-Ind. Biog., 152-53; DGF56, 24, 34, 35, 37; C de D, 1955-58; C de S, 1976-82, 1964-70; HA, 1 Sept. 1980, 7-8.

Soberón y Parra, Galo

a-1896. b-Chilpancingo, Guerrero. c-Early education unknown; preparatory studies at the National Preparatory School; medical degree, National School of Medicine, UNAM, with a thesis on typhus, 1921; Professor of Parasitology, National School of Medicine, UNAM. d-Alternate Federal Deputy from the State of Querétaro, Dist. 4, 1924-26; *Federal Deputy* from the State of Guerrero, Dist. 2, 1937-40. e-None. f-Delegate of the Department of Health, Iguala, Guerrero; Director of the Federal Health Office; Director of the Technical Office for the Eradication of Malaria; special ambassador of the Mexican government in France and in Germany. g-None. i-Married Carmen Acevedo; father of *Guillermo Soberón*, secretary of Health, 1982, and *Jorge Soberón*, Senator, 1976-80. j-None. k-International expert on malaria. l-C de D, 1937-40.

Solana (Morales), Fernando

a-Feb. 8, 1931. b-Federal District. c-Early education unknown; studies in civil engineering, National School of Engineering, UNAM, 1948-52; studies in philosophy, School of Philosophy and Letters, UNAM, 1955; degree in political science and public administration, School of Political and Social Sciences, UNAM, 1964, with an honorable mention; Professor of Economic Organization and Mexican Public Administration, National School of Economics, UNAM, 1965-66; Professor of World Politics, 1964-65, Government and Politics of State of México, 1967-70, Political Science, 1970, Society and Politics of Contemporary Mexico, 1971-72, Political Science, 1973-74, and Political Analysis of Public Finance, 1976, School of Political and Social Sciences, UNAM; Professor of Theory and Politics, Graduate School, UNAM, 1973- ; Director of the Seminar of Public Administration, UNAM, 1965-68;

Secretary General of UNAM, 1966-70. d-None. e-Member of the advisory board of the IEPES of PRI. f-Researcher in international economic problems, National Finance Bank, 1961-65; member of the Committee on Public Administration, Secretariat of the Presidency, 1965-66; Subdirector of Planning and Finance, CONASUPO, 1970-76; Managing Director of Industries, CONASUPO, 1975-76; *Secretary of Industry and Commerce,* 1976-77; *Secretary of Commerce,* 1977; *Secretary of Public Education,* 1977-82; Director General of Banamex, 1982-88; *Secretary of Foreign Relations,* 1988-93; *Secretary of Public Education,* 1993-94. g-Representative of the faculty of the School of Political Science, UNAM, 1975-79; adviser to the National Sugar Producers Union, 1964-66. h-Journalist, 1952-66; editor of *Transformación,* 1963-64; Director of Informac, S.A., 1965-66; member of the Board of the National Productivity Council, 1966-70; Subdirector of *Mañana;* author of many works on public administration. i-Collaborator of *Javier Barros Sierra;* student of *Víctor Flores Olea;* nephew of Daniel Morales Blumenkron, newspaper editor; nephew of *Guillermo Morales Blumenkron,* governor of Puebla; son of Fernando Solana Castillo, industrialist, and Concepción Morales Blumenkron; son-in-law of *Adrián Lajous Martínez;* brother, Luis Javier, was coordinator of social affairs for the presidency; married Roberta Lajous. j-None. k-None. l-*Plural,* Dec. 1977, 97-98; *Excélsior,* 13 May 1977, 6, 10 Dec. 1977, 13, 1; HA, 31 Jan. 1977, 19; WNM, 217; HA, 6 Dec. 1976, 22; *Excélsior,* 3 Dec. 1976, 15; 14 Oct. 1982, 26; DBGM, 466; letter; DBGM89, 337; DBGM92, 358.

Solís Manjarrez, Leopoldo
a-Sept. 2, 1928. b-Federal District. c-Early education unknown; economics degree, National School of Economics,

UNAM, 1948-52; graduate studies in macroeconomic models, Yale University, 1957-59; Professor of International Trade, Technological Institute of Mexico, 1960-62; Professor of Macro and Micro Economic Theory, Monetary Theory, Growth Theories, and Economic Development, Center for Economic and Demographic Studies, Colegio de México, 1962-70; Visiting Professor, Princeton University, 1975-76; Researcher, Center for Economic and Demographic Studies, Colegio de México, 1976. d-None. e-None. f-Director of the Department of Economic Studies, Bank of Mexico, 1964-70; Director, Joint Commission of Economic and Social Planning, Secretariat of the Presidency, 1970-75; *Subsecretary of Commercial Planning,* Secretary of Commerce, 1977; *Subdirector General of the Bank of Mexico,* 1976-85; Director General of Banca Confia, 1982; Coordinator of Economic Advisers, Presidency of Mexico, 1985-88; 1988-94. g-None. h-Author of various articles and books on economics; member of the National College, 1976; member of the Executive Board of the Latin American Institute of Economic and Social Planning, Santiago, Chile, 1971-74; President of the Board of Directors, International Bank, 1973-74; adviser, Cía Minera Autlán, 1977-82. i-Son of Jorge Solís Avendaño, surgeon, and Emilia Manjarrez Gasca; brother, Marco Aurelio, was a director general of the Secretariat of Commerce and Industrial Development; mentor to *Hugo Cervantes del Río, Manuel Camacho, Emilio Lozoya, Ernesto Zedillo,* and *Francisco Gil Díaz.* j-None. k-None. l-Letters; Enc. Mex., XI, 1977, 451; *Excélsior,* 5 Sept. 1982, 20; IEPES; DBGM, 401; DBGM, 87, 372.

Solorzano, Roberto A.
a-July 20, 1904. b-Colima, Colima. c-Primary studies in Colima; secondary

studies at the Colegio Francés La Salle; preparatory studies from the National Preparatory School; law degree, National School of Law, UNAM, 1930. d-*Federal Deputy* from the State of Colima, Dist. 1, 1949-52, member of the Tariff and Foreign Trade Committee, the Gran Comisión, the General Accounting Office Committee; *Senator* from Colima, 1952-58, member of the Second Tariff and Foreign Trade Committee, the Treasury Committee, and the Second Constitutional Affairs Committee. e-None. f-Attorney for the Workers of the Mexican Light and Power and Streetcar Company, 1930-45; Director of the Trolley Car Company of the Department of the Federal District. g-None. h-Practicing lawyer. i-Classmate of *Miguel Alemán* and *Manuel Ramírez Vázquez* at the National School of Law. j-None. k-None. l-Ind. Biog., 153-54; DGF51, I, 20, 29, 30, 34; C de D, 1949-52, 91; DGF56, 5, 8, 9, 11, 12.

Solorzano Juárez, Carlos Enrique
a-July 15, 1942. b-Morelia, Michoacán. c-Early education unknown; business administration degree, School of Accounting and Administration, UNAM, 1964-68; degree in public administration, International Institute of Public Administration, France, 1971-72, with a thesis on improving human resources. d-None. e-Joined PRI, 1966. f-Head, Department of Organization and Systems, Secretariat of Industry and Commerce, 1968-71; Head, Department of Organization and Methods, Division of Expenditures, Secretariat of the Treasury, 1973-75; Chief of Advisers, Subsecretary of Expenditures, Secretariat of the Treasury, 1976; General Coordinator of Regional Delegations, Secretariat of the Treasury, 1976; Chief of Technical Advisers, Subsecretary of the Budget, Secretariat of Programming and Budget, 1977-81; General Coordinator of Budget Control, Secretariat of

Programming and Budget, 1981-82; Coordinator General of Budgeting, Department of Federal District, 1982-83; *Oficial Mayor of the Department of the Federal District*, 1983-86; *Secretary General of Social Development*, Department of the Federal District, 1986-88. g-None. h-None. i-Son of Jesús Solorzano Castrejón, businessman, and Esperanza Juárez Ortega; married Susana Teresita Ibarrola Cortés. j-None. k-None. l-DBGM, 402; HA, 27 May 1986, 22; DBGM87, 374.

Somuano López, Rubén Dario
a-May 29, 1909. b-Ocotlán de Morelos, Oaxaca. c-Early education unknown; graduated as a 2nd Lieutenant in infantry, Heroic Military College; diploma, Higher War College; Professor of Infantry Tactics and Military History, Heroic Military College; Professor of General Tactics and Tactics of Information and Military History, Higher War College; Chief, Pedagogical Section in Military Geography and Military History, Heroic Military College; technical adviser, Heroic Military College. d-*Federal Deputy* from the State of Oaxaca, Dist. 9, 1979-82. e-None. f-*Oficial Mayor of the Secretariat of National Defense*, 1973-75. g-None. h-None. i-Related to general Somuano López, director Higher War College, 1961. j-Career army officer; Military Attaché to Chile; Chief of the Technical Section, Department of Rural Defenses; Director of Security, Department of Military Industry; Director of Archives and Correspondence, Secretariat of National Defense; Secretary of the Presidential Staff; Subchief of Staff, Secretariat of National Defense; rank of Division General; Subdirector of Finances, Institute of Social Security of the Armed Forces, 1977-79. k-None. l-Rev. de Ejer., 1953; MGF, 175; C de D, 1979-82.

Soto Alba, Francisco
a-Nov. 18, 1927. b-Hidalgo. c-Early
education unknown; completed secondary studies; private accounting degree,
1944-45. d-*Plurinominal Federal
Deputy* from PAN, 1982-85, member of
the Information and Complaints
Committee, and the Radio, Television,
and Film Commmittee. e-Joined PAN,
1958; President of the District PAN
Committee, Dolores Hidalgo, Guanajuato, 1963; adviser to the National
Committee of PAN, 1965; adviser to the
state committee of PAN, 1967; candidate for federal deputy from Dist. 1,
State of Guanajuato, 1964, 1967, 1979,
1982; candidate for local deputy to the
State Legislature of Guanajuato, 1976;
candidate for governor of Guanajuato,
1979. f-None. g-President of Canacintra, Northern Region, State of
Guanajuato, 1967-70. h-Businessman.
i-Son of José Jesús Soto and María del C.
Alba.; married Lucilia Sánchez. j-None.
k-None. l-Directorio, 1982-85; Lehr,
579; C de D, 1982-85; DBGM, 600.

Soto Guevara, Carlos
(Deceased 1957) a-Feb. 2, 1897.
b-Puebla, Puebla. c-Early education
unknown; law degree, University of
Puebla, 1927; professor of languages,
1919-21, in New York City. d-Member
of the City Council, Puebla, Puebla;
Local Deputy to the State Legislature of
Puebla, 1925-26; Federal Deputy from
the State of Puebla, 1932-34; *Alternate
Senator* from the State of Puebla, 1934-
39. e-None. f-Agent of the Ministerio
Público, Hermosillo, Sonora; Director of
the Department of Economic Statistics,
Secretariat of the Economy, 1931-32;
Justice of the Superior Tribunal of
Justice of the Federal District and
Federal Territories, 1939-42; Justice of
the Federal Tax Court, 1942-57.
g-None. j-None. k-None. l-DP70,
2015; C de S, 1934-40; C de D, 1932-34;
DGF51, I, 550; DGF56, 552.

Soto Izquierdo, Enrique
a-Dec. 13, 1935. b-Cusihuiriáchi, Chihuahua. c-Primary studies at the Víctor
María Flores School in Cusihuiriáchi
and in the Miguel de Unamuno School
in the Federal District; secondary
studies at the Secondary School No. 3,
Federal District; preparatory studies at
the National Preparatory School No. 1;
legal studies, National School of Law,
UNAM, 1954-59, graduating in 1961;
professor of law and economics,
UNAM, 1965- . d-*Federal Deputy* from
the Federal District, No. 23, 1976-79,
member of the Agrarian Affairs Committee, the Scientific and Technological
Development Committee, Physical
Education Subcommittee, the Fourth
Tourism Development Committee, the
Fourth Housing Development Commit-
tee, the Second Government Commit-
tee, the Credit Section of the Treasury
Committee, and the Juvenile Study
Committee; *Federal Deputy* from the
State of Chihuahua, Dist. 3, 1982-85,
Secretary of the Gran Comisión,
member of the Government and
Constitutional Affairs Committee,
member of the Budget and Public
Accounts Committee. e-Orator, *Adolfo
López Mateos* presidential campaign,
1958; Director of *La República* (official
magazine of PRI), 1968-70; General
Delegate of the CEN of PRI, various
states; Subdirector of Legal Affairs of
the IEPES of PRI, 1981-82. f-Lawyer,
Department of Legal Affairs, Secretariat
of Government, 1962-78; Director, Department of Saline Waters, Secretariat
of Human Dwellings and Public Works,
1977; Director General of the National
Institute of Youth, 1971-76. g-Member
of the Society of Students of Chihuahua, School of Law, UNAM, 1954-55;
President, Society of law Students,
1956; Member of the Technical Advisory Council of the CNC, 1963. h-Sub-
champion of oratory at the National
Preparatory School, 1952; international

oratory champion of the *El Universal* contest, 1957; translated the Mexican Constitution into English and French for the Senate, 1961; published the first trilingual (English, French, and Spanish) edition of the Mexican Constitution, 1962; Director of the Sunday Supplement of Culture for *El Día* and *El Gallo Illustrado*, 1965-70. i-Student leader at the National Preparatory School with *Alfredo Bonfil, Pedro Vázquez Colmenares,* and *Pindaro Urióstegui,* 1952-53; son of engineer Enrique Soto, a Constitutional Deputy, and Joséfina Izquierdo; married Luz María Magaldi Aguilar. j-None. k-None. l-HA, 12 Nov. 1973; Enc. Mex., XI, 1977, 500; HA, 19 Feb. 1979, V-VI; *Excélsior,* 5 Sept. 1976, 1; D de C, 1976-79, 5, 15, 22, 43, 45, 56, 58, 77; C de D, 1982-85; Lehr, 102; Directorio, 1982-85; HA, 1 Mar. 1982, 13; DBGM, 606; Lehr, 102.

Soto (Martínez), Ignacio
(Deceased 1962) a-1890. b-Bavispe, Sonora. c-Early education unknown; no degree. d-*Governor of Sonora,* Sept. 1, 1949, to Sept. 1, 1955. e-None. f-None. g-None. h-Businessman in grains; owner of several industries in Sonora; early investor in the cement industry in Hermosillo and Mazatlán. j-None. k-None. l-DP70, 2014; DGF51, I, 92; Alonso, 219.

Soto Máynes, Oscar
a-Oct. 16, 1904. b-Valle de Allende, Chihuahua. c-Primary studies at Ciudad Jiménez, Chihuahua; secondary studies in Mexico City; preparatory studies at the National Preparatory School; law degree, National School of Law, UNAM, 1928. d-*Federal Deputy* from the State of Chihuahua, Dist. 1, 1949-50, member of the Administration Committee and the First Grand Jury; *Governor of Chihuahua,* 1950-55. e-None. f-Local judge, State of Chihuahua; Judge, Superior Tribunal of Justice,

State of Veracruz; Judge, Superior Tribunal of Justice, State of Chihuahua; Attorney General of the State of Chihuahua; Judge, First Appeals Court; adviser to the Private Secretary to the President of Mexico, 1946-48. g-None. i-Member of the "Alemán generation" at UNAM; close friend of *Miguel Alemán* since childhood, when he lived with the Alemán family; tied by marriage to the Terrazas-Creel families in Chihuahua; mother ran a boarding house; brother, *Roberto Soto Máynez,* was a federal deputy from Jalisco, Dist. 2, 1946-49. j-None. k-Took leave from the governorship after a minor riot and popular campaign against him; accused in the press of graft; precandidate for senator from Chihuahua, 1970. l-DGF51, I, 20, 34, 89; HA, 29 Aug. 1955, 16; Anderson; *Excélsior,* 10 Aug. 1955; Scott, 277; C de D, 1949-52, 91; Hoy, 12 Feb. 1955, 23; DGF47; Hoy, 21 Mar. 1970, 4; NYT, 10 Aug. 1955, 13; HA, 25 Oct. 1954, 15; letter; Almada, 1968, 505.

Soto Resendiz, Enrique
a-Apr. 15, 1927. b-Tecosautla, Hidalgo. c-Primary studies in Tecosautla; secondary studies at the Military Institute Benjamín N. Velasco, Querétaro; preparatory studies at the Laurents Institute, Monterrey, Nuevo León; law degree from the National School of Law, UNAM. d-*Federal Deputy* from the State of Hidalgo, Dist. 5, 1970-73, member of the Ninth Section of the Legislative Studies Committee, the Rules Committee, and the First Tax Committee. e-Participated in the first and second oratory contests sponsored by PRI, 1949-50, winner of first and second place in the State of Hidalgo and second and fourth for Mexico; Director of Youth Action of PRI in Hidalgo, Mexico, and the Federal District; Official Orator of the *López Mateos* presidential campaign, 1958; delegate to various PRI conventions; General Coordinator of

the Popular Program Boards of PRI for
Hidalgo; Secretary of Organization of
PRI in Hidalgo; Secretary General of the
State Committee of PRI in Hidalgo;
Subsecretary of Organization of the
CEN of PRI, 1973-74. f-Subdirector of
the Offices of Government, Department
of the Federal District; Subdirector of
the Rules and License Inspection Office,
Government Division, Department of
the Federal District; Director of the
Special Tax Department, State of
Hidalgo. g-Technical adviser to the
CNC. h-Practicing lawyer. j-None.
k-None. l-Directorio, 1970-72; C de D,
1970-72, 137.

Soto Reyes, Ernesto
(Deceased Apr. 29, 1972) a-Apr. 16,
1899. b-Puruándiro, Michoacán.
c-Secondary studies at the Colegio
Primitivo; preparatory studies at the
Colegio de San Nicolás, Morelia,
Michoacán; professional studies at the
Colegio de San Nicolás and at UNAM;
no degree. d-Member of the City
Council of Morelia, 1921-22; Mayor of
Morelia, Michoacán, 1921; Federal
Deputy from the State of Michoacán;
Senator from the State of Michoacán,
1934-40; president of the Senate, 1935;
president of the National Revolutionary
Block. e-Founding member of the
Michoacán Socialist Party, 1917;
President of the PNR in Michoacán,
1929-32; Secretary of the CEN of the
PNR, 1932-34; member of *Lázaro
Cárdenas's* presidential campaign
committee, 1933-34; *Secretary of
Agrarian Action of the CEN of the PNR,*
1935-36. f-Private Secretary to the
Governor of Michoacán, 1929; Member
of the Federal Electoral Commission,
1936; Minister to Paraguay, 1941-43;
Ambassador to Venezuela, 1943-46, to
Uruguay, 1946, to Panama, 1964-65, to
Haiti, 1965, and to Turkey, 1967-68.
g-None. h-Author of several books.

i-Close personal friend of *Lázaro
Cárdenas* and *Francisco Múgica*;
member of the *Múgica* political group;
nephew of *Alberto Bremauntz*; brother,
Arturo, was active in politics; mother,
Abigail Reyes, ran the first student
boarding house in Morelia. j-None.
k-Leader of the Michoacán radicals in
the Senate; led the fight to defeat *Portes
Gil's* candidates for the Senate, which
eventually caused *Portes Gil* to resign
on Aug. 19, 1936, as President of the
CEN of the PNR; head of the National
Orientation Committee in favor of
General *Henríquez Guzmán*, 1951-52.
l-DPE65, 27; Kirk, 141; EBW46, 54;
Excélsior, 30 Apr. 1972; Morton, 334,
26, 19-20; González Navarro, 122;
López, 1044; Casasola, V; Bremauntz,
56, 59, 101.

Sousa (Gordillo), Mario
a-Apr. 7, 1903. b-Veracruz, Veracruz.
c-Primary studies in Veracruz, prepara-
tory studies at the National Preparatory
School; law degree, National School of
Law, UNAM, 1925, economics degree,
National School of Economics, UNAM,
1940; LLD, National School of Law,
UNAM, 1950; professor, National
School of Law, UNAM; Professor of
Economics, UNAM, 1925-38; Director,
National School of Economics, UNAM,
1938-40. d-None. e-Secretary of the
National Federation for Renovation, in
support of General Obgreón for presi-
dent, 1927. f-Economic adviser,
National Bank of Ejido Credit; Chief,
Legal Department, Secretariat of
Agriculture; Chief, Legal Department,
Secretariat of Labor; Chief, Institute of
Rural Economy, Secretariat of Agricul-
ture; Secretary of the National Workers
Bank for Industrial Development; Pri-
vate Secretary to the Rector of UNAM,
Roberto Medellín, 1933; *Subsecretary of
Industry and Commerce*, 1940-42;
Director General of the Government

Printing Office, 1942-46; *Head of the Department of Agrarian Affairs and Colonization*, 1946-52. g-None. h-Writer for the magazine *Hoy*; author of articles on economics. i-Knew *Eduardo Bustamante* at UNAM; student assistant to *Manuel Gómez Morín*; close friend of Enrique González Aparicio; father a commissioner in Veracruz. j-None. k-None. l-WWM45, 113; DP70, 2386; *Hoy*, 14 Dec. 1940; DGF51, I, 465; DGF51, II, 165, 181; DGF50, II, 129, 139; López, 1045; Illescas, 622.

Stephens García, Manuel
a-June 2, 1925. b-Bellavista, Nayarit. c-Primary studies at the Benito Juárez School, Bellavista, Nayarit; secondary studies at the Normal School of Jalisco and the Normal Institute of Sciences, Nayarit; teaching certificate from the Higher Normal School of México, Mexico City; secondary school teacher. d-*Federal Deputy* from the State of Nayarit, Dist. 1, 1961-64, member of the Plaints Committee and the General Means of Communication Committee; *Federal Deputy* (Party Deputy from the PPS), 1970-73, member of the National Lands and Resources Committee, the First Public Education Committee, the Second Tax Committee, and the Military Health Committee; *Plurinominal Federal Deputy* from the PCM, 1979-82. e-Secretary of Press and Publicity of the PPS, 1961-68; Secretary General of the PPS in the Federal District; cofounder of the Party of the Mexican People (PPM), 1977; member, Executive Committee, PPM, 1977-78; Executive Secretary of the PPM, 1977-78. f-Director of Foreign Secondary Schools, Tuxpan, Nayarit. g-Secretary of Union Education of Local 20 of the SNTE, Nayarit. h-None. j-None. k-Candidate of the PPS for senator from the Federal District, 1964; candidate of

the PPS for Governor of Nayarit; first federal deputy from the PPS in Nayarit. l-C de D, 1961-63, 92, 1970-72, 137; Directorio, 1970-72; C de D, 1979-82.

Suárez (Aranzolo), Eduardo
(Deceased Sept. 19, 1976) a-Jan. 3, 1895. b-Texcoco, México. c-Primary studies at the Colegio del Estado de México, and at the Colegio Williams, Mexico City; preparatory studies from the National Preparatory School, 1908-12; law degree from the National School of Law, UNAM, 1913-17; Professor of Juridical Sociology, National School of Law, UNAM, 1916; Professor of Civil Procedures, National School of Law, UNAM, 1917; Professor of Mercantile Law, School of Business, UNAM, 1917; Professor of Industrial Law and General Theory of the State, UNAM, 1920-32. d-None. e-None. f-Oficial Mayor in charge of the Secretary General of Government, State of Hidalgo, 1917-19; President of the Board of Conciliation and Arbitration of the Federal District, 1926; Assistant Lawyer, Mexican-United States General Claims Commission, 1926-28; Assistant Agent, Mexican-British Claims Commission, 1928-29; technical adviser, Legal Department, Secretary of Foreign Relations, 1929-30, member of the Mexican-French Claims Commission, 1930; member of the Mexican delegation to the International Monetary Conference, 1934; *Secretary of the Treasury*, 1935-40, 1940-46; *Ambassador to Great Britain*, 1965-70; President of the Federal Board of Conciliation and Arbitration. g-None. h-Member of the Drafting Commission, General Banking Law, 1932; Member of the Technical Commission, International Waters Commission (Mexican-United States); technical adviser to PEMEX, the National Finance Bank, and the National Railroads of Mexico; Director of the Mexican-North Ameri-

can Institute of Cultural Relations,
1959-61. i-Father a notary and lawyer;
great uncle Julián Villagrán was a
general in the insurgent army of Nicolás
Bravo; married Leonor Vázquez,
widowed, married Luz María Dávila;
mentor to *Antonio Carrillo Flores*; son,
Eduardo Suárez Dávila, was subsecretary of the treasury, 1982-88. j-None.
k-Ran for local deputy in Hidalgo, 1920,
election disputed, and won by his friend
Javier Rojo Gómez; offered an appointment as Justice of the Supreme Court
and Subsecretary of Government by
Emilio Portes Gil. l-Kirk, 168; DGF51,
II, 5; Peral, 779; DGF50, II, 10; HA, 30
July 1945; WWM45, 114; DP70, 1076;
DPE65, 26; Enc. Mex., XI, 1977, 509;
López, 1046; NYT, 26 Oct. 1942, 28;
HA, 30 July 1943, 38, 27 Sept. 1976, 7;
DBGM, 404; DBGM89, 341.

Suárez (Dávila), Francisco
a-Apr. 20, 1943. b-Federal District.
c-Early education unknown; law studies
from the National School of Law,
UNAM, 1961-65, with a degree on
"Juridical Study of the Juridical Person-
ality," 1965; MA in economics, Kings
College, Cambridge, 1965-67; postgraduate work in economics, University
of Paris, 1968-69, University of Chicago,
1972; Professor of Economics, UNAM,
1970-72, and at Autonomous Technological Institute of México, 1971- .
d-None. e-Subsecretary of International
Economic Affairs, CEN of PRI, 1981-82.
f-Economist, Technical Office of the
Director General, Bank of Mexico,
1970-71; Manager, Internal Economic
Affairs, Bank of Mexico, 1977-78; General Manager of International Economic
Affairs, Bank of Mexico, 1978-80; Director of Financial Programming and External Financing, National Finance Bank,
1980-82; *Subsecretary of the Treasury*,
1982-88. i-Son of *Francisco Suárez
Aransolo*, Secretary of the Treasury,
1935-46, and Luz Dávila; married Diana

Mogollón Abad. j-None. k-None.
l-*Excélsior*, 4 Dec. 1982, 14; Q es QAP,
107-08; DBGM, 404; DBGM89, 341.

Suárez Molina, José Luis
b-Tula, Hidalgo. c-Early education
unknown; law degree. d-*Federal
Deputy* from the State of Hidalgo, Dist.
2, 1952-55, member of the Gran Comisión; *Federal Deputy* from the State of
Hidalgo, Dist. 2, 1961-64. e-President of
Regional Committee of PRI, State of
Hidalgo, 1951; President of the National
Youth of the CEN of PRI, 1951.
f-*Interim Governor of Hidalgo*, 1976-78.
g-None. i-Close to *Guillermo Rossell*,
who served as his alternate federal
deputy; political enemy of *Jorge Rojo
Lugo*. j-None. k-Practically exiled from
the state of Hidalgo by *Jorge Rojo Lugo*.
l-*Excélsior*, 24 Dec. 1979, 23; C de D,
1952-55, 1961-64; Pérez López, 463.

Suárez (Ruiz), Marcos Manuel
a-Jan. 5, 1935. b-Cuernavaca, Morelos.
c-Primary studies at the Colegio de
México, Mexico City; secondary studies
at Secondary School No. 2, Mexico
City; studies at Loyola College, Mon-
treal, Canada; engineering degree, MIT,
Boston, Massachusetts; completed
fourth year of law at the National
School of Law, UNAM. d-Substitute
Mayor of Cuernavaca, 1966-68; Local
Deputy to the State Legislature of
Morelos, 1968-70; *Federal Deputy* from
the State of Morelos, Dist. 1, 1970-73,
member of the Artisans Committee, the
Public Works Committee, the Public
Housing Committee, and the Gran
Comisión; Majority Leader of the
Chamber of Deputies, 1973. e-Secretary
of Housing of the CEN of CNOP, 1975-
76. f-Executive Director of Tourism
Development, State of Morelos; *Oficial
Mayor of Labor*, 1976-78. g-Founding
member of the Platform of Mexican
Professionals. h-None. i-Friend of
Pedro Ojeda Paullada since the foun-

ding of the Platform of Mexican Professionals. j-None. k-Precandidate for governor of Morelos, 1974. l-*Excélsior*, 26 Dec. 1974, 15; Directorio, 1970-72, C de D, 1970-73, 138.

Suárez Torres, Gilberto
a-Feb. 5, 1912. b-Oaxaca, Oaxaca. c-Primary studies at the Pestalozzi School, Oaxaca, Oaxaca; secondary studies at the Institute of Arts and Sciences of Oaxaca; law degree, National School of Law, UNAM, 1932-37. d-*Senator* from the State of Oaxaca, 1970-76, member of the Gran Comisión, president of the Second Government Committee and First Secretary of the Rules Committee. e-General Delegate of the CEN of PRI. f-Secretary of the Second Judicial District of Oaxaca, 1933-34; local judge, Oaxaca, Oaxaca, 1934-35; Consulting lawyer to the Chief of Police, Oaxaca, 1935-46; agent of the Ministerio Público, Office of the Attorney General for the Federal District, 1946-52; Subdirector of the Department of Federal Security, Secretariat of Government, 1952-58; *Assistant Attorney General of México* (2), 1958-64; *Attorney General for the Federal District and Federal Territories*, 1964-70. g-None. h-Practicing lawyer, 1935-46. i-Married María de la Luz Herrera. j-None. k-None. l-*Libro de Oro*, xl; DPE65, 211; DGF56, 89; HA, 22 Dec. 1958, 8; D de Y, 2 Dec. 1964, 2, 9 Dec. 1958, 1; *Por Qué*, 4 Dec. 1969, 7; letter.

T

Talamantes, Gustavo L.
(Deceased Nov. 22, 1958) a-Aug. 10, 1891. b-Hacienda de Roncesvalles, Matamoros, Chihuahua. c-Primary studies, Hidalgo del Parral; agricultural engineering degree, College of Agricultural of Ciudad Juárez (founding student). d-Mayor of Ciudad Juárez,

Chihuahua, 1916; Senator from the State of Chihuahua, 1930-34; *Governor of Chihuahua*, 1935-40. e-*Secretary of Agrarian Action of the CEN of the PNR*, 1935-36. f-Delegate of the National Agrarian Commission, Secretariat of Agriculture, 1924; Director, Agricultural Ejido Bank, Durango; Manager of the National Ejido Bank, Durango; Director of the Federal Treasury Office, Aguascalientes, Aguascalientes, 1930; Inspector General, Secretariat of Agriculture, 1940s. g-President of the Agrarian Commission of the State of Chihuahua, 1920-24. h-Director, *El Sol de Aguascalientes*. i-Classmate of *Alfredo Chávez* at college. k-Imposed Col. *Alfredo Chávez* as his successor over PRM's choice of *Fernando Foglio Miramontes* by running him on the Independent Revolutionary Party of Chihuahua. l-*Siempre*, 3 Dec. 1958, 6; Peral, 783; Anderson, 74-76; C de S, 1930-34; Almada, 582; Almada, 1968, 512.

Talán Ramírez, Raúl Eric
a-Jan. 9, 1942. b-Federal District. c-Early education unknown; electrical engineering degree from IPN with a thesis on the IBM computer, 1959-65; MA in computing from the National Center of Calculation, IPN; MA in electrical engineering, Center for Research and Advanced Studies, IPN, 1968; Ph.D. in engineering, UCLA, 1973; assistant, Computer Center, UCLA, 1973; Professor, Higher School of Mechanical and Electrical Engineering, IPN, 1965-78; Systems Analyst, National Center of Calculation, IPN, 1964-65; *Director General of IPN*, 1985-88. d-None. e-None. f-General Delegate of the Secretariat of Public Education to Quintana Roo, 1978-79; Director General of Accreditation and Certification, Secretariat of Public Education, 1979-81; Technical Secretary of Global Programming and Administrative Improvement, Secretariat of Public

Education, 1981-82; *Subsecretary of Education and Technical Research*, Secretariat of Public Education, 1988-93. g-None. h-None. i-Son of Raúl Talán González, government employee, and María del Refugio Ramírez López, normal teacher; married Manijeh Esrhaghi Godsinia. j-None. k-None. l-QesQAP, 323; *Excélsior*, 4 Dec. 1985, 5; DBGM, 404; DBGM92, 362; DBGM89, 342.

Talavera López, Abraham
a-July 16, 1949. b-Tenango del Valle, México. c-Early education unknown; degree in International Relations, Center of International Studies, Colegio de México, 1967-69, with a thesis on writers and the Cuban revolution; courses from the Colegio de México; postgraduate work in Mexico and abroad; researcher, Library of Congress, Washington, D.C., 1972; professor, Autonomous University of the State of México, 1969. d-*Federal Deputy* from the State of México, Dist. 12, 1973-76; *Plurinominal Federal Deputy* from PRI, 1991-94. e-Joined PRI, 1967; Director of Youth of PRI, State of México, 1969-71; Director General of the CEPES of PRI, State of México, 1974; General Delegate of the CEN of PRI to Campeche, 1976; Director General of the IEPES of PRI, 1989-91. f-Adviser, State of México, 1974; adviser to the Director of the National Bank of Public Works and Services, 1977; Delegate of the Department of the Federal District to Venustiano Carranza, 1977; Director of Political and Social Research, Secretariat of Government, 1979-80; *Oficial Mayor of Government*, 1980-82; Ambassador to Guatemala, 1985-87. g-None. h-None. i-Son of Raúl Talavera Mondragón, public official and farmer, and Crispina López Mondragón Navas. j-None. k-None. l-HA, 14 July 1980, 15; DBGM89, 377-78:DBGM92, 585.

Tamayo (Castillejos), Jorge L.
(Deceased Dec. 17, 1978) a-Aug. 8, 1912. b-Oaxaca, Oaxaca c-Primary and secondary studies in Oaxaca and in Mexico City; preparatory studies in mathematics and physical sciences, National Preparatory School, Mexico City, 1930-32; civil engineering degree, National School of Engineering, UNAM, October, 1932-36; founder of the School of Irrigation; member of the Governing Board of UNAM; Professor of Regional Geography, Economic Geography, Geological Resources and Necessities of Mexico, Superior Normal School and the Workers University, Mexico City; professor, School of Philosophy and Letters, UNAM, 1943; assistant, National School of Engineering, 1934-35. d-None. e-Member of the Popular Party; member of the PRM until 1944. f-Director of the Water Department of the Lagunera Irrigation District, 1935-37; Director of Technical Water Inspections, Valle de México, 1937-38; engineer, Secretariat of Hydraulic Resources, 1939-43; Comptroller, Mexicano Railroads, 1946-49; Comptroller, National Railroads of Mexico, 1947-49; Technical Consultant to the Economic Commission for Latin America, 1950; Director General of the Tuxtepec Paper Company, 1973-78; Executive Secretary of the Papaloapan Commission, 1974-78. g-Student leader at the National School of Engineering, 1935. h-Author of dozens of books; Sales Manager, Mechanical Equipment, S.A., 1951-56. i-Married Martha López Portillo, cousin of *José López Portillo*; father of *Jorge Tamayo*. j-None. k-Resigned from the PRM after he felt unjustly denied of being elected a federal deputy, 1944; candidate for governor of Oaxaca several times. l-HA, 25 Dec. 1978, 16;*Excélsior*, 9 Oct. 1978, 12; Enc. Mex., XII, 1977, 1; *Excélsior*, 19 Dec. 1978, 4.

Tamayo (López Portillo), Jorge
a-July 17, 1937. b-Oaxaca, Oaxaca
c-Early education unknown; economics
studies, National School of Economics,
UNAM, 1955-59, graduating in 1960,
with a thesis on integration in the state
of Oaxaca; graduate studies at Georgetown University, 1960; graduate studies
at the Central School of Planning and
Statistics, Varzovia, Poland, 1962-63;
Assistant Professor to *Mario Ramón
Beteta* in Economic Theory, 1961-63;
Professor of Planning, National School
of Economics, UNAM, 1964-73;
Professor and Director of the Seminar
on the Economics of Production, 1968-
70; Secretary General of the National
School of Economics, UNAM, 1965-67.
d-None. e-Joined PRI, 1970; *Secretary
of the IEPES of the CEN of PRI, 1981.*
f-Subdirector General of the Central
Light and Power Company, Mexico
City, 1970-76; *Subsecretary of Internal
Trade*, Secretariat of Commerce, 1976-
81; Subdirector General, National Finance Bank, 1981-82; Corporate Director, Sidermex, 1982-83; General Coordinator of Comisariats, Secretariat of the
Controller General, 1983-88; Director
General of Concarril, 1988-92; Director
General of Railroads, Secretariat of
Communications and Transportation,
1992-94. g-President of the National
College of Economists, 1974. i-Son of
Martha López Portillo, cousin of *José
López Portillo*, and *Jorge L. Tamayo*, a
member of the Popular Party, famous
geographer and Executive Director of
the Papaloapan Commission, 1974-78;
married Isabel Castroparedes Ortiz, economist. j-None. k-None. l-Letter; *Excélsior*, 9 Oct. 1978, 12; DBGM92, 363.

Tame Shear, Amado
a-Apr. 8, 1927. b-Federal District.
c-Early education unknown; engineering degree, Mexico City. d-Alternate
Federal Deputy (Party Deputy of the

PPS), 1964-67; *Plurinominal Federal
Deputy* from the PPS, 1979-82. e-Member of the Mexican Communist Party,
1949-60; joined the PPS, 1960; Secretary
of Educational Policy of the Central
Committee of the PPS. f-None.
g-None. j-None. k-Candidate of the
PPS for Federal Deputy from Dist. 33,
Federal District, 1979. l-HA, 16 Apr.
1979, V.

Tamez (Cavazos), Ramiro
(Deceased) a-Jan. 18, 1889. b-General
Terán, Nuevo León. c-Primary studies
in General Terán; secondary and
preparatory studies at the Colegio Civil,
Monterrey; medical degree from the
National School of Medicine, UNAM.
d-Mayor of General Terán, Nuevo León;
local deputy to the State Legislature of
Nuevo León; Interim Governor of Nue-
vo León; 1922-23; Director of Coordinating Services, State of Nuevo León;
Senator from the State of Nuevo León,
1940-46, President of the Consular and
Diplomatic Service Committee, member of the Health Committee, alternate
member of the tariff and Second Foreign
Trade Committee. e-None. f-Secretary
General of Government of the State of
Nuevo León, 1936-39, under Governor
Anacleto Guerrero. g-None. h-Author
of several amendments to the Federal
Labor Law concerning strikes dealing
with workers employed in public
services; practicing physician, 1946-68.
i-During the Revolution, he became
friends with Dr. *Francisco Castillo
Nájera* and *Aurelio Manrique*; met
Antonio Díaz Soto y Gama at UNAM;
brother, Nicandro, was a senator and
deputy from Nuevo León; son of Porfiro
Tamez and Modesto Cavazos; married
Margarita Rodríguez. j-Left Medical
School in his third year, 1911, to participate in the Revolution with other medical students; Francisco Villa had a great
affection for him because he saved a

friend's life. k-President Obregón forced him from office as Governor of Nuevo León in 1923; Tamez went into exile and practiced medicine in San Benito, Texas, 1924-35; he returned to Mexico in 1936. l-C de S, 1940-46; PdM, 362; Peral, 785; letter; López, 1055.

Tapia Camacho, Manlio Fabio
a-Sept. 18, 1928. b-Veracruz, Veracruz c-Primary studies in the Xicotencatl School; secondary and preparatory studies at the Illustrious Preparatory School of Veracruz, 1941-45; law degree, School of Law, May 18, 1951, Professor of Agrarian Law, 1951-64, Secretary of the School of Law, and Professor of Civil Law, 1951-64, all at the University of Veracruz, professor at the secondary school, Vespertina Veracruz, and at the normal and preparatory schools, Veracruz, 1953-64. d-Local Deputy to the State Legislature of Veracruz, 1959-62; *Alternate Senator*, 1964-68, but replaced Senator *Murillo Vidal* from 1968 to 1970, as Senator from Veracruz; Mayor of Veracruz, 1964-67. e-Member of PRI since 1947; Director of the official PRI newspaper, *El Constitu-cionalista*; President of PRI in Veracruz, 1960-62. f-Director of Publicity, Department of Health, State of Vera-cruz; assistant in the office of the Secretary General of Government of Veracruz; Group Secretary for the Board of Conciliation and Arbitration of the State of Veracruz; Director of the Legal Department of the State of Veracruz, 1956-59; Judge of the Superior Tribunal of Justice of Veracruz, 1962-64; Private Secretary to the Secretary of Agricul-ture, *Bernardo Aguirre*, 1970-73; Private Secretary to the Governor of Chihua-hua, *Bernardo Aguirre*, 1974-77. g-Law-yer for the League of Agrarian Commu-nities of the State of Veracruz. h-As a student, worked for the Judicial Police of Veracruz; State of Veracruz oratory champion from the University of

Veracruz, 1950; national subchampion of Revolutionary Oratory; founder of several magazines; professional newspa-perman since student days. i-Son of a school teacher; studied under *Angel Carvajal* and *Fernando Román Lugo* at the University of Veracruz. j-None. k-None. l-C de S, 1964-70; DBM68, 594; letter; DAPC, 1977; *Excélsior*, 11 Aug., 1978, 23.

Tapia Freyding, José María
(Deceased 1969) a-May 16, 1896. b-Nogales, Sonora. c-Early education unknown; technical military studies, New York; no degree. d-Federal Deputy from Baja California del Norte, Dist. 1, 1926-28, member of the Gran Comi-sión; *Senator* from the State of Baja California del Norte, 1958-64, President of the Mail and Telegraph Committee and of the First National Defense Committee, member of the Committee on Taxes, the Military Justice Commit-tee, and the War Materials Committee; Vice President of the Senate, Sept., 1961. e-None. f-Chief of Staff of the Secretariat of National Defense, 1928; Chief of Staff of President *Emilio Portes Gil*, 1929; Governor and Military Commander of Baja California del Norte, 1929-30; Director General of Federal Retirement and Pensions; Director General of Public Charities, 1932-35; Consul General, New York City; Director General of the Mails, 1944; Chief of Staff, Secretariat of National Defense, 1952; Director General of Customs; Director General of the National Army-Navy Bank, 1964-69. g-None. h-None. j-Fought in the Revolution, 1913-20; fought against General Maytorena; fought against Victoriano Huerta, 1913; career army officer; member of the staff of *Abelardo Rodríguez*, 1920; fought against Adolfo de la Huerta, 1923; Brigadier General, May 16, 1929; reached rank of Division General; Chief of Staff for Baja Califor-

nia del Norte, Nayarit and Sinaloa; Commander of the 25th Military Zone, Puebla, Puebla, 1952; Commander of the 1st Infantry Regiment; Commander of the 6th Military Region, Tijuana, 1956. k-None. l-C de S, 1961-64, 70; Peral, 785; D070, 2045; Func., 122; Rev. de Ejer., Apr.-June 1952, 134.

Taracena, Antonio
a-Jan. 17, 1901. b-Villahermosa, Tabasco c-Primary studies in a public school, Villahermosa; preparatory studies at the National Preparatory School, 1918-21; law degree, National School of Law, UNAM, May 21, 1926; Professor of Criminal Law, National School of Law, UNAM, 1930-35; Professor of Labor Law, School of Law, University of Guanajuato, 1940-41; Professor of Civics and Ethics, Juárez Institute of Tabasco, 1943-44. d-*Senator* from the State of Tabasco, 1946-52, member of the Legislative Studies Committee, the Electric Industry Committee, the Public Works Committee and the Second Balloting Group. e-None. f-Scribe in a criminal court, 1923-26; Assistant Attorney General of Baja California del Sur, 1926; Agent of the Ministerio Público in the Federal District, 1926-28; Attorney General of the State of Tabasco under Governor *Noé de la Flor Casanova*, 1943-46; Judge of the Superior Tribunal of Justice of the Federal District and Federal Territories, 1963-70. g-None. h-Practicing lawyer, 1928-43, 1952-63; author of the Penal Code of Tabasco. i-Son of a businessman; related to Salome Taracena, poet from Tabasco. j-None. k-Involved in the trial of José León Toral, assassin of General Obregón, 1928. l-Letters; López, 1056; DGF51, I, 7, 11-14; Santamaría, 262-63.

Tejeda (Olivanes), Adalberto
(Deceased Sept. 8, 1960) a-Mar. 28, 1883. b-Chicontepec, Veracruz. c-Primary studies in the Cantonal School, Chicontepec; preparatory studies at the National Preparatory School, Mexico City; engineering studies, National School of Engineering; no degree. d-Deputy to the Constitutional Congress from the State of Veracruz, Dist. 4, 1916-17; Senator from the State of Veracruz, 1918-20; Governor of Veracruz, 1920-24; Governor of Veracruz, 1928-32. e-Candidate for President of Mexico on the Communist Party Ticket, 1934. f-Secretary of Communications and Public Works, Dec. 1, 1924, to Aug. 25, 1925; Secretary of Government, 1925-28; *Ambassador to France*, 1936-37; Ambassador to Guatemala, 1937-38, to Spain, 1938-39, 1940-41, and to Peru, 1942–48. g-None. h-None. i-Son, Luis Tejeda Tejeda, served under his father in Spain and became a consul in the Mexican Consulate Service, 1961; mentor to Fabio Manlio Altamirano; son of Entiquia Olivares. j-Maderista during the Revolution; Chief of Staff of the Eastern Division under General *Cándido Aguilar*; fought Victoriano Huerta; head of Military Operations for the North but never wore a uniform; rank of Brigadier General, 1948. k-Did not attend the Constitutional Congress because of military activities and personal affairs; caudillo of the State of Veracruz during the 1920s; Brandenburg considered him an Inner Circle favorite of President Calles, 1924-28. l-DP70, 2064; Scott, 122; Brandenburg, 63; Peral, 787; DBM68, 595; López, 1058; Michaels, 28-29; Enc. Mex., XII, 1977, 34.

Telleache (Merino), Ramón
(Deceased Feb. 22, 1972) a-May 3, 1914. b-Villahermosa, Tabasco c-Primary studies in Villahermosa; secondary studies in Puebla; preparatory studies at the National Preparatory School; law degree from the National School of Law, UNAM, 1940. d-Mayor of Frontera, Tabasco, 1965-67. e-None. f-Agent of the Ministerio Público of the Office of

the Attorney General of the Federal District, 1940-43; Substitute President of the Federal Board of Conciliation and Arbitration, 1944-47; *Subsecretary of Livestock*, 1970-72. g-President of the Livestock Association of Frontera, Tabasco (3 times); Delegate to the National Federation of Cattlemen; member of the Executive Council, State Cattlemen's Association, Tabasco. h-Involved in cattle ranching in Tabasco since 1947; Secretary and Treasurer of the Tabasco Credit Union. j-None. k-None. l-HA, 14 Dec. 1970, 21; D del S, 23 Feb. 1972, 1.

Téllez Benoit, María Emilia
a-Dec. 27, 1921. b-Washington, D.C. c-Primary studies in Washington, D.C.; secondary studies in Rome; law degree from the National School of Law, UNAM, 1947, with a thesis on "The Continental Shelf;" Assistant Professor of Public International Law, National School of Law, UNAM, 1946; Assistant Professor, Public International Law and General State Theory Seminar, UNAM, 1946-47, 1958-61; Professor of International Public Law, Women's University of Mexico, 1949-50; Professor of International Public Law, National School of Law, UNAM, 1957-58. d-None. e-None. f-Career Foreign Service officer; joined the Foreign Service, Apr. 1, 1946, with the rank of Vice Consul; Assistant in the Office of Protocol, Secretariat of Foreign Relations, 1946; lawyer for the Department of Legal Affairs, Secretariat of Foreign Relations, 1946; Director of the Post-War Section, Secretariat of Foreign Relations, 1946-48; Director of the United States and Canada Section, Secretariat of Foreign Relations, 1948-55; Director of the Europe, Asia, and Africa Department, Secretariat of Foreign Relations, 1958-59; Director of the Department of American Affairs, Secretariat of Foreign Relations, 1959; Director of the Depart-

ment of Information, Secretariat of the Presidency, 1959; Third Secretary, Washington, D.C., 1947-48; Vice Consul, Washington, D.C., 1947-48; Second Secretary, Havana, Cuba, 1955-58; Director General of International Organizations, Secretariat of Foreign Relations, 1964-68; Subdirector General of International Organizations, 1961-64; *Oficial Mayor of the Secretariat of Foreign Relations*, 1970-76; *Subsecretary of Special Studies and International Affairs*, Secretariat of Foreign Relations, 1976-82. g-None. h-None. i-Father, Manuel C. Téllez, was Secretary of Government and Secretary of Foreign Relations, 1931-32; attended UNAM with *Luis Echeverría* and *José López Portillo*. j-None. k-She was the first woman Oficial Mayor in a Mexican cabinet. l-HA, 14 Dec. 1970, 20; DPE61, 17; *Libro de Oro*, xxv; letter.

Téllez Cruz, Agustín
a-Nov. 15, 1918. b-Guanajuato, Guanajuato c-Early education unknown; law degree, National School of Law, UNAM, 1938-42, with a thesis on amparo; professor, School of Law, University of Hidalgo, 1945-46. d-*Senator from the State of Guanajuato*, 1982-88. e-Joined PRI, 1966. f-Secretary of the Second Judicial District, Hidalgo, 1944-46; Secretary of Judicial District, Puebla, 1946-47; lawyer, Relator "B", 1947-48; Director, Office of Law Compilation, Supreme Court, 1949; Secretary of Studies and Accounts, Supreme Court, 1949; Judge, District Court, Chihuahua, Sonora and the Federal District, 1951-58; Judge, Collegiate Court, Puebla, 1960-64; Director General of Legal Services, Department of the Federal District, 1965-74; Director General of Juridical and Governmental Affairs, Department of the Federal District, 1974; *Supernumerary Justice of the Supreme Court*, 1974-75; *Justice of the Supreme Court*, 1975-77; *President of*

the Supreme Court, 1977-82; *Interim Governor of Guanajuato*, June 26, 1984, to 1985; personal representative of president *Carlos Salinas* to the Vatican, 1990-94. g-President, Federation of University Students of Hidalgo, 1936. h-None. i-Son of Agustín Téllez López, supreme court justice, and Elena Cruces Sánchez; married Rosa María Straffon Rabling. j-None. k-None. l-Almanaque of Mexico, 1982, 77; Protag., 335; HA, 9 July 1984, 25; *Excélsior*, 26 Dec. 1981, 16; letter; Lehr, 176; DBGM89, 345; DBGM, 608.

Téllez Oropeza, Esperanza
a-1920s. b-Zacatlán, Puebla c-Primary studies in the Benito Juárez School, Zacatlán; completed secretarial studies, Oliver Pestalozzi Academy, Mexico City, 1931; teacher, Oliver Pestalozzi Academy. d-*Federal Deputy* from the State of Puebla, Dist. 10, 1958-61, member of the Library Committee and the Committee on the Radio and Television Industry. e-None. f-Personal secretary to *Enrique Rodríguez Cano*, Secretary of the Presidency, 1952-56; employee, Administrative Department, Secretariat of the Presidency, 1956-58. g-Employee of the National Teachers Union, 1937. j-None. k-First female deputy from the state of Puebla. l-Func., 327; C de D, 1958-61, 92.

Tello (Baurraud), Manuel
(Deceased Nov. 27, 1971) a-Nov. 1, 1898. b-Zacatecas, Zacatecas c-Primary studies at the Christian Brothers School, Zacatecas; secondary studies at the Instituto Científico, Zacatecas; preparatory studies at the National Preparatory School; law studies at the Escuela Libre de Derecho and at the National School of Law, UNAM; no degree. d-*Senator* from the State of Zacatecas, 1964-70. e-None. f-Joined the Foreign Service, 1923; Vice Consul, Brownsville, Texas, 1924; Vice Consul,

Nuevo Laredo, 1925; Consul, Antwerp, 1925-27; Consul, Berlin and Hamburg, 1927-29; Consul, Yokohama, 1930-33; Alternate Mexican delegate to the League of Nations, 1934-37; Mexican Delegate to the League of Nations, 1938-41; Director General of the Diplomatic Service and Political Affairs, Secretariat of Foreign Relations, 1942-43; *Oficial Mayor of Foreign Relations*, 1943-44; *Subsecretary of Foreign Relations*, 1944-48; *Subsecretary-in-Charge of the Secretariat*, 1948-51; *Secretary of Foreign Relations*, 1951-52; *Ambassador to the United States*, 1952-58; *Secretary of Foreign Relations*, 1958-64. g-None. h-Author of several books on foreign relations. i-Student of *Manuel J. Sierra* at UNAM; close friendships with *Vicente Sánchez Gavito, José Gorostiza* and *Jaime Torres Bodet*; married Guadalupe Macías; son, *Manuel Tello Macías*, became Ambassador to Great Britain in 1976; son, *Carlos*, was appointed Secretary of Programming and Budgeting, 1976-77; father, a rancher. j-None. k-None. l-HA, 10 Aug. 1951, 14; DGF56, 126; WWW70-71, 894; EBW46, 128; HA, 6 Dec. 1971, 22, 8 Dec. 1958, 25; WWMG, 38; WWM45, 116; DPE70, 7; STYRBIWW54, 1046; López, 1059; NYT, 29 Nov. 1971, 42; LA, 3 Dec. 1976; letter.

Tello Macías, Carlos
a-Nov. 4, 1938. b-Geneva, Switzerland. c-Primary and secondary at various public and private schools; BS degree from Georgetown University, 1955-58; MS degree from Columbia University, 1958-59; economics degree, King's College, Cambridge University, 1961-63; Assistant Professor of Modern Economic Systems, National School of Economics, UNAM, 1960-61; Professor of the Seminar on Foreign Trade, School of Political Science, UNAM, 1964; researcher, Colegio de México, 1963-64; Professor of Economic Theory, Colegio

de México, 1964-70; Professor of Economic Doctrines, National School of Economics, UNAM, 1966-75; Professor of the Revision of Economic Concepts, CEMLA, Inter-American Development Bank; Researcher, National School of Economics, UNAM, 1983-84; Guest Scholar, Woodrow Wilson Center for International Scholars, Washington, D.C., 1984; Visiting Researcher, Center for Mexican-United Studies, UCSD, La Jolla, 1984-85. d-None. e-None. f-Economist, Department of External Savings, National Finance Bank, 1959-60; economist, Governing Board of State Organizations and Enterprises, 1960-61; adviser to *José López Portillo*, Subsecretary of the Presidency, 1965-70; *Subsecretary of Revenues*, Secretariat of the Treasury, 1975-76; Subdirector General of Credit, Secretariat of the Treasury, 1971-75; *Secretary of Programming and Budget*, 1976-77; Director General of Financiera Nacional Azucarera, 1978-82; *Director General of the Bank of Mexico*, 1982; Ambassador to Portugal, 1987-89; President of the Executive Council of Solidarity, 1989-90; Ambassador to Russia, 1990-94. g-None. h-Author of many economic works. i-Son of *Manuel Tello*, Secretary of Foreign Relations, 1958-63, and Guadalupe Macías Viadero; brother of *Manuel Tello Macías*, Ambassador to Great Britain, 1977-79; married to Catalina Díaz Casasús. j-None. k-Resigned as Secretary of Programming and Budget because of policy disagreements with *Julio Moctezuma Cid* and *José López Portillo*; not a member of PRI; *López Portillo* personally chose him as his undersecretary when he headed the treasury ministry. l-*Excélsior*, 4 Jan. 1975, 10, 1 Dec. 1976; *El Día*, 1 Dec. 1976; *Excélsior*, 17 Nov. 1977; LA, Nov. 1977; HA, 13 Jan. 1975, 9, 6 Dec. 1976, 24; DPE71, 32; WSJ, 3 Sept. 1982, 3; HA, 13 Sept. 1982, 42; letters; LA, 17 Set. 1982, 3, 6; DBGM92, 365.

Tello Macías, Manuel
a-Mar. 15, 1935. b-Geneva, Switzerland. c-Primary and secondary education at the Colegio Benavente (Christian Brothers Boarding School), Puebla; preparatory studies at the Cristóbal Colon School, Mexico City; undergraduate studies at Georgetown University, Washington, D.C., in the Foreign Service Program; studies at UNAM. d-None. e-None. f-Joined the Foreign Service with the rank of Vice Consul, 1957; rank of Third Secretary, 1960; rank of Second Secretary, 1962; rank of First Secretary, 1964; rank of Counselor, September, 1966; rank of Minister, October 15, 1969; Subdirector of the Department of International Organizations, Secretariat of Foreign Relations, 1967-70; Director General of International Organizations, Secretariat of Foreign Relations, 1970-72; Director-in-Chief of International Organizations, 1972-75; Director-in-Chief, Bilateral Political Affairs, Secretariat of Foreign Relations, 1975-76; *Ambassador to Great Britain*, 1976-79; *Subsecretary of Multilateral Relations*, 1979-82; Permanent Representative to International Organizations, Geneva, 1982-88; *Ambassador to France*, 1989-94. g-None. h-None. i-Son of *Manuel Tello*, Secretary of Foreign Relations, 1958-63; brother of *Carlos Tello Macías*, Secretary of the Presidency, 1976-77. j-None. k-None. l-HA, 20 Jan. 1975, 9, 11 June 1979, 9; letter; DBGM92, 366.

Tena, Felipe de Jesús
(Deceased 1958) a-1873. b-Panindícuaro, Puruándiro, Michoacán. c-Secondary studies at the Colegio de San Simón, Zamora, Michoacán; preparatory studies at the Seminario de Morelia; law degree, School of Law, University of Michoacán, July 24, 1899; Professor of Law, University of Michoacán; Director of the School of Law, University of Michoacán; Professor of Mercantile

Law, National School of Law, UNAM, 1930. d-Local deputy to the State Legislature of Michoacán, 1911. e-None. f-Secretary General of Government of the State of Michoacán, 1911, under Governor Miguel Silva; Director of the Legal Department, Secretariat of Agriculture; Director of the Legal Department, Secretariat of Government; *Justice of the Supreme Court of Mexico*, 1941-43. g-None. h-Member of the Editorial Committee writing the new Commercial Code; translator of various legal works; author of works on commercial law. i-Father of Supreme Court Justice *Felipe Tena Ramírez*; father a lawyer; married Sara Ramírez. j-None. k-One of Mexico's outstanding jurists. l-DP70, 2072; letter; Enc. Mex., XII, 1977, 53.

Tena Ramírez, Felipe
a-Apr. 23, 1905. b-Morelia, Michoacán c-Early education unknown; law degree, Escuela Libre de Derecho, May 18, 1929, with a thesis on "The Foundation of Law, From Individualism to Socialism"; LLD, National School of Law, UNAM, 1950; Professor of Civil Proceedings, National School of Law, UNAM, 1931-64; Professor of Constitutional Law, National School of Law, UNAM. d-None. e-Consultant to the IEPES of PRI, 1982. f-*Supernumerary Justice of the Supreme Court*, 1947, 1951-56; *Justice of the Supreme Court*, 1957-69. g-None. h-Author of law books. i-Son of Supreme Court Justice *Felipe de J. Tena* and Sara Ramírez; married María Gómez. j-None. k-None. l-*Justicia*, Dec., 1966; WNM, 224.

Terán Mata, Juan Manuel
a-Mar. 2, 1917. b-Tampico, Tamaulipas c-Primary studies in Tampico; secondary studies in the Federal District; preparatory studies at the National Preparatory School, Mexico City; law

degree with honorable mention from the National School of Law, UNAM, 1939; MA in philosophy, UNAM, 1941; Ph.D. in philosophy from UNAM, 1954 (magna cum laude); professor at the National Preparatory School since 1937; Professor by Competition of Law and Political Philosophy, National School of Law, UNAM; Professor of the Theory of Knowledge, Normal School; Professor of Legal Philosophy, School of Philosophy and Liberal Arts, UNAM. d-*Federal Deputy* from the State of Tamaulipas, Dist. 1, 1952-55, member of the Legislative Studies Committee, the Military Justice Committee, the Budget and Accounts Committee (3rd year), the Constitutional Affairs Committee, and the First Section of the Credentials Committee; *Senator* from the State of Tamaulipas, 1958-64, member of the Gran Comisión, the Special Legislative Studies Committee, the First Tariff and Foreign Trade Committee, the First Justice Committee, the Second Petroleum Committee, and the Committee on Taxes; President of the Second Constitutional Affairs Committee. e-None. f-Member of the legislative studies committee, Secretariat of Public Education; head of the Department of University Studies, Secretariat of Public Education; Private Secretary to the Director of the Mexican Delegation to UNESCO, *Jaime Torres Bodet*, 1945; President of the Advisory Council of the Secretariat of the Navy; Director General of the Professions Division, Secretariat of Public Education, 1955-57; President of the Advisory Council of the Secretariat of the Navy, 1965-70. g-None. h-Author and notable legal philosopher. i-Student of Antonio Caso; married Olga Contreras; son of Manuel Terán and Encarnación Mata. j-None. k-None. l-Func., 373; DGF56, 302; DPE65, 55; C de D, 1952-54, 51; C de S, 1961-64, 71; WNM, 224; DP70, 775.

Terán Terán, Héctor
a-Apr. 3, 1931. b-Moctezuma, Sonora.
c-Early education unknown; business
administration degree, Technological
Institute of Higher Studies of Monte-
rrey, 1952. d-Local Deputy to the State
Legislature of Baja California, Dist. 3,
1980; *Plurinominal Federal Deputy*
from the PAN, 1985-88; *Senator* from
Baja California, 1991-97. e-Joined PAN
as a member of the youth sector, 1952;
President of the Regional Committee of
PAN, State of Baja California (twice);
Secretary of Publicity of Youth Sector of
PAN; Coordinator of Salvador Rosas
Magallón's campaign for governor of
Baja California; Editor of *El Debate* of
PAN; Delegate of the CEN of PAN to
Sonora; candidate of PAN for city
council of Mexicali, for federal deputy
from Baja California, 1964, for senator
from Baja California, 1970, for mayor of
Mexicali, 1971, and for governor of Baja
California, 1977; precandidate for PAN
presidential nomination, 1981; candi-
date of PAN for governor of Baja
California, 1983; adviser to the CEN of
PAN, 1985-88; adviser to PAN in Baja
California, 1985-88; member of the
CEN of PAN, 1985-88. f-None.
g-None. i-Married Alma Curella.
j-None. k-Persecuted and imprisoned
for political activities; first opposition
party member elected to the state
legislature. l-*La Nación*, 16 Sept. 1981;
HA, 6 June 1983, 32-33; Protag., 336;
DBGM87, 574.

Terán Torres, Héctor
a-Feb. 4, 1922. b-Zitácuaro, Michoacán.
c-Early education unknown; law degree,
National School of Law, UNAM;
Professor of Law, National School of
Law, UNAM. d-*Federal Deputy* from
the State of Michoacán, Dist. 8, 1976-
79. e-None. f-Lawyer, Office of the
Attorney General of the Federal
District; Judge (criminal division),
Federal District; First Assistant Attor-

ney General of the Federal District,
1975-76; Justice of the Superior Tribunal of Justice of the Federal District,
1971-75. g-None. j-None. k-None.
l-*Excélsior*, 1 Sept. 1976, 1C; C de D,
1976-79.

Terán (Zozaya), Horacio
(Deceased 1970) a-1905. b-Ciudad
Victoria, Tamaulipas c-Law degree,
National School of Law, UNAM.
d-*Governor of Tamaulipas*, 1951-57.
e-None. f-Agent of the Ministerio
Público; Second Civil Judge, Mexico
City; Penal Judge, Eighteenth Court
District, Mexico City; Civil Judge,
Tampico; Director of the Legal Depart-
ment, Department of the Federal
District; *Oficial Mayor of the Secre-
tariat of Government*, 1946-50; Del-
egate of the National Council of
Tourism, San Antonio, Texas, 1970.
g-None. i-Law School companion of
Miguel Alemán. j-None. k-None.
l-DGF56, 101; DP70, 2096; *Siempre*, 19
Sept. 1956, 10; DGF47, 71; HA, 25 Oct.
1954, 15; Casasola, V.

Terrazas Lozaya, Samuel
a-Apr. 7, 1924. b-Federal District
c-Early education unknown; no degree.
d-*Senator* from the State of Veracruz,
1970-76, member of the Gran Comisión, President of the First Petroleum
Committee, First Secretary of the
Second Labor Committee, and Second
Secretary of the Second Tariff and
Foreign Trade Committee. e-None.
f-None. g-Member of the CTM, 1950;
Secretary of Education of the Petroleum
Workers Union of the Mexican Republic, 1962; Treasurer of the STPRM,
1964-66; Secretary General of the
STPRM, Poza Rica, Veracruz, 1966-68.
i-First cousin married to *Pedro
González Azcuaga*, president of PARM,
1973-75. j-None. k-None. l-C de S,
1970-76, 86; MGF73; PS, 5982; Guerra
Leal, 365.

Terrones Benítez, Alberto
(Deceased Dec. 28, 1981) a-June 3, 1887. b-Villa de Nombre de Dios, Durango. c-Primary studies in Nazas, Topoia and Durango, Durango, under his father; preparatory studies at the Juárez Institute, Durango, 1900; preparatory studies in engineering, National Preparatory School; studies toward a degree in mining engineering, National School of Engineering, UNAM; law degree, Juárez Institute, Dec. 10, 1910, with a specialty in mining labor law. d-Deputy to the Constitutional Convention at Querétaro from the State of Durango, Dist. 6, 1916-17; Alternate Federal Deputy from the State of Durango, Dist. 4, 1920-22, 1922-24; Federal Deputy from the State of Durango, Dist. 6, 1924; Senator from the State of Durango, 1924-26; Provisional Governor of Durango, 1929-30; *Senator* from the State of Durango, 1952-58, member of the Indigenous Affairs Committee, the Special Legislative Studies Committee; President of the Special Committee on Small Agricultural Property, President of the First Mines Committee and First Secretary of the Military Justice Committee; *Senator* from the State of Durango, 1964-70. e-None. f-Lawyer, Attorney General's Office; official of the Department of Agrarian Affairs. g-Organized the Agrarian Union of Durango, 1917. h-Practicing lawyer, Mexico City. i-Father was a school teacher; brother of General Adolfo Terrones Benítez, Director of the Infantry, Secretariat of National Defense, 1956. j-None; married María Lanone; son, José, served as president of Canacintra. k-Removed as provisional governor of Durango after attempting to implement stronger pro-agrarian reforms. l-C de D, 1922-24, 34, 1920-22, 34, 1924-26, 35; C de S, 1924-26; Ind. Biog., 155; DGF56, 6, 8, 9, 11, 12, 14; *Excélsior*, 29 Dec. 1981, 10.

Tiburcio González, Adrián
(Deceased Sept. 21, 1972) a-June 22, 1907. b-Alvarado, Veracruz. c-Primary and secondary studies in Veracruz; preparatory studies in Veracruz; naval studies at the Fernando Siliceo Nautical School; Professor of Algebra, Analytical Mechanics and Physics, School of Engineering, UNAM; Professor at the National Military College. d-*Federal Deputy* from the State of Veracruz, Dist. 11, 1967-70. e-Member of the Authentic Party of the Mexican Revolution; orator for *Lázaro Cárdenas*, 1939-40. g-Founder of the General Federation of Labor; Secretary General of the CTM in Veracruz. h-Seaman by profession. i-Father in the navy and later a successful businessman; personal friend of *Lázaro Cárdenas*; married Mercedes Pérez. j-Captain in the navy; naval inspector; adviser to the port captain, Veracruz. k-Headed a dissident faction of PARM, 1962; candidate for federal deputy numerous times. l-MGF69, 96; C de D, 1967-69; HA, 2 Oct. 1972, 64; López, 1067; *Excélsior*, 29 Sept. 1974.

Todd Pérez, Luis Eugenio
a-Oct. 22, 1935. b-Monterrey, Nuevo León. c-Early education unknown; medical degree, School of Medicine, Autonomous University of Nuevo León, 1953-58; resident, Nutritional Hospital of Mexico, 1961; resident, Kidney Division, Washington University Hospital, 1962-63; resident, Kidney Division, Georgetown University Hospital, 1963-64; professor, School of Medicine, Autonomous University of Nuevo León, 1959-60; Director, Metabolic Unit, University Hospital, Nuevo León, 1965-88; Dean, School of Nursing, Autonomous University of Nuevo León, 1968; Rector, Autonomous University of Nuevo León, 1973-79. d-None. e-Joined PRI, 1961. f-Chief of Coordination, Public Health Services, State of

Nuevo León, 1979-82; *Subsecretary of Higher Education and Scientific Research*, Secretariat of Public Education, 1988-92; Ambassador to UNESCO, 1992-94. g-None. h-Practicing physician, 1960- . i-Son of Hiram Todd Grajales, mechanical engineer, and Carmen Pérez Maldonado Garza; married Elvira Lozano González. j-None. k-None. l-DBGM89, 349; DBGM92, 367-68.

Toledo Corro, Antonio
a-Apr. 1, 1919. b-Escuinapa, Sinaloa. c-Primary and secondary studies in Sinaloa; no degree. d-Local Deputy to the State Legislature of Sinaloa, 1952; Mayor of Mazatlán, Sinaloa, 1957-62; Mayor of Mazatlán, 1970-76; *Federal Deputy* from the State of Sinaloa, Dist. 4, 1976-78, coordinator of the deputies from the CNC sector, 1976; *Governor of Sinaloa*, 1980-86. e-Participant in the presidential campaigns of *Adolfo López Mateos*, 1958, *Gustavo Díaz Ordaz*, 1964, and *Luis Echeverría*, 1970. f-Director of the National Grain Promotion Program, Juchitlan Irrigation District; Director of Rural Mechanization, Secretariat of Agrarian Reform; *Secretary of Agrarian Reform*, June 9, 1978-80. g-President of the Chamber of Commerce of Mazatlán, 1957; Delegate of the Livestock Association of Southern Sinaloa; member of the National Livestock Federation. h-Rancher; owner of an agricultural machinery business. i-Married Estela Ortiz; part of the *Francisco Merino Rábago* camarilla. j-None. k-Precandidate for governor of Sinaloa against *Leopoldo Sánchez Celis*, 1963, suffered political ostracism; strongest precandidate for governor of Sinaloa against *Alfonso Calderón Velarde*, 1974; *Adolfo López Mateos* praised him as an outstanding mayor of Mazatlán; *Excélsior* accused him of being a large landholder in El Rosario region. l-*Excélsior*, 28 Aug. 1976, 1C,

10 June 1978, 1, 4, 8, 18; *The News*, 10 June 1978, 2; *Proceso*, 12 June 1978, 7; *Excélsior*, 27 Apr. 1980, 4.

Topete Ibañez, Rosendo
(Deceased) a-1892. b-Jicaltepec, Veracruz. c-Primary studies in Martínez de la Torre, Veracruz; secondary studies in Tlapacoyan, Veracruz; studied business and accounting, Tlapacoyan, Veracruz. d-Local Deputy to the State Legislature of Veracruz under Governor *Adolfo Ruiz Cortines*, 1947-50; *Federal Deputy* from the State of Veracruz, Dist. 4, 1955-58, President of the Gran Comisión, member of the First Government Committee; *Senator* from the State of Veracruz, 1958-64, member of the Gran Comisión, the Second National Defense Committee, the Second Petroleum Committee, the Special Livestock Committee, and the Consular and Diplomatic Service Committee; President of the Special Hydraulic Resources Committee. e-Assistant to the treasurer of the Pro *Avila Camacho* Political Committee, 1940; official of the *Adolfo Ruiz Cortines* campaign, 1952. f-Treasurer General of Veracruz under Governor *Adolfo Ruiz Cortines*, 1944-47; Chief of the Presidential Offices under *Adolfo Ruiz Cortines*, 1952-55. g-None. h-Businessman, 1929-30, 1946. i-Brother of Ricardo Topete, federal deputy under President Calles; uncle of *Flavio Romero de Velasco*. k-None. l-Func., 387; C de S, 1961-64, 71; DGF56, 29, 33, 30; Ind. Biog., 155-57.

Torres Bodet, Jaime
(Deceased 1974) a-Apr. 17, 1902. b-Federal District. c-Preparatory studies at the National Preparatory School, graduating, 1917; law degree, National School of Law, UNAM, 1918-22; instructor of free preparatory course in general literature, 1920; Secretary of the National Preparatory School under Ezequiel Chávez, 1920; Professor of Art

History, National Preparatory School, 1922-23; Professor of French Literature, School of Philosophy and Letters, UNAM, 1925-29. d-None. e-None. f-Private Secretary to José Vasconcelos, Rector of UNAM, 1921; Director, Department of Libraries, Secretariat of Public Education, 1922-24; joined the Foreign Service, 1929; Second Secretary, Spain, 1929-31; First Secretary of the Legation, Paris, 1935-36; Secretary, Buenos Aires, 1934-35; Chargé d'Affaires, Holland, 1932-34; Director of the Diplomatic Service, Secretariat of Foreign Relations, 1936-37; Chargé d'Affaires, Brussels, Belgium, 1938-40; *Subsecretary of Foreign Relations,* 1940-43; *Secretary of Public Education,* 1943-46; *Secretary of Foreign Relations,* 1946-48; Secretary General of UNESCO, 1949-52; *Ambassador to France,* 1953-58; *Secretary of Public Education,* 1958-64; Ambassador-at-Large, 1970-71. g-None. h-National Prize for Literature, 1966; founded and published *Contemporáneos,* 1928-31, which included such authors as Xavier Villaurrutia and *Salvador Novo;* head of the Mexican delegation which formed UNESCO, 1945; head of the Mexican delegation to the Bogota Conference, 1948; writer and poet, published first book at age 16. i-Studied under *Alfonso Caso* at UNAM, 1918; founding member of the Ateneo de la Juventud, 1918, which included *Luis Garrido* and *José Gorostiza;* studied with *Rafael de la Colina* at preparatory and at UNAM; classmate of *Salvador Novo;* attended UNAM with Daniel Cosío Villegas. j-None. k-Member of the Revolutionary family, 1940-48. l-HA, 8 Dec. 1958, 26; WWMG, 39; Daniels, 108-09, 140-41; Brandenburg, 178, 80; IWW, 1231; WWM5, 117; DGF56, 126; HA, 11 Oct. 1972, 18-21; Peral, 798; HA, 4 Oct. 1971, 18; Novo, 166; STYRBIWW54, 1054; letters; Enc. Mex., XII, 1977, 193-94.

Torres Chavarría, Celia
a-June 3, 1928. b-Iztapaluca, México. c-Primary and secondary studies in Mexico City; studies in journalism and labor law; five years of special studies at the Conservatory of Music of the National Institute of Fine Arts; law degree, Ibero-American University, 1979-83. d-*Federal Deputy* from the Federal District, Dist. 25, 1976-79, member of the Public Foodstuffs Committee, the Agrarian Affairs Committee and the Development of Social Security and Public Health Committees; *Federal Deputy* from the Federal District, Dist. 6, 1988-91. e-Member of the PPS, 1957-88; member of the National Liberation Movement, 1959; joined the PRD, 1989; member of the CEN of the PRD. f-Representative of the Women of Indigenous Origin to the Secretariat of Agrarian Reform and the Department of the Federal District; Director of the Indigenous Cultural Center, Secretariat of Public Education. g-None. i-Daughter of Julio Torres, peasant leader in the Valle del Tenango, and Julia Chavarría García; recruited to PRI by *Rodolfo González Guevara;* married to Fernando Sánchez Ramírez, a lawyer. j-None. k-None. l-D de C, 1976-79, 3, 5, 37; HA, 31 May 1976, 10-11; *Excélsior,* 3 Sept. 1976; DBGM89, 548.

Torres Gaitán, Ricardo
a-Dec. 1, 1911. b-Calcoman, Michoacán. c-Economics degree from the National School of Economics, UNAM, Apr. 12, 1944, with a thesis on Mexican monetary policy; Assistant Professor of Organization and Financing of Private Enterprise, 1943; Assistant Professor of Credit Operations and Institutions, 1944-49; Chief of Labs, UNAM, 1944-49; Professor of International Trade Theory, UNAM, 1947-77; Director of the National School of Economics, 1953-59, and Professor of the Seminar on Economic Development, 1963-77, all

at the National School of Economics, UNAM; member of the Governing Board, UNAM, 1962-74. d-None. e-None. f-Researcher, Committee on Tariffs and Subsidies for Foreign Trade, 1944-45; Chief of the Banking Department, Secretariat of the Treasury, 1946; Director of the Department of Administration and Development of Enterprises, National Finance Bank, 1947-52; Director of the Institute of Economic Research, UNAM, 1950-52; Director of Statistics, Secretariat of Industry and Commerce; *Oficial Mayor of Industry and Commerce*, 1952-53; Director General of the National Ejidal Bank, 1958-64; adviser, Mexican Institute of Foreign Trade, 1971-76; adviser, Secretariat of Agriculture and Hydraulic Resources, 1977-82. g-None. i-Professor of *Julio Faesler Carlisle*, director general of the Mexican Institute of Foreign Trade, 1970-76; relative of *Carlos Torres Manzo*. j-None. k-Supported *Carlos Torres Manzo* for Governor of Michoacán, 1974. l-D de Y, Dec. 1958; HA, 15 Dec. 1958, 5; letter; JSH, 402-04.

Torres Landa, Juan José
(Deceased June 16, 1980) a-Apr. 16, 1911. b-Hacienda El Saucillo, Cuerámaro, Guanajuato. c-Primary and secondary studies in León, Guanajuato; preparatory studies from the University of Guanajuato, León, Guanajuato; law degree, National School of Law, UNAM, 1937, with a thesis on the regulation of marriage; Director, Normal School of León, 1938. d-*Federal Deputy* from the State of Guanajuato, Dist. 2, 1949-52, member of the Second Administrative Committee, the First Treasury Committee, and the Consular Service and Diplomatic Committee; *Governor of Guanajuato*, 1961-67. e-Joined PNR, 1935; General Delegate of PRI to Baja California, 1968-70; General Delegate to the CEN of PRI to Michoacán, 1978.

f-Director of the Preparatory Schools of Guanajuato, 1943-44; Ambassador to Brazil, 1970-74. g-Member, League of Workers and Peasants, 1929; president of the Society of Preparatory Students, University of Guanajuato, 1931; founder and president of the Vanguard of Revolutionary Guanajuato Students, 1935; student leader, 1933 strike at UNAM; delegate of the first convention of the CNOP of PRI, 1943. h-Practicing lawyer, León, 1935-55. i-Son, Juan José Torres Landa García, was a precandidate for Federal Deputy, 1976; son, Sergio Torres Landa, was a director general of the secretariat of public works, 1977; son, *Juan Ignacio*, was a federal deputy from Guanajuato, 1991-94; married Mara Teresa García; son of Hermión Torres Aranda and Ana María de Landa y Yermo; uncle, Hilaron, was an industrialist; grandfather, Hermión Torres Aranda, a large landowner. j-None. k-*Por Qué* alleges he left the state of Guanajuato 1500 million pesos in debt after the fiasco of his Plan Guanajuato; *Por Qué* also claims he was involved in several land scandals. l-C de D, 1949-51, 92; *Por Qué*, 18 Sept. 1968, 32ff; *Hoy*, 13 Mar. 1971, 10; *Por Qué*, 4 Dec. 1969, 20, 22; *Excélsior*, 7 Nov. 1978, 13; Torres Martínez, 189, 206; HA, 23 June 80, 12; Almanaque de México, 500; DBGM92, 589.

Torres Manzo, Carlos
a-Apr. 25, 1923. b-Coalcomán, Michoacán. c-Primary studies, Ignacio Manuel Altamirano School, Uruapan, Michoacán, 1937-41; secondary studies, Boarding School of Workers' Children, Zamora, Michoacán, 1942-44; preparatory studies, National Preparatory School, Mexico City, 1945-46; economics degree, National School of Economics, UNAM, 1947-52, with a thesis on the pure theory of international trade; thesis received recognition from the Bank of Mexico; graduate studies,

London School of Economics, 1955-57; diploma from the Government of Japan for studies in Tokyo on economic planning and free trade; Professor of Literature, Etymology, History of Economic Thought, Economic Theory, and International Trade, National School of Economics, UNAM, 1958-70. d-*Governor of Michoacán*, 1974-80. e-Joined PRI, 1947; Director of the Foreign Commerce Studies Commission, IEPES of the CEN of PRI; campaigned for *Luis Echeverría* for president by presenting reports on tourism, the electrical industry, and industrialization; Director of the IEPES of PRI, 1987. f-Librarian, secondary school of Zamora, 1944-45; employee of the Secretariat of Education, 1946-47; warehouseman, Commerce Bank, 1947; Technician, Secretariat of National Properties, 1947-49; supervisor, Secretariat of Industry and Commerce, 1952-54; economist, Secretariat of Industry and Commerce, 1958; economist, National Ejido Bank, 1959-61; Director, Department of Commercial Policy, Secretariat of Industry and Commerce, 1961-64; Supervisor, Department of Commercial Policy, Secretariat of Industry and Commerce, 1952-54; Manager of Conasupo, 1964-70; *Secretary of Industry and Commerce*, 1970-74. g-President of the Federation of University Students, 1950; Secretary General of the League of Revolutionary Economists of the CNOP of PRI; President of the College of Economists, 1970-71; Director of the Association of Small Business Banks. h-Researcher, Institute of Investigations, National School of Economics, UNAM, 1958-64; author of many articles on economic subjects for *El Nacional* and *Prensa Gráfica*. i-Studied under *Eduardo Bustamante* and *Ricardo Torres Gaitán* at UNAM; as a student at UNAM, knew *Jorge de la Vega Domínguez* and *Jesús Silva Herzog Flores*. j-None. l-Letters; HA, 7 Dec. 1970, 24; *Hoy*, 9

Jan. 1971, 4; *Excélsior*, 19 Jan. 1974, 8; Enc. Mex., Annual, 1977, 546; Enc. Mex., XII, 195; HA, 16 Sept. 1974, 36.

Torres Mesías, Luis

a-Mar. 26, 1916. b-Mérida, Yucatán c-Primary and secondary studies in Mérida; teaching certificate; no degree. d-Mayor of Mérida, Yucatán, 1959-60; *Federal Deputy* from the State of Yucatán, Dist. 1, 1961-64, member of the Gran Comisión, member of the Public Works Committee and the Budget and Accounts Committee; *Governor of Yucatán*, 1964-70. e-President of the Regional Committee of PRI for Yucatán, 1956-58; member of the PRI student political group in Yucatán, Juventudes Sociales. f-Secretary General of Government of the State of Yucatán, Feb. to Oct., 1958, under Governor *Agustín Franco Aguilar*. g-None. h-None. j-None. k-Unpopular gubernatorial candidate; opposed José Vallejo Novelo; member of the *Ernesto Novelo Torres* group. l-*Informes*, 1964-70; C de D, 1961-63, 93; D de Y, 24 Nov. 1964, Q es Q, 242-43; Richmond, 395; *Siempre*, 23 Oct. 1963, 93; *Novedades*, 5 Aug. 1963.

Torres Ortiz, Pedro

(Deceased) a-May 13, 1887. b-Colima, Colima. c-Primary studies in Colima; no degree. d-Mayor of Zamora, Michoacán; Mayor of Purandiro, Michoacán; Mayor of Ciudad Guzmán, Michoacán; *Governor of Colima*, Nov. 1, 1939, to Oct. 31, 1940; *Senator* from the State of Colima, 1934-39. e-Candidate of Cooperative Party for governor, 1923; formed own political party, Only Revolutionary Front of Colima, 1939, to oppose Gen. *Santa Ana*; supported Gen. *Miguel Henríquez Guzmán*, 1945; supported Gen. *Miguel Henríquez Guzmán*, 1951. f-Provisional Governor of Colima, 1931. g-None. h-None. j-Career army officer; Commander of the 57th Cavalry

Regiment; joined the Revolution, 1914; initially opposed Carranza; supported Carranza, 1920; supported General Maycotte in Oaxaca against Obregón, 1923; rank of Brigadier General, Oct. 1, 1942. k-Political opponent of *Miguel G. Santa Ana;* in exile in the United States, 1923. l-Letter; Peral, 800-01; López, 1081; Moreno, 84.

Torres Pancardo, Oscar
(Deceased Sept. 9, 1983) a-May 20, 1935. b-Poza Rica, Veracruz. c-Completed primary and secondary studies; no degree. d-*Federal Deputy* from the State of Veracruz, Dist. 3, 1979-82; Mayor of Poza Rica, Veracruz, 1983. e-None. f-None. g-Joined the Petroleum Workers Union, 1961; Secretary of Conflicts of Local 30 of the STPRM, 1967-69; Secretary of Bargaining of Local 30 of the STPRM, 1969-71; President of the General Council of Vigilance of the STPRM, 1970-73; Secretary of Interior and Accords of Local 30 of the STPRM, 1973-75; Secretary General of Local 30 of the STPRM, 1976-77; Secretary General of the Union of Petroleum Workers of the Mexican Republic, 1977-79; President of the Congress of Labor, 1977-78; Secretary General of Local 30 of the STPRM, 1979-83. h-Joined PEMEX as a laborer, 1952; assistant plumber, Department of Production and Gas, PEMEX, 1961. i-Married Olivia Plascencia. j-None. k-Foul play suspected in his death. l-HA, 10 July 1978, 9; C de D, 1979-82

Torres Ramírez, Víctor Manuel
a-Jan. 12, 1928. b-Tecolótlan, Jalisco c-Early education unknown; law studies, National School of Law, UNAM, 1954-58, graduating with a thesis on constitutional liberties and social dissolution violations, 1961; studies, Colegio de México, 1960-69; professor of law, National School of Law, UNAM, 1966-67. d-*Federal*

Deputy from the State of Jalisco, Dist. 11, 1982-85, member of the Agrarian Reform and the Foreign Relations Committees. e-Joined PRI, 1964; adviser, IEPES of PRI, 1973-76. f-Legal adviser to the Subsecretary of Colonization and National Lands, Department of Agrarian Affairs, 1963-65; Director, Office of Land Titles, Department of Agrarian Affairs, 1967-68; Secretary, Advisers Center, Secretariat of Agriculture; adviser, Secretary of Agrarian Reform; *Secretary General of the Department of Agrarian Affairs, 1970-75; Subsecretary of the Secretariat of Agrarian Reform, 1975-76;* Subdelegate of Labor, Secretariat of Labor, 1978-79. g-Legal adviser to the Secretary General of the CTM, 1981-83; Auxiliary Secretary of Agrarian Action, CNC, 1968-70; member, Technical Council, CNC, 1968-82; adviser, Union of Sugar Cane Workers, 1979-83. h-General Manager, Administradora General de Inmuebles, S.A. i-Brother nominated as PRI candidate for mayor of Puerto Vallarta; son of Agustín Torres Olmedo and Soledad Ramírez Villaseñor; married Julieta Bueno Soria. j-None. k-None. l-Directorio, 1982-85; *Excélsior,* 3 Nov. 1976, 4; Lehr, 236; DBGM, 611.

Torres Sánchez, Enrique
(Deceased Apr. 2, 1965) a-Feb., 1903. b-Nazas, Durango. c-Primary and secondary studies in Durango, Durango; preparatory studies at the National Preparatory School; law degree from the National School of Law, UNAM, 1927. d-*Governor of Durango, 1950-56.* e-None. f-Judge of the Superior Tribunal of Justice of Durango, 1932-35. g-None. h-Practicing lawyer. i-Student with *Miguel Alemán, Mariano Azuela, Eduardo Bustamante, Angel Carvajal, Manuel Sánchez Cuen,* and *Horacio Terán Z.* at UNAM in the 1920s. j-None. k-Murdered. l-HA, 25 Oct. 1954, 15; DGF56, 92.

Torres Torija, José
(Deceased 1952) a-1885. b-Federal
District. c-Early education unknown;
medical degree, School of Medicine,
UNAM, 1908; Professor of Clinical
Surgery and Legal Medicine, School of
Medicine, UNAM; *Secretary General of
UNAM*, 1940-42; member of the Gover-
ning Board of UNAM. d-None. e-None.
f-Oficial Mayor of the Department of
Public Health; Director of the Juárez
Hospital, 1921. g-None. h-Physician at
the Juárez Hospital, 1908-48; author of
many medical books; President of the
Mexican Academy of Medicine, 1929.
j-None. k-None. l-Enc. Mex., 12, 196;
López, 1002; DP70, 2156; Q es Q, 584.

Tovilla Cristiani, Homero
a-Oct. 13, 1940. b-Comitán de Domínguez, Chiapas c-Early education
unknown; economics degree, National
School of Economics, UNAM, 1958-62;
Ph.D. in public administration and
political science, UNAM, 1967-70;
professor of economics, National School
of Economics, UNAM, 1963-65.
d-*Federal Deputy* from the State of
Chiapas, Dist. 3, 1976-79, 1982-85,
member of the Programming, Budgeting, and Public Accounts Committee
and member of the Inspection Committee of the General Accounting Office.
e-Joined PRI, 1961. f-Director of
Business Studies Section, Department
of Marketing and Statistics, National
Diesel Company, 1962-66; Subdirector
of Statistics Department, UNAM;
Subdirector General of Administration,
UNAM, 1966-70; Manager of Operations and of Administration, Conasupo,
1970-75; Director of Administration and
Public Relations, Fertimex, 1976-82.
g-Secretary of Organization, League of
Revolutionary Economists, 1974-75;
Special Delegate of CNOP to Querétaro;
Oficial Mayor of CNOP, 1975-76.
h-None. i-Son of Gustavo Tovilla
Morales, public official, and Consuelo

Cristiana Abarca, businesswoman;
married Estela María Lara Díaz. j-Rank
of Corporal. l-C de D, 1976-79, 1982-85;
Directorio, 1982-85; Lehr, 87.

Toxqui Fernández de Lara, Alfredo
a-Aug. 5, 1913. b-Cholula, Puebla
c-Primary studies at the José María
Lafragua School, Puebla; secondary
studies in Puebla; preparatory studies at
the University of Puebla; medical
degree, University of Puebla, Oct. 1940,
with a thesis on autochemotherapy;
professor, School of Medicine, University of Puebla, Professor of General
Surgery, IMSS Hospital, Puebla.
d-Substitute Councilman of Puebla,
1948-51; Local Deputy to the State
Legislature of Puebla; *Federal Deputy*
from the State of Puebla, Dist. 3, 1955-
58, member of the Second Public
Education Committee, the Second
Balloting Committee, and the Military
Health Committee; *Senator* from the
State of Puebla, 1970-74, member of the
Gran Comisión, First Secretary of the
Immigration Committee and President
of the Insurance Committee; *Governor
of Puebla*, 1975-81; *Senator* from the
State of Puebla, 1988-91. e-Secretary
General of PRI in Puebla; Official
Orator of PRI, 1948; cofounder of the
CEPES in Puebla; President of the
Regional Committee of PRI in Puebla.
f-Director of Sanitorium No. 1, IMSS
Regional Hospital; Director of IMSS
Clinics No. 1 and 2; Subdirector of
Government for the State of Puebla,
1966-67; Oficial Mayor of Puebla, 1967.
g-General delegate of the CNOP of PRI
to Puebla, 1957; Secretary General of
the CNOP for Puebla, 1957-63; member
of the student directorate at preparatory
school at the University of Puebla,
1933; Secretary of the University of
Puebla Student Federation, 1934.
h-Winner of the First Prize in Oratory at
the University of Puebla, 1938; Intern,
General Hospital, Puebla; Medical

Director of the Green Cross, Puebla, 1940-44. j-None. k-None. l-DBP, 679-80; C de D, 1955-57; DGF56, 27, 32, 35, 37; letter; CyT, 679-80; C de S, 1970-76, 87; Ind. Biog., 157-58.

Trejo Hernández, Melquiades
a-Dec. 10, 1918. b-Puebla, Puebla. c-Primary studies only; no degree. d-Local Deputy to the State Legislature of Puebla, 1960-63; Councilman from Puebla, 1957-60; *Federal Deputy* from the State of Puebla, Dist. 1, 1964-67, member of the Textile Industry Committee and the First General Means of Communication Committee; *Federal Deputy* from the State of Puebla, Dist. 1, 1970-73, member of the Public Assistance Committee, the Small Industries Committee, and the First General Means of Communication Committee. e-None. f-Representative before Group 1, Central Board of Conciliation and Arbitration, State of Puebla, 1963-64. g-Secretary of Labor and Conflicts of Local 120, Textile Workers Union of the Mexican Republic, 1946; Secretary General of Local 120 of the Textile Workers Union of the Mexican Republic, 1948; Delegate of the CTM of Puebla to the CTM, 1950; Secretary of Finances, CTM of the State of Puebla, 1951-54; Secretary of Labor and Conflicts of the CTM of the State of Puebla, 1954-57; Secretary of Labor of the CTM for the State of Puebla, 1957-66. h-Textile worker. j-None. k-None. l-C de D, 1970-72, 138; C de D, 1964-66, 87, 95; Directorio, 1970-72.

Treviño (González), Jacinto B.
(Deceased Nov. 6, 1971) a-Sept. 11, 1883. b-Ciudad Guerrero, Coahuila. c-Primary studies in Ciudad Guerrero and in the Colegio Hidalgo and Colegio Bolívar, Monterrey; preparatory studies at the Colegio Civil of Monterrey, enrolled in the National Military College, Dec. 26, 1901, graduated as an indus-

trial engineer with the rank of artillery Lieutenant, Dec. 6, 1908. d-Constitutional Deputy, 1916-17; Federal Deputy from Coahuila; *Senator* from the State of Coahuila, 1952-58, member of the Second Foreign Relations Committee, the Public Welfare Committee, and the Gran Comisión. e-Supporter and organizer of the pro-*Almazán* Revolutionary Committee for National Reconstruction, 1939-40; founder and *President of PARM*, 1957-65. f-Oficial Mayor of the Secretariat of War, 1914; Secretary of Industry, Commerce and Labor, June 6 to Nov. 30, 1920; Director of Mexican Free Ports, 1957-66. g-None. h-None. i-Son-in-law of Col. Lauro Carrillo, governor of Chihuahua, 1887-92; son of Francisco Z. Treviño, colonel in the National Guard, and Trinidad González; married María Carrillo Gutiérrez; father of Salvador F. Treviño, a mining engineer. j-Rank of 2nd Captain, 1910; member of Madero's staff, 1911; organized the 25th Irregular Regiment, Saltillo, Coahuila, 1912; fought General Huerta, 1913; rank of Major; Chief of Staff for Carranza, 1913; rank of Colonel, June 8, 1913; Brigadier General, June 5, 1914; rank of Brigade General, 1915; rank of Division General, Dec. 22, 1915; General in Chief of the forces against Francisco Villa, 1916; Military Commander of Chihuahua, 1916; supported Obregón against Carranza, 1920; supported De la Huerta; supported Escobar, 1929; Commander of the 1st Brigade of the 1st Division of the Army of the Center, 1914. k-First signer of the Plan of Guadalupe, Mar. 26, 1913; supported the De la Huerta movement, 1923; jailed, 1923-25; opposed Obregón's reelection, 1927; supported Escobar rebellion, 1929; in exile, 1929-36; returned to Mexico, rejoined the army, 1940, at the rank of Division General, 1941; precandidate for Governor of Coahuila, 1957. l-DGF56, 8, 9; HA, 15 Nov. 1971; Peral, 806; Enc.

Mex., Annual, 1977, 597-98; Ind. Biog., 159; Moreno, 195-200; WNM, 228.

Treviño Martínez, Jorge A.
a-Nov. 2, 1935. b-Monterrey, Nuevo León. c-Early education unknown; law degree, National School of Law, UNAM, 1952-56, graduating with an honorable mention; Ph.D. in administrative law, University of Paris, 1959-63; postgraduate studies in public finance, University of Rome, 1962-63; Professor of Economics, 1963-65, Professor of Business, 1965-66, and Professor of Law, 1983, all at the Autonomous University of Nuevo León; Professor of Finances and Administration, ITESM, Monterrey, 1968-69. d-*Federal Deputy* from the State of Nuevo León, 1982-85; *Governor of Nuevo León*, 1985-91. e-Joined PRI, 1958. f-Secretary, Federal Tax Court, 1957-59; Tax Adviser, Governor of Nuevo León, 1968-70; Assistant Treasurer General of Nuevo León, 1970-73; Regional Tax Administrator, Secretariat of the Treasury, Nuevo León, 1973-82. g-None. h-Legal adviser, law firm, 1963-72. i-Son of Dr. Luis J. Treviño, pediatrician, and Julia Martínez Ugarte; married Cristina Larralde Laguera; met *Miguel de la Madrid* at UNAM. j-None. k-None. l-DBM68, 607; Lehr, 343; *Excélsior*, 17 Mar. 1985, 1; DBGM, 612; DBGM89, 748.

Treviño Ríos, Oscar
c-Primary, secondary, and preparatory studies in Monterrey, Nuevo León; law degree from the National School of Law, UNAM, 1929-34. d-None. e-None. f-Director General of Legal Affairs, Secretariat of Foreign Relations, 1946-52, 1952-58; *Assistant Attorney General of Mexico* (1), 1958-62; *Attorney General of Mexico*, 1962-64. g-None. h-Practicing lawyer. i-Married Guadalupe Serrato. j-None. k-None. l-Letter; DGF47, 89; HA, 22 Dec. 1958, 8; D de Y, 9 Dec. 1958, 1; DGF56, 150.

Treviño Zapata, Norberto
a-1911. b-Matamoros, Tamaulipas c-Early education unknown; medical degree, National School of Medicine, UNAM; Professor of Medicine, National School of Medicine, UNAM. d-*Federal Deputy* from the State of Tamaulipas, Dist. 2, 1952-55, President of the Gran Comisión, member of the First Government Committee; *Governor of Tamaulipas*, 1957-63. e-None. f-Director General of the National Institute for the Protection of Infants, 1970-72; Ambassador to Italy, 1972-76. g-Delegate to the 10th National Student Congress, 1933; Delegate to the Student University Federation, 1933-34; President of the Student Association of the National School of Medicine, 1933-34. h-Practicing physician. i-Political mentor of *Emilio Martínez Manatou*, with whom he practiced medicine. j-None. k-None. l-Hayner, 211; Sebastián Mayo, 70; Ind. Biog., 102; HA, 21 June 1976, 20; Morton, 67; HA, 8 Dec. 1958, 42, 23 Oct. 1972, 21.

Trigo (Cortínez), Octavio Marciano
(Deceased Dec. 1, 1973) a-Nov. 2, 1885. b-Veracruz, Veracruz. c-Primary and secondary studies in Veracruz, Veracruz; preparatory studies at the School of Law, Jalapa; law degree, School of Law, Jalapa, Veracruz; Professor of Labor Law, National School of Law, UNAM. d-Federal Deputy from the State of Chihuahua, Dist. 3, 1918-20, 1932-34. e-None. f-Agent of the Ministerio Público of the Attorney General of Mexico, Judge of the Superior Tribunal of Justice, and Public Defender, each in the states of Chihuahua and Coahuila; District Court Judge; Secretary General of Veracruz, 1911; Interim Governor of Chihuahua; *Justice of the Supreme Court*, 1936-40. g-None. h-Author of a federal labor law book, 1937; practiced law with Manuel Zamora after graduation. i-Married

Angelina Gómez; son, Oscar, served as a general manager of Syntex; son, Gaspar, served as a secretary to several supreme court justices; son of Gaspar Trigo and Dolores Cortínez. j-Fought in the Revolution under Pablo González, 1913; fought with Francisco Murguía; member of Carranza's staff. k-Precandidate for Governor of Veracruz, 1937, was prevented from campaigning after a grave injury suffered in an automobile accident. l-Novo35, 216; HA, 10 Dec. 1973, 16; López, 1095; Pasquel, 388; Illescas, 469-70, 728.

Truchuello, José María
(Deceased 1953) a-Apr. 29, 1880. b-Querétaro, Querétaro c-Primary, secondary and preparatory studies, Querétaro; law degree, University of Querétaro; Professor of Constitutional Law, School of Law, University of Querétaro. d-Governor of Querétaro, 1920-23; Deputy to the Constitutional Convention of Querétaro, 1916-17, from the State of Querétaro; Secretary of the Constitutional Convention. e-None. f-Syndic to the City Council of Querétaro, Querétaro; public defender, Querétaro; Secretary of the First Civil Judicial District of Querétaro, Querétaro; consulting lawyer to the government of the State of Querétaro; Judge of the Superior Tribunal of Justice of the State of Querétaro; Secretary General of Public Instruction of the State of Querétaro; Justice of the Supreme Court, 1917-18; President of the Superior Tribunal of Justice of the Federal District and Federal Territories; *Justice of the Supreme Court*, 1935-40. g-President of the Student Association, University of Querétaro. i-Related to J. Manuel Truchuelo, senator from Querétaro, 1922-25. j-None. k-Initiated the idea of dividing the Supreme Court into four divisions. l-DP70, 2176; López, 1096; Noriega, 477.

Trueba Barrera, Eduardo
a-Jan. 25, 1920. b-Mérida, Yucatán. c-Primary studies in Felipe Carrillo Puerto Public School, Mérida; secondary studies in Agustín Vadillo Ciero Public School; preparatory studies at the Free Preparatory School of Yucatán; degree in pharmaceutical chemistry, School of Chemistry, University of Yucatán, 1948. d-*Federal Deputy* from the State of Yucatán, Dist. 1, 1964-67. e-Member of PAN. f-Secretary of the Board of Material, Moral and Civic Improvement, Mérida. g-Secretary General of the Secondary School Student Circle, 1937-38; President of the Student Circle, School of Chemistry, University of Yucatán, 1944-45; President of the Parents Union of Yucatán, 1963-64; various positions in the National Chamber of Pharmaceutical Industries, Yucatán, 1955-65. h-Chemist. j-None. k-None. l-Directorio, 1964-67; C de D, 1964-67.

Trueba Rodríguez, Salvador
a-Apr. 5, 1922. b-Toluca, México. c-Early education unknown; law degree, National School of Law, UNAM, 1948; professor, Free School of Law, 1954-57. d-None. e-Joined PRI, 1980. f-Private Secretary to the Director General of the National Finance Bank, *Antonio Carrillo Flores*, 1947-50; Director, Office of Liquidation of Credit Institutions, Secretariat of the Treasury, 1950-54; Director of Legal Affairs, National Finance Bank, 1976-77; *Oficial Mayor of the Secretariat of the Treasury*, 1977-80; *Subsecretary of Tax Investigation*, Secretariat of the Treasury, 1980-82; Director General of Financiera Nacional Azucarera, S.A., 1983-88, 1988-94. g-Director General of the National Union of Sugarcane Producers, 1972-74; Director General of the Coordinating Council of Entrepreneurs, 1975-76. h-Private practice as a lawyer, 1954-75. i-Son of Domingo Trueba Mercado,

lawyer, and María Rodríguez Guillén; married Susana Fournier Vogel. j-None. k-None. l-*Excélsior*, 8 Apr. 1980, 23, 9 Apr. 1980, 22; HA, 21 Apr. 1980, 21; DBGM, 419; DBGM87, 388; DBGM92, 373.

Trueba Urbina, Alberto
a-Sept. 19, 1906. b-Campeche, Campeche. c-Primary studies, Campeche Institute; preparatory studies at the Instituto Campechano; law degree from the University of the Southeast, Mérida, Dec. 1927; Professor of Law, National School of Law, UNAM, 1937-45. d-*Federal Deputy* from the State of Campeche, Dist. 1, 1940-43, member of the First Constitutional Affairs Committee and the Fourth Labor Committee; *Federal Deputy* from the State of Campeche, Dist. 1, 1949-52, member of the Legislative Studies Committee (1st and 2nd years), and the First Labor Committee; *Senator* from the State of Campeche, 1952-55; *Governor of Campeche*, 1955-61. e-None. f-Civil and Criminal Judge, Mérida, Yucatán, 1928-29; Attorney General for Yucatán, 1930; Lawyer, Office of the Attorney General for the Federal District, 1935; Assistant Director, Department of Social Security, Federal District Department, 1936; President of the Federal Board of Conciliation and Arbitration for the Federal District, 1937-38; Adviser to the Presidency, 1944-45. g-Director of the Legal Department, Mexican Federation of Labor, 1944. h-Adviser to the Mexican delegation to the United Nations, San Francisco, 1945; author of widely used texts on law. i-Son, Jorge, a professor of law at UNAM and coauthor with his father of a 1972 book on labor law. j-None. k-None. l-D del S, 1 Dec. 1940, 1; D de Y, 26 June 1937, 1; C de D, 1949-51, 92; G of M, 10-11; WWM45, 118-19; DGF56, 6, 90; Peral, 808; C de D, 1940-42, 21.

Trujillo García, Mario
a-Jan. 21, 1920. b-Villahermosa, Tabasco. c-Primary and secondary studies in Villahermosa; preparatory studies in social science at the National Preparatory School; law degree, National School of Law, UNAM. d-*Federal Deputy* from the State of Tabasco, Dist. 1, 1967-70, member of the Petroleum Committee; *Senator* from the State of Tabasco, 1970-71; *Governor of Tabasco*, 1971-77. e-Delegate of the CEN of PRI to the State of México and Guerrero; President of PRI in Guerrero; official of CNOP. f-Managing Director of the Santa Rosalía Mill; adviser to the State of Tabasco; Director General of Social Welfare, Secretariat of Labor, 1951; Private Secretary to the Secretary of Labor; Director of the National Sugar Industry Commission, 1978-82. g-None. i-Nephew of *Francisco Trujillo Gurría*, Governor of Tabasco, 1939-43; son of Juan Trujillo Gurría, mayor of Villahermosa and brother of *Francisco Trujillo Gurría*. j-None. k-None. l-*Excélsior*, 11 Oct. 1978, 22; HA, 6 Sept. 1971; C de D, 1967-70, 82; DGF51, I, 400; Almanaque of Mexico, 44.

Trujillo Gurría, Francisco
(Deceased) a-1900. b-Villahermosa, Tabasco c-Secondary education in Mexico City; law degree. d-Federal Deputy from the State of Tabasco, 1928-30; *Senator* from the State of Tabasco, 1934-39; *Governor of Tabasco*, 1939-43. e-None. f-Subsecretary of Government of the State of Tabasco; Secretary of Government of the State of Tabasco, 1931-35; Provisional Governor of Tabasco, 1931; *Secretary of Labor*, 1943-46. g-None. h-Special diplomatic mission to Europe for *Lázaro Cárdenas*. i-Relative of *Ernesto E. Trujillo Gurría*, federal deputy from Tabasco, 1943-46; became friend of *Manuel Avila Camacho* when he was zone commander of Tabasco, 1932-33; cousin of *Alfonso Gutiérrez Gurría*,

senator from Tabasco, 1940-46; uncle of
Mario Trujillo García, governor of Tabasco, 1971-77; brother of Juan Trujillo,
mayor of Villahermosa. j-Member of
the Constitutional Forces. k-None.
l-HA, 12 Mar. 1943, 11; WWM45, 119;
letter; Enc. Mex., V, 45; Peral, 808-09;
NYT, 3 Mar. 1943, 4; López, 1097;
Almanaque of Tabasco, 154.

Tudón Hurtado, Luis
a-June 21, 1904. b-Ciudad del Maíz, San
Luis Potosí. c-Primary studies, Benito
Juárez School, Ciudad del Maíz; no
secondary studies; no degree. d-*Federal
Deputy* from the State of San Luis Poto-
sí, Dist. 4, 1964-67, 1970-73. e-None.
f-Coordinator of Government, Central
Region, State of San Luis Potosí, 1925;
Director of Purchasing, Secretary of
Agriculture; Director of Regulations,
Department of the Federal District.
g-Secretary of the League of Agrarian
Communities, San Luis Potosí.
h-None. i-Personal assistant to
Saturnino Cedillo; married María
Flores. j-Joined the Revolution, 1916.
k-None. l-C de D, 1964-67; Directorio,
1970-73; C de D, 1970-73.

U

Ugarte, Gerzáyn
(Deceased July 31, 1955) a-Jan. 13,
1881. b-Terrenate, Tlaxcala. c-Primary
studies in Huamantla, Tlaxcala; preparatory studies at the University of Puebla, Puebla; school teacher. d-Federal
Deputy from the State of Tlaxcala, Dist.
2, 1914-16; Local Deputy to the State
Legislature of Tlaxcala, 1908; Deputy to
the Constitutional Convention from the
Federal District, Dist. 3, 1916-18; Senator from the State of Tlaxcala, 1918-20;
Senator from the State of Tlaxcala,
1920-24; *Senator* from the State of Tlaxcala, 1946-52, member of the Foreign
and Domestic Trade Committee, the

Gran Comisión, the First National
Defense Committee, the First Instruc-
tive Section of the Grand Jury and the
First Balloting Group. e-Supported
General Bernardo Reyes for Vice
President of Mexico; member of the
Antireelectionist Party; campaigned for
Francisco Madero. f-Private Secretary
to Próspero Cahuantzi, Governor of
Tlaxcala; Minister to Venezuela,
Colombia and Ecuador, 1918-20; Sub-
director of Inspectors, Traffic Depart-
ment, Federal Highway Police, 1935-40;
Director of the Department of Traffic,
Federal Highway Police, 1940-46, 1952-
55. g-None. h-Director of *El Liberal*
with Venustiano Carranza. i-Son of
Apolinar Ugarte and Dolores Rodríguez.
j-Member of the Staff of Venustiano
Carranza, 1914-15; rank of First Captain, 1915. k-Representative of General
Arnulfo Gómez in the United States,
1927; representative of General Gonzalo
Escobar in the United States, 1929; had
to leave school to work in the textile
factories of Puebla and Tlaxcala.
l-DGF51, I, 8-14; C de S, 1946-52; DP70,
320; PS, 6098; Noriega, 479.

Ulloa Ortiz, Manuel
(Deceased May 30, 1975) c-Combined
secondary and preparatory studies at the
National Preparatory School, 1924-28;
law degree, National School of Law,
UNAM, 1928-32; Professor, National
School of Law, UNAM, 1934-69.
d-None. e-Member of the CEN of PAN,
1939-49; author of numerous pamphlets
for PAN. f-None. g-Founder of the
National Union of Catholic Students,
1931. h-Subdirector General of the
Bank of Mexico and London. i-Son of
lawyer Manuel G. Ulloa; greatly
influenced by *Manuel Gómez Morín*,
his law school professor; among his
students was *José González Torres*,
President of PAN, 1958-62. j-None.
k-None. l-Letter; Mabry.

Unzueta Lorenzana, Gerardo
a-Aug. 3, 1925. b-Tampico, Tamaulipas
c-Early education unknown; one year of
legal studies; two years of studies at the
National School of Plastic Arts. d-*Plurinominal Federal Deputy* from the
Communist Coalition of the Left, 1979-
82, member of the Social Security and
the Department of the Federal District
Committees. e-Joined the PCM, 1946;
member of the Central Committee and
the Executive Committee of the
Mexican Communist Party, 1960;
Director of the official paper of the
PCM, 1960-63. f-None. g-Organizer of
the General Union of Workers and
Peasants. h-Director of *La Voz de
México*, 1979-81. j-None. k-None.
l-Protag., 341; C de D, 1979-82.

Uranga Gutiérrez, Luis E.
a-Jan. 21, 1947. b-Chihuahua, Chihuahua. c-Early education unknown;
college degree. d-None. e-None.
f-Assistant to the Coordinator and
Subcoordinator, 1968-69, Assistant to
the General Subcoordinator, 1969-71,
Assistant to the Director General, 1971-
72, and Chief, Office of Promotion,
1972-73, all of the National Tourism
Council; adviser, Private Fund for
Tourism Development, 1976; Director
General of Promotion, National Tourism Council, 1976-79; *Subsecretary of
Operations*, Secretariat of Tourism,
1980-82. g-None. j-None. k-None.
l-Protag., 341; DAPC, 1981, 141.

Urbina y Frías, Salvador
(Deceased Sept. 12, 1961) a-June 4,
1885. b-Mexico City. c-Primary studies
at a private school and public school
No. 5, Mexico City; secondary studies,
Colegio de Joaquín Noreña; preparatory
studies, National Preparatory School;
law degree, National School of Law,
UNAM, 1902-07, with a thesis on the
conflict of administrative laws in
international law; Professor of Political

Economy, National School of Law,
UNAM, 1912; Professor of Civil
Proceedings, National School of Law,
UNAM. d-*Senator* from the Federal
District, 1952-58. e-None. f-Agent of
the Ministerio Público of the District
Court of Durango, 1909; Oficial Mayor
of the Supreme Court of Mexico, 1910-
12; First Agent of the Ministerio Públi-
co, 1913; First Agent of the Ministerio
Público, Office of the Attorney General
of Mexico, 1914; Presidential negotiator
to Carranza, 1914; Director of the
Advisory Department, Secretariat of the
Treasury, 1915-16; Oficial Mayor of the
Secretariat of the Treasury; Attorney
General of Mexico; Justice of the
Supreme Court of Mexico, 1923-35;
President of the Supreme Court, 1929-
34; Subsecretary of the Treasury, 1922,
Interim Secretary of the Treasury, 1922;
Justice of the Supreme Court, 1940;
President of the Supreme Court, 1941-
46, 1946-51; Director of the National
Lottery, 1958. g-None. h-Delegate to
the Pan American Conference, 1928;
private law practice, 1914-15, 1935-40;
founder and principal author of *Mexican
Petroleum Review*, 1915. i-Son of
Manuel Urbina, a physician; married
Leticia Bolland. j-None. k-Gruening
considered him completely honest as a
public official in the 1920s. l-Gruening,
504; WWM45, 119; DGF56, 6; Peral,
811; EBW46, 411; DGF47, 29-30; DP70,
2201; HA, 14 Dec. 1951, 6; Ind. Biog.,
160-61; Enc. Mex., XII, 1977, 277.

Urquizo (Benavides), Francisco L.
(Deceased Apr. 6, 1969) a-Oct. 4, 1891.
b-San Pedro de las Colonias, Coahuila
c-Primary education in Torreón,
Coahuila; secondary education at the
Liceo Fournier, Mexico City; no degree.
d-None. e-None. f-Oficial Mayor of the
Secretariat of War; Subsecretary of War
(in charge of the ministry), 1920; Director of the Federal Office of the Treasury,
Pachuca, Hidalgo; Bureau Director, Se-

cretariat of the Treasury, 1930-34; Chief
of Staff, Secretariat of National Defense;
Subsecretary of National Defense,
1940-45; *Secretary of National Defense,*
1945-46; Director of the Military
Industry Department, 1952-58. g-None.
h-Author of many books and articles on
the history of the Revolution. i-Parents
were campesinos; he was forced into the
Federal Army for disobeying the
hacendado; friend of *Matías Ramos
Santos* and *Marcelino García Barragán.*
j-2nd Lieutenant in the Federal Army,
1911; joined Madero, 1913; Brigadier
General, 1920; Chief of Military
Operations in Veracruz, 1918; Military
Zone Commander, 1938-40; member of
the Presidential Council for National
Defense, 1959-69. k-Retired from the
Army but later rejoined, reaching the
rank of Division General. l-WWM45,
119; DBM68, 612; DGF56, 529; *Hoy,* 19
Apr. 1969, 8; DP70, 1104-05;
STYRBIWW54, 299; Peral, 814; Strode,
261; EBW46, 1148; *Siempre,* 4 Feb.
1959, 6; Enc. Mex., XII, 1977, 279-80.

Uruchurtu, Ernesto Peralta
a-Feb. 28, 1906. b-Hermosillo, Sonora.
c-Primary studies in Alamos, and at the
Escuela Normal, Hermosillo, Sonora;
secondary studies at the Escuela
Normal, Hermosillo; law studies,
National School of Law, UNAM, 1925-
29, degree in 1931. d-None. e-Auxiliary
Subsecretary during the *Alemán*
presidential campaign, 1946; *Secretary
General of the CEN of PRI,* 1946; first
party position, 1937; State Chairman of
the Regional Committee of PRI, Sonora.
f-Justice of the State Supreme Court of
Sonora under Governor Yocupicio;
Judge, State Court, Nogales, Sonora;
agent of the Ministerio Público of the
State of Sonora; adviser, Department of
Legal Affairs, Secretariat of Agriculture
and Livestock; legal adviser to the
National Bank of Ejido Credit; Director,
Department of Legal Affairs, Secretariat

of Agriculture; Director of the Legal
Department, National Bank of Ejido
Credit, 1940-46; *Subsecretary of
Government,* 1946-51; *Secretary of
Government,* Oct. 14, 1951-52; *Head of
the Federal District,* 1952-58, 1958-64,
1964-66. g-None. h-Practicing lawyer,
Ciudad Obregón, 1937; practicing
lawyer, 1967-70. i-Son of Dr. *Gustavo
A. Uruchurtu,* Senator from Sonora,
1946-52, and María Luisa Peralta;
attended UNAM with *Miguel Alemán,
Antonio Carrillo Flores, Andrés Serra
Rojas,* and *Alfonso Noriega;* nephew of
Francisco Martínez Peralta, Federal
Deputy from Sonora. j-None.
k-Precandidate for the PRI presidential
nomination, 1958, but considered too
close to the right wing; precandidate for
Governor of Sonora, 1972; resigned as
Head of the Federal District in the
midst of an anti-corruption campaign
after the mishandling of a squatters'
affair; precandidate for Governor of
Sonora, 1978. l-D del S, 6 Dec. 1946;
HA, 15 Feb. 1952, 3; *Quién Será,* 136-
37; Morton, 63; Q es Q, 592; HA, 7 Dec.
1964, 21; DGF56, 465; HA, 8 Dec. 1958,
30, 2 Nov. 1964, 30; WWMG, 39-40;
Excélsior, 23 Nov. 1977, 18; HA, 16
Aug. 1946; NYT, 28 July, 1957, 2, Scott,
78; WNM, 230.

Uruchurtu, Gustavo A.
b-Hermosillo, Sonora c-Medical degree
(Surgeon), National School of Medicine,
UNAM. d-Federal Deputy from the
Federal District, Dist. 15, 1928-30;
Senator from the State of Sonora, 1946-
52. e-None. f-Director of Hygenic
Education, Secretariat of Public Educa-
tion; Director of the Department of
Disinfection, General Hospital, Mexico
City. g-None. h-Author of numerous
articles on medical subjects; specialist
in urology; internship at the General
Hospital, Mexico City i-Father of
Ernesto P. Uruchurtu, Head of the
Department of the Federal District,

1952-66; married María Luisa Peralta.
j-None. k-None. l-C de S, 1946-52;
Peral, 814; López, 1105.

Urzua Flores, María Guadalupe
a-Dec. 12, 1922. b-San Martín Hidalgo,
Jocotepec, Jalisco. c-Primary studies at
the Joséfa Ortiz de Domínguez School,
San Martín Hidalgo; secondary studies
in Guadalajara, Jalisco, and at the Rural
Normal School, Zocoalco de Torres;
studies at the Pedro J. Vizcarra School of
Commerce and Accounting, Guadalajara, Jalisco (3 years). d-Council-
woman of San Martín Hidalgo, 1953-55;
Federal Deputy from the State of
Jalisco, Dist. 11, 1955-58, member of
the Second Government Committee
and the Second Balloting Committee;
Federal Deputy from the State of
Jalisco, Dist. 10, 1964-67, member of
the Public Assistance Committee and
the National Lands Committee; *Federal
Deputy* from the State of Jalisco, Dist.
9, 1970-73, member of the First Ejido
Committee, the Small Agricultural
Properties Committee, and the National
Lands Committee; *Federal Deputy* from
the State of Jalisco, Dist. 9, 1976-79.
e-Secretary of Women's Action for PRI,
San Martín Hidalgo, 1948-50; member
of the National Women's Council of
PRI, 1958-60; Subdirector of the
National Women's Directorate of PRI,
1965. f-Ejido Commissioner for San
Martín Hidalgo, Jalisco; Secretary of the
Civic and Moral Improvement Board,
San Martín Hidalgo, 1949-52; Solicitor
for the Department of Plaints, Office of
Agrarian Affairs, Secretariat of the
Presidency, 1961-63. g-Founding
member of the CNC, 1938; Secretary of
Women's Action, Peasants Committee,
San Martín Hidalgo, 1951-53; Secretary
of Women's Action, League of Agrarian
Communities and Peasants, Jalisco,
1938, 1951-53, 1966-69; Secretary of
Women's Action, CEN of the CNC,
1953-56, 1958, 1964-67. h-Nurse, Green

Cross, Mexico City, and in Guadalajara.
j-None. k-Served more times as a
federal deputy from 1955 to 1979 than
any other Mexican woman. l-Directorio, 1970-72; C de D, 1955-57, 1970-72,
139, 1964-66, 78, 94; DGF56, 25, 34, 35;
C de D, 1976-79, 80; Ind. Biog., 161-62.

Uscanga Uscanga, César
b-Ignacio de la Llave, Veracruz.
c-Secondary studies at Secondary School
No. 3, Mexico City; preparatory studies
at the National Preparatory School;
chemical engineering degree, National
School of Biological Sciences; teacher at
the Rafael Dondé School; Director of
the Rafael Dondé School. d-None.
e-None. f-Director of Technical,
Industrial, and Commercial Schools,
Secretariat of Public Education; Subdirector of Technical, Industrial, and
Foreign Schools, Secretariat of Public
Education; Director of Technological
and Industrial Education, Secretariat of
Public Education, 1970-74; *Subsecretary
of Intermediate, Technical, and Higher
Education*, Mar. 15, 1974 to 1976;
Subsecretary of Technical Education,
1977; Adviser to the Secretary of Public
Education, 1977-82. g-None. j-None.
k-None. l-HA, 25 Mar. 1974, 10;
DPE71, 106; DAPC, 1977, 71; *Excélsior*,
16 June 1976, 4.

V

Valadés, José C.
(Deceased 1976) a-Dec. 10, 1902.
b-Mazatlán, Sinaloa. c-Early education
unknown; preparatory studies at the
University of Guadalajara and the Free
Preparatory School, Mexico City;
studies at Saint Vincent College, Los
Angeles, California; studies at the
National Homeopathic College, Mexico
City; no degree; Professor of History,
UNAM, 1941-45. d-None. e-Secretary
of the Latin American Bureau of the

Third Communist International, 1922; supported José Vasconcelos for president, 1929; Secretary General of the Federation of the Peoples Parties, 1946. f-Private Secretary to the Secretary of Foreign Relations, *Ezequiel Padilla*, 1940-42; Ambassador to Lebanon, Iran and Syria, 1952-53; Ambassador to Colombia, 1953-56; Ambassador to Uruguay, 1956-57; Ambassador to Portugal, 1963-66. g-Founder and director of the World Youth Organization, 1920; organizer of the Communist Youth Organization; secretary general of a labor union, 1921. h-Author of dozens of books; Director of *El Correo de Occidente*, Mazatlán, 1942-45. i-Son of Francisco Valadés, a successful pharmacist, and Inés R. Valadés; grandfather, Juan Jacobo Valadés, an important man of letters, physician, and weathly businessman; members of his father's family were actively involved in Sinaloan politics; son, *Diego Valadés Ríos*, was a subsecretary of health, 1984. j-None. k-Skirius, 205; WWM45, 120; Enc. Mex., XII, 1977, 290-91; DBGM, 422.

Valadés Ríos, Diego
a-May 8, 1945. b-Mazatlán, Sinaloa. c-Primary studies at Modern Gymnasium José Pedro Varela, Bogotá, 1950-56; secondary and preparatory studies, Colegio Franco Español. 1956-62; legal studies, Clasical University, Portugal, 1963-66; law degree, National School of Law, UNAM, 1967-69, with a thesis on social law; researcher, Institute of Legal Research, UNAM, 1970-81; professor, National School of Law, UNAM, 1973-79; Director General of Cultural Publicity, UNAM, 1973-76; general counsel, UNAM, 1977-80; Coordinator of Humanities, UNAM, 1981-87. d-None. e-Joined PRI, 1962. f-Auxiliary Legal Coordinator, Coordinator of Health Services, Presidency of Mexico, 1981-82; Director General of Legal Affairs, Secretariat of Government, 1982-84;

Subsecretary of Health Regulation, Secretariat of Health, 1984-85; Secretary General of Government, State of Sinaloa, 1987-88; Ambassador to Guatemala, 1988; Coordinator of Legal Affairs, Department of the Federal District, 1988-91; *Secretary General of Metropolitan Coordination*, Department of the Federal District, 1991-92; *Attorney General of Justice of the Federal District*, 1992-94. g-None. h-None. i-Son of *José C. Valadés*, historian and ambassador, and Inés Rios Flores; married Patricia Galeana Herrera, teacher. j-None. k-None. l-DBGM, 422; *El Nacional*, 23 June 1992, 29; DBGM92, 376.

Valadez Montoya, Baltazar Ignacio
a-June 2, 1944. b-Puebla, Puebla. c-Primary studies completed; studies in journalism from the Carlos Septién García School, 1966-68. d-*Plurinominal Federal Deputy* from the PDM, 1982-85, member of the Human Dwellings and Public Works Committee and the Foreign Relations Committee. e-Secretary of Peasant Action, National Sinarquist Union, 1965-67; Head of the National Sinarquist Union, Federal District, 1965-67; Director of the weekly paper *Orden* of the National Sinarquist Union, 1967-70; founding member of the PDM, 1970; candidate of the PDM for Federal Deputy from the Federal District, Dist. 30, 1979-82; candidate of the PDM for governor of Puebla, 1980; Secretary of Organization of the National Sinarquist Union, 1980-82. f-None. g-None. i-Married Martha Silvia Tavera. j-None. k-None. l-Lehr, 567; Directorio, 1982-85; C de D, 1982-85.

Valadez Montoya, Miguel José
a-Mar. 22, 1949. b-Aguascalientes, Aguascalientes. c-Primary and secondary studies in Aguascalientes; preparatory studies in Aguascalientes; law degree, National School of Law,

UNAM, August 1, 1976; Professor of Law, Carlos Septién García School of Journalism. d-*Federal Deputy* (Party Deputy from the PDM), 1979-82. e-Secretary of Labor Action of the Mexican Democratic Party, 1979. f-Lawyer, Legal Department, Secretary of Communications and Transportation, 1979. g-None. h-None. j-None. k-None. l-HA, 12 Feb. 1979, 23; C de D, 1979-82.

Valdemar Lima, Hilda Luisa
a-Apr. 17, 1940. b-Puebla, Puebla. c-Completed secondary studies; teaching certificate; English teacher, Belisario Domínguez Higher Normal School, 1972-77. d-Local Deputy to the State Legislature of Puebla, 1977-80; *Alternate Federal Deputy* from the State of Puebla, Dist. 1, 1976-79; *Federal Deputy* from the State of Puebla, Dist. 1, 1982-85, member of the Social Security and the Labor and Social Welfare Committees. e-None. f-None. g-Member of the Radio Workers Union; Secretary of Organization and Publicity, 27th Delegation, SNTE, Puebla; Secretary of Social Action of the CTM, Puebla, 1972-83; Secretary of Workers Action, ANFER, Puebla, 1976-81; Subdirector of Information, CEN of ANFER, 1981-82; Secretary General of the Workers Federation of Women's Organizations, Puebla, 1982. h-Radio announcer, Gold Stars Station, Puebla, 1975-82. i-Daughter of Luis Valdemar González, railroad worker, and Consuelo Lima Sánchez, social worker and teacher; widow of Roberto Camacho Sologuren, public accountant. j-None. k-None. l-Directorio, 1982-85; Lehr, 378; C de D, 1982-85; Lehr, 378; DBGM, 614.

Valdés, José Ramón
a-Aug. 31, 1888. b-Santiago Pasquiaro, Durango. c-Primary and secondary studies in Durango; no degree. d-Federal Deputy from the State of Durango, Dist. 1, 1928-30; Substitute Governor of Durango, 1930-31; Federal Deputy from the State of Durango, Dist. 5, 1930-32, member of the Gran Comisión; *Substitute Governor of Durango*, 1947-50. e-None. f-Inspector of Police, Durango; Oficial Mayor of the Federal Auditor's Office, Secretariat of the Treasury; Oficial Mayor of the Chamber of Deputies. g-None. h-None. j-Commander of military forces in Durango; rank of Colonel. k-None. l-HA, 6 Feb. 1948, 8; Peral, 820; López, 1109.

Valdés (González Salas), Renata María
a-July 6, 1938. b-Federal District. c-Early education unknown; degree in Industrial Relations, Ibero-American University, 1962-64; MA, Sorbonne, Paris, 1965; professor, Ibero-American University, 1966-82. d-None. e-None. f-Office Head, Transportation Service, Pemex, Paris, France, 1967-72; Manager, International Trade, Maya International, S.A., 1972-77; Director, Special Telephone Information Service, Teleinformation Service of Mexico, S.A., 1977-80; Assistant Manager of Corporate Banks, Foreign Trade Bank, 1982; *Oficial Mayor of Tourism*, 1982-86. g-None. h-Director of Personnel, Rodecarga, S.A., 1966-67. i-Daughter of Fernando Valdés Villarreal, surgeon, and Renée González Salas; married Alejandro Danón Gattegno, industrialist. j-None. k-First woman graduate of a private university to reach the position of oficial mayor. l-Q es QAP; DBGM, 423.

Valdés Ornelas, Oscar
a-Oct. 22, 1922. b-Guadalajara, Jalisco. c-Early education unknown; medical studies in veterinary medicine from the Military Medical School, 1931-33, and from the National School of Veterinary Medicine, UNAM, 1934-35, graduating from UNAM, 1935; professor, postgraduate program, National School of Biological Sciences, IPN, 1941-51;

Secretary, 1948-49, Professor of General
Pathology and Infectious Diseases,
1951-67, Dean, 1954-59, all at the
National School of Veterinary Medi-
cine, UNAM; Director, National
Institute of Livestock Research, 1962,
1965-67. d-None. e-None. f-Veterinar-
ian, State of Sonora, 1936, State of
Coahuila, 1937, and at Livestock
Institute, Secretariat of Agriculture and
Livestock, 1937-45; *Subsecretary of
Livestock*, 1962-65; Director General of
Animal Health, Secretariat of Agricul-
ture and Hydraulic Resources, 1981;
Subsecretary of Livestock, 1981-82,
1982-84. g-None. h-Author of many
scientific works on livestock; Alternate
President of the Board of Albamex, S.A.,
Nutrimex, S.A., and Fermex, S.A.. i-Son
of Ceferino Valdés Cepeda, business-
man, and Amparo Ornelas Anguiano;
married Gertrud Krieg Beschta. j-None.
k-None. l-Q es QAP, 212; DPE65, 98;
HA, 3 Aug. 1981, 24; DGF66, 28;
DBGM, 423-24.

Valdez Montoya, Alfredo
a-1921. b-Ahome, Sinaloa. c-Early
education unknown; studies in economics, National School of Economics,
UNAM; economics degree, School of
Economics, University of Guadalajara,
1943. d-*Governor of Sinaloa*, 1969-74.
e-None. f-Employee of the Secretariat
of Public Education; employee of the
Secretariat of the Treasury; Treasurer of
the State of Sinaloa, 1968. g-None.
i-Married Judith Gaxiola, related to
Francisco Gaxiola. j-None. k-Accused
by *Proceso* of representing large landowners' interests in Sinaloa as governor.
l-*Proceso*, 7 Aug. 1978, 12; DNED, 255.

Valenzuela Ceballos, Mariano
a-July 26, 1908. b-Mapimi, Durango.
c-Early education unknown; completed
two years of studies in labor law; no degree. d-*Federal Deputy* from the State
of Chihuahua, Dist. 2, 1952-55; *Federal

Deputy* from the State of Chihauhua,
Dist. 1, 1967-70. e-None. f-None.
g-None. i-Married Aniceta García.
j-None. k-None. l-C de D, 1967-70;
Directorio, 1967-70; C de D, 1952-55.

Valenzuela (Esquerro), Gilberto
a-Dec. 1, 1922. b-Federal District.
c-Primary studies, St. Patrick School, El
Paso, Texas; secondary studies, English
School and Colegio Francés Morelos,
Mexico City; civil engineering degree,
National School of Engineering,
UNAM, 1947. d-None. e-None.
f-Director, Office of Paving, Department
of Public Works, Department of the Federal District, 1952-53; Chief, Technical
Department, Controller, Department of
the Federal District, 1953; adviser, Head
of the Department of the Federal District, *Ernesto P. Uruchurtu*, 1953; Subdirector of the Department of Construction, Department of Public Works,
Department of the Federal District,
1955-58; Subdirector General of Public
Works, Department of the Federal District, 1958-59; Director General of Public Works, Department of the Federal
District, 1959-64; *Secretary of Public
Works*, 1964-70; *Secretary of Works and
Services*, Department of the Federal
District, 1978-79. g-None. h-Consulting engineer for Ford, Bacon, and Davis;
private engineering practice; engineer
for National Railroads of Mexico;
consulting engineer to the Department
of Public Works, 1953. i-Student of
Antonio Dovalí Jaime at the National
School of Engineering and later worked
with him in several positions; brother of
Raúl Valenzuela Esquerro, Subdirector
General of the Consular Service,
Secretariat of Foreign Relations, 1967;
son of *Gilberto Valenzuela*, Secretary of
Government, 1923-25 and Justice of the
Supreme Court, 1953-60. j-None.
k-None. l-HA, 7 Dec. 1964, 19; DGF56,
467; *Hoy*, 12 July 1969, 10; DBM68,
615; WWMG, 40; *El Universal*, 1 Dec.

1964; *Libro de Oro*, xxxiv; D de Y, 2 Dec. 1964, 2; HA, 5 Dec. 1977, 3, 9 Jan. 1978, 25; *Excélsior*, 10 Feb. 1978, 5.

Valenzuela (Galindo), Gilberto
(Deceased Feb. 9, 1978) a-Apr. 27, 1891. b-Sahuaripa, Sonora. c-Primary studies in Sonora under Epifanio Vieyra; preparatory studies at the Boys Liceo, Guadalajara, Jalisco; law studies, National School of Law, UNAM, 1910-14, law degree; Director, Bacanora Elementary School, 1906. d-Local Deputy to the State Legislature of Sonora, 1916. e-Candidate for president, 1928; supported Geneneral *Almazán* for president, 1940. f-Governor of Sonora, 1916-17; Subsecretary in charge of Government, 1920; Secretary of Government, 1922-25; Minister to England, 1925-28; *Justice of the Supreme Court*, 1953-60. g-President of the Literary Center of the Fiat Lux Preparatory School, Guadalajara; founded the Student Antireelectionist Union, 1910. h-None. i-Father of *Gilberto Valenzuela Esquerro*, Secretary of Public Works, 1964-70; son of Federico Valenzuela and Eustaquia Galindo; married Olga Esquerro. j-Joined the Constitutionalists under Carranza in Veracruz, 1914; chief military instructor, Jalapa, Veracruz; agent of the Ministerio Público, Military Attorney General; opposed Carranza, 1920; supported the Escobar movement, 1929. k-In exile, Mesa, Arizona, 1929; offered post of Justice of the Supreme Court, 1928, but broke ties with Calles; offered post of Secretary of Foreign Relations by *Emilio Portes Gil*, 1929, but refused. l-López, 1111-1112; *Excélsior*, 10 Feb. 1978, 5; Balboa, 46; Meyer, No. 12, 93.

Valero (Becerra), Ricardo
a-Nov. 29, 1942. b-Federal District. c-Early education unknown; studies in political science, School of Political and Social Science, UNAM, 1961-63; degree

in international relations, Colegio de México, 1964-66; MA in international relations, Colegio de México, 1967-68, with a thesis on the "Fundamentals and Tendencies in the Foreign Policy of Brazil"; Professor of Political Science, Center for International Studies, Colegio de México; Professor of Political Science, School of Political and Social Science, UNAM; Professor of Political Science, Autonomous Metropolitan University. d-*Plurinominal Federal Deputy* from the PRD, 1991-94. e-Director, *Linea*, CEN of PRI, 1975-76; Secretary of the National Consultation Committee of Ideology and Programs of the CEN of PRI, 1976; Subsecretary of International Affairs of the CEN of PRI, 1981-82; *Secretary of International Affairs of the CEN of PRI* 1982; joined the PRD, 1989; Secretary of Foreign Relations of the CEN of the PRD, 1989-93. f-Chief, Department of Studies, Division of Documents and Presidential Addresses, Secretariat of the Presidency, 1971; Subdirector of Studies, Division of Documents and Presidential Addresses, Secretariat of the Presidency, 1972; Director General of Documents and International Affairs, Secretariat of Labor, 1972-76; Coordinator of the Center of Documentation, Secretariat of Government, 1978; Director General of the Government Printing Office, 1978-82; *Subsecretary of International Cooperation*, Secretariat of Foreign Relations, 1985-88. g-None. h-None. i-Son of Francisco Valero Recio, lawyer and military officer, and Eugenia Becerra Vila; married Nuria Pie Contisoch, psychologist. j-None. k-None. l-IEPES; Protag., 346; Q es QAP; DBGM87, 394; DBGM92, 595; DBGM, 427.

Vallejo, Demetrio
(Deceased Dec. 24, 1985) a-1910. b-Espinal, Tehuantepec, Oaxaca. c-Completed three years of primary; self-educated. d-*Plurinominal Federal*

Deputy from PSUM, 1985. e-Militant, Socialist Unified Action, with Valentín Campa and Hernán Laborde (later Workers Peasant Party); cofounder of the Mexican Workers Party with *Heberto Castillo*, 1974; Secretary of Organization, Mexican Workers Party, 1974-83. f-None. g-Began labor organizing in Coatzacoalcos, Veracruz, 1934; active in the CTM under *Vicente Lombardo Toledano*; Secretary General of the Federation of Petroleum Workers of the South; organizer, National Petroleum Workers Union; Secretary General of the STFRM, 1958-59. h-Employee, Express Department, National Railroads of Mexico, Coatzacoalcos, Veracruz, 1958. i-From a Zapotec family. j-None. k-Directed the 1958-59 railroad workers strike; imprisoned under the social dissolution law, 1959-70; removed from post in the Mexican Workers Party, 1983. l-Protag., 346; HA, 21 Mar. 1983, 7, 7 Jan. 1986, 14; *Excélsior*, 26 Dec. 1985, 1.

Valles Vivar, Tomás
a-Oct. 31, 1900. b-Camargo, Chihuahua. c-Primary studies in Camargo; secondary studies in Camargo; no degree. d-*Federal Deputy* from the State of Chihuahua, Dist. 1, 1943-46; *Senator* from the State of Chihuahua, 1958-64, member of the First Credit, Money, and Credit Institutions Committee, the First Tariffs and Foreign Trade Committee, President of the First Mines Committee and the Special Livestock Committee. e-None. f-Treasurer of the National Railroads of Mexico; *Director General of Conasupo*, 1952-56; minister to Lisbon, Portugal, 1956-57. g-None. h-Businessman in Camargo; livestock dealer. j-None. k-Resigned from Conasupo because of internal policy disputes on imports and food prices, Mar. 10, 1956. l-Func. 163; C de S, 1961-64, 71-72; D de Y, 6 Dec. 1952, 1; NYT, 11 Mar. 1956, 24.

Valner Onjas, Gregorio
a-June 26, 1929. b-Toluca, México. c-Primary studies in Toluca; medical degree, National School of Medicine, UNAM, 1954; postgraduate studies in psychiatry and psychoanalysis, Mexican Psychoanalytical Association, and the University of Chicago; Professor of Psychoanalysis, UNAM; Professor of Psychoanalysis, Mexican Association of Psychotherapy, 1967-69. d-None. e-Joined PRI as a member of the IEPES, 1970; member of the Advisory Council of the CEPES of the State of México; Coordinator of Advisers to the IEPES in public housing; Director of the CEPES of the Federal District during *José López Portillo's* presidential campaign, 1975-76. f-President of the Regulatory Commission on Land Tenure, State of México, 1970-75; *Subsecretary of Public Housing*, 1977-82. g-Founding Director General of the Institute of Urban Action and Social Integration, State of México, 1970. h-Practicing physician, Benito Juárez General Hospital, Mexico City; physician, Central Military Hospital; physician, National Institute of Nutrition; intern, National Institute of Cardiology and Michael Reese Hospital (Chicago). i-Son of Kissel Valner and Cecilia Onjas. j-None. k-President, Human Rights Commission, United Nations, Mexico, 1980-81. l-Letter; DAPC, 72.

Varela Mayorga, Juan. J.
a-May 1, 1915. b-Huejúcar, Jalisco. c-Primary studies at the Zaragoza School, Zacatecas, Zacatecas; secondary studies at the Institute of Sciences, Zacatecas (3 years); preparatory studies at the National Preparatory School, Federal District (2 years); studies at the National School of Law, UNAM; no degree. d-Council member in León, Guanajuato, 1952-54; Mayor of Fresnillo, Zacatecas; local deputy to the State Legislature of Guanajuato; *Federal*

Deputy from the State of Guanajuato, Dist. 4, 1964-67; *Federal Deputy* from the State of Guanajuato, Dist. 6, 1970-73, member of the Second Public Education Committee and the Legal Complaints Committee (1st year); *Federal Deputy* from the State of Guanajuato, Dist. 3, 1976-79, member of the Second Labor Committee, the Complaints Committee, the Pension Subcommittee and the Cooperatives Development Commitee. e-None. f-General Inspector of Alcohol, Industry, and Commerce, State of Guanajuato. g-Secretary General of the CTM in Guanajuato, 1962; Secretary General of Local 12 of the Union of Cement Workers, León, Guanajuato; Secretary to the Secretary General of the Cement Workers Union. h-Technician for Portland Cement. i-Married Olga Flores. j-None. k-None. l-C de D, 1970-72, 139, 1964-66; Directorio, 1970-72; C de D, 1976-79, 81; *Excélsior*, 31 Aug. 1976, C1.

Vargas Bravo, David
a-Jan. 2, 1913. b-San Luis Potosí, San Luis Potosí. c-Primary education in Mexico City; secondary studies at the Felipe Carrillo Puerto Night School, Mexico City; preparatory studies at the National Preparatory School in social sciences; law degree, National School of Law, UNAM, 1953. d-*Senator* from the State of San Luis Potosí, 1952-58, President of the Second Labor Committee, member of the First Instructive Section of the Grand Jury; First Secretary of the Electrical Industry Committee and Second Secretary of the Railroad Committee. e-None. f-Director, Electrical Department, Director of Real Property, Director of the Legal Department, Assistant to the Controller General, Subdirector and Director of Finances, and General Attorney, all for the National Railroads of Mexico. g-Cofounder of the National Railroad

Workers Union (later the STFRM), 1931; Secretary of Local 16 of the STFRM; general representative of the STFRM, 1938; representative of labor on the Federal Board of Arbitration and Conciliation, 1948; Secretary General of the STFRM, 1951-54. h-Began working for the National Railroads of Mexico as a laborer, 1927; later an electrician. i-Active in the Unified Socialist Action group with *Valentín Campa*. j-None. k-Forced into exile, 1954-58, for union political activities. l-*Proceso*, 18 Dec. 1976, 18-19; HA, 1 Feb., 1954, 6-7; Ind. Biog., 163; DGF56, 7, 9, 11, 13.

Vargas de Garza Montemayor, Carlota
a-Feb. 8, 1943. b-Monterrey, Nuevo León. c-Early education unknown; economics degree, University of Nuevo León, 1960-65; MA in economics, University College, London, 1965-67; Professor of Economics and Macro Economics, University of Veracruz, 1968-69; Professor of Economics at the Technological Institute of Higher Studies of Monterrey; Researcher, Center for Economic Research, University of Nuevo León. d-Alternate Local Deputy to the State Legislature of Nuevo León, 1973-76; *Federal Deputy* from the State of Nuevo León, Dist. 1, 1976-79; *Federal Deputy* from the State of Nuevo León, Dist. 3, 1982-85, member of the Treasury and the Government Properties and Industrial Development Committees. e-Special Delegate of PRI in Teziutlán, Puebla, 1977; Special Delegate of PRI in León, Guanajuato, 1979. f-Director of the Department of Economic Studies, Division of Planning, 1971-73, Oficial Mayor, 1973-75, and Secretary of Economic Development, 1980-82, all for the State of Nuevo León; g-Secretary of Industry and Commerce, CNOP, Nuevo León, 1980. h-Author of various articles on urban planning. i-Daughter of Carlos Francisco Vargas de León,

surgeon, and Carlota Garza. j-None.
k-None. l-*Excélsior*, 27 Aug. 1976, 1C;
C de D, 1976-79, 1982-85; Directorio,
1982-85; Lehr, 340; Almanaque of
Nuevo León, 27; DBGM, 618.

Vargas Saldaña, Mario
a-Mar. 13, 1935. b-Boca del Río,
Veracruz. c-Early education unknown;
law degree, National School of Law,
UNAM. d-Mayor of Veracruz; *Federal
Deputy* from the State of Veracruz,
Dist. 11, 1964-67, 1973-76, 1982-85,
member of the Gran Comisión, Secre-
tary of the Government and Constitu-
tional Affairs Committee, and member
of the Rules Committee; *Federal
Deputy* from the Federal District, Dist.
30, 1988-91, member of the Govern-
ment and Constitutional Affairs
Committees. e-General Delegate of the
CEN of PRI to Sonora and Nuevo León;
General Delegate of the CEN of PRI to
Coahuila, 1982; Secretary General of
PRI in Sinaloa, Veracruz, and the
Federal District; *Secretary General of
the CEN of PRI*, 1982-84. f-General
Coordinator of Relations, Secretariat of
Public Relations; representative of the
government of Veracruz before the
Technical Council of the Secretariat of
Public Education; Director of Political
and Social Research, Secretariat of Gov-
ernment. g-None. h-None. j-None.
k-None. l-HA, 20 Dec. 1982, 6; Direc-
torio, 1982-85; Lehr, 502; C de D, 1964-
67, 1973-76, 1982-85; DBGM89, 555.

Vasconcelos, Eduardo
(Deceased Apr. 26, 1953) a-Oct. 11,
1895. b-Oaxaca, Oaxaca. c-Primary
studies in Oaxaca; secondary and
preparatory studies at the Instituto of
Arts and Sciences of Oaxaca; law degree
from the National School of Law,
UNAM, 1910 with a thesis on Article
123; professor at the Preparatory School
of Chilpancingo, Guerrero; professor at
the Institute of Arts and Sciences of

Oaxaca, professor at Institute of
Sciences and Letters, Toluca, México.
d-Local deputy to the State Legislature
of Oaxaca; Federal Deputy from the
State of Oaxaca, Dist. 1, 1920-22, 1922-
24, President of the Chamber of De-
puties, 1921. e-Founder of the Socialist
Student Party, 1912. f-Secretary of
Government, Baja California del Norte,
1917; Secretary General of Government
of the State of México, 1926; Attorney
General of Guerrero, 1925-26; Legal
Adviser to the cities of Chilpancingo,
Cuernavaca and Toluca; *Justice of the
Supreme Court*, 1940-46, 1947; Minister
to Italy, 1935-36; Oficial Mayor of the
Secretariat of Government, 1930-32;
Secretary of Government, 1932-34;
Secretary of Public Education, May 9,
1934, to Nov. 30, 1934; *Interim Gover-
nor of Oaxaca*, 1947-50. g-None.
h-None. i-Nephew of José Vasconcelos,
Secretary of Education, 1920-23; son of
Joaquín Vasconcelos. j-Joined the
Revolution under General Mosta in
Sinaloa, 1915; fought under General
Benjamín Hill, 1919. k-None.
l-Gaxiola 90, etc.; Hayner, 214; Enc.
Mex., 42; STYRBIWW54, 1070; Peral,
832-33; López, 1123.

Vasconcelos de Berges, Justina
a-Jan. 1, 1905. b-Toris, Sonora. c-Early
education unknown; teaching certificate; concert diploma, National Conservatory of Music; studies at UNAM;
representative of the School of Music to
the University Council, UNAM.
d-*Federal Deputy* from the State of
Oaxaca, Dist. 5, 1964-67. e-Joined PRI,
1940. f-Director of the National
Institute for the Protection of Children,
Oaxaca, 1964. g-Founder and President
of the Union of Women's Associations;
founder and Secretary General of the
Alliance of Women in Mexico; President of the Womens' Committee of Ex-
Students of the Institute of Oaxaca;
member of the National Newspaper

Editors Union. i-Father a military officer. j-None. k-None. l-Directorio, 1964-67; C de D, 1964-67.

Vásquez Avila, Fernando
a-Sept. 21, 1891. b-Río Verde, San Luis Potosí. c-Early education unknown; graduated with an engineering degree, National Military College; Professor of Math, IPN. d-*Federal Deputy* (Party Deputy from PARM), 1967-70. e-Member of PARM; Vice-president of PARM. f-None. g-None. h-None. i-Friend of General *Juan Barragán*, President of PARM, 1965-74, since boyhood. j-Career military officer; fought in the Revolution; rank of Brigadier General, Feb. 1, 1942; Director of Military Engineering, Secretariat of National Defense. k-None. l-C de D, 1967-70; Directorio, 1967-70.

Vázquez Colmenares, Pedro
a-Nov. 2, 1934. b-Tuxtepec, Oaxaca. c-Early education unknown; Law degree, National School of Law, UNAM, 1960; Professor of Sociology, National Preparatory School, 1959-65; Professor by opposition in Penal Law and Sociology, National School of Law, UNAM, 1962-65; Subdirector of Scholarly Services, UNAM; Director of the National Preparatory School No. 2. d-*Governor of Oaxaca*, 1980-85. e-Subdirector of Youth Action, Regional Executive Committee of PRI for the Federal District, 1955; Oficial Mayor of PRI in the Federal District, 1975-76. f-Agent of the Ministerio Público, Attorney General of Mexico, 1959-64; Private Secretary to the Oficial Mayor of Labor, 1960-63; Private Secretary to the Governor of Baja California del Sur, *Hugo Cervantes del Río*, 1965-70; Private Secretary to the Secretary of the Presidency, *Hugo Cervantes del Río*, 1970-71; *Oficial Mayor of the Secretariat of the Presidency*, 1971-73; Director General of Airports, 1973-74;

Subsecretary of New Population Centers, Secretariat of Agrarian Reform, 1976; Director General of Aero México, 1976-80; Director General of Investigations and National Security, Secretariat of Government, 1985-88; Ambassador to Guatemala, 1988-94. g-President of the National Federation of University Students, 1956; President of the National Association of Law Students, 1957. h-Member of the National Association of Lawyers since 1964; directed conferences at the Schools of Law in Guatemala and El Salvador. i-Son of *Genaro Vázquez*, secretary of labor, and Amparo Colmenares Garmendia; brother, *Genaro Vázquez Colmenares*, served as a Federal Deputy from Oaxaca, 1961-63; married Ana María Guzmán Rodríguez, lawyer. j-None. k-Lost as a precandidate for Governor of Oaxaca, 1974; lost as a precandidate for senator from Oaxaca, 1976. l-HA, 1 Nov. 1971, 5; *Tiempo Mexicano*, 56; *Excélsior*, 16 Oct. 1975, 12; HA, 5 Dec. 1977, 30, 12 Apr. 1976, 32; *Excélsior*, 29 Jan. 1974, 13; HA, 19 Apr. 1980, 32; DBGM89, 363; DBGM92, 382.

Vázquez del Mercado, Antonio
a-Nov. 2, 1903. b-Distrito Federal. c-Primary studies in Puebla, Puebla; enrolled in the Naval Academy, Apr. 8, 1917; Director of the Naval College, 1941. d-*Plurinominal Federal Deputy* from PARM, 1979-82. e-Vice President of PARM, 1977-79. f-Gerente of the Navy Department, Petróleos Mexicanos, S.A.; Secretary General of the Department of the Navy, 1940-41; Naval Attaché to Washington, D.C. 1948; Director General of Fishing and Related Industries, Secretariat of Industry and Commerce, 1960-64; *Secretary of the Navy*, 1964-70. g-None. h-None. i-Son, Antonio, was a director general of the Naval Administrative School; married to Lucia Muñoz de la Guardia. j-Career naval officer;

rank of navy Lieutenant, 1928; commander of the coast guard ship Guaymas, 1928; commander of the naval garrison, Islas Marías, 1929; rank of Captain, Dec. 29, 1943; Director General of the Merchant Marine, 1947-48; rank of Commodore, Dec. 29, 1946; Commander of the 4th Naval Zone; rank of Admiral, 1956; Commander of the Fleet, 1956; rank of Rear Admiral. k-Precandidate of PARM for federal deputy, 1978. l-WWMG, 40; DGF56, 386; HA, 7 Dec. 1964, 18; D de Y, 2 Dec. 1964, 2; DPE61, 65; *Excélsior*, 2 July 1977, 15; HA, 16 Apr. 1979, I; C de D, 1979-82.

Vázquez Nava, María Elena
a-July 1, 1954. b-Federal District. c-Early education unknown; sociology degree, School of Political and Social Sciences, UNAM, 1973-75; economics degree, National School of Economics, UNAM, 1974-77, with a thesis on impact of oil revenues on tax policy; special studies in programming and finance policy, International Monetary Fund, 1979. d-None. e-Joined PRI, 1979; member of the Advisory Council of the IEPES of PRI, 1986; *Secretary of Finances of the CEN of PRI*, 1987-88. f-Analyst and department head, Department of Analysis and Federal Financing, Secretariat of Programming and Budgeting, 1975-79; Auxiliary Subdirector of Tax Analysis and Public Sector Financing, Secretariat of Programming and Budgeting, 1979-81; Technical Coordinator of the Division of Budget Policy, Secretariat of Programming and Budgeting, 1982; Director General of Public Works Standards, Secretariat of Programming and Budgeting, 1982-84; Coordinator General of Federal Public Administration Modernization, Secretariat of Programming and Budgeting, 1984-85; Technical Secretary of Intersectorial Committee of Civil Services and Public Works, Secretariat of

Programming and Budgeting, 1985-87; *Secretary of the Controller General*, 1988-94. g-None. h-None. i-Daughter of Pedro Vázquez López, physician, and María Elena Nava de la Vega, English teacher; married Alfredo Valdés Gaxiola, economist. j-None. k-None. l-DBGM92, 384-85.

Vázquez (Osequerra), Gabino
(Deceased) a-1889. b-Morelia, Michoacán. c-Preparatory studies at the Colegio de San Nicolás, Morelia; law degree, Colegio de San Nicolás, 1924-29; Rector of the Colegio de San Nicolás. d-Federal Deputy from the State of Michoacán, Dist. 1, 1932-34; *Federal Deputy* from the State of Michoacán, Dist. 5, 1964-67. e-Member of the National Committee for *Lázaro Cárdenas's* presidential campaign, 1933-34; Secretary General of the PNR, 1934. f-Judge of the Superior Court of the State of Michoacán; Provisional Governor of Michoacán, 1930-31; Secretary General of Government of the State of Michoacán, 1930-32; Attorney General of Michoacán; personal representative of General *Cárdenas* to the committee writing the 1934 Agrarian Code; *Head of the Department of Colonization and Agrarian Affairs*, 1934-40. g-None. i-Married Consuelo Alfano; classmate with *Alberto Bremauntz* and *José María Mendoza Pardo* at the Colegio de San Nicolás; uncle of *Luis Ignacio Vázquez Cano*, a subsecretary of the Secretariat of the Controller General, 1989. j-None. k-None. l-Peral, 47, 48; Kirk, 3, 118; Gáxiola, 448; Peral, 834; López, 1127; Bremauntz, 93; Meyer, 227.

Vázquez Pallares, Natalio
(Deceased Mar. 26, 1981) a-Jan. 5, 1913. b-Coalcomán, Michoacán. c-Preparatory studies at the Colegio de San Nicolas de Hidalgo, Morelia, Michoacán; studies in law, University of Gua-

dalajara and from the School of Law, University of Michoacán; law degree, National School of Law, UNAM; Rector of the University of Michoacán, 1939. d-*Federal Deputy* from the State of Michoacán, Dist. 8, 1949-52, member of the Editorial Committee, the Legislative Studies Committee, the Petroleum Committee, and the Second Constitutional Affairs Committee; Secretary of the Second Constitutional Affairs Committee (2nd year); *Senator* from the State of Michoacán, 1958-64, member of the Gran Comisión, the National Lands Committee, the Special Legislative Studies Committee, and the Lands and Natural Resources Committee; substitute member of the First Labor Committee; President of the Agriculture and Development Committee and the Second Ejido Committee. e-Adviser to PRI, 1981. f-Various judgeships in the state of Michoacán; private secretary to the Governor of Michoacán; Attorney General of Michoacán; Ambassador to Yugoslavia, 1965-68; agrarian adviser No. 4, Department of Agrarian Affairs and Colonization, 1970-72; Subdirector General of the National Fund for Ejido Development, 1973-75; Director General of the Center of Historical Studies of Agrarianism in Mexico, Secretariat of Government, 1980. g-Leader of the Federation of Socialist Students of the West; director of Unified Socialist Youth of Mexico. i-Son of Natalio Vázquez Sánchez, rancher, and Reinalda Pallares. k-Supported *Cuauhtémoc Cárdenas* for Governor of Michoacán, 1973; precandidate for Governor of Michoacán, 1962; resigned as ambassador, 1968. l-Func., 267; C de S, 1961-64, 72; C de D, 1949-51, 93; DGF51, 23, 32, 35; DPE65, 32; DPE71, 130; NYT, 20 May 1962, 30; DBM68, 618; *Excélsior*, 30 Oct. 1973, 12; Enc. Mex., XII, 310; HA, 6 Apr. 1981, 2 June 1980, 15; DBM68, 618.

Vázquez Pérez, Francisco
a-Apr. 25, 1904. b-Chilpancingo, Guerrero. c-Early education unknown; law degree, Free School of Law, 1922, with an honorable mention, 1st prize during the 1917-20 classes; 2nd prize, 1921 class. d-None. e-None. f-President of the Committee to Revise the Health Code, 1933; Director, Legal Services Department, Department of Health, 1931-34; *Oficial Mayor of the Department of Agrarian Affairs*, 1935; Oficial Mayor of the Department of Indigenous Assistance, 1937; President of the Committee on the Organization of Territorial Properties, 1935-39; Secretary, Federal Electoral Commission, 1960. g-None. i-Son of General Francisco Vázquez de Hurtado and Enriqueta Pérez; married Magdalena Fernandez Díaz. j-None. k-None. l-WNM, 232-33.

Vázquez (Quiroz), Genaro Vicente
(Deceased May 6, 1967) a-1892. b-Oaxaca, Oaxaca. c-Secondary studies, Institute of Arts and Sciences of Oaxaca; law degree, National School of Law, UNAM. d-Federal Deputy from the State of Oaxaca, Dist. 3, 1918-20, 1922-24, 1924-26, member of the Gran Comisión; Federal Deputy from the Federal District, Dist. 7, 1926-28; Senator from the State of Oaxaca, 1930-32; Interim Governor of Oaxaca, 1925-28. e-Secretary General of the PNR, 1930; General Delegate of the PNR to the State of Oaxaca, 1930. f-Director of the Consultation Department, Secretariat of Government; Secretary General of the Department of the Federal District; *Secretary of Labor*, 1935-37; *Attorney General of Mexico*, 1937-40; *Justice of the Supreme Court*, 1935 and 1952. g-None. h-Author of legislation for Indian groups in Mexico. i-Son *Pedro Vázquez Colmenares* was subsecretary of the Secretariat of Agrarian Reform, 1976; son *Jenaro Vázquez*

Colmenares was a federal deputy from Oaxaca, 1961-63. j-None. k-Precandidate for Governor of Oaxaca, 1939; founder of the Department of Indigenous Affairs; political enemy of Colonel *Constantino Chapital*, governor of Oaxaca, 1936-40. l-D del S, 21 June 1937; DP70, 2230; Peral, 835; D de Y, 22 June 1937, 2; López, 1128; Enc. de Mex., 12, 308; *Excélsior*, 14 Mar. 1974, 11.

Vázquez Ramírez, Celso
a-July 28, 1913. b-Hueyapan, Santiago Tuxtla, Veracruz. c-Primary studies in Tlacotalpan; secondary studies in Alvarado, Veracruz; preparatory studies in Veracruz; graduated from the National Military College, 1938-41; professor, Heroic Military College. d-*Federal Deputy* from the State of Veracruz, Dist. 11, 1958-61, member of the Forest Affairs Committee, the First National Defense Committee, the War Materiels Committee, the Social Welfare Committee and the Complaints Committee; *Federal Deputy* from the State of Veracruz, Dist. 13, 1967-70, member of the Internal Trade Committee, the First National Defense Committee, the Military Industry Committee, the Foreign Relations Committee, and the Military Justice Committee; *Alternate Federal Deputy* from the State of Veracruz, Dist. 13, 1979-82; *Federal Deputy* from the State of Veracruz, Dist. 13, 1982-85, member of the Information Committee, the Complaints Committee, the National Defense Committee and the Tourism Committee. e-Joined the PNR, Aug. 10, 1938. f-Chief of Services, Presidential Staff, 1946-52. g-President of the student society at his preparatory school. h-None. i-Married Carmen Enrique; son of Policarpo Vázquez Camacho, cattle rancher, and Francisca Ramírez Crespo; married María del Carmen Enríquez Chávez. j-Career army officer; rank of Colonel, Dec. 17, 1957; Subdirector, Arms and Munitions

Department, Secretariat of National Defense; Commander of the 1st Marine Infantry Battalion; Director of Artillery, Secretariat of the Navy; Director of Infantry, Secretariat of National Defense; rank of Division General. k-None. l-Func., 398; PS; C de D, 1958-61, 94, 1967-70, 61, 75, 80, 86, 1982-85, 1979-82; Directorio, 1982-85; Lehr, 504; DBGM, 619.

Vázquez Rojas, Genaro
(Deceased Feb. 2, 1972) a-June 10, 1931. b-San Luis Acatlán, Guerrero. c-Primary studies in Guerrero; primary teaching certificate from the National Teachers School, 1950; preparatory studies in law at the National Preparatory School. d-None. e-Organizer of the political organization known as the Comite Cívico Guerrerense, which rallied support in opposition to the government of General *Caballero Aburto* in Guerrero, 1960-61; head of various guerrilla groups in the State of Guerrero, 1968-72. f-School teacher at School No. 5, Federal District, 1957; left teaching because of political activities, 1960. g-Student leader at the National Teachers School; delegate of the Independent Peasant Federation (CCI) to Guerrero, 1961. h-None. i-Son of peasants; married to Consuelo Solís, a teacher. j-None. k-The Comité Cívico Guerrerense helped students to organize strikes against the state government in Guerrero, 1961, which eventually forced the Federal Government to remove *Caballero Aburto* as governor; captured at MLN headquarters in Mexico City, 1967, and imprisoned in Iguala until 1968, when he escaped in Apr. after his group attacked the prison; responsible for the much publicized kidnapping of the Rector of the University of Guerrero, *Jaime Castrejón Díaz*; died in the Public Hospital of Morelia from head fractures as a result of an automobile accident; his supporters and some

critics of the Mexican government maintain he was killed by the army. l-HA, 14 Feb. 1972, 14-15.

Vázquez Segura, María Antonia
a-June 13, 1955. b-Arteaga, Michoacán. c-Early education unknown; law degree, University of Michoacán, 1975-80; school teacher; professor, Agricultural-Technological Institute of Morelia, 1980. d-*Federal Deputy* from the State of Michoacán, Dist. 13, 1982-85. e-Joined PRI, 1970; representative of PRI to the local elections in Ciudad Hidalgo, Michoacán, 1981. f-Assistant to Salvador Gudiño Cervantes, President of the Regional Commission of Minimum Wages, 1975-77; adviser to the Legal Services of Michoacán, 1977-78. g-Legal adviser to the League of Agrarian Communities of Michoacán, 1979-80; Secretary of Women's Action of the CCE of the League of Agrarian Communities of Michoacán, 1980; Secretary General of the National Group of Revolutionary Women, Michoacán, 1982. h-Lawyer, Ramos Santillán Law Firm, 1978-79. i-Daughter of José Vázquez Chávez Chávez, farmer, and María de Jesús Segura Ramírez. j-None. k-None. l-Directorio, 1982-85; C de D, 1982-85; Lehr, 310; DBGM,619.

Vázquez Soto, Jesús
a-July 13, 1932. b-Vega Larga, San Pedro de la Colonias, Coahuila. c-Early education unknown; agricultural engineering degree, National School of Agriculture, 1952-58; diploma in photographic interpretation, Rural University of Brazil; special courses, Forestry Institute, Oxford University, 1963. d-None. e-None. f-Director General of Protection and Reforestation, Secretariat of Agriculture, 1971-72; *Subsecretary of Forestry and Fauna*, 1972-76; Director General of Forestry Operations, Tuxtepec Paper Factory, Oaxaca, 1977-80; Director General of Reforestation,

Secretariat of Agriculture and Hydraulic Resources, 1982-83. g-None. h-Technical Forestry Director, Fibracel, S.A., Ciudad Valles, San Luis Potosí, 1966-70; consultant in forestry, private sector, 1980-82. j-None. k-None. l-*Excélsior*, 8 Jan. 1972; HA, 19 Jan 1972, 26; Q es QAP, 242; DPE70, 70.

Vázquez Torres, Ignacio
a-Aug. 13, 1939. b-Sauz de Méndez, Pénjamo, Guanajuato. c-Early education unknown; law studies, National School of Law, UNAM, 1957-61, graduating with a thesis on the law and nonrenewable natural resources, Aug. 12, 1961. d-*Federal Deputy* from the State of Guanajuato, Dist. 15, 1967-70, member of the National Properties and Resources Committee, the Budget and Accounts Committee and the General Means of Communication Committee; *Federal Deputy* from the State of Guanajuato, Dist. 8, 1973-76; *Alternate Senator* from the State of Guanajuato, 1976-80, in functions as senator, 1980-82; *Federal Deputy* from the State of Guanajuato, Dist. 7, 1979-82. e-Youth Director of PRI, Penjámo, Guanajuato, 1958; Secretary of Agrarian Action of the National Youth Committee of PRI, 1962; Auxiliary Secretary of the CEN of PRI, 1972; General Delegate of the CEN of PRI to the State of Veracruz, México, Yucatán, Jalisco, Zacatecas, Hidalgo, Nayarit and Puebla; *Secretary of Organization of the CEN of PRI*, 1982. f-Director General of Political and Social Research, Secretariat of Government, 1976-78; *Oficial Mayor of Government*, 1978-79; Director of Delegates of the Secretariat of Public Education, 1982-83; General Coordinator of Educational Decentralization, Secretariat of Public Education, 1983-86; Delegate of the Department of the Federal District, Cuauhtémoc, 1988-90; General Coordinator of Distribution and Supplies, Department of the Federal District,

1990-93. g-Secretary of Youth Action of the CEN of the CNC, 1962; Auxiliary Secretary of the CEN of the CNC, 1964. h-None. i-Son of Miguel Vázquez Guzmán, farmer, and María Socorro Torres Hermosillo; married Irma Lucia Chavolla Hernández. j-None. k-None. l-DAPC, 73; C de D, 1973-76, 1967-70, 60, 83, 90; PS, 6250; *Excélsior*, 8 June 1979, 4, 12; Almanaque of Guanajuato, 32; Q es QAP, 325; DBGM89, 365; DBGM, 433; DBGM92, 386.

Vázquez Vela, Gonzalo
(Deceased Sept. 28, 1963) a-Nov. 7, 1894. b-Jalapa, Veracruz. c-Primary studies in Veracruz; preparatory studies at the University of Veracruz, Jalapa; law degree, National School of Law, UNAM. d-*Governor of Veracruz*, 1932-35. e-Member of the League of Professionals and Intellectuals of the PRM. f-Subsecretary General of Government of the State of Veracruz, 1920; Secretary General of Government of the State of Veracruz, 1920, under *Cándido Aguilar*; Secretary General of Government of the State of Veracruz, 1928-32, under *Adalberto Tejeda*; Oficial Mayor of the Secretariat of Government, 1929-32; *Secretary of Public Education*, June 17, 1935, to Nov. 30, 1940. g-None. h-Advisor to various businesses, the President of Mexico, and the National Mortgage Bank; manager of Aseguradora Mexicana. i-Protégé of *Adalberto Tejeda*; son of lawyer Manuel Vázquez. j-None. k-None. l-DP64, 1537; DP70, 2234; *Excélsior*, 18 June 1935; Dulles, 629; Gaxiola, 167-68; *Hoy*, 4 Nov. 1939, 18; Michaels, 128; Meyer, 13, 280; Heldt, 226; Pasquel, Jalapa, 667-668.

Vega Alvarado, Renato
a-Jan. 19, 1937. b-San Miguel de Allende, Guanajuato. c-Primary studies, Alvaro School, Culiacán, Sinaloa; secondary and preparatory studies, University of Sinaloa; agricul-

tural engineering degree, Higher School of Agriculture, Ciudad Juárez, Chihuahua, with a thesis on the cultivation of tomatoes in the Culiacán Valley, 1960. d-*Federal Deputy* from the State of Sinaloa, Dist. 3, 1970 to Sept. 28, 1972, member of the Administrative Committee (2nd year), the Agricultural Committee, the Fourth Ejido Committee, and the Agricultural Development Committee; President of the Chamber of Deputies, 1972; *Federal Deputy* from the State of Sinaloa, Dist. 9, 1985-88; *Governor of Sinaloa*, 1993- . e-Technical adviser in public administration to the CEPES of PRI in Sinaloa; General Delegate of the CEN of PRI to Jalisco, 1982-85; Secretary General of PRI in the Federal District, 1975-76; General Delegate of the CEN of PRI to Yucatán, 1982. f-Agent of the National Ejido Credit Bank, Sinaloa; agent of the Agricultural Credit Bank, Jalisco; Manager, Agricultural Banks, Jalisco and Veracruz, 1962-65; *Oficial Mayor of the Department of Federal District*, Aug. 9, 1972-75; Director General of Population, Secretariat of Government, 1976-79; Director of Immigration, Secretariat of Government, 1979; *Subsecretary of Agrarian Affairs*, Secretariat of Agrarian Reform, 1986-88, 1988-92. g-Subsecretary of Workers Action of the Central Executive Committee of the Mexican Agronomy Society; President of the Mexican Agronomy Society in Martínez de la Torre, Veracruz, and in Los Mochis, Sinaloa; Secretary General of the Mexican Agronomy Society, Jalisco; member of the CEN of the Political Committee of the CNC, 1971-74; General Delegate of the CNC to Yucatán, 1971. h-Agricultural extension agent, States of México and Jalisco. i-Son of General Renato Vega Amador, former Chief of Police of the Federal District and Director General of Traffic, and Graciela Alvarado Valdés; married

Juana María Carrillo Hernández. j-None. k-Precandidate for Governor of Sinaloa, 1974; precandidate for Senator from Sinaloa, 1981. l-Directorio, 1970-72; HA, 13 Sept. 1971, 10; C de D, 1970-72, 139-40; HA, 21 Aug. 1972, 13; *Excélsior*, 10 Aug. 1972, 10; HA, 9 Oct. 1972, 12; *Excélsior*, 20 Feb. 1974; DAPC, 1977; *Excélsior*, 26 Dec. 1981, 16, 14 Apr. 1982, 23.

Vega García, Antonio
a-Jan. 4, 1909. b-Santa Inéz Zacatelo, Tlaxcala. c-Early education unknown; no degree. d-*Federal Deputy* from the Federal District, Dist. 3, 1946-49; *Federal Deputy* from the State of Tlaxcala, Dist. 2, 1976-79. e-Campaigned in various elections for federal deputy and for senator; delegate from Tlaxcala to the PRI Basic Plan of Government, 1976-82; founder and president of the National Railroads Political Committee of PRI. f-None. g-Director of Statistics, STFRM. j-None. k-None. l-C de D, 1946-49; MGF49, 6; *Excélsior*, 3 Sept. 1976, 1C; C de D, 1976-79.

Vega Macías, José Guadalupe
a-June 13, 1926. b-Ahualulco, San Luis Potosí. c-Completed primary studies, Colegio Cristóbal Colón; some secondary studies. d-Local Deputy to the State Legislature of San Luis Potosí, Dist. 3, 1972-75; member of the City Council of Soledad Díez Gutiérrez, San Luis Potosí; *Federal Deputy* from the State of San Luis Potosí, Dist. 2, 1976-79; Mayor of Soledad Díez Gutiérrez, 1980-82; *Federal Deputy* from the State of San Luis Potosí, Dist. 2, 1982-85, member of the Information and Complaints Committee and the Labor and Social Welfare Committee. e-Joined PRI, 1952; Secretary of Labor Action of PRI, San Luis Potosí. f-Attorney for the Defense of Labor, San Luis Potosí; Director, Department of Labor and Social Welfare, San Luis Potosí. g-Representa-tive of labor on the Board of Conciliation and Arbitration; Assistant Secretary of the Textile Workers Union of Mexico, 1975-81; Secretary General of the CTM in San Luis Potosí, 1982. h-Textile worker; laborer. i-Son of José Refugio Vega Mora, administrator, and Agustina Macías; married María Cruz Escobedo Nieto. j-None. k-None. l-Directorio, 1982-85; C de D, 1982-85; Lehr, 417; C de D, 1976-79; DBGM, 620.

Vega Memije, Carlos Javier
a-Jan. 21, 1948. b-Chilpancingo, Guerrero. c-Early education unknown; law degree, with honors, National School of Law, UNAM, 1967-71; MA, UNAM, 1974; LLD, National School of Law, UNAM, 1975; Assistant Professor of Political Structure of the State, Graduate Division, UNAM, 1975-76; Professor of Constitutional Law, National School of Law, UNAM; professor, Ibero-American University, 1985. d-*Federal Deputy* from the State of Guerrero, Dist. 1, 1988-91. e-Technical Secretary of the IEPES of PRI, 1986-87; Director of the IEPES of PRI, Guerrero, 1987. f-Secretary, 12th Criminal Judicial District, Mexico City; Director General of Administration, National Warehouses; Controller General of National Warehouses; Secretary of the Board of National Warehouses; Assistant to the Private Secretary to the President of Mexico, 1981-82; *Private Secretary to the President of Mexico, José López Portillo*, 1982; Subdelegate of Government, Department of the Federal District, 1983-84; Secretary of Administrative Development, State of Guerrero, 1987-88; Secretary General of Government of the State of Guerrero, 1991-93. g-None. h-None. i-Worked in several posts with his mentor, *Roberto Casillas Hernández*; son of Juan Manuel Vega García, retailer, and Carlota Memije Pastor; married María Teresa Adame Navarro, teacher. j-None. k-None.

l-*Excélsior*, 13 Aug. 1982, 4; HA, 23 Aug. 1982, 8; DAPC81; DBGM89, 557; DBGM92, 846.

Véjar Vázquez, Octavio
(Deceased Nov. 10, 1974) a-Apr. 20, 1900. b-Jalapa, Veracruz. c-Primary and secondary studies at the Escuela Práctica, Jalapa; preparatory studies at the Colegio Preparatoria under Salvador Díaz Mirón and the National Preparatory School; law degree, National School of Law, UNAM, Dec. 6, 1923; LLD, National School of Law, UNAM; Professor of Aeronautic Law, School of Military Aviation; Professor of Military Law, National School of Law, UNAM; professor, National War College; professor, National Military College. d-None. e-Founder of the National Independent Democratic Party, 1944; member of the National Coordinating Committee of the Popular Party, 1947-48; Vice President of the Popular Party (PPS), 1951; Interim President of the Popular Party, 1949, 1952. f-Public defender; agent of the Ministerio Público; Justice, Superior Tribunal of Military Justice; Prosecuting Attorney of Military Justice; *Attorney General of the Federal District and Federal Territories*, 1940-41; *Secretary of Public Education*, Sept. 12, 1941, to Dec. 22, 1943. g-None. h-Practicing attorney, 1923; President of the Post War Studies Commission, 1943; member of the committee in charge of writing the second Six Year Plan, 1940. i-Close friend of José Vasconcelos; uncle of physician Carlos Véjar Lacave, Ambassador to Finland, 1964-65; brother of Pedro Véjar Vázquez, military engineer and chief of federal highways, 1932; son of Pedro Véjar Gómez and María Vázquez. j-None. k-Detained in the military prison of Tlatelolco, 1952, for ostensibly disobeying a superior's military order, raising the issue of whether or not career officers were really free to

participate in politics. l-*Hoy*, 20 Sept. 1941; WWM45, 123; Millon, 156; EBW46, 568; Peral, 841-42; Correa, 2; Kirk, 335, 148-55; Strode, 374-75; D del S, 2 Dec. 1940, 1-6; González Navarro, 161; López, 1134; NYT, 12 Sept. 1941, 8; Raby, 63; *Excélsior*, 12 Nov. 1949; HA, 18 Nov. 1974, 10; NYT, 15 Apr. 1952, 18 Apr. 1952, 5; *Excélsior*, 11 Nov. 1974, 20; Illescas, 603-04; WNM, 233; Pasquel, 673-74.

Velasco, Miguel Angel
a-Apr. 30, 1903. b-Jalapa, Veracruz. c-Completed primary studies; no degree; Professor of the History of the Labor Movement in Mexico, Workers University, 1964-77. d-None. e-Member of the Federation of Communist Youth, 1926; joined the PCM, 1927, resigned his membership, 1943; member of the CEN of the PCM, 1928-43; cofounder and member of the Unified Socialist Action, 1945-50, and of the Mexican Workers and Peasant's Party, 1955; member of the National Committee of the PPS, 1963-68; founder of the Movement of Socialist Action and Unity (MAUS), 1970; Secretary General of the MAUS, 1977-82; candidate of the leftist coalition for federal deputy and for governor of Veracruz, 1979. f-None. g-Began union activity as an official in the Bakers Workers Union, 1919; Secretary of Acts, Bakers Workers Union, 1921; founder of the Federation of Workers and Peasants Unions in Córdoba, Veracruz, 1925; organizer, Only Chamber of Labor of Nuevo León, 1932; peasant organizer, Lombardia and New Italy haciendas, 1933; representative of the Only Federation of Unions, 1935; member of the first CEN of the CTM, 1936. i-None. j-Fought against de la Huerta in Jilotepec, 1923; member of the staff of *Heriberto Jara*. k-Imprisoned many times; prisoner on Islas Marías, 1932. l-Enc. de Mex., 12, 314-15; Protag., 349.

Velasco Curiel, (Fernando) Francisco
a-Sept. 15, 1917. b-Cuauhtémoc, Colima. c-Primary studies, Gertrudis Bocanegra School, Colima, Colima; preparatory studies, National Preparatory School; law degree, National School of Law, UNAM, Apr. 28, 1944, with a thesis on cooperatism in Mexico and other countries. d-*Senator* from the State of Colima, 1958-61, member of the Economics and Statistics Committee, the First Ejido Committee, and the Agricultural Development Committee; substitute member of the Agriculture and Development Committee; *Governor of Colima*, 1961-67. e-General Delegate of the CEN of PRI to Jalisco, Guanajuato, Colima, and Querétaro. f-Director, Federal Automobile Registration Department, Secretariat of Industry and Commerce; Director, Department of Special Studies and Administrative Affairs, Secretariat of the Treasury, 1952-58. g-None. i-Student of *Eduardo Bustamante* at UNAM; school companion of *Antonio Salazar Salazar*, senator from Colima, 1958-64; sister Clotilde Velasco Curiel married Francisco Vizcaíno Fernández, father of Rafael Vizcaíno, a director of administration, Public Works Bank. j-None. k-None. l-WWMG, 40; DBM70, 558; DGF56, 164; letter; Func., 146; DBGM87, 410.

Velasco Ibarra, Enrique
a-June 28, 1927. b-Acámbaro, Guanajuato. c-Primary studies at a public school and at the Colegio Franco-Español, 1933-36; secondary and preparatory studies, Colegio Francés; completed preparatory studies at the National Preparatory School; law degree, National School of Law, UNAM, 1944-48 with an honorary mention; highest grades of his generation at the National School of Law, 1947; Professor of Political Philosophy, School of Political and Social Sciences, UNAM, 1962-65; professor, Graduate School of

Business Administration, UNAM, 1958; member of the Governing Board of UNAM, 1974; Professor of General Theory of the State, National School of Law, UNAM, 1958-66. d-*Governor of Guanajuato*, 1979-84. e-None. f-Director of the Banking Section, Secretariat of the Treasury, 1956; General Attorney for the Mexican Tobacco Company, 1960-61; Private Secretary to the Rector of UNAM, *Ignacio Chávez*, 1962-66; Subdirector General of Planning of the Secretariat of the Presidency, 1966-70; Auxiliary Secretary General of UNAM, 1970-73; Coordinator of Planning and Development, UNAM, 1973; Director General of Administration, Secretariat of the Treasury, 1974-75; *Oficial Mayor of the Secretariat of the Treasury*, 1975-76; *Private Secretary to President José López Portillo*, 1976-78. g-Executive Secretary of the Industrial Center for Productivity, 1956-60. h-Author of many works; researcher, Institute of Comparative Law, UNAM, 1959-62; practicing lawyer, 1949-55. i-Longtime collaborator of *José López Portillo*. j-None. k-Reportedly handled *López Portillo's* personal finances as his secretary; forced to resign as governor, June 26, 1984. l-*El Día*, 1 Dec. 1976; *Proceso*, 4 Dec. 1976, 27; LA, 15 Dec. 1978, 388; HA, 25 Dec. 1978, 39; *Excélsior*, 1 Dec. 1976; Almanaque of Guanajuato, 25.

Velasco Lafarga, Ernesto
a-Nov. 14, 1911. b-Tampico, Tamaulipas. c-Primary studies, Colegio San Borja, Colonia del Valle, Mexico City; preparatory, Colegio "La Salle" and the Colegio Morelos, Mexico City; engineering degree from the School of Mining and from the School of Engineering, UNAM, May 9, 1935. d-*Federal Deputy* (Party Deputy from PAN), 1970-73, member of the Sugar Industry Committee, the Department of the Federal District Committee, and the

Second Section of the Agrarian Affairs Committee. e-Active member of PAN since 1939; head of PAN in Mazatlán, Sinaloa; Director of PAN for the 17th District, Federal District. f-Head of the Board of Civic and Moral Improvement, Mazatlán, Sinaloa; adviser to the City of Mazatlán; engineer for the National Mortgage Bank, 1935; engineer for the National Irrigation Commission, 1936-37; Superintendent and resident engineer, Irrigation Works, Ixmiquilpan, Hidalgo, 1938-47. g-Adviser to the National Chamber of Construction Industries. h-Civil engineer. j-None. k-Candidate for Federal Deputy from the Federal District, Dist. 17, 1967. l-Directorio, 1970-72; C de D, 1970-72, 139.

Velasco Suárez, Manuel
a-Dec. 18, 1915. b-San Cristóbal de las Casas, Chiapas. c-Primary, secondary, and preparatory studies in San Cristóbal de las Casas; medical degree, National School of Medicine, UNAM, 1933-39; studies in Orthopedic Surgery, University of Iowa, 1940; studies in neurology and neurosurgery, Harvard University, and at Massachusetts General Hospital, 1941-42; studies in neuropathology, George Washington University, Washington, D.C., 1942-43; Professor, National School of Medicine, UNAM, 1944-70; Professor of Neurosurgery, National School of Medicine, UNAM, 1959-70; Professor of Clinical Surgery, National School of Medicine, UNAM, 1950-59. d-*Governor of Chiapas*, 1970-76. e-Joined PRI, 1952. f-Neurosurgeon, Juárez Hospital, Mexico City, 1948-63; Director, Neuropsychiatric Assistance, Secretariat of Health, 1951-59; Director, Neuro and Neurosurgery Services, Juárez Hospital, 1958-63; founder and Director of the National Neurology Institute, 1952-70; Director General of the Neurological, Mental Health and Rehabilitation Division, Secretariat of Health, 1958-70. g-None.

h-Author of numerous works in his specialty. i-Physician and close friend to *Luis Echeverría*; son of lawyer José Manuel Velasco Balboa; married Elvira Siles Aguilera; father-in-law of *Manuel Camacho*, head of the Federal District Department; was in business with Camacho's father and General *Jesús Lozoya*. j-None. k-Founder of numerous hospitals in Mexico City. l-DPE65, 151; DPE61, 111; letter; WNM, 234-35; DBC, 261-63.

Velázquez Carmona, Manuel
a-Mar. 12, 1945. b-Federal District. c-Early education unknown; legal studies, National School of Law, UNAM, graduating in 1968; graduate studies in law, National School of Law, UNAM, 1971; Professor of Constitutional Law, National School of Law, UNAM, 1969-84; Professor of Constitutional Law, National School of Political and Social Science, UNAM, 1971-72; Professor of the Theory of the State, National School of Law, UNAM. d-None. e-Member of the National Executive Council of PRI Youth, 1965; Subsecretary of Organization of the National Youth Committee of PRI, 1965; Secretary of Planning of the National Youth Committee of PRI, 1965; Auxiliary Secretary of the CEN of PRI, 1969; Director of Voter Registration and Electoral Action of PRI, 1969. f-Private Secretary to the Director General of the Olympic Organizing Committee, *Pedro Ramírez Vázquez*, 1967-69; adviser to the Director General of Legal Affairs, Secretariat of Communications and Transportation, 1969-70; adviser to the Oficial Mayor of the Secretariat of the Presidency, 1970-71; adviser to the Attorney General of Mexico, 1971-72; Subdirector General of Documentation and Presidential Speeches, Secretariat of the Presidency, 1972-73; Subdirector General of Legal Affairs and Presidential Legislation,

Secretariat of the Presidency, 1973-75; Director General of Legal Affairs and Legislation, Secretariat of the Presidency, 1976-76; Director General of Legal Affairs and Legislation, Secretariat of Public Works, 1976-77; *Subsecretary of Real Property and Urban Works*, 1981-82; adviser to the Secretary of Health, 1983. g-Director of Electoral Action of the CEN of CNOP, 1972. h-None. i-Son of Ezequiel Velázquez Carmona, public accountant, and Sofía Carmona Barrera, public official; married Orlanda Yamilet Garrido Vargas. j-None. k-None. l-DAPC81, 19; DAPC77, 74.

Velázquez de Alba, Elpidio G.
(Deceased Nov. 14, 1977) a-May 12, 1892. b-San Juan de Guadalupe, Durango. c-Primary and secondary studies in the state rural schools of Durango; studied at the Military Academy of Mexico. d-*Governor of Durango*, 1941-44. e-None. f-Assistant Director, Administrative Department, Secretariat of National Defense; Director of the War Materiels Department, Secretariat of National Defense, 1935. g-Member of the Durango Chamber of Commerce. h-General merchant in Durango; first employment as a factory laborer before 1910. i-Son of Severiano Velázquez, industrial worker. j-Joined the Revolution in 1910 under Aguirre Benavides, with the rank of 2nd Lieutenant; Assistant Chief of Staff for General *Lázaro Cárdenas*, 1933; Chief of Staff for various Revolutionary Generals; Commander of the 55th Regiment; Commander of the 64th Regiment; rank of Brigadier General, 1939; rank of Division General, Nov. 20, 1968. k-None. l-WWM45, 123; Peral, 847-48; EBW46, 1135; *Hoy*, 4 May 1940, 13; López, 1138; Casasola, V; Rev. de Ejer., Nov. 1968, 53; Enc. de Mex., Annual, 241.

Velázquez de la Parra, Manuel
a-Mar. 1, 1937. b-Federal District. c-Early education unknown; economics degree, National School of Economics, UNAM, with a thesis on economic aspects of budget expenditures of the Department of the Federal District, 1964; seminar, World Bank, Washington, D.C., 1969; Professor of Political Economy, Institute of Political Education, PRI, 1974. d-None. e-Technical Secretary of the Housing Committee of the IEPES of PRI, 1981-82. f-Analyst, Secretariat of the Treasury Group, Bank of Mexico, 1965-70; adviser to the Subdirector of Finances, Pemex, 1971-72; Financial Subdirector of Housing, Director General of Credit, Secretariat of the Treasury, 1972-76; adviser on housing, Secretariat of the Treasury, 1972-82; Director General of the Housing Fund (FOVI), Bank of Mexico, 1972-82; *Subsecretary of Housing*, Secretariat of Urban Development and Ecology, 1982-84; Director General of the Technical Secretariat of the Cabinet, 1984-88. g-None. h-Employee, insurance company, Monterrey, 1953-55; employee, Hilaturas Lourdes, 1955-62. i-Worked with *Miguel de la Madrid* early in his career. j-None. k-None. l-IEPES; Q es QAP, 274; DBGM, 436; DBGM89, 370; HA, 30 July 1984, 14.

Velázquez Jaaks, Luis
a-June 21, 1936. b-Distrito Federal. c-Primary studies at the Orozco y Berra and Damián Carmón Schools, Mexico City; secondary studies in Mexico City; preparatory studies from the National Preparatory School No. 1; law degree, National School of Law, UNAM; Professor of the Sociology of Education and Economic Policy, Pasteur Institute. d-*Federal Deputy* from the Federal District, Dist. 14, 1970-73, member of the Department of the Federal District Committee, the Labor Section of the Legislative Studies Committee and the

Promotion and Development of Sports Committee; *Federal Deputy* from the Federal District, Dist. 37, 1979-82. e-Assistant Director of the National Youth Sector of PRI, 1960-70. f-Employee, Federal Electric Commission; legal adviser, La Forestal, 1973-76; Legal Director, Tlalnepantla, 1974-76; legal adviser, Secretariat of Labor, 1978-79. g-Employee, Archives, CTM, 1956-58; President of the Subcommittee on Youth of the Congress of Labor, 1960-64; general cashier, CTM, 1960; adviser, International Labor Organization; Secretary of Social Action of the CTM, 1968-74; Secretary General of the National Youth Sector of the CTM, 1960-70. i-Nephew of long-time CTM leader, *Fidel Velázquez*; son of *Gregorio Velázquez*, four-time federal deputy from México. j-None. k-None. l-Directorio, 1970-72, 140, 1970-73, 140; C de D, 1979-82.

Velázquez Sánchez, Fidel
a-Apr. 2, 1900. b-Villa Nicolás Romero, México. c-Primary studies in Villa Nicolás Romero, completed, 1914; no degree. d-*Senator* from the Federal District, 1946-52, 1958-64, member of the Department of the Federal District Committee, the Social Welfare Committee, the First Labor Committee, the First Balloting Committee, the First Instructive Section of the Grand Jury. e-Representative of labor to PRI. f-None. g-Began union activities on the El Rosario ranch; Secretary of Interior of the Union of Milk Industry Workers, 1921; Secretary General of the Union of Milk Industry Workers for the Federal District, 1929; member of the Executive Committee of the Federation of Mexican Labor, 1936-40; Secretary of Organization and Propaganda, CEN of the CTM, 1936; founding member of the General Federation of Mexican Workers and Farmers, 1933; *Secretary*

General of the Mexican Federation of Labor, 1940-46; *Secretary General of the CTM*, 1946-52, 1952-58, 1958-64, 1964-70, 1970-76, 1976-82; 1982-88, 1988-94. h-Worked as a field laborer, in a lumberyard, and on a hacienda; employed as a milkman. i-Close personal friend of *Lauro Ortega* and *Jesús Yurén*; parents, Gregorio Velázquez Reyna and Herlinda Sánchez Chávez, were farmers; married Nora Quintana Perera; brother, *Gregorio*, was Secretary General of the CTM for Mexico and a federal deputy, 1955-58; nephew, *Luis Velázquez Jaaks*, was a federal deputy, 1970-73. j-None. k-Brandenburg puts him in the Inner Circle of influence, 1940-46; one of the most powerful labor leaders in Mexico; founded the Milk Industry Workers Union with *Alfonso Sánchez Madariaga*; cofounder of the General Federation of Mexican Workers and Farmers (CGOCM) with *Vicente Lombardo Toledano*. l-WWW70-71; HA, 7 Feb. 1972, 12-14; Brandenburg, 80, 93; Johnson, 68; Morton, 47, 90; C de S, 1946-52; Padgett, 170-72; C de S, 1961-64, 72-73; Strode, 373; Kirk, 90-93; Enc. Mex., XII, 1977, 318; López, 1138; HA, 20 Oct. 1950; *Excélsior*, 22 May 1973, 19, 16 Mar. 1973, 22; Alonso, 192; WNM, 235.

Velázquez Sánchez, Gregorio
a-Mar. 5, 1910. b-Villa Nicolás Romero, Mexico. c-Primary studies in a public school, Mexico City; secondary studies at Night Secondary School No. 5, Mexico City; no degree. d-Local Deputy to the State Legislature of México, 1940-42; *Federal Deputy* from the State of México, Dist, 1, 1943-46; *Federal Deputy* from the State of México, Dist. 5, 1949-52, member of the Administration Committee and the Budgets and Accounts Committee; *Federal Deputy* from the State of México, Dist. 5, 1955-58, member of the Economics and Statistics Committee, the Second Balloting

Committee and the General Accounting Office Committee; *Federal Deputy* from the State of México, Dist. 2, 1967-70, member of the Tenth Section of the Legislative Studies Committee, the General Accounting Office Committee and the Social Welfare Committee. e-Secretary of Labor Organizations of PRI in the State of México, 1946. f-Supervisor of Theaters, Department of the Federal District, 1938-40. g-Founder of the Regional Organization of the CTM in Tlalnepantla; representative of the CTM to the International Labor Organization Meeting on Social Security, Rio de Janeiro, 1952; Delegate of the CTM in Mexico, 1946. h-Began working at the La Sirena Iron Works, 1924; milk industry employee, 1925; employee of the National Railroads of Mexico, 1932-38. i-Brother of *Fidel Velázquez Sánchez*, Secretary General of the CTM; father of *Luis Velázquez Jaaks*, federal deputy from the Federal District, 1970-73, 1979-82; parents were peasants. j-None. k-Federal deputy from the State of México more times between 1934 to 1979 than any other Mexican. l-Ind. Biog., 164-65; C de D, 1949-42, 94, 1955-58; DGF56, 25, 32, 34-35; C de D, 1967-70, 68, 78, 83.

Velázquez Torres, Consuelo
a-Aug. 21, 1922. b-Ciudad Guzmán, Jalisco. c-Studied singing at the age of four under Ramón Serratos and Aurora Garibay; continued studies under Serratos at the Normal School of Music, Mexico City, graduating as a piano teacher, 1939. d-*Federal Deputy* from the Federal District, Dist. 36, 1979-82. e-Joined PRI, 1940. f-None. g-None. h-Notable Mexican singer; composer; wrote internationally famous song "Bésame Mucho." i-Married Mariano Rivera Conde, artistic director at RCA Victor. j-None. k-None. l-C de D, 1979-82; Romero Aceves, 1740-41.

Ventura Valle, Angel
A-July 27, 1939. b-Cuernavaca, Morelos. c-Early education unknown; economics degree, National School of Economics, UNAM, 1959-63, with a thesis on reconstituted milk as a means of increasing the Mexican market; professor, University of the Valle de México, 1966-68; professor, School of Accounting and Administration, University of Morelos, 1972-74. d-*Senator* from the State of Morelos, 1976-82, Secretary of the Permanent Committee of Congress, 1976-82; *Senator* from the State of Morelos, 1991-97. e-Joined PRI, 1960; member, Advisory Council of the IEPES of PRI, 1981-82. f-Analyst, Secretary of the Presidency, 1963-65; Secretary of Economic Promotion, State of Morelos, 1970-76; Secretary of Budgeting and Finance, State of Morelos, 1988-91. g-President of the Revolutionary Youth of CNOP, State of Morelos, 1960-62; President of the Technical Council of CNOP, 1981-82. h-None. i-Son of Angel Ventura Neri, surgeon, and Estela Valle Segura; married Graciela Dávalos Villa. j-None. k-None. l-IEPES; C de S, 1976-82; DBGM92, 599-600.

Verdugo Quiroz, Leopoldo
a-Mar. 1, 1898. b-Alamos, Sonora. c-Primary studies in Alamos; no degree. d-*Senator* from the State of Baja California del Norte, 1952-58, President of the Public Health Committee, First Secretary of the Social Security Committee and the Agricultural and Development Committee and Second Secretary of the Administration Committee. e-None. f-Director of Customs, Mexicali; Director of the Customs Officers, Mexicali, Matamoros and Veracruz. g-None. j-Fought in the Revolution as an enlisted man. k-None. l-Ind. Biog., 166-67; DGF56, 5, 9, 13; C de S, 1952-58.

Verduzco Rios, Leobardo
a-1945. b-Zamora, Michoacán. c-Primary studies in Morelia; secondary studies in Mexico City; law degree, National School of Law, UNAM; professor at the National Polytechnic Institute. d-None. e-Joined PARM, 1970; Secretary of Information and Publicity of the Executive Committee of PARM; Secretary of Information, Press, and Publicity of the Regional Committee of PARM for the Federal District, 1979. f-None. g-None. h-Administrator, National Center of Industrial Technical Instruction. j-None. k-Candidate for federal deputy from PARM. l-HA, 7 May 1979, I.

Verges (Xochihua), Juan Víctor
a-1913. b-Federal District. c-Preparatory studies at the National Preparatory School; economics degree, National School of Economics, UNAM, 1939-42, graduating in 1944 with a thesis on military insurance. d-None. e-None. f-Director of Technical Administrative Organizations, Secretariat of Government Properties; Director General of Administration, Secretariat of Government Properties, 1951-55; Subdirector General of Administration, Secretariat of Government, 1956-61; Director General of Administration, Secretariat of Government, 1965-68; *Oficial Mayor of Government Properties*, 1968-70. g-None. j-None. k-None. l-EN de E, 265; DGF51, I, 445; DPE61, 11; DGF56, 83; DPE65, 13.

Vicencio Tovar, Abel C.
a-Nov. 4, 1925. b-México. c-Early education unknown; law degree, National School of Law, UNAM, 1952, with a thesis on the citizen and public rights; professor, UNAM. d-*Federal Deputy* from the Federal District, Dist. 17, 1964-67, member of the Labor Section of the Legislative Studies Committee; *Federal Deputy* (Party Deputy from

PAN), 1973-76; *Plurinominal Federal Deputy* from PAN, 1979-82, 1988-91. e-Joined PAN, October, 1958; *Secretary General of the CEN of PAN*, 1960-61; member of the CEN of PAN, 1969; *President of the CEN of PAN*, 1978-84. f-Lawyer, Secretariat of Public Works. g-None. h-Practicing lawyer. i-Brother of *Astolfo Vicencio Tovar*, Secretary General of PAN, 1961-66; son of Gustavo A. Vicencio, Justice of the Supreme Court, 1926-28; husband of *María Elena Alvarez*, party deputy from PAN, 1976-79; uncle of *Gustavo A. Vicencio Acevedo*, Plurinominal Federal Deputy, 1982-85. j-None. k-None. l-C de D, 1973-76, 29, 1964-67, 84; Mabry; letter; C de D, 1979-82; HA, 20 Feb. 1984, 16; DBGM89, 559.

Vicencio Tovar, Astolfo
a-Mar. 20, 1927. b-Federal District. c-Primary studies; completed secondary and preparatory studies; completed four years of a CPA program, School of Business and Banking, Mexico City, 1948-52. d-*Federal Deputy* (Party Deputy from PAN), 1967-70; *Plurinominal Federal Deputy* from PAN, 1982-85, member of the Trade and the Budget and Public Accounts Committee; *Plurinominal Federal Deputy* from PAN, 1988-91. e-Joined PAN, 1947; Chief of PAN, 6th District, Federal District, 1958-60; Secretary General of the Regional Committee of PAN in the Federal District, 1960-62; member of the CEN of PAN, 1961-70; member of the regional council of PAN and delegate of the CEN of PAN to the State of México, 1969-75, 1981-82; National Director of Electoral Campaigns for PAN, 1966-68; President of the Regional Committee of PAN, State of México, 1969-70; *Secretary General of the CEN of PAN*, 1961-66; director of the 1970 PAN presidential campaign. f-None. g-None. h-Assistant accountant, branch bank of Banamex, 1952-55; assistant

accountant, Titan Carton Co., 1952-55; General Administrator, Flagasa, S.A., 1958-73; President, ASLIC Advertising Agency, 1971- . i-Son of Gustavo A. Vicencio Copado, Justice of the Supreme Court, 1926-28, and former Rector of the Institute of Arts and Sciences of México, Toluca, and Dolores Tovar Ortiz; brother of *Abel Vicencio Tovar*, President of PAN, 1978; good friend of *José González Torres*, president of PAN, 1959-62; married María del Carmen Acevedo; father of *Gustavo A. Vicenco Acevedo*, Plurinominal Federal Deputy, 1982-85; grandfather, Celso, was a senator and judge. j-None. k-Candidate of PAN for federal deputy, 1958; candidate of PAN for senator from the State of México, 1964; candidate for Mayor of Naucalpan, México, 1969. l-Mabry; C de D, 1967-70; letter; PS, 6336; C de D, 1982-85; Directorio, 1982-85; Lehr, 578; DBGM, 621.

Viesca Palma, Jorge
(Deceased Oct. 1952) b-Saltillo, Coahuila. c-Early education unknown; law degree, National School of Law, UNAM. d-*Federal Deputy* from the State of Hidalgo, Dist. 1, 1949-52, member of the Mines Committee. e-None. f-*Private Secretary to the President of Mexico, Miguel Alemán*, 1946-49. g-None. h-Owner of Rancho Atotonilco el Grande. i-Knew *Miguel Alemán* as a law school student. j-None. k-None. l-C de D, 1949-52, 19, 94; Pérez López, 496.

Vildosola Almada, Gustavo
a-Sept. 15, 1905. b-Alamos, Sonora. c-Primary studies in Mexicali; secondary and preparatory studies in Hermosillo, Sonora; no degree. d-*Senator* from the State of Baja California del Norte, 1958-64, member of the Gran Comisión, First Secretary of the National Properties Committee, Second Secretary of the Economy and Statistics Commit-

tee, and member of the Second Balloting Group. e-None. f-None. g-President of the Chamber of Industries, Baja California del Norte; President of the Regional Agricultural Union, Baja California del Norte; President of the Highway Association of Baja California del Norte. h-Businessman. j-None. k-None. l-Func., 123; C de S, 1961-64, 73.

Villa Michel, Primo
(Deceased Aug. 22, 1970) a-Nov. 7, 1893. b-Ciudad Carranza, Jalisco. c-Primary and secondary studies at the Colegio de la Inmaculada, Zapopan, Jalisco; preparatory studies at the Instituto San José, Guadalajara, Jalisco; law studies, School of Law, University of Guadalajara; law degree, National School of Law, UNAM. d-None. e-None. f-Judge of the lower court of Sonora, 1915; Public Defender, Nogales, Sonora, 1917; Federal Public Defender for the State of Sonora, 1920; Director of Records, Secretariat of Government, 1923; Oficial Mayor, Secretariat of Industry and Commerce, 1923-24; Subsecretary of Government, 1925; Secretary General of the Department of the Federal District, 1925-26; Head of the Department of the Federal District, 1927-28; Ambassador to Germany, 1929; Subsecretary of Industry and Commerce, 1930-32; Secretary of Industry and Commerce, 1932-34; Ambassador to Uruguay, 1935; *Ambassador to Great Britain*, 1937-38; Ambassador to Japan, 1939-41; First Secretary of the Mexican Embassy, Washington, D.C., 1941-43; *Oficial Mayor of the Secretariat of Government*, 1944-45; *Secretary of Government*, 1945-46; Ambassador to Canada, 1947-51, to Guatemala, 1952-53, to Syria, 1956-57, to Luxemburg, 1959-60, to Belgium, 1960-64. g-Secretary, National Chamber of Commerce. h-Delegate to many international conferences; manager, Petróleos

Mexicanos; Director, National Institute of Housing; Director of the Bulletin of Federal Statutes, Secretariat of Government, 1923. i-Son, Primo Jr., was Director of the Department of Primary Statistics, Investment Commission, 1956; married María Dávila. j-None. k-None. l-WWM45, 125; DP64, 1968; DP70, 2266; D de Y, 23 Aug. 1970; Correa, 360; STYRBIWW54, 1074; EBW46, 128; DPE61, 20; Peral, 859; López, 1162; NYT, 15 May 1938, 36, 27 July 1954, 10, 24 Dec. 1941, 3, 3 Dec. 1942; HA, 5 July 1946, 4; Enc. Mex., XII, 1977, 404-05; Medina, No. 20, 48.

Villa Salas, Avelino B.
a-Nov. 16, 1940. b-El Paso, Texas. c-Early education unknown; agricultural engineering degree, National School of Agriculture, Chapingo, 1963; studies in Stockholm. d-None. e-None. f-Director, Calculations and Statistics, Department of Photometry and Inventories, National Institute of Forestry Research, 1965-68; Subdirector General of the National Forestry Inventory, 1968-72; Chief, Department of Technical Services, National Institute of Forestry Research, 1972-73; Director, National Institute of Forestry Research, 1977-80; Director General of Research and Forestry Education, Secretariat of Agriculture and Hydraulic Resources, 1980; *Subsecretary of Forestry and Fauna*, 1980-82. j-None. k-None. l-Protag., 352; *Excélsior*, 11 Mar. 1980, 4.

Villa Treviño, Jorge
a-1930. b-Federal District. c-Early education unknown; law degree, National School of Law, UNAM, with a thesis on gambling and the law, 1963. d-None. e-*Secretary of Press and Publicity of the CEN of PRI*, Aug. 3, 1972-75; member of various commissions for the IEPES and the CNOP; active in the presidential campaign of *Luis Echeverría*; joined PRI, 1957. f-Member, Department of

Publicity, Secretariat of Public Works, 1955-56; adviser to the administration of the Federal Post Office, 1968; Subdirector (A) of PIPSA. g-None. h-Cofounder of the magazine *Voz* with *Mario Moya Palencia*; editor of the magazine *Ferronales*, official publication of the National Railroads of Mexico. j-None. k-None. l-HA, 14 Aug. 1972, 11-12; *Hoy*, 19 Aug. 1972, 65; *Excélsior*, 4 Aug. 1972, 4-5.

Villalobos Chaparoo, Florentina
a-Apr. 17, 1931. b-Parral, Chihuahua. c-Primary and secondary studies in Parral; special studies in journalism, Carlos Septién García School of Journalism, 1958-62; scholarship to study in Spain, 1963; teaching certificate; studies in private accounting; preparatory school teacher; teacher in private accounting courses, various private schools, Chihauhua, 1948-78. d-*Federal Deputy* from the State of Chihuahua, Dist. 2, 1964-67; *Plurinominal Federal Deputy* from PAN, 1982-85, member of the Radio, Television and Film Committee and the Labor and Social Welfare Committee. e-Joined PAN, 1956; member of the Municipal Committee of PAN, Parral, 1963-67; regional adviser to PAN in Chihuahua, 1967-71; national adviser to PAN, 1967-82; candidate of PAN for Mayor of Parral, 1968; candidate of PAN for Senator from Jalisco, 1976; President of the Regional Committee of PAN, Chihuahua, 1971; Coordinator of the National Feminine Committee of PAN, 1980. f-None. g-Leader of Catholic Action, 1951-57. h-Wrote for *El Correo de Parral*, 1964-67; wrote for *Señal*, 1960-61. i-Daughter of Tomás Villalobos Loya, civil engineer, and Elvira Chaparro; married Carlos Pineda Flores, lawyer. j-None. k-None. l-C de C, 1964-67; Directorio, 1964-67; Lehr, 644; C de D, 1982-85; DBGM, 625.

Villalobos (Mayar), Antonio
(Deceased Dec. 27, 1965) a-Dec. 16,
1894. b-Distrito Federal. c-Preparatory
studies at the National Preparatory
School, Mexico City; law degree, National School of Law, UNAM. d-Federal
Deputy from the State of Oaxaca, 1918-
20; Federal Deputy from the Federal
District, Dist. 4, 1934-35; *Senator* from
the Federal District, 1940-46, First Secretary of the Department of the Federal
District Committee, and president of
the First Constitutional Affairs Committee. e-Private secretary to the
President of the PNR, *Lázaro Cárdenas*,
1930-31; Secretary General of the CEN
of the PNR, 1934-35; *President of the
CEN of the PRM*, 1940-46. f-Agent of
the Ministerio Público; Judge of the
District Court of San Luis Potosí, La
Paz, Aguascalientes, Zacatecas, Pachuca, and Tijuana, 1927-30; Secretary General of Government to Governor *Jesús
Agustín Castro*, State of Oaxaca, 1915-
16; Secretary General of the State of
Durango, under Governor *Jesús Agustín
Castro*, 1921-24; Attorney for Military
Justice; Oficial Mayor of the Secretariat
of Government; *Secretary General of
the Department of the Federal District*,
1935-37; Secretary General of Government of Baja California del Norte, 1933-
34, under General *Agustín Olachea
Aviles*; *Secretary of Labor and Social
Welfare*, 1937-40; Ambassador to Brazil,
1946-52; President of the Federal Board
of Conciliation and Arbitration for the
Federal District, 1952-58. g-None.
h-Member of the Commission for the
Adjustment of the Public Debt, Secretariat of the Treasury. j-Joined the
Revolution under General *Jesús Agustín
Castro* in Veracruz, 1914. k-Brandenburg places him in the Inner Circle from
1940-46. l-WWM45, 126; *Polémica*,
1969, 71; DGF56, 559; DP70, 2269;
letter; Peral, 861; HA, 5 Nov. 1943, 35;
Brandenburg, 80; STYRBIWW54, 1074;
López, 1160; NYT, 3 Dec. 1940, 12.

Villalobos Rivera, Haydée Aide Eréndira
a-Mar. 13, 1948. b-Guadalajara, Jalisco.
c-Early education unknown; CPA
degree, University of Guadalajara;
degree in business administration,
University of Guadalajara; studies
toward an MA in public administration,
Monterrey Institute of Higher Studies;
Professor of Public Administration,
University of Guadalajara, 1974-82.
d-*Federal Deputy* from the State Jalisco,
Dist. 12, 1982-85, member of the
Treasury Committee and the Program
and Budgeting Committee. e-Joined
PRI, 1970; Subdirector of Patrimony of
the CEN of ANFER of PRI. f-Oficial
Mayor of the State of Jalisco, 1977-82.
g-Member of the Technical Council of
CNOP; General Delegate of CNOP to
Guadalajara, 1983. h-Auditor, Olavarría
and Associates, CPA Firm, 1970;
General Controller, Tequila Products of
Jalisco, 1964-73; General Controller,
Regional Chamber of Tequila Indus-
tries, 1967-73. i-Daughter of Carlos
Villalobos Díaz, public accountant, and
Irene Rivera Espinosa. j-None. k-None.
l-C de D, 1982-85; Directorio, 1982-85;
Lehr, 237; DBGM, 625.

Villalpando Núñez, Sara
a-Mar. 11, 1939. b-Jiquilpan, Michoacán. c-Completed secondary studies;
studies in business. d-*Federal Deputy*
from the Federal District, Dist. 19,
1982-85, member of the Department of
the Federal District Committee, the
Information and Complaints Committee, and the Health and Welfare Committee; *Federal Deputy* from the Federal
District, Dist. 6, 1988-91; Representative of District 18 to the Assembly of
the Federal District, 1991-94. e-Joined
PRI, 1961; labor delegate from the 6th
PRI district, Federal District. f-None.
g-Secretary of the Committee for Sports
Promotion of the CTM of the Federal
District; Secretary of Organization and
Propaganda of the Union of Drugstore,

Drug, and Laboratory Workers; member of the CEN of Women's Organizations of the CTM of the Federal District. h-None. i-Daughter of Enrique Villalpando Magallón, public official. j-None. l-Directorio, 1982-85; C de D, 1982-85; Lehr, 137; DBGM92, 627-28; DBGM89, 560.

Villarreal, Antonio I.
(Deceased Dec. 16, 1944) a-July 3, 1879. b-Lampazos, Nuevo León. c-Secondary education at the Normal School of San Luis Potosí and Monterrey; primary teaching certificate, Normal School of Monterrey; teacher in Monterrey normal schools. d-None. e-Three-time candidate for President of Mexico, the last time in 1934; Secretary of the Organization Committee for the Mexican Liberal Party, Saint Louis, Missouri, 1906. f-Consul General for President Madero in Barcelona, Spain, 1912-13; Secretary of Agriculture, June 1, 1920 to Nov. 26, 1921. g-Reopened the Casa del Obrero Mundial, 1914. h-Writer for the Liberal newspaper *Regeneración*, published by Juan Sarabia and Ricardo Flores Magón, 1904. i-Relative of General Zuazua, Commander of the Northern Armies during the War of the Reform; good friend of José Vasconcelos during the Revolution; married Blanca Sordo; son of Próspero Villarreal and Ignacia González. j-Leader of a revolt in Las Vacas, Coahuila, 1908; joined the Revolution, 1910; rank of Colonel, 1910; rank of Brigade General, 1913, supported the Plan of Guadalupe; Governor and Military Commander of the State of Nuevo León; First President of the Convention of Aguascalientes, 1914; supported Carranza until 1920; supported De la Huerta, 1923; supported Generals Serrano and Gómez, 1927; supported General Escobar, 1929; rank of Division General, Nov. 16, 1940. k-Imprisoned for publishing *El Liberal* in Nuevo León, 1906; went into exile,

1920, 1923, 1929; imprisoned several times. l-DP70, 2274; Peral, 863; Womack, 202-03; López, 1163; Enc. Mex., XII, 1977, 407; Almanaque of Nuevo León, 100-101; Morales Jiménez, 19-22.

Villarreal, Rafael
b-Soto la Marina, Tamaulipas. c-Primary and secondary studies at public schools in Tamaulipas; medical degree, Military Medical College. d-Local Deputy to the State Legislature of Tamaulipas; *Governor of Tamaulipas*, 1933-35. e-None. f-None. g-None. h-Physician. i-Parents were peasants. j-Physician to military forces in Ciudad Victoria, Tamaulipas. k-None. l-Letter.

Villarreal Arrambide, René Patricio
a-Jan. 3, 1947. b-Monterrey, Nuevo León. c-Early education unknown; economics degree, University of Nuevo León, 1964-69, with a thesis on "External Desequilibrium in the Industrialization of Mexico, 1929-75, a Structuralist Focus"; MA in economics, Colegio de México, 1969-71; Ph.D. in economics, Yale University, 1972-75; professor, Anáhuac University, 1971-72; Professor of Economics, Autonomous Technological Institute of Mexico, 1975; Professor of Economics, Colegio de México, 1978-79. d-None. e-None. f-Adviser, Director of Projects and Industrial Programs, National Finance Bank, 1971-72; adviser, Subsecretary of the Treasury, 1974-75; adviser, Secretary of Government Properties, 1975; adviser, Subsecretary of Foreign Trade, Secretary of Commerce, 1977-82; Director of International Finances, Secretariat of the Treasury, 1977-79; Subdirector General of Planning, Secretariat of the Treasury, 1979-82; Technical Secretary, Committee of Industrial Development for Government Plannning, 1982; *Subsecretary of Industrial and Commercial Planning*, Secretariat of Trade and Industrial Development, 1983-85; Gen-

eral Coordinator of the Center of Project Development and Evaluation, Secretariat of Energy, Mines, and Government Industries, 1985-88; Director General of Pipsa, 1988-94. g-Secretary of Interior, National Council of Economists, 1981-83. h-None. i-Son of Patricio Villarreal Quintanilla, businessman, and Esther Arrambide Páez; married Norma Rocío. j-None. k-None. l-Q es QAP, 191; letter; DBGM, 441; DBGM89, 373-74; DBGM92, 394; letter.

Villarreal Caravantes, Guillermo
a-Jan. 10, 1921. b-Durango, Durango. c-Economics degree, Superior School of Economics, National Polytechnic School, 1943; Professor of Economics, Superior School of Economics, IPN, 1953-70; member of the Advisory Commission of the Superior School of Economics. d-None. e-None. f-Economist, Secretary of the Treasury, 1938-45; economist, Secretariat of Agriculture, 1954-70; economist, Conasupo, 1954-70; economist, Department (Regulatory) of Acquisitions, Secretariat of National Patrimony, 1954-70; economist, Bank of Mexico, 1954-70; Oficial Mayor of the Federal Electric Commission, 1970-71; *Director General of the Federal Electric Commission*, 1971-72. g-None. h-Author of numerous economic studies. i-Married Alicia Chávez, physician. j-None. k-None. l-HA, 7 Dec. 1970, 27; HA, 12 Apr., 1971; WNM, 237; Lajoie, 237.

Villarreal Guerra, Américo
a-Apr. 3, 1931. b-Ciudad Victoria, Tamaulipas. c-Early education unknown; civil engineering degree, National School of Engineering, UNAM, 1949-53, with a thesis on drainage systems. d-*Senator* from the State of Tamaulipas, 1982-88, president of the Agricultural Committee; *Governor of Tamaulipas*, 1987-93. e-Joined PRI, 1956; adviser to the IEPES of the

CEN of PRI, 1981-82. f-Chief of Small Irrigation Works, Secretariat of Hydraulic Resources, Tamaulipas, 1956-60; Subdirector of Small Irrigation Works, Secretariat of Hydraulic Resources, 1960-67; Director of Hydraulic Resources, Secretariat of Hydraulic Resources, 1970-76; Director General of Hydraulic Works and Agricultural Engineering for Rural Development, Secretariat of Agriculture and Hydraulic Resources, 1976; *Subsecretary of Hydraulic Infrastructure*, Secretariat of Agriculture and Hydraulic Resources, 1976-80. g-Member of the Liberal Youth of Tamaulipas, 1946-48; member of the Liberal Youth of Mexico, 1949-53. h-None. i-Son of Emilio Villarreal Villarreal, businessman, and Oralia Guerra Hinojosa, businesswoman; married Beatriz Anaya Guerrero. j-None. k-Member of the national champion track team, 1946-48, and national high jump champion, 1951. l-DBGM92, 849; IEPES; Lehr, 465-66; C de S, 1982-88; DBGM, 627; DBGM89, 755.

Villaseñor (Angeles), Eduardo
(Deceased Oct. 15, 1978) a-Sept. 13, 1896. b-Angamacutiro, Villa Unión, Michoacán. c-Primary studies in Angamacutiro; preparatory studies at the Colegio de San Nicolás de Hidalgo, Morelia, Michoacán; studies at the University of London; two years of study in engineering; three years of study in law; graduate studies in philosophy; never formally received a degree; Professor of Economics, National School of Agriculture, 1921-25; Professor of International Trade, National School of Economics, UNAM. d-None. e-None. f-Director, Department of Cooperative Societies, National Agricultural Bank, 1926-28; Director of Economic Statistics, British-Mexican Claims Commission, 1928-29; Secretary, British-Mexican Claims Commission, 1928-29; Commercial Attaché, Mexican Delegation, London,

1929-31; Director of the Consular Department, Secretariat of Foreign Relations, 1931-32; Director, Department of Printing and Publicity, Secretariat of Finance, 1932; member, National Banking Commission, 1932-33; Secretary, National Council of Economics, 1932-34; Secretary, Board of Directors, National Mortgage Bank of Urban and Public Works, 1932-34; Consul General, New York City, 1935; Director of the National Bank of Agricultural Credit, 1936-37; *Subsecretary of the Treasury*, Jan. 17, 1938, to 1940; *Director General of the Bank of Mexico*, 1940-46. g-Leader of the student movement at the Colegio de San Nicolás de Hidalgo, Morelia; Alternate Delegate to the International Congress of Students, Mexico City, 1921. h-Author of many books on economic questions in Mexico; cofounder of the Fondo de Cultura Económica, 1934; President of the Banco del Atlántico, 1949-65; President of the Bank of Mexico City, 1966-70. i-Brother, Roberto, was Director General of the National Institute of Forestry Research; married Margarita Urueta; friends since the 1920s with *Eduardo Suárez, Manuel Gómez Morín*, and *Daniel Cosío Villegas*; father was a small store keeper. j-None. k-None. l-Letter; EBW46, 311; Peral, 865; Kirk, 174-76; Strode, 394; D de Y, 18 Jan. 1938, 1; WWM45, 126; Simpson, 368; Novo35, 196; López; HA, 23 Oct. 1978, 13; NYT, 16 May 1945, 11; HA, 16 Apr. 1945, 34.

Villaseñor (Martínez de Arredondo), Víctor Manuel
(Deceased, Dec. 1981) a-Dec. 23, 1904. b-Distrito Federal. c-Professional studies at the University of Southern California, 1921-24; studies at Cornell University; specialized studies, University of Michigan, 1924-26; law degree, University of Michigan, 1926; law degree, National School of Law,

UNAM, 1929; founder with *Lombardo Toledano* of the Worker's University, 1936; Director of the Karl Marx Workers University, 1936-40. d-None. e-Founder and President of the Socialist League, 1944; Secretary General of the Partido Popular, 1948-49. f-Lawyer, Mexico-United States Claims Commission, 1929-33; delegate, Seventh Pan American Conference, 1933; legal adviser, Mexican Ambassador, Washington, D.C., 1934; Director of Archives, Secretariat of the Treasury, 1934; member, National Council of Higher Education, 1935-38; Director, Department of the Six-Year Plan, Secretariat of Government, 1939-40; Director of the Siderúrgica Nacional, 1949-52; Director General of the Constructora Nacional de Carros de Ferrocarril, 1952-58; Director General of Diesel Nacional, 1959-70; *Director General of National Railroads of Mexico*, 1971-73. g-Founding member of the CTM; representative of the CTM in Zurich, 1939. h-Member of the National Council of Scientific Investigation; Director of *Futuro*, 1936-40; Director General of Siderúrgica Nacional, 1964-70. i-Longtime friend of *Narciso Bassols* and, in his youth, of *Vicente Lombardo Toledano*; practiced law with Luis Cabrera, 1927-28; father, Manuel F. Villaseñor, was an engineer and federal deputy under Madero; grandfather was a senator and supreme court justice under Porfirio Díaz; married Martha de la Portilla. j-None. k-Participated in the IX Olympic Games, Amsterdam, 1928; champion in the 400 meters; candidate for Federal Deputy, 1943. l-Millon, 156; HA, 7 Dec. 1970, 26-27; WWM45, 126; *Hoy*, 13 Mar. 1971, 10; HA, 19 Apr. 1971, 16; letters; Enc. Mex., XII, 1977, 408.

Villaseñor Saavedra, Arnulfo
a-July 19, 1928. b-Guadalajara, Jalisco. c-Early education unknown; legal studies, National School of Law, UNAM,

1947-48, graduating from the School of Law, University of Guadalajara, 1949-51; professor, University of Guadalajara; professor, Feminine University of Guadalajara. d-*Federal Deputy* from the State of Jalisco, Dist. 8, 1967-70; *Senator* from the State of Jalisco, 1976-80; Mayor of Guadalajara, 1980-82; *Federal Deputy* from the State of Jalisco, Dist. 14, 1985-88. e-Joined PRI, 1950; General Delegate of the CEN of PRI to Chihuahua and Durango, 1968; General Delegate of the CEN of PRI to Jalisco, 1972-76; President of PRI, Jalisco, 1972-76. f-Oficial Mayor of the City of Guadalajara, 1953; Secretary of the City of Guadalajara, 1954; Chief, Legal Department, City of Guadalajara, 1962; Private Secretary to the Governor of Jalisco, 1967; Secretary of Finances, State of Jalisco, 1992-94. g-None. h-None. i-Son of Tomás Villaseñor and Isaura Saavedra Padilla; married Teresa Fierro García. j-None. k-None. l-DBGM87, 586; DBGM92, 850.

Villegas (Lora), Otilio
(Deceased Aug. 10, 1961) a-Dec. 13, 1888. b-Jacala, Hidalgo. c-Primary studies in Jacala, Hidalgo; no degree. d-Mayor of Jacala, Hidalgo, 1922-23; Federal Deputy from the State of Hidalgo, Dist. 11, 1928-30, Dist. 6, 1932-34; *Federal Deputy* from the State of Hidalgo, Dist. 6, 1940-43. e-None. f-*Interim Governor of Hidalgo*, 1940-42. g-None. j-Joined the Revolution as a Lieutenant, 1913; rank of Colonel, 1913; rank of Brigadier General, 1916; commander of forces in Hidalgo; commander of forces in Puebla, 1918; supported the Plan of Agua Prieta, 1920; supported de la Huerta forces against the government, 1923-24. k-None. l-Peral; Pérez López, 503-04; C de D, 1940-43, 1932-34, 1928-30.

Villegas Nájera, Dora
a-June 19, 1934. b-Gómez Palacio, Chihuahua. c-Early education un-

known; completed preparatory studies; completed nursing studies, Escuela Justo Sierra, Ciudad Cuauhtémoc, Chihuahua, 1975. d-Member of the City Council of Ciudad Juárez, 1977-80; *Federal Deputy* from the State Chihuahua, Dist. 8, 1982-85, member of the Industrial Development and Property Committee, the Human Dwellings and Public Works Committee, and the Labor and Social Welfare Committee. e-Joined PRI, 1953; Secretary of Organization of the ANFER of PRI, Ciudad Juárez, Chihuahua, 1976-79; Secretary of Social Action of the Executive Committee of ANFER of PRI of Chihuahua, 1979-82; Secretary General of ANFER of PRI in Ciudad Juárez, Chihuahua, 1979-82. f-None. g-Secretary of Political Action of the CTM in Chihuahua, 1978-82; Alternate Secretary of Labor of the CTM, 1980; Secretary General of the Union of Assembly Workers of Ciudad Juárez, 1982-89. i-Daughter of Basilio Villegas Pineda, laborer, and Eduarda Nájera López; married Angel Montañez Magdaleno, white collar worker. j-None. k-None. l-Lehr, 108; Directorio, 1982-85; C de D, 1982-85; DBGM, 627.

Villegas Piña, José Isabel
a-Mar. 2, 1938. b-Ciudad Lerdo, Durango. c-Completed primary school; studies in private accounting, Banking and Business School, Ciudad Lerdo. d-*Plurinominal Federal Deputy* from PAN, 1982-85, member of the Complaints and Information Committee. e-Joined PAN, 1968; Secretary of PAN, Lerdo, Durango, 1969-72; President of PAN, Lerdo, Durango, 1972-74; candidate of PAN for alternate federal deputy, 1973; candidate of PAN for Federal Deputy from Durango, Dist. 11, 1979; candidate of PAN for mayor of Lerdo, 1979; regional adviser to PAN in Durango, 1982; national adviser to PAN, 1982. f-None. g-President of the

Parents Association of the Ricardo
Flores Magón Secondary School, Lerdo,
Durango, 1978-80. h-Accountant,
Juárez Furniture Store; businessman.
i-Son of Juan Villegas Castro and María
de la Luz Piña. j-None. k-None.
l-Directorio, 1982-85; Lehr, 584; C de D,
1982-85.

Viramontes de la Mora, Oralia Estela
a-June 12, 1938. b-Ríoverde, San Luis
Potosí. c-Early education unknown;
architecture degree, University of
Guadalajara, 1956-61; courses at the
School of Plastic Arts, University of
Guadalajara; courses at the Women's
University of Mexico, Mexico City;
member of the Board of Directors,
Professor of Interior Design, 1962-74,
Director, Technical Department,
Interior Decorating Division, 1963-76,
and Secretary General, 1976-77, all at
the Women's University of Guadalajara.
d-Member of the City Council of
Guadalajara, 1979-82; *Federal Deputy*
from the State of Jalisco, Dist. 13, 1982-
85, member of the Human Dwellings
and Public Works Committee, the
National Defense Committee and the
Ecology Committee. e-Joined PRI,
1971. f-None. g-None. j-None.
k-None. l-C de D, 1982-85; Directorio,
1982-85; Lehr, 238; DBGM84, 628.

Viramontes Paredes, José Salvador
a-Dec. 15, 1930. b-Ciudad Serdán,
Puebla. c-Early education unknown;
studies in architecture, IPN, 1952-53;
Professor of Architecture, School of
Architects of Morelos, 1960. d-*Plurino-
minal Federal Deputy* from PAN, 1982-
85. e-Joined PAN, 1965; candidate of
PAN for Alternate Federal Deputy,
1973; candidate of PAN for Senator
from Morelos, 1976; President of the
Regional Committee of PAN for
Morelos, 1975-78; national adviser to
PAN, 1975-78. f-Janitor, Department

Head, Post Office Department, Federal
District, 1944-51; agent, Secretariat of
Health and Welfare, Cuernavaca, 1977.
g-Coordinator, Christian Family
Movement, 1960-68. h-Owner, Art and
Construction Company, 1969-80; owner
and manager, Exclusive Crafts, 1976-80;
Superintendent of Construction, Río
Tijuana & Co. Business Center, 1980-
81. i-Son of Salvador Antonio
Viramontes Paredes, public official, and
Carmen Paredes Vázquez; married
María Elizabeth Leonor Montejo.
j-None. k-None. l-Directorio, 1982-85;
Lehr, 555; C de D, 1982-85; DBGM, 628.

Vista Altamirano, Flavio César
a-Mar. 7, 1922. b-Jalapa, Veracruz.
c-Early education unknown; legal
studies, University of Veracruz, Jalapa,
1939-42, graduating in 1943 with a
thesis on "The Criminal Judge";
professor, School of Business and Law,
University of Veracruz, 1957-64;
professor, National School of Law,
UNAM, 1968-71. d-*Federal Deputy*
from the State of Veracruz, Dist. 5,
1964-67, Vice President of the Gran
Comisión, Vice President of the
Chamber, Dec., 1964; member of the
Legislative Studies Committee, Third
Section on Criminal Affairs; the First
Government Committee; the Budget
and Accounts Committee (1st year); the
Foreign Relations Committee. e-Joined
PRI, 1947; Secretary General of the
CNOP of the PRI of Veracruz, 1962-65;
Secretary of Interior of the CNOP, 1965-
68; *Secretary of Political Action for the
CEN of PRI*, 1964-65; Oficial Mayor of
PRI, 1968-70. f-President of the Board
of Conciliation and Arbitration,
Orizaba, Veracruz, 1944; Secretary, First
Criminal Court, Federal District, 1946-
47; Agent of the Ministerio Público of
the Criminal Courts for the Federal
District, 1947-56; Judge of the State
Supreme Court of Veracruz, 1956-62;

Oficial Mayor of the State of Veracruz, 1962-64; *Oficial Mayor of the Department of the Federal District*, 1970-71; Director General of Legal Affairs, Secretariat of Agrarian Reform, 1982. g-None. h-None. i-Son of Francisco Vista Criscuela, businessman, and Blidah Lucila Altamirano Flores; married Dora Pérez Barrientos. j-None. k-None. l-HA, 14 Dec. 1970, 25; DBM70, 570; C de D, 1964-66, 57; DBGM, 444.

Vital Jáuregui, Ignacio
a-Oct. 18, 1929. b-Fresnillo, Zacatecas. c-Early education unknown; civil engineering degree, University of Guadalajara, 1947-52. d-*Plurinominal Federal Deputy* from the PDM, 1982-85. e-Joined the National Sinarquista Union, 1947; joined the Sinarquista Youth in Jalisco, 1949; Director, Sinarquista Youth in Jalisco, 1951-52; Regional Director of the Popular Force of the National Sinarquista Union; joined the PDM, 1976; President of the PDM in Sinaloa, 1970-74; candidate of the PDM for governor of Sinaloa, 1980; national adviser to the PDM, 1981-89. f-Engineer, Secretariat of Health, 1967-69. g-None. h-Director of Vitmar Construction Company, 1973- . i-Son of Anastasio Vital Enríquez and Micaela Jáuregui Jiménez; married Magdalena Martín Romo. j-None. k-None. l-Directorio, 1982-85; Lehr, 652; C de D, 1982-85; DBGM, 628.

Vivanco García, Pedro
a-June 29, 1915. b-Alvaro Obregón, Michoacán. c-Early education unknown; no degree. d-Mayor of Poza Rica, Veracruz; *Federal Deputy* from the State of Veracruz, Dist. 3, 1952-55, 1964-67. e-None. f-None. g-Director of Local 30, Petroleum Workers Union, Poza Rica, Veracruz; *Secretary General of the National Petroleum Workers Union*, 1959-61; Secretary of Social

Action of the CTM, 1966. h-Petroleum worker. j-None. k-None. l-C de D, 1952-55, 1964-67.

Vivanco (Lozano), José S.
a-Mar. 29, 1899. b-Linares, Nuevo León. c-Primary studies in Monterrey; secondary studies at the Colegio del Sagrado de Corazón de Jesús in Monterrey, Nuevo León; studies in business administration; no degree. d-*Senator from the State of Nuevo León, 1946-52.* e-None. f-Treasurer of the State of Nuevo León, 1939-46; Secretary General of Government of the State of Nuevo León, 1952; *Substitute Governor of Nuevo León, 1952-55; Director General of Conasupo, 1956-58;* Director General of the National Border Program, 1966-69. g-None. h-Sales agent in Monterrey, 1939. i-Son of Manuel Vivanco. j-None. k-None. l-DGF47, 21; HA, 28 Sept. 1945, xvi; DBM68, 629; PdM, 395-96; letter; NYT, 14 Mar. 1956, 27.

Vivanco Montalvo, Isabel
a-July 31, 1934. b-Distrito Federal. c-Primary studies at the Lorenzo Rosales School, Mexico City; secondary studies at the Technical Secondary School No. 2, IPN; no degree. d-*Alternate Federal Deputy* from the Federal District, Dist. 6, 1976-79; *Federal Deputy* from the Federal District, Dist. 29, 1979-82. e-None. f-None. g-Representative of Labor Sector, 20th District, Mexico City; member of the CTM. i-Daughter of Vicente Vivanco and Remedios Montalvo; married Javier Gaeta Vázquez. j-None. k-None. l-Romero Aceves, 742; C de D, 1976-79, 1979-82.

Viveros Pérez, Ernesto
(Deceased Apr. 1953) b-Tetepango, Hidalgo. c-Early education unknown; teaching certificate; teacher. d-Federal Deputy from the State of Hidalgo, Dist.

4, 1930-32; Mayor of Pachuca, Hidalgo, 1932-33; *Governor of Hidalgo*, 1933-37. e-None. f-Director of Tax Collecting, Pachuca, Hidalgo; Treasurer General of the State of Hidalgo. g-None. j-None. k-None. l-C de D, 1930-32; Pérez López, 506.

Vizcaíno Murray, Francisco
a-Oct. 31, 1935. b-Guaymas, Sonora. c-Early education unknown; accounting degree, Certified Public Accountant, UNAM, 1956-61, with "Some Aspects of Fractioning"; MA degree, School of Business and Administration, National Polytechnic Institute, 1964-65; Ph.D. in Administrative Sciences, School of Business and Administration, National Polytechnic School, 1965; professor, School of Business and Administration, UNAM; professor, School of Business and Administration, IPN. d-None. e-None. f-Fiscal adviser to the Secretary of Industry and Commerce, 1967; Auditor General of the Department of Agrarian Affairs, 1965-70; financial adviser to the State of Durango, 1968-70; *Secretary General of the IMSS*, 1970; Subdirector General of Accounting for IMSS, 1971-72; *Subsecretary of the Environment, Secretariat of Health*, 1972-76; Director of the Institute of Nuclear Energy, 1977-79; Director General of Mexican Uranium, 1979-82; Director General of Food Industry, Department of the Federal District, 1982-84. g-None. h-Accountant, Roberto Casas Alatriste Firm, 1956-58; general auditor, Inmobiliaria y Comercial Bustamante, 1959-60; vice president of Firma Vizcaíno, 1960-70; representative of Mexico to various international conferences on the environment. i-Protégé of *Manuel B. Aguirre*; son of Faustino Vizcaíno Valdez, public official, and Rosalina Murray Garay, teacher; married Yvonne Marianne Larrazolo. j-None. k-Precandidate for Governor of Sonora, 1973, 1978.

l-Letter; HA, 14 Aug. 1972, 14; *Excélsior*, 6 Jan. 1973, 23 Nov. 1977, 18, 10 Sept. 1978, 12, 11 Aug. 1978, 1, 11; Q es QAP, 454; DBGM, 444-45.

Vizcarra, Rubén
(Deceased Aug. 19, 1948) a-Nov. 28, 1892. b-Colima, Colima. c-Primary studies in Colima, Colima; teacher certificate, National Normal School, Aug. 30, 1914, on a government scholarship; CPA degree, National Cash Register Co., 1926-30; Professor of Publicity and Sales, Business School, Havana, Cuba, 1930-33. d-Federal Deputy from the Federal District, Dist. 13, 1922-24; *Senator from the State of Colima*, 1946-52. e-None. f-Inspector, Military Instruction, National Preparatory School, Preparatory Boarding School, Normal School and Higher Schools, 1916; administrative inspector, Mexico City Government, 1919; technical administrative inspector, Secretariat of Public Education, 1919. g-None. h-Manager, Rex Publishing Co., Havana, Cuba, 1924-25; agent, National Cash Register Co., San Clara, 1926-30. i-Descendant of historian Ignacio G. Vizcarra. j-Joined the Revolution with a group of students from the Casa M. de Lara, 1913; joined the forces of Major Paulino Navarro Blanca, Sinaloa, 1915; Constitutionalist, 1915-17; member of the Council of War, Mexico City, 1917; retired with the rank of Lt. Colonel, 1917; imprisoned during Plan of Agua Prieta, Guadalajara, May 11, 1920. k-Imprisoned by Victoriano Huerta, 1913. l-Romero Aceves, 211-213; C de D, 1922-24, 33; C de S, 1946-52.

W

Warman (Gryj), Nathan
a-Jan. 1, 1930. b-Federal District. c-Early education unknown; architectural degree, School of Architecture,

UNAM, 1950; economics degree, National School of Economics, UNAM, 1955; post graduate studies, University of Manchester, 1961; post graduate studies, University of Glasgow, 1963; fellow, United Nations, 1960-63; professor, University of Glasgow, 1963-71; professor, Colegio de México. d-None. e-None. f-Economist, Secretariat of the Treasury, 1955-74; Subdirector, Department of Tariffs, Secretariat of the Treasury, 1957-59; Director, Department of Special Studies, Division of Financial Studies, Secretariat of the Treasury, 1959-60; Coordinator of Research for Mexico, Economic Commisson for Latin America, 1971-74; Director General of Credit, National Sugar Finance Bank, 1974-76; *Subsecretary of Industrial Development*, Secretariat of Government Properties, 1976-82. g-None. h-None. i-Part of *Emilio Mújica Montoya*'s group at UNAM; brother of Arturo Warman, director general of the National Indigenous Institute, 1988; brother, José, held position in the Secretariat of Commerce and Industry; son of Issac Warman Langman, merchant, and Elena Gryj Moses. j-None. k-None. l-*Excélsior*, 29 Feb. 1980, 13; Protag., 357.

Wimer (Zambrano), Javier
a-Jan. 6, 1933. b-Federal District. c-Early education unknown; law degree, National School of Law, UNAM, 1952-56; postgraduate studies in philosophy, UNAM, 1952-56; Ph.D., Sorbonne, University of Paris, 1956-58. d-None. e-None. f-Adviser to the President of Mexico, 1959-64, 1970-76; cultural attaché, Mexican Embassy, San José, Costa Rica, 1966-67, Buenos Aires, Argentina, 1967-70; Coordinator of Audiovisual Education, Secretariat of Public Education, 1976-78; joined the Foreign Service, 1980; Director General of Archives, Libraries and Publications, Secretariat of Foreign Relations, 1979-81; Ambassador to Yugoslavia and Albania, 1981-82; *Subsecretary (2) of Government*, 1982-84; Director, Free Textbook Commission, 1984-88, 1988-89. g-None. h-Director, *Nueva Política* magazine, 1973-82; Director General, National Council of Cultural and Recreation for Workers, 1974-76; Director of Espiral Publications, S.A., 1977-81; Director General of the Latin American Center for Political Studies, 1977-81. i-Son of Esperanza Zambrano Sánchez, famous poet, and Miguel Wimer Toscano, surgeon; married Angelina del Valle Fuentes, sociologist; part of the *Medio Siglo* group with *Porfirio Múñoz Ledo*, served as co-director of the magazine; classmate of *Miguel de la Madrid*. j-None. k-None. l-*Excélsior*, 22 Aug. 1983, 7; Q es QAP, 26; IEPES; DBGM, 447; DBGM89, 377.

Wolpert Barraza, Enrique
a-Aug. 18, 1939. b-Culiacán, Sinaloa. c-Primary studies at the Miguel Hidalgo School, Tijuana, Baja California, 1945-51; secondary studies at the Special Studies School No. 29, Tijuana, 1951-54; preparatory studies at the public preparatory school, Tijuana, 1954-56; medical degree, National School of Medicine, UNAM, 1957-62; specialization in internal medicine, National Nutrition Institute, 1964-67; studies in gastroenterology, May Clinic, Rochester, 1967-70; professor, National School of Medicine, UNAM, 1973; professor, National Nutrition Institute, 1973, 1985. d-None. e-None. f-Department head, National Nutrition Institute, 1971; *Subsecretary of Health Services*, Secretariat of Public Health, 1988- . g-None. h-Practicing physician. i-Son of Leon Wolpert Franck, businessman, and Manuel Barraza Pereda; married Rossa Kkrui Alfaro, psychologist. j-None. k-None. l-DBGM89, 378; DBGM92, 397.

Y

Yáñez Centeño, Francisco José
a-Dec. 19, 1909. b-Villa de Alvarez, Colima. c-Primary studies at the Hidalgo School, Colima; secondary studies at the Ramón R. de la Vega School, Colima; teaching certificate from the Normal School of Colima, 1924-29; law degree, School of Law, University of Guadalajara, Jan. 28, 1935, with a thesis on the importance of international law in international relations; Professor of Colima History, Political Economy, Economic Problems of Mexico and Spanish Literature, Popular University of Colima, 1941-51; Professor of Introduction to Law, General Theory of the State, Philosophy of Law, School of Law, University of Colima. d-*Alternate Federal Deputy* from the State of Colima, Dist. 1, 1946-48; Local Deputy to the State Legislature of Colima, 1948-51. e-None. f-Secretary of the City Council of Manzanillo, Colima, 1939-40; Judge, Superior Tribunal of Justice of Colima, 1940-41; President, Arbitration and Conciliation Board of Colima, 1941; Penal Judge, Colima, 1941; Chief of Public Defenders of Colima, 1947-48; *Interim Governor of Colima*, Mar. 18-31, 1951. g-None. h-Editor in Chief of *Horizonte*, Colima; editor of *El Heraldo*, Guadalajara. i-Son of Leonardo Yáñez Centeño Córdoba and Sara Rangel Arroyo; son, Francisco José, was a director general in the Secretariat of Agrarian Reform, 1992; married Hermelinda Cabrera Gudiño. j-None. k-None. l-C de D, 1946-49; Romero Aceves, 213-15; DBGM92, 398.

Yáñez Ruiz, Manuel
a-1903. b-Huehuetoca, Hidalgo. c-Primary studies in Tulancingo; secondary studies in Tulancingo; preparatory studies at the National Preparatory School; law degree from the National

School of Law, UNAM, June 2, 1926, with a specialty in fiscal legislation. d-*Federal Deputy* from the State of Hidalgo, Dist. 2, 1958-61, member of the Legislative Studies Committee (4th Section), the Tax Committee, and the Budget and Accounts Committee; substitute member of the Foreign Relations Committee. e-None. f-Judge of the First Instance, Mextitlan, Hidalgo, 1926-27; judicial conciliator, Pachuca, Hidalgo, 1927-28; Judge of the Second Penal Court, Pachuca, 1927-28; Judge of the Second Penal Court, Pachuca, 1928-29; Judge of the First Instance, Tulancingo, Hidalgo, 1929-30; Judge of the Civil Court, Pachuca, 1930-31; Judge of the Superior Tribunal of Justice of the State of Hidalgo, 1931; President of the Conciliation and Arbitration Board of Hidalgo, 1933; Secretary General of Government of the State of Hidalgo under Governor *Rojo Gómez*, 1937-40; Treasurer of the Federal District, 1940-44; Representative of the Central Zone before the National Arbitration Commission, Secretariat of the Treasury, 1946-53; Director General of Domestic Taxes, Secretariat of the Treasury, 1953-58; *Justice of the Supreme Court*, 1961-64, 1965-70, 1971-73. g-President of the National Student Federation, 1925. i-Political protégé of *Javier Rojo Gómez*; descendant of Mariano Yáñez, Secretary of the Treasury in the 19th century; married María Teresa Crespo; son of Carlos Yáñez Ortiz de Montellano and Esther Ruiz Beckar. j-None. k-None. l-Func., 231; C de D, 1958-60, 9; DGF56, 165; letter; *Justicia*, June, 1968; WNM, 245; HA, 26 Nov. 1973, 10.

Yáñez (Santos Delgadillo), Agustín
(Deceased Jan. 17, 1980) a-May 4, 1904. b-Guadalajara, Jalisco. c-Primary and secondary studies in Guadalajara; preparatory studies in Guadalajara; law degree, University of Guadalajara, Oct. 15, 1929, with a thesis "Towards an

American International Law"; professor, Preparatory School José Paz Camacho, Guadalajara, 1926-29; professor, Preparatory School, University of Guadalajara, 1931-32; normal school teacher, Guadalajara, 1923-29; professor at UNAM, 1932-42; professor, Women's University of Mexico, 1946-50; professor of Spanish and Literature, National Preparatory School, 1932-76 (with leaves); founder and Director of the Institute of the State of Nayarit, 1930-31; Professor of Literary Theory, School of Philosophy and Letters, UNAM, 1942-53, 1959-62. d-*Governor of Jalisco,* 1953-58. e-Member of the Political Education Section of the IEPES of PRI, 1972. f-Director of Radio Educational Extension Programs, Secretariat of Public Education, 1932-34; Director of Primary Education for the State of Nayarit, 1930-31; Assistant Director and Director of the Library and Economic Archives, Secretariat of the Treasury, 1934-52; President of the Editorial Committee of UNAM, 1944-47; President of the Technical Council of Humanistic Research, UNAM, 1945-52; adviser to the Secretariat of the Presidency, 1959-62; Special Ambassador to Argentina, 1960; *Subsecretary of the Presidency,* 1962-64; *Secretary of Public Education,* 1964-70; President of the Free Textbook Commission, 1978-79. g-Member of the Mexican Catholic Youth Association with *Efraín González Luna* in the 1920s. h-Member of the Education Committee of UNAM, 1945-52; major Mexican novelist and author of many literary studies. i-Parents were peasants; married Olivia Ramírez Ramos. j-None. k-Sympathetic to the Cristero movement in Jalisco, 1928-29; supported José Vasconcelos, 1929; candidate for Director of the National Preparatory School, Aug. 1944, but did not win. l-DBM68, 633-34; WWMG, 41; Johnson, 183; HA, 10 July, 1972, 10; DGF56, 94; IWW67-68, 1341; Correa,

255; Peral, 873; DEM, 13-14; Enc. Mex., XII, 1977, 433-34; letter; López, 1172-73; HA, 17 Dec. 1973, 30; *Excélsior,* 19 Jan. 1980, B1, 3.

Yocupicio (Valenzuela), Román
(Deceased 1950) a-Feb. 28, 1890. b-Masiaca, Alamos, Sonora. c-Primary education in Masiaca; no degree. d-Mayor of Navojoa, Sonora, 1921-23. e-None. f-*Substitute Governor of Sonora,* 1937-39. g-None. h-Farmer, 1929. i-Son of a Yaqui Indian, Juan Yocupicio, and Paulina Valenzuela. j-Joined the Revolution, 1909; first action was at Alamos, Sonora, 1910; joined the Constitutional Army, 1913; fought in the battle for Culiacán, Oct. 23, 1913; fought Francisco Villa at Celaya, 1915; rank of Major, 1915; special escort to General Obregón, 1915; fought in the battle of Puebla, Jan. 1915; opposed the Convention of Aguascalientes, 1914-15; fought against De la Huerta, Ocotlán, Jalisco, 1923; supported General Escobar against the Federal Government, 1929; reached rank of Division General. k-Unsympathetic to *Cárdenas's* agrarian reform program in his state, supported the interests of industrialists and large landowners; the CTM accused him of being a fascist. l-DP70, 2312; Millon, 134; *Annals,* Mar. 1940, 18; Peral, 874-75; NYT, 17 July 1938; NYT, 20 Aug. 1938, 4; Almanaque de Sonora, 130; de Parodi, 45-53.

Yurén Aguilar, Jesús
(Deceased Sept. 22, 1973) a-Jan. 1, 1901. b-Federal District. c-Primary studies in the Federal District; studies in business administration in the Federal District; left school in 1915; no degree. d-*Federal Deputy* from the Federal District, Dist. 9, 1937-40, Dist. 8, 1943-46; *Senator* from the Federal District, 1952-58, member of the Gran Comisión, the Second Navy Committee, the Securities Committee, and the Legal Studies Committee; *Senator* from the Federal

District, 1964-70. e-*Secretary of Labor Action of the CEN of PRI*, 1958-64. f-Driver for the Department of the Federal District; head of the Chauffeurs Department of the Department of the Federal District. g-Began union activity, 1922; head of the Sanitation Workers of the Department of the Federal District; organized the workers central in the Federal District, 1928; leader of the Street Cleaners and Transportation Workers Union, 1929; chief of the Mexican delegation to the International Labor Conference, Geneva, 1938; First Secretary of the Federation of Workers of the Federal District, 1941-43; member of the executive committee of the CTM, 1952; Secretary General of the Federation of Workers of the Federal District, 1949-73. h-Worked for El Aguila Petroleum Company. i-Married Blanca Guerrero; early labor ally of *Vicente Lombardo Toledano*; political supporter of *Fidel Velázquez* since 1941; founded the CTM with *Fidel Velázquez, Fernando Amilpa*, and *Alfonso Sánchez Madariaga* in 1936; co-founder with *Fidel Velázquez* of the Federation of Workers of the Federal District, 1941. j-Fought in the Constitutionalist Army under Carranza, 1920. k-None. l-C de S, 1952-58; C de D, 1937-39; C de S, 1964-70; C de D, 1943-45; DGF56, 6, 8, 11, 13, 14; HA, 30 Sept. 1973, 18; Ind. Biog., 168.

Z

Zamora, Adolfo

b-Nicaragua. c-Preparatory studies at the National Preparatory School, Mexico City, 1921-24; irregular studies at the School of Liberal Arts and the Law School, Sorbonne, Paris, 1926-30; completed legal studies at the National School of Law, UNAM, 1931; law degree, Jan. 1932, with a thesis on the "Birth and Death of the Bourgeois

State"; professor at the Higher School of Commerce and Administration, National Polytechnic Institute, 1931-40; Professor of Social Welfare at UNAM. d-None. e-None. f-Technician, Department of Social Welfare, Secretariat of Labor, 1932; President of the Editorial Committee of the Social Security Law, 1932-40; lawyer for the National Urban Mortgage Bank of Public Works, 1933; founder and Director of the Office of Municipal Studies, National Urban Mortgage Bank of Public Works; Director of the Legal Department, National Urban Mortgage Bank of Public Works; founder and Director General of the Housing Development Bank, 1946; Subdirector of the National Urban Mortgage Bank of Public Works, 1947; Director General of the National Urban Mortgage Bank of Public Works, 1947-53. g-None. h-Author of the 1941 Social Security Law approved by Congress; author of several articles on social security; wrote for José Vasconcelos's magazine, *Antorcha*; lawyer for the Federal Comptroller General, 1932; investigator for the Institute of Social Investigations, UNAM, 1930. i-Friend of *Antonio Ortiz Mena* in preparatory school. j-None. k-None. l-Letter; DGF47; *Excélsior*, 26 Aug. 1981, 18.

Zamora Verduzco, Elías

a-Nov. 3, 1946. b-Cuauhtémoc, Colima. c-Early education unknown; degree in political science and public administration, National School of Political and Social Sciences, UNAM, 1974-77; studies in accounting, IPN. d-Mayor of Manzanillo, Colima, 1983-85; *Governor of Colima*, 1985-91. e-Joined PRI, 1965; Secretary of Sports Action of the CEN of PRI, 1965; Auxiliary Secretary of Organization of the CEN of PRI, 1979. f-Auxiliary Director General, Banobras, 1966-72; Housing Supervisor, Banobras, 1972-74; Assistant Manager, Villa Coapa Development, Banobras, 1975-76; General Administrator, Vicente Guerrero Housing Unit, Department of the Federal District, 1978-79; General Administrator, Ermita Zaragoza Housing Unit, Department of the Federal District, 1979. g-Auxiliary Secretary, Youth Sector, CNC, 1968-70. h-None. i-Son of Salvador Zamor Vizcaíno, laborer, and Petra Verduzco Contreras; married Elba Cecilia Vega Ochoa, teacher. j-None. k-None. l-*Excélsior*, 21 Jan. 1985, 6, 18 Jan. 1985, 12; DBGM89, 756-57.

Zapata Loredo, Fausto
a-Dec. 18, 1940. b-San Luis Potosí, San Luis Potosí. c-Primary studies, Niños Heroes School, San Luis Potosí; secondary studies at the Normal School of San Luis Potosí; preparatory studies from the University of San Luis Potosí; legal studies from the School of Law, University of San Luis Potosí, 1958-61, no degree; studies at the World Press Institute, Macalester College, Minnesota, 1964; seminars, Cornell University, New York; Professor of the Informational Sciences, School of Political and Social Sciences, UNAM, 1967-68. d-*Alternate Federal Deputy* from the State of San Luis Potosí, Dist. 4, 1967-70, but in functions, 1968-70; *Senator* from the State of San Luis Potosí, 1976-82; *Governor of San Luis Potosí*, 1991 (Oct. 1-9). e-Member of the National Council of the PRI; campaigned for *Antonio Rocha* during his gubernatorial campaign, 1967; National Press Coordinator for the presidential campaign of *Luis Echeverría*, 1970. f-*Subsecretary of the Presidency*, 1970-76; Ambassador to Italy, 1977; Ambassaador to China, 1987. g-Secretary of Press and Publicity for the National Farmers Federation, 1965. h-Reporter for *La Prensa*, Mexico City; Assistant Director and Director of Information, *La Prensa*, 1962-65; columnist, *Excélsior*, 1986-87. i-Son of Fausto Zapata Delgadillo and María

Concepción Loredo de Avila; married Laurie Gershenson Shapiro. j-None. k-The first Subsecretary of Information for the Secretariat of the Presidency; elected as an Alternate Deputy but replaced *Guillermo Fonseca Alvarez*, 1968-70; precandidate for governor of San Luis Potosí, 1984; forced to resign as governor of San Luis Potosí after nine days because of public protests atainst election fraud. l-*Hoy*, 19 Dec. 1970, 4; HA, 14 Dec. 1970, 23; MGF69, 95; LA, 3 Dec. 1976, 3; *Excélsior*, 27 July 1984, 20; *El Nacional*, 10 Oct. 1991, 1.

Zapata Portillo de Manrique, Ana María
a-June 22, 1915. b-Cuautla, Morelos. c-Completed primary studies. d-*Federal Deputy* from the State of Morelos, Dist. 2, 1958-61, member of the Library Committee and the Agrarian Committee. e-Began political activities, 1934; Secretary of Women's Action of PRI for the State of Morelos. f-Syndic for the City Council of Cuautla, Morelos. g-President of the National Union of Revolutionary Women; Secretary of Women's Action of the League of Agrarian Communities. i-Related to Emiliano Zapata. j-None. k-First female deputy elected from the state of Morelos. l-Func., 283; C de D, 95.

Zapata Vela, Carlos
c-Preparatory studies at the National Preparatory School; law degree, National School of Law, UNAM, with a thesis on the "Socialization of Land," 1931. d-*Federal Deputy* from the Federal District, Dist. 10, 1940-43, Secretary of the Preparatory Groups, member of the Second Constitutional Affairs Committee, the First Government Committee and the Political Control Committee; *Federal Deputy* from the Federal District, Dist. 11, 1961-64, member of the Credit, Money and Institutions of Credit Committee and the Second Balloting Committee.

e-Member of the Legal Section of the Advisory Body to the National Revolutionary Bloc of the Senate, 1937. f-Subdirector of the National Agricultural Credit Bank, 1946-50; *Ambassador to the USSR*, 1967-69. g-None. h-Director of the Institute of Friendship and Inter-Cultural Exchanges, USSR -Mexico, 1974. i-Assistant to General *Jara.* j-None. k-Leader of the 1929 Strike Movement at UNAM; editor of the National Preparatory School newspaper, *Avalancha*; Marxist. l-NYT, 24 May 1964, 3; DGF47, 354; DGF49, 468; C de D, 1961-63, 95, 1940-42, 22, 46, 51; DGF49, 468; Novo35, 570.

Zárate Albarrán, Alfredo
(Deceased Mar. 8, 1942) a-Aug. 21, 1900. b-Tamascaltepec, México. c-Primary studies while working to help parents; no degree. d-*Federal Deputy* from the State of México, Dist. 9, 1937-40; *Senator* from the State of México, 1940-41; *Governor of México*, 1941-42. e-None. f-Employee, Mixed Judicial District, First Appeals Division, Tamascaltepec; agent of the Ministerio Público, Temascaltepec. g-None. i-Son of Angel Zarate Huerta and Natalia Albarrán Cuevas, peasants; father had a tiny business in Real de Arriba, México. j-None. k-Assassinated by Fernando Ortiz Rubio, police inspector and president of the State Legislature of México; his assassination renewed the political career of *Isidro Fabela* who replaced him as governor. l-Correa, 134; NYT, 7 Mar. 1942, 5; *Hoy*, Dec. 1940, 64-65; HA, 8 Jan. 1943, 5 Mar. 1942; Siliceo, 202-03.

Zárate Aquino, Manuel
a-Dec. 25, 1911. b-Yanhuitlán, Nochixtlán, Oaxaca. c-Early education unknown; normal teaching certificate, 1929-33; certificate in primary education, Normal Urban School, Mar. 27, 1946; legal studies at the University of Oaxaca (Benito Juárez), 1943-49,

graduating with a thesis on the unconstitutionality of the civil administrative boards, 1955; professor at the Institute of Arts and Sciences of Oaxaca, 1948-74; professor at the Normal Urban School, Oaxaca. d-Member of City Council, Oaxaca, Oaxaca, 1933, 1936-38; *Federal Deputy* from the State of Oaxaca, Dist. 6, 1964-67, President of the Chamber, Nov., 1964, secretary of the Gran Comisión, member of the First General Means of Communication Committee, the Second Constitutional Affairs Committee, the Editorial Committee, and Secretary of the Legislative Studies Committee; *Governor of Oaxaca*, 1974 to Mar. 3, 1977. e-Member of the Oaxacan Socialist Party, 1929; President of the Economic, Social, and Planning Council of PRI for the *López Mateos* presidential campaign, 1958; former member of the PPS. f-Penal judge, Oaxaca, Oaxaca, 1958-60; President of the Superior Tribunal of Justice of Oaxaca, 1960-64, 1969-74. g-Secretary General of Local 22 of the SNTE, 1951; Secretary General of the FSTSE, State of Oaxaca, 1949-52. i-Personal friend of *Víctor Bravo Ahuja*, Secretary of Public Education, 1970-74; son of Manuel Zárate Ramírez and Carmen Aquino. j-None. k-PRI candidate for Governor of Oaxaca, 1974; his candidacy surprised most political observers; political enemy of *Jesús Robles Martínez* during his union activities in the SNTE in the 1950s; resigned from the governorship. l-*Excélsior*, 14 Mar. 1974, 11, 15 Mar. 1974, 17; C de D, 1964-67, 81, 83, 92, 95; *Excélsior*, 4 Mar. 1977; HA, 14 Mar. 1977, 20; *Excélsior*, 11 Aug. 1978, 4.

Zárate Pineda de Lino, Irma
a-Dec. 23, 1939. b-Toluca, México. c-Early education unknown; secondary teaching certificate, Normal School, Toluca, México, 1958; kindergarten certificate, Higher Normal School, Toluca, 1962; primary teacher, 1959;

teacher, Girls Normal School, 1961.
d-*Federal Deputy* from the State of
México, Dist. 4, 1982-85, member of the
Public Education Committee, the
Tourism Committee, and the Radio,
Television and Film Committee. e-Secretary of the local electoral committee
of PRI; Delegate of ANFER of PRI to
senatorial elections; Secretary General
of the ANFER of PRI in the State of
México, 1981-86. f-Director of the Department of Artistic Activities, Division
of Public Education, State of México,
1969-81. g-Secretary of Finances,
SNTE, State of México. h-None. i-Widow of Manuel Lino Velázquez, career
military; daughter of Manuel Zárate
Rodríguez, public official, and Consuelo
Pineda Moreno, teacher. j-None.
k-None. l-C de D, 1982-85; Directorio,
1982-85; Lehr, 260; DBGM, 630.

Zavala, Silvio
a-Feb. 7, 1909. b-Mérida, Yucatán.
c-Preparatory studies at the University
of the Southeast, Mérida, Yucatán; law
degree, National School of Law,
UNAM, 1931; LLD from the Central
University of Madrid, 1931-33, on a
fellowship; Professor, History of Social
Institutions of America, School of
Philosophy and Letters, UNAM, 1945;
founder, Director, and Professor, Center
of Historical Studies, Colegio de
México, 1940-56; lectured at Columbia
University, Princeton University and
the University of Pennsylvania under a
grant from the Carnegie Endowment for
International Peace; Guggenheim
Fellow, Library of Congress, 1938-40;
Rockefeller Foundation Fellow, 1944.
d-None. e-None. f-Researcher, His-
panic American Section, Center of
Historical Studies, Madrid, Spain, 1933-
36; Secretary, National Museum,
Mexico City, 1937-38; Director,
Mexican Historical Series of Unedited
Works, 1938-40; Director, National
Museum of History of Mexico, 1946-54;

Director, Educational and Cultural
Section, United Nations, 1947; Cultural
Adviser, Mexican Embassy, Paris,
France, 1954-58; Permanent Delegate of
Mexico to UNESCO, 1956-62; President
of the Colegio de México, 1963-66;
Ambassador to France, 1970-75.
g-Member of the National College.
h-Director of the *Revista de Historia de
América*, 1938. i-Married María
Castelo Biedma; son of Arturo Závala
Castillo and Mercedes Vallado García;
disciple of Rafael Altamirano; studied
under *Daniel Cosío Villegas*. j-None.
k-National Prize in Letters, 1969.
l-Letters; Enc. Mex., XII, 1977, 569-70;
López, 1188; WNM, 247-48; B de M,
267-68; WWM45, 129; JSH, 436-438.

Zebadua (Liévano), José Humberto
a-Mar. 14, 1921. b-San Cristóbal Las
Casas, Chiapas. c-Primary studies in
San Cristóbal; secondary studies in
Mexico City; BA degree from Holy
Cross College, Worcester, Massachusetts. d-*Federal Deputy* from the State
of Chiapas, Dist. 2, 1958-61, member of
the Legislative Studies Committee, the
Fourth Ejido Committee and the First
General Means of Communication
Committee. e-Joined PAN, 1957.
f-None. g-None. h-Businessman.
j-None. k-Elected as Alternate Federal
Deputy from the Federal District, Dist.
6, but replaced *Antonio Zoreda Cebada*
as the deputy from Chiapas. l-Func.,
155; C de D, 1958-61, 95.

Zedillo Ponce de Léon, Ernesto
a-Dec. 27, 1951. b-Federal District.
c-Primary and secondary studies at
public schools, Mexicali, Baja California; preparatory studies, IPN Vocational
School No. 5, 1967-69; economics
degree, Higher School of Economics,
IPN, 1969-72; special studies in human
resources, University of Bradford, 1973;
MA in economics, Yale University;
Ph.D. in economics, Yale University,

1974-78, with a thesis on the external public debt in Mexico; Professor, Higher School of Economics, IPN, 1973-74, 1978-80; Professor, Colegio de México, 1981-83. d-None. e-Joined PRI, 1971; director of *Luis Donaldo Colosio's* presidential campaign, 1993-94; replaced *Luis Donaldo Colosio* as PRI presidential candidate following Colosio's assassination. f-Economic Researcher, Division of Economic and Social Planning, Secretariat of the Presidency, 1971-74; economist, 1978-82, Assistant Manager, Economics and Treasury Research, 1982-83, and Director, Ficorca, 1983-87, all at Bank of Mexico; *Subsecretary of Planning and Budget Control*, Secretariat of Programming and Budget, 1987-88, under *Pedro Aspe; Secretary of Programming and Budgeting*, 1988-92; *Secretary of Public Education*, 1992-93. g-Not an activist leader, but participated in the 1968 student movement while at IPN Vocational School No. 5. h-None. i-Son of Rodolfo Zedillo Castillo, contractor, and Martha Alicia Ponce de León; disciple of *Leopoldo Solís*, who supervised him at the secretariat of the presidency; classmate of *Jaime Serra Puche*, Yale University; came in contact with *Carlos Salinas de Gortari* as an analyst in Presidency, 1972. j-None. k-None. l-DBGM89, 385; *Proceso*, 13 Jan. 1992, 13; DBGM92, 402.

Zepeda Torres, David
a-May 30, 1924. b-Mazatlán, Sinaloa. c-Early education unknown; pilot, Nautical School, Mazatlán; naval engineering degree, Heroic Naval Military School of the Pacific, Mazatlán, 1941-45; Continental Defense Course, Inter-American Defense College, Washington, D.C., 1967-68; staff and command diploma, Center for Higher Naval Studies, 1970; professor, Center for Heroic Naval School, 1957-61; Director, Center for Higher Naval Studies, 1973-

75. d-None. e-None. f-*Subsecretary of the Navy*, 1988-94. g-None. h-None. i-Son of Pablo Zepeda Contreras, small businessman, and Irene Torres Hernández; married Irma Concepción Girón Lacunza. j-None. k-None. l-Section Chief, Staff, Secretariat of the Navy, 1966-67, 1968-70; Aide, Naval Attaché, United States, 1967-68 Subchief of Staff, Secretariat of the Navy, 1970-73; Commander, Second Naval Zone, Puerto Cortés, 1975-77; Inspector, Secretariat of the Navy, 1978-79; Director General of Services, Secretariat of the Navy, 1979-82; Naval Attaché, Lima, Peru, 1983-85; Inspector and Controller General of the Navy, 1986-88. k-None. l-DBGM87, 418; DBGM89, 385; DBGM92, 403.

Zermeño Araico, Manuel
a-Oct. 26, 1901. b-Guadalajara, Jalisco. c-Primary and secondary studies in Guadalajara; graduated from the Naval Academy of Veracruz; professor at the Higher War College; Director of the Naval School of Mazatlán. d-None. e-Vice President of PARM, 1977. f-Adviser to the Chief of Staff under President *Cárdenas*, 1935-39; Chief of Staff for the Navy, 1946-47; Naval Attaché to the Mexican Embassy, Washington, D.C., 1941-45; Director General of the Fleet, Secretariat of the Navy, 1951-55; Ambassador to Norway, 1955-58; *Secretary of the Navy*, 1958-64. g-None. h-Author of various works on naval subjects. i-Married María Antonia del Peón. j-Career naval officer; joined the navy, 1917; put down a revolt in Frontera, Tabasco, Apr. 22, 1924; fought against the de la Huerta Rebellion, 1923; rank of Frigate Captain, 1940; rank of Navy Captain, 1943; rank of Commodore, 1946; Commander of the 3rd Naval Zone, Veracruz (3 times); Commander of the Anahuac Unit; served on the corvette *Záragoza*; rank of Rear Admiral, 1950; rank of

Vice Admiral, 1952; rank of Admiral, 1952; Adjutant General of the Naval College at Veracruz; retired from active duty, 1967. k-None. l-D de Y, 2 Dec. 1958, 7; HA, 8 Dec. 1958, 30; DGF56, 128; DGF47, 234; D de S, 3 Dec. 1952, 1; Func.; HA, 19 Mar. 1979, VI; *Excélsior*, 2 July 1977, 15.

Zertuche Múñoz, Fernando
a-Feb. 3, 1936. b-Federal District. c-Early education unknown; law degree, National School of Law, UNAM, 1961; developed a course in methodology and historical research, Colegio de México; Professor of Sociology and Constitutional Law, Women's University of Mexico, 1957-58; researcher for the Seminar of History, Colegio de México, 1959-60; Professor of History of the Mexican Revolution, 1968-70; Professor of Labor Law, School of Accounting and Administration, UNAM, 1962-64. d-None. e-Director, Fondo para la Historia de las Ideas Revolucionarias en México, PRI, 1976-78. f-Director of the Department of Labor Relations, Teléfonos de México, S.A., 1961-66; Assistant Secretary of the Technical Council of the IMSS, 1966-70; *Oficial Mayor of Labor*, 1970-74; President of the Federal Board of Conciliation and Arbitration, 1974-76; *Secretary General of the IMSS*, 1976-82; *Subsecretary "A" of Labor*, 1982-85. g-None. h-Executive Secretary of *Medio Siglo*, 1956-58, founded by *Porfirio Múñoz Ledo*. i-Married to Martha Sánchez Servín; son of Albino Zertuche Carrillo, engineer, and Sofia Múñoz Amparo. j-None. k-None. l-HA, 14 Dec. 1970, 23; DPE71; letters; *Excélsior*, 14 June 1974, 19; Q es QAP; DBGM, 452.

Zevada (Martínez de Castro), Ricardo José
(Deceased Oct. 25, 1979) a-July 5, 1904. b-Federal District. c-Primary studies in Colima and in Mexico City; law degree, National School of Law, UNAM, 1925; Professor of Administrative Law, UNAM, 1927-34. d-None. e-None. f-Chief of Lawyers, Committee to Liquidate Old Banks, 1930-32; chief lawyer, National Mortgage Bank of Urban and Public Works, 1932-34; Director General of Credit, Secretariat of the Treasury, 1934-36; financial adviser to Ambassador *Narciso Bassols*, London, 1936-37; Director, Department of Credit, National Bank of Ejido Credit, 1937-38; Executive Director of the Commodities Market Regulatory Commission, 1938-40; member of the Editorial Committee for the Second Six-Year Plan, 1940; Founder and Director General of the National Savings Bank, 1941-52; *Director General of the National Bank of Foreign Trade*, 1952-58, 1958-64, 1965; President of the Board of Directors, National Savings Bank, 1965-76. g-None. h-Book clerk at UNAM; author of many works on Mexico; founder of the National Bank of Ejido Credit, 1936; practicing lawyer with *Narciso Bassols*, 1925-34; founding stockholder of GE of Mexico and many other companies. i-Friend of *Antonio Martínez Báez* at UNAM; close personal friend of *Narciso Bassols*; son of a mining engineer, Alfonso María Zevada Baldenebro, and Catalina Martínez de Castro de la Vega; grandfather, Ricardo Martínez de Castro, was a senator; married Guadalupe Moreno Garcini, daughter of railroad engineer; uncle, José María Zeveda, married *Francisco González de la Vega*'s aunt; mentor to *Miguel de la Madrid* in his early career. j-None. k-None. l-Letter; González Navarro, 161; WWM45, 129; Enc. Mex., XII, 1977, 572-73; Linajes, 293-94; *Excélsior*, 27 Oct. 1979, 2.

Zierold Reyes, Pablo
b-Federal District. c-Early education unknown; degree in veterinary medicine, UNAM, 1938; Professor, School of

Veterinary Medicine, UNAM, 1957-65; Director of the School of Veterinary Medicine, UNAM, 1965. d-None. e-None. f-Veterinarian, Secretariat of Agriculture and Livestock (fourteen years); *Subsecretary of Livestock,* Secretariat of Agriculture, 1975-76. g-None. h-President of the Third and Fourth Pan American Veterinary Congresses. j-None. k-None. l-*El Universal,* 27 June 1975, 2; *The News*; HA, 7 July 1975, 20.

Zincúnegui Tercero, Leopoldo
a-Feb. 23, 1895. b-Zinapécuaro, Michoacán. c-Secondary studies at the Scientific and Literary Institute of Toluca, México; preparatory studies at the National Preparatory School, Mexico City; law degree, National School of Law, UNAM. d-Federal Deputy from the State of Michoacán, Dist. 4, 1918-20, 1920-22; Federal Deputy from the Federal District, Dist. 1, 1924-26; Federal Deputy from the State of Michoacán, Dist. 4, 1926-28, Dist 4, 1928-30; *Alternate Federal Deputy* from the State of Michoacán, Dist. 11, 1937-40; *Federal Deputy* from the State of Michoacán, Dist. 11, 1940-43, member of the Permanent Commission, 1940, member of the Protocol Committee, the First Balloting Committee, the Rules Committee, and the First Instructive Section of the Grand Jury. e-None. f-Judge of the Civil Registry, Mexico City; Federal Inspector for the Secretariat of the Treasury; Subdirector of the Technical Industrial Department, Secretariat of Public Education. g-None. h-Author of several works. i-Grandson of General Miguel Zincúnegui, Governor of Michoacán in the 1850s; governor Miguel Silva was his patron. j-None. k-None. l-Peral, 886-87; DP70, 2345; C de D, 1937-39, 1940-42, 47, 53, 55, 59; López, 1190-91; C de D, 1918-20, 1920-22, 1924-26, 1926-28, 1928-30; Dicc. Mich., 492.

Zorrilla (Carcaño), Manuel
a-1921. c-Early education unknown; engineering degree; Director of the Graduate School of Mechanical and Electrical Engineering, IPN, 1968; Director of the Electronics and Communication Engineering Curriculum, IPN, 1970. d-None. e-None. f-*Director General of the National Polytechnic Institute,* 1970-76. g-President of the Mexican Association of Engineers. h-None. j-None. k-Remained on good terms with the students during the 1968 strike. l-HA, 6 Sept. 1971, 21; HA, 21 Dec. 1970, 72; Glade and Ross, 178.

Zorrilla de la Garza, Carlos
a-Apr. 7, 1922. b-Monterrey, Nuevo León. c-Early education unknown; legal studies, National School of Law, UNAM, 1941-45, graduating in 1946; post graduate studies in American law, University of Louisiana, 1946-47; Professor of Institutions and Credit Operations, Autonomous Technological Institute of Mexico, 1960-63. d-None. e-None. f-Subdirector of Finances, Pemex, 1967-70; Director of Finance, Sahagún Industrial Complex, 1970-75; adviser to the Director General of the IMSS, 1975-77; Chief, Sectoral Unit Coordination, Secretariat of Government, 1977-78; Director of Credit, National Finance Bank, 1978-82. g-None. h-Subdirector of Trusts, Bancomer, 1947-53; lawyer, Monterrey Glass Group, 1953-56; Manager of Trusts, Bancomer, 1956-63; Subdirector General of Crédito Minero y Mercantil, S.A., 1963-68. i-Son of Carlos Zorrilla Gómez, lawyer, and Josefina de la Garza Evia; married María Guadalupe Sada de la Garza; cousin of *Pedro Zorrilla Martínez.* j-None. k-None. l-Letter.

Zorrilla Martínez, Pedro Gregorio
a-July 30, 1933. b-Monterrey, Nuevo León. c-Primary, secondary, and preparatory studies in Monterrey; first year of

law studies, Law School, University of
Nuevo León; legal studies at the
National School of Law, 1950-54, law
degree, Oct. 27, 1955; LLD from the
School of Law and Economic Sciences,
University of Paris, 1956-58; Ph.D.,
Dec. 2, 1958; postgraduate work in
economic planning and public finance,
University of London and at the
International Academy at The Hague,
1958; Professor of Public Administra-
tion and Economic Development,
National Preparatory School; Professor
in the Ph.D. program of the School of
Political and Social Sciences, UNAM,
1967-73; Professor of Administrative
Law, Ibero-American University, 1966-
67; Professor of Labor Law, School of
Social Workers, 1959-60; guest profes-
sor, CEMLA, 1967-70; visiting profes-
sor, St. Mary's University, San Antonio,
Texas; Professor of Administrative
Theory, National School of Law,
UNAM, 1959-84. d-*Governor of Nuevo
León*, 1973-79. e-Professor at the
Institute of Political Training, PRI.
f-Legal adviser to the Federal Board for
Decentralized Agencies; Secretary to
the Third Division, Superior Tribunal of
Justice of the Federal District, 1955;
Director General of Population, Secre-
tariat of Government, 1970-71; Secre-
tary General of the State of Tamaulipas,
1968; adviser to the Secretariat of the
Presidency, 1980-82; Subdirector of
Legal Counsel, Secretariat of the
Presidency, 1965; General Attorney for
the National Border Program, 1961;
legal adviser, Secretariat of National
Patrimony, 1961; Commissioner of the
Public Administration Commission,
Secretariat of the Presidency, 1964-68;
*Oficial Mayor of the Department of the
Federal District*, 1971-72; *Attorney
General of the Federal District and
Federal Territories*, Aug. 9, 1972-73.
g-None. h-Considered an expert on
administrative theory. i-Brother,
Rodrigo, is an architect; assistant to

Horacio Flores de la Peña, impressed
Octavio Senties as an adviser to the
11th Interparliamentary Reunion
between Mexico and the United States;
married María Concepción Velasco
Laddaga; son of Pedro Zorrilla Gómez,
lawyer, and María Aurora Martínez
Lozano; compadre of *Miguel de la
Madrid*. j-None. k-As Secretary
General of Government under Governor
Ravize, Zorrilla Martínez actually
served as governor for a year when
Ravize was ill, giving him the opportu-
nity to meet *Luis Echeverría* in 1969.
l-B de M, 269-70; HA, 13 Sept. 1971, 21
Aug. 1972, 13; *Excélsior*, 10 Aug. 1972,
10, 8 Mar. 1973, 14; HA, 13 Aug. 1973,
33; letter; Q es Q, 77, 243-44; Enc. Mex.,
Annual, 1977, 547-48; DBGM, 453-44.

Zubirán (Anchondo), Salvador
a-Dec. 23, 1898. b-Federal District.
c-Preparatory studies at the National
Preparatory School, Mexico City, 1913-
16; medical degree, National School of
Medicine, UNAM, 1923; advanced
studies at Harvard University and
Brigham Hospital, 1924-25; Professor of
Medicine, Graduate School, UNAM,
1946-66; Professor of Therapeutics,
1925-27, Professor of Clinical Medicine,
1934-67, and Professor Emeritus, 1967,
all at the National School of Medicine,
UNAM. d-None. e-None. f-Director,
Office of Food and Drink, Secretariat of
Health, 1931-35; member of the
presidential study commission, 1935-
37; First Director of the Department of
Child Welfare, 1937-38; *Subsecretary of
Health*, 1938-40 (in charge of the
secretaryship, 1938-39); *Subsecretary of
Health*, 1940-43; *Rector of UNAM*,
1946-48; Director General of the
National Industry of Pharmaceutical
Chemicals, 1949-52; Director, Dietetics
Service, General Hospital, 1943-45;
Director of the Hospital for Nutritional
Diseases, 1949-64; Director of the
Institute of Nutrition, Secretariat of

Health, 1964-70. g-None. h-Author of various medical studies. i-Personal friend of *Gustavo Baz* since preparatory school days; personal physician to Presidents Calles, *Cárdenas*, and *Avila Camacho*; son of José María Zubirán and María Anchondo; married Ana María Villarreal. j-None. k-Resigned from the Rectorship of UNAM after students rioted and held him prisoner in his own office. l-Novo, 173; D de Y, 25 June 1937, 1; DGF50, 348; DPE61, 114; D de S, 2 Dec. 1940, 1, 6; letter; DPE65, 153; Simpson, 354-55; Hayner, 247; letter; Enc. Mex., XII, 1977, 595; López, 1194; WNM, 249.

Zuckermann Duarte, Conrado
(Deceased Aug. 8, 1984) a-Nov. 7, 1900. b-Mérida, Yucatán. c-Preparatory studies at the National Preparatory School, Mexico City, 1913-16; medical degree, National School of Medicine, UNAM, Aug. 22, 1924; professor, National School of Medicine, UNAM, 1928-37; graduate studies in various hospitals. d-None. e-None. f-Intern, General Hospital, Mexico City, 1924-36; Director of Interns, General Hospital, 1936; Clinical Assistant, National School of Medicine, UNAM, 1924-27; Clinical Investigator, Cancer Section, Department of Health, 1925-27; Surgeon and Director, Mexican Clinic of Surgery and Radiotherapy; Director of the National Campaign against Cancer, 1941-43, 1970-76; *Subsecretary of Welfare*, Mar. 1, 1960, to 1964. g-None. h-Book clerk as a student at UNAM; author of various articles on surgery and medicine; received many awards for his work on cancer. i-Married Carmen Quintero; son of Alberto Zuckermann Handler and Carmela Duarte. j-None. k-None. l-Letter; DPE61, 109; Peral, 889; WWM45, 130; DBM70, 580; López, 1195; *Excélsior*, 8 Aug. 1984, 35.

Appendixes

Appendix A

Supreme Court Justices, 1935–1993

1935
President:[*] Daniel V. Valencia
Presidents:[+] *José Ortiz Tirado, Francisco H. Ruiz,* Alonso Aznar Mendoza, *Xavier Icaza y López Negrete*
Members: *Rodolfo Asiaín,* Abenamar Eboli Paniagua, *Hermilo López Sánchez, Sabino M. Olea, Rodolfo Chávez S.,* Luis Basdresch, Daniel Galindo, *Alfonso Pérez Gasca, Genaro V. Vázquez,* Alfredo Iñarritu, Agustín Aguirre Garza, *Octavio M. Trigo, José María Truchuelo, Vicente Santos Guajardo,* Jesús Garza Cabello, *Salomón González Blanco*

1936
President: Daniel V. Valencia
Presidents: *Francisco H. Ruiz,* Luis Basdresch, Alonso Aznar Mendoza, Daniel Galindo
Members: Abenamar Eboli Paniagua, *Xavier Icaza y López Negrete, Rodolfo Chávez S.,* Alfredo Iñarritu, *Vicente Santos Guajardo,* Jesús Garza Cabello, *Salomón González Blanco, José Ortiz Tirado, Sabino M. Olea, Hermilo López Sánchez, José María Truchuelo, Rodolfo Asiaín, Octavio M. Trigo,* Agustín Gómez Campos, *Alfonso Pérez Gasca,* Agustín Aguirre Garza

1937
President: Daniel V. Valencia
Presidents: *Francisco H. Ruiz,* Luis Basdresch, Alonso Aznar Mendoza, Daniel Galindo
Members: Abenamar Eboli Paniagua, *Xavier Icaza y López Negrete, Rodolfo Chávez S.,* Alfredo Iñarritu, *Vicente Santos Guajardo,* Jesús Garza Cabello, *Salomón González Blanco, José Ortiz Tirado, Sabino M. Olea, Hermilo López Sánchez, José María Truchuelo, Rodolfo Asiaín, Octavio M. Trigo,* Agustín Gómez Campos, *Alfonso Pérez Gasca,* Agustín Aguirre Garza

1938
President: Daniel V. Valencia
Presidents: *Francisco H. Ruiz,* Luis Bascresch, *Fernando López Cárdenas,* Alonso Aznar Mendoza
Members: Abenamar Eboli Paniagua, *Alfonso Pérez Gasca, Rodolfo Chávez S.,* Jesús Garza Cabello, *Octavio M. Trigo, José Ortiz Tirado, Salomón González Blanco, Hermilo López Sánchez, Sabino M. Olea, Rodolfo Asiaín, Vicente Santos Guajardo,* Agustín Aguirre Garza, Alfredo Iñarritu, Agustín Gómez Campos, *Xavier Icaza y López Negrete, José María Truchuelo*

[*] The President serves as the chief justice of the Supreme Court.
[+] The Mexican Supreme Court is divided into criminal, administrative, civil, and labor divisions. A president presides over each.

1939
President: Daniel V. Valencia
Presidents: *Francisco H. Ruiz*, Alonso Aznar Mendoza, *Fernando López Cárdenas, Rodolfo Chávez S.*
Members: Abenamar Eboli Paniagua, Jesús Garza Cabello, *José María Truchuelo, José Ortiz Tirado*, Luis G. Caballero, *Hermilo López Sánchez*, Agustín Gómez Campos, *Rodolfo Asiaín, Sabino M. Olea*, Agustín Aguirre Garza, *Octavio M. Trigo*, Luis Basdresch, *Salomón González Blanco, Xavier Icaza y López Negrete, Alfonso Pérez Gasca*

1940
President: Daniel V. Valencia
Presidents: *Francisco H. Ruiz*, Alonso Aznar Mendoza, *Fernando López Cardenas, Rodolfo Chávez S.*
Members: Abenamar Eboli Paniagua, Jesús Garza Cabello, *José María Truchuelo, José Ortiz Tirado*, Luis G. Caballero, *Hermilo López Sánchez*, Agustín Gómez Campos, *Rodolfo Asiaín, Sabino M. Olea*, Agustín Aguirre Garza, *Octavio M. Trigo*, Luis Basdresch, *Salomón González Blanco, Xavier Icaza y López Negrete, Alfonso Pérez Gasca*

1941
President: *Salvador Urbina*
Presidents: *José Ortiz Tirado, Hilario Medina, Gabino Fraga Magaña, Roque Estrada*
Members: *Antonio Islas Bravo, Hermilo López Sánchez, Fernando de la Fuente*, Carlos L. Angeles, *Nicéforo Guerrero Mendoza*, José Rebolledo, *Eduardo Vasconcelos, Emilio Pardo Aspe, Alfonso Francisco Ramírez, Manuel Bartlett Bautista*, Tirso Sánchez Taboada, *Teófilo Olea y Leyva, José María Mendoza Pardo, Felipe de J.*

Tena, Franco Carreño, Octavio Mendoza González

1942
President: *Salvador Urbina*
Presidents: Carlos L. Angeles, *Emilio Pardo Aspe, Gabino Fraga Magaña, Eduardo Vasconcelos*
Members: *Antonio Islas Bravo*, José Rebolledo, *Fernando de la Fuente, Manuel Bartlett Bautista, Nicéforo Guerrero Mendoza, Teófilo Olea y Leyva, Alfonso Francisco Ramírez, Felipe de J. Tena*, Carlos I. Meléndez, *Octavio Mendoza González*, José María Mendoza Pardo, *José Ortiz Tirado, Franco Carreño, Hilario Medina, Hermilo López Sánchez, Roque Estrada*

1943
President: *Salvador Urbina*
Presidents: José Rebolledo, *Felipe de J. Tena, Franco Carreño, Hermilo López Sánchez*
Members: *Antonio Islas Bravo, Octavio Mendoza González, Fernando de la Fuente, José Ortiz Tirado, Nicéforo Guerrero Mendoza, Hilario Medina, Alfonso Francisco Ramírez, Roque Estrada*, Carlos I. Meléndez, Carlos L. Angeles, *José María Mendoza Pardo, Gabino Fraga Magaña, Manuel Bartlett Bautista, Emilio Pardo Aspe, Teófilo Olea y Leyva, Eduardo Vasconcelos*

1944
President: *Salvador Urbina*
Presidents: *Fernando de la Fuente, Hilario Medina, Alfonso Francisco Ramírez, Antonio Islas Bravo*
Members: *Nicéforo Guerrero Mendoza, Eduardo Vasconcelos*, Carlos I. Meléndez, *Angel Carvajal,*[*] *Manuel Bartlett Bautista*, Agustín Mercado Alarcón, *Teófilo Olea y Leyva, Vicente Santos Guajardo, Octavio Mendoza*

---

[*]*Angel Carvajal* was nominated in 1944 and resigned the same year. This accounts for the listing of 17 members, instead of the usual 16.

González, Luis G. Corona, *José Ortiz Tirado*, José Rebolledo, *Roque Estrada, Franco Carreño, Carlos L. Angeles, Hermilo López Sánchez, Emilio Pardo Aspe*

1945
President: *Salvador Urbina*
Presidents: *Teófilo Olea y Leyva*, Carlos I. Meléndez, *Octavio Mendoza González, Eduardo Vasconcelos*
Members: *Nicéforo Guerrero Mendoza,* Luis G. Corona, *Manuel Bartlett Bautista*, José Rebolledo, *José Ortiz Tirado, Franco Carreño, Roque Estrada, Hermilo López Sánchez*, Carlos L. Angeles, *Fernando de la Fuente, Emilio Pardo Aspe, Alfonso Francisco Ramírez, Agustín Mercado Alarcón, Hilario Medina, Vicente Santos Guajardo,Antonio Islas Bravo*

1946
President: *Salvador Urbina*
Presidents: *José Ortiz Tirado, Vicente Santos Guajardo, Manuel Bartlett Bautista*, Luis G. Corona
Members: *Nicéforo Guerrero Mendoza, Fernando de la Fuente, Roque Estrada, Alfonso Francisco Ramírez*, Carlos L. Angeles, *Hilario Medina, Emilio Pardo Aspe, Antonio Islas Bravo*, Agustín Mercado Alarcón, *Teófilo Olea y Leyva,* José Rebolledo, *Octavio Mendoza González, Franco Carreño*, Carlos I. Meléndez, *Hermilo López Sánchez, Eduardo Vasconcelos*

1947
President: *Salvador Urbina*
Presidents: Carlos L. Angeles, Agustín Mercado Alarcón, *Franco Carreño,*

Antonio Islas Bravo
Members: *Nicéforo Guerrero Mendoza, Teófilo Olea y Leyva, Roque Estrada, Octavio Mendoza González, Emilio Pardo Aspe*, Carlos I. Meléndez, *José* Rebolledo, *Eduardo Vasconcelos, Hermilo López Sánchez, José Ortiz Tirado, Fernando de la Fuente, Manuel Bartlett Bautista, Alfonso Francisco Ramírez, Vicente Santos Guajardo, Hilario Medina*, Luis G. Corona
Supernumerary:[*] *Felipe Tena Ramírez*

1948
President: *Salvador Urbina*
Presidents: *Luis Chico Goerne, Roque Estrada, Alfonso Francisco Ramírez, Mariano Ramírez Vázquez*
Members: *Nicéforo Guerrero Mendoza,* Carlos I. Meléndez, Carlos L. Angeles, *José Ortiz Tirado, Emilio Pardo Aspe, Manuel Bartlett Bautista*, José Rebolledo, *Vicente Santos Guajardo, Fernando de la Fuente*, Luis G. Corona, *Hilario Medina*, Agustín Mercado Alarcón, *Teófilo Olea y Leyva, Franco Carreño, Octavio Mendoza González, Hermilo López Sánchez*

1949
President: *Salvador Urbina*
Presidents: José Rebolledo, *Vicente Santos Guajardo, Nicéforo Guerrero Mendoza, Hermilo López Sánchez*
Members: *Emilio Pardo Aspe*, Luis G. Corona, *José Ortiz Tirado*, Agustín Mercado Alarcón, *Fernando de la Fuente*, Franco Carreño, *Hilario Medina, Luis Chico Goerne, Teófilo Olea y Leyva, Alfonso Francisco Ramírez, Octavio Mendoza González, Roque Estrada*, Carlos I. Meléndez,

[*] A supernumerary is not assigned to any of the four divisions of the Court, but is called upon to sit on a case when another minister is ill or on leave of absence. Often the supernumeraries may be the source of new ministers of the Court when one resigns or dies. A list of supernumeraries does not appear regularly throughout the appendix, because they are not always listed in official records and their names are not available on a consistent year-by-year basis.

Enrique Pérez Arce, *Manuel Bartlett Bautista, Mariano Ramírez Vázquez*

1950
President: *Salvador Urbina*
Presidents: Luis G. Corona, *Roque Estrada, Octavio Mendoza González Agapito Pozo*
Members: *José Ortiz Tirado, Luis Chico Goerne, Fernando de la Fuente, Alfonso Francisco Ramírez, Hilario Medina,* Armando Z. Ostos, *Teófilo Olea y Leyva, Luis Díaz Infante,* Carlos I. Meléndez, José Rebolledo, *Manuel Bartlett Bautista, Nicéforo Guerrero Mendoza,* Agustín Mercado Alarcón, *Vicente Santos Guajardo, Franco Carreño, Hermilo López Sánchez*

1951
President: *Salvador Urbina*
Presidents: *Teófilo Olea y Leyva,* Carlos I. Meléndez, *Manuel Bartlett Bautista, Armando Z. Ostos*
Members: *José Ortiz Tirado,* José Rebolledo, *Fernando de la Fuente, Vicente Santos Guajardo, Hilario Medina, Hermilo López Sánchez,* Agustín Mercado Alarcón, Luis G. Corona, *Franco Carreño, Octavio Mendoza González, Luis Chico Goerne, Agapito Pozo, Alfonso Francisco Ramírez, Roque Estrada, Luis Díaz Infante, Arturo Martínez Adame*
Supernumeraries: *Felipe Tena Ramírez, Gabriel García Rojas, Angel González de la Vega, Mariano Azuela, Rafael Matos Escobedo*

1952
President: *Roque Estrada*
Presidents: *Luis Chico Goerne,* Agustín Mercado Alarcón, *Octavio Mendoza González, Luis Díaz Infante*
Members: *José Castro Estrada, Vicente Santos Guajardo, Gabriel García Rojas, Hilario Medina, Arturo Martínez Adame, Alfonso Francisco Ramírez, Alfonso Guzmán Neyra, Rafael Rojina*

Villegas, José Rivera Pérez Campos, Genaro V. Vázquez, Luis G. Corona, *Edmundo Elorduy, Agapito Pozo, Ernesto Aguilar Alvarez, Franco Carreño, Teófilo Olea y Leyva*
Supernumeraries: *Angel González de la Vega, Felipe Tena Ramírez, Juan José González Bustamante*

1953
President: *Hilario Medina*
Presidents: *José Ortiz Tirado, Gabriel García Rojas, Alfonso Francisco Ramírez, Arturo Martínez Adame*
Members: Luis G. Corona, *Vicente Santos Guajardo, Luis Chico Goerne, José Castro Estrada, Teófilo Olea y Leyva, Rafael Rojina Villegas, Franco Carreño, Alfonso Guzmán Neyra, Nicéforo Guerrero Mendoza, Gilberto Valenzuela, Octavio Mendoza González, Luis Díaz Infante, José Rivera Pérez Campos, Agapito Pozo, Agustín Mercado Alarcón,* Vacancy
Supernumeraries: *Angel González de la Vega, Mariano Azuela, Juan José González Bustamante, Rafael Matos Escobedo, Felipe Tena Ramírez*

1954
President: *José Ortiz Tirado*
Presidents: *Luis Chico Goerne, José Castro Estrada, José Rivera Pérez Campos,Alfonso Guzmán Neyra*
Members: Luis G. Corona, *Luis Díaz Infante, Teófilo Olea y Leyva, Agapito Pozo, Franco Carreño, Genaro Ruiz de Chávez, Nicéforo Guerrero Mendoza, Mariano Ramírez Vázquez, Octavio Mendoza González Hilario Medina,* Agustín Mercado Alarcón, *Alfonso Francisco Ramírez, Vicente Santos Guajardo, Gabriel García Rojas, Gilberto Valenzuela, Arturo Martínez Adame*
Supernumeraries: *Felipe Tena Ramírez, Mariano Azuela, Angel González de la Vega, Rafael Matos Escobedo, Juan José González Bustamente*

1955

President: *Vicente Santos Guajardo*
Presidents: *Genaro Ruiz de Chávez, Mariano Ramírez Vázquez, José Rivera Pérez Campos, Agapito Pozo*
Members: *Teófilo Olea y Leyva, Alfonso Francisco Ramírez, Franco Carreño, Gabriel García Rojas, Nicéforo Guerrero Mendoza, Arturo Martínez Adame, Octavio Mendoza González,* Luis Chico Goerne, *Agustín Mercado Alarcón, José Castro Estrada, Gilberto Valenzuela, Alfonso Guzmán Neyra, Luis Díaz Infante, Rodolfo Chávez S., Hilario Medina, Mario G. Rebolledo*
Supernumeraries: *Mariano Azuela, Juan José González , Felipe Tena Ramírez, Rafael Matos Escobedo, Angel González de la Vega*

1956

President: *Vicente Santos Guajardo*
Presidents: Agustín Mercado Alarcón, *Gilberto Valenzuela, Octavio Mendoza González, Mario G. Rebolledo*
Members: *Franco Carreño, José Castro Estrada, Nicéforo Guerrero Mendoza, Alfonso Guzmán Neyra, Luis Díaz Infante, Rodolfo Chávez S., Hilario Medina, Agapito Pozo, Alfonso Francisco Ramírez, Mariano Ramírez Vázquez, Gabriel García Rojas, José Rivera Pérez Campos, Arturo Martínez Adame, Genaro Ruiz de Chávez, Luis Chico Goerne, Carlos Franco Sodi*
Supernumeraries: *Mariano Azuela, Juan José González, Felipe Tena Ramírez, Rafael Matos Escobedo, Angel González de la Vega*

1957

President: *Hilario Medina*
Presidents: *Rodolfo Chávez S., Vicente Santos Guajardo, Franco Carreño, Luis Díaz Infante*
Members: *Luis Chico Goerne, José Rivera Pérez Campos, Alfonso Francisco Ramírez, Genaro Ruiz de Chávez,* *Gabriel García Rojas, Carlos Franco Sodi, Arturo Martínez Adame, Felipe Tena Ramírez, José Castro Estrada,* Agustín Mercado Alarcón, *Alfonso Guzmán Neyra, Octavio Mendoza González, Agapito Pozo, Gilberto Valenzuela, Mariano Ramírez Vázquez, Mario G. Rebolledo*
Supernumeraries: *Mariano Azuela, Juan José González, Angel González de la Vega, Rafael Matos Escobedo*

1958

President: *Agapito Pozo*
Presidents: *Luis Chico Goerne, Alfonso Guzmán Neyra, Alfonso Francisco Ramírez, Arturo Martínez Adame*
Members: *Gabriel García Rojas, Octavio Mendoza González, José Castro Estrada, Gilberto Valenzuela, Mariano Ramírez Vázquez, Juan José González, José Rivera Pérez Campos, Rodolfo Chávez S., Angel González de la Vega Franco Carreño, Carlos Franco Sodi, José López Lira, Felipe Tena Ramírez, Angel Carvajal,* Agustín Mercado Alarcón, *Manuel Rivera Silva*
Supernumerary: *Rafael Matos Escobedo*

1959

President: *Alfonso Guzmán Neyra*
Presidents: *Juan José González Bustamante, Gabriel García Rojas, Felipe Tena Ramírez, Angel González de la Vega*
Members: *Agapito Pozo, Agustín Mercado Alarcón, Luis Chico Goerne, Octavio Mendoza González, Arturo Martínez Adame, Gilberto Valenzuela, Rafael Matos Escobedo, Rodolfo Chávez S., José Castro Estrada, Franco Carreño, Mariano Ramírez Vázquez, José López Lira, José Rivera Pérez Campos, Angel Carvajal, Carlos Franco Sodi, Manuel Rivera Silva,*

1960
President: *Alfonso Guzmán Neyra*
Presidents: *Juan José González Bustamante, José Castro Estrada, Felipe Tena Ramírez, Angel Carvajal*
Members: *Gabriel García Rojas, José Rivera Pérez Campos,* Alberto R. Vela, *Carlos Franco Sodi, Mariano Azuela,* Agustín Mercado Alarcón, *Agapito Pozo, Octavio Mendoza González, Luis Chico Goerne, Gilberto Valenzuela, Arturo Martínez Adame, Franco Carreño, Rafael Matos Escobedo, José López Lira, Mariano Ramírez Vázquez, Manuel Rivera Silva*

1961
President: *Alfonso Guzmán Neyra*
Presidents: *Juan José González Bustamante, José López Lira, José Rivera Pérez Campos, Agapito Pozo*
Members: Agustín Mercado Alarcón, *Mariano Ramírez Vázquez,* Alberto R. Vela, *Gabriel García Rojas,* Manuel Rivera Silva, *Mariano Azuela, Angel González de la Vega, María Cristina Salmorán,* * *Rafael Matos Escobedo, José Castro Estrada, Felipe Tena Ramírez, Adalberto Padilla Ascencio, Octavio Mendoza González, Angel Carvajal, Franco Carreño,* Manuel Yáñez Ruiz, *José Castro Estrada*

1962
President: *Alfonso Guzmán Neyra*
Presidents: *Juan José González Bustamante, Mariano Ramírez Vázquez, Octavio Mendoza González, Agapito Pozo*
Members: *José Rivera Pérez Campos, Mariano Azuela,* Agustín Mercado Alarcón, *María Cristina Salmorán,* Alberto R. Vela, *José Castro Estrada,* Manuel Rivera Silva, Adalberto Padilla Ascencio, *Angel González de la Vega, Angel Carvajal, Rafael Matos Escobedo,* Manuel Yáñez Ruiz, Felipe

*First woman on the Supreme Court.

Tena Ramírez, Rafael Rojina Villegas, Franco Carreño, Vacancy, *José Castro Estrada*

1963
President: *Alfonso Guzmán Neyra*
Presidents: *Juan José González Bustamante, Mariano Azuela, Franco Carreño, Agapito Pozo*
Members: *Octavio Mendoza González, José Castro Estrada, Mariano Ramírez Vázquez, Pedro Guerrero Martínez, José Rivera Pérez Campos, María Cristina Salmorán,* Agustín Mercado Alarcón, *Adalberto Padilla Ascencio,* Alberto R. Vela, *Angel Carvajal, Manuel Rivera Silva, Manuel Yáñez Ruiz, Angel González de la Vega, Rafael Rojina Villegas, Felipe Tena Ramírez, Mario G. Rebolledo*
Supernumeraries: *Alberto González Blanco, Raúl Castellano Jiménez*

1964
President: *Alfonso Guzmán Neyra*
Presidents: *Angel González de la Vega, Rafael Rojina Villegas, Pedro Guerrero Martínez, Agapito Pozo*
Members: *Mariano Azuela, María Cristina Salmorán, Octavio Mendoza González, Adalberto Padilla Ascencio, Mariano Ramírez Vázquez, Angel Carvajal, José Rivera Pérez Campos, Manuel Yáñez Ruiz, Agustín Mercado Alarcón, Enrique Martínez Ulloa, Manuel Rivera Silva, Abel Huitrón y Aguado, Felipe Tena Ramírez, Jorge Iñarritu, Mario G. Rebolledo Fernández, José Castro Estrada*
Supernumeraries: *Alberto González Blanco,* Ramón Cañedo Aldrete, *Raúl Castellano Jiménez, José Luis Gutiérrez*

1965
President: *Agapito Pozo*
Presidents: *Manuel Rivera Silva, Enrique Martínez Ulloa, Jorge Iñarritu,*

Manuel Yáñez Ruiz
Members: *Angel González de la Vega,*
Mariano Azuela, Agustín Mercado
Alarcón, *José Castro Estrada, Mario G.*
Rebolledo Fernández, Rafael Rojina
Villegas, Abel Huitrón y Aguado, Angel
Carvajal, Octavio Mendoza González,
Alfonso Guzmán Neyra, José Rivera
Pérez Campos, María Cristina
Salmorán, Felipe Tena Ramírez,
Adalberto Padilla Ascencio, *Pedro*
Guerrero Martínez, Mariano Ramírez
Vázquez
Supernumeraries: *Raúl Castellano*
Jiménez, José Luis Gutiérrez, Alberto
González Blanco, Ramón Cañedo
Aldrete

1966
President: *Agapito Pozo*
Presidents: *Abel Huitrón y Aguado, José*
Castro Estrada, Felipe Tena Ramírez,
Manuel Yáñez Ruiz
Members: *Manuel Rivera Silva,*
Mariano Azuela, Jorge Iñarritu, Rafael
Rojina Villegas, Enrique Martínez
Ulloa, Angel Carvajal, Agustín
Mercado Alarcón, *Alfonso Guzmán*
Neyra, Mario G. Rebolledo Fernández,
María Cristina Salmorán, José Rivera
Pérez Campos, Adalberto Padilla
Ascencio, *Pedro Guerrero Martínez,*
José Luis Gutiérrez, Mariano Ramírez
Vázquez, Octavio Mendoza González
Supernumeraries: *Raúl Castellano*
Jiménez, Ezequiel Burguete Farrera,
Alberto González Blanco, Ernesto Solís
López, Ramón Cañedo Aldrete

1967
President: *Agapito Pozo*
Presidents: *Mario G. Rebolledo*
Fernández, Mariano Ramírez Vázquez,
José Rivera Pérez Campos, Manuel
Yáñez Ruiz
Members: *Abel Huitrón y Aguado,*
Rafael Rojina Villegas, Felipe Tena
Ramírez, Angel Carvajal, José Castro
Estrada, Alfonso Guzmán Neyra,

Manuel Rivera Silva, María Cristina
Salmorán, Jorge Iñarritu, Ezequiel
Burguete Farrera, Enrique Martínez
Ulloa, Ramón Cañedo Aldrete, *Octavio*
Mendoza González, Pedro Guerrero
Martínez, Mariano Azuela, Vacancy
Supernumeraries: *Raúl Castellano*
Jiménez, Ernesto Solís López, *Alberto*
González Blanco

1968
President: *Agapito Pozo*
Presidents: *Ezequiel Burguete Farrera,*
Mariano Ramírez Vázquez, Octavio
Mendoza González, Ramón Cañedo
Aldrete
Members: *Mario G. Rebolledo*
Fernández, Mariano Azuela, José Rivera
Pérez Campos, Rafael Rojina Villegas,
Manuel Yáñez Ruiz, Angel Carvajal,
Abel Huitrón y Aguado, Alfonso
Guzmán Neyra, Felipe Tena Ramírez,
María Cristina Salmorán, Manuel
Rivera Silva, Ernesto Aguilar Alvarez,
Jorge Iñarritu, Ernesto Solís López,
Enrique Martínez Ulloa, Pedro
Guerrero Martínez
Supernumeraries: *Raúl Castellano*
Jiménez, Salvador Mondragón Guerra,
Alberto Orozco Romero, Luis Felipe
Canudas Orezza

1969
President: *Alfonso Guzmán Neyra*
Presidents: *Ernesto Aguilar Alvarez,*
Ernesto Solís López, *Pedro Guerrero*
Martínez, Angel Carvajal
Members: *Ezequiel Burguete Farrera,*
Jorge Iñarritu, Mariano Ramírez
Vázquez, Enrique Martínez Ulloa,
Ramón Cañedo Aldrete, *Alberto Orozco*
Romero, Mario G. Rebolledo
Fernández, Mariano Azuela, José Rivera
Pérez Campos, Rafael Rojina Villegas,
Manuel Yáñez Ruiz, María Cristina
Salmorán, Abel Huitrón y Aguado,
Carlos del Río Rodríguez, *Felipe Tena*
Ramírez, Manuel Rivera Silva
Supernumeraries: *Raúl Castellano*

Jiménez, Alberto Jiménez Castro, *Salvador Mondragón Guerra*, Antonio Capponi Guerrero, *Luis Felipe Canudas Orezza*

1970
President: *Alfonso Guzmán Neyra*
Presidents: *Manuel Rivera Silva, María Cristina Salmorán, Carlos del Río Rodríguez, Mariano Azuela*
Members: *Ezequiel Burguete Farrera, Mariano Ramírez Vázquez,* Mario G. Rebolledo Fernández, Rafael Rojina Villegas, Abel Huitrón y Aguado, Enrique Martínez Ulloa, Ernesto Aguilar Alvarez, Ernesto Solís López, *Alberto Jiménez Castro, Ramón Cañedo Aldrete, Jorge Iñarritu, Manuel Yáñez Ruiz,* Jorge Saracho Alvarez, *Salvador Mondragón Guerra, Pedro Guerrero Martínez, Angel Carvajal*
Supernumeraries: Antonio Capponi Guerrero, *Raúl Castellano Jiménez,* J. *Ramón Palacios Vargas, Alfonso López Aparicio, Luis Felipe Canudas Orezza, Euquerio Guerrero López*

1971
President: *Alfonso Guzmán Neyra*
Presidents: *Ezequiel Burguete Farrera, Mariano Ramírez Vázquez,* Alberto Jiménez Castro, Ramón Cañedo Aldrete
Members: *Mario G. Rebolledo Fernández, Rafael Rojina Villegas, Abel Huitrón y Aguado, Enrique Martínez Ulloa,* Ernesto Solís López, *Manuel Rivera Silva, Manuel Yáñez Ruiz, Carlos del Río Rodríguez, Salvador Mondragón Guerra, Jorge Iñarritu, Angel Carvajal,* Jorge Saracho Alvarez, *María Cristina Salmorán, Pedro Guerrero Martínez, Mariano Azuela*
Supernumeraries: *Euquerio Guerrero López, Raúl Castellano Jiménez*

1972
President: *Alfonso Guzmán Neyra*
Presidents: *Ezequiel Burguete Farrera, Mariano Ramírez Vázquez,* Alberto Jiménez Castro, Ramón Cañedo Aldrete
Members: *Mario G. Rebolledo Fernández, Rafael Rojina Villegas, Abel Huitrón y Aguado, Enrique Martínez Ulloa, Ernesto Aguilar Alvarez,* Ernesto Solís López, *Manuel Rivera Silva, Manuel Yáñez Ruiz, Carlos del Río Rodríguez, Salvador Mondragón Guerra, Jorge Iñarritu, Angel Carvajal,* Jorge Saracho Alvarez, *María Cristina Salmorán, Pedro Guerrero Martínez, Mariano Azuela*
Supernumeraries: *Euquerio Guerrero López, Raúl Castellano Jiménez*

1973
President: *Alfonso Guzmán Neyra*
Presidents: *Ezequiel Burguete Farrera, María Cristina Salmorán, Jorge Iñarritu,* J. *Ramón Palacios Vargas*
Members: *Mario G. Rebolledo Fernández, Mariano Ramírez Vázquez, Manuel Rivera Silva, Rafael Rojina Villegas, Abel Huitrón y Aguado, Enrique Martínez Ulloa, Ernesto Aguilar Alvarez, Ernesto Solís López, Pedro Guerrero Martínez,* Ramón Cañedo Aldrete, *Carlos del Río Rodríguez, Salvador Mondragón Guerra,* Alberto Jiménez Castro, *Euquerio Guerrero López, Antonio Rocha Cordero,* Jorge Saracho Alvarez
Supernumeraries: Antonio Capponi Guerrero, *David Franco Rodríguez, Alfonso López Aparicio, Raúl Cuevas Mantecón, Arturo Serrano Robles*

1974
President: *Euquerio Guerrero López*
Presidents: *Ernesto Aguilar Alvarez, Enrique Martínez Ulloa, Antonio Rocha Cordero,* Ramón Cañedo Aldrete
Members: *Mario G. Rebolledo Fernández, Ernesto Solís López, Manuel Rivera Silva,* J. *Ramón Palacios Vargas,*

Abel Huitrón y Aguado, David Franco Rodríguez, Ezequiel Burguete Farrera, María Cristina Salmorán, Pedro Guerrero Martínez, Jorge Saracho Alvarez, Jorge Iñarritu, Salvador Mondragón Guerra, Carlos del Río Rodríguez, Alfonso López Aparicio, Alberto Jiménez Castro, *Rafael Rojina Villegas*
Supernumeraries: Antonio Capponi Guerrero, *Agustín Téllez Cruz, Arturo Serrano Robles, Fernando Castellanos Tena, Raúl Cuevas Mantecón*

1975
President: *Euquerio Guerrero López*
Presidents: *Manuel Rivera Silva, David Franco Rodríguez, Carlos del Río Rodríguez,* Ramón Cañedo Aldrete
Members: *Ernesto Aguilar Alvarez, Agustín Téllez Cruz, Eduardo Langle Martínez, Juan Moisés Calleja García, Abel Huitrón y Aguado, Alfonso López Aparicio, Mario G. Rebolledo Fernández, María Cristina Salmorán, Antonio Rocha C.,* Jorge Saracho Alvarez, *Jorge Iñarritu, Salvador Mondragón Guerra,* Alberto Jiménez Castro, *J. Ramón Palacios Vargas, Arturo Serrano Robles, Rafael Rojina Villegas*
Supernumeraries: *Raúl Cuevas Mantecón, Fernando Castellanos Tena, Raúl Lozano Ramírez,* Livier Ayala Manzo

1976
President: *Mario G. Rebolledo Fernández*
Presidents: *Ernesto Aguilar Alvarez, María Cristina Salmorán, Salvador Mondragón Guerra, Arturo Serrano Robles*
Members: *Raúl Cuevas Mantecón, David Franco Rodríguez, Manuel Rivera Silva, J. Ramón Palacios Vargas, Fernando Castellanos Tena,* Ramón Cañedo Aldrete, *Antonio Rocha C., Alfonso López Aparicio, Eduardo*

Langle Martínez, Juan Moisés Calleja García, Jorge Iñarritu, Raúl Lozano Ramírez, Carlos del Río Rodríguez, Jorge Saracho Alvarez, *Agustín Téllez Cruz,* José Alfonso Abitia A.
Supernumeraries: *Atanasio González Martínez, Jorge Olivera Toro, Francisco Pavón V., Luis Felipe Canudas Orezza, Gloria León Orantes*

1977
President: *Agustín Téllez Cruz*
Presidents: *Mario G. Rebolledo Fernández, Alfonso López Aparicio, Eduardo Langle Martínez, Raúl Lozano Ramírez*
Members: *Ernesto Aguilar Alvarez, Manuel Rivera Silva, Fernando Castellanos Tena, Antonio Rocha C., Jorge Iñarritu, Carlos del Río Rodríguez, Arturo Serrano Robles, Salvador Mondragón Guerra, Atanasio González Martínez, Raúl Cuevas Mantecón, J. Ramón Palacios Vargas,* José Alfonso Abitia A., *María Cristina Salmorán,* de Tamayo, *Julio Sánchez Vargas, Juan Moisés Calleja García, David Franco Rodríguez*
Supernumeraries: *Gloria León Orantes, Jorge Olivera Toro, Francisco H. Pavón V., Luis Felipe Canudas Orezza,* Roberto Ríos Elizondo

1978
President: *Agustín Téllez Cruz,*
Presidents: *Mario G. Rebolledo Fernández, Alfonso López Aparicio, Eduardo Langle Martínez, Raúl Lozano Ramírez*
Members: *Fernando Castellanos Tena, Manuel Rivera Silva, Jorge Iñarritu, Antonio Rocha C., Arturo Serrano Robles, Carlos del Río Rodríguez, J. Ramón Palacios Vargas, Atanasio González Martínez, María Cristina Salmorán, Raúl Cuevas Mantecón,* José Alfonso Abitia A., *Juan Moisés Calleja García, David Franco Rodríguez, Julio Sánchez Vargas, Gloria León Orantes,*

Francisco Pavón V.
Supernumeraries: *Jorge Olivera Toro,*
Roberto Ríos Elizondo, Luis Felipe
Canudas Orezza

1979
President: *Agustín Téllez Cruz*
Presidents: *Mario G. Rebolledo*
Fernández, Alfonso López Aparicio,
Eduardo Langle Martínez, Raúl Lozano
Ramírez
Members: *Fernando Castellanos Tena,*
Manuel Rivera Silva, Jorge Iñarritu,
Carlos del Río Rodríguez, Arturo
Serrano Robles, Atanasio González
Martínez, J. Ramón Palacios Vargas,
Raúl Cuevas Mantecón, María Cristina
Salmorán, José Alfonso Abitia A., Juan
Moisés Calleja García, Julio Sánchez
Vargas, David Franco Rodríguez, Gloria
León Orantes, Francisco Pavón V., Jorge
Olivera Toro
Supernumeraries: *Tarsicio Marquez*
Padilla, Enrique Alvarez, Manuel
Gutiérrez de Velasco, Ernesto Díaz
Infante, Santiago Rodríguez Roldán

1980
President: *Agustín Téllez Cruz*
Presidents: *Mario G. Rebolledo*
Fernández, Juan Moisés Calleja García,
Eduardo Langle Martínez, Gloria León
Orantes
Members: *Manuel Rivera Silva, Raúl*
Lozano Ramírez, Francisco Pavón V.,
Jorge Olivera Toro, J. Ramón Palacios
Vargas, Fernando Castellanos Tena,
José Alfonso Abitia A., Raúl Cuevas
Mantecón, Jorge Iñarritu, David Franco
Rodríguez, Arturo Serrano Robles, Julio
Sánchez Vargas, Carlos del Río
Rodríguez, Alfonso López Aparicio,
Atanasio González Martínez, María
Cristina Salmorán
Supernumeraries: *Manuel Gutiérrez de*
Velasco, Tarsicio Marquez Padilla,
Santiago Rodríguez Roldán, Ernesto
Díaz Infante, Enrique Alvarez del
Castillo

1981
President: *Agustín Téllez Cruz*
Presidents: *Antonio Rocha Cordero,*
José Alfonso Abitia A., Salvador
Mondragón Guerra, Julio Sánchez
Vargas
Members: *J. Ramón Palacios Vargas,*
Francisco Pavón V., Fernando
Castellanos Tena, Juan Moisés Calleja
García, Raúl Cuevas Mantecón,
Eduardo Langle Martínez, Jorge
Iñarritu, David Franco Rodríguez,
Arturo Serrano Robles, Jorge Olivera
Toro, Carlos del Río Rodríguez, Alfonso
López Aparicio, Atanasio González
Martínez, María Cristina Salmorán,
Gloria León Orantes, Mario G.
Rebolledo Fernández
Supernumeraries: *Manuel Gutiérrez de*
Velasco, Tarsicio Marquez Padilla,
Santiago Rodríguez Roldán, Ernesto
Díaz Infante, Enrique Alvarez del
Castillo

1982
President: *Mario G. Rebolledo*
Fernández
Presidents: *Juan Moisés Calleja García,*
Eduardo Langle Martínez, Gloria León
Orantes, Jorge Iñarritu
Members: *Francisco Pavón V., Jorge*
Olivera Toro, J. Ramón Palacios
Vargas, Fernando Castellanos Tena,
Raúl Cuevas Mantecón, Alfonso López
Aparicio, David Franco Rodríguez, Julio
Sánchez Vargas, Carlos del Río
Rodríguez, Atanasio González
Martínez, María Cristina Salmorán,
Manuel Gutiérrez de Velasco, Santiago
Rodríguez Roldán, Arturo Serrano
Robles, *Ernesto Díaz Infante, Enrique*
Alvarez del Castillo
Supernumeraries: *Tarsicio Marquez*
Padilla, Salvador Martínez Rojas, *Luis*
Fernández Delgado, Víctor Manuel
Franco Pérez

1983
President: *Jorge Iñarritu*
Presidents: *Juan Moisés Calleja García, Eduardo Langle Martínez, Gloria León Orantes, Mario G. Rebolledo Fernández*
Members: *Francisco Pavón V., Jorge Olivera Toro, J. Ramón Palacios Vargas, Fernando Castellanos Tena, Raúl Cuevas Mantecón, Alfonso López Aparicio, David Franco Rodríguez, Julio Sánchez Vargas, Carlos del Río Rodríguez, Atanasio González Martínez, María Cristina Salmorán, Manuel Gutiérrez de Velasco, Santiago Rodríguez Roldán,* Arturo Serrano Robles, *Ernesto Díaz Infante, Tarsicio Marquez Padilla*
Supernumeraries: *Luis Fernández Delgado,* Salvador Martínez Rojas, *Guillermo Guzmán Orozco,Víctor Manuel Franco Pérez*

1984
President: *Jorge Iñarritu*
Members: *Juan Moisés Calleja García, Eduardo Langle Martínez, Gloria León Orantes, Fausta Moreno Flores, Fran-cisco Pavón V., Jorge Olivera Toro, J. Ramón Palacios Vargas, Fernando Castellanos Tena, Raúl Cuevas Mantecón, Alfonso López Aparicio, David Franco Rodríguez, Mariano Azuela Guitrón, Carlos del Río Rodríguez, Atanasio González Martínez, María Cristina Salmorán, Manuel Gutiérrez de Velasco, Santiago Rodríguez Roldán, Luis Fernández Doblado, Ernesto Díaz Infante, Tarsicio Márquez Padilla*
Supernumeraries: Salvador Martínez Rojas, *Felipe López Contreras, Guillermo Guzmán Orozco,Víctor Manuel Franco Pérez*

1985
President: *Jorge Iñarritu*
Members: *Victoria Adato Green,* Santiago Rodriguez Roldán, *Luis Fernández Doblado,* Raúl Cuevas Mantecón, *Francisco Pavón V., Fausta Moreno Flores, Atanasio González Martínez,* Carlos de Silva Nava, *Manuel Gutiérrez de Velasco, Noé Castañón León, Ernesto Díaz Infante, Fernando Castellaños Tena,* Sergio Hugo Chapital, *Mariano Azuela Guitrón, Ulises Schmill Ordóñez, José Martínez Delgado, Felipe López Contreras, David Franco Rodríguez, Jorge Olivera Torre, Carlos del Río Rodríguez*
Supernumeraries: *Martha Chávez Padrón,* Carlos García Vázquez, *Guillermo Guzmán Orozco, Víctor Manuel Franco Pérez, Leopoldino Ortiz Santos*

1986
President: *Jorge Iñarritu*
Members: *Victoria Adato Green,* Santiago Rodriguez Roldán, *Luis Fernández Doblado,* Raúl Cuevas Mantecón, *Francisco Pavón, Vasconcelos, Fausta Moreno Flores, Atanasio González Martínez,* Carlos de Silva Nava, *Manuel Gutiérrez de Velasco, Noé Castañón León, Ernesto Díaz Infante,* Juan Díaz Romero, Sergio Hugo Chapital, *Mariano Azuela Guitrón, Ulises Schmill Ordóñez,* José Martínez Delgado, *Felipe López Contreras,* José Manuel Villagordoa *Jorge Olivera Torre, Carlos del Río Rodríguez*
Supernumeraries: *Martha Chávez Padrón,* Carlos García Vázquez, *Guillermo Guzmán Orozco, Víctor Manuel Franco Pérez, Leopoldino Ortiz Santos*

1987
President: *Carlos del Río Rodríguez*
Members: *Victoria Adato Green,* Santiago Rodríguez Roldán, *Luis Fernández Doblado, Raúl Cuevas Mantecón, Francisco Pavón V., Fausta Moreno Flores, Atanasio González Martínez,* Carlos de Silva Nava, *Manuel Gutiérrez de Velasco, Noé Castañón*

León, Ernesto Díaz Infante, José
Manuel Villagordoa, Sergio Hugo
Chapital, Mariano Azuela Guitrón,
Ulises Schmill Ordóñez, José Martínez
Delgado, Felipe López Contreras, Juan
Díaz Romero, Angel Suárez Torres,
Jorge Olivera Torre,
Supernumeraries: Martha Chávez
Padrón, Carlos García Vázquez,
Guillermo Guzmán Orozco, Víctor
Manuel Franco Pérez, Leopoldino Ortiz
Santos

1988
President: Carlos del Río Rodríguez
Members: Victoria Adato Green,
Santiago Rodríguez Roldán, Luis
Fernández Doblado, Raúl Cuevas
Mantecón, Francisco Pavón V., Fausta
Moreno Flores, Atanasio González
Martínez, Carlos de Silva Nava, Manuel
Gutiérrez de Velasco, Noé Castañón
León, Ernesto Díaz Infante, José
Manuel Villagordoa, Samuel Alba
Leyva, Sergio Hugo Chapital, Ulises
Schmill Ordóñez, José Martínez
Delgado, Felipe López Contreras, Juan
Díaz Romero, Angel Suárez Torres,
Mariano Azuela Guitrón
Supernumeraries: Martha Chávez
Padrón, Carlos García Vázquez,
Guillermo Guzmán Orozco, Víctor
Manuel Franco Pérez, Irma Cué Sarquis

1989
President: Carlos del Río Rodríguez
Members: Victoria Adato Green,
Santiago Rodriguez Roldán, Luis
Fernández Doblado, Salvador Rocha
Díaz, Francisco Pavón Vasconcelos,
Fausta Moreno Flores, Atanasio
González Martínez, Carlos de Silva
Nava, Clementina Gil Guillén, Noé
Castañón León, Ignacio Magaña
Cárdenas, José Manuel Villagordoa,
Samuel Alba Leyva, Sergio Hugo
Chapital, Ulises Schmill Ordóñez, José
Martínez Delgado, Felipe López
Contreras, Juan Díaz Romero, Angel

Suárez Torres, Mariano Azuela Guitrón,
Martha Chávez Padrón, Carlos García
Vázquez, Guillermo Guzmán Orozco,
Irma Cué Sarquis, José Antonio Llanos
Duarte

1990
President: Carlos del Río Rodríguez
Members: Victoria Adato Green,
Santiago Rodriguez Roldán, Luis
Fernández Doblado, Salvador Rocha
Díaz, Fausta Moreno Flores, José
Antonio Llanos Duarte, Atanasio
González Martínez, Carlos de Silva
Nava, Clementina Gil Guillén, Noé
Castañón León, Ignacio Magaña
Cárdenas, José Manuel Villagordoa,
Samuel Alba Leyva, Sergio Hugo
Chapital, Ulises Schmill Ordóñez,
Miguel García Domínguez, Felipe López
Contreras, Juan Díaz Romero, Mariano
Azuela Guitrón, Luis Gutiérrez Vidal,
Martha Chávez Padrón, Carlos García
Vázquez, Guillermo Guzmán Orozco,
Irma Cué Sarquis

1991
President: Ulises Schmill Ordóñez
Members: Victoria Adato Green,
Santiago Rodriguez Roldán, Luis
Fernández Doblado, Ignacio Moisés Cal
y Mayor, Fausta Moreno Flores, José
Antonio Llanos Duarte, Atanasio
González Martínez, Carlos de Silva
Nava, Clementina Gil Guillén, Noé
Castañón León, Ignacio Magaña
Cárdenas, José Manuel Villagordoa,
Samuel Alba Leyva, Sergio Hugo
Chapital, José Trinidad Lanz Cárdenas,
Miguel García Domínguez, Felipe López
Contreras, Juan Díaz Romero, Mariano
Azuela Guitrón, Luis Gutiérrez Vidal,
Martha Chávez Padrón, Carlos García
Vázquez, Guillermo Guzmán Orozco,
Irma Cué Sarquis

1992
President: *Ulises Schmill Ordóñez*
Members: *Victoria Adato Green,
Santiago Rodriguez Roldán, Luis
Fernández Doblado,* Ignacio Moisés Cal
y Mayor, *Fausta Moreno Flores,* José
Antonio Llanos Duarte, *Atanasio
González Martínez,* Carlos de Silva
Nava, *Clementina Gil Guillén, Noé
Castañón León,* Ignacio Magaña
Cárdenas, José Manuel Villagordoa,
Samuel Alba Leyva, Sergio Hugo
Chapital, José Trinidad Lanz Cárdenas,
*Miguel García Domínguez, Felipe López
Contreras,* Juan Díaz Romero, *Mariano
Azuela Guitrón,* Luis Gutiérrez Vidal,
Martha Chávez Padrón, Carlos García
Vázquez, *Guillermo Guzmán Orozco,
Irma Cué Sarquis,* Miguel Montes
García

1993
President: *Ulises Schmill Ordóñez*
Members: *Victoria Adato Green,
Santiago Rodríguez Roldán, Luis
Fernández Doblado,* Ignacio Moisés Cal
y Mayor, *Fausta Moreno Flores,* José
Antonio Llanos Duarte, *Atanasio
González Martínez,* Carlos de Silva
Nava, *Clementina Gil Guillén, Noé
Castañón León,* Ignacio Magaña
Cárdenas, José Manuel Villagordoa,
Samuel Alba Leyva, Sergio Hugo
Chapital, José Trinidad Lanz Cárdenas,
*Miguel García Domínguez, Felipe López
Contreras,* Juan Díaz Romero, *Mariano
Azuela Guitrón,* Luis Gutiérrez Vidal,
Martha Chávez Padrón, Carlos García
Vázquez, *Guillermo Guzmán Orozco,
Irma Cué Sarquis,* Miguel Montes
García

Appendix B

Senators, 1934–1997

1934-40 (36th and 37th Legislatures)

State	Senator	Alternate
Aguascalientes	*Vicente L. Benítez* J. Jesús Marmolejo	J. Isabel Durón
Campeche	Carlos Góngora Gala *Angel Castillo Lanz*	
Chiapas	*Juan M. Esponda* Gustavo R. Marín	
Chihuahua	Julián Aguilar G. *Angel Posada*	Jesús Lugo
Coahuila	*Alberto Salinas Carranza* *Nazario S. Ortiz Garza*	Francisco Rivera
Colima	*Manuel Gudiño* *Pedro Torres Ortiz*	
Distrito Federal	*José María Dávila* *Ezequiel Padilla*	José Torres Ch.
Durango	*Domingo Arrieta* Alejandro Antuna López	
Guanajuato	*Ignacio García Téllez* David Ayala	*Nicéforo Guerrero*
Guerrero	Miguel F. Ortega Román Campos Viveros	
Hidalgo	Polioptro F. Martínez Antonio Cadena	Juvencio Nochebuena

Jalisco	Fernando Basulto Limón *J. Jesús González Gallo*	
México	Manuel Riva Palacio *Antonio Romero*	Armando P. Arroyo Luis Ramírez de A.
Michoacán	*Ernesto Soto Reyes* *Luis Mora Tovar*	Juan S. Picazo
Morelos	Elías Pérez Gómez *Benigno Abúndez*	Alfonso R. Sámano *Elpidio Perdomo*
Nayarit	José Alejandro Anaya Guillermo Flores Muñoz	Tomás López
Nuevo León	Federico Idar *Julián Garza Tijerina*	Manuel Pérez Mendoza
Oaxaca	*Wilfrido C. Cruz* *Francisco López Cortés*	José Pérez Acevedo
Puebla	Bernardo L. Bandala *Gonzalo Bautista*	*Carlos Soto Guevara* Tirso Sánchez T.
Querétaro	Gilberto García Ignacio L. Figueroa	Fidencio Osornio Noradino Rubio
San Luis Potosí	*Gonzalo N. Santos* Eugenio B. Jiménez	Marcelino Zúñiga
Sinaloa	Cristóbal B. Bustamante *Rodolfo T. Loaiza*	Agustín G. del Castillo
Sonora	Camilo Gastélum Jr. Francisco L. Terminel	Andrés H. Peralta
Tabasco	Augusto Hernández Olive *Francisco Trujillo Gurría*	*Salomon González Blanco* Bartolomé Flores
Tamaulipas	*Francisco Castellanos Jr.* Manuel Garza Zamora	
Tlaxcala	Félix C. Rodríguez *Mauro Angulo*	Joaquín Ballina Vela
Veracruz	*Miguel Alemán Valdés* *Cándido Aguilar*	José Murillo

Yucatán	*Bartolomé García Correa* Gualberto Carrillo Puerto	Laureano Cardos Ruz
Zacatecas	*Leobardo Reynoso* Luis R. Reyes	

1940-46 (38th and 39th Legislatures)

State	Senator	Alternate
Aguascalientes	Ramón B. Aldana *Enrique Osornio Camarena*	Abelardo Reyes S.
Campeche	*Eduardo R. Mena Cordova* Pedro Tello Andueza	
Chiapas	F. Gustavo Gutiérrez R. *Emilio Araujo*	
Chihuahua	*Eugenio Prado Proaño* Benjamín Almeida Jr.	
Coahuila	Joaquín Martínez Chavarría *Damián L. Rodríguez*	José María Hernández
Colima	*Miguel G. Santana* Conrado Torres Ortiz	
Distrito Federal	*Alfonso Sánchez Madariaga* *Antonio Villalobos Mayar*	
Durango	*Salvador Franco Urías* Máximo García	
Guanajuato	*Celestino Gasca* *Rafael Rangel Hurtado*	
Guerrero	*Nabor A. Ojeda* *Arturo Martínez Adame*	
Hidalgo	*Vicente Aguirre* *José Lugo Guerrero*	*Fernando Cruz Chávez*
Jalisco	*Estéban García de Alba* *Abraham González Rivera*	
México	*Alfonso Flores M.* *Alfredo Zarate Albarrán*	Augusto Hinojosa

Michoacán	*Antonio Mayes Navarro*	
	J. Trinidad García	
Morelos	*Fernando Amilpa*	
	Jesús Castillo López	
Nayarit	*Luis Aranda del Toro*	
	Evaristo Jiménez Valdez	
Nuevo León	Dionisio García Leal	
	Ramiro Tamez	
Oaxaca	*Eleodoro Charis Castro*	
	Fernando Magro Soto	
Puebla	*Noé Lecona*	Narciso Guarneros
	Rosendo Cortés	
Querétaro	Carlos Ortega Zavaley	Isidro Zuñiga Solórzano
	José Pérez Tejeda	
San Luis Potosí	*Gilberto Flores Muñoz*	
	León García Pujou	
Sinaloa	*Gabriel Leyva Velázquez*	Arturo Arcaraz
	Alejandro Pena	
Sonora	*Alejo Bay*	
	Francisco Martínez Peralta	
Tabasco	Huberto Sala Rueda	Tito Livio Calcaneo
	Alfonso Gutiérrez Gurría	
Tamaulipas	Genovevo Martínez P.	
	Abel Oseguera Alvarez	
Tlaxcala	Samuel Hoyo Castro	Gerardo Juárez
	Rafael Avila Bretón	
Veracruz	*Vidal Díaz Muñoz*	
	Adolfo E. Ortega	
Yucatán	*José Castillo Torre*	
	Florencio Palomo Valencia	
Zacatecas	*Enrique Estrado*	Lamberto Elías
	Adrián Morales Salas	

1946-52 (40th and 41st Legislatures)

State	Senator	Alternate
Aguascalientes	*Edmundo Gámez Orozco* José González Flores	*Salvador Gallardo D.* Gonzalo Padilla Díaz
Campeche	*Pedro Guerrero Martínez* Fernando Berrón Ramos	José María Guerrero López Mauro Pérez
Chiapas	*Efraín Aranda Osorio* *Efraín Lazos*	Rafael Gómez Manuel Borges
Chihuahua	*Alfredo Chávez* *Antonio J. Bermudez*	*Teófilo R. Borunda* *Manuel López Dávila*
Coahuila	*Raúl López Sánchez* *Manuel López Güitrón*	*Ricardo Ainslie R.* Manuel de León Lodoza
Colima	*Rubén Vizcarra* Melitón de la Mora	Antonio Tirado Mayagoitia Carlos Alcaraz Ahumada
Distrito Federal	Carlos I. Serrano *Fidel Velázquez S.*	Juan José Rivera Rojas Emiliano Barrera Esqueda
Durango	*Maríno Castillo Najera* *Atanasio Arrieta García*	Fernando Alvarez Lozoya Juan Manuel Tinoco
Guanajuato	*Federico Medrano Valdivia* *Roberto Guzmán Araujo*	*José Rivera Pérez C.* José Lanuza Araujo
Guerrero	*Donato Miranda Fonseca* *Ruffo Figueroa Figueroa*	Andrés Jaimes Francisco Díaz y Díaz
Hidalgo	*Alfonso Corona del Rosal* *José Gómez Esparza*	Gregorio Hernández Joel Pérez
Jalisco	Miguel Moreno Padilla J. Jesús Cisneros Gómez	Justo González Manuel Romero Rojo
México	*Gabriel Ramos Millán* *Adolfo López Mateos*	Malaquías Huitrón *Salvador Sánchez Colín*
Michoacán	*Félix Ireta Viveros* *Ricardo Ramírez G.*	José Torres Caballero Roberto E. Rodríguez
Morelos	*Elpidio Perdomo García* Carlos López Uriza	Manuel Aranda José Balbuena

Nayarit	*Candelario Miramontes* *José Limón Guzmán*	Ricardo Marín Ramos Jesús Mora Yáñez
Nuevo León	*Juan Manuel Elizondo* *José S. Vivanco*	Francisco Vela González Rodolfo Gaitán
Oaxaca	*Manuel R. Palacios* Armando Rodríguez Mújica	Demetrio Flores Fagoaga *Manuel Mayoral Heredia*
Puebla	Alfonso Moreyra Carrasco *Gustavo Díaz Ordaz*	Agustín Hernández D. Mariano Rayón Aguilar
Querétaro	Gilberto García Navarro *Eduardo Luque Loyola*	José E. Calzada Antonio Pérez Alcocer
San Luis Potosí	*Fernando Moctezuma* *Manuel Alvarez López*	*Antonio Rocha Jr.* *Pablo Aldrett*
Sinaloa	*Fausto A. Marín* Vacant	Guillermo Osuna y Osuna Vacant
Sonora	Antonio Canale *Gustavo A. Uruchurtu*	Manuel Gándara Jr. *Noé Palomares Navarro*
Tabasco	*Antonio Taracena* *Adelor D. Sala*	Luis León Olivos Jesús Lombardini
Tamaulipas	Eutimio Rodríguez *Magdaleno Aguilar*	José Cárdenas Vázquez Ladislao Cárdenas Jr.
Tlaxcala	*Mauro Angulo* *Gersáyn Ugarte*	*Ezequiel M. García* Baltasar Maldonado
Veracruz	*Fernando López Arias* *Fernando Casas Alemán*	José Fernando Villegas Alfonso Palacios L.
Yucatán	*Gonzalo López Manzanero* *Ernesto Novelo Torres*	Adalberto Aguilar Osorio Félix Rosado Iturralde
Zacatecas	*Jesús B. González* Salvador Castañedo R.	J. Jesús María García M. Valente Lozano

1952-58 (42nd and 43rd Legislatures)

State	Senator	Alternate
Aguascalientes	*Pedro de Alba* *Aquiles Elorduy*	Roberto Díaz Joaquín Cruz Ramírez

Baja California	*Leopoldo Verdugo Quiroz* *Esteban Cantú Jiménez*	Jesús Montaño Monge Manuel Quiroz Labastida
Campeche	*Rigoberto Otal Briseño* *Alberto Trueba Urbina*	Raúl Loyo y Loyo *Manuel Pavón Bahaine*
Chiapas	Rodolfo Suárez Coello *Julio Serrano Castro*	Héctor Yáñez Alejandro Rea Moguel
Chihuahua	*Teófilo R. Borunda* *Oscar Flores*	Salvador González R. Luis de la Garza O.
Coahuila	*Jacinto B. Treviño* *Gustavo Cárdenas Huerta*	Domingo Ortiz Garza Rafael Duarte Núñez
Colima	*Rafael S. Pimentel* *Roberto A. Solórzano*	*Salvador G. Govea* Jorge Alvarez Gutiérrez
Distrito Federal	*Jesús Yurén Aguilar* *Salvador Urbina*	José López Peral *Jesús Lozoya Solís*
Durango	*Francisco González de la V.* *Alberto Terrones Benítez*	Alfonso Pérez Gavilán Francisco Celis M.
Guanajuato	*Luis I. Rodríguez* *Francisco García Carranza*	*Rafael Corrales Ayala* Vicente García González
Guerrero	*Alfonso G. Alarcón* *Emigdio Martínez Adame*	*Alfonso L. Nava* *Caritino Maldonado Pérez*
Hidalgo	*Raúl Fernández Robert* *Alfonso Cravioto*	Eduardo Manzano *Julián Rodríguez Adame*
Jalisco	*Silvano Barba González* *Saturnino Coronado O.*	Guillermo Ramírez Valadez Luis Ramírez Meza
México	*Alfredo del Mazo Vélez* *Juan Fernández Albarrán*	Hermilo Arcos Pérez Eulalio Núñez Alonso
Michoacán	*David Franco Rodríguez* *Enrique Bravo Valencia*	Ignacio Ochoa Reyes José Garibay Romero
Morelos	*Norberto López Avelar* *Fausto Galván Campos*	*Felipe Rivera Crespo* Nicolás Zapata
Nayarit	*Emilio M. González* *Esteban B. Calderón*	Manuel Villegas Arellano Francisco García Monteros

Nuevo León	*Anacleto Guerrero Guajardo*	Félix González Salinas
	Rodrigo Gómez Gómez	*Roberto A. Cortés Muñiz*
Oaxaca	*Alfonso Pérez Gasca*	Ernesto Meixueiro
	Rafael E. Melgar	Darío L. Vasconcelos
Puebla	*Luis C. Manjarrez*	Alfonso Castillo Borsani
	Guillermo Castillo Fernández	Félix Guerrero Mejia
Querétaro	*José Figueroa Balvanera*	Enrique Montes Dorantes
	Manuel González Cosío	Francisco Rodríguez A.
San Luis Potosí	*Antonio Rocha*	Jesús Noyola
	David Vargas Bravo	Benito Noyola
Sinaloa	*Macario Gaxiola Urías*	*Jesús Gil Ryathga*
	Jesús Celis Campos	Humberto Bátiz Ramos
Sonora	*Fausto Acosta Romo*	Antonio Quiroga Rivera
	Noé Palomares Navarro	Francisco Enciso Mezquita
Tabasco	*Marcelino Inurreta*	Salvador Camelo Soler
	Agustín Beltrán Bastar	Felipe Ferrer Trujeque
Tamaulipas	*Raúl Gárate L.*	José López Cárdenas
	Manuel Guzmán Willis	Crisóforo Barragán Albino
Tlaxcala	*Higinio Paredes Ramos*	*Anselmo Cervantes H.*
	Miguel Osorio Ramírez	Maximiliano Cervantes Pérez
Veracruz	*Roberto Amorós Guiot*	*Isauro Acosta García*
	José Rodríguez Clavería	Hermenegildo J. Aldana
Yucatán	*Efraín Brito Rosado*	*Víctor Mena Palomo*
	Antonio Médiz Bolio	Armando Medina Alonso
Zacatecas	*Brigido Reynoso*	Roberto del Real
	Lauro G. Caloca	Gonzalo Castañedo

1958-64 (44th and 45th Legislatures)

State	Senator	Alternate
Aguascalientes	*Manuel Moreno Sánchez*	J. Guadalupe López Velarde
	Alfredo de Lara Isaacs	María Araiza López
Baja California	*José María Tapia Freyding*	Jorge Riva Palacio
	Gustavo Vildósola Almada	Francisco Dueñas Montes

Campeche	*Fernando Lanz Duret*	Luis Felipe Martínez M.
	Nicolás Canto Carrillo	*José Dolores García A.*
Chiapas	*José Castillo Tielemans*	J. Guadalupe Hernández
	Abelardo de la Torre G.	Marcelina Galindo Arce
Chihuahua	*Rodrigo M. Quevedo Moreno*	Valente Chacón Vaca
	Tomás Valles V.	Jaime Canales Lira
Coahuila	*Vicente Dávila Aguirre*	*Rafael Carranza H.*
	Federico Berrueto Ramón	*Salvador Hernández Vela*
Colima	*Antonio Salazar Salazar*	*Roberto Pizano Saucedo*
	Francisco Velasco Curiel	Raymundo Anzar Nava
Distrito Federal	*Hilario Medina Gaona*	Raoul Fournier Villada
	Fidel Velázquez Sánchez	*Joaquín Gamboa Pascoe*
Durango	*Carlos Real*	Pablo Avila de la Torre
	Enrique Dupré Ceniceros	*Abdon Alanís Ramírez*
Guanajuato	*Jesús López Lira*	*José López Bermúdez*
	Vicente García González	Efrén Alcocer Herrera
Guerrero	*Caritino Maldonado*	Francisco Vázquez Añorve
	Carlos Román Celis	*Jorge Soberón Acevedo*
Hidalgo	*Julián Rodríguez Adame*	*Carlos Ramírez Guerrero*
	Leónardo M. Hernández M.	Agustín Mariel Anaya
Jalisco	*Mariano Azuela*	Elías Mendoza González
	Guillermo Ramírez Valadez	Marcos Montero Ruiz
México	*Abel Huitrón y Aguado*	Felipe J. Sánchez
	Maximiliano Ruiz Castañeda	*Mario Colín Sánchez*
Michoacán	*Manuel Hinojosa Ortiz*	Lauro Pallares C.
	Natalio Vázquez Pallares	Norberto Vega Villagómez
Morelos	*Porfirio Neri Arizmendi*	Antonio Flores Mazari
	Eliseo Aragón Rebolledo	Gonzalo Pastrana Castro
Nayarit	*Alberto Medina Muñoz*	Ricardo Gómez García
	Enrique Ledón Alcaraz	Amador Cortés Estrada
Nuevo León	*Angel Santos Cervantes*	*Napoleón Gómez Sada*
	Eduardo Livas	*Margarita R. García*

Oaxaca	*Rodolfo Brena Torres*	Manuel Rivera Toro
	Ramón Ruiz Vasconcelos	Nicolás Grijalva Mirón
Puebla	*Donato Bravo Izquierdo*	Carlos Vergara Soto
	Rafael Moreno Valle	José Ignacio Morales Cruz
Querétaro	*Rafael Altamirano Herrera*	Avertano Mondragón Ochoa
	Domingo Olvera Gámez	Realino Frías Rodríguez
San Luis Potosí	*Juan Enrique Azuara*	Agustín Olivo Monsiváis
	Pablo Aldrett Cuéllar	Jacinto Maldonado V.
Sinaloa	*Teófilo Alvarez Borboa*	Enrique Riveros Castro
	Leopoldo Sánchez Celis	Héctor Manuel López Castro
Sonora	*Guillermo Ibarra*	Ernesto Salazar Girón
	Carlos B. Maldonado	Manuel Torres Escobosa
Tabasco	César A. Rojas	Diógenes Zurita Suárez
	Julián A. Manzur O.	Joaquín Bates Caparroso
Tamaulipas	*Emilio Martínez Manautou*	Rafael Sierra de la Garza
	Juan Manuel Terán Mata	*Manuel A. Ravizé*
Tlaxcala	*Francisco Hernández y H.*	Raúl Juárez Carro
	Samuel Ortega Hernández	Ricardo Velázquez Vázquez
Veracruz	*Roberto Gómez Maqueo*	*Ferrer Galván Bourel*
	Rosendo Topete Ibáñez	Manuel Meza Hernández
Yucatán	*Edgardo Medina Alonso*	J. Enrique Millet Espinosa
	Antonio Mena Brito	Artemio Alpízar Pacheco
Zacatecas	*Mauricio Magdaleno*	Bernardo del Real de León
	José Rodríguez Elías	Salvador Esparza Gutiérrez

1964-70 (46th and 47th Legislatures)

State	Senator	Alternate
Aguascalientes	*Alberto Alcalá de Lira*	José Ramírez Gámez
	Luis Gómez Zepeda	Roberto Díaz Rodríguez
Baja California	*Hermenegildo Cuenca Díaz*	Milton Castellanos Everado
	José Ricardi Tirado	Eduardo Tonella Escamilla
Campeche	*María Lavalle Urbina*	Carlos Cano Ruiz
	Carlos Sansores Pérez	*Ramón Marrero Ortiz*

Chiapas	*Andrés Serra Rojas*	Gustavo Lescieur López
	Arturo Moguel Esponda	Amadeo Narcia Ruiz
Chihuahua	*Luis L. León Uranga*	*Ricardo Carrillo Durán*
	Manuel Bernardo Aguirre S.	Mariano Valenzuela Ceballos
Coahuila	*Eulalio Gutiérrez Treviño*	Raymundo Córdoba Zúñiga
	Florencio Barrera Fuentes	Ramiro Peña Guerra
Colima	*Jesús Robles Martínez*	Alberto Larios Gaytán
	Alfredo Ruiseco Avellaneda	Crescencio Flores Díaz
Distrito Federal	*Luis González Aparicio*	*Renaldo Guzmán Orozco*
	Jesús Yurén Aguilar	*Rodolfo Echeverría Alvarez*
Durango	*Alberto Terrones Benítez*	*Carlos Real Encinas*
	Cristóbal Guzmán Cárdenas	*Ignacio Castillo Mena*
Guanajuato	*Juan Pérez Vela*	Virginia Soto Rodríguez
	Manuel Moreno Moreno	*Eliseo Rodríguez Ramírez*
Guerrero	*Baltasar R. Leyva Mancilla*	*Jerónimo Gomar Suástegui*
	Ezequiel Padilla Peñaloza	*Moisés Ochoa Campos*
Hidalgo	*Oswaldo Cravioto Cisneros*	Carlos Raúl Guadarrama M.
	Manuel Sánchez Vite	*Federico Ocampo Noble*
Jalisco	*Salvador Corona Bandín*	Luis Ramírez Meza
	Filiberto Rubalcaba Sánchez	José G. Mata López
México	*Fernando Ordorica Inclán*	Alejandro Arzate Sánchez
	Mario C. Olivera Gómez T.	Eduardo Arias Nuville
Michoacán	*J. Jesús Romero Flores*	Manuel López Pérez
	Rafael Galván Maldonado	Jesús Arreola Belmán
Morelos	*Diódoro Rivera Uribe*	Ramón Hernández Navarro
	Antonio Flores Mazari	Luis Flores Sobral
Nayarit	*Alfonso Guerra Olivares*	Raúl Llanos Lerma
	J. Ricardo Marín Ramos	*Rogelio Flores Curiel*
Nuevo León	*Armando Artega Santoyo*	*Santiago Roel García*
	Napoleón Gómez Sada	José Ovalle Morales
Oaxaca	*José Pacheco Iturribarría*	*Rodolfo Sandoval López*
	Raúl Bolaños Cacho	Manuel Martínez Soto

Puebla	*Gonzalo Bautista O'Farrill*	Eduardo Naude Anaya
	Eduardo Cué Merlo	Jorge Vergara Jiménez
Querétaro	*Eduardo Luque Loyola*	Alfonso Alexander Hernández
	Manuel Soberanes Muñoz	*Fernando Espinosa Gutiérrez*
San Luis Potosí	*Juan José González B.*	*Florencio Salazar Méndez*
	Jesús N. Noyola Zepeda	Adalberto Tamayo López
Sinaloa	*Manuel Sarmiento Sarmiento*	Canuto Ibarra Guerrero
	Amado Estrada Rodríguez	Héctor González Guevara
Sonora	*Juan de Dios Bojórquez León*	*Mario Morúa Johnson*
	Alicia Arellano Tapia	Fernando Pesqueira Juvera
Tabasco	*Gustavo A. Rovirosa Pérez*	José Leonides Gallegos A.
	Fausto Pintado Borrego	Fernando Hernández Loroño
Tamaulipas	*Magdaleno Aguilar Castillo*	Manuel Guerra Hinojosa
	Antonio García Rojas	Alfonso Barnetche González
Tlaxcala	*Ignacio Bonilla Vázquez*	Rafael Minor Franco
	Luciano Huerta Sánchez	José Hernández Díaz
Veracruz	*Rafael Murillo Vidal*	*Manlio Fabio Tapia Camacho*
	Arturo Llorente González	Martín Díaz Montero
Yucatán	*Rafael Matos Escobedo*	*Ramón Osorio Carbajal*
	Carlos Loret de Mola	Rubén Marín y Kall
Zacatecas	*Manuel Tello Baurrand*	*Fernando Pámanes Escobedo*
	José González Varela	Aurelio López de la Torre

1970-76 (48th and 49th Legislatures)

State	Senator	Alternate
Aguascalientes	*Miguel A. Barberena Vega*	*Augusto Gómez Villanueva*
	Enrique Olivares Santana	Roberto Díaz Rodríguez
Baja California	*Ramón Alvarez Cisneros*	Pablo Villarino
	Gustavo Aubanel Vallejo	Adolfo Ramírez Méndez
Campeche	*Ramón Alcalá Ferrera*	Rubén Selem Salum
	Carlos Pérez Cámara	Enrique Escalante Escalante
Chiapas	Ramiro Yáñez Cordova	*Edgar Robledo Santiago*
	Juan Sabines Gutiérrez	María Celorio Vda. de Rovelo

Chihuahua	*José I. Aguilar Irungaray*	José Pacheco Loya
	Arnaldo Gutiérrez Hernández	Samuel I. Valenzuela
Coahuila	*Braulio Fernández Aguirre*	Mauro Berrueto Ramón
	Oscar Flores Tapia	Pedro González Rivera
Colima	*Roberto Pizano Saucedo*	Alfonso García Franco
	Aurora Ruvalcaba Gutiérrez	Miguel Trejo Ochoa
Distrito Federal	*Martín Luis Guzmán*	Alfonso Sánchez Silva
	Alfonso Sánchez Madariaga	Luis Díaz Vázquez
Durango	*Salvador Gámiz Fernández*	Salvador Nava Rodríguez
	Agustín Ruiz Soto	Hortensia Flores Varela
Guanajuato	*José Rivera Pérez Campos*	Ramón López Díaz
	José Castillo Hernández	Alfonso Sánchez López
Guerrero	*Rubén Figueroa Figueroa*	Ismael Andraca Navarrete
	Vicente Fuentes Díaz	José Guadalupe Solis G.
Hidalgo	*Raúl Lozano Ramírez*	*Rafael Anaya Ramírez*
	Germán Corona del Rosal	Vicente Trejo Callejas
Jalisco	*Javier García Paniagua*	Vicente Palencia Murillo
	Ignacio Maciel Salcedo	*Renaldo Guzmán Orozco*
México	Félix Vallejo Martínez	Manuel Huitrón y Aquado
	Francisco Pérez Ríos	Sixto Noguez Estrada
Michoacán	*J. Jesús García Santacruz*	Gerardo Jiménez Escamilla
	Norberto Mora Plancarte	María Teresa Calderón C.
Morelos	*Elpidio Perdomo García*	Ignacio Guerra Tejeda
	Francisco Aguilar Hernández	Marcos Figueroa Ocampo
Nayarit	*Rogelio Flores Curiel*	Santos Ramos Contreras
	Emilio M. González Parra	Pedro López Díaz
Nuevo León	*Luis M. Farías*	Arnulfo Guerra Guajardo
	Bonifacio Salinas Leal	Hilario Contreras Molina
Oaxaca	*Celestino Pérez Pérez*	Mario Melgar Pacchiano
	Gilberto Suárez Torres	*Diódoro Carrasco Palacios*
Puebla	*Guillermo Morales Blumenkron*	*Guadalupe López Bretón*
	Alfredo Toxqui F. de Lara	Enrique Martínez Marquez

Querétaro	*Arturo Guerrero Ortiz*	Ricardo Rangel Andrade
	Salvador Jiménez del Prado	José González Olvera
San Luis Potosí	*Florencio Salazar Martínez*	Juan Antonio Ledesma
	Guillermo Fonseca Alvarez	Carlos Manuel Castillo
Sinaloa	*Alfonso G. Calderón Velarde*	Ramón F. Iturbe
	Gabriel Leyva Velázquez	Mateo Camacho Ontiveros
Sonora	*Benito Bernal Miranda*	Ramón Angel Amante E.
	Alejandro Carrillo Marcor	Benjamín Villaescusa R.
Tabasco	*Pascual Bellizzia Castañeda*	Hernán Robelo Wade
	Enrique González Pedrero	Máximo Evia Ramón
Tamaulipas	*Enrique Cárdenas González*	José Bruno del Río Cruz
	José C. Romero Flores	José María Vargas Pérez
Tlaxcala	*Vicente Juárez Carro*	Guillermo Villeda Hernández
	Nicanor Serrano del C.	Estéban Minor Quiroz
Veracruz	*Samuel Terrazas Zozaya*	Daniel Sierra Rivera
	Rafael Arriola Molina	*Juan Maldonado Pereda*
Yucatán	*Francisco Luna Kan*	Hernán Morales Medina
	Víctor Manzanilla Schaffer	Francisco Repetto Milán
Zacatecas	*Calixto Medina Medina*	Manuel Ibarguengoitia L.
	Aurora Navia Millán	Abundio Monsiváis García

1976-82 (50th and 51st Legislatures)

State	Senator	Alternate
Aguascalientes	*Rodolfo Landeros Gallegos*	*Roberto Díaz Rodríguez*
	Héctor Hugo Olivares V.	José de Jesús Medellín M.
Baja California	*Celestino Salcedo Monteón*	Rafael García Vázquez
	Roberto de la Madrid R.	*Oscar Baylón Chacón*
Baja California del Sur	*Alberto A. Alvarado A.*	Prisca Melgar de Tuchmann
	Marcelo Rubio Ruiz	*Víctor M. Liceaga Ruibal*
Campeche	*Carlos Sansores Pérez*	Rosa María Martínez D.
	Fernando Rafful Miguel	Joaquín E. Repetto Ocampo
Chiapas	*Salomón González Blanco*	Roberto Corzo Gay
	Horacio Castellanos Coutio	María G. Cruz Aranda

Chihuahua	*Oscar Ornelas Kuckle*	Santiago Nieto Sandoval
	Mario Carballo Pasos	Federico Estrada Meraz
Coahuila	*Eliseo F. Mendoza Berrueto*	*Oscar Ramírez Mijares*
	Gustavo Guerra Castanos	Ramiro Ruiz Madero
Colima	*Griselda Alvarez P. de Leon*	Aquileo Díaz Virgen
	Antonio Salazar Salazar	Roberto Anzar Martínez
Distrito Federal	*Hugo Cervantes del Río*	Luis del Toro Calero
	Joaquín Gamboa Pascoe	Rodolfo Martínez Moreno
Durango	*Ignacio Castillo Mena*	Antonio Calzada Guillén
	Tomás Rangel Perales	Felipe Ibarra Barbosa
Guanajuato	*Euquerio Guerrero López*	*Ignacio Vázquez Torres*
	Jesús Cabrera Muñoz Ledo	Adolfo González Aguado
Guerrero	*Jorge Soberón Acevedo*	Luis León Aponte
	Alejandro Cervantes Delgado	Rubén Uriza Castro
Hidalgo	*Humberto A. Lugo Gil*	Juan Sánchez Roldán
	Guillermo Rossell de la L.	José Luis Suárez Molina
Jalisco	*José María Martínez R.*	*María Guadalupe Martínez*
	Arnulfo V. Saavedra Reyes	*Rodolfo Flores Zara*
México	*Leonardo Rodríguez Alcaine*	Ignacio Guzmán Garduño
	Gustavo Baz Prada	Humberto Lira Mora
Michoacán	*Cuauhtémoc Cárdenas S.*	José Luis Escobar Herrer
	Guillermo Morfín García	José Berber Sánchez
Morelos	*Angel Ventura Valle*	Bernardo Heredia Valle
	Javier Rondero Zubieta	Roque González Urriza
Nayarit	Leobardo Ramos Martínez	Félix Torres Haro
	Daniel Espinosa Galindo	José Manuel Rivas Allende
Nuevo León	*Napoleón Gómez Sada*	José Díaz Delgado
	Federico Amaya Rodríguez	Adrián Yáñez Martínez
Oaxaca	*Eliseo Jiménez Ruiz*	*Rodolfo Alavez Flores*
	Jorge Cruickshank García	Mario Vázquez Martínez
Puebla	*Horacio Labastida Muñoz*	Ignacio Cuauhtémoc Paleta
	Blas Chumacero Sánchez	Marco A. Rojas Flores

Querétaro	*Rafael Camacho Guzmán* *Manuel González Cosío*	*César Rubén Hernández E.* Telésforo Trejo Uribe
Quintana Roo	Vicente Coral Martínez José Blanco Peyrefitte	José E. Azueta Orlayneta Hernán Pastrana Pastrana
San Luis Potosí	*Carlos Jongitud Barrios* *Fausto Zapata Loredo*	Rafael A. Tristán López Francisco Padrón Puyou
Sinaloa	*Hilda J. Anderson Nevares* *Gilberto Sebastián Ruiz A.*	Silvestre Pérez Lorens César A. López García
Sonora	*Juan José Gastelum Salcido* *Adolfo de la Huerta Oriol*	*Alejandro Sobarzo Loaiza* Juan A. Ruibal Corella
Tabasco	*David Gustavo Gutiérrez R.* *Carlos Pellicer Cámara*	Antonio Ocampo Ramírez Nicolás Reynes Berezaluce
Tamaulipas	*Morelos Jaime Canseco G.* *Martha Chávez Padrón*	Fernando García Arellano Enrique Fernández Pérez
Tlaxcala	*Jesús Hernández Rojas* Rafael Minor Franco	Joaquín Cisneros Fernandez Alvaro Salazar Lozano
Veracruz	*Silverio R. Alvarado A.* Sergio Martínez Mendoza	Angel Gómez Calderón Delia de la Paz Rebolledo
Yucatán	*Víctor Manuel Cervera P.* *Graciliano Alpuche Pinzón*	Efraín Zumárraga Ramírez Martín García Lizamas
Zacatecas	*Jorge Gabriel García Rojas* *José Guadalupe Cervantes C.*	José Bonilla Robles *Arturo Romo Gutiérrez*

1982-88 (52nd and 53rd Legislatures)

State	Senator	Alternate
Aguascalientes	Andrés Amador Valdivia A. *Roberto Casillas Hernández*	
Baja California	*Alfonso Garzón Santibáñez* *María del Carmen Marquez*	
Baja California del Sur	Armando Trasvina Taylor Guillermo Mercado Romero	
Campeche	Rafael Armando Herrera M. *Renato Sales Gasque*	

Chiapas	Manuel Villafuerte Mijangos *José Patrocinio González G.*
Chihuahua	*José Refugio Mar de la Rosa* José Socorro Salcido Gómez
Coahuila	*Francisco José Madero González* *Raúl Castellano Jiménez*
Colima	*Javier Ahumada Padilla* *Socorro Díaz Palacios*
Distrito Federal	*Hugo B. Margáin* *Abraham Martínez Rivero*
Durango	*Miguel González Avelar* *José Ramírez Gamero*
Guanajuato	*Agustín Téllez Cruz* *Gilberto Muñoz Mosqueda*
Guerrero	*Guadalupe Gómez Maganda* Filiberto Vigueras Lázaro
Hidalgo	*Adolfo Lugo Verduzco* *Luis José Dorantes Segovia*
Jalisco	*Heliodoro Hernández Loza* *Ramón Martínez Martín*
México	*Yolanda Senties de Ballesteros* Héctor Joaquín Hernández
Michoacán	*Antonio Martínez Báez* *Norberto Mora Plancarte*
Morelos	*Antonio Riva Palacio López* *Gonzalo Pastrana Castro*
Nayarit	Rigoberto Ochoa Zaragoza *Celso H. Delgado Ramírez*
Nuevo León	*Raúl Salinas Lozano* *Raúl Caballero Escamilla*
Oaxaca	*Andrés Henestrosa* *Heladio Ramírez López*

Puebla	Alfonso Zegbe Sanen
	Angel Aceves Saucedo

Querétaro   *Silvia Hernández de Galindo*
                Mariano Palacios Alcocer

Quintana Roo   *Miguel Borge Martín*
                Alberto E. Villanueva S.

San Luis Potosí   *Gonzalo Martínez Corbala*
                José Antonio Padilla S.

Sinaloa   Ernesto Millán Escalante
                Juan Millán Lizarraga

Sonora   *Jorge Díaz Serrano*
                Fernando Mendoza Contreras

Tabasco   *Humberto Hernández Haddad*
                Salvador Neme Castillo

Tamaulipas   *Salvador Barragán Camacho*
                Américo Villarreal Guerra

Tlaxcala   Faustino Alba Zavala
                Héctor Vázquez Paredes

Veracruz   *Manuel Ramos Gurrión*
                Mario Hernández Posadas

Yucatán   *Myrna Hoyos de Navarrete*
                Víctor Manzanilla Schaffer

Zacatecas   Rafael Cervantes Acuña
                Arturo Romo Gutiérrez

1988-1997 (54th, 55th, and 56th Legislatures)[*]

State	Senator	Alternate
Aguascalientes	*Héctor Olivares Ventura*	Jesús A. López Velarde Campa
	Benjamín Zarzoza Díaz	
	Jorge Rodríguez León	

---

[*]Mexico has recently staggered its election of senators. The first senator listed served a six-year term from 1988-1994; the second senator's term began in 1988 and ended in 1991; the third senator will serve from 1991 to 1997.

Baja California	César Moreno Martínez *Margarita Ortega Villa* *Héctor Terán Terán*	Luis. R. González Cruz
Baja California del Sur	Raúl Carillo Silva Gustavo Almaraz Montaño Antonio B. Manríquez Guluarte	Jorge Vargas Meza
Campeche	Jorge A. Vega Camacho Francisco Solís Rodríguez *Carlos E. Sales Gutiérrez*	Jesús M. Flores Hernández
Coahuila	*Oscar Ramírez Mijares* Gaspar Valdés Valdés *Rogelio Seguy Montemayor*	Alicia López de la Torre
Colima	Roberto Aznar Martínez Graciela Larios Rivas Ramón Serrano Ahumada	Ramón A. Núñez de la Mora
Chiapas	Antonio Melgar Aranda Blanca Ruth Esponda Eduardo Rincón Robledo	César R. Nauman Escobar
Chihuahua	*Saúl González Herrera* *Alonso Aguirre Ramos* Artemio Iglesias Miramontes	José López Villegas
Distrito Federal	*Porfirio Muñoz Ledo* *Ifigenia Martínez Hernández* *Manuel Aguilera Gómez*	*Luz Lajous y Vargas*
Durango	*Maximiliano Silero Esparza* *Héctor Mayagoitia Domínguez* *Angel S. Guerrero Mier*	Judith Murgía Corral
Guanajuato	José de Jesús Padilla Martín A. Montaño Arteaga Roberto Suárez Nieto	Héctor Hugo Flores Varela
Guerrero	Netzahualcóyotl de la Vega Antonio Jaimes Aguilar *Rubén Figueroa Alcocer*	Israel Soberanis Nogueda
Hidalgo	*Humberto A. Lugo Gil* *Julieta Guevara Bautista* *Jesús Murillo Karam*	Orlando Arvizu Lara

Jalisco	Justino Delgado Caloca *María E. Scherman Leaño* *José L. Lamadrid Suaza*	Sofía Valencia Abundis
México	*Leonardo Rodríguez Alcaine* *Jesús Alcántara Miranda* Mauricio Valdés Rodríguez	Heberto Barrera Velásquez
Michoacán	Roberto Robles Garnica Cristóbal Arías Solís Víctor M. Tinoco Rubi	Emma Mondragón Navarrete
Morelos	*Jesús Rodríguez y Rodríguez* *Hugo Domenzáin Guzmán* Angel Ventura Valle	Alfonso Cerqueda Martínez
Nayarit	*Emilio M. González Pana* *Julián Gascón Mercado* *Salvador Sánchez Vázquez*	Antonio Gómez Chumacero
Nuevo León	*Alfonso Martínez Domínguez* Jesús R. Canavati Tafich María Elena Chapa Hernández	César Lazo Hinojosa
Oaxaca	*Idolina Moguel Contreras* Luis Martínez Fernández *Diodoro H. Carrasco Altamirano*	Manuel Díaz Cisneros
Puebla	*Blas Chumacero Sánchez* *Alfredo Toxqui Fernández* Germán Sierra Sánchez	Carlos Grajales Salas
Querétaro	Ernesto Luque Feregrino *Enrique Burgos García* *Silvia Hernández Enríquez*	Luis Alvarez Septién
Quintana Roo	José González Castro María C. Sangri Aguilar Mario E. Villanueva Madrid	José E. Godoy Hernández
San Luis Potosí	*Carlos Jonguitud Barrios* Fernando Silva Nieto Carlos Jiménez Macías	Blanca S. Ruiz Ruedas
Sinaloa	*Salvador Esquer Apodaca* Mario Niebla Alvarez Gustavo A. Guerrero Ramos	José Luis Leyson Castro

Sonora	*Luis Donaldo Colosio* Ramiro Valdés Fontes	Rubén Díaz Vega
Tabasco	Nicolás Reynés Berezaluce *Roberto Madrazo Pintado* *Manuel Gurría Ordóñez*	Jesús A. León Estrada
Tamaulipas	Ricardo Camero Candiel Laura A. Garza Galindo *Manuel Cavazos Lerma*	*Enrique Cárdenas González*
Tlaxcala	Alberto Juárez Blancas Alvaro Salazar Lozano José A. Cruz Alvarez Lima	Ernesto García Sarmiento
Veracruz	Alger León Moreno Julio Patiño Rodríguez *Miguel Alemán Velasco*	Eduardo R. Thomae Domínguez
Yucatán	Dulce María Sauri Riancho Gonzalo Navarro Báez Carlos H. Sobrino Sierra	Carlos R. Calderón
Zacatecas	Gustavo Salinas Iñiguez Eliseo Rangel Gaspar *Arturo Gutiérrez Romo*	Ricardo Monreal Avila

Appendix C

Federal Deputies, 1937–1993

1937-40 (37th Legislature)

State	Deputy	Alternate
Aguascalientes	1. Ramón B. Aldana	J. Concepción Rodríguez
	2. Pedro Quevedo	Carlos R. Ramos
Baja California del Norte (Territory)	1. Hipólito Rentería	Ramón M. Hernández
Baja California del Sur (Territory)	1. Adán Velarde	Manuel Gómez
Campeche	1. *Héctor Pérez Martínez*	*Pedro Guerrero Martínez*
	2. Ignacio Reyes Ortega	Emilio M. Pérez Arroyo
Chiapas	1. Gil Salgado Palacio	Gustavo López Gutiérrez
	2. *Rafael P. Gamboa*	Adolfo C. Corzo
	3. *Emilio Araujo*	Armando Guerra A.
	4. *Efraín Aranda Osorio*	Carlos Albores C.
	5. A. Fuentevilla Jr.	José Orantes
Chihuahua	1. *Eugenio Prado*	Leobardo Chávez
	2. *Guillermo Quevedo M.*	Tito Herrera Rojas
	3. *Francisco García C.*	Enrique Acosta E.
	4. Ismael C. Falcón	Ignacio León
	5. Carlos Terrazas	Justino Loya
Coahuila	1. Tomás Garza Felán	Apolonio Martínez
	2. Juan Pérez	Fernando Rivera
	3. *Damián L. Rodríguez*	Manuel Rodríguez F.
	4. Emilio N. Acosta	Arturo V. Ibarra M.
Colima	1. *José Campero*	Rafael C. Ceballos
	2. Pablo Silva	Julio Santa Ana

Distrito Federal	1. *José Muñoz Cota*	Juventino Aguilar
	2. Salvador Ochoa Rentería	Roberto Aguilera C.
	3. J. Maximino Molina	Juan de Dios Flores
	4. José Escudero Andrade	Rafael Cárdenas R.
	5. Francisco Sotomayor R.	Fernando Carrillo
	6. Francisco Martínez V.	Manuel Ramos Z.
	7. *F. Amilpa y Rivera*	Sebastián Pavia González
	8. Luis S. Campa	Erasmo Reséndis
	9. *Jesús Yurén Aguilar*	Miguel Fraire
	10. Miguel Florés Villar	Rodolfo Moralés Alamilla
	11. J. Jesús Rico	Francisco Vargas Rivera
	12. *León García*	*Aarón Camacho López*
Durango	1. Alfredo Mena	Rafael R. Torres
	2. Tomás Palomino Rojas	José García Gutiérrez
	3. Ernesto Calderón R.	Emilio Bueno
	4. Manasio Arrieta	Jesús M. Rosales
Guanajuato	1. Benigno Arredonde Rivera	Tomás Soria
	2. *Celestino Gasca*	Baltázar Villalpando
	3. *José Hernández Delgado*	Adelaido Gómez
	4. J. Jesús Guzmán Vaca	Sebastián Ortiz Hernández
	5. Francisco Vallejo	Luis Chabolla
	6. Manuel L. Farías	J. Jesús Franco
	7. *José Aguilar y Maya*	Adolfo Martínez Guerrero
	8. Antolín Piña Soria	Antonio Bucio
	9. Pascual Alcalá	Víctorio Florés Paz
	10. Federico Hernández A.	José T. Arvide
Guerrero	1. Francisco S. Carreto	Moisés H. Villegas
	2. *Galo Soberón y Parra*	Job R. Gutiérrez
	3. Bolívar Sierra	Pedro Popoca
	4. Miguel Andréu Almazán	Alberto Méndez
	5. *Nabor A. Ojeda*	Jesús Rodríguez Maldonado
	6. Feliciano Radilla	Julio Diego
Hidalgo	1. Daniel C. Santillán	*Eleázar Canale*
	2. Honorado Austria	Napoleón Pérez Chávez
	3. Agustín Olvera	Nicolás Solís
	4. *Vicente Aguirre*	Marciano Viveros
	5. *José Lugo Guerrero*	Felipe Estrada
	6. Leopoldo Badillo	Luis F. Flores
	7. Eduardo B. Jiménez	Felipe Castillo
Jalisco	1. J. Jesús Ocampo	Anacleto Tortolero
	2. Guillermo Ponce de León	Juan I. Godínez
	3. Marcelino Barba González	Antonio González Alatorre
	4. Miguel Moreno	Jesús L. Pérez
	5. Luis Alvarez del Castillo	José Romero Gómez

	6. Rodolfo Delgado	José Aguilera
	7. *Margarito Ramírez*	Manuel Basulto Limón
	8. David Pérez Ruflo	Vicente P. Fajardo
	9. *César Martino*	Fructuoso Arreola
	10. Alfredo Cuéllar Castillo	Ladislao Velasco
	11. Manuel Palomera Calleja	Arturo B. Gómez
	12. J. Rosalio Ahedo	Pedro G. Narváez
	13. J. Teobaldo Pérez	Juan Manuel Sánchez Robles
México	1. Gonzalo Peralta A.	Sidronio Choperena
	2. Alfredo Sánchez Flores	Javier Salgado
	3. Carlos Aguirre	Miguel Espejel Villagrán
	4. José L. Rosas	Estanislao Mejía
	5. Antonio S. Sánchez	José Jiménez
	6. Efrén Peña Aguirre	Angel Aguilar
	7. *Alfonso Florés M.*	Leopoldo Quiroga
	8. Joaquín Mondragón	Darío Nava
	9. *Alfredo Zarate Albarrán*	Felipe Estrada
	10. Jesús Mondragón Ramírez	Juan Albarrán
Michoacán	1. Elías Miranda G.	José Montejano
	2. Aurelio Munguía H.	Pedro S. Talavera
	3. Alfonso García González	Felipe Anguiano
	4. José M. Cano	Antonio Soto Aldaz
	5. Ernesto Prado	Conrado Magaña
	6. *Baltazar Gudiño*	Francisco Zepeda Maciel
	7. Rafael Vaca Solorio	J. Guadalupe Rojas
	8. Leopoldo O. Arias	Matilde Pimentel
	9. Juan Guajardo H.	Arturo Pineda H.
	10. José Zavala Ruiz·	Luiz Mora Gómez
	11. Jaime Chaparro	*Leopoldo Zincúnegui Tercero*
Morelos	1. Andrés Duarte Ortiz	Zeferino Ortega
	2. Gregorio Carrillo	Juan Lima
Nayarit	1. *Luis Aranda del Toro*	*Candelario Miramontes*
	2. José Angulo Araico	Marcos Jiménez
Nuevo León	1. Manuel Flores	José Ojeda
	2. *Miguel Z. Martínez*	Julián V. Domínguez
	3. *Dionisio García Leal*	Eliséo B. Sánchez
	4. Hilario Contreras Molina	Margarito Osorio
Oaxaca	1. *Heliodoro Charis Castro*	Cuberto Chagoya
	2. Arturo Vado	Heriberto Jiménez
	3. Carlos Santibáñez	Ildefonso Zorrilla
	4. *Jorge Meixueiro*	Antonio Sumano
	5. Maximino González Fernández	Luis Mora Rojas

	6. *Alfonso Francisco Ramírez*	Jacobo Ramírez Gómez
	7. Antolín Jiménez	Enrique E. Sumano
	8. Adán Ramírez López	Ignacio Gamboa Zebadúa
	9. Ranulfo Calderón Sánchez	Adelaido Ojeda
	10. Benito Zaragoza	*Dagoberto Flores Betancourt*
	11. Félix de la Lanza	Delfino Cruz
Puebla	1. Juan Salamanca V.	Carlos M. Mora
	2. Mauricio Ayala L.	Porfirio Martínez
	3. *Froylán C. Manjarrez*	Luciano M. Sánchez
	4. Miguel Hidalgo Salazar	Pedro L. Romero
	5. Francisco Hernández	Marcos Fuentes
	6. Agustín Huerta	Jesús Guerrero
	7. Julián Cacho	Rafael Herrera A.
	8. Rosendo Cortés	*Sacramento Joffre Vázquez*
	9. Luis Viñals León	*Fausto M. Ortega*
	10. *Rafael Molina Betancourt*	Adán M. Vázquez
	11. Luis Lombardo Toledano	Benigno Campos
	12. Lindoro Hernández A.	Alberto Jiménez
Querétaro	1. Emiliano Siurob	José D. Luque
	2. *Noradino Rubio Ortiz*	Genaro Canto
Quintana Roo (Territory)	1. Diódoro Tejero	Pedro Pérez Garrido
San Luis Potosí	1. *Víctor Alfonso Maldonado*	Valentín Narváez
	2. Epifanio Castillo	Florencio Galván T.
	3. Francisco Arellano B.	Julio Muñoz Ontañón
	4. Josué Escobedo	Ignacio Cuéllar
	5. Arnulfo Hernández Z.	Pedro Izaguirre
	6. José Santos Alonso	Tomás Oliva B.
	7. Alfonso R. Salazar	Andrés Zárate Sánchez
Sinaloa	1. Raúl Simaneas	Miguel Sandoval A.
	2. *Gabriel Leyva Velázquez*	Eligio Samaniego
	3. *Ramón F. Iturbe*	Jesús P. Cota
	4. J. Ignacio Lizárraga	Antonio Topete
Sonora	1. Humberto Obregón	Ramón M. Real
	2. *Francisco Martínez P.*	Elías A. Salazar
	3. Ricardo G. Hill	Antonio C. Ramos
Tabasco	1. *Alfonso Gutiérrez Gurría*	Enrique Becerra Martínez
	2. Carlos Domínguez López	Felipe Trejo
Tamaulipas	1. *José Cantú Estrada*	Alberto Cárdenas
	2. Juan Rincón	Bernardo Turrubiates
	3. Ignacio Alcalá	Gonzalo Zaragoza

Tlaxcala	1. Alberto Ríos Conde	Andrés C. Jiménez
	2. *Francisco Mora Plancarte*	Juan Rodríguez
Veracruz	1. *Manuel E. Miravete*	Aureliano Azuara
	2. Manuel Jasso	Vicente Gutiérrez
	3. *Adolfo Ruiz Cortines*	Antonio Pulido
	4. Odilón Montero	Leandro García
	5. *Jesús M. Rodríguez*	Gerónimo García
	6. Demetrio Gutiérrez	Efrén Aburto
	7. Alfonso Pérez Redondo	Juan Alarcón García
	8. Adolfo E. Ortega	Crispín Vargas
	9. Silvestre Aguilar	José Zúñiga
	10. Santos Pérez Abascal	Bonifacio Seyde Molina
	11. Manuel Ayala	
	12. Rodolfo T. Márquez	Sebastián Fabián
	13. Joaquín Jara Díaz	Rafael Escobar Pérez
	14. Luis R. Torres	Benjamín E. Lule
Yucatán	1. Miguel A. Menéndez Reyes	Manuel López Amábilis
	2. *Víctor Mena Palomo*	René Almeida
	3. Alvaro Pérez Alpuche	Tomás Briceño
	4. Agustín Franco V.	Germán Pech
Zacatecas	1. Luis Florés G.	Tomás Hernández
	2. Daniel Z. Duarte	Tomás Zapata
	3. *Enrique Estrada*	Heraclio Rodríguez
	4. M. Vázquez del Mercado	Onésimo Ramírez

1940-43 (38th Legislature)

State	Deputy	Alternate
Aguascalientes	1. Benjamín Reséndiz	Andrés M. Esquivel
	2. Vicente Madrigal Guzmán	Carlos M. Ramos
Baja California del Norte (Territory)	1. Blas Valdivia	Simón Flores
Baja California del Sur (Territory)	1. Isidro Domínguez Cota	Jesús Adarga
Campeche	1. *Alberto Trueba Urbina*	José del Carmen González
	2. Ramón Berzunza Pinto	Barbaciano Chuc
Chiapas	1. *Mariano Samayoa*	Ramiro J. Farrera
	2. Angel Corzo Molina	Gustavo Lazos G.
	3. Guillermo Malpica Esponda	José Domingo Meza
	4. Antonio Cachón Ponce	Rubén Blaneo
	5. Jesús M. Ramírez	Arturo Mendoza

Chihuahua	1. Rogelio Sánchez Corral	Epifanio de Anda
	2. Valento Chacón Baea	Lorenzo Oropeza
	3. Jesús U. Melina	J. Trinidad Sáenz
	4. *Manuel Bernardo Aguirre*	Carlos Enríquez Ch.
	5. Rafael F. Lazo	Anselmo Ramos
Coahuila	1. Pedro Cerda	Enrique Guzmán
	2. Genaro S. Cervantes	Manuel Arenas
	3. Arturo Carranza	Manuel Pérez Bernea
	4. Carlos Samaniego G.	Domingo Márquez
Colima	1. *Manuel Gudiño*	José C. Fuentes
	2. *Jesús Michel Espinosa J.*	Rubén Vizcarra
Distrito Federal	1. Lamberto Zúñiga	Clemente S. Suárez
	2.	
	3. Rafael Cárdenas	Luis Yurén
	4. Alfonso Peña Palafox	Félix Cortés
	5. Carlos M. Orloineta	Fidel Guerrero
	6. César M. Cervantes	Salvador López Abitia
	7. *Alejandro Carrillo*	Ramón Castilleja
	8.	
	9. Luis Quintero Gutiérrez	Rafael Gaona
	10. *Carlos Zapata Vela*	Estanislao Martínez
	11. Jesús de la Garza	Gonzalo Elizalde
	12. *Aarón Camacho López*	Octaviano Núñez
Durango	1. Enrique Carrola Antura	Severo Reyes
	2. Mariano Padilla	Mariano Borrego
	3. *Braulio Meraz Nevárez*	Alberto Pérez E.
	4. Manuel Solórzano Soto	Margarito González
Guanajuato	1. J. Buenaventura Lara	Amado Arenas
	2. Rafael Rionda	Juan H. Díaz
	3. *Ricardo Acosta V.*	J. Cruz Sánchez
	4. Joaquín Madrazo	Ignacio Castro
	5. Ernesto Gallardo S.	Alberto González B.
	6. Rafael Otero y Gama	Abundio Toral
	7. Arnulfo Rosas	Arnulfo López Orozco
	8. Adolfo Martínez G.	Dionisio Castilla
	9. Reynaldo Lecona Soto	Alfredo Guerrero Tarquín
	10. Fausto Villagómez	Emilio García
Guerrero	1. Mario Lasso	Francisco Amigón
	2. *Rubén Figueroa*	Mucio Cárdenas
	3. Amadeo Meléndez	Ramiro Cruz Manjarrez
	4. Alfredo Córdoba Lara	Rafael Mendoza G.
	5. J. Jesús Muñoz Vergara	Roberto Arzate Olea
	6. Antonio Molina Jiménez	Marcos Sánchez

Hidalgo	1. José Pérez Jr.	Ignacio Hidalgo Quesada
	2. *Leonardo M. Hernández*	Casimiro Benítez
	3. Gumersindo Gómez	*José Gómez Esparza*
	4. Gregorio Hernández	Felipe Contrera
	5. *Alfonso Corona de Rosal*	Jesús Martínez
	6. Otilio Villegas	Erasto Olguín
	7. *Juvencio Nochebuena*	Pedro Vélez
Jalisco	1. Juan I. Godínez	Emilio Gutiérrez Durán
	2. Catarino Issac	J. Jesús Silva Romero
	3. Manuel Martínez Sicilia	Emilio González Gutiérrez
	4. Ismael M. Lozano	José Ana Castañeda
	5. Lucio González Padilla	Pablo Esqueda
	6. Felipe R. Díaz Rodríguez	José I. Chávez Nuño
	7. Fernando Basulto Limón	Moisés Chávez Hernández
	8. J. Jesús Cisneros Gómez	José María Chávez
	9. J. Jesús Landeros	Ramón Urzúa
	10. Jaime Llamas	José Ramírez
	11. Martiniano Sendis	Candelario Loreto
	12. Alfonso G. Cebalius	Miguel Rosales
	13. *Juan Gil Preciado*	Eliseo Navarro
México	1. Adolfo Manero	Joaquín González Aragón
	2. Raúl Serrano T.	Luis Martínez
	3. Ignacio Gómez Arroyo	José Enríquez Infante
	4. Juan N. García	Pedro Posada
	5. Tomás Pérez R.	Justo Martínez
	6. *Porfirio Ramírez*	Amador Mora
	7. José Hernández Mota	Martín Velázquez
	8. Antonio Mancilla Bauza	Gabriel Maldonado
	9. Daniel Tenorio	Felipe Estrada
	10. Armando P. Arroyo	Ignacio Bustamante
Michoacán	1. José Molina	Luis G. Zumaya
	2. Pablo Rangel Reyes	Sabino Cruz
	3. Pascual Abarea Pérez	J. Encarnación Castillo
	4. José Alfaro Pérez	Ignacio Torres Espinosa
	5. Ignacio Urbina Mercado	José Torres
	6. Juan S. Picazo	Genaro Guerrero
	7. Ramón Medina	Manuel Magaña
	8. Luis Ordorica Cerda	Dunstano Morfín Pérez
	9. Ignacio Ramírez Palacios	Silviano Díaz Barriga
	10. Heli M. López	David Soto
	11. *L. Zincúnegui Tercero*	Tiburcio Correa Medina
Morelos	1. *Porfirio Neri Arizmendi*	José Cuevas
	2. Ignacio Acevedo	Matías Polanco

Nayarit	1. *Candelario Miramontes*	Luis Rivera
	2. *Emilio M. González*	José C. Villaseñor
Nuevo León	1. J. Refugio F. Rodríguez	Ramón Villarreal
	2. Leandro Martínez L.	Gregorio Lecca
	3.	
	4. Maximino Reyna	Marcos Quintanilla
Oaxaca	1. Fernando de Gyves Pineda	José B. Calvo
	2. Manuel Rueda Magro	Francisco Jiménez
	3. Hermenegildo Luis	Rosendo Pérez
	4. *Demetrio Bolaños Espinosa*	Zeferino Canseco
	5. Manuel Chávez	Genaro Ramos
	6. Adalberto Lagunas Calvo	Flavio Pérez Gasca
	7. Adelaido Ojeda Caballero	Benigno Cisneros
	8. Luis E. Velasco	Cupertino Zárate
	9. Carlos R. Balleza Jr.	Vicente Castillo Ramírez
	10. Ignacio Gamboa Zebadúa	Rosendo Mendoza
	11. Narciso Medina Estrada	Javier R. Villar
Puebla	1. Martín Torres	Eustasio Mozo
	2. *Blas Chumacero*	Juan F. Rojas
	3. Bernardo Chávez V.	Jacinto Natario
	4. Tomás Covarrubias	Agustín Bayón
	5. Fernando S. Romero	José Solís
	6. *Aarón Merino Fernández*	Eustolio Tapia
	7. Gabriel Cuevas Víctoria	Rafael Rodríguez Meza
	8. Antonio Portas	Rafael Argüelles
	9. *Luis Vázquez Lapuente*	Manuel González Aguirre
	10. Julio Lobato M.	Abelardo Bonilla
	11. *Emilio Gutiérrez Roldán*	Gabriel Herrera G.
	12. *Antonio Nava Castillo*	Roberto M. L. Castelán
Querétaro	1. Alfredo F. Díaz Escobar	Medardo Trejo
	2. Enrique Montes	Félix Méndez
Quintana Roo (Territory)	1. Raymundo Sánchez Corral	Ricardo Villanueva
San Luis Potosí	1. *Florencio Salazar*	Fidel Cortés
	2. J. Delfino Moreno	J. Félix Reyes
	3. Benjamín Gutiérrez R.	José María P. Peláez
	4. Luis Aguilera	Alfredo Garfías
	5.	
	6. Luis Márquez Ricano	Domingo Candelario
	7. Herminio Salas	J. Guadalupe Espinosa
Sinaloa	1. José Jiménez Acevedo	Jesús García
	2. Rafael Granja Lizárraga	José Medina Velázquez

	3. Cuauhtémoc Ríos Martínez	Jesús Osuna P.
	4. Modesto Antimo	Zeferino Urías
Sonora	1. Jacinto López	Antonio M. Cano
	2. Ramón M. Durón	Rafael A. Moraga
	3. Miguel A. Salazar	Antonio C. Encinas
Tabasco	1. Rogelio Castañares Jamet	Juan Mendoza Valles
	2. Ulises González Blengio	Jaime Cancino Tadeo
Tamaulipas	1. *Hugo Pedro González*	José H. Hernández
	2. *Silverio Meza P.*	Florentino Guevara
	3. Benjamín Zapata	Salvador Ortiz Silva
Tlaxcala	1. Miguel Moctezuma	Abraham Rojas
	2. Ezequiel Selley	Armando Flores Cárdenas
Veracruz	1. Alfredo S. Sarrelangne L.	Zenón González Ortiz
	2. Salvador González	Onofre Morales
	3. *César Garizurieta*	Ricardo D. González
	4. Leandro García	Vicente Calderón M.
	5. Eduardo S. Arellano	Rosalino Jiménez
	6. Josafat Melgarejo	Ignacio R. Ojeda
	7. *Fernando López Arias*	José García
	8. Julio López Silva	Ascención Vázquez Arenzano
	9. Gonzalo Casas Alemán	Andrés Cerón H.
	10. Ramón Camarena Medina	Ricardo Rodal
	11. Jesús Arizmendi	José C. González
	12. *Eduardo Hernández Cházaro*	Rafael Arriola Molina
	13. José Ch. Ramírez	Ramón B. Prieto
	14. Bernardino F. Simeneen	José Pera
Yucatán	1. José M. Bolio Méndez	Humberto Lara y Lara
	2. Carlos Jordán Arjona	Emilio Pacheco
	3. *Antonio Betancourt Pérez*	Hernán Moralés Medina
	4. Juan Manuel Torres	Ernesto Alcocer Osorno
Zacatecas	1. *Aurelio Pámanes Escobedo*	Mauricio Castillo
	2. Carlos Ponzio M.	José Fernández Cortés
	3. *Leobardo Reynoso*	Salvador Castañedo
	4. Paulino Pérez	J. Jesús Valencia
	5. Antonio Ramírez	Salvador Mora

1943-46 (39th Legislature)

State	Deputy	Alternate
Aguascalientes	1. Voided	Voided
	2. *Manuel Moreno Sánchez*	Felipe Hernández
Baja California del Norte (Territory)	1. Eduardo Garza Senande	José Inés Oviedo
Baja California del Sur (Territory)	1. Adán Velarde	Benito Beltrán Beltrán
Campeche	1. *Pedro Guerrero Martínez*	Alfredo Ferráez
	2. Arcadio Ché Cunché	Francisco Alvarez Barrett
Chiapas	1. *Andrés Serra Rojas*	Tomás Martínez
	2. *Juan M. Esponda*	Filberto Santiago Flores
	3. José Pantaleón Domínguez	Humberto Pascacio Gamboa
	4. Francisco José Burelo	David Pérez N.
	5. Rafael Jiménez Bolán	Julio Muñoz Castillo
Chihuahua	1. *Tomás Vallés V.*	Carlos Sánchez Rubio
	2. Gustavo Chávez	Felipe González N.
	3. *Teófilo Borunda*	Alberto C. Castillo
	4. *Guillermo Quevedo Moreno*	Francisco Millán Millán
Coahuila	1. Francisco López Serrano	Alejandro V. Soberón
	2. Ubaldo Veloz A.	Eduardo B. Alvarado
	3. *Raúl López Sánchez*	Andrés Montoya
	4. Víctor M. Bosque	Secundino Ramos y Ramos
Colima	1. Rubén Vizcarra	José S. Benítez
	2. Carlos Alcaraz Ahumada	Miguel S. Fuentes
Distrito Federal	1. Francisco Linares T.	Fortunato Reyes II
	2. *Carlos A. Madrazo*	*Marcelino Inureta*
	3. Filemón Manrique	Antioco Ramírez
	4. *Ruffo Figueroa Figueroa*	Manuel E. Trejo
	5. J. Leonardo Flores Vázquez	Carlos L. Díaz y Díaz
	6. Juan Best Gareta	Luis Martínez Mezquida
	7. Pedro Téllez Vargas	Francisco Mayorga
	8. *Jesús Yurén Aguilar*	Rafael Gaona
	9. Roberto Aguilera Carbajal	Nemesio Fuentes Fuentes
	10. Antonio Ulibarri	Eugenio de la Torre Gómez
	11. *Sacramento Joffre Vázquez*	Emiliano Aguilar
	12. Leopoldo Hernández	Bonifacio Moreno Jr.

Durango	1. José Donaciano Sosa	Juan B. Nájera
	2. Miguel Breceda	Domingo Garibaldi
	3. *Marino Castillo Nájera*	Miguel Arrieta
	4. Juan Manuel Tinoco	Marcelo Chairez
Guanajuato	1. Fernando Mora	Luis Carreón
	2. Luis Madrazo Basuri	Justo Pedroza
	3. *Federico Medrano Valdivia*	Ciro Aree
	4. *Fernando Díaz Durán*	J. Jesús L. Vargas
	5. José R. Velázquez Nuño	Antonio Bucio
	6. *Francisco García Carranza*	Antonio E. Pérez
	7. *Guillermo Aguilar y Maya*	Miguel Hernández Garibay
Guerrero	1. José María Suárez Téllez	Angel Tapia Alarcón
	2. Carlos F. Carranco Cardoso	Alberto Salgado Cuevas
	3. Isauro López Salgado	Odilón C. Flores
	4. Ramón Mata y Rodríguez	Ignacio Víctoria
	5. *Donato Miranda Fonseca*	Arquímides Catalán Guevara
Hidalgo	1. Daniel Olguín Díaz	Pánfilo Hernández
	2. *Ramón G. Bonfil*	Gorgonio Rodríguez
	3. *Víctor M. Aguirre*	Felipe Contreras Ruiz
	4. *Raúl Lozano Ramírez*	Manuel Lara Salguero
	5. Adolfo Lugo Guerrero	Luis de la Concha
Jalisco	1. Alberto Velázquez	J. Jesús Macías Pérez
	2. Miguel Moreno Padilla	J. Martín del Campo
	3. *Heliodoro Hernández Loza*	Manuel Ayala Pérez
	4. Fidencio Vázquez Cerda	Guillermo Lara Mendoza
	5. Adalberto Oriega Huizar	Procopio Domínguez
	6. Ignacio Luis Velázquez	Aurelio Arrayo
	7. Jorge Contreras Bobadilla	Narciso Martínez
	8. José de Jesús Lima	Cosme Morán
	9. W. Partida Hernández	J. Ascención Andrade Berumen
México	1. *Gregorio Velázquez Sánchez*	Antonio Galván Albarrán
	2. *Antonio Manero*	Agustín González Argüelles
	3. Juan José Rivera Rojas	Arturo Chávez Vázquez
	4. José D. Izquierdo	Agustín Albarrán
	5.	
	6. Federico S. Sánchez	Ernesto Domínquez
	7. *Juan Fernández Albarrán*	Fernando Pruneda Batres
	8. *Octavio Sentíes G.*	Felipe Estrada
	9. *Gabriel Ramos Millán*	Bartolomé Requena González
Michoacán	1. *Ricardo Ramírez Guerrero*	Melesio Aguilar Ferrera
	2. Salvador Ochoa Rentería	Homero Areiniega

	3. Agustín Otero Gutiérrez	Antonio Licca Luna
	4. Francisco de P. Jiménez	Silverio Ceja
	5. José Zavala Ruiz	Alfredo Ayala
	6. Diego Hernández Topete	José Concepción Padilla
	7. Jesús Torrés Caballuo	J. Jesús Bantista
	8. Gabriel Chávez Tejeda	Salvador Méndez
Morelos	1. Manuel Aranda	Mayolo Alcazar
	2. *Eliseo Aragón Rebolledo*	Arturo M. Cortina
Nayarit	1. Alberto Tapia Carrillo	Alfonso Llanos Ramírez
	2. G. Castañeda Landózuri	José María Narváez
Nuevo León	1. Rodolfo Gaytán	Zacarías Villarreal
	2. *Julián Garza Tijerina*	J. Cruz Acevedo
	3. *Carlos F. Osuna*	Delfino García Sáenz
	4. Hilario Contreras Molina	Isaac Medina
Oaxaca	1. Alberto Ramos Sesma	Julio Gómez López
	2.	
	3. Demetrio Flores Fagoaga	Rogelio Jiménez
	4. *Melquiades Ramírez*	Rafael Pineda León
	5. *Octavio Reyés Spíndola*	Fernando León Díaz
	6. *Francisco López Cortés*	Manuel Castellanos
	7. *Norberto Aguirre*	Salvador Velázquez
	8. José Larrazábal González	Ricardo Vázquez Echeverría
Puebla	1. *Gustavo Díaz Ordaz*	Agustín Huerta
	2. Mariano Rayón	Gustavo Romero Aldaz
	3. *Antonio J. Hernández*	Rigoberto González
	4. *Cosme Aguilera Alvarez*	Jacobo Ojeda
	5. Andrés Robago Castellanes	Enrique Pacheco G.
	6. Alfonso M. Moreyra	Miguel Bárcena
	7. José Manuel Gálvez	Jorge W. Sánchez
	8. Luis Huidobro	Javier N. Luna
	9. Carlos I. Betancourt	Alvaro Lechuga
Querétaro	1. *Eduardo Luque Loyola*	Antonio Martínez Montes
	2. Gilberto García	*Domingo Olvera Gámez*
Quintana Roo (Territory)	1. A. González Villarreal	Francisco Cordero Núñez
San Luis Potosí	1. Luis Jiménez Delgado	*Antonio Rocha*
	2. *Pablo Aldrett*	Manuel Chávez
	3. Víctor Alfonso Maldonado	*Enrique Parra Hernández*
	4. *Fernando Moctezuma*	Manuel García
	5. *Ismael Salas*	Ignacio Moralea
	6. Manuel Alvarez	Emilio López R.

Sinaloa	1. Rosendo G. Castro	Conrado Ochoa
	2. Fausto A. Marín	Enrique Pera G.
	3. *Bernardo Norzagaray*	Miguel Navarro Franco
Sonora	1. Jesús M. Figueroa	Carlos Escardante
	2. Herminio Ahumada Jr.	Jesús María Suárez, Jr.
	3. Saturnino Saldívar	Edmundo Olachea
Tabasco	1. Nicolás Quintana V.	Bertino Madrigal Camelo
	2. Ernesto E. Trujillo Gurría	Rafael León Cáceres
Tamaulipas	1. Félix Cabanas Hernández	Antonio de León
	2. *Graciano Sánchez*	Martín Martínez
	3. Saúl Cantú Balderas	Francisco Romero Cortés
Tlaxcala	1. *Mauro Angulo*	Ricardo Altamirano
	2. Adalberto Santillán	Agustín López
Veracruz	1. Manuel Jasso	Melitón T. Pólito
	2. *Rafael Murillo Vidal*	*Silverio R. Alvarado*
	3. José Fernández Gómez	Nieves Martínez
	4. Gorgonio Quesnel Acosta	Fulgencio Arellano
	5. *Juan Cerdán*	Fernando Campos
	6. *Silvestre Aguilar*	Fernando de la Garza
	7. Genaro Lapa	Arnulfo Sánchez
	8. *Cándido Aguilar*	Vicente Romero
	9. Rodolfo Tiburcio Márquez	José A. Lemus
	10. Carlos I. Serrano	José Luis Tejeda
	11. *Benito Coquet*	Delfino Beltrán
	12. Manuel Martínez Ch.	Pablo S. Piña
Yucatán	1. Mauricio Escobedo Granados	Esteban Durán Rosado
	2. *Efraín Brito Rosado*	Alfonso Baquerio Cantón
	3. Laureano Cardós Ruz	Pedro Pérez Chávez
	4. Alvaro Vivas Marfil	Adalberto Aguilar
Zacatecas	1. Rafael López W.	José Fernández Cortés
	2. Pánfilo Natera Jr.	Manuel Zamudio
	3. *Brígido Reynoso*	José García Ortega
	4. Jesús M. García Martínez	Abraham R. Frías

1946-49 (40th Legislature)

State	Deputy	Alternate
Aguascalientes	1. *Aquiles Elorduy*	Salvador Hernández Duque
	2. Roberto J. Rangel	Reynaldo Negrete

Baja California
del Norte (Territory)   1. *Braulio Maldonado*   Ignacio Gutiérrez Argil

Baja California
del Sur (Territory)   1. *Antonio Navarro Encinas*

Campeche   1. Manuel J. López Hernández   Eduardo Negrín B.
                        2. *Carlos Sansores Pérez*   Pedro Balán

Chiapas   1. Antonio Cachón Ponce   Eduardo Sánchez Chanona
                        2. Ramón Franco Esponda   Manuel Castellanos Cancino
                        3. Gil Salgado Palacios   Cicerón Trujillo Fernández
                        4. José Castañón   Conrado de la Cruz Albores
                        5. Gonzalo López López   Salvador Durán Pérez

Chihuahua   1. *Eugenio Prado*   Benito E. Romero
                        2. Undecided   Undecided
                        3. Luis R. Legarreta   Estanislao Apodaca
                        4. *José López Bermúdez*   José Ramón García

Coahuila   1. *Federico Berrueto Ramón*   Antonio Zamora
                        2. León V. Paredes   Juan M. Borjón
                        3. José de Jesús Urquizo   Santiago Aguirre
                        4. Federico Meza Zúñiga   Francisco Moreno

Colima   1. José S. Benítez   *Francisco J. Yáñez*
                        2. *J. Jesús Espinosa Michel*   José Serratos

Distrito Federal   1. Manuel Peña Vera   Juan Reyés Ch.
                        2. *Lauro Ortega Martínez*   Bartolo G. Sanabria
                        3. *Antonio Vega García*   Trinidad Morales Dávila
                        4. *Alfonso Martínez D.*   Luis R. Velasco
                        5.
                        6. Leobardo Wolstano Pineda   Alonso Echánove Acereto
                        7. César M. Cervantes   Leonilo Salgado Figueroa
                        8. *Juan Gutiérrez Lascuraín*   Francisco García Sáinz
                        9. *Fernando Amilpa Rivera*   Fernando Jiménez C.
                       10. *Manuel Orijel Salazar*   Adán Montaño
                       11. Víctor Herrera González   José Villanueva Aguilera
                       12. Trinidad Rosales Rojas   Enrique Yáñez D.

Durango   1. J. Guadalupe Bernal   Armando Gómez Navarrete
                        2. J. Encarnación Chávez   Francisco Landeros
                        3. Ramiro Rodríguez Palafox   Fernando Arenas Esquivel
                        4. Eulogio V. Salazar   Jesús García Escobar

Guanajuato   1. *Ramón V. Santoyo*   Luciano Landeros
                        2. *Luis Díaz Infante*   *Enrique Gómez Guerra*

3. Pascual Aceves Barajas — J. Jesús Rotunno Soto
4. Ernesto Gallardo S. — Daniel Hernández
5. Manuel Alemán Pérez — Alfonso Sánchez Castañeda
6.
7. Manuel Rocha Lasseaul Z. — José Antonio de la Vega

Guerrero
1. Angel Tapia Alarcón — Margarito S. Ortiz
2. *Nabor A. Ojeda* — Francisco Urióstegui
3. Alberto Jaimes Miranda — Adolfo Arce
4. Alejandro Gómez Maganda — Antonio Rosas Abarca
5. Alejandro Sánchez Castro — Jesús Rodríguez Maldonado

Hidalgo
1. David Cabrera Villagrán — Francisco Soto G.
2. Galileo Bustos Valle — *Quintín Rueda Villagrán*
3. Felipe Contreras Ruiz — Camilo Serrano Angeles
4. *Juvencio Nochebuena* — Jesús Pérez
5. *Fernando Cruz Chávez* — Vicente Trejo

Jalisco
1. Rodolfo González González — José Montés de Oca
2. Roberto Soto Máynez — Angel Dávalos Rodríguez
3. J. Ramón Hidalgo Jaramillos — Avelino Castellón Lara
4. Ramón Castellanos Camacho — Ignacio Nava
5. Francisco Torres Rojas — Aureliano Navarro R.
6. Arturo Guzmán Mayagoitia — Ramón González
7. José María Ibarra G. — Amado Madrigal
8. Jaime Llamas García — Pomposo Preciado
9. *Abraham González Rivera* — Alfredo Trejo Romero

México
1. Esteban Marín Chaparro — Antonio García Lobera
2. *Gustavo Castrejón y Chávez* — Alfonso García Ortega
3. Francisco Sánchez Garnica — Roberto Cornejo Cruz
4. *David Romero Castañeda* — Domingo Rivas Chávez
5. *Fernando Guerrero Esquivel* — Ernesto López Soriano
6. Mucio Cardoso Jr. — Hermilo Arcos Pérez
7. Santiago Velasco — Anselmo Dávila Gámez
8. Fernando Riva Palacio — Antonio Peña Navarrete
9. Salvador Mena Rosales

Michoacán
1. Francisco Núñez Chávez — David Gutiérrez H.
2. *Francisco Mora Plancarte* — Eleuterio Páramo
3.
4. *Enrique Bravo Valencia* — Francisco Vega Ramírez
5. *Víctoriano Anguiano* — Luis Martínez
6. Miguel Ramírez Munguía — Primitivo Gómez
7. Horacio Tenorio — Antonio Güijosa Mercado
8. Luis Ordorica Cerda — Carlos Loreto Martínez

Morelos	1. Porfirio Palacios	Manuel Ocampo
	2. Nicolás Zapata	Leobardo Alanís
Nayarit	1. Antonio Pérez Cisneros	José Stephens
	2. Angel Mesa López	Federico González Gallo
Nuevo León	1. *Antonio L. Rodríguez*	Francisco Morales
	2. *Armando Arteaga y Santoyo*	Rodolfo Jiménez
	3. Santos Cantú Salinas	Ismael Leal Galán
	4. Simón Sepulveda	Enedino Martínez
Oaxaca	1. Efrén Ortiz Bartolo	Agustín Carballo
	2. Francisco Eli Sigüenza	Rafael Díaz Hernández
	3. Martíno Rojas V.	Jacinto Reyes
	4. Nemesio Román Guzmán	Manuel Oseguera Sarmiento
	5. Alfonso Patiño Cruz	Artemio Guzmán Garfias
	6. Manuel Sodi del Valle	Jorge O. Acevedo
	7. Fernando Magro Soto	Wulfrano Estevez
	8. Vicente J. Villanueva	Jenaro Ramos
Puebla	1. *Blas Chumacero Sánchez*	Francisco Márquez
	2. Ricardo Luna Morales	Luis C. Manjarrez
	3. Agustín Pérez Caballero	Nemesio Viveros R.
	4. Ruperto Sánchez Taboada	Raymundo Ramírez
	5. Miguel Barbosa Martínez	Erasto Enríquez
	6. Bernardo Chávez Velázquez	Andrés Hernández Méndez
	7. Fausto M. Ortega	Salvador Vega Bernal
	8. *José Ricardi Tirado*	Benjamín Méndez Luna
	9. Luis Márquez Ricano	Samuel Lechuga Méndez
Querétaro	1. Pablo Muñoz Gutiérrez	*Manuel González Cosío*
	2. Enrique Montés Dorantes	Rómulo Vega M.
Quintana Roo (Territory)	1. Manuel Pérez Avila	Antonio Erales Abdelnur
San Luis Potosí	1. *Florencio Salazar*	Manuel Vázquez Cerda
	2. Ignacio Gómez del Campo	Aurelio Guerrero
	3. Agustín Olivo Monsiváis	Eugenio Quintero
	4. *Jesús Medina Romero*	
	5. Francisco Purata Herrera	Felipe Raga González
	6. Miguel Moreno Ibarra	Erasto Roque
Sinaloa	1. *Alfonso G. Calderón*	Francisco R. Verduzco
	2. Armando Molina Trujillo	Jesús Ledón Ruiz
	3. Miguel Gaxiola y V.	Cuauhtémoc Ríos M.

Sonora	1. *Francisco Martínez Peralta*	Antonio Vázquez Corzo
	2. Jesús María Suárez, Jr.	Jesús María Preciado
	3. Rafael Contreras Monteón	Alejo Gastélum
Tabasco	1. Manuel Antonio Romero	Rafael Barjau Díaz
	2. Manuel Flores Castro Jr.	Candelario Rosada Muñoz
Tamaulipas	1. Antonio Yáñez Salazar	Basilio Ramos
	2. Bernardo Turrubiates	Pablo Villanueva
	3. Antonio Salmón Ortiz	Zenaido Romero
Tlaxcala	1. Moisés Rosalio García	Fidel Camacho Era
	2. José Estrada Romero	Luis Granillo A.
Veracruz	1. Rafael Herrera Angeles	José Osorio Cruz
	2. Josué Benignos Hideroa	Pedro L. Menéndez
	3. Rafael Gómez	José Abraham Rubio
	4. Ernesto Núñez Velarde	Gustavo Lavalle G.
	5. Fernando Campos Montes	Ezequiel Domínguez
	6. Ramón Camarena Medina	Angel Luis Archer
	7. *Daniel Sierra Rivera*	Luis Fernández Olarzábal
	8. Francisco Sarquís Carriedo	Alfonso Colina
	9. Ricardo Rodal Jiménez	Gustavo Huerta
	10. *Rafael Arriola Molina*	Raúl Zamorano Márquez
	11. *Vidal Díaz Muñoz*	Abelardo Maldonado
	12. Bulmaro A. Rueda	Fermín León Tello
Yucatán	1. Humberto Carrillo Gil	Francisco Acosta
	2. Carlos Villamil Castillo	Eustaquio Blanco
	3. Rafael Cebada Teneiro	Javier Magaña Zapata
	4. Gaudencio Peraza E.	Gaspar García Rodríguez
Zacatecas	1. Jesús Aguirre D.	Francisco E. García
	2. Lorenzo Hinojosa	
	Rodríguez	Ramón Meza R.
	3. Joel Pozos León	Alfredo U. Márquez
	4. Alfonso Hernández Torres	Luis de la Fuente

1949-52 (41st Legislature)

State	Deputy	Alternate
Aguascalientes	1. Jesús Avila Vázquez	Luis García Cortés
	2. Salvador Luévano Romo	José Santos Reyna Martínez
Baja California		
del Norte (Territory)	1. *Ricardo Alzalde Arellano*	Mariano Córdova de la Torre

Baja California
del Sur (Territory)   Vacant

Campeche   1. *Alberto Trueba Urbina*   Fernando Turriza Peña
                  2. Alberto Perera Castillo   Antonio Chablé Caamal

Chiapas   1. *Valentín Rincón Coutiño*   Manuel Orduña
                  2. J. Rodolfo Suárez Coello   Carmen M. Morales
                  3. Emilio Zebadúa Robles   Roberto Castañón de la Vega
                  4. *Miltón Castellanos E.*   Alfonso Macías Zebadúa
                  5. Felipe Pagola Reyes   Román Reyés Velázquez

Chihuahua   1. *Oscar Soto Máynez*   Oscar Ornelas Armendáriz
                  2. José Aguilar Irungaray   Jesús Alvirez Mendoza
                  3. *Teófilo R. Borunda*   Guillermo Salas Nájera
                  4. Esteban Uranga   Armando Esquivel

Coahuila   1. Evelio H. González Treviño *Florencio Barrera Fuentes*
                  2. Juan Magos Borjón   *Braulio Fernández Aguirre*
                  3. Fernando Vargas Meza   Adán A. Rocha Sánchez
                  4. Ramón Quintana Espinosa   Félix Zavala López

Colima   1. *Roberto A. Solórzano*   Jorge Ochoa Gutiérrez
                  2. *Salvador González Ventura* Antonio Morentín Rocha

Distrito Federal 1. *Rafael S. Pimentel*   Fortunato Reyes H.
                  2. José Tovar Miranda   Francisco Hernández Navarro
                  3. Adolfo Omaña Avelar   J. Jesús Jiménez Torres
                  4. *Francisco Fonseca García*   Mario Guerrero
                  5. J. Leónardo Flores   J. Jesús Bautista
                  6. *Gabriel García Rojas*   Efrén Franco Lugo
                  7.
                  8. *Alfonso Sánchez Madariaga* J. Jesús Palacios
                  9. Uriel Herrera Estúa   Javier Rodríguez Ascorve
                 10. Eduardo Facha Gutiérrez   José Cortina Goribar
                 11. *Aarón Camacho López*   Gregorio Flores Torres
                 12. *Enrique Rangel Meléndez*   Angel Velázquez Gómez

Durango   1. Enrique Campos Luna   Jesús López de la Cruz
                  2. *Carlos Real Encinas*   Felipe Gutiérrez
                  3. Gustavo Durón González   Epifanio Alanís Navar
                  4. *Armando del Castillo F.*   Efraín Acosta García

Guanajuato   1. *Rafael Corralés Ayala*   Rodrigo Vázquez
                  2. *Juan José Torres Landa*   Enrique Mendoza Ortiz
                  3. *Vicente Salgado Páez*   J. Refugio Acosta
                  4. *Francisco García Carranza* Martín Zuloaga Vargas
                  5. *Benjamín Méndez Aguilar*   Fernando Lizardi

	6. J. Jesús Yáñez Maya	Pedro Espinosa Martínez
	7. Melitón Cárdenas V.	Moisés Rangel Huerta
Guerrero	1. Lamberto Alarcón Catalán	Domingo Adame Vega
	2. *Alfonso L. Nava*	Heberto Aburto Palacios
	3. Nicolás Wences García	Rogelio Aranda González
	4. Mario Romero Lopetegui	Rafael Jaime Silva
	5. *Caritino Maldonado Pérez*	Gonzalo A. Carranza
Hidalgo	1. *Jorge Viesca y Palma*	Roberto Quezada
	2. Miguel Angel Cortés	Manuel Castelán
	3. *Víctor M. Aguirre C.*	César Tovar Angeles
	4. Domitilo Austria García	Carlos Manuel Andrade
	5. *Quintín Rueda Villagrán*	Luis de la Concha Paulín
Jalisco	1. *Saturnino Coronado O.*	Salvador Sánchez Sigala
	2. Manuel Ayala Pérez	Genaro Salazar Vega
	3. *Jaime Robles Martín C.*	Angel Oyarzábal
	4. Angel Ruiz Vázquez	Daniel Celso Zacarías
	5. Luis F. Ibarra Plascencia	Isidro Camacho Contreras
	6. *Guillermo Ramírez Valadez*	Felipe Torres Polanco
	7. *Francisco Galindo Ochoa*	Pedro Rodríguez González
	8. Edmundo Sánchez Gutiérrez	Fidencio Cobián Regalado
	9. Jorge Saracho Alvarez	José María Guillén
México	1. Rafael Suárez Ocaña	Antero González Torrescano
	2. Tito Ortega Sánchez	David Martínez García
	3. Roberto Ocampo González	Apolonio Rojas Güereque
	4. Enrique González Mercado	Luis Millán Boissón
	5. *Gregorio Velázquez Sánchez*	J. Guadalupe Angeles B.
	6. Eulalio Núñez Alonso	Salvador Maldonado Rodea
	7. *Abel Huitrón y Aguado*	Luis Berrueta Valencia
	8. *Raúl Serrano Tellechea*	Felipe Avila Sil
	9. Daniel Moreno Castelán	Luis Pozos Quiroz
Michoacán	1. Norberto Vega Villagómez	Leopoldo Carrasco Sandoval
	2. Gonzalo Chapela	Manuel García Padilla
	3. Alfonso Reyes Hernández	José Solorio Zaragoza
	4. *David Franco Rodríguez*	Maximino Padilla Hernández
	5. Martín Rivera Godínez	J. Trinidad Hernández Herrera
	6. *Salvador Pineda*	Roberto Antúnez Vázquez
	7. Matías Rebollo Telles	Andrés Rojas Herrera
	8. *Natalio Vázquez Pallares*	Fernando Urena Méndez

Morelos	1. Julián González Guadarrama	Celestino Alvear Muñoz
	2. *Norberto López Avelar*	Nabor Galicia González
Nayarit	1. Francisco García Montero	Otilio Díaz Quintero
	2. *Emilio M. González*	Nazario Meza Peña
Nuevo León	1. *Pablo Quiroga Treviño*	Pedro Escamilla Flores
	2. Antonio Coello Elizondo	Felipe Florés Mancilla
	3. *Juan José Hinojosa*	Juventino García Villagómez
	4. Alfredo Garza Ríos	Mauro Reyes
Oaxaca	1. Graciano Pineda Carrasco	Julio Gómez López
	2. Ernesto Meixueiro	Alfredo D. Altamirano M.
	3. *Alfonso Pérez Gasca*	Raúl Bolaños Cacho
	4. Carlos R. Balleza Jr.	Daniel Carbajal Rodríguez
	5. Leopoldo Florés Zavala	Benjamín Bolaños Jiménez
	6. Efrén Dávila Sánchez	Cirilo R. Luna
	7. *Norberto Aguirre*	Cirino Pérez Aguirre
	8. Alberto Mayoral Pardo	*Rodolfo Alavez Flores*
Puebla	1. Francisco Márquez Ramos	José A. Centeno Rodríguez
	2. Luis Cruz Manjarrez	Salvador Díaz Valdivia
	3. Nemesio Viveros Rodríguez	Miguel Munive Alvarado
	4. Undecided	Undecided
	5. Alfredo Reguero Gutiérrez	Alvaro Lechuga Cabrera
	6. Salvador Martínez Aguirre	Edmundo Meza Zayas
	7. Luis Núñez Velarde	Alejandro Macip Alcántara
	8. Francisco Landero Alamo	Armando Cortés Bonilla
	9. Eduardo Vargas Díaz	Evencio Cabrera Tello
Querétaro	1. *Manuel González Cosío*	Ricardo Rivas Maldonado
	2. David Rodríguez Jáuregui	Rosalio Herrera Maldonado
Quintana Roo (Territory)	1. Abel Pavía González	Antonio Erales Abdelnur
San Luis Potosí	1. *Antonio Rocha Jr.*	José de la Luz Cerda
	2. Pedro Pablo González	Agapito Beltrán Pérez
	3. Fidel Cortés Carranco	Francisco González Arellano
	4. Nicolás Pérez Cerrillo	J. Guadalupe Martínez Sánchez
	5. Ignacio Moralés Altamirano	Macario Balderas
	6. *J. Jesús N. Noyola*	Manuel Toledano Zugasti
Sinaloa	1. Samuel Cabrera Castro	José I. Liera López
	2. Teódulo Gutiérrez Laura	Abraham Hernández Ochoa
	3. Othón Herrera y Cairo	Manuel Sánchez Guerra

Sonora	1. *Noé Palomares Navarro*	Felipe Arriola Gándara
	2. Ignacio Pesqueira F.	Teodoro O. Paz
	3. Leobardo Limón Márquez	Juan Francisco Olguín
Tabasco	1. Agustín Beltrán Bastar	Salomón Quintero Carrillo
	2. Mario S. Colorado Iris	Andrés Salagurría
Tamaulipas	1. Lauro Villalón de la Garza	Indalecio Esquivel
	2. Agustín Aguirre Garza	Manuel Florés Montalvo
	3. Manuel Jiménez San Pedro	Tomás López Rico
Tlaxcala	1. *Joaquín Cisneros*	Juan F. Pérez Amador
	2. *Francisco Hernández y H.*	J. Caridad Martínez
Veracruz	1. Melitón T. Pólito	Roberto Roblés Nava
	2. *Enrique Rodríguez Cano*	Vitelio Ruiz Gómez
	3. *César Garizurieta E.*	Roberto Núñez y Domínguez
	4. *Rafael Murillo Vidal*	Antonio Islas Morín
	5. Rafael Ortega Cruz	Encarnación Contreras Fuentes
	6. *Silvestre Aguilar*	Jesús Castelán
	7. Vicente Luna Campos	Ernesto Bravo Pozos
	8. *Hermenegildo J. Aldana*	Juan Herrera Soriano
	9. *José Rodríguez Clavería*	Raúl Barcelata Aldama
	10. José Fernández Villegas	Octaviano Corro R.
	11. Francisco Turrent Artigas	Armando Pavón Moscoso
	12. Carlos Real	Gabriel E. Morales
Yucatán	1. Humberto Esquivel Medina	Miguel F. Vidal Rivero
	2. *José Castillo Torre*	Gabriel Ferrer Mendiolea
	3. *Efraín Brito Rosado*	Aurelio Velázquez
	4. Samuel Espadas Centeno	Antonio Fernández Vivas
Zacatecas	1. Blas Bocardo	Arnulfo Torres González
	2. David Valle Camacho	José Rosso Martínez
	3. *José Minero Roque*	*Mauricio Magdaleno*
	4. Roberto T. Amezaga	*José E. Rodríguez Elías*

1952-55 (42nd Legislature)

State	Deputy	Alternate
Aguascalientes	1. Luis T. Díaz	Francisco González Sánchez
	2. Benito Palomino Dena	Fernando Ramos Jáuregui
Baja California	1. *Braulio Maldonado Sánchez*	Francisco Benítez Méndez

	2. *Aurora Jiménez de Palacios*[1]	Onésimo López Alvarez
Baja California del Sur (Territory)	1. Guillermo Corssen Luna	Lamberto Verdugo López
Campeche	1. *Fernando Lanz Duret*	Hermilo Sandoval Campos
	2. Leopoldo Sales Rovira	Emilio Ceh Gamboa
Chiapas	1. Roque Vidal Rojas	Omelino Villator
	2. *Abelardo de la Torre G.*	Adolfo Celerino López Carpio
	3. *Juan Sabines Gutiérrez*	Eduardo Tovar Armendáriz
	4. Nephtali Nucamendi Serrano	Francisco Fernández Aguilar
	5. Salvador Durán Pérez	Pablo Coeto Rosales
Chihuahua	1. Genaro R. Martínez	Miguel R. Esquivel
	2. Mariano Valenzuela C.	Raúl Soto Reyes
	3. Pedro Díaz González	David M. Chávez Guerra
	4. Luis González Herrera	Justino Loya Chávez
	5. Hipólito Villa Rentería	Lorenzo Torres H.
Coahuila	1. *Rafael Carranza H.*	Jesús Santos Cepeda
	2. José Villarreal Corona	Antonio Alonso Hernández
	3. Antonio Marmolejo Barrera	José Ma. Rangel Abúndiz
	4. Feliciano Morales Ramos	Jorge Frías Ruiz
Colima	1. Jorge Huarte Osorio	Emiliano Ramírez Suárez
	2. *Jesús Robles Martínez*	*Roberto Pizano Saucedo*
Distrito Federal	1. Pedro Julio Pedrero Gómez	Ignacio Capistrán Lazcano
	2. *Juan José Osorio Palacios*	Leopoldo López Muñoz
	3. *Felipe Gómez Mont*	Patricio Aguirre Andrade
	4. Alberto Hernández Campos	Jorge Riva Palacio
	5. *José María L. A. Ruiz Z.*	Francisco Hernández Mavarro
	6. Narciso Contreras	Manuel Barroso Petris
	7. Mariano Ordorica Burgos	Antonio Aguilar Sandoval
	8. *Rómulo Sánchez Mireles*	Margarito Curiel Sosa
	9. Javier de la Riva	Adolfo Guevara Pren.
	10. Antonio Rivas Ramírez	Víctor Manuel Avila Romero
	11. *Eugenio Ibarrola Santoyo*	Ignacio Limón Maurer
	12. Heriberto Garrido Ordóñez	Carlos Couto Alba
	13. Fidel Ruiz Moreno	Alfonso Hermoso Nájera
	14. Juventino Aguilar Moreno	Juan Ramírez
	15. Luis Quintero Gutiérrez	Alfonso Trejo Chávez
	16. Ramón Cabrera C.	Angel Ortega Acosta

[1]First female deputy in Mexican history.

	17. *Alfonso Martínez Domínguez*	Ramón Romero Gómez
	18. *Rodolfo Echeverría Alvarez*	Mario Córdova Curtis
	19. Enrique Marcúe Pardiñas	Juan Negrete López
Durango	1. Máximo Gámiz Fernández	Jesús Cisneros Roldán
	2. *Enrique Dupré Ceniceros*	Jesús María Romo Romo
	3. Ramiro Rodríguez Palafox	Edilberto Aguirre Medina
	4. *Braulio Meraz Nevárez*	Pedro Dávila de la O.
Guanajuato	1. J. Jesús Lomelín M.	Ignacio Vázquez Sánchez
	2. Herculano Hernández D.	Antonio Castro
	3. Cayetano Andrade López	Antonio Ramírez Maldonado
	4. Ezequiel Gómez Hernández	Maximiano Villafaña Ibarra
	5. Ernesto Gallardo Sánchez	Salvador Alvarado Vargas
	6. Vicente Muñoz Castro	Luis Solís Múgica
	7. Oliverio Ortega	Ocatavio Lizardi Gil
	8. Rodrigo Moreno Zermeño	Juan Anselmo Serrano D.
Guerrero	1. Pedro Ayala Fajardo	Heliodoro Salgado Valencia
	2. Jesús Mastache Román	Alberto Salgado Cuevas
	3. Heberto Aburto Palacios	*Carlos Román Celis*
	4. José Gómez Velasco	Mario de la O. Téllez
	5. *Damaso Lanche Guillén*	José Ventura Neri
Hidalgo	1. Librado Gutiérrez	Eduardo Vergara
	2. *José Luis Suárez Molina*	Gorgonio de la Concha M.
	3. *José María de los Reyes*	Leónardo Ramírez
	4. *Juvencio Nochebuena*	Juan Ramírez Reyes
	5. Antonio Ponce Lagos	Pedro Caravantes
Jalisco	1. *Rodolfo González Guevara*	Miguel de Alva Arroya
	2. Ramón Garcilita Partida	Martín Coronado Ramón
	3. J. Jesús Ibarra Navarro	Flavio Gutiérrez Casillas
	4. *Ramón García Ruiz*	Elías Gómez Rodríguez
	5. *Abraham González Rivera*	José Gutiérrez Zermeño
	6. J. Jesús Cordero Mendoza	Jesús Navarro González
	7. *Filiberto G. Rubalcaba S.*	Salvador Hernández Mata
	8. Fidencio Vázquez Cerda	Manuel Zamora Negrete
	9. Alfredo Medina Guerra	Francisco Torres Flores
	10. J. Jesús Landeros Amézola	Sergio Corona Blake
	11. Angel F. Martínez G.	Salvador Chávez Magaña
México	1. *Roberto Barrios Castro*	Jesús Alarcón Moreno
	2. *Manuel Martínez Orta*	Francisco Moguel Martínez
	3. *Fernando Guerrero Esquivel*	Adolfo Ramírez Fragoso

	4. Hilario Carrillo Gasca	Jesús Sánchez Lara
	5. *Francisco Pérez Ríos*	Jesús García Lovera
	6. Carlos Garduño González	Eduardo Betancourt Aguilar
Michoacán	1. Fernando Ochoa Ponce de L.	Cayetano Vivanco Reyes
	2. Aquiles de la Peña Ortega	Francisco Núñez Chávez
	3. *Agustín Arriaga Rivera*	Cresencio Cruz Morales
	4. *Daniel P. Mora Ramos*	J. Jesús Magaña Ortiz
	5. Miguel Pinedo Gil	Angel Ayala Alfaro
	6. *Manuel Hinojosa Ortiz*	Alberto Pérez Villanueva
	7. Raúl de la Puente Díaz	Abelardo Sierra Sánchez
	8. Francisco Chávez González	Roberto López Maya
	9. Juan Figueroa Torres	Jacinto Hernández González
Morelos	1. Lorenzo R. Jiménez	Manuel Díaz Leal
	2. Porfirio Palacios	Vicente Lahera
Nayarit	1. José Angulo Araico	Juventino Espinosa Jr.
	2. Bernardo M. de León	Ricardo Gómez García
Nuevo León	1. Caleb Sierra Ramos	Donato González Castillo
	2. José Carrera Franco	Gil Páez Cardona
	3. Eugenio Morales Núñez	Ernesto Serna Villarreal
	4. Jesús Garza Cantú	Isauro S. Santos
	5. *Arturo Luna Lugo*	J. Refugio Solís
Oaxaca	1. *Heliodoro Charis Castro*	Mariano Escobar Barrientos
	2. Eustorgio Cruz Aguilar	Hermenegildo Luis Pérez
	3. *Manuel Aguilar y Salazar*	Víctor Díaz Hernández
	4. *Jacobo Aragón Aguillón*	Angel Galindo N.
	5. Gilberto Alamirano H.	Emilio Morales Angulo
	6. Cirilo R. Luna	Agustín Solano
	7. *Miguel García Cruz*	Manuel Martell Gómez
	8. Manuel Sodi del Valle	José A. Salinas Narváez
	9. Crisanto Aguilar Pérez	Antonio J. Pérez Córdoba
Puebla	1. *Blas Chumacero Sánchez*	Jesús Ramos Rodríguez
	2. Angel Pacheco Huerta	Jesús H. Ramírez
	3. *Antonio Montes García*	Esaú Torres Pastrana
	4. Luis H. Jiménez	Virginio Ayaquica Nava
	5. Leopoldo Rivera González	Miguel Angel Godínez
	6. Mario Andrade Balseca Lara	Benito Guzmán Cid
	7. Arnulfo Valdés Rodríguez	Ernesto Rodríguez Orea
	8. Carlos Díaz Pumarino	Benjamín Guzmán
	9. *José Ricardi Tirado*	José María Arroyo
	10. Alberto Jiménez V.	Elías Cortés González

Querétaro	1. Eduardo Ruiz Gutiérrez	Ricardo Rivas Maldonado
	2. *Manuel Soberanes Muñoz*	Samuel Palacios Borja
Quintana Roo (Territory)	1. Antonio Erales Abdelnur	Alfonso Godoy Castillo
San Luis Potosí	1. Agustín Olivo Monsiváis	J. Jesús Blanco Vega
	2. *Pablo Aldrett Cuéllar*	Héctor Mendoza de la Rosa
	3. Alfonso R. García	Adalberto Torres Rodríguez
	4. Jorge Ferretis	Jacinto Maldonado Villaverde
	5. Alfonso Viramontes G.	Primitivo Contreras Ugalde
Sinaloa	1. Miguel León López	Tomás Romanillo Rodrigo
	2. Félix López Montoya	Porfirio López Mejía
	3. Amado Ibarra Corral	Andrea Mariscal Vda. de V.
	4. *Bernardo Norzagaray Angulo*	Alberto Tripp Flores
Sonora	1. Jesús Lizárraga Gastélum	Jesús Siqueiros Moreno
	2. Jesús María Suárez Arvizu	Benito de la Ree
	3. Rafael Contreras Monteón	Manuel V. Quintana
Tabasco	1. Ernesto Brown Peralta	José María Valenzuela O.
	2. Federico Jiménez Paoli	Aristides Pratts Salazar
Tamaulipas	1. *Juan Manuel Terán Mata*	Francisco Morales Núñez
	2. *Norberto Treviño Zapata*	Aureliano Caballero G.
	3. Juan Báez Guerra	José Jesús Betancourt
	4. Antonio H. Abrego	Eligio Contreras Maldonado
Tlaxcala	1. Ezequiel Selley Hernández	Agustín García Quintos
	2. *Emilio Sánchez Piedras*	Cenobio Pérez Romero
Veracruz	1. José Pólito Morales	
	2. Leónardo Silva Espinosa	Lázaro Vargas Segura
	3. *Pedro Vivanco García*	Alberto Bache Herrera
	4. Manuel Zorrilla Rivera	Agustín G. Alvarado
	5. Manuel González Montes	David de la Medina
	6. Lorenzo Azúa Torres	Miguel Domínguez
	7. Agustín Ramírez Romero	Manuel Abascal Sherwell
	8. Manuel Meza Hernández	Aurelio Moreno Serna
	9. *Roberto Gómez Maqueo*	Donaciano Caballero
	10. Juan Chiunti Rico	Angel Estrada Loyo
	11. José Ch. Ramírez	Rafael Barreiro Gutiérrez
	12. Felipe L. Mortera Prieto	Francisco Rocha Ruiseco
Yucatán	1. *Ramón Osorio y Carvajal*	Rubén Frías Bobadilla
	2. Antonio Bustillos Carrillo	Jorge Martínez Ríos
	3. Fernando Vargas Ocampo	Mauricio Escobedo Granados

Zacatecas	1. Alfredo Lozano Salazar	Carlos Zorrilla Enciso
	2. Cornelio Sánchez Hernández	J. Jesús Vela Ruiz
	3. *José Rodríguez Elías*	Fidel B. Serrano
	4. Alfredo Muñoz Cervantes	Francisco Olvera Peralta

1955-58 (43rd Legislature)

State	Deputy	Alternate
Aguascalientes	1. Edmundo L. Bernal Alonso	María del Carmen Martín
	2. *Alberto Alcalá de Lira*	*Alfredo de Lara Isaacs*
Baja California	1. Emilio Hernández Armenta	Roberto Cannet González
	2. Guilebaldo Silva Cota	Abelardo Rodríguez Ortega
Baja California del Sur (Territory)	Vacant	
Campeche	1. Tomás Aznar Alvarez	Felipe Rubio Ortiz
	2. *Carlos Sansores Pérez*	Porfirio Reyna Salazar
Chiapas	1. Guadalupe Fernández de L.	Fernán Pavia Farrera
	2. Jesús Argueta López	Francisco S. Becerra Pérez
	3. Octavio Esponda Rovelo	Esteban Jiménez Miranda
	4. *Marcelina Galindo Arce*[2]	Martiniano Jacob M.
	5. Gamaliel Becerra Ochoa	Roberto Mandujano Herrera
Chihuahua	1. Leónardo Revilla Romero	Andrés Quezada Pallares
	2. Manuel Villa Atayde	Feliciano Morales García
	3. *Jesús Sanz Cerrada López*	Raúl García Baca
	4.	
	5. *Guillermo Quevedo Moreno*	Adolfo Baca García
Coahuila	1. Carlos Valdés Villarreal	Tomás Algaba Gómez
	2. Amador Robles Santibáñez	Salvador Hernández Rodríguez
	3. Jesús Rodríguez Silva	Eduardo Dávila Garza
	4. Antonio Hernández Méndez	Juan F. Villarreal
Colima	1. *Antonio Salazar Salazar*	J. Jesús Plascencia Ortiz
	2. *Roberto Pizano Saucedo*	Crispín Casián Zepeda
Distrito Federal	1. César Velázquez Sánchez	Arturo Esponda Gallegos
	2. Roberto Herrera León	Jacinto González Mejía
	3. *Patricio Aguirre Andrade*	Guillermo Martínez Estape

[2] First female deputy from the State of Chiapas.

4. Salvador Carrillo E.   *Joaquín del Olmo Martínez*
5. *Alfonso Sánchez Madariaga*   Francisco Robles Rodríguez
6. *Baltázar Dromundo Chorné*   Javier Salgado Estrada
7. Ricardo Velázquez Vázquez   Guillermina García Cruz M.
8. José Gutiérrez Díaz   Miguel Conde Rodríguez
9. *Manuel Sierra Macedo*   Julián Aguilar Fernández
10. José Rodríguez Granada   Francisco Iturbe Madero
11. *Francisco Aguirre Alegría*   Feliciano Montero Abasolo
12. Juan Gómez Salas   Evaristo Orozco López
13.
14. Ramón Castilleja Zárate   Salvador Padilla Flores
15. Jorge Ayala Ramírez   Aristeo Ponce Huerta
16. *Luis M. Farías*   Tomás González Arias
17. *Alfonso Ituarte Servín*   Ubaldo Vargas Martínez
18. Julio Ramírez Colozzi   Eulalio Cabañas González
19. Marcelino Murrieta   Emiliano Aguilar Garcés
      Carreto

Durango
1. *Carlos Real Encinas*   Macedonio Rodda Córdoba
2. Manuel García Santibáñez   Francisco Galindo Chávez
3. Juan Pescador Polanco   Ismael Mora
4. Pablo Picharra Esparza   Ismael Mora Hernández

Guanajuato
1. *Rafael Corrales Ayala E.*   Bernardino Aguilar Montano
2. Enrique Mendoza Ortiz   José Hidalgo Quiroz
3. Gonzalo Maldonado C.   Francisco Granados González
4. Manuel Padilla Villa   Aurelio García Sierra
5. Alfonso Fernández Monreal   Florencio Orozco Quiroz
6. *José López Bermúdez*   Manuel Rosillo Morales
7. Jesús Madrigal Yáñez   Miguel Roncal Gener
8. *Agustín Arroyo Damián*   Juan Flores Echeverría

Guerrero
1. *José Inocente Lugo Lagunas*   Augusto Lozano Hernández
2. *Jorge Soberón Acevedo*   Faustino Rivera Díaz
3. *Carlos Román Celis*   Alvaro Negrete Pérez
4. Gustavo Rueda Medina   Florencio Encarnación Urzúa
5. Aarón Peláez Salazar   Rodolfo Rodríguez Ramos

Hidalgo
1. *Julián Rodríguez Adame*   Andrés Manning Valenzuela
2. *Manuel Sánchez Vite*   Angela Barrientos Montiel
3. *Carlos Ramírez Guerrero*   Ignacio Mora Piña
4. Agustín Mariel Anaya   Florentino Gómez Estrella
5. Miguel Gómez Mendoza   Gabriel Parrodi Casaux

Jalisco
1. *Ignacio González Rubio*
2. Aurelio Altamirano G.   José Montes de Oca Avalos
3. Marcos Montero Ruiz   Luis Escobar Reyes
4. Diego Huizar Martínez   J. Jesús Toledo Villegas
5. Agustín Pineda Flores   Isidro Alférez Espinosa

	6. *Francisco Rodríguez Gómez*	Flavio Ramírez Alvarez
	7. *Carlos Ramírez Ladewig*	José Bracamontes Ortega
	8. *Flavio Romero de Velasco*	Pedro Parra Centeño
	9. David Pérez Rulfo	*Luis Javier Luna B.*
	10. *María Guadalupe Urzúa F.*[3]	Alfredo Trejo Romero
	11. *Francisco Galindo Ochoa*	José Ramos Gómez
México	1. José Guadalupe Cisneros	Hermenegildo Castro Padilla
	2. Luis Berroeta Valencia	Benito Monroy Ortega
	3. Leopoldo Trejo Aguilar	Abel González Marino
	4. *Mario Colín Sánchez*	Alfonso Valencia Medrano
	5. *Gregorio Velázquez Sánchez*	Juan Gómez Mondragón
	6. *Albertina Ezeta Remedios*[4]	Margarita Colín Mondragón
	7. Rubén Osuna Pérez	Arcadio Escalante Cortés
	8. *Leónardo Rodríguez Alcaine*	Santiago Montes Cerros
Michoacán	1. Enrique Aguilar González	María Dolores Pacheco G.
	2. Agustín Carreón Florián	María Dolores Tregoni de R.
	3. Antonio Arriaga Ochoa	Víctoriano Cázares Sánchez
	4. *Conrado Magaña Cerda*	José María Cano Ramos
	5. Alfonso Sánchez Flores	Luis Patiño Carrillo
	6. Roberto González Zamudio	Cornelio Méndez Gómez
	7. *Salvador Pineda Pineda*	Adolfo Arias Ochoa
	8. José Campuzano Ramírez	Emilio Padilla García
	9. José Garibay Romero	David Pérez Zepeda
Morelos	1. *Federico Sánchez Navarrete*	Cristóbal Rojas Romero
	2. *Benigno Abúndez Chávez*	Antonio A. Pliego Noyola
Nayarit	1. Felipe Ibarra Partida	José María Zamorano Aguirre
	2. Manuel Villegas Arellano	Joaquín Hernández Curiel
Nuevo León	1. Angel Lozano Elizondo	Luis Díaz de León Arrieta
	2. Leopoldo Banda Romero	Jesús Malacara García
	3. Rafael González Montemayor	Heliodoro Lozano González
	4. *Margarita García Flores*[5]	Roberto M. González G.
	5. J. Ascensión Charles Luna	Dustano Muñiz Leija
Oaxaca	1. Adolfo Gurrión Gurrión	Bulmaro Antonio Rueda
	2. Graciano Federico H.	Zeferino González Diego

[3] First female deputy from the State of Jalisco.
[4] First female deputy from the State of México.
[5] First female deputy from the State of Nuevo León.

	3. *Raúl Bolaños Cacho G.*	*Fernando Gómez Sandoval*
	4. Marcos Carrillo Cárdenas	Rufino López González
	5. *Melquiades Ramírez S.*	Federico Ramírez Juárez
	6. Manuel Cantú Méndez	*Antonio López y López*
	7. Fidel López Sánchez	Manuel Hernández Hernández
	8. Angel G. Arreola Martínez	Leopoldo Jiménez Córdova
	9. *Ramón Ruiz Vasconcelos*	Guillermo Meixueiro Salgado
Puebla	1. Salvador Lobato Jiménez	Rodolfo Arriaga Martínez
	2. *Manuel Rivera Anaya*	Carlos Rosas Mendoza
	3. *Alfredo Toxqui Fernández*	Heriberto Genis Solís
	4. *Antonio J. Hernández J.*	Salvador Serrano Ramírez
	5. Eduardo Rodríguez Méndez	Irene Ramírez Benavides
	6. *Amador Hernández González*	Alberto Víctoria Arenas
	7. *Fernando Cueto Fernández*	Alfonso Valderrama González
	8. Jesús López Avila	José Cid Sánchez
	9. Javier Ruperto Bonilla C.	Francisco Albarrán Cortés
	10. José Ignacio Morales Cruz	Bernardo González Muñoz
Querétaro	1. Román Esquivel Pimentel	Domingo Olvera Gámez
	2. Rosalio Herrera Maldonado	Palemón Ledesma Ledesma
Quintana Roo (Territory)	1. Gastón Pérez Rosado	Tiburcio May Uh
San Luis Potosí	1. *Jesús Medina Romero*	Miguel Angel Alvarez S.
	2. Félix Dauajare Torres	Santiago Lara Jara
	3. Rodolfo Rico Díaz	Perfecto Domínguez Hernández
	4. José de la Luz Blanco G.	Narciso García Tovar
	5. Jacinto Maldonado V.	Domingo Luis Rocha Rangel
Sinaloa	1. Eliseo Galaviz Bernal	Ramón López Gutiérrez
	2. Manuel Luna Quintero	Luis Gutiérrez Figueroa
	3. Joaquín Duarte López	Alejandra Retamoza Reynaga
	4. *Leopoldo Sánchez Celis*	Mateo Camacho Ontiveros
Sonora	1. Luis Mendoza López	Santos Sánchez Ochoa
	2. *Emiliano Corella Molina*	Francisca Córdoba Macalpín
	3. Saturnino Saldivar Alcalá	Eulalio Vázquez Cota
Tabasco	1. Joaquín Bates Caparroso	Roberto Núñez Martínez
	2. *Agapito Domínguez*	José del Carmen Palma
Tamaulipas	1. José Cruz Contreras Gamboa	Cipriano Montemayor González
	2. *Emilio Martínez Manautou*	Bernardo Reyes Flores

| | 3. Jesús Betancourt Vergara | Florentino López Mireles |
| | 4. Ignacio Pacheco León | Rafael Salinas Medina |

| Tlaxcala | 1. Raúl Juárez Carro | Ricardo Altamirano Flores |
| | 2. *Samuel Ortega Hernández* | Antonio de la Lanza M. |

Veracruz	1. *Raymundo Flores Fuentes*	Raúl Lince Medellín
	2. Antonio Pulido Cobos	Alvaro Lorenzo Fernández
	3. Telésforo Reyes Chargoy	Luis Salas García
	4. *Rosendo Topete Ibáñez*	Prisciliano Nava Vay
	5. Raúl Navarro Chanes	Mario de la Garza Castro
	6. Telésforo Contreras Solano	José de Jesús Solís Tapia
	7. Antonio García Molina	Carlos Hernández Fabela
	8. *Hesiquio Aguilar Marañón*	José Zúñiga Acevedo
	9. Juan Malpica Mimendi	Juan Méndez Martínez
	10. *Hermenegildo J. Aldana*	Auxilio M. Tejeda
	11. Rubén B. Domínguez	Agustín Ortega Santos
	12. Francisco Rocha Ruiseco	Armando Velázquez Vázquez

Yucatán	1. Carlos R. Castillo C.	Alfredo Canto López
	2. Aurelio Carrillo Puerto	Alberto Peniche Barrera
	3. José Manuel López Lliteras	Gustavo Flota Rosas

Zacatecas	1. Roberto del Real Carranza	Alfonso José Cardona Peña
	2. Gonzalo Bretado Sánchez	Rafael Yáñez Sosa
	3. Fidel B. Serrano	Francisco Rodríguez Haro
	4. *Fernando Pámanes Escobedo*	Abundio Monsiváis García

1958-61 (44th Legislature)

State	Deputy	Alternate
Aguascalientes	1. Heriberto Béjar Jáuregui	Manuel Jiménez Hernández
	2. *Enrique Olivares Santana*	Rafael Reyes Rangel
Baja California del Norte (Territory)	1. *Ricardo Alzalde Arellano*	Rafael Gómez García
	2. Germán Brambila Gómez	José Carmen Moreno Ramírez
Baja California del Sur (Territory)	1. Alejandro D. Martínez R.	Bartolo Geraldo Camacho
Campeche	1. *José Ortiz Avila*	Eduardo Negrín Baeza
	2. Carlos Cano Cruz	María Reyes Ortiz
Chiapas	1. *Juan Sabines Gutiérrez*	*Máximo Contreras Camacho*
	2. Antonio Zoreda Cebada	Jorge Octavio Cepeda Ramos
	3. Francisco Argüello C.	Francisco Quiñones León

	4. Esteban Corzo Blanco	Augusto Castellanos Hernández
	5. Juan Trinidad López	Jorge Chamlati Trinidad
Chihuahua	1. *Miguel A. Olea Enríquez*	J. Bonifacio Fernández F.
	2. José R. Muñoz Espinosa	Raúl Soto Reyes
	3. Marcos Flores Monsiváis	J. Ascención Tarelo García
	4. *Arnaldo Gutiérrez H.*	José Peña Flores
	5. *Alfredo Chávez V. Jr.*	Jesús Sagarñaga Alarcón
Coahuila	1. *Florencio Barrera Fuentes*	Raúl Malacara Flores
	2. Manuel Calderón Salas	Julio Vega Arreola
	3. Pablo Orozco Escobar	Octavio Villa Coss
	4. Daniel Hernández Medrano	Jaime Borjón Valdés
Colima	1. Othón Bustos Solórzano	Héctor Dueñas Aguilar
	2. Tomás Bejarano Figueroa	*Jorge Lang Islas*
Distrito Federal	1. Antonio Aguilar Sandoval	Juan Antonio Sámano Oláez
	2. *Joaquín de Olmo Martínez*	Juan Federico Villalpando
	3. *Felipe Gómez Mont*	José Bayón Arciniega
	4. Ramón Villarreal Vázquez	Luis Díaz Vázquez
	5. *José María Leoncio A. Ruiz*	Víctor Manuel Avila Romero
	6. *Marta Andrade del Rosal*	*José Humberto Zebadua*
	7. Manuel Moreno Cárdenas	José Alvarez Garduño
	8. *Emilio Gandarilla Avilés*	Rosa Gómez de Dávila
	9. *Arturo López Portillo*	Manuel Zenteno Cuevas
	10. Roberto Gavaldón Leyva	Alfonso Acevedo Belbouis
	11. J. Jesús López González	Rafael Montaño Montes de Oca
	12. Adán Hernández Rojas	Alberto Martínez Carrero
	13. Gastón Novelo Von Glumer	Luisa Martínez de Castelazo
	14. Rafael Buitrón Maldonado	Salvador Lecona Santos
	15. *Juan José Osorio Palacios*	Manuel Núñez Villegas
	16. Rubén Marín y Kall	Filemón Tapia Hernández
	17. Gonzalo Peña Manterola	Mariano Chávez López
	18. *Antonio Castro Leal*	Justo Olmedo Martínez
	19. Emiliano Aguilar Garcés	*Oscar Ramírez Mijares*
Durango	1. José Guillermo Salas A.	Guadalupe Camacho
	2. Ricardo Thompson Rivas	Francisco Torres García
	3. *Enrique W. Sánchez García*	Fernando Barraza Aguilar
	4. Ezequiel Nevárez Ramírez	Ramón Ortiz Serrato
Guanajuato	1. Manuel Tinajero Orosio	Pablo Arenas Sánchez
	2. *Enrique Gómez Guerra*	Pedro Lona Quezada
	3. Antonio Lomelí Garduño	Daniel Bravo Hernández
	4. *Aurelio García Sierra*	J. Jesús Aguirre Reynoso

	5. *Fernando Díaz Durán*	Juan Pérez Vela Rosa
	6. *Vicente Salgado Páez*	Rosa González de Carmona
	7. Javier Guerrero Rico	Salvador Montes Redondo
	8. Luis Ferro Medina	Juan Pons Pons
Guerrero	1. *Moisés Ochoa Campos*	Andrés Alarcón Rojas
	2. Macrina Rabadán Santana[6]	Elodia Salgado Figueroa
	3. Enrique Salgado Sámano	Antonio Sánchez Molina
	4. Mario Castillo Carmona	Guillermo Leyva Ventura
	5. Herón Varela Alvarado	Efraín Guillén de la Barrera
Hidalgo	1. Andrés Manning Valenzuela	Adalberto Cravioto Meneses
	2. *Manuel Yáñez Ruiz*	Antonio Hernández García
	3. *Federico Ocampo Noble P.*	Heberto Malo Paulín
	4. Francisco Rivera Caretta	Norberto Hernández Arenas
	5. Martiniano Martín Alvarez	Guillermo Barcena B.
Jalisco	1. Luis Ramírez Meza	Primitivo Tolentino Mancilla
	2. *María Guadalupe Martínez*	Juan Ramírez García
	3. *Porfirio Cortés Silva*	Felipe López Prado
	4. *Carlos Guzmán y Guzmán*	Rodrigo Ortega Anzures
	5. *José Pérez Moreno*	Salvador Quezada Ramírez
	6. Tito Padilla Lozano	Jesús Navarro González
	7. Vacancy	Vacancy
	8. José Luis Martínez R.	David Alvarez Miramontes
	9. *José María Martínez R.*	José Mendoza Cortés
	10. *Sebastián García Barragán*	Alejandro Soltero Vidrio
	11. José de Jesús Castro R.	Raúl Rojas Ruiz
México	1. Enrique Tapia Aranda	Raúl Mancera Alfaro
	2. *Manuel Martínez Orta*	Eduardo Soberanes Romero
	3. Sidronio Choperena Ocariz	Pedro B. Noguez Becerril
	4. *Fernando Guerrero Esquivel*	Filiberto Cortés Ponce
	5. *Francisco Pérez Ríos*	Angel Celorio Lujambjo
	6. *Carlos Hank González*	Francisco García Rubio
	7. Benito Contreras García	Silvano Ortega Sánchez
	8. Graciana Becerril Bernal	Guillermo García Alcántara
Michoacán	1. Jesús Ortega Calderón	Ignacio Tapia Fernández
	2. Adolfo Gandara Barón	Manuel García Mendoza
	3. *Daniel T. Rentería Acosta*	Carlos Grajeda Rodríguez
	4. José García Castillo	José Luis Villegas Magaña
	5. *Baltázar Gudiño Canela*	Salvador Valdez Ayala
	6. José R. Castañeda Z.	Antonio Iñiguez Canela

[6] First female deputy from the State of Guerrero.

	7. Silvestre García Suazo	María Pérez Ríos
	8. Horacio Tenorio Carmena	Indalecio Peña Reyes
	9. Rubén Vargas Garibay	Salvador Méndez Solórzano

Morelos
1. Manuel Castillo Solter — Jesús Galindo Pichardo
2. *Ana María Zapata Portillo* — Francisco Sánchez Benítez

Nayarit
1. Salvador Arámbul Ibarra — Genoveva Suárez
2. Pedro Luna Mercado — José Ramírez Rodríguez

Nuevo León
1. *Leopoldo González Sáenz* — Alfonso Garza y Garza
2. Rosalio Delgado Elizondo — José Ovalle Morales
3. Aarón S. Villarreal V. — Jocobo Domínguez Lacea
4. Antonio Garza Peña — *Carolina Morales Farías*
5. Ramón Berzosa Cortés — Pedro Hernández Tovar

Oaxaca
1. *Andrés Henestrosa Morales* — Francisco Luis Castillo
2. Jenaro Maldonado Matías — Eufrosino Sánchez Moreno
3. *Federico Ortiz Armengol* — José Morales Paz
4. Antonio Acevedo Gutiérrez — Agustín Domínguez Herrera
5. Bulmaro A. Rueda — Samuel López Martínez
6. Enrique Sada Baigts — Carlos Merino Camarillo
7. *Manuel Hernández Hernández* — Antonio Velasco Ortiz
8. Adán Cuéllar Layseca — *Jesús Guzmán Rubio*
9. *Jacobo Aragón Aguillón* — Carlos Innés Acevedo

Puebla
1. *Blas Chumacero Sánchez* — Juan Galindo Quintero
2. Porfirio Rodríguez Flores — Norberto Espinosa Ceron
3. *Miguel García Sela* — Sebastián Cordero Jiménez
4. Salvador Serrano Ramírez — Miguel Munive Alvarado
5. *Antonio López y López* — Jesús Benavides Bazán
6. Joaquín Paredes Román — Perfecto de los Santos V.
7. Carlos Trujillo Pérez — Alfonso Valderrama González
8. *José Ricardi Tirado* — Carlos Viveros Castillo
9. Amando Cortés Bonilla — José de la Llave Arroyo
10. *Esperanza Téllez Oropeza*[7] — Alfonso Sosa Domínguez

Querétaro
1. Luis Escobar Santeliees — Rafael Ayala Echavarri
2. Palemón Ledesma Ledesma — Vacancy

Quintana Roo (Territory)
1. Félix Morel Peyefitte — Julio Mac H.

San Luis Potosí
1. *Francisco Martínez* — Pedro Pablo González
2. *Manuel Moreno Torres* — José Rodríguez Alvarez N.

---

[7] First female deputy from the State of Puebla.

	3. Juan Díaz Macías	Galdino Martínez Rodríguez
	4. Ignacio Aguiñaga Castañeda	Roberto Iglesias García
	5. Joaquín Guzmán Martínez	Simitrio Sagahón Domínguez
Sinaloa	1. *Samuel Castro Cabrera*	Nicolás Mariscal Mariscal
	2. Arcadio Camacho Luque	Pablo Rubio Espinosa
	3. José Concepción Carrillo	Alejandro Gaxiola Ramos
	4. *Aurora Arrayales*[8]	Modesto Antimo Rivas
Sonora	1. José A. Montaño Torres	*Alicia Arellano Tapia*
	2. Benito Bernal Domínguez	Ciro Arce Fonseca
	3. Aurelio García Valdés	Matías Méndez Limón
Tabasco	1. *María Luisa Rosado de H.*	José Luis Gallegos Avendano
	2. Hilario García Canul	Cándido Rivera Cortázar
Tamaulipas	1. Tiburcio Garza Zamora	Ruperto Villarreal
		Montemayor
	2. Pompeyo Gómez Lerma	Silvestre Mata Carrizales
	3. Aureliano Caballero G.	Leopoldo de la Fuente Núñez
	4. Carlos Parga González	Pedro Castañeda Zúñiga
Tlaxcala	1. *Emilio Sánchez Piedras*	Nicolás López Galindo
	2. *Crisanto Cuéllar Abaroa*	María Guadalupe Juárez C.
Veracruz	1. Manuel Herrera Angeles	María Lucía Molina de Lince
	2. Germán Granda García	Florencio T. Cobos Ovando
	3. Raúl Lara Mendoza	Manuel Salas Castelán
	4. Antonio Marroquín Carlón	Diego Arrazola Becerra
	5. *Salvador Olmos Hernández*	Luis E. Murillo
	6. Humberto Celis Ochoa	Aristeo Rivas Andrade
	7. Samuel Vargas Reyes	Angel Contreras Cerrilla
	8. Rafael Espinosa Flores	Rubén Calatayud Balaguero
	9. *Arturo Llorente González*	Ismael Lagunes Lastra
	10. Octaviano Coro Ramos	José Antonio Tejeda Panama
	11. *Celso Vázquez Ramírez*	Manuel Malpica Mortera
	12. Felipe L. Mortera Prieto	Delfino Santos Fernández
Yucatán	1. *Eduardo José Molina C.*	Humberto Lizcano Ríos
	2. Gustavo Flota Rosas	Mario Ceballos Novelo
	3. José Vallejo Novelo	Bruno Mezquita Cisneros
Zacatecas	1. Jaime Haro Rodríguez	Ana María Segura Dorantes
	2. Antonio Ledesma González	José Acevedo Solís
	3. Hugo Romero Macías	Valentín Rivero Azearraga
	4. Leandro Castillo Venegas	Antonio Betancourt
		Hernández

[8] First female deputy from the State of Sinaloa.

1961-1964 (45th Legislature)

State	Deputy	Alternate
Aguascalientes	1. Manuel Trujillo Miranda	Joaquín Díaz de León Gil
	2. Carmen María Araiza López	Camilo López Gómez
Baja California	1. Gustavo Arévalo Gardoqui	*Alfonso Garzón Santibáñez*
	2. *Gustavo Aubanel Vallejo*	Alfonso Siordia Dávales
	3. Luis González Ocampo	Quintín Hurtado Olivares
Baja California del Sur (Territory)	1. *Antonio Navarro Encinas*	*Alberto Alvarado Arámburo*
Campeche	1. *Manuel Pavón Bahaine*	Armida del Carmen Reyes R.
	2. *Carlos Sansores Pérez*	Genaro Espadas Barrera
Chiapas	1. *Rafael P. Gamboa Cano*	Oscar Rueda Escobar
	2. Amadeo Narcía Ruiz	Abraham Aguilar Paniagua
	3. Romeo Rincón Serrano	Pedro J. Cancino Gordillo
	4. *Máximo Contreras Camacho*	Enrique Cruz Vals
	5. Gustavo Lescieur López	José Oscar Castellanos J.
	6. *Arturo Moguel Esponda*	María Celorio Rovelo
Chihuahua	1. *Manuel Bernardo Aguirre*	Francisco Romo Ortiz
	2. *José I. Aguilar Irungaray*	Manuel Primo Corral
	3. *Ricardo Carrillo Durán*	Roberto Delgado Urias
	4. Esteban Guzmán Vázquez	Armando B. Chávez M.
	5. Fernando Figueroa Tarango	Enrique Miramontes Maldonado
	6. *Carlos Chavira Becerra*	Manuel Pazos Cano
Coahuila	1. Salvador González Lobo	Nemesio López Ramos
	2. *Braulio Fernández Aguirre*	Rodolfo Siller Rodríguez
	3. Félix de la Rosa Sánchez	Pedro Tijerina Ortegón
	4. Esteban Guzmán Vázquez	Oscar Brown Gutiérrez
Colima	1. Carlos Gariby Sánchez	Juan Hernández Pizano
	2. *Alfredo Ruiseco Avellaneda*	Herminio Malaga Rojas
Distrito Federal	1. Jorge Abarca Calderón	Haidé Espinosa Segura
	2. Francisco García Silva	Darío García González
	3. *Javier Blanco Sánchez*	José Luis Aristi Garay
	4. Neftalí Mena Mena	Alfonso Ortiz Martínez
	5. Agustín Vivanco Miranda	Alberto Morales Jiménez
	6. *Rodolfo Echeverría Alvarez*	Tomás Covarrubias Blancas

7. Guillermo Solórzano G.	Miguel Cubián Pérez
8. Javier González Gómez	Gustavo Reyes Cruz
9. Mercedés Fernández Austri	Luis del Moral Flores
10. *Manuel Alvarez González*	Miguel Rendón Blanco
11. *Carlos Zapata Vela*	María Guadalupe Santoyo
12. *Rodolfo García Pérez*	Juan Aguilar Castro
13. Carlos L. Díaz	Humberto Antúnez Barrera
14. *Romulo Sánchez Mireles*	*Norberto Mora Plancarte*
15. *Francisco Aguirre Alegría*	Ramiro Ruiz Madero
16. Salvador López Avitia	Juan José Castillo Mota
17. Gonzalo Castellot Madrazo	José M. de la Peña Hernández
18. *Joaquín Gamboa Pascoe*	Pedro Guerrero Manríquez
19. Salvador Carrillo E.	Alejandro Arzate Sánchez
20. *Renaldo Guzmán Orozco*	Juan Gómez Salas
21. *Oscar Ramírez Mijares*	Santiago Mar Zúñiga
22. *María Guadalupe Rivera M.*	Jorge Aurelio Rocha C.
23. Antonio Vargas MacDonald	Fernando González Piñón
24. Humberto Santiago López	Margarita Rodríguez Meza

Durango	1. *Oscar Valdés Flores*	María Zataraín del Valle
	2. Gonzalo Salas Rodríguez	Amador Pérez Ramírez
	3. *Agustín Ruiz Soto*	Antonio Martínez Rivas
	4. *José Antonio Ramírez M.*	Jesús Samaniego Nevárez

Guanajuato	1. Virginia Soto Rodríguez	Luis Macías Luna
	2. Enrique Aranda Guedea	J. Guadalupe Carreño Rangel
	3. Rodrigo Moreno Zermeño	Romeo Rincón Serrano
	4. Manuel B. Márquez Escobedo	José E. Bravo Aranjo
	5. *Eliseo Rodríguez Ramírez*	Margarito Juárez Rizo
	6. *Juan Pérez Vela*	Cirilo Bravo Bravo
	7. *Manuel Moreno Moreno*	Isauro Zúñiga Flores
	8. *José López Bermúdez*	Carlos Lira Leyva
	9. *Enrique Rangel Meléndez*	Roberto Arteaga Saavedra

Guerrero	1. Salvador Castro V.	*Vicente Fuentés Díaz*
	2. María López Díaz	Ismael Pineda Flores
	3. Leopoldo Ortega Lozano	Humberto Nájera Gómez Cana
	4. Gabriel Lagos Beltrán	Martín Sánchez Rodríguez
	5. Simón Guevara Ramírez	Abel García Garnelo
	6. Luis Vázquez Campos	Rubén Maurilio Vázquez

Hidalgo	1. Jorge Quiroz Sánchez	Samuel Zenteño Ramírez
	2. *José Luis Suárez Molina*	Antonio Ramírez Pérez
	3. Daniel Campuzano Barajas	Rodrigo Ordóñez Mejía

	4. Contrán Noble Pérez R.	Joaquín Calva Olguín
	5. *Jorge Rojo Lugo*	Anatolio Romero Trejo

Jalisco	1. *José Luis Lamadrid Sauza*	Roberto S. Weeks López
	2. *Miguel de Alba Arroyo*	Amalia Mendoza Trujillo
	3. *Flavio Romero de Velasco*	José G. Armas González
	4. José Félix Zermeño Venegas	J. Concepción Guzmán Guzmán
	5. Guillermo Mayoral Espinosa	Salvador Guerrero Gómez
	6. Francisco Rodríguez Gómez	Carlos Anaya Gómez
	7. *J. Jesús González Cortázar*	Alfredo Gutiérrez Rivera
	8. *Filiberto Ruvalcaba S.*	Salvador Avalos Alvarado
	9. *Salvador Corona Bandín*	Clemente Nuño Guerrero
	10. José Guadalupe Mata López	Guillermo Preciado Gómez
	11. Florentino Robles Flores	Salvador Ruesga García
	12. Agustín Coronado Gutiérrez	Gustavo de la Torre Arias

México	1. Abraham Saavedra Albíter	Fernando Macedo Estrada
	2. David López Sención	Wenceslao Rangel
	3. Heliodoro Díaz López	Clara del Moral Ramírez
	4. Benito Sánchez Henkel	Víctor Javier Guadarrama
	5. Eduardo Arias Huville	Faustino Sánchez Pinto
	6. Daniel Benítez Villalpando	Leonel Domínguez Rivero
	7. Federico Nieto García	Armando Becerril Estrada
	8. Silverio Pérez Gutiérrez	Marciano Trueba Ruiz
	9. Froylán Barrios Villalobos	Jesús Arana Morales

Michoacán	1. Daniel Franco López	Antonio Chávez Sámano
	2. Agustín Carreón Florián	Guillermo Chávez Cordoba
	3. Rafael Morelos Valdés	Antonio Lara López
	4. Luis Aguilar Garibay	Nabor Servín Orozco
	5. *Enrique Bravo Valencia*	Jorge Hernández Miranda
	6. Juan Velasco Vargas	Enrique Bautista Adame
	7. Eligio Aguilar Ortiz	Salvador Rosales Angelés
	8. Melchor Díaz Rubio	Lázaro Correa Osornio
	9. Elías Pérez Avalos	David Pérez Zepeda

Morelos	1. *Diódoro Rivera Uribe*	Susana Peralta Colín
	2. Alfonso Muñoz	Joel Hernández Ramos

Nayarit	1. *Manuel Stephens García*	Genaro Navarro Rivera
	2. Leopoldo T. García Esteves	Flavio Gómez Hernández

Nuevo León	1. Noé G. Elizondo Martínez	Francisco Morales Morales
	2. José Carmen Rodríguez P.	Ramiro González Moya

	3. *Virgilio Cárdenas García*	Filiberto Villarreal Ayala
	4. *Armando Arteaga Santoyo*	Leónides Cueva Cantú
	5. Dustano Muñiz Leija	José Antonio Garza Garza
Oaxaca	1. Pío Ortega Grapaín	José Julio Hernández C.
	2. Manuel Orozco Mendoza	Antonio Figueroa Jiménez
	3. *Norberto Aguirre*	Ernesto Miranda Barriguete
	4. Jenaro Vázquez Cruz	*Rodrigo Bravo Ahuja*
	5. Melitón Vargas Martínez	Emilio Alvarez Moguel
	6. Heriberto Camacho Ambrosio	Miguel Morán Ramírez
	7. Enrique Pacheco Alvarez	Gilberto Cruz Pantoja
	8. Manuel Sodi del Valle	Manuel Iglesias Meza
	9. Everardo Gustavo Varela S.	Fernando Castillo Castillo
Puebla	1. Francisco Márquez Ramos	Andrés Rojas Romero
	2. *Juan Figueroa Velasco*	Andrés Funes Méndez
	3. Ciriaco Tista Montiel	Enrique Zamora Palafox
	4. *Antonio J. Hernández*	*Eleazar Camarillo Ochoa*
	5. *Gonzalo Bautista O'Farrill*	Irene Godínez Orta
	6. *Amador Hernández González*	Gabriel Domínguez y D.
	7. Ezequiel Meza Zayas	Guillermo Martínez Anaya
	8. Luis Viñals Carsi	Rodolfo Garcés Mauardón
	9. Benjamín Méndez Luna	Luis Rivera León
	10. Jorge Vergara Jiménez	Israel Gómez Díaz
Querétaro	1. *Eduardo Luque Loyola*	Alfonso Alexander H.
	2. Teófilo Gómez Centeño	Arturo Domínguez Paulín
Quintana Roo (Territory)	1. Delio Paz Angeles	Pedro Salazar González
San Luis Potosí	1. Alfonso Guerrero Briones	Nicolás Vázquez Cruz
	2. Aurelio Guerrero Carreón	Rafael Yrizar Ruiz
	3. Baltasar Ruiz Jiménez	Avelino de León Guevara
	4. Fidel Nieto Flores	Gregorio Martínez Narváez
	5. Sixto García Pacheco	Hugo Arnoldo Gómez Rivas
Sinaloa	1. *Ernesto Alvarez Nolasco*	José María Robles Quintero
	2. *Manuel Sarmiento Sarmiento*	Manuel de Jesús García C.
	3. María del Refugio Báez S.	Alejandra Retamoza Reynaga
	4. Joaquín Noris Saldaña	J. Bartolo González Zúñiga
Sonora	1. Jesús Ortiz Ruiz	María Cruz Serrano C.
	2. *Alicia Arellano Tapia*	Jorge Flores Valdés
	3. Gilberto Borrego Zamudio	Raymundo López Lerma
	4. Gerardo Campoy Campoy	Román Argüelles Obregón

Tabasco	1. *Manuel R. Mora Martínez*	José del Carmen Méndez A.
	2. Voltaire Merino Pintado	Roberto Rosado Sastre
Tamaulipas	1. Advento Guerra Barrera	Oscar Herrera Flores
	2. *Antonio García Rojas*	Marciano Aguilar Mendoza
	3. Juan José Domene Flor	Pantaleón de los Santos C.
	4. Manuel Guerra Hinojosa	Isidro Gómez Reyes
	5. Ricardo Camero Cardiel	J. Guadalupe Silva Ochoa
Tlaxcala	1. *Anselmo Cervantes H.*	Filemón Sánchez Hernández
	2. Bernardo Ceballos Gómez	Salvador Espejel Espejel
Veracruz	1. Rafael Santibáñez F.	Gilberto Valenzuela Vera
	2. *Jesús Reyes Heroles*	Lázaro Vargas Segura
	3. José Viñas Zunegui	Raymundo Villegas Sánchez
	4. Carlos V. Torres Torija	Amado Ceja Galindo
	5. Eduardo S. Arellano	Gonzalo Anaya Jiménez
	6. Martín Díaz Montero	Daniel Parra García
	7. Irene Bourell Galván[9]	Abraham D. Contreras García
	8. Miguel Angel Rodríguez R.	Nicolás García Hernández
	9. Rubén Hernández y H.	Gilberto Tenorio Cortés
	10. Joaquín Calatayud González	Pascual González Rojas
	11. Vicente Ortiz Lagunes	Emilio Aguirre Campos
	12. *Gonzalo Aguirre Beltrán*	Humberto M. Fentanes Cunco
	13. Amadeo González Caballero	Arturo M. Vargas Sánchez
	14. José Vasconcelos Morales	Guillermo Rodríguez Morfín
Yucatán	1. *Luis Torres Mesías*	Juan de Dios Ancona Fierros
	2. Manuel Pasos Peniche	Joaquín Reyes Andrade
	3. *Carlos Loret de Mola*	Melchor Sozaya Raz
Zacatecas	1. Alfonso Méndez Barraza	Benito López Mauricio
	2. J. Jesús Saucedo Meléndez	Juan Manuel Carrillo Berumen
	3. *Guadalupe Cervantes C.*[10]	Aurelio López de la Torre
	4. Antonio Betancourt H.	José Leal Langoria

1964-67 (46th Legislature)

State	Deputy	Alternate
Aguascalientes	1. Antonio Femat Esparza	Jorge Díaz de León
	2. *Augusto Gómez Villanueva*	Enrique Torres Calderón

[9] First female deputy from the State of Veracruz.
[10] First female deputy from PAN.

Baja California	1. José Luis Noriega Magaña	Dionisio Mirales Corral
	2. *Salvador Rosas Magallón*	Fausto Cedillo López
	3. Luis Mario Santana Cobián	Rogelio Zepeda Villaseñor

| Baja California del Sur (Territory) | 1. *Alberto Arámburo Alvarado* | Crisóforo Salido Almado |

| Campeche | 1. *Carlos Pérez Cámara* | Rodolfo Dorantés Salazar |
| | 2. *José D. García Aguilar* | Felipe Ehuán Yeh |

Chiapas	1. Jesús Cancino Casahonda	*Martha Luz Rincón C.*
	2. Abraham Aguilar Paniagua	Héctor Salinas Gómez
	3. *Jorge de la Vega Domínguez*	Jorge Guillén Ortiz
	4. Gilberto Balboa Escobar	Ignacio Lara Peñagos
	5. José León Cruz	Oscar Chapa Castañón
	Alberto Orduña Culebro	Ovidio de la Rosa López
	6. Alfonso González Blanco	Mario Balboa Robles

Chihuahua	1. *Saúl González Herrera*	Amador Campoya Almazán
	2. *Florentina Villalobos C.*	Román Pineda Casas
	3. Raúl H. Lezama Gil	Salvador de la Torre Grajales
	4. Pedro N. García Martínez	Armando González Soto
	5. *Arnaldo Gutiérrez H.*	Carlos Enríquez Chávez
	6. José Martínez Alvídrez	Esperanza Domínguez de M.

Coahuila	1. Tomás Algaba Gómez	José Dimas Galindo V.
	2. Alfonso Reyes Aguilera	Francisco Pérez Gutiérrez
	3. Francisco Padilla R.	Gonzalo Navarro Chávez
	4. *Mauro Berrueto Ramón*	Amado Flores Peña
	5. *Argentina Blanco Fuentes*	Juan José Elguezabal P.

| Colima | 1. Mario Llerenas Ochoa | Juan Eusebio Mejía |
| | 2. Rafael Paredes | Antonio Suárez Orijel |

Distrito Federal	1. *Arturo López Portillo*	Magdaleno Gutiérrez Herrera
	Francisco Quiroga F.	Agustín Velázquez Uribe
	2. *Felipe Gómez Mont*	*Hiram Escudero Alvarez*
	Arnulfo Vázquez Trujillo	Macario Gutiérrez Navarro
	3. *Enrique Ramírez y Ramírez*	Alfonso Gutiérrez Gutiérrez
	4. Salvador Rodríguez Leija	Consuelo Grajales Caracas
	5. *Everardo Gámiz Fernández*	Raúl Macías Guevara
	6. Luis Ignacio Santibáñez P.	Eduardo Field Romero
	7. Francisco Ortiz Mendoza	Leonides Guadarrama Jiménez
	Jesús Hernández Díaz	Héctor Guillermo González G.

8. *Juan Landerreche Obregón*   René Ostos Mora
    Manuel Orijel Salazar   Francisco Prieto Herrera
9. Federico Estrada Valera   *José Blas Briseño Rodríguez*
    Emilio Gandarilla Aviles   Blas Nieto Valdez
10. *Juan Moisés Calleja*   José C. Salinas Vázquez
11. Jorge Avila Blancas   Héctor Federico Ling A.
    Luis Priego Ortiz   Tito Pequeño Pedroza
12. *Marta Andrade del*   Miguel Barrera Fernández
    Rosal[11]
13. *Hilda Anderson Nevárez*   Leopoldo Arias Ochoa
14. Manuel Contreras Carrillo   Manuel Morales Vargas
15. Rodolfo Rivera Rueda   *Pedro Luis Bartilotti P.*
16. *Jorge Garabito Martínez*   Carlos Oropeza Gómez
    Ramón Zentella Asencio   Guillermo Prieto Sánchez
17. *Alejandro Carrillo Marcor*   Gabriel Sánchez Gómez
    Abel Carlos Vicencio Tovar   Nicolás González Rodríguez
18. Enrique Torres Calderón   José Oropeza Cerón
19. Rafael Estrada Villa   Rubén Alvarez del Castillo
    Marciano González V.   Guillermo Márquez Panteón
    Salvador Padilla Flores   José Gamboa Paredes
20. Roberto Guajardo Tamez   Nehemías González Chimal
    Antonio Martínez Manatou   Manuel Esquivel Cisneros
21. *Miguel Covián Pérez*   Dimas Martínez Ramos
22. *Gonzalo Martínez*   Miguel Hernández Labastida
    Corbalá
    Jacinto G. Silva Flores   Arturo Tinajero Contreras
23. *Adolfo Christlieb Ibarrola*   Ascención Almaraz Espinosa
    Fernando González Piñón   Tomás Ordaz Padilla
24. Bonifacio Moreno Tenorio   J. Félix González Organo

Durango
1. *Angel Rodríguez Solórzano*   *Joséfina Lugo de Rueda L.*
2. Jesús José Reyes Acevedo   Jesús Ibarra Rayas
3. *Enrique Wenceslao*   Rodolfo Reyes Soto
    Sánchez
4. *Braulio Meraz Nevárez*   J. Inés Rodríguez Díaz

Guanajuato
1. J. Jesús Orta Guerrero   Matilde Rangel López
    Jaime L. Dantón Rodríguez   Antonio Arellano González
2. Luis Manuel Aranda Torres   José Ayala Frausto
3. Domingo Camarena López   Efrén Pérez Guajardo
4. *Juan J. Varela Mayorga*   Vicente López Díaz
5. *Vicente Salgado Páez*   Enrique Fernández Martínez
6. *Luis H. Ducoing Gamba*   J. Jesús Arroyo Celedón
7. *Enrique Gómez Guerra*   José Jiménez Díaz
8. *Ricardo Chaurand Concha*   Manuel Hernández Tamayo
    Agustín Arroyo Damián   Luis Martínez Aguado
9. Antonio Vázquez Pérez   Alfredo Guerrero Tarquín

[11] First female deputy from the Federal District.

Guerrero	1. *Vicente Fuentés Díaz*	María Teresa Bernal C
	2. *Rubén Figueroa Figueroa*	Daniel Molina Miranda
	3. *Miguel Osorio Marbán*	Antonio Sánchez Molina
	4. Rafael Camacho Salgado	Darío Estevés Legua
	5. Arquimedés Catalán Guevara	Crisóforo Alvarez Iriarte
	6. Juan Francisco Andraca M.	Faustino García Silverio
Hidalgo	1. Humberto Velasco Aviles	Hilario Ortega Portillo
	2. Domingo Franco Sánchez	Raúl Vargas Ortiz
	3. Herberto J. Malo Paulín	Leornardo Vega Pérez
	4. *Raúl Lozano Ramírez*	Gustavo Castillo Díaz
	5. Jaime López Peimbert	Jesús Hernández Trejo
Jalisco	1. *Raúl Padilla Gutiérrez*	José Vicente Palencia M.
	2. *Guillermo Ruiz Vázquez*	José Guadalupe Rodríguez P.
	Heliodoro Hernández Loza	J. Ventura Flores Navarro
	3. *Rubén Moheno Velasco*	Abel Galván Chávez
	4. Francisco Silva Romero	Rafael Madrigal Vázquez
	5. *Carlos Ramírez Ladewig*	Víctor Manuel Márquez H.
	6. Raúl Alvarez Gutiérrez	Guillermo Muñoz Hernández
	7. Gregorio Contreras Miranda	José Martín Barba
	8. Constancio Hernández A.	Juan Valdivia Gómez
	9. Vicente Madrigal Guzmán	José de Jesús Rubio Neri
	10. José María Martínez R.	*Salvador Aguilar Vázquez*
	11. *Francisco Villafaña C.*	*María Guadalupe Urzua Flores*
	12. *José de Jesús Limón Muñoz*	Javier Michel Vega
México	1. Juan de Dios Osuna Pérez	Ernesto Gómez Gómez
	2. *Francisco Pérez Ríos*	*Leónardo Rodríguez Alcaine*
	3. Enrique González Vargas	Gildardo Herrera Gómez Tagle
	4. Guillermo Molina Reyes	Enrique Castañeda Ornelas
	5. *Mario Colín Sánchez*	Maximino Pérez Cámara
	6. *Jesús Moreno Jiménez*	Ernestina González Cano
	7. José Chiquillo Juárez	Rodolfo Ruiz Pérez
	8. Raúl Legaspi Donis	Enrique Chávez Montes de Oca
	9. Enedino Ramón Macedo	Bernardo Aragón Sánchez
Michoacán	1. *Celia Gallardo González*	José Alvarado Vega
	2. Enrique López Narango	José Rodríguez Espinosa
	3. *Roberto Chávez Silva*	J. Jesús Sánchez Ortiz
	Ernesto Reyes Rodríguez	Alfredo Pimentel Ramos
	4. Domingo García López	José Arroyo Domínguez
	5. *Gabino Vázquez Oseguera*	Héctor Pantoja Vázquez
	Miguel Estrada Iturbide	Alfonso Arias Sánchez

	6. Enrique Bautista Adame	Guillermo Navarro Quiroz
	7. *José Servando Chávez H.*	Wilfrido Ruiz Balderas
	8. Raúl Reyes Hernández	Pedro Rubio Sataray
	9. *J. Jesús García Santacruz*	Lorenzo Escobar Béjar
Morelos	1. *Gonzalo Pastraña Castro*	Esther Galván Figueroa
	2. Antonio Pliego Noyola	Adalberto Sámano Salgado
Nayarit	1. Eugenio Cárdenas Andrade	Luis Romero Castillo
	2. *Marina Núñez Guzmán*[12]	Saturnino González Ismerio
Nuevo León	1. *Leopoldo González Saenz*	Fulberto Chavarría Treviño
	2. Arnulfo Treviño Garza	Hilario Salazar Tamez
	Pedro Reyes Velázquez	Félix Lazcano Elizondo
	3. Guillermo Ochoa Rodríguez	José González Alvarado
	4. *Alfonso Martínez Domínguez*	Antonio Garza Ayala
	5. Ricardo Covarrubias	Anastasio Santana Martínez
Oaxaca	1. *Jorge Cruickshank García*	Crisóforo Chinas Mendoza
	Andrés Henestrosa Morales	José María Luna Martínez
	2. *Eliseo Jiménez Ruiz*	Wilfrido Sánchez Contreras
	3. Juan I. Bustamante V.	María Toledo de Ramírez
	4. Aurelio Fernández Enríquez	Pedro Castillo Estrada
	5. *Justina Vasconcelos de B.*	Diódoro Carrasco Palacios
	6. *Manuel Zárate Aquino*	José Manuel Alvarez Martín
	7. *Rodolfo Alavéz Flores*	Ignacio Montes Martínez
	8. Gustavo Martínez Trejo	Heriberto Pérez Aguirre
	9. Jesús Torres Márquez	Fernando Moncada Díaz
Puebla	1. Melquiades Trejo Hernández	José Gómez Salinas
	2. *Manuel Rivera Anaya*	Dionisio del Razo Espinosa
	3. *Pablo Solís Carrillo*	Filemón Pérez Cázares
	4. Rigoberto González Flores	Salvador Serrano Ramírez
	5. Enrique Marín Retif	Ruperto Zafra Hernández
	6. Rodolfo Rossano Fraga	Felipe Balderrama García
	7. Eloy Linares Zambrano	Federico Hernández Cortés
	8. Alfonso Castillo Borzani	Gloria Rodríguez de Campos
	Vicente Lombardo Toledano	Luis Martínez Aguado
	9. Jorge Rubén Herta Pérez	José Guevara Minor
	10. *Guillermo Morales B.*	Ramón Herrera Cravioto
Querétaro	1. *Arturo Guerrero Ortiz*	Antonio Pesa Peña
	2. Arturo Domínguez Paulín	J. Concepción Vega Pérez

[12] First female deputy from the State of Nayarit.

Quintana Roo (Territory)	1. Luz M. Zaletade Elsner[13]	José Antonio Ascencio N.
San Luis Potosí	1. *Juan Barragán Rodríguez*	José Martínez Castro
	Diana Torres Ariceaga	Alvaro Salguero Franco
	2. José Rodríguez Alvarez	Pedro Delgado Calzada
	3. Miguel Gascón Hernández	J. Guadalupe Martínez Sánchez
	4. *Luis Tudón Hurtado*	Mauro Gutiérrez Compeán
	5. Librado Bicavar García	Julián Pozos Caro
Sinaloa	1. *Samuel Castro Cabrera*	Carlos Beltrán Flores
	2. Humberto Morales Corrales	Pedro Mondaca Robles
	3. Joaquín Salgado Medrano	Rigoberto Arriaga Ruiz
	4. Francisco Alarcón Fregoso	Jorge Luis Osuna y Osuna
Sonora	1. Manuel Duarte Jiménez	Luis Mendoza López
	2. *Faustino Félix Serna*	Alfonso Reyna Celaya
	3. *Manuel Bobadilla Romero*	Mario Moraga Bórquez
	Jacinto López Moreno	Florentino Ríos Barragán
	4. Rodolfo Velázquez Grijalva	Ofelia Arredondo Corral
Tabasco	1. *Manuel Gurría Ordóñez*	Manuel Ramón Ramón
	2. Rosendo Taracena Alpuín	Luis Antonio Zurita Zurita
Tamaulipas	1. Luis G. Olloqui Guerra	Julia García Soto
	Mariano González Gutiérrez	Virgilio Barrera Fuentes
	2. Angel J. Lagarda Palomares	Víctor Vargas Cuéllar
	3. Ladislao Cárdenas Martínez	Gregorio Soto Guerrero
	4. Lauro Rendón Valdez	Darío Manuel Hernández C.
	5. *Salvador Barragán Camacho*	José Bruno del Río Cruz
Tlaxcala	1. *Tulio Hernández Gómez*	Faustino Zempoaltecatl T.
	2. Luis Granillo Astorga	Cenobio Pérez Romero
Veracruz	1. Raúl Lince Medellín	Andrés Tovar González
	2. Francisco Rodríguez Cano	José Fernández Gómez
	3. *Pedro Vivanco García*	Eleazar Pulido Valdez
	4. César del Angel Fuentes	Julio César Gutiérrez C.
	5. *Fluvio Vista Altamirano*	Bricio Rincón Hernández
	6. *Mario Hernández Posadas*	Juan H. Sánchez Hernández
	7. *Serafín Iglesias Hernández*	Abraham Contreras García
	8. Agustín González Alvarado	Cándido G. Rojas Cruz
	9. *Miguel Castro Elías*	Agustín de Jesús Valerio
	Ramón Rocha Garfias	Hermenegildo Lobato Cerón
	10. Pastro Murguía González	Víctor Manuel Ocampo M.

[13] First female deputy from the State of Quintana Roo.

	11. *Mario Vargas Saldaña*	Manuel Hernández Delgado
	12. José Antonio Cobos	Cipriano Villasaña Jiménez
	Panamá	
	13. Ramiro Leal Domínguez	Lucio Martínez Salas
	14. Pablo Pavón Rosado	Brigida Rodríguez Fuster
Yucatán	1. *Eduardo Trueba Barrera*	Miguel F. Vidal Rivero
	Fidelia Sánchez de M.	Bibiano Segura León
	2. Fabio Espinosa Granados	Magda Bauza Romero
	3. *Francisco Luna Kan*	Pablo Caamal
Zacatecas	1. *Aurora Navia Millán*	J. Cruz Guerrero Encinas
	2. Adolfo Rodríguez Ortiz	Arturo Ortiz Arechar
	3. José Muro Saldívar	Angel Estrada González
	4. *Pedro Ruiz González*	Antonio Cortés Hurtado

1967-70 (47th Legislature)

State	Deputy	Alternate
Aguascalientes	1. *Francisco Guel Jiménez*	Juan Romo Hernández
	2. *J. Refugio Esparza Reyes*	J. Guadalupe Delgado de L.
Baja California	1. Francisco Muñoz Franco	Guillermo Cannet González
	2. *Gustavo Aubanel Vallejo*	Joséfina Vázquez Calderón
	3. *Celestino Salcedo Monteón*	Nicolás Bojorquez Ayala
Baja California del Sur (Territory)	1. *Angel César Mendoza A.*	Fortunato García Yuen
Campeche	1. *Ramón Alcalá Ferrera*	Sixto Sosa Almeida
	2. *Manuel Pavón Bahaine*	Pascual Hernández
Chiapas	1. *Martha Luz Rincón C.*	Romeo Noriega Chamlati
	2. Roberto Coello Lescieur	Augusto Castellanos Hernández
	3. *Edgar Robledo Santiago*	Armando Chacón Antonio
	4. Daniel Robles Sasso	Adrián Contreras Romero
	5.	
	6. *José Patrocinio González*	José Oscar Moscoso Moscoso
Chihuahua	1. Mariano Valenzuela C.	Ofelia Báez Duarte
	2. Pablo Picharra Esparza	Juan Antonio Sánchez Monge
	3. Guillermo Quijas Cruz	Rafael Veloz Alatorre
	4. Armando B. Chávez Montañez	Alfredo Caraveo Martínez
	5. Everardo Escárcega López	Rubén Montaño Camarena
	6. Armando Bejarano Pedroza	Alfredo Rohana Estrada

Coahuila	1. *José de las Fuentes R.*	Carlos Gutiérrez Salazar
	2. Heriberto Ramos González	Daniel Martínez Peral
	3. Juan Manuel Berlanga	Eladio Perales Herrera
	4. Feliciano Morales Ramos	María del Pueblito Villarreal
Colima	1. Ricardo Guzmán Nava	Agustín González Villalobos
	2. Ramiro Santa Ana Ugarte	Inocencio Palomares Sánchez
Distrito Federal	1. *Pedro Luis Bartilotti Perea*	Andrés Díaz Vadia
	2. José del Valle de la C.	Miguel Angel Celis Ponce
	3. Ernesto Quiñones López	Ramiro Rodríguez Gutiérrez
	4. *Octavio A. Hernández G.*	César Velázquez Sánchez
	5. *Gilberto Aceves Alcocer*	Graciela Valles Griego
	6. *Ignacio Castillo Mena*	Tomás Covarrubias Blancas
	7. *Jorge Durán Chávez*	José Luis Sánchez Díaz
	8. *Eleuterio Macedo Valdez*	Hernán Estrada Unda
	9. *Javier Blanco Sánchez*	Aurora Fernández Fernández
	10. *Manuel Alvarez González*	Luis Mayén Ruiz
	11. Pedro Rosas Rodríguez	Leonor Ferrón de Madera
	12. Martín Guaida Lara	J. Jesús Jiménez Torres
	13. *Joaquín Gamboa Pascoe*	Enrique Melgarejo Phario
	14. Alberto Briceño Ruiz	*Carlos Jongitud Barrios*
	15. Enrique Bermúdez Olvera	Eduardo Gutiérrez Evia
	16. Fernando Córdoba Lobo	Arturo Marín Oropeza
	17. *Raúl Noriega Ondovilla*	Alberto Pérez Azpeitia
	18. *Joaquín del Olmo Martínez*	Rodolfo Martínez Moreno
	19. Adolfo Ruiz Sosa	*Roberto González Torres*
	20. Ignacio Guzmán Garduño	Sebastián González Galván
	21. *Oscar Ramírez Mijares*	José Luis Preciado G.
	22. *María Guadalupe Aguirre S.*	Francisco Javier Ogarrio P.
	23. *Hilario Galguera Torres*	Joaquín Ventura Mosso
	24. María Elena Jiménez Lozano	Ernesto Aguilar Cordero
Durango	1. *Agustín Ruiz Soto*	Carlos Leónardo Ruiz Piña
	2. J. Natividad Ibarra Rayas	Francisco Navarro Veloz
	3. Juan Antonio Orozco Fierro	Andrés Calvo Ramírez
	4. *José Antonio Ramírez M.*	J. Bernabé Silvestre F.
Guanajuato	1. Daniel Chowell Cázares	Gabriel Pérez Saavedra
	2. *José Castillo Hernández*	Herón Aíza Torres
	3. Andrés Sojo Anaya	Rafael García Meza
	4. *Fernando Díaz Durán*	Roberto Rodríguez Ramírez
	5. *Ignacio Vázquez Torres*	María de la Luz Bravo G.
	6. Adolfo Meza Arredondo	Gilberto Muñoz Mosqueda
	7. *María Contreras Martínez*	Pedro Mandujano Mendoza

	8. Manuel Orozco Yrigoyen	Ezequiel Nieto González
	9. *Enrique Rangel Meléndez*	Raymundo Patlán Amador

Guerrero

1. Juan Pablo Leyva Cordoba — Altagracia Alarcón Sánchez
2. Humberto Acevedo Astudillo — Rafael Reyes Ramírez
3. Alberto Díaz Rodríguez — Filiberto Vigueras Lázaro
4. *Israel Nogueda Otero* — Alfonso Argudín Alcaraz
5. Eusebio Mendoza Avila — Leandro Alvarado Vázquez

Hidalgo

1. *Adalberto Cravioto Meneses* — Abundio Rodríguez Reséndiz
2. Raúl Vargas Ortiz — Luis Barrios Saldierna
3. Sergio Butrón Casas — Daniel Campuzano Barajas
4. José Gonzalo Badillo — René Espinosa Sagaón
5. *Humberto A. Lugo Gil* — Aurelio Gómez Membrillo

Jalisco

1. Adalberto Padilla Quiroz — David Alvarez Viramontes
2. *Miguel de Alba Arroyo* — Miguel Arroyo García
3. José María García P. — Adalberto Gómez Rodríguez
4. *Felipe López Prado* — Roberto Neri Rodríguez
5. *Leopoldo Hernández Partida* — José Santos Salas Aparicio
6. *Alfonso de Alba Martín* — Elías Muñoz S. Alba
7. *Renaldo Guzmán Orozco* — J. Jesús González Martín
8. *José de Jesús Bueno A.* — Guillermo Jiménez González
9. *Ignacio González Rubio* — Clemente Nuño Guerrero
10. *Luis Javier Luna B.* — Alfredo González Vargas
11. *Sebastián García Barragán* — Esquivel Paz Espinosa
12. *Guillermo Cosío Vidaurri* — Enrique Salgado Vega

México

1. Arturo Flores Mercado — José Santaolaya Consuelo
2. *Gregorio Velázquez Sánchez* — Guillermo Choussal V.
3. Fernando Suárez del Solar — Javier Hinojosa Trigos
4. *Ignacio Pichardo Pagaza* — José Gil Valdez
5. Faustino Sánchez Pinto — David Maldonado Rodea
6. Leonel Domínguez Rivero — Juan Monroy Ortega
7. *Leonardo Rodríguez Alcaine* — Agustín Chávez Magallón
8. *Antonio Bernal Tenorio* — Guillermo Pérez Calva
9. Angel Bonifaz Ezeta — Gonzalo Barquín Díaz

Michoacán

1. *María Guadalupe Calderón* — Marco Antonio Aguilar C.
2. Pedro Rubio Zataray — J. Jesús García Bucio
3. José Encarnación Tellitud — Víctor Cázares Sánchez

	4. José Valdovinos Garza	José Rodríguez López
	5. Carlos Grajeda Rodríguez	Jesús Alcazar Quiroz
	6. Roberto Reyes Pérez O.	Santiago Vargas Reyes
	7. *Norberto Mora Plancarte*	Aureliano Martínez B.
	8.	
	9. Guillermo Morfín García	Mario Cortés García
Morelos	1. Javier Bello Yllanes	José Nares Alvarez
	2. *Elpidio Perdomo García*	Abel Sánchez Aguilar
Nayarit	1. *Roberto Gómez Reyes*	Pedro López Díaz
	2. *Emilio M. González Parra*	Simón Pintado Carrillo
Nuevo León	1. Pedro F. Quintanilla	Mario Jasso Grimaldo
	2. *Luis M. Farías*	Julio Camelo Martínez
	3. *Virgilio Cárdenas García*	Saturnino Torres Sena
	4. Graciano Bortoni Urteaga	Mario Canales Sáenz
	5. Eloy Treviño Rodríguez	Juan Saldaña Muñiz
Oaxaca	1. Macedonio Benítez Fuentes	Fortino Paulo Hernández
	2. Juvencio Molina Valera	Wilfrido Luis Pérez M.
	3. Jorge F. Iturribarría	Ernesto Miranda Barriguete
	4. *Rodrigo Bravo Ahuja*	Saturnino Mendoza García
	5. *Diódoro Carrasco Palacios*	Federico Ramírez Juárez
	6. *Dagoberto Flores B.*	David Morán Maceda
	7. *Manuel Hernández y H.*	Virginia Cisneros Reyna
	8. Manuel Iglesias Meza	León Oloarte Espinosa
	9. Fernando Moncada Díaz	Fernando Castillo Castillo
Puebla	1. *Blas Chumacero Sánchez*	Juan Hernández Cardel
	2. Atilano Pacheco Huerta	Agustín Castillo Flores
	3. Alfonso Meneses González	Elías Rivera Sánchez
	4. *Antonio J. Hernández J.*	Miguel Munive Alvarado
	5. *Cosme Aguilera Alvarez*	José Guadalupe Ramírez V.
	6.	
	7. Esteban Rangel Alvarado	Gonzalo Pacheco Navarro
	8. René Tirado Fuentes	Porfirio Camarena Sánchez
	9. *Humberto Díaz de León*	Gonzalo Cruz Pérez
	10. Horacio Hidalgo Mendoza	Abraham Fosado Gutiérrez
Querétaro	1. José Arana Morán	Alberto Fernández Riveroll
	2. Enrique Redentor Albarrán	Enrique Rabell Trejo
Quintana Roo (Territory)	1. Eliezer Castro Souza	Alejandro Tamay Ancona
San Luis Potosí	1. Jorge Márquez Borjas	Gabriel Echenique Portillo
	2. Francisco Padrón Puyou	Adalberto Lara Núñez

	3. *Florencio Salazar Martínez*	Rodolfo Ortiz Reyes
	4. *Guillermo Fonseca Alvarez*	*Fausto Zapata Loredo*
	5. José de Jesús González L.	J. Refugio Zavala Rodríguez
Sinaloa	1. *Alfonso G. Calderón V.*	Froylán Rodríguez Cota
	2. Mateo Camacho Ontiveros	Jesús María Cervantes Atondo
	3. Miguel Leysón Pérez	José Herrera Mares
	4. *Ernesto Alvarez Nolasco*	Juan Tirado Osuna
Sonora	1. Ignacio Guzmán Gómez	Fernando Peña Benítez
	2. *Guillermo Núñez Keith*	Jesús Reyes Lamas
	3. Francisco Villanueva C.	Francisco Arispuro Calderón
	4. *Carlos Armando Biebrich T.*	Juan Pedro Camou Cubillas
Tabasco	1. *Mario Trujillo García*	Cecilio Antonio Pedrero G.
	2. *Agapito Domínguez Canabal*	Luz Zalaya de García
Tamaulipas	1. Antonio Guerra Díaz	Luis Rocha Acosta
	2. Cristóbal Guevara Delmas	Juan Mendoza López
	3. Jesús Elías Elías	Antonio Caballero González
	4. *Elvia Rangel de la Fuente*	Isaías Rodríguez Oñate
	5. Candelario Pérez Malibrán	Miguel Hernández Lemus
Tlaxcala	1. Nicolás López Galindo	Angel Méndez Cano
	2. Germán Cervón del Razo	Héctor Vázquez Paredes
Veracruz	1. Héctor Cequera Rivera	Julio Contreras Sáins
	2. *Silverio Ricardo Alvarado*	Miguel López Lince
	3. *Heriberto Keohoe Vincent*	Miguel Rivadeneyra Herrera
	4. Julio César Gutiérrez C.	Leocadio Azúa Torres
	5. *Rodolfo Virúes del Castillo*	Simitrio Amador Ballinas
	6. Raúl Olivares Vionet	Reyna Oyarzábal de Caraza
	7. *Acela Servín Murrieta*	Crispino Ruiz Contreras
	8. Helio García Alfaro	Delfino Rosas Nolasco
	9. *Daniel Sierra Rivera*	Gustavo Mayorga Daza
	10. *Hesiquio Aguilar Marañón*	Pascual González Rojas
	11. Román Garzón Arcos	Adolfo Sánchez Guzmán
	12. Mariano Ramos Zarrabal	Julio Castillo Pitalúa
	13. *Celso Vázquez Ramírez*	Jonas Bibiano Landero
	14. Rafael Cárdenas Lomelí	Gabino Reyes Alafita
Yucatán	1. *Rubén Encalada Alonzo*	María Luisa Loza Rivas
	2. *Julio Bobadilla Peña*	Jorge Gasque Gómez
	3. *Víctor Manzanilla Schaffer*	Pablo Medina Acosta

Zacatecas	1. *Calixto Medina Medina*	Enrique Mendoza Figueroa
	2. *Rosa María Ortiz de C.*	Nicolás Márquez Acosta
	3. Antonio Ruelas Cuevas	J. Jesús de León Luna
	4. Juan Martínez Tobias	Gabino Díaz Díaz

1970-73 (48th Legislature)

State	Deputy	Alternate
Aguascalientes	1. Luciano Arenas Ochoa	Luis Gilberto de León Pedroza
	2. Baudelio Lariz Lariz	J. Refugio Jiménez Luévano
Baja California	1. Francisco Zarate Vidal	Carlos Rubio Parra
	2. Marco Antonio Bolaños C.	Héctor Lutteroth Camou
	3. *Alfonso Garzón Santibáñez*	Luis Ayala García
Baja California del Sur (Territory)	1. Rafael Castillo Castro	Antonio Verdugo Verduzco
Campeche	1. *Rafael Rodríguez Barrera*	Jorge Muñoz Icthé
	2. *Abelardo Carrillo Zavala*	Lilia González Vda. de A.
Chiapas	1. José Casahonda Castillo	Ariosto Oliva Ruiz
	2. Angel Pola Berttolini	Hermilo Flores Gómez
	3. *Maximo Contreras Camacho*	Rogerio Román Armendáriz
	4. *Eloy Morales Espinosa*	Hugo Calderón Vidal
	5. Antonio Melgar Aranda	Pantaleón Orella Machique
	6. *Octavio Cal y Mayor Sauz*	Daniel González Damas
Chihuahua	1. Ramiro Salas Granado	Humberto Martínez Delgado
	2. *Diamantina Reyes E.*	Manuel Garfio Chaparro
	3. Mario Jáquez Provencio	Fernando Pacheco Parra
	4. Armando González Soto	Antonio Barrio Mendoza
	5. Abelardo Pérez Campos	Homero Corral Piñón
	6. *J. Refugio Mar de la Rosa*	J. Refugio Rodríguez R.
Coahuila	1. Gustavo Guerra Castaños	José Cruz Salazar
	2. Luis Horacio Salinas A.	Horacio Gutiérrez Crespo
	3. Aureliano Cruz Juárez	Jesús Barraza Rentería
	4. *Salvador Hernández Vela*	Conrado Marines Ortiz
Colima	1. José F. Rivas Guzmán	Jorge Arellano Amezcua
	2. José Ernesto Díaz López	Fidel Nando Vázquez
Distrito Federal	1. León Michel Vega	Antonio Cueto Citalán
	2. Mauricio Martínez Solano	Francisco Pérez Turlay
	3. *José Luis Alonzo Sandoval*	Eleazar T. Cruz R.
	4. *Octavio Sentíes Gómez*	Carlos Hernández Márquez

	5. Raúl Gómez Pedroso Suzán	Marina Masso Soto
	6. Jorge Báeza Rodríguez	Ignacio Colunga Mones
	7. Jaime Fernández Reyes	Jesús Araujo Hernández
	8. *Manuel Orijel Salazar*	Francisco Rivera Muñoz
	9. *Aurora Fernández F.*	Arturo Romo Gutiérrez
	10. *Juan Moisés Calleja G.*	Ofelia Castillas Ontiveros
	11. Juan Rodríguez Salazar	José Luis Lobato Campos
	12. Ignacio Sologuren Martínez	José Servién Bolaños
	13. Leopoldo Cerón Sánchez	Isaac Díaz Ramírez
	14. *Luis Velázquez Jaacks*	Carlos Onofre Hernández R.
	15. Roberto Dueñas Ramos	Alvaro Roldán Olvera
	16. Rafael Argüelles Sánchez	Marie Edith Arróniz de F.
	17. *Cuauhtémoc Santa Ana S.*	Joaquín Ortiz Lombardini
	18. Rodolfo Martínez Moreno	Jesús Anlen López
	19. *Hilda Anderson Nevárez*	Samuel Mora Zamudio
	20. Oscar Hammeken Martínez	Juan Canales Pérez
	21. J. Héctor Ayala Guerrero	Teófilo Aguilar Riojas
	22. *Guillermina Sánchez Meza*	Juan Villarreal López
	23. Ignacio F. Herrerías M.	Ruffo Pérez Pleigo
	24. Tarsicio González G.	Raúl García Olvera
Durango	1. Manuel Aguilera Tavizón	Pedro Avila Nevárez
	2. Manuel Esquivel Gámez	Leobardo Martínez Amador
	3. Francisco Navarro Veloz	Rodolfo Reyes Soto
	4. Jacinto Moreno Villalba	Zacarías Luna Antuna
Guanajuato	1. Vicente Martínez S.	Manuel Barajas Morales
	2. Antonio Hernández Ornelas	Rafael Avila Pérez
	3. José Arturo Lozano Madrazo	Taurino Murillo Navarro
	4. Roberto Sánchez Dávalos	Francisco Robles Acosta
	5. Bonifacio Ibarra Morales	Juan Flores Aguilar
	6. *Juan J. Varela Mayorga*	J. Guadalupe Enríquez M.
	7. J. Jesús Arroyo García	Luis Martínez Aguado
	8. Roberto Suárez Nieto	Constantino Olalde Moreno
	9. *Luis H. Ducoing Gamba*	Manuel Martínez Maldonado
Guerrero	1. *Moisés Ochoa Campos*	Elías Cuahtémoc Tabares J.
	2. Jaime Pineda Salgado	Lorenzo Román Adán
	3. Ramiro González Casales	Albino Macedo Rivera
	4. Rogelio de la O Almazán	Franco Núñez Ramírez
	5. Ramón Uribe Urzúa	Primitivo Solano R.
	6. José María Serna Maciel	José María Robles de la Cruz
Hidalgo	1. Darío Pérez González	María Cristina Alvarez de S.
	2. Antonio Hernández García	Ricardo Avila Yáñez
	3. Humberto Cuevas Villegas	Fernando León Hernández
	4. *Abel Ramírez Acosta*	María Isabel Fayad
	5. *Enrique Soto Reséndiz*	Adolfo Langenschet

Jalisco	1. José Carlos Osorio Aguilar	Enrigue Rosales Shamón
	2. *María Guadalupe Martínez*	Juan Ramírez García
	3. Genaro Cornejo Cornejo	Raúl Bracamontes Gutiérrez
	4. *Porfirio Cortés Silva*	Miguel Nuño Casillas
	5. *Humberto Hiriart Urdanivia*	Alfonso Lozano González
	6. *Rubén Moheno Velasco*	Ernesto Ríos González
	7. José Martín Barba	Rigoberto González Quezada
	8. *Arnulfo Villaseñor S.*	J. Guadalupe Covarrubias Iba
	9. *Oscar de la Torre Padilla*	Oscar Navarro Franco
	10. *José Ma. Martínez R.*	Adolfo Medrano Rebolledo
	11. *María Guadalupe Urzúa F.*	Manuel Robles Morán
	12. Abel Salgado Velasco	Francisco Márquez Hernández
México	1. Alberto Hernández Curiel	Marciana Valdespino S.
	2. *José Delgado Valle*	Ma. de Carmen Colín Pouche
	3. Rafael Riva Palacio	Florentino Rebollo Velázquez
	4. Alfonso Solleiro Landa	Alfredo Ramos Zúñiga
	5. Enrique Díaz Nava	María Martínez Rivera
	6. Guillermo Olguín Ruiz	Habacuc Acosta Ayala
	7. Jesús Martínez Cabrera	Cuahtémoc Sánchez Barrales
	8. *Mario Colín Sánchez*	Alfonso Funes Tiarado
	9. Román Ferrat Sola	Juan Ortiz Montoya
Michoacán	1. Salvador Reséndiz Arreola	Angel Bolaños Guzmán
	2. J. de Jesús Arroyo Alanís	Moisés Martínez Muñoz
	3. *Esvelia Calderón Corona*	Amador Reyes Tinajero
	4. *Daniel Mora Ramos*	Antonio Pérez Zavala
	5. Ignacio Gálvez Rocha	Miguel García Vega
	6. Agapito Hernández H.	J. Jesús Rangel Aguilar
	7. Julio Antonio Gallardo O.	Delia Vélez Romero
	8. Roberto Estrada Salgado	Martha Arana Peñaloza
	9. Ildefonso Estrada Jacobo	Rafael Martínez Infante
Morelos	1. *Marcos Manuel Suárez Ruiz*	Raúl Arana Pineda
	2. *Filomeno López Rea*	Otilio Rivera Almada
Nayarit	1. Salvador Díaz Coria	José Félix Torres Haro
	2. *Celso H. Delgado Ramírez*	Eugenio Plantillas Grajeda
Nuevo León	1. *Santiago Roel García*	Carlos Canseco González
	2. Francisco Cerda Muñoz	Flavio Perales Galván
	3. Pedro Beceira Chávez	Manuel Flores Varela
	4. *Arturo de la Garza G.*	Fortunato Zuazua Zertuche
	5. *Carolina Morales Farías*	Gorgonio García Bernal

Oaxaca	1. *José Estefan Acar*	Gudelia Pineda Luna
	2. *Rodolfo Alavez Flores*	Aurelio Ramírez García
	3. Alberto Canseco Ruiz	Genoveva Medina de Márquez
	4. Mario Prieto Sánchez	Juan Bueno Lázaro
	5. Francisco Rosado Lobo	Magdaleno Villegas Domínguez
	6. Ramón Mendoza Cortés	Mauro Gómez Ruiz
	7. Fernando Castillo Castillo	Reynaldo Daza de Jiménez
	8. Abdón Ortiz Cruz	Ma. Guadalupe Pérez B.
	9. Jesús Rojas Villavicencio	Eloísa Ortiz de Contreras
Puebla	1. Melquiades Trejo Hernández	Adolfo García Camacho
	2. *Juan Figueroa Velasco*	Manuel Pérez Hernández
	3. Francisco Vázquez O.	Antonio Montes García
	4. *Eleazar Camarillo Ochoa*	Agustín Pérez Caballero
	5. Rodolfo Sánchez Cruz	Jesús Salmorán Malpica
	6. *Fernando Cueto Fernández*	Conrado Tapia Cardoso
	7. Carlos Trujillo Pérez	Federico Hernández Cortés
	8. Alberto Guerrero C.	Armando González Sánchez
	9. Sixto Uribe Maltos	Octavio Manzano Díaz
	10. Julio Abrego Estrada	Isidro Herrera Maldonado
Querétaro	1. *Consuelo García Escamilla*	Pedro Jesús Montiel
	2. *Alfredo V. Bonfil Pinto*	Manuel García Mancebo
Quintana Roo (Territory)	1. Hernán Pastrana Pastrana	Delio Paz Angeles
San Luis Potosí	1. Ramiro Robledo Treviño	Ruth Arvides Sánchez
	2. Juan Pablo Cortés Cruz	Eduardo Rocha Pérez
	3. Salvador Díaz Macías	José Víctor García Villar
	4. *Luis Tudón Hurtado*	Raymundo Escobar Nieto
	5. Tomás Medina Ponce	Angel Martínez Manzanares
Sinaloa	1. *Salvador Esquer Apodaca*	Efraín Robles Robles
	2. Marco Antonio Espinosa P.	Emeterio Carlón López
	3. *Renato Vega Alvarado*	Víctor Manuel Gandarilla C.
	4. Alejandro Ríos Espinosa	Angel Villalpando Brizuela
Sonora	1. Jesús Gámez Soto	José Luis Aguilar
	2. Enrique Fox Romero	Jesús Enríquez Burgos
	3. *Manuel R. Bobadilla Romero*	Heraclio Sotelo Leal
	4. Javier R. Bours Almada	Enrique Rubio Canedo
Tabasco	1. Manuel Piñera Morales	Cirilo Rodríguez Torres
	2. Rubén Darío Vidal R.	Justo Priego Alipi

Tamaulipas	1. Donaciano Muñoz Martínez	José Pérez Cardona
	2. Gerardo Ballí González	Gregorio Perales de la Garza
	3. *Agapito González Cavazos*	Francisco de la Fuente
	4. Marciano Aguilar Mendoza	Esperanza Quijano Herrera
	5. Cirilo Rodríguez Guerrero	Martín Aguirre Márquez
Tlaxcala	1. J. Dolores Díaz Flores	Héctor Cano Cano
	2. *Ma. de los Angeles Grant*	Wilulfo Candía Monter
Veracruz	1. Raymundo Flores Bernal	Sofía Maza de De León
	2. *Noé Ortega Martínez*	Antonio San Juan Rodríguez
	3. Salvador Verónica Sánchez	Luis de la Tejera Piña
	4. Mario V. Malpica Bernabé	Luis Salas García
	5. Agustín Alvarado González	Marco Antonio Ramírez Luzuria
	6. Ignacio González Rebolledo	Frida Pabello de Mazzott
	7. José Román Mortera Cuevas	Angel Gómez Calderón
	8. Juan Zurita Lagunes	Pascual Cuacua Mendoza
	9. Santiago Villalvazo M.	Angel Castro Ruiz
	10. Marco Antonio Ros Martínez	Ulpiano Gómez Vargas
	11. Roberto Avila González	Gervasio Triana Arano
	12. Ignacio Altamirano Marín	Onésimo Sentíes Cué
	13. Hilario Gutiérrez Rosas	Ernestina Gutiérrez Reyes
	14. Sergio Martínez Mendoza	Rafael Córdoba García
Yucatán	1. *Orlando Valencia Moguel*	Pedro Silveira Rodríguez
	2. Alejandro Peraza Uribe	Rita María Medina de Catín
	3. Jorge Carlos González R.	Bartolomé Moo Dzib
Zacatecas	1. Raúl Rodríguez Santoyo	José Ma. Pino Méndez
	2. Nicolás Márquez Acosta	Francisco Arellano Macías
	3. J. Jesús Yáñez Castro	Salvador López Olmos
	4. J. Jesús Bárcenas Gallegos	Patricio García Pérez

Party Deputies (PAN)[*]
[*]Party deputies, and later plurinominal deputies (with a complicated formula), represent parties achieving a certain percentage of votes in the national election. Therefore, since they are not elected by district, they are listed beneath the party they represent. Currently, 300 deputies are elected on the basis of a contested district, and 200 as plurinominal representatives of their parties.

Guillermo Báeza Somellera	*Magdaleno Gutiérrez Herrera*
Alfonso Orozco Rosales	*Bernardo Batiz Vázquez*
Miguel Hernández Labastida	*Francisco José Peniche Bolio*
Mayo Arturo Bravo Hernández	*Guillermo Islas Olguín*
Jesús Rojo Pérez	*José Blas Briseño Rodríguez*

Juan Landerreche Obregón
Hiram Escudero Alvarez
Inocencio Sandoval Zavala
Juan Manuel López Sanabria
Jorge Garabito Martínez

Guillermo Ruiz Vázquez
Miguel López González
Roberto Flores Granados
Ernesto Velasco Lafarga
José Melgarejo Gómez

Party Deputies (PPS)

Felipe Cerecedo López
Jesús Luján Gutiérrez
Simón Jiménez Cárdenas
Emilia Dorado Baltázar
Manuel Stephens García

Francisco Hernández Juárez
Jorge Cruickshank García
Francisco Ortiz Mendoza
Maximiliano León Murillo
Alejandro Gascón Mercado

Party Deputies (PARM)

Juan Barragán Rodríguez
Héctor Rentería Acosta
Laura Peraldi Ferrino

Roberto Herrera Giovanini
Fortino A. Garza Cárdenas

1973-76 (49th Legislature)

State	Deputy	Alternate
Aguascalientes	1. José de Jesús Medellín M.	Adelina Hernández de V.
	2. Higinio Chávez Marmolejo	Gilberto Calderón Romo
Baja California	1. Federico Martínez Manatou	Margarita Ortega Villa
	2. Rafael García Vázquez	Manuel Trasvina Pérez
	3. *Celestino Salcedo Monteón*	Jorge Moreno Bonet
Baja California del Sur (Territory)	1. Antonio Carrillo Huacuja	Agapito Duarte Hernández
Campeche	1. Rosa M. Martínez Denegri	Mario Boeta Blanco
	2. Luis Fernando Solís Patrón	Ismael Estrada Cuevas
Chiapas	1. Carlos Moguel Sarmiento	Enrique Enciso Solís
	2. Rafael Moreno Ballinas	Jorge Paniagua Herrera
	3. Fedro Guillén Castañón	Roberto Bonifaz Caballero
	4. Nereo González Camacho	Miguel Hernández Gómez
	5. Jaime J. Coutino Esquina	Norberto de Gives Goches
	6. María G. Cruz Aranda	Darvelio Macosay Luna
Chihuahua	1. Julio Cortázar Terrazas	Normando Perales Ramírez
	2. Luis Parra Orozco	Juan Heredia Arteaga
	3. *Francisco Rodríguez Pérez*	Roberto Delgado Urías
	4. Luis Fuentes Molinar	Fernando Martínez Tafoya
	5. Angel González	Alfredo González Brondo
	6. Ernesto Villalobos Payán	Artemio Iglesias Miramontes

Coahuila	1. *Jesús Roberto Dávila Narro*	Gasper Valdez Valdez
	2. Francisco Rodríguez Ortiz	Ma. del Carmen Arreola Robles
	3. Arnoldo Villarreal Z.	José Alvarez Alfaro
	4. Jesús López González	Oswaldo Villarreal Valdez
Colima	1. Daniel A. Moreno Díaz	Crispín Casián Zepeda
	2. Jorge A. Gaitán Gudiño	Hilario Contreras López
Distrito Federal	1. Guillermo G. Vázquez A.	Alfonso del Rosal Andrade
	2. *Angel Olivio Solís*	Víctor Manuel Avila Romero
	3. *Ofelia Casillas Ontiveros*	Gilberto Villegas Ralda
	4. Efraín H. Garza Flores	Leopoldo Núñez Flores
	5. Hilario Punzo Morales	Carlos Molina Osorio
	6. Concepción Rivera Centeño	Graciano Morales Ortiz
	7. Jorge Durán Chávez	María Elena Márquez Rangel
	8. *Carlos Dufoo López*	*Silvia Hernández Enríquez*
	9. Daniel Mejía Colín	Leonardo Ochoa Mérida
	10. Simón García Rodríguez	Gloria Carrillo Salinas
	11. *Juan José Hinojosa H.*	René Martínez Tinajero
	12. Alberto Juárez Blancas	Rafael Meneses Narváez
	13. *Javier Blanco Sánchez*	Reyes Roldán Moreno
	14. *Onofre Hernández Rivera*	Roberto Valdez Amezquita
	15. Luis González Escobar	Mario Berumen Ramírez
	16. Luis del Toro Calero	Graciela Valles de Moctezuma
	17. José Humberto Mateos Gómez	Carlos Hidalgo Cortés
	18. *Joaquín del Olmo Martínez*	Salustio Salgado Guzmán
	19. José María Ruiz Zavala	Jesús Ibarra Tenorio
	20. Ricardo Castañeda G.	Aurora Larrazolo Flores
	21. Mariano Araiza Zayas	Janitzio Mújica Rodríguez
	22. *Arturo González Cosío Díaz*	José N. Iturriaga de la F.
	23. *Carlos Madrazo Pintado*	Rosalinda Núñez Perea
	24. *Rodolfo Echeverría Ruiz*	Marcelo Bolaños Martínez
	25. Luis Adolfo Santibáñez B.	Manuel Jiménez Guzmán
	26. *Carlos Sansores Pérez*	Guadalupe Rivera Marín
	27. Ernesto Aguilar Cordero	Víctor Manuel Tommasi N.
Durango	1. María Aurelia de la Cruz	José Ramón Hernández Meraz
	2. Jesús José Gamero Gamero	Francisco Javier Morales F.
	3. Víctor Rocha Marín	Francisco Javier Cueto A.
	4. José María Rivas Escalante	María Cristina Arreola Rocha
Guanajuato	1. *Jaime L. Dantón Rodríguez*	Aurora Guerrero Olivares
	2. *Carlos Martín del Campo*	Salvador Muñoz Padilla
	3. Antonio Torres Gómez	Guillermo Liceaga Díaz

	4. *Tomás Sánchez Hernández*	José Luis Vázquez Camarena
	5. José Luis Estrada D.	J. Jesús Gómez León
	6. *Gilberto Muñoz Mosqueda*	Alfredo Carrillo Juárez
	7. Francisco González M.	Humberto Soto Morales
	8. *Ignacio Vázquez Torres*	Sergio Tovar Alvarado
	9. José Mendoza Lugo	Silvestre Bautiste López
Guerrero	1. Luis León Aponte	Florencio Salazar Adame
	2. Píndaro Urióstegui Miranda	Efigenia Márquez Rodríguez
	3. *Alejandro Cervantes D.*	Alicia Buitrón Brugada
	4. Graciano Astudillo Alarcón	Vicente Rueda Saucedo
	5. Ismael Andraca Navarrete	Angelina Morlet Leyva
	6. *Gustavo N. Ojeda Delgado*	Constantino Flores Peña
Hidalgo	1. Rafael Cravioto Muñoz	Augusto Ponce Coronado
	2. Oscar Bravo Santos	Enrique Gutiérrez Escobedo
	3. María Estela Rojas de Soto	Daniel Campuzano Barajas
	4. Javier Hernández Lara	Antonio Flores Roldán
	5. Ismael Villegas Rosas	Francisco Escamilla Velázquez
Jalisco	1. *Reyes Rodolfo Flores Z.*	Genaro Muñiz Padilla
	2. Gilberto Acosta Bernal	Reynaldo Dueñas Villaseñor
	3. Guillermo A. Gómez Reyes	Javier Antonio Chávez Anaya
	4. Marcos Montero Ruiz	Pedro Martínez López
	5. Amelia Villaseñor y V.	José Luis Leal Sanabria
	6. Héctor Castellanos Torres	José Luis Peña Loza
	7. *Gilberto Aceves Alcocer*	J. Merced Valle Navarro
	8. Rafael Gómez García	Enrique Chavero Ocampo
	9. *Flavio Romero de Velasco*	Luis Albino Reyes Robles
	10. Ramón Díaz Carrillo	José Munguía Rodríguez
	11. *José Luis Lamadrid Sauza*	José Ramírez Ruelas
	12. Francisco Márquez H.	Jesús Octavio Urquides V.
	13. Carlos Rivera Aceves	Daniel Aguirre Cortines
México	1. Sergio L. Benhumea Munguía	Juan Ugarte Cortés
	2. Jesús García Lovera	Hiram García Garcés
	3. Jorge Hernández García	Bricio Escalante Quiroz
	4. Alfonso Gómez de Orozco	José Luis García García
	5. Javier Barrios González	Oscar González César
	6. *Jesús Moreno Jiménez*	Juan Monroy Ortega
	7. *Leonardo Rodríguez Alcaine*	José Antonio Rivas Roa
	8. Humberto Lira Mora	Fernando Rivapalacio
	9. Cuahtémoc Sánchez B.	Angel García Bravo
	10. Sixto Noguez Estrada	Miguel Pérez Guadarrama
	11. María de la Paz Becerril	Angel Otero Rivero
	12. Abraham Talavera López	Javier Pérez Olagaray

	13. Mario R. de Chávez García	Luis Manuel Valle Caro
	14. Pedro García González	Abel Domínguez Rivero
	15. María Martínez Rivera	Rogelio Torres Galicia
Michoacán	1. Gustavo Garibay Ochoa	Salvador Ruiz García
	2. *Jorge Cañedo Vargas*	Macario Castro Apastillado
	3. *Antonio Martínez Báez*	Miguel García Flores
	4. José Alvarez Cisneros	Rodolfo Ramírez Trillo
	5. José Luis Escobar Herrera	Roberto Garibay Ochoa
	6. Octavio Peña Torres	Manuel Cruz Díaz
	7. María Villaseñor Díaz	José Octavio León Infante
	8. Francisco Valdés Zaragoza	Antonio Chávez Samano
	9. Rafael Ruiz Béjar	Vicente Sánchez Cervantes
Morelos	1. José Castillo Pombo	Ubaldo Palacios Betancourt
	2. Roque González Urriza	David Pacheco Saucedo
Nayarit	1. Joaquín Canovas Puchades	José Angel Cerón Alba
	2. Anselmo Ibarra Beas	José Luis Béjar Fonseca
Nuevo León	1. *Margarita García Flores*	Ramiro Martínez Lozano
	2. Raúl Gómez Danés	Ricardo Ayala Villarreal
	3. *Gerardo Cavazos Cortés*	Gilberto Montero Rodríguez
	4. *Leopoldo González Sáenz*	Rosendo González Q.
	5. Ramiro Rodríguez Cabello	Eleazar Bazaldúa Bazaldúa
	6. Francisco Javier Gutiérrez	Rogelio Emilio González
	7. Julio Camelo Martínez	Laura Hinojosa de Domeno
Oaxaca	1. Cecilio de la Cruz Pineda	Josafat Espinosa Rodríguez
	2. Jorge Reyna Toledo	Wilfrido Luis Pérez Méndez
	3. Hugo Manuel Félix García	Ricardo Hernández Casanova
	4. Antonio Jiménez Puya	Guadalupe Castro Moreno
	5. *Diódoro Carrasco Palacios*	Maclovio Rodríguez Pérez
	6. Jaime Esteva Silva	Víctor Espíndola Loyola
	7. *José Murat Casas*	Fernando Mimiaga Sosa
	8. José Rivera Arreola	Moisés Cabrera Téllez
	9. Efrén Ricárdez Carrión	*Genoveva Medina de Márquez*
Puebla	1. Miguel Fernández del Campo	Rosalia Ramírez de Ortega
	2. Alejandro Cañedo Benítez	María del Rosario Huerta L.
	3. Matilde del Mar Hidalgo	Marcelino Naranjo Santillán
	4. *Lino García Gutiérrez*	Moisés Alonso Amador
	5. José Octavio Ferrer Guzmán	Armando García Mendoza
	6. Rafael Pedro Cano Merino	Silvino Jiménez Pérez
	7. Nefthalí López Páez	Venustiano Andrade del C.
	8. Enrique Zamora Palafox	Samuel Herrera Alvarado

	9. *Horacio Labastida Muñoz*	Arturo Alonso Hidalgo
	10. *Guillermo Jiménez Morales*	Angel Esquitín Lechuga
Querétaro	1. José Ortiz Aranda	José Borbolla Patiño
	2. Telésforo Trejo Uribe	Severiano Pérez Enríquez
Quintana Roo (Territory)	1. *Jesús Martínez Ross*	Sebastián Uc Yam
San Luis Potosí	1. Ernesto Báez Lozano	María de Jesús Mena de Zavala
	2. Adalberto Lara Núñez	Claudio Díaz Díaz
	3. Angel Rubio Huerta	Jorge Amaya Verástegui
	4. Vicente Ruiz Chiapetto	Roberto Guerrero Guerrero
	5. Rafael Tristán López	Leonardo Zúñiga Azuara
Sinaloa	1. Silvestre Pérez Lorenz	Raúl Miguel Otondo Sánchez
	2. María Edwigis Vega Padilla	Pablo Moreno Cota
	3. Fernando Uriarte Hernández	Rafael César Borbón Ramos
	4. *Salvador Robles Quintero*	Jesús Arnoldo Millán
	5. Ignacio Carrillo Carrillo	Juan Manuel Inzunza Lara
Sonora	1. Ramiro Oquita y Meléndrez	Pedro Zamora López
	2. *Alejandro Sobarzo Loaiza*	Rita Silvina Agramont
	3. Jesús Enríquez Burgos	*Fernando Elías Calles*
Alvarez		
	4. Gilberto Gutiérrez Quiroz	José Rosario Ruelas
Tabasco	1. Feliciano Calzada Padrón	Armando León Franyutti
	2. *Humberto Hernández Haddad*	Alfredo Domínguez H.
	3. Julián Montejo Velázquez	Elvira Gutiérrez de Alvarez
Tamaulipas	1. Carlos Enrique Cantú Rosas	Gilberto Ortiz Medina
	2. Gilberto Bernal Mares	Silvestre Mata Carrizales
	3. Juan Báez Guerra	Lorenzo Méndez Soto
	4. Jesús Elías Piña	Eustolia Turrubiates Guzmán
	5. Gabriel Legorreta V.	Manuel Méndez Villagrana
	6. Jorge A. Torres Zárate	Diego Vidal Balboa
Tlaxcala	1. Esteban Minor Quiroz	Ernesto García Sarmiento
	2. Aurelio Zamora García	Héctor Vázquez Paredes
Veracruz	1. *Silverio R. Alvarado A.*	Francisco Romero Azuara
	2. *Demetrio Ruiz Malerva*	Olga Ruiz de Oviedo
	3. Ignacio Mendoza Aguirre	José Lima Cobos

	4. *Patricio Chirinos Calero*	Antonio Martínez García
	5. *Rafael Hernández Ochoa*	Juan Pablo Prom Lavoignet
	6. José L. Melgarejo Vivanco	Carlos Domínguez Millán
	7. Delia de la Paz Rebolledo	René León Márquez
	8. *Lilia Berthely Jiménez*	Marco Vinicio Méndez C.
	9. Rogelio García González	Carlos Hernández Fabela
	10. *Modesto A. Guinart López*	Eustaquio Sosa Barba
	11. *Mario Vargas Saldaña*	Juan Zomoano Aragón
	12. *Fidel Herrera Beltrán*	César Fentanes Méndez
	13. *Serafín Domínguez Fermán*	Alfredo Vielma Villanueva
	14. David Ramírez Cruz	Pablo Martín Cruz Hernández
	15. *Manuel Ramos Gurrión*	Manuel Pérez Escalante
Yucatán	1. *Víctor Cervera Pacheco*	Horacio Herve Rodríguez
	2. Hernán Morales	Nelly Guadalupe Valencia B.
	3. Efraín Ceballos Gutiérrez	Augusto Briseño Contreras
Zacatecas	1. Luis Arturo Contreras S.	Consuelo Garibaldi Castillo
	2. *Arturo Romo Gutiérrez*	José Haro Avila
	3. Filiberto Soto Solís	Salvador Enríquez Cid
	4. Alfredo Rodríguez Ruiz	Abel Chaires Báez

Party Deputies (PAN)

Graciela Aceves de Romero	Carlos Gómez Alvarez
Alfredo Oropeza García	Jorge Báeza Somellera
Héctor G. González García	*Eugenio Ortiz Walls*
Alvaro Fernández de Cevallos Ramos	*Manuel González Hinojosa*
Margarita Prida de Yarza	Armando R. Calzada Ramos
José Eduardo Limón León	Lorenzo Reynoso Ramírez
José Angel Conchello Dávila	Alberto A. Loyola Pérez
Federico Ruiz López	Alejandro Coronel Oropeza
José de Jesús Martínez Gil	*José de Jesús Sánchez Ochoa*
Fernando Estrada Sámano	Gerardo Medina Valdez
Abel Carlos Vicencio Tovar	

Party Deputies (PPS)

Belisario Aguilar Olvera	Miguel Hernández González
Pedro Bonilla Díaz de la Vega	Ezequiel Rodríguez Arcos
Lázaro Rubio Félix	Javier Heredia Talavera
Salvador Castañeda O'Connor	Mario Vázquez Martínez

Party Deputies (PARM)

Alejandro Mújica Montoya	*Jesús Guzmán Rubio*
Juan C. Peña Ochoa	Rubén Rodríguez Lozano
Alicia Mata Galarza	Héctor Guillermo Valencia M.

1976-79 (50th Legislature)

State	Deputy	Alternate
Aguascalientes	1. *Jesús Martínez Gotari*	Rosa Guerrero de Reyes
	2. Camilo López Gómez	Camilo López Gómez
Baja California	1. Ricardo Eguía Valderrama	Guadalupe Trejo de Conteras
	2. Alfonso Ballesteros Pelayo	Mario Mayans Concha
	3. *Alfonso Garzón Santibáñez*	Ma. de la Lz Mangas G.
Baja California del Sur	1. Víctor M. Peralta Osuna	Antonio Flores Mendoza
	2. Agapito Duarte Hernández	Gloria Davis de Benzinger
Campeche	1. *Abelardo Carrillo Zavala*	Rubén Uribe Aviles
	2. Jorge Muñoz Icthe	Nery Granados Martínez
Chiapas	1. *Jaime Sabines Gutiérrez*	Luis Manuel Zuarth Moreno
	2. J. Fernando Correa Suárez	Antonio Pérez Pérez
	3. *Homero Tovilla Cristiani*	Javier Pinto y Pinto
	4. Manuel Villafuerte M.	Adrián Contreras Romero
	5. Gonzalo A. Esponda Zebadua	Salvador Durán Pérez
	6. Leonardo León Cerpa	Adán Lara Beltrán
Chihuahua	1. Alberto Ramírez Gutiérrez	Tomás García García
	2. Oswaldo Rodríguez González	Silverio García Bustillos
	3. José Estrada Aguirre	Luis J. Vidal Quiñones
	4. Juan E. Madera Prieto	José Moreno Cruz
	5. Artemio Iglesias M.	Germán Hernández Domínguez
	6. *José R. Mar de la Rosa*	Irma Aceves de Galindo
Coahuila	1. *José de las Fuentes R.*	Guadalupe González Ortiz
	2. Carlos Ortiz Tejeda	Fernando Roque Villanueva
	3. Fernando Cabrera Rodríguez	Enrique Meave Muñiz
	4. Julián Muñoz Uresti	Ariel Cueto Rodríguez
Colima	1. *Ramón Serrano García*	Guillermo Cedano Castillo
	2. Fernando Moreno Peña	Isidro Estrada Díaz

Distrito Federal	1. Eduardo Andrade Sánchez	Luis Rendón de Lara
	2. José Salvador Lima Zuño	Manuel Gutiérrez Montoya
	3. *Carlos Riva Palacio V.*	Leonardo Salas Valenci
	4. *Enrique Ramírez y Ramírez*	Fernando Crocker Solórzano
	5. Miguel Molina Herrera	María Geniz Paredes
	6. Alfonso Rodríguez Rivera	*Isabel Vivanco Montalvo*
	7. Ma. Elena Marqués de T.	Rosa Lilia Rosas Pons
	8. Julio C. Mena Brito A.	Francisco Peña Avila
	9. *Venustiano Reyes López*	Consuelo Marqués de V.
	10. Gloria Carrillo Salinas	Antonio Fuentes Aguilar
	11. Jaime Aguilar Alvarez	Noé Marcos Lazcano Rivero
	12. Miguel López Riveroll	Salvador Villaseñor Franco
	13. *Rodolfo González Guevara*	Raquel Ocharán de Sánchez
	14. Jorge Mendicutti Negrete	Rosa Ma. de la Peña García
	15. *Juan J. Osorio Palacios*	Fernando Zamora López
	16. *Silvia Hernández*	Alfonso Argudín Laria
	17. Héctor Hernández Casanova	Héctor Gutiérrez de Alba
	18. Hugo Díaz Velázquez	José Hererra Arango
	19. *Abraham Martínez Rivero*	Raimundo Baldamís Peláez
	20. Jesús González Balandrano	José Sánchez Miranda
	21. *Marta Andrade de Del Rosal*	Manuel Granados Chirino
	22. *Ifigenia Martínez Hernández*	Ernesto García Herrera
	23. *Enrique Soto Izquierdo*	Guadalupe Salazar de Zamora
	24. *Enrique Alvarez del C.*	Juan Balanzario Díaz
	25. *Celia Torres de Sánchez*	Humberto Casillas Padilla
	26. Humberto Serrano Pérez	Pablo León Orta
	27. Hugo R. Castro Aranda	*Xochil Elena Llarena*
Durango	1. *Angel S. Guerrero Mier*	Zina Ruiz de León
	2. *Maximiliano Silerio Esparza*	Carlos Cruz Molina
	3. Salvador Reyes Nevares	Rodolfo Reyes Soto
	4. *José Ramírez Gamero*	Vicente Soria Barbosa
Guanajuato	1. Esteban M. Garaíz	Lucio Loyola González
	2. *Enrique Gómez Guerra*	Félix Vilchis Ríos
	3. *Juan J. Varela Mayorga*	J. Dolores Urbieta H.
	4. *Miguel Montes García*	Cirilo Soto Barajas
	5. Aurelio García Sierr	Rubén García Farias
	6. Alfredo Carrillo Juárez	Luis Rosiles Flores
	7. Enrique León Hernández	Isidro Hernández Gómez
	8. Graciela Meave Torrescano	Carlos Chaurand Arzate
	9. Donaciano Luna Hernández	Alfredo Zavala Ramírez

Guerrero	1. Isaías Gómez Salgado	Isidro Mastache Suárez
	2. Isaías Duarte Martínez	Gustavo Martínez Martínez
	3. Miguel Bello Pineda	Rafael García Vergara
	4. *Hortensia Santoyo de García*	Efrén Díaz Castellanos
	5. Reveriano García Castrejón	Javier Jiménez Vázquez
	6. Salustio Salado Guzmán	Eloy Polanco Salinas
Hidalgo	1. Ladislao Castillo F.	Elvia Fernández Segovia
	2. *Luis J. Dorantes Segovia*	Rubén Vargas Torres
	3. Efraín Mera Arias	Alvaro Cortés Azpeitia
	4. José A. Zorrilla Pérez	Nicandro Castillo Gómez
	5. Vicente J. Trejo Callejas	José Guadarrama Márquez
Jalisco	1. *Guillermo Cosío Vidaurri*	Jamie Alberto Ramírez
	2. Reynaldo Dueñas Villaseñor	Agapito Isaac López
	3. Félix Flores Gómez	Antonio Brambilia Meda
	4. *Porfirio Cortés Silva*	Ricardo Moreno Delgado
	5. José Mendoza Padilla	Gabriel Ponce Miranda
	6. Rigoberto González Quezada	Salvador Huerta Herrera
	7. *Cecilia Martha Piñón Reyna*	José María Rodríguez G.
	8. Ricardo P. Chávez Pérez	Juan Valdivia Gómez
	9. *María G. Urzúa Flores*	Raúl Juárez Valencia
	10. Francisco J. Santillán O.	Lorenzo Zepeda Uribe
	11. Héctor F. Castañeda J.	Gregorio Velez Montes
	12. Rafael González Pimienta	Antonio Zepeda Pacheco
	13. Jesús A. Mora López	Miguel Armando Naranjo
México	1. *Gildardo Herrera Gómez T.*	Filemón Salazar Bueno
	2. *Joséfina Esquivel de Q.*	Federico Osorio Hernández
	3. *José Delgado Valle*	Bricio Escalante Quiroz
	4. *Arturo Martínez Legorreta*	Miguel Portilla Saldaña
	5. José Martínez Martínez	Julio Garduño Cervantes
	6. Rosendo Franco Escamilla	Antonio Solanes Oviedo
	7. Julio Zamora Bátiz	Francisco Meixhueiro Soto
	8. Armando Labra Manjarrez	Martha Elena Reyes
	9. Juan Ortiz Montoya	Albino Pazos Téllez
	10. José Luis García García	Carlos Cortés Ocaña
	11. Guillermo Choussal V.	Fernando de Moral Bermúdez
	12. Ceclio Salas Gálvez	Ignacio Legaria Ramírez
	13. Pedro Avila Hernández	J. Concepción Silva German
	14. Armando Hurtado Navarro	Rodolfo González Martínez
	15. Héctor Ximénez González	Saúl Rayón Vázquez
Michoacán	1. Nicanor Gómez Reyes	María de la Luz Vera
	2. Antonio Jaimes Aguilar	Abel Pérez Guzmán

	3. Raúl Lemus García	Natalio Flores Lázaro
	4. Roberto Garibay Ochoa	J. Tariacuri Cano Soria
	5. Jaime Bravo Ramírez	José María Montejano
	6. Eduardo Estrada Pérez	Salvador Castillo Núñez
	7. Juan Rodríguez González	Adimanto Vladimir Hernández
	8. *Héctor Terán Torres*	Luis Yarza Solórzano
	9. Roberto Ruiz del Río	Valente Genel Manzo
Morelos	1. *Antonio Riva Palacio López*	Simona Rico de Urueta
	2. *Filomeno López Rea*	Leopoldo Rivas Pizano
Nayarit	1. Ignacio Langarica Quintana	Fausto Ramos Cervantes
	2. María Hilaria Domínguez A.	Simón Pintado Carrillo
Nuevo León	1. *Carlota Vargas de M.*	Roberto Garza González
	2. Heriberto D. Santos Lozano	Guillermo Guzmán
	3. *Raúl Caballero Escamilla*	Alfonso Treviño González
	4. Eleazar Ruiz Cerda	Zenén Ramírez Villalba
	5. *Arturo Luna Lugo*	Salvador Capistrán A.
	6. *Jesús Puente Leyva*	Alfonso Ayala Villarreal
	7. Roberto Olivares Vera	Felipe Zambrano Páez
Oaxaca	1. Lucía Betanzos de Bay	Tomás Vicente Martínez
	2. Gustavo Santaélla Cortés	Tadeo Cruz López
	3. Ericel Gómez Nucamendi	Fortino Pérez Medina
	4. Ernesto Aguilar Flores	Serafín Aguilar Franco
	5. Luis C. Jiménez Sosa	Magdaleno Villegas D.
	6. *Heladio Ramírez López*	Fidel Herrera Salbuena
	7. *Zoraida Bernal de Badillo*	Irma Pineiro Arias
	8. Julio Esponda Solana	Honorina Betanzos de Chunga
	9. Raúl Bolaños Cacho Guzmán	Benjamín Juana Fernández
Puebla	1. Nicolás Pérez Pavón	*Hilda Luisa Valdemar*
	2. Jorge E. Domínguez Ramírez	Melquiades Morales Flores
	3. *Antonio Montes García*	Adoración Youshimatz
	4. *Antonio J. Hernández J.*	Salvador Zavala V.
	5. *Sacramento Jofre Vázquez*	Jesús Reyes Nieto
	6. Antonio Tenorio Adame	Felipe Valderrama G.
	7. *Guadalupe López Bretón*	José Isabel Alonso C.
	8. Jesús Sarabia y Ordóñez	Armando González Sánchez
	9. Manuel Rivera Anaya	Jorge Murat Macluf
	10. Adolfo Rodríguez Juárez	Marcos Gutiérrez Garrido

| Querétaro | 1. Eduardo D. Ugalde Vargas | María Luisa Medina |
| | 2. Vicente Montes Velázquez | Severiano Orduña Ocaña |

| Quintana Roo | 1. Carlos Gómez Barrera | Faride Cheluja de Aguilar |
| | 2. Emilio Oxte Tah | Salvador Ramos Bustamante |

San Luis Potosí	1. Roberto Leyva Torres	Juan Manuel Fortuna T.
	2. *J. Guadalupe Vega Macías*	J. Refugio Guerrero A.
	3. *Víctor A. Maldonado M.*	J. Guadalupe Martínez
	4. Héctor González Larraga	Petrolino Lara Núñez
	5. Eusebio López Sáinz	Saúl Azua Jacob

Sinaloa	1. Erasmo U. Avila Armenta	Tolentino Rodríguez Félix
	2. Felipe Armenta Gallardo	Miguel Ahumada Cortés
	3. *Rafael Oceguerra Ramos*	José Carlos Loaiza
	4. *Antonio Toledo Corro*	Leonardo Peraza Zamudio
	5. Patricio Robles Robles	Gustavo Félix Beltrán

Sonora	1. *Ricardo Castillo Peralta*	Raúl Corella Ruiz
	2. Augusto C. Tapia Quijada	Alfonso García Gallegos
	3. José Luis Vargas González	José Antonio Ruiz González
	4. Bernabe Arana León	Rubén Duarte Corral

Tabasco	1. Luis Priego Ortiz	Elvira Gutiérrez de Alvarez
	2. Roberto Madrazo Pintado	Edgar Méndez Garrido
	3. Francisco Rabelo Cupido	Manuel de Jesús Martínez

Tamaulipas	1. Abdón Rodríguez Sánchez	Francisco Martínez Cortés
	2. Oscar Mario Santos Gómez	Diodora Guerra Rodríguez
	3. *Agapito González Cavazos*	Moisés Lozano Padilla
	4. *Aurora Cruz de Mora*	Luis Quintero Guzmán
	5. *Fernando San Pedro Salem*	Rogelio Carlos Caballero
	6. Julio D. Martínez R.	Armando García Peña

| Tlaxcala | 1. Nazario Romero Díaz | Raymundo Pérez Amador |
| | 2. Antonio Vega García | Salvador Domínguez Sánchez |

Veracruz	1. Guilebaldo Flores Fuentes	Roberto Mendoza Medina
	2. Pericles Namorado Urrutia	Toribio García Lorenzo
	3. Emilio Salgado Zubiaga	Vanancio Caro Benavides
	4. Manuel Gutiérrez Zamora	Guadalupe Solares de M.
	5. Seth Cardena Luna	Lucía Méndez Hernández
	6. Carlos M. Vargas Sánchez	Sara Luz Quiros Ruiz
	7. Daniel Nogueira Huerta	Benjamín Domínguez Rivera
	8. Celeste Castillo Moreno	Miguel Angel Yunes Linares
	9. Mario Martínez Dector	Rosa María Martínez Nájera
	10. Pastor Murguía González	Armando García Lebres
	11. Miguel Portela Cruz	Raúl Ramos Vicarte
	12. *Mario Hernández Posadas*	Miguel Aguirre Lavalle

	13. Francisco Cinta Guzmán	Víctor White Fonseca
	14. Juan Meléndez Pacheco	Simeón Chinas Valdiviesco
	15. Eduardo Thomae Domínguez	Plinio Priego Gutiérrez
Yucatán	1. *Mirna E. Hoyos de Navarrete*	Carlos Velázquez Franco
	2. *Carlos R. Calderón Cecilio*	Alvaro Hernando Brito A.
	3. *Víctor Manzanilla Schaffer*	Noé Antonio Peniche P.
Zacatecas	1. Gustavo Salinas Iñíguez	Albino Tizcareno H.
	2. Crescencio Herrera Herrera	Lorenzo Ruvalcaba C.
	3. José Leal Longoría	Juvenal Rivas Zacarías
	4. Julián Macías Pérez	Honorio Pérez Marín

Party Deputies (PAN)

Gonzalo Altamirano Dimas   *Guillermo Islas Olguín*
Fausto Alarcón Escalona   Rosalba Magallón Camacho
Miguel Campos Martínez   Teodoro Ortega García
Jorge Garabito Martínez   *Francisco J. Peniche Bolio*
Sergio Lujambio Rafols   José Ortega Mendoza
José L. Martínez Galicia   Ma. E. Alvarez Vicencio
Francisco Pedraza Villarreal   Adrián Peña Soto
Ramón Garcilita Partida   Jacinto G. Silva Flores
Carlos G. De Carcer Ballesca   Juan Torres Cipres
Miguel Hernández Labastida

Party Deputies (PPS)

Rafael Campos López   *Marcela Lombardo de Gutiérrez*
Víctor Manuel Carrasco   Ildefonso Reyes Soto
Felipe Cerecedo López   *Jesús Luján Gutiérrez*
Román Ramírez Contreras   Francisco Ortiz Mendoza
Alberto Contreras Valencia   *Héctor Ramírez Cuéllar*
Francisco Hernández Juárez

Party Deputies (PARM)

Saúl Castorena Monterrubio   Arcelia Sánchez de Guzmán
Manuel Hernández Alvarado   *Pedro González Azcuaga*
Raúl Guillén Pérez Vargas   Apolinar Ramírez Meneses
Fortino A. Garza Cárdenas   Eugenio Soto Sánchez
Edilio Hinojosa López

1979-82 (51st Legislature)

State	Deputy	Alternate
Aguascalientes	1. Roberto Díaz Rodríguez	Epigmenio García Avila
	2. Gilberto Romo Nájera	Andrés Valdivia Aguilera
Baja California	1. *José Luis Andrade*	Ambrosio A. Vaca Castro
	2. Juan Villapando Cuevas	Leónor Rosales
	3. Luis Ayala García	David Ojeda Ochoa
	4. Rodolfo Fierro Márquez	Cruz Arellano Espinosa
	5. *María del Carmen Márquez*	Juan Pablo Calderón Lomas
	6. Rafael García Vázquez	Rafael Sáinz Moreno
Baja California del Sur	1. Armando Trasvina Taylor	Gilberto Márquez Fisher
	2. Ramón Ojeda Suárez	Alfredo Polanco Holguín
Campeche	1. Rafael Armando Herrer M.	Gabino Cruz Cisneros
	2. José E. Vázquez Ríos	Eraclio Soberanis
Chiapas	1. *Rafael P. Gamboa Cano*	Aurea Suárez de Cortázar
	2. Pedro P. Zepeda Bermúdez	Manuel Burguete Estrada
	3. Leyver Martínez González	Rubén Domínguez Domínguez
	4. Salvador de la Torre G.	Edín Barrios de León
	5. Jaime J. Coutiño Esquina	Trinidad Cesarea Chamlati
	6. Alberto Ramón Cerdio Bado	Alfonso Pérez Martínez
	7. Antonio Cueto Citalán	Jorge Montesinos Melgar
	8. Juan Alberto Irán Cuesy	
	9. César Augusto Santiago R.	Jorge de Jesús Ramírez
Chihuahua	1. *Margarita Moreno Mena*	Vicente Gassón Chávez
	2. Jesús Chávez Báeza	José Merced Vences
	3. René Franco Barreno	Ignacio Rodríguez Varela
	4. Miguel Lerma Candelario	Jesús Acosta Polanco
	5. Enrique Pérez González	Fernando Babraza Barrera
	6. Enrique Sánchez Silva	Primitivo Campos Gutiérrez
	7. Demetrio B. Franco D.	Oscar Adolfo Martínez V.
	8. Mario Legarreta Hernández	Sergio Vázquez Olivas
	9. *Rebeca Anchondo Vda. de R.*	Cruz Castro Vigil
	10. Alfonso J. Armendáriz D.	Roberto Avila Rede
Coahuila	1. Jorge Masso Masso	José Guadalupe Zuno
	2. Juan Antonio García Villa	Jorge Zermeño Infante
	3. Rafael Ibarra Chacón	
	4. Angel López Padilla	María del Consuelo Villarreal
	5. Conrado Martínez Ortiz	

	6. *Francisco J. González M.*	Alonso Hernández Hernández
	7. Lorenzo García Zarate	Marcelino Ramírez Mani
Colima	1. Agustín González V.	*Javier Ahumada Padilla*
	2. Arnaldo Ochoa González	Vicente Montes Salazar
Distrito Federal	1. Carlos Dufoo López	Clyde Connor Wood
	2. *Angel Olivo Solís*	
	3. Hugo Domenzaín Guzmán	Florentino Ruiz Mora
	4. Rodolfo Siller Rodríguez	Domingo Alapizco Jiménez
	5. Juan Araiza Cabrales	Florencio Salazar Adame
	6. Daniel Mejía Colín	Graciano Morales Ortiz
	7. David Reynoso Flores	Ramón Alvarez Aguirre
	8. *Lidia Camarena Adame*	Ramón Corona Alvarez
	9. *Gonzalo Castellot Madrazo*	Octavio Ponce Rojas
	10. Ignacio Zúñiga González	María Luisa Castañeda
	11. *Manuel G. Parra y Prado*	María del Carmen Parras N.
	12. Roberto Castellanos Tovar	Juan Carlos Vargas Rocha
	13. Joel Ayala Almeida	Luis Jorda Galena
	14. Eduardo Anselmo Rosas	Ignacio Jacinto Huepna
	15. José Herrera Arango	Arturo Aguirre Salazar
	16. Jorge Flores Vizcarra	Arcadio Carbajal
	17. Rubén Figueroa Alcocer	Susana Godoy Castrillón
	18. Leobardo Salgado Arroyo	María Tirado y Valle
	19. Francisco Simeano y Chávez	Mario Bandala Serrano
	20. Ricardo I. Castañeda G.	Melesio López Ojeda
	21. Enrique Gómez Corchado	Ernesto Valles Favela
	22. Enrique González Flores	Emilio Serrano Jiménez
	23. Cuauhtémoc Anda Gutiérrez	Ubaldo Ruiz Suárez
	24. Carlos Robles Loustaunau	Ernesto Aguilar Apis
	25. *María Eugenia Moreno Gómez*	Moisés R. Bueyes y Oliva
	26. Marcos Medina Ríos	Rafael Gutiérrez Moreno
	27. Humberto Olguín y Hermida	Miguel Angel Gutiérrez Torres
	28. Carlos Romero Deschamps	José Valdez Navarro
	29. *Isabel Vivanco Montalvo*	Francisco Cortés Campos
	30. Roberto Blanco Moheno	Abel Ochoa Carlín
	31. *Ofelia Casillas Ontiveros*	Luis Rodríguez Damián
	32. Joaquín Alvarez Ordóñez	Emilio Kawage Vera
	33. Miguel Angel Camposeco C.	Linda Alma Bravo M.
	34. Carlos Hidalgo Cortés	Ricardo Sánchez Aguilar
	35. Arturo Robles Aparicio	César Velázquez Sánchez
	36. *Consuelo Velázquez Torres*	Alfonso Cipres Villarreal
	37. *Luis Velázquez Jaacks*	Federico Durán Linan

		38. *Tristán M. Canales Najjar*	Jesús Cruz Chávez
		39. *Antonio Carrillo Flores*	Ildefonso S. Pérez
		40. Mario A. Berumen Ramírez	Lorenzo Madero Rodríguez

Durango
1. Luis Angel Tejada Espino — Pedro Avila Nevárez
2. *Eduardo López Faudoa* — Cuahtémoc Ontiveros López
3. *Armando del Castillo Franco* — Nicolás Quintero Montgomery
4. Miguel A. Fragoso Alvarez — Abdón Alanís González
5. Gonzalo Salas Rodríguez — *María Albertina Barbosa*
6. Praxedis Nevárez Cepeda — José Miguel Castro Carrillo

Guanajuato
1. *Rafael Corrales Ayala* — Daniel Ramos Hernández
2. Rafael Hernández Ortiz — Federico Plascencio Fonseca
3. Juan Rojas Moreno — Luz María Aguilar Gómez
4. Martín Montaño Arteaga — Juan Martínez Santoyo
5. Jorge Martínez Domínguez — Miguel Ruteaga Rocha
6. *Gilberto Muñoz Mozqueda*
7. *Ignacio Vázquez Torres* — Serafín Rodríguez Guzmán
8. *Ofelia Ruiz Vega* — Miguel López Duthoy
9. *Guadalupe Rivera Marín* — Federica Herrera
10. Guillermo González Aguado — Eduardo Aguayo Juárez T.
11. Andrés Sojo Anaya
12. Raúl Moreno Mújica — Gerardo Martínez Moreno
13. Enrique Betanzos Hernández — Cirilo Tapia León

Guerrero
1. Herón Varela Alvarado — Federico Miranda Castañeda
2. Porfirio Camarena Castro — Silva Portillo Zeñon
3. Aristeo Roque Jaimes Núñez — Custodiojas Domínguez Morales
4. *Guadalupe Gómez Maganda* — César Varela Blanco
5. Ulpiano Gómez Rodríguez
6. H. Israel Martínez Galeana — Ulises Estrada Vázquez
7. Jorge Montufar Araujo — Rutilio Arias Acevedo
8. Filiberto Vigueras Lázaro — Antonio Díaz Salgado
9. José María Serna Maciel — Ladislao Sotelo Bello
10. *Dámaso Lanche Guillén* — Aureliano Ballinas Salas

Hidalgo
1. Adolfo Castelán Flores — Arturo Avila Marín
2. *José Ernesto Gil Elorduy* — Orlando Arvizu Lara
3. *María Amelia Olguín Vargas* — Raúl Angeles González
4. *Jesús Murillo Karam* — Irene Albarrán Hernández
5. José Guadarrama Márquez — Venancio Contreras Plata
6. Manuel Rangel Escamilla — Pedro Flores Hernández

Jalisco

1. Eduardo Avina Bátiz	Juan Enrique Ibarra Pedroza
2. Agapito Isaac López	Eduardo Arias Hernández
3. Adalberto Gómez Rodríguez	Luis Ernesto Uribe Casillas
4. Octavio R. Bueno Trujillo	María del Carmen Mercado
5. Manuel Ojeda Orozco	Jesús María Pinto Herrera
6. Juan D. Castañeda Ceballos	Jesús Delgado Pérez
7. *Ignacio González Rubio V.*	Joel Fernández González
8. Gabriel González Acero	*Rodolfo Flores Zaragoza*
9. José María Sotelo Amaya	Mario A. Rosales Anaya
10. Javier Michel Vega	Antonio Sánchez Ramírez
11. Ismael Orozco Loreto	Gustavo Villaseñor García
12. Luis R. Casillas Rodríguez	José A. Flores Ruiz
13. Juan Delgado Navarro	Gregorio Godoy Magaña
14. *Francisco Rodríguez Gómez*	J. Guillermo Vallarta Plata
15. Enrique Chavero Ocampo	Amparo Rubio
16. Carlos Rivera Aceves	Jorge Ramón Quiñones Ruiz
17. Margarita Gómez Juárez	Nicolás de Jesús Orozco R.
18. *Felipe López Prado*	Roberto Ramírez Maldonado
19. Carlos Martínez Rodríguez	Rosalio Gómez Tapia
20. Antonio Ruiz Rosas	Vidal González Durán

México

1. Juan Ugarte Cortés	Fernando Ayala Alcocer
2. Armando Neyra Chávez	Arturo Mercurio Hernández
3. Alberto Rábago Camacho	Jorge Bobadilla Alvarez
4. *José Merino Manón*	Sabino Lujano Lara
5. Antonio Huitrón Huitrón	Horacio Gaza Morales
6. Guillermo Olguín Ruiz	Juan Monroy Ortega
7. Jorge A. Díaz de León V.	Armando Becerril Estrada
8. Mauricio Valdés Rodríguez	
9. Eugenio Rosales Gutiérrez	Joséfina Vélez de Saldaña
10. Antonio Mercado Guzmán	Francisco Javier Balderas
11. Héctor Jarquín Hernández	Francisco Maldonado Tirado
12. Lorenzo Valdepeñas Machuca	Daniel Alcantara Pérez
13. Fernando Leyva Medina	Héctor San Román Arriaga
14. Juan Martínez Fuentes	Erasmo Osornio Alcantara
15. *Graciela Santana Benhumea*	Mariano Garrido Trejo
16. *Yolanda Sentíes de B.*	Delia Correa González
17. Herberto Barrera Velázquez	Carlos A. Castañeda Hernández
18. Enrique Jacob Soriano	Salvador Navarro González
19. Humberto Lira Mora	Elizabeth Barrera de Macías
20. José Antonio Rivas Roa	Flor Elena Pastrana Villa
21. *Alfredo Navarrete Romero*	Roberto Paredes Gorostieta
22. *María Elena Prado Mercado*	Antonio Rebollo Altuna
23. Juan Alvarado Jacco	Emilio Alvarado Guevara

	24. Francisco J. Gaxiola Ochoa	Silvano Morales Pérez
	25. Leonel Domínguez Rivero	Alberto Ortiz F.
	26. *Elba E. Gordillo Morales*	Carlos Corona Arreguín
	27. *Ignacio Pichardo Pagaza*	María Elisa Garzón Franco
	28. Odón Madariaga Cruz	Rogelio Vargas Soriano
	29. Fernando Riva Palacio I.	Aarón Ruviera Almaraz
	30. Vicente Coss Ramírez	José Aguilera Hernández
	31. Héctor Moreno Toscano	Estanislao Duarte Villegas
	32. *Jesús Alcantara Miranda*	Mario Enrique Vázquez
	33. José Luis García Montiel	Crisóforo Lozano Portillo
	34. José María Téllez Rincón	Clemente Samudio Sauza
Michoacán	1. Marco A. Aguilar Cortés	Juan Sandoval Gallegos
	2. José Luis Lemus Solís	Federico Hernández Rodríguez
	3. *Norberto Mora Plancarte*	Luis Corral Medrano
	4. *Humberto Romero Pérez*	Luis Torres Arias
	5. Javier Zepeda Romero	Roberto Gutiérrez Gómez
	6. Rafael Ruiz Vejar	Octaviano Alanís Alanís
	7. Raúl Pineda Pineda	María Guadalupe Méndez
	8. Luis Coe Guichard	Artemio Yáñez
	9. Alfonso Quintero Larios	Constatino Ortiz Tinoco
	10. Jaime Genovevo Figueroa	Moisés Martínez Muñoz
	11. *Leticia Amezcua de Sánchez*	Ignacio Alvarado García
	12. Abimael López Castillo	Heriberto González Díaz
	13. José L. González Aguilera	Inocente García Carrillo
Morelos	1. David Jiménez González	Quintín R. Manrique Barenque
	2. Francisco Pliego Nava	
	3. *Gonzalo Pastrana Castro*	Gloria Ulloa Villanueva
	4. *Lauro Ortega Martínez*	Juan Salgado Brito
Nayarit	1. Alberto Tapia Carrillo	Reynaldo Pacheco Sánchez
	2. *Emilio M. González Parra*	Javier Carrillo Casas
	3. Carlos Serafín Ramírez	Alejandro González Sánchez
Nuevo León	1. Fernando de Jesús Canales	Catalina Garza González
	2. Juan C. Camacho Salinas	Héctor G. González Martínez
	3. *Luis Medina Peña*	Rebeca Rodríguez Valdez
	4. Filiberto Villarreal Ayala	Simón López Guerra
	5. José Faud González Amille	Virgilio Reyna Martínez
	6. *Luis M. Farías*	Lucio Andrés Tijerina
	7. Andrés Montemayor H.	Maltilde Olivares Rojas
	8. Francisco Valero Sánchez	José H. Villaneuva Moreno
	9. María Amparo Aguirre H.	Juan Cantú Rodríguez
	10. Adalberto Núñez Galaviz	Francisco Rafael Treviño
	11. Armando Thomae Cerna	Gilberto Támez Rodríguez

Oaxaca	1. José Murat Casas	Lucio Guzmán Jiménez
	2. Leandro Martínez Machuca	Israel Martínez García
	3. Elezar Santiago Cruz	Rubén Vasconcelos Beltrán
	4. Rosalino P. López Ortiz	
	5. *Genoveva Medina de Márquez*	Moisés Molina Becerril
	6. Alicio R. Ordoño González	
	7. Aurelio Mora Contreras	Francisco Alonso Sosa
	8. *Norberto Aguirre Palancares*	Juan Arturo López Ramos
	9. *Rubén Darío Somuano López*	Quintín Galguera Barrera
	10. Ignacio Villanueva Vázquez	José Estefan Acar
Puebla	1. *Angel Aceves Saucedo*	Víctor Manuel Fernández
	2. Víctoriano Alvarez García	Julieta Mendivil
	3. Melitón Morales Sánchez	
	4. *Eleazar Camarillo Ochoa*	Roberto Maldonado Aguilar
	5. Juan Bonilla Luna	Celso Delgado Farciet
	6. *Amador Hernández González*	Refugio Salcedo Chávez
	7. *Elizabeth Rodríguez de C.*	Domingo Bautista Luna
	8. Guillermo Melgarejo P.	Ricardo Mendizábal Banda
	9. Constantino Sánchez Romano	Lorenzo Rivera Galindo
	10. Alfonso Zegbe Sanen	Uriel Martí Radoni
	11. *Guillermo Jiménez Morales*	Miguel Rojas Pedraza
	12. Francisco S. Díaz de R.	Olegario Valencia Portillo
	13. Rodolfo Alvarado Hernández	Francisco Coronel Rodríguez
	14. Melquiades Morales Flores	Julio Heberto Calderón
Querétaro	1. *Fernando Ortiz Arana*	Alejandro Esquivel Rodríguez
	2. Federico Flores Tavares	José Guadalupe Flores Cabello
	3. Rodolfo L. Monroy Sandoval	Alfredo García Pacheco
Quintana Roo	1. *Pedro Joaquín Coldwell*	Salvador Ramón Bustamante
	2. Primitivo Alonso Alcocer	Leonel Fausto Villanueva
San Luis Potosí	1. *Antonio Rocha Cordero*	Gualberto Meléndez Cruz
	2. Antonio Sandoval González	Irene Cadena de Lozano
	3. José R. Araujo de Angel	Quintín Rodríguez González
	4. Angel Martínez Manzanares	Vicente Olvera Fontanelli
	5. Bonifacio Fernández Padilla	Amado Olguín García
	6. Guillermo Medina de los S.	Librado Ricabar García
	7. José Ramón Martel López	Joaquín Guzmán Martínez

Sinaloa	1. *Salvador Esquer Apodaca*	Rodolfo Higuera González
	2. Francisco Alarcón Fregoso	Jesús María Cervantes Atondo
	3. Jesús Enrique Hernández C.	Jorge Guillermo Félix R.
	4. Héctor E. González Guevara	Herculano Rojas Farías
	5. Palemón Bojórquez Atondo	Ignacio Fajardo Arroyo
	6. Fortino Gómez Mac Hattón	Gildardo Vega Castro
	7. Baldomero López Arias	Gabriel López Rojo
	8. *María del Rosario Hernández*	Arnulfo Rosas Encinas
	9. José Carlos de Saracho C.	Antonio Yamaguchi
Sonora	1. Luis Antonio Bojórquez S.	Ana Silvia Sánchez
	2. Alejandro Sobarzo Loaiza	Norberto Ortega Hinojosa
	3. Hugo Romero Ojeda	Florentino López Tapia
	4. Rubén Duarte Corral	Guillermo Peña Enríquez
	5. Salomón Faz Sánchez	Carlos H. Arvizu Apodaca
	6. Fernando Mendoza Contreras	Trinidad Sánchez Leyva
	7. Carlos Amaya Rivera	Armando García Herrera
Tabasco	1. Angel A. Buendía Tirado	Rubén Magaña Méndez
	2. Angel M. Martínez Zentella	Roberto Limonchi Wade
	3. Carlos Mario Piñera y Rueda	Laureano Naranjo Cobián
	4. *Humberto Hernández Haddad*	Australia Camacho
	5. Hernán Rabelo Wade	Vicencio Mandujano Peralta
Tamaulipas	1. Pedro Pérez Ibarra	Wenceslao Lozano Rendón
	2. Ernesto D. Cerda Ramírez	Ismael García Cortés
	3. Miguel Treviño Emparán	Rogelio García Lerma
	4. Jaime Báez Rodríguez	José Antonio Martínez Torres
	5. Joaquín Contreras Cantú	Javier González Alonso
	6. Hugo Eduardo Barba Islas	Francisco Galván Malo
	7. José Bruno del Río Cruz	
	8. Pedro Reyes Martínez	
	9. Enrique Fernández Pérez	Enrique Morales Barrios
Tlaxcala	1. Salvador Domínguez Sánchez	Alfredo Cortés Herrera
	2. *Beatriz E. Paredes Rangel*	Daniel Corona Sánchez
Veracruz	1. Gustavo Gámez Pérez	Julio Melo Sánchez
	2. *Demetrio Ruiz Malerva*	
	3. *Oscar Torres Pancardo*	María Eva Izaguirre Camacho
	4. Gonzalo Anaya Jiménez	Armando Hernández Mercado
	5. *Lucía Méndez Hernández*	Manuel Huesca Alarcón
	6. Luis Porte Petit	Onésimo Fernández Campos
	7. Carlos Roberto Smith Véliz	Francisco Marín Domínguez

	8. Hesiquio Aguilar de la P.	Porfirio Pérez Olivares
	9. *Miguel Castro Elías*	Gersón López Maldonado
	10. Silvio Lagos Martínez	Gudelina del Socorro Reyes
	11. *Juan Maldonado Pereda*	
	12. Gonzalo Vázquez Bravo	Roque Spinoza Foglia
	13. *Marco A. Muñoz Turnball*	Celso Vázquez Ramírez
	14. *Sebastián Guzmán* *Cabrera*	Guadencio Pérez Montalvo
	15. Francisco Mata Aguilar	Felipe Balderas Gutiérrez
	16. *Fidel Herrera Beltrán*	Raúl Pazzi Seguera
	17. *Manuel Ramos Gurrión*	
	18. *Noé R. Ortega Martínez*	Venancio Caro Benavides
	19. Gonzalo Morgado Huesca	Germán Muñoz Reyes
	20. Gonzalo Sedas Rodríguez	Leonardo Tepixtle Apace
	21. *Carolina Hernández Pinzo*	Rafael Lira Morales
	22. *Rosa M. Campos Gutiérrez*	Tomás Montoya Pereyra
	23. Enrique Carrión Solana	Ismael Miranda Hernández
Yucatán	1. Federico Granja Ricalde	Rolando Castillo Calderón
	2. Gonzalo Navarro Báez	Antonio García Canul
	3. Jorge Jure Cejín	Roque Castro González
	4. Roger Miltón Rubio Madera	Emilia Cime de Dzul
Zacatecas	1. *Arturo Romo Gutiérrez*	Carlos Mier Macías
	2. Hermenegildo Fernández A.	Alberto Márquez Olguín
	3. Rafael Cervantes Acuña	Daniel Dávila García
	4. Gonzalo García García	Feliciano Ambriz Hernández
	5. *Aurora Navia Millán*	Eliseo Rangel Gaspar

Plurinominal Deputies (PAN)

Graciela Aceves de Romero	José Gregorio Minondo
Esteban Aguilar Jáquez	Salvador Morales Muñoz
David Alarcón Zaragoza	Rafael Moreles Valdes
Rafael Alonso y Prieto	Rafael Gilberto Morgan
Carlos Amaya Rivera	Adalberto Núñez Galaviz
Francisco J. Aponte Robles	Antonio Padilla Obregón
Armando Avila Sotomayor	*Eugenio Ortiz Walls*
David Bravo y Cid	Delfino Parra Banderas
Luis Calderón Vega	*Alberto Pettersen Biester*
Fernando de J. Canales	Carlos Pineda Flores
Carlos E. Castillo	*Marta Cecilia Piñón Reyna*
Luis Castañeda Guzmán	Manuel Rivera del Campo
Juan de Dios Castro Lozano	Augusto Sánchez Losada
Alvaro Elías Loredo	Carlos Stephano Sierra
Hiram Escudero Alvarez	Francisco Ugalde Alvarez
Juan Antonio García Villa	Raúl Velasco Zimbrón
Jesús González Schmal	*Abel C. Vicencio Tovar*
Edmundo Gurza Villarreal	Esteban Zamora Camacho

María del Carmen Jiménez
Juan Landerreche Obregón
Juan Manuel López Sanabria
Miguel Martínez Martínez

José J. Jiménez Velasco
Héctor Federico Ling Altamirán
Pablo Emilio Madero Beldén

Plurinominal Deputies (PCM)

Valentín Campa Salazar
Antonio Becerra Gaytán
Ramón Danzos Palomino
Santiago Fierro Fierro
Alejandro Gascón Mercado
Pablo Gómez Alvarez
Sabino Hernández Téllez
Roberto Jaramillo Flores
Luis Fernando Pedraza M.

Gilberto Rincón Gallardo
Othón Salazar Ramírez
Manuel Arturo Salcido Beltrán
Juventino Sánchez Jiménez
Carlos Sánchez Cárdenas
Manuel Stephens García
Gerardo Unzueta Lorenzana
Arnaldo Martínez Verdugo

Plurinominal Deputies (PPS)

Cuahtémoc Amezcua Dromundo
Belisario Aguilar Olvera
Ernesto Rivera Herrera
Martín Tavira Urióstegui
Juan Manuel Elizondo
Benito Hernández García

Ezequiel Rodríguez Arcos
Lázaro Rubio Félix
Humberto Pliego Arenas
Amado Tame Shear
Gilberto Velázquez Sánchez
Hildebrando Gaytán Márquez

Plurinominal Deputies (PST)

América Abaroa Zamora
Jesús Ortega Martínez
Pedro René Etienne Llano
Juan Manuel Rodríguez G.
Loreto Hugo Amao González

Manuel Terrazas Guerrero
Adolfo Mejía González
Graco Ramírez Garrido Abreu
Jorge Amador Amador
Juan Manuel Elizondo Cadena

Plurinominal Deputies (PDM)

José Valencia González
Roberto Picón Robledo
José E. Guzmán Gómez
José M. Valadez Montoya
Adelaida Márquez Ortiz

Luis Cárdenas Murillo
Felipe Pérez Gutiérrez
Gumersindo Magaña Negrete
Juan Aguilera Azpeitia
Luis Uribe García

Plurinominal Deputies (PARM)

Antonio Vázquez del Mercado
Carlos Enrique Cantú Rosas
Rodolfo Delgado Severino
Luis Laberto Gómez Grajales

Juan Manuel Lucía Escalera
Rafael Carranza Hernández
Ricardo Flores Magón y López
Antonio Gómez Velasco

Jesús Guzmán Rubio   Ramiro Lupercio Medina
Enrique Peña Bátiz   Horacio Treviño Valdez

1982-85 (52nd Legislature)

State	Deputy	Alternate
Aguascalientes	1. Heriberto Vázquez Becerra	Ofelia Castañeda Velez
	2. *Héctor H. Olivares Ventura*	Jesús Guerrero Escobedo
Baja California	1. José Ignacio Monge Rangel	Margarita Ortega de Romo
	2. Martiniano Valdez Escobedo	Agustín Pérez Rivero
	3. José Luis Castro Verduzco	Angelica Valdez de Matéus
	4. Gilberto Gutiérrez Banaga	José Santana Peraza
	5. *Leonor Rosales Rodríguez*	Gilberto Portugal Gilberto
Baja California del Sur	1. Jesús Murillo Aguilar	Eréndira Real Castro
	2. Alberto Miranda Castro	Alvaro Gerardo Higuera
Campeche	1. Jorge Dzib Sotelo	Carlos Enrique Sierra y B.
	2. *Abelardo Carrillo Zavala*	Elia María Cervera Rejón
Chiapas	1. Enoch Casasino Casahonda	Tito Rubín Cruz
	2. Areli Madrid Tovilla	Jorge Mario Lescieur Talavera
	3. *Homero Tovilla Critiani*	José Javier Culebro
	4. *Oralia Coutiño Ruiz*	Manuel Carballo Bastard
	5. Faustino Roos Mazo	José Antonio Puig Lastra
	6. Humberto Púlido García	Manuel Vera Morales
	7. Sami David David	Carlos Octavio Castellanos
	8. Germán Jiménez Gómez	Mario Aceituno Ramos
	9. Eloy Morales Espinoza	José Pascacio Méndez
Chihuahua	1. Miguel Angel Acosta Ramos	Pedro Domínguez Alarcón
	2. Alfonso Cereceres Peña	Juan Manuel Villela Ríos
	3. *Enrique Soto Izquierdo*	Luis Jesús Vidal Quiñones
	4. *Francisco Rodríguez Pérez*	Ramón Belmonte Gómez
	5. Samuel Díaz Olguín	Felicitas Trejo Uribe
	6. Diógenes Bustamante Vela	Miguel Angel Díaz Ochoa
	7. Juan M. Terrazas Sánchez	Benjamín Palacios Perches
	8. *Dora Villegas Nájera*	Jesús Flores Andrade
	9. R. Servando Portillo Díaz	Lilia Romero García
	10. Miguel Angel Olea Enríquez	Joel Ochoa Rubio
Coahuila	1. Abraham Cepeda Izaguirre	José López Molleda
	2. Víctor González Avelar	Alicia López de la Torre
	3. Enrique Neavez Muñiz	Gilberto Cortés Reyna
	4. Lucio Lozano Ramírez	Hilario García Arellano

		5. *Oscar Ramírez Mijares*	Ramón Verduzco González
		6. Enrique Agüero Avalos	Lauro Quintanar Ortega
		7. Juan A. García Guerrero	Lucilia Gómez Barrera
Colima		1. Humberto Silva Ochoa	Rodrigo Vergara Arellano
		2. Ramón Serrano García	Raúl Oscar Gordillo Lozano
Distrito Federal		1. *Pedro L. Bartilotti Perea*	Carolina O'Farril Tapia
		2. Rodolfo García Pérez	Miriam del Carmen Jure Cejín
		3. Carlos Jiménez Macías	Adolfo Juárez Ortega
		4. Domingo Alapizco Jiménez	Mercedes Cortés Montes de Oca
		5. Miguel A. Morado Garrido	Carlos Jiménez Lizardi
		6. Venustiano Reyes López	Venustiano Reyes López
		7. José de Jesús Fernández A.	María Angelica Luna Para
		8. Juan Saldaña Rosell	Salvio Herrera Lozano
		9. Arturo Contreras Cuevas	Gilberto Valencia Diez
		10. Manuel Osante López	Alma Elizabeth del Río
		11. Enrique León Martínez	Alicia Sánchez Jara
		12. Wulfrano Leyva Salas	Rebeca Arenas Martínez
		13. *Hilda Anderson Nevárez*	Juan Carlos Quiroz Tovar
		14. Alvaro Brito Alonso	Consuelo Enciso Vieyra
		15. *Juan José Osorio Palacios*	María del Carmen Gutiérrez
		16. José Aguilar Alcerreca	Juan Rodríguez González
		17. Guillermo Dávila Martínez	José María Reyes Gutiérrez
		18. Joaquín del Olmo Reyes	Alberto Márquez Azcano
		19. *Sara Villalpando Núñez*	Jesús Obregón Nava
		20. Mateo de Regil Rodríguez	Juana Elena Martínez Mújica
		21. *Evarado Gámiz Fernández*	Francisco Elizondo Mendoza
		22. José Carreño Carlón	Alredo A. Mena Alfaro
		23. Servio Tulio Acuña	Guillermo Morales Rosas
		24. Daniel Balanzario Díaz	Valentín Reyes Torrijos
		25. Jesús Salazar Toledano	Carlos Bello Zornoza
		26. *Ignacio Cuauhtémoc Paleta*	Inocencio Valenzo Miranda
		27. *Xóchitl Llarena de Guillén*	José Luis López Torres
		28. Antonio Osorio León	Ernesto Juárez Frías
		29. *Manuel Alvarez González*	Bertha Martínez Garza
		30. Esteban Núñez Perea	María Emilia Farías Mackey
		31. María L. Calzada de Campos	Julio Chon Yong
		32. *Luz Lajous de Madrazo*	Julián García Sánchez
		33. José Parcero López	Jamila Hermelinda Olmedo
		34. Netzahualcóyotl de la Vega	María del Carmen Carreño
		35. Armida Martínez Valdez	José de Jesús Hernández T.
		36. Armando Corona Boza	María Elena García Olalde
		37. Alfonso Valdivia Ruvalcaba	Armando Lazcano Montoya
		38. Alejandro Posadas Espinosa	Juan José Castro Justo

	39. Alicia P. Sánchez Lazcano	*Everardo Moreno Cruz*
	40. *Norma López Cano*	José Leonardo Rosado Azcuaga
Durango	1. Zina Ruiz de León	José Francisco Solís M.
	2. Jesús Ibarra Reyes	Elisa Ortega Ruiz
	3. *María Albertina Barbosa E.*	María Elisa Hernández López
	4. *Maximiliano Silerio Esparza*	Benjamín Avila Guzmán
	5. Juan Arizmendi Hernández	María Teresa Campa Mendoza
	6. Cirino Olvera Espinoza	Rosario Sáenz López
Guanajuato	1. *Enrique Fernández Martínez*	Roberto Zarate Torres
	2. *Carlos Machiavelo Martín*	Rodrigo Moreno Rodríguez
	3. Juan Valera Mayorga	Heliodoro Villanueva Chávez
	4. Luis Vaquera García	Enrique León Hernández
	5. Rubén García Farías	Manuel Vargas Vargas
	6. Javier Martínez Aguilera	Isidro Conríquez Aguilar
	7. Alvaro Uribe Salas	Pedro Herrera Herrera
	8. *Luis Dantón Rodríguez*	Alfonso Torre Vázquez
	9. *Salvador Rocha Díaz*	Jaime Martínez Tapia
	10. Rubén Pérez Espino	Alejandro Aboytes Patiño
	11. Rodolfo Padilla Padilla	Rodolfo Rea Avila
	12. Sergio Lara Espinoza	José Guadalupe Flores López
	13. José Luis Caballero C.	Rubén Serrano Villagómez
Guerrero	1. Zotico García Pastraña	María de la Angeles Nava R.
	2. José Martínez Morales	Juan Manuel Santamaria
	3. Rafael Armenta Ortiz	Rafael Catalán Valdez
	4. *Rosa Maretha Munuzuri*	Evaristo Sotelo Brito
	5. Mario González Navarro	Bernardino Vielma Heras
	6. Adrián Mayoral Bracamontes	José Calleja Bernal
	7. Eloy Polanco Salinas	Yolanda Escobar Torres
	8. Luis Jaime Castro	Hilario Enrique Martini C.
	9. Efraín Zúñiga Galeana	Zefernio Nieto Avendano
	10. Rubén Pérez Espino	Simón Alfonso Guevara R.
Hidalgo	1. Juan Mariano Acoltzín V.	Paulino Merced Chávez M.
	2. *Julieta Guevara Bautista*	José Alejandro Spíndola Y.
	3. César Humberto Vieyra S.	José Martínez Martínez
	4. *Onofre Hernández Rivera*	Eliseo Espinoza Herver
	5. *Humberto Lugo Gil*	Alberto Aranda del Villar
	6. *Antonio Ramírez Barrera*	Mauricio Villarreal Moreno
Jalisco	1. *José Luis Lamadrid Sauza*	Francisco Javier Besso O.
	2. Ramiro Plascencia Loza	Ana Isabel Dueñas Durán

3. José Luis Peña Loza — Beatriz Sánchez Aldama
4. *María del Carmen Mercado* — Amador González Navarro
5. *Leopoldo Hernández Partida* — Alejandro Ontiveros Gómez
6. Luis Garfías Magaña — Abraham Aldana Aldana
7. José Rosas Gómez Luna — Manuel de la Torre Gutiérrez
8. Sergio M. Beas Pérez — Francisco López Calderón
9. *Bertha Lenía Hernández* — Ricardo Ramírez Meléndez
10. Francisco Galindo Musa — José Luis Ortiz García
11. *Víctor M. Torres Ramírez* — Jorge González Villanueva
12. *Aide H. Villalobos R.*
13. *Oralia Estela Viramontes* — Raúl Juárez Valencia
14. *José L. Martínez Rodríguez* — Francisco Camacho Gutiérrez
15. Héctor Perfecto Rodríguez — Francisco Javier Flores R.
16. Héctor A. Ixtlahuac G. — Alfredo Cadena Villanueva
17. Nicolás Orozco Ramírez — Alma Guadalupe Salas Montiel
18. Alfredo Barba Hernández — Teresa Hernández Villalobos
19. Oscar Chacón Iñíguez — Rubén Munguía Jasso
20. Rafael García-Sancho Gómez — Rafael García Sancho Gómez

México

1. Roberto Rubi Delgado — Víctor Manuel Segura Catalán
2. *Gerardo Cavazos Cortés* — Paula Camacho Villaseñor
3. Hugo Díaz Velázquez — José Silva Jarquín
4. *Irma Zarate de Lino* — Gabriel Gama Flores
5. Antonio Velez Torres — Emma Salinas López
6. Guillermo Vargas Alarcón — Luis Trujillo Arana
7. Luis René Martínez S. — Isaac Bueno Soria
8. Gustavo Pérez Pérez — María de Jesús Gonzáles Melo
9. Moisés Raúl López Laines — José Luis Avalos Zuppa
10. *Josefina Luévano Romo* — José Israel Hidalgo Alipi
11. Luis Mayén Ruiz — Mario Enrique Vázquez H.
12. Maurilio Hernández G. — Emiliano Nava Rodríguez
13. Miguel Angel Sáenz Garza — Armando Andrade Sánchez
14. Martín Téllez Salazar — Agustín Zurita Serrano
15. *Gildardo Herrera Gómez T.* — Gabriel Ramos Millán F.
16. *Arturo Martínez Legorreta* — Antonia Ramona Pastrana G.
17. Apolinar de la Cruz Loreto — Olga Delgado Ocampo de E.
18. José Armando Gordillo M. — Amado Olvera Castillo
19. Ernesto Andónegui Luna — Francisco Meixueiro Soto
20. José Ruiz González — María Teresa Flores Calderón
21. Hugo Díaz Tome — Francisco Vargas García
22. *José Luis García García* — Virgilia Noguera Corona
23. Juan de Dios Salazar S. — Teresa Navarro de Mendoza
24. José Lucio Ramírez Ornelas — Miguel Pérez Guadarrama
25. Juan Herrera Servín — Pablo Muñoz Aguilera
26. Leonardo González Valera — Jorge Fidel Cruz Solano

	27. Carlos Barrios Honey	Juan Linas Rivera
	28. Alonso Gaytán Esquivel	María Amparo Flores Guevara
	29. Eleazar García Rodríguez	Benigno López Mateos
	30. Guillermo Fragoso Martínez	Wilfredo Isidro Muñoz Rivera
	31. Enrique Riva Palacio G.	Salomón Ramos Pacheco
	32. Raúl Vélez García	Encarnación C. Díaz Rodríguez
	33. Manuel Nogal Elorza	Rito Yesas Fragoso
	34. María E. Alvarado Carrillo	Claudio Muñoz Franco
Michoacán	1. Francisco Xavier Ovando H.	José Encarnación Tellitud R.
	2. *Jorge Cañedo Vargas*	Pompeyo Pérez Sandoval
	3. Raúl Lemus García	J. Socorro Rodríguez Vera
	4. Hermenegildo Anguiano M.	Lino Cruz Fuentes
	5. Guillermo Villa Avila	José Felipe Herrera García
	6. Rubén Vargas Martínez	Manuel Cruz Díaz
	7. Cristóbal Arias Solís	José López Méndez
	8. Ignacio Olvera Quintero	Enrique Sánchez Velasco
	9. Juan Villegas Torres	Francisco Navarro Robles
	10. Eulalio Ramos Valladolid	Amador Hurtado Mota
	11. Armando Ballinas Mayez	
	12. José Cervantes Acosta	
	13. Ma. Antonia Vázquez Segura	Salvador Zúñiga Andrade
Morelos	1. Juan Salgado Brito	Simona Rico González
	2. Heladio Gutiérrez Ortega	Delfino Castro Quintero
	3. Lorenzo García Solís	Ricardo Dorantes San Martín
	4. Emma Víctoria Campos F.	Florentino Ayala Figueroa
Nayarit	1. Antonio Pérez Peña	Bertha Jáuregui González
	2. Ignacio González Barragán	Anabella Sandoval Acosta
	3. Juan Medina Cervantes	Angel Ocedgueda Cuevas
Nuevo León	1. Alberto Santos de Hoyos	José Luis Cantú Velázquez
	2. Juventino González Ramos	Jesús Pasquel Avila
	3. *Carlota Vargas Garza*	Javier Galindo Mora
	4. Homero Ayala Torres	Antonio Flores Garza
	5. Eleazar Bazaldúa Bazaldúa	Rigoberto de la Garza G.
	6. *Jorge Treviño Martínez*	Arturo Cantú Garza
	7. Ricardo Cavazos Galván	Gloria Manrique de Ortega
	8. Antonio Medina Ojeda	José de Jesús González T.
	9. Alejandro Lambretón Narro	Zoila Sepúlveda Garza
	10. *Luis E. Todd Pérez*	Anastasio Villareal Arreola
	11. Guillermo Garza Luna	Rodolfo Escarzaga Rodríguez
Oaxaca	1. Raúl Enríquez Palomec	Javier Fuentes Valdivieso
	2. Artemio Meixueiro S.	Anastasio Pérez Castelanos

	3. *María Encarnación Paz*	Carmelo Sánchez Sánchez
	4. Odilia Torres Avila	Francisco Fernández Arteaga
	5. Luis Martínez Fernández	Abundio Martínez Reyes
	6. Jorge Luis Chávez Zarate	Saúl Castro Díaz
	7. Antonio Fabila Meléndez	Taurino Angeles Lázaro
	8. Pedro Salinas Guzmán	Tadeo Cruz López
	9. Serafín Aguilar Franco	Heliodoro Ríos Arrelanes
	10. *Joséph Estefan Acar*	Francisco Carlos Villalobos
Puebla	1. *Hilda Luisa Valdemar Lima*	David Flores Rivera
	2. Guillermo Pacheco Pulido	José González Salgado
	3. Efraín Trujeque Martínez	Marcial Pérez Torres
	4. *Lino García Gutiérrez*	Prisciliano L. Pintle Reyes
	5. Olegario Valencia Portillo	Miguel Herrera Ramos
	6. Wulfrano Ascención Bravo	Joaquín Vázquez Salas
	7. *María I. Serdán Alvarez*	Jesús Morales Flores
	8. Jaime Alcántara Silva	Darío Maldonado Casiano
	9. Luis Aguilar Cerón	Arcelia Amador Gutiérrez
	10. *Mariano Piña Olaya*	Raúl Alarcón Guarnos
	11. Javier Bolaños Vázquez	Antonio Castelán Guarneros
	12. Manuel R. Villa Issa	Felipe de Jesús Guerrero R.
	13. Víctor Manuel Carreto	Justino Cortés Cazales
	14. *Sacramento Joffre V.*	José Oscar Aguilar G.
Querétaro	1. *Angélica Paulín Posada*	Luis Herrera Castañón
	2. Ramón Ordaz Almaraz	Ramón Ordaz Almaraz
	3. Ernesto Luque Feregrino	Joaquín Ferrer Fernández
Quintana Roo	1. Sara Esther Musa de M.	Octavio Ascensio Reynoso
	2. Javier Sánchez Lozano	María Esther Namur Suárez
San Luis Potosí	1. *Víctor Alfonso Maldonado*	Juan Ramiro Robledo Ruiz
	2. *José Guadalupe Vega*	Joel Ramírez Díaz
	3. Odilón Martínez Rodríguez	Carlos Gama Morales
	4. Gerardo Ramos Romo	María Eugenia Olvera R.
	5. Eusebio Ordaz Ortiz	María Hortensia Flores V.
	6. *Leopoldo Ortiz Santos*	Alfonso Lastras Ramírez
	7. Helios Barragán López	Rebeca Guevara de Terán
Sinaloa	1. Angel Sandoval Romero	Raúl Lizárraga Rojo
	2. Homobono Rosas Rodríguez	Jesús Homobono Rosas R.
	3. Jesús Manuel Viedas E.	Jesús Manuel Viedas E.
	4. Germinal Arámburo C.	María Esther Lizárraga G.
	5. *Rafael Oceguera Ramos*	Marco Antonio Sánchez M.
	6. Rodolfo López Monroy	Juvencio Robles Gámez
	7. Maclovio Osuna Balderrama	José Angel Velázquez Parra
	8. Saúl Ríos Beltrán	Teófilo Mejía López
	9. Manuel Tarriba Rojo	

Sonora	1. Luis Héctor Ochoa Bercini	Sandra Elena Bojórquez Lara
	2. Alfonso Molina Ruibal	María del Carmen Calles B.
	3. Florentino López Tapia	Gregorio Alvarado
	4. *Manlio Fabio Beltrones R.*	Horacio Vega Soto
	5. *Ricardo Castillo Peralta*	Marcelino Camarillo M.
	6. Rubén Castro Ojeda	José Encarnación Alfaro
	7. Ramiro Valdez Fontes	Adrián Manjarrez Díaz
Tabasco	1. Amador Izúndegui Rullán	Oscar Alberto Priego G.
	2. Oscar Cantón Zetina	Juan Antonio Solís Avalos
	3. Andrés Sánchez Solís	César Jiménez Velázquez
	4. Manuel Llergo Heredia	María Elena de la Cruz
	5. María G. García Serra	Marcos Quintero Buendía
Tamaulipas	1. Ascención Martínez Cavazos	Rafael Reyes Orbe Reséndiz
	2. Federico Hernández Cortés	Amaro Garza Villarreal
	3. Heriberto Batres García	Servando Hernández Camacho
	4. Abdón Martínez Hinojosa	Salvador Guerrero Zorrilla
	5. Roberto González Barba	
	6. Benito Ignacio Santamaría	
	7. Mario Santos Gómez	Ezequiel Alvarez Cornejo
	8. *Manuel Cavazos Lerma*	Ernesto Guajardo Maldonado
	9. *Martha Chávez Padrón*	Ignacio de la Llave Ramos
Tlaxcala	1. José A. Alvarez Lima	José Antonio Alvarez Lima
	2. *Alma Inés Gracia de Z.*	Abraham Mora Amador
Veracruz	1. Antonio Murrieta Necoechea	Guilebaldo Flores del Angel
	2. Rogelio Carballo Millán	Pedro Hernández Maldonado
	3. Mauro Melo Barrios	Adoraím Aldana Pérez
	4. Edmundo Martínez Zaleta	Guadalupe Solares Bausa
	5. Alfonso Arroyo Flores	Simitrio Amador Ballinas
	6. Salvador Valencia Carmona	Leopoldo Castillo Rodríguez
	7. Servando Díaz Suárez	Edmundo Portilla Martínez
	8. José Nassar Tenorio	Arturo Parra Zapata
	9. *Daniel Sierra Rivera*	Carlos Corpi Corpi
	10. Jorge M. Porte Petit	Hugo Hernández Muñoz
	11. *Mario Vargas Saldaña*	Librado Trujillo Serrano
	12. *Irma Cué Sarquís*	Gustavo Arroniz Zamudio
	13. *Celso Vázquez Ramírez*	Clemente Suriano Mateo
	14. Wilfrido Martínez Gómez	Rubén Urdapilleta Moreno
	15. Carlos Brito Gómez	Ramón Hernández Toledo
	16. Héctor Sánchez Ponce	Fidela García Rivera
	17. Elpilia Excelente Azuara	Juan Cristóbal Cespedes
	18. *Silverio R. Alvarado*	Antonio Bustillos Carcamo
	19. Roque Spinoso Foglia	Seth Cardena Luna

	20. Ramón Ojeda Mestre	Demetrio Ernesto Espinosa
	21. Amador Toca Cangas	Harry Jackson Sosa
	22. *Serafín Domínguez Ferman*	Luis Díaz del Castillo R.
	23. Manuel Solares Mendiola	Noé Cadena Grajeda
Yucatán	1. *Víctor Cervera Pacheco*	Horacio Herbe Rodríguez
	2. José Pacheco Durán	Rosa Elena Baduy
	3. *Carlos R. Calderón Cecilio*	Roberto Pinzón Alvarez
	4. Dulce María Sauri Riancho	Lindbergh Mendoza Díaz
Zacatecas	1. *Genaro Borrego Estrada*	Raúl Flores Muro
	2. Antonio Herrera Bocardo	Alfredo González Aguirre
	3. Roberto Castillo Aguilar	Eulogio Quirarte Flores
	4. Jesús Ortiz Herrera	Gumaro Elías Hernández Z.
	5. *Ana María Maldonado P.*	Pedro Garza Bárcenas

Plurinominal Deputies (PAN)

José González Torres	*Bernardo Bátiz Vázquez*
Juan Vázquez García	*Gerardo Medina Valdez*
Marco Antonio Fragoso Fragoso	*Manuel Iguíiz González*
José Viramontes Paredes	*Jorge Alberto Ling Altamirano*
José Juan Hinojosa	Francisco González Garza
Arturo Trujillo Parada	*Javier Blanco Sánchez*
María Teresa Orduño Gurza	*Astolfo Vicencio Tovar*
Francisco Soto Alba	*Carlos Chavira Becerra*
Alberto González Domene	Luis Torres Sarranía
José Isable Villegas Piña	*Emma Medina Valtierra*
Gustavo Arturo Vincencio A.	Esperanza Espinoza Herrera
Salvador Romero Estrada	Luis Enrique Sánchez Espinoza
Graciela Gutiérrez de Barrios	Luis J. Prieto González
Roger Cicero MacKinney	Angel Mora López
Rubén Darío Méndez Aquino	Fabián Basaldúa Vázquez
Paulino Aguilar Paniagua	Arnoldo Garate Chapa
Miguel Gómez Guerrero	José Haddad Interián
Manuel Zamora y Duque	*Felipe Gutiérrez Zorrilla*
Jesús Salvador Larios Ibarra	Alfonso Méndez Ramírez
Rodlofo Peña Farber	Miguel Angel Martínez Cruz
Javier Moctezuma y Coronado	Gabriel Salagado Aguilar
Juan Millán Brito	Juan Molina Rodríguez
José Guadalupe Esparza López	Pablo Castillón Alvarez
Andrés Cazares Camacho	*Florentina Villalobos de Pineda*
Francisco Calderón Ortiz	

Plurinominal Deputies (PSUM)

Iván García Solís
Salvador Castañeda O'Connor
José Dolores López Domínguez
Víctor González Rodríguez
José Encarnación Pérez Gaytán
Pedro Bonilla Díaz de la Vega
Samuel Meléndez Luévano
Florentino Jaimes Hernández

Rolando Cordera Campos
Arnaldo Córdova
Edmundo Jardón Arzate
René Rojas Ayala
Héctor Sánchez López
Raúl Rea Carvajal
Daniel Angel Sánchez Pérez
Jesús Lazcano Ochoa

Plurinominal Deputies (PDM)

David Orozco Romo
David Lomeli Contreras
Juan López Martínez
Margarito Benítez Durán
María de Jesús Orta Mata
Ignacio Vital Juáregui

Baltázar Ignacio Valadez Montoya
José Augusto García Lizama
Ofelia Ramírez Sánchez
Francisco Javier Alvarez de la F.
Enrique Alcantar Enríquez
Raymundo León Ozuna

Plurinominal Deputies (PST)

Rafael Aguilar Talamantes
Mariano López Ramos
Ignacio Moreno Garduño
Ricardo Antonio Covela Autrey
Pablo Sánchez Puga
Alberto Salgado Salgado

Raúl Rodolfo López García
Antonio Ortega Martínez
Cándido Díaz Cerecedo
César Humberto González Magallón
Domingo Esquivel Rodríguez

Plurinominal Deputies (PPS)

Francisco Ortiz Mendoza
Héctor Ramírez Cuéllar
Jorge Cruickshank García
Juan Gualberto Campos Vega
Cresenio Morales Orozco

Jesús Luján Gutiérrez
Alfredo Reyes Contreras
Viterbo Cortés Lobato
Juan Ruiz Pérez
Sergio Quiroz Miranda

1985-88 (53rd Legislature)

State	Deputy	Alternate
Aguascalientes	1. Alfredo González González	
	2. *Miguel Angel Barberena Vega*	
Baja California	1. Luis Ignacio López Moctezuma	
	2. Rafael Sáinz Moreno	
	3. Enrique Pelayo Torres	
	4. *Margarita Ortega Villa*	

5. Rogelio Preciado Cisneros
6. Jorge Salceda Vargas

Baja California
del Sur

1. *Víctor Manuel Liceaga Ruibal*
2. Eligio Soto López

Campeche

1. Elizabeth Cuevas Melken
2. Pedro López Vargas

Chiapas

1. Eduardo Robledo Rincón
2. César Augusto Santiago Ramírez
3. Homero Díaz Córdova
4. Blanca Esponda Espinosa
5. Antonio Melgar Aranda
6. Ilse Sarmiento Gómez
7. Humberto Andrés Savala Peña
8. Oscar Ochoa Zepeda
9. Sergio Armando Valls Hernández

Chihuahua

1. Eduardo Turati Alvarez
2. Jacinto Gómez Pasilla
3. Undecided
4. Oscar Luis Rivas Munos
5. Alfonso Aguirre Ramos
6. *Fernando Báeza Meléndez*
7. Doroteo Zapata García
8. Edelberto Galindo Martínez
9. Fernando Abarca Fernández
10. José Bernardo Ruiz Ceballos

Coahuila

1. *Eliseo Francisco Mendoza Berrueto*

2. *Braulio Manuel Fernández Aguirre*
3. Daniel Castaño de la Fuente
4. Rodolfo Jiménez Villarreal
5. Gaspar Valdés Valdés
6. Heriberto Ramos Salas
7. Gonzalo Padilla Fuentes

Colima

1. Ma. Concepción Barbosa Hernández
2. Alfonso Santos Ramírez

Distrito Federal

1.
2.
3.
4. Rafael López Zepeda
5. Rafael Lozano Contreras
6. José Herrera Arango

7. Javier Garduño Pérez
8. Adrián Mora Aguilar
9. Armando Lozano Montoya
10. Jaime Aguilar Alvarez
11. Julio Valenzuela Herrera
12. Joaquín López Martínez
13. Federico Liñan Durán
14. Lorenzo Silva Ruiz
15. Javier Pineda Serino
16. Francisco Berlin Valenzuela
17. *Guillermo Fonseca Alvarez*
18. Alfonso Godínez López
19. Luis Altamirano Cuadros
20. Antonio Punzo Gaona
21. *Ofelia Casillas Ontiveros*
22. Juan J. Castillo Mota
23. *Juan José Bermer Martino*
24. Federico Granja Ricalde
25. *Santiago Oñate Laborde*
26. *Manuel G. Parra Prado*
27. Gilberto Nieve Jenkins
28. Agustín Bernal Villaneuva
29. *Juan Moisés Calleja García*
30. María Emilia Farias Mackey
31. *Fernando Ortiz Arana*
32. Fernando Ulibarri Pérez
33. Jaramilla Olmedo de Garcilita
34. Alfonso Reyes Medrano
35. Manuel Monarres Valenzuela
36. Manuel Jiménez Gúzman
37. *Gonzalo Castellot Madrazo*
38. *Sócrates Rizzo García*
39. Juan J. Castro Justo
40.

Durango
1. Alfonso Joel Rosas Torres
2. Cristóbal García Ramírez
3. Francisco Gamboa Herrera
4. José Ramón García Soto
5. *Angel Sergio Guerrero Mier*
6. Joel Lleverino Reyes

Guanajuato
1. Nestor Rául Luna Hernández
2. Undecided
3. Héctor Hugo Varela Flores
4. Jesús Gutiérrez Seoviano
5. *Eliseo Rodríguez Ramírez*
6. Alberto F. Carrillo Flores
7. Arturo Ruiz Morales

8. Jaimes Martínez Jasso
9. María Luisa Mendoza Romero
10. Felipe C. Domínguez Villanueva
11.
12. Mario Murillo Morales
13. Juan A. Araujo Urcelay

Guerrero

1. Humberto Salgado Gómez
2. Porfiro Camarena Castro
3.
4. Amin Zarur Menez
5. Rueben Robles Catalán
6. Agustín Villavicencio A.
7. Félix Liera Ortiz
8. Pindaro Urióstegui Miranda
9. *Gustavo N. Ojeda Delgado*
10. Jorge Montúfar Araujo

Hidalgo

1. *Germán Corona del Rosal*
2. Roberto Valdespino Castillo
3. Amelia Olguin Vargas
4. Juan C. Alva Calderón
5. José G. Badillo Ortiz
6. *Jesús Murillo Karam*

Jalisco

1. Santiago Camarena Flores
2. Justino Delgado Caloca
3. *María E. Scherman Leaño*
4. *Porfirio Cortés Silva*
5. Alma G. Salas Montiel
6. Jorge Sanroman Quiñones
7. Alejandro Ontiveros Gómez
8. *Rodolfo Flores Zaragoza R.*
9. Rafael González Pimienta
10. Francisco Contreras Contreras
11. Javier Michel Díaz
12. Francisco García Castellón
13. Francisco J. Morales Aceves
14. *Arnulfo Villaseñor Saavedra*
15. Félix Flores Gómez
16. Antonio Brambila Meda
17. Jesús González Cortazar
18. David Serrano Acosta
19. Samuel Orozco González
20. Héctor C. Hernández Allende

México

1. Enrique Martínez Orta
2. Eduardo Lecanda Lujambio
3. Alberto Rábago Camacho

4. Laura Pavón Jaramillo
5. Regina Reyes Retana
6. Juan M. Tovar Estrada
7. Agustín Leñero Bores
8. Jorge Díaz de León
9. *Jesús Alcántara Miranda*
10. Eugenio Rosales Gutiérrez
11. Heriberto Serrano Moreno
12. Luis Pérez Díaz
13. Luis M. Orci Gandara
14. Eduardo Hernández Mier
15. Héctor Ximénez González
16. Enrique González Isunza
17. Abelardo R. Alaniz González
18. Sergio Mancilla Guzmán
19. Guadalupe Ponce Torres
20. Serafin Roa Sánchez
21. Pedro Zamora Ortiz
22. Guillermo Altamirano Conde
23. Juan Alvarado Jacco
24. Gustavo A. Robles González
25. José Delgado Valle
26. Dionisio Moreno Cortés
27. Ricardo Regalado Hernández
28. Jorge Flores Solano
29. José Salinas Navarro
30. *Marcela González Salas P.*
31. José E. Alfaro Cazares
32. Gerardo Fernández Casanova
33. Miguel Angel Herrerias
34. Lauro Rendón Castrejón

Michoacán
1. Macario Rosas Zargoza
2. Antonio Correa López
3. Raúl Castellanos Martínez B.
4. José Berber Sánchez
5. Roberto Ruiz del Río
6. Rafael Ruiz Béjar
7. J. Ascención Busto Velasco
8. Abimael López Castillo
9. Juan C. Velasco Pérez
10. Janitzio Mújica Rodríguez
11. Rosalba Buenrostro López
12. Leonel Villalobos Chávez
13. Ignacio Ramos Espinoza

Morelos
1. David Jiménez González
2. Raúl Ramírez Chávez

           3. Elvia Lugo de Vera
           4. Ruben Román Sánchez

Nayarit

1. José Félix Torres Haro
2. Leobardo Ramos Martínez
3. Enrique Medina Lomeli

Nuevo León

1. Javiero Lobo Morales
2. Amilcar Aguilar Mendoza
3. Jesús Ricardo Canavati Tafich
4. Isaias Vázquez Mendoza
5. Jesús Siller Rojas
6. Graciano Bortoni Urteaga
7. Ricardo Flores Caballero R.
8. Pedro Ortega Chavira
9. Humberto Cervantes Vega
10. Rolando Castillo Gamboa
11. Gloria J. Mendiola Ochoa

Oaxaca

1. Mario Bustillos Villalobos
2. Mauro Rodríguez Cruz
3. Jesús E. Martínez Alvarez
4. Alberto Pérez Mariscal
5. Rodolfo Linares González
6. Ricardo Hernández Casanova
7. Oswaldo García Criollo
8. Patricia Villaneuva Abrajan
9. Leonel Rojas Medina
10. Alfredo López Ramos

Puebla

1. *Blas Chumacero Sánchez*
2. Amado Llaguno Mayaudon
3. *Guadalupe López Bretón*
4. *Eleazar Camarillo Ochoa*
5. Víctor H. Islas Hernández
6. Miguel Romero Sánchez
7. Melquiades Morales Flores
8. Dario Maldonado Casiano
9. Heriberto Morales Arroyo
10. Rodolfo Budib Lichtle
11. Germán Sierra Sánchez
12. José M. López Arrollo
13.
14. Antonio Tenorio Adame

Querétaro

1. Edmundo González Llaca
2. Ezequiel Espinosa Mejia
3. Augusto Guerrero Castro

Quintana Roo	1. Ma. Cristina Sangri Aguilar
	2. Salvadro Ramos Bustamante
San Luis Potosí	1. Teófilo Torres Corzo
	2. Marcelino Rodríguez Silva
	3. Antonio Sandoval González
	4. Rosa M. Armendáriz Muñoz
	5. Alberto Mercado Araiza
	6. Alfonso Lastras Ramírez
	7. Román González Ayala
Sinaloa	1. *Salvador Esquer Apodaca*
	2. Marco A. Espinosa Pablos
	3. Mario Alfonso Niebla A.
	4. *Diego Valadés Ríos*
	5. José A. Pescador Osuna
	6. *Salvador Robles Quintero*
	7. María Luisa Solís Payán
	8. Adrián González García
	9. *Renato Vega Alvardo*
Sonora	1. Jorge Acedo Samaniego
	2. *Alicia Arellano Tapias*
	3. Heleno de Anda López
	4. Andrés Pacheco Moreno
	5. *Luis Donaldo Colosio Murrieta*
	6. Ismael Torres Díaz
	7. Francisco Villanueva Casteló
Tabasco	1. Nicolás Reynes Berezaluce
	2. Manuel Urrutia Castro
	3. Homero Pedrero Priego
	4. José E. Beltrán Hernández
	5. Oscar Llergo Heredia
Tamaulipas	1. Undecided
	2. Emilio Cordero García
	3. Undecided
	4. Diego Navarro Rodríguez
	5. Joaquín Contreras Cantú
	6. Luis Nájera Olvera
	7. Marciano Aguilar Mendoza
	8. Gerardo Gómez Castillo
	9. Aureliano Caballero González
Tlaxcala	1. *Beatriz E. Paredes Rangel*
	2. Samuel Quiroz de la Vega

Veracruz	1. Guilebaldo Flores del Angel
	2. Alberto S. Mañueco Guzmán
	3. Americo Rodríguez García
	4. Guadalupe Solares Bauza
	5. Nicolás Callejas Arroyo
	6. Héctor Yunes Landa
	7. Carlos R. Smith Velez
	8. María A. Munguía Archundia
	9. Sergio Roa Fernández
	10. Dante A. Delgado Rannauro
	11. Juan Maldonado Pereda
	12. Isidro Pulido Reyes
	13. Hesiquio Aguilar de la Parra
	14. *Sebastián Guzmán Cabrera*
	15. Héctor Sen Flores
	16. Demetrio Ruiz Malerva
	17. Héctor Aguirre Barragán
	18. Rebeca Arenas Martínez
	19. Cirilo Rincón Aguilar
	20. Pastor Muguia González
	21. Rafael García Anaya
	22. Federico Fernández Fariña
	23. Oscar Aguirre López
Yucatán	1. Rodolfo A. Menéndez M.
	2. José Nerio Torres Ortiz
	3. Wilbert Chi Góngora
	4. Renán Solís Aviles
Zacatecas	1. Irene Ramos Dávila
	2. Pedro Goytia Robles
	3. Eliseo Rangel Gaspar
	4. Manuel Monreal Zamarripa
	5. José Luis Galaviz Cabral

Plurinominal Deputies (PAN)

Xavier Abreu Sierra
Carlos A. Acosta González
Juan Alcocer Bernal
Gonzalo Altamirano Dimas
Víctor G. Alvarez Herrera
Pablo Alvarez Padilla
Alejandro Cañedo Benítez
Juan de D. Castro Lozano
José Angel Conchello Dávila
Jaime Delgado Herrera
Jesús Galván Muñoz
Ricardo F. García Cervantes

Pablo Ventura López
Ubaldo Mendoza Ortiz
Sergio T. Meza
María E. Morelos
Jorge E. Ortiz G.
Javier Paz Zarza
Héctor Pérez Plazola
Humberto E. Ramírez
Humberto Rice García
Federico Ling Altamirano
Cecilia Romero Castillo
Consuelo Botello

Jesús González Schmal
María del C. Jiménez Méndez
Enrique G. Jiménez Remus
Salvador Landa Hernández

Rubén Rubiano Reyna
María E. Silva Alvarez
Germán Tena Orozco
Héctor Terán Terán

Plurinominal Deputies (PPS)

Cuauhtémoc Amezcua Dromundo
Vicente Calvo Vázquez
Manuel Fernández Flores
Hildebrando Gaytán Márquez
Gabriela Guerrero Oliveros
Francisco Hernández Juárez

Héctor Morquecho Rivera
Adner Pérez de la Cruz
Indalecio Sáyago H.
Martín Tavira Urióstegui
Víctor M. Jiménez Osuna

Plurinominal Deputies (PST)

Jorge Amador Amador
José A. Aguirre Romero
Agustín M. Alonso Raya
César A. del Angel Fuentes
José F. Flores Gutiérrez
Magdalena García Rosas

Jesús H. Noriega C.
José G. Piñero López
Graco L. Ramírez G.
María S. del Río Herrera
Beatriz Gallardo Macias
Máximo de León Garza

Plurinominal Deputies (PSUM)

Jorge Alcocer Villanueva
Pablo J. Pascual M.
Ramón Danzos Palomino
Leopoldo de Gyves
Gerardo Unzueta Lorenzana
L. Arturo Whaley Martínez

Arnoldo Martínez Verdugo
José L. Sánchez González
Manuel Terrazas Guerrero
José C. Valenzuela
Eraclio Zepeda Ramos
Demetrio Vallejo Martínez

Plurinominal Deputies (PMT)

Eduardo Acosta Villeda
Heberto Castillo Martínez
Oswaldo N. Harris Muñoz

Miguel E. Valle
José Luis Díaz Moll
Alejandro Gascón Mercado

Plurinominal Deputies (PRT)

Rubén Aguilar Jiménez
Rosario Ibarra de Piedra
Rosalía Peredo Aguilar

Ricardo A. Pascoe
Pedro J. Peñaloza
Efraín J. Calvo Zarco

Plurinominal Deputies (PARM)

Enrique Bermúdez Olvera
Héctor Calderón Hermosa
Jaime Castellanos Franco
María de la Luz Gama
Gregorio Macías Rodríguez

Jorge Masso Masso
Nabor Camacho Nava
Reyes Fuentes García
Juan M. Lucía Escalera

Plurinominal Deputies (PDM)

Carlos Barrera Auld
Roberto Calderón Tinoco
José T. Cervantes Aguirre
Juan de Dios Colli Mas
Leonardo Durán Juárez
Jaime Haro Rodríguez

Antonio Monsiváis Ramírez
Lorenzo Serrano Gutiérrez
Gustavo I. Valenzuela
Magadaleno Yáñez H.
Jesús Zamora Flores
Homero Díaz Mota

1988-91 (54th Legislature)

State	Deputy	Alternate
Aguascalientes	1. Manuel González Díaz	Silvia E. Avila Chávez
	2. *Augusto Gómez Villanueva*	Pedro González G.
Baja California	1. Jesús A. Hernández Montaño	Nirvana Estrada Ojeda
	2. Bernardo Sánchez Ríos	Magdalena Saucedo Gómez
	3. Luis González Ruiz	María Ramírez García
	4. Miguel Díaz Muñoz	Leticia Castellano
	5. René O. Treviño Arredondo	Franciscana Krauss
	6. Mercedes Erdmann Baltazar	Martín G. Aguirre R.
Baja California del Sur	1. José Luis Parra Rubio	Oscar M. López Arvizu
	2. Antonio B. Manríquez	Gabriel Renero Lara
Campeche	1. Eraclio Soberanis Sosa	Camilo Massa Pérez
	2. Jorge E. Minet Ortiz	Humberto Curmina Barrera
Chiapas	1. Antonio Pariente Algarín	Manuel de la Torre
	2. Javier López Moreno	José Ebodio Penago
	3. José J. Culebro Siles	Roberto J. Fuentes
	4. Sami G. David David	Adrián Contreras Romero
	5. César R. Naumann E.	Antonio de Jesús Díaz
	6. Romeo Ruiz Armento	José Darvelio Nacossay
	7. Neftalí Rojas Hidalgo	Teófilo Ponce Figueroa
	8. Leyber Martínez González	José C. Suriano
	9. Areli Madrid Tovilla	Manuel Huerta Rivera

Chihuahua	1. Esquipulas David Gómez R.	José A. Delgado S.
	2. Rafael Chávez Rodríguez	Martín Rentería Sánchez
	3. Miguel A. Corra Olivas	Francisco J. Galindo
	4. Santiago Rodríguez de Valle	Silvia Iglesias
	5. Jorge E. Sandoval Ochoa	José A. Comadurán
	6. María G. López Alvarez	María Pérez Domínguez
	7. Carlos Barranco Fuentes	Tito Terrazas
	8. Eliher Flores Prieto	David Rodríguez Torres
	9. Rebeca Anchondo Fernández	Armando Villarreal
	10. Artemio Iglesias Miramontes	Oscar Leos Mayagoitia
Coahuila	1. Enrique Martínez y Martínez	José G. Guardiola Ledezma
	2. Alicia López de la Torre	Juan S. Aldape Huerta
	3. Benigno Gil de los Santos	Hildabrando Lafuente
	4. *Rogelio Montemayor Seguy*	Carlos Juarigui
	5. Ignacio Dávila Sánchez	Leopolda García Duarte
	6. Humberto Roque Villaneuva	José Ortiz Barroso
	7. Noé F. Garza Flores	Pedro Herrera Soto
Colima	1. *Socorro Díaz Palacios*	Ramón Carrillo Ramírez
	2. Juan Mesina Alatorre	J. Jesús Caballero G.
Distrito Federal	1. Jaime Aviña Zepeda	Miguel García Colorado
	2. *Onofre Hernández Rivera*	Eugenio Albuerne Piña
	3. Juan F. Díaz Aguirre	Rogelio Zamora Barradas
	4. Jesús Anlen López	Gustavo D. Morales
	5. Ramón Choreño Sánchez	María E. Corona Marín
	6. Sara Villalpando	Luis F. Canudas
	7. Jaime Fernández Sánchez	Gabriel Vázquez Jiménez
	8. Ignacio López Tarso	Manuel Sosa Acosta
	9.	
	10. Jorge Gómez Villarreal	Juan A. Preza
	11. José Humberto Aguilar	Jaime Mariano del Río
	12. Fernando Sologuren Bautista	Arturo Villaroel
	13. *Hilda Anderson Nevares*	Aarón Elí Herrera
	14. Serafín Ramírez Ramírez	Carlos A. Arce
	15. Pedro Alberto Salazar	José A. Barrera
	16. Arturo Ocampo Villalobos	Héctor Gonzáez Reza
	17. José Luis Luego Tamargo	José Félix Manzano
	18. María C. Esqueda Llanes	Víctor M. Guevara
	19. Eleazar F. Cervantes Medina	Rogelio Rosas Nolasco
	20. Sóstenes Melgarejo Eraga	Gabriel Llamas Mougardín

	21. Víctor M. Sarabia Luna	Héctor F. Ortega P.
	22. María del R. Guerra Díaz	Gilberto Hernández
	23. Esther Kolteniuk Toyber	J. Juan López Durán
	24. *Guillermo Jiménez Morales*	Francisco J. Aguirre
	25. Demetrio Javier Sodi	Alberto Nava Salgado
	26. Jorge F. Schiaffino Isunza	Armando Jurado Alarid
	27. Juan J. Hernández Trejo	Oscar E. Hernández
	28. Adolfo Barrientos Parra	José de Jesús Herce
	29. *Guillermo Islas Olguín*	Maria G. Bojorges
	30. *Mario Vargas Saldaña*	Isaías Miranda Romero
	31. José L. Salfonso Sampayo	Víctor M. Palacios
	32. Joaquín Alvarez y Ordoñez	Saúl Molina Montes
	33. Carlos Martín Jiménez	Jaime Luis Morett
	34. *Juan José Osorio Palacios*	José A. Femat Flores
	35. José I. Cuauhtémoc Paleta	Gabriel Guerra
	36. Federico Ruiz López	Ernesto Salas Tejeida
	37. Miguel Aroche Parra	Ignacio Avila Campos
	38. *Marcela Lombardo Gutiérrez*	Justino Barrios
	39. *Luis A. Medina Peña*	María E. Silva
	40. Alvaro Garcés Rojas	Luis C. Delgadillo
Durango	1. Joaquín Garduño Vargas	Gabriela Irma Avelar
	2. J. Natividad Ibarra	Severo Barraza
	3. Rubén Hernández Higuera	Martín Silvestre
	4. María A. Barbosa Espinosa	Roberto Retana
	5. Jesús Leodegario Soto	Javier Covarrubias
	6. Lázaro Pasillas Rodríguez	Juan M. Calderón
Guanajuato	1. *Miguel Montes García*	Luis A. Muñoz
	2. Elías Villegas Torres	Francisco J. Fonseca
	3. Vicente Fox Quezada	Héctor Ortiz Martínez
	4. Antonio del Río Abaunza	Arnulfo Hinojosa
	5. Rubén García Farías	José L. Padilla
	6. *Gilberto Muñoz Mosqueda*	José González Ramírez
	7. Alvaro Uribe y Salas	Luis A. Tinajero
	8. Guillermo Nieto Almeida	Simitrio Celedón
	9. María E. Valiente Govea	María C. Escobedo
	10. Everardo Vargas Zavala	Wolstano Franco
	11. José Pedro Gama Medina	Francisco Martín Valdez
	12. Jorge García Henaine	Víctor M. Martínez
	13. María del C. Moreno	David López Espitia
Guerrero	1. *Carlos J. Vega Memije*	David Guzmán Maldonado
	2. Filiberto Vigueras Lázaro	Felipe Cardona Marino
	3. Valdemar Soto Jaimes	Angel Pérez Palacios
	4. *Guadalupe Gómez Maganda*	Ricardo Morlet
	5. Blas Vergara Aguilar	Javier A. Jiménez

	6. Juan Albarrán Castañeda	Salvio Herrera
	7. Pedro Lagunas Román	Miguel Terrazas
	8. Jaime Castrejón Díez	Hilario C. Flores
	9. María Inés Solís González	Eladio Palacios
	10. *Rubén Figueroa Alcocer*	Juan Muñoz Caballero
Hidalgo	1. Esthela Rojas de Soto	Justino H. Mercado
	2. Alberto Assad Avila	Isaías Vera Avelino
	3. César H. Vieyra Salgado	María G. Silva
	4. Orlando Arvizu Lara	Víctor Azuara
	5. J. Gregorio Bonilla Chávez	Prisciliano Gutiérrez
	6. Rodolfo Ruiz y Pérez	Ismael León Viveros
Jalisco	1. Blanca Leticia Escoto	Ivette Henry
	2. José A. Chávez Martínez	Carlos F. Arias
	3. Silviano Urzua Ochoa	Efrén Atilano López
	4. María del C. Mercado Chávez	Amador González
	5. Héctor A. Ixtlahuac Gaspar	Javier Avila Mares
	6. Julián Orozco González	Víctor M. Alba
	7. Juan Enrique Ibarra Pedroza	Alfonso Gutiérrez
	8. Margarita Gómez Juárez	Alfredo Becerra
	9. Francisco Galindo Mesa	Francisco J. Moya
	10. Francisco J. Santillán	María Esther Fletes
	11. Ismael Orozco Loreto	Francisco Espinosa
	12. Ramiro Hernández García	Máximo Martínez A.
	13. César Coll Carabias	María C. Solórzano
	14. Jose M. Martínez Aguirre	Herbert Taylor
	15. Gregorio Curiel Díaz	Paulino López Leaño
	16. Jesús Oscar Navarro Gárate	José Luis Ayala
	17. Sofía Valencia Abundis	Benito Villagómez
	18. Antonio Alvarez Esparza	Jorge Linares G.
	19. Oscar Chacón Iñiguez	José de J. Ramírez
	20. Raúl O. Espinoza Martínez	Catalino González
México	1. Sara Esthela Velázquez	Ceclia E. López
	2. Héctor Jarquín Hernández	*Oscar Espinosa Villarreal*
	3. Octavio Moreno Toscano	Bernabé Valdez Ceijas
	4. Agustín Gasca Pliego	Enrique R. Gómez
	5. Jaime Almazán Delgado	Arturo Osornio Sánchez
	6. Francisco Javier Santos	Ricardo Martínez
	7. Luis Martínez Souberville	Roberto Flores G.
	8. Alfonso Alcocer Velázquez	Manuel Sandoval
	9. Rafael P. Garay Cornejo	Aurelio Salinas
	10. José Luis Salcedo Solís	Gabino Román Calles
	11. Javier Gaeta Vázquez	Félix García Hernández
	12. Fernando A. García Cuevas	Francisco Tello
	13. *Carlos Real Encinas*	Reyes A. Silva
	14. José de J. Miramontes	Mireya Mondragón

	15. Martha P. Rivera Pérez	Carlos Vargas G.
	16. Jesús de la Cruz Martínez	José Luis Chávez
	17. Fernando Barrera Velázquez	Virgilio Vélez T.
	18. *Astolfo Vicencio Tovar*	Raúl Durán Domínguez
	19. *Mario Ruiz de Chávez*	Luis Mayén Ruiz
	20. José Ruiz González	Javier L. Chávez
	21. Cecilio Barrera Reyes	Juan Pascual Ramos
	22. Francisco J. López González	Florencio Catalán
	23. Enrique Riva Palacio	Rodrigo Rangel G.
	24. J. Jesús Ixta Cerna	Fernando Padilla R.
	25. Delfino Ronquillo Nava	Miguel Rodríguez R.
	26. Maurilio Hernández González	Gerardo Dorantes
	27. Mauricio Valdés Rodríguez	José Avalos Zuppa
	28. Teresa Navarro y Ramírez	Manuel Cañedo Arce
	29. Guadalupe M. García Rivas	Perfecto Martínez
	30. Isaac Bueno Soria	Francisco Hernández
	31. Cuauhtémoc Anda Gutiérrez	Sara Cruz Olvera
	32. Margarita Sánchez Gavito	Silvano Rivera L.
	33. Ruth Olvera Nieto	Alvaro Ramírez Chávez
	34. Juan Ugarte Cortés	Pascual F. Camacho
Michoacán	1. Octavio Ortiz Melgarejo	Angel Bravo Cisneros
	2. Humberto Urquiza Marín	Ignacio Ocampo
	3. Carolina Escudero	J. de Jesús Bautista
	4. Alfredo Torres Robledo	Enrique Aguiñaga
	5. Rodolfo Paniagua Alvarez	Javier Ríos Ramírez
	6. Francisco Kuri Pérez	Antonio Luguna
	7. Roberto Garibay Ochoa	Juan Torres Martínez
	8. Hiram Rivera Teja	Pablo Cruz Parra
	9. Raúl Reyes Ramírez	Marcelo Valencia
	10. Vicente L. Coca Alvarez	María M. Terrazas
	11. Pablo García Figueroa	Onofre Vázquez
	12. Isidro Aguilera Ortiz	Sergio González C.
	13. Rafael Melgoza Radillo	Manuel Santamaría
Morelos	1. Mario Rojas Alba	Alejandro Díaz J.
	2. Saturnino Solano Pérez	Ignacio Guerra T.
	3. Carlos E. Sánchez Mendoza	Luciano Domínguez
	4. Pablo Torres Chávez	Otilio Rivera Navarro
Nayarit	1. *Salvador Sánchez Vázquez*	Jorge Verdín López
	2. Ignacio González Barragán	Arturo Calderón
	3. Olga López Castillo	Rafael Mascorro Toro
Nuevo León	1. Benjamín Clariond Reyes	Juan J. Belmares
	2. Luis H. Hinojosa Ochoa	Silvia Mirella G.

	3. Felipe Onofre Zambrano	César Flores Garza
	4. Agustín Serna Servín	Ramiro Guerra
	5. Eleazar Bazaldúa Bazaldúa	Trinidad García R.
	6. Napoleón Cantú Cerna	Javier A. Solís
	7. Ismael Garza T. González	Fernando Sánchez L.
	8. Rosalío Elías Zúñiga	Miriam Garza Hernández
	9. María E. Chapa Hernández	Francisco Plata G.
	10. Yolanda M. García Treviño	Humberto González
	11. *Raúl Caballero Escamilla*	Israel Rojas Galván
Oaxaca	1. *José Murat Casab*	Darbien S. Rasgado
	2. Artemio Meixuéiro	Hipólito Splinker
	3. *Raúl Bolaños Cacho Guzmán*	Alvaro Jiménez Soriano
	4. Juan José Moreno Sada	Juan Sosa Benítez
	5. *Diódoro Carrasco Palacios*	Alfonso Terán García
	6. Eloy Argos García Aguilar	Alejandro León M.
	7. María T. Chagoya Méndez	Serafín Cruz Santiago
	8. Cirila Sánchez Mendoza	Moisés M. Toscano
	9. Jorge González Ilescas	Heladio F. Ordaz Luna
	10. Jorge Camacho Cabrera	José L. Vázquez
Puebla	1. Carlos V. M. Carreto	Oscar Lerín Martínez
	2. Carlos E. Grajales Salas	América Soto López
	3. César Alfonso Neri Avila	Octaviano A. Mino
	4. Serafín Sánchez Campos	Alfonso Domínguez L.
	5. Cupertino Alejo Domínguez	Celso Delgado Farcier
	6. Eillebaldo García de la C.	Adolfo Gil García
	7. Francisco Salas Hernández	Ramón Meza Báez
	8. Ricardo Mendizábal Bando	Rafael Landa
	9. Alejandro Paredes Jurado	Serafín Soto Espinoza
	10. Narcisco A. Amador Leal	Valdemar Cabrera
	11. Miguel A. Quiroz Pérez	María Lucero Saldaña
	12. Marco A. Rojas Flores	Sergio F. Reguero
	13. Amado Roberto Moreno Nava	Pascual M. Alamirra
	14. María de los A. Moreno B.	Sebastián G. Centeño
Querétaro	1. María E. Martínez Carranza	José L. Aguilera
	2. Octaviano Camargo Rojas	J. Jesús Llamas
	3. Benjamín E. Rocha Pedraza	Martha Prado Ugalde
Quintana Roo	1. Elina Elfi Coral Castilla	Agustín Mata González Patrón
	2. Isidoro V. Mendoza de la C.	Daniel Cuxim Pech

San Luis Potosí	1. Guillermo Delgado Robles	Marco A. Navarro
	2. José G. Vega Macías	Ma. del Socorro Vázquez
	3. Emilio de J. Ramírez G.	Juan Miranda Uresti
	4. Miguel Martínez Castro	Hugo Ariel Acuña
	5. Fructuoso López Cárdenas	Abel Vázquez Castillo
	6. *Gonzalo Martínez Corbalá*	Juana González Ortiz
	7. Rebeca Guevara de Terán	Julio D. Domínguez
Sinaloa	1. Ramón Alejo Valdez	Mario O. Zamora
	2. Juan Burgos Pinto	José J. Armenta
	3. Jorge del Rincón Bernal	Mercedes Murillo
	4. Juan Rodolfo López Monroy	Roberto López García
	5. Martín Gavica Garduño	Jorge A. López
	6. María Eduwiges Vega Padilla	Pedro R. Peña
	7. David Miranda Valdez	Miguel Sotelo Burgos
	8. Jesús A. Aguilar Padilla	José L. Malverde
	9. Pablo Moreno Cota	María D. Galindo
Sonora	1. Armando López Nogales	Elías A. Freig
	2. Manuel Robles Linares	Elizabeth Estrada
	3. José I. Martínez Tadeo	José Flores Orduño
	4. Juan M. Verdugo Rosas	Ernesto J. Talamante
	5. Víctor H. Celaya Celaya	María C. Bejarano
	6. Sergio J. Torres Serrano	José R. Moreno
	7. Ramiro Valdez Fontes	Manuel Martínez M.
Tabasco	1. Gustavo Rosario Torres	Yolanda del C. Osuna
	2. Darvín González Ballina	Julio César Pérez
	3. Joaquín Ruiz Becerra	José A. Pedrero
	4. Zoila Victoria León	Fernando Morales M.
	5. Freddy Chable Torno	Carlos M. Rovirosa
Tamaulipas	1. Enrique Leobardo Reséndez	Arnulfo Tejeda Lara
	2. Jorge Constantino Barba I.	José Elías Leal
	3. Miguel Treviño Emparan	Mauro P. Longoría
	4. Jaime Rodríguez Inurrigarro	Jacobo de León
	5. Alvaro H. Garza Cantú	Juana Elda Mellado
	6. Julián Murillo Navarro	Honorio Olvera B.
	7. Bernardino Canchola H.	Saturnino Méndez
	8. *Manuel Cavazos Lerma*	Gilberto Aguilar B.
	9. Raúl García Leal	Marcelo Salazar G.
Tlaxcala	1. Félix Pérez Amador	Nely M. Ramírez M.
	2. Jesús Pelcastre Rojas	J. Pascual Grande

Veracruz
1. Carlos Herrera Rodríguez   Juan C. Céspedes
2. Graciela P. Gómez   Francisco Bautista
   Rodríguez
3. Vicente Sequera Mercado   Luis Sánchez Gómez
4. Edmundo Martínez Zaleta   Florencio Azúa Gallegos
5. Gustavo Moreno   Fernando Ortega H.
6. Ricardo Olivares Pineda   Carmelo Flandes A.
7. Dionisio E. Pérez Jácome   Fernando López V.
8. Fernando Córdoba Lobo   Guillermo E. Loera
9. Alberto Andrade Rodríguez   José E. Cruz Arellano
10. Adalberto Díaz Jácome   Enrique Ramos Rodríguez
11. Rodolfo Duarte Rivas   Enrique Levet Orozpe
12. Gilberto Uscanga Medina   Ambrosio Paz Valle
13. Humberto Peña Reyes   Angel Gutiérrez C.
14. Vicente Torres Ruíz   Tomás D. Hernández
15. Marco A. Castellanos   Carlos Pérez Carballo
16. Nicodemus Santos Luck   Frumencio Ochoa
17. Antonio Cruz Sánchez   Rafael Guzmán Osorio
18. Francisco Sánchez   Balfrén Gonález M.
    Rodríguez
19. Luis A. Pérez Fraga   Guillermo de la Rosa
20. Jorge Sierra Gallarado   Adán Lozano Meza
21. Américo J. Flores Nava   Armando López Rosado
22. Susana Torres Hernández   Pedro G. Rivera
23. Rosa E. Guízar Villa   Elidoro Merlín Alor

Yucatán
1. Ana Rosa Payán Cervera   Miguel A. Díaz H.
2. Carlos R. Calderón Cecilio   Irma M. López Godoy
3. Noé A. Peniche Patrón   Raymundo E. Bobadilla
4. Eric L. Rubio Barthell   Alonso de J. Pereira

Zacatecas
1. Julián Ibarguengoytia   Bertha Torres Valdés
2. Ricardo Monreal Avila   Antonio Ramos M.
3. Victorio de la Torre   José Flores Basurto
4. Carlos Pavón Campos   Celestino Tobanche
5. José M. Ríos Núñez   Guillermo Ulloa C.

Plurinominal Deputies (PAN)

Pedro César Acosta Palomino   Alfredo M. Arenas Rodríguez
Carlos M. Aguilar Camargo   Eduardo Arias Aparicio
Noé Aguilar Tinajero   *Bernardo Bátiz Vázquez*
Miguel Angel Almaguer Zárate   Jesús Bravo Cid de León
Donaciano Amrbosio Velasco   José F. Bueno Carrera
Gerardo de J. Arellano Aguilar   Francisco de J. Cabrera
Luisa Calderón Hinojosa   Roger Cicero MacKinney
Constantino Cirilio Palacios   Eleazar G. Cobos Borrego
Carlos E. Castillo Peraza   María T. Cortés Cervantes
Luis A. Delgado Esteva   Rodolfo Elizondo Torres

Alejandro Díaz Pérez Duarte
Matías S. Fernández Gavaldón
José A. Gándara Terrazas
José González Morfín
Víctor Guerrero González
Miguel Hernández Labastida
José Herrera Reyes
Jorge A. Ling Altamirano
José A. Luna Mijares
Enrique Martínez Hinojosa
Gerardo Medina Valdez
Juan J. Medrano Castillo
Eugenio Ortiz Walls
Teresa Ortuño Gurza
Manuel Ponce González
Américo A. Ramírez Rodríguez
María G. Rodríguez Carrera
Benito F. Rossell Isaac
Leopoldo H. Salinas Gaytán
José de J. Sánchez Ochoa
María del C. Segura Rangel
Astolfo Vicencio Tovar

Hiram Escudero Alvarez
José Zeferino Esquerra
Gildardo Gómez Verónica
Horacio González de las C.
Leobardo Gutiérrez G.
Magdaleno G. Gutiérrez
José N. Jiménez M.
Pedro R. López Alarid
Ramón Martín Huerta
Alonso Méndez Ramírez
José R. Medina Padilla
Ambrosio Montellano Bustos
Ruth Olvera Nieto
Ramiro Pedroza Torres
Ceferinio Ramos Nuño
Rosalía Ramírez
Mario A. Riojas
Jesús R. Rojo Gutiérrez
Espiridión Sánchez
María L. Sarre Navarro
Abel C. Vicencio Tovar
Gaudencio Vera Vera

Plurinominal Deputies (PRI)

Alberto J. Ahumada Padilla
Guerrero Chávez Herrera
Guillermo Garza Luna
Alfonso Garzón Santibáñez
Horacio Labastida Muñoz
José Luis Lamadrid Sauza
Judith Murguía Corral
José de Jesús Pérez
Adalberto J. Porte Petit
Salvador Revueltas Olvera
Eleazar Ruiz Cerda
Eugenio Soto Medina
Hermenegildo Anguiano
Abraham Martínez Alvarez

Cecilio de la Cruz Pineda
Vicente Fuentes Díaz
Napoleón Gómez Sada
Andrés Henestrosa Morales
Luz Vargas Lajous
José T. Lanz Cárdenas
Augusto Ponce Coronado
Liborio Pérez Elorriaga
José H. Pulido García
Jaime Sabines Gutiérrez
Melchor de los Santos
Antonio Martínez Báez
Guillermo Castellanos

Plurinominal Deputies (PPS)

Belisario Aguilar Olvera
Modesto Cárdenas García
Jesús A. Carlos Hernández
Abigail Cruz Lázaro
María P. Hernández Oliva
Luis Jacobo García
Heray Lescieur Molina

Lauro Zepeda Seguro
Leonel Godoy Rangel
Héctor Colio Galindo
Tomás Gutiérrez Narváez
Armando Ibarra Garza
Julio Jácome López
Gregorio L. Domínguez

Jesús Luján Gutiérrez
José Marín Rebollo
Carmen Mercado Téllez
Crescencio Morales Orozco
Sergio Quiroz Miranda
Ernesto Rivera Herrera
Mario Vázquez Martínez
Cecilia Torres Chavarría
Nicolás Salazar Ramírez

Manuel Marcué Pardiñas
Herón Maya Anguiano
Félix Mercado Téllez
Francisco Ortiz Mendoza
Román Ramírez Contreras
Gloria Rodríguez Aceves
Jorge Martínez y A.
Alejandro Martínez C.

Plurinominal Deputies (PMS)

Rodolfo A. Armenta Scott
Amalia D. García Medina
Pablo Gómez Alvarez
Alberto Anaya Gutiérrez
Gerardo Avalos Lemus
Daniel López Nelio
Carlos Navarrete Ruiz
Patricia Olamendi Torres
José A. Ríos Rojo
Margarito Ruiz Hernández

Osiris S. Cantu
Marcos C. Cruz
Juan N. Guerra Ochoa
Virgilio Escamilla
Carlos E Bracho
Ciro Mayén Mayén
Jesús Ortega Martínez
Reynaldo Rosas Domínguez
José del C. Rosado

Plurinominal Deputies (PFCRN)

Rafael Aguilar Talamantes
Víctor M. Avalos Limón
José J. Enríquez Félix
Pedro R. Etienne Llano
Jesús A. Fernández Gardea
Armando Herrera Guzmán
Mariano Leyva Domínguez
Odón Madariaga Cruz
Catalino Mendoza Vázquez
Francisco Navarro Montenegro
Tomás Pedroza Esparza
Juan M. Rodríguez González
José E. Rojas Bernal
Alexander Santos Alvarez
Paula Vargas Florencio
Ignacio Castillo Mena
Manuel López Zorilla

José L. Alonso Sandoval
Francisco Chávez Alfaro
Armando Duarte Moller
Israel F. Galan Baños
Juana García Palomares
Roberto Jaramillo Flores
Pedro M. Cruz López
José N. Madrigal Gómez
José A. Montes V.
José M. Pelayo Lepe
Raúl F. Plascencia
Alfredo Pliego Aldana
Manuela Sánchez López
Gregorio Urias Germán
Rubén Venadero Valenzuela
Rommel Contreras Flores
Rosalio Wences Reza

Plurinominal Deputies (PARM)

Alberto Bernal González
Francisco Castañeda Ortiz
Humberto Esqueda Negrete

Leopoldo López Muñoz
María T. Dorantes Jaramillo
Manuel P. Estévez

Luis Gambino Heredia
Juan Jaime Hernández
Erasmo López Villarreal
Alfredo Monsreal Walkinshaw
José Pérez Fontecha
David Ramírez Márquez
Lorenzo Ruiz Gómez
Horacio Treviño Valdez
Rafael Yudico Colín
Teodoro Altmirano Robles

Ramón Garza Rodríguez
Ernesto A. Jiménez
José F. Melo Torres
Gilberto Ortiz Medina
Oscar M. Ramírez Ayala
Salvador Miranda Polanco
Lorenzo Treviño Santos
Ismael Yáñez Centeño
Héctor Beltrán Manriquez

1991-94 (55th Legislature)

State	Deputy	Alternate
Aguascalientes	1. Armando Romero Rosales	Marta Gallardo Topete
	2. Javier Rangel Hernández	Jorge H. González Martínez
Baja California	1. José Ramírez Román	René Arturo Gómez Michel
	2. José de Jesús González R.	Miguel Delfín Castro
	3. Rogelio Appel Chacón	Miguel Valadés Ríos
	4. Francisco J. Cital Camacho	Rigoberto Cárdenas Valdés
	5. Miguel E. Enciso Clark	Enrique G. Fernández Ortega
	6. Carlos Tomás Esparza	Juan Meneses Jiménez
Baja California Sur	1. Guillermo Mercado Romero	Yolanda Robinson Manríquez
	2. Mario Vargas Aguilar	Juan Hernández Villanueva
Campeche	1. Luis Alberto Fuentes Mena	Alejandra Ramírez Romero
	2. Francisco Puga Ramayo	Mario A. Berlin Mijangos
Coahuila	1. Oscar Pimentel González	Jesús Santos Méndez
	2. Francisco José Dávila	Sanjuana Martínez Cortinas
	3. Fidel Hernández Puente	Ana P. Ramos de los Santos
	4. Jesús M. Ramón Valdez	Irma Elizondo Ramírez
	5. Gaspar Valdez Valdez	Ascención Montelongo González
	6. Mariano López Mercado	Irma Mayela Adame Aguayo
	7. Javier Guerrero García	Jesús Alberto Pader Villareal
Colima	1. Rigoberto Salazar Velasco	Guillermo Torres Hernández
	2. Graciela Larios Rivas	Raúl Macías Villaseñor
Chiapas	1. Antonio García Sánchez	Dora Fanny León Narcía
	2. Cuauhtémoc López Sánchez	Emilia González Arrazate
	3. Juan C. Bonifaz Trujillo	Alberto Sánchez López
	4. Orbelín Rodríguez Velasco	Valente Ordóñez Ruiz
	5. José A. Aguilar Bodegas	Jorge Rodríguez Casahonda
	6. Marlene C. Herrera Díaz	Alberto A. Rebora González

	7. Jorge F. Montesinos Melgar	Teresa Paniagua Jiménez Cruz
	8. Ricardo López Gómez	Roger de Coss Corzo
	9. Octavio Elías Albores Cruz	Aymir Moreno Solís
Chihuahua	1. Fernando Rodríguez Cerna	Marco A. Guevara García
	2. Edmundo Chacón Rodríguez	Gabriel H. Sepúlveda Reyes
	3. Carlos Morales Villalobos	Jesús Limón Alonso
	4. Oscar René Nieto Burciaga	Gerardo Hernández Ibarra
	5. Pablo I. Esparza Natividad	Gustavo López Ibarra
	6. Jaime Ríos Velasco Grajeda	Manuel A. Valenzuela Colomo
	7. Socorro Eloy Gómez Panda	Juan José Baca Herrera
	8. José L. Canales de la Vega	Artemisa Márquez Haro
	9. Luis C. Rentería Torres	Martín R. Payán Lugo
	10. Israel Beltrán Montes	Odorico Vázquez Bernal
Distrito Federal	1. José A. Ruiz de la Herrán	Raúl Marroquín Segura
	2. Rafael Peña Farrera	Socorro Gutiérrez Rejón
	3. *Gloria Brasdefer Hernández*	Irene Estrada Valente
	4. Domingo Alapizco Jiménez	Mario Alberto Pérez Manzo
	5. Filiberto Paniagua García	Leobardo Beltrán
	6. Marco A. Fajardo Martínez	María C. Serrano Morales
	7. Julio Alemán	Alicia Ramos Zepeda
	8. Fernando Lerdo de Tejada	Cristina Alcayaga
	9. Alfonso Sáinz de la Maza	Jorge García Rodríguez
	10. Manuel Solares Mendiola	René Chico Méndez
	11. José A. González Fernández	Esperanza Hernández Sánchez
	12. Roberto Castellanos Tovar	Rogelio Gasca Hernández
	13. Anibal Pacheco López	Manuel Manzo Ortega
	14. José G. Rodríguez Rivera	Alejo M. González
	15. Armando Lazcano Montoya	Juan Carlos Flores
	16. Paloma Villaseñor Vargas	Anastacio García
	17. Javier Garduño y Pérez	Ignacio Contreras
	18. Alfonso Godínez y López	Edgar Vázquez Iturbe
	19. Eduardo F. Trejo González	Enrique Tello
	20. Silvestre Fernández Barajas	Teresa Martínez Rodríguez
	21. *Everardo Gámiz Fernández*	Juan Manuel Lucia
	22. Juan José Castillo Mota	María Pia Castillo
	23. Alfonso Rivera Domínguez	Epifanio Rosales
	24. Alfredo Villegas Arreola	Sergio Amezcua
	25. Alberto Nava Salgado	Soledad Salazar
	26. Alberto Celís Velasco	Antonio Mora
	27. Silvia Piñal Hidalgo	Antonio Flores
	28. Luis Beltrán Salgado	Lucio Ibarra
	29. *Juan Moisés Calleja García*	Concepción Salinas

30. Benjamín González Roaro	José C. Solano
31. Manuel Jiménez Guzmán	Guadalupe León
32. *Rodolfo Ruiz Echeverría*	Gustavo Terrazo
33. Victoria Reyes Reyes	Mario Morales
34. Manuel Díaz Infante	Fernando F. Castro
35. Manuel Monarres Valenzuela	Luis Ordaz Marquez
36. Felipe de Jesús Muñoz	Patricia Roel Luna
37. Fernando Espino Arevalo	Raúl Tello Becerril
38. Amado Treviño Abatte	Ubaldo Poblete Cruz
39. *Salvador Quintero Robles*	Alberto Monterde
40. José Merino Castrejón	Joaquín Alvarado

Durango

1. Armando S. González	Carlos Miguel Guereca Díaz
2. José M. Castro Carrillo	María de la Luz Tovar Montelongo
3. Francisco Gamboa Herrera	Gabino Rutiaga Fierro
4. Benjamín Avila Guzmán	Ramón Martínez González
5. Gabriela Irma Avelar V.	Ismael A. Hernández Deraz
6. Jesús Molina Lozano	José Luis F. González Achem

Guanajuato

1. Francisco A. Arroyo Vieyra	Ricardo Azuela Espinoza
2. Alejandro Gutiérrez de V.	David Zúñiga Arenas
3. Luis Arturo B. Torres	Leticia Villegas Nava
4. Francisco J. Alvarado A.	José L. Rojas Navarro
5. Juvenal Medel	César G. Quezada Guerra
6. Ernesto Botello Martínez	J. Soledad Guevara Sánchez
7. Rafael Sánchez Leyva	Enrique Oliveros Jiménez
8. Mauricio Wolnitzer Clark	Francisco J. Ramírez Martínez
9. Juan I. Torreslanda García	Martha E. Tello Castillo
10. José Azanza Jiménez	J. Javier Castellanos Avalos
11. Luis Fernández Vega	Patricia M. A. Sánchez Junquera
12. José G. Enríquez Magaña	Miguel Zavala Alcantar
13. Martín Santos Gómez	Cecilia Novoa Guzmán

Guerrero

1. Florencio Salazar Adame	Jesús Herrera Vélez
2. Porfirio Camarena Castro	Antonio Cabrera Rivera
3. Hugo Arce Norato	Hesiquio Bravo Fernández
4. Fernando Navarrete M.	Mónica G. Leñero Alvarez
5. Juan José Castro Justo	Bonifacio F. Cruz Merino
6. Angel H. Aguirre Rivero	Andrés Manzano Añorve
7. *Gustavo N. Ojeda Delgado*	César J. Varela Blanco
8. Luis Taurino Jaime Castro	Antonio Díaz Salgado
9. Efraín Zúñiga Galeana	Pedro Magaña Ruiz
10. *Jesús Ramírez Guerrero*	Héctor Vicario Castrejón

Hidalgo

1. María de la Luz Guevara B.	Jorge Conde Gómez
2. José Guadarrama Márquez	María R. Llaca Colchado

Jalisco		
	3. *José E. Gil Elourduy*	Patricio E. Briseño Castillo
	4. Joel Guerrero Juárez	Jorge L. López del Castillo
	5. *Germán Corona y del Rosal*	Alejandro Rivera Cela
	6. Juan Carlos Alva Calderón	Hilario Aviles Lugo

Jalisco

1. Jorge Leobardo Lepe García — Guillermo Sánchez Arrellano
2. Francisco Ruiz Guerrero — Enrique Reyes Vizcarra
3. *Adalberto Gómez Rodríguez* — Samuel Romero Valle
4. *José Alberto Cortés García* — Armando Arciniega González
5. Samuel Fernández Avila — Francisco J. Púlido Alvarez
6. Juan A. Serrano González — Martín Lozano Villalobos
7. J. Socorro Velázquez H. — Martina Márquez Loza M.
8. Eliázer Ayala Rodríguez — Manuel Velázquez Gutiérrez
9. Enrique Chavero Ocampo — César Ramón López Jara
10. Alejandro Ontiveros Gómez — José A. Mata Bracamontes
11. Bertha O. González Rubio — Francisco J. Iñíguez García
12. Rafael González Pimienta — Alfredo Gómez Gómez
13. Juan J. Bañuelos Guardado — Mario Ramón Méndez López
14. José M. Correa Ceseña — Fernando Quirarte Gutíerrez
15. Raúl Juárez Valencia — Quintín Vázquez García
16. *María E. Scherman Leaño* — José de J. Ramírez Ornelas
17. Bernardo Gutíerrez Ochoa — Francisco J. Guizar Macías
18. Alfredo Barba Hernández — Joel González Ibarra
19. J. Jesús Núñez Regalado — Jorge Bernal Zepeda
20. Jesús Enrique Ramos Flores — Felipe Hernández Castro

México

1. Fernando R. Odorica Pérez — Hilario Salazar Cruz
2. Eduardo Lecanda y Lujambio — Jorge Espinoza Cruz
3. Armando Neyra Chávez — Tito Castillo González
4. Laura H. Pavón Jaramillo — Alfonso Gómez Aguirre
5. Crescencio Pérez Garduño — Carlos Castro Vilchis
6. Luis C. Riojas Guajardo — Armando Dorantes Montes
7. María E. Cásares Esquibel — Guillermo González Martínez
8. Roberto Ruiz Angeles — Jesús Genaro Arroyo García
9. Moisés Armenta Vega — Ernesto Aguilar Hernández
10. Cupertino Juárez Gutiérrez — Martín Márquez Sandoval
11. Rafael Maldonado V. — Noé Cadena Grajeda
12. Pablo Casas Jaime — Victor A. López Martínez
13. Antonio Huitrón Vera — Antonio Lara Vázquez
14. Amador Monroy Estrada — Pablo Bazáñes García
15. Felipe Medina Santos — Daniel Reyes Valencia
16. Arturo Montiel Rojas — Miguel A. Terrón Mendoza
17. Rodrigo A. Nieto Enríquez — Fidel Chávez Guzmán
18. Francisco Gárate Chapa — Alejandra Cuevas Núñez
19. Enrique A. Jacob Rocha — Rafael de Celis y Contreras
20. Roberto Soto Prieto — Carlos Embriz Gómez

21. Javier Barrios González   Fausto Antonio Urbán Velasco
22. Rafael G. Bernal Chávez   María del R. Ramírez Sánchez
23. Jaime Serrano Cedillo   Herlindo Miguel Urieta
24. Salomón Pérez Carrillo   Manuel Quezada Romero
25. José Benigno López Mateos   Ana María Pérez Serrano
26. Luis Pérez Díaz   J. Ascención Piña Patiño
27. Jorge René Flores y Solano   Hermilo Martínez Vega
28. José Salinas Navarro   Luis A. Contreras Salazar
29. Angel García Bravo   Juan Cruz Garfías
30. Sara Cruz Olvera   Isidoro Cruz Torres
31. Juan Adrián Ramírez García   Fernando Mendieta Acosta
32. José A. Torres Martínez   Guadalupe Mino Luna
33. Leodegario López Ramírez   José Luis Pedro Mondragón Paz
34. Fidel González Ramírez   José Modesto Ortiz Prado

Michoacán

1. Jorge Mendoza Alvarez   Beatriz Ontiveros Fernández
2. Julían Rodríguez Sesmas   Luis Quintana Pérez
3. José J. G. Flores Alonzo   Ezequiel Cruz Pérez
4. Eduardo Villaseñor Peña   Efraín Zavala Cisneros
5. Mariano Carreón Girón   J. Hugo Francisco Miranda Mora
6. Anacleto Mendoza Maldonado   Silvano Carbajal Fuentes
7. Hernán V. Pineda Arellano   Mario Cardona Mendoza
8. José A. Orihuela Barcenas   María de los A. Gaytán Contreras
9. Jaime Calleja Andrade   Abel Palominos Casillas
10. Carlos Avila Figueroa   Rubén Pérez Gallardo Ojeda
11. Alfredo Anaya Gudiño   Jorge Chavolla Espinoza
12. Medardo Méndez Alfaro   Victor Manuel Silva Tejeda
13. José F. Moreno Barragán   José Godoy Vargas

Morelos

1. Rodolfo Becerril Straffón   María Cristina Ríos Meraza
2. Julio Gómez Herrera   Clemente Raymundo Llera Peña
3. Tomás Osorio Aviles   Jorge R. R. Escalante Ferrer
4. Felipe Ocampo Ocampo   Luz Gómez Domínguez

Nayarit

1. Rigoberto Ochoa Zaragoza   Juan Alonso Romero
2. Víctor J. Canovas Moreno   Juan Jiménez Segura
3. José R. Navarro Quintero   José Luis Santana Pérez

Nuevo León

1. José R. Treviño Salinas   Felipe Enríquez Hernández
2. José Basaldúa González   Santiago Villareal Aguilar
3. Oscar F. Herrera y Hosking   Eloy Higinio Marroquín Garza
4. Juan Morales Salinas   Bernardino Serna González

	5. Jaime Rodríguez Calderón	José Belem Mendoza Guzmán
	6. *Arturo de la Garza G. Jr.*	Jaime de la Garza Guzmán
	7. Eloy Cantú Segovia	Armando Leal Ríos
	8. Gloria J. Mendiola Ochoa	Margarito Muñoz Garza
	9. Erasmo Garza Elizondo	Agustín F. de Asis Basave Benítez
	10. *Rogelio Villareal Garza*	Simitrio Javier Torres de la Peña
	11. Andrés Silva Alvarado	Juana María Martínez Galván
Oaxaca	1. Porfirio Montero Fuentes	Francisco Javier García López
	2. Vitálico Coheto Martínez	Rafael R. Bermúdez Santos
	3. *Jorge Iturribarría Bolaños*	Reveriano Andrés Chagoya Corres
	4. Antonio Sacre Ebrahim	Margarito Quintana Perdomo
	5. Armando D. Palacios García	Emilia García Guzmán
	6. Rafael S. Vera Cervantes	Mario Guadalupe Mendoza Chávez
	7. Antonia I. Piñeyro Arias	Rosalio Mendoza Cisneros
	8. Nahum I. Zorrilla Cuevas	Santiago Silverio Fernández
	9. Claudio M. Guerra López	Benjamín Hernández Silva
	10. Francisco Felipe Angel V.	Abel Camacho Villalobos
Puebla	1. Raúl Pardo Villafaña	Crescenciano España Morales
	2. Rafael Cañedo Benítez	Victor Emanuel Díaz Palacios
	3. *Julieta Mendivil Blanco*	José Luis Domínguez Bermudes
	4. Eleázar Camarillo Ochoa	Felipe Flores Mena
	5. José P. Alarcón Hernández	Fidencio Romero Tobón
	6. Marco A. Haddad Yunes	Luis Ascención Carrera
	7. Melquiades Morales Flores	María E. Rodríguez y Muñoz de C.
	8. Pedro Jaime Olivares	Felipe Ruiz Rojas
	9. Jorge R. Sánchez Juárez	María I. A. Muñoz Molina
	10. Alberto Jiménez Arroyo	Ardelio Vargas Fosado
	11. Eduardo Cué Morán	José Luis Pichón Rivera
	12. Guillermo Pacheco Púlido	Omar Alvarez Arronte
	13. David. S. Montesino Marín	Vicente Raúl Soriano Castillo
	14. Jesús Saravia Ordoñez	Darío Balderas Hernández
Querétaro	1. *Fernando Ortiz Arana*	José Domingo Olvera Cervantes
	2. Gil Mendoza Pichardo	Juan Aurelio Higuera Gómez
	3. J. Guadalupe Martínez M.	Juan José Montoto Rangel
Quintana Roo	1. Joaquín E. Hendricks Díaz	Nahum Fuentes Morales
	2. Sonia Magali Achach Solís	Sebastián Segundo Canul Tamayo

San Luis Potosí	1. Alfredo Lujambio y Rafols	Roberto Ramos Palomo
	2. Felipe Rodríguez Grimaldo	Leonides Martínez Martínez
	3. Jorge V. Mejía Tobías	Antonio Juárez Berrones
	4. Jesús M. del Valle F.	Julio Hernández López
	5. Antonio Esper Bujaidar	Juan Acosta Cerón
	6. Horacio Sánchez Unzueta	José Manuel Medellín Milán
	7. Felipe A. Torres Torres	Norberto L. Jonguitud Azuara
Sinaloa	1. Jesús O. Falomir Hernández	María Elena Torres Ruiz
	2. Alberto López Vargas	Ramiro Rojo López
	3. Humberto Gómez Campaña	Alicia Montaño Villalobos
	4. Juan S. Millán Lizarraga	Armando Zamora Canizalez
	5. Jesús A. Millán Trujillo	María Elisa Meza Rochín
	6. Manuel Valdez Sánchez	Manuel Angel López Castro
	7. Miguel Sotelo Burgos	Juan Bautista Camacho Rivera
	8. Eduardo Cristerna González	José Abel Camacho Calderón
	9. Víctor Gandarilla Carrasco	Eleázar Robledo Sicairos
Sonora	1. Guillermo Hopkins Gámez	Alejandro Silva Hurtado
	2. Ovidio Pereyra García	Ricardo Acedo Samaniego
	3. Julián Luzanilla Contreras	Francisco J. Villaseñor Maytorena
	4. Arsenio Duarte Murrieta	Manuel Horacio Vega Soto
	5. Luis Moreno Bustamante	Roberto Díaz Gallardo
	6. Víctor R. Burtón Trejo	Gilberto J. Gutiérrez Sánchez
	7. Miguel A. Murillo Aispuro	María del Rosario Oros Ibarra
Tabasco	1. *Roberto Madrazo Pintado*	Francisco A. Rabelo Cúpido
	2. Héctor Argüello López	María de Lourdes Bolívar Gorra
	3. Mario Rubicel Ross García	Juan Córdova Candelero
	4. Jesús M. Martínez de E.	María de los A. Frías Sánchez
	5. Gladys Ethel G. Cano Conde	Rubén Magaña Méndez
Tamaulipas	1. Horacio E. Garza Garza	Rubén Miranda Villalva
	2. Oscar Leubbert Gutérrez	José A. Gutiérrez García
	3. Tomás J. Yarrington R.	Benjamín J. López Aguirre
	4. Laura A. Garza Galindo	Isidro Ruiz Sandoval
	5. Ma. del C. Bolado del Real	María Doris Hernández Ochoa
	6. Jesús Suárez Mata	Manuel Carrillo Chávez
	7. Manuel Muñoz Rocha	María Adelaida de la C. Moreno
	8. Hugo A. Araujo de la Torre	Ernesto Rodríguez Garza
	9. Arturo H. Saavedra Sánchez	Javier Villareal Salazar

Tlaxcala	1. Héctor Israel Ortiz Ortiz	Eligio Chamorro Vázquez
	2. Alvaro Salazar Lozano	José G. S. Pintor Castillo
Veracruz	1. Gustavo Gámez Pérez	Pedro Muñoz Pérez
	2. José Manuel Pozos Castro	Ezequiel Castañeda Nevárez
	3. Edmundo Sosa López	Fermín Ceballos Torres
	4. Arturo Nájera Fuentes	Irma Reyes Palomino
	5. Celestino M. Ortiz Denetro	María Magdalena Marín Aguirre
	6. Rubén Pabello Rojas	Maria de Lourdes Ramírez Cárdenas
	7. Salvador Valencia Carmona	Conrado Rafael Arenas Contreras
	8. Miguel A. Yunes Linares	Noemi Zoila Guzmán Lagunes
	9. Isaías A. Rodríguez Vivas	Raúl Vázquez Santos
	10. Juan Antonio Nemi Dib	Virginia Rodríguez Villanueva
	11. Guillermo J. González Díaz	Rafael Gutiérrez Cristo
	12. *Fidel Herrera Beltrán*	Manuel Santos Pérez
	13. Jorge Uscanga Escobar	Omar Manzur Asad
	14. Pablo Pavón Vinales	Daniel Cárdenas Barajas
	15. Fernando A. Charleston S.	Adrián Grijalva Ramos
	16. Guillermo Díaz Gea	Oscar Rolando Ricardi García
	17. Rufino Saucedo Márquez	María Ignacia Larios Pazarán
	18. Juan Bustillos Montalvo	Pedro Martín Turrubiates Martínez
	19. Froylan Ramírez Lara	Pablo A. Llaguno Cabañas
	20. Ignacia García López	José Luis Olguín Martínez
	21. Ramón Ferrari Pardiño	Rosa María Somohano Hernández
	22. *Gustavo Carvajal Moreno*	Angel Torres Málaga
	23. Luis A. Beauregard Rivas	Rafael Merlín Alor
Yucatán	1. Luis Humberto Correa Mena	Rafael Alberto Castilla Peniche
	2. Fernando Romero Ayuso	Carlos Daniel Salomón y Barbosa
	3. José Feliciano Moo y Can	Ruyluz Alcocer Rosado
	4. José I. Menducuti Pavón	Rubén Higinio Rodríguez y Moguel
Zacatecas	1. José M. A. Olvera Acevedo	Milagros del C. Hernández Muñoz
	2. José E. Bonilla Robles	Miguel Rocha Wiver
	3. Pedro de León Sánchez	Antonio Sandoval Luna
	4. Celestino Tobanche Alonso	Samuel Delgado Díaz
	5. José Escobedo Domínguez	Roberto Luévano Silva

Plurinominal Deputies (PAN)

Diego Fernández de Cevallos
Francisco José Paoli Bolio
Luis González Pintor
Gonzalo Altamirano Dimas
Felipe de Jesús Calderón Hinojosa
Salvador Abascal Carranza
Diego Heriberto Zavala Pérez
Alfredo Ling Altamirano
Juan de Dios Castro Lozano
Rubén Raymundo Gómez Ramírez
Humberto Pedro Flores Cuéllar
Francisco Javier Salazar Saenz
Sergio César Alejandro Jáuregui Robles
Lucás Adrián del Arenal Pérez
María Cristina Hermosillo Ramírez
Andrés Barba Barba
J. Benigno Aladro Fernández
José Antonio Alba Galván
Hiram Luis de León Rodríguez
Daniel de la Garza Gutiérrez
Pablo Emilio Madero Belden
Luis Humberto Correa Mena
Fernando Lugo Hernández
Arturo Núñez Pardo
Juan Huesca Pérez
Fernando Estrada Sámano
Luisa Urrecha Beltrán
José G. Tarcisio Rodríguez Martínez
Quinardo Meléndrez Montijo
Germán Alberto Petersen Biester
Marco Antonio García Toro
María Guadalupe Salinas Aguila
Julio Eustaquio López Valenzuela
Pedro Macías de Lara
Luis Felipe Bravo Mena
José Luis Durán Reveles
Salvador López Sánchez
Concepción Rosas de la Luz
José Luis del Valle Adame
Salomón Miranda Jaimes

Ana Teresa Aranda Orozco
Victor Martín Orduña Muñoz
José A. Gómez Urquiza de la M.
Fauzi Hamdan Amad
Marco Humberto Aguilar Coronado
Fernando F. Gómez Mont Urueta
Emilio Badillo Valseca
Gilberto Zapata Frayre
Jorge Zermeño Infante
José de Jesús Rafael Puga Tovar
Victor Manuel Martínes Fourcans
Napoleón Gallardo Ledesma
Alberto Miguel Martínez Mireles
Joel Arce Pantoja
Manuel Rivera del Campo
Jorge Sánchez Muñoz
Patricia Alina Terrazas Allen
Eduardo Constantino Torres Campos
Lydia Madero García
Hugo Sergio Palacios Laguna
Gonzalo Guajardo Hernández
Luis Silverio Suárez Ancona
Luis Alberto Rejón Peraza
Arturo Fuentes Benavídez
Enrique Gabriel Jiménez Remus
Raúl Velasco Gómez
Rafael Gilberto Morgan Alvarez
Esteban Zamora Camacho
José Guillermo Orendaín Guerrero
Arnuflo Vázquez Ramírez
Diego Velázquez Duarte
Juan Luis Calderón Hinojosa
Roderico Tapia Ruiz
Héctor Pérez Plazola
Juan Enrique Caballero Peraza
José Raúl Hernández Avila
Francisco Aguilar Salinas
Alfredo Castillo Colmenares
Joaquín Martínez Gallardo

Plurinominal Deputies (PRI)

Pedro Ojeda Paullada
Miguel Angel Sáenz Garza
Ramón Mota
Carlos Antonio Romero Deschamps

María de los A. Moreno Uriegas
Angel Aceves Saucedo
José M. González Avelar
Leonel Reyes Castro

Jaime Luis Dantón Rodríguez
Lorenzo Duarte García
Sebastían Guzmán Cabrera
Manuel Garza González
Juan José Rodríguez Prats
José Antonio Valdivia
José Fausto de los Palos Solana
Eduardo Rafael Aviña Batiz
Abraham Talavera López
Félix Miguel Osorio Marbán
Trinidad Reyes Alcaras

Juan Ramiro Robledo Ruiz
César Augusto Santiago Ramírez
Blanca Ruth Esponda Espinosa
José Antonio González Curi
Layda Elena Sansores San Román
Amador Rodríguez Lozano
J. Jesús González Gortázar
Oscar Garzón Garate
Jaime Ignacio Muñoz y Domínguez
Enrique Sada Fernández
Cesareo Morales García

Plurinominal Deputies (PPS)

Cuauhtémoc Amezcua Dromundo
Héctor Ramírez Cuéllar
Héctor Morquecho Rivera
Heli Herrera Hernández
Rigoberto Arriaga Ruiz
Francisco Juárez Hernández

Gabriela Guerrero Oliveros
Hildebrando Gaytán Marquez
Jorge Tovar Montañez
Juan Gualberto Campos Vega
Martín Tavira Urióstegui
Juan Jacinto Cárdenas García

Plurinominal Deputies (PRD)

Oscar Ricardo Valero Recío Becerra
René Juvenal Bejarano Martínez
Evangelina Corona Cadena
Guillermo Flores Velasco
Martha Patricia Ruiz Anchondo
Emilio Becerra González
Raymundo Cárdenas Hernández
Elipidio Tovar de la Cruz
Manuel R. Huerta Ladrón de Guevara
Domingo Alberto Martínez Reséndiz
Miguel Cuitlahuac Vázquez Hidalgo
Carlos González Durán
Miguel Angel León Corrales
José Octaviano Alaniz Alaniz
Jesús Humberto Zazueta Aguilar
Alejandro Luévano Pérez
Othón Salazar Ramírez
Salomón Jara Cruz
Eloí Vázquez López
Josafat Arquimides García Castro
Luis Raúl Alvarez Garín

Gilberto Rincón Gallardo y Meltis
Francisco Javier Saucedo Pérez
Jorge Alfonso Calderón Salazar
José Martín del Campo Castañeda
Enrique Rico Arzate
Jorge Torres Castillo
Atalo Sandoval García
Liliana Flores Benavides
Jorge Modesto Moscoso Pedrero
Salvador Juárez García
Cristóbal Arias Solís
Martha Maldonado Zepeda
José Camilo Valenzuela
Juan Ramón López Tirado
Rosa Albina Garavito Elías
Alejandro Encinas Rodríguez
Julio César García Hernández
Guillermo Sánchez Nava
Juan Hernández Mercado
Rufino Rodríguez Cabrera

Plurinominal Deputies (PFCRN)

Nicolás Olivos Cuéllar
Javier Centeño Avila
José María Téllez Rincón
Teodulo Martínez Vergara
Abundio Ramírez Vázquez
Eberto Croda Rodríguez
Demetrio Hernández Pérez
José de Jesús Berrospe Díaz
José Ramos González
Alberto Marcos Carrillo Armenta
Odilón Cantú Domínguez
Demetrio Santiago Torres

Jorge Oceguera Galván
Rodolfo Toxtle Tlamani
Pedro Terrazas Guerrero
Israel González Arreguín
Rafael Fernández Tomás
Tomás González de Luna
Luisa Alvarez Cervantes
Rodolfo Barbosa Rodríguez
Félix Bautista Matías
Tomás Correa Ayala
Juan Manuel Huezo Pelayo

Plurinominal Deputies (PARM)

Adolfo Alberto Kunz y Bolaños
Roberto García Acevedo
Yolanda Elizondo Maltos
Estanislao Pérez Hernández
Manuel Laborde Cruz
Francisco Felipe Laris Iturbide
Javier Marcelino Colorado Púlido
Gonzalo Cedillo Váldez

Alfredo Castañeda Andrade
Leonides Samuel Moreno Santillán
Carlos Enrique Cantú Rosas
Romeo Flores Leal
Servando Antonio Hernández
  Camacho
Cecilia Guadalupe Soto González
Francisco Dorantes Gutiérrez

Appendix D

Directors of Federal Departments, Agencies, and Banks, 1935–1992

Attorney General of Justice for the Federal District

Attorney General of Justice

Castellano Jiménez, Jr., Raúl	18 June 1935-31 Dec. 1937
Coutiño, Amador	4 Jan. 1938-11 Jan. 1940
Ornelas Villarreal, Antonio	12 Jan. 1940-14 June 1940
García, Luis G.	15 June 1940-30 Nov. 1940
Vejar Vázquez, Octavio	1 Dec. 1940-12 Sept. 1941
Castellanos, Francisco	12 Sept. 1941-30 Nov. 1946
Franco Sodi, Carlos	1 Dec. 1946-30 Nov. 1952
Aguilar y Maya, Guillermo	1 Dec. 1952-15 Oct. 1956
Acosta Fuentes, Ignacio	25 Oct. 1956-30 Nov. 1958
Román Lugo, Fernando	1 Dec. 1958-30 Nov. 1964
Suárez Torres, Gilberto	1 Dec. 1964-30 Nov. 1970
García Ramírez, Sergio	1 Dec. 1970-9 Aug. 1972
Zorrilla Martínez, Pedro	9 Aug. 1972-14 Dec. 1972
Castellanos Coutiño, Horacio	15 Dec. 1972-3 Mar. 1976
Narváez Angulo, Fernando	4 Mar. 1976-30 Nov. 1976
Alanís Fuentes, Agustín	1 Dec. 1976-30 Nov. 1982
Adato de Ibarra, Victoria	1 Dec. 1982-26 Dec. 1985
Sales Gasque, Renato	27 Dec. 1985-30 Nov. 1988
Morales Lechuga, Ignacio	30 Nov. 1988-June, 1991
Montes García, Miguel	June 1991-21 June 1992
Valadés Ríos, Diego	22 June, 1992-

Attorney General of the Republic

Attorney General

Guerrero, Silvestre	18 June 1935-25 Aug. 1936
Vázquez, Genaro V.	21 June 1937-30 Nov. 1940
Aguilar y Maya, José	1 Dec. 1940-30 Nov. 1946
González de la Vega, Francisco	1 Dec. 1946-30 Nov. 1952
Franco Sodi, Carlos	1 Dec. 1952-1955
Gutiérrez, José Luis	1955
Aguilar y Maya, José	29 Oct. 1955-30 Nov. 1958

López Arias, Fernando	1 Dec. 1958-1962
Treviño Ríos, Oscar	1962-30 Nov. 1964
Rocha, Antonio	1 Dec. 1964-1967
Sánchez Vargas, Julio	1967-Aug. 1971
Ojeda Paullada, Pedro	Aug. 1971-30 Nov. 1976
Flores Sánchez, Oscar	1 Dec. 1976-30 Nov. 1982
García Ramírez, Sergio	1 Dec. 1982-30 Nov. 1988
Alvarez del Castillo, Enrique	1 Dec 1988-June 1991
Morales Lechuga, Ignacio	June 1991-3 Jan. 1993
Carpizo, Jorge	4 Jan. 1993-

Assistant Attorney General

Santos Guajardo, Vicente	1934-21 June 1937
Ramírez Vázquez, Mariano	22 June 1937-30 Nov. 1940
Matos Escobedo, Rafael	Dec. 1946-1950
Canudas Orezza, Luis Felipe	1951-1952
Gutiérrez y Gutiérrez, José L.	Dec. 1952-30 Nov. 1958
Treviño Rios, Oscar	1 Dec. 1958-1962
Vacant	1962-1964
Franco Rodríguez, David	1 Dec. 1964-1973
Rosales Miranda, Manuel	1973-30 Nov. 1982
Baeza, Fernando	1 Dec. 1982-1986
García Domínguez, Miguel Angel	1986-1988
Polo Uscanaga, Abraham Antonio	1988-1991
González de la Vega, René José Angel	1991-

Assistant Attorney General (2)

Carvajal, Angel	Aug. 1936-24 Feb. 1944
Corrales Ayala, Rafael	Dec. 1946-1949
Canudas Orezza, Luis F.	1949-1951
Santoyo, Víctor Ramón	Dec. 1952-1957
Acosta, José Luis	1957-30 Nov. 1958
Suárez Torres, Gilberto	Dec. 1958-30 Nov. 1964
Acosta Romo, Fausto	Dec. 1964-1967
Sánchez Vargas, Julio	1967
Rosales Miranda, Manuel	1967-1973
Alba Leyva, Samuel	1 Jan. 1974-30 Nov. 1982
Porte Petit, Luis Octavio	1 Dec. 1982-1988
Reyes Tayaba, Jorge	1986-1988
Barreto Rangel, Gustavo	1988-1991
Andrade Sánchez, Eduardo	1991-

Bank of Mexico

Director General

Robles, Gonzalo	1935-30 Dec. 1935
Montes de Oca, Luis	31 Dec. 1935-6 Sept. 1940
Villaseñor Angeles, Eduardo	7 Sept. 1940-30 Nov. 1946

Novoa, Carlos	1 Dec. 1946-30 Nov. 1952
Gómez, Rodrigo	1 Dec. 1952-14 Aug. 1970
Fernández Hurtado, Ernesto	18 Sept. 1970-30 Nov. 1976
Romero Kolbeck, Gustavo	1 Dec. 1976-17 Mar. 1982
Mancera Aguayo, Miguel	18 Mar. 1982-2 Sept. 1982
Tello Macías, Carlos	2 Sept. 1982-30 Nov. 1982
Mancera Aguayo, Miguel	1 Dec. 1982-1 Dec. 1988
Mancera Aguayo, Miguel	1 Dec. 1988-

Subdirector General (1)

Espinosa Porset, Ernesto	1938-1970
Bello, Daniel J.	1971-1976
Solís, Leopoldo	1976-1985
Borja Martínez, Francisco	1985-

Department of the Air Force

Chief

Fierro, Roberto	1935-36
Rojas Razo, Samuel C.	1937-38
Salinas Carranza, Alberto	1939-40
Fierro, Roberto	1940-41
	1941-46
Cárdenas Rodríguez, Antonio	1946-52
Viétiz y V., Alberto	1952-54
Cruz Rivera, Alfonso	1954-59
Fierro, Roberto	1959-64
Vergara, Jose C.	1964-70
Salido Beltrán, Roberto	1970-76
Berthier Aguiluz, Héctor	1976-82
Mendoza Marquez, Miguel	1982-88
Acosta Jiménez, Fermín	1988-91
Ahuja Fuster, Héctor Vicente	1991-

Department of the Federal District

Head

Hinojosa, Cosme	18 June 1935-3 Jan. 1938
Siurob, José	4 Jan. 1938-23 Jan. 1939
Castellano, Raúl	24 Jan. 1939-30 Nov. 1940
Rojo Gómez, Javier	1 Dec. 1940-30 Nov. 1946
Casas Alemán, Fernando	1 Dec. 1946-30 Nov. 1952
Uruchurtu, Ernesto P.	1 Dec. 1952-14 Sept. 1966
Corona del Rosal, Alfonso	21 Sept. 1966-30 Nov. 1970
Martínez Domínguez, Alfonso	1 Dec. 1970-14 June 1971
Sentíes, Octavio	15 June 1971-30 Nov. 1976
Hank González, Carlos	1 Dec. 1976-30 Nov. 1982

Aguirre Velázquez, Ramón	1 Dec. 1982-30 Nov. 1988
Camacho Solís, Manuel	1 Dec. 1988-29 Nov. 1993
Aguilera Gómez, Manuel	30 Nov. 1993-

Secretary General of Government (Secretary General "A", 1978-83; Secretary of Government, 1974-78; Secretary General 1935-73)

Villalobos Mayar, Antonio	1935-19 June 1937
Priani, Alfonso	1937-39
Corona, Gustavo	1939-30 Nov. 1940
Sánchez, Antonio	1 Dec. 1940-30 Nov. 1946
Carrillo Marcos, Alejandro	1 Dec. 1946-30 Nov. 1952
Cándano y García de la Mata, José	1 Dec. 1952-54
Quirasco, Antonio M.	4 June 1954-2 June 1956
García Torres, Arturo	16 Oct. 1956-23 Sept. 1966
González Guevara, Rodolfo	24 Sept. 1966-30 Nov. 1970
Hernández, Octavio A.	1 Dec. 1970-17 May 1979
Gurría Ordóñez, Manuel	30 May 1979-30 Nov. 1982
Maldonado Pereda, Juan	1 Dec. 1982-22 Mar. 1984
Moreno Rodríguez, Rodrigo	23 Mar. 1984-20 Oct. 1985
Cosío Vidaurri, Guillermo	21 Oct. 1985-30 Nov. 1988
Aguilera Gómez, Manuel	1 Dec. 1988-1991
Martínez Alvarez, Jesús	1991-23 June 1992
Ebrard Casaubon, Marcelo Luis	23 June 1992-

Secretary of Works and Services (Secretary General "C," 1970-73)

Reta Martínez, Carlos	1 Dec. 1970-Jan. 1973
Ríos Elizondo, Roberto	Jan. 1973-30 Nov. 1976
Gómez de Orozco, Alfonso	1 Dec. 1976-2 Jan. 1978
Valenzuela, Gilberto	2 Jan. 1978-27 Mar. 1979
Santa Ana, Cuauhtémoc	28 Mar. 1979-30 Nov. 1982
Guerrero Villalobos, Guillermo	1 Dec. 1982-4 Jan. 1984
Nissan Rover, Simón	5 Jan. 1984-1985
Noreña Casado, Francisco	1985-30 Nov. 1988
Ruiz Fernández, Daniel	1 Dec. 1988-

Secretary General of Planning and Evaluation (Secretary General (B) 1970-73; 1978-83)

González Blanco Garrido, José P.	1 Dec. 1970-1973
Gurría Ordóñez, Manuel	1978-29 May 1979
Mondragón Hidalgo, Gustavo	30 May 1979-30 Nov. 1982
González de Aragón, Arturo	1 Dec. 1982-30 Nov. 1988
Beristaín Iturbide, Javier	1991-

Secretary General (D) 1970-73

Ríos Elizondo, Roberto	1 Dec. 1970-73

Secretary General of Protection and Maintainance (1984)

Mota Sánchez, Ramón	1984-30 July 1986
Ramírez Garrido Abréu, José Domingo	31 July 1986-1988
Tapia Aceves, Santiago	1991-

Secretary General of Social Development (1984)

Bustani Hid, José	1984-1986
Solórzano, Carlos E.	15 May 1986-30 Nov. 1988
Moreno Toscano, Alejandra	1 Dec. 1988-

Secretary General of Metropolitan Coordination (1992)

Martínez Alvarez, Jesús	23 July 1992-

Oficial Mayor

Ruíz Cortines, Adolfo	1935-37
González Villarreal, Marciano	1937-38
González Herrejón, Carlos	1940-46
González Cárdenas, Antonio	1946-52
López Arias, Fernando	1952
García Torres, Arturo	1952-55
Aguilar Velasco, Fernando	1958-64
Coudurier, Luis	1964-66
Lerdo de Tejada, Guillermo	1966-70
Vista Altamirano, Fluvio	1970-71
Zorilla Martínez, Pedro	1971-72
Vega Alvarado, Renato	1972-75
Jiménez San Pedro, Manuel	1975-76
Garduño Villavicencio, Jesús	1976-82
Bustani Hid, José	1982-84
Solórzano, Carlos E.	1984-86
Espinosa Palacios, Lino	1986-88
Salcedo Aquino, Roberto	1988-

Department of Health (1930-43)

Head

Siurob, José	19 June 1935-4 Jan. 1938
Andrew Almazán, Leonides	17 Jan. 1938- 4 Aug. 1939
Siurob, José	5 Aug. 1939-30 Nov. 1940
Fernández Manero, Víctor	1 Dec. 1940-15 Oct. 1943

Federal Electric Commission

Director General

Páez Urquidi, Alejandro	1946-52
Ramírez Ulloa, Carlos	1952-58
Moreno Torres, Manuel	1958-64

Martínez Domínguez, Guillermo	1 Dec. 1964-30 Nov. 1970
Villarreal Caravantes, Guillermo	1 Dec. 1970-8 Aug. 1972
López Portillo, José	9 Aug. 1972-29 May 1973
Farrell, Arsenio	29 May 1973-30 Nov. 1976
Cervantes del Río, Hugo	1 Dec. 1976-12 July 1980
Escofet, Alberto	13 July 1980-30 Nov. 1982
Hiriart Balderama, Fernando	1 Dec. 1982-4 Mar. 1988
Eibeshutz, Juan	5 Mar. 1988-30 Nov. 1988
Guerrero Villalobos, Guillermo	1 Dec. 1988-

Federal Highways and Bridges and Adjacent Entrances and Exits (Federal Entry Roads)

Director General

Pedrero, Andrés	1958-July 1959
Cervantes del Río, Hugo	July 1959-May 1965
Patiño, Ernesto	May 1965-Oct. 1965
Sánchez Teruel, Jorge	Oct. 1965-Dec. 1970
Bernal, Antonio	Dec. 1970-30 Nov. 1976
Calderón, Héctor M.	1 Dec. 1976-30 Nov. 1982
Gutiérrez Barrios, Fernando	1 Dec. 1982-28 Apr. 1988
López Mendoza, Sergio	29 Apr. 1986-30 Nov. 1988
Martínez Villicaña, Luis	1 Dec 1988-3 Jan. 1993
Petricioli, Gustavo	4 Jan. 1993-

Institute of Insurance and Social Services for Federal Employees (1959) (Director General of Pensions and Retirement, 1925-58)

Director

Liekens, Enrique	1935-40
Manrique de Lara Hernández, A.	1940-45
Gamboa, Rafael P.	1945-46
García de Alba, Esteban	1946-52
Pizarro Suárez, Nicolás	1952-64
Sánchez Mireles, Rómulo	1964-70
Robledo Santiago, Edgar	1970-75
Sánchez Vázquez, Salvador	1975-76
Jongitud Barrios, Carlos	1976-79
Sansores Pérez, Carlos	1979-79
Riva Palacio, Carlos	1979-82
Carrillo Castro, Alejandro	1982-88
Lozoya Thalman, Emilio	1988-93
Martínez Corbalá, Gonzalo	1993-

Mexican Institute of Social Security (1943)

Director General

Santos Guajardo, Vicente	19 Jan. 1943-1 Jan. 1944
García Téllez, Ignacio	1 Jan. 1944-30 Nov. 1946
Díaz Lombardo, Antonio	1 Dec. 1946-30 Nov. 1952
Ortiz Mena, Antonio	1 Dec. 1952-30 Nov. 1958
Coquet Laguna, Benito	1 Dec. 1958-30 Nov. 1964
Alatriste, Sealtiel	1 Dec. 1964-25 Jan. 1966
Morones Prieto, Ignacio	26 Jan. 1966-30 Nov. 1970
Gálvez Betancourt, Carlos	1 Dec. 1970-26 Sept. 1975
Reyes Heroles, Jesús	27 Sept. 1975-30 Nov. 1976
Farrell, Arsenio	1 Dec. 1976-30 Nov. 1982
García Sáinz, Ricardo	1 Dec. 1982-30 Nov. 1988
García Sáinz, Ricardo	1 Dec. 1988-31 Dec. 1990
Gamboa, Emilio	1 Jan 1991-28 Apr. 1993
Borrego Estrada, Genaro	29 Apr. 1993-

Secretary General

García Cruz, Miguel	22 Jan. 1943-21 Dec. 1958
Orozco Uruchurtu, José Manuel	22 Dec. 1958-4 Jan. 1965
Alvarez del Castillo, Enrique	5 Jan. 1965-25 Apr. 1966
Muñoz Ledo, Porfirio	26 Apr. 1966-1 Dec. 1970
Vizcaíno Murray, Francisco	2 Dec. 1970-13 Dec. 1970
Ríos Elizondo, Roberto	14 Dec. 1970-26 Sept. 1971
López Faudoa, Eduardo	27 Sept. 1971-7 Dec. 1976
Zertuche Muñoz, Fernando	8 Dec. 1976-30 Nov. 1982
Fraga Mouret, Gabino	1 Dec. 1982-Apr 1985
Rabasa Gamboa, Emilio	1985-30 Nov. 1988
Doporto Ramírez, Héctor	1 Dec 1988-31 Dec 1990

Mexican Petroleum Company (Petróleos Mexicanos) (1938)

Director General

Cortés Herrera, Vicente	1938-40
Buenrostro Ochoa, Efraín	Dec. 1940-Nov. 1946
Bermúdez, Antonio J.	Dec. 1946-Nov. 1958
Gutiérrez Roldán, Pascual	Dec. 1958-Nov. 1964
Reyes Heroles, Jesús	Dec. 1964-Nov. 1970
Dovalí Jaime, Antonio	Dec. 1970-Nov. 1976
Díaz Serrano, Jorge	Dec. 1976-5 June 1982
Moctezuma Cid, Julio	6 June 1981-30 Nov. 1982
Beteta, Mario Ramón	1 Dec. 1982-Feb. 1987
Rojas Gutiérrez, Francisco José	1 Feb. 1987-30 Nov. 1988
Rojas Gutiérrez, Francisco José	1 Dec. 1988-

National Bank of Foreign Commerce (1937)

Director General

López, Roberto	16 May 1937-20 Jan. 1950
Parra Hernández, Enrique	21 Jan. 1950-8 Dec. 1952
Zevada, Ricardo José	9 Dec. 1952-1 Feb. 1965
Armendáriz, Antonio	2 Feb. 1965-11 Dec. 1970
Alcalá Quintero, Francisco	12 Dec. 1970-26 Apr. 1979
Lajous Martínez, Adrián	1979-30 Nov. 1982
Phillips Olmedo, Alfredo	1 Dec. 1982-30 Nov. 1988
Soto Rodríguez, Humberto	1 Dec. 1988-

National Company of Public Commodities CONASUPO (National Distributor and Regulator, 1941; Mexican Export-Import Company, 1949)

Director General

Trejo, Amado J.	1941-Aug. 1943
Ortiz Garza, Nazario S.	1943-46
Cinta, Carlos M.	1947
Ampudia, Eduardo	1950-52
Valles Vivar, Tomás	Dec. 1952-10 Mar. 1956
Vivanco, José S.	13 Mar. 1956-1958
Rodríguez Adame, Julián	1958
Amorós Guiot, Roberto	1 Dec. 1958-30 Nov. 1964
Hank González, Carlos	1 Dec. 1964-1969
Mondragón Hidalgo, Gustavo	1969-30 Nov. 1970
de la Vega Domínguez, Jorge	1970-11 Feb. 1976
Díaz Ballesteros, Enrique	12 Feb. 1976-30 Nov. 1976
González Cosío, Manuel	1 Dec. 1976-3 May 1979
Díaz Ballesteros, Enrique	4 May 1979-30 Nov. 1982
Costamalle, José E.	1 Dec. 1982-30 Nov. 1988
Ovalle Fernández, Ignacio	1 Dec. 1988-

National Finance Bank (Nacional Financiera)

Director General

Mesa Andraca, Manuel	1934-35
Espinosa de los Monteros, Antonio	1936-45
Carrillo Flores, Antonio	1945-52
Hernández Delgado, José	1 Dec. 1952-30 Nov. 1970
Martínez Domínguez, Guillermo	Dec. 1970-11 Jan. 1974
Romero Kolbeck, Gustavo	11 Jan. 1974-30 Nov. 1976
Ibarra, David	1 Dec. 1976-17 Nov. 1977
Espinosa de los Reyes, Jorge	23 Nov. 1977-30 Nov. 1982
Petricioli, Gustavo	1 Dec. 1982-1986
Marcos Giacomán, Ernesto	1986-30 Nov. 1988

Páramo Díaz, Juan José   1 Dec. 1988-1991
Espinosa Villarreal, Oscar   1991-

National Railroads of Mexico (1941)

General Manager
Hernández, Pablo Mario	1941-2 Jan. 1941
Estrada, Enrique	3 Jan. 1941-3 Nov. 1942
Ramírez, Margarito	4 Nov. 1942-16 Feb. 1944
Ortiz, Andrés	17 Feb. 1944-18 Jan. 1945
Hernández, Pablo M.	6 Feb. 1945-30 Nov. 1946
Palacios, Manuel R.	1 Dec. 1946-30 Nov. 1952
Amorós, Roberto	1 Dec. 1952-30 Nov. 1958
Méndez Aguilar, Benjamin	1 Dec. 1958-30 Nov. 1964
Sandoval Rodríguez, Eufrasio	1 Dec. 1964-30 Nov. 1970
Villaseñor, Víctor Manuel	1 Dec. 1970-7 May 1973
Gómez Zepeda, Luis	7 May 1973-30 Nov. 1982
Cota, Eduardo	1 Dec. 1982-7 Apr. 1986
Méndez Savage, Roberto	8 Apr. 1986-30 Nov. 1988
Orozco Sosa, Carlos	1 Dec. 1988-

Private Secretary to the President (Chief of Staff)

Private Secretary
Rodríguez, Luis I.	1935-37
García Téllez, Ignacio	1937-38
Castellano Jiménez, Raúl	3 Jan. 1938-24 Jan. 1939
Leñero, Agustín	1939-40
González Gallo, J. Jesús	1940-46
Viesca y Palma, Jorge	1946-52
Olmos, Salvador	1952-58
Romero Pérez, Humberto	1958-64
Cisneros, Joaquín	1964-70
Ovalle Fernández, Ignacio	1970-13 Nov. 1972
Bremer Martino, Juan José	14 Nov. 1972-4 Oct. 1975
Gil Elorduy, Ernesto	4 Oct. 1975-30 Nov. 1976
Velasco Ibarra, Enrique	1 Dec. 1976-14 Dec. 1978
Casillas, Roberto	15 Dec. 1978-Mar. 1982
Martínez Vara, Andrés	Mar. 1982-13 Aug. 1982
Vega Mimije, Carlos Juan	13 Aug. 1982-30 Nov. 1982
Gamboa Patrón, Eduardo	1 Dec. 1982-30 Nov . 1988
Massieu Berlanga, Andrés	1 Dec. 1988-

Secretariat of Agrarian Reform (Department of Agrarian Affairs and Colonization, 1959-75; Agrarian Department, 1934-58)

Secretary

Vázquez, Gabino	18 June 1935-30 Nov. 1940
Foglio Miramontes, Fernándo	1 Dec. 1940-19 Jan. 1944
Barba González, Silvano	20 Jan. 1944-30 Nov. 1946
Sousa, Mario	1 Dec. 1946-30 Nov. 1952
Villaseñor Luquín, Cástulo	1 Dec. 1952-30 Nov. 1958
Barrios, Roberto	1 Dec. 1958-30 Nov. 1964
Aguirre Palancares, Norberto	1 Dec. 1964-30 Nov. 1970
Gómez Villanueva, Augusto	1 Dec. 1970-26 Sept. 1975
Barra García, Félix	27 Sept. 1975-30 Nov. 1976
Rojo Lugo, Jorge	1 Dec. 1976-8 June 1978
Toledo Corro, Antonio	9 June 1978-28 Apr. 1980
García Paniagua, Javier	29 Apr. 1980-18 Mar. 1981
Carvajal Moreno, Gustavo	19 Mar. 1981-30 Nov. 1982
Martínez Villicaña, Luis	1 Dec. 1982-2 Feb. 1986
Rodríguez Barrera, Rafael	3 Feb. 1986-30 Nov. 1988
Cervera Pacheco, Víctor	1 Dec. 1988-

Secretary General (1935-75)

Villafuerte, Clicerio	1935-40
Rodríguez Adame, Julián	1940-44
Teusser, Salvador	1945-46
Gándara Machorro, Manuel J.	1 Dec. 1946-1950
Villaseñor Luquín, Cástulo	1950-30 Nov. 1952
López Bermúdez, José	1 Dec. 1952-1955
Carranza Hernández, Rafael	1955-30 Nov. 1958
Noguera Vergara, Arcadio	1 Dec. 1958-30 Nov. 1964
Alcérreca García Peña, Luis G.	1 Dec. 1964-30 Nov. 1970
Torres Ramírez, Víctor M.	1 Dec. 1970-30 Nov. 1976

Secretary General of Colonization (1958-64)

López Serrano, Francisco	1958-30 Nov. 1964

Secretary General of the New Ejido Population Centers (1964-82)

Franco Bencomo, Joaquín	1 Dec. 1964-30 Nov. 1970
Chávez Padrón de Velázquez, Marta	1 Dec. 1970-Apr. 1976
Vázquez Colmenares, Pedro	Apr. 1976-30 Nov. 1976
Mora, Prudencio	1 Dec. 1976-18 June 1978
Armienta Calderón, Gonzalo	19 June 1978-30 Nov. 1982

Secretary General of Legal Affairs (1971-75)

Canudas Orezza, Luis Felipe	1971-75

Secretary General of Organization and Ejido Development (1971-76)

Reyes Osorio, Sergio	1971-30 Nov. 1976

Secretary General of Agrarian Development (1975-78)
Garza González, Manuel   1 Dec. 1976-31 July 1978

Subsecretary of Agrarian Action (1975-82) [*]
Osorio Marbán, Miguel   1 Dec. 1976-18 June 1978
Galván Bouver, Ferrer   19 June 1978-30 Nov. 1982

Subsecretary of Organization and Development (1980)
Cosío Vidaurri, Guillermo   4 Dec. 1980-1981
Rodríguez Barrera, Rafael   1981-82
Paredes, Beatriz   1 Dec. 1982-1985
Barceló Rodríguez, Víctor Manuel   1985-30 Nov. 1988
Ocaña García, Samuel   1 Dec. 1988-May, 1992
Gordillo de Anda, Gustavo   May, 1992-

Subsecretary of Planning and Agricultural Infrastructure (1981-85)
Martínez Villicaña, Luis   1981-30 Nov. 1982
Robles Quintero, Salvador   1 Dec. 1982-24 July 1985

Subsecretary of Agrarian Affairs (1981)
Fonseca Alvarez, Guillermo   1981-30 Nov. 1982
Rodríguez Barrera, Rafael   1 Dec. 1982-2 Feb. 1986
Vega Alvarado, Renato   1986-30 Nov. 1988
Vega Alvarado, Renato   1 Dec. 1988-1992
López González, Armando   1992-

Oficial Mayor
Vázquez Pérez, Francisco   1935
Teusser, Salvador   1936-40
Valero, Pedro S.   1940-46
Mendieta y Nuñez, Lucío   1946-48
Fernández Albarrán, Juan   1948-52
Garizurieta, César   1952-58
Badillo García, Román   1958-64
Varela, Everardo G.   1964-70
Esparza Reyes, José R.   1970-74
Olivares Ventura, Héctor   1974-76
del Campo, Gustavo Martín   1976-80
González Cosío, Arturo   1980-81
Guerrero del Castillo, Eduardo   1981-82
Fox Cruz, Miguel Angel   1982-86
Ampudia Herrera, Jorge   1986-88
Murillo Karam, Jesús   1988-91
Pineda Pineda, Raúl   1991-

[*] Most subsecretaries joining a new presidential administration are appointed in
the middle of December, although the government often uses the December 1 date
as the official point of tenure.

Secretariat of Agriculture and Hydraulic Resources (Secretariat of Agriculture and Livestock, 1946-76; Agriculture and Development, 1917-46)

Secretary

Cedillo, Saturnino	11 June 1935-16 Aug. 1937
Parres, José A.	16 Aug. 1937-30 Nov. 1940
Gómez, Marte R.	1 Dec. 1940-30 Nov. 1946
Ortiz Garza, Nazario	1 Dec. 1946-30 Nov. 1952
Flores Muñoz, Gilberto	1 Dec. 1952-30 Nov. 1958
Rodríguez Adame, Julián	1 Dec. 1958-30 Nov. 1964
Gil Preciado, Juan	1 Dec. 1964-30 Nov. 1970
Aguirre, Manuel Bernardo	1 Dec. 1970-2 Jan. 1974
Brauer Herrera, Oscar	2 Jan. 1974-30 Nov. 1976
Merino Rabago, Francisco	1 Dec. 1976-30 Nov. 1982
García Aguilar, Horacio	1 Dec. 1982-18 July 1984
Pesqueira Olea, Eduardo	19 July 1984-30 Nov. 1988
de la Vega Domínguez, Jorge	1 Dec. 1988-3 Jan. 1990
Hank González, Carlos	4 Jan. 1990-

Subsecretary of Agriculture (1934-1984, 1990-)

Parres, José A.	1 Dec. 1934-16 Aug. 1937
Foglio Miramontes, Fernando	16 Aug. 1934-1940
Vázquez del Mercado, Francisco	10 Jan. 1940-30 Nov. 1940
González Gallardo, Alfonso	1 Dec. 1940-30 Nov. 1946
Merino Fernández, Jesús	1 Dec. 1946-1954
Patiño Navarrete, Jesús	1 Dec. 1958-30 Nov. 1964
Acosta Velasco, Ricardo	1 Dec. 1964-30 Nov. 1970
Ramírez Genel, Marcos	1 Dec. 1970-Oct. 1972
Brauer Herrera, Oscar	Oct. 1972-2 Jan. 1974
Martínez Medina, Lorenzo	2 Jan. 1974-30 Nov. 1976
Ortega, Benjamín	1 Dec. 1976-1978
Amaya Brondo, Abelardo	1978-30 Nov. 1982
Mercado Flores, Ignacio	1 Dec. 1982-1984
Enríquez Rubio, Ernesto	1990-

Subsecretary of Livestock (1940-82, 1988-)

Liera B., Guillermo	1 Dec. 1940-30 Nov. 1946
Flores Sánchez, Oscar	1 Dec. 1946-30 Nov. 1952
Ortega Martínez, Lauro	1 Dec. 1952-30 Nov. 1958
Mercado García, Daniel	1 Dec. 1958-30 Nov. 1964
Valdés Ornelas, Oscar	1 Dec. 1964-14 Sept. 1965
Guzmán Willis, Manuel	14 Sept. 1965-30 Nov. 1970
Telleache Merino, Ramón	1 Dec. 1970-22 Feb. 1972
Reta Petterson, Gustavo A.	23 Feb. 1972-26 June 1975
Zierold Reyes, Pablo	27 June 1975-30 Nov. 1976
Fernández Gómez, Rubén	1 Dec. 1976-23 July 1981
Valdés Ornelas, Oscar	23 July 1981-30 Nov. 1982
Enríquez Rubio, Ernesto	1988-90
Reta Petterson, Gustavo Adolfo	1990-

Subsecretary of Forest Resources and Fauna

Castro Estrada, José	1951-31 Nov. 1951
Hinojosa Ortiz, Manuel	1 Dec. 1952-30 Nov. 1958
Beltrán Castillo, Enrique	1 Dec. 1958-30 Nov. 1964
Palomares Navarro, Noé	1 Dec. 1964-30 Nov. 1970
de la Garza Ollervides, Eulogio	1 Dec. 1970-8 June 1972
Vázquez Soto, Jesús	9 June 1972-30 Nov. 1976
Cárdenas, Cuauhtémoc	1 Dec. 1976-1 Mar. 1980
Villa Salas, Avelino B.	10 Mar. 1980-30 Nov. 1982
Castaños Martínez, León Jorge	1 Dec. 1982-1986
Villa Issa, Manuel Rafael	1986-1988
Hernández Ochoa, Rafael	1988-3 Jan. 1990
Mondragón y Kalb, Manuel	4 Jan. 1990-

Subsecretary of Hydraulic Infrastructure (1977-88)

Villarreal Guerra, Américo	1977-Dec. 1981
Robledo Cabello, Luis	Dec. 1981-30 Nov. 1982
González Villareal, Fernando	1 Dec. 1982-30 Nov. 1988

Subsecretary of Planning (1977)

Cruickshank García, Gerardo	1977-9 Mar. 1980
Highland Gómez, Mario	10 Mar. 1980-30 Nov. 1982
Muñoz Vázquez, Jesús	1 Dec. 1982-84
Acevedo Valenzuela, Narciso	1984-88
Gordillo de Anda, Gustavo	1988-91
Téllez Kuenzler, Luis Manuel	1991-

Oficial Mayor

Castillo, Epífano	1935-37
Florencio, Antonio	1937-39
Liera, Guillermo	1940
Gómez, Andrés E.	1946-51
Barrera Fuentes, Florencio	1951-52
Gómez, Andrés E.	1952-58
Uranga Prado, Esteban	1958-64
Palomares, Noé	1964
Sánchez de Velasco, Abraham	1964-70
Pérez Vela, Juan	1970-72
Barraza Allande, Luciano	1972
Bucio Alanís, Lauro	1972-76
Highland Gómez, Mario	1976-80
Rocha Bandala, Juan F.	1980-82
Enríquez Rubio, Ernesto	1982-83
Díaz de Vargas, María Esther	1983-1984
Sierra Olivares, Carlos	1984-88
Aguilera Noriega, Jorge	1988-90
Rojas Cabrera, Alfredo	1990-

Secretariat of Commerce and Industrial Development (Secretariat of Commerce, 1976-82; Secretariat of Industry and Commerce, 1958-76; Economy, 1947-58; National Economy, 1936-46)

Secretary

Sánchez Tapia, Rafael	18 June 1935-31 Dec. 1937
Buenrostro, Efraín	3 Jan. 1938-30 Nov. 1940
Gaxiola, Francisco	1 Dec. 1940-30 June 1944
Serrano, Gustavo	1 July 1944-30 Nov. 1946
Ruíz Galindo, Antonio	1 Dec. 1946-20 Oct. 1948
Martínez Báez, Antonio	21 Oct.1948-30 Nov. 1952
Loyo, Gilberto	1 Dec. 1952-30 Nov. 1958
Salinas Lozano, Raúl	1 Dec. 1958-30 Nov. 1964
Campos Salas, Octaviano	1 Dec. 1964-30 Nov. 1970
Torres Manzo, Carlos	1 Dec. 1970-18 Jan. 1974
Campillo Sáinz, José	18 Jan. 1974-30 Nov. 1976
Solana, Fernando	1 Dec. 1976-8 Dec. 1977
de la Vega Domínguez, Jorge	9 Dec. 1977-30 Nov. 1982
Hernández Cervantes, Héctor	1 Dec. 1982-30 Nov. 1988
Serra Puche, Jaime José	1 Dec. 1988-

Subsecretary (1935-76)

Santillán, Manuel	1935-36
Moctezuma, Mariano	1936-38
Sousa, Mario	1940-42
Rolland, Modesto C.	1942-30 Nov. 1946
Parra, Manuel Germán	1 Dec. 1946-7 June 1948
Sánchez Cuen, Manuel	23 Oct. 1948-30 Nov. 1952
Pérez Duarte, Constantino	1 Dec. 1952-56
Segura y Gama, David	1956-30 Nov. 1958
García Reynoso, Plácido	1 Dec. 1958-30 Nov. 1970
Campillo Sáinz, José	1 Dec. 1970-18 Jan. 1974
Becker Arreola, Juan G.	18 Jan. 1974-30 Nov. 1976

Subsecretary of Foreign Trade (Trade, 1959-76)

Díaz Arias, Julián	1959-Sept. 1961
Margáin, Hugo B.	Sept. 1961-30 Nov. 1964
Cano Luebbert, Sergio	1 Dec. 1964-30 Nov. 1970
Mendoza Berrueto, Eliseo	1 Dec. 1970-23 Feb. 1976
Hernández Cervantes, Héctor	24 Feb. 1976-30 Nov. 1982
Bravo Aguilera, Luis	1 Dec. 1982-30 Nov. 1988
Blanco Mendoza, Herminio A.	1 Dec. 1988-1990
Noyola de Garagorri, Pedro J.	1990-

Subsecretary of Industry and Foreign Investment (1988)

Sánchez Ugarte, Fernando	1 Dec. 1988-

Subsecretary of Fishing (1971-77)

Medina Neri, Héctor	1971-30 Nov. 1976
Rafful Miguel, Fernando	1 Dec. 1976-77

Subsecretary of Commercial Planning (1976-78; 1982-85)

Solís, Leopoldo	1 Dec. 1976-1977
Díaz Ballesteros, Enrique	1 Jan. 1978-1 Dec. 1978
Villarreal Arrambe, René	1 Dec. 1982-1985

Subsecretary of Domestic Trade and Foodstuffs (Regulation and Foodstuffs (1978-85)

Díaz Ballesteros, Enrique	1 Dec. 1978-3 May 1979
Pérez Jácome, Dionisio E.	23 May 1979-30 Nov. 1982
Cano Escalante, Francisco	1 Dec. 1982-1985
Díaz Ballesteros, Enrique	1 Dec. 1988-1989
Carrión Rodríguez, Eugenio P.	1989-

Subsecretary of Internal Trade (1976)

Tamayo, Jorge	1 Dec. 1976-1981
Franco Díaz, Efrén	Apr. 1981-1985
Sánchez Jiménez, Jesús	1985-30 Nov. 1988

Subsecretary of Regulation of Foreign Investment and Technology Transfer (1985)

Armendáriz Etchegaray, Manuel B.	1985-30 Nov. 1988

Subsecretary of Industrial Development (1985)

María y Campos Castello, Mauricio	1985-30 Nov. 1988

Oficial Mayor

Padilla, Guillermo C.	1935-36
Sánchez Cuen, Miguel	1936-37
Bernard, Miguel	1937-38
Sánchez Cuen, Manuel	1939-40
Cebada, Manuel J.	1940-41
Avila Camacho, Rafael	1942-46
Muñoz Turnball, Marco	1946-49
Márquez Padilla, Tarciscio	1949-52
Torres Gaitán, Ricardo	1952-58
Díaz Arias, Julián	1958-59
Margáin, Hugo B.	1959-61
Rodríguez Gómez, Francisco	1964-70
Fabre del Rivero, Carlos	1970-76
Duahlt Kraus, Miguel	1976-80
Aguilera Noriega, Jorge	1980-82
López Munguía, Agustín	1982-88
Carrión Rodríguez, Eugenio F.	1988-89
Argüelles Díaz González, Antonio	1989-

Secretariat of Communications and Transportation (1959)

Secretary

Buchanan, Walter Cross	1 Jan. 1959-30 Nov. 1964
Padilla Segura, José A.	1 Dec. 1964-30 Nov. 1970
Méndez Docurro, Eugenio	1 Dec. 1970-30 Nov. 1976
Mujíca Montoya, Emilio	1 Dec. 1976-30 Nov. 1982
Félix Valdés, Rodolfo	1 Dec. 1982-30 Nov. 1984
Díaz Díaz, Daniel	1 Dec. 1984-30 Nov. 1988
Caso Lombardo, Andrés	1 Dec. 1988-29 Apr. 1993
Gamboa, Emilio	29 Apr. 1993-

Subsecretary

Ramírez Caraza, Juan Manuel	1 Jan. 1959-30 Nov. 1964
Méndez Docurro, Eugenio	1 Dec. 1964-30 Nov. 1970
Barrientos, Javier A.	1 Dec. 1970-30 Nov. 1976
Barbarena, Miguel A.	1 Dec. 1976-1981
de Garay y Arenas, Fernando	1981-2 Sept. 1985
Caso Lombardo, Andrés	5 Sept. 1985-14 May 1986
Patiño Guerrero, Gustavo	15 May 1986-30 Nov. 1988
Patiño Guerrero, Gustavo	1 Dec. 1988-

Subsecretary of Broadcasting (1970-76)

Herrera, Enrique	1 Dec. 1970-11 June 1971
Alvarez Acosta, Miguel	Oct. 1972-30 Nov. 1976

Subsecretary of Ports and Merchant Marine (1977-82)

Velarde Bonnin, José Juan	1 Dec. 1976-30 Nov. 1982

Subsecretary of Communication and Technical Development (1982)

Jiménez Espríu, Javier	1 Dec. 1982-1 Nov. 1988
Mier y Terán Ordiales, Carlos	1 Dec. 1988-1992

Subsecretary of Infrastructure (1988)

Mahbub Matta, Víctor Manuel	1 Dec. 1988-

Oficial Mayor

Medina Urbizo, Eduardo	1959-64
Fabela, Ramón	1964-70
Pérez Abreu Jiménez, Juan	1970-73
Bobadilla Peña, Julio	1973-76
Altamirano Calderón, Carlos	1976-82
Patiño Guerrero, Gustavo	1982-86
Luna Traill, Jaime	1986-88
León García, María Eugenia de	1988-

Secretariat of the Controller General (1983)

Secretary

Rosas Gutiérrez, Francisco	1983-6 June 1987
Pichardo Pagaza, Ignacio	7 Jan. 1987-30 Nov. 1988
Vázquez Nava, María Elena	1 Dec. 1988-

Subsecretary "A"

Pichardo Pagaza, Ignacio	1983-6 June 1987
Val Blanco, Enrique del	Mar. 1987-30 Nov. 1988
Val Blanco, Enrique del	1 Dec. 1988-1990
Vázquez Cano, Luis Ignacio	1990-

Subsecretary "B"

Robles Segura, Raúl	1983-May 1987
González González, Eduardo	May 1987-30 Nov. 1988
Vázquez Cano, Luis Ignacio	1 Dec. 1988-1990
Giordano Gómez, Salvador	1990-

Oficial Mayor

Ponce de León, Javier	1983-1987
Miranda Pasquel, Raúl	Mar. 1987-30 Nov. 1988
Casas Guzmán, Francisco J.	1 Dec. 1988-1991
Rodríguez Hernández, Antonio	1991-

Secretariat of Energy, Mines and Government Industries (Secretariat of Property and Industrial Development, 1977-82; Secretariat of Government Properties, 1947-77)

Secretary

Caso, Alfonso	1 Jan. 1947-9 Jan. 1949
Rangel Couto, Hugo	9 Jan. 1949-1 Aug. 1951
Carvajal, Angel	1 Aug. 1951-30 Nov. 1952
López Lira, José	1 Dec. 1952-30 Nov. 1958
Bustamante, Eduardo	1 Dec. 1958-30 Nov. 1964
Corona del Rosal, Alfonso	1 Dec. 1964-15 Sept. 1966
Franco López, Manuel	21 Sept. 1966-30 Nov. 1970
Flores de la Peña, Horacio	1 Dec. 1970-2 Jan. 1975
Alejo, Javier	3 Jan. 1975-30 Nov. 1976
Oteyza, José Andrés	1 Dec. 1976-30 Nov. 1982
Labastida Ochoa, Francisco	1 Dec. 1982-17 Apr. 1986
del Mazo Vélez, Alfredo	21 Apr. 1986-4 Mar. 1988
Hiriart Balderrama, Fernando	5 Mar. 1988-30 Nov. 1988
Hiriart Balderrama, Fernando	1 Dec. 1988-

Subsecretary of State Industry, 1977-87 (Subsecretary, 1947-77)

Carvajal, Angel	1947
Rangel Couto, Hugo	1947-30 Nov. 1952

López Arias, Fernando	Dec. 1952-53
Barocio Barrios, Alberto	1953-30 Nov. 1958
Alatriste, Sealtiel	1 Dec. 1958-30 Nov. 1964
González Guevara, Rodolfo	1 Dec. 1964-23 Sept. 1966
Langle Martínez, Eduardo	1966-68
De la Torre Grajales, Abelardo	1968-30 Nov. 1970
López Portillo, José	1 Dec. 1970-9 Aug. 1972
García Ramírez, Sergio	9 Aug. 1972-30 Apr. 1973
Rafful Miguel, Fernando	30 Apr. 1973-Mar. 1976
Cebreros, Alfonso	Mar. 1976-30 Nov. 1976
García Sáinz, Ricardo	1 Dec. 1976-16 Nov. 1977
Hiriart Balderrama, Fernando	23 Nov. 1977-28 Jan. 1978
García Ramírez, Sergio	29 Jan. 1978-29 Dec. 1981
Arroyo Marroquín, Romarico	1 Dec. 1982-1987

Subsecretary of Nonrenewable Resources (1958-78)

Franco López, Manuel	1 Dec. 1964-21 Sept. 1966
De la Peña Porth, Luis	1 Dec. 1970-2 Mar. 1973
Leipen Garay, Jorge	5 Mar. 1973-29 Jan. 1978

Subsecretary of Real Property and Urbanization (1958-77)

Rossell de la Lama, Guillermo	1959-30 Nov. 1964
Medellín, Jorge L.	1 Dec. 1964-30 Nov. 1970
Moctezuma Díaz Infante, Pedro	1 Dec. 1970-30 Nov. 1976
Martínez Corbalá, Gonzalo	1 Dec. 1976-3 Feb. 1977

Subsecretary of Mines (Mines and Energy, 1978-87)

Hiariart Balderrama, Fernando	30 Jan. 1978-30 Nov. 1982
Mendoza Berrueto, Eliseo	1 Dec. 1982-1 Mar. 1985
Escofet Artigas, Alberto	May 1987-1988
Elías Ayub, Alfredo	1 Dec. 1988-

Subsecretary of Energy (1985)

Alcudia García, José Luis	1985-1988
Escofet Artigas, Alberto	1 Dec. 1988-1991
Aburto Avila, José Luis	1991-

Subsecretary of Government Transformation Industries, 1982-1988 (Industrial Development, 1976-82)

Warman, Natán	1976-30 Nov. 1982
Barriero Pereda, Mario	1 Dec. 1982-1986
Laris Alanís, Eugenio	1986-1988

Oficial Mayor

Lazo, Carlos	1947-49
Silva, Leonardo	1949-52
López Arias, Fernando	1952-53
Gómez Esparza, José	1953-58
Rossell de la Lama, Guillermo	1958-59

Orozco González, Juan	1959-64
de la Torre Grajales, Abelardo	1964-68
Verges X., Juan Víctor	1968-70
Guzmán Bracho, Roberto	1970-75
Merino Mañon, José	1975-76
Sordi Sodi, Antonio	1976-82
Lincón Baca, Clemente	1982-86
Almada López, Carlos F.	1986-88
Paz Sánchez, Fernando	1988-

Secretariat of Fishing (Department of Fishing, 1977-82)

Head

Rafful Miguel, Fernando	1 Jan. 1977-30 Nov. 1982
Ojeda Paullada, Pedro	1 Dec. 1982-30 Nov. 1988
Moreno, María de los Angeles	1 Dec. 1988-21 May 1991
Jiménez Morales, Guillermo	22 May 1991-

Subsecretary of Fishing Development (1977-85)

Yáñez Ramos, Alfonso	1977-82
Calderón V., Alfonso G.	1982-24 July 1985

Subsecretary of Fishing Infrastructure (1977-85)

Urbina Peña, Rubén	1977-82
Castro y Castro, Fernando	1982-85

Subsecretary (1985)

Castro y Castro, Fernando	1985-88
Jusidman Rapoport, Clara	1988-

Secretariat of Foreign Relations

Secretary

González Roa, Fernando	17 June 1935-18 June 1935
Ceniceros, José Angel	18 June 1935-30 Nov. 1935
Hay, Eduardo	30 Nov. 1935-30 Nov. 1940
Padilla, Ezequiel	1 Dec. 1940-10 July 1945
Tello, Manuel	10 July 1945-31 Aug. 1945
Castillo Nájera, Francisco	1 Sept. 1945-30 Nov. 1946
Torres Bodet, Jaime	1 Dec. 1946-24 Nov. 1948
Tello, Manuel	24 Nov. 1948-30 Nov. 1952
Padilla Nervo, Luis	1 Dec. 1952-30 Nov. 1958
Tello, Manuel	1 Dec. 1958-30 Mar. 1964
Gorostiza, José	30 Mar. 1964-30 Nov. 1964
Carrillo Flores, Antonio	1 Dec. 1964-30 Nov. 1970
Rabasa, Emilio O.	1 Dec. 1970-28 Dec. 1975
García Robles, Alfonso	29 Dec. 1975-30 Nov. 1976

Roel, Santiago	1 Dec. 1976-16 May 1979
Castañeda, Jorge	16 May 1979-30 Nov. 1982
Sepúlveda Amor, Bernardo	1 Dec. 1982-30 Nov. 1988
Solana, Fernando	1 Dec. 1988-29 Nov. 1993
Camacho Solís, Manuel	29 Dec. 1993-

Subsecretary (Bilateral Affairs) (A)

Ceniceros, José	16 June 1935-30 Apr. 1936
Beteta, Ramón	12 May 1936-30 Nov. 1940
Torres Bodet, Jaime	1 Dec. 1940-31 Dec. 1943
Santos Guajardo, Vicente	3 Jan. 1944-June 1944
Tello, Manuel	1 July 1944-30 Nov. 1951
Guerra, Alfonso	30 Nov. 1951-1 July 1953
Gorostiza, José	1 July 1953-30 Nov. 1964
Fraga Magaña, Gabino	1 Dec. 1964-30 Nov. 1970
González Sosa, Rubén	1 Dec. 1970-30 Nov. 1976
de Olloqui, José Juan	1 Dec. 1976-June 1979
Tello Macías, Manuel	22 June 1979-30 Nov. 1982
de Rosenzweig, Alfonso	1 Dec. 1982-30 Nov. 1988
González Gálvez, Sergio	1 Dec. 1988-1992
Rozental Gutmán, Andrés	Apr. 1992-

Subsecretary (B) of Multilateral and Cultural Affairs

Campos Ortiz, Pablo	1 June 1960-1 Apr. 1964
García Robles, Alfonso	1 Apr. 1964-30 Nov. 1970
Gallástegui, José S.	1 Dec. 1970-30 Nov. 1976
de Rosenzweig, Alfonso	1 Dec. 1976-30 Nov. 1982
Flores Olea, Víctor	1 Dec. 1982-30 Nov. 1988
Rozental Gutmán, Andrés	1 Dec. 1988-1992
Barros Valero, Javier	Apr. 1992-

Subsecretary (C) of International Cooperation (1982) Special Studies and International Affairs (1976)

Castaneda, Jorge	12 Jan. 1976-30 Nov. 1976
Téllez Benoit, María	1 Dec. 1976-30 Nov. 1982
Valero, Ricardo	1 Dec. 1982-30 Nov. 1988
Valero, Ricardo	1 Dec. 1988-1992
Green Macías, María del Rosario	Apr. 1992-

Subsecretary of Economic Affairs (D) (1978-82)

Sánchez Meza de Solís, Guillermina	1978-June, 1979
Navarrete, Jorge Eduardo	June, 1979-1982

Oficial Mayor

Sierra, Manuel J.	1935-36
Hidalgo, Ernesto	1936-42
Campos Ortiz, Pablo	1944-46
Guerra, Alfonso	1946-51
Lelo de Larrea, José	1951-52

Campos Ortiz, Pablo	1952-57
Darío Ojeda, Carlos	1957-64
Gallástegui, José	1965-70
Téllez Benoit, María	1970-76
Sánchez Meza de Solís, Guillermina	1976-78
Garza Plaza, Adrián	1978-79
González Martínez, Aida	1979-82
González Salazar, Roque	1982-88
Núñez Urquiza, Carlos	1988-92
Icaza González, Carlos Alberto de	1992-

Secretariat of Government

Secretary

Barba González, Silvano	18 June 1935-24 Aug. 1936
Guerrero, Silvestre	25 Aug. 1936-31 Dec. 1937
García Téllez, Ignacio	4 Jan. 1938-30 Nov. 1940
Alemán, Miguel	1 Dec. 1940-17 June 1945
Villa Michel, Primo	18 June 1945- 30 Nov. 1946 *Pérez*
Martínez, Héctor	1 Dec. 1946-13 Feb. 1948
Uruchurtu, Ernesto P.	13 Feb. 1948-29 June 1948
Ruiz Cortines, Adolfo	30 June 1948-12 Oct. 1951
Uruchurtu, Ernesto P.	13 Oct. 1951-30 Nov. 1952
Carvajal, Angel	1 Dec. 1952-30 Nov. 1958
Díaz Ordaz, Gustavo	1 Dec. 1958-18 Nov. 1963
Echeverría Alvarez, Luis	19 Nov. 1963-10 Nov. 1969 *Moya*
Palencia, Marío	11 Nov. 1969-30 Nov. 1976
Reyes Heroles, Jesús	1 Dec. 1976-16 May 1979
Olivares Santana, Enrique	17 May 1979-30 Nov. 1982
Bartlett Díaz, Manuel	1 Dec. 1982-30 Nov. 1988
Gutiérrez Barrios, Fernando	1 Dec. 1988-3 Jan. 1993
González Blanco Garrido, Patrocinio	4 Jan. 1993-

Subsecretary of Government and Political Development (1988)

Arroyo Ch., Agustín	12 Sept. 1935-4 Jan. 1938
Santos Guajardo, Vicente	4 Jan. 1938-30 Nov. 1940
Casas Alemán, Fernando	1 Dec. 1940-17 June 1945
Pérez Martínez, Héctor	18 June 1945-30 Nov. 1946
Uruchurtu, Ernesto P.	1 Dec. 1946-30 Nov. 1952
Ortiz Tirado, José María	1 Dec. 1952-5 Feb. 1953
Román Lugo, Fernando	6 Feb. 1953-30 Nov. 1958
Echeverría Alvarez, Luis	1 Dec. 1958-15 Nov. 1963
Hernández Ochoa, Rafael	1 Dec. 1964-30 Nov. 1970
Gutiérrez Barrios, Fernando	1 Dec. 1970-30 Nov. 1982
Dávila Narro, Jesús	1 Dec. 1982-2 Jan. 1985
Elías Calles, Fernando	12 Jan. 1985-30 Nov. 1988
Beltrones Rivera, Manlío Favio	1 Dec. 1988-12 Mar. 1991

Núñez Jiménez, Arturo	13 Mar. 1991-2 Jan. 1993
Canales Najjar, Tristán	3 Jan. 1993-

Subsecretary of Population (1988)
Subsecretary 2 (1958-1988)

Gálvez Betancourt, Carlos	30 Nov. 1964-68
Moya Palencia, Marío	1 July 1969-10 Nov. 1969
Biebrich Torres, Carlos	1 Dec. 1970-22 Dec. 1972
García Ramírez, Sergio	30 Apr. 1973-30 Nov. 1976
Echeverría, Rodolfo	1 Dec. 1976-14 Aug. 1978
Lamadrid, José Luis	15 Aug. 1978-21 May 1979
González Guevara, Rodolfo	22 May 1979-30 Nov. 1982
Wimer, Javier	1 Dec. 1982-July, 1984
Pérez Correa, Fernando	July, 1984-30 Nov. 1988
Limón Rojas, Miguel	1 Dec. 1988-2 Jan. 1993
García Villalobos, Jorge R.	3 Jan. 1993-

Subsecretary of Civil Protection (1988)
Subsecretary 3 (1978-1988)

García Paniagua, Javier	15 Aug. 1978-29 Apr. 1980
Rivera Pérez Campos, José	30 Apr. 1980-30 Nov. 1982
Carrillo Olea, Jorge	1 Dec. 1982-30 Nov. 1988
Rabasa Gamboa, Emilio	1 Dec. 1988-12 Mar.1991
Pérez Jácome, Dionisio Eduardo	13 Mar. 1991-2 Jan. 1993
Díaz Palacios, Socorro	3 Jan. 1993-

Oficial Mayor

Barba González, Silvano	1934-35
García de Alba, Esteban	1935-40
Ruiz Cortines, Adolfo	1940-44
Villa Michel, Primo	1944-45
Guzmán Araujo, Roberto	1945-46
Coquet Laguna, Benito	1946
Terán Zozaya, Horacio	1946-51
Rodríguez Cano, Enrique	1951-52
Román Lugo, Fernando	1952-53
Díaz Ordaz, Gustavo	1953-58
Palomares Navarro, Noé	1958-64
Gálvez Betancourt, Carlos	1964-65
Murillo Vidal, Rafael	1965-68
Heredia Ferráez, Jorge	1968-70
Ibarra Herrera, Manuel	1970-76
Lamadrid, José Luis	1976-78
Vázquez Torres, Ignacio	1978-79
Hernández Gómez, Tulio	1979-80
Talavera López, Abraham	1981-82
Corrales Ayala, Rafael	1982-
Cavazos Lerma, Manuel	1985-1988

Ponce Coronado, Augusto   1988-1993
Cantú Segovia, Eloy   1993-

Secretariat of Health and Welfare (1938)

Secretary
Hernández Alvarez, Enrique   3 Jan. 1938-2 Nov. 1938
Guerrero, Silvestre   24 Jan. 1939-30 Nov. 1940
Baz, Gustavo   1 Dec. 1940-30 Nov. 1946
Gamboa, Rafael P.   1 Dec. 1946-30 Nov. 1952
Morones Prieto, Ignacio   1 Dec. 1952-30 Nov. 1958
Alvarez Amezquita, José   1 Dec. 1958-30 Nov. 1964
Moreno Valle, Rafael   1 Dec. 1964-15 Aug. 1968
Aceves Parra, Salvador   17 Aug. 1968-30 Nov. 1970
Jiménez Cantú, Jorge   1 Dec. 1970-2 Mar. 1975
Navarro Díaz de León, Gines   2 Mar. 1975-30 Nov. 1976
Martínez Manatou, Emilio   1 Dec. 1976-4 June 1980
Calles, Marío   5 June 1980-30 Nov. 1982
Soberón, Guillermo   1 Dec. 1982-30 Nov. 1988
Kumate, Jesús   1 Dec. 1988-

Subsecretary (1938-58)
Zubirán, Salvador   1938-43; in charge 1938-39
Martínez Báez, Manuel   18 Oct. 1943-1 Mar. 1946
Mondragón Guerra, Salvador   Mar. 1946-30 Nov. 1946
Morones Prieto, Ignacio   1 Dec. 1946-31 Dec. 1947
Argil Camacho, Gustavo   1 Jan. 1948-30 Nov. 1952
Pesqueira y D'endara, Manuel E.   1 Dec. 1952-30 Nov. 1958

Subsecretary of Assistance (1958-1982)
Castro Villagrana, José   1 Dec. 1958-27 Jan.1960
Zuckermann, Conrado   1 Mar. 1960-30 Nov. 1964
Aceves Parra, Salvador   1 Dec. 1964-21 Oct. 1968
Loyo Díaz, Mauro   21 Nov. 1968-30 Nov. 1970
Campillo Sáinz, Carlos   1 Dec. 1970-30 Nov. 1976
Gual Castro, Carlos   1 Dec. 1976-3 July 1980
Beltrán Brown, Francisco   4 July 1980-30 Nov. 1982

Subsecretary of Research and Development (1982-84)
Laguna, José   1 Dec. 1982-1984

Subsecretary of Health Services (Health, 1959-1982)
Bustamante, Miguel   1959-30 Nov. 1964
Martínez García, Pedro D.   1 Dec. 1964-30 Nov. 1970
Guzmán Orozco, Renaldo   1 Dec. 1970-30 Nov. 1976
Calles, Marío   1 Dec. 1976-4 June 1980
Chávez Peón, Federico   5 June 1980-30 Nov. 1982
Fernández Varela, Héctor   1 Dec. 1982-1985

Kumate, Jesús	1985-30 Nov. 1988
Wolpert Barraza, Enrique	1988-

Subsecretary of Planning 1982-1988)

Isoard, Carlos Alfredo	1 Dec. 1982-1983
Ruiz Massieu, José Francisco	1983-1986
Ruiz de Chávez, Manuel H.	1986-1988

Subsecretary of Coordination and Development (1991)

Sepúlveda Amor, Jaime	1991-

Subsecretary of Health Regulation and Development (1984)

Valadés Ríos, Diego	1984-1985
Martuscelli Quintana, Jaime	1985-1988
Juan López, Mercedes	1988-

Subsecretary of the Environment (1972-82)

Torres H., Marco Aurelio	20 Jan. 1972-25 Jan. 1972
Vizcaíno Murray, Francisco	26 Jan. 1972-30 Nov. 1976
Romero Alvarez, Humberto	1 Dec. 1976-3 July 1980
López Portillo, Manuel	4 July 1980-30 Nov.1982

Oficial Mayor

Treviño, Julio César	1935-37
López Lira, José	1937-39
Mondragón, Octavio S.	1940-45
Pasquel Jiménez Unda, Leonardo	1945-46
Morones Prieto, Ignacio	1946
Argil Camacho, Gustavo	1946-48
Guzmán, Jr., Saturnino	1949-52
Mayoral Pardo, Demetrio	1952-58
de la Riva Rodríguez, Javier	1958-64
Maldonado Pérez, Caritino	1965-69
López Faudoa, Eduardo	1970-71
Soto Prieto, Roberto	1971-76
Hernández Rizo, José	1976-80
González Torres, Roberto	1980-82
Ruiz Massieu, Francisco	1982-83
González Fernández, José Antonio	1983-85
Ortega Lomelín, Roberto	1985-88
García Pérez, Gabriel	1988-92
Fonseca Alvarez, Guillermo	1992-

Secretariat of Hydraulic Resources (1947-77)

Secretary

Orive Alba, Adolfo	1 Jan. 1947-30 Nov. 1952
Chávez, Eduardo	1 Dec. 1952-25 Apr. 1958

Echegaray Bablot, Luis   25 Apr. 1958-30 Nov. 1958
Del Mazo Vélez, Alfredo   1 Dec. 1958-30 Nov. 1964
Hernández Terán, José   1 Dec. 1964-30 Nov. 1970
Rovirosa Wade, Leandro   1 Dec. 1970-21 Aug. 1976
Robles Linares, Luis   22 Aug. 1976-31 Dec. 1976

Subsecretary (A) of Construction
Riquelme, Eugenio   1 Jan. 1947-30 Nov. 1952
Echegaray Bablot, Luis   1 Dec. 1952-30 Nov. 1958
Colín Varela, Alfredo E.   1 Dec. 1958-30 Nov. 1964
Aguilar Chávez, Salvador   1 Dec. 1964-30 Nov. 1970
Robles Linares, Luis   1 Dec. 1970-31 Dec. 1976

Subsecretary (B) of Operations (1964-76)
Barnetche González, Alberto   1 Dec. 1964-30 Nov. 1970
Amaya Brondo, Abelardo   1 Dec. 1970-30 Nov. 1976

Subsecretary of Planning (1970-76)
Cruickshank, Gerardo   1 Dec. 1970-30 Nov. 1976

Oficial Mayor
Cardénas Huerta, Gustavo   1947-52
Pérez Moreno, José   1952-58
Castrejón y Chávez, Gustavo   1958-64
Ibarra, Guillermo   1964-70
Castaños Patoni, Fernando   1970-76

Secretariat of Labor and Social Welfare

Secretary
Vázquez, Genaro   18 June 1935-18 June 1937
Villalobos, Antonio   19 June 1937-21 Jan. 1940
Arroyo Ch., Agustín   21 Jan. 1940-30 Nov. 1940
García Téllez, Ignacio   1 Dec. 1940-16 Jan. 1943
Palacios, Manuel R.   16 Jan. 1943-28 Feb. 1943
Trujillo Gurría, Francisco   1 Mar. 1943-30 Nov. 1946
Serra Rojas, Andrés   1 Dec. 1946-30 Nov. 1952
López Mateos, Adolfo   1 Dec. 1952-18 Nov. 1957
González Blanco, Salomón   18 Nov. 1957-30 Nov. 1970
Hernández Ochoa, Rafael   1 Dec. 1970-11 Sept. 1972
Muñoz Ledo, Porfirio   12 Sept.1972-26 Sept. 1975
Gálvez Betancourt, Carlos   27 Sept. 1975-30 Nov. 1976
Ojeda Paullada, Pedro   1 Dec. 1976-14 Oct. 1981
García Paniagua, Javier   14 Oct. 1981-28 Dec. 1981
García Ramírez, Sergio   29 Dec. 1982-30 Nov. 1982
Farell Cubillas, Arsenio   1 Dec. 1982-30 Nov. 1988
Farell Cubillas, Arsenio   1 Dec. 1988-

Subsecretary (A) (1940)

Cantu Estrada, José	1935-37
Padilla, Florencio	1937-40
Santos Guajardo, Vicente	1940-Jan. 1943
Palacios, Manuel R.	1943-Apr. 1946
Serrano Castro, Julio	Apr. 1946-30 Nov. 1946
Ramírez Vázquez, Manuel	1 Dec. 1946-48
Canale Muñoz, Eleazar	Oct. 1948-30 Nov. 1952
González Blanco, Salomon	1 Dec. 1952-30 Nov. 1958
Santos Coy Perea, Julio	1 Dec. 1958-30 Nov. 1970
Llorente González, Arturo	1 Dec. 1970-30 Nov. 1976
Carvajal, Gustavo	1 Dec. 1976-10 Aug. 1978
Echeverría, Rodolfo	15 Aug. 1978-29 Dec. 1981
Ruiz de Chávez, Arturo	30 Dec. 1981-30 Nov. 1982
Zertuche Muñoz, Fernando	1 Dec. 1982-15 Oct. 1985
Gomezperalta Damirón, Manuel	16 Oct. 1985-30 Nov. 1988
Gomezperalta Damirón, Manuel	1 Dec. 1988-

Subsecretary (B) Social Welfare

Canales Valverde, Tristán	Dec. 1964-30 Nov. 1970
Alanís Fuentes, Agustín	1 Dec. 1970-30 Nov. 1976
González López, Guillermo	1 Dec. 1976-1981
Cosío Vidaurri, Guillermo	1981-1982
Lozoya T., Emilio	1 Dec. 1982-30 Nov. 1988
Bonilla García, Jesús Javier	1 Dec. 1988-1991
Samaniego Breach, Norma	1991-

Oficial Mayor

Ortiz Armengol, Federico	1935-36
Olive, Issac	1937-39
Rivera Pérez Campos, José	1940
Lanuza Araujo, Agustín	1940-46
González Blanco, Salomón	1946-52
Quirasco, Antonio M.	1952-53
Aguirre Zertuche, Santiago	1953-58
Candiani, Guillermo	1958-61
Canales Valverde, Tristán	1961-64
Hori Robaina, Guillermo	1965-70
Zertuche Muñoz, Fernando	1970-74
Uribe Castañeda, Manuel	1974-76
Suárez, Marcos Manuel	1976-78
Brasdefer Hernández, Gloria	1978-82
Bastarrachea Sabido, Jorge	1982-88
Mendoza Hernández, Raúl	1988-90
López Araiza Orozco, Mario	1990-

Secretariat of National Defense

Secretary

Figueroa, Andrés	18 June 1935-17 Oct. 1935
Avila Camacho, Manuel	17 Oct. 1935-17 Jan. 1939
Castro, Jesús Agustín	23 Jan. 1939-30 Nov. 1940
Macías Valenzuela, Pablo E.	1 Dec. 1940-11 Sept. 1942
Cárdenas, Lázaro	11 Sept. 1942-27 Aug. 1945
Urquizo, Francisco	1 Sept. 1945-30 Nov. 1946
Limón, Gilberto R.	1 Dec. 1946-30 Nov. 1952
Ramos Santos, Matías	1 Dec. 1952-30 Nov. 1958
Olachea Aviles, Agustín	1 Dec. 1958-30 Nov. 1964
García Barragán, Marcelino	1 Dec. 1964-30 Nov. 1970
Cuenca Díaz, Hermenegildo	1 Dec. 1970-30 Nov. 1976
Galván López, Félix	1 Dec. 1976-30 Nov. 1982
Arévalo Gardoqui, Juan	1 Dec. 1982-30 Nov. 1988
Riviello Bazán, Antonio	1 Dec. 1988-

Subsecretary

Avila Camacho, Manuel	1935-1 Nov. 1937
Corral, Blas	1 Jan. 1938-39
González Villareal, Marciano	1939-40
Urquizo, Francisco	1940-31 Aug. 1945
Limón, Gilberto R.	1 Sept. 1945-30 Nov. 1946
Gárate Legleu, Raúl	10 Dec. 1946-17 Apr. 1947
González Lugo, Jesús	1947-49
Calles Pordo, Aureo L.	1949-52
Guinart López, Modesto A.	1 Dec. 1952-30 Nov. 1958
Flores Torres, Juan	1 Dec. 1958-30 Nov. 1964
Gastélum Salcido, Juan José	1 Dec. 1964-30 Nov. 1970
Gomar Suástegui, Jerónimo	1 Dec. 1970-21 Jan. 1972
Sandoval Castarrica, Enrique	1972-May, 1975
Camargo, Héctor	1975-76
de la Fuente Rodríguez, Juan A.	1 Dec. 1976-13 Dec. 1979
Portillo Jurado, Héctor	16 Jan. 1980-30 Nov. 1982
Guerrero, Marco Antonio	1 Dec. 1982-30 Nov. 1988
Ochoa Toledo, Alfredo	1 Dec. 1988-

Oficial Mayor

Avila Camacho, Manuel	1934-35
Corral Martínez, Blas	1936-37
Orozco Camacho, Miguel	1937-39
González Villarreal, Marciano	1939-40
Montes Alanís, Federico	1940-40
Sánchez, J. Salvador	1940-41
Corral Martínez, Blas	1941-44
Ruiz Camarillo, Leobardo	1945-46
Cabrera Carrasquedo, Manuel	1946-48

Leyva Velázquez, Gabriel	1948-50
López Sánchez, Arturo	1951-52
Corsen León, Adolfo E.	1952-53
Leyva Mancilla, Baltásar	1953-58
Pámanes Escobedo, Fernando	1958-64
Gurza Falfán, Alfonso	1965-65
Pérez Ortiz, Basilio	1965-70
Corona Mendioroz, Arturo	1970-73
Somuano López, Rubén Darío	1973-75
Carduño Canizal, Leopoldo	1975-76
Ochoa Palencia, Arturo	1976-77
Mardegaín Simón, Antonio	1977-80
Moguel Cal y Mayor, José	1980-83
López Flores, Arturo	1983-88
Juárez Carreño, Raúl	1988-

Secretariat of the Navy (1940)

Secretary

Gómez Maqueo, Roberto	1 Jan. 1940-31 Dec. 1940
Jara, Heriberto	1 Jan. 1941-30 Nov. 1946
Schaufelberger, Luis F.	1 Dec. 1946-8 Oct. 1948
Coello, David	8 Oct. 1948-20 Oct. 1949
Pawling, Alberto J.	21 Oct. 1949-6 Feb. 1952
López Sánchez, Raúl	7 Feb. 1952-30 Nov. 1952
Sánchez Taboada, Rodolfo	1 Dec. 1952-1 May 1955
Poire Ruelas, Alfonso	2 May 1955-22 Dec. 1955
Gómez Maqueo, Roberto	23 Dec. 1955-2 Apr. 1958
Meixueiro Alexandre, Héctor	7 Apr. 1958-30 Nov. 1958
Zermeño Araico, Manuel	1 Dec. 1958-30 Nov. 1964
Vázquez del Mercado, Antonio	1 Dec. 1964-30 Nov. 1970
Bravo Carrera, Luis	1 Dec. 1970-30 Nov. 1976
Cházaro Lara, Ricardo	1 Dec. 1976-30 Nov. 1982
Gómez Ortega, Miguel A.	1 Dec. 1982-30 Nov. 1988
Schleske, Mauricio	1 Dec. 1988-18 July 1990
Ruano Angulo, Luis Carlos	19 July 1990-

Subsecretary

Vázquez del Mercado, Antonio	1 Jan. 1940-30 Nov. 1940
Blanco, Othón P.	5 Dec. 1940-30 Nov. 1946
Schaufelberger, Luis F.	1 Dec. 1946-8 Oct. 1948
Pawling, Alberto J.	9 Oct. 1948-30 Nov. 1952
Poire Ruelas, Alfonso	1 Dec. 1952-30 Nov. 1958
Orozco Vela, Oliverio F.	1 Dec. 1958-30 Nov. 1964
Fritsche Anda, Oscar	1 Dec. 1964-2 July 1965
Aznar Zetina, Antonio J.	13 July 1965-30 Nov. 1970
Cházaro Lara, Ricardo	1 Dec. 1970-30 Nov. 1976

Montejo Sierra, José M.	1 Dec. 1976-30 Nov. 1982
Martínez Najera, Humberto	1 Dec. 1982-30 Nov. 1988
Zepeda Torres, David	1 Dec. 1988-

Oficial Mayor

Muñoz Medina, Lorenzo	1935-40
Valencia, Roberto Laurencio	1940-46
Pérez Zavala, Cuauhtémoc	1946
Coello Ochoa, David	1946-47
Lagos Beltrán, Gabriel	1948-52
Montalvo Salazar, Gonzalo	1952-54
Meixueiro, Alexandre	1955-58
Luque Salanieva, Víctor	1958
Otal Briseño, Rigoberto	1958-64
Castro y Castro, Fernando	1964-70
Cubría Palma, José Luis	1970-76
Artigas Fernández, Marío	1976-82
Piaña Lara, Fernando	1982-86
López Sotelo, Carlos	1986-88
Rodríguez Jurado, Rodolfo	1988-91
Díaz González Roca, Omar	1991-

Secretariat of Programming and Budget (1976-92) (Secretariat of the Presidency, 1958-76; Confidential Secretary, 1946-58)

Secretary

Amorós, Roberto	July 1946-30 Nov. 1946
De la Selva, Rogerio	Dec. 1946-30 Nov. 1952
Rodríguez Cano, Enrique	1 Dec. 1952-55
Coquet Laguna, Benito	1956-30 Nov. 1958
Miranda Fonseca, Donato	1 Dec. 1958-30 Nov. 1964
Martínez Manautou, Emilio	1 Dec. 1964-30 Nov. 1970
Cervantes del Río, Hugo	1 Dec. 1970-3 Oct. 1975
Ovalle Fernández, Ignacio	4 Oct. 1975-30 Nov. 1976
Tello Macías, Carlos	1 Dec. 1976-16 Nov. 1977
García Sáinz, Ricardo	17 Nov. 1977-16 May 1979
De la Madrid, Miguel	17 May 1979-29 Sept. 1981
Aguirre Velázquez, Ramón	30 Sept. 1981-30 Nov. 1982
Salinas de Gortari, Carlos	1 Dec. 1982-Oct. 1987
Aspe, Pedro	Oct. 1987-30 Nov. 1988
Zedillo, Ernesto	1 Dec. 1988-1992

Subsecretary of Evaluation, 1976-82 (Subsecretary, 1948-76)

Amorós, Roberto	1 Jan. 1948-13 Nov. 1951
Coquet, Benito	1 Dec. 1952-56
Ortiz Mena, Raúl	1 Dec. 1958-61
Yáñez, Agustín	1961-64
Ortiz Mena, Raúl	15 Dec. 1964-6 Nov. 1968

López Portillo, José	Nov. 1968-30 Nov. 1970
Muñoz Ledo, Porfirio	1 Dec. 1970-14 Nov. 1972
Ovalle Fernández, Ignacio	14 Nov. 1972-4 Oct. 1975
Bremer, Juan J.	4 Oct. 1975-30 Nov. 1976
Alegría Escamilla, Rosa	1 Dec. 1976-13 Aug. 1980
López Portillo, José Ramón	18 Aug. 1980-Oct. 1981
Sbert, José María	Oct. 1981-30 Nov. 1982

Subsecretary of Programming (Information, 1970-76)

Zapata Loredo, Fausto	1970-25 Feb. 1976
Jiménez Lazcano, Mauro	26 Feb. 1976-30 Nov. 1976
Pasquel Moncayo, Eduardo	1 Dec. 1976-26 Jan. 1978
Cebreros Murillo, Alfonso	26 Jan. 1978-May. 1979
Labastida Ochoa, Francisco	May, 1979-30 Nov. 1982
Páramo Díaz, Juan José	1 Dec. 1982-30 Nov. 1988
Gasca Neri, Rogelio	1 Dec. 1988-1992

Subsecretary of Budget Control and Planning (1982-88)

| Castillo Ayala, Javier | 1 Dec. 1982-1985 |
| Aspe Armella, Pedro C. | 1985-1987 |

Subsecretary of Developmental Planning (1982-86)

| Montemayor Seguy, Rogelio | 1 Dec. 1982-1986 |

Subsecretary of Planning (1988-92)

| García Alba Iduñate, Pascual | 1 Dec. 1988-1992 |

Subsecretary of Regional Development (1982-86)

| Camacho Solís, Víctor Manuel | 1 Dec. 1982-1986 |

Subsecretary of Programming and Budgeting of Social and Rural Development (1982-92)

| Moreno Uriegas, María de los Angeles | 1 Dec. 1982-30 Nov. 1988 |
| Rojas Gutiérrez, Carlos | 1 Dec. 1988-1992 |

Secretariat of Public Education

Secretary

Vázquez Vela, Gonzalo	18 June 1935-30 Nov. 1940
Sánchez Pontón, Luis	1 Dec. 1940-11 Sept. 1941
Véjar Vázquez, Octavio	12 Sept.1941-20 Sept.1943
Torres Bodet, Jaime	22 Dec. 1943-30 Nov. 1946
Gual Vidal, Manuel	1 Dec. 1946-30 Nov. 1952
Ceniceros, José A.	1 Dec. 1952-30 Nov. 1958
Torres Bodet, Jaime	1 Dec. 1958-30 Nov. 1964
Yáñez, Agustín	1 Dec. 1964-30 Nov. 1970
Bravo Ahuja, Víctor	1 Dec. 1970-30 Nov. 1976
Muñoz Ledo, Porfirio	1 Dec. 1976-8 Dec. 1977

Solana, Eduardo	9 Dec. 1977-30 Nov. 1982
Reyes Heroles, Jesús	1 Dec. 1982-19 Mar. 1985
González Avelar, Manuel	25 Mar. 1985-30 Nov. 1988
Bartlett Díaz, Manuel	1 Dec. 1988-1992
Zedillo, Ernesto	1992-29 Nov. 1993
Solana Morales, Fernando	29 Nov. 1993-

Subsecretary General (1921-76)

Moctezuma, Mariano	1934-35
Lucío Argüelles, Gabriel	1935-36
Chávez Orozco, Luis	1936-38
Nicodemo, Francisco	1938-40
Arreguín, Enrique	1 Dec. 1940-11 Sept. 1941
Bonilla Cortés, Roberto T.	12 Sept. 1941-30 Dec. 1943
Sánchez Hernández, Tomás	31 Dec. 1943-30 Nov. 1946
Chávez, Leopoldo	1 Dec. 1946-47
Merino Fernández, Aaron	7 Jan. 1948-30 Nov. 1952
Gómez Robleda, José	1 Dec. 1952-54
Sandoval Vallarta, Manuel	1954-30 Nov. 1958
Enríquez Coyro, Ernesto	1 Dec. 1958-30 Nov. 1964
Berrueto Ramón, Federico	1 Dec. 1964-30 Nov. 1970
Bonfil, Ramón G.	1 Dec. 1970-30 Nov. 1976

Subsecretary of Higher Education and Scientific Investigation (Subsecretary of Intermediate, Technical and Higher Education, 1958-76)

Bravo Ahuja, Víctor	1958-68
Ortiz Macedo, Luis	Feb. 1969-30 Nov. 1970
Mayagoitia Domínguez, Héctor	1 Dec. 1970-15 Mar. 1974
Uscanga Uscanga, César	15 Mar. 1974-28 Dec. 1977
Mendoza Berrueto, Eliseo	2 Jan. 1978-30 Nov. 1982
Flores Valdés, Jorge	1 Dec. 1982-1985
Velasco Fernández, Rafael	1985-30 Nov. 1988
Todd Pérez, Luis Eugenio	1 Dec. 1988-1992
Gago Huguet, Antonio	Jan. 1992-

Subsecretary of Education and Technical Research (1978)

Massieu Helguera, Guillermo	Apr. 1978-June 1979
Carranza, José Antonio	June 1979-30 Nov. 1982
Valerio Ortega, Manuel	1 Dec. 1982-30 Nov. 1988
Talán Ramírez, Raúl Eric	1 Dec. 1988-

Subsecretary of Culture and Recreation (Subsecretary of Popular Culture and Educational Extension, 1976-78)

Flores Olea, Víctor	1 Dec. 1976-14 Nov. 1978
Díaz de Cossío, Roger	15 Nov. 1978-30 Nov. 1982
Bremer, Juan José	1 Dec. 1982-3 Mar. 1985
Durán Solís, Leonel	4 Mar. 1985-23 Apr. 1986
Reyes Vayssade, Martín	24 Apr. 1986-30 Nov. 1988

Subsecretary of Sports (1981-85) (Subsecretary of Youth and Sports 1976-78)

García Ramírez, Sergio	1 Dec. 1976-11 Jan. 1978
Mondragón y Kalb, Manuel	20 Jan. 1981-30 Nov. 1982
Alanís Camino, Fernando	1 Dec. 1982-24 July 1985

Subsecretary of Cultural Affairs (1958-76)

Castillo Ledón, Amalia	1958-30 Nov. 1964
Magdaleno, Mauricio	1 Dec. 1964-30 Nov. 1970
Aguirre Beltrán, Gonzalo	1 Dec. 1970-30 Nov. 1976

Subsecretary of Educational Planning (Planning, 1971-82)

Díaz de Cossío, Roger	1971-30 Nov. 1976
Bonilla García, Javier	1 Dec. 1976-28 Dec. 1977
Rosenblueth, Emilio	29 Dec. 1977-30 Nov. 1982
Medina, Luis	3 Dec. 1983-30 Nov. 1988

Subsecretary of Middle Education (1980)

Caballero Caballero, Arquímedes	8 July 1980-30 Nov. 1988
Caballero Caballero, Arquímedes	1 Dec. 1988-May 1989
Liceaga Angeles, Jesús Ulises	May 1989-

Subsecretary of Elementary Education (1981)

Noguera Vergara, Arcadio	20 Jan. 1981-30 Nov. 1982
Moguel Contreras, Idolina	1 Dec. 1982-30 Nov. 1988

Subsecretary of Basic Education (1992)

Guevara Niebla, Gilberto	20 July 1992-

Subsecretary of Educational Services for the DDF (1992)

Pescador Osuna, José Angel	20 July 1992-

Oficial Mayor

Molina Betancourt, Rafael	1934-36
Nicomedo, Francisco	1937-38
Pérez H., Arnulfo	1938-40
Enríquez Coyro, Enrique	1944-46
Merino Fernández, Aaron	1946-48
Fraga Magaña, Santiago	1948-52
Miranda Basurto, Angel	1952-53
Echeverría, Luis	1954-57
López Dávila, Manuel	1958-61
Aguilera Dorantes, Mario	1961-70
Barbosa Heldt, Antonio	1970-73
Hedding García, Marcelo	1973-76
López Mestre, Severo	1976-80
Maliachi Velasco, Eduardo	1980-86
Lara Sáenz, Leoncio	1986-1988
Hernández Torres, José de Jesús	1988-92
Moctezuma Barragán, Esteban	1992-

Secretariat of Social Development (Secretariat of Urban Development and Ecology, 1983-92; Secretariat of Public Works and Dwellings, 1976-83; Communication and Public Works, 1891-1958; Public Works, 1958-76)

Secretary

Múgica, Francisco J.	18 June 1935-22 Jan. 1939
Angulo, Melquiades	23 Jan. 1939-30 Nov. 1940
De la Garza Gutiérrez, Jesús B.	1 Dec. 1940-28 Sept. 1941
Avila Camacho, Maximino	29 Sept. 1941-17 Feb. 1945
Martínez Tornel, Pedro	28 Feb. 1945-30 Nov. 1946
García López, Agustín	1 Dec. 1946-30 Nov. 1952
Lazo, Carlos	1 Dec. 1952-5 Nov. 1955
Buchanan, Walter Cross	8 Nov. 1955-30 Nov. 1958
Barros Sierra, Javier	1 Dec. 1958-30 Nov. 1964
Valenzuela Jr., Gilberto	1 Dec. 1964-30 Nov. 1970
Bracamontes, Luis Enrique	1 Dec. 1970-30 Nov. 1976
Ramírez Vázquez, Pedro	1 Dec. 1976-30 Nov. 1982
Javelly Girard, Marcelo	1 Dec. 1982-10 Mar. 1985
Carrillo Areña, Guillermo	11 Mar. 1985-Mar. 1986
Camacho Solís, Víctor Manuel	Mar. 1986-1988
Fraga Mouret, Gabino	1988-30 Nov. 1988
Chirinos Calero, Patricio	1 Dec. 1988-12 Apr. 1992
Colosio, Luis Donaldo	13 April 1992-28 Nov. 1993
Rojas Gutiérrez, Carlos	29 Nov. 1993-

Subsecretary of Public Works, 1976-82 (Subsecretary, 1935-76)

Cortés Herrera, Vicente	1935-6 Apr. 1938
Angulo, Melquiades	1938-23 Jan. 1939
Santillán, Manuel	1939-30 Nov. 1940
Cortés Herrera, Vicente	Dec. 1940-41
Betancourt, Carlos I.	1941-43
Martínez Tornel, Pedro	1943-46
Dovalí Jaime, Antonio	1 Dec. 1946-30 Nov. 1952
Buchanan, Walter C.	1 Dec. 1952-30 Nov. 1958
Bracamontes, Luis E.	1 Dec. 1958-30 Nov. 1964
Espinosa Gutiérrez, Fernando	23 Dec. 1964-3 Apr. 1966
Félix Valdés, Rodolfo	1966-30 Nov. 1982
Díaz Díaz, Daniel	1 Dec. 1982-30 Nov. 1984

Subsecretary of Public Works (1946-58)

Mayoral Heredia, Manuel	1946-50
González, Enrique M.	1950-52
Bracamontes, Luis E.	1952-58

Subsecretary of Ecology, 1983-92 (Subsecretary of Real Property and Urban Works, 1976-83; Subsecretary B, 1972-76)

Etcharren Gutiérrez, René	26 Jan. 1972-30 Nov. 1976
González Sáenz, Leopoldo	1 Dec. 1976-
Velázquez Carmona, Manuel	-30 Nov. 1982

Barcenas Ibarra, Alicia	1 Dec. 1982-30 Mar. 1986
Reyes Luján, Sergio	31 Mar. 1986-25 May 1992

Subsecretary of Housing and Property (1992) (Subsecretary of Housing, 1983-92; Subsecretary of Human Dwellings, 1977-83)

Valner, Gregorio	1977-1982
Velázquez de la Parra, Manuel	1 Dec. 1982-1984
Arroyo de Yta, Fernando	1984-85
Fraga Mouret, Gabino	1985-88
Chávez Martínez, Humberto	1988-92
Phillips Olmedo, Alfredo	26 May 1992-

Subsecretary of Urban Development and Infrastructure (Subsecretary of Urban Development, 1983-92)

Eibenschutz Hartman, Roberto	1983-5 May 1986
Covarrubias Gaitán, Francisco	6 May 1986-25 May 1992
Soberanes Reyes, José Luis	26 May 1992-

Subsecretary of National Properties (1976-77)

Martínez Corbalá, Gonzalo	1 Dec. 1976-3 Feb. 1977

Subsecretary of Regional Development (1992)

Rojas Gutiérrez, Carlos	26 May 1992-29 Nov. 1993

Oficial Mayor

Anglie L., J. Enrique	1935-40
Betancourt, Carlos I.	1940-41
Ortega, Fausto M.	1942-45
Ostos, Guillermo	1946-52
Rocha Sagaón, Gustavo	1953-64
Ríos Elizondo, Roberto	1964-70
Caso Lombardo, Andrés	1970-76
Madrazo Pintado, Carlos	1976-78
Ramírez Delrich, José	1978-82
Arroyo de Yta, Fernando	1982-84
González González, Eduardo	1985-88
Salcedo Aquino, Roberto	1987-88
Bernal Gutiérrez, Andrés Marco A.	1988-92
Reséndiz Contreras, Rafael	1992-

Secretariat of Tourism (Department of Tourism, 1959-75)

Secretary

García González, Alfonso	1 Jan. 1959-2 Dec. 1961
Aguilar, Manuel	2 Dec. 1961-6 July 1962
González de la Vega, Francisco	7 July 1962-30 Nov. 1964
Salvat Rodríguez, Agustín	1 Dec. 1964-30 Nov. 1970
Olachea Borbón, Agustín	1 Dec. 1970-2 Nov. 1973

Hirschfield Almada, Julio	3 Nov. 1973-30 Nov. 1976
Rossell de la Lama, Guillermo	1 Dec. 1976-13 Aug. 1980
*Alegría Escamilla, Rosa**	14 Aug. 1980-30 Nov. 1982
Enríquez Savignac, Antonio	1 Dec. 1982-30 Nov. 1988
Hank González, Carlos	1 Dec. 1988-3 Jan. 1990
Joaquín Coldwell, Pedro	4 Jan. 1990-

Secretary General (1959-76)

Sánchez Juárez, Delfín	1959-60
Aguilar, Manuel	1961
Corrales Ayala, Rafael	1962-64
De la Huerta Oriol, Adolfo	Dec. 1964-74
De la Torre Padilla, Oscar	1974-30 Nov. 1976

Subsecretary of Tourism and Planning (1976-85)

Enríquez Savignac, Antonio	1 Dec. 1976-Nov. 1977
Ortiz Salinas, Antonio	Nov. 1977-1980
Guerra Quiroga, Ricardo	1980-1982
Dondé Escalante, Pedro	1 Dec. 1982-24 July 1985

Subsecretary of Operations (1976)

Herrerias, Armando	1 Dec. 1976-1980
Uranga Gutiérrez, Luis	1980-82
Morones Ochoa, Alejandro	1 Dec. 1982-30 Nov. 1988
Gurría Ordóñez, Manuel	1 Dec. 1988-Jan. 1990
Orozco Loreto, Ismael	Jan. 1990-

Subsecretary of Promotion and Development (Development, 1979-88)

de Santiago, Manuel	4 Apr. 1979-30 Nov. 1982
Grimm González, Guillermo	1 Dec. 1982-30 Nov. 1988
Padilla Couttolenc, Ezequiel	1 Dec. 1988-Jan. 1990
Kiehnle Mutzenbecher, Bruno A.	Jan. 1990-

Secretariat of the Treasury and Public Credit

Secretary

Suárez, Eduardo	18 June 1935-30 Nov. 1946
Beteta, Ramoó	1 Dec. 1946-30 Nov. 1952
Carrillo Flores, Antonio	1 Dec. 1952-30 Nov. 1958
Ortiz Mena, Antonio	1 Dec. 1958-16 Aug. 1970
Margaín, Hugo B.	17 Aug. 1970-29 May 1973
López Portillo, Jóse	29 May 1973-26 Sept. 1975
Beteta, Mario Ramón	27 Sept. 1975-30 Nov. 1976
Moctezuma Cid, Julio Rodolfo	1 Dec. 1976-16 Nov. 1977
Ibarra, David	17 Nov. 1977-15 Mar. 1982

* First woman to reach cabinet rank in Mexico.

Silva Herzog F., Jesús	16 Mar. 1982-16 July 1986
Petriccioli, Gustavo	17 July 1986-30 Nov. 1988
Aspe, Pedro Carlos	30 Nov. 1988-

Subsecretary (1934-58)

Buenrostro Ochoa, Efraín	1934-16 Jan. 1938
Villaseñor, Eduardo	17 Jan. 1938-8 Sept. 1940
Espinosa de los Monteros, Antonio	9 Sept. 1940-30 Nov. 1940
Beteta, Ramón	1 Dec. 1940-2 Oct. 1945
Silva Herzog, Jesús	3 Oct. 1945-30 Nov. 1946
Bustamante, Eduardo	1 Dec. 1946-30 Mar. 1949
González de la Vega, Angel	1949-50
Iturriaga Alarcón, Bernardo	1950-30 Nov. 1952
Armendáriz, Antonio	1 Dec. 1952-30 Nov. 1958

Subsecretary of Credit (1946)

Mancera Ortiz, Rafael	1946-30 Nov. 1958
Rodríguez y Rodríguez, Jesús	1 Dec. 1958-30 Nov. 1970
Beteta M., Mario Ramón	1 Dec. 1970-26 Sept. 1975
De la Madrid, Miguel	29 Sept. 1975-17 May 1979
Silva Herzog F., Jesús	22 May 1979-15 Mar. 1982
Enríquez Savignac, Antonio	16 Mar. 1982-30 Nov. 1982
Suárez Davila, Francisco	1 Dec. 1982-30 Nov. 1988
Ortiz Martínez, Guillermo	1 Dec. 1988-

Subsecretary of Expenditures (1958-76)

Camaño Muñoz, Enrique	1958-30 Nov. 1970
Isoard, Carlos A.	1 Dec. 1970-3 Feb. 1976

Subsecretary of Revenues

Garduño, Eduardo	1958-61
Romero Castaneda, David	1961-64
Alcalá Quintero, Francisco	1 Dec. 1964-30 Nov. 1970
Petricioli, Gustavo	1 Dec. 1970-10 Oct. 1974
Alejo, Javier	10 Oct. 1974-3 Jan. 1975
Pichardo Pagaza, Ignacio	1 Dec. 1976-16 Jan. 1978
Prieto Fortún, Guillermo	17 Jan. 1978-16 July 1986
Serra Puche, Jaime	17 July 1986-30 Nov. 1988
Gil Díaz, Francisco	1 Dec. 1988-

Subsecretary of Tax Inspection (1972-85)

Cárdenas González, Enrique	19 Jan. 1972-29 May 1974
Ruiz Almada, Gilberto	29 May 1974-25 Feb. 1976
Carrillo Olea, Jorge	26 Feb. 1976-30 Nov. 1976
Reyes Retana, Oscar	1 Dec. 1976-6 June 1979
Acosta Lagunes, Agustín	6 June 1979-1980
Trueba Rodríguez, Salvador	1980
Valles González, María del Rosario	1980-30 Nov. 1982
Madrazo, Ignacio L.	1 Dec. 1982-24 July 1985

Subsecretary of Banking (1982-86)
Sales Gutiérrez, Carlos   1 Dec. 1982-16 July 1986

Subsecretary of Budget Control (1992)
Ruiz Sacristán, Carlos   1992-

Subsecretary of International Financial Affairs (1989)
Gurría Treviño, José Angel   1989-

Subsecretary of Programming and Budgeting (1992)
Gasca Neri, Rogelio   1992-

Oficial Mayor
Cárdenas, J. Raymundo   1935-40
Martínez Sicilia, Manuel   1946-49
Iturriaga Alarcón, Bernardo   1950
Noriega, Raúl   1951-58
Sierra, Manuel J.   1958-64
Cordera Pastor, Mario   1964-70
Riba Ricón, Luis   1970-75
Velasco Ibarra, Enrique   1975-76
Azuara Salas, Enrique   1976-77
Trueba Rodríguez, Salvador   1977-80
Madrazo Reynoso, Ignacio   1980-82
Foncerrada Moreno, Juan   1982-86
Mendoza Hernández, Raúl   1986-88
Sánchez Gochicoa, Antonio   1988-

Appendix E

Ambassadors to the United Kingdom, the United States, France, Russia, OAS, Cuba, and the United Nations, 1935–1993

UNITED KINGDOM

Andreu Almazán, Leonides	1 Jan. 1935-3 Dec. 1935
Bassols, Narciso	4 Jan. 1936-4 Jan. 1937
Villa Michel, Primo	1937-38
No Relations	1938-42
Rosenzweig Díaz, Alfonso de	21 Jan. 1942-14 Feb. 1945
Jiménez O'Farrell, Federico	15 Feb. 1945-10 Mar. 1952
de Icaza, Francisco A.	11 Mar. 1952-55
Vacant	1955-57
Campos Ortiz, Pablo	4 July 1957-17 Jan. 1961
Armendáriz, Antonio	18 Jan. 1961-3 May 1965
Suárez, Eduardo	4 May 1965-70
Sánchez Gavito, Vicente	1970-73
Margáin, Hugo B.	1973-76
Tello Macías, Manuel	1976-25 June 1979
De Olloqui, José Juan	1979-82
Cuevas Canciano, Francisco	1982-88
Sepúlveda Amor, Bernardo	1988-93

UNITED STATES

Castillo Najera, Francisco	1935-45
Espinosa de los Monteros, Antonio	1945-49
De la Colina, Rafael	1949-52
Tello, Manuel	1952-58
Carrillo Flores, Antonio	1958-64
Margaín, Hugo B.	31 Dec. 1964-Aug. 1970
Rabasa, Emilio O.	Sept. 1970-Dec. 1970
De Olloqui y Labastida, José Juan	1971-76
Margáin, Hugo B.	1976-82
Sepúlveda Amor, Bernardo	1982
Espinosa de los Reyes, Jorge	1982-88
Petricioli Iturbide, Gustavo	1988-92
Montaño Martínez, Jorge	1992-

FRANCE

Gómez, Marte R.	1935-36
Tejeda, Adalberto	1936-37
Ruiz C., Leobardo	1937-38
Bassols, Narciso	1938-39
Rodríguez, Luis I.	1939-40
Aguilar, Francisco J.	1940-41
Bósquez, Gilberto	1941-45
Ríos Zertuche, Antonio	1945-46
Rosenzweig Díaz, Alfonso	1946
Fernández Manero, Víctor	1946-51
Jiménez O'Farrill, Federico	1951-53
Torres Bodet, Jaime	1953-58
Morones Prieto, Ignacio	1958-65
Apodaca Osuna, Francisco	1965-70
Zavala, Silvio	1970-75
Fuentes, Carlos	1975-77
Flores de la Peña, Horacio	1977-82
Castaneda, Jorge	1982-88
Tello Macías, Manuel	1989-

RUSSIA (1942)

Quintanilla, Luis	1942-45
Bassols, Narciso	1945-46
Sánchez Pontón, Luis	1946
Joublanc Rivas, Luciano	1946-48
Rennou Hay, Germán L.	1948-51
Alemanza Gordoa, Ricardo	1952-53
Rosenzweig Díaz, Alfonso de	1953-60
Iturriaga Suaco, José	1961-66
Zapata Vela, Carlos	1967-69
González Salazar, Roque	1973-75
Flores Olea, Víctor	1976-77
Martínez Aguilar, Rogelio	1977-79
Salinas Lozano, Raúl	1979-80
Carrillo Flores, Antonio	1980-81
Romero Kolbeck, Gustavo	1982
Flores de la Peña, Horacio	1982-88
Bremer Martino, Juan José	1988-90
Tello Macías, Carlos	1990-

OAS (1945)

Quintanilla, Luis	1945-58
Sánchez Gavito, Vicente	1959-65
de la Colina, Rafael	1965-86
Icaza González, Eusebio Antonio de	1986-91

Oñate Laborde, Santiago	1991-92
Carrillo Castro, Alejandro	1992-

CUBA

Cravioto, Alfonso	1934-38
Reyes Spíndola, Octavio	1938-39
Romero, José Rubén	1939-43
Ceniceros, José Angel	1944-47
Coquet, Benito	1947-52
Bosquez, Gilberto	1953-64
Pamanes Escobedo, Fernando	1964-67
Covián Pérez, Miguel	1967-70
Maldonado, Víctor Alfonso	1970-75
Flores, Edmundo	1975
Delgado Ramírez, Celso	1975-76
Madero Vázquez, Ernesto	1976-80
Martínez Corbala, Gonzalo	1980-82
Echeverría Ruiz, Rodolfo	1982-85
Ovalle Fernández, Ignacio	1987-88
Castellano Jiménez, Raúl	1988-90
Moya Palencia, Mario	1990-

UNITED NATIONS (1946)

Padilla Nervo, Luis	1946-52
de la Colina, Rafael	1952-58
Padilla Nervo, Luis	1958-64
Cuevas Canciano, Francisco	1965-71
García Robles, Alfonso	1971-75
Cuevas Canciano, Francisco	1976-79
Muñoz Ledo, Porfirio	1979-85
Moya Palencia, Mario	1985-89
Montaño Martínez, Jorge	1989-92

Appendix F

Governors, 1935–1993

AGUASCALIENTES

Osornio Camarena, Enrique	1 Dec. 1932-30 Nov. 1936
Alvarado, Juan G.	29 June 1937-30 Nov. 1940
Del Valle, Alberto	1 Dec. 1940-30 Nov. 1944
Rodríguez Flores, Jesús M.	1 Dec. 1944-30 Nov. 1950
Games Orozco, Edmundo	1 Dec. 1950-July 1953 (died in office)
Palomino Dena, Benito	9 Sept. 1953-30 Nov. 1956
Ortega Douglas, Luis	1 Dec. 1956-30 Nov. 1962
Olivares Santana, Enrique	1 Dec. 1962-30 Nov. 1968
Guel Jiménez, Francisco	1 Dec. 1968-30 Nov. 1974
Esparza Reyes, J. Refugio	1 Dec. 1974-30 Nov. 1980
Landeros Gallegos, Rodolfo	1 Dec. 1980-30 Nov. 1986
Barberena, Miguel Angel	1 Dec. 1986-30 Nov. 1992
Granados Roldán, Otto	1 Dec. 1992-

BAJA CALIFORNIA (TERRITORY OF BAJA CALIFORNIA DEL NORTE 1936-52)

Magaña, Gildardo (Lt.Col.)	21 Aug. 1935-18 Feb. 1936
Gavira, Gabriel	19 Feb. 1936-15 Aug. 1936
Navarro Cortina, Rafael (Gen.)	16 Aug. 1936-22 Feb. 1937 (resigned)
Sánchez Taboada, Rodolfo (Lt.Col.)	23 Feb. 1937-31 July 1944 (leave)
Rico Islas, Juan Felipe (Gen.)	2 Aug. 1944-20 Dec. 1946
Aldrete, Alberto V.	20 Dec. 1946-Oct. 1947 (resigned)
García González, Alfonso	1947-30 Nov. 1953
Maldonado, Braulio	1 Dec. 1953-30 Nov. 1959
Esquivel Méndez, Eligio	1 Dec. 1959-64 (died in office)
Aubanel Vallejo, Gustavo	18 Dec. 1964-31 Oct. 1965
Sánchez Díaz, Raúl	1 Nov. 1965-31 Oct. 1971
Castellanos, Milton Everardo	1 Nov. 1971-31 Oct. 1977
De la Madrid, Roberto	1 Nov. 1977-31 Oct. 1983
Leyva Mortera, Xicotencatl	1 Nov. 1983-3 Jan. 1989
Báylon Chacón, Oscar	4 Jan. 1989-31 Oct. 1989
Ruffo Appel, Ernesto	1 Nov. 1989-

BAJA CALIFORNIA DEL SUR (TERRITORY UNTIL 1975)

Domínguez, Juan (Gen.)	1932-Oct. 1937
Pedrajo, Rafael M. (Lt. Col.)	1937-40
Múgica, Francisco J. (Gen.)	1940-45
Olachea Aviles, Agustín (Gen.)	1945-56 (resigned)
Flores, Petronilo (Gen.)	14 Apr. 1956-4 Apr. 1957 (died in office)
Rebolledo, Luciano M. (Lt. Col.)	1957-Dec. 1958 (resigned)
Salinas Leal, Bonifacio (Gen.)	1958-11 Apr. 1965 (resigned)
Cervantes del Río, Hugo	20 Apr. 1965-70
Agramont Cota, Félix	1970-75
Mendoza Arámburo, Angel César	1975-1981
Alvarado, Alberto Andrés	1981-1987
Liceaga Ruibal, Manuel	1987-1993

CAMPECHE

Mena Cordova, Eduardo	16 Sept. 1935-15 Sept. 1939
Pérez Martínez, Héctor	16 Sept. 1939-15 Sept. 1943
Lavalle Urbina, Eduardo J.	16 Sept. 1943-15 Sept. 1949
López Hernández, Manuel J.	16 Sept. 1949-15 Sept. 1955
Trueba Urbina, Alberto	16 Sept. 1955-15 Sept. 1961
Ortiz Avila, José (Col.)	16 Sept. 1961-15 Sept.1967
Sansores Pérez, Carlos	16 Sept. 1967-3 Mar. 1973 (leave)[*]
Pérez Camara, Carlos	3 Mar. 1973-15 Sept. 1973
Rodríguez Barrera, Rafael	16 Sept. 1973-15 Sept. 1979
Echeverría Castellot, Eugenio	16 Sept. 1979-15 Sept. 1985
Carrillo Zavala, Abelardo	16 Sept. 1985-15 Sept. 1991
Azar García, Jorge Salomón	16 Sept. 1991-

CHIAPAS

Grajales, Victorio R. (Col.)	1932-22 Sept. 1936 (dissolution of powers)
Coutiño, Amador	23 Sept. 1936-15 Dec. 1936
Gutiérrez Rincón, Efraín A.	15 Dec. 1936-30 Nov. 1940
Gamboa, Rafael P.	1 Dec. 1940-30 Nov. 1944
Esponda, Juan (Gen.)	1 Dec. 1944-Jan. 1947 (resigned)
Lara, César (Gen.)	1947-30 Nov. 1948
Grajales, Francisco J. (Gen.)	1 Dec. 1948-30 Nov. 1952
Aranda Osorio, Efraín	1 Dec. 1952-30 Nov. 1958
León Brindis, Samuel	1 Dec. 1958-30 Nov. 1964
Castillo Tielemans, José	1 Dec. 1964-30 Nov. 1970
Velasco Suárez, Manuel	1 Dec. 1970-30 Nov. 1976
De la Vega Domínguez, Jorge	1 Dec. 1976-8 Dec. 1977

[*] The term *leave* indicates that a governor has been granted permission by the state legislature to leave his office, usually for a period of six months, either for personal or political reasons. In rare cases, a governor may be granted successive six-month leaves and later return to office. See Manuel Sánchez Vite, Governor of Hidalgo, for such a case.

González Blanco, Salomón	9 Dec. 1977-Jan. 1980
Sabines Gutiérrez, Juan	Jan. 1980-30 Nov. 1982
Castellanos, Absalón (Gen)	1 Dec. 1982-30 Nov. 1988
González Blanco, José Patrocino	1 Dec. 1988-3 Jan. 1993
Elmar Selser, Jalmer	4 Jan. 1993-

CHIHUAHUA

Quevedo, Rodrigo M. (Gen.)	1932-3 Oct. 1936
Talamantes, Gustavo L.	4 Oct. 1936-39
Prado Proano, Eugenio	1939-3 Oct. 1940
Chávez, Alfredo (Col.)	4 Oct. 1940-3 Oct. 1944
Folgio Miramontes, Fernando	4 Oct. 1944-3 Oct. 1950
Soto Maynes, Oscar	4 Oct. 1950-Aug. 1955 (leave)
Lozoya Solís, Jesús	10 Aug. 1955-3 Oct. 1955
Borunda, Teófilo R.	4 Oct. 1955-3 Oct. 1962
Giner Durán, Praxedes	4 Oct. 1962-3 Oct. 1968
Flores Sánchez, Oscar	4 Oct. 1968-3 Oct. 1974
Aguirre, Manuel Bernardo	4 Oct. 1974-3 Oct. 1980
Ornelas Kuckle, Oscar	4 Oct. 1980-19 Sept. 1985 (leave)
González Herrera, Saúl	20 Sept. 1985-3 Oct. 1986
Baéza Meléndez, Fernando	4 Oct. 1986-3 Oct. 1992
Barrio, Francisco	4 Oct. 1992-

COAHUILA

Váldés Sánchez, Jesús	1 Dec. 1933-30 Nov. 1937
Rodríguez Triana, Pedro V.	1 Dec. 1937-1 Nov. 1941
Cevera, Gabriel R.	15 Nov. 1941-30 Nov. 1941
López Padilla, Benecio (Gen.)	1 Dec. 1941-30 Nov. 1945
Cepeda Dávila, Ignacio	1 Dec. 1945-47 (committed suicide)
Valero, Vicente	23 July 1947-1947
Ainslie, Ricardo	1947-Mar. 1948 (resigned)
Faz Riza, Paz (Gen.)	Mar. 1948-5 June 1948
López Sánchez, Raúl	6 June 1948-30 Nov. 1951
Cepeda Flores, Ramón	1 Dec. 1951-30 Nov. 1957
Madero González, Raúl (Gen.)	1 Dec. 1957-30 Nov. 1963
Fernández Aguirre, Braulio	1 Dec. 1963-30 Nov. 1969
Gutiérrez Treviño, Eulalio	1 Dec. 1969-30 Nov. 1975
Flores Tapia, Oscar	1 Dec. 1975-10 Aug. 1981 (resigned)
Madero González, Francisco J.	10 Aug. 1981-30 Nov. 1981
de las Fuentes Rodríguez, José	1 Dec. 1981-30 Nov. 1987
Mendoza Berrueto, Eliseo	1 Dec. 1987-30 Nov. 1993

COLIMA

Saucedo, Salvador	20 Nov. 1931-21 Aug. 1935 (dissolution of powers)
Campero, José	21 Aug. 1935-9 Nov. 1935
Santa Ana, Miguel (Gen.)	10 Nov. 1935-31 Oct. 1939
Torres Ortiz, Pedro (Col.)	1 Nov. 1939-31 Oct. 1943
Gudiño Díaz, Manuel	1 Nov. 1943-31 Oct. 1949

González Lugo, J. Jesús (Gen.)	1 Nov. 1949-31 Oct. 1955
Chávez Carrillo, Rodolfo	1 Nov. 1955-31 Oct. 1961
Velasco Curiel, Francisco	1 Nov. 1961-3 Oct. 1967
Silva García, Pablo	1 Nov. 1967-31 Oct. 1973
Ramírez García, Leonel	1 Nov. 1973-31 Dec. 1973
Noriega Pizano, Arturo	1 Jan. 1974-31 Dec. 1979
Alvarez, Griselda	1 Jan. 1980-31 Dec. 1985
Zamora Verduzco, Elías	1 Jan. 1986-31 Dec. 1991
de la Madrid Virgen, Carlos	1 Jan. 1992-

DURANGO

Real, Carlos	1932-31 Dec. 1935 (dissolution of powers)
Ceniceros, Severino (Gen.)	1 Jan. 1936-Aug. 1936 (resigned)
Calderón Rodríguez, Enrique	Aug. 1936-40
Velázquez, Elpidio G. (Gen.)	1940-44
Corral Martínez, Blas (Gen.)	15 Sept. 1944-30 Apr. 1947 (died in office)
Celís M., Francisco	30 Apr. 1947-18 Sept. 1947
Valdés, José Ramón	19 Sept. 1947-14 Sept. 1950
Torres Sánchez, Enrique	15 Sept. 1950-14 Sept. 1956
González de la Vega, Francisco	15 Sept. 1956-3 July 1962 (resigned)
Dupré Ceniceros, Enrique	15 Sept. 1962-4 Aug. 1966 (dissolution of powers)
Rodríguez Solorzano, Angel	1966-14 Sept. 1968
Páez Urquidi, Alejandro	15 Sept. 1968-14 Sept. 1974
Mayagoitía Domínguez, Héctor	15 Sept. 1974-14 Dec. 1979
Gámiz Fernández, Salvador	15 Dec. 1979-14 Sept. 1980
Del Castillo Franco, Armando	15 Sept. 1980-14 Sept. 1986
Ramírez Gamero, José	15 Sept. 1986-14 Sept. 1992
Silero Esparza, Maximiliano	15 Sept. 1992-

GUANAJUATO

Yáñez Maya, Jesús	16 Dec. 1935 (dissolution of powers)
Fernández Martínez, Enrique	18 Dec. 1935-20 Apr. 1937
Rodríguez, Luis I.	21 Apr. 1937-27 Apr. 1938 (leave)
Rangel Hurtado, Rafael	27 Apr. 1938-39
Rodríguez, Luis I.	1939-25 Sept. 1939
Fernández Martínez, Enrique	26 Sept. 1939-25 Sept. 1943
Hidalgo, Ernesto	26 Sept. 1943-8 Jan. 1946 (dissolution of powers)
Guerrero Mendoza, Nicéforo	10 Jan. 1946-22 Sept. 1947 (resigned)
Castorena, J. Jesús	22 Sept. 1947-29 Oct. 1948
Díaz Infante, Luis	30 Oct. 1948-25 Sept. 1949
Aguilar y Maya, José	26 Sept. 1949-25 Sept. 1955
Rodríguez Gaona, J. Jesús	26 Sept. 1955-25 Sept. 1961
Torres Landa, Juan José	26 Sept. 1961-25 Sept. 1967
Moreno, Manuel M.	26 Sept. 1967-25 Sept. 1973
Ducoing Gamba, Luis Humberto	26 Sept. 1973-25 Sept. 1979

Velasco Ibarra, Enrique	26 Sept. 1979-26 June 1984 (resigned)
Téllez Cruz, Agustín	27 June 1984-25 Sept. 1985
Corrales Ayala, Rafael	26 Sept. 1985-25 Sept. 1991
Medina Plascencia, Carlos	26 Sept. 1991- (interim)

GUERRERO

Guevara, Gabriel R. (Gen.)	25 Mar. 1933-5 Nov. 1935 (dissolution of powers)
Lugo, José (Gen.)	5 Nov. 1935-31 Mar. 1937
Berber, Alberto F. (Gen.)	1 Apr. 1937-18 Feb. 1941
Carraco Cardoso, Carlos	19 Feb. 1941-30 June 1941
Catalán Calvo, Rafael	30 June 1941-31 Mar. 1945
Leyva Mancilla, Gabriel (Gen.)	1 Apr. 1945-31 Mar. 1951
Gómez Maganda, Alejandro	1 Apr. 1951-21 May 1954 (dissolution of powers)
Arrieta M., Darío L.	21 May 1954-31 Mar. 1957
Caballero Aburto, Raúl (Gen.)	1 Apr. 1957-3 Jan. 1961 (dissolution of powers)
Martínez Adame, Arturo	Jan. 1961-31 Mar. 1963
Abarca Alarcón, Raimundo	1 Apr. 1963-31 Mar. 1969
Maldonado Pérez, Caritino	1 Apr. 1969-17 Apr. 1971 (died)
Nogueda Otero, Israel	Apr. 1971-31 Jan. 1975 (dissolution of powers)
Olea Muñoz, Javier	Feb. 1975-1 Apr. 1975
Figueroa, Rubén	1 Apr. 1975-31 Mar. 1981
Cervantes Delgado, Alejandro	1 Apr. 1981-31 Mar. 1987
Ruiz Massieu, Francisco	1 Apr. 1987-31 Mar. 1993
Figueroa Alcocer, Rubén	1 Apr. 1993-

HIDALGO

Viveros, Ernesto	1933-37
Rojo Gómez, Javier	1937-40
Villegas, Ofilio (Gen.)	1940-41
Lugo Guerrero, José	1941-45
Aguirre, Vicente	1945-31 Mar. 1951
Rueda Villagrán, Quintin	1 Apr. 1951-31 Mar. 1957
Corona del Rosal, Alfonso (Gen.)	1 Apr. 1957-4 Dec. 1958 (resigned)
Cravioto, Oswaldo	6 Dec. 1958-31 Mar. 1963
Ramírez Guerrero, Carlos	1 Apr. 1963-31 Mar. 1969
Sánchez Vite, Manuel	1 Apr. 1969-Dec. 1970 (leave)
Serna, Donaciano	Dec. 1970-May 1972
Sánchez Vite, Manuel	May 1972-31 Mar. 1975
Miranda Andrade, Otoniel	1 Apr. 1975-29 Apr. 1975 (dissolution of powers)
Lozano Ramírez, Raúl	May 1975-Aug. 1975
Rojo Lugo, Jorge	Aug. 1975-1 Dec. 1976 (leave)
Suárez Molina, José Luis	3 Dec. 1976-1 June 1978
Rojo Lugo, Jorge	2 June 1978-31 Mar. 1981
Rossell de la Lama, Guillermo	1 Apr. 1981-31 Mar. 1987

Lugo Verduzco, Adolfo	1 Apr. 1987-31 Mar. 1993 *Murillo*
Karam, Jesús	1 Apr. 1993-

JALISCO

Topete, Everardo	1 Mar. 1935-39
Barba González, Silvano	1939-43
García Barragán, Marcelino	1943-17 Feb. 1947 (removed)
Coronado Organista, Saturino	17 Feb. 1947-28 Feb. 1947
González Gallo, Jesús	1 Mar. 1947-28 Feb. 1953
Yáñez, Agustín	1 Mar. 1953-28 Feb. 1959
Gil Preciado, Juan	1 Mar. 1959-4 Dec. 1964 (resigned)
Muñoz, José de Jesús	Dec. 1964-28 Feb. 1965
Medina Asencio, Francisco	1 Mar. 1965-28 Feb. 1971
Orozco Romero, Alberto	1 Mar. 1971-28 Feb. 1977
Romero de Velasco, Flavio	1 Mar. 1977-28 Feb. 1983
Alvarez del Castillo, Enrique	1 Mar. 1983-30 Nov. 1988
Rodríguez Gómez, Francisco	1 Dec. 1988-28 Feb. 1989
Cosío Vidaurri, Guillermo	1 Mar. 1989-2 May 1992 (resigned)
Rivera Aceves, Carlos	3 May 1992-

MÉXICO

Solorzano, José Luis	1933-27 June 1936 (resigned)
López, Eucario	3 July 1936-15 Sept. 1937
Labra García, Wenceslao (Col.)	16 Sept. 1937-15 Sept. 1941
Zárate Albarrán, Alfredo	16 Sept. 1941-5 Mar. 1942 (assassinated)
Gutiérrez, José L.	8 Mar. 1942-15 Mar. 1942
Fabela, Isidro	16 Mar. 1942-15 Sept. 1945
Del Mazo Vélez, Alfredo	16 Sept. 1945-15 Sept. 1951
Sánchez Colín, Salvador	16 Sept. 1951-15 Sept. 1957
Baz, Gustavo	16 Sept. 1957-15 Sept. 1963
Fernández Albarrán, Juan	16 Sept. 1963-15 Sept. 1969
Hank González, Carlos	16 Sept. 1969-15 Sept. 1975
Jiménez Cantú, Jorge	16 Sept. 1975-15 Sept. 1981
del Mazo González, Alfredo	16 Sept. 1981-18 Apr. 1986
Baranda, Alfredo	21 Apr. 1986-15 Sept. 1987
Beteta, Mario Ramón	16 Sept. 1987-7 Sept. 1989
Pichardo Pagaza, Ignacio	11 Sept. 1989-15 Sept. 1993
Chuayffet, Emilio	16 Sept. 1993-

MICHOACÁN

Ordorico Villamar, Rafael (Gen.)	18 June 1935-15 Sept. 1936 (provisional)
Magaña, Gildardo (Gen.)	16 Sept. 1936-13 Dec. 1939 (died in office)
Magaña Cerdo, Conrado	13 Dec. 1939-15 Sept. 1940
Ireta Viveros, Félix (Gen.)	16 Sept. 1940-15 Sept. 1944
Mendoza Pardo, José María	16 Sept. 1944-26 Aug. 1949
Rentería, Daniel T.	1949-15 Sept. 1950
Cárdenas del Río, Damaso	16 Sept. 1950-15 Sept. 1956
Franco Rodríguez, David	16 Sept. 1956-15 Sept. 1962

Arriaga Rivera, Agustín	16 Sept. 1962-15 Sept. 1968
Gálvez Betancourt, Carlos	16 Sept. 1968-15 Sept. 1971
Chávez Hernández, José	16 Sept. 1971-15 Sept. 1974
Torres Manzo, Carlos	16 Sept. 1974-15 Sept. 1980
Cárdenas Solorzano, Cuauhtémoc	16 Sept. 1980-15 Sept. 1986
Martínez Villicaña, José Luis	16 Sept. 1986-3 Dec. 1988
Figueroa Zamudio, Jaime Genovevo	4 Dec. 1988-15 Sept. 1992
Villaseñor Peña, Eduardo	16 Sept. 1992-6 Oct. 1992 (leave)
Chávez, Ausencio	7 Oct. 1992-

MORELOS

Bustamante, José Refugio	1934-6 May 1938 (dissolution of powers)
Sámano, Alfonso (Col.)	6 May 1938-16 May 1938
Perdomo, D. Elpidio (Gen.)	17 May 1938-16 May 1942
Castillo López, Jesús	17 May 1942-17 May 1946
Escobar Muñoz, Ernesto	18 May 1946-17 May 1952
López de Nava, Rodolfo (Gen.)	18 May 1952-17 May 1958
López Avelar, Norberto (Col.)	18 May 1958-17 May 1964
Riva Palacio, Emilio	18 May 1964-17 May 1970
Rivera Crespo, Felipe	18 May 1970-17 May 1976
León Bejarano, Armando	18 May 1976-17 May 1982
Ortega, Lauro	18 May 1982-17 May 1988
Riva Palacio, Antonio	18 May 1988-

NAYARIT

Parra, Francisco	1 Jan. 1934-31 Dec. 1937
Espinosa Sánchez, Juventino (Gen.)	1 Jan. 1938-31 Dec. 1941
Miramontes, Candelario	1 Jan. 1942-31 Dec. 1945
Flores Muñoz, Gilberto	1 Jan. 1946-31 Dec. 1951
Limón Guzmán, José	1 Jan. 1952-31 Dec. 1957
García Montero, Francisco	1 Jan. 1958-31 Dec. 1963
Gascón Mercado, Julián	1 Jan. 1964-31 Dec. 1969
Gómez Reyes, Roberto	1 Jan. 1970-31 Dec. 1975
Flores Curiel, Rogelio	1 Jan. 1976-31 Dec. 1981
González Parra, Emilio	1 Jan. 1981-31 Dec. 1987
Delgado, Celso H.	1 Jan. 1988-

NUEVO LEÓN

Quiroga, Pablo	1933-27 Sept. 1935
Morales Sánchez, Gregorio (Gen.)	28 Sept. 1935-36
Guerrero, Anacleto (Gen.)	1936-39
Salinas Leal, Bonifacio	1939-43
Arteaga y Santoyo, Armando	1943-44
De la Garza, Arturo B.	1944-49
Morones Prieto, Ignacio	4 Oct. 1949-Dec. 1952
Vivanco, José S.	Dec. 1952-3 Oct. 1955
Rangel Frías, Raúl	4 Oct. 1955-3 Oct. 1961
Livas Villarreal, Eduardo	4 Oct. 1961-3 Oct. 1967
Elizondo, Eduardo A.	4 Oct. 1967-June 1971 (resigned)

Farías, Luis M.	June 1970-3 Oct. 1973
Zorrilla, Pedro	4 Oct. 1973-3 Oct. 1979
Martínez Domínguez, Alfonso	4 Oct. 1979-3 Oct. 1985
Treviño Martínez, Jorge A.	4 Oct. 1985-3 Oct. 1991
Rizzo, Socrates	4 Oct. 1991-

OAXACA

García Toledo, Anastasio	1 Dec. 1932-30 Nov. 1936
Chapital, Constatino (Col.)	1 Dec. 1936-30 Nov. 1940
González Fernández, Vicente (Col.)	1 Dec. 1940-30 Nov. 1944
Sánchez Cono, Edmundo (Gen.)	1 Dec. 1944-19 Jan. 1947
Vasconcelos, Eduardo	20 Jan. 1947-30 Nov. 1950
Mayoral Heredia, Manuel	1 Dec. 1950-31 July 1952 (dissolution of powers)
Cabrera Carrasquedo, Manuel (Gen.)	1 Aug. 1952-1 Oct. 1955
Pacheco Iturribarría, José (Gen.)	11 Oct. 1955-30 Nov. 1956
Pérez Gasca, Alfonso	1 Dec. 1956-30 Nov. 1962
Brena Torres, Rodolfo	1 Dec. 1962-30 Nov. 1968
Bravo Ahuja, Víctor	1 Dec. 1968-30 Nov. 1970 (resigned)
Gómez Sandoval, Fernando	1 Dec. 1970-30 Nov. 1974
Zárate Aquino, Manuel	1 Dec. 1974-3 Mar. 1977 (resigned)
Jiménez Ruiz, Eliseo (Gen.)	4 Mar. 1977-30 Nov. 1980
Vázquez Colmenares, Pedro	1 Dec. 1980-30 Nov. 1986
Ramírez López, Heladio	1 Dec. 1986-30 Nov. 1992
Carrasco, Diodoro	1 Dec. 1992-

PUEBLA

Mijares Palencia, José (Gen.)	1933-31 Jan. 1937
Avila Camacho, Maximino (Gen.)	1 Feb. 1937-3 Jan. 1941
Bautista, Gonzalo	1 Feb. 1941-31 Jan. 1945
Betancourt, Carlos I.	1 Feb. 1945-31 Jan. 1951
Avila Camacho, Rafael	1 Feb. 1951-31 Jan. 1957
Ortega, Fausto M.	1 Feb. 1957-31 Jan. 1963
Nava Castillo, Antonio (Gen.)	1 Feb. 1963-30 Oct. 1964 (resigned)
Merino Fernández, Aarón	1 Nov. 1964-31 Jan. 1969
Moreno Valle, Rafael	1 Feb. 1969-Apr. 1972 (leave)
Bautista O'Farrill, Gonzalo	14 Apr. 1972-8 Mar. 1972 (resigned)
Morales Blumenkron, Guillermo	9 Mar. 1973-31 Jan. 1975
Toxqui Fernández, Alfredo	1 Feb. 1975-31 Jan. 1981
Jiménez Moreno, Guillermo	1 Feb. 1981-31 Jan. 1987
Piña Olaya, Mariano	1 Feb. 1987-31 Jan. 1993
Bartlett Díaz, Manuel	1 Feb. 1993-

QUERÉTARO

Rodríguez Familiar, Ramón (Gen.)	1 Oct. 1935-30 Sept. 1939
Rubio Ortiz, Noradino	1 Oct. 1939-30 Sept. 1943
Pozo, Agapito	1 Oct. 1943-17 Apr. 1949
Luque Loyola, Eduardo	18 Apr. 1949-30 Sept. 1949
Mondragón, Octavio S.	1 Oct. 1949-30 Sept. 1955

Gorráez, Juan C.	1 Oct. 1955-30 Sept. 1961
González Cosío, Manuel	1 Oct. 1961-30 Sept. 1967
Castro Sánchez, Juventino	1 Oct. 1967-30 Sept. 1973
Calzada, Antonio	1 Oct. 1973-30 Sept. 1979
Camacho Guzmán, Rafael	1 Oct. 1979-30 Sept. 1985
Palacios Alcocer, Mariano	1 Oct. 1985-30 Sept. 1991
Burgos García, Enrique	1 Oct. 1991-

QUINTANA ROO (TERRITORY UNTIL 1975)

Melgar, Rafael E.	17 Jan. 1935-14 Dec. 1940
Guevara, Gabriel R. (Gen.)	15 Dec. 1940-44
Ramírez, Margarito	30 Mar. 1944-Jan. 1959 (resigned)
Merino Fernández, Aarón	16 Jan. 1959-Nov. 1964
Mendoza Becerra, Eligio	Nov. 1964-19 Mar. 1965
Figueroa, Ruffo	20 Mar. 1965-14 May 1967 (resigned)
Rojo Gómez, Javier	2 June 1967-31 Dec. 1970 (died in office)
Gutiérrez Ruiz, David Gustavo	7 Jan. 1971-4 Apr. 1975
Martínez Ross, Jesús	4 Apr. 1975-3 Apr. 1981
Joaquín Coldwell, Pedro	4 Apr. 1981-3 Apr. 1987
Borge Martín, Miguel	4 Apr. 1987-3 Apr. 1993
Villanueva Madrid, Mario	4 Apr. 1993-

SAN LUIS POTOSÍ

Anaya, Aurelio G.	1935-36
Hernández Netro, Mateo (Col.)	26 Sept. 1936-22 May 1938
Rivas Guillén, Genovevo (Gen.)	26 May 1938-39
Pérez Gallardo, Reynaldo (Gen.)	1939-19 Aug. 1941 (dissolution of powers)
Jiménez Delgado, Ramón (Gen.)	20 Aug. 1941-25 Sept. 1943
Santos, Gonzalo N.	26 Sept. 1943-25 Sept. 1949
Salas, Ismael	26 Sept. 1949-25 Sept. 1955
Alvarez López, Manuel	26 Sept. 1955-Jan. 1959 (resigned)
Martínez de la Vega, Francisco	2 Apr. 1959-25 Sept. 1961
López Dávila, Manuel	26 Sept. 1961-25 Sept. 1967
Rocha, Antonio	26 Sept. 1967-25 Sept. 1973
Fonseca Alvarez, Guillermo	26 Sept. 1973-25 Sept. 1979
Jongitud Barrios, Carlos	26 Sept. 1979-25 Sept. 1985
Salazar Martínez, Florencio	26 Sept. 1985-24 May 1987
Ortiz Santos, Leopoldino	25 May 1987-25 Sept. 1991
Zapata Loredo, Fausto	26 Sept. 1991-9 Oct. 1991
Martínez Corbalá, Gonzalo	10 Oct. 1991-18 Oct. 1992
Torres Corzo, Teófilo	18 Oct. 1992-18 May 1993
Sánchez Unzueta, Horacio	18 May 1993-

SINALOA

Páez, Manuel	1933-16 Dec. 1935 (dissolution of powers)
Leyva Velázquez, Gabriel (Gen.)	17 Dec. 1935-15 Sept. 1936
Delgado, Alfredo (Gen.)	16 Sept. 1936-15 Sept. 1940

Loaiza, Rodolfo (Col.)	16 Sept. 1940-20 Feb. 1944 (assassinated)
Cruz, Ricardo Teodoro	1944-31 Dec. 1944
Macías Valenzuela, Pablo E. (Gen.)	1 Jan. 1945-31 Dec. 1950
Pérez Arce, Enrique	1 Jan. 1951-Feb. 1953 (resigned)
Aguilar Pico, Rigoberto	19 Aug. 1953-31 Dec. 1956
Leyva Velázquez, Gabriel (Gen.)	1 Jan. 1957-31 Dec. 1962
Sánchez Celis, Leopoldo	1 Jan. 1963-31 Dec. 1968
Váldez Montoya, Alfredo	1 Jan. 1969-31 Dec. 1974
Calderón Velarde, Alfonso	1 Jan. 1975-31 Dec. 1980
Toledo Corro, Antonio	1 Jan. 1981-31 Dec. 1986
Labastida Ochoa, Francisco	1 Jan. 1987-31 Dec. 1992
Vega Alvarado, Renato	1 Jan. 1993-

SONORA

Ramos, Ramón	1 Sept. 1935-16 Dec. 1935 (dissolution of powers)
Gutiérrez Cázares, Jesús	(Gen.) 17 Dec. 1935-3 Jan. 1937
Yocupicio, Román	4 Jan. 1937-31 Aug. 1939
Macías Valenzuela, Anselmo (Gen.)	1 Sept. 1939-31 Aug. 1943
Rodríguez, Abelardo L.	1 Sept. 1943-Apr. 1948 (leave)
Sobarzo, Horacio	Apr. 1948-31 Aug. 1949
Soto, Ignacio	1 Sept. 1949-31 Aug. 1955
Obregón, Alvaro	1 Sept. 1955-31 Aug. 1961
Encinas Johnson, Luis	1 Sept. 1961-31 Aug. 1967
Félix Serna, Faustino	1 Sept. 1967-31 Aug. 1973
Biebrich Torres, Carlos A.	1 Sept. 1973-25 Oct. 1975 (resigned)
Carrillo Marcar, Alejandro	25 Oct. 1975-31 Aug. 1979
Ocaña García, Samuel	1 Sept. 1979-31 Aug. 1985
Félix Valdes, Rodolfo	1 Sept. 1985-31 Aug. 1991
Morúa Johnson, Mario	1 Sept. 1991-1 Oct. 1991
Fabio Beltrones, Manlio	1 Oct. 1991-

TABASCO

Lastra Ortiz, Manuel	1935-23 July 1935 (dissolution of powers)
Calles, Aureo (Gen.)	24 July 1935-36
Fernández Manero, Víctor	1936-31 Dec. 1938
Trujillo Gurría, Francisco	1 Jan. 1939-31 Dec. 1943
De la Flor Casanova, Noé	1 Jan. 1944-31 Dec. 1947
Santamaría, Francisco J.	1 Jan. 1948-31 Dec. 1952
Bartlett Bautista, Manuel	1 Jan. 1953-22 Mar. 1955 (leave)
Orrico de los Llanos, Miguel (Gen.)	23 Mar. 1955-31 Dec. 1958
Madrazo, Carlos	1 Jan. 1959-31 Dec. 1964
Mora, Manuel R.	1 Jan. 1965-31 Dec. 1970
Trujillo García, Mario	1 Jan. 1971-31 Dec. 1976
Rovirosa Wade, Leandro	1 Jan. 1977-31 Dec. 1982
González Pedrero, Enrique	1 Jan. 1983-31 Dec. 1988
Neme Castillo, Salvador	1 Jan. 1989-28 Jan. 1992
Gurría Ordóñez, Manuel	1 Feb. 1992-

TAMAULIPAS

Villarreal, Rafael	5 Feb. 1935-20 Nov. 1935 (resigned)
Canseco, Enrique	16 Aug. 1935-4 Feb. 1937
Gómez, Marte R.	5 Feb. 1937-4 Feb. 1941
Aguilar Castillo, Magdaleno	5 Feb. 1941-4 Feb. 1945
González, Hugo P.	5 Feb. 1945-10 Apr. 1947 (dissolution of powers)
Gárate Legleu, Raúl	17 Apr. 1947-4 Feb. 1951
Terán Z., Horacio	5 Feb. 1951-4 Feb. 1957
Treviño Zapata, Norberto	5 Feb. 1957-4 Feb. 1963
Balboa Gojón, Praxedis	5 Feb. 1963-4 Feb. 1969
Ravize, Manuel A.	5 Feb. 1969-4 Feb. 1975
Cárdenas González, Enrique	5 Feb. 1975-4 Feb. 1981
Martínez Manatou, Emilio	5 Feb. 1981-4 Feb. 1987
Villarreal Guerra, Américo	5 Feb. 1987-4 Feb. 1993
Cavazos Lema, Manuel	5 Feb. 1993-

TLAXCALA

Bonilla, Adolfo	1933-37
Candia, Isidro (Col.)	1937-41
Cisneros Molina, Joaquín	1941
Santillán, Manuel	1941-Aug. 1944 (resigned)
Angulo, Mauro	1944-14 Jan. 1945
Avila Bretón, Rafael	15 Jan. 1945-14 Jan. 1951
Mazarrasa, Felipe	15 Jan. 1951-14 Jan. 1957
Cisneros Molina, Joaquín	15 Jan. 1957-14 Jan. 1963
Cervantes Hernández, Anselmo	15 Jan. 1963-14 Jan. 1969
Bonilla Vázquez, Ignacio (Gen.)	15 Jan. 1969-19 Jan. 1970 (died in office)
Cuéllar Abarca, Crisanto	Jan. 1970-Apr. 1970
Huerta Sánchez, Luciano	Apr. 1970-14 Jan. 1975
Sánchez Piedras, Emilio	15 Jan. 1975-14 Jan. 1981
Hernández Gómez, Tulio	15 Jan. 1981-14 Jan. 1981
Paredes, Beatriz	15 Jan. 1987-11 Apr. 1992
Quiroz, Samuel	11 Apr. 1992-14 Jan. 1993
Alvarez Lima, José Antonio	15 Jan. 1993-

VERACRUZ

Vázquez Vela, Gonzalo	1 Dec. 1932-1935 (leave)
Robolledo, Guillermo	3 July 1935-30 Nov. 1936
Alemán V., Miguel	1 Dec. 1936-39 (resigned)
Casas Alemán, Francisco	1939-30 Nov. 1940
Cerdán, Jorge	1 Dec. 1940-30 Nov. 1944
Ruiz Cortines, Adolfo	1 Dec. 1944-48
Carvajal, Angel	1948-30 Nov. 1950
Muñoz T., Marco A.	1 Dec. 1950-30 Nov. 1956
Quirasco, Antonio M.	1 Dec. 1956-30 Nov. 1962
López Arias, Fernando	1 Dec. 1962-30 Nov. 1968
Murillo Vidal, Rafael	1 Dec. 1968-30 Nov. 1974

Hernández Ochoa, Rafael	1 Dec. 1974-30 Nov. 1980
Acosta Lagunes, Agustín	1 Dec. 1980-30 Nov. 1986
Gutiérrez Barrios, Fernando	1 Dec. 1986-30 Nov. 1988
Delgado Ranuro, Dante	1 Dec. 1988-30 Nov. 1992
Chirinos, Patricio	1 Dec. 1992-

YUCATÁN

Alayola Barrera, César	2 Feb. 1934-5 Oct. 1935 (resigned)
López Cárdenas, Fernando	5 Oct. 1935-30 June 1936
Palomo Valencia, Florencio	1 July 1936-31 Jan. 1938
Canto Echeverría, Humberto	1 Feb. 1938-31 Jan. 1942
Novelo Torres, Ernesto	1 Feb. 1942-31 Jan. 1946
González Beytia, José	1 Feb. 1946-Sept. 1951 (resigned)
Esquivel Medina, Humberto	1951- 31 Jan. 1952
Marentes Miranda, Tomás	1 Feb. 1952-15 June 1953 (resigned)
Mena Palomo, Víctor	18 June 1953-31 Jan. 1958
Franco Aguilar, Agustín	1 Feb. 1958-31 Jan. 1964
Torres Mesias, Luis	1 Feb. 1964-31 Jan. 1970
Loret de Mola, Carlos	1 Feb. 1970-31 Jan. 1976
Luna Kan, Francisco	1 Feb. 1976-31 Jan. 1982
Alpuche Pinzón, Graciliano (Gen.)	1 Feb. 1982-15 Feb. 1984 (resigned)
Cervera Pacheco, Víctor	16 Feb. 1984-31 Jan. 1988
Manzanilla Schaffer, Víctor	1 Feb. 1988-14 Feb. 1991 (resigned)
Sauri Riancho, Dulce María	15 Feb. 1991-

ZACATECAS

Ramos Santos, Matías	28 Nov. 1932-15 Sept. 1936
Banuelos, J. Félix	16 Sept. 1936-15 Sept. 1940
Natera, Pánfilo	16 Sept. 1940-15 Sept. 1944
Reynoso, Leobardo	16 Sept. 1944-15 Sept. 1950
Minero Roque, José	16 Sept. 1950-15 Sept. 1956
García, Francisco E.	16 Sept. 1956-15 Sept. 1962
Rodríguez Elías, José	16 Sept. 1962-15 Sept. 1968
Ruiz González, Pedro	16 Sept. 1968-15 Sept. 1974
Pámanes Escobedo, Fernando	16 Sept. 1974-15 Sept. 1980
Cervantes Corona, José	16 Sept. 1980-15 Sept. 1986
Borrego Estrada, Genaro	16 Sept. 1986-12 Apr. 1992
León Sánchez, Pedro	12 Apr. 1992-15 Sept. 1992
Romo, Arturo	16 Sept. 1992-

Appendix G

Rectors and Directors General of the National Universities, 1935–1993

National Autonomous University of Mexico/Universidad Nacional Autónoma de Mexico (UNAM) (founded 1551)

Rector

Ocaranza Carmona, Fernando	26 Nov. 1934-17 Sept. 1935
Chico Goerne, Luis	24 Sept. 1935-21 June 1939
Baz, Gustavo	21 June 1939-3 Dec. 1940
De la Cueva y de la Rosa, Mario	3 Dec. 1940-17 June 1942
Brito Foucher, Rodulfo	18 June 1942-27 July 1944
Caso y Andrade, Alfonso	15 Aug. 1944-24 Mar. 1945
Fernández Macgregor, Genaro	24 Mar. 1945-4 Mar. 1946
Zubirán Anchondo, Salvador	4 Mar. 1946-23 Apr. 1948
Garrido Díaz, Luis	23 Apr. 1948-14 Feb. 1952
Carrillo Flores, Nabor	14 Feb. 1952-13 Feb. 1961
Chávez Sánchez, Ignacio	13 Feb. 1961-5 May 1966
Barros Sierra, Javier	5 May 1966-5 May 1970
González Casanova, Pablo	5 May 1970-8 Dec. 1972
Soberón, Guillermo	3 Jan. 1973-1981
Rivero Serrano, Octavio	1981-1984
Carpizo MacGregor, Jorge	2 Jan. 1985-2 Jan. 1989
Sarukhán, José	3 Jan. 1989-

Secretaries General   **(1935-1988)**

Gual Vidal, Manuel	1935-38
De la Cueva, Mario	1938-40
Torres Torrija, José	1940-42
Noriega, Alfonso	1942
Ramírez Moreno, Samuel	1942-44
Jiménez Rueda, Julio	1944
García Maynez, Eduardo	1944-46
González Castro, Francisco	1946-47
Rivera Pérez Campos, José	1947-48
González Bustamante, Juan José	1948-52
Carranca y Trujillo, Raúl	1952-53
Del Pozo, Efrén C.	1953-61
Mantilla Molina, Roberto	1961-66

Solana Morales, Fernando	1966-70
Madrazo Garamendi, Manuel	1970-72
Pérez Correa, Fernando	1972-81
Béjar Navarro, Raúl	1981-84
Narro Robles, José	1985-88

National Polytechnic Institute/Instituto Politécnico Nacional (founded 1937)

Director General

Medellín Ostos, Roberto	1937
Bernard, Miguel	1938-39
Cerrillo Valdivia, Manuel	1940
Massieu, Wilfrido	1940-42
Laguardia, José	1942-43
Sandoval Vallarta, Manuel	1943-46
Alvarado Pies, Gustavo	1946-48
Guillot Schiaffino, Alejandro	1948-50
Ramírez Caraza, Juan Manuel	1950-53
Hernández Corzo, Rodolfo	1953-56
Peralta Díaz, Alejo	1956-59
Méndez Docurro, Eugenio	1959-63
Padilla Segura, José Antonio	1963-64
Massieu Helguera, Guillermo	1964-70
Zorrilla, Manuel	1970-12 Dec. 1973
Gerstl Valenzuela, José	13 Dec. 1973-14 Dec. 1976
Viñals, Sergio	15 Dec. 1976-13 Dec. 1979
Mayagoitía Domínguez, Héctor	14 Dec. 1979-30 Nov. 1982
Garza Caballero, Manuel	6 Dec. 1982-3 Dec. 1985
Talán Ramírez, Raúl Eric	4 Dec. 1985-Dec. 1988
Joffre Velásquez, Oscar Javier	Dec. 1988-

Appendix H

National Executive Committees of the PNR, PRM, and PRI, 1935–1993

National Revolutionary Party (Partido Nacional Revolucionario, PNR)

18 JUNE 1935

President	*Emilio Portes Gil*
Secretary General	*Ignacio García Téllez*
Labor Secretary	*Gustavo Talamantes*
Agrarian Secretary	*Ernesto Soto Reyes*
Press Secretary	*Roque Estrada*
Economic Secretary	*Rodolfo T. Loaiza*
Education Secretary	*David Ayala*
Organization Secretary	Juan Ignacio García
IEPES Secretary	*Julián Garza Tijerina*

27 AUG. 1936

President	*Silvano Barba González*
Secretary General	*Estéban García de Alba*
Labor Secretary	*Arnulfo Pérez H.*
Agrarian Secretary	*Antonio Mayés Navarro*
Press Secretary	*Gilberto Bosques S.*
Organization Secretary	*Wenceslao Labra*
Economic Secretary	Julián Aguilar G.
Education Secretary	*Gilberto Flores Muñoz*
IEPES Secretary	Enrique Calderón

1937

President	*Silvano Barba González*
Secretary General	*Gilberto Flores Muñoz*
Labor Secretary	*Arnulfo Pérez H.*
Agrarian Secretary	*Antonio Mayés Navarro*
Education Secretary	*Gilberto Bosques S.*
Press Secretary	*Rafael Molina Betancourt*
Organization Secretary	*Wenceslao Labra*
Economic Secretary	Julián Aguilar G.
IEPES Secretary	Enrique Calderón

Party of the Mexican Revolution(Partido Revolucionario Mexicano, PRM)

2 APR. 1938

President	*Luis I. Rodríguez*
Secretary General	*Estéban García de Alba*
Labor Secretary	*Alfonso Sánchez Madariaga*
Agrarian Secretary	*León García*
Popular Secretary	*Leopoldo Hernández Partida*
Military Secretary	*Edmundo Sánchez Cano*
Press Secretary	*Gilberto Bosques S.*
Finance Secretary	Elías Miranda

19 JUNE 1939

President	*Heriberto Jara*
Secretary General	*Gustavo Cárdenas Huerta*
Finance Secretary	Carlos Serrano
Popular Secretary	*Leopoldo Hernández Partida*
Agrarian Secretary	*León García*
Labor Secretary	*Alfonso Sánchez Madariaga*
Military Secretary	*Edmundo Sánchez Cano*
IEPES Secretary	*Alejandro Carrillo*
Press Secretary	*Serafín Iglesias Hernández*

2 DEC. 1940

President	*Antonio I. Villalobos*
Secretary General	*Gustavo Cárdenas Huerta*
Labor Secretary	*Fernando Amilpa*
Agrarian Secretary	*Sacramento Joffre Vázquez*
Popular Secretary	*Antonio Nava Castillo*
Military Secretary	*Alfonso Corona del Rosal*

1943

President	*Antonio Villalobos*
Secretary General	Florencio Padilla
Agrarian Secretary	Francisco Cruz Chávez
Labor Secretary	*Fernando Amilpa*
Popular Secretary	*Antonio Nava Castillo*
Finance Secretary	Ismael Salas

Institutional Revolutionary Party (Partido Revolucionario Institucional, PRI)

19 JAN. 1946

President	*Rafael P. Gamboa*
Secretary General	*Ernesto P. Uruchurtu*
Labor Secretary	*Fernando Amilpa*
Agrarian Secretary	*Francisco Martínez Peralta*
Popular Secretary	*Rafael Murillo Vidal*
Political Secretary	Jesús Lima

| Political Secretary | Augusto Hinojosa |
| Finance Secretary | *Sealtiel Alatriste* |

5 DEC. 1946

President	*Rodolfo Sánchez Taboada*
Secretary General	*Teófilo R. Borunda*
Agrarian Secretary	Jesús Molina Urquidi
Labor Secretary	*Blas Chumacero Sánchez*
Popular Secretary	*Ernesto Gallardo*
Political Secretary	*Fernando López Arias*
Political Secretary	*Norberto López Avelar*
Finance Secretary	Guillermo M. Canales
Press Secretary	*Luis Echeverría Alvarez*
IEPES Secretary	*Armando Arteaga y Santoyo*
Women's Secretary	*Margarita García Flores*
Youth Secretary	*Antonio Mena Brito*

1 MAR. 1949

President	*Rodolfo Sánchez Taboada*
Secretary General	*José López Bermúdez*
Agrarian Secretary	Jesús Molina Urquidi
Labor Secretary	*Blas Chumacero Sáncez*
Popular Secretary	Ernesto Gallardo
Political Secretary	*Fernando López Arias*
Political Secretary	Rafael Arriola Molina
Finance Secretary	Guillermo M. Canales
Press Secretary	*Luis Echeverría Alvarez*
Oficial Mayor	Manuel Jasso

1 JULY 1951

President	*Rodolfo Sánchez Taboada*
Secretary General	*José López Bermúdez*
Agrarian Secretary	*Vicente Salgado Páez*
Labor Secretary	*Blas Chumacero Sánchez*
Popular Secretary	Ernesto Gallardo
Political Secretary	*Fernando López Arias*
Political Secretary	*Norberto López Avelar*
Oficial Mayor	Manuel Jasso
Finance Secretary	*Francisco Galindo Ochoa*
Press Secretary	*Luis Echeverría Alvarez*
Youth Secretary	*Agustín Arriaga Rivera*
IEPES Secretary	*Armando Arteaga Santoyo*
Women's Secretary	*Margarita García Flores*

3 JUNE 1952

President	*Rodolfo Sánchez Taboada*
Secretary General	*Adolfo López Mateos*
Agrarian Secretary	*Vicente Salgado Páez*

Labor Secretary	*Alfonso Sánchez Madariaga*
Popular Secretary	Angel Luis Archer
Political Secretary	*Fernando López Arias*
Political Secretary	*Salvador Pineda*
IEPES Secretary	*Armando Arteaga Santoyo*
Press Secretary	*Luis Echeverría Alvarez*
Youth Secretary	*Antonio Mena Brito*
Women's Secretary	*Margarita García Flores*
Oficial Mayor	Manuel Jasso

JULY 1952

President	*Rodolfo Sánchez Taboada*
Secretary General	*José Gómez Esparza*
Labor Secretary	*Alfonso Sánchez Madariaga*
Agrarian Secretary	*Vicente Salgado Páez*
Popular Secretary	Angel Luis Archer
Political Secretary	*Fernando López Arias*
Political Secretary	*Norberto López Avelar*
IEPES Secretary	*Armando Arteaga y Santoyo*
Youth Secretary	*Antonio Mena Brito*
Women's Secretary	*Margarita García Flores*
Finance Secretary	*Agustín Salvat*
Press Secretary	*Moisés Ochoa Campos*

4 DEC. 1952

President	*Gabriel Leyva Velázquez*
Secretary General	Gilberto García Navarro
Agrarian Secretary	*Magdaleno Aguilar*
Labor Secretary	*Fidel Velázquez*
Popular Secretary	*Caritino Maldonado*
Political Secretary	*Emigdio Martínez Adame*
Political Secretary	*Rodolfo González Guevara*
Finance Secretary	*Agustín Salvat*
Press Secretary	*Moisés Ochoa Campos*
IEPES Secretary	*Armando Arteaga y Santoyo*
Women's Secretary	*Margarita García Flores*
Youth Secretary	*Antonio Mena Brito*

5 JAN. 1953

President	*Gabriel Leyva Velázquez*
Secretary General	*José Gómez Esparza*
Agrarian Secretary	*Vicente Salgado Páez*
Labor Secretary	*Alfonso Sánchez Madariaga*
Popular Secretary	Jorge Saracho
Political Secretary	*Emigdio Martínez Adame*
Political Secretary	*Rodolfo González Guevara*
Women's Secretary	*Margarita García Flores*
IEPES Secretary	*Armando Arteaga Santoyo*

Press Secretary   *Moisés Ochoa Campos*
Youth Secretary   *Antonio Mena Brito*
Finance Secretary   *Agustín Salvat*

1 APR. 1953
President   *Gabriel Leyva Velázquez*
Secretary General   Gilberto García Navarro
Agrarian Secretary   *Magdaleno Castillo*
Labor Secretary   *Fidel Velázquez*
Popular Secretary   *Caritino Maldonado*
Political Secretary   *Emigdio Martínez Adame*
Political Secretary   *Rodolfo González Guevara*
Finance Secretary   *Agustín Salvat*
Oficial Mayor   *Carlos Real Félix*
IEPES Secretary   *Armando Arteaga Santoyo*
Youth Secretary   *Antonio Mena Brito*
Press Secretary   *Moisés Ochoa Campos*
Women's Secretary   *Margarita García Flores*
Organization Secretary   *Arcadio Noguera Vergara*

26 APR. 1956
President   *Agustín Olachea Avilés*
Secretary General   *Rafael Corrales Ayala*
Agrarian Secretary   *Magdaleno Aguilar*
Labor Secretary   *Fidel Velázquez*
Popular Secretary   *Caritino Maldonado*
Political Secretary   *Francisco Galindo Ochoa*
Finance Secretary   *Agustín Salvat*
Press Secretary   *Moisés Ochoa Campos*
Women's Secretary   *Margarita García Flores*
Oficial Mayor   *Carlos Real Félix*
Organization Secretary   *Arcadio Noguera Vergara*

15 MAY 1956
President   *Agustín Olachea Avilés*
Secretary General   Gilberto García Navarro
Popular Secretary   *Caritino Maldonado*
Agrarian Secretary   *Magdaleno Aguilar Castillo*
Labor Secretary   *Fidel Velázquez*
Political Secretary   *Emigdio Martínez Adame*
Political Secretary   *Francisco Galindo Ochoa*
Finance Secretary   *Agustín Salvat*
Press Secretary   *Moisés Ochoa Campos*
Oficial Mayor   *Carlos Real Félix*

4 DEC. 1958
President   *Alfonso Corona del Rosal*
Secretary General   *Juan Fernández Albarrán*

Agrarian Secretary	*Magdaleno Aguilar Castillo*
Labor Secretary	*Jesús Yurén*
Popular Secretary	*Antonio Mena Brito*
Political Secretary	Luis Vázquez Campos
Political Secretary	*Fernando Díaz Durán*
Finance Secretary	*Agustín Salvat*
Press Secretary	*Francisco Galindo Ochoa*
Women's Secretary	*Margarita García Flores*
Oficial Mayor	*Salvador Pineda*
Organization Secretary	*Abelardo de la Torre G.*

1962

President	*Alfonso Corona del Rosal*
Secretary General	*Juan Fernández Albarrán*
Agrarian Secretary	*Magdaleno Aguilar Castillo*
Labor Secretary	*Jesús Yurén*
Popular Secretary	*Alfonso Martínez Domínguez*
Political Secretary	*Antonio Salazar Salazar*
Political Secretary	*Manuel M. Moreno*
Organization Secretary	*Abelardo de la Torre G.*
Finance Secretary	*Agustín Salvat*
Oficial Mayor	*Salvador Pineda*

JAN. 1964

President	*Alfonso Corona del Rosal*
Secretary General	*Manuel M. Moreno*
Agrarian Secretary	*Magdaleno Aguilar*
Labor Secretary	*Jesús Yurén*
Popular Secretary	*Alfonso Martínez Domínguez*
Political Secretary	*Rafael Moreno Valle*
Political Secretary	*Manuel Bernardo Aguirre*
Organization Secretary	*Abelardo de la Torre G.*
Press Secretary	*Francisco Galindo Ochoa*
Finance Secretary	*Agustín Salvat*
Oficial Mayor	*Salvador Pineda*

4 DEC. 1964

President	*Carlos A. Madrazo*
Secretary General	*Lauro Ortega Martínez*
Agrarian Secretary	*Leopoldo Hernández Partida*
Labor Secretary	*Blas Chumacero Sánchez*
Popular Secretary	*Renaldo Guzmán Orozco*
Political Secretary	*Armando Arteaga y Santoyo*
Political Secretary	*Fluvio Vista Altamirano*
Organization Secretary	*Fernando Díaz Durán*
Finance Secretary	*José Espinosa Rivera*
Press Secretary	*José Luis Lamadrid*
IEPES Secretary	*Octaviano Campos Salas*

APRIL 1965

President	*Carlos A. Madrazo*
Secretary General	*Lauro Ortega*
Agrarian Secretary	*Leopoldo Hernández Partida*
Popular Secretary	*Renaldo Guzmán Orozco*
Labor Secretary	*Blas Chumacero*
Political Secretary	*Armando Arteaga Santoyo*
Political Secretary	*Fluvio Vista Altamirano*
Organization Secretary	*Fernando Díaz Durán*
Press Secretary	*José Luis Lamadrid*
Finance Secretary	*José Espinosa Rivera*
Youth Director	*Rodolfo Echeverría Ruiz*
IEPES Secretary	Carlos Andrade Muñoz

22 NOV. 1965

President	*Lauro Ortega Martínez*
Secretary General	*Fernando Díaz Durán*
Agrarian Secretary	*Amador Hernández González*
Labor Secretary	*Blas Chumacero Sánchez*
Popular Secretary	*Renaldo Guzmán Orozco*
Political Secretary	*Cristóbal Guzmán Orozco*
Political Secretary	*Rubén Moheno Velasco*
Organization Secretary	*Oswaldo Cravioto Cisneros*
IEPES Secretary	Carlos Andrade Muñoz
Press Secretary	Noé G. Elizondo
Finance Secretary	Juan Antonio Orozco

JULY 1966

President	*Lauro Ortega*
Secretary General	*Fernando Díaz Durán*
Organization Secretary	*Oswaldo Cravioto Cisneros*
Agrarian Secretary	*Amador Hernández*
Popular Secretary	*Renaldo Guzmán Orozco*
Labor Secretary	*Blas Chumacero Sánchez*
Political Secretary	*Cristóbal Guzmán Cárdenas*
Political Secretary	*Rubén Moheno Velasco*
Press Secretary	Noé G. Elizondo
IEPES Secretary	Ignacio Machorro

27 FEB. 1968

President	*Alfonso Martínez Domínguez*
Secretary General	*Enrique Olivares Santana*
Agrarian Secretary	*Augusto Gómez Villanueva*
Labor Secretary	*Blas Chumacero Sánchez*
Popular Secretary	*Renaldo Guzmán Orozco*
Political Secretary	*Cristóbal Guzmán Cárdenas*
Political Secretary	*Víctor Manzanilla Schaffer*
Organization Secretary	*José Ricardo Tirado*
Finance Secretary	*Pedro Luis Bartilotti B.*

Press Secretary	*Humberto Lugo Gil*
IEPES Secretary	*Jorge de la Vega Domínguez*
Oficial Mayor	*Flavio Vista Altamirano*
Women's Action	*María Lavalle Urbina*

4 DEC. 1970

President	*Manuel Sánchez Vite*
Secretary General	*Vicente Fuentes Díaz*
Agrarian Secretary	*Alfredo V. Bonfil*
Labor Secretary	*Blas Chumacero Sánchez*
Popular Secretary	*Julio Bobadilla Peña*
Political Secretary	*Salvador Gamíz Fernández*
Political Secretary	*Cuauhtémoc Santa Ana*
Organization Secretary	*Carlos Jongitud Barrios*
Finance Secretary	*Abel Ramírez Acosta*
Press Secretary	René Viñet López
IEPES Secretary	*Jorge de la Vega Domínguez*
Oficial Mayor	*Rodolfo Echeverría Ruiz*
Political Education Secretary	*Enrique González Pedrero*
Social Action Secretary	*Enrique Cárdenas González*

21 FEB. 1972

President	*Jesús Reyes Heroles*
Secretary General	*Enrique González Pedrero*
Agrarian Secretary	*Alfredo V. Bonfil*
Labor Secretary	*Blas Chumacero Sánchez*
Popular Secretary	*Julio Bobadilla Peña*
Political Secretary	*Enrique Olivares Santana*
Political Secretary	*Luis H. Ducoing*
Organization Secretary	*Rafael Rodríguez Barrera*
Finance Secretary	Sergio L. Benhumea
Press Secretary	*Víctor Manzanilla Schaffer*
IEPES Secretary	*Santiago Roel*
Oficial Mayor	*Rodolfo Echeverría Ruiz*
Political Education Secretary	*Arturo González Cosío*
Social Action Secretary	Alejandro Peraza Uribe

16 MAR. 1973

President	*Jesús Reyes Heroles*
Secretary General	*Enrique González Pedrero*
Subsecretary General	*Carlos Sansores Pérez*
Oficial Mayor	*Rodolfo Echeverría Ruiz*
Agrarian Secretary	*Celestino Salcedo Monteón*
Labor Secretary	*Blas Chumacero Sánchez*
Popular Secretary	*Oscar Flores Tapia*
Political Secretary	*Enrique Olivares Santana*
Political Secretary	*Luis H. Ducoing*
Organization Secretary	*Miguel Angel Barberena*
Political Education Secretary	*Arturo González Cosío*

Press Secretary — *Jorge Villa Treviño*
Social Action Secretary — *José Luis Lamadrid*
Finance Secretary — Sergio L. Benhumea
Political Subsecretary — *Salvador Gamíz Fernández*
Political Subsecretary — *Humberto Hiriart Urdanivia*
Organization Subsecretary — *Enrique Soto Reséndiz*
Press Subsecretary — *Ernesto Alvarez Nolasco*
IEPES Secretary — *Horacio Labastida*

APR. 1975

President — *Jesús Reyes Heroles*
Secretary General — *Miguel Angel Barberena*
Oficial Mayor — *Rodolfo Echeverría Ruiz*
Agrarian Secretary — *Celestino Salcedo Monteón*
Labor Secretary — *Blas Chumacero Sánchez*
Popular Secretary — *David Gustavo Gutíerrez R.*
Political Secretary — *Enrique Olivares Santana*
Political Secretary — *Carlos Sansores Pérez*
Organization Secretary — *Fidel Herrera Beltrán*
Political Education Secretary — *Arturo González Cosío*
Press Secretary — *Ernesto Alvarez Nolasco*
Finance Secretary — Sergio L. Benhumea
Social Action Secretary — *José Luis Lamadrid*
IEPES Secretary — *Julio Rodolfo Moctezuma C.*

4 MAR. 1976

President — *Porfiro Muñoz Ledo*
Secretary General — *Augusto Gómez Villanueva*
Oficial Mayor — *Rodolfo Echeverría Ruiz*
Agrarian Secretary — *Celestino Salcedo Monteón*
Labor Secretary — *Blas Chumacero Sánchez*
Popular Secretary — *David Gustavo Gutíerrez R.*
Political Secretary — *Carlos Sansores Pérez*
Political Secretary — *Enrique Olivares Santana*
Organization Secretary — *Leopoldo González Sáenz*
Political Education Secretary — *Arturo González Cosío*
Press Secretary — *Pedro Ramírez Vázquez*
Finance Secretary — Severo López Mestre
Social Action Secretary — *Carlos Jongitud Barrios*
IEPES Secretary — *Julio Rodolfo Moctezuma C.*

9 DEC. 1976

President — *Carlos Sansores Pérez*
Secretary General — *Juan Sabines Gutíerrez*
Oficial Mayor — *Miguel Covián Pérez*
Agrarian Secretary — *Celestino Salcedo Monteón*
Labor Secretary — *Blas Chumacero Sánchez*
Popular Secretary — *José de las Fuentes R.*
Political Secretary — *Joaquín Gamboa Pascoe*

Political Secretary	*Augusto Gómez Villanueva*
Organization Secretary	*Alberto Alvarado Aramburo*
Political Education Secretary	José Murat
Press Secretary	*Humberto Lugo Gil*
Finance Secretary	*Tristán Canales Najjar*
Social Action Secretary	*Onofre Hernández Rivera*
IEPES Secretary	*Luis Dantón Rodríguez*

28 JULY 1978

President	*Carlos Sansores Pérez*
Secretary General	*Gustavo Carvajal Moreno*
Subsecretary General	*Enrique Alvarez del C.*
Oficial Mayor	*Miguel Covián Pérez*
Agrarian Secretary	*Oscar Ramírez Mijares*
Agrarian Subsecretary	*Alfonso Garzón Santibañez*
Popular Secretary	*José de las Fuentes R.*
Political Secretary	*Joaquín Gamboa Pascoe*
Political Secretary	*Rodolfo González Guevara*
Organization Secretary	*Humberto Lugo Gil*
Labor Secretary	*Blas Chumacero Sánchez*
Labor Subsecretary	*Antonio J. Hernández*
Press Secretary	*Rodolfo Landeros Gallegos*
International Affairs Secretary	*Alejandro Sobarzo*
IEPES Secretary	*Alejandro Cervantes D.*

27 OCT. 1979

President	*Gustavo Carvajal*
Secretary General	*José de las Fuentes R.*
Political Secretary	*Joaquín Gamboa Pascoe*
Political Secretary	*Lauro Ortega*
Oficial Mayor	*Humberto Lugo Gil*
Agrarian Secretary	*Oscar Ramírez Mijares*
International Affairs Secretary	*Rafael Rodríguez Barrera*
Ideological Divulgation Secretary	*Sergio Guerrero Mier*
Labor Secretary	*Blas Chumacero Sánchez*
Popular Secretary	*Carlos Riva Palacio*
Press Secretary	*Rodolfo Landeros*
Organization Secretary	*Víctor Cervera Pacheco*
Political Education Secretary	Víctor Manuel Barceló
Social Action Secretary	*José Luis Andrade Ibarra*
Finance Secretary	Eduardo Guerrero del C.
IEPES Secretary	*Guillermo Fonseca Alvarez*

JAN. 1981

President	*Gustavo Carvajal Moreno*
Secretary General	*José de las Fuentes R.*
Oficial Mayor	*Rafael Rodríguez Barrera*
Agrarian Secretary	*Víctor Cervera Pacheco*
Labor Secretary	*Blas Chumacero Sánchez*

Popular Secretary	*Humberto Lugo Gil*
Political Secretary	*Joaquín Gamboa Pascoe*
Organization Secretary	José Luis Sandoval
Political Education Secretary	Víctor Manuel Barceló
Electoral Action Secretary	Humberto Romero Cándano
Ideology Secretary	*Sergio Guerrero Mier*
Press Secretary	Manuel García Murillo
Social Action Secretary	*José Luis Andrade Ibarra*
International Affairs Secretary	*Carlos Madrazo Pintado*
Sports Development Secretary	Félix Flores Gómez
Finance Secretary	Eduardo Guerrero del C.
IEPES Secretary	*Carlos Torres Manzo*

8 MAY 1981

President	*Javier García Paniagua*
Secretary General	*Guillermo Cosío Villegas*
Agrarian Secretary	*Víctor Cervera Pacheco*
Popular Secretary	*Humberto Lugo Gil*
Political Secretary	*Lauro Ortega*
Political Secretary	*Joaquín Gamboa Pascoe*
Political Education Secretary	*Arturo Romo Gutíerrez*
Ideological Divulgation Secretary	Guillermo Morfín García
Social Action Secretary	Ramón Martínez Martín
Finance Secretary	*Florencio Salazar Martínez*
Oficial Mayor	*Arturo González Cosío*
Labor Secretary	*Blas Chumacero Sánchez*
Organization Secretary	*Ignacio Vázquez Torres*
Electoral Action Secretary	Carlos Sánchez Dosal
Press Secretary	Jaime Canseco Morelos
Director of IEPES	*Jorge Tamayo*
International Affairs Secretary	*José Luis Andrade Ibarra*

15 OCT. 1981

President	*Pedro Ojeda Paullada*
Secretary General	*Manuel Bartlett Díaz*
Subsecretary	*Hilda Anderson Nevares*
Oficial Mayor	*Adolfo Lugo Verduzco*
Agrarian Secretary	*Víctor Cervera Pacheco*
Labor Secretary	*Blas Chumacero Sánchez*
Political Secretary	*Joaquín Gamboa Pascoe*
Political Secretary	*Lauro Ortega Martínez*
Organization Secretary	*Silvia Hernández*
Electoral Action Secretary	Guillermo González López
Press Secretary	*Miguel González Avelar*
Finance Secretary	*Francisco Rojas Gutiérrez*
International Affairs Secretary	*Ricardo Valero Becerra*
Sports Development Secretary	Gamaliel Ramírez Andrade
Director of the IEPES	*Carlos Salinas de Gortari*

DEC. 1982

President	*Adolfo Lugo Verduzco*
Secretary General	*Mario Vargas Saldaña*
Subsecretary	*Hilda Anderson Nevares*
Oficial Mayor	*Guillermina Sánchez Meza*
Agrarian Secretary	*Víctor Cervera Pacheco*
Electoral Action Secretary	Fausto Villagómez Cabrera
Labor Secretary	*Blas Chumacero Sánchez*
Political Secretary	*Miguel González Avelar*
Political Secretary	*Humberto Lugo Gil*
Organization Secretary	*Manuel Garza González*
Finance Secretary	Jorge Thompson Aguilar
Social Action Secretary	*Ramón Martínez Martín*
Popular Secretary	*Enrique Fernández Martínez*
International Affairs Secretary	*Humberto Hernández Haddad*
Sports Development Secretary	Antonio Murrieta Necoechea
Press Secretary	Alfredo Nolasco Cabral
Ideology Secretary	*Ricardo Carrillo Arronte*

OCT. 1986

President	*Jorge de la Vega Domínguez*
Secretary General	*Irma Cué de Duarte*
Oficial Mayor	*Maximiliano Silerio E.*
Agrarian Secretary	*Héctor Hugo Olivares V.*
Labor Secretary	*Blas Chumacero Sánchez*
Popular Secretary	*Guillermo Fonseca Alvarez*
Political Secretary	*Antonio Riva Palacio López*
Political Secretary	Nicolás Reynés Berezaluce
Organization Secretary	*Pedro Joaquín Coldwell*
Electoral Action Secretary	*Patricio Chirinos Calero*
Political Education Secretary	*Arturo Núñez Jiménez*
Ideological Divulgation Secretary	*Juan José Bremer Martino*
Promotion Secretary	*Manlio Fabio Beltrones R.*
Information Secretary	*Otto Granados Roldán*
Social Action Secretary	Antonio Jaimes Aguilar
International Affairs Secretary	*Alejandro Sobarzo Loaiza*
Sports Development Secretary	Raúl González Rodríguez
Finance Secretary	*Maria Elena Vázquez Nava*

DEC. 1988

President	*Luis Donaldo Colosio M.*
Secretary General	*Rafael Rodríguez Barrera*
Oficial Mayor	*Héctor Hugo Olivares V.*
Agrarian Secretary	*Maximiliano Silerio E.*
Labor Secretary	Rigoberto Ochoa Zaragoza
Popular Secretary	*Silvia Hernández*
Political Secretary	*Emilio M. González*
Political Secretary	*Guillermo Jiménez Morales*
Organization Secretary	*Roberto Madrazo Pintado*

Political Education Secretary   *Luis Medina Peña*
Electoral Action Secretary   *César A. Santiago Ramírez*
Ideological Divulgation Secretary   *Santiago Oñate Laborde*
Information Secretary   Rafael Reséndiz Contreras
Social Action Secretary   Javier López Moreno
International Affairs Secretary   Romeo Flores Caballero
Sports Development Secretary   Sandalio Sáinz de la Maza
Finance Secretary   *Dulce María Sauri Riancho*

DEC. 1990
President   *Luis Donaldo Colosio M.*
Secretary General   *Rafael Rodríguez Barrera*
Organization Secretary   Jesús Salazar Toledano
Regional Coordination Secretary   *Carlos Armando Biebrich*
Electoral Action Secretary   *César A. Santiago Ramírez*
Social Administration Secretary   *Ignacio Ovalle Fernández*
International Affairs Secretary   *Roberta Lajous Vargas*
Information Secretary   Rafael Reséndiz Contreras
Finance Secretary   *Carlos Sales Gutiérrez*

MAY 1992
President   *Genaro Borrego Estrada*
Secretary General   *Beatriz Paredes Rangel*
Organization Secretary   Genovevo Figueroa Zamudio
Regional Coordination Secretary   *Héctor Hugo Olivares V.*
Electoral Action Secretary   Amador Rodríguez Lozano
Social Administration Secretary   María Elena Chapa
International Affairs Secretary   *Roberta Lajous Vargas*
Information Secretary   Héctor González Pérez
Finance Secretary   *Miguel Alemán Velasco*

1993
President   *Fernando Ortiz Arana*
Secretary General   *José Luis Lamadrid Sauza*
Organization Secretary   Genovevo Figueroa Zamudio
Regional Coordination Secretary   Melchor de los Santos
Electoral Action Secretary   Amador Rodríguez Lozano
Social Administration Secretary   María E. Chapa Hernández
Information Secretary   Héctor González Pérez
International Affairs Secretary   *Roberta Lajous Vargas*
Finance Secretary   *Carlos Sales Gutiérrez*

Appendix I

Presidents and Secretaries General of the National Action Party and Presidents of the Party of the Democratic Revolution, the Cardenista Front for National Reconstruction Party, the Authentic Party of the Mexican Revolution, the Popular Socialist Party, and the Mexican Democratic Party, 1939–1993

National Action Party (1939)

Presidents

Manuel Gómez Morín	1939-40
Juan Gutiérrez Lascuraín	1949-56
Alfonso Ituarte Servín	1956-59
José González Torres	1959-62
Adolfo Christlieb Ibarrola	1962-69
Ignacio Limón Maurer	1968-69
Manuel González Hinojosa	1969-72
José Angel Conchello Dávila	1972-75
Efraín González Morfín	1975
Manuel González Hinojosa	1975-78
Abel Vicencio Tovar	1978-84
Pablo Emilio Madero Beldén	1984-87
Luis H. Alvarez	1987-93
Luis Castillo Peraza	1993-

Secretaries General (1939-1983)

Roberto Cossío y Cossío	1939-51
Raúl Velasco Zimbrón	1954-57
José González Torres	1957-58
Abel Vicencio Tovar	1960-61
Astolfo Vicencio Tovar	1961-66
Ignacio Limón Maurer	1966-68
Juan Manuel Gómez Morín	1969-72
Bernardo Bátiz Vázquez	1972-75
Raúl J. González Schmal	1975-78
Alfonso Arronte Domínguez	1978-81
Raúl J. González Schmal	1981-83

Party of the Democratic Revolution (1989)

President

Cuauhtémoc Cárdenas	1989-93
Porfirio Muñoz Ledo	1993-

Cardenista Front for National Reconstruction Party (1988)

President
Rafael Aguilar Talamantes   1988-

Authentic Party of the Mexican Revolution

Presidents
Jacinto B. Treviño   1954-64
Juan Barragán Rodríguez   1964-74
Pedro González Azcuaga   1974-75
Antonio Gómez Velasco   1975-79
Antonio Vázquez del Mercado   1979
Jesús Guzmán Rubio   1979-80
Fortino A. Garza Cárdenas   1980-83
Jesús Guzmán Rubio   1983-84
Carlos Enrique Cantú Rosas   1984-93
Juan Jaime Hernández   1993
Rosa María Martínez de Negri   27 July 1993-

Popular Socialist Party (Popular Party, 1948-60)

Presidents
Vicente Lombardo Toledano   1948-68
Jorge Cruickshank García   1968-89
Indalecio Sayago Herrera   1989-

Mexican Democratic Party (1975-88)

Presidents
Ignacio González Gollaz   1975-78
Gumercindo Magaña Negrete   1978-88

Appendix J

Secretaries General of the CTM, CNC, FNOC, FSTSE, STPRM, and SUTERM, 1935–1993

Mexican Federation of Laborers (Confederación de Trabajadores de México, 1936)

Lombardo Toledano, Vicente	Feb. 1936-24 Feb. 1941
Velázquez, Fidel	25 Feb. 1941-46
Amilpa, Fernando	1946-49
Velázquez, Fidel	1949-

National Farmers Confederation (Confederación Nacional Campesina, 1938)

Sánchez, Graciano	15 July 1938-30 Dec. 1942
Leyva Velázquez, Gabriel	31 Dec. 1942-28 May 1947
Barrios, Roberto	29 May 1947-May 1950
Gándara, Manuel J.	May 1950-21 Jan. 1952
Galván, Ferrer	22 Jan. 1952-1953
Azua Torres, Lorenzo	1953-20 July 1954
Luna Lugo, Arturo	21 July 1954-18 Jan. 1957
Flores Fuentes, Raymundo	19 Jan. 1957-26 Aug. 1959
Hernández y Hernández, Francisco	27 Aug. 1959-26 Aug. 1962
Rojo Gómez, Javier	27 Aug. 1962-25 Aug. 1965
Hernández, Amador	26 Aug. 1965-21 Sept. 1967
Gómez Villanueva, Agusto	Oct. 1967-Dec. 1970
Bonfil, Alfredo V.	Dec. 1970-25 Jan. 1973
Salcedo, Celestino	Feb. 1973-1977
Ramírez Mijares, Oscar	27 Aug. 1977-Aug. 1980
Cervera Pacheco, Víctor	Aug. 1980-Aug. 1983
Hernández Posadas, Mario	Aug. 1983- Aug. 1986
Oivares Ventura, Héctor Hugo	Aug. 1986-Aug. 1988
Silerio Esparza, Maximiliano	1988-91

National Front of Organizations and Citizens (Frente Nacional de Organizaciones y Ciudadanos), United Citizens in Movement (Une Ciudadanos en Movimiento, 1989-93), National Federation of Popular Organizations (ConfederaciónNacional de Organizaciones Populares, 1943-89)

Nava Castillo, Antonio	1943-46
Murillo Vidal, Rafael	1946
Gallardo, Ernesto	1946-49
Archer, Angel Luis	1949-52
Maldonado Pérez, Caritino	1952-58

Vázquez Campos, Luis	1958-61
Martínez Domínguez, Alfonso	1961-65
Guzmán Orozoco, Renaldo	1965-71
Bobadilla Peña, Julio	1971-72
Flores Tapia, Oscar	1972-75
Gutiérrez Ruiz, David G.	1975-76
De la Fuentes Rodríguez, José	1976-79
Riva Palacio, Carlos	1979-80
Lugo Gil, Humberto A.	1980-82
Mendoza Aramburu, Angel C.	1982-83
Fernández Martínez, Enrique	1983-87
Fonseca Alvarez, Guillermo	1987-89
Hernández Enríquez, Silvia	1989-93
Barberena, Miguel Angel	1993-

Federation of Government Employees' Unions (Federacion de Sindicatos de Trabajadores al Servicio del Estado, 1938)

Patiño Cruz, Francisco	1938-40
Jaramillo, Cándido	1940-42
Villanueva, Ignacio	1942
Galaviz, Gabriel	1942
Herrera Angeles, Rafael	1943-44
Figueroa Figueroa, Ruffo	1944-47
Soto Ruiz, Armando	1947-50
Martínez Domínguez, Alfonso	1950-53
Aguirre Alegría, Francisco	1953-56
De la Torre Grajales, Abelardo	1956-59
Sánchez Mireles, Rómulo	1959-64
Robles Martínez, Jesús	1965
Bernal, Antonio	1965-67
Robledo Santiago, Edgar	1967-70
Aceves Alcocer, Gilberto	1970-75
Sánchez Vargas, Salvador	1975-76
Espinosa Galindo, Daniel	1976-77
Riva Palacio, Carlos	1977-79
Dorantes Segovia, Luis José	1980-83
Parra Prado, Manuel Germán	1983-86
Domenzaín Guzmán, Hugo	1989-

Petroleum Workers Union (Sindicato de Trabajadores Petroleros de la Republica Mexicana, 1936)

Soto Innes, Eduardo	1936-37
Gray, Juan	1938
López T., Rafael	1938-39
Martínez, Aurelio	1939
Suárez R., Rafael	1940-41
Salmón, Antonio	1942-43
Gutiérrez, Isidoro	1944-45
Ortega, Jorge R.	1946

Abrego, Antonio H.	1947
Ibañez, Eulalio N.	1948-49
Martínez, Demetrio	1950-51
López Naranja, Enrique	1952-53
Pacheco León, Ignacio	1954-55
Mortera Prieto, Felipe	1956-58
Vivanco García, Pedro	1959-61
Hernández Galicia, Joaquín	1962-64
Cárdenas Lomeli, Rafael	1965-67
Terrazas Zozaya, Samuel	1968-70
Barragán Camacho, Salvador	1971-73
Martínez Mendoza, Sergio	1974-76
Kehoe Vincent, Heriberto	1977
Torres Pancardo, Oscar	1977-79
Barragán Camacho, Salvador	1981-84
Sosa Martínez, José	1985-88
Guzmán Cabrera, Sebastián	1989-

Union of Electrical Workers (Sindicato Unico de Trabajadores Electristas de la República Mexicana, 1944)

Pérez Rios, Francisco	1944–27 Mar. 1975
Rodríguez Alcaine, Leonardo	28 Mar. 1975–

A Selected Bibliographical Essay

Earlier bibliographical sources on public figures in Mexico have been characterized by their unavailability, inaccuracy, and lack of information. In general, the sources used in this work can be divided into four types: privately published directories, public directories, magazines and newspapers, and monographs and biographies, which are not discussed individually because they are of value only for information about a single person. The following essay attempts to describe the strengths and shortcomings of a selective list of works that have proved most useful as sources for this book.

Privately Published Directories

The English-language sources of privately published directories that are useful in gathering biographical information on Mexican public figures are limited to a small number. The two most important publications of this type were both published in 1946, which limits their usefulness to persons prominent enough to have been included before that date. These two works are the *Who's Who in Latin America* (Stanford: Stanford University Press) and the *Biographical Encyclopedia of the World* (New York: Institute for Research in Biography). The first of the two works has been published in three editions (1935, 1940, 1945–1950), with the two first editions covering Latin American personalities in one volume, and the last edition devoting a single volume to Mexico in 1945. Even though the first two editions assist the reader interested in Mexico by including an index of names by country, the third and final edition is by far the most useful because of the larger number of Mexicans included. (An indication of the state of scholarship on biography of Latin American leaders is illustrated by the fact that Blaine Ethridge Press reprinted this edition in 1971 just as it had appeared from 1945 to 1950.) The 1946 volume on Mexico, under the editorship of Ronald Hilton, is the most accurate English-language source published since 1935. The *Biographical Encyclopedia of the World* went through five editions, changing its title at midpoint to *World Biography* in 1948. The three most valuable editions are the third, fourth, and fifth, 1946, 1948, and 1954, respectively, because they contain more Mexican and Latin American personalities. Like the *Who's Who in Latin America*, the *Biographical Encyclopedia of the World* is quite accurate and contains political personages at all levels. However, its great disadvantage is that the Mexicans are dispersed among other nationalities and the 1946 edition is not in alphabetical order.

A newer source, however, and useful because of its breadth and accuracy, is Lucien Lajoie's *Who's Notable in Mexico* (Mexico, 1972). Although not widely available, it contains many political leaders from recent decades who were living at the time of publication. Unfortunately, no further volumes were published. An attempt was made to replicate this work with a book entitled *Who's Who in Mexico 1987* (Washington, D.C.: Worldwide Reference, 1987). Although the title is in English, the biographies are in Spanish, and the selection is uneven, as is true of most privately published Spanish-language directories. This work does contain a useful index of names by occupation.

The only attempt that has been made since 1946 to provide a guide to Mexican public figures has been the work of Marvin Alisky. The most important of a series of small pamphlets put out by the Arizona State University Center for Latin American Studies is his *Who's Who in Mexican Government* (Tempe, 1969), which contains only about a dozen biographies of any length. The listings for the rest of the individuals give only the most recent or present position held, sometimes state of birth, and the type of university education. Most of this information is duplicated much more completely in the various Mexican government organizational manuals (excepting state of birth). Other publications by Alisky, notably the *Guide to the Government of the Mexican State of Sonora* (Tempe, 1971), do contain some relevant biographical information on governors, incomplete though they may be.

Of the standard world *Who's Who* sources, the most useful is the *International Year Book and Statesmen's Who's Who*. All editions of this work are helpful because they normally list the cabinet members, supreme court justices, and governors holding office at the time of publication. The earlier editions also include diplomatic posts, information that is helpful in tracing Mexicans with foreign service careers. The 1954 edition is particularly generous with the amount of biographical data on prominent Mexicans, but the coverage is quite limited and superficial. *Who's Who in the World, 1971-1972* (Marquis) contains short, outdated, and very brief Mexican biographies, a characteristic continued in the subsequent editions.

The two most readily available Spanish-language sources and the most useful are the *Diccionario Porrúa* (Mexico: Editorial Porrúa) and the *Diccionario biográfico de México* (Monterrey: Editorial Revesa). The first is a standard reference work of Mexican biography, geography, and history, published in numerous editions. The limitations of the *Diccionario Porrúa* are that it contains only persons who have died, and many of the biographies, while generally accurate, are incomplete and lack dates for the position held by the individual. However, the *Diccionario Porrúa* does contain one of the few published sources of the cabinet positions with the names of those who held them and their tenure in office. It also contains a considerable amount of historical information describing political affairs and the men who took part in them, making it one of the best sources for tracing Mexican political families.

The second work, the *Diccionario biográfico de México*, is the most complete up-to-date general *Who's Who* published in Mexico, and it has been issued in two editions, 1968 and 1970. The 1968 edition is far more useful for public figures since the 1970 volume tends to be padded with duplicates of the biographies in the first volume. It is more complete than the *Diccionario Porrúa* for individual biographies, but tends to be very uneven in coverage, including losing candidates for federal deputy but omitting many cabinet members and governors.

The only other general Mexican source published in the last fifty years is the *Diccionario biográfico mexicano* by Miguel Angel Peral. Peral's dictionary could have been excellent, but it must be used with some care because of numerous inaccuracies about birthdates and legislative sessions. If the researcher keeps these limitations in mind, however, Peral provides the most complete coverage of the officeholders available from 1935 to 1945, and his 1947 supplemental volume brings old biographies up to date and adds many new ones.

A more specific and unusual source is the *Quién es quién en la nomenclatura de la cuidad de México* (Mexico, 1962) by Carlos Morales Díaz, which has gone through two editions, the most recent being 1971. This is a fascinating book, and, as the title indicates, it includes persons whose names have been used somewhere in Mexico City to name streets, parks, or public places. Although the persons included usually have died, this is not always the case. The biographies are generally quite complete and very accurate.

One of the best single sources, but one limited to a certain group of public figures, is the book by Sergio Serra Domínguez and Roberto Martínez Barreda entitled *México y sus funcionarios* (Mexico: Litográfico Cárdenas, 1959). Available at the University of Texas's Benson Library, it contains biographies of nearly all cabinet members, senators, and federal deputies serving under President Adolfo López Mateos in 1958. While many of the biographies contain laudatory rhetoric by the authors, many include difficult to obtain information on political friendships and educational background. A newer work of this type, probably the finest Spanish-language scholarly work published on political biographies in Mexico, is Volker G. Lehr's *Manual biográfico del congreso de la unión, LII legislatura* (Mexico: UNAM, 1984). This incorporates detailed biographical information on all senators and deputies as well as their committee assignments. It is extremely carefully cross-indexed, an unusual feature in Mexican publications. An antecedent of this specific type of work is Arturo R. Blancas and Tomás L. Vidrio's *Indice biográfico de la XXLIII legislatura federal* (Mexico, 1956), which contains biographical information about members of the 1955–1958 federal legislature, but is not readily available. Finally, although not dealing with public figures specifically, Víctor Díaz Arciniega has compiled extensive information on all of Mexico's national prizewinners in the sciences and arts from 1945 through 1990, many of whom qualify for inclusion in a political directory. *Premio nacional de ciencias y artes (1945–1990)* includes a list of prizewinners by year and a general index.

Encyclopedias provided another source of biographical information. The standard *Diccionario Enciclopedia UTEHA* (Mexico: UTEHA, 1950) contains many biographical sketches, but these are rather short. The newer *Enciclopedia de México* (Mexico: Enciclopedia de México, S.A., 1976) has been revised and expanded by José Rogelio Alvarez, and now includes numerous, excellent biographies in its twelve volumes. The 1977 yearbook also includes detailed biographies of all governors currently in office. The *Enciclopedia de México* contains a complete list of cabinet members and their tenure in office from independence to 1977. It is extremely accurate. Unfortunately, there are no plans to bring out a newer edition. The other important reference works are those by Juan B. Iguiniz, Mexico's leading biographical source material on thousands of prominent figures in Mexican history. The work, entitled *Bibliografía biográfica mexicana* (Mexico: UNAM, 1969) is a detailed, annotated work of biographical source material on thousands of prominent figures in Mexican history. The book is extremely useful as a starting point for biographical research because it is cross-indexed, with a complete alphabetical list of the names of Mexican personalities followed by the page on which a biographical source appears for that individual. Even more useful for the North American researcher, with many of the same features, is Sara de Mundo Lo's *Index to Spanish American Collective Biography, Mexico* (Boston: G. K. Hall, 1982), a cross-indexed work by name and directory field. This work is especially helpful because the editor has identified those libraries that hold each of the directories indexed.

Other works in Spanish are limited either by geography, such as state directories, or by subject, such as directories of writers. A great deal of searching can produce state dictionaries (usually published early in the century, such as Eduardo Bolio Ontiveros, *Diccionario histórico, geográfico y biográfico de Yucatán* [Mexico, 1945]), or more recent social and business directories (such as Raúl Vázquez Galindo, *Quién es quién en Durango, 1966–1967*). Such works vary considerably in quality and coverage, and their availability is generally quite limited to Mexican libraries. The most useful of all social directories is the *Libro de oro de México*, which was published annually from 1924 to 1973, when it ceased publication. It is valuable because it lists higher-level officeholders by position, with their wives, and gives the latest official and home addresses of each person. It was one of the best sources for locating prominent individuals of former administrations who continue to maintain a residence in Mexico.

Public Directories

Public directories are confined to Spanish-language sources. The most readily available sources are various government organization manuals published over the years. The first serious attempt of the government to publish such a manual was the one-volume *Directorio del gobierno federal*, published by the federal government in 1947. In 1948, it was republished in two volumes, the first contained judicial, legislative, and executive branch positions, and the second, decentralized agencies, companies, and banks. This *Directorio* was published in a similar fashion each year until 1951. Extremely well indexed, these manuals contain a position as well as name index and a complete listing of most positions in the federal government from bureau chief on up. In 1956, the manual was published in a larger, one-volume version that again contained the names and positions of officeholders in all three branches of government, indexed in the same fashion. The most complete collection of these manuals in the United States is in the Department of State library, Washington, D.C., and the Columbus Memorial Library, Pan American Union.

In 1961, the government issued a new manual entitled *Directorio del poder ejecutivo federal*, published under the Secretariat of the National Patrimony and available at the University of Florida library. Unfortunately, while very complete for the cabinet agencies, the manual did not include an administrative history of each agency or department, nor a description of the legal powers of the administrative units as was true in the manuals issued from 1947 to 1956. The 1961 manual, however, did contain the dual person and position index, that made it easy to use. In 1965, the government produced another manual under the same title which followed the format of the 1961 edition. In 1969, the Secretary of the Presidency published the *Manual de organización del gobierno federal, 1969–1970*, which followed the format of the 1956 guide, containing all branches of government and administrative descriptions. Unfortunately, however, the number of officeholders listed under each agency was limited to only the highest levels, and there was no index of names. In 1971, the government issued a manual under the title, *Directorio del poder ejecutivo federal*, and it reverted to the 1961 and 1965 editions in format and content. But in 1972, this was followed with a loose-leaf version, and in 1973, replacement pages for the original. López Portillo's administration published a cross-indexed directory of cabinet agency directors in 1977, but it is very limited in the depth of the positions covered.

In 1982, the federal government became seriously interested in disseminating information about its public figures. Encouraged by then president Miguel de la Madrid, the executive branch published its own *Quién es quién en la administración pública de México* (1982), containing biographies of executive branch officials from the rank of *oficial mayor* on up. This administration set up a Unidad de la Crónica Presidencial to provide better documentation of public activities, including public servants. Under the initial coordination of Flor de María Hurtado and, more recently, Rosa Pretelín, the government has published four successive directories, 1984, 1987, 1989, 1992, entitled *Diccionario biográfico del gobierno mexicano*, copublished with the Fondo de Cultura Económica. Each edition includes improvements over the previous volume. The scope of the volumes is quite broad and includes top officials of all state governments, as well as the three branches of the federal government. The biographies are indexed by name and by government area. These biographies, which are generally excellent, are based on questionnaires sent to each individual qualifying for inclusion. In the executive branch, it extends down to director generals of departments, thus providing a broad sweep of trends occurring in public life. These are the first directories to include a consistent source of information at the state level and a selective group of top military officers.

Some state governments have published imitations of the federal manuals, but these are not readily available in Mexico or the United States. Individual agencies have also published small directories, but the only agency directory with valuable biographical data that the author has encountered is the *Programa de becas y datos profesionales de los becarios*, published by the Bank of Mexico in 1961 to describe the educational backgrounds and careers of most of its scholarship holders up to the publishing date (available at the Columbus Memorial Library). Many of these individuals have since become prominent public figures. The data are quite accurate, but vary in completeness from one individual to the next, partly due to the fact most individuals had only just begun their careers at the date of publication. The author has also obtained some excellent, unpublished directories from the Institutional Revolutionary Party, generally during the presidential campaigns of 1982 and 1988.

The other major government source has been the official directories for individual legislatures of both houses of Congress. For the most part, these must be obtained through private sources or from the Congressional Library in Mexico City. The Library of Congress in Washington, D.C., and the Benson Library at the University of Texas each holds only two individual legislative directories published in this century. They list the legislator by state, district, name, and committee assignments. Since the 1930s, these directories have been published under the title of *Directorio de la cámara de diputados* or *senadores* followed by the name of the legislature. In addition to these published directories, the lower chamber has occasionally put together an unpublished directory with biographical information filled in by the deputies or their assistants. Unfortunately, these are not readily available even to the researcher in Mexico, and the author cannot determine if they exist for past legislatures other than the 1955–58, 1970–73, 1982–85, and 1985–88 legislatures. These would be extremely useful if available, since they are very detailed and accurate.

Magazines and Newspapers

Among the periodical sources of biographical data, credit must also be given to *Tiempo* (*Hispano Americano* in the United States) as the most useful. It had the best coverage of lower-level officials and governors, and it regularly took note of resignations and appointments. At one time or another it devoted a cover story to each cabinet officer. During the beginning months of the 1964–1982 administrations, it provided biographical information on subsecretaries and *oficiales mayores*. The main limitation of *Tiempo* is its lack of an index and the fact that it was not published during the first two years of this study.

In terms of usefulness, *Hoy*, *Siempre*, and other Mexican weeklies, with the exception of *Proceso*, trail far behind *Tiempo*. While *Hoy* has a regular weekly feature covering events of the past week, including anecdotes about public figures, biographical notes are not very frequent. *Siempre*, like *Hoy*, usually limits biographical notes to occasional stories about individuals. For consistently critical views about the behavior of many government officials, *Por Qué!* was the best source, although it did not contain any biographical notes per se. More recently, *Proceso* has played this role and is the most widely read political magazine critical of the government. It often supplies details about a career or personal ties unavailable elsewhere. The most accurate newspaper source is *Excélsior*, which attempts to cover resignations and appointments with the same regularity as did *Tiempo*. The "Frentes Políticos" section is a source of fascinating information, especially at election time, about the political careers of many people. A new English-language weekly, *El Financiero International*, frequently profiles various top political leaders. The obituaries placed at the end of the first section of *Excélsior* are about the only means of determining recent deaths of public officials, unless the person is notable enough to receive mention in the press. While there is no obituary index for Mexican newspapers, the *New York Times Obituary Index* occasionally does include a Mexican, usually a person involved in foreign affairs. Anyone receiving coverage in the *New York Times* would also receive attention in the Mexican papers at approximately the same date. As is true of Mexican periodicals, there are no Mexican newspaper indexes of any type, a fact that limits the usefulness of these publications.

A new source that provides discussion of political activities as well as some information about public leaders is the *Análisis Político*, a survey of major newspapers that is published by the Mexican Institute of Political Studies in Mexico. *Polémica*, an official publication of the PRI, has had some biographies of former PRI party presidents, but it contains mostly articles and speeches by party members. Last, publications by individual institutions often have biographical data on their more distinguished members. Probably the most notable of such publications is *La Justicia*, which since 1962 has published a detailed biography each month of a well-known Mexican from a variety of fields.

Monographs and Biographies

Monographs of Mexico would, of course, provide an endless list of sources. The bibliography of sources cited includes neither individual biographies nor monographs that may have had relevant information for two or three persons whose biographies appear in this work. Most monographs are readily available, well known by students and scholars, and indexed for easy use. The reason so few have been cited is that they usually deal with a person's notable political activities, not with career data appropriate for this directory. Six works deserve to be mentioned because they have dealt with politicians' careers in greater detail than do standard works. Two are in English: John W. F. Dulles, *Yesterday in Mexico* (Austin: University of Texas Press, 1961) and Ernest Gruening, *Mexico and Its Heritage* (New York: D. Appleton-Century, 1928). Both books, unfortunately, deal only with Mexico before the late 1930s. Gruening, who had access to frank reports of government agents, has some career comments unequaled in other sources. Furthermore, he deals with state governments and political activities in those states in more detail than any other writer since 1928 and does an excellent job of tracing personal political ties. Dulles's account is full of anecdotes, often provided by persons who were still living at the time he researched the book. His work is useful from a biographical standpoint because it contains some unusual information about selected individuals.

The four other books are in Spanish: James Wilkie and Edna Wilkie, *México visto en el siglo xx* (Mexico: Instituto Mexicano de Investigaciones Económicas, 1969), Salvador Novo, *La vida en México en el periodo presidencial de Lázaro Cárdenas* (Mexico: Empresas Editoriales, 1964) and his *La Vida en México en el periodo presidencial de Miguel Alemán* (Mexico: Empresas Editoriales, 1967), and Javier Hurtado's "Familias, política y parentesco: Jalisco, 1919–1991" (unpublished, University of Guadalajara, 1993). The Wilkie volume is a frequently cited but, I fear, not a frequently used collection of taped and edited interviews with a number of distinguished public figures in Mexico. Not only are the biographical data of the interviewees in great abundance, but comments about their careers and friendships with other well-known Mexicans contribute to understanding their personal development and later participation in Mexican public life in this century. The Novo works, basically a collection of articles he wrote for newspapers under the regimes of Cárdenas and Alemán, contain a great deal of anecdotal information that completes some biographies and determines contacts and friendships among the men and women in the directory. The best recent work on political careers, and the most detailed ever undertaken on the importance of family ties, is that of Javier Hurtado, which examines in close detail the interconnected familial linkages among Mexican politicians at the state, local, and national levels from the important western state of Jalisco. This case study demonstrates the extensiveness and importance of kinship and sanguinal ties in Mexican politics.

Probably the greatest source of information has been correspondence to the author and interviews by the author. These sources deserve some comment. During the last two decades, I wrote to more than six hundred individuals who themselves qualified for inclusion in this book or who had information about others who should be included. During that time, over three hundred replies provided a substantial amount of information contained in the biographical section, as well as in the appendixes. Many governmental and nongovernmental agencies assisted me with detailed lists of officeholders and their dates in office. PAN headquarters, for example, sent me a number of biographies of various party leaders. Correspondents have ranged from the dean of Notre Dame University, where one of the biographees graduated, to a living ex-president of Mexico. Much of the information contained in this directory comes from unpublished sources and therefore remains uncited except for the word *letters* in the source section.